TO HEAL A NATION

ERS · THOMAS J DOSTAL · JAMES A FRANCIS
WARD R GRUSCZYNSKI · HERBERT C HEINTZ
KINARD · PAUL F KO
· MICHAEL J LAWR
· DAVID E NELSON
LD W PARMLEY
RYAN · STEVEN R
HN J SCHMID
ALAN P ST
ALLEN Jr · G
IS J CANNITO
RICHARD E GENEST
WILH
MAN R HETZEL
EST
MUSKETT
NG Jr
RAYCHEL
DIN
E ROBICHAU
MARSHA
TRUEX · KEN
BOGACZ
OY L B
J LEDB
MESON
E SHO
AUDILL
CHA
UGHTY

TO HEAL A NATION

THE VIETNAM VETERANS MEMORIAL

Jan C. Scruggs and Joel L. Swerdlow

INTRODUCTION BY HOWARD K. SMITH

HarperPerennial
A Division of HarperCollins*Publishers*

A previous edition of this book was published in 1985 by Harper & Row, Publishers, Inc.

First HarperPerennial edition published 1992.

Designed by Ernie Haim

Library of Congress Cataloging-in-Publication Data

Scruggs, Jan C.
To heal a nation.

"Perennial Library."
1. Vietnam Veterans Memorial (Washington, D.C.)
2. Washington (D.C.)—Monuments. 3. Scruggs, Jan C.
I. Swerdlow, Joel L. II. Title.
F203.4V54S37 1986 959.704'3 84-48191
ISBN 0-06-092344-X

92 93 94 95 96 RRD 10 9 8 7 6 5 4 3 2 1

This book is dedicated to my wife, Rebecca Scruggs. Her love and encouragement never failed during the difficult times that I faced in the struggle for the Vietnam Veterans Memorial.

Jan C. Scruggs

After watching thousands of men risk mutilation and death in the trenches during World War I, the British physician Charles McMoran Wilson, himself decorated for bravery, thought he finally understood courage.

"Courage," he said, "is a moral quality. It is not a chance gift of nature like an aptitude for games. It is a cold choice between two alternatives, the fixed resolve not to quit, an act of renunciation which must be made not once but many times by the power of the will. Courage is will power."

I have been privileged to share a special closeness with one man while he demonstrated such courage.

Under the worst of times, when the angels themselves had started to weep, he never lost his resolve, his humor, or his grace.

A book about the young men and women who served in Vietnam is properly dedicated to such a person.

His courage reaches out to all those who still endure the pains of war, to those whose lives will bear the burden of future wars, and to everyone whose life may be threatened by circumstances such as serious illness. "Love each other now," this courage says. "Enjoy each day, and remember that acts of kindness and loyalty, no matter how small they may seem, can defeat life's most dirty devices."

With love and admiration, for my brother,
Paul Heshel Swerdlow, M.D., Ph.D.

Joel L. Swerdlow

But we . . . shall be remembered;
We few, we happy few, we band of brothers;
For he to-day that sheds his blood with me
Shall be my brother; . . .

William Shakespeare
Henry V

Contents

Foreword

It was a cold, wintry night in Washington, D.C. More than four inches of snow was on the ground and more was falling steadily as the wind gusted. Nights like that are times when the only place to be is indoors. I ventured out to the most amazing place in the nation's capital.

The Jefferson and Lincoln Memorials were empty. Yet well past midnight, in weather as bad as weather gets in Washington, the Vietnam Veterans Memorial was not alone. Visitors were there to experience the quiet power and majestic beauty that sets this memorial apart from all others in America.

The visitors were perhaps hoping to experience America's most visited memorial without bus loads of tourists around. Maybe that is what makes this memorial different. The Wall is not just another monument that one drops by to admire while on a three-day tour of Washington. Rather it is something to be experienced. The Wall can make you feel compassion, sadness, patriotism, anger, or love. Gazing into the names of 58,000 men and women killed in Vietnam while seeing your own reflection in the polished granite brings about profound feelings for you, the visitor, to experience.

The experience of seeing the names is an emotional one for those of us who saw the horrors of combat in Vietnam. Never shall I be able to walk past the name of Michael Hrutkay without feeling pain. He died laying down rifle fire so a small group of soldiers could escape from an ambush. I was one of those soldiers. Michael is on panel 16 West, line 45.

Maya Lin's simple design is recognized internationally as an American architectural triumph. The names are engraved not alphabetically but in chronological order. Therefore those who died together in battle are forever together on The Wall. The visitors who took part in those battles are taken back in time as they see those names. They begin to heal at a memorial built to heal a nation.

More than ten years have passed since bulldozers and heavy construction equipment went to work excavating the area on the Mall now graced by the Vietnam Veterans Memorial. The annual visitors are counted not in the thousands or tens of thousands, but in the millions.

Some have compared the Memorial to a hybrid combining attributes of Mecca and the Wailing Wall of Jerusalem. All faithful Moslems feel the need to make a pilgrimage to Mecca. Those of the Jewish faith go to Jerusalem and partake of the tradition of placing written prayers between the cracks of Israel's Wall. How similar this is to the tradition of placing items at the Vietnam Veterans Memorial. Just as Mecca and Jerusalem's Wailing Wall harken the faithful, so too does the Vietnam Veterans Memorial beckon those who were touched by Vietnam.

Few people remember that this Memorial was nearly a casualty of Washington politics when a group of powerful men tried to stop "The Black Gash of Shame and Sorrow" from ever being built. There were some who could not understand how an unconventional memorial could honor the unselfish service of Vietnam veterans. That story and more is in the book that you are about to read and enjoy.

In closing, let me just give you something to mull over. In 1979 a former army corporal, a "C" student in college who was a low-ranking employee at the Department of Labor, decided to build a national memorial. Despite seemingly insurmountable obstacles the memorial was built. When you finish this book take a look at your life. Look at your dreams. Then look into your heart and find the courage to contribute to making this a better country and a better world.

Jan C. Scruggs

Introduction

HISTORIANS REGARD THE CIVIL WAR as America's most traumatic experience and the Great Depression as second most. A strong minority believes our searing war in Vietnam is third, and some even think it should displace number two. The Depression was, after all, not very divisive; we were almost all in the same waterlogged boat, and hard times had a strangely unifying effect. Vietnam, on the other hand, is still an inflamed wound it hurts to touch, and partisans are still ready to tear at one another over the subject when it is resurrected from a dark place in our past.

Abraham Lincoln was the hero of the first trauma, though his effort to bind up wounds was aborted by assassination. Franklin Roosevelt was the hero of the second, though it was his furious activity rather than the immediate results that made us feel better. The hero of the third trauma is a young man, nowhere nearly presidential, named Jan Scruggs, who was struck by an idea in the middle of a night.

The sheer folly of the project that Scruggs and friends so boldly set for themselves makes this an adventure story with nearly as many unlikely escapes from extinction as an Indiana Jones adventure. First off, they planned to achieve their purpose by erecting, of all things, a monument—in a city sinking under the weight of monuments and wanting no more.

The monument would at once honor all veterans of the war, soothe and inspire veterans still living, conciliate the dissidents, and put the country at long last at peace with its recent past. What manner of bronze or marble could achieve aims so excessively ambitious and contradictory?

The monument would not be in some obscure place like the Ben Franklin and Daniel Webster monuments, which stand unnoticed in corners of Pennsylvania Avenue. It would be located where people could not avoid seeing it even if they so wished—on the sacred Mall between the great memorials to Lincoln and Washington. What unthinking Secretary of the Interior would ever agree to let cloutless amateurs have such a priceless piece of real estate for so impossible a use?

As Scruggs and company gathered support, the supporters divided into relentless camps, each threatening to undo the whole project unless its tastes dominated the Memorial. One camp consisted of the modern symbolists, who wanted a V-shaped black granite wall with the name of every single soldier who died in Vietnam engraved on its shiny surface. The second camp was made up of traditional representationalists, who wanted bronze statues of soldiers that looked like bronze statues of soldiers. To save their project, the vets had to agree to both, though the antithetical combination might cancel the effect of each.

This story of how a young man without special influence led the collection of over eight million dollars (with not a penny from the government), won the prize location, gained strong supporters (and alienated others just as strong), melded two themes into one, and oversaw the completion of the whole thing—this whole true narrative may renew one's faith that individuals and their dreams do count.

The final result has a quality of magic. The monument has indeed united the spirits of all who have visited it. It has begun the healing of a nation. If you see it, you are compelled by some mysterious force to touch it, to feel the names on the granite surface.

Far from being incongruous, the bronze soldiers unite with the granite wall in one haunting theme. It is as if a disembodied voice has said to the figures, "Soldier, before you is the roll of those who shall not return alive. Read it and know your fate." The expressions on the bronze faces, weary but intent, seeming to search the roll of names on the wall, are unlike those on any representational monument ever made.

When you, the visitor, pass before the granite slabs and read the names, you suddenly see beyond the names the faces of living Americans, moving, looking, touching, whispering—and in their midst your own face reflected in the shining mirror. It seems to say, Vietnam was not theirs alone, it is all of ours; if you wish peace, love them.

Howard K. Smith

PART ONE

1985 and Beyond

IT IS A PLACE FOR PEOPLE. You can feel alone or linked as never before with the people you love. You can feel uncomfortable or exhilarated. The Memorial dictates nothing.

This seeming simplicity is deceptive. The names keep you from remaining indifferent. You become part of them, and they become part of you. They search for something within you, and they stimulate you to search for something with greater meaning than yourself.

Many people come to see a special name. Every day someone leaves a flag, a flower, a snapshot, a memento, a poem, or a personal note.

Most visitors have no particular vet in mind. They come because they know that the Memorial has something important to offer.

These visitors include both the generation that got America involved in Vietnam and the Vietnam generation: 9 million men and women who served in the military and 30 million women and 20 million men who never served.

Always, there are countless young people—members of the post-Vietnam generation upon whom America depends to fight its wars.

Most of these young people know little about Vietnam. A child of draft age in 1986 was not born until three years after U.S. Marines first landed at Da Nang. For a six-year-old in 1985, Vietnam seems as far back as George Washington or Abraham Lincoln.

So they ask questions. Why is this here? Who are these names? What did they do? Why did they die? Did you know them? What does it mean to me?

PART TWO

1979–1980

1

THE BEGINNING

IN MARCH OF 1979, Jan Scruggs, a 29-year-old former rifleman with the U.S. Army 199th Light Infantry Brigade, went to see a movie entitled *The Deer Hunter,* notorious for its explicit, bloody depiction of death and cruelty.

Scruggs became upset, not by the combat scenes, but because of the scenes showing blue-collar youth in a Pennsylvania coal town. They were the people who had believed in their country, which then abandoned them when the war went sour—the people he'd seen suffer and die in Vietnam.

That night, Scruggs couldn't sleep. At 3:00 A.M. he was alone in the kitchen with a bottle of whiskey. Mortar rounds hit. Twelve men were unloading an ammunition truck. An explosion. Scruggs came running. By instinct, he pulled the first-aid bandage from his trousers. Organs and pieces of bodies were scattered along the ground. They belonged to his friends. He had only one bandage. He stood and screamed for help.

The flashbacks ended, but the faces continued to pile up in front of him. The names, he thought. The names. No one remembers their names.

"I'm going to build a memorial to all the guys who served in Vietnam," Scruggs told his wife the next morning. "It'll have the name of everyone killed."

She smiled. But days later, when he was still talking about a memorial, she started to worry. He was having delusions. Even his close friends were expressing their concern to her. "Is there something wrong with Jan?" they asked. The best thing, she figured, was to let this play out.

DOUBEK AND WHEELER

Scruggs heard about a meeting of Vietnam veterans planning activities for a week in their honor proclaimed by Congress. It would provide the perfect time to announce plans for the memorial, so Scruggs went to discuss his plans.

Forty vets attended. Scruggs laid out his dream. They would build a memorial with the name of every GI killed in Vietnam—a delayed victory parade, a powerful symbol of national reconciliation. They'd accept no government money. Dollars would flow in from the American people.

The others listened carefully and then told Scruggs that he was a bit naive. The country would never do it. Besides, at a time when vets went on hunger strikes to protest inadequate care and benefits, who needed a memorial?

Scruggs was hurt and shocked. He had thought it was a brilliant idea and that he would leave the room with forty volunteers.

As Scruggs left, a serious-looking former Air Force officer who had served in Da Nang in 1969 handed Scruggs a business card. "You ought to form a nonprofit corporation," the man said. He was an attorney named Bob Doubek who had grown tired of day-to-day legal humdrum. The number of people who took the dream seriously had doubled: to two.

The ex-infantryman needed time to devise a plan, so he took two weeks off without pay from his job in the Labor Department. He called UPI, and a sympathetic reporter suggested that Scruggs hold a press conference.

Scruggs had never even seen a press conference, but on May 28 he stood in a National Press Club conference room, explained his dream, and told a dozen reporters that "the only thing we're worried about is raising too much money."

He really thought this was true. Once the country read about the memorial, nearly everyone would send money, and within two or three months at the most, there would be $1 million—which would be enough to do the job.

During the next month, Scruggs rushed down to the post office every day at noon to see how much money the publicity from his press conference had generated. A few dollars did come in. The donations were never large, averaging five or ten dollars. Five dollars from an unemployed Vietnam vet. A man living on Social Security sent three dollars. A young girl sent ten dollars in memory of her father. One man described his paratrooper brother who had survived combat, only to commit suicide six years after returning home. An Air Force wife said her husband had flown 433 combat missions and never said one word about them. A former POW said his scars brought him no bitterness. A 20-year-old college student wrote about growing up with dread that his government would make him die in a place he did not understand.

Mostly the letters carried names: my buddies, my brother, my son, my husband, my father. Help him be remembered. Keep his death from remaining meaningless.

"When my best friend was killed and his body sent home, I was requested by his family to escort the body home," wrote a combat medic. "In Philadelphia, someone saw the casket being put on the plane and said to me, 'Well, there's another Vietnam stiff.' "

Another Vietnam vet wrote, "All we want is for people to recognize the sacrifices and contributions they made because the country they love told them it was right." One check came with only a torn piece of paper on which the name of a dead GI was written. "Don't waste time and money writing back to us," one person told Scruggs. "Just keep working."

But a memorial cannot be built with emotions. You need money, and for that more publicity was essential. Scruggs called the wire services, and they agreed that his fund-raising problems were newsworthy. A few days later, Scruggs sat back with a beer and turned on the *CBS Evening News.* Near the end of the broadcast, Roger Mudd reported—with a knowing smile—that the organization formed to build a national memorial to Vietnam veterans had gathered the grand sum of $144.50.

Scruggs knew that the entire country now saw him as just another Vietnam vet who couldn't make it. It didn't feel good.

Later that night, things got worse. A comedian on a network program made fun of Scruggs. It was a good joke, and the audience laughed.

Vacationing with his family in South Carolina, Washington attorney Jack Wheeler didn't laugh. Wheeler was a graduate of West Point, Yale Law School, and the Harvard Business School, and a Vietnam vet. For years, he had been fighting the national amnesia that had turned Vietnam into a nonevent. Wheeler knew that the war had dramatically changed America, and yet the nation had forsaken its soldiers even before combat ended. Wheeler's efforts had centered around successfully establishing the Southeast Asia Memorial at West Point. The Academy's own desire to forget had been so strong that even Wheeler's extensive connections in military, law, government, and corporate circles had barely kept the project alive. And now Scruggs, a former infantryman, a grunt, a man out of nowhere, was popping up on television, saying he wanted a *national* memorial.

The West Pointer knew what to do. God, he believed, often used an imaginative and humorous grace to work His will.

Wheeler called Scruggs.

A week later, Scruggs, Doubek, and Wheeler met. "It can be done," Wheeler said. "Let me call some people."

RECRUITING

For Vietnam veterans, coming home from Vietnam was not the way John Wayne had promised.

You weren't a hero.

You had gone over there filled with images of John F. Kennedy, Hollywood movies, and Sergeant Rock comic books, and you did your duty, even though few of these images matched the muck and the moral confusion in Asia.

Then they put you on an air-conditioned plane with smiling stewardesses, and suddenly the war was over. It happened so quickly.

"Wash up," one vet's mother said. "Your welcome-home dinner is just about ready."

He looked at his hands. Mud from Vietnam was still under his fingernails.

You also came home alone, with no sense of completion.

You were safe, yet the killing continued. You might write a few letters to friends, but you lost touch. You never learned what happened to them, even whether they were alive or dead.

Back home, no one wanted to hear what you'd been through. If people saw you in uniform they might spit, call you a murderer, or—most painfully—ask why you were stupid enough to go. And if you'd been seriously wounded and were lucky enough to return with only a leg or an arm missing, someone might come up and say, "Served you right."

Even ten years after you came back, the easiest way to clear a room was to mention Vietnam. Friends and family only wanted you to quietly and happily join their sanitized, safe lives. "I was shocked," one vet said, "not by the fact that no one cared, but that no one even talked about it."

Many vets who thought the war had no lasting effect on them eventually discovered a hardening rage within whatever could be defined as their souls. It hurt to go fight a war and then have to sneak in the back door of the country at night.

This shared pain, coupled with a continued sense of obligation to brothers-in-arms, bound vets together.

Thus, Wheeler received a warm response when he made his calls to Vietnam vets. Corporate lawyers, congressional aides, lobbyists, business executives, engineers—all gathered in early August to hear Scruggs, Doubek, and Wheeler describe the dream. Many attended a few meetings, listened carefully, decided it would be impossible, and drifted away. Others, men Wheeler called the "horses," stayed.

They were former enlisted men and former officers, experienced, smart, expert in organizing, and not afraid of either hard work or conflict.

They were willing to invest thousands of hours of time for no pay and little public recognition. Their motivation was mixed, ranging from an idealistic sense of duty to a desire to destroy all vestiges of the "baby-killer" image.

Beneath it all, were the names of those who had not come home. Wheeler expressed it best:

> We live in hope that in the final day
> we will see our brothers again,
> face to face, where they shall know
> us and we them, and we will not be
> strangers.

Scruggs and Doubek incorporated the Vietnam Veterans Memorial Fund as a nonprofit organization in April 1979. During the following summer and fall, the vets began to organize the VVMF. Ironclad financial management and cash-accounting controls were established. The VVMF, however, was an open organization. Any vet or interested citizen who wanted to suggest ideas or get involved could easily do so.

They agreed upon a timetable: 1980—obtain land for the Memorial; 1981—finish raising money; 1982—construct the Memorial; Veterans Day 1982—dedicate the Memorial.

No listing of the vets who worked for the Fund could be complete. Some had joined earlier than others and some were staff members—but all shared and sweated for the dream.* Chief among them were: Bob Frank, John Woods, Sandie Fauriol, John Morrison, Ron Gibbs, Bill Jayne, Paul and Heather Haaga, Dick Radez, Art Mosley, George "Sandy" Mayo, Don Schaet, Bob Carter, Kathie Kielich, and Karen Doubek. All had their own skills; each made more than one invaluable contribution. Many had been wounded and decorated for bravery in Vietnam. With what lay ahead, all would live by the dictum suggested by John Morrison, a former Army captain who lost one eye in combat. "As long as they're not shooting at you," he said, "there's little to fear."

Several important patterns began to emerge. They never discussed their personal views about what the Vietnam War meant, whether it should have been fought, whether proper tactics were used, what they thought of the antiwar movement, or why America lost. They knew that the war had been too complex, and had gone on for too long, for their views to be unanimous. There was no need to replay the passions of the 1960s and early 1970s.

Also unspoken was the pessimism each vet felt about whether they could meet their self-imposed deadlines. Scruggs, Doubek, and Wheeler kept saying it could be done. But no monument had ever been built in Washington without extraordinary delays. Even something as seemingly simple as a memorial to Abraham Lincoln had been started in 1867 and completed in 1922. Money had to be raised. A design had to be commissioned. A bill had to pass Congress. Approval had to be obtained from

*For more details about key individuals and a longer list of names, see "Roll Call of Honor" at the end of the text.

various public commissions. You'll be lucky if you've got this done by the end of the decade, some thought. But no one ever said such things out loud.

In addition to raising money, the group identified two principal obstacles: the old and powerful antiwar movement, which would seek to destroy anything that memorialized America's Vietnam policy; and the Washington bureaucracy, the endless labyrinth of congressional committees, art commissions, and federal agencies that would suffocate any new idea—no matter how virtuous—if it threatened their notions of how things should be done.

In their enthusiasm, the vets could not know that their worst obstacle, which would nearly destroy their much-loved memorial, had not yet surfaced.

Wheeler and Scruggs exchanged handwritten notes during this period. "The need is not for a vindictive examination of the record," Wheeler wrote. "I see the need this way: Very likely our own generation will be forced to consider committing American troops to combat. In making the policy judgment, we have to do our best to avoid the faulty reporting and thinking, both inside and outside of government, that went on in our country regarding Southeast Asia from 1946–1975. . . . Speaking personally, I think we have to try because, aside from my religious faith, that is the only way I can find meaning in the death of my friends."

Scruggs never enjoyed philosophizing. He wrote Wheeler a short response: "We've got something very good here. Enclosed are envelopes and stationery. Write anyone, ask for anything."

Although he was the son of a milkman in rural Maryland and had no contacts within Washington's power structure, Scruggs decided to do some recruiting of his own.

First stop was his U.S. senators. Scruggs had high expectations. After all, what sort of politician could refuse to honor veterans? Scruggs wandered into the office of Maryland Republican Charles McC. Mathias, Jr. A summer intern took careful notes, and said someone would call back. When Scruggs left, he knew two things for sure: that the Fund only had $144.50, and that no one really seemed to care about the Memorial.

On August 4, 1979, the telephone rang: Come see Mathias.

Doubek and Scruggs explained to the senator that the Memorial would be strictly nonpolitical, that hawks and doves could agree to honor service and sacrifice. They emphasized that they wanted no tax dollars. They would raise every dollar themselves. They just wanted Congress to give them land.

Mathias, who had opposed America's involvement in Vietnam, was a master politician. He believed that America did not like to deal with pain, especially when it was responsible for that pain. He knew there would be no political benefit from embracing Vietnam vets. But he also knew that the vets had been short-changed. Much had been expected of them, and too little had been given in return.

He looked at Scruggs and Doubek carefully. Their sincerity was obvious. As the conversation continued, the senator's voice lost some of its formality. He settled back in his chair and kept asking for more information. The dream had another recruit.

Scruggs also tried to recruit the President of the United States.

The presidential aide in charge of veterans affairs, a former schoolteacher who had never served in the military, listened quietly as Scruggs outlined his plans for national reconciliation. "Would the current Commander-in-Chief be interested in giving his support?" Scruggs asked.

"Put it in writing."

Scruggs's letter carried his passion. "Having the American people finance the memorial," he wrote, "will be in effect a delayed victory parade, a permanent reminder of how much the nation, however belatedly, cared for its sons and daughters who served during a most difficult and dangerous time."

After several weeks and a half-dozen calls from Scruggs, the answer arrived. "There is a strict White House policy to not endorse any fund-raising efforts," the aide explained. "Please accept my apologies for the delay in responding."

A short time later, the Washington Police Department's fraud unit—the bunko squad—called Scruggs. A congressional staff member had called the White House to see if the Vietnam Veterans Memorial Fund was a legitimate organization, and the White House had apparently passed the question on to the police. So now the cops wanted to know all about Scruggs.

When Wheeler heard about this, he called his Atlanta friend A. D. Frazier, who had served as a White House adviser during the early days of the Carter Administration. Within forty-eight hours, the Fund received a call from Dean Phillips, who had won the Silver Star in Vietnam and was special assistant to Veterans Administration chief Max Cleland. "I was on long-range patrols, with the 101st Airborne," Phillips said. "Wounded. . . . You've got a great idea. What's your schedule? I'll be right over."

NEXT TO THE LINCOLN MEMORIAL

As the summer of 1979 ended, a top official of the Fine Arts Commission, the most powerful government agency that would have to approve the Memorial, suggested that the most logical site for a Vietnam Veterans Memorial would be across the Potomac River from Washington, on the road leading to Arlington Cemetery. Scruggs and Wheeler drove out there. It was sterile and deserted. Cars filled with tourists rushed by on their way to somewhere else. No one ever stopped.

"That spot is unacceptable," they reported back to Doubek. "We mustn't let them stick our memorial in such an out-of-the-way place. It must be where people will see it."

But what could they do? Washington had a well-established procedure for deciding where memorials went. When Congress authorized the Memorial, it would instruct the appropriate authorities to figure out the best place for it. And the appropriate authorities were already telling the vets to start thinking about a location that provided more insult than honor.

Mathias had a solution: Bypass the federal bureaucracies. Have Congress pass legislation giving Vietnam vets a specific piece of land. This approach involved obvious dangers. Offended bureaucrats could kill the Memorial. The risk, Mathias reassured the vets, was worth it.

In September 1979, Doubek, Wheeler, Scruggs, and three National Park Service officials waited just off the Senate floor for a meeting with Mathias. The official produced a map of Washington with all park land marked in green.

"Landscaped solution," Wheeler said, "A garden-type approach. We want to create the Memorial but without removing the land from its use by the people."

The senior official nodded. "Great," he said. "That's important. That's right."

Mathias arrived, shook hands all around, and looked at the map. He agreed with everyone present that the site should be prominent, and he said he liked the landscape approach. Then he put his thumb on the map.

"How about this?" He was looking at the Park Service representative. "What do you think?"

The official stifled a gulp. "Sure is a good site, Senator."

Wheeler and Doubek looked down at the senator's thumb. It was on the Mall, in a place called Constitution Gardens, right next to the Lincoln Memorial.

Once the possibility of this site entered the vets' consciousness, it seemed overwhelmingly logical. Right at the foot of the Lincoln Memorial—what a spot! No one could ignore it. Members of Congress would see it every morning as they drove to work. Presidents would see it whenever they ventured forth from the White House. Everyone in America, especially Vietnam vets themselves, would know that a special honor had been granted. The symbolism was perfect. If the Vietnam Veterans Memorial was to help bind the nation's—and their generation's—wounds, what better place than in the shadow of Abraham Lincoln?

Mathias suggested that the vets inform the National Capital Memorial Advisory Committee—whose members included each government body that had to approve memorials in and around Washington—of their intentions. There was a clear danger, Mathias noted, that the Committee would react negatively, thereby damaging the chances that legislation could get through Congress. But the Committee members had to be faced eventually, and it was better to do so at an early stage.

On October 24, the Committee sat patiently as Doubek explained the dream:

> The Vietnam war has been the collective experience of the generation of Americans born during and after World War II. . . . Over 2.7 million Americans served in Vietnam. More than 57,000 died* and over 300,000 were wounded. . . . The Vietnam Veterans Memorial is conceived as a means to promote the healing and reconciliation of the country after the divisions caused by the war. . . . It will symbolize the experience of the Vietnam generation for the generations which follow.

*At the time that the Vietnam Veterans Memorial was being planned and constructed, the official total for U.S. military personnel killed in Vietnam was 57,939, eight of whom were women. Since then, the Department of Defense has added more names to its official listing, so the total now exceeds 58,000.

Although the meeting closed with an invitation to return in January and present an updated report, Committee members told Doubek and Scruggs that they would oppose site-specific legislation.

The Fund's plans called for a Veterans Day 1979 press conference during which Mathias and several dozen other senators would announce that they were introducing a bill granting the vets two acres next to the Lincoln Memorial. Its bipartisan co-sponsors included Republican Barry Goldwater, who ran for President in 1964 as a hawk, and Democrat George McGovern, who ran for the nation's highest office as a dove in 1972. All would be endorsing the belief that Vietnam veterans could be honored without commenting on America's Vietnam policy; the warrior could be separated from the war.

Several weeks before the press conference, the first potentially serious crisis arose. A former Marine officer named James Webb requested permission to show a draft of the legislation to Congressman John Hammerschmidt of Arkansas, a conservative Republican who sat on the House Veterans Affairs Committee.

Webb's request made sense. The vets had few contacts in the House, and they had no one like Mathias rounding up support. They needed all the new friends they could find. Furthermore, they trusted Webb, who had written a widely read Vietnam novel.

A few days later, Webb called Doubek. The former Marine was proud to report progress. That very day, Hammerschmidt had introduced the legislation in the House. Webb read aloud from the congressman's statement, which concluded by arguing that "nine or ten years ago our media brought great attention and dignity to the notion of dissent when others in the Vietnam-era age group gathered on the Mall to protest the war. . . . Now it is their [the Vietnam veterans'] turn to gather on the Mall."

Doubek felt sick as he listened. However innocent his motivations, Hammerschmidt could have robbed the scheduled Veterans Day press conference of its news value. Far worse, his their-turn-on-the-Mall comment could outrage the antiwar people, arouse their active opposition, and kill the Memorial before it got started.

Few of the vets slept well that night. Over breakfast they felt better. The morning newspapers had ignored Hammerschmidt.

On Thursday, November 8, 1979, the VVMF's Senate sponsors held a press conference to announce that twenty-six senators were co-sponsoring their bill. "A location on the Mall is symbolically appropriate," Senator Mathias told reporters. "We can all recall when the Mall was the battleground of opinion and dissent regarding America's role in Vietnam. Its proximity to the Lincoln Memorial is also fitting, for not since the Civil War had this Nation suffered wounds and divisions as grievous as those endured over Vietnam."

Rumors flew. The Memorial was a Republican trick to embarrass the Carter Administration. A group of New Right radicals wanted to glamorize Vietnam.

But an article by Scruggs appearing in the *Washington Post* that Sunday placed the VVMF's motives clearly on the public record:

> Serving with an Army Infantry company from 1969 through 1970 was an experience one does not forget, especially on Veterans Day [Scruggs wrote]. About 90 percent of my company was drafted. The massive protests against the war by then did little to help sagging morale. Yet if the war was unpopular at home, it was probably liked even less by those whose fate it was to serve in Vietnam. It was a year-long nightmare. Half the men in my company were killed or wounded. . . . Several months before leaving Vietnam I spent four hours of my life 50 feet from a North Vietnamese machine gun emplacement. A dozen American youths were pinned down; several were wounded. We were able to retreat as one fellow exposed himself to the enemy gunners and drew their fire. He held his own for the few crucial minutes needed to retreat with our wounded. Then came his screams. . . . We knew we were watching the man who had given his life for us die a horrible, excruciating death. We also knew he had a wife in Pennsylvania. . . . The bitterness I feel when I remember carrying the lifeless bodies of close friends through the mire of Vietnam will probably never subside. I still wonder if anything can be found to bring any purpose to all the suffering and death.

Scruggs closed with a poem—"The Young Dead Soldiers," by Archibald MacLeish. "We were young," it read. "We have died. Remember us."

Several days later, a reporter called Scruggs. From his questions and comments, Scruggs could tell that the man was strongly antiwar. "You're real egomaniacs," the reporter finally said. "You're building a memorial to yourselves."

"If I sat around waiting it would never happen," Scruggs replied. The irony hit. People being memorialized usually did not do it themselves. Yet here were Vietnam vets building a memorial to honor service to a country that *still* seemed anxious to forget. What the hell, he figured. It had been that kind of war.

2

MONEY

MONEY WAS THE PROBLEM. A September 1979 plan for a test fund-raising letter required $20,000—far more than the Fund's total assets. The only full-time staff member was Doubek, who accepted the position of executive director in December 1979 at a salary that cut his income in half; and the VVMF's offices, opened on January 1, 1980, consisted of a ten-by-ten-foot room that looked like a telephone booth.

Scruggs's audacity, bred by naiveté, still fueled the Fund. Figuring that you get money from rich people, he wrote to Senator John W. Warner (R-Va), who was then married to actress Elizabeth Taylor. "Senator, let me get to the point," Scruggs wrote. "I'm asking you to donate the tax-deductible five thousand dollars we need to begin producing fund-raising materials for the many people who are now requesting them. If you can't afford this big a donation, perhaps you could give us a noninterest loan for a year."

In Washington, people simply do not write to U.S. senators and ask for interest-free loans. But Scruggs did not even pause for amenities or apologies. "I don't mean to rush you," he told Warner, "but we need an answer soon. . . . We need your help. How about it?"

If Scruggs had approached Warner with the proper sophistication, the letter probably would have elicited a polite yet firm rejection. But

Warner had volunteered for military duty in World War II and Korea, and as Secretary of the Navy during much of the Vietnam War he had signed orders sending thousands of Marines and sailors into the combat zone. Scruggs's let's-just-do-it attitude reminded Warner of his own youth. Within days, the vets were sitting in Warner's office.

"I'll help you raise the first year's budget," Warner told the vets. He said their best bet was to get money from defense contractors—companies that had profited from the Vietnam War. He would be happy to invite them to a fund-raising reception.

Warner, however, warned the vets that some people would say they were going after "blood money." For several days, discussion among the vets was heated. Then a consensus emerged. With a million-dollar memorial to build, and only a few thousand dollars in hand, too much concern about image would be an unaffordable luxury. Blood money was not attractive, but why call it that? And if it was blood money, so what? They had it coming. It had been their blood.

Scruggs called Warner and told him to arrange the reception.

Meanwhile, veterans groups started to rally around the Memorial. In August 1979, the American Gold Star Mothers—about half of whose members had lost a son in Vietnam—had initiated a letter-writing campaign urging Congress to support the Memorial. Twenty-five hundred dollars, the largest contribution to date, came in from the Veterans of Foreign Wars. The American Legion, the Marine Corps League, the Retired Officers Association, the National Guard Association, and numerous other groups endorsed the Fund, and publicized it in their newsletters. Momentum seemed to be building.

Five days before Christmas of 1979, Warner hosted an 8:00 A.M. breakfast at his Georgetown home. Scruggs, Doubek, Wheeler, several other vets, and Washington representatives of about a dozen major defense contractors sipped coffee and made small talk in the living room. It had high ceilings, gold-colored carpets, and an original Monet. The men wore business suits, and Elizabeth Taylor wore a pink robe and white slippers with tassels on the toes.

At 8:30, Warner called the meeting to order. He and Mathias praised the project, and then introduced Scruggs. Realizing that this might be the only opportunity to get big money quickly, Scruggs tried to make the arms manufacturers feel that their contribution would be more important than combat duty. "Our obligation to build this Memorial," he said, "is perhaps the most important thing any of us will ever do."

Warner ended the gathering by writing a personal check for $1,000 and telling the defense contractors to get their dollars flowing to the Fund. They all said they would report back to their corporate headquarters and await instructions.

Eventually, the breakfast yielded over $40,000, but fear that defense industry money would flood the Fund never proved to be justified. Most corporations which had profited financially from the war never demonstrated any special willingness to contribute—even when approached directly.

In late 1979, Doubek learned that an article in *Parade* magazine would mention the Fund and give its address for donations. *Parade* had 20 million readers, so the Fund thought it prudent to organize volunteers to answer all the calls that would come in, and to spend $250 for 10,000 envelopes and thank-you letters.

The response: few calls and, at most, 50 pieces of mail.

The letters came from elderly people and in childish scrawl, on fancy stationery and on scraps of paper, from all parts of the country, from those who fought and from those who did not know one veteran. The letters carried pride, anger, bitterness, patriotism, nostalgia. Many told eloquent and intimate stories of pain and sacrifice.

The Fund had touched a nerve that stretched across the entire political spectrum.

"Steve was only twenty years old, brave and patriotic," one man wrote. "He was fresh out of high school and too young to know better. They sent what they said were Steve's remains back in a box. Our neighborhood has never been the same since, and his parents' sadness has made them old before their time. It is a well-known saying that old men send young men to war. We hope that this memorial will stand to honor our veterans, but also will stand as a warning for those old men who even now are trying to drag us into another useless war."

Another person wrote that "those who chose to disgrace their national heritage and now take pride in 'having ended the war in Vietnam' already have their monument—the bodies of the men, women, and children now resting in the bottom of the South China Sea. The boat people of Southeast Asia."

A desperate desire for contact and shared grief was apparent. But the thousands of unused thank-you letters spoke even more loudly. Dollars would not just come rolling in. If they wanted to raise enough for a memorial, they would have to work very, very hard.

Although professional fund-raisers warned that Vietnam would not sell well, the vets decided that the best way to raise money would be through mass mailings, which would give millions of people a chance to be part of a "people's memorial." They formed a National Sponsoring Committee that included First Lady Rosalynn Carter and former President Gerald Ford, Bob Hope, Nancy Reagan, William C. Westmoreland, novelist James Webb, and Admiral James J. Stockdale, who had been one of America's most prominent Vietnam POW's. These names appeared on the letterhead of a 200,000-piece test mailing that went out in early 1980.

Ten thousand dollars to help make the mailing possible came from Texas billionaire H. Ross Perot. Throughout the Vietnam War, Perot had taken a strong interest in the well-being of Vietnam vets. He had loaded thousands of Christmas turkeys onto a jumbo jetliner and tried to fly them to Hanoi to serve America's POW's. North Vietnam never let the plane land, but worldwide publicity forced them to improve treatment of the captured Americans. Perot had also provided financial assistance to many POW families. He was a tough-minded, take-charge, self-made man widely respected by Vietnam vets.

Bob Hope signed the letter, which read in part: "All of us, regardless of how we felt about the war, can participate in building this memorial that says we care about the men and women who fought in Vietnam. If you give $20, it will sponsor the name of one Vietnam war veteran who gave his life in service to our country."

Most of the 200,000 names on the mailing lists came from mainly conservative, patriotic organizations, but several thousand names from a McGovern-for-President committee were also included.

Normally, half the money raised by mail arrives during the first three weeks. The vets waited. Nothing came in. One of the people who worked on the mailing relieved some of the pressure by telling her friends about the project. Virtually all had been antiwar, so she expected that they would talk about how wrong and dirty the war had been. She prepared to fight back, to describe how lucky she felt to be working with the vets. Without exception, however, her friends had the same reaction: "The

Memorial's a great idea. How do I contribute?"

Then the responses starting arriving. Within a month, the vets could make an assessment. A group like the VVMF, with no organized support, normally loses money on its first mailing; the best it could hope for was to get some publicity, to begin to compile a list of contributors, and to break even. But the VVMF's response rate turned out to be 1.12 percent, and the average gift was $17.93—an unusually high figure. By the end of March, the 200,000 solicitations had yielded $36,768, for a profit of approximately $6500.

George McGovern's name, however, caused problems. Although his 1972 campaign contributors donated to the Memorial, each week hundreds of letters came back with McGovern's name circled. One angry note said, "I would have given you money, but this man is why we lost the war and I won't support you until you drop him." One of the nation's large corporations had promised to give $5,000. When its president saw McGovern's name, he dropped the amount to $500.

The vets faced a decision: Should they remove the senator's name from their letterhead?

"We cannot give away our integrity," Doubek argued. "Reconciliation may be a lofty goal, but without reconciliation the Memorial will never succeed."

No one disagreed. McGovern's name stayed.

One million more pieces of mail went out with a slight change. In the revised version, Bob Hope quoted an article Scruggs had written for the *Washington Star* in 1979: "On my return from Vietnam, still in uniform, a group of people my own age booed and made obscene gestures at us. This experience was painful, but others suffered far worse than I. One veteran—an amputee—was told straight out, 'It serves you right for going there.' "

For all their idealism, the vets could not escape reality. If this mailing failed, the VVMF might have to fold. The results were still in doubt late in April 1980, when James J. Kilpatrick wrote in his nationally syndicated column, "The bitterness engendered by Vietnam may never be forgotten. The sacrifice at least should be remembered. . . . In the 16 years I have been writing this column, I don't believe I ever have urged contributions to a particular cause. I do now."

Normally, newspaper appeals—even when they provide an address—produce little money. No matter how committed they are, people want envelopes in which to place their checks: no envelope, no contribution.

Two days after the Kilpatrick column appeared, the Fund received a half-dozen letters citing Kilpatrick as their reason for giving.

It was only six letters, but it was an important sign. Within a few weeks, the Fund had received over $60,000 from Kilpatrick's readers. Any doubts about the Memorial's fund-raising potential could now be dismissed. Thus, final results of the mailing came as no surprise. Net income was $120,000—more than enough to keep fund-raising efforts alive. Experts knew of no similar mailing that had ever done so well.

THE LETTERS

The Memorial could not be built without money. It could never mean anything without the tens of thousands of letters that accompanied this money:

> My son was killed and I can't bring it up during a party.
>
> I did not expect a ticker-tape parade when I returned to the States, but I have served my country faithfully.
>
> I hope this monument will be built in my lifetime.
>
> I am grateful that you have taken the time to do something that will honor so many brave people.
>
> Our son did not come home to us.
>
> From the grandmother, 87-years-old, of a Marine who lost both legs in Vietnam.
>
> For my son, so he can ask the questions I'll never be able to answer.

Look at the sheer whimsy of it all. They are dead. I am not.

My son, an only child, who wanted to fly and to eventually become a doctor, was lost in Vietnam. He left a little 15 month old girl and a lovely wife.

The whole town turned out for the funeral for he was the only boy who died there from this small town—but there it ended. There is no recognition of his death anywhere so far as the town he grew up in is concerned.

In memory of my son, who died after saving the life of his shipmate. He was 18 years old.

I hope your memorial can heal many of the hurts that that unfortunate war has caused. It lies there like unfinished business.

The memorial is long overdue, and I will be awaiting the day I can travel to Washington to see it.

He joined the Marines when he was seventeen, he was eighteen when he was killed. It has been very hard for me to write this letter.

Thank you for remembering.

He didn't die there; he just died inside.

He was my only grandson.

We always attend the services at the cemetery, especially Memorial Day and Veterans Day.

It will give us great comfort to know that this sacrifice was not in vain.

For the war I hated and the friends I loved and lost. Let us never forget the waste of war.

My brother suffered greatly due to the isolation and bullshit and, seven years after his separation, remains quite distant from his near family and has few friends.

Besides honoring the War Dead, the monument may also symbolize the wrecked hopes, dreams, and lives of all the War's victims' families, friends and loved ones.

Anyone who died in that fiasco is a hero in my eyes.

Those boys, God Bless, were give a very *Rotten* deal.

I opposed the war. I marched (and prayed) for peace. I counseled C.O.'s. But I will never, never forget what so many gave of what they had for what they believed. And many of these, tragically, were the best we had.

Fourteen days after arriving there he was killed.

Thank you for remembering your buddies.

I don't have any money to send right now so at least for the time being I hope you'll accept what little I have—my heart—my pride in those brave people who gave so much.

The memorial is a stupid thing when so many of the surviving veterans are so sick and suffering with no place to turn to.

A monument to such an infamous event can only serve to augment the bitterness of those who were sucked into this unwholesome affair by reminding them that they, too, could have precluded their misery by having evaded the draft like the wiser ones did. . . . Let's not perpetuate the memory of such dishonorable events by erecting monuments to them.

What have you done to clean up filthy V.A. hospitals?

I for one am getting very very tired of hearing about the poor Vietnam veterans. To me you are a bunch of crying babies.

Don't build us a memorial. Instead, every year invite each of us to a classroom to discuss what it was like.

Letters that opposed the Memorial showed as much pain as those that supported it. A growing sense of just how deeply this pain ran through America kept the vets who were working for the Fund going through eleven-hour days and six-day workweeks. Their personal lives shrank and disappeared. Many became obsessed. They had to get the Memorial built by November 1982.

3

THE ANTIWAR MOVEMENT

BACK IN LATE 1979, the VVMF learned that their anticipated foe—the antiwar movement—was awakening. Of all the thousands of letters the *Washington Post* received, the newspaper's editors had chosen to publish an attack on the notion of a veterans memorial.

"The tens of thousands of young Americans who were forced—through the draft—to fight the immoral war certainly deserve better treatment today and adequate recognition of their suffering," it read. "[But] if this memorial is to serve any positive purpose, it must include all war resisters who were imprisoned for resisting the draft. This is the minimum, the very least that must be demanded."

This appeared to be merely a beginning. The antiwar movement, which had expended so much energy organizing such effective opposition to the war, seemed poised to launch an intellectual and political assault on the Memorial. From one perspective, who could blame them? Vietnam had been the war everyone loved to hate. The Fund's desire for reconciliation, its argument that the warrior could be honored without honoring the war, would seem like a paltry public relations ploy once antiwar passion descended over Congress.

Furthermore, the vets knew they were at least one generation too soon. If history taught any lesson about memorials, it was that they could not be built until passions had cooled and everyone who had directly experienced the events being memorialized had passed from the scene.

Feelings about the Vietnam War, which had ended only 48 months before Scruggs had set out to build a memorial, were still red hot. America had forgotten the vets, but it had not forgotten its longest war. Frustration, finger-pointing, and contradictory lessons bred by a decade of television images were all imbedded in the nation's psyche.

A government advisory commission that evaluates ideas for memorials provided evidence that the antiwar movement might have some surprising allies. In early January, the vets presented their plans. They figured that the representative of the Pentagon would offer the strongest support.

When it came time for questions, the military man said, in effect, "Why should we build a memorial to losers?"

Sensitive to the emotional minefield they were approaching, Wheeler in a February 6, 1980, memo warned his colleagues that they should never take a political position or express views on Vietnam-related subjects. To Wheeler, the stakes were far greater than simply building a memorial. "We have become," he said, "trustees of a portion of the national heart."

UNANIMOUS SUPPORT FROM THE U.S. SENATE

Senate hearings on the Memorial were scheduled for March 1980, and the vets saw plenty of trouble ahead.

The National Park Service wanted Congress to give the Secretary of the Interior power to place the Memorial anywhere in Washington he wanted, subject to approval by the Fine Arts Commission.

It had some powerful allies. J. Carter Brown, the prestigious Fine Arts Commission chairman, had already warned that legislation giving the vets a specific site would set a dangerous precedent—that if the Vietnam vets got their way, Washington would soon be cluttered with memorials honoring every group powerful enough to pressure Capitol Hill.

J. Carter Brown's logic was persuasive, and most of the vets knew that he was right. But they didn't care. Let others worry about problems with future memorials. Vietnam vets were a unique case. An extraordinary site for their memorial was not too much to ask. If anything, it was too little.

Furthermore, site location was *the* issue, more important even than the design. To leave power over site selection in the hands of the Interior Secretary would be to wait for years until the bureaucracy reached a decision; such a delay could easily kill the Memorial, something that many people in Washington obviously hoped would happen. One powerful man in the House of Representatives, for example, was already saying in public that Vietnam vets were crybabies who should receive *less* from the government. It could mean a memorial shoved off onto some forgotten and insulting site. Vietnam vets would get shortchanged again. It could also mean a serious, perhaps fatal, handicap for fund-raising. To raise several million dollars for a memorial on the Mall was a difficult but not impossible challenge. To request money for a memorial to be placed on some unspecified and potentially obscure location would be foolish. No one would give.

The vets wanted the land in Constitution Gardens. It was their one uncompromisable demand.

In Washington, when you want something very badly you do not come right out and tell people how important it is to you. Instead, you ask for other things and then grudgingly give them away until you are left with what you wanted in the first place.

The vets had devised two major giveaways. They asked for two acres right at the foot of the Lincoln Memorial. In reality, they would have been happy with fifty square feet. And they asked that the Secretary of the Interior be given only a consulting role. In truth, the Fund was willing for the Interior Secretary or anyone else to have power over virtually anything. He could have veto power over design, fund-raising procedures, even how the fund was organized—just so long as he could not take away their land.

For a while, the vets hoped that the Carter Administration would be their ally in their battle for legislation that would give them the land they so desperately wanted. Like a majority of the Senate, Carter was a Democrat. In a close vote, he could make the difference. Then Dean Phillips at the Veterans Administration called to say that VA administrator Max

Cleland would testify in favor of the Memorial, but the Carter Administration would take no public position on whether the legislation should designate a site. The vets would be on their own.

Senators Mathias and Warner searched for more co-sponsors. They made a good team: Mathias liberal and antiwar, Warner conservative and hawkish. They had a strong case. What could be more benign than a no-cost-to-the-taxpayer memorial honoring veterans? Liberals, conservatives, and moderates, Republicans and Democrats, would all benefit politically from endorsing the Fund. No organized opposition existed. And yet most senators refused to sign up as co-sponsors. Days before the March 12, 1980, hearings before the Senate Subcommittee on Parks, Recreation and Renewable Resources, the number of co-sponsors for the Mathias bill seemed frozen at 45.

Something significant, however, was changing in the chemistry of America.

On the surface, the spring of 1980 was not a time for romance or heroism. Unemployment and inflation climbed steadily into double digits. Night after night, television screens showed hostile Iranian mobs screaming obscenities as U.S. diplomats were held hostage for still another day. Thousands of boat people were dying off the shores of Indochina. Invading Soviet troops were settled into Afghanistan, openly defying an outraged and apparently impotent America.

Americans wanted to regain control over their place in the world, and all of a sudden the use of force—sending GI's to clean out the enemy—seemed attractive in a way it had not since at least the mid-1960s. Sensing this new mood, both houses of Congress were in the midst of approving defense spending bills larger than the President had requested, the first time this had happened since the end of the war in Vietnam.

The role of Vietnam vets in this new national mood remained unclear. The country could choose one of two contradictory attitudes toward them. A frustrated public could turn even further away from vets who had fought the nation's only unsuccessful war. Voters could demand billions more for new missiles and manpower, but not a penny more for those perceived to represent past mistakes. Or, remembering that the real world did indeed demand that young men be willing to fight, the nation could embrace and honor 2.7 million citizens who had recently answered the call to arms.

One person who knew which way the country would—and should—go was Stan Kimmitt, Secretary of the Senate.

Kimmitt had two sons who had served in Vietnam. He knew how the average GI had sacrificed plenty and received little in return. He also knew that the Secretary of the Senate must never try to persuade a senator to support or oppose any legislation. So Kimmitt acted on his own. Quietly, with great efficiency, he made sure that every senator took the time to read and consider the Vietnam Veterans Memorial legislation. Late in the last afternoon before the Senate hearings, Scruggs received a telephone call from a congressional aide who had remained indifferent to the Memorial. The aide sounded shocked. "Something unprecedented is going on," he said. "My boss is now on board. You guys are winning big."

That night, Scruggs answered his phone at home. He recognized the voice of another Capitol Hill aide, one who supported the Memorial. The friend sounded very happy. "You now have eighty-eight co-sponsors," he said.

The U.S. Senate respected Stan Kimmitt.

The vets met early on the morning of the hearings to once again practice answering the tough questions they expected.

"How much money do you have?" some senator would ask.

"About $25,000," they'd have to reply.

"And how much do you think this Memorial will cost?"

"About $2 or $2.5 million."

"Then how do you expect to build it?"

"Once we get the land and some good publicity, our efforts to date indicate that we will not have a major problem. We'll be able to get the money."

This was weak, but the best they could do.

Fifteen minutes before the hearings were scheduled to begin, Scruggs and a suitcase full of documents were in his car, and he couldn't find a parking place. He pulled into a parking lot reserved for senators. A guard approached.

"Listen, goddamn it, I've got to testify before the U.S. Senate for the Vietnam Memorial," Scruggs said. "I'm late. Hearings start in seven minutes."

The guard laughed. "Third Marines. Two tours." He motioned Scruggs into a senator's parking spot. "Get the hell in there."

The hearings opened with an encouraging surprise. Among the witnesses was a freshman senator from South Dakota, Larry Pressler. Pressler was a skilled orator who had been educated at Oxford, but his voice quivered as he described a recent experience:

"I was doing an interview on an entirely different subject during a press conference and a reporter asked me about my background. I mentioned that I was a military veteran of the Vietnam conflict and he immediately interrupted—Did you kill any people or participate in any assassination groups? I replied, No, I hadn't. But the distressing thing was I found myself going on the defensive immediately. . . . It seems a veteran who served in the military in Vietnam is constantly on the defensive. Many of them have told me that they simply say they weren't involved in combat. . . . I hope," Pressler concluded, "[that this Memorial] will help allow all veterans to finally come home."

Senator Warner also appeared as a witness. We must build this Memorial immediately, Warner told his colleagues, because once passions have cooled America might be all too willing to forget those who served so well.

The National Park Service, however, had little use for emotion. "We recommend," its representative told the committee, "that the resolution be amended to strike a reference to a specific site."

Three weeks later, the committee, by a unanimous vote, recommended that the vets receive two acres right at the foot of the Lincoln Memorial.

By the end of April, the Fund had 95 Senate co-sponsors. Scruggs called the remaining five. "We have ninety-nine co-sponsors," he told each of them. "Associated Press wants to know who the holdout is. What should I tell them?" Within hours, 100 senators—the entire U.S. Senate—had signed up.

In a mid-April letter to Mathias, the Park Service said: "Since the proposed memorial is of great significance, does not memorialize a single person or event, but rather a 10-year period of our Nation's history, and is envisioned as a landscaped solution emphasizing horizontal elements, we concur [that] a site in Constitution Gardens is preferable."

At the same time, the vets used one of their giveaways; they dropped objections to legislative language that specified that the Secretary of the Interior, the Fine Arts Commission, and the National Capital Planning Commission would have to approve "the design and plans" before construction could begin. This strengthened role for the Secretary of the Interior seemed reasonable. At worst, the vets figured, it would introduce some bureaucratic hassles—a small price to pay for their land. It was springtime in Washington, and the November cold—with its presidential election and the possibility of a new Interior Secretary—seemed far, far away.

On April 30, 1980, Scruggs was at his desk at the Labor Department when Doubek called. "Be over in the Senate gallery at three-thirty," Doubek said. "They're going to be voting on our bill."

Scruggs was wearing his usual work clothes—a western shirt, jeans, and cowboy boots. He rushed out to a clothing store and tried on a sport jacket, slacks, and dress shirt. They made him look the way a man lobbying the U.S. Senate is supposed to look. The store manager sensed a quick sale. To hell with it, Scruggs decided, as he tossed everything back on the rack. To hell with the whole system. We're just getting some measly land for a memorial to guys who served. The hell with the clothes.

About a dozen vets gathered in the Senate gallery. Some were unemployed, happy to have a purpose for the afternoon; others were highly paid lawyers whose work schedules seldom allowed such unplanned interruptions. But this moment was too good to miss. Senator Robert Byrd (D-W Va) stood up and explained that, as majority leader of the U.S. Senate, tradition bound him not to co-sponsor legislation, but that he was making an exception in this case so that each and every U.S. senator would be a co-sponsor.

Less than seven minutes later, the bill had passed.

The vets hugged and slapped each other on the back. They had achieved the impossible. Now George Washington, Thomas Jefferson, and Abraham Lincoln would have some new neighbors—every GI who served in America's most hated war.

TROUBLE IN THE HOUSE

In the House of Representatives, the Fund had no Mathias, no Warner, and no Stan Kimmitt.

As of April 15, 1980, the vets had only 177 co-sponsors—107 Democrats and 70 Republicans—some of whom had been persuaded by unemployed Vietnam vets who wandered from office to office talking to staff members.

The effort needed new momentum, so on March 5, 1980, the vets and several congressmen—whose political ideologies ranged from liberal to conservative—held a press conference to announce reintroduction of the legislation. At this conference, Scruggs attempted to prevent a heated House debate by emphasizing that the Memorial would "stand as a symbol of our unity as a nation and as a focal point for all Americans regardless of their views on Vietnam, for remembering the tragedies wrought by the conflict—and the lessons taught us."

One of the press conference participants was Representative Don Bailey (D-Pa), a former college football player who had won a Silver Star while serving as an infantry officer in Vietnam. Like Hammerschmidt, Bailey had been brought in by Webb. When it was his turn to speak, Bailey started talking about how the Memorial should not promote reconciliation. Within a few sentences, he was shouting. America, he said, had lost the war because of those who protested against it. The Memorial should be a patriotic answer to such disgusting behavior.

Wheeler later warned Scruggs, "Stay away from Bailey."

The vets followed this advice, and never again sought out the congressman. But something in the emotionalism of Bailey's performance had been disturbing. He did not look like a man who would just go away.

Bailey, however, was not the vets' most serious problem in the House. Some Democrats opposed the Memorial because they thought it implied that the Carter Administration had not done enough for Vietnam vets. But with the help of House majority leader Jim Wright (D-Tex), and Libraries and Memorials Subcommittee chairman Lucien N. Nedzi (D-Mich), the legislation seemed to be gliding toward approval before Memorial Day 1980, the deadline for the Fund's million-piece mailing. With House and Senate passage in hand, the fund-raising appeal would have irreplaceable momentum.

Hearings in the House had none of the drama of the Senate. The representatives' chief concern seemed to be that the Memorial would require too many tax dollars for maintenance. Scruggs reassured them that as a result of the Memorial the National Park Service would have less grass to mow. One congressman joked that it should be located in his district in New Jersey.

On May 20, hours before Congress would recess for the Memorial Day holiday, Nedzi asked that the Memorial bill be put on the unanimous consent calendar—which meant that it would be passed as a pro forma matter without debate or vote.

A slightly stooped, broad-shouldered man stood up on the floor of the House. It was Phillip Burton (D-Cal), who had been a strong antiwar leader since the mid-1960s. As chairman of the subcommittee with jurisdiction over public lands, he was also a leading expert on national parks. Burton refused to agree to unanimous consent, and demanded that the bill be referred to his committee for full hearings.

Minutes later, Nedzi left the House floor to confer with Doubek.

"Burton's offering two acres, but not where you want them," Nedzi said. "You can take it, or take a chance that you'll get nothing."

"I'll take the two acres."

The House unanimously passed the bill as amended by Burton. It spoke only of "a site in the District of Columbia."

Since the House and Senate versions differed, the matter would have to be settled in a conference committee, where representatives from each legislative body would meet in closed session to select compromise language. As a matter of tradition, the full House and Senate would quickly pass whatever their conferees agreed upon.

Thus, when Congress went into recess for Memorial Day, the vets still did not have their land.

The vets considered attacking Burton, who apparently wanted to kill the Memorial in conference. It would be a good trick; the public would never see any member actually vote against the Memorial. It would just get lost in the shuffle.

The message from their supporters on the Hill, however, was clear: Burton loves a fight. He's a master parliamentarian. Don't take him on. His maneuver may seem unfair to you, and it may even mean a long, debilitating delay. But even his enemies regard him as a man of great principle. Yes, through this one ploy, the bill could get lost for years. If that happens, don't worry. Don't be in such a rush. If you want a memorial just anywhere, you can get it. But you want to get on the Mall, and that's playing with fire. Be patient. It takes time to get things done in Washington. It could even take ten years to get your memorial. You're young. Hang in there.

The warriors decided not to fight. They followed the same strategy they'd used when Bailey had attacked them from the right. They simply reiterated their dream of national reconciliation.

"From the beginning," Doubek told reporters, "we have seen a prominent site as a significant part of this effort, and we see Constitution Gardens as an appropriate place for this symbol of national reconciliation. We thought it was right for Congress to designate the site and we thought everyone was in agreement that the Monument should be in an area that was the site of massive demonstrations, near the Lincoln Memorial, which also symbolizes reconciliation."

Scruggs taped a Chinese proverb next to his telephone: "If you can be patient in one moment of anger, it will save you a hundred days of sorrow." He planned to follow strictly this advice. It never occurred to him that more than one hundred days of sorrow lay ahead anyway.

MEMORIAL DAY 1980

Memorial Day ceremonies at the Tomb of the Unknown Soldier at Arlington National Cemetery represent a ritual healing for the country, a time of taps, bands, dress uniforms, a time to cry in public and to renew the collective commitment to never forget men who died for their country.

On Memorial Day 1980 at Arlington, Miss America sang "The Star-Spangled Banner," and soldiers wearing sparkling belt buckles and spotless uniforms marched. Most of the several thousand people who attended were middle-aged and elderly men, and the atmosphere was one of moral certainty. Their wars had been clear-cut, and their dead had died for undeniably justifiable reasons. Their small talk concerned not doubts or anger but what they saw as the death of old-fashioned patriotism. If any of them noticed that the word "Vietnam" was never mentioned in the official services, they did not complain.

Across the Potomac River, the VVMF held services on the Constitution Gardens site that Congress had not yet given them. About 400 people, mostly young men in their late twenties and early thirties, attended. Many were in wheelchairs, or were missing arms. Some were blind. Some wore jungle fatigues, boonie hats, and faded uniforms. Others had on suits and ties, with medals and colorful ribbons pinned on in neat rows. Scattered among these young men were older couples and children.

They listened as Mathias quoted from Lincoln's Second Inaugural Address, inscribed on the nearby Lincoln Memorial: "Let us strive . . . to bind up the nation's wounds; to care for him who shall have borne the battle, and for his widow and his orphan."

Mathias stopped speaking and looked directly into the faces before him, to read what they were trying to say. "In any fair and compassionate consideration of the ordinary fighting man in Vietnam," the senator continued, "the question of the morality of the war must be laid aside. . . . Time has a way of reconciling us to history. Wounds heal. Divisions mend. Americans have at last come to feel that our nation and its institutions emerged from the crucible of Vietnam strengthened and purged."

What Mathias noticed most about the crowd was the physical contact. Couples held hands or hugged children. And the ex-GI's stood in tight clusters, as though sheer body proximity would help them share whatever emotions they felt.

The next speaker was retired Brigadier General George B. Price, who had been one of the nation's ranking black officers. In the military, he had been known for his courage, and for his belief that an officer should ask his men to show courage in attacking the enemy, not in defending untenable positions. Sometimes this attitude got Price in trouble with the top brass in Vietnam, but it generated a fierce loyalty from his men. Indeed, as he approached the podium, some of the Vietnam vets, all of whom had been out of the military for at least ten years, reflexively snapped to attention. The crowd cheered as Price called Vietnam vets "the best we had," victims of "the absence of a national purpose."

The U.S. Army field band played "The Battle Hymn of the Republic," and Wheeler stepped to the microphone.

"There's no more sacred part of a person than his name," the VVMF chairman said. "We have to start remembering real, individual names."

Then members of the audience came up to the microphone, one by one, to say the name of someone they had lost. My son. My husband. My father. My fiancé. My brother. My childhood friend. My buddy. My classmate. We still love them. We still remember.

On the news that evening, viewers saw an empty field but one that was filled with tears and spoken memories. The next day's newspapers carried stories about the first Memorial Day services at a national level to honor Vietnam's dead. Many found it curious that the vets wanted to link the words "honor" and "Vietnam." Most quoted bitter, angry veterans who considered the services to have been "too little, too late." Their wounds had been festering for over a decade. For a GI who said, "When I came home I was laughed at," it would take more than nice words from a politician and a former general to begin the healing.

When reporters called to do follow-up stories, Scruggs talked about two letters the Fund had recently received. One read: "I would have given but I do not like reconciliation [with those who opposed the war]." The other said: "I lost my brother in that war, and I hate everything about it."

If we can get each of those people to send in just a few bucks, Scruggs told the reporters, then we'll be successful.

On May 30, President and Mrs. Carter invited 200 Vietnam veterans to a ceremony marking the first Vietnam Veterans Week. Carter had tears in his eyes as he read aloud from journalist Phil Caputo's description of his friend Lieutenant Walter Levy:

> You embodied the best that was in us. You were part of us, and a part of us died with you, the small part that was still young, that had not yet grown cynical, bitter and old with death. Your courage was an example to us, and whatever the rights and wrongs of the war, nothing can diminish the rightness of what you tried to do. Yours was the greater love. You died for the man you tried to save, and you died pro patria.
>
> You were faithful. Your country is not. As I write this, eleven years after your death, the country for which you died wishes to forget the war in which you died. Its very name is a curse. There are no monuments to its heroes, no statues in small-town squares and city parks, no plaques and wreaths and memorials. For plaques and wreaths and memorials are reminders, and they would make it harder for your country to sink into the amnesia for which it longs. It wishes to forget and it has forgotten.

Sitting far back in the audience, Scruggs smiled. "Just you wait," he whispered to his wife. "Levy's name will be on the Mall a couple of blocks from here."

4

THE VETS GET THEIR LAND

THE VETS STILL HAD TO DEAL WITH Representative Burton, whom they saw as the point man for the antiwar movement, which was finally emerging into full view.

The Carter White House offered no help, but Ron Gibbs and Bob Doubek were finally able to arrange a private meeting with Burton.

"It's just like the Gulf of Tonkin Resolution," the congressman said. He opened a filing cabinet and pulled out a thick file. "It's all in here. LBJ talked me into supporting quick passage. It needed more study, and so does your bill. I won't make the same mistake twice."

The vets explained how their memorial was aimed at reconciliation, *not* reopening old wounds. They finally won Burton over with one simple sentence: "George McGovern is on our sponsoring committee."

The House-Senate conference committee adopted the Senate version of the bill, giving the VVMF their land near the Lincoln Memorial.

The bill said that two acres in Constitution Gardens should be set aside for a memorial "in honor and recognition of the men and women of the Armed Forces of the United States who served in the Vietnam war."

It gave power of approval over the design to the Fine Arts Commission and the National Capital Planning Commission—and the Secretary of the Interior.

On June 24, 1980, Senator Mathias hosted a reception in the Senate caucus room to celebrate the conference committee's action. Dozens of senators mingled with Vietnam veterans, including a Navy officer who had once been a POW in North Vietnam. "The Vietnam veteran doesn't really want anything special," he told the *Washington Post.* "Just someone to shake his hand, pat him on the back, tell him thanks."

In his remarks, Scruggs thanked the Fund's early supporters and told his fellow vets, "Have a good time, because this may be your only chance to have a U.S. senator buy you a drink."

One week later, about 150 members of Congress, representatives of veterans organizations, and Vietnam vets, many in wheelchairs, endured 100-degree heat in the Rose Garden as they watched President Jimmy Carter sign legislation giving the vets two acres on the Mall.

"A long and painful process has brought us to this moment today," Carter said. "Our nation was divided by this war. For too long we have tried to put that division behind us by forgetting the Vietnam War, and, in the process, we ignored those who bravely answered their nation's call. . . . We are ready at last to acknowledge more deeply and also more publicly the debt which we can never fully pay to those who served."

The Memorial, he predicted, would stand as a "reminder of the past, what was lost, and a reminder of what we learned."

Generous as Carter's words were, the ceremony created the impression that the White House had pushed the bill through Congress. This angered the vets, as did the apparent White House decision to bury news coverage of the Memorial by choosing that same day to release a quarter-million-dollar Veterans Administration study on public attitudes toward the Vietnam War. Over 90 percent of all Vietnam vets told the pollsters they were proud they had served, and 55 percent of all Vietnam vets said they would "serve again if requested." Although most vets now said the United States should have stayed out of Vietnam, they demonstrated a surprisingly strong faith in the U.S. government. Contrary to media images, the vets were neither drug addicts nor violence-prone psychopaths. By most measures, they were just like other Americans.

The vets were not surprised to see one particular statistic: 62 percent of the American people said that those who fought in Vietnam "were made suckers."

Another finding jumped out. According to the poll, less than half of the vets said they received a warm welcome home from friends and family.

After the bill-signing ceremony, reporters asked Scruggs about the design. "We do not seek to make any statement about the correctness of the war," he said. "Rather, by honoring those who sacrificed, we hope to provide a symbol of national unity and reconciliation."

Judging from news stories that followed, the journalists found this answer satisfactory. Nothing in the notion of an apolitical memorial indicated to them that any problems might lie ahead. Yet the news media were tough-minded. A *New York Times* editorial, for example, called the bill-signing ceremony "not a commonplace occurrence in any nation—commemorating a war that wasn't won."

Many vets who attended the ceremony and who followed events in the newspapers were dissatisfied. They thought that Carter should have provided fewer nice words and more money for veterans programs. A VA study and land for a memorial just would not be enough. Unemployment among Vietnam vets was high. Counseling centers were crowded. Medical benefits were inadequate. Agent Orange, a chemical defoliant that contained one of the most powerful cancer-causing agents known to man, seemed to be creating peculiar problems. Between 1962 and 1970, the United States had sprayed over 10.6 million gallons of Agent Orange over South Vietnam—so much that the poison had soaked into the ground and entered the drinking water. Military manuals had said that it was "relatively non-toxic to man and animals." Now, years after the fighting had ended, thousands of Vietnam vets were suffering body sores, mood changes, malfunctioning joints, hair loss, fatigue, and, most mysteriously, fatal cancers almost never found in young men. "I died in Vietnam, only I didn't know it," said one victim.

Vietnam seemed to be creating a new type of war widow: the woman whose husband had come back in one piece only to die an anonymous death years later. Even worse, Vietnam had become the first war to reach into the nation's maternity wards. Wives of men who had served in Indochina were giving birth to dead babies and to babies with genetic abnormalities of the heart, spine, and extremities. So young women began to live with a numbing dread: Should they risk having children?

The government's answer was that no definitive proof existed. The vets knew, however, that if the government admitted that Agent Orange had caused this carnage, then the U.S. taxpayer and the corporations that manufactured Agent Orange would be liable for billions of dollars in damages.

In this context, the argument that Vietnam vets needed money more than memorials had much truth to it. Indeed, three years before he conceived of the Memorial, Scruggs had appeared before a U.S. Senate committee and described a questionnaire he had sent to over 600 Vietnam vets attending college. He had discovered that more than half of the 233 who replied felt that duty in Vietnam had caused them major employment, health, or psychological problems. Alienation was so high that some combat vets even refused Civil Service preferences rather than admit they had served in Vietnam. His recommendation—that the federal government should meet its responsibilities by funding veterans programs—had elicited nothing more than polite nods on Capitol Hill. But Scruggs knew that the trade-off was not a Memorial in place of adequate aid. Just the opposite was true. Reconciliation and justice could come only in steps. Once Congress and the country honored the dead, and once they recognized the value of service in Vietnam, then the road would be open to meeting the other real needs of the war's survivors and their families.

Furthermore, many of the Vietnam veterans' needs could not be met with money: needs of the spirit, the longing for respect, wounds that were simultaneously on the surface and too deep to see. Healing these wounds would cost the American people only a simple thank-you.

MONEY AGAIN

Most of the vets now saw money as their major, and the only remaining, problem.

A handshake from the President was nice, but by the day of the Rose Garden ceremony the Fund had raised only about $250,000.

The late-1979 and early-1980 efforts had demonstrated that the core of their support was going to be small contributors who could be reached only through direct mail—one of the most expensive vehicles for fund-raising. Another million-piece mailing was planned for November.

On July 2, the day after the Rose Garden ceremony, Scruggs called H. Ross Perot.

Scruggs liked Perot. He and the Texan had spoken several times on the telephone, and Scruggs found him to be sincere and easily accessible. At one point, however, Perot had said that he himself had tried to get a Vietnam veterans memorial built in Washington. Funds would have come through a nationwide fund-raising campaign that would have had schoolchildren—Perot had called them "the future warriors of America" —helping out. Perot's plan had not gone very far, and he'd told Scruggs that it would be embarrassing to have a 29-year-old with no resources succeed where he'd failed.

Now, as Scruggs explained the need for more funds, Perot said he would not give any more money at that time. But he offered a provocative suggestion: Scruggs should call former government officials who got America involved in Vietnam. "Ask them for money," Perot said. "It was their war too."

Scruggs loved it. The Memorial should have a healing effect for all Americans. As much as the vets, perhaps more, these people were in need of healing.

How do you find the people who designed America's war policy? One easy call, Scruggs figured, would be to a man whose name was still in the newspapers, World Bank president Robert S. McNamara—Secretary of Defense from 1961 to 1968, when U.S. troop commitment in Vietnam rose from several thousand to over half a million.

When Scruggs told McNamara's secretary what the call was about, the former Defense Secretary came on the line.

"We need big bucks," Scruggs explained.

McNamara promised he'd put the former corporal in touch with those who could help. "Drop me a note and then we'll talk again," McNamara said.

The next day, Scruggs wrote McNamara a letter. A week later, Scruggs called and left a message. He kept leaving messages over the next two months. He never heard from McNamara again.

In mid-July, Scruggs received a call from a man who identified himself as an interested citizen. "They've removed the marker for the

Vietnam vet at the Tomb of the Unknown Soldier," the man said.

Scruggs knew that several years earlier a spot had been designated for a Vietnam war soldier and that a stone had been laid. No body had been interred, because government regulations required 80 percent of a set of unidentifiable remains, and no Vietnam remains met this requirement. But what government functionary would dare remove the stone? The stranger's story seemed unbelievable.

The next day, the man showed up at Scruggs's office with photographs. The two-and-a-half-ton tombstone had indeed been lifted out. Only a terrible truth remained: The parents, children, and friends of Vietnam veterans who saved their money and traveled to Arlington to honor their dead had nothing.

PART THREE

1980–1981

5

THE DESIGN COMPETITION

THROUGHOUT THE SUMMER AND FALL of 1979, the VVMF had also focused on what sort of memorial to construct.

Certain basic notions were fixed. Scruggs contributed the concept that had been with him from the beginning: the names.

From Wheeler came the "landscaped solution" theme, putting the Memorial in a "spacious garden setting" and making it horizontal so that it would not awkwardly compete with the Lincoln Memorial and Washington Monument.

The vets saw three options: to design the Memorial themselves, to pay several firms to submit designs and then choose the best, or to hold a design competition.

Scruggs, Wheeler, Webb, and Doubek were befriended by a 35-year-old Washington sculptor named Frederick Hart, who specialized in representational art. Although he said he had been gassed in antiwar demonstrations, Hart wanted very much to do the Memorial. He had apprenticed under Felix de Weldon, sculptor of the Iwo Jima Memorial, and felt he would be able to capture what he called the angst of war.

In late September the VVMF board decided to conduct some sort of competition, so it rejected Hart's principal concept: "a pavilion structure, with design influenced by elements of a Buddhist pagoda . . .

containing two works of sculpture, one a realistic depiction of two soldiers and the second a more abstract form of plexiglass with internal images."

The reason they finally decided on an open competition was that this would fit in with the American spirit of solving problems through fair and open contests, and would give the American people an opportunity to speak out about what sort of memorial they wanted.

It was also dangerous. What if the design jury chose a winner that was totally insensitive to the vets' feelings?

Wheeler, assessing emotions and deep divisions left over from Vietnam, warned of another danger. To promote healing, a design would have to open and clean old wounds. In the process, it would cause anger. "Whatever design we come up with will be one thousand degrees hot. There will be a fight."

In July 1980, the Fund hired Paul D. Spreiregen as their professional adviser in organizing the competition. Spreiregen had written the definitive book on the subject, had personally supervised numerous competitions, and was recognized as a leading authority.

One primary goal in forming the jury was to obtain a design that would move quickly and smoothly through the official approval process. Lurking over them was the ghost of the Franklin D. Roosevelt Memorial. In 1958, Congress had approved a memorial honoring the four-term President. A distinguished jury, an internationally acclaimed competition, and promises of federal funds had, by 1960, produced a winning design that the jury called "a mirror of our present-day culture." But for the next two decades, bureaucratic in-fighting and debate over the design froze the project on the drawing board. Millions of dollars and thousands of man-hours had been invested, and nothing had happened.

Spreiregen said that the VVMF could have Vietnam vets, Gold Star Mothers, or wives of men still missing in action sit on the jury. This could help guarantee a suitable winner, but carried several clear risks. Other jurors might defer too much to the opinions of a Vietnam vet, who could describe the feeling of combat but would not necessarily know how to look at two-dimensional plans and visualize a three-dimensional memorial. Besides, Vietnam vets and their families were pluralistic. How could you find one representative individual or even a representative sample?

The other possibility was to select a world-class jury composed *entirely* of the most prominent professionals available. Such a jury might select an unacceptable winner. It would, however, attract world-class competitors. It would also make the winning design easier to defend. If vets picked the winner, then antiwar people, the design community, and the dreaded federal commissions might be more likely to attack their memorial.

This issue so divided board members that they sometimes stood and screamed at each other during meetings. In one session, Wheeler pounded the table with his fist, insisting that women and blacks—groups deeply affected by the war—also be represented. Another time, Dick Radez argued, "We've got to have Vietnam veterans so we can get what we want."

"What *do* we want?" Doubek asked.

No one could answer.

The feeling among many board members was that if one vet was included on the jury it should be Scruggs. But Scruggs himself found the whole issue boring. "Let's put the names on the Mall and call it a day," he said.

The problem floated around during the summer of 1980. At one point, a possible solution seemed to be finding vets who were also qualified professionals. Doubek called James Webb. "We haven't decided yet how we'll structure the jury, but we're thinking of including a humanist. Would you be interested?" Doubek asked.

Webb replied that he'd rather leave that job to people with knowledge of art and architecture.

Finally in September a compromise was reached. The jury would include only the most prominent professionals, but the Fund would carefully screen and interview potential jurors to make sure they demonstrated sufficient sensitivity to what service in Vietnam had meant. The vets did not care about jurors' views of the war so long as each juror supported the vets.

To protect themselves, the vets also discussed a stipulation that a figurative sculpture had to be part of the winning design. Such sculptures dated back to antiquity and had withstood the test of time; people related well to them. In the end, however, this stipulation was dropped. The competition was to be thoroughly democratic, which meant not mandating the inclusion or exclusion of any particular idea.

After a lengthy, detailed interviewing process, an extraordinarily prestigious jury—Pietro Belluschi, Harry M. Weese, Garrett Eckbo, Hideo Sasaki, Richard H. Hunt, Constantino Nivola, James Rosati, and Grady Clay—emerged. Included were leaders in the fields of sculpture and landscape architecture. Its members knew war and suffering from personal experience. Among them were combat vets of two world wars. Others had endured fascism before escaping to freedom.

Wheeler made a reading list of books by vets and about Vietnam for the jury. One of its themes came from an exchange in the screenplay of Nikos Kazantzakis's *Zorba the Greek:*

> "Why do the young men die? Why does anybody die? Tell me."
>
> "I don't know."
>
> "What's the use of all your damn books? If they don't tell you that, what the hell do they tell you?"
>
> "They tell me about the agony of men who can't answer questions like yours."

Press attention focused on what the winning design might be. "If this memorial is to be a symbol of reconciliation," *Washington Post* critic Wolf Von Eckardt said, "it must reconcile established notions of 'good art' and popular notions of 'meaningful art.' "

Von Eckardt noted that Americans resist art that is emotionally moving. Not so in Europe, he said. As an example, he cited an Italian memorial, "an enormous granite slab hovering above rows upon rows of stone coffins [that] hold the remains of Italian villagers held hostage and then murdered by the Nazis."

He said the "the simplest yet most haunting memorial . . . is nothing but a dark space built of rough boulders. It is the Hall of Remembrance on Har Harikaron in Jerusalem. On its somber mosaic floor are inscribed the names of 21 of the largest Nazi death camps."

Von Eckardt concluded: "None of these is 'good art' or popular art, abstract or representational, 'modern' or 'traditional.' They are simply powerful ideas translated into a powerful emotional experience."

On Saturday, September 27, 1980. Doubek sat in the office, alone. He was the vet most worried about details, the step-by-step man who always made sure that the VVMF did everything it had to do. He felt there was too much to do and too little time to do it; it was like hanging on to an airplane fuselage by one's fingertips and slowly slipping off. The VVMF needed a statement of purpose for its design competition, and he began to write on a yellow legal pad. Later, after other vets had suggested changes, this draft emerged as the best, most eloquent explanation of what the Memorial was all about:

> While debate and demonstrations raged at home, these servicemen and women underwent challenges equal to or greater than those faced in earlier wars. They experienced confusion, horror, bitterness, boredom, fear, exhaustion, and death.
>
> In facing these ordeals, they showed the same courage, sacrifice, and devotion to duty for which Americans traditionally have honored the nation's war veterans in the past.
>
> The unique nature of the war—with no definite fronts, with vague objectives, with unclear distinctions between ally and enemy, and with strict rules of engagement—subjected the Vietnam soldier to unimaginable pressures.
>
> Because of inequities in the draft system, the brunt of dangerous service fell upon the young, often the socially and economically disadvantaged.
>
> While experiences in combat areas were brutal enough in themselves, their adverse effects were multiplied by the maltreatment received by veterans upon their return home. . . .
>
> The purpose of the Vietnam Veterans Memorial is to recognize and honor those who served and died. It will provide a symbol of acknowledgment of the courage, sacrifice, and devotion to duty of those who were among the nation's finest youth.
>
> The Memorial will make no political statement regarding the war or its conduct. It will transcend those issues. The hope is that the creation of the Memorial will begin a healing process.

Names of the jurors and the statement of purpose were released to the public in early November.

Reaction was overwhelmingly positive. No art critic, no veterans organization, no public official, no Vietnam vet questioned the jury's credentials. No one said it was too liberal or too conservative, too traditional or too modern. The presence of such men simply seemed a victory, an honor to all those who served in Vietnam.

But storm warnings did appear. A *Cincinnati Enquirer* art critic noted, for example, that a glorious, Iwo Jima–type memorial would not work for Vietnam: "[This is] not because there was no victory or because the citizens of the United States held divergent views about American policy in Vietnam, but because the people back home had a chance to watch the war on TV. They saw for themselves that war was not just a matter of flying banners, gallant marches and flashing swords."

And award-winning war correspondent Peter Braestrup laughingly asked what sort of memorial could possibly emerge from their reconciliation theme. "What are you going to do?" he asked Scruggs, Doubek, and Bill Jayne over lunch. "Show a hippie hugging a Marine?"

One day in November, shortly after the news media carried details of the upcoming competition, three Yale University undergraduates drove down to Washington. One of their professors had assigned designing a Vietnam veterans memorial as a classroom project, so they wanted to examine the Memorial site. It was cold, yet the sky was blue and clear. The only other people around were several Frisbee players.

After a few minutes, one of the students decided that the way to build a memorial would be to cut open the earth and to have stone rise up as part of the healing—something that would be like two hands opening to embrace people. She saw the Mall as a living thing that should not be disrupted or destroyed.

She also thought about death. To her, it was an abstract concept. She was 20 years old, and no one she loved had ever died.

MONEY

In late 1980 and early 1981, money—and not the design competition—was the Fund's chief concern. Without enough money, no design, no matter how wonderful, could be built.

Dick Radez had spent the summer of 1980 analyzing the VVMF's fund-raising needs. At a November 1980 board meeting, he made a detailed presentation of how fund-raising worked and what the Fund's real needs would be. Flip charts and flow diagrams highlighted his main points.

"The bottom line," he said, "is that this organization will never build a memorial with the current fund-raising goal of two and a half million dollars. Not on that site of land. Our fund-raising effort must raise between six and ten million dollars. Maybe seven would do it."

Seven million dollars! Sandie Fauriol, a fund-raising professional who had just been hired, realized that her burden had just tripled. But she could not argue. Radez's figures spoke for themselves.

Scruggs chose a long way home that night. He needed time to think. A $10 million project? How could they get that kind of money? Rob a bank? Accept government funds? Send out 40 million pieces of mail? There just wasn't any easy way.

The Fund continued to rely on a fund-raising letter signed by Bob Hope. Its theme was simple: "I hope you share my pride in honoring these young men and women who gave so willingly when their country called."

One million copies of the Bob Hope letter went out on Veterans Day 1980. The goal was to mail another five million in the next twelve months.

As had occurred with all previous mailings, the checks came flowing back. One boy, who had been five years old when his father died in Vietnam, sent $250 he'd been saving for college. "Just promise that my mother and I can come to the dedication and see my dad's name," he said.

"Today is my son's birthday—he would be thirty-one years old," a woman wrote. "He lost his young life in Vietnam on April 15, 1968. I hope his name will be inscribed in memory of my love for him."

The mass mailings and publicity about the Memorial also generated a wide range of grassroots fund-raising activity. A professional race car driver gathered pledges for every lap he drove in the Indianapolis 500. A seventh-grade English class raised $634.75. A cash-poor Texas rancher pledged all proceeds from the eventual sale of two zebu cattle. One vet purchased an M-16 rifle for $400, sold $1,000 in raffle tickets, and mailed in the profits. In Florida young women in bikinis stopped cars at red lights and asked for money. All across the country, dinner dances, bingo games, bake sales, garage sales, concerts, and walkathons—thousands of them organized by local American Legion and VFW chapters—kept the dollars flowing in.

But not all vets supported the concept of a memorial. One winner of three Purple Hearts was traveling across the country making parachute jumps to help publicize the need for vets counseling and jobs programs. He told reporters that the idea for a memorial was a "crock." The best memorial, he said, "is to compensate us and treat us [decently]."

Scruggs loved such opposition. That was what the Memorial was all about. Get out there and kick ass. Make the country care.

THE HOSTAGES RETURN

Ever since 1979, professional fund-raisers had been warning that Vietnam vets were not hot. You'd have better luck raising funds for handicapped kids or cancer research, the pros said.

But the nation's attitude was changing. Since 1975, Americans had been seeing real baby-killers in Cambodia, so the days of calling every Vietnam vet a "baby-killer" seemed to be ending. Americans had also seen thousands of boat people risk suffering and death to escape the North Vietnamese communists—the people America's GI's had stood up to fight.

Indeed, during the 1980 presidential campaign, Republican Ronald Reagan called service in Vietnam "an act of moral courage" in a "noble cause." Although many voters still regarded such views as heresy, Reagan won.

Then, on January 20, 1981, the day Reagan was inaugurated, Iran released the 52 Americans it had been holding hostage. Over 1,200 media personnel greeted them in West Germany, climaxing 444 days of press attention that had transformed each hostage into a national hero.

This media overload broke the silence of nearly a decade. Until January 1981, America's agreement with its vets seemed to be: Don't ask the vets about Vietnam, and they won't talk about it.

Now the men who fought no longer found this arrangement acceptable.

"On the television, in the papers, every time one turned the dial on a radio, there was some new piece of thanks to the hostages for having sat out 444 days of their lives," James Webb wrote in the *Washington Post.* "Free baseball tickets forever—good seats. Free trips to Florida. Here is a hostage calling home. There is a hostage jogging. Here is a congressman proposing special benefits, gold medallions. Gold medallions? Parades. Yes, real motorcar parades. . . . Honest . . . none of us [Vietnam vets] really had the audacity to expect we might get free baseball tickets when we got back. But at least you could have noticed that we went."

Across the country, envy, hurt, anger, and anguish came out. Vets holding up "What About Agent Orange?" signs during parades for the hostages. Vets talking to each other for the first time since combat ended. Vets calling newspapers. "It's damned unfair," one Massachusetts vet complained in a story that received national circulation. "I walk with a limp, from the shrapnel, and it got to the point where I'd say I got it in a car accident rather than say I was a vet. It's funny. I come back feeling like a fool and they come back feeling like heroes." Another vet told reporters, "They got a parade. The only thing we got was a burnt steak at the discharge station."

Families of vets also demanded that the nation notice their pain. One woman whose son had died in Vietnam found old wounds causing new pain. Like thousands of others, she wrote to the VVMF. "On one occasion when I took a package to the post office to be sent to him, not knowing if he would ever receive it," she said, "I was told by the postal clerk that anyone in Vietnam didn't deserve to get a package."

Scruggs was in the crowd as tens of thousands of Washingtonians cheered the returning hostages. There were flags, fireworks, tears, and schoolchildren with handmade signs. The crowd roared as each hostage's name was read off. It was like a Hollywood extravaganza.

Scruggs looked over at the vacant site where the Vietnam Veterans Memorial might stand someday. He thought about what it would be like to read off 58,000 names. The country will remember, he promised himself. The country will remember.

The hostages were heroes that unified America. Their welcome home, Vietnam Veterans of America chief Bobby Muller told reporters, "provides the nation an opportunity to reflect on all Americans who in times of national stress have put their lives on the line."

Slowly, the media—and the American people—began to respond. "The returning hostages served to unite us in a time when we needed it," wrote *Atlanta Constitution* columnist Bob Ingle. "So while we feel that way, let's get on with the memorial for the people who deserve it. No man or woman should ever be ashamed of serving this country, much less have to lie about it."

The owner of one elegant New York City restaurant closed it to the public and invited 50 vets and their friends and families to a special thank-you dinner. Red, white, and blue ribbons hung from the ceiling as the owner served salmon mousse and champagne. A table for two was left empty in honor of those who died and those who had killed themselves since returning home. But the most telling moment came before the first guest arrived. When the restaurateur told her chef, a man she had known for many years, about her plans, the chef started to cry. "Madame," he said, "I had a son killed in Vietnam."

Amid the emotions, it was hard to tell just how much—if at all—this new mood was helping fund-raising. Then the first figures were ready. Money was coming in at a much faster pace. The average contribution and the percentage of those who contributed increased dramatically. The Ayatollah Khomeini was helping to solve the Fund's money problems.

One other important shift had taken place in America. As of January 1981, for the first time in at least a quarter-century, conservatives controlled the executive and legislative branches of the federal government. Liberals were in a political tailspin. Senator Edward M. Kennedy had been defeated in his 1979–80 quest for the White House. George McGovern and other leading antiwar spokesmen had been defeated in their re-election campaigns.

The new Secretary of the Interior was an archconservative named James Watt, whom columnist George F. Will described as "a man to whom conflict . . . is the syrup on the flapjack of life."

Watt had to grant a construction permit before the Memorial could be built. He had never served in the military. But he described himself as a strong patriot, and there seemed to be no cause for concern.

ENTRIES

Opportunities like this did not come along very often. For an entry fee of $20, someone would win $20,000, and their work would be placed on the Mall for as long as the United States of America continued to exist. Anyone who was an American citizen could enter.

During January, the entries trickled in. From their registration forms, it was clear they included the nation's best architects, designers, and artists. By February, entries were arriving at the rate of several hundred a week. Anonymity was strictly observed. Contestants taped their names in sealed envelopes on the back of their submissions, which were given a number and stored in a warehouse. They remained forbidden fruit, unopened.

When the March 31 deadline arrived, the Fund had received 1,421 entries—probably more than any other open art competition in history. If set side by side, the submissions would stretch for 1.3 miles.

Such a response confirmed that the Memorial had touched a nerve in the American imagination, but it also created a serious logistical problem. The entries had to be unpacked and hung at eye level for the jury to examine, but no warehouse in the capital area was large enough to hold all of them. Vietnam vet Joseph Zengerle, then an assistant secretary of the Air Force, saved the day. He arranged for the Fund to use a gigantic hangar at Andrews Air Force Base, just outside Washington. This location was especially attractive because the Air Force could provide round-the-clock security guards for the Memorial designs. It was not unreasonable to think that some antiwar or antimilitary group might want to burn them or blow them up as a symbolic protest.

At Yale, the young architecture student had submitted her ideas to the class for discussion. She had created what she called an "architectural pun," a row of falling dominoes in front of a wall of names. The other students convinced her that these stones cluttered the design. They also tried to get her to change the color of the stone from black to white.

When he examined her clay model carefully, Professor Andrus Burr said he liked her basic conception, but that she "had to make the angle mean something." He also encouraged her to make the listing of the names chronological.

The student saw her design more as "visual poetry" than as a work of architecture. In all, work on it took less than six weeks.

On the last day that entries could be submitted, a friend gave her a ride to the post office so she could mail her design to Washington.

6

APRIL 26, 1981: NATIONAL DAY OF RECOGNITION

ON FEBRUARY 24, 1981, President Reagan presented the Congressional Medal of Honor to Roy P. Benavidez, a retired Army sergeant. It had been lost in bureaucratic red tape for over a decade. Like most of the other 239 Medals of Honor awarded for Vietnam service, it was being given to a soldier who risked everything for his fellow GI's. On May 2, 1968, Benavidez had saved eight Green Berets, while he himself was seriously wounded and experiencing heavy enemy fire. "They [the vets] were greeted by no parades, no bands, no waving of the flag they so proudly served," Reagan said. "It's time to show our pride in them and and thank them."

A few weeks later, the President once again asked America to honor its Vietnam vets. He officially proclaimed April 26 a National Day of Recognition for Veterans of the Vietnam Era.

Despite emotions generated by the hostage release, the Day of Recognition generated little public response. Only 50 people turned out in Philadelphia; a ceremony in Minneapolis attracted less than 100 people.

To help draw attention to the Vietnam Memorial, two vets—one former infantryman and one former paratrooper—walked 818 miles from Jacksonville, Illinois, to the Mall in Washington, D.C. American Legion posts along the way gave them food, shelter, and moral support; and at the Ohio-Indiana border they were joined by Homer Tutor, whose son had been killed in Vietnam. "My wife and I want to see our son's name on the monument," he explained. He had intended only to cross Ohio with the two ex-GI's, but stayed all the way to Washington.

About 150 people, including vets on crutches and in wheelchairs, joined the walkers as they crossed the Potomac. "It would have been nice to have a bigger reception for these guys," Scruggs told reporters. "Well, maybe the Americans killed in Vietnam don't mean that much to a lot of people." He looked at the small crowd. Representatives of veterans organizations were there, but where were the senators and congressmen, and generals and admirals?

"I don't know what is wrong with us," a CBS commentator noted. "President Reagan [is] trying to cut out a measly twelve million dollars that supports neighborhood outreach centers that help Vietnam vets who still can't adjust to what happened to them on our behalf. And Vietnam Veterans Recognition Day gets no recognition.

"A lot of us hated the war, but I never thought we hated our fellow citizens whom we sent out there to do the fighting for us. . . . If all the people who go through Arlington so reverently every day would send a dollar to the Memorial Fund, we could erase part of the stain of dishonor our forgetting these veterans has brought to us."

THE JURY DELIBERATES

On Friday, March 14, businessman Ross Perot announced that he would underwrite the design competition—at a cost of $160,000. "They served with honor and are every bit as much heroes as are the veterans of every war since the American Revolution," he told reporters.

Some of the vets were upset. Acting on his own, Scruggs had solicited and accepted a sizable contribution. From one perspective, this was great. For a small organization, no $160,000 donation could be easily ignored. But Perot's generosity might make him feel he had a special license to comment on whatever design was eventually selected.

On the day the entries were trucked to Andrews AFB, Doubek realized that an unforeseen problem had to be solved. Pigeons were living in the empty hangar and would drop their waste on the artwork. A suggestion was made: "Buy some pellet guns and the guards will take care of it while on duty," the officer suggested.

The jury was scheduled to conduct its deliberations from Monday, April 27, to Friday, May 1, when it would present its recommendation to the VVMF.

On Sunday evening, April 26, the Fund hosted a dinner for volunteers and jurors and their spouses at a fancy restaurant. It was a way to say thank you for the thousands of unpaid work hours. Doubek had warned everyone not even to hint at what sort of memorial was wanted, so the evening was filled with much joking and small talk. But unspoken fears dominated the veterans' thinking. They had given an extraordinary responsibility to men they barely knew, most old enough to be their fathers or grandfathers. What if the the jury came up with something lousy? Or controversial? Or insulting? Anything could happen. Plenty could go wrong.

The dinner's highlight came when one juror became drunk. He rambled on about war and death, and then tried to drink his chocolate mousse.

Right before the evening ended, Scruggs gave the jurors a pep talk. "Do your best," he said. As he left the room, Scruggs thought, These guys are the same age as the people who sent us to 'Nam.

On Monday morning, the jurors met and selected Grady Clay, editor of *Landscape Architecture* and an expert on urban development, as their chairman.

For one hour they reviewed the competition requirements and discussed the principles behind the Memorial. It was to make no political statement, and it was to promote healing.

They then spread out to examine the 1,421 entries, each of which had been hung at eye level for easy viewing. The proposed memorials came in all shapes, including circles, semicircles, squares, Corinthian columns, miniature Lincoln memorials, and peace signs. There were towers, hovering helicopters, a giant Army helmet, mausoleums, abstract figures, and obelisks. Each juror had committed himself to examine every entry at least once.

That evening, a friend of one of the juror's bumped into him at their hotel in Georgetown.

"What's the quality of the entries?" the friend asked.

"About what you'd expect."

"How's it going?"

"Very strange. One keeps haunting me."

By noon on Tuesday, 1,189 submissions had been eliminated. The remaining 232 were placed together for further examination and discussion.

That evening, the juror once again saw his friend. The juror shook his head. "It's still haunting me," he said.

The only VVMF official to enter the hangar during this period was Doubek, who made sure that the the jurors received whatever logistical backup they needed. He was able to see the process of elimination, and knew something strange was happening. Number 1026 kept surviving the cut. He looked at 1026 over and over again. For the life of me, I can't figure out what it is, he kept thinking.

Scruggs did not sleep well that week. Every night he would come home and ask his wife, Becky, "What if this fails? What if Wheeler was right and a vet should have been on the jury? What if this group of old fellows screws us with some abstract avant-garde work of art that no one can relate to? What if we let everyone down?"

She could only reply, "Don't worry so much. Things have always worked out."

By Thursday, the jury was down to the final 39 entries. Fifteen would receive honorable mention. There would be a third place finisher, a runner-up, and a winner.

Number 1026 generated the most comments: "There's no escape from its power." "A confused age needs a simple solution." "Totally eloquent." "He knows what he's doing, all right." "Presents both solitude and a challenge." "No other place in the world like that." "As though the ground had subsided away, leaving the rock on which are the names." "Shielded from street noise." "People come and experience it, not merely look at it." "Looks back to death and forward to life." "Note the reflectiveness." "Symbolizes the slow start and slow finish to the war in Vietnam." "It's easy to love it." "Visitors can come here and pay homage." "Not a thing of joy, but a large space for hope." "Quiet, a place speaking of acceptance." "Reverential." "Shows the evolution of the war."

When they finished a detailed discussion of the final three, Grady Clay polled the jurors. The unanimous winner was Number 1026.

He polled the jury again: 1026.

Spreiregen spoke to both Doubek and Scruggs that night.

"Do we have a beauty?" Scruggs asked.

"I think so. The jury was unanimous. But I feel a little uneasy about how you may react."

Scruggs drove with Don Schaet through a heavy rainstorm to Andrews AFB on Friday morning. As they entered the hangar, they saw rows and rows of designs hung on metal braces. It was breathtaking. The competititors had obviously invested an extraordinary amount of time and talent. Even the bad designs seemed to be in good taste. People had put heart and soul into their efforts. You could tell just from looking.

Scruggs walked off by himself to calm down. The Memorial was really going to happen! The names were going up on the Mall!

A flapping sound distracted him. Flopping along the floor was a wounded, bloody pigeon.

Jack Wheeler, Bob Doubek, Sandie Fauriol, John Woods, Bob Frank, Art Mosley, George Mayo, Karen Doubek, Kathie Kielich, Don Schaet, and Jan Scruggs sat on metal chairs facing the jurors.

Paul Spreiregen stood and described the process by which a winner had been selected. The words poured out. "Unanimous decision." "One of the most profound memorials ever built." "Exciting."

A juror went behind the curtain and brought out the number-three design, which would receive a $5,000 award. Scruggs recognized the work of Frederick Hart. It was great. Beautiful. He could not wait to see the next one.

The second-place winner, which would receive $10,000, looked weird to Scruggs. It was like a giant pile of twisted steel dumped on two marble pillars.

He pushed deeper into his chair, and felt good. The next one would be a winner, a great design.

Then it came. A big bat. A weird-looking thing that could have been from Mars. Scruggs smiled. Maybe a third-grader had entered the competition and won. All the Fund's work had gone into making a huge bat for veterans. Maybe it symbolized a boomerang—the names of dead GI's bouncing back right in front of the White House and Congress—where it had all begun.

Silence hit. One second. Two seconds. Three seconds.

Wheeler felt the confusion around him. It was hard to envision the pastel sketches as finished stone. But he began to see it: massive, longer than a football field. Every name. *Every* name.

The moment was slipping away. It was time for commitment. "This is a work of genius," Wheeler said.

The group applauded.

Jury chairman Grady Clay had joined Spreiregen in explaining the winner: "Of all the proposals submitted, this most clearly meets the spirit and formal requirements of the program. . . . This memorial with its wall of names becomes a place of quiet reflection and a tribute to those who served their nation in difficult times. . . . All who come here can find it a place of healing. . . . The designer has created an eloquent place where the simple setting of earth, sky, and remembered names contains messages for all who will know this place."

Spreiregen pointed out that the honorable mentions came from a solid geographic cross-section of America—Iowa, Texas, Michigan, Arizona, California, New York, New Jersey, Virginia, Minnesota, Indiana, Maryland . . .

The vets then asked some tough questions. How will GI's who did not die be honored? How will we explain this strange design to the public? How will it affect fund-raising? How much will it cost to construct?

The jurors worked hard to explain their decision. The design, they said, would stand the test of time. It was not a retreat to past notions of glory. It was not a *war* memorial; it was a memorial to honor service. But it would be controversial.

Some of the jurors' answers were were less than satisfying. The design, they said, was still at the idea stage. During "design refinement" the vets could make adjustments, such as adding an inscription to honor all of those who served.

The vets immediately recognized that they had a tremendous public relations problem. The drawings looked terrible. At least five minutes of explanation were necessary before the design could be understood. "If people say we're putting up a black hole," Wheeler warned, "we're going to get murdered."

"Great art is a complex matter," Clay responded. "All great works furnish material for endless debate. We are certain this will be debated for years to come. This is healthy and ought to be expected. All knowledge cannot be self-explaining in two seconds."

The jurors thought one enemy lay waiting: government bureaucrats who would "chew up" the design during the approval process.

The vets had expected that the winner would be a prominent professional working with a prestigious firm. Doubek looked up Number 1026. "Maya Ying Lin." An Oriental name. She was 21 years old. She lived in New Haven, Connecticut. Wheeler recognized the address. An undergraduate residence at Yale.

Doubek shouted, "This started as one man's dream. Let's hear what he thinks."

Scruggs walked to the front. "Well," he said, "I really like it. It's a great memorial." He kept smiling as everyone clapped and cheered. But he was thinking, It's weird and I wish I knew what the hell it is.

The vets could have rejected the design. Or they could have told the jury, Thanks for your recommendation, we want to think about it. Instead, they voted unanimously to endorse the jury's action. Most were already convinced that they had a great work of art.

"Do you really think this thing is going to go over with the general public?" Scruggs whispered to John Woods.

"You would be surprised how sophisticated the general public really is."

"I sure as hell hope you're right."

MAYA YING LIN

Maya Lin never expected to win.

She felt the American people would never accept a memorial that said war is sad. She also knew that she had not presented her ideas with any professional polish. Her grade in the class had been a B. In virtually everything else, she received A's.

A call came from someone named Schaet. "Don't get excited, and please don't tell anyone about this call," he said. "We're coming up to talk to you."

She still could not understand.

The VVMF knew that selling the design concept would be extremely important. Maya Lin, whoever she was, would need a crash course in how to handle a Washington press conference.

The same day that Doubek called her, Memorial Fund staffers Sandie Fauriol, Don Schaet, and Kathie Kielich flew to New Haven. They met Maya Lin in her dormitory room. She sat and fingered her pork-pie hat—the type Frank Lloyd Wright had worn—while Schaet discussed how important the Memorial was.

"Come on," Kielich finally said. "Tell her."

Schaet took a deep breath. "You've won. First prize."

Maya Lin continued to finger the hat and showed no emotion.

She arranged to postpone one of her final exams, and the next day she flew down to Washington.

Everyone in the VVMF office applauded and cheered when she walked in. She just smiled.

Maya Lin spent the weekend rehearsing for the press conference at which her design would be unveiled. The vets learned more about her. She had been born in 1959, the year of the first official American combat casualty in Vietnam; she had been nine years old when the Tet offensive occurred; she cared little about politics and knew little about the war in Vietnam. She had grown up in the small college town of Athens, Ohio, where her parents settled after fleeing mainland China when it fell to the communists in 1949. Although she came from a family with a long artistic line—her grandparents had socialized with H. G. Wells, E. M. Forster, Thomas Hardy, and Bertrand Russell—she considered herself a typical Midwesterner. She had grown up with no sense of ethnic identity, and as a teenager worked at McDonald's.

The vets liked her. She was smart and sincere. That she was young, an amateur, Oriental, and a woman would only help the Memorial by demonstrating how open the competition had been. But the seeds for future trouble were planted early. At lunch, Scruggs explained to her how important it was to meet the Veterans Day 1982 goal for dedicating the Memorial. "You're all so militaristic," she responded.

On May 3, Scruggs was in San Francisco to speak at the Independent Petroleum Association of America about the Memorial. His telephone rang at 8:30 A.M. It was Ross Perot. "What's the design?"

No one was supposed to discuss the winner until the press conference. But Scruggs had to make a quick decision. Perot had already donated nearly $160,000. He was a heavy hitter. Scruggs described Maya Lin's design.

"You've made a big, big mistake," Perot said. "It'll only be nice for the guys who died."

Suddenly, a shouting match seemed to start. "It's not heroic," Perot said.

"Yes, it is."

"It's something for New York intellectuals."

"You don't understand."

"It's twenty-first-century art."

"That's only what you think."

Scruggs was very upset. It was not every day that he fought with a billionaire. He called Senator Warner and told him what had happened. "Don't worry," Warner said. "Perot's opinionated. Just keep charging forward, working on getting enough money."

On Wednesday, May 6, wire service keys clicked in news bureaus across Washington:

> *Event:* Announcement of winning design of a memorial to be placed on the Mall to honor Vietnam veterans; to be announced by Vietnam Veterans Memorial Fund.
>
> *Time:* 10:30 AM
>
> *Location:* American Institute of Architects, 1735 New York Avenue, NW, Washington, DC.

Several dozen reporters, including numerous camera crews, showed up. Doubek pulled back the sheet covering a model of the design, and Maya Lin read a statement explaining it. All the journalists applauded.

On the surface, the press conference went very well. Maya Lin was direct in answering questions. Why was it black? Why is it underground? The design, she said, "evokes feelings, thoughts, and emotions. . . . It does not scream anything. It is strong in its understatement. It is strong in its simplicity. It is not a banner's blaring. It is not loud. I do not think that makes it less beautiful. It is different."

"Does it make a difference, you being Oriental?" someone asked.

"I don't see why it should," she responded.

The applause and the ease were deceptive. By the time they picked up the next day's newspapers, the vets knew they had made at least four mistakes.

First, the model, which had been specially made for the press conference, did not photograph well. It was supposed to show how the design would look in its final three-dimensional form. Instead it looked like Maya Lin's rendition: two black lines.

Second, Scruggs said, "The Memorial says exactly what we wanted to say about Vietnam—absolutely nothing." He meant that the design was absolutely apolitical. It was a stupid comment. It sounded as though the design did not honor the vets' service.

Maya Lin also made an innocent yet deadly statement. Explaining how the design concept evolved, she said, "I wanted to describe a journey—a journey which would make you experience death." This prompted many people to conclude that the Memorial only honored those vets who died in Vietnam—leaving unhonored the nearly 2.7 million who served and survived.

And Doubek too made an error. *Washington Post* reporter Henry Allen, himself a Vietnam veteran, asked, "Is the word 'Vietnam' on the Memorial?" The truthful answer was that Maya Lin's design did not mention Vietnam, and that the vets needed time to discuss what, if any, inscription should be added.

But Doubek said, "Is George Washington's name on the Washington Monument?"

These mistakes did not seem serious amid the avalanche of favorable press reaction. The *New York Times* proclaimed that the design's "extreme dignity and restraint honors these veterans with more poignancy, surely, than more conventional monuments. . . . This design seems to capture all of the feelings of ambiguity and anguish that the Vietnam War evoked in this nation."

The *Washington Star* said, "There is pride, as well as a reconciliation, in the memorial. The men who fought honorably in Vietnam are themselves honoring their comrades, but inviting us to share as we may not have, as a nation and as individuals."

The *Cleveland Plain Dealer* noted the "understated brilliance of the design." The *Christian Science Monitor* called it "a visual document of frozen passions." The Albuquerque, New Mexico, *Tribune* said it "will speak more eloquently to future generations than the most grandiose and imposing monuments." Wolf Von Eckardt of the *Washington Post* said, "It seemed too much to expect that a worthy memorial could emerge from the mess that was Vietnam. But it did."

Of the nation's major critics, only the *Chicago Tribune*'s Paul Gapp attacked the design. He called it inane, an erosion control project. "We have been told [by other critics] that Miss Lin's design is perfect because it reflects the feelings of ambiguity Americans have about the Viet Nam War," Gapp wrote. "It is not my impression, however, that anybody has ambiguous feelings about the 57,692 men and women who *died* in the war. The memorial's message should be about *them* should it not?"

Gapp predicted that "the Vietnam memorial as presently envisioned will never be built (even assuming that the $7 million will be raised, which itself is doubtful)."

The Fund expected some criticism no matter what sort of design it selected. Every major memorial in Washington seemed to have caused some sort of fight. The Washington Monument had been called ugly and the work of an architect with nothing else to do. The Jefferson Memorial was called "academic, dreary and pompous" by the commission that selected its chief architect. The Lincoln Memorial had triggered bitter arguments between Northern and Southern congressmen. "In nearly 200 years of trying, we have discovered no universal solution to the complex problem of designing a public monument or memorial that is aesthetically satisfying and symbolically appropriate," Benjamin Forgey of the *Washington Post* now noted.

War memorials were not exempt. Many stimulated opposition from the men being honored. In 1882, for example, an elaborate new sculpture honoring Civil War veterans was unveiled. "I have only one fault to find," General Philip H. Sheridan said. "It's fireproof." Several years later, a Northern sculptor won a competition to design a statue of General Robert E. Lee, to be erected in the former Confederate capital of Richmond. General Jubal A. Early promptly promised to "get together all the surviving members of the Second Corps and blow it up with dynamite." Another competition was held.

A Vietnam veterans memorial bore a special burden. It had to satisfy audiences with conflicting needs and expectations. It was for Vietnam veterans and their families, and also belonged to the vast majority of Americans who were never directly affected by Vietnam. It had to meet the emotional needs of the Vietnam generation, yet also stimulate and educate generations who would know Vietnam only through history books. Furthermore, there was no such thing as "the war in Vietnam." There had been many wars. The people back home had fought about

Vietnam while their soldiers fought in Vietnam. And the soldiers themselves had vastly differing opinions and experiences. Some had served in combat; others had been safe and comfortable throughout their tours. Some had arrived in Indochina during the idealistic anything-is-possible years. Others had risked their lives long after America had clearly demonstrated lack of either ability or will to win. Some vets saw the war as a principled and necessary defense of freedom; others viewed it as a mistaken policy pursued via stupid military tactics.

On top of all this, the design was difficult to comprehend. Even experienced, trained experts sometimes needed lengthy explanations before they could understand what the Memorial would be. And even then they often came away with different images. They called it a body count on the Mall, a wound in Mother Earth, and an open book. Such ambiguity, however, was part of the design's strength.

It did not dictate a point of view. Instead, it used the names as a common denominator. Every veteran and every American could find reason to honor those who loved their country enough to serve it during difficult times.

The anticipated dissent did not emerge. Members of Congress examined the model at a special Capitol Hill showing, and all apparently came away with praise. In fact, Armed Services Committee chairman John Tower (R-Tex) later said that the design did more than honor vets. It reminded everyone that America should never again send her sons to fight a war she did not intend to win.

The publications of most veterans organizations carried pictures of Maya Lin's creation, and asked members to contribute to the VVMF. The most emotionally significant vote of support came from the American Gold Star Mothers, whose official publication commented by reprinting a *New York Times* editorial:

> It used to be much simpler to build a monument. The roll of honor on bronze tablets, or the statue of the fallen warrior holding a flag appeared predictably on the village green. Anonymous generals and unknown soldiers furnish innumerable traffic islands. Forgotten heroes dot the nation's parks. The uniform changes, the heroes sit or stand or occasionally ride a horse, but the message remains the same: a noble cause well served.
>
> Nowadays, though, patriotism is a complicated matter.

> Ideas about heroism, or art, for that matter, are no longer what they were before Vietnam. And there is certainly no consensus yet about what cause might have been served by the Vietnam War.
>
> But perhaps that is why the V-shaped, black granite lines merging gently with the sloping earth make the winning design seem a lasting and appropriate image of dignity and sadness. It conveys the only point about the war on which people may agree: that those who died should be remembered.

The Gold Star Mothers were not asking for glory. They knew the reality of war. They wanted their sons to be remembered and honored, not to have died in vain. They wanted future generations to look at their sons' names and ponder service, sacrifice and commitment—the grand ideals without which a democracy cannot long survive.

Within a week, the American people started to register their opinion. Fund-raising, especially among veterans groups, flourished. When a weekend radiothon began at a major shopping center at 3:00 P.M. on a Friday, the vets agreed they'd be happy with $35,000. By 6:00 P.M. on Sunday, they had $250,000.

Only hours into the radiothon, the broadcasters were mobbed. Vets and their families stopped by to tell their stories. Former POW's came to plead for funds. Fathers brought their children to give small change and dollars. People signed over Social Security and disability checks. A young Marine whose best friend had died in his arms came by because he had to see it for himself. A vet arrived wearing the uniform he'd hidden since his return from combat. Another wore medals that had been in a bottom drawer. Nonvets came in with grocery bags filled with cash they'd collected at parties. Cars on nearby highways stopped and people lined up at telephone booths to make pledges. It was emotional and magic and somewhat unbelievable. "What *is* going on out there?" a reporter asked Scruggs. He could only answer, "Hooray, America."

The magic continued. A third-grade class sold T-shirts to raise money in honor of Mike Frey, a Vietnam vet who had been totally paralyzed when he was nineteen. In a ceremony held in the Pottstown, Pennsylvania, town square, they gave Scruggs over $1,000. Speaking through a tube inserted in his windpipe, Mike sent the children a message. "I was aware there was danger over there," he said. "I suppose I believe in patriotism, and that's why I enlisted. I'm glad I did."

Tens of thousands of letters containing checks arrived. Many were from former antiwar activists, whom the VVMF had once considered their most likely opponents. "There are those of us who might have fought because of our age, but we didn't because of what we believed," said one letter writer. "We know what happened to those who fought—and to ourselves. We watched, we hurt, we cried. We know who died for us."

But the public had no legal power over the design. The Fine Arts Commission and other federal agencies could examine Maya Lin's work and tell the vets to start all over again. The approval process offered little predictability and no guarantees. The FDR Memorial, which had been fully funded by Congress, had been slowly dying for decades at agencies that refused to grant approval.

Remarkably, no problems appeared for the Vietnam Veterans Memorial. On July 20, after public hearings, Fine Arts Commission chairman J. Carter Brown wrote to the vets that the Commission had "voted unanimously to approve the proposed memorial." Brown was known as the nation's "arbiter of excellence," a man who would not compromise, and who called the Mall "sacred turf." Thus, when he said that "the design has a simplicity and sense of dignity that befits an important memorial for this site and complements the character of the park," the vets had won a tremendous victory.

On August 6, also after open hearings, the National Capital Planning Commission unanimously approved the design.

Of course, as with all architectural projects, design development would be needed before final approval could be granted by the Fine Arts Commission and the National Capital Planning Commission. Maya Lin's rudimentary drawings had to be transformed into an actual memorial.

Maya Lin lacked the experience and professional skills needed to complete the project by herself. Indeed, trained architects explained to her that they never could have created her design, because they would have known about all the difficulties involved in actually building such a memorial.

Thus, the VVMF hired the Washington architecture firm headed by Kent Cooper and William Lecky, who had worked on Washington's Dulles Airport, the National Zoo, and other complex projects. The firm, in turn, hired Maya Lin as a design consultant.

Foremost among the problems was where to actually put the Memorial. Congress had given two acres of land. Maya Lin had devised a design with one wall facing the Washington Monument, and the other pointing toward the Lincoln Memorial. It could go anywhere in the two acres.

Cooper and Maya Lin spent hours walking up and down the site searching for the sweet spot, the exact right place. There were no rules to go by; it had to come from the gut. They would stop, stretch out ribbon the length of the Memorial, and move it around. When they found a place that looked good, they'd stake out the ribbon and go to the top of the Washington Monument to see how it looked.

Ten feet in any given direction could make a huge difference. It changed the foreground and background, the whole sense of the Memorial.

When they found a spot that looked as though it might be good, they left the stakes in overnight. The next morning, the stakes were gone. The National Park Service had removed them. That afternoon they again found what seemed like the perfect place, so they drove their stakes in close to the ground so the Park Service wouldn't notice they were there.

Searching for hours the next day produced nothing. The stakes were too low to the ground. "There's only one thing we can do," Cooper said. "Let's start back from the beginning and try to find the perfect place." They paced and tested angles and finally found the ideal spot. Then they knelt down to put in new stakes. There, right in front of them, were the missing stakes.

Other problems they solved included providing access for the handicapped, devising a small trip wall so people would not walk off the top, and placing a slight curve along the top so that the walls would not seem to be tilting backwards.

Cooper also devised a design with panels of names that could be replaced in case political extremists ever bombed the Memorial as a symbolic protest against the U.S. government.

He never conceived of the Memorial, however, as being especially popular, and always envisioned it as a deserted—although beautiful—part of the Mall.

Over at the Interior Department, Secretary Watt had the power to disapprove the design if he acted within ninety days. As the paperwork passed through routine channels at Interior, he raised no objections.

Each of the vets was developing his own opinion of Maya Lin's design. Some had started out not liking it. A sense of discipline, of faith in the process through which it had been selected, prompted them to give it the benefit of the doubt. Then, as the summer of 1981 passed, each developed an emotional attachment to the design. The more they thought about it, the more they liked it. Their interpretations were different, yet all somehow the same. The Memorial would always be a place where you could express love. It would remind the country that it could never escape responsibility for its actions. It would place the Vietnam veteran fully within the scope of American history.

They did not know that the hard part was only beginning.

7

THE VETS AND MAYA LIN

THE VETS had not set out to contribute a great work of art to America. Their only goal was to honor those who served. As far as they were concerned, Maya Lin's design had nothing to do with minimalism, modernism, or any other school of artistic endeavor. Her design worked, and that was all they cared about. They best understood Maya Lin not by trying to categorize her but by examining the influences that had worked upon her.

She had never taken a college-level history course. She had never read a book or seen a TV film clip about Vietnam. And she had never read *All Quiet on the Western Front, A Farewell to Arms,* or any of the other basic literature on war.

She told reporters, "I don't read the papers. I just ignore the world. It's like everything is up in my head [with] no real concrete experiential reality." Her favorite writer was the Argentine Jorge Luis Borges, who wrote stories with titles such as "Everything and Nothing," "The Modesty of History," and "A New Refutation of Time."

The artists she most admired were Dan Flavin, Robert Irwin, and James Turrell—selected because their work featured imaginative utilization of light.

Her mother called her a "modern American," and yet Maya Lin devised a design in which many experts saw a strong Oriental influence. Oriental philosophy, for example, often describes life and death as part of a continuous circle. Likewise, Maya Lin described her design as a circle. One part is the two arms of the wall. The final segment of the circle is the living person who visits, and through his presence fills in the part of the circle that has been omitted.

Whatever had shaped her, Maya Lin's work clearly fit in with America's changing tastes in war memorials. When seen from this perspective, her design was not so startling.

The traditional war memorial had demonstrated a strong Greek or Roman influence, often with allegorical images such as an eagle for strength and courage, palm leaves for victory, and a woman in a long dress for peace. After the Civil War, Walt Whitman said that the traditional war memorial was outdated, a prediction apparently confirmed by the designs that followed World War I—and which had the greatest influence on Maya Lin. She cited one in particular. Located in Thiepval, France, it is the memorial to the dead of the Somme offensive. It has a great arch, with arch tunnels along two axes, which are inscribed with 73,000 names. It is a geometric abstraction that is sensitive to the surrounding landscape, and which greets visitors like a great scream.

Maya Lin, who studied this memorial before entering the VVMF design competition, said the arch at Thiepval was a "journey from violence to serenity"—a description that closely parallels her explanation of the Vietnam Veterans Memorial.

The combination of geometric form and names to honor service in war was also used by Yale University. Virtually every day she was at Yale, Maya Lin walked past the walls inscribed with the names of other Yale students who died in America's wars. She was present when Yale University dedicated the Vietnam portion of this memorial.

Despite their initial liking of her, Maya Lin and most of the vets did not get along. Perhaps this was inevitable. A generational gap separated the designer from the vets. Her generation was a clean slate; theirs had been defined by a cataclysmic event. They could not understand her detachment. She did not seem to feel emotions, and sometimes wondered aloud whether she was "too cold and cynical" in her approach to death. To her, it still seemed to be an abstraction, a design problem. Perhaps such detachment was necessary to create the design, but it did not help her relationship with the vets, each of whom loved people whose names were going on the wall.

She had long hair and wore jeans and an oversized man's shirt; even at press conferences she often dressed like what she was: a young undergraduate. "As long as you look like a hippie, you'll be treated like a hippie," one vet said. "Don't change your appearance for us. Do it for your design."

Sometimes she listened. Often she complained—"You're treating me like a little girl"—and did what she wanted.

All of this could have been overcome, but the possessiveness felt by Maya Lin and the vets could not. She thought it was her design. They believed they defined the Memorial through the competition guidelines and through the majestic location they had obtained. Her contribution had been crucial, even essential, but it did not make the Memorial *hers.*

Publicity added to the problem of possessiveness. Maya Lin became an instant national celebrity. The media called it "her memorial," and the vets would pick up newspapers and see her picture and read the news that she had been sighted in Washington's chic Georgetown section. Yet these same newspapers would carry nothing about vets and what was happening to them.

Maya Lin did have vaguely defined legal rights to preserve her original creation. So some of the vets worked hard to explain the two major changes they wanted.

First, her design called for names to be listed in the chronological order of their death. Maya Lin argued that chronological listing was essential to her design. The wall would read like an epic Greek poem. Vets would find their story told, and their friends remembered, in the panel that corresponded with their tour of duty in Vietnam. Locating specific names with the aid of a directory would be like finding bodies on a battlefield.

Some vets initially disagreed. If some 58,000 names were scattered along the wall, anyone looking for a specific name would wander around for hours and then leave in frustration. One solution seemed obvious: List everyone in alphabetical order.

But when the vets examined a two-inch-thick Defense Department listing of Vietnam casualties, their thinking changed. There were over

600 Smiths; 16 people named James Jones had died in Vietnam. Alphabetical listing would make the Memorial look like a telephone book engraved in granite, destroying the sense of profound, unique loss that each name carried.

They admitted she was right.

A more serious disagreement concerned an inscription. Maya Lin thought an inscription would rob the names of their emotional power. The vets, however, demanded an inscription. The Memorial had to explicitly honor *all* vets who had served in Vietnam. Maya Lin resisted.

"This is very serious stuff," Wheeler said. "Emotions are running high."

"I must protect the integrity of my design," she responded.

"There are going to be changes, Maya," Wheeler shouted. "You'd better understand that."

Eventually, the vets convinced her that a prologue and an epilogue would build upon the chronological listing.

Despite resolution of these two problems, the issue of who controlled the Memorial was never resolved, and communication between the vets and Maya Lin slowly deteriorated throughout 1981. She never asked, "What is combat like?" or "Who were your friends whose names we're putting on the wall?" And the vets, in turn, never once explained to her what words like "courage," "sacrifice," and "devotion to duty" really meant.

The VVMF solicited advice on the inscription from dozens of people, ranging from General William Westmoreland to former enlisted men.

The vets rejected "police action" and "conflict"; whether or not officially declared, Vietnam had been a *war.* They also eliminated language such as "fight for freedom" and "never again." The Memorial had to be kept strictly nonpolitical.

The final inscription, completed in early October 1981, was a group effort:

> *Prologue:* In honor of the men and women of the Armed Forces of the United States who served in the Vietnam War. The names of those who gave their lives and of those who remain missing are inscribed in the order they were taken from us.

> *Epilogue:* Our nation remembers the courage, sacrifice, and devotion to duty and country of its Vietnam veterans. This memorial was built with private donations from the American people.

Some of the vets wanted the Prologue and Epilogue to be large and gilded in gold. But Kent Cooper convinced them they were wrong. "No word, no letter," he said, "should be more important or more noticeable than any name."

BLACK GASH OF SHAME

The vets wanted a noncontroversial, apolitical memorial. Maybe this was naive. Vietnam had been America's most controversial, politicized war.

They wanted one memorial to "symbolize the experience of the Americans who fought in Vietnam." Maybe this was idealistic. Too many experiences were festering in too much leftover repressed emotion.

They wanted to list the dead. Maybe this was asking for unnecessary trouble. Any reminder that real people die in war inevitably angers those who see war as a playing field for heroes.

What they wanted had seemed so simple. Maybe too much blood had been shed for it to have worked out that way.

In any event, the controversy, predicted by Wheeler back in 1979, finally arrived.

The first rumblings had started close to home. Shortly after Maya Lin's first press conference, James Webb—who had considered himself unqualified to sit on the jury—said Maya Lin's design was unacceptable. "Why is it black?" he asked. "Why is it underground?"

Wheeler urged Webb to wait, "to give the design time to grow on you." Webb agreed.

That same week, a former VVMF volunteer named Tom Carhart—who had entered his own design in the competition—showed up. "Oh, boy," he said to Doubek, "what did you guys do?"

As soon as he left, Doubek dug out Carhart's entry. It showed an officer holding a dead young GI up to heaven as though in sacrifice. The officer was standing in a huge Purple Heart.

The early volunteers involved with the Vietnam Veterans Memorial stand in the U.S. Capitol with members of Congress. Left to right: Murray McCann; Lieutenant Commander Jerry Bever, USN; Bill Marr; Senator Patrick Leahy (D-Vt); Ron Gibbs; Senator Charles McC. Mathias, Jr. (R-Md); Senator Robert J. Dole (R-Kan); Jan C. Scruggs (in blue jeans); Tom Carhart; Senator Dale Bumpers (R-Ark); Robert W. Doubek; Arthur C. Mosley; unidentified man; John P. Wheeler III; G. William Jayne; and Bruce Spiher. SENATE PHOTOGRAPHER

Senator George S. McGovern, whose name was once synonymous with the antiwar movement, became an early supporter of the Memorial honoring Vietnam vets. Senator McGovern is shown here at lunch with Jan C. Scruggs, founder of the Memorial effort. SENATE PHOTOGRAPHER

Bob Hope, champion of GI's in three wars, meets with the leaders of the Memorial effort in Washington's Kennedy Center. Bob Hope signed the fund-raising letter that was sent to more than 12 million Americans. Left to right: Bob Hope, VVMF project director Robert W. Doubek, chairman of the board John P. Wheeler III, treasurer Robert H. Frank, and Jan C. Scruggs. RICHARD BRAATEN

The introduction of legislation designating two acres on the Mall for a National Vietnam Veterans Memorial took place on November 8, 1979. The legislation's sponsors hoped that the Memorial would become a symbol of gratitude to the Americans who served in the nation's longest war and a symbol of national reconciliation after the divisive conflict. Left to right: Senator John W. Warner (R-Va), Congressman John Paul Hammerschmidt (R-Ark), Senator Charles McC. Mathias, Jr. (R-Md), and Jan C. Scruggs. SENATE PHOTOGRAPHER

President Jimmy Carter signs into law the legislation that gave two acres of land for the National Vietnam Veterans Memorial. The ceremony took place in the White House Rose Garden on July 1, 1980, nearly eight months after the bill was introduced. JOAN MARCUS

The leaders of the Memorial effort unanimously approve the winner of the design competition, which attracted more entries than any such competition ever held. Standing is Paul Spreiregen, professional adviser to the competition. On his left are the seven jurors, all nationally prominent architects and sculptors. On Spreiregen's right are the staff and directors of VVMF who unanimously approved the design. Left to right: Robert W. Doubek, John O. Woods, Jan C. Scruggs, George W. Mayo, John P. Wheeler III, Arthur C. Mosley, Colonel Don Schaet, USMC (Ret), and Robert H. Frank. VVMF

Distinguished American diplomat and former ambassador to Vietnam Ellsworth Bunker was a major supporter of the Memorial and was especially active in fund-raising. He is shown here at the corporate victory luncheon, celebrating the groundbreaking and the success of the corporate effort. Left to right: Ellsworth Bunker, VVMF fund-raising director Sandie Fauriol, and John P. Wheeler III. STEVE ANDERSON

VA administrator Max Cleland, a triple amputee from the Vietnam War, became involved with the Memorial in 1979. Cleland later testified before Congress on behalf of the legislation that would donate government land for the Memorial. Left to right: Jan C. Scruggs, VVMF volunteer publicity chairman G. William Jayne, VA administrator Max Cleland, Robert W. Doubek, and George W. Mayo.
VETERANS ADMINISTRATION

Maya Ying Lin, then a 21-year-old undergraduate at Yale University, displays her winning design, which called for two walls of polished black granite engraved with the names of the 58,000 American casualties from the Vietnam War. The design later became the focus of a heated national controversy. Left to right: Jan C. Scruggs, Maya Ying Lin, and Robert W. Doubek. VVMF

Corporate leaders formed a special advisory board to help raise funds for the Memorial. American corporations eventually raised $1.5 million under the leadership of former LTV president Paul Thayer. Left to right: John McElwee, president of John Hancock Insurance; Jan C. Scruggs; Senator John W. Warner (R-Va); Senator Charles McC. Mathias, Jr. (R-Md); Sandie Fauriol; and Paul Thayer, VVMF's corporate advisory board chairman.
SENATE PHOTOGRAPHER

A Vietnam veteran is overcome with emotion after the groundbreaking ceremony on March 26, 1982. Other veterans try to comfort him. Because of delays in getting Department of Interior Secretary James G. Watt's go-ahead to begin construction, there was concern that the Memorial might not be completed in time for the National Salute to Vietnam Veterans in November.
S. J. STANISKI

At the site of the Vietnam Veterans Memorial, plans are being made for construction despite the highly politicized effort to stop the Memorial. Left to right: VVMF architect of record Kent Cooper; John Marquart and Bill Choquette of the Gilbane Building Company; Maya Ying Lin, designer; Robert W. Doubek; and Bill Lecky, Cooper-Lecky Partnership. VVMF

American Legion Commander Al Keller presents a check for over one million dollars to Jan C. Scruggs to help build the Vietnam Veterans Memorial. AMERICAN LEGION

The 1.9 million-member Veterans of Foreign Wars presents a check on December 22, 1981, to the Vietnam Veterans Memorial Fund. In attendance was Rocky Bleier, who recovered from disabling wounds received while in Vietnam and went on to play in the Super Bowl as a Pittsburgh Steeler. Left to right: VFW Commander Arthur J. Fellwock; Rocky Bleier; Jan C. Scruggs; and Miriam Watson, the VFW's president of the ladies auxiliary. VVMF

The unveiling of the first panel of names placed on the Memorial wall occurred on July 22, 1982. Four families came to the brief ceremony. To the right of Jan C. Scruggs is Vietnam veteran Congressman John P. Murtha (D-Pa) and retired chaplain James Kingsley. VVMF

This photograph shows the Vietnam Veterans Memorial under construction in September 1982. The Memorial was opened to the public just a few days before the November 13, 1982, dedication. GILBANE BUILDING COMPANY

This veteran has his sleeve pinned to his chest with a Purple Heart earned when he lost his arm in Vietnam. He awaits the dedication ceremony.
U.S. NAVY

A mother and her son pause in remembrance and respect for a casualty of the Vietnam War. SMITHSONIAN INSTITUTION

A kneeling child softly touches the name of a serviceman who gave his life in Vietnam years before she was born.

A mother grieves as she remembers her son, a highly decorated pilot, who gave his life in Vietnam.
SMITHSONIAN INSTITUTION

A former Green Beret hugs Bill Menard, a Sioux Indian, with whom he served in Vietnam. Menard had presented the Green Beret with a sacred warrior's pouch that he had carried for courage and good luck during his year of Vietnam combat.
JANET CENTURY

American Indians from the Inter Tribal Association hold a ceremony on November 12, 1982, dedicating the Memorial to the Great Spirit. During the ceremony ancient warrior chants were sounded as the names of Indians slain in the war were called out. At the conclusion eyewitnesses watched in awe as the clouds overhead suddenly parted.
LARRY CENTURY

Among those watching the parade marchers pass by the reviewing stand on their way to the dedication ceremony were American Legion Commander Al Keller (far left) and Maya Ying Lin. In front, Paul Cheremeta of the Paralyzed Veterans of America and Bobby Muller, founder of the Vietnam Veterans of America, watch from their wheelchairs. TYL ASSOCIATES

Items left at the Memorial included this handmade beaded cross, left by American Indians.
SMITHSONIAN INSTITUTION

A crowd of 150,000 gathers at the Vietnam Veterans Memorial prior to the dedication ceremony on November 13, 1982.
SMITHSONIAN INSTITUTION

General William C. Westmoreland embraces Bob Wieland, a double amputee from the Vietnam War, at a reception held on November 12, 1984. Wieland was walking across the United States on his hands to raise funds for needy children.
TYL ASSOCIATES

On the morning of the dedication ceremony three Vietnam veterans sleep in front of the walls that bear the names of their friends. The crutches of one veteran lie alongside them. SMITHSONIAN INSTITUTION

A mother and her children show pride in and respect for Vietnam veterans as they watch the historic parade prior to the Memorial's dedication ceremony. SMITHSONIAN INSTITUTION

Moments after the Memorial dedication a joyful John P. Wheeler III embraces Brigadier General George Price, USA (Ret), as Senator John W. Warner (R-Va) looks on.
SMITHSONIAN INSTITUTION

Overcome with emotion during a visit to the Memorial on November 13, 1982, a man holds his daughter.
U.S. NAVY: ALL HANDS

A U.S. Marine stands erect and salutes during the dedication ceremony. SMITHSONIAN INSTITUTION

Frederick Hart's sculpture of three American soldiers in Vietnam was unveiled at the site of the Memorial in November 1984. NEESHAN NATALCHAYAN

General John W. Vessey, chairman of the Joint Chiefs of Staff, congratulates Jan C. Scruggs, after presenting him with an award for gallantry and with the Good Conduct Medal, which he earned in Vietnam fourteen years earlier, in 1969. With Jan is his wife, Becky. DEPARTMENT OF DEFENSE

Wheeler, Mosley, and Carhart had been classmates at West Point. Carhart called Mosley. "I just can't live with this," he said. "There have been a lot of us who've been looking for a memorial to celebrate and glorify the Vietnam veteran."

Then, on September 18, 1981, the *National Review* called the Memorial "Orwellian glop."

"Okay, we lost the Vietnam War," the magazine said. "Okay, the thing was mismanaged from start to finish. But the American soldiers who died in Vietnam fought for their country and for the freedom of others and they deserve better than the outrage that has been approved as their memorial. . . . the Reagan Administration should throw the switch on this project, whether through executive action or a bill in Congress."

The *National Review* carried great weight with the so-called New Right—which included Interior Secretary James Watt and many members of Congress. What if they took the magazine's suggestion seriously? Congress could pressure Watt into killing the Memorial. Worse, Watt might not need much pushing. He considered himself a superpatriot. He was tough, and he was willing to cause controversy. He had already said in public that all U.S. citizens fell into two categories, "liberals and Americans." Thus, he might grandstand against liberal influence in the arts and insist upon an American memorial imbued with his views of patriotism.

The VVMF could have rallied its troops, most of whom believed that the Memorial was well on its way to a problem-free dedication in November 1982. Allies on Capitol Hill, in the White House, and in veterans organizations could have been alerted. The extensive network of vet volunteers could have been mobilized. But the VVMF, its overworked seven-person staff focusing on fund-raising and construction plans, did not launch a counteroffensive.

On October 13, 1981, the Fine Arts Commission was scheduled to review granite samples—a boring, routine, construction detail. When Fund officials arrived, they found the hearing room overflowing with journalists, including television camera crews. This was the first time television had covered any hearings involving the Memorial. The reason: Tom Carhart, wearing a three-piece suit with two Purple Hearts pinned on, was waiting to testify.

In his statement, Carhart called the Memorial "a black gash of shame." The phrase had a nice ring to it, and numerous newspapers—including the *New York Times*—prominently reprinted portions of his testimony.

Fund officials tried to contain the damage. "There's a lot of anger and there's a shortage of things to show your anger about," Scruggs told reporters. "We get some of the misdirected anger."

It did not work. Journalists paid little attention to Scruggs, while Carhart received front-page treatment. It did not matter that Carhart represented only himself, or that he had waited for over six months to complain about a competition that he himself had entered and lost. Carhart was creating news: angry Vietnam vet against the art establishment; Vietnam veterans getting screwed again; an impending civil war among Vietnam vets. It made an interesting story. People who had never before heard about the Vietnam Veterans Memorial began to think it was a black gash of shame.

From a historical perspective, the criticism of Maya Lin's design followed a well-established pattern. "What is really fascinating about the history of monument building in this city," Benjamin Forgey wrote in the *Washington Post*, "is that in almost every case, whether the product resulted from a competition or a commission, certain clear divisions occur: Professional standards versus popular taste, modernity versus tradition, abstract symbolism versus realist representation."

In television appearances, newspaper interviews, visits to Congress, and telephone conversations with vets across the country, Fund officials tried to explain why criticism such as Carhart's was factually incorrect:

"The Memorial is below ground, denoting shame."

Not true. It will be cut in a hillside and will enjoy a clear line of sight to the Washington Monument and the Lincoln Memorial. It will have a southern exposure, so it will be sunny all day. Lowering the wall makes it possible for everyone to read every name.

"There is no flag. This dishonors those who died fighting for that flag."

Most war memorials do not have flags.

"It is black, a color of shame."

The Seabee and the Iwo Jima memorials have black granite, and no one says this denotes shame. White stone would not work, because visitors could not read the names, especially in the sunlight. As General William Westmoreland notes, "Polished black granite is more handsome than any other possible stone."

"It forms the antiwar 'V' peace sign."

This is not a "V." One arm of the Memorial will point toward the Lincoln Memorial; the other will point toward the Washington Monument. The angle is 125 degrees. No human hand could form a "V" at such an angle.

"It is a tombstone, honoring only those who died."

It will be contemplative, not death-oriented. The names of all 2.7 million who served cannot be engraved. Who would deny special treatment for those who died or remain missing? An inscription will honor all Vietnam vets.

"It is unheroic."

Heroism is in the eyes of the beholder. There is plenty of heroism in those names. Wait until you see them right there on the Mall with Washington, Jefferson, and Lincoln.

"It should be representational."

Maybe. But a great nonrepresentational work of art emerged victorious from an extremely fair, open competition. Furthermore, the names are a representational symbol that everyone will understand and honor. The American people watched the Vietnam War on television. They do not need a representation of what they already know. They need something to help them see the veterans they have managed to ignore.

"The names on the wall will have no rank or service designation."

This is a memorial to human beings, not a military symbol. They are all Americans, and they all made an equal sacrifice to their country. No other designation is necessary.

"The word 'Vietnam' is not mentioned."

Incorrect. It will be prominently featured in an inscription.

"It will become the site of future antiwar demonstrations."

All demonstrations, pro- or antiwar, will be banned. It is a place to honor veterans.

WATT ACTS

Attacks continued throughout November and December.

Carhart circulated a memo within the White House and Interior Department carrying false charges that a member of the jury had been involved with communists.

Webb resigned from the National Sponsoring Committee and tried to get other vets to join him. Westmoreland refused, saying, "Beauty is in the eyes of the beholder."

Figuring that Webb must have written to every Vietnam vet on the Sponsoring Committee, Scruggs called former Admiral James J. Stockdale, who had been a senior American prisoner of war in Vietnam and had received the Congressional Medal of Honor. They had talked several times before. Stockdale had been nice, but always too busy to learn more about the Memorial or to offer anything but his name on the letterhead.

"Admiral, I realize that you've received Webb's letter," Scruggs said. "It is unfortunate that there is disagreement about the design, but I'd like to explain."

Build the Memorial rising and white, Stockdale said. Make it inspiring.

Scruggs tried to explain the beauty of polished black granite and that the Memorial would not be hidden underground.

The telephone went dead. James Stockdale, who had endured years of North Vietnamese torture in the name of freedom, had hung up on him.

Only Stockdale joined Webb. Gerald Ford, Rosalynn Carter, Bob Hope, Nancy Reagan, Jimmy Stewart, William C. Westmoreland, and every other member of the National Sponsoring Committee remained firmly on the side of the Memorial.

It was a strange public relations war. Opponents found sanctuary in faceless rumor and innuendo. Denials, no matter how well documented, only escalated the conflict.

The press played an important role. Vets attacking the Memorial were big news; vets explaining and praising it were boring. A Vietnam vet on the West Coast suggested that the Memorial should be a three-story black plastic M-16 rifle stuck upside down in the ground. Although he had no artistic credentials and no backing, newspapers across the country carried his smiling picture. Likewise, the *Washingtonian* magazine gossip page referred to "Vietnam, America's most unpopular war and the nation's most divisive monument."

Although the vets restrained their desire to counterattack, eloquent voices spoke out in defense of Maya Lin's design. "It is a pity that this voluntary undertaking should recently have been slowed by controversy over the memorial design," wrote syndicated columnist James J. Kilpatrick. "Let me venture my own opinion. This will be the most moving war memorial ever erected."

Washington Post critic Wolf Von Eckardt wrote, "Carhart . . . says the jury should have consisted of war veterans, as if a beauty contest should be judged only by beauties . . . those bothered by abstract design might consider that grand obelisk, the Washington Monument. We have come to love it. Someday the Vietnam Memorial, too, may win the hearts and minds of the American people."

A *National Review* article denounced that magazine's "premature evaluation" of the Memorial. It will be "beautiful, imposing, and fitting," the article concluded.

The most meaningful statements of support continued to come from the American people. Veterans organizations sponsored bingo games, bake sales, garage sales, dinner dances, and other activities that generated millions of dollars. Hundreds of thousands of veterans and their families had been exposed to considerable adverse publicity about Maya Lin's design, and yet they continued to donate their time and their dollars.

A retired Army colonel raised $819 from pledges after running the New York City Marathon. He wore a camouflage T-shirt reading "Vietnam Veterans Memorial Fund" and was cheered along the entire 26-mile 385-yard route. An unemployed Vietnam vet studied Maya Lin's design and then mailed in $65. VA hospitals and vet centers conducted "pass the helmet" fund-raising campaigns.

In Mattoon, Illinois, under the guidance of 86-year-old World War I veteran Alf Thompson, over 1,500 people participated in a two-hour parade that honored Vietnam veterans. Scruggs served as parade marshal. Afterwards, he was the featured guest at a VFW lunch. Three Vietnam vets were there, and all expressed support for the Memorial. "Everything that Vietnam touches seems to go sour," one said sadly. "I may never have the money to get to D.C., but it would make me feel good to know that my buddies' names are up there." Parents of a dead Vietnam vet also shook his hand. "Don't let them stop you, Jan," the father said. "Those folks in Washington are always fooling around with anything good. Don't let 'em do it this time."

The most tense time in fund-raising came in October. Small donations continued to come in, but Sandie Fauriol had expected corporate donations in the $50,000 range.

She examined the mail every day, looking for the large envelopes that would include corporate checks. There were only smaller personal envelopes. Had the controversy cut off corporate funds? Finally, in December, the big envelopes started to arrive. Many of America's most prestigious corporations—including Getty Oil, LTV, AT&T, Rockwell International, Aetna Life Insurance, Boeing, Exxon, MCA, Time Inc., American Express, and Pepsico—sent sizable checks.

On December 22, the Veterans of Foreign Wars held a press conference at the National Press Club in Washington to present a four-foot-long check for $180,000. An opponent of the Memorial had warned VFW officials that "you'll lose every Vietnam veteran member if you give the Fund money." But the VFW did not like to be threatened; its officials also knew that the membership supported Maya Lin's design. To make its position absolutely clear, VFW national commander Arthur J. Fellwock flew in to personally present the check.

Former Pittsburgh Steeler football star Rocky Bleier also participated. Bleier had served as a grunt in Vietnam, where he was wounded in both legs. Doctors had said he'd never walk normally again. But he fought back, and had been a star running back on the 1975 Super Bowl winner.

Scruggs picked Bleier up at the airport right before the press conference. The 200-pound former private hugged the former corporal, who was now down to 140 pounds. "What the hell are you letting those guys do?" Bleier asked. "Let's go get 'em."

After the press conference, Doubek led the way as two men carried out a new six-by-seven-foot model used to explain the Memorial. As he walked past two swinging doors, a camera crew waved for him to step aside. They were waiting for someone important.

Doubek recognized who it was. Henry Kissinger.

The former Secretary of State already had his overcoat on and seemed in a hurry. "What's that?" he asked Doubek.

"That's a model for the Vietnam Veterans Memorial."

"Is that the design that's causing all the controversy?"

Doubek started to say, It's not really controversial, but he stopped himself. "Yes, that's the one."

"Well, how does it go?"

Using the model, Doubek described how the names would be inscribed and how the walls would be situated between the Lincoln Memorial and the Washington Monument.

"It's very moving," Kissinger said.

Two days later, a personal check from Kissinger for $500 arrived.

One individual, James Watt, continued to hold life-or-death power over the Memorial.

VFW executive director Cooper T. Holt, one of Washington's smartest political observers, called Scruggs with a warning: Ronald Reagan's people could not satisfy some of his conservative supporters on abortion and school prayer. With congressional elections scheduled in less than a year, the White House just might throw them a bone—the Vietnam Veterans Memorial.

In late December, conservative Republican congressman Henry Hyde of Illinois, a prominent spokesman for right-wing causes, launched what he called his "Christmas offensive." Along with 27 colleagues he signed a letter to all Republicans in the House asking that they write to President Reagan requesting that Interior Secretary Watt not grant construction approval for the Memorial.

Reporters called Scruggs for a comment. "What all this goes to prove," he said, "is that this country is not recovered from the war. When people start ganging up on a guy who's just trying to honor Vietnam veterans, I think it's a lot more than aesthetics. It shows we need to do a lot more healing."

At a late December VVMF board meeting, Don Schaet suggested

that when the Memorial was ready for dedication, a national salute to Vietnam veterans should be held. It would have a parade and days of festivities.

Everyone got excited. A cleansing ritual. A welcome home to the warriors. A way to diffuse grief by special remembrance of the dead. A celebration of life. A public opportunity for the country to show its feelings.

"Why talk about a national salute when there might not be a memorial?" someone asked.

"There will never be another time in history when we have this opportunity," Wheeler said. "The Memorial can be dedicated right on schedule—November 1982."

They were buried in negative publicity. And some of the nation's most powerful political figures seemed poised to destroy their memorial. Yet the board voted unanimously to hold a parade on November 13, 1982, honoring all Vietnam veterans.

On January 4, 1982, a letter from Watt arrived. In technical legal language, its message was clear. Watt had put the Memorial on hold until further notice.

Late one night, Scruggs went to the Mall and walked up to the statue of Abraham Lincoln.

They were losing their memorial. How did it happen? The competition had been fair. No one had complained. The jury had done a good job. After the negative publicity, art critics had gone back and examined all 1,421 entries. They had concluded that Maya Lin's was by far the most brilliant.

An angry group of less than a dozen men wanted to politicize the Memorial. It was easier to destroy than to create. Much easier. Wheeler had once remarked that a few angry men could shape history through their will to destroy. Look at what had happened to Lincoln. The dream of a memorial was about to die.

Scruggs looked up at Lincoln. The Civil War had been America's bloodiest conflict, and yet this memorial carried no sense of violence. It was nonpolitical. Nothing favored the North or the South. Nothing said that slavery was morally wrong. Or that the Civil War was right. Like Maya Lin's design, it provided a sense of history, it was simple, and it relied on words. People could read Lincoln's Gettysburg Address and

Second Inaugural Address, think about the words, stand quietly, and let the feelings flow. They could come away different than when they arrived.

Maya Lin's design would do the same thing. Its words were the names. Even those who wanted glory had only to pick a name at random. Who could deny the glory in a young man willing to risk—and give—his life for his country?

The American people would not tolerate censorship. They would not permit anyone to tell them what to think—particularly about anything as important as all those young soldiers who died in Vietnam.

The Memorial would be built. Let the American people come here with their children. Let the children ask tough questions. Who were those people whose names we're seeing? What did they do? What does it mean?

PART FOUR

1982

8

THE DECISION TO COMPROMISE

THE MEMORIAL SEEMED TO BE CRUMBLING. Rumors bombarded Fund headquarters. More and more congressmen were joining the opposition. Nancy Reagan would drop off the Sponsoring Committee. President Reagan was about to kill the Memorial.

Scruggs wanted to call a staff meeting and tell everyone not to worry, that the situation was under control. But he could not. It was not true.

Some 58,000 GI's were, in death, what they had been in life: pawns of Washington politics.

The Vietnam Veterans Memorial had at first seemed to be drawing surprisingly *little* hostile fire. With 230 million Americans and 2.7 million Vietnam vets, some dissent was inevitable no matter what design had been selected. There were bound to be those who wanted a different design. But there had been no groundswell of opposition. Despite their extraordinary influence, critics seemed limited to a small group in Washington who had energized the far right in Congress and the Reagan Administration. These opponents had used the mass media to spread misinformation and arguments that a large number of Americans believed.

This small group wanted to use the Memorial to say to the war's opponents, "You were wrong. You have blood on your hands." They wanted to take an undeclared war that had oozed on and off the center stage of American life and transform it into a John Wayne movie. They wanted the Memorial to make Vietnam what it had never been in reality: a good, clean, glorious war seen as necessary and supported by a united country.

They seemed unable to understand or show respect for those—including many who had bled in Vietnam—who had legitimate views different from their own. And they especially could not understand someone like Maya Lin, who said, "I honestly don't have thoughts on the war."

Undoubtedly, most of the opponents were sincere. It's hard to lose the war you fought as a youth, especially when it was not your fault; and it's impossible to forget your debt to the dead and your admiration for those whose bravery was wasted. Yet they displayed a surprising intensity and a deadly passion. They loved the idea of a memorial, but hated Maya Lin's design. Their vehemence came from a belief that the stakes were extraordinarily high. "The memorial," Webb later wrote, "will occupy a permanence in the national mindset, with an even greater power than history itself. History can be re-evaluated. New facts can be discovered, leading to different interpretations. But a piece of art remains, as a testimony to a particular moment in history, and we are under a solemn obligation to get that moment down as correctly as possible."

Somehow, a new form of national amnesia seemed to be at the heart of the opposition's motivation and strength. Novelist Tim O'Brien, a Vietnam combat vet, described this new amnesia best in an essay published in late 1981.

> It would seem that time and distance erode memory. We adjust, we lose the intensity. . . . For many of us, years later, Vietnam is seen with a certain tempered nostalgia. A half-remembered adventure. We feel, many of us, proud of having "been there," forgetting the terror, straining out the bad stuff, focusing on the afterimage. . . . We have forgotten, or lost the energy to recall, the terribly complex and ambiguous issues of the Vietnam War. . . . What to fight for? When, if ever, to use armed forces as instruments of foreign policy? What regimes to support, and how, and under what conditions? To what extent and by what means do we, as a nation, try to make good on our beliefs and

> principles—opposing tyranny, preserving freedoms, resisting aggression? . . .
>
> We're all adjusted. The whole country. And I fear that we are back where we started.
>
> I wish we were more troubled.

Some of those who opposed the design managed to muster a sense of humor. Columnist R. Emmet Tyrrell, for example, asked for a statue that included "the statisticians preparing their graphs for Secretary of Defense Robert McNamara. . . . How about [one] depicting [Jane Fonda] as she responded to the POW's stories of torture in communist prison camps?"

However, the stakes were too high for much humor. Vietnam had been the dominant event of a generation that had, as Jack Wheeler pointed out, been "touched with fire." The war had changed the nation's image of itself and its role in the world. The nation had gained maturity, and lost moral certainty; it had gained experience, but lost confidence.

In this context, the Vietnam Veterans Memorial had a special obligation: to affirm that in an age of doubt and selfishness millions of men found their country worth fighting—and dying—for.

To engage in revisionism, to say that Vietnam had been glorious, would be a lie. Such revisionism would miss the lessons, miss the mistakes, and make the sacrifices and deaths doubly meaningless.

Soldier of Fortune magazine said it best: A memorial should "remind and inspire the living."

Many members of the VVMF hated to sit back and let a small group destroy the Memorial. They wanted to energize Congress; after all, opponents of the design constituted only an ideologically isolated minority. They wanted to hold a press conference and return Perot's money, since the Texas businessman was emerging as one of the most forceful opponents of Maya Lin's design. They wanted to publicize quotes from the published writings of James Webb and other opponents in order to document their views on politics and war. They wanted to remind the country that many congressmen who had signed Representative Hyde's letter had *not* supported vets on key issues such as counseling, Agent Orange, and job training. They wanted to activate the arts community, and to ask the American Legion, Veterans of Foreign Wars, Gold Star Mothers, and other groups to counterattack.

It was tempting.

But the VVMF's theme was reconciliation. How could this be

achieved if the Fund itself escalated a divisive battle against fellow vets? Vietnam vets had enough problems. They had fought a war on the same side, and they should stick together now that national indifference had forced them to build their own memorial and organize their own welcome-home parade.

The VVMF needed a compromise, some way to bring the dissidents onto the team. So they asked Senator Warner to invite supporters and opponents of the Memorial to a private meeting at which they would resolve all differences amid feelings of shared patriotism.

The meeting was set for 3:00 P.M. on January 27, 1982.

As the VVMF waited for this meeting, a bittersweet triumph came. Money had always been the Fund's greatest concern. Now the totals for 1981 became available. The vets had met the goal they had set back in 1979: to complete fund-raising by the end of 1981. They had over $8 million, counting a $1 million American Legion pledge—more than enough to build their memorial. Over 650,000 people had given ten dollars or less.

Yet it was not a time for celebration.

"If we ever have a groundbreaking ceremony," chief fund-raiser Sandie Fauriol said, "I'd like to be the one who gives the command."

"Sure," one of the vets responded. "If it ever happens."

JIMMY MOSCONIS

In mid-January, the telephone rang at the Scruggs home.

"Jayun, you've got a tiger by the tail up there," a voice with a deep Southern accent said. It was Jimmy Mosconis, the sergeant in charge of Scruggs's mortar platoon. Mosconis had seen a TV network newscast about Scruggs and Watt, and had called to offer encouragement. "You need to get that old Watt out of the way," Mosconis said. "We've got to get the names of those boys up there where they belong. Remember the day Claude got it? Jesus, there were so many of 'em killed. We're just lucky as hell our ass didn't get killed back in '69. Jayun, you just keep fightin'."

Scruggs had last spoken to Mosconis in the field. An inexperienced officer had led them into an ambush. Claude, a GI from Iowa, had been walking point. A claymore mine had put hundreds of holes through his head and chest. The company had taken a dozen other casualties. In an ambush the next day, shrapnel from a rocket grenade had torn into Scruggs, who was bleeding and losing consciousness while watching Mosconis—himself wounded—risk his life to save another GI. Mosconis was a courageous straight shooter. Support from a man like that meant a lot.

ADDING A STATUE

Things were moving quickly.

On January 12, *60 Minutes* called to say they were planning a story on the Memorial. They wanted cooperation, honesty, and openness. The air date had not yet been set.

The next day, Ross Perot and an aide showed up in Washington. Perot wanted to pay for a Gallup Poll of all Vietnam vets to see what they thought of Maya Lin's design. It was an interesting notion. But how could a fair poll be done about a memorial that was not yet built? You would wind up with a hundred different groups pushing a hundred different designs—and there would be no memorial. "Great idea," Scruggs said. "They should have done a Gallup Poll in the war zone to see who wanted to keep on fighting and who wanted to go home."

Hours after talking to Perot, the vets and jury chairman Grady Clay met with Watt to explain the design. Watt was noncommital.

Late that week, senior White House staff members examined the VVMF's large model of Maya Lin's design. Some liked it; some did not. No one wanted to kill it. And no one wanted to defend it. They seemed to view the whole issue as a problem that would not go away.

On January 26, Doubek and Scruggs meet with Henry Hyde, their chief congressional opponent. Hyde looked at their slides, smiled, and called Maya Lin's design "impressive." He did not promise to stop attacking them.

In the meantime, letters kept pouring in to the key player, Secretary of the Interior James Watt:

From former U.S. ambassador to South Vietnam Ellsworth Bunker: "The proposed Memorial would be a distinguished and fitting mark of the respect we owe them."

From the editor of the Marine Corps *Gazette:* "We published detailed information on the selected memorial design and found wide acceptance for it among our 30,000 readers."

From John G. McElwee, president of the John Hancock Mutual Life Insurance Company: "In my efforts to raise funds [for the Memorial], I've had only two negative comments about the design in over 500 industry contacts."

From former Marine combat officer Shaun Sheehan, senior vice president of the National Association of Broadcasters: "This organization endorsed with great enthusiasm the Vietnam Veterans Memorial. Broadcasters through radiothons, public service announcements, talk shows, and news coverage have played a major role in helping launch this most worthy project. An adamant group of arch-conservatives stands between successful completion of this fitting monument and continued rancor and counterproductive debate."

From Stanley Resor, Secretary of the Army under Presidents Johnson and Nixon: "[The design is] excellent."

Pressure also came from the press. "Fortunately for the country," the *Baltimore Sun* noted, "thousands of people—including General William Westmoreland and hundreds of local chapters of the American Legion and the Veterans of Foreign Wars—disagree [with right-wing critics]. There is a shrill, whining, and mischievous tone to the criticism."

Columnist James J. Kilpatrick said, "I happen to believe that the war was just as Ronald Reagan described it in August 1980: It was indeed a 'noble cause.' In the end the cause was lost, but that tragic fact cannot obscure the motivation or denigrate the sacrifice. If this contemplative memorial prompts visitors to reflect on the price of defending freedom, so be it. . . . Viewing it, each of us may remember what he wishes to remember—the cause, the heroism, the blunders, the waste."

The Berwick, Pennsylvania, *Enterprise* wrote, "History has not yet placed its hand on the Vietnam War and our country's involvement, and it will be years before the passions and resentments and bitternesses associated with the war will be placed in proper perspective on the pages of history books. But do we have to wait that long? . . . The site has been set aside, the funds are available, the memorial design has been chosen and construction could be started at the flick of a switch. We think Watt and the detractors with whom he stands should step out of the way and let the memorial rise. We're also certain that's the way most Americans today feel, too."

Spontaneous support also sprang up in Congress. Republican Representative Lawrence J. DeNardis of Connecticut, for example, circulated a "Dear Colleague" letter citing "an odor of mischief in this last-minute attempt to discredit the Vietnam veterans' design selection process."

DeNardis reminded his fellow members of Congress that "the Commodore Barry American Legion Post in Berwyn, Illinois, in Congressman Hyde's District, conducted a walkathon to raise funds for the memorial, on November 26th, over six months after the design was revealed."

The most eloquent messages, however, came from so-called ordinary vets: Do not politicize our memorial, they said. It's not the memorial's job to judge the rights and wrongs of Vietnam. It is a living memorial, helping to end the disgraceful attitudes toward us. The design is simple and sensitive, people-oriented. The nation must always remember the terrible price we paid for nothing. Do not meddle.

Forty-eight hours before the Warner meeting was scheduled to begin, the VVMF received a warning from a key congressional aide. "Perot is in town," the aide said. "He's brought a lot of ex-POW officers. They're calling the smaller veterans groups. It's going to be stacked in favor of a small minority. You're walking into a trap."

The vets considered asking Senator Warner to postpone the meeting. But postponement would anger the Memorial's opponents, heating emotions that needed to be cooled. The decision, filled with risk, was: Let's go ahead.

The vets faced another critical decision. Should they invite Maya Lin? It had been difficult to persuade her to make even technical adjustments in her design. What if she refused any accommodation with the opponents? "It's incredible how possessive I am about the memorial," Maya Lin had recently told the *Washington Post.* "It's like my art is my babies."

On January 27, 1981, the day of the meeting, she was in a station wagon, accompanying the large model of the Memorial to New York City, where it would be shown on the ABC program *Good Morning America* the next day.

The meeting began on schedule. About 100 people crowded into the Senate Committee on Veterans Affairs hearing room. Opponents, who arrived in groups, outnumbered advocates by about four to one. The American Legion and the Veterans of Foreign Wars, which together represented nearly 5 million veterans, had only four people present. Ross Perot had arrived with at least ten people. The trap was set to spring.

The VVMF made a slide presentation outlining the fairness of the process through which Maya Lin's design had been selected, and emphasizing how well it would work on the Mall. VVMF officials suggested placing a flag at the Memorial site.

Then the opponents and their allies stood one by one and repeated the familiar list of demands. The Memorial had to be white. Black meant only shame. It had to be above ground. There should be a Gallup Poll. It had to be more patriotic. Many read from identical three-by-five cards. Some of those who opposed the design carried tremendous moral credibility. Alabama Senator Jeremiah Denton, for example, had been a leader of America's Vietnam POW's.

But some of those who now stood to criticize the design had never served in Vietnam—even though they used the pronoun "we" when referring to Vietnam veterans.

Finally, Scruggs could not stand it any longer. He was on his feet. "This is all rehearsed! We could have brought hundreds of our vet volunteers and Gold Star Mothers. We thought we were going to talk things over, not get ambushed."

He pointed at each of the men who had just spoken. "Where were you during the past three years? Why didn't you help? Why are you trying to destroy this Memorial now that it's ready to be built?"

Then he stopped. Schaet, Doubek, and others from the VVMF were shaking their heads. He was making a fool of himself, exactly what the Memorial's opponents wanted.

The former corporal sat, and the three-by-five card readings continued, cut off only by a calm yet impassioned voice. "I have heard your arguments," General George Price, one of America's highest-ranking black officers said. "I remind all of you of Martin Luther King, who fought for justice for all Americans. Black is not a color of shame. I am tired of hearing it called such by you. Color meant nothing on the battlefields of Korea and Vietnam. We are all equal in combat. Color should mean nothing now."

After that, no one mentioned making the wall white.

The battle continued for hours. Sometimes everyone shouted. A heavy cloud of smoke hung between the table and ceiling. No one asked for a break, and few people slipped out to search for restrooms.

At 7:30 P.M., General Mike Davison stood. He had been a strong, active supporter of the VVMF from the beginning. "Look," he said, "this has gone on for too long. Let's be reasonable. Why don't we just add a statue to the design, improve the inscription, and add a flag?"

Warner started waving his arms. "We've got it," he shouted. "Let's pull together. Let's make a compromise."

The deal was made by voice vote. Opponents agreed to halt their political efforts to block groundbreaking. The VVMF would pull out all design competition entries containing works of figurative sculpture. Slides of these sculptures would be reproduced and distributed to the principal attendees for their review. The statue would be discussed at a second meeting, scheduled for March 11.

Some of the vets felt dirtied. A national memorial was being designed via a back-room deal. They were giving away some of their integrity. Thus, in the rush to get home, it was convenient not to think about Maya Lin.

Scruggs flew to New York City, and on *Good Morning America* the next day he explained that changes would be made in the design, bringing Vietnam veterans together once again.

Maya Lin confronted him backstage. "Jan, what changes?"

"There's gonna be a flag."

"What else?"

"There's gonna be a little statue somewhere."

She tightened her lips and walked away.

At a lunch several days later, the vets told Maya Lin, "Don't worry. A statue won't screw up your design. You can fight it if you want, but not now, please. We need to start construction."

"I know there was nothing you could do," Maya Lin said. "You had to compromise with them."

"Aesthetically, the design does not need a statue, but politically it does," Scruggs said.

Maya Lin seemed to agree.

In her private moments, the designer knew she was becoming more cynical. An earlier idea, really a joke, had been to submit a competition entry in which the area of the Memorial was left empty, and every day at a set time a plane would come by and drop napalm. Now the idea did not seem so bad.

The Yale undergraduate knew that if she talked with outsiders she could fire up the opposition and destroy the Memorial. Although numerous journalists tried to reach her, she honored the VVMF's request and did not speak to the press.

THE CONSTRUCTION PERMIT

A White House aide who attended the January 27 meeting concluded in his official summary that "there is no reason to hold up the plan to break ground by March 1."

Opponents felt otherwise. Some sensed that if the wall was completed before the statue, then the American people might see no need for a statue. Some were afraid that the VVMF would not honor its agreement, or that the Fine Arts Commission or National Capital Planning Commission would kill the statue and flag. After all, the Fine Arts Commission in its original July 1981 approval of Maya Lin's design had warned that its "essential simplicity [should] be kept" and that "there should be no obtrusive visual elements." Others hated Maya Lin's design so much that they wanted to kill it through endless delays.

Anti-Memorial pressure continued. A letter to Watt signed by Henry Hyde and over three dozen other representatives, for example, called her design a "black ditch."

Memorial supporters did not remain inactive. A telegram to Watt from the VFW's national commander read: "Our nation has never given the honor and respect due Vietnam veterans. Now the nation is giving them respect, and I urge you to do the same by approving this Memorial."

American Legion national commander Jack W. Flynt flew to Washington for the sole purpose of meeting with Watt to discuss groundbreaking for the Memorial. He reported that a sampling of 200 Vietnam veteran Legionnaires, all with distinguished military and civilian records, found that *all* overwhelmingly supported groundbreaking. "The American Legion is hardly a hotbed of flag-burning or veteran-snubbing, so you'd think any U.S. War Memorial that could pass the Legion's muster would be pretty good," read a *Baltimore Sun* editorial. "Let's get on with it."

On February 4, the vets met with Watt to report progress. The Secretary congratulated them on the compromise and said he was now "inclined" to approve groundbreaking. He also said that the design was "a terrible political statement."

After leaving Watt's office, Scruggs showed Watt's press secretary a statement that he planned to issue to the wire services. The press secretary approved it, and UPI and Associated Press quickly carried a story quoting Scruggs as saying that Watt "just agreed to let us begin construction." The stories also had an ad lib quote from Scruggs: "Bring on the bulldozers."

Late that afternoon Scruggs received a call from Watt. "You're worse that the environmentalists," Watt screamed. "What's this crap about bulldozers on the Mall? I can just see what the environmentalists will do with that."

"Well, you could just blame it on me."

Scruggs's comment only seemed to incense Watt. The screams came faster and at a higher pitch. "There are two hundred ways that I can kill that design and I am tempted to prove that to you." Watt was a wild man —and he held life-and-death power over the Memorial.

One week later, the VVMF sent Watt a letter reaffirming their commitment to the compromise and documenting that they had enough money to complete construction. "We respectfully request your formal approval . . . so that we may proceed to break ground on schedule during the first week of March."

Monday. Tuesday. Wednesday. No answer from Watt. The March 1 deadline was slipping away. The VVMF called Interior. Watt and his aides never called back. The American Legion called Watt. Still no response. One of the basic rules in Washington is that when a group as powerful as the Legion calls, you at least listen politely. Watt just let the message slips pile up. On Friday, February 19, the VVMF called Watt again and again. If the March 1 groundbreaking was to occur, a construction permit was needed right away.

"If that son of a bitch doesn't give us a construction permit, we'll go after him," Scruggs told VVMF staff members. "We'll have a press conference and bring in Gold Star Mothers, the VFW, the American Legion. He'll wish he had a thousand environmentalists on a hunger strike outside Interior. We'll give a 'Vets for Jim Watt's Resignation' rally."

"We have been set up," Wheeler said. "Something's wrong at Interior."

Four o'clock came, then five. They waited until six-thirty, and went home feeling defeated. Another week had gone by with no response from

Watt. Something was up. Someone had gotten to him. On February 25, Watt wrote to the Fine Arts Commission and the National Capital Planning Commission saying, in effect, "I won't give a construction permit until you approve the statue and flag."

Two days later, the *Washington Post* reported: "Supporters of the Memorial had hoped to have it completed in time to be dedicated on Veterans Day, November 11, but that now seems unlikely."

Scruggs called Elliot Richardson, one of the capital's most respected public figures. The former Secretary of Defense, who had won two Purple Hearts during World War II, had been helping the VVMF with political advice and fund-raising contacts. "Watt may be playing games with you," Richardson said. "This may be a delay designed to be permanent. This may be the right time to fight Watt, but be very cautious. A wrong move could cause an irretrievable loss. Be mindful of the discretion given Watt under your legislation. Build up a record of reasonableness in your dealings with him. Do everything you can to avoid a fight, but remember the principle of time on target."

Time on target. Richardson was going back to his military days. It meant that all fire—mortars, artillery, planes, everything—strikes a designated target at the same moment, giving your enemy little time to take cover or to fire back.

"What will happen if it comes to that?" Scruggs asked.

"I'll be with you all the way. Call me at home any time."

On March 1, the originally scheduled day of groundbreaking, the VVMF board of directors held an emergency meeting. They still had no groundbreaking permit. Scruggs, Doubek, and a few others wanted to declare all-out war on Watt—let the country know that he alone was stopping the Vietnam Veterans Memorial. Too much had been happening behind the scenes.

Wheeler disagreed. "We could go for the kill," he said. "But if the Memorial is going to stand for healing, then we can't breathe hate into it. We'll get the statue approved, and prove to Watt that we keep our promises. That's the best way to honor vets."

The Board voted to follow Wheeler's and Richardson's advice. They would avoid a fight, while working hard to obtain approval from the Fine Arts Commission and the National Capital Planning Commission for the statue and flag.

That night, Wheeler arrived home around midnight. His wife was up. Six years earlier, their daughter, Katie, had been born with a partially unformed trachea, possibly a result of his exposure to Agent Orange during service in Vietnam. She had to sleep every night attached to an electronic alarm designed to ring if she stopped breathing. Tonight the alarm was not working. Wheeler wrapped a blanket around himself and pulled a chair up to her bed. He would keep watch.

Katie was a strong and courageous little girl, full of humor, a perfect reminder that battles over a memorial had to be kept in perspective. But by the time dawn broke, Wheeler had repeatedly replayed the board's decision not to fight back. The VVMF was giving extra time and opportunity to those who were so passionately commited to killing Maya Lin's design. That decision, no matter how idealistic, still seemed correct. Its dangers, however, were obvious. In life, the good guys did not always win.

Three days later, on March 4, the National Capital Planning Commission approved the statue and flag, in concept, but warned that these additions must "be located and designed so as not to compromise or diminish the basic design of the memorial as previously approved."

In its report to Watt, the National Capital Planning Commission indicated it would have preferred *no* additions to Maya Lin's design, but that it was responding to the political situation.

Five days later, on March 9, the Fine Arts Commission similarly approved the statue and flag, in principle.

Although approval for a statue that had not been designed was highly unusual, Watt *still* did not issue the construction permit. Then the VVMF understood: The second meeting—to select the statue—was scheduled for March 11. The Memorial's opponents had obviously persuaded Watt to wait until after this meeting. If they did not get their way, they would have him kill the Memorial.

Ross Perot sat next to Scruggs when the meeting began, and shortly made it clear that, once again, he controlled the majority. The VVMF had walked into another ambush.

By voice vote, the agenda was quickly changed. Instead of reviewing 80 slides of statues that had been submitted as part of the original design competition, the meeting focused on where to put the flag and statue. This was at best silly. Only the Fine Arts Commission and National Capital Planning Commission had power to choose a location for the flag and statue. But the debate went on for hours.

Architect Kent Cooper argued that there was no need to "adorn the Memorial with patriotic claptrap." He tried to explain that the American flag was too powerful a symbol to be located too close to the wall. Not realizing that politics had long since replaced art as the chief battleground, he called the flag, in architect's jargon, "a long stringy object."

This only enraged people like Sybil Stockdale, wife of the former POW who had resigned from the VVMF. "Let's put art where it belongs," she said. "In the art museums."

Maya Lin stood silently in the back of the room. She looked small and out of place in a room full of swearing vets.

At one point, Warner asked her, "What do you think of the ideas on placement being discussed?"

She could have said, The statue is a ridiculous idea, or, You'll never get away with it, or, I'll fight you all the way and you'll lose.

But she was in an alien environment, without allies, facing people whose passions sometimes made them seem to verge on violence. Her voice sounded timid. "If you're going to do this," she said, "it should be done in an integrated, harmonious way."

When someone made a motion to throw out Maya Lin's design and start over again, Perot silently shook his head no, and the motion was defeated. But by voice vote, the opponents backed a motion to have the flag at the center of the two walls, with the statue somewhere in the triangle formed by the walls.

At Perot's suggestion, a majority also agreed to form an ad hoc committee to choose the statue.

Design opponent Milt Copulos wrote in a newspaper article, "Something remarkable happened. Veterans split over the issue realized that the project was in jeopardy, and chose to set aside their preconceptions and come together in an effort to develop a consensus. . . . Some might argue that these changes are mere symbols, and hardly worth the pain and anguish they caused. But soldiers fight for symbols—symbols that embody the principles in which they believe.

"Pain, however, is often a necessary part of healing, and in a very real sense, the healing process for the wounds of Vietnam began. . . . The wall of the memorial could have been a wall between us. Instead, it became a bridge."

Some people, however, still tried to convince Watt *not* to issue a construction permit. They wanted approval from the Fine Arts Commission and the National Capital Planning Commission for specific placement of the statue and flag before a construction permit was issued. Others obviously still wanted to kill Maya Lin's design. An assistant secretary of Interior, for example, told Doubek that he'd been informed it would be criminal to issue a permit for the wall of names.

Scruggs went to see Senator Warner, the man who had forged the compromise. "It's now or never," Scruggs said. "We've got to have that permit."

"We'll get it," Warner said. He grabbed Scruggs's arm. "Once those shovels are in the ground, this episode is over."

Telephone lines connecting Congress, the White House, and the Interior Department were put to heavy use. Washington's power brokers were once again assessing whether the Vietnam vets should be given their memorial.

The moment of truth had arrived. "What Arthur Miller said of people in his play *After the Fall* seems equally true of nations," Vietnam vet Joseph Zengerle wrote in the *Washington Post.* " 'One must finally take one's life in one's arms.' "

At 11:00 A.M. on Monday, March 15, Doubek called from the National Park Service headquarters. "I've got it," he said. "I've got the damned permit!"

Everyone at the office cheered. Wheeler brought over a bottle of champagne. When it was empty, he reminded everyone that Watt still could be persuaded to revoke the permit. "Get the construction crews on the site," he said. "Now!"

The construction foreman was a combat vet. He stood with Scruggs out on the Mall.

"Do you know what it looks like after a B-52 raid?" Scruggs asked.

"I know a little about that."

Scruggs nodded toward the beautifully manicured grass where the Memorial would stand.

"Can you make this look like one of those raids? Can you give us a lot of holes all over the place that no one could ever fill?"

The foreman smiled. "Sure. I've had plenty of practice."

If Watt ever tried to revoke the construction permit, he would have a lot of explaining to do.

STOUGHTON, MASSACHUSETTS

Several days after the construction permit was issued, Scruggs flew to Stoughton, Massachusetts, whose militia in 1775 had been one of the first to volunteer for the Revolutionary Army.

Television camera crews from Boston greeted him, and a crowd of Vietnam veterans hustled him into a waiting car with a homemade "Welcome Jan Scruggs" sign on the side. Inside the car, he was handed a beer, which he drank as a police escort led the six-car motorcade at 75 miles per hour.

It was the handiwork of former helicopter gunner Billy Large and VFW Post 1645, known as "The Post with a Heart."

Large told Scruggs exactly what he thought about the Memorial: "You are kicking ass, you crazy SOB. You are getting the names where they belong. You know, we never heard of the Memorial until some veterans started saying it was a hole in the ground. I couldn't believe it. Vietnam veterans getting something. We had to pull together, so we decided to raise some money for that hole in the ground."

The next morning there was a parade through town to commemorate withdrawal of the last American troops from Vietnam. It was a good old-fashioned parade, with veterans groups from all over New England, a firing detail from the Massachusetts National Guard, soldiers in colonial costumes, and Vietnam Gold Star parents. Afterwards, there was a memorial service, and a $5,000 check was presented to the VVMF. Speeches were given. A bugler played taps.

Billy Large, his voice breaking with emotion, read a poem that he had composed:

> My country called. . . . Yes I was there.
> You tell me now there is no job here.
> Twenty years old . . . I've just come home.
> Not figuring at all I'm still alone. . . .
> I ask myself with a mixed-up mind, to see what I have left behind.
> Friends and comrades eighteen and brave, so many now in a makeshift grave.
> The cries of death heard throughout the night. A stupid war they wouldn't let us fight.

Wreaths were laid, salutes were given, and the colors were presented. Then a Vietnam vet walked to the podium. "Simeon J. B. Bergman," he said.

There was a pause and from somewhere behind the podium the town-hall bell, which had been cast by Paul Revere, tolled once.

"Kevin Clancy."

The bell tolled again.

"Paul Czerwon."

This continued for nine names, Stoughton's sons killed in Vietnam.

People bowed their heads and wept.

Stoughton was what it was all about. People who worked in factories and went to church and raised kids and believed in America. The land of the free that made a mistake sometimes. This was who the Memorial was for. It wasn't for Jim Watt, Texas billionaires, generals, or politicians. It was for these people.

PREPARING THE PANELS

Maya Lin did not understand why the VVMF was in such a rush. Some 58,000 people had given their lives and countless others had given their limbs in a war that lasted over ten years. Couldn't the VVMF at least take the time to do things right? They were building a "McMonument," a fast-food memorial. Perhaps it would be best to do things very slowly. It had taken ten years for all the men whose names were on the Memorial to die. Perhaps inscribing their names should take at least as long. They should erect an empty granite wall, and then let the country watch, name by name, year by year, as the death toll mounted.

She had promised to remain silent until the groundbreaking permit was issued. But she had told them, "Once construction on the Mall begins, I'll do what I have to do."

In the meantime, preparation of the granite had started. Because all black granite quarried in the United States has prominent gray veins, the VVMF's supply came from a quarry near Bangalore, India. While the VVMF juggled Washington politics, 30 trucks drove across snow-covered roads to Barre, Vermont, to deliver 3,000 cubic feet of granite to Natavi & Sons and Granite Industries of Vermont, Inc. Indian laborers had quarried the granite, which weighed 210 pounds per cubic foot, by hand.

The job: Transform these granite blocks into about 150 panels, each three inches thick, 40 inches wide, and varying in height from ten feet eight inches to eight inches.

A massive high-speed diamond-tipped saw cut the granite into slices like pieces of bread.

The slices were polished, using first a series of bricks and then a felt buffer covered with tin oxide, which is much finer than talc. The stone now had a glossy shine.

Guided by computer-generated drawings, workers then fabricated the stone, cutting it into panels. They had little room for error. If they broke or incorrectly cut any of the panels, more granite would have to be sent from the same quarry in India. No one knew how much, if any, was still available.

There was another reason to worry. Black granite is formed by volcanic action of the earth. It is impossible to see fractures in such stone until it is polished; most work, therefore, must be done before you learn if it is wasted. In late winter, workers saw what they feared: major fractures in some of the stone. A telex went out to India: "Send another shipment immediately."

Once completed, the panels had to be shipped to the Binswanger Glass Company of Memphis, Tennessee, where the names would be sandblasted on. To prevent scratching the glossy surface, each panel was wrapped in four-foot-wide adhesive tape and placed on a specially air-cushioned flatbed truck.

By mid-May, the panels started arriving in Memphis.

Maya Lin was not happy. She knew that finished panels would begin arriving on the Mall within 60 to 90 days. She had to make a decision. Should she do nothing, or should she fight the statue?

People kept saying things to her like "You're young. You don't know what you've designed." She considered the addition of a statue to be a desecration, but whenever she asked about it, they told her not to worry. No matter how she dressed or acted, she felt treated like a little girl.

And she, in turn, believed that the vets did not understand what they were building. They thought the Memorial was only going to be beautiful. They did not understand what it would really be. At one point, for example, Doubek asked her, "What will happen when people first see it?"

She swallowed and said something encouraging. She wanted to say, They'll cry.

9

GROUNDBREAKING

FRIDAY, MARCH 26, 1982, was sunny, cold, and windy in Washington.

A 500-foot red ribbon was stretched along the ground, one arm pointing toward the Washington Monument, the other toward the Lincoln Memorial. One hundred and twenty shovels, one each for 120 vets representing all 50 states and all veterans organizations, were placed along the ribbon.

Several thousand spectators stood to the left of the podium. The press section was overflowing.

Because of the VVMF's instructions that bulldozers rip apart the site, the entire area was filled with inch-thick mud.

Vietnam veterans, top officials from virtually every veterans organization in America, Gold Star Mothers, notables such as Ambassador Ellsworth Bunker, and just plain GI's, including Scruggs's old buddy Jimmy Mosconis, were waiting with their shovels.

VA deputy administrator Charles Hagel scribbled some notes as others spoke. But as he approached the podium, he crumpled the paper. He had been awake much of the night trying to write out his thoughts. But they were too tied up with emotions, not the sort of thing he could wrestle down onto cold, impersonal paper.

"This is a particularly poignant week for me," Hagel said. Something about his face and the tenseness of his body immediately caught the audience's attention. "I served in the Ninth Division at the Mekong Delta, with my brother Tom, for one year in 1968. It was this week, fourteen years ago, that my brother Tom and I were crossing a river on patrol when the first squad of our company tripped claymore mine trip wires, and the first squad ahead of my brother and me was killed. The names of those squad members will be part of the 57,000 names remembered and inscribed in this Memorial. And I think it's essential that we also remember the 2,500 MIA's that are all part of this Memorial. . . .

"We also must know, and understand, that there is no glory in war, only suffering. That's why we recognize those who have gone before us and that's why we continually try and understand and learn from wars."

Army chaplain Max D. Sullivan gave the benediction: "May this be a holy place of healing for the conflicting emotions of that terrible, divisive war, conflicting feelings of laughter and the tears, the fun and the fears, the caring, the cruelty, the loving, and, oh, yes, the pride."

The crowd cheered and sang "God Bless America." As they left, most saved the official program: "2,700,000 served," it said, "300,000 were wounded, 75,000 were disabled, 57,000 died, and more than 2,000 remain unaccounted for. . . . *They are not forgotten.*"

All the fine emotions generated by groundbreaking could not hide signs of future trouble. VA administrator Robert Nimmo refused to give VA employees an hour off to attend the ceremonies, even though these workers had received time off to honor the Washington Redskins football team when they won the Super Bowl. As shovels were breaking ground, Nimmo himself was playing at a nearby golf course, a good indication that the Reagan Administration was perhaps distancing itself from the Memorial.

Another important person who chose not to attend was Maya Lin. Pain, resentment, and anger resulting from the statue compromise had alienated her from the VVMF. She was honoring her word about remaining silent, and had also grown tired of dodging reporters with questions about the statue. "I just want to be far away," she told one of the vets.

On her day of great personal triumph, Maya Lin was out of town.

Journalists reported that some vets liked the idea of a statue and some did not. Most vets seemed to share the views of Thomas G. Suprock, a partially disabled former helicopter pilot who represented Rhode Island:

"Further arguments are meaningless. . . . I don't need a memorial to remember their sacrifice, as I am sure no other Vietnam vet or their families need to be reminded. But certainly the people of this country do [need reminding] now and 300 years from now."

The groundbreaking also attracted considerable editorial comment. "It could not have come at a more appropriate time, for this nation, a time when we face very difficult questions being tossed about concerning America's standing among its foes and its allies," the Mountain Home, Arkansas, *Baxter Bulletin* said. "There is not now, and probably never will be a consensus of opinion about what America should have done in Vietnam. . . . Only those who were there can be counted upon to voice opinions from which we can draw wisdom, and guidance in the future. Many of those are silenced because they are embittered by their treatment upon return home, and by controversies at home as they fought abroad. The U.S. policymakers need to listen."

After the ceremonies, the VVMF hosted a thank-you reception in the U.S. Capitol for members of Congress and major corporate contributors.

Suddenly shouts came from the doorway. Fatigue-clad vets, their combat boots covered with mud, pushed through the door. They'd driven all night from New England to attend the ceremonies. Who had the right, they shouted, to exclude them?

A violent confrontation between the vets and Capitol Hill police seemed likely. Someone could easily get hurt, and then the story would be on every front page in America, confirming that Vietnam vets were indeed untamed psychopaths. But Senator Warner put his arm around the biggest vet. "Fellas," the senator said, "I'm going to take you to a real good lunch. Follow me."

As soon as he could slip away from the reception, Scruggs went to find those vets. He was angry. They had screwed up just when things were working out. God knows what trouble they'd caused after leaving with Warner. They looked as though they were upset enough to do anything. But he found them in a private dining room, laughing, eating steak, and pounding Warner on the back.

Scruggs walked away worried. If a simple groundbreaking ceremony almost provoked violence, what would happen when hundreds of thousands of vets arrived in November for the Salute? A lot of anger had been building up for years. They could just rip the place apart.

THE SCULPTURE PANEL

Later that week, Wheeler drafted a charter for the sculpture panel. Their assignment was to recommend a sculptor, a statue design, and locations for the flag and statue to the VVMF board. In forming the panel, the VVMF followed the same strategy as before: Get opponents on the team. James Webb and Milt Copulos from the opponents vs. Art Mosley and Bill Jayne, who supported Maya Lin's design. "Two and two," Wheeler said. "There's no majority. They either agree or they fail."

At its first meeting, all four members of the panel agreed that the statue should reflect ordinary Vietnam vets—who they were and what they did. "It should also make the wall more accessible," Jayne said. "It should be prideful, but not glorify war."

The panel interviewed Frederick Hart, the sculptor who had been part of the creative team which had placed third in the original design competition. He was unquestionably an artist of considerable talent who possessed one other attractive attribute: He had played his politics well. Unlike Maya Lin, who never tried to learn about Vietnam, Hart had spent considerable time studying the war and talking with its veterans. He had nurtured a relationship with most of the key players, including Scruggs, Doubek, Wheeler, and especially Fund adversary James Webb.

Hart told the panel what sort of statue he envisioned: true to life, capturing the feeling of closeness and camaraderie shared by Vietnam vets. Nothing huge, not a fighting statue, and certainly not the toy soldiers that some people wanted. Something that would neither obscure nor compete with Maya Lin's design.

Still worried that the statue had been conceived in a closed-door compromise, Mosley called the original jurors and asked what they thought. He was able to reach all but one. The jurors seemed to feel that a statue *could* be added if that was politically necessary, but none was enthusiastic about such an addition.

On May 17, Hart and the sculpture panel agreed that "one figure was just too lonely, and could not interact with the Memorial in a way that would be most effective." They authorized him to work with three figures, and to "begin work on a fully refined bronze model of the sculpture approximately 16 inches high showing all details."

The day after meeting with the sculpture panel, Hart was sitting with a handful of modeling clay at his dining-room table. He knew that his statue had to capture the brotherly love, intimacy, and camaraderie that vets had shared in combat. But how? He had gotten to the point where he had tried too hard. He had played out ideas, read books, talked with hundreds of vets. And yet he was back at point zero. The modeling clay did nothing.

Slowly, his fingers starting moving. Hours later, he was on the telephone with sculpture panel members. The six-inch statue in front of him looked *exactly* right. "I think I've got it," he said. "I think I've got it."

On June 17, the panel members saw it, and felt for an instant they were back in Vietnam. Like *Red Badge of Courage* author Stephen Crane, Hart had never served in the military. Yet he captured the feelings and the texture of combat. The statue reminded the vets of their youth and of friends who never came back. It showed fear and courage and the heroism of endurance.

The three soldiers, however, did reveal the limitations of strictly representational art. There was a white, a black, and a Hispanic. All were young and all looked like infantrymen. Pilots, sailors, native Americans, Orientals, nurses, and other groups would not be represented. The VVMF could only hope that pressure for "equality" did not begin. Such pressure to turn Hart's work into a mob scene could kill the statue—and with it the Memorial.

While Hart sculpted a presentation model of the statue, work on the Memorial continued. Construction workers were driving 140 concrete pilings 35 feet into bedrock, and Doubek supervised compilation of names. The criterion for including a name on the wall was clear: Executive orders from Presidents Johnson and Nixon had specified Vietnam, Laos, Cambodia, and coastal areas as a combat zone. If the Defense Department, acting in accordance with these directives, considered an individual to be a Vietnam fatality or to be missing in action, his name would be included.

Many cases were heartbreaking. Some veterans had been slowly dying from war-related causes for fifteen years. Some were in comas. Some had died in training or on the way to Indochina. At least one Vietnam POW had committed suicide shortly after returning home.

Who should go on the wall? The VVMF could only rely on the Department of Defense: Vietnam fatalities were whomever the U.S. government designated. Heartbreak notwithstanding, nothing could be done about the rest.

A further problem came with the possibility that government records might be inconsistent, inaccurate, or incomplete. This possibility forced the Fund, under the direction of Doubek, to spend several months cross-checking casualty lists to make sure every eligible name was included. Another two months' effort went into guaranteeing that each name was spelled correctly. The VVMF paid to have personnel at the military archives in St. Louis pull out each fatality's individual folder and double-check the spelling of his name on the final fatality list.

There seemed to be little room for error. Once the names were engraved on granite, they could not be erased. But a ragged edge on each line was left so there would be room for several hundred additions.

As Doubek worked, *60 Minutes* correspondent Morley Safer came in with a camera crew.

There was no way to know what the *60 Minutes* story would say or when it would be broadcast. "We like to keep our distance until the work is done," an official explained.

Because the media had already exaggerated and encouraged the split among vets, the VVMF was worried. Whenever *60 Minutes* got involved, the stakes were especially high. The program attracted about 30 million viewers.

60 Minutes cameras also followed progress of the granite panels. In Memphis, workers at Binswanger Glass produced two 40-by-48-inch sample stones, cut to specifications set by architect Kent Cooper.

The names were engraved through a complicated process. Each stone was cleaned, painted with chemicals, and allowed to dry overnight. It was then covered with a photo negative that was an exact stencil of the names in the order in which they would appear on the wall. Then it was exposed to a light, left for a short time, washed, and sandblasted. Next, it was examined for pinholes, improperly formed letters, and other imperfections.

Many tedious problems had to be solved. Only slow, trial-and-error work on test panels could reveal the proper balance of chemicals and exposure to light. Furthermore, cutting the letters too deep cast a shadow. Much experimentation revealed that the engraving was 20/1000th of an inch too much. The thickness of a strand of hair could spoil the Memorial.

Other key problems included which grit of sand—actually, aluminum oxide—to use. Fine sand produced smooth but not-so-light letters; coarser sand made letters lighter, but grainier and not as legible. Architect Kent Cooper finally decided to use smooth letters. The angle of sandblasting also had to be determined. Standing straight in front of the panel produced uniform valleys in the middle of the letters; standing off to the side provided slanted valleys.

And finally, the distance that sandblasters stood from the panels had to be determined. Standing too close created irregular edges; standing too far left the letters too shallow.

As he tested for the best depth of letters and angle of engraving, Cooper continually asked the workmen to move the 400–500-pound test panels out onto the parking lot. He had to see how light would fall on the polished black granite surface.

The workers were accustomed to handling glass, and knew that the granite would shatter if dropped. They bent over the panels and moved slowly as they laid the slabs next to each other out in the parking lot.

One day Cooper noticed something strange as soon as the workmen stepped back. The sky was on the ground. Clouds were moving. Color, texture, shading, and depth—all in clear, soft impressionistic tones—were mirrored on the black granite.

Maya Lin had insisted on black granite in part because it was "reflective"—owing to the presence of mica. Neither the jurors nor anyone who worked on the wall had considered this attribute to be especially important. Now, as he stared down at clouds, Cooper felt his heart pounding.

Kent Cooper's final decision: To maximize legibility, use very fine grit sand, do the blasting from straight in front, and stand about 18 inches away, so the letters would have maximum depth with no shadow. The letters would be .53 inches high and .015 inches deep.

Sandblasting was done by humans rather than machines, because even a few seconds of a malfunctioning or jammed machine could ruin an entire panel.

Sandblasters dressed in hot rubber diving suits with fresh cool air coming in the helmet worked one at a time. They were mostly students from a local art school. Concentration was essential. If they moved faster to the left than to the right, the panel would be streaked—something that would be apparent only later when it was carried outside. Different parts of the granite had different hardness, so it was often necessary to stop and use a micrometer to check the depth of the letters. If a letter was too deep, for any reason, a panel would be ruined, and there were only three spare panels.

One particularly emotional moment came when a woman whose brother had died in Vietnam engraved his name.

PLANNING THE SALUTE

Preparing for the Salute continued at a 14-hour-a-day pace.

Staff members visited local military installations to learn how parades were organized. Doing things right involved incredible detail. The Army alone had over 300 units, each with its own flag.

Plans called for a National Salute to Vietnam Veterans from November 10 to 14, what the VVMF billed as "a big national thank-you." It would entail the work of at least 500 volunteers.

Wednesday, November 10: A 24-hour-a-day vigil at National Cathedral would begin. Over 250 volunteers would read aloud every name on the wall. This would last more than 50 hours. In the evening, there would be the Entertainers' Salute to Vietnam Veterans at Constitution Hall.

Thursday: Vietnam Veterans of America, issue-oriented workshops; ceremonies at Arlington Cemetery; Red Cross special POW reception; unit reunion registration; concert by the U.S. Army band.

Friday: VFW open house; panel on Agent Orange and panel on post-traumatic stress disorder; Gold Star open house; American Legion open house; VVMF thank-you to volunteers.

Saturday: Parade down Constitution Avenue to the Memorial.

Sunday: Religious ceremonies nationwide in remembrance of all who served.

To conduct such an elaborate series of activities over a five-day period involved many risks. A crazy individual, provoked by the crowds and the emotions, could start shooting. Thousands of angry vets, spurred by what they considered to be callous treatment on issues such as Agent Orange, could storm the VA headquarters. Rumors even suggested that the Salute could be like the famed World War I Bonus Army, which had ended in bloodshed.

The risk, however, would have to be taken. When else would Vietnam's veterans have another chance? They had already been home for ten years and had been ignored the whole time.

Although at least 100,000 people were expected, lack of publicity continued to worry the Salute's organizers. Millions of veterans and their families would suffer a new hurt: They would hear about the Salute only *after* it had happened.

The current Commander-in-Chief, Ronald Reagan, could help on this front, and the vets made numerous efforts to enlist him as honorary chairman of the Salute. But the White House seemed unable to respond. The vets' inability to plan for a dedication of the Memorial also made publicity difficult. James Watt's groundbreaking permit had stated that the statue and flag "must be completed prior to any dedication." By accepting this permit, the VVMF had pledged *not* to push for dedication.

The Fund did the best it could through press conferences and mass mailings. The response highlighted how desperately the American people wanted the Salute. Hundreds of volunteers showed up at VVMF headquarters. And a young girl in North Carolina wrote, "I can't tell you how happy your letter made my daddy. We didn't know about the memorial. I would like to see my daddy in the parade. Could my daddy be in the parade? Please tell me if there is anything special he should wear."

MAYA LIN ATTACKS

Things seemed to be going well until the morning of July 7. Milt Copulos called Scruggs at home. "Have you seen the *Post?*" he asked.

In a story headlined "Maya Lin's Angry Objections," she had broken her silence: "This farce has gone on too long. . . . I have to clear my own conscience. . . . Past a certain point it's not worth compromising. . . . They are keeping me uninformed . . . in an isolation chamber. . . . I was told, 'If you don't agree, we're gonna can the whole thing right now.' It was a real power play blackball. I kept asking myself, 'Is it worth getting built if you have to sell out?' It [groundbreaking] was a really tough time for me. I just ran away, left the country. I probably should have fought."

Her views on Frederick Hart left little to the imagination: "I can't see how anyone of integrity can go around drawing mustaches on other people's portraits."

Maya Lin argued that Hart had entered the initial competition and lost; that he had found a back door to the Mall; that a small group of men had subverted the democratic process; and that politics had won over art. "It's really disillusioning," she said.

"She finds it particularly ironic," the *Post* reported, "that the veterans, 'who say they fought in Vietnam to defend freedom,' find her understated, 'think-what-you-will' design so distressing."

Copulos already had a firm idea of how to respond. "We should tell Maya, 'No statue, no wall,' " he said to Scruggs. He mentioned that Watt could revoke the construction permit at any time.

"Everything will be O.K.," Scruggs said. "We'll get the statue, don't worry."

Maya Lin's statement was an opening salvo in what journalists soon labelled an "art war." Robert N. Lawrence, president of the American Institute of Architects called the addition of Hart's statue "ill conceived," a "breach of faith," and a "dangerous precedent." Paul Spreiregen, who had organized the design competition, called Hart's statue an "outrageous desecration." Juror Harry Weese told reporters, "It's as if Michelangelo had the Secretary of the Interior climb onto the scaffold and muck around."

Such statements were only the surface evidence of an intense behind-the-scenes effort to convince the Fine Arts Commission that it should disapprove the statue.

Heavy firepower, however, was also lining up on the other side. Watt, for example, called for "a heroic sculpture."

"Design aesthetics," he warned the Fine Arts Commission, "are a secondary concern."

60 Minutes added to the tension. Reporters and producers interviewed Perot, Carhart, and other principals, trying to stimulate comments. "Mr. Perot is very emotional and very upset about this project," one producer told Scruggs.

The VVMF did not need another fight with the billionaire.

In the meantime, Maya Lin retained a nationally famous law firm. Her legal position was unclear. The design competition rules specified that the VVMF retained the right to resolve all disagreements. But a growing body of legal precedents had given artists considerable control over changes in their works. A lawsuit by Maya Lin would also generate considerable publicity, arousing the artistic, liberal, and antiwar communities. She might even obtain a temporary injunction, which could stall the project for years.

Wheeler tried to head off a confrontation by telling her lawyers, "Most of us are here because we remember men who did not come home alive. We're trying to do the right thing. Do you have any ideas that can help us?"

The lawyers remained noncommittal.

Ironically, Maya Lin and the Memorial's opponents had one goal in common: They all wanted to delay dedication. James Webb was arguing that the construction fence should stay up until the statue and flag were in place—sometime in 1983 or 1984. Perot called to ask that the VVMF cancel its Salute, and threatened to sue. Maya Lin wanted the VVMF to wait a few years until the pressure died down and to then build the Memorial without a statue.

The VVMF wanted only one thing: to have every name on the Mall by Veterans Day 1982, as planned.

THE FIRST PANEL ON THE MALL

The vets were afraid that the assault by Maya Lin would prompt the sometimes unpredictable James Watt to cancel the construction permit. "We have to get one of the finished panels on the Mall," one vet suggested. "Any attempt to remove it would then trigger an emotional and political firestorm."

In early July, a call went out to Memphis: "We need a finished panel right away."

Six panels were ready, but the problem was finding a flatbed truck with the necessary air shock absorbers. Desperate calls finally produced results, and late one night the 3,000-pound panel began its journey across Tennessee and Virginia. Engineers and a crane were waiting on the Mall, and within hours it was installed on the concrete backing that now stretched at the foot of the Lincoln Memorial.

The human element also had to be in place. Once they knew which panel was being sent, the VVMF tried to find the parents of GI's whose names appeared on it. They began by looking up names in the Washington and Baltimore telephone books. Most calls were wasted, but then they found a Gold Star Mother. "I loved him so much," she said. "Yes, of course, we'll be there. All of our family will be there."

Three other families were found. None mentioned the controversy or the need for a statue and flag. Seeing the son's name was all each wanted.

On July 22, about 24 hours after the panel arrived in Washington, several dozen reporters mingled with parents, family members, and vets who had heard about the upcoming ceremony.

Men working at the site took off their hardhats and stood silently as Emogene Cupp, whose son had been buried on his twentieth birthday, released a rope that held a blue velvet sheet over the panel with 665 names.

Scruggs introduced the parents and announced who their sons were. Then each family walked up to the panel and left one long-stemmed red rose.

The families also did something unexpected. *They touched the stone.* Even a six-year-old girl walked calmly through the adults and reached up to an uncle she had never met. The touches were more than soft. They were gentle, filled with feeling—as if the stone were alive.

Nobody can stop the dream now, Scruggs thought. The names are up. Washington and Lincoln are no longer alone—665 Vietnam vets have joined them. Try and stop us now, James Watt. A battalion of grunts is ready and waiting.

Later that night, an ex-Marine who had attended the ceremony wrote to Scruggs: "Reflecting on what had transpired during this morning, I recalled a personal experience in Vietnam. Stationed near a medical unit with a helicopter pad for evacuation of the dead and wounded, the memory came to mind of marines wrapped in black bags waiting to be flown out by helicopter. I remember how tenderly the bodies were lain by their comrades, something approaching love or tenderness of a higher plane of one comrade for another."

Work on engraving the panels continued throughout the summer. Project architect Carla Corbin, who worked for Kent Cooper, spent much of this time flying back and forth between Memphis and Washington. One day, a man sat next to her and asked what all her blueprints were about. As soon as he heard it was the Vietnam Veterans Memorial, he said he was a Vietnam combat vet, that he knew about the controversy, and that he wanted to hear all about the wall.

Something about the emotion in his voice made Corbin open up. She stopped talking only after the plane had landed. My God, she suddenly thought, what if he hates it?

The man's voice broke. "I'm very honored," he said. He turned away and started to cry.

Workmen installing the panels on the Mall had a special problem. Whenever the gate opened to let a truck in or out, someone would try to sneak past the eight-foot construction fence. Once inside, they often refused to leave, even when warned they could get hurt.

Other people, many of whom had come from out of town, simply stood outside the fence waiting for a glimpse of the wall. Usually, construction workers made special allowances for family members and vets. An older man explained that he wanted to see his son's name. He found it, and stood there clear-eyed and staring. But when he recognized nearby names, people his son had mentioned in letters home, the man started to sob.

A Navy pilot in uniform brought a Purple Heart. "It belonged to my brother," he explained. "He and I flew together. I'd like you to put it in with the concrete that's being poured."

The pilot saluted as the medal disappeared into the wall.

10

WORKING TOWARD THE SALUTE

THE VVMF ASKED VETS to send in preregistration forms for the Salute. As of Labor Day, not one had been received.

To stimulate interest, the vets called NBC, ABC, and CBS. The answer: If your events turn out to be really good, we'll show up. For now, forget it.

But work on the Salute continued under the direction of Sandie Fauriol. Letters to all state and territorial governors requested that they proclaim the Salute to be Vietnam Veterans Week, and that they organize official delegations in the parade. Veterans organizations were briefed. Volunteers were recruited. Unit reunions were planned. Participation by civic organizations, the Veterans Administration, the District of Columbia government, the Red Cross, the USO, the U.S. Park Police, bus companies, Amtrak, and all major airlines was coordinated. Publicity packets were prepared. Bands were contacted. Construction of floats began. Scripts were written for the parade announcers. Maps and directions for bus drivers were compiled. Arrangements were made for press facilities, podiums, and portable toilets. Parade marshals were selected. Bleacher seats were rented. Staging areas were established. Radio communications systems were set up. Appropriate parade permits were requested, and an appeal was made for permission to have Vietnam-era helicopters and jets fly over the parade.

Word was getting out, and letters kept coming in.

From a former Marine: "I saw much pain and agony and death. For those who are unable, I would like to say, thank you for caring."

From a former paratrooper: "The Memorial has led me to seek out the small notebook which I carried in Vietnam, and to read again the names of soldiers in my company killed in action. . . . The sadness that comes from remembering them alive, laughing, working, soldiers at war [is overwhelming]."

From a former grunt: "If I can touch the name of my friends who died, maybe I will finally have time to react. Maybe I will end up swearing, maybe crying, maybe smiling, remembering a funny incident. Whatever it is, I will have time and the focal point to do it now. There just wasn't the emotional time in Nam to know what happened."

From a former platoon commander: "I once again studied the photographs of my young troopers, and wept. The sadness of their tragic deaths overcame me. And once again the hatred of and bitterness toward three former Presidents, Secretaries of State and Defense, countless numbers of gutless members of Congress, and an apathetic and uncaring public, well up inside me. It will be totally unjust if any politician in office between 1965 and 1975 is allowed near the Memorial."

From a VA hospital patient: "All I ever asked for was a little thank you for the time I spent in my nation's service. Maybe this will be it."

From a friend of a Vietnam vet: "At Peyton Randolph Elementary School, John Thompson played the infield, usually third base. A little heavy, he hit right-handed with power. Slow on the bases, usually quiet and friendly. And now John Thompson's name will be on our Vietnam Veterans Memorial. Thank you for the opportunity to express the grief, to relieve the pain and the tears. And to remember his fight."

From an antiwar person: "Although I opposed the war with all my heart, it was the fault of our politicians. The men who died and were wounded were needless sacrifices our country should nevertheless honor and respect for individual valor, courage and heroism."

From someone who escaped the draft: "I never served in the military and for this reason I've always had a feeling I did not do my part, but for those who served in Vietnam, particularly those who lost their lives, I say 'thank you and I'm sorry.' "

The poet William Blake once noted that mankind imprisons itself in "mind-forged manacles." All across America, manacles of the mind were slipping open. Frustration and anger were dissolving into introspection and acceptance.

The Memorial, although not yet constructed, had already started doing its work.

THE POLITICAL FIGHT CONTINUES

One of the major problems for Salute organizers was that they could not announce that the Memorial would be dedicated.

James Watt and opponents of Maya Lin's design wanted to delay dedication until after the statue and flag were in place. For the most part, they insisted that the statue be right in front of the wall and that the flag fly from the wall's apex. Anything less, they seemed to feel, should be reason enough to kill the whole thing. If the placement is not done correctly, someone at Interior warned, then we'll "shut down the construction site."

The statue and flag, however, could not be placed anywhere without careful thought. Architect Kent Cooper, for example, warned that the juncture of the walls was too "weak a location for a powerful symbol such as the American flag. . . . The casual placement looks more like an oversized putting green."

The American Legion, Veterans of Foreign Wars, AMVETS, Vietnam Veterans of America, and other veterans groups added pressure with their demands that dedication take place on Veterans Day 1982, no matter what the status of the statue and flag.

Robert W. Spanogle, national adjutant of the American Legion, told the VVMF board on September 9 that "failure to dedicate the Memorial in November of 1982 will be a breach of good faith with the citizens of this nation. More importantly . . . a delay . . . will stand as the final insult to those who served and have already waited too long for their rightful place in history."

Legionnaires, according to Spanogle, were organizing car caravans and other means of transportation "for not only Vietnam veterans but for mothers and fathers, uncles and aunts and children. [They] are coming to dedicate the most significant national shrine erected in this century.

We cannot deny them that right. In fact, with the momentum now established, I do not believe the dedication can be stopped."

In other words, thousands and thousands of vets and family members would break down the construction fence and dedicate the Memorial with their love, tears, and prayers. With or without Watt's permission, it would be a People's Dedication.

The American Legion had muscle to back up its notions of morality. Legionnaires—making an average contribution of nine dollars—had raised $1 million for the Memorial. The message from them now seemed clear: No dedication, no dollars.

At the end of the VVMF board meeting, Wheeler reported what Webb wanted: Leave the fence around the wall, or at least leave one panel out to show that the wall is not ready to be dedicated. Then go ahead with the Salute.

Wheeler also reminded his colleagues that they had promised James Watt not to push for a dedication until the statue was ready. "We're a bunch of guys in a birch canoe surrounded by piranhas," he said. "If just one of us breaks the canoe, we fall in."

"Fine," said Fauriol. "Let Webb choose the panel to be left out, and have him call the mothers of the guys whose names are being kept off the wall."

"Let's invite Watt to watch Vietnam vets tear down the fence," someone else suggested.

By overwhelming vote, with only Wheeler dissenting, the board decided to join those who demanded a dedication.

THE STATUE IS UNVEILED

In mid-September, Maya Lin and her attorney accepted an invitation to see the statue before the press conference at which it would be unveiled.

She walked up to the statue, stared at it, and started to walk around it. She said nothing.

To the vets, she looked bruised and angry. They respected her courage, and were ready to fight her if they had to.

She left after only a few minutes.

Later interviews published in *Art in America* magazine revealed the depth of difference between the two artists.

Hart: "I don't like blank canvases. Lin's memorial is intentionally not meaningful. It doesn't relate to ordinary people, and I don't like art that is contemptuous of life."

Lin: "Three men standing there before the world—it's trite. It's a generalization, a simplification. Hart gives you an image—he's illustrating a book."

On September 20, Frederick Hart pulled back a tarpaulin covering a two-foot-high model of the statue.

"One senses the figures as passing by the treeline and caught in the presence of the wall, turning to gaze upon it almost as a vision," he said. "There is about them the physical contact and sense of unity that bespeaks the bonds of love and sacrifice that is the nature of men at war. And yet they are each alone."

To the vets, the statue looked true. Boonie hat. Facial expressions. Fatigues. Helmet. Dog tags in a boot. Way of holding weapons. The men were strong, yet vulnerable. Committed, yet confused. Wheeler told reporters that the sons and daughters of men killed in Vietnam would look at the statue and say, "This is my father. I never saw him alive. But he wore those clothes. He carried that weapon. He was young. I see now, and know him better."

Some critics praised Hart's work, while others agreed with the *Boston Globe*'s assessment that it was "a Starsky and Hutch pose" in a design resembling " 'Socialist-realist' Stalinist sculpture in Moscow." Most reporters, however, reacted to the statue only in its overall political context. Nationally syndicated columnist Ellen Goodman, for example, wrote that the Memorial would now be "a classic example of art by committee." The London *Economist* said, "This 'improvement' would make the V-shaped memorial more like other memorials, but it cannot make Vietnam more like other wars." *New York Times* critic Paul Goldberger wrote, "To try to represent a period of anguish and complexity in our history with a simple statue of armed soldiers is to misunderstand all that has happened, and to suggest that no lessons have been learned."

A day after the unveiling, a James J. Kilpatrick column appeared in the nation's newspapers. He had walked through the mud to see the construction site. "Gradually the long walls . . . came into view,"

Kilpatrick wrote. "Nothing I had heard or written had prepared me for the moment. I could not speak. I wept. . . . This memorial has a pile driver's impact. No politics. No recriminations. Nothing of vainglory or of glory either. For 20 years I have contended that these men died in a cause as noble as any cause for which war was ever waged. . . . Never mind. The memorial carries a message for all ages: this is what war is all about."

Then Kilpatrick noted what was perhaps the Memorial's strongest attribute: "On this sunny Friday morning, the black walls mirrored the clouds of a summer's ending and reflected the leaves of an autumn's beginning, and the names—the names!—were etched enduringly upon the sky."

Another visitor to the site was Frank McCarthy, president of the Vietnam Veterans Relief Foundation (now the Vietnam Veterans Agent Orange Victims, Inc.) "I must admit that when I first viewed the artist's sketch, I was not impressed," he wrote in *The Stars and Stripes.* "In fact, I did not like the design, and sat at my desk to write a protest. . . . Last week I was in Washington on business and was fortunate enough to visit the construction site of the memorial. Although it is only half completed, its size and strength are awesome. One cannot comprehend the reality of this memorial by looking at artist's sketches. Nor can one feel the many emotions that arise upon viewing the names."

THE FINE ARTS COMMISSION ACTS

The Fine Arts Commission was scheduled to meet on Wednesday, October 13. On Sunday, October 10, *60 Minutes* ran its segment on the Memorial.

A group of friends came over to watch at the Scruggs home. They cheered when the segment entitled "Lest We Forget" began. The room soon quieted.

60 Minutes showed Americans the heavy political pressure that had built around the Memorial, but it divided the story neatly into good guys and bad guys. Perot and Watt were the bad guys. Maya Lin and the art establishment were the good guys. Washington's politicians had joined the bad guys. Everyone was ganging up on Maya Lin. Morley Safer highlighted one of the story's ugliest aspects: racism. Some vets did not like the idea of a memorial designed by an Oriental, prompting Safer to ask, "Was it the design that provoked such controversy or the designer, who was a student, a woman, an American, a Chinese-American?"

"I think it is, for some, very difficult for them," Maya Lin responded. "I mean they sort of lump us all together, for one thing. What is it? There is a term used. I first heard it maybe two years ago. It's called a gook."

Three days later, on the morning the Fine Arts Commission was scheduled to meet, the *Washington Post* prominently featured a long story about the Memorial by Tom Wolfe.

Wolfe, one of the leading writers to come out of the 1960s, specialized in narratives that slashed into whatever celebrity or social norm happened to be in vogue. He had never displayed any special interest in Vietnam or in veterans, but he did strongly favor representational art; indeed two of his most recent books had called modern art a fraud and attacked modernist architects.

In his *Post* story, Wolfe made it seem as though Carhart and Webb had initiated and organized the VVMF. He called the wall "a tribute to Jane Fonda," and said soldiers like Scruggs were "proles," a phrase which in George Orwell's novel *1984* referred to "dumb masses." But the writer saved his greatest passion for the jurors who had selected Maya Lin's design. He called them the "Mullahs of Modernism," and explained that "by the late 1940s the universities were turning out students who acted as if modernism were encoded in their genes. You could put a gun at the temple of one of the new breed and you couldn't make him sculpt a realistic figure of a soldier to put up on a pedestal."

Such writing was entertaining, provocative, and convincing. By the time they finished Wolfe's piece, readers would believe that Webb, Carhart, and their various friends had worked long and hard on the Memorial only to have it stolen by the spineless, mindless Mullahs.

Both *60 Minutes* and Tom Wolfe raised important questions. What is the relationship between popular and elite art? How should public art be selected? How should an artist's integrity be protected? Yet at the same time, these prestigious journalistic voices were distorting events rather than reporting them. It was impossible to guess what effect this might have on the Fine Arts Commission. Perhaps none. Or perhaps the Commission would recoil and conclude that the only responsible response to racism and to direct assaults on the arts community was to kill Hart's statue.

After they crowded past television cameras to find seats in the Fine Arts Commission hearing room, the VVMF and its opponents joined forces in arguing for authorization of the statue and flag.

James Webb, who had fought so hard against Maya Lin's design: "[You must] allow all those who served in Vietnam to feel that they are honored when they visit the site."

General Michael Davison, who had first suggested the statue and flag as a compromise: "This statue is breathtaking, because Frederick Hart, out of his genius, has captured that unique bond that ties men together in the face of danger."

Jack Wheeler: "Grief means looking at the truth and brings at times anger at the loss, and the anger takes different forms in each person. The hardest part of the job of building the Vietnam Veterans Memorial is to face the anger involved as our country does this work."

Some anger, however, seeped through. Ex-Marine David DeChant, who served three tours in Vietnam, told the commissioners, "Over the last several years, I have observed the process that has left me [with] . . . anger because of the individuals who speak out against the memorial design allegedly in the name of their Vietnam brothers, anger because of the individuals who are not veterans who threatened and attempted to dictate their wills through their power and money for spite and their own ego satisfaction, [and] anger for those who still wish to make a political statement about the war through the memorial. . . ."

Henry F. Arnold, designer of Constitution Gardens, spoke out strongly against Hart's work: "The proposed undistinguished, made-to-order statue is a sentimental response to a difference of opinion. The result is more likely to serve as a memorial to pettiness and corruptive endeavor. . . . It might be prudent and appropriate for the Commission to delay their decision until each member . . . and the detractors have had the chance to visit the Memorial, after it is completed, and experience the mysterious power of this unprecedented work of art."

Maya Lin, however, made the most powerful antistatue statement: "I [appeal] to the Commission to protect the artistic integrity of the original design. What is realistic? Is any one man's interpretation better able to convey an idea than any other's? Should it not be left to the observer? The original design gives each individual the freedom to reflect upon the heroism and sacrifice of those who served. It is symbolic of the freedom this country stands for. . . . It is a living park, a symbol of life

—the life of the returning veteran, who sees himself reflected within the time, within the names."

Everyone was sincere and held strong convictions. Many had waited hours to testify. Both opponents and supporters of the statue raised valid issues. But as the day ended, the time for argument was over. The Fine Arts Commission had to make a tough decision.

J. Carter Brown led the other commissioners to the Memorial site, where workers waited with an eight-foot styrofoam model of the statue. The workers moved this model back and forth in front of the wall as the commissioners stood back and discussed what to do. This continued for nearly an hour.

"We understand, I think, the dimensions of this decision," Brown said as soon as everyone returned to the hearing room. "I think it is not lost on us as human beings or as citizens of the United States the degree to which there is a felt need in this country for healing. . . . [The Mall] is sacred soil that is right next to our dearest and greatest patriotic memorials. And to put anything there is about the highest honor that this country can bestow."

The vets were sweating. These sounded like rosy three-dollar words for rejecting the statue.

"It is extraordinarily moving," Brown continued. "I think the litany of those names is enough to bring enormous emotions to everyone's heart, emotions of pride and of honor in the sacrifices that have been made in serving this country."

The Fine Arts Commission chairman then announced that by unanimous vote the Commission found the statue "acceptable," but that both the statue and flag were granted conditional approval, with the precise location of each subject to further study.

J. Carter Brown had walked safely through the political and artistic minefield. By refusing to place these new elements as demanded by the opponents, he avoided outraging Maya Lin and her allies in the arts community, effectively ending the threat posed by her lawsuit.

"In a funny sense the compromise brings the memorial closer to the truth," Maya Lin later wrote. "What is also memorialized is that people still cannot resolve that war, nor can they separate the issues, the politics, from it."

At the same time, by accepting the statue, Brown gave the Memorial's opponents no excuse to destroy it. What would Watt do now? No matter how much he might hate Maya Lin's design, his only option was to permit dedication.

A THREAT TO BLOW IT UP

At the VVMF, workdays stretched into fifteen and sixteen hours. Publicity was picking up. Special fund-raising efforts helped pay for television and radio ads. The Army agreed to supply tents for vets with nowhere to sleep. The government granted permission for flyovers by helicopters and F-4's. Honeywell donated computers so vets could find friends who also came to town for the Salute. The VVMF office stayed open seven days a week. Additional staff was hired.

Then, on October 19, just three weeks before the National Salute, word from James Watt arrived: Go ahead and dedicate the Memorial.

When workmen put the final panel of names in place, the construction fence was replaced by a small portable picket fence, which, in turn, was removed on November 10. Bright new sod from Florida was trucked in.

One mother visited the wall and wrote an open letter to her son:

> I didn't know what to expect or what my reactions would be at seeing this black wall. I just had to go. . . .
>
> The weather was unseasonably warm and sunny when we arrived in Washington, D.C. We got out of the car and started walking toward this Memorial. I could feel pulled toward this black wall and yet my feet didn't want to move. I was so scared. I was afraid I would find [your] name on this wall and yet I was afraid that maybe some mistake had been made and the name was left out. . . . [Then I saw it.] My heart seemed to stop. I seemed to tremble. I shook as though I was freezing. My teeth chattered. I felt as though I couldn't get my breath. God, how it hurt! . . . From the wall, like a mirror reflecting through my blurry tears, I seemed to see faces. Then I realized it was not the faces of the ones who had died, but of the living, who were here, like me, to find the name of a loved one.

Twenty-four hours before the National Salute, Doubek gave a briefing on the Memorial for counselors who would be available to help vets. As he spoke, Doubek had no idea how his audience was responding. Most were combat vets. Webb, Carhart, Perot, and others had been insisting for over a year that such people overwhelmingly rejected the Memorial, that they felt insulted. It was impossible to guess what they were thinking. They just stared at him.

When Doubek finished, the counselors asked a few questions. Doubek responded, and there was silence. Then, slowly, as though they did not want the moment to end, they all stood and applauded.

A workman used a hooked knife to clean the lines where the panels with names touched each other. He worked slowly and carefully. When he was finally satisfied, he took rags from his back pocket and wiped away the tiny spots of glue left over from the protective covering that had encased the granite during shipment.

At the VVMF offices, hundreds of calls were coming in every hour. Vets from all over the country wanted to learn about their Salute. Then one call made everyone stop. "We're going to blow up the Memorial," a man said.

The threat could not be ignored. In a nation where people shoot Presidents, a memorial would not be immune. The Fund called local police, the U.S. Park Police, and the FBI. Many were Vietnam veterans who expressed a special interest in providing protection. Furthermore, as word of the threat spread, groups of ex–Green Berets volunteered to stand 24-hour-a-day guard duty.

The names on the wall would not be alone.

PART FIVE

November

1982

11

GETTING THERE

FROM 1776 to 1982, large numbers of veterans had encamped in the nation's capital only twice. On Sunday, September 18, 1892, Washington, D.C., welcomed approximately 100,000 Union veterans who came for a reunion. Forty years later, during the Great Depression, at least 30,000 World War I veterans and their families came to demand advance payment of benefits awarded for wartime service. Two vets and a child died when tanks, soldiers on horseback, and bayonets forced them out of town.

Now, in November 1982, veterans and their families from all over America were once again gathering. It was exciting and spontaneous, with a momentum that defined itself.

"I will be in Washington for the dedication," one vet wrote. "I will not be there to tell tales of terror in the skies over Hanoi. I won't be representing anyone but a handful of ghosts whose blurry names and strangely boyish faces needed to be welcomed home."

A Vietnam vet sold his washer and dryer to get money for plane fare.

A vet got out of bed one night and told his wife, "I've got to go to Washington."

A vet walked 3,000 miles to Washington in combat fatigues and carrying a full combat pack, just as he had 12 years earlier in Vietnam.

A vet whose twin brother had died in Vietnam walked 1,255 miles to Washington.

A vet hitchhiking to Washington fell asleep, and awoke at the airport with a paid airline ticket in his pocket.

A vet told his wife about the Salute.

"You're going, of course," she said.

"Can we afford it?"

"Does that make any difference? You were there, you should go."

A vet put a sign reading " 'Nam Vet to D.C" in the back window of his car. People honked and waved.

A group of vets checked out of a VA hospital, penniless. A Congressional Medal of Honor winner took out a personal loan to rent a bus for them.

A Midwestern couple heard about the Salute on TV just after finishing dinner. They rushed to clear the table, loaded the dishwasher, switched it on, and went out to the door to D.C.

A bus bearing 40 vets broke down down in Columbus, Ohio. The repair bill was $1,500. The maintenance shop foreman said, "My son is a Vietnam vet," and refused payment.

All across America, such buses—along with airplanes and car caravans—became rolling barracks, as the men drifted into Washington from Boston, Cleveland, Dallas, Denver, and San Francisco; and from Stroud, Oklahoma; Fergus Falls, Minnesota; Jessup, Iowa; Bethel, Connecticut; and all the other towns and cities whose sons had served.

"It was as if they were all drawn by the same ghostly bugle," a newspaper in Beaumont, Texas, noted.

As they traveled, they made up songs and remembered how great it was to get C rations—pound cake and peaches.

They were afraid they would not be able to find the names they wanted. They were afraid they would cry. They were afraid they would be disappointed once again. They did not know what to expect.

Families and friends, virtually anyone whose life had been touched by a Vietnam vet, heard the same bugle.

"They say that you never forget your first love," a woman wrote to her local newspaper. "In 1957, when I was a teenager . . . he was slim and dark with a really nice smile. Overcoming his shyness, he invited me to a party, I took my 45's in a small gray cardboard box with a plastic handle. Our favorite record was Bobby Helms's 'Special Angel.' He carried the box and held my hand as we walked. It was beautiful, and it was romantic. We were very young (and, no doubt, very naive), but we were very happy.... Although we talked a lot and kissed a lot... the romance didn't last long. His family [moved away]. I never saw him again. Years later, escaping the drudgery of caring for my infant son, I went to the movies with my sister. We ran into an acquaintance who told us that he had been killed in Vietnam. In spite of all the rhetoric about America forgetting, from that day on I never have. . . . I will go to Washington and try to find his name on the Memorial. I hope I'll be able to touch it."

COMING HOME

Most GI's came home from Vietnam in one of two ways. The best was to reach your DEROS, date of expected return from overseas. For others, the trip was more complicated. Their remains were placed in rubberized canvas bags, zippered shut, and often stacked like firewood at collection points.

At the mortuary, the bodies were logged in, cleaned, fingerprinted, and kept in a walk-in refrigerator until identification could be confirmed. Then they were embalmed, issued new ID tags, and shipped to the United States, where they were dressed in a new uniform at the port of entry. Back in Vietnam, the body bags were washed in preparation for the next men.

Homecoming for vets, dead or alive, was mostly lonely. Few people had noticed when you left, and fewer expressed interest when you returned. Vietnam was on the newspaper front pages, yet somehow it was dirty, best left alone.

But now, as hundreds of thousands of people from every part of the country converged on Washington, as priests at the National Cathedral prepared a chapel for the Candlelight Vigil of Names, America was finally ready to welcome home its sons.

VIGIL

The vigil was scheduled from 10:00 A.M. Wednesday, November 10, to midnight of Friday, November 12.

At either end of the chapel was a large slow-burning candle. There were twelve rows of seats, red roses, and the soft echoes that followed each breath and each footstep.

It was a simple ceremony: Volunteers worked in half-hour shifts reading the names, throughout the day and night. Every fifteen minutes there was a pause for prayer.

For weeks, volunteers had been practicing their allotted names. The hardest part was preparing not to cry, so that each name could be read loudly and clearly. Pronunciation was also a problem; and a Polish priest, a Spanish teacher, and a rabbi supplied expert advice.

"Rhythmic Spanish names. Tongue-twisting Polish names, guttural German, exotic African, homely Anglo-Saxon names," wrote *Newsweek* editor-in-chief William Broyles, who served in Vietnam as a Marine infantry lieutenant. "Chinese, Polynesian, Indian, and Russian names. They are names which run deep into the heart of America, each testimony to a family's decision, sometime in the past, to wrench itself from home and culture to test our country's promise of new opportunities and a better life. They are names drawn from the farthest corners of the world and then, in this generation, sent to another distant corner in a war America has done its best to forget. But to hear the names being read . . . is to remember. The war was about names, each name a special human being who never came home."

When you lost a son in Vietnam, you did everything you could to never forget anything about him. You made yourself remember conversations and scenes over and over again. You studied family photographs and realized there were far too few. You climbed to the attic and opened the cedar chest in which he'd stored his things. You touched the American flag that had come home with him, and you reread letters of condolence from the President.

So much had been taken from you, so you clung to the one thing they could never take away, something that had been with you since the joy of his birth: his name.

As they were read in the chapel, each name was like a bell tolling. Each ripped through the heart, into old wounds that could heal only after they were reopened.

They were read in alphabetical order, from Gerald L. Aadland of Sisseton, South Dakota, to David L. Zywicke of Manitowoc, Wisconsin.

Time slots when names would be read were announced, so their sound could reach across America to people who loved them. In Oklahoma, for example, at the exact moment her son's name was being said out loud, a woman stopped feeding her chickens and whispered a prayer.

Families and friends crowded into the Cathedral, where they waited, with cold hands and thumping hearts, for the precious moment. The father of an infantryman who had died in 1968 at age 19 explained to the volunteer reader: "It is important to have other people hear his name."

Another reader asked a mother if she would like to say her son's name when the time came. "You won't cry, will you?" the reader said.

The woman sat and waited, noting how every name was read slowly and clearly and with feeling—as if to say, We know your pain. We know this was a very special person who did not want to die.

She became tense as her time approached. Thoughts and emotions had to be forced aside. The reader nodded, and she stood, and in a loud, clear voice said her son's name in the crowded chapel, and added, "Our son."

Shortly afterwards, another woman rushed in late, so her son's name was read again. As she sat alone, a vet took her hand. Tears ran down his cheeks. They hugged and never said a word.

A journalist asked one vet who had just read names what it all meant to him. "I hope," he said, "that the Vietnam Veterans Memorial constantly reminds those who make foreign policy decisions of the costs of those decisions, and that it reminds the American people that they are ultimately responsible for what their government does."

A Medal of Honor winner who had volunteered to read names lasted five minutes before he broke down. He read the rest of the names on his knees.

"ONE HELLUVA PARTY"

It was, said one vet, "one helluva party."

Vets were everywhere. They wore fatigues, ribbons, medals, cowboy hats, baseball caps, headbands, leather jackets, and regular business clothes. Their handmade signs, T-shirts, and pins read "I Prayed for Survival, but Forgot Peace of Mind," "Vietnam Veterans Never Forget," "2nd Place, Southeast Asia War Games, 1961–1974," "Remember POW-

MIAs," "Agent Orange Destroys," and "Never Again."

People walking along the sidewalk shook their hands. Bartenders gave them free drinks. Taxi drivers refused payment for rides. When they entered restaurants, people stood and cheered. Construction workers waved flags and banners. No one protested when vets sang loud enough to block out everything but happy memories. Hotels let them sleep in corridors and drink beer in lobbies, which the *Village Voice* described as "wall-to-wall grunts."

Where cooperation could not be found, the VVMF provided encouragement. One major hotel, for example, did not have a ramp for the handicapped. The manager said it would take weeks to have such a ramp installed. Scruggs told a volunteer to call the manager and to say, "I'm with ABC News and we've heard about your problem. We want to get a camera crew down there to get a picture of those vets." Within hours, vets in wheelchairs had joined their buddies inside.

It was a time for decompression. For remembering youth and innocence. For talking and thinking. For telling the story of the guy who walked point instead of you and died. For seeing a familiar face and shouting, "Is that you! Is that really you?" For saying you had been so afraid your wife would leave you. For breaking down. For finding that piece of yourself that had been missing.

The language was firefight, humping the boonies, roundeye, Momma San, bird, blooper, zapped, wasted, fire base, dustoff, Puff the Magic Dragon, gunship, ARVN, Ruff Puffs, R and R, APC, incoming, clicks, slick, lifers, LP, Alpha Papa Charlie, the Red Paint Brush, fire in the hole, RPG, and freedom bird.

The places and battles were Da Nang, Qui Nhon, Quang Tri, Route 13, Ben Het, Hill 875, War Zone D, Lang Vei, River Valley, Se San, Interstate 9, Tet, Nui Ba Ho, My Tho, Con Thien, DMZ, Khe Sanh, Xuan Loc, the Delta, Bien Hoa, Hue, Dong Ha, Hamburger Hill, Dak To, Hill 881, Phu Bai, Chu Lai, An Loc, Com Lo, Duy Xien, Quang Tri, and Cholon. But the sentence said most often was "Welcome home, brother."

After many beers, a vet said he had won the Medal of Honor but had been afraid of how people would react. To the cheers of an entire bar, he opened his suitcase, took out the medal with its blue ribbon, and put it on for the first time.

A stonecutter adds the finishing touch to the Vietnam Veterans Memorial by engraving the year 1959 on the wall. The casualties are listed in chronological, not alphabetical, order on the 492-foot-long Memorial, beginning with the first casualties in 1959 and ending with the final casualties in 1975. ROBERT DOUBEK

In November 1982 the National Salute to Vietnam Veterans began with a vigil at the National Cathedral, at which the names of the 58,000 American casualties were read by volunteers, as family members waited and listened. NICK SEBASTIAN

Veterans like this one came from all across America to see, and often to touch, the names of their fallen friends. SAL LOPES

Often relatives of Vietnam War dead leave flowers, photographs, medals, and articles of clothing near the name of a loved one.
JANET CENTURY

The mother of a U.S. pilot killed in the war holds his picture next to his name.
NICK SEBASTIAN

The widow and children of a war casualty search for his name on the polished granite wall, and when they find it, embrace. This poignant scene takes place almost every day.
JANET CENTURY

A member of the VFW makes a "rubbing" of a casualty's name on the wall by placing a piece of paper over the name and rubbing it with a pencil. Visitors often take rubbings to families who have not yet been to the Memorial. SAL LOPES

Jubilant Vietnam veterans from every state and U.S. territory join hands and raise their arms as they march to their Memorial and to the dedication ceremony on November 13, 1982. The armed forces provided a flyover by Vietnam-era helicopters and jet aircraft during the parade. LARRY FORD

This group of veterans, the fighting Irish of South Boston, came to march in the parade wearing ties and jackets and red carnations, and displaying a replica of the South Boston Memorial, one of the first in the nation dedicated to Vietnam veterans. LARRY FORD

An army nurse pushes the wheelchair of a double amputee, one of hundreds of wheelchair veterans who took part in the ceremonies.
JANET CENTURY

A veteran of World War I from Joliet, Illinois, reverently bears the American flag that was once draped over the coffin of his son, who was killed in action in the Korean War. MEDFORD TAYLOR

This Vietnam veteran and his dog carry on their backs the equipment they used on the long walk from Vermont to Washington that they undertook as a tribute to fallen comrades. LARRY FORD

Vietnam veterans from Illinois, one of the largest contingents in the parade, are led by Sam Davis (the sandy-haired man third from the right), a recipient of the Medal of Honor. SMITHSONIAN INSTITUTION

The parade made Vietnam veterans feel like triumphant warriors returning home—although most had returned over a decade earlier to a country trying hard to forget its most unpopular war. The parade was organized by Colonel Kelvin Hunter, USA (Ret), who worked overtime for six months as an employee of the Vietnam Veterans Memorial Fund. LARRY FORD

Two women who lost sons cheer as the war's survivors march by. On the left is Ruth Frye; on the right is Katherine Mannion, whose son held off a large enemy force single-handedly for nearly an hour until he was killed by a North Vietnamese soldier. MEDFORD TAYLOR

Veterans from Virginia, including those in wheelchairs and those still on active duty with the armed forces, line up for the parade in the staging area. MEDFORD TAYLOR

This red, white, and blue float carries singing "Young Vets" from Palo Alto, California, who worked for months to raise the funds needed for their opportunity to take part in the historic parade and who entertained the crowds with patriotic songs as part of a program at a VA hospital. LARRY FORD

Local Washington, D.C., residents came by the thousands to cheer on the vets, with some displaying "Welcome Home" signs which captured the spirit of the day and which, for many of the marchers, represented the first time the nation had expressed its gratitude to them.
NICK SEBASTIAN

As the parade ended, a crowd of over 150,000 gathered for the dedication ceremony at the Memorial. In the background is the Capitol.
AMERICAN SERVICEMEN'S LIFE INSURANCE

As soon as the brief, dignified ceremony had ended, the crowd rushed over the fences and descended upon the wall. It was an unforgettable moment, as relatives and friends of those who never returned, as well as thousands of veterans, were drawn to the nation's most moving memorial.
JANET CENTURY

The ceremony began with the presentation of the flags of every state and U.S. territory by military personnel in dress uniforms. In the background is the Washington Monument.
AMERICAN SERVICEMEN'S LIFE INSURANCE

Following the dedication, volunteer guides wearing yellow hats assisted people searching for names on the Memorial. Volunteer guides have been at the Memorial every day since November 1982.
MEDFORD TAYLOR

Three Marine Corps veterans search the wall for the name of a friend, their intensity a mirror of their emotions. NICK SEBASTIAN

Friends and families of war casualties touch and photograph the names of those they have lost. Many observers speak of the visitors' "communion with the dead" and of the Memorial as a place to remember and to heal the wounds of the soul. NICK SEBASTIAN

The profile of a mother who lost a son is reflected in the wall, as she makes a rubbing of his name to take home as a reminder of the young man who went to war. SAL LOPES

Vietnam veteran Terry McConnell, an ex-Marine, came from Ohio to hold the American flag at the Memorial for over 50 hours in honor of America's prisoners of war and those missing in action.
SMITHSONIAN INSTITUTION

A child holds a rose next to the name of a casualty from a war that ended before she was born. Guides report that children visiting the Memorial often ask the innocent question "Why did these people have to die?"
MEDFORD TAYLOR

The urge to touch the name of a loved one on the wall is often overwhelming. This woman is given an assist so that she can reach the name of a young soldier who, in the words of Abraham Lincoln, gave his "last full measure of devotion."
MEDFORD TAYLOR

The morning after the dedication ceremony the wall was lined with wreaths and flowers, which, in this photograph, made it seem transparent.
MEDFORD TAYLOR

The Washington Monument is reflected in the wall above the wreaths and personal mementos left by visitors during the dedication ceremony to honor the 58,000 Americans killed in the war. SAL LOPES

A veteran's hand reaches out to place a flower next to the name of a friend. The Memorial has become a meeting ground where Vietnam veterans seeking names often encounter friends from wartime service.
NICK SEBASTIAN

At night, lights seem to make the Memorial come alive.
CAROLOU MARQUET

A man in a wheelchair slowly pushed his way through a bar that was filled to capacity. At first, no one noticed him. Slowly, the noise diminished, and then people reached out to touch him.

An ex-medic was walking down the sidewalk when someone grabbed him. "You remember me?" the man said.

"No."

"Well, I was shot up pretty bad. Take a closer look."

"Sorry, brother, I still don't know you."

"Well I remember *you,* man. You saved my ass. Thanks."

Another medic sat in a corner crying. He pushed away everyone who tried to console him. "I should have saved more," he kept saying. "I should have saved more."

Former Marines crowded a hotel ballroom for their reunion. There was much hugging and pounding on the back and asking, "Who were you with?" "When were you there?" "How were you wounded?" Over the noise, a voice shouted names, units, and times into a microphone in a effort to help people find each other. Then someone walked up to the microphone, and yelled, "Corpsman, corpsman, corpsman, corpsman." Within a minute, everyone started to chant. The room rocked—"corpsman, corpsman, corpsman"—in tribute to Navy medics who so often risked their own lives to save Marines.

Many vets complained about the mass media: "We had a fire [in my home town] a couple of weeks ago. This guy carries out a seventy-nine-year-old lady; they did a beautiful article on it. At the very end of the story, the guy said he did more heroic things in Vietnam. If he had started the fire, you would have known right from the beginning of the story he was a Vietnam veteran."

It was not unusual for reporters and photographers to cry as they covered the Salute.

Mothers and fathers pressed among the vets, searching for men who had fought in the unit in which their sons had died. They touched the vets, seeking a living link with their sons, and they pleaded for answers. "Yes, ma'am," the vets said, "we had a real tough fight, and we got caught in the crossfire." Or, "Yes, sir, of course everyone dies instantly when a helicopter crashes."

Sometimes the answers came out so fast they were honest.

On a shuttle bus from Arlington Cemetery, a woman stopped all ex-Marines and asked, "Were you on the DMZ?"

"I was there."

She named her son.

"Hey, I knew him. We'd just met and we were chatting for maybe fifteen or twenty minutes, and then a bullet whizzed past my ears. I turned to say, 'Hey, I never heard one that close,' and it had gone right into his forehead."

On Friday, November 12, the Vietnam Veterans of America organized a forum on Agent Orange. One vet talked about his five children with birth defects. When he went to the VA for help, the clerk had said, "Oh, another one of you."

The vet looked around at the vets crowded into the hearing room. "I paid my taxes and I fought for this country and I've been treated like dirt," he said.

Everyone stood and cheered and shouted.

Counselors worked sixteen hours a day talking to vets about their resentment and anger. Flashbacks and prolonged crying spells were not unusual.

But even with over 150,000 vets in town, there was no violence.

The entire city of Washington became a giant troopship bringing the boys home.

THE WALL

All week the American people discovered the wall.

At night they used matches and cigarette lighters and burned torches of rolled newspapers to find names. Volunteers stayed until dawn passing out flashlights. One father struck match after match, and then said to his wife in a hushed voice, "There's Billy."

They always touched the names. Fingertips traced out each letter. Lips said a name over and over, and then stretched up to kiss it.

Sunlight made it warm to the touch. Young men put into the earth, rising out of the earth. You could feel their blood flowing again.

Perhaps by touching, people regained a sense of life; or perhaps they finally came to peace with death.

We're with you, they said. We never forgot.

The panels of names were like mirrors. The more you looked, the deeper inside you saw. The names floated all around you, along with the clouds.

"As you saw your living reflection mixed with the names, a strong bond, a sharing, came forth."

"As I looked at and touched the names, a jolt went through me that rendered me stationary for a couple of seconds. It was as though time had stopped."

"I wouldn't have been born if Daddy had died in Vietnam."

"The names reach out and grab you and they scream, 'I don't want to be here!' "

"All the little children looking for their fathers' names. God!"

"It's depressing, but the war was depressing."

"What a waste. All those boys died, and for what? For fighting a war they had no way of winning."

"How did it happen? Why? Why does it hurt so much? Why my son?"

"The waste. The waste."

"I hate the reason he died."

"I never expected it to be passionless," Maya Lin explained to reporters. "The piece was built as a very psychological memorial. It's not meant to be cheerful or happy, but to bring out in people the realization of loss and a cathartic healing process. A lot of people were really afraid of that emotion; it was something we had glossed over."

A small group of protesters arrived shouting slogans denouncing the Vietnam War. Hundreds of Vietnam vets surrounded them. Violence seemed likely. Then the vets started to sing "God Bless America." The protesters looked embarrassed and left.

The vets had their own rituals of remembrance.

A vet carried a paper bag and a pack of cigarettes as he approached the wall. He found a name and took a beer out of the bag. He snapped open the beer, poured some on the ground, and drank the rest without pausing to breathe. He lit a cigarette, and smoked it slowly. Then he moved on to another name until the six-pack was gone.

A vet took out a bottle of whiskey and a dozen shot glasses. He stood in front of a name, saluted, filled all the glasses, drank them rapidly, saluted again, and left.

A vet struggled to keep ten candles lit. The wind kept blowing them out. Others vets stood around to block the wind. No one asked questions.

A small group of vets scattered the ashes of a comrade who had committed suicide. Another group arrived with a large American flag, and planted it in front of the wall.

"I want my daughter to see it," one man said. "I want her to stand up and be proud that her father fought."

Vets read the wall like an epic poem about the war in Vietnam: "There are the names of the guys who took bullets for me." "There's my whole platoon together!" "That's the day my helicopter went down." "Shit, here's half my platoon." "Ten guys died on the day I got hit."

One volunteer guide had her arm around a vet as she led him along the wall and showed him three names. The vet was shaking and crying. At a fourth name, he ran his fingers along the letters and cried out, "I loved him, and I love this wall."

A former medic searched for the name of a GI he had worked to save. Images of this man suffering had haunted the medic for years. "He lived! He lived!" the medic screamed. "I can't find the name."

Other vets found names of people they thought had made it home.

"Why am I here now, no longer young, with even less answers than I had then?" one vet wrote. "My name could have been on that wall. Six inches lower and I wouldn't have a leg. One man to the left and Sergeant Masso would be here and I'd be up there. I had no more right to life than they. What would they feel now if we had traded places? Would they have used their 14 years more wisely than I?"

Many vets went to the wall alone. They were afraid they would hate it, and afraid of the memories it would bring back. The smells. The filth. The horror. The loneliness. The sadness.

After seeing the wall, however, they needed each other, so they gathered in little groups. Men who had been strangers cried together. Many hugged. You have to touch the wall, they said to each other. They had never before been more strong or more fragile.

Promises to friends that they would never be forgotten had now been kept.

PARADE

To parade coordinator Kelvin Hunter, the parade was a living link to the wall, a strong statement that the Salute was a beginning and not an end. The vets were "Marching Along Together Again"—into the future.

At 5:00 A.M. on Saturday it was raining, with thunder and lightning. By six the rain stopped. The weather, however, remained cloudy, cold, and windy.

About 15,000 Vietnam vets gathered for an old-fashioned parade down Constitution Avenue to the Memorial. There were color guards, a colonial fife and drum corps, grand marshals, floats, cadets from the military academies, and soldiers, sailors, and Marines in dress uniform. Wind made the flags snap loudly.

At places along the parade route spectators stood three and four deep; many were waving American flags, applauding, reaching out to shake hands, and shouting, "Welcome home," "Thank you," and "We love you." Some wore old antiwar buttons. Others held children up so they could see. "I'm Proud My Daddy's a Vietnam Vet," said one placard.

The parade was carried live on Cable Network News, and covered extensively by the three major TV networks. Some vets and their families who could not attend kept three or four television sets going at the same time so they would not miss anything.

It was the largest parade in Washington since John F. Kennedy's funeral, and a parade like the nation had never seen before.

Men in wheelchairs led most state delegations. The vets who followed them had long and short hair, even ponytails. Some wore three-piece suits with shoulder patches attached by safety pins. Many wore faded, torn segments of uniforms. There were boonie hats, steel helmets, bowling team shirts, canes, crutches, wheelchairs, and vets pushing baby carriages. One unemployed vet spent his last $68 on a suit. "I came proud," he told reporters. Another vet who had just arrived in town carried his suitcase. A Gold Star Mother ran out to join her son's division. A float was a tiger cage holding a prisoner of war to remind Americans of the 2,500 still missing in action.

The vets sauntered, strolled, strutted, limped, and rolled. For some of the wounded, the march was painful. For nearly two hours, they let only pride show.

Many men purposely kept the lines crooked. No more military bullshit, they announced. But then they found themselves unconsciously getting in step out of respect for dead comrades. Up and down the ranks, GI's started counting cadence.

They locked arms, holding hands, and chanted, "Vietnam vets, Vietnam vets."

They gave V signs, and thumbs-up signs. One clasped his hands above his head, shouting, "We're home! We're home!"

They sang "The Battle Hymn of the Republic" and "America the Beautiful," and they cheered their former field commander General William Westmoreland. Many wore buttons that stated, "I'D DO IT AGAIN," but the anger came through in the placards:

WE KILLED, WE BLED, WE DIED FOR WORSE THAN NOTHING.

57,000 KILLED IN VAIN. SHAME, HORROR, DECEIT, TREACHERY.

AGENT ORANGE VICTIMS OF NEW JERSEY.

NEXT TIME, LET US WIN IT.

NO MORE WARS. NO MORE LIES.

WHY WERE THE PRIVILEGED EXEMPT?

I NEED A JOB.

Navy and Air Force F-4's and Army helicopters flew over. When they heard the wop-wop-wop, the marchers cheered. "Thanks for the ride, man," they shouted. "Thanks for the ride."

"Thank you," a woman kept shouting to the marchers.

A vet pointed to her and said, "Thank *you.*"

"No," she said. "We thank *you.*"

Both started to cry.

A former helicopter pilot was walking at the edge of the parade when a woman stepped up and said, "Welcome home." He was stunned, unable to move. He had never realized how badly he had needed those words.

Another woman drove to Washington with a huge sign. She felt embarrassed and almost left it in her car, but at the last minute she decided to hold it up for the marchers to see: "I came to thank those who came home, and to keep alive the memory of my nephew and his 57,939 comrades." Throughout the parade, vets waved and gave her the thumbs-up sign. Some fell into her arms and wept.

A man from the crowd ran out to shake the hand of a vet in a wheelchair.

Some vets stood among the spectators. "Join us! Join us! Join us!" their comrades called.

One Vietnam vet in an old uniform with a chestful of ribbons stood behind several rows of spectators. The marchers saw him, jumped across the barricade, and embraced him. In tears, he joined the parade.

At the end of the parade, many vets threw their hats in the air and cheered. "How do you explain the feelings when you embrace a brother and you feel your heart beat against his heart?" one said.

Another said, "I could almost hear the chains clinking as they fell off us."

The cousin of one vet came up to him and said, "I envy you."

When was the last time anyone said that to a Vietnam vet?

A letter to the *Washington Post* read:

> I never expected that at the age of 37 I would want to march in a parade, or touch and hug other guys like myself, or be able to cry—and see unknown thousands of guys like me doing the same thing. . . .
>
> I challenge the *Post* to pick up the momentum that we brought to Washington, and realistically and truthfully examine the many serious problems that still face some Vietnam veterans: unemployment or underemployment; suicide, drug abuse, crime, prisons and alcoholism; the toxic defoliants issue; job training and counseling efforts; and the myriad of issues involved in being a handicapped person and the rehabilitation process.
>
> I also challenge Vietnam veterans who, to date, have not been involved in helping our brothers, to start doing something positive.

DEDICATION

All through the Thursday and Friday before the dedication ceremony, a vet had stood by the wall holding the American flag.

A police officer came up and said, "The United States of America is having a ceremony here. You'll have to take down that flag."

"You'll have to ask them," the vet responded, pointing to at least 10,000 vets who were shouting encouragement to him as they waited for the ceremony to begin.

The police officer looked out over the crowd. "O.K.," he said. "The flag looks fine right where it is."

An emotional crowd of over 150,000 gathered for the dedication. People climbed trees for a better view, and pushed past guards to get closer to the wall.

"Wait," Scruggs said. "We've waited over ten years. We can wait another hour." The crowd cheered.

A small group of vets stood off to the side and listened as the Marine Band played. They began to sing along very softly, and people nearby joined in.

Before the ceremony, the children of No Greater Love, who had lost their fathers in Vietnam, laid roses at each panel of the Memorial. According to their creed, "No greater love can be shown than when men and women so live and die that their friends may be free."

At 2:00 P.M., Air Force chaplain Owen J. Hendry gave the invocation: "Your presence is felt in this place as a mighty wind, O God, echoing again the words once spoken by your prophet Isaiah, 'I have called you by name, you are mine.' Keep them close to you, O God, in your eternal peace."

In his speech, Senator Warner said, "We Americans must face the sober lessons of history. We learned a terrible lesson from the Vietnam War—a lesson which we must never forget. We learned that we should never again ask our men and women to serve in a war which we do not intend to win. We learned that we should not enter a war unless it is necessary for our national survival. We learned that, if we do enter such a war, we must support our men and women to the fullest extent of our powers."

American Legion commander Al Keller asked everyone to join hands "in a silent pledge to care for the children of vets who died in Vietnam."

Billy Ray Cameron, national junior vice-commander-in-chief of the VFW, quoted from the Tomb of the Unknown Soldier in Edinburgh,

Scotland: "They shall not grow old, as we that are left grow old. Age shall not worry them, nor years condemn. At the going down of the sun and in the morning we shall remember them."

General John Vessey, chairman of the Joint Chiefs of Staff, had been asked to sit on the rostrum. He refused, explaining that all ranks were equal on the wall and should be equal during dedication. Vessey stood in the crowd among the former enlisted men.

At 2:55, the crowd sang "God Bless America," and then paused for a moment of silence. "Ladies and gentlemen," Scruggs said, "the Vietnam Veterans Memorial is now dedicated."

Minutes later, the fences that had been erected for crowd control were crushed as the 150,000 surged forward to the wall, which waited like a pair of a pair of outstretched arms.

The people and the wall met.

Standing. Sitting in wheelchairs. Stretching up. Leaning over the top. Holding each other. Kneeling. Walking back and forth. Crying. Smiling. Staring. In silence. Talking. Weeping. Hugging. Discovering. Remembering. Promising.

At one moment, three hands reached up to touch a name, and then held on to each other as they were lowered.

Nearby, a father led his two small children to the wall and made them touch a certain name. "Don't ever forget that man," he said. "Don't you ever forget him. If it were not for that man, you would never be here. Don't ever forget."

Further along the wall, a man wearing a Purple Heart stood and stared at the names. A woman came up, touched him on the shoulder, and said, "Thank you." He started to weep.

Next to this vet, someone had stuck in the ground a sign that said, "Honor the Dead, Fight Like Hell for the Living."

Each person had a moment of discovery. To them, at that moment, the wall was alive, and in the midst of it all, a lone GI stood at the top of the wall, put a bugle to his lips, and played taps. The notes came out slow and strong, mournful and hopeful.

Later that evening, thousands of people were still there. The wall had been transformed—claimed by people with flags, wreaths, photographs, crosses, flowers, poems, notes, medals, personal items, and pieces of uniforms. The objects were tokens of grieving, of greeting, and of letting go.

A guide was helping a vet find the name of a buddy he'd last seen when they were both seriously wounded. They could not find it in the book that listed the names alphabetically. Was there a bureaucratic foul-up? Had the name been omitted by mistake? "Maybe you are remembering or spelling it incorrectly," the guide said.

"No," the vet insisted. "I've got the name right." Finally, they went to the point on the wall that represented the exact day when the vet and his friend had been wounded. They bumped into another guide with another vet who had his eyes fixed on the wall, his fingers tracing names. Soon, four sets of fingers were searching. They didn't find what they were looking for, and the fingers were slowly lowered.

The vets turned to leave and saw each other. They stared.

The stare continued. Then came screams. They had been looking for each other's name etched in the granite.

Journalists and cameras carried the emotions into virtually every American home.

"The TV cameras loved the black slabs," a newspaper reporter noted. "They would return again and again to the names. . . . In doing this, the cameras caught a remarkable tableau. People were standing and kneeling by the slabs, people were leaning on crutches and sitting in wheelchairs by the slabs, and most of them were doing the same thing: they were touching the names.

"Some hands were seen stroking the names determinedly, as if there were life in them. Sometimes the fingers would reach and pull away, as if the stone were hot. Many of the people were weeping."

"When you touch a friend's name on the stone," one vet later explained, "for a magical moment you are suspended halfway between heaven and earth . . . with them again. Then you back off and see his name and your reflection in the polished granite."

It was an honest reflection, which gave the Memorial special meaning. No matter how you looked at it, you always saw yourself reflected back among the names. No matter who you were, you could no longer deny that you shared responsibility. You realized that you had to learn from this war, and that you could not escape its pain. The wall challenged you to match the courage of the men who fought.

"Never mind the often-discussed public policy 'lessons' of the war," the Quincy, Massachusetts, *Patriot Ledger* said. "These will be recorded in history books—and kept alive in public debate. What the history books do not record, and what politicians almost always ignore, is the human sacrifice of Americans who served in Vietnam. Dedication of the Memorial closes the chapter of denial. It could end years of bitterness. It should be a balm for wounds that were too long in healing."

Before the Salute began, an Associated Press reporter wrote, "Wouldn't it be something if the reunion of the old Southeast Asia hands turned out to be as unpredictably successful as the GAR [Grand Army of the Republic] encampment held in the nation's capital a decade or so after the Civil War, when the whole town in the old photographs seemed to be one big bivouac, or at least as lively and majestic as the great old American Legion parades of my youth?"

His wish came true. There had been a lot of love and emotion, and maybe a little too much drinking; but there were no incidents and no arrests.

Many vets stayed in Washington. For them, it was not yet over. Weeks after the Salute ended, they could still be seen kneeling at the wall.

A FINAL PRAYER

On the weekend of November 13–14, veterans and their families all over America took the pulpit to lead prayers for America's sons, for reconciliation, and for the country.

At Washington's National Cathedral, the Reverend Theodore H. Evans asked worshippers to pray "that by remembering we may become a living memorial."

By Sunday evening, at the homes of those who worked on the Memorial and the Salute, telephones sat silent for the first time in over two years. There were no crises and no impossible deadlines, so they could relax.

Most had forgotten how.

Around the country, the work of the Memorial was just beginning.

Vietnam vets were changing the way they felt about themselves; many experienced a healing, which, one vet said, "has been one helluva long time coming."

On his way home from the Salute, one vet wore his Combat Infantry Badge, Purple Hearts, and other ribbons.

"What are those?" someone asked.

He explained each.

"Why are you wearing them?"

"I'm proud to be a Vietnam vet."

Friends and family members visited graves they had neglected for years. Neighbors asked questions and really seemed interested in the answers. Schoolteachers gave assignments that involved Vietnam. Speeches by civic leaders and politicians emphasized that service in Vietnam made young men community assets. Fellow workers surprised Vietnam vets by decorating their offices with flowers and flags.

One vet returning from the Salute walked into his house and set down his suitcase. His wife came running up from the basement. With tears in her eyes, she smiled and ran over and put her arms around him. "Welcome home," she said. "Welcome home."

Epilogue

THOMAS J DOSTAL · JAME
D R GRUSCZYNSKI · HERBE
RD · PAUL F KO
VID E NELSON
· STEVEN R

Epilogue

IN EARLY 1983, government commissions decided to put the statue and flag in an entrance plaza leading to the wall. The flag began flying from its 60-foot staff in mid-1983. At its base are emblems of the five services. The statue was installed on Veterans Day 1984.

Lights, five permanent name-location guidebooks, and an expanded walkway have been added.

The Memorial now belongs to the U.S. government. Over 650,000 people paid for it with their private contributions.

As work was completed, some of the opponents publicly accused the VVMF of financial impropriety, a charge repudiated by a major federal audit of Fund records. Opponents also tried unsuccessfully to get Congress to pass a law placing the statue in front of the walls. They may forever continue their war on Maya Lin's design. Somehow their anger about the Vietnam War, rather than turning toward healing, seems transformed into permanent hatred.

Over five million people visited the Vietnam Veterans Memorial during its first two years. It is the second most visited memorial in the nation's capital. On some days, over 20,000 people come. Late at night, at dawn, someone is *always* there.

Most visitors touch the wall or hug each other. They linger and talk, and carry part of it away with them. *U.S. News & World Report* called it in late 1983, one year after its dedication, "the most emotional ground in the nation's capital."

Black granite does not wear out. Hundreds and thousands of years from now, people can still touch the names.

People are awed, perhaps most of all, by its reflectiveness. Jack Wheeler, in a prayer on Veterans Day 1983, said:

> Who among us
> was not touched,
> or even wounded, in some way by the Vietnam War?
> The walls shine like mirrors.
> So we begin to see hurts inside us, too,
> when we see our own reflections
> in the walls.

The Memorial does not dictate any emotion or political view. The more you look, the more you'll see.

Is healing happening?

If so, Vietnam vets have led the way.

Is it helping Vietnam vets?

The country can no longer ignore them.

Is it helping nonvets?

They now know that healing begins only when you look deeply into yourself and when you honor those who have suffered on your behalf.

Is America more at peace with its own history and better able to control its future?

Americans are learning that to forget too easily only increases pain and invites repetition of past mistakes.

F. Scott Fitzgerald once wrote, "Show me a hero and I will write you a tragedy."

Maybe Vietnam vets are forever condemned to be the most tragic of all heroes—those whose bravery was wasted.

"No!" the Memorial shouts. "It must not be." The names rise from the earth. Even on the coldest days they are somehow warm. They speak. To their buddies. To their wives and children. To mothers, fathers, brothers, and sisters. To all young Americans who must prepare for future wars.

To all the politicians.
To all the generals.
To everyone who tries to understand:

. . . We were young. We have died. Remember us.

. . . We have done what we could but until it is finished it is not done.

. . . We have given our lives but until it is finished no one can know what our lives gave.

. . . Our deaths are not ours; they are yours; they will mean what you make them.

. . . Whether our lives and our deaths were for peace and a new hope or for nothing we cannot say; it is you who must say this.

. . . We leave you our deaths. Give them their meaning.

We were young. . . . We have died. Remember us.

Roll Call of Honor

Roll Call of Honor

IN ADDITION TO HONORING those who served in Vietnam, the Vietnam Veterans Memorial was intended to help heal the divisions in the country caused by the war. Accordingly, we did not seek an edifice financed by passionless tax dollars. Our memorial had to be paid for by private contributions in a largely volunteer effort organized by people whose principal reward would be knowing they had honored those whom the nation had managed to ignore.

Hundreds of thousands of people responded with their time, energy, money, hard work, idealism, and ideas. Their success speaks for itself. Long after we have gone, the names of Americans killed in their youth will live on as part of the nation's memory.

It is impossible to even list all the organizations and people who have earned a thank-you. But some individuals, by virtue of their extraordinary dedication and sacrifice, their intelligence, sincerity, and toughness, and their good old-fashioned problem-solving abilities, deserve special mention. They are presented in alphabetical order.

Colonel Robert A. (Bob) Carter enlisted as a rifleman in the South Carolina Army National Guard upon graduation from high school, then completed 33 years of military service, primarily as a jet fighter pilot in the USAF. Colonel Carter served in high-level USAF command and staff positions, completing over 100 missions in Vietnam, and won numerous awards in a distinguished military career. He became the VVMF's executive vice president in April 1982 and directed day-to-day activities, budgeted and provided financial management, formulated public relations strategy, organized staff activities, and guided the construction process. His organizational and planning experience kept "the train on the track," and as business manager for the statue, he helped ensure completion of the Memorial by Veterans Day 1984, in time for conveyance to the U.S. government. A native of South Carolina, Colonel Carter is a graduate of The Citadel and George Washington University in Washington, D.C. He and his family—Wanda, Sarah Ann, and Robert, Jr.—reside in Alexandria, Virginia.

David A. Christian, one of the most decorated soldiers of the Vietnam War, came to the rescue of the Vietnam Veterans Memorial twice under very difficult circumstances. He has earned our continual admiration for his courageous efforts on our behalf.

Karen Kendig Doubek, an Air Force brat, came to the VVMF in March 1981 as a volunteer, and then, in April, was hired as assistant campaign director. As ACD she researched and coordinated the massive fund-raising efforts. Later, as deputy director of the National Salute to Vietnam Veterans, she coordinated the "welcome home" offered by the Washington, D.C., private sector (hotels, retail stores, businesses, and transportation companies) as well as many of the week's events. She and Bob Doubek met and married while working on the project.

Robert W. Doubek, an attorney with a background in corporate, construction, and procurement law, was a cofounder of the VVMF. Our project director and corporate secretary until completing his work in June 1983, he served as our executive director from December 1979 until February 1981. Doubek's dedication and contributions were prodigious. He became our first employee at great financial sacrifice and served as our sole salaried staff member for over nine months. He secured the support of the major veterans organizations and coordinated passage of our authorizing legislation. He initiated our direct-mail campaign and directed the design competition. As project director, he superintended the lengthy and complex process of obtaining federal approval of the design, organized the design and construction team, and oversaw the timely completion of the Memorial. He was responsible for verifying the completeness and accuracy of the names inscribed on the walls and later initiated the name locator directories and the National Park Service volunteer guide program. Finally, he organized and managed the Memorial's dedication ceremony and many other public events.

Sandie Fauriol in October of 1980 was a thirty-year-old woman, an Army brat who had worked once before as a fund-raiser. She was hired as the director of the Memorial's fund-raising effort. She took on this huge task and directed a flawless, creative, and unquestionably successful fund-raising campaign. Yet another challenge awaited. She agreed to direct the National Salute to Vietnam Veterans, which in five days in 1982 welcomed home America's Vietnam veterans, who had been waiting for over ten years to hear the words "thank you." No one rose to the occasion the way Sandie did.

Our treasurer, Bob Frank, CPA, provided his extraordinary business talent to the decisions made by the VVMF. If there was ever a way to save money or do a job more efficiently, he found it. Bob devised VVMF's financial controls, took part in numerous contract negotiations, and unselfishly gave of himself and his time. His talent for business and the generous use of the resources of Frank, Stefanou and Company were a great asset to the VVMF.

Ron Gibbs, who served as an Army captain in Vietnam, became involved in the early effort to gain passage of the legislation. He spent many hours walking the halls of Congress. After the legislative work was completed, Ron assisted with the fund-raising effort and design competition. He never asked for public recognition or acclaim. His only desire was to see the 58,000 names inscribed in a place of honor.

Kathie Kielich became VVMF's administrative aide in September 1980 and stayed until the final staff phasedown in July 1984. She is a hard-working, organized, and talented woman, and none of us at the VVMF will ever forget her ability to resolve the difficult challenges that faced an overworked office staff.

George "Sandy" Mayo, also a Vietnam veteran, was among the earliest volunteers. His quiet manner was never shaken by the emotional turmoil that engulfed the project. When others, including myself, became unnerved as a result of being in the center of a national controversy, Sandy would calmly help us to put things into perspective.

John Morrison, who had been seriously wounded in Vietnam, consistently showed sound judgment throughout the project. When the legislation was introduced, he logged over 400 hours as a volunteer, taking time from his law practice to lobby Congress on our behalf. He took on many difficult tasks and without fail showed his integrity, wit, and courage.

Dick Radez, a banker who is a graduate of West Point and Harvard, provided invaluable advice and assistance in the development of a comprehensive plan for financing the Memorial. His later work in developing a political strategy to keep the Memorial from being destroyed was particularly significant. Dick is a man of great integrity and extraordinary managerial skill.

Colonel Don Schaet, USMC (Ret) was VVMF's first executive vice president. He is a true leader. In the spirit of the Marine Corps, he led by example. Working six-day weeks and leaving the office late with a stack of letters to answer at home, he worked at VVMF during our most difficult year, when everything was riding on our ability to raise the needed money and remove the political obstacles.

Tom Shull, a West Pointer on the White House staff, volunteered to be an intermediary between the different groups in the design dispute. He was asked by the White House senior staff to do what he could to help reconcile the differences. He kept the White House informed of all the key facts. In the thankless role of peacemaker, he was a catalyst in the compromise of incorporating a statue. Given the difficult situation, his commitment took faith and a certain reckless courage. He was effective because he kept his word, was easy to get along with, and kept passion and emotion in check.

John Wheeler, chairman of our board of directors, gave several thousand hours of volunteer time to the project. His adept political and managerial decisions were crucial. He had to spend many nights on the phone and much time away from his family in order to get the job done. For Jack, the project was a great personal burden. It included facing raw anger and attempts at intimidation from opponents of the design. Everyone who visits the Memorial owes Jack a debt of gratitude for his perseverance and unselfishness and for the sacrifices he made in order to honor the men and women who served in Vietnam. When first told about the dream of a memorial, he said, "It can be done. Let me call some people." He is a West Pointer, and he made his words come true. His book *Touched with Fire: The Future of the Vietnam Generation* is provocative and important.

John Woods's last memory of Vietnam is of being in a helicopter riddled by bullets, plummeting to the earth. He became actively involved with the VVMF and used his expertise as a designer/structural engineer to both build and defend the Memorial. John unselfishly volunteered his time to help with many projects and spent a great deal of effort in helping the Vietnam Veterans Memorial to become a reality.

Gratitude is due the families of those who became involved in this demanding project. To the wives, husbands, and children of the staff and board of directors of the VVMF, a hearty thanks.

Just as many individuals made sacrifices, so did many organizations become actively involved. The American Legion and the Veterans of Foreign Wars, for example, made special efforts, but many other groups also helped to build the Memorial. This is just a partial list: The AMVETS, the American Gold Star Mothers, Air Force Association, Air Force Sergeants Association, American Veterans Committee, Association of the U.S. Army, Blinded Veterans Association, First Air Cavalry Association, 1st Division Association, 199th Light Infantry Brigade Association, 3rd Marine Division Association, 173rd Airborne Brigade Association, 101st Airborne Division Association, Congressional Medal of Honor Society, D.A.V., Fleet Reserve Association, Jewish War Veterans, Legion of Valor, Marine Corps League, Marine Corps Association, 1st Marine Division Association, Military Order of the Purple Heart, Military Order of the World Wars, National Association of the Uniformed Services, National Fundraising Lists, Naval Reserve Association, Non-Commissioned Officers Association, Paralyzed Veterans of America, Special Forces Association, Reserve Officers Association, Veterans of the Vietnam War, Vietnam Veterans of America, Williams and Connolly. Many others are deserving of mention. To each we give our thanks.

The Vietnam Veterans Memorial is, in the words of journalist Hugh Sidey, "A Tribute to Sacrifice." There were many sacrifices made by unselfish people who gave of their time and talent to ensure that the names of over 58,000 Americans would be in a place of honor. To all who sacrificed for these men and women, we give our thanks. And to those who gave their lives for our country, we pledge that we will never forget.

Edward H. Able, Jr.
Sheryl Abraham
Lee Adriani
Frederick Ahearn
Karen Ahern
Joe L. Allbritton
Chuck Allen
Sandra Alley
Maj. Gary Allord, USMC
Everett Alvarez, Jr.
Steve Anderson
Debbie Webb Angello
Jim Angello
George Appleby

Richard Armitage
Henry A. Arnold
Robert L. Ashworth
Jerry Atchison
Frank Athanason
Charles H. Atherton

Pearl Bailey
Richard Bain
Howard H. Baker, Jr.
James Baker
Andrej Balanc
Adriana Barbieri
Robert Barnett
Marion Barry
Carol Bates
Lucius D. Battle
Wilbur N. Baughman
Pietro Belluschi
Capt. John Bender
Virginia Bensheimer
John Benson
Kenneth Berez
R. Christian Berg
Tom Bettag
Lt. Cdr. Jerry Bever, USN
Tony A. Bevinetto
Livingston Biddle
Max J. Bielke
Arthur S. Blank
Rocky Bleier
Bill Boe
Rubin Bonilla
David E. Bonior
Randy Bordelon
Frank Bosch
Sheila Brady
Peter Braestrup
Judy Bridgett
Olivia Brooks
Debbie Brown
J. Carter Brown
Joe Brown
Sgt. Maj. Robert L. Brown, Jr., USA
William Broyles
Christoper Buckley
Davis Buckley
Dale Bumpers
Ellsworth Bunker
J. Thomas Burch
Carol Burnett
August A. Busch III
George Bush
James Butera

Billy Ray Cameron
Ross Cameron
Jose Cano
Phillip Caputo
Elliott Carroll
J. Bryan Carter
Jimmy Carter
Peggy Carter
Rosalynn Carter
Col. Matthew P. Caulfield, USMC
Larry Century
Steve Champlin
Jane Chandler
Seth Chandler
Paul Cheremeta
David Childs
Shirley A. Chisholm
William H. Choquette
William P. Clark
Grady Clay
Max Cleland
Ron Cohen
William Colby
Col. Francis C. Conaty, Jr., USA (Ret)
Chuck Conconni
Bob Conley
Caryle Connolly
W. Kent Cooper
Carla Corbin
Phyllis Corbitt
Lt. Gen. Charles A. Corcoran, USA (Ret)
Baltazar Corrada
Bill Corson
Howard Cosell
Craig A. Coulter
John Coventry
G. B. Craighill
Christopher Crane
Roger Craver
Warren Creech
Helen Cronkite
Keith Cunningham
Emogene Cupp
George Cusick
James Madison Cutts

John C. Danforth
Charles D. Daniel
Richard Darman
Thomas A. Daschle
Lt. Gen. Frederick Davidson, USA, (Ret)
Patrick B. Davis, Jr.
Gen. Michael S. Davison, USA (Ret)
Anthony Day
James P. Dean
David DeChant
Dennis DeConcini
Glenn DeMarr
Lawrence DeNardis
James DeSorbo
Grant Dillman

Robert J. Dole
Pete V. Domenici
Pegi Donovan
Mary Lou Dowling
Hugh Drescher
Harry DePuente Duane
Jerry Dufault
Lupe Duke
Paul Dunn
Elbridge Durbow
David F. Durenburger

Garrett Eckbo
Lt. Col. William D. Eckert, USAF
Bob Edgar
Jeanne Edmunds
Ed Egan
Claude Engle
Joan Englehardt

Chris Farlekas
Georges Fauriol
Mike Feinsilber
Richard T. Feller
Arthur J. Fellwock
Jack Ferrebee
Manus J. Fish, Jr.
Victor Fisher
Betty Fishman
Mack Flemming
Herbert E. Fletcher
Jack W. Flynt
Gerald R. Ford
A. D. Frazier
Leta Frazier
Allen Freeman
Bill Frenzel
Mike Frey
William K. Friedman
Jonathan Friendly
Ruth Frye
Richard Fuller

Frances Garth
Robert J. George
Quinto Gesiotto
Phil Geyelin
Col. Joseph Gleason, USA
Lt. Col. James W. Gleisner, USA
Alan Glickman
Capt. Bobby E. Glisson, USAF
Al Goergins
Arnold Goldstein
Barry M. Goldwater
Raymond Grace
Don Graff
Rocky Granato
Harry Gray
Paul D. Gray
Barbara Green
Robert Gresham
Reginald W. Griffith
Ann Mills Griffiths
Susan Grimes

Heather Sturt Haaga
Paul Haaga
Lt. Col. Frank Hadl, USAF
Charles T. Hagel
David L. Hamilton
Michael P. Hamilton
John Paul Hammerschmidt
Norman Hannah
Ernest Harper
Husher Harris
Frederick E. Hart
Gary Hart
Thomas Harvey
Richard Harwood
Augustus Hawkins
S. I. Hayakawa
Maj. Gen. Thomas Jay Hayes, III, USA (Ret)
Thomas J. Haynes
Jock B. Hazeltine
Monica Healy
Tom Hebert
Lee Hediger
Chaplain Owen J. Hendry, USAF
Brig. Gen. James Herbert, USA (Ret)
Jay Hersch
Theodore Hesburgh
Donald Paul Hodel
Jeanne B. Hodges
Francis S. M. Hodsoll, USA (Ret)
Wayne Hoffman
Harry Holland
Cooper T. Holt
Bob Hope
Bruce Hopkins
William P. Horn
Jan Howard
Hal W. Howes
Jim Hubbard
Patricia Hudson
Patricia Hughes
John Hummel
Pat Hunsaker
Richard Hunt
Col. Kelvin Hunter, Jr., USA

Peter A. Iovino
Charles Itte
Maj. Bob Ivany, USA

G. William Jayne
Chelette Johnson
Beverly M. Jones
Gen. David C. Jones, USAF (Ret)
Maj. Mel Jordan, USAF
Vernon Jordan
Sandra Jorgensen

Robert Kee
Gary Keefe
Al Keller
Levy Kelly
Margee Kendig
Robert E. Kendig
James J. Kilpatrick
J. Stanley Kimmitt
Robert M. Kimmitt
Addie King
Fred King
Jean King
Larry King
Chaplain E. James Kingsley, USA
Lane Kirkland
Henry Kissinger
Earl Kittleman
Cliff Knesel
Pete Koeppen, Jr.
Michael J. Kogutek
Stanley E. Kolbe, Jr.
Ted Koppel
Mylio Kraja
Burt R. Kubli
David Kupferschmid

Jonathan F. Ladd
Bob Lafferty
L. Bruce Laingen
Marcia Landau
Bill Large
Carmella LaSpada
Kay Lautman
William Lecky
Steve Leer
Alan Leighton
Carl Levin
Jerome Levinrad
Lt. Cdr. Donald Lewis, USN
Russell B. Light
Maya Ying Lin
Robert Livingston
Clarence Long
Robin Luketina

Lt. Gen. Leroy Manor, USAF (Ret)
Gordon Mansfield
Donna Marlene
Walter Marquardt
John Marquart
William A. Marr, Jr.
Joan Mashburn
Charles McC. Mathias, Jr.
Larry Matthews
Murray McCann
Colman McCarthy
Phil McCombs
Col. James A. McDonnell, USAF (Ret)
John McElwee
Robert C. McFarlane
George S. McGovern
Jim McHenry
Candace McKee
AMCS David Meaney, USN
John Meek
Edwin Meese
Joel Meisner
Bill Menard
Richard Merryman
Donald B. Meyer
Joseph Miller
Kenneth W. Miller
Paul C. Miller
Robert F. Miller
Walter F. Mondale
Gillespie V. Montgomery
Robert Moody
Will Moore
Jimmy Mosconis
Arthur C. Mosley, Jr.
Bobby Muller
J. Richard Munro
Ruth Murdoch
David J. Murphy
Mark Murray
John Murtha
Joe Musolino

Ruth Nadeau
John F. Nash, Jr.
Silvio Nativi
Lucien N. Nedzi
William I. Newman
Wayne Newton
Robert Nimmo
Pamela Nissman
Constantino Nivola
Chris Noel
Robert W. Nolan
Peggy Noonan
Frances Norton

George Oberlander
Gordon Ochenrider

Terrence O'Donnell
Susan O'Hara
Jack Olsen
Walter Osborne

Jan Padden
Leon Panetta
Lester Paquin
John Parrinello
John Parsons
Patrick Pellerin
Charles Perry
Don Pfeiffer
Dean Phillips
Roberta Pilk
Peter Pitcher
John D. Pitney
Michael Pittas
David Place
Richard Pounds
Jack Powell
Edmund G. Pratt
Larry Pressler
Brig. Gen. George B. Price, USA (Ret)
Lt. Col. Tom Price, USA
David Priddy
Kathryn Purchase

Nancy Reagan
Dennis H. Reeder
Marie Reid
Rabbi Arnold E. Resnicoff, USN
Stanley R. Resor
Lt. Thomas Reynolds, USMC
Elliot L. Richardson
Dallas Ricker
Phillip Riggin
Charles S. Robb
Richard G. Robbins
Maj. Gen. J. Milnor Roberts, USA (Ret)
Harry G. Robinson III
David Rockefeller
James Rogan
Edgar D. Romig
Vicki Roney
Joseph Ronsisvalle
James Rosati
William F. Ruback
Dennis Rude
James A. Rubin
Steve Runge
Morgan Ruph
Dean Rusk

Barbara L. Sadoff
Morley Safer
Kelly Sander
Hideo Sasaki
Jim Sasser
Sarah Saunders
Sherry Saville
Regina Saxton
Helen M. Scharf
Julian Scheer
Harrison Schmidt
James H. Schofield
Louise N. Scruggs
Donna Seay
Robert F. Semple
Chris Shand
Don Shannon
Marjorie L. Share
Daniel H. Shear
Shaun Sheehan
Bill Sherard
Donald Sherman
Lt. Col. Bob Shields, USA
Helen Shipman
Robert Shullman
Don Sider
Hugh Sidey
Steven Silver
Melanie Silverberg
Alan K. Simpson
Donald M. Skinder
Ed Small
Austin Smith
Jack Smith
Murray L. Smith
Nikki Smith
P. Daniel Smith
Priscilla Smith
Ruth Somers
Robert W. Spanogle
Barry Speare
Dewey Spencer
W. Bruce Spiher
Paul Spreiregen
Robert T. Stafford
Sylvester Stallone
Brian Stanley
Julie Stanton
Willie Stargell
Roger Staubach
Peter Stefanou
Don Steffen
Jimmy Stewart
Lawrence J. Stingcomb
John Stitak
Helen Stuber
George Sullivan
Chaplain Max D. Sullivan, USA

J. R. Sungenis
Walter S. Surrey
Steven Swan
Stanley W. Swain
Edward Sweeny
Paul Heshel Swerdlow
Cynthia Szady

Elizabeth Taylor
John Terzano
Robert Terzo
Brian Thacker
Paul Thayer
Alf Thompson
Adm. William Thompson, USN
Lynn Thonus
Mary Tillotson
Edward Timperlake
John G. Tower
Kevin C. Troy
Garry Trudeau
Arnold Trujillo
Homer Tutor

Steve Umin
Lloyd N. Unsell

Sumner Vale
Anthony R. Vallance
Rob Van Akin
Cyrus R. Vance
Linda Van Devanter
Renne Vaught
Gen. John W. Vessey, Jr., USA
Wolf Von Eckardt

Andrew Wahlquist
John E. Wain
John T. Walker
Marty Walsh
Harry N. Walters
Grace Warman
John W. Warner
Paul Warren
Miriam Watson
Harry M. Weese
Carol Welu
Gen. William C. Westmoreland, USA (Ret.)
Clyde Wheeler
Elisa DesPortes Wheeler
Francis Whitebird
Fran Wigglesworth
Maj. Dennis Wightman, USAF
Robert Wilderotter
Regina Wilk
George F. Will
Edward Bennett Williams
Thomas Williams
Kathy Wilson
Col. Minter L. Wilson, USA (Ret)
T. A. Wilson
John L. Winkel
Jim Witek
Ernest Wittenberg
Mary Jane Wood
R. James Woolsey
Gary Wright
Jim Wright
Ethel Wyman

Jerry Yates

Marilyn Zahn
Joseph C. Zengerle
Charles B. Zucker

Included in this Roll Call of Honor are the names of those who helped make this book possible. Particular among them is Patricia Hersch, who made invaluable contributions to the research, conceptualization, and editing of this book. Before working on the book, Pat knew no one who had served in Vietnam, but she is part of the generation touched in their youth and forever changed by the war. A mother of three sons—Michael, Jamie, and Eric—she brought personal understanding of the stakes of war. Pat's close relationship with the Memorial is important because it symbolizes the fact that *every* American, not just veterans and their families, is part of the healing and learning process which transcends Vietnam and its veterans and goes right to the heart of what America is and what it will be as a nation. As journalist and author Michael Herr wrote in *Dispatches*: "Vietnam, Vietnam, we've all been there."

Jan C. Scruggs

Directory of Names

The following are the names of the American men and women who made the supreme sacrifice in Southeast Asia between 1957 and 1975. They are listed alphabetically, and the location of each name on the Vietnam Veterans Memorial is given.

NAME	STATE	PANEL NO.	LINE NO.
AADLAND GERALD L	SD	63W	14
AALUND JAMES DOWNING	TX	13W	66
AAMOLD DANIEL LAWRENCE	MN	08W	124
AARDE JAMES RAYMOND	WA	13E	95
AARON CHARLES EDWARD	MA	11W	98
AARON EUGENE ALLEN	FL	07W	43
AARON MICHAEL PETER	TX	48W	10
AARON RICHARD ALAN	DC	05W	80
AARON THOMAS MILTON JR	PA	22W	37
AARONSON WILLIAM F IV	FL	05W	54
AASEN DAVID KIM	WA	25E	27
ABARA JOSE GENE	NJ	37E	76
ABBATE RICHARD CLARK	IL	62E	15
ABBATE ROSARIO RUSSEL	NY	18E	38
ABBATEMARCO JOHN BENJAMIN	NJ	10W	30
ABBIE DONALD PAUL	CA	44W	34
ABBOTT CARROLL DAVID	TN	11E	125
ABBOTT DAVID FRANCIS	VA	16W	16
ABBOTT DENIS EUGENE	PA	06E	129
ABBOTT EDWARD DONALD	CA	55E	37
ABBOTT GUY FRANCIS	CO	32W	87
ABBOTT HAROLD WAYNE	IN	39E	68
ABBOTT JAMES EDWARD	LA	12W	110
ABBOTT JAMES MICHAEL	TN	26W	42
ABBOTT JAMES TERRY	IN	05W	38
ABBOTT JOHN	CA	06E	124
ABBOTT JOHN WILLIAM	IN	24W	100
ABBOTT PAUL DENNIS	WI	28E	89
ABBOTT RAYMOND LAWRENCE	PA	24E	65
ABBOTT ROBERT ESTEN JR	MO	56E	34
ABBOTT ROBERT WILLIAM	NY	04E	19
ABBOTT STEVEN GLENN	MN	58E	29
ABBOTT TERRY MICHAEL	NH	40E	57
ABBOTT WALLACE ADRION	TN	12E	16
ABDELLAH BRUCE ALLYN	ME	02W	50
ABDULLAH GHALIB AHMED	NY	35E	84
ABEL ARNOLD GORDON	IN	34E	13
ABEL CHARLES SEABORN	KY	10E	89
ABENE CHARLES FREDERICK	NJ	38W	9
ABERNATHY DANIEL OWEN	NJ	47W	58
ABERNATHY JIMMY EDD	NC	33W	35
ABERNATHY ROBERT LLOYD	MO	04E	19
ABERNATHY ROBERT WILLIAM	MD	42E	59
ABERNETHY REGINALD JOE	NC	04W	65
ABERNETHY WILLIAM FORMAN	FL	23E	96
ABEY GEORGE WAYNE	PA	06E	13
ABEYTA ERNEST	CA	23W	34
ABEYTA JERRY DELBERT	NM	55W	17
ABEYTA TONY GENEVEVO	CO	02E	74
ABINA ROBERT THOMAS	CA	31E	8
ABLE DAVID FLOYD	TX	25E	41
ABLER JAMES LYNN	IA	10W	77
ABLES ELMER ROBERT LEE JR	CA	28E	71
ABMEYER KENNETH RONALD	OK	20E	99
ABNER CARL EDWARD	CA	32E	66
ABNEY DANIEL THOMAS JR	FL	25W	114
ABOLINS JANIS	IA	35W	32
ABOLTIN RICHARD D	MA	08E	114
ABRAHAM ARLEY GEORGE	WV	44W	44
ABRAHAM JAMES JOSEPH	PA	41W	50
ABRAHAM PAUL HAROLD	TX	28W	106
ABRAHAM PAUL LEONARD	CA	53E	44
ABRAHAM ROOSEVELT JR	NC	20W	105
ABRAHAMSON GARY LEE	IA	07W	75
ABRAM JAMES HENRY	LA	04W	114
ABRAMOFF ARTHUR JOHN	NJ	14E	56
ABRAMOSKI LEO BERT	MI	01E	59
ABRAMS JOHN ALAN	IL	13E	129
ABRAMS JOHN LEON	MN	52W	21
ABRAMS LEWIS HERBERT	NJ	30E	83
ABRAMS SAMUEL JR	FL	19W	7
ABRAMS TIMOTHY C JR	AL	13E	112
ABRAMSON ANDREW JOHN	OR	17W	107
ABREU-BATISTA MIGUEL A JR	NY	56E	34
ABRUZESE ANTHONY JOSEPH	NY	10E	34
ABRUZESE ROBERT ALEXANDER	NY	15W	101
ABRUZZESA MICHAEL JOHN JR	NY	45W	59
ABSHEAR WILLIAM WALLACE	MD	30W	61
ABSHIRE RICHARD FRANKLIN	LA	53E	44
ABSTON JAMES ESTUS JR	AL	15E	102
ACALOTTO ROBERT JOSEPH	PA	05W	122
ACERET PEPITO RIVERA	HI	15W	34
ACEVEDO HECTOR SANTOS	NY	10E	6
ACEVEDO RICHARD JOSEPH	CA	28E	71
ACEVEDO ROBERTO	NY	32W	18
ACEVEDO-MILLAN ANGEL LUIS	PR	16W	129
ACEVEDO-RECHANI RAFAEL	PR	03E	121
ACHAS ROBERT JOHN	IL	01E	95
ACHER ROBERT PAUL JR	IN	18W	18
ACHESON CHARLES RALPH	KS	30E	52
ACHICA EDDIE	CA	09E	121
ACHISON TIMOTHY EUGENE	OR	15W	12
ACHOE LEEVERNE RICHARD	OH	57W	34
ACHOR TERRENCE WILLIAM	CA	42E	60
ACHORD DAVID PAUL	LA	22W	115
ACHTERHOFF JAMES PATRICK	MI	45E	18
ACKER HERMAN CAROL	LA	01W	76
ACKER ODELL BERNARD PATE	NC	18W	63
ACKERMAN BILL R	UT	12W	54
ACKERMAN DANIEL LEVERNE	NV	49E	7
ACKERMAN DAVID ALAN	NH	60W	24
ACKERMAN DAVID FOLEY	NJ	21W	68
ACKERMAN DENNIS CARLTON	LA	40W	41
ACKERMAN EDWIN ARTHUR JR	MN	32W	57
ACKERMAN JAMES CARROLL JR	OH	45E	53
ACKERMAN JOHN ROBERT	IN	03E	64
ACKERMAN LEONARD MICHAEL	MI	12W	24
ACKERMAN MAXIE EDWARD	MI	41E	15
ACKERMAN REX WILLIAM	IN	26W	5
ACKERMAN ROGER CARL HENRY	WI	56E	20
ACKERMAN THOMAS ALAN	NJ	45W	35
ACKERSON VENCEN	OK	30W	35
ACKLEY GERALD LEVIE	CA	21E	41
ACKWOOD WALTER JAMES	NY	11E	120
ACORD EWELL EDGEL	WV	19E	2
ACOSTA DANIEL	CA	12E	57
ACOSTA GERMAN PORTACIO		02E	18
ACOSTA JAMES ARTHUR JR	LA	52W	33
ACOSTA JESSE RODRIQUEZ	TX	01E	115
ACOSTA JOHN MICHAEL	CA	35E	2
ACOSTA JOHN WAYNE	AR	50W	16
ACOSTA JOSE FRANCISCO	KS	27E	35
ACOSTA LOYD DEAN	CA	18W	88
ACOSTA-ROSARIO HUMBERTO	PR	47W	30
ACRE LAWRENCE DALE	WA	17W	53
ACREE BILLIE RAY	IN	64E	10
ACREE ROGER LEE	OH	23E	68
ACTON DAVID AUGUST	IN	23E	9
ACTON GERALD RICHARD	MI	25W	58
ACTON MARION FRANKLIN	AL	06E	96
ACTON TOM PERRY	TX	66E	5
ACUFF EDDIE DUANE	TX	22W	115
ACUNIA EDGAR	CA	30W	51
ADACHI THOMAS YUJI	CA	11W	34
ADAIR DALLAS TYLER JR	AZ	52E	13
ADAIR HARVEY GENE	CA	46E	43
ADAIR SAMUEL YOUNG JR	GA	01W	24
ADAIR THURMAN	OK	13E	57
ADAIR WILLIAM MICHAEL	WA	14W	6
ADAKAI LEO JOE	ID	20W	105
ADAM BARRY L	PA	21E	103
ADAM HOSEA DENNIS	LA	07E	79
ADAM JOHN QUINCY	KS	65E	6
ADAM RAYMOND ALVIN	SD	01E	49
ADAME ARTHUR PINA	TX	10W	78
ADAME GILBERT JIMMIE	CA	48E	38
ADAMES SANTIAGO D JR	TX	44W	8
ADAMITZ IAN WILLIAM	FL	31E	89
ADAMO RICHARD CHARLES	NY	41E	58
ADAMOLI ROWLAND JOSEPH	PA	02E	53
ADAMS ARTHUR LLOYD JR	CO	47W	36
ADAMS AUGUSTUS	MS	03W	60
ADAMS BERT MORRIS III	TX	26W	76
ADAMS BOYED TIMOTHY	FL	26W	16
ADAMS CARL TURNER	TX	44E	64
ADAMS CARROLL EDWARD JR	RI	10W	21
ADAMS CHARLES HENRY	GA	06W	58
ADAMS CHARLES WESLEY	NY	20W	111
ADAMS CLARENCE CLIFTON	WI	32W	10
ADAMS CLARENCE MATTUE	MI	33E	5
ADAMS DARRIUS WAYNE	WV	54E	42
ADAMS DAVEY MARLIN	MS	36W	9
ADAMS DAVID LEE	MI	21E	20
ADAMS DAVID LEE	MI	48W	51
ADAMS DAVID VERNON	MI	35W	86
ADAMS DENNIS MICHAEL	PA	31W	87
ADAMS DONALD BEN JR	VA	23E	84
ADAMS DWANE LONNIE	SC	35W	86
ADAMS DWIGHT LEE	TN	43W	1
ADAMS EDDIE MARTIN	MA	39W	46
ADAMS EDWARD CODY	WV	50E	10
ADAMS EMMITT COLON	KY	05E	54
ADAMS ERHARD JIMMIE	NC	06W	33
ADAMS FRANK DAVID	LA	49W	28
ADAMS FRANK HOUSTON	TN	12W	34
ADAMS GEORGE DAYTON	NM	06E	135
ADAMS GEORGE FRANCIS	MA	45E	17
ADAMS GEORGE GAYRAL	TX	50E	36
ADAMS GEORGE HARTWELL	NY	12W	126
ADAMS GILLES DAVID	CA	44E	56
ADAMS GLENN ARTHUR	IA	10W	21
ADAMS HARLAN FLOYD	MO	22E	28
ADAMS HERBERT NORMAN	GA	07E	43
ADAMS HUGHIE DARELL	TX	01E	40
ADAMS JAMES CLARENCE	WV	38W	70
ADAMS JAMES CONRAD	AL	11W	78
ADAMS JAMES EDWARD	CA	15E	68
ADAMS JAMES HENRY	KY	27W	43
ADAMS JAMES LINDELL	CA	44W	34
ADAMS JAMES RICHARD	TN	18E	67
ADAMS JAMES ROBERT	FL	45E	36
ADAMS JERRY DEAN	IN	39E	79
ADAMS JESSE LEWIS	SC	38W	22
ADAMS JOHN K	NM	17E	48
ADAMS JOHN LOUIS	NC	52W	13
ADAMS JOHN ROBERT	CA	29E	46
ADAMS JOHN TERRY	OK	08E	50
ADAMS JOHN WILBURN	CA	01W	25
ADAMS JOSEPH	LA	59E	17
ADAMS JOSEPH BOYCE	SC	48W	21
ADAMS KENNETH STANLEY	CA	30E	68
ADAMS KENNEY MILTON JR	TX	38W	63
ADAMS LARRY	MI	40E	72
ADAMS LARRY EARL	MS	54W	14
ADAMS LEE AARON	CA	06E	122
ADAMS LEE CHESTER	WI	50E	44
ADAMS LEE SCOTT	PA	48E	26
ADAMS LEON HENRY	CA	23W	116
ADAMS MERRITT	NC	07W	51
ADAMS MICHAEL DRUE	TX	32W	63
ADAMS MICHAEL EDWARD	IL	30E	21
ADAMS MICHAEL EUGENE	WA	43W	11
ADAMS MICHAEL THOMAS	NM	26W	109
ADAMS NEIL JR	GA	03W	118
ADAMS NORMAN EDWARD	OK	34E	66
ADAMS OLEY NEAL	MO	08E	55
ADAMS PAUL EDWIN	CA	50E	36
ADAMS PAUL VERNON	MI	13W	90
ADAMS PETER ROBERT	MA	23W	24
ADAMS PHILIP FRANCIS	NY	30E	68
ADAMS PHILIP J	PA	05W	38
ADAMS PHILLIP CURTIS	NJ	11W	99
ADAMS RAYMOND SPENCER	UT	32E	61
ADAMS RICHARD LEE	OH	15E	43
ADAMS RICHARD LYLE	MO	16W	44
ADAMS RICKY FAY	CA	42E	12
ADAMS ROBERT JAMES	IN	08W	50
ADAMS ROBERT LEE JR	PA	12E	16
ADAMS ROBERT LELAND	PA	06E	130
ADAMS ROGER DEAN	OH	22E	96
ADAMS RONALD M	MD	32E	90
ADAMS RONALD WYATT	CO	35E	13
ADAMS RONNIE LEE	TX	39E	16
ADAMS ROSCOE DAVID	TX	50W	21
ADAMS ROYCE HORACE	FL	27W	79
ADAMS RUSSELL BYRD	GA	33W	90
ADAMS RUSSELL LEE	DC	28E	52
ADAMS SAMUEL	FL	03E	8
ADAMS SPENCER	AL	39E	42
ADAMS STANLEY LEE	OH	16W	25
ADAMS STEADMON JR	NC	06E	9
ADAMS STEPHEN HAMILTON	MD	44E	64
ADAMS STEVEN HAROLD	IA	11E	85
ADAMS STEVEN JACK	OH	16E	6
ADAMS TED WANE	TX	12E	76
ADAMS TERRANCE DEAN	TX	04E	117

NAME	STATE	PANEL NO.	LINE NO.
ADAMS TERRY LEE	NC	23E	68
ADAMS THOMAS B	DE	42E	60
ADAMS THOMAS EDWARD	NY	33E	6
ADAMS THOMAS EDWARD	KS	31W	75
ADAMS WALTER LEE	AL	21E	82
ADAMS WAYNE ROGER	OH	29E	103
ADAMS WILLIAM CARL	KS	19W	99
ADAMS WILLIAM EDWARD	CO	03W	54
ADAMS WILLIAM ERNEST	CA	41E	34
ADAMS WILLIAM J	OH	33E	55
ADAMS WILLIAM JAMES	IA	24W	35
ADAMS WILLIAM JR	NY	50E	44
ADAMS WILLIAM OTHELLO JR	SC	65W	3
ADAMS WILLIAM RAYMOND	IL	17W	60
ADAMS WILLIAM RICHARD	OH	34W	39
ADAMS WOODROW WILLIAM	NY	32W	75
ADAMSKI DENNIS JAMES	WI	22E	9
ADAMSON DONALD BRUCE	MI	05E	63
ADAMSON FRANK LESLIE	KY	02E	16
ADAMSON LARRY ONEAL	AL	17W	33
ADAY RICHARD DONALD	OR	17E	33
ADAY ROBERT LEE	CA	17W	111
ADCOCK BILLY ANTHONY	TN	41W	3
ADCOCK RICHARD LYNN	CA	30W	71
ADCOX RONNIE DARNELL	NC	16E	6
ADDAIR KYLE ASHCOM	AR	32W	87
ADDICE FRANK PAUL	NJ	49E	18
ADDINGTON ROYCE LEE	OK	06W	52
ADDINGTON ZACK TAYLOR	GA	61E	7
ADDIS BILLY WAYNE	SC	11W	29
ADDIS FRANCIS RAY	PA	09W	67
ADDIS JERRY LEROY	NC	56W	34
ADDISON HARVEY CHARLES	CA	55W	32
ADDISON JOHN EDWARD	PA	32E	67
ADDISON O'NEAL	AL	07E	22
ADDISON RICHARD EDWARD JR	NY	48W	36
ADDUCI JOHN JOSEPH	IL	16W	113
ADE DWIGHT I	MI	12W	54
ADENIR RESTITUTO POBLETE		03E	4
ADES ARNOLD ALVIN	MN	54W	39
ADGER WILLIE HOWARD	NC	37E	79
ADIKAI ALVIN JR	AZ	04W	45
ADIUTORI RICHARD	NY	35W	86
ADKINS BOBBY RAY	WV	21W	5
ADKINS CARL EDWARD	OK	31E	42
ADKINS CHARLES L	OH	36E	64
ADKINS CHARLES LELAND	CO	39W	31
ADKINS DONALD WAYNE	VA	28E	18
ADKINS HENRY DALE	OH	03W	51
ADKINS JAMES DALE	OH	23W	108
ADKINS JOHN	OH	48E	38
ADKINS KENNETH DALE	WV	06W	65
ADKINS LLOYD MARVIN JR	OH	21E	2
ADKINS MARVIN JARRELL	WV	24E	13
ADKINS MICHAEL DUANE	OH	05W	101
ADKINS NORMAN DALE	OH	11W	48
ADKINS RONALD EUGENE	NE	46W	55
ADKINS TERRY LEE	IL	25W	45
ADKINS WAYNE LAWRENCE	GA	17W	89
ADKISON CARL ELMUS	AL	19W	7
ADKISSON JAMES WILLIE	CO	11E	54
ADLER HENRY	NE	37E	17
ADLER TOM ROBERT	DC	03W	52
ADLER WOODROW DENNIS	NM	30E	87
ADOLF LARRY EUGENE	NE	57E	12
ADRIAN JOSEPH DANIEL	NJ	16E	67
AERTS DAVID LEE	MI	36W	43
AESCHLIMAN DAVID KEITH	MI	14W	37
AFFLERBACH MARK	PA	04W	30
AGAR ANTHONY PHILIP	NY	25W	16
AGAR ROBERT LEE	WV	28E	94
AGARD ROWLAND NATHANIEL	NY	18W	127
AGARD TIMOTHY CHARLES	WI	40E	17
AGATHER FREDERIC GUSTAVE	MN	23W	34
AGAZZI DAVID MICHAEL	NY	27E	26
AGEE JOHN CHARLES	OH	15E	112
AGIUS VINCENT JAMES	WI	18E	38
AGNES MANOLO BRIONES		03W	99
AGNEW JAMES WILLIAM	MO	27W	4
AGRI JOSEPH JOHN JR	MA	26W	5
AGRI SALVATORE JR	MA	48E	56
AGUADO ROBERT CHARLES	IL	22E	9
AGUAYO OSCAR JR	AZ	31E	96
AGUGLIARO MATTHEW JOHN	NY	32E	56
AGUIAR JUAN DANIEL	CA	44E	43
AGUILAR ADOLFO	TX	44E	46
AGUILAR ARMANDO	TX	15E	11
AGUILAR ARNOLD	TX	51E	15
AGUILAR DOMINGO IGNACIO	NY	31E	62
AGUILAR JAMES DANIEL	AZ	03W	42
AGUILAR MIKE JOHN	CA	01W	15
AGUILAR NICK ALFRED JR	TX	12W	110
AGUILAR OSCAR	CA	01W	15
AGUILAR PEDRO RAMIREZ	TX	31E	21
AGUILAR REIMUNDO	TX	19E	124
AGUILAR ROBERT	TX	18E	32
AGUILAR RUDOLPH RENE	CA	03E	33
AGUILERA DANIEL	CA	13W	76
AGUILLON FELIZARDO CUENCA	CA	01W	122
AGUILLON JOSE JESUS	TX	25W	59
AGUIRRE ARTHUR CECILIO	TX	14E	78
AGUIRRE CARLOS CRUZ	NM	41E	6
AGUIRRE FIDEL JOE	TX	30W	98
AGUIRRE FILBERTO JR	AZ	25E	45
AGUIRRE GEORGE	CA	16E	99
AGUIRRE JOSEPH ANTHONY	CA	34W	81
AGUIRRE RAYMOND	CO	12W	47
AGUON JOSE QUINATA	GM	61W	9
AHART WILLIAM JUNIOR	IN	14W	16
AHERN BRIAN PAUL	MA	33E	63
AHERN JOHN BERNARD	CA	44E	64
AHERN RAYMOND JOSEPH JR	PA	38W	63
AHERN ROBERT PAUL	NH	28W	89
AHINZOW TONY	IL	22E	122
AHLBERG THOMAS OLIVER	ID	11W	94
AHLFIELD ALAN PAUL	IL	01W	71
AHLMEYER HEINZ JR	NY	19E	77
AHLSTROM ROBERT ERNEST	TX	18W	45
AHLUM WILLIAM JOHN	PA	28W	16
AHOUSE WILLIAM C	GA	58W	1
AHRENDSEN DENNIS LYNN	IA	45W	47
AHRENS JAMES JOHN	WI	22W	84
AHRENS RUSSELL GEORGE	NY	04W	57
AHUNA ABRAHAM KAALELE	HI	61E	21
AIAU HARVEY CHADWICK K	MD	12W	2
AIGELDINGER ELDRIDGE CHAR	PA	10E	49
AIKEN DAVID ROSS	MD	11E	2
AIKEN LARRY DELARNARD	NY	20W	42
AIKEN LEROY BENJAMIN	NY	01W	6
AIKEN WILLIAM LESLIE	NY	06W	55
AIKEY TIMOTHY WAYNE	PA	04E	51
AIKIN GEORGE LEE	DE	17W	53
AILES WILLIAM EUGENE	OH	31E	62
AILI DAVID E	MI	31E	83
AILSTOCK JIM LAMARR JR	TX	46E	26
AINSWORTH JOHN MATHEW JR	CT	22E	94
AINSWORTH KENNETH JOHN	LA	36E	64
AIREY GEORGE VERNON JR	MI	57E	12
AIRLIE WILLIAM CLARK	MI	10W	63
AITKEN DEAN L	UT	11W	96
AITON GERALD DAVID	WA	52E	45
AJSTER JOSEPH ROBERT	IL	41W	9
AKAMU ALBERT KAIWI	CA	57E	12
AKANA FRANKLIN RANDOLPH	HI	06W	72
AKE HOMER LEE JR	TN	42E	46
AKEHURST HOWARD DAVID	WA	37E	47
AKEL RICHARD LOUIS	FL	63E	4
AKER JEFFREY SCOTT	KY	34E	66
AKERLEY DENNIS	NY	17W	123
AKERS ARVEL DEWIT	KY	04E	57
AKERS DENNIS OWEN	KY	60W	14
AKERS E G JR	VA	09W	121
AKERS EDWARD DARRELL	VA	04E	63
AKI FRANCIS CLAYBURN JR	HI	39W	69
AKIN JOHN VINCENT	TX	57W	22
AKIN RICHARD ARTHUR JR	OR	45W	30
AKINS ADRIAN ALAN	AL	17W	118
AKINS CHARLES JAMES	NY	37W	44
AKINS DONALD WAYNE	OK	23W	116
AKINS JAMES FRANKLIN	TN	20E	42
AKINS RONALD PAUL	OH	41E	15
AKINS SAMUEL LEROY	CA	44W	44
AKKERMAN DUANE CHARLES	ID	28E	77
AKSTIN JAMES MICHAEL	CA	19E	91
ALAGNA PETER LEONARD	CA	34W	63
ALAIMO HOWARD JAMES	NY	62W	4
ALAIMO JOHN CHARLES	PA	27W	35
ALAKULPPI VESA JUHANI	WA	60E	7
ALAMED WILLIAM ROBERT JR	MA	13W	102
ALAMEDA WILLIAM KAPENA	HI	40W	70
ALAMO GABRIEL RALPH	NJ	01E	57
ALANDT CHARLES BYRON	MI	16E	6
ALANIZ AMADO JR	TX	04W	94
ALANIZ BENITO	CO	16E	109
ALANIZ BENITO V	TX	41W	71
ALANIZ FEDERICO JR	CA	22W	37
ALANIZ LUIS ANGEL	TX	14W	102
ALANIZ PAUL GILBERT JR	TX	58E	29
ALANIZ RAYMOND	TX	37W	15
ALARCON ARTURO FRAGOSO	CA	29W	42
ALBA JESSIE CHARLES	TX	70E	1
ALBANESE JOHN ERNEST JR	NY	66E	5
ALBANESE LEWIS	WA	12E	131
ALBANESE LUIGI FRANK	WA	35E	43
ALBANESE ROBERT	NJ	21W	50
ALBANO PAUL EDWARD	NY	17E	59
ALBAREZ SEFERINO JR	TX	57W	7
ALBASIO JOHN A		20W	53
ALBERICI MICHAEL	NY	47W	59
ALBERT DANIEL JOHN	NH	38W	22
ALBERT DAVID	NJ	18W	35
ALBERT LOUIS BASIL JR	ME	17W	48
ALBERT PETER	MA	20E	39
ALBERT RAYMOND HOWARD JR	CA	43W	44
ALBERT RICHARD PATRICK	ME	19W	76
ALBERT SERGIO EDITH	NY	21E	93
ALBERT WILLIAM DAVID	IL	21W	115
ALBERTINI JAMES CHRISTOPH	MA	39E	16
ALBERTINI JOSEPH ALFRED	CA	27E	56
ALBERTON BOBBY JOE	CA	07E	126
ALBERTS DANIEL LOUIS	IN	17E	77
ALBERTS FRANCIS JOHN	NJ	10E	49
ALBERTS JOHN CHARLES	IL	07E	64
ALBERTS ROGER DUANE	ND	37E	30
ALBERTSON BERNARD GEORGE	PA	04W	130
ALBERTSON DONALD NORMAN	MI	39W	46
ALBERTSON ROBERT ALLEN	MI	29E	18
ALBERTSON RONALD DALE	MI	51W	29
ALBI LOUIS VICTOR JR	MD	34W	46
ALBIETZ RAYMOND PETER	NJ	14E	65
ALBRECHT ADOLPH WILLIAM	TX	52W	13
ALBRECHT GEORGE HENRY	PA	01E	73
ALBRECHT JOSEPH ALFRED	MA	50W	47
ALBRIGHT BUCK EDWARD	AZ	24W	80
ALBRIGHT JAMES MILTON	IL	16E	50
ALBRIGHT JOHN SCOTT II	WV	36W	13
ALBRIGHT PETER HENRY	FL	10E	34
ALBRIGHT TERRY LEE	WI	17W	47
ALBRIGHT TERRY ROBERT	WV	07W	125
ALBRIGHT WALTER LEROY	PA	17E	33
ALBRITTON GERALD WAYNE	FL	23W	49
ALBRITTON JOHNNY BOYD	LA	27E	26
ALBRITTON KENNETH HOSEA	NC	36E	45
ALBURY LELAND W JR	FL	08E	106
ALCANTAR FRANK COSME	CA	02E	94
ALCOCER-MARTINEZ HECTOR M	PR	14E	19
ALCOCK RONNIE GILMAN	NC	24W	27
ALCORN DALE ROBERT JR	CA	18W	45
ALCOS LARRY MELVIN	HI	32W	41
ALDAG WILLIAM ARTHUR	NY	13W	50
ALDAM KEVIN GERRY	MA	21W	22
ALDAY DANNY WADE	FL	57W	16
ALDAY FRANK TISNERO	AZ	41E	58
ALDERIDGE JAMES CURTIS	TN	31W	31
ALDERMAN ANDREW ALBERT	KS	16E	99
ALDERMAN JAMES MURIEL	NY	15W	101
ALDERMAN WILFORD HARLESS	VA	32W	87
ALDERMAN WINFRED	NC	20E	14
ALDERN DONALD DEANE	SD	09W	101
ALDERSON BENJAMIN ROBERT	CA	22W	30
ALDERSON MICHAEL EDWARD	MI	16E	55
ALDERSON TERRY HOWARD	TX	55E	37
ALDERSON THOMAS EARL	ND	42W	65
ALDOUS LILO ELMER	UT	44W	60
ALDRED JAMES VINCENT	MI	17W	93
ALDRICH DAVID ALAN	OH	47E	7

NAME	STATE	PANEL NO.	LINE NO.
ALDRICH JOHN HERRICK	WY	22W	95
ALDRICH LAWRENCE LEE	TX	55E	37
ALDRIDGE HERBERT RAY	IA	43E	12
ALDRIDGE NEIL WAYNE	IL	21E	60
ALDRIDGE WILLIE GENE	KY	37W	78
ALECK JOHN IRA	NV	30W	62
ALEGRE DANIEL ALBERT	CA	13W	66
ALENCASTRE ANTHONY ALBERT	CA	49E	50
ALERT ROBERT JOSEPH JR	IN	25W	27
ALESHIRE KENNETH EDWARD	PA	41E	47
ALESHIRE RONALD LEE	CA	56W	16
ALEWINE LEMUEL LENOEL	TX	28E	18
ALEX CHARLES RAY	CA	16W	78
ALEXANDER BARRY KENNETH	SC	18W	124
ALEXANDER BOBBY RAY	AL	29E	104
ALEXANDER CALVIN EUGENE	NJ	31W	99
ALEXANDER CARL THEODORE	IN	35W	63
ALEXANDER CHARLES PHILLIP	TN	15E	67
ALEXANDER DALLAS C JR	OH	01W	106
ALEXANDER DAVID HAROLD	ME	36W	28
ALEXANDER DAVID J JR	AL	51W	2
ALEXANDER DAVID LEE	PA	05W	80
ALEXANDER DEWEY LEE	TX	11E	106
ALEXANDER DONALD RAY	NM	28W	7
ALEXANDER ELEANOR GRACE	NJ	31E	8
ALEXANDER ELTON HARROLD	TN	18W	36
ALEXANDER GEORGE W JR	NM	11E	43
ALEXANDER J H	TN	05E	127
ALEXANDER JAMES BLAIR JR	OH	01E	87
ALEXANDER JAMES HINES	IN	14W	110
ALEXANDER JAMES PATRICK	IL	04W	107
ALEXANDER JASPER MARION	OH	30W	17
ALEXANDER KERRY	FL	46W	55
ALEXANDER LAURIE LEON	IN	10E	3
ALEXANDER MICKEY ROY	OK	17W	99
ALEXANDER NICHOLAS RICHAR	IA	38W	70
ALEXANDER RICHARD CARL	PA	07W	54
ALEXANDER ROBERT	DC	57E	13
ALEXANDER ROBERT DAVID	DE	20E	52
ALEXANDER ROBERT EMMET	CA	39E	56
ALEXANDER ROBERT LEE	TN	16W	7
ALEXANDER ROBERT SAMUEL	PA	12W	86
ALEXANDER ROGER DALE	NC	16W	92
ALEXANDER ROY M	IL	45E	37
ALEXANDER SAMMIE EDWARD	TX	10W	55
ALEXANDER STAMATIOS G JR	TX	27W	61
ALEXANDER TERRY LEE	WA	10E	34
ALEXANDER WILLIAM LEE	MI	23W	24
ALEXANDER WOODROW	NY	12W	50
ALFANO RODNEY ARTHUR	MA	36E	64
ALFERINK JERRY LAVERN	OH	31W	70
ALFEROFF IVAN	NY	06E	61
ALFONSO JOHN	NJ	23E	93
ALFONSO RONALD JOSEPH	NY	29W	34
ALFORD GEORGE ALLEN JR	TX	50W	40
ALFORD MARK CARL	CA	18W	26
ALFORD MICHAEL LYNN	CA	53E	27
ALFORD TERRY LANIER	TX	16W	26
ALFORD THOMAS EARL III	LA	37W	16
ALFORD ULYSSES	NC	09E	8
ALFRED BRUCE CROCKLIN	GA	32E	67
ALFRED GERALD OAK JR	WA	13E	31
ALFRED THOMAS SAMUEL	CA	51E	35
ALFREDSON WILLIAM RICHARD	MI	11W	5
ALFSTAD KENNETH ORVILLE	WA	11E	38
ALGAARD HAROLD LOWELL	MN	04W	20
ALGARIN-RIVERA RAFAEL ANG	PR	04E	98
ALGER GEORGE BERKLEY	CO	37W	9
ALGIRE ROGER DEAN	OH	38W	63
ALHO ANTONIO LOPEZ	CT	28W	42
ALI ARFIEN CLIFFORD	NJ	05E	53
ALICEA DAVID	NY	46W	55
ALICEA ISRAEL	NY	15E	13
ALICEA MANUEL JR	NY	08E	103
ALICEA MIGUEL ANGEL CRUZ	PR	02W	118
ALICEA ROBERT	NY	42W	52
ALICEA-SERRANO DAVID	PR	24W	27
ALINCIC RONALD ELI	PA	41W	50
ALIPIO LESTER WARREN	HI	05W	114
ALIVENTO FRANCIS DOMINICK	NY	27W	35
ALKIRE THEODORE A JR	WV	12E	98
ALL CARL KELLY	IN	61W	24
ALLAGONEZ RODOLFO P	HI	19W	65
ALLAIRE JOHN KEVIN	SC	41W	21
ALLAN DONALD EUGENE JR	OH	34W	46
ALLARD MICHAEL JOHN	WI	25E	67
ALLARD PAUL EDWARD	PA	26W	7
ALLARD RICHARD MICHAEL	MI	25E	36
ALLARD VAL GENE	MA	37E	17
ALLAWAY DONALD	NJ	07E	79
ALLBRIGHT RONALD HARRISON	TX	11W	53
ALLDRIDGE GALE ARTHUR	MN	27E	56
ALLEE RICHARD KENNETH	NY	36W	55
ALLEN ADRIAN LAURENCE	TN	17W	54
ALLEN ANDREW AUGUSTUS III	TX	41E	34
ALLEN ANTHONY	PA	23E	48
ALLEN BILLIE ALVIN	MS	12E	9
ALLEN BOBBY KENNETH	IL	34E	51
ALLEN BRUCE JOSEPH	NY	23E	24
ALLEN CHANNING JR	NY	15E	38
ALLEN CHARLES DAVID JR	TX	04W	53
ALLEN CHARLES DELMAR JR	OH	20E	109
ALLEN CHARLES ERVIN	VA	50E	26
ALLEN CHARLES FRANKLIN II	KY	02E	105
ALLEN CHARLES RICHARD	MO	04E	47
ALLEN DALE CHARLES	OH	22E	67
ALLEN DAN S III	TN	29E	79
ALLEN DAN STEVEN	TN	10E	24
ALLEN DANIEL WEBSTER JR	TX	04W	26
ALLEN DANNY RAY	MS	12W	2
ALLEN DAVID ANDREW	CA	08W	68
ALLEN DAVID MARTIN	GA	07W	122
ALLEN DEAN BROOKS	NY	20W	13
ALLEN DENNIS WAYNE	IL	52W	11
ALLEN DONALD RAY	TX	50E	44
ALLEN DONALD WILLIAM JR	WI	36E	64
ALLEN DOUGLAS MELVIN	DC	37W	20
ALLEN EARNEST JR	TX	19W	116
ALLEN EDDIE HUGH	TX	65W	3
ALLEN EDDIE JAMES	IN	25E	27
ALLEN EDWARD JAMES	IN	61E	6
ALLEN EDWIN CHARLES	FL	21W	115
ALLEN ELVIN L	MO	43E	51
ALLEN EUGENE	NY	04W	43
ALLEN EVERETT ALBERT	MA	24E	13
ALLEN FRANCIS MONROE JR	MA	14W	91
ALLEN FREDDIE LEE	LA	22E	82
ALLEN GARY	OK	26W	51
ALLEN GARY CHARLES	CA	05E	97
ALLEN GARY JOHN	NJ	39W	39
ALLEN GARY LEE	FL	58E	29
ALLEN GERALD WILLIAM	NY	41E	6
ALLEN GRANVILLE JOEL JR	AL	66E	6
ALLEN GUS	GA	08W	45
ALLEN HENRY GERHARDT	AZ	16W	113
ALLEN HENRY LEWIS	FL	12W	44
ALLEN HERBERT MARSHALL	FL	56W	31
ALLEN HERVEY HARRIS	VA	21E	20
ALLEN HOWARD LLOYD	IL	04E	32
ALLEN JACK LEE	IN	14E	13
ALLEN JAMES HARLEN	AR	04W	93
ALLEN JAMES JOSEPH	PA	60W	14
ALLEN JAMES LOUIS	TX	03E	22
ALLEN JAMES OTIS	IN	05E	53
ALLEN JAMES WARREN JR	OH	29E	46
ALLEN JAMES WILLIAM	KY	51E	35
ALLEN JERRY JOE	CA	09W	67
ALLEN JERRY L	NE	25E	21
ALLEN JESSE WAYEN	OH	24E	58
ALLEN JOE EBERT	MS	67E	3
ALLEN JOHN BAXTER	PA	30E	87
ALLEN JOHN DOSS	TX	10W	88
ALLEN JOHN FRANKLIN	KY	29W	76
ALLEN JOHN LEE	MO	20W	99
ALLEN JOHN WILLIS	TX	23E	72
ALLEN JOHNNY JR	AL	09W	109
ALLEN JON ANTHONY	NC	16W	123
ALLEN JOSEPH HAROLD	CA	50E	10
ALLEN KEITH DOBSON JR	ME	27W	70
ALLEN KEITH WESLEY	TX	28E	7
ALLEN KENNETH	KY	32E	84
ALLEN KENNETH JEFFREY	OH	38E	22
ALLEN LARRIE CORNELIUS	MI	08W	128
ALLEN LARRY DEAN	CO	13E	107
ALLEN LARRY HUGH	CA	43W	24
ALLEN LARRY MICHAEL	GA	09W	62
ALLEN LEONARD PETER	NY	06W	58
ALLEN LUECO JR	OH	13E	95
ALLEN LYLE ERNEST JR	MI	52E	45
ALLEN MARK ERWIN	NC	02W	101
ALLEN MELVIN ARLEIGH	OR	63E	4
ALLEN MELVIN LEE	IL	19E	34
ALLEN MERLIN RAYE	WI	22E	86
ALLEN OTIS LEE	MO	67W	8
ALLEN PAUL JAMES	MN	49E	18
ALLEN RAYMOND	GA	05E	130
ALLEN RAYMOND EUGENE	MO	25E	21
ALLEN REX THOMAS	CA	07W	7
ALLEN RICHARD C	PA	30E	21
ALLEN RICHARD GRAHAM	CA	05E	98
ALLEN RICHARD JAMES	MI	61E	22
ALLEN RICHARD LEE	NM	33W	75
ALLEN ROBERT CHRISTIAN	NV	62W	12
ALLEN ROBERT CLYDE	LA	15E	103
ALLEN ROBERT EUGENE	OK	27E	104
ALLEN ROBERT JOHN	RI	38E	42
ALLEN ROBERT SAMUEL	NJ	54E	42
ALLEN ROBERT WARREN	AL	02E	103
ALLEN RONALD JOSEPH	LA	31W	87
ALLEN RONALD PAUL	MN	32E	67
ALLEN RONALD STEWART III	OK	32E	34
ALLEN ROY	PA	41E	34
ALLEN ROY RANSOM	NJ	06E	27
ALLEN SAMUEL R	OH	20E	4
ALLEN SANFORD THOMAS	NC	57E	13
ALLEN TERRANCE W	MI	55E	38
ALLEN TERRY DE LA MESA JR	TX	28E	18
ALLEN TERRY ERNEST	NY	42E	60
ALLEN TERRY JAMES	CA	19E	9
ALLEN TERRY JR	GA	55W	20
ALLEN TERRY LEE	OR	58W	5
ALLEN TERRY LEE ODIS	MO	22E	35
ALLEN THOMAS	OH	19E	114
ALLEN THOMAS BARRY	MS	30E	61
ALLEN THOMAS RAY	OK	24E	53
ALLEN WAYNE ANDERSON	CA	39W	25
ALLEN WAYNE CLOUSE	MA	14W	22
ALLEN WILLIAM CORDELL JR	TN	22E	56
ALLEN WILLIAM EUGENE	PA	15W	108
ALLEN WILLIAM JOHN	MI	32W	75
ALLEN WILLIAM JR	FL	27W	28
ALLEN WILLIAM ORLANDO	FL	05E	63
ALLEN WILLIAM TERRY	AL	31E	32
ALLENBERG JAMES PATTEE	AZ	06W	128
ALLENDER FRANK ROSS JR	CA	22E	120
ALLENDORF MICHAEL GEORGE	KS	29W	3
ALLERBY MILTON RICHARD JR	MA	58W	21
ALLES JAMES KENNETH	IL	58E	18
ALLESSIE JOSEPH	PA	38W	60
ALLEY DON EARL	TN	10E	69
ALLEY DONALD RAY	VA	36W	13
ALLEY DOUGLAS DWIGHT	DE	05E	78
ALLEY GERALD WILLIAM	ID	01W	103
ALLEY JAMES HAROLD	FL	02W	130
ALLEY LONNIE DOUGLAS	VA	46E	26
ALLEY MICHAEL MORRIS	MO	39E	1
ALLEY WILLIE WARNIE	VA	18W	18
ALLGOOD FRANKIE EUGENE	KS	46E	26
ALLGOOD RONALD KEVIN	UT	07W	105
ALLING JOHN STEPHEN JR	NY	38W	64
ALLINSON DAVID JAY	MT	09E	129
ALLISON ARTHUR RICHARD	MA	20W	4
ALLISON DARRELL GENE	NY	14W	129
ALLISON GEORGE BRIAN	OK	52E	29
ALLISON JAMES SAMUEL	TX	40W	60
ALLISON JOHN ROBERT	SC	40E	57
ALLISON SAM STEPHEN	TX	52W	4
ALLISON STEPHEN HARRIS	NC	17W	93
ALLISON WILLIAM EDWIN	IN	22E	94
ALLMAN HENRY HAYDEN	IL	08E	90
ALLMAN JONATHAN WAYNE	CA	26W	17
ALLMERS ROBERT ROGER	WI	15W	45
ALLMEYER FREDERICK ALLEN	IL	23W	81
ALLMOND BARRY KENNETH	TX	01W	23
ALLOWAY CLYDE DOUGLAS	NH	09W	22
ALLPORT JAMES SHERWOOD	MD	53E	44

NAME	STATE	PANEL NO.	LINE NO.
ALLRED FRANK LEROY JR	CA	30E	87
ALLRED JAMES HERBERT	ID	01E	38
ALLRED ORIN LARRY	AZ	03E	41
ALLRED REX CHARLES	CA	25W	92
ALLSBROOK WILLIAM I JR	NC	07W	105
ALLSOPP STEPHEN ALLISON	NY	55E	38
ALLSTOTT MARK JOSEPH	IN	37E	17
ALLUM DANIEL E	PA	02E	137
ALLUMS ALLEN WAYNE	AL	25W	8
ALLUMS FREDERICK LARRY	AL	43E	40
ALLWOOD JOSEPH WAYNE BRYA	FL	24E	53
ALM RICHARD ANDREW	WA	04E	127
ALMAGUER BENJAMIN FRANCIS	IL	44E	4
ALMANZA JOHN JERALD	CA	25E	45
ALMANZA JUAN	TX	26E	41
ALMANZA PABLO	IL	21E	55
ALMANZA RICKY JEROME	IL	45W	30
ALMANZAR IGNACIO JR	TX	02E	33
ALMARAZ RONALD PAUL	CA	04E	136
ALMASY ROBERT	PA	11W	82
ALMEIDA EDWARD JOSEPH	MA	02E	31
ALMEIDA JOE JR	CA	25W	34
ALMEIDA RICHARD HENRY	MA	19E	20
ALMEIDA RUSSELL VIVEIROS	MA	04E	29
ALMENDARIZ SAMUEL	TX	23E	55
ALMON WILLIAM RUSSELL	ME	50W	33
ALMONEY JOHN STANLEY	PA	19E	20
ALONGI MICHAEL PETER JR	IL	40W	70
ALONZO JULIAN	TX	19E	124
ALONZO LUIS	CA	01W	61
ALONZO MANUEL BUSTOS	TX	29W	50
ALPHIN TALMADGE HORTON JR	VA	47W	36
ALSEVER MICHAEL HADWIN	NY	06W	109
ALSMAN WILLIAM FRANKLIN	IN	42E	47
ALSTED STEPHEN PAUL	IA	05E	98
ALSTON ADELL ARIE	NC	08E	83
ALSTON BENNIE	NC	32E	19
ALSTON BILLY CLYDE	TN	27W	84
ALSTON CHARLES EDWARD	NC	04E	86
ALSTON ERNEST JR	NC	08E	63
ALSTON FRANKLIN JR	NY	08E	96
ALSTON MACK ARTHUR	NC	26E	64
ALSTON RUBEN CLEVELAND	FL	04E	52
ALSTON WILLIE EDWARD	NY	60E	17
ALSUP STEPHEN JOHN	RI	12W	99
ALSUP TERRY DANE	VA	23E	72
ALTAMIRA LUIS ANTONIO	TX	08W	73
ALTERWISHER ARTHUR CARL	NY	10E	127
ALTHOFF RODNEY EUGENE	PA	12E	17
ALTHOUSE EARL IRVIN	PA	42E	12
ALTIERI ALLAN JOSEPH	CA	08E	83
ALTIZER ALBERT HAROLD	WV	17W	49
ALTMAN DAVID BRANTLEY	GA	27E	57
ALTSCHAFFL STEPHEN ALLEN	NE	05W	56
ALTUS ROBERT WAYNE	OR	02W	71
ALURA RUDOLFO RESTA	WA	13W	80
ALVARADO ALFRED FREDERICK	CA	25E	94
ALVARADO LEONARD LOUIS	CA	19W	7
ALVARADO RAMIRO	TX	41E	47
ALVARADO RAUL JR	TX	30W	18
ALVARADO-RIVERA JERONIMO	PR	31E	68
ALVAREZ ALEX JIM	CA	23W	94
ALVAREZ BERNARDO RODRIGUEZ	MI	03W	6
ALVAREZ CHARLES ALLEN	CA	39E	56
ALVAREZ ESTEBAN MORALES	AZ	08E	128
ALVAREZ FRANCISCO	TX	38W	54
ALVAREZ GEORGE CALDERON	CA	24E	102
ALVAREZ GUADALUPE MASIAS	TX	26E	40
ALVAREZ IGNACIO JR	TX	38E	64
ALVAREZ JIMMIE MARRON	CA	37W	20
ALVAREZ JOSE CARMEN	CA	26W	97
ALVAREZ JOSE RICARDO L	AZ	39W	6
ALVAREZ JULIAN MARTINEZ	TX	14E	55
ALVAREZ MICHAEL BYRON	CA	51E	15
ALVAREZ ROBERT	TX	17E	33
ALVAREZ-BUZO ELIAS	PR	03E	54
ALVAREZ-DELGADO LUIS F	NY	13E	73
ALVAREZ-TAPIA JOSE LUIS	PR	42E	26
ALVERAZ CYRIL ANTHONY	CA	41W	71
ALVERSON ROBERT WARREN JR	TX	07W	105
ALVES MOSES LOPES	NJ	17W	65
ALVEY ALFRED ELI JR	KY	30W	72
ALVEY RONALD LOUIS	KY	27E	52
ALVIS DONALD DEAN	IN	38E	42
ALVIS ROY GENE	IL	12E	58
ALVORD RONNIE EUGENE	KS	43E	2
ALWAN HAROLD JOSEPH	IL	15E	103
ALWAY HARRY L	NC	23E	66
ALWINE RAY ERNEST	PA	38E	43
ALY LESLIE MORGAN	MO	18W	99
ALYEA WALTER JOHN	AZ	50W	47
AMADOR DIEGO	IL	34W	47
AMADOR ERNEST BALDONADO	TX	09E	121
AMADOR RAYNALD JIMENZ	OH	04E	63
AMADOR SEVERIANO	TX	62W	4
AMANN MARK THOMAS	MO	19W	7
AMANTEA SAMUEL DONALD	PA	27E	67
AMARAL MATTHEW PERRY III	MA	31E	90
AMATO DENNIS FLOYD	OH	03E	115
AMATO EDWARD MATHEW	NY	16E	127
AMATO MICHAEL JOHN	NY	19E	102
AMATO RICHARD C	CA	04E	63
AMBROGI ALLEN ROBERT	PA	23W	94
AMBROSE EDWARD	AL	19W	105
AMBROSE GREGORY FRANCIS	NY	44E	56
AMBROSE JAMES WILLIAM III	IL	33W	23
AMBROSE LOUIS ALLEN	NJ	06E	27
AMBROSINI JOHN STEVEN	IL	35E	66
AMBROSIO FRANK CARL	NY	26W	81
AMBROSIO JOSEPH GEORGE	OH	42W	25
AMBRUSO RICHARD DICK	CT	37W	9
AMBURGEY ALFRED JUNE	VA	10E	35
AMEIGH JAMES KEITH	IN	21W	5
AMEJKA JOSEPH EDWARD	NJ	39W	42
AMENDOLA JAMES JOSEPH	NJ	20W	68
AMENDOLA WILLET RANKIN	NY	29E	8
AMERINE KENT L	KS	09E	96
AMERSON CARLTON	GA	15E	38
AMES ALEXANDER AUDREY	NY	40W	61
AMES GARY DENNIS	OR	31E	62
AMES JAMES DAVID	MO	60E	13
AMES RONALD EDWARD	MI	17E	69
AMES THOMAS ROBERT	NY	02E	23
AMESBURY HARRY ARLO JR	IL	01W	7
AMESCUA STEVEN EPEFANIO	CA	60E	18
AMEY SAMUEL ALLEN	CA	02W	53
AMHEISER DAVID JAMES	OH	07W	20
AMICK FREDDY L	WV	17E	83
AMICK RICHARD MICHAEL	TN	25W	59
AMICK TIMOTHY DAVID	FL	06W	47
AMISON ROOSEVELT JR	CA	16E	42
AMISONE FUIFUITAUA	HI	14E	7
AMMANN ALBERT FRANK	KS	07W	64
AMMERMAN ROSCOE	WI	02E	102
AMMON GLENDON LEE	IN	10E	126
AMMON WILLIAM RESOR	OH	50E	10
AMMONS WALTER NORRIS	VA	05E	31
AMODIAS OSVALDO	FL	03E	67
AMOROSO FRANCIS BRADFORD	DE	25E	92
AMOS FLOYD LEHMAN	GA	20E	4
AMOS JAMES ALBERT	MS	20W	53
AMOS JOE	PA	28E	99
AMOS THOMAS HUGH	MO	01W	4
AMOS WILLIAM LEE	WV	24E	4
AMOS WILLIE FRANK	GA	18E	46
AMOSS RUSSELL MONROE	MD	35E	85
AMRHEIN HERBERT FRANKLIN	MO	20W	13
AMSPACHER ROBERT ALAN	OK	36W	75
AMSPACHER WILLIAM H JR	CA	01E	130
AMSTUTZ WILLIAM JOSEPH JR	MO	05E	19
AMUNDSON DALE HARLAN	ND	40W	56
ANABLE HAROLD JAMES	NY	18E	47
ANANIAN JOHN MOSES	CA	17W	20
ANASIEWICZ RICHARD JOSEPH	NJ	09E	31
ANASTASIO VINCENT JOHN	MD	37W	20
ANAYA GEORGE MICHAEL	NM	12W	59
ANDERS CHARLIE	WV	03E	67
ANDERS EDWARD JAMES	CA	02E	13
ANDERS HERMAN E JR	NY	16E	127
ANDERS JOEL GARY	MN	46E	27
ANDERS JOHN ROYLE	MI	10W	111
ANDERS JOHN WILLIAM	MO	04W	98
ANDERS RICHARD ALAN	OH	49E	50
ANDERS ROBERT LEROY	MN	33W	36
ANDERSEN ANDREW CARL	NY	57E	13
ANDERSEN BARRY FRANK	MI	03E	106
ANDERSEN BUEL EDWARD	NE	26W	17
ANDERSEN CURTIS LEE	SD	44W	44
ANDERSEN MARTIN WEIGNER	CT	25E	15
ANDERSEN MICHAEL NILE	CA	43W	59
ANDERSEN REESE MARK	ID	26W	6
ANDERSEN WILLIAM T JR	CA	54W	25
ANDERSON ALFRED EARL	KS	29E	35
ANDERSON ALTO JR	FL	58W	31
ANDERSON ARCHIE	SC	41E	58
ANDERSON ARTHUR JAMES	FL	32W	87
ANDERSON ARTIS WESLEY	GA	07E	66
ANDERSON BILLY RAY	NC	05W	44
ANDERSON BOYD WELLINGTON	NY	11E	96
ANDERSON BRUCE CARLYLE	MN	20W	4
ANDERSON CARL EDGAR	MA	02E	114
ANDERSON CHARLES C JR	WA	17E	16
ANDERSON CHARLES E	OH	39E	57
ANDERSON CHARLES E JR	WV	15E	56
ANDERSON CHARLES EUGENE	WA	05E	112
ANDERSON CHARLES LEON	WA	20E	24
ANDERSON CHARLES RICHARD	DE	04W	18
ANDERSON CHARLES T JR	WA	12E	58
ANDERSON CLINTON H JR	CA	22E	122
ANDERSON CLINTON RUSSELL	CA	05E	59
ANDERSON CURTIS STEWART	ME	34W	19
ANDERSON DALE ARTHUR	OR	09W	3
ANDERSON DALE EDWARD	WI	40E	50
ANDERSON DANIEL LEONE	SD	46W	11
ANDERSON DARRELL EUGENE	MN	28W	23
ANDERSON DAVID ANTHONY	MT	39W	6
ANDERSON DAVID BRUCE	IA	47E	7
ANDERSON DAVID BRUCE	MN	27W	14
ANDERSON DAVID GEORGE	MT	43E	24
ANDERSON DAVID MICHAEL	FL	37E	77
ANDERSON DAVID PAUL	NY	49E	28
ANDERSON DELMER	KY	34E	40
ANDERSON DENIS LEON	KS	34E	27
ANDERSON DENNIS KEITH	MN	60E	18
ANDERSON DENNIS WILLIAM	NE	13E	31
ANDERSON DONALD LEROY JR	CA	10E	111
ANDERSON DONNIE WRAY	NC	03W	86
ANDERSON DOUGLAS RAY	NY	09W	114
ANDERSON DOYLE TRAVIS	WA	54W	14
ANDERSON EARL ERNEST	OH	22W	115
ANDERSON EDWARD	MA	60E	7
ANDERSON EDWARD EUGENE	LA	11E	80
ANDERSON EDWIN P	CA	27W	36
ANDERSON ELTON GENE	WY	39W	15
ANDERSON ERIC ARNOLD	NY	58W	1
ANDERSON ERLING ALTON	WI	22E	35
ANDERSON EVERETT LEE	CT	01E	88
ANDERSON EVERETT ROBERT	CO	03E	14
ANDERSON FRANCIS ALAN	IL	46E	61
ANDERSON FRANKLIN EMMETT	GA	45W	18
ANDERSON FRANKLIN VANCE	OR	61E	22
ANDERSON GARY	GA	06W	89
ANDERSON GARY JOHN	AZ	10W	63
ANDERSON GEORGE DONALD	OH	35E	28
ANDERSON GEORGE JOHN	PA	54W	34
ANDERSON GEORGE ROGERS	MO	48W	21
ANDERSON GEORGE ROLAN	MT	41W	20
ANDERSON GERALD ROBERT	WI	37E	17
ANDERSON GORDON GUY	MN	09W	67
ANDERSON GREGORY LEE	IL	14W	73
ANDERSON HARRY WILLIAM JR	MA	41W	28
ANDERSON HENRY JR	NY	28E	78
ANDERSON HERBERT R	MN	34E	57
ANDERSON HOWARD D	FL	32E	67
ANDERSON IVY THOMAS	FL	17E	48
ANDERSON JACK HERBERT	MT	18E	17
ANDERSON JACK WILLIAM JR	WI	25E	90
ANDERSON JAMES	PA	19E	21
ANDERSON JAMES ALBERT	PA	40E	35
ANDERSON JAMES BARTON	ID	35E	29
ANDERSON JAMES BOYD	CA	57E	13
ANDERSON JAMES DWIGHT	KY	19W	43
ANDERSON JAMES EDWARD	CA	29E	13
ANDERSON JAMES GERALD	PA	11W	94
ANDERSON JAMES HOWARD	CA	45W	47
ANDERSON JAMES JR	CA	15E	112

NAME	STATE	PANEL NO.	LINE NO.
ANDERSON JAMES K	UT	08W	84
ANDERSON JAMES RICHMOND	KS	38E	43
ANDERSON JAMES THEODORE	OH	29W	27
ANDERSON JOHN AUSTIN	NY	59E	16
ANDERSON JOHN ERNEST	GA	20W	27
ANDERSON JOHN H JR	PA	70W	1
ANDERSON JOHN KEITH	MI	20W	120
ANDERSON JOHN LOUIS	NE	23E	97
ANDERSON JOHN PERRY	MI	22E	94
ANDERSON JOHN STEVEN	IA	16W	26
ANDERSON JOHNNIE LEE	MN	27W	53
ANDERSON JOHNNY MAC	TX	39W	42
ANDERSON JULIAN RAYE	NC	26W	17
ANDERSON JUSTIN KENNETH	IL	36W	60
ANDERSON KENNETH RAY	OK	23E	24
ANDERSON KENNETH TERRY	CA	22W	115
ANDERSON KENT STUART	CA	18W	18
ANDERSON LANNIE RAY	KS	14W	124
ANDERSON LARRY	NY	39E	16
ANDERSON LARRY EDWARD	WA	51E	46
ANDERSON LARRY JAMES	GA	05W	15
ANDERSON LARRY MICHAEL	IA	28E	18
ANDERSON LARRY WAYNE	MD	09W	81
ANDERSON LEE DAVID	NE	05E	69
ANDERSON LEE E	AZ	02E	90
ANDERSON LEON JR	MS	37E	1
ANDERSON LEWIS CARL	IL	14E	66
ANDERSON LUCIUS JR	FL	44E	44
ANDERSON LYNN DENNIS	WA	30W	18
ANDERSON MARCUS PETER	NJ	49W	18
ANDERSON MARK ANTHONY	MN	20E	93
ANDERSON MARK STEVEN	IL	25W	24
ANDERSON MARLYN RONALD	MN	38E	74
ANDERSON MELVIN WALLACE	MN	12E	131
ANDERSON MEREDITH GLENN	IL	11W	62
ANDERSON MICHAEL FRANCIS	IL	67E	4
ANDERSON MICHAEL PATRICK	NY	38E	69
ANDERSON MILLARD RAY	OH	24W	92
ANDERSON MITCHELL LESTER	MT	02E	40
ANDERSON NORMAN RALPH	OH	33E	11
ANDERSON OLIVER	GA	54E	22
ANDERSON PETER NEWELL	NY	31E	8
ANDERSON PHILLIP RUSSELL	FL	39W	77
ANDERSON RAL JEFRO JR	IN	30W	51
ANDERSON RALPH TOMMY	FL	53E	44
ANDERSON RANDALL BRUCE	IL	34E	73
ANDERSON RICHARD ALLEN	TX	19W	110
ANDERSON RICHARD ANDREW	NY	21E	116
ANDERSON RICHARD GUNNAR	IL	50E	3
ANDERSON RICHARD LEE	WI	26W	42
ANDERSON RICHARD MERIDITH	MI	38E	64
ANDERSON RICHARD WILBUR	WA	28W	7
ANDERSON ROBERT CARL	DE	37E	3
ANDERSON ROBERT DALE	MI	01W	80
ANDERSON ROBERT DOUGLAS	CA	27E	26
ANDERSON ROBERT EUGENE	CA	52E	45
ANDERSON ROBERT GARY	MN	20E	71
ANDERSON ROBERT JAMES	FL	63W	2
ANDERSON ROBERT KEITH	AZ	37W	22
ANDERSON ROBERT LEE	NY	24W	81
ANDERSON ROBERT RALPH	UT	16E	88
ANDERSON ROBERT WILLIAM	IL	27E	67
ANDERSON ROGER CHARLES	IL	47W	59
ANDERSON ROGER WILBUR JR	MN	06W	100
ANDERSON RONALD CARLIS	GA	54E	30
ANDERSON RONALD DAVID	NY	17E	116
ANDERSON RONALD STANLEY	OR	02W	118
ANDERSON RONNIE COLEMAN	KY	12E	116
ANDERSON ROY JR	AL	06W	111
ANDERSON ROY L	OK	38E	43
ANDERSON STEPHEN ARTHUR	IL	11E	12
ANDERSON STEVE	NJ	21W	91
ANDERSON STEVEN RAY	OH	17E	30
ANDERSON STEVEN RICHARD	NY	40E	20
ANDERSON TERRANCE WESLEY	CA	13W	98
ANDERSON THOMAS EDWARD	AK	01E	12
ANDERSON THOMAS LESLIE	WI	15W	77
ANDERSON VERNON RAY JR	TX	06W	135
ANDERSON VICTOR EDWARD	ID	04E	122
ANDERSON VINCENT CRAIG	CA	01W	75
ANDERSON VON STEVEN	LA	14W	92
ANDERSON WALTER EVAN JR	KY	44E	4
ANDERSON WALTER GILMORE	OR	40E	50
ANDERSON WALTER H	SC	06E	116
ANDERSON WARREN CHARLES	NE	08W	113
ANDERSON WARREN LEROY	MI	06E	135
ANDERSON WARREN LESTER	CA	04E	68
ANDERSON WAYNE MARSHALL	WA	15W	23
ANDERSON WAYNE RICHARD	IA	09W	87
ANDERSON WENDELL WARREN	DC	46W	26
ANDERSON WILLIAM ALLISON	AL	16W	36
ANDERSON WILLIAM EDGAR JR	PA	27E	83
ANDERSON WILLIAM EDWARD	ID	09E	92
ANDERSON WILLIAM EDWARD	OH	38E	43
ANDERSON WILLIAM JOHN JR	OH	19W	105
ANDERSON WILLIAM JOSEPH	WI	37E	32
ANDERSON WILLIAM JR	CO	50E	13
ANDERSON WILLIAM JR	WI	07W	7
ANDERSON WILLIAM LEE	PA	24W	114
ANDERSON WILLIAM MARK	FL	33E	63
ANDERSON WILLIAM OLIN	CA	21W	79
ANDERSON WILLIAM THEODORE	NC	46W	11
ANDERTON SAMUEL LEE	PA	40E	57
ANDINO NELSON	NY	19W	28
ANDLER MARION BRYAN	NM	09W	36
ANDO CURTIS TADASHI	WY	13E	112
ANDRADA WILFREDO BALAGOT	HI	18W	118
ANDRADE EDWARD JAMES	MA	25E	80
ANDRADE ELISEO A JR	PR	27E	4
ANDRADE JOHN DUTRA	RI	11E	34
ANDRADE KENNETH SOARES	HI	41E	47
ANDRADE RICHARD	AZ	33W	46
ANDRADE ROBERT D	HI	20W	9
ANDRADE ROBERT SOARES	HI	05E	21
ANDRE CARL VAL	IL	42E	27
ANDRE DOUGLAS VERNON	PA	03E	125
ANDRE HOWARD VINCIENT JR	TN	21W	80
ANDREASEN ROBERT WAYNE	NJ	03E	117
ANDREASSI CIRO JOHN	WA	23E	66
ANDREOTTA GLENN URBAN	MO	48E	50
ANDREOZZI VICTOR PATRICK	RI	26E	98
ANDRES KEITH JOHN	IL	29E	9
ANDRESEN HAAKON WILLY	UT	20E	71
ANDRESEN SCOTT FREDERICK	MA	25W	93
ANDRESEN TERRY LEE	MO	16W	72
ANDREW DENNIS RICHARD	PA	06E	28
ANDREW JOSEPH CARLISLE	KY	39E	79
ANDREWS ALAN WAYNE	NY	17E	16
ANDREWS ARTHUR LEE	FL	31W	48
ANDREWS CHRISTOPHER	FL	31E	29
ANDREWS CLIFTON BISHOP	AL	09E	72
ANDREWS COLEY L	AL	13E	60
ANDREWS DALE CHARLES	MI	56E	34
ANDREWS DAVID LYNN	OH	46W	56
ANDREWS DENNIS DEE	PA	52W	26
ANDREWS FRED EUGENE	AR	33E	34
ANDREWS GEORGE ROBERT	DC	17W	80
ANDREWS HORACE	GA	11W	99
ANDREWS HOWARD RIVERS JR	AL	11W	16
ANDREWS JAMES EDWARD	NY	54W	40
ANDREWS JERRY LYNN	TN	58E	18
ANDREWS JOHN MICHEAL	OH	19E	4
ANDREWS LAWRENCE THEODORE	MA	28W	103
ANDREWS MICHAEL ALLEN	OH	40E	35
ANDREWS MICHAEL WAYNE	NC	37W	44
ANDREWS OTIS ELIZA	IL	06W	115
ANDREWS ROBERT LEE JR	AZ	64E	12
ANDREWS ROBERT P	IL	10E	62
ANDREWS ROBERT WARREN JR	NV	24W	29
ANDREWS RONALD L	CA	27E	68
ANDREWS STUART MERRILL	CT	05E	98
ANDREWS VAUN	CA	27E	62
ANDREWS WALTER EUGENE JR	NY	12W	41
ANDREWS WILBERT ISOM	RI	07E	29
ANDREWS WILLIAM ALBERT	MD	44E	13
ANDREWS WILLIAM LARRY	TX	15E	38
ANDREWS WILLIAM LARRY	MS	12W	45
ANDREWS WILLIAM RICHARD	OR	11E	48
ANDREWS WILLIS NORWOOD	OH	04W	130
ANDREYKA THEODORE E JR	AZ	25E	94
ANDRISANO FRANK JR	NJ	30E	21
ANDRUS CARL JOSEPH	MI	33W	18
ANDRUS DANIEL FRANCIS	UT	58W	21
ANDRUS FLOYD EDWARD III	NY	12W	3
ANDRUS WILLIAM EDWARD	WI	26E	77
ANDRY HILAIRE ALBERT JR	LA	35E	14
ANDRYSIAK FRANCIS HOWARD	NY	34E	13
ANDUHA HOWARD J	HI	09E	3
ANDUJAR CHARLES MANUEL	NJ	22W	40
ANELI JOHN ROBERT	PA	24E	85
ANELLA JAMES DAVID	CA	13W	83
ANELLO BRUCE FRANCIS	PA	62W	4
ANGE CARMELLO JR	OH	52E	2
ANGE RONALD EDWARD	VA	07E	92
ANGEL MICHAEL EUGENE	CA	30W	18
ANGEL TOMMIE RAY	MI	10W	93
ANGELIDES JAMES JOSEPH	NY	10E	99
ANGELL ALAN FRANCIS	MA	51W	16
ANGELL MARSHALL JOSEPH	VA	01E	37
ANGELL VAUGHN MARVIN	UT	34E	73
ANGELLEY GERALD DWAIN	CA	26W	6
ANGERMAN DONALD EDWARD	MI	52E	27
ANGERMILLER JAMES ALLEN	TX	14E	125
ANGERSTEIN MICHAEL EDWARD	TX	28E	78
ANGERT PAUL EDWARD	PA	11W	65
ANGLE PETER JASON	VA	54W	26
ANGLIM ADRIAN JAMES	MI	10E	35
ANGLIM PATRICK EMMETT	CA	32E	84
ANGLIN GEORGE LARRY	NC	42W	44
ANGLIN ROBERT LEE	WV	28W	56
ANGRISANI CHARLES JOSEPH	NY	40W	17
ANGSTADT RALPH HAROLD	PA	11E	85
ANGUIANO RUBEN	TX	32W	24
ANGUIANO TONY	TX	03W	112
ANGUS CLARENCE RAY	VA	24E	112
ANGUS WILLIE JAMES	TN	36E	64
ANKNEY SAMUEL FREDERICK	MI	42W	8
ANKROM EVERETT LEE	WV	12W	91
ANKRUM GLENN EUGENE	IN	35E	85
ANNABLE JEFFREY DALE	FL	30E	95
ANNIS CHARLES DOUGALS	CA	12W	110
ANNIS ROBIN RICHARD	CA	27W	8
ANNOS GEORGE RICHARD	CA	20E	5
ANSELL JOHN ARTHUR JR	MD	53E	44
ANSELMO WILLIAM FRANK	CO	30W	62
ANSLOW WALTER HAROLD	FL	45E	53
ANSPACH ROBERT ALLEN	MO	31E	79
ANTE JAMES LOUIS	KY	25E	91
ANTEAU KARL THOMAS	OH	08W	64
ANTER ALBERT GABRIEL	RI	17E	69
ANTHONY ASHER AUBREY	NC	23E	49
ANTHONY BENJAMIN JONES	LA	06W	81
ANTHONY BOBBY DEAN	NC	33W	23
ANTHONY CAREY C	AR	35E	85
ANTHONY CARL THOMAS	LA	16E	127
ANTHONY CHARLIE C	FL	25W	59
ANTHONY DAVID MARSHALL	GA	15E	112
ANTHONY GERALD DOUGLAS	TN	26W	96
ANTHONY JOHN EDWARD	CA	08W	123
ANTHONY JOSEPH ROY	LA	05W	94
ANTHONY LIONEL S	CA	16E	15
ANTHONY PAUL WAYNE	NC	12W	105
ANTHONY RAYMOND F JR	NE	02W	114
ANTHONY WARD LEROY	OH	50E	25
ANTILL MICHAEL EVAN	IA	32E	84
ANTLE MICHAEL LOUIS	OK	11W	108
ANTOGNINI JOSEPH III	CA	36W	83
ANTOINE DENNIS LLOYD	WI	23E	97
ANTOL DAVID	MI	32E	29
ANTOLINI JAMES VINCENT	WV	57E	18
ANTON TERRY LYNN	SC	17E	119
ANTONACE JOHN JR	PA	53W	31
ANTONE FRANK GEORGE	CA	32E	49
ANTONELLI JOSEPH PAUL	PA	14W	32
ANTONELLY CHARLES JOSEPH	PA	03E	23
ANTONIO CATALINO B JR	HI	01W	67
ANTONIO JOHNNIE JR	NM	32E	67
ANTONITIS GEORGE FRANKLIN	NC	31E	28
ANTONOVICH RICHARD ROBERT	MN	56W	21
ANTRIM TOMMY EDWARD	IA	38E	20
ANTU JUAN	TX	58W	5
ANTUNANO GREGORY ALFRED	CA	03W	114
ANTWINE RONALD MICHAEL	NY	10W	30
ANZALDUA ALBERTO TORRES	TX	20W	121
ANZALDUA OSCAR	TX	25E	60
ANZELONE PAUL ROBERT	MD	38E	43

NAME	STATE	PANEL NO.	LINE NO.
APELLIDO RAYMOND HUGH	CA	07W	75
APEROCHO REGALADO M D		13W	80
APLAND RICHARD BRUCE	MN	34W	35
APODACA JACK MICHAEL	CA	19W	36
APODACA PETER MICHAEL	CA	21E	20
APODACA VICTOR JOE JR	CO	21E	75
APOLINAR FORTINO JAMES	AZ	33E	25
APONTE EDWIN	NJ	18E	117
APPELHANS RICHARD DUANE	MT	28E	15
APPERSON GERALD FRANKLIN	SD	35W	53
APPLE GLENN WILSON	OH	11E	65
APPLEBURY MELVIN LYNN	OR	30W	18
APPLEBY IVAN DALE	CA	27E	63
APPLEBY RICKEY EUGENE	CA	43E	64
APPLEGATE DONALD LEE	OH	32E	68
APPLEGATE JOSEPH CHARLES	IN	36E	65
APPLEGATE KENNETH CHARLES	CA	18E	117
APPLEGATE NEWELL F SR	KS	04W	114
APPLEGATE PAUL ORBEN	AZ	04W	134
APPLEGATE ROSS	NJ	46E	27
APPLETON DANNY ELBERT	CA	17W	99
APPLETON JOHN BURDETTE	KY	18E	117
APPOLONIA JOHN JOSEPH	RI	62W	4
APRILLIANO ANJELO JOSEPH	NY	52E	13
APUTEN LESLIE GEORGE	MI	60E	18
AQUINO RAYMOND JOHN	IL	14W	45
ARAGON ALONSO JR	CA	56E	19
ARAGON HENRY T	HI	25E	32
ARAGON JOSE RUBEN	CO	01E	115
ARAGON JOSEPH MANUEL	AZ	18E	44
ARAGON RUEBEN THOMAS	CO	02W	20
ARAKAKI WAYNE ALLEN	HI	01E	56
ARAMBULA PAUL TEJEDA	CA	44E	28
ARANDA EUGENE LEONARD	OK	02E	93
ARANDA ISMAEL BENITO	CO	18W	13
ARANDA JUAN FRANCISCO	TX	06W	28
ARANDA-SANTOS EDUARDO	PR	47E	19
ARANN RICHARD MAXWELL	VA	21W	5
ARAUJO ABELARDO	NM	17E	114
ARAUJO ROBERT JOSEPH	NY	27E	106
ARAUJO RUDOLPH ERNEST	MA	15W	76
ARB FRANCIS LOREN	KS	21E	25
ARBEIT MARTIN IRVING	NC	06W	80
ARBOGAST CARL FRANCIS JR	MI	25W	93
ARBOGAST RANDALL	WV	21E	20
ARBUTHNOT JAMES MALCOLM	KS	06E	61
ARCAND DONALD LEONARD	MA	02E	70
ARCENEAUX HERBERT JOHN JR	LA	15E	56
ARCHBOLD JOHN CHRISTOPHER	NH	23W	94
ARCHER ALLEN H	VT	17E	16
ARCHER DAN WILLIE JR	TN	23E	73
ARCHER DANNY LEE	WA	09W	121
ARCHER JESSE HAROLD	TN	30W	98
ARCHER RICHARD CHARLES	MA	27E	8
ARCHER SANFORD KIM	MT	37E	77
ARCHIBALD DENNIS	IL	60W	24
ARCHIBALD GARY MICHAEL	IN	50E	25
ARCHULETA JESUS MAGIN	UT	14E	47
ARCHULETA JOSEPH	NM	27E	8
ARCHULETA RODOLFO JOSE	UT	37W	54
ARCHULETTA RAY ADAM	CO	26E	21
ARD BOBBY JOE	MS	18E	118
ARD HENRY	AL	11E	132
ARD HOWARD CARLTON	FL	19W	58
ARD RANDOLPH JEFFERSON	FL	04W	30
ARDENEAUX GARY JAMES	LA	24E	13
ARDIS JOHN COLEMAN	SC	11E	100
ARDOIN ROBERT GLEN	LA	20W	84
ARELLANO ANTHONY WILLIAM	NM	51W	16
ARELLANO LE ROY FRED	CA	55W	17
ARENAS MANUEL V JR	TX	52W	3
ARENAS REYNALDO	MI	35W	10
ARENS DAVID LE ROY	WA	21E	111
ARENS FREDERICK V JR	MA	67E	4
ARENS TIMOTHY GEORGE	WI	42W	52
ARENT KENNETH JACOB	CA	29E	8
AREY WILLIAM NOVAK	PA	61E	22
ARGENTA ALLEN CHARLES	CT	21W	97
ARGENTI ROBERT LEE	RI	08W	33
ARGENZIO NESTOR LORENZO	NY	02E	119
ARGY EDWARD WILLIAM	MA	34E	13
ARIAS LUCIANO	CO	28W	32
ARIAS RICHARD	CA	33W	5
ARIAS WILLIAM CIP JR	CA	06W	85
ARIAZ EDWARD JOSEPH	IL	44E	65
ARIENS RICKY MICHAEL	IN	02W	43
ARIMENTO JOSEPH A	NY	12E	111
ARIZMENDEZ DANIEL MICHAEL	MI	63W	2
ARKIE VALLANCE GALEN	AZ	25E	91
ARKOETTE PETER ALLAN	MA	24W	36
ARLENTINO DUDNEY NELSON	AZ	31E	58
ARLINE SOLOMAN DAVID JR	GA	15E	73
ARMATO SALVATORE JOSEPH	NY	06W	56
ARMBRUSTER ANTHONY CLARK	TX	35W	59
ARMENDAREZ MIKE	CA	16E	57
ARMENIO ROBERT WILLIAM	NY	20W	53
ARMENTA HERIBERTO	CA	05E	98
ARMENTA RUBEN MAXIMO	CA	17E	69
ARMENTO FRANKLIN CHARLES	NJ	44E	56
ARMENTROUT CHARLES F	MD	10W	78
ARMENTROUT RAYMOND LEE	WV	05W	131
ARMENTROUT STANLEY WILLIA	OH	39W	72
ARMES BOBBY WAYNE	WV	20W	91
ARMES REXIE LEO	TN	12E	72
ARMIJO FRANK CHARLES	NM	19W	43
ARMITAGE ROBERT LAYMON	WA	14E	115
ARMITAGE THOMAS LEON	WI	32W	18
ARMITSTEAD STEVEN RAY	CA	29W	58
ARMLIN LOREN AARON	NY	16E	56
ARMOND ROBERT LAURENCE	CA	02E	13
ARMOR LOYDE DEAN	MO	34E	13
ARMS JAMES WALTER	IL	27E	68
ARMS WILLIE DEWITT	TN	11W	120
ARMSTEAD GREGORY VAN	MD	06E	59
ARMSTEAD JAMES DOUGLAS JR	NY	38W	13
ARMSTEAD LOUIS ELTON	NC	28E	107
ARMSTEAD ROCKY D	TX	17W	39
ARMSTRONG ATWELL ASBELL	GA	37W	84
ARMSTRONG BARRY LEE	IL	14W	92
ARMSTRONG BILLY CARL	OK	51E	16
ARMSTRONG BILLY STANLEY	AR	57W	34
ARMSTRONG BRUCE ELLIS	TN	12W	126
ARMSTRONG CHARLES JOSEPH	MD	16W	114
ARMSTRONG DEAN EDWARD	OK	19E	103
ARMSTRONG DONALD GLENN	CA	12W	78
ARMSTRONG DOUGLAS WAYNE	IN	38W	22
ARMSTRONG EDWIN LAWRENCE	OK	46E	27
ARMSTRONG EUGENE GERALD SR	NC	07E	17
ARMSTRONG EVERETT	TN	14E	126
ARMSTRONG FRANK ALTON III	LA	27E	58
ARMSTRONG HAROLD KINGSLEY	NY	03W	19
ARMSTRONG HERBERT ELBRIDG	ME	02W	27
ARMSTRONG HERMAN ROBERT	IL	10E	25
ARMSTRONG JAMES HAROLD	TN	28W	32
ARMSTRONG JAMES LEONARD	OK	04W	117
ARMSTRONG JOHN HENRY	CA	17E	33
ARMSTRONG JOHN WILLIAM	TX	29E	55
ARMSTRONG JOSEPH LARRY	KY	04W	111
ARMSTRONG KENNETH DANIEL	CA	52W	16
ARMSTRONG LEVI LESTER	OR	20W	121
ARMSTRONG MICHAEL DAVID	OH	43W	59
ARMSTRONG PEDER WALTER	WA	46E	52
ARMSTRONG RAYMOND	OH	49E	38
ARMSTRONG RICHARD TED	NC	08E	41
ARMSTRONG ROBERT DALE	TN	34W	14
ARMSTRONG ROBERT GEORGE	NY	01E	67
ARMSTRONG SHERMAN FELTON	OK	08W	110
ARMSTRONG TERRY LEE	MS	39W	7
ARMSTRONG WALTER LEE	AZ	31E	96
ARMSTRONG WARDELL LESTER	KY	41W	33
ARMSTRONG WILLIAM L	IN	05E	5
ARMSTRONG WILLIAM PRESTON	TX	50W	52
ARMWOOD JESSE JAMES	NY	65W	3
ARNADO FREDRICO	HI	16E	33
ARNALL ROBERT D	CA	05W	12
ARNAUD GARY WAYNE	LA	35W	42
ARNDT CRAIG ALAN	CO	43E	51
ARNDT ROBERT DARRELL	WA	24E	14
ARNESON KEITH SAM	OR	11W	78
ARNESON MARCUS EUGENE	IL	03W	43
ARNETT FRANCIS IENATIUS	NY	39E	16
ARNETT JAMES DOUGLAS	KS	44W	61
ARNETT MAHLON RONNIE	IN	14W	114
ARNETT RAY JR	OH	06W	38
ARNEY RANDALL NAVE	WA	52W	17
ARNIOTIS DIMITRIOS G	NY	28W	56
ARNN JOHN OLIVER	AZ	04E	39
ARNOLD ALLEN RAY	IA	30W	62
ARNOLD DANIEL RAYMOND	FL	25W	93
ARNOLD DAVID BRUCE	IL	29W	3
ARNOLD DAVID L	FL	06E	62
ARNOLD DAVID MORGAN	DE	52W	33
ARNOLD DONALD EDWARD	IL	62W	19
ARNOLD DONALD RAY	NC	28W	56
ARNOLD GARY WAYNE	FL	49E	19
ARNOLD GEORGE DALE	OH	15E	124
ARNOLD HAROLD	AL	10E	75
ARNOLD JAMES	SC	22E	35
ARNOLD JAMES EDWARD	IN	41W	34
ARNOLD JOE EDDY	IL	41W	34
ARNOLD JOHN CRAIG	IL	16E	117
ARNOLD KENNETH HAROLD	OK	16E	33
ARNOLD KENNETH W	IL	57E	14
ARNOLD LARRY FRANKLIN	SC	25E	46
ARNOLD LOUIS BROWARD	FL	28E	95
ARNOLD LOUIS GEORGE WASHI	MI	30E	37
ARNOLD MAJOR JR	IN	05E	96
ARNOLD MOSES ANTHONY	GA	36E	65
ARNOLD ODIS DANIEL	CA	01E	3
ARNOLD PHILLIP FRED	GA	10W	55
ARNOLD REID CARLTON	FL	26E	5
ARNOLD RICHARD EARL	KS	04E	105
ARNOLD RICHARD W	ME	06E	2
ARNOLD ROBERT	FL	48W	36
ARNOLD ROBERT DWAIN	WI	06E	120
ARNOLD ROBERT JOSEPH	OH	18W	88
ARNOLD ROBERT MILTON JR	TX	48W	21
ARNOLD ROBERT WILLIAM	MI	24W	73
ARNOLD ROBIN LEE	IL	09E	65
ARNOLD RODNEY KEITH	OR	11W	48
ARNOLD ROY LEE	AZ	26W	105
ARNOLD STEVEN ERNEST	MO	17W	39
ARNOLD WILLARD DAVID	GA	15E	16
ARNOLD WILLIAM HENRY	TX	27E	68
ARNOLD WILLIAM TAMM	WI	12E	84
ARNOTT DAVID BRUCE	NY	29W	75
ARNOVITZ RICHARD MICHAEL	PA	18W	10
ARNTZ WILLARD LEE	NJ	41W	71
ARNWINE EDWARD RAY	TX	47W	59
ARONCE JOSEPH CHARLES	TX	41W	9
ARONHALT CHARLES E JR	MD	20E	20
ARONHALT LARRY DUANE	FL	13W	77
ARQUERO ELPIDIO ALLEN	HI	19E	77
ARQUILLO JOHN DOMINICK	OH	17W	72
ARRAIZ JAMES PAUL	CA	24E	14
ARRANTS MICHAEL LORRELL	TX	14W	82
ARREDONDO JESSIE	TX	27W	47
ARREDONDO JOSE MARIA R	CA	03W	58
ARREDONDO THOMAS ALFRED	CA	18E	55
ARREGUIN JOE	CA	19E	124
ARREY FRANK JR	CA	10E	127
ARRIAGA TONY R	HI	07E	31
ARRIBI DONALD	NJ	23W	95
ARRIES JAMES MICHAEL	WI	17E	83
ARRIGONI RONALD LOUIS	MN	13E	113
ARRINGTON JOHN ROBERT	IN	32E	68
ARRINGTON JOSEPH PHILLIP	AZ	14E	84
ARRINGTON SAMUEL W JR	AL	14E	126
ARROWOOD JAMES OSCAR	MD	44W	44
ARROYO JOSE FRANCISCO	TX	22W	95
ARROYO RAMON JAIME	NY	30W	62
ARROYO-BAEZ GERASIMO	PR	28W	25
ARROYO-BRENES GILBERT D	FL	26W	42
ARROYO-SIERRA FELIX JR	PR	24W	27
ARRUDA RICHARD HATHAWAY	MA	44W	34
ARSENAULT RICHARD ROLAND	MA	01W	33
ARSENEAU GALEN LEROY	IL	16E	6
ARTAVIA JOSEPH GREGORY	CA	46E	2
ARTEAGA JOHN J	WI	07W	51
ARTHINGTON MARVIN S	TX	06W	85
ARTHUR ALLEN LEE	IL	28E	78
ARTHUR GREGORY KENNETH	OK	45E	17
ARTHUR JAMES RAYMOND	OH	13E	129
ARTHUR JESSE JAMES III	GA	18W	57
ARTHUR JOHNNY	NM	03W	71
ARTHUR LAWRENCE KENNETH	NY	64W	4

NAME	STATE	PANEL NO.	LINE NO.
ARTHUR RICHARD THORNTON	WV	43E	64
ARTHUR WILLIAM PRESCOTT	GA	09W	67
ARTIS HERBERT J	NC	03W	90
ARTIS VERNON DARYLE	DC	21W	80
ARTKOP ARTHUR JAMES	CT	24W	28
ARTMAN GARY RAY	OK	05E	44
ARTMAN JAMES BOYD	IL	36W	85
ARTMAN TIMOTHY HAROLD	FL	33E	78
ARVESETH BRENT LARSEN	UT	20W	17
ARVIDSON JAMES WARREN	MN	50W	47
ARVIDSON KENNETH ARVID	MN	05E	3
ARVIN CARL ROBERT	MI	27E	68
ARVISO HERBERT	NM	17W	119
ARVIZU XAVIER AMADO	CA	31W	31
ARWOOD LARRY RANDALL	TN	29E	55
ARZUAGA JOAQUIN	NY	19E	42
ASADA RONALD KAZUO	CA	35W	63
ASANOMA FRANCISCO M	GM	06W	30
ASBECK GREGORY JOSEPH	OH	12W	3
ASBRIDGE LARRY GENE	IL	24E	102
ASBURY BENTON FRANCIS	IN	10W	123
ASBURY DAVID CHARLES	MO	21W	11
ASBURY DONNIE DEWAYNE	MI	08W	102
ASCHENBRENER ERVIN G JR	CA	30E	22
ASCHENBRENNER DENNIS DALE	SD	22E	94
ASCHER JAMES ALLAN	IL	35W	52
ASEP MICHAEL	NY	07W	45
ASH EDWARD GARLAND JR	VA	51W	23
ASH FREDERIC NATHANIEL	FL	30W	41
ASH JOHN SILVY	AL	15W	15
ASH PAUL ENGLISH JR	KY	13W	25
ASH PAUL MICHAEL	IN	39E	61
ASH ROBERT EVERETT	KY	52W	3
ASH RONALD KEITH	OH	02E	111
ASH RONNIE EDWARDS	PA	12W	34
ASHALL ALAN FREDERICK	MT	46W	56
ASHBROOK DELMER VIRGIL	KY	29W	65
ASHBURN JERRY ALLEN	WI	22W	62
ASHBURN RONALD WAYNE	TN	22W	11
ASHBY CLAYBORN WILLIS JR	KY	39E	69
ASHBY DONALD ROBERTS SR	VA	14E	52
ASHBY JAMES WESLEY	MN	21E	25
ASHBY JEDD EDWARD	OK	46W	46
ASHCRAFT HARRY DANIEL	KY	24W	63
ASHE RONALD A	CT	01W	60
ASHECRAFT JAMES ARTHUR	NC	13E	88
ASHENFELTER ALAN WAYNE	IL	08W	104
ASHER ALAN	NY	25W	59
ASHER DENNY LYNN	OH	26W	68
ASHER FRANK LOUIS	OH	08W	37
ASHER HAROLD E	OK	05W	15
ASHER JAMES LOUIS	WI	22W	17
ASHER ROBERT FRANKLIN	TX	42W	52
ASHER SAMUEL EARL	TN	11W	53
ASHER SAMUEL QUENTON	OH	13E	82
ASHERMAN ALDON MACAY JR	PA	07E	114
ASHFORD BILL JR	MO	29W	94
ASHFORD DAVE EDWARD	MI	32E	19
ASHFORD GREGORY MICHAEL	CA	02W	1
ASHFORD HENRY LEWIS	TX	32W	87
ASHFORD HOWARD HERRELL	NJ	42E	47
ASHFORD JAMES ANTHONY	OK	61E	22
ASHLEY CHARLES R JR	GA	04E	86
ASHLEY EUGENE JR	NC	37E	77
ASHLEY FRANKLIN D II	WV	29W	94
ASHLEY UPTON FINLEY	VA	12E	12
ASHLEY WILLIE FRANK	VA	27E	23
ASHLINE PAUL STUART	VT	06E	62
ASHLOCK CARLOS	PA	19E	91
ASHMAN JOHN FREDERICK	PA	04E	35
ASHMORE LAURENCE RAY	TX	43E	20
ASHNAULT RAYMOND JOHN	NJ	19W	65
ASHTON CURTIS MORRIS	TX	15W	96
ASHTON DONALD MILLARD JR	MA	32W	10
ASHTON JAMES ODELL	TX	58W	1
ASHTON NORMAND JOSEPH JR	MA	07E	58
ASIP EDWARD VINCENT	NY	19E	55
ASIRE DONALD HENRY	CA	13E	20
ASKAM ROBERT EUGENE	OH	22W	62
ASKEW THOMAS EARL	AL	16W	129
ASKIN JAMES FREDERICK	FL	09E	44
ASLETT ALLAN THEO	ID	17W	12

NAME	STATE	PANEL NO.	LINE NO.
ASMUSSEN GLENN EDWARD	DC	05E	5
ASMUTH ROBERT LABUDDE JR	NJ	08W	54
ASP FRANK WALTER	MN	35E	58
ASPER IVAN RICHARD JR	IN	05W	104
ASPEY DARRELL WAYNE	MO	13W	60
ASPINALL WILLIAM ALBERT	NY	26E	64
ASPLUND MARCUS RAY	AZ	48W	5
ASQUITH WILLIAM ROBERT	MO	06W	70
ASSELIN LEO ROGER	ME	22W	30
ASSELTA CHARLES CARL	NJ	45E	17
AST STEVEN VINCENT	KS	04W	16
ASTLEY JOHN MICHAEL	IA	21E	57
ASTON BLAKE EDWARD	TX	07W	97
ASTON JAMES MICHAEL	TX	29W	75
ASTON JAY STEVEN	OH	03W	109
ASTON LYLE GLENN	WV	28W	88
ASUNCION HENRY FRANCE	CA	38W	70
ATCHER HAROLD ALLEN	KY	02E	14
ATCHISON JAMES MITCHELL	MD	12W	127
ATCHLEY KEITH NOEL	WA	49E	19
ATEN WARNELL EUGENE	IL	32W	57
ATER ROBERT ALLAN	OH	08W	117
ATHANASIOU RONALD S	TX	14W	50
ATHERDEN LESTER ROBERT	CT	05E	100
ATHERTON FRANK WILLIAM	PA	49E	38
ATHEY BURDER SMITH III	GA	09W	75
ATKINS DAVID BRUCE	NJ	18W	22
ATKINS DON LARRY	GA	25W	59
ATKINS DOUGLAS PAUL	MI	08W	58
ATKINS DOYLE	CA	34W	13
ATKINS JAMES	KS	17W	39
ATKINS JOHN	NJ	20E	53
ATKINS JOSHUA ABRAHAM III	DC	18E	89
ATKINS MATTHEW DAVID III	MI	16E	130
ATKINSON FRANKLIN G JR	NJ	26W	96
ATKINSON FREDERICK GEORGE	MA	09E	8
ATKINSON GERALD THOMAS	IA	13W	115
ATKINSON GLEN LAWRENCE	ID	33W	46
ATKINSON HOWARD	PA	32W	88
ATKINSON JERRY DOYLE	CA	47E	8
ATKINSON JOHN F JR	NY	29E	26
ATKINSON ROBERT LOUIS JR	MI	28W	42
ATKINSON ROGER CARL	WI	41E	35
ATKINSON ROGER DALE	VA	27E	105
ATKISON CHARLES LEON	MO	18W	119
ATKUCUNAS EDWARD	PA	25W	40
ATOLE FLOYD SAMUEL	NM	32W	69
ATON PAUL DOUGLAS	KY	50W	29
ATOR JOHNNIE WAYNE	IL	33W	91
ATOR RICHARD DENNIS	WA	13W	84
ATTARIAN ALAN	NJ	18W	92
ATTERBERRY EDWIN LEE	TX	24E	102
ATTERIDGE LEON JOSEPH JR	RI	44E	33
ATUATASI SA JR	CA	27W	61
ATWELL DONALD WILLIAM JR	FL	15W	97
ATWELL ROBERT WAGNER	NY	45E	45
ATWELL WILLIAM ALBERT	AZ	50W	17
ATWOOD CHARLES AARON JR	FL	37W	73
ATWOOD DAWSON JESSE	IN	42W	22
ATWOOD DOUGLAS EDWARD	UT	27E	79
ATWOOD RICHARD	OH	49E	19
AU HOY EARL CHUI MUN	HI	32W	75
AU KEITH WARREN	OH	11W	63
AUBAIN JOSEPH AUGUSTINA	PR	02W	74
AUBAIN ROY ANTONIO	VI	35W	32
AUBERT THOMAS CLIFFORD	CA	27E	83
AUCOIN ROBERT JOSEPH	MA	50W	17
AUD FRANCIS MATTHEW	MD	14W	68
AUDILET FRANKLIN DELANO	TX	47E	29
AUE OTTO WAYNE	FL	41W	63
AUEN DAVID OLIVER	PA	59W	18
AUER EDUARD ADOLPH	OH	26E	91
AUFIERE ARMAND JAMES	PA	14E	84
AUGE DAVID CHARLES	MN	35E	19
AUGUST FRANK JOHN	LA	10E	20
AUGUSTINAS WALTER PETER	NY	04E	127
AUGUSTINE FRANK FRANCIS	RI	17W	14
AUGUSTUS DAVID RYAN	MD	33W	52
AUKLAND LEO CURTIS	SD	26E	41
AULD ROGER MARTIN JR	CA	26W	29
AULETTI PETER PAUL	NY	08W	24

NAME	STATE	PANEL NO.	LINE NO.
AULL EARL DUBOIS	LA	03E	68
AULT DANIEL LEE	PA	49W	38
AULTMAN GREGORY WAYNE	IL	06W	33
AUMAN ERVIN LEWIS	NE	57W	22
AUMILLER AARON BUCKLEY	PA	07E	22
AURADY MICHAEL VICTOR	OH	51W	47
AUSBERN JOHN RAYMOND	OK	37W	27
AUSBORN DONALD EUGENE	AL	49W	50
AUSBROOKS RICHARD DAVID	KY	27W	55
AUSMUS ROBERT ARTHUR	OH	53W	15
AUSTERMANN RAYMOND A JR	MO	17E	90
AUSTIN ALBERT DELGADO JR	AZ	26W	59
AUSTIN CARL BENJAMIN	OR	03E	119
AUSTIN CHARLES DAVID	CT	18E	89
AUSTIN EDDIE PAUL	CA	18E	55
AUSTIN EDWARD PAUL	MI	12E	5
AUSTIN ELLIS ERNEST	MI	06E	125
AUSTIN GLENN FREDERIC	MI	13W	91
AUSTIN JAMES EARL	IN	05W	114
AUSTIN JAMES FRANKLIN	VA	12W	129
AUSTIN JOSEPH CLAIR	WV	16E	109
AUSTIN LARRY D	CA	54W	22
AUSTIN LARRY DEAN	IA	04W	85
AUSTIN MICHAEL FRANCIS	LA	39E	79
AUSTIN MICHAEL PAUL	MA	05W	73
AUSTIN OSCAR PALMER	AZ	32W	88
AUSTIN PAUL JASPER JR	DC	07W	23
AUSTIN RILEY CLAYTON	TX	56W	11
AUSTIN ROBERT	CA	29E	103
AUSTIN ROLLIN RANDOLPH	NM	65W	3
AUSTIN SCOTTY GENE	MI	18W	108
AUSTIN STEPHEN EDWARD	CA	58W	1
AUSTIN TOM LEW	OH	07E	47
AUSTIN TYRONE WAGNER	MO	54E	1
AUSTIN VICTOR LEROY	MI	35W	1
AUSTIN VIRIL LEE	VA	16E	109
AUSTIN WILLIAM EUGENE	NC	08W	72
AUSTIN WILLIAM KENNETH	WA	02W	8
AUSTIN WILLIAM OLEN	TX	41W	56
AUSTIN WILLIE JR	AL	11W	66
AUSTON KENNETH JOE	CA	13W	115
AUTEN DONALD EUGENE	NC	08W	68
AUTEN FRANK LEROY	NM	52W	26
AUTEN NORMAN DWANE	TX	19W	58
AUTON BOBBIE MAXSEN	NC	20E	88
AUTORINO JOSEPH G JR	NY	16W	86
AUTREY JAMES HAROLD	TX	26W	17
AUVE CHARLES PAUL	FL	15W	46
AUWARTER EARL DEAN	MN	27E	63
AUXIER JERRY EDWARD	WV	50W	29
AVALOS ALBERTO ANGEL	TX	08E	96
AVANT JOE LYNN	MS	04W	45
AVANT SHERMAN	IL	04W	69
AVELLA JOHN JOSEPH	FL	52W	3
AVELLEYRA JOHN WILLIAM	MD	21E	3
AVERA JOHN ADAMS	OK	12W	113
AVERILL CRAIG PHILIP	NC	46E	27
AVERITTE WILLIAM CLAYTON	TX	50E	11
AVERY ALLEN JAMES	IA	05E	31
AVERY ALLEN JONES	MA	02W	130
AVERY DON WAYNE	IL	08W	96
AVERY GERALD LAWRENCE	MI	42E	27
AVERY HARVEY CHARLES	AR	29W	75
AVERY JAMES LINWOOD	DC	30W	62
AVERY JOHN MARK	AL	40W	59
AVERY JOHN PAUL	TN	27E	105
AVERY KENNETH VARSALL	WA	19E	55
AVERY LEWIS EUGENE	OH	17E	101
AVERY MARVIN DOUGLAS	OH	31W	75
AVERY RALPH LEE	MI	29E	27
AVERY ROBERT DOUGLAS	NC	54E	23
AVERY RONNIE G	AL	46W	36
AVERY WILLIAM CALVIN	GA	17W	35
AVEY EVERAL FLOYD	AR	67W	8
AVGERINOS GEORGE RICHARD	IL	30W	51
AVILA JESUS V	CA	35E	29
AVILA JOHN MANUEL	CA	19E	103
AVILA JUAN JR	TX	07W	58
AVILA MANUEL JR	CA	12E	58
AVILA RAFIEL	TX	50W	47
AVILA THOMAS ROBERT	KS	33E	63
AVILES ALFREDO EDWARDO	NY	18W	66

NAME	STATE	PANEL NO.	LINE NO.
AVILES ANIBAL FELIPE JR	NY	05E	113
AVILES PETER	NY	22E	91
AVILES-AVILES JUAN PASCUA	PR	16E	128
AVINGTON LARASETT EARL JR	IL	08E	128
AVOLESE PAUL ANDREW	NY	23E	25
AVORE MALCOLM ARTHUR	ME	02E	39
AWALT JIMMY ARDELL	TX	51W	29
AXFORD JOSEPH WILLIAM	MI	21E	30
AXSOM HOBART JR	WA	29W	34
AXTON EDWIN EVERETTE	CA	22W	17
AYALA EDUARDO	TX	12E	58
AYALA GEORGE HERMAN	MI	17W	125
AYALA GILBERT JR	CA	35E	19
AYALA TONY JOHN	TX	49W	46
AYALA-MERCADO JUAN	PR	30W	41
AYALA-REYES WILFREDO	PR	22W	62
AYD JACQUE JOSEPH	MD	20E	20
AYDLETT JAMES QUINEL	OH	09E	16
AYER HERLEY JR	MO	34E	61
AYERS CARL BRACY JR	IL	18W	5
AYERS CHARLES DAVID	FL	21W	16
AYERS DANNY R	FL	44W	55
AYERS DARRELL EUGENE	WA	12W	19
AYERS DAVID WILLIAM	CA	08W	34
AYERS DENNIS MICHAEL	PA	36W	60
AYERS DOUGLAS EDWARD	CT	04W	72
AYERS EDWARD FRANKLIN	MD	27W	23
AYERS GEORGE BERNARD	PA	51E	44
AYERS HAROLD GENE	TN	08E	96
AYERS JAMES WESTLEY	SC	20E	110
AYERS JAREL WAYNE	MO	13E	103
AYERS JOHNNIE MARVIN	WV	34W	19
AYERS LESLEY STEVEN	AL	38E	20
AYERS RICHARD LEE	IA	11W	12
AYERS WILLIAM HERSCHEL	GA	23W	69
AYLOR CHARLES VINCENT	CA	23E	55
AYLOR GERALD LEON	AR	20E	56
AYLWORTH RANDAL RAY	MI	20E	81
AYRES ALBERT BOYD	NY	15E	81
AYRES CHARLES HASKELL	TN	34W	55
AYRES GERALD FRANCIS	DE	01W	44
AYRES JAMES HENRY	TX	05W	21
AYRES JESSE STEPHEN	TX	57W	34
AYRES WILLIAM FRANCIS	NJ	05E	82
AZARA CHARLES F JR	OH	10E	32
AZBELL JAMES ALLEN	IL	32W	88
AZBILL ROY GORDON	CA	01E	79
AZLIN LUKE JUNIOR	OK	23W	81
AZNOE KENNETH EUGENE	CA	11W	34
AZORE DAVID	TX	55E	38
AZZARITO FRANK ANTHONY JR	CT	37E	3
BAADE CLIFFORD KEITH	NE	06W	111
BAADE ROBERT RICHARD II	CA	18W	81
BAAL CARL THOMAS	PA	03E	39
BABB KENNETH ALVIN	VA	08E	33
BABB RICHARD CLARK JR	IL	15W	113
BABBAGE EWING COTTRELL	KY	04E	102
BABBITT WALTER LEE JR	NJ	21E	3
BABCOCK DENNIS LEE	WI	23W	5
BABCOCK JOHN RICHARDS	CA	36W	38
BABCOCK RONALD LESTER	AZ	04W	8
BABEL DWIGHT FABIAN	WI	18W	36
BABERS HENRY DENNIS	FL	26E	87
BABEY DAVID PAUL	NY	17W	89
BABIARZ EDWARD MARTIN	IL	50W	40
BABICH JOHN MICHAEL	IL	08W	41
BABICH NIKOLA	WI	65W	4
BABICH RONALD GREGORY	MT	21E	31
BABIN CLARENCE JOSEPH JR	LA	31W	42
BABIN JACOB BENEDICT JR	MA	04W	79
BABIN THOMAS DALTON JR	LA	33E	34
BABINSACK JOHN DAVID	PA	55W	17
BABSON MARK ALBERT JR	TN	17W	79
BABULA ROBERT LEO	PA	10E	52
BABULJAK STEPHEN	FL	37W	37
BABYAK ANDREW JOHN JR	OH	48E	56
BABYAK LAWRENCE JOSEPH	CA	15W	2
BACA FRANK MARTIN	CA	13W	61
BACA GABRIEL	NM	27E	57
BACA ISIDRO	NM	25E	22
BACA JOHNNY LAWRENCE JR	NM	37E	17
BACA RICHARD DAVID	CA	22W	84
BACCA RONALD VICTOR	UT	03E	4
BACCUS JIMMY DEVER	CA	09E	83
BACH COLIN JAMES	NJ	40W	17
BACH JOHN JOSEPH III	VA	26W	12
BACH LAWRENCE EDWARD	PA	22E	67
BACH LYMAN CONRAD	WI	23W	41
BACH MICHAEL ROBERT	OH	37W	60
BACHELOR DON RAY	CA	49W	7
BACHER MARK WARREN	CA	10W	60
BACHERT RICHARD CHARLES	MI	36W	55
BACHLEDA BERND	CT	44E	24
BACHMAN ALBERT CARL JR	PA	09W	26
BACHMAN CHARLES W JR	CT	17W	24
BACHMAN PAUL JOHN	OH	37E	47
BACHMAN ROGER JOSEPH	NJ	16W	94
BACHMANN LYNN JR	NY	12E	53
BACHUS JOSEPH RICHARD	OH	12E	38
BACIK VLADIMIR HENRY	TX	25E	48
BACKEBERG BRUCE BURTON	MT	10E	116
BACKEN DENNIS D	CA	05E	34
BACKER WILLIAM PAUL	ND	34E	33
BACKES BRUCE RICHARD	NJ	54E	42
BACKHAUS STEVEN EUGENE	NE	15W	76
BACKLUND JAMES VICTOR	MN	42E	13
BACKMAN ROBERT EUGENE	CA	11W	63
BACKUS KENNETH FRANK	NY	20E	81
BACKY THOMAS ALAN	MO	38E	44
BACO JOHN	NY	07E	41
BACON BARNARD	GA	10W	38
BACON CLIFTON LEROY	VT	07E	29
BACON NILON KAY	TN	66W	1
BACON PAUL DAVID	NJ	01W	35
BACON ROBERT FRANKLIN	NJ	20W	9
BACON WILLIAM IVOR TENNEY	NY	22E	82
BACORN KEITH RAY	OH	35E	43
BACOT DOUGLAS MONROE	SC	46E	2
BACOTE MOSES JUNE	FL	64W	4
BACZALSKI JOSEPH	CT	12E	49
BADAVAS THOMAS EDWARD	NJ	15E	67
BADCOCK ROBERT	MA	52E	27
BADER ARTHUR EDWARD JR	NJ	37W	9
BADER WILLIAM EDWARD	MI	55W	25
BADGER BRUCE LYLE	VT	47E	40
BADGER THOMAS ALBERT	MO	35E	65
BADGETT LEAGRANT	AL	02W	22
BADGLEY DALE ERNEST	OH	61W	19
BADLEY JAMES LINSDAY	OR	46E	43
BADOLATI FRANK NEIL	NH	04E	105
BADON JOHN WAYNE	OH	25E	10
BADOSTAIN TIMOTHY ERNEST	CA	16W	124
BADSING MICHAEL TERRANCE	IL	02E	76
BADWAY VICTOR WOLF JR	KS	13W	40
BAER GLENN CHARLES	PA	24E	111
BAER HERMAN JOHN	MN	26E	110
BAER MAX IRWIN	IN	29W	86
BAER RANDALL THOMAS	MI	08W	27
BAER WILLIAM CLAY	TX	64E	2
BAETZEL ROBERT ALLEN	IL	29W	95
BAFILE JOHN ANTHONY	CA	40E	36
BAGAASON GERALD BENNETT	MN	10E	79
BAGASOL ALEJANDRO BIRRI		42W	38
BAGEN RONALD S	OH	38E	75
BAGENSTOSE TOM JAY	PA	25E	67
BAGGARLY JIMMY RAY	KY	29E	18
BAGGETT CHARLES RICHARD	AR	13W	66
BAGGETT CURTIS FRANKLIN	NC	37E	47
BAGGETT FRANK ALLEN	CA	42W	53
BAGGETT JOSEPH BRADSHAW	FL	04E	18
BAGGETT WAYNE CARLOS	FL	04W	117
BAGGS WILLIAM F JR	PA	27W	47
BAGLEY DENNIS	NJ	21W	68
BAGLEY JACK LAWRENCE	MO	06W	24
BAGLEY JERRY	GA	18E	90
BAGLINI THOMAS EDWARD	RI	65W	4
BAGLIO RICHARD ANTHONY	CA	16E	34
BAGNAL LUTHER NETTLES III	NC	05W	75
BAGNALL ROBERT SALMON	CT	34E	40
BAGO JOHN STEVEN	OH	13E	114
BAGSHAW JAMES MALCOLM	PA	25E	80
BAGSHAW WILLIAM MICHAEL	NY	41E	35
BAHL RICHARD HOWARD JR	IL	14W	35
BAHL ROBERT FRANCIS JR	PA	33E	63
BAHL WALTER TIMOTHY	CO	37W	27
BAHNSEN KENT EUGENE	NE	30E	53
BAHR DENNIS KEITH	NE	10E	18
BAHR RICHARD DUNCAN	VA	43E	41
BAHRKE RUSSELL LEROY JR	WI	08W	106
BAILEY ALFRED LEON JR	CA	47W	14
BAILEY ALLEN CHARLES	NE	05E	99
BAILEY ARTHUR WILLIAM JR	CT	26W	89
BAILEY BERNARD PHILLIP	CA	19W	105
BAILEY BOBBY LEE	MS	08W	19
BAILEY BYRLE BENNETT	NE	24W	101
BAILEY CARROLL JAMES	NC	40W	36
BAILEY CHARLES CLIFFORD	KS	61W	9
BAILEY DAVID ORIN	MI	06E	93
BAILEY DENNIS MICHAEL	NY	08W	123
BAILEY DERWIN MICHAEL	OH	16W	26
BAILEY DONALD G	NY	02W	103
BAILEY DONALD RAY	DE	04W	96
BAILEY DOUGLAS GRANT	NC	48E	14
BAILEY ELLIS MILLER	TX	27E	87
BAILEY EVERETTE ROLAND	KY	40W	26
BAILEY FLOYD CLARK	IL	58E	20
BAILEY FRED EARL	FL	08E	9
BAILEY FRED MCKINLEY	NY	22W	116
BAILEY GENE THOMAS	GA	46E	27
BAILEY GEORGE EDWARD	VA	06W	109
BAILEY GEORGE LEROY	ME	35W	7
BAILEY JAMES ALBERT	PA	07W	122
BAILEY JAMES ALVIN	GA	33E	55
BAILEY JAMES ANTHONY	IN	16W	97
BAILEY JAMES DANIEL	NC	34W	20
BAILEY JAMES EDWIN	OK	01E	63
BAILEY JAMES RAY	TN	04E	2
BAILEY JESSE THOMAS JR	VA	04E	132
BAILEY JOHN EDWARD	MN	07E	44
BAILEY JOHN HOWARD	AL	19E	3
BAILEY JOHN J	MI	14E	4
BAILEY JOHN SPENCER JR	KY	20W	33
BAILEY JON	ME	31W	32
BAILEY JOSEPH DANIEL	KY	02E	127
BAILEY JOSEPH JR	IL	16E	118
BAILEY JOSEPH THOMAS	NY	40E	17
BAILEY KENNETH DEAN	VT	28W	7
BAILEY KENNETH NORMAN JR	NY	12W	95
BAILEY LARRY EUGENE	AZ	28W	23
BAILEY LARRY WILLIAM	GA	11E	34
BAILEY LELAND ALSTON	MD	18W	116
BAILEY LORING M JR	CT	13W	129
BAILEY MICHAEL A	OH	58E	29
BAILEY MICHAEL WILSON	AR	33W	11
BAILEY RAE ARVID	NY	06W	6
BAILEY RAYMOND	IL	02E	109
BAILEY ROBERT BENTON	CA	20E	5
BAILEY ROY DEE	TX	08E	110
BAILEY SCOTT JAY	UT	34W	4
BAILEY TERRY JOE	CA	04W	122
BAILEY THOMAS EARL	PA	22E	95
BAILEY THOMAS HAROLD	AR	55E	38
BAILEY TOLLIE	MD	18W	52
BAILEY WILLIAM EUGENE	TN	04W	34
BAILEY WILSON PAUL	AR	08W	113
BAILY PHILLIP RAY	OH	29W	4
BAIN BRUCE ARNOLD	MI	07W	51
BAIN THOMAS ARTHUR	NY	01E	65
BAINES TOMMIE	NY	04W	4
BAINTER NEAL VINCENT	CA	08W	99
BAIR CHARLES JACOB	FL	04E	106
BAIR DONALD RAY	SC	14E	126
BAIR ROBERT VOLNIE	WI	14E	107
BAIRD ALBERT FRANKLIN	MI	05E	92
BAIRD JACKIE RANDLE	OH	21E	64
BAIRD JAMES STEPHEN	MA	13W	13
BAIRD JOHN ROBERT JR	IL	32W	75
BAIRD MICHAEL HARRY	TX	14W	110
BAIRD ROBERT STANLEY	CA	26E	98
BAIRD RONALD EUGENE	CA	55E	38
BAITINGER DAVID JAMES	WI	17W	86
BAIZ LEE THOMAS	NY	08W	64
BAIZE GARY CECIL	IL	48W	51
BAJIN ENVER	NY	06W	67
BAKA JAMES ALEXANDER	ME	27W	105
BAKER ALLEN JAMES	TX	60W	25

NAME	STATE	PANEL NO.	LINE NO.
BAKER ALTON EUGENE	CA	03E	10
BAKER AQUILA	AR	07E	79
BAKER ARTHUR DALE	TX	01E	102
BAKER BARRY JAY	CA	29E	56
BAKER BERNARD GERALD	PA	49W	18
BAKER BILLY RAY	TX	11W	71
BAKER BOBBY GENE	MI	18W	77
BAKER BOBBY RUSSELL	OH	27W	85
BAKER BRUCE ALLAN	VT	09E	65
BAKER CHARLES ALFRED	NY	10E	86
BAKER CHARLES OAKES II	ME	57W	22
BAKER CLARENCE EUGENE	SC	06W	97
BAKER CURTIS EVERETT	IL	42E	60
BAKER CURTIS RICHARD	AR	17E	60
BAKER DANNY RAY	AR	22W	62
BAKER DAVID	PA	16E	109
BAKER DAVID	NC	28E	89
BAKER DAVID RICHARD	PA	19W	84
BAKER DAVID WALLACE	WA	07W	71
BAKER DENNIS RALPH	PA	17W	93
BAKER DON CARTER	MN	06E	70
BAKER DONALD	PA	58W	6
BAKER DONALD ALLEN	OH	10W	107
BAKER DONALD LEE	IL	02E	9
BAKER DONALD LEE	CA	26E	5
BAKER DUANE SCOTT	WA	21E	60
BAKER EDGAR JR	OH	45E	45
BAKER EDWARD GLEN	OK	49W	18
BAKER EDWARD JEFFREY	IL	12W	86
BAKER ELBERT JAMES JR	GA	21W	97
BAKER ELDON ALLEN	IN	52E	13
BAKER ELWOOD	OK	22E	56
BAKER ELWOOD CHARLES	OH	06W	128
BAKER ERNEST AUSTIN JR	AL	64E	11
BAKER EUGENE JR	IL	49W	11
BAKER EVERDENE JR	NC	21E	65
BAKER FRANKIE GUY	OK	04W	24
BAKER FREDERICK NORMAN	MD	02E	9
BAKER GARRY WAYNE	OK	50W	29
BAKER GARY BRUCE	NY	21E	43
BAKER GARY PAUL	MO	10W	16
BAKER GEORGE ARTHUR	NJ	33W	12
BAKER GEORGE WAYNE	GA	09W	31
BAKER GERALD D	TN	24E	76
BAKER GERALD OTIS	CO	35W	87
BAKER HARRY E JR	MI	12W	61
BAKER HARVEY WAYNE	NC	02W	94
BAKER HOWARD RANOLD	FL	23W	82
BAKER ISIAH III	LA	05E	99
BAKER JACK AMOS	PA	08E	46
BAKER JACK LESLIE	IL	26W	23
BAKER JACK MARVIN	MT	07W	39
BAKER JAMES HOWARD JR	MD	08E	25
BAKER JAMES MICHAEL	OH	44W	56
BAKER JERALD LAVERN	PA	46E	28
BAKER JERRY	MI	38W	22
BAKER JERRY SCRUGGS	AL	43E	65
BAKER JESSE RUTLEDGE	SC	25E	10
BAKER JOHN HOUSTON	TX	54W	8
BAKER JOHN THOMAS	CA	17W	72
BAKER JOHN WESLEY JR	GA	36W	79
BAKER JON ALLEN	NJ	60E	8
BAKER JON DOUGLAS	IL	19E	55
BAKER JOSEPH WILLIAM	PA	43E	40
BAKER JOSEPH WRIGHT	PA	27E	68
BAKER KENNETH ALVIN	MA	38W	32
BAKER KENNETH EARL JR	TX	45E	53
BAKER LA BROSSIE LUCIEN	OH	19W	111
BAKER LARRY JAMES	NY	10E	102
BAKER LINWOOD LEE	MA	03W	114
BAKER MELVIN	AL	33E	78
BAKER MICHAEL DEAN	NY	01W	5
BAKER MICHAEL O'BRIEN	NM	23W	41
BAKER MICHAEL RAY	MO	33E	44
BAKER MICHEAL ROGER	TN	37W	27
BAKER PAUL JOSEPH	NY	28W	78
BAKER PAUL WILLIAM	OH	36W	75
BAKER PHILIP KENNETH	MI	44W	34
BAKER PHILIP LOU	IA	30W	18
BAKER RAFTKEITH EROS	IL	39E	28
BAKER RAYMOND DELMAR	AL	43W	1
BAKER RAYMOND JOHN	MN	04W	39
BAKER REGINALD	IL	54E	1
BAKER RENNIE JOE JR	MO	21W	97
BAKER RICHARD ALLAN	OH	34W	4
BAKER RICHARD THOMAS	CO	05W	114
BAKER ROBERT BENTON JR	TX	07W	127
BAKER ROBERT JOHN	IL	21W	105
BAKER ROBERT LEE	IN	58E	3
BAKER ROBERT LEE	ME	06W	85
BAKER ROBERT NELSON	CA	40E	51
BAKER ROBERT OLIVER JR	CA	02W	94
BAKER RONALD	MD	34E	73
BAKER RONALD BOYSEN	PA	14W	119
BAKER RONALD RAY	CA	23W	69
BAKER RUSTON LEE	MI	48W	37
BAKER SAMUEL J	FL	11E	100
BAKER SAMUEL THEODORE	OH	02E	126
BAKER SAMUEL THOMAS	WA	24W	1
BAKER STANLEY LOYD	CO	37E	77
BAKER STANLEY MARTIN	VT	20E	53
BAKER STANLEY WELLINGTON	CA	09E	9
BAKER STEVEN DEWITT	CA	64W	5
BAKER THOMAS HARRY	MI	15E	67
BAKER THOMAS HUGH	OK	39W	15
BAKER THOMAS MICHAEL	MO	63E	4
BAKER TONY ANDERSON	CA	53W	15
BAKER VERNON HOWARD II	CT	22E	5
BAKER VERNON R	MD	17E	97
BAKER VINCENT B	AZ	29E	64
BAKER WALLACE EDWIN	OH	04E	49
BAKER WAYNE ROLAND	TX	10E	33
BAKER WILLIAM EMANUEL	MI	24E	111
BAKER WILLIAM S	DE	50W	4
BAKER WILLIE CECIL	MO	25E	56
BAKER WILLIE JAMES	MS	16E	56
BAKER WILLY SCOTT	TN	12E	72
BAKEWELL RONALD CHARLES	PA	50W	48
BAKKE LARRY NEIL	MI	23W	95
BAKKE TONY LEE	MN	09E	110
BAKKEN WILLIAM DONALD	WI	32W	18
BAKKIE DONALD KEITH	CA	58E	29
BALADES DAVID ZAVALA	CA	41E	58
BALAI ANDRES	HI	36W	28
BALAMOTI MICHAEL DIMITRI	NY	16W	114
BALAZY GEORGE STEPHEN	NY	02E	81
BALBIRNIE JAMES FREDERICK	CA	08E	78
BALCH JAMES IVERSON	CA	19E	21
BALCOE CHARLES WALTER DEW	WV	27E	26
BALCOM JOEL ARNOLD	MO	16W	22
BALCOM RALPH CAROL	WA	07E	61
BALDAUF FREDERICK WILLIAM	PA	05W	28
BALDAUF RAYMOND JOSEPH	OH	32W	30
BALDERA BARTOLOME ALFONSO	NY	40E	51
BALDINI MICHAEL LOUIS	LA	09W	81
BALDINO FRANCIS	PA	39W	63
BALDIZON-IZQUIERDO CARLOS A	CA	20W	107
BALDON RUDY LEE	OR	16W	51
BALDONADO SECUNDINO	NM	01E	117
BALDONI LINDSAY DAVID	MI	25E	29
BALDRIDGE JOHN ROBERT JR	TN	16W	97
BALDWIN CHARLES LEROY	MI	19W	124
BALDWIN CLARENCE JAY	NY	67E	5
BALDWIN CLIFTON ADAIR	TX	17W	24
BALDWIN GERALD LEE	NY	53W	32
BALDWIN GERALD LEE	ID	15W	49
BALDWIN HENRY PHILIP	MI	29W	75
BALDWIN JOHN FRANK	IA	35W	80
BALDWIN KENNETH MAYNARD	IA	48W	37
BALDWIN LARRY DEAN	CA	28W	7
BALDWIN LARRY GLENN	AL	07W	76
BALDWIN MICHAEL RICHARD	NJ	44W	35
BALDWIN NELLO JR	TX	05W	29
BALDWIN NORMAN EARL	FL	46W	28
BALDWIN ORVAL ARTHUR	WI	17W	38
BALDWIN PETER NELSON	NY	46E	52
BALDWIN ROBERT EARL	TX	37E	47
BALDWIN ROBERT LANOUE	WI	17E	77
BALDWIN ROBERT LLOYD	MD	29W	65
BALDWIN ROY LEE	IL	25W	60
BALDWIN SANDERS RAY	VA	15W	86
BALDWIN SCOTT DOUGLAS	MN	23W	41
BALDWIN TERRY LYMAN	MA	49W	21
BALDWIN WILLIAM CLARENCE	IL	63E	4
BALDWIN WILLIAM MCKINLEY	NY	10E	3
BALDWIN WILLIAM ROBERT	SC	01W	103
BALENTINE ROLAND JR	KS	27E	44
BALES CHARLES ROBERT	KS	47W	25
BALES RICHARD LEE	NY	37W	37
BALES RONALD EUGENE	NE	04W	125
BALES SHAREL EDWARD	CO	25E	61
BALFOUR DENNIS R	VA	10E	82
BALFOUR WILLIAM JAY	IA	26E	109
BALISTERI CODY ALLEN	OH	11E	107
BALITCHIK MICHAEL JOSEPH	PA	52E	13
BALITSARIS JOHN BOMAR	TN	23W	70
BALKIT DONALD	PA	52E	2
BALL ALBERT THOMAS	VA	02W	30
BALL ARTHUR WYMAN	TX	51E	35
BALL CHARLES HOMER	OH	13E	66
BALL CLYDE JAMES	KY	08W	68
BALL DAVID MARTIN	TX	20W	84
BALL DWIGHT HERBERT	OH	12W	86
BALL EDWARD MEARL	OH	03W	11
BALL GARY WAYNE	NH	52W	38
BALL HARRISON BRUCE	MI	26E	87
BALL JAMES EDWARD III	VA	22E	122
BALL JAMES MARVIN	CA	07W	67
BALL JIMMY REX	AL	07E	113
BALL JOHN ROBERT	WV	02E	14
BALL LESLIE ARNOLD	OR	47E	19
BALL LUTHER EDWARD JR	FL	27W	70
BALL MERLIN EUGENE	KS	16E	75
BALL MICHAEL EDWARD	KY	04W	130
BALL MICHAEL HENRY	MS	07E	6
BALL MICHAEL ROGER	IA	28W	42
BALL ROBERT	OH	58W	17
BALL ROBERT LEE	NJ	56W	17
BALL ROSCOE WILLET JR	WV	28W	8
BALL THOMAS ELROY JR	OH	29E	23
BALL THOMAS LESLIE SNIDER	WA	31E	8
BALLANCE EDMOND TELLO	FL	03W	67
BALLANCE ELBERT ANDREW	NC	44E	65
BALLANCE NORMAN L III	FL	16E	128
BALLAND ERNEST CLAUDE	WY	10W	93
BALLANGER ENOCH ANDREW	GA	21E	8
BALLANTINE RICHARD REED	NE	41E	47
BALLARD ADAM DAVID	CO	18E	73
BALLARD CARL HERSHEL	OK	01E	25
BALLARD EDWARD HARDING	NC	16E	56
BALLARD GERALD ROY	TX	48W	37
BALLARD GILBERT FLOYD	GA	23E	84
BALLARD JOHN RICHARD	FL	10E	55
BALLARD MEL ROY	CA	50E	36
BALLARD MELVIN	IL	16E	56
BALLARD NORMAN CASEY	FL	35E	65
BALLARD PAUL ALLEN	OH	34W	40
BALLARD ROBERT IRVING	LA	37E	3
BALLARD ROBERT LEE	CA	33W	53
BALLARD RONNIE EDSEL	AR	33E	15
BALLAUF CHARLES ALAN	CA	23E	25
BALLAY JAMES VINCENT	MO	10W	21
BALLENGER CARL AUGUSTUS	KY	28E	42
BALLEW ARTHUR CLAY	AL	54W	22
BALLEW CHESTER LLOYD	OK	10W	63
BALLEW HENRY HERSCHEL	IL	47W	37
BALLEW HENRY JR	GA	20W	53
BALLEW PATRICK DEWEY	LA	35W	45
BALLEW ROLAND LEE	IL	49E	38
BALLHEIM RICHARD ALAN	IA	35E	52
BALLIN JOE MAGDALENO JR	CA	10E	99
BALLINGER JAMES ARTHUR	IN	35E	85
BALLINGER TIMOTHY J	MI	24W	92
BALLINGER WILLIAM JOSEPH	NE	65W	4
BALLOU CHARLES DAVISON	PA	39W	31
BALLOU DAVID ALLAN	FL	47W	25
BALLREE EMMETT EUGENE	NC	19E	34
BALMER ROBERT OLIVER	NJ	03E	102
BALMER WAYNE ASHLEY	PA	03E	10
BALOG LOUIS ROBERT	MI	37E	18
BALSLEY ROBERT F JR	TX	39W	72
BALTERS STEPHEN A JR	CA	21E	41
BALTEZORE THEODORE ELLIS	SD	22W	95
BALTHAZOR RICHARD JOHN	WI	25E	27
BALUKONIS RICHARD CHARLES	PA	31E	28
BALZARINI DAVID RAYMOND	PA	34W	35

NAME	STATE	PANEL NO.	LINE NO.
BALZER MICHAEL ARLIN	VA	16E	128
BAMBRICK RICHARD GEORGE	NJ	48E	50
BAMFORD GEORGE ARTHUR	OR	13W	99
BAMFORD THOMAS CAMPBELL	CA	49W	21
BAMVAKAIS JOHN ROBERT JR	MO	27E	23
BAN HERMAN HALEMANU	HI	15W	124
BANAGA SALVADOR M L JR	CA	38E	47
BANAR MARVIN DALE	OH	31E	22
BANASZYNSKI RICHARD MICHA	WI	40W	31
BANCROFT PHILIP SEAN	PA	42W	45
BANCROFT STEPHEN WAYNE	MO	08W	65
BANCROFT WILLIAM W JR	IN	06W	56
BANDA MACARIO S	TX	32W	10
BANDELIER HOWARD WAYNE	IN	50E	25
BANDY CURTIS ELBERT	CO	55E	39
BANDY LARRY GENE	IL	50W	40
BANDY MICHAEL J	LA	46E	28
BANDY RAYMOND DOUGLAS	VA	36W	20
BANEK LAWRENCE BENJAMIN	RI	42W	26
BANEY CHARLES LYNN	IN	28E	11
BANEY WILLIAM GERALD JR	KY	51E	35
BANG JAMES CURTIS	MN	57E	14
BANGERT BYRON ALLEN	MN	04W	16
BANGERT ROGER CARL	MN	34W	55
BANGERT STEPHEN RAY	IL	15E	130
BANGLOS GARY ALAN	CA	35E	85
BANGS CHRISTOPHER DELBERT	CA	28W	106
BANGS LAWRENCE GENE	WA	05W	10
BANISTER JOHN EDWARD	IL	27W	92
BANKOWSKI ALFONS ALOYZE	CT	01E	1
BANKOWSKI JOHN FRANCIS	MI	14E	84
BANKS DAVID LENOX	WI	26W	17
BANKS DINGUS JR	OH	37E	18
BANKS FLOYD JACKSON	IL	15W	31
BANKS HENRY DUANE	AZ	52W	26
BANKS IRVIN SYLVESTER	VA	17E	119
BANKS JAMES C	MI	25E	49
BANKS JAMES R	TX	17E	120
BANKS JOHN LAWRENCE III	MN	06E	59
BANKS LARRY CLAYTON	IN	29E	37
BANKS LAVINE JOHN	LA	03E	68
BANKS MICHAEL FRANCIS	SC	18W	52
BANKS RAY CARROL	TX	36E	65
BANKS RICHARD ANTHONY	OH	52W	38
BANKS RICHARD ROOSEVELT	NC	08E	110
BANKS RICHARD STEVEN	MI	52E	32
BANKS ROBERT ALAN	CA	25W	27
BANKS ROBERT ALLEN	OH	13W	125
BANKS ROBERT LEE	PA	10E	50
BANKS STERLING CLARK	VA	54E	30
BANKS VINCENT NORVELL	SC	31W	63
BANKSTON RONALD NEIL	TX	56E	34
BANNA WILLIAM THOMAS JR	NY	48W	21
BANNACH GERALD JOSEPH	WI	11E	8
BANNER STEVE ARTHUR	CA	43E	3
BANNING JAMES HENRY JR	CT	43E	3
BANNISTER HOWARD WILLIAM	WV	23E	48
BANNISTER RICHARD WAYNE	TN	32E	68
BANNISTER RUSSELL REID	MI	25E	61
BANNON GARY CLIFFORD	KS	20E	53
BANNON PAUL WEDLAKE	AL	21W	105
BANNON WILLIAM JOHN JR	CT	27W	54
BANOVEZ MICHAEL JOSEPH JR	WI	09E	31
BANSAVAGE JOHN GEORGE	NY	06E	55
BANTA LANNY WILSON	KY	33W	12
BANTA MICHAEL DEAN	AK	07W	105
BANUELOS ALBERT A JR	CA	43W	33
BAPP RONALD DALE	IN	40E	17
BAPTISTA PAUL ALIPIO	CA	11W	120
BAPTISTE MICHAEL BRADFORD	FL	41E	15
BARAN BRUNO	IL	29W	42
BARANCZYK ALBIN ANTON	WI	07E	67
BARANOSKI JOHN FRANK	NJ	40E	36
BARANOWSKI BISHOP SKIP	NY	21W	80
BARASH LOUIS ABBEY	NY	36W	79
BARB MANVILLE LAWRENCE	OH	28E	95
BARBA PHILLIP JOSE	CA	06W	72
BARBARE JAMES MICHAEL	SC	45W	39
BARBARIA LOUIS JOSEPH	NY	12W	28
BARBARINO ANTHONY ADAMS	PA	33W	55
BARBEE FRANK LEROY	SC	10E	55
BARBEE GARRY DWIGHT	NC	20W	88

NAME	STATE	PANEL NO.	LINE NO.
BARBEE JERRY PAUL	TN	53W	16
BARBEE JOHN WESLEY	TN	49W	18
BARBEE LARRY HULAN	SD	23W	82
BARBEE RICHARD LORDY	CA	03W	40
BARBEE THOMAS JOSEPH	OK	14E	72
BARBEE WILBERT RAY	NC	44E	57
BARBER BARRY MORRIS	NV	36W	79
BARBER BOB	OK	46W	46
BARBER BOBBY JOE	TN	17E	60
BARBER BOBBY LEE	NC	29E	8
BARBER CHADWICK MC FALL	AL	35W	53
BARBER CHRISTOPHER JAMES	NY	54E	42
BARBER DAVID EDWIN	CA	59W	18
BARBER DAVID LEON	PA	15W	76
BARBER DAVID LYNN	MT	52E	33
BARBER ERNEST LEE	IL	38W	70
BARBER ERNEST McDONALD	AL	07W	15
BARBER FLOYD EDWARD	OH	23W	5
BARBER GEORGE L III	TX	42E	60
BARBER HARRY ADELBERT	IA	52W	8
BARBER HENRY EDWARD JR	TX	17W	108
BARBER JOHNIE RAY	MO	35E	53
BARBER LONNIE	NC	13E	88
BARBER MANNIE ALFRED	GA	12W	91
BARBER MELVIN	CA	10E	18
BARBER MORRIE CURTISS	FL	31W	32
BARBER RICHARD JOSEPH	MI	11W	120
BARBER ROBERT FRANKLIN	WA	02E	85
BARBER ROGER LEE	CA	21E	96
BARBER RONALD LEE	OR	18E	79
BARBER SIDNEY EMERY	CT	31E	32
BARBER THOMAS DAVID	CO	45E	7
BARBERA PETER	NY	15E	13
BARBERY ROBERT NELSON	NY	35E	59
BARBIERE CHARLES LOUIS	NY	25W	60
BARBOLLA RICHARD ANTHONY	TX	38W	23
BARBOSA ALVARO	LA	06W	115
BARBOSA-OYOLA EUGENIO	PR	11W	120
BARBOSA-VILLAFANE ANTONIO	PR	04E	136
BARBOUR JAMES C JR	VA	46W	36
BARBOUR JAMES WESLEY	NY	60W	15
BARBOUR JOHN RAMAGE	NM	25E	95
BARBRE SAMUEL DAVID	GA	18W	23
BARBURY JOHN	UT	38E	20
BARCA JOHN JR	NY	28W	8
BARCALOW RONALD RICHARD	MI	23E	94
BARCELONA RALPH ANTHONY	IL	22W	38
BARCENA BOBBY JOHN	HI	15E	103
BARCHAK JOHNNIE F JR	TX	15E	112
BARCKLOW LAWRENCE ANTHONY	NY	12E	118
BARCLAY FREDERICK ALLEN	MD	54E	42
BARD MICHAEL	MI	58W	23
BARDACH ALAN JENSEN	IN	33E	78
BARDACH ROBERT ERLE	IL	27E	105
BARDEN ARNOLD WINFIELD JR	CA	02W	20
BARDEN EDWARD	NC	23E	118
BARDEN HOWARD LEROY	OH	14E	99
BARDET RAYMOND FREDERIC	NJ	64W	5
BARDON BRUCE HAROLD	IL	11W	56
BARDUSON DAVID JULIEN	MN	46E	2
BARE WILLIAM ORLAN	OK	24E	4
BAREFIELD BOBBY JOE	AZ	07E	109
BAREFIELD JAMES ARTHER	AL	01W	29
BARELA BARTOLO AMADOR JR	CO	12W	54
BARELA IGNACIO	NM	21E	31
BARETTI ALAN GEORGE	NY	45E	37
BARFIELD JERRY	FL	21W	87
BARFIELD JOHN R	MS	38E	44
BARFIELD LARRY BRUCE	FL	27W	70
BARGA SAMMY A	OH	07E	67
BARGAHEISER LAWRENCE GILB	OH	49W	18
BARGAR RICHARD M	OH	48E	22
BARGE FREDERICK DOUGLAS	AL	23W	95
BARGER FERDINAND ORA JR	CA	45W	35
BARGER GEORGE HAYES	PA	34W	56
BARGER IVAN LLOYD JR	OK	07W	3
BARGER KENNETH ALLEN	PA	05W	94
BARGER LARRY EARL	NV	46E	28
BARGER LEE MELLINGTON	TX	65E	4
BARGER PHILLIP DENNIS	TX	39W	46
BARGMANN GILBERT RAY	ND	22W	84
BARGY MORRIS LEE	OH	03E	117

NAME	STATE	PANEL NO.	LINE NO.
BARHAM LARRY GENE	MO	37E	48
BARICKMAN LEON ROSS	MN	20W	54
BARIGLIO RICHARD LOUIS	NY	16W	51
BARILI PETER LINO	MI	05W	127
BARILLO JOSEPH WILLIAM	NY	23E	16
BARISIC LAWRENCE WILLIAM	NY	16E	99
BARKER BOBBY LEE	IL	12W	64
BARKER DANA RANDOLPH	CA	32W	24
BARKER ELVIS GORDON	OR	01E	94
BARKER FLOYD JR	KY	17E	16
BARKER FRANK AKELEY JR	CT	57W	6
BARKER GARY LEE	CA	28E	19
BARKER GREG ALLEN	MI	19W	7
BARKER HOWARD CLEVELAND	FL	12E	17
BARKER JACK LAMAR	GA	04W	59
BARKER JAMES HAROLD	OR	13E	106
BARKER JEDH COLBY	NJ	26E	99
BARKER JEFFREY LAWRENCE	NJ	21E	72
BARKER JERRY EDWIN	WA	18W	100
BARKER JOHN WAYNE	IN	16E	1
BARKER KENNETH MONROE	WV	46E	2
BARKER LARRY DALE	OK	32W	88
BARKER LARRY LEE	MO	26E	39
BARKER OSCAR JR	GA	03E	68
BARKER PAUL LEROY	ME	54E	23
BARKER RAY MILTON	PA	19W	90
BARKER ROBERT LEE JR	CA	48E	23
BARKER STEPHEN PETER	WA	34E	51
BARKER WILLIAM GAYLAND	IA	20W	54
BARKFELT DAVID WILLIAM	CA	30E	22
BARKLEY EARL DUANE	PA	02W	64
BARKLEY JESSE LOUIS	IL	44W	14
BARKLEY KENNETH PAUL JR	MD	16W	61
BARKLEY KENNETH RAY	PA	28W	16
BARKLEY KIRK OWEN	MI	08W	96
BARKLEY LAWRENCE WILLIAM	OH	29E	37
BARKLEY STEPHEN RICHARD	CA	10W	89
BARKSDALE CULLEN JR	IN	27E	27
BARKSDALE JAMES WILLIAM	FL	03E	23
BARKSDALE JERRY DEAN	KS	35E	86
BARKSDALE WILLIAM HOWARD	AL	29W	4
BARLEEN THOMAS LYLE	CA	18E	19
BARLETT RALPH HARRY JR	IL	29E	69
BARLOW CLARK EUGENE	NY	51E	27
BARLOW EDWARD ARNOLD	KY	25W	46
BARLOW JEFFREY LAWRENCE	MI	05W	68
BARLOW JESSIE LEE	GA	26E	5
BARLOW ROSS OWEN	TX	55W	4
BARMMER TIMOTHY MICHAEL	CT	35E	65
BARNABY DAVID W	MI	19E	21
BARNABY ROLAND NATHANIEL	GA	52W	17
BARNARD GARY ADRIAN	IL	11E	12
BARNARD GARY MICHAEL	CA	22E	95
BARNARD HAROLD EDWARD	MD	03W	68
BARNARD LARRY WAYNE	TN	39E	17
BARNARD LEON EDWARD	TN	29W	35
BARNARD LEWIS CECIL	AL	09E	31
BARNARD RICHARD GEORGE	NY	36W	61
BARNARD THOMAS WALTER	OK	44W	1
BARNER LARRY KENNETH	PA	09E	96
BARNES AARON ANDRE JR	NC	35W	2
BARNES ALFRED	NJ	25W	60
BARNES ALFRED JR	DC	19W	28
BARNES ALLAN GEORGE	SC	55E	39
BARNES ALLEN ROY	AZ	59E	16
BARNES BARRIE VANE	MD	07E	31
BARNES BERNARD	GA	03W	68
BARNES BRUCE MICHAEL	IL	19W	8
BARNES CEPHAS JR	FL	04E	13
BARNES CHARLES PETER	TX	55W	11
BARNES CHARLES RONALD	PA	29W	50
BARNES CLARENCE EDWARD	TN	06E	97
BARNES DANNY CLEON	WA	13E	119
BARNES DARRYL VERDUE	LA	35W	32
BARNES DAVID GREGORY	WI	55E	1
BARNES DAVID THOMAS	PA	52E	33
BARNES DONALD ALBON	IL	03E	68
BARNES DONALD JOSEPH	PA	21E	60
BARNES ERIC MARVIN	CT	17E	41
BARNES FRANCIS ARCHER	CA	46E	13
BARNES GALE LYNN	MI	23W	108
BARNES GARY ALAN	NY	48W	52

NAME	STATE	PANEL NO.	LINE NO.
BARNES GARY LESTER	MN	23W	116
BARNES GEORGE LEE	MI	38W	32
BARNES HAROLD DUANE	NE	04E	48
BARNES HERBERT SPENCER	OK	03W	41
BARNES ISIAH JR	NC	33W	46
BARNES JACKSON DILLON	TN	33W	30
BARNES JAMES ALAN	MI	13W	18
BARNES JAMES FREDERICK	WY	12E	32
BARNES JAMES WILLIAM JR	NY	18E	51
BARNES JIMMY ONEAL	MI	23E	34
BARNES JOE WILSON	SC	15E	89
BARNES JOHN ANDREW III	MA	29E	84
BARNES JOHN HENRY	MO	29E	80
BARNES JOHN HOWARD	MD	46E	44
BARNES JOHN LUMSDEN	FL	34E	73
BARNES LAURIE EUGENE	OH	27W	54
BARNES LAWRENCE MERRIDITH	NJ	32E	68
BARNES LEROY		09E	41
BARNES LEROY FRANCIS	CT	10E	27
BARNES MARK ALBERT	NY	42W	26
BARNES MARVIN DONALD	CA	31W	87
BARNES MERRILL	VA	24W	109
BARNES MICHAEL ALLEN	PA	33W	53
BARNES MITCHELL ODELL	TN	03W	59
BARNES RICHARD FRANK	NY	05E	44
BARNES RICHARD LEIGH	CA	23W	61
BARNES RICHARD LOUIS	AL	09W	90
BARNES ROBERT CROZIER JR	IL	63W	14
BARNES ROBERT EUGENE	WY	59W	19
BARNES ROBERT LEE	GA	09E	9
BARNES ROBERT SEWELL	NY	26E	21
BARNES RODGER GLYNN	FL	28E	78
BARNES ROY DWIGHT	CA	02W	46
BARNES SHELDON ORA	TX	26W	68
BARNES STEPHEN WESTLEY	TX	08W	26
BARNES THOMAS JACKSON JR	KY	21W	87
BARNES TOMMY LEE	IL	28W	16
BARNES TOMMY LEE	GA	14W	119
BARNES WALTER EDWARD	PA	34W	20
BARNES WALTER FRASIER	CA	53E	9
BARNES WILLIAM ACKER	AZ	15W	41
BARNES WILLIAM CAREL JR	MI	37E	18
BARNES WILLIAM EDWARD	NC	14W	11
BARNES WILLIE JAMES	IL	36E	45
BARNETT ALAN LYNN	OR	03E	16
BARNETT BENJAMIN FRANKLIN	AZ	43W	60
BARNETT BILLIE JOE JR	MO	29E	38
BARNETT CARL EUGENE	NE	12W	66
BARNETT CARL TAYLOR	IN	10W	60
BARNETT CHARLES EDWARD	TX	01W	29
BARNETT CLIFFORD C JR	IN	18E	90
BARNETT DAVID WILLIAM	TN	11W	82
BARNETT DONALD EUGENE	AL	28W	42
BARNETT EUGENE MELVIN	OH	49W	7
BARNETT GARY JOE	KS	12W	28
BARNETT GARY KEITH	OK	16W	35
BARNETT GLENDON ROMAN	NH	21E	100
BARNETT IRIA DANIEL	OR	31W	63
BARNETT JEFF THOMAS SR	TN	05W	47
BARNETT JIMMY DALTON	TX	46E	28
BARNETT JOHN DANIEL JR	PA	32E	20
BARNETT JOHN FRANK	CA	08W	30
BARNETT KENNETH LEE	FL	01W	35
BARNETT MELVIN DONALD	WA	02W	24
BARNETT MEREDITH LEE	OH	06W	42
BARNETT PAUL WAYNE	OK	35W	23
BARNETT ROBERT RUSSELL	TX	06E	91
BARNETT SAMUEL HOYT	PA	05W	59
BARNETT STEVEN PAUL	CA	22W	30
BARNETT STUART LEE	AR	07W	8
BARNETT THOMAS MARTIN	IN	07W	91
BARNETT TONEY ANTHONY	SC	24E	14
BARNETTE FRED EDWARD	VA	18E	90
BARNETTE ROY GRANT	SC	34W	56
BARNETTE WALLACE WAYNE	NC	22E	95
BARNEY ALEXANDER LORENZO	NY	10E	82
BARNEY LUTHER	NM	02W	90
BARNEY TERENCE EDWARD	NE	29W	58
BARNHART BEVERLY LEE	WA	27W	54
BARNHART CARL RAY	IL	30E	83
BARNHART EARL EDWARD JR	OH	70W	1
BARNHART JACK ADRIAN	NJ	46W	37
BARNHART JOHN LOUIS	SC	29E	87
BARNHART OTTO PHILIP	MD	26W	29
BARNHART ROGER ALAN	PA	06W	116
BARNHILL GLEN ROBERT	WA	35E	2
BARNHILL JAMES EUGENE	NY	45W	47
BARNHILL LARRY M	MD	13E	13
BARNHILL ROBERT EUGENE	NE	06W	44
BARNHOLDT TERRY JOE	CA	28W	78
BARNHOUSE DARREL EMERSON	CA	48W	21
BARNICK CHARLES EDWARD	MN	17W	125
BARNITZ DOUGLAS WANNER	OH	23W	61
BARNS LAWRENCE RAY	TX	12W	16
BARNUM GARY LANE	OK	45E	53
BARNUM WAYNE ALAN	MT	37W	61
BARNWELL JACKIE WAYNE	TX	05W	119
BARNWELL RAY MAX	AR	05E	112
BARON DOUGLAS KEN	CA	43W	51
BARON FRANCIS VINCENT	MN	40W	9
BARON FRANTZ MARIO	NY	16E	118
BARONE SANDRO NICHOLAS	VA	11W	5
BARONOWSKI MICHAEL ALEXAN	PA	12E	128
BAROTT WILLIAM CHAUNCEY	PA	12E	17
BAROVETTO JOHN LAWRENCE	CA	33E	63
BARR ALLAN VAUGHN	OK	26W	30
BARR EDWARD NASUESAK	AK	26W	105
BARR ELMER EDWARD	PA	28W	88
BARR JAMES DAVID	NC	45E	17
BARR JOHN FREDERICK	AR	28E	33
BARR JUNIOR WAYNE	VA	65E	4
BARR MICHAEL MCKEE	IA	46E	61
BARR ROBERT CHARLES	PA	16W	55
BARR ROBERT H	WI	20W	54
BARR TERRY LEE	KS	19W	52
BARR THOMAS M	AK	25W	60
BARR WILLIAM JAMES	PA	52W	38
BARR WILMA J	TX	22E	119
BARRAGAN REYNALDO LEON JR	CA	15W	84
BARRAGY WILLIAM JOSEPH	IA	07E	22
BARRAS GREGORY INMAN	MS	36W	41
BARREIROS SILVINO FERNAND	CT	35E	44
BARRERA GILBERTO	TX	22E	95
BARRERA JOSE GILBERT	CA	06W	52
BARRERA MANUEL	CA	14E	13
BARRERA RAUL ROY JR	CA	16W	114
BARRERA TOMAS ANTONIO	TX	45W	40
BARRERAS FRANK III	CA	16E	118
BARRETO LUIS JR	LA	29E	67
BARRETT ANDREW RYAN	MN	07W	16
BARRETT CHARLES ARTHUR II	WV	23E	108
BARRETT CHARLES WESLEY	CA	16E	68
BARRETT CLARE ARNOLD	IL	12W	92
BARRETT DAVID MORRIS	OR	38W	56
BARRETT DONALD	GA	11W	73
BARRETT DONALD RICHARD	IN	19W	58
BARRETT DREW JAMES III	PA	30W	84
BARRETT FREDERICK HARRY	CA	18W	45
BARRETT GEORGE DWAYNE	KS	45E	37
BARRETT GEORGE PATRICK	MI	28E	78
BARRETT JAMES ALLEN	PA	11E	67
BARRETT JOHN DANIEL	TX	06W	53
BARRETT JOHN HAROLD	GA	11W	78
BARRETT LARRY WAYNE	IN	47E	45
BARRETT MICHAEL BARRY	CA	38E	20
BARRETT MICHAEL OWEN	GA	22E	90
BARRETT ROBERT LEE JR	CA	29W	65
BARRETT STANLEY FOSTER	MI	18E	99
BARRETT STANLEY HOWARD	NY	07W	109
BARRETT STEPHEN CLARK	NY	35E	29
BARRETT THOMAS A	TN	60E	8
BARRETT THOMAS J JR	LA	03E	51
BARRETT WILLIAM KATHMAN	KY	02E	128
BARRICK BENJAMIN LUTHER	KY	18E	33
BARRICK HAROLD EUGENE	PA	48E	50
BARRIGA ARTURO	AZ	11E	63
BARRIMOND ERROL MICHAEL	NY	54E	1
BARRINGER ARDREY WATTS JR	NC	58W	6
BARRINGTON ALVIS T JR	VA	02W	41
BARRINGTON PAUL V JR	FL	19W	28
BARRIOS BERNARD	NJ	06E	88
BARRIOS JAMES PATRICK	CA	35W	74
BARRIOS MARCELLO NUNEZ	CA	19W	21
BARRITT WILLIAM EMMETT	MS	08W	110
BARRITT WILLIAM STEPHEN	OH	15W	57
BARRON DANNY LANCE	AL	20W	96
BARRON FLORENTINO CIPRIAN	NE	20E	20
BARRON JEFFREY MICHAEL	CA	31W	42
BARRON JOHN ELDREW	PA	34E	33
BARRON ROBERT BRUCE	TX	39W	46
BARROW ERIC B JR	FL	10E	18
BARROW MICHAEL EDWARD	OR	22W	116
BARROW THOMAS MELVIN JR	GA	18E	90
BARROWS IRVING DONALD	LA	51E	16
BARRS SHELTON FERRELL	SC	18W	127
BARRUS DAVID WILLIAM	MI	12W	59
BARRY CRAIG NICHOLAS	NY	12W	123
BARRY EDWARD FRANCIS	NY	32W	36
BARRY GEORGE FRANCIS JR	MA	10W	83
BARRY JAMES MICHAEL	MA	02W	134
BARRY JOHN FRANKLIN	NY	07E	115
BARRY KENNETH DONALD	OR	33E	79
BARRY ROBERT JAMES	OH	42W	45
BARRY ROBERT OWEN	NY	20E	5
BARRY THOMAS R	NY	16E	74
BARSCH JOHN PAUL	NJ	32E	69
BARSCHOW WILLIAM MARCUS	OH	01E	101
BARSLOW KENNETH WILLIAM	NY	34E	33
BARSOM GEORGE KASPER III	AL	01W	3
BARTA ROBERT CHARLES	IA	22E	95
BARTALOTTI ALFONSO PAUL	CA	30E	95
BARTASCH WALTER	PA	17W	39
BARTEK DONALD EUGENE	OH	14W	92
BARTELL LARRY MICHAEL	MO	36W	79
BARTELL MICHAEL RICHARD	OR	43W	24
BARTELME MICHAEL PAUL	WI	19E	9
BARTELS GARY LESLIE	MN	06W	128
BARTELS NORMAN WILLIAM	IL	40W	31
BARTELS STEPHEN DONALD	CA	29E	56
BARTH BRUCE GEORGE	MI	05E	8
BARTH THOMAS FREDRICK	CA	24W	57
BARTH WAYNE ROBERT	CA	18E	78
BARTHELMAS WILLIAM J JR	OH	02E	44
BARTHELME ALBERT LEWIS JR	MD	11W	5
BARTHOL JEFFREY CLAYTON	PA	30W	35
BARTHOLOMEW CHARLES RICKY	IA	45E	45
BARTHOLOMEW DAVE MARTIN	LA	33E	1
BARTHOLOMEW DAVID RUSSELL	PA	56W	31
BARTHOLOMEW HARRY ROBERT	PA	33E	25
BARTHOLOMEW MICHAEL M	CA	20W	42
BARTHOLOMEW RICHARD D JR	WI	32W	21
BARTHOLOMEW ROGER JAY	OR	38W	70
BARTHOLOMEW TILMEN VERGES	LA	19W	18
BARTHOLOMEW WILLIAM H JR	PA	14W	60
BARTKOWSKI GREGORY JOSEPH	WI	40W	56
BARTLE BARRY GEORGE	FL	64W	5
BARTLE RICHARD PAUL	MO	10E	131
BARTLEBAUGH DENNIS LEE	CA	18W	118
BARTLETT ARTHUR FRANCIS	MA	35W	18
BARTLETT ARTHUR WAYNE SR	TX	31W	42
BARTLETT BRUCE EUGENE	FL	47W	16
BARTLETT CHARLES DENNIS	MA	49W	28
BARTLETT DAVID ALLAN	OH	28E	71
BARTLETT DONALD HAROLD	ME	40W	61
BARTLETT DONNIE STEPHEN	AL	13W	109
BARTLETT JAMES B	NH	08E	117
BARTLETT JOHN REX	CA	34W	30
BARTLETT LARRY PAUL	WA	14W	16
BARTLEY DON LAVERNE	VA	23W	109
BARTLEY DONALD RAY	IN	29W	75
BARTLEY HOWARD LYNN	TX	28E	107
BARTLEY JOHN PETER	OH	01E	18
BARTLEY KENNETH LEONARD	MD	22W	30
BARTLEY RALPH GILBERT JR	IL	07W	109
BARTLEY RICHARD LOUIS	IN	35E	86
BARTLEY WALTER CARL JR	OH	11W	4
BARTLING TERRY NOBLE	OK	55W	25
BARTLOW GARY WILLIAM	CA	09E	31
BARTLOW RICHARD LEE	IA	54E	1
BARTMAN STEVEN DOUGLAS	CA	35W	53
BARTMESS GARY WAYNE	IA	06W	15
BARTOCCI JOHN EUGENE	NY	45W	12
BARTOCK DAVID	PA	16E	50
BARTOLF NOEL MICHAEL	NY	04E	49
BARTOLINA ERNEST E JR	ND	33W	75
BARTON ALAN KEITH	MI	08W	63

NAME	STATE	PANEL NO.	LINE NO.
BARTON DAVID ALLEN	AL	04W	4
BARTON DENNIS MICHAEL	IA	24E	14
BARTON HAROLD BRUCE	CA	25E	10
BARTON JAMES EUGENE	AZ	05W	132
BARTON JAMES JOHN	NJ	22W	102
BARTON JAMES LEE	WY	27W	28
BARTON JAMES PAUL	MO	16E	109
BARTON JAMES RAYBON	TX	10W	38
BARTON JAMES WESLEY	TX	55E	1
BARTON JERE ALAN	CA	09W	23
BARTON JIM ALBERT	MT	25W	20
BARTON JIMMIE WOODROW	SD	03E	68
BARTON LANCE BRYAN	VA	32E	61
BARTON LARRY DEAN	OH	16E	128
BARTON MICHAEL GEORGE	SC	09E	19
BARTON NORMAN LEE	IL	20W	106
BARTON ROBERT JAMESON	FL	02W	42
BARTON ROBERT W JR	NY	13E	129
BARTON VAL E	CA	46E	3
BARTON VIRGIL WAYNE	CA	02E	64
BARTON WILL PAGE II	WA	08E	25
BARTONE JOHN PATRICK	VA	08W	19
BARTRAM FORREST LA WAYNE	TX	61E	6
BARTRAM GERALD EDWARD	IL	16E	42
BARTZ GARY EUGENE	WY	06E	11
BARTZ ROGER CHARLES	NE	15W	26
BARUTH DAVID ARTHUR	MN	11E	117
BARUZZI MARCO JOSEPH	OH	14E	110
BARZAN JOHN JOSEPH	NY	11E	12
BASALLA DONALD ALBERT	OH	30E	88
BASCO HARVEY LEE	LA	29W	42
BASCO JOSEPH FLOYD JR	FL	18E	55
BASDEN DENNIS EARL	NC	55E	39
BASDEN JERRY DON	TX	03E	21
BASEHORE HAROLD EDWARD JR	PA	11W	39
BASEY DWIGHT LEROY	IN	12E	86
BASHAM EDWARD RAY	KY	13E	31
BASHAM HAROLD LAWTON	TN	37W	3
BASHAM JAMES DARRYL	IN	10E	73
BASHAW DAVID	NJ	08E	15
BASILE PATRICK LYNN	CA	21W	98
BASILIERE RALPH	MA	07E	67
BASINGER RICHARD LOUIS	OH	19E	92
BASNETT JERRY DALE	MO	19E	92
BASNIGHT RALPH WOOD	VA	06W	73
BASON WILLIAM ALFRED II	AL	04E	136
BASS BUDROW JR	LA	42E	13
BASS CHARLES WILLIAM	IA	03E	69
BASS DAVID HARUM	NC	18E	118
BASS DUNCAN EDWARD JR	FL	12E	84
BASS GARY NOLAN	CA	09E	73
BASS GEORGE CLINGER	TX	04W	26
BASS HARRY WAYNE JR	OH	53W	16
BASS JACKIE DENNIS	GA	23W	24
BASS JAMES HENRY JR	TN	34E	83
BASS JOE HARRELL	TX	28E	99
BASS JOHN DABNEY	VA	07W	84
BASS RONALD WAYNE	VA	16E	77
BASS ROY LEE	AL	14W	2
BASS SEYMOUR R	NJ	60E	8
BASS WILLIAM THOMAS JR	MI	20W	17
BASSETT ROY DOUGLAS JR	FL	15W	71
BASSIGNANI WILLIAM JOHN	VT	19W	58
BASSO MICHELE	NY	38E	20
BAST ALBERT FRANK JR	MN	15W	49
BAST PAUL G	MI	02W	103
BASTARACHE FIDELE JOSEPH	MA	65W	5
BASTIAN MICHAEL FRANCIS	NJ	35W	19
BASTYR DOUGLAS BRUCE	CA	31W	43
BATCHELDER WILLIAM KIMBAL	MA	20E	81
BATCHELDER WILLIAM ROBERT	ME	02E	6
BATCHELOR CHARLES EDWARD	TN	10W	93
BATCHELOR JOHN ELSEY JR	MS	27W	28
BATCHELOR MARTIN T JR	NC	31W	43
BATCHELOR MAX WAYNE	IN	27E	47
BATCHER LARRY GENE	FL	07W	127
BATEMAN JAMES AUSTIN	IL	24W	24
BATEMAN JAMES RONALD	MS	43E	65
BATEMAN JAMES TERENCE	OR	13W	21
BATEMAN JESSIE RAYMOND	AR	17W	100
BATEMAN MARK ANDREW	AZ	27E	43
BATEMAN NEIL ELLIS	NY	19E	125

NAME	STATE	PANEL NO.	LINE NO.
BATEMAN RAYMOND	MO	53W	32
BATEMAN WILLARD THURMAN	TX	30E	53
BATES BRIAN WILLIAM	AZ	39E	79
BATES CARL CALVIN JR	AR	19W	53
BATES GLEN DOUGLAS	NJ	29E	9
BATES HARRY E	KY	37W	61
BATES JAMES EDWARD	CA	70W	1
BATES JAMES JOHN	NY	16E	110
BATES JAMES LEON	MD	63W	14
BATES LARRY LEE	IL	38W	48
BATES MELVIN CARROLL JR	MD	07W	20
BATES NORMAN WILLIAM	KY	34E	13
BATES PAUL JENNINGS JR	AZ	03W	127
BATES RICHARD STANLEY	NJ	10E	104
BATES ROBERT ANTHONY	IL	11E	96
BATES ROBERT JR	MD	21W	98
BATES ROBERT MICHAEL	NY	29E	56
BATES ROBERT W	MO	25E	4
BATES RONALD JOSEPH	NJ	20W	79
BATES TERRY HOYTE	AR	40W	36
BATES VIRGIL JAY JR	IL	03W	128
BATES WAYNE SHERWOOD	CA	33E	55
BATESEL DENNIS GORDON	MO	07W	8
BATH ELDRIDGE JACK	CA	43E	3
BATH JOHN MICHAEL	CT	43W	45
BATISTA-RODRIGUEZ JORGE L	NY	54W	1
BATISTE CLEVELAND JR	LA	20E	71
BATISTE JOHN MILLIAN	LA	07E	106
BATOR WILLIAM HENRY	OH	13E	26
BATOZYNSKI CHARLES HENRY	MI	43E	13
BATSON JAMES CHARLES	CT	17E	48
BATSON MICHAEL OLAN	TX	15E	38
BATSON ROBERT FILMORE	TX	02E	54
BATSON WAYLAND JESS	NC	18E	74
BATT DARYLE WAYNE	IA	26W	59
BATT MICHAEL LERO	OH	29W	50
BATT ROGER LEE	IL	34E	47
BATTAGLIA AUGUST THOMAS	IL	49E	39
BATTAGLIA CHRISTOPHER PAU	CA	50E	11
BATTAGLIA PHILIP J JR	FL	40W	63
BATTEL ANTHONY BRIAN	NJ	14W	73
BATTEN JAMES EARNEST	VA	24E	58
BATTERSON JOHN PEDDIE JR	NY	22W	84
BATTERTON TROY HILLIS	KY	12W	106
BATTIEST ANDREW	CA	55W	32
BATTIN DARRELL GENE	MI	17W	39
BATTISTA ANTHONY JOSEPH	PA	06E	116
BATTISTA FRANCIS DUANE	NJ	29E	70
BATTLE HAROLD JAMES	AL	03E	42
BATTLE JOHN HENRY	FL	02W	10
BATTLE JOSEPH CHRISS	TX	41E	15
BATTLE RONALD KENNETH	FL	29W	86
BATTLE ULYSSES	IL	32W	52
BATTLE WILLIAM ALFRED	DC	53W	32
BATTLES CHARLES EDWARD	OH	21W	30
BATTLES TROY CLEVELAND	IL	33E	55
BATTON CURTIS LEE	NC	42W	14
BATTS LARRY	IL	02W	121
BATTS PERCILL	MO	14W	129
BATTS WILLIAM GEORGE	FL	18W	23
BATTY DENNY ALBERT	CA	31E	83
BAUCHIERO HAROLD	CA	25E	18
BAUCHMANN EARL JOHN	CT	10E	116
BAUCOM JAMES FREDERICK	MI	41E	58
BAUDER JAMES REGINALD	CA	10E	126
BAUER ALFRED	NJ	34W	13
BAUER CARL TIMOTHY	IL	11W	29
BAUER CHARLES JAMES JR	NY	36E	65
BAUER CRAIG ARLEN	IL	13W	43
BAUER CURTIS DEAN	CA	04W	72
BAUER DARYL CHARLES	OH	29W	4
BAUER GREGORY CHARLES	NY	30E	37
BAUER JAMES NEIL	CA	20E	84
BAUER JAMES PHILLIP	MO	14E	78
BAUER JOSEPH FREDERICK JR	MD	31W	64
BAUER KAROL RAYMOND	PA	18E	118
BAUER KENNETH LEROY	MN	04E	80
BAUER LAWRENCE EDWARD	KS	26W	81
BAUER LEO ALLEN	SD	02E	80
BAUER LEONARD WILLIAM	WI	11W	20
BAUER RICHARD GENE	AK	16W	26
BAUER ROBERT ERNEST	NY	07W	91

NAME	STATE	PANEL NO.	LINE NO.
BAUER ROBERT LOUIS	MI	61E	22
BAUER STEVEN ROBERT	MN	33W	91
BAUER TIMOTHY PAUL	OH	31W	64
BAUER WILLIAM HENRY	NY	26W	89
BAUER WILLIAM LYLE	OR	07E	15
BAUERLE FREDRICK E III	KY	52E	33
BAUGH CHARLES LEE	LA	39E	42
BAUGH FRED OTIS JR	PA	09E	61
BAUGH LARRY MICHAEL	IN	16W	7
BAUGHMAN JOHN OLIVER	KS	26W	6
BAUGHMAN RONALD GENE	IN	33W	46
BAUGHMAN WESLEY GENE	OR	55E	1
BAUGHN PHILIP WAYNE	OH	17W	93
BAUM DAVID MICHALE	IN	06W	104
BAUM DOUGLAS BRUCE	CA	30E	13
BAUM MICHAEL EDWARD	IL	08W	27
BAUM MICHAEL LEE	CA	26E	91
BAUM RORY MICHAEL	MO	20W	62
BAUMAN CHARLES W	OR	07E	79
BAUMAN RICHARD LEE	OH	04W	54
BAUMANN LANNY ROSS	NE	20W	62
BAUMANN LUDWIG GEORGE	NJ	33W	18
BAUMANN OTTO WILLIAM JR	NJ	13E	89
BAUMANN RENE GEORGES	CA	55E	1
BAUMBERGER RICHARD L JR	OH	25W	4
BAUMER JAMES CHARLES	OH	14W	51
BAUMERT BRENT JOHN	ID	06E	135
BAUMGARDNER DAVID LEON	CA	05E	112
BAUMGARDNER DUANE ROY	CA	23W	43
BAUMGARDNER THOMAS EDI JR	TX	03W	69
BAUMGARNER RAYMOND ERVIN	NC	29W	35
BAUMGART ROBERT LEE	WI	55E	39
BAUN DAVID ELROY	PA	08E	110
BAURLE MATTHEW JOHN	NY	23W	13
BAUSCH BARRY RALPH	NY	25W	60
BAUSCH DAVID ALAN	NJ	01W	29
BAUTISTA JESUS ESTRADA	AZ	55E	1
BAUZA-PEREZ JUAN	PR	35W	57
BAWAL ROBERT JOSEPH	MI	31E	43
BAX BERNARD HERMAN	MO	11W	129
BAXLEY BOBBY	NC	17W	80
BAXLEY DENNIS WAYNE	CA	08W	97
BAXTER BOBBIE RAY	MO	13W	55
BAXTER BRUCE RAYMOND	MA	29E	47
BAXTER DENNIS WARREN	NJ	14E	78
BAXTER IVERY LEE	CA	08W	97
BAXTER JAMES COLON	FL	45W	4
BAXTER JERRY	CA	28W	57
BAXTER JOHN STANLEY	MI	46W	37
BAXTER KENNETH CARL	IA	53E	27
BAXTER LARRY LEE	MO	25W	61
BAXTER PETER WALTER	NY	08E	114
BAXTER ROGER BRUCE	TX	11W	108
BAXTER TERRY DON	OK	11W	120
BAXTER TERRY LEE	FL	47E	58
BAY RONALD STEPHEN	AZ	13W	56
BAYES THOMAS JOSEPH	NY	48E	38
BAYLES GERALD WILLIAM	CA	07E	130
BAYLES STEPHEN ERNEST	CA	16W	51
BAYLISS PAUL M	VA	12E	36
BAYLOR ARTHUR JEROME	MD	06E	93
BAYLOR HAROLD BOOKER T	OH	62E	14
BAYNE JAMES TERENCE	OK	10E	112
BAYNE MICHAEL JOHN	AZ	04W	84
BAYNES ERNEST JOHN	CT	43W	11
BAYONET THOMAS WYLIE	FL	40W	70
BAYRON BENEDICTO PIOSALAN	HI	03E	64
BAYS LEE R	CA	15E	38
BAYS PAUL EUGENE	WV	01E	89
BAYSINGER DONALD FREEMAN	WA	30W	84
BAZA JOSEPH CRUZ	CA	45E	37
BAZAN ISIDRO SIGFREDO	NM	53W	16
BAZAR PAUL THOMAS	NE	26W	18
BAZEL MICHAEL GEORGE	IL	11W	48
BAZELL FRANK DAVID	CA	15E	124
BAZEMORE EARL SHERMAN	MD	46W	26
BAZEMORE THOMAS WAYNE	ME	19W	76
BAZEMORE WILLIAM HODGES	VA	26W	24
BAZULTO SALVADOR	CA	27E	92
BAZZINOTTI CHARLES A	MA	10W	31
BAZZLE DAVID WAYNE	NC	29W	51
BEACH ARTHUR JAMES	CA	06E	25

NAME	STATE	PANEL NO.	LINE NO.
BEACH DEAN L	MI	41W	21
BEACH FLOYD IRVY	IA	15W	89
BEACH HAROLD DEAN	NC	25W	27
BEACH LEO ALBERT JR	MI	07W	82
BEACH MYRON STANLEY JR	NY	23E	40
BEACH SAM FESTIS JR	AZ	34E	61
BEACHAM EDWARD EARL	MS	66W	1
BEACHAM WARREN LEE	NC	30W	9
BEADLE HARRY JOSEPH JR	PA	61W	10
BEADNELL WILLIAM LEE	VA	15W	101
BEAGLE FRANCIS WAYNE	OH	04E	53
BEAGLE HOWARD EUGENE	NY	18E	8
BEAL GEORGE WILLIE JR	OH	10W	48
BEALE GEORGE EUGENE	OH	43E	13
BEALE MILLS III	VA	25W	46
BEALE ROBERT BOUGHTON	NY	16E	99
BEALIN TROY	LA	12E	118
BEALL CHARLES RICHARD	FL	43E	13
BEALL ROGER CLOYCE	IA	34W	90
BEALL TYSON VANCE	CA	25W	9
BEALL WILLIAM EARNEST JR	CO	51W	5
BEALS ALLEN MACY	IL	17E	83
BEALS CHARLES ELBERT	IN	03W	103
BEALS LAWRENCE FREDERICK	MA	41E	16
BEALS MICHAEL ALLEN	MI	52W	35
BEALS RONNIE HERBERT	CA	32E	90
BEALS STEPHEN CARL	TX	38W	64
BEAM EARNEST LEE	OR	10E	86
BEAM ERNEST EUGENE	OK	41E	47
BEAM JACK EVAN	OH	13E	66
BEAM RAYMOND	GA	44W	45
BEAM RAYMOND GLENN	IL	34W	31
BEAM ROGER LEROY	PA	35E	36
BEAMAN ROBERT JON	CT	23W	50
BEAMAN RONALD RALPH	CA	21W	21
BEAMON THEODORE M	DC	03E	109
BEAMON THOMAS KEITH	CA	51E	36
BEAMS JAMES WOODSON	NE	24E	4
BEAN CHRISTOPHER JOHN	MA	23W	117
BEAN DAVID ELTON	PA	19W	36
BEAN DONALD WAYNE	MO	44E	13
BEAN EUGENE JR	LA	07W	96
BEAN GEORGE TYRUS	IL	18E	52
BEAN GUY ROBERT	ME	40E	72
BEAN JAMES FRANCIS	TX	23E	98
BEAN JIMMY DALE	TX	28W	32
BEAN JOHN ROBERT	FL	06W	89
BEAN KENYON ELROY	ND	20E	39
BEAN LARRY DAVID	UT	05W	60
BEAN RICHARD RAYMOND	OH	19E	69
BEAN STEPHEN LOUIS	ME	67E	4
BEANE HAROLD GEORGE JR	NY	43E	40
BEANNER ROBERT RANDOLPH	PA	58E	30
BEAR CHARLES MARTIN	OR	22W	18
BEAR DONALD EARL	OK	53W	42
BEARD ALEXANDER	AL	41W	56
BEARD ASBERRY JR	MS	18W	36
BEARD BILLIE LESTER	CA	01E	9
BEARD CHARLES C	TN	50E	44
BEARD CHARLES RAY	CO	38W	23
BEARD DONALD WAYNE	TX	01E	75
BEARD JACK ALLEN	MD	37E	31
BEARD JEFFREY LEE	OH	41W	9
BEARD LEON	VA	33W	18
BEARD LEON	KY	30W	84
BEARD WILLIAM ARTHUR	CT	30W	71
BEARDEN LEE V	AL	13E	95
BEARDEN RICHARD DEWAYNE	AL	04E	106
BEARDSLEE TERRY HUGH	MI	40W	22
BEARDSLEY JEFFREY RANDOLP	PA	38W	6
BEARDSLEY JEFFREY THOMAS	CA	13W	40
BEARDSLEY RONALD ALLEN	CA	40W	61
BEARDSLEY WILLIAM BURDON	MI	04W	60
BEARE CHARLES HAWKINS	AR	18W	118
BEARFIELD CLUSTER LEE	TN	35W	87
BEARGEON DAN WILLIAM	WA	09E	72
BEARWALD ORLAND ORRIN	WI	02E	77
BEARY DANIEL WARREN	MT	19E	115
BEASLEY DONNIE RAY	KY	16E	83
BEASLEY EDGAR HUNTER	MS	12E	12
BEASLEY EDWARD RUSSELL	TX	29W	35
BEASLEY GEORGE HUTCHINSON	AL	21W	80
BEASLEY JAMES OTIS	CO	27E	63
BEASLEY JAMES TERRY	FL	10E	45
BEASLEY JOHNNIE HAROLD	FL	55E	2
BEASLEY LUZON	MS	47E	8
BEASLEY MERRILL VAN	FL	14E	102
BEASLEY MICHAEL LAWRENCE	PA	22E	96
BEASLEY ODELL DANIEL	AR	25W	98
BEASLEY PERCY JR	IN	25E	41
BEASLEY PHILIP ARTHUR	ID	42W	45
BEASLEY ROY CLAUDE	OH	14W	64
BEASLEY WILLIAM RONALD	ID	11E	12
BEATON ROBERT LOUIS	AL	05E	59
BEATTIE DAVID ROWLAND	NJ	10E	112
BEATTIE ERICK WALTER	NY	14W	70
BEATTY DEWEY LLOYD	WA	24E	14
BEATTY DONALD EDWARD	NY	65W	4
BEATTY FREDERICK LEE	PA	05W	135
BEATTY JAMES RUSSELL	OH	19W	105
BEATTY JERRY ALLEN	PA	43E	13
BEATTY LEONARD JR	IL	38W	16
BEATTY THOMAS WILLIAM	MI	03W	73
BEATTYS LAWRENCE VICK	KY	35W	32
BEATY ARTHUR LEE	TX	58E	30
BEATY JEFFREY LANDIS	WI	15E	39
BEAUBIEN WILLIAM ALEXIS	MA	30E	53
BEAUCHAMP ALBERT ALLEN	MI	29W	51
BEAUCHAMP ERNEST MICHAEL	VA	16E	16
BEAUCHAMP JOHN HENRY JR	MD	06E	14
BEAUCHAMP KEVIN PATRICK	FL	52E	30
BEAUCHAMP RAYMOND FREDERI	OH	34W	90
BEAUDETTE LARRY MICHAEL	CA	11W	99
BEAUDOIN GAETAN JEAN GUY	NH	19W	116
BEAUFORD SAMUEL P	GA	56E	35
BEAUFORD WILLIS JR	MA	43E	13
BEAULIEU LEO VERNON	MN	07E	64
BEAULIEU NORMAND LOUIS	MA	21E	31
BEAUMONT HERBERT MICHAEL	NJ	29W	58
BEAUMONT ROBERT EUGENE	CA	33W	53
BEAUMONT WARREN MARTIN	PA	49E	28
BEAUPRE GILBERT THOMAS	NH	28E	64
BEAUREGARD KENNETH EDWARD	MA	05E	113
BEAUREGARD RICHARD MAURIC	RI	03W	11
BEAUREGARD SILVESTER	TN	48E	38
BEAVER HEARNE W	CT	09E	35
BEAVER JAMES CLARKE	IL	16W	26
BEAVER JAMES HAROLD	FL	44E	65
BEAVER JOHN DOUGLAS	MI	43E	51
BEAVER MAX RUSSELL	OK	39E	16
BEAVER MICHAEL HUGH	IA	15W	106
BEAVER ROBERT LYNN	OH	10W	78
BEAVER WESLEY	MI	29W	43
BEAVERS CHARLES EVAN	GA	28E	13
BEAVERS CHRISTOPHER WAYNE	IL	20E	21
BEAVERS FRANK ARVIS	WV	39E	28
BEAVERS JAMES DAVID	AL	01W	118
BEAVERS ROBERT ALLEN	TX	02W	4
BEAVERSON HAROLD A JR	TN	21E	20
BEBO WAYNE RICHARD	MI	11W	121
BEBUS CHARLES JAMES	MN	01W	99
BECANNEN BARRY J	MI	47W	37
BECERRA JAVIER	TX	18E	52
BECERRA RUDY MORALES	TX	12W	37
BECHARD JOHN COWIE	NY	41W	3
BECHARD RAYMOND JOSEPH	ME	30W	84
BECHTEL HERBERT STEPHEN	OH	10E	35
BECHTEL STEPHAN LEROY	KY	38E	75
BECHTOLD FRANCIS SCOTT	NY	39E	69
BECK CARL GARY	PA	18W	36
BECK DAVID MICHAEL	GA	25W	61
BECK EDGAR PETER JR	NY	05W	15
BECK EDWARD CHARLES	IL	27E	27
BECK EDWARD EUGENE JR	OH	20W	119
BECK GLEN RAY	MI	62W	19
BECK GREGORY GEORGE	CA	24W	36
BECK JAMES ROBERT	PA	40W	23
BECK JERRY DON	TX	27W	23
BECK JOHN ROBERT	NY	45W	4
BECK JOHN THERON	AL	41E	6
BECK JOSEPH ROBERT JR	PA	28E	72
BECK LARRY MONROE	OK	34W	63
BECK MARTIN ROBERT	FL	20W	38
BECK MICHAEL JAMES	CO	61W	20
BECK MICHAEL RAY	WY	06E	56
BECK NORMAN ELMER	IL	28W	17
BECK PATRICK FRANCIS	IL	02E	69
BECK RICHARD JAMES	PA	49W	7
BECK RICHARD JAMES JR	IL	60E	8
BECK ROBERT JAMES	WI	43W	24
BECK ROBERT MILTON	WI	27W	9
BECK STEVEN LEE	CA	44W	45
BECK TERRENCE DANIEL	WI	32E	29
BECK TERRY LEE	PA	17W	24
BECK WINFIELD WESLEY	FL	39E	17
BECKER CHARLES WARNER	IL	18W	83
BECKER GARY EDWARD	IL	66W	1
BECKER HARRY MATHIAS	MT	50W	41
BECKER HOWARD JOHN JR	IL	03W	107
BECKER JAMES CHRISTOF	TX	08W	113
BECKER JAMES FRANCIS	AZ	23W	19
BECKER JOHN BERTRAM	KY	46W	37
BECKER JOHN JOSEPH JR	OH	10E	12
BECKER JOHN PAUL	WI	11W	83
BECKER LESTER ERWIN	IL	03E	118
BECKER MICHAEL PAUL	NE	59W	19
BECKER THOMAS ALEXANDER	PA	30W	51
BECKER THOMAS LEWIS	WI	39W	25
BECKER TOMMY JOE	MI	01W	2
BECKER WALTER WARD	TX	22W	71
BECKER WILLIAM JOHN	NY	14W	16
BECKERMANN FRED B JR	CA	08E	122
BECKERS JOHN PAUL	SD	23W	82
BECKETT JOHN WESLEY	NM	33E	15
BECKETT RONALD LEE	MI	18E	99
BECKHAM JERRY LEE	OK	20E	39
BECKLEY GEORGE EDWARD	MS	09W	17
BECKMAN DOUGLAS MARTIN	VA	05W	32
BECKMAN KENNETH BRYANT	TN	14W	24
BECKMAN ROBERT CARL	NY	16W	55
BECKMAN ROBERT CHARLES	MI	19W	65
BECKMANN LOUIS MARTIN	MO	29W	58
BECKMEYER FREDRICK HALL	IL	37E	18
BECKNER JAMES MALCOLM	VA	01E	66
BECKSTED RONALD JAMES	OH	04W	84
BECKWITH EDWARD COE	LA	49E	29
BECKWITH HARRY MEDFOR III	MI	04W	72
BECKWITH RICHARD EARL	NY	42E	2
BECKWITH WALTER LEE JR	FL	13W	87
BECKWITH WILLIAM ARNOLD	OR	53W	11
BECKWITH WILLIAM HENRY	MN	43E	65
BECKWORTH HARLEY DANIEL	GA	03E	69
BEDAL ARTHUR EUGENE	CA	01E	26
BEDARD BARRY JOSEPH	CA	16W	114
BEDDINGFIELD GEORGE CLYDE	NC	13E	23
BEDDOE PAUL MELVIN JR	OR	35E	2
BEDELL JAMES WAYNE	IN	21W	73
BEDFORD CHARLES	TX	33W	75
BEDFORD WILLIE	WI	11W	89
BEDGOOD JAMES DOUGLAS	LA	19E	103
BEDGOOD JIMMY	GA	55E	39
BEDIENT ROSS EDWARD	NY	08W	14
BEDKER ROBERT	VA	10E	69
BEDNAR STEPHEN ANDREW	PA	03W	107
BEDNAREK JONATHAN BRUCE	NY	01W	27
BEDNARZ WILLIAM WALTER	IL	20E	5
BEDOLLA JOSEPH LOPEZ	CA	35E	30
BEDRA THEODORE FRANK	CA	07W	8
BEDROCK ALAN	NJ	10W	111
BEDROSIAN DAVID PETER J	MA	16W	72
BEDROSSIAN GEORGE J	RI	57E	14
BEDSOLE CHARLES ARTHUR	MD	56W	11
BEDSWORTH BILLIE MICHAEL	CA	15W	127
BEDWELL SAMMIE LEE	TN	04E	117
BEDWELL WAYNE JOSEPH	NY	56E	1
BEDWORTH GRIFFITH BRONSON	CT	31E	9
BEE ROSS MICHAEL	ID	14E	52
BEEBE JERRY RAY	MN	23E	16
BEEBE LARRY CHARLES	PA	26W	105
BEEBE LARRY DWAYNE	MI	14W	51
BEEBE RICHARD WILLIAM	NY	07W	118
BEECH HARRY DAVID JR	PA	27W	92
BEECHE RAFAEL EDUARDO	CA	09E	31
BEECHER QUENTIN RIPPETOE	IN	21E	93
BEECHING EARL PETER	NY	24W	73
BEECK RONALD MARVIN	IA	48E	23

NAME	STATE	PANEL NO.	LINE NO.
BEECY GREGORY WILLIAM	MA	07W	125
BEEDY GEORGE	OH	06W	90
BEEK ERWIN	NY	30E	13
BEEK JOHN LAWRENCE	CA	14W	82
BEELER CLIFFORD DOIL	OK	14E	121
BEELER GEORGE FREDRICK	MO	08W	61
BEELER RUSSELL RICHARD	IL	13W	72
BEENE JAMES ALVIN	CA	11E	48
BEER MERLIN GAIL	IN	16W	57
BEERES GEORGE KEVIN	NJ	05E	24
BEERS CARL WILLIAM JR	MO	35W	23
BEERS EDWARD NELSON	PA	66E	6
BEERS JACK BLAINE	TN	27W	28
BEESLER CHARLES WILLIAM	OH	20W	94
BEESLEY GARY EVANS	MO	22E	36
BEESON MORRIS SAMPSON	LA	28W	8
BEESON ROBERT BRUCE	NE	19E	35
BEESON ROBERT HENRY JR	CO	21E	8
BEESON WILLIAM DALE	IN	38W	64
BEGAN JOHN LESTER	OH	48W	22
BEGAYE EDDIE CHARLES	NM	20E	100
BEGAYE FELIX DOHALTAHE	NM	31E	70
BEGGS LARKIN MCDONALD JR	FL	07E	44
BEGGS TERRY KENT	TX	03W	65
BEGLAU DAVID BERNARD	OR	03W	112
BEGLEY BURRISS NELSON	KY	13E	13
BEGLEY JACK PERRY JR	OK	04W	118
BEGLINGER THOMAS EDWIN	NY	11E	35
BEGNOCHE REGINALD PETER	VT	18W	31
BEGODY HAROLD L	AZ	39E	28
BEGOSH MARTIN JOHN	MD	48W	37
BEGOTKA JOSEPH LLOYD	WI	35E	43
BEHAN WILLIAM GERALD	PA	58E	4
BEHAR DANIEL SIMON	IL	24W	57
BEHLKE GERALD DENNIS	WI	20E	81
BEHM CHARLES JOEL JR	OH	53E	9
BEHM CHRIS ROGER	FL	02W	30
BEHM DANIEL LOUIS	MI	14W	61
BEHM STANLEY WILLIAM	CA	60E	18
BEHNFELDT ROGER ERNEST	OH	01W	68
BEHNKE RICHARD CARL	WI	28W	96
BEHRENS PETER CLAUS	MO	06W	105
BEHRENS THOMAS MARTIN	IA	40W	61
BEHRENS WILLIAM CHARLES	WI	35E	86
BEHRENT MARK SYLVESTER	WI	09W	56
BEHRNS RICHARD JOHN	IL	23E	108
BEIER ELROY EUGENE	ND	55E	2
BEIERLE THOMAS LAWRENCE	IL	37E	77
BEILE FRED	MO	16E	75
BEILFUSS EDWARD ALAN JR	WI	28E	107
BEIRNE MICHAEL JAMES	IL	19E	77
BEITLICH JOHN WILLARD	WI	17W	119
BEJARANO ADOLFO MARTINEZ	TX	41W	51
BEKIEMPIS THOMAS CHESTER	NJ	17E	60
BEKSI WILLIAM JOSEPH	NJ	15W	26
BELANCIN GEORGE JOHN	PA	45W	30
BELAND WILLIAM ANTHONY	IL	20E	109
BELANDER DONN WHITNEY	UT	15W	76
BELANGER ALBERT LEE	ME	18W	77
BELANGER GEORGE	ME	11E	102
BELANGER GEORGE HENRY	MA	37W	20
BELANGER JOSEPH KENNETH L	ME	01E	84
BELANGER PAUL EDWARD	ME	35W	87
BELARDE BENJAMIN JOSEPH	CO	46E	28
BELARSKI RONALD DALE	PA	07W	3
BELASCO CHARLES THEODORE	NY	48W	37
BELCHAK PAUL JR	IL	62W	20
BELCHER FRANK EDWARD	MI	59W	19
BELCHER FRED ARTHUR	NJ	44W	45
BELCHER GLENN ARTHUR	ND	33E	6
BELCHER HERBERT EUGENE	GA	28W	96
BELCHER JORDAN	KY	52E	33
BELCHER ROBERT ARTHUR	LA	28W	65
BELCHER ROBERT WINSLOW	MA	49E	19
BELCHER ROLAND	OH	34E	4
BELCHER STEPHEN EDWIN	MD	27W	14
BELCHER TED	WV	12E	86
BELCHER TOMMY JOE	OH	01E	88
BELCHER VERNON EUGENE	IL	50W	38
BELDEN LARRY GENE	KS	20W	46
BELDING CARL FRANK JR	WA	32W	88
BELEW GREG BLAINE	UT	37E	78
BELEY JERRY	OH	25E	81
BELFIELD ANDREW LEE	NC	32W	89
BELFLOWER JAMES H	GA	26W	42
BELFORD JOHN ARTHUR	MI	32W	11
BELICOSE RICHARD J	NJ	20E	53
BELINGE RICHARD LEWIS	MO	46E	29
BELINSKI JAMES GERALD	MI	54W	26
BELKNAP HARRY JOHN	NC	08E	78
BELKNAP RONALD LEE	CA	09E	110
BELL ALBERT LEE	TX	15W	34
BELL ARTHUR FREDERICK	MS	25W	61
BELL CHARLES ARTHUR	PA	06E	13
BELL CHARLES MARTIN	KS	33E	25
BELL CHRISTOPHER HIAWATHA	NC	44E	65
BELL CHRISTOPHER JAMES	MD	24W	114
BELL DAVID LEROY	HI	32W	31
BELL DAVID LYNN	TN	23W	109
BELL DAVID THOMAS	OH	55W	6
BELL DAVID TOMIE	AL	15E	93
BELL DEAN ALLAN	MO	45W	47
BELL DEXTER	MI	43W	60
BELL DONNELL	IL	41E	16
BELL DOYLE LYNN	TX	32E	16
BELL EDGAR DEWAYNE	OK	45E	7
BELL EDWARD ALLEN	CA	37W	28
BELL EDWARD JAMES	TX	18E	67
BELL ELIAS JR	MI	02E	36
BELL ELVIE JR	NC	31W	89
BELL GARY JOSEPH	FL	42E	61
BELL GEORGE A JR	MD	05E	73
BELL GEORGE BENJAMIN	NM	12E	112
BELL GERALD DEAN	CA	23W	19
BELL GILBERT STEVENS JR	ME	36W	17
BELL HARDY LEE	TX	12E	118
BELL HARRISON	TX	08W	19
BELL HENRY DANIEL JR	CA	14W	82
BELL HOARD CLAYTON	CA	39E	28
BELL HOLLY GENE	TX	14W	73
BELL HOMER B JR	TN	60E	18
BELL JAMES B JR	FL	19E	3
BELL JAMES EDWARD	MI	51E	27
BELL JAMES EVERRETT	CA	61W	20
BELL JAMES LYLE	KY	18E	83
BELL JAMES WILLIAM	IL	32W	47
BELL JEROME	AL	48W	22
BELL JERRY LEE	TN	17E	17
BELL JERRY W	IL	07E	79
BELL JIM GLENN JR	NV	40W	59
BELL JOE EDGAR	OH	15E	8
BELL JOHN DARVIN	GA	09W	59
BELL JOHN HENRY	IL	05E	112
BELL JOHN JR	FL	02E	54
BELL JOHN MARTIN	CA	49E	39
BELL LARRY DEAN	IL	03E	40
BELL LARRY GENE	NJ	19W	127
BELL LEO JR	IL	23E	115
BELL LEON EARL	NJ	22E	94
BELL LEONARD JONATHEN	NY	58E	19
BELL LEROY LEMUEL	FL	19W	124
BELL LESLIE RAVEN	TX	19W	124
BELL LESTER	FL	16E	50
BELL LEWIS DOUGLAS	TX	05E	113
BELL MALCOLM FRANK	FL	25W	46
BELL MARK WAYNE	CA	23W	117
BELL MARVIN EARL	AR	09W	102
BELL MARVIN VINCENT	NC	43W	58
BELL MICHAEL DEAN	TX	38W	54
BELL NEWTON THOMAS JR	SC	19W	58
BELL OLIVER JR	FL	27E	105
BELL OSCAR CHARLIE JR	AZ	09E	54
BELL PAUL M	TN	04E	88
BELL REGINALD CONRAD	NC	50E	11
BELL RICHARD WILLIAM	PA	17W	24
BELL ROBERT GRAHAM	TX	01E	116
BELL ROGER DALE	NC	45W	35
BELL RONALD EUGENE	MO	58W	6
BELL RUBEN JR	FL	33E	42
BELL SAMUEL WAYNE	CA	25W	35
BELL STEVEN ALLEN	IN	28W	18
BELL THOMAS LYNN	IN	16E	128
BELL WAYNE MORRIS	MI	41W	52
BELL WILLIAM	PA	26E	77
BELL WILLIAM BRENT	NJ	28W	57
BELL WILLIAM JR	VA	02W	88
BELLACH LOUIS WILLIAM JR	NY	27E	18
BELLAIRE JOHN MICHAEL	MI	16W	61
BELLAMY ANTHONY RODNEY	ID	55E	3
BELLAMY JOHN MICHAEL	CA	23W	70
BELLAMY LARRY RONALD	FL	39W	25
BELLAMY PAUL ROBERT	OR	35E	2
BELLAMY ROBERT LEE	FL	45E	53
BELLAMY ROLAND ROBERT	NY	45E	61
BELLAMY SIMMIE JR	SC	05E	78
BELLAMY WESLEY EARL	KY	23E	81
BELLANGER JOHN GEORGE	MN	39E	29
BELLANT FRANK LEROY	MI	25E	55
BELLEMARE ANDRE REMI	NY	33W	5
BELLER WILLIAM RUSSELL JR	KS	18E	118
BELLERIVE DAVID LESLIE	MA	34W	36
BELLES JOHN DAVID	IL	41W	56
BELLETTI ANTHONY JOHN	PA	40W	17
BELLEW GUY LESTER	GA	27E	98
BELLILE WILLIAM MARVIN	WI	23W	117
BELLINGER RONALD LEE	NY	54W	40
BELLINO PAUL GEORGE	MA	24W	36
BELLOMO TERRENCE JOHN	CA	45E	48
BELLOMY WILLARD GORDON	AL	48W	38
BELLRICHARD LESLIE ALLEN	CA	20E	54
BELLWOOD RICHARD ROY	NY	34W	73
BELNAP GLEN DEAN	CA	32E	29
BELON MARC BRADLEY	CA	10W	38
BELONGER DENNIS MICHAEL	WI	20W	17
BELSAR KENNETH RAY	PA	34E	65
BELSLY STEVEN DALE	IL	26W	89
BELT ARTHUR LAVINE	AL	35W	23
BELT CECIL DELBERT JR	OK	34E	66
BELT MARVIN MARK	NY	04E	39
BELT ROBERT ERIC	TX	24W	2
BELTON CALVIN	CT	22E	123
BELTON JAMES	SC	03E	29
BELTON RAY	NC	13E	115
BELTON THEODORE	SC	45E	38
BELTRAM AUGUSTINE JR	TX	28E	13
BELTRAN ANASTACIO HERNAND	TX	15E	47
BELTRAN FRANK JOSEPH	NY	49W	46
BELTRAN ROBERT JOSEPH	CA	07W	127
BELTRAN ROBERT LEON	CA	36W	10
BELTZ JOHN DAVID	MO	12E	17
BELVEAL JAMES ALLEN	CA	30E	22
BELVER DAVID EUGENE	RI	32W	89
BEM WALTER PAUL	PA	26W	81
BEMBENEK MARLIN EDWIN	MN	11E	117
BEMBOOM HERBERT DONALD	MO	08W	1
BEMBRY SNYDER PATTISHALL	GA	03E	69
BEMIS EARLE JOHN	GA	23W	35
BENADUM RICHARD DENNIS	CA	16E	129
BENAIM GILBERT ALBERT	LA	14W	33
BENAK JOSEPH FRANK	FL	15W	47
BENALLIE DAVID HOWARD	UT	17W	60
BENAVENTE DAVID GUERRERO	GM	03E	110
BENAVIDEZ BENJAMIN JOHN	NM	04W	121
BENAVIDEZ TRINO BALTAZAR	TX	15W	15
BENBOW EVANS JR	NY	25W	93
BENCH CLIFFORD EUGENE	OH	04W	52
BENCHER ALVIN KENNETH		54W	36
BENDER GARY DEAN	IA	22W	56
BENDER GERNOT	GA	28W	32
BENDER IVYL RAY	IA	37E	48
BENDER LARRY WARREN	WI	62W	5
BENDOR JOHN LEE	CA	29W	4
BENDORF DAVID GLEN	WI	20E	54
BENEDETT DANIEL ANDREW	WA	01W	129
BENEDETTI DENNIS EUGENE	MI	12E	131
BENEDETTI VINCENT MARIO	RI	03W	43
BENEDICT JOSEPH WAYNE	FL	34E	74
BENEDICT ROBERT JOHN	WI	30W	71
BENEDIK NORMAN FLORIAN	PA	16W	68
BENEFIEL DUDLEY JAMES JR	IL	23W	5
BENEGAS VINCENT JOSEPH	CA	18E	55
BENES WAYNE JOSEPH	CA	41W	73
BENFIELD DON CURTIS	GA	17E	120
BENFORD JONAS	IL	47W	5
BENGE LARRY WAYNE	TX	42E	15
BENGE SAMUEL EDWARD	IN	23W	50

NAME	STATE	PANEL NO.	LINE NO.
BENGE THOMAS CLAYTON	IN	22E	60
BENGEN ARTHUR BURTON	WA	16W	11
BENGTSON FRANK WALTER	MA	03W	25
BENGTSON ROBERT DAVID	MN	28W	78
BENICEK JAMES MILTON	WI	07W	100
BENICEWICZ RICHARD C	CT	29W	96
BENIEN JOHN DAVID	OK	32W	24
BENIGNI ALFREDO	PA	41E	59
BENISHEK FREDERICK LEE	WI	23W	95
BENITEZ JUAN	TX	02E	124
BENITEZ RAFAEL RIVERA	PR	05W	86
BENITEZ-RIVERA JOSE EMILIO	PR	55W	17
BENJAMIN FREDDIE JAMES	LA	30E	22
BENJAMIN GARY THOMAS	MA	18W	57
BENJAMIN JEFFERY JAMES	CO	10W	94
BENJAMIN KENNETH ROGER	MA	31E	63
BENJAMIN PHILLIP ERNEST	MD	35W	25
BENJAMIN RICHARD	AL	37E	48
BENJAMIN ROBERT LEE	LA	07E	92
BENJAMIN ROBERT WILLIAM	HI	39W	11
BENKE RONALD JOHN III	MD	05E	41
BENKERT PAUL ANTHONY	WA	13E	120
BENN PHILIP CRAIG	NJ	46E	40
BENN WILLIAM PAUL	NJ	23W	82
BENNEFELD STEVEN HENRY	KS	24E	15
BENNER FRED ALFRED	IL	06E	108
BENNETT ANTHONY HERCULES	OK	24E	117
BENNETT ANTHONY LEE	AZ	62W	8
BENNETT BENJAMIN F JR	LA	17W	116
BENNETT BENTFORD	NC	08E	81
BENNETT BILLY JOE	TN	25E	81
BENNETT BRIAN JOHN	CA	08W	114
BENNETT BRUCE ROLLA	ID	10E	70
BENNETT CHARLES DUANE	GA	53W	32
BENNETT CHARLES EDWIN	TX	37E	78
BENNETT CHARLES HERMAN	NC	16E	7
BENNETT CLIFFORD RAYMOND	NY	35E	65
BENNETT CLIFTON E	CA	09E	110
BENNETT CLYDE JAMES	KY	16W	3
BENNETT DAN MICHAEL	WI	36W	10
BENNETT DANIEL JOSEPH	CA	02E	38
BENNETT DANIEL MORRIS	FL	12E	70
BENNETT DANIEL MURPHY	AL	07W	16
BENNETT DARL D	OH	07E	127
BENNETT DONALD CASPER	OH	04W	84
BENNETT DONALD CHARLES JR	PA	42E	2
BENNETT DONALD LEE	MI	16E	56
BENNETT DONALD LUCIAN	CA	02E	82
BENNETT DOUGLAS ALVIN	WV	18W	13
BENNETT DWIGHT FARWELL JR	IL	31E	2
BENNETT DWIGHT LLOYD	OK	24E	53
BENNETT EDWARD DALE	IN	58W	17
BENNETT FRANK EVERETT	RI	01E	100
BENNETT GEORGE DEWEY	NC	20E	110
BENNETT GEORGE ROGERS	GA	52E	13
BENNETT GEORGE WILLY JR	TX	11W	108
BENNETT HAROLD GEORGE	AR	01E	79
BENNETT HOWARD DUNCAN	FL	37E	3
BENNETT JACOB	AL	52W	40
BENNETT JAMES HARRELL JR	MO	28E	100
BENNETT JAMES HARVEY	KY	39E	42
BENNETT JAMES STEPHEN	GA	53E	9
BENNETT JERRY CLAUD	OK	26E	77
BENNETT JOHN ARTHUR	GA	18W	92
BENNETT JOHN JAY	NY	13W	73
BENNETT JOHN WILLIE	OH	17W	76
BENNETT JOSEPH RICHARD	PA	51E	44
BENNETT KENNETH DEVON	MI	10W	21
BENNETT LARRY DARRALL	OK	41W	72
BENNETT MARTIN LEE	IA	41E	59
BENNETT MARVIN DALE	TX	14E	85
BENNETT MELVIN LESLIE	AL	04E	122
BENNETT MICHAEL E	NH	28E	107
BENNETT PHILIP MARK	CA	10W	22
BENNETT PRENTICE J	TN	52W	40
BENNETT RICHARD BOYCE	UT	26W	96
BENNETT RICHARD CHARLES	IL	24E	98
BENNETT RICHARD JAY	NY	25W	61
BENNETT ROBERT DAVID	OH	01E	14
BENNETT ROBERT ELWOOD III	NJ	31E	85
BENNETT ROBERT HORACE	MS	06W	38
BENNETT ROBERT LEWIS	FL	24E	15
BENNETT ROBERT LLOYD	CA	32W	89
BENNETT ROBERT M	CA	20E	127
BENNETT ROBERT VERNON	LA	58E	19
BENNETT RONALD DAVID	LA	28E	72
BENNETT STEVEN LOGAN	LA	01W	51
BENNETT THOMAS EVANS	MA	04W	2
BENNETT THOMAS WARING JR	MS	01W	103
BENNETT THOMAS WILLIAM	WV	32W	10
BENNETT VICTOR RAYMOND JR	OH	04W	84
BENNETT WAYNE	AZ	10W	55
BENNETT WILLIAM GEORGE	AL	25E	81
BENNETT WILLIAM RAYMOND	AZ	12E	131
BENNEY KENDAL LEE JR	MI	25E	18
BENNING WILLIAM DONAVAN	PA	01E	113
BENOIST WILLIAM F III	IL	07W	33
BENOIT FRANCIS ARTHUR	MN	16E	88
BENOIT GARLAND DAVE	LA	12W	16
BENOIT PAUL BRIAN	VA	15W	3
BENOIT ROBERT CHARLES JR	MI	18W	53
BENOSKI JOSEPH JR	AL	12W	48
BENSBERG ROBERT TRAME	CO	24W	114
BENSE JOHN FREDERICK JR	PA	18E	40
BENSON ALBERT DU WARD	IA	21W	68
BENSON ALLAN CAMERON	IL	25W	61
BENSON ARNOLD JR	PA	25E	114
BENSON DALE EARL	IA	14E	31
BENSON DAVID EUGENE	GA	02E	86
BENSON DENNIS GUY	MA	36W	67
BENSON GERALD ALLEN	WI	36W	43
BENSON GUYE RAYMOND	TX	16E	129
BENSON JOSEPH	OH	25E	4
BENSON JOSEPH HENNING	MT	17W	49
BENSON KEITH LLOYD	CA	28E	102
BENSON LEE DAVID	CA	45E	10
BENSON MARTIN JOSEPH	MN	13W	57
BENSON RAYMOND EDDIE	WY	18E	74
BENSON ROBERT JOHN	MI	48E	23
BENSON ROBERT WILLIAM	CA	36W	47
BENSON STANLEY J	OR	07E	1
BENT GORDON WILLIAM	MI	16W	68
BENTFELD JOHN JOSEPH	OH	14E	107
BENTFORD ANANIAS	AL	10W	112
BENTLEY BORIS ROMAN BENJA	CA	24E	70
BENTLEY COBBIE JAMES	AL	26E	78
BENTLEY DUANE RUSSELL	OR	25E	36
BENTLEY JAMES E JR	TN	41E	16
BENTLEY WALTER EARL	CT	29E	1
BENTON ARNOLD RAY	IN	04W	13
BENTON BENJAMIN PERRY	NC	34W	31
BENTON CARROLL JOE	MO	03W	73
BENTON CHARLIE CORBETT	NC	09W	123
BENTON GREGORY REA JR	CA	24W	81
BENTON HENRY	FL	07E	92
BENTON HENRY EDWIN JR	NC	48W	32
BENTON JAMES AUSTIN	TN	18E	100
BENTON JOHNNY WILLIAM	ID	38W	54
BENTON JOSEPH TATEM	NC	05E	44
BENTON ROBERT DANIEL	AZ	11E	125
BENTON THOMAS HOWARD	CA	26E	110
BENTSON PETER MORGAN	CT	01W	55
BENTSON RUSSEL DEAN	UT	28E	72
BENVENUTO THEODORE F JR	NY	19W	8
BENWAY JAMES DWIGHT	WI	09E	9
BENZ ROBERT JOSEPH	NY	44W	45
BENZE PATRICK HENRY	NE	28W	42
BENZEL RICHARD DALE	OR	01E	14
BENZING BRUCE MARTIN	FL	30E	37
BERAN FRANK HENRY III	TX	20E	54
BERAN NICHOLAS MICHAEL JR	IL	22E	64
BERANEK CHARLES SYLVESTER	WI	57W	16
BERANEK DEAN MITCHELL	WI	23E	109
BERARD JAMES EUGENE	CA	15E	29
BERBERT KARL ROBERT	CA	04W	107
BERBLINGER KENNETH MICHAE	IL	02W	55
BERCIER KENNETH SANDFORD	MT	14W	74
BERDAHL DAVID DONALD	ND	02W	98
BERDY MICHAEL EDWARD	NY	32E	61
BERECH LAWRENCE PAUL	WA	19E	42
BEREK MICHAEL STANLEY	IL	23E	68
BERENDS JAMES	MD	32W	90
BERENWICK WILLIAM MICHAEL	NJ	15E	39
BERESIK EUGENE PAUL	MA	62W	5
BERG BRUCE ALLAN	WA	03W	125
BERG DALE RUSS	NY	27E	27
BERG GARY RICHARD	MI	37W	48
BERG GEORGE PHILLIP	NJ	05W	114
BERG GERALD LEROY	PA	08E	117
BERG HAROLD EDWARD JR	ND	14E	110
BERG HAROLD PETER	IA	29W	59
BERG JOHN STEPHEN	NJ	23E	73
BERG JOHN VERNON	NC	40W	56
BERG JULIAN WINSLOW	MN	26W	30
BERG MYRON WALDO	CA	12W	106
BERG RALPH RUSSELL	MA	43E	40
BERG RAY WILLIAM JR	CA	51E	28
BERG ROGER LEE	MI	07E	22
BERG THOMAS ALAN	MN	23W	82
BERGAN MERLIN HERMAN	KS	49W	50
BERGANTZEL ALBION JOE	IA	04W	12
BERGE JAMES MAYNARD	OR	35E	13
BERGEN JAMES THOMAS III	TX	36E	45
BERGENSTEIN DENNIS PAUL	OH	19E	21
BERGER BARRY HOWARD	MD	05W	36
BERGER CARL STEPHEN JR	ND	12W	87
BERGER DIXIE CARL	TX	52E	46
BERGER DONALD JOSEPH	NY	15W	101
BERGER ELDIN GEORGE JR	PA	17W	54
BERGER GERALD DAVID	KS	49W	12
BERGER JOHN EDWARD	OH	41E	48
BERGER LORAN LEON	NV	34W	81
BERGER NICHOLAS ALLEN	IL	06W	111
BERGER RAYMOND REX	WI	06W	17
BERGER ROBERT FRANCIS	NY	11W	121
BERGERA DEE	UT	03W	76
BERGERON DOUGLAS HUGH	OR	39W	15
BERGERON ROBERT JAMES	MA	41W	3
BERGERON ROY LOUIS	LA	11W	12
BERGERON SIMEON JOSEPH A	MA	29W	42
BERGERSON JOHN FRANCIS	WA	14E	94
BERGESS FREDERICK WILSON	SC	17E	41
BERGEVIN CHARLES LEE	CT	47W	37
BERGFELDT DAVID EDWARD	NM	15W	85
BERGFIELD PHILLIP REX	IL	03W	97
BERGIN GERARD FRANCIS	MA	46W	37
BERGIN THOMAS JAMES	NY	01E	46
BERGMAN CLIFTON BALLANTYN	VA	27E	108
BERGMAN JACK STEPHEN JR	MD	01W	76
BERGQUIST ERIC EMANUEL	TX	20W	54
BERGQUIST VERNON GAIL	IA	09W	42
BERGREN THOMAS HOWARD	CA	58E	19
BERGSTROM WALLACE CARL JR	CT	33W	76
BERHOWE MARVIN RICHARD	MO	16W	83
BERINGER MICHAEL AUGUST	MN	03E	106
BERKEBILE JACK	PA	38W	40
BERKERY MICHAEL WAYNE	NJ	37E	31
BERKFIELD THOMAS DUDLEY	MI	37W	72
BERKHEIMER DENVER JOSEPH	OH	65E	5
BERKHOLTZ LARRY WAYNE	WI	07W	102
BERKHOLZ DAVID DENNIS	MI	14E	99
BERKSON JOSEPH MIKE	IL	01W	10
BERLANGA RAFAEL ANGEL	NY	03E	51
BERLETT THEODORE JAMES	NE	01E	5
BERMEA VICTOR D	TX	07E	115
BERMEJO RICHARD ISMAEL	PR	15E	112
BERMINGHAM DANIEL JOSEPH	NY	47W	37
BERMINGHAM JAMES CHARLES	NE	02E	114
BERMUDEZ JESUS ROJAS	CA	03E	11
BERMUDEZ JOSE DAVID JR	NY	39W	31
BERMUDEZ-PACHECO ENRIQUE	PR	24E	93
BERMUDEZ-QUINONES LUDIN	PR	13E	33
BERN HAROLD STANLEY	OR	26E	6
BERNAL ENRIQUE MUNOZ	TX	43E	41
BERNAL JOSE ROLANDO	IL	48E	38
BERNAL RAYMOND JR	CA	12E	130
BERNAL VINCENT	NE	02W	74
BERNARD CHARLES LOUIS JR	IL	26E	42
BERNARD DONALD LEE	OK	18E	90
BERNARD GUY NORTH	WA	42E	27
BERNARD HENRY WILFRED JR	CT	24E	15
BERNARD JOHN EDWIN	NY	21E	117
BERNARD RAMON	PR	03E	51
BERNARD RANDALL BRUCE	CA	02W	22
BERNARD RODNEY ROYCE	MI	60W	14
BERNARD THEODORE DANIEL	ME	44E	58

NAME	STATE	PANEL NO.	LINE NO.
BERNARD THOMAS D	TN	57W	34
BERNARD VINCENT	MA	43W	51
BERNARD WILLIAM ERWIN	GA	33E	58
BERNARD-ROBLES ANTONIO RA	NY	03E	51
BERNARDY THOMAS G	TX	33E	15
BERNER EDGAR DAVIDSON	IL	11W	66
BERNESKI LAWRENCE AUGUSTI	PA	28E	13
BERNEY TERRY LYNN	NE	17W	21
BERNHARDT ROBERT EDWARD	VA	01W	116
BERNHARDT WAYNE WILLIAM	NY	58W	22
BERNHART CARL HANS	OH	44E	65
BERNHEISEL DAVID ARNOLD	MI	39E	69
BERNIER ROGER JEROME	MN	13W	43
BERNING ROBERT RAYMOND	KY	10W	112
BERNING THOMAS JOSEPH	KY	10W	133
BERNOSKA WAYNE GARY	IN	30W	44
BERNREUTHER WALTER JOHN	NY	48E	14
BERNSTEIN ALAN MARTIN	NY	29W	95
BERNSTEIN BRUCE BRYANT	CA	33W	62
BERNSTEIN JACK	NY	30W	98
BERNSTEIN JOEL	PA	10E	35
BERNSTEIN LESLIE PAUL	NY	16E	75
BERNTSEN ROBERT	NY	19E	93
BERRIER DANNY CLARENCE	TX	13W	61
BERRIER KENNETH CLAY	NC	61E	24
BERRIER TOMMY JOE	KS	19W	48
BERRIGAN BRENDON JAY	SD	50W	4
BERRIO JOHN ANTHONY	MA	21W	5
BERRIOS JOHN RICHARD	FL	30E	96
BERRIOS MICHAEL	NY	32E	7
BERRIOS-GARCIA RAFAEL	PR	17W	40
BERRIOS-RIVERA JESUS M	PR	06W	103
BERRISFORD RONALD E	MA	15E	16
BERRY ALAN WAYNE	MA	14W	92
BERRY CHARLES RAY	TX	14W	117
BERRY CHARLIE E	GA	56W	11
BERRY DAVID JOE	CA	52E	33
BERRY DAVID LOYALL	TX	09E	51
BERRY DONALD CARL	KY	33W	46
BERRY ELMER EUGENE	MO	05E	78
BERRY FLOYD JOSEPH JR	PA	15E	8
BERRY JACK ALBERT	TX	25E	95
BERRY JACKIE WAYNE	LA	38E	64
BERRY JAMES CRAIG	MI	29E	87
BERRY JAMES E	MI	22E	5
BERRY JAMES F	CA	35W	57
BERRY JAMES GRAYSON	WV	02E	115
BERRY JOE CLEVELAND	GA	42W	3
BERRY JOHN ALVIN	CO	37W	44
BERRY KENNETH BERYL	OK	33E	56
BERRY KURTIS AUREL	IN	21W	68
BERRY LARRY MICHAEL	IL	09E	55
BERRY LOUIS EDWARD	VI	34E	34
BERRY MALCOLM CRAYTON	CT	08E	106
BERRY MICHAEL GEORGE	CA	34E	34
BERRY MICHAEL LEWIS	IN	28W	17
BERRY PAUL L	FL	34E	14
BERRY RALPH THOMAS	CA	35E	86
BERRY ROBERT ERVA	CT	11E	67
BERRY ROBERT LESTER	ME	45E	17
BERRY RONALD LEE	WV	20W	121
BERRY ROY VERNON JR	CA	39E	79
BERRY TIMOTHY DALE	OH	14E	8
BERRY TOMMY LOYD	TX	44W	61
BERRY VANCE ALYN	TX	48E	14
BERRY WILLIAM AARON	CA	26E	99
BERRY WILLIAM ANTHONY	OH	16E	18
BERRY WILLIAM ARTHUR	GA	35E	86
BERRY WILLIAM MC KINLEY	IN	43W	51
BERRYMAN LUTHER CLARK	KY	42W	31
BERRYMAN WILLIAM ERNEST	AL	06W	111
BERSTLER BILL LAVERN	IA	22W	63
BERTA ROBERT DEWITT	IN	31E	85
BERTAGNA LAWRENCE JOSEPH	CA	20W	54
BERTHEL JOHN JOSEPH	NY	08E	107
BERTHIAUME PAUL DAVID	MA	04E	35
BERTHOUX DALE PORTER	IL	30E	88
BERTOLINO FRED GORDON	IL	22E	9
BERTOLOZZI PAUL CHARLES	IL	24E	68
BERTOMEN NARCISO JR	CA	03E	39
BERTRAM DAVID MICHAEL	KY	57W	22
BERTSCH BRENT JOHN	CA	61E	23

NAME	STATE	PANEL NO.	LINE NO.
BERTSCH KENNETH RAY	OH	10E	90
BERTSCHINGER DENNIS LEE	WI	17E	60
BERTULLI ALFRED LEON	MA	29E	25
BERUBE KENNETH ALLEN	MA	24E	99
BERUBE RICHARD	ME	27E	106
BERUMEN JUAN BOSCO	CA	16W	2
BERWEGER ALLAN FREDERICK	WI	19E	77
BERWERT PATRICK MICHAEL	KS	46E	14
BERZINEC WILLIAM EDWARD	OH	50W	34
BESCH ROBERT DEAN	MN	12W	111
BESCHEN JAMES	NJ	09E	35
BESKE WILLIAM HENRY JR	MI	24W	92
BESS BENNY DALE	OK	46W	37
BESS CHARLES RAY	WV	05W	47
BESS SAMUEL	NC	03E	14
BESSENT SAMUEL ALONZO	IL	26W	46
BESSON LAWRENCE EUGENE	LA	12E	17
BESSOR BRUCE CARLTON	VA	25W	94
BEST ANDREW THOMAS	AR	08E	95
BEST ARTHUR	NC	04W	102
BEST BILLY HOWARD	MD	30W	19
BEST CAREY EDWIN	MI	04E	99
BEST CHARLES HYMAN	NY	26W	109
BEST GARY ALLEN	IL	17W	126
BEST HUGH ELROY III	NC	33W	13
BEST HUGH VICTOR	TX	16E	76
BEST NEAL IRA	SC	30E	37
BEST OLIVER ADRIAN JR	NY	25W	9
BEST PATRICK WALLACE	WI	25W	94
BEST RICHARD JAMES JR	MT	18W	53
BEST RONALD LEE	OH	56W	31
BEST THOMAS EMANUEL	NY	27W	14
BESTMANN CHARLES EDWARD	NY	38W	82
BESZE GYORGY JANOS	IL	10E	35
BETANCOURT GABRIEL	CA	26E	91
BETANCOURT JAMES	NY	18W	109
BETANCOURT-MOJICA CARLOS	NJ	05E	9
BETCHEL DAVID BROOKS	CA	30E	38
BETEBENNER DAVID LEE	MO	56E	1
BETHARDS EDWARD WAYNE	CA	05W	39
BETHEA CHARLES DUNCAN	NC	11W	129
BETHEA HENRY	NY	30W	35
BETHEA JIMMY CARLTON	SC	07E	107
BETHEA LUTHER JR	SC	48W	5
BETHEA RAYMOND LEWIS	NY	30W	84
BETHEA TROY	WA	22W	84
BETHEA WILLIAM HENRY III	MD	20E	100
BETHEL JAMES WALTER	WV	09E	55
BETHUNE ROBERT EDWIN	OH	14E	14
BETLEYOUN GOLA CALVIN	GA	40E	72
BETTELYOUN PERCY JR	SD	64W	5
BETTENCOURT DANIEL F JR	CA	45E	45
BETTENCOURT DANIEL STEPHE	MA	19E	69
BETTENCOURT JOHN FRANCIS	MA	29E	104
BETTGER GENE LYLE	CA	13E	70
BETTIS JAMES WILLIAM	OK	44E	24
BETTIS JOHN CALVIN	VA	20E	93
BETTIS NORMAN RADEAN	IA	33W	28
BETTS ALBERT LEON	MD	36E	65
BETTS DAVID PAUL	WA	28E	79
BETTS LARRY LE ROY	AK	16W	104
BETTS TERRY WADE	MI	56E	19
BETTY CLAUDE CHARLES	MA	28E	33
BETZ ROBERT JOSEPH	NJ	01E	88
BETZ SAMUEL	OR	20W	100
BEUKE DENNIS ARTHUR	IL	27E	87
BEUSTER RONALD LEE	IL	04E	136
BEUTEL ROBERT DONALD	IL	02W	73
BEUTLER RONALD EUGENE	OR	03W	104
BEVAN JERRY EUGENE	MN	07W	69
BEVARD BOBBY LEE	CA	19W	8
BEVELS LEONARD LEROY	TX	30E	74
BEVERFORD TIMOTHY WAYNE	CA	20W	63
BEVERHOUDT CLARENCE VEREN	VI	03E	69
BEVERIDGE DOUGLAS JAMES	CT	33W	91
BEVERLY FRANCIS M	NY	20W	38
BEVERLY WILLARD FRANKLIN	SC	10E	75
BEVICH GEORGE MICHAEL JR	PA	13E	9
BEVIER MELVIN EDWARD	OH	38W	54
BEVILACQUA RENATO MARTIN	OH	58W	2
BEWLEY THOMAS EUGENE	OH	13W	40
BEXLEY ROBERT EDWARD	AL	04E	118

NAME	STATE	PANEL NO.	LINE NO.
BEY NELSON	NY	30W	41
BEYDA IRWIN	FL	31W	88
BEYER EDWARD HUGO	TX	12W	111
BEYER THOMAS JOHN	ND	50W	34
BEYER WILLIAM ARTHUR	WI	14E	102
BEYERLING JAMES LEROY	MD	29E	70
BEYL DAVID ROBERT	IN	08W	27
BEYRAND JOHN MICHAEL	PA	24E	93
BEZEAU RICK WILLIAM	OH	58E	30
BEZECNY JOHN WILLIAM	IL	56E	35
BEZEGA MICHAEL STEPHEN	NJ	09W	77
BEZENSKI STEVEN MICHAEL	PA	46E	29
BEZOLD STEVEN NEIL	MO	40W	52
BIA MICHAEL HOWARD	AZ	60W	25
BIAGINI MARK FREDERICK	GM	01W	42
BIALKOWSKI JOHN JOSEPH	NY	22E	56
BIANCHINI MICHAEL LINN	CA	05E	113
BIANCONI NICHOLAS CHARLES	PA	23E	115
BIAS CLIFFORD	WV	48E	39
BIBBS LEONARD JEROME	IL	09E	91
BIBBS WARREN LARRY	NJ	53W	32
BIBBS WAYNE	IL	01W	40
BIBBY JOHN FRANCIS	SD	37E	31
BIBER GERALD MACK	NE	01E	3
BIBER JOSEPH FRANK	CA	43W	33
BIBERDORF DENNIS FLOYD	MT	23W	50
BIBEY DWAIN LEE	OH	33W	76
BIBLER WILSON E JR	CA	15E	82
BICE DOUGLAS WYATT	MI	29W	27
BICE JIMMIE RAY	AL	25W	94
BICE QUINTON MORGAN	TX	27E	106
BICKEL BARRY WAYNE	IN	21W	105
BICKEL ROBERT JOHN	NY	29E	27
BICKFORD RALPH NEVIN	KS	28W	8
BICKFORD RICHARD OLIVER	CT	41W	72
BICKFORD THOMAS WAYNE	MI	03W	105
BICKLE JIMBOB	CA	64E	11
BICKLEY WILSON CHARLES	SC	10E	61
BIDART DAVID LOUIS	NV	43E	3
BIDDLE DANIEL ELLIS	IN	19E	9
BIDDLE JOSEPH LENORD	NJ	30W	10
BIDDULPH THOMAS ARTHUR	GA	40W	41
BIDWELL BARRY ALAN	PA	03W	80
BIEBER EDWARD L	CT	28E	53
BIEDIGER LARRY WILLIAM	TX	14E	94
BIEDRON ANDREW ALBERT JR	IL	26W	6
BIEDRON MICHAEL PETER	IN	33W	5
BIEGEL ROBERT CHARLES	IL	35E	87
BIEGERT RONALD LEE	MN	13W	129
BIEHL GARY LADD	FL	19E	21
BIEHL JAMES ALBERT	OH	17W	37
BIEHL LESTER OSCAR JR	WI	02E	72
BIEHL OSCAR JR	CT	21E	17
BIEHN MAURICE JOHN	MI	27E	79
BIEKER CARL JOSEPH	CO	22W	85
BIELEK RUDOLPH JOHN JR	PA	34E	40
BIELICKI GREGORY CHESTER	NY	12E	86
BIEMERET ARTHUR THOMAS	CA	13W	110
BIENEMAN JOHN CHARLES	IL	48W	38
BIENKOWSKI WALTER JOSEPH	NY	02E	98
BIERBAUM LAWRENCE ANTHONY	IL	10W	117
BIERLEIN PATRICK M R	NJ	49E	28
BIERLINE THOMAS RALPH	PA	06W	70
BIERMA LYNN SEATON	NE	18E	91
BIERMAN CARROLL MONROE JR	CA	01E	131
BIERNACKI JAMES RICHARD	CA	44E	44
BIEROWSKI REINER WALTER	WI	08E	64
BIES EDWARD ALAN	MI	63E	5
BIESANTZ HOWARD STANLEY	NJ	32W	89
BIESER KARL ROY	CA	43W	67
BIESIADA RICHARD EDWARD	NJ	64E	11
BIEVER WILLIAM DENNIS	SD	23E	90
BIFARETI JOHN ANTHONY JR	MD	61E	23
BIFFLE JOE LESLIE JR	TX	35E	3
BIFFLE WILLIAM CALVIN	TN	18W	116
BIFOLCHI CHARLES LAWRENCE	MA	33E	79
BIGELOW LAWRENCE CARROLL	NY	12W	95
BIGELOW PAUL LEE	MI	44E	57
BIGELOW RALPH WILLIAM	NY	10W	78
BIGELOW ROBERT FRANCIS	MA	26E	58
BIGELOW RONNIE O	OR	40E	36
BIGGER CALVIN HART	IN	41E	35

NAME	STATE	PANEL NO.	LINE NO.
BIGGERS LEWIS LAMAR	GA	46W	26
BIGGERSTAFF HENRY CHARLES	VA	58E	4
BIGGS DAVID OWEN	KY	22W	17
BIGGS EARL ROGER	WV	34E	57
BIGGS JAMES EDWARD	TN	11E	54
BIGGS JIMMY DEAN	MO	37W	54
BIGHAM CHARLES FREDERICK	NJ	25E	81
BIGHAM THEODORE LEWIS	UT	51W	47
BIGLEY CHRISTOPHER JOHN	PA	03W	44
BIGLEY GEORGE CARL	IL	01E	81
BIGLEY RICHARD RAY	NE	03E	106
BIGLIENI CHARLES ROBERT	MO	04W	23
BIGTREE JAMES VICTOR	NY	04E	63
BIHLMEYER JAMES ROY	MI	18E	28
BILBO WILLIAM JOHN JR	PA	46W	26
BILBREY EDMOND DAVID	NM	04W	36
BILDEN HARLAN TILPHER	IA	22E	91
BILDUCIA CONRADO FRANCISC	AZ	42E	62
BILENSKI JOHN CHARLES	NJ	54W	40
BILES CALVIN WEBB	AR	32E	69
BILES MICHAEL LYNN	AZ	16W	83
BILKO TIMOTHY JAMES	PA	02E	129
BILLEAUD WAYNE JAMES	LA	03W	79
BILLEAUD WILLIS J JR	LA	51W	16
BILLER HAROLD DOUGLAS	MD	31W	43
BILLERO MICHAEL JAMES JR	NJ	10E	3
BILLHIMER GARY ARTHUR	CA	18E	38
BILLIE LARRY ROGERS	AZ	11E	66
BILLINGHAM FREDERICK A JR	NJ	41E	16
BILLINGS DAVID VERN	PA	04E	56
BILLINGS JAMES ARTHUR JR	NY	64E	11
BILLINGS KEMPER SWANSON	NC	11E	126
BILLINGS TERRENCE ROY	OH	08W	58
BILLINGS WILL DANNY	AL	06W	42
BILLINGSLEA DAMON EARL	OH	31E	40
BILLINGSLEY RICHARD WAYNE	CA	10E	36
BILLINGSLY LEE WAYNE	KS	01W	58
BILLIOT RUDOLPH JOHN	LA	32E	34
BILLIPP NORMAN KARL	WI	25W	9
BILLS KENNETH DALE	TN	08W	129
BILLS LYLE PRESTON	IA	61E	23
BILLS RUFUS WILSON	TX	24E	71
BILMER KRIS	WI	22W	116
BILONTA LARRY KILITO	HI	32E	7
BILOTTA RICHARD GALE	NY	04E	118
BILSIE EDWARD ORVILLE	WA	31E	9
BILY WILLIAM CHARLES	IL	03W	72
BINA THOMAS MELVIN	MN	44W	14
BINDER CALVIN WILLIAM II	IA	09W	101
BINDER FREDRICK MARLTON	WA	08E	99
BINDER GARY LEE	KS	27E	98
BINDER PAUL LAROY	WI	14W	38
BINDER QUENTIN WAYNE	MI	36E	70
BINEGAR BENJAMIN H JR	IL	33W	53
BINGAMON DAVID LEE	OH	52W	14
BINGENHEIMER JAMES	NJ	04W	48
BINGER GERALD A	NJ	01E	82
BINGHAM CHESTER ELMEARL	IN	26W	24
BINGHAM DAVID ANDREW	MA	35E	10
BINGHAM DAVID RICHARD	CT	54E	2
BINGHAM DENNIS WILLIAM	IA	20W	10
BINGHAM KLAUS YRURGEN	HI	03W	28
BINGHAM MICHAEL FRANCIS	PA	08E	103
BINGHAM ORAN LOTHIER	UT	03W	125
BINGHAM TONY RAY	NC	03W	14
BINGLEY JOHN LEE JR	SC	45E	8
BINGMAN PETER RUBEN	OH	10E	28
BINGMAN RONALD HOWARD	CA	45W	35
BINION CURTIS ESTILL	WV	08E	132
BINION THOMAS	AL	06E	59
BINK JAMES CLEVELAND JR	NY	20W	100
BINKLEY STEVEN RAY	KY	42W	38
BINKLEY STUART MARSHALL	MI	03W	91
BINKO GEORGE	MD	32E	68
BINKOWSKI RONALD JOHN	MI	15W	69
BINNS DAVID RICHARD	CA	60E	19
BINNS GEORGE MICHAEL	WA	30W	19
BINSTOCK PETER JR	ND	35W	24
BINTLIFF RONNIE HANKINS	FL	12E	46
BIONDI JOHN MICHAEL	MD	21E	8
BIONDILLO JOHN CARL	OH	24E	5
BIONDO MARTIN	MO	45E	33
BIRCH DANIEL PATRICK	CA	05E	99
BIRCH JOEL RAY	AZ	01W	97
BIRCH JOHN MACY	CA	12W	3
BIRCH LARRY WAYNE	KY	31E	70
BIRCH THOMAS H	NJ	40E	72
BIRCHAK FRANCIS JOSEPH	PA	35W	69
BIRCHIM JAMES DOUGLAS	CA	39W	69
BIRCO JOSE GOTERA		04E	63
BIRD CHARLES WESLEY	MI	27E	106
BIRD DANNIE LEON	KS	35W	87
BIRD GEORGE ALLISON III	GA	31E	9
BIRD HAROLD ALVIN	CA	02E	86
BIRD JACKIE DEAN JR	TX	19W	91
BIRD JOHN THOMAS	NJ	11E	43
BIRD KENNETH ROBERT	CA	27W	29
BIRD KIM SOVEREEN	LA	13E	42
BIRD LEONARD ADRIAN	DE	52W	21
BIRD MICHAEL ALAN	IN	27E	106
BIRD MICHAEL DE VERNE	TX	16E	118
BIRD THOMAS ARNOLD JR	PA	06E	28
BIRDEN LEE ROY	CA	34E	14
BIRDSALL THOMAS EDDY	MI	12E	58
BIRDSELL GEORGE DAVID	CA	08E	51
BIRDSELL GORDON DOUGLAS	FL	26W	110
BIRDWELL GEORGE ALFRED	FL	10W	94
BIRDWELL MICHAEL DEL	CA	38W	55
BIRELEY KENNETH PAUL	PA	22E	123
BIRENBAUM BERNARD	NY	03E	52
BIRKET SCOTT LEE	CA	01W	76
BIRKHOLZ ROBERT EARL	IN	08W	10
BIRKLAND WILEY COLE	MT	06E	6
BIRKS JAMES P	OK	67E	4
BIRKY HAROLD EDWIN	IA	05W	68
BIRMINGHAM EDWARD ARNOLD	VT	27E	40
BIRMINGHAM TERRY WAYNE	AR	33E	16
BISCAILUZ ROBERT LYNN	CA	24E	50
BISCAMP MARVIN LYNN	NE	02W	135
BISCHOF WOLFRAM WALTHER	DE	15E	24
BISCHOFF EDWARD ALLEN	PA	14W	28
BISCHOFF JOHN MALCOLM	SC	01E	3
BISCHOFF JOHN WILLIAM	NE	24E	71
BISE ROGER ALLEN	WV	05E	28
BISH LEONARD THOMAS	PA	20E	5
BISHOP DALE ALAN	IL	18E	21
BISHOP DANIEL EDWARD	CA	01E	104
BISHOP DANNY RAY	TX	13W	121
BISHOP EDGAR LEE	GA	14W	16
BISHOP EDWARD JAMES JR	CT	11W	66
BISHOP JAMES ARTHUR	AL	27W	29
BISHOP JAMES FRANKLIN	IL	02W	27
BISHOP JAMES LOUIS	KS	22W	116
BISHOP JAMES MATTHEW	SC	19E	77
BISHOP JAMES WALTER	IL	15W	49
BISHOP JOSEPH ADRIAN	GA	43W	33
BISHOP MARK RONALD	FL	24E	15
BISHOP MICHAEL RICHARD	CA	36W	28
BISHOP RICHARD LAVERN	CA	11E	32
BISHOP ROGER EARL	KY	46W	11
BISHOP ROGER WAYNE	MD	18W	53
BISHOP RONALD BURK	MO	18W	100
BISHOP RONNIE HAROLD	OH	13E	80
BISHOP ROSTEN WAYNE	FL	07E	93
BISHOP RUSSELL LAVERNE	CA	06E	28
BISHOP TED JASON	TX	14W	111
BISHOP THOMAS WAYNE	IN	60E	21
BISHOP WILLIAM BUEL II	TN	17W	104
BISHOP WILLIAM WAYNE	IL	18E	47
BISHOP WOODROW WILSON JR	AL	25W	4
BISJAK HOWARD ROBERT	AZ	35E	65
BISONETT LAWRENCE EDWARD	NY	35E	3
BISSAILLON FRANCIS HENRY	MA	11E	43
BISSELL WILLIAM RONALD	MD	65E	5
BISSEN HOWARD MATTHEW	IA	33E	79
BISZ RALPH CAMPION	FL	24E	78
BITEL BEN STANLEY	NY	52E	46
BITNER DANNY LEE	VA	45W	4
BITTENBENDER DAVID FRITZ	NY	23E	25
BITTING JACK	PA	52E	2
BITTINGER ROBERT LEE JR	MD	27W	98
BITTLE DOUGLAS ROBERT	KS	22W	102
BITTNER DARREL GENE	IA	25W	20
BITTNER ROBERT EDWARD JR	CT	17W	12
BITTON GARY W	ID	01E	35
BIVENS FREDERICK WOOD JR	MD	18E	118
BIVENS HERNDON ARRINGTON	NY	11W	5
BIVETTO CHARLES FRED	NY	17E	83
BIXBY JACK DENTON	MN	04E	49
BIXBY THOMAS EUGENE	NY	46E	44
BIXBY VIRGIL MARTIN	IA	08W	41
BIXEL KENNETH BRUCE	OH	36W	25
BIXEL MICHAEL SARGENT	FL	01W	83
BIXLER MARTIN EDWARD	PA	42W	65
BIZZELL RAYMOND ALBERT	MS	14E	19
BJERKE GLEN ALLEN	WI	24E	66
BJORKE ERLE LAWRENCE	MN	28E	7
BLAAUW JAMES EVART	MI	45E	54
BLACK CHARLES DUFFY	IL	18E	21
BLACK DAVID FORREST	SC	28W	32
BLACK DE WAYNE RODNEY	OH	15E	124
BLACK DENNIS BEDELLE	LA	61E	23
BLACK DENNIS WALTER	IN	03E	69
BLACK HARRY ELSWORTH	CT	20W	70
BLACK HARVEY	GA	40W	23
BLACK JIMMY P	AL	01W	124
BLACK JOHN ENOCH	OK	47E	45
BLACK LARRY PAUL	AL	32E	46
BLACK LEWIS DAVIS	IL	51W	2
BLACK MARK RYAN	IN	24E	108
BLACK MARK STEPHEN	WA	06E	62
BLACK NOLAN EUGENE	WI	16W	3
BLACK PAUL JR	OH	50W	4
BLACK PAUL VERNON	CA	04W	13
BLACK PERRY GRAY	NC	08W	76
BLACK RALPH ROLAND	MI	59E	17
BLACK ROBERT DENNIS JR	FL	05W	39
BLACK ROBERT JACOB	PA	11E	75
BLACK ROBERT JAMES JR	PA	34E	75
BLACK RODNEY JOE	NM	26W	96
BLACK RONALD LEE	IL	26E	54
BLACK VICTOR LEE	TX	06W	15
BLACK WALTER CURTIS JR	OK	35W	7
BLACK WILLIAM RAY	TN	30W	72
BLACKBURN DAVID RAY	FL	30E	82
BLACKBURN EDMOND SMITH JR	OK	05W	91
BLACKBURN ELBERT FRANK	CA	16E	88
BLACKBURN FREDDIE ANDRAY	KY	33E	81
BLACKBURN HARRY LEE JR	VA	01W	16
BLACKBURN HUGH FRANK	SC	19E	78
BLACKBURN JERRY EDWARD	TX	30E	75
BLACKBURN RICHARD VINCENT	MN	05W	39
BLACKBURN WILLIAM ALFRED	TN	16W	56
BLACKBURN WILLIAM KENDALL	KY	19W	48
BLACKERBY RALPH W	IN	20E	89
BLACKFORD JOHN MELVIN	WA	23W	95
BLACKFOX ROBERT LEE	OK	13W	22
BLACKMAN DAVID RAWSON III	OR	30E	53
BLACKMAN LARRY PAUL	IA	15E	53
BLACKMAN THOMAS JOSEPH	WI	58E	4
BLACKMAN THOMAS LEE	TX	12E	18
BLACKMER WILLIAM EDWARD	MI	35E	13
BLACKMON DAVID OTIS	FL	06E	133
BLACKMON DENNIS GLENN	AL	28E	39
BLACKMON EDWARD GEE	TX	12E	40
BLACKMON JAMES ARTHUR	NY	10W	10
BLACKMON JAMES WILLIE	LA	08W	74
BLACKMON JOHNNY	MI	19E	42
BLACKMON KENNETH LEON	TX	34E	14
BLACKMON WILLIAM B JR	PA	05W	52
BLACKMOND PHILLIP CORNELI	NC	03W	37
BLACKNER CRAIG SLADE	WY	04E	132
BLACKSHEAR JAMES GUY	FL	45E	8
BLACKSMITH RONALD RAY	MI	04W	102
BLACKSTEN BILLY JOE	MO	37E	18
BLACKSTEN RONALD LEE	IN	39E	17
BLACKSTON DONALD LAMAR	AL	22W	96
BLACKWATER DWIGHT THOMAS	AZ	03W	82
BLACKWELDER KIT	OR	18E	67
BLACKWELL FREDERIC DELANO	OH	22W	86
BLACKWELL JAMES LISMAN JR	IN	28E	19
BLACKWELL JOHN WILLIE	NC	27W	27
BLACKWELL JOSEPH CARLTON	MS	06W	90
BLACKWELL KENNETH	PA	54E	2
BLACKWELL KENNETH G	AZ	27W	36
BLACKWELL KENNETH HORACE	FL	12E	59

NAME	STATE	PANEL NO.	LINE NO.
BLACKWELL MILTON	VA	23W	61
BLACKWELL ROBERT LAWRENCE	SC	06W	100
BLACKWELL ROY JAMES JR	SC	30E	22
BLACKWELL THOMAS MICHAEL	OH	32W	57
BLACKWELL WILLIAM ALLEN	WV	20E	21
BLACKWOOD GORDON BYRON	CA	20E	128
BLADEK JOHN EMERY	PA	26W	43
BLADES THOMAS NELSON	MD	61W	20
BLADES WILLIAM CEACON III	MA	19E	55
BLAESE RONALD PAUL	WI	23E	109
BLAGDON EDWIN ELLIS	CA	40W	70
BLAGG PATRICK EARL	KY	27W	61
BLAHA THOMAS JOHN	WI	38E	21
BLAIN DENNIS KNUTE	ME	42W	9
BLAIN JAMES ALLEN	UT	25W	9
BLAINE JAMES GRAHAM	WA	39E	42
BLAIR ALAN LEE	NY	33E	16
BLAIR ANTHONY BURDETTE	OR	19W	92
BLAIR CHARLES DOUGLAS	FL	10W	38
BLAIR CHARLES EDWARD	VA	45E	33
BLAIR DONALD D		26W	38
BLAIR DONALD RAY	TX	04E	58
BLAIR GERALD ALLAN	RI	24W	81
BLAIR IVY LOUIS	MS	58E	30
BLAIR JOSEPH R L	ME	21E	100
BLAIR KENNETH NEAL	KY	63W	2
BLAIR KENNETH RAY	GA	49W	50
BLAIR PATRICK LYNN	TX	29W	95
BLAIR ROCKY LEE	CA	40W	48
BLAIR RONNIE	OH	41W	38
BLAIR TERRY LEE	MO	04W	30
BLAIR THOMAS ARTHUR	TX	20W	62
BLAIR THOMAS GEORGE JR	VA	03W	58
BLAIR WILLIAM EARL	OH	52W	14
BLAIR WILLIAM WEBB JR	OK	36W	55
BLAIS ROBERT LAWRENCE	MA	33W	24
BLAKE ARMIN JOCHAIM	CO	28W	8
BLAKE DALE ADAMS	MA	12W	24
BLAKE DANNY LEE	MD	47W	15
BLAKE EDWARD ALOYSIUS	MS	01E	69
BLAKE JACK PATRICK	TX	36W	47
BLAKE JAMES WILLIAM	OH	20W	91
BLAKE JOHN CHARLES	VT	12W	28
BLAKE L C	TX	03E	110
BLAKE RICHARD THOMAS	MO	20W	69
BLAKE ROGER LEE	MD	22E	75
BLAKE RONALD EARL	RI	02E	3
BLAKE TIMOTHY MORGAN	WV	03E	52
BLAKE WAYNE VALGEEN	IL	08W	81
BLAKE WILLIAM H JR	MA	37E	48
BLAKELEY ROY JAMES	TX	02E	42
BLAKELY BRUCE WILLIAM	TN	09W	26
BLAKELY JOSSLYN F JR	AL	11E	107
BLAKELY MARTIN GEORGE	CA	64E	3
BLAKELY MELFORD KEITH	OK	35W	63
BLAKELY WILLIAM	CA	39E	29
BLAKENEY GREGORY ALLEN	MD	10W	94
BLAKESLEE THOMAS WAYNE	OH	37W	21
BLAKEY HOWELL FRANK	VA	12W	121
BLAKEY MICHAEL ARCHIE	CA	35W	87
BLAKLEY EDWIN JR	TN	33W	19
BLAKLEY JAMES AUBREY	TN	22E	67
BLALACK JIMMY DALE	TN	40W	62
BLALOCK GHERALD EDWARD	TX	61E	24
BLALOCK HARRY LAMAR	NC	47E	46
BLALOCK JAMES TERRELL	AL	48E	23
BLALOCK JOHN HILTON	MS	47E	29
BLALOCK WALTER ROGERS	TX	16E	26
BLANCHARD ANDRUS JAMES	LA	14W	30
BLANCHARD DAVID MELVIN	OR	62E	15
BLANCHARD JAMES A	RI	16E	111
BLANCHARD THOMAS JOSEPH	CT	49W	23
BLANCHARD WILLIAM GEORGE	NY	06E	28
BLANCHETT STEPHEN PAUL	PA	16E	34
BLANCHETTE GUY ANDRE	NH	19W	117
BLANCHETTE MICHAEL R	AZ	08W	58
BLANCHETTE RAYMOND	CT	05E	99
BLANCHFIELD MICHAEL R	IL	21W	50
BLANCHFIELD RICHARD ALLEN	MD	06E	62
BLANCO CHARLES JOSEPH	PA	10E	123
BLANCO HERIBERTO	TX	37W	4
BLANCO JOHN ALEXANDER JR	IL	36W	32
BLAND GARY PAUL	IL	02E	92
BLAND ISAAC	KS	45E	37
BLANDEN JAMES D	MS	32E	16
BLANDIN RAYMOND WELLINGTO	SC	35W	37
BLANDING AARON	SC	12E	65
BLANDING HENRY ARTHUR	NY	41W	44
BLANDING JOHN WESLEY	VA	23W	13
BLANDINO HOWARD	MI	14W	77
BLANDON GILBERT	MD	14W	114
BLANEY THOMAS ARTHUR	CA	10E	24
BLANK FRANK HUFFORD	PA	02E	54
BLANK ROBERT GERDES	WI	36W	55
BLANKENSHIP CHARLES HERMA	MD	23E	25
BLANKENSHIP CLAYTON MITCH	WV	01W	83
BLANKENSHIP DENCIL RAY	WV	06W	8
BLANKENSHIP DONALD LEE	CA	31W	88
BLANKENSHIP DONALD RAY	OH	53W	34
BLANKENSHIP EDGAR WILLIAM	OH	44E	32
BLANKENSHIP GODFRED	VA	17E	48
BLANKENSHIP JACKIE LEE	WV	22W	116
BLANKENSHIP JAMES ARLIA	CA	33E	6
BLANKENSHIP JAMES ORIS	MO	34E	4
BLANKENSHIP JAMES THOMAS	OK	40W	26
BLANKENSHIP JEWELL C	KY	30W	71
BLANKENSHIP LARRY J	AL	37E	31
BLANKENSHIP LEROY IRVIN	WA	28W	101
BLANKENSHIP OVIE EARCIL	OH	15E	93
BLANKS CLARENCE	MS	19E	35
BLANKS THOMAS LEE	GA	15W	124
BLANKS TONY PAGE	VA	15E	60
BLANKSMA GERRIT LYNN	MN	70W	1
BLANN STEPHEN	FL	32W	42
BLANSCET MICHAEL JOHN	KS	09W	18
BLANTIN ERIC GEORGE	CT	16W	97
BLANTON BILL EDWARD	OH	03W	6
BLANTON BURTON ALEXANDER	SC	06E	62
BLANTON CALVIN JR	OH	17W	119
BLANTON CLARENCE F	OK	44E	13
BLANTON JAMES LEE JR	TN	25W	94
BLANTON JOHN JAMES	MD	10E	45
BLANTON KENNETH GENE	MO	16E	129
BLANTON MICHAEL MERLE	OR	08E	132
BLANTON RICHARD PATRICK	IN	26W	81
BLANTON RUSSELL LEE	OH	23E	73
BLANTON WALTER CLAY	OH	42W	34
BLAS ANTHONY MARTIN M	GM	13W	117
BLAS FRANK	SC	14W	42
BLASEN RICHARD LEE	IL	21E	41
BLASINGAME NORMAN LEE	CA	47E	8
BLASKIS JAMES LAWRENCE	OH	24E	15
BLASKO JAMES DEE	IN	26W	89
BLASKO PETER PAUL JR	NC	39W	36
BLASKOVICH STEVE JR	IN	09W	26
BLASKOWSKI RICHARD L	MI	06W	105
BLASSIE MICHAEL JOSEPH	MO	01W	23
BLATNICK RODGER ALAN	CO	38W	69
BLATTEL DAVID LEE	MO	55E	2
BLATZ RUSSELL KEITH	VA	33E	79
BLATZ THOMAS LEE	KY	04W	105
BLAUT ROBERT JR	KY	32W	90
BLAUVELT RALPH LEIGH	IL	33W	24
BLAUWKAMP ARLYN JAY	MI	34E	34
BLAVAT JAMES NORBERT	WI	27W	79
BLAYLOCK BERYL STANLEY	TN	52E	14
BLAZ JAMES LUJAN	GM	21E	65
BLAZONIS PETER VINCENT	MA	22W	72
BLEA MICHAEL DELANO	NV	25W	94
BLEA ROBERT DANIEL	CO	34E	14
BLEACHER RONALD THOMAS	DE	42W	38
BLEDSOE DONALD RAY	KY	29W	43
BLEDSOE HOWARD TYRONE	IL	09W	123
BLEDSOE MILARD LUTHER E	TN	41W	38
BLEEKER LARRY DEAN	IA	28E	72
BLEIGH ALFRED HARLEN JR	WV	38E	44
BLEND CLIFFORD CRAIG JR	MD	14W	2
BLENKINSOP WILLIAM DARWIN	ID	07W	21
BLESSING LYNN	PA	01W	129
BLESSING WILLIAM STANTON	CO	27E	92
BLESSMAN WILLIAM DAVID	CA	21E	117
BLETSCH WILLIAM PETE	TX	12W	3
BLEVINS ANTHONY JAMES	CA	47W	45
BLEVINS DANNY EUGENE	TN	44E	57
BLEVINS DANNY EUGENE	KY	13W	26
BLEVINS FRANK LEE	MO	09E	110
BLEVINS HIRIS WAYNE	AR	22W	63
BLEVINS HOWARD CALVIN	NC	06E	97
BLEVINS HUGH BRADLEY JR	VA	26W	68
BLEVINS JAMES EVERETT	OH	17E	70
BLEVINS JAMES ROBERT	IN	12E	26
BLEVINS LURAL LEE III	PA	48W	22
BLEVINS RICHARD LEWIS	OK	36E	45
BLEVINS RONALD WAYNE	VA	57W	16
BLEVINS THOMAS A K	HI	06E	88
BLEVINS THOMAS LEE JR	NJ	23W	24
BLEWETT ROY ROGER	IA	12E	26
BLEWITT WILLIAM A JR	PA	56W	32
BLEXRUDE GORDON H	WI	08E	39
BLEYTHING LARRY DEAN	IA	27W	105
BLICKENSTAFF JOSEPH W JR	PA	06W	131
BLINDER RICHARD BART	CA	16E	1
BLINER JOHN EDWARD	CA	21W	123
BLISARD REX WAYNE	AR	35W	58
BLISS BENJAMIN CHARLES	MO	25W	35
BLISS THOMAS ROBERT	PA	24W	115
BLISSETT JIMMIE RAY	TX	34E	57
BLISSETT ROBERT ALLEN	MI	31E	9
BLITCH BERNARD L	KS	10E	99
BLOCHER RUSSELL GLEN	OR	05W	84
BLOCK WILLIAM JOHN	OR	39E	2
BLOCKER MURRIE LEE	LA	34E	14
BLODGETT DAVID WILMER	NY	02E	106
BLODGETT DOUGLAS RANDOLPH	VA	50E	44
BLOEMHARD ANTON D	NY	41E	6
BLOHM RONALD ROY	WI	44W	14
BLOMFELT DANIEL JOHN	MI	55E	2
BLOMSTROM WAYNE ALDEN	TX	12W	122
BLONDIN MICHAEL ANTHONY	MI	12W	55
BLOODSWORTH LARRY WILL	TX	21E	82
BLOODWORTH DONALD BRUCE	CA	08W	47
BLOOM DARL RUSSELL	PA	01E	71
BLOOM LAWRENCE CLIFFORD	NH	35E	36
BLOOM RICHARD MCAULIFFE	CA	10E	123
BLOOM RONALD KEITH	CO	35W	24
BLOOM RONALD NORMAN	PA	50W	48
BLOOM STEVEN GARY	IN	16E	39
BLOOMER DONALD HUGH	WA	12W	65
BLOOMER JERRY ROBERT	IN	10E	88
BLOOMER TERRY LEE	IL	45W	30
BLOOMFIELD HARRY GENE	FL	39E	43
BLOOMFIELD MICHAEL LEE	MI	10W	56
BLOOMFIELD NORMAN HUBERT	NM	21W	98
BLOOMFIELD WILLIAM DAVID	OH	23W	42
BLOSCHICHAK JOHN RODMAN	PA	09W	67
BLOSKY GENE ORVILLE	CA	28W	39
BLOSSER ROBERT KEITH	OH	03W	52
BLOSSEY RAYMOND ROBERT	MI	17W	110
BLOSSOM STEVEN CARL	MI	49W	12
BLOTTENBERGER MICHAEL J	MD	13W	70
BLOTZER EDWARD JOSEPH	PA	27E	79
BLOUGH DAVID ANTHONY	MA	32E	90
BLOUGH ROBERT DEAN	OH	26E	21
BLOUNT GARY GEORGE	LA	10E	75
BLOUNT JAMES CURTIS	GA	41E	16
BLOUNT JOHN WILLIAM	GA	08W	15
BLOUNT JOHNIE LEE JR	CT	08E	129
BLOUNT ROBERT LARRY	LA	26E	91
BLOW JAMES LYNELL JR	VA	08W	81
BLOWERS RICHARD LYLE	CA	14W	37
BLOYER SHELDON EUGENE	IN	40E	1
BLUBAUGH THOMAS EDWARD	IA	02E	35
BLUDWORTH MICHAEL VERNON	AZ	13W	31
BLUE JAMES EARL	NC	48W	28
BLUE JONATHAN JR	NY	30E	88
BLUE RONALD MICHAEL	TX	10W	89
BLUME DALE L	CA	60E	8
BLUME GERARD JAMES JR	MI	38W	23
BLUMER EDWARD EUGENE	IL	29E	38
BLUMER KRIS	WI	21W	12
BLUMER WILFORD LEE	IL	45W	12
BLUNKALL EARL JEROME	TN	46W	38
BLUNN DAVID LEE	CO	13E	130
BLUNT PAUL BOREN JR	TX	15W	124
BLUNT SAMUEL	TX	33E	80
BLY PERCY EUGENE JR	VA	07W	63

NAME	STATE	PANEL NO.	LINE NO.
BLY ROBERT TILDON	OH	30E	38
BLYSTONE THOMAS MICHAEL	IN	24E	66
BLYTHE TERRY LEE	MS	03E	112
BOADO EMIL E	NC	35W	88
BOAL STEVEN	WY	17W	111
BOAN JIMMY E	SC	05E	70
BOARD STEPHEN DOUGLAS	WV	28W	78
BOARDMAN CURTIS	UT	10W	68
BOARDMAN DAVIS JAMES	NY	36E	48
BOARDMAN EDWARD ALLEN	MD	47E	29
BOARDMAN MICHAEL KENNETH	MO	23E	90
BOAT MICHAEL TERRY	IA	19W	91
BOATMAN ELMER LEE	MO	10E	113
BOATMAN LARRY NEAL	OK	21E	41
BOATRIGHT WILLIAM ARVEL	AR	01W	16
BOATWRIGHT GEORGE OLIVER	MS	13W	18
BOATWRIGHT JACKLIN MEGGS	AR	25E	95
BOATWRIGHT RAYMOND LAVOY	FL	04E	80
BOATWRIGHT TOMMY LEE	NY	07E	7
BOAZ DONALD JOE	TX	49E	29
BOAZ KENNETH WAYNE	IL	17E	120
BOB CHESTER	LA	48E	14
BOBANICH JOSEPH A JR	OH	11W	23
BOBB JOHN FRANKLIN	KY	51W	38
BOBBITT ARTHUR	CA	49E	50
BOBBITT GARLAND CLAUDE	MD	06E	18
BOBBITT JERRY KEITH	CA	04W	99
BOBBITT WILLIAM E G	VA	40E	57
BOBE RAYMOND EDWARD	AL	29W	51
BOBIAN RALPH DANIEL	CO	32E	20
BOBKOVICH STEPHEN JOSEPH	OH	42E	13
BOBLETT MACK CLIFFORD	WV	31W	76
BOBO CHARLES GLEN	AL	05W	86
BOBO EDWARD LEE	AR	25E	22
BOBO JOHN PAUL	NY	17E	70
BOBO LEON NELSON	MO	10W	74
BOBO WILLIAM CHARLES	OH	21W	87
BOBOWSKI JAN EDWARD JR	NY	48E	39
BOBULA JEFFREY LOUIS	PA	16W	69
BOCANEGRA FELIX RAMON	CA	60W	14
BOCANEGRA HUGO ARTHUR	CA	24E	54
BOCANEGRA ROJELIO	IL	21E	55
BOCEK LEONARD JOSEPH	MD	05E	93
BOCHE GARY ALLEN	NJ	58E	4
BOCHNEWETCH SHERMAN II	NY	13W	66
BOCK JERRY CHARLES	IL	25W	95
BOCK JIMMIE VAN	CA	24W	63
BOCKBRADER JERRY ALLAN	OH	64E	3
BOCKEWITZ CARL EDWARD	MO	15E	113
BOCOOK RONALD EDWARD	OH	12E	59
BODA JAMES ALBERT	CA	18E	112
BODAHL JON KEITH	ID	16W	61
BODAMER MICHAEL ANTHONY	NV	20E	39
BODDEN TIMOTHY ROY	IL	21E	42
BODDIE JAMES EDWARD	OH	03W	43
BODE ROBERT RUSSELL	HI	08E	134
BODELL KENNETH A	UT	06E	2
BODELL LARRY ALLEN	MI	32W	57
BODENSCHATZ JOHN EUGEN JR	CA	10E	52
BODIN ALLEN JAMES	LA	06W	85
BODIN DANIEL ROGER	MN	40E	36
BODINE ROBERT LEE	IL	44E	66
BODISH JAMES ROBERT	PA	07W	67
BODISON JAMES CALVIN	SC	35E	66
BODNAR GEORGE JOSEPH	OH	48W	16
BODNAR JOSEPH A	OH	63E	5
BODZICK WILLIAM JOSEPH	MI	13E	2
BOECK GARY RAYMOND	MN	05W	28
BOEGLI STEVEN WARREN	TX	10W	17
BOEHLER JAMES LEONARD	WI	25E	22
BOEHM ALLEN THOMAS	OH	03W	6
BOEHM BRADLEY WAINWRIGHT	AZ	34E	4
BOEHM LARRY JOE	TX	32W	75
BOEHM RICHARD JOHN	ND	04W	85
BOEHM WILLIAM EUGENE	IL	33W	60
BOEHM WILLIAM JOSEPH	MD	22E	36
BOEHNE STEPHEN BRUCE	IN	13W	122
BOEING RONALD FRANK	WI	01W	71
BOELZNER ROBERT CRAIG	CA	12E	126
BOESE ROBERT LEE	KS	24W	81
BOESHART RICHARD JOSEPH	IA	31E	96
BOESKOOL ROBERT RAY	MI	09W	18

NAME	STATE	PANEL NO.	LINE NO.
BOETCHER HAROLD EDWARD	CA	08E	64
BOETJE WILLIAM WAYNE	IL	58W	17
BOETS PETER QUIRINUS JR	CA	19E	103
BOETTCHER WALTER R JR	CA	31E	43
BOETTGER TERRI MARTIN	WI	32E	8
BOEVER DAVID RICHARD	MO	48W	22
BOFFMAN ALAN BRENT	VA	04W	57
BOGACZ JAMES MITCHELL	MA	19W	124
BOGARD JACK CROSBY	OH	37E	31
BOGARD LONNIE PAT	LA	01W	24
BOGART CHARLES ROBERT	GA	39W	57
BOGER RHINE HART	FL	31E	71
BOGGESS EDWARD JAMES	ID	35W	2
BOGGESS RALPH M III	OH	18W	63
BOGGS CHARLES EDWARD	WV	16E	26
BOGGS CHARLES WILSON	MN	11E	107
BOGGS CLIFFORD ALLEN	CA	34E	34
BOGGS DAVID LEONARD	TX	32E	69
BOGGS DONNIE REX	MO	11W	54
BOGGS IRA C JR	OH	05E	31
BOGGS JIMMIE WAYNE	OK	44W	14
BOGGS PASCHAL GLENN	GA	25E	49
BOGGS ROBERT SIDNEY	WV	11W	66
BOGGUESS MAURICE	IL	40E	57
BOGIAGES CHRISTOS C JR	FL	30W	10
BOGLE DENNIS DEAN	OK	15W	3
BOGUE JEFFREY LYNN	NV	16W	61
BOGUSKI PAUL ARTHUR	OK	56W	32
BOHAN PATRICK JOHN	IL	08W	6
BOHANNON EDWARD JEAN	AZ	20E	71
BOHANNON JOHN CALVIN	OK	14E	102
BOHANNON RONALD	OH	26W	13
BOHLER ROBERT RONALD	CA	04E	6
BOHLIG JAMES RICHARD	CA	19W	65
BOHLSCHEID CURTIS RICHARD	ID	21E	91
BOHMER ROBERT JAMES	WI	20E	89
BOHN DAVID J	UT	11E	48
BOHNER LEONARD ALLEN	CA	19E	92
BOHNSACK JOHN EDWARD	IN	32W	36
BOHNWAGNER PETER PAUL	NY	06W	22
BOHON RONALD EUGENE	MO	17E	27
BOHRER LEROY PRESTON	VA	16E	43
BOHRMAN MICHAEL DENNIS	WI	10W	133
BOICE LARRY LEE	IN	31E	71
BOICOURT JESS BURTON JR	ID	44E	14
BOICOURT ROBERT C	IL	08E	74
BOIS CLAIRE RONALD ALAN	AZ	25E	41
BOIS RENE ARMAND	RI	36W	28
BOIS RICHARD JOSEPH	MA	30W	63
BOISE RICHARD HOWARD	NY	15W	3
BOIVIN EDWARD J	ME	12E	113
BOJANEK ROBERT ARTHUR	NY	06W	97
BOJARSKI GEORGE JOSEPH	MI	16E	43
BOJORQUEZ SISTO BOJORQUEZ	AZ	34E	5
BOKINA ROBERT JOHN	NY	09E	73
BOLAK THEODORE NICHOLAS	MI	50W	17
BOLAN EDWARD WILLIAM	OH	32W	76
BOLAN ROBERT LOUIS	MD	08W	48
BOLAND DENNIS MICHAEL	OH	15W	92
BOLAND JAMES ROBERT	NJ	05E	70
BOLAND MELVIN LYNN	MS	37W	44
BOLAND WILLIAM JOSEPH JR	IL	54W	14
BOLDEN CARL EUGENE	TX	13E	102
BOLDEN DANIEL HYMAN	TX	22W	18
BOLDEN ROLLIE LEE	OR	03E	70
BOLDING BENJAMIN FOREST	OK	32W	36
BOLDING EDGAR LEE	MI	35E	87
BOLDING LANNY ROSS	TN	15E	39
BOLDT CHARLES DAVID	MN	27E	8
BOLDUC DANIEL ALPHONSE		20W	69
BOLEN FREEMAN	MS	47E	19
BOLEN JACKIE EVERRETT JR	WV	28E	19
BOLES FLETCHER W II	AL	26W	97
BOLES HARRY LEE	SC	17W	33
BOLES JOEY LEE	CA	23W	25
BOLES ROBERT MADISON	GA	07W	45
BOLES WARREN WILLIAM	MA	34E	66
BOLEY RONALD MARTIN	OH	18E	56
BOLGER LAWRENCE JOSEPH	PA	22E	68
BOLHOUSE DEAN FRANKLIN	SD	35W	19
BOLICH KENNETH CHARLES	PA	03E	70
BOLIN DANNY ARNOLD	OH	06E	121

NAME	STATE	PANEL NO.	LINE NO.
BOLIN DANNY LEE	IN	24E	73
BOLIN FORREST LEE	OK	37E	48
BOLINDER ARNOLD LEE	UT	54E	23
BOLING CHARLES GEORGE	GA	25W	20
BOLING CHARLES L	OH	11E	79
BOLING LESLEY JR	AR	37W	28
BOLLINGER ARTHUR RAY	IL	01W	114
BOLLINGER NEAL GEORGE	PA	43W	12
BOLLMAN DONALD WARREN	IL	15E	125
BOLLMAN ROBERT NORMAN	IL	08W	121
BOLLMAN ROBERT VINSON	OK	42W	15
BOLMAN DENNIS LOUIS	OH	26E	42
BOLSON JAMES JOSEPH	NY	37W	28
BOLSTER CHRISTOPHER ORAN	CA	36W	13
BOLSTER DAN ARTHUR	WA	02W	95
BOLT AUGUST FERREL	KY	54W	26
BOLTE WAYNE LOUIS	OK	02W	127
BOLTER KENT ROBERT	MI	51E	5
BOLTON ANDERSON DON	TX	34W	78
BOLTON BILLY CARROLL	TX	35E	66
BOLTON DAN ARTHUR JR	TN	26W	82
BOLTON DAVID JOSEPH	CA	56W	1
BOLTON DENNIS LEWIS	CA	33W	5
BOLTON DENNIS OPAL	IN	18E	47
BOLTON JESSE JAMES	TN	05E	76
BOLTON MELVIN	GA	25W	20
BOLTON WAYNE FRANKLIN	MN	34W	20
BOLTON WILLIE EDWARD	MS	29W	95
BOLTZ RICHARD LEONARD	NJ	15E	113
BOLTZE BRUCE EDWARD	MI	01W	80
BOLYARD LARRY CHARLES	FL	52E	34
BOMAR FRANK WILLIS	FL	06W	133
BOMBERRY GREGORY LEE	NY	45W	48
BONACCI LAWRENCE LOUIS	MI	41W	10
BONANNO FREDERICK M	FL	14E	96
BONAPART PAUL	NY	29W	43
BOND DAVID ARTHUR	AZ	04W	85
BOND FRANCIS ARTHUR	MA	09W	68
BOND GEORGE ALAN	OH	41W	28
BOND LAWRENCE FREDRICK	UT	58W	6
BOND RICHARD WILLIAM	MA	05E	129
BOND RONALD DALE	ND	44E	14
BOND RONALD LESLIE	NJ	02W	31
BOND THEODORE CHARLES	OH	56W	1
BOND WILLIAM ROSS	MD	12W	65
BONDERER THOMAS EDWARD	MO	53E	27
BONDI CHARLES NICK	OK	32W	31
BONDROWSKI DARREL ANTHONY	PA	38E	44
BONDS BYRON DEAN	IN	18E	56
BONDS CHARLES EDWARD	NC	42E	27
BONDS MICHAEL DAVID	MO	03W	24
BONE LOSSIE FRANKLIN	TX	13W	34
BONE ROBERT LYNN	TX	36W	43
BONEBRIGHT ROBERT ALLEN	IL	24W	37
BONERT RONALD JOSEPH	IL	21E	100
BONESTEEL DAVID LARRY	MI	21W	73
BONESTROO KENNETH WAYNE	IA	05W	80
BONETTI FREDDIE ALLEN	TX	34W	31
BONETTI PAUL JOSEPH	IL	57W	6
BONEY ALLEN LEWIS	NC	10W	40
BONEY BERNARD	NY	43E	51
BONEY WILLIAM	TX	39E	57
BONGARTZ CHARLES JOSEPH	PA	52E	27
BONGO ANTHONY	HI	24W	59
BONHAM THEODORE R JR	NC	55E	3
BONIFANT SAMUEL HAROLD	OH	54E	30
BONIFAZI GERARD REX	TX	09W	57
BONILLA HERMINIO AMELIO	IL	14W	32
BONILLA-VIERA FELIPE	PR	05E	70
BONILLAS GUILLERMO TRUJIL	AZ	08E	130
BONIN BOBBY JOE	TX	28E	64
BONINE THOMAS MARVIN	NJ	23W	50
BONJOUR KEVIN EARL	CA	07W	8
BONKO DONALD RAYMOND	OH	03E	114
BONNARENS FRANK OWEN	MO	43W	33
BONNEAU DEAN LOUIS	WI	11W	94
BONNELL GEORGE H III	OH	12E	62
BONNELL LARRY GENE	IN	18E	83
BONNELL WILLIAM LAWRENCE	MA	21E	86
BONNER CHARLES LARRY	TN	44E	57
BONNER DON W	AR	37W	28
BONNER FREDERICK NEIL	NJ	35W	11

NAME	STATE	PANEL NO.	LINE NO.
BONNER IKE OTHEL	OH	60W	7
BONNER JOHN SIDNEY JR	TX	10W	123
BONNER JOSEPH	MI	63E	5
BONNER ROGER LEE JR	GA	11E	32
BONNER WILLIAM EDWARD	GA	15W	97
BONNER WILLIAM ROBERT	CA	09W	71
BONNET CHRISTOPHER	VA	22E	5
BONNETT EUGENE EDWARD	NY	13E	42
BONNETT GEORGE FABIAN	MD	19W	49
BONNETT SHERL KENT	OH	36W	43
BONNETTE PAUL EUGENE	MA	38W	55
BONNEY ALAN WAYNE	PA	20E	100
BONNEY JOHN CLAIR	MI	47E	46
BONNICI ROBERT JOHN	MI	41W	61
BONNIE LEWIS ELI	IN	12E	40
BONO BEN DOMINIC	MO	19E	115
BONVENTRE THOMAS S	NY	21W	58
BONZO JOHN CLIFTON	UT	01E	32
BOOBAR LARRY DANIEL	ME	18W	46
BOOCHKO VICTOR	IL	47W	6
BOOE GARY MICHAEL	NC	09W	37
BOOKER ALBERT N	TX	26W	43
BOOKER HARVEY WATKINS	LA	51E	28
BOOKER JERRY LABORN	IN	51E	28
BOOKER JIMMY	MI	30W	51
BOOKER JOSEPH OTIS	VA	28E	33
BOOKER TERRY WAYNE	IN	17W	54
BOOKER THOMAS ARTHUR	AL	34E	11
BOOKOUT CHARLES FRANKLIN	OK	09W	117
BOOKS JAY KARL	PA	12E	78
BOOLIN CLARENCE HENRY	KS	28W	9
BOOMSMA ROGER ALLEN	CA	49E	39
BOON MURLIN EUGENE	OK	14E	55
BOONE ALAN RANSOM	IA	02W	43
BOONE DANNY LEE	KY	63E	4
BOONE DENNIS CLAYTON	NC	45W	23
BOONE JAMES ARTHUR	IL	19E	10
BOONE JOHN THOMAS	VA	27W	47
BOONE RANDOLPH ERNELL	NC	35E	87
BOONE ROBERT EDWARD	NY	45W	48
BOONE WILLIAM EDWARD	VA	40E	17
BOONE WILLIAM EDWARD	NC	07W	128
BOONE WILLIAM EDWARD IV	AL	27W	15
BOOR ALAN SCOTT	IL	07W	54
BOORAS PETER WILLIAM	NY	10E	25
BOORMAN JAMES EDWARD	PA	18E	100
BOOTH EMMETT LEE	CA	21E	86
BOOTH GARY PRESTON	WA	05W	1
BOOTH HERBERT W JR	FL	01E	13
BOOTH JAMES ERVIN	CA	55W	20
BOOTH JOHN BINGHAM	TX	25E	46
BOOTH JOHN ROBERT	PA	07E	64
BOOTH LAWRENCE RANDOLPH	VA	17W	83
BOOTH ROY ROBERT	TX	20E	128
BOOTH STEPHEN FLOYD	IN	43E	41
BOOTH TERRY LYLE	PA	17W	80
BOOTH WALTER CLAY	WI	28W	43
BOOTH WILLIAM DOUGLAS	PA	10W	22
BOOTHE BAY BENTON	PA	48W	16
BOOTHE RONALD CHARLES	NY	23W	5
BOOTS CURTIS EUGENE	ND	41W	10
BOOTS JAMES ALLEN	CA	39W	59
BOOTS STEPHEN ELDON	IA	05W	30
BOOTY LARRY OVEID JULIAN	LA	04E	118
BOOTZ CLARK T		07W	112
BOOZE DELMAR GEORGE	NE	04E	84
BOOZER DON ALLEN	MS	43E	3
BORAH DANIEL VERNOR JR	IL	01W	75
BORAWSKI JAMES DAVID	MO	19E	22
BORCHARD LEONARD E JR	IA	46E	14
BORCHART WILLIAM H	IL	32E	42
BORCHERS CARL WILHELM	MI	03W	68
BORCZYK STEPHEN ZBIGNIEW	IL	15E	39
BORCZYNSKI FREDERICK EARL	NY	42W	15
BORDEAUX JAMES PRESTON JR	VA	44W	61
BORDEN CHARLES E	NY	24E	116
BORDEN JAMES ARTHUR	TN	25W	16
BORDEN LAWRENCE THOMAS	MA	10E	90
BORDEN MURRAY LYMAN	NC	11E	69
BORDEN TIMOTHY ZANE	NJ	13W	129
BORDER WILLIAM EDWARD	OH	06E	108
BORDERS DARELD NORVAL	KS	54W	35

NAME	STATE	PANEL NO.	LINE NO.
BORDERS JOHN WILLIAM JR	CA	43E	51
BORDERS WARDELL	FL	60E	19
BORDES ANDREW MORLEY	IL	03W	120
BORDNER WILLIAM HAROLD	OH	05E	40
BORDUAS RAYMOND ARTHUR	ME	60W	8
BOREN JIMMY FLOYD	KY	03E	70
BOREN TOM EDWIN	GA	08E	29
BORENSTEIN BORIS FRANZ M	LA	30E	83
BOREY DAVID CHRISTOPHER	MA	19E	103
BORG JOHN MICHAEL	FL	22W	111
BORG MICHAEL ROYCE	AZ	07W	128
BORGEN CARL LEE	CA	47W	59
BORGENS JERRY LEE	CO	16E	72
BORGER ROBERT LEE	OH	12E	108
BORGES JOSEPH WILLIAM	RI	25W	21
BORGES MICHAEL EDWARD	CA	12W	78
BORGMAN NORRIS RAY	IN	14W	2
BORGMAN RICHARD LEE	ND	42E	47
BORICK JOSEPH JAMES	PA	18E	105
BORIEO RICHARD DAVID	AZ	06E	108
BORJA DOMINGO R S	CA	15E	67
BORJA JUAN SANTOS	GM	03W	15
BORKHOLDER JERRY M	IN	22W	104
BORLAND DENNIS ALLEN	NY	36W	71
BORMAN JERALD ALLEN	IN	47E	58
BORNEMAN DEAN ALLEN	IA	14W	58
BORNHEIMER RICHARD IRVING	NY	50W	48
BORNMAN DONALD WAYNE	IL	33E	44
BORNSTEIN ANTON THOMAS	WA	20E	40
BOROMISSZA CSABA FERENC	OH	07E	45
BORON DAVID JOSEPH	OH	25W	62
BORONSKI JOHN ARTHUR	MA	12W	37
BOROSKI ANTON WALTER	TX	21W	16
BOROSS LASZLO JR	NJ	35E	87
BOROVICK RICHARD JOHN	MA	35W	19
BOROWICZ KENNETH	NY	36E	66
BOROWSKI JOHN C	IL	23E	40
BOROWSKI RAYMOND JOHN	MI	20E	54
BOROWSKI TADEUSZ JAN	IN	60W	8
BOROWSKI WAYNE ROY	NC	04W	102
BOROWSKY CHARLES GEORGE	NC	11E	64
BORQUEZ LAWRENCE GABE	CA	34W	73
BORR JEFFREY	MI	18W	60
BORREGO ANTHONY J	NJ	23E	9
BORREGO EDWARD LEE	CA	17W	80
BORREGO LUIS CARLOS JR	TX	24W	14
BORREGO-RUIZ FRANCISCO J	TX	12W	99
BORRELL CLIFFORD GLENN	PA	41E	7
BORRERO-SANCHEZ JOSE LUIS	PR	17W	108
BORROUSCH DEAN WALTER	MI	13W	31
BORRUSO JOSEPH JR	CA	06W	22
BORS JOSEPH CHESTER	NY	52E	34
BORSAY PETER SAMUEL	WV	23W	25
BORSCHEL LARRY DEAN	IA	04E	3
BORST LEROY J JR	IL	15E	30
BORT HARRY JULIAN	MD	08W	48
BORTLE JONATHAN R	NY	18W	36
BORTON ROBERT CURTIS JR	MI	10E	53
BORYSZEWSKI STEPHEN J	NY	27W	47
BORZYCH DAVID RUSSELL	WI	12W	95
BOSBERY DONALD CHARLES	CA	27W	54
BOSCH ERIC ALAN	CA	15W	97
BOSCH JOHN ARTHUR	NY	47W	15
BOSCO FRANK JOSEPH	RI	22W	102
BOSENBARK SAMUEL GAROLD	MI	23W	83
BOSH ANTHONY ROBERT	CA	10E	73
BOSHEERS JAMES LARRY	TN	53E	27
BOSKO MICHAEL JOHN JR	NJ	11E	120
BOSLEY JAMES GILBERT	WV	25E	81
BOSOWSKI MICHAEL ALAN	MI	13W	13
BOSS CHARLES FREDRIC	MI	23E	73
BOSS ROBERT LEON	MA	07E	32
BOSSE LAURIER GERARD	RI	66E	6
BOSSER JOHNNY STEVE	CO	19W	127
BOSSIE KENNETH JAMES	ME	08E	33
BOSSIO GALILEO FRED	WA	09E	85
BOSSMAN PETER ROBERT	NY	11E	12
BOSSOM JOHN AUSTIN	OR	15W	9
BOSSONG FRANK W	NY	30W	36
BOST MICHAEL JAMES	MI	19E	115
BOSTICK BENJAMIN R IV	KY	07W	91
BOSTOCK JAMES EDWARD	NY	14E	122

NAME	STATE	PANEL NO.	LINE NO.
BOSTON CHARLES EDWARD	AR	04E	6
BOSTON DONALD EARL	AL	17E	114
BOSTON GROVER WESLEY	OK	54E	2
BOSTON HARRY JAMES	NC	34E	51
BOSTON JAMES JR	FL	24W	91
BOSTON JOHNNY B	MS	06E	79
BOSTON KENNETH DEAN	MO	14W	129
BOSTON LEO SYDNEY	CO	07E	7
BOSTON RONALD	NY	22E	96
BOSWELL BRADLEY LLOYD	PA	07W	65
BOSWELL DAVID HENRY	NY	43E	14
BOSWELL JOE ROSCOE	MO	34W	74
BOSWELL JOHNNIE LEE	GA	03E	52
BOSWELL RICHARD WELDON JR	TX	15W	69
BOSWELL WILLIAM HENRY	IL	49E	51
BOSWORTH DAVID RUSSELL	ME	40E	36
BOSWORTH RAYMOND PAUL JR	TX	53W	7
BOSWORTH RICHARD LEE	OH	39E	60
BOSWORTH TERRY LEE	CA	04W	94
BOTELLO JUAN JOSE	TX	23E	68
BOTES GEORGE	IL	63E	5
BOTHWELL WILLIAM DAVID	TX	07W	88
BOTT RUSSELL PETER	MA	13E	3
BOTTAN DANIEL JACQUES	CA	46W	56
BOTTESCH JOHN RICHARD	PA	09E	36
BOTTOM A J	IL	14E	31
BOTTOMS HAROLD GENE	IL	26W	7
BOTTS DAVID MARTIN	MN	47W	6
BOTTS ROBERT EUGENE	OH	45W	40
BOTTS THOMAS H	OH	02E	74
BOUCHARD MICHAEL LORA	MT	36W	48
BOUCHARD MICHAEL PHILIP	MA	09W	3
BOUCHARD PETER JOSEPH	MA	28W	65
BOUCHARD RICHARD GEORGE	NH	18W	112
BOUCHARD ROGER HAROLD	MI	08W	87
BOUCHARD WILLARD J JR	MA	02W	4
BOUCHER ROBERT CHARLES	PA	26W	13
BOUCHET ROBERT LOUIS	MA	49W	46
BOUCHEZ DANNY PHILLIP	IL	46E	3
BOUDRA KILBERN DEAN	AR	25W	95
BOUDREAU JOHN HENRY	MI	19E	55
BOUDREAUX ALLEN JOHN	CA	64E	12
BOUDREAUX JIMMY DALE	MS	17W	119
BOUDREAUX KENNETH CHARLES	LA	09E	1
BOUDREAUX LEE JOSEPH JR	LA	13E	3
BOUGHNER GARY WILLIAM	MI	35W	8
BOUINGTON JOHNNY WILLIAM	LA	03E	113
BOUKNIGHT CALVIN	DC	03E	64
BOULE THOMAS MICHAEL	NY	27W	8
BOULLION ELLIAS	LA	02E	98
BOULWARE GEORGE WALTER	MI	02W	17
BOULWARE SHERMAN JAMES	OH	61E	23
BOUNDS GARY LEE	MD	55E	3
BOURDAGE NELSON JOSEPH	MI	43E	6
BOURDEAU GERALD LEE	CT	12E	26
BOURDEAU VINCENT CARMEN	NY	12E	25
BOURG MILLER JOHN	LA	08E	91
BOURGEOIS LEROY ANTHONY	TX	02E	12
BOURGEOIS WILFRID NARCISS	MA	01E	61
BOURNE GEORGE LEANDER	RI	20W	106
BOURNE JOHN NOLAN	UT	62W	20
BOURNE LAWRENCE GILBERT	MO	40W	62
BOURNE RICHARD E	NY	32E	49
BOURQUE BRADLEY JOHN	LA	36W	32
BOURQUE VALMORE WILLIAM	MA	01E	67
BOURRAGE I V	MS	15E	68
BOUSHELE GARY RAY	ID	17W	123
BOUSLEY DONALD GEORGE	MI	36W	63
BOUSQUET JAMES ESTREM	IA	26W	38
BOUSQUET ROBERT GEORGE	MA	02E	54
BOUTON JEFFERY DALE	FL	18E	56
BOUTON WILLIAM INNES JR	SC	35W	53
BOUTTRY CHARLES EDWARD	NY	24W	1
BOUTWELL AMOS HAYES	FL	38E	21
BOUYER JAMES EARL	AL	28W	101
BOVA EDWARD JAMES	MI	37E	49
BOVAN PAUL CLAYTON	MI	12W	102
BOVE HARMON JOSEPH JR	VT	13W	80
BOVE ROGER GERHARD	VA	21W	110
BOVINETTE CHARLES E JR	MI	05W	127
BOVIO RICHARD STEPHEN	TX	13W	61
BOW MICHAEL WAYNE	TX	13W	80

NAME	STATE	PANEL NO.	LINE NO.
BOWARD KENNETH WILLIAM	WV	14W	2
BOWCUTT SCOTT CANNON	UT	16E	129
BOWDEN BYRON BILL	CA	23W	25
BOWDEN CARLYLE MILLER III	VA	27W	93
BOWDEN JAMES EDWARD	WA	45W	36
BOWDEN JAMES LEE	NC	47W	15
BOWDEN JAMES RONALD	GA	54E	31
BOWDEN JOHN WESTLEY	NC	62W	5
BOWDEN LEE ANDREW	NC	48E	23
BOWDEN RICKY LYNN	AR	14W	119
BOWDERN ROBERT JAMES JR	MO	52E	27
BOWDISH KEVEN WAYNE	OR	66W	1
BOWDLER GARY LEE	NY	18W	53
BOWDREN JAMES IGNATIUS JR	PA	06W	75
BOWE ROBERT WILLIAM	FL	26W	106
BOWE THOMAS JOHN	CT	30W	72
BOWELL TERRANCE LEE	CO	13W	70
BOWEN ARCHIE SHERROD	FL	01E	27
BOWEN BILLY ROY	TX	45E	18
BOWEN CLIFTON LEE	TN	44W	56
BOWEN DONALD	NY	34E	74
BOWEN DUANE CURTIS	CA	23W	6
BOWEN GROVER	OH	18W	119
BOWEN GROVER CLEVELAND	WA	32W	69
BOWEN HAMMETT LEE JR	FL	21W	21
BOWEN HARVEY LEWIS JR	GA	05E	70
BOWEN HOWARD LEWIS	NY	12E	40
BOWEN JOHN JR	WV	07W	80
BOWEN JOHN LEWIS	CA	21W	17
BOWEN LARRY HANSEN	NJ	23W	96
BOWEN LARRY WILLIAM	CA	39W	39
BOWEN MARVIN WHITNER	SC	34E	66
BOWEN MATTHEW ANDERSON	SC	03W	24
BOWEN RALPH EDWARD	MI	27E	52
BOWEN RAYMOND LEWIS JR	NY	04E	84
BOWEN ROLAND MICHAEL	GA	35E	87
BOWEN STANLEY E	WA	22E	90
BOWEN THOMAS RAY	CA	12W	65
BOWENS FRANK	FL	09W	62
BOWENS JAMES TERRY	MI	12E	119
BOWENS TOMMY	TX	06W	76
BOWER HOWARD JAMES JR	MI	04W	102
BOWER IRVIN LESTER JR	PA	17W	44
BOWER JIMMY CHARLES	IL	35W	81
BOWER JOSEPH EDWARD	NV	02E	47
BOWERS BRADLEY D	OK	53W	7
BOWERS BRUCE ELLIOT	MI	18E	39
BOWERS DANNY WARD	MI	10W	107
BOWERS DONALD IRA	PA	08E	51
BOWERS EDGAR LEE	NC	52W	40
BOWERS GROVER COLEMAN JR	SC	14W	24
BOWERS JAMES DALE	PA	08E	117
BOWERS JAMES DAVID	TN	67E	5
BOWERS JAMES E	VA	10E	16
BOWERS JAMES RICHARD JR	NC	13W	91
BOWERS JEROME EARL	OH	18W	13
BOWERS JEROME EDWARD JR	PA	11W	20
BOWERS JOHN MICHAEL	MD	06E	28
BOWERS LARRY HUTTON	OH	31E	63
BOWERS RICHARD ALAN	CA	58E	30
BOWERS RICHARD LEE	WI	28W	23
BOWERS RICHARD SAULERS	IA	04W	13
BOWERS STEVEN WAYNE	NY	24E	5
BOWERS WILLIAM JAMES	PA	43E	52
BOWERSMITH CHARLES GEORGE	OH	29E	27
BOWERSOCK STEVEN EDWARD	OH	01W	16
BOWERSOX CHARLES W JR	PA	22E	96
BOWLEN HAROLD DAVID	AL	02W	69
BOWLER SHELDON DON	UT	30E	61
BOWLES BRUCE GREGORY	ID	34W	4
BOWLES DWIGHT POLLARD	VA	03E	14
BOWLES FRANK JOSEPH	VA	23E	38
BOWLES HARRY OWEN	KS	02W	40
BOWLES LLOYD LANE	IL	10W	129
BOWLES THEOPHILUS	CA	29W	35
BOWLIN PAUL MADISON	VA	23W	109
BOWLIN ROBERT JOE	IL	35W	46
BOWLING BRADLEY	KY	65W	5
BOWLING DAVID BICKNEL	MD	15W	93
BOWLING GARY DEAN	OH	48W	23
BOWLING JAMES WISDOM	IN	37W	54
BOWLING JOHN RAYMOND SR	VA	11E	132
BOWLING JOSEPH PERRY	KS	38E	75
BOWLING ROY HOWARD	CA	03E	70
BOWMAN ARTHUR BAILEY JR	NY	44W	14
BOWMAN BARRY ALAN	OR	02W	40
BOWMAN BRICKIE JR	MI	01E	123
BOWMAN BRUCE ALLEN	CO	04W	32
BOWMAN CLARENCE JR	IN	56W	17
BOWMAN CURTIS	SC	19W	53
BOWMAN DANIEL RAYMOND	GA	33E	80
BOWMAN DAVID FRANK	MI	30E	96
BOWMAN DAVID LLOYD JR	MN	37E	51
BOWMAN DAVID WINSLOW	MA	01E	101
BOWMAN DONALD ROBERT	KS	38E	21
BOWMAN FRANK	SC	56W	1
BOWMAN HAROLD E	OK	52W	38
BOWMAN HARRY THOMAS II	NJ	57E	14
BOWMAN JACK ALLEN	IN	39W	77
BOWMAN JAMES EDGAR	TN	55E	3
BOWMAN JAMES ERNEST	OH	21W	30
BOWMAN JAMES LAVERN	MI	46E	52
BOWMAN JESSE CARL	KY	28W	43
BOWMAN JOHN DAVID III	PA	05E	20
BOWMAN JOHN OTTO	OR	25W	9
BOWMAN JOSEPH B	VA	38E	21
BOWMAN JOSEPH GEORGE JR	MI	29W	96
BOWMAN JOSEPH MICHAEL	PA	40W	62
BOWMAN LARRY EARL	OH	24E	111
BOWMAN LESLIE VON	IN	40W	71
BOWMAN LESTER ELWOOD JR	PA	51W	29
BOWMAN MELVIN	SC	11W	109
BOWMAN MICHAEL LEE	OH	17W	25
BOWMAN PAUL BARKLEY	MI	14W	83
BOWMAN PAUL JR	CA	21E	103
BOWMAN REGINALD ALONZO	MD	61E	24
BOWMAN RICHARD ALAN	DE	09W	31
BOWMAN ROBERT CARLOSS	FL	04E	86
BOWMAN ROBERT EARL	KY	25W	35
BOWMAN ROBERT EUGENE	OH	33E	16
BOWMAN ROBERT MICHAEL	DE	08E	107
BOWMAN ROBERT WAYNE	PA	29W	43
BOWMAN ROGER DALE	VA	48W	17
BOWMAN RONALD LEON	MO	10E	28
BOWMAN RUDY GORDON	OH	16E	34
BOWMAN STEPHEN WESLEY	CA	61W	10
BOWMAN TOMMY RAY	MI	42W	26
BOWMAN WILLIAM PARKER	IL	40W	9
BOWMAN WILLIAM THOMAS	OH	01E	111
BOWMAN WILLIS SHEPHERD JR	PA	09E	72
BOWYER ARTHUR J	MD	07E	47
BOWYER REX ALLAN	WV	36E	46
BOX HOUSTON CLIFFORD JR	CA	33E	16
BOX JOHN ROBERT	CA	18W	60
BOXLER CHARLES EVERETT	DE	17W	126
BOYANOWSKI JOHN GORDON	PA	02W	87
BOYCE ALTON	AR	66W	1
BOYCE EUGENE RUSSELL	SC	44W	35
BOYCE GARY LEE	IN	01W	108
BOYCE JAMES FRANKLIN	NJ	34W	41
BOYCE JOHN FRANKLIN	AZ	10E	6
BOYCE JOHN MERTON	OR	42E	27
BOYCE LAWRENCE STEVEN	CA	25W	35
BOYCE McDONALD E	MD	51E	16
BOYCE SAMUEL MINOR	AR	37E	49
BOYCE TERRY LAWRENCE	IL	40E	1
BOYD ANANIAS	AL	63W	3
BOYD BILLY RAY	CA	21E	42
BOYD BRADLEY MONROE	CA	63W	14
BOYD CHARLES	MS	32W	36
BOYD DAVID LEROY	NJ	38E	45
BOYD DAVID STEWART	NY	12E	70
BOYD DON GAYNOR	MI	15E	113
BOYD ERNEST JR	IL	63W	3
BOYD GERALD DAVID	CT	22E	31
BOYD HURLEY MILLARD	OH	28W	107
BOYD JAMES	NC	41E	59
BOYD JAMES P	TX	17E	115
BOYD JOHN JOSEPH JR	TN	13W	130
BOYD JOHN LEE	CA	42W	15
BOYD RANDALL JAMES	TX	03W	65
BOYD RICHARD EUGENE	KS	46E	14
BOYD RICHARD KLEMM JR	PA	28E	72
BOYD ROBERT CARL	CA	13E	71
BOYD ROBERT RAY	TN	20E	12
BOYD ROBERT WHITE	ME	27E	98
BOYD ROGER WILLIAM	IL	66E	6
BOYD ROY BRADLEY	MO	28W	79
BOYD SAM HENRY	SC	64W	5
BOYD SAMUEL JR	NJ	60W	25
BOYD SAMUEL LEE JR	OK	41W	34
BOYD STEPHEN LESLIE	NY	08W	78
BOYD THOMAS MASSIE III	TX	59E	16
BOYD WALTER	VA	01W	132
BOYD WAYNE	SC	47E	46
BOYD WILBURN HUGH	IL	08E	96
BOYD WILLIAM DEMARR	CA	13E	115
BOYDEN THOMAS ROBERT	NJ	32E	8
BOYDSTON OSCAR DAN	CA	25W	95
BOYE HENRY JOSEPH JR	NJ	62W	5
BOYER ALAN LEE	MT	46E	52
BOYER BARNEY EVANS	CA	02E	78
BOYER BRUCE E	RI	21E	31
BOYER CHARLES DENNIS	NY	55W	11
BOYER CHARLES GOODHUE	MT	43E	14
BOYER CHARLES THOMAS	OH	57E	14
BOYER DAVID EUGENE	PA	22E	82
BOYER DENNIS MICHAEL	MO	11W	29
BOYER DONALD WILLIAM	CA	29E	104
BOYER JAMES ALAN	IL	08W	76
BOYER JAMES IRVIN	PA	02E	83
BOYER JAMES ROGER	MO	26E	111
BOYER JOHN WILLIAM	OH	26E	87
BOYER LARRY DEAN	IL	14W	51
BOYER LARRY EUGENE	AL	33W	36
BOYER LARRY EUGENE	PA	24W	101
BOYER MICHAEL DAVID	OR	22W	72
BOYER MONTY DOYAL	NM	07W	43
BOYER ROBERT LEE	CA	32E	84
BOYER RONALD EARNEST	IL	33W	91
BOYER STEPHEN GREGORY	SD	62W	20
BOYER STEVEN HESS	PA	03E	125
BOYER THOMAS MICHAEL	MI	07W	125
BOYER WAYNE DOUGLAS	WV	37E	49
BOYER WILLIAM KLINE	IA	08W	10
BOYETT GARY RODNEY	FL	14E	31
BOYETT PAUL DEWAYNE	OK	52E	14
BOYEV PETER KESTUTIS	IL	11W	54
BOYKIN KENNETH LEE	TX	04W	37
BOYKIN PRENTIS BARNEY JR	WA	42E	61
BOYKIN ROBERT THOMAS	VA	20E	54
BOYKINS RANDY RONELL	AZ	30W	85
BOYLE DAVID JOSEPH	CA	05E	31
BOYLE FRANCIS MICHAEL	NY	06E	38
BOYLE HARRY LEWIS	CA	51W	38
BOYLE JAMES PATRICK	IL	50E	26
BOYLE JAMES ROBERT	PA	35W	8
BOYLE JOHN ALEX	ID	34W	83
BOYLE MICHAEL PETER	WA	49W	36
BOYLE RICHARD EUGENE	TX	18E	21
BOYLE ROBERT RAY	NE	40E	37
BOYLE WILLIAM	PA	13W	67
BOYLES DONALD RAY	OK	16W	104
BOYLES JERRY LEE	MO	50E	36
BOYLESS JOSE JULIO	MI	14E	85
BOYNTON CHARLES B JR	MD	50E	11
BOYNTON FRANK	GA	02E	86
BOYTER GEDDES CHARLES JR	SC	54W	26
BOZARTH ALVIN RAY	CA	24E	106
BOZARTH TERANCE M	OH	40E	58
BOZEMAN CHARLES LEE	AR	45E	18
BOZEMAN DWIGHT ERVYN	GA	57E	15
BOZEMAN PERRY LEONARD	CA	29W	4
BOZIER WILLIE JR	NY	08W	1
BOZIKIS RONALD HENRY	MO	17W	116
BOZINSKI JOHN MICHAEL	WI	19W	43
BOZZELLO FRANK MARIO	WA	24E	108
BRAASCH GARY WILLIAM	MN	11E	55
BRAATZ CURTISS EDWARD	MI	38W	23
BRABANT WILLIAM ANDREW	NY	41W	28
BRABO HENRY	CO	19W	9
BRACE BRUCE WAYNE	CA	12W	59
BRACEY LESTER	NY	01W	13
BRACK DAVID ALLAN	CO	23W	35
BRACK HARRY HUBERT JR	KS	02W	47
BRACKEN ALAN LEE	PA	14W	64

NAME	STATE	PANEL NO.	LINE NO.
BRACKENS JOE JEFFERSON	LA	35W	41
BRACKER DAVID EUGENE	FL	10E	18
BRACKETT EVERETT LEE	OH	10E	100
BRACKETT FRANK	IL	31E	43
BRACKIN RANDY CARROLL	AL	07W	29
BRACKINS ALLEN	GA	06E	132
BRACKINS VERNON EDWARD	CA	10E	56
BRADBERRY ARTHUR MILTON	AL	28W	89
BRADBERRY DUDLEY FRANCIS	TX	02W	22
BRADBURY STEVEN WAYNE	KS	21W	110
BRADDOCK STEPHEN LEE	TX	35E	88
BRADEE GARY LEROY	FL	56E	20
BRADEN TERRY LEE	MO	14E	68
BRADFORD ALLEN ROYAL	KS	56E	20
BRADFORD CHARLES MARSHALL	KY	11E	43
BRADFORD EDWARD LEWIS	OK	59W	19
BRADFORD ELLSWORTH SMITH	IL	17W	65
BRADFORD JOHN LESLIE	TN	20W	82
BRADFORD JOHN TRAVIS	TX	11E	117
BRADFORD KIRBY WAYNE	TN	14E	79
BRADFORD LEONARD EDWARD	PA	35W	2
BRADFORD RODNEY	IL	43W	6
BRADFORD SHERMAN DUANE	CA	34W	81
BRADFORD TERRILL EDWARD	TN	03W	17
BRADFORD THOMAS JOHNSON	MI	54E	2
BRADFORD WILLIAM JONATHAN	CA	03W	120
BRADFORD WILLIE B	AR	43E	65
BRADLE JAMES DENNIS	WI	08W	101
BRADLEY ALFRED LEE	OK	07W	88
BRADLEY DAVID MICHAEL	WA	22E	96
BRADLEY DENNIS DALE	WA	10E	131
BRADLEY FRANKLIN S JR	TX	38E	45
BRADLEY GERALD GREGORY	MA	34W	4
BRADLEY GIVEN WEST	KY	38E	75
BRADLEY GLEN WAYNE	OR	02E	34
BRADLEY GLENN MARTIN	KY	18W	124
BRADLEY JAMES	SC	05E	4
BRADLEY JAMES JEROME	NY	05E	113
BRADLEY JOHN ALLAN	PA	37E	78
BRADLEY JOSEPH KEITH	TN	26E	6
BRADLEY KENNETH EUGENE	TN	66W	2
BRADLEY KENNETH RAY	SC	37E	49
BRADLEY KENNETH ROBERT	IN	41E	59
BRADLEY LARRY ALAN	TX	14W	7
BRADLEY LARRY GRANT	TN	35W	76
BRADLEY LOREN EUGENE	IL	07E	7
BRADLEY LOUIS LLOYD JR	LA	61E	6
BRADLEY MARTEE JR	MI	37W	61
BRADLEY MICHAEL LEE	CA	07W	95
BRADLEY RAY EUGENE	CA	15E	40
BRADLEY RICHARD ALLEN	TN	08E	62
BRADLEY RICHARD BURTON	NY	03E	64
BRADLEY RICKY CURTIS	AR	33W	36
BRADLEY ROBERT NEAL	MI	16E	129
BRADLEY ROBERT RICHARD	WA	26W	6
BRADLEY ROBERT TIMOTHY	MI	04W	82
BRADLEY RUBIN FLETCHER	AL	02E	23
BRADLEY STANLEY THOMAS	GA	28W	66
BRADLEY SYLVAN KEITH	MO	12E	49
BRADLEY THOMAS JAMES	MN	22W	85
BRADLEY THOMAS R	NC	06W	75
BRADLEY TYRONE CARLOS	AL	05W	86
BRADLEY WILLIAM MARTIN	NY	27E	33
BRADLEY WOODROW WILSON JR	NC	40W	75
BRADMAN JOHN FREDRIC	NJ	13W	26
BRADNER JACK RAY	VA	07E	61
BRADSBY KERNELL PERSONE	VA	26W	89
BRADSHAW CONLEY ARLEN	TN	61W	10
BRADSHAW DAVID ALFORD	OK	39W	63
BRADSHAW DAVID ALLEN	MI	26E	22
BRADSHAW FAYBERT RAY	TX	02E	40
BRADSHAW FLOYD LEE III	GA	03W	77
BRADSHAW HENRY LEE	CA	49W	50
BRADSHAW JAMES THOMAS	IL	16E	108
BRADSHAW JESSE JOHN	NC	36W	32
BRADSHAW PAUL LESLIE	WA	04W	16
BRADSHAW ROBERT S III	TX	14W	129
BRADSHAW THEODORE JACKSON	AR	07E	93
BRADSHER ROBERT JR	DC	08W	17
BRADY DANIEL WILLIAM	PA	22E	97
BRADY DAVID HARVEY	TN	07W	46
BRADY EDWARD FRANCIS III	NJ	10W	22
BRADY EDWARD MARK	NY	23E	17
BRADY JAMES ALFRED SR	TN	54W	35
BRADY JAMES GREGORY	CA	38W	71
BRADY JAMES HOMER	FL	10W	129
BRADY JAMES PATRICK	WA	22W	72
BRADY JOHN JAMES	WA	47E	46
BRADY JOHN PATRICK JR	NY	16W	27
BRADY JOSEPH CLINTON	TX	04E	14
BRADY JOSEPH JAMES	MI	51E	44
BRADY JOSEPH MARTIN	WV	14E	122
BRADY MICHAEL EDWIN	NY	29W	42
BRADY MICHAEL ERVAN	NH	14E	90
BRADY MICHAEL JOHN	MA	32W	90
BRADY ROBERT JAMES	NJ	20E	40
BRADY SHERMAN C	MS	59E	17
BRADY TERRY PHILIP	FL	42W	38
BRADY THOMAS GERALD	CA	30E	53
BRADY THOMAS PAUL	CA	23E	107
BRADY THOMAS RICHARD	NY	06W	34
BRAEUTIGAN MICHAEL L	NV	20E	13
BRAGA JOHN PAUL JR	RI	35E	88
BRAGER ROY LEE	TX	66W	4
BRAGG CLAUDE EDWARD	SC	33W	91
BRAGG DONNIE JAY	VA	15W	57
BRAGG FRED GARLAND JR	OH	23E	55
BRAGG JOE EDDY	KY	24W	1
BRAGG JOHN ROBERT	IN	23W	83
BRAGG PAUL JOSEPH	NE	21W	123
BRAGG RAYMOND DALE	WV	13W	15
BRAGG ROGER DALE	WA	27W	36
BRAGGS ROOSEVELT JUNIOR	OH	09W	12
BRAGHINI ROBERTO JR	KY	55W	39
BRAGUE EDWIN STEVEN JR	NJ	13E	120
BRAICO NICHOLAS JOHN	IL	11W	99
BRAID JOHN EDWARD	MI	22W	117
BRAINERD FLEMING B III	OH	01E	124
BRAIS JIMMY GENE	WA	09E	120
BRAITHWAITE ARNIM N	NY	21W	123
BRAKE BOYD LAWERENCE	KY	30W	41
BRAM AARON L	IL	13E	49
BRAM RICHARD CRAIG	OH	02E	31
BRAMAN DONALD LEON	CT	01E	15
BRAME CLARENCE RAY	NC	07E	93
BRAMLET WILLIE JOE	TX	05E	112
BRAMLETT HOWARD WAYNE JR	AL	05W	14
BRAMSEN DAVID EUGENE	OR	20W	75
BRAMWELL RAYMOND SANDERS	TN	08W	132
BRANAM LARRY ANTHONY	TN	12W	19
BRANAM RONNIE FRANKLIN	TN	49E	8
BRANAMAN KENNETH MERLE	IN	09E	36
BRANAUGH LARRY JAMES	CO	51E	5
BRANCATO JOHN HARRISON JR	IL	37E	81
BRANCATO MICHAEL GEORGE	CA	02E	111
BRANCATO PETER JOSEPH JR	NY	08E	46
BRANCH CHARLES ARTHUR	MN	42W	53
BRANCH DAVID WESLEY	FL	11E	55
BRANCH FREDDIE ISIDORE	NM	07E	67
BRANCH GEORGE ALLEN	LA	48W	38
BRANCH JAMES	NY	32W	24
BRANCH JAMES ALVIN	IL	02E	75
BRANCH LOUIS WILLIAM	FL	33E	64
BRANCH WILLIAM ANDERSON	NJ	09W	18
BRANCHEAU DANIEL ALLAN	MI	02W	2
BRANCHEAU FRANCIS EMIL II	MI	19W	69
BRANCIO DAVID MIKE	CO	51E	36
BRAND JOSEPH WILLIAM	IL	10E	14
BRAND THOMAS RICHARD	MI	02E	54
BRAND WILLIAM EDWARD	WA	11E	100
BRANDBORG JOHN RALPH	MN	28W	9
BRANDENBURG CHARLES FRANK	MD	24E	79
BRANDENBURG DALE	MD	01W	114
BRANDENBURG STEVEN KEITH	IN	48W	52
BRANDENBURG VERLIN RICHARD	IN	19E	49
BRANDES KENNETH NEIL	NY	47W	25
BRANDES THOMAS GLENN	WI	03E	70
BRANDOM THOMAS M JR	MO	26W	43
BRANDON DARWIN OTHEL	OH	08W	53
BRANDON DAVID BRUCE JR	OR	07E	115
BRANDON JAMES BYRD	IL	37E	4
BRANDON JAMES MILES JR	VA	16E	99
BRANDON JESSE L	NC	15E	125
BRANDON PHILLIP MICHAEL	OH	04W	30
BRANDON TOMMIE	MI	40E	1
BRANDT FREDRICK KEITH	MI	05W	13
BRANDT GEAROLD LEE	KS	22W	11
BRANDT KEITH ALLAN	WA	04W	57
BRANDT RICHARD CARL	MA	13E	17
BRANDTS HARLAN RAY	IA	42E	28
BRANES EDUARDO PAUL	NY	18E	52
BRANHAM HARRY WALTER	VA	16E	107
BRANHAM JAMES JEROME	IL	19W	9
BRANHAM JOHNNY THOMAS	SC	23E	93
BRANHAM ROY LEE	MI	19E	89
BRANIGAN LAWRENCE ANTHONY	PA	44E	24
BRANIN MICHAEL FRANCIS JR	NJ	39W	58
BRANK IRA CHARLES	KY	02W	21
BRANN DANA E	MA	03E	65
BRANNAN JAMES CURTIS	LA	28W	96
BRANNEN JAMES ROBERT	GA	10E	123
BRANNFORS ERIC ARTHUR	OR	13E	89
BRANNING WILBUR RALPH JR	TX	43W	1
BRANNOCK JERRY W	NC	31E	80
BRANNOM MORRIS II	TX	32W	76
BRANNON CLAYTON CHARLES	FL	48W	23
BRANNON DAVID CRAIG	MI	16W	2
BRANNON GARY MICHAEL	OK	28W	33
BRANNON HARRY G	NJ	10E	6
BRANNON JAMES EDWARD	WI	28W	33
BRANNON JOHN LESLIE	OR	03W	133
BRANNON PAT GERARD	OH	02W	47
BRANNON PAUL DEWITT	AL	11W	67
BRANNON PHILLIP ARTHUR	TX	10E	96
BRANNON WALTER LEE	SC	47E	8
BRANOCK WILLIAM MICHEAL	MD	15E	61
BRANSCUM ARLIS RAY	AR	14W	114
BRANSON DANIEL ALEXANDER	KY	49E	51
BRANSON DAVID RUSSELL	OH	16W	27
BRANSON JAMES ALLAN	CT	10E	84
BRANSON JERRY LEON	MO	10E	116
BRANSON RALPH ALTON JR	MO	45E	8
BRANSTROM DAVID JOSEPH	NE	13E	20
BRANT DAVE WILLIAM	MI	41W	62
BRANT DONALD GENE	NY	40E	37
BRANT RICHARD F JR	GA	14W	3
BRANTLEY ALEXANDER BRYANT	FL	22W	18
BRANTLEY DAVID WATSON	GA	59W	19
BRANTLEY JOHN ARTHUR	IL	21E	117
BRANTLEY LEROY	SC	28W	66
BRANTLEY LESTER J	VA	19W	76
BRANTLEY MARK CURTIS	CA	09W	71
BRANTLEY TROY ELLIS JR	GA	03W	135
BRANTLEY WILLIAM OSLER JR	MS	16W	127
BRANTMEIER BERNARD GEORGE	WI	09W	90
BRANTNER WAYNE EUGENE	PA	29W	51
BRANYAN PAUL F JR	DE	31E	71
BRASCHE GERALD WILLIAM	IL	11E	1
BRASHEAR WILLIAM JAMES	CA	25W	21
BRASHEARS LARRY FRANKLIN	MD	53E	10
BRASHEARS RONALD LEE	MO	23W	70
BRASHER JIMMY MAC	TX	28E	33
BRASIER CHARLES DAVID	OK	21W	115
BRASILE TERRENCE CARMINE	NY	20W	106
BRASINGTON JACK WILLIAMS	SC	40E	51
BRASS BASIL PLANE	FL	10E	14
BRASS PAUL ROBERT	IL	06W	119
BRASSFIELD ANDREW THOMAS	OH	12W	100
BRASWELL BOBBY JOE	TX	05E	32
BRASWELL BOBBY MCRAY	NC	23E	56
BRASWELL DANNIE GLENN	IN	08E	33
BRASWELL DONNY JOE	GA	08W	8
BRASWELL JAMES EARL	NC	39W	46
BRASWELL JAMES HILLIARD	NJ	16W	104
BRASWELL JAMES PORTER JR	NY	26E	42
BRATCHER CHARLIE ARUCE	KY	40E	1
BRATCHER CLIFFORD SHERAN	TX	09E	44
BRATHWAITE ROGER CLAYTON	NY	20W	5
BRATRSOVSKY GERALD JOHN	CO	28W	66
BRATTAIN THOMAS LAIRD	OR	38W	82
BRATTON DARRELL DWANE	AR	65E	5
BRATTON FREDDY LAMAR	CA	10W	119
BRATTON JOHN LESLIE	LA	39W	48
BRATTON ROY DONALD	SC	20W	94
BRATZ WAYNE ALLEN	WI	29W	5
BRAUBURGER EVERETT W	ID	20W	38

NAME	STATE	PANEL NO.	LINE NO.
BRAUGHTON CLYDE B JR	OH	35E	88
BRAULT DENNIS JAMES	MA	09W	93
BRAUN EDWARD RAYMOND	WY	51W	23
BRAUN HARRY WALKER JR	IL	63E	5
BRAUN MICHAEL WILLIAM	WI	66W	2
BRAUN PAUL JOSEPH	CT	18E	105
BRAUNER HENRY PAUL	NJ	02W	121
BRAVIN JOSEPH SIMON	NY	43W	25
BRAWNER FRANK EDWARD	KY	35W	32
BRAXTON JAMES HAROLD	AZ	16E	100
BRAXTON JOHN ALAN	PA	20W	48
BRAY ARNOLD REX	TX	26W	59
BRAY BERNARD	NY	10W	94
BRAY CHARLES EDWIN JR	CT	08W	2
BRAY ERVIL THOMAS	KY	24E	17
BRAY RALPH OSCAR JR	KS	21W	105
BRAY RICHARD LOYD III	FL	40W	41
BRAY RONNIE LEE	NC	10E	28
BRAY WILLIAM ROBERT	NC	27E	79
BRAYBOY BRYANT JR	PA	03E	29
BRAYBROOKE CHRISTOPHER	NJ	27E	73
BRAYE LLOYD HERBERT	NY	08E	84
BRAZEN HAROLD J	PA	04E	54
BRAZIER JOHN KENNETH	MD	60W	25
BRAZIK RICHARD	OH	24E	1
BRAZZEAL TED OLAND	TX	70W	1
BRDA JUSTIN PAUL	MI	10W	112
BREAULT RODERICK WAYNE	NY	31E	2
BREAUX LEONARD	LA	37E	19
BREAUX SHELTON L	LA	13E	20
BRECH RICHARD LEE	SD	23W	42
BRECK GARY ANTHONY	CA	63W	3
BRECKENRIDGE FRANKLIN U	VA	06W	88
BREDA DENNIS JOHN	CA	16E	110
BREDBURY PETER MALCOLM	MA	03E	121
BREDE ROBERT WILLIAM	MN	29E	104
BREDENKAMP DAVID JOE	NE	23W	96
BREDESEN DAVID JOHN	WI	24W	14
BREECE WILLIAM WARREN JR	PA	37W	45
BREEDEN CLIFFORD LYNN JR	MI	28E	19
BREEDEN ROBERT PORTNER	NC	26E	88
BREEDEN WILLIAM RAYMOND	PA	46E	5
BREEDING EUGENE JR	MI	19E	10
BREEDING MICHAEL HUGH	KS	14W	130
BREEDING WAYNE PETER EARL	MO	02E	114
BREEDLOVE CURTIS	NC	25W	62
BREEDLOVE RODNEY ALLEN	WV	18E	56
BREEN DAVID THOMAS	PA	35W	75
BREEN GERALD JAMES	NJ	16E	19
BREES WILLIAM MARION JR	IN	41W	29
BREFCZYNSKI EDWARD JOSEPH	WI	38E	64
BREGLER JOHN RAMSEY	FL	06W	4
BREHM TOMMY JOE	OR	55W	4
BREIGHTMYER WILLIAM DENNIS	PA	55E	2
BREINER STEPHEN EUGENE	IN	42W	5
BREITENBACH BERNARD PAUL	CA	38E	65
BREITNITZ LAWRENCE W	FL	42W	4
BRELAND CECIL DOUGLAS	MS	07E	32
BRELAND LEO MEYERS	MS	26W	52
BRELLENTHIN MICHAEL JOHN	NJ	41E	17
BREMERMAN DALE VINCENT JR	FL	15E	125
BREMMER DWIGHT AMOS	TN	02W	87
BREMS PATRICK JOHN	NJ	06E	70
BRENCICH WILLIAM JOSEPH	IL	31W	88
BRENDEL LARRY WILLIAM	IA	15E	77
BRENDEN NORRIS LEE	MN	37E	32
BRENES NERY JACINTO	PR	35E	14
BRENES-ESCOBAR JOSE	PR	48E	24
BRENKE FREDRICK JOSEPH	MN	22E	72
BRENKER ECKHARD GERHARD	PA	56E	35
BRENN HARRY MILTON	ID	18E	21
BRENNAN CHARLES EUGENE	PA	26E	6
BRENNAN GARY O	PA	14E	47
BRENNAN HERBERT OWEN	NE	30E	88
BRENNAN JAMES ALOYSIUS	MO	35E	88
BRENNAN JAMES FRANCIS JR	PA	15W	128
BRENNAN JAMES JOHN	NY	38E	45
BRENNAN JOHN FRANCIS	PA	03E	52
BRENNAN JOHN PATRICK	NJ	17W	54
BRENNAN STEPHEN JOHN	CT	21W	123
BRENNAN THOMAS JOHN	MA	56W	17
BRENNAN TIMOTHY FRANCIS	NY	29E	38
BRENNAN WILLIAM ROBERT	NY	25E	113
BRENNEMAN RICHARD EUGENE	PA	28W	44
BRENNER DAVID ALDEN	KS	47E	30
BRENNER DAVID GEORGE	KS	57W	6
BRENNER KENNETH JAMES	KS	28W	79
BRENNER LARRY RAY	AZ	09W	109
BRENNER RICHARD IRVING	NJ	27W	70
BRENNING RICHARD DAVID	NE	20W	46
BRENNO WESLEY CRAIG	ND	17E	60
BRENT DAVID ALLISON	IL	58E	31
BRENT EDMUND DAVID JR	MD	08E	74
BRENT GERALD ROBERT	IL	35E	43
BRENT LARRY THOMAS	PA	34E	57
BRENTON MICHAEL JOSEPH	CA	08W	110
BRENTON PRENTICE FAY	WA	16E	43
BRENWALL KENNETH WAYNE	WI	17E	17
BRERETON RAYMOND JAMES	NJ	41E	35
BRESE ANTHONY ARTHUR	NY	05W	8
BRESHEARS ALAN WAYNE	KS	19W	9
BRESHEARS KENNETH LESTER	CA	17E	77
BRESHEARS RONALD CHRIS	CA	32E	85
BRESKI JOSEPH JR	PA	23W	83
BRESLIN PATRICK JOHN	PA	02W	42
BRESNAHAN ALAN RAY	IA	22W	30
BRESNAHAN WILLIAM JOHN JR	MA	20E	110
BRETCHES RAYMOND DEAN	CA	33E	11
BRETON HAROLD GEORGE	ME	32W	90
BRETSCHNEIDER HANS KARL	NJ	09E	9
BRETT ROBERT ARTHUR JR	OR	01W	75
BRETT ROBERT RAYMOND	DC	40E	58
BREUER ANTHONY JOSEPH	WI	42E	28
BREUER DONALD CHARLES	NY	01W	91
BREUER LOUIS KARL IV	TX	01W	47
BREWER ARTHUR LOGAN	MA	40W	9
BREWER BOBBIE HERALD	AL	13W	7
BREWER DALE CONNARD	IL	31E	3
BREWER DON RAYLAN	OH	29W	27
BREWER EDWARD JOSEPH	NY	37E	50
BREWER ELZA MORTON JR	VA	29E	70
BREWER GARDNER	MA	26E	69
BREWER GEORGE HENRY	CA	41W	22
BREWER GRADY LEE	GA	19W	9
BREWER JAMES DALE	OH	16E	127
BREWER JAMES EUGENE	IN	37W	61
BREWER JAMES LEWIS	TN	11E	107
BREWER JESSIE SEYMORE	MS	27E	38
BREWER JOHN NEWTON	CA	34E	27
BREWER JOHN WILLIS JR	MI	03W	24
BREWER MICHAEL LEON	MD	57E	15
BREWER RICHARD DENNIS	TX	11W	83
BREWER SAMMY L	TN	59E	17
BREWER SAMUEL WALTER	CT	10E	53
BREWER THOMAS COLEMAN JR	SC	05E	78
BREWER THOMAS NEAL	TX	33E	64
BREWER THOMAS RICHARD	PA	13W	130
BREWER WILLIAM GLENN	NC	49W	12
BREWER WILLIAM JACKSON JR	KY	10W	39
BREWINGTON DANNIE JAMES	NC	09E	36
BREWINGTON HARVEY JR	NC	15E	3
BREWSTER CARL WARDEN	OH	03W	71
BREWSTER GLENN RICHARD	NJ	13W	125
BREWSTER OLLIS	AL	59E	17
BREWTON JOHN COOKE	AL	14W	28
BREZINSKI CHARLES ANTHONY	NY	34W	82
BRIALES MIGUEL EUGENIO	NY	25W	21
BRIC WILLIAM HENRY III	CA	47W	38
BRICE ERIC PARKER	NC	60W	8
BRICE ROBERT KENNETH	PA	20E	40
BRICE RONNIE	CA	05W	54
BRICE WILLIAM FRANCIS JR	NJ	65W	5
BRICKER CHARLES WILLIAM	IL	19E	10
BRICKER WILLIAM EDWARD	GA	64W	6
BRICKEY BARRY WAYNE	VA	17E	90
BRICKHOUSE EMANUEL KRIS	NY	21E	117
BRICKHOUSE WILLIE T JR	VA	32E	61
BRICKLE DONALD LEVER	SC	21W	6
BRICKMAN DEWAINE LAWRENCE	MN	05W	47
BRICMONT FRANCIS PETER JR	CA	59E	18
BRIDDELL CHARLES LILLETON	MD	34W	20
BRIDENBAKER PATRICK G R	NY	23E	9
BRIDGE JOSEPH LEONARD	PA	16E	19
BRIDGE WILLIAM DAVID	NY	09W	57
BRIDGEFORD WILLIAM MICHAEL	PA	34E	25
BRIDGEMAN BILLY WAYNE	KY	54E	22
BRIDGERS DOUGLAS STEPHEN	KY	06W	97
BRIDGES BERRY JOE	CA	21E	100
BRIDGES CECIL BENNY	TX	24E	16
BRIDGES ERNEST LARRY	IN	47E	59
BRIDGES FRED J JR	AR	29W	17
BRIDGES JERRY GLEN	TN	40W	6
BRIDGES LESTER	NJ	15E	56
BRIDGES LONNIE	LA	33W	83
BRIDGES PHILLIP WAYNE	CA	03W	94
BRIDGES R B JR	GA	57W	23
BRIDGES RICHARD HAMILTON	SC	18E	39
BRIDGES ROBERT EARL	CT	21E	117
BRIDGES ROBERT JAN JR	SD	40E	18
BRIDGES WILLIAM EARL JR	TN	32E	42
BRIDGES WILLIAM LEE	LA	37E	19
BRIDGES WILLIE GENE	FL	51E	16
BRIDGETT PAUL EDWARD	MD	07W	8
BRIDGMAN CLEAVELAND FLOYD	MA	12W	65
BRIED ROBERT ALLAN	IL	16E	130
BRIERLY JAMES KENNETH	CA	36W	10
BRIESACHER MARVIN CARROLL	MN	02W	85
BRIESE STEPHEN CRAIG	IA	08W	92
BRIGGS DAVID IVAN	NY	38W	40
BRIGGS ERNEST FRANK JR	TX	33E	44
BRIGGS EVERETTE WAYNE	VA	28W	56
BRIGGS FRANK HOWARD		17W	90
BRIGGS GORDON MICHAEL	WA	07E	115
BRIGGS JAMES RAYMOND	WA	21W	11
BRIGGS LARRY ISHMUEL	CA	33E	44
BRIGGS RONALD DANIEL	PA	33W	70
BRIGGS THOMAS HAROLD C	CA	38E	21
BRIGHAM ALBERT	GA	13E	42
BRIGHAM JAMES WOODROW JR	FL	34W	20
BRIGHAM ROBERT GENE	CO	33E	64
BRIGHT BILLIE WAYNE	AL	29E	70
BRIGHT PAUL GLEN	OH	04W	16
BRIGHT RALPH NORTH	FL	11W	30
BRIGHT RICHARD	CA	09E	51
BRIGHT RICHARD HALL	OR	15W	54
BRIGHT ROY EVERETT	AR	27W	98
BRIGHT THOMAS JR	MO	29W	17
BRIGHTER JERRY KAOPUA	HI	13W	43
BRIGHTMAN DONALD LAVOYCE	OK	22W	51
BRIGHTMAN HARRY PHILLIP	KY	15E	93
BRIGHTMAN MICHAEL DENNIS	IL	16W	7
BRIGMAN BILLY DEAN	NC	14E	42
BRIGMAN JOHNNIE LEE	SC	23W	13
BRIGNAC JOSEPH PAUL	LA	43E	14
BRILES JAMES WALTER	OR	07E	115
BRILEYA DAVID ALAN	VT	21E	86
BRILLO ALBERT JR	PA	29E	2
BRIM JOHN LARUE	VA	17E	66
BRIMM JOHN M	IL	33E	25
BRIMMER DELBERT ELLERY	MI	21W	35
BRINCKMANN ROBERT EDWIN	NJ	12E	18
BRINDLE WILLIAM VICTOR	IN	24E	16
BRINDLEY THOMAS DREW	MN	34E	83
BRINE CHRISTOPHER DAREING	MA	18E	33
BRINEGAR BARRY LYNN	IN	05W	86
BRINES GERALD RAYMOND	WI	23E	82
BRING JOHN DALE	NE	20W	117
BRINK JAMES RICHARD	CA	13E	43
BRINKER KENNETH RAY	IL	27W	105
BRINKEY LARRY HOWARD	MI	25W	13
BRINKLEY ROBERT THOMAS	TN	17E	49
BRINKMAN JAMES MARTIN III	TN	47E	30
BRINKMAN ROBERT JAY	IA	27W	70
BRINKMEYER JOHN WILLIAM	ND	38W	71
BRINKOETTER JAMES ALBERT	AZ	41W	17
BRINKS KENNETH LEE	MI	25W	62
BRINSON HUBERT F	GA	15W	128
BRINZO ANDREW J III	PA	60E	19
BRISCOE CHARLES	OH	33E	26
BRISCOE CHESTER JR	IN	69W	1
BRISCOE JOHN ARNOLD	MD	35E	36
BRISCOE LARRY	CO	56E	2
BRISCOE LOUIE DON JR	TX	23E	49
BRISENO JOHNNY CHARLES	OK	09W	62
BRISKIN ROGER STEVEN	PA	17E	77
BRISS MARVIN CLARENCE	ND	23W	6

NAME	STATE	PANEL NO.	LINE NO.
BRISSETTE RONALD JOSEPH	RI	08E	34
BRISTER BILLY MAC	TX	65E	5
BRISTER JAMES STANLEY	OH	18W	75
BRISTOL CLARENCE FRANK	MT	19W	9
BRISTOL GUY RAY	WA	13W	73
BRISTOW GLENN TRUMAN	IL	17E	101
BRISTOW NORMAN KENNETH	FL	50W	5
BRISUDA STEPHEN CHARLES	PA	02E	100
BRITO ALFONSO ANTONIO	NY	05W	62
BRITT AQUILLA FRIEND	CA	28E	64
BRITT BILLY WINFORD	GA	33E	16
BRITT CHARLES JACKSON	MD	02W	124
BRITT DAN MICHAEL	NC	29W	65
BRITT HOWARD LINTON	FL	22E	28
BRITT JAMES JAY	TN	35W	13
BRITT JAMES LINWOOD	NC	14W	116
BRITT KENNETH JOHN	GA	38W	55
BRITT RONALD JEROME	IL	29E	20
BRITT TED DENNIS	GA	47E	14
BRITT WYMAN GENE	NC	20W	94
BRITTAIN DANIEL SPENSER	MD	07E	124
BRITTAIN JAMES HAROLD	NC	17E	78
BRITTAIN JOSEPH BRUCE	IN	06W	38
BRITTEN LAWRENCE ALAN	CA	06E	63
BRITTEN ROGER GEORGE	NJ	03E	110
BRITTENUM OSCAR LEE JR	IL	15W	61
BRITTIAN CHARLES HENRY JR	GA	23W	78
BRITTINGHAM ELMORE JR	DE	17E	41
BRITTINGHAM LINDEN WAYNE	DE	42E	13
BRITTLE ADRIAN COOGIE JR	FL	43W	51
BRITTON BERNARD BRUCE	NY	25E	18
BRITTON GARY WILLIAM	OR	10W	60
BRITTON MILTON DONALD	MI	01E	8
BRITTON MURRY LAWRENCE	CA	23W	42
BRITTON SHERRICK CAMDEN	CA	49E	8
BRITTON STEVEN MICHAEL	OH	33W	54
BRITTON THOMAS WESLEY JR	NY	07E	116
BRITTON WILLIAM DAVID	MS	26W	112
BRITTON WILLIAM NED	OH	43E	41
BRITZ RONALD JOSEPH	MD	18W	26
BRIX JOHN ELMER	WA	38W	55
BRIX ROBERT CARL	IN	04E	13
BRIXEN GARY MAURICE	WI	30E	54
BRIZZOLI LOUIS EMIDIO	PA	20E	6
BROACH EARL DAVID	TX	08W	78
BROAD WILLIAM RAY	OK	14E	90
BROADBECK JOHN GILBERT	CA	18E	91
BROADHEAD DAVID J	UT	05E	9
BROADHEAD JACK PHILLIP	AL	31E	22
BROADHURST RICHARD EDWARD	CT	02E	48
BROADNAX WILLIE LEE	NC	30E	55
BROADSTON SCOTTY RAY	AZ	09W	12
BROADTMAN HENRY ROBERT JR	LA	34W	82
BROADY TERRY LEE	IN	66W	2
BROBST JAMES ROBERT	OH	05W	104
BROCHETTI FRANK THOMAS	PA	02W	133
BROCK ARNOLD LEE	KY	18E	67
BROCK DANIEL LEE	GA	13W	70
BROCK DILLARD	OH	26E	42
BROCK EDWARD LEE	AL	56E	1
BROCK EDWARD LEROY	WA	13E	66
BROCK HARRY GILES	TX	12E	72
BROCK JAMES ALBERT	GA	27W	15
BROCK JAMES BARRETT	MI	47E	19
BROCK JAMES PATRICK	OH	04E	6
BROCK JAMES WALTER III	AL	29E	18
BROCK JOHN HARRY	TN	01W	52
BROCK LARRY DEE	OK	26W	60
BROCK MARVIN ZION JR	FL	18E	33
BROCK PERCY GUY JR	MS	01W	51
BROCK RANDY HOFFMAN	GA	37E	78
BROCK ROBERT LEE	UT	10W	89
BROCK TERRANCE LEE	MO	35W	33
BROCK THOMAS DEAN	SC	43W	67
BROCK WILLIAM TONY	OK	29E	69
BROCKER THOMAS GEORGE	CA	55E	3
BROCKINGTON CURTIS	CA	08E	123
BROCKMAN FRANCIS CARL III	CA	01W	32
BROCKMAN JOHN NELSON	OR	39E	2
BROCKMAN PHILLIP LLOYD	PA	62W	6
BROCKMAN RICHARD BELTON	SC	14E	42
BROCKMAN ROBERT DAVID	FL	57W	23
BROCKMAN VERNDEAN ARTHUR	MO	01E	34
BROCKMANN ROBERT JAMES	NJ	11E	55
BROCKMEIER THOMAS MICHAEL	OH	13W	91
BROCKMEYER DELBERT RAY	IL	61W	23
BROCKS EVERETT LEWIS	MI	11W	99
BROCKWAY RANDALL LAWRENCE	IA	32W	89
BROCKWELL LEYBURN W JR	SC	19E	3
BRODA RICHARD DALE	VA	03E	102
BRODERICK PATRICK EMMET	IL	27E	2
BRODEUR DAVID LEE	VI	03E	125
BRODHAGEN FREDERICK HAROL	WI	17E	33
BRODIE RAYMOND HERBERT JR	NY	26W	110
BRODNIK FRANKLIN VINCENT	CA	05E	76
BRODRICK STEVEN PARKER	CA	37W	84
BRODT JAMES HENRY	FL	01E	23
BROEFFLE IVAN CLIFFORD	IL	57E	15
BROEGELER HERMAN C III	VA	24E	59
BROEKHUIZEN ALLEN PAUL	NY	42W	53
BROENNEKE LEONARD LEE	ID	03W	75
BROERMAN BARRY BERNARD	OH	18E	13
BROGAN ROBERT HENRY	OH	31W	43
BROGDON DONALD RAY	FL	56E	1
BROGDON MARGIE	NY	21E	9
BROGOITTI BRUCE CLAYTON	CA	48W	52
BROMLEY ALBERT LEROY	PA	54W	35
BROMLEY EDWARD LEWIS	MI	23E	34
BROMLEY THOMAS EDWARD	IL	15E	65
BROMMANN HENRY RICHARD	FL	43E	14
BROMS EDWARD JAMES JR	PA	50W	41
BRONAKOSKI JAMES DENNIS	PA	18E	100
BRONCZYK LAWRENCE JOSEPH	MN	58E	31
BRONKEMA JOHN MITTCHEL	WI	16E	43
BRONSON RANDY K	ID	25W	104
BRONSON RICHARD TERRY	MN	54W	1
BRONSON THOMAS CARL	NC	02E	69
BROOKE EARL THOMAS	MD	37W	21
BROOKENS WILLARD JR	CA	17E	101
BROOKER DANIEL SCANLON	FL	02W	67
BROOKHART GARY LEE	IA	25W	27
BROOKINS DAVID EVERETT	IN	33W	24
BROOKINS FREDDIE	PA	43E	14
BROOKINS ZACKRIE JR	PA	13E	103
BROOKS ALLEN	IL	11E	121
BROOKS AMBROSE H JR	NC	18W	58
BROOKS ANDRE MAURICE	NY	56E	35
BROOKS BARTON W	KS	41E	17
BROOKS BENJIMAN	CA	03E	99
BROOKS CARL RAYMOND	KY	04E	49
BROOKS CHARLES ALLEN	MI	09W	52
BROOKS CHARLES EDWARD	OH	05E	63
BROOKS CHARLES EDWARD	TX	13W	95
BROOKS CHRISTOPHER EUGENE	NC	08E	122
BROOKS CLARENCE HERBERT	OR	24E	71
BROOKS DAVID LEE	SC	09W	114
BROOKS DAVID LEE JR	OH	01W	30
BROOKS DAVID LEROY	FL	50W	21
BROOKS DAVID T	MI	30E	13
BROOKS DAVID WILLIAM	NJ	39W	32
BROOKS DONALD RAY	GA	41W	38
BROOKS EDWARD ALLEN	MO	24W	58
BROOKS FRANKLIN EUGENE	MO	13E	26
BROOKS GREGORY PAUL	FL	41W	10
BROOKS GUY FRANKLIN	WA	36E	66
BROOKS HESSIE ALLEN	TN	05W	57
BROOKS JACKIE RAY	OR	07W	83
BROOKS JAMES EDWARD	TX	12W	20
BROOKS JAMES FOSTER	AL	24E	112
BROOKS JAMES FRANCIS JR	PA	07E	89
BROOKS JAMES HARRISON JR	WV	11W	48
BROOKS JAMES LLOYD	VA	38W	24
BROOKS JAMES ROY JR	SC	02E	55
BROOKS JERRY EDWARD	OH	14E	103
BROOKS JESSIE MICHAEL	AL	04W	16
BROOKS JIMMIE LYNN	FL	04E	22
BROOKS JOHN HENRY RALPH	ME	25W	95
BROOKS JOHN RICHARD	PA	50E	45
BROOKS JOHN WESLEY	PA	17W	72
BROOKS JOHN WOODRUFF	GA	29E	47
BROOKS LARRY EUGENE	MI	07W	41
BROOKS LARRY LEE	MO	31W	32
BROOKS LAWRENCE ARTHUR	CA	21E	66
BROOKS LEE MURRAY	LA	36W	71
BROOKS LEON RAY	GA	36W	32
BROOKS LONNIE ALLAN	VA	54E	23
BROOKS LYLE GIBSON	ME	42W	38
BROOKS MAURICE	TX	30E	10
BROOKS MONTE D	VA	04E	86
BROOKS NICHOLAS GEORGE	NY	15W	117
BROOKS RAYMOND AUGUSTA	DC	10E	36
BROOKS RICHARD ALBERT	NH	52E	9
BROOKS RICHARD W III	PA	32E	85
BROOKS RICHARD WILLIAM	MA	45W	36
BROOKS ROBERT EVERETT	MA	18E	47
BROOKS ROY MAURICE	TN	09E	55
BROOKS STEVEN KARL	FL	21W	74
BROOKS STEVEN RANDALL	IN	44W	45
BROOKS TERRY HUDGINS	VA	55W	33
BROOKS THOMAS JOSEPH	WV	12E	49
BROOKS THOMAS JR	GA	21W	80
BROOKS WALTER HARM JR	NY	22E	97
BROOKS WHEELER DAVID	IA	03W	83
BROOKS WILLIAM FRANCIS	CT	12W	12
BROOKS WILLIAM LEE	AL	23W	83
BROOKS WILLIAM LESLIE	TX	11W	34
BROOKS WILLIAM ROGER	AR	54E	31
BROOKS WILLIE LEWIS	GA	13E	57
BROOKSHIRE GEORGE DEWEY	CA	18W	19
BROOM ERNEST ODELL	OH	34E	27
BROOM PHILLIP WARD	NC	29E	14
BROOME CECIL ANGUS JR	NH	07E	110
BROOME THOMAS EDWARD	WI	22E	75
BROOME WADE LAMAR	TN	54W	13
BROOMFIELD TED DEWAINE	LA	12E	59
BROPHY DANIEL RALPH	CA	55W	25
BROPHY DENNIS JAMES	NJ	04E	106
BROPHY JAMES JOHN	NY	07E	93
BROPHY MARTIN EARL	NY	55E	4
BROPHY PATRICK JOSEPH	PA	27E	37
BROQUIST STEVEN ANDRE	IL	19E	115
BROSE ALBERT C	IL	20E	21
BROSE STEPHAN ROBERT	MN	23W	61
BROSHEAR SARGENT J	FL	43W	60
BROSIUS DONALD EDWARD	PA	51W	9
BROSNAN RANDY DALE	MI	09E	65
BROSSMAN EDGAR JAMES	TX	41E	59
BROSTROM DAVID CHARLES	CA	09E	126
BROTHEN ROBERT ALVIN	ND	31W	76
BROTHERS BENJAMIN M III	FL	22E	26
BROTHERS GERALD JOHN	CA	27E	93
BROTZ DANNY RAY	MI	18E	119
BROTZMAN MICHAEL RAY	CA	14E	20
BROUGHMAN RALPH WAYNE	VA	01E	85
BROUGHT DALE EDWARD	PA	20E	55
BROUGHTON ROBERT BALLARD	OH	23W	70
BROUGHTON WILLIAM ERNEST	OH	08W	125
BROUHARD MALCOLM KEITH	IN	12E	113
BROULLON ANTHONY JOSEPH	NY	18W	58
BROUMAS ANDRE GEORGE	OH	18W	26
BROUMLEY TERRY HUGH	TX	22E	23
BROUSE PAUL ANDREW	OH	26W	76
BROUSSARD ANDREW RICHARD	LA	16E	7
BROUSSARD GERALD GENE	LA	25W	36
BROUSSARD LEO JAMES JR	LA	18W	74
BROW CHRISTOPHER	NY	31W	64
BROWDER JEROME ALBERT JR	TN	03W	134
BROWDER PAUL ROGER	SC	10W	56
BROWER DONALD HARRY	NJ	16E	104
BROWER PATRICK EARL	WA	34W	21
BROWER RALPH WAYNE	OH	29E	56
BROWN ALBERT LEE	MI	25E	28
BROWN ALBERT LEE	GA	05W	52
BROWN ALEXANDER CAMERON	CT	16W	111
BROWN ALFRED LEE	PA	19E	80
BROWN ALVIN RAY	CA	41E	45
BROWN ANDREW THOMAS	NY	43W	2
BROWN ANTHONY BARTOW	AZ	60W	25
BROWN ARLO FRANK	ID	14E	26
BROWN ARTHUR DANIEL	OH	21W	105
BROWN ARTHUR LEROY SR	MA	32W	52
BROWN AUBREY SHAWN	FL	16E	7
BROWN BARRETT CHAMBERLAND	CA	19W	91
BROWN BARRY EDWARD	CA	04W	130
BROWN BARRY LEE	FL	02W	41
BROWN BARRY LYNN	IL	55E	4

NAME	STATE	PANEL NO.	LINE NO.
BROWN BENJAMIN FREEMAN JR	FL	20W	24
BROWN BENTON	GA	17W	111
BROWN BILLY EDWARD	TX	24E	54
BROWN BILLY JAMES	IL	49E	29
BROWN BILLY RAY	TX	66W	2
BROWN BOBBY GENE	IL	31E	9
BROWN BOBBY JAMES	AL	42W	45
BROWN BOBBY JOE	IN	24E	16
BROWN BOBBY RAY	IN	22W	45
BROWN BRIAN CHARLES	MN	15E	61
BROWN BRIAN DALE	TX	01E	116
BROWN BRUCE EDWARD	CA	23W	50
BROWN BRUCE GILBERT	IL	41W	22
BROWN BRUCE WADLEIGH	NH	44W	35
BROWN BYRON LEA	FL	38E	45
BROWN CARL	AL	12E	84
BROWN CARL LEE	AL	46W	11
BROWN CHARLES	MS	31W	88
BROWN CHARLES CHUCK	IL	08E	96
BROWN CHARLES EDWARD	AK	31E	43
BROWN CHARLES EDWARD JR	VA	12E	9
BROWN CHARLES LYNN	CA	25W	62
BROWN CHARLES NORMAN	ME	23E	49
BROWN CHARLES PATRICK	MI	64E	12
BROWN CHARLES PAUL	NJ	16E	43
BROWN CHARLES WILLIAM JR	OH	16E	117
BROWN CHARLES WILLIAM JR	VA	63W	3
BROWN CHARLES WILLIS E	DC	47W	25
BROWN CHRIS JR	SC	04W	76
BROWN CLARENCE	MO	08W	132
BROWN CLARENCE ARTHUR	TX	15E	73
BROWN CLARENCE F JR	NC	14W	77
BROWN CLEMMIE JR	CA	07W	119
BROWN CLINTON RAY	TX	07E	88
BROWN CLYDE ALVIN	IL	10W	112
BROWN COLBURN	AL	18E	18
BROWN CURTIS CHARLES	TX	52W	33
BROWN CURTIS LEE	GA	36W	43
BROWN DALE FRAZIER	TN	24W	28
BROWN DANIEL L	MO	13E	80
BROWN DANIEL MARTIN	FL	20W	63
BROWN DANIEL MARTIN	NY	03W	65
BROWN DARIUS E	KY	11E	70
BROWN DARIUS LLEWLYN DEMA	DC	13E	71
BROWN DAVID ALAN	MI	23W	109
BROWN DAVID ALLEN	OH	52E	14
BROWN DAVID CARLTON	VA	45W	60
BROWN DAVID CHAPPELL	NC	35E	88
BROWN DAVID CLARENCE	IN	03W	69
BROWN DAVID DEE JR	AK	50E	12
BROWN DAVID GRANT	IN	02E	123
BROWN DAVID HAROLD	TN	26E	42
BROWN DAVID LYNN	PA	45E	16
BROWN DAVID PETER	MI	05E	41
BROWN DAVIS FREEMAN	FL	65E	5
BROWN DENNIS ADRAIN	GA	17W	76
BROWN DENNIS EARL	OR	24E	16
BROWN DENNIS EDWARD	IA	08E	34
BROWN DENNIS LEE	WI	54W	14
BROWN DENNIS RICHARD	MN	27E	98
BROWN DENNIS WILLIAM	IL	22E	9
BROWN DERRIS	NC	42W	26
BROWN DEWEY HEARRELL JR	TX	16E	19
BROWN DEWITT WILCOX III	IN	04W	94
BROWN DIEROTHER	MO	36E	61
BROWN DON CHARLES	CA	19W	117
BROWN DONALD ALAN	AZ	08W	68
BROWN DONALD CALVIN	NY	34E	34
BROWN DONALD GENE	TX	18E	56
BROWN DONALD GEORGE	TX	16E	50
BROWN DONALD HUBERT JR	CA	02E	51
BROWN DONALD LEROY	ME	12E	53
BROWN DONALD LYNN	CA	40W	23
BROWN DONALD RAY	FL	06E	88
BROWN DONALD WAYNE	IN	35W	24
BROWN DONALD WILLIAM	GA	47W	38
BROWN DONNIE WAYNE	NC	43W	45
BROWN DOUGLAS	GA	28E	102
BROWN EARL CARLYLE	NC	16W	114
BROWN EARL FREDERICK	WV	04E	106
BROWN EARNEST CAESAR	LA	17E	84
BROWN EARNEST WAYNE	TX	54E	2
BROWN EDDIE JR	GA	03E	65
BROWN EDDIE STEPHEN	OH	45W	12
BROWN EDDIE WAYNE	KY	39W	74
BROWN EDGAR CLARENCE	VA	02E	10
BROWN EDWARD DEAN JR	NC	02E	44
BROWN EDWARD FREDERICK JR	NY	14W	130
BROWN EDWARD LEE	NY	22E	97
BROWN EDWARD WALLACE JR	WV	19E	3
BROWN EDWIN FAY	WI	34E	15
BROWN ELMER WILLIAM	VA	48E	24
BROWN ELYVIN LAVERNE	IL	36E	46
BROWN EMMETT RUBEN	PA	24W	15
BROWN ERNEST JAMES	NC	12W	41
BROWN ERNEST LYKURGUS JR	TN	13W	51
BROWN EUGENE	FL	10W	63
BROWN EUGENE ONEIL	VA	07W	130
BROWN FRANK LESTER	OH	42E	47
BROWN FRANK MONROE JR	PA	10E	116
BROWN FRED EDWARD	OH	29W	43
BROWN FRED JR	TX	10E	6
BROWN GALE LEE	CA	26W	68
BROWN GALEN CHARLES	MO	25W	96
BROWN GARDNER JOHN	ME	19W	117
BROWN GARY LEE	OH	12W	111
BROWN GARY WAYNE	CA	42W	55
BROWN GARY WAYNE	FL	11W	100
BROWN GENE WESLEY	IA	23E	34
BROWN GEORGE ALLEN	NY	04E	127
BROWN GEORGE ARTHUR	VA	25W	62
BROWN GEORGE LAWRENCE	VA	30W	42
BROWN GEORGE MICHAEL	CA	27E	104
BROWN GEORGE R	FL	46E	53
BROWN GEORGE WASHINGTON	NY	35W	81
BROWN GERALD AUSTIN	TX	20E	6
BROWN GERALD BERNARD	MD	23W	71
BROWN GERALD FRANCIS	NJ	61W	10
BROWN GERALD KEITH	FL	43E	41
BROWN GERALD RAY	CA	52E	46
BROWN GORDON CURTISS	IL	63E	6
BROWN GORDON RICHARD	OK	01E	32
BROWN GREGORY LYNN	OH	28E	39
BROWN HANSEL	NC	08E	118
BROWN HAROLD MILTON	KY	22W	17
BROWN HARON LEE II	WV	31E	90
BROWN HARRY LEE	MO	38W	24
BROWN HARRY WILLIS	SC	39E	2
BROWN HARVE EDWARD	MO	13E	3
BROWN HARVEY LEE III	MO	30E	38
BROWN HERMAN	VA	03E	29
BROWN HERMAN FRANK	FL	29W	5
BROWN HERMAN JR	LA	07E	4
BROWN HOWARD EUGENE JR	MO	14W	17
BROWN HUGH BERNARD III	AL	51W	16
BROWN IRAN COURTLAND	VA	23W	13
BROWN IRVIN	SC	36E	66
BROWN IRVING JOHN JR	LA	02W	39
BROWN JACK MONTGOMERY JR	DC	09E	38
BROWN JACKIE RAY	OH	11E	28
BROWN JAMES ANDERSON II	GA	26W	38
BROWN JAMES ARTHUR	NY	27W	23
BROWN JAMES AUSTON	TN	08W	104
BROWN JAMES AZALOU JR	NY	10E	80
BROWN JAMES BRENT	PA	14W	88
BROWN JAMES DAVID	TX	01W	85
BROWN JAMES DOUGLAS	TX	40E	51
BROWN JAMES EDWARD	CA	23E	84
BROWN JAMES FREDERICK	PA	30E	83
BROWN JAMES GARLAND	TX	08E	132
BROWN JAMES GREGORY	TX	33W	83
BROWN JAMES HENRY JR	SC	19W	84
BROWN JAMES HOMER	AL	32E	34
BROWN JAMES JR	LA	07W	67
BROWN JAMES LEE	SC	32E	20
BROWN JAMES LEE JR	AR	39E	17
BROWN JAMES LEROY	NC	52W	17
BROWN JAMES MICHEAL	OH	43E	4
BROWN JAMES PATRICK	IL	21W	27
BROWN JAMES PHILLIP	AL	12E	59
BROWN JAMES RICHARD	MO	09E	61
BROWN JAMES RONALD	TX	29E	38
BROWN JAMES RONALD	AZ	03W	126
BROWN JAMES SCOTT	AZ	58E	4
BROWN JAMES THARPE JR	GA	02E	17
BROWN JAMES TRULY	MD	05E	79
BROWN JAMES WARREN	NH	06E	2
BROWN JAMES WILLIAM	TX	06E	84
BROWN JEFFREY JOSEPH	NJ	30E	63
BROWN JIMMIE DONOVAN	MI	17W	83
BROWN JIMMY RAY	TX	57E	15
BROWN JOE DAVID	GA	35E	53
BROWN JOE HENRY	MS	41E	17
BROWN JOE MAC	CA	07W	71
BROWN JOEL ANDREW	NY	16E	51
BROWN JOEL KENTON	IN	40E	1
BROWN JOHN ALPHONZO	VA	07E	23
BROWN JOHN CHARLES	TX	38W	71
BROWN JOHN HENRY	AL	02W	44
BROWN JOHN MARSHALL III	NC	06E	92
BROWN JOHN PATRICK	OR	64E	11
BROWN JOHN STEPHEN	IN	56W	32
BROWN JOHN THOMAS	NY	36E	46
BROWN JOHN WAYNE	MS	09W	68
BROWN JOHNNIE LEE	MS	04E	87
BROWN JONATHAN	FL	37W	21
BROWN JOSEPH CLINTON	MD	09E	90
BROWN JOSEPH GORDON	OR	05W	115
BROWN JOSEPH L JR	FL	60W	26
BROWN JOSEPH M	MI	46E	29
BROWN JOSEPH MARTIN LEROY	NC	07W	48
BROWN JOSEPH ORVILLE	CT	06E	122
BROWN JOSEPH RAYMOND	IL	43W	2
BROWN JOSEPH WHELTON III	VA	06E	108
BROWN JULIUS LAVERN	TX	20W	47
BROWN KARL ANTHONY	TN	17E	66
BROWN KARL EUGENE	NY	13W	22
BROWN KENNETH EARL	LA	27W	54
BROWN KENNETH HYRUM	UT	22E	60
BROWN KENNETH LAVERN	KS	06W	34
BROWN KENNETH LLOYD	WY	23E	40
BROWN KENNETH RAY	NM	01W	11
BROWN KENNETH RAYMOND	MA	24E	79
BROWN KENNETH WILLIAM	PA	15W	15
BROWN LARRY	FL	34W	45
BROWN LARRY ALLEN	AL	16W	128
BROWN LARRY DONALD	NV	30W	72
BROWN LARRY LEE	OK	12W	106
BROWN LARRY LYNN	UT	04W	125
BROWN LARRY PAUL	TX	39W	33
BROWN LARRY WAYNE	FL	37E	32
BROWN LAURENCE GORDON	CA	08W	61
BROWN LAWRENCE GEORGE	NY	03E	123
BROWN LAWRENCE JAMES	PA	37W	54
BROWN LESTER EUGENE	OR	35E	89
BROWN LONNIE JR	NC	18W	64
BROWN LOUIS	AR	27W	15
BROWN MANCE	FL	12W	87
BROWN MARC ALAN	CA	18E	57
BROWN MARCUS JR	MD	25E	55
BROWN MARION C	IN	06E	14
BROWN MARK LARRY	NH	17W	12
BROWN MARSHALL EDWARD	TN	18E	21
BROWN MARSHALL JASON	CA	45W	48
BROWN MARTIN	PA	24W	81
BROWN MARVIN H	OR	32W	90
BROWN MAX EUGENE JR	MI	14E	126
BROWN MELVIN BERNARD	DC	48E	51
BROWN MERLE DEWAYNE	OH	04W	118
BROWN MICHAEL DEAN	UT	11W	57
BROWN MICHAEL FRANCIS	MD	11W	109
BROWN MICHAEL GEORGE	UT	30W	63
BROWN MICHAEL GREGORY	CA	22E	76
BROWN MICHAEL PAUL	PA	30E	88
BROWN MICHAEL R	CA	13E	95
BROWN MICHAEL WADE	CO	08W	78
BROWN NATHANIEL	NC	11E	132
BROWN NED RAYBURN	TN	41E	7
BROWN NEIL SHIPP	UT	26W	97
BROWN NICHOLSON	DC	10E	104
BROWN NORMAN DALE	FL	23W	83
BROWN OWEN DAVIS JR	TX	28W	43
BROWN PAUL O'NEAL	AL	12E	94
BROWN PETER H		11E	64
BROWN RALPH WAYNE	PA	03E	71
BROWN RANDOLPH JR	CA	32W	19

NAME	STATE	PANEL NO.	LINE NO.
BROWN RAYMOND	IN	37E	79
BROWN RAYMOND	IL	28W	88
BROWN RAYMOND EARL	OR	04E	66
BROWN RAYMOND LEE	NY	38W	14
BROWN REX LEE	OK	44W	46
BROWN RICHARD	NY	21E	3
BROWN RICHARD ALBERT	CA	55E	4
BROWN RICHARD ALLEN	OH	46W	38
BROWN RICHARD ALLEN	DC	36W	33
BROWN RICHARD ALLEN	CA	29W	59
BROWN RICHARD ALLEN	OH	09W	114
BROWN RICHARD CHARLES	NY	42E	29
BROWN RICHARD CRAIG	CT	44E	4
BROWN RICHARD GORDON	MN	21E	100
BROWN RICHARD JAMES	NJ	28E	73
BROWN RICHARD LEE	CA	19W	28
BROWN RICHARD SAMUEL	OH	53W	16
BROWN RICHARD STEVEN	WY	48E	39
BROWN RICHARD TYRONE	CA	18E	91
BROWN RICK SAMUEL	AZ	05W	30
BROWN ROBERT	LA	05E	114
BROWN ROBERT ALLEN	NC	12W	20
BROWN ROBERT ALLON	TX	21W	68
BROWN ROBERT ALVA II	CA	43W	45
BROWN ROBERT EDWARD	IL	16E	118
BROWN ROBERT GUY	PA	06E	29
BROWN ROBERT IRWIN	NY	48W	10
BROWN ROBERT JAY	WA	48W	23
BROWN ROBERT JOSEPH JR	NY	08W	41
BROWN ROBERT LEE	MI	52E	14
BROWN ROBERT LEE	NY	03W	57
BROWN ROBERT LESLIE	PA	08W	123
BROWN ROBERT LEWIS	GA	14E	79
BROWN ROBERT MACK	VA	01W	90
BROWN ROBERT MAURICE	DC	63W	4
BROWN ROBERT MAXWELL JR	NC	04E	13
BROWN ROBERT NUGENT	IN	02W	44
BROWN ROBERT RAY	TX	27E	36
BROWN ROBERT RAYMOND	MT	15W	12
BROWN ROBERT WILSON JR	MD	41E	36
BROWN ROGER	NY	27W	44
BROWN ROGER ALLEN	PA	36W	39
BROWN ROGER CLINTON	NJ	38W	14
BROWN ROGER DAVID	MA	19W	43
BROWN ROGER LOUIS	CA	35W	14
BROWN ROGER RAY	GA	15W	93
BROWN ROGER THOMAS	PA	47E	9
BROWN RONALD A	CA	24W	82
BROWN RONALD DOUGLAS	OH	42W	53
BROWN RONALD HOWARD	CA	37E	79
BROWN RONALD LEE	WV	37E	50
BROWN RONALD LEE	VA	38E	45
BROWN RONALD LEWIS	NY	43W	25
BROWN ROSS ANDREW	TX	07E	125
BROWN RUSSELL LEE	CA	15W	85
BROWN SAMUEL JUNIOUS	SC	14E	126
BROWN SHERRILL VANCE	PA	09E	14
BROWN STANLEY ALTON	NY	16W	11
BROWN STEVEN ALAN	FL	22E	123
BROWN STEVEN EUGENE	IL	23W	19
BROWN STEVEN MERLE	NY	14W	11
BROWN SYLVESTER LEWIS	NC	41W	56
BROWN SYRES MATTSON	MI	09W	7
BROWN TANNER MARTIN JR	CA	15W	117
BROWN TERRANCE LEE	IL	27W	23
BROWN TERRY LEE	GA	02W	112
BROWN THAL ANTHONY	OK	47W	38
BROWN THEODORE	KY	25E	55
BROWN THEODORE JR	PA	35E	3
BROWN THOMAS	NY	20E	55
BROWN THOMAS EDWARD	IL	07E	7
BROWN THOMAS EDWARD	NC	38W	55
BROWN THOMAS EDWARD		15W	15
BROWN THOMAS FRANCIS JR	MD	17W	60
BROWN THOMAS LOUIS	CO	27W	44
BROWN THOMAS MICHAEL	PA	32W	91
BROWN THOMAS RICHARD	MN	09W	82
BROWN THOMAS TAD	UT	24E	88
BROWN TIMOTHY JOHN	OR	10W	120
BROWN TOM WILLIE	IN	03E	124
BROWN TOMMY LEE	GA	24W	1
BROWN TYRONE	NJ	34E	67
BROWN VAUGHN LEE	IN	53W	42
BROWN VERNON JR	AR	56W	17
BROWN WALTER	PA	23E	84
BROWN WALTER EVANS JR	AL	28W	33
BROWN WALTER OTHO JR	TX	32E	20
BROWN WALTER STONEMAN	MN	09E	55
BROWN WALTER WILLIAM	IL	03E	21
BROWN WARREN FRED	LA	23W	42
BROWN WARREN GENE	MI	43E	15
BROWN WARREN KEITH	IA	52W	26
BROWN WARREN RICHARD	NH	40E	58
BROWN WAYNE GORDON II	WA	01W	56
BROWN WENDELL LEE	WV	11W	67
BROWN WERNER CURT II	DE	42W	39
BROWN WILBUR RONALD	NC	04E	134
BROWN WILLIAM ANTHONY	NY	12W	57
BROWN WILLIAM ARTHUR	MI	16E	130
BROWN WILLIAM B	FL	23E	107
BROWN WILLIAM EDWARD	OH	32W	19
BROWN WILLIAM ERNEST	OH	39W	69
BROWN WILLIAM FLOYD	WA	04E	41
BROWN WILLIAM FRANKLIN	OH	48E	24
BROWN WILLIAM HENRY	AR	29W	5
BROWN WILLIAM HENRY JR	IL	28W	107
BROWN WILLIAM JOSEPH	PA	20E	55
BROWN WILLIAM JOSEPH	MD	32E	69
BROWN WILLIAM JOSEPH	NY	16W	86
BROWN WILLIAM LENNINGTON	MI	02E	33
BROWN WILLIAM LEO	FL	38E	65
BROWN WILLIAM LEROY	PA	35W	2
BROWN WILLIAM THEODORE	CA	16W	22
BROWN WILLIAM WESLEY	LA	05E	99
BROWN WILLIE	FL	26W	38
BROWN WILLIE LEE	VA	20E	40
BROWN WILLIE LEE JR	FL	30W	72
BROWN WILLMATT	GA	07E	67
BROWN WILSON BOYD	SC	54W	14
BROWN-BEY LANCASTER	MI	42W	54
BROWNE EARL FREDERICK	NY	28W	67
BROWNE EDWARD RAYMOND	CA	24E	5
BROWNE FRANK HAROLD II	TX	34W	21
BROWNE GORDON FRANCIS	NY	54W	22
BROWNE RAY BURMASTER	VA	01E	41
BROWNE RICHARD ALLAN	LA	27W	77
BROWNE ROBERT GODWIN	TX	14W	119
BROWNE WALTER D	HI	20W	85
BROWNFELD PHILIP	NY	16E	88
BROWNING BILL GWINN	GA	08W	34
BROWNING CLEVELAND	GA	24W	82
BROWNING DENNIS JAMES	WA	18W	127
BROWNING FRANK LEON	TX	02W	4
BROWNING GARY LEE	KS	43W	25
BROWNING GEORGE EDWARD	WV	28W	66
BROWNING GEORGE ROBERT	KY	22W	72
BROWNING JOHN C	WA	32W	91
BROWNING LEROY JACK	DC	55W	26
BROWNING MICHAEL LOUIS	CA	28E	59
BROWNING PERRY NATHAN	VA	20W	69
BROWNING RAYMOND VENSON	KS	27E	93
BROWNING ROBERT EUGENE	SC	25E	91
BROWNING WILLIAM FRANK	CA	09W	121
BROWNLEE CHARLES RICHARD	CO	36W	71
BROWNLEE KENNETH DUANE	AZ	34W	56
BROWNLEE ROBERT LEON	TX	38W	14
BROWNLEE ROBERT WALLACE JR	IL	01W	6
BROWNLOW ERNEST R III	TN	07W	54
BROWNOTTER LAWRENCE DEAN	ND	30E	13
BROXTON ARTHUR JR	FL	07E	132
BROYER CLIFTON LEE	MA	31W	89
BROYLES ALVIN KLASON JR	TN	01E	110
BROYLES FREDERICK PHILLIP	TN	07W	92
BROYLES IVAN JOSEPH	CA	06E	125
BROYLES LANHAM ODELL	CA	11E	30
BROYLES RICHARD ALAN	OH	12W	51
BROZ GEORGE MICHAEL	WA	32E	69
BROZICH ANTHONY GEORGE	IL	03W	17
BRUBAKER DONALD DEAN	OR	02W	28
BRUBAKER HAROLD RAYMOND	TN	43W	60
BRUBAKER JOSEPH HAROLD JR	PA	33W	54
BRUBAKER MAX L	IN	10E	36
BRUBAKER NORMAN CURTIS	VA	60E	19
BRUBAKER THOMAS GEORGE	CA	05W	7
BRUCE DANIEL DEAN	IN	31W	99
BRUCE DAVID RAYMOND	WA	15W	76
BRUCE DENNIS RAY	CA	06E	37
BRUCE DENNY LOWELL	IA	12E	18
BRUCE HENRY McDONALD	MD	49W	7
BRUCE JEFFREY RICHARD	NY	32W	3
BRUCE LEE RAYMOND JR	MD	35W	69
BRUCE RICHARD BERT	MD	29W	68
BRUCE RICHARD PETER	OH	44E	24
BRUCE ROBERT	NY	18W	77
BRUCE ROBERT GRAHAM	WA	03W	42
BRUCE RONALD DWIGHT	OH	18E	44
BRUCE SAMMY BRYAN	TX	18E	47
BRUCE SAMUEL JR	FL	34E	67
BRUCE WILLIAM JACK	CA	31W	89
BRUCH DONALD WILLIAM JR	NJ	07E	7
BRUCHER ANDREW CARL	NY	17E	97
BRUCHER JOHN MARTIN	OR	32W	52
BRUCK DONALD WILLIAM	NY	40W	9
BRUCK THOMAS FREDERICK	OH	04E	61
BRUCKART DONALD LEE	CA	28W	96
BRUCKER LESLIE L JR	OH	46W	11
BRUCKNER DONALD RICHARD	OH	33E	64
BRUCKNER HOWARD RUSSELL	NY	19W	59
BRUCKNER PATRICK LOUIS	CA	53E	10
BRUDER JAMES ROBERT	PA	41E	17
BRUDERER STEVEN LEE	UT	32E	8
BRUE EDWARD JAMES	IA	01W	63
BRUECK RICHARD ALLEN	MI	13W	99
BRUESKE HARRY DIETRICH	IL	34W	56
BRUGGEMAN DAVID CHARLES	PA	02W	126
BRUGMAN PAUL FRANK	MA	29E	27
BRUHN GARY WILLIAM	CA	17W	111
BRUHN JAMES WILLIAM	NE	12E	72
BRUIN JOHN WILLIAM	KY	05W	132
BRULE GORDON JOSEPH JR	NY	27E	4
BRULE RICHARD CHARLES	RI	10W	69
BRULL MICHAEL JOSEPH	KS	25W	25
BRULTE ROBERT FRANCIS JR	PA	39E	43
BRUM PETER	MI	55E	4
BRUMAGEN ARTHUR	KY	12E	113
BRUMBAUGH JOHN LOUIS JR	WV	32W	91
BRUMET ROBERT NEWTON	ID	01E	48
BRUMFIELD RICHARD LYNN	LA	23W	6
BRUMFIELD STEPHEN MICHAEL	VA	01W	52
BRUMLEY BOB GENE	CA	05E	45
BRUMLEY JOHNNY EDWARD	TX	15E	93
BRUMLEY MERRELL EUGENE JR	TX	05W	64
BRUMMER MICHAEL LEE	IL	03W	3
BRUMMET PAUL DOUGLAS	CA	13W	77
BRUNAT MICHAEL F	CA	07E	32
BRUNCKHORST ROBERT L JR	NE	07W	134
BRUNDAGE MICHAEL LESTER	OH	19W	39
BRUNDRETTE RICHARD E JR	MA	01W	93
BRUNELLE JOSEPH E	NY	07E	25
BRUNER DAVID	OK	24W	2
BRUNER MARK LEROY	CA	21W	98
BRUNET ELDRIDGE MICHAEL	LA	27E	18
BRUNGARD GUY JOSEPH	FL	17E	66
BRUNING DAVID KENNETH	MI	42E	61
BRUNKE RICHARD JOSEPH	WI	04E	16
BRUNN CHRIS FREDRICK	NY	32W	48
BRUNN RICHARD CONRAD	NJ	31W	43
BRUNN WILLIAM EDWARD	PA	34E	74
BRUNNER DONALD RALPH	IL	12E	18
BRUNNER GARY EDWARD	WI	22W	120
BRUNNER HANS WOLFGANG	IL	46E	61
BRUNNER MICHAEL CARL	OH	49W	38
BRUNNER MICHAEL JAMES	WI	34E	5
BRUNNER O D	CA	54E	1
BRUNNOW RICHARD ALBERT	NJ	45W	23
BRUNO EDWARD	NY	20W	106
BRUNO PAUL JOSEPH	CT	02E	31
BRUNO ROGER LEE	WV	17E	84
BRUNO VITO VINCENT	OH	13E	32
BRUNS ROBERT HARRIS	OK	31E	32
BRUNS VERLYN CARL	IA	14W	25
BRUNSON DAVID LEROY	SC	07E	56
BRUNSON GAZZETT BEN JR	IL	69W	2
BRUNSON JACK WALTER	NY	03W	59
BRUNSON LANCE DUNHAM	MD	24E	82
BRUNSON LOUIS	FL	24W	87

NAME	STATE	PANEL NO.	LINE NO.
BRUNSON ROBERT WADE	AL	07W	124
BRUNT ARTHUR LEE	GA	42E	14
BRUNTON STEPHEN CORNELL	CA	48W	38
BRUPBACHER ROBERT MICHAEL	LA	23W	84
BRUSH RICHARD BERNARD	NY	27W	4
BRUSKE GARY LEE	MI	15E	125
BRUSO RICHARD NORMAN	MA	05W	104
BRUST GLENN ROY	NY	35E	66
BRUSTER WILLIAM EARL	SC	43W	25
BRUSTMAN DOUGLAS JOHN	NY	19W	28
BRUTON CARL LEON	MO	11W	2
BRUTON JOHNNY LEE	NC	14E	14
BRUTSCHER RONALD WAYNE	WA	36W	83
BRUX GARY H	WI	11E	51
BRUYERE PETER NORBERT		10W	94
BRUZNACK NICHOLAS EDWARD	PA	26E	81
BRYAN AUBREY ALLEN	VA	49E	8
BRYAN BLACKSHEAR M JR	DC	26E	111
BRYAN CHARLES WILLIAM	TX	34E	83
BRYAN CLIFFORD EDWARD	OH	35E	29
BRYAN DAN E	IL	38E	22
BRYAN DAVID ANDREW	OH	06W	80
BRYAN DAVID GRADEY	GA	08E	34
BRYAN FRANKLIN DELANO	AL	31W	48
BRYAN HECTOR WARREN	PA	06E	70
BRYAN JAMES MICHAEL	MI	19E	115
BRYAN JERRY WAYNE	OH	52E	34
BRYAN JOHN ALLEN	IN	10E	112
BRYAN LARRY MICHAEL	MI	21W	43
BRYAN LAWRENCE GEORGE	OH	43W	2
BRYAN LIONEL JOHN JR	NY	04E	53
BRYAN PATRICK		09W	12
BRYAN ROBERT LAMARR	MI	08W	14
BRYANT ALVIA GRADY	TX	33E	11
BRYANT BOBBY RAY	KS	11E	35
BRYANT CEASAR	FL	13E	49
BRYANT CHARLIE PAUL JR	MI	26W	13
BRYANT CHRISTOPHER	OK	61E	24
BRYANT CREED LORENZIO	CT	44W	21
BRYANT CULLIE WILSON	FL	34E	40
BRYANT DAVID ALTON	IN	38W	71
BRYANT DAVID BANKS	VA	10E	4
BRYANT DAVID EDWIN JR	OH	38E	22
BRYANT DAVID EUGENE	GA	06W	8
BRYANT DAVID THEODORE	NJ	26E	44
BRYANT DONALD RAY	OH	08E	100
BRYANT EMMETT JOSEPH	LA	01E	86
BRYANT FRANCIS LEON	IL	29E	93
BRYANT FREDDIE JAMES	GA	43E	52
BRYANT GARY RAY	SC	04E	87
BRYANT GEORGE EDWARD	GA	12E	46
BRYANT JAMES CLINTON	NC	50E	26
BRYANT JAMES ROBERT	OH	02W	113
BRYANT JAMES ROY	SC	40E	72
BRYANT JAMES WESLEY	WA	10E	75
BRYANT JERRY	SC	18W	37
BRYANT JERRY HAROLD	NM	14E	79
BRYANT JOHN DARRALL	FL	06W	114
BRYANT JOHNNY LEON	TN	24W	74
BRYANT KENNETH MARK	KY	36W	75
BRYANT LARRY KENNETH	OK	64E	9
BRYANT MAURICE HERBERT	MS	03W	69
BRYANT MELVIN GENE	LA	07W	102
BRYANT MICHAEL STEVEN	IL	14E	85
BRYANT NELTON RAYMOND	MS	02E	103
BRYANT PELLUM JR	NY	09E	77
BRYANT PHILIP SHERWOOD	ME	63W	4
BRYANT RICHARD WAYNE	WV	22E	76
BRYANT ROBERT ELMER	PA	10E	90
BRYANT ROGER JERREL	AL	12E	60
BRYANT ROGER SMITH	VA	14E	47
BRYANT RONALD WILLIAM	MI	37E	50
BRYANT ROSCOE EDWARD	MD	41E	48
BRYANT RUSSELL DAVID JR	LA	37E	4
BRYANT SAMUEL EDWARD	NC	43W	12
BRYANT SIDNEY LEE JR	WA	11E	121
BRYANT SOLOMON HERBERT	NJ	17W	2
BRYANT THOMAS MELVIN	VA	22W	32
BRYANT TINSLEY	VA	04E	6
BRYANT WALTER TARVER	TN	29W	96
BRYANT WILLIAM J JR	AZ	15E	13
BRYANT WILLIAM JOHN	IN	25E	10

NAME	STATE	PANEL NO.	LINE NO.
BRYANT WILLIAM MAUD	MI	28W	24
BRYAR JOHN JOSEPH	IL	17E	27
BRYDUN BOHDAN PETER	NJ	31E	71
BRYNELSEN THOMAS ALLEN	IL	19E	35
BRYSON JOHNNY RAY	GA	33E	64
BRYSON ROBERT EUGENE	NY	17E	49
BRYSON TERRY ADAM	NC	14W	93
BRZEZINSKI BERNARD FRANCI	FL	03W	91
BUAN LEE BJARNE	MN	20E	55
BUBALA RICHARD FRANCIS	IN	06E	97
BUBAR RICHARD PERLEY	ME	01E	70
BUCCILLE RICHARD GARY	PA	15W	72
BUCHANAN BENJAMIN JOHN J	NY	15W	114
BUCHANAN CHARLES C	VA	19W	127
BUCHANAN CHARLES DON	VA	24W	52
BUCHANAN ELMER LEVERNE	IN	11E	8
BUCHANAN GARY WAYNE	OK	16W	124
BUCHANAN GILBERT EDWARD	IN	50E	39
BUCHANAN HERMAN DALE	TX	15W	46
BUCHANAN JACK LYNN	KS	25E	76
BUCHANAN JAMES ELSON	MS	16W	22
BUCHANAN JEFFREY LYNN	IN	39W	64
BUCHANAN JOHN GARY	IN	05W	4
BUCHANAN JOSEPH MICHAEL	WA	29W	27
BUCHANAN JOSEPH WILLIAM	VA	39W	58
BUCHANAN ROBERT BUTLER	MD	56W	17
BUCHANAN ROBERT DAVID	VA	27E	107
BUCHANAN ROGER ALLAN	OH	17E	56
BUCHANAN RONALD IVAN	IA	20W	21
BUCHANAN ROY OTIS	PA	20W	111
BUCHANAN WAVERIE HUGH	MA	16E	100
BUCHECK ROBERT MARTIN	CA	18W	116
BUCHER BERNARD LUDWIG	IL	58E	31
BUCHER HARRY LUTHER	PA	10W	4
BUCHNER JAMES IRVING	NY	35E	14
BUCHY JAMES LOUIS	FL	44E	32
BUCIOR ANDREW ZBIGNIEW	NJ	48E	15
BUCK ARTHUR CHARLES	OH	34E	27
BUCK FRANK HENRY	NJ	32E	34
BUCK HOLLIS WINFIELD	ME	52E	28
BUCK JAMES MARION	OK	35E	43
BUCK PAUL JOHN	NJ	06E	52
BUCK ROBERT RONALD	OH	32W	91
BUCK WILLIAM ANDREW JR	NC	23W	61
BUCKA WALTER HERBERT JR	PA	14W	106
BUCKELEW EARNEST JACK	TX	31W	76
BUCKHOLDT LEO BUDDY	CA	08E	51
BUCKINGHAM KEITH CHARLES	MN	31W	44
BUCKLER TERRY WAYNE	MI	08E	59
BUCKLES DONALD RAY	NE	35E	56
BUCKLES RICHARD DEAN	IL	05W	112
BUCKLES RICHARD LEE	CA	21W	106
BUCKLES WILLIAM THOMAS	FL	37E	50
BUCKLEW DENNIS	OH	02W	4
BUCKLEY CARL DWAYNE	IL	06E	96
BUCKLEY CHARLES JOSEPH	PA	36W	55
BUCKLEY FRANCIS RICHARD	CA	04E	20
BUCKLEY JAMES ANDREW	KY	35W	2
BUCKLEY JIMMY LEE	IA	25E	22
BUCKLEY LOUIS JR	MI	07E	94
BUCKLEY MAC CURTIS	TX	53W	16
BUCKLEY MICHAEL FRANK	NY	19E	104
BUCKLEY ROBERT EARL	AL	16E	16
BUCKLEY ROBERT WALTER	NY	24W	58
BUCKLEY THOMAS EDWARD	NY	43W	2
BUCKLEY VICTOR PATRICK	VA	15W	61
BUCKLEY WILLIAM ROBERT	PA	08E	113
BUCKMASTER MICHAEL GENE	OK	16W	48
BUCKNER ANTHONY EUGENE	MO	29E	56
BUCKNER ROBERT OLEN JR	TX	31E	43
BUCKNER RUSSELL DON	NC	22W	18
BUCKRIDGE MARVIN DOUGLAS	KS	25E	10
BUCKWALTER JAY Q III	PA	61W	10
BUCZOLICH PAUL JOSEPH	MI	30W	19
BUCZYNSKI GREGORY THOMAS	NJ	08E	30
BUDAHAZY JAMES DONALD II	MD	55W	26
BUDBILL GERALD JACOB	OH	34W	64
BUDDE LARRY JOHN	IA	24W	36
BUDDI THOMAS LOUIS	IA	13W	95
BUDKA DAVID JOHN	MD	04E	118
BUDKA RICHARD WALTER	NY	32E	56
BUDZINSKI LAWRENCE JOSEPH	MO	26W	38

NAME	STATE	PANEL NO.	LINE NO.
BUEHLER LEON CHRIST	IL	47E	59
BUEHLER ROBERT HENRY	CA	43W	60
BUELL CRAIG HAROLD	MO	39E	2
BUELL KENNETH RICHARD	IL	01W	73
BUELL NORMAN JOSEPH	HI	05E	100
BUENDIA JUAN VILLEGAS	TX	23E	82
BUENTELLO LEONEL	TX	39E	29
BUERK WILLIAM CARL	CA	04W	118
BUESCHER JOHN FRANCIS	KY	07W	92
BUFF CHARLES FREDERICK	FL	21E	61
BUFF WILLIAM REINHART	IL	10E	57
BUFFIN NICHOLAS JAY	IN	54W	26
BUFFINGTON FRED	GA	54W	25
BUFFINGTON LARRY DANIEL	MO	11W	100
BUFFINGTON SAMMY	GA	32E	61
BUFORD ALPHA LEE	OK	29E	47
BUFORD LARRY GRAHAM	TN	31E	10
BUFORD LEROY	TN	18E	44
BUFORD RALPH JOSEPH	LA	09W	18
BUGAJSKY KERRY MICHAEL	IL	34E	74
BUGAR JOSEPH EDWARD JR	PA	19W	77
BUGARIN BENJAMIN	CA	26W	60
BUGGER CURTIS BURKE	UT	35E	3
BUGGS NATHANIEL JR	MD	49W	3
BUGMAN DAVID CHARLES	PA	11W	63
BUGNI FLORIAN ANTHONY JR	MI	66E	6
BUGOSH WILLIAM	MD	14W	37
BUHOLTZ TONY LEE	FL	28W	9
BUHR THOMAS FREDERICK	IN	66E	5
BUILAERT FRANCOIS JOSEPHI	MA	07E	124
BUIS DALE R		01E	1
BUIS DALE R		01E	1
BUJALSKI DAVID ALLAN	ND	24E	112
BUKALA DANIEL SCOTT	MI	32E	34
BUKER BRIAN LEROY	ME	12W	96
BUKOVINSKY ANDREW THOMAS	NY	42W	15
BUKOWSKI DAVID FREDERICK	NY	25W	96
BUKOWSKI RONALD	NJ	54E	3
BULGER JOHN DAVID	MA	12E	65
BULIFANT ROGER DEAN	MI	05E	84
BULIN JERRALD JOSEPH	WI	33W	19
BULKLEY DAVID JUSTUS	WI	44W	5
BULL BILLY BRUCE	IA	08W	48
BULL KENNETH R	NE	27W	98
BULL ROBERT GEORGE II	NY	46W	27
BULLA ROBERT FRANKLIN JR	NC	14W	56
BULLARD ALLEN ANTHONY JR	NC	15W	61
BULLARD CHARLES DORIAN	TX	33W	12
BULLARD CURTIS HERMAN	OK	08E	64
BULLARD HOWARD	TX	18E	74
BULLARD KARL LEE	FL	56E	2
BULLARD KENNY WAYNE	AL	07E	85
BULLARD STEPHEN EUGENE	TN	01W	120
BULLARD THOMAS C	FL	35W	69
BULLARD VICTOR WALKER JR	CA	34W	47
BULLARD WILLIAM HARRY	CA	10E	36
BULLEN LAWRENCE RANDOLPH	MD	46W	30
BULLER RENE ALDO	TX	28W	57
BULLERDICK GARY ALLEN	MO	14W	101
BULLIN VERNON TERRY	NC	36W	84
BULLINGTON FREDERICK CURT	VA	07E	125
BULLINGTON JAMES ALLEN	CA	19E	48
BULLIS KRAG COLT SR	CA	04W	105
BULLIS STANLEY ALLEN	IL	51E	36
BULLOCH JAMES GRADY	NM	09W	42
BULLOCH SAMUEL VIEL JR	GA	31E	72
BULLOCK DAN	NY	23W	96
BULLOCK DENNIS JOHN	PA	07W	55
BULLOCK GARY EDWIN	AK	14E	99
BULLOCK GLEN F	PA	11E	65
BULLOCK HERSHEL JOE SR	TX	47W	15
BULLOCK LARRY ALAN	KY	13E	106
BULLOCK LEON DANIEL	FL	44W	61
BULLOCK MARVIN A J	NC	61E	6
BULLOCK NATHANIEL	NC	14E	32
BULLOCK RICHARD WILLIAM	VA	07E	68
BULLWINKEL ALDEN JOHN	NJ	18W	66
BULMAN WILLIAM CHARLES	NY	30E	6
BULMER ROBERT ARTHUR	NJ	48W	11
BULPITT JOHN A	RI	07E	4
BULTHUIS WILLIAM NELSON	IL	05W	1
BULTMAN ROY JAMES	IL	10E	62

NAME	STATE	PANEL NO.	LINE NO.
BUMGARNER BRUCE HOWARD	CA	31E	85
BUMGARNER THOMAS EDWARD	CA	24W	2
BUMILLER ROBERT OSCAR	MO	49W	35
BUMP THOMAS EDWARD	MI	53E	33
BUMPUS RONALD LEE	MA	24E	71
BUMSTEAD DONALD ROYCE	MI	43E	15
BUNCH CLAUDE MARVIN	AL	01E	116
BUNCH FRANCIS JOSEPH	PA	06W	31
BUNCH IVOR ECAROL	NC	08E	97
BUNCH JAMES GEORGE JR	KS	27W	43
BUNCH LARRY DALE	MO	17W	94
BUNCH RAYMOND LEE JR	CA	53W	17
BUNCH WILLIAM LLOYD	CA	15W	101
BUNDAGE CECIL ODELL	CA	42W	15
BUNDY GLENN EDWARD	IN	13W	67
BUNDY LINCOLN E	CA	24W	37
BUNDY MARK STEPHEN	IN	14W	62
BUNDY NORMAN LEE	FL	10E	72
BUNDY WAYNE PHILIP	NY	42W	66
BUNGARTZ FREDERICK WILLIA	WI	39E	29
BUNK FRANCIS XAVIER	NY	06W	50
BUNKER DAVID ELVIN	NH	29E	87
BUNKER PARK GEORGE	IL	05W	14
BUNKER WILLIAM REUBEN III	TX	01E	11
BUNN BENJAMIN JR	DC	18E	58
BUNN DONALD WAYNE	IN	23W	96
BUNN JAMES ALBERT	FL	36E	66
BUNN JERRY ARTHUR	IA	20W	5
BUNNER LESTER EARL	WV	10W	48
BUNNIS RICARD THOMAS	MN	23E	69
BUNTE WILLIE EARL	TX	10E	70
BUNTING BERTRAM ARNOLD	VA	39E	2
BUNTING DENNIS LAMAR	FL	10E	104
BUNTING RONALD DELL	IA	38E	68
BUNTING WILLIAM JOSEPH	DE	10W	101
BUNTION CHARLES WAYNE	MO	02W	125
BUNYEA WALTER CLIFFORD JR	NM	29E	38
BUONAIUTO JAMES JOSEPH	NY	38W	64
BUONO MATTHEW JOSEPH	NY	47E	59
BURBACH RICHARD	WI	37E	79
BURBAGE RAYMOND DOUGLAS	CA	40E	51
BURBEY EUGENE LEROY	WI	18W	124
BURCH CLIFFORD GARLAND	MD	23E	38
BURCH DAVID CARROLL	NC	45W	31
BURCH DAVID FELIX	VA	23W	51
BURCH HENRY	NY	08E	34
BURCH JAMES EDWARD	IN	20E	21
BURCH JAMES ROBERT JR	FL	45E	8
BURCH KENNETH EDWARD RAY	AL	03E	71
BURCH KENNETH EUGENE	GA	20W	128
BURCH STEVEN RALPH	MN	04W	23
BURCHARD MARK WAYNE	CA	16W	86
BURCHELL EDGAR BROWER III	NY	08E	5
BURCHETT GEORGE ELMER	IL	02E	87
BURCHETT LONNIE MORRIS	VA	52W	9
BURCHETT TIMOTHY GORDON	WA	21W	31
BURCHFIELD JIMMY FRED	TX	29W	91
BURCHFIELD JOE STUART	ME	02W	82
BURCHWELL ASHLAND FREDERI	TX	40E	18
BURCIAGA ALBERT	TX	52E	3
BURCIAGA ROBERT	CA	06E	88
BURCK WILFRIED	MI	18E	100
BURD DOUGLAS GLENN	VA	20W	82
BURD GEORGE JAMES	NJ	36W	67
BURD HARMON CHARLES	PA	05E	64
BURDEN JOHN CURTIS	KY	25E	4
BURDETT CLARENCE HENRY	SC	41E	64
BURDETT EDWARD BURKE	GA	30E	13
BURDETTE CLIFFORD GERALD	WV	06W	28
BURDETTE HILBURN M JR	SC	08W	11
BURDETTE JAMES RONALD	WV	10E	28
BURDETTE LANNY JOE	MD	39W	25
BURDETTE LARRY WAYNE	TN	22E	6
BURDETTE ROBERT LEE	WV	17E	43
BURDICK BRIAN HARRY	NY	36W	44
BURDICK DANIEL JOSEPH	NY	37W	28
BURDICK DOUGLAS JOHN	MI	41E	48
BURDICK HOWARD EARL	NY	66W	3
BURDICK WILLIAM F JR	CT	58W	6
BURFOOT PHILLIP DUANE	CA	23W	96
BURFORD JOHN SHELBY	MO	25E	67
BURGAMY ERNIE LEE	GA	53W	8
BURGANS RICHARD	NJ	02E	106
BURGARD PAUL EDWARD	OR	60W	26
BURGDORFER STEPHEN WALTER	PA	04W	27
BURGE BEN CARLOS	TX	38W	32
BURGE FREDERICK	DC	55E	4
BURGE THOMAS GUY	CA	33W	5
BURGENER GERALD EUGENE	IL	40W	10
BURGER DIETER HANS	IL	25E	113
BURGERT ROBERT	WI	01E	18
BURGESON THOMAS JON	IA	31W	32
BURGESON VERNON WALTER	WA	50E	25
BURGESS ALEX LEROY	NY	40E	18
BURGESS CLEATIS LYNN	GA	06W	9
BURGESS DAVID ROY	NY	04E	81
BURGESS DONALD RAY	OK	31E	86
BURGESS GARRY LEE	WV	08E	62
BURGESS JOHN	NC	27W	105
BURGESS JOHN B	MA	29E	1
BURGESS JOHN HARLIE JR	TX	08W	81
BURGESS JOHN LAWRENCE	MI	09W	104
BURGESS JOHN PETER	OH	27E	23
BURGESS LAWRENCE DEAN	KS	09W	18
BURGESS RAYMOND ARTHUR	CT	38E	65
BURGESS RICHARD ALBERT	MN	13W	26
BURGESS ROBERT HOWARD	CA	21W	111
BURGESS RUBEN ANTHONY	LA	40E	73
BURGESS RUSSELL DAVID	TX	52E	15
BURGESS SCOTT M	MI	27E	14
BURGESS STANLEY WAYNE	NV	25W	36
BURGESS TITUS LEVEN	SC	13E	3
BURGESS WILLIAM C JR	GA	23W	65
BURGETT BOYCE DALE	AR	33W	24
BURGETT JOSEPH SCOTT	IL	37E	32
BURGOON WILLIAM PAUL	OH	34E	74
BURGOS JUAN R	NY	31E	90
BURGOS-CRUZADO ANGEL LUIS	PR	56E	2
BURGOS-TORRES BENJAMIN	PR	05W	104
BURGOYNE JAMES JOSEPH	IL	13W	73
BURIAN DENNIS WAYNE	PA	37W	55
BURICH JOHN ANTHONY JR	CA	31W	89
BURINDA JOSEPH FRANK JR	PA	31W	76
BURINGRUD RICHARD ALLEN	ND	23W	117
BURK JIMMY REA	TX	15W	9
BURK TERRY PAUL	TX	08W	11
BURKART CHARLES KENTON JR	PA	55W	18
BURKART CHARLES WILLIAM JR	NY	08E	44
BURKE CHARLES MORRIS	LA	39E	29
BURKE DAVID MOY JR	CT	11W	67
BURKE DENNIS EDWARD	RI	37E	50
BURKE EARL FREDERICK	PA	37E	76
BURKE GARY LEE	MN	49E	8
BURKE HOWARD D	WA	44W	8
BURKE JAMES EDWARD	OH	13W	7
BURKE JAMES FRANCIS JR	NY	24E	58
BURKE JAMES ROBERT	OH	54E	3
BURKE JOHN JOSEPH	NY	37E	30
BURKE JOHN MARTIN	MA	29W	87
BURKE JOHN PATRICK	CA	15E	30
BURKE JOHN ROLAND	FL	21E	60
BURKE JOHN WALTER	NC	28E	14
BURKE JOSEPH SCOTT	TX	05W	105
BURKE KEVIN GAIL	IA	38W	14
BURKE LARRY ERWIN	NV	13E	124
BURKE MARION McCLAIN	FL	30W	63
BURKE MARSHALL JR	PA	09E	4
BURKE MICHAEL JOHN	IL	11E	90
BURKE PATRICK KEVIN	MA	47E	9
BURKE ROBERT ALLEN	NY	43W	12
BURKE ROBERT CHARLES	IL	61E	24
BURKE ROGER VINCENT PAUL	CT	14E	127
BURKE ROY JEFFREY	PA	15W	75
BURKE THOMAS CHARLES	NY	14W	130
BURKE THOMAS JAMES	MA	20E	82
BURKE WALTER FRANCIS	NY	33W	61
BURKE WALTER LAVERTE	NY	38W	33
BURKE WILLIAM DAVIDSON JR	CA	22W	72
BURKE WILLIAM ERVIN III	OR	06E	37
BURKE WILLIAM GREGORY	NJ	28W	96
BURKE WILLIAM JAMES JR	CA	25W	63
BURKELL GENE MICHAEL	MI	52E	14
BURKES BRUCE WAYNE	OH	60W	15
BURKES DAVID E	IL	04E	87
BURKES DAVID RONALD JR	IL	54W	8
BURKES JOSEPH	MI	52E	3
BURKETT CLOYCE ORAL JR	KS	27E	69
BURKETT CURTIS EARL	AR	05W	120
BURKETT EDWARD DALE	NY	06W	84
BURKETT ELIJAH WALLACE	MS	21W	91
BURKETT GARY LEE	OK	12W	3
BURKETT HAROLD ELMER	PA	04E	122
BURKETT JOSEPH WILLIAM	OK	01E	58
BURKETT SCOTT McCLELLAND	PA	27E	69
BURKETT WILLIAM OMER	IN	27W	93
BURKEY KERMIT EDWARD	CA	21E	86
BURKHALTER RALPH JR	VA	26W	18
BURKHARDT LARRY JAMES	MT	65W	5
BURKHARDT THOMAS ALAN	PA	20E	128
BURKHARDT WILLIAM JAMES	NY	27E	93
BURKHART EUGENE WAYNE	CA	13E	63
BURKHART MICHAEL JAMES	IL	67E	5
BURKHART RONALD WAYNE	OR	46E	29
BURKHART WALTER GUY	FL	16W	56
BURKHART WILLARD HARLEY	KY	33W	61
BURKHEAD DANNY DALE	KY	27E	57
BURKHEAD JERRY CLARK	VA	38E	22
BURKHEART GEORGE WILLIAM	TN	02E	74
BURKHOLDER LARRY GENE	IN	17W	44
BURKS GARY ALLEN	VA	18E	112
BURKS HARMON WAYNE	TN	35E	66
BURKS JAMES CARL	MS	30W	22
BURKS LEROY JR	TX	12E	2
BURKS VIRGIL JR	MO	26W	43
BURLESON CLARENCE PAUL	CA	30W	85
BURLESON GARNEY JR	NC	05W	66
BURLESON JOHN ALLAN	OK	40W	17
BURLESON MICHAEL FINNIE	TX	63E	6
BURLEY CLARENCE JOHN	MD	17E	49
BURLILE THOMAS EDWARD	OH	03E	52
BURLINGAME STEPHEN FRANK	CA	16E	67
BURLINGAME WYNNE LEONARD	WI	59W	20
BURLINGHAM ROBERT GENE	RI	27E	57
BURLOCK KENNETH GEORGE JR	NC	18W	100
BURNAM STEVEN WAYNE	KS	39W	15
BURNELL SAM JUNIOR	CO	04E	61
BURNES ROBERT WAYNE	OK	15W	128
BURNETT CHARLES C JR	MO	19E	116
BURNETT CURTERS JOSEPH	MO	06W	75
BURNETT DAVID LEIGH	CA	27W	15
BURNETT DONALD FREDERICK	AL	37E	51
BURNETT DOUGLAS MCARTHUR	MI	07E	134
BURNETT EDWARD DENZEL	OK	01W	16
BURNETT GARY RAY	MO	43E	4
BURNETT JAMES SANDFORD JR	NY	34W	91
BURNETT JOSEPH DARRYL	CA	12E	111
BURNETT KENNETH MAURICE	NC	18E	13
BURNETT PAUL WAYNE	FL	06W	122
BURNETT RICHARD JAMES	GA	42E	14
BURNETT SHELDON JOHN	NH	04W	31
BURNETT WILLIAM A	VA	04E	45
BURNETT WILLIAM ROBERT	MI	14E	8
BURNETTE ARCHIE JR	WA	35E	89
BURNETTE FREDDIE LEE	NC	13E	83
BURNETTE GARY RAY	PA	55W	20
BURNETTE GARY WAYNE	OH	23E	90
BURNETTE MICHAEL ROBERT	TX	27W	79
BURNEY CHARLIE LEE	GA	22E	60
BURNEY DAVID FRANK	FL	29E	27
BURNEY ELMO JR	NY	15E	65
BURNEY JAMES LARRY	MI	33E	80
BURNEY MARVIN	MD	12E	53
BURNEY NILES	WA	21E	60
BURNHAM DONALD DAWSON	AL	36E	67
BURNHAM JOSEPH FRANCIS	NJ	63E	6
BURNHAM MASON IRWIN	OR	01W	4
BURNHAM NEIL ROBERT	MA	36W	33
BURNHAM RICHARD FLOYD JR	GA	54W	27
BURNHAM ROGER CLARK	VT	30W	10
BURNITE BARRY TYSON	PA	03E	71
BURNLEY DILLARD REED	VA	04E	127
BURNLEY EARL ROSEMOND JR	MS	61E	6
BURNLEY JOHN MOORE	AR	14W	99
BURNOR LEE ERVIN	MI	33W	54
BURNS BENNY CHARLES	TN	44E	14
BURNS BERNARD JOHN JR	PA	37E	51

NAME	STATE	PANEL NO.	LINE NO.
BURNS CHARLES CALVIN	TN	21E	26
BURNS CHARLES STUART III	NJ	11E	25
BURNS DARRELL EDWARD	WA	09W	82
BURNS DEAN HARRY	CA	47E	20
BURNS DEWEY RAY JR	TX	18W	77
BURNS EARL KENNETH JR	MA	12E	119
BURNS ERNEST DOOM	NY	21W	115
BURNS ERVIN L	KY	22E	36
BURNS FREDERICK JOHN	NY	32E	56
BURNS GERALD RAY	OK	12E	40
BURNS HOWARD FRANK	IN	49W	46
BURNS HOWARD MICHAEL	MI	16W	72
BURNS HOWELL WAYNE	TN	02W	86
BURNS JAMES ARTHUR	CT	18W	78
BURNS JAMES DAVID	CA	26W	52
BURNS JAMES EDWARD	NY	31E	57
BURNS JAMES LYNN	MT	32E	35
BURNS JAMES PATRICK	IL	45W	24
BURNS JAMES PHILLIP	NY	21E	57
BURNS JAMES T	NY	20E	21
BURNS JOHN D JR	TX	14E	9
BURNS JOHN FRANCIS	OH	11E	91
BURNS JOHN JAMES JR	NY	14W	124
BURNS JOHN PATRICK	AZ	02E	28
BURNS JOHN ROBERT	TN	09E	105
BURNS JOHN ROBERT JR	MO	35E	44
BURNS JUNIOR R	IN	28E	14
BURNS KEN DWIGHT	CA	06W	56
BURNS LEONARD WESLEY	FL	11E	86
BURNS LUTHER	SC	60W	15
BURNS MARTIN JAMES	IL	05W	75
BURNS MARVIN MELTON	FL	22W	117
BURNS MICHAEL CHRISTOPHER	MA	31W	44
BURNS MICHAEL EDWARD	CA	08W	11
BURNS MICHAEL PAUL	TX	20W	79
BURNS MICHAEL THOMAS	CA	18W	46
BURNS MICHEAL ALLEN	TX	53E	10
BURNS MORRIS EUGENE	IN	15E	18
BURNS RICHARD ALLEN	CA	31W	89
BURNS ROBERT ALLEN	MN	11W	30
BURNS ROBERT EDWARD	MA	19E	104
BURNS ROBERT GEORGE	LA	42E	28
BURNS ROCKY AUGUST	NY	13W	61
BURNS RONDAL LEE	TN	22W	56
BURNS STEVEN CRAIG	MN	03W	35
BURNS THOMAS RAYMOND	WI	20E	110
BURNS VICTOR LEE	LA	22E	68
BURNS WALTER	SC	27E	4
BURNS WENDELL MELVIN	WA	18W	46
BURNS WILLIAM CARL JR	CA	25E	95
BURNSED RANDELL HEATHE	OK	56E	20
BURNSIDE DERRILL LEE	AZ	03W	23
BURNSIDE DONALD RAY	MS	40W	27
BURNSIDE DONALD WAYNE	MN	47E	30
BUROFF LANNY HOWARD	IL	09W	124
BURR DANIEL LEE	WI	45E	8
BURR GEORGE WALLACE	UT	66W	3
BURR ROBERT GLENN	NC	39E	17
BURR STEWART SAMUEL	NJ	26W	30
BURRAGE WAYNE R	NC	23W	97
BURRELL CHARLES FRANKLIN	OR	17W	60
BURRELL GEORGE HARRY	MI	36W	48
BURRELL PHILIP EDWARD	MA	34E	27
BURRELL ROBERT GEORGE	NY	09E	96
BURRELL ROBERT LANSING	NY	34E	62
BURRI MIGUEL RAMON	CA	13E	58
BURRIER PAUL THOMAS	MD	12W	62
BURRIS BERNES EDWARD	NY	55E	5
BURRIS DONALD DEANE JR	PA	15W	81
BURRIS FRANKLIN IVAN JR	FL	49W	35
BURRIS FREDERICK	NY	16E	21
BURRIS JOHN CHARLES	AR	10W	123
BURRIS JOSEPH SAMUEL III	IL	18W	67
BURRIS LEONARD CHARLES	CA	15E	61
BURRIS REGINALD WAYNE	DE	19W	66
BURRIS ROY NEIL	NC	41E	48
BURRIS VICTOR ANTONIEO	CA	28W	67
BURRISS JOHNNY LEE	MS	16W	92
BURROLA SAMMY JR	CA	42W	9
BURROUGH JESSE CLARENCE	TX	47E	59
BURROUGHS EMANUEL FERO	GA	39E	43
BURROUGHS JAMES MICHAEL	GA	20E	55

NAME	STATE	PANEL NO.	LINE NO.
BURROUGHS JUDGE JR	NY	09E	111
BURROUGHS ROBERT JAMES	NJ	27E	107
BURROUGHS ROBERT NELSON	OH	53W	42
BURROUGHS TED WILLIAM JR	MI	32E	42
BURROUGHS ULYSSES G	SC	14E	122
BURROUGHS WALTER L	OH	07E	68
BURROW LEONARD	MO	10E	104
BURROWS MARVIN EUGENE	FL	48E	24
BURROWS ROBERTS PATON	MD	07W	134
BURROWS ROGER THOMAS	KY	58W	17
BURRUANO SAMUEL VINCENT	MO	20W	35
BURSAW CLARENCE HERBERT	MN	17E	41
BURSE TYRONE GREGORY	PA	09E	107
BURSIS JOSEPH THOMAS JR	NJ	37W	29
BURSON DAVID RICHARD	CA	33E	26
BURT GLEN GEORGE	NV	19E	106
BURT JAMES HOWARD	AL	37W	55
BURT MICHAEL DAVID	MA	07E	130
BURT WILLIAM ROBERT JR	NY	21W	98
BURTNESS ALAN CLARENCE	WA	32W	64
BURTON BERT ELLIS	IL	31W	76
BURTON CECIL W	OH	05E	120
BURTON CHRISTOPHER LEONAR	NY	52W	21
BURTON DENNIS LEE	IN	08E	118
BURTON DONALD RUSSELL	PA	06E	74
BURTON ERNEST	KY	53E	10
BURTON FRANK THOMAS	IN	04W	109
BURTON FRED DOUGLAS	VA	30W	19
BURTON HAROLD	NC	30E	54
BURTON HAROLD RAY	KY	10W	95
BURTON HARRY PAYNE		27W	71
BURTON HENRY LEE	SC	11W	2
BURTON HORACE LEE	AR	04W	27
BURTON JACK EDWIN	TN	52W	41
BURTON JAMES ALLEN	MS	58W	22
BURTON JAMES ARTHUR	IL	34W	69
BURTON JAMES BILLY	TX	22W	38
BURTON JAMES EDWARD JR	CO	13W	77
BURTON JOHN LEE	MD	17W	3
BURTON JOHN THOMAS	TN	62E	15
BURTON JOHNNY EDWARD	OH	15E	56
BURTON JOHNNY RAY	MS	43E	65
BURTON LUTHER WILLIAM	VA	03E	11
BURTON ROBERT THOMAS	TX	37W	21
BURTON SAMUEL NURRELL	PA	14W	130
BURTON STEPHEN E	RI	11E	6
BURTON STEVEN DALE	IN	47E	20
BURTON THEODORE HUGHES	PA	26W	52
BURTON THOMAS JOHN	FL	38W	15
BURTON THOMAS LEE	OK	31W	99
BURTON WILLIAM JR	SC	15E	125
BURTON WILLIAM RUSSELL JR	NJ	03E	71
BURWELL LANGDON GATES	MA	37E	4
BURZAWA JOHN ANDREW JR	IL	35E	30
BUSBY CHARLES FRANCIS	IN	11E	100
BUSBY MONTE REX	AL	34E	28
BUSBY RICHARD CURTIS JR	TX	54W	22
BUSBY RONALD DEAN	OH	49W	28
BUSBY SAM WILLIAM	AL	31W	77
BUSBY STEPHEN LEE	WA	12W	91
BUSBY WILLIAM LEON	KY	35E	89
BUSBY WILLIAM RUSSELL	GA	45W	24
BUSCEMI ANTHONY PETER	NY	35W	11
BUSCH ELWIN HARRY	MO	21E	77
BUSCH ERIC PETER	IL	08W	90
BUSCH JOHN EDWARD	NJ	14E	14
BUSCH JON THOMAS	OH	21E	73
BUSCH THOMAS LEOPOLD III	NJ	19W	84
BUSCHKE JOHN ALLEN	WI	32W	91
BUSCHLEITER WALTER DENNIS	MI	22E	122
BUSCHMANN JOHN RICHARD	NY	28W	43
BUSEN JAMES LOA	IL	17W	44
BUSENLEHNER RICHARD THOMAS	TX	30E	38
BUSH CECIL FLOYD	LA	31W	77
BUSH EDWARD L	KS	16E	119
BUSH ELBERT WAYNE	MS	01W	109
BUSH FRANK KENNETH	PA	10W	39
BUSH GILBERT BYRON	WY	07E	39
BUSH JAMES	AL	11W	78
BUSH JAMES EDWARD	TN	05E	100
BUSH JAMES HOWARD JR	GA	32E	18
BUSH JOHN ROBERT	FL	51W	47

NAME	STATE	PANEL NO.	LINE NO.
BUSH JOSEPH KERR JR	TX	32W	3
BUSH LEE RANDALL	MI	60W	26
BUSH MARK JOEL	CA	09W	77
BUSH MILTON JACKSON	GA	24W	36
BUSH NATHANIEL	MD	17W	25
BUSH OTIS LEE	FL	27E	2
BUSH PAUL WILLIAM	PA	45E	54
BUSH PEARL	KY	58E	19
BUSH ROBERT EDWARD	CT	06E	43
BUSH ROBERT IRA	WI	08E	25
BUSH STEVEN CLARENCE	MO	61W	20
BUSH THOMAS BURKE	OK	45W	4
BUSH THOMAS EDWARD	MA	38W	24
BUSHARD WILLIAM DEAN	MI	23W	117
BUSHAY BYRON HALEY	CA	12E	19
BUSHEY FRANK HARRY	NJ	49E	8
BUSHEY PETER B	NY	32E	42
BUSHEY WILLIAM TIMOTHY	NY	18W	88
BUSHNELL BRIAN LEE	OR	12W	111
BUSHONG DONALD RICHARD	MI	52W	26
BUSICK LARRY RUSSELL	MI	07W	76
BUSINDA CHARLES ARTHUR	PA	11W	23
BUSKEY ORRIE JULIUS	NY	09E	111
BUSS ROGER LEE	WI	01E	83
BUSS RONALD FRANK	CA	46W	12
BUSSE DANIEL DEAN	SD	45W	18
BUSSE DONALD GENE	MI	10W	74
BUSSELMAN DUANE LORENZ	NE	46W	27
BUSSEY JIMMY LEE	GA	14E	127
BUSSEY MARVIN WILLIAM	OH	19E	10
BUSTAMANTE ARTHUR	CA	34E	41
BUSTAMANTE GILBERTO	FL	18W	67
BUSTAMANTE MICHAEL ANDREW	CA	16W	48
BUSTAMANTE PAUL	NM	43W	2
BUSTAMANTE STANLEY R JR	CA	49W	24
BUSTLE MACK C JR	NC	13W	95
BUSTOS CANDELARIO PATRICK	WY	25W	36
BUSTOS GREGORIO C	IN	54W	40
BUSTOS MIKE GARCIA	IN	02E	21
BUSUTTIL JOSEPH	MI	33E	2
BUSWELL ROBERT DALE	OR	20W	47
BUTCHER BRUCE EDWARD	KY	04W	125
BUTCHER DAVID AUSTIN	OH	11W	129
BUTCHER DAVIS CARROLL	TX	24W	2
BUTCHER DEWEY FRANK	UT	19W	10
BUTCHER GALE W JR	CA	14W	11
BUTCHER JOHN HENRY JR	CA	18E	33
BUTCHER LARRY R	WV	15E	93
BUTCHER REUBEN	NY	07E	58
BUTE DONALD LEROY	IL	19E	3
BUTGEREIT LARRY DUANE	MI	14E	9
BUTKUS ALAN PAUL	IL	49E	28
BUTLER ALBERT CHARLES	MS	28W	9
BUTLER ALBERT JR	TX	22E	36
BUTLER ALLEN LEROY	PA	15E	18
BUTLER BENNY LEE	IL	20E	13
BUTLER CHARLES GILMAN JR	MD	24E	59
BUTLER CHARLES KING	VA	15W	102
BUTLER CHARLES LEWIS	MI	01W	48
BUTLER DAVID LEROY	CA	05W	44
BUTLER DENNIS LEE	MI	05W	26
BUTLER DEWEY RENEE	DC	21W	116
BUTLER DONALD RAY	KY	44W	35
BUTLER DOYLE LEROY JR	PA	38E	75
BUTLER EARLIE JAMES JR	FL	06E	6
BUTLER EDWARD WAYNE	CA	09E	55
BUTLER ELMO LARRY	OK	52E	46
BUTLER FRED III	FL	32W	76
BUTLER GARY WILLIAM	CA	02W	18
BUTLER GEORGE RICHARD	IL	20E	6
BUTLER GERALD EUGENE	MI	15W	72
BUTLER GERALD THOMAS	MI	11W	27
BUTLER GORDON	LA	42W	39
BUTLER GREGORY WILLIAM	NJ	15E	126
BUTLER HARRY WILLIAM	MI	61W	21
BUTLER HENRY	TX	10E	7
BUTLER JAMES CLIFFORD JR	NY	69W	1
BUTLER JAMES EDWARD	NC	12W	24
BUTLER JAMES MICHAEL	FL	08W	48
BUTLER JIMMIE JOE	MO	16W	11
BUTLER JOHNNIE ELMER	SC	07E	32
BUTLER JOSEPH MILTON	CA	04E	36

NAME	STATE	PANEL NO.	LINE NO.
BUTLER KENNETH ALLAN JR	CA	51W	38
BUTLER KENNETH DORAN	OR	33E	65
BUTLER LARRY DON	CA	45W	24
BUTLER LARRY WAYNE	WA	18E	91
BUTLER LAWRENCE JOSEPH	WI	27W	8
BUTLER LINNELL	SC	30W	65
BUTLER LIONEL SR	WA	37E	79
BUTLER MERLE FLOYD II	NY	31W	32
BUTLER PETER MARK	NY	35E	89
BUTLER RANDOLPH TODD	FL	34E	5
BUTLER ROBERT D	TX	10E	96
BUTLER ROBERT EARL	TN	34E	90
BUTLER ROBERT EDWARD	NY	12E	132
BUTLER ROBERT HERMAN JR	IN	09E	32
BUTLER ROBERT LEE	IL	46E	30
BUTLER RUSSEL E	WA	51W	23
BUTLER STEVEN ANDREW	NY	52W	46
BUTLER TERRENCE EDWIN	NY	48W	52
BUTLER THOMAS J JR	NY	09E	36
BUTLER THOMAS LYNN	KY	62W	20
BUTLER WILBERT RUDOLPH	DE	05E	9
BUTLER WILLIAM GRANT JR	PA	53E	28
BUTLER WILLIAM SANFORD JR	NC	12E	19
BUTLER WINSTON JR	DC	05W	26
BUTOROVIC STEVE	CA	54E	3
BUTSKO ALBERT MICHAEL	OH	26E	43
BUTT GARY		04W	103
BUTT HERBERT HAMBLY JR	VA	35E	59
BUTT RICHARD LEIGH	VA	12E	53
BUTTENBAUM GARY RICHARD	NJ	19E	69
BUTTERFIELD CALVIN FRANKL	IL	62W	6
BUTTERFIELD DOUGLAS HOLMAN	CA	21E	57
BUTTERFIELD MARVIN JEAN	CA	18W	10
BUTTERFIELD ROBERT A	MI	01E	107
BUTTERWORTH DONALD H	MD	21W	12
BUTTON DONALD B	SC	67E	5
BUTTON HOWARD EARL	NY	35E	89
BUTTON MONTY DUWAYNE	OR	19E	22
BUTTRY DAVID EUGENE	KY	21W	69
BUTTRY RICHARD RUSSELL	CA	06W	66
BUTTS DARRELL WAYNE	KS	22E	36
BUTTS GARY RICHARD	PA	24W	101
BUTTS GEORGE LESSIE	OK	21W	116
BUTTS JERRY EUGENE	CA	24E	111
BUTTS JOHN MICHAEL	CA	54W	27
BUTTS LONNIE R	AL	19E	125
BUTTS ROY JOHN	NY	15W	34
BUTTZ HAROLD WARREN	IA	41W	64
BUTZ CLAIR BERNARD	PA	14W	3
BUTZ ROBERT ALLEN	PA	02E	20
BUURSMA DAVID	MI	38E	46
BUXTON DALE RYAN	ME	08W	74
BUXTON DELOS RICHARD	OR	21W	106
BUYNOSKI LAWRENCE J III	MI	22W	11
BUYS KENNETH ALLEN	CA	42E	47
BUZA FREDERICK ANDREW	PA	20E	56
BUZZARD LARRY B	CA	49W	3
BUZZARD LLOYD LYNN	TX	22W	85
BUZZELL RICHARD HOWARD	MA	06W	131
BYAM MICHAEL LEROY	CA	11E	38
BYARS EARNEST RAY	TX	24E	50
BYARS JERRY DAN	TX	24E	17
BYARS RICHARD SCOTT	CO	35E	10
BYARS STEVE EUGENE	FL	28W	17
BYASSEE NORMAN KELLY	AZ	13W	56
BYE ROBERT ANTHONY	FL	33W	47
BYERLY JAY MARTIN	PA	11W	109
BYERS CLAYTON HENRY JR	OH	20E	93
BYERS EASLEY PHILLIP JR	NC	15W	85
BYERS JAMES NORMAN	MD	14E	55
BYERS JAMES ROBERT JR	NC	62W	6
BYERS JERRY DUANE	WY	15E	126
BYERS JERRY WALTER	SC	42E	28
BYERS KENNETH EDWARD	CA	17E	97
BYERS MELVIN JOHN	MI	37E	49
BYFORD GARY D	MT	12E	98
BYFORD LARRY STEPHEN	TX	22E	52
BYHAM DAN RAE	PA	32W	58
BYINGTON STEVEN L	MT	52W	21
BYLER STEPHEN HAWLEY	TX	29E	57
BYLINOWSKI MICHAEL DAVID	NV	31E	46

NAME	STATE	PANEL NO.	LINE NO.
BYLON JOHN LOUIS	IL	15E	78
BYNOE MIGUEL ANTONIO	NY	02W	19
BYNUM ALANSON GARLAND	TX	17E	27
BYNUM FRANKLIN D	GA	22E	78
BYNUM NEIL STANLEY	OK	17W	119
BYOUS MARCUS RANDOLPH	OH	25W	36
BYRD ALTON DOYLE	MS	07W	68
BYRD ARTHUR MALCOLM	TX	21E	42
BYRD BILLIE	NC	35W	3
BYRD BOBBY JOHN	CA	47W	6
BYRD CHARLES	CA	69W	1
BYRD CLIFFORD LAMONT	CT	02W	12
BYRD DOUGLAS EVERETT	MS	07W	119
BYRD EATTERSON JR	IL	10W	112
BYRD ELMER DON	OK	25E	113
BYRD GARY DEAN	MO	27E	99
BYRD GEORGE BENJAMIN JR	FL	18E	119
BYRD GEORGE ELLIS	VA	15E	94
BYRD GUY ALBERT	AL	17E	102
BYRD HUGH MCNEIL JR	KY	35W	58
BYRD JAMES CARMEN	CA	25W	37
BYRD JAMES EDWARD	NC	12W	79
BYRD JAMES EDWARD JR	TN	61W	21
BYRD JAMES THOMAS	NC	15E	113
BYRD LONNIE VERNON	AL	38W	41
BYRD NATHANIEL	FL	03E	53
BYRD NOLAN DARYL	MD	37W	29
BYRD NORMAN CECIL	MD	27W	80
BYRD RALPH	TN	05E	9
BYRD RALPH EUGENE	SC	29E	103
BYRD REGINALD TYRONE	FL	18W	67
BYRD VINSON	NC	23E	17
BYRD WALTER FRANK JR	GA	37W	37
BYRD WILLIAM LARRY	GA	09W	19
BYRNE CONAL JOSEPH JR	PA	26E	99
BYRNE JAMES PATRICK	OH	16E	39
BYRNE JAMES RONALD	CA	19W	29
BYRNE JEFFREY R	NJ	40E	2
BYRNE JOHN PATRICK	NJ	26W	82
BYRNE JOSEPH HENRY	IL	44E	33
BYRNE JOSEPH LEON JR	PA	09E	45
BYRNE PAUL RANDOLPHE	VA	13E	32
BYRNE WAYNE EUGENE	VT	27W	93
BYRNES RALPH WILLIAM	NY	44W	15
BYRNES ROBERT HOWARD	IL	60E	20
BYRNES ROBERT JOHN	NY	43W	61
BYRNES ROBERT SCOTT	CA	38E	46
BYRNS GERALD WINSTON JR	OK	11W	57
BYRON MICHAEL JOSEPH	MA	42W	66
BYRUM DONALD EDWARD	OH	08E	103
BYSTEDT DAVID JOHN	OR	04E	64
BYUS ROGER LEE	WV	16W	115
CAAMANO LEONARD OLGUIN	AZ	17W	14
CABALA DUANE JACOB	MI	20W	5
CABALLERO DAVID JOE	TX	51E	44
CABALLERO GILBERTO JR	TX	23E	17
CABALLERO HENRY JOHN	NY	21W	50
CABALLERO JOSE LUIS	TX	04E	3
CABANA JOHN BISHOP JR	NH	17E	66
CABANAYAN ALBERT	HI	05E	114
CABANO GEORGE ANGELO JR	CA	42W	66
CABARUBIO JAMES	TX	22W	73
CABBAGESTALK EUGENE	PA	14E	9
CABE DENNIS STEWART	GA	20W	33
CABE JOHNNY DWAIN	NM	61W	21
CABE PAUL PHILIP	TN	04W	108
CABELL DARRELL LEE	WV	40E	2
CABLE RICHARD ALLEN	IN	21E	101
CABLES GORDON LEONARD	CT	16E	119
CABNESS DERRICK CLIFFORD	DC	36E	1
CABOT ANTHONY JOHN JR	PA	21W	36
CABRAL ANIBAL SYLVIA JR	MA	34W	74
CABRAL JAMES ANTHONY JR	MA	19W	10
CABRAL JOHN JOSEPH	MA	01W	43
CABRAL PAUL ANTHONY	RI	29W	66
CABRERA ANDY ANASTACIO	NM	33E	26
CABRERA EDWARD A	NM	21E	57
CABRERA JOAQUIN PALACIOS	GM	29E	28
CABRERA JOHN WAIKANE	HI	08E	79
CABRERA LOUIS XAVIER JR	IL	08E	60
CABRERA-RODRIGUEZ CANDIDO	PR	47E	46
CABRERA-RODRIGUEZ MARCELI	PR	13E	103

NAME	STATE	PANEL NO.	LINE NO.
CABRINI JOHN RICHARD	MO	21E	17
CABY BILLY RAY	IL	09E	9
CACCIA CARL HENRY	MI	05W	127
CACCIOLA DOMENICO	NY	20E	110
CACCIOTTOLO NEIL JOSEPH	IL	19E	78
CACCIUTTOLO MICHAEL	NY	51E	36
CACERES ADALBERTO	NY	38E	76
CACERES EDGARDO	WA	07E	51
CACIOPPO JOHN RICHARD	NY	15E	103
CADE BRUCE WAYMAN	MI	17E	115
CADEAU ROBERT KENNETH	FL	20E	100
CADELL ERNEST WOODY JR	TX	14E	32
CADENHEAD RANDALL JAMES	IN	07E	71
CADENHEAD THEODORE L	NY	13W	102
CADIEUX THOMAS PAUL	IL	03W	27
CADILLE FREDERICK FRANK	NY	03E	125
CADORETTE MICHAEL JOHN	MA	37W	55
CADWALLADER PATRICK A	OR	15W	73
CADWELL ANTHONY BLAKE	MT	28E	19
CADY BRIAN THOMAS	NY	34E	51
CADY DOUGLAS MICHAEL	MI	34W	69
CADY GARY ROBERT	WA	06W	11
CADY MICHAEL MORRIS	WA	39E	45
CADY STEPHEN MICHAEL	MO	07W	131
CAFFARELLI CHARLES JOSEPH	PA	01W	91
CAFFERY HOWARD EUGENE	MO	09W	103
CAFFEY MICHAEL ALEXANDER	MI	08W	99
CAFIERO LESTER VINCENT JR	NY	13W	115
CAFRELLI ALFRED BENNETT	PA	51E	16
CAGLE ALLEN JAMES	GA	22E	60
CAGLE RANDY GRAHAM	GA	18W	70
CAGLEY JAMES NELSON	MO	12E	111
CAGNACCI JOSEPH MARIO	CA	16E	39
CAGUIMBAL PEPITO	CA	11E	35
CAHALANE MICHAEL JOSEPH	OH	20E	94
CAHALL EDWIN LEWIS	FL	58W	7
CAHALL JAMES WARREN	MO	14E	32
CAHELA GERALD ALAN	AL	43W	68
CAHILL CARL THOMAS	OH	23W	35
CAHILL DANIEL FRANCIS	MI	31W	33
CAHILL GEORGE EUGENE	NH	25E	65
CAHILL KEVIN ARTHUR	MA	27E	93
CAHILL PAUL MATTHEW	MA	12W	95
CAHILL WILLIAM JOSEPH	MA	06W	7
CAHOON GLYNN THOMAS	NC	22W	11
CAHOON HERMAN CURTIS	NC	02W	45
CAHOON MORGAN LANE	NC	14W	124
CAIL GLENN ALFRED	SC	15W	97
CAIL JOHN EDWARD JR	GA	07E	42
CAIN ALLEN	FL	18W	92
CAIN CARL DENNIS	LA	30W	52
CAIN DENNIS REED	IA	40W	18
CAIN DOUGLAS MICHAEL	IA	52W	27
CAIN FORREST EARL	IL	24E	80
CAIN FREDERICK CHARLES	HI	06E	133
CAIN GLENNIE WAYNE	MO	27W	36
CAIN JAMES CALWINN	TX	07W	16
CAIN JAMES DOUGLAS	TX	52E	34
CAIN JERRY MAURICE	MO	05E	17
CAIN JIMMY RAY	TX	16W	36
CAIN LEWIS RODNEY	VA	38W	10
CAIN MICHAEL JOSEPH	CO	48E	39
CAIN PORTER RAY	WV	07E	51
CAIN ROBERT DANIEL	MI	28E	53
CAIN ROBERT EMMET	NY	10W	68
CAIN ROBERT JR	SC	12E	114
CAIN ROBERT KEITH II	CA	03W	59
CAIN RODGER KENNETH	WA	30E	54
CAIN WILLIAM MICHAEL	TX	19E	56
CAINES FREDERICK ALFRED	NY	15W	109
CAIQUEP JOSE	CA	33E	45
CAIRES CLYDE JOSEPH	HI	16E	8
CAIRNS ROBERT ALEXANDER	CA	08E	55
CALABRIA DAVID MICHAEL	TX	25E	5
CALAMIA JACK	NY	17W	94
CALANDRINO MICHAEL THOMAS	IL	31W	44
CALDERON CESARIO	TX	12E	19
CALDERON FELIX ANTONIO	CA	27W	63
CALDERON JULIO ALFREDO	CA	35E	13
CALDERON LOUIS OSCAR	CA	01W	86
CALDERON RICHARD TORRES	AZ	12W	106
CALDERON-PACHECO JOSE A	PR	23W	62

NAME	STATE	PANEL NO.	LINE NO.
CALDWELL ALLEN HAYES	GA	16W	87
CALDWELL CHARLES WARREN E	KY	37W	61
CALDWELL DONALD PATRICK	MD	47W	59
CALDWELL EDWARD CLARK III	NY	13W	36
CALDWELL EVERETTE BRENT	CA	09W	19
CALDWELL FLOYD DEAN	MO	02W	87
CALDWELL GARY LESLIE	OH	07E	105
CALDWELL HENRY JR	AL	30W	10
CALDWELL HUGH PINSON JR	MI	25W	63
CALDWELL JAMES BRUCE	OR	44W	15
CALDWELL JOE	AZ	12E	82
CALDWELL LARRY EUGENE	OK	12W	20
CALDWELL LARRY GAIL	NE	57E	15
CALDWELL MERLIN FRANCIS	TX	20E	82
CALDWELL RICHARD BRUCE JR	FL	59E	18
CALDWELL ROBERT EDWARD	NC	41E	60
CALDWELL TIMOTHY BRUCE	WA	25E	80
CALDWELL WILLIAM JAMES	SC	08E	34
CALDWELL WILLIAM MILES	OH	12W	130
CALE JAMES MARTIN	DC	01E	116
CALENDER MARSHALL LEE	AL	31W	77
CALENTINE RONALD LEE	OH	47W	39
CALEY MICHAEL SHANE	OH	46W	1
CALFEE JACK WAYNE	FL	62W	20
CALFEE JAMES H	TX	44E	14
CALHOON DONALD EUGENE	LA	49E	9
CALHOUN DURL GENE	LA	08W	34
CALHOUN EDWIN GERALD	TX	04W	76
CALHOUN FRANCHOT TONE	AL	67E	5
CALHOUN JOHN CALDWELL	MA	33E	68
CALHOUN JOHNNY C	GA	46E	45
CALHOUN JOSEPH	MI	20E	22
CALHOUN LARRY GENE	AR	62E	14
CALHOUN PATRICK PALMER	GA	01E	104
CALHOUN ROBERT DARRELL	CA	31W	88
CALHOUN RODERICK WESLEY	GA	13W	40
CALHOUN STEVEN BRIAN	NY	24W	37
CALHOUN WILLIAM STEVE	TX	34E	84
CALIBOSO ROBERT MALUENDA	HI	05E	114
CALIFF JAMES PATRICK	IL	05W	127
CALKINS BYRON THOMAS	CO	23W	25
CALKINS CODY RAY	IL	21W	106
CALKINS DAVID EARL	OH	29E	39
CALKINS VIRGIL ALLEN JR	OR	21W	81
CALL DANA ROBERT	MA	60W	14
CALL GERALD LEE	MD	25W	27
CALL JIMMY OWEN	TN	33W	54
CALL JOHN GRANVILLE	GA	26E	6
CALL JOHN HENRY III	MD	02W	130
CALL RICHARD JOSEPH	CA	47E	59
CALLAGHAN DENNIS PATRICK	NY	11W	109
CALLAGHAN THOMAS LEONARD	CA	20W	63
CALLAHAM JOHN MARSHALL JR	CA	58E	5
CALLAHAN BILL D	NC	32W	92
CALLAHAN CHARLES L III	RI	51W	26
CALLAHAN CLIFTON EUGENE	SC	05W	79
CALLAHAN CLYDE	OH	32W	92
CALLAHAN DANIEL DAVID	MA	41E	17
CALLAHAN DAVID FRANCIS JR	VT	43W	68
CALLAHAN DAVID PATRICK	PA	23W	71
CALLAHAN MARSHALL EUGENE	NC	46W	58
CALLAHAN MICHAEL JOHN	PA	29E	47
CALLAHAN MICHAEL PATRICK	NJ	23W	97
CALLAHAN PATRICK RICHARD	MI	23E	34
CALLAHAN RAYMOND W JR	PA	32W	92
CALLAHAN THOMAS FRANCIS	MO	39W	79
CALLAHAN WELBORN A JR	GA	16E	7
CALLAN GEORGE ALLAN	NJ	30W	42
CALLAN PHILIP MICHAEL	CA	11E	44
CALLAN ROBERT THOMAS	OH	06W	124
CALLANAN JOHN V	FL	29W	5
CALLANAN RICHARD JOSEPH	CA	04E	56
CALLANDER CECIL EUCLED	NY	05W	36
CALLAWAY ALLAN BROOKS	GA	32W	69
CALLAWAY LEWIS ANDRES III	GA	33W	7
CALLAWAY MICHAEL ROGERS	TX	45E	46
CALLAWAY McARTHUR	OH	46E	14
CALLE-ZULUAGA FERNANDO	CA	59E	20
CALLEN JAMES GRANT	PA	14E	32
CALLEN RICHARD JAMES	CA	09E	111
CALLER MICHAEL JAY	KY	25E	56
CALLERY WILLIAM THOMAS	MA	05E	59

NAME	STATE	PANEL NO.	LINE NO.
CALLIES MARLIN JOSEPH	SD	53W	33
CALLIES TOMMY LEON	SD	20W	82
CALLIHAN BLAINE EDWARD	NY	43W	52
CALLIHAN LYNDAL RAY	MO	46W	58
CALLINAN WILLIAM FRANCIS	ME	12E	53
CALLIS DAVID GEORGE	CA	06E	29
CALLIS JAMES HAROLD	VA	24E	80
CALLISON DONALD JOSEPH	TX	14E	9
CALLISON JIMMY RAY	OK	06W	76
CALLISTER ARTHUR ALLEN	UT	33W	42
CALLIVAS GUST	MN	03E	106
CALLOWAY HARDY EUGENE	FL	29W	66
CALLOWAY LARRY JAMES	OH	11E	13
CALLOWAY PORTER EARL	LA	44E	15
CALLOWAY RONALD DUANE	OR	03W	87
CALLWOOD GLADSTON	NY	58W	22
CALMESE ALBERT	MO	08W	58
CALP ALBERT FRANKLIN	LA	02E	48
CALPH GENE ELWOOD	CA	22E	37
CALTON DENNIS ARNOLD	WI	04W	37
CALVERLEY ANTHONY GEORGE	WI	09E	24
CALVILLO ROBERT JESS	CA	15E	113
CALVIN GLENN HENRY	OK	38E	65
CALVIN STANLEY DEAN	KS	13W	41
CALVITTI DAVID	OH	25E	113
CALZIA FRANK VINCENT	CA	58E	5
CAMA DENNIS ROCCO	NJ	26W	7
CAMACHO DAVID BITANGA	GM	65E	6
CAMACHO GREGORIO MENO	GA	42W	19
CAMACHO RODRIGUEZ PEDRO J	PR	48W	11
CAMARENA-SALAZAR EDUARDO	CA	02E	85
CAMARGO JUAN HIPOLITO	TX	22W	38
CAMARILLO FELIPE DURAN	TX	47E	47
CAMARILLO FERNANDO JR	TX	63W	4
CAMAROTE MANFRED FRANCIS	PA	30E	37
CAMBAS VICTOR BYRON	LA	09W	93
CAMBRELEN JAIME	NY	28E	7
CAMBRON JOSEPH TERRY	KY	51W	48
CAMBY STEVE LEWIS	NC	15E	18
CAMDEN FRANCIS EDWARD JR	MD	14E	55
CAMDEN JOHNNIE ROGER	KS	52W	27
CAMERLENGO JOSEPH VINCENT	NY	17W	94
CAMERLENGO MICHAEL DENNIS	MA	16W	17
CAMERO SANTOS	CA	28E	22
CAMERON BOBBY WAITS	AL	19E	48
CAMERON DARRELL ADEN	NY	12W	51
CAMERON GERALD WAYNE	TX	22W	117
CAMERON JAMES FREDERICK	GA	18W	78
CAMERON JAMES LUTHER	MI	30W	99
CAMERON JOHN IRWIN	NY	04E	132
CAMERON KENNETH ROBBINS	CA	20E	22
CAMERON ROBERT CHARLES	OH	21W	17
CAMERON ROBERT JOHN	CA	33W	6
CAMERON ROGER SLETTEN	SD	36E	1
CAMERON THOMAS STEWART	GA	08E	35
CAMERON VIRGIL KING	TX	09E	85
CAMERON WILLIAM BURR	MI	34E	15
CAMINO JOHN EDWARD	PA	21E	112
CAMIRE PAUL JOSEPH	NH	20E	100
CAMMARATA SALVATORE	NY	14E	116
CAMP ANTHONY LORIN	GA	23W	62
CAMP JACK	TX	15W	12
CAMP JAMES DALE	IA	33W	54
CAMP JAMES STEVEN	SC	14E	36
CAMP JOHN HOLMES JR	DC	18W	67
CAMP JOHN WAYNE	GA	29W	44
CAMP WILLIAM GORDON	CA	39W	26
CAMPA JOHN JOSEPH	IL	23E	97
CAMPAIGNE JERRY ALAN	CA	01E	21
CAMPANELLO DARRELL EDWARD	MD	61W	21
CAMPANIELLO ANTHONY VICTO	NY	32E	20
CAMPBELL ALEXANDER JR	NC	06W	11
CAMPBELL ALLIE WILLIAM	IL	03E	42
CAMPBELL ANDREW J	KY	06E	97
CAMPBELL BILLY WAYNE	SC	23W	35
CAMPBELL BRIAN EUGENE	IL	69W	1
CAMPBELL CARLIN MARTIN JR	CA	22E	37
CAMPBELL CLYDE WILLIAM	TX	31W	99
CAMPBELL COYTE DAVID	NC	52E	34
CAMPBELL DAVID DANA	OH	03W	28
CAMPBELL DAVID GRAHAM	MI	10W	133
CAMPBELL DAVID JAMES	OH	08W	129

NAME	STATE	PANEL NO.	LINE NO.
CAMPBELL DAVID LAVERN	IA	60E	20
CAMPBELL DONALD	IL	13E	104
CAMPBELL DONALD A	MI	55E	5
CAMPBELL DONALD ALLEN	OH	44W	8
CAMPBELL DONALD BRUCE	PA	50W	23
CAMPBELL DONALD DUANE	WA	09W	114
CAMPBELL DONALD R	NV	29E	42
CAMPBELL DONNY RAE	NC	45W	5
CAMPBELL DOUGLAS JOHN	FL	06W	34
CAMPBELL DWIGHT STANLEY	OK	15E	73
CAMPBELL EARNEST EUGENE	OH	61W	21
CAMPBELL EDGAR ALLEN	OK	32E	21
CAMPBELL EUGENE CHARLES	CA	25E	49
CAMPBELL FRANCIS DUNCAN	OR	34W	13
CAMPBELL FRANK WILLIS JR	VA	62W	21
CAMPBELL GEORGE	MA	46E	3
CAMPBELL GEORGE ALLEN	GA	36E	46
CAMPBELL GEORGE LEE	MI	18E	28
CAMPBELL GEORGE SAMUEL	MI	24E	2
CAMPBELL GIOVANNI HENRY	WI	22W	31
CAMPBELL GORDON ALLAN	GA	34E	15
CAMPBELL IVAN J	TX	38W	33
CAMPBELL JACK	IL	11E	28
CAMPBELL JACK DONALD	CA	26W	30
CAMPBELL JACK EDWIN	MD	34W	56
CAMPBELL JAMES CLYDE	NC	17W	14
CAMPBELL JAMES HENRY JR	IL	46E	30
CAMPBELL JAMES LEE	CA	08W	16
CAMPBELL JAMES ROBERT	NE	52E	28
CAMPBELL JERRY ALBERT	TN	62W	21
CAMPBELL JERRY RAY	NC	02E	21
CAMPBELL JERRY WAYNE	NC	23E	118
CAMPBELL JIMMY LEE	OK	14W	125
CAMPBELL JOHN ALLEN	MO	24E	107
CAMPBELL JOHN DREW	IL	03E	107
CAMPBELL JOHN RUSSELL	IL	35W	58
CAMPBELL JOSEPH	RI	37E	51
CAMPBELL JOSEPH TIMOTHY	MA	57W	23
CAMPBELL KEITH ALLEN	VA	15E	8
CAMPBELL KENNETH	IL	38E	46
CAMPBELL LARRY GENE	MO	25E	14
CAMPBELL LEONARD WAYNE	KY	27E	99
CAMPBELL MICHAEL	FL	02E	123
CAMPBELL MICHAEL FRANCES		52E	15
CAMPBELL PATRICK FRANCIS	NJ	11E	59
CAMPBELL PERCY LEROY	PA	12E	32
CAMPBELL RANDALL KENNETH		01E	109
CAMPBELL RANDALL M III	NJ	12E	88
CAMPBELL REED EARL	UT	15W	52
CAMPBELL RICHARD MICHAEL	SC	56E	20
CAMPBELL ROBERT CRAWFORD	MO	31E	72
CAMPBELL ROBERT DEAN	CA	20E	40
CAMPBELL ROBERT JOHN	CA	30W	20
CAMPBELL ROBERT JOSEPH	PA	04E	32
CAMPBELL ROBERT LEWIS	KY	33E	13
CAMPBELL ROBERT MERRILL	NC	34W	91
CAMPBELL ROBERT WAYNE	TN	37E	32
CAMPBELL RONALD EDWARD	KY	10W	22
CAMPBELL RONALD GATES	FL	34E	84
CAMPBELL RONALD JACOB	PA	52E	3
CAMPBELL RONALD STEVEN	TX	22W	63
CAMPBELL STANLEY CLAUS	MI	10E	39
CAMPBELL STEPHEN MANTON	GA	09E	45
CAMPBELL STEVE DANIEL	AZ	25E	5
CAMPBELL THOMAS ALLEN	AL	08W	6
CAMPBELL THOMAS DAVID	GA	07E	116
CAMPBELL THOMAS EDWARDS	CA	22E	28
CAMPBELL THOMAS EUGENE	OK	17W	126
CAMPBELL THOMAS FRANCIS	NY	48E	56
CAMPBELL THOMAS JOHN D	AL	21W	64
CAMPBELL THOMETT DARTHAN	TN	08E	10
CAMPBELL TOMMIE JOE	IN	08E	123
CAMPBELL WARREN DANE	NC	28E	53
CAMPBELL WILLIAM ARTHUR	FL	42W	9
CAMPBELL WILLIAM EDWARD	TX	33W	12
CAMPBELL WILLIAM EUGENE	IL	20W	85
CAMPBELL WILLIAM H III	MA	32E	62
CAMPBELL WILLIAM HENRY	WV	01E	96
CAMPBELL WILLIAM L JR	MO	14W	11
CAMPBELL WILLIAM LADD	MD	16E	8
CAMPBELL WILLIAM ROGER	PA	60W	26
CAMPBELL WILSON	NC	07W	52

NAME	STATE	PANEL NO.	LINE NO.
CAMPEAU FRANCIS	NJ	24E	17
CAMPEN GARY LYNN	WA	37E	33
CAMPESTRE ALBERT JOHN	NY	62E	1
CAMPFIELD ALBERT L	IN	35E	14
CAMPFIELD MELVIN	GA	62E	15
CAMPION EUGENE MICHAEL	MN	39E	18
CAMPOS JOSE BALLENTINE	TX	35W	88
CAMPOS LARRY PAUL	NM	13E	8
CAMPOS LUIS BARRON	TX	49E	39
CAMPOS LUIS HECTOR	TX	02W	27
CAMPOS MAGNO	HI	03E	30
CAMPOS MICHAEL WILLIAM	PA	46E	30
CAMPOS RICARDO	TX	44E	58
CAMPOS RICHARD FREDERICK	CA	13E	15
CANADA CLYDE LEE ROY	CA	16W	3
CANADA GEORGE JR	AL	07E	61
CANADA SAM JR	TX	08E	60
CANADY DEE OKEY NELSON	OK	16W	78
CANADY ROY BILLY	NY	11E	79
CANADY TROY VERNAL	KS	12W	130
CANALES DAVID JOSEPH	AZ	07E	100
CANALES REFUGIO	TX	39W	7
CANALES VICTOR JOEL	MI	60W	15
CANAMARE GEORGE JOSEPH	NY	33W	83
CANAN HAROLD JEFFREY	NY	26E	70
CANAPP GARY EDWARD	MD	56E	34
CANAS ROBERTO LUIS	OH	05W	65
CANAVAN MARTIN JOSEPH JR	CA	28W	78
CANCEL PEDRO O	CT	13E	123
CANCEL RAMON PENA	IN	56W	18
CANCELLIERE FRANK ANTHONY	NJ	29W	44
CANCILLA NICHOLAS	PA	28W	44
CANDEAS JOSEPH EDWARD	MA	10E	37
CANDELARIA RAUL	TX	37E	33
CANDELAS JOHN FRANK	CA	48E	15
CANDIANO JOSEPH PAUL	MA	29E	80
CANDLER DONALD PRIESTER	TX	20W	111
CANDLER GREGORY JAMES	CA	28E	64
CANDRL BRUCE CHARLES	MO	08W	16
CANDY JOHN ELTON	PA	41W	44
CANELAKES PETER JOSEPH	IL	25E	73
CANFIELD BOYD	KS	46W	47
CANFIELD JESSE DEFOREST	MI	14W	39
CANFIELD LEON	OK	31E	64
CANFIELD MATTHEW M JR	CT	38W	56
CANIDATE JAMES ELLIS	AL	27E	93
CANIFF JOHN R	OH	12E	27
CANIFORD JAMES KENNETH	MD	02W	121
CANLAS SEBASTIAN PIADOCHE		05E	24
CANN DOUGLAS ALLEN	MA	54W	35
CANN HORACE	MI	28E	79
CANNADA BRIAN JEFFREY	IL	56E	2
CANNADAY MICHAEL D	VA	13E	107
CANNADY WOODROW MICHAEL	GA	07W	83
CANNAN DENNIS CHARLES	NY	06W	20
CANNATA GEORGE ANTHONY JR	NY	06E	63
CANNING RICHARD BRUCE	TN	17W	35
CANNINGTON JAMES B JR	MD	14E	26
CANNION WILLIAM	AL	45W	48
CANNITO DENNIS JOHN	NJ	19W	117
CANNIZZARO VINCENT JUNIOR	NY	15E	95
CANNON BRUCE ALTON	GA	02W	11
CANNON EDWARD EUGENE	FL	17E	70
CANNON EMORY STEPHEN	FL	34E	28
CANNON FRANCIS EUGENE	AZ	33E	80
CANNON GEORGE ELMER SR	NC	20W	102
CANNON HENRY TUCKER	FL	03E	30
CANNON JOHN HENRY	FL	36E	67
CANNON JOHN WAYNE	TX	07W	57
CANNON KEVIN GEORGE	PA	48E	1
CANNON LARRY GEORGE	AL	37E	4
CANNON RALPH	TN	32W	11
CANNON ROBERT BYREL	OH	45E	9
CANNON ROBERT EARL	PA	40W	41
CANNON RONALD LAMAR	GA	17W	66
CANNON SHAWN GLEN	NY	08W	97
CANNON STEVEN LEE	WA	19E	78
CANNON WILLARD SPARKS III	MA	11W	67
CANNON WILLIAM EUGENE	PA	06E	24
CANO JOSE RAMON	TX	34W	4
CANOVA RICHARD JOHN	MA	11E	55
CANOY ERVIN PRESTON JR	MS	37W	16

NAME	STATE	PANEL NO.	LINE NO.
CANRIGHT STEVEN CRAIG	CA	40W	41
CANTER RONALD M	TX	04E	1
CANTER WILLIAM LINDLEY	FL	23E	73
CANTERBURY MARVIN DEWAYNE	WV	32W	94
CANTLER DENNIS RICHARD	MD	45E	38
CANTLON JOHN EDWARD JR	MI	12E	114
CANTOHOS RODNEY SALVADOR	HI	39E	18
CANTRELL GERALD WAYNE	VA	27W	9
CANTRELL JAMES WESLEY	SC	12E	73
CANTRELL JERRY DALE	AR	20W	75
CANTRELL KEITH NOLAND	TX	34W	64
CANTRELL LESLIE HOWARD	TN	05E	19
CANTRELL LEWIS EDWARD	AL	18E	112
CANTRELL PHILLIP GENE	CA	32E	43
CANTRELL ROBERT OWEN	FL	05E	24
CANTU ADAM	TX	14W	103
CANTU ERNESTO SOLIZ	TX	30E	38
CANTU ESIQUIO AIRNALDO	OH	17E	49
CANTU FELIPE JR	OR	41E	7
CANTU FLORENTINO JR	TX	40E	52
CANTU REFUGIO JOSE	TX	16E	19
CANTWELL KENNETH JAMES	TX	52W	38
CANUP FRANKLIN HARLEE JR	NC	14E	26
CANUP WILLIAM DAVID	IN	48E	24
CAPANDA ROBERT JOHN	MI	57E	16
CAPASSO JOHN ALAN	MD	11W	121
CAPE JERRY	SC	18E	83
CAPEL JOHN BRUCE	IL	07E	51
CAPELLE GERALD CARL	WI	01E	99
CAPERS LEE MARVIN	NY	34E	5
CAPEZIO FRANCIS JOHN	WI	43E	15
CAPITANI DANIEL CARL	PA	15W	62
CAPLAN DAVID LEON	NC	08W	74
CAPLAN LAURENCE CURTIS	MO	63W	3
CAPLING ELWYN REX	MI	43W	33
CAPODANNO VINCENT ROBERT	HI	25E	95
CAPORALE MICHAEL JOSEPH	NJ	50E	45
CAPOZZI ANTHONY LOUIS	NY	39E	57
CAPPAERT JON M	GA	32E	91
CAPPARELLI GEORGE GUY	NJ	53E	28
CAPPELLI CHARLES EDWARD	RI	30E	6
CAPPELLO DANIEL PETER	PA	31E	44
CAPPS WALTER ROBERT	NC	03W	121
CAPRARO CLAUD WILLIAM	CO	37W	29
CAPRIGLIONE ANTHONY	NY	08E	118
CAPRIO MICHAEL JAMES	NY	20W	47
CAPUANO FRANK PHILIP	NY	39E	30
CAPUANO GEORGE ANTHONY	CA	09W	87
CAPUANO PAUL RICHARD	MA	06E	70
CAPUTO JAMES WILLIAM	NY	08E	103
CAPUTO MICHAEL ANTHONY SR	PA	16W	41
CAPUTO MICHAEL JOHN	CA	29W	66
CAPUTO RICHARD P	CT	43W	61
CARA ROBERT JOSEPH	PA	22E	10
CARABALLO HECTOR LUIS	NY	13W	84
CARABALLO-GARCIA MEGDELIO	PR	03E	75
CARABBA RICHARD ALOYSIUS	NY	17W	12
CARABEO LEONARD	AZ	52E	35
CARACCILO ANTHONY J JR	NY	05W	120
CARAMELLA PAUL DOANE	CA	25E	41
CARANASIOS EVANGELOS K	IN	37W	4
CARAPEZZA RICHARD ALLAN	NY	31W	99
CARAS FRANKLIN ANGEL	UT	18E	105
CARAVELLO VINCENT JAMES	NY	64E	12
CARAVETTA LARRY ANTHONY	IL	65W	5
CARAWAY EARNEST WESLEY	TX	38E	66
CARAWAY JOHNNIE J	CA	23W	118
CARAWAY THOMAS GLENN	TX	30E	100
CARBAJAL ADRIAN DAVID	LA	26W	43
CARBAJAL CARLOS GUZMAN	CA	46W	12
CARBAJAL RUBEN JOSE	TX	16W	56
CARBAJAL-AZMITIA RENE	NY	51W	17
CARBAUGH WOODROW FRANKLIN	MD	60W	15
CARBONE RICHARD	NY	24W	52
CARCLAY JACK CRAIG	MI	54E	23
CARD WAYNE NORMAN	CA	15E	40
CARDEN ALBERT PARKER	WV	03W	88
CARDEN CHARLIE ALFRED	NJ	07E	116
CARDENAS ARNOLDO J	IL	08E	111
CARDENAS DANIEL JR	CA	48W	38
CARDENAS JOE CANDELARIA R	AZ	41W	51
CARDENAS JOSEPH ARTHUR	CO	10W	68

NAME	STATE	PANEL NO.	LINE NO.
CARDENAS LEROY ROBERT	WY	23W	62
CARDENAS MANUEL II	MN	16E	39
CARDENAS PAUL H JR	TX	14W	85
CARDENAS RAMIRO	IL	41E	48
CARDENAS RUDY	TX	66W	3
CARDER DENZIL MASON JR	OH	25E	41
CARDIFF THOMAS N JR	PA	13E	96
CARDIN WILLIS GLEN	CA	37E	52
CARDINAL DAVID CHARLES	NY	47E	30
CARDINAL GARRYL DAVID	MN	39W	40
CARDINAL WAYNE MEDDIE	MI	28E	48
CARDINALE JAMES ANTHONY	CA	48E	15
CARDINALI RICHARD WILLIAM	MA	52E	35
CARDONA GABRIEL JR	NY	37W	38
CARDONA RONALD WILLIAM	MA	21W	69
CARDOSA CRECENCIO	TX	49E	9
CARDOT JOHN ANDREW	NY	09E	126
CARDWELL ERNEST DANIEL	VA	06W	3
CARDWELL HENRY WATERS	AL	26W	30
CARDWELL JAMES MELVIN	CA	04W	135
CARDWELL JOHNNIE WAYNE	OK	13E	2
CARDWELL TYREE	PA	24W	1
CARDY BRUCE LEE	CO	17W	44
CAREW FARRELL RICHARD	NY	25E	67
CAREY BARTON WAINWRIGHT	KS	46E	30
CAREY BRUCE LEO	NY	40E	2
CAREY CHARLES B	GA	17W	72
CAREY DANIEL EDWARD	IL	19W	43
CAREY DANIEL LESTER	VA	20W	38
CAREY DAVID LEE	OH	43E	52
CAREY FRANKLIN LEE	VA	28E	7
CAREY JAMES DOUGLAS JR	FL	34W	5
CAREY JAMES EDWARD	PA	18E	57
CAREY JERRY MICHAEL	NC	09W	98
CAREY JOHN DOUGLAS	OR	09E	27
CAREY JOHN JR	CA	24E	11
CAREY JOHN LEROY	PA	39E	18
CAREY JOHN PATRICK JOSEPH	PA	25E	46
CAREY MICHAEL WILLIAM	CA	20E	111
CAREY ROGER GARYLEE	MN	27E	107
CAREY RONALD DUANE	IN	13W	84
CAREY THOMAS JOSEPH	IN	14E	79
CAREY WILLIAM JAMES	NY	28W	67
CARGILE CLAUDE HARMON	AL	10W	95
CARIVEAU WILLIAM JOSEPH	CA	09W	93
CARKIN HARVEY MCKEE	VA	15E	33
CARL ARTHUR JACK	CA	40W	18
CARLAN JACK MORRIS	GA	24E	17
CARLBORG ALAN GEORGE	AZ	07W	99
CARLE GARY LEE	IN	20E	82
CARLETON RONALD DEE	CA	02W	74
CARLEY MICHAEL JOHN	CT	15E	103
CARLEY RAYMOND MONTELL	CA	08E	82
CARLEY TIMOTHY LYNN	KS	28W	44
CARLI DAVID ARTHUR	CA	42E	48
CARLIN DAVID ALLEN	CA	34W	13
CARLIN JAMES COOK	NY	12W	65
CARLIN STEPHEN BERNARD	NY	35W	58
CARLISI IGNATIUS	NY	08E	52
CARLISLE BILLY PAT	MS	12W	66
CARLISLE LARRY DEXTER	FL	58W	22
CARLISLE THOMAS G II	NY	46E	61
CARLO GILBERT	NY	51W	30
CARLOCK JOHN RONALD	CA	33E	45
CARLOCK RALPH LAURENCE	IL	16E	16
CARLONE JOHN JOSEPH II	IL	04E	41
CARLONI JAMES FRANCIS	NY	15W	16
CARLOS STEPHEN G	HI	43E	41
CARLOUGH GEORGE GERALD	NJ	34W	57
CARLOZZI ROBERT MATTHEW	MD	28E	79
CARLQUIST BRIAN FIZTGERAL	UT	03E	72
CARLS TERRY ALAN	IL	13E	104
CARLSON CARL LEONARD	MN	49E	29
CARLSON DAVID LAWRENCE	CT	12E	27
CARLSON DENNIS ALLEN	IA	27E	107
CARLSON DONALD LE ROY	MN	50W	41
CARLSON FREDERICK JOSEPH	NY	42W	16
CARLSON GARY LEE	WA	37W	4
CARLSON GARY WILLIAM	MA	22W	85
CARLSON JAMES BLAIN	OR	47W	26
CARLSON JAMES CLARK	CA	38W	40
CARLSON JOHN EDWARD	IL	18W	93

NAME	STATE	PANEL NO.	LINE NO.
CARLSON JOHN WERNER	IL	13E	18
CARLSON PAUL VICTOR	MN	15E	18
CARLSON PETER JOHN	WI	19E	89
CARLSON RICHARD ALLAN	CA	67E	5
CARLSON RICHARD ARNOLD	MN	34W	36
CARLSON RICHARD BUCK	ID	12E	19
CARLSON RICHARD LEE	NJ	32E	85
CARLSON RICHARD THEODORE	AZ	09W	31
CARLSON VERNELL DWIGHT	MN	13E	80
CARLSON WAYNE LOUIS	NY	19W	117
CARLSON WILLIAM EUGENE	MN	39W	64
CARLTON DANNY E	TN	03E	72
CARLTON DAVID JAMES	MN	24E	59
CARLTON JAMES EDMUND JR	AL	18E	39
CARLTON LAVALLE ERNEST	OH	03E	30
CARLTON RANDALL MARK	NJ	32W	69
CARLUCCI ANTHONY JACK	NY	16W	98
CARLYLE ARCHIE MONROE	NC	27E	14
CARLYLE DONALD RICHARD	MO	34W	69
CARMACK JOHN EDWARD	LA	19E	92
CARMAN JAMES CONRAD	OH	14W	88
CARMAN ROBERT LEON	TX	49W	38
CARMICHAEL ALFRED JR	AL	12E	49
CARMICHAEL DALE EUGENE	IN	18E	83
CARMICHAEL GERALD LANE	WA	11E	76
CARMICHAEL HENRY ELLIS JR	IL	41W	10
CARMICHAEL ROBERT EDWARD	VA	15W	117
CARMICHAEL SAMUEL LEE	IL	30E	14
CARMODY JAN ARTHUR	NY	56W	1
CARMODY ROBERT J	NY	28E	79
CARMODY TIMOTHY LEE	NY	46W	12
CARMONA EFREN	CA	48E	39
CARMONA JESSE JR	MI	54E	24
CARMONA-MEDINA RAFAEL CEC	PR	03E	42
CARN ROBERT MARION JR	PA	02E	69
CARNAHAN STEPHEN MICHAEL	NM	17E	91
CARNEGIE THOMAS EDWARD	CT	50E	37
CARNELL ARCHIE DENNIS	SC	03W	25
CARNELL PATRICK J	PA	28E	64
CARNELL TALMADGE WAYNE	IL	26E	57
CARNES DONALD LLOYD	MI	53E	28
CARNETT DENNIE LYNN	MO	10W	89
CARNEVALE DAVID JAMES	CA	03E	53
CARNEY GEORGE AUSTIN	NJ	47W	15
CARNEY JAMES PATRICK JR	CT	31W	77
CARNEY JOHN CHARLES	PA	64W	6
CARNEY JOSHUA ELI	OK	05W	98
CARNEY ROBERT ARTHUR	OH	37W	29
CARNEY THOMAS EARL	PA	08E	48
CARNEY TYRONE EDWARD	CA	56W	12
CARNEY WALTER JOHN	NY	22W	38
CARNINE STEPHEN MICHAEL	IN	49W	51
CARNLEY RUDY AVON	FL	23W	14
CARNLINE TROY MONROE	LA	19E	22
CARNOSKE ROBERT THOMAS	MO	15E	94
CAROLAN TIMOTHY JOHN	IL	22W	73
CARON BERNARD JOHN		38E	46
CARON WAYNE MAURICE	MA	50W	22
CAROTA JOHN THOMAS	MA	26E	6
CAROTHERS CECIL WAYNE	PA	44W	21
CAROTHERS RICHARD LEE	TN	13E	49
CAROVILLANO ROBERT	NJ	17E	42
CARPENTER BILL DUAYNE	UT	10W	4
CARPENTER CHARLES	CA	32E	21
CARPENTER CHARLES EDWARD	OH	31W	33
CARPENTER CHARLES EDWARD	GA	21W	17
CARPENTER CLIFFORD LEE	OH	09E	46
CARPENTER CLINTON R JR	MA	43E	16
CARPENTER DAVID CLYDE	NM	07E	32
CARPENTER DONALD EUGENE	NE	11W	45
CARPENTER DOUGLAS JOE	AR	17E	42
CARPENTER EDDIE DEAN	KY	16W	69
CARPENTER FRED W	IN	22E	76
CARPENTER FRED WILLIAM	NY	40W	37
CARPENTER GARY RALPH	CA	35E	67
CARPENTER GEORGE WHITNEY	NY	15E	54
CARPENTER HOWARD B	OH	16E	26
CARPENTER HOWARD R JR	IN	40E	2
CARPENTER JAMES ALVIN	SC	29W	37
CARPENTER JESSE DALE	IN	32W	92
CARPENTER KENNETH BRAXTON	MS	33E	17
CARPENTER KENNETH HAROLD	OH	32E	11
CARPENTER NICHOLAS MALLOR	OH	55W	26
CARPENTER RALPH R JR	IL	39W	7
CARPENTER RAMEY LEO	OK	28W	97
CARPENTER RAYMOND EARL	WA	40E	37
CARPENTER ROGER LEE	SC	49E	51
CARPENTER ROGER NELVIN	CA	04W	132
CARPENTER SAMUEL DAVID	OH	07E	68
CARPENTER SCOTT MARSHALL	CA	44W	15
CARPENTER TERRY WAYNE	OH	07E	68
CARPENTER THOMAS JR	AL	34E	15
CARPENTER TOMMY LEE	IN	35E	14
CARPENTER WALTER ANDREW	NY	30W	73
CARPENTER WILLIAM H JR	PA	32E	70
CARPENTER WILLIAM JOHNNY	GA	62W	21
CARPENTER WILLIAM JR	OH	12E	12
CARPENTIER LUCIEN GERARD	RI	50W	5
CARPER EDDIE DEAN	WV	28W	33
CARPER JOHN WILLIAM JR	OR	09W	115
CARPER LORING WILLIAM JR	VA	07E	69
CARR ALVIN	MI	43E	15
CARR BENNY GILLIS	KY	26E	81
CARR BERTRAM ANTHONY	KY	23W	35
CARR CLINT EDWIN	LA	01W	16
CARR DANIEL LEE	NE	44W	15
CARR DANNIE ARTHUR	TN	21W	50
CARR DENNIS ROBERT	PA	44E	66
CARR DONALD GENE	TX	03W	101
CARR ERNEST RAY	KY	45W	12
CARR FREEMAN ABRAHAM	VT	18W	93
CARR GEORGE DARE	TX	22W	73
CARR GEORGE JOSEPH	WI	21E	9
CARR GEORGE LEE	MI	50W	22
CARR GERALD REID	PA	33W	76
CARR GREGORY VERNON	CA	47W	6
CARR HAROLD EDWARD	TN	05W	43
CARR JAMES ALLEN	OH	20W	55
CARR JAMES OTIS	MI	07W	69
CARR JAMES WILLIAM	VA	52W	3
CARR JOHN PARM III	CA	02W	54
CARR LEN E	NY	05E	41
CARR LON GALE	NY	50W	5
CARR MARTIN CODY	IL	11W	22
CARR MICHAEL PETER	NY	23E	109
CARR ROBERT GEORGE	IL	22W	73
CARR ROBERT HARDY	PA	19E	22
CARR ROBERT HOWARD JR	PA	08E	48
CARR ROGER JAMES	CA	08W	65
CARR STEPHEN DOUGLAS	VT	07W	10
CARR WILLIAM LEE JR	WV	51W	10
CARRA ANTHONY	IA	58W	2
CARRANO JACKIE ANDREW	CA	51E	28
CARRANZA HORACIO	TX	42E	29
CARRANZA MARTIN	CA	20E	101
CARRASCO ARTHURO	CA	23W	118
CARRASCO DANIEL	CA	26W	97
CARRASCO RALPH	AZ	28E	20
CARRASQUILLO SOLTERO REINALDO	CT	20W	73
CARRASQUILLO-DENTON ALBERTO	PR	38E	22
CARRATURO FREDERICK JAMES	NY	20E	82
CARRELL LARRY DALE	IL	28E	90
CARRICARTE LOUIS ANTHONY	FL	01E	36
CARRICO CHESTER CALVIN JR	MO	14W	88
CARRICO CLYDE ROBERT	ID	15W	71
CARRICO DAVID AARON	IN	18E	28
CARRIER ALBERT JOSEPH III	MI	19W	91
CARRIER DANIEL LEWIS	CA	21E	31
CARRIERE OSCAR ROLAND	CA	10E	14
CARRIKER GRADY ISIAIAH JR	NC	31E	86
CARRILLO ARNOLDO LEONEL	TX	33E	69
CARRILLO GEORGE J JR	CA	14E	127
CARRILLO JIMMY	CA	12W	116
CARRILLO JOE JR	AZ	56E	35
CARRILLO JOSE CASTANEDA	CA	16W	40
CARRILLO JUAN	TX	15W	66
CARRILLO MELVIN	NM	42E	48
CARRILLO RICHARD	CA	67E	6
CARRINGTON FRED EMERY	IL	14W	125
CARRINGTON THOMAS WILLIAM	IA	19W	13
CARRION JOSE ANTONIO	OH	20W	107
CARRIZALES DIONISIO G	TX	11W	109
CARROLA EDWARD	CA	12E	65
CARROLL BAXTER COLIDGE	NC	04E	68
CARROLL DAVID	PA	25E	91
CARROLL DOUGLAS	KY	10W	45
CARROLL DWIGHT WAYNE	TN	67E	6
CARROLL FERGUS JOSEPH	PA	56W	18
CARROLL FRANK JEROME	CO	28W	102
CARROLL GERALD FORD	CO	25E	32
CARROLL JAMES JOSEPH	FL	11E	48
CARROLL JAMES NATHAN III	OH	55E	5
CARROLL JAMES RICHARD	PA	41W	51
CARROLL JOE DAVID	GA	48W	39
CARROLL JOHN LEONARD	GA	01W	90
CARROLL JOHN THOMAS	CA	27E	87
CARROLL JOSEPH FRANCIS	MA	13E	58
CARROLL JOSEPH KENNETH	MD	31W	64
CARROLL KENNETH AUTRY	WV	58E	5
CARROLL KEVIN JAMES	NY	15E	19
CARROLL LARRY DAVID	GA	30W	85
CARROLL LARRY MARTIN	FL	38W	48
CARROLL MANUEL LEROY	IN	10E	116
CARROLL MAX EDWARD	NC	06W	21
CARROLL MICHAEL	NY	10E	59
CARROLL MICHAEL DAVID	TX	45E	18
CARROLL PATRICK HENRY	MI	16W	19
CARROLL PATRICK JOHN	WI	39W	58
CARROLL PETER RICHARD	CA	34W	5
CARROLL RAYMOND FRANK	RI	05W	94
CARROLL ROBERT HUGH	MT	58E	31
CARROLL ROGER EUGENE	IA	16W	4
CARROLL ROGER WILLIAM JR	MO	01W	74
CARROLL ROY ARNOLD	GA	26W	24
CARROLL SAMUEL T JR	NC	08W	35
CARROLL THOMAS J	MI	52E	15
CARROLL TIMOTHY MICHAEL	CA	30W	85
CARROLL WALTER JACKSON	FL	11E	121
CARROLL WESLEY WOMBLE III	TX	14W	72
CARROLL WILLIAM EUGENE	IL	46E	44
CARRUTH DAVE SCOTT JR	NY	07W	21
CARRUTHERS EDWARD ANTHONY	NV	27E	22
CARSON ALAN DALE	TX	42E	61
CARSON BRADLEY JAMES	NY	26E	88
CARSON CARL LEE	PA	46E	62
CARSON CHAD LEONARD	ID	15W	45
CARSON CHARLES N JR	AL	12E	3
CARSON CLARENCE JASPER JR	CA	12W	95
CARSON DAVID RICKEY	WV	36E	1
CARSON EDWIN EVERETT	MN	40W	10
CARSON JOHN HARVEY	TX	60W	16
CARSON LAWRENCE HOWARD	MO	62W	6
CARSON MERVYN MAURICE	IL	15E	31
CARSON OMER PRICE	KY	06W	112
CARSON PAUL DAVID	IA	13W	130
CARSON PAUL ROLAND	MA	02W	35
CARSON RICHARD JAMES	MA	16E	119
CARSON RICHARD RAY	IL	04W	85
CARSON RUSSELL BERTON	OH	21W	81
CARSON TYRONE BRUCE	MO	01E	128
CARSON WILLIAM D	CT	13E	78
CARSTARPHEN HAROLD JR	AL	11W	129
CARSTENS GARY AMOS	CO	17E	120
CARSTENS THOMAS HENRY	OH	40W	36
CARSTENS THOMAS JAMES	WI	24E	110
CARTAGENA-ACOSTA MOISES	PR	19W	29
CARTER ALAN GLEN	WA	64W	6
CARTER ANDERSON JR	MD	19E	10
CARTER ARDON WILLIAM	TX	05E	1
CARTER BRUCE LANDON	OR	44W	21
CARTER BRUCE WAYNE	FL	20W	107
CARTER CHARLES IRA	KY	23E	79
CARTER CLIFFORD RUSSELL	MI	31E	86
CARTER CLYDE ELMER JR	OK	36E	47
CARTER CLYDE RAY JR	NC	40W	53
CARTER CLYDE WALTER	FL	26E	91
CARTER D C	CT	16W	62
CARTER DANIEL JR	IL	16W	62
CARTER DAVID EDWARD	OH	20W	121
CARTER DENNIS RAY	CA	10E	53
CARTER DONALD ODELL	DC	03W	37
CARTER DONALD SUMINGUIT	GM	35W	63
CARTER DUANE ELWOOD	NY	29E	14
CARTER EDWARD EUGENE	OH	51E	5

NAME	STATE	PANEL NO.	LINE NO.
CARTER ERNEST LEE	OK	12E	36
CARTER ERNEST MACK	OH	23E	9
CARTER EUGENE	NC	13W	70
CARTER FRANKIE NATHANIEL	MI	54E	31
CARTER FRED DOUGLAS JR	TX	69W	2
CARTER FRED JOSHUA	SC	16W	33
CARTER FREDERICK THOMAS	RI	14E	14
CARTER GARY DON	TX	24W	101
CARTER GARY MICHAEL	TN	47E	47
CARTER GEORGE ALBERT	MD	42W	27
CARTER GEORGE WILLIAM	FL	01W	5
CARTER GERALD LYNN	OR	05W	64
CARTER GILL LESTER	LA	25E	5
CARTER GLENN	PA	44W	15
CARTER GREG ROY	CA	05W	90
CARTER GREGORY	OH	43W	68
CARTER GREGORY	FL	17W	70
CARTER HAMP JR	AL	61W	22
CARTER HAROLD E	GA	32W	70
CARTER HARRY GIBSON	AL	21E	18
CARTER HARVEY WILLIAM	MD	37W	29
CARTER HUBERT CLAYTON	OH	31E	63
CARTER JACK DAVID	AZ	28W	34
CARTER JACKIE CHARLES	CA	40W	71
CARTER JAMES BASIL	FL	05W	110
CARTER JAMES DEVRIN	MI	57W	7
CARTER JAMES DOUGLAS JR	TX	21E	65
CARTER JAMES LOUIS	CA	04E	134
CARTER JAMES WILLIAM	CO	06W	128
CARTER JERALD WAYNE	AL	02W	74
CARTER JERRY DONALD	NC	08E	16
CARTER JERRY RAY	MO	22E	82
CARTER JIMMY	LA	35W	75
CARTER JIMMY EARL	NC	22E	68
CARTER JOE EDDIE	MS	32E	50
CARTER JOHN E JR	IA	13W	14
CARTER JOHN LEWIS	SC	54W	42
CARTER JOHNNIE JR	FL	58E	31
CARTER JOSEPH JR	FL	06W	65
CARTER KENNETH ROBERT	MA	09E	91
CARTER L C	MS	24W	63
CARTER LARRY REAUMAINE	GA	07W	25
CARTER LEONARD ALEXANDER	VA	18E	8
CARTER LEONARD JAMES	IL	21E	73
CARTER LESLIE DEAN JR	CA	20W	47
CARTER LESLIE LOUIS	ND	54W	27
CARTER LINWOOD CHARLES JR	VA	06W	14
CARTER MARK JERALD	FL	62E	15
CARTER MERLE KEITH	OK	28E	49
CARTER MICHAEL BOYD	CA	15E	78
CARTER MICHAEL STEPHEN	IN	13W	18
CARTER MILFORD DONAVIN	LA	17E	97
CARTER NATHANIEL EARL III	AL	03E	113
CARTER OTIS	KS	07W	101
CARTER PAUL C JR	MA	36E	1
CARTER PAUL DEAN	KY	03W	56
CARTER PAUL LAMAR	FL	16E	1
CARTER RALPH DWAIN	OH	10E	79
CARTER RALPH WINFIELD	IL	18E	78
CARTER REGINALD F JR	DC	15E	126
CARTER RICHARD ALBERT	PA	22E	86
CARTER RICHARD KENNETH	WI	30E	23
CARTER RICHARD THOMAS	VA	14W	59
CARTER ROBERT HENRY JR	NC	24W	115
CARTER ROBERT JEROME	VA	26W	52
CARTER ROBERT LESTER	OH	29E	28
CARTER ROBERT NEL	NJ	38E	46
CARTER RODNEY BALAAM	CA	11E	107
CARTER RONALD JAMES	OH	25W	46
CARTER RONALD LEE	TN	10E	14
CARTER ROY LYNN	OH	10W	69
CARTER SHELBY M	LA	11W	130
CARTER STANLEY ALAN	WA	27W	85
CARTER STEVE DWAYNE	TX	17W	36
CARTER TERREL ELBERT	FL	14E	33
CARTER TERRY ALFRED	MI	14W	74
CARTER THOMAS ANTHONY	FL	29E	96
CARTER THOMAS JAMES	CA	29E	70
CARTER THOMAS LEE	CA	39W	42
CARTER THURL GUY III	CA	40W	71
CARTER TIMOTHY GENE	NV	21W	122
CARTER VERNON THOMAS JR	FL	04E	7

NAME	STATE	PANEL NO.	LINE NO.
CARTER WALLACE SPERGON	PA	18W	108
CARTER WALTER CORBIN	MD	26W	60
CARTER WENDELL LOUIL	CA	21E	96
CARTER WILLIAM ALLEN	IN	32E	29
CARTER WILLIAM EDWIN	OH	18W	93
CARTER WILLIAM THOMAS	SC	12E	50
CARTER ZANE AUBRY	ME	24E	72
CARTHAGE OTIS JR	AL	15W	102
CARTIER VICTOR JOHN	MO	27W	36
CARTLAND DONALD NORMAN	IL	18W	37
CARTLEDGE ALBERT J III	TX	24W	115
CARTNEY PATRICK CYRIL	PA	36E	1
CARTONIA CARMEN PAUL	NY	12E	23
CARTRETTE HARRY KENNETH	NC	20E	111
CARTWRIGHT BILLIE JACK	TX	04E	34
CARTWRIGHT JAMES HOWARD	TX	05W	32
CARTWRIGHT JAMES WARREN	OR	20E	89
CARTWRIGHT JIMMY	AR	01E	55
CARTWRIGHT JOHN STANBOROU	NJ	19E	35
CARTWRIGHT MICHEAL GLENN	OH	15E	40
CARTWRIGHT PATRICK G	NV	05W	70
CARTWRIGHT RALPH WINDALL	VA	03E	53
CARTWRIGHT RICHARD CORTEZ	OH	40W	71
CARTWRIGHT ROBERT MICHAEL	MA	16E	130
CARTWRIGHT RONALD JOSEPH	OR	27E	63
CARTWRIGHT THOMAS CLARK	NY	22E	64
CARUOLO RICHARD ANTHONY	RI	06E	41
CARUSO DAVID RAYMOND	OH	58E	32
CARUSO THOMAS EDWARD	CA	18W	128
CARUTHERS THOMAS HOWARD	TX	06E	121
CARVAJAL FRANCISCO TERONI	NY	11W	100
CARVAJAL JOSEPH CARLOS	CA	44E	15
CARVALHO GILBERT	MA	44W	61
CARVALLO CESAR EDUARDO	NY	22E	97
CARVEN RUPERT SADLER III	MA	05E	100
CARVER BILLY KAY	OK	17E	120
CARVER BOBBY DON	CA	31E	44
CARVER HAROLD LEROY	MO	17E	102
CARVER HARRY FRANKLIN	IN	49E	13
CARVER JERRY DEWAYNE	AL	09W	93
CARVER JERRY LEON	AL	31E	20
CARVER RANDALL ALLEN	MI	09W	110
CARVER RICHARD ALAN	CA	15E	33
CARVILLE JOHN JOSEPH	MA	07E	16
CARWITHEN ALBERT MORGAN	WV	33E	45
CARY WILLIE B	AL	09E	51
CASALE JAMES ERNEST	MA	07E	116
CASALETTO EDWIN JAMES	MA	21E	9
CASARES MANUEL	CA	60W	26
CASAREZ RAUL	OH	18E	78
CASAS BONNIE PATALINGHUNG		04E	99
CASE CHARLES CECIL	IA	25W	63
CASE DANIEL CHARLES	KS	12W	123
CASE DAVID DUANE	NY	02E	84
CASE EDWIN HARRY	SD	40W	72
CASE GLENN EDWARD	CA	35W	24
CASE JAMES GILBERT	MD	26W	97
CASE JAMES RUSSELL	KY	11W	43
CASE ORSON HOWARD	NY	09E	21
CASE ROBERT DON	CA	35W	53
CASE THOMAS FRANKLIN	GA	07E	127
CASE THOMAS JOSEPH	NY	19E	69
CASE THURLE EUGENE JR	CA	12W	4
CASEBOLT HENRY CLAYTON	MO	05E	84
CASERIO CHARLES DOMINIC	NM	02W	15
CASEY DANIEL GENE	CA	20W	63
CASEY DANNY CURTIS	OR	48W	5
CASEY DANNY VANN	NC	28W	24
CASEY DAVID WARRINGTON	PA	62E	16
CASEY DENNIS LEE	MT	22E	6
CASEY DONALD FRANCIS	TN	55W	20
CASEY EDDY RAY	UT	28W	43
CASEY FRANCIS JOSEPH	NY	11E	129
CASEY GEORGE WILLIAM	MA	09W	126
CASEY JAMES PATRICK	MA	24W	37
CASEY JOHN MICHAEL	TN	46E	14
CASEY JOHNNY DALE	GA	55W	11
CASEY LEO CARL JR	MS	14W	12
CASEY LIAM SOUEPH	CA	17E	91
CASEY MAURICE ALOYSIUS	OH	07E	107
CASEY MICHAEL DALE	OK	14W	59
CASEY MICHAEL JAMES	MA	45E	18

NAME	STATE	PANEL NO.	LINE NO.
CASEY PAUL WILLIAM	NY	19E	125
CASEY RICHARD WILLIAM	CA	38W	71
CASEY ROBERT MICHAEL	NJ	61E	7
CASEY THOMAS JEROME JR	NY	32W	42
CASEY THOMAS MICHAEL JR	MA	32W	42
CASEY TOM GAYLE	AZ	40W	32
CASH BENNY DALE	AL	53E	10
CASH DAVID MANFRED	CA	39E	43
CASH JAMES RONALD	MO	21W	27
CASH JERRY MICHAEL	TN	23E	17
CASH JOHN HAROLD JR	ME	58E	32
CASH MORRIS ELTON	HI	51E	36
CASHDOLLAR GLENN FRANCIS	WV	46E	15
CASHLEY JOHN EDWARD	PA	59E	19
CASHMAN CORNELIUS JAMES	OH	19W	10
CASHMAN HAROLD EDWARD JR	PA	36E	2
CASIANO JUAN	NY	15E	114
CASIAS CHRISTOPHER	CA	32W	93
CASIAS HENRY ELOY	CO	37E	19
CASILLA-VAZQUEZ MANUEL JR	NY	33E	65
CASILLO CARMINE	NY	43E	42
CASINO JOSEPH WALTER	MI	05W	71
CASLER JOSEPH DUANE	CO	06W	25
CASNER LEWIS EDGAR JR	MD	08W	31
CASON DAVID ALLAN	CA	07W	103
CASON GEORGE GILBERT JR	MO	62W	6
CASON WILLIAM ARNOLD	IA	32E	70
CASP MICHAEL ALLEN	PA	29E	94
CASPER FREDERICK RAYMOND	WI	57E	16
CASPER RICHARD ALLEN	MN	21E	7
CASPER RONALD JEROME DENT	CA	42E	48
CASPERSEN ROBERT P II	WI	29E	98
CASPOLE RALPH WARREN	MA	08E	1
CASS ANTHONY MAC	NM	20E	111
CASS FRANK LEE	NH	04W	37
CASS WILLIAM DAVID	NY	27E	5
CASSANO DANIEL	IL	34W	21
CASSANO RICHARD ANTHONY	NY	52E	35
CASSATA ORRIN JOSEPH	IL	26E	22
CASSEL KENNETH WAYNE	SC	40W	62
CASSEL RONALD ROY	PA	20E	22
CASSELL KEVIN RAY	TX	51E	21
CASSELL ROBIN BERN	AZ	23E	74
CASSELL RONALD BRETT	MD	29W	96
CASSELMAN RODNEY WILLARD	CA	09E	105
CASSERLY JOSEPH MICHAEL	MN	15E	31
CASSIDY DAVID ALEXANDER	CT	38W	33
CASSIDY DONALD THOMAS	NY	12E	16
CASSIDY JEFFREY TYRONE	DE	30W	99
CASSIDY JOSEPH J JR	PA	45E	38
CASSIDY MICHAEL OLIVER	OH	33W	47
CASSIDY MICHAEL PATRICK	MI	23E	67
CASSIDY PATRICK CHRISTIAN	IL	32E	17
CASSIDY RAYMOND SENTER	NY	18E	78
CASSIDY WILLIAM EDWARD	MD	67E	6
CASSIN FRANK ANDREW JR	PA	07W	1
CASSIN RICHARD ALBERT	CT	19E	35
CASSMEYER VICTOR PAUL JR	MO	18W	60
CASSUBE RICHARD HUGH	FL	05E	59
CAST THOMAS EDWARD	MI	32E	70
CASTAGNA JOSEPH PHILIP	NY	36W	56
CASTALDI JAMES	NJ	34E	38
CASTALDO CLEMENT SAM	IL	07E	116
CASTANEDA BENJAMIN BELTRAN	CA	01E	83
CASTANEDA BENJAMIN FRANK	CA	42W	16
CASTANEDA EUGENE	HI	24E	102
CASTANEDA HUGO CARLOS	CA	52W	2
CASTANON ALFREDO	TX	11E	6
CASTEEL JAMES DENNIS	TN	15W	66
CASTELDA ANDREW THOMAS	VA	16E	71
CASTELLANO SAMUEL RODGER	MA	45W	5
CASTELLANOS JUAN CARLOS	NY	34E	75
CASTELLANOS SANTOS JR	IL	03W	127
CASTELOT ROBERT SHEEHAN	NH	58W	22
CASTILLO ANTONIO GONZALES	TX	22W	102
CASTILLO APOLINAR JR	TX	21W	64
CASTILLO ARTHUR JOHN	CA	16W	52
CASTILLO CHARLES MIKE	CA	26E	99
CASTILLO DANIEL SANDUAL	MI	14E	66
CASTILLO DAVID RIVAS	CA	16W	87
CASTILLO ERASMO CAMARGO	TX	21E	86
CASTILLO GEORGE RALPH	OK	35E	20

NAME	STATE	PANEL NO.	LINE NO.
CASTILLO GREGORIO PEDRO	CA	18W	119
CASTILLO JOHN JAMES	MI	27E	94
CASTILLO JOSE	CA	23E	97
CASTILLO JOSE JAIME	TX	08W	93
CASTILLO LEONARD BALDOMIR	HI	24W	2
CASTILLO LOUIS	IL	12E	98
CASTILLO MANOLITO WISCO		01E	98
CASTILLO MANUEL ANGEL	CA	51W	2
CASTILLO MANUEL GRIJALVA	CA	26E	7
CASTILLO PHILLIP	IN	09W	62
CASTILLO RICHARD	TX	02W	121
CASTILLO THOMAS	CA	20W	83
CASTILLO-LIMA BENJAMIN	NY	03E	43
CASTLE HAL CUSHMAN JR	VA	26W	69
CASTLE LARRY FLOYD	OH	12E	126
CASTLE ROBERT EDWARD	CA	12W	28
CASTLE ROGER ALLEN	WV	15E	82
CASTLE RUSSELL LEONARD	VA	22E	97
CASTLE VIRGIL LEE	OH	20W	117
CASTLEBERRY BILLIE MAC	OK	02E	111
CASTLEBERRY JAMES ANDREW	TX	62W	7
CASTLEBERRY JIMMIE LYNN	CA	17W	76
CASTLEBERRY ROY LEE	GA	20E	94
CASTLEMAN RICKEY DON	FL	08E	107
CASTO CLARENCE LEROY	OH	12E	66
CASTON JAMES CALVIN	TX	02E	49
CASTOR JAMES WILLIAM	KS	19W	29
CASTRO ALFONSO ROQUE	CA	16W	27
CASTRO ERNESTO F JR	TX	49W	19
CASTRO JESSE ROMERO	CA	16E	44
CASTRO JOAQUIN	MD	40E	2
CASTRO JOE	CA	01W	123
CASTRO JORGE ARTURO	CA	49E	51
CASTRO JOSE ANTONIO		34W	31
CASTRO JUAN JOSE	CA	06E	41
CASTRO JUAN PASCUAL R	GM	29W	96
CASTRO LOUIS	CA	27W	71
CASTRO REINALDO ANTONIO	CA	18E	100
CASTRO-CARRASQUILLO MIGUEL	PR	07E	132
CASTRO-MORALES RAMON	PR	36W	33
CASTRO-RAMOS JUSTINO ENRI	PR	18E	78
CASWELL EDWIN DOUGLAS	KY	32W	93
CASWELL EUGENE WILLIAM	MI	07E	112
CASWELL KENNETH LEE	MI	16W	62
CASWELL RAYMOND M	TX	35E	30
CASWELL ROBERT LYNN	MI	47E	47
CATALANO GEORGE FRANCIS	NY	24E	50
CATALANO SAM JR	CO	20W	121
CATANZARITI RONNIE S	NY	22E	28
CATE WILLIAM EARL	NH	10E	96
CATELLI CHARLES JOHN	CA	35W	33
CATES GARY RAY	TN	39E	3
CATES NORMAN GENE	IL	40W	72
CATES NORMAN LOUIS	VA	34W	21
CATES ROBERT MATHEW JR	NV	48W	5
CATES WILLIAM LLOYD	AZ	30E	69
CATHER TERRENCE JAY	NY	10E	61
CATHERMAN ROBERT RAY	NY	23W	99
CATHEY J B	SC	40E	4
CATINO STEVEN LYNN	CA	14W	119
CATLIN NORMAN RICHARD	IL	16E	89
CATLIN THOMAS DAVID	OH	09W	87
CATLING ROBERT PHILIP	NJ	08E	123
CATLING WILLIE B	MS	54W	35
CATO HERBERT HUGO III	SC	47E	38
CATO ROBERT O'NEAL	FL	46W	12
CATO WILLIE FRED	FL	17W	73
CATOIR JOSEPH GEORGE P JR	LA	55W	33
CATON GERALD LEWIS	VA	19W	53
CATON LEONARD ROGER	MT	30W	73
CATRON GARRY WAYNE	CA	40W	62
CATT JOSEPH FRANCIS JR	CA	57E	16
CATTERSON RONALD GENE	CO	54W	16
CATTON JOHN LESLIE	IL	21E	32
CAUBLE ARTURO ALVARADO	TX	30W	36
CAUCCI STEVEN RICHARD	PA	08W	84
CAUDILL BILLY JOE	IN	19W	127
CAUDILL DONNIE WAYNE	OH	29W	28
CAUDILL ELMON C II	OH	06W	90
CAUDILL JAMES	OH	48W	39
CAUDILL ORVILLE	KY	29E	99
CAUDILL ORVILLE	OH	02W	29
CAUDILL ROGER DALE	KY	18E	113
CAUDILLO JOSEPH	CA	19E	22
CAUDILLO PEDRO JAIME	TX	63E	6
CAUGHEY JAMES EDWARD	IN	01E	61
CAUGHMAN McKINLEY JR	NY	16E	44
CAULDER DURWOOD	SC	50W	17
CAULEY AUBREY	AL	09E	126
CAULEY EUGENE JR	FL	15W	55
CAULEY ROGER DALE	KY	56E	19
CAULTON WILLIE RICHARD	IL	35E	41
CAUSEY BEN ELMORE JR	AL	39E	30
CAUSEY DAVID LOUIS	CA	19W	77
CAUSEY JOHN BERNARD	IL	05E	77
CAUSEY WILLIAM HARVEY	SC	06E	97
CAUTHEN CALDWELL M JR	PA	43E	42
CAUTHEN FRANK REGINALD	NC	52W	17
CAUTHEN HENRY CLAY SR	MS	24E	54
CAUTHERN ROGER ROBERT	CT	29E	47
CAUTHRON R G	OK	52W	4
CAVALARATOS GEORGE ANASTA	NY	51W	2
CAVALLI ANTHONY FRANK	NY	08E	103
CAVALLIN LESTER MELVIN	WA	18W	19
CAVANAGH ARTHUR	NY	04E	64
CAVANAGH MICHAEL HOWARD	OR	23W	42
CAVANAUGH EDWARD JOSEPH	MA	03W	117
CAVANAUGH JAMES VINCENT	RI	32W	52
CAVANAUGH JOHN CHARLES	IL	31E	72
CAVANAUGH RICHARD FRED	OR	38E	19
CAVANAUGH THOMAS JAMES	CT	43W	34
CAVANAUGH WILLIAM THOMAS	RI	01E	48
CAVAROCCHI JOSEPH	PA	19E	104
CAVARZAN DUANE EARL	CA	22E	76
CAVAZOS DANIEL GUTIERREZ	TX	24E	17
CAVAZOS MARTIN	TX	19E	42
CAVAZOS REYNALDO ROY	WA	05E	46
CAVAZOS RONALD THOMAS	MI	48E	1
CAVENDER JIM RAY	CA	16W	27
CAVER JOHN WAYNE	TX	28E	102
CAVICCHI JAMES HENRY JR	MA	06E	31
CAVIN DOUGLAS JAMES	TX	43W	52
CAVIN STEVEN IKE	VA	40W	63
CAVINEE RONALD C	OH	05E	79
CAVINS SAMUEL McARTHUR	WV	42W	45
CAVIS DAVID JUDE	MI	40E	58
CAWLEY JAMES PATRICK	PA	52E	3
CAWLEY PATRICK FRANCIS	MN	10W	74
CAWLEY RICHARD ERNEST	MO	49E	39
CAWLEY ROBERT WILLIAM	MT	44E	44
CAWLEY WILLIAM BRACE JR	IN	42E	29
CAWTHORNE WILLIAM BAYLES	GA	01E	56
CAYCE JOHN DAVID	TX	29E	80
CAYEY EDWARD CECIL JR	NY	12E	82
CAYFORD PHILLIP J JR	ME	45E	54
CAYLOR RANDY LEE	NY	03W	119
CAYSON ALVIN LLOYD	KY	42E	29
CAYWOOD GARY STEVEN	WA	53E	28
CAZANAS-DIAZ EDWARDO ENRI	RI	13E	120
CAZARES JAMES STEVEN	OK	26E	33
CAZIN RICHARD PAUL	WY	46W	1
CEARNEL HARRY LEE	NC	13W	110
CECH LEROY CHARLES	MT	09W	68
CECIL ALAN BRUCE	OK	18W	119
CECIL JACK WILSON	CA	04E	128
CECIL ROBERT RANDALL	MI	01W	56
CECIL ROGER DALE	AR	23E	69
CEDERLUND RONALD MICHAEL	IL	45W	31
CEDERSTROM DAVID ORIN	UT	21E	9
CEGIELSKI RICHARD JOSEPH	OH	53W	17
CELANO FRANK ANTHONY	CA	05W	60
CELESTE RAYMOND	NY	03E	107
CELLETTI JERRY	IL	46W	38
CELMER LAWRENCE JOSEPH	NY	16E	104
CEMELLI SALVATORE PETER	NJ	13E	20
CENTENO CHARLES MANUEL	CA	11E	21
CENTENO EDWARD LOUIS	CA	22E	53
CENTENO HERMINIO GENOVA	NY	06W	44
CENTER ROBERT LEE	CA	23E	49
CENTERS WILLIAM P JR	KY	20E	71
CEPEDA JUAN DUENAS	GM	09E	85
CERENE AMBROSE JOSEPH	PA	30E	39
CERES THOMAS ALLEN	FL	21W	92
CERIO JOSEPH ANTHONY	NY	10W	78
CERIONE JAMES STANLEY III	IL	38E	23
CERNA NARCISO REZA JR	TX	09E	21
CERRA RICHARD RALPH	WI	49W	22
CERRANO LOUIS FRANCIS JR	NY	18E	67
CERRATO NICHOLAS FRANK	NJ	25W	37
CERRONE JOSEPH CARMEN JR	MA	48W	39
CERVANTES GEORGE ANDREW	CA	18E	119
CERVANTES GERALD	CA	42E	2
CERVANTEZ EDWARD EDDY	IL	35E	67
CERVANTEZ JUAN JOSE	TX	14E	4
CERVANTEZ LUIS GODINEZ	UT	21W	106
CERVELLINO CARMINE ANTHON	NY	01E	50
CERVERA MICHAEL BERNARD	NJ	37E	4
CESAR RICHARD ALLEN	IA	03E	5
CESTARE JOSEPH ANGELO	NY	51E	5
CESTARIC JOSEPH ANTHONY	PA	04E	20
CEVALLOS ROBERT G	TX	25W	65
CHABERT GARY AUGUST	LA	51E	17
CHABOT DON WILLIAM	CA	06E	9
CHABOT RICHARD EARL	CT	04E	7
CHACALOS GEORGE MANUAL	WV	44E	33
CHACE GEORGE HENRY	MA	11E	93
CHACON DAVID ANDREW	CO	32W	76
CHACON RIGOBERTO COTO	CA	02E	37
CHACON ROBERT REINHARD	CA	35W	41
CHADEE NYROON	NY	37W	45
CHADWICK BILLY RAYMOND	KS	22W	63
CHADWICK FRANK W JR	MA	12E	130
CHADWICK JAMES EDWARD	OH	19E	128
CHADWICK KENNETH RAY	TX	16E	89
CHADWICK LEON GORDON III	NC	12E	70
CHAFFEE VAN	OH	20E	101
CHAFFIN ALLAN RAY	AL	19E	125
CHAFFIN CLARENCE RAY	TX	40W	53
CHAFFIN DONALD ALAN	IN	15E	82
CHAFFIN THOMAS WILLIAM	MI	20E	6
CHAFFIN WILLIAM T III	TN	18W	5
CHAFFINS ERNEST JR	KY	41E	36
CHAHOC DAVID KEITH	OH	42W	27
CHAIRA FRANCISCO PERAZA	AZ	11E	60
CHALAKEE RUDY YORK	OK	44E	4
CHALLBERG CURTIS PAUL	IL	19W	91
CHALLENER ROBERT JOSEPH	PA	35W	37
CHALMERS DEMPSEY JR	MS	50E	37
CHALOU RONALD DAVID	MI	21W	111
CHAMAJ ANDREW PETER	PA	09E	22
CHAMBERLAIN ALLEN B	FL	15E	31
CHAMBERLAIN CARL EUGEN	TN	32E	85
CHAMBERLAIN DALE STEWART	CA	07W	91
CHAMBERLAIN HENRY	TX	29W	28
CHAMBERLAIN LESLIE ALLEN	PA	22E	23
CHAMBERLAIN MICHAEL JOHN	NY	10W	95
CHAMBERLAIN RICHARD MORRI	DE	55W	11
CHAMBERLAIN ROBERT F	NM	11E	54
CHAMBERLAIN ROY WARNER JR	MI	17E	27
CHAMBERLIN DENNIS DEAN	WI	09W	93
CHAMBERLIN GEORGE E JR	FL	01E	50
CHAMBERLIN HOWARD ARTHUR	NH	26E	59
CHAMBERS BILLY CLAYTON	OK	26W	60
CHAMBERS CHRISTOPHER LEE	OR	47W	38
CHAMBERS CORNELIUS J B	FL	17E	95
CHAMBERS DAVID WAYNE	TX	47E	47
CHAMBERS DONALD EDWARD	OH	12W	79
CHAMBERS ERNEST L JR	DC	20E	53
CHAMBERS HARVEY ROBERT JA	KY	16E	55
CHAMBERS HILLMAN GLEN	NJ	50W	12
CHAMBERS JACKIE DEAN	OK	62W	21
CHAMBERS JAMES DOUGLAS	IL	41E	60
CHAMBERS JAMES LARRY	OH	56E	36
CHAMBERS JAMES THOMAS	TX	38E	23
CHAMBERS JAMES WAYNE	TN	26E	81
CHAMBERS JERRY LEE	OK	65E	4
CHAMBERS JOHN LUTHER	TX	48E	1
CHAMBERS JOHNNY A	WA	13E	124
CHAMBERS JOSEPH LEE	AR	07W	30
CHAMBERS LESTER EUGENE	TX	41E	18
CHAMBERS LORANZEY PAUL	OK	22W	103
CHAMBERS OSCAR EDWARD	AL	16E	34
CHAMBERS PAUL RICHARD	AL	09E	22
CHAMBERS RAYMOND EARL	IN	26E	82
CHAMBERS RICHARD ALAN	MI	43W	12
CHAMBERS RICHARD THOMAS	NY	36W	61

NAME	STATE	PANEL NO.	LINE NO.
CHAMBERS ROBERT JOHN	PA	39E	18
CHAMBERS ROBERT O	AL	45W	48
CHAMBERS ROBERT STANLEY	ID	30E	75
CHAMBERS SAMUEL P III	IL	02E	23
CHAMBERS STEVEN DOYLE	CA	19E	78
CHAMBERS THOMAS BEEB	TN	32E	8
CHAMBERS TOMMIE ALLEN	TX	50E	26
CHAMBERS UDELL	MO	55W	11
CHAMBERS-QUIROZ GEORGE	NY	09W	77
CHAMBLEE DANIEL LEE	GA	02W	69
CHAMBLEE DICKEY	TN	33E	7
CHAMBLEE JIMMIE LADON	AL	09W	80
CHAMBLEE WILLIAM DONALD	FL	08W	54
CHAMBLEY THEODORE ROOSEVE	NY	02E	124
CHAMBLIN DONALD RAY JR	NC	43E	52
CHAMBLISS JIMMY LEE	OH	14W	28
CHAMBLISS LUTHER	GA	19E	79
CHAMBLISS ROGER RIDGELY	MI	01W	86
CHAMPAGNE THOMAS EUGENE	MA	18W	81
CHAMPION CHARLES DON	TX	46W	47
CHAMPION GERALD ALAN	MO	21E	21
CHAMPION JAMES ALBERT	TX	03W	8
CHAMPION JOSEPH	GA	16E	130
CHAMPION WAYNE WILLIAM	MN	58E	32
CHAMPLIN JOHN ROBERT	KY	04W	57
CHAN PETER	CA	01W	75
CHANDLER ANTHONY GORDON	GA	56W	1
CHANDLER CHARLES	NY	27W	106
CHANDLER CHARLES PERRY	OH	21W	81
CHANDLER CHARLES WILLIAM	MO	26W	54
CHANDLER CONNIE LEROY	IA	03E	102
CHANDLER JEROME DEE	NE	38W	73
CHANDLER JOE WAYNE	MO	17E	56
CHANDLER LARRY DELYNN	AL	27W	62
CHANDLER LARRY TOM	OR	24E	80
CHANDLER LEONARD ONEAL	AL	42E	61
CHANDLER QUINNEN T JR	OK	27E	36
CHANDLER ROBERT HUGHESTON	CA	20E	111
CHANDLER ROBERT LARRY	TN	35W	42
CHANDLER RONALD EUGENE	OH	07W	9
CHANDLER THOMAS J JR	TN	06E	9
CHANDLER THOMAS LEROY	SC	13W	50
CHANDLER WILLIAM GARY	PA	01W	62
CHANEY ARTHUR FLETCHER	VA	54E	24
CHANEY DAVID GLENN	KY	07W	26
CHANEY DAVID LEE	VA	33E	12
CHANEY DAVID MICHAEL	CA	18E	33
CHANEY DONALD LEE	CA	34E	62
CHANEY DOUGLAS DALE	CA	51W	38
CHANEY ELWOOD DAVID JR	DC	28E	20
CHANEY LARRY WILLIAM	AL	02W	34
CHANEY MICHAEL WAYNE	IN	39W	47
CHANEY NORMAN J	CA	45W	24
CHANEY ROY LEE	IN	05W	16
CHANEY STEPHEN JOHN	OH	18W	129
CHANEY THOMAS CLIFFORD	CA	13W	87
CHANNEL BILLY GENE	MO	04W	115
CHANNON BUDDY EUGENE	TX	30W	85
CHAP DE LAINE ARNOLD A JR	CA	58W	23
CHAPA ARMANDO JR	CA	37E	52
CHAPA LORENZO JR	TX	17W	120
CHAPARRO-VILLANUEVA GERMAN	PR	06E	84
CHAPEL HOSY	IN	04E	119
CHAPIN CHARLES CLARK	CA	14W	3
CHAPIN JOEL HENRY	MA	27E	99
CHAPLIN LAWRENCE	SC	37E	80
CHAPMAN ANDEE JR	AL	01W	35
CHAPMAN BILLY	GA	66E	7
CHAPMAN BILLY GENE	WV	19W	1
CHAPMAN CECIL LEROY	NC	16E	51
CHAPMAN CHARLES DANE	MI	28E	102
CHAPMAN CLINTON	MS	67E	6
CHAPMAN DAVID LEE	OK	07E	80
CHAPMAN DAVID THOMAS	MS	24W	92
CHAPMAN GARRY RAYMOND	OK	55E	5
CHAPMAN GARY MICHAEL	MN	38W	56
CHAPMAN GARY WAYNE	IN	37W	73
CHAPMAN GEORGE ANTHONY	WI	02W	2
CHAPMAN HENRY LEE	WV	24W	92
CHAPMAN JERRY JUNIOR	IL	51E	6
CHAPMAN JOHN RICHARD	VA	12W	28
CHAPMAN JOHN ROY	IN	17E	95
CHAPMAN JOHN THOMAS	WI	33E	80
CHAPMAN JOHNNY HOWARD	ID	03W	135
CHAPMAN KURTIS NOLAN	KS	57E	16
CHAPMAN LARRY LEE	IN	50E	26
CHAPMAN MAURICE P JR	MD	26E	95
CHAPMAN PETER HAUDEN II	OH	02W	130
CHAPMAN ROBERT L	NC	36E	67
CHAPMAN RODNEY MAX	MI	32W	53
CHAPMAN RONALD	MS	33W	28
CHAPMAN RONALD JAMES	PA	14W	106
CHAPMAN SHERMAN JR	NJ	08E	79
CHAPMAN SIDNEY DAVID	IL	20E	6
CHAPMAN THOMAS TODD	OH	37W	79
CHAPMAN WARREN NELSON	NY	55W	26
CHAPMAN WILLIAM JR	PA	60E	20
CHAPMAN WILLIE JAMES	AL	24W	3
CHAPP ROBERT ANTHONY	CA	18E	25
CHAPPEL LUTHER MALCOLM	KY	22W	86
CHAPPELL DANIEL L	TX	02E	135
CHAPPELL EDWARD LEWIS	IL	29W	59
CHAPPELL JOHN MONROE	MO	04E	20
CHAPPELL KENNETH LEE	VA	32E	70
CHAPPELL KENNEY DEAN	LA	28E	53
CHAPPEY JOHN MICHAEL	IN	13W	110
CHARBONEAU LEROY HARLAND	MI	23E	56
CHARD SALUM EDWARD JR	NJ	19W	127
CHARETTE MARK OWEN	WA	48E	25
CHARITY EDWARD JR	DC	28E	79
CHARLAND ROGER OVIDE	MA	47W	39
CHARLES BILLY	GA	15E	5
CHARLES DAN EUGENE	IN	42E	48
CHARLES EARL EUGENE	OH	17W	54
CHARLES EDWARD WILLIAM	AR	22W	73
CHARLES FRANCIS	PA	43W	52
CHARLES MICHAEL LANE	VA	42E	49
CHARLES NICHOLES WILLIAM	MI	69W	2
CHARLES RONALD	OH	22E	98
CHARLES RONNIE JOE	CA	46E	15
CHARLES TERRY LEE	FL	18W	112
CHARLESWORTH CHAD ALLEN	CA	13W	53
CHARLESWORTH JAMES W JR	OH	10W	17
CHARLEY MICHAEL JOHN	PA	55E	5
CHARLIE PETER	NM	08W	93
CHARLTON JERRY DEAN	AR	28E	65
CHARLTON JOHN WILLIAM	FL	18E	2
CHARNETZKI PAUL FREDERICK	ND	37E	80
CHARNOPLOSKY JOHN ANDREW	WV	02W	67
CHARTERS GEORGE W JR	PA	08W	76
CHARTIER RAYMOND ALLEN	VA	16W	98
CHARVET PAUL CLAUDE	WA	17E	1
CHASE CHARLES JOSEPH	CA	58W	23
CHASE CLARENCE LAWRENCE	ME	25E	22
CHASE CURTIS EDWARD	MA	19E	48
CHASE FREDDIE NICKLYS	MA	29W	36
CHASE GARY LEE	MI	19E	11
CHASE JAMES FRANCIS	ME	36W	33
CHASE JOHN JOSEPH	MD	21E	65
CHASE JOHN LENWOOD	MD	37W	4
CHASE LEO CURTIS JR	FL	03E	53
CHASE MARK RICHARDSON	CA	01E	95
CHASE MICHAEL LYN	OH	09W	12
CHASE OLIVER C JR	NY	02E	42
CHASE RAYMOND HOWARD JR	PA	29E	65
CHASE ROBERT KENDRICK	MA	36W	67
CHASE RUSSELL DAVID	MI	37E	19
CHASE TERRY A	IA	03E	76
CHASE VERNON GLENN	IA	05E	58
CHASE VICTOR EDWARD	FL	06E	116
CHASE WALTER WILLIAM	MA	27W	9
CHASIN STEPHEN C	GA	10W	39
CHASON THEODORE JOSEPH	DE	27E	69
CHASSER RAYMOND MICHAEL	OH	19E	126
CHASSION PHILIP RONALD	MA	36E	73
CHASTAIN DONNIE RAY	SC	13W	67
CHASTAIN GERALD EDWARD	SC	12E	108
CHASTAIN WOODROW BEAL	SC	03W	132
CHASTANG JOHNELL LAVERNE	AL	03W	27
CHASTANT RODNEY RENE	AL	40W	18
CHASTEEN ROGER WILSON	MO	19E	79
CHASTINE KENNETH FOSTER	IL	41E	18
CHATBURN JOSEPH THOMAS	PA	29W	51
CHATBURN THOMAS W III	OR	08E	35
CHATELAIN RAY AUGUSTINE	TX	24E	50
CHATFIELD DANIEL H	IA	61E	7
CHATFIELD WENDELL OLIVER	CA	08E	19
CHATMAN NATHANIEL	PA	29E	87
CHATMAN TYRONE	FL	19W	44
CHATMON CHARLES LOUIS	GA	08E	118
CHATMON NATHAN EUGENE	MI	13E	131
CHATOS WALTER ALEX JR	WI	18E	34
CHATTEN MARYLAND	VA	04E	36
CHATTERTON DAVID ROGER	ID	23E	85
CHATTIN AL JUNIOUS	WV	06E	47
CHAUDOIN ROBERT CONN	CA	04W	82
CHAVARIE NORMAN JOSEPH	ME	20W	27
CHAVARRIA JOHN MAREZ	CO	13W	83
CHAVES ALLEN FRED	AZ	19E	36
CHAVES JOHN CLIFFORD	MA	12W	122
CHAVEZ ANTONIO GONZALEZ	IL	19E	11
CHAVEZ CARLOS JR	CA	09W	90
CHAVEZ DANIEL JOSEPH	NM	06W	78
CHAVEZ DAVID CRUZ	NM	14W	36
CHAVEZ EDUARDO	CA	12E	99
CHAVEZ FILIBERTO	OH	58E	32
CHAVEZ FREDDIE PAUL	NM	30W	99
CHAVEZ GARY ANTHONY	NY	08W	68
CHAVEZ GILBERT MICHAEL	CO	31W	33
CHAVEZ GLEN ALEX	NM	08W	129
CHAVEZ GREGORY ANTON	CO	11W	110
CHAVEZ JESUS ERNEST JR	CA	51W	24
CHAVEZ JOHN MANUAL	TX	18W	128
CHAVEZ PAUL EDWARD	MT	55E	6
CHAVEZ RAFAEL ALBERT	TX	09W	63
CHAVEZ ROBERT L	AZ	12W	41
CHAVEZ RUBEN G	TX	03E	72
CHAVEZ RUDOLFO	CA	30E	96
CHAVIRA STEPHEN	CA	03W	57
CHAVIS ALPHONZO LINWOODEL	NC	24W	115
CHAVIS BRADLEY	NC	15E	94
CHAVIS HENRY LEWIS	NY	06W	106
CHAVIS RONNIE	SC	07W	35
CHAVOUS ALVIN RICHARDSON	PA	28E	45
CHAVOUS SAMUEL CALHOUN JR	FL	48E	1
CHEADLE HAROLD LEE JR	OH	47W	39
CHEANEY PRUITT HENRY	FL	09E	65
CHEARNLEY JOSEPH MICHAEL	OH	58W	7
CHEATHAM JAMES MICHAEL	KY	15W	53
CHEEK DONALD KIRBY	NC	37W	62
CHEEK JAMES WILLIAM	TX	27E	9
CHEEK KENNETH NORRIS	PA	20E	22
CHEEK PHILIP DUANE	IA	03W	110
CHEEK RICHARD ALLAN	IL	26E	74
CHEEK ROBERT MICHAEL	IN	41W	68
CHEEK ROGER DALE	NC	48W	39
CHEEKS JOHN HERBERT	NJ	18E	110
CHEESEMAN ALAN B	MA	08W	106
CHEIVES CALVIN L	VA	06E	63
CHEMIS CHARLES ROBERT	OH	02E	124
CHENAULT ROBERT GLEN	TX	36E	2
CHENAULT THOMAS DUDLEY	TX	03W	7
CHENEY DANIEL BERNARD	WA	35W	42
CHENEY DAVID PAUL JR	TN	24W	37
CHENEY RICHARD DANIEL	MA	25W	28
CHENEY WILLIAM CHARLES	NY	33E	7
CHENIS MARK CONSTANT	CT	41W	68
CHENOWETH AUSTIN RAY	CO	34W	5
CHENOWETH IRVING S III	IL	27W	71
CHEPELY GENE E	IL	05E	9
CHERNEY PETER FREDERICK	CA	36E	67
CHEROFF MICHAEL	CA	19E	56
CHERRICK JAMES WESTON	NY	09E	22
CHERRSTROM RONALD PAUL	CA	26E	22
CHERRY ALLEN SHELDON	MO	24E	95
CHERRY CHARLES EDWARD	FL	21E	9
CHERRY DANIEL PARKS	CA	01W	83
CHERRY DAVID EARL JR	NC	25W	63
CHERRY ERVIN BENJAMIN	MD	03W	59
CHERRY JAMES EDWARD	MS	37W	10
CHERRY JAMES L	TX	07E	80
CHERRY JERRY LEE	TN	56E	36
CHERRY WILLIAM LOUIS	VA	13E	3
CHERRY WILLIAM TEMEN JR	CA	26E	74
CHERVONY EDDIE EDWIN	CA	55E	6
CHESEBROUGH FREDERIC READ	RI	16E	91

NAME	STATE	PANEL NO.	LINE NO.
CHESEBROUGH JOHN LANE	SC	18W	100
CHESHIRE ALLEN DONIHUE	GA	33W	36
CHESHIRE GARY ALLEN	MO	14W	81
CHESLEY EUGENE NATHANIEL	MD	05E	4
CHESLEY LEONARD GEORGE JR	MA	49E	19
CHESNUT GERRY GEORGE	UT	31E	23
CHESNUTT CHAMBLESS M	AR	02E	98
CHESNUTT JEFFERSON CLIFFORD	TN	19E	56
CHESS LLOYD ALLEN	WV	38W	64
CHESSER HARRY EDWARD	GA	08W	114
CHESSER ROBERT RICHARD	VA	02W	70
CHESSHER CHARLES MICHAEL	FL	67E	6
CHESTER ALVIN	AZ	02E	27
CHESTER DENNIS EDWARD	CA	46E	44
CHESTER HENRY J JR	MI	44E	44
CHESTNUT JOSEPH LYONS	TN	07W	132
CHESTNUT LELAND McLANE	SC	10W	10
CHEVALIER HENRY ANTHONY	MA	24W	3
CHIACCHIO JOSEPH S JR	CA	20W	47
CHIAGO GREGORY BURKHART	AZ	38W	33
CHIALASTRI THOMAS ANTHONY	CT	26W	18
CHIARELLO VINCENT AUGUSTUS	NY	09E	85
CHIASERA AUGUST JR	NY	14E	103
CHICANTEK ANDREW JAMES	WI	63W	4
CHIFOS WILLIAM LEWIS	IN	51E	28
CHILCOTE BRYAN MICHAEL	OH	41W	57
CHILCOTT RONALD HARRY	CA	51E	37
CHILD CHARLES CHRISTOPHER	MA	16W	4
CHILD RONALD WILLIAM	MO	55E	6
CHILDERS ESTILL LEE	MO	11E	6
CHILDERS JAMES STANLEY BE	CA	15E	32
CHILDERS JOHN KENNETH	MT	34W	47
CHILDERS MELVIN RONALD	AZ	18W	100
CHILDERS PHILLIP DON	AL	01E	125
CHILDERS ROGER DALE	WV	10E	90
CHILDERS STEPHEN ANDREW	IL	14E	52
CHILDERS VIRGIL EUGENE	AL	45E	9
CHILDERS WILLIAM STEVEN	AK	35W	25
CHILDRESS BENJAMIN V JR	TN	12W	64
CHILDRESS BILLY W	TX	54W	5
CHILDRESS CALVIN BUSTER	MS	02W	44
CHILDRESS CALVIN JEFFERY	MD	30W	99
CHILDRESS GEORGE W	MO	23E	109
CHILDRESS IVY GALE	TN	55W	33
CHILDRESS J M	AR	14W	98
CHILDRESS LEWIS CLAYTON	IL	29E	104
CHILDRESS MARTIN DEAN	OH	19W	10
CHILDRESS ROBERT JR	TN	10W	22
CHILDRESS ROBERT MORRIS	PA	50W	12
CHILDRESS WILBUR HERBERT	WA	01W	4
CHILDS BOBBY RAY	SC	56E	1
CHILDS CHRISTOPHER J III	ME	10W	4
CHILDS FORREST CLIFFORD	OK	07W	52
CHILDS VANDIVER L	TN	18E	34
CHILTON RICHARD KENNETH	OH	38W	56
CHILVERE ROBIN LEE	MI	18E	119
CHIMERI LOUIS	NY	55E	6
CHIMINELLO THOMAS JAMES	TX	28E	95
CHIN ALEXANDER SCHELEPH	MD	40E	58
CHING STEVEN SAM CHOY	HI	17E	68
CHINN JAMES RUSSELL	OH	48E	57
CHINO GERALD GREGORY	NM	46E	3
CHINQUINA ROBERT NORRIS	MD	08W	61
CHIPCHASE PHILIP GRANT	NY	21E	103
CHIPMAN RALPH JIM	UT	01W	106
CHIPP DONALD WARREN JR	WY	06W	53
CHISHOLM ALEXANDER	NY	26E	43
CHISHOLM DAVID ANDREW	MA	44E	58
CHISHOLM HOWARD	NY	13E	50
CHISHOLM JAMES	GA	40E	73
CHISHOLM JOSEPH CHARLES	MI	25W	64
CHISHOLM RONALD LEE	FL	19E	89
CHISKO JOSEPH JOHN	PA	09W	31
CHISLOCK LEONARD JAMES	CA	05E	54
CHISOLM ALEXANDER	SC	51E	29
CHISOLM ARTHUR LEE	SC	44E	5
CHISOLM RONALD	NY	11W	94
CHISUM DAVID	CA	48W	23
CHITKO BENJAMIN ALBIN	WI	10E	100
CHITTESTER NORMAN PHILIP	PA	32W	76
CHITTUM RONALD HENRY	VA	03E	100
CHITTWOOD JAMES PHILLIP	MO	20W	69
CHITWOOD FRED ALLEN JR	MO	47W	16
CHITWOOD HAROLD LYNN	TN	13W	46
CHITWOOD JERRY MICHAEL	OK	67E	7
CHITWOOD ROY DUKE	TX	20E	22
CHITWOOD WAYNE CECIEL	WI	35E	21
CHIVERS JAMES LEE	OH	57W	30
CHLEWA JOHN	IL	18E	113
CHLOUPEK MELVIN EUGENE	OR	41E	60
CHMEL DENIS MICHAEL	OH	57W	23
CHMIEL ANDREW	MI	11E	70
CHMIEL DONALD GEORGE	AK	07W	3
CHMIEL LARRY VINCENT	MD	21E	32
CHMIEL MARK ANTHONY	WI	14E	69
CHMURA MICHAEL LOUIS	CT	02E	125
CHO HERBERT POK DONG	CA	42W	13
CHOATE RANDALL BINGHAM	CA	49W	3
CHOCK LINUS GERARD K	HI	12E	128
CHOI WILLIAM DAVID	CA	41E	36
CHOMEL CHARLES DENNIS	IN	21E	87
CHOMYK WILLIAM	NY	51E	29
CHOPPA RICHARD ANTHONY	OH	31E	96
CHOPPER FRANKLIN DELANO	MT	21E	96
CHOQUETTE ROBERT G JR	CT	09W	124
CHORLINS RICHARD DAVID	MO	14W	25
CHOW CALVIN KEALOHAOKALAN	HI	06E	29
CHOWKA ANDREW DANIEL	CT	44E	45
CHRAN RICKEY LEE	MI	52E	28
CHRIN JOHN STEPHEN	PA	02W	38
CHRISCO EUGENE	NC	07E	29
CHRISCOE CHARLES RICHARD	NC	28E	65
CHRISMAN REX GORDON	CA	45W	13
CHRISS BRAD DONALD	FL	29W	76
CHRISS GARY DOYLE	OK	03W	31
CHRIST DONALD ALFRED	WI	11E	129
CHRISTEN RONALD ARTHUR	NY	15W	89
CHRISTENBURY GARY STEVEN	NC	38E	66
CHRISTENSEN ALLEN DUANE	SD	02W	128
CHRISTENSEN ALVIN PETER	SD	56W	18
CHRISTENSEN BRUCE ARDEN	MN	05W	90
CHRISTENSEN DALE ELLING	UT	12W	79
CHRISTENSEN DICK HOOTEN	UT	41W	14
CHRISTENSEN EDWARD JOHN	CT	20E	23
CHRISTENSEN HAROLD ROY	CA	22W	86
CHRISTENSEN JAN PAUL	MN	34W	5
CHRISTENSEN JOHN MICHAEL	UT	02W	135
CHRISTENSEN QUENTON LEE	UT	32W	64
CHRISTENSEN ROGER LEE	MO	02W	84
CHRISTENSEN WARREN LEE	UT	05E	85
CHRISTENSEN WILLIAM MURRE	MT	05E	93
CHRISTENSEN WILLIAM RAY	IL	34W	37
CHRISTENSON DANIEL BRIAN	WA	62E	16
CHRISTENSON WILLIAM B	NJ	21W	92
CHRISTENSON WILLIAM LEE	MN	09W	126
CHRISTER EUGENE MERL	CA	36W	25
CHRISTESON LEONARD WAYNE	KS	49W	51
CHRISTIAN BRUCE CALVIN	WA	44W	1
CHRISTIAN DANIEL KIETH	OH	50E	12
CHRISTIAN DAVID MARION	KS	01E	129
CHRISTIAN LYTELL B	AL	44E	32
CHRISTIAN PETER KARL J	TX	12W	106
CHRISTIAN ROBERT M JR	NV	27W	55
CHRISTIAN RUSSELL THOMAS	MA	08E	1
CHRISTIAN TED HOWARD	WV	27E	94
CHRISTIAN THOMAS BARRY	WV	49W	19
CHRISTIAN VERNON WEBB JR	OH	47W	6
CHRISTIANO JOSEPH	NY	04E	36
CHRISTIANSEN BERNHARD M	NJ	27W	62
CHRISTIANSEN EUGENE F	CA	33W	70
CHRISTIANSEN JOHN E JR	IA	09E	77
CHRISTIANSEN ROBERT DOUGLAS	OK	32W	70
CHRISTIANSEN THOMAS LEE	MN	24W	28
CHRISTIANSON DAVID B	CA	30W	99
CHRISTIANSON PETER BUGBEE	MA	27W	4
CHRISTIANSON RONALD F	CA	30W	20
CHRISTIE DENNIS RAY	CA	21E	87
CHRISTIE DONALD	NJ	22W	39
CHRISTIE EDWARD EUGENE	OK	08E	19
CHRISTIE JAMES MILLER	GA	53E	28
CHRISTIE LARRY EDWARD	NY	[illegible]8W	57
CHRISTIE ZANE	TX	06W	20
CHRISTJOHN PAUL EMERSON	WI	44W	8
CHRISTMAN JERRY NOLAN	AZ	59W	20
CHRISTMAN LAWRENCE PAUL	AZ	12W	100
CHRISTMAN RONALD S H	PA	41E	60
CHRISTMAN WILLIAM J III	MD	32W	77
CHRISTMAS LOYE THOMAS	FL	01E	41
CHRISTMAS MICHAEL LYNN	SC	25W	10
CHRISTMAS PAUL	NJ	35E	44
CHRISTOFFER VERNON H JR	MI	36E	21
CHRISTOFFERSON SCOTT ANDREW	MO	27E	77
CHRISTOPHER ADOLPHUS	AZ	21W	123
CHRISTOPHER ANTHONY PHILLIP	CA	02E	67
CHRISTOPHER SAMUEL JR	SC	25W	28
CHRISTOPHER WAYNE EDWARD	MD	44W	22
CHRISTOPHERSEN KEITH ALLEN	MN	01W	111
CHRISTOPHERSON DAVID LYN	MN	10W	48
CHRISTY ALBERT GEORGE JR	CT	32W	4
CHRISTY ALBERT KRISUNAS	PA	06E	17
CHRISTY DONALD RAY	CA	21E	32
CHRISTY GILMORE WILSON	OK	14E	127
CHRISTY JAMES ARTHUR	OH	10E	14
CHRISTY RICHARD NEIL II	OH	02W	107
CHRISTY RICHARD THOMAS	CA	57W	16
CHRONISTER JAMES VIRGIL	IL	19E	2
CHRUPCALA WALTER JOHN	NJ	50E	3
CHRYSLER MEDFORD ADARINE	CA	22E	98
CHRYSTYNYCZ THEODORE	IL	35E	53
CHUBB JOHN JACOBSEN	CA	04W	60
CHUBB RICHARD CHARLES	PA	29W	36
CHUBBUCK MICHAEL FRANCIS	NY	61W	22
CHULCHATSCHINOW WALERIJA	PA	32E	54
CHUN REGINALD WUNG YETT	HI	33E	34
CHUNG DOUGLAS KAMKEE	HI	35W	75
CHUNGES JERRY MICHAEL	IL	16E	100
CHUNKO GEORGE DAVID	CA	18W	78
CHURAN RONALD BRUCE	TX	18W	10
CHURCH ALVIN RAY	NC	39E	3
CHURCH JIMMY KERMIT	OH	24W	101
CHURCH JOHN LEONARD	CA	36E	2
CHURCH LEVAN ARLIN	CA	24E	59
CHURCH RALPH LEE	NE	03W	73
CHURCH REX FILLMORE	OH	28W	17
CHURCH RICKY WAYNE	MI	19W	44
CHURCH ROBERT EDWARD	NJ	61E	7
CHURCH STEVEN ANTHONY	WA	05E	116
CHURCH WILLIAM MALCOM	IL	29W	95
CHURCHILL CARL RUSSELL	ME	11W	90
CHURCHILL LAWRENCE JEFFREY	CA	28E	34
CHURCHILL RAYMOND JOHN	WI	09E	105
CHURCHILL STEVE JOHN	IL	20E	26
CHURCHILL THOMAS HENRY	TX	17W	36
CHURCHILL WENDELL EUGENE	OK	09E	92
CHURCHWARD STEVEN DEAN	IN	29W	44
CHURCHWELL DONALD WALTER	AL	18W	81
CHUTE STEPHEN FORREST	CA	62E	16
CHUTER JOHN DAVIS	TX	07E	38
CHUTIS JOHN VINCENT	PA	18E	119
CHWAN MICHAEL DANIEL	NJ	02E	99
CIALLELLA JOHN WILLIAM	NJ	39W	78
CIARFEO GLENN THOMAS	CA	62W	21
CIBOROWSKI THOMAS PAUL	NY	18E	2
CICCHIANI WALTER ANTHONY	PA	53E	11
CICERO FEDELE ANTHONY	IL	22E	98
CICHON WALTER ALAN	NJ	47E	9
CICIO ROBERT DANIEL	NY	50E	12
CIECURA THOMAS PAUL	MI	31E	32
CIESIELKA MICHAEL J JR	PA	37W	72
CIESIELSKI STANLEY M	CT	09W	46
CIFELLI DOMINIC JOSEPH	NY	18E	106
CIGAR FREDDIE JOE	CA	55E	6
CIMORELLI JOHN JOSEPH JR	PA	56W	20
CINCOTTA THOMAS ANTONE	CA	21W	27
CINKOSKY DAVID EDWARD	ID	03W	123
CINOTTI RALPH SILVIO	CT	17W	128
CINTINEO GIACOMO JAMES	AZ	13E	78
CINTRON JIMMIE DUAYNE	CA	18E	66
CINTRON-MENDEZ WILFREDO	PR	40W	75
CIPRIANI ALAN BRADLEY	NM	21E	10
CIRIELLO BASIL LINCOLN	MA	40W	10
CIRILLO PHILIP M	NY	34E	84
CIRUTI JAMES DAVID	LA	18E	106
CISAR THOMAS CHARLES	IN	06W	116
CISNEROS CHARLES CASTULO	NM	09W	78

NAME	STATE	PANEL NO.	LINE NO.
CISNEROS JOSE B	CA	21W	106
CISNEROS MARIO ALVAREZ	CA	30E	23
CISNEROS ROY	TX	44W	22
CISTARO RUDOLPH V JR	IL	37E	9
CIUPINSKI JAMES MICHAEL	IL	40W	72
CLACK CECIL JAMES	SC	35W	15
CLACK HOWARD LEE	OH	32W	70
CLAEYS EDWARD ORAN	CA	20E	13
CLAFLIN RICHARD AMES	KS	24E	2
CLAGGETT JOHN ALLEN	MO	10W	69
CLAIBORNE DELL ROSS	TX	33E	81
CLAIR JAMES THOMAS	IL	33E	26
CLAIRE KENNETH WILLIAM	CA	41E	18
CLAMPFFER ROBERT LEE	PA	56E	2
CLANCY CRAIG MICHAEL	IL	22W	74
CLANCY DENNIS PATRICK	MI	41E	61
CLANCY JOSEPH A	IL	03E	38
CLANCY TERRANCE BURTON	MI	25W	28
CLANCY WILLIAM EDWARD	MA	18W	93
CLANTON CHARLES BENJAMIN	AL	17E	42
CLANTON HOWARD	IN	11E	132
CLANTON LARRY JACK	CA	45E	61
CLANTON LOUIS LAMAR	AL	53W	43
CLAPP GARY LYN	MI	46W	27
CLAPPER GEAN PRESTON	PA	32E	91
CLARBOUR DONALD ALAN	IL	16W	37
CLARDY JAMES DONALD	SC	27E	14
CLARDY JASPER DUEL	TN	04E	43
CLARE BERNARD ERROYL	NY	07E	51
CLARE RICHARD STEVEN	IL	20W	28
CLARK ALLEN HOWELL	SC	03W	117
CLARK ANTHONY LAURENCE	MI	10W	79
CLARK ARTHUR	GA	14W	96
CLARK ARTHUR BOYD	FL	15W	47
CLARK BARRY EDWIN	NJ	06W	116
CLARK BARRY ROBERT	OH	18W	37
CLARK BILLY EARL	GA	62W	22
CLARK BILLY FLOYD	CO	36W	20
CLARK BOBBY DEAN	AL	30W	86
CLARK BOBBY JOE	TN	49W	51
CLARK BRADLEY ELLIS	NJ	48E	1
CLARK BRADLEY RUSSELL	NY	56E	36
CLARK BRIAN DALE	OH	11E	65
CLARK BRIAN JAMES	FL	61W	22
CLARK BRUCE ALAN	RI	34W	47
CLARK CHARLES	SC	03W	116
CLARK CHARLES CHAPMAN	NE	12E	3
CLARK CHARLES EDWARD	FL	09E	10
CLARK CHARLES EDWARD	TN	14E	52
CLARK CHARLES II	FL	41W	22
CLARK CHARLES RONALD	KY	52W	18
CLARK CLYDE JR	GA	20E	7
CLARK CONN KAY	ID	20W	79
CLARK DALE LEE	MO	10E	19
CLARK DANNY TAYLOR	VA	35W	69
CLARK DAVID LEROY	OR	43W	52
CLARK DAVID LLOYD	OR	25E	42
CLARK DENNIS EUGENE	MS	08W	19
CLARK DENNIS McCOY	VA	17W	108
CLARK DONALD E JR	VA	06E	41
CLARK DONALD EUGENE	CA	37E	52
CLARK DONALD ROBERT	OH	03E	39
CLARK DORIS WAYNE	AL	60E	20
CLARK DOUGLAS MARK	MN	41W	3
CLARK DOYLE WAYNE	CA	39W	53
CLARK EARL GLENN	TX	07E	69
CLARK ERNEST LEE	CA	24W	64
CLARK EUGENE PAUL	NC	19W	11
CLARK FRANCIS EVERETTE	AL	19E	11
CLARK FRANCIS WILLIAM	CO	06E	19
CLARK FREDERICK RALPH	CT	17W	3
CLARK GARY LEE	IN	21W	6
CLARK GARY RICHARD	CA	31E	44
CLARK GARY VAUGHN	TX	15W	66
CLARK GEORGE ARTHUR	CO	07E	23
CLARK GEORGE EDWARD JR	TN	28E	42
CLARK GEORGE WILLIAM	CT	67E	8
CLARK GRANT LEROY	ID	03E	5
CLARK HARLOW GARY JR	GA	05E	128
CLARK HENRY PATRICK	IL	09W	63
CLARK HOWE KING JR	TX	24W	82
CLARK ISAAC NATHANIEL	FL	52W	41
CLARK J C JR	AL	02E	66
CLARK JAMES EARL	NY	03E	16
CLARK JAMES GENIUS	MS	20E	101
CLARK JAMES LEE	CA	56E	3
CLARK JAMES LEE	OH	20W	42
CLARK JAMES LESTER	GA	33W	61
CLARK JAMES MCKENZIE	NY	10E	123
CLARK JAMES NELSON	MI	23W	118
CLARK JAMES ROGER	OH	13W	26
CLARK JAMES THOMAS	MI	02E	53
CLARK JAMES THOMAS	MI	18W	19
CLARK JAMES WOODFORD	NV	24W	115
CLARK JERRY DOUGLAS	IN	49E	20
CLARK JERRY FURMAN	NY	22E	29
CLARK JERRY PROSPER	IA	04E	16
CLARK JERRY WAYNE	MI	56E	21
CLARK JESSE LEWIS II	AZ	06E	109
CLARK JIMMY RAY	TN	54E	31
CLARK JOHN CALVIN II	TX	15W	26
CLARK JOHN HOWARD JR	FL	43E	15
CLARK JOHN JAMES	WA	10W	133
CLARK JOHN JOSEPH	TN	28W	79
CLARK JOHN MICHAEL	GA	02W	64
CLARK JOSEPH THAXTER	WA	32E	62
CLARK KENDALL HANSON	NE	40E	59
CLARK KERRY EDWARD	NV	25E	11
CLARK LARRY GENE	AL	37E	19
CLARK LARRY GENE	MO	57W	24
CLARK LARRY MONROE	MD	36E	68
CLARK LARRY RAY	KS	22W	85
CLARK LAWRENCE	IN	11E	86
CLARK LAWRENCE EDWARD	KY	11E	65
CLARK LEM	GA	03W	66
CLARK LONNIE WARREN	CA	40E	73
CLARK LORENZO	TN	13E	48
CLARK LORINZER PAUL JR	OH	29E	99
CLARK LUGENE JACKIE	MI	02E	95
CLARK MAURICE	AR	01W	41
CLARK MELVIN E	NY	37W	79
CLARK MICHAEL BURRISS	CA	38W	41
CLARK NATHANIEL BUSTER	IL	52E	15
CLARK NORMAN HARVEY	MN	36W	39
CLARK PAUL FRANKLIN	FL	32W	93
CLARK PAUL LESLIE	CA	26E	9
CLARK PHILIP SPRATT JR	WA	01W	104
CLARK PHILLIP HENRY	WI	05E	100
CLARK PHILLIP LESLIE	FL	13W	99
CLARK RALPH E	OH	35E	67
CLARK RAYMOND CHARLES	CA	13E	60
CLARK RAYMOND GORDON	TN	40W	23
CLARK REUBEN L JR	PA	08E	19
CLARK RHONNIE LEE	NC	39W	78
CLARK RICHARD	AL	34W	91
CLARK RICHARD CHAMP	WA	28E	59
CLARK RICHARD CROSBY	IL	03E	100
CLARK RICHARD DEWYATT	MT	10E	37
CLARK RICHARD GARLAND	AZ	13E	125
CLARK RICHARD THOMAS	MI	44W	46
CLARK ROBERT ALAN	CA	01W	110
CLARK ROBERT ARTHUR	WV	36W	49
CLARK ROBERT LEE	AL	05E	70
CLARK ROBERT LEE	AR	07E	23
CLARK ROBERT LEWIS	IN	01E	117
CLARK ROBERT NELSON JR	IN	16E	16
CLARK ROBERT SAMUEL JR	MS	49E	29
CLARK ROGER DALE	OH	11E	129
CLARK ROGER WILLIAM	VT	23E	40
CLARK RONALD BLAIR	IA	44W	1
CLARK RONALD CLEVELAND	GA	22E	39
CLARK RONALD EMERY	IA	60E	9
CLARK RONNIE LEE	KS	41E	18
CLARK ROOSEVELT	AR	55W	12
CLARK ROY EDWARD	WV	24W	93
CLARK STANLEY SCOTT	CA	32W	31
CLARK STEPHEN WILLIAM	CA	54E	24
CLARK STEVEN EUGENE	IN	38E	47
CLARK TERRY DESMOND	NC	24W	93
CLARK TERRY LEE	PA	29E	57
CLARK TERRY RICHARD	IN	30E	23
CLARK THOMAS	GA	33W	47
CLARK THOMAS EDWARD	OH	10E	37
CLARK THOMAS EDWARD	PA	33W	84
CLARK THOMAS ELMER	OH	16W	4
CLARK THOMAS JR	LA	36W	48
CLARK THOMAS LEE JR	PA	20W	108
CLARK THOMAS OSBORN	NY	23E	97
CLARK THORNE M III	CA	22E	37
CLARK TIMOTHY EUGENE	AR	13E	67
CLARK TIMOTHY RICHARD	KS	21E	73
CLARK TOMMIE JOE	TX	36W	29
CLARK VINCENT ALLEN	IN	46W	38
CLARK WALTER LEVON	MI	28E	95
CLARK WILLIAM HOWARD JR	MI	14W	59
CLARK WILLIAM JEROME III	IL	31E	10
CLARK WILLIAM JR	GA	01W	76
CLARK WILLIAM MARSHALL	FL	02W	109
CLARK WILLIAM MARTIN	IA	08W	81
CLARK WILLIAM STEPHEN	FL	50W	22
CLARK WILLIE C	CA	54E	3
CLARKE CLIFFORD LESLI III	NJ	02W	23
CLARKE CORNELL RICHARD R	OH	29W	28
CLARKE DAVID ERROL	FL	02W	109
CLARKE EDWARD ALLEN	PA	25W	96
CLARKE FRED LEE	NC	36W	14
CLARKE GEORGE WILLIAM JR	VA	28E	14
CLARKE IRVIN JR	NY	05E	79
CLARKE JAMES PHILLIP	TX	50E	37
CLARKE JOHN KEARNAN	CT	16E	27
CLARKE KENNETH GEORGE JR	VA	30W	86
CLARKE KEVIN MICHAEL	MI	23E	48
CLARKE LEE TILSON	VA	49W	28
CLARKE RITSON LEWIS Y	NY	18E	106
CLARKE ROBERT WAYNE	OR	46W	27
CLARKE WALTER KIRT	CA	52E	46
CLARKE WILLIAM MOSBY JR	VA	65E	6
CLARKE WILLIAM VICTOR	MI	49W	38
CLARKEN THOMAS HENRY III	NJ	43W	34
CLARKIN FRANCIS THOMAS	NY	05E	130
CLARKSON GERALD JOSEPH	FL	44W	1
CLARKSON JAMES LA FAYETTE	GA	15W	12
CLARKSON JAY OWEN	MO	11W	5
CLARY JOHN WILLARD	SC	17E	67
CLASEN MICHAEL ROY	CA	46W	12
CLASPILL LARRY VERNAL	MO	37E	33
CLASSEN EARL THOMAS	AZ	37E	20
CLATFELTER ROBERT DENNIS	IL	22W	31
CLAUD PERNELL RUSSELL	VA	23E	56
CLAUSE MICHAEL ALLEN	LA	30W	42
CLAUSEN HARLAND GENE JR	CA	16E	67
CLAUSEN HUGH CONRAD	WA	10E	131
CLAUSEN LAWRENCE C	FL	15E	34
CLAUSSEN HENRY ROBERT	IA	63W	4
CLAVERIE RICHARD LEE	MO	42E	62
CLAVIER DAVID MICHAEL	MI	33E	34
CLAVIO PETER ANTHONY JR	NY	61W	11
CLAW PETER YAZZIE	AZ	48E	18
CLAWSON RODGER DEAN	MI	09E	37
CLAWSON WILLIAM K	IN	31E	90
CLAXTON CHARLES PETER	IL	32E	91
CLAXTON RICHARD REX	MO	22W	39
CLAY AMBROSE WILKIE J JR	TN	56E	21
CLAY CHARLES EDWARD	MO	31W	65
CLAY CHRISTOPHER ELLIOTT	MI	57W	16
CLAY DOYLE GREGORY	IL	41E	18
CLAY EDWARD ROGER	IN	58W	18
CLAY EUGENE LUNSFORD	TX	29E	57
CLAY HERMAN ALLEN JR	TX	12W	112
CLAY JAMES HENRY	PA	33E	26
CLAY JAMES WILFORD	MI	23W	14
CLAY KAROL	IL	49W	39
CLAY MELVIN EUGENE	TX	33W	30
CLAY RAYMOND	OK	26E	99
CLAY RUSSELL LELAND	CA	04W	91
CLAY WILLIAM CLIFTON III	NC	18E	18
CLAYBAUGH JAMES BRADLEY	ID	28W	79
CLAYBORN BILLY JOE	AR	37W	30
CLAYBORNE MILTON GAY	PA	61E	5
CLAYBROOK LARRY DEAN	IL	14E	85
CLAYBURN MERRELL J	WY	26E	82
CLAYBURN RONNIE LEE	KY	23W	97
CLAYCOMB CLARENCE J	PA	34E	41
CLAYPOOL GEORGE ROBERT	OH	49W	51
CLAYPOOL RHONDAL GENE	IL	40E	3
CLAYTON ALFRED PATRICK	NY	37W	62

NAME	STATE	PANEL NO.	LINE NO.
CLAYTON BENNIE CLIFFORD	MO	17W	100
CLAYTON BENNY DEAN	SC	39W	16
CLAYTON BILLY JACK	FL	11E	38
CLAYTON BRIAN DOUGLAS	NJ	38W	33
CLAYTON CECIL ROGER	IA	09W	53
CLAYTON CURVIN	NC	07W	60
CLAYTON DAVID NELSON	MD	01E	88
CLAYTON GARY EVERET	OK	33E	17
CLAYTON GEORGE DONALD	NJ	29E	39
CLAYTON GEORGE MILTON JR	VA	41W	4
CLAYTON JESSE NATHANIEL	FL	28E	80
CLAYTON JOHN WILLIAM	IL	12E	94
CLAYTON MICHAEL MARSHALL	UT	51E	6
CLAYTON TOMMY MAKIN	CA	10W	98
CLEARWATER NORMAN WILBUR	NY	32E	75
CLEARWATERS CHRISTOPHER L	WA	05W	123
CLEARY JAMES WILLIAM	ME	26W	76
CLEARY PETER MCARTHUR	CT	01W	81
CLEAVE LONNIE LEONARD	TN	60W	16
CLEAVELAND MELVIN RAY	TX	04W	43
CLEAVER DONALD GENE	MO	42W	69
CLEAVER FRANCIS CRAIG	PA	21E	10
CLEAVES MICHAEL DAVID	CA	01W	5
CLEELAND DAVID	NY	09E	73
CLEEM LARRY LLOYD	CA	33E	65
CLEEREMAN DAVID FRANK	WI	33W	13
CLEFISCH DUANE ALAN	IA	18W	10
CLEGG LESTER HOWARD	DC	05E	85
CLELAND RONALD LOUIS	IN	06W	45
CLELAND THOMAS LEONARD	MI	23E	49
CLEM EDWARD	OH	28E	73
CLEM THOMAS DEAN	IN	54E	24
CLEM THOMAS SAMUEL	VA	28E	90
CLEMENCIA JEAN ROGER JR	DC	29W	5
CLEMENS MICHAEL JOSEPH	IA	13E	130
CLEMENS ROGER O	NY	43W	34
CLEMENT GREGORY C	TX	15E	78
CLEMENT JAMES WILFRED	VA	13W	110
CLEMENT NEWTON STEVE	AR	09W	82
CLEMENTS DAWSON	GA	42W	66
CLEMENTS GARY MAXWELL	AR	20W	100
CLEMENTS JAMES WALTER	OR	25E	15
CLEMENTS LONNIE EDWARD	GA	08E	64
CLEMENTS MARSHALL EDWARD	IL	16E	76
CLEMENTS MILO DEAN	NE	30W	86
CLEMENTS RANDALL KELVIN	AL	02W	27
CLEMENTS RICHARD BART	OK	42W	54
CLEMENTS ROBERT ANDREW	KY	16W	112
CLEMENTS ROBERT STEVEN	WA	15W	3
CLEMENTS WALTER LEE	GA	16E	72
CLEMENTS WAYNE DOUGLAS	NJ	40E	59
CLEMENTS WILLIAM RICHARD	CA	11E	106
CLEMENTZ RICHARD JOSEPH	OH	35E	67
CLEMMER DERRELL W	OK	43W	45
CLEMMON EDWARD L	MO	32E	17
CLEMMONS DOUGLAS FRANK	FL	28E	80
CLEMMONS JACK ELLIOTT	AL	04E	22
CLEMONS EDWARD	FL	33W	76
CLEMONS JAMES NOEL	MS	32E	50
CLEMONS JOSEPH	FL	13E	26
CLEMONS LARRY RAYMOND	FL	36E	2
CLEMONS WILLARD LEE	KY	12W	87
CLEMSON GERALD RICHARD	OH	38E	23
CLENDENEN CHARLES CURTIS	CA	18E	44
CLENDENEN RICHARD DEAN	IA	24E	17
CLENDENIN CHARLES FISHER	IA	21W	31
CLENNON EDWARD FRANCIS	IL	24W	102
CLERKIN JOSEPH	NY	27W	48
CLESTER DOUGLAS ARTHUR	IN	08E	42
CLEVE REGINALD DAVID	MO	04W	66
CLEVELAND ALBERT FRANKLIN	AL	18E	39
CLEVELAND BRENT PHILLIP	AL	02W	53
CLEVELAND CLARK EDWARD	GA	26E	70
CLEVELAND DAVID LUHVER	PA	19E	56
CLEVELAND HARDY EDWARD	AR	02W	55
CLEVELAND JAMES	CA	15E	56
CLEVELAND JAMES ARTHUR	WA	51W	17
CLEVELAND LANCE JOSEPH	WA	08E	118
CLEVELAND LARRY MICHAEL	CA	17W	107
CLEVELAND RICHARD GROVER	FL	39W	78
CLEVELAND RONALD	GA	04W	94
CLEVELAND WALTER K	TX	54E	3

NAME	STATE	PANEL NO.	LINE NO.
CLEVENGER DANIEL JOHN	CO	48E	47
CLEVENGER WILLIAM HENRY	IN	23W	84
CLEVER LOUIS JOHN	PA	33W	61
CLEVERLEY WILLIAM BERT	MI	08W	61
CLEWLOW ROBERT LEE	IN	43E	66
CLIBURN HALQUA DALE	TN	09W	94
CLICKNER LEE FULTON	PA	17W	116
CLICKNER MICHAEL DUANE	MN	12W	122
CLIFCORN JAMES RICHARD	TX	18E	25
CLIFFORD GARY ALAN	IN	44E	66
CLIFFORD GEORGE HENRY	MI	20W	48
CLIFFORD HAROLD JOHN	CA	66W	3
CLIFFORD JON IRVING	ME	05E	130
CLIFFORD MICHAEL JAMES	PA	21E	96
CLIFFORD MICHAEL WILLIAM	CT	38W	15
CLIFFORD WILLIAM HENRY	AZ	06W	18
CLIFTON KENNETH CHARLES	OR	33W	55
CLIFTON LAYNE FARELL	OR	19E	70
CLIFTON MANCOL RAYMOND	CA	36W	39
CLIFTON RANDY LEE	TN	02W	85
CLIFTON ROBERT HARRISON	MO	02W	49
CLIFTON TERRY W	FL	38W	15
CLIFTON WILLIAM A	AR	54W	3
CLIME RALPH JOHN	MI	22W	86
CLIMER DAVID LEROY	OH	08W	93
CLINARD CHARLES WAYNE	TX	01W	77
CLINCH JOSEPH RUSSLE	IL	10W	120
CLINE CHARLES WILLIAM	GA	40E	59
CLINE CURTIS ROY	MI	18W	108
CLINE DONALD LEO	AL	27W	15
CLINE JOSEPH OLIVER III	TX	49W	39
CLINE MARCUS EUGENE	LA	55W	28
CLINE PAUL HAROLD	FL	37E	52
CLINE ROBERT LOUIS	MI	33E	35
CLINE RODNEY BARRETTE	MI	28E	45
CLINE RONALD GREER	OH	11W	48
CLINE WILLIAM LOUIS	GA	13W	7
CLINGER GUY WESLEY JR	PA	21E	118
CLINGER WILLIAM C III	PA	31W	33
CLINGERMAN JOSEPH ALLAN	OH	56E	3
CLINGLER STANLEY MELVIN	IN	28W	44
CLINTON DEAN EDDIE	IL	21E	87
CLINTON LARRY ELZA VAN	OH	09E	102
CLIREHUGH ROBERT W JR	CA	26W	24
CLITTY CHARLES GUST	MN	58W	21
CLODFELTER DARREL JAY	IN	05W	42
CLODFELTER GARY REID	NC	24W	11
CLOKES ROBERT	NY	37W	38
CLONEY WILLIAM THOMAS III	MA	45W	60
CLOPTON KENNETH RAY	MS	22E	98
CLORE LEE WILLIAM	NY	05W	39
CLOSE DONALD EDWARD	CA	01E	114
CLOSE FLOYD EUGENE	OK	25E	96
CLOSE SANFORD JR	FL	34W	74
CLOSSER HENRY VERNON	AR	02W	70
CLOSSON JAMES STANLEY	NY	35W	75
CLOTFELTER MARK DENNIS	FL	22W	57
CLOUD HARRY JAMES	FL	33W	25
CLOUD JOSEPH JR	CA	30E	69
CLOUD MILAM EDWARD	GA	29W	76
CLOUD RONALD MYRON	MN	53W	8
CLOUGH ARTHUR EDWARD	NH	13W	26
CLOUGH BRUCE EDWARD	DE	50W	48
CLOUGH DONNIE JOE	IL	18W	61
CLOUGH KENNETH RICHARD	NM	35W	46
CLOUGH TONY	PA	11W	54
CLOUSE DUANE LEON	MI	24W	102
CLOUTIER DAVID WILLIAM	MA	21E	61
CLOUTIER ROBERT LOUIS	WI	07E	94
CLOVER LIONEL TIMOTHY	MD	65E	6
CLOVER WILLIAM FRANK JR	IN	19E	93
CLOVIS FRANKLIN	GA	38E	23
CLOWE ROBERT EARL	WA	25E	15
CLOWER HUGH JR	OK	12W	12
CLUBBS CHARLES EARL	MO	22W	111
CLUKEY ROBERT LEOPOLD JR	ME	21E	119
CLUNE BRIAN J	NY	09E	111
CLUTE MICHAEL ALLEN	NY	32W	48
CLUTTER CARL NORMAN	CA	25W	21
CLYDESDALE CHARLES FREDRI	PA	01E	96
CLYMER DENNIS LEE	IL	08W	27
COACHMAN JAMES LEE JR	NY	24E	112

NAME	STATE	PANEL NO.	LINE NO.
COADY ROBERT FRANKLIN	LA	34W	31
COAKLEY WILLIAM FRANCIS	MA	09E	132
COALSON STEPHEN EDWARD	CA	33E	66
COALSTON ECHOL W JR	TN	35E	3
COAST ALBERT FRANK	OK	04W	135
COATES DONALD LEROY	OR	04E	128
COATES EMORY THERON	IL	07W	39
COATES FLOYD BURNETT	VA	12W	41
COATES HARRY JAY JR	SD	16W	27
COATES JAMES RUSSELL	NC	43W	12
COATES JOHN WAYNE	KY	07E	44
COATES KENNETH WILLIAM	MI	37E	33
COATES PAUL JAMES	NY	63W	15
COATES ROBERT EDMUND	NY	37E	80
COATES RONALD PERRY	OH	09E	65
COATES STERLING KITCHENER	PA	22E	101
COATS CHARLES ALEX	CA	47W	39
COATS CHARLES THOMAS	OR	65W	4
COATS DOUGLAS	AL	25E	67
COATS JAMES PRESTON	OH	04E	87
COATS LARRY DALE	ID	45W	31
COATS WILLIAM G	SC	21E	26
COAXUM THEODORE	SC	40E	60
COBARRUBIAS ROBERTO	CA	49W	22
COBARRUBIO LOUIS ANTONIO	PA	25E	5
COBB ALBERT JR	PA	25W	22
COBB BRUCE ALAN	PA	46E	15
COBB CHARLES MICHAEL	TX	12W	96
COBB EARL RUSSELL	WV	25E	96
COBB GEORGE LEE	SC	66W	3
COBB HUBBARD DON	TX	34E	47
COBB JAMES PAUL	NY	05W	105
COBB JOHN WESLEY	CA	05E	16
COBB JOHNNY RAY	IL	08W	6
COBB MILFORD EUDENE	OK	24W	82
COBB PAUL FREDERICK	VA	61E	7
COBB RAYMOND	LA	44W	48
COBB ROBERT JAN	IA	45W	36
COBB RONALD DAVID	MO	52E	47
COBB ROY WILLIAM	FL	13W	5
COBB THERON WALLACE	AZ	38W	48
COBB TYLER WILLIAM JR	CA	34E	6
COBB WILLIS	OH	07W	119
COBBLEY EARL WILLIAM JR	UT	60W	8
COBBS RALPH BURTON	IL	08E	55
COBEIL EARL GLENN	MI	29E	23
COBLE CLYDE WAYNE	TX	05W	71
COBLE JAMES THOMAS	NC	24W	15
COBLEY WARREN W	MI	09E	4
COBOS ALFRED	CA	20E	101
COBURN CLYDE RALPH	ID	31E	68
COBURN WILLIAM H	VA	05E	64
COCA ANDREW	NM	34E	47
COCCHIARA JAMES STEPHEN	MA	05E	98
COCHRAN AARON WASHINGTON	AL	09E	108
COCHRAN CHARLIE LYNN	MS	18W	14
COCHRAN GARY DUANE	VA	03W	26
COCHRAN ISOM CARTER JR	TX	66E	7
COCHRAN JAMES CLIFFORD	AR	49E	51
COCHRAN LARRY ALAN	AZ	32W	11
COCHRAN MICHAEL DALE	CA	29E	39
COCHRAN PATRICK SHELDON	TX	25E	23
COCHRAN PAUL JEFFEREY	OR	53E	29
COCHRAN ROBERT EDMUND	TX	44E	6
COCHRAN ROBERT FISHEL JR	MS	02E	55
COCHRAN ROBERT McLAIN JR	FL	27W	29
COCHRAN ROY BENJAMIN	NC	44E	66
COCHRAN SCOTT EDWARD	OR	24W	114
COCHRAN VERNON TERRY	NC	22E	37
COCHRAN WILLIAM SHERWOOD	GA	12E	32
COCHRANE BLANCHARD WARD	RI	07E	51
COCHRANE DEVERTON C	MA	09W	59
COCHRANE GREGG LAWRENCE	CA	17W	3
COCHRANE JOHN FLOYD	MI	11E	102
COCKERHAM JOHN WILLIE JR	CA	19W	118
COCKERL JAMES CALVIN	NY	24W	52
COCKRELL JAMES WARREN JR	MS	66W	4
COCKRELL WILBERT R	TX	28E	34
CODDING RAY EDWIN	CO	40W	10
CODDINGTON JAMES PATRICK	TN	06W	47
CODRINGTON STEPHAN	NY	59E	18
CODY CLYDE TERRY	FL	36E	47

NAME	STATE	PANEL NO.	LINE NO.
CODY FRANCIS WARREN	OR	31W	44
CODY HOWARD RUDOLPH	MS	01E	35
CODY PETER GIRARD	MI	17E	34
CODY ROBERT DEAN	IN	33W	25
CODY WESLEY OTERIA	AR	07W	9
CODY WILLIAM DE BRECE	IL	28W	57
COE BENNY BOB	OK	04E	4
COE HEWETT FRANK EVASTUS	SC	01E	9
COE KENNETH EUGENE	KS	22E	99
COE PAUL THOMAS	CA	06W	58
COE RONALD RAY	OH	52W	22
COEN HARRY BOB	WY	58E	32
COEN LOVELL FRANKLIN	KY	26W	82
COEN ROGER LEE	NE	06W	15
COEN WILLARD GILSON	WA	31W	77
COERS BARRY BRYANT	AL	19W	111
COFER ARTHUR WILLIAM	IL	30W	100
COFER EVERETTE EARL	MS	12W	87
COFER JAMES TERRELL	GA	24W	38
COFFARO ANTHONY CHARLES	NJ	13E	82
COFFELT BOBBY J	TX	10E	7
COFFEY BILLY RAY	TX	02W	75
COFFEY EDWARD AUBREY	PA	24E	99
COFFEY EDWARD VINCENT	NY	47W	14
COFFEY JERRY EAIRD	IL	10E	94
COFFEY JESSE J	TN	06E	71
COFFEY RICHARD ARTHUR	CA	03E	17
COFFEY ROBERT ALLEN	KY	31W	45
COFFEY ROBERT DANIEL	KY	04W	79
COFFEY ROBERT WILLIAM	IN	15E	40
COFFEY STEVEN LYNN	AZ	07W	18
COFFEY WILLIAM LOUIS	TN	04W	29
COFFIELD JOHN DAVID	PA	04E	80
COFFIN DONALD A	NY	34E	75
COFFIN JEFFREY ALAN	AZ	06W	76
COFFINO THOMAS PAUL	NY	07W	60
COFFMAN CHARLES EUGENE	IL	37W	84
COFFMAN CLYDE LEE	MO	12W	91
COFFMAN DOUGLAS DAVIS	OR	24E	106
COFFMAN FREDDIE LEE	WV	24W	3
COFFMAN ROGER LEROY	OH	13W	111
COFFROTH ALFRED PATRICK L	WA	36E	3
COFIELD EDWARD CHARLES JR	DC	29W	52
COFIELD JESSIE CLIFFORD	GA	26E	65
COFRAN WILLIAM EARL	IL	45E	19
COFRANCESCO LOUIS J JR	NJ	44W	67
COGDELL WILLIAM KEITH	IN	14E	42
COGDILL RANDY RALPH	TN	28E	90
COGGESHALL WILLIAM AYER	MA	15E	88
COGGINS JAMES TERRY	GA	54W	8
COGGINS LARRY FRANKLIN	NC	28E	99
COGGINS TERRY LEE	TX	54W	27
COGGINS WILLIAM RAY	TN	13W	31
COGHILL JOHN WESLEY	IL	19E	104
COGHILL MILO BRUCE	VA	01E	5
COGILL PETER	MA	15E	88
COHAN STEPHEN	FL	40E	18
COHEN CHARLES MITCHELL	PA	16W	87
COHEN GARY MARTIN	MA	04W	37
COHEN GERALD	NY	51E	17
COHEN HARRY	IL	02E	40
COHEN LOUIS GEORGE	PA	54E	4
COHEN ROBERT BRUCE	CA	59E	1
COHEN SHELDON ROBERT	MA	07E	117
COHEN SIDNEY	NJ	03E	53
COHN WILLIAM PAUL JR	CT	40W	10
COHRON JAMES DERWIN	IA	34E	35
COILEY CHARLES ROBERT	ME	06W	97
COIN GREGORY CLEVELAND	MI	21E	82
COINER CHARLES FREDRICK	NJ	05E	96
COIT LEON	MD	30W	100
COKER BILLY LEE	SC	16W	115
COKER DAVID LANGSTON JR	LA	04W	72
COKER DENNIS SANDERS	GA	30W	10
COKER DOUGLAS CARROLL	AR	25E	68
COKER HORTON SISLER JR	WA	11E	80
COKER JAMES LEE	AZ	39E	3
COKER RONALD LEROY	NE	28W	24
COKER SAMUEL EARL	AL	03E	48
COKER TROY ORION	TX	18W	93
COKLEY GARY WAYNE	WA	06W	34
COKLEY TROY WESLEY	GA	26E	100
COLANGELO GEORGE PEYTON	FL	32E	21
COLANTUONO WAYNE ALBERT	NJ	28E	42
COLASUONNO VINCENT	NY	32W	19
COLASURDO JOSEPH PETER	NJ	35W	25
COLATRUGLIO ROBERT F	MI	09W	71
COLBAUGH HOWARD LEBRON	GA	02W	75
COLBERT DOUGLAS ROBERT	NY	15E	40
COLBERT GEORGE H	UT	28E	53
COLBERT JAMES HAMILTON	PA	04W	13
COLBERT JOHN WAYNE	MO	38W	41
COLBURN DENVER DEWEY JR	FL	33E	81
COLBURN RICHARD EUGENE	NY	03W	7
COLBY BRIAN LYNN	MI	15E	114
COLDEBERG DONALD RAY	IN	16E	8
COLDIRON DALE WILLIAM	IN	29W	52
COLDREN ELDON DEAN JR	IL	44W	22
COLDREN THOMAS L	AR	20E	90
COLE BILLY JOE	KY	50E	12
COLE CLAUDE JR	TX	38W	15
COLE DENNIS WAYNE	WA	25E	49
COLE EMERSON PAUL	OH	46E	56
COLE EMILE	LA	34E	47
COLE ERNEST WESLEY	MD	37E	80
COLE FRED VINCENT	VA	10W	23
COLE GORDON EUGENE	MI	48W	11
COLE JAMES WILLIAM	PA	21W	111
COLE JERRY JEROME	OR	62W	22
COLE JERRY RICHARD	MI	33W	6
COLE JOHN HENRY	MA	39W	42
COLE JOHN MATTHEW	PA	13E	11
COLE JOHN MICHAEL	KY	01W	51
COLE JON	AZ	07W	60
COLE LEGRANDE OGDEN JR	CT	22E	86
COLE MARVIN EUGENE	OH	63W	5
COLE MARVIN RAY	AR	15E	68
COLE MOZIE LEE	MS	12E	66
COLE MURIL STEVEN	NE	17W	21
COLE NATHAN JOHN JR	OH	04E	58
COLE PATRICK LERVILLE	NY	14W	100
COLE PHELON HERMAN	WA	33E	81
COLE RAINER LOUIS	MD	12W	87
COLE RANDALL EARL	VA	45E	62
COLE RAYMOND ALLEN	MT	32W	93
COLE RICHARD MILTON JR	NY	01W	44
COLE RICHARD WILSON	FL	22W	86
COLE ROBERT EARL	TX	47E	9
COLE ROBERT KENNETH	IN	10W	60
COLE ROBERT LEROY	IN	57E	16
COLE ROBERT OWEN	CA	28W	79
COLE ROGER DALE	WV	06W	53
COLE SAM JR	CA	57E	17
COLE THOMAS STEPHEN	IL	52E	28
COLE TIMOTHY JR	GA	41W	72
COLE WAYNE MICHAEL	CA	14W	12
COLE WILLIAM NOEL	PA	21E	118
COLE WILLIAM WINSTON	MI	30E	69
COLE WILLIE JR	OK	08E	35
COLEGATE WILLIAM KARL	IL	38E	23
COLEGROVE ROBERT HOWARD	KY	48E	51
COLEMAN ARTHUR JR	MS	51W	17
COLEMAN BILLIE LEE	KY	02W	44
COLEMAN BOBBY WALTER	TX	18E	13
COLEMAN BONNIE LEE	MI	38E	47
COLEMAN CHARLES LOYD	KY	62W	7
COLEMAN CLARENCE BERNARD	NY	08W	132
COLEMAN CLARENCE LEROY	IN	01E	89
COLEMAN DANIEL	IL	31W	33
COLEMAN DONALD HUSTON	CA	39E	18
COLEMAN DONNIE	GA	26E	22
COLEMAN GARY TERRENCE	CA	23E	56
COLEMAN GEORGE	AL	59E	19
COLEMAN GEORGE WILLIAM	NJ	45E	9
COLEMAN JAMES EDWARD	MO	20E	111
COLEMAN JAMES FRANCIS	MO	42E	2
COLEMAN JAMES IVORY	IL	17W	94
COLEMAN JAMES JR	FL	08E	97
COLEMAN JAMES LARRY	TX	20W	55
COLEMAN JIMMY LEE	AL	30W	53
COLEMAN JOEL DANIEL	PA	07E	29
COLEMAN JOHN LEE	NC	51E	17
COLEMAN JOHN THOMAS	GA	32W	5
COLEMAN JOSHUA	LA	11W	12
COLEMAN LARRY HAROLD	IN	33W	76
COLEMAN LAWRENCE BARBE JR	NC	03W	131
COLEMAN LENARD	GA	44E	25
COLEMAN LEO ALFRED	NY	06W	7
COLEMAN LONALD RAY	MO	05W	87
COLEMAN LOUIS WILSON JR	MS	20E	23
COLEMAN LYNN BAILEY	MS	63E	6
COLEMAN MICHAEL JOHN	IL	35E	44
COLEMAN McARTHUR	OH	06E	63
COLEMAN OLAN DAN	SC	05W	95
COLEMAN OLIVER JR	FL	16W	11
COLEMAN PETER MICHAEL	PA	36E	3
COLEMAN PHILLIP RODNEY	KY	11E	126
COLEMAN RALPH	FL	06E	98
COLEMAN RICHARD	IL	06E	59
COLEMAN RICHARD CLYDE	KY	63E	7
COLEMAN RICHARD FREEMAN	OH	23E	98
COLEMAN ROBERT JOSEPH	MA	21W	36
COLEMAN ROBERT LAURENCE	NY	11W	121
COLEMAN ROBERT LEWIS	OK	10W	95
COLEMAN RONALD ALLEN	MD	61W	11
COLEMAN RONALD DEAN	FL	53W	33
COLEMAN RONALD JOHN	MN	02W	91
COLEMAN THOMAS KEITH	WV	35E	44
COLEMAN WILBERT EVANE	NY	38W	15
COLEMAN WILLIAM FRANK	OH	50E	12
COLEMAN WILLIE JR	TN	14E	66
COLEMAN WYMAN BYRD	SC	41W	29
COLES ALEXANDER JR	NJ	14E	69
COLES GEORGE EUGENE JR	NJ	15E	78
COLES HOWARD FRANKLIN JR	NY	35E	39
COLES KYLE J	UT	41E	61
COLES LEONARD ASHWORTH	NY	24W	24
COLES VINCENT SAMSON	NJ	61E	8
COLEY BILLY JOHN	TX	01E	39
COLEY BRUCE EDWARD	NJ	21W	74
COLFACK LLOYD ARTHUR	WA	46E	15
COLFORD DARRELL LEE	IL	06W	45
COLGAN DANIEL PAUL	TX	41W	22
COLGAN GEORGE BURTON III	VA	15W	12
COLGLAZIER DONALD ROBERT	NC	14W	43
COLICCHIO PETER	NY	39E	44
COLITO JAMES MARTIN JR	WA	26E	78
COLL DENNIS JOSEPH	NJ	30W	20
COLL JOHN THOMAS JR	NJ	30E	7
COLL WILLIAM PATRICK	PA	26E	65
COLLAMORE ALLAN PHILIP JR	MA	14E	116
COLLAZO CARLOS MANUEL	NY	22W	18
COLLAZO RAPHAEL LORENZO	CA	04W	96
COLLENE CHARLES EDWARD	OH	19E	93
COLLER WILFORD PAUL	NY	07E	89
COLLETT PAUL RAYMOND JR	TX	36E	68
COLLETT ROBERT LEE JR	KY	11W	79
COLLETTE CURTIS DAVID	CT	08E	55
COLLETTE ROGER CHARLES	LA	07E	23
COLLETTO ALBERT V JR	PA	19W	11
COLLEY MICHAEL IRA	AL	18E	120
COLLIER ALONZO CARLTON	GA	69W	2
COLLIER CHARLES MICHAEL	VA	20W	106
COLLIER CHARLEY HOLTON	TX	03E	54
COLLIER DONALD EARL	MI	35W	88
COLLIER GENE FRANCIS	MD	48E	51
COLLIER GEORGE EDWARD	MS	01E	9
COLLIER GERALD JAMES	MI	11E	76
COLLIER JAMES ALLEN	NC	29E	71
COLLIER JAMES WILLIAM	NY	17E	98
COLLIER JERRY LAMAYNE	AL	37E	80
COLLIER JOHN STANFORD	NC	41E	61
COLLIER JUNIUS COLUMBUS	TN	42E	29
COLLIER LARRY EUGENE	GA	53W	8
COLLIER LAWRENCE HENRY	TN	28E	20
COLLIER NOAH CHANDLER JR	GA	11E	108
COLLIER RAYMOND LYN	ME	24W	83
COLLIER STEVEN EDWARD	CT	40W	42
COLLIER TIMOTHY LYNN	CA	40E	18
COLLIER TONY WAYNE	TX	25E	15
COLLIER WILLIAM FLOYD	TN	05E	45
COLLIER WILLIE LESTER	AL	08E	84
COLLINA GEORGE WILLIAM	MA	07W	41
COLLINGSWORTH DELNO BILLY	IN	07E	125
COLLINS ALBERT	GA	10E	66
COLLINS ALBERT EUGENE	OK	43E	4

NAME	STATE	PANEL NO.	LINE NO.
COLLINS ARLIE RAY	MO	27W	71
COLLINS ARLIN DARRELL	MO	46W	47
COLLINS ARNOLD	NY	31E	33
COLLINS BILLY G	AZ	34E	48
COLLINS BRIAN PATRICK	MA	44W	34
COLLINS BRUCE WAYNE	CA	48W	16
COLLINS CHARLES ALLEN	NC	03E	73
COLLINS CLAUDE LAVERNE	SC	25E	82
COLLINS CLAYTON	WV	03E	21
COLLINS CLINT	CA	56E	36
COLLINS CLYDE CECIL	KY	49E	9
COLLINS DAVID BURR	KY	22W	87
COLLINS DAVID JIM	OH	21W	41
COLLINS DAVID LEE	IN	22W	57
COLLINS DAVID LEROY	NV	36E	47
COLLINS DONALD CLIFTON	MO	08W	106
COLLINS DOUGLAS WOODROW	GA	47W	16
COLLINS EDWARD W III	PA	56E	3
COLLINS ELTON BRADLEY	IN	35W	8
COLLINS ELZIE J JR	KY	05E	50
COLLINS EUGENE	VA	31E	44
COLLINS FLOYD EUGENE JR	GA	27E	80
COLLINS FRANCIS LEO	OR	21E	58
COLLINS FRANKLIN THOMAS	GA	21E	55
COLLINS GARY DEAN	KS	42W	34
COLLINS GARY EDWARD	OH	33W	6
COLLINS GEORGE PORTEOUS	MN	31W	65
COLLINS GUY FLETCHER	FL	44E	33
COLLINS HAROLD DUANE	IN	45W	24
COLLINS HARRIS LESTER	TX	52E	15
COLLINS HORACE CLEVELAND	FL	01E	88
COLLINS JACK LARELL	IA	14E	55
COLLINS JAMES ALFRED	IL	34E	84
COLLINS JAMES BRUCE	WA	42W	10
COLLINS JAMES FREW	PA	05W	93
COLLINS JAMES GILBERT	PA	58E	19
COLLINS JAMES WILFORD	TN	09E	79
COLLINS JEROME LISTON	AL	23W	20
COLLINS JOHN CALVIN	NC	67E	7
COLLINS JOHN JAMES	PA	29E	71
COLLINS JONATHAN III	CA	27W	16
COLLINS JULIUS JR	SC	08E	123
COLLINS LARRY ELBERT	VA	16W	115
COLLINS LARRY RICHARD		26W	90
COLLINS MARK PAINE		64E	12
COLLINS MARSHALL BARB	TX	01W	63
COLLINS MICHAEL	NY	17W	3
COLLINS MICHAEL HOWARD	FL	20E	112
COLLINS MICHAEL LEE	IL	18W	26
COLLINS MICHAEL RAYMOND	CA	04W	21
COLLINS MICHAEL STEPHEN	OR	40E	59
COLLINS MICHAEL TIMOTHY	PA	32E	9
COLLINS NATHANIEL	NY	21E	21
COLLINS NOBLE JR	TX	41E	19
COLLINS RALPH RAYMOND JR	OH	59E	19
COLLINS RAY	IL	26E	92
COLLINS RICHARD FRANK	CA	16W	108
COLLINS RICHARD GLEN	CA	12E	27
COLLINS ROBERT KNAPP	OR	04E	1
COLLINS ROBERT ORVILLE	WV	14W	100
COLLINS RODNEY D	NC	04W	10
COLLINS RODNEY RAY	WV	17W	112
COLLINS RONALD CHARLES	IN	15W	58
COLLINS ROSS WILLARD JR	VA	28W	80
COLLINS SYLVESTER	MI	13W	73
COLLINS THEOTHIS	NJ	48W	52
COLLINS THOMAS EDWARD	NY	07E	126
COLLINS THOMAS RUSSELL JR	MI	21W	69
COLLINS THOMAS TIMOTHY	MA	03W	106
COLLINS TOBY ERNEST	DE	58W	23
COLLINS VERNEL	IL	11W	72
COLLINS WALTER MONROE	NY	06E	116
COLLINS WILLARD MARION	IL	05E	131
COLLINS WILLIAM ANDERSON	NC	30E	14
COLLINS WILLIAM DANIEL	KY	24E	18
COLLINS WILLIAM ELICE JR	TX	14E	69
COLLIS GERALD ALAN	MI	63W	15
COLLISTER JERRY LEE	IA	41E	19
COLLOPY JOHN PATRICK	MA	23E	74
COLLUM WILLIAM EDWARD	FL	03W	4
COLLUMS BOBBY G	AR	01W	125
COLLYER DALE ELWYN	MI	35W	58

NAME	STATE	PANEL NO.	LINE NO.
COLN RAY EUGENE	OH	28E	101
COLOMBERO JAMES STEPHEN	CA	23W	6
COLOMBO GARY LEWIS	WA	43E	16
COLON ALBERTO	NY	40E	37
COLON HARRY JOSEPH	NY	22W	103
COLON LUIS ANGEL	NY	41E	7
COLON-DIAZ JUAN	PR	09W	103
COLON-MOTAS ESTEBAN	GA	20E	23
COLON-PEREZ ABRAHAM LINCO	NY	42E	49
COLON-RIVERA JOSE RAMON	PR	47W	16
COLON-RODRIGUEZ GOLGUIS	PR	15W	113
COLON-SANTOS RAFAEL	NJ	11W	16
COLONE RONALD JAMES	IN	52E	6
COLONNA PHILIP GEORGE	NY	58W	3
COLOPY STEPHEN LYNN	OH	18E	74
COLORIO JOSEPH	NY	19W	11
COLOSANTI NORMAN EDWARD	ME	33E	47
COLOTTI JOSEPH LEONARD	NY	18E	48
COLQUHOUN TED D	OR	43W	52
COLSON BRUCE NORMAN	NY	49W	12
COLSON DONALD REGINALD	LA	38E	76
COLSON RONALD SANDERS	KY	29W	97
COLSTON EDWARD JEROME	MI	21E	87
COLSTON LOUIS JR	AL	27E	107
COLTER KENNY LAWRENCE	NY	39E	58
COLTMAN WILLIAM CLARE	PA	01W	76
COLTON MICHAEL NORRIS	MN	20W	63
COLUNGA GEORGE	TX	30W	20
COLVIN DAVID	IN	06E	53
COLVIN GENE FRANCIS	NY	22E	91
COLVIN GERALD SELAH	VT	21W	81
COLVIN PAUL SILVEY	VA	24E	59
COLVINS RONALD EARL	IL	39W	47
COLWELL KEITH	KY	16W	108
COLWELL PAUL	KY	06W	112
COLWELL RONALD LEE	MI	44W	57
COLWELL WILLIAM KEVIN	NY	04E	36
COLWYE JAMES LEON	AR	05W	63
COLYEAR CURTIS CRAIG	CA	08W	118
COLYER WILLIAM WALTER	KY	10W	56
COMACHO PETER FRANK JR	CA	46W	38
COMBER DAVID WAYNE	PA	05W	105
COMBEST JERRY WAYNE	TX	47W	16
COMBS ALFRED HENRY JR	CA	02E	17
COMBS ALLAN EUGENE	CA	08E	26
COMBS CHARLES	KY	15E	114
COMBS CLIFFORD DALE	MO	31W	45
COMBS DAVID JOHN	PA	10W	108
COMBS DENNIS ALAN	OH	21E	111
COMBS EDWARD ALTON	KY	33E	7
COMBS FARRISH	IL	15W	58
COMBS JACKIE RANDALL	WA	30E	7
COMBS JAMES MILES	CA	11W	121
COMBS JAMES STEPHEN	OH	40E	60
COMBS JOHN ASHER	OH	59W	20
COMBS JOHN BEECHLY	AL	27W	106
COMBS KENNETH DALE	CA	46W	39
COMBS LEE ROY	OH	28W	58
COMBS LOWELL THOMAS	TX	39E	30
COMBS PAUL REX	WA	35E	4
COMBS PHILLIP EUGENE	MO	25W	36
COMBS THOMAS EUGENE	OH	17E	102
COMBS TYRONE	OH	23E	56
COMBS VIRGIL CARLYLE	OK	32W	53
COMEAUX JOSEPH BERNILLE	TX	25E	37
COMER HOWARD BRISBANE JR	FL	16W	115
COMER WILLIAM MARVIN JR	KS	36E	47
COMFORT RAY THOMAS	PA	49E	40
COMIS LARRY MELVIN	MI	12W	37
COMLY WILLIAM ALVIN	NJ	13W	111
COMPA JOSEPH JAMES JR	OH	02E	4
COMPTON DOUGLAS	KY	41W	45
COMPTON FRANK RAY	VA	06E	29
COMPTON JOHNNIE RAY	AL	41W	11
COMPTON LORN DAVID	WV	48E	3
COMPTON MICHAEL JOSEPH	MN	10E	20
COMPTON ROBERT WILLIAM	CA	25W	64
COMPTON WILLIAM EDGAR III	CA	25E	14
COMSTOCK ARTHUR EDWIN JR	NY	10E	58
COMSTOCK ROBERT JAMES	IA	43E	66
CONANT GREGORY C	NM	39E	3
CONAWAY GARY LEE	IL	28E	59

NAME	STATE	PANEL NO.	LINE NO.
CONAWAY LAWRENCE YERGES	OH	11W	90
CONAWAY LONDON	GA	27W	4
CONAXIS NICHOLAS S	MA	55E	7
CONCANNON FRANCIS BRYANT	MD	16E	60
CONCANNON JAMES P JR	PA	43W	53
CONCANNON JOHN FRANCIS	MA	07E	23
CONCANNON RICHARD NEIL	IA	05W	105
CONCEPCION FRANCISCO JR	HI	03E	72
CONCEPCION-CHAPMAN JIMMY		51W	24
CONCEPCION-NIEVES DAVID	PR	09W	37
CONCHOLA BENITO	TX	33W	92
CONDE-FALCON FELIX M	IL	27W	9
CONDIT DOUGLAS CRAIG	OR	30E	89
CONDIT WILLIAM HOWARD JR	OH	22W	117
CONDON FRANK ALLOYSIUS	GA	60W	27
CONDON JAMES GREGORY III	MA	08E	71
CONDON ROBERT EUGENE	NE	34E	67
CONDON RUSSELL WILLIAM	TX	01E	121
CONDREAY ERVIN LEE	CO	26E	82
CONDREY GEORGE THOMAS III	GA	56E	37
CONDY LADD ROBERT	CO	05E	37
CONE JOHN MILTON	IA	16W	87
CONE LEROY	FL	58E	5
CONE LLOYD ALFORD	SC	56E	37
CONE REGINALD LOUIS	NJ	11E	19
CONELLY MITCHELL PAULLIS	FL	62W	22
CONEY LAWRENCE NELSON	IL	54W	41
CONFER MICHAEL STEELE	NE	11E	65
CONGER JOHN EDWARD JR	OH	34W	91
CONGIARDO THOMAS DEAN	IL	11E	60
CONGLETON ROY ELSWORTH	NC	01E	78
CONKEL THOMAS EUGENE	OH	37W	38
CONKLE JOE THOMAS	GA	24W	58
CONKLIN BERNARD	NY	09E	88
CONKLIN JOSEPH PETER	NY	38E	47
CONKLIN LARRY JAMES	NY	28W	18
CONKLIN MICHAEL LEE	MI	09W	88
CONKLIN RICHARD DOUGLAS	CT	57W	24
CONKLIN RONALD RAYMOND	NY	37W	30
CONKLIN THOMAS ARTHUR	OH	20E	112
CONKRIGHT JAMES EDWARD	KY	17W	94
CONLAN BRIAN DALY JR	NJ	14E	76
CONLEY ALEX BOYD	VA	37W	30
CONLEY BILLY GENE	KY	15E	55
CONLEY DAVID LEE	MI	07W	46
CONLEY EUGENE OGDEN	OH	14E	60
CONLEY GERALD DONALD	PA	64W	6
CONLEY GREEN	AZ	06E	109
CONLEY JAMES GRADY	GA	02W	63
CONLEY LARRY RAY	MI	07W	131
CONLEY MICHAEL FRANCIS	NY	21E	22
CONLEY MONROE JASON	OH	06W	25
CONLEY ROBERT ALAN	UT	29W	28
CONLEY ROBERT FRANK	CA	43W	55
CONLEY ROBERT L	IN	36E	47
CONLEY RONALD CLARENCE	PA	27W	44
CONLEY SYLVESTER E JR	NC	44E	5
CONLEY TERRY LEWIS	CA	21E	111
CONLEY THEODORE R JR	NC	37W	8
CONLEY WILLIAM THOMAS	PA	40E	54
CONLIN JEFFREY FRANCIS	CA	43E	16
CONLIN PETER EDWARD	NY	51E	17
CONLIN RICHARD JOSEPH	PA	36W	20
CONLON JOHN FRANCIS III	PA	05E	101
CONN DAVID BRUCE	CA	13E	60
CONN DONALD WARREN JR	CO	08E	26
CONN FRANKLIN L	WV	03E	42
CONN JAMES DOUGLAS	TX	14W	38
CONN RONALD RAY	TX	13E	82
CONNACHER RONNIE EDWARD	TX	06E	30
CONNEL DAVID ARNOLD	TX	07W	120
CONNELL CHARLES ANTHONY	FL	12W	24
CONNELL EDWIN DOUGLAS	NC	48E	52
CONNELL JAMES JOSEPH	DE	09E	22
CONNELL JOHN ALEXANDER	NC	47W	7
CONNELL MICHAEL JOSEPH	PA	13W	87
CONNELL OSCAR ALLEN	AL	12W	17
CONNELL THOMAS MICHAEL	IN	25W	96
CONNELL VAUGHN DAVID	NY	29W	87
CONNELLY EDWARD WALTER JR	MA	55E	7
CONNELLY PATRICK ALLEN	WI	56W	32
CONNELLY RICHARD JOHN	CA	13W	61

NAME	STATE	PANEL NO.	LINE NO.
CONNELLY SAMUEL GERALD	IN	59E	19
CONNER DAVID LELAND	WV	07W	69
CONNER DONNIE RAY	MO	01W	116
CONNER EDWIN RAY	TX	10W	48
CONNER EUGENE JOSEPH	IA	36E	3
CONNER GERALD WILLIAM	NJ	40E	39
CONNER IDUS JAMES	FL	51W	48
CONNER JACK WILLIAM	CA	12W	92
CONNER JEROME	TN	14E	76
CONNER JESSIE WENDELL	GA	30E	1
CONNER KENNETH LEE	TN	22W	45
CONNER LORENZA	GA	28E	80
CONNER MELVIN HUBBARD JR	CA	28W	99
CONNER MICHAEL RAY	TN	11W	34
CONNER PATRICK	IL	20E	112
CONNER PAUL ALLAN	FL	45E	19
CONNER ROGER LEROY	KY	08E	19
CONNER STEPHEN GRANT	TX	15W	47
CONNER THOMAS EARL	IL	05E	129
CONNERS LEE ALEXANDER	NY	14W	32
CONNERS RALPH WILSON JR	DC	24W	74
CONNEVEY LAYNE HALE	TX	18W	31
CONNIFF THOMAS JOSEPH	CA	03W	72
CONNOLLY GEORGE THOMAS	CA	06W	114
CONNOLLY KEVIN THOMAS	FL	36W	48
CONNOLLY MICHAEL DENNIS	NY	56E	37
CONNOLLY RICHARD	MA	36E	3
CONNOLLY TERRENCE CHARLES	NY	17W	126
CONNOLLY THOMAS CHARLES	IL	67E	7
CONNOLLY VINCENT JOHN	TX	12E	20
CONNOR CHARLES RICHARD	UT	40W	48
CONNOR FRANCIS JOSEPH	PA	47W	17
CONNOR GLENN MARSHALL	VA	56E	36
CONNOR JAMES FRANCIS JR	MA	05W	95
CONNOR JAMES KENNETH	WV	42W	67
CONNOR JOHN JR	NC	05E	26
CONNOR PATRICK JAMES	IL	07W	48
CONNOR PETER MICHAEL	OH	16W	28
CONNOR PETER SPENCER	NJ	05E	129
CONNORS DAVID THOMAS	MI	47E	39
CONNORS FERGUS FRANCIS JR	CT	21E	87
CONNORS JACK LEE	MI	19W	85
CONNORS PATRICK JOSEPH	MI	10E	57
CONOLLY SIDNEY MCLEAN JR	TX	56W	18
CONOVER CHARLES RAYMOND	IN	07W	30
CONRAD ANDREW CHARLES JR	MI	24E	94
CONRAD CARLOS WADE	AR	08E	107
CONRAD GEORGE DEWEY JR	FL	20W	85
CONRAD HARRY FLOYD	NJ	16E	76
CONRAD JOHN WILLIAM	OH	06W	59
CONRAD MARTIN JAMES	NY	10E	55
CONRAD PAUL LEWIN	OH	07E	107
CONRAD ROY EUGENE	CA	28E	63
CONRADY MICHAEL JOSEPH	OH	62W	22
CONRARDY RICHARD JOHN	KS	09W	110
CONROY MICHEAL EUGENE	NY	27E	33
CONROY PATRICK J	NY	48E	15
CONROY PAUL AMES JR	NY	17E	27
CONROY RONALD LEE	KS	42W	67
CONRY DENNIS	MA	26W	82
CONRY JOHN TIMOTHY	AZ	01W	15
CONSAVAGE RALPH EDWARD	MI	43E	42
CONSOLVO JOHN WADSWORT JR	VA	01W	14
CONSTANDE DONALD	MA	09E	129
CONSTANTINE MICHAEL EUGEN	MA	45W	25
CONSTANTINI FRANK J JR	CA	22E	29
CONSTANTINO CLIFFORD JOHN	NJ	18W	31
CONSTIEN JOHN RICHARD W	OK	19W	11
CONTARINO DONALD ALLEN	MA	19W	37
CONTESTABILE DANIEL J	MA	55E	7
CONTI ANTHONY NOAH	PA	52W	34
CONTI ROBERT FREW	PA	16W	115
CONTINO RAYMOND FRANK	CT	10W	49
CONTRERAS BENITO JR	CA	45W	18
CONTRERAS JOHN JENARO	CA	35E	4
CONTRERAS JUAN LEONARDO	TX	24W	15
CONTRERAS MIGUEL ZARAGOZA	CA	23E	93
CONTRERAS PABLO GUERECA	TX	14E	56
CONTRERAS RICHARD AGUIRRE	AZ	40E	60
CONTRERAS VALERIANO DAVID	TX	22W	51
CONTREROS ALBERT D JR	NY	38W	16
CONVERSE PHILIP HOWELL	TX	22E	99
CONVERSON TYRONE	LA	07W	30
CONVERY JOSEPH FRANCIS JR	PA	37E	51
CONWAY EDWARD JOHN	MI	17E	34
CONWAY JAMES BENNETT	TN	06E	105
CONWAY JAMES THADDEUS	OH	11W	49
CONWAY JASPER RAY	NC	12E	99
CONWAY JOHN JAMES	MA	16E	100
CONWAY JOSEPH QUINTON	PA	10E	61
CONWAY LEROY	NY	23W	118
CONWAY RAYMOND LESTER	VA	36E	48
CONWAY RAYMOND TERRENCE	FL	43W	34
CONWAY TERRY MIKEL	CA	07W	128
COODY GEORGE LA FAYETTE	MS	25W	10
COOK ALBERT ELMORE	IL	61W	11
COOK AUDREY JULIUS	MD	56W	19
COOK AUSTIN BRUCE	CA	23E	82
COOK BERNARD JAMES	IL	43W	13
COOK BILLY LEE	IL	51W	3
COOK CALVIN LEON	FL	30E	69
COOK CHARLES	GA	11W	40
COOK CHARLES FRANCIS	MI	28W	67
COOK CHARLES HERMAN	MO	36E	48
COOK CHARLES JOSEPH	CA	56E	21
COOK CHARLES JR	CA	52W	4
COOK CHARLES ROBERT	OH	36W	80
COOK CHARLES WILLIAM	IA	03W	91
COOK CHRISTOPHER CORWIN	CA	03W	108
COOK CLINTON ARTHUR	AK	11W	63
COOK CURTIS KEITH JR	MI	27W	106
COOK DAVID RICHARD	MD	16W	41
COOK DAVID SAMUEL	WV	52W	14
COOK DELFIN HILARIO	MI	42W	27
COOK DELMAR FREDRICK	WA	20E	7
COOK DENNIS LYNN	IN	56E	3
COOK DENNIS PHILIP	CA	06E	89
COOK DONALD ESTEL	CO	08E	20
COOK DONALD GILBERT	NY	01E	80
COOK DONALD JAMES	LA	25W	64
COOK DONALD MICHAEL	MI	40W	42
COOK DONALD RICHARD	TN	06W	22
COOK DONALD WARREN	IN	12W	51
COOK DOUGLAS ALEX	OR	19W	128
COOK DWIGHT WILLIAM	IA	01W	74
COOK EARL LLOYD	OH	21W	91
COOK GARRY KENDELL	TN	15E	114
COOK GEORGE KENNETH	CA	16E	76
COOK GLENN RICHARD	NC	17W	100
COOK HAROLD CLARENCE	FL	25E	96
COOK JAMES BLACK	IA	49W	3
COOK JAMES EDWARD	SC	06E	129
COOK JAMES JOHN	MI	12W	130
COOK JAY ALAN	MO	56E	3
COOK JERRY ROBERT	GA	21E	118
COOK JIMMIE DEE	FL	30W	42
COOK JIMMY LEE	AZ	22E	29
COOK JOEL LESLIE	MI	15W	85
COOK JOHN DALE	IN	08E	44
COOK JOHN EDWARD	AR	17W	100
COOK JOHN I	SC	14E	94
COOK JOHN PATRICK	NY	48W	23
COOK JOHN PHILLIP	CA	32W	53
COOK JOHN W	CA	42E	3
COOK JOHN WILLIAM JR	GA	42E	3
COOK JOSEPH FRANCIS	MA	58E	5
COOK KELLY FRANCIS	IA	29E	65
COOK KENNETH LYNN	TX	41E	61
COOK LARRY DAVIDSON	AL	47W	26
COOK LARRY DEAN	OK	51W	24
COOK LESLIE	PA	43E	42
COOK LESTER CHARLES	TX	17W	14
COOK LEWIS COLLIN	OR	20E	23
COOK MARLIN CURTIS	AL	04E	106
COOK MARVIN JR	AR	34W	82
COOK MELVIN BRUCE	OR	28E	20
COOK MICHAEL DEAN	CA	06E	73
COOK MICHAEL FRANK	CA	09E	86
COOK MILTON	MI	49W	54
COOK NATHANIEL	TX	23W	20
COOK PATRICK HENRY JR	GA	49E	40
COOK PETER ALLAN	MA	11W	122
COOK PETER BROWN JR	MS	27E	58
COOK PETER EVERETT	IA	18E	68
COOK RANDALL VINCENT	NY	21E	10
COOK RAYMOND LEE	NY	55E	9
COOK ROBERT EDWARD	MO	48E	25
COOK ROBERT EMERY	PA	09W	12
COOK ROBERT PAUL	CA	28E	80
COOK ROBERT WILKINSON	MD	20E	112
COOK ROGER JOHN	NY	14E	33
COOK RONALD JOHN	AZ	67E	7
COOK SCOTT HOWARD	MO	33E	2
COOK THOMAS RAY JR	PA	50W	12
COOK THOMAS STANLEY	NY	52E	47
COOK TIMOTHY ANDREW	MI	18W	116
COOK WEYMAN TERRY	MS	30W	52
COOK WILLIAM DONALD JR	CA	13E	50
COOK WILLIAM HAROLD	WA	46E	30
COOK WILLIAM RICHARD	MN	52E	35
COOK WILMER PAUL	MD	32E	43
COOK WILSON LEE	MD	15E	104
COOKE CALVIN COOLIDGE JR	DC	01W	7
COOKE CALVIN EDWARD	VA	24W	74
COOKE CHARLES THOMAS	VA	33E	27
COOKE DOUGLAS RUDOLPH	VA	44E	66
COOKE EDDIE BOYD JR	SC	13E	60
COOKE ERNEST FRISSELL JR	VA	40W	72
COOKE HAROLD THOMAS	CA	08E	35
COOKE LARRY HOUSTON	CA	26W	7
COOKE PAUL DONALD	LA	30W	20
COOKE ROBERT ALLEN	CA	18W	128
COOKE ROBERT MORRIS	VA	08E	64
COOKS MELVIN EUGENE	TX	03E	72
COOKSON ROBERT MERLE	MA	31W	90
COOL MARK DOUGLAS	WV	42E	28
COOLER SIDNEY HOMER	SC	33E	45
COOLEY DAVID LEO	VA	51E	29
COOLEY DICKEY LARUE	VA	13W	32
COOLEY HARVEY LYNN	TX	56E	4
COOLEY JAMES EDWARD	MD	14W	48
COOLEY LOUIS NEWTON JR	IA	32E	9
COOLEY MONTE RAY	TX	45E	19
COOLEY OCIE DANIEL	CA	23E	98
COOLEY ORVILLE DALE	WY	34E	58
COOLEY ROBERT KARL	CT	10W	123
COOLEY RONALD MARVIN	IN	20E	56
COOLEY SHELBY EMERSON	OH	58E	6
COOLEY WILLIAM	MA	05E	20
COOLS JAMES HARVEY	MI	25E	77
COOMBS DAN L F III	KS	06W	132
COOMER RICHARD ROSS	CA	40W	45
COOMES JOSEPH ANTHONY	KY	26E	100
COOMES WILLIAM MICHAEL	KY	04E	134
COON CALVIN KERMIT	OH	43W	32
COON DAVID WILLIAM	NY	05W	52
COON JAMES THOMAS	KY	29E	65
COON JESSE JAMES	PA	51E	37
COON JOHN LEMOINE	NY	66E	7
COON KEITH DAVID ED WILL	KS	39E	58
COON MICHAEL RAY	TX	32W	42
COONE GEORGE W JR	TN	39W	47
COONEY JAMES	NY	12W	112
COONEY JAMES HENRY	CA	22E	123
COONEY PHILLIP BERNARD	IL	17W	20
COONEY THOMAS JOSEPH	IL	41E	20
COONON DANIEL JAMES	PA	41W	31
COONROD ARNOLD LEE	OH	33E	27
COONROD ROBERT LEE	CA	46W	48
COONS CHESTER LEROY	ND	39E	69
COONS CLIFFORD KENT	AZ	24E	112
COONS GREGORY MAC	IA	13W	14
COONS HENRY ALBERT	NY	41E	61
COONS PETER MICHAEL	CA	20E	101
COONS RICHARD WILLIAM	PA	14W	130
COONS ROBERT WAYNE	NY	10W	64
COOPER ALEXANDER	PA	29E	19
COOPER ANDREW JONES	VA	19E	105
COOPER ARCHIE LEE	NC	26E	22
COOPER AVERY LEE	IL	21E	42
COOPER CALVIN EMANUEL	SC	23W	6
COOPER CARL DALTON	KY	06W	34
COOPER CHARLES EDWARD	KS	06E	114
COOPER CURTIS	GA	08W	114
COOPER DANIEL DEAN	OR	02W	104
COOPER DAVID ARTHUR	IN	14E	42

NAME	STATE	PANEL NO.	LINE NO.
COOPER DAVID H II	PA	17E	42
COOPER DAVID LAWRENCE	OR	19E	105
COOPER DONALD NATHANIEL	CA	41E	62
COOPER DONALD RAY	CA	27W	37
COOPER EDWARD THOMAS	IA	29W	8
COOPER EDWIN EARL	CA	15E	82
COOPER FAY KENNY	SC	24E	103
COOPER GARY RAY	FL	39W	36
COOPER GARY ROBERT	MO	30E	23
COOPER GEORGE GRADY	TX	14E	60
COOPER GERALD ALLAN	MI	07W	89
COOPER HERMAN LEE	AL	11E	60
COOPER HOWARD KENNETH	IN	39W	47
COOPER IRA DAUNETTE	LA	37W	73
COOPER JAMES ARTHUR	GA	15W	71
COOPER JAMES ENNIS	GA	56E	37
COOPER JAMES RALPH	NY	40W	63
COOPER JAMES RAYMOND	KS	19E	79
COOPER JAMES RICHARD	CA	03W	33
COOPER JAMES WILLIAM	TX	48E	57
COOPER JAMES WILLIAM	VA	63E	7
COOPER JEFFREY LANCE	AL	03W	34
COOPER JOE	LA	02W	14
COOPER JOHN OLIN III	DC	28E	73
COOPER JOHN RANDOLPH JR	GA	54W	8
COOPER JOSEPH HENRY JR	NY	08E	71
COOPER KENNETH WILLIAM	CO	09W	126
COOPER LEONARD DEAN	IA	17W	87
COOPER MAURICE ALAN	IN	43E	66
COOPER MICHAEL LINN	WV	46W	1
COOPER MILES DENNIS	MI	12E	87
COOPER NAPOLEN KELLY	NC	15E	27
COOPER OSCAR EDMOND	MD	03E	105
COOPER OTIS JR	TX	52W	18
COOPER RICHARD LEE	MO	44W	62
COOPER RICHARD WALLER JR	MD	01W	95
COOPER ROBERT GEAN	CA	48W	13
COOPER ROBERT LEE	NC	24W	64
COOPER ROBERT WAYNE	FL	20W	112
COOPER ROBERT WESLEY	TX	32E	43
COOPER ROCKY LEE	MI	02W	102
COOPER ROGER DALE	KY	17E	121
COOPER ROGER EDWARD	WV	14E	5
COOPER ROY ELDON	CA	50W	34
COOPER TERRY LEE	OH	36W	61
COOPER TOMMY DALE	OK	13W	130
COOPER ULYSSES CORNELIUS	GA	09E	32
COOPER WILLIAM EARL	GA	06E	131
COOPER WILLIAM MORRIS	AL	45W	60
COOPER WILLIE A	GA	05E	71
COOPER WILLIE GENE	TN	54W	9
COOPER WILLIE JAMES	LA	14E	4
COOPERWOOD JACK J III	TN	23E	57
COOREMAN RAYMOND ROBERT	MN	05W	10
COOTS JACKIE	KY	21W	17
COPACK JOSEPH BERNARD JR	IL	01W	103
COPAS ARDIE RAY	FL	10W	23
COPE CHARLES ALFRED	MO	60E	20
COPE CHARLES RICKY	TX	19W	1
COPE ROBERT JOE	WA	18E	48
COPE STANLEY SMITH JR	PA	11E	118
COPELAND ARTHUR PERRY	MI	32E	35
COPELAND DAVID LEE	GA	17W	22
COPELAND EUGENE	TN	31W	64
COPELAND JAMES ALAN	NC	39W	36
COPELAND JAMES RANDALL	GA	34W	74
COPELAND JERRY DON	OK	44W	22
COPELAND JERRY DON	MI	13W	126
COPELAND JOE MIKEL	TX	40E	38
COPELAND LARRY ODELL	NC	52E	47
COPELAND MELVIN	MI	46W	57
COPELAND NORMAN OTTIS	MO	37E	39
COPELAND RALPH A	ND	03E	48
COPELAND ROBERT	MO	13E	43
COPELAND SAMUEL CHAMPION	AL	23W	97
COPELAND WILLIAM E II	KS	06E	47
COPENHAVER GREGORY SCOTT	MD	01W	130
COPLEY BRUCE	OH	22W	103
COPLEY HENRY EUGENE JR	IL	09W	49
COPLEY WILLIAM MICHAEL	CA	39W	72
COPLIN SCOTT RONDAL	OH	11W	30
COPP BARRY ALAN	TX	40W	51

NAME	STATE	PANEL NO.	LINE NO.
COPP THOMAS ELLIOTT	CA	13W	5
COPPAGE GEORGE HERMAN III	DE	60E	21
COPPEDGE LAWRENCE	NJ	22W	15
COPPERNOLL DAVID WILLIAM	CA	14W	11
COPPLE RAMON ALLEN	LA	11E	108
COPPO PATRICK BRIAN	MI	58W	7
CORBETT DONALD JUNE	GA	25W	96
CORBETT ISAAC JOSEPH	GA	17W	45
CORBETT LINWOOD CALVIN	NY	29E	31
CORBETT MARK CHARLES	NY	15W	97
CORBETT THOMAS LOUIS	VA	30E	39
CORBIERE AUSTIN MORRIS		07E	42
CORBIN ANDREW PHILLIP	NJ	52E	4
CORBIN DONALD LEE	NJ	09E	112
CORBIN NORMAND ALFRED		20W	100
CORBIN RONALD JAMES	CA	32W	70
CORBIN RUSSELL BIGBEE JR	TN	37E	81
CORBIN THOMAS BERRY	FL	33E	12
CORBIN WILLIAM JENNINGS	MD	20E	41
CORBITT DEWAYNE	FL	43W	13
CORBITT GILLAND WALES	CO	24E	5
CORBITT WALLACE THOMAS	VA	34W	91
CORBO AL DOUGLAS	OK	41W	57
CORCORAN BRUCE ANTHONY	KS	16E	110
CORCORAN DAVID JAMES	ND	21W	11
CORCORAN EDWARD JOSEPH	PA	11E	81
CORCORAN EDWARD WALTER	NY	03W	4
CORCORAN KEVIN	NJ	67E	8
CORCORAN RICHARD FRANCIS	NJ	59W	20
CORCORAN WILLIAM RICHARD	FL	48W	34
CORDEAU EDWARD RICHARD	MA	43E	42
CORDELL RALPH DURWARD	GA	14E	33
CORDELL TERRY DENVER	FL	01E	13
CORDER JAMES RUSSELL	WV	66E	7
CORDERO JULIAN GARZA	TX	07E	2
CORDERO WILLIAM EDWARD	CA	02E	15
CORDIA MICHAEL JAMES	MO	45E	38
CORDINER DUANE GORDON	WA	06W	120
CORDLE CHARLES LINWOOD	VA	13W	22
CORDLE DONALD CALVIN	GA	06W	128
CORDON RALPH BRENT	ID	03W	21
CORDOVA CHRIS B	NM	03W	31
CORDOVA JAMES THOMAS H	LA	01E	83
CORDOVA JOHN BARELAS	TX	04E	3
CORDOVA OSCAR	NY	34W	70
CORDOVA RICHARD JOE	CO	26W	60
CORDOVA ROBERT JAMES	NE	35E	45
CORDOVA RUTILIO PROFIRIO	CO	25E	61
CORDOVA SAM GARY	CA	01W	69
CORE DERRICK	OH	22W	63
CORE JAMES ALBERT	NY	28E	80
CORES THOMAS RICHARD II	TX	59W	20
COREY GEORGE EDWARD	KY	09E	66
COREY JAMES ALLEN	WI	42E	30
COREY WILLIAM GEORGE	PA	01E	28
CORFIELD STAN LEROY	NM	19E	4
CORFMAN DARYL RAYMOND	OH	10E	4
CORK CLIFFORD MARKWOOD	WV	29W	18
CORK RAYMOND LEE JR	WI	31E	33
CORKERN JERRY WAYNE	LA	12E	119
CORKILL ROBERT ARNOLD	TX	07E	117
CORL FRANKLIN MATTHEW JR	PA	07W	60
CORLE JOHN THOMAS	PA	04E	1
CORLETT GERALD ERNEST	OH	12W	4
CORLEW ROY KENNETH	NY	52W	18
CORLEY CLARENCE ALTON JR	LA	17W	15
CORLEY JERRY WAYNE	MN	56E	21
CORLEY JOHN THOMAS JR	NY	44W	2
CORLEY ROBERT HAL	IL	06E	22
CORLEY THOMAS EUGENE	OH	37E	52
CORMIER EDWARD JAMES	MA	16W	120
CORMIER EUGENE FRANCIS	MA	26E	111
CORMIER FRANCIS JOSEPH	TX	30E	7
CORMIER MELVIN GLENN	LA	07E	56
CORMIER RONALD RAYMOND	NH	18E	57
CORMIER WILLIS	TX	28W	9
CORN JACK ALVIN	GA	40W	18
CORNEJO ALFRED JOSEPH	CA	25E	19
CORNELISON JOSEPH MICHAEL	CO	26W	53
CORNELIUS JOHNNIE CLAYTON	AZ	54W	2
CORNELIUS MERLIN G JR	IL	50W	12
CORNELIUS SAMUEL BLACKMAR	TX	01W	119

NAME	STATE	PANEL NO.	LINE NO.
CORNELL DONALD FREDERICK	OH	38W	41
CORNELL EDWARD MICHAEL	CA	23E	10
CORNELL RICKY LYNN	CA	39W	66
CORNELL ROBERT LESLIE	FL	18E	120
CORNELL STEVEN THOMAS	NY	25E	96
CORNETT CARLOS WAYNE	KY	57E	17
CORNETT CHARLES RANDELL	OK	46W	13
CORNETT DONALD C	LA	03E	73
CORNETT GREGORY DOUGLAS	KY	24W	38
CORNETT JAMES MITCHELL	TN	06E	43
CORNETT ROGER LARRY	UT	26E	95
CORNISH LARRY IRVING	NY	21W	99
CORNISH RUSSELL HUBARD	NJ	49E	30
CORNMAN CHARLES NORMAN	PA	35W	88
CORNS BOBBY LARRY	VA	22E	10
CORNS RONALD FREEMAN	FL	25E	5
CORNWELL HARRY JAY	IA	41E	62
CORNWELL JOHN BRUCE	NY	21W	88
CORNWELL LEON LAWRENCE JR	PA	19E	56
CORNWELL LEROY JASON III	AZ	02W	13
CORNWELL THOMAS GLENN	MI	18W	78
CORO BERNARD LOUIS	ME	02W	29
CORONA DOMINIC ANTHONY	CA	09E	86
CORONA FRANK RODRIQUEZ	CA	11W	83
CORONA JOEL	TX	06W	45
CORONA RUDOLPH RALPH III	CA	20E	58
CORONADO ROBERT	TX	05W	128
CORONIS MARTIN JAMES	NH	23E	50
CORP JERRY MARSH	MO	11W	30
CORPUS DAVID JOSEPH	AZ	10W	4
CORR CLIFFORD WAYNE	KS	04W	85
CORR JOHN GEYER	CT	32E	85
CORR PAUL JR	CA	22W	19
CORRALES RICHARD MENDOZA	TX	48E	40
CORREA ANGEL MERESI	NJ	22E	65
CORREA LUIS FELIPE	NY	22E	61
CORREA MICHAEL STEVEN	NY	11W	40
CORREA-MORALES FRANCISCO	PR	06E	129
CORREIA DA SILVA HELDER A	NJ	05E	16
CORRELL JOSEPH CLAIR	PA	04E	66
CORRELLO SCOTT DENNIS	OH	58W	2
CORRIE GARY ALLEN	CA	25W	64
CORRIE MARK LANE	CA	08E	16
CORRIGAN DANNY JOSEPH	IL	25E	19
CORRIGAN MICHAEL JOSEPH	CA	41W	4
CORRIVEAU GERARD	MA	05W	30
CORRIVEAU RICHARD THOMAS	ME	21W	99
CORRY CHARLES MICHAEL	GA	50E	3
CORSI BOBBY GLYNN	OH	10E	26
CORSINO EDDIE NELSON	OH	18W	101
CORSON RICHARD P	NY	05E	101
CORSON TERRY CHARLES	ME	44W	2
CORTES-CASTILLO JUAN	PR	36W	1
CORTES-ROSA RAMON	FL	31E	97
CORTEZ ALBERT ROMERO	CA	09W	21
CORTEZ ALBERTO GUTIERREZ	TX	26W	69
CORTEZ JOSE G	TX	38E	47
CORTEZ JUAN ESQUIVEL	TX	34W	5
CORTEZ RICHARD	CA	13E	15
CORTOR FRANCIS EDWIN JR	MO	17W	100
CORWIN EDWIN HUGH	OH	36W	61
CORWIN FRANCIS HENRY JR	MA	34W	6
CORWIN JOHN JAMES II	IN	27W	98
CORWIN MICHAEL HARRY	FL	10W	56
CORYELL MICHAEL NOBLE	CA	11E	130
CORZINE BOBBY WAYNE	TX	14E	61
COSBY DAVID FRANKLIN	VA	44E	45
COSGRAVE GARY WAYNE	MD	19E	93
COSGRIFF PAUL LEONARD	PA	40W	11
COSGROVE CHESTER	NJ	39W	78
COSGROVE COURTNEY JAMES	OH	21W	31
COSOM LEVERN	SC	47E	47
COSSA WILLIAM EDWARD JR	CA	21E	21
COSSEY JOHN DWANE	MI	20W	18
COSSEY RICKY FAY	KY	36W	39
COSSINS JACK EDWARD	NV	22E	10
COSSON WILBUR LYNN	FL	23E	27
COSTA MARIO	NJ	52W	18
COSTA ROBERT JOSEPH	MA	31W	98
COSTA WILLIAM CARL	CA	23W	98
COSTANTINO RONALD JOSEPH	IL	29E	1
COSTANZA KENNETH DAVID	NY	17W	5

NAME	STATE	PANEL NO.	LINE NO.
COSTANZO RALPH PAUL	CT	28E	8
COSTELLO GEORGE SIMONDS	HI	04E	32
COSTELLO JEREMIAH FREDERI	MD	01W	117
COSTELLO LAWRENCE R	KS	12E	3
COSTELLO RUSSELL RALPH	FL	07W	37
COSTELLO STEPHEN RANDALL	OK	20W	5
COSTIN CHARLES GREY	NC	40W	73
COSTLEY LARRY LEE	MI	42W	67
COSTNER JOHNNY PHILLIP	SC	06W	49
COSTON RICHARD JAMES	CA	17W	95
COTA ERNEST KENO	CA	60E	9
COTE DONALD RICHARD	WA	31E	33
COTE ROBERT FRANCIS	MA	17E	102
COTE ROBERT PAUL	CA	10W	74
COTES MICHAEL EUGENE	MI	17W	86
COTHRAN CURTIS EDGAR	FL	26E	34
COTNER MORRISON AUTHER	AR	18E	106
COTNEY ELMER EUGENE	AL	11E	30
COTTEN JAMES L JR	KY	23E	35
COTTEN LARRY WILLIAM	TN	13W	99
COTTEN OLLIE RAY	MI	02E	55
COTTEN ROBERT BRYAN	TX	24E	18
COTTENIER ROBERT WILLIAM	RI	25E	96
COTTER JOHN REDMOND	MI	27E	84
COTTER KENNETH JAMES	WI	12W	100
COTTER RICHARD LANE	MA	32W	4
COTTERELL JACK PATRICK	CA	35E	30
COTTERILL MICHAEL	NY	26W	44
COTTERMAN HARRY ANDREW	OH	10W	49
COTTET DUANE LEE	MT	40W	73
COTTIN LELAND RICHARD	TX	08E	65
COTTINGHAM DUANE ROGER	WA	57W	7
COTTINGHAM JOHN EDWARD	KY	18W	128
COTTMAN ROBERT LEE	MD	40W	2
COTTO MODESTO JR	NY	36E	3
COTTON CHARLES MICHAEL	TX	56W	32
COTTON MICHAEL	LA	41E	36
COTTON MOSES M	MS	05E	25
COTTON THOMAS III	TX	12E	52
COTTON THOMAS WAYNE	AL	31E	86
COTTRELL DARRELL WAYNE	IN	54E	32
COTTRELL DUANE ALLAN	IA	02W	24
COTTRELL JOHN NELSON	MI	34W	36
COTTRELL SIDNEY ALLEN	OH	02W	34
COTTRELL THOMAS LEE	CA	35E	11
COTTRELL THOMAS LEWIS	WI	28W	80
COTTRELL TIMOTHY JAMES	OH	46W	39
COTTRELL WILLIE JAMES	AL	34E	16
COTTRILL GEORGE W JR	OH	08E	51
COUCH FREDDIE LEE	AR	47W	7
COUCH GAYLORD MARTIN	OK	23W	7
COUCH GEORGE M	TN	01W	10
COUCH HAROLD EUGENE	NC	29E	80
COUCH JACKY RAY	MO	34E	35
COUCH JAMES ROBERT	PA	20W	24
COUCH JULIAN WAYNE	GA	15E	78
COUCH LESLIE CRAIG	PA	05E	17
COUCH MICHAEL ALFRED	OR	37E	81
COUCH ROBERT EDWARD	GA	35W	8
COUCH ROY EVERETT	AR	14W	111
COUCH STEVEN WILLIAM	UT	15E	114
COUGHLIN ARTHUR RAYMOND	AL	27E	43
COUGHLIN JOHN PETER	MA	41W	62
COUGHLIN PATRICK CHARLES	MI	48E	57
COUICK ROGER LYNN	NC	39E	69
COUILLARD BRUCE ALVIN	MN	45E	38
COUK KARL HENRY	OH	26E	43
COULOMBE FRANCIS JOSEPH	MA	20W	62
COULON JOHN GERARD JR	NY	44W	22
COULSON THOMAS EUGENE	CA	16E	110
COULT GERRY DON	MO	03W	111
COULTER DONALD CLAY	TN	24E	86
COULTER ROBERT LLOYD	OR	54W	2
COULTHART GERALD FRANK	ND	26W	69
COUNCILL ARTHUR COBY III	CA	22W	103
COUNIHAN MICHAEL BRENDAN	MA	40W	73
COUNTAWAY JOHN ALDEN JR	MA	56E	37
COURCHANE DALE LOUIS	WA	06E	73
COURSON CHARLES TRUITT	TX	06E	51
COURTEAU EDWARD GERARD	CA	17E	115
COURTEMANCHE CALLEN JAMES	CA	36E	10
COURTNEY ALLEN WESLEY JR	TX	62E	1
COURTNEY JAMES IRA	KS	08E	20
COURTNEY JIMMY DARRELL	TN	20W	43
COURTNEY JOE RAY JR	CA	65E	6
COURTNEY MICHAEL JOSEPH	OH	07W	21
COURTNEY RONNIE	OK	40W	73
COURTNEY TERENCE FRANCIS	IL	01W	11
COURTRIGHT MICHAEL EUGENE	AZ	26W	61
COURVILLE ROGER MARVIN	MT	24W	38
COUSAR WILLIAM JAMES	GA	26W	24
COUSETTE JOSEPH	AL	12E	87
COUSIN MOSES JAMES	MI	59E	19
COUSIN ROBERT LEE	GA	58W	2
COUSINEAU HENRY CONRAD	MA	33E	35
COUSINS MERRITT THOMAS	IA	23E	35
COUTO JIMMIE MICHAEL	MA	39E	19
COUTRAKIS GEORGE	CA	22E	99
COUTU RENE RAYMOND	RI	25E	49
COUTURE JOHN VICTOR	NY	35W	25
COUTURIAUX EUGENE JR	IL	31W	90
COVARRUBIAS JUAN ALONSO	TX	28W	24
COVELLA JOSEPH FRANCIS	NY	04E	52
COVENY DAVID PAUL	NY	27E	33
COVER BOBBY CECIL	AR	46W	47
COVER LAWRENCE LEROY	CA	02W	21
COVERT RICHARD DEAN JR	CA	05W	102
COVEY CHARLES ALLEN	IN	10W	11
COVEY ELWOOD D JR	NY	13E	96
COVEY GENE TRACY	IL	51E	23
COVEY JAMES HERBERT	MI	22W	103
COVEY JERRY K	OK	26E	100
COVEY LAWRENCE LAVERN	NE	03E	48
COVEY WILLIAM F JR	CT	02E	25
COVINGTON CLAUDE HENRY	NY	51E	37
COVINGTON DARELL LEE	IN	23W	118
COVINGTON DONALD LINCOLN	NC	21W	81
COVINGTON HOBART EARL	TN	31W	65
COVINGTON HOPSON	PA	32E	91
COVINGTON LAWRENCE CORNEL	NJ	33E	79
COVINGTON RORY ARN	PA	42E	3
COVINGTON WILLIAM LEE	GA	13E	120
COWAN AARON DAVIS	IL	11E	121
COWAN ALPHONSO DEDRICK	FL	20W	46
COWAN DANNY ALLEN	CA	02W	47
COWAN DARRELL WAYNE	OK	05W	73
COWAN HARLEY RICHARD	WA	52E	16
COWAN HAROLD EUGENE	IL	09W	82
COWAN JAMES ALTON JR	GA	22W	74
COWAN JOHN R	NY	06E	1
COWAN PAUL ALLEN	CA	24W	28
COWAN ROBERT LE RHEA III	OK	25W	64
COWAN SAMUEL PAIGE JR	KS	50E	37
COWART DAVID LAWRENCE	PA	27E	9
COWART JOHN WAYNE	MS	33W	6
COWDELL MELVIN THOMAS	UT	24W	25
COWDEN LESLIE LAWRENCE	MN	37E	8
COWDRICK HORACE W JR	NY	29E	88
COWELL JAMES EDWARD	IL	62W	7
COWELL RICHARD JOHN	CA	13W	102
COWELL ROBERT BLANCO	CA	13E	61
COWEN CHRISTOPHER	NJ	52W	37
COWEN HAROLD EDWARD	MO	02W	21
COWLES GARY TWYMAN	NE	18E	79
COWLEY BENNYE WARREN	TX	32W	93
COWLEY JEFFRY EDWARD	TX	04W	125
COWLEY THOMAS REGINALD	OH	10E	53
COWSERT KENNETH WILLIAM	MO	13W	103
COX ALLAN LAMAR	GA	09E	93
COX CARL	UT	17E	34
COX CHARLES CLAYBOURN	NC	03E	17
COX CHARLES EDWARD	AL	03E	73
COX CHARLES STANLEY	NC	51E	37
COX CHARLES WILLIAM	KY	06W	112
COX CHESTER GARVIS	KY	13E	50
COX CLAUDIE LEE	TX	02W	12
COX DANIEL FRANKLIN	AK	05W	45
COX DANIEL RONEN	IL	23E	2
COX DAVID AUSTIN	ME	62E	1
COX DAVID LEE JR	PA	09E	20
COX EARNEST LEE	WV	18E	84
COX EDWARD ERLIN JR	LA	32W	36
COX EDWARD JAN	PA	04E	84
COX ELBERT ELISAH JR	VA	53E	29
COX EUGENE THOMAS	NY	21W	36
COX EVERETT FREDERICK	IN	36W	72
COX FRANCIS PATRICK	NY	35E	67
COX FRANK WILLIAM JR	NY	52W	27
COX FREDDIE JAMES JR	CA	57E	17
COX FREDIE RAY	MI	33E	46
COX GARY ALLEN	CA	23W	71
COX GARY DEAN	KS	39W	78
COX GARY LEE	TX	10W	31
COX GARY WAYNE	IN	23W	7
COX GARY WAYNE	CA	20W	112
COX GEORGE JOSE	VA	44E	45
COX GEORGE MARION II	MD	42W	16
COX GEORGE TOLLOVAR	FL	17E	42
COX GERALD WAYNE JR	UT	59E	1
COX GREGORY ELLIS	CA	33E	35
COX HAROLD ANTHONY	RI	21W	74
COX HENRY THOMAS	VA	08W	107
COX HOWARD MAX	IA	40E	60
COX JACKSON ELLIOTT	GA	17E	41
COX JAMES ALAN	NY	40W	63
COX JAMES ALLEN	MO	24W	38
COX JAMES BLAINE	WV	32E	87
COX JAMES MICHAEL	VA	20W	30
COX JAMES WILLIAM	OR	60W	16
COX JEHU JUNIS JR	MD	39E	30
COX JIMMIE DON	FL	17W	55
COX JIMMY RICHARD	NC	60E	9
COX JOHN DAVIES JR	AZ	54W	41
COX JOHN DENNIS II	NC	12E	41
COX JOSEPH LEE	TN	04W	132
COX JOSEPH WILLIAM	SC	18W	74
COX LARRY CHARLES	CO	40E	60
COX LARRY JAMES	CA	11E	70
COX LEON DAVID	ND	24W	28
COX LESTER WAYNE	FL	57E	17
COX LEWIS EARL	OK	10W	64
COX MACK CECIL	FL	03E	73
COX MARTIN	MO	06E	92
COX MICHAEL JOHN	MI	51E	44
COX MICHAEL LOU JR	MI	20W	96
COX MICHAEL MILTON	CA	18W	27
COX MITCHELL EDWARD	KY	09E	58
COX NATHANIEL JR	NC	12W	17
COX OMMIE TRUMAN JR	TX	32E	9
COX RAYMOND PRATER	OH	30E	1
COX RICHARD LEIGH	MN	24W	116
COX RICHARD PAUL	CA	12W	33
COX ROBERT IVAN	PA	18W	14
COX ROGER DALE	SC	15W	102
COX ROY ALLEN	TX	57E	20
COX RUBE ARTHUR JR	KY	35E	45
COX SHERBERT LEON	VA	18W	129
COX STANLEY GILBERT	OK	07E	80
COX STERLING EDWARD	TN	34W	6
COX TIMOTHY ROBERT	OH	16E	72
COX WILLIAM GAYLE	KY	04W	91
COX WILLIAM JOSEPH	MI	11E	72
COY BEN	TX	22E	24
COY BENJAMIN D JR	IN	25E	68
COY DWIGHT CLIFFORD JR	TX	46W	28
COY JAMES ANTHONY	GA	02E	7
COY JESSIE EDDIE LEE	FL	53W	8
COYE ROGER HERBERT	NY	13E	18
COYLE GARRY	NJ	05E	32
COYLE GARY JOSEPH	NY	33W	77
COYLE GERALD A	PA	01W	125
COYLE GERARD	PA	40W	11
COYLE HUGH	NJ	53W	33
COYLE JAMES MICHAEL	NJ	01E	62
COYLE JOHN	NJ	17E	67
COYLE LAVERNE DARTON	LA	06W	101
COYLE RICHARD DENNIS	PA	30W	52
COYMAN PETER R	FL	01E	107
COYNE KEVIN MARK	MD	59W	21
COYNE WILLIAM FRANCIS	OH	14E	9
COZAD JERRY LEE	NE	10W	49
COZAD WILLIAM MORRIS	IA	10W	31
COZART ROBERT GORDON JR	LA	12W	24
CRABB BRUCE WAYNE	WI	44W	23
CRABB WINFORD R	CA	57E	18
CRABBE FRANK EDWARD		05E	40

NAME	STATE	PANEL NO.	LINE NO.
CRABBE ROBERT JOHN	MI	18E	45
CRABTREE DAVID ALLEN	TN	12E	111
CRABTREE GEORGE RONALD	TN	12W	88
CRABTREE HARVEY C JR	TN	22W	87
CRABTREE JAMES OTIS	MO	02E	1
CRABTREE MICHAEL ANDREW	OR	30E	14
CRABTREE RANDALL LEWIS	IN	11W	54
CRABTREE ROBERT ANDREW	VA	29E	94
CRABTREE STEPHEN C	TN	27E	9
CRABTREE VARISE HELTON JR	WV	41W	45
CRADDOCK CARY	FL	07E	24
CRADDOCK FRED BURKETT JR	AR	25E	61
CRADDOCK RANDALL JAMES	OK	01W	98
CRADEUR DOUGLAS JOSEPH	LA	55E	9
CRAFT CLAYTON ANDREW	WV	48E	51
CRAFT EZRA DELANO	MD	64W	6
CRAFT GRAYSON	MS	36W	36
CRAFT HARLAN MERDEAN	TX	29W	18
CRAFT HAROLD GLEN	MI	11W	83
CRAFT JAMES	TX	39W	73
CRAFT JAMES ADOLPH	MI	30W	2
CRAFT JAMES DAVID	AL	50E	45
CRAFT JOSEPH RODNEY	WV	12E	73
CRAFT ROBERT LEE	UT	04E	8
CRAFT TOMMY LEWIS	PA	14E	33
CRAFT WILLIAM EDWARD	WV	27E	9
CRAFTON JAMES J	PA	03E	23
CRAGAR JAMES LEROY	MI	02E	129
CRAGG GERALD	IL	30E	2
CRAGHEAD THOMAS JAMES JR	VA	37E	20
CRAGIN ROBERT STUART JR	NY	41E	36
CRAIG BENJAMIN JR	NY	41E	62
CRAIG BRUCE KEITH	MI	50E	11
CRAIG CHARLES OWEN JR	IL	32W	92
CRAIG CLAYTON GEROME	AL	06W	129
CRAIG DAVID III	PA	01E	84
CRAIG DEAN JOHN	MD	32E	14
CRAIG DICKEY	IN	06W	9
CRAIG EDWARD JOSEPH	NJ	35E	37
CRAIG EDWARD LEE	KS	14W	88
CRAIG GARY RAYMOND	CA	56E	4
CRAIG HARRY LEE	IL	62E	16
CRAIG JAMES HERBERT	MO	10W	84
CRAIG JAMES LARRY	LA	05W	30
CRAIG JAMES LEWIS JR	FL	01W	82
CRAIG JIMMY LEON	KS	27E	27
CRAIG JOHN PHILIP	VA	23W	84
CRAIG MERLIN JOSEPH	LA	19W	118
CRAIG MICHAEL DENNIS	CA	54E	4
CRAIG ODELL	IL	25W	4
CRAIG PHILIP CHARLES	NY	23E	1
CRAIG REX LEE	KS	17E	102
CRAIG ROBERT MITCHELL	SC	23E	118
CRAIG ROGER GENE	WV	11W	90
CRAIG THOMAS EDWARD	CA	21E	32
CRAIG THOMAS RICHARD JR	GA	38E	24
CRAIG WAIN PERRY	TX	14W	71
CRAIG WAYNE SHELBY	VA	03W	58
CRAIG WILLARD D	VA	12E	87
CRAIG WILLIAM ANDERSON	IN	08W	85
CRAIG WILLIAM HOVER JR	FL	06E	18
CRAIG WILLIAM THOMAS JR	MI	30W	73
CRAIGE AMOS MARK	PA	07W	128
CRAIGHEAD TERRY DEAN	MO	09E	95
CRAIGMYLE FLOYD JOSEPH	OR	16W	22
CRAIN CARROLL OWEN JR	TN	16E	39
CRAIN CHARLES ERNEST	CA	22E	99
CRAIN JOSEPH DEWEY JR	MS	15E	23
CRAIN ROBERT VICTOR	AL	16E	83
CRAIN RONALD EDWARD	AR	23E	57
CRAIN TRAVIS GLEN	KY	12E	94
CRAM ROY ROBERT	OR	54E	4
CRAMBLET HOWARD EARL	CA	25W	65
CRAMER DAVID ARTHUR	WI	40E	59
CRAMER DONALD JAMES JR	MI	42W	67
CRAMER DONALD MARTIN	MO	05W	26
CRAMER HARRY G	PA	01E	78
CRAMER HENRY LEE	OR	09E	102
CRAMER JAMES WALLACE	PA	42W	27
CRAMER JEFFREY THOMPSON	OH	46W	13
CRAMER PARKER DRESSER	NY	01E	22
CRAMER ROBERT MICHAEL	MO	33E	81
CRAMPTON GARY LEE	OH	41E	62
CRAN JAMES A	MN	16E	76
CRANDALL BRET FLETCHER	UT	28W	89
CRANDALL CHARLES EVERETT	IN	36E	4
CRANDALL GREGORY STEPHEN	WA	05W	115
CRANDALL JOHN PAUL	IL	17E	1
CRANDALL RODNEY ALLEN	MI	56E	4
CRANDALL RONALD JAY	NY	22E	53
CRANDALL TIMOTHY ALLEN	CA	39W	79
CRANDALL WAYNE STEPHENS	NY	36W	49
CRANDELL JAMES LEE	MI	38W	34
CRANE CHARLES HENRY	HI	09E	37
CRANE DAVID CHAUNCEY	NY	50W	48
CRANE DEAN DENNIS	WI	22E	29
CRANE DENNIS	NJ	57W	24
CRANE DONALD ELLIS	PA	03E	73
CRANE DONALD LEONARD	IN	21E	3
CRANE JOHN LA VERNE	MI	40W	42
CRANE PHILIP MATT II	MI	54W	2
CRANE ROBERT BRENDEN	WA	28E	73
CRANE ROBERT IRVING	CA	42E	14
CRANE RODNEY LANE	NV	30W	86
CRANE WILLIAM JOSEPH II	MO	02W	101
CRANE WILLIAM RANDALL	OR	15W	69
CRANEY LESLIE LEE	ME	47E	48
CRANFORD CHARLES RYA	NC	09W	23
CRANFORD LARRY EDWARD	NC	07E	108
CRANFORD THOMAS WILLIAM	CA	57E	18
CRANMER FOSTER	CA	15W	31
CRANSON ROBERT DORIAN	ME	06W	129
CRAPO RONALD CARL	CA	15E	82
CRAPSE WAYNE FRANKLIN	SC	39E	19
CRARY DAVID WAYNE	TX	36E	68
CRARY JOSEPH WILLIAM	ND	10W	108
CRARY MORRELL JOSEPH	OR	29E	1
CRASE LIONEL RUSSELL	MT	48E	40
CRAUN GALE EUGENE	OR	50E	13
CRAVEN ANDREW JOHNSON	NC	59E	1
CRAVEN DONALD RAY	TX	44W	35
CRAVEN FLOYD CARL	TN	25E	97
CRAVEN GARY ALAN	MA	07W	36
CRAVEN JAMES EVERETT III	TX	37E	53
CRAVEN LEONARD ISLER	IN	05E	25
CRAVENS DANNY CAROL	OH	18W	109
CRAVENS ROBERT MILTON JR	IL	48W	24
CRAVENS THOMAS LLOYD	OH	11W	110
CRAVER DENNIS LINN	IA	04W	9
CRAVER DENNIS MARTIN	IA	03W	13
CRAVEY JOHN JAMES	AL	13W	84
CRAW DONALD DWIGHT JR	CA	07W	92
CRAWFORD ANDY PAUL	NY	37E	81
CRAWFORD BILLY MAX	FL	12E	32
CRAWFORD BOBBY DEAN	IL	34E	16
CRAWFORD CHARLES HUGH	OH	21E	10
CRAWFORD CHARLES J JR	NJ	38E	44
CRAWFORD CHARLES MARION	OH	03W	44
CRAWFORD CLAUDE LEE	CA	30E	39
CRAWFORD CURTIS EUGENE	NY	15E	115
CRAWFORD DAVID WESLEY	NM	67E	8
CRAWFORD DOUGLAS JAY	NY	05W	132
CRAWFORD GALE VERNON	TN	07E	47
CRAWFORD GORDON LEE	IN	05W	71
CRAWFORD HAROLD JEROME	GA	22W	19
CRAWFORD JAMES DAVID	TN	09W	47
CRAWFORD JAMES EDWARD	TN	22E	69
CRAWFORD JAMES EUGENE	AR	12W	38
CRAWFORD JAMES J	MO	02W	103
CRAWFORD JAMES PATRICK	CA	66W	2
CRAWFORD JOHN CALVIN	NY	16E	51
CRAWFORD JOHN NELSON JR	MO	08W	90
CRAWFORD JOHNNY RAY	IN	27E	57
CRAWFORD LAWRENCE BERNARD	MI	27E	5
CRAWFORD LAWRENCE JOE	IL	10W	96
CRAWFORD LOWELL LAVAIN	IA	28W	107
CRAWFORD MICHAEL ALAN	OK	02W	75
CRAWFORD REMBERT JR	NC	37E	34
CRAWFORD RICHARD	FL	37W	55
CRAWFORD RICHARD ALLEN	IL	03E	5
CRAWFORD RICHARD WAYNE	NY	26E	7
CRAWFORD ROBERT DEAN	MO	28E	60
CRAWFORD STANLEY WENDEL	CA	12W	130
CRAWFORD STEPHEN EARL	OH	61E	8
CRAWFORD TERRY LEE	OR	31W	78
CRAWFORD WALTER NORMAN	GA	32W	19
CRAWFORD WILLIAM DON	NC	44E	33
CRAWFORD WILLIAM LLOYD	OK	11E	96
CRAWFORD WILLIAM THOMAS	MO	01E	117
CRAWLEY LAWRENCE ERWIN	NC	04W	134
CRAWLEY ROBERT LEO	WI	33E	82
CRAWN RONALD MARCEL	OR	11E	13
CRAWSHAW STEEVE ALEXANDER	KS	25W	10
CRAYNE KENNETH EUGENE	NE	06W	101
CRAYTHORNE ROBERT EARL	OK	22E	10
CREAGER RONALD LEE	MI	12W	29
CREAGHEAD CLARENCE	AL	24W	74
CREAL CARL MARTIN	CA	26W	16
CREAMER ALBERT EUGENE	SC	27W	85
CREAMER CHARLES FORAK III	IN	06W	87
CREAMER FRANCIS P	NY	17W	80
CREAMER JAMES EDWARD JR	CT	51E	18
CREAR WILLIS CALVIN	AL	05W	105
CREASON JESS WILLIAM JR	ID	52E	16
CREASON RICHARD EARL	IN	29E	19
CREASON W K UTAH	CA	24W	52
CREASY JERRY N	IN	19W	66
CREECH BILLY GENE	GA	30W	52
CREECH PHILLIP GENE	KY	13W	73
CREECH ROBERT JR	VA	52W	22
CREECH WILLIAM OWEN JR	IL	05W	64
CREECY LARRY RAYMOND	TX	48E	16
CREED BARTON SHELDON	NY	04W	43
CREED BERNARD JAMES	MA	03E	74
CREED EDWARD GAFFNEY	TX	08E	91
CREEK HENRY LEE	TX	11E	44
CREEK THOMAS ELBERT	TX	32W	25
CREEKMORE JESSE CARL	TN	14W	97
CREEL DAVID DE WITT	MS	38W	72
CREEP GUY BARE JR	PA	37W	51
CREGON KEVIN FRANCIS	NY	32W	94
CREIGHTON PAUL BAREN	TN	51E	45
CRELIA BILLY DUANE	AR	13W	18
CREMER RONALD MARVIN	FL	21W	107
CRENSHAW JAMES LEE	TX	24E	18
CRENSHAW JOE EDWARD	AL	06W	112
CRENSHAW OLLIE EDWARD JR	TN	02W	121
CRENSHAW WILLIAM ANDERSON	AL	19E	36
CRESCENZ MICHAEL JOSEPH	PA	38W	16
CRESPIN ARTHUR	NM	41E	7
CRESPO JOSE	NY	31W	90
CRESSEL TERRY WALKER	VA	55W	27
CRESSEY DENNIS CLARKE	WY	01W	25
CRESSEY JAMES DANIEL JR	ME	35W	81
CRESSMAN PETER RICHARD	NJ	01W	114
CREVELING ZED CONNOR	WA	06E	98
CREW CARL JOSEPH	MD	28W	24
CREW JAMES ALAN	PA	29E	66
CREWS CHARLES RICHARD	FL	30E	42
CREWS JOHN DIVINE JR	NJ	61W	11
CREWS JOHN HUNTER III	NC	65E	7
CREWS JOHN W JR	WV	15W	62
CREWS PHILIP MARVIN	TN	42E	49
CREWS ROBERT LOUIS	FL	65E	7
CREWS THOMAS FRANKLIN	AL	56E	4
CRIBB EDWARD BERNARD	AZ	01E	27
CRIBB FLOYD ALLEN	SC	04E	107
CRIBBS JAMES WESLEY	TX	19E	57
CRIBBS MARTIN JOSEPH	NY	17W	116
CRIBELAR MICHAEL DEAN	MI	34E	28
CRICHTON CHARLES FREDERIC	IL	48W	17
CRICHTON ROBERT GARY	WY	08W	24
CRICK DALE EUGENE	AZ	32W	11
CRICKENBERGER RICHARD WAY	VA	66W	4
CRIDER JAMES WALTER	NC	09W	88
CRIDER RUSSELL DUANE	AZ	53E	29
CRIGGER HENRY GLEAVES	VA	29E	99
CRIGGER RELL JR	WV	33W	37
CRIKELAIR JOHN FRANCIS	NJ	20W	101
CRILLY DAVID ANTHONY	CA	23W	98
CRIM CHARLES RAY	TX	49W	6
CRIPE DENNIS WRAY	IN	32W	65
CRIPE JACK LESTER	MI	22E	38
CRIPE MERL L	CA	12E	87
CRIPE TOMMIE MAX	IN	06E	119
CRIPPS GEORGE WARREN	DE	04E	68

NAME	STATE	PANEL NO.	LINE NO.
CRISCI LARRY ANTHONY	NY	20E	13
CRISE PERRY ROCCO	NY	50W	12
CRISMAN WILLIAM HAROLD	MI	03E	115
CRISMON LONNIE JOE	AR	43E	66
CRISP JIMMY WAYNE	TX	23W	71
CRISP JOHN DAVID III	NC	26E	7
CRISP JOHN HAROLD	GA	25W	65
CRISP THOMAS MIKELL	KY	07W	39
CRISP WILLIAM HENRY	OK	04E	31
CRISSELL EARL LEON JR	NY	15E	126
CRISSEY HARRY ELIAS JR	MD	07E	85
CRIST KENNETH LEE	OH	47E	31
CRIST KENNETH ROY	KS	36W	34
CRIST STEPHEN EDWARD	OH	18W	112
CRISTMAN FREDERICK LEWIS	NC	04W	58
CRISWELL GEORGE DAVID	IN	21W	65
CRISWELL JAMES JOSEPH	PA	46W	48
CRISWELL RICHARD K III	PA	49W	39
CRISWELL ROBERT REED	CA	43E	4
CRITCHFIELD REECE A JR	OH	35E	4
CRITCHFIELD WILLIAM ROBER	NJ	32E	71
CRITELLI ALFRED JOSEPH	NJ	36W	1
CRITES FRANKLIN THOMAS	MI	03W	75
CRITES RAYMOND	IL	24W	3
CRITES RICHARD LEE	OH	28E	21
CRITES ROBERT LINCOLN JR	CA	22W	104
CRITTENBERGER DALE J	DC	18W	101
CRITZER RONAL EDWARD	VA	52E	47
CROCCO WALTER VINCENT	MA	28W	66
CROCE JOHN JOE	FL	16W	108
CROCE ROBERT JAMES	MA	09E	22
CROCKER DAVID ROCKWELL JR	NY	24W	29
CROCKER DAVID STEPHEN	OR	07E	94
CROCKER DENNIS OWEN	ME	48W	31
CROCKER DENTON WINSLOW JR	NY	08E	6
CROCKER DONALD JACK	LA	23E	74
CROCKER EVANS BLANE JR	TX	54E	4
CROCKER JAMES NORRIE JR	NC	21W	82
CROCKER RICHARD ANTHONY	PA	02W	115
CROCKETT CHARLES D JR	TX	54W	11
CROCKETT DELMAR LEE JR	AR	15E	57
CROCKETT FREDDIE ISIASH	VA	56E	4
CROCKETT JAMES BRANNAH	GA	51E	37
CROCKETT JAMES LARRY	AL	54W	27
CROCKETT JOEL	AR	26E	111
CROCKETT STANLEY GENE	OK	05W	20
CROCKETT TRAVIS RICHARD	TX	36W	67
CROCKETT WILLIAM JAMES	NM	01W	68
CROCKRAN JAMES	MO	42E	62
CRODY KENNETH LLOYD	IN	01W	55
CRODY RONALD ISAAC	AL	34W	21
CROFFORD CLINTON E	AL	22E	82
CROFT JIMMY O'NEAL	SC	58W	3
CROKE ROBERT STANLEY	CA	52E	28
CROLEY JAMES ROBERT	TX	09E	37
CROMIE MICHAEL JOHN	MI	38W	6
CROMWELL EARL LEE	FL	04E	36
CROMWELL ROBERT WALTER	FL	36W	1
CRON JODY ALLEN	PA	45E	33
CRONE CARL RICHARD	TX	44W	36
CRONE DONALD EVERETT	CA	05W	106
CRONE GARY LEE	PA	35E	58
CRONIN BRIAN JOHN	CT	01E	75
CRONIN DAVID MICHAEL	IL	58W	23
CRONIN JAMES RUSSELL	AZ	16E	77
CRONIN JOHN EARL	IL	19E	116
CRONIN WILLIAM BERNARD	WV	18E	101
CRONK PAUL MARVIN JR	MA	30E	1
CRONK RICHARD EDWARD	MI	02E	65
CRONKHITE CHRISTOPHER	CT	18E	9
CRONKRITE CHARLES LIGON	TX	22E	24
CRONKRITE WOODROW CHARLES	MD	26E	43
CRONRATH STEVEN MARK	PA	11W	44
CROOK ELLIOTT	AZ	01W	26
CROOK JAMES PEYTON	CA	38E	76
CROOK JIMMY RAY	GA	21E	42
CROOK OREN LEE	MO	13W	87
CROOK THOMAS HARRY	WI	32W	94
CROOK THOMAS HIRAM	MO	62E	1
CROOK WILLIAM FELTON JR	AR	46W	39
CROOKS DOUGLAS EUGENE	IA	04W	101
CROOKS EDWARD TAUL	KY	09E	102
CROOKS LESTER LOIS	LA	05E	17
CROOKS RONALD LEE	NC	21E	66
CROOM HUBERT	MS	29E	81
CROOM MARION JR	DC	14W	45
CROOM RUFUS RAY	GA	18E	52
CROON GALE WALTER	IL	36W	10
CROPPER CURTIS HENRY	CA	12W	96
CROPPER RAY D	PA	40E	38
CROSBY ARTHUR ALLEN JR	CT	30W	1
CROSBY BRUCE ALLEN JR	NY	02W	125
CROSBY CHARLES DAVID	FL	27W	82
CROSBY FREDERICK PETER	FL	01E	129
CROSBY GERALD LEE	MD	08E	104
CROSBY HERBERT CHARLES	OK	14W	22
CROSBY JACKIE LAWRENCE	SC	29W	18
CROSBY JAMES ALLEN	CA	33E	56
CROSBY JAMES EDWARD	NC	17W	4
CROSBY LOUIS JOHN	MO	09W	115
CROSBY RICHARD ALEXANDER	WA	31E	23
CROSBY ROBERT BARRY	MS	13W	56
CROSBY ROBERT LEROY	MA	17W	9
CROSBY ROBERT MICHAEL	TX	40W	23
CROSBY ROLAND CLEMON	NC	57E	1
CROSBY ROLIN JAMES	DE	02W	63
CROSE JAMES CHARLES	WV	26W	7
CROSE RONALD ALAN	IL	30E	75
CROSIER CARL ROGER	WV	16E	119
CROSIER STEVEN SEBASTIAN	WA	08W	61
CROSLEY CHARLES RAYMOND	NY	10E	88
CROSS ARIEL LINDLEY	IA	52W	41
CROSS AVIN EUCLID	NC	11W	16
CROSS BENNIE LEE	IL	16E	34
CROSS EDWARD JOHN	OH	44E	67
CROSS FRANK WARREN	VA	44W	62
CROSS FREDERICK WILLARD	VA	08W	124
CROSS GARY LEE	MO	27W	44
CROSS HERBERT TERRELL	LA	48E	52
CROSS HUGH W	CA	24E	18
CROSS JAMES EMORY	OH	11W	44
CROSS JOSEPH ALEXANDER	PA	12E	73
CROSS LARRY EDWARD	IN	14E	127
CROSS MONROE WARD	CA	30E	54
CROSS SAMMY JOE	OK	39W	43
CROSS THOMAS JOHN	MO	15W	113
CROSSEN MICHAEL O	CA	21E	104
CROSSLAND RICHARD GUINN	TX	05E	10
CROSSLEY EUGENE	MI	40W	61
CROSSLEY JOSEPH	OH	18E	68
CROSSLEY MICHAEL LEE	TX	04W	84
CROSSLEY ORMAN LEE JR	NY	11E	55
CROSSMAN GREGORY JOHN	MI	52E	4
CROSSMAN MELVIN EUGENE	CO	31E	86
CROSSMAN WILLIAM HARRY	MI	21E	118
CROSSON GERALD JOSEPH JR	NY	61E	8
CROTHERS DANNY KAY	OH	32W	25
CROTHERS HOWARD ROBERT	WV	53E	29
CROTTS DONALD COLEMAN	SC	57W	7
CROTWELL BYRON HUGH	MS	04E	68
CROUCH ALBERT B	IA	10W	60
CROUCH JACK EMANUEL JR	IL	11E	6
CROUCH JIMMY LEELAND	TX	02E	94
CROUCH NATHAN EUGENE	MI	34W	92
CROUSE EDGAR FRANKLIN JR	VA	08W	34
CROUSE JEFFREY CHARLES	CA	23E	118
CROUSE JOHN RAYMOND	OH	55E	8
CROUSE LESLIE DEWAYNE	IA	45W	13
CROUSON MICHAEL LEE	ID	13E	26
CROUT KENNETH MILES	WA	17E	115
CROUTER ROBERT	NJ	64E	3
CROW CHARLES CURTIS	CA	49E	40
CROW DAVID LYNN	LA	07E	89
CROW DAVID REID IV	MS	27W	44
CROW EDWARD DAVID	GA	60E	9
CROW ENNIS EUGENE	NM	33E	17
CROW JAMES DENNIS	AZ	26W	61
CROW JESSIE FRANKLIN	WV	63E	7
CROW KENNETH LELAND	AR	11W	20
CROW LARRY EDWIN	MO	17W	66
CROW LINDSEY HOUSTON	MO	03E	100
CROW RAYMOND JACK JR	UT	02W	119
CROW RODGER PINKNEY	AL	07W	24
CROW THOMAS M	NC	03E	2
CROWDER HAROLD EDWARD	AR	30W	21
CROWDER HERBERT HAROLD	VA	14E	43
CROWDER HYLAN LYNN	MS	47W	38
CROWDER JOSEPH BERKLEY	VA	09E	129
CROWDER MICHAEL	AR	35W	37
CROWDER NEAL STEVEN	MO	04W	43
CROWDER RAYMOND D JR	PA	22E	10
CROWE CARL WAYNE	CA	10W	101
CROWE CHARLES DOUGLAS	TN	09E	27
CROWE DOUGLAS D	MA	42E	62
CROWE HAROLD MICHAEL	TX	03W	49
CROWE KEVIN ROBERT	MA	23W	71
CROWE RICHARD EYRE	CA	07E	117
CROWE RONALD GARY	AL	22W	19
CROWELL ARTHUR ALBERT	ME	66W	4
CROWELL ROGER BRIAN	NJ	36E	4
CROWELL SAMUEL GERALD	AL	13E	104
CROWLEY CARL LESLIE	WI	16W	28
CROWLEY JAMES ALLEN II	MA	41W	66
CROWLEY JOHN EDWARD	NY	08W	99
CROWLEY LELAND STEPHEN JR	UT	28W	102
CROWLEY RALPH HEMAN	MI	24W	113
CROWLEY ROBERT EDWARD	UT	48W	17
CROWTHER DONALD DAVID	MA	60E	19
CROXDALE JACK LEE II	LA	30E	23
CROXEN RICHARD LYNN	CA	04E	3
CROY JOHN LEE	IN	24W	74
CROY WILLARD WINSTON	GA	14W	12
CROY WILLIAM MARK	IN	10E	7
CROZIER DAVID PAUL	MD	23E	40
CRUCE CLAYTON LEON	FL	02E	15
CRUCE LEONARD ERWIN	NM	60W	27
CRUDEN DONALD JOSEPH	NJ	32E	71
CRUDO RICHARD FRANK	NY	21W	44
CRUGNOLA MARIO CHARLES JR	CT	24E	18
CRUICKSHANK WILLIAM ROY	FL	30W	100
CRUISE KENNETH T JR	CA	25W	97
CRUITT MICHAEL DOUGLAS	AL	35E	4
CRULL DALE ALTON	IL	52E	16
CRULL RAYMOND H	MI	12W	45
CRUM CURTIS RAY	OH	37W	16
CRUM DARYL WAYNE	CA	45E	19
CRUM DUANE	IL	03W	129
CRUM EDWARD WALDREN	IL	37E	53
CRUM ROBERT H JR	TX	07E	100
CRUM STEVEN VINCENT	IA	19W	29
CRUMBAKER LARRY HOMER	OH	17E	70
CRUMLEY ELDON GENE	NE	21W	44
CRUMLEY HARRY RICHARD	IA	04E	87
CRUMM WILLIAM JOSEPH	NY	23E	26
CRUMP BUCKNER JR	KY	21E	66
CRUMP CHARLES ALVIN	TX	20E	112
CRUMP ERSKINE LOGAN	CA	32W	37
CRUMP JACK VANN	AL	24W	83
CRUMP JESSIE LEE	KY	11E	121
CRUMP VICTOR LINCOLN	MD	31E	3
CRUMPTON EUGENE HAYWARD	GA	06W	36
CRUSE GARY ROBERT	GA	48W	40
CRUSE GEORGE LARRY	KS	54E	4
CRUSE JAMES DALE	KY	57W	24
CRUSE MICHAEL LEE	KY	32W	77
CRUSE STANLEY JOE	OK	09W	129
CRUSIE WILLIAM MICHAEL JR	NY	23W	84
CRUTCHER JOE ALBERT	FL	28E	21
CRUTCHER TERRY LYNN	IL	21W	6
CRUTCHFIELD CHARLES ELLIS	IL	05E	117
CRUTCHFIELD TERRY WAYNE	TN	58W	18
CRUTCHLEY DONALD CLAIR	MD	04E	22
CRUTHIRD GEORGE W	IL	37E	53
CRUTTS RALPH JOEL	MI	24W	38
CRUZ CARLOS RAFAEL	PR	32E	91
CRUZ EDWARD CRUZ	GM	56W	2
CRUZ ENRIQUE SALAS	GM	31W	78
CRUZ FRANK	WA	22W	74
CRUZ FRANK BRYAN	MI	24E	5
CRUZ JESUS ROSAS	OH	15E	104
CRUZ JOHNNY MANUEL	CA	24W	75
CRUZ JOSE MANUEL	NY	11E	90
CRUZ JOSEPH AGUIGUI	GM	07E	8
CRUZ JOSEPH WILLIAM	GM	24E	106
CRUZ LUIS	NY	49W	39
CRUZ LUIS ANTONIO	NY	06W	38

NAME	STATE	PANEL NO.	LINE NO.
CRUZ LUIS PHILIP	NY	26W	98
CRUZ OSCAR	CA	09E	66
CRUZ PEDRO AFLAGUE	GM	20E	82
CRUZ PETE FRANK	CA	38E	24
CRUZ RAPHAEL	CA	01E	28
CRUZ RICHARD PEREZ	TX	16E	119
CRUZ SAM	NM	27E	94
CRUZ TONY	AZ	18W	27
CRUZ VIRGIL GALAN	TX	02E	97
CRUZ-CRUZ RAFAEL	PR	32W	11
CRUZ-LEBRON GASPAR	PR	19W	66
CRUZ-VAZQUEZ ANGEL MANUEL	PR	52W	4
CRYAN KENNETH MICHAEL	CA	54E	32
CRYAR MICHAEL GEORGE	CA	07E	101
CRYDER ROBERT D	TX	45W	49
CRYSEL KENNETH LEE	OH	39E	44
CRYSTER JAMES PERRY III	PA	29E	94
CRYTZER RALPH WOODWARD JR	OH	19E	36
CUASITO RONALD PEREZ	GM	18W	38
CUBBAGE CLIFTON	DE	61E	8
CUBERO HECTOR	NY	27E	94
CUBIT BILLY RAY	IL	30E	62
CUCCIA DOMINICK LAWRENCE	NY	10W	120
CUCCINELLI ROBERT ALVANDR	NJ	52W	41
CUCH WILBERT WAYNE	UT	66W	4
CUDE HERSHEL DUANE JR	CO	02W	19
CUDLIKE CHARLES JOSEPH	MI	24W	39
CUDNIK EDMUND VICTOR	MI	36W	80
CUDWORTH ALBERT WAYNE	NY	47E	48
CUE CARL JAMES	NV	19E	11
CUE WILLIAM CHARLES	OH	50W	49
CUELLAR JULIAN CASTILLO	TX	06E	73
CUELLAR PILAR JOSEPH	CA	40W	36
CUEVAS FRANK OSCAR	IN	57W	7
CUEVAS-RIVERA ERNESTO	PR	13W	7
CUFF DICK E	IA	45E	39
CUFF DONALD MERRITT	DE	59W	21
CUKALE JOHN ANTHONY JR	WY	04W	9
CULBERTH ROBERT LEE JR	FL	31E	10
CULBERTSON GARY MORTEN	NE	41W	51
CULBERTSON SAMUEL KENT	CA	58E	18
CULBREATH JOHNIE KING	FL	01E	113
CULHANE GERALD AUGUSTINE	NY	26E	59
CULL HERMAN RAY	IN	21E	77
CULLEN DENNIS JOHN	CA	08E	91
CULLEN KENNETH ARTHUR	FL	18E	2
CULLEN MARK JAMES	NY	31E	63
CULLEN RICHARD IVORY	PA	66E	7
CULLEN RICHARD LEE	IA	36E	68
CULLEN THOMAS JOSEPH	NY	29E	49
CULLERS RONALD KENNETH	MO	09E	23
CULLETON CARSON GREGORY	IL	50W	5
CULLINAN JOHN PATRICK	CT	34E	16
CULLINS ALVIN	FL	26E	23
CULLISON BARRY ANDREWS	IN	17E	78
CULLNAN LARRY LAWRENCE	CO	52W	42
CULLUM DENNIS OWEN	OK	62E	1
CULOTTA ANTHONY THOMAS	OH	39W	58
CULP DAVID JR	NC	47E	9
CULP EVERETT T	IN	28W	58
CULP JOHN PAUL	SC	36E	68
CULP KARL HOWARD	TX	27W	93
CULP RICHARD THOMAS	OH	34W	22
CULP THOMAS DALE	OH	26E	55
CULPEPPER ALLEN ROSS	LA	24W	39
CULSHAW DONALD IGNATIUS	MN	36W	62
CULVER ALFONZIE	AL	27E	88
CULVER ARCHIE GLENN	TX	20W	28
CULVER DARYL CHESTER	TN	49W	22
CULVER DICK DAVIS	TX	18E	84
CULVER PHILIP LEE	MA	56E	21
CULVER RAYMOND WALTER	CO	02W	13
CULVER ROBERT WAYNE	CA	12W	12
CULVER WILLIAM RONALD	TX	14W	106
CULVERHOUSE LEON THOMAS	CA	23W	51
CULVEY KENNETH LEROY	SC	23E	69
CULWELL JAMES RONALD	OH	16W	78
CULWELL JIMMY LEE	TX	33W	13
CUMBEE JIMMY DEAN	GA	23W	51
CUMBERLAND PAUL ANTHONY	MD	31W	78
CUMBERPATCH JAMES R JR	MD	08E	79
CUMBIE HAROLD ERVIN	AR	30E	55

NAME	STATE	PANEL NO.	LINE NO.
CUMBIE WILLIAM THOMAS	FL	33W	92
CUMBO LINWOOD RAY	NC	33W	80
CUMBRY JOHN EDWARD	TX	48W	24
CUMISKEY JAMES LEE	OK	21E	97
CUMMINGS CHARLES HENRY	MA	13W	115
CUMMINGS CHESTER ARTHUR	MA	19E	23
CUMMINGS DALLAS DEWEY	IN	40E	3
CUMMINGS DANIEL TERRY	NJ	14E	43
CUMMINGS DAVE JR	TN	34E	16
CUMMINGS DAVID GUY	CA	31W	65
CUMMINGS DAVID NEWTON	OR	19E	117
CUMMINGS DONALD LOUIS JR	CA	31E	57
CUMMINGS HAROLD VAN JR	MS	11W	3
CUMMINGS HAROLD WARREN JR	MA	31E	33
CUMMINGS JAMES BARTON JR	CA	16E	77
CUMMINGS JAMES E JR	VA	39W	53
CUMMINGS JAMES EDWARD	NY	32W	94
CUMMINGS JAMES EDWARD	FL	10W	49
CUMMINGS JAMES LONEL	MS	65W	6
CUMMINGS JAMES THOMAS JR	IL	47E	10
CUMMINGS KENNETH THOMAS	NY	18W	31
CUMMINGS LONZO SILAS	WV	32W	4
CUMMINGS NATHANIEL	AR	58W	7
CUMMINGS PAUL JOSEPH JR	FL	41W	57
CUMMINGS RALPH RONALD	NH	12W	17
CUMMINGS RICHARD MICHAEL	PA	14E	24
CUMMINGS ROBERT GEORGE JR	NY	10E	105
CUMMINGS ROGER WAYNE	IN	26W	13
CUMMINGS RONALD EUGENE	CA	04E	7
CUMMINGS STEPHEN WILLIAM	MA	27W	85
CUMMINGS THOMAS FRANCIS	PA	52E	16
CUMMINGS WILLIAM LARRY	FL	28E	45
CUMMINS JOHN RUDOLPH JR	NM	10E	105
CUMMINS LANNY DEE	CA	62E	2
CUMMINS RICHARD LEROY	SD	17W	61
CUMMINS STEVEN TRAVIS	FL	21W	107
CUMMINS THOMAS WAYNE	CA	25W	65
CUNDIFF ROBERT EUGENE	KY	46E	31
CUNEEN MICHAEL RAY	PA	06E	84
CUNEO ANDRA JR	CA	07E	5
CUNEO STEVE CLYDE	WA	22E	91
CUNNANE DENNIS THOMAS	PA	36E	4
CUNNINGHAM BILLY	AR	25E	11
CUNNINGHAM BRUCE EDWARD	PA	38E	24
CUNNINGHAM BRUCE WAYNE	CO	30E	39
CUNNINGHAM CAREY ALLEN	AL	24E	66
CUNNINGHAM CARL EDWIN	KS	20W	5
CUNNINGHAM CHARLES ROBERT	OH	28W	97
CUNNINGHAM CLARENCE BENO	NY	40W	27
CUNNINGHAM DAVID CARSON	CA	17E	34
CUNNINGHAM DENNIS ANTHONY	MI	19W	85
CUNNINGHAM DENNIS LANE	TX	45E	9
CUNNINGHAM DONNIE LEE	MO	06W	67
CUNNINGHAM EDWARD	NY	43W	3
CUNNINGHAM GEORGE MICHAEL	CA	42W	4
CUNNINGHAM JACOB H III	NC	15E	28
CUNNINGHAM JAMES ANDREW	TN	17E	17
CUNNINGHAM JAMES EARL	TN	07E	9
CUNNINGHAM JAMES LEON	IA	15E	104
CUNNINGHAM JERRY MAX	MI	14W	25
CUNNINGHAM JESSE J JR	AR	55W	27
CUNNINGHAM JOHN EDD JR	TN	49E	30
CUNNINGHAM JOSEPH W JR	CA	10W	19
CUNNINGHAM KENNETH LEROY	IL	17W	33
CUNNINGHAM KENT ALAN	WI	40W	73
CUNNINGHAM LARRY ALFONSO	DC	26W	82
CUNNINGHAM LARRY LA MONT	MS	37W	30
CUNNINGHAM LEONARD DWIGHT	TN	13W	116
CUNNINGHAM LOUIS JAMES	SD	04E	27
CUNNINGHAM NORMAN NORTHRO	CA	42W	4
CUNNINGHAM PRINCE CHARLES	NY	05E	10
CUNNINGHAM RICHARD IRA	NE	26W	61
CUNNINGHAM RICHARD SAVAGE	MD	10W	39
CUNNINGHAM ROBERT JAMES	MA	08W	6
CUNNINGHAM ROBERT MAURICE	IL	27W	106
CUNNINGHAM RONALD CHARLES	MN	38W	72
CUNNINGHAM STEPHEN EARL	OH	19W	100
CUNNINGHAM STEPHEN RAE	CO	44E	25
CUNNINGHAM WALTER WAYNE	MI	28E	102
CUNNINGHAM WELLS ELDON	MO	10E	15
CUNNINGHAM WILLIAM LEDFOR	WI	42E	14
CUNNINGHAM WILLIAM NEAL	VA	15W	102

NAME	STATE	PANEL NO.	LINE NO.
CUNNION MICHAEL ALFRED	NY	09E	23
CUOZZO FRANK XAVIER	CA	19E	79
CUPP ERNEST BRYAN	AL	17E	103
CUPP JOHN CHARLES	IN	57W	8
CUPP ROBERT WILLIAM	VA	60W	27
CUPPLES GARY CURTIS	AR	21E	26
CURBOW BILLY JOE	AR	33W	92
CURCI ANTHONY BOY	CA	30W	11
CURD RICHARD LOWELL	WV	25E	6
CURETON JOHNNY JACOB JR	SC	19W	1
CURETON RONNIE CHARLES	MO	45E	62
CURIEL SAM TRINIDAD	TX	26E	7
CURL FRANKLIN NEWTON	MT	39W	40
CURL ROBERT GRAHAM	MI	15W	16
CURLEE JOHNNIE M	OH	06E	37
CURLEE ROBERT LEE JR	NC	02E	4
CURLESS EUGENE JEROME JR	NY	46E	15
CURLEY ALBERT ALLEN	NM	17E	70
CURLEY RAYMOND NELSON	CA	37E	34
CURLEY ROOSEVELT C JR	MI	23E	98
CURRAN DANIEL JOSEPH	MI	28W	89
CURRAN JAMES R	AZ	16E	111
CURRAN JOHN DEHAAS	AZ	03W	54
CURRAN MICHAEL PATRICK	OH	22W	12
CURRAN PATRICK ROBERT	IL	17W	18
CURRAN PAUL WILLIAM	MA	16E	8
CURRAN PHILIP ROBERT	OH	25E	56
CURRAN ROBERT BRUCE	IL	03W	123
CURRENCE EVERETT AUSTIN	WV	09E	73
CURRENCE WILLIAM ALLEN	CA	34W	6
CURRETHERS JEFF	MI	16E	100
CURRIE ANDREW	TN	23E	1
CURRIE ANTHONY EUGENE	TX	11W	6
CURRIE GEORGE CRAWFORD	CT	55W	18
CURRIE JAMES JR	SC	46W	48
CURRIER GERALD FRANCIS	MA	12E	20
CURRIER GORDON LEROY JR	MO	36E	4
CURRIER PHILIP BUCHANAN	VT	34W	13
CURRIER RICHARD JAMES JR	FL	09E	66
CURRIN JERRY WAYNE	NC	17E	71
CURRY ALVIN CHRISTOPH	VA	03W	44
CURRY DICKIE CARSON	VA	08W	63
CURRY DOUGLAS RAY	TX	09W	55
CURRY FRANCIS MICHAEL	NY	04W	48
CURRY GEORGE DEVER	NJ	09E	93
CURRY GLENN VERNARD	MI	05E	45
CURRY HOVEY RICE	PA	33E	82
CURRY JACK HENRY	CT	36W	68
CURRY JAMES JOSEPH	MA	28W	102
CURRY JIMMY DOUGLAS	CA	26E	100
CURRY JIMMY LEE	GA	52E	35
CURRY KEITH ROYAL WILSON	WV	05W	33
CURRY LARRY EDWARD	VA	52W	34
CURRY M L	MS	37E	34
CURRY MARVIN ELLIS	MO	03E	8
CURRY RICHARD JOHN	PA	32W	94
CURRY ROBERT ERVEN	CA	13E	104
CURRY ROBERT LOUIS	MA	17E	71
CURRY ROY JERRY	OR	22W	74
CURRY WENDELL PAUL	PA	17W	45
CURRY WILBUR JR	NY	03E	54
CURRY WILLIAM RIEVES	KY	53W	26
CURTIN DONALD LEO	MA	22W	87
CURTIN JAMES CHRISTOPHER	IL	35E	37
CURTIN JOHN GERALD	CT	18E	89
CURTIN JOHN HENRY	IL	33E	17
CURTIN JOHN III	NJ	46W	28
CURTIS ALAN DENNIS	RI	15W	31
CURTIS BERNARD EUGENE	MD	08E	120
CURTIS BRUCE WAYNE	MI	31W	45
CURTIS DAVID ALLEN	NY	22W	57
CURTIS DAVID LEE	ID	03W	79
CURTIS FREDERICK N	MA	23W	7
CURTIS GARY ALLEN	TN	15E	42
CURTIS GARY STILLMAN	CA	24E	109
CURTIS GREGORY PAUL	WA	31E	90
CURTIS HAROLD GENE	TN	17W	95
CURTIS HENRY THOMAS II	VA	51E	41
CURTIS HERBERT RAY	TX	38W	24
CURTIS JAMES MARVIN	ID	39W	70
CURTIS JERRY JAMES	AR	19W	66
CURTIS JOSEPH PAUL	MD	06W	126

NAME	STATE	PANEL NO.	LINE NO.
CURTIS LARRY GENE	TN	33W	30
CURTIS RICHARD	CA	31E	84
CURTIS ROBERT JOHN	OH	05W	13
CURTIS ROGER DALE	CA	26W	33
CURTIS RONALD GAY	WA	05W	131
CURTIS TERRY MELVIN	MI	39E	3
CURTIS THOMAS GUY JR	FL	35E	20
CURTIS THOMAS MICHAEL	WI	16W	17
CURTISS EDWIN HARRY	PA	07W	134
CURTTRIGHT LARRY BRENT	CA	31W	90
CUSHEN KENNETH	CT	31E	97
CUSHING DAVID ROY	TX	20E	114
CUSHMAN CLIFTON EMMET	ND	11E	13
CUSHMAN HAROLD EDWARD	NY	19W	92
CUSHMAN JOHN ROBERT	MI	16E	120
CUSHMAN KENNETH GEORGE	PA	44W	46
CUSICK MICHAEL PETER	NY	38W	56
CUSSINS LOUIS WADE	MI	40E	3
CUSSON THOMAS LEE	CA	09W	72
CUSTEN HENRY DAVID	MD	32W	97
CUSTER GEORGE PAUL	WV	20E	83
CUSTODE RALPH	NJ	17W	87
CUSUMANO ANTHONY MICHAEL	NY	33W	30
CUTBIRTH KENDELL DWAYNE	TX	15E	89
CUTBIRTH RICHARD EUGENE	MO	64W	7
CUTCHINS ROLAND A	VA	17E	49
CUTHBERT BRADLEY GENE	IA	38W	41
CUTHBERT GEORGE RICHARD	MI	12W	55
CUTHBERT LOWRY TAYLOR	CA	17W	6
CUTHBERT STEPHEN HOWARD	CA	01W	52
CUTINHA NICHOLAS JOSEPH	FL	42E	30
CUTLER DONALD EARL	IN	25E	91
CUTLER JAMES IRVING	MI	35W	3
CUTLER RALPH LOUIS	MI	26W	44
CUTLER RICHARD ALLEN	IL	20W	28
CUTRELL NICKEY WADE	NC	34W	6
CUTRER FRED CLAY JR	MS	01E	60
CUTRER MARVIN EUGENE	LA	20E	13
CUTRI MICHAEL JOHN	NY	64W	7
CUTSHALL DAVID WARREN	SD	43E	52
CUTSHAW WILLIAM	TN	04E	76
CUTTER WILLIAM SCOTT	OK	31E	28
CUTTING JERRY WOODROW	IA	05W	62
CUTTING WILLIAM STANLEY	NH	47E	31
CWIKLA LEROY WALTER	WI	17E	50
CWIOK FRANK JOHN	IL	12W	20
CYGON STANLEY JOHN	NJ	47E	48
CYMBALSKI KENNETH JULIAN	MD	21W	92
CYR LAWRENCE JOSEPH	ME	33E	82
CYR PAUL LEO	ME	18E	115
CYR RANSOM CRAIG	WA	64W	7
CYR WAYNE CLIFTON	ME	56E	22
CYR WILLIAM JOSEPH	MA	36E	5
CYR WILLIAM LOUIS	MT	12E	41
CYRÁN RICHARD EDWARD	NJ	23W	84
CYSEWSKI GARY FRANCIS	MN	44W	23
CZAJAK DANIEL JOSEPH JR	NY	41W	4
CZAJKOWSKI JOSEPH VERBERT	MD	65E	7
CZARNECKI STEVEN CHARLES	CA	35W	11
CZARNOTA CHRISTOPHER ZENO	NJ	04W	65
CZARNY WILLIAM EUGENE	IN	19E	71
CZECHOWSKI JOHN LOUIS JR	AZ	51E	18
CZERWIEC RAYMOND GEORGE	IL	28W	59
CZERWONKA AUGUST EMIL	IL	52W	22
CZERWONKA PAUL STEVEN	MA	58E	6
CZZOWITZ THOMAS EUGENE	PA	02E	79
D'ADAMO ALBERT L JR	NJ	28W	67
D'ADAMO JOHN JR	NJ	38E	66
D'AGOSTINO JOHN	NY	30E	40
D'AGOSTINO JOHN R JR	WI	53E	11
D'AGOSTINO NORMAN THOMAS	NY	39E	27
D'AGRELLA MICHAEL LOUIS	TX	17W	40
D'AIELLO MICHAEL DENNIS	CA	27E	43
D'AMBRA JOSEPH NICK	NY	57E	18
D'AMICO FRANK ANTHONY	MA	06E	109
D'AMICO PHILIP ANTHONY JR	PA	48W	40
D'AMICO ROBERT JOSEPH	NY	24E	58
D'ANGELICO JOSEPH MICHAEL	NY	15W	117
D'ANGELO RAYMOND ANTHONY	NY	64W	7
D'EMANUELE ROBERT PAUL	CA	43W	3
D'ENTREMONT LARRY AIME	ME	30E	40
D'EUSTACHIO THOMAS GERARD	NY	36E	45

NAME	STATE	PANEL NO.	LINE NO.
D'ORSAY DOUGLAS HAROLD	MA	02E	18
DA COSTA JACK RICHARD	CT	15W	16
DA PONTE ANTHONY	NJ	64W	7
DAANE DOUGLAS JACK	WI	10W	129
DABBERT WILLIAM CARL	IL	21W	28
DABBS ALAN COURTNEY	TX	48W	53
DABNEY HAROLD THOMAS	CO	34W	6
DABNEY RICHARD EARL JR	TX	08E	1
DABON NATHANIEL	IL	28E	8
DABONKA JOHN ANTHONY	NJ	14E	107
DABREU DANIEL JOHN	MA	60W	8
DACANAY FRANCISCO DE LA C		14E	20
DACEY BERTRAND JAHN	NY	26W	61
DACUS FREDDIE LOUIS	TX	06W	53
DACUS WILLIAM FLOYD	AR	11W	49
DACY JAMES WESLEY	OK	45W	32
DADANTE LEONARD JOHN	OH	02E	78
DADISMAN GORDON ALAN	OH	08W	90
DADISMAN MICHAEL RAYMOND	DE	09W	88
DAFFER JOSEPH JOHN	CA	44E	5
DAFFIN GARY ROBERT	MD	43W	3
DAFFRON JIMMY SHERMAN	OR	12E	73
DAFFRON THOMAS CARL	IL	13W	27
DAFLER DEAN BLAIN	OR	11W	6
DAGGER CARL RICHARD	OH	62E	2
DAGLEY GARY GENE	NE	25W	46
DAGNON MICHAEL ERWIN	IL	17W	96
DAHILL DOUGLAS EDWARD	OH	27W	99
DAHL ALBERT EUGENE	IL	59E	18
DAHL JAMES STEPHEN	WI	60E	9
DAHL KENNETH ALAN	CA	05W	37
DAHL LARRY GILBERT	OR	05W	132
DAHL TIMOTHY ALLEN	WI	17W	20
DAHL WILLIAM JOHN	MN	15W	89
DAHLIN DAVID COURTNEY	CA	44W	36
DAHLMAN GEORGE CLARENCE	WI	27W	106
DAHM RALPH ALBERT	WI	38E	24
DAHMS LARRY ALBERT	IA	06W	66
DAHR JOHN WESLEY	PA	13E	125
DAIELLO VINCENT THOMAS	NY	36W	49
DAIGLE BENNETT JOSEPH	ME	07W	106
DAIGLE BRADLEY TIMOTHY	LA	15E	3
DAIGLE JAMES CHARLES	MA	10W	40
DAIGLE JOSEPH DEWEY	LA	27E	99
DAIGLE LOUIS VINNIE	NY	42W	46
DAIGNEAULT JOSEPH RICHARD	MA	64E	3
DAIGREPONT ROBERT LYNN	LA	54W	34
DAIL WILLIE FRED JR	TN	33E	7
DAILEY BILLY JACKSON	MO	10E	131
DAILEY BOBBY RAY	IL	06W	134
DAILEY DAVID LEON	WA	10W	69
DAILEY DOUGLAS VINCENT	MI	36W	14
DAILEY FRANCIS EDWIN	AL	08E	24
DAILEY GEORGE FREDERICK	WI	07E	52
DAILEY GERALD LEE	NY	04E	64
DAILEY HAROLD CARL II	TX	46W	62
DAILEY JAMES ALBERT	KY	30E	14
DAILEY JERRY MICHAEL	TX	23W	72
DAILEY KEVIN MELBOURNE	CA	17E	28
DAILEY LARRY EUGENE	WV	13W	67
DAILEY PAUL MARION	WV	11W	79
DAILEY RONALD CHARLES	OH	21E	10
DAILEY WILLIAM GRANT JR	IL	18E	113
DAILY DAVID CHRISTOPHER	WA	34E	16
DAILY SAM WEBSTER	OK	11E	44
DAILY THOMAS BLAKE	CA	20E	72
DAINS PAUL LELAND	MO	37W	62
DAINS ROGER ALLAN	MI	51E	29
DAIR ALBERT JOSEPH	LA	43W	26
DAISHER DAVID CHARLES	OH	49W	52
DAL PAZZO ANTHONY JR	CA	01W	113
DALBERG DEAN LAVERNE	WI	43E	5
DALE BENNIE	AZ	59E	3
DALE CAROL DEAN	NC	12W	17
DALE CHARLES ALVA	AZ	02E	2
DALE CHARLES RICHARD	MD	05E	64
DALE CHESTER DONALD	NM	40W	76
DALE DENNIS HUMPHREY	MD	06W	73
DALE DONALD MILTON	IL	39E	44
DALE GEORGE LOUIS	NH	56E	5
DALE JAMES MILTON	MO	16W	98
DALE TERRENCE MICHAEL	IN	40E	61

NAME	STATE	PANEL NO.	LINE NO.
DALENTA ZBIGNIEW JOSEF	CA	04W	9
DALEY DANIEL WILLIAM	NJ	53E	29
DALEY GERALD CHARLES	NJ	21W	36
DALEY MICHAEL JAMES	NJ	16E	89
DALEY PAUL MICHAEL	MA	25E	37
DALEY RAYMOND COYLE	NH	54W	41
DALEY RICHARD JOHN	MA	25W	10
DALEY ROBERT F	MA	18W	94
DALEY RONALD PAUL	MA	01W	77
DALEY TERRENCE JOSEPH	OH	07E	117
DALEY WALTER RALPH	MA	14E	103
DALEY WALTON GARLAND	NY	31W	45
DALEY WILLIAM	IL	33W	13
DALEY WILLIAM MICHAEL	MA	31E	28
DALGLIESH MARK ANTHONY	TX	20E	24
DALHOUSE JOHN DUDLEY	AL	54W	41
DALIE LOUIE FRANK	IL	23W	73
DALKE BURTON WARD	NY	25W	11
DALLAPE TERRY LEE	IL	20W	75
DALLAS RICHARD HOWARD	TN	18E	101
DALMAN LEONARD JAMES	MO	59E	1
DALOLA JOHN FRANCIS III	PA	11E	56
DALRYMPLE LESLIE AARON	ME	16W	98
DALRYMPLE ROGER EARL	CA	30E	7
DALRYMPLE WILLIAM RAY	WA	20E	113
DALTON BILL NORMAN	UT	38E	24
DALTON CLARENCE ELMER JR	CO	29E	39
DALTON DAVID JAMES	FL	19E	116
DALTON DONALD EVERETT	OR	23W	14
DALTON EDWARD JOSEPH JR	MA	10E	4
DALTON GORDON THOMAS	OH	32E	71
DALTON JAMES ALBERT	NJ	45W	5
DALTON JAMES GILBERT	OK	14W	28
DALTON JAMES WENDALL	OH	32W	58
DALTON JOHN	NJ	42W	46
DALTON JOHN MICHAEL	IL	12E	99
DALTON MAJOR ROY JR	WV	13E	107
DALTON MICHAEL FRANCIS	MO	60E	10
DALTON MICHAEL JOSEPH	MO	16W	73
DALTON MICHAEL MORAN	RI	03W	71
DALTON RANDALL DAVID	IL	03W	113
DALTON ROBERT ALAN	OH	29W	97
DALTON ROBERT LE ROY	CA	15W	16
DALTON ROBERT LLOYD	MI	05W	120
DALTON THEODORE HUBERT	PA	40W	74
DALTON TOUSSAINT O JR	MD	06W	15
DALY EUGENE THOMAS JR	MA	39W	7
DALY JAMES JOSEPH	NY	07W	69
DALY JOSEPH FRANCIS	PA	18E	74
DALY RICHARD VINCENT	NY	50W	19
DALY TIMOTHY	NJ	14E	111
DAMATO PAUL JOHN JR	MA	05W	4
DAMBECK ROBERT CARL	PA	23E	26
DAMERON LARRY RAY	NC	15W	47
DAMERON ROBERT WOODROW	VA	54E	32
DAMEWOOD DONNIE LEE	TN	47W	26
DAMIAN ALLAN JAMES	GM	22E	69
DAMIANO LEROY EDWARD	ID	39E	4
DAMITIO MARTIN LEO	WA	25W	97
DAMM THOMAS WILLIAM	WI	09W	126
DAMMER WILHELM KARL	NY	55E	8
DAMON MICHAEL PATRICK	CA	05W	113
DAMRON WILLIAM THOMAS	FL	37W	10
DAMROW OLIVER PIERCE	MI	23E	50
DAMSCHEN RICHARD A JR	WA	47W	17
DAMSGARD CHARLES DE WAYNE	MN	13E	21
DANA ROGER JOSEPH	MA	59E	20
DANAY JERRY LEE	IL	04W	40
DANBERRY CHARLES LABAW	NJ	66E	8
DANCE ALAN	NY	10E	100
DANCE JACK RAY	IN	34W	32
DANCE LAWRENCE RUSSELL	VA	03W	35
DANCE ROBERT LYNN	CA	20W	112
DANCER WALTER JAMES	FL	54E	24
DANCHETZ LESTER	NJ	30W	86
DANCY ARTHUR LEE	NC	14E	71
DANDO THOMAS J	NJ	16E	111
DANDRIDGE ALBERT	MS	40E	19
DANDURAND JAY THOMAS	NJ	13W	116
DANDY CURTIS E	CO	56E	5
DANEHART EDWIN RUSSELL	WV	25W	22
DANFORD JAMES ISAH E	FL	13E	121

NAME	STATE	PANEL NO.	LINE NO.
DANGBERG ROBERT LEE	NE	11W	20
DANIEL ANDREW JAMES	NY	36E	69
DANIEL CANTRELL MONRO III	GA	03W	19
DANIEL CHARLES LINCOLN	VA	36E	5
DANIEL ELIJAH JR	AL	11E	97
DANIEL FRED JACOBO	AZ	22W	31
DANIEL FREDDIE LAWS	OH	21W	22
DANIEL JAMES LEE	TN	25E	82
DANIEL JAMES ROBERT	GA	22W	87
DANIEL JOHNNIE LINCOLN	SC	11E	44
DANIEL JOHNNIE LLOYD	CA	62W	7
DANIEL MATHIS	IL	43E	43
DANIEL OLLIE JAMES	MS	27W	24
DANIEL ROBERT G	AL	29W	52
DANIEL STEPHEN ARTHUR	TX	27W	21
DANIELL THOMAS FRED	GA	17W	95
DANIELLES DEIGHTON ALONZO	PA	26E	44
DANIELS BRUCE WILLIAM	CA	28W	80
DANIELS CARL STEPHEN	LA	03E	17
DANIELS CHARLES E	NY	45E	54
DANIELS CHARLES WESLEY JR	OK	27E	19
DANIELS CHARLIES E	MI	05E	79
DANIELS CHRISTOPHER MICHAEL	NJ	37E	5
DANIELS CURTIS RAY	MO	23W	14
DANIELS DANNY EARL	SC	38E	27
DANIELS DAVID RICHARD	NY	15E	126
DANIELS DONALD EDWARD	NC	05E	32
DANIELS EARL JR	GA	22E	65
DANIELS EDWARD EARL	VA	39W	20
DANIELS EDWARD STEVEN	NJ	08E	52
DANIELS ELDRIDGE MAURICE	IL	35W	25
DANIELS FRANCIS ANTHONY M	PA	64W	8
DANIELS GARY LEONARD	FL	52E	47
DANIELS GEORGE HOWARD II	WA	18W	32
DANIELS GEORGE W JR	PA	07W	120
DANIELS HARLAN EUGENE	CA	12W	122
DANIELS HAROLD DWAINE	TX	50E	13
DANIELS JAMES AURTHUR	CT	11E	39
DANIELS JAMES DENNIS	GA	11E	91
DANIELS JAMES MICHAEL	KS	26E	23
DANIELS JAMES RICHARD	NC	20W	55
DANIELS JOHN FRANCIS JR	PA	17E	93
DANIELS JOHNIE NATHANIEL	AR	15E	32
DANIELS JOSEPH RAY JR	OH	36W	48
DANIELS JOSEPHUS	NC	21W	36
DANIELS JOSHUA MARICE	NJ	05W	55
DANIELS LARRY DEAN	NC	54E	32
DANIELS LARRY PHILLIP	CA	12W	102
DANIELS LAWRENCE EDWARD	IL	09E	66
DANIELS LEROY BUDDY	PA	33W	37
DANIELS LUNAS JONAS	NC	39E	44
DANIELS MARK FRANCIS	MI	29W	66
DANIELS PAUL FREEMAN JR	MS	63E	7
DANIELS RAYMOND LOUIS	LA	48W	10
DANIELS REX MARTIN	NY	04W	128
DANIELS RICHARD CARLTON	NC	22W	118
DANIELS RICHARD GALE	OH	44W	23
DANIELS ROBERT BLAINE	NC	20E	128
DANIELS RUSSELL GLEN	AZ	06W	66
DANIELS THOMAS JAMES	CA	26E	82
DANIELS THOMAS RAY	MN	32W	64
DANIELS TOMMY LEON	CA	32E	62
DANIELS WALTER EUGENE	AL	12E	73
DANIELS WILLIAM ALVIN JR	TX	22W	104
DANIELS WILLIAM JR	CA	24W	4
DANIELS WILLIAM MARCUS	OH	39E	44
DANIELSON BENJAMIN FRANKLIN	MN	15W	26
DANIELSON CHARLES F JR	PA	16W	12
DANIELSON LEE ROGER	WI	34E	35
DANIELSON MARK GILES	CO	01W	44
DANILUCK PETER JOSEPH	NY	42W	16
DANISON JOSEPH WILLIAM	OH	18W	79
DANKERT ROBERT SHELDON	MI	23W	72
DANKOWSKI JAMES HILLARY	MI	21W	12
DANN DAVID BRIAN	WI	12E	41
DANNA JOSEPH JOHN JR	NJ	06W	124
DANNA SAMUEL DON	CA	12E	66
DANNEELS ROBERT HAROLD	MI	08E	91
DANNER JESSIE JAMES	MS	66W	5
DANOWSKI DAVID LEE	PA	05E	83
DANOWSKI THOMAS GEORGE	NJ	36W	44
DANSBY CHARLES M	TX	01E	108
DANSBY EMMIT CHARLES	AR	59E	2
DANSER GARY RICHARD	CA	23E	93
DANTZLER KENNETH JAMES	NC	17E	84
DANTZLER WILL ROY	MS	02W	76
DARBY JAMES MICHAEL	LA	42E	48
DARBY JIMMY EARL	AL	23E	41
DARBY JOHN FREDERICK III	FL	33W	27
DARBY PAUL	LA	05W	48
DARCY EDWARD JOSEPH	ME	32E	92
DARCY JAMES LEO	MT	17E	111
DARCY MICHAEL CHAVEZ	CA	07E	58
DARDAR CLARENCE JR	LA	30E	76
DARDEAU OSCAR MOISE JR	LA	30E	14
DARDEN CLAUDE JR	DC	33E	27
DARDEN LARRY EUEL	FL	47E	31
DARDEN OTIS JAMES	CA	33W	47
DARDEN PAUL L JR	NC	57E	1
DARDEN WILLIAM HENRY	MI	24W	93
DARGAN JEFFREY LYNN	DC	57W	8
DARLINE JOSEPH A III	NH		
DARLING ALBERT JAMES III	NY	19E	79
DARLING DENNIS THOMAS	AZ	04W	60
DARLING FRANK MAXWELL	WY	51E	6
DARLING GEORGE ROBERT	ME	08E	52
DARLING JOHN EDWARD JR	MI	10W	61
DARLING LARRY WAYNE	IN	40E	19
DARLING LLOYD THOMAS	NY	45W	49
DARLING ROBERT HARRY	PA	29E	28
DARLING ROLLAND EUGENE JR	MI	37W	79
DARLING THOMAS DUANE	TN	16E	120
DARNALL DON EDWARD	OR	11E	97
DARNELL DANA CORNELL	SC	18E	91
DARNELL GEORGE RICHARD	NY	21E	77
DARNELL GEORGE W JR	OH	57E	18
DARNELL HAROLD DALE	TX	14W	48
DARNELL JIMMY ALLEN	MO	39E	19
DARNELL MICHAEL EDWARD	TN	14W	25
DARNELL WILLIAM EUGENE	IN	45E	33
DARR AARON LEE	IL	13W	116
DARR CHARLES EDWARD	AR	01W	98
DARRAH GARY KOYLE	CA	62W	22
DARRAH MICHAEL LEE	NV	02W	38
DARRETT TYRONE	TX	23E	85
DARRIGAN RAYMOND MAURICE	MA	14E	128
DARRISAW CURTIS	GA	32W	95
DARROW DONNIE LEN	MO	31E	10
DART DANNY JOE	OK	61W	22
DART LAWRENCE MICHAEL	IA	16W	42
DART WALTER JOSEPH JR	NY	23W	98
DARTT PAUL RICHARD	VT	40W	27
DARTY OMER GENE	KS	04E	7
DARVILLE EDWARD R III	FL	48W	39
DARWIN JAMES DAVID	AL	18W	79
DASARO AGOSTINO WILLIAM	NY	15E	41
DASCOMBE RONALD EUGENE	PA	20W	18
DASEN GERALD RANDAL III	OH	16W	73
DASH DAVID WINTHROP	SC	11W	83
DASH SAMUEL LEE JR	NY	25E	98
DASHER GARY JOHN	OK	27W	72
DASHNAW JOHN MYRON	NY	36E	69
DASHNER GILFORD FRANK	MA	43W	26
DASHO GEORGE ALBERT F JR	IL	27W	48
DASILVA RAYMOND M JR	PA	57E	1
DASTOLI JOSEPH PETER	MD	10W	123
DATENA VINCENT ANTHONY	NY	42E	49
DAU KENNETH RUSSELL	MN	31E	97
DAUBENDIEK RAYMOND M	CO	01W	26
DAUBER JERRY MARTIN	NY	38W	72
DAUBERT EDWARD LYNN	PA	43W	53
DAUBERT WILLIAM JOHN	MD	27W	48
DAUCH GARY LEONARD	OH	40W	74
DAUGHERTY CECIL	KY	18W	116
DAUGHERTY DENNIS MICHAEL	IL	13W	81
DAUGHERTY DONALD D	CA	06E	109
DAUGHERTY EVERETT L JR	MO	41W	43
DAUGHERTY JAMES ALEXANDER	PA	57E	13
DAUGHERTY JAMES OLIVER JR	VA	27W	9
DAUGHERTY RALPH OLEN JR	GA	41W	70
DAUGHERTY RICHARD LAWRENCE	IL	46W	26
DAUGHERTY ROBERT LEE	TX	02W	112
DAUGHERTY RONNIE JOE	TN	67E	8
DAUGHERTY THOMAS LEE ROY	OH	16W	125
DAUGHERTY WILLIAM DON	TN	14E	117
DAUGHERTY WILLIAM STANLEY	IN	21E	43
DAUGHTON JOSEPH D JR	CA	39E	19
DAULTON JAMES HAROLD	KY	13E	43
DAULTON WILLIAM MANSON	IN	06W	18
DAUNIS JOSEPH	MI	28E	43
DAUPHINE ROBERT JR	LA	13E	108
DAUT CHARLES WILLIAM	PA	19E	57
DAUTEN FREDERICK W JR	CT	12W	91
DAUTREMONT DENNIS DALE	IA	33E	27
DAVAN BENEDICT MAHER	ME	29W	59
DAVENPORT ALBERT ASHLEY	NY	33W	37
DAVENPORT BARD ELTON	ME	28W	58
DAVENPORT CHARLES E II	FL	46E	4
DAVENPORT DAVID D JR	SC	14E	122
DAVENPORT DONALD GENE	WA	09E	61
DAVENPORT GEORGE C JR	NC	17W	36
DAVENPORT JAMES DONALD	AL	24E	90
DAVENPORT JAMES HUEY	AL	14E	61
DAVENPORT JAMES MICHAEL	OH	24W	93
DAVENPORT JOHN CHARLES	MI	29W	59
DAVENPORT JOHN JUNIOR	KS	02E	46
DAVENPORT JOHN SANFORD	OK	26W	69
DAVENPORT RICHARD	NY	04E	119
DAVENPORT ROBERT DEAN	MO	28W	68
DAVENPORT ROBERT MALCUM	CA	33W	77
DAVENPORT ROGER DALE	TX	02W	66
DAVERN MATTHEW JOHN	NJ	07E	39
DAVES DENNIS LEE	NC	07W	61
DAVES DONALD CHARLES	SC	29E	99
DAVEY GLEN VINCENT	WV	23E	26
DAVEY LOREN KEITH	OK	53E	11
DAVI JOSEPH NICHOLAS	CT	10E	131
DAVID CHARLES EDWARD JR	OH	45W	31
DAVID GARY CHARLES	PA	04W	13
DAVID HAROLD LUCIEN JR	LA	52W	27
DAVID JEFFREY JAY	PA	22E	69
DAVID MICHAEL DENNIS	CA	57W	24
DAVID ROBERT	NM	64E	13
DAVIDENKO DANIEL JOSEPH	IL	16W	52
DAVIDHEISER STANLEY JR	PA	17E	61
DAVIDOVE ERNEST FREDERIC	CA	39E	20
DAVIDSON CHARLES ALLEN	AZ	11W	130
DAVIDSON CHARLES LEON	WI	05E	131
DAVIDSON DAVID ARTHUR	MD	07W	112
DAVIDSON DENNIS ROBERT	OH	49E	20
DAVIDSON DONALD FREDERICK	LA	01E	29
DAVIDSON GERALD WAYNE	TN	01E	56
DAVIDSON JAMES RICHARD	IN	42E	62
DAVIDSON JOHN CLARK	VA	37W	30
DAVIDSON JOHN WAYNE	VA	63E	7
DAVIDSON MICHAEL JOHN	WI	19E	93
DAVIDSON MICHAEL MURRAY	MI	33W	92
DAVIDSON ROBERT GRIFFIN	MD	11E	49
DAVIDSON RONALD LARRY	FL	35W	59
DAVIDSON RONALD LEE	OH	49W	12
DAVIDSON THOMAS JAMES	MI	51E	38
DAVIDSON VERBIN EUGENE	TN	27W	90
DAVIDSON WILLIAM GALAN	MI	29E	71
DAVIDSON WILLIAM JAMES JR	PA	35E	53
DAVIE BOOKER T JR	AL	14W	115
DAVIE RODNEY OWEN	IL	24E	54
DAVIE THOMAS EARL JR	OK	20E	72
DAVIES ALFRED JOHN JR	MI	50W	29
DAVIES ARTHUR JR	NV	18E	101
DAVIES DAVID MARSHALL	WA	06E	74
DAVIES DONALD PAUL		21W	32
DAVIES EDWARD EARL	NM	25E	28
DAVIES JOSEPH EDWIN	VA	63E	8
DAVIES KEITH RICHARD	NY	07W	24
DAVIES ROBERT JOHN	WI	24E	19
DAVIES STEPHEN GEORGE	MO	03W	58
DAVIES TIMOTHY SCOTT	AL	09E	45
DAVILA ALFREDO	NY	65W	6
DAVILA FRANK	NY	22E	99
DAVILA GUILLERMO JR	TX	21W	17
DAVILA JOSE	TX	67E	7
DAVILA TEODORO	TX	18E	107
DAVILA-TORRES MAXIMILIANO	PR	10W	80
DAVINO THOMAS ALPHONSE	IL	54W	41
DAVIS AARON JR	NY	05W	98
DAVIS ABRON EARL	OH	35W	69

NAME	STATE	PANEL NO.	LINE NO.
DAVIS ALAN EUNICE	CA	04W	63
DAVIS ALBERT	AL	51E	18
DAVIS ALBERT J	OH	26W	83
DAVIS ALBERT JACKSON	CA	34W	22
DAVIS ALBERT LEE	NC	17W	95
DAVIS ALFRED LEE	CA	13E	83
DAVIS ANDREW JAMES JR	GA	22E	56
DAVIS ARNEL J JR	MI	22E	76
DAVIS ARTHUR LAVELLE	NC	52E	36
DAVIS ARTHUR LEROY	NC	59E	20
DAVIS ARTHUR RAYMOND	NY	21W	22
DAVIS AUBREY GUY	TN	34W	92
DAVIS BENNY EARL	TX	34W	64
DAVIS BENTLEY THOMAS	FL	06W	49
DAVIS BILLY CHARLES	GA	26W	39
DAVIS BILLY SYLVESTER	MI	14E	56
DAVIS BLAKELY IRVING JR	FL	24E	19
DAVIS BRENT EDEN	CA	06E	19
DAVIS BRUCE	LA	05E	101
DAVIS BUREN RAY	OK	03E	74
DAVIS CARL RAYMOND	MO	34E	67
DAVIS CARLOS RAY	CA	45E	54
DAVIS CECIL LEROY	AL	45E	19
DAVIS CHARLES AUGUSTUS	PA	28E	65
DAVIS CHARLES CECIL	MO	19E	23
DAVIS CHARLES EDWARD	CA	34E	75
DAVIS CHARLES EDWARD JR	SC	29W	60
DAVIS CHARLES EUGENE	KS	52E	36
DAVIS CHARLES HENRY	NJ	35W	75
DAVIS CHARLES OWEN	NC	07E	41
DAVIS CHARLES R JR	OH	03E	11
DAVIS CHARLES WILLIAM	VA	08E	134
DAVIS CHARLES WILLIAM	AL	27E	58
DAVIS CHARLIE ANTHONY	NC	35W	46
DAVIS CHARLIE BROWN JR	KY	11W	34
DAVIS CHRISTOPHER WILMER	ND	16E	104
DAVIS CLAUD ALBERT	AR	14W	51
DAVIS CLIFFORD GORDON	TX	18E	120
DAVIS CLIFFORD MORRIS JR	MO	13W	91
DAVIS CLIFTON ANTHONY	LA	43W	53
DAVIS CLIFTON HENRY	VA	50E	45
DAVIS CLYDE	IL	03W	36
DAVIS CORNER MACK	SC	01W	48
DAVIS CURRY BARRY	AL	44W	8
DAVIS DALE L E	MI	39E	43
DAVIS DALE LEROY	CA	41W	67
DAVIS DANIEL RICHARD	GA	19W	59
DAVIS DANNY CRAIG	CA	14W	120
DAVIS DARYL LEE	NC	31E	10
DAVIS DAVID LEE	IA	29W	87
DAVIS DENNIS DEAN	MD	19W	128
DAVIS DON EDDIE	MO	23E	85
DAVIS DON EDWARD	AR	51E	18
DAVIS DONALD ALLEN	AZ	10W	89
DAVIS DONALD VANCE	NC	23E	118
DAVIS DOUGLAS ONEILL	MI	40E	61
DAVIS DUANE MICHAEL	OH	31W	34
DAVIS DUANE ROSS	CA	27W	62
DAVIS DUDLEY	CO	13W	116
DAVIS EDGAR FELTON	NC	43W	13
DAVIS EDGAR SYLVESTER	TX	26E	8
DAVIS EDWARD DANIEL	NM	13E	89
DAVIS EDWARD LEE	TX	18W	58
DAVIS EDWARD THOMSON JR	CA	16W	124
DAVIS EDWIN PHILLIP	CT	60E	10
DAVIS ELIGAH LAMAR	GA	12W	96
DAVIS ELLSWORTH I JR	MS	13E	24
DAVIS ELMER NEAL	MD	26E	92
DAVIS ELTON JR	TX	17W	18
DAVIS ELWOOD WILLIAM JR	OH	03E	74
DAVIS EMMETT LARUE	FL	24W	93
DAVIS EMMETT LEE	AL	23W	43
DAVIS EMMETT RAY	KS	12E	108
DAVIS ERLE FLETCHER	DC	17W	127
DAVIS ERNEST J JR	MI	16W	104
DAVIS ERNEST PETTWAY	FL	54W	9
DAVIS ERNEST RAY	NY	08W	22
DAVIS EUGENE FESTER	IL	51W	30
DAVIS EVERARD AARON	NY	34E	41
DAVIS EVERETT	IN	44E	34
DAVIS FLOYD ROBERT	AZ	01E	20
DAVIS FRANCIS JOHN	IA	01W	42

NAME	STATE	PANEL NO.	LINE NO.
DAVIS FRANK EDWARD	MS	42W	39
DAVIS FRANK JR	LA	17W	90
DAVIS FREDERIC HUTCHISON	MI	23W	98
DAVIS GAIL LEE	MO	03E	51
DAVIS GARRY DON	IL	11E	6
DAVIS GARY JAMES	CA	18W	101
DAVIS GARY LYNN	AZ	15W	121
DAVIS GARY RAY	OH	62E	16
DAVIS GENE EDMOND	IN	06E	5
DAVIS GENE THOMAS	OH	03E	39
DAVIS GEORGE LEWIS JR	NC	32W	95
DAVIS GEORGE NATHAN	VA	51W	30
DAVIS GERALD ARTHUR	MI	02W	8
DAVIS GERALD EDWARD	PA	23E	74
DAVIS GLENN EDWIN	IL	55E	8
DAVIS GLENN PHILLIP	IL	59E	20
DAVIS HARLAND M JR	NJ	01W	53
DAVIS HAROLD MICHAEL JR	MI	34W	32
DAVIS HARRIS VONZELL	LA	21E	65
DAVIS HARRY K	AZ	20E	72
DAVIS HARRY LEE	CO	17E	98
DAVIS HERBERT CARSON	GA	39E	45
DAVIS HOLBERT EUGENE	VA	27E	52
DAVIS HUGH MOZELL	VA	51W	30
DAVIS J C	TN	06W	42
DAVIS JAMES	NY	63W	15
DAVIS JAMES ALBERT	FL	59E	18
DAVIS JAMES ALLEN	CA	59E	20
DAVIS JAMES DEAN	NE	04W	99
DAVIS JAMES GREGORY	NY	34W	22
DAVIS JAMES LEE	GA	21W	69
DAVIS JAMES LEONARD	MI	12W	25
DAVIS JAMES LEROY	GA	03E	43
DAVIS JAMES MARK	AZ	11W	130
DAVIS JAMES MIKE	CA	09W	37
DAVIS JAMES NORRIS	MD	62E	2
DAVIS JAMES ROBERT	TX	21W	88
DAVIS JAMES THOMAS	TN	01E	4
DAVIS JAMES THOMAS	KS	23E	35
DAVIS JAMES THOMAS	TN	39E	45
DAVIS JAMES W	MS	44E	14
DAVIS JAMES WELDON	TX	53W	8
DAVIS JAMES WILLIAM	MI	19W	29
DAVIS JEFFREY ALAN	IN	45W	49
DAVIS JEFFREY LYNN	CA	11W	13
DAVIS JERALD C C	IL	26W	44
DAVIS JERRY LLOYD	GA	46W	18
DAVIS JERRY REED	MS	33W	45
DAVIS JERRY VANOID	GA	24E	20
DAVIS JERRY WILLIAM	OK	13E	89
DAVIS JOE MASON	IL	51W	32
DAVIS JOHN ALLEN	CO	06E	98
DAVIS JOHN B III	NC	09E	4
DAVIS JOHN CALVIN	CO	07W	44
DAVIS JOHN CLAYTON JR	OH	45W	13
DAVIS JOHN CLINTON	NE	26W	69
DAVIS JOHN EDWARD	TN	27E	84
DAVIS JOHN EDWARD	NE	31E	87
DAVIS JOHN EDWIN	CA	45W	5
DAVIS JOHN ENGLISH	MD	05W	48
DAVIS JOHN GAYLEALON	GA	30E	76
DAVIS JOHN HENRY	NY	29E	14
DAVIS JOHN HENRY	NY	32W	95
DAVIS JOHN K	SC	15E	94
DAVIS JOHN LARRY	PA	18E	57
DAVIS JOHN LAWRENCE	KS	46W	57
DAVIS JOHN LOUIS	OK	09W	43
DAVIS JOHN MICHAEL	WV	19W	49
DAVIS JOHN PAUL	TN	35W	69
DAVIS JOHN POWERS	IN	02E	42
DAVIS JOHN SEVIER	TX	07E	58
DAVIS JOHN TRAVIS	TN	23W	7
DAVIS JOHN WESLEY	TX	44W	46
DAVIS JOHN WILLIAM	IL	23E	1
DAVIS JOHNNIE WALTER	NC	57E	19
DAVIS JOHNNY F	AR	22W	46
DAVIS JON ERIC	TX	19W	103
DAVIS JOSEPH EDWARD JR	PA	39W	11
DAVIS JOSEPH WILLIAM	FL	13W	18
DAVIS KELLY RAY	OR	09W	119
DAVIS KENNETH	OH	31W	45
DAVIS KENNETH JOE	TN	33W	55

NAME	STATE	PANEL NO.	LINE NO.
DAVIS KINSEY ARTHUR	NC	49W	46
DAVIS LARRY FRANKLIN	GA	07W	64
DAVIS LARRY KENT	CA	29W	67
DAVIS LAWRENCE ARNOLD	MD	51W	3
DAVIS LEONARD DOUGLAS	AZ	09E	96
DAVIS LEONARD RAY	AZ	01W	2
DAVIS LEROY JR	TX	62W	7
DAVIS LESTER RAY	TN	39W	64
DAVIS LEWIS ANTHONY	SC	04W	54
DAVIS LEWIS JR	MI	26E	44
DAVIS LUTHER EUGENE	TN	10W	96
DAVIS MARCUS RAYMOND	KY	12W	92
DAVIS MARTIN JOSEPH	PA	50W	49
DAVIS MARVIN HOMER	TX	07E	44
DAVIS MARVIN ROYCE	GA	31E	97
DAVIS MELVIN ERNEST	LA	09W	19
DAVIS MELVIN GILMORE	MD	14E	61
DAVIS MICHAEL DE-WAYNE	MO	12W	4
DAVIS MICHAEL EDWARD	NY	02E	128
DAVIS MICHAEL EDWARD	AL	53W	17
DAVIS MICHAEL FRANK	NC	22W	31
DAVIS NEVITT DIEALL	LA	26E	82
DAVIS PAUL PATRICK	OH	48E	25
DAVIS PHILIP GEORGE	OH	47W	39
DAVIS PORTER THAD	MS	03E	114
DAVIS RANDALL MARK	IN	60W	11
DAVIS RANDOLPH	MS	12E	12
DAVIS RANDY MAYO	SC	10W	31
DAVIS RAY ELBERT	OK	11E	118
DAVIS RAY GENE	OK	21W	117
DAVIS RAY RENE	CA	30W	1
DAVIS RAYMOND ALEXANDER	UT	05E	25
DAVIS RAYMOND CARL	MO	14E	111
DAVIS RAYMOND RANCE	LA	01W	77
DAVIS REX ALLEN	IL	44W	16
DAVIS RICARDO GONZALEZ	NM	29W	87
DAVIS RICHARD BOUCHE JR	TX	14W	125
DAVIS RICHARD GLEN	WA	29E	2
DAVIS RICHARD HAROLD	TN	11W	72
DAVIS RICHARD JOHN	MN	19E	80
DAVIS RICHARD JR	NY	42W	27
DAVIS RICHARD LARRY	PA	33W	77
DAVIS RICHARD LEE	CO	22W	111
DAVIS RICHARD LLOYD	WI	46W	28
DAVIS RICHARD ROBERT	MA	23E	26
DAVIS RICHARD SHIRLEY JR	MA	60W	27
DAVIS RICHARD WAYNE	NJ	35W	33
DAVIS ROBERT ALLEN	IN	22E	38
DAVIS ROBERT ARNOLD	PA	03E	54
DAVIS ROBERT CHARLES	TX	54W	9
DAVIS ROBERT CHARLES	NJ	28W	18
DAVIS ROBERT DENNIS	OH	44E	15
DAVIS ROBERT EUGENE	IN	46E	31
DAVIS ROBERT FORD	TX	03W	101
DAVIS ROBERT HENRY	OH	58W	24
DAVIS ROBERT JOSEPH	IL	42W	54
DAVIS ROBERT JULIAN JR	MD	24E	86
DAVIS ROBERT LEWIS	KY	03E	74
DAVIS ROBERT NELSON	IL	07E	1
DAVIS ROBERT ORLIFF	TX	09E	129
DAVIS ROBERT ROY	IA	14W	128
DAVIS ROBERT SCOTT	CA	29W	97
DAVIS ROBERT WENDELL	OK	18E	92
DAVIS ROBERT WILSON	OH	51W	10
DAVIS RODNEY MAXWELL	GA	26E	8
DAVIS ROLAND K	SC	35E	30
DAVIS ROLLIN DUANE	IA	54E	31
DAVIS RONALD	IN	49E	9
DAVIS RONALD CALEB	IL	17E	50
DAVIS RONALD CHARLES	NH	14W	59
DAVIS RONALD EUGENE	AR	45W	25
DAVIS RONALD L	NC	02E	99
DAVIS RONNIE DEAN	IL	56W	19
DAVIS RONNIE LEE	SC	21W	74
DAVIS ROY HENRY	CA	31W	34
DAVIS SAMUEL LUTHER	NC	48E	25
DAVIS SAMUEL M	MS	27E	89
DAVIS SAMUEL VERNELL	CA	35W	3
DAVIS SHERMAN PONDEXTER	NC	09W	114
DAVIS STANLEY ROY	NY	62E	2
DAVIS STEPHAN ANDREW	TX	02W	95
DAVIS STEPHEN WINFIELD	MA	25E	11

NAME	STATE	PANEL NO.	LINE NO.
DAVIS STEVE	MO	51E	45
DAVIS STEVE CLAYTON	TX	20E	72
DAVIS STEVEN FREDERICK	LA	56E	22
DAVIS SYLVESTER	OH	34W	64
DAVIS TERRY LEE	OH	15E	83
DAVIS TERRY LEE	IL	52W	34
DAVIS THEODORE H	PA	15E	95
DAVIS THOMAS ARTHUR	MI	27W	107
DAVIS THOMAS J III	LA	69W	1
DAVIS THOMAS JOEL	CA	51E	38
DAVIS THOMAS JOSEPH	NV	09W	90
DAVIS THOMAS RAYMOND	MD	33W	25
DAVIS THOMAS WARREN	NC	25W	103
DAVIS TOM JR	FL	46E	16
DAVIS WALTER EMERSON	OK	24W	15
DAVIS WALTER SCOTT	CA	45W	13
DAVIS WARREN K	VA	20W	18
DAVIS WAYNE ROBERT	MA	08W	129
DAVIS WENDLE CLYDE	UT	20E	102
DAVIS WESLEY WAYNE	AZ	07W	97
DAVIS WILBERT CLAUDE	MO	02E	120
DAVIS WILLIAM DEWITT	GA	31E	80
DAVIS WILLIAM EDWARD JR	NC	04E	8
DAVIS WILLIAM FORREST	FL	17W	49
DAVIS WILLIAM FRANCIS JR	AL	19W	128
DAVIS WILLIAM JEWEL JR	MS	37W	31
DAVIS WILLIAM LOUIS	NY	14E	56
DAVIS WILLIAM R	MS	11E	97
DAVIS WILLIAM RUSSELL	RI	10E	24
DAVIS WILLIAM SHELDON III	NJ	10E	117
DAVIS WILLIAM STANLEY	CA	07W	83
DAVIS WILLIAM TERRELL	FL	46W	48
DAVIS WILLIAM THOMAS	NH	46W	13
DAVIS WILLIAM THOMAS	WV	42W	6
DAVIS WILLIAM W JR	FL	44E	58
DAVIS WILLIAM WALTER JR	MA	23E	26
DAVIS WILLIAM WESLEY	OR	11W	84
DAVIS WILLIE CECIL	CT	24W	52
DAVIS WILLIE EDWARD	TX	05E	45
DAVIS WILLIE JAMES	SC	21W	117
DAVIS WILLIE JR	IL	21E	104
DAVIS WILLIE LOUIS	AL	23E	69
DAVIS WILLIE SONNY	MI	41W	45
DAVIS WILSON	SC	09W	32
DAVIS WOODROW JR	SC	57W	25
DAVIS YALE REZIN JR	KS	38W	10
DAVISON DAVID MICHAEL	CA	15W	27
DAVISON DENNIS ALLEN	TX	04W	4
DAVISON GUY ALLEN	WA	46W	13
DAVISON JACKIE LEE	CO	29W	74
DAVISON LARRY CHARLES	IL	23W	98
DAVISON NORMAN RAY	OH	01E	35
DAVISON ROBERT GAYLE	MI	13E	52
DAVISON WILLIAM A JR	PA	05E	54
DAVOULT GAYLON DARYL	OK	22E	83
DAW CECIL ERNEST	LA	08E	91
DAW JERRY LORENZO	AZ	21E	73
DAWES DANIEL LEE SR	NC	52W	4
DAWES JOHN JAMES	CA	07E	29
DAWES WILLIAM LE GRAND	AL	17W	90
DAWKINS BENJAMIN TALLY	NC	45W	49
DAWKINS CALVIN DONALD	SC	31E	87
DAWKINS CLARENCE JR	SC	45E	64
DAWSON ANDREW LEE	IL	37E	20
DAWSON CLYDE DUANE	WI	06E	41
DAWSON DANIEL GEORGE	CA	01E	71
DAWSON DANIEL MILLARD	PA	15W	58
DAWSON DANNY LEE	WV	12W	116
DAWSON DENNIS EUGENE	IL	32W	25
DAWSON DONALD EDWARD JR	DE	38E	48
DAWSON EUGENE	WV	20E	14
DAWSON FRANK ARTHUR	CA	39E	70
DAWSON FRANK WILLIAM	OH	12W	38
DAWSON HAROLD CARL JR	WV	24W	53
DAWSON JAMES VERNON	KY	20W	6
DAWSON JOHN ROBERT	MI	28E	81
DAWSON LAWRENCE MICHAEL	WA	23E	98
DAWSON MICHAEL DALE	IL	10W	52
DAWSON MICHAEL DAVID	TN	22W	64
DAWSON NORMAN EDWARD JR	CT	09E	27
DAWSON PAUL GLEN	CA	02E	7
DAWSON ROBERT CLARK	NC	09W	63
DAWSON STEVEN JAMES	NJ	43W	13
DAWSON THOMAS JOE JR	CA	24E	19
DAWSON THOMAS PHILLIP	GA	22W	19
DAWSON WAYNE EUGENE	IL	13E	61
DAWSON WILLIAM JOHN	CA	19W	66
DAY ARTHUR MICHAEL	PA	25W	22
DAY BILLY BROWN	TN	05E	59
DAY CALVIN SYLVESTER	DC	33W	31
DAY CHARLES KEITH	OH	35W	70
DAY CHARLES TYRONE	AL	10E	63
DAY CLINTON LEE	OK	23W	119
DAY DENNIS IRVIN	OK	02W	60
DAY DENNIS PATRICK	PA	36E	69
DAY DOUGLAS WAYNE	CA	11W	110
DAY EDWARD	MI	47E	48
DAY EDWARD	PA	46W	28
DAY JERROLD BERNELL	UT	13W	8
DAY JOLLY J	OK	15W	17
DAY KEVIN LLOYD	CA	32W	26
DAY MICHAEL ROBERT	TN	33E	82
DAY OSCAR ALFRED	NY	11W	90
DAY PETER EVAN	CA	20E	128
DAY ROY JUNIOR	MO	01W	10
DAY STEPHEN WAYNE	CO	12E	132
DAY TERRY BUCKLES	UT	42W	39
DAY WENDELL LEWIS	PA	25E	6
DAY WESLEY DAVID	MI	30E	89
DAYAO ROLANDO CUEVAS		17W	25
DAYHOFF RALPH PAUL	PA	49W	52
DAYRINGER HAROLD V JR	NC	02E	84
DAYTON JAMES LESLIE	IL	57E	1
DAYTON JOHN EMERY	IN	11W	122
DAYTON WILLIAM CLARENCE	MD	15E	89
DAZEY THOMAS FRANCIS JR	WI	48E	57
DAZEY WILLIAM LESLIE JR	WA	35E	68
DE ABRE JAMES MICHAEL	CA	27E	94
DE AMARAL CHARLES F JR	CA	02E	105
DE ANGELIS ADAMO ERMINO	NJ	16W	8
DE ANGELIS DOMINIC A	NY	03E	54
DE ANGELIS DOMINIC JOHN	NY	06W	3
DE ANGELIS RICHARD NICHOL	CT	41W	66
DE ARO STEPHEN WAYNE	CA	25W	63
DE BARBER JOHN THOMAS	CT	11E	81
DE BAULT JOE ROBERT	TX	21E	104
DE BERNARDO FRANK JR	CT	12E	78
DE BOARD BLAINE A JR	PA	13E	96
DE BOARD ROBERT DARRELL	OH	33W	84
DE BOCK JOHN ALBERT	WI	24E	72
DE BOER LAWRENCE NEIL	MI	10W	11
DE BOER WILLIAM SYLVESTER	MN	35W	7
DE BOLT MICHAEL LLOYD M	CA	16W	109
DE BONO ANTHONY JAY	NY	35W	57
DE BOW EDWARD CARL	PA	29W	67
DE BRULER JAMES PAUL	MO	07E	94
DE BUSK MICHAEL EUGENE	IN	34E	85
DE BUTTS DANIEL FRENCHY	OR	23E	50
DE CAMP MICHAEL DAVID	OH	25E	97
DE CARLO GENNARO JOSEPH	IL	25E	50
DE CARLO JAMES ANTHONY	CT	12W	88
DE CELLE ROBERT EUGENE II	CA	05W	128
DE CORA ELLIOTT LEO	WI	48W	24
DE COSTE DAVID ANTHONY	IL	34E	85
DE CRAENE ALAN CHARLES	IL	13W	19
DE CROSTA JOSEPH FRANCIS	NJ	34E	75
DE CUBELLIS CARMEN JR	RI	16W	1
DE DIE ROGER ALLEN	MI	16W	116
DE DOMINIC ROBERT MARIO	NY	20E	14
DE FAZIO PHILLIP FRANK	PA	44W	23
DE FILIPPIS LARRY DALE	ID	12E	60
DE FOOR FREDDIE CARVIAL	NM	13W	62
DE FOOR VICTOR LEE	TX	08W	7
DE FORD DALE DARREL	NE	06E	133
DE FORD ELMO LEE	ID	07E	17
DE FORGE DAVID HENRY	CT	30W	73
DE FOSSE THOMAS GLENN	OH	42E	63
DE FRANCO JAMES CLINTON	NY	13W	41
DE FRANGE MARK JOHN	OH	21W	12
DE FRIES GAYLORD KILA	HI	20W	83
DE GALLEY JEROME ANTHONY	WI	28W	97
DE GARMO GORDON EARL	NJ	38W	72
DE GENNARO JOSEPH	NY	04E	88
DE GRAF DICK	WA	54W	36
DE GRAW CHARLES IVAN	CA	39W	20
DE GRAY JERRY FREDERICK	WI	28E	21
DE HAAS PETER	NJ	45W	60
DE HART SOLOMON WILLIAM	PA	31E	45
DE HERRERA BENJAMIN DAVID	CO	30E	24
DE HERRERA PEDRO	CO	20W	112
DE HIMER MARTIN JAMES	NY	13W	111
DE HOMMEL HANK JOHN CONRA	MI	30E	89
DE JARNETT GEORGE WESLEY	OH	42E	3
DE JEAN CHARLES ODEN III	LA	09E	10
DE JESSA JOSEPH CARMINE	NJ	17E	50
DE JESUS COLON JOSE CELS	NJ	49W	22
DE JESUS JOAQUIN	FL	07E	33
DE JESUS MUNOZ ALEJANDRO	PR	47E	31
DE JESUS SANCHEZ ANIBAL	PR	16E	77
DE JESUS-ROSA RAUL	PR	09W	78
DE LA CRUZ FERNANDO	TX	12W	4
DE LA HOZ CARLOS A M	NY	65E	7
DE LA PAZ ABEL JOSEPH	CA	32W	95
DE LA PAZ HILARIO JR	TX	03E	55
DE LA PENA GILBERT	CA	47E	48
DE LA ROSA GUMESINDO	TX	16W	62
DE LA ROSA JESUS JR	TX	09E	37
DE LA ROSA LARRY A JR	CA	41E	19
DE LA TORRE JOSE MANUEL	CA	22W	74
DE LA TORRE LUIS	CA	05E	41
DE LAAT DAVID WILLIAM	WI	09W	43
DE LACY MICHAEL CHARLES	CA	03E	65
DE LAGARZA EMILIO A JR	IN	12W	121
DE LAIGLE THEUS EVERETTE	GA	41E	62
DE LANGE JACK PETER	WI	30W	42
DE LAPP WILLIAM C III	CA	43E	53
DE LARA FRANKLIN VICTORY	FL	66E	8
DE LASSUS CHARLES EDWARD	MO	42W	28
DE LAUGHDER DAVID LEE	KS	18E	52
DE LEON GUILLERMO JR	TX	33E	46
DE LEON HERMAN BORJA	GM	53E	30
DE LEON JESUS HERNANDEZ	TX	13W	126
DE LEON MARIO ONTIVERO	TX	20E	56
DE LEON MARIO P	TX	19W	59
DE LEON RAFAEL JR	TX	27W	86
DE LEON RODOLFO	IL	39E	30
DE LISA WILLIAM JOSEPH	PR	49E	30
DE LOACH DAVID LLOYD	GA	20W	85
DE LOACH LLOYD DWAIN	TX	22E	38
DE LONG EVERETT EUGENE JR	FL	03W	119
DE LONG JERALD STEVEN	WI	07W	128
DE LONG RONALD LAWRENCE	TN	16W	37
DE LONG WILLARD JR	OH	17W	12
DE LOOZE JERALD FREDERICK	NY	31E	91
DE LORA PEDRO ASCENCION	NM	20W	107
DE LORENZO FRED JOSEPH JR	MA	19W	11
DE LORENZO PHILIP T JR	MA	47W	26
DE LORENZO RONALD	NJ	25W	65
DE LOS RIOS PABLO G PEREZ JR	TX	10W	96
DE LUCA RAYMOND PAUL	VA	54W	5
DE LUCA SEBASTIAN EDWARD	NC	03W	89
DE LUCA THOMAS STEVEN JR	NY	27W	24
DE LUNA MANUEL JR	TX	39W	73
DE MAGNIN MICHAEL ANDRE R	NJ	16W	12
DE MARCHES JOHN THOMAS	KY	17W	112
DE MARCHI FRANK JR	NY	06E	83
DE MARCO FRANK JOHN	CA	25E	62
DE MARCO PATRICK THOMAS	PA	35W	81
DE MARCUS JERRY DENNIS	CA	20W	64
DE MARIA FRANK F JR	NY	22W	19
DE MARINIS THOMAS JOSEPH	NY	24W	39
DE MARIS RICHARD ORIN	MA	14E	33
DE MARR JOHN CHARLES JR	MD	50W	49
DE MARSICO MICHAEL JAMES	NY	11E	32
DE MASI MICHAEL ARMOND	AZ	08W	11
DE MATA BRUNO WALTER	WI	31W	83
DE MATTIO MARIO FRANK	NJ	45E	15
DE MECURIO ROCCO J	NJ	12W	68
DE MELLO BRYAN JOE	CA	18W	109
DE MELLO CLYDE LAWRENCE	CA	38E	48
DE MELLO ROBERT BRUCE	CA	21E	43
DE MEOLA RAYMOND WARREN	NY	24W	4
DE MEY JOHN	MD	22W	96
DE MICHAEL DENNIS JOHN	NY	16E	57
DE MICHELLE CRAIG NORMAN	NY	31W	78
DE MILIO LAWRENCE	PA	24W	29

NAME	STATE	PANEL NO.	LINE NO.
DE MOE RAYMOND ROGER	WI	17E	43
DE MORE KENNETH EDWARD JR	NJ	15W	49
DE MUNDA GERALD ANTHONY	NY	30E	89
DE MUTH RICHARD LAWRENCE	MA	03W	16
DE NARDIS CLAUDE CHARLES	NY	21W	22
DE NARDO FRANK MICHAEL JR	CA	40W	27
DE NARDO JOSEPH FREDERICK	CO	01W	89
DE NAVA JOHN JOSEPH	CO	34E	52
DE NICOLA ALLEN	FL	15E	19
DE NIKE STEVE SPENCER	MI	05W	15
DE NISCO THOMAS JOSEPH	NY	56E	5
DE PALMA THOMAS CARMINE	RI	24W	76
DE PEW VERNON EUGENE	WA	20E	57
DE PRIEST DARRELL JAMES	MS	61E	8
DE PRIEST DAVID REED	ND	46E	16
DE PRIEST DAVID WAYNE	VA	35E	68
DE PRIEST JOHN THOMAS	AL	27W	107
DE PROFIO MICHAEL ALLEN	MA	18E	39
DE RIGGI ANTHONY	NJ	10E	76
DE RISO LESTER MICHAEL	RI	22E	38
DE ROO JOHN ALBERT	CA	14W	3
DE ROO LANCE AARON	CA	12W	96
DE ROSA JOSEPH WILLIAM	IL	18E	25
DE ROSE GERALD LOUIS	NJ	47E	20
DE RUBEIS FERNANDO	NY	21W	6
DE RUE DAVID JOHN	NY	22E	100
DE SANTIS STEPHEN ANTHONY	CT	18W	74
DE SHURLEY GEORGE ROBERT	NM	47E	20
DE SIMONE ALFRED	NJ	21W	6
DE SOTO ERNEST LEO	AR	27W	62
DE SULLY MAX FRANCIS JR	OR	23W	62
DE TAMBLE THOMAS GLENN	MI	13E	32
DE VASIER BILLY KIETH	AR	27E	14
DE VAULT MARVIN ANDREW	NY	32W	64
DE VEGA DUANE ALFRED	NY	32W	10
DE VEGTER PAUL ANTHONY	CA	20W	117
DE VERE MONTE RAOUL	WA	14W	22
DE VILLE FRANCIS XAVIER	OH	35W	76
DE VINNEY ROBERT EUGENE	MN	15W	35
DE VOE MICHAEL EUGENE	TX	07E	101
DE VOE ROBERT LEE	PA	29E	48
DE VORE EDWARD ALLEN JR	CA	45E	20
DE VOS WILLIAM MARINUS	NY	40E	3
DE VRIES KEITH ALLEN	MI	18W	6
DE WAAL HOWARD JACOB	UT	31E	80
DE WALD JOHN FRANCIS	NY	27E	47
DE WALT VICTOR MONROE	PA	06W	49
DE WATER PATRICK LEE	WA	44W	2
DE WEESE RONALD GENE	MO	16W	73
DE WEESE WILLIAM CHARLES	IN	52E	16
DE WILDE PETER F JR	MI	30W	43
DE WINDT CHARLES ROSS	WI	16W	127
DE WISPELAERE REXFORD JOH	NY	16W	116
DE WITT DAVID CHARLES	IA	10E	63
DE WITT JAMES PHILLIP	CO	02E	56
DE WITT LAWRENCE	NY	39W	40
DE WITT SPOTSWOOD	VA	13E	67
DE WOLF DALE LEE	NE	01W	115
DE WULF PATRICK THOMAS	MI	08W	35
DE YOUNG ABE RICHARD	MI	19E	11
DEACON JAMES DALA	GA	04W	37
DEAL FLOYD ANDREW	AZ	27W	29
DEAL FRANCIS WILMER JR	IL	17W	33
DEAL GARETH JOHN	SD	11E	81
DEAL LARRY KEITH	IN	08E	115
DEAL OLIVER EVANS JR	CA	16W	12
DEAL TERRY WAYNE	NC	01W	77
DEAL WILLIAM LEANDER	NJ	01E	15
DEAN ALAN JAMES	IL	17E	105
DEAN ALBERT	WI	07E	57
DEAN ANTHONY WILLIAM	IN	15W	41
DEAN CARL ANDREW	MD	18W	118
DEAN CARL EARLY JR	IL	16W	130
DEAN CHARLES ROBERT JR	PA	07E	101
DEAN CHRISTOPHER J JR	FL	07E	47
DEAN DONALD BING	ME	34W	82
DEAN DONALD CHESTER	MO	17W	25
DEAN GLENN FREDRICK	WI	46W	39
DEAN HOWARD HADDEN	KY	14E	79
DEAN JAMES HOWARD	WV	15W	77
DEAN JAMES ROBERT JR	FL	15W	109
DEAN JAMES WILLIAM	RI	27W	80

NAME	STATE	PANEL NO.	LINE NO.
DEAN KENNETH BERNARD	MI	34E	52
DEAN KENNETH LEE JR	OH	01E	106
DEAN LARRY LAMARR	OH	13E	125
DEAN LAWRENCE CHARLES	AR	01W	67
DEAN MICHAEL FRANK	CA	09W	103
DEAN ROBERT WILLIAM	VA	21W	99
DEAN RONALD PHILIP	WV	51E	19
DEAN SIMON JR	TN	26W	76
DEAN TERRY LEE	MO	07W	81
DEAN THOMAS	NC	11E	51
DEAN THOMAS JOLLEY	NY	34E	6
DEAN THOMAS JOSEPH III	PA	21E	17
DEAN THOMAS NELSON	DC	55E	8
DEAN THOMAS WILLIAM	WV	13W	103
DEAN WILLIAM EDWARD	OH	44E	34
DEAN WILLIAM MEARL	IL	01E	61
DEAN WOODIE JUNIOR	MI	40W	74
DEANE MICHAEL LINDSEY	MA	67E	8
DEANE WILLIAM LAWRENCE	FL	01W	109
DEARBORN PATRICK JOHN		29E	9
DEARDEN ALLEN KENNETH	NY	20E	24
DEARDORFF HEROLD TROY	CA	12E	60
DEARING JERRY WAYNE	CA	35E	37
DEARING LARRY GENE	OH	33E	82
DEARING PHILIP RAY	SC	03W	41
DEAS CHARLES MILTON	AL	05W	95
DEASEL JAMES JEROME JR	MD	21E	43
DEATHERAGE DENNIS RAY	TX	04W	112
DEATHRAGE DON LE ROY JR	MO	21E	119
DEATON CARL WOODROW	OK	02E	135
DEATON CHARLES THOMAS	OR	17W	15
DEATON JACK JOE	IN	13E	50
DEATON JOHN CLAUD	OK	34W	14
DEAVER FREDERICK KENNETH	IA	10E	28
DEAVER JACK	CA	27E	70
DEAVERS KENNETH LAMAR JR	MD	15E	4
DEBATES WILLIAM ARTHUR	IL	28W	102
DEBICKERO DENNIS RALPH	IL	02W	63
DEBLASIO RAYMOND VINCE JR	NY	03W	80
DEBNER DENNIS ERWIN	MN	15W	121
DEBO WILLIAM LOUIS	OH	49W	47
DEBOLD REGIS PETER	PA	11E	67
DEBOLT WILLARD CLINTON	IN	12W	62
DEBREW JAMES EDWARD	NC	10W	11
DEBUSK RAY B JR	TX	13E	67
DECAIRE JACK LEONARD	FL	02W	59
DECAREAUX NORMAN E JR	LA	09E	111
DECESARO JACK JR	IL	37E	53
DECHENE ROBERT NORMAND	ME	26E	83
DECK PATRICK A JR	MD	01W	63
DECKER ALLAN GEORGE	FL	46W	14
DECKER BERTON	NY	29W	36
DECKER DAVID FRANKLIN	NY	27W	72
DECKER DAVID JOHN	PA	30E	24
DECKER DEWEY RUSSELL	MI	24W	15
DECKER GERALD ANTHONY	ND	27W	48
DECKER JOSEPH NICHOLAS	OH	30W	21
DECKER MELVIN JEROME	MN	52E	29
DECKER MICHAEL THOMAS	NY	33W	92
DECKER ROBERT HUGH	WI	28E	34
DECKER STEVEN WILLIAM	MD	43W	26
DECKER TEE WALLACE	AR	07E	45
DECKER WAYNE AUSTIN	IN	57W	8
DECKER WILLIAM BERNARD	OH	49W	14
DECKER WILLIAM THOMAS JR	OH	42W	34
DECOTA WALTER JOSEPH	RI	10E	15
DECOW MELVIN DALE	KS	69W	2
DEDEAUX ALDON JAMES	MS	29E	81
DEDEK JOHN FRANCIS	NY	32W	77
DEDMAN JULIAN DEAN	CA	26W	31
DEDMAN LESLIE PAUL	AL	12E	60
DEDMAN RONALD EUGENE	NV	30W	87
DEDMAN TONY	IL	07E	69
DEDMON DONALD CLAY	IL	02E	4
DEDMORE GERALD GLEN JR	OR	56W	19
DEDON CHARLES BERLIN	LA	21W	50
DEDRICK DWIGHT A	NY	36E	5
DEE KENNETH SAMUEL	NY	13W	77
DEEBLE JAMES FREDERICK	CA	11W	21
DEEDRICK CHARLES ORVIS JR	MN	22E	38
DEEDS LELAND SAMUEL	MO	59E	21
DEEDS RICK DUANE	MI	34E	85

NAME	STATE	PANEL NO.	LINE NO.
DEEL STONEY LEE	VA	23W	119
DEEN DAVID KEITH	FL	12E	46
DEENY MICHAEL FRANCIS III	PA	64E	13
DEER TERRY LOUIS	OK	07W	113
DEERE CHARLES KENNETH	OK	55E	8
DEERE DONALD THORPE	TX	07E	69
DEERING GALE EDWARD	MI	48W	53
DEERINWATER BRUCE EDWARD	OK	34W	74
DEES CURTIS CLEVELAND	TX	25W	4
DEES EDGAR ALLEN JR	AL	30W	73
DEES JERRY RICHARD	AZ	20W	55
DEESE DANNY EUGENE	FL	51W	38
DEESE JACK DEMPSEY	GA	66W	5
DEESE JAMES EDWARD JR	NC	41E	37
DEESON MICHAEL DANIEL	FL	30E	89
DEETER DAVID KIM	OH	50E	45
DEETER JACK EARL	PA	16W	120
DEETER MICHAEL ALAN	OH	37E	78
DEETZ BILL WAYNE	MN	40E	19
DEEVERS DONALD JAMES	OK	24W	102
DEFELICE LAWRENCE JOSEPH	NY	31W	65
DEFENBAUGH FRANKLIN D	WI	06W	90
DEFENBAUGH KENNETH LEROY	IA	11W	85
DEFER RICHARD HENRY	MI	02W	43
DEFER WILLIAM CHARLES	MI	34W	75
DEFIBAUGH MICHAEL THOMAS	MD	10E	76
DEFORREST RONALD C	MA	26W	44
DEGE RAYMOND WILLIAM III	NJ	11W	122
DEGEN ROBERT	NY	05W	33
DEGEN ROBERT PAUL	WA	30E	40
DEGENAARS BRADLEY RICHARD	NJ	46W	47
DEGEROLAMO ANTHONY JR	PA	37E	34
DEGNER HAROLD PAUL	TX	29W	60
DEGNIS JAMES EDWARD	MA	56W	19
DEGROOT MAARTEN	CA	06E	58
DEHART DONNIE RAY	TX	18E	113
DEHART JACKIE CLYDE	VA	18W	6
DEHERRERA RAYMUNDO F	CA	16E	120
DEHN ARTHUR ANDREW	MN	10W	101
DEHNER GEORGE EDWARD	IA	40W	2
DEHNKE DALE WILLARD	CA	03W	39
DEIBEL EDWARD PAUL III	MD	07W	35
DEICHELMANN SAMUEL MACKAL	AL	45W	49
DEIHL JOHN PERRY	IL	38W	24
DEIKE ROBERT JAMES	OH	56E	22
DEINLEIN LEONARD PETER	MA	30W	1
DEISHER LAWRENCE JAMES	PA	08E	26
DEITCH DAVID	NY	22W	87
DEITCHLER RUSSELL FLOYD	MT	51E	45
DEITEMEYER THOMAS PAUL	IN	15E	19
DEITMAN EDWARD	NJ	24W	27
DEITRICK GEORGE DOUGLAS	CA	22W	118
DEITSCH CHARLES EDWARD	FL	40W	6
DEITZ GORDON JAMES JR	MD	02E	26
DEITZ THOMAS MITCHELL	MD	29W	67
DEKKER DAVID ROSS	MI	04W	128
DEKKER GEORGE WILLIAM	CA	27E	5
DEL CAMP ADRIAN LEROY	WI	42E	63
DEL CASTILLO MARCO OSCAR	CA	57E	19
DEL GRECO VICTOR JR	CT	13W	74
DEL GUIDICE GREGORY	NJ	19W	30
DEL JESUS CARRERAS EFRAIN	PR	10E	94
DEL ROSARIO JOSEPH JESUS	HI	26W	90
DEL TERZO COLOMBO PHIL	NY	43W	13
DEL VALLE SANCHEZ ALEJO	PR	19W	44
DELA CRUZ FREDERICO V	GM	19W	77
DELA HOUSSAYE ARTHUR J JR	LA	36E	5
DELACERDA ANTONIO H JR	TX	40W	63
DELACROIX WILLIE JAMES	LA	15W	109
DELANEY ALBERT LEE	MS	21W	44
DELANEY DONNEY	TN	23W	63
DELANEY HERALD LEE	IL	53E	30
DELANEY JAMES PATRICK	OH	02W	64
DELANEY JAMES PERRY	AZ	36W	44
DELANEY JOHN PATRICK III	OH	50W	34
DELANEY KENNETH LEON	FL	13W	8
DELANEY RICHARD LAWRENCE	VT	23W	99
DELANEY THOMAS ALAN	CA	12W	33
DELANEY WARREN C	GA	26W	44
DELANGE FREDERIC R	NJ	05E	26
DELANO DARWIN JAMES	NH	38W	65
DELANO HENRY HARRISON	TX	09E	56

NAME	STATE	PANEL NO.	LINE NO.
DELANO JIMMY LYNN	OR	44E	34
DELANO MERWIN A JR	ME	06E	18
DELANO PETER FRANK	NY	15E	14
DELANO THOMAS FRANCIS	CA	08W	58
DELAPHIANO JOE B	MI	08W	7
DELAPLAINE DONALD LYNN	NY	03W	92
DELAPLANE JAMES CHARLES	IN	50E	27
DELASANDRO DENNIS FRANCIS	NJ	13E	89
DELCAMBRE TERRY LEE	TX	28W	97
DELEHANT THOMAS FRANCIS	IA	03W	44
DELEIDI RICHARD AGUSTINE	CA	33W	77
DELGADO CARLOS MARTINEZ	TX	05W	123
DELGADO CHRISTOPHER GEORG	TX	39E	70
DELGADO FRANCISCO H	TX	16W	45
DELGADO FRANCISCO PENA	CA	11W	122
DELGADO GILBERT TREVINIO	TX	48W	40
DELGADO JOHN PEDRO	CA	52W	5
DELGADO JOSE ALEJANDRO	CA	20W	43
DELGADO LE ROY FRED JR	CO	15E	54
DELGADO MICHAEL JULIAN JR	IL	06E	37
DELGADO RAY	CA	33E	2
DELGADO RAYMOND RODRIGUEZ	CA	30W	1
DELGADO REINALDO LUIS	NY	13E	115
DELGADO RICHARD FALCON	CA	36E	21
DELGADO ROBERT MONTOLVE	UT	02W	113
DELGADO RUBEN	IL	04E	119
DELGADO-CLASS LUIS	PR	62E	2
DELGADO-MARIN ARTURO	OH	31E	11
DELIKAT EDWARD JOHN JR	NJ	10W	31
DELISLE RODNEY JEROME	ME	21W	69
DELL GEORGE DOUGLAS	IA	55W	33
DELL KENNETH JOHN	PA	39W	21
DELL THOMAS CARL	NY	10E	94
DELL'ANGELO DAVID JOSEPH	MI	42W	67
DELL'ARENA RICHARD M	NJ	12W	66
DELLAMANDOLA GREGORY JOHN	CA	29E	73
DELLAPINA CHRISTOPHER L	PA	28W	89
DELLECKER HENRY FLOYD	AZ	02W	65
DELLINGER CHARLES AVERY	NC	35E	59
DELLINGER CHARLES HILTON	PA	50W	49
DELLINGER ROBERT LARRY	NC	40W	42
DELLOS SAMUEL LEE	WY	05E	5
DELLVON WILLIAM GRANT	MI	23E	35
DELLWO THOMAS ALBERT	MT	04W	48
DELMARK FRANCIS JOHN DUNC	UT	02E	55
DELMONT JAMES LOVES	MA	09W	37
DELONG JOE LYNN	TN	20E	20
DELOZIER DAVID VINCENT	PA	06W	67
DELOZIER JOHN ADRIAN	AZ	32E	92
DELP KENNETH HARVEY	CA	06E	134
DELP RONALD MARVIN	IN	41W	72
DELPH JERRY	VA	18E	107
DELPH SCOTT CLAYMON	IN	55W	12
DELPHIN BARRY RONAL	FL	16E	120
DELRIE JAMES EDWARD	LA	22E	65
DELUCA GEORGE ABRAHAM	NJ	02E	51
DELVERDE RONALD LEON	MA	42W	10
DELY WILLIAM	WV	08E	44
DEMALINE JOHN THOMAS	FL	10E	57
DEMALINE PAUL ALLEN	OH	08W	118
DEMARA JUAN JOSEPH	CA	43E	5
DEMARCO BILLY JOE	NM	09W	19
DEMARCO MICHAEL GREGORY	NY	49E	20
DEMATTEIS DAVID KELL	IL	42E	30
DEMBOSKI STANLEY T	NJ	05E	101
DEMBY GEORGE ALLEN	MD	29W	6
DEMERJIAN STEPHEN HAIG	IL	35W	52
DEMERS ARTHUR EMILE JR	NH	22E	100
DEMERS RICHARD ARTHUR	NH	28E	14
DEMERS RICHARD WILFRED	MA	09E	23
DEMERSON JOE EDDIE	TX	29W	97
DEMETRIS VASILIOS	NY	31W	34
DEMGEN ROBERT NICHOLAS	MI	17W	85
DEMINGS DAVID EUGENE	OK	25W	66
DEMKO LEONARD RICHARD	PA	37E	34
DEMMON DAVID STANLEY	CA	02E	2
DEMOND DONALD ALLEN R	MI	15W	9
DEMORE MICHAEL GEORGE	CT	19W	77
DEMOREST DAVID KEITH	MI	30E	1
DEMOROW ALAN GEORGE	MI	09W	7
DEMORY RAYMOND FRANK	TX	14E	111
DEMPS HENRY VAN	FL	10E	26
DEMPSEY GARY LEE	DE	15W	114
DEMPSEY JACK ISHUM	MT	08E	56
DEMPSEY JACK TAYLOR	OK	17E	50
DEMPSEY RONALD LEE	IN	41E	63
DEMPSEY THERON SPENCER	FL	06E	20
DEMPSEY WARREN LEIGH	NM	03E	122
DEMSEY WALTER EDWARD JR	NJ	05W	115
DENCY KARL PETER	IL	37W	55
DENEEN EARL MERRILL	MN	26W	61
DENEEN JOHN FRANKLIN JR	PA	34W	57
DENGLER JOHN LEO	NY	41E	63
DENHAM GAIL JR	FL	38E	66
DENHAM JAMES VIRL	KY	54W	23
DENHOFF ALAN BRIAN	NY	26W	62
DENHOFF THOMAS EDWARD	FL	35E	29
DENHOFF WILLIAM MICHAEL	WA	07E	24
DENIG JOSEPH HENRY	OH	08W	125
DENIPAH DANIEL DEE	AZ	32E	86
DENISOWSKI STANLEY GEORGE	NY	41W	39
DENKINS FRED JR	OH	11W	90
DENLEY BILLY WAYNE	MS	17W	127
DENLINGER DAVID WOOD	CA	31W	66
DENMAN WILLIAM LUTHER	CA	12E	27
DENMARK ROBERT LEE	CA	02W	93
DENNA DAVID RAMIRO	CA	08W	84
DENNANY JAMES EUGENE	MI	16W	63
DENNARD MACK JR	FL	18W	109
DENNEY ALAN WAYNE	AZ	21E	118
DENNEY DONALD GENE	NM	57W	17
DENNEY JIMMIE BRYSON	AL	10E	15
DENNEY TERRY LEE	OH	18W	61
DENNEY WILLIAM HERMAN JR	WV	33W	37
DENNING DWIGHT THOMAS	NC	35E	38
DENNING NEAL ALBERT	NC	07E	52
DENNING THOMAS GEORGE	IN	16E	1
DENNIS BLAIR EDWARD	CA	17E	17
DENNIS BOBBIE JEFFERSON	NC	11E	86
DENNIS CHARLES	TX	38W	65
DENNIS DAN MICHAEL	TX	19E	105
DENNIS DANIEL MAURICE	IN	21W	107
DENNIS DAVID ALAN	IN	39W	53
DENNIS DELMAR CLAUDE	SC	27W	45
DENNIS DOUGLASS J	NM	38E	25
DENNIS HAYVARD JR	CA	29E	28
DENNIS JAMES WALTER JR	AL	06E	20
DENNIS JERRY ALLEN	NC	06W	31
DENNIS JOHN ALLEN	MO	62W	8
DENNIS LARRY WAYNE	TX	18W	119
DENNIS MARK V	OH	09E	23
DENNIS PAUL JONES	TX	19E	36
DENNIS PAUL LESLIE	PA	52E	4
DENNIS RICHARD LESTER	ID	31E	63
DENNIS RONALD GENE	IN	15W	89
DENNIS THADDEUS	DC	04W	118
DENNIS WALTER KENON	GA	14W	131
DENNIS WILLIAM EARL	AL	55W	12
DENNIS WILLIAM R III	KS	16E	104
DENNIS WILLIAM ROY	PA	50E	46
DENNIS WILLIE ROSS	OH	34E	41
DENNISON CORTLAND ELLIS	KY	55E	9
DENNISON JAMES RICHARD	NY	33E	12
DENNISON RICHARD SAMUEL	DE	04W	23
DENNISON TERRY ARDEN	WA	09E	37
DENNULL EDWARD MICHAEL	OH	20W	28
DENNY CHARLES EDWARD	IL	26E	100
DENNY DAVID LESTER	IN	11E	89
DENNY JACKIE LEE	CA	05W	77
DENNY JERRY DAVID	WA	14W	83
DENNY LAWRENCE EDWARD	IL	09E	66
DENNY RICHARD EMERSON JR	MN	35E	59
DENNY ROGER EDWARD	LA	29W	6
DENSLOW GEORGE ROBERT	NY	38E	25
DENSON FLOYD CORNELIUS	AR	08E	65
DENSON JERRY EDWARD	TN	42W	28
DENT BILLY RAY	TX	43W	3
DENT BRUCE JAMES	AZ	41E	9
DENT GARY LYNN	CA	05W	20
DENT MICHAEL EARL	IN	13E	51
DENT WILLIAM LORANCE	NC	29W	97
DENTINO MERLE ALLEN	IL	09W	103
DENTON ARTHUR GERALD	WI	03W	133
DENTON BOBBY LEE	TX	27W	72
DENTON DAVID ANDREW	CA	55W	21
DENTON DENNIS ALAN	KS	18W	101
DENTON GREGORY JOHN D	FL	20W	64
DENTON GUY THOMAS	VA	12W	4
DENTON MANUEL REYES	TX	01E	29
DENTON NORRIS JAMES	TX	08E	129
DENTON RANDALL MORRIS	MA	20W	69
DENTON ROBERT ANTHONY	TX	11W	110
DENTON SIDNEY EDWARD	LA	21E	97
DEOCAMPO GREGORIO MANESE	CA	18E	58
DEORIO WILLIAM JOSEPH JR	CT	48W	53
DEPAUL MICHAEL JOSEPH S	NJ	04W	54
DEPP CHARLES WILLIAM	IN	10E	86
DEPREO WALLACE JOSEPH	MS	02W	41
DERAGON MICHAEL HENRY	ME	19W	37
DERBY EARL LEE	MN	18E	42
DERBY PAUL DAVID	WI	39W	77
DERBYSHIRE JAMES WILBERT	NJ	27W	86
DERDA JAMES MICHAEL	NM	27W	29
DERENBURGER RONALD HAL	MT	34E	67
DERHEIM KENNETH LEE	MT	04E	28
DERIG PATRICK MARTIN	CA	47E	20
DERKSEMA WILLIAM ARTHUR	WA	12E	46
DERMONT DONALD EUGENE JR	IL	06E	98
DEROCHER FREDERICK GEORGE	MA	36W	10
DEROSIER LAURIER DON	ME	31E	28
DEROSIER MICHAEL DOUGLAS	FL	10E	117
DEROSIER RICHARD TERRANCE	NH	15W	121
DEROSIER THOMAS ALBERT	MA	23E	27
DERRICK ALVIN JOSEPH	SC	33W	47
DERRICK BRUNSON A SR	SC	04W	34
DERRICK RANDY WAYNE	OK	36W	14
DERRICK ROBERT ALLEN	MI	06W	36
DERRICKSON THOMAS G II	CA	27E	97
DERRICO JACK EDWARD	PA	46E	31
DERRIG MICHAEL JAMES	IL	46W	42
DERRILL CARROLL EDWARD	MD	37W	62
DERRINGTON EARMON RAY	IL	18W	32
DERRITT EDDIE RAY	KS	07E	19
DERRY DAVID WAYNE	TN	45E	55
DERRYBERRY ABRAHAM R III	LA	43E	43
DERVISHIAN SARKIS	CA	09W	32
DES LAURIERS PHILIP GENE	MN	20W	117
DES ROCHERS JAMES BRIAN	IL	36E	6
DESCHAINE NORMAND CAMILLE	ME	59W	21
DESCHAMPS RAMON	AZ	09E	32
DESCHENES JAMES GEORGE	ME	39W	73
DESCHENES MICHAEL HUBERT	ME	43W	3
DESCHENES THOMAS ALFRED	MA	22E	37
DESCO DENNIS A	MI	06E	98
DESCOTEAUX MAURICE CLAUDE	NH	25E	15
DESILETS WILLIAM J	CA	33E	46
DESILLIER RICHARD GILL	CT	10W	32
DESKINS RONALD DEAN	WA	27W	4
DESMARAIS DONALD ROGER	MA	17W	105
DESMARAIS GEORGE PHILIP	NH	46E	53
DESMOND JOSEPH FRANCIS	MA	39W	36
DESMOND RAY GLEN	CA	04W	108
DESMORE LAWRENCE	NY	30W	100
DESO BERTRAM ANTHONY	NY	42E	14
DESOCIO DANIEL JOSEPH	NY	09W	72
DESORMEAUX HARRY HENRY	MI	62E	3
DESPARD JEROLD VIRGIL	IA	24E	19
DESPER RICHARD LINCOLN	MA	31W	66
DESROCHERS ROBERT ALAN	MA	38W	10
DESSELLE RICHARD JUDE	LA	19E	4
DESSELLE THOMAS WILLIAM	TX	38W	23
DETERS DAVID STEPHEN	MO	19W	12
DETMER DONALD GARY	FL	15E	104
DETOMASO CHARLES PHILIP	NY	18E	114
DETREMPE BARRY VICTOR	IL	32W	4
DETRICK DONALD GLEN	PA	05W	48
DETRICK GARY GENE	OH	27W	72
DETRICK ROBERT LLOYD	CA	38W	14
DETRIXHE JAMES B W	PA	05E	71
DETWILER LAWRENCE R JR	PA	19W	92
DEUEL CHARLES FRANK	WI	42E	13
DEUEL WILLIAM TOWNSLEY	IL	11E	30
DEUERLING WILLIAM JOSEPH	FL	23E	41
DEUSEBIO FRANK CESARE	NY	45E	20
DEUSO CARROLL JOSEPH	VT	06W	122
DEUTER RICHARD CARL	IL	16W	109

NAME	STATE	PANEL NO.	LINE NO.
DEUTSCH BERNARD FRANCIS	IA	20W	18
DEUTSCH HENRY ALBERT	FL	01E	113
DEVANEY BRIAN JOHN	IN	10W	120
DEVANEY JAMES PRICE	NC	13W	68
DEVERALL GEORGE NOBLE	VA	49E	10
DEVEREAUX REESE	IL	07E	33
DEVERS DAVID RONALD SR	OH	09E	132
DEVERS LESLIE ALLEN JR	CA	47E	30
DEVERS PAUL ANTHONY	NY	02E	50
DEVIK DAVID RALF	WA	38E	66
DEVINCENT EDWARD J JR	MD	06E	38
DEVINE CAMERON JOSEPH	NM	34W	92
DEVINE DAVID EUGENE	OH	55E	7
DEVINE FRANCIS STANLEY JR	PA	54E	5
DEVINE JOHN WILLIE	GA	16E	120
DEVINE RICHARD DANIEL JR	MA	34E	17
DEVINE RICHARD WILLIAM	NY	07W	1
DEVINE THOMAS EDWARD	NY	15W	62
DEVINS RICHARD CHARLES	MI	38W	82
DEVLIN JOSEPH WILLIAM	NY	13W	96
DEVLIN THOMAS ROGER	NJ	04E	102
DEVNEY JAMES ROBERT	WI	20W	18
DEVOE DAVID FRANCIS	MA	12E	36
DEVOE DOUGLAS WAYNE		41W	15
DEVOR KENNETH LEE	PA	38E	67
DEVORE CRAIG JESSE	NJ	53W	42
DEVORE KENNETH ROY	CA	36W	72
DEVORE RICHARD E	IN	33E	46
DEVORE WILLIAM ROBERT	WA	12E	126
DEW EDWARD EARL	NC	40E	4
DEW HENRY LOUIS	ME	06E	122
DEW JAMES JUNIOR	NC	43W	61
DEW PAUL ROBERT	MI	34W	14
DEW ROBERT EARL	NC	07W	24
DEWANE RICHARD ALLEN	NY	15E	115
DEWAR JAMES CRAIG	PA	25W	37
DEWBERRY JERRY DON	OK	53W	17
DEWEESE BILLY CLARENCE	OH	04E	88
DEWEY DANNY LEE	MI	09W	13
DEWEY ERIC MELVIN	CA	24E	20
DEWEY JAMES ELLIOTT	PA	17E	98
DEWEY LARRY RICHARD	NY	03W	53
DEWINE ROBERT BRUCE	OH	03W	34
DEWITT DAVID EUGENE	PA	46E	16
DEWLEN MICHAEL LEE	TX	58W	24
DEWVEALL JERALD GLENN	TX	34W	75
DEWYEA RONALD RICHARD	NY	21W	31
DEXTER BENNIE LEE	OR	07E	42
DEXTER HERBERT J	IL	02E	86
DEXTER RICHARD AUGUSTINE	CO	54W	36
DEXTER RONALD CLIFFORD	SD	10E	117
DEXTER RONALD JAMES	TX	21E	43
DEXTER VAUGHN LEROY	PA	22E	100
DEXTRAZE RICHARD PAUL		26W	31
DEYERMOND WARREN CHARLES	MA	21W	116
DEYNEKA CARL	NY	24W	94
DEYO ROBERT WILBUR JR	IA	30E	7
DI ANTONIO MARTIN M JR	NJ	17E	71
DI BARI LOUIS SCOTT	CA	18W	37
DI BARTOLOMEO RONALD J	PA	06W	52
DI BERARDINO PERRY	MA	43W	4
DI CAPRIO PAUL JOSEPH	NY	62E	3
DI CAVALLUCCI VICTOR	NJ	42E	3
DI DOMIZIO JOHN	NY	25E	97
DI FATE RALPH DOUGLAS	NY	43E	43
DI FIGLIA FRANK ANTHONY	CA	28W	44
DI FINIZIO LOUIS CARL	NY	07W	36
DI GENNO MICHAEL	MD	29W	6
DI GREGORIO JOSEPH	NY	11W	6
DI GUARDIA ALEXANDER NICH	NY	28E	73
DI LANDRO JOSEPH JOHN	NY	17E	1
DI LORENZO RAYMOND JOHN	KS	14W	111
DI MARZIO MARTIN JOHN	IL	13W	128
DI NAPOLI JOHN JR	NJ	60E	10
DI NAPOLI MICHAEL JOSEPH	CA	32E	50
DI NUNZIO CARL LAWRENCE JR	NY	28W	10
DI PASQUANTONIO MICHAEL	DE	14W	103
DI PIETRO ROBERT JOHN	MI	03W	118
DI REDA ROBERT J	MA	06E	63
DI RITA GENE	MI	31E	71
DI ROBERTO ROBERT	NY	13E	47
DI SANTI RAYMOND JAMES	PA	10W	32
DI SANTIS WILLIAM RICHARD	IL	11W	6
DI SAPIO DONALD ANTHONY	NY	08E	44
DI STEFANO RONALD MICHAEL	PA	02E	112
DI TOMMASO ROBERT JOSEPH	NY	09E	86
DI TULLIO FRANCO ANTONIO	MA	23W	63
DIAKOW ROBERT	NY	21W	88
DIAL JAMES WILLIAM	TN	56E	5
DIAL ROBERT LEWIS	NC	06E	9
DIAMOND CHARLES EDWARD	PA	14W	93
DIAMOND STEPHEN WHITMAN	NY	09E	38
DIAMOND WILLIAM T JR	IL	26E	74
DIAN DON FAUROT	MO	51E	38
DIANA-DIAZ JOSE RAMON	PR	60E	10
DIANDA CASIMIRO	AZ	30E	40
DIANI FRANCO	NJ	07W	76
DIAS RALPH ELLIS	PA	16W	63
DIAZ ALEJANDRO	NY	65E	7
DIAZ ANGEL LUIS	CT	28E	90
DIAZ BENITO JR	MI	28W	90
DIAZ DANIEL	CA	33E	83
DIAZ EDWARD REYES	GM	08W	20
DIAZ FRANCISCO	NY	60E	21
DIAZ GARY MICHAEL	CA	37E	20
DIAZ GILBERT	NY	35E	54
DIAZ JOSE RENTERIA	TX	27W	62
DIAZ PEDRO	NY	46W	48
DIAZ RAFAEL ANGEL	NY	06W	98
DIAZ-COLLAZO MIGUEL ANGEL	PR	39E	20
DIAZ-DOMENECH JUAN A	PR	18W	128
DIAZ-ROMAN CARMELO	PR	28W	102
DIBB STEPHEN KEITH	WI	09E	51
DIBBERT BERNARD WAYNE	WA	01E	129
DIBBLE GORDON JOHN	CA	28E	54
DIBBLE MORRIS FREDERICK	NY	03E	126
DICE CARL RICHARD	NY	15W	39
DICE ROBERT FLOYD	OH	12W	12
DICESARE ANTHONY JR	NJ	22E	69
DICK ALAN JAY	FL	54E	5
DICK BOYCE RAY	KY	57E	19
DICK BRUCE DAVID	MA	25W	28
DICK MANUEL LEVI	CA	08W	84
DICK SAMUEL EUGENE	HI	05W	4
DICK TIMOTHY MORGAN	PA	31E	80
DICK WILLIAM EDWARD JR	PA	43W	44
DICKASON CLYDE LEROY	AR	35W	70
DICKE DENNIS MICHAEL	IL	03W	75
DICKEN PERRY JR	IL	49E	20
DICKENS DAVID RUDOLPH	AL	03E	11
DICKENS DELMA ERNEST	GA	01W	98
DICKENS ELMER WILLIAM	HI	13E	32
DICKENS FREDDIE DALE	MO	41W	68
DICKENS JACKIE LEE	WV	23W	41
DICKENS JAMES AARON	VA	15E	8
DICKENS ODELL	NC	31W	46
DICKENS PHIL JACKSON	NC	31E	91
DICKENS RUSSELL W	MD	15E	115
DICKENSON LLEWELLYN PAUL	WI	26W	106
DICKERHOFF TERRY WAYNE	IN	28W	103
DICKERSON BERNARD W JR	IA	58W	24
DICKERSON CHARLES C JR	FL	27W	40
DICKERSON DAVID DOWNING	DC	15W	47
DICKERSON DOUGLAS R JR	NJ	24E	113
DICKERSON GEORGE EVERETT	KY	15E	41
DICKERSON HAROLD	IN	29E	71
DICKERSON JAMES CAROL	VA	48W	24
DICKERSON JAMES EGBERT	MD	50E	27
DICKERSON JOHN GREEN III	IN	11E	49
DICKERSON OMER PAUL	MO	31E	33
DICKERSON RICCARDO BURTON	IN	12E	13
DICKERSON ROBERT BOLT III	MD	03W	21
DICKERSON STANLEY HEMAN	NY	19W	59
DICKERSON THOMAS GERALD	GA	38W	42
DICKERSON TOMMY EUGENE	MD	19E	23
DICKERSON WILLIAM CLINT	AZ	25W	97
DICKEY ALAN EVERETT	MI	16W	99
DICKEY CHARLES C JR	FL	17E	78
DICKEY CHARLES JOSEPH	NH	53W	33
DICKEY DERREL KEITH	KS	08W	45
DICKEY DOUGLAS EUGENE	OH	17E	50
DICKEY FORREST PITTMAN	MO	12E	132
DICKEY GARY LYNN	KS	02E	43
DICKEY JAMES MARCELL	TN	03W	108
DICKEY JAMES WHEELER	VA	06W	14
DICKEY THOMAS ROBERT	MA	32W	5
DICKEY WILLIAM RONALD	OH	20W	122
DICKEY WILLIAM WALTER	IL	32W	96
DICKIE GUY DOUGLAS	PA	38E	25
DICKINSON DANIEL ALBERT	KS	03E	135
DICKINSON DAVID THOMAS	CO	31E	45
DICKINSON EUGENE HAROLD	VT	20E	72
DICKINSON JOHN ALBERT	NY	44W	36
DICKINSON LESLIE A JR	ME	37E	5
DICKINSON ROBERT CHARLES	DC	54W	28
DICKINSON THOMAS MORTON	TN	22E	57
DICKMAN DAVID MICHAEL	OH	37W	84
DICKS MARVIN MERLE	MI	14E	61
DICKSON EDWARD ANDREW	PA	01E	85
DICKSON ERIC VOUGHN	CO	62W	8
DICKSON GROVER LEE	LA	12E	54
DICKSON JIM LEE	OR	31W	66
DICKSON KENNETH ODELL	TN	07W	106
DICKSON MARK LANE	MI	44E	67
DICKSON ROBERT LEE	CO	37E	5
DICKSON RONALD GEORGE	MO	07W	2
DICKSON THOMAS GEORGE	CA	13W	53
DICKSON WILLIAM DOUGLAS	CA	32E	54
DICKUS MICHAEL JOHN	IN	08W	27
DICUS RICHARD LEE	MO	14W	7
DIDAMO RALPH ANTHONY JR	NY	04E	52
DIDASKALOU GEORGE ARTHUR	MI	25E	92
DIDIER JOHN PAUL JR	IL	12W	45
DIDURYK MYRON	NJ	11W	44
DIEBALL DENNIS RAY	CA	29E	2
DIECKMAN JAMES HENRY	MI	34W	12
DIECKMANN JOHN E	OH	07E	80
DIEDERICH JOHN LEO	KS	47W	40
DIEDRICH JAMES NICHOLAS	WI	13W	27
DIEDRICH ROBERT JAMES	WI	53E	11
DIEDRICKSEN ALAN LEE	CT	22E	100
DIEFENBACH LARRY ARTHUR	IN	33E	46
DIEFENDERFER THOMAS EDWAR	CA	54E	5
DIEFFENBACH ROBERT W JR	DE	41W	72
DIEHL DANA EDWARD	PA	37W	79
DIEHL HARRY G	CA	22W	75
DIEHL PATRICK REGAN	OH	24W	64
DIEHL ROBERT ERNEST	PA	30W	12
DIEHL STANLEY GENE	FL	08W	41
DIEHL WILLIAM CALVIN JR	OK	29E	40
DIEKEMA ARNOLD RAYMOND	MI	38W	42
DIEMLER RICHARD LEE	PA	30W	36
DIERS RICHARD WALTER	FL	38W	16
DIERYCK JAMES LEO	MN	02E	63
DIETZ DIETER WALTER	PA	12E	119
DIETZ DONALD WILLIAM	AR	18W	105
DIETZ GARY PHILIP	FL	33E	83
DIETZ LAWRENCE ALFRED II	CA	24E	7
DIETZ LEWIS RAY	OR	05E	32
DIETZ WALLACE JAMES	SC	49E	30
DIETZ WOLF-DIETER	CA	45W	36
DIEU GARY ALLEN	WA	14E	90
DIEUDONNE CARROLL STEPHEN	MD	53W	21
DIEZ ISAAC ANDREW JR	LA	21E	26
DIFFENDERFER TERRY EUGENE	PA	54W	23
DIGGS JOHN FRANCIS	CA	49W	39
DIGGS MICHAEL RONELL	VA	53E	12
DIGGS WILLIAM FRANKLIN	MI	18W	88
DIGSBY LEROY	FL	58W	18
DIKEMAN LARRY ERNEST	OR	23W	25
DIKER GEORGE JR	NY	20E	96
DILALLO JOHN LAWRENCE	NY	01W	48
DILBECK LONNIE ADKEN	AL	35W	15
DILE STEVEN ORLANDO	PA	14W	74
DILGER HERBERT HUGH	NY	17W	25
DILIBERTO KIM MICHAEL	NY	19W	53
DILL GARVIN WAYNE	AR	10W	96
DILL JAMES ARTHUR	SC	49E	27
DILLARD BERNARD	IL	09E	38
DILLARD DONALD GARY	WA	19W	12
DILLARD HAROLD JEROME	NJ	20E	102
DILLARD JAMES BRYAN	NC	37W	31
DILLARD JAMES L III	FL	44W	47
DILLARD JERRY ALLEN	VA	41W	66
DILLARD JOHN ALBERT B JR	LA	10W	23
DILLARD JOHN EDWARD	MO	41E	49

NAME	STATE	PANEL NO.	LINE NO.
DILLARD TERRY LEE	TN	50W	18
DILLARD THOMAS MANUEL	AL	05E	53
DILLENDER WILLIAM EDWARD	FL	04W	60
DILLENSEGER BERNARD GUY J	VA	02W	10
DILLER JAY THOMAS	PA	11W	110
DILLETT LENO RENALDO	NY	03W	11
DILLEY DANA ALLEN	OH	13W	126
DILLINDER RANDY EUGENE	MI	31E	72
DILLMAN ROGER L	VA	64E	13
DILLMAN WAYNE THOMAS	PA	38E	25
DILLON DAVID ANDREW	CA	09E	45
DILLON DENNIS EARL	PA	61W	11
DILLON DENNIS JAMES	CA	09W	82
DILLON DONALD EUGENE	KS	23E	17
DILLON FRANCIS THOMAS	NJ	18E	114
DILLON GEORGE ALFRED CHED	CA	49E	52
DILLON JACK HOWARD	OR	08W	65
DILLON JAMES DALE	FL	48E	57
DILLON PATRICK MAURICE	IA	15W	69
DILLON RAYMOND LAWRENCE	NY	47E	49
DILLON RICHARD HALL JR	AR	63E	8
DILLON WILLIAM JERRY	IL	22E	11
DILLOW JERRY WAYNE	WV	48E	51
DILLS RONALD EUGENE	IN	11W	122
DILLWORTH EARL JR	AL	19E	4
DILMORE JOHN HARRY	PA	12W	79
DILWORTH ARTHUR WILLIAM	MS	53W	18
DILWORTH HENSLEY MCFADDEN	MS	17E	71
DIMAGARD WILLIAM CHARLES	OH	46E	53
DIMICK HARLEY DANIEL	OR	24W	94
DIMITT ROBERT VICTOR	KS	40W	31
DIMMER MICHAEL PHILLIP	AZ	15W	111
DIMMERLING ROME EDWARD	OH	51E	6
DIMMITT FRANK ROBERT	OR	42E	49
DIMOCK JAMES ALBERT JR	TX	24W	39
DIMOND ALVIN JAMES	IL	02E	7
DIMOULAS CHRISTY TED	NY	32E	92
DINAN DAVID THOMAS III	NJ	29W	62
DINDA MICHAEL JOSEPH	CT	15W	106
DINE JAMES CHARLES	IL	20W	117
DINEEN THOMAS GERARD JR	PA	24E	98
DINEEN TIMOTHY JOHN	CA	37E	35
DINES JEFFERY THOMAS	IA	14E	20
DINGELDEIN DONALD GLEN	WI	10E	92
DINGER JAMES ROBERT	MI	05E	41
DINGLE EARL	SC	27E	58
DINGMAN MILFRED HAROLD	IL	29W	6
DINGUS CARL	IN	37E	6
DINGUS JOHN WILLIAM JR	TN	42W	54
DINGUS MICHAEL JOE	MO	31E	45
DINGWALL JOHN FRANCIS	NY	02E	31
DINKINS MICHAEL GARY	FL	32W	70
DION LAURENT NORBERT	RI	25E	6
DION THOMAS JAMES	MI	20W	48
DIONNE DONALD THOMAS SR	CA	01W	122
DIONNE ROBERT PAUL	NH	02E	37
DIORIO MARK STEVEN	CA	13W	56
DIPACE RALPH JOSEPH	NY	28E	103
DIPERT MARVIN LEE	IN	20W	13
DIPHILLIPO ROCCO	ME	04W	45
DIPOLO ROLAND FORREST	FL	22W	20
DIREEN KEVEN THOMAS	NM	50E	46
DIRICKSON MARION LEE	OK	21E	41
DIRNBERGER LAWRENCE ANDRE	MO	15E	89
DISCEPOLO ANTHONY ALBERT	OH	68E	1
DISCHERT JAMES RICHARD	IL	02E	118
DISCHHAUSER DIETER HERBER	NY	03W	9
DISHEROON BILLY WAYNE	TX	03W	136
DISHMAN DOUGLAS EDWARD	VA	44E	34
DISHMAN JERRY	OH	28W	45
DISHMAN WILLIAM ANDREW	KY	18E	38
DISMAYA EDDIE JR	CA	49W	29
DISMUKE ALBERT ROYCE	GA	42E	50
DISMUKES RAYMOND KYLE	AL	16W	120
DISON EDWARD DEAN	TN	16E	8
DISPENSIERO DOUGLAS LOUIS	CA	16E	85
DISRUD DAVID A	MN	42W	68
DISSELKOEN DONALD GENE	IL	23W	72
DISSINGER GARY FRANK	PA	28E	81
DISTEFANO FERDINANDO	NY	41E	8
DITCH DAVID KENNETH	IA	44E	35
DITORO WILLIAM FENTON	NY	13E	121

NAME	STATE	PANEL NO.	LINE NO.
DITSON LYMAN RICHARD	CO	33W	93
DITTMER DAVID ALLEN	MO	27W	107
DITTMER LEWIS ALLEN	UT	48W	53
DITZFELD BOBBIE LEE	MO	35E	20
DIVENS MELVIN	IL	68E	1
DIVES THOMAS LAMONTE JR	CA	20W	86
DIX CRAIG MITCHELL	MI	04W	54
DIX DONALD ANDREW	CO	01W	95
DIX STANLEY WESLEY	LA	23E	109
DIXON ALONZO LENORD	IL	65E	8
DIXON CARL DEAN	MI	11W	130
DIXON CARLTON LEO	GA	02W	97
DIXON CECIL F	NJ	23E	1
DIXON CHARLES ALVIN	FL	37W	80
DIXON CORDIE LEE	SC	05E	32
DIXON DAVID ALLEN	NY	19E	126
DIXON DAVID ERNEST	FL	59W	21
DIXON DAVID LEE	IN	21E	32
DIXON DAVID LLOYD	OR	42W	35
DIXON DONALD WAYNE	GA	39E	58
DIXON FRAZIER THOMAS	SC	15W	21
DIXON GALE WILLIAM	IN	65E	13
DIXON JAMES C	MS	18E	101
DIXON JESSE JAMES	NC	16E	7
DIXON JOHN ALANSON	NY	23W	14
DIXON JOHN HENERY	VA	61E	9
DIXON JOHN T	PA	08E	26
DIXON LEE ARTICE	AL	29E	40
DIXON LEE CHRIS	CA	04E	56
DIXON LELAND FRANCIS	AL	05E	115
DIXON LEO CHESTER	AL	10E	37
DIXON LINDEN BROOK	MD	28E	81
DIXON LOUIS KRIMMIT	AL	28W	58
DIXON MARK HANNAY	CT	26W	76
DIXON MICHAEL KENNETH L	CA	24W	64
DIXON MIKLE EUGENE	NC	03W	41
DIXON MORRIS FRANKLIN JR	FL	19E	70
DIXON PATRICK MARTIN	IL	23W	7
DIXON RICHARD LEE	IL	34W	14
DIXON ROBERT DALE	FL	23W	51
DIXON ROGER ALLEN	VA	34W	22
DIXON STEPHEN DOUGLAS	PA	19E	80
DIXON TERRENCE GLADE	FL	17E	121
DIXON TOMMY JOE	AR	29W	44
DIXON WARREN MITCHELL	KY	39E	45
DIXON WILLIAM ALFRED JR	TX	21E	11
DIXON WILLIAM ALLEN	MD	14W	80
DIZE GEORGE HARLAND	MD	39E	31
DLUGOKINSKI EDMUND VALENT	MI	12E	87
DLUZAK DAVID MARTIN	IN	43E	5
DOADES FLOYD EUGENE	IN	02E	56
DOAK STANLEY WAYNE	NE	17W	15
DOAK TOMMY ALLEN	OH	03E	74
DOAN LESTER ALLAN	MT	40W	11
DOAN TERRY WAYNE	KY	04W	65
DOANE GEORGE ALFRED	CA	21E	21
DOANE JAMES ABRAHAM	HI	17W	120
DOANE MICHAEL LEO	MT	46E	45
DOANE STEPHEN HELDEN	NY	28W	34
DOBASH JOHN ERNEST	NY	26W	45
DOBBIN LOUIS DAVID II	MA	20E	24
DOBBINS FREDDIE JUNIOR	NC	37W	80
DOBBINS GARY LEE	OH	47W	17
DOBBINS ISAIAH ANTHONY	NJ	15E	4
DOBBS DONEL JOE	AR	02W	115
DOBBS GERALD THOMAS	TN	30E	24
DOBBS JIMMIE LEE	IL	12E	36
DOBBS ROBERT ARTHUR	TX	24W	83
DOBBS RONALD GENE	MO	54E	5
DOBBS RONALD STEPHEN	MI	43E	16
DOBISH JAMES THOMAS	WI	20E	57
DOBOSZ DAVID GEORGE	WI	09W	72
DOBRENZ LAWRENCE CARL	WI	11E	102
DOBRINSKA THOMAS EARL	WI	38E	67
DOBROSKI JOHN LEE	TX	05W	52
DOBRY STEVEN LOUIS	OK	09W	32
DOBRZYNSKI RAYMOND PAUL	DE	44E	35
DOBSON CAREY LEE	PA	24W	64
DOBSON CECIL LEE	KY	13W	126
DOBSON JAMES CARLINE	KY	11E	73
DOBY CARL LEE	NC	55W	27
DOBY HERB	OR	14E	116

NAME	STATE	PANEL NO.	LINE NO.
DOBY JOHN WILLIAM	CO	37E	53
DOBYNES JOSEPH JAMES	AL	28W	59
DOBYNS RUSSELL MARTIN JR	GA	25W	37
DOCK RAYMOND LEE JR	CA	22W	57
DOCKERY ROOSEVELT GEORGE	NY	14W	100
DOCKERY STEVE JULIUS	TN	43W	35
DOCKSTADER RANDELL L	UT	39W	32
DOCTOR GARY DEAN	NY	11E	56
DODD BILLY FRANCIS	CA	14W	120
DODD CHARLES DAVID	GA	02W	63
DODD DANNY JOE	WV	32W	12
DODD EDDIE LEROY	TX	04W	75
DODD JAMES ERWIN	MD	13W	96
DODD JAMES WILLIAM	FL	53E	1
DODD JOSEPH JAMES	NY	19E	57
DODD LAWRENCE ADDINSON	TX	42E	15
DODD LAWRENCE RUDIN	CA	20E	113
DODD RICHARD EUGENE	OK	05W	16
DODD RICHARD WILLIAM	IL	08W	31
DODDS LARRY FLOYD	MS	24W	58
DODDY VICTOR LOUIS	PA	51W	3
DODE FRED RICHARD	IL	30E	55
DODGE EDWARD RAY	VA	01E	80
DODGE GREGORY ALEXIS	CA	08W	2
DODGE JEFFREY BRUNS	NY	11W	49
DODGE JEWELL FLETCHER	AR	23E	50
DODGE MICHAEL JAMES	MI	22W	46
DODGE RONALD WAYNE	CA	20E	14
DODGE WARD KENT	KS	23E	13
DODSON BILLY	TN	07E	17
DODSON DAVID LEE	CA	08E	16
DODSON DAVID PAUL	GA	35E	31
DODSON ERNEST DEAN	KS	35W	24
DODSON FREDDY DEAN	TX	01E	56
DODSON JACK LEROY	ID	20E	113
DODSON JERRY LEE	IL	41E	19
DODSON JOHN LARRY	OH	09E	56
DODSON LEONARD	NY	29W	67
DODSON PAUL ALONZO SR	DC	03W	94
DODSON ROBERT GERALD	NJ	53W	34
DODSON SEAN PAUL	TN	05E	101
DODSON WESLEY ELLSWORTH	PA	28E	21
DODSON WILLIAM NEAL JR	MO	54W	9
DODSWORTH ROBERT LEE	IL	49E	43
DOEBERT PHILLIP RAY	MO	25W	66
DOEDEN NICOLAUS AUGUST	NE	01E	132
DOELGER-LANDIVAR HERMANN	FL	45E	10
DOERING LLOYD DOUGLAS	VA	45W	60
DOERING ROBERT	PA	11W	79
DOERRMAN CHARLES ELLSWORT	PA	01E	22
DOEZEMA FRANK JR	MI	36E	6
DOGGETT EDWARD JOSEPH	IL	02W	45
DOGGETT RONALD THOMAS	MO	60E	11
DOHERTY GUY WOODS	LA	50W	22
DOHERTY JOHN WILLIAM	NJ	22E	100
DOHERTY MARTIN STEPHEN	NY	15W	23
DOIG DOUGLAS WILLIAM	MA	13E	90
DOIKE JOHN TOSHIO	HI	09E	36
DOILEY ARTHUR LEROY JR	NY	48W	40
DOIRON WILFRED ALCIDE	OK	08E	74
DOKE JAMES ALLEN	OK	06E	44
DOKES CHARLES WILLIE	AR	13W	62
DOLAN DAVID PATRICK	CA	34W	82
DOLAN HASKELL JUNIOR	LA	07W	103
DOLAN JAMES EDWIN	MA	10W	96
DOLAN JIMMY MICHAEL	NJ	19W	106
DOLAN THOMAS ALBERT	MD	03W	127
DOLAN THOMAS WILLIAM III	MA	22W	31
DOLAN WILLIAM JOHN	CT	50E	35
DOLBOW BRUCE EDWARD	DE	46W	14
DOLBY MELVIN LESTER	PA	48E	40
DOLEN JIMMIE ALAN	WA	55E	9
DOLIBER EDGAR SNOW	MA	07E	24
DOLIK PAUL EDWARD	IL	13W	48
DOLIM STEVEN FRANCIS JR	CA	60W	27
DOLIN DANNY JOSEPH	WV	10E	82
DOLL JEROME NORMAN	WI	23W	26
DOLLAR EUGENE DOYCE	WI	04E	88
DOLLARD JAMES	SC	29W	44
DOLLENS HAROLD RAY	MO	01E	97
DOLOUGHTY JAMES CORNELIUS	PA	21W	88
DOLVIN JAMES RICHARD	NY	22W	75

NAME	STATE	PANEL NO.	LINE NO.
DOMAN BENJAMIN VICTOR	IL	07W	80
DOMAN HAROLD ARTHER	PA	30E	90
DOMBROSKI DARRYL TOD	OH	25W	28
DOMER GLENN WILSON	PA	27W	72
DOMIAN EDWARD THOMAS JR	PA	04E	107
DOMIANO PETER PAUL	NY	08E	115
DOMINE MANUEL DE LEON	OK	06W	20
DOMINGUEZ CARLOS	TX	59E	21
DOMINGUEZ ERNESTO	CA	08E	15
DOMINGUEZ FRANK L	AZ	39W	64
DOMINGUEZ JOE REINI	TX	34E	68
DOMINGUEZ MICHAEL CHARLES	CA	16E	89
DOMINGUEZ MICHAEL GENE	CO	10W	113
DOMINGUEZ MICHAEL J	AZ	10E	82
DOMINGUEZ ROBERTO	TX	34W	75
DOMINGUEZ-CORTES ELIEZER	PR	41W	34
DOMINIAK HOWARD STANLEY	IL	18E	79
DOMINIAK MARIAN J JR	WI	32E	43
DOMINICK CHARLIE JUNIOR	GA	52W	42
DOMINIQUE GARY MARK	FL	10W	40
DOMINKOWITZ MICHAEL JOHN	NY	25W	97
DOMKE PAUL LOUIS	MI	23E	99
DONA BIENVENIDO GENIZA		06E	42
DONAGHY EDGAR STOMS	PA	01E	116
DONAHE WARREN LEE	CA	14W	12
DONAHOE DAVID JOHN	WI	28E	90
DONAHUE CHRISTOPHER C	MA	24W	53
DONAHUE JAMES ALLAN	IL	08W	129
DONAHUE JAMES T JR	IL	26E	111
DONAHUE JOHN JOSEPH	MA	64W	8
DONAHUE JOHN THOMAS	MN	10W	79
DONAHUE MORGAN JEFFERSON	VA	36W	14
DONAHUE RICHARD EARLE	IA	11E	108
DONAHUE ROBERT WILLIAM JR	PA	16W	130
DONAHUE WELLINGTON MARTIN	MD	12E	33
DONALD HARMON ODELL JR	MS	14W	115
DONALD HOWARD ARTHUR	PA	21E	73
DONALD ROBERT CYRILL	NC	15E	54
DONALDSON DARRELL WAYNE	TX	30W	87
DONALDSON DONALD ROBERT	PA	13W	103
DONALDSON EVERETTE LEROY	MD	01E	55
DONALDSON HERBERT C JR	MI	28E	95
DONALDSON JAMES ALLEN	MO	43W	35
DONALDSON LAWRENCE GERARD	PA	31W	46
DONALDSON ROBERT D	MD	04E	122
DONALDSON STEVEN ELLIS	MA	27W	16
DONATHAN RICHARD PETE	CO	09E	121
DONATIELLO JERRY RICHARD	NJ	30E	40
DONATO PAUL NICHOLAS	MA	39E	70
DONAVAN TIMOTHY CHARLES	PA	25W	66
DONAWAY ROBERT HUGHES	DE	19W	59
DONDERO ROBERT ALFRED	MA	16W	37
DONER PATRICK RALPH	VT	24E	76
DONESKI HENRY JOHN	CT	34E	17
DONICS WILLIAM CALDWELL	PA	24W	16
DONKER LEO MICHAEL	FL	06E	79
DONLAN RICHARD MICHAEL	VA	31W	90
DONLON MICHAEL PATRICK	NY	08E	10
DONNAL JOHN ANDREW	IL	24E	60
DONNELL JAMES PATRICK	TN	04E	86
DONNELL LAWRENCE HENRY	MD	21E	78
DONNELL PETER FRANCIS	VA	52E	17
DONNELL ROBERT A II	NY	06W	67
DONNELLAN DANIEL PAUL	WA	15E	57
DONNELLY ALAN CHARLES	NY	39W	65
DONNELLY DAVID	IL	33E	12
DONNELLY JAMES VOELKEL	DE	06E	48
DONNELLY JAMES WARREN JR	MO	20W	97
DONNELLY JOHN JOSEPH III	PA	09W	83
DONNELLY RAYMOND PETER	CT	01W	57
DONNELLY VERNE GEORGE	CA	01W	73
DONOHO WILFORD LYNN	IL	17W	40
DONOHOE CHARLES VINCENT	NY	06W	43
DONOHUE FRANCIS CHARLES	CT	15E	127
DONOHUE FRANCIS DAVID	PA	36W	84
DONOHUE JOHN MARTIN	MI	43W	4
DONOHUE RONALD FRANCIS	IN	47W	40
DONOHUE STEPHEN SCOTT	OK	63W	5
DONOHUE WILLIAM EDMOND	NY	35E	45
DONOVAN ARTHUR EDMUND	NY	14E	76
DONOVAN DENNIS GEORGE	PA	04W	120
DONOVAN JOHN DENNIS	NJ	63E	8

NAME	STATE	PANEL NO.	LINE NO.
DONOVAN JOSEPH MICHAEL	NY	16E	20
DONOVAN LEROY MELVIN	CO	01E	121
DONOVAN MICHAEL G III	NY	35E	4
DONOVAN MICHAEL JOHN	IL	59W	21
DONOVAN MICHAEL LEO	KS	02W	31
DONOVAN PAMELA DOROTHY	MA	53W	43
DONOVAN PATRICK JOHN	CA	16W	33
DONOVAN PETER MICHAEL	NY	45W	13
DONOVAN ROBERT JOHN	NY	12E	46
DONOVAN ROBERT MARTIN	RI	60E	21
DONOVAN THOMAS EDWARD	CT	45E	62
DONOVAN THOMAS STEPHEN	MA	21E	44
DONOVAN TOMMY CLAYTON II	CA	35W	46
DONOVAN WILLIAM JOSEPH	NY	03W	114
DONSTAD JAMES MARVIN	WI	33W	53
DOODY ALBERT CHARLES	NY	10E	79
DOODY DOUGLAS WILLIAM	OH	36E	6
DOODY THOMAS PATRICK	CO	05W	87
DOOLEY DENNIS LYNN	IL	12E	50
DOOLEY JAMES EDWARD	VT	28E	48
DOOLEY MICHAEL BANION	CA	46W	14
DOOLEY RICHARD LEE	OR	31E	97
DOOLEY ROBERT ELLIS	MS	40E	61
DOOLITTLE GARY WAYNE	OH	41W	71
DOOLITTLE JON HILIARE	NE	11W	111
DOOLITTLE RONALD LEE	OR	03W	27
DOOLITTLE RONALD LOUIS	CA	40W	2
DOOM CHARLES LEONARD	KY	19E	23
DOORNBOS DON MICHAEL	KS	39E	31
DOOSE GARY LEE	TX	18E	84
DOPP GARY RUSSELL	WI	11E	13
DOPP RICHARD ERNEST	OH	21W	32
DORAN JAMES DONALD	NJ	38W	65
DORAN PATRICK MICHAEL	CA	15E	57
DORAN SEAN TIMOTHY	CA	28W	68
DORAN THOMAS E	AL	10E	63
DORAN TIMOTHY PATRICK	OH	51W	24
DORAN WILLIAM JOSEPH	NY	26E	34
DORCHAK GEORGE ROBERT	PA	45W	61
DORE GARY AUSTIN	KY	03W	50
DORFMAN WILLIAM DAVID	AL	05E	131
DORIA ALDO ANTHONY	CT	44W	9
DORIA RICHARD ALBERT	NY	19W	67
DORING LARRY ALLEN	MN	23E	41
DORIO JOHN WILLIAM ALLEN	NJ	40W	32
DORITY RICHARD CLAIR	ME	02W	60
DORMAN CHARLES DUDLEY	CA	59E	2
DORMAN DANIEL GENE	CA	03W	106
DORMAN DARREL GENE	MN	07E	117
DORMAN DONALD RALPH	MD	15E	41
DORMAN GEORGE STANTON	OR	20W	95
DORMAN MICHAEL RODNEY	TX	26W	45
DORN MICHAEL LEWIS	PA	34W	36
DORN PHILIP KENNETH	NJ	08E	6
DORNAK LEONARD EDWARD	TX	33E	83
DORNBERGH WILLIAM L JR	CA	20E	113
DORNELLAS RICHARD ALLISON	FL	14W	71
DORNER ROBERT ANDREW	NY	06E	44
DORNON CHARLES WILLIAM	KS	22W	75
DORONZO PAUL FRANK	CO	14W	83
DOROUGH JERRY EUGENE	AL	38W	10
DORR GERALD ANDREW	ME	14E	90
DORR GERALD BRIAN	MA	18E	28
DORRIES CARL WAYNE	TX	36E	6
DORRIS CLAUDE HESSON	KY	33E	66
DORRIS CURTIS EUGENE	TN	06E	73
DORRIS DAVID WALTER	MT	50E	37
DORSCH RICHARD STEPHEN	PA	37E	81
DORSE ROBERT EDWARD JR	MI	14W	7
DORSETT HARRY CLINTON	IN	36W	11
DORSETT ROY GEREAD	AZ	54W	15
DORSEY CARLITO LADORES	CA	12E	99
DORSEY CECIL EVERETT	IL	11E	7
DORSEY DENNIS	IL	39E	45
DORSEY EDWARD ROBERT	CT	24E	19
DORSEY GARDNER	MD	15W	118
DORSEY GEORGE HARRY JR	MI	15E	83
DORSEY HARRY JAMES	SC	35W	81
DORSEY JAMES R JR	MD	26W	53
DORSEY JAMES VERNON JR	DC	33W	61
DORSEY LEWIS R G	KS	44E	25
DORSEY ROBERT LEE	GA	10E	12

NAME	STATE	PANEL NO.	LINE NO.
DORSEY ROGER	GA	07E	45
DORSEY WILLIAM BANFIELD	NY	12E	94
DORSEY WILLIAM TIMOTHY	NY	09W	115
DORSHAK ROBERT JOSEPH	IN	46W	14
DOSECK RICHARD ALLEN	OH	30W	100
DOSS HAROLD CONWAY JR	LA	27E	52
DOSS LARRY DONNELL	TN	43W	45
DOSS LUTHER JAMES JR	MD	11W	72
DOSS RAYMOND	KY	11E	126
DOSS ROBERT WILLIAM	VA	01E	109
DOSSETT JAMES EDWIN	IL	27E	52
DOSSETT JOHN ADRIAN JR	MO	09W	43
DOSTAL THOMAS JEROME	IA	19W	111
DOSTER HENRY JAMES	NY	05E	115
DOTEN ROBERT ALAN	MA	05W	25
DOTSON DENNIS WILLIAM	CA	09W	13
DOTSON DONALD LUTHER	TN	04E	107
DOTSON EUGENE LEWIS	CA	34W	32
DOTSON JEFFERSON SCOTT	VA	20W	118
DOTSON MICHAEL LEE	GA	21E	11
DOTSON MICHAEL ROBERT	MI	22E	101
DOTSON RICHARD WAYNE	KY	05W	8
DOTSON WILLIAM THOMAS III	TX	07W	76
DOTTER EDWIN EARL	KS	23W	20
DOTY CHARLES	LA	29E	48
DOTY CLAIR DUANE	MI	01E	51
DOTY JAMES MARSHALL	WV	08W	72
DOTY LOYAL BARON	WV	38E	48
DOTY VAUGHN ORMON	NY	35W	82
DOTY WESLEY GEORGE	NJ	44W	36
DOUBERLY JAMES ODEN	GA	14E	20
DOUCET LEON NORMAND	NH	14E	122
DOUCET WILLIAM BRADLEY	CA	10W	50
DOUD NORMAN KENT	CT	52W	34
DOUGAN CHARLES GARVIN	MO	11W	101
DOUGAN MICHAEL JAMES	CT	08W	126
DOUGANS EMMETT ARTHUR	DC	09E	10
DOUGHER THOMAS EDWARD	NY	18E	120
DOUGHERTY JOHN CHRISTIAN	IN	57E	19
DOUGHERTY KENNETH EUGENE	MO	16E	83
DOUGHERTY KIRBY JON	SD	45W	18
DOUGHERTY LON JR	TN	13W	41
DOUGHERTY ROBERT JOSEPH	NJ	22E	29
DOUGHERTY THEODORE ALOYIS	PA	30E	76
DOUGHTIE CARL LOUIS	NC	02E	4
DOUGHTIE RONALD EDWARD	PA	01W	39
DOUGHTY JAMES ALDEN	MA	19W	128
DOUGHTY ROBERT THOMAS	NJ	13E	32
DOUGLAS CARL SCOTT	NC	30W	11
DOUGLAS CHARLES MAC	CA	17E	17
DOUGLAS CLARK ROBERT	NY	16W	56
DOUGLAS DELBERT	OH	18W	61
DOUGLAS DONALD DAVID	WA	09W	63
DOUGLAS DWIGHT SAMUEL	VA	14W	97
DOUGLAS FRANK FREDERICK	PA	10E	105
DOUGLAS HARVEY JAMES	ME	34W	32
DOUGLAS JAMES DALE	IN	40E	4
DOUGLAS JAMES THOMAS	TN	33W	71
DOUGLAS JOHNNIE LAMAR	FL	57W	17
DOUGLAS JOHNNIE LEE	CA	37E	20
DOUGLAS LARRY WAYNE	MI	12W	107
DOUGLAS LESLIE FORREST JR	MS	09W	104
DOUGLAS PAUL MELVYN	MS	40E	52
DOUGLAS ROBERT EDWARD JR	NY	29E	94
DOUGLAS TERRY LEE	IL	50W	22
DOUGLAS THOMAS EVAN	OH	03E	107
DOUGLAS WILLIAM LOWELL JR	OH	09E	23
DOUGLASS GERALD TYLER JR	CA	41E	20
DOUILLETTE WILLIAM R JR	NH	13W	12
DOUSE JAMES LOUIS	SC	04E	37
DOVE JACK PARIS SR	VA	23E	57
DOVER GEORGE RICHARD	IN	22W	88
DOVER JOHNNY LEWIS JR	SC	09W	13
DOW ROBERT MELVIN	NM	01W	96
DOWD CARTER WAYNE	GA	12W	66
DOWD FRANCIS JOSEPH JR	CT	44E	34
DOWD JOHN ALOYSIUS	NJ	19W	30
DOWD LAWRENCE KENT	MA	19W	1
DOWD THOMAS BROWN	NY	15E	127
DOWD THOMAS JOSEPH	PA	15W	77
DOWD WILLIAM DAVID	WA	33E	47
DOWDELL MARVIN	GA	11E	76

NAME	STATE	PANEL NO.	LINE NO.
DOWDELL STEPHEN	CA	20W	64
DOWDS ROBERT RAOUL	MA	11W	100
DOWDY JAMES RAY	IL	19E	23
DOWDY MITCHEL ANTHONY	GA	02W	136
DOWDY RUFUS JOHN	VA	29E	29
DOWDY WILLIAM	TN	08E	80
DOWELL GARY LOUIS	KY	02E	137
DOWELL GILBERT	NY	04W	23
DOWJOTAS GERALD JAY	IL	03W	92
DOWLING CLIFFORD FRANKLIN	OR	03W	115
DOWLING FRANCIS ELLSWORTH	ND	28E	21
DOWLING JEAN PIERRE	WI	04E	107
DOWLING JESSE WILLARD	OK	61W	22
DOWLING JOHN ROBERT	IA	56W	33
DOWLING ROBERT MOFFETT	WA	04E	67
DOWLING WILLIE JR	NJ	16E	57
DOWNARD CLYDE DAVID JR	KY	40W	28
DOWNEY CHARLES ROBERT JR	PA	20E	14
DOWNEY CLAY EDWARD	OH	15E	19
DOWNEY EARL GARLAND	PA	02E	22
DOWNEY EDWARD FRANCIS JR	OH	05W	128
DOWNEY EDWARD JOSEPH JR	MA	49E	21
DOWNEY GERALD JOSEPH	NY	35W	54
DOWNEY JOHN FRANCIS JR	NY	43W	26
DOWNEY MICHAEL WAKEFIELD	MA	22E	91
DOWNEY PATRICK H	IL	41E	8
DOWNEY STEPHEN WOOD	CO	43E	16
DOWNIN RAYMOND CHARLES	NY	46E	53
DOWNING DAVID ALLEN	IN	16E	57
DOWNING DONALD WILLIAM	WI	25E	113
DOWNING DUANE AULDON	MI	32W	96
DOWNING JAMES LESLIE	MO	16W	38
DOWNING JOHN FREDERICK	CA	11W	13
DOWNING JOHN LESLIE	AZ	55E	9
DOWNING JOSEPH HENRY JR	NC	38E	67
DOWNING LESTER EARL	NC	26W	77
DOWNING MICHAEL WILLIAM	IN	47E	49
DOWNING WILLIAM KELLY	OK	19E	24
DOWNS ARTHUR MITCHELL	GA	11E	83
DOWNS CARL LESTER	AR	42E	4
DOWNS CHARLES MILTON	LA	32W	59
DOWNS EDWARD JOSEPH	DC	50W	23
DOWNS EDWIN ALFAY	OR	25W	66
DOWNS JACK DENNIS	CA	48E	25
DOWNS JAMES LARRY	AL	13W	91
DOWNS JERRY WAYNE	IN	10E	117
DOWNS LLOYD J	DE	22W	88
DOWNS VERNON LEROY JR	AL	45E	62
DOWNS WILLIAM GEORGE JR	IA	42E	45
DOXEY JAN DEAN	FL	40E	61
DOYE RICKY LEE	IL	55E	7
DOYLE ALBERT BARCINAS	GM	14E	60
DOYLE DAVID LEE	OH	16W	92
DOYLE HOWARD L	MI	31E	91
DOYLE JOHN FRANCIS	CT	10E	37
DOYLE JOSEPH CLARENCE	PA	41E	63
DOYLE LARRY R	MN	32E	92
DOYLE MICHAEL CHARLES	IL	12E	36
DOYLE MICHAEL WALTER	NY	30W	74
DOYLE MICHAEL WILLIAM	PA	01W	69
DOYLE PATRICK LAWRENCE	MN	28E	8
DOYLE PATRICK MICHAEL	WA	06E	50
DOYLE RAYMOND E JR	PA	01E	21
DOYLE REX WAYNE	TX	62E	3
DOYLE ROBERT WALTER	DE	33E	47
DOYON PAUL FRANCIS	MA	20E	24
DOZIER DEBROW	MS	08E	2
DOZIER JAMES EDWARD	MI	10E	38
DOZIER JERALD LEON	TX	02E	121
DOZIER JOBIE CLAYTON	NM	15E	83
DOZIER JOHN TILLMAN II	GA	03W	80
DOZIER WILLIE CLAY	SC	28W	34
DRABY LEROY JUNIOR	MI	26E	34
DRAEGER WALTER FRANK JR	WI	01E	100
DRAEMER CHARLES EDWARD	NC	63W	15
DRAGONE JAMES VINCENT	NY	05W	3
DRAGOSAVAC DAVID GEORGE	PA	12W	66
DRAGOTI JAMES ROBERT	NY	03E	75
DRAHER CLIFFORD EARL	OH	15W	71
DRAIN HOWARD ELMER	SD	02W	115
DRAK ROBERT	PA	23W	85
DRAKE CARL WILSON	OH	09W	65
DRAKE CLANCY GEORGE	WA	04E	4
DRAKE DAVID LAWRENCE JR	MA	06E	24
DRAKE DONALD JOSEPH	PA	38W	82
DRAKE DONALD WILLIAM	NJ	13E	104
DRAKE EARLE AVON	CA	24E	82
DRAKE GLENN FRANKLIN	PA	04E	122
DRAKE JOHN DE WITT	CA	06W	12
DRAKE JOHN PETER	NY	01E	59
DRAKE MICHAEL JOSEPH	MI	15W	62
DRAKE MICHAEL LEON	MI	64W	8
DRAKE MICHEAL JOHN	FL	16E	9
DRAKE RICHARD GUY	CA	36W	34
DRAKE RICHARD KENNETH JR	MA	35E	68
DRAKE RODNEY GEORGE	IL	14E	14
DRAKE ROGER KENNETH	OH	40W	24
DRAKE STEVEN COLE	MO	33E	56
DRAKE TIMOTHY CALVIN	MD	10W	11
DRAKEN OTTO JAMES	NV	12W	67
DRAKES CLARENCE EARL	MS	25E	97
DRANE JOHN WILBUR	AZ	25W	66
DRANE WILBERT RAY	MS	08W	11
DRAPER CLIFFORD ARVIN	NE	47W	40
DRAPER MARION LEON	UT	12E	3
DRAPER MARK GREGORY	IN	08W	42
DRAPER ROBERT DALE	AZ	24E	66
DRAPER WILFRED	AZ	52E	17
DRAPER WILLIAM LLOYD	VA	39E	70
DRAPER WILLIAM MICHAEL	NY	58W	7
DRAPP ROBERT GEORGE	WI	06W	63
DRAUGHN THOMAS EDWARD	LA	34W	47
DRAUGHON ISAAC RAY	NC	52W	22
DRAUT CHARLES BERNARD JR	MO	15W	71
DRAVES LARRY DANIEL	IN	19E	12
DRAVIS JAMES STEVENS JR	PA	20W	86
DRAWDY RYLAND WHITNEY	FL	02E	55
DRAY DONALD BARRY	NY	26E	70
DRAZBA CAROL ANN ELIZABET	PA	05E	46
DRAZER THOMAS STEPHEN	IN	04E	107
DREA TERRANCE LEE	WI	14W	51
DREHER RICHARD E	OH	02W	119
DREIER MARK STEVEN	IA	23W	43
DRENNEN NILS ARDEN	PA	16E	67
DRESHER HARRY EVERETT JR	OK	27E	88
DRESSEL KENNETH HAROLD	MN	35E	31
DRESSEN DOUGLAS STANLEY	MN	20W	13
DRESSLER EMMETT L	PA	03E	71
DREW EDWARD JOSEPH II	IA	33E	56
DREW JAMES LEE	MO	23W	8
DREW JOSEPH LAWRENCE	MA	04E	40
DREW KENNETH LEE	OR	54W	15
DREW ROBERT DEARHART	MI	39W	43
DREW THEODORE GLENN	ME	10W	23
DREW THOMAS FRANCIS	NY	21E	11
DREWES RICHARD CHARLES	NJ	36W	34
DREWICZ ROBERT CHARLES	OH	36W	56
DREWRY NOLAN FRANKLIN	TX	05E	130
DREYER THEODORE HENRY	NY	24E	66
DRIGGERS ARTHUR M JR	SC	23E	99
DRIGGERS JERRY TRUMAN	SC	28W	90
DRIGGERS VESTIE TIMOTHY	PA	37W	5
DRINKARD DANNY GEORGE	MI	04W	135
DRINKHOUSE JOHN WATTS	LA	30E	15
DRINNON BEDFORD LEE	OK	02W	94
DRINSKI DAREN LEE	IN	28W	98
DRISCOLL FRANCIS MURTAUGH	MA	42E	4
DRISCOLL JOHN RAYMOND III	CA	21W	58
DRISCOLL PAUL RICHARD	MA	40W	64
DRISCOLL VICTOR MICHAEL	TX	21E	44
DRISKELL LARRY RAY	IA	09E	127
DRISKILL JERYL FRANKLIN	IL	20W	19
DRIVER DALLAS ALAN	VA	07W	122
DRIVER JOHN CECIL		27W	99
DRIVERE RICHARD JOSEPH	PA	44W	16
DRIZA STANLEY WILLIAM	PA	32E	43
DROB DAVID MICHAEL	MI	51W	31
DROBENA MICHAEL JAMES	TX	32W	96
DROHOSKY EDWARD DANIEL	IN	20E	114
DROIGK MARTIN WAYNE	TX	20W	29
DROSD WALTER LLOYD	MD	64W	8
DROSZCZ DANIEL PATRICK	IL	46W	40
DROUGHT DAVID LEE	WI	33E	7
DROUHARD PETER AUGUST	KS	21W	117
DROWN DAVID ALAN	MA	17E	56
DROWN LARRY GENE	OH	42W	10
DROWN LYLE EUGENE	ID	27W	86
DROWN SAMUEL ROBERT	WV	16E	27
DROWN TERRY FRANCIS	ME	22W	20
DROZ DONALD GLENN	MO	27W	63
DROZDZ STANISLAW JOSEPH	NJ	19W	77
DRUM THOMAS	NY	13W	81
DRUMMOND AUSTIN LEON	SC	07E	88
DRUMMOND EMANUEL FRANK JR	FL	11E	2
DRUMMOND PAUL ROBERT	RI	06E	37
DRURY JACKY LEE	GA	14W	106
DRUSCHEL WILLIAM LENORD	IL	41W	57
DRUZINSKI KARL WALTER	NY	04W	65
DRY MELVIN SPENCE	NY	01W	38
DRYDEN MICHAEL THEODORE	OK	60E	21
DRYDEN RALPH MARION JR	HI	50W	23
DRYE JACK LEE	AZ	13W	22
DRYER RICHARD EUGENE	CA	37W	45
DRYNAN ARTHUR W	TX	08E	20
DRYOEL DONALD L	IL	06E	131
DRYSDALE CHARLES DOUGLAS	AL	34W	83
DU BEAU GERALD EUGENE	IL	20W	43
DU BOIS GREG ALAN	NV	57E	1
DU BOIS RICHARD FRANCIS	LA	23W	20
DU BOSE LARRY DOUGLAS	NC	39W	11
DU CHARM PAUL MEDORE	DC	20W	55
DU LONG FRANKLIN ROOSEVEL	WI	52E	36
DU MOND ROLAND DENNIS	PA	23E	18
DU PLESSIS RICHARD JAMES	PA	03W	119
DU PONT JAMES CAMIL	OH	07W	71
DU PONT RALPH PETER JR	NY	01W	25
DU VALL DEAN ARNOLD	IN	06E	3
DUART BILLIE D	IA	02W	1
DUARTE GERALD MICHAEL	CA	45W	50
DUARTE JOHN	TX	01E	17
DUARTE JOHN FRANK JR	CA	17W	27
DUBACH GARY LYNN	OH	32W	31
DUBB DEWAIN V	WA	29E	29
DUBBELD ORIE JOHN JR	FL	04W	18
DUBBS RAYMOND ARTHUR	PA	44E	5
DUBE ANDRE LOUIS	ME	10E	29
DUBE PETER LEE	ME	24E	67
DUBIA LAWRENCE NORMOND	NH	14W	100
DUBIEL PETER PHILIP	CT	25W	67
DUBOSE DOUGLAS SCOTT	FL	10E	33
DUBOSE FRED CLINTON III	AL	33E	17
DUCAT BRUCE CHALMERS	MD	13E	4
DUCAT PHILLIP ALLEN	IN	11E	13
DUCE ROGER L	CA	58E	15
DUCHARME RICHARD EDWARD	RI	27E	38
DUCHNOWSKI JOHN PAUL	OH	03E	21
DUCK CURTIS LAMAR	CA	15E	41
DUCK WILLIAM WHITBY	FL	27E	43
DUCKER RONALD DWIGHT	SC	42E	50
DUCKETT ARLEN JACKSON JR	FL	05E	64
DUCKETT CURTIS LEE	IL	22E	53
DUCKETT JOSEPH L JR	DC	19E	116
DUCKETT LARRY THOMAS	TX	05W	29
DUCKETT RONALD WARREN	IN	05E	64
DUCKETT THOMAS ALFRED	PA	12E	10
DUCKETT THOMAS ALLEN	GA	06W	116
DUCKWORTH JAMES EDWARD	AL	07W	26
DUCOMMUN RONALD LLOYD	CA	16W	78
DUCOTE LONNIE JOSEPH JR	TX	24E	107
DUDASH JOHN FRANCIS	NJ	18E	92
DUDDY CHARLES STEVEN	PA	35W	15
DUDEK JOSEPH WALTER	IL	34E	52
DUDEK RICHARD ALAN	MI	41W	22
DUDLEY BRUCE WESLEY JR	SC	35E	15
DUDLEY CARL DOUGLAS JR	NC	22E	69
DUDLEY CHARLES GLENDON	MT	02E	22
DUDLEY DONALD KIETH	UT	52E	17
DUDLEY FOREST EDD	IL	13E	71
DUDLEY GARY WILLIAM	KS	35W	88
DUDLEY HARVEY JR	OH	16W	105
DUDLEY JOHN MITCHELL	PA	24E	20
DUDLEY LAWRENCE WESLEY JR	TX	27W	16
DUEL EDWARD KENNETH	CT	40W	11
DUELK JOSEPH DAVID JR	NY	57W	17
DUELLMAN HENRY RALPH	WI	32W	5
DUEMAN MERLE L	CA	26E	83

NAME	STATE	PANEL NO.	LINE NO.
DUEMLING RALPH NELSON	CA	08W	121
DUENAS JOSE BAMBA	GM	04E	18
DUENAS JUAN LEON GUERRERE	CA	19W	104
DUENAS ROBERTO CERVANTES	CA	19W	67
DUENSING JAMES ALLYN	CA	01W	113
DUER THOMAS WADE	IL	51W	40
DUESSENT CHARLES PAUL	CA	14W	131
DUFAULT JAMES RAYMOND	CT	17W	70
DUFAULT JAMES RICHARD	ME	08E	74
DUFAULT PAUL	MA	09W	64
DUFF BARRY WILLIAM	MD	07E	95
DUFF JACK CECIL JR	MO	17E	115
DUFF PHILLIP RANDALL	GA	01W	53
DUFF ROBERT DARREL	MO	05W	33
DUFFER ERIC THOMAS	TN	30W	1
DUFFETT EDWARD STEPHEN	MA	26E	88
DUFFETT JAMES HENRY JR	MD	10E	114
DUFFEY GERALD THOMAS	CA	53W	18
DUFFEY JERRY NORMAN	MI	02W	86
DUFFIELD JOHN DAVID LOCKW	CA	42E	4
DUFFIN REY L	UT	30E	8
DUFFNER WILLIAM FRANK	NY	10W	79
DUFFORD PAUL EDWARD	PA	31E	64
DUFFY DANIEL BENJAMIN JR	MA	06E	131
DUFFY DANIEL WALTER	NY	02E	69
DUFFY DONALD RAYMOND JR	MA	04E	46
DUFFY FRANCIS JOSEPH	CA	19E	90
DUFFY JAMES PATRICK JR	OH	24W	102
DUFFY JOHN	NJ	52E	36
DUFFY JOHN EVERETT	ME	12W	92
DUFFY KEITH WILLIAM	NY	40W	74
DUFFY LAWRENCE RICHARD	MA	31E	3
DUFFY MICHAEL BERNARD	WA	31W	34
DUFFY PATRICK EDWARD	AL	31E	68
DUFFY THOMAS BENEDICT JR	IL	22E	39
DUFFY THOMAS KNOWLES	FL	01W	8
DUFFY VINCENT EDWARD	CA	12W	5
DUFRESNE WILLARD J JR	MN	24W	4
DUGAN BEN GOOLMAN	NM	21W	58
DUGAN EDWARD MICHAEL	NE	09W	4
DUGAN JOHN FRANCIS	NJ	04W	60
DUGAN JOHN FREDERICK	NY	20E	113
DUGAN KEVIN HOWARD	NY	43W	14
DUGAN KEVIN JOHN	NY	59W	1
DUGAN PATRICK JAMES	PA	32W	48
DUGAN THOMAS WAYNE	PA	36W	14
DUGAS JOSEPH GERALD	LA	24E	20
DUGAS MICHAEL JEAN	CA	19W	92
DUGGAN GARY LEE	WA	28W	103
DUGGAN THOMAS PATRICK	CA	33W	7
DUGGAN WILLIAM JOSEPH	CA	13E	118
DUGGAN WILLIAM YOUNG	TX	02W	93
DUGGER ALFRED	OH	31E	45
DUGGER DOUGLAS ALAN	MI	35W	11
DUGGER JAMES DOWEL JR	PA	01W	82
DUGNESS PETER	NY	10E	19
DUHE BYRON RANDALL	CA	36E	6
DUHY HARVEY ALBERT JR	MA	22W	88
DUKE ALAN RAY	CA	56W	2
DUKE BILLY WAYNE	AL	28W	68
DUKE DOUGLAS OVYLE	OK	36W	49
DUKE GEORGE G	TX	09E	67
DUKE LARRY WADE	GA	13W	103
DUKE THOMAS WAYNE	SC	45E	20
DUKEHART STEPHEN ERNEST	CA	13E	74
DUKELOW CORNELIOUS P II	KS	34W	57
DUKES ARTHUR ROGER JR	FL	52W	42
DUKES GEORGE BENNIE	SC	54W	23
DUKES PAUL DOUGLAS	LA	18W	14
DUKES ROY RAYMOND	MI	04W	18
DUKES THOMAS LESTER	FL	21W	111
DULAC MALCOLM CYRIL	ME	55E	10
DULAK RAYMOND ROBERT JR	TX	10W	23
DULAY SALVADOR REDILLA	CA	04E	76
DULEBOHN DENNIS LEE	OH	36W	62
DULEN RENDLE	OH	57E	19
DULIK THOMAS WILLIAM	OH	69W	3
DULIN ZETTIE J C	IN	11W	57
DULL EDWARD JAMES	MA	47W	17
DULLEY KENNETH LAWRENCE	CA	25W	11
DULYEA BARRY H	MI	50E	38
DUMAS DAVID DONALD	NY	40W	43
DUMAS LONNIE EUGENE	OK	05W	14
DUMAS OLIVER DEWITT	GA	10E	38
DUMAS SAMUEL ALEXANDER	TN	13W	111
DUMAS WILLIAM RICHARD	OH	14E	95
DUMDEI CHARLES MARION	MN	36W	39
DUMIN PAUL MICHAEL	CT	30E	90
DUMKE ALLEN WILLIAM	WI	17W	96
DUMOND DAVID EDWARD	NY	26E	83
DUMONT ROGER JOSEPH	MA	28W	68
DUNAGAN JIMMY LYN	CA	02W	99
DUNAGAN MICHAEL DENNIS	AZ	18W	19
DUNAJ WILLIAM ANTHONY	MI	23W	51
DUNAWAY GORDON HERBERT	AL	09E	130
DUNAWAY JAMES ROBERT	DC	10W	113
DUNAWAY ROBERT LEON JR	TX	08W	130
DUNBAR ALLEN SEVARN	TX	46W	57
DUNBAR CLARENCE WILSON	KY	32W	37
DUNBAR DOYLE DANIEL	MT	27W	86
DUNBAR JOHN MICHAEL	IL	30E	41
DUNBAR ROBERT	IL	32W	42
DUNBAR ROBERT SIDNEY	WA	10W	124
DUNBAR ROY WILLIAM JR	WI	24W	25
DUNCAN ANDREW MCARTHUR	MI	09E	106
DUNCAN BENJAMIN WAYNE	GA	04W	66
DUNCAN BOYCE LOWRANCE JR	TX	35E	15
DUNCAN CHARLES EDWARD	IN	54W	10
DUNCAN DONALD ROBERT	KY	12E	114
DUNCAN EDWARD FRANCIS	OR	05E	131
DUNCAN GALVIN LEE	OK	25E	98
DUNCAN GARY BERYL	MO	35E	15
DUNCAN GLENN CHRISTIE	GA	11W	91
DUNCAN HERMAN DERL	AR	51W	3
DUNCAN JAMES EDWARD	WV	04W	19
DUNCAN JAMES HENRY	FL	15E	4
DUNCAN JAMES PAUL	OK	05W	68
DUNCAN JAMES ROBERT	CA	25E	82
DUNCAN JOHN DAVID	MA	19W	67
DUNCAN JOSEPH WILLIE	NC	13W	8
DUNCAN KENNETH EUGENE	KY	07E	69
DUNCAN KURT WILLIAM	MN	43W	35
DUNCAN LEON TIMOTHY	NY	22W	64
DUNCAN LLOYD ALVAN	OR	31E	68
DUNCAN MITCHELL JEROME	LA	32E	35
DUNCAN ONNIE DAVID	GA	07W	9
DUNCAN PHILLIP ALLEN	MS	16W	116
DUNCAN RICHARD WINERFRED	CA	29E	48
DUNCAN ROBERT LEE	TN	27E	58
DUNCAN ROBERT RAY	FL	46W	57
DUNCAN ROGER EVANS	OK	45E	10
DUNCAN RONNIE MARSHALL	NC	02E	115
DUNCAN ROY WILLIAM	CA	41E	63
DUNCAN THOMAS DAVID	AL	03E	11
DUNCAN TIMOTHY JOSEPH	CA	41W	4
DUNCAN WALTER EARL JR	OH	20E	57
DUNCAN WILLIAM ARTHUR	MO	16W	99
DUNCAN WILLIAM BRADLEY	AK	36E	7
DUNCAN WILLIAM JAY	IL	61W	12
DUNCAN WILLIAM M	KY	23E	99
DUNDAS JERRY RICHARD	MI	55E	10
DUNDAS MICHAEL C	FL	10E	7
DUNDAS STEVEN WILLIAM	AZ	30W	43
DUNEMAN ALLEN EUGENE	IA	38W	73
DUNES ALBERTO JR	TX	39W	48
DUNFORD DAVID WILLIAM	WV	32W	96
DUNFORD FRANK BELLEW III	KY	28E	48
DUNGEE RUDOLPH FRANCIS	PA	15E	24
DUNGEY RIM MICHAEL	CA	25E	46
DUNHAM BOBBY JOE	AR	35W	59
DUNHAM BRUCE JOEL	VA	23W	119
DUNHAM RICHARD FRANCIS	NY	17E	28
DUNIFER DELFERD BENJAMIN	WI	36E	69
DUNIGAN JERRY WAYNE	KY	12E	60
DUNITHAN THOMAS LAWRENCE	WV	59W	1
DUNKEL MICHAEL ROBERT	MN	41W	23
DUNKENBERGER DAVID GEORGE	NY	27E	70
DUNKIN JAMES EDGAR JR	CA	39W	7
DUNKLE JAMES ROBERT	PA	25W	98
DUNLAP DARRELL EDWARD	WV	38E	26
DUNLAP FRANCIS EDWARD JR	PA	27W	80
DUNLAP JERRY	AR	35W	26
DUNLAP JOHN CORNELIUS	NC	18E	2
DUNLAP JOHN TURNER III	PA	53E	4
DUNLAP JOHN WALTER	TX	53W	26
DUNLAP LAWRENCE DAVID JR	IL	21E	26
DUNLAP RAYMOND EARL	TX	37E	54
DUNLAP RICHARD LANCE	TN	44E	25
DUNLAP WILBUR TURBY	PA	01E	31
DUNLAP WILLIAM CHARLES	AZ	15W	17
DUNLOP JOHNSTON	NY	50E	13
DUNLOP THOMAS EARL	FL	02W	131
DUNMORE ONEAL	SC	27E	5
DUNN CARL EDWARD	OH	07W	4
DUNN CHARLES CLIFFORD	MI	42E	63
DUNN CREIGHTON ROBERT	CA	11E	126
DUNN DAVID HAMILTON	MT	21W	124
DUNN DONALD LEORY	CA	19W	37
DUNN DONALD LOUIS	OK	05W	95
DUNN GARY WAYNE	NE	64E	4
DUNN GERALD	NY	23E	35
DUNN GREGORY LYNN	CA	29E	88
DUNN JAMES HARLOW III	VA	26W	31
DUNN JOE DANIEL	TX	42E	15
DUNN JOSEPH PATRICK	MA	39E	31
DUNN JOSEPH WESLEY	MA	09E	32
DUNN LARRY	IL	38W	25
DUNN LAURENCE JOHN	IL	10E	38
DUNN LESSELL JR	LA	27E	36
DUNN MERL THOMAS JR	CT	19E	70
DUNN MICHAEL EDWARD	IL	35E	38
DUNN MICHAEL JOHN	NY	34E	76
DUNN MICHAEL ROY	MA	28W	34
DUNN MORRIS GORDON	VA	45W	14
DUNN RALPH ALLEN	CO	01E	56
DUNN RALPH GERALD	AL	32W	43
DUNN RICHARD EDWARD	CT	01W	7
DUNN ROBERT TERRENCE	MO	40W	28
DUNN ROBERT WAYNE	TX	44W	36
DUNN TEDDY REX	TX	21E	22
DUNN WAYLAND JR	NC	10E	3
DUNNAVANT JAMES M JR	TN	08W	28
DUNNE GERARD JOSEPH	NY	46W	14
DUNNE PAUL HUBERT JR	MA	16W	94
DUNNEBACK MICHAEL ARTHUR	MI	30W	43
DUNNING DENNIS GYMAN	MS	01W	17
DUNNING TIMOTHY CHARLES	CA	40W	71
DUNNING WILLIAM MARTIN	CT	09W	78
DUNSING DENNIS PAUL	CA	56E	5
DUNSMORE FRANK MELVIN JR	MD	15W	118
DUNSMORE LEO PAUL	RI	39E	4
DUNTON JAMES G	MA	01E	74
DUNTZ RONALD DE VERE	IA	30W	53
DUNYON DAVID PHERRAL	UT	50W	18
DUPELL ROBERT JOSEPH JR	PA	14W	107
DUPERE EDWARD JOSEPH	MA	32W	96
DUPERE JOSEPH RENE	RI	03E	43
DUPERE PAUL ANDREW	MA	24E	20
DUPERRY PETER ALFRED	CA	30W	11
DUPLAGA JOHN STANLEY	WV	24E	21
DUPLECHAIN ANDRUS FLOYD	LA	07W	98
DUPLESSIE ALEXANDER WILLI	PA	03W	108
DUPLESSIS GEORGE LLOYD	LA	31E	23
DUPONT ERNEST THOMAS	WV	14E	101
DUPONT KENNETH FRANCIS	OR	35W	54
DUPRE CHARLES VAUGHN	NY	29W	28
DUPRE LARRY DAVID	NY	16W	12
DUPRE NORMAN LEE	TX	11E	19
DUPREE BENNY RAY	GA	17W	55
DUPREE BILL JAKE	GA	26W	62
DUPREE DOUGLAS	TX	37W	62
DUPREE WILBERT SHELBY JR	NY	04W	86
DUPREY ARTHUR RAYMOND	NY	48W	25
DUPREY DANNY LEE	ME	18W	124
DUPUIS CLEMENT ARTHUR	CT	28W	98
DURALL ROBERT MICHAEL	AL	08W	130
DURAN ALFONSO MARQUEZ	CO	20W	48
DURAN AMIE JACOB	CO	53E	32
DURAN ELOY	CO	05E	33
DURAN ERNEST LOUIS	CO	08E	35
DURAN IGNACIO	TX	63W	15
DURAN JUAN CHAIRES JR	CA	41W	57
DURAN PABLO	CA	43E	5
DURAN RICHARD LOSOYA	NM	29W	29
DURAN SALVADOR GUTIERREZ	TX	10W	69
DURAN STEVE GONZALES	NM	02E	56

NAME	STATE	PANEL NO.	LINE NO.
DURANCEAU DAVID MARIUS	ME	23E	27
DURAND DENNIS CHARLES	MI	03W	54
DURAND PAUL LIONEL	RI	17E	28
DURANT FORBIS PIPKIN JR	OK	44E	6
DURANT RICHARD HENRY	NY	13W	116
DURANT WILLIE	PA	34E	62
DURBIN ROBERT VERNON	WV	24E	80
DURBIN RONALD WAYNE	MD	66W	5
DURBIN THOMAS FREDERICK	CA	26E	101
DURDEN TROY	FL	07W	134
DURELL ALGER EDGAR JR	CA	17E	110
DURFLINGER ROLLAND LEON	IL	15W	31
DURHAM DAVID TERRELL	KY	52W	27
DURHAM DWIGHT MONTGOMERY	OK	27W	48
DURHAM GEORGE RAY	OH	13E	67
DURHAM HAROLD BASCOM JR	GA	28E	20
DURHAM JAMES CLAUDE JR	MI	43W	4
DURHAM JAMES WILLIAM JR	DC	37E	82
DURHAM JOHN ALBERT	OH	33W	55
DURHAM JOHN MELVIN	MI	54E	32
DURHAM OLIVER EARL	TX	38W	73
DURHAM RHONALD LEE	KY	10W	5
DURHAM SAMUEL RAY	CA	21E	78
DURHAM THOMAS WYATT	VA	28W	59
DURHAM VAN LESLIE	WA	42W	39
DURHAM WILLARD DUANE JR	NY	23E	110
DURHAM WILLIAM JAMES	OH	19W	30
DURKIN JOSEPH WILLIAM JR	CT	07E	101
DURLIN JOHN STEWART	PA	09W	83
DURLING JOSEPH A III	NH	26E	23
DURO IGNACIO ESCOBAR	WA	26W	90
DUROY ALLEN JACQUES	CA	04W	133
DURR BRIAN FRANCIS	NY	38E	26
DURR LAVALL	CA	06E	106
DURRETT THADDEUS	NY	49W	52
DURRWACHTER HERMAN K JR	PA	01E	4
DURST JOHN BERNARD	WV	62W	8
DURST LARRY BLAINE	PA	40W	57
DURTKA GERALD WILBERT	MI	16W	4
DURYEA ARNOLD MAX	NY	38E	48
DUSART KENNETH WALTER	NY	40W	2
DUSBABEK GLENN HENRY	TX	56W	33
DUSBABEK JOHN ROBERT	MN	04E	132
DUSCH GEORGE EDWARD	AZ	32W	77
DUSCH PARIS DALE	KY	03E	55
DUSCHEK RUDI HERMANN	FL	18E	18
DUSING CHARLES GALE	SC	03E	8
DUSSEAU ALBERT EUGENE	MI	31E	72
DUSSEAU JERRY JAMES	MI	14E	21
DUSSEAU RICHARD FRANK	MI	30W	43
DUSZYNSKI ANDREW JOSEPH	MI	13W	43
DUTCHER JIMIE DALE	NY	25E	37
DUTCHER LEONARD EARL	WI	61W	13
DUTCHES WILLIAM GEORGE	NJ	08E	46
DUTHU ROY ANTHONY	LA	04E	108
DUTKIEWICZ ROBERT JOHN	OH	04W	126
DUTRA ROBERT LEONARD	CA	54W	15
DUTRO RICHARD THOMAS	WA	56W	33
DUTTON BERNARD F JR	MA	53W	9
DUTTON CHARLES MATHEW	NY	48E	52
DUTY ANTHONY	KY	23W	99
DUTY CHARLES HOWARD	TN	18E	120
DUTY EDWARD	WV	30W	63
DUTY MELVIN DAROLD	MI	12E	33
DUVAL MICHAEL EUGENE	CA	10W	120
DUVALL GARY LEE	FL	22E	83
DUVALL RANDOLPH JR	KY	27E	88
DVORATCHEK THOMAS ANTHONY	IL	02E	108
DWIGGINS DONALD HOMER JR	NC	16W	49
DWIGHT WILLIAM LAMAR	GA	31E	23
DWORACZYK WALLACE STANLEY	TX	20E	84
DWORNIK VALENTINE MARION	MI	23W	8
DWYER ALFRED THOMAS	TX	35E	68
DWYER DALE DON	WI	22E	6
DWYER LAWRENCE LEE JR	TX	17W	83
DWYER MATTHEW MURICE JR	NJ	41E	63
DWYER MICHAEL ALLEN	KY	20W	79
DWYER PATRICK PETER	PA	09E	32
DWYER PATRICK WILLIAM	CA	24W	65
DWYER ROBERT KEEFE	CT	23E	74
DWYER ROBERT MARTIN	NY	20E	89
DWYER THOMAS D	CT	01W	125
DWYER THOMAS RICHARD	MA	21W	70
DYBVIG NED TURNER	OH	56W	2
DYCE DONALD MYRON	OH	17W	120
DYCHES CHARLES HENRY	SC	47E	10
DYCKS RONALD KING	OH	20W	48
DYCUS RICKEY DALE	CA	23W	43
DYCZKOWSKI ROBERT RAYMOND	NY	06E	129
DYDYNSKI STEPHEN MICHAEL	MD	14E	62
DYE DANIEL GROVER	CA	02W	47
DYE DANIEL ROBERT	RI	41W	51
DYE DANNY DAVID	CA	07E	70
DYE DAVID ALAN	OH	19E	92
DYE EDWARD PHILLIP	OH	28E	22
DYE HENRY ALBERT JR	WA	29W	7
DYE JAMES CLETUS	CA	01E	53
DYE JAMES HERBERT	OH	25W	98
DYE LARRY CLAY	KY	17E	61
DYE MELVIN CARNILLS	MI	40E	19
DYE RALPH VICTOR JR	TN	19E	12
DYE RONALD HARVEY	WV	50W	49
DYE TIMOTHY ELDEN	OH	27W	30
DYER ALLEN JOHN	OH	03W	109
DYER BLENN COLBY	ME	18E	103
DYER BRUCE HERBERT	WA	66E	8
DYER DAVID WAYNE	CA	33E	66
DYER DENNIS EARL	CA	62E	3
DYER FREDERICK LEE	CA	54W	36
DYER GLENN CHARLES	NC	01E	69
DYER HARRY GORDON	NM	08E	104
DYER IRBY III	TX	13E	4
DYER JAMES RICHARD	CA	02E	48
DYER JAY CEE	MI	41E	37
DYER JEFFERY STEPHEN		27W	63
DYER JOSEPH FRANCIS JR	PA	30E	15
DYER LARRY EUGENE	MD	14W	100
DYER MARTIN BARRY JR	NY	18W	113
DYER ORRIN LEONARD JR	NH	37E	6
DYER RICHARD	RI	09W	104
DYER TERRY BROOKS	CA	15W	93
DYER WILLFORD LEON	TN	50E	46
DYER WILLIE GENE	FL	21E	44
DYKE CHARLES EARL	PA	17E	61
DYKE KENNETH	NY	24E	21
DYKE ROBERT LOUIS	CA	11E	108
DYKE STANTON RICHARD	NY	38E	48
DYKEMA ROSS ALLEN	MI	31E	29
DYKES CLEVELAND E	MI	32W	53
DYKES FRANK FAYETE	MO	43E	17
DYKES LONNIE ALLEN	WY	09W	37
DYKES MONTE DALE	TX	18W	6
DYKES RICHARD MONROE	CA	17E	110
DYKES ROBERT LEE JR	GA	38E	26
DYKES WILLIAM FRANK	TN	28E	96
DYMERSKI ALFRED JOHN	NY	14E	34
DYRDAHL RAYMOND ERNEST	UT	31E	45
DYRESON DONALD LEE	OR	39E	46
DYSON CHARLES E JR	PA	05E	65
DYSON LESLIE MILTON JR	MD	46W	40
DYVIG ARTHUR HARRIS JR	WA	09E	73
DZIARCAK WILLIAM WALTER	NY	43E	17
DZIEDZIC MARK ROBERT	WI	44E	67
DZIENCILOWSKI JAMES	NY	37E	21
DZIENGEL MICHAEL PETER	MN	17W	73
DZIWISZ FRANK EDWARD JR	IL	11E	21
EADDY ISHMELL	CT	33E	83
EADE RAYMOND FREDRICK	CA	28W	25
EADEN WILLIAM HENRY	TX	03E	42
EADIE GORDON PATTERSON	MI	24E	113
EADS DENNIS KEITH	IL	11W	40
EADS JOHN PATRICK	MO	14E	21
EADS RUSSELL WADE	MI	26W	110
EADS WALTER TASMAN	VA	24E	21
EAGLESON ROBERT WILLIAM	OR	44E	6
EAGLIN JOHN HENRY	TX	06E	99
EAKER DENNIS KEITH	PA	10E	105
EAKIN HOWARD MAXWELL JR	PA	01E	23
EAKIN SHELTON LEE	AR	09E	79
EAKINS CHARLES ADRAIN	KY	20E	14
EAKINS MARION TROY	IL	23E	50
EAKINS MELVIN WARREN	OH	26W	98
EALEY DOUGLAS	NJ	40W	2
EALEY WILLIS EDWARD	IL	06W	62
EALUM CARREL GORUM	FL	44W	16
EALY CARL	OH	09W	26
EALY WILLIAM DANIEL	IL	43W	46
EAMICK BRUCE ALLEN	IN	20W	112
EANS LAWRENCE GEORGE	PA	36W	1
EARICK JAMES ALLEN	OH	24E	21
EARL MICHAEL RANDALL	NM	15W	98
EARLE JOHN STILES	MA	09W	78
EARLENBAUGH DANIEL LEE	MI	10E	46
EARLES ARTHUR JAMES	GA	33E	45
EARLES FRED THOMAS	CA	08E	65
EARLEY CLARENCE ANDREW	NY	29W	29
EARLEY JOHN RICHARD	CA	26W	70
EARLEY WILEY B	TX	24W	53
EARLL DAVID JOHN	TX	11E	95
EARLS LARRY DON	TN	13E	108
EARLY HOWARD LEE	LA	32W	58
EARLY JAMES MICHAEL	OH	19W	85
EARLY WILLIAM DAIL	OH	18E	121
EARLYWINE GARY JAMES	IA	13W	27
EARNEST CHARLES M	AL	01W	92
EARNEST JAMES DALE	TX	20W	38
EARNEST JUNIOR BARNETT	AR	37W	49
EARNEST WILLIE LEE	MS	13E	51
EARNESTY JOHN WILLIAM	PA	13E	33
EARNHARDT CLIFFORD JERRY	VA	12W	130
EARP BILLY WAYNE	AL	20W	122
EARP MICHAEL LEE	ID	22W	75
EASLEY DAVID ROY	MS	12W	112
EASLEY DENNIS BOYD	TX	09E	46
EASLEY LEONARD EUGENE	TX	24E	109
EASLEY ODELL	IL	19W	67
EASLEY SAMUEL HARRISON II	VA	64W	8
EASLEY TIMOTHY	NY	17E	1
EASON DOUGLAS DUKE	NC	02W	70
EASON EDWIN RAYMOND	CA	01E	72
EASON JOSEPH MILTON	MD	03W	19
EASON JOSHUA WAY	AR	14E	76
EAST FRANKLIN	WV	01W	9
EAST JAMES BOYD JR	OK	26W	53
EAST LEON NELSON	VA	28E	22
EAST MELVIN DOUGLAS	WA	27E	108
EAST VERNON WAYNE	PA	31W	91
EASTER DENNY RAY	PA	05W	43
EASTERLING EARL K	LA	18E	68
EASTERN JOE BUTLER	MI	29W	67
EASTHAM MARTIN PHILLIP	IL	08E	65
EASTMAN ALLAN JOHN	MA	16W	50
EASTMAN EVERETT ALLAN	IL	24E	54
EASTMAN JESSE GEORGE	NY	06E	38
EASTMAN THOMAS DELL	MN	07E	30
EASTON DAVID EVERETT	IL	04W	38
EASTON DAVID STEARNS	PA	57E	2
EASTON JOHN WILLIAM	CA	42W	10
EASTON ROBERT GLENN	CA	20W	6
EATMAN EARNEST JR	AL	49W	52
EATMON EDDIE RAY	NC	11W	84
EATMON JAMES LARKIN	OK	06E	128
EATON BOBBY LYNN	TX	09E	108
EATON BRUCE HORACE	CA	22E	119
EATON CLIFFORD LYMAN	NY	60W	16
EATON CURTIS ABBOT	RI	10E	4
EATON DAVID LEE	OH	30E	54
EATON EMMANUEL LLOYD	IL	11E	118
EATON GARY CLIFTON	NC	10W	108
EATON GEORGE ELWOOD	PA	26W	53
EATON JACK	LA	17E	1
EATON JERRY ARNOLD	OH	10W	56
EATON MARK HASKIN	MS	03W	131
EATON NORMAN DALE	OK	35W	82
EATON ROBERT LEROY	NE	33W	55
EATON TOMMY RAY	IN	36W	34
EATON WILLIAM ALBERT	AK	11W	21
EAVES CARROLL WAYNE	IL	53W	34
EAVES FRANK GEORGE	GA	68E	1
EAY RUDY EDEJER	GM	42W	61
EBALD MICHAEL LEO	PA	16E	9
EBBINGA HERMAN GERALD	MN	21E	119
EBBS RALPH ELDON	OR	32W	53
EBEL WILLIAM EARNEST	OH	11E	7
EBEL WILLIAM MICHAEL	MI	38W	65
EBERHARDT PHILLIP JOHN	WI	33E	83

NAME	STATE	PANEL NO.	LINE NO.
EBERHARDT WILLIAM HENRY	NJ	02E	71
EBERHART SAMUEL HOUSTON	GA	05W	77
EBERLE RONALD EARL	FL	54W	15
EBERT CHARLES DANDRIDGE	PA	51W	10
EBERT MICHAEL LEROY	IN	45E	46
EBRIGHT WILLIAM RAYMOND O	OH	59W	1
EBRON LINWOOD EARL	NC	19E	78
EBY EDWARD LEE	PA	33W	31
ECCARD HARRY LEE	PA	18E	48
ECHANIS JOSEPH YGNACIO	OR	16W	33
ECHEVARRIA JOSE ANIBAL JR	NY	23W	72
ECHEVARRIA RAYMOND LOUIS	NY	11E	39
ECHOLS ALVIN	MI	12E	125
ECHOLS DAVID ALLEN	OH	24E	76
ECHOLS ROBERT EDWIN	GA	23E	57
ECHOLS TIMOTHY DAVID	OH	13W	127
ECKELL JOHN W	KS	55E	10
ECKENROAD RONNIE LEE	PA	29W	77
ECKENRODE DANIEL EDNEY	CA	14W	29
ECKENRODE DAVID JOHN	PA	51W	25
ECKENRODE MARCUS RICHARD	CA	64E	13
ECKER ROBERT RAYMOND	PA	14E	123
ECKER TERRY LEE	MD	25E	56
ECKERDT CHRISTIAN JOHN JR	MI	17E	34
ECKERFELD MICHAEL DAvID	OH	42W	17
ECKERT HAROLD LEE JR	P	27	108
ECKERT RONALD LEE	PA	07E	70
ECKES WILLIAM CARL	ND	16E	51
ECKHART LEON DELBERT	PA	15E	88
ECKHART RUSS EUGENE	KS	21E	11
ECKL THOMAS ANTHONY	CA	40E	38
ECKLE STEPHEN JOHN	OH	49E	30
ECKLES JAMES PATRICK	MI	19W	12
ECKLEY WAYNE ALVIN	OR	32E	92
ECKLUND ARTHUR GENE	AZ	27W	6
ECKMAN KENNETH WAYNE	UT	52W	12
ECKOFF DALE ARNOLD	CA	33W	49
ECKSTEIN RODGER DEAN	MT	27E	38
ECKVALL RICHARD ALLEN	CO	06E	48
ECONOMOUS GEORGE J JR	UT	50E	5
ECTON HARRY LEON	MD	36E	7
ECTOR JERRY	OH	53W	18
EDDEN GEORGE EDWARD	MT	48E	16
EDDLEMAN ROYCE EDSEL	SC	51E	19
EDDY EDMUND FRANCIS	CT	06E	56
EDDY GARRETT EDWARD	WA	07W	103
EDDY JERRY WAYNE	WV	10E	46
EDDY JOHN ARTHUR	OK	07E	24
EDDY JOHN DAVID	MI	02W	96
EDDY RICHARD NELSON	NY	32E	71
EDDY THOMAS EARL	TX	08E	97
EDELMAN IRWIN LEON	NY	32W	54
EDELSTEIN ROY L	WI	48W	12
EDEN CHESTER WADE	KY	15E	42
EDENFIELD RONALD DAVID	FL	21E	119
EDENTON HIRAM EURIAS JR	VA	07W	85
EDER ROBERT OTTO	OH	15W	3
EDER WILLIAM JOHN	MD	37W	80
EDGAR ROBERT JOHN	FL	37E	35
EDGAR TERRECE EUGENE	CA	61W	23
EDGE DENNIS EUGENE	OR	36W	1
EDGE JAMES HAMPTON	NC	05E	115
EDGE PAUL JOSEPH	MA	35E	68
EDGEMON JAMES EDWARD	TX	04W	86
EDGERLY JOHN WALLACE	MI	09E	130
EDGERTON ARTHUR DONALD JR	CA	48W	34
EDGERTON WILLIAM T JR	NC	27E	95
EDGREN THOMAS GORDON	IL	08W	93
EDIE KURT CHARLES	CA	19E	24
EDINGER JAMES GARD	MI	29E	9
EDINGTON PAUL RICHARD	TX	19E	94
EDLEY GEORGE STEVEN	NJ	07E	3
EDMOND COIL JR	NE	20E	25
EDMOND PAUL ROBERT	MN	23W	119
EDMOND THOMAS ALLEN	CT	58W	3
EDMONDS ARTHUR LEE JR	OH	39E	20
EDMONDS JAMES THOMAS	NC	33W	62
EDMONDS JERRY BAXTER JR	TN	05W	16
EDMONDS JOSEPH	MA	49E	52
EDMONDS LAWRENCE NATHANIEL	WV	07E	57
EDMONDS MONZIE DURREL	MI	38E	76
EDMONDS WILLIAM ORVILLE	OK	23E	2

NAME	STATE	PANEL NO.	LINE NO.
EDMONDSON HAROLD T JR	SC	04E	119
EDMONDSON WILLIAM ROTHROC	MO	07E	127
EDMONSON BOBBY	MS	18W	19
EDMUND EDWARD JOSEPH	TX	22W	64
EDMUNDS CALVIN	VA	30W	28
EDMUNDS ROBERT CLIFTON JR	VA	40W	43
EDNEY DAVID LEE	TN	44E	35
EDNEY DONALD WAYNE	AR	33W	56
EDRIS RICHARD JOHN	OH	12E	3
EDSALL JAMES	PA	50W	18
EDWARDS ANTHONY JOHN	TX	49W	7
EDWARDS AUSTIN IVAN	SC	30W	21
EDWARDS BERNARD W JR	PA	57W	10
EDWARDS BILLY MARCUS	LA	07E	50
EDWARDS BOBBY BRANCE	CA	36W	72
EDWARDS CHARLES DAVID	OK	27E	63
EDWARDS CHARLES HAROLD JR	MN	04W	91
EDWARDS CHARLES KENNETH	OH	17W	96
EDWARDS CHARLES LEE	TN	05E	115
EDWARDS CHARLES M	AR	08E	92
EDWARDS DANIEL LYNN	WV	49W	43
EDWARDS DANIEL WINSLOW JR	NM	15W	85
EDWARDS DENNETTE A III	FL	41E	38
EDWARDS DONALD MAC	CA	32W	95
EDWARDS DOUGLAS GLYN	MO	29W	88
EDWARDS EDWIN RAY	SC	42E	50
EDWARDS EUGENE	NY	06W	98
EDWARDS FREDDIE LEE JR	AL	13W	42
EDWARDS FREDFOR	SC	47W	26
EDWARDS GARY LEE	TN	12W	48
EDWARDS GARY STEPHEN	IN	14E	54
EDWARDS GEORGE FREDERICK	CT	44E	6
EDWARDS GEORGE RAY FAYFIE	MI	20E	15
EDWARDS GILBERT	TN	18E	48
EDWARDS HARRY JEROME	SC	02W	98
EDWARDS HARRY SANFORD JR	GA	11E	91
EDWARDS JAMES HERBERT	RI	18E	9
EDWARDS JAMES MERTON	SC	49W	29
EDWARDS JAMES WALTER	IL	09E	33
EDWARDS JERRALD LEROY	CA	25E	82
EDWARDS JOHN H JR	GA	37E	54
EDWARDS JOHN JAY	NY	05E	102
EDWARDS JOHN LEONARD	CA	27E	99
EDWARDS JOHN NEWT	KY	27W	16
EDWARDS JOHN PAUL	MD	65W	6
EDWARDS JOHN THOMAS	OH	24E	21
EDWARDS JOHNNY LAWRENCE	CA	29W	99
EDWARDS JOSEPH	PA	14E	52
EDWARDS JOSEPH WILLIAM	AL	36W	44
EDWARDS KENNETH MILES	MI	15E	115
EDWARDS KINNETH GLENN	TX	30E	55
EDWARDS LEON GEORGE	MI	44E	25
EDWARDS PAUL WILLIAM	CT	20W	10
EDWARDS R V	LA	10E	29
EDWARDS RANDOLPH A	NY	37E	82
EDWARDS RICHARD JR	FL	39W	40
EDWARDS RICHARD LYON	OH	40W	24
EDWARDS ROBERT JAMES	MS	28E	8
EDWARDS ROBERT THEODORE	CA	14E	21
EDWARDS ROBERT WAYNE	MI	18E	107
EDWARDS RODNEY CLINTON	MI	18E	2
EDWARDS ROGER WAYNE	MI	15E	20
EDWARDS RONALD CHARLES	NY	17W	73
EDWARDS ROY WILLIAM	TX	34E	35
EDWARDS STEVEN FRANK	IA	14W	42
EDWARDS TED LAVERN	PA	21E	4
EDWARDS TED WILLIS	NC	36E	69
EDWARDS THOMAS CLIFFORD	FL	08E	92
EDWARDS THOMAS RAY	OH	55W	4
EDWARDS THOMAS WILLIAM	NY	05E	115
EDWARDS WILLIAM EDGAR	SC	47E	39
EDWARDSON DAVID R	IA	22E	77
EFAW ROBERT T	PA	02E	120
EFIRD FRANKLIN D ROOSEVELT	AR	38W	34
EGAN DONALD JASON JR	NY	15E	20
EGAN EDWARD THOMAS JR	MA	18E	58
EGAN FRANCIS XAVIER	NY	01W	96
EGAN JAMES THOMAS JR	NJ	04E	81
EGAN STANLEY JOSEPH	MA	16W	111
EGAN TIMOTHY JAMES	IL	22E	39
EGAN WILLIAM PATRICK	TX	07E	8
EGBERT DALE EDWARD	IA	30E	76

NAME	STATE	PANEL NO.	LINE NO.
EGGE ERIC CRAIG	MN	27E	105
EGGENBERGER WILLIAM GARY	NJ	25W	98
EGGER JOHN CULBERTSON JR	OK	29E	14
EGGER WALTER JACOB	OH	45E	55
EGGERS CHARLES RONALD	OH	02W	93
EGGERT RUSSELL WILLIAM	OH	55E	10
EGGERT SAM	NM	25W	37
EGGLESTON DAVID LEROY	VA	15W	77
EGGLESTON HARRY H	PA	10E	124
EGGLESTON ROBERT	AL	03W	87
EGGLESTON ROBERT RICHARD	CA	08E	92
EGGLESTON RODNEY LEE	OH	28E	99
EGLIN CHARLES WILLIAM III	NY	39E	49
EGLINSDOERFER LARRY JAMES	MI	23W	99
EGLY SHELLY	IN	18E	92
EGOLF CARL M	MD	13E	78
EGOLF KLAUS DIETER	CA	41E	60
EGOLF RODGER LEE	IN	05E	65
EGYED GERALD LEONARD	MI	41W	58
EHLERS DOUGLAS GARY	TX	06W	31
EHLERS LARRY DEAN	IL	02W	19
EHLERS LONNEY LEWIS	MI	21E	27
EHLERS ROBERT FREDERICK	MN	11E	93
EHNES RICHARD LEE	MT	12W	29
EHNIS KENNETH PAUL	MI	40E	19
EHRHART MELVIN GRAYSON	PA	26W	70
EHRLICH DENNIS MICHAEL	NJ	14E	53
EHRMENTRAUT JOHN E JR	NY	01E	108
EIBER ROBERT ALLAN	TX	02E	19
EICHBAUER EARL KENT	UT	24E	90
EICHELBERGER BARRY LEE	PA	29W	88
EICHELBERGER STEPHEN JOHN	ND	20E	7
EICHELER GARY ERNEST	OH	15W	121
EICHENAUER THOMAS LYNN	IN	48W	12
EICHER MERLE CLAYTON JR	PA	35E	5
EICHHORN MONTY JAY	MI	18W	113
EICKHOLT ROBERT LEO	OH	28E	49
EICKLEBERRY ROBERT DONALD	IL	32W	97
EIDEN EDWARD VALENTINE JR	WI	27W	55
EIDSMOE NORMAN EDWARD	SD	35E	39
EIDSON RONALD LEE	MO	21W	99
EIDSON SAMUEL ARLEN	AL	03E	30
EIDUKAITIS GEDIMINAS JUST	OH	20E	41
EIGHMIE RONALD WILLIAM	VA	43W	53
EILAND GRADY LOUIS	AL	08W	59
EILER LINDEN DALE JR	IN	52E	4
EILERS ANTHONY MICHAEL	MI	03W	69
EILERS DENNIS LEE	IA	04E	37
EINARSON LOWELL GREEMER	ND	10E	59
EISAMAN DALE LEON	PA	29W	68
EISCHEID THOMAS JOHN	IA	66E	8
EISENACHER CHARLES JOHN	CA	37E	58
EISENBEISZ ROBERT ARTHUR	WA	05W	95
EISENBERGER GEORGE JOE BU	OK	03E	126
EISENBRAUN DAVID LAWRENCE	OH	43W	14
EISENBRAUN WILLIAM FORBES	CA	02E	27
EISENHART GUY LEE	PA	43E	53
EISENHOUR DWIGHT DAVID	NE	23E	2
EISENHOUR GLENN R	IL	29E	88
EISENHOUR JAMES DOYLE	KS	48W	40
EISENHOWER WILLIAM JACK	PA	59E	6
EISERT HAROLD BERNARD JR	NY	14W	17
EISMAN JAMES FREDRICK	CA	34W	32
EISNER JAMES WILLIAM	NY	12E	13
EISTER WILLIAM	NJ	37E	54
EITEL DENNIS	WI	20W	24
EITEL JACK ORVAL	KS	02E	31
EKART PAUL DAVID	IA	35E	38
EKLOFE SAMUEL ALVIN	IA	31W	46
EKLUND MARK JAMES	MN	03W	124
EKLUND PAUL HERBERT	WA	03E	101
EKSTADT JOHN MILTON	MI	30E	84
EKWELL THOMAS JANES	NY	31E	11
EL HONDAH DOVE	IL	05E	65
ELA ALAN DAVID	MA	34W	33
ELAM JOHN JR	TN	04W	48
ELAM WALTER ALAN	NY	25W	15
ELAND JOHN FREDERICK	MI	25W	67
ELBEN MICHAEL WILLIAM	IL	40E	20
ELBERT GEORGE STEVEN	NY	50E	27
ELBERT JOE A	WA	44W	47

NAME	STATE	PANEL NO.	LINE NO.
ELBRACHT WILLIAM MICHAEL	CA	21W	12
ELCHERT JAMES MELVIN	OH	21E	119
ELDER ALLEN THOMAS JR	TX	16W	12
ELDER EUGENE	NY	30W	52
ELDER GRADY LEE	GA	08E	36
ELDER HOWARD LEE	TX	09W	130
ELDER JAMES BRYAN JR	CO	13E	96
ELDER WILLARD FRANCIS	FL	04E	41
ELDERS ERNEST FRANKLIN	NC	29W	88
ELDRED ROBERT EDWARD	GA	02W	32
ELDRIDGE DONALD LEE	ID	42W	28
ELDRIDGE JAMES WILBUR	KS	20E	41
ELDRIDGE ROBERT BURCH	SC	16W	33
ELDRIDGE THOMAS CHARLES	LA	36W	15
ELDRIDGE THOMAS FARRELL	NY	04E	44
ELDRIDGE WETZEL LONNIE	OH	64W	9
ELDRIDGE WILLIAM FRANKLIN	KY	50E	38
ELENBAAS JACK	MI	21E	74
ELENBURG ALVIN ROBERT	AL	01W	17
ELENBURG JAMES WALTER	AL	07E	95
ELFENBEIN ERNIE JON	NJ	27E	59
ELFLEIN MICHAEL FREDRICK	NY	25E	73
ELFORD GARY EUGENE	OR	03E	5
ELGAARD ROBERT JAMES	KS	14E	123
ELGIN ROBERT GERALD	CA	48E	2
ELIA GARY LAWRENCE	NY	34E	85
ELIA REESE CURRENTI JR	CA	49W	29
ELIA ROBERT A	CT	39E	20
ELIAS JUAN ANGEL	AZ	63W	5
ELIAS PORFIRIO ELIAS	CA	21E	111
ELIASON WENDELL THEO	CA	01E	98
ELICHKO DEAN JOSEPH	NJ	04E	88
ELIE LEONARD WAYNE	LA	17E	103
ELIOT BRUCE JR	NY	42E	30
ELISOVSKY DAVID HENRY	AK	04E	83
ELIZONDO DAVID	TX	04W	58
ELIZONDO FREDERICK H	IL	21E	61
ELKIN JAMES FREEMAN	OK	09W	104
ELKINS BRUCE CLINTON	NC	06W	59
ELKINS FRANK CALLIHAN	NC	11E	68
ELKINS GEORGE ANDREY	KY	17W	55
ELKINS JAN AVERY	NY	40W	36
ELKINS JEROME	CA	02E	67
ELKINS ROGER LYNN	OK	32W	48
ELKINS WAYNE ROBERT	ME	17W	36
ELKINTON MICHAEL	CA	51W	3
ELL ALLEN CHARLES	MT	05W	69
ELLARD CLAUDE ERNEST JR	AL	17W	49
ELLEDGE DON THOMAS	TX	10E	17
ELLEDGE KEITH O'NEIL	MN	13E	44
ELLEDGE MICHAEL STEWART	AR	51W	48
ELLEDGE WAYNE CLARENCE	TX	41W	58
ELLEFSON DAVID JOHN	OR	11W	49
ELLEN WADE LYNN	VA	01W	5
ELLENBERGER CAREY WAYNE	IN	14E	15
ELLENDER TERRY LEE	LA	17E	121
ELLENSON JEROME WILLIAM	ND	34E	20
ELLENWOOD STEPHEN A JR	WA	47W	40
ELLER CHARLES LEROY	NC	03E	75
ELLER JOHN ARTHUR	VA	47W	40
ELLER LAWRENCE WILLIAM	NC	49E	10
ELLERBE JIMMIE LOUIS	NC	17E	103
ELLERBE LONNIE JR	NC	48W	5
ELLERBROCK MARVIN CHARLES	OH	19E	48
ELLERD CARL JOSEPH	TX	17W	26
ELLERMAN GARRY RONALD	MO	58E	20
ELLING ROGER WILLIAM	WA	42W	54
ELLINGER FRANKLIN MAX	IN	49W	52
ELLINGER VICTOR LEE	VA	06W	80
ELLINGSON JAMES EARL	ME	34W	33
ELLINGSON JOEL ARDEN	ND	22E	65
ELLINGTON HERBERT L	VA	20E	39
ELLINGTON KENNETH JULIAN	IL	27W	37
ELLIOT ARTHUR JAMES II	ME	35W	3
ELLIOT ROBERT MALCOLM	MA	39E	31
ELLIOTT ANDREW JOHN	CA	09W	32
ELLIOTT ANTHONY EDWIN	GA	35E	69
ELLIOTT ARTHUR FLOYD	OR	35E	69
ELLIOTT BILLY RONALD	OK	03E	55
ELLIOTT BROCK DENNIS	CA	20E	114
ELLIOTT CHARLES HENRY JR	VA	47W	17
ELLIOTT DAVID RAY	CA	23W	43
ELLIOTT DONALD LYLE	MA	20W	122
ELLIOTT EDWIN ELLIS	ME	18E	13
ELLIOTT ERNEST LEE	AL	55W	5
ELLIOTT FRANK WILLIAM	IL	57E	20
ELLIOTT GEORGE L III	VA	43E	17
ELLIOTT GERALD LEE	IL	65E	8
ELLIOTT JAMES LEE	NC	15E	41
ELLIOTT JERRY W	MS	35E	5
ELLIOTT JULIUS R	TX	59E	8
ELLIOTT LARRY WILBERT	MO	39E	31
ELLIOTT LAVAUGHN	KY	53W	34
ELLIOTT LEROY	PA	19E	57
ELLIOTT NORMAN JR	VA	01E	93
ELLIOTT PHILLIP ALLEN	MI	13W	103
ELLIOTT RAYMOND LESTER	MD	14E	34
ELLIOTT RICHARD	NY	12W	79
ELLIOTT ROBERT JOE	KS	02W	12
ELLIOTT ROBERT THOMAS	AR	01W	98
ELLIOTT ROBERT THOMAS III	AK	44W	9
ELLIOTT ROBERT WILLIAM	NJ	08W	97
ELLIOTT THAROLD WASHINGTO	SC	19E	12
ELLIOTT THOMAS MCCLURE	TX	17E	2
ELLIOTT TOMMY GENE	IL	19W	100
ELLIOTT VANDERBILT JR	VA	29W	7
ELLIOTT WILLIAM KARL	IL	26E	34
ELLIS ADOLPHUS	PA	42E	15
ELLIS ALDWIN ARDEAN JR	OR	27E	64
ELLIS ALFRED	IL	21E	18
ELLIS ALTON LEE	FL	30W	87
ELLIS ALTON STARLING	FL	25W	18
ELLIS BAXTER HARRISON	NC	25E	16
ELLIS BENNEL	IL	02E	94
ELLIS BILLY JOE	TN	33E	27
ELLIS CHARLES PAUL	NJ	10E	90
ELLIS CHARLES WESTLEY JR	AR	17W	4
ELLIS CLARENCE EDWARD	WV	34W	22
ELLIS CONEY	AR	59W	22
ELLIS DENNIS FLOYD	CA	29W	76
ELLIS DONALD RAY	AZ	20E	57
ELLIS EARL WAYNE	MO	03W	85
ELLIS FRANK JOSEPH G JR	NY	28W	34
ELLIS FRED MILTON	ME	15W	107
ELLIS GENE HOWARD JR	CA	24E	117
ELLIS GEORGE LEMUEL	MD	09E	106
ELLIS GEORGE WALTER	CA	33E	84
ELLIS HARRY JOSEPH III	NJ	44E	45
ELLIS HERMAN JR	IN	27E	47
ELLIS JAMES ALVIN	CA	01E	22
ELLIS JAMES FRANCIS	WA	65W	6
ELLIS JAMES LEE JR	GA	29E	29
ELLIS JAMES MARION	SC	25W	4
ELLIS JERRY NORMAN	MN	53W	9
ELLIS JESSE LEONARD	OH	33W	13
ELLIS JOE HENRY	GA	35W	59
ELLIS JOHN MICHAEL	NY	21W	92
ELLIS JOHN PATRICK	GA	41E	64
ELLIS KENNETH WARREN	MA	02W	26
ELLIS LARRY WAYNE	NC	18W	124
ELLIS MAURICE STEPHEN	NC	28E	22
ELLIS MELVIN RUPERT	WA	11E	76
ELLIS MICHAEL LE ROY	CA	30E	24
ELLIS OTIS RANDOLPH JR	VA	17E	61
ELLIS PRESTON HENRY	FL	09W	59
ELLIS RANDALL LEE	WV	06W	47
ELLIS RANDALL SHELLEY	SC	27W	107
ELLIS RAYMOND	PA	02E	99
ELLIS RAYMOND DEAN	SC	10W	17
ELLIS RICHARD LEIALOHA K	HI	01E	11
ELLIS ROBERT EARL	IN	13W	27
ELLIS ROBERT LEE	OH	20W	64
ELLIS ROBERT WAYNE	IN	42E	4
ELLIS ROGER ALLEN	WI	32E	62
ELLIS RONALD LEE	IN	43E	17
ELLIS RUSSELL HAROLD	OH	33W	31
ELLIS STEVEN JOHN	OR	03W	73
ELLIS SYLVESTER	MS	11W	111
ELLIS WALTER EUGENE	OH	26E	83
ELLIS WALTER GENE MERVIN	FL	17E	2
ELLIS WILLIAM JR	SC	08E	84
ELLIS WILLIAM RICHARD	AL	06W	59
ELLIS WILLIAM WALTER III	FL	19W	100
ELLISON ALTON LEON	GA	17W	33
ELLISON CHARLIE MELVIN	NC	31W	79
ELLISON GREG BENSON	NY	34W	23
ELLISON JASPER JR	NJ	57W	19
ELLISON JESSE ROGER	TX	31W	34
ELLISON JOHN COOLEY	UT	17E	35
ELLISON NEVADA LARRY	MI	27E	53
ELLISON RICHARD WRIGHT	MA	05W	111
ELLISON ROBERT LOOMIS	MI	24E	22
ELLISON WAYNE EDWIN	TX	11E	7
ELLISON WILBERT ALLEN	TX	38W	54
ELLISON WILLIE JR	AR	26E	83
ELLMAN JOSEPH RAYMOND	WA	08E	26
ELLSWORTH ELMER EDWARD	NY	28E	91
ELLSWORTH JAMES OLIVER	CA	60W	16
ELLSWORTH LAWRENCE	CA	38W	57
ELLSWORTH MARK ALLEN	IA	42W	11
ELLSWORTH NEIL ROBERT	MA	18E	22
ELLSWORTH RICHARD ALLEN	IN	21W	7
ELLSWORTH ROBERT WAYNE	CO	49E	31
ELLWOOD EUGENE LEE	OH	02E	102
ELLYSON ARCHIE MERLIN	WV	14E	76
ELMAN DAVID HERBERT	NJ	06E	64
ELMANDORF ARTHUR DEWEY	NY	52W	9
ELMORE ALLAN LADD	CA	06E	30
ELMORE CLAUDE EUGENE	AL	23E	57
ELMORE DONALD ROBERT	AZ	24E	60
ELMORE GARY LEWIS	MI	03E	30
ELMORE HUGH WILLIAM	PA	06E	48
ELMORE KENNETH GLENN	MT	16W	73
ELMORE LARRY EUGENE	MO	46E	31
ELMORE ROBERT LOVIS	SC	50E	38
ELMORE WILLIAM H JR	TX	25E	82
ELMY MICHAEL LEE	MI	19E	70
ELROD DAVID LAMAR	GA	20W	33
ELROD JAMES THOMAS	GA	09E	121
ELROD JIMMY CHARLES	AL	31E	57
ELROD WAYMON CLAY	TN	35W	26
ELROD WILLIAM CARROLL JR	GA	04W	123
ELSBERND DAVID DUANE	ND	18W	61
ELSENBURG WILLIE EDWARD	TX	10W	108
ELSENRATH JOHN JOE	KS	28W	80
ELSHIRE TERRY MICHAEL	MT	20E	73
ELSON JEFFREY CHARLES	CA	19W	37
ELSTEN WILLIAM JAMES	OR	35W	37
ELSTON JACKIE LINDELL	OK	52E	36
ELSTON ROBERT FRANKLIN	IN	11W	72
ELSTON ROY DAVID JR	OH	46E	54
ELSWICK JAMES TIPTON JR	VA	25W	67
ELSWICK LEX	IL	12E	27
ELSWICK ROBERT WAYNE	OH	44E	67
ELTING STEVEN VERNON	MI	18W	120
ELTRINGHAM WILLIAM DAVID	PA	37E	54
ELWART PAUL DEAN	MI	25W	67
ELWELL DONOVAN KEITH	ME	15E	89
ELWELL MICHAEL REID	MN	38E	26
ELY DANIEL GERARD	GA	31W	70
ELYEA SIDNEY JOHN	IL	04E	132
ELZA RONALD LEE	IL	21E	93
ELZINGA LARRY LA VERN	MI	49W	4
ELZINGA RICHARD GENE	OR	12W	45
ELZY JOHN CALVIN III	MN	03E	65
EMANUEL WILLIAM FREDERICK	LA	09W	110
EMBREE RONALD EUGENE	IA	14W	17
EMBREY DAVID NORMAN	VA	47W	27
EMBREY GRADY KEITH	GA	02E	91
EMBREY RALPH CURTIS II	KS	12W	131
EMBREY RICHARD LYNN	AZ	49E	40
EMBRY WILLIAM ESSIE	IL	31E	34
EMBRY WILLIAM ROBERT JR	IL	39W	26
EMCH JAMES KENNETH	WA	08W	65
EMEIGH MICHAEL GEORGE	MI	20W	10
EMERINE JERRY OWEN	CA	09W	118
EMERLING JOHN PATRICK	NY	03E	103
EMERSON ERVIN JUNIOR	WV	10E	105
EMERSON JAMES WAYNE	WA	10E	38
EMERSON PHILIP BLAINE	MI	19E	126
EMERSON ROBERT LOYD	KY	08E	16
EMERSON STEWART CHARLES	MD	41W	52
EMERSON TOM	OK	28W	25
EMERSON WAYNE HERSCHEL	CA	21W	32
EMERSON WILLIAM	MA	38W	16
EMERT TOMMIE D	TX	01E	77

NAME	STATE	PANEL NO.	LINE NO.
EMERTON WILLIS WAYNE	TX	27E	80
EMERY CHARLES HENRY JR	NY	17W	15
EMERY DONALD CARLTON	OR	46E	45
EMERY JOE LOUIS	KS	36W	80
EMERY LOUIS CRAIG	ID	12W	5
EMERY OWEN RAY	OH	15E	73
EMERY ROBERT EDWARD	IL	04E	4
EMERY ROBERT LEWIS	MI	15W	102
EMERY STEPHEN BRADFORD	MA	11W	95
EMINETH NORMAN ANTHONY	ND	10W	79
EMMANS WILLIAM ROBERT	VA	11W	30
EMMART JAMES LEE	IN	08E	65
EMMERT CHARLES WILLIAM	OH	22W	75
EMMERT JAMES RICHARD	WV	22E	39
EMMETT GARY WILLIAM	OK	05E	116
EMMONS JOHN WARREN JR	TX	09W	53
EMMONS JUDSON WAYNE	FL	32E	71
EMMONS THOMAS KENNETH	CO	05E	116
EMOND DAVID BRUCE	CT	53W	18
EMORY CHARLES ROBERT	VA	17E	2
EMORY ILLINOIS JR	IL	25E	46
EMORY THERMON HENRY JR	TN	13W	57
EMRATH JOHN PHILLIP	KY	30W	74
EMRICH ROGER GENE	FL	30E	8
EMRICK ERVIN JUNIOR	MO	25W	47
EMRICK STEVEN ERIC	WV	39E	58
EMRO ROBERT BENNETT	NH	18E	45
ENARI MARK NIGGOL	CA	13E	4
ENBODY MICHAEL WILLIAM	CA	39E	4
ENCARNACION-BETENCOURT JESUS	PR	29W	80
ENCARNACION-COLON JESUS M	PR	13W	64
ENCINAS ESEQUIEL MARTINEZ	CA	01W	43
ENCZI RAYMOND MICHAEL	OH	40W	64
ENDERBY ROBERT FRANCIS	IL	21E	66
ENDERIZ VICTOR ANTHONY	CA	31E	23
ENDERLE CLYDE WILSON	OH	12W	20
ENDICOTT DANNY G	OH	22W	104
ENDICOTT FRANKLIN DAVID	ID	25E	97
ENDICOTT MICHAEL LEE	MO	24E	80
ENDICOTT RICHARD LEROY	WY	53E	11
ENDRESS WILLIAM JAMES	OH	09W	94
ENDSLEY KENNETH RICHARD	CA	21E	33
ENEDY ROBERT JOHN	CA	53E	12
ENFINGER KENNETH EARL	AL	23W	109
ENGBERSON ROBERT LEWIS	CA	07E	34
ENGEBRETSON GARY LYNN	WA	43E	17
ENGEBRETSON LARRY DOUGLAS	WA	08W	14
ENGEDAL JOHN	NJ	29W	98
ENGEL ALLEN NORBERT	WI	22E	11
ENGEL GERALD WILLIAM	MI	06E	121
ENGEL GREGORY CHARLES	CA	20W	39
ENGEL HARVEY LEROY	NE	06E	1
ENGEL MEIR	PA	01E	77
ENGEL RODNEY LOUIS	NE	19W	60
ENGEL TERENCE DEAN	MN	01E	117
ENGELHARD ERICH CARL	OH	22W	111
ENGELHARDT ALBERT ALOIS	NY	44E	67
ENGELHARDT GARY WAYNE	IN	06W	5
ENGELHART LESLIE EUGENE	WA	22E	24
ENGELMAN RICHARD GEORGE	AZ	07E	19
ENGELMAN THOMAS ALMET	CA	17W	123
ENGELMEIER JAMES FRANCIS	PA	22W	32
ENGELSEN ROBERT ALLEN	IL	53E	30
ENGEN ROBERT JOSEPH	CA	05W	115
ENGESSER DANNY WRAY	IL	25E	73
ENGLAND GARY LLOYD	NY	31E	40
ENGLAND MICHAEL	GA	30W	21
ENGLAND RICHARD ALAN	IL	21W	107
ENGLAND ROBERT BLAIR II	CA	35E	59
ENGLAND RONALD LEE	CA	10E	121
ENGLAND STEVEN GLENN	ID	05W	106
ENGLAND TONIE LEE JR	TX	17E	2
ENGLANDER LAWRENCE JESSE	CA	54E	5
ENGLE CHARLES EDWIN	IN	05W	130
ENGLE DARRELL LEROY	CA	36W	68
ENGLE PHILLIP HENRY	TN	36W	34
ENGLE RICHARD EUGENE	NY	36E	70
ENGLE RUSSEL WARREN	NJ	22E	39
ENGLERT JAMES RAYMOND	OH	43W	4
ENGLISH CARVER JOSEPH JR	LA	04E	54
ENGLISH DARYL LEE	CT	36W	80

NAME	STATE	PANEL NO.	LINE NO.
ENGLISH DENNIS LAVERNE	AL	19W	85
ENGLISH ERNEST ERVIN	TX	11W	44
ENGLISH GLENN HARRY JR	PA	07W	44
ENGLISH JAMES PATRICK	MA	18E	68
ENGLISH MARK LEO	IA	13E	58
ENGLISH PHILIP DOMINIC K	HI	39W	32
ENGLISH ROBERT PRESTON	AR	37W	63
ENGLISH RUBEN	PA	21E	33
ENGLISH STEVE CRAIG	WA	05W	98
ENGLISH WILLIAM WELTON JR	GA	11E	81
ENGMAN DARWIN HAROLD	WA	07E	33
ENGRAM RANDAL CLYDE	FL	11E	39
ENGREN RUSSELL ALAN	MN	10E	38
ENGROFF RICHARD CHARLES	PA	27E	80
ENGS RUSSELL LARNED III	IL	57E	20
ENGSTROM BRUCE EINAR	NY	37E	6
ENGSTROM LOREN EUGENE	CA	39W	59
ENIX JACK GENE	OH	59W	1
ENLOW PHILIP JAMES	KS	16W	13
ENMAN DEVON MARDIC	MA	07W	57
ENMON DAVID J	TX	21E	104
ENNERS RAYMOND JAMES	NY	43W	26
ENNIS JAMES LESTER	WV	02W	105
ENOS BLAINE WILBERT JR	PA	14W	83
ENOS LEONARD ARVIN	AZ	20E	102
ENOS ROBERT RAYMOND JR	MI	05W	43
ENQUIST ARTHUR JOHN	NE	58W	18
ENRICO ENRIQUE THOMAS	WA	22W	76
ENRIGHT ROBERT EARL	AZ	35W	12
ENRIQUEZ LUCAS R	CA	21W	124
ENRIQUEZ NICHOLAS BEN	CA	29E	1
ENRIQUEZ TERRY MICHAEL	CA	30E	8
ENSELL JOHN ROBERT	OH	29E	40
ENSIGN WALTER LYMAN JR	OH	62E	17
ENSLEY RONALD JOHN JR	TN	29E	14
ENSSLIN OTTO ROBERT	WI	18E	68
ENTRICAN DANNY DAY	MS	03W	39
ENYEART RAYMOND R JR	CA	05W	26
ENZ HARVEY GORDON	MN	28W	10
ENZINNA JOHN JOSEPH	NY	46E	4
EOFF WILLIAM BRADFORD JR	OK	54W	28
EPHLAND GUY BERNARD JR	NC	65W	6
EPHRAIM EDDIE LEE	TX	45E	46
EPHRIAM DAVID BURNELL	CA	10E	79
EPIFANIO NEAL DAVID	NJ	18W	27
EPLEY KENNETH KEITH	FL	26W	70
EPLEY ROGER LEE	CA	12E	54
EPLIN JAMES LEONARD	WV	39W	59
EPPERSON CHARLES WILLIAM	FL	50W	41
EPPERSON ROY ALLEN	AZ	15W	4
EPPERSON STEVEN GILL	AR	13W	41
EPPERSON THOMAS EDWARD	VA	03W	70
EPPINGER GEORGE	NJ	12E	99
EPPLEY GERALD VERNON	OH	09E	107
EPPS CECIL WAYNE	VA	38E	49
EPPS CLINTON HURANSO	MO	03W	120
EPPS HERSCHEL LEE JR	IL	14E	43
EPPS JAMES	NY	24W	16
EPPS JOE HERBERT	TX	14E	26
EPPS LAMONT GEORGE	MD	29E	88
EPPS PATRICK BEVERLY	NY	40W	64
EPPS RICHARD MAYNARD	VA	06E	48
EPPS TITUS LEE	TX	06W	53
EPSTINE LARRY DAVID	PA	01W	10
EQUI RUSSELL LLOYD	CT	34W	83
ERB KARL FRIEDRICK	IN	20E	57
ERB PATRICK DOUGLAS	CA	04W	48
ERBENTRAUT STEVEN CHARLES	MA	30W	87
ERBES JOHN HENRY	MN	31W	79
ERBLAND NORMAN JOSEPH	OH	42E	30
ERBY LESTER	MS	66W	5
ERDELY RALPH GABRIEL	MA	07E	52
ERDMAN DALE ARTHUR	WI	12W	103
ERDOS DENNIS KEITH	OH	13E	51
ERENSTOFT DAVID KARL	NY	13W	96
ERFORD DENNIS CHARLES	OH	37W	73
ERFORD JOHN LEWIS JR	OH	18W	53
ERHART MICHAEL DAVID	OH	26W	83
ERICKSON ALAN CLIFFORD	WA	24E	22
ERICKSON DAVID WAYNE	MN	45E	1
ERICKSON DONALD THEODORE	CA	09E	97
ERICKSON HOWARD W JR	IL	26W	83

NAME	STATE	PANEL NO.	LINE NO.
ERICKSON JOSEPH FRANK	MI	13W	48
ERICKSON KENT DOUGLAS	MN	04W	91
ERICKSON LEONARD DANIEL	CA	48E	40
ERICKSON MARVIN LE ROY	WI	34W	63
ERICKSON PHILIP CHARLES	CA	35W	82
ERICKSON RICHARD ANTON	MN	14E	72
ERICKSON ROBERT DALE	WI	14E	21
ERICKSON RUSSELL MARTIN	IL	51W	49
ERICKSON THOMAS GUSTAV	MN	12E	114
ERICKSON WILLIAM L JR	WA	17W	43
ERICSON GARY WAYNE	IL	15W	128
ERICSON WILLIAM F II	CT	21W	124
ERIKSEN ALF EDWARD	NY	23W	97
ERKES WILLIAM JAMES JR	PA	14W	7
ERLANDSON DANIEL KENNETH	MA	05W	52
ERLING WILLIAM NELS JR	IL	26E	8
ERNHART STUART JAMES	IN	04E	96
ERNSBERGER RANDALL WAYNE	AZ	29E	13
ERNST EDWARD JOSEPH	CA	15E	57
ERNST GARY JOSEPH	MO	21E	120
ERNST RALPH HERMAN	MO	03E	75
ERSCHOEN ARTHUR RAYMOND	CA	12E	41
ERSKINE ALBERT	NY	31W	66
ERTEL LOREN LESLIE	WI	27E	84
ERTL RICHARD LOUIS	MN	24E	55
ERVIN BAXTER FRENCH	OH	25E	23
ERVIN CHARLES DWAYNE	OK	24W	116
ERVIN CLIFFORD LEON	AL	50W	34
ERVIN DONALD FRANK	NC	28W	86
ERVIN GARY LEE	OH	14W	46
ERVIN GLEN OTIS	CA	37E	6
ERVIN GREGORY ALLEN	CA	21E	11
ERVIN JAMES WILBUR	CA	03E	75
ERVIN JERRY GLENN	TN	30W	78
ERVIN JERRY LYNN	TX	23W	110
ERVIN JOHN LEE	IL	07W	26
ERWIN ARTHUR ALBERT	OR	23E	41
ERWIN DANNY MAX	TN	04E	69
ERWIN DONALD EDWARD	IN	42W	61
ERWIN EARL JR	AL	42E	4
ERWIN HUBERT AARON	LA	13E	82
ERWIN LYAL HANCIL	IN	01E	82
ERWIN RICHARD EUGENE	TX	49E	21
ERWIN YOUEAL DEAN	TN	20W	29
ESBENSEN CHARLES JOSEPH	PA	13E	27
ESCAGEDA JESUS	CA	37W	21
ESCALANTE DOMINGO JR	CA	15E	42
ESCALERA RICHARD MEDINA	CA	05W	16
ESCALLIER STEVE LOUIS	ND	16W	8
ESCAMILLA JOSE	TX	05E	22
ESCAMILLA JOSEPH	CA	34W	23
ESCANDON JOE ALEXANDER	TX	12W	45
ESCANO JUANITO MAIQUEZ	GM	10W	74
ESCARENO ARMANDO LEO	MI	29E	81
ESCH FRANK RYAN	IL	06E	38
ESCHBACH CHARLES LINWOOD	MI	04E	89
ESCOBAR EDWARD ANGIANO	CA	19E	12
ESCOBAR JESUS GUTIERREZ	CA	55W	34
ESCOBAR JOSEPH SANCHEZ	CA	21E	33
ESCOBAR SANTIAGO HERRERA	CA	01W	28
ESCOBEDO DANIEL	CA	35E	45
ESCOBEDO JULIAN JR	TX	18W	20
ESCOBEDO ROBERTO	TX	45W	36
ESCOTT KENNETH ROBERT	CA	55W	12
ESHLEMAN DENNIS CHARLES	PA	33W	14
ESKEW CURTIS DEAN	MO	24E	22
ESKEW RONNIE JOE	CA	35E	15
ESKRIDGE JAMES EARL	IL	06W	80
ESKRIDGE WARREN REED	VA	33W	7
ESMAN DAVID HARM	MI	25E	56
ESNAULT JEAN CLAUDE T E	NY	01E	38
ESPARZA FELIX JR	TX	07E	70
ESPARZA ISRAEL	TX	19W	49
ESPARZA JOHN PAUL JR	MN	37E	55
ESPARZA JOSEPH DAVID	CA	03W	57
ESPARZA MALCOLM MARCELLIN	CA	49W	21
ESPARZA NICHOLAS JR	TX	26W	14
ESPENSHIED JOHN LEE	OH	17W	101
ESPINOSA ELLIS CASIANO	IL	13E	51
ESPINOSA JUAN	PR	04W	49
ESPINOSA MIKE	TX	44E	5
ESPINOSA VICENTE T	GM	28W	59

NAME	STATE	PANEL NO.	LINE NO.
ESPINOZA ALFONZO LOUIS JR	CA	04W	120
ESPINOZA MARTIN	TX	47W	7
ESPINOZA VICTORIANO JR	TX	34E	6
ESPONOZA MIKE PATRICIO	CA	47W	41
ESPOSITO FRANK CARL	NY	16E	58
ESPOSITO JAMES MICHAEL	NJ	40W	32
ESPOSITO WILLIAM	NY	22E	30
ESPOSITO WILLIAM JR	NY	03E	40
ESPY JOHNNIE BEE	NJ	59W	22
ESQUEDA ANTONIO ALVARADO	NM	14E	73
ESQUEDA ARTHUR DIAZ	CA	26E	101
ESQUIERDO JOHNNY RAYMOND	TX	17W	6
ESQUILIN-ORTIZ ERROL W	PR	48W	56
ESQUIVEL JAIME	CA	19E	105
ESSARY GEORGE ARTHUR	TN	59W	22
ESSARY JAMES	MO	14E	43
ESSARY MARTIN WILLIAM JR	TX	17W	96
ESSER LAWRENCE ROBERT	ND	29W	18
ESSIG PHILLIP JOHN	IL	48W	17
ESSLER RONALD HENRY	MN	30E	69
ESSLINGER WILLIAM BERTUS	WY	21E	27
ESSMANN ROBERT CHARLES	WI	23W	85
ESTEIN DALTON MAIN	TX	48E	26
ESTELLA ANTHONY JOHN	SC	28E	54
ESTEN JOHN ERNEST	CT	34E	85
ESTEP EARL B	WV	42W	61
ESTERGREN JAMES HOWARD	NJ	19E	94
ESTERLY LAWRENCE ALAN	OH	20W	14
ESTERS CHARLES JR	FL	14E	97
ESTERS FREDDIE	WV	23E	18
ESTES BRIAN ROBERT	CA	30W	11
ESTES DENNIS REX	CA	30E	84
ESTES DONALD CARTHEL	AL	08E	84
ESTES DOUGLAS DALE	TN	37W	63
ESTES EDWARD STANLEY	TX	39E	20
ESTES JERRY DUANE	ID	05E	6
ESTES KENNETH	OH	27W	17
ESTES MERLE EDWARD	KY	02E	7
ESTES NEDWARD CLYDE JR	GA	14W	38
ESTES WALTER O	MI	30E	24
ESTEVES FERNANDO BARCINAS	GM	13W	14
ESTEVES-NEGRON ANTONIO	PR	03W	93
ESTOCIN MICHAEL JOHN	PA	18E	92
ESTOK MICHAEL DAVID	CA	19E	105
ESTRADA ADOLFO MEDARDO	PR	37W	34
ESTRADA CARLOS ALBERT JR	TX	12W	21
ESTRADA DAVID	VA	17E	51
ESTRADA ESTEBAN PENA	TX	35E	62
ESTRADA GUILLERMO	IN	33E	8
ESTRADA JUAN VARGAS	TX	34W	14
ESTRADA MARIO PEREDA	CA	42W	4
ESTRADA MAXIMINO	CA	04W	76
ESTRADA RANDOLPH PHILLIP	CA	60E	22
ESTRADA RICHARD ALLEN	NE	49E	45
ESTRADA ROY LEE	CA	45E	20
ESTRADA-COSTAS HERMAN	PR	03E	123
ESTRIDGE CURTISS	KY	07W	9
ETCHBERGER RICHARD	PA	44E	15
ETHERIDGE COLIE JR	SC	61W	12
ETHERIDGE HAMPTON A III	AR	21W	124
ETHERIDGE JAMES RALPH	GA	40E	73
ETHERIDGE MICHAEL RAYMOND	CO	16W	49
ETHERTON STEVEN PAUL	CO	22W	39
ETHINGTON GLENN RAY	KY	05W	56
ETSITTY VAN	NM	61W	3
ETTEL HENRY C JR	IN	23W	99
ETTER PAUL QUAMMEN	MI	37W	63
ETTZ MICHAEL CHARLES	NJ	28E	54
EUBANK CHARLES HORTON	PA	10W	75
EUBANKS CARL MARCUS	MS	16E	77
EUBANKS DEWEY MAYNARD	NC	22W	118
EUBANKS GEORGE F	WV	31E	57
EUBANKS JOE WOFFORD	NC	01W	34
EUBANKS RANDOLPH	FL	32W	97
EUBANKS RAYMOND CARL JR	TN	32E	53
EUCKER FRANKLIN CHARLES	NJ	09E	67
EUDALY F M	TX	29W	52
EUKEL DAVID DEAN	GA	38E	26
EULER MICHAEL DAN	IN	07E	85
EULITT LEONARD ELZY	OK	38E	49
EUNICE RONALD LEE	IL	09E	33
EUSTACE ARTHUR BARNETT JR	IL	02E	20
EUSTAQUIO JOSEPH MARTIN	GM	29W	98
EUTSLER JOHN WESLEY	OH	33W	25
EUTSLER JOHNNY NEIL	IN	21W	124
EVANCHO RICHARD	PA	46E	31
EVANGELISTA FRANK PAUL	NY	30W	13
EVANOFF ALVIN LEE	IL	06W	110
EVANS ALBERT	GA	35E	5
EVANS ALFRED KINDELL	TX	17E	91
EVANS ALONZA	SC	10E	91
EVANS ANDREW C	AL	07E	48
EVANS BENNETT EDWARD	WY	46W	7
EVANS BILLY KENNEDY JR	VA	37W	45
EVANS CECIL VAUGHN	MD	45W	61
EVANS CHARLES JAMES	GA	23E	110
EVANS CHARLES MICHAEL	IL	14E	53
EVANS CHRIS STEVEN	CA	23E	51
EVANS CLARENCE LOVICE	TX	36E	7
EVANS CLEVELAND JR	AR	44E	35
EVANS CLIFFRED MELVIN	WA	58W	8
EVANS CLIVE LEROY	OK	25E	98
EVANS CLYDE SAMPSON	OH	24W	65
EVANS CURTIS NEIL	OR	45W	25
EVANS DANNY LEO	OK	08W	100
EVANS DAVID LYNN	OR	40W	28
EVANS DAVID PAUL	RI	12W	112
EVANS DONALD ALLEN	KS	35E	69
EVANS DONALD JERRY	PA	07E	118
EVANS DONALD LYNN	LA	03W	97
EVANS DONALD PATRICK	MI	38W	17
EVANS DONALD RAY	CA	53E	30
EVANS DONALD WARD JR	CA	14E	85
EVANS DOUGLAS McARTHUR	AL	24W	39
EVANS EDWARD LOUIS	TX	09W	38
EVANS ERIC WILLIAM	NY	13E	40
EVANS ERNEST	SC	51W	17
EVANS FREEMON	GA	37W	38
EVANS GARFIELD	CA	41E	37
EVANS GARY GENE	ID	57W	8
EVANS GARY LEE	KY	18W	27
EVANS GEORGE AUGUSTA	NY	35W	76
EVANS GEORGE FREDRICK	MA	31W	91
EVANS GERALD BRUCE	KS	03E	76
EVANS GERALD LEE	AR	04W	11
EVANS GORDON EDWARD	PA	14W	29
EVANS GREGORY JAMES	MI	40E	3
EVANS HAYDN	NJ	62W	5
EVANS HENRY ELMER	TX	02W	90
EVANS HENRY FRANKLIN	SC	24W	40
EVANS HERMAN	AL	07W	52
EVANS JAMES JOSEPH	KS	01E	100
EVANS JAMES LARRY	AL	17E	18
EVANS JAMES WILLIAM	OH	17E	43
EVANS JEFFERY WILLIAM	IL	40W	20
EVANS JEFFREY ALAN	MD	45W	50
EVANS JERRY BRIAN	NY	44W	23
EVANS JERRY DEWAIN	NY	40E	73
EVANS JERRY THOMAS	AL	54E	33
EVANS JOE	IL	64E	4
EVANS JOE FRANKLIN	OH	44E	15
EVANS JOHN DOUGLAS	MA	36E	66
EVANS JOHN HARPER JR	NY	08W	90
EVANS JOHN R	PA	24E	12
EVANS JOHN TROY	OK	15E	24
EVANS JOHNNIE LEE	AL	15E	83
EVANS JOHNNY LEE	LA	40W	48
EVANS JOSEPH GEORGE JR	PA	05E	116
EVANS LARRY EDGAR	OH	30W	74
EVANS LLOYD WILLIAM JR	TX	50W	38
EVANS LONEY JR	NC	41W	11
EVANS LONNIE BERNARD	VA	30E	76
EVANS LONNIE DALE	LA	27W	49
EVANS MICHAEL EUGENE	GA	41W	39
EVANS MICHAEL JOHN	CA	23W	85
EVANS MICHAEL THOMAS	NC	52E	17
EVANS NORMAN FRANCIS	OR	06W	80
EVANS PAUL MICHAEL	NY	35W	33
EVANS PAUL OLYNN	SD	13E	71
EVANS PAUL RAYMOND	GA	55E	10
EVANS RAY FRANCIS	NV	11W	91
EVANS RAYMOND E	CO	42W	35
EVANS RICHARD ALLEN JR	MO	46W	58
EVANS RICHARD WAYNE	FL	08W	14
EVANS ROBERT DAVID	TX	26E	8
EVANS ROBERT DILLON	FL	28W	59
EVANS RODNEY JOHN	AL	20W	14
EVANS ROGER DALE	WV	32E	21
EVANS RONALD D	OH	13E	80
EVANS RONALD LEE	OH	03W	17
EVANS RUSSELL	GA	23W	26
EVANS RUSSELL IRWIN	IN	19E	106
EVANS SAMMY GRAY	AR	18E	58
EVANS SAMUEL JAMES	NJ	38W	25
EVANS THOMAS C	AL	19E	51
EVANS THOMAS J JR	VA	15E	127
EVANS THOMAS JAMES	MN	08E	56
EVANS THOMAS JOHN	MI	39W	32
EVANS VANCE MARTIN	IA	17W	108
EVANS WADDEL	KY	19E	90
EVANS WALTER C	PA	27E	100
EVANS WARD CECIL	ND	33W	84
EVANS WILLARD JAMES	OH	34W	83
EVANS WILLIAM ANTHONY	WI	30W	12
EVANS WILLIAM LARRY	TN	21E	66
EVELAND JOSEPH NORMAN	WI	15W	62
EVELAND MARK W	WA	19W	49
EVELAND MICKEY EUGENE	CA	02W	50
EVENHUS GERALD WALLACE	OR	10E	100
EVENSON EDDIE LEE	MN	28W	17
EVENSON MICHAEL ARTHUR	ND	42E	31
EVEREST ROBERT K III	GA	10W	39
EVERETT BOBBY JOE	LA	19W	78
EVERETT CLARENCE E	GA	13E	96
EVERETT EVERETT WHITE	TX	51W	31
EVERETT GARY WAYNE	TX	36W	62
EVERETT JAY LEROY	PA	20W	43
EVERETT JERRY DON	AR	28E	103
EVERETT LAUREN RAY	IA	02W	41
EVERETT LEROY	FL	32E	21
EVERETT LUCIOUS LIONEL	MI	13E	24
EVERETT MARK ROSS	WA	22E	98
EVERETT NORMAN ROY	NJ	14W	64
EVERETT ROCKFORD GREY	MS	49E	31
EVERETT STANLEY OLIVER	WA	22W	46
EVERETT TONY	OK	13E	118
EVERHART WILLIAM JOSEPH	KS	01E	34
EVERSGERD MARLIN CHRIS	IL	16E	110
EVERSGERD NORMAN LEE	IL	48W	41
EVERSULL ANTHONY PATRICK	CA	54E	33
EVERT BARRY EDWARD	NJ	15E	4
EVERT LAWRENCE GERALD	WY	29E	48
EVERTS DENNIS LEE	CA	62E	3
EVERTS JACK CHARLES	UT	11W	72
EVILSIZER DAVID NATHANIEL	IL	06E	114
EVILSIZOR RALPH RAYMOND	OH	16W	69
EVITT WAYNE LEE	GA	08E	66
EWALD RICHARD CLAYTON	MN	40W	53
EWALD ROBERT CLARENCE	CA	56W	19
EWALD WOODROW JOHNSEN JR	MN	18W	68
EWALT DONALD THOMAS	OH	40E	4
EWART JOHN ANDREW	CA	17E	28
EWING ARTHUR RICHARD	NY	27E	19
EWING DAVID JAMES	MI	24W	75
EWING JERRY LEE	MI	29W	98
EWING JERRY LEW	CA	24W	29
EWING KENNETH GENE	MO	16W	109
EWING LON BARRY	CA	63E	18
EWING MICHAEL LEE	IA	58W	24
EWING RONALD ARTHUR	MT	54W	10
EWING TIMOTHY DAVID	CA	13E	51
EWOLDT ROBERT EDWIN	IA	37E	55
EX DAVID LEE	MI	09W	47
EXNER FRED ANTONY III	CA	16W	99
EXPOSE HENRY RAY	MS	07W	10
EXUM EDMUND GARDNER JR	PA	21E	44
EXUM EZEKEIL THEODORE	FL	15E	74
EXUM NEIL HARRIS	RI	51E	19
EYER KENNETH JONES JR	NC	25W	38
EYLER ALLAN DOUGLAS	IN	26W	31
EYNON JOHN PATRICK	CA	11E	44
EYRING KENNETH ROBERT	TX	29W	77
EYSTER GEORGE SENSENY JR	WV	04E	72
EZELL BURLEY DEAN	OK	34E	6
EZELL DONNIE D	MO	01E	108
EZELL WILLIAM BENJAMIN	LA	38W	7

NAME	STATE	PANEL NO.	LINE NO.
FABACHER SAZIN DALE	TX	06W	134
FABER THOMAS WALTER	WI	21W	15
FABIAN WILLIAM HILRIC	WA	39W	65
FABRIS CHRIS FRANK	IL	09E	74
FABRISI PAUL EUGENE	CT	20W	64
FABRIZIO JAMES	CT	23E	41
FACCHINI STEPHEN DALE	CA	31W	35
FACCIO ROBERT DANIEL	NY	41W	52
FACER RICHARD MICHAEL	UT	06W	31
FACKRELL CLINTON BLAIR	CA	06E	109
FACONDINI RICHARD MICHAEL	CT	03E	126
FACTORA DOUGLAS GEORGE	HI	59E	21
FACULAK GARY J	MI	06W	124
FAEHNRICH DAVID RAYMOND	MN	25E	50
FAGE ROBERT FREDERICK JR	CA	11W	63
FAGERLIND MERLE KEITH JR	IA	31E	34
FAGGETT CHARLES EARL	TX	14E	95
FAHEY JOSEPH MICHAEL JR	TX	01E	6
FAHEY WILLIAM PAUL	PA	15E	115
FAHRENBRUCH RICHARD L	CO	47E	49
FAHRENHORST THOMAS KENNET	MO	49W	13
FAHRNI DALE ALLEN	WI	25W	16
FAIDLEY JOHN CHARLES	VA	14E	86
FAILS EDWARD LEE JR	OH	22E	11
FAIN GARY LEE	TX	36W	68
FAIN JAMES LEONARD	KY	05E	60
FAIR RONALD	PA	34E	68
FAIRBOTHAM ROBERT LAWRENC	MI	45W	40
FAIRCHILD DAVID ACEL	ID	04E	133
FAIRCHILD DENNIS MELVIN	IN	34W	7
FAIRCLOTH ARTHUR CRAIG	GA	18W	97
FAIRCLOTH ELLIS LOVINE	GA	57E	2
FAIRCLOTH HENRY FLOYD	GA	28W	58
FAIRCLOTH JOHNNIE WILLIAM	GA	02E	87
FAIRCLOTH JULIUS CLYDE	MO	41W	64
FAIRCLOTH RICHARD DWAYNE	NM	46W	58
FAIRES ROBERT DON	OK	35E	38
FAIRFIELD DENNIS HOWARD	IL	20E	41
FAISON EARL JR	MD	17E	91
FAISON EVERSON BENJAMIN	SC	16W	73
FAITH WALTER DANIEL	NJ	41E	8
FAKIN ZLATKO M		01E	99
FAKO JOHN STEPHEN	NY	06W	3
FALARDEAU JOSEPH ERNEST	MA	47W	41
FALATO JOSEPH ANTHONY	NJ	15E	32
FALCK CARL LEONARD JR	WA	12E	66
FALCO ANTONIO	MA	26W	87
FALCON ANIBAL	CT	49W	13
FALCONBURY EARL FERN	IN	29W	36
FALCONE JOHN PAUL JR	NH	29E	72
FALDERMEYER HAROLD JOHN	NY	01W	23
FALEAFINE SISIFO	HI	34E	17
FALER ALLEN LEE	WY	54E	33
FALES PHILIPPE B	CA	16W	83
FALK DAVID JOHN	MI	11W	27
FALK FREDERICK JOHN JR	CT	35E	39
FALK GARY DAVID	OH	35W	33
FALK RICHARD WILLIAM	PA	43W	61
FALK THOMAS EDWARD	NY	40E	61
FALKENAU ROBERT ARTHUR	DE	15W	32
FALKNER RUFUS PERRY JR	GA	02W	51
FALLER JOEL EDWARD	PA	25E	28
FALLON MICHAEL JAMES	NJ	65W	7
FALLON PATRICK MARTIN	PA	21W	59
FALLON THOMAS J JR	NY	08E	14
FALLOON EDWIN JOSEPH	IL	02E	95
FALLOWS ROBERT LANE	NC	13W	57
FALLSTICH JAMES ROLAND	PA	51W	4
FALWELL DONALD WAYNE	VA	19E	24
FAMILIARE ANTHONY JOHN	PA	28E	22
FANCHER JIMMIE ALVIN	TX	56E	11
FANELLA LAWRENCE ANDREW	NY	23W	52
FANFA ANTHONY JOHN	CA	27W	30
FANIS GEORGE NICHOLAS JR	IL	31E	64
FANKBONER DANIEL ROSS	IN	15W	35
FANKHAUSER CARROLL E	IA	02E	82
FANN DANNY WAYNE	GA	25W	93
FANNIN BRYANT D	MD	29E	99
FANNIN CLAYTON ALLEN	CA	01E	16
FANNING EDWARD CHARLES	NJ	22W	51
FANNING HUGH MICHAEL	TX	28E	103
FANNING JOSEPH PETER	NY	36W	15
FANNING MARTIN VINCENT	NM	03W	7
FANNING MICHAEL FRANCIS	MA	35E	15
FANNING RICHARD HENRY	SC	03W	13
FANNING THOMAS F JR	TX	21W	111
FANNING THOMAS GARRET	WA	19E	49
FANT LAWRENCE L	MO	19E	70
FANT RUSSELL THOMAS	CT	33W	48
FANTE ROBERT GERALD	MI	49W	19
FANTLE SAMUEL III	SD	33E	47
FANUA FIAPAI JR	CA	37W	63
FARAN DANIEL EDWARD	CA	19W	106
FARAWELL GEORGE THOMAS	NJ	29W	68
FARBRO MILLARD WADE	OK	30E	77
FARDEN KENNETH ROY	CA	43W	4
FARELLI LAWRENCE JOHN	MA	40E	4
FAREWELL ROGER WILLIAM	TX	03W	98
FARHAT ALAN JAMES	MI	21E	120
FARINARO GUIDO	NY	50W	37
FARLEY ANDREW SIMMONS JR	DC	23W	52
FARLEY DAVID LITTLEHALE	ME	27E	81
FARLEY GARY LEE	OH	29E	81
FARLEY JAMES CABELL	TN	30E	41
FARLEY JOHN HARLAND	MI	23W	44
FARLEY MARSHALL COLIN	CA	26E	92
FARLEY MICHAEL LEE	IN	12W	117
FARLEY MICHAEL MARION	NE	02W	55
FARLEY PATRICK MICHAEL	RI	42W	55
FARLEY ROBERT JERRY SR	TX	30E	8
FARLEY WILLIAM DANIEL	MO	20E	89
FARLOW CRAIG LEE	OH	01W	26
FARLOW GARY ALLAN	OH	19E	94
FARLOW RANDALL LEE	IA	43W	14
FARMER BOBBY GENE	GA	21W	92
FARMER CHARLES EDWARD	MD	27E	53
FARMER CHARLIE WILL JR	GA	22W	22
FARMER HARRY EARL	FL	15W	118
FARMER JAMES BRYON II	VA	45E	1
FARMER JAMES DALE	TX	01W	111
FARMER JAMES GORDON	KY	27E	80
FARMER JOSEPH LYLE	TN	33E	8
FARMER MICHAEL LEE	NJ	48E	2
FARMER MICHAEL MELVIN	CT	39W	20
FARMER NEIL PHILIP	IN	27W	55
FARMER THOMAS HOYT	OR	03W	70
FARMER THOMAS LEONARD	CO	10W	90
FARMER WILLIAM HOKE JR	NC	21E	12
FARMER WILLIAM NIAL	MI	43W	68
FARMER WILLIE JR	NC	27E	27
FARNER JON MICHAEL	IL	19E	24
FARNHAM ALLEN STEARNS	CT	35W	8
FARNHAM ROBERT DALE	IA	14W	32
FARNOW JERE DOUGLAS	NV	43E	18
FARNSWORTH JOHN JOSEPH JR	PA	06W	56
FARNSWORTH NEVIN O JR	PA	17W	104
FARO JAMES ELLIS	MI	45W	61
FARR DAVID EARL	CA	14W	68
FARR DAVID LEROY	NY	30E	30
FARR JACK GRAHAM	MS	02E	44
FARRAR ERROLD RUFUS	NY	15W	86
FARRAR JAMES EDWARD JR	NC	08E	27
FARRELL ALBERT JAMES JR	NY	13W	117
FARRELL BRUCE CHARLES	CA	01E	30
FARRELL CHARLES DOUGLAS	MA	61W	12
FARRELL DANIEL FRANCIS	IL	05W	90
FARRELL GERALD MARTIN	NY	19E	12
FARRELL KENNETH JAMES	NY	33E	35
FARRELL MICHAEL CHARLES	MI	20E	25
FARRELL MICHAEL JAMES	LA	28E	23
FARRELL TIMOTHY CHARLES	NE	14W	125
FARRELL WILLIAM DOUGLAS	IA	34W	57
FARRELL WILLIAM PETER	NY	31E	73
FARREN MARK	WA	11W	31
FARRIER GERALD WYATTE	AR	24E	22
FARRINGTON HERBERT L III	PA	19E	4
FARRINGTON ROBERT DEAN	MO	15W	48
FARRIOR BILLY RANDY	TN	05W	8
FARRIS BLAKE WILEY JR	VA	35E	69
FARRIS DALE WAYNE	TX	02W	126
FARRIS DENNIS BARRY	WY	35W	74
FARRIS DENNIS CLAUDE	OK	05W	135
FARRIS GARY BRUCE	OK	01W	32
FARRIS GEORGE K	IN	11E	108
FARRIS MICHAEL J	MO	42E	50
FARRIS NORMAN CARL	MA	12E	100
FARRIS WILLIAM FARRELL	IL	37E	55
FARRO STANLEY DALE	MI	33W	78
FARROW DAVID ASHBY	VA	07E	57
FARROW FRANKIE LEE	VA	46E	4
FARROW JAMES EUGENE	TX	37W	80
FARTO CARLOS ANGEL	FL	13E	18
FARVOUR WILLIAM HAROLD	WI	32W	43
FASCHING LEROY JAMES	MT	12W	67
FASNACHT DAVID ANTHONY	MN	23E	75
FASSEL GARY CARL	NY	24W	116
FASSITT ERIC RICHARD	MA	33E	56
FAST ROGER THEODORE	MN	48W	54
FASTH KENNETH LEE	MN	24E	22
FATICA ROBERT JOSEPH	OH	15W	122
FAUCETT GARY LEE	NY	17E	84
FAUGHN ISSAC DAVID	LA	15W	35
FAUGHT DAVID LAWERANCE	MI	09E	121
FAUGHT FRANK EDWIN	OK	36E	7
FAUGHT WILLIAM AVENER JR	VA	08W	51
FAUL KENNETH WAYNE	OH	40W	48
FAULCONER DAVID ROSS	WA	10E	88
FAULK PAUL	NY	26W	45
FAULK THEODORE ALPHONSE	LA	35E	20
FAULKNER ARNOLD JOE	OR	06E	38
FAULKNER CHARLES LONG	VA	12E	119
FAULKNER EARL EUGENE	IN	53W	9
FAULKNER ELMER LEE JR	DE	56W	20
FAULKNER JAMES THOMAS	NC	02E	118
FAULKNER LARRY ALLEN	OH	20E	15
FAULKNER LARRY FREEMAN	ME	23E	67
FAULKNER MAURICE	IL	16E	20
FAULKNER MICHAEL ANTHONY	CA	45W	64
FAULKNER MICHAEL LEE	OH	07E	40
FAULKNER RICHARD J	DE	41E	20
FAULKNER TROY DAVID	TX	26W	32
FAULKS DANIEL CLYDE JR	CA	32E	62
FAULKS WILLIE JAMES	AL	46W	58
FAULL CLIFFORD LEONARD	MI	48E	2
FAUSER RUSSELL JAY JR	NY	39E	46
FAUST TIMOTHY RAY	GA	12W	127
FAVATA SAM JOSEPH	CA	51W	25
FAVERTY ALVIS RAY JR	OH	48W	41
FAVOR JOHN ROBERT	MI	35E	21
FAVOR ROBERT FRANCIS		15W	63
FAVORS BOBBY LEE	KY	05E	1
FAVOURITE RONALD LEE	OH	54E	6
FAVROTH CHARLES	NY	29E	81
FAVUZZA LOUIS ANTHONY	MA	11W	67
FAWBUSH STEVEN LEE	KY	08W	48
FAWCETT DONALD JAMES	PA	08E	123
FAWKS ERNEST EUGENE	PA	42E	50
FAY MICHAEL ANDREW	CA	46E	32
FAY PATRICK DENNIS	CA	44W	16
FAY RICHARD EUGENE	PA	08W	31
FAY ROBERT JOSEPH	MA	03E	4
FAZZAH GEORGE RICHARD	CA	16W	84
FAZZINO JAMES DOUGLAS	OH	58W	24
FEAGAN MICHAEL JOHN	VA	32E	35
FEARN GUY VICTOR	OH	03W	33
FEARNO JOSEPH BARNETT	KS	06E	30
FEARS THOMAS JEFFERSON	IN	05E	95
FEASTER WILLIAM NEWCOMER	NH	11E	109
FEATHERSTON CLIO C JR	CA	32W	54
FEATHERSTON FIELDING W III	OH	15W	109
FEATHERSTONE RICHARD ALLI	NJ	38E	27
FEBO-BETANCOURT IVAN ROBE	NY	48E	22
FEBUS OCTAVIO	NY	08E	84
FECK DANIEL EDWARD	OH	26W	77
FECTEAU GENE EDWARD	CT	52W	14
FECTEAU RALPH BARNARD JR	NH	66E	8
FEDASCH PETER	NY	54W	15
FEDDEMA CHARLES JOHN	MN	16E	20
FEDDER FRED ANDERSON	WI	20W	118
FEDELE JOHN ANTHONY	LA	15W	50
FEDER LLOYD ARTHUR	WI	35W	38
FEDERLINE AUDLEY M JR	SC	12E	88
FEDEROWSKI ROBERT ALLAN	IL	68E	1
FEDLER BRUCE JEROME	IA	43W	14
FEDOR ANDREW	NJ	16E	90
FEDOR TERRENCE EUGENE	PA	40E	20

NAME	STATE	PANEL NO.	LINE NO.
FEDOROFF ALEXANDER	CA	40E	38
FEDRO JAMES RAY SR	TX	53E	31
FEE DONALD FRED	VA	23E	99
FEE EDWARD FRANCIS JR	TX	23E	1
FEE PHILYAW	KY	06E	99
FEEHERY RICHARD JOSEPH	PA	20E	73
FEELEY EUGENE JOSEPH JR	MA	44W	47
FEEMAN JAMES OSCAR	PA	39E	58
FEEMSTER COLINNA	OH	10E	60
FEENEY JAMES TERRANCE	MI	33W	38
FEENEY JOSEPH MICHAEL	NJ	02W	36
FEESER JOHN RAYMOND	PA	11W	101
FEEZEL HAROLD EUGENE	IL	43W	54
FEEZELL DAN GUINN	IL	08W	104
FEEZER JOHN HARVEY	MD	52W	28
FEGAN ROBERT MATHEW	IN	22W	76
FEGAN RONALD JAMES	NY	01E	103
FEGATELLI PETER FRANK	RI	25W	38
FEGELY TERRY GRANT	PA	13E	116
FEHRENBACH THERON CARL II	LA	12W	101
FEIERABEND PETER MATTHEW	WI	01E	43
FEIGENBUTZ TERRENCE R	CA	36E	48
FEINAUER WAYNE OWEN	UT	35W	89
FEIRO RICHARD DALE	WA	43E	66
FEISTNER STEPHEN ELY	NJ	27E	70
FEIT CHRISTIAN FRANZ III	PA	35E	31
FEKETE JAMES CHARLES	OH	21E	104
FELAND THEODORE GLEN	CA	01E	3
FELCH ARLEIGH FRANCIS	WI	24E	81
FELD RAYMOND GENE	PA	33W	38
FELDEN ANTHONY WAYNE	NY	15W	73
FELDER JESSE CLARANCE	NJ	08E	107
FELDHAUS JOHN ANTHONY	TN	11E	60
FELDHAUS THOMAS VINCENT	CO	17W	101
FELDMANN BARRY EDWARD	MO	31E	73
FELICIANO GILBERT	OH	23E	2
FELICIANO NOEL JESUS	NY	21E	18
FELIX-TORRES JUAN RAMON	PR	44W	62
FELKAMP RONALD ALLEN	IL	06W	14
FELKER GREGORY WAYNE	MI	05W	4
FELKINS WILBURN DANIEL	AZ	02E	45
FELKNER DAVID WILLIAM	CA	14W	26
FELL CARL EUGENE	PA	08E	104
FELL DANIEL BOONE	IA	08W	31
FELL DAVID GLEASON	OH	40W	75
FELL EDWARD WILLIAM JR	MD	52W	42
FELL GEORGE FRANCIS JR	MA	10W	84
FELLENZ CHARLES RICHARD	WI	16W	116
FELLER DAVID KENT	LA	53E	12
FELLERS ROGER WAYNE	TX	15W	118
FELLINGER WILLIAM G JR	NY	20E	25
FELLOWS ALLEN EUGENE	MN	45E	39
FELLOWS DAVID THOMAS	NY	18W	64
FELLOWS ROBERT DAWYNE	OR	11E	14
FELLS WILLIAM HENRY	DC	04W	65
FELSHAW JOHN ARTHUR	NY	35E	45
FELSHER JOHN ALFRED	MS	22W	64
FELT DAVID LEVANT	CA	02E	53
FELT RICHARD WAYNE	OH	21W	51
FELTER ROBERT CHARLES	NY	04E	11
FELTNER GERALD LEE	IA	03E	5
FELTON GARLAND PARIS	VA	06W	54
FELTON MELVIN JAMES	WA	05W	91
FELTON RUBY EDWARD III	CA	16E	27
FELTON THOMAS MOODY	MS	21W	116
FELTON WALTER	PA	07E	70
FELTS DAN OWEN	AZ	07W	76
FELTS EUGENE JR	GA	35W	4
FELTY JAMES LEE	SC	40E	20
FELTY ROY LEE	KY	20W	101
FELTZ KEITH A	OH	30E	2
FELVER GALE HERBERT	NJ	09E	86
FENCEROY LOUIS EARL	LA	24W	65
FENCEROY WILLIAM CHARLES	LA	15E	90
FENDLEY JOEL DAVID	TX	24E	94
FENECH EMMANUEL SALVATORE	MI	18E	92
FENELEY FRANCIS JAMES	MI	07E	48
FENENGA TERRY HOWARD	SD	28E	36
FENKO STEVE BRIAN	OH	23E	69
FENN DANIEL RICHARD	WA	07W	61
FENN MELVIN B	CA	43E	18
FENNELL ALTON JIMMY	GA	33E	84

NAME	STATE	PANEL NO.	LINE NO.
FENNELL ROBERT HARRY	PA	12W	62
FENNELL WALTER HENRY	NC	43W	27
FENNELL WILLIAM ERVIN	FL	47W	18
FENNER MARK WILLIAM	IN	24W	94
FENNER STANLEY STEWART	PA	21W	82
FENNESSEY DAVID LEE	NY	20E	56
FENNEWALD DANIEL FRANK	MO	54E	25
FENNEY DOUGLAS JAMES	MN	13E	113
FENNIMORE GREGORY SCOTT	IN	30E	41
FENSTERMACHER RONALD LEE	WV	09E	67
FENTER CHARLES FREDERICK	AZ	01W	99
FENTON JAMES WILLIARD	AZ	07W	21
FENTON ROBERT ALLEN	CA	07E	28
FENTON WILLIAM CHARLES JR	CT	28W	45
FENTRESS LEON AUBREY	VA	14W	89
FENUSH THOMAS PAUL	PA	21W	99
FERA JOHN ANTHONY	MA	45E	20
FERBOS STANLEY	LA	23E	99
FERDIG RICHARD CHARLES	WI	24E	77
FERDIG RUSSELL NORMAN	SD	44W	2
FERENCE EDWARD PAUL	MA	03E	43
FERENCE MICHAEL WILLIAM	IL	30E	41
FERGUSON AARON FLOYD	UT	41W	23
FERGUSON BENNY HAROLD	SC	21W	44
FERGUSON BLAINE M	CA	14E	4
FERGUSON DAVID CHARLES	OH	30W	45
FERGUSON DENNIS DEAN	IA	06E	24
FERGUSON DENNIS WAYNE	MN	18W	102
FERGUSON DEWEY LINDON	TX	08E	20
FERGUSON DONALD PORTER	CT	34E	41
FERGUSON DOUGLAS DAVID	WA	15W	110
FERGUSON EARL	GA	28W	69
FERGUSON EDWARD KENNETH	CA	23E	2
FERGUSON GARY SCOTT	MI	09E	103
FERGUSON JAMES ALLEN	WA	46W	29
FERGUSON JAMES DONAHUE	MO	55E	11
FERGUSON JAMES P	TX	38E	27
FERGUSON JERRY ROGER	TN	57W	9
FERGUSON JOHN EDWARD	NC	21E	74
FERGUSON KEVIN LEE	NJ	28E	14
FERGUSON LATNEY DEAN	MO	39W	26
FERGUSON LEROY	SC	57E	20
FERGUSON LOWELL VERNON JR	FL	03W	7
FERGUSON LYNN MICHAEL	OH	16E	27
FERGUSON MARION FRANKLIN	MI	39E	46
FERGUSON MARK ANDREW	CA	10E	106
FERGUSON MERL WAYNE	CA	24E	6
FERGUSON MICHAEL LYNN	TN	16W	130
FERGUSON MICHAUEL DON	CA	44E	46
FERGUSON PETER CLARENCE	CT	59W	22
FERGUSON RALPH	OH	62W	8
FERGUSON RANDALL EUGENE	MO	02E	47
FERGUSON RICHARD EUGENE	CA	25E	68
FERGUSON RICHARD HAROLD	NY	57W	17
FERGUSON RICHARD LEE	TN	06W	118
FERGUSON ROBERT FRANCIS	PA	09E	10
FERGUSON RONALD BRUCE	MT	27W	73
FERGUSON RONALD DENNIS	CA	03E	55
FERGUSON SAMUEL	MS	16E	84
FERGUSON TED SCOTT	WI	51W	33
FERGUSON THOMAS ALTON	TX	44E	16
FERGUSON THOMAS BERNARD	ME	47E	10
FERGUSON THOMAS WAYNE	TX	43E	43
FERGUSON WALTER JR	NY	47W	41
FERGUSON WALTER LEE	MI	01W	94
FERGUSON WARREN JOHN JR	CA	13W	34
FERGUSON WAYNE ARDELL	OR	56W	2
FERGUSON WHITNEY T III	CT	29W	7
FERGUSON WILLIAM BOYD	CA	37W	49
FERGUSON WILLIAM EDWIN	AL	36W	84
FERGUSON WILLIAM GLEN	IN	24E	107
FERGUSON WILLIAM GLEN JR	ME	42W	55
FERGUSON WILLIE C JR	OK	41W	45
FERGUSSON ROBERT C L	CA	29E	49
FERN JOHN CHARLES	MI	12W	5
FERNAN WILLIAM	WA	50W	41
FERNANDEZ DANIEL	NM	05E	46
FERNANDEZ DENNIS	IL	53W	9
FERNANDEZ EARL WILLIAM	CA	25E	112
FERNANDEZ EUGENIO E JR	TN	57E	17
FERNANDEZ GARY DENNIS	NY	33E	77
FERNANDEZ JAMES THOMAS	IL	31W	91

NAME	STATE	PANEL NO.	LINE NO.
FERNANDEZ JORGE L	NY	08E	21
FERNANDEZ MANUEL ANSELMO	CA	01W	53
FERNANDEZ MANUEL FORTUNATO	NY	02E	92
FERNANDEZ MARGARITO JR	TX	29W	68
FERNANDEZ MAXIMO PAULITE		08E	14
FERNANDEZ RENE	NY	17E	84
FERNANDEZ REYNALDO SALINE	TX	20E	42
FERNANDEZ ROBERT SANCHEZ	CA	01E	122
FERNANDEZ SANTANA S JR	TX	26W	18
FERNANDEZ WILLIAM MATTHEW	TX	05W	119
FERNANDEZ XAVIER	CA	12E	132
FERNANDEZ-LESTON ENRIQUE	FL	33E	66
FERNHOFF CURTISS	NY	21W	100
FERO RONALD MILLER	NY	04E	30
FEROUGE RONALD WALTER	CA	24W	5
FERRA-FLORES PEDRO	FL	23E	10
FERRALEZ RICHARD	CA	66W	7
FERRANTE GILBERT	CA	09E	132
FERRARA MICHAEL JOHN	NY	43E	18
FERRARI ARNOLD JAY	CA	47E	21
FERRARO DAVID ALLEN	PA	08E	111
FERRAZZANO JOHN RAYMOND	NY	41W	69
FERREBEE RUSSELL EDWIN	WV	12E	114
FERRELL BILLY	MI	10W	117
FERRELL CHARLES ELTON	OK	15W	32
FERRELL CHARLES REGINALD	SC	25E	42
FERRELL HUGH JAMES	VA	34E	32
FERRELL JAMES LEE	IL	16W	52
FERRELL JOHN WESLEY	TN	14E	47
FERRELL MARK JR	PA	06E	22
FERRELL TENNIS CRISPIAN	FL	17E	3
FERRELL WALTER LARRY	WA	34W	92
FERRELL WILLIAM ALFORD	TN	03E	76
FERRELLI ROBERT THOMAS	NJ	45E	21
FERREN JERRY WAYNE	MO	42E	15
FERRIL JOHN HENRY II	NY	23E	25
FERRIS DELMER LEE	IA	01E	89
FERRIS ROBERT CLARK	MA	14E	26
FERRO JAMES	MA	07E	110
FERRO JOSEPH	OH	40W	57
FERRO PHILIP ANTHONY	CA	23E	51
FERRON FRANCIS RAYMOND JR	MA	16E	51
FERRUGGIA RICHARD GEORGE	NJ	27E	70
FERRULLA ROBERT SAMUEL	CA	29E	88
FERRY DANIEL SAMUEL	OH	10E	63
FERRY DAVID LYNN	AK	47W	27
FERRY RAY LEONARD III	CT	49E	55
FERZACCA MICHAEL	MI	17E	95
FESER JEFFERY EVAN	WA	60W	17
FESKEN WILLIAM	NJ	19E	13
FESPERMAN HAROLD PHILIP	NC	13W	8
FESSENDEN ROGER ALLEN	IL	56E	22
FETHEROLF JOHN LAWRENCE	OH	03W	111
FETHEROLF LARRY STEVEN	GA	15E	42
FETNER HAROLD EVERETT	NY	20E	58
FETT DENNIS JAMES	NJ	38W	73
FETTER KENNETH LLOYD	NY	40E	38
FETTERMAN GLENN LEROY	MI	28W	90
FETTKETHER GERALD THOMAS	IA	15E	8
FETTUCCIA FRANK	NY	42E	16
FETTY CLARENCE EDWARD	OH	30W	102
FETZER TERRY LEE	WY	55W	12
FEUCHT JAMES DONALD	LA	56E	22
FEW SAMUEL ARTHUR	KS	47W	8
FEWELL CHESTER DECATUR	NC	13E	130
FEWELL JOHN PHILLIP JR	IN	04E	102
FEWELL TIMOTHY FLOYD	CA	09W	32
FEWLASS CALVIN JOE	MI	21W	44
FEY GLENN THOMAS	PA	55E	12
FIALKO DAVID ANDREW JR	CT	39W	65
FICARA JOSEPH	NY	26W	18
FICKLER EDWIN JAMES	WI	34W	23
FICKLIN ERIC	MS	52E	5
FICKLIN EXCELL	MS	61E	9
FICKLIN GEORGE RAY	CO	19E	13
FICKLING ROY EDWARD	GA	16W	130
FICKUS JOHN ZANG	MD	39W	53
FIDEL HONORIO MORAN JR	CA	24E	94
FIDIAM AARON GREGORY JR	NY	01E	117
FIDUCIOSO STEPHANO JAMES	NJ	29E	8
FIEBELKORN MARCUS GUY	CO	62E	13
FIECHTER JOHNNY PATTON	KY	63W	5

NAME	STATE	PANEL NO.	LINE NO.
FIEDLER DREW	CT	41W	52
FIEDLER GARY JAMES	WI	04W	108
FIEDLER JOHN JUNIOR	WI	24E	23
FIEGLE GERALD WILLIAM	IN	55E	11
FIELD GARY EDGAR	NY	06W	87
FIELD JAMES ROLAND	CA	18W	38
FIELD LEON ROY	NJ	36W	15
FIELD MICHAEL FINLAY	VA	28E	15
FIELDEN WAYNE SAMUEL	TX	22E	11
FIELDER CALVIN	TN	38W	10
FIELDER DONALD REED II	MI	18E	69
FIELDER JOHN LIONEL	NC	19W	30
FIELDER PAUL WESLEY	NE	10E	97
FIELDER ROBERT FLETCHER	VT	05E	96
FIELDING CRAIG PYPER	UT	12W	67
FIELDING DAVID ANDREW	CA	53W	34
FIELDING WAYNE JAMES	PA	46E	32
FIELDS ABRAHAM LINCOLN	NC	03E	55
FIELDS ANTHONY THOMAS	DC	26E	8
FIELDS BOBBY GEORGE	KY	07W	83
FIELDS BOBBY JENE	GA	04W	45
FIELDS CHARLIE	FL	30W	22
FIELDS CLINTON ANGELO	MD	19E	57
FIELDS DANIEL LEE	CO	08E	124
FIELDS ELMER EUGENE	OK	24W	94
FIELDS FREDERICK LEE	FL	06W	98
FIELDS GARRISON DAVID	IN	07W	61
FIELDS HERMAN THURSTON	GA	19W	38
FIELDS JAMES BENJAMIN	OK	27E	28
FIELDS JAMES EDWARD	NY	22E	24
FIELDS JAMES LEWIS	AL	17E	67
FIELDS JAMES RONALD	AL	24W	29
FIELDS JAMES THOMAS	MI	32W	37
FIELDS JERRY	KY	54E	6
FIELDS JERRY L	TN	07E	133
FIELDS JOHN CURTIS	OK	54W	23
FIELDS JULIAN THOMAS	KY	62E	17
FIELDS KELLY	KY	69W	3
FIELDS KENNETH WAYNE	FL	18W	68
FIELDS LARRY EDWARD	OH	23E	70
FIELDS LLOYD JR	VA	06E	110
FIELDS LONNIE DALE	KY	06W	42
FIELDS MICHAEL DAVID	NY	25W	67
FIELDS PETER WHITMAN	NC	05E	85
FIELDS ROBERT JR	GA	17W	55
FIELDS ROBERT LOUIS III	IL	04E	99
FIELDS ROBERT WAYNE	FL	28W	45
FIELDS RONALD CLARK	OH	37E	21
FIELDS RONALD ELWOOD	SC	07W	102
FIELDS SAMUEL JR	TX	12W	88
FIELDS SHERMAN ROBERT JR	NC	62E	4
FIELDS WILLIAM MICHAEL	AL	25W	68
FIELDS WILLIE JR	VA	49W	23
FIELDS WILLIE STEPHEN	GA	48W	54
FIELLER RICHARD BURDICK	NY	04E	108
FIERRO ALEJANDRO FRANCISC	CA	21E	33
FIESLER ROBERT NATHAN	AZ	04W	115
FIESTER GLEN ALAN	IL	07W	46
FIESZEL CLIFFORD WAYNE	TX	42W	47
FIFE JAMES HERBERT JR	WA	09E	112
FIFFE JOHN CHARLES	NY	57E	2
FIFFE RICHARD LEE	KS	29W	88
FIGUEREDO CARLOS	NY	04E	103
FIGUEROA ADAN	NY	25E	11
FIGUEROA ALBERT MARTINEZ	TX	38W	11
FIGUEROA ANGELO	IL	27W	24
FIGUEROA ANTHONY H JR	AZ	22W	88
FIGUEROA CABALLERO FERNANDO	PR	19E	106
FIGUEROA FERNANDO	IL	02W	100
FIGUEROA FRANK NUNEZ	CA	13W	44
FIGUEROA JAVIER PUENTES	CA	35E	54
FIGUEROA JOSE JUAN	PR	31E	73
FIGUEROA JUAN JAVIER	PR	23W	119
FIGUEROA MICHAEL ANGEL	PA	43W	35
FIGUEROA-MELENDEZ EFRAIN	PR	30W	41
FIGUEROA-PEREZ CRISTOBAL	PR	36E	70
FIKE ARTHUR HARRY	FL	10E	19
FIKE DANIEL EUGENE	PA	41W	73
FIKE ROGER WESLEY	IL	13W	27
FIKE RONALD EDWARD	TX	22E	77
FIKE ROSS FRANCIS	MD	20E	7

NAME	STATE	PANEL NO.	LINE NO.
FIKE RUSSELL LARRY	FL	24E	23
FIKE THOMAS EUGENE	MD	02W	84
FILES ALBERT CLIFTON JR	CA	17E	43
FILIBERTI RUSSELL LOUIS	NY	22E	11
FILIPIAK PETER JAN	CA	41E	19
FILIPPELLI ALFRED ANDREW	NY	42W	17
FILIPPELLI JOHN MARIO	CA	39W	16
FILIPPI GERALD FRANCIS	CA	07W	80
FILIPPI JOHN CHARLES	OH	31E	44
FILKINS RONALD MARION	MO	09E	46
FILLERS DONALD JAY	TN	01E	125
FILLIATOR RICHARD ANTHONY	OH	05E	54
FILLINGIM THURMAN ELBY	FL	17E	92
FILLION WILLIAM HENRY	MI	10W	50
FILLMAN WALTER CHARLES SR	OR	06E	92
FILLMORE RONALD RICHARD	CA	16E	121
FILPI JOHN TAYLOR	IL	14E	100
FINA RICHARD CARL	WI	68E	1
FINAN ROBERT EDWARD	NH	27W	93
FINCH FORDHAM E JR	SC	14E	21
FINCH JOHN WEBSTER	KS	02E	25
FINCH LAMONT WILKERSON	AL	13E	90
FINCH MELVIN WAYNE	VA	02W	125
FINCH MICHAEL THOMAS	MS	26E	55
FINCH PATRICK DALE	IL	23W	63
FINCH TERRY DEAN	OR	35E	39
FINCHAM WILLIAM EDWARD	VA	17W	61
FINCHER CECIL FRANKLIN JR	AR	14E	73
FINCHER DONALD B	AR	13W	127
FINCHER JULIAN A JR	OH	14E	69
FINCHER LARRY LEONARD	WA	46W	56
FINCHUM JACK WILLARD	IN	24E	6
FINDLAY ROBERT BRUCE	OR	54E	6
FINDLAY WILLIAM THOMAS	PA	06W	26
FINDLEY ROBERT DENNIS	TX	09E	130
FINDLEY ROBERT GAYLORD	PA	44E	46
FINE NORMAN ELLSWORTH JR	PA	34E	68
FINERTY MICHAEL ROY	OK	44E	58
FINGER DAVID HAROLD	NY	20W	101
FINGER SANFORD IRA	NY	02W	51
FINK HUBERT JOSEPH	NY	22E	12
FINK PHILIP RUSH	TN	48W	6
FINK RICHARD ELWOOD	PA	13E	121
FINK ROBERT ALTON	CA	66E	9
FINK WILLIAM MICHAEL	NY	12W	80
FINKE STEPHEN PAUL	MO	11W	101
FINKEL CHARLES	NY	25E	98
FINKEL KENNETH IAN	GA	26E	95
FINKEL WILLIAM ARTHUR	OH	10E	53
FINLAY EDWARD ARTHUR	NY	32E	9
FINLEY CHARLES RICHARD	MO	49E	21
FINLEY DICKIE WAINE	MO	40W	11
FINLEY GUY MARVIN	VA	31E	46
FINLEY LELAND PATRICK	CA	58E	6
FINLEY MICHAEL PAUL	IL	19E	58
FINLEY NICK ALLISON	TN	15W	63
FINLEY RAYMOND PATRICK	ID	27E	36
FINLEY VALARIAN LAWRENCE	ND	23W	8
FINLEY WILLIAM EDWARD	GA	33W	38
FINN ALBERT MAURICE	PA	07W	77
FINN JAMES NORMAN	NH	12E	20
FINN MICHAEL BLAKE	IL	20W	29
FINN WILLIAM ROBERT	LA	02W	91
FINNEGAN DAVID GARTH	PA	24W	40
FINNEGAN DENNIS WILLIAM	NY	01W	86
FINNEGAN JOHN JOSEPH	NY	21E	4
FINNEGAN ROBERT MICHAEL	NY	36E	7
FINNERTY FRANCIS M JR	NJ	39W	79
FINNEY ARTHUR THOMAS	FL	09E	93
FINNEY BOBBY LEE	MA	22E	40
FINNEY CHARLES ELBERT	MS	29W	60
FINNEY HAROLD JAMES JR	GM	22W	102
FINNEY JAMES JR	NY	08W	78
FINNEY STEPHEN	VA	13E	90
FINNICUM JOHN OTIS	OH	08E	2
FINSTERWALDER RICHARD KEI	NY	12E	109
FINTER GEORGE AIKMAN	NY	13W	68
FINZEL JAMES WARREN	MN	13W	87
FINZER BENJAMIN B	IL	10E	91
FIORENTIN JOHN VELCO	CA	03E	110
FIPPS EUGENE	NC	24E	109
FIRAK ANTHONY MARIAN	IL	16W	42

NAME	STATE	PANEL NO.	LINE NO.
FIREBAUGH ROBERT ANTHONY	MO	33W	19
FIRKUS JAMES RONALD	MN	03W	4
FIRMIN MITCHELL LAWRENCE	LA	42W	28
FIRMNECK ALLAN PAUL	CT	18E	69
FIRST MICHAEL BRUCE	OH	05W	87
FIRTH ALLEN EDWARD	VA	28E	34
FIRTH CHARLES VERNON	IN	49W	13
FIRTH THOMAS ELWOOD	NJ	02E	56
FISCH DAVID ALAN	IA	20E	7
FISCHBACH ALLAN RUSSELL	OH	02E	76
FISCHER ADAM	MS	14E	111
FISCHER DONALD ERNEST	PA	06W	9
FISCHER GEORGE ARTHUR	IL	47E	31
FISCHER GEORGE WARREN JR	NY	49W	4
FISCHER GREGORY JAMES	CA	13E	83
FISCHER GREGORY WILLIAM	OH	40E	62
FISCHER JAMES ROBERT	WI	23E	110
FISCHER JOHN RICHARD	PA	10E	80
FISCHER JOSEPH DENNIS	ND	24W	83
FISCHER KENNETH EDWARD	FL	54W	42
FISCHER LOUIS HAROLD	NY	36E	8
FISCHER NORMAN CHARLES	IL	03W	4
FISCHER RICHARD WILLIAM	WI	33E	84
FISCHER ROBERT PHILIP	NJ	37W	38
FISCHER ROY SCOTT	FL	41W	34
FISCHER THEODORE LAUER	PA	06E	24
FISCHER WAYNE HENRY	IL	35W	51
FISCHIO JOHN ANTHONY	OH	43E	18
FISER DIETER JAMES	OH	02W	16
FISH FRED KEITH	MN	56E	23
FISH GEORGE WILLIAM JR	OH	38W	34
FISH GLENN CHARLES	MT	46W	40
FISH GORDON ALIDEAN	MO	05W	30
FISH JOSEPH KENNETH	VT	40E	20
FISH WILLIAM ARRON	CA	20E	25
FISHBACK WILLIAM EDWARD	MO	44W	9
FISHBECK JAY JOHN	FL	04W	79
FISHENDEN ARTHUR ERIC	NY	23E	117
FISHER ARTHUR	NY	06W	73
FISHER CARL NELSON JR	NE	11W	57
FISHER CARROLL DEAN	WV	06W	45
FISHER DALE CHARLES	PA	32W	80
FISHER DANNY JAY	OH	32E	30
FISHER DARRELD EDWARD	OH	11W	55
FISHER DAVID FRANCOIS	OH	32E	93
FISHER DAVID HERBERT	OH	40W	19
FISHER DAVID LUTHER	IL	05E	38
FISHER DAVID R	IN	18E	9
FISHER DAVID WAYNE	IL	28E	54
FISHER DENNIS FAY	MO	08W	35
FISHER DENNIS FRANKLIN	CA	25E	98
FISHER DENNIS WAYNE	AR	35W	4
FISHER DONALD ELLIS	OR	32E	93
FISHER DONALD GARTH	PA	11W	35
FISHER DONALD JAY	MD	31W	79
FISHER DUAINE KARL	PA	20E	25
FISHER EDWARD STEPHAN	CA	20E	114
FISHER EDWIN FREDERICK	PA	04W	131
FISHER ERIC ANDERS	MA	32W	44
FISHER FRANK CLARK	NY	25E	50
FISHER HARRY	TN	13E	47
FISHER HENRY LEE	KS	22E	6
FISHER JAMES ELTON	MI	45E	39
FISHER JAMES LOUIS	TX	03E	76
FISHER JAMES ROY	PA	60E	22
FISHER JAMES TED	WA	10W	113
FISHER JIMMY LEE	CA	29E	100
FISHER JOHN WILLIAM	CA	08W	2
FISHER LA MARR	CA	10E	21
FISHER MARSHALL WAYNE	OH	53W	9
FISHER OTIS SYLVESTER	IL	12E	61
FISHER RANDY LEE	IA	07W	103
FISHER RICHARD JAMES	NY	26W	77
FISHER RICHARD OTIS	OH	26E	44
FISHER RICKIE DAVIS	CA	31E	34
FISHER ROBERT GENE	CA	45E	21
FISHER ROBERT LEROY	IN	18W	113
FISHER RONALD EZELL	NY	39W	79
FISHER RONALD JAY	OH	05W	133
FISHER ROYAL CLIFTON JR	TX	03E	17
FISHER THOMAS GAYLON	OH	32W	25
FISHER THOMAS WILLIAM	PA	25E	99

NAME	STATE	PANEL NO.	LINE NO.
FISHER WILLIAM JOHN	MT	10E	132
FISHLEIGH ROBERT JUNIOR	OR	07W	89
FISK BARRY KEVIN	NY	42W	17
FISK RICHARD OWEN	MI	36W	29
FITCH DANNIE	LA	10W	32
FITCH DELLWYN ALLEN	ME	49E	21
FITCH EARL FREDERICK	MO	42E	31
FITCH GARY RAY	IL	36E	70
FITCH PHILIP	OH	05E	114
FITCH RONALD JAMES	MI	17E	103
FITCH RONALD RUSSELL	ME	38W	17
FITCH WILLIAM ANDREW	KY	18W	102
FITCHETT REGINALD WILLIAM	CA	03W	82
FITEZ HARRY SAMUEL JR	MD	35E	39
FITTON CROSLEY JAMES JR	CT	42E	5
FITTS CHARLES MILTON	TX	01E	16
FITTS GERALD LAMPLEY	AR	36E	8
FITTS RICHARD ALLAN	MA	37W	10
FITTS RICHARD LEE JR	KY	57W	25
FITZGERALD DAVID BARTLETT	WI	04W	108
FITZGERALD DAVID EDWARD	IL	20W	86
FITZGERALD GEORGE RICHARD	CT	10E	106
FITZGERALD HOWARD KIM	UT	28W	18
FITZGERALD JOHN FRANCIS	MA	49E	32
FITZGERALD JOHN W JR	KY	31E	87
FITZGERALD JOSEPH EDWARD	MA	21E	21
FITZGERALD MANFRED WILLY	TN	32W	65
FITZGERALD MARK JOSEPH	MA	02W	110
FITZGERALD MICHAEL THOMAS	IA	36E	8
FITZGERALD PATRICK VINCEN	NY	58E	18
FITZGERALD PAUL L JR	GA	28E	23
FITZGERALD ROBERT MICHAEL	NY	10W	130
FITZGERALD RONALD EUGENE	WA	11W	123
FITZGERALD TERENCE PATRIC	CA	20E	114
FITZGERALD WILLIAM CHARLE	VT	24E	86
FITZGERALD WOODROW MELVIN	VA	01E	33
FITZGIBBON RICHARD BERNAR	MA	02E	77
FITZGIBBON THOMAS GEORGE	NY	12E	61
FITZGIBBONS JOHN FRANCIS	MA	38W	57
FITZGIBBONS PAUL EDWARD	MA	59E	21
FITZHUGH ROBERT PAUL	CO	14W	46
FITZMAURICE TIMOTHY GEORG	IL	57E	20
FITZPATRICK CURTIS L JR	IL	11E	32
FITZPATRICK JOHN DOUGAL	WI	12E	88
FITZPATRICK MICHAEL THOMAS	MA	09E	14
FITZPATRICK PETER THOMAS	MI	05E	54
FITZPATRICK THOMAS M	OH	27W	108
FITZPATRICK WALTER JOSEPH	MA	16E	9
FITZSIMMONS JAMES PATRICK	CA	20E	26
FITZSIMMONS LARRY LEE	TX	45E	21
FITZSIMMONS PATRICK G	CA	07W	1
FITZWATER JOHN CURTIS	WV	35W	63
FIUME JAMES ROCCO	NY	24W	40
FIVELSON BARRY FRANK	IL	05W	106
FIX MICHAEL DAVID	MN	47W	41
FIX WILLIAM LEROY	CA	52E	17
FJERSTAD DAVID ORSON	SD	15E	104
FLABBI GARY BERNARD	MD	11E	100
FLACK REGINALD	NJ	20E	58
FLADGER RALPH SAMUEL	CA	20W	19
FLADRY LE ROY EDWARD	PA	30E	70
FLAGELLA JAMES POTITO	OH	26W	110
FLAGG ALTON ONEIL	TX	12E	112
FLAGG JAMES EDWARD	AR	04E	22
FLAGIELLO RICHARD JAMES	PA	25W	68
FLAHERTY KEVIN GREGORY	DE	29E	19
FLAHERTY KEVIN MICHAEL	NY	07E	125
FLAHERTY PAUL JAMES	NJ	35W	47
FLAHERTY ROGER ELLIS	ME	17E	110
FLAHERTY STEVE	SC	28W	35
FLAHERTY WILLIAM F III	MO	46W	40
FLAHIVE THOMAS FRANCIS	PA	11E	101
FLAHIVE WILLIAM JOSEPH JR	NY	36E	8
FLAMENT HOWARD L	IL	16W	34
FLAMMER TIMOTHY MATTHEW	KY	22E	120
FLANAGAN DAVID DALE	NE	35E	46
FLANAGAN GEORGE FRANCIS	NH	33E	35
FLANAGAN RUSSELL DAVID	MT	31W	91
FLANAGAN SHERMAN E JR	MD	51W	25
FLANAGAN TOM	MS	13E	130
FLANAGAN WARREN JUNIOR	WV	47E	21
FLANDERS DANNY GEORGE	PA	61W	23
FLANDERS LEON D	SC	08E	56
FLANIGAN JOHN DAVID	OH	30E	8
FLANIGAN JOHN NORLEE	FL	19W	67
FLANIGAN ROBERT MORRIS	MI	26W	77
FLANIGAN THOMAS F II	NY	44W	62
FLANIGAN WESLEY ELMER	TN	32W	97
FLANINGAM DAVID EUGENE	IL	24E	6
FLANNERY BRIAN MICHAEL	IL	13W	28
FLANNERY DAVID ELWOOD	MI	28W	60
FLANNERY JAMES KENNETH	PA	11W	13
FLANNERY MICHAEL EDWARD	CA	30E	9
FLANNERY ROBERT EDWARD JR	CA	19E	24
FLANNIGAN PHILLIP WAYNE	IL	26W	83
FLANSAAS DANIEL ROBERT	CA	23E	70
FLASHNER KENNETH MICHAEL	LA	13W	68
FLASKAMP JOHN EUGENE	IN	69W	3
FLATLEY THOMAS MICHAEL	IL	31E	64
FLATTERY RICHARD T JR	IA	64E	4
FLAVIN PATRICK JAMES	NY	20E	23
FLECK GARY LEE	OH	09W	94
FLECK GREGORY LAMAR	IN	25W	29
FLECK ROBERT LEE	WV	28E	40
FLECK WILBERT CLEMENS	ND	20W	56
FLEEK CHARLES CLINTON	KY	24W	116
FLEENER NICK ULYSSES	AK	08W	65
FLEER ROBERT DEAN	CA	38E	27
FLEETWOOD DONALD LOUIS	IA	31E	73
FLEISCHER DAVID ABRAM	IL	36W	29
FLEISCHMANN DALE FRANK JR	CA	09W	20
FLEISCHMANN MARTIN A	KY	24E	6
FLEITMAN GLENN RAY	TX	23W	110
FLEMING BERNARD JOHN	CA	42E	63
FLEMING CHARLES ROGER	NC	09E	38
FLEMING DENNIS K	OH	39E	32
FLEMING DUNCAN HARTWELL	CT	21E	44
FLEMING HORACE HIGLEY III	FL	58E	6
FLEMING JAMES MARTIN	MI	20W	6
FLEMING JERRY	IL	56W	20
FLEMING JOHN FREDERICK	OR	18E	114
FLEMING JOHN J	MI	02E	99
FLEMING JOHN JAMES	IL	09E	58
FLEMING KENNETH CLAIR JR	OH	55W	13
FLEMING LARRY JR	SC	04E	76
FLEMING MICHAEL JOHN	MN	13W	57
FLEMING MORRIS LAFOND	NY	55E	11
FLEMING PATRICK JAY	MT	24E	113
FLEMING PAUL DENNIS	MA	35W	47
FLEMING PHILLIP HARRY	NC	28W	25
FLEMING RAYMOND E JR	OH	11E	1
FLEMING RICHARD ALAN	IL	34W	23
FLEMING SIDNEY WADE	TX	14E	86
FLEMING THOMAS RYAN	VA	44E	24
FLEMING WILLIAM ELGIN JR	MS	06W	73
FLEMING WILLIAM GORDON JR	KY	10E	106
FLEMING WILLIE JAMES	TN	06W	2
FLEMISTER HUGH ROBERT	FL	27E	64
FLESHER RUSSELL RAY	OH	36E	70
FLESHMAN RANDY ALLEN	OH	03W	119
FLESKES DAVID ALLEN	IA	47W	41
FLETCHER BRUCE JAMES	OR	35E	31
FLETCHER CHARLES EUGENE	MI	17E	18
FLETCHER DAVID FOSTER	IL	57E	2
FLETCHER DONALD EDWARD	NC	20W	52
FLETCHER DONALD FRANK	TN	40W	64
FLETCHER DONNITH HOWARD	FL	09W	103
FLETCHER GUY TALMADGE JR	MD	27W	55
FLETCHER HERMAN RAY	TN	34E	17
FLETCHER JAMES FERRELL	MI	36W	62
FLETCHER JERRY	TN	59E	6
FLETCHER JOHN EARL	LA	39W	65
FLETCHER KENNETH JACK	TX	14E	131
FLETCHER KIM WILLIAM	CA	58W	18
FLETCHER LAWRENCE EUGENE	VA	11W	123
FLETCHER LON M	NM	02E	107
FLETCHER PETER	NH	34E	86
FLETCHER RANDALL SCOTT	CT	46W	1
FLETCHER ROBERT MELVIN	KY	59E	1
FLETCHER ROBERT WENDELL	OH	20W	65
FLETCHER THOMAS THERON	IL	17W	116
FLICKINGER JAMES EDWARD	CA	27E	88
FLICKINGER JAMES HERBERT	CA	19E	25
FLIEGER GERARD JOHN	NY	21W	37
FLIEGER HAROLD NORMAN	OR	06W	112
FLIEGER HARRY GREGG	WA	11W	130
FLINN JOHN LEROY	CA	21W	45
FLINT RALPH PRESTON JR	MD	21E	4
FLINT RAYMOND LLOYD	NY	31W	46
FLINT TROY LEE	LA	10W	24
FLINT WILLIAM JOHN	MA	45W	18
FLINT WILLIAM NEIL	FL	38E	49
FLINT WINFIELD SCOTT	ID	19E	117
FLIPPEN HENRY COAKLEY	MI	66E	9
FLIZANES VAUGHN PAUL	PA	28E	59
FLOHR GEORGE JR	CA	41W	11
FLONNOY FRANK WARREN JR	OH	26W	39
FLONORY ORLANDO	MD	25E	55
FLOOD CHARLES DALE	OH	44E	6
FLOOD JOHN JOSEPH JR	PA	49W	47
FLOOD JOHN PATRICK JR	MA	31E	67
FLOOD MICHAEL HAROLD	IL	27W	8
FLOOD THOMAS BERNARD	MA	06E	30
FLOOD WILLIAM JAMES JR	MA	04W	38
FLORA LARRY VINSON	OH	26E	23
FLORANG LARRY DEAN	NE	14W	36
FLOREN JIMMY ERIK	OR	29E	29
FLORENCE DEXTER BUSH	AR	01W	85
FLORES ANTONIO JR	TX	18E	28
FLORES ARTHUR MERINO	TX	51W	25
FLORES BENNY SAN NICOLAS	GM	07E	70
FLORES CHARLE CORDOVA	NM	57E	21
FLORES DANIEL	CA	11W	73
FLORES DANIEL PORRAS	TX	38W	73
FLORES DAVID	PA	06E	24
FLORES DAVID CRUZ	GM	01W	17
FLORES DOUGLAS	HI	08E	132
FLORES EDWARDO	CA	28W	38
FLORES FELIX FRANK	CA	59W	1
FLORES FIDENCIO JR	OR	03W	4
FLORES FLORENTINO	TX	07W	10
FLORES FRANCISCO JOHN	ID	20E	73
FLORES GUADALUPE	TX	26W	26
FLORES JERRY	NM	04W	27
FLORES JIMMY	TX	44E	16
FLORES JOSE ANIBAL	IL	27E	19
FLORES JOSE DEJESUS	CA	09E	74
FLORES JOSE LUIS	CA	19W	12
FLORES JOSE MARIA	TX	18E	14
FLORES JUAN JR	TX	43E	5
FLORES MANUEL SOLARES	AZ	15E	42
FLORES MANUEL SOTO	IN	36E	8
FLORES MONICO JR	CA	38W	65
FLORES RAMON AGUILAR	TX	41W	23
FLORES RAMON JR	OH	10W	97
FLORES RAUL	TX	09E	108
FLORES RAYES CISNEROS	TX	03E	7
FLORES RICHARD JAVIER	CA	58E	7
FLORES ROBERT JR	OH	17W	65
FLORES ROBERT LEE	AZ	31E	98
FLORES ROBERTO C	TX	08W	37
FLORES VICTOR JR	TX	02E	56
FLORES-JIMENEZ ANGEL RAMO	NY	30E	41
FLOREZ FRANK OCHOA JR	OH	02E	137
FLOREZ REYNALDO B	CA	22E	65
FLOREZ TONY MANUEL	CO	09W	130
FLORIO FRANK	NY	32E	86
FLORIO ROLAND LOUIE	NY	48W	17
FLORY ROBERT LESTER JR	IN	18E	29
FLOTT CHARLES LAWRENCE	MD	01W	36
FLOURNOY CHARLES KAISER	NE	47E	21
FLOURNOY JEFFERY DONALD	IL	27E	70
FLOURNOY MAURICE W	TX	01E	1
FLOURNOY PAUL DOUGLAS	FL	48E	41
FLOWER CARL DAVID	CA	21E	22
FLOWERS DANIEL THOMAS	NY	11E	122
FLOWERS EDGAR ALLEN	SD	28W	98
FLOWERS FLOYD TYRONE	PA	14E	34
FLOWERS LAWRENCE BUFORD	GA	27E	36
FLOWERS MILTON EUGENE	NC	63W	5
FLOWERS RALPH EUGENE JR	IL	16W	79
FLOWERS WILLIAM EDWARD TH	GA	01E	36
FLOWERS WILSON NATHENIAL	CA	31E	3
FLOYD ALAN GREGORY	GA	41E	64
FLOYD ALVIN WINSLOW	GA	12W	80
FLOYD BOGARD LAFAYETTE	MO	45E	1

NAME	STATE	PANEL NO.	LINE NO.
FLOYD CHARLES GRADY	TN	10W	108
FLOYD DAVID ALLEN	LA	30W	2
FLOYD EDWIN ZEKE	KY	52W	14
FLOYD GARLAND DALE	CA	21W	52
FLOYD GEORGE ALLEN	CA	02W	17
FLOYD JAMES MILTON	TX	18W	94
FLOYD JAMES WALTER	NC	02E	115
FLOYD JOHN DOUGLAS	AL	37W	45
FLOYD KENNETH WAYNE	NC	56E	23
FLOYD LARVON	TX	57W	18
FLOYD LONNIE ALLEN	TN	14E	27
FLOYD MELVIN FRANKLIN	TX	09E	112
FLOYD PAUL EDWARD JR	MA	11E	73
FLOYD ROBERT EUGENE	OH	53E	26
FLOYD ROBERT GENE	FL	12W	67
FLOYD ROBERT WILSON	NC	14W	78
FLOYD ROGER LEE	VA	03E	43
FLOYD RONALD JAMES	DC	33W	93
FLUHARTY DONOVAN RUSSEL	PA	24W	58
FLUMERE KEITH MICHAEL	MA	44E	16
FLURRY JAMES DURWARD	TN	26W	98
FLYINGHORSE@ CONRAD LEE	SD	07W	26
FLYNN BILLY WAYNE	NC	14E	70
FLYNN DANIEL JOSEPH	NY	69W	3
FLYNN DANIEL LEOPOLD	WA	12W	67
FLYNN FREDERICK HAROLD	NY	42W	53
FLYNN GARY FRANCIS	MA	26E	65
FLYNN GEORGE EDWARD III	LA	01E	64
FLYNN HAROLD BROWN	LA	03W	126
FLYNN JAMES GERALD	CT	23W	32
FLYNN JIMMY EDWIN	KY	29E	100
FLYNN JOHN HENRY	IL	16E	52
FLYNN MICHAEL FRANK	TX	17E	116
FLYNN RAYMOND JOSEPH JR	OH	06W	127
FLYNN RAYMOND PATRICK	LA	01E	41
FLYNN ROGER JOHN	WI	15W	70
FLYNN WILLIAM PATRICK	NY	64W	9
FLYNN WILLIAM VINCENT	FL	18W	117
FLYNT JAMES WILLIAM III	NC	30E	25
FLYTE FORREST JAY	PA	59W	2
FOAD MELVIN EUGENE	IL	29E	9
FOARD WALLACE BILLANY JR	FL	54E	6
FOBAIR ROSCOE HENRY	CA	02E	43
FODARO THOMAS ANTHONY	NY	04E	69
FODEN JOHN JOSEPH	NY	35E	31
FOELL GERALD LLOYD	IA	21E	47
FOERSTER RAYMOND CARL	TX	16W	39
FOGARD RONALD DEAN	MN	56W	20
FOGARTY GEORGE ALLEN	IA	12E	61
FOGARTY JOHN JOSEPH III	IA	34W	75
FOGG ALBERT RANDOLPH III	CA	37E	55
FOGG DAVID BRUCE	ME	14W	107
FOGG DAVID EDWARD	CO	21W	65
FOGLE LARY DALE	IN	04E	30
FOGLEMAN GEORGE EDWARD	IL	10W	18
FOGLEMAN JAMES OLIN	NC	24W	40
FOGLEMAN JOHNNY	IN	45W	25
FOGLER LEWIS JOHN	MD	19E	5
FOHT STEPHEN CRAIG	IL	09W	7
FOILES FRANCIS IVAN	OK	65W	7
FOLCK BENJAMIN THOMAS	IN	63E	8
FOLDEN THOMAS	FL	28W	10
FOLDVARY JOHN JR	MI	45E	10
FOLEY BRENDAN PATRICK	NY	30E	77
FOLEY BRIAN ROBERT	NY	05W	83
FOLEY CHARLES DANIEL	NM	10W	84
FOLEY DOUGLAS LEE	VA	02E	72
FOLEY JAMES RICHARD	IL	05E	71
FOLEY JAMES WILLIAMS	NE	35E	37
FOLEY JOHN JOSEPH III	NJ	21E	88
FOLEY LONNIE DEE	CA	03W	32
FOLEY MARTIN FRANCIS	MA	26W	90
FOLEY ROBERT JOHN JOSEPH	PA	46W	58
FOLEY ROBERT MICHAEL	MA	29E	10
FOLEY ROBERT PAUL	MA	36E	71
FOLEY ROBERT RAYMOND JR	MA	39W	48
FOLEY THOMAS HAROLD	WI	02W	82
FOLEY WILLIAM LOYD	OK	50W	18
FOLGER JOHN VINCENT	NJ	25W	98
FOLKERS LA VOUGHN HERMAN	WI	15E	119
FOLKS EDWARD LEROY	PA	23E	79
FOLLAND MICHAEL FLEMING	VA	21W	51
FOLLETT ALLAN EUGENE	MO	31E	79
FOLLETTE FREDERICK JOHN	MA	26W	98
FOLLON WILLIAM ELLYN	IA	14W	93
FOLMAR HARRIS ALAN	GA	59W	2
FOLMAR MASON OPHELIA	CA	39W	65
FOLSOM ROBERT ELMER	CA	26E	92
FOLSOM TERENCE J	CA	14W	59
FOLTZ PAUL RAYMOND	IN	02W	45
FOLZ GARY LEE	WI	15W	48
FOMBY JIMMY LEE	TX	15W	38
FONDA PETER FRANCIS	NY	56W	18
FONES PAUL MARK	DE	34E	18
FONGER LYNDSEY FRANK	UT	05E	60
FONSECA JOHN	IL	54W	2
FONSECA MICHAEL JEROME	KS	28E	81
FONSECA-VARGAS HORACIO A	FL	10W	24
FONT MANUEL LOUIS	NJ	10E	7
FONTAINE JOHN ALBERT	MA	06E	131
FONTAINE LARRY LEE	NE	12E	37
FONTAINE MICHAEL ARTHUR	LA	35W	68
FONTAINE NORMAND EDWARD	MA	57E	2
FONTANA ADAM ANTHONY	PA	58E	7
FONTANEZ-VELEZ JOSE LUIS	PR	12E	20
FONTENOT CHESTER JOSEPH C	LA	62E	4
FONTENOT GARY PAUL	LA	24E	103
FONTENOT HAROLD	LA	24E	23
FOOTE FERNANDO VICENTE	NY	25E	99
FOOTE PETER WELLESLEY	MA	35E	80
FOOTE WALTER BRUCE	AZ	13W	88
FORAME PETER CHARLES	VA	02W	89
FORAN JOSEPH PAUL	WI	15E	43
FORAN PATRICK JOSEPH	NY	14E	128
FORAN WILLIAM PATRICK	IL	05E	93
FORBES ARTHUR KIRKS	IL	24W	59
FORBES HARRY BURKLEY	VA	08E	108
FORBES KEVIN LYNN	NY	62E	17
FORBES MICHAEL	TX	22W	118
FORBES PAUL GLENN JR	CA	22E	101
FORBES RICHARD ALLAN	CA	16W	69
FORBES THOMAS LEROY	GA	26E	59
FORBES WALTER HENRY III	MA	17E	3
FORBUSH ROBERT WALDRON JR	NY	19E	25
FORCE DAVID LEE	CA	05E	131
FORCE RODGER DENNIS	NY	30W	22
FORCK MICHAEL RICHARD	MO	30W	64
FORCUM KEVIN PAUL	WA	03W	63
FORD ALLEN D	CO	32E	63
FORD ALVIN WALLACE	AR	35W	47
FORD BERNARD FRANCIS	IL	23E	10
FORD BILLY KEITH	WV	52E	37
FORD BOB JOE JR	LA	15W	77
FORD BOB W	TX	01W	125
FORD CHARLES EDWARD	GA	20W	35
FORD CHARLES EVANS	SC	08E	36
FORD CHARLES JESSE	TN	05E	134
FORD CHARLES LEWIS	VA	11E	14
FORD CHARLES WALKER	AL	17E	110
FORD CHARLES WAYNE	KY	25W	68
FORD CLIFFORD EUGENE JR	AL	58W	8
FORD DAVID TODD	CA	19W	78
FORD DONALD LEE	WY	38W	35
FORD DOUGLAS OAKLEY	NJ	05W	37
FORD EARL EUGENE	CA	07W	81
FORD EDWARD	AL	37W	73
FORD ERNEST DOW	CA	16W	84
FORD FREDDIE DARREL	TN	33E	67
FORD GEORGE B	TN	04E	97
FORD GLENN EDWARD	AL	38W	25
FORD GLENN JESSE III	MI	35W	47
FORD HAROLD ANDREW	PA	20E	83
FORD HAROLD JOSEPH	AR	10W	124
FORD HENRY HARRISON JR	NC	13E	37
FORD JACKIE LEWIS	NC	10W	68
FORD JERRY STEVENSON	NC	06W	18
FORD JOSEPH A III	KS	03E	94
FORD KENNETH ALLISON JR	OH	15W	63
FORD KENNETH LAVERNE	IL	23W	100
FORD KENNETH RAYMOND	WV	19W	128
FORD LEONARD DAVID	FL	05E	28
FORD MANZELLE ALAN	IA	37E	82
FORD MARSHALL H	NH	33E	67
FORD MELVIN	KY	09E	61
FORD MICHAEL EUGENE	IL	69W	3
FORD OMAR RAY	NE	11E	114
FORD PATRICK OSBORNE	CA	55W	13
FORD RALPH LEE	FL	29E	24
FORD RANDOLPH WRIGHT	FL	55W	5
FORD RAYMOND LEE	KY	06E	60
FORD RAYMOND SYLVESTER	KY	05E	55
FORD RICHARD EDWARD	NJ	14W	42
FORD RICHARD WAYNE	CA	31W	39
FORD RICHARD WILLIAM	OK	04W	58
FORD ROBERT	AL	14W	89
FORD RUSSELL THOMAS	FL	19E	94
FORD STEPHEN ROMO	IL	26E	55
FORD THOMAS VINCENT JR	MI	15E	43
FORD VICTOR JAMES	PA	07E	8
FORD WALLACE ADDISON	WV	68E	2
FORD WILLIAM	NC	28E	54
FORD WILLIAM WALLACE	TN	35W	64
FORDHAM BENJAMIN STEPHEN		50E	3
FORDHAM JERRY LEE	GA	19W	30
FORDHAM JOHN LA VERNE	IL	21W	51
FORDHAM KENNETH CHARLES	GA	38E	27
FORDHAM RUSSELL CARRELL	GA	18W	32
FORDI MICHAEL JOSEPH	MA	57E	3
FORDYCE RAY	MO	10E	12
FORE ALEXANDER	NJ	19E	36
FORE JAMES EDWARD	IN	15W	84
FORE JAMES LARRY	NC	08W	28
FORE WILLIAM C	SC	15E	16
FOREE JOSEPH HERMAN	OH	08E	47
FOREHAND JERRY	FL	21E	105
FOREMAN AUBURN WOOD JR	AL	04E	18
FOREMAN BOBBY LEE	KY	23E	27
FOREMAN DWIGHT GARY	DC	16W	105
FOREMAN JAMES LEE	IN	20E	26
FOREMAN JOHN WILLIAM	NY	15W	103
FOREMAN ROBERT JR	LA	12W	46
FOREMAN ROGER EARL	ND	20W	14
FOREMAN TAYLOR W JR	MS	39E	59
FOREMAN TERRY WILLIAM	IA	10W	90
FOREMAN THOMAS ALLEN	ID	34W	41
FOREST DONALD STEVEN	NY	28W	45
FORESTER RICHARD THOMAS	WA	30W	93
FORET KENNETH JOHN	LA	31E	46
FORGET RONALD EDMOND	MA	58W	3
FORGETTE DUANE GARTH	NM	02W	21
FORGUE GERALD HENRY	CT	40W	57
FORK NORMAN KERMIT	NE	17W	9
FORKL ROBERT WAYNE	NY	35E	70
FORKUM GARRY MICHAEL	TN	36W	62
FORMAN CLARENCE GENE	OK	08E	60
FORMAN LEWIS MICHAEL	MI	31W	35
FORMAN WILLIAM STANNARD	MN	04E	82
FORMEY JERRY BERNARD	DC	18E	93
FORMICA GARY PETER	NJ	07W	110
FORNEY ALVIN CARVER	IN	02E	71
FORNEY DENNIS RAY	OK	22W	96
FORREST JIMMIE LEE	MS	27W	17
FORREST MONTE WAYNE	KS	08W	85
FORREST STEPHEN CALEB	CA	08E	129
FORRESTER CARL JAMES	PA	04E	128
FORRESTER JOEL WAYNE	AL	24W	53
FORRESTER JORDEN DUWAYNE	OK	03E	76
FORRESTER LAWRENCE BRADFO	CA	02W	21
FORRESTER RONALD WAYNE	TX	01W	106
FORRISTAL RUSSELL PATRICK	OH	19W	31
FORRY JEFFREY SCOTT	OH	29W	88
FORS GARY HENRY	WA	32E	44
FORSBACH RONALD CARL	TX	08E	97
FORSBERG DOUGLAS BRUCE	MN	31W	46
FORSBERG JAY EDWARD	MI	22E	101
FORSHEY JOHN DANIEL	FL	16E	9
FORSHEY ROBERT ERNEST	CA	37E	55
FORSMAN JAMES ESKEL	NJ	14E	111
FORSYTHE DALE RICHARD	PA	14W	46
FORSYTHE DAVID ALLEN	TX	44W	63
FORSYTHE THOMAS LYNN	TX	15W	78
FORT JEROME	VA	45W	25
FORT MELVIN FRANK	TN	03E	76
FORT RAYMOND JR	AR	25E	50
FORTE FREDERICK C JR	FL	13W	44
FORTE GERALD WAYNE	AR	26W	107

NAME	STATE	PANEL NO.	LINE NO.
FORTE OLLIE	NC	58W	25
FORTE RICHARD JOSEPH	MA	36W	68
FORTE RICHARD MICHAEL	NY	11W	57
FORTENBERRY EDWARD EUGENE	MS	15E	37
FORTENBERRY JAMES RICHARD	TX	07W	86
FORTIN ROBERT GENE	SD	02W	15
FORTNER FREDERICK JOHN	CA	28E	23
FORTNER GARY DUANE	TX	48E	26
FORTNER JOHN LYNWOOD	FL	13W	99
FORTNEY KENDALL THOMAS	WI	43E	18
FORTUNE RODGER LEE	CA	20E	115
FOSBURG RICK HAROLD	MI	56E	28
FOSNAUGH CAREY ALLEN	OH	14W	61
FOSS DANIEL ARTHUR	ME	32W	5
FOSS DUANE JOHN	MN	27E	108
FOSS JOSEPH RALPH	ME	01E	101
FOSSETT NORMAN ARCHIE	MD	42E	51
FOSTER ALBERT DEAN	IA	25W	38
FOSTER ALFONZA	OH	07W	18
FOSTER BENNY EDWARD	IN	07E	110
FOSTER BILLY RAY	LA	08E	49
FOSTER BILLY REX	KY	52E	18
FOSTER BYRON JAMES	MI	03E	31
FOSTER CARL	NJ	15E	9
FOSTER CARL RICHARD	IA	49W	47
FOSTER CLEVELAND	NY	06E	82
FOSTER CURTIS LAMARR	IN	01E	132
FOSTER DANIEL JOHN	NY	32W	58
FOSTER DANIEL WILLIAM	CT	29E	82
FOSTER DAVID DAN	ME	35W	38
FOSTER DONALD RAY	CO	28E	65
FOSTER DOUGLAS EUGENE	OH	61E	9
FOSTER DOUGLAS GENE	WA	44W	63
FOSTER DOYLE	TN	04W	76
FOSTER DWIGHT DUNARD	MI	20W	113
FOSTER EARL WILLIAM JR	SC	04E	77
FOSTER EDDIE DALE	CA	37W	63
FOSTER EVERETT EDWARD	NY	23E	94
FOSTER FRANK	MS	27E	108
FOSTER GARY JACK	ID	08E	6
FOSTER GARY NEIL	UT	35E	38
FOSTER GEORGE	NY	23E	100
FOSTER GEORGE ARTHUR III	NM	37W	5
FOSTER GERALD ANTHONY	DC	54W	28
FOSTER GLENN WILCOX JR	UT	26E	101
FOSTER HADLEY	TX	29W	36
FOSTER ISIAH	FL	06E	42
FOSTER JAMES BYRD JR	SC	04W	46
FOSTER JAMES CLAIR	NY	40E	17
FOSTER JAMES EARNEST	TX	40W	19
FOSTER JAMES LESTER	NM	63E	9
FOSTER JAMES WILBUR	OR	18E	9
FOSTER JEAN CLIFTON	TX	38W	25
FOSTER JIMMIE LEE	IA	05E	71
FOSTER JOE ALBERT JR	AL	18W	120
FOSTER JOHN MICHAEL	CA	28W	23
FOSTER JULIUS CARTWRIGHT	WV	40E	62
FOSTER LARRY AUSTIN	NC	11W	131
FOSTER LARRY EDWARD	TN	36W	80
FOSTER LARRY RAY	OR	23E	70
FOSTER LAWRENCE EUGENE	CA	07E	101
FOSTER MARK ANTHONY	IL	14W	89
FOSTER MARVIN LEE	TX	29W	52
FOSTER MARVIN RAY	TX	13E	8
FOSTER PAUL HELLSTROM	CA	27E	108
FOSTER PAUL LEONARD	TN	32E	93
FOSTER ROBERT ENOCH JR	ME	07E	8
FOSTER ROBERT EUGENE	NY	05E	132
FOSTER ROBERT L	TX	44W	63
FOSTER ROBERT LEE	CA	07E	71
FOSTER SAMUEL EDWARD	SC	46E	4
FOSTER SHELBY GENE	WV	17W	41
FOSTER STEEN BRUCE	IL	10W	40
FOSTER STEVEN JOEL	NJ	46W	2
FOSTER THOMAS EUGENE	MO	25W	99
FOSTER THOMAS RICHARD	WA	17W	123
FOSTER TIMOTHY K	HI	24W	109
FOSTER TOMPKINS GRIFFEN	FL	07E	108
FOSTER TONY CURTIS	PA	15W	27
FOSTER WILLIAM EARL JR	OH	44W	37
FOSTER WILLIAM HENRY	MD	51W	25
FOSTER WILLIE FRANK	SC	42E	63

NAME	STATE	PANEL NO.	LINE NO.
FOSTER WILLIE JAMES	GA	68W	1
FOTI PAUL JOHN	NY	04W	70
FOUCHE PAUL JERRY	GA	08W	7
FOUGHT PAUL EARL JR	PA	40W	6
FOULK PAUL FREDERICK	PA	18W	54
FOULKE JEFFREY HOWARD	CA	32W	31
FOULKS CHARLES JR	NJ	32W	59
FOULKS RALPH EUGENE JR	CA	33E	47
FOUNDS GERALD DEAN	KS	01E	85
FOUNTAIN KENNETH LOREN	GA	35W	34
FOURMENTIN GREGG R	AZ	47E	50
FOURNET DOUGLAS BERNARD	LA	54E	33
FOURNIER JOSEPH DAVID	ME	22W	64
FOURNIER NELSON EDWARD	NY	54E	6
FOUS JAMES WILLIAM	NE	60E	11
FOUST DONALD CHARLES	IN	46E	32
FOUST KENNETH EDWARD	OH	18W	38
FOUST MICHAEL THORNTON	CA	13E	21
FOUTZ KENNETH LEE	OH	11W	111
FOUTZ MICHAEL GEORGE	OR	14W	52
FOWBLE ROBERT L JR	OH	12E	13
FOWLER CLAUDIE	CT	21W	100
FOWLER DANIEL CHARLES	CA	18E	107
FOWLER DAVID ALLEN	OH	14W	42
FOWLER DONALD LEON	MO	29W	7
FOWLER DONALD RANDALL	GA	50W	42
FOWLER EUGENE RUSSELL	IN	01E	109
FOWLER JAMES ALAN	ND	01W	38
FOWLER JAMES EDWARD	MI	29W	7
FOWLER JAMES HARRELL	OK	17E	104
FOWLER JAMES ISIAH JR	KS	49W	8
FOWLER JAMES JEWEL	MO	17W	26
FOWLER JAMES ROBERT	GA	11W	44
FOWLER JOE LYNN	IA	24W	25
FOWLER JOEL CAROL	FL	20E	73
FOWLER JOHN KENNETH	MI	16W	57
FOWLER KENNETH W	IN	26W	48
FOWLER LARRY EUGENE	NC	15E	73
FOWLER LARRY LYNN	PA	16W	127
FOWLER LAWRENCE EUGENE	IN	12E	35
FOWLER LEWIS LOREN	CA	07W	131
FOWLER MICHAEL EDWARD	GA	21W	37
FOWLER ROBERT ALLEN	AL	54E	33
FOWLER ROY GILLMAN	VA	17W	26
FOWLER THOMAS LEE	NE	19W	38
FOWLER VICTOR ORIN JR	WA	11E	86
FOWLER VIRGIL JAMES	WA	57E	21
FOWLER WILL LEE DENNIS	TN	21E	12
FOWLER WILLIAM EDWARD	MD	02E	33
FOWLER WILLIAM HOLT III	CA	30E	25
FOWLER WILLIAM RAY	GA	19E	80
FOWLKE EARNEST WESLEY	UT	40E	21
FOWNER JACOB HENRY	NM	07E	17
FOX AMOS OLIVER	AL	51E	38
FOX BERNARD LYLE	IL	50E	38
FOX CARL JAMES	AL	04E	108
FOX CHARLES BURTON JR	NV	52W	5
FOX CHARLES NATHAN	IN	01E	118
FOX CRAIG JAMES	WA	11W	101
FOX DAVID NELSON	NY	05W	87
FOX DEAN FRANKLIN	UT	16E	35
FOX EDWARD HAROLD	TX	02E	87
FOX GARY DUANE	WY	68E	2
FOX GARY REGAN	TN	18E	53
FOX GARY WAYNE	PA	18E	121
FOX GERALD LAWRENCE	NY	23E	58
FOX HOWARD THOMAS	OH	31W	47
FOX JAMES CARL	CA	28W	90
FOX JAMES DARRYL	GA	14W	48
FOX JOHN WILLIAM	PA	47E	49
FOX LARRY ROSS	NY	36W	49
FOX LEON VINCENT	MS	13E	58
FOX LORENZO	NC	07W	29
FOX PHILLIP CARROL	MI	11E	70
FOX REINIS	FL	41W	23
FOX RICHARD HERBERT	GA	40E	5
FOX RICHARD W B JR	VA	33E	31
FOX ROBERT ALAN	IL	19W	60
FOX ROBERT CHARLES	FL	37W	46
FOX ROBERT LYNN JR	NC	37W	10
FOX RONALD LEE	IL	33E	84
FOX THOMAS AMISS	VA	56E	6

NAME	STATE	PANEL NO.	LINE NO.
FOX THOMAS JOSEPH	NY	03E	44
FOX THOMAS JOSEPH JR	CA	10W	5
FOXE GEORGE	NC	03E	56
FOXWORTH ARTHUR	NJ	17W	127
FOXWORTH ROGER CHRISTOPHE	MI	33E	84
FOXX RICHARD L	SC	01E	13
FOY JERRY	PA	03W	56
FOY JOHN CARL	NC	51W	48
FOY MICHAEL JOSEPH	CT	39W	11
FOY STEVEN JOSEPH	IN	36W	44
FOY THOMAS LAMAR	GA	19E	80
FOY THOMAS WALTER	MD	60E	22
FOZZARD ROBERT LEE	IL	10W	70
FRACIONE FREDERICK R	TX	05W	19
FRACKER DOUGLAS MONROE	MI	39E	46
FRADY DAVID WAYNE	NC	03W	136
FRADY HARVIE RENA	GA	14W	68
FRAGOSA-GARCIA ANGEL LUIS	PR	16E	75
FRAGUA GEORGE LEONARD	NM	13E	78
FRAHM WILBER DALE	IL	10W	130
FRAHMAN LAWRENCE JOHN	SD	08E	119
FRAIN KENNETH MICHAEL	IN	29W	6
FRAKER ROGER LEE	PA	46W	40
FRAKES DWIGHT GLENN	CA	01E	94
FRAKES JERRY ALLEN	IA	19W	49
FRAKES KENNETH DEAN	CA	22E	12
FRAKES ROBERT LEE	IL	01W	112
FRAKES WILLIAM DOUGLAS	IN	09W	115
FRALEY CHARLES ALBERT	GA	12W	107
FRALEY CLAYTON EUGENE	MD	30W	53
FRALEY DAVID FORREST	OH	19E	71
FRALEY EUGENE THOMAS	MI	35E	5
FRALEY EZEKIEL JR	KY	07W	69
FRALEY GARY THOMAS	IN	14E	80
FRALEY LANDER RAY	DC	10E	83
FRALEY WILLIAM CLIFFORD	KY	08E	133
FRALICKS LARRY DOUGLAS	TX	18W	32
FRAMBES JOHN MALHON	NJ	21E	88
FRANCAVILLA JOHN FRANCIS	WA	49E	1
FRANCE MACK LEMUL JR	TN	07E	33
FRANCE PHILLIP STANLEY	MD	27E	109
FRANCE RICHARD WAYNE	TX	38E	25
FRANCE RONALD LYNN	CT	29W	18
FRANCE WILLIAM RICHARD	OH	26E	9
FRANCEWAR JOHN EDWARD	LA	35W	41
FRANCIES DOLROY	LA	15W	13
FRANCIS CARRIS MICHAEL	OH	12W	38
FRANCIS DAVID ANTHONY	MA	25E	23
FRANCIS JAMES AUGUSTUS	VI	19W	111
FRANCIS JAMES PATRICK	CA	24W	117
FRANCIS JOHN FREDRIC		11E	109
FRANCIS JOHN PAUL	MI	21E	45
FRANCIS JOHN VINCENT	IL	14W	120
FRANCIS JOSEPH WILLIAM JR	NJ	18E	3
FRANCIS LARRY EDWARD	VA	12W	131
FRANCIS LINDELL	MO	30W	88
FRANCIS MICHAEL JAMES	MI	27E	33
FRANCIS OSCAR THOMAS	GA	11W	45
FRANCIS PAUL JAMES	GA	12W	51
FRANCIS STEVEN DAVID	CA	14E	62
FRANCIS TERRANCE DEAN J	IN	35W	64
FRANCIS THOMAS EARL	NJ	26E	59
FRANCIS WILLIAM JOSEPH	MI	13W	100
FRANCIS WILLIE JR	LA	03E	105
FRANCIS WILLIE JR	LA	08E	71
FRANCISCO DARRYL GRANT	MI	22W	39
FRANCISCO JAMES LEONARD	NJ	33W	62
FRANCISCO PATRICK PHILLIP	AZ	18E	93
FRANCISCO SAN DEWAYNE	WA	38W	57
FRANCISCO WILLIAM JR	NJ	35W	64
FRANCK RALPH HENRY JR	WA	57W	25
FRANCKOWIAK JOSEPH RALPH	CA	50W	18
FRANCO CHARLES STEPHEN	NY	08E	16
FRANCO FRANCISCO	CA	42E	51
FRANCOLINI JOSEPH DAVID	CT	17E	18
FRANGELLA FRANK A	FL	19W	54
FRANK EDWARD ROY SR	MT	20E	26
FRANK HAROLD LEROY	WA	09W	130
FRANK HARRY BERNARD JR	GA	22E	77
FRANK JOHNSON FRANCIS	NC	05E	79
FRANK NEAL RAY	MN	10W	50
FRANK RICHARD WAGNER II	MA	15W	72

NAME	STATE	PANEL NO.	LINE NO.
FRANK RODNEY GALE	WA	43E	6
FRANK THOMAS PAUL	IA	02W	58
FRANK TIMOTHY GEORGE	PA	11W	43
FRANKE BERNARD LEE	IL	20E	94
FRANKE WILLIAM THOMAS	NJ	32W	64
FRANKEL JOHN PAUL	CA	12E	20
FRANKEN ARLIN DALE	IA	20W	10
FRANKENSTEIN JACKIE	OH	59W	2
FRANKHAUSER CHRIS WALTER	OH	57E	21
FRANKIEWICZ PHILIP ROBERT	IL	32W	26
FRANKLIN AMOS LEE	WA	59E	22
FRANKLIN CHARLES EDWARD	OH	10E	4
FRANKLIN CHARLES ROBERT	FL	50E	27
FRANKLIN CLARENCE RICHARD	AL	04W	117
FRANKLIN DOUGLAS M	VA	24E	60
FRANKLIN EUGENE	FL	54E	7
FRANKLIN EUGENE DELANO	TN	02E	17
FRANKLIN FLOYD STANLEY	MO	12W	59
FRANKLIN GARRY LYNN	NC	09W	90
FRANKLIN GEORGE STEVE	CA	06E	74
FRANKLIN IRA MELTON JR	AL	30W	53
FRANKLIN JAMES ANTHONY	AL	29W	19
FRANKLIN JAMMIE VAN	CA	24E	2
FRANKLIN JEFF LEE JR	CA	22W	40
FRANKLIN JEROLD	MS	08W	69
FRANKLIN JOHN ALVIN	GA	52E	18
FRANKLIN JOHN HENRY	CA	06E	30
FRANKLIN KEITH KOY	NY	10W	24
FRANKLIN LAWRENCE ANDRE	WA	02E	115
FRANKLIN MARVIN LYLE JR	OK	25E	74
FRANKLIN PHILIP GILBERT	PA	53E	12
FRANKLIN ROBERT ORME	PA	02E	83
FRANKLIN WILLIAM E JR	TN	14E	128
FRANKLIN WILLIAM JOHNSON	MI	07W	68
FRANKLIN WILLIE	MI	27E	109
FRANKOWIAK ROBERT JOSEPH	MI	31W	91
FRANKS ANTHONY L	SC	24E	90
FRANKS BARRY RICHARD	CA	34W	23
FRANKS DAVITT JOHN	OH	18W	120
FRANKS ERNEST RICHARD	VA	29W	37
FRANKS IAN JACK	NY	45E	63
FRANKS JOHN HOWDEN	FL	04W	115
FRANKS JOSEPH RONALD	MI	38W	25
FRANKS MONROE	FL	17W	22
FRANKS WARREN GAMALIEL JR	NC	09W	57
FRANKS WILLIAM J	PA	15E	91
FRANSEN ALBERT MERK JR	NV	21W	45
FRANSEN RONALD CLIFFORD	MN	45E	46
FRANTA MICHAEL JOHN	IL	10W	84
FRANTZ CURTIS RUSSELL	PA	16W	105
FRANTZ LARRY EDWARD	PA	46W	59
FRANTZ MAXWELL STOWELL	NY	09E	56
FRANTZ WILLIAM DAVID	PA	41W	69
FRANZ BRUCE RONALD	CO	15W	50
FRANZINGER KURT WALTER JR	WV	22W	32
FRAPPIEA FRED C H JR	VT	45E	55
FRASCA RICHARD PATRICK	NY	40E	52
FRASCH ROBERT LOUIS	MO	08W	126
FRASER DOUGLAS PAUL	CT	53W	26
FRASER RONALD MONTE	MN	44W	56
FRASER THOMAS EDWIN	MI	12W	92
FRASER WILLIAM GEORGE	NH	32E	86
FRASHER GARY DEAN	IA	11W	131
FRASHER JOSEPH EDWARD	OH	01W	66
FRASIER DENNIS WILLARD	NY	20E	115
FRASURE HURSHEL	OH	05E	50
FRATELLENICO FRANK ROCCO	NY	08W	124
FRATTALI MICHAEL ANGELO	CA	04W	91
FRATTO MICHAEL JOHN	CT	26W	98
FRATUS EDWARD FRANCIS	NH	15W	41
FRAUSTO NOLBERTO JR	TX	37E	6
FRAVEL DAVID WARD	OH	39E	70
FRAWLEY WILLIAM DAVID	MA	05E	93
FRAY EARL RICHARD	OR	36W	15
FRAZE JERRY WAYNE	TX	44E	26
FRAZEE GEORGE HOWARD JR	OH	01E	125
FRAZELLE DONALD JEROME	NC	04W	63
FRAZER FREDRICK HARRY	AZ	38W	72
FRAZER KENNETH CHARLES	IL	44W	9
FRAZER RONALD LLOYD	IN	68E	2
FRAZIER ALBERT WILLIAM	MO	31E	34
FRAZIER BARRON ALLEN	NC	25E	11
FRAZIER BARRY LYNN	PA	53E	31
FRAZIER CHARLIE JR	CO	09E	10
FRAZIER EDWARD LEE	TX	39E	32
FRAZIER FLOYD MILTON	NC	01E	6
FRAZIER FLOYD WENDELL JR	OK	02W	44
FRAZIER FRED RAYMOND JR	OK	33W	84
FRAZIER GARY LEE	MS	08W	130
FRAZIER GARY VIRGIL	ID	42E	31
FRAZIER GENE ALLEN	OK	50W	13
FRAZIER JERRY RAY	IA	31W	67
FRAZIER JOHN DUDLEY	OK	60E	22
FRAZIER JOHNNIE LEE	TX	24E	23
FRAZIER KEITH EUGENE	PA	27E	100
FRAZIER LEROY	CT	11E	33
FRAZIER PAUL REID	WI	45W	32
FRAZIER REX LEONARD	CA	06W	47
FRAZIER RICHARD BERYL	MT	05W	123
FRAZIER RICHARD JACOB	MI	05W	133
FRAZIER RONALD LEON	MO	49E	1
FRAZIER TIMOTHY JOSEPH JR	NY	59W	2
FRAZIER ULYSSES VAN	GA	11E	52
FRAZIER WILLIE JAMES	GA	25W	5
FREASIER THOMAS HALL	TX	13W	23
FRECH THOMAS WILLIAM	NJ	06W	101
FRECHETTE FRANCIS GERALD	MA	22W	65
FRECHETTE TERRY ALLEN	MI	50W	15
FREDA ARTHUR ANTHONY JR	MA	10E	66
FREDA NORMAN ALAN	MI	33W	26
FREDA ROBERT	FL	07W	63
FREDENBERG RALPH	WI	51E	45
FREDERICK ARTHUR DONALD	SC	40E	62
FREDERICK CHARLES EMMETT	OH	04E	123
FREDERICK CLIFTON JR	KY	14E	66
FREDERICK DAVID ADDISON	OH	24E	51
FREDERICK DOUGLAS LLOYD	FL	49W	53
FREDERICK JAMES CARL	FL	30E	25
FREDERICK JOHN WILLIAM JR	IL	03E	136
FREDERICK LAMAR DONALD	OH	05E	80
FREDERICK PETER JOSEPH	NY	16E	84
FREDERICK STEVEN EDWARD	FL	33W	19
FREDERICK WILLIAM V	OH	23E	10
FREDERICKSON EARL WARREN	MN	01W	47
FREDERICKSON PAUL LOWELL	MI	57E	21
FREDRICK BRIAN RANDALL	FL	35W	76
FREDRICKSEN ALLAN MARCUS	WA	63E	10
FREDRICKSON ALAN DOUGLAS	MI	18E	3
FREDRICKSON GERALD GEORGE	MN	24E	23
FREDSTI STEFFAN MICHAEL	CA	18E	25
FREDWELL GARCLEE M	MO	46W	59
FREE JOHNNY WAYNE	TX	03W	121
FREE LAWRENCE CAMERON	IN	11E	68
FREEBERG RANDALL ROGER	MN	25E	28
FREED DAVID BRUCE	NJ	43W	35
FREED ROBERT THOMAS	IL	16E	9
FREEDLE FRANK LOUIE	CA	50E	46
FREELAND CHARLES JEFFERY	OH	25W	38
FREELAND GEORGE EDWARD	PA	13E	80
FREELAND GUY THOMAS	AR	01E	74
FREELAND TROIT DONOVAN	IL	08W	107
FREEMAN ARDENIA	FL	29E	29
FREEMAN BOBBY	GA	49W	53
FREEMAN CHARLES LLOYD	NC	43W	27
FREEMAN CHESTER LEON	AR	13E	10
FREEMAN DARELL GOODWIN	CA	03E	107
FREEMAN DAVID FRANKLIN	MO	07W	64
FREEMAN DAVID HAROLD	AL	11E	68
FREEMAN DAVID MICHAEL	CT	19W	1
FREEMAN DONALD VERN	IN	27E	44
FREEMAN EARNEST TAYLOR	NC	25W	68
FREEMAN EUGENE LARRY JR	FL	50E	28
FREEMAN FLEMMON PAUL	AR	05E	71
FREEMAN FURNACE JR	NY	29W	37
FREEMAN GARRY DON	AL	14E	15
FREEMAN GARY	VA	22W	118
FREEMAN GENE	NC	37W	10
FREEMAN GLENN WAYNE	WV	33E	85
FREEMAN IVEL DOAN	CO	16E	44
FREEMAN JAMES PAUL	TX	55E	11
FREEMAN JEFFREY ALEXANDER	OH	12W	107
FREEMAN JIMMY GRANT	AL	28W	25
FREEMAN JOHN OLIVER	OK	10E	127
FREEMAN JOSEPH LLOYD JR	SC	30W	19
FREEMAN JOSEPH WARREN JR	OH	24W	4
FREEMAN LESTER	NY	39E	47
FREEMAN MARTIN LEE	ME	16E	10
FREEMAN MOULTON LAMAR	FL	25W	99
FREEMAN OLLIE CURTIS	TX	58E	20
FREEMAN RANDALL GAYLORD	IA	06W	120
FREEMAN REX BRADFORD	OK	42E	31
FREEMAN RICHARD BARTON	CA	01W	86
FREEMAN ROBERT GLENN	NC	61E	9
FREEMAN ROBERT LEE	MI	24W	40
FREEMAN RONALD WILLIAM	NY	35W	19
FREEMAN ROY ELDON JR	IN	07E	42
FREEMAN RUBE ALFRED	GA	01E	21
FREEMAN SAMUEL DIGGES III	CT	13E	121
FREEMAN STEVEN FORREST	TX	31E	3
FREEMAN WALTER DAVID	OR	37W	22
FREEMAN WILLARD	NY	06W	46
FREEMAN WILLIE LEE	GA	65W	7
FREESE ELMER EUGENE	MN	38W	42
FREESTONE DAVID EDWARD	TX	19W	124
FREESTONE SPENCER SCOTT	MI	39E	47
FREESTONE WILLIAM FREDRIC	IA	08E	133
FREGIA ROBERT RANDY	CO	36W	15
FREGOSO MARCO AURELIO	CA	18W	1
FREIDT JAMES CHRISTIAN	ND	27E	89
FREILING JOHN RICHARD JR	CA	24E	91
FREISE MELVIN JOHN	IL	26W	32
FREITAG DIETER KUNO	NJ	01W	17
FREITAG KENNETH LEE	LA	07E	18
FREITAS ROBERT EDWIN	CA	22W	104
FRENCH ALBERT LEROY	NY	09E	122
FRENCH ALLEN GEORGE	IL	10E	8
FRENCH DAVID LEE	OH	33E	12
FRENCH DENNIS	AZ	17W	10
FRENCH DOUGLAS ROBERT	TX	09E	51
FRENCH FRED	CA	07W	86
FRENCH JOY TRINT	IL	57E	21
FRENCH WILLIE JR	NC	31E	98
FRENCL MICHAEL JAMES	IL	31W	67
FRENDLING EDWARD JOSEPH	IL	28W	100
FRENG MARSHALL FRANKLIN	MD	30E	62
FRENG STANLEY JON	SD	08E	56
FRENIER FREDERICK IRVING	WA	17E	56
FRENYEA EDMUND HENRY	CA	04E	83
FRENZELL HERBERT ERNEST	CA	14E	62
FREPPON JOHN CHARLES	KY	31E	80
FREPPON JOHN DENNIS	OH	33W	38
FRERICKS LOUIS WAYNE	IL	29W	19
FRESE MICHAEL ALBERT	IL	10W	113
FRESE STEVEN ROBERT	NY	44W	24
FRET-CAMACHO JUAN ALBERTO	PR	14W	46
FREUDENTHAL RICHARD HOLT	VA	22E	87
FREUND CARTER JOHN	IL	31W	92
FREUND ERNEST ELWOOD JR	IN	36E	9
FREUND TERRENCE JAY	WI	11E	109
FREUND WILLIAM CARL	OH	20E	26
FREY DANIEL ALAN	CA	14W	131
FREY DEAN LEE	CA	11W	24
FREY DONALD	MO	02E	114
FREY JESSE CLIFFORD	CA	13W	53
FREY JOHN HARVEY	LA	15W	21
FREY WILLIAM AUSTIN	PA	44W	63
FREY WILLIAM JOSEPH	PA	47E	50
FREYNE BERNARD ANTHONY	NY	16E	52
FRIAR FREDDIE LYNN	AR	16E	44
FRICK EDSALL A	CA	39W	16
FRICK JOHN ALAN	CA	19E	13
FRICKE EUGENE MARSHALL	WI	03W	24
FRICKE PATRICK LOYAL	IA	04W	31
FRIDAY LORRENCE TEALOA	PA	48E	41
FRIDDLE GLENN MARK	FL	09E	120
FRIDDLE KENNETH CLAYTON	GA	11E	62
FRIED DOUGLAS LAWRENCE	MT	27E	9
FRIED VERN JACOB	SD	37E	82
FRIEDHOFF DENNIS PATRICK	IA	46W	41
FRIEDMANN GARY WAYNE	PA	16E	58
FRIEL BRUCE GARY	CA	27W	86
FRIEL JOHN CHARLES	TX	24E	116
FRIEL JOSEPH AUGUSTUS	MA	10E	127
FRIEL LUSTER CLARK	WV	06E	114
FRIEND GARY RALPH	OR	07W	51
FRIEND RICHARD ALLEN	CA	46E	4

NAME	STATE	PANEL NO.	LINE NO.
FRIERSON EDDIE TYREE	TX	51W	4
FRIERSON KENNETH	SC	14W	64
FRIES DANIEL LESLIE	MI	06W	9
FRIES DANNY JOE	IA	08W	42
FRIES DENNIS JEROME	IL	28E	74
FRIESE MICHAEL KEITH	IL	34E	36
FRIESE WILLARD JOHN	IA	06E	29
FRIESNER ROGER HUNTER	MI	22E	101
FRIESON SAMUEL JEROME	IL	44E	57
FRIGAULT JOSEPH O		20E	15
FRILEY ARTHUR TIMOTHY	OH	39E	59
FRILLING JEROME RAYMOND	OH	07W	102
FRINK JOHN WESLEY	NM	02W	127
FRINK PAUL JOSEPH	MA	12W	103
FRINK RICHARD W	NY	57E	8
FRINK STEVEN ARTHUR	WA	50W	13
FRISBEE DENNIS WAYNE	CA	40E	5
FRISBIE JARED ARTHUR	NY	19W	68
FRISBIE WALTER CHARLES	NY	02W	49
FRISBY CHARLES LEE	IL	53E	12
FRISCHMANN DAVID JOSEPH	WI	14E	103
FRISK JOHNNY EARL	MO	49W	8
FRISK ROBERT JOHN	RI	46E	44
FRITS ORVILLE BILL	CA	20E	58
FRITSCH ANDREW JOSEPH III	PA	08W	100
FRITSCH THOMAS WILLIAM	CT	58E	7
FRITSCHE ROBERT JR	CA	50E	4
FRITTER JOHN WILLIAM	MO	16W	74
FRITTS FREDERIC WILLIAM	TX	08E	108
FRITTS LOUIE GENE	WA	02E	103
FRITZ ALVIN RAY	TX	32W	32
FRITZ DAVID URBAN	MN	46W	41
FRITZ GERALD W	TX	01W	125
FRITZ JERALD DUANE	MI	08E	111
FRITZ LAUREN DEAN	MN	15W	89
FRITZ LEONARD EUGENE	AZ	30E	2
FRITZ MARTIN CHARLES	PA	36W	2
FRITZ NICHOLAS HEFER	NY	42E	16
FRITZ RAYMOND WILBERT JR	NJ	27E	47
FRITZE TIM LAVERN	IA	56W	33
FRITZER THOMAS ALBERT JR	CT	17W	73
FRITZGERALD LARRY JOHN	MI	35E	5
FRIZZELL MARSHALL RAY	VT	05E	55
FRIZZELL RONALD EUGENE	IL	09E	130
FRODSHAM EDWARD THOMAS DA	WA	08E	27
FROE GEORGE WASHINGTON	WV	18E	3
FROEHL PAUL A	MI	65E	8
FROEHLICH LAURENCE E	MI	01W	126
FROEHLICH NORBERT LOUIS	ND	35E	70
FROLICH LESLIE JAMES	NJ	39E	4
FROMANT KENNETH B	OH	23E	75
FROMM RONALD ALBERT	IL	12E	4
FROMME FREDERICK W JR	CA	19E	71
FRONGILLO JOHN RALPH	MA	24W	30
FRONTELLA MELVIN LAWRENCE	CA	04E	22
FROSIO ROBERT CLARENCE	FL	12E	61
FROSSARD WILLIAM JOHN	IL	07W	86
FROST BOBBY GENE	TX	14W	120
FROST CARLTON ANDREW	ME	63E	9
FROST DANA STANLEY	MA	06E	122
FROST FRANK RUDOLPH III	CT	21E	88
FROST GERALD JAMES	NH	58W	2
FROST HERBERT CORNELIUS	CA	22W	106
FROST JAMES ALLEN	AR	39W	26
FROST MICHAEL DENNIS	WA	42E	31
FROST RAPHEAL JOHN	ND	36W	50
FROST RICHARD HAMMOND	FL	33E	36
FROST ROBERT DEAN	OK	13W	44
FROST WOODY JOE	TX	27E	109
FROWNER EDWARD	AL	23W	20
FRUECHTENICHT CARL LEE	KY	12W	80
FRUHLING DALE ERVIN	NE	19W	12
FRY BILLY G	CA	04E	128
FRY GEORGE HAROLD	NY	21W	100
FRY JAMES HUGH	MI	15W	110
FRY JAMES RAY JR	CA	56W	36
FRY JOSEPH PATTON	PA	12E	82
FRY NASH	OK	10W	59
FRY RICHARD LEROY	PA	30W	53
FRY ROLLAND KEITH	KS	26W	99
FRY STEPHEN MICHAEL	CA	27W	63
FRY WALTER ALLEN	IN	38W	17

NAME	STATE	PANEL NO.	LINE NO.
FRYAR BRUCE CARLTON	NJ	15W	118
FRYAR GLASCO JUNIOR	NC	09E	97
FRYC DAVID CHARLES	NE	16E	27
FRYE ALFRED ALLEN	MS	01E	84
FRYE BOBBY SAM	AL	55E	12
FRYE CLIFFORD KENNETH	MN	23E	51
FRYE DANNY LEE	OH	30E	90
FRYE DONALD PATRICK	CA	23E	90
FRYE EARL WAYNE	KY	46E	32
FRYE GARY NELSON	NC	63E	9
FRYE HERBERT ALANSON	VA	24E	24
FRYE JAMES KENNETH	IL	31E	20
FRYE JOHN R	NY	21W	93
FRYE KEVIN MARK	FL	08W	62
FRYE LOUIS ARTHUR	PA	40W	43
FRYE MICHAEL BRUCE	IN	33W	19
FRYE RICHARD ALAN	CA	10E	46
FRYE STARR FREDERICK	UT	06W	125
FRYE TERRANCE DONALD	CA	18E	84
FRYER BENNIE LAMAR	CA	01W	107
FRYER CHARLES WIGGER	OK	09E	109
FRYER EDWARD ALBERT JR	NY	39W	33
FRYER ROBERT RISLEY	CA	35E	40
FRYER WILLIE JAMES	FL	10E	29
FRYMAN JAMES OMER	IN	43W	27
FRYMAN ROY ALLEN	CA	19W	106
FUCHS GREGORY GERALD	OH	23W	63
FUCHS JAMES LEE	SD	37E	56
FUCHS RICHARD ELLSWORTH	OH	14E	10
FUCHS WILLIAM JR	WI	05E	85
FUDGE JOHN T	AR	20W	29
FUELLHART ROBERT HOWARD	PA	02E	51
FUENTES ANTONIO MORILLIA	CA	16W	79
FUENTES FRANCISCO	NY	63E	9
FUENTES HECTOR	CA	22E	102
FUENTES ROBERT MARTINEZ	TX	25W	47
FUERST GEORGE JOSEPH	NY	16W	87
FUGATE DALE LEROY	IL	03E	39
FUGATE GARLAND G	OH	13E	108
FUGETT HENRY J	MI	27E	109
FUHRMAN JAMES FRANCIS	MT	33E	36
FUHRMAN JAMES MICHAEL	PA	14W	111
FUHRMAN ROBERT MICHAEL	PA	03W	5
FUHRMAN TERRY LEE	IN	49E	52
FUHRMAN WILLIAM RALPH	IL	01E	106
FUJIMOTO DONALD SHUICHI	CA	56W	12
FUJIMOTO MASAICHI	HI	17E	92
FUJITA MELVIN SHOICHI	HI	21W	45
FUKUNAGA RODNEY TAMOTSU	HI	27W	45
FULCHER DOUGLAS EDWARD	VA	48E	2
FULCHER JOHN HENRY	VA	11E	7
FULFORD JIMMY DON	AR	52W	18
FULFORD JOHN THOMAS	FL	20E	42
FULFORD VARL ESTON	FL	08E	14
FULGHAM EDWARD BRAXTON JR	FL	22W	119
FULGHAM JOE HUGH	MS	08W	76
FULGHUM JACKIE JUNIOR	AL	03E	6
FULGHUM JOE RAYMOND JR	TN	14E	107
FULK BILLIE HOWARD JR	MO	63W	15
FULK DALE STEVEN	IN	18W	68
FULK JAMES WESLEY	IN	01W	63
FULK MICHAEL RAYMOND	IL	02E	103
FULKERSIN ROBERT DOUGLAS	TX	51E	19
FULKERSON ROBERT ALAN	IN	27W	37
FULKERSON ROGER ALAN	NY	42W	11
FULKS CHARLES EUGENE	KY	15W	35
FULLAM JOHN JOSEPH JR	NY	31E	73
FULLAM WAYNE EUGENE	TN	27E	64
FULLAWAY LAWRENCE LEE	WA	49E	21
FULLER CARIO	AR	18E	3
FULLER CARROLL BRUCE	CA	40E	5
FULLER CHARLES MCDONALD	OH	25W	11
FULLER DENNIS EARL	CA	34E	76
FULLER EUGENE EDWARD	MN	06E	74
FULLER EUGENE OTTO	WI	44W	9
FULLER FLOYD EDWARD JR	MS	10W	64
FULLER GARY LEROY	OH	15E	105
FULLER GEORGE RONALD	GA	40E	21
FULLER HERMON EUGENE JR	MI	11E	14
FULLER JAMES E	IL	08E	74
FULLER JAMES LARRY	IL	39W	12
FULLER JAMES RAY	TX	01W	99

NAME	STATE	PANEL NO.	LINE NO.
FULLER JOEL	MS	12E	13
FULLER JOHN F	NY	32E	44
FULLER JOHN LUTHER JR	GA	17E	28
FULLER JOHNNIE CHESTER	DC	20E	27
FULLER JOHNNY THOMAS	GA	42W	46
FULLER LARRY LEE	OH	12E	10
FULLER MICHAEL ALLAN	NY	22W	32
FULLER MICHAEL BRUCE	OK	58W	8
FULLER MICHAEL DAVID	IA	32E	72
FULLER ROBERT GENE	OR	19E	126
FULLER ROBERT JOHN	DE	16W	52
FULLER ROBERT JOSEPH	OH	23W	26
FULLER RONALD FRANCIS	RI	09W	126
FULLER STANLEY CARL	CA	36W	11
FULLER THOMAS LEE	CO	20W	80
FULLER TIMOTHY	CO	43E	53
FULLER WILLIAM OTIS	TX	25E	47
FULLERTON FRANK EUGENE	GA	50W	17
FULLERTON FRED SAMUEL JR	PA	57E	3
FULLERTON GLEN LEE	WV	03W	96
FULLERTON JAMES PRICE	CA	29W	29
FULLERTON JOHN JOSEPH JR	MA	36E	9
FULLERTON RONNIE JOE	TX	35W	76
FULLILOVE WILLIE KETCHERY	IL	23E	58
FULLMER ROBERT MICHAEL	ND	23W	85
FULLUM DARRYL BLAKE	OH	46E	5
FULMER NICHOLAS JOSEPH	PA	12E	61
FULMER RONNIE DALE	MS	14W	78
FULTON CHARLES EDWARD	TN	01E	81
FULTON CLARENCE	MD	47W	7
FULTON JOHNNY LEE	OR	10W	5
FULTON KENNETH LIGE	MI	39E	47
FULTON RONALD JOE	WA	14W	84
FULTS LAWRENCE ARTHUR JR	AZ	44E	35
FULTZ MICHAEL KENT	IL	24W	5
FULWIDER DANIEL RAYMOND	IN	33E	85
FUNCK ALFRED	IN	17E	29
FUNDERBURK RUPERT A JR	NC	19W	85
FUNELLI RICHARD ARTHUR JR	PA	14E	34
FUNES DAVID JOHN	GM	02W	36
FUNICELLI ERNEST D JR	NJ	29E	15
FUNK BRUCE ELLIOTT	PA	26W	99
FUNK DALE LEE	MI	03E	113
FUNK EMMONS EDWARD JR	OH	27W	53
FUNK JOE ALBERT II	WV	20E	102
FUNK JOSEPH JOHN	NY	34W	41
FUNK LESLIE HAROLD JR	WA	27E	59
FUNK ROBERT NELSON	NY	17W	120
FUNKE THOMAS GEORGE	ID	40W	72
FUNKHOUSER CARL T	IN	10E	13
FUNN GARY FRANCIS	HI	09E	122
FUNSTON JOSEPH ERNEST	IL	46W	15
FUQUA GARY JAMES	WY	04W	52
FUQUA HARRY IVAN JR	KS	42E	5
FUQUA JAMES F	FL	39E	21
FUQUA JOHN EDWARD	TN	04E	123
FUQUA ROBERT LEE JR	OH	28E	23
FURCH JOE HENRY	AZ	30E	96
FURGERSON JAMES MURPHY	KY	12W	55
FURLONG EDWARD FRANCIS JR	NY	21E	67
FURLONG WILLIAM ROBERT JR	MD	32E	22
FURMAN EDMUND	LA	19W	92
FURNEY WILLIS LEE	GA	16E	44
FURNISH THOMAS HAROLD	FL	13W	32
FURPHY KENT PALMER	TX	12E	62
FURR DONALD MICHAEL	NC	53W	33
FURR FREDERICK EDWARD	AR	26W	77
FURR JAMES HENRY	NC	07E	95
FURR WILLIAM RENARD	IN	04W	114
FURROW SHERMAN ALVIN JR	VA	41W	29
FURSE WARREN RANDOLPH	SC	31W	92
FURSTENWERTH ROBERT EDWAR	WA	02W	91
FURTADO EDWARD JR	MA	60E	22
FUSCO PAUL RICHARD	NY	52W	39
FUSILE MARK LOUIS	OH	37W	31
FUSON JACK ANTHONY	OH	23E	30
FUSS ROBERT EDWARD	NE	52E	26
FUSS THEODORE FRANK	OH	24E	67
FUSSELL FELTON ROGER	FL	23W	85
FUSSEY GENE PAUL	MI	17W	45
FUSSNER ALLEN GEORGE	MO	42W	55
FUTO JOHN ANTHONY	OH	18W	23

NAME	STATE	PANEL NO.	LINE NO.
FUTRELL GARY THOMAS	AR	07E	68
FYALL VERNON ROBERT	SC	39W	26
FYAN RUSSELL RICKLAND	MI	52E	18
FYFFE THOMAS CLEO	TX	51W	48
FYOCK TERRY LOUIS	PA	61W	20
GA NUN PAUL HUNTINGTON	NJ	24W	41
GAA JOSEPH WILLIAM JR	HI	05W	45
GAARDER DAVID EIDNES	OH	35W	47
GABALDON TONY EIDDIE	CA	25E	99
GABANA ROBERTO LAY		47W	27
GABBARD THOMAS JEFFERSON	KY	17W	15
GABBERT DENNIS ERWIN	CA	25E	77
GABBIN FRED LEE	CO	28W	69
GABEL GARY LEE	OH	36E	71
GABLE ARLAN DEAN	ND	23E	42
GABLE CHESTER LEWIS	TX	05E	24
GABLE ROBERT LEE	PA	26E	78
GABLE RONALD HOWARD	OH	50W	4
GABORIAULT SANFORD RENE	VT	56E	6
GABRIEL CHARLES DAVID	TX	13E	118
GABRIEL GARRY LEE	ID	32E	72
GABRIEL HERBERT JAMES	TX	13E	95
GABRIEL JAMES JR	HI	01E	8
GABRIEL JOEL LYNN	OR	32W	12
GABRIEL MEREDITH ALTON	CA	33E	36
GABRIEL VINCENT JAMES JR	NJ	20E	83
GABRYS STEPHEN MICHAEL	NY	26W	79
GABURO GEORGE W	NJ	28E	96
GACHES CHARLES WILLIAM	TX	01W	74
GADDA ANTHONY JOSEPH JR	NJ	12E	33
GADDIE DAVID JR	NC	07W	111
GADDIS FRED AUSBUN	GA	12E	21
GADDIS JONATHAN ROYAL	GA	41E	8
GADDIS RALPH ARNOLD	LA	09W	79
GADDY WILLIE GENE	GA	42W	40
GADIE BOBBY GLYNN	NC	06E	31
GADSON EDDIE DEAN	KS	57E	3
GADZIALA GARY LEE	NM	58E	7
GAERTNER BYRL WILLIAM	MN	62E	17
GAETH JOHN CEPHAS	NE	51W	17
GAFFANEY RICHARD JAMES JR	ND	52W	22
GAFFIGAN ROBERT MICHAEL	MD	06W	23
GAFFNEY EDWARD ALBERT	MD	53E	1
GAFFNEY MICHAEL FRANCIS	IL	24E	24
GAFFNEY McARTHUR	MO	23W	73
GAFFNEY RONALD SEFTON	FL	01E	93
GAFTUNIK ROBERT ERNEST	CA	19W	111
GAFTUNIK STEVEN JOHN	CA	46E	45
GAGE JAMES ROBERT	TX	37W	39
GAGE JOHN THOMAS	NE	15W	63
GAGE MICHAEL ARTHUR	CA	08W	107
GAGE NORMAN GLENN	TX	13W	48
GAGE ROBERT HUGH	OH	08E	124
GAGLIANO FRANK F	IL	15E	43
GAGLIARDI GREGORY	NY	26E	23
GAGLIARDO FRANK ANDREW	NY	03E	6
GAGNE BERTRAND RONALD	ME	19W	93
GAGNE DALE FRANCIS	MN	23E	58
GAGNE DONALD	MA	12E	21
GAGNE JOSEPH JAMES	MN	07W	77
GAGNE LOUIS PHILLIP JR	MA	11E	30
GAGNE RENALD LUDGER	CT	33W	38
GAGNE ROBERT OMER	MA	24E	12
GAGNIER WILLIAM JOSEPH	MN	44W	24
GAGNON JOHN EDGAR	ME	36E	48
GAGNON JOSEPH DENNIS	ME	08W	130
GAGNON MORRIS DOMINIQUE	ME	22E	30
GAGNON PATRICK JOHN	MI	18E	85
GAGNON PERCY CHARLES	ME	12W	35
GAHAGAN JAMES MILAN	WI	34W	24
GAIDIS ALFRED JAMES	CT	10W	11
GAILEY ALLEN DALE JR	UT	26E	24
GAILLIARD HERMAN BERNARD	SC	27E	100
GAINER GARY LEE	WV	06W	116
GAINER JOHN ROBERT	OK	20W	65
GAINES ALLAN JOSEPH	AL	48E	41
GAINES BERNARD LAVERNE	PA	46E	5
GAINES BYRON ADAMS JR	FL	32E	86
GAINES CHARLES A	FL	07E	95
GAINES CHARLES JERRY	MS	12E	95
GAINES DOUGLAS JR	FL	43W	5
GAINES GREGORY RANDALL	GA	56E	23
GAINES JAMES JR	NJ	33W	39
GAINES MARVIN JEROME	NC	38W	66
GAINES MELVIN CLYDE	CA	16E	10
GAINES PHILIP FALCONA	OK	49E	31
GAINES PHILLIP RAY	IL	20E	115
GAINES THOMAS GALE	GA	38E	76
GAINES THOMAS LEE JR	IL	30W	4
GAINES WILLIAM FRANKLIN	OK	23E	100
GAINES WORDELL	AL	45E	55
GAINGER JOHN B	NC	20W	43
GAINOUS JOHN CHARLES	FL	20E	27
GAISER JAMES ALFRED	PA	16W	42
GAISER LEWIS BERNARD	NY	22E	70
GAITHER CURTIS	MO	11W	84
GAITHER THOMAS MARK	VA	14W	52
GAJAN ALTON LOUIS	NY	04E	54
GAJDOSIK ERNEST WAYNE	TX	15E	65
GALABIZ JOHN ROSALEZ	CA	53W	43
GALAMBOS JOSEPH GARY	CA	01E	49
GALAN DAVID LUIS	CA	04E	89
GALAN RICHARD	FL	30E	77
GALANTE RONALD ALFRED	NY	35E	20
GALARZA RUDOLPH JOSEPH	IL	03E	77
GALARZA-QUINONES JOSE M	PR	24W	83
GALATA JOHN MICHAEL	PA	33E	57
GALATI JAMES FRANCIS	PA	47E	21
GALBAVY GEORGE RICHARD	IL	17E	98
GALBRAITH HUGH CAMPBELL	TN	09E	67
GALBRAITH MARVIN EARL	WA	46E	45
GALBRAITH MICHAEL JOSEPH	NY	08E	14
GALBRAITH RAYMOND CLARENC	PA	02E	4
GALBRAITH RUSSELL DALE	OH	36W	2
GALBREATH BOBBY FRANK	TX	39E	59
GALBREATH ROBERT GENE	NH	02W	110
GALBREATH TERRELL ROBERT	NM	09W	100
GALBRETH EMME R II	TX	01W	118
GALE ALVIN RICHARD	MA	33W	6
GALE DAVID LEE	CA	19E	94
GALEA MICHAEL	NY	35W	38
GALENO ANTHONY MICHAEL	NY	25E	20
GALES JAMES LENARD	NC	20E	115
GALEY JAMES NORBERT	IN	41E	64
GALIANA RUDOLPH STEVEN	CA	18E	57
GALINDEZ MANUEL ANTONIO	NY	56W	2
GALINDO EDWIN GENE	OK	54E	34
GALINDO EVERARDO JR		20W	49
GALINDO GUADALUPE JR	TX	19W	106
GALKA VINCENT EDWARD	PA	02W	92
GALKOWSKI JAMES LEONARD	PA	22W	52
GALL ROBERT JOSEPH	NY	26E	44
GALLAGHER ARTHUR TERRY	CA	15W	50
GALLAGHER DANIEL F	WI	07W	52
GALLAGHER DANIEL PATRICK	PA	34W	48
GALLAGHER DONALD LOUIS	WI	37E	56
GALLAGHER FRANK R	IN	10E	21
GALLAGHER GEORGE FRANCIS	VT	25E	62
GALLAGHER GERALD THOMAS	NY	38E	67
GALLAGHER JOHN HENRY	GA	12E	62
GALLAGHER JOHN JOSEPH	PA	15W	66
GALLAGHER JOHN MICHAEL	NJ	26E	70
GALLAGHER JOHN THEODORE	CT	33E	48
GALLAGHER JOSEPH THOMAS	PA	40E	39
GALLAGHER LARRY HERBERT	NY	50W	5
GALLAGHER MICHAEL JOSEPH	NY	28E	23
GALLAGHER MICHAEL PATRICK	MI	20E	73
GALLAGHER PATRICK	NY	17E	71
GALLAGHER PATRICK JOSEPH	NY	27E	19
GALLAGHER PHILIP S III	MA	02W	86
GALLAGHER RAYMOND LEROY	MT	42E	32
GALLAGHER RICHARD	PA	43E	53
GALLAGHER ROBERT PATRICK	RI	16W	63
GALLAGHER WILLIAM JOSEPH	KY	02E	121
GALLANT FRANK JAMES	MA	21E	27
GALLANT HENRY JOSEPH	FL	02E	36
GALLANT ROGER PAUL	ME	14E	27
GALLANT ROY DALE	OH	18E	26
GALLARDO ARMANDO	TX	18E	79
GALLARDO ERNESTO R	TX	46W	59
GALLARDO JOHNNY JOE	CA	13W	63
GALLAUGHER DARRYL ALAN	OH	42E	64
GALLAWAY WILLIAM DENNIS	OH	11W	45
GALLEGO LAWRENCE	HI	27E	49
GALLEGO MICHAEL	AZ	17W	41
GALLEGOS GABRIEL	CA	08E	66
GALLEGOS OSCAR CONANDO	TX	58E	20
GALLEGOS STEVEN	IL	35W	15
GALLERY RICHARD MULROY	NY	54E	7
GALLINA ANTHONY JOSEPH	MO	07W	77
GALLION DAVID ANDREW	FL	10W	24
GALLION GAYLEN RAY	CA	26W	8
GALLIS STEVE SAMUEL JR	MI	17E	61
GALLMAN SAMUEL III	PA	17E	35
GALLO PETER JOSEPH	CA	47E	10
GALLOW RYAN JUDE	TX	39W	79
GALLOWAY ARTHUR LEE JR	VA	04W	83
GALLOWAY CLARENCE	IL	05E	16
GALLOWAY DENIS WAYNE	MO	11E	102
GALLOWAY EMMITT	NY	35E	46
GALLOWAY GEORGE K JR	OH	38W	1
GALLOWAY ROBERT GLENN	KY	61W	14
GALLOWAY SAM HARRIS	GA	36E	9
GALLUP ROBERT DARYL	OH	02E	10
GALPIN RONALD DAVIS	MI	58E	20
GALUTZ JAMES ANTHONY	NY	18E	53
GALVAN RICARDO	OH	35W	12
GALVEZ JOE ANGEL	CA	43W	27
GALVEZ TOM	AZ	65W	7
GALVEZ-PASTRANA MANUEL	PR	13W	56
GALVIN JAMES PATRICK	CA	12E	132
GALVIN RALPH FORRESTER	CA	02E	44
GALVIN RONALD EDMOND	IL	16E	40
GALYAN TROY ALEXANDER	NC	30E	39
GAMBER ROBERT ALLEN	PA	45W	50
GAMBILL CHARLES RICHARD	IL	14W	43
GAMBINO JOSEPH JR	NY	01W	116
GAMBINO MICHAEL JAMES	MA	07W	83
GAMBLE BOBBY GENE	TN	33W	93
GAMBLE CHARLES F JR	AK	17W	127
GAMBLE DAVID JOHN	PA	16W	38
GAMBLE DAVID LESLIE	OH	09E	57
GAMBLE DEXTER NUNTON JR	OK	37W	80
GAMBLE HARRY PAUL	CA	02E	1
GAMBLE HENRY HWEY	FL	17E	114
GAMBLE JAMES HENRY	AL	32E	63
GAMBLE PHILIP LYLE JR	MA	24W	110
GAMBLE RONALD RICHARD	PA	54E	25
GAMBLE WILLIAM H	PA	08E	44
GAMBOA DAVID HERCLIFF JR	NY	27W	17
GAMBOTTO LARRY LOUIS	MI	44W	47
GAMBRELL FRANKLIN DOUGLAS	SC	05E	33
GAMBRELL JOHN LAWRENCE	GA	15E	65
GAMELIN ERNEST ULRIC JR	NH	40W	24
GAMET RANDOLPH MERL	MO	26E	27
GAMMON LARRY JAMES	IL	03W	40
GAMMONS HARLAN KENNETH JR	NC	14W	17
GAN LEONARDO MEDINA		17W	26
GANCI SAMUEL JOSEPH	MS	02E	8
GANDIL ROBERT PATRICK	NJ	13E	58
GANDOLFO PHILIP NICK	MI	32E	87
GANDY CLAUDDELL	FL	07E	48
GANDY KENT ELLSWORTH	CT	09E	132
GANDY MICHAEL L	KS	46E	62
GANION THOMAS FRANCIS	IL	23E	100
GANLEY RICHARD OWEN	NH	16W	117
GANNON EUGENE RICHARD	NY	49E	22
GANNON GERALD WILLIAM	NY	15E	64
GANNON JOHN PATRICK	WI	22E	70
GANOE BERMAN JR	FL	12W	38
GANT EDDIE DEAN	MS	45E	21
GANT HERMAN EUGENE	OH	35W	26
GANTT GRADY JR	NY	45E	21
GANTT JOHNNY EDWARD	GA	46E	32
GANTT SAMUEL LEE	AL	06W	84
GANTZ KARL RAY	OH	04W	14
GANZY ALLAN ALPHONSA	NY	08E	85
GANZY CLYDE WAYNE	FL	30W	12
GAPINSKI ROBERT VICTOR	NY	21W	82
GAPP ALVIE WAYNE	SD	21E	67
GARAMILLO ELDON	NE	33E	18
GARANT ROBERT OLIVER	TN	09E	86
GARAPOLO FRANK WILLIAM	IL	65W	7
GARBER CHARLES WILLIAM JR	VA	49E	1
GARBER EDWIN SIDNEY	WA	17E	78
GARBER WAYNE ARTHUR	IL	03W	76

NAME	STATE	PANEL NO.	LINE NO.
GARBETT JIMMY RAY	FL	07W	122
GARCIA ABEL D JR	TX	19E	58
GARCIA ALBARO QUEZADA	ID	09W	88
GARCIA ALEJANDRO JR	TX	13E	97
GARCIA ANDRES	TX	04E	73
GARCIA ANDRES	NM	01W	132
GARCIA ANDREW PEREZ	CA	33W	84
GARCIA ANGEL ANTONIO	CA	35E	54
GARCIA ANTONIO	IL	13E	52
GARCIA ANTONIO	TX	53E	31
GARCIA ANTONIO	PA	30W	44
GARCIA ANTONIO MENDEZ	CA	30W	12
GARCIA ANTONIO VARGAS	TX	49W	40
GARCIA ARNOLD FALCON	CA	21W	117
GARCIA ARTHUR MARTINEZ JR	AZ	14W	111
GARCIA ARTURO	TX	28E	24
GARCIA AUGUSTO JOSE	TN	52W	42
GARCIA BENJAMIN	NY	14W	64
GARCIA CARLOS HILL	TX	12W	131
GARCIA CHRISTOPHER	CA	51W	31
GARCIA CLIVE JR	AZ	16W	124
GARCIA CRECENCIO CASAREZ	TX	51E	45
GARCIA DAVID ADAME	TX	59E	22
GARCIA DAVID BENEDICTO	CO	05E	10
GARCIA DAVID JOSE	NM	10W	102
GARCIA DAVID Z	TX	08E	17
GARCIA DOMINGO YBBARA	CA	17W	66
GARCIA EDDIE LEONARD	NM	21W	37
GARCIA EDELMIRO LEONEL SR	TX	03W	33
GARCIA EDILBERTO	CA	17E	72
GARCIA EDUARDO JR	TX	45E	22
GARCIA EDWARD	NY	08E	27
GARCIA EDWARD LEE	CO	30W	22
GARCIA EDWARD MARC	NY	02W	7
GARCIA EMILIO GAMBOA	TX	35E	16
GARCIA ENRIQUE LORENZO JR	WA	33E	85
GARCIA FRANCISCO	TX	15E	74
GARCIA FRANCISCO M JR	NM	26W	53
GARCIA FRANK JOSEPH	CA	18E	3
GARCIA FRANK JR	MT	24E	77
GARCIA GEORGE ARRIAGA	TX	21E	112
GARCIA GILBERTO	TX	07W	30
GARCIA GREGORIO M	CA	09E	91
GARCIA HENRY JR	CA	25W	38
GARCIA HENRY R	TX	31E	74
GARCIA HERIBERTO ARNALDO	TX	01E	71
GARCIA ISAAC RAMIREZ JR	CA	44W	2
GARCIA ISIDRO	NM	13W	130
GARCIA JAMES RONALD	LA	21E	120
GARCIA JEROME	CA	55W	35
GARCIA JERRY FRANK	NE	50E	28
GARCIA JESSE EULOJIO	TX	54E	7
GARCIA JESUS MARIA	CO	44W	24
GARCIA JOE CECILIO	NM	18E	121
GARCIA JOE ROBERT	TX	23W	63
GARCIA JOHN	CA	05E	3
GARCIA JOHNNY PHILLIP	CA	06W	104
GARCIA JOSE	TX	39W	43
GARCIA JOSE GILBERTO	TX	53W	18
GARCIA JOSE JR	TX	23W	57
GARCIA JOSE OSCAR	MO	13W	117
GARCIA JOSEPH ANDREW	NV	36E	9
GARCIA JUAN	TX	15E	94
GARCIA JUAN MANUEL	AZ	30E	42
GARCIA JUAN RAFAEL	NY	03E	77
GARCIA JUAN REFUGIO	IL	54W	2
GARCIA LARRY ROBERT	AZ	10W	61
GARCIA LEANDRO	NY	36E	71
GARCIA LOUIS MAGIN	NM	46E	16
GARCIA LUDIN	NY	54W	28
GARCIA LUPERTO	NM	54W	5
GARCIA MANUEL MENDEZ JR	CA	24E	12
GARCIA MARCAS JOSE	CA	17W	86
GARCIA MARCIAL BONDOC	CA	60W	9
GARCIA MELESSO	CA	28E	24
GARCIA MIGUEL JR	TX	06E	128
GARCIA MIGUEL RAMOS	FL	13W	84
GARCIA NICKOLAS GASTELUM	CA	26W	25
GARCIA OSCAR	TX	11E	122
GARCIA PEDRO CORDOVA	CA	14W	57
GARCIA PEDRO GALLARDO	TX	43W	27
GARCIA PEDRO INCARNACION	TX	17E	43

NAME	STATE	PANEL NO.	LINE NO.
GARCIA RAMON	NM	47W	42
GARCIA RAUL JR	TX	15W	119
GARCIA RAYMOND CHARLES	OH	54W	42
GARCIA RAYMOND IGNACIO	CA	66W	6
GARCIA RAYMOND JR	CA	30E	15
GARCIA RICARDO MARTINEZ	TX	04W	58
GARCIA RICHARD	CA	08E	17
GARCIA RICHARD	TX	14E	97
GARCIA RICHARD	TX	47E	21
GARCIA RICHARD CALUDE	CA	26W	106
GARCIA ROBERT	TX	26E	71
GARCIA ROBERT IRA	NY	07W	106
GARCIA SALVADOR BORREGO	TX	43E	4
GARCIA STEVEN VARGAS	AZ	31W	50
GARCIA WILLIAM	CA	12E	4
GARCIA WILLIE JR	CO	37E	56
GARCIA-DIAZ JUAN ENRIQUE	PR	30W	89
GARCIA-FIGUEROA JUAN F	PR	60W	17
GARCIA-GARAY JUAN	CA	12W	131
GARCIA-MALDONADO JOSE I	PR	18E	129
GARCIA-SOTO JERONIMO	PR	20E	115
GARCIAPAGAN RAFAEL	PR	05W	69
GARCILLE DAVID LEE	LA	03W	123
GARD DANNY D	TX	41E	65
GARD JAMES BARRY	IN	56E	6
GARDELIS NICHOLAS LEWIS	NY	12W	88
GARDELL CLIFFORD McCARTHY	CO	33W	39
GARDELLA MARK JEFFREY	WA	06E	25
GARDELLA WILLIAM KIRBY	MA	22E	61
GARDENHIRE JIMMY MARYLAND	CA	26W	19
GARDINER ROBERT PAUL	CA	21W	60
GARDINER ROY WILLIAM	UT	11W	21
GARDNER ALAN DAVID	PA	09W	98
GARDNER ALEN LOUIS	NY	18E	69
GARDNER BOBBY RAY	NC	24E	90
GARDNER DANIEL ELI	OK	31E	74
GARDNER DAVID ERNEST	NH	36W	2
GARDNER EDDIE AUGUSTUS	MS	53E	13
GARDNER FRANK MAYNARD	RI	11E	109
GARDNER FRED MICHAEL	AL	24E	72
GARDNER GERALD LEE	IA	14W	93
GARDNER GLENN VIRGIL	CA	12E	116
GARDNER GORDON DWIGHT	CA	33W	48
GARDNER JACK ELROY	CA	07E	89
GARDNER JAMES ALTON	TN	05E	11
GARDNER JAMES DALE	FL	09W	76
GARDNER JAMES EDWARDS	MI	11E	71
GARDNER JAMES LEE	OR	04E	133
GARDNER JOHN GARRETT	NC	21E	45
GARDNER LARRY WAYNE	PA	14E	62
GARDNER LAWRENCE LEE	NV	28E	66
GARDNER MARION LORA	OK	25W	99
GARDNER MICHAEL JOHN	MN	66W	6
GARDNER PHILLIP D	TX	23W	86
GARDNER RICHARD GEORGE	DC	11W	45
GARDNER ROBERT CHARLES	IL	48W	25
GARDNER ROBERT EUGENE	AL	50E	46
GARDNER ROBERT LINLEY	OH	50W	35
GARDNER ROBERT LOUIS	NH	01E	9
GARDNER ROBERT WAYNE	MD	11W	58
GARDNER ROY EDWARD	AL	16E	58
GARDNER SAMUEL RAY	KS	55E	12
GARDNER STEPHEN MARK	WA	54W	10
GARDNER WILHIMON	NY	19W	118
GARDNER WILLIAM HUGH JR	AL	09E	97
GARDNER WILLIE JR	AL	05W	99
GAREISS KURT WILLIAM	MD	01E	94
GAREY ROBERT EARLE	NV	07E	133
GARGUS FRANCIS BERTON	IL	19W	78
GARGUS ROY PHILLIP	TX	23W	64
GARI STEPHEN LOUIS	NY	02W	4
GARIBAY GUADALUPE B L	CA	16E	1
GARIEPY CRAIG BARRY	NY	22E	57
GARIEPY ROBERT DAVID	MA	54E	34
GARIS GARY WILLIAM	PA	05E	60
GARIS LE ROY DELANO M	PA	22W	12
GARITY CHARLES JOSEPH JR	NY	19W	13
GARLAND CONLEY R	VA	13E	121
GARLAND DENNIS	PA	11E	61
GARLAND MARCELLUS JR	PA	51W	18
GARLAND RONALD EDWARD	NY	06W	50
GARLEY FRANK ELOY	NM	25W	22

NAME	STATE	PANEL NO.	LINE NO.
GARLICK RICHARD LEE	IL	42E	16
GARLICK RODGER LYNN	MD	29W	60
GARLO MICHAEL	NY	19W	78
GARMAN THOMAS ALFRED	VA	31W	35
GARMS PETER HENRY	PA	39W	70
GARNER BOYD GRAYSON	MN	16E	68
GARNER ERNEST LEROY	AR	09W	76
GARNER GARY HAROLD	MO	14W	3
GARNER IRA L	MS	29E	30
GARNER JACKIE WAYNE	AL	42E	51
GARNER JOHN HENRY	SC	21E	12
GARNER JOHNNIE LINTON	TX	25E	83
GARNER LARRY ARTHUR	IL	24E	51
GARNER LARRY D	UT	19W	10
GARNER LYDES JAY JR	OR	26E	9
GARNER RICKEY DEAN	TX	05E	116
GARNER RONALD LEE	VA	32W	71
GARNER RONALD RAY	FL	22W	52
GARNER WILLIAM DONALD	SC	18E	22
GARNER WILLIAM ROGER	NC	21W	82
GARNER WILLIE FRANK	AL	58E	21
GARNES JACK ALLEN	CO	02W	56
GARNET OWEN NIEL	FL	36E	9
GARNETT ISIAH CALVIN	LA	07W	10
GARNETT LEON JR	DC	11W	95
GARNETT REUBEN LOUIS JR	PA	05E	102
GARNICA ANDY	CA	34E	86
GARRAHAN ERNEST EDWARD	NY	35W	12
GARRAPY DAVID EARL	NM	10E	36
GARRARD JESSIE JEROME	OH	21W	18
GARRETSON RICHARD EUGENE	IN	02W	75
GARRETT ALFRED DOUGLAS	LA	40W	43
GARRETT ALLEN MATTHEW	OK	11W	6
GARRETT ALLEN MORGAN	NY	07E	71
GARRETT ALONZO	SC	12W	123
GARRETT DAVID FRANK	IN	26E	101
GARRETT DONALD WAYNE	GA	25W	68
GARRETT ERNEST WILLIAM	GA	55W	27
GARRETT EUGENE JR	TX	06E	99
GARRETT FRANK DAVID	TX	03E	1
GARRETT HENRY WAYNE	VA	17W	22
GARRETT HOWARD	MS	10E	100
GARRETT JACKY LEROY	SC	34E	6
GARRETT JAMES MICHAEL	KS	15W	4
GARRETT JONATHAN WAYNE	MI	15W	16
GARRETT LAWRENCE CASEY	CA	37W	11
GARRETT LEROY JR	TX	02E	123
GARRETT LLOYD EARL	SC	12E	100
GARRETT MAURICE EDWIN JR	PA	02W	47
GARRETT MICHAEL SHERIDAN	CA	41E	37
GARRETT MICHAEL STEVEN	WV	30W	36
GARRETT NORMAN RAY	TX	01E	92
GARRETT RICHARD B	IA	33W	78
GARRETT ROBERT EUGENE	GA	09E	109
GARRETT ROBERT GILMER	VA	32W	5
GARRETT ROBERT JUNIOR	NC	09W	33
GARRETT ROBERT LEE	OH	40W	19
GARRETT ROGER LEE	VA	19E	126
GARRETT THOMAS C III	LA	07E	102
GARRETT THOMAS STEVEN	TX	47W	43
GARRETT TOMMIE	GA	04E	23
GARRICK JERRY ARTHUR	MI	28W	90
GARRIDO ROBERT JACOB	NJ	56E	6
GARRIGAN JOHN L	IL	31E	34
GARRIGUS HARRY	TN	20W	113
GARRINGER DAVID FRANK	CA	38W	49
GARRINGER JAN DOUGLAS	IL	13W	19
GARRIS GEORGE ROBERT	PA	29W	45
GARRIS MICHAEL ANTHONY	MD	08E	36
GARRISON CARL FRANKLIN	AL	12E	10
GARRISON DANIEL LEE	OH	13E	81
GARRISON EARL STANLEY	ME	16E	10
GARRISON GEORGE ALBERT	TN	50W	38
GARRISON LARRY ALLEN	IA	52W	43
GARRISON NOEL KEITH	IN	20W	10
GARRISON RONALD MILLARD	OH	05W	58
GARRISON RUSSELL G	NJ	26E	34
GARRISON WILLIAM LAWRENCE	NY	19E	106
GARRITY ANDREW JAMES	NY	27E	39
GARRITY EUGENE JOSEPH JR	PA	32W	97
GARRITY JAMES JEFFREY	PA	25E	99
GARRITY WILLIAM JOHN JR	MT	11E	110

NAME	STATE	PANEL NO.	LINE NO.
GARRITY WILLIAM KENNETH	IN	14W	89
GARRON LAWRENCE E JR	MA	43W	54
GARSIDE FREDERICK THOMAS	MA	01E	2
GARSIDE THOMAS EDWARD	MI	16E	79
GARSKI KENNETH JAMES	WI	12W	51
GARST WALIS WARREN	WY	16W	95
GARSTKIEWICZ WALTER J JR	PA	14W	21
GARTEN JAMES RAY	MI	05W	57
GARTH CLYDE JR	MS	40W	37
GARTH JESSIE JAMES	TN	04W	70
GARTH RAYMOND	AL	29E	89
GARTH ROBERT WILTON JR	GA	11E	2
GARTLAND THOMAS	PA	55E	11
GARTNER ROBERT FREDRICK	MN	02W	3
GARTON TOMMY RAY	CA	21E	105
GARVEN CHARLES DANIEL	OH	41W	23
GARVEN WAYNE ERIC	OH	24W	102
GARVER PHILLIP EUGENE	CA	35E	32
GARVEY DONALD JESS JR	MO	17W	16
GARVEY VINCENT FRANCIS	PA	11E	56
GARVICK DERYL RAY	MN	39E	59
GARY CYE	NY	15W	122
GARZA ANTONIO	OH	17W	34
GARZA ANTONIO GUERRA JR	TX	20E	83
GARZA ARNOLD GARZA	CA	12W	48
GARZA CARL EDWARD	TX	45E	10
GARZA DAVID	TX	16W	95
GARZA ELIAZAR EFRIEN	TX	08E	119
GARZA FRANCISCO	TX	18E	40
GARZA GENARO	TX	05W	133
GARZA HENRY ALLEN	TX	12E	44
GARZA JOHN ANGEL	CA	09W	94
GARZA JOSE JR	TX	16E	58
GARZA JOSE JR	TX	24W	41
GARZA JOSE SALUSTINO	TX	48E	2
GARZA MARCELLO C JR	TX	53E	13
GARZA MARGARITO	TX	22E	102
GARZA PABLO BENITEZ	TX	16W	98
GARZA RAMON	TX	24E	24
GARZA RICHARD JR	CA	21W	41
GARZA VICENTE	TX	33E	85
GASCON GARY LYNN	NY	29E	2
GASE JAMES FLORIAN	OH	19W	13
GASKA LAWRENCE LEONARD	IL	42E	51
GASKIN DAVID WILLIAM	FL	56W	3
GASKINS DARRELL FREDERICK	NC	21E	88
GASKINS LARRY LEE	OH	27E	71
GASKINS WILBUR CORNELL	NC	50E	38
GASKO ROBERT JOHN JR	NJ	14W	49
GASPAR ALFRED JOHN	MA	24E	24
GASPARD CLAUDE JOSEPH JR	NJ	64E	4
GASPERICH FRANK JOHN JR	IL	05W	81
GASS CHARLES LEE	NM	28E	35
GASSAWAY AMBROSE	LA	21W	59
GASSELING JAMES LEE	WA	17W	49
GASSEN STEVEN CARL	IL	43W	62
GASSER DONALD LEROY	CA	25E	62
GASSER JAMES EDWARD	MI	20W	75
GASSMAN FRED ALLEN	FL	07W	113
GASSMAN GERALD LYNN	OH	27E	109
GASSNER LARRY MICHAEL	OR	10W	124
GAST WILLIAM RAYMOND	FL	44W	16
GASTELUM EUGENE	CA	26W	99
GASTON JOHN RUFUS JR	DC	37W	5
GASTON JUAN	NY	31W	47
GASTON ROSS ALLEN	AL	17E	116
GASTON STANLEY STEPHEN	PA	35W	59
GATES ALBERT HENRY JR	NY	13W	92
GATES ALFRED ALAN	CA	33W	78
GATES JAMES WALTER	GA	47W	8
GATES JAMES WAYNE	LA	06E	89
GATES MONTE LEROY	PA	10W	102
GATES RICHARD PALMER	NY	32W	26
GATES ROBERT ALFRED	FL	35E	40
GATES ROBERT SIDNEY	MA	15W	103
GATEWOOD CHARLES HUE	IL	62W	9
GATEWOOD CLARENCE MELVIN	VA	15W	21
GATEWOOD GERALD PETER	CA	49W	29
GATHMAN GORDON KAYE	NE	07W	77
GATLIFF LARRY ALLEN	OR	08W	46
GATLIN IVAN WEBSTER	TX	21E	12
GATLIN JERRY GENE	IL	18W	89

NAME	STATE	PANEL NO.	LINE NO.
GATTI DENNIS ALBERT	NY	19W	93
GATTI DENNIS JOSEPH	NJ	10W	113
GATTI GARY FRANCIS	CA	24E	101
GATTIS CHARLES MANLEY JR	IL	23E	11
GATTO DANIEL ARTHUR	NY	23W	86
GATTON DAVID RAY	SD	13E	97
GATWOOD MICHAEL OWEN	OH	07E	89
GATWOOD ROBIN FREDERIC JR	NC	02W	128
GAU LOUIS ELLIE	CA	47W	8
GAUCH DAVID ALAN	OH	35W	89
GAUCHE DAVID PETER	OR	24W	53
GAUDET THOMAS WILFRED	NH	26W	19
GAUDREAU CHARLES ARTHUR	MA	57W	9
GAUGHAN AUSTIN MICHAEL	PA	44E	59
GAUGHAN ROGER CONRAD	MA	19E	5
GAULEY JAMES PAUL	OK	14E	5
GAULOCHER FRANCIS LEROY	IA	46E	5
GAULT ALAN ROBERT	PA	49E	10
GAULT BILL EDGER	CA	30E	100
GAULT CLINTON MONROE JR	AZ	40W	49
GAUNA DANIEL JR	TX	24W	16
GAUS BRADLEY KENT	IL	12W	5
GAUSE BERNARD JR	AL	01W	130
GAUSE CHARLIE	MI	10E	101
GAUTHIER BRIAN JAMES	LA	02E	35
GAUTHIER DENNIS LEE	MI	16W	8
GAUTHIER GERALD ALAN	WI	14W	49
GAUTHIER GERALD PAUL	LA	33E	18
GAUTHIER GERARD LOUIS JOS		25E	99
GAUTNEY EARL	AL	28E	58
GAUTREAU REGINALD JOSEPH	MA	37E	56
GAUTZ WAYNE JACOB	MI	18E	85
GAUVIN PETER JOSEPH	MA	03W	128
GAUVIN ROGER EDWARD	ME	01E	46
GAVARIA GEORGE LOUIS	IL	13E	1
GAVIA JOSEPH JESS	CA	26W	39
GAVILAN-TORRES WILFREDO	PR	06W	3
GAVIN EZRA	IL	42E	64
GAWEL JOHN LEONARD	MI	29W	53
GAWEL WALTER L	OH	46E	3
GAWORSKI FRANCIS XAVIER	DE	12W	117
GAY ALBERT LUMMIS JR	VA	40W	75
GAY ALVIN LEON	UT	28W	101
GAY CHARLES ELBERT	NY	36W	25
GAY CURTIS TAYLOR	PA	35E	70
GAY DAVID AUSTIN	OH	19W	53
GAY DONALD COLEMAN	KY	06W	11
GAY EDDIE GILBERT	FL	34W	48
GAY GARY PAUL	PA	04E	99
GAY HAROLD CORNELL	NC	06W	11
GAY HERBERT LYMAN	OK	24W	30
GAY JAMES NATHANIEL	SC	20W	32
GAY JOHN BEN	GA	28E	66
GAY KENNETH RAY	KY	35E	21
GAY LONNIE JAMES	CA	68W	2
GAY MARVIN EDWARD	KY	39W	53
GAY WAYNE OLIVER	TN	17E	29
GAY WILLIAM ELLIS JR	GA	10W	121
GAYER KENNETH EUGENE	CA	30W	101
GAYLES LORENZA	KY	10E	64
GAYLOR GERALD H	FL	04E	82
GAYLORD DOUGLAS DRUE	MO	29W	53
GAYLORD GORDON MANSON	IL	12W	100
GAYMAN JOHN DUFF	GA	13E	27
GAYMON STEPHEN H	CA	08E	5
GAYNE JEFFREY LEE	AZ	09W	53
GAYNOR JAMES THOMAS	CA	39E	47
GAYNOR KURTIS LANE	WA	09W	55
GAYOSSO JOE FRANK	CA	03W	44
GAYTAN EDWARD RAY	TX	26E	43
GAYTAN HUGO ARAUX	CA	02W	38
GAZAR GUILLERMO	NY	24E	7
GAZAWAY CHARLIE TIDWELL	GA	04W	21
GAZDAGH JAMES ALEX	CA	23E	36
GAZZE JAMES ALBERT	IL	29W	19
GEAR GARY WAYNE	CA	10W	70
GEARHART DONALD LEE	PA	46E	5
GEARHART MICHAEL EUGENE	SD	07E	64
GEARHEART MIKE DUANE	MO	27W	99
GEARHEART RALPH ALLAN	OH	66W	6
GEARING WILLIAM CARL JR	NY	24W	54
GEARY HARRY EUGENE	WI	21E	45

NAME	STATE	PANEL NO.	LINE NO.
GEARY JOHN MICHAEL	NY	19E	95
GEARY JOHN WESLEY	NY	11E	25
GEARY ROBERT FRANCIS JR	NY	09E	62
GEARY WILLIAM STANLEY	PA	27W	17
GEBBIE RONALD JACKSON	NY	31W	79
GEBHARD ROY ALLEN	PA	13E	38
GEBHART CARL MERLIN JR	CA	07E	13
GEBHART DONALD WILLIS	NJ	31E	11
GEDDES KERRY RICHARD FOST	NY	34E	68
GEDDINGS JOHN HUGHIE	SC	05W	53
GEDDIS HENRY LEO JR	FL	33E	2
GEDEON RUSSELL EUGENE	IL	15W	35
GEE ALAN TIMOTHY	CA	17W	86
GEE EUGENE PAUL	NC	12W	97
GEE GREGORY JOSEPH	CA	19W	54
GEE LE ROY	IL	52W	5
GEE MacARTHUR G	VA	60W	17
GEE PAUL STUART	WI	34E	58
GEE RAYMOND LEON JR	IL	55E	12
GEER ROBERT SAMPSON	KY	06W	98
GEER STEPHEN JAMES	CT	09W	43
GEERDES DONNIE ADELBERT	MN	57W	9
GEHL MICHAEL ARTHUR	IL	28W	18
GEHLER RONALD CHARLES	SD	15E	32
GEHLING DONALD ANTON	MN	28E	1
GEHRIG JAMES MONROE JR	PA	02E	12
GEHRKE DARRELL DEAN	NE	32E	63
GEHRKE GARY BERNARD	WI	34W	48
GEHRT MICHAEL DAVID	IA	06W	81
GEIB ALLEN	NJ	35E	40
GEIB JEFFERY LYNN	OH	19W	112
GEIER WILLIAM MICHAEL	IL	22E	12
GEIGER CHARLES RICHARD	FL	18W	37
GEIGER FRANCIS EDWARD	ND	02E	43
GEIGER GARY GEORGE	PA	04W	76
GEIGER ISADORE SAMUEL JR	FL	55E	12
GEIGER LARRY FREDERICK	WI	18E	93
GEIGER LAWRENCE	PA	08W	130
GEIGER LAWRENCE RAYMOND	CO	10W	40
GEIGER ROBERT CHARLES	CA	10W	17
GEIGER WALDEMAR JOHN	OH	23W	120
GEIGER WALTER THOMAS	NY	20E	42
GEILEN DONATUS JOSEPH	KY	15E	116
GEIS RANDALL HAROLD	WI	03W	115
GEIS WILLIAM CHARLES	IL	04E	102
GEISE DELL CONLEY	WI	14E	80
GEISE MICHAEL DAVID	IN	42E	65
GEISEN JOHN BENNETT JR	CT	11E	110
GEISER DAVID JEROME	CA	11W	55
GEISERT CHARLES PRICE	TX	16W	28
GEISSINGER ALAN GWINN	DE	21W	100
GEIST STEPHEN JONATHAN	MD	27E	15
GEISTER MICHAEL LEWIS	NH	12W	5
GELB ALAN STUART	NY	62E	17
GELDIN JEFFREY LEE	OH	23W	44
GELIEN WALTER JOHN	CA	03E	1
GELINAS JOSEPH ARMAND ROG	NH	27E	89
GELL JACK EARL	SC	03E	49
GELLER CHARLES GREGORY	IL	41E	20
GELLER ROBERT EARL	DC	24E	24
GELLERMAN KENNETH GILBERT	CA	17E	57
GELONEK ROBERT EUGNE JR	IL	15E	68
GELUSO SALVATORE ANTHONY	NY	21W	82
GEMAS TERRY DALE	CA	13E	97
GEMBORYS JOHN CHESTER	MA	24E	51
GEMMATI ORONZO	IL	48E	26
GENAU CLARENCE HAROLD JR	NY	33E	13
GENCHI BERNARDINO FRANCIS	NY	20W	33
GENDEBIEN WILLIAM RAYMOND	PA	02E	136
GENDRON ROBERT MICHAEL	CA	27W	80
GENERAL CARL LEWIS	FL	50W	50
GENERAL LESLIE NEIL	NY	53E	31
GENES LUTHER ALLEN	SC	07W	58
GENESEO LOUIS J	ME	20W	39
GENEST RICHARD EDGAR	NH	19W	118
GENITTI CHARLES THOMAS	MI	14W	131
GENNOCRO ANTHONY ANGELO	PA	07E	5
GENOVESE CARMINE VINCENT	NJ	07E	40
GENS JONATHON LEE	MN	52E	29
GENSEMER DAVID DANIEL III	AR	04E	118
GENTH GARY ROY	IN	32W	58
GENTILE HAROLD FRANCIS	NY	55W	5

NAME	STATE	PANEL NO.	LINE NO.
GENTILE JAMES RAYMOND	NY	28W	45
GENTINNE THOMAS HENRY	MI	25W	69
GENTKOWSKI JOHN STEVEN	OH	04W	134
GENTLE CLYDE GLENN	AL	24E	99
GENTRY BILL W	WA	32W	37
GENTRY BOBBY LEE	KY	21W	83
GENTRY CHARLES EDWARD	MD	28E	96
GENTRY DAVID ANTHONY	TX	27E	28
GENTRY DENNIS WAYNE	GA	07W	61
GENTRY HENRY JR	KS	03E	126
GENTRY JERRY WAYNE	GA	29E	57
GENTRY JIMMIE FERREL	AR	56W	20
GENTRY LENNIS CLYDE	TN	14W	57
GENTRY LEROY JAMES	NC	25W	5
GENTRY MICHAEL DALE	NC	07W	115
GENTRY OSCAR JR	AL	58W	31
GENTRY ROBERT BARRY	FL	05W	87
GENTRY ROBERT LEVETT	SC	23E	85
GENTRY TERRANCE NEIL	WV	19W	112
GENWRIGHT McKENZIE W	NC	18W	27
GENZLER AUGUST HENRY	MO	37E	21
GEOGHAGEN GEORGE EDDIE	FL	04E	49
GEOGHEGAN GERALD DALY	NJ	10E	113
GEOGHEGAN JOHN L	NY	03E	56
GEOGHEGAN PETER DANIEL	NY	08E	30
GEORGE CHARLES MICHAEL	MO	06W	51
GEORGE CLAUDE MARVIN	IN	60W	17
GEORGE D C	LA	14E	66
GEORGE EDWARD LEE	OR	06E	99
GEORGE EMMITT ROOSEVELT	SC	29E	24
GEORGE FRANK DANIEL	IL	24E	86
GEORGE GARY RICHARD	PA	30W	64
GEORGE GERALD LEE JR	CO	30E	25
GEORGE GORDON MILTON JR	CO	23W	120
GEORGE HEZEKIAH	NY	08E	2
GEORGE JAMES EDWARD JR	TX	38E	28
GEORGE JOHN WESLEY	DC	43W	14
GEORGE JOHN WILLIAM	TN	02W	72
GEORGE KENDALL EMANUEL	NY	13E	4
GEORGE LEO ALLEN	OH	35W	38
GEORGE LOUIS AARON	MI	30W	2
GEORGE MICHAEL DEAN	TX	21E	56
GEORGE MICHAEL THEODORE	PA	34E	42
GEORGE RAYMOND JAMES	CA	04W	49
GEORGE RICHARD EUGENE	CA	03E	110
GEORGE S W	OK	09E	45
GEORGE STEPHEN FREDERICK	PA	15W	103
GEORGE WILLIAM MICHAEL	OH	03W	40
GEORGE-PIZARRO ARTHUR	NY	30W	101
GEORGES JERRY HAROLD	CA	17E	29
GERAGHTY MERRILL THOMAS	AZ	45W	50
GERALD BOZY	MI	06E	99
GERALD DANA LEON	ME	16E	58
GERALD GEORGE ADEN	VA	45W	50
GERALD RAEFORD JAMES JR	NC	24W	59
GERALD WILSON TRUMAN	NC	20E	15
GERARD LAWSON DOUGLAS	CA	21E	45
GERBER LEROY LYNN	OH	25E	23
GERBER MICHAEL EUGENE	KS	24W	117
GERCZ FRANCIS GARY JR	WI	35E	32
GERDES ALBERT BRUNO JR	LA	36W	50
GERDESMEIER JOHN ALOIS	MN	48W	25
GERDON ROY CLINTON	FL	42E	32
GEREAU RICHARD NORMAN	MI	05E	117
GERG THOMAS ARTHUR	WI	14E	15
GERHARDT ERNEST KAY	CA	02E	87
GERHARDT KEITH EDWARD	OH	26E	71
GERKEN RALPH BERNARD	IA	23E	11
GERLACH PAUL EDGAR	WI	35E	70
GERLACH STEVEN HENRY	IL	46E	33
GERMAIN JAMES THOMAS	NY	06W	26
GERMAIN PHILIP MICHAEL	VT	36E	49
GERMAN BROMLEY HOWARD	CT	33E	57
GERMANY FRANKLYN WALLACE	MI	51W	4
GERMEK JOHN ALAN JR	PA	44W	47
GERNERT EDWARD HARRY	PA	21W	37
GERO EDWARD W	MA	40E	62
GERO JOHN ANTHONY	CA	54W	16
GEROME MICHAEL ANTHONY	CA	56E	23
GERONIMO CHARLES ANTHONY	FL	59E	3
GERONZIN ANSON THORNE JR	IA	22W	119
GEROU JAMES ALLAN	WI	50E	28

NAME	STATE	PANEL NO.	LINE NO.
GERRISH ALAN ROBERT	MA	45W	61
GERRY JERRY L	NV	02E	108
GERRY PETER JAMES	MA	20W	65
GERRY RONALD LEE	NE	04E	54
GERSHEN HOWARD DEXTER	CA	15E	79
GERSHNOW STEVEN ANDREW	NY	51W	4
GERSPACH PETER JOSEPH III	NY	20E	102
GERSTEL DONALD ARTHUR	IL	01W	71
GERSTEL HOWARD MARTIN	NY	27E	48
GERSTENLAUER PETER F	NY	35W	64
GERSTHEIMER HEINRICH	MI	48E	3
GERSTNER RONALD EDWARD	MI	06W	47
GERTEN RONALD EUGENE	MI	05W	17
GERTH PETER HUDSON	WA	09W	108
GERTSCH JOHN GARY	PA	20W	19
GERTSEN ROGER LEE	IA	06E	70
GERTZEN FRED	PA	37W	64
GERVAIS DONALD PETER	TN	53E	31
GERWATOWSKI JOSEPH	NJ	34E	76
GERWIG RONALD EUGENE	PA	25E	12
GESSEL GREG LOW	OR	26E	71
GEST DENNIS EUGENE	IN	34W	58
GETCHELL PAUL EVERETT	ME	35W	82
GETLIN MICHAEL PETER	IL	17E	72
GETMAN CHARLES LESTER	IL	09E	38
GETTELFINGER THOMAS J	IN	04W	126
GETTER JAMES LEE	AR	04W	52
GETTER WAYDELL	TX	47W	27
GETTINGS GUY CLIFTON	IN	18E	93
GETTY DENNIS ALAN	MI	26E	9
GETZ PAUL ROBERT	NV	16W	8
GETZ ROBERT WILLIAM	IL	23W	36
GEURIN STEPHEN BURL	TX	23W	86
GEUY JAMES ROBERT	OH	21W	100
GEVARA RAY JR	NE	27E	71
GEYER JAY FRANKLIN	PA	17E	121
GEYER LEROY CLYDE	CA	56W	16
GEYER RICHARD WEBB	WA	01E	24
GFELLER JOHN HERBERT	KS	40E	21
GHAHATE LUTHER ANDERSON	NM	40W	12
GHAIS TAHER FATHI	MA	48E	3
GHEE JAMES FITZROY	MD	15W	45
GHEER JAMES MELVIN	OR	40W	64
GHELLI THOMAS ALFRED	MA	34E	18
GHERARDINI SERGIO JOHN	NY	36E	10
GIACOBBE ANGELO	NJ	48W	54
GIACOBELLO FRANK A JR	PA	21E	101
GIACONE JOHN ALBERT JR	NY	41W	35
GIACOPPO STEVEN JR	NY	52W	35
GIAMBRONE RICHARD LAWRENC	PA	47E	32
GIAMMARINO VINCENT FRANK	NY	54W	7
GIANELLI ANTHONY	CT	04E	78
GIANNANGELI ANTHONY ROBER	PA	02W	127
GIANNELLI ALAN ROBERT	NY	44W	56
GIANNELLI GIUSEPPE	CA	15E	43
GIANNINI MICHAEL ANTHONY	PA	16E	90
GIARDINA STEFANO	NY	09W	38
GIBBINS ROBERT WAYNE	CA	52W	5
GIBBLE ALVIN RALPH	PA	46E	33
GIBBONS BRIAN FRANCIS	NY	17E	3
GIBBONS CLAUDE ROBERT	OK	04W	109
GIBBONS DARRELL LEE	VA	27E	89
GIBBONS JOHN MICHAEL	NY	14W	131
GIBBS CHARLES EDWARD	NY	56E	7
GIBBS CLIFFORD WARREN	MO	27E	10
GIBBS HAROLD DOUGLAS	NY	08E	115
GIBBS IRA EUGENE	IN	05W	17
GIBBS ISREAL	SC	47W	8
GIBBS JACK RONALD	TN	06W	90
GIBBS JERRY DON	TX	35W	9
GIBBS KENNETH SAMUEL	GA	25E	100
GIBBS KITCHELL SNOW	MI	24W	41
GIBBS MATHEW	NY	24E	77
GIBBS MICHAEL GERALD	TN	18E	85
GIBBS RAYMOND ANDREW	TX	19E	95
GIBBS SAMUEL DAVID	TX	25E	100
GIBBS WILLIAM ARNOLD	MN	44W	25
GIBBS WILLIAM HARLEY JR	IL	53W	19
GIBBS WILLIAM JR	SC	38W	74
GIBEL RAYMOND	PA	20W	56
GIBERSON JERRY GUY	IA	09W	72
GIBILTERRA CHARLES J JR	PA	33W	39

NAME	STATE	PANEL NO.	LINE NO.
GIBIS MICHAEL E	MD	37W	64
GIBLER DONALD GENE	MO	05W	115
GIBLIN WALTER EDMUND JR	NY	23E	91
GIBNER GEORGE THOMAS	TX	21W	37
GIBNEY ALLEN RICHARD	WI	57E	22
GIBSON ALTON GEORGE	OH	34W	48
GIBSON AUSTIN DALE	OK	51W	18
GIBSON BRUCE STEWART	MI	18W	72
GIBSON BURRELL	OH	22E	40
GIBSON CARL REED	VA	53E	13
GIBSON CLIFFORD MICHAEL	PA	19W	50
GIBSON CORNELL HARRISON	VA	46E	62
GIBSON DALE HENRY	IL	09E	97
GIBSON DAVID	SC	62E	18
GIBSON DAVID PARKER	KS	17E	121
GIBSON DONALD FREDERICK	IL	10E	46
GIBSON DONALD LEE	DE	51W	10
GIBSON EDDIE CARL	OH	23E	58
GIBSON ERNEST	TN	09E	112
GIBSON HAROLD LEE	WY	21E	78
GIBSON HARRY HUTCHISON	NC	29W	98
GIBSON HERMAN DANNY	WV	16W	38
GIBSON JAMES DONALD	SC	20W	56
GIBSON JAMES THURMAN	KY	56W	21
GIBSON JAMES VAL	OH	09W	1
GIBSON JOE BILL	IN	12W	104
GIBSON JOHN	GA	37E	82
GIBSON JOHN A	MO	30E	84
GIBSON JOHN ARTHUR IV	IL	62E	4
GIBSON JOHN BROWN JR	FL	30W	2
GIBSON JOHN CHRISTOPHER	MD	50W	21
GIBSON JOHN EDDIE	OH	42W	40
GIBSON JOHNNY ALLISON	TX	28W	91
GIBSON KEITH EDWARD	MI	24W	117
GIBSON LAWRENCE EDWARD	IN	39E	32
GIBSON LONNIE LOWELL	TN	17W	16
GIBSON MICHAEL THURSTON	VA	16W	130
GIBSON OTHA DOUGLAS	OK	55W	34
GIBSON PETER	FL	25W	39
GIBSON RAYMOND ALBERT	MI	17W	84
GIBSON RICHARD HOPKINS	TX	24E	25
GIBSON RONALD WARREN	OH	16W	45
GIBSON ROWLAND EDWARD	IN	14E	67
GIBSON ROY ALLEN	NM	29E	30
GIBSON ROY LEE	TX	53E	13
GIBSON SILAS EUGENE	SC	36E	71
GIBSON STEVIE RAY	KY	16E	84
GIBSON TERRELL	NC	23W	100
GIBSON THOMAS MICHAEL	OR	28W	69
GIBSON WALTER CARL	CO	24E	25
GIBSON WALTER LEWIS	CA	18E	22
GIBSON WALTER MURRAH	GA	17W	127
GIBSON WILLIAM ARTHUR	MS	41E	20
GIBSON WILLIAM TERRY	PA	56W	21
GIDDENS HORACE GILBERT JR	AL	36E	71
GIDDENS LA VON	MI	56E	7
GIDDINGS ALBERT HUGH	VA	47W	27
GIDDINGS CLYDE ARTHUR	CO	26W	62
GIDDINGS JOHN PATRICK	MI	46E	33
GIDEON RICHARD EDWARD	NY	36E	72
GIDEON WILBURN CHASTAIN	TX	47W	42
GIDVILAS MICHAEL	CT	26E	24
GIEBE RICHARD JOHN	IL	29E	57
GIEBELL FLOYD STEPHEN	PA	16W	8
GIEGEL JAMES LLOYD	NJ	10W	102
GIEJC ALEXANDER	WI	39E	59
GIER DAVID JULIAN	HI	06E	5
GIERAK GEORGE GREGORY JR	NY	08E	47
GIERMAN WALTER EDWARD II	FL	27W	94
GIES MARVIN ARTHUR	NC	34W	48
GIESE MICHAEL EVERETT	WI	04W	105
GIESECKE JERRY DON	TX	15W	70
GIESEN WALLACE LEE	WI	37E	83
GIETZEN GENE THOMAS	ND	24W	65
GIFFARD SAMUEL POOKEAOKAL	HI	04E	89
GIFFORD DAVID RANDOLPH	OH	32E	9
GIFFORD GREGORY ALLEN	MT	38E	28
GIFFORD HOWARD M	CA	46E	62
GIFFORD LARRY HOWARD	OR	58W	8
GIFFORD ROBERT ALLEN	NY	37E	7
GIFFORD WILLIAM GARY	AZ	62W	9
GIGLIO PHILIP	NY	31W	6

NAME	STATE	PANEL NO.	LINE NO.
GIGLIOTTI MICHAEL	PA	55W	5
GIGNAC RAYMOND ALBERT	MA	34E	76
GIITTINGER RICHARD FREDER	NE	32E	32
GIL CORNEL	IN	13E	90
GILBERT CARL EDWARD	TN	14W	4
GILBERT DAVID ARTHUR	PA	11E	82
GILBERT DON RAY	TX	37E	7
GILBERT FRANKLIN BRADLEY	MD	32W	37
GILBERT FRANKLIN DELANO R	TX	05E	85
GILBERT GERALD FREDERICK	IN	46E	54
GILBERT GLENN RAYMOND	NY	08W	82
GILBERT HAROLD JEFFREY	MA	15E	20
GILBERT HARVEY WOODFORD	IA	09E	133
GILBERT JACK DEAN	CO	06E	83
GILBERT JACK RICHCARDO	IL	08W	79
GILBERT JAMES CAROLL	TN	29W	19
GILBERT JAMES MICHAEL	IA	25W	47
GILBERT JAMES SILAS	VA	12E	84
GILBERT LARRY	NY	12W	68
GILBERT LAWRENCE JOSEPH	PA	24E	25
GILBERT PATRICK JOSEPH	NY	12E	95
GILBERT PAUL ARTHUR	PA	05E	50
GILBERT PAUL FARIS	TX	01W	44
GILBERT RICHARD JOSEPH	MA	24E	103
GILBERT RICHARD LEE	MI	60E	10
GILBERT STANLEY DONALD	MN	28E	24
GILBERT THOMAS ORVAL	CA	07E	133
GILBERT TRUMAN JAMES W	MS	15W	86
GILBERTSON ALAN DALE	MN	04W	103
GILBERTSON CARL LOUIS	CA	12W	12
GILBERTSON LARRY RUSSELL	MN	23W	120
GILBERTSON RICKY MARK	WI	19E	25
GILBERTSON TERRY ALAN	WI	41E	65
GILBERTSON VERLAND ANSEL	CA	28E	24
GILBREATH GRANT MADISON	MI	18E	14
GILBREATH RICHARD ARTHUR	CT	09E	57
GILBRECH RUSSELL EARL	IN	14W	4
GILBRETH DON RILEY	CA	02W	16
GILCH JAMES XAVIER	NJ	09E	52
GILCHRIST FRANK R JR	IL	20W	76
GILCHRIST RICKY DEAN	NJ	03W	87
GILCHRIST ROBERT MICHAEL	CO	11E	56
GILDER LEWIS C	AL	25E	92
GILDOW THOMAS JOSEPH	OH	33W	56
GILE JOSEPH THOMAS JR	MA	11E	56
GILES BARNEY MCKINLEY JR	MS	06E	84
GILES CLAUDE VERNOR	GA	13W	19
GILES CLEM CALVIN	FL	61W	12
GILES DENNIS LEE	MI	42W	5
GILES FRANKLIN N JR	NJ	46E	46
GILES GARY LYN	CA	09W	1
GILES JAMES	CA	09W	30
GILES LEONARD EARL	AL	21E	33
GILES WILLIE JR	AL	42E	16
GILFORD JAMES A	TX	03E	84
GILGENBERG JOHN DANIEL	IL	19E	81
GILGER WILLIAM GRANT III	OH	31E	57
GILIN GARY JOSEPH	MI	59E	22
GILKER JOHN VICTOR	AR	21W	7
GILKEY TIMOTHY WILLIAM	PA	53W	19
GILL DAVID EUGENE	IN	02E	73
GILL DAVID ROYDEN	OH	22W	119
GILL DONALD WADE JR	VA	16W	63
GILL JOSEPH GEORGE	OH	55E	13
GILL KENNETH LEE	WV	10W	117
GILL LEWIS BERNARD	NC	16W	17
GILL RICHARD DENZIL JR	ND	09E	52
GILL ROBERT EARL	AL	27W	94
GILL THOMAS PATRICK III	RI	15W	36
GILL WILLIAM DANIEL	NY	07E	105
GILL WILLIAM RALPH JR	TN	10E	80
GILL-BEY MEHMET ALI	NY	13E	4
GILLARD GARY LEE	WA	24W	16
GILLARD MICHAEL	LA	64E	4
GILLASPIE LARRY ALAN	OR	28W	46
GILLASPIE PAUL THOMAS	KS	06W	86
GILLASPY EDWARD ANDREW	CA	57E	22
GILLASPY THOMAS DAVID	MS	09W	127
GILLEAN GARY LEWIS	IL	26E	35
GILLEN FREDRICK PAUL	PA	19W	13
GILLEN JOHN ALOYSIUS	IL	24W	94
GILLEN ROBERT C	NY	33E	57

NAME	STATE	PANEL NO.	LINE NO.
GILLEN THOMAS ELDON	KS	13W	28
GILLERAN DENNIS MICHAEL	OR	19W	100
GILLES ALAN CLARK	CA	35W	54
GILLESPIE ALBERT ALOYSIUS	OH	63E	10
GILLESPIE DANIEL CRAIG	VT	18E	107
GILLESPIE GEORGE ALLEN	MN	16W	17
GILLESPIE JAMES ROY	MI	34E	36
GILLESPIE JOE	TX	26E	55
GILLESPIE LLOYD DEAN	TX	41W	35
GILLESPIE MARTIN L JR	MA	06E	31
GILLESPIE ROBERT JAMES JR	MA	49W	47
GILLESPIE ROY PAINTER	KY	29E	24
GILLESPIE WILBERT LEE	PA	15W	92
GILLETT DONALD CHARLES	LA	30W	101
GILLETT JERRY CECIL	WI	09W	7
GILLETTE WILLIAM JAMES	NY	10E	80
GILLEY CHARLES TEDDY	TX	02W	1
GILLEY RICHARD ALAN	NY	36E	10
GILLHAM JAN ROYCE	NE	36E	72
GILLHAM RICHARD GERALD	NE	35W	65
GILLIAM DAVID LEE	NC	45E	1
GILLIAM GEORGE HARVEY	MD	47E	50
GILLIAM JOHN PERRY	CA	05E	80
GILLIAM KENNETH RAY	KY	31W	47
GILLIAM LARRY EDWARD	VA	06W	104
GILLIAM MARTIN GALE	CA	07W	125
GILLIAM RICHARD	PA	29W	77
GILLIAM ROBERT WENDELL	CA	11E	57
GILLIAM RONALD STUART	MD	61W	23
GILLIAM TERRY LYNN	AR	20W	19
GILLIAM THOMAS EDWARD	OH	25E	28
GILLIAND JERRY WILLIAM	NC	33E	57
GILLIARD EDWARD LEE	MS	30W	11
GILLIES JAMES FRANCIS	NY	08W	90
GILLIES ROBERT KNELL	NJ	26W	19
GILLILAND DENNIS ELBERT	AZ	05W	123
GILLILAND GEORGE ERNEST	OR	01W	72
GILLILAND JOHN HENRY III	CA	27E	71
GILLINGHAM RICHARD KIRK	NY	20E	39
GILLINGHAM WILLIAM DAVID	PA	21W	121
GILLINGS JOHNNY RAY	TX	15W	22
GILLIS GARY WAYNE	FL	27W	30
GILLIS HAROLD THOMAS	PA	19E	81
GILLISPIE LARRY WAYNE	KY	66E	9
GILLISPIE LUCION JR	MS	25E	23
GILLMAN DONALD STANDLEY	FL	44E	16
GILLMER STEVEN MARTIN	WA	61W	23
GILLOCK RAYMOND RICHARD	TX	46E	54
GILLS LEWIS CLARENCE	VA	48W	25
GILLUM RICKEY LEAROY	OH	14E	48
GILLY RONALD ALAN	CT	22E	87
GILMAN FREDERICK EUGENE	IL	12W	6
GILMER CHARLIE MACK	VA	20E	90
GILMER GILES WILSON	VA	24W	5
GILMOR DAVID LEE	CA	06W	125
GILMORE ANTHONY	TX	08E	80
GILMORE EUGENE THOMAS	MS	05W	55
GILMORE HARLON JOE	TX	34W	64
GILMORE JAMES ROBSON JR	SC	23W	44
GILMORE KENNETH DEE	TX	04E	123
GILMORE MICHAEL DOUGLAS	NC	27W	10
GILMORE PETER WARREN	CA	10W	90
GILMORE ROBERT ERVIN	NC	32W	22
GILMORE RONALD	AL	30E	96
GILMORE STANLEY RAY	MO	36W	50
GILMORE WILLIAM ALAN	LA	26E	24
GILMORE WILLIAM ALLEN	OK	15E	68
GILMORE WILLIAM F JR	OK	15W	128
GILPIN JAY BARRY	PA	30W	64
GILPIN TERRY LEE	PA	08W	77
GILRAY ROBERT BRUCE JR	NJ	45W	62
GILREATH JAMES R	OH	11W	73
GILREATH LUTHER VERMONT	TN	03E	65
GILROY WILLIAM THOMAS	NY	24E	25
GILSINGER FREDERICK M JR	IN	39W	59
GILSON MICHAEL ANTHONY	CA	05E	103
GILSON TIMOTHY LAWRENCE	IL	31W	1
GILSTRAP DANNY LYNN	TX	40E	62
GILSTRAP DWIGHT ONEAL	SC	18E	108
GIMBERT MARTIN JOSEPH	VA	34W	81
GINAL RICHARD	MI	43E	43
GINART DONALD FRANCIS	LA	23W	52

NAME	STATE	PANEL NO.	LINE NO.
GINDER RICHARD SAMUEL	WA	42E	51
GINDLESBERGER GERALD THOM	FL	03W	21
GINES MANUEL LOUIS	CA	61W	1
GINGERICH GREGORY RAY	CA	20E	103
GINGERY JOHN BERNARD	PA	52E	37
GINN DAVID LANDRELL	SC	02W	60
GINN JAMES MICHAEL	VA	07W	10
GINN MICHAEL PATRICK	FL	11W	45
GINTER DENNIS HARRY	IL	08E	108
GINTER EDWARD JOHN	PA	15E	95
GIOIA JOHN ALBERT	NY	09W	33
GIORDANO ANDREW MIX	NY	25E	100
GIORDANO DANIEL J III	NJ	24W	41
GIORDANO JOSEPH CHARLES	NY	03E	44
GIORDANO RALPH JOSEPH	MA	07W	52
GIORGIANNI JON JOSEPH	PA	25E	83
GIOVANACCI RICHARD ALLEN	CA	23E	85
GIOVANNELLI GARY LEE	CA	13W	8
GIPE J RANDALL	PA	04E	55
GIPNER GORDON PHILLIP	MI	31W	67
GIPSON BILLY EDWIN	IN	08E	10
GIPSON CHARLES DONNETTE	AL	01W	33
GIPSON CLARENCE FREDDIE	MI	17E	95
GIPSON F G JR	TX	11E	73
GIPSON GAYLON G	TX	28E	8
GIPSON GEORGE WESLEY	FL	51W	18
GIPSON HOWARD WAYNE	IL	05W	26
GIPSON R W	TX	36W	83
GIPSON RICKY DUANE	CA	37W	64
GIPSON ROBERT PAUL	GA	06E	14
GIPSON RONNIE LEE	KY	01W	59
GIRARD CHARLES JACK	SC	14W	40
GIRARD CHARLES PIERRE	CA	30W	88
GIRARD CHRISTIAN GEORGE	VA	27W	37
GIRARDO DAVID LAVERNE	CO	26W	106
GIRARDOT FRANCIS MICHAEL	MI	15W	63
GIRDNER ROBERT ORAL	KS	48E	3
GIRETTI ANTHONY ALFRED	NY	29W	77
GIROD JOHN ALTON JR	LA	05E	58
GIROIR PAUL GERARD	LA	26E	112
GIROLIMON LOUIS MARIO	MA	58W	19
GIRON FRANCISCO	CO	17W	34
GIRON MARK JOSEPH	OH	24W	5
GIROUARD YVON ELDMOND	NH	24W	84
GIROUX RONALD	MA	13E	90
GIRSCH ROBERT EDWARD	IL	48E	16
GIRTANNER JULES T	NJ	10E	46
GISCHER GERALD MARION	IL	48W	41
GISE DONALD RICHARD	PA	41W	4
GISH BENNY THOMAS	MO	21W	88
GISH CALVIN ROBERT	IN	09W	110
GISH HENRY G	PA	44E	16
GISH JAMES EDWARD	IN	28E	66
GIST TOMMY EMERSON	OK	62E	22
GITHENS RICHARD EARL	IL	63W	6
GITTENS ERIC EUGENE	GA	16W	21
GIULIANI RICHARD ANTHONY	NY	26E	88
GIUNTA MICHAEL ANTHONY	IL	27W	38
GIUSTA JOSEPH MICHAEL	MI	09W	1
GIVEN FRANK A	MO	02E	135
GIVEN MARTIN GEHRING	MA	38W	26
GIVENS BILLY R	KY	52E	5
GIVENS DAVID JERRY	MI	18W	14
GIVENS ROGER LEE	IL	14W	84
GIVENS ROY NATHANIEL	VA	20W	70
GLADDEN JAMES TAYLOR JR	KS	09W	47
GLADDEN MICHAEL JAY	TX	30E	42
GLADDING DANIEL GEORGE	NY	57E	22
GLADNEY HAROLD SAMUEL	MI	30W	44
GLADNEY JOHN WILLIE	NY	21W	59
GLADU ROBERT JOSEPH	MO	09W	108
GLAESMAN RICHARD E	SD	26E	74
GLANCY LEE ODAY III	CA	46W	29
GLANDON GARY ALVEN	TN	07E	110
GLANTON ALBERT THOMAS	OH	29W	29
GLANVILLE JOHN TURNER JR	NJ	08E	47
GLASCO DAVID MAX	MI	20W	56
GLASFORD MICHAEL RICHARD	WA	50W	29
GLASGOW ROBERT LEE	PA	20W	39
GLASPER JOHN JAMES	IN	02E	39
GLASPER WILLIAM LAWRENCE	LA	38E	28
GLASPEY RICKY MAURICE	IA	15W	93

NAME	STATE	PANEL NO.	LINE NO.
GLASPIE WILLIAM HAROLD	CA	55W	13
GLASS ARTHUR	AL	04W	108
GLASS BILLY WAYNE	TN	11W	24
GLASS DONALD ROBERT	CA	28W	69
GLASS PHILLIP SCOTT	KY	03W	34
GLASS WALTER LEWIS	IL	01E	44
GLASSBURN JOE RICHARD	IN	21W	101
GLASSBURN MARVIN EDWARD	IN	06E	31
GLASSCOCK CARL LEE	TX	10E	39
GLASSCOCK DAVID LEWIS	TX	17E	67
GLASSCOCK TERRY LEE	IN	27W	24
GLASSER JOHN MICHAEL	MA	10E	97
GLASSEY JOHN GIRARD	NY	27W	87
GLASSFORD GARY BRUCE	IL	07W	55
GLASSON WILLIAM ALBERT JR	CA	06E	106
GLASSPOOLE RANDALL JOHN	WY	03W	43
GLATFELTER LARRY EUGENE	PA	08W	42
GLAUDE RICHARD PAUL	ME	21E	82
GLAWE THOMAS DUANE	IL	08E	52
GLAWSON GEORGE HOWARD JR	NJ	03W	60
GLAZAR AARON ZANE HOWARD	FL	43W	68
GLAZE JERRY WAYNE	TX	37W	39
GLAZE KENNETH LEE	KS	10E	29
GLAZEBROOK FRANCIS E JR	IA	26E	35
GLAZER HERBERT JAY	NY	45W	62
GLEAR GARY LEE	MO	33W	48
GLEASON ARTHUR A	NY	18E	4
GLEASON DANIEL WARD	MI	31W	1
GLEASON DENNIS STEPHEN	NJ	46E	33
GLEASON LARRY FRED	PA	55E	13
GLEATON HOMER LAYNE	SC	28W	35
GLEATON MELVIN ROSCOE	IL	02W	125
GLECKLER STEPHEN DONALD	OR	20W	70
GLEGG JAMES EDWARD	IN	44W	3
GLEGHORN JERRY WAYNE	OK	37E	84
GLEI ROGER LEE		21W	125
GLEIM ARTHUR FREDERICK JR	CA	08W	82
GLEISINGER STANLEY RICHAR	OH	12E	124
GLEIXNER WILLIAM ALLEN	PA	40E	63
GLENDENNING FRANK BARD	MO	13W	57
GLENN CHARLES JOSEPH III	PA	23E	28
GLENN CHARLES PHILLIP	AR	36W	63
GLENN DENNIS RAY	IA	21E	12
GLENN DONALD NELSON	SC	50W	42
GLENN EDWARD FRANCIS JR	NY	08W	49
GLENN EDWARD RALPH JR	MD	14E	43
GLENN GEORGE EARL JR	PA	27E	10
GLENN HAYLEN FOSTER	VA	06W	28
GLENN JACKIE D	MO	01W	126
GLENN LIVINGSTON	GA	31E	68
GLENN MICHAEL O'ROY	FL	34E	58
GLENN MICHAEL ROBERT	GA	14W	126
GLENN RANDY JACK	NC	21E	105
GLENN RICHARD J	AL	38E	28
GLENN ROBERT LEE JR	LA	52E	37
GLENN WILLIAM STUART	OH	04W	66
GLESENKAMP JOHN CARR	MI	38E	49
GLESSING FERDINAND W JR	NY	33E	28
GLICKMAN DONALD ERIC	PA	04E	8
GLIDDEN ARTHUR	NY	12E	47
GLIDDEN RICHARD CUNNINGHA	MA	15E	24
GLIDDEN ROBERT WAYNE	MN	51E	6
GLIM RALPH THEODORE	NY	06W	122
GLIME DONALD EUGENE	MI	43W	10
GLINES ALLEN BRUCE	UT	33E	28
GLINIEWICZ RICHARD F	MA	23W	26
GLINNEN EDDIE DANIEL	NY	14W	26
GLISSON JAMES EDWIN	KY	37W	11
GLISSON JOHNNY WILLIAM	GA	17W	16
GLOER DAVID LAWRENCE	LA	51W	26
GLORE STEPHEN LESLIE	WA	39W	48
GLORIOSO JOHN ANTHONY	PA	53E	13
GLOSSUP LOWELL THOMAS	TN	03W	42
GLOVER ARTHUR WAYNE	TN	01E	43
GLOVER CALVIN CHARLES	OH	65E	8
GLOVER DAVID CYRIL	MO	18E	34
GLOVER DONALD LAWRENCE	GA	34E	76
GLOVER DOUGLAS J	NY	40E	21
GLOVER EDWARD LEE	OK	47E	10
GLOVER FRED RICHARD	FL	47E	50
GLOVER FREDDIE BEE	AL	10E	5
GLOVER HAROLD LEE	NC	38W	42

NAME	STATE	PANEL NO.	LINE NO.
GLOVER JAMES ALBERT	DE	21E	22
GLOVER JAMES LEAR JR	MO	46W	52
GLOVER JOHN	RI	04W	112
GLOVER LARRY	NY	10E	124
GLOVER LARRY RAY	IN	17W	47
GLOVER LAWRENCE WALTER	AL	18W	14
GLOVER MANZIE JR	NJ	10E	118
GLOVER RALPH LEWIS	PA	34W	75
GLOVER RAYMOND EDWARD	WV	33W	78
GLOVER ROBERT BRANCH	AL	13E	105
GLOVER ROSCOE JR	PA	43W	61
GLOVER WILLIE EDWARD	GA	49E	10
GLOWACKI DANIEL NORBERT	NY	53W	10
GLOWACKI EUGENE THOMAS	OH	14E	62
GLOWE STEPHEN	MI	20W	122
GLOWIAK FRANK ANTHONY	PA	11E	118
GLUECKSTEIN WILLIAM ROBER	WI	04E	108
GLYNN AARON GEORGE	NJ	19E	81
GLYNN DENNIS WAYNE	KS	44W	37
GLYNN JOHN JOSEPH JR	NY	25W	16
GLYNN MICHAEL JOSEPH	MN	15E	116
GLYNN PETER JOHN	NY	24W	65
GLYNNE MICHAEL THOMAS	NY	07E	113
GMACK JOHN ROBERT	WI	10W	114
GNANN HENRY MOUZON	GA	17W	77
GNIADEK ROBERT JOSEPH	IL	34W	92
GNIEWEK KENNETH STANLEY	MI	07W	38
GOACHER CARL FRANKLIN	AR	16W	57
GOAD ROBERT LEE	MN	33W	1
GOAR LARRY L	CA	07E	112
GOBBLE CHARLES HARTSELL	TN	25E	114
GOBBO JERRY WAYNE	CO	31W	92
GOBER BILLY WILLIE	GA	33E	36
GOBER CHARLES WESLEY JR	TX	08E	6
GOBER CLARENCE JR	PA	09W	94
GOBER RONALD BERNARD	TX	26E	71
GOBLE NORMAN ROBERT	NJ	30E	55
GOBLE PATRICK MICHAEL	TX	56E	24
GOC PAUL STEPHEN JR	NE	22W	46
GOCZAL FREDERICK	NJ	45W	40
GODBEY EDGAR	KY	54W	28
GODBEY SAMUEL EDWARD	IN	21W	125
GODBOLDT WILLIE FRANK	FL	03E	56
GODBOUT RICHARD GERALD	NH	33E	2
GODDARD MYRON THOMAS	IL	16E	105
GODDARD ROBERT GORDON	OK	20E	116
GODDARD ROCKFORD WAYNE	CO	08E	21
GODDARD RONALD WILLIAM	WA	05E	102
GODDEAU THOMAS ARTHUR	NY	22E	87
GODEN RICHARD WALTER	MD	28W	10
GODERRE JOHN ROGER	ME	07E	95
GODETTE MICHAEL SPENCER	NC	44W	10
GODFREY BARRY WILLIAM	NH	07W	4
GODFREY BILLY LAMAR	GA	31E	91
GODFREY CHARLES FAIRCHILD	NJ	15W	113
GODFREY GASTON DAVID	NC	06E	20
GODFREY JAMES WALTER	ME	18E	34
GODFREY JOHN JR	NY	39E	32
GODFREY JOHN LARIMORE	IN	12E	100
GODFREY JOHNNY HOWARD	AZ	04E	64
GODFREY JOHNNY LEE	FL	08W	28
GODFREY McVINCENT JR	OH	44W	48
GODFREY PARKER KEITH	OH	33W	1
GODFREY WILLARD ANSEL	WI	15E	4
GODFREY WILLIAM ROLLAND	NJ	17W	61
GODFROY RALPH DONALD	GA	18W	6
GODINES MIKE MORA	CA	31W	79
GODINEZ ALEJANDRO RAY	CA	22E	70
GODING ROBERT EARLE	ME	30W	22
GODLEY LOUIS HENRY	NY	24W	111
GODLEY RALEIGH LEE	MO	07E	103
GODMAN EARL ARTHUR	MD	23W	8
GODOWNS ROY WILLARD	GA	15W	114
GODOY PETER JR	CA	27W	30
GODSEY DANNY RAY	IN	22E	66
GODSEY JAMES FREDERICK	KS	25E	37
GODSEY JAMES MARVIN	WA	09E	28
GODWIN HARRY M	AR	05E	102
GODWIN JAMES OLIVER	NC	17W	26
GODWIN JAMES R	CA	37E	7
GODWIN JOHNIE REESE JR	AL	37W	5
GODWIN JOSEPH SAMUEL	CA	06E	92

NAME	STATE	PANEL NO.	LINE NO.
GODWIN KENNETH RAY	NC	14W	84
GODWIN RAYMOND WILLARD	IL	22E	12
GODWIN SOLOMON HUGHEY	AR	37E	35
GODWIN STANLEY MAURICE	FL	20E	27
GODWIN WILLIAM RILEY	AL	31E	11
GOEBEL MARVIN E	OH	26E	84
GOEBEL RUPERT WATSON JR	NC	30W	23
GOEBEL THOMAS ANTHONY	IL	06W	23
GOECKNER EUGENE FRANKLIN	IL	12E	21
GOEDDE ROBERT JOSEPH	MO	26W	54
GOEDEKER WILLIAM HOWARD	PA	25E	37
GOEDEN GENE WILLIAM	OR	16E	101
GOEGLEIN JOHN WINFRED	MO	09W	104
GOELLER MICHAEL DENNIS	CA	23W	36
GOELZ EDWARD CHARLES	IL	24E	2
GOELZ FRANK GERALD	PA	44E	7
GOELZ STEVEN WILLIAM	MN	04W	2
GOEN MARTIN DOUGLAS	IN	04W	110
GOEN RICHARD DEAN	GA	50W	50
GOEREE WIM	CA	13W	96
GOERS LOUIS LLOYD	IL	18E	58
GOETHE SPENCER ALAN	IL	12W	80
GOETSCH THOMAS AUGUST	TN	01W	73
GOETSCH WAYNE AUGUST	CA	37E	56
GOETT JOHN KENNETH	CT	17W	120
GOETZ JAMES GORMON	MO	16E	90
GOETZER JOSEPH JAMES JR	NY	22W	96
GOFF ALAN SHERMAN	CA	03W	102
GOFF AUBREY JR	KY	36E	10
GOFF CHARLES MITCHELL	IN	26E	101
GOFF DALTON TRURO	PA	26E	35
GOFF FLOYD HAROLD	NJ	04W	5
GOFF HENRY LARRY	VA	68W	1
GOFF KENNETH B JR	RI	25E	38
GOFF LARRY ALLEN	MI	36W	56
GOFF ROGER EARL	VA	18E	108
GOFF STANLEY ARTHUR	AZ	07W	95
GOFFREDO MICHAEL ANTHONY	IN	24E	85
GOFORTH CHARLES DAVID	VA	47E	11
GOFORTH JACKIE LEE	MO	08E	100
GOGGAN HERBERT GARY	TX	05E	33
GOGGIN JOHN PHILIP	NY	18W	68
GOGGIN PAUL STEPHEN	WV	35E	70
GOGGIN RICHARD JAMES	ME	03W	13
GOHAGIN JAMES RAYFORD	AL	25W	99
GOHEEN RICHARD H	IN	18E	29
GOI LOUIS CHARLES	FL	45E	22
GOIAS EVERETT WILLIAM	CA	03E	31
GOINES ROBERT	NJ	03E	126
GOING WALLACE	OK	36W	69
GOINGS JOSEPH HUBERT JR	GA	19E	117
GOINS BILLY LEE	OK	36W	2
GOINS CHESTER LEON	CA	19W	44
GOINS GERALD	OK	39E	4
GOINS GORDON L	OH	34E	18
GOINS HUGH CRAIG	OH	26E	24
GOINS MICHAEL RAY	MO	47W	8
GOINS WILLIAM HARRISON	TN	41E	38
GOLASZEWSKI WALTER	PA	09W	23
GOLBERG LAWRENCE HERBERT	MN	09E	112
GOLC JOSEPH LOUIS JR	IN	18W	69
GOLD EDWARD FRANK	CA	04E	34
GOLD ERIC STUART	NC	35W	38
GOLD FRED EDWARD	TN	18W	125
GOLD ROBERT JOSEPH	OH	15E	95
GOLDA EDWARD	NY	42W	46
GOLDBERG BENJAMIN NILES	MD	60E	23
GOLDBERG HOWARD STANLEY	NJ	13E	83
GOLDBERG JOSEPH A	NJ	01E	10
GOLDBERG STEWART B	MD	20W	49
GOLDBERG WILLIAM JACOB	FL	38E	49
GOLDBIN CHARLES HENRY	CA	02W	22
GOLDEN BARRY LEIGH	MO	28W	103
GOLDEN CALVIN JR	IL	56W	21
GOLDEN DONALD LEWIS	MS	06W	98
GOLDEN GEORGE KENNETH	AL	28W	69
GOLDEN HAROLD	FL	03E	31
GOLDEN JACK DUANE	NE	41W	58
GOLDEN JIMMY LEE	AR	52W	15
GOLDEN JOHN MICHAEL	CA	55W	34
GOLDEN KENNETH D JR	FL	06E	81
GOLDEN KENNETH EDWARD	OH	36E	72

NAME	STATE	PANEL NO.	LINE NO.
GOLDEN MERVIN DENNIS	ID	58W	8
GOLDEN ROBERT WALTER	MN	08E	62
GOLDEN RONALD DUANE	WI	47W	7
GOLDEN WILLIAM JOSEPH	FL	10W	12
GOLDER EDWARD ENOCH III	MD	40W	32
GOLDHAGEN BOBBY GENE	TX	14E	22
GOLDING JAMES RICHARD	FL	38W	43
GOLDING JERRY BOGGIE	NC	15E	44
GOLDMAN SAMMY WAYNE	LA	13W	71
GOLDMEYER CHARLES HENRY	CA	17W	7
GOLDSBERY JOHN ALLEN II	IL	61W	24
GOLDSBORO STEVEN MICHAEL	NJ	15E	9
GOLDSMITH CARL EDWARD JR	WV	32W	4
GOLDSMITH DANIEL ERIC	CA	66W	6
GOLDSMITH DAVID PETER	NY	42E	64
GOLDSMITH DONALD LAWRENCE	SC	38W	42
GOLDSMITH MILTON	NC	13W	74
GOLDSMITH ROGER DWIGHT	WI	23E	110
GOLDSTEIN STEVEN VICTOR	NY	41E	38
GOLEBIEWSKI RONALD FRANK	PA	44E	36
GOLEMBIEWSKI WALTER EDWAR	MI	41W	52
GOLEMBSKI PAUL JOSEPH	NJ	22E	102
GOLEMON FLOYD EDWARD JR	TX	17W	101
GOLIGHTLY ROLLIN EUGENE	FL	32E	87
GOLL DAVID ROBERT	IA	10W	41
GOLLAHON GENE RAYMOND	OH	02E	51
GOLLAHON JOHN DAVID	GA	54W	23
GOLLIDAY WILLIAM FRANK	IA	19W	107
GOLLIHER PATRICK CARL	CA	35W	26
GOLLING CHARLES RONALD	OH	47W	42
GOLMON JIMMY DARWIN	LA	13E	63
GOLOMBESKI WALTER BILLY	MI	08W	66
GOLON WAYNE LEONARD	NJ	37E	35
GOLSH STEPHEN ARTHUR	CA	12W	29
GOLSON ANTHONY	SC	13W	77
GOLWITZER RONALD ANTHONY	NY	47W	28
GOLZ JAMES ROLAND	OR	35E	46
GOLZ JOHN BRYAN	IL	11W	35
GOMES ALLEN EDWARD	HI	42W	68
GOMES MICHAEL CHARLES	CA	11W	7
GOMEZ ANDRES ARMANDO R	CA	34E	18
GOMEZ ARMONDO ABEL	IL	40E	39
GOMEZ ATANACIO JR	TX	49E	41
GOMEZ BASILIO	TX	56W	21
GOMEZ ERNEST LAWRENCE	CO	37W	74
GOMEZ EVELIO ALFRED	MI	08W	124
GOMEZ FELIDELPHIO BENJIMI	CO	07E	80
GOMEZ FRANK	WI	47W	42
GOMEZ GELASIO NICANOR JR	VT	53E	32
GOMEZ HAROLD	IN	15E	69
GOMEZ HENRY	CA	27E	39
GOMEZ JESSIE YUTZE	AZ	13E	52
GOMEZ JESUS EPHRAIM JR	NY	37W	5
GOMEZ JOSE MANUEL	TX	19E	37
GOMEZ JOSEPH JAMES	NV	04W	40
GOMEZ LAMBERT ANSELMO	CA	38E	54
GOMEZ MANUEL JOSEPH	CA	50E	28
GOMEZ MARGARITO RODRIQUEZ	CO	03W	112
GOMEZ OSCAR JOE	TX	14W	117
GOMEZ RAYMUNDO	TX	17E	85
GOMEZ RICARDO JOSE	FL	22W	12
GOMEZ ROBERT	CA	03E	56
GOMEZ ROBERT ARTHUR	FL	11W	40
GOMEZ ROBERT RAZO	CA	12E	78
GOMEZ STEVE	FL	68W	1
GOMEZ VALENTINE BERMEA JR	TX	12W	123
GOMEZ XAVIER	TX	14W	12
GOMEZ-BADILLO DAVID	PR	30W	13
GOMEZ-DIAZ RIGOBERTO	CA	19W	60
GOMEZ-MESA LUIS G	NY	45W	19
GOMEZ-RIVERA JUAN	PR	50E	47
GOMEZ-ROBLES TOMAS	PR	23W	52
GOMEZGUTIERREZ MANUEL	CA	03W	118
GOMOLICKE LEONARD MICHAEL	CA	21W	117
GONANO JAMES MARTIN	PA	30W	88
GONCE RAY LONNIE	IL	11E	90
GONDER KENNETH WALTER	NJ	10W	64
GONDERMAN FRANK LEE	CA	08E	100
GONNEVILLE ROBERT ROLAND	MA	29E	58
GONSALEZ LUIS MARTINEZ	CA	19W	94
GONSALEZ MARIO	TX	13W	85
GONSALVES AUGUST JR	MA	60W	17

NAME	STATE	PANEL NO.	LINE NO.
GONSALVES GEORGE GREART	OR	33E	48
GONTERO ROBERT CLYDE	PA	21W	18
GONZALES AGAPITO JR	TX	49E	41
GONZALES ALEXANDER	HI	26E	25
GONZALES ARTURO PEREZ	TX	35W	42
GONZALES CARLOS LUIS	NY	42E	16
GONZALES CARLOS M	CA	22W	52
GONZALES DAVID	CA	12W	29
GONZALES DOMINGO RAUL	TX	51E	19
GONZALES EDWARDO JOSE	TX	20E	58
GONZALES ELIGIO RICE JR	TX	59W	2
GONZALES FELIX G JR	TX	25W	99
GONZALES FRANK CAVOSOS	TX	43W	62
GONZALES GERARDO HOLQUIN	AZ	36W	69
GONZALES JESUS ANTONIO	CO	05W	56
GONZALES JIM ROY	CA	54W	29
GONZALES JIMMY	CA	05E	38
GONZALES JOE JULIAN	CA	37W	49
GONZALES JOSE BERNARDINO	NM	13E	24
GONZALES JOSE LUNA JR	TX	07W	37
GONZALES JUAN E	CA	05W	64
GONZALES LUIS GARCIA JR	TX	56W	14
GONZALES MANUEL	TX	31W	67
GONZALES MANUEL MARTINEZ	TX	31E	74
GONZALES MERCED HERMAN	CA	12E	127
GONZALES MICHAEL FILBERT	CO	16W	117
GONZALES NICHOLAS VALERIA	MI	37W	64
GONZALES OSCAR CRUZ	TX	14W	65
GONZALES PAUL ALFRED	CA	64W	9
GONZALES PAUL GUTTERREZ	TX	22W	20
GONZALES PEDRO CHAVARRIA	TX	52W	46
GONZALES RICHARD CASTILLO	CA	55E	13
GONZALES ROBERT	CA	18W	1
GONZALES ROY JR	TX	05E	117
GONZALES SANTIAGO RODRIGUEZ	TX	15E	105
GONZALES TOM JR	UT	31E	58
GONZALES TOMAS	TX	50E	47
GONZALES-MADERA ANGEL L	PR	35W	56
GONZALEZ ALBERT	CA	51W	39
GONZALEZ ALFREDO	TX	37E	21
GONZALEZ AMADOR L	TX	19E	25
GONZALEZ AMALIO	OH	06E	134
GONZALEZ ANDRES AVALOS	OH	65E	9
GONZALEZ BENITO REYNA	TX	19E	116
GONZALEZ BERNARDINO JR	CA	17E	110
GONZALEZ CARLOS	CA	48W	32
GONZALEZ CARLOS SAAVEDRA	TX	07E	16
GONZALEZ CONRAD NICHOLAS	NY	33E	67
GONZALEZ DENNIS	IL	17W	50
GONZALEZ DOUGLAS DAVID	MO	57W	18
GONZALEZ FRANCISCO HERNAN	NJ	27E	71
GONZALEZ FRANCISCO JR	IL	19W	68
GONZALEZ GUADALUPE	TX	12W	38
GONZALEZ HECTOR	FL	50W	6
GONZALEZ HECTOR MANUEL	TX	45W	26
GONZALEZ JESUS	TX	16E	28
GONZALEZ JESUS ARMANDO	TX	50E	47
GONZALEZ JOAQUIN CHRISTOP	CA	47W	9
GONZALEZ JOSE ALBERTO	CA	11W	123
GONZALEZ JOSE JESUS	TX	21E	88
GONZALEZ JOSE LUIS	AZ	31W	47
GONZALEZ JUAN ANTONIO	TX	20E	42
GONZALEZ JUAN JOSE	TX	21E	105
GONZALEZ LARRY EUGENE	AL	32E	35
GONZALEZ PABLO RENE	TX	23E	86
GONZALEZ PEDRO ACEVEDO	TX	14W	52
GONZALEZ RAMIRO MEDINA	TX	28W	98
GONZALEZ RAMON HERNANDEZ	NY	39E	25
GONZALEZ RICHARD	CA	57E	3
GONZALEZ ROBERT	NY	47E	49
GONZALEZ ROBERT ESPINOZA	CA	66E	9
GONZALEZ RODOLFO GUADALUP	TX	12E	56
GONZALEZ RODOLFO MARCIANO	TX	12E	70
GONZALEZ VICTOR JR	IL	40E	76
GONZALEZ VINCENTE RAMIREZ	TX	34E	11
GONZALEZ WILFREDO LOUIS	WI	41W	11
GONZALEZ-DROZ EDUARDO	PR	06E	39
GONZALEZ-LOPEZ ADOLFO	PR	04W	4
GONZALEZ-MALDONADA MANUEL	PR	02E	130
GONZALEZ-MARTINEZ ANGEL L	PR	58W	9
GONZALEZ-MORALES ROBERTO	PR	40W	1
GONZALEZ-PEREZ ARAMIS	PR	07E	118

NAME	STATE	PANEL NO.	LINE NO.
GONZALEZ-RIVERA MIGUEL A	PR	32W	78
GONZALEZ-RODRIGUEZ RAMON	PR	20E	43
GONZALEZ-SANCHEZ ROBERTO	PR	17W	27
GONZALEZ-VELEZ JOEL HUMBE	PR	36E	72
GOOCH CALVIN LIONEL	TX	58E	21
GOOCH JERRY DALE	MI	23E	119
GOOCH WESLEY LEE	KS	34E	36
GOOD BILLY DUANE	WV	01E	52
GOOD CURTIS	CT	15W	107
GOOD JOHN DUDLEY	OK	11E	68
GOOD KENNETH NEWLON	CA	01E	15
GOOD LARRY DEAN	MI	21E	58
GOOD PAUL EUGENE	PA	22E	12
GOOD RAY LYNN	PA	33W	60
GOOD ROBERT SAYE JR	SC	04W	44
GOODALE JOSEPH DANIEL JR	GA	28W	68
GOODALE LEON RUSSELL JR	CT	31W	67
GOODALE THOMAS LEE	MO	36W	63
GOODALL EARL WAYNE	MI	08E	28
GOODALL HERMAN GLENDAEE	KY	55E	14
GOODCHILD RAYMOND LEE	MI	01W	85
GOODE GEORGE SHERMAN	IN	18W	64
GOODE JACK DEE	KS	51E	20
GOODE RODNEY MICHAEL	KY	30W	3
GOODELL JIMMY LEON	OK	09W	38
GOODEN GERALD LYNN	MO	13E	71
GOODEN JOHNNIE	DC	47W	43
GOODEN MICHAEL ANTHONY	CA	09E	24
GOODEN WILLIAM ELLIOTT	IL	22W	32
GOODFELLOW CARL RAYMOND	LA	32E	50
GOODHEART WILLIAM	NY	45E	39
GOODHUE MARLIN JAMES	FL	23E	3
GOODIN DANIEL EUGENE	NY	03W	134
GOODIN SYDNEY UEL	NY	14E	128
GOODINE DAVID ROBERT	CA	17W	84
GOODING LLOYD LEE	NM	11E	2
GOODING ORANGE	VA	30W	64
GOODING WILLIAM PHILIP	NJ	19W	54
GOODIRON RONALD CHRISTY	ND	41E	66
GOODLETT JOHN FLETCHER	VA	18W	94
GOODLIN JERRY LEE	CA	23W	36
GOODMAN BARRY JASON		15E	24
GOODMAN BRUCE TED	NY	36W	21
GOODMAN CHARLES EDWARD	TX	56W	11
GOODMAN CHARLES OBADATH	TN	38E	50
GOODMAN DONNIELL	PA	28E	35
GOODMAN EDWARD LEE	VA	49E	31
GOODMAN EDWARD LEON	MD	17W	84
GOODMAN GREG FREDRIC	CA	16E	121
GOODMAN JACK LANCE	FL	01E	25
GOODMAN JAMES A	TX	53W	35
GOODMAN JAMES DONALD	AR	13E	131
GOODMAN KENNETH VIRGIL	MN	35E	21
GOODMAN LAWRENCE RAY JR	CA	19W	93
GOODMAN MARVIN FOY JR	FL	06E	23
GOODMAN NORMAN ELAN	MI	35W	89
GOODMAN RAYMOND LEE	VA	58W	31
GOODMAN RICHARD LEE	IA	37W	31
GOODMAN ROBERT JAMES	PA	41W	12
GOODMAN ROBERT ONNIE JR	WV	02W	33
GOODMAN RUSSELL CLEMENSEN	UT	15E	65
GOODMAN THOMAS HILL JR	TN	65W	8
GOODNER ROBERT EUGENE	KS	24W	66
GOODNESS KENNETH GLEN	WI	19W	38
GOODNIGHT JACKIE LEE	IN	18W	38
GOODNIGHT PETER RAY	CA	07W	125
GOODNO KEVEN ZANE	MN	01W	84
GOODRICH EDWIN RILEY JR	NY	16E	68
GOODRICH JEFFERY CAMON	KY	03W	22
GOODRICH JOHN MATTHEW	TX	51E	7
GOODRICH THOMAS WENDELL	NY	20E	116
GOODSELL BRUCE LYNN	ID	05W	29
GOODSELL OWEN DAVID	NY	14E	75
GOODSELL WILLIAM JOSEPH	WA	08E	51
GOODSON CARL BRADFORD	WV	12W	101
GOODSON JOSEPH ALAN	SC	30W	36
GOODSON THOMAS HENRY	FL	62W	9
GOODSPEED WILLIAM HUNTER	OH	31E	58
GOODWIN ALVIN MAYNARD	FL	24E	60
GOODWIN BOB JACK	KS	25E	90
GOODWIN CHARLES BERNARD	TX	02E	78
GOODWIN CHARLES RAY	TX	17E	2

NAME	STATE	PANEL NO.	LINE NO.
GOODWIN DANNY ERIC	MA	25E	38
GOODWIN FORREST	MS	16E	2
GOODWIN JACK LEROY	OR	44E	7
GOODWIN JOHN MASON	OH	29W	77
GOODWIN PAUL VENON	AL	25W	100
GOODWIN PHILIP BENJAMIN	MA	14W	103
GOODWIN RAYMOND RAY	LA	16E	10
GOODWIN ROBBIN ADAIR	CA	09E	103
GOODWIN RONALD NELIONAL	SC	03W	113
GOODWIN WILLIAM FRANKLIN	MO	30W	64
GOODWINE ISOM JUNIOR	FL	15W	98
GOOGINS DOUGLAS E JR	ME	34E	48
GOOLSBY JAMES RUEL	FL	22W	12
GOOLSBY WILLIAM RAY JR	TX	07W	65
GOONAN PAUL EDWARD JR	OH	25W	100
GOOSEN ROBERT HENRY	MI	13W	122
GOOSSENS MATTHEW RAYMOND	IL	25E	77
GOPP THOMAS ALAN	OH	24E	72
GORAL GERALD EUGENE	MI	26W	84
GORALSKI LEO STANLEY	IL	37W	74
GORBE VAUN ARLEN	MI	07W	113
GORBEY JACK EUGENE	WV	43E	53
GORDIAN LARRY BERNARD	NY	24E	103
GORDILS LOUIS ALFREDO	NY	23W	36
GORDON ALVIN JR	AR	33W	62
GORDON ARTHUR MELVIN	MS	03E	113
GORDON CHARLES A	FL	54W	6
GORDON CLEVELAND WILLIAM	PA	01E	40
GORDON DARWIN DALE	IL	46E	6
GORDON DRANNON RAY	OK	16W	34
GORDON ERNEST LEE	AL	25W	100
GORDON GARY GENE	TX	50W	23
GORDON GERALD ELLIOTT	DC	39E	57
GORDON GLENN ALLYN	WA	26W	84
GORDON GLENN RAYMOND	MA	30W	23
GORDON GUY LEE	WA	13E	91
GORDON HENRY JOE	IL	34E	36
GORDON HUBERT ELTON	CO	22E	61
GORDON HUBERT HASKEL JR	AR	44E	7
GORDON JAMES BERNARD L JR	DC	13W	23
GORDON JAMES EDWARD	OH	13E	108
GORDON JAMES LEWIS	MI	19W	86
GORDON JAMES THOMAS	NJ	39E	71
GORDON JIMMIE LEE	LA	30W	44
GORDON JOHN HEBER	CA	33W	31
GORDON JOHN PATRICK JR	NY	37E	21
GORDON JOHN SWAIN	KS	29E	100
GORDON JOHNNY LEE	CA	13E	41
GORDON LAWRENCE LEE	IN	11W	111
GORDON MARVIN EDWARD	IA	26E	84
GORDON OTIS JR	FL	01E	72
GORDON RICHARD DALE	IN	54W	10
GORDON ROBERT JERRY	ID	27W	87
GORDON ROGERS STUART	MI	21W	7
GORDON THOMAS LESLIE	AL	22E	13
GORDON WAYNE VICTOR	MI	22E	61
GORDON WILLIAM SAMUEL	DC	36E	10
GORDON WYATT CECIL	IN	36E	4
GORDY JESSE ARNEL	TX	31E	58
GORDY MICHAEL EDWARD	MD	27W	108
GORE CALVIN THOMAS	GA	01W	36
GORE DAVID EDWARD	CA	66E	9
GORE DONALD EARL	CA	08E	97
GORE EVERETT JR	WV	16W	121
GORE FREDDY RAY	IN	23E	67
GORE GREGORY	NY	32E	30
GORE HAROLD DOUGLAS	MS	62W	9
GORE HORACE ROSCOE	SC	20E	27
GORE JAMES BENJAMIN	NC	16E	90
GORE JAMES RAYMOND	MT	09W	83
GORE JERRY	CA	20W	126
GORE KENNETH ALRIC	NC	21E	46
GORE PAUL EDWIN	NC	17W	27
GORE THOMAS	TX	56E	24
GOREE CARLTON TRAVIS	AL	45W	40
GOREE WILLIE VANN	AR	28E	24
GORGES RICHARD JOHN	WI	13W	6
GORHAM MARC CHARLES	OR	35W	9
GORHAM RUDOLPH	NC	25E	62
GORHAM WALTER PRESTON	VA	01E	20
GORMAN EDWARD T III	KS	61E	9
GORMAN HENRY WILLIAM	PA	34E	52

NAME	STATE	PANEL NO.	LINE NO.
GORMAN KEVIN TERRENCE	IL	20E	59
GORMAN PAUL JAMES	MA	50W	35
GORMICAN DAVID C	FL	21W	107
GORMLEY JAMES	NY	41E	9
GORMLEY PAUL LEO JR	MA	04E	24
GORNEY JERRY EDWARD	OH	19E	104
GOROSPE LEONARD GORDON	HI	09E	130
GORRELL DAVID EUGENE	MO	17E	116
GORRERA GEORGE MEDFORD JR	MD	29W	89
GORRILL THOMAS ROY	MA	28W	107
GORSCHBOTH ROLAND ALLEN	MD	44W	24
GORSICH JAMES TONY	CA	46E	33
GORSKE ROBERT EDWARD	FL	10W	75
GORSLENE TERRY EUGENE	OH	14W	13
GORSUCH WILLIAM DALE	WI	17W	27
GORTON DAVID ATOIGUE	GM	02W	67
GORTON GARY BRUCE	NY	05E	41
GORTON JACK BURT	CA	62E	4
GORTON RALPH SHOUP III	ID	65W	8
GORTON THOMAS FREDERICK	OH	01E	36
GORVAD PETER LAWRENCE	CA	30W	74
GORVET WILLIAM ANTHONY	OH	19W	118
GOSCH LARRY GENE	IA	23W	86
GOSCH THOMAS CHARLES	CA	42E	17
GOSCHKA LARRY HERMAN	MI	13W	1
GOSE ELVIN WAYNE	IN	45E	22
GOSELIN ROBERT MARTIN	IL	09W	13
GOSEN LAWRENCE DEAN	MN	51W	39
GOSHORN EDWARD FRANCIS	LA	22W	76
GOSHORN WALTER L	PA	13E	108
GOSLIN GREGG MICHAEL	WI	29E	82
GOSNELL JACK MARTIN	MD	16E	111
GOSNELL ODIS LEON	IL	45E	46
GOSNEY DURWARD DEAN	AZ	01E	65
GOSS BERNARD JOSEPH	NY	06E	129
GOSS CLARENCE EUGENE	AZ	38W	34
GOSS DANNY LEON	AR	10W	97
GOSS HEZEKIAH JR	MI	04E	73
GOSS JACK EUGENE II	MO	21E	46
GOSS JAMES SPURGEON	NC	15E	116
GOSS JEFFERY ALAN	UT	68E	4
GOSS JEFFREY KENNETH	NY	30W	24
GOSS LARRY JO	IN	39E	32
GOSS RICHARD DEAN	CA	01E	63
GOSS WARREN JUDGE	VA	37W	49
GOSSAGE DOUGLAS EUGENE	MO	42W	17
GOSSARD DAVID EUGENE	OH	26E	96
GOSSE JOSE C	CA	09E	43
GOSSELIN JAMES EDWARD	PA	36E	72
GOSSELIN PHILIP LYN	KS	50W	23
GOSSELIN ROBERT JOSEPH	VA	10W	102
GOSSETT HERSHEL LEE WALTO	TN	43W	62
GOSSETT WILLIAM O	AZ	06E	14
GOSSMAN KERRY RAY	MN	06W	2
GOSWICK LARRY EUGENE	GA	51E	7
GOSWICK WESLEY IRA	FL	20E	27
GOSZEWSKI THOMAS WALTER	MO	06W	86
GOTCHER LARRIE JACK	CA	45E	55
GOTT HERBERT D III	NY	03W	28
GOTT JOHN JOSEPH JR	DE	36W	40
GOTT RODNEY HERSCHEL	FL	33W	65
GOTTHARDT ROBERT WILLIAM	NJ	59E	3
GOTTI GALE EDWARD	CA	21E	67
GOTTIER ROBERT CARL	PA	06W	81
GOTTSCHALK WILLIAM HENRY	IL	19E	95
GOTTWALD GEORGE JOSEPH JR	MA	36E	73
GOUCHER EDWARD LOUIS	OK	25E	100
GOUDE CHARLES MELVIN	SC	12E	59
GOUDEAU JEFF JR	OK	04E	14
GOUDELOCK FORREST	GA	50E	47
GOUDELOCK WILLIAM ROGER	CA	45E	22
GOUDY GARY ROY	OH	38W	35
GOUDY RICHARD LEE	KS	02E	49
GOUGER WILLIAM DAVID JR	MI	32W	12
GOUGH HURSHELL HARRY	OK	40E	37
GOUGH LINWOOD	PA	68W	1
GOUGH STANFORD MORRIS	OR	48E	52
GOUGH WILLIAM LYLE	IL	30W	54
GOULD CARLTON EDGAR	NY	22E	30
GOULD CARLYLE LEROY	MI	13E	131
GOULD EDWARD DEAN	AR	18E	59
GOULD FRANK ALTON	NY	01W	99

NAME	STATE	PANEL NO.	LINE NO.
GOULD JOHNNY WAYNE	FL	18E	40
GOULD WARREN LEE	WV	10E	118
GOULD WILLIAM ANDREW	CA	28W	91
GOULD WILLIAM C JR	MA	28W	81
GOULD WILLIAM IRVING	NY	15E	57
GOULDIN THOMAS MILTON	VA	16W	92
GOULET RONALD DAVID	MI	33E	28
GOULET RONALD MARCEL	CT	17W	9
GOURDINE LARRY RONALD	SC	42E	52
GOURLAY BRUCE ANDREW	IN	25W	47
GOURLEY LAURENT LEE	IA	20W	118
GOVAN ROBERT ALLEN	DC	17E	85
GOWER WILLIAM RAY	MO	09E	87
GOWERS THOMAS ANTHONY	IN	10W	75
GOWIN HARRY DALE	IL	22W	76
GOYNE ALLEN BENJAMIN JR	IL	17W	27
GOZDAN MICHAEL STEPHEN	PA	27E	60
GRABBE JOHN ALBERT	IN	30W	54
GRABER GARY DAVID	MN	19W	78
GRABER JOHN ALLEN JR	KS	16E	90
GRABER SCOTT THOMAS	OH	03W	132
GRABLE MICKEY RAY	IL	09E	74
GRABOSKEY EDWARD ELLIOTT	MI	03E	1
GRABOW OTTO CHARLES	NY	20E	28
GRABOWSKI JAN JOSEPH JR	NJ	17E	3
GRACE DENNIS FREDERICK	NY	13W	111
GRACE EARLEY CARTER	OH	05W	116
GRACE JAMES WILLIAM	LA	22W	46
GRACE LARRY	TX	24W	30
GRACE LARRY EDWARD	AL	24E	25
GRACE MARTIN JOSEPH JR	KS	66W	6
GRACE WILLIAM EDWARD	NC	48E	3
GRACHTRUP JOHN NORBERT	MI	13E	27
GRADECKI GLENN RICHARD	WI	15W	107
GRADEL JOSEPH	PA	18E	114
GRADOVILLE CHARLES EDWARD	IA	21E	112
GRADY JAMES WILLIAM	TN	06E	64
GRADY JERRY EDWARD	CA	56E	7
GRADY LEO FRANCIS	MA	02W	29
GRAEBNER SIEGFRIED LOUIS	NY	51W	31
GRAESER CALVIN KYRLE JR	PA	16E	59
GRAF ALBERT STEPHEN	NJ	18W	6
GRAF BARRY WADE	AR	29W	99
GRAF JOHN GEORGE	CA	16W	79
GRAFF ALLEN MICHAEL	CA	24W	95
GRAFF JAMES HOWARD	IL	11E	39
GRAFF PAUL ARNOLD	CA	24W	105
GRAFF THOMAS GEORGE	OH	18E	121
GRAFFE PAUL LEROY	WA	17W	34
GRAFT TERRY GENE	IN	18W	15
GRAFTON JAMES CALVIN	MS	14W	57
GRAGNANI THOMAS J	MO	13E	14
GRAHAM ALAN RAY	TX	32W	78
GRAHAM ALBERT F JR	CT	06W	21
GRAHAM ALBERT JR	CA	21E	34
GRAHAM ALLEN UPTON	AL	01W	82
GRAHAM ANNIE RUTH	NC	48W	12
GRAHAM ARMAND ROY	NY	13E	83
GRAHAM BARRY FRANCIS	NJ	08W	79
GRAHAM BARRY LEE	PA	46E	34
GRAHAM BENNIE JOE	MS	29W	8
GRAHAM BRADFORD MARK	WA	02W	68
GRAHAM BRUCE ELLIOT	VA	10W	102
GRAHAM BURDETTE DELROY	NY	28E	40
GRAHAM CHARLES HERBERT	AR	37E	22
GRAHAM CHARLES WAYNE	KY	44E	26
GRAHAM DAVID BRUCE	CA	33W	85
GRAHAM DAVID DEL	MI	58E	21
GRAHAM DAVID TIESON JR	NJ	02E	93
GRAHAM DENNIS LEE	KS	46E	54
GRAHAM DONALD TERRY	MN	12W	33
GRAHAM EARL CLAYTON	SC	03E	56
GRAHAM EARNEST WILMER	TX	31W	1
GRAHAM FLOYD JR	NY	37W	32
GRAHAM GENTRY	NC	05E	72
GRAHAM GEORGE RICHARD	IL	01E	51
GRAHAM GILBERT JAMES	CA	27E	24
GRAHAM GORDON J	MI	28E	66
GRAHAM HARLAN LEE	NE	40W	57
GRAHAM HAROLD EDWARD	WV	55W	21
GRAHAM HARVEY GENE	IN	10W	61
GRAHAM HENRY HERNDON	DC	40E	63

NAME	STATE	PANEL NO.	LINE NO.
GRAHAM JAMES	NY	03E	127
GRAHAM JAMES ALBERT	MD	21E	46
GRAHAM JAMES EVERETT JR	PA	11E	7
GRAHAM JAMES HENRY	CA	17W	55
GRAHAM JAMES SCOTT	PA	19E	38
GRAHAM JOHN HARRY	CA	15E	116
GRAHAM JOHN MEIGS	KY	05W	48
GRAHAM JOHNNIE JR	NY	19W	44
GRAHAM JOHNNIE LEE JR	LA	26W	54
GRAHAM JOSEPH HAROLD	LA	63W	16
GRAHAM KENNETH ERROL	OH	03E	31
GRAHAM LARRY ALONZA	GA	22W	65
GRAHAM LARRY ELLSWORTH	WA	27W	99
GRAHAM MICHAEL ALLAN	NC	07W	117
GRAHAM MORRIS	LA	28E	66
GRAHAM PATRICK JOHN	MN	52E	5
GRAHAM RICHARD FRANCIS	NY	06E	53
GRAHAM RICHARD SCOTT	PA	16E	2
GRAHAM ROBERT LEE	SC	61W	2
GRAHAM ROBERT LEE	NM	51W	18
GRAHAM ROBERT LEE	MN	22W	76
GRAHAM ROBERT OWEN	KY	32E	93
GRAHAM ROGER LEE	AL	22W	12
GRAHAM ROY WAYNE	CA	24W	59
GRAHAM SAMUEL HENRY II	NY	07E	3
GRAHAM SEBERN EMLIS JR	MO	12E	22
GRAHAM STEVEN LOUIS	CA	53W	19
GRAHAM TERRY DURAND	FL	28W	70
GRAHAM THOMAS JR	GA	33W	1
GRAHAM WENDELL JOHN M JR	WA	23W	36
GRAHAM WILLIAM RICHARD	VA	05E	126
GRAJEWSKI JERRY FRANCIS	VA	42W	11
GRALLA DONALD MICHEAL	CA	30E	26
GRAMLICK MICHAEL F	CA	20W	56
GRAMMAR WILLIAM MICHAEL	OK	20E	59
GRAMMER HENRY BRIAN	VA	24E	99
GRANADO-AVILES ALFREDO D	PR	37W	17
GRANADOS RICHARD	CA	43E	6
GRANAHAN JOHN WILLIAM	MA	23E	11
GRANATH JOHN EDWARD JR	IL	11W	111
GRANATO FRANK	NY	17E	18
GRANBERRY JOHNIE FRANKLIN	FL	22W	67
GRANDAHL JACK WILLIAM	MI	39E	21
GRANDE JOSEPH JOHN JR	NY	15E	127
GRANDE ROBERT JOSEPH	NY	32E	17
GRANDEA AMBROSIO SALAZAR	MD	21E	97
GRANDPRE EDWARD FREDERICK	CT	34W	7
GRANDSTAFF BRUCE ALAN	WA	20E	28
GRANELLE AMEDEE GEORGE JR	CA	37W	49
GRANEY DONALD CARYL	CA	15E	83
GRANGE ARTHUR CHARLES	IL	35E	32
GRANGER DALE GENE	MN	42W	68
GRANGER FLOYD IRA JR	LA	35W	60
GRANGER WILLIE EARL	NJ	49W	4
GRANIELA JOSE ANTONIO JR	NY	48W	25
GRANILLO HENRY	CA	25E	29
GRANNAN MICHAEL STEPHEN	CA	04E	8
GRANOFF ROBERT HOWARD	NY	15E	90
GRANSBURY GERALD ARLEN	CA	53E	17
GRANT ANDREW CARL	MI	08W	87
GRANT ARTHUR JOHN JR	IL	18E	34
GRANT BENJAMIN DAVIS	TX	36E	49
GRANT BILL WAYNE	MO	45E	56
GRANT CHARLES ROBERT	IN	29W	30
GRANT CREIGHTON ROONEY	MA	04E	119
GRANT DALE EUGENE	IA	68W	2
GRANT DENNIS HOWARD	CO	28E	84
GRANT ED NATHAN LOUIS	GA	25E	100
GRANT GENE TYNDALL	DE	63W	6
GRANT GOLLIE LEO	NC	10E	118
GRANT HERBERT RAYMOND	CA	31W	1
GRANT HOUSTON JR	GA	32E	51
GRANT JACKYA KEDERIS	IL	14E	90
GRANT JAMES MICHAEL	IN	15W	58
GRANT JAMES WOOD	FL	56E	24
GRANT JERRY	LA	31E	74
GRANT JOHNNIE	FL	05E	11
GRANT JOSEPH XAVIER	MA	12E	67
GRANT KELLUM WARREN	NY	54E	34
GRANT MELVIN LEE	NV	19W	38
GRANT NORMAN WILLIAM JR	MA	47W	43
GRANT PHILLIP	SC	17E	85

NAME	STATE	PANEL NO.	LINE NO.
GRANT PHILO DERRICK III	GA	65W	8
GRANT ROBERT EARL	AR	30W	75
GRANT ROBERT LEE	TX	23W	37
GRANT ROBERT WILLIAM	IL	50E	5
GRANT STEPHEN LEE	CA	26E	9
GRANT STEPHEN MITCHELL	FL	57W	25
GRANT THOMAS	SC	31E	64
GRANT THOMAS RICHARD	OH	04E	103
GRANT WARREN HARVEY JR	CA	22E	102
GRANT WAYNE AUGUSTUS	NJ	28E	74
GRANT WESLEY ONEAL	LA	21W	83
GRANT WILLIAM RICHARD	CA	47W	43
GRANT WILLIE JR	LA	17E	3
GRANT WILLIE JR	CA	45E	39
GRANTHAM ELY JR	MS	11W	35
GRANTHAM JOSEPH M III	NC	20E	48
GRANTHAM ROBERT EUGENE	CA	04W	32
GRANTHAM ROY EUGENE	TN	22E	77
GRANVILLE RONALD LESTER	MA	42W	28
GRASER JOHN WILLIAM	MD	65W	8
GRASS LAWRENCE GEORGE	IL	25E	74
GRASSER ARTHUR	MT	20W	101
GRASSER HAROLD PHILLIP	PA	45W	11
GRASSI CLEMENT JOHN	PA	57W	25
GRASSI ERNEST JOSEPH	NY	37W	74
GRASSI LAWRENCE GARY	PA	37E	35
GRASSIA JOSEPH JR	NJ	30W	88
GRASSL KENNETH JOSEPH	WI	35E	60
GRASSO ANTHONY JOHN	IL	25E	57
GRASSO JOHN M JR	CT	03E	115
GRASSO PAUL DAVID	NY	46E	34
GRASSO PAUL VINCENT	MA	54E	34
GRATEN FREDERICK DUNHAM	OR	49E	22
GRAU ANTONIO AMBROSIO	NJ	07W	24
GRAUERT HANS HERBERT	NY	29E	15
GRAUSTEIN ROBERT STEWART	ME	01W	99
GRAVEL BOBBY JOE	CA	48E	26
GRAVELINE RICHARD PAUL	CT	44W	10
GRAVER RAYMOND CHARLES JR	NY	12W	97
GRAVES CARTER LEE	NC	28W	35
GRAVES DONALD LAVERNE	NY	26E	25
GRAVES EDWARD STEPHEN	MN	05E	83
GRAVES FRANK	DC	08E	108
GRAVES GARY EVERETT	AZ	39W	48
GRAVES GEORGE W III	TN	40E	39
GRAVES HAROLD LEONARD	CA	12E	120
GRAVES JAMES EDDIE	KY	40W	75
GRAVES JAMES LEROY	NC	09E	11
GRAVES JEHOVAH	SC	35E	71
GRAVES JERRY LEE	MO	50W	24
GRAVES LARRY	GA	12W	80
GRAVES LEONARD OLSEN	WA	44W	25
GRAVES MICHAEL LEROY	SC	22E	102
GRAVES RANDOLPH EDWIN	GA	09W	130
GRAVES RICHARD CAMPBELL	MA	20E	105
GRAVES STANLEY EDWIN JR	TX	41E	49
GRAVES TERRENCE COLLINSON	NY	39E	71
GRAVES THOMAS LAWRENCE	CA	16W	88
GRAVES WILLIAM BOYD	WY	23E	107
GRAVES WILLIAM D	MD	13E	122
GRAVES WILLIAM RALPH JR	NC	13W	131
GRAVIL JOHN ALLEN	CT	20E	59
GRAVITTE CONNIE MACK	NC	08E	56
GRAVLEY JAMES THOMAS	VA	34W	70
GRAVROCK STEPHEN HOWARD	CA	01W	58
GRAY ALLEN RAY	IL	05W	39
GRAY ARTHUR POWELL IV	VA	08W	31
GRAY ASA PARKER JR	MI	25W	100
GRAY BERNARD LEROY	CA	01E	18
GRAY BOBBY ELMER	FL	09W	127
GRAY CARL AVERY	NC	03E	116
GRAY CARLTON COE	OR	10W	61
GRAY CHARLES GONZIE	MD	22W	105
GRAY CHARLES HOWARD JR	NC	07W	27
GRAY CHARLIE	NC	09E	67
GRAY CHRISTOPHER JAMES	WA	15W	78
GRAY CLARENCE HENRY	OH	02E	107
GRAY CLIFFORD	GA	08W	20
GRAY DALE ALAN	AZ	07W	77
GRAY DANNY MICHEAL	AR	40W	57
GRAY DAVID ARTHUR	IL	18E	26
GRAY DELACY	AL	15E	79

NAME	STATE	PANEL NO.	LINE NO.
GRAY DOUGLAS TAYLOR III	VA	15W	41
GRAY EDWARD JAMES	NJ	46W	16
GRAY EDWIN MICHAEL	IL	29E	58
GRAY FRANCIS GARFIELD	MD	51E	7
GRAY FREDDY LYNN	TN	21E	78
GRAY GARY GERALD	PA	19W	119
GRAY GEORGE ALBERT	PA	52W	5
GRAY GEORGE CHRISTIAN	PA	28W	81
GRAY GERALD ALFRED	IL	05W	120
GRAY GERALD DAN	CO	11W	27
GRAY GREGORY VAUGHAN	AR	36E	4
GRAY HAROLD EDWIN JR	NY	02E	48
GRAY HAROLD LEROY	MO	37E	7
GRAY HAROLD PAUL	PA	39E	60
GRAY HARVEY DUNCAN	WI	55E	13
GRAY HERBERT HOOVER	GA	30E	42
GRAY JAMES	AZ	07E	127
GRAY JAMES ANTHONY	NY	12W	93
GRAY JAMES H	OH	07E	52
GRAY JAMES JUNIUS	NC	23E	75
GRAY JAMES KENNETH	TX	11E	110
GRAY JAMES T	TN	01E	108
GRAY JESSE ALEXANDER	TN	01E	54
GRAY JIMMIE DELL	TN	11E	35
GRAY JOHN PATRICK	WI	62W	9
GRAY JOHN TERRY	MS	27W	30
GRAY KENNETH MERVIN	CA	10W	70
GRAY LARRY GENE	MI	14E	44
GRAY LEONARD CLARENCE JR	CA	14E	48
GRAY MICHAEL DOUGLAS	TX	43E	19
GRAY NEWTON MORGAN JR	IA	64E	5
GRAY PAUL HOUSTON	IA	15E	84
GRAY RALPH	NY	17E	18
GRAY RAYMOND ANTHONY	OH	27W	38
GRAY RAYMOND HENRY	DC	06W	91
GRAY RICHARD ARLINGTON	TX	21E	78
GRAY RICHARD JOSEPH	MA	03W	74
GRAY RICHARD KEY	NC	18W	81
GRAY RICHARD PAUL	OR	35E	71
GRAY RICHARD TENNEY	VA	01W	118
GRAY ROBERT ALLEN	IN	04E	23
GRAY ROBERT EDWARD	KY	43W	28
GRAY ROBERT LEE	NJ	09W	57
GRAY ROBERT LYNDON	IL	30E	97
GRAY ROBERT ROGER	MA	38E	67
GRAY ROBERT VERNON	OH	18W	10
GRAY RONALD K	OH	08E	92
GRAY RONALD LEONARD	IL	25W	69
GRAY ROSCOE CONKLIN JR	DC	32W	48
GRAY ROY VIRGIL	MO	11W	58
GRAY RUZELL	TX	62W	10
GRAY SAMUEL	VA	31E	81
GRAY SEVIER JR	AR	11W	35
GRAY STEPHEN FRANCIS	ME	03W	26
GRAY TERRY ADAM	OR	34E	52
GRAY THOMAS ALAN	NY	15E	58
GRAY THOMAS EDWARD	MI	25W	47
GRAY THOMAS EDWARD M JR	ME	15E	85
GRAY WALTER RAY	KY	02E	3
GRAY WARREN	CA	58E	7
GRAY WILBUR LEWIS JR	IN	42E	32
GRAY WILLIAM EARL	NY	14E	129
GRAY WILLIAM GEORGE	FL	22W	119
GRAY WILLIAM RUSSELL JR	NY	33W	7
GRAYS DEMETRIUS JEROME	MO	25W	39
GRAYSON HERMAN LEE	LA	25W	5
GRAYSON JERELL LEE	MO	03E	77
GRAYSON JOE EDWARD	NY	35W	65
GRAYSON RAMON LEE	AL	11W	101
GRAYSON REID ERNEST JR	MT	36W	84
GRAYSON RONNIE PAUL	AL	35W	39
GRAYSON SAMUEL A III	MS	06W	91
GRAYSON WELBY HERBERT III	VA	18W	1
GRAYSON WILLIAM RONALD	CA	06E	71
GRAZIANO ANDREW ALBERT	NY	05E	46
GRAZIER RUSSELL ALLAN	NY	24E	26
GRAZIOSI FRANCIS GEORGE	NY	14W	22
GRCICH NICK JIM	IN	16E	121
GREANY VIRGIL RAYMOND	ND	01E	64
GREATHOUSE JULIUS JR	TX	13E	52
GREATHOUSE ROBERT CHARLES	KS	17W	70
GREAVU BILLY JOEL	OH	13W	104

NAME	STATE	PANEL NO.	LINE NO.
GREB JAMES J	MO	49E	52
GREBBY ROBERT WILLIAM	WI	07W	81
GRECO ERIC JOSEPH	LA	24W	4
GRECO LEE ATTILIO	CA	13E	15
GRECO MICHEL JACK	IL	18W	61
GRECO STEVEN JAMES	FL	20W	39
GRECU MICHAEL JOHN	CA	19W	93
GREEF LAWRENCE DAY	OR	19W	13
GREEFF REMI HENDRICUS	UT	33W	22
GREELEY DENNIS ANTHONY	PA	15W	1
GREELEY MICHAEL JEFFERSON	OR	20E	116
GREELEY TIMOTHY MARTIN	NY	08W	51
GREELEY VERNE MILTON	NH	23E	18
GREEN ALLEN RUSSELL	MO	62E	5
GREEN ARTHUR HAYWOOD		24E	72
GREEN ARTHUR WILLIAM	IL	11E	14
GREEN AUTRY	TX	13E	16
GREEN BERNARD ALAN	CA	09E	43
GREEN BILLY MONROE	CA	08E	85
GREEN CANEY	NC	10E	8
GREEN CARL FRED	NY	58E	8
GREEN CARL JOHN JR	OR	26W	39
GREEN CHARLES DEE	WA	22W	20
GREEN CHARLES JR	IL	25E	47
GREEN CHARLES VERNON	CA	14W	89
GREEN CLAUDE HEWITT	NY	49E	1
GREEN CLIFFORD NEWTON	CA	12W	29
GREEN CLYDE RAY	TX	25W	69
GREEN CRAIG STEVEN	OR	16W	95
GREEN DALLAS EUGENE	TN	09E	39
GREEN DAVID HARRY JR	SC	38E	50
GREEN DAVID NATHANIEL JR	SC	23E	115
GREEN DENNIS BLAINE	KS	34W	37
GREEN DENNIS JOSEPH	WI	20W	113
GREEN DONALD ALBIE	GA	15E	54
GREEN DONALD CARL	MN	07E	127
GREEN DONALD EDWARD	CA	45E	56
GREEN DONALD GEORGE	CA	03E	66
GREEN DOUGLAS BARTON III	NJ	34E	28
GREEN EDDIE	MD	08E	14
GREEN EDWARD JR	SC	28W	35
GREEN ERNEST	IL	13E	40
GREEN EUGENE	GA	61E	10
GREEN FRANK CLIFFORD JR	TX	01W	55
GREEN FREDDIE WALLACE	NC	05E	51
GREEN GARRY GEORGE	CO	43W	46
GREEN GEOFFREY EMMONS	MI	02E	78
GREEN GEORGE CURTIS JR	IN	06W	106
GREEN GEORGE RICHARD JR	NY	25W	5
GREEN GERALD	CO	02E	81
GREEN HAROLD ALFRED	GA	09W	59
GREEN IVAN IVORY	IL	27W	38
GREEN JAMES ARVIL	OK	09W	64
GREEN JAMES DAVID	AR	13E	97
GREEN JAMES EDWARD	IA	17E	72
GREEN JEFFREY WALLACE	KY	40E	39
GREEN JEREMIAH	FL	55W	5
GREEN JERRY L	AZ	44E	26
GREEN JEWELL ROBERT	GA	28W	36
GREEN JIMMIE RAY	OK	38W	74
GREEN JIMMIE WAYNE	FL	27E	100
GREEN JIMMY CARROLL	NC	41W	73
GREEN JIMMY LEON	TX	34W	41
GREEN JOE WORTH	WY	12W	68
GREEN JOHN JR	NY	07E	107
GREEN KENNETH GERALD	MI	37W	32
GREEN KENNETH LEON	AZ	27E	28
GREEN KENNETH LESLIE	IL	27E	10
GREEN KISH LEMONT	CA	22W	52
GREEN LARRY	NY	35W	60
GREEN LARRY	MD	14W	101
GREEN LARRY EDWARD	MI	46E	42
GREEN LARRY VERNARD	MI	45E	22
GREEN LAURENCE BURTON	UT	39W	27
GREEN LEO FRANK JR	NJ	19W	14
GREEN LUTHER JR	KS	06W	117
GREEN MARTIN L JR	VA	25W	48
GREEN MELVIN	TX	19W	14
GREEN MELVIN JR	NC	25W	69
GREEN MELVIN LOUIS	DC	18E	85
GREEN MELVIN RICKEY	OH	37W	6
GREEN MICHAEL FRANK	ID	44E	7
GREEN MICHAEL WAYNE	CA	25W	54
GREEN MILFRED RAY	TX	05W	75
GREEN MOSES	NY	16E	10
GREEN NORMAN DUANE	NE	40E	5
GREEN NORMAN MORGAN	DC	34E	7
GREEN OTIS	NJ	33W	56
GREEN PHELBON MICHAEL	OH	06W	91
GREEN PHILLIP WILLIAM JR	NC	09W	50
GREEN RALPH LA VERNE	MI	43W	28
GREEN RICHARD AL	IL	55E	14
GREEN RICHARD ALBERT	VT	02W	83
GREEN RICHARD HERSHEL	NY	16W	88
GREEN RICHARD JR	NY	44W	63
GREEN ROBERT BAILEY	TX	11E	104
GREEN ROBERT CARL JR	KY	36W	56
GREEN ROBERT CARRELL	ID	04W	55
GREEN ROBERT EARL	TX	40E	74
GREEN ROBERT EARL	MS	10W	24
GREEN ROBERT EUGENE	MA	29W	61
GREEN ROBERT JAMES	NV	19E	58
GREEN ROBERT PAUL	MA	64W	9
GREEN ROBERT WILLIAM	MT	13E	125
GREEN RODNEY R	SD	32W	54
GREEN RONALD FRANK	GA	42W	17
GREEN ROY COLYN	CA	15E	79
GREEN STANLEY NORRIS	GA	38W	26
GREEN STEVEN LYNN	MN	15W	119
GREEN THOMAS FREDERICK	CA	02W	51
GREEN THOMAS HENRY	GA	21W	89
GREEN THOMAS OWEN	MD	03E	117
GREEN TIMOTHY JOSEPH	AR	14W	120
GREEN TIMOTHY LEE	IA	11W	123
GREEN VERNON ANDREW	PA	04W	2
GREEN WALTER JR	MD	28W	10
GREEN WESLEY	OK	31E	29
GREEN WILBUR LEON	TN	25W	22
GREEN WILLIAM HERSCHELL	AR	23W	110
GREEN WILLIE F	OH	27E	48
GREEN WILLIE FRANK	FL	28W	46
GREEN WILLIE JR	AR	11E	39
GREENDYKE GERALD BRUCE	OH	37E	7
GREENE ALLEN JOSEPH	VT	33W	63
GREENE ARTHUR WILLIE	FL	14E	56
GREENE BEN JOHN	IL	56E	24
GREENE BENNY DOYCE	NC	12W	131
GREENE BILLY RAY	TX	54E	34
GREENE BRADFORD BARTON	FL	19E	90
GREENE BRUCE BRIANT	PA	36W	16
GREENE BRUCE GREGORY	PA	13W	23
GREENE CALVIN ARTHUR	NC	32E	22
GREENE CARL MADASON	IL	26E	112
GREENE CHARLES EDWARD	GA	02W	104
GREENE CHARLES RICHARD	NY	09E	113
GREENE CHARLES WILLIAM	OH	17E	31
GREENE DANNY MARVIN	WV	19E	71
GREENE DONALD BRICE	FL	07W	21
GREENE DONALD JOSEPH	MA	50W	30
GREENE EDWARD EUGENE	NC	13E	109
GREENE EDWARD LEONARD	CA	30E	42
GREENE ELLIS DAVID	CO	10W	84
GREENE FREDDY	TN	55W	18
GREENE FREDERICK DAVID	MI	08W	37
GREENE JAMES ETHERIDGE JR	AL	25W	48
GREENE JAMES LEONARD JR	CT	35E	71
GREENE JERRY LANE	NC	16W	125
GREENE JESSIE FLOYD JR	MI	28E	92
GREENE JOE WILLIAM	OH	37E	57
GREENE JOHN EDWARD	GA	02W	114
GREENE JOHN MARVIN	NC	28W	26
GREENE JOHN PRESTON	NJ	03E	127
GREENE JOHN WAYNE	AR	53W	10
GREENE JOSEPH	NY	57E	22
GREENE KENNETH JOHN	NJ	44E	55
GREENE KENNETH LAWRENCE	MA	22E	40
GREENE KEVIN LESLIE	NJ	42W	29
GREENE LAWRENCE DOUGLASS	KY	35E	71
GREENE LLOYD EARLE JR	WV	43W	36
GREENE LLOYD ROLLAND	MO	39W	21
GREENE LLOYD VINCENT	NJ	03E	31
GREENE PAUL HARRISON	OH	05E	96
GREENE PHILIP F	VT	42E	5
GREENE RAYMOND MILLER	MS	12W	97
GREENE RICHARD EDWARD JR	RI	22E	40
GREENE RICHARD HAYWARD	NY	17W	105
GREENE RICHARD HENRY	IL	38W	11
GREENE ROBERT EARL	CA	38W	1
GREENE RONNIE GENE	NC	20W	25
GREENE TERRY WILLARD	NC	04W	126
GREENE WILBUR	SC	04W	114
GREENE WILLIE	GA	26E	108
GREENFIELD GUY EMERY	OR	36E	11
GREENFIELD JOHN ARTHUR	MD	51E	29
GREENFIELD KENNETH EUGENE	WV	30E	62
GREENHALGH LARRY DEE	ID	29W	61
GREENHALGH TERRY LYNN	WA	36W	63
GREENHOUSE RONALD RAPHAEL	MI	06W	91
GREENIDGE MICHAEL RODNEY	NY	47E	22
GREENLAW ALAN HEALD	CA	22W	77
GREENLEAF JOSEPH GALES	MA	02W	136
GREENLEE DUANE THEODORE	OH	10E	39
GREENLEE JAMES EDWARD	OH	18E	108
GREENLEE STEVEN JOSEPH	TX	11W	84
GREENLEY JON ALFRED	ND	04E	56
GREENMAN DREW MARLIN	TX	21W	59
GREENO GERALD THOMAS JR	MT	16W	1
GREENSAGE ROY LEE	TX	25E	83
GREENSPAN RICHARD	NJ	39W	43
GREENSTREET ROBERT LOWELL	CA	03W	55
GREENWALD DENNIS	MI	30E	48
GREENWALD RONALD ALBERT	WA	39E	5
GREENWAY ROGER KENNETH	CA	15W	114
GREENWELL JOSEPH EDWARD	KY	33W	14
GREENWELL WILLIAM LEONARD	TN	39E	60
GREENWOOD BRUCE JOHN	WI	45W	39
GREENWOOD DALE EDWARD	TX	30W	65
GREENWOOD FRANCIS DAVID	IN	32E	72
GREENWOOD GEORGE R W K	HI	29E	24
GREENWOOD JAMES WILLIAM	TX	12W	21
GREENWOOD PAUL JOHN	NY	34E	62
GREENWOOD ROBERT ROY JR	VA	01W	70
GREER CHARLES ROBERT	KS	17E	4
GREER DENNIS DALE	CA	28W	46
GREER EDMOND JUNIOR	OK	57W	9
GREER FRANK MICHAEL	MI	34W	50
GREER HARRY CHARLES	MS	11W	40
GREER LARRY WAYNE	AL	18E	59
GREER LAWRENCE FREDERICK	PA	33W	39
GREER MATTHEW ERNEST	FL	55E	14
GREER MONROE	TX	39W	66
GREER RALPH JERRY	LA	21W	65
GREER ROBERT LEE	CA	01E	54
GREER WADE ANTHONY	TX	16W	34
GREER WAYNE STEVENSON	PA	37E	57
GREESON DAVID CURTIS	FL	16W	42
GREESON JOHN EGBERT	FL	51W	32
GREETAN ROGER WILLIAM	WI	23E	86
GREEVER HAROLD LEE	WV	27W	73
GREGA GEORGE WILLIAM	PA	16W	18
GREGG DANIEL LEE	TN	37W	64
GREGG JOHNNY GLEN	TX	38W	66
GREGG JOSEPH GENE	OH	30E	26
GREGG ROBERT STANLEY	IL	30W	88
GREGO PHILLIP HARRY	IA	10E	29
GREGOIRE DAVID EDWARD	MA	45E	40
GREGOIRE JOHN RICHARD	IL	17E	92
GREGOIRE MILES ROBERT	ME	54W	32
GREGORASH LON PAUL	WI	03W	81
GREGORIUS GEORGE	CA	53E	14
GREGORIUS MICHAEL JON	WI	19W	14
GREGORY ALFRED RAYMOND	CO	20E	84
GREGORY BOB LEROY	OK	33E	67
GREGORY CHARLES CLARK	ID	24E	26
GREGORY CHARLES LESTER	PA	36E	11
GREGORY DAVID	NJ	12E	1
GREGORY DAVID CLARK	MS	14E	73
GREGORY EULAS FAY	FL	45E	63
GREGORY FRANCISCO	CT	26W	52
GREGORY FRANK EDWIN	PA	59W	3
GREGORY GLENARD JAY	IL	26W	15
GREGORY HENRY	OH	39E	71
GREGORY HERBERT LEE III	FL	36E	11
GREGORY JAMES OTTO JR	NC	08E	129
GREGORY JOHN HENRY JR	FL	02W	26
GREGORY MACK EDWARD	CA	20E	59

NAME	STATE	PANEL NO.	LINE NO.
GREGORY PAUL ANTHONY	VA	08W	51
GREGORY PHILIP LEE	MO	34E	18
GREGORY ROBERT ARTHUR	MI	43W	36
GREGORY ROBERT RAYMOND	MO	13E	5
GREGORY SHERMAN WILLIAM	VA	23W	73
GREGORY THOMAS ESTON	NY	57W	26
GREGORY THOMAS JR	MD	23E	36
GREGORY WILLIAM ROBERT	AL	23W	120
GREGOVICH PAUL MICHAEL	OH	23E	75
GREGSON THOMAS ROBERT	MI	30W	75
GREIFE DALE EDWARD	MO	09W	38
GREIGER DONALD LEONARD	WI	15W	17
GREILING DAVID SCOTT	MI	51W	49
GREILING JOHN FREDRICK	NY	10E	83
GREINER DONALD HENRY	NY	39W	64
GREINER GARY JAMES	MT	25W	100
GREINKE NEIL NORMAN	WI	18W	69
GREISEN THOMAS ANDREW	WI	23W	64
GREKELA WILLIAM EINO	MI	55E	13
GRELLA DONALD CARROLL	NE	04E	43
GRELLA PATRICK MARTIN	WV	17W	96
GRENHAM LAWRENCE ALPHONSE	MA	45E	7
GRENIER JOSEPH KENT	MO	07W	37
GRENIER RONALD LOUIS	WI	50W	50
GRENNAY WILLIAM EFREN	MI	35E	71
GRENSBACK THEODORE E JR	IL	20W	39
GRENZEBACH EARL WILFRE JR	NY	19E	95
GRESCH FREDERICK WILLIAM	MA	34W	7
GRESENS JOHN CARL	NY	13E	118
GRESHAM WILBERT JAMES	OK	16E	40
GRESHAM WILLIAM THOMAS JR	MS	20W	86
GRESHAMER LEON G	WI	38E	28
GRESKOWIAK ROBERT	WI	01E	115
GRESSEL JOHN VINCENT	MI	50W	30
GRETENCORD DEAN LEE	KS	27E	15
GRETH ROBERT EUGENE	PA	25W	69
GRETHEN GALEN DEAN	IA	06E	117
GRETTEN HENRY ARTHUR	IA	05E	29
GREVILLE LEONARD GEORGE	CA	21W	74
GREWELL LARRY IRWIN	WA	16W	117
GREY JAMES WILLIAM	CA	04E	17
GREY RODNEY CHARLES	CA	06W	118
GRIBBIN JAMES MICHAEL	CA	12W	13
GRIBBLE RAY NEAL	IN	28E	25
GRIBBLE ROBERT MARSHALL	NC	04W	92
GRIBLER DONALD ROSS	IN	04E	89
GRICE LARRY JAMES	PA	25E	51
GRIEGO CLARENCE	CA	36E	49
GRIEGO ELOY SANTIAGO JR	CO	23E	51
GRIEGO JESUS	NM	52W	39
GRIEGO JOHN FRANK RAY	NM	14E	27
GRIEGO RICHARD EDWARD	NM	28W	81
GRIEME RICHARD JOSEPH	NC	09W	72
GRIENER JAMES G	FL	22W	52
GRIER JIMMY LEE	TX	39W	16
GRIER LAIFELT	NY	26E	78
GRIER RICHARD EUGENE	OH	41E	52
GRIER RONALD EUGENE	NY	66W	7
GRIESER PHILIP LEE	OH	24W	41
GRIEVE MICHAEL A	MI	36E	11
GRIFASI JAMES ANTHONY	NY	12W	46
GRIFFEE THOMAS LYNN	CO	28E	49
GRIFFEY JAMES RAY	IL	04E	59
GRIFFEY TERRENCE HASTINGS	IA	07E	110
GRIFFIN ALLAN GEORGE	PA	15E	74
GRIFFIN ALLEN AVERY	MS	46W	41
GRIFFIN BOBBY RONALD	GA	28E	43
GRIFFIN BRADFORD THOMAS	NY	26E	62
GRIFFIN BRUCE FRANKLIN	OH	07E	96
GRIFFIN CARLTON	GA	10E	127
GRIFFIN CEPHUS JR	TX	48E	16
GRIFFIN CHARLES FARRELL	MI	36W	16
GRIFFIN DALE ANTHONY	AK	44E	46
GRIFFIN DAVID SCOTT	FL	28E	74
GRIFFIN DONALD ORTHEL	MO	16E	101
GRIFFIN DOUGLAS HOLTZ	TX	37E	57
GRIFFIN EUGENE	FL	02W	5
GRIFFIN FRANCIS LEKIRKLAS	SC	36E	49
GRIFFIN FRED ANDREW JR	NC	17W	4
GRIFFIN GARLAND ALEX JR	GA	34E	19
GRIFFIN GARY O'NEAL	MT	24W	84
GRIFFIN GERALD CHARLES	NE	01E	12
GRIFFIN GERALD LEE JR	CA	12W	88
GRIFFIN HALLIA LEON JR	NY	22W	57
GRIFFIN HAROLD DEXTER	NC	21E	13
GRIFFIN JAMES DONALD	GA	10W	124
GRIFFIN JAMES LLOYD	TN	20E	43
GRIFFIN JAMES ROGER	FL	10E	101
GRIFFIN JAMES T JR	TX	46W	2
GRIFFIN JIMMY RICHARD	TN	01E	20
GRIFFIN KEITH D	KS	16E	89
GRIFFIN KENNETH WAYNE	TX	05W	13
GRIFFIN LEANDER	NY	02E	132
GRIFFIN LEVESTER	IL	30E	62
GRIFFIN LOUIS FREDRICK	CA	31W	42
GRIFFIN MARION TRACY	NC	03W	104
GRIFFIN OSCAR LEE	GA	16W	92
GRIFFIN PATRICK JOSEPH	KS	48W	41
GRIFFIN ROBERT	MA	50W	42
GRIFFIN ROBERT ALLEN	TX	21W	60
GRIFFIN ROBERT EUGENE	TN	14W	117
GRIFFIN RODNEY LYNN	MO	11W	85
GRIFFIN RONALD DEVONE	NC	51E	20
GRIFFIN RONALD LEWIS	OH	54W	16
GRIFFIN ROY LEE JR	NC	47E	11
GRIFFIN RUDOLPH WILLIAM	NY	08W	77
GRIFFIN SAMMIE	PA	04E	23
GRIFFIN THEDORE STEVEN	MA	57W	26
GRIFFIN THOMAS B JR	MA	33E	13
GRIFFIN THOMAS DWAIN	NC	09W	73
GRIFFIN WALTER JOE LOUIS	TX	22W	77
GRIFFIN WILLIAM DONALD II	MI	06W	122
GRIFFIS JAMES LARRIAN	FL	36E	49
GRIFFIS JOSEPH E	GA	15E	90
GRIFFIS MICHAEL DANIEL	PA	27W	31
GRIFFIS ROBERT DALE	OH	40E	21
GRIFFIS WILLIAM A III	TX	14W	62
GRIFFIS WILLIAM ARLAND	GA	68W	1
GRIFFITH DALE EUGENE	KY	23W	100
GRIFFITH EDWARD WILSON	AR	25W	48
GRIFFITH ERIC LAWRENCE	LA	06W	101
GRIFFITH JOE EDD	TN	49E	41
GRIFFITH JOHN GARY	MO	44E	29
GRIFFITH JOHN HOWARD	NY	04E	128
GRIFFITH LARRY DONALD	PA	14W	18
GRIFFITH MICHAEL LYNN	OH	45W	51
GRIFFITH MICKEY EUGENE	CA	12W	81
GRIFFITH PERRY WITT	CO	40W	3
GRIFFITH RICHARD OWEN	NV	41W	35
GRIFFITH RICHARD WAYNE	WV	22E	103
GRIFFITH ROBERT ELWIN	TX	30W	23
GRIFFITH ROBERT SMITH	GA	40E	32
GRIFFITH ROGER DALE	WV	33E	36
GRIFFITH THURSTON A JR	NM	01E	82
GRIFFITH TONY LEE	TN	33W	63
GRIFFITH WILLIAM CHAPIN	CA	36W	25
GRIFFITH WILLIAM WILLIS	MN	27W	99
GRIFFITH WILLIE ROGER	VA	20E	28
GRIFFITHS RAYMOND CARSON	CA	08E	130
GRIFFITHS ROBERT BRYNLEY	CA	26E	7
GRIFFY VIRGIL D	OH	03E	117
GRIGGS BRENT IKE	TX	09E	46
GRIGGS EDWARD LOUIS III	MI	31W	2
GRIGGS HARLEY FRANKLIN	SC	51E	39
GRIGGS MICHAEL ALLEN	MD	50W	50
GRIGGS STEVEN THOMAS	CA	08W	85
GRIGSBY BARRY N	CA	39E	60
GRIGSBY JOE WALTER	MO	37E	83
GRIGSBY MARK WELDON	MA	19W	60
GRIJALVA DAVID CENTENO	NM	18E	102
GRIJALVA GERONIMO LOPEZ	AZ	45W	37
GRILLO JOSEPH JOHN JR	CT	60W	9
GRILLO LAWRENCE HUGH	CT	23W	8
GRILLY DAVID A	CA	23W	100
GRIM MALCOLM JONATHAN	NJ	14W	60
GRIMENSTEIN JOHN PAUL JR	PA	30W	3
GRIMES ALVIN	LA	25W	101
GRIMES CARL WAYNE	WI	01E	51
GRIMES GARY DEMPSY	TX	18E	63
GRIMES GARY LYNN	TX	09W	52
GRIMES GARY W		02E	86
GRIMES JOHN LEONARD	VA	10W	124
GRIMES JOHN R	KY	15E	58
GRIMES LLOYD HAROLD II	GA	07W	89
GRIMES MICHAEL	MO	27E	64
GRIMES MICHAEL BRYAN	CA	17E	19
GRIMES RANDOLPH CLINTON	NY	42W	11
GRIMES THOMAS ALLEN	IN	33E	88
GRIMM MICHAEL JOSEPH	NC	09W	127
GRIMMETT JON LESLIE	NC	35E	21
GRIMSHAW DANNY LEE	WA	47W	43
GRIMSLEY LEE ELDRIGE	AL	04W	128
GRIMSTAD SIGARD RICHARD	NJ	63E	10
GRINDOL PHILLIP WAYNE	IL	52E	5
GRINDSTAFF THOMAS JACKSON	TN	29W	99
GRINE PAUL RAY	PA	46W	41
GRINER JAMES GRAY	FL	22W	53
GRINER JOHN ARTHUR	NJ	14W	117
GRINER THOMAS EUGENE	PA	32E	22
GRINNELL GEORGE ALLEN	CA	20W	30
GRINNELL RICHARD RALPH	ME	19W	94
GRINNELL THOMAS D III	VA	10E	64
GRISAFE MICHAEL F JR	CA	23W	86
GRISAFI JOSEPH	PA	01W	80
GRISARD JOHN ROBERT	NJ	06W	70
GRISBY DON LEE	TX	21E	97
GRISBY GARY BERNARD	AZ	55W	27
GRISHAM CHARLES COLE	TN	36E	50
GRISMER EDGAR JOSEPH	KY	45W	62
GRISSETT EDWIN RUSSELL JR	TX	04E	82
GRISSETTE PRELOW	NC	30E	26
GRISSOM GARY L	MO	28E	68
GRISSOM HAROLD GLENN	TN	11W	58
GRISSOM JOHNNY PAUL	AR	30W	89
GRIST WILLIAM ANTHONY	PA	64W	9
GRISWOLD GARY CLIFFORD	CT	28E	1
GRISWOLD SCOTT CRAIG	CA	34W	70
GRITTE ROBERT JOSEPH	MA	16E	16
GRITTS WILLIAM ARCHIE	OK	57W	9
GRITZ TOBY RICHARD	CA	12W	42
GRIX THOMAS E	NJ	31E	98
GRIZZLE CHARLES WENDLE	MO	29E	66
GRIZZLE WENDELL RAY	TX	11E	33
GROAT RICHARD JAMES	MI	42E	5
GROAT WAYNE DOUGLAS	MI	33W	39
GROENE DAVID	IL	37W	50
GROF ROBERT LESTER	MI	04W	115
GROFF DENNIS ALLEN	WI	31W	92
GROFF RONALD HOWARD	PA	22E	61
GROGAN BRYAN EUGENE	NC	02E	27
GROGAN KEVIN DOUGLAS	OR	04W	136
GROH CHARLES DIETER	NY	35W	19
GROHMAN JOHN JOSEPH	NJ	45E	56
GROMPONE JAMES JOHN	NY	35W	42
GRONAU DAVID JAMES	MI	28E	9
GRONBORG MARTIN WAYNE JR	NE	02W	10
GRONEWOLD LARRY MARSHALL	IA	46E	16
GRONOWSKI THEODORE JR	MI	09E	52
GRONSKY DALE ANDRE	OH	12W	81
GROOM ALAN DAVIS	MI	17W	66
GROOM ROBERT ROXBURGH	MD	29E	72
GROOMES MURIEL STANLEY	MD	39W	8
GROOMS CHARLES EARL JR	OH	29W	78
GROOMS JIMMIE LEE	SC	53E	30
GROOMS RICHARD JAMES	GA	45E	11
GROOMS ROBERT LEE	OH	02W	14
GROOMS RONALD KEITH	FL	56W	22
GROOMS WILLIAM DAVID	OH	56W	3
GROOVER JAMES COMPTON	MS	32E	10
GROOVER JOHN WILLIAM O	MI	05E	33
GROOVER RICHARD ANTHONY	FL	06E	25
GROS RONNIE LEE	IL	28E	67
GROSCOST ROBERT MILLARD	OH	16W	4
GROSE THOMAS NEIL	MT	31W	44
GROSHONG ALLEN EBERLY	VA	48E	52
GROSS ALAN HARRY	MI	10W	85
GROSS BILLY MONROE	GA	51W	39
GROSS COLUMBUS VIRGLE	IN	03W	45
GROSS GARY WAYNE	OH	36W	30
GROSS JAMES DAVID	CA	61E	10
GROSS JIMMY RAY	NC	30W	3
GROSS JOHN ALBERT	WI	03W	115
GROSS LARRY MICHAEL	IL	64E	13
GROSS MARK IRWIN	NY	07W	131
GROSS MICHAEL ANTHONY	CA	09W	50
GROSS OLLIE JAMES	OH	26W	32

NAME	STATE	PANEL NO.	LINE NO.
GROSS RICHARD ALBAN	MI	45W	31
GROSS ROBERT HENRY	MI	31E	74
GROSS RODGER THOMAS	IL	22E	77
GROSS STEPHEN RUSSELL	GA	23W	87
GROSS VICTOR MAHLON	NJ	27E	64
GROSS WAYNE WILLIAM	IA	48W	54
GROSSE CHRISTOPHER A JR	TX	46E	54
GROSSHART ROBERT STEVEN	MO	58W	25
GROSSLIN GAILEN CHEEK	OK	26E	92
GROTH DENNIS ARTHUR	MN	40W	3
GROTH STEPHEN JAMES	ND	23E	58
GROTH WADE LAWRENCE	MI	39E	5
GROTH WILLIAM GEORGE	OH	23E	116
GROTHAUS DARYL ROBERT	IN	09W	111
GROTHAUS ROBERT JOHN II	KS	60E	11
GROTHE LEWIS DANIEL	CA	14E	5
GROTTKE EDWIN REYNOLDS JR		17W	77
GROTZKE ALLEN FREDERICK	WI	16W	79
GROUF JACK STEVEN	NY	11W	123
GROVE CORDELL	CA	21W	41
GROVE EARL RUSSELL	MN	18E	9
GROVE KENNETH ARNOLD	MI	16W	28
GROVE KENNETH EDWARD	MD	13E	47
GROVE LOUIS CANCIAN	NJ	35E	73
GROVE NORMAN DOYAL	CA	26E	75
GROVE RICHARD CRAIG	AL	06E	64
GROVE ROBERT WOODROW	WY	01E	92
GROVE STANLEY COLVILLE	PA	39E	60
GROVE STEVEN EUGENE	MO	07W	111
GROVE WALTER BRENNEMAN JR	IL	61W	1
GROVER DANIEL LAWRENCE	MA	07W	22
GROVER GENE DELANO	OH	41W	39
GROVER ROBERT JOHN	MI	16W	28
GROVER THOMAS ROY	NJ	33W	40
GROVES DAVID LIVINGSTONE	WV	45E	11
GROVES DENNIS MICHAEL	KY	29W	53
GROVES FERGUS COLEMAN II	KY	01E	5
GROVES JAMES DOUGLAS	KY	01W	17
GROVES LOWELL ROGER	OH	30W	54
GROVES RONALD LEE	IN	32W	12
GROVES WILLIAM E	WA	31E	12
GROVNER ALLEN JEROME	GA	50W	13
GROW GARY LEE	OH	31E	12
GROW GARY WARREN	MI	28W	72
GROW LA MOINE EUGENE	IN	12E	78
GRUBB DONALD LEE	TN	21W	83
GRUBB EARL GILBERT	NM	19E	127
GRUBB GARY HOWARD	WV	34E	53
GRUBB KENNETH WILLIAM	WA	24W	84
GRUBB PETER ARTHUR	NY	26E	84
GRUBB STEVE FREEMAN	VA	23W	9
GRUBB WILMER NEWLIN	PA	04E	97
GRUBBS GAREY LEE	CA	24W	117
GRUBBS GARY EUGENE	NC	16W	18
GRUBBS GEORGE EDWARD	IN	47E	11
GRUBBS JERRY ROE	MS	51E	7
GRUBBS ROGER WAYNE	VA	43W	46
GRUBE TERRY LEE	IN	11E	118
GRUBER CLEMENT BRADLEY	SC	43E	54
GRUBER FREDERICK LOUIS	CA	37W	16
GRUBER JOHN HENRY	CA	03W	52
GRUBER MARTIN STEVE JR	OH	49W	30
GRUBER MICHAEL ALFRED	WI	03E	127
GRUBER MILTON DARRELL	OH	61W	24
GRUCA PETER ALAN	NJ	16W	109
GRUD THOMAS ANTHONY	IL	32E	58
GRUDZINSKI WILLIAM THOMAS	WI	11E	94
GRUEBER RANDALL ROMAN	NE	19E	81
GRUENWALD MICHAEL JEROME	SD	29W	8
GRUEZKE JAMES A	MI	04E	35
GRUGAN JOSEPH PATRICK	PA	02E	20
GRUHN ROBERT AYERS	NY	25W	101
GRULKE BARRY RICHARD	MI	22W	77
GRUMLING RONALD GARY	PA	15E	117
GRUNBERG RICHARD HENRY	NY	13E	10
GRUNDER ROLAND JOHN	OH	30E	77
GRUNDMAN ROBERT FRANCIS	MN	11E	19
GRUNDY ANTHONY WARREN	OK	53W	35
GRUNDY DALLAS GEORGE	CA	12E	28
GRUNDY JAMES LEROY JR	CA	01W	104
GRUNEWALD BRUCE WALTER	IL	43E	54
GRUNEWALD JEROME E	WI	60W	9
GRUNSTAD STANLEY LLOYD	WA	51W	10
GRUSCZYNSKI EDWARD ROY	WI	19W	112
GRUTSCH JOHN WILBUR JR	MO	57E	22
GRYDER MICHAEL STEVEN	WA	13W	28
GRYZEN GARY M	MI	15W	53
GRZEGOREK JAMES ANDREW	NY	43E	19
GRZESKOWIAK WALDEMAR S	CA	06W	49
GUADAGNO GUY PAUL	RI	16E	59
GUAJARDO HILARIO H	TX	19E	5
GUARALDI THOMAS JOSEPH	CA	20E	8
GUARD MARTIN WILLIAM	CA	52E	29
GUARDADO DANIEL	CA	48E	4
GUARDADO RUDOLPH	CA	30W	3
GUARDINO STEPHEN ANTHONY	PA	34E	86
GUARIENTI RALPH	CA	39W	54
GUARINO RAYMOND BLAISE	CT	17E	51
GUARINO SALVATORE	NJ	11E	2
GUASP GARY ARNALDO	NY	55E	14
GUAY HERVE JOSEPH	ME	61W	12
GUBBELS STANLEY DONALD	NE	28E	43
GUBBINS EUGENE	IL	44E	36
GUCK RALPH STEPHEN	MN	06W	91
GUCOFSKI STEPHEN DOUGLAS	FL	04W	66
GUCWA JOSEPH JOHN	NY	51W	11
GUDE MARVIN JOSEPH	FL	23W	44
GUDEN THOMAS CHARLES	WI	22E	62
GUDISWITZ EUGENE RICHARD	MO	09W	64
GUDLESKE GUSTAVE FRANKLIN	WI	24E	60
GUELIG PAUL JOSEPH	WI	11W	46
GUENETTE PETER MATHEW	NY	62E	18
GUENTHER BERT MARRION JR	CA	06W	62
GUENTHER CARLYLE	MN	55E	14
GUENTHER JOHN CARL JR	CA	21W	32
GUENTHER JOSEPH ELLIS	OH	41W	24
GUENTHER TERRY ELMER	IL	13W	115
GUENTHER THOMAS ANDREW	NJ	13W	11
GUENTHER WILLIAM RICHARD	MI	45W	51
GUENTZEL LARRY RAY	TX	22E	57
GUERETTE ROLAND PHILIPPE	ME	13E	43
GUERIN JOHN PETER	CA	08E	10
GUERIN ROBERT LOUIS	OH	07E	96
GUERIN WALTER THOMAS	IL	05E	11
GUERRA BERT III	OH	17E	104
GUERRA DARIO DAVID	NJ	38W	43
GUERRA GEORGE JR	TX	65E	9
GUERRA JERRY EUGENE	CA	25E	57
GUERRA RAUL ANTONIO	CA	27E	71
GUERRA ROBERT ROCHA	TX	22W	96
GUERRA-HERNANDEZ RENE	CA	33E	67
GUERRERO ANDREW CASTRO	TX	06W	127
GUERRERO FRANK ROBERT	CA	09W	4
GUERRERO JESSE	TX	12E	116
GUERRERO JOSE F JR	CA	14W	22
GUERRERO JOSEPH DONALD	IN	05E	6
GUERRERO PEDRO ROSARIO		10E	47
GUERRERO RICHARD JOSEPH	CA	60E	11
GUERRERO RICHARD JR	TX	25E	101
GUERRERO VICTOR MANUEL	CA	16W	79
GUERRERO VINCENT FEJA	GM	30W	75
GUERRERO WILEY	TX	29E	82
GUERTIN DONALD ALAN	MA	34W	24
GUEST DANIEL	NC	46W	59
GUEST DOUGLAS WILLARD JR	PA	48E	41
GUEST EDWARD ROBERT	PA	25E	38
GUEST GARY RICHARD	MA	24W	116
GUEST JAMES WALKER	PA	40E	40
GUEST RAYMOND CALVIN	CA	44E	59
GUEST ROGER THOMAS	MS	19W	119
GUEVARA ERVELL MADRID	CA	08E	75
GUEVARA IRINEO	CA	35W	70
GUEX BRUCE JOHN	WI	30W	54
GUFFEY JAMES DALE	OK	43E	19
GUGLIELMONI TIMOTHY P	CA	20E	94
GUICHAUD FRANK JOHN	NY	20E	95
GUIDA PAUL ANTHONY	MA	01W	111
GUIDRY MICHAEL JAMES	LA	03W	135
GUILD ELIOT FRANKLIN	NH	34E	86
GUILD LEROY J JR	OK	16E	78
GUILETTE LEONALD GEORGE	WI	07W	126
GUILLAUME NORMAN E JR	KY	12E	82
GUILLEN DAVID LAWRENCE	CA	30W	13
GUILLEN GILBERTO LUIS JR	TX	15E	117
GUILLEN JOHN DAVID	KS	14W	93
GUILLEN PHILLIP O	CA	36E	73
GUILLERMIN LOUIS FULDA	PA	53E	14
GUILLET ANDRE ROLAND	CT	07E	81
GUILLORY BUD AUGUSTINE	LA	16E	40
GUILLORY EARL J	LA	66E	10
GUILLORY EDWARD JOSEPH	LA	22E	6
GUILLORY GERALD JAMES	LA	17W	90
GUILLORY HUBIA JUDE	LA	52E	5
GUILLORY JAMES CLIFTON	CA	04E	41
GUILLORY WENDELL	LA	50E	13
GUILLORY WILLIAM ALLEN	LA	23E	91
GUILMET DANIEL J	WA	04E	23
GUILMETTE DENNIS MICHAEL	MI	25W	70
GUILMETTE JOSEPH JR	MA	22W	58
GUIMOND PAUL DANIEL	MA	11E	122
GUIMOND PAUL GERALD	IL	08W	16
GUIN EDGAR JAMES	NC	26E	102
GUINN ALLAN	OK	14E	80
GUINN FREDDIE RAY	TN	31W	7
GUINN JIMMY HORACE	IL	17E	95
GUINN JOSEPH WADE	TN	05W	9
GUINN ROBERT GEORGE	MI	09W	7
GUIRE JOHN CHARLES	AR	15W	17
GUIST JOHN JOSEPH	OH	20E	15
GUITTAR DONALD HARVEY	MO	31E	75
GUKICH MICHAEL MARTIN	WI	19E	58
GULA PAUL RICHARD	PA	47E	11
GULASH DAVID JOHN	MI	26E	60
GULBRANDSEN ROBERT EIVEND	NY	27W	94
GULBRANTSON DAVID ARLIN	IL	49W	13
GULDAN JOHN ANTHONY	IL	08W	79
GULEY DAVID ANTHONY	NY	49W	40
GULICH DENNIS FRANSIC	MI	41E	21
GULIE JAMES PATRICK	CA	40W	12
GULLA DENNIS JAMES	MI	33W	48
GULLART SAMMY MANUEL	CA	10W	103
GULLEDGE ERNEST PEPPER JR	MS	09E	122
GULLETT GORDON ELDON	TX	07E	111
GULLETT KENNETH RAY	OR	02W	2
GULLEY HOUSTON	MI	21W	45
GULLEY PERCY LEE JR	AL	28W	107
GULLEY RONALD WALTER	IL	02E	112
GULLEY WILLIAM JEFFERY	UT	09W	43
GULLIKSEN HOWARD WAYNE	AK	35E	72
GULLIVER JOHN JOSEPH	NY	22E	83
GULLIXSON RICHARD OWEN	OR	42W	40
GULLUNG JOSEPH FRANK III	LA	48E	27
GULSETH SHELDON LEE	MN	04W	14
GUM EDWARD SHERIDAN	KY	32W	78
GUMBERT ROBERT WILLIAM JR	OH	09W	79
GUMM ROBERT HUGH JR	WV	06W	56
GUMMERE DAVID DEE	CA	07E	9
GUMP TERRY LEWIS	OR	27W	73
GUNDAKER FRANK JOSEPH	NJ	09E	93
GUNDER DENNIS ANTHONY	IA	46W	2
GUNDERSON DAVID CRAIG	IA	11W	101
GUNDERSON GERALD JAMES	MN	46E	34
GUNDERSON GUNDER PETER RI	ND	03E	111
GUNDERSON JAMES JOHN	WI	16W	80
GUNDERSON MELVIN WILLARD	WI	19E	71
GUNDERSON RICKIE NORMAN	MN	32W	59
GUNDERSON THOMAS LA VON	MN	08W	121
GUNDOLF STEVEN DEAN	OH	17E	72
GUNHUS GORDON MARLO	MN	12W	55
GUNN ALAN WENDELL	TX	39E	6
GUNN ALBERT LEONARD	MO	57W	28
GUNN CHARLEY EDWARD	TX	16E	91
GUNN DANIEL MCNEIL	TX	09E	62
GUNN GEORGE BRUCE	NY	29E	72
GUNN TERRY SIDNEY	AL	13E	97
GUNNELL DALE ALAN	NC	26E	10
GUNNELLS WILLIAM ASHLEY	SC	02W	110
GUNNELS MICHAEL DAVID	AL	17W	9
GUNNING LEO BRENT	NY	48E	4
GUNSET WILLIAM FRANCIS	MA	57W	26
GUNSTER DAVID JAMES	NJ	59W	3
GUNTER ALVIN FLYNN	TN	28W	70
GUNTER CALVIN DOUGLAS	VA	03W	94
GUNTER MELVIN WISTER	AL	03E	77
GUNTER WILLIAM ANTHONY JR	LA	25E	83
GUNTER WILLIAM CLAYTON	FL	21E	61

NAME	STATE	PANEL NO.	LINE NO.
GUNTHER CLARENCE M JR	WV	25E	83
GUNTHER JOHN JACOB	FL	44E	43
GUNTHER ROBERT LOUIS	OH	30E	70
GUPTON RICHARD CHARLES	CA	19E	49
GURDCILANI BORIS WALTER	NJ	19W	101
GURLEY THOMAS	AL	23E	94
GURNIAS NICKALAS PEREZ	CA	08W	107
GUROVICH JOHN EDWARD	CT	16W	49
GURR HERMAN LEROY	FL	14E	34
GURTLER CHARLES RONALD	KS	06E	126
GURULE RICHARD ALBERT	NM	40W	19
GURVITZ JEFFERY	IL	42E	8
GURWITZ LEONARD ZACHARY	CA	49W	53
GUSEMAN WILLIAM E III	PA	14E	78
GUSMAN FRED GRABIEL JR	TX	24W	5
GUSTAFSON BRUCE GORDON	WA	15W	53
GUSTAFSON DENNIS RUSSEL	WI	26W	111
GUSTAFSON DONALD LEE	OK	19E	58
GUSTAFSON EDWARD LEE	IL	40W	74
GUSTAFSON JAMES ERNEST	MN	51E	30
GUSTAFSON RANDALL JOHN	NY	39E	33
GUSTIN ANTHONY JOHN	ME	09E	4
GUTEKUNST JOHN THOMAS	PA	12W	30
GUTHRIDGE JOHN HOWARD	PA	18W	7
GUTHRIE ARCHIE LEE	CT	20E	8
GUTHRIE CHARLES LARRY	GA	28W	11
GUTHRIE DANNY EUGENE	GA	48E	27
GUTHRIE DENNIS HAROLD	OK	34W	65
GUTHRIE EDWARD F	OK	54E	9
GUTHRIE FRANK LYNN	TX	19E	117
GUTHRIE HAROLD LEE	NC	01E	11
GUTHRIE ROBERT ELDRIDGE	TN	13W	68
GUTHRIE ROBERT FRED	WY	04E	123
GUTHRIE STEVEN ALLEN	CA	36E	12
GUTHRIE THOMAS LEON	IN	51W	11
GUTIERREZ ALBERT R JR	TX	46W	2
GUTIERREZ ARTURO B	TX	25W	48
GUTIERREZ CHRISTOPHER	MO	08W	35
GUTIERREZ ERISTEO JR	TX	41W	39
GUTIERREZ ERNEST LEMAS	CA	17E	109
GUTIERREZ FERNANDO	TX	52E	29
GUTIERREZ GEORGE JR	TX	02E	71
GUTIERREZ HENRY L JR	MI	33W	31
GUTIERREZ JOE MARIA	CO	40E	5
GUTIERREZ JOSE ANTONIO	TX	04E	103
GUTIERREZ JUAN FEDERICO	NM	23E	70
GUTIERREZ LOUIS SAM	OH	03E	100
GUTIERREZ OSCAR G	MI	44E	17
GUTIERREZ RAUL CAMPOS	TX	21E	13
GUTIERREZ RAUL GRIMALDO	TX	33E	68
GUTIERREZ RAYMOND RAMIREZ	CA	24W	117
GUTIERREZ-OLIVERAS ELVING P	PR	46W	15
GUTIERREZ-VELAZQUEZ JOSE D	PR	44W	46
GUTKE RONALD LAWRENCE	WI	18W	113
GUTLOFF EDWARDO LEOPOLD	NY	17E	51
GUTLOFF PETER EMMANUEL	NY	17W	88
GUTOWSKI WALTER JOSEPH	IL	20W	97
GUTRICK DONALD MAURICE	MD	51E	46
GUTTILLA CHARLES RICHARD	GA	15E	66
GUTTMANN JOHN PETER JR	IL	30W	101
GUY ALLEN EDWARD	IL	46W	29
GUY BENNY ROSS	AL	37W	20
GUY GEORGE ALLEN	CA	19W	60
GUY GEORGE ANDREW	MI	27E	72
GUY LEONARD ALLEN	PA	40W	32
GUY THOMAS EDWARD	PA	18W	58
GUYER ALBERT MARSHALL	KS	17E	126
GUYER RONALD LYNN	AL	07E	108
GUYER WILLIAM HARRIS	OH	04E	108
GUYETT GEORGE ERVIN	IL	57E	24
GUYMON ALAN RUSSELL	CA	48E	16
GUYTON MELVIN	MI	29W	8
GUZMAN JUAN ARAUJO	CA	33E	28
GUZMAN PETER DAVID	CA	14W	74
GUZMAN PHILLIP JR	CA	19W	14
GUZMAN REYNALDO	NM	04E	89
GUZMAN-LUGO EDUARDO	PR	12E	62
GUZMAN-PAGAN JORGE LUIS	PR	34W	83
GUZMAN-RIOS ANTONIO	PR	59E	3
GUZZETTI MICHAEL T JR	MA	09W	95
GUZZO ALFREDO	MI	54W	16
GWALTNEY GERALD WAYNE	VA	31W	2

NAME	STATE	PANEL NO.	LINE NO.
GWINN MICHAEL JAMES	CA	51W	18
GWINN RICHARD ALFRED	FL	17W	10
GYDESEN GREGORY ALLEN	MI	06W	126
GYORE ALLAN RONALD	NY	30W	44
GYULVESZI THEODORE LOUIS	MI	32W	6
HAAG RICHARD HAROLD JR	MI	29W	8
HAAK WILLIAM LEWIS	TN	20W	44
HAAKE DAVID OSCAR	IL	19W	14
HAAKENSEN DAVID ARNOLD	MT	11E	130
HAAKENSON KENNETH WAYNE	WI	44E	40
HAAKENSON ROBERT W JR	NE	01W	84
HAAKINSON WILLIAM H III	CA	11W	21
HAAN DOUGLAS JOHN JR	IL	36W	50
HAARWALDT ERWIN JOHN	NJ	16E	121
HAAS CHARLES GEORGE	FL	14E	10
HAAS FREDERICK WILLIAM	CA	39E	47
HAAS HARRY JAMES	MN	49W	53
HAAS KENNETH DANIEL	WI	24E	81
HAAS LEON FREDERICK	NJ	01W	57
HAAS MAURICE JOHN	WI	45W	6
HAAS RAY IRA	PA	46E	55
HAAS RUSSELL CARL	WI	42E	32
HAAS THOMAS VENCENT	PA	15W	90
HAASE DELBERT WAYNE	IN	28E	35
HABADA TOM	IL	15W	9
HABBLETT EDWARD F JR	PA	10W	61
HABECKER GERALD LLOYD	PA	34W	49
HABEN MERLE WILLIAM	OH	18W	120
HABER CHARLES HARRY JR	NJ	17E	19
HABERLEIN CRAIG	CA	22W	88
HABERMAN DAVID	OH	50E	14
HABERMAN NOLAN DONALD	IL	34E	48
HABETS GREGORY LEE	MT	28W	46
HABUREY EDWARD JAMES	CT	16E	45
HACEK JAMES DAVID	IL	42W	18
HACK BENNY GLEN	TX	03E	113
HACK RONALD GORDON	NY	44W	17
HACKER KURT ERIC	IL	60W	18
HACKER RONALD VENTION	OH	27W	5
HACKER THOMAS EWALD	TX	29W	19
HACKETT CHARLES K JR	CO	11W	51
HACKETT DANIEL HAROLD	FL	22W	97
HACKETT DAVID SPENCER	PA	18E	122
HACKETT HARLEY B III	SC	51W	49
HACKETT JAMES EDWARD	FL	01W	40
HACKETT JAMES FRANCIS JR	WI	14W	74
HACKETT ROBERT E	IN	30E	84
HACKETT WILLIAM CLAYTON	PA	21W	21
HACKETT WILLIAM RALPH JR	IL	28E	82
HACKLEMAN LARRY L	MO	39E	5
HACKLEY LAWRENCE EARL	VA	01E	25
HACKNEY DONNIE LEE	WV	19W	68
HACKNEY RONALD WAYNE	IN	05W	69
HACKNEY TATE TALMAGE III	MD	55W	18
HACKWORTH CHARLES LEHMAN	AR	20W	57
HACKWORTH DWIGHT LEE	TX	16E	17
HADDEN HERBERT MICHAEL	FL	08W	115
HADDEN ROBERT BRUCE	MO	10E	5
HADDICK HAROLD WILLIAM	DE	25E	29
HADDIX DOUGLAS BOYD	OH	09E	122
HADDOCK ARTHUR	OR	51W	39
HADDOCK EDWARD	NJ	35E	54
HADDOCK LOUIS EDWARD JR	NC	11E	36
HADDOX GEORGE HENRY	MS	14E	22
HADLEY GARY PATRICK	MO	45E	1
HADLEY JAMES STANTON JR	IL	54E	7
HADLEY JEROME CECIL	CA	27E	15
HADLEY JOSEPH AUSTIN	CA	37W	26
HADLEY LEO LARRY	KS	48W	12
HADLEY SHERRY JOE	FL	65W	8
HADLEY STEPHEN JAMES	NJ	03W	36
HADLEY STEPHEN WAYNE	IN	55W	4
HADLEY THOMAS JOSEPH	NC	37W	50
HADLEY VERLON	AL	02E	57
HADLEY WILLIAM YANCEY	GA	31E	35
HADNOT RICHARD LEE	TX	18E	79
HADNOTT GARY ANDERSON	TX	07E	124
HADSOCK WILLIAM ALFRED	FL	48W	41
HADZEGA GEORGE STEPHEN	CA	57W	26
HAEFNER DAVID ALLEN	MN	55E	16
HAEFNER DAVID RAYMOND	PA	32E	63
HAEGELE DAVID PETER	ND	33W	85

NAME	STATE	PANEL NO.	LINE NO.
HAEGELE WOLFGANG ALBRECHT	NE	19E	128
HAERLE JEFFREY WILLIAM	MN	59E	22
HAGA JOSEPH CLAYTON	FL	28W	36
HAGAN JOHN ROBERT	GA	25W	11
HAGAN ROBERT ALBERT JR	IN	40W	24
HAGARA LESLIE PAUL	PA	50E	14
HAGE MARK KELLOGG	MI	49W	14
HAGEDORN LAWRENCE RAYMOND	IA	17E	122
HAGEL RICHARD WILLIAM	CA	55E	15
HAGELSTEIN JAMES DAVID	NJ	13W	9
HAGEMAN JOEL THOMAS	KS	04W	40
HAGEMEIER THOMAS VANCE	NV	21W	51
HAGEN CRAIG LOUIS	CA	02E	5
HAGEN JAMES JOSEPH	MO	31E	20
HAGEN JAMES ROBERT	WI	01E	78
HAGEN JEROME ALFRED	MN	14E	27
HAGEN LOREN DOUGLAS	ND	03W	125
HAGEN RONALD JAMES	WI	18W	102
HAGEN THOMAS FRANK	CA	14W	117
HAGER HAROLD EUGENE	NM	33E	57
HAGER JACK LEONARD	OH	22W	21
HAGER ROBERT LEE JR	NC	18W	125
HAGER THOMAS GARY	MI	09W	59
HAGERICH WILLIAM CLYDE	FL	13W	35
HAGERMAN ROBERT WARREN	IL	29E	30
HAGERTY PATRICK MICHAEL	OH	23W	27
HAGERTY WILLIAM THOMAS	MA	30E	43
HAGEY CLARENCE E	WV	07E	81
HAGGARD DARRELL LYNN	AR	36W	50
HAGGARD THOMAS EDWARD	LA	16E	121
HAGGARD WILLIAM ELMER	TN	14W	52
HAGGERTY EDWARD CHARLES	WY	11W	85
HAGIE MICHAEL WADE	IL	23W	110
HAGINS GREY LYNN	PA	22W	33
HAGL EDWARD JOSEPH	MT	44E	47
HAGLAGE ANDREW MARTIN	OH	33W	56
HAGLUND VICTOR MILFORD JR	CO	16W	74
HAGMAN RICHARD HAROLD	NM	01W	26
HAGOOD JOHN ROBERT	NE	16W	13
HAGSTROM RONALD EDWIN	IL	17W	28
HAGUE GERALD CHARLES	WI	20E	59
HAGY JOSEPH ROBERT JR	KY	17W	112
HAHN BRUCE EDWARD	MI	11W	112
HAHN DENNIS FRANCIS	IL	40E	6
HAHN GARY GORDON	CA	31E	46
HAHN HARLAN LESLIE	CA	31W	35
HAHN JEFFREY CHARLES	NJ	27E	89
HAHN LEON HENRY JR	PA	61E	10
HAHN MICHAEL DUANE	IA	48W	42
HAHN PAUL EDWARD	CA	25E	33
HAHN RAYMOND GEORGE JR	OH	21E	120
HAHNER GEORGE LAWRENCE JR	IL	25E	77
HAIDER JAMES FRANCIS	SD	23W	120
HAIDER JAMES MICHAEL	MN	23E	59
HAIDER MICHAEL EDWARD	MN	18W	94
HAIFLEY MICHAEL FIRESTONE	OH	01W	107
HAIGHT STEPHEN HAROLD	NY	10W	5
HAIGLER CECIL MORRIS	GA	53E	14
HAIL WILLIAM WARREN	CA	02E	47
HAILE DONALD JACK	ID	38E	50
HAILE RICHARD GUSTAVE JR	FL	10W	121
HAILEY JERRY LEE	MO	09E	68
HAILEY JOSEPH CARLTON	MO	19E	117
HAILEY MARK STEVEN	NC	08W	85
HAILEY ODDIE C	TX	22E	53
HAIN GEORGE ANTON	IL	06W	16
HAIN ROBERT PAUL	AZ	34E	19
HAINES ADHERENE LOUIS	SC	02E	107
HAINES CRAIG WARD	WV	13W	23
HAINES DENNIS ALLEN	IA	14W	97
HAINES GLENN BRANSON JR	TX	30W	54
HAINES JOHN CHARLES JR	NJ	16E	35
HAINES JOHN LODA	MI	43E	19
HAINES MICHAEL SCOTT	IL	59W	3
HAINES PAUL ALLEN	OH	06E	74
HAINES ROBERT FREDERICK	NH	25E	51
HAINES ROBERT LEE	PA	22E	103
HAINES WILLIAM ALLEN JR	OH	01W	9
HAINING PAUL LINN	CO	08W	46
HAINLEY WILLIAM ROBERT	OH	12W	56
HAINS ANTHONY JOSEPH JR	LA	14W	97
HAIR ROBERT LEE	FL	41E	49

NAME	STATE	PANEL NO.	LINE NO.
HAIRE BENJAMIN WAYNE	GA	24W	59
HAIRE CARSON EARL	LA	04E	66
HAIRSTON CHARLES MCKINLEY	WV	44E	7
HAIRSTON CLIFTON ODELL	NY	14E	80
HAIRSTON JIMMY LEE	DC	51W	49
HAIRSTON JOHNNY MICHAEL	VA	12E	112
HAIRSTON MELVIN LEE	PA	04E	70
HAITHCOX RICHARD ALLEN	NC	10W	57
HAJMAN PETER OSCAR	WI	16W	63
HAKE DAVID TERRANCE	WA	12E	117
HAKE WILBUR O	MI	36W	51
HAKES CLARENCE DEAN	MN	04W	2
HAKES CLIFFORD EDWARD	CA	15E	117
HAKES JAMES DANIEL JR	CO	07E	61
HALBACH BRUCE CHARLES	IA	06W	71
HALBAUER DAVID MICHAEL	MN	02E	122
HALBERT EDWARD JOSEPH	MO	20W	70
HALBERT LEROY ERNEST JR	CA	05W	17
HALBERT PATRICK HENRY	LA	14W	68
HALBOWER HARLOW KENNETH	KS	04E	50
HALCOMB CARLTON BARRY	CO	39E	33
HALE CHARLES CHAPLIN JR	VA	37E	83
HALE HAROLD LELAND	CO	17E	29
HALE HENRY MAURICE STAFFO	TX	33E	8
HALE HOLLIS RAY	GA	36E	67
HALE JOHN DOUGLAS	KY	04W	32
HALE JOHN JR	OH	27W	78
HALE LANNY EARL	TX	38E	29
HALE MICHAEL DAVID	IN	48W	42
HALE PAUL EDWARD	IL	22E	78
HALE RALPH DAVID II	PA	31E	69
HALE ROBERT LAWRENCE	TX	29E	60
HALE TERRELL WILLIAM	TX	49W	36
HALE TERRY ALLEN	TX	06W	37
HALE VICTOR	KS	37W	65
HALE WILLIAM EARL	IN	59W	3
HALE WILLIAM ROBERT	AR	24W	6
HALE WILLIAM THOMAS	TX	41W	45
HALEN JAMES PAUL	NY	15W	82
HALES RAYMON DRAPER	UT	20W	19
HALEY CLIFFORD EUGENE	TX	12W	60
HALEY GARLAND GENE	TX	55E	15
HALEY GARY ROBERT	MI	33W	63
HALEY HARRISON LEROY	CA	66W	7
HALEY JACK WAYNE	OK	46E	6
HALEY JERRY RANKIN	LA	37E	5
HALEY JOHN MATTHEW JR	NJ	25E	77
HALEY PATRICK LAWRENCE	IL	18E	45
HALEY TOMMY WAYNE	OK	19E	106
HALFMAN BLAKE HENRY	WI	39E	71
HALFORD CALVIN DOUGLAS	MS	10E	64
HALFORD CHARLES E	IL	19E	118
HALFORD MICHAEL DEAN	TX	21E	58
HALGRIMSON MARLOYE KEITH	MN	25W	70
HALIBURTON MICHAEL R		08W	93
HALIBURTON NATHANIEL JR	TX	66W	5
HALL ACIE DAVID	TN	04E	7
HALL ADOLPHUS JR	AL	16W	107
HALL ALBERT	OH	06W	88
HALL ALFRED FLOYD	PA	14W	18
HALL ARVEL HUGH	GA	11E	21
HALL BILLIE ALLEN	OK	05E	132
HALL BLUCHER RAY	VA	43E	19
HALL BOYCE LEE	SC	37W	81
HALL BROWNIE	KY	13E	74
HALL BRUCE	TX	32E	72
HALL BYRON ROYCE	AL	21W	112
HALL CHARLES EDWARD	FL	36E	12
HALL CHARLES WAYNE	GA	39W	33
HALL CHARLES WILLIAM JR	TX	37W	65
HALL CHAUNCEY IKE	MO	61W	24
HALL CHESTER GENE	KY	10W	5
HALL CLARENCE	KY	30E	43
HALL CLARENCE JAY	NY	17W	47
HALL CLYDE	WV	06E	128
HALL DAVID CHARLES	PA	34W	36
HALL DAVID COLIN	MA	25E	62
HALL DAVID EMERSON	IN	10E	13
HALL DAVID LEE	IL	12E	4
HALL DAYLE RAYMOND	MI	05W	78
HALL DEAN ELLSWORTH	MI	15W	103
HALL DELBERT EUGENE	IL	11W	58
HALL DENNIS GAYLE	KY	17W	95
HALL DENNIS LEE	NC	22E	78
HALL DONALD	KY	13W	62
HALL DONALD ALLEN JR	MI	07W	92
HALL DONALD DALE	OH	09W	23
HALL DONALD JOE	OK	14E	129
HALL DONALD WILFORD	LA	06E	100
HALL EDWARD SENIOR	ME	16E	52
HALL ELMORE LAWRENCE	GA	17W	50
HALL FRANK JR	TN	15W	81
HALL FREDRICK MERVYN	NC	27W	63
HALL GARY ALBERT	VT	46W	59
HALL GARY C	AR	01W	121
HALL GARY DODDS	UT	42E	64
HALL GARY L	KY	01W	130
HALL GARY NEAL	OK	52E	30
HALL GARY VAN	TN	31W	80
HALL GEORGE MICHAEL	IN	36E	50
HALL GEORGE THOMAS	MO	25W	29
HALL HARLEY HUBERT	WA	01W	112
HALL JACKIE BURL	TX	12E	42
HALL JACKIE WAYNE	GA	34E	42
HALL JAMES ALBERT	OH	02E	33
HALL JAMES BUCKNER	MD	33E	37
HALL JAMES EUGENE	NC	46W	15
HALL JAMES HAYES	FL	37W	11
HALL JAMES HENRY	NY	18W	125
HALL JAMES KENNETH	CA	31W	36
HALL JAMES LUTHER	NC	28W	103
HALL JAMES MICHAEL	KY	35W	15
HALL JAMES OSCAR JR	CA	22W	105
HALL JAMES SHREVE	NC	09E	87
HALL JAMES WAYNE	CA	01W	84
HALL JEFFERSON DAVIS	AL	06E	94
HALL JEFFERY H	MI	56W	34
HALL JERRY RAY	FL	28E	35
HALL JIMMY WILLIAM	SC	21E	67
HALL JOHN DEAN	FL	41E	65
HALL JOHN LOUIS	TN	11E	57
HALL JOHN STANLEY	TX	19W	38
HALL JOHN STERLING	MD	13E	74
HALL JOSEPH LINDSEY	AR	04W	136
HALL KENNETH ROBERT	NH	06E	132
HALL KENNETH WALTER	NH	55W	28
HALL KIMBER LYNN	WA	03W	65
HALL LAVLE JIMMY	AL	14E	88
HALL LEONARD JOHN	CA	28W	51
HALL LEWIS STEVEN	CA	05W	37
HALL LINDY ROLAND	PA	18E	93
HALL MARVIN LOUIS	MS	02W	110
HALL MICHAEL JENNINGS	IN	33E	86
HALL MICHAEL JIM	TX	26E	87
HALL MICHAEL ROBERT	FL	08E	71
HALL MILTON LEE	FL	19E	53
HALL PATRICK LINDSEY	FL	34E	29
HALL PERRY WOODROW AMES	GA	15W	98
HALL PRESTON LEE	TN	14W	71
HALL RICHARD DAVID	CA	43E	44
HALL RICHARD JAMES	NC	43E	12
HALL RICHARD LE ROY	NE	48W	26
HALL RICKEY WAYNE	IN	19W	101
HALL RICKY GENE	IA	24E	67
HALL ROBERT EDWARD	VA	37E	22
HALL ROBERT JAMES	CO	32W	50
HALL ROBERT JOSEPH	IN	15E	105
HALL ROBERT KENNETH	OH	33W	56
HALL RONALD HUGH	AL	03W	94
HALL RONNIE ELMON	IN	06E	56
HALL ROY RAY	OK	04W	123
HALL SAMUEL CHRISTIAN	OH	24W	57
HALL SAYWARD NEWTON JR	ME	01E	106
HALL STEPHEN THOMAS	IN	26W	84
HALL THEODORE CROSSMAN	KY	30W	55
HALL TIMOTHY JOHN	WA	31W	36
HALL VAUGHN O'NEIL	DE	24W	84
HALL VINCENT JOSEPH	LA	15W	36
HALL WALTER LOUIS	ME	02E	5
HALL WALTER RAY	CA	04W	66
HALL WARREN STUART	MN	14W	40
HALL WILLIAM GARDINER	MI	46E	6
HALL WILLIAM GARY	TN	30E	101
HALL WILLIAM JR	PA	18W	113
HALL WILLIE LEE JR	NY	36W	2
HALL WILLIS R	NE	44E	17
HALL WORLEY WAYNE	TN	17E	57
HALLADAY JOHN ANTHONY	NJ	18W	82
HALLAM DURWOOD MICHAEL	TX	26E	35
HALLAS JOSEPH MICHAEL	OH	24E	117
HALLBERG CARL RAYMOND	WI	20E	28
HALLBERG ROGER C	CA	17E	35
HALLENBECK TED B	VA	01W	115
HALLER LEROY CLAYTON	PA	62W	10
HALLETT ROBERT J	MA	33E	8
HALLEY RUSSELL LOUIS	IA	12E	100
HALLEY WILSON FITZGERALD	IN	38W	74
HALLIDAY GARY DEAN	CA	04W	77
HALLMAN PAUL TRUVILLE	GA	37E	22
HALLOCK DOUGLAS PAUL	NY	18E	122
HALLOCK WILBUR LEWIS J JR	FL	56W	34
HALLOW DONALD WILLIAM	PA	31W	2
HALLOWELL ALBERT GEORGE	MI	11E	79
HALLOWS DANIEL JOHN	NY	09W	83
HALLSTROM CHARLES MAURY	SD	07W	89
HALMAN JOHN HENRY JR	OH	65E	9
HALPENNY JERRY LEE	WV	41W	58
HALPIN DAVID PAUL	NY	42W	35
HALPIN MICHAEL PATRICK	NJ	34E	77
HALPIN RICHARD CONROY	CA	02W	122
HALPIN WILLIAM FRANCIS	IL	11E	87
HALSELL JOHN EDMOND	AR	51W	4
HALSEY JOHN CALVIN	GA	03W	114
HALSEY MacDONALD BROOKE	NJ	20W	30
HALSTEAD BENNY RAY	WV	07W	9
HALSTEAD LEE MICHAEL	MI	42W	41
HALSTEAD MICHAEL CLAY	AR	04E	28
HALSTEAD STEPHEN LLOYD	GA	46E	6
HALSTEAD WAYNE EDWIN	CA	22E	24
HALT ARDON	TX	39W	21
HALVERSON ALVIN LEONARD	WI	14W	121
HALVERSON GARY JOSEPH	WI	44W	25
HALVORSEN DONALD KELCEY	NJ	19E	118
HALVORSON ERNEST JOSEPH	CA	01E	68
HAM GEOFFREY LAWRENCE	PA	22E	78
HAM TERRELL THOMAS	SC	29W	9
HAM WOODROW WILSON JR	NC	05E	103
HAMACHER WILLIAM BERNARD	NJ	65E	11
HAMBLETON BARRY N	OH	02E	88
HAMBLETON HARRY B III	WI	44W	64
HAMBLETON MARK EVAN	HI	07W	72
HAMBLETT ROBERT BRYANT	VA	16W	64
HAMBLIN RICHARD ALAN	OH	26E	102
HAMBLIN RONALD B	AZ	23E	94
HAMBRICK HAROLD MICHAEL	CA	02E	116
HAMBRICK JAMES JR	GA	39W	47
HAMBURG McARTHUR	MS	45E	23
HAMBY CLYDE RANDALL	CA	65E	9
HAMBY JACKIE DWAYNE	AR	20W	65
HAMBY JIMMY WAYNE	MS	64E	14
HAMBY KIRBY LYNN	GA	58W	3
HAMBY LANNY MAYES	GA	17W	77
HAMBY PAUL CHARLES JR	SC	12E	33
HAMEL TEDDY LEON	IN	16W	121
HAMEL WAYNE DOUGLAS	MA	37E	36
HAMES BOBBY JOE	SC	03E	57
HAMES HENRY MC NEAL T JR	OR	37W	46
HAMES LAWRENCE EVERETT	MI	40E	6
HAMET DENNIS JOSEPH	MD	13E	91
HAMIL LOUIS WILLIAM	TX	46E	46
HAMILL WRIGHT BARTWYN	OR	03E	17
HAMILTON AMBERS ANDREW	TX	05W	81
HAMILTON ANDREW LEROY	NY	18E	69
HAMILTON AUGUST FRANKLIN	TX	20W	76
HAMILTON BERT ABNER JR	MO	13W	88
HAMILTON CHARLES GARY	NY	26E	25
HAMILTON CHARLES HENRY	VA	10W	50
HAMILTON CHARLES ODEAN	WA	21W	41
HAMILTON CHARLES RAYMOND	IL	06W	83
HAMILTON DAVID ALLEN	OH	28E	1
HAMILTON DAVID KENNETH	MA	51W	26
HAMILTON DENNIS CLARK	IA	33E	49
HAMILTON DICK DALE	IN	47W	18
HAMILTON DONALD PAUL	AR	22E	70
HAMILTON DONALD PHILIP	DE	32E	22
HAMILTON DOUGLAS BLAKE	MO	18E	77

NAME	STATE	PANEL NO.	LINE NO.
HAMILTON EARLIE C JR	CA	17E	19
HAMILTON EDWARD	FL	07E	71
HAMILTON EDWARD SAMUEL	KY	20W	28
HAMILTON EUGENE DAVID	AL	04E	123
HAMILTON FLOYD WAYNE	OK	07E	105
HAMILTON FOSTER	PA	55E	15
HAMILTON GEORGE BARKER	PA	41W	66
HAMILTON GEORGE KIRTLAND	FL	32W	20
HAMILTON GEORGE W JR	PA	52W	15
HAMILTON GERALD LOUIS	NE	08W	84
HAMILTON GILBERT LEE	CO	36E	73
HAMILTON GLENN ANTHONY	CA	20W	49
HAMILTON JAMES EDWARD	GA	36E	50
HAMILTON JAMES LEON	OK	40W	43
HAMILTON JAMES RICHARD	MI	47W	18
HAMILTON JAMES V	LA	27E	19
HAMILTON JAMES WILLIAM JR	LA	18E	85
HAMILTON JEFFREY GILES	OH	45E	56
HAMILTON JOHN DAVID JR	NY	28W	27
HAMILTON JOHN SMITH	NM	18E	48
HAMILTON JOSEPH THOMAS	PA	03E	32
HAMILTON KYLE STEVENS	VA	04W	86
HAMILTON LARRY EDWARD	OK	37W	50
HAMILTON LEON GONZA JR	DC	54E	8
HAMILTON MARCUS JAMES	OH	07W	16
HAMILTON MARK LELAND	GA	03W	122
HAMILTON MICHAEL EUGENE	MO	61E	10
HAMILTON MICHAEL GEORGE	IN	10E	72
HAMILTON MILBERT WALTER	MN	17W	117
HAMILTON PAUL GEORGE JR	IA	31E	87
HAMILTON PAUL JR	MI	02E	103
HAMILTON RICHARD ELMER	NM	01E	12
HAMILTON RICHARD LENARD	MI	04W	6
HAMILTON ROBERT DAVID	TX	01W	52
HAMILTON ROBERT E LEE	TN	33E	86
HAMILTON ROBERT LEE JR	TX	42W	35
HAMILTON ROBERT RICHARD	OH	42W	40
HAMILTON ROBERT THEODORE	NY	32W	12
HAMILTON ROGER DALE	MD	18E	59
HAMILTON ROLAND CHARLES	CA	20W	34
HAMILTON RONALD JOAQUINE	OH	13W	44
HAMILTON RONALD LLOYD	OH	22E	53
HAMILTON RUSSELL LEE	OH	07E	25
HAMILTON THOMAS SCOTT	KY	32W	38
HAMILTON TIMOTHY MCKEE	IL	62E	5
HAMILTON ULYS FORD	AL	42W	47
HAMILTON VIRGIL VERN	FL	23W	21
HAMILTON WALTER WADE	PA	08W	54
HAMILTON WAYNE DAVID	PA	37W	65
HAMILTON WILLIAM EUGENE	AZ	27E	28
HAMILTON WILLIE CHARLES L	KY	38W	35
HAMILTON WINSTON CLINTON	SC	31E	29
HAMLET BERNARD JR	IN	24W	30
HAMLET JAMES LEWIS	WI	21E	83
HAMLETT BYRON DWAYNE	TN	16E	52
HAMLIN DARRELL L	IA	01W	126
HAMLIN RALPH GERALD JR	MA	03E	118
HAMLIN ROBERT WAYNE	GA	33W	63
HAMLIN WILLIAM LLOYD	TX	22E	54
HAMLIN WILLIAM ROBERT	WA	01E	74
HAMM ADOLPH BRINKMAN JR	NY	43W	62
HAMM DONALD CURTIS	AL	41W	35
HAMM EDDIE DEAN	TN	26E	26
HAMM FRANKLIN ALVIN	AR	06W	71
HAMM GERALD EUGENE BOOTH	AR	40W	76
HAMM HARRY DAVID	MD	48W	42
HAMM JAMES EDWARD	CO	44E	47
HAMM JOHN WILLIAM	KY	09E	7
HAMMAC JOSEPH EARL	AL	21E	112
HAMMACK CAL THOMAS	IN	33W	14
HAMMACK LESLIE TOBIAS	IN	16W	99
HAMMACK ORLA DANIEL	OH	09W	23
HAMMAN LEE THOMAS	CA	29W	78
HAMMAN THOMAS RALPH	FL	01W	43
HAMMAR JAMES LEROY	CA	27E	34
HAMMARSTROM ARTHUR F JR	MI	02E	43
HAMMEL KENNETH DALE	IA	08W	49
HAMMEL RALPH LEWIS	PA	43E	44
HAMMER BILLY GENE	AL	02E	9
HAMMER RICHARD JOSEPH	MN	30E	2
HAMMER ROBERT RALPH	CA	60E	11
HAMMER ROBERT WAYNE	OK	62E	18
HAMMER WILLIAM JOHN	NY	04W	44
HAMMERBECK EDWARD COX	VA	18W	4
HAMMERSCHLAG WALTER LUDWI	NY	13E	21
HAMMERSLA JAMES RUSSELL	MD	36W	35
HAMMERSTROM RONALD ROY	MN	31E	56
HAMMETT DAVID A	IL	06E	100
HAMMETT RICHARD LEE	CA	38W	74
HAMMOCK JERRY WENDELL	TN	62E	5
HAMMON GERALD EDMUND JR	NY	41W	14
HAMMOND BILLY JOE	GA	02W	119
HAMMOND CAREY JR	GA	25E	101
HAMMOND CHARLES WELDON	MI	58W	13
HAMMOND DENNIS WAYNE	MI	38E	29
HAMMOND EARL NEWSOM	TX	16E	122
HAMMOND FRANK DALE	NV	14W	60
HAMMOND HERBERT LEE	GA	51E	30
HAMMOND JACK MICHAEL	WA	28E	35
HAMMOND JULIAN DICKIE JR	MS	11E	110
HAMMOND KEITH TAIT	PA	25W	5
HAMMOND KENNETH JOE	CA	03E	107
HAMMOND LAWRENCE CLAIR	OH	01E	16
HAMMOND LAWRENCE THEODORE	MD	04E	77
HAMMOND LELAND EMANUEL	SC	11E	66
HAMMOND LLOYD MARTIN JR	CA	15W	73
HAMMOND PETE B	IL	18W	82
HAMMOND RICHARD MARK	NY	40E	6
HAMMOND RUSSELL EARL	PA	03E	22
HAMMOND TERRY MICHAEL	MI	02W	6
HAMMOND TIMOTHY ROWLEY	NY	37E	36
HAMMONDS JAMES ROBERT	AL	53E	32
HAMMONDS ROY LEE	TX	15W	124
HAMMONS HERBERT DON	OK	39E	61
HAMMONS JAMES LUTHER	TX	56E	7
HAMMONS PHILIP	KY	20W	35
HAMMONTREE BILLY LEON	LA	21E	4
HAMNER CHARLES	AL	50W	38
HAMNER JOHN ALBERT	AL	15E	25
HAMNER LEON	MS	37E	8
HAMNER MICHAEL KEITH	OH	43W	36
HAMNER THEODORE S III	AL	31W	80
HAMNER WALTER SCOTT	LA	31W	2
HAMPSHIRE ROBERT CLOYCE	OH	50E	28
HAMPTON CHARLES VERNON JR	LA	36E	12
HAMPTON DAVID CONRAD	OK	09E	113
HAMPTON DAVID LEE	IL	44E	36
HAMPTON DELL GENE	MS	08E	80
HAMPTON EDMOND	LA	39E	33
HAMPTON ENOCH	FL	18W	58
HAMPTON FRED LEE	MS	62W	10
HAMPTON FREDERICK JORDAN	FL	43E	20
HAMPTON HENRY GARFIELD	CA	19E	118
HAMPTON HORACE ALVESTER	GA	06E	55
HAMPTON ISAAC DE VAND	LA	52W	43
HAMPTON JOHN EDISON	KY	08E	80
HAMPTON MICHAEL DEWAYNE	AR	21W	8
HAMPTON ORVILLE	KY	24W	95
HAMPTON OTIS JAMES	NY	03E	77
HAMPTON RALPH LAMAR	LA	14W	30
HAMPTON ROBERT POST JR	PA	09W	101
HAMPTON STEVEN AARON	IN	36W	25
HAMPTON WALTER JAMES	TN	13W	117
HAMRICK BENJAMIN NEAL	WV	09E	113
HAMRICK DONALD RALPH	NC	04W	38
HAMRICK EDWARD JOSEPH	WV	14W	26
HAMRICK JAMES MADISON JR	MD	02W	108
HAMRICK KENNETH JAMES	WV	19W	39
HAMSMITH ALLAN FREDRICK	MN	51W	32
HAN CHARLES WILLIAM	MT	38W	17
HANAWALD LEN MARTIN	NM	18W	28
HANBURY DAVID DELANY	CA	27W	108
HANCOCK CHARLES EDWARD	CA	18W	64
HANCOCK EDWARD DEAN	OH	30E	62
HANCOCK EUGENE SCOTT	FL	31W	36
HANCOCK GERALD QUINN	KY	32W	43
HANCOCK JERRY EDWARD	MO	05W	12
HANCOCK JESSE LEROY	WA	04E	109
HANCOCK JOHN ALBERT	NJ	15W	38
HANCOCK JOHN DAVID	TX	37W	65
HANCOCK WILLIAM EDGAR	WV	15E	5
HANCOCK WILLIAM HOWARD II	NE	53E	14
HANCOCK WILLIAM TYLER	GA	48E	27
HAND FRANK EDWARD III	TX	47E	32
HAND LARRY EDWARD	MS	13W	35
HAND WILLIAM HARRY	OH	19W	79
HANDEL LIBERO CHARLES	OH	18W	20
HANDERHAN PAUL WAYNE	NJ	11W	50
HANDLEY ANTHONY WILLIAM	AR	38E	29
HANDLEY CRAIG WILLIAM	NY	34E	63
HANDLEY HOWARD BROWN	AL	44W	48
HANDLEY TERENCE ARNOLD	OR	06W	12
HANDLON JERRY LEE	IN	09E	11
HANDLY EDWARD CLARENCE	IN	04E	90
HANDRAHAN EUGENE ALLEN	MN	41W	40
HANDSHUMAKER LLOYD E JR	KS	24W	30
HANDY EDWARD LA MONT	OR	32W	65
HANDY TODD ARTHUR	OH	42E	40
HANDY WALTER ELMER	WY	44E	36
HANEY BOBBY GENE	MI	13W	127
HANEY KEITH EUGENE	OH	03W	11
HANEY PERRY EUGENE	TX	58E	8
HANEY ROBERT ALAN	MN	18W	11
HANEY ROBERT BRUCE JR	IA	11W	91
HANEY THOMAS WILLIAM	MN	10E	5
HANEY WILLIAM DAVID	MI	25E	33
HANEY WILLIAM THOMAS	MI	17W	87
HANEY WILLIAM THOMAS	MO	09W	118
HANGER JACK DENNIS	CA	17E	4
HANIK RAYMOND CONRAD	IL	51W	5
HANIOTES STEVEN MICHAEL	OH	20E	16
HANKAMER GREGORY L	CA	01W	126
HANKERSON JIMMIE	NC	54W	40
HANKINS ALBERT RAY	TN	03W	26
HANKINS BRUCE LYNN	AZ	06W	63
HANKINS GREGORY EUGENE	FL	31W	3
HANKINS JOEL RICHARD	AL	04W	80
HANKINS THOMAS FRED	PA	41W	46
HANKINS THOMAS MAURICE	TN	03W	126
HANKISON TOMMY LEE	FL	59E	22
HANKS DANNY DEAN	LA	13W	78
HANKS ERNEST BEAUEL III	CA	27E	34
HANKS JOSEPH HENRY III	PA	36W	24
HANLAN ALLEN DEWEY	OH	49E	10
HANLEY JOHN JOSEPH	WA	68W	2
HANLEY KEVIN CARROLL	RI	43W	15
HANLEY LARRY JAMES	WA	16W	29
HANLEY RICHARD WILLIS	PA	50W	13
HANLEY TERENCE HIGGINS	ME	33E	11
HANLEY THOMAS JOSEPH	NY	01E	70
HANLIN GARY LEON	MO	45E	49
HANLON GEORGE MARTIN	MA	13E	122
HANLON JAMES PAUL	NJ	31W	80
HANLON MARTIN JOSEPH	PA	05W	11
HANN CHARLES EDWARD	OH	09W	79
HANN DAVID LEE	TN	02W	34
HANN DAVID MICHEL	CA	05E	103
HANN GAROLD ARTHUR	OR	06E	31
HANNA DAVID RUSSELL	OH	18W	28
HANNA DONALD RAY	AZ	52E	6
HANNA ELGIE GEORGE	MI	45E	40
HANNA GARY W	MD	36E	12
HANNA KENNETH	SC	37E	83
HANNA MARVIN JIM	WV	58E	21
HANNA ROBERT	PA	08E	27
HANNA ROCKY WADE	WA	35W	70
HANNA WILLIAM ANTHONY	AR	31W	92
HANNAH BYRON MARK	OH	06W	11
HANNAH CHARLES MITCHELL	WV	56W	3
HANNAH FREDDIE JARREL	KY	39W	21
HANNAH SAMUEL JAMES	OH	59W	22
HANNAMAN ROBERT ALLEN	OH	48W	32
HANNEMAN MICHAEL IRVIN	WA	43W	54
HANNIBAL JAMES EDWARD	CA	34W	84
HANNIGAN JOHN EDWARD III	CA	03E	32
HANNIGAN THOMAS M JR	PA	17E	82
HANNIGAN TIMOTHY CHARLES	NY	49W	23
HANNIGAN UDO	NJ	50E	39
HANNIGAN WILLIAM FRANCIS	NY	12W	39
HANNING DONALD JERRY	MI	01W	71
HANNINGS WILLIAM ELWOOD	PA	59W	3
HANNO MARTIN LARRY	NY	30E	77
HANNON PATRICK JOSEPH	CO	10E	67
HANNON PATRICK KEITH	PA	56W	3
HANNON RICHARD LAMAR	SC	26W	8
HANRAHAN JEROME M JR	IL	18E	122

NAME	STATE	PANEL NO.	LINE NO.
HANRATTY THOMAS MICHAEL	CO	21E	89
HANS NEIL RONALD	PA	03E	12
HANSARD JAMES BURL	TX	40W	24
HANSARD JOHN WILLIAM III	NC	52W	33
HANSBROUGH LYLE CLEVELAND	WI	29W	61
HANSCOM JOHN WILLIAM	MA	16E	2
HANSELMAN CHARLES LEON	MI	34E	19
HANSELMAN ROBERT ALAN	MI	32E	44
HANSELMAN ROBERT LOYD	IN	22W	65
HANSEN BARRY ANDRE	WY	05E	128
HANSEN BERNARD TIMOTHY	MN	58W	9
HANSEN CRAIG HAYES	ID	22W	97
HANSEN DONALD CHARLES JR	IL	28E	1
HANSEN DONALD D	KY	08E	85
HANSEN EDWARD ROBERT	CT	07E	128
HANSEN GERALD STEVEN	WA	49E	2
HANSEN JOHN CURRIE	OR	21W	125
HANSEN JOHN MARK	MO	41W	58
HANSEN LESTER ALAN	CO	19W	32
HANSEN LOWELL C	AL	24E	83
HANSEN LYLE WAYNE	IL	59E	3
HANSEN MARK JOHN	CA	26W	54
HANSEN PETER MYKAL	MA	31E	4
HANSEN PETER RAYMOND JR	MN	37E	57
HANSEN RANDY LEE	ND	27W	24
HANSEN ROBERT GREG	NE	08W	91
HANSEN ROBERT WARREN	ID	25W	39
HANSEN STANLEY RAYMOND	WI	10W	75
HANSEN STEPHEN MICHAEL	WA	40E	40
HANSEN WILLIAM JAMES	CA	53W	26
HANSEY MITCHEL CAREY	ND	36W	21
HANSHAW EDWARD PAUL	NY	14E	100
HANSHEW FRED NEWTON JR	IN	16E	78
HANSLEY TIMOTHY WHARTON	OH	21W	75
HANSON ALAN MORRIS	MN	22E	104
HANSON CLYDE WENDELL	AL	05W	96
HANSON DANNY LEROY	ND	30W	75
HANSON DARRELL WAYNE	MN	09W	1
HANSON DENNIS GORDON	MN	39W	59
HANSON EDWARD MAYNARD	OR	18W	79
HANSON HOWARD EMERSON JR	IA	33E	86
HANSON JACK DELE JR	UT	14W	57
HANSON JAMES RICHARD	MN	11E	25
HANSON JOHNNIE RAY	CT	29W	78
HANSON KENNETH GREGORY	CA	28E	100
HANSON LOWELL RAY	TX	47W	18
HANSON MICHAEL LEROY	IL	54E	8
HANSON ROBERT	NJ	61W	1
HANSON ROBERT TAFT JR	OH	04E	135
HANSON STEPHEN PAUL	CA	21E	46
HANSON STEVEN REED	ND	02W	25
HANSON TERRANCE RANDALL	MN	45W	51
HANSON THOMAS PATTERSON	FL	25E	114
HANSON WILLIAM HENRY	WI	44W	37
HANSSEN WILLIAM DENNIS	MN	59E	21
HANTZ HERMAN EUGENE	IN	61W	24
HANVEY ROBBY DAVID	TX	09W	33
HAO JOSEPH N	HI	01E	72
HAP EDWARD FRANK	IN	09E	46
HAPPEL JERRY LEE	MO	12E	42
HARAH FRANK A	PA	49W	4
HARALDSON DAVID ALAN	CA	20E	74
HARALSON WILLIAM SCOTT	WA	60W	11
HARAN RORY TIMOTHY T	CA	23W	72
HARANO ALLEN HIDEO	CA	37E	57
HARBAUGH ROY ARBEN JR	PA	48W	54
HARBER STEPHEN JAMES	MN	09W	111
HARBERT CHARLES WALTER	MD	59E	4
HARBERT RONALD VINCENT	OK	54W	16
HARBIENKO ANDREW	NJ	32W	6
HARBIN CARL ROSS JR	OH	10E	39
HARBIN GARY LEE	IL	13E	21
HARBIN MONTY LEWIS	WA	05W	131
HARBISON ROY F	WA	05E	117
HARBISON SHERRON EVERETT	MI	55E	15
HARBORD ANTHONY GORDON	CA	33W	1
HARBOT FREDERIC RICHARD	FL	26W	70
HARBOTTLE JAMES LAVERN	AZ	47W	18
HARBOUR DEXTER DUANE	KS	13W	35
HARBOUR THOMAS JAMES	CA	61W	13
HARDEE JOSEPH EDWARD	SC	15W	38
HARDEE JOSEPH ROBERT	CA	14W	107

NAME	STATE	PANEL NO.	LINE NO.
HARDEN DANIEL DAVID	TN	03E	12
HARDEN DONALD LEWIS	OR	58E	8
HARDEN JAMES ARNO	WA	14E	44
HARDEN JOHN MERRILL	IL	05E	103
HARDEN LARRY OWEN	PA	05W	27
HARDEN ROBERT WESLEY JR	GA	03E	32
HARDENBROOK ROBERT HOMER	OR	24E	61
HARDER ERWIN JOHN	MN	26W	78
HARDER STEPHEN	IN	29W	9
HARDESTY EDWIN HOWARD JR	KY	32W	43
HARDESTY MICHAEL OWEN	MD	45W	51
HARDESTY RICHARD LEE	IN	19W	15
HARDESTY ROBERT JOE	IN	13E	84
HARDESTY ROBERT WARREN	CA	45E	2
HARDIE ANTHONY ROY	MO	03E	2
HARDIE CHARLES DAVID	TX	24E	6
HARDIG TERRY NEIL	IL	34W	49
HARDIMAN KEVIN BARRY	MA	32E	93
HARDIMAN LA FRANCIS	NY	29E	89
HARDIMON EARNEST JR	IL	09W	64
HARDIN CURTIS LEVENCE	SC	25W	70
HARDIN DENNIS IVAN	OH	53E	32
HARDIN HAROLD MORRIS	KY	08W	51
HARDIN JAMES RICHARD	TX	13W	33
HARDIN JOHN EDGAR	VA	11E	110
HARDIN KENNETH ALLEN	KY	49E	2
HARDIN PHILLIP RALPH	AR	11W	112
HARDIN RAYMOND HOWARD	DC	20W	80
HARDIN RICHARD ALLEN	KY	20E	60
HARDIN WILLIAM RICHARD	NJ	04E	109
HARDING CHARLES CLIFFORD	MD	15E	11
HARDING DAVID LEE	CA	13W	28
HARDING EVERETTE EUGENE	NC	17E	4
HARDING JOHN CHARLES JR	NC	37W	65
HARDING JOHN H	AR	27E	72
HARDING STEVE ALDMAN	GA	52E	18
HARDING TERRY ALAN	CA	20E	103
HARDING THOMAS FORD	WA	29E	66
HARDING WARREN GUTHRIE JR	CA	41E	65
HARDISON ALLEN CARSON	GA	36E	73
HARDISON CHARLES HERBERT	TN	45W	41
HARDISON OSCAR	NC	33E	37
HARDISON ROBERT SMITH	TN	28W	60
HARDMAN DEAN WILLIAM	UT	07W	57
HARDMAN JAMES ALLEN	CA	39W	36
HARDMEYER LOWELL GEORGE	ND	09W	38
HARDT ROSS ERLE	MN	13W	5
HARDWICK EDWARD MAHLON	CT	22W	89
HARDWICK JIMMY WAYNE	KY	40W	33
HARDWICK ROBERT CUSPERT	GA	10W	32
HARDWICK ROCKNE LAMAR	TX	36W	56
HARDWICK TOMMY	FL	66E	10
HARDWICK WILLIAM HIXSON	TX	12E	115
HARDY ABRAHAM LINCOLN	TX	29E	82
HARDY ARTHUR HANS	MA	02W	114
HARDY BUFORD	KY	30W	102
HARDY CHARLES McRAE	AZ	48W	26
HARDY DAVIS EDWIN	TX	41W	24
HARDY FRANK EARLE	VA	21E	14
HARDY FRED DOUGLAS	CA	13E	21
HARDY HERBERT FRANCIS JR	ME	01E	45
HARDY JERRY RAY	CA	39W	49
HARDY JOHN CHARLES	MO	47E	50
HARDY JOHN KAY JR	CA	27E	95
HARDY JOSEPH EDGAR	OH	16W	117
HARDY KEITH L	UT	18E	4
HARDY LARRY JOSEPH	WA	60E	16
HARDY LINCOLN	AZ	33W	40
HARDY PHILLIP DEAN	NC	22W	21
HARDY ROOSEVELT JR	CT	31W	3
HARDY THOMAS DOUGLAS	MS	40W	19
HARDY WARREN JR	AL	21E	111
HARDY WILLIE CHARLES	MI	43W	15
HARE ANGUS LAYAFETTE	FL	28E	82
HARE DAYTON LEO JR	DC	12E	4
HARE JOHN HENRY	MS	02W	75
HARE JOHN THOMAS	MD	31W	48
HARE MICHAEL JAMES	CA	21E	120
HARE MICHAEL KENNETH	CA	47E	11
HAREFORD BASIL LEE	VA	54W	42
HARFF WILLIAM HENRY JR	WI	52E	37
HARGENS DAVID ALLEN	NE	24W	95

NAME	STATE	PANEL NO.	LINE NO.
HARGER CHARLES F JR	OK	52W	6
HARGER DON R	IA	25E	6
HARGETT JOHN JR	MA	13E	116
HARGIS DANNY WAYNE	TX	23W	21
HARGRAVE JOHN KING	PA	17E	85
HARGRAVE KENNETH LEE	TX	15E	33
HARGRAVE STEPHAN LEE	IL	18W	75
HARGRAVE TRACY WALLACE	NY	46E	17
HARGRAVES MANCE KENNETH	DC	17E	122
HARGRAVES MURVYN EUGENE	CA	08W	53
HARGREAVES JOHN JAMES	OH	14W	4
HARGROVE DALE VERNON	NJ	06W	23
HARGROVE JAMES MABRON	AL	11E	28
HARGROVE JAMES WELDON	TX	11E	87
HARGROVE JOSEPH N	NC	01W	130
HARGROVE LANE KORNEGAY	PA	51E	20
HARGROVE OLIN JR	AL	28E	25
HARGROVE TEDDY EARL	OK	22W	38
HARGROVE WILLIAM EUGENE	TN	25E	114
HARGROVE WILLIAM S	TX	01W	91
HARIG DEAN ALLEN	NE	11W	16
HARING KARL RICHARD	IL	42W	3
HARING WALTER WALTON	PA	15E	44
HARJO KENNETH DEWAYNE	OK	16W	91
HARKANSON JAMES PHILLIP	PA	40E	6
HARKE LARRY ARNOLD	WA	32E	22
HARKER JACK ALBERT JR	UT	22W	1
HARKER ROBERT DALE	IL	25W	7
HARKEY RONALD LYNN	NC	32W	78
HARKINS EDISON AMOS III	IN	08W	69
HARKINS ROBERT CHARLES	TX	28E	67
HARKLESS JAMES ANTHONY	LA	07E	113
HARKNESS THOMAS JONES JR	MI	50W	39
HARLAMERT MICHEAL RAY	MO	47W	9
HARLAN JOHN ALVIN	TN	23E	61
HARLAN RICHARD ELLIOTT	TX	04W	49
HARLAND WAYNE LYNN	TX	53E	32
HARLESS CARL CLARENCE	FL	42E	65
HARLEY DONNIE RAY	IN	23W	1
HARLEY JOHN LEWIS	CA	10W	109
HARLEY LEE DUFFORD	VA	07E	81
HARLEY MICHAEL NATHAN	NY	21E	4
HARLEY ROBERT LEE	MS	01W	72
HARLOW CLARENCE LOUIS	TX	30E	26
HARLOW DAVID HUGH	MS	12W	62
HARLOW JOHN BRAYTON JR	OH	42W	68
HARLOW REX DOUGLAS	KY	21W	38
HARMAN CHARLES DAVID	CO	24E	2
HARMAN CURTIS JOSEPH	MD	21E	121
HARMAN ROBERT HENRY	PA	37W	50
HARMON ALPHONSO LEE	MD	29E	89
HARMON ARTHUR	MS	53W	26
HARMON CAREY DEAN	AZ	52E	19
HARMON CHARLES	MI	06E	47
HARMON DANIEL LEE	AK	21E	34
HARMON DANIEL WILLIAM	WA	09E	68
HARMON DENNIS GUY	PA	06E	112
HARMON DENNIS LEROY	MI	09E	52
HARMON EDEWIN CLEO	AR	13W	20
HARMON FLOYD STEVE	NC	05E	72
HARMON JAMES CRAIG	SD	20W	123
HARMON JAMES EDWARD	GA	19E	59
HARMON JERRY WILSON	AR	08E	2
HARMON LEWIS ANDREW	GA	51E	39
HARMON NORMAN MARK	CA	31W	4
HARMON PAUL OLIVER JR	OH	62W	10
HARMON RAY MELVIN	KY	15E	69
HARMON WAYNE CLARK	CA	20E	43
HARMS FREDERICK W JR	IL	10W	12
HARMS GARY LA MONTE	CA	46W	29
HARMS LLOYD	IA	48W	42
HARMS LOWELL EUGENE	MI	13E	8
HARNDEN JIM LAWRENCE	CA	31E	75
HARNED GARY ALAN	PA	12W	39
HARNED RICHARD DOUGLAS	NY	47W	42
HARNER DAVID IRA	WA	29E	100
HARNER RICHARD EDWARD JR	PA	37E	22
HARNESS ANTHONY GENE	MT	28W	87
HARNESS JAMES WILLIAM	TX	39W	58
HAROULAKIS ANDRE	OH	03E	103
HARP DONALD EUGENE	OH	31E	46
HARP DOUGLAS RAY	IN	48E	17

NAME	STATE	PANEL NO.	LINE NO.
HARP MICHAEL LEE	MD	19W	86
HARP THOMAS ALEXANDER	KY	25E	6
HARP WILLIAM	FL	07W	37
HARPER ALLAN G	GA	28W	60
HARPER BILLY FRANK	MS	32W	20
HARPER BILLY NEAL	IN	13E	98
HARPER CLARENCE EUGENE JR	GA	15W	107
HARPER DENNIS JR	WV	13E	33
HARPER DONALD EUGENE JR	IN	16E	91
HARPER EDWARD BENJAMIN	MS	29E	72
HARPER GEORGE DALE	MO	14W	90
HARPER GREGORY ALEXANDER	MI	64E	14
HARPER HAROLD OWEN	MI	07W	58
HARPER JAMES CECIL JR	GA	25W	101
HARPER JIMMY CHESTER	MO	17E	122
HARPER JOHN CURTIS	MS	43W	46
HARPER JOHN DAVID JR	GA	46E	17
HARPER JOSEPH JAMES	FL	11W	91
HARPER LARRY NEIL	AR	26W	8
HARPER MARVIN	MO	06E	6
HARPER MONTE RAY	CA	22E	13
HARPER RALPH LEWIS	IN	59W	4
HARPER RICHARD EARL	AL	04E	66
HARPER RICHARD K	MA	01E	121
HARPER RICHARD WALKER	NY	36E	12
HARPER ROBERT EDWARD	TX	07W	132
HARPER STEVEN FRANCIS	TN	53W	10
HARPER TERRY L	VA	06E	32
HARPER THOMAS O JR	PA	31E	47
HARPER TIMOTHY VAUGHN	MN	05W	113
HARPER TONY	FL	20W	76
HARPER WILLIAM CLYDE	TN	02E	116
HARPER WILLIAM MICHAEL	MO	26E	84
HARPER WILLIE JR	MS	09E	11
HARR GERRY ARTHUR	OR	03W	98
HARR MICHAEL EDWIN	TN	27W	87
HARRA LEE HAMILTON	MN	33W	20
HARRELL DON CLAIR	IA	28E	67
HARRELL DONALD AUGUSTUS	AR	48E	17
HARRELL J D	TX	07E	25
HARRELL JAMES ELMORE	IN	17E	68
HARRELL JAMES RANDOLPH	TX	38W	43
HARRELL JOHN REHILL	VA	38W	17
HARRELL LENWOOD THOMAS	CT	55E	15
HARRELL LOVETT LEE	NY	41W	6
HARRELL RAYMOND DALE	VA	14W	84
HARRELL ROGER PARRY	FL	20W	70
HARRELL RONNIE	AL	40E	22
HARRELL SAMUEL	FL	01W	18
HARRELL SAMUEL MORGAN	NC	04W	49
HARRELL STANLEY MOORE	FL	40W	76
HARRELL STEPHEN CARL	CA	21W	52
HARRELL WILLIAM FRANKLIN	GA	37W	74
HARRELSON OLIVER YATES	NC	14W	62
HARRIES JIMMY RIED	WI	55W	34
HARRIGAN GREGORY MICHAEL	MN	26W	39
HARRIGAN LAWRENCE COLBURN	NY	09E	7
HARRILL RANDY ALTON	NC	22E	40
HARRILL RONALD WILLIAM	SC	15E	61
HARRIMAN ALAN BATES	MA	01E	62
HARRIMAN EUGENE HOWARD	NH	32E	51
HARRINGTON CHARLES J	TN	50E	51
HARRINGTON CLIFTON WILLIA	NC	03E	32
HARRINGTON FREDERICK E JR	MA	40W	18
HARRINGTON GEORGE M	CO	17E	114
HARRINGTON HUGH LEE	AR	52W	6
HARRINGTON IRIS HILTON	LA	23W	37
HARRINGTON JAMES A JR	NY	46E	55
HARRINGTON JOHN CHARLES	MI	60W	10
HARRINGTON JOHN DANIEL	MA	16W	57
HARRINGTON JOHN DEE	AZ	33W	57
HARRINGTON JOHN MILTON	NC	10E	118
HARRINGTON KYLE TURNER	PA	11E	61
HARRINGTON PATRICK JAMES	FL	53E	27
HARRINGTON PAUL VINCENT	MS	17E	98
HARRINGTON TIMOTHY MICHAE	CA	33W	63
HARRINGTON WILLIAM FREDER	ME	38E	32
HARRIS ABRAHAM	SC	27E	100
HARRIS ALLAN LYNN	CA	02W	5
HARRIS BENJAMIN	AL	23W	64
HARRIS BENJAMIN HARRY	PA	12E	37
HARRIS BILLY DEAN	TX	47W	44

NAME	STATE	PANEL NO.	LINE NO.
HARRIS BOBBY GLENN	TX	04W	56
HARRIS BRUCE RANDALL	IN	33E	18
HARRIS BURNIE	IN	07E	81
HARRIS CALVIN	LA	21W	108
HARRIS CARL ALLEN	MI	34E	36
HARRIS CARL COLEMAN	AL	19W	79
HARRIS CARL E	SC	03E	57
HARRIS CHARLES EDWARD	VA	34E	48
HARRIS CHARLES LOUIS	PA	18W	38
HARRIS CHARLES RICKEY	MS	03W	113
HARRIS CLEVELAND SCOTT	AL	42E	6
HARRIS CLINTON EUGENE JR	GA	29E	49
HARRIS CURTIS RAY	NC	24W	6
HARRIS DAVID STANLEY	OH	28W	26
HARRIS DEAN ALLEN	CA	05W	67
HARRIS DENNIS DAY	OR	11E	71
HARRIS DOYLE LEE	MI	21E	67
HARRIS EARL WAYNE	TN	41E	65
HARRIS EDDIE CLAYTON	TX	39E	21
HARRIS EDGAR	GA	09W	95
HARRIS EDWARD JAMES JR	OH	34E	12
HARRIS EDWARD LAWRENCE	MI	02W	10
HARRIS EDWARD LEON	AL	49E	31
HARRIS EDWARD LEWIS	MN	30W	3
HARRIS EDWARD LOUIS	PA	09E	11
HARRIS ELTON ODIS	TX	08E	60
HARRIS ERVIN ELLIS	OH	37W	6
HARRIS EUGENE	NC	51E	20
HARRIS FRANK CAY	AL	49W	40
HARRIS GARY BLUITT	AL	47E	32
HARRIS GEORGE WILLIAM	CT	20E	116
HARRIS GLENN ALVIN	IL	15E	69
HARRIS GRADY HERSHALL	FL	49W	30
HARRIS GREGORY JOHN	OH	08E	42
HARRIS HAL	MI	18W	82
HARRIS HARLIN JR	FL	09E	97
HARRIS HAROLD LEE	NC	11E	94
HARRIS HAROLD RAY	MO	12W	25
HARRIS HARRY JAMES	IL	37W	46
HARRIS HARRY KENDALL JR	PA	03W	115
HARRIS HARVEY C	WA	14E	5
HARRIS HARVEY JR	IL	35E	46
HARRIS ISAAC	GA	44W	37
HARRIS JACK HAROLD	WI	11E	111
HARRIS JACK JR	VA	18W	95
HARRIS JACK M	CA	18E	26
HARRIS JACK MARSTON	CA	19E	127
HARRIS JACKIE LOUIS	VA	16E	3
HARRIS JAMES BRADDOCK	MO	03W	8
HARRIS JAMES CRAIG	IN	05W	71
HARRIS JAMES FRANKLIN	OH	13E	63
HARRIS JAMES LARRY	GA	24W	84
HARRIS JAMES LOUIS	MD	68W	2
HARRIS JAMES RONALD	AR	46W	41
HARRIS JAMES THOMAS	GA	13E	63
HARRIS JAMES WALDEN JR	OH	51W	5
HARRIS JEFFREY LYNDOL	MD	01W	18
HARRIS JERRY BRUCE	NC	05E	55
HARRIS JERRY LEE	AL	42W	41
HARRIS JESSE LEE	WA	12E	88
HARRIS JESSE LEE	IL	23E	81
HARRIS JESSIE EARL	IL	36E	13
HARRIS JIMMY	KY	03E	78
HARRIS JIMMY LEO	KY	46W	49
HARRIS JOHN CARLOS	TN	02E	42
HARRIS JOHN HENRY JR	NE	20W	57
HARRIS JOHN JAMES	KS	45E	11
HARRIS JOHN LEE JR	MD	26E	105
HARRIS JOHN OLIVER	NY	17E	4
HARRIS JOHNNIE DARRIEL	NC	46E	34
HARRIS JOSEPH RANDAL	KY	16W	117
HARRIS JOSEPH RICHARD	FL	02W	133
HARRIS KENNETH RAY	KY	22W	40
HARRIS KENNETH WARD	KY	29E	58
HARRIS LANTIE LAWRENCE JR	NJ	41W	46
HARRIS LARRY CORNELIOUS	VA	15E	117
HARRIS LARRY RAY	TN	33W	14
HARRIS LAWRENCE HUBERT	MN	11E	76
HARRIS LEE RUSSELL	MO	34W	24
HARRIS LESLIE EARL JR	TN	55E	16
HARRIS LEWIS CRAIG	MT	29W	9
HARRIS LYNN ARDEN	IN	13E	125

NAME	STATE	PANEL NO.	LINE NO.
HARRIS MARVIN	GA	08E	100
HARRIS MATTHEW N JR	PA	01E	126
HARRIS MAX GILBERT	TX	10E	64
HARRIS MICHAEL LEO	CA	04W	67
HARRIS MICHAEL LEROY	IN	16W	18
HARRIS MICHAEL PAUL	IL	45E	63
HARRIS MICHAEL R JR	KY	24E	3
HARRIS MICHAEL STEVENS	MO	04E	4
HARRIS NATHANIEL	AL	28E	36
HARRIS NED HENRY	TX	09W	127
HARRIS NOEL AUSTIN JR	AR	12W	33
HARRIS PATRICK JAMES	IL	05E	46
HARRIS PAUL WINIFORD	OH	16E	72
HARRIS PERRY LEE	GA	14E	95
HARRIS PHILIP ANTHONY	MI	12W	112
HARRIS PRENTISS JR	IL	23W	27
HARRIS RANDALL LYNN	AR	05W	88
HARRIS REUBEN BEAUMONT	OH	06E	106
HARRIS RICHARD FLAMOND	MS	37W	56
HARRIS RICKEY ELTON	OH	20W	95
HARRIS ROBERT DUANE	IA	16W	29
HARRIS ROBERT EARL	CA	57E	23
HARRIS ROBERT ERNEST	IA	12E	47
HARRIS ROBERT EUGENE	KY	65E	10
HARRIS ROBERT GEORGE	MA	49E	32
HARRIS ROBERT JOHN	MO	27W	17
HARRIS ROBERT LEE	KS	18W	32
HARRIS ROBERT TAYLOR	AR	21E	121
HARRIS ROBERT WILLIAM	IL	43W	69
HARRIS RODNEY CARSWELL	FL	03E	12
HARRIS ROLAND LORENZO	MI	33W	71
HARRIS RONALD LEE	PA	34W	37
HARRIS ROY EDWARD	CT	08W	54
HARRIS ROY GREEN JR	NY	26E	96
HARRIS RUSSELL LEE	UT	32W	14
HARRIS SAMUEL GARY	OH	09E	52
HARRIS STEPHEN WARREN	MO	11W	35
HARRIS STEVE WESTLEL	MD	10E	8
HARRIS TERRENCE L	MI	05W	5
HARRIS THOMAS WYATT	FL	45W	56
HARRIS VERN ALLEN	SD	44W	64
HARRIS WALTER	NJ	10E	124
HARRIS WESLEY HOMER JR	LA	16W	18
HARRIS WILLIAM DEXTER	KY	01W	120
HARRIS WILLIAM LAWRENCE	MI	41E	66
HARRIS WILLIAM LEE	WA	18E	108
HARRIS WILLIAM LEE	TN	54W	10
HARRIS WILLIAM THOMAS	TX	01E	30
HARRIS WILLIAM THOMAS	TN	30W	43
HARRISON ALBERT LEWIS	LA	11W	114
HARRISON BILLY GERALD	TN	14W	43
HARRISON BILLY JOE	TN	10E	33
HARRISON BUFFARD CLIFTON	OK	22W	97
HARRISON CELISTER JR	IL	17E	111
HARRISON CHARLES E JR	NY	08W	54
HARRISON CHARLES FRANCIS	NY	17E	19
HARRISON CHIP RUSSELL	AZ	49E	11
HARRISON CLEOPHIS	AL	29E	15
HARRISON DANA ALAN	IL	49W	23
HARRISON DANIEL WALLACE	VA	09W	1
HARRISON DONALD	NY	13E	5
HARRISON DONALD LEE	GA	40W	53
HARRISON DONALD LEWIS	IN	03E	57
HARRISON DOUGLAS LEE	VA	47E	39
HARRISON EDWARD TERRY JR	CA	26E	70
HARRISON FOSTER EARL	CA	21W	22
HARRISON GEORGE ROBERT	WY	18E	75
HARRISON HARRY TODD	IA	30W	23
HARRISON HERMAN CLYDE JR	NJ	37W	56
HARRISON JAMES RICHARD	CA	30W	89
HARRISON JAMES ROY	TX	25W	70
HARRISON JIMMIE RAY	IL	44E	47
HARRISON JIMMY KEN	KS	16W	13
HARRISON JOHNNY	NY	07E	71
HARRISON JOSEPH	GA	24E	94
HARRISON JOSEPH WAYNE	LA	12E	120
HARRISON LARRY GENE	NC	04W	7
HARRISON LARRY THOMAS	GA	13W	32
HARRISON LONNIE HUGHLEN	GA	22W	13
HARRISON PAUL ALVIN	AR	54E	8
HARRISON PAUL JAMES	CA	07E	96
HARRISON PAUL LEROY	MD	17E	104

NAME	STATE	PANEL NO.	LINE NO.
HARRISON PAUL RAYMOND	OH	58W	25
HARRISON RANDOLPH MONROE	WV	49E	41
HARRISON RICHARD DARRELL	WV	31E	91
HARRISON RICHARD EARL	TN	20E	60
HARRISON RICKY GENE	GA	47W	44
HARRISON ROBERT ALAN	NY	14W	26
HARRISON ROBERT ALLEN	NC	05W	21
HARRISON ROBERT HEERMAN	NY	01W	44
HARRISON ROBERT LOUIS	MA	64E	15
HARRISON RONALD EDWARD	NM	64E	5
HARRISON RONALD EUGENE	OH	07E	81
HARRISON SAMMY RAY	AR	19E	13
HARRISON THEODORE JR	IL	39W	49
HARRISON THOMAS EDWARD	IL	55W	6
HARRISON THOMAS NORMAN	MI	08E	75
HARRISON WALTER CORNEL JR	TN	02W	15
HARRISON WILLIAM H III	VA	01W	77
HARRISON WILLIAM MILAM	TX	33W	74
HARROLD PATRICK KENDAL	KS	15W	27
HARROTT RICHARD LEONARD	TX	60E	23
HARROW DAVID NELSON	OH	21W	93
HARRY CLIFFORD ROBERT	IL	02E	130
HARSANYI JIMMY ROGER	WV	04E	99
HARSCH RODNEY CECIL	OR	02W	2
HARSHBARGER ERIC THOMAS	ID	16W	13
HARSHMAN STEPHEN WARD	OH	22E	103
HARSON EDWARD EARL JR	TX	29E	2
HARSSON JERRY DON	AR	31W	93
HARSTER RAYMOND JAMES	NY	40W	53
HART BENNY EUGENE	TX	04W	105
HART DANIEL LESTER	OR	16W	88
HART DAVID MELDRUM	MD	19E	81
HART DONALD WAYNE	WA	24E	55
HART ERNEST DWIGHT JR	CA	03W	79
HART FRED D	GA	13E	109
HART GREEN LEE	MO	27E	81
HART GREG EUGENE	WA	11E	111
HART JOSEPH BRENDAN	NY	05W	133
HART JOSEPH FELDER	SC	26W	70
HART JOSEPH LESLIE	WY	15E	90
HART JOSEPH LESTER	CA	12W	56
HART LARRY EUGENE	PA	16E	91
HART MELVIN ELLSWORTH	MN	07E	25
HART RANDOLPH GUY JR	LA	04W	11
HART RAYMOND LEONARD	MI	15E	28
HART ROBERT WILLIAM	IL	08W	118
HART RONALD DAVID	WA	15E	54
HART SAMUEL NICHOLAS	IL	30W	24
HART TEDDY MYRLE	LA	22E	66
HART THOMAS TRAMMELL III	FL	01W	99
HART VERNON	GA	03W	132
HART WILLIAM DARRYL	PA	35E	46
HART WILLIAM EDMOND LEE	TN	30W	55
HART WILLIAM JOSEPH JR	KY	25E	57
HARTEAU JAMES PETER	WI	06E	89
HARTENHOFF DUANE LELAND	GA	24W	42
HARTER DENNIS MICHAEL	WI	20W	91
HARTER FRANCIS WILLIAM	IN	06W	48
HARTER JAMES WILSON	MI	25W	70
HARTER ROBERT LOUIS	FL	30W	13
HARTER WILLIAM AARON	IN	39E	5
HARTGEN WILLIAM CLAYTON	PA	24E	27
HARTIGAN LARRY ANTHONY	IL	31W	3
HARTKEMEYER JOHN RAYMOND	OH	36W	35
HARTL JOSEPH MICHAEL	IL	10W	79
HARTLAGE JOHN PETER III	MA	43E	54
HARTLAND CHARLES LEE	CA	10E	76
HARTLEY CHRISTOPHER ROBER	MA	61W	19
HARTLEY DAVID WILLIAM	OH	07E	30
HARTLEY JOHN THOMAS	NY	46W	49
HARTLEY ROBERT CARL	OH	51W	5
HARTLEY ROBERT JOSEPH	MA	64E	7
HARTLEY WILLIAM LEE	TN	10E	30
HARTMAN BENJAMIN C JR	TN	43W	36
HARTMAN BRUCE BRADLEY	WI	35W	60
HARTMAN DARRELL ELMER	SD	25W	49
HARTMAN DONALD OWEN	MO	22W	1
HARTMAN EUGENE WINFIELD	MD	45W	52
HARTMAN FRED ANDREW JR	IL	26W	45
HARTMAN GARY RICHARD	NY	18E	59
HARTMAN HENRY WILBURN	TX	36E	13
HARTMAN HOWARD JOHN	MI	46W	60
HARTMAN JOHN WILLIAM	CA	31E	12
HARTMAN MARVIN LEO	WA	37W	66
HARTMAN NICHOLAS MARK	CA	12E	83
HARTMAN RICHARD DANNER	NJ	23E	86
HARTMAN ROBERT GLENN	CA	17W	22
HARTMAN THOMAS JOSEPH	PA	16W	93
HARTMAN TIMOTHY JAMES	TX	25E	101
HARTMAN VERNON LYNN JR	VA	27E	88
HARTMAN WILLIAM TAYLOR	CA	34E	86
HARTNELL RICHARD MIGUEL	CA	09E	90
HARTNESS AARON	TX	56E	24
HARTNESS DONALD HARRY	MI	59W	26
HARTNESS GREGG	TX	38W	66
HARTNESS ROGER DALE	OK	08W	7
HARTNETT MICHAEL GERALD	MA	18E	102
HARTNEY JAMES CUTHBERT	FL	33E	48
HARTOGH DAVID MICHAEL	IA	18W	54
HARTPENCE DENNIS RAY	OH	50E	48
HARTRY OTIS LAMONT	MI	48W	26
HARTSFIELD BILLY JACOB	FL	12W	48
HARTSOCK LONNIE D	IA	09E	88
HARTSOCK ROBERT WILLARD	MD	31W	3
HARTSOE DAVID EARL	PA	20E	60
HARTSON STANLEY GERALD	FL	01E	6
HARTSUFF LEO FRANCIS	MI	18W	54
HARTUNG CHARLES LEONARD	MN	14W	4
HARTUNG THOMAS EDWARD	IL	05E	72
HARTWELL HAROLD JAMES	LA	12W	42
HARTWELL PATRICK ALAN	IN	09W	13
HARTWELL ROBERT ALLEN	NY	30E	15
HARTWELL WILLIAM RAYMOND	IN	34E	19
HARTWICK BILLY WAYNE	AR	05W	33
HARTWICK FLOYD WAYNE JR	MO	23E	75
HARTY DAVID LEWIS	CA	52E	18
HARTY THOMAS JOHN	WA	14E	35
HARTZ JOSEPH EDWARD	NY	43E	20
HARTZEL GERALD LESTER	PA	11W	27
HARTZELL DONALD F JR	PA	13W	59
HARTZELL SAMMY LOWELL	IL	06E	1
HARTZHEIM JOHN FRANCIS	WI	41E	49
HARVELL McKINLEY H JR	VA	06W	51
HARVELL RICHARD KENEFICK	NH	27E	28
HARVEY ALAN DARYL	FL	19W	2
HARVEY CARMEL BERNON JR	IL	22E	30
HARVEY CHARLES EDWARD	IL	06E	100
HARVEY CLEVELAND RAY	VA	06W	67
HARVEY DARNELL	IN	21W	13
HARVEY EUGENE DAVID	VA	22E	57
HARVEY GARY WAYNE	WA	19W	61
HARVEY JACK ROCKWOOD	ME	01W	93
HARVEY JEFFERY ARNOLD	CA	26W	63
HARVEY LARRY DREW	OK	02E	104
HARVEY LARRY WAYNE	KS	02W	118
HARVEY LAWRENCE DANIEL	NE	25W	71
HARVEY MICHAEL ANTHONY	WI	30W	4
HARVEY MICHAEL GAIL	CA	22E	54
HARVEY NEIL EDWARD	CA	15W	67
HARVEY OCTAVIANO MARTINEZ	NM	12E	80
HARVEY PAUL EUGENE	PA	12W	56
HARVEY RANDALL LLOYD	AR	30W	75
HARVEY RAYMOND	IL	24E	117
HARVEY ROBERT GEORGE	IA	49W	40
HARVEY ROBERT LEON	OK	15E	95
HARVEY THOMAS PRESTON	WV	03W	78
HARVILLE LAWRENCE	WV	58E	8
HARVIN JIMMIE LEE	FL	40E	40
HARVIN JIMMIE LEE	SC	39W	40
HARWELL GARY CURTIS	AL	18W	39
HARWELL RONALD EUGENE	GA	07W	33
HARWOOD JAMES ARTHUR	TX	05W	45
HARWOOD WILLIAM PHILLIP	IL	44W	3
HARWORTH ELROY EDWIN	MN	07E	128
HASDORFF DENTON JOSEPH	TX	58W	32
HASELBAUER JOHN IRVINE	NY	38E	29
HASELTON JOHN HERBERT	VT	01W	23
HASENBECK PAUL ALFRED	MO	18E	60
HASENFLUG JAMES MICHAEL	NY	16W	52
HASFORD JOHN LAWRENCE JR	MI	53W	27
HASH JAMES RICHARD	IN	24W	66
HASH JONATHAN PAUL	IN	19W	15
HASHAGEN WILLIAM LOUIS	NJ	04W	24
HASHIN JOSEPH MICHAEL JR	PA	20W	101
HASKELL CHARLES WESLEY	CA	65E	10
HASKELL LLOYD BURTON JR	ME	09E	29
HASKETT EDWARD O DAY	FL	45W	6
HASKINS DONALD DEAN	IA	03E	9
HASKINS HARRY DONALD	OH	07E	8
HASKINS JOHN MERLE	AZ	26E	93
HASKINS MICHAEL WAYNE	CA	36E	50
HASKO RONALD JON	WI	46E	46
HASLAM ALBERT WILLIAM	RI	13W	131
HASLET THOMAS EARL	CA	11W	124
HASLINGER PAUL MICHAEL	OR	08E	47
HASPER CHARLES MARTIN	IA	01E	40
HASS STEPHEN CRAIG	IA	22E	30
HASSELL NORMAN WINSTON	NY	61W	1
HASSELL ULYSSES C	MS	24W	75
HASSELL WILLIAM ROBERT	NC	15W	70
HASSELMAN WILLIAM GEORGE	CA	03W	18
HASSENGER ARDEN KEITH	OR	04E	37
HASSETT JAMES PETER	KS	09W	16
HASSEY PAUL ELIAS	MA	06E	56
HASSLER CHARLES EDWARD JR	VA	15E	91
HASSLER FREDRICK ANDREW	TN	15W	110
HASSLER HARVEY JOE	OR	22W	97
HASTE RODGER DALE	IN	32E	44
HASTINGS ANDREW LALONE	MO	05E	102
HASTINGS BOBBY GENE	AR	30E	43
HASTINGS CARLETON PHILIP	NY	56W	22
HASTINGS DAVID LYNN	DE	20W	14
HASTINGS MICHAEL KENNETH	NV	42E	18
HASTINGS STEVEN MORRIS	CA	50W	44
HASTINGS THOMAS WILLIAM	MI	25W	49
HASTREITER RICHARD JAMES	IN	13E	44
HASTY WILLIAM DONALD	AL	06E	75
HASUIKE SKYLER LANCE	CA	07E	65
HASZ ROBERT LEE	WI	24E	26
HATA GLENN LEE	CA	04W	101
HATADA FRED KAWAILANI MAS	HI	36E	13
HATCH KENNETH NEAL	FL	17W	4
HATCH LARRY G	MN	17E	122
HATCH RICHARD LEE	CA	33E	29
HATCHER ANTHONY DWIGHT	KY	65E	10
HATCHER CARLOS RANDALL	GA	05E	95
HATCHER CHARLES LAVERNE	OR	46E	35
HATCHER CLAYBURN MCGEE	MD	26W	46
HATCHER DAVID LEE	NY	06W	54
HATCHER JAMES LEWIS	WV	06W	57
HATCHER JERRY DEAN	IA	17E	123
HATCHER KENNETH MARVIN	SC	04W	134
HATCHER LARRY DAVIS	VA	49E	22
HATCHER RICHARD ANTHONY	GA	24E	26
HATCHER ROBERT LEE	FL	15W	38
HATCHETT EUREY LEE	IN	08E	124
HATCHETT KYLE HENRY	NY	02E	65
HATFIELD BILLY T	AL	01E	58
HATFIELD BOBBY RAY	MI	40E	22
HATFIELD CHARLES DAVID	FL	09E	74
HATFIELD DRUEY LEE	WV	04W	86
HATFIELD GARY CLARK	NE	16E	122
HATFIELD JACK	OH	23W	73
HATFIELD JIMMY DALE	MO	27E	15
HATFIELD JOHN FREDERICK	OH	26W	90
HATFIELD LARRY DEAN	TX	13E	41
HATFIELD MICHAEL JAMES	MI	12W	33
HATFIELD WOODWARD S JR	TX	11E	74
HATH JAMES STUART	MI	45W	41
HATHAWAY JOHN HOOPER	FL	17W	66
HATHAWAY STEPHEN WORTH	AZ	43E	44
HATHAWAY STEVE	FL	22W	119
HATHAWAY WALTER SAMUEL	FL	26W	111
HATHCOCK LARRY CECIL	NC	18W	120
HATHORN CHARLES LEE JR	MS	27W	31
HATHORNE JAMES COLEMAN JR	KY	39W	62
HATISON JEFFREY STEPHEN	WV	22E	103
HATLE THEODORE MAGNUS	SD	22W	120
HATLESTAD RICHARD L	CA	01E	21
HATLEY EDDIE LEE	CA	28W	47
HATLEY JOEL CLINTON	NC	04W	24
HATTABAUGH PAUL RUSSEL	IN	06E	76
HATTEN GEORGE EDWARD	GA	19E	48
HATTER JEROME GERALD	IL	16W	2
HATTER LARRY RICHARD	NY	05W	116
HATTING WILLIAM THEODORE	IA	15W	82

NAME	STATE	PANEL NO.	LINE NO.
HATTON FRANKLIN DELANO R	TX	39E	21
HATTON JAMES L	IN	11E	64
HATTON RANDOLPH EDWARD		39W	66
HATTON ROBERT WILLIS	OH	12E	67
HATTON RUSSELL ODELL	MI	04E	129
HATTON WILTON NEIL	TX	33W	64
HATTORI MASAKI	CA	45E	63
HATZELL MICHAEL MAXWELL	CA	24W	69
HAUCK JAMES MICHAEL	OH	36E	13
HAUER LESLIE JOHN	MI	30E	15
HAUER ROBERT DOUGLAS	MA	07W	39
HAUF JERRY WAYNE	OH	11E	92
HAUG EARL WARREN	WA	38E	68
HAUG FRED GUNDER	CA	27W	107
HAUG RONALD LEE	KS	13W	5
HAUGABOOK WILLIE CLARENCE	GA	21W	89
HAUGEN ALAN ROBERT	CA	48E	27
HAUGEN EDWARD JOHN	MN	29W	20
HAUGEN WARREN GEORGE JR	NC	38W	26
HAUGER KEVIN JEFFREY	TX	02W	71
HAUGH JAMES CURTIS	IN	46E	46
HAUGHT GARY LEE	WV	18W	102
HAUGHT HOWARD THADDEUS JR	WV	31W	93
HAUKENESS GLENN S JR	WI	22W	89
HAUPERT WILLIAM JOHN	MN	54W	36
HAUPT RONALD JOHN	WI	21W	75
HAUPT WILLIAM HENRY III	NY	35W	4
HAUSCHILDT CHARLES LEE	MN	31E	65
HAUSCHILDT JOHN CHARLES	IL	02E	107
HAUSCHULTZ JERRY LEE	WI	15W	27
HAUSER RAYMOND EDWARD	CA	04W	132
HAUSER ROBERT CHARLES	NJ	11E	8
HAUSER VINCENT VANALSTYNE	CA	31E	47
HAUSERMAN LEONARD STEPHEN	OH	06E	64
HAUSHERR CHARLES RAYMOND	OR	05W	134
HAUSMAN HENRY RICHARD JR	OH	23W	1
HAUSRATH DONALD ARTHUR JR	CA	38E	77
HAUSS JAMES ROBERT	NY	07E	48
HAUSWIRTH GERALD RICHARD	WI	13W	127
HAVARD MICHAEL JOHN	IL	19W	86
HAVAS STEPHEN LAWRENCE	MD	49W	4
HAVEARD DAVID MARSHALL	AL	09W	127
HAVEL DONALD JAMES	TX	04W	99
HAVEL MICHAEL DENNIS	MA	21W	18
HAVEL RICHARD THOMAS	CA	38W	1
HAVEMANN JAMES EDWARD	TX	01E	65
HAVENS ALAN DALE	CO	35W	77
HAVENS DANIEL LEE	IL	32E	86
HAVENS KENNETH GAGE	NY	17W	101
HAVER DALE HARRY	NJ	27W	56
HAVERKAMP AUSTIN WILLIAM	TX	42W	35
HAVERLAND MARK JOSEPH JR	WV	24W	66
HAVERS LARRY RONALD	NY	28E	96
HAVILAND ROY ELBERT	NY	01W	113
HAVLICK JOHN CHARLES	OK	48E	17
HAVLIK RICHARD ALLAN	IA	20W	20
HAVNAER RALPH MILTON	NC	55W	35
HAVRANEK MICHAEL WILLIAM	MT	21E	89
HAWCO RICHARD JOSEPH	NY	14W	68
HAWES JAMES DALE	GA	03E	40
HAWES ROBERT CARLBERN	CA	51E	7
HAWES WAYNE LINDSAY		35W	16
HAWK CHARLES EDWARD	PA	18E	49
HAWK JAMES RICHARD	AL	12W	60
HAWK JEFFREY ALLEN	CA	30E	26
HAWK JESSE VIRGINIUS III	IL	57W	18
HAWK MICHAEL ALLEN	WA	20W	20
HAWK RANDALL LEE	AZ	27W	49
HAWK RAY GLENWOOD	PA	50W	24
HAWKER TOMMY MELVIN	VA	01W	78
HAWKEY LOUIE ELMER	IL	20W	113
HAWKING THOMAS HOWARD	CA	10E	101
HAWKINS ALBERT WILLIAM	OH	62E	5
HAWKINS ANTHONY	PA	17E	62
HAWKINS ARTHUR LEE JR	OH	45E	23
HAWKINS ARTHUR LOREN JR	CA	29E	66
HAWKINS CHARLES E JR	PA	24W	66
HAWKINS DANNIE LEE	AL	10W	117
HAWKINS DEN JUNIOR	NC	57E	4
HAWKINS DON ALBERT	CA	29E	3
HAWKINS DONALD DALE	WA	48W	55
HAWKINS EDGAR LEE	TX	02E	91
HAWKINS FELIX BOYD	VA	22E	83
HAWKINS GARY WAYNE	KY	28E	60
HAWKINS GORDON ABNER	TN	58W	25
HAWKINS HAROLD FREDRICK	MI	22W	77
HAWKINS HENRY B JR	NY	29E	100
HAWKINS JERRY PAVEY	IL	01E	97
HAWKINS JOHN LEE JR	OK	33W	93
HAWKINS JOHN LEWIS JR	OH	10E	8
HAWKINS JOHNNY LEE	VA	15W	125
HAWKINS JONATHON JEFFREY	IN	41W	40
HAWKINS KENNETH JEROME	FL	58W	25
HAWKINS MICKEY LEE	CO	14W	4
HAWKINS NORMAN LEVERN	NY	06E	100
HAWKINS PHILIP III	TX	60E	23
HAWKINS RALLS	GA	12E	100
HAWKINS ROBERT CARROLL	NC	58W	32
HAWKINS ROBERT LEWIS	AZ	13W	42
HAWKINS STARLING G	TX	02W	97
HAWKINS TERRY LEE	OH	21W	118
HAWKINS THOMAS G	AZ	29E	30
HAWKINS WAYNE R	PA	60W	1
HAWKINS WILLIAM EDWARD	KY	10W	103
HAWKINS WILLIAM HENRY	SC	09E	68
HAWKINS WILLIE GEORGE JR	TX	05E	134
HAWKINS WILLIE HOWARD JR	NC	07W	16
HAWKS ROBERT JAMES	IL	25W	23
HAWKS RONNIE LEE	MO	15W	103
HAWLEY DONALD REY	TX	04E	20
HAWLEY JACK ALLEN	OH	12W	117
HAWLEY JOHN HARRISON	IN	18E	14
HAWLEY KENNETH BRUCE	WI	09E	131
HAWLEY KENNETH RAY	TX	12W	81
HAWLEY LAWRENCE CHESTER	FL	33W	85
HAWLEY ORIL WILLIAM	WA	45W	10
HAWLEY PETER SHELDON	MI	07W	126
HAWLEY RICHARD A JR	PA	11W	112
HAWLEY ROGER LEE	OH	28W	70
HAWORTH WILLIAM HARRY	PA	20E	103
HAWRYSHKO DAVID WILLIAM	PA	31W	80
HAWS HOMER HOWARD	IN	50E	4
HAWSEY KENNETH	LA	10E	8
HAWTHORN JOHN EDMON	TX	54E	8
HAWTHORNE ANDREW GEORGE	AL	08W	72
HAWTHORNE GENE	AZ	07E	25
HAWTHORNE JAMES LYNWOOD	VA	57W	18
HAWTHORNE MARVIN DALE	TX	24E	117
HAWTHORNE RICHARD WILLIAM	NY	26E	60
HAWTHORNE WILLIAM ALLEN	KS	30E	43
HAWYER DONALD ROBERT	MI	57W	27
HAY GERALD WAYNE	OH	11W	46
HAY JAMES STEWART	NY	58E	22
HAYASHIDA HERBERT REIJI	MN	50E	48
HAYDEN GLENN MILLER	CA	39E	71
HAYDEN HAROLD RICHARD	VA	66E	10
HAYDEN JOHN JOSEPH JR	MA	16W	105
HAYDEN JOHN LOREN	CA	14E	57
HAYDEN JON JAMES	DE	24E	116
HAYDEN MICHAEL PYM	MI	50E	14
HAYDEN NEIL WILLIAM	CA	24W	42
HAYDEN RALPH PARKER	FL	56E	7
HAYDEN ROBERT ALLEN	WA	68E	2
HAYDEN TROY RAY	VA	46E	6
HAYDEN WILLIAM LYLE	CA	25W	101
HAYDON PAUL DEARING	KY	30W	76
HAYEN EDWARD GARDNER II	CA	01W	57
HAYES ALBERT JUDSON	FL	15E	28
HAYES BILLY CHARLES	NC	37E	83
HAYES BOBBY LEE	KY	15E	3
HAYES BRUCE ROBERT	NY	63W	6
HAYES CHRISTOPHER LYNN	KY	46W	42
HAYES DALE LAMONT	MI	01W	18
HAYES DAN DAVID	CA	48W	26
HAYES DANNY CARLTON	OH	42W	18
HAYES DANNY MARTIN	WV	19E	13
HAYES DAVID ANTHONY	CA	29E	49
HAYES DAVID BARTOW	GA	08W	14
HAYES DENNIS LEO	CA	12W	42
HAYES DONALD RAY	TX	56E	9
HAYES DWIGHT	OR	14W	107
HAYES EARL MARSHALL	NC	28W	36
HAYES FRANCIS JOSEPH JR	NJ	60E	23
HAYES FRED JOE	CA	49E	42
HAYES GARRY LEE	MO	26W	91
HAYES GEORGE E	KS	05E	33
HAYES GEORGE FRANKLIN	KY	44E	26
HAYES HAROLD UTAH	MO	08W	69
HAYES HARRY ELLIS	AL	12W	62
HAYES HILTON JR	NC	41W	24
HAYES IVEY JACKSON	GA	27W	10
HAYES JAMES EDWARD	FL	15W	64
HAYES JAMES JR	LA	11E	119
HAYES JEREMIAH MICHAEL JR	NJ	19W	15
HAYES JESSE BOYD	TN	35W	60
HAYES JOHN COOK	NE	02W	40
HAYES JOHNNY VANCE	AL	27E	15
HAYES JOSEPH D	CA	03W	74
HAYES JOSEPH FRED	NJ	13E	122
HAYES KENNETH FRANCIS	LA	09W	4
HAYES LAWRENCE ALLEN	AL	20W	91
HAYES LEROY ANTHONY	MD	29E	19
HAYES LYLE DENNIS	MN	06W	83
HAYES LYNN CAROL	TN	20E	16
HAYES MICHAEL JOHN JR	NJ	29W	37
HAYES NEIL BURGESS JR	MI	10W	80
HAYES NELSON LLOYD	MI	04E	129
HAYES PATRICK JOHN	WI	15W	13
HAYES PHILLIPS III	LA	41E	21
HAYES QUENTIN	FL	57E	23
HAYES RAY ALLEN	TN	43W	15
HAYES RICHARD EDWARD	MD	30E	90
HAYES ROBERT GARY	NC	35W	65
HAYES ROBERT WAYNE	IN	17W	45
HAYES RONALD MORRIS	WA	20E	74
HAYES THOMAS	NM	36W	81
HAYES THOMAS JAY IV	VA	50E	29
HAYES TIMOTHY LEE	IN	05E	6
HAYES TRISTAN WHITNEY	MA	43W	15
HAYES WAYNE MICHAEL	WI	23E	18
HAYES WAYNE NORMAN	CA	15E	117
HAYES WILLARD FAYETTE	VA	41E	66
HAYES WILLIAM ALLEN	IL	59W	4
HAYES WILLIAM JOHN	NY	35W	21
HAYES WILLIAM THOMAS	NY	19E	14
HAYES WILLIE JAMES	MS	15W	119
HAYLETT LARRY CLARENCE	PA	14E	10
HAYMAN ARCHIE ANDREW	OH	47E	39
HAYMES RICHARD SCOTT	MO	51W	49
HAYNER CLAIRE LOWELL	CA	02E	130
HAYNES ALBERT RANDELL	PA	49W	41
HAYNES BARTON EDWARD	NJ	28E	49
HAYNES BOBBY GENE	TN	18W	46
HAYNES CHARLES F	NY	01W	60
HAYNES CLIFFORD EARL JR	PA	24W	110
HAYNES DENNIS HAROLD	NC	35W	70
HAYNES FREDDIE NEIL	MS	16W	64
HAYNES GARRY DWIGHT	WV	37W	74
HAYNES JAMES EDWARD	IN	30E	78
HAYNES JIMMY LAWRENCE	NY	02W	54
HAYNES JOHN ONA	AZ	24E	27
HAYNES JOHN WALLACE	SC	03W	82
HAYNES MARTIS LEON	TX	09E	113
HAYNES MICHAEL WAYNE	WV	11W	7
HAYNES RICHARD WAYNE	WV	25W	71
HAYNES ROBERT EMMETT	PA	29E	72
HAYNES ROBERT MARION JR	TX	17W	41
HAYNES RON JACKSON	TN	18W	39
HAYNES SIDNEY JR	MO	44W	57
HAYNES VERNON LEE	IA	01E	118
HAYNES WILLIAM THOMAS	OH	04E	129
HAYNIE GALEN EARL	UT	18W	129
HAYNIE ROBERT RAY	MO	63W	16
HAYS CLIFTON WALTER	KS	03E	40
HAYS GALE JACKSON	WV	11E	87
HAYS GEORGE BURNS	IL	21E	97
HAYS JOHN HULSEY	FL	39W	37
HAYS KENNETH DOUGLAS	MI	33W	1
HAYS ROBERT BRADFORD	TX	08W	37
HAYS THOMAS EARL	OK	23W	21
HAYS WAYNE ALLEN	OH	43W	28
HAYS WILLIAM BRIAN	LA	31E	12
HAYSLIP BOBBY VERNON	GA	20E	43
HAYTON BRENT ALLAN	TX	06W	77
HAYWARD ARNOLD COURTNEY	NJ	21W	101
HAYWARD DAVID ROY	LA	04W	67

NAME	STATE	PANEL NO.	LINE NO.
HAYWARD ERNEST	NC	02E	134
HAYWARD GEORGE ERNEST	OH	33W	64
HAYWARD JOHN KENT	FL	36W	35
HAYWARD LEWIS MORRISON	PA	44E	37
HAYWARD PHILLIP BRUCE	NJ	13E	38
HAYWOOD DONALD RAY	KY	25W	19
HAYWOOD GLENNON	LA	15W	90
HAYWOOD JAZREAL LEVITE	KS	43E	6
HAYWOOD MOSES JR	IN	04W	19
HAYWOOD ROGERS LEMANDER	LA	23W	15
HAYWORTH DENNIS TRUMAN	TN	11E	25
HAZARD JAMES JOSEPH	MA	10W	70
HAZEL LOUIS	CA	01W	54
HAZELTON HERMAN	LA	21W	101
HAZELWOOD JOHN EDWARD	KS	64W	12
HAZELWOOD THOMAS GERALD	AR	41E	66
HAZEN PAUL GORDON	MI	11E	3
HAZEN RONALD L	IN	11W	68
HAZLE BRUCE EDWIN	SC	17W	10
HAZLETT ROBERT DALE	IN	52W	43
HAZLEY MELVIN	MO	04W	40
HAZLIP CHARLES EDWARD	IL	40W	54
HAZZARD FRANKLIN GEORGE	MA	20E	28
HAZZARD LOUIS TIMOTHY	OH	34E	7
HEAD BILLY RAY	GA	24W	54
HEAD DAVID FREEMAN	MI	34W	58
HEAD DAVID NEIL	KS	05W	124
HEAD MARVIN JR	AL	34E	29
HEAD NOBLE THOMAS	MO	40W	44
HEADLEY CHARLES PAUL	TN	39E	75
HEADLEY FRANK EBERLY IV	CA	47E	32
HEADLEY JOHN BRYANT	RI	29E	10
HEADRICK VERNON LEON	TN	43W	41
HEADRICK WILLIAM DAVID	MO	55W	6
HEAGGANS THURSTON CONRAD	NC	06W	62
HEAGY JAMES WILLIAM	PA	37W	50
HEAL HENRY ALBERT JR	ME	51E	30
HEAL MICHAEL JOSEPH	CA	15E	118
HEALEY JAMES JAY	IL	12E	13
HEALEY JOHN JOSEPH JR	CT	15W	27
HEALEY ROBERT CHARLES JR	NJ	49E	42
HEALY JOSEPH	NY	31E	29
HEALY LOUIS GLENN	MT	53W	19
HEALY RICHARD JOHN	OH	34E	48
HEALY THOMAS EDWARD	OH	09W	27
HEALY THOMAS MICHAEL	MN	21E	68
HEAPS CHARLES WILLIS	PA	17E	123
HEAPS JOHN WAYNE	IL	44W	56
HEARD EARNEST JR	GA	20W	108
HEARD HOWARD CHARLES	MO	22W	13
HEARD JAMES BENEDICT	MD	13W	62
HEARD JAMES CORNEL	PA	56W	22
HEARD JAMES ROBERT JR	AL	42W	18
HEARD ROBERT LOUIS	AL	41E	21
HEARN KENNETH LEE	IN	19E	118
HEARNE MAURY WILLIAM	CA	16W	5
HEARNS ROGER CHARLES	MI	27E	101
HEARNS WILLIAM VAN	IL	24E	51
HEARON TERRY SHAVON	SC	19E	95
HEARSCH JOHN PATRICK JR	MI	07W	4
HEASLEY EDWARD FRANCIS	PA	03W	34
HEASTER ROY DWIGHT	WV	09E	28
HEASTON DONALD LEROY	CA	10E	30
HEATER DANIEL NEIL	IN	13W	117
HEATER LARRY STEVEN	WV	37W	17
HEATER PAUL LEO	NV	10E	30
HEATH BRIAN CHARLES	FL	22W	97
HEATH CHARLES EDWARD	AL	10E	26
HEATH DOUGLAS RANDOLPH	LA	49E	42
HEATH ISAAC EDWARD	CA	29W	66
HEATH JAMES ROBERT	PA	07E	118
HEATH JOSEPH EMERSON	ME	40W	54
HEATH KENNETH EDWARD	AL	17W	109
HEATH LLOYD LAVERN	IN	19E	14
HEATH MICHAEL FREDERICK	FL	23W	27
HEATH NED ARTHUR	MI	45W	52
HEATH RICHARD FARLEY	TX	12W	132
HEATH RUSSELL JAMES	WA	43W	5
HEATH RUSSELL M	PA	02E	107
HEATHCOTE CLIFFORD S JR	NJ	10E	65
HEATHERLY DARRELL W	TN	21E	61
HEATHERLY GEORGE GLEN	TN	24W	6
HEATON TOMMY CALVIN	GA	27W	100
HEAVER BRIAN TRACY	IL	41W	46
HEAVIN WILLIS RAY	TX	19E	25
HEAVNER LARRY KEITH	NC	19E	107
HEAVRIN MARK THOMAS	IN	07W	70
HEBERT ALTON JOHN	LA	03W	111
HEBERT CALVIN RAYMOND JR	LA	05E	60
HEBERT CARROLL JAMES	LA	12E	129
HEBERT DAVID NELSON	WA	17W	117
HEBERT FREDERICK CONRAD	VA	02W	31
HEBERT JAMES III	LA	23W	1
HEBERT MELVIN DERWARD JR	OR	41W	5
HEBERT ROBERT W	NY	27E	72
HEBERT RODGER DALE	TX	57W	27
HEBERT SYRIAC JR	AR	12W	68
HEBERT YVON ANDRE	NH	14E	44
HEBRON CHARLES EDWARD	TX	36E	13
HECIMOVICH ROBERT ALLEN	IL	13E	122
HECK DAVID WILLIAM	CO	40E	6
HECK NORMAN WALTER JR	MI	01E	74
HECK RICHARD MICHAEL	MO	11E	52
HECK RONALD DAVID	NJ	14W	65
HECKLER FREDRICK MERRIMAN	CA	45W	32
HECKMAN CLARENCE ALVIN	MI	30W	65
HECKMAN LAWRENCE EUGENE	OR	36E	60
HECKWINE PETE GERALD	IL	31W	4
HECTOR GEORGE ANTHONY JR	PA	14W	43
HEDBLUM DAVID ARTHUR	WA	23E	3
HEDDEN HAROLD C JR	TN	24W	42
HEDDEN ROGER DALE	IN	49W	53
HEDEMANN WAYNE HOWARD	HI	10W	32
HEDERMAN PATRICK SHAWN	CA	47W	44
HEDGE BILLY WAYNE	IN	03E	108
HEDGE ROBERT BLANCHARD	MA	41E	38
HEDGECOCK DONALD GENE	IL	16W	38
HEDGER JAMES ROBERT	MI	37E	22
HEDGES DANIEL MACOM	AR	07W	61
HEDGLIN MILES BRADLEY	PA	28W	36
HEDGPATH WILLIAM THOMAS	OH	18E	94
HEDIN GARY ORVILLE	MN	34E	19
HEDLUND PETER BURR	MN	38E	50
HEDSTROM HARVEY NORMAN	MN	24W	31
HEEKIN TERRY GENE	CA	16E	2
HEEMAN GARY LEE	PA	34W	7
HEEN LARRY MICHAEL	WA	05W	5
HEEP WILLIAM ARTHUR	CA	46W	2
HEERDT RANDY LEIGH	NY	18E	102
HEEREN DARREL WAYNE	CA	33E	68
HEERMAN DENNIS RAY	IA	13W	92
HEESACKER VICTOR ROMAN	NE	64E	14
HEETER JAMES RALPH	WV	48W	42
HEETHER JAMES JOSEPH II	MI	10E	118
HEFFERNAN DANIEL JOSEPH	IL	18E	80
HEFFERNAN THOMAS FRANCIS	PA	04E	69
HEFFNER DENNIS WAYNE	IN	48W	26
HEFFNER KEITH DARRELL	PA	04W	17
HEFFNER STEVEN CLINTON	KS	52E	19
HEFFRON JAMES BROOKS	NJ	10E	58
HEFLIN GLENN ELDEN	CA	37W	51
HEFLIN JOHN DARRACOTT	TX	25E	84
HEFNER FRANCIS JOE	CA	65W	9
HEFNER JAMES JOSEPH	NY	48W	55
HEFT NORMAN ANTHONY	IL	10E	30
HEFTY JOHN ELLSWORTH	IN	46E	17
HEGGAN DONALD ERNEST	NJ	51W	19
HEGGEN GREGORY LYNN	CO	40W	76
HEGGEN KEITH RUSSELL	IA	01W	100
HEGLER FLOYD JR	AR	42E	33
HEGLER MOSE JR	AL	32E	72
HEGWOOD WILLIAM DAVID	NC	22W	111
HEIBEL DANIEL JOSEPH	MO	24E	103
HEIDE HENRY NICHOLAS II	FL	15W	4
HEIDEBRECHT DALE ROGER	OK	18W	23
HEIDEMAN THOMAS EDWARD	IL	06W	19
HEIDEN CARL WILLIAM	WI	27E	6
HEIDER ANDREW L	WI	59E	23
HEIDER DONALD GEORGE	WA	33W	26
HEIDER WILLIAM STEPHEN	WI	19W	50
HEIDERICH DANIAL GUY	OK	15W	104
HEIDRICH GREGG WILLIAM	OH	18W	121
HEIFNER EDWARD WILLIAM	OH	35E	32
HEIFNER KENNETH RICHARD	OH	31W	3
HEIGHTLAND ORVILLE W JR	OH	40E	7
HEIHN DENNIS RAY	CA	10E	68
HEIKA JOHN ALLEN	NY	09E	122
HEIL BRUCE HUPPERT	NJ	04W	35
HEIL JACKIE PHILLIP	CO	07W	89
HEIL LOUIS GEORGE	OH	55W	21
HEIL RICHARD EDWARD	CA	46E	17
HEILIG ROBERT FRANK JR	IL	17W	84
HEILMAN WILLIAM EMORY	PA	55E	16
HEIM JAMES PHILLIP	OH	26W	32
HEIM RICHARD WAYNE	CA	31W	48
HEIMAN JOSEPH EDWARD	WA	37E	36
HEIMAN SHERLIN ANDREW	IL	37W	11
HEIMARK DON RAY	CA	12W	68
HEIMBOLD JAMES REEVE	CA	06W	106
HEIMES RICHARD THEODORE	SD	35E	72
HEIN ANTHONY	NJ	49W	23
HEIN CHARLES JOHN JR	IA	11W	131
HEIN GARY LLOYD	IA	15W	32
HEIN RICHARD AUGUST	UT	19E	72
HEIN ROBERT CHARLES	CA	04W	126
HEINDSELMAN MICHAEL JAMES	WA	08W	22
HEINE CHARLES EDWARD	PA	35W	26
HEINECKE RONALD MATHIAS	WI	48W	43
HEINEMEIER CHARLES THOMAS	IL	19W	86
HEINEN EDGAR PAUL	TX	10E	65
HEINMILLER ROBERT LYNN	CA	30W	13
HEINRICH GREGORY ALLEN	WI	26W	111
HEINRICH MICHAEL	IL	10W	62
HEINSELMAN THEODORE E	FL	28W	48
HEINTZ HERBERT CHARLES	OR	19W	112
HEINTZ NED RICHARD	OH	10W	50
HEINTZ RONALD ARTHUR	OR	10E	132
HEINTZ WAYNE DOUGLAS	CA	58W	19
HEINZ DENNIS RALPH	NY	11W	13
HEINZ DONALD E	WI	23E	11
HEINZ JOHN DIETRICH	NE	04W	70
HEINZ PAUL WALTER	WI	42E	17
HEINZ ROGER WILLIAM	CT	15W	42
HEINZE KELLY K	NJ	02E	74
HEINZMAN PETER GEORGE	SD	17W	128
HEISE THOMAS HOWARD	IL	25W	39
HEISEL RODNEY G		13W	111
HEISELMAN JOHN GERALD	IA	43E	20
HEISER DAVID FRANKLIN	PA	33W	40
HEISER DUANE KENNETH	NY	06E	10
HEISER EDWARD MICHAEL	OH	54W	11
HEISER JOHN LOUIS	MI	30W	24
HEISER ROBERT ALLEN	WI	25E	29
HEISER TERRY RICHARD	OH	25W	71
HEISKELL LUCIUS LAMAR	TN	14E	129
HEISSE EDWIN	TN	03W	8
HEISSENBUTTEL PETER HERMA	NY	36E	74
HEISSER KENNETH HAROLD	AZ	19E	43
HEISTER RICHARD EUGENE	NM	01E	130
HEITGER MICHAEL LYNN	IN	44W	37
HEITMAN STEVEN WAYNE	IN	44E	39
HEITMANN KENNETH HARRY	IA	12W	42
HEITNER DENNIS EDWARD	NY	09W	50
HEIZER GARY PAUL	FL	28W	60
HEIZER JERRY HOGUE	VA	26E	10
HELBER LAWRENCE NEAL	OH	04E	84
HELBERT ROY LEE	VA	05W	96
HELD JOHN WAYNE	IN	50E	29
HELD KEITH ARTHUR	PA	10W	130
HELEMS KENNETH EUGENE	TX	07E	9
HELFENSTINE SAMUEL JAMES	OH	34E	20
HELGESON DALE GEORGE	CA	30W	4
HELGESON ELLIS EUGENE JR	OH	43E	20
HELIKER RUSSELL JAMES	MI	56E	25
HELKA GLENN OWEN	MI	45W	41
HELLAND JERRY IRVEN	MN	05E	4
HELLARD RICHARD W JR	MA	49W	8
HELLBACH HAROLD JAMES	LA	20E	44
HELLENBRAND DAVID PETER	WI	37W	17
HELLER DAVID JUNIOR	CO	22E	41
HELLER EMERSON E	PA	26W	46
HELLER IVAN LOUIS	IL	41W	46
HELLER MICHAEL LEO	IA	13W	35
HELLER ROBERT LEE	CA	33E	65
HELLMAN KENNETH RAYMOND	CA	65W	9
HELLMANN GERALD M JR	KY	12W	123

NAME	STATE	PANEL NO.	LINE NO.
HELLWIG STEVEN LOUIS	WA	35E	6
HELLYER WILLIAM EDWARD	IL	23E	86
HELM CARL BENJAMIN	KY	55W	26
HELM DAVID EARL	TX	29E	66
HELM DAVID FRANKLIN	VA	09W	27
HELM HERSCHEL PITTMAN JR	MS	10E	113
HELM WILLIAM CARROLL	IL	21W	101
HELMICH GERALD ROBERT	NH	16W	64
HELMICK ALAN DALE	WV	11W	3
HELMICK DUANE A	WI	55E	16
HELMKE DARREL BRUCE	MN	49E	32
HELMS JERRY DONALD	SC	03W	19
HELMS JOHN RAY	CO	07W	92
HELMSTETLER MICHAEL DAVID	NC	56W	31
HELRIEGEL DAVID	CO	18E	35
HELRING CARL JOHN	PA	12W	89
HELSEL PAUL ELROY JR	OH	05E	83
HELSEL RODNEY GLENN	MO	13W	112
HELSLEY GREGORY PHILLIP	MT	51W	39
HELSTROM KENNETH JAMES	NY	29E	40
HELT HARRY PHILIP JR	NY	05E	103
HELTON DONALD LEONARD	OH	14E	48
HELTON DONALD TERRY	NC	17E	96
HELTON DWAYNE	OH	44W	48
HELTON GLEASON CAY	KY	12W	60
HELTON JAMES CARLOS	TN	18E	40
HELTON JAMES EDWARD	AR	04E	73
HELTON JOHN KENNETH	GA	23E	18
HELTSLEY JOSEPH JUSTIN	OH	22W	58
HELTSLEY PAUL R III	OH	01E	58
HELVESTON ROBERT FULTON	FL	14E	116
HELVEY JOE DEAN	OK	62E	18
HELWIG ROGER DANNY	CO	18W	69
HEMBREE JAMES THOMAS JR	GA	08W	16
HEMBREE JAMES VERNON	IN	26E	10
HEMBREE RONALD GENE	NC	64W	10
HEMER JOSEF	NY	29E	94
HEMKE DAVID LEE	PA	14W	84
HEMMEL CLARENCE JOSEPH	MO	28E	48
HEMMINGS SEAFORD NATHANIE	NY	04E	12
HEMMINGSON NELS IVAR	IL	09W	60
HEMMINGWAY CHARLES LYNN	KS	21E	98
HEMMITT TERRY EUGENE	MO	11E	36
HEMNES ROBERT BERNARD	WA	08E	17
HEMP STUART FRANKLIN	VA	19W	94
HEMPEL BARRY LEE	CA	58E	8
HEMPEL CHARLES ROBERT JR	NY	03E	9
HEMPEL THOMAS EUGENE	NE	21W	125
HEMPHILL CRAIG MANSFIELD	WA	32W	44
HEMPHILL DAVID WAYNE	IN	38W	43
HEMPHILL FREDRICK H	MN	34E	49
HENAGHAN WILLIAM FREDERIC	NY	01W	18
HENASEY HAROLD	NJ	53E	1
HENCE WILLIAM WASHINGTON	WA	61W	13
HENDEE LARRY KEITH	IL	40W	65
HENDERLIGHT BUDDY EUGENE	IL	17W	102
HENDERSHOTT THOMAS EDWARD	MI	20E	76
HENDERSON ANTHONY JOSEPH	LA	34E	87
HENDERSON ARTHUR FRANKLIN	CA	26W	11
HENDERSON BILLY HUGH	GA	43E	21
HENDERSON BRUCE DALE	TN	27W	56
HENDERSON CARL	PA	16W	64
HENDERSON CHARLES CLIFTON	LA	25E	42
HENDERSON CHARLES EDWARD	PA	13E	43
HENDERSON DAVID B JR	TX	39W	16
HENDERSON DERRICK	IN	39W	17
HENDERSON DONNELL	TN	21E	27
HENDERSON EARL	WA	11W	13
HENDERSON EDWARD E JR	FL	54W	37
HENDERSON FRANK HAREL	CA	32E	94
HENDERSON FREDERICK HOWAR	NY	12E	14
HENDERSON GARLIN JERIS JR	CA	13W	118
HENDERSON GARY LLOYD	NY	05E	132
HENDERSON GREG NEAL	MT	04W	115
HENDERSON HAL KENT	MT	20W	86
HENDERSON HENRY F III	NY	39E	72
HENDERSON HUGHLEN	CA	04E	100
HENDERSON ISAAC LEE	TX	51W	32
HENDERSON JACK JR	IL	61E	10
HENDERSON JAMES D	FL	14E	103
HENDERSON JOHN LESLIE	OH	35W	65
HENDERSON JOHN MICHAEL	CA	19E	14

NAME	STATE	PANEL NO.	LINE NO.
HENDERSON JONATHAN	IL	59E	4
HENDERSON KAYLE DEAN	CA	21W	70
HENDERSON LEON	FL	45E	11
HENDERSON MARION F	OK	29E	49
HENDERSON MONTE EUGENE	IL	52W	10
HENDERSON MONTIE H JR	SC	42W	55
HENDERSON RALPH LEE	DC	13E	98
HENDERSON RICKY DONALD	MI	36E	14
HENDERSON ROBERT CAUFIELD	NY	33E	37
HENDERSON ROBERT KNAPP JR	OK	09W	68
HENDERSON ROBERT LEE	SC	17E	4
HENDERSON ROBERT LEE	NC	09W	56
HENDERSON ROBERT MICHAEL	PA	36E	14
HENDERSON ROGER LEO	OR	06E	32
HENDERSON ROY JOHN	MA	06E	10
HENDERSON RUFUS Q	MO	45E	40
HENDERSON STEPHEN CONRAD	IL	18W	82
HENDERSON TIMOTHY	OK	49E	22
HENDERSON TOMMY RAY	CA	04W	19
HENDERSON WILLIAM GLADE	UT	21E	74
HENDERSON WILLIAM ROY	OH	34W	65
HENDERSON WILLIAM WAYNE	VA	26W	62
HENDERSON WILLIE	TX	12W	21
HENDLE DAVID WALLACE	OH	61E	11
HENDON JOHN LEWIS	AL	10W	33
HENDON WILLIAM ATTLEE	OK	12E	34
HENDRICK LARRY EMERSON	WV	06W	29
HENDRICKS CLARENCE O III	OH	58W	4
HENDRICKS EUGENE WILLIAM	NJ	40W	12
HENDRICKS HARRY LANN	OH	21E	95
HENDRICKS JAMES THOMAS	CT	41W	17
HENDRICKS STEPHEN EDWARD	IN	05W	42
HENDRICKS STERLING CRAIG	TX	18E	49
HENDRICKS STEVEN WAYNE	IA	03W	55
HENDRICKS TERRY ALAN	CA	29E	40
HENDRICKSON ALAN EUGENE	CA	24E	73
HENDRICKSON CURTIS LYNN	MN	23W	100
HENDRICKSON GARY ARLAND	KS	15E	127
HENDRICKSON GAYLORD BLAIN	KS	60W	21
HENDRICKSON GERALD RAY	MI	30E	90
HENDRICKSON LONNIE HILTON	ID	27W	5
HENDRICKSON MICHAEL FRANC	MT	50W	6
HENDRICKSON PATRICK RAYMO	MN	38W	35
HENDRICKSON WESLEY PAUL	MN	32W	20
HENDRIX CHARLES RODNEY	KY	61E	11
HENDRIX EARNEST L	AR	24E	51
HENDRIX ELWOOD RANDALL	MO	26E	60
HENDRIX JERRY WAYNE	KS	01W	55
HENDRIX JOHN RUSSELL	IL	48E	17
HENDRIX KENNETH LEVON	MS	24E	7
HENDRIX KENNETH WAYNE	OH	06W	23
HENDRIX PAUL GEORGE	AL	09E	21
HENDRIX ROBERT EDWARD	NY	33W	26
HENDRY DAVID EUGENE	TX	07W	117
HENESY HAROLD THOMAS	FL	55E	16
HENGELS RAYMOND GEORGE	IL	25E	101
HENISS FRANK AMOS	PA	02E	77
HENJYOJI GRANT HIROAKI	OR	30W	76
HENK JAMES LYNN	NE	45E	47
HENKE KENNETH LEE	WI	16W	45
HENKE RICHARD ARTHUR	IL	10W	33
HENKE VERNON LEE	WI	20E	44
HENLEY AUBREY RUDOLPH		48W	55
HENLEY CHARLES RAY	MI	52W	35
HENLEY ROY LEE	MS	43W	62
HENLING RICHARD RAY	AZ	11E	122
HENLY CARL O'NEAL	TX	20W	37
HENN JOHN ROBERT JR	MA	01W	30
HENN NORVILLE MARTIN JR	MO	26W	107
HENNEBERG ROBERT JOSEPH	CA	09E	80
HENNEBERRY JAMES CALVIN	MA	02E	25
HENNEGHAN ROBERT LEE	SC	17W	13
HENNEN PATRICK ERNEST	MN	11W	131
HENNESSEY ARTHUR F JR	MA	01E	104
HENNESSEY JAMES DALE	MI	22W	77
HENNESSY DANIEL A	PA	13E	91
HENNESSY STEPHEN THOMAS	MN	08W	100
HENNING ARTHUR ROBERT	WI	55E	17
HENNING DOUGLAS ALLEN	NY	52W	43
HENNINGER HOWARD WILLIAM	CA	06E	3
HENNINGER JOHNIE MICHAEL	IN	21E	62
HENNINGER KENTON ELWOOD	OH	30W	63

NAME	STATE	PANEL NO.	LINE NO.
HENNINGSEN REID CHARLES	IL	14W	8
HENREY RICHARD DEE	CA	27E	10
HENRICH BRUCE JAMES	MI	02E	57
HENRICH MYLLIN GERALD	IA	09W	83
HENRICH RICHARD FREDERICK	NY	20E	90
HENRICKS CHARLES DRAYTON	CA	28W	19
HENRICKS DONALD MERLE JR	IL	11E	14
HENRICKS FRED CARL	CA	09W	60
HENRICKSON COMBLY HANIBAL	CA	36E	14
HENRICKSON JAN VICTOR	DE	49W	54
HENRICKSON KEITH RICHARD	WA	26E	88
HENRY ANDREW L	MS	04E	72
HENRY BERNARD JAMES	MI	18W	114
HENRY BISMARK WASHINGTON	DC	38E	51
HENRY CLARENCE IVORY	LA	14E	91
HENRY DANIEL BENEDICT	NY	36E	14
HENRY DANIEL LEE	AZ	32W	25
HENRY DAVID ALAN	CA	10E	119
HENRY DAVID FRANKLIN	TX	22E	19
HENRY DAVID PAUL	TX	17W	7
HENRY DENNIS LEE	KY	19W	107
HENRY DONALD RAY	IN	26E	10
HENRY EDWARD DOUGLAS	VT	39W	27
HENRY EDWARD EARL	TN	42E	65
HENRY EPHRIAM JR	IL	13E	8
HENRY EUGENE EARL	NY	37E	58
HENRY FRANCIS GILBERT	CA	36E	51
HENRY FREDERICK JOHN	CA	23W	73
HENRY GEARLD ALBERT	AR	19W	61
HENRY GEORGE D JR	AR	08W	108
HENRY GEORGE EDWARD	TN	19W	119
HENRY GEORGE WARD JR	WV	25E	114
HENRY GERALD EDWARD	IL	25W	71
HENRY GERALD RUSSELL	CA	23E	28
HENRY HOWARD BOYD	MD	16W	64
HENRY JAMES EDWARD	MA	17E	51
HENRY JIMMY LYNN	TN	25W	29
HENRY JOHN PATRICK	NJ	13W	104
HENRY LEONARD IRA	PA	07E	34
HENRY LINDY EDWARD	FL	18E	108
HENRY NELSON PAGE	TN	28E	91
HENRY ROBERT GREGORY	CA	55W	35
HENRY ROBERT JOHN	NV	18E	94
HENRY RONALD JEROME	CA	18E	98
HENRY SCOTT D	CA	48W	12
HENRY SCOTT ORVILLE	PA	03E	57
HENRY STEPHEN MICHAEL	MA	21E	105
HENRY TERRY LYNN	PA	10W	6
HENRY THOMAS CARMEN	MI	46E	62
HENRY WALTER MAURICE	WA	47W	44
HENRY WILLIAM JAMES	NY	02E	84
HENRY WILLIAM JAMES	SC	09E	98
HENRY WILLIAM RICHARD	CA	28E	1
HENRY WILLIE LEE	GA	48W	43
HENS JOHN MICHAEL	NY	11E	40
HENSEL DAVID WILLIAM	PA	10W	51
HENSEL ERNEST VICTOR JR	VA	15E	55
HENSEY LAWRENCE LOUIS JR	IL	11W	24
HENSHAW LARRY ROY	OK	11W	79
HENSHAW PATRICK LEE	WA	32E	23
HENSHAW THOMAS STOW	CA	32E	23
HENSINGER ARTHUR JAMES	PA	30E	84
HENSLEE JAMES EUGENE	OK	28E	67
HENSLEY A G	TN	17E	79
HENSLEY GAREY LEE	SC	26E	75
HENSLEY GARY LEE	MI	29E	15
HENSLEY GETER ALFRED	NC	29E	82
HENSLEY JACKIE VERNON	CO	34W	84
HENSLEY JAMES CURTIS	IL	18W	125
HENSLEY JAY THOMAS	OH	19E	52
HENSLEY JOHN	CA	23W	44
HENSLEY JOHN THOMAS	FL	11E	57
HENSLEY LEROY	CA	15E	11
HENSLEY MARK ALAN	MT	07W	73
HENSLEY MEDFORD S JR	IL	25E	50
HENSLEY RAYMOND ALBERT	IA	62E	5
HENSLEY RICHARD DAVID	CT	11E	66
HENSLEY RONNIE LEE	WV	11W	36
HENSLEY SHELBY GLEASON	VA	05W	90
HENSLEY THOMAS TRUETT	LA	45E	11
HENSLEY WAYNE GEORGE	WA	41W	46
HENSON ALVAH WORRELL JR	MD	38W	1

NAME	STATE	PANEL NO.	LINE NO.
HENSON CHARLES KENNETH	IL	46E	46
HENSON CLARK LEE JR	MO	56W	3
HENSON CLIFTON	KY	32E	94
HENSON FRANK THEODORE	NY	01W	18
HENSON GEORGE RICHARD	TX	01W	48
HENSON GWYN THAXTON	IL	45W	19
HENSON JOHN MICHAEL	CA	25W	29
HENSON LARRY KEITH	SC	25W	23
HENSON LESLEY HERBERT	CA	19W	37
HENSON ROGER LEE	MO	32E	73
HENSON THOMAS GEORGE	NY	03E	44
HENTHORN ALVA DEAN	OH	59W	4
HENTHORN HARRY THOMAS	IN	07W	22
HENTSCHEL ROBERT EDWARD	NY	32E	73
HENTZ RICHARD JAY	WI	04W	21
HENZE RANDALL ALLEN	IN	40E	63
HEPBURN WILLIAM BARTON	ID	10E	31
HEPLER FRANK MONROE	PA	59E	4
HEPNER STEPHEN THOMAS	AZ	19E	14
HEPPEN GEORGE HENRY JR	IN	20E	74
HEPPLER JAMES HOWARD	MA	07W	27
HERALD CLABE JR	OH	12E	42
HERALD ROBERT	FL	44W	64
HERALD SHERRILL NEWTON	KY	41W	5
HERBERT DAVID EDWIN	ID	08E	119
HERBERT LARRY EUGENE	OH	34E	53
HERBERT REGINALD MILMEN	NY	33W	32
HERBST THOMAS WILLIAM	CA	21W	93
HERBSTRITT RONALD LEE	PA	08E	90
HERCHKORN RICHARD RONALD	CA	05E	87
HERD RONALD WARD	TX	08W	85
HERD THOMAS LEON	CA	41E	66
HERDEBU DAN LEON	ND	44E	8
HERDERICK CHRISTOPHER ERV	CA	28E	25
HEREAU DANNY EDWARD	KY	52E	19
HEREDIA MIGUEL	CA	34W	42
HERENDON DAVID MACK	GA	29E	19
HERFEL LAURENCE JOHN	WI	41E	14
HERGERT THOMAS MALCOLM	IL	01E	45
HERIAUD FREDERICK CHARLES	IL	03E	78
HERIN JAMES EDWARD	IA	16W	5
HERING JAMES ALFRED	MI	53E	1
HERING MARK RICHARD	NY	30E	27
HERING ROBERT HENRY	WI	48W	55
HERING WILLIAM ARTHUR	MN	27W	49
HERINGHAUSEN ARTHUR J JR	OH	38W	18
HERINGTON JOHN DONOVAN	IL	07W	11
HERIOT THEODORE S JR	VA	22W	40
HERKINS THOMAS FRANKLIN	OH	46W	3
HERLIHY JOHN HENRY JR	NY	06E	3
HERMAN ALLAN JOSEPH	IL	26E	45
HERMAN CLYDE RUSSEL	VA	03E	23
HERMAN LAWRENCE JOHN III	AL	11W	124
HERMAN ROBERT CURTIS	PA	27W	108
HERMANN GREGORY WILLIAM	MI	01W	2
HERMANN LOUIS VINCENT JR	PA	18W	7
HERMANOWICZ JOHN JOSEPH	IL	19E	52
HERMANSON GARRY W	NJ	01W	121
HERMANSON STEPHEN MARK	CA	37E	58
HERMOSILLO JOSEPH REFUGIO	CA	29W	10
HERMS KLAUS JURGEN	CA	05E	104
HERMSEN MICHAEL EDWARD	WI	28W	11
HERN WILLIAM BURCH	NM	07W	98
HERNANDEZ ALEX JAMES	AZ	34E	20
HERNANDEZ ALEXANDER VERA	CA	10E	74
HERNANDEZ ANTONIO	TX	52W	44
HERNANDEZ ANTONIO BENAVIDEZ	TX	45W	32
HERNANDEZ ARTHUR	TX	04W	99
HERNANDEZ CLEMENTE DANIEL	CA	15E	44
HERNANDEZ DEMETRIO LOMELI	CA	27E	72
HERNANDEZ FELIPE	CA	19W	112
HERNANDEZ FELIX	NY	10E	95
HERNANDEZ FRANK SANCHEZ	CA	11W	112
HERNANDEZ HERIBERTO SEGOVIA	TX	37W	46
HERNANDEZ HUMBERTO ROBLES	AZ	19W	42
HERNANDEZ JOE JR	CO	13E	109
HERNANDEZ JOHN ALBERT	TX	11W	73
HERNANDEZ JOSE G	TX	18E	75
HERNANDEZ JOSE JR	TX	12W	132
HERNANDEZ JOSEPH J JR	WI	38W	11
HERNANDEZ JULIO ALFONSO	CA	60W	1
HERNANDEZ JULIO JR	NY	29W	45

NAME	STATE	PANEL NO.	LINE NO.
HERNANDEZ LOUIS PETER	CA	05E	117
HERNANDEZ MANUEL	NY	30E	91
HERNANDEZ MANUEL JR	TX	26W	71
HERNANDEZ MARCOS	TX	03E	6
HERNANDEZ NOEL BARBARO	FL	05W	48
HERNANDEZ PEDRO ALEXANDRO	CA	36E	51
HERNANDEZ PEDRO JR	NY	13E	64
HERNANDEZ PHILLIP	CA	24W	6
HERNANDEZ RAMON ANTONIO	CA	06W	85
HERNANDEZ RAMON N	TX	34W	58
HERNANDEZ RAMON S JR	CA	45W	6
HERNANDEZ RAMON SANCHEZ	MI	42E	65
HERNANDEZ RAYMOND RODRIGUEZ	TX	41W	21
HERNANDEZ RENE ZAROGOZA	CA	36E	74
HERNANDEZ REYES C JR	CA	53E	33
HERNANDEZ REYNALDO CASTILLO	CA	03E	78
HERNANDEZ RICHARD	TX	18E	122
HERNANDEZ ROBERT	TX	52W	10
HERNANDEZ ROBERT REYES	TX	21E	46
HERNANDEZ ROLANDO	TX	65E	10
HERNANDEZ RUDOLPH VILLALPANE	TX	02E	28
HERNANDEZ SALOME	NM	32E	87
HERNANDEZ STEVEN	MN	40E	40
HERNANDEZ VICTOR REYES	CA	41W	73
HERNANDEZ WILLIAM ANTHONY	TX	35W	43
HERNANDEZ-CARRASQUI JAIME	PR	08W	88
HERNANDEZ-CARRION GILBERT	NY	45E	47
HERNANDEZ-FELICIANO DAMAS	PR	35E	22
HERNANDEZ-PENA AUDELIZ	NJ	18E	14
HERNANDEZ-RIVERA ANGEL L	PR	17W	128
HERNANDEZ-RODRIGUEZ RUBENEDID	PR	06W	42
HERNANDEZ-SOTO ANTONIO	PR	14E	10
HERNANDEZ-VELEZ ALBERTO	PR	42W	47
HERNDON ARTHUR ROBERT	TX	15W	78
HERNDON DONALD LEE	VA	40E	40
HERNDON HARRY H	TX	41W	73
HERNDON RICKY LYNN	MI	21E	79
HERNDON ROBERT EDWARD	CA	11W	102
HERNDON THOMAS HAYDEN	MI	09W	111
HERNDON W COLE	WA	44W	25
HEROD ARTHUR WEINMANN	NY	41E	50
HEROLD ERIC GARY	WA	02W	66
HEROLD RICHARD WALTER	NY	01W	69
HEROY DEWEY WILLIAM	IN	21W	75
HERR JAY DONALD	PA	25E	19
HERRADA GABRIEL	MI	39W	66
HERRANDO ROGER DANIEL	MI	14E	107
HERREID ROBERT DALE	IL	41W	40
HERRELL DANIEL BRUCE	CA	28E	55
HERREN EVERETT DELOY	GA	14W	71
HERREN RONALD WAYNE	GA	65W	9
HERRERA AURELIO GARZA	TX	64E	14
HERRERA BEN LOPEZ	TX	49W	41
HERRERA FELIPE	TX	43W	46
HERRERA FRANCISCO	TX	06E	60
HERRERA FRANK G	AZ	62E	19
HERRERA FRANK VINCENT	WI	48E	4
HERRERA FREDERICK DANIEL	NM	28W	36
HERRERA JESSE EMIL	TX	09E	11
HERRERA JIMMIE ANDREW	MI	14E	73
HERRERA JOSE BABAUTA	GM	40E	41
HERRERA JOSE BENJAMIN	NM	34E	87
HERRERA LARRY	CA	11W	85
HERRERA LOUIS ANTHONY	CO	46W	60
HERRERA MANUEL	CO	06E	32
HERRERA MANUELITO LEOPOLD	CO	41E	21
HERRERA MICHAEL WARD	CA	18E	10
HERRERA MOISES ROMERO JR	TX	16W	19
HERRERA NARCISO FRANCIS	NM	08E	119
HERRERA PHILLIP ARNOLD JR	CA	10E	78
HERRERA RAMIRO JR	TX	26E	112
HERRGESELL OSCAR	CA	01W	59
HERRICK BENNETT JAMES	MO	46E	17
HERRICK DENNIS HALDANE	MO	08W	110
HERRICK HENRY TORO	CA	03E	57
HERRICK JAMES WAYNE JR	IA	17W	124
HERRIMAN RONNIE LEE	KS	20W	44
HERRIN CLIFFORD RAY	TN	16E	122
HERRIN DELMAR JOYCE JR	CA	13W	9

NAME	STATE	PANEL NO.	LINE NO.
HERRIN HENRY HOWARD JR	MA	33E	13
HERRIN LARRY FRANKLIN	PA	08E	66
HERRING ALFRED JIMMY JR	SC	07W	78
HERRING BILLY DALE	MO	03W	45
HERRING BOYD LEMUEL	VA	43E	54
HERRING BRADY WILLIAM	SC	43W	5
HERRING DAVID BOUNDS	AL	24W	103
HERRING ELIJAH JR	GA	30W	89
HERRING HAROLD JOERENZO	FL	54W	11
HERRING JOHN HOWARD	NC	53W	19
HERRING JOHN WILLIE	FL	06W	49
HERRING PEDRO	NC	10W	80
HERRING STEVEN WAYNE	CA	23W	74
HERRING THOMAS FOREST	IL	06W	127
HERRING THOMAS LEANDRA	VA	31E	24
HERRING WILLIAM EARL	VA	23E	28
HERRINGTON CARWAIN L	TX	10W	62
HERRINGTON CHARLES EDWARD	TX	03E	58
HERRINGTON JEROME	GA	04E	90
HERRINGTON RAYMOND NEIL	MI	13E	61
HERRINGTON RICHARD LEE JR	MI	10W	64
HERRINGTON RONNIE JOE	LA	04E	79
HERRITZ EVERETT AUGUST	CO	23E	76
HERRMANN WALTER EDWIN III	CA	13E	44
HERROLD NED RAYMOND	NJ	07E	128
HERRON DENNIS	OH	62W	10
HERRON JOSEPH SAMUEL	MN	05E	104
HERRON LEE ROY	TX	32W	78
HERRON PATRICK	PA	26E	10
HERRON ROCKWELL SELDEN	NJ	17E	44
HERSCHBACH DAVID EDWARD	IL	29W	99
HERSCHBACH PAUL DELL	OK	40E	52
HERSEY CARROLL FRANKLIN	NH	24W	42
HERSHAN WILLIAM	NY	44E	59
HERSHBERGER DAVID HARPER	VA	34E	17
HERSHBERGER GARY PATRICK	FL	16W	121
HERSHEY CHARLES THOMAS	PA	39W	60
HERSHISER DAVID OWEN	CO	35W	34
HERSHMAN KENNETH	PA	04E	109
HERSHNER DENNIS L	CA	17E	57
HERST WILLIAM DONALD JR	TX	30E	44
HERTEL RODGER RAY	ND	41E	37
HERTLEIN GEORGE B III	GA	51E	46
HERTRICK DONALD JOSEPH	PA	39W	37
HERTZ ALLEN CONRAD	PA	01E	132
HERTZ ROBERT DALE	CO	05W	43
HERTZLER RICHARD DALE	CA	26W	71
HERVAS AARON KAMALA	AL	30E	44
HESFORD PETER DEAN	CT	45E	47
HESKETT BRUCE WILLIAM	WA	09W	101
HESKETT JAMES EARL	KS	33E	68
HESKETT JERRY WAYNE	OH	24W	75
HESLER STEVEN EUGENE	OH	35W	12
HESS DALE JOSEPH	OH	53E	15
HESS FREDERICK WILLIAM JR	MO	28W	81
HESS GENE KARL	DE	08E	57
HESS JACK WAYNE	NV	49E	32
HESS JAMES DONALD	OR	59E	23
HESS KENNETH CHARLES	PA	33W	89
HESS KERRY EUGENE	KS	23W	74
HESS LARRY LEROY	PA	03E	78
HESS PAUL J JR	PA	12E	54
HESS PHILLIP HOWARD	NJ	13E	72
HESS ROBERT JAY	CA	50E	36
HESS THOMAS G	WV	11W	91
HESS ZAN	TX	29E	89
HESSE CHARLES THOMAS	IA	51W	40
HESSE GEORGE BERNARD	NY	43W	54
HESSELSCHWARDT HERMAN ALO	OH	51E	43
HESSING JAMES WILLIAM	WI	10W	85
HESSION PATRICK B	FL	56E	8
HESSLER JAMES JOHN	TX	07E	18
HESSMAN RONALD ANTHONY	CA	28E	100
HESSOM ROBERT CHARLES	CA	05E	114
HESSON DANNY ROBERT	WV	17W	61
HESSON JIMMY DALE	TN	14E	63
HESSON JOSEPH LEONARD III	NJ	20W	123
HESSON LARRY DEAN	TN	16E	11
HESSON RONALD EUGENE	WV	12E	14
HESTER CHARLES RICHARD	LA	09W	105
HESTER ELVESTER JR	NC	39E	6
HESTER GUY WILSON JR	MS	07W	119

NAME	STATE	PANEL NO.	LINE NO.
HESTER JIMMY CARROLL	NC	36W	72
HESTER JOE EDD	KY	33W	93
HESTER LEO CLAUDE	CA	16E	52
HESTER LEO CLAUDE JR	FL	16W	19
HESTER MARTIN DAVID	GA	27E	53
HESTER STEVEN LEWIS	GA	13W	35
HESTER VANESTER LAMAR	FL	29E	89
HESTER WILLIAM WALTER	PA	54W	29
HESTERLEE RAY WESLEY	GA	36W	51
HESTLE ROOSEVELT JR	FL	08E	134
HETLAND RONALD LEE	IL	33E	86
HETRICK CARL POST	FL	53W	20
HETRICK GERALD EVERETT	MI	52W	19
HETRICK RAYMOND HARRY	PA	05E	72
HETTERLY JOHN DONALD SR	FL	04E	90
HETTICH ALAN JOSEPH	KY	49E	32
HETTICH DONALD LEE	FL	31E	4
HETTINGER ROBERT LANCE	MD	33W	94
HETZEL NORMAN RALPH	NJ	19W	119
HETZER JOSEPH EDWARD JR	PA	04E	55
HETZLER LARRY GLEN	LA	38W	57
HETZLER RAYMOND CURTIS	DE	13W	63
HEUER JERRY WAYNE	WI	50E	4
HEUER MICHAEL WAYNE	MN	06E	126
HEUSEL ALBERT FRANCIS JR	NY	46E	7
HEUSTON GERALD WILFORD	PA	06E	6
HEVERN RUSSELL JAMES E	MT	35W	48
HEVLE DAVID EUGENE	SD	17E	123
HEWETT RICHARD ALFRED	NC	46E	55
HEWIT RUSSEL HOWARD JR	OH	34W	49
HEWITSON PAUL CRAWFORD	CA	52W	23
HEWITT AUBREY LAURENCE	GA	21E	45
HEWITT BRIAN CHARLES	FL	19E	82
HEWITT BURL DENTON	OH	59E	23
HEWITT CHARLES GLEN	FL	12W	52
HEWITT RALEIGH L II	WI	29E	95
HEWITT ROBERT EUGENE	OH	15W	55
HEWITT SAMUEL EUGENE	IN	06E	41
HEWITT THOMAS THEODORE	KS	09W	111
HEWITT WILLIAM FRANK	OK	09E	1
HEWLETT DENNIS HENRY	PA	27E	72
HEWLETT JAMES JOSEPH	PA	64E	15
HEYDINGER LAUREN JOSEPH	OH	38E	51
HEYDORN CHARLES GEORGE	OH	51W	40
HEYDT RICHARD BROWN	PA	16E	59
HEYEN JOHN EUGENE	IN	38W	28
HEYER EDWARD E	AL	21E	121
HEYER WALTER EARL JR	MI	18W	82
HEYMACH HAROLD FRANK	NJ	43E	54
HEYNE RAYMOND THOMAS	WI	58E	9
HEZEL KARL D	NJ	30E	9
HIATT BARRY CLINTON	CA	13W	81
HIBBARD GARY EDWARD	PA	26E	16
HIBBARD RONALD EDWARD	TN	41W	35
HIBBLER JOE JR	AR	42W	72
HIBBLER RICHARD WAYNE	TX	14W	18
HIBBS ROBERT JOHN	IA	05E	118
HIBLER RUSSELL CRANSTON	WA	12W	60
HIBPSHMAN WILLIAM EARL	AK	21W	13
HICE ROBERT KENNETH	PA	18E	23
HICKERSON JERRY WARNER	IA	18W	46
HICKEY EDWARD ROBERT	PA	30W	45
HICKEY JAMES PHILIP	MA	23W	2
HICKEY JAMES W	NY	30E	91
HICKEY JERRY THOMAS	TN	05W	37
HICKEY JOHN JOSEPH	WI	26W	42
HICKEY JOHN PATRICK	FL	09E	77
HICKEY JOHNNY	TN	08E	85
HICKLEN GRAHAM RAY	TX	18E	41
HICKMAN ARTHUR EDWARD	MO	04E	1
HICKMAN DALLAS EDWIN	OH	06E	20
HICKMAN DAVID ALAN	CA	19E	37
HICKMAN DAVID ALLEN	FL	15W	24
HICKMAN JAMES RUSH	WV	04E	46
HICKMAN JOSHUA	OK	21E	34
HICKMAN RANDALL SHERWOOD	NC	06E	8
HICKMAN ROBERT DAVE	WV	04E	8
HICKMAN ROBERT EUGENE	OH	54W	29
HICKMAN STEVEN MURDOCK	MS	30W	24
HICKMAN THOMAS STEVEN	IN	07W	11
HICKMAN VINCENT JOSEPH	NY	01E	40
HICKMAN WANDLE LEWIS	OH	23E	59
HICKOK ROGER ALAN	CA	10W	57
HICKOX ROBERT DAVIS	WA	52W	35
HICKS ARCHIE EVERETT	WV	17W	4
HICKS BENNY JOE	FL	41W	48
HICKS CARMAN KEETON	IN	19E	72
HICKS CHARLES DARNELL JR	CA	13W	104
HICKS CHARLES LEE	KY	12E	101
HICKS CHARLES WAYNE	NC	31E	98
HICKS DAN SELLMAN	VA	43E	44
HICKS DAVID LEE	CA	07W	81
HICKS DONALD	AZ	54W	24
HICKS DONALD GENE	IN	40E	74
HICKS EARLIE HENRY JR	GA	50E	39
HICKS ELVIS GORMEN	TN	04E	97
HICKS EUGENE STANLEY	CA	34E	58
HICKS FRANK EDWARD	CA	34W	37
HICKS GARY DALE	NC	45E	4
HICKS GENE DANIEL	RI	34E	77
HICKS GLEN RAY	OK	50W	42
HICKS HIAWATHA	MI	51E	20
HICKS JAMES BEN	AR	09W	88
HICKS JAMES LARRY	TN	20W	83
HICKS JAMES ROBERT	PA	21E	89
HICKS JAMES RUSSELL	MN	04W	27
HICKS JEFFREY LYNN	MO	38W	18
HICKS JIMMY ISHMAEL	WA	12W	56
HICKS JOHN MITCHELL	NC	19E	118
HICKS JOSEPH LONNIE	NJ	23E	3
HICKS KENNETH WAYNE	NC	56W	34
HICKS LARRY DAVID	MO	07W	87
HICKS LEROY	NJ	02E	86
HICKS LESLIE CLYDE	ME	04W	18
HICKS LEVIL	TX	21W	31
HICKS MANUEL ARTLAN JR	TN	17E	79
HICKS MICHAEL EUGENE	CA	22W	21
HICKS NORMAN EDWARD JR	MD	62W	11
HICKS PAUL EVERETT	OK	43E	21
HICKS PAUL J	TN	19E	43
HICKS PRENTICE WAYNE	AL	28W	37
HICKS RANDOLPH TRUMAN	TN	01E	126
HICKS ROBERT LYLE	IL	65E	10
HICKS SHELDON WAYNE	ME	23W	101
HICKS SILAS LUCAS JR	MD	26W	106
HICKS STEVEN GARY	CA	65E	11
HICKS TERRIN DINSMORE	MD	48W	18
HICKS WILBUR LEE	FL	31W	93
HICKS WILLIAM DONALD	PA	01E	118
HICKS WOODIE LEE	AL	04E	90
HICKSON LEONARD MARTIN	AZ	24W	42
HIDALGO JAMES YBARRA	TX	32E	10
HIDAY THOMAS MICHEAL	IN	31W	4
HIDO RICHARD LEE	OH	08E	108
HIEBER JACK JEAN	IA	09E	82
HIEBERT JOHN MICHAEL	KS	02W	82
HIEBERT LYNN GREGORY	MN	68E	3
HIEMENZ JAMES BORLAND	FL	19W	39
HIEMER JERRY ALLAN	TN	03E	78
HIENSMAN STEVEN LANCE	IL	09W	98
HIERLMEIER DONALD ALVIN	WI	39E	61
HIGBEE CHARLES E JR	SC	35W	82
HIGBEE GARY LEE	MI	49W	29
HIGBEE ROBERT DANIEL	PA	09E	123
HIGDON DAVID DARRIN JR	NJ	06E	112
HIGDON JIMMY RAY	OK	12W	122
HIGDON LEONARD THOMAS	GA	10W	75
HIGDON RALPH TAYLOR	VA	42W	69
HIGGERSON TOMMY DOYLE	MO	15E	128
HIGGINBOTHAM HAROLD S	FL	37E	8
HIGGINBOTHAM JOHN BILL	TX	13W	1
HIGGINBOTHAM LARRY GENE	CA	30W	2
HIGGINBOTHAM MICHAEL JOE	TX	09W	27
HIGGINBOTHAM OSCAR K JR	GA	48W	18
HIGGINBOTHAM RICHARD LEE	AL	12W	124
HIGGINBOTHAM ROBERT M	MD	24W	6
HIGGINBOTHAM WILLIAM R	NC	05W	114
HIGGINBOTHAN ALLEN L	IN	06E	75
HIGGINS DENNIS EDWARD	NY	04E	79
HIGGINS DENNIS MICHAEL	MA	22E	28
HIGGINS DENNIS MICHAEL	WA	02W	65
HIGGINS EDWARD C III	NY	30E	91
HIGGINS EDWARD HUBERT	FL	59W	4
HIGGINS EDWIN RAY	AZ	10E	91
HIGGINS HERSHEL	MO	35E	16
HIGGINS JEROME	OH	16W	62
HIGGINS JERRY WAYNE	AL	15E	58
HIGGINS JOHN FRANCIS	MI	37W	66
HIGGINS JOHN IGNATIUS JR	CA	28E	2
HIGGINS JOHN LAWRENCE	NY	46E	18
HIGGINS KENNETH LEE	ME	13W	36
HIGGINS MATTHEW	PA	16E	78
HIGGINS MERLE ROBERT	PA	23W	74
HIGGINS PATRICK ALBERT	CA	58E	9
HIGGINS ROY JOHN JR	AZ	05E	118
HIGGINS THOMAS ANDREW	IN	18W	23
HIGGINS WILLIAM PATRICK	IA	15W	104
HIGGINSON LARRY CRAIG	NV	44W	64
HIGGS DANNY TRENT	MI	05E	126
HIGGS DAVID A	WA	01W	126
HIGGS RALPH EDWARD	VA	43E	21
HIGH LARRY JAMES	NJ	27E	3
HIGH RONALD CLYDE	OK	45W	14
HIGH THEODORE W IV	GA	10W	45
HIGHBERGER FRED DEAN JR	PA	17W	121
HIGHFILL REX WHEELER	MO	15E	20
HIGHFILL ROBERT RAY	CA	29W	78
HIGHLAND BYRON GRANT	MI	15E	69
HIGHLAND FOREST G JR	OH	09W	95
HIGHLANDER MICKY RAY	KY	48W	33
HIGHLEY RAYMOND HOWARD	WV	36W	7
HIGHSMITH GRANT HAMLY	CA	15W	55
HIGHSMITH JAMES ARTHUR	IL	04W	99
HIGHT CHARLES BENNY	CA	26W	91
HIGHT DAVID KEITH	CT	08E	111
HIGHT WILLIAM REID	SC	40E	74
HIGHTOWER ALFRED JR	NC	38W	49
HIGHTOWER GEORGE MALCOLM	WA	07E	52
HIGHTOWER JAMES LARRY	KY	11E	97
HIGLEY LYNNFORD HARLOW	KS	35W	60
HIGMAN JOHN EVERETT	WA	03E	58
HIGUERA MANUEL	CA	30W	23
HILB-SCHELEIN ARNOLD	PR	31W	48
HILBERT CHARLES ALLEN	KY	24W	76
HILBERT JERRY LEE	KY	68E	3
HILBRICH BARRY WAYNE	TX	09W	33
HILBURGER MICHAEL J	NY	19E	5
HILDEBRAND ALFRED DEAN	OK	35W	34
HILDEBRAND HERBERT S	AR	27W	87
HILDEBRANDT DANIEL ALAN	NJ	39E	22
HILDEBRANDT JAMES GEORGE	WI	51W	5
HILDEN ANDREW J	MN	14E	108
HILDENBRAND CHARLES JOHN	OH	22E	13
HILDENBRAND LESLIE IAN	PA	02E	50
HILDERBRAND RONALD LEE	OK	19E	49
HILDERBRANT PHILLIP JAY	MI	08W	72
HILDRETH DAVID WAYNE	NH	27W	81
HILERIO ALBERT JR	FL	23W	9
HILERIO-PADILLA LUIS A N	NY	16W	69
HILEY THOMAS CHARLES	NE	36E	14
HILFIKER HERBERT ALLEN	NE	03E	135
HILGART RICHARD PETER	IL	20E	44
HILKIN LAWRENCE ARCHIE	IA	27W	25
HILL ALAN JR	MO	10W	103
HILL ALLAN BRUCE	CA	35W	54
HILL ALVESTER	NC	15E	128
HILL ALVIN GENE	FL	22E	41
HILL ANDREW LAMAR	DC	08W	62
HILL ARTHUR SINCLAIR JR	CA	04E	45
HILL ARTHUR STANLEY JR	DE	30W	37
HILL BILLY DAVID	NV	35E	6
HILL CARL LEE JR	NC	48E	4
HILL CARL WAYNE	AR	31W	49
HILL CHARLES DALE	MO	19E	127
HILL CHARLES HERMAN	WI	08E	75
HILL CHARLIE III	MS	28W	97
HILL CHESTER EUGENE	AR	32W	6
HILL CLARENCE MITCHELL	FL	34W	37
HILL CLEABERN WILLIAM JR	TN	25W	101
HILL DALE ARTHUR	NY	64E	15
HILL DALE EVAN	CA	52E	37
HILL DAVID ALLEN	MA	32W	26
HILL DAVID NOEL	IL	42E	33
HILL DAVID WILLIAM	PA	09E	62
HILL DENNIS EUGENE	IN	29E	48
HILL DOUGLAS WAYNE	OK	23E	100

NAME	STATE	PANEL NO.	LINE NO.
HILL EDDIE LEE JR	AL	03E	18
HILL EDWIN CHARLES	FL	14E	22
HILL ELMER DEAN	MS	52E	38
HILL ERNEST JAMES	NY	52W	28
HILL EUGENE DONALD	MO	39W	43
HILL EUGENE JOHN JR	NJ	47W	44
HILL FOSTER EUGENE	OK	54E	8
HILL FRANK ALLEN III	RI	20W	91
HILL GARY	MO	43W	18
HILL GARY PAUL	VT	53E	33
HILL GERALD RAY	PA	23W	64
HILL GERALD WILLIAM	OH	05W	31
HILL GORDON CLARK	WA	09W	105
HILL HENRY JR	MN	47W	45
HILL HERMAN LINWOOD	NY	31E	69
HILL HOWARD SCOTT	PA	24W	85
HILL HUGH GILBERT JR	NY	27W	18
HILL IRVIN HUGH	TX	35W	89
HILL IVORY JR	LA	53W	35
HILL JAMES EDWARD	MS	08E	36
HILL JAMES EDWARD	AR	19E	14
HILL JAMES LEROY	TX	61W	13
HILL JAMES LOUIS	LA	61E	11
HILL JAMES MARSHALL	LA	39E	48
HILL JAMES WALLACE JR	NY	58E	22
HILL JERRY DWAIN	AL	39W	66
HILL JERRY JAMES	MN	68E	3
HILL JERRY L	OH	29E	30
HILL JERRY WILLIAM	OK	19W	79
HILL JIMMY ARNOLD	MD	11W	79
HILL JIMMY LEE	FL	08W	20
HILL JOE LAWRENCE	OR	09E	105
HILL JOHN CHARLES	NJ	42E	17
HILL JOHN EDWIN	VA	12W	103
HILL JOHN KENNY	MS	46W	39
HILL JOHN MICHAEL	KY	19W	93
HILL JOHN RICHARD	PA	11W	58
HILL JOHN ROBERT	CA	22E	13
HILL JOHN ROBERT	CA	31W	36
HILL JOHN WALTER III	AZ	29E	73
HILL JOHN WESLEY JR	KY	30W	102
HILL JOSEPH ARNOLD	IL	64W	10
HILL LAMONT DOUGLAS	OH	16E	28
HILL LARRY EDWIN	GA	34E	53
HILL LEROY	DC	03E	32
HILL LONNIE O'NEAL	TN	25E	63
HILL MARVIN CHARLES	WA	20E	103
HILL MAURICE RICHARD	CA	02E	24
HILL MICHAEL ALAN	AZ	01W	56
HILL MICHAEL WAYNE	CA	04W	40
HILL MICKEY WILLIAM	NC	29W	98
HILL ORVILLE EDWARD	NY	33W	78
HILL PAUL JEWELL	OH	59E	4
HILL PAUL WAYNE	CA	27E	16
HILL PETER ALAN	CA	38E	77
HILL PHILLIP ANDREW	MI	38W	11
HILL RALPH OWEN	SC	11W	50
HILL RANDALL STEVEN	CA	52W	23
HILL RAYFORD JEROME	TX	17W	28
HILL RAYMOND LEE	TN	04E	120
HILL RICHARD ALFRED	NY	17E	79
HILL RICHARD ALLEN	UT	51E	30
HILL RICHARD DALE	TX	01E	36
HILL RICHARD GARFIELD	MD	15W	42
HILL RICHARD KENNETH	DE	06E	51
HILL ROBERT ALLEN	OH	08E	22
HILL ROBERT ALLEN	OH	12W	68
HILL ROBERT HARDY JR	MI	09W	14
HILL ROBERT LA VERNE	MI	11E	87
HILL ROBERT MORRIS	MS	03E	58
HILL ROBERT OREN JR	PA	07W	95
HILL ROBERT WILSON	IL	16E	78
HILL RODNEY DEAN	CA	27E	65
HILL RONALD ALLEN	IL	26W	91
HILL RONALD JAMES	OR	06W	61
HILL RONALD LEE	PA	40E	63
HILL SAMUEL TONY	NC	62W	16
HILL SID	DC	51W	40
HILL STERLING HAROLD	MI	66W	7
HILL THOMAS	TX	65W	10
HILL THOMAS ARTHUR	CT	22W	1
HILL THOMAS MARVIN JR	AL	14W	121
HILL THOMAS WAYNE	MD	40E	74
HILL TOMMY EDWARD	TN	05E	34
HILL TYRONE	NJ	59E	4
HILL VERTIS JAMES JR	SC	12E	42
HILL VICTOR C	NY	16E	20
HILL WILLIAM B JR	AL	10E	70
HILL WILLIAM ERNEST	FL	02E	94
HILL WILLIAM LEE	NC	04W	46
HILL WILLIAM LEO	SD	53E	33
HILL WILLIAM OMER	WV	13E	33
HILL WILLIAM RAY	WI	18E	35
HILLARD WILLIAM JAMES II	NY	29W	45
HILLER MICHAEL JAMES	AZ	24E	87
HILLEY ROBERT LEE	AL	33E	55
HILLIARD DONALD RAY	IL	08W	114
HILLIARD JAMES FRANCIS	MI	24W	110
HILLIARD JAMES GILBERT	FL	20W	123
HILLIARD JOSEPH ROLLINS	TX	03E	79
HILLIARD ROBERT RICHARD	OH	39W	73
HILLIARD WILLIAM EARL	TX	22E	104
HILLIN DOUGLAS WAYNE	TX	49W	41
HILLMAN COLEMAN GEE	TN	31E	27
HILLMAN JOSEPH III	AL	51W	30
HILLMAN RONALD ARWED	TX	55E	19
HILLMAN RONALD JOSEPH	NY	32W	59
HILLS CLARENCE S	AZ	42E	34
HILLS EARL H	OR	43E	21
HILLS JOHN RUSSELL	IN	05E	34
HILLS RICKY J	NY	08W	66
HILLSGROVE BARRY MALCOLM	NH	47E	12
HILLYER LOUIS	ND	33E	68
HILMES STEVEN LEE	KS	45W	26
HILT RICHARD MICHAEL	MN	32W	26
HILTE FRANK ELTON	PA	38E	51
HILTERBRAN DANNY LEE	OK	08W	66
HILTON DANIEL JEROME	IA	42W	11
HILTON DAVID LYNN	OH	30E	78
HILTON EUGENE JR	OH	60W	1
HILTON ROBERT LARIE	MD	06E	7
HILTON STEPHEN RANDOLPH	SC	46W	15
HILTS DAMION RANDOLPH	NY	05E	45
HILTZ JAMES FREDERICK	MA	01E	28
HILYARD JAMES HAROLD	MI	49W	47
HILYER BROADUS DALE	AL	41E	8
HIMEBAUGH LEE EDWARD	MI	65W	9
HIMES BERNARD MALCOLM	PA	62E	6
HIMES CLYDE STEVEN	MD	66W	7
HIMES EARL W	PA	30W	45
HIMES EDWARD LOUIS	TN	02W	51
HIMES JACK LANDEN	AZ	05E	80
HIMES LLOYD ALLEN	PA	36E	15
HIMES MICHAEL BRUCE	AL	26E	25
HIMES STEPHAN CARL	IN	20E	95
HIMLER ROBERT JOHN	ND	46W	3
HIMMELREICH HARRY EDWARD	NJ	02E	116
HIMMER LAWRENCE	CA	50E	14
HIMMERICK MICHAEL DUANE	ND	17E	111
HINCEWICZ EDWARD JOSEPH	PA	04E	69
HINCH JAMES GARY	TX	22E	14
HINCKLE JAMES NELSON	OK	43E	21
HINCKLEY CHARLES ALBON	MA	46E	18
HINCKLEY WILLIAM K JR	MA	24E	27
HINDERKS GREGG CLIFTON	MO	21W	32
HINDERMAN ANDREW JACOB	OH	02E	81
HINDMAN TOMMY IVAN	IA	11W	113
HINDS KENNETH WILLIAM	OH	08W	12
HINDS STEPHEN JOHN	MN	49E	42
HINE GLEN DOUGLAS	MA	07E	18
HINER FRANKLIN JOE	UT	55W	35
HINERMAN WILLIAM RUSSELL	OH	10E	112
HINES ARTHUR	GA	38E	72
HINES GEORGE MCDONALD	KY	14W	13
HINES JAMES ROOSEVELT	IL	03E	79
HINES JOE RAYMOND	FL	65E	11
HINES JOHN CHARLES	NY	07W	1
HINES JOHN LESTER	VA	26E	75
HINES JOHN THOMAS	SC	35W	71
HINES JOHN WAYNE	OH	07W	87
HINES JONNY	CT	10W	80
HINES LESLIE EDMUND III	WA	46W	3
HINES LOUIS CLARK	MS	10E	128
HINES NAMON JR	TX	22E	57
HINES PHILIP BLAINE	KS	09E	1
HINES PHILLIP MASON	KS	20E	44
HINES RALPH EARLE	MA	15E	62
HINES RANDY VICTOR	MI	03W	82
HINES RONALD DICKERSON	TX	01E	50
HINES TERRI LIEGH	IN	22E	104
HINES VAUGHN M	CA	29E	50
HINES WILBURT NATHAN	AR	37W	51
HINES WILLIAM CARROLL	NC	03W	120
HINES WILLIAM JOSEPH	NY	24E	87
HINES WILLIAM LINCOLN JR	MD	05E	17
HINGLETON EUGENE JR	SC	41W	29
HINGSTON WILLIAM E JR	MA	14E	74
HINKEL DANIEL KENNETH	OH	28W	47
HINKLE CARL RODMAN	IN	35W	4
HINKLE DOUGLAS LEE	OH	31W	4
HINKLE JACK LEE	OH	50E	14
HINKLE JAMES MELVIN	IL	02W	46
HINKLE JOHN WARREN	MI	38W	26
HINKLE KENNETH DANIEL	KY	58W	19
HINKLE MARK GORDON	MT	03E	14
HINKLE NORMAN LEE	MN	51E	33
HINKLE TERRY LEE	OH	38W	49
HINKLE TERRY RICHARD	PA	48W	6
HINKLE WILLIAM CECIL	IL	30E	56
HINKLEY STEPHEN	MA	56E	8
HINKSTON ROBERT FRANCIS	CA	37W	75
HINMAN DWIGHT EARL	IA	55W	21
HINNANT BENJAMIN LOWELL	PA	56E	8
HINNANT KENNETH LEE	TN	49E	42
HINO MICHAEL LYNN	SC	02W	58
HINOJOSA FERNANDO AMYO	TX	07E	18
HINOJOSA JOSE ANTONIO	TX	41E	55
HINOJOSA MARCOS	TX	56W	22
HINOJOSA RUDOLPH JR	FL	21W	30
HINSCHBERGER LAWRENCE K	MN	21W	7
HINSDALE GERALD CLINTON	VA	03W	94
HINSLEY EARNEST RICHARD	TX	28E	103
HINSON ALVIN CRAWFORD	NJ	25W	71
HINSON BERT HOWARD	WA	34E	53
HINSON DON	NY	36W	61
HINSON HERBERT STEPHEN	OH	05W	49
HINSON JAMES HARVEY	FL	22E	120
HINSON JOHN ROBERT	SC	25E	1
HINSON RALPH LEON	GA	04E	21
HINSON REGGIE WESTEL	IN	13W	36
HINSON RONALD DOUGLAS	SC	50E	15
HINSON THOMAS ALLEN	TX	20W	57
HINSON WILLIAM RONALD	NC	45W	19
HINTERLONG LEO EDWARD	OH	09E	53
HINTHER GARY ROGER	MT	54W	17
HINTON CHARLES COLEMAN JR	CA	14W	78
HINTON DENNIS EDWARD	CO	55E	17
HINTON DENNIS RAY	IN	02W	36
HINTON JIMMIE DAVID	MS	02W	11
HINTON LUTHER ANDERSON	VA	21W	18
HINTON OVERTIS JR	AR	63E	10
HINTON RICHARD	NY	08E	66
HINTON RODNEY GENE	KS	37E	84
HINTZ JAMES RAYMOND	MI	17E	5
HINTZ JAMES WESLEY	MI	18E	10
HINZ DAVID LEE	TX	47E	4
HINZPETER ALAN ROLF	ND	02W	11
HIPKE HARRY ALLAN	WI	02E	79
HIPKINS COLIN KEITH	IA	26E	11
HIPP JOSEPH EARNEST	GA	04E	64
HIPPACH MICHAEL HARVEY	UT	14W	36
HIPPIE BRADFORD JOHN F	NJ	63W	6
HIPPLE DUANE ALLEN	PA	31W	68
HIPPO DENNIS WILLIAM	PA	34W	24
HIRANO OWEN TETSUMI	HI	17W	56
HIRES THOMAS MICHAEL	CA	15W	90
HIRNI TROY EDWARD II	MO	36E	15
HIROKAWA ROCKY YUKIO	CA	13W	96
HIRSCH MARSHALL RAYMOND	IL	05E	58
HIRSCHI CRAIG W	ID	07W	65
HIRSCHLER RALPH DEAN JR	CO	44E	17
HIRSCHMANN FREDERICK III	CA	26E	78
HIRST KENNETH LEWIS JR	NY	19E	107
HIRST ROBERT LEE	PA	03E	79
HIRTLE HAROLD HERMAN	MA	11E	43
HIRTLER ERNEST LLOYD	MO	04W	63

NAME	STATE	PANEL NO.	LINE NO.
HISAW TEDDY LEE JR	OK	28E	91
HISCOCK STEPHEN MAYO	GA	05W	134
HISE JAMES HAMILTON	IA	17E	44
HISEY JOHN EDWIN	OH	20W	71
HISEY TYRONE WADE	OH	06E	64
HISLE GARY LEE	KY	24W	85
HISSONG HARRY LEAVERN	IL	19E	43
HITCHCOCK LEE CHARL	IN	26E	45
HITCHCOCK RALPH JOHN	FL	55E	17
HITCHCOCK RAYMOND R JR	MD	55W	28
HITCHCOCK TILLMON POWELL	TN	18E	94
HITCHCOCK WILLIAM F	MA	27W	87
HITCHENS LAWRENCE EDWARD	DE	24W	31
HITCHINS LLOYD LYNN	IL	31E	87
HITE FRANKLIN DANIEL	PA	16E	72
HITER VIRGIL LEMAR	OH	32E	10
HITES ALLEN LYNN	OH	19W	113
HITES ROGER ALLEN	IA	14E	35
HITESHUE FRANK RICHARD	PA	06W	59
HITRO BERNARD GEORGE JR	NY	35W	65
HITSON FREDERICK ALTON	CA	16E	59
HITT ROY MARVIN JR	AL	03E	18
HITTINGER FRANCIS R JR	VA	43E	67
HITZELBERGER GEORGE	MD	06E	25
HIUKKA GERALD ALLEN	OR	34E	42
HIVELY BENNIE RAY	AR	03W	8
HIVELY DANIEL RICHARD	OH	08W	7
HIVELY GUY RICHARD	WV	36E	74
HIVELY ROBERT LYNN	NY	22W	89
HIX KEITH EUGENE	MO	11E	61
HIX RICHARD LAWSON	AR	22E	8
HIX WILLIAM COLQUETH JR	FL	33W	64
HIXSON CARL EDWARD	PA	33E	48
HIXSON RANDALL LEE	TN	13E	84
HJORTH WILLIAM HAROLD	MI	03W	45
HLADIK HAROLD HERBERT	KS	32W	49
HLAVACEK GLENN JOHN	IL	18E	4
HO ALVIN JOCK	HI	32W	38
HOADLEY GARY ELLIS	CA	49W	5
HOADLEY LARRY FRANCIS C	MI	45W	19
HOAG EARL THOMAS	MI	30W	76
HOAG JAMES DEAN	GA	22W	89
HOAG PAUL RICHARD JR	NY	59E	23
HOAGE GERALD CURTIS	OR	36W	3
HOAGLAND GEORGE A III	AZ	04E	109
HOAGLAND JEFFREY KAY	VA	11W	46
HOAR JOHN MICHAEL	NJ	05E	29
HOARE THOMAS JOSEPH JR	NY	34E	68
HOBACK DOUGLAS EDWARD	WV	36E	75
HOBAN CHARLES JOHN III	IL	25E	29
HOBAN MICHAEL NOEL	WA	49W	13
HOBART GLENN EDWARD III	MA	35W	48
HOBBS CECIL R JR	MI	48E	4
HOBBS CHARLES MICHAEL	MO	30W	4
HOBBS DOUGLAS ERNEST	CA	10W	51
HOBBS GARY LEE	CA	14W	72
HOBBS GARY LYNN	TX	16E	122
HOBBS GLEN THOMAS	OH	43E	22
HOBBS KIMMEY DEAN	TX	49E	11
HOBBS LARRY L	AZ	16E	59
HOBBS RONALD ROBERT	DC	36W	21
HOBBS RONALD WAYNE	MI	05E	26
HOBERT WILLIAM JOSEPH	WA	09E	98
HOBSON CHRISTOPHER MARK	CO	10W	85
HOBSON JOHN KING	NE	37W	81
HOCH LARRY DEAN	PA	25W	12
HOCHMUTH BRUNO ARTHUR	TX	29E	95
HOCHSTETLER TERRY LYNN	OH	01W	40
HOCHSTETTER JAMES JAY	MN	22W	117
HOCK LELDON EDWIN JR	WA	32W	20
HOCK RICHARD JAMES	OH	02W	98
HOCK ROBERT WILLIAM	IL	19W	2
HOCK RONALD FRANCIS	NY	09E	91
HOCK STEPHEN LOUIS	OR	24E	27
HOCKADAY JIMMY LEON	TX	09E	127
HOCKENBERRY EDWIN CLOYD	PA	19W	61
HOCKENBERRY JOSEPH LESTER	PA	17E	92
HOCKENSMITH DAVID BAKER	KY	06W	54
HOCKER NORMAN ROGER	CO	19E	127
HOCKER WILLIAM EDDIE	NC	26E	1
HOCKETT DAVID ALLEN	IN	13W	36
HOCKETT JAMES RAYMOND	IL	43W	63
HOCKNELL HENRY ROBERT JR	NJ	29E	50
HOCKRIDGE JAMES ALAN	NY	01W	82
HOCUTT LARRY KEITH	AL	28W	82
HODAL ROBERT JOHN	MI	42E	65
HODEL MARK EDWARD	CA	47E	22
HODGE ANDREW HERMAN	FL	12E	4
HODGE CHARLES EDWARD	IL	43E	55
HODGE CHARLES LYNN	NV	28W	91
HODGE CLAUDE ARTHUR	NY	20E	16
HODGE DENNIS RAY	OH	26E	65
HODGE EDWARD L	MI	05E	128
HODGE JAMES EDWARD	OH	49E	40
HODGE JOHN DAVID	CA	05W	113
HODGE KENNETH RAY	TN	12W	69
HODGE MICHAEL ALLARD	WI	37E	54
HODGE MICHAEL LEONARD	MI	22W	78
HODGE RONALD ELLSWORTH	MI	11W	22
HODGE RUSSELL ADDISON	KY	39W	73
HODGE THOMAS WAYNE	IL	35E	22
HODGE WILLIAM JOHN	MA	13W	68
HODGE WILLIAM REUBEN	FL	31W	4
HODGES BENNIE E	AL	54W	6
HODGES BERNARD	NC	06W	110
HODGES CARL FREDERICK JR	NC	50W	1
HODGES DAVID LAWTON	MD	27E	66
HODGES DWIGHT	MS	36W	69
HODGES ERNEST MAEHUE	NY	55W	28
HODGES FERMAN BOBBY	AL	17W	128
HODGES GARY STEPHEN	NC	37W	81
HODGES HARKLES LEROY	SC	51W	40
HODGES HARRY GAINES	TN	34E	49
HODGES HOMER LEE JR	TX	44W	10
HODGES JAMES DALE	AL	68W	2
HODGES JOSEPH	GA	54W	42
HODGES KENNETH ALLEN	WA	39W	67
HODGES LARRY LEON	TN	29W	9
HODGES LEE ROY	TX	28E	15
HODGES RAYMOND LEON JR	OK	07W	18
HODGES RICHARD PRESTON	GA	32W	79
HODGES ROBERT GENTRY	TN	38W	57
HODGES RUFUS WELDON	TX	34W	24
HODGES TEDDY MERLIN JR	ID	23W	87
HODGES TERRY ALAN	NC	48W	55
HODGES WESLEY EUGENE	TX	40E	75
HODGES WILLIAM JEFFREY	MD	37W	39
HODGES WILLIAM JESSE SR	MO	07W	80
HODGKIN FOREST CLAYTON	ME	16W	80
HODGKINS GUY MERRILL	NM	10E	65
HODGSKIN JAMES G JR	FL	19W	61
HODGSON CECIL J	TX	04E	109
HODGSON DOUGLAS RALPH	IA	19E	50
HODOROWSKI RAYMOND	OH	16E	28
HODSON CHARLES HERBERT JR	VA	36W	72
HODSON VICTOR M	WA	27W	81
HOECKELBERG THOMAS JOE	IN	36W	68
HOEFFS JOHN HARVEY	CA	12E	127
HOEKER JOSEPH ALAN	MI	18W	83
HOEL RONALD EDWIN	WA	09E	33
HOELSCHER JOHN MICHAEL	TX	05E	51
HOEME FORREST DEAN	KS	16E	57
HOENIGES THOMAS LEO	IL	21E	74
HOERNER RAYMOND DALE	MT	14E	5
HOEWELER JAMES EDWARD	OH	23E	11
HOFER RUSSELL GENE	CA	50W	19
HOFER THOMAS EDWARD	IN	27W	49
HOFF DENNIS WAYNE	MN	52E	6
HOFF MICHAEL GEORGE	OR	14W	8
HOFF MICHAEL GORDON	MI	40W	76
HOFF RONALD ALVIN	IN	20W	6
HOFF SAMMIE DON	TX	10E	57
HOFFEDITZ DONALD RAY	MO	12W	127
HOFFERT DAVID EDGAR	OH	38W	6
HOFFLER RICHARD WILLIAM	VA	18W	15
HOFFMAN ALLAN ROY	MN	22E	70
HOFFMAN CARL DEAN	OH	12E	47
HOFFMAN CHARLES DAVID	WV	06W	39
HOFFMAN CHARLES EDWIN	TX	38E	51
HOFFMAN DANIEL ROBERT	IL	02W	36
HOFFMAN DAVID PAUL	MO	13W	58
HOFFMAN DAVID R	IL	55W	34
HOFFMAN DENNIS EUGENE	PA	21E	36
HOFFMAN DONALD ROBERT	OH	56W	22
HOFFMAN DOUGLAS ELMER	IA	33W	40
HOFFMAN EDWIN EARL	IL	26W	71
HOFFMAN FREDRICK JEAN	CA	27E	53
HOFFMAN IRWIN LEWIS	NY	04E	70
HOFFMAN JAMES MICHAEL	MS	61W	14
HOFFMAN JOHN DANIEL	PA	06E	75
HOFFMAN JOHN PAUL	OK	02W	3
HOFFMAN KENNETH JAMES	NY	50W	6
HOFFMAN LEROY DAVID	WI	38W	34
HOFFMAN LYNN ARTHUR	PA	51W	32
HOFFMAN MELVIN ELMER	MI	20E	95
HOFFMAN ROBERT ALLEN	IL	20W	80
HOFFMAN RODNEY LOUIS	CO	24E	106
HOFFMAN RONALD THOMAS	CO	04W	28
HOFFMAN RONNIE JOE	TX	39E	5
HOFFMAN SHULER ADOLF	SC	37E	36
HOFFMAN TERRY ALAN	IN	48W	56
HOFFMAN WILLIAM DAVID	KS	48E	27
HOFFMANN CHARLES J III	FL	18E	10
HOFFMANN RICHARD ALFONCE	IL	43W	37
HOFFMANN ROBERT JAMES	NJ	23W	53
HOFFMANN THOMAS MARTIN	NJ	24W	54
HOFFNER WAYNE HENRY	IA	52E	19
HOFMANN EARL FREDERICK	IL	13W	28
HOGAN BILLY JACK JR	MO	06W	92
HOGAN DARRELL	KY	02W	56
HOGAN DAVID CLEVELAND	GA	34W	58
HOGAN EDWARD JOSEPH	NY	24W	67
HOGAN GARY LEE	AZ	36W	69
HOGAN GORDON LEE	IL	17E	79
HOGAN JERRY FRANKS	AL	14E	63
HOGAN JOHN BERNARD	NY	39E	48
HOGAN JOHN LAWRENCE	NH	04W	86
HOGAN JOHN WESLEY	IL	43E	55
HOGAN KRAIG SEWELL	CA	43E	44
HOGAN RADFORD DOUGLAS	CO	04E	90
HOGAN WALTER DE WAYNE	NV	30E	9
HOGAN WILLIAM FRANCIS JR	KY	16E	78
HOGANS WALTER JIM	AL	17W	41
HOGARTH RICHARD DOUGLAS	OH	07E	34
HOGBIN RONNIE ELLIS	FL	24W	103
HOGE FRANK LEE	OH	39E	72
HOGEMAN CARROLL GENE	LA	12E	120
HOGENBOOM DENNIS NORMAN	NY	09W	20
HOGENMILLER FRANK	PA	39W	70
HOGGARD JAMES LUTHER	VA	09E	29
HOGGATT JOHN ANDREW	WA	49E	22
HOGGATT JOSEPH LEE	TX	27E	59
HOGGE DOUGLAS WARREN	VA	08E	10
HOGGE MICHAEL LEE	KY	23E	82
HOGLE RICHARD LEE	WI	08E	45
HOGLUND GARY WILLIAM	MN	20E	16
HOGLUND MICHAEL AUGUST	MI	29E	65
HOGSTON ROGER LEE	OH	15E	62
HOGUE JOHN MICHAEL	WA	51W	41
HOHMAN DANIEL JOHN	OH	05W	124
HOHMAN JOHN MICHAEL	FL	23W	27
HOHMAN LARRY LOUISE	PA	15W	32
HOHN RODNEY ALLEN	MI	25W	6
HOHSTADT JIMMY ROSS	NM	27E	81
HOJNACKI ROBERT FRANK	IL	02W	23
HOJNOWSKI STANLEY BERNARD	PA	20W	102
HOKE MICHAEL THOMAS	AK	32E	41
HOKENSON WAYNE ALLEN	KY	47E	22
HOLAN ROBERT ANDREW JR	MN	28W	26
HOLBROOK BENNIE H	OH	18E	121
HOLBROOK CARL EUGENE	GA	22E	62
HOLBROOK CHARLES ALLEN	IL	42W	47
HOLBROOK GARY WAYNE	MI	37E	84
HOLBROOK HORACE ALVIE	AL	19E	96
HOLBROOK JAMES NEWTON	OK	02E	110
HOLBROOK JAMES WENDELL	CA	64W	10
HOLBROOK JEFFREY LYNN	IN	40E	41
HOLBROOK JERRY RAY	KY	24E	3
HOLBROOK VERNON GLEN	AL	16W	53
HOLBROOK WILLIAM R	OH	06E	10
HOLCK PAUL ALAN	AZ	26E	89
HOLCMAN MORRIS ELIOT	IL	49W	8
HOLCOMB DANIEL	GA	40E	41
HOLCOMB DANIEL JENNINGS	CA	17E	5
HOLCOMB DOYLE	TN	22E	41
HOLCOMB JAMES LEE	WV	12E	5

NAME	STATE	PANEL NO.	LINE NO.
HOLCOMB JOHN NOBLE	OR	37W	32
HOLCOMB JOHN PALMORE	MD	53E	15
HOLCOMB MELVIN DOUGLAS	CA	23E	19
HOLCOMB REBEL LEE	KS	03E	33
HOLCOMB ROBERT EARL	MN	15E	46
HOLCOMBE THOMAS MARVIN	CA	51E	21
HOLDAWAY GUY	VA	37W	46
HOLDBROOKS THOMAS BERNARD	TX	32E	87
HOLDEMAN ROBERT EUGENE	IN	30E	85
HOLDEN ALFRED JEFFERSON	AL	04E	120
HOLDEN DAVID CHARLES	MA	15E	118
HOLDEN ELMER LARRY	OK	58W	9
HOLDEN JAMES EDWARD	DE	03E	79
HOLDEN JOHN PARKER II	PA	49E	23
HOLDEN LOWELL DEAN	MI	26E	75
HOLDEN ROBERT FRANKLIN	IL	56E	25
HOLDEN THOMAS JAMES	NJ	11E	97
HOLDEN WILLIAM DAVID	MA	15E	44
HOLDER CARL LEWIS	SC	35W	27
HOLDER FREDRICK LEE	MO	34W	15
HOLDER HENRY EMIL JR	TX	34W	49
HOLDER JAMES EDWARD	OK	11E	15
HOLDER JAMES EDWARD	NC	08W	127
HOLDER KENNETH LEROY	PA	19E	72
HOLDER LEONARD DONALD	TX	45E	47
HOLDER RANDOLPH CHESTER	FL	01E	126
HOLDER SAMUEL LOYD	OK	29W	10
HOLDERBAUM JOHN ARTHUR	MI	49W	38
HOLDERBY VERLIN DON	OK	41E	21
HOLDERMAN BRUCE EDWARD	CA	13E	91
HOLDING DARRELL EUGENE	OK	35W	83
HOLDITCH ROBERT WILSON		21W	45
HOLDREDGE DAVID LEE	CA	34W	15
HOLDWAY DAVID KEITH	MD	19E	26
HOLEMAN RAY WALTER	OH	11E	3
HOLEMAN RONALD STEVEN	CA	21W	112
HOLEMAN WARREN DALE	CA	02W	1
HOLES JASON AIREAL	WA	59W	4
HOLEYFIELD ROBERT ERIE	TN	52E	38
HOLGUIN FRANK JOHN	CA	01E	47
HOLGUIN ISMAEL	TX	37E	84
HOLGUIN JOSE JR	TX	15E	128
HOLGUIN LUIS GALLEGOS	CA	05W	22
HOLIAN GARY LEE	IL	03W	129
HOLIDAY MICHAEL LEONARD	MI	36E	15
HOLIEN RICHARD PAUL	WA	08E	112
HOLIFIELD FLOYD JR	NC	23E	28
HOLJES FREDERICK Y	NJ	45E	57
HOLKE DONALD STEVEN	WA	29E	58
HOLKEM JIMMY RAY	AL	07W	30
HOLL GEORGE WILLIAM	NY	39W	44
HOLLADAY GEORGE ALFRED	OR	23E	76
HOLLAND CARLTON JAKE	WY	01E	86
HOLLAND CHARLES JAMES	NJ	25E	13
HOLLAND CHARLES RALPH	TN	32E	23
HOLLAND CLARENCE MICHAEL	VA	30W	55
HOLLAND CLAYTON MONROE JR	PA	35E	24
HOLLAND DAVID HERMAN	PA	20E	74
HOLLAND DOUGLAS C	IA	18E	4
HOLLAND DOUGLAS DEAN	IA	34E	58
HOLLAND EDDIE HERMAN	GA	33E	49
HOLLAND FARIS E	OH	40W	65
HOLLAND FRANK RODNEY	PA	17E	35
HOLLAND GARY DAVID	PA	38E	51
HOLLAND GARY R	OK	49E	33
HOLLAND JAMES LARRY	AL	40E	63
HOLLAND JOHN HENRY	VT	18E	109
HOLLAND JOHNNY ROBERT	NE	13E	38
HOLLAND JOSEPH PHILLIP	CT	36E	51
HOLLAND KERMIT W JR	VA	12W	34
HOLLAND LAWRENCE THOMAS	CA	02E	9
HOLLAND LUEY VERNON	CA	36E	15
HOLLAND MELVIN A	WA	44E	21
HOLLAND ROBERT JOSEPH	AL	14W	49
HOLLAND ROBERT LOW	TX	21E	101
HOLLAND ROBERT VERNON	VA	60W	10
HOLLAND RUSSELL JAMES	NM	31W	49
HOLLAND VERNON EDWARD	KY	04E	24
HOLLAND WAYNE BIZZLE	NC	40W	37
HOLLAND WILLIAM DELBERT	TX	33E	8
HOLLAND WILLIAM L JR	NJ	44E	27
HOLLAND WILLIE J	KY	29E	24

NAME	STATE	PANEL NO.	LINE NO.
HOLLANDSWORTH EDDIE DEAN	TX	13E	50
HOLLAR COURTNEY PRICE JR	PA	01E	51
HOLLAR HOWARD ESLIE	VA	43E	22
HOLLAWAY PHILIP STEPHEN	AL	31E	92
HOLLE JOHN WILLIAM	TX	21W	42
HOLLEDER DONALD WALTER	NY	28E	25
HOLLEMAN JOE EARL	TX	28W	47
HOLLENBACH DONALD WALTER	NY	30E	63
HOLLENBACH KENNETH RALPH	PA	04E	100
HOLLENBACH MERLIN CHARLES	PA	32E	44
HOLLENSHEAD WINSTON GEORG	LA	16E	111
HOLLER CARL WAYNE	OH	56W	4
HOLLER ROGER EMIL	MN	11W	102
HOLLER ROGER GUY	PA	05W	49
HOLLEY BOBBY ROY	CA	09E	39
HOLLEY GLYNN BYRON	TX	15W	93
HOLLEY LARRY DOUGLAS	NM	24E	26
HOLLEY PAUL RICHARD	OH	55E	17
HOLLEY ROBERT GORDON	OK	47W	45
HOLLEY ROBERT STANLEY III	MD	21W	52
HOLLEY TILDEN STEWART	TX	34E	87
HOLLIDAY BERNARD	IL	54W	29
HOLLIDAY CLYDE LEE	CA	20W	49
HOLLIDAY CRIS	MS	23W	15
HOLLIDAY JAMES WILLIS	PA	11E	20
HOLLIE ROBERT LEE JR	IL	53W	27
HOLLIFIELD FORREST HUGHY	NC	08W	69
HOLLIFIELD HAROLD DEAN	NC	08W	111
HOLLIFIELD ROGER DALE	VA	20W	123
HOLLIFIELD SAMUEL F JR	NC	33E	69
HOLLIFIELD VERNON GILBERT	SC	10E	39
HOLLIMAN TED DELANE JR	NC	32E	73
HOLLIMON BILLY MICHAEL	AL	43E	6
HOLLINGER GREGG NEYMAN	ID	02W	88
HOLLINGSWORTH DON RAY	TX	19E	37
HOLLINGSWORTH GARY LYNN	MO	03W	40
HOLLINGSWORTH HAL T	ID	04E	74
HOLLINGSWORTH JERRY G JR	SC	61E	11
HOLLINGSWORTH JOHN ANDREW	AR	20E	44
HOLLINGSWORTH JOSEPH K	MS	26W	8
HOLLINGSWORTH MICHAEL DEN	FL	37E	28
HOLLINGSWORTH NICHOLAS LE	IL	53E	15
HOLLINGSWORTH RICHARD LEE	MI	04E	59
HOLLINGSWORTH VERNICE	FL	18E	45
HOLLINGWORTH DAVID MCLEAN	CO	56W	12
HOLLIS JAMES AUGUSTUS	AL	42W	61
HOLLIS JAMES FAY	WA	01W	36
HOLLIS JAMES SHELTON	CA	13E	72
HOLLIS JOHN EDWARD	TX	06W	51
HOLLIS THEODORE ROBERT	TX	64E	15
HOLLIS THOMAS WILLIAM	IL	35E	54
HOLLISTER HOMER WARREN	PA	33W	40
HOLLISTER JOHN FREDERICK	AZ	09W	98
HOLLMAN DAVID LEE	IN	18W	109
HOLLMEN WILLIAM HARRY	AZ	52E	38
HOLLOMAN CLETUH JR	IL	56E	8
HOLLOPETER RAYMOND RICHARD	IN	29E	71
HOLLOWAY CHARLES EDWARD	FL	01E	15
HOLLOWAY EDWIN NEWLIN III	PA	16E	79
HOLLOWAY FREDDY LEE	AR	22W	21
HOLLOWAY JAMES OWENS JR	NJ	48E	5
HOLLOWAY JOHN MARSHALL	OK	32W	32
HOLLOWAY JOHNNY RAY	MS	05E	104
HOLLOWAY LARRY DANIEL	LA	16W	84
HOLLOWAY LYLE D	MO	07E	118
HOLLOWAY MICHAEL JAMES	IL	19W	31
HOLLOWAY MICHAEL SCOTT	MI	04W	87
HOLLOWAY PAUL DAVID	FL	14E	97
HOLLOWAY RICHARD ALTON	TX	31E	24
HOLLOWAY THOMAS EUGENE	IN	27W	64
HOLLOWELL DALE MITCHELL	TN	04W	33
HOLLOWELL WILLIAM BYARD	AL	17E	35
HOLLWEDEL CHARLES WILLIAM	IL	24E	27
HOLLY CHARLIE DELNO	TX	10E	13
HOLLY GEORGE JOSEPH III	NV	35E	22
HOLLY RONNIE	CA	01W	66
HOLM ALAN HANS	WA	03W	21
HOLM ARNOLD EDWARD JR	CT	01W	40
HOLM DENNIS LEE	SD	20E	84
HOLM DONALD HENRY	IA	30E	16
HOLMAN ADAM JR	WA	22W	53
HOLMAN BOBBY FOSTER	TX	33E	39

NAME	STATE	PANEL NO.	LINE NO.
HOLMAN CLARENCE LEANEAL	NC	16W	29
HOLMAN DONALD WOODS	AR	13W	104
HOLMAN GERALD ALLAN	MI	13E	44
HOLMAN MARSHALL DANIEL	MI	02E	34
HOLMAN RAYMOND CLARK	CT	22W	58
HOLMAN RICHARD JEROME	OR	23W	74
HOLMAN SAMUEL L	MD	03E	79
HOLMES ALLAN WILLIAM	AZ	01W	66
HOLMES BILLY RAY	WV	53W	1
HOLMES CLEVELAND	FL	35E	72
HOLMES DAVID	NY	03E	28
HOLMES DAVID HUGH	MA	06E	10
HOLMES DAVID WILLIAM	TN	09E	39
HOLMES EARNEST PAUL JR	AL	39E	48
HOLMES EDWARD WAYNE	TN	13W	118
HOLMES FREDERICK LEE	CA	02W	92
HOLMES HAROLD	NJ	42E	52
HOLMES HAROLD ANTHONY	GA	08W	35
HOLMES HUGH BRYANT	CA	21W	8
HOLMES JACK EUGENE	KS	15W	98
HOLMES JAMES CECIL	OH	45W	52
HOLMES JAMES MICHAEL	MS	40W	20
HOLMES JAMES ROBERT	MO	12W	56
HOLMES JERRY LEONARD	CA	21E	22
HOLMES JIM HENRY	MI	10W	80
HOLMES JOHN HARRIS	MS	32E	30
HOLMES JOHN HENRY	SC	06W	101
HOLMES JOHN LEE	OR	58W	32
HOLMES JOSEPH	GA	17W	84
HOLMES KEITH DANIEL	AR	06W	134
HOLMES LARRY LAMAR	GA	24W	43
HOLMES LEONARD HUGH	AL	33W	48
HOLMES LESTER EVAN	IA	20E	81
HOLMES LINWOOD MCCOY	NC	10E	119
HOLMES LONNIE MICHAEL	IN	21E	106
HOLMES MICHAEL DOUGLAS	MO	27W	81
HOLMES NATHAN	GA	42E	17
HOLMES NORMAN WARD	WA	38E	52
HOLMES PHILLIP HEASE JR	LA	08E	21
HOLMES ROBERT HAROLD	MO	11E	52
HOLMES ROBERT THOMAS	IL	18W	79
HOLMES RODGER DALE	IN	31W	49
HOLMES RONALD EUGENE	MD	31E	47
HOLMES SAM JR	FL	03W	34
HOLMES SAMMY LEE	FL	21E	121
HOLMES TERRY WAYNE	KY	33E	3
HOLMES THOMAS EUGENE	SC	16W	39
HOLMES WILLIAM DAVID	VA	03W	2
HOLMGREN ROY JAY	CA	09W	64
HOLMON ALPHONZO JR	SC	36E	51
HOLOKA JOHN CHARLES	PA	09E	57
HOLOVITS LASZLO	CA	27E	3
HOLROYD JAMES LAWRENCE	KS	18E	4
HOLSCLAW GARY ARTHUR	CA	22E	104
HOLSINGER GARY OLSON	OH	42E	65
HOLSOMBACK FRANK NOLAN	LA	27E	95
HOLST FREDERICK AUGUST	IA	07W	120
HOLSTEIN JOHN L	CA	13E	98
HOLSTER TIMOTHY	MA	12E	5
HOLSTIUS MICHAEL JOHN	CA	25E	84
HOLSTON ARVELL BERNARD	MI	12W	25
HOLSTON PAUL	MI	42W	29
HOLSWORTH JAMES MICHAEL	MO	16E	60
HOLT ALLEN LEE	KS	02E	28
HOLT BILLY JOE	TX	07E	118
HOLT CLARENCE RAY	MO	38E	65
HOLT CLAY JR	MO	46W	49
HOLT CRAIG BARKER	RI	66W	8
HOLT DANIEL JAMES	WA	34W	33
HOLT DAVID RODNEY	NC	38W	7
HOLT DENNIS EDWARD	TN	06E	65
HOLT EDWARD EUGENE	NY	45E	48
HOLT GARY RICHARD	WA	08E	85
HOLT HERSCHEL CYLE	TN	09E	103
HOLT JACK ENGLISH	GA	13E	106
HOLT JAMES	MS	59W	5
HOLT JAMES CHARLES	CA	37W	39
HOLT JAMES RICHARD	AR	37E	36
HOLT JAMES WILLIAM	AR	37E	84
HOLT JOHNNY SAMUEL	NC	34W	58
HOLT MARSHALL MYRON JR	IA	05E	95
HOLT MERRIL	WV	09W	73

NAME	STATE	PANEL NO.	LINE NO.
HOLT RAYMOND CLYDE	CA	05W	11
HOLT RICHARD ANCIL	GA	59W	5
HOLT ROBERT ALAN	MA	43W	37
HOLT RONALD WALTER	TX	10W	12
HOLTE BRENT ARTHUR	CA	26E	102
HOLTE MARK DELANE	MN	15E	14
HOLTE ROGER ALLEN	MN	37W	16
HOLTHOFF WILLIAM HENRY	IL	17E	5
HOLTMAN JOHN THOMAS	MO	25E	84
HOLTOM MARK RICHARD	KS	07W	93
HOLTON GARY DENNIS	CA	53W	1
HOLTON JOHN THOMAS JR	FL	53W	35
HOLTON LEON G	GA	02E	112
HOLTON LOUIS ALEXANDER JR	MD	19E	82
HOLTON ROBERT EDWIN	MT	33W	14
HOLTON STANLEY GENE	AZ	49W	54
HOLTORF DENNIS WAYNE	IA	15W	4
HOLTREY DANIEL PERRY	MI	19W	86
HOLTSCHNEIDER GEORGE ALEX	MO	14W	18
HOLTZ ALFRED JOSEPH JR	WI	54W	37
HOLTZ LARRY WILLIAM	NE	12E	62
HOLTZ MICHAEL LEE	CA	17W	56
HOLTZ PAUL AUGUST	NE	34W	38
HOLTZCLAW GARY EARL	KY	26W	99
HOLTZCLAW PHILIP BRUCE	GA	04W	38
HOLTZCLAW THOMAS J III	GA	18E	60
HOLTZHOUSER RONALD LEE	MO	50E	4
HOLTZLANDER DOYLE EDWARD	MI	07E	1
HOLTZMAN EDWARD MONROE	PA	32W	13
HOLTZMAN RONALD LEE	VA	25E	38
HOLUPKO LON MICHAEL	MI	21W	93
HOLYCROSS RICHARD LAKE	OH	26E	45
HOLZ GARY LEROY	WA	27E	73
HOLZ JOHN FREDERICK	PA	32E	23
HOLZAPFEL NORBERT PAUL	PA	38E	52
HOLZER BOBBY LEE	AR	07W	33
HOLZER RICHARD EUGENE JR	MO	20W	83
HOLZHEIMER DENNIS ALLEN	WA	34W	76
HOLZKNECHT BERNARD LEE	IN	19W	3
HOLZMAN MICHAEL WILLIAM	CA	42E	17
HOM CHARLES DAVID	CA	25E	7
HOMBEL RAY EARL	WA	19W	15
HOMER ERNEST CRAIG	PA	39W	74
HOMER WARD ELLIOTT	PA	29W	78
HOMEYER FREDERICK	NY	06E	121
HOMINICK HOWARD HUGH	NY	52E	30
HOMMEL DANIEL JOHN	NY	68W	3
HOMMEL DAVID ELSON	PA	30E	56
HOMSCHEK ROBERT WILLIAM	PA	04W	105
HOMSLEY IVAN D	TX	36E	15
HOMSLEY VICTOR JORY	AR	15E	118
HOMSTAD MILO STEVEN	MN	53W	10
HOMUTH RICHARD WENDAL	CA	20E	90
HON JOHNNY JOE	IL	60E	12
HONAKER RALPH	KY	23W	87
HONAKER RAYMOND KERMIT JR	GA	45W	14
HONAKER WILLIE ELSWORTH H	IN	02E	75
HONAN JOSEPH PAUL	PA	13W	23
HONCHAROFF GENE EDWARD	ND	66W	8
HONDA KAORU	HI	25E	92
HONDEL WILLIAM JAMES	WI	44E	37
HONEA STANLEY RAY	WA	19W	106
HONEK KENNETH JEROME	MN	47E	51
HONEY RICHARD LANCE	TX	16W	38
HONEYCUTT BENJAMIN ALLEN	TX	54E	9
HONEYCUTT BLAINE LEROY	KS	30W	89
HONEYCUTT BURLON TALMAGE	NC	16E	79
HONEYCUTT DONALD EUGENE	MI	58E	22
HONEYCUTT JAMES DON	TX	08E	60
HONEYCUTT JAMES EARL	AR	39E	75
HONLEY JIMMIE CARROL	LA	12E	95
HONNOLD STEPHEN JEFFRY	MO	22E	103
HONOUR CHARLES M JR	GA	05E	47
HONRATH JON ROY	CA	25E	7
HONSE GEORGE EMILE	VA	13E	126
HONSINGER TIMOTHY L	TX	10E	86
HOOD BUDD EDWARD	OH	15E	118
HOOD CARLTON HARVEY	GA	65W	10
HOOD CHARLES ALAN	OH	19W	15
HOOD CHARLES EARNEST	AL	28E	67
HOOD CHARLES PERRY JR	TX	15W	50
HOOD DALE ROBERT	OH	04W	111
HOOD DERALD JOE	MO	06W	132
HOOD DON RICHARD	UT	02E	101
HOOD ERNEST ERVIN	CA	35E	22
HOOD EUGENE	AL	14W	29
HOOD JAMES GARY	VA	29E	83
HOOD JERRY WAYNE	OH	18E	122
HOOD JOHN EDWARD	OK	43E	67
HOOD RAYMOND	MI	06E	10
HOOD RICHARD E JR	FL	22E	41
HOOD ROGER WILLIAM	MT	27W	73
HOOD RUFUS	TX	33E	69
HOOD TERRANCE LEE	AZ	10W	25
HOOD WILLIAM WILLIS	MO	15E	118
HOOGTERP STEPHEN JOSEPH	MI	41W	47
HOOK CHARLES WAYNE	MD	21E	121
HOOK MARK LOREN	OH	46W	49
HOOK ROBERT W	TX	32W	21
HOOK WILLIAM FOSTER JR	PA	50W	46
HOOK WILLIAM WREN	IN	40E	22
HOOKER JOHN ARTHUR	SC	44E	8
HOOKER SANDY LEE	IL	36W	76
HOOKS DAYTON JOSEPH	SC	59W	23
HOOKS DENNIS RAYE	IL	20E	9
HOOKS RALPH MICHAEL	KY	18W	15
HOOKS WILEY DEAN	GA	10W	6
HOOP ROBERT GENE	IL	59E	23
HOOPAUGH LONNIE ELWOOD	NC	32W	13
HOOPENGARNER BENJAMIN L JR	MI	37W	56
HOOPER BARRY WAYNE	CA	43E	7
HOOPER HENRY JAMES	NC	05E	104
HOOPER JOHN JOSEPH	CA	08W	74
HOOPER JULIAN R	AR	25E	68
HOOPER STEVEN DALE	KY	28W	11
HOOPER VINS RONALD	NJ	22E	41
HOOPER WARD LAWRENCE JR	CA	15W	42
HOOPER WILLIE JR	VA	07W	33
HOOPII BERNARD PALENPA JR	HI	13E	38
HOOPS FRANKLIN WERNER JR	FL	59W	5
HOOS WILLIAM ARTHUR JR	IN	05E	34
HOOSIER ROGER KEITH	KY	16E	91
HOOTS DOUGLAS JAMES	IL	25E	110
HOOTS RICHARD MAXWELL	NY	29E	59
HOOVER ALVIN R III	WA	41W	47
HOOVER EDWARD LEE	NC	43E	45
HOOVER GERALD DONALD	MI	07E	102
HOOVER GORDON WOOD	NY	36E	16
HOOVER JAMES	OH	03E	12
HOOVER MELVIN SYLVESTER	WV	21E	62
HOOVER MICHAEL J	MD	30E	1
HOOVER REX MICHAEL	IN	43W	16
HOOVER ROGER JOSEPH	MI	31E	21
HOOVER THOMAS EUGENE	OH	27W	31
HOOVER THOMAS LEE	AR	27E	20
HOOVER WILLIAM CLIFTON	CA	02E	5
HOOVER WILLIE JR	AL	01W	42
HOPE MICHAEL CLINT	OK	09W	24
HOPE RICHARD MICHAEL	CT	07W	113
HOPE SAMUEL JR	OH	29W	35
HOPES GLENN CHALFANT	PA	32E	94
HOPEWELL DONALD CLEMENT	FL	32E	73
HOPKINS AARON MILTON	MD	08E	85
HOPKINS ALVIN JR	OK	09E	91
HOPKINS CHESTER LEE	ME	19E	96
HOPKINS DANNY LEE	MD	23W	37
HOPKINS DAVID LEE	PA	50W	43
HOPKINS DAVID MICHAEL	WV	07W	98
HOPKINS EDWARD ARTHUR	WA	27W	10
HOPKINS GARY WAYNE	TX	53W	20
HOPKINS IRVIN JAMES	PA	11E	30
HOPKINS JACK MAYNARD	MI	05E	95
HOPKINS JAMES EARL	NC	61W	2
HOPKINS JAMES FREDRICK	NY	11W	95
HOPKINS JAMES HARRISON	GA	23W	64
HOPKINS JOHN EDWARD	DC	08E	120
HOPKINS JOSEPH LEE JR	NC	42W	62
HOPKINS LEROY JR	AZ	28E	55
HOPKINS MARION MARSHALL	NJ	27E	48
HOPKINS MICHAEL EDWARD	VA	08E	129
HOPKINS MICHAEL WAYNE	VA	13W	51
HOPKINS MYLON RAY	SC	22W	21
HOPKINS PAUL ROBERT	NY	19W	54
HOPKINS PERRY BERNARD	GA	16W	5
HOPKINS RAYMOND LEE	CO	41W	12
HOPKINS RICHARD LEE	OH	25W	72
HOPKINS ROBERT E	CT	37E	23
HOPKINS ROBERT LOUIS	TX	05E	6
HOPKINS RONALD FRANK	WA	14W	13
HOPKINS THOMAS	NY	38W	27
HOPKINS WALLACE W JR	NV	27E	43
HOPKINS WILLIAM EDWARD	CO	29W	68
HOPKINS WILLIAM KENIS	MD	36W	21
HOPKINS WILLIAM ROBERT	KY	53W	42
HOPPE PATRICK BERT	CA	24E	67
HOPPER BARRY VORRATH	PA	14W	65
HOPPER DANIEL EUGENE	FL	28E	91
HOPPER EARL PEARSON JR	AZ	34E	20
HOPPER GERALD LEE	OR	24E	94
HOPPER JAMES JR	NC	22W	13
HOPPER JOSEPH CLIFFORD	TN	01W	12
HOPPER LARRY CHARLES	CA	49E	43
HOPPER RICHARD WHAN	PA	46E	24
HOPPER WILLIAM CARL	TN	43E	45
HOPPERS MICHAEL EUGENE	MO	68W	3
HOPPOUGH DENNIS KARL	NY	20W	9
HOPPS GARY DOUGLAS	FL	05E	22
HOPSON FREDERICK WAYNE	NY	09W	73
HOPSON JAMES HARVEY	MI	17E	5
HOPSON ROE JR	KY	10W	130
HOPSON WILLIAM DOUGLAS	VA	08E	15
HORACE ALBERT C JR	TX	25E	63
HORAL THOMAS GLEN	CA	23W	74
HORAN JOHN WILLIAM	NY	23W	75
HORAN LEO JOSEPH	MA	05E	47
HORCAJO ROBERT ALBERT	CA	31W	5
HORCHAR ANDREW ANTHONY JR	PA	12W	111
HORCHEM NELSON LEPORT JR	IL	28W	91
HORDERN DAVID JAMES	NY	30W	90
HORGAN DUANE FRANK	CO	65E	11
HORINEK BRIAN ANTHONY	OK	05W	15
HORINEK DONALD EDWARD	KS	47W	45
HORLBACK FRANCIS D	SC	23E	70
HORN ALAN MURRAY	CA	21W	33
HORN ALEC HENRY	WI	34W	15
HORN CHARLES HENRY	WA	18E	22
HORN DAVID MICHAEL	OH	23E	59
HORN DAYMON DONALD	KY	03E	135
HORN DONALD FRANCIS	NY	18W	24
HORN DOUGLAS LEE	MO	05W	103
HORN EDWARD ANDREW JR	OH	26W	91
HORN EMMETT HARVEY	TX	01E	78
HORN JACOB ANDREW	KY	17E	19
HORN JERRY VERNE	AK	26E	79
HORN JOHN ELIA	HI	13E	52
HORN MICHAEL LEE	WV	63W	6
HORN RAYMOND LEON	IL	01E	111
HORN RONALD DAVID	NM	42W	69
HORNADAY RALPH JR	FL	46E	47
HORNBACK RICHARD JERRY	OR	24W	31
HORNBAKER KENNETH EUGENE	PA	40E	22
HORNBROOK RONALD RAY	LA	03E	66
HORNBUCKLE ALTON LEE	TN	01E	81
HORNBUCKLE CLARENCE E JR	KY	59W	5
HORNBURGER WILLIE ROGERS	MS	25W	49
HORNBY DAVID EUGENE	IN	06E	80
HORNBY THOMAS FRANK	NJ	06E	20
HORNE AUSTIN ALBERT	PA	31E	47
HORNE KENNETH RAY	FL	05E	26
HORNE LAMAR	GA	16E	68
HORNE STANLEY HENRY	CA	34E	49
HORNE WAYNE MORRIS	NY	39W	67
HORNELAS ISMAEL FERNANDO	NE	27W	38
HORNER ALBERT LEROY	OH	32E	73
HORNER CARL NICHOLAS M	CA	45W	62
HORNER HERBERT DAVID	TN	09W	14
HORNER LARRY MARK	PA	08W	2
HORNER MARK ROLAND	SD	13W	14
HORNER MICHAEL MERVIN	OR	29E	3
HORNER WALTER DENNIS	NJ	19E	59
HORNER WILLIAM	NC	02E	34
HORNSBY JOHN R	KY	30W	76
HORNSTEIN EDMUND HENRY	RI	06E	107
HORNYAK JOHN JOSEPH	NY	04E	56
HORRELL GERALD ROBERT	CA	35W	39
HORRIDGE FREDERICK RAYMON	CA	41W	59

NAME	STATE	PANEL NO.	LINE NO.
HORSKY ROBERT MILVOY	IA	04E	12
HORSLEY LA MONTE VAN	MI	57E	23
HORSLEY LARRY FRANK	AL	44W	3
HORSLEY RICHARD WAYNE	CA	40W	58
HORSMAN GEORGE LESLIE II	OK	33E	58
HORSMAN JOSEPH BERNARD	KY	12W	42
HORSPOOL ROBERT KENT	UT	47E	22
HORST PHILLIP METZ	MS	09W	105
HORST ROBERT LOUIS	MO	02W	131
HORTON ALBERT HUGH	CA	30E	91
HORTON BARRY DEVERE	WA	30W	24
HORTON CHARLES BRENT	MO	25E	102
HORTON CHARLES RONALD	IN	40E	53
HORTON DANIEL EUGENE	NV	15E	16
HORTON DONALD MULLALY	PA	31W	80
HORTON DONNIE EDWARD	TN	11W	73
HORTON FLOYD MONROE	CT	06E	65
HORTON FRED HOWARD	CO	05E	118
HORTON HARRY WADE JR	TX	32E	45
HORTON JAMES HARRISON	WV	29W	10
HORTON JOHN MARTIN JR	NY	40W	3
HORTON JOHN RICHARD	NY	46E	35
HORTON MARSHAL LYNN	CA	13E	78
HORTON ROBERT BERNARD	MD	53W	35
HORTON RUBEN LEE	WI	65W	9
HORTON STANLEY	NC	26E	96
HORVATH ANDREW	NJ	17E	20
HORVATH CHARLES WILLIAM	PA	26E	45
HORVATH ROBERT JOHN	CO	43E	22
HORVATH WAYNE STANLEY	OH	21W	38
HORVATH WILLIAM FRANCIS	PA	18E	22
HORWITZ STANLEY LOUIS	PA	11E	94
HOSAKA ISAAC YOSHIRO	CA	01W	30
HOSE HERMAN BATER JR	HI	29W	37
HOSE JOHN WALLACE JR	AL	27E	20
HOSEA MICHAEL LEE	TX	16W	9
HOSEA WILLIAM HADLEY	IN	17E	67
HOSEY SANDRA	TX	43E	22
HOSEY TOMMY BRYAN	MS	61W	2
HOSFORD LARRY DELANO	KY	40W	44
HOSKEN JOHN CHARLES	OH	12W	39
HOSKING CHARLES ERNEST JR	NJ	17E	5
HOSKINS ALVIN	OH	05E	22
HOSKINS CHARLES LEE	KS	05W	111
HOSKINS DANNY	OH	68W	3
HOSKINS DONALD RUSSELL	IN	01W	7
HOSKINS GARY LEE	OK	19W	16
HOSKINS GEORGE JR	PA	24W	95
HOSKINS GOMER DAVIS JR	TN	17E	51
HOSKINS HAROLD ORION	MI	38E	2
HOSKINS JOHN THOMAS	LA	56E	9
HOSKINS ROBERT EDWARD	WA	38W	58
HOSKINS ROBERT LEE JR	VA	05E	80
HOSKINS ROBERT SULLIVAN	WV	53E	33
HOSKINS SHELDON DALE	ID	41W	24
HOSKINSON HARRY RONALD	DC	04E	15
HOSKINSON ROBERT EUGENE	OR	09E	87
HOSKO GARY LYNN	MI	29W	79
HOSLER FRANKLIN EUGENE	NC	06E	83
HOSNANDER CARL E	MA	48E	17
HOSNEDLE ALAN ROGER	MI	29W	20
HOSTEN CLIFFORD ARTHUR	NY	02W	50
HOSTETTER STUART GLEN	LA	22W	22
HOSTIKKA RICHARD AUGUST	WA	13W	74
HOSTUTTLER HERMON R	WV	03E	58
HOTALING DENNIS MICHAEL	NY	04W	70
HOTCHKISS KENNETH EUGENE	TX	36E	16
HOTCHKISS LEROY CASE III	TX	17E	111
HOTCHKISS MICHAEL JENNING	CA	24E	95
HOTTELL JOHN A III	NY	09W	128
HOTTENROTH JAMES RANDALL	CA	28E	9
HOTTINGER FRED LEE	CA	19E	107
HOUCHIN DARCY ALLEN	IN	29W	69
HOUCK ALLEN PAUL	PA	49W	8
HOUCK EARL FRANKLIN JR	IN	32W	43
HOUCK LAWRENCE EMANUEL II	PA	33W	57
HOUCK STEPHEN CHARLES	WA	54W	30
HOUDASHELT FRANCIS GERALD	FL	33E	18
HOUG DOUGLAS DUANE	IA	13E	91
HOUGH MATTHEW	SC	05E	65
HOUGH MICHAEL PETER	MI	50E	39
HOUGHTALING FLOYD W III	NY	40W	77
HOUGHTION ROBERT CHARLES	LA	14E	35
HOUGHTON JAMES CURTIS	CA	32E	10
HOULDITCH JULIUS C JR	AL	18W	47
HOULE DANNY WILLIAM	WI	27W	64
HOULE KIRK EDWARD	IL	38E	1
HOULE ROBERT KENNETH	RI	38W	59
HOULIHAN JOHN RICHARD	MA	23E	19
HOUNSHELL JEFFREY DAVID	GA	37W	11
HOURIGAN MICHAEL PATRICK	CA	61W	2
HOURIGAN WILLIAM JOSEPH	NY	13E	31
HOUSE ALTON	NC	53W	6
HOUSE DOUGLAS ARTHUR	TN	45W	52
HOUSE GEORGE JONATHAN	IN	38E	77
HOUSE JOHN ALEXANDER II	NY	22E	87
HOUSE JOHN CHARLES	AR	31E	98
HOUSE JOHN K	TX	53E	34
HOUSE JOHN LEE	TX	12W	48
HOUSE OSCAR LEE	MO	49W	9
HOUSE RICHARD ALLAN	NY	32E	14
HOUSE WILLIAM HANDSOME	MD	01E	41
HOUSE WILLIS FRANCIS	MD	29W	30
HOUSEHOLDER RICHARD WAYNE	OH	26W	112
HOUSEHOLTER TERRY AUGUST	KS	22W	120
HOUSER CARL RAY	MO	26W	71
HOUSER CHARLES MILTON	NC	27E	101
HOUSER CLYDE RICHARD JR	PA	21E	98
HOUSER DAVID ROBERT	OH	02W	41
HOUSER DORIAN JAN	CA	19E	82
HOUSER JERRY LEE	CA	20E	75
HOUSH ANTHONY FRANK	IL	50E	48
HOUSH RICHARD HENRY	MO	17E	36
HOUSKER HAROLD DEAN	MN	38W	66
HOUSLEY CHARLES LARRY	TN	32E	30
HOUSLEY JAMES DAVID	AR	11W	7
HOUSMAN ROBERT CHARLES	IL	15W	70
HOUSTON ALEX RAY	NC	28E	68
HOUSTON BENNIE LEE	IL	17E	123
HOUSTON ELWOOD LAYTON	VA	53W	28
HOUSTON J H	IA	15E	105
HOUSTON JOHN DAVIS JR	CA	50E	29
HOUSTON JOHN LUCIUS	FL	01E	57
HOUSTON JOHN ROBERT	MO	03W	95
HOUSTON JOHN WESLEY	AR	05E	30
HOUSTON LATHAN	MS	37W	81
HOUSTON MARK JOSEPH	IN	03W	95
HOUSTON MARVIN LYNN	AR	58W	9
HOUSTON RICHARD PAUL	OH	30E	91
HOUSTON THOMAS EUGENE	TX	14E	70
HOUSTON WILLIAM JOSEPH	PA	43W	63
HOUTZ JOSEPH MERLE	MO	53W	1
HOUX LESTER JR	OH	26E	45
HOVANCIK ANDREW M JR	PA	23E	80
HOVANEC DONALD FRANCIS	NJ	21W	75
HOVENDEN DARREL LEROY	NE	21E	47
HOVER JOHN MICHAEL	TN	56W	4
HOVEY VERNON FLETCHER III	NY	09W	14
HOVIS RONALD LEE	IN	36W	40
HOVLAND RICHARD DALE	ND	36E	16
HOWARD A W JR	OK	36W	84
HOWARD BILLY	FL	06E	39
HOWARD BRUCE LEE	TX	31E	75
HOWARD CHARLES EMORY	KS	54W	30
HOWARD CHARLES VINCENT	MI	08E	120
HOWARD CHESTER THEO JR	MS	14W	49
HOWARD CLARENCE WILLIAM	AL	04E	124
HOWARD CLAUDE	OH	20E	116
HOWARD DAVID LAFATE	SC	02E	29
HOWARD DAVID LEROY	IN	26E	71
HOWARD DAVID RAY	OH	49W	22
HOWARD DAVID TERRELL	CA	23W	75
HOWARD DONNELL	TN	42W	12
HOWARD DOUGLAS ALLEN	WA	02W	110
HOWARD DWANE GENE	CA	26W	19
HOWARD EDWARD EMANUEL	AL	12W	124
HOWARD ELI PAGE JR	NY	19W	68
HOWARD ERNEST	TN	34E	42
HOWARD GARY EDWARD	FL	56E	25
HOWARD GENE JAY	WI	47E	39
HOWARD GEORGE DOUGLAS	MS	17W	56
HOWARD GLEN EUGENE	IL	15W	64
HOWARD GREGORY MARSHALL	VA	09E	124
HOWARD HARLEY MICHAEL	VA	37W	32
HOWARD HARVEY RICKERT	VT	28E	15
HOWARD HAZE III	GA	08E	124
HOWARD HORACE	PA	36E	57
HOWARD JAMES BYRON	CA	59W	5
HOWARD JAMES EDWARD JR	HI	29E	10
HOWARD JAMES GEORGE JR	TX	10W	130
HOWARD JAMES J	AL	03E	12
HOWARD JAMES RAY	MI	29E	59
HOWARD JAMES T	FL	12W	117
HOWARD JAMES VAN	TN	40W	58
HOWARD JIMMIE	GA	18E	75
HOWARD JIMMY LEE	LA	40W	6
HOWARD JULIUS JAKE JR	SC	43E	7
HOWARD LAWRENCE EDWARD	IL	25E	1
HOWARD LAWRENCE PAIGE JR	PA	03E	29
HOWARD LEON GAYE	KY	15E	79
HOWARD LEWIS JR	GA	09W	128
HOWARD LUTHER HARRIS	NC	22E	87
HOWARD MARK THOMAS	MO	30E	2
HOWARD MICHAEL DAVID	OK	27W	74
HOWARD RALPH ARTHUR	NH	14W	121
HOWARD RAY JR	TX	51W	41
HOWARD ROBERT BAILEY	CO	20W	102
HOWARD ROBERT CLARENCE	PA	29E	20
HOWARD ROBERT LOUIS	CT	22W	13
HOWARD RODGER DALE	NC	33W	85
HOWARD RONALD HERBERT	GA	29W	53
HOWARD ROY LEE	GA	28W	19
HOWARD ROY WILLIAM	LA	50W	50
HOWARD SAMUEL HENRY	IN	31E	24
HOWARD STEVEN DALE	KS	01W	87
HOWARD SYDNEY CLAUDE	CA	29W	38
HOWARD SYLVESTER JOSEPH	DE	41W	62
HOWARD TAYLOR BROOKS JR	NY	50E	39
HOWARD THEODORE	AL	27E	44
HOWARD WALTER JOHN JR	MT	42W	46
HOWARD WALTER LEE	TX	15E	69
HOWCOTT HENRY GRANT	NY	36E	16
HOWDEN ROBERT WILSON	NY	41E	67
HOWE CHARLES LEE	NY	46E	35
HOWE FRANCIS EDWARD	NC	23E	80
HOWE FRANK ROBERT	NY	32W	65
HOWE HARVEY GRANT JR	IN	14E	91
HOWE JAMES DONNIE	SC	11W	113
HOWE JOHN ALLAN	MI	16W	74
HOWE LARRY WAYNE	CA	50W	43
HOWE LEROY CHARLES	NY	19E	107
HOWE OLAN JOSEPH	TX	12W	97
HOWE SIDNEY A	AR	52E	38
HOWE STEVEN TIMOTHY	NV	17W	16
HOWE THOMAS JOHN	VA	41W	18
HOWELL A T	TX	09E	4
HOWELL ADRIAN EALON	MS	31E	35
HOWELL BEN WILLIS	GA	64W	10
HOWELL CALVIN LAMAR JR	GA	31W	5
HOWELL CARTER AVERY	NC	02W	113
HOWELL CASCO DEVAUGHN	NC	09E	47
HOWELL CHARLES DENNIS	IN	28W	11
HOWELL DANNY RAY	WV	38E	77
HOWELL DONALD EDWARD	CA	01W	19
HOWELL DUANE GEORGE	CO	04W	53
HOWELL DWIGHT BRINSON	GA	03W	136
HOWELL DWIGHT SANFORD	TX	49W	14
HOWELL EDWARD MICHAEL	OH	18E	41
HOWELL ERNEST RICHARD	NC	03W	20
HOWELL GATLIN JERRYL	CA	23E	28
HOWELL HAL KENT	WV	42W	41
HOWELL HANCIL EVERT JR	IN	10W	103
HOWELL JAMES LAURENCE	FL	13W	85
HOWELL JAMES RILEY	AZ	07E	53
HOWELL JOHN WILLIAM	TN	05W	106
HOWELL KENNETH RALPH	NC	34E	53
HOWELL LARRY L	MO	26W	71
HOWELL MICHAEL WAYNE	CA	19E	52
HOWELL PERCY WRAY	TX	01E	23
HOWELL PHILIP	VA	03E	80
HOWELL PRESTON LEE	AL	57E	23
HOWELL RALPH	NC	06W	84
HOWELL RANDALL DUMON	TX	10E	50
HOWELL ROBERT LEE	IN	32W	6
HOWELL ROBERT LEE	SC	06W	104
HOWELL ROBERT MALICHI JR	TX	09E	103

NAME	STATE	PANEL NO.	LINE NO.
HOWELL ROLAND HAYES	MS	17E	87
HOWELL SAMMIE	SC	14E	86
HOWELL WILLIAM ERAY	MS	11W	124
HOWELL WILLIAM GLENN	NC	19W	119
HOWER THOMAS ALLEN	MI	37W	32
HOWERTER BRUCE G	IL	39E	6
HOWERTER EARL EVERETT JR	CO	17W	90
HOWERTON JERRY RUSSELL	OH	31W	5
HOWES DOUGLAS GREGORY	UT	12W	13
HOWES GEORGE ANDREWS	IN	14W	23
HOWES ROGER HAYDEN	IL	30W	76
HOWIE LLOYD GEORGE	WI	10W	45
HOWIE NORMAN PERRY JR	NC	20E	60
HOWIE RICHARD S	NC	09E	24
HOWISON CALVIN DANIEL	TX	24E	28
HOWISON GRAHAM HENRY	TX	21W	112
HOWLAND HOWARD P JR	TN	55W	6
HOWLAND JOHN CHARLES	IL	15E	12
HOWLAND LEROY LARKIN	NM	16W	99
HOWLE ERNEST CLARENCE	SC	31W	49
HOWLETT NORMAN LOCKE JR	MA	47E	12
HOWLEY WESLEY CHARLES JR	WA	09W	97
HOWZE CHARLES CROCKETT	SC	15W	17
HOWZE DAVID JR	MI	33W	57
HOXWORTH WALTER BRUCE	OH	30W	77
HOY ROBERT ELVIN	VA	26W	62
HOYER MICHAEL GERARD	PA	02E	71
HOYEZ JAMES KENNETH	OR	44W	25
HOYLE WAYNE ROGER	NC	33W	26
HOYT ARTHUR JAMES	ME	57W	27
HOYT ERVIN JAMES	NE	52E	4
HOYT LARRY LEONARD	NY	38E	68
HOYT LAWRENCE WILLIAM	NY	10W	76
HOYT NORMAN LEE ROY	MI	10E	128
HOYT VICTOR RONALD	MI	13E	84
HRDLICKA DAVID LOUIS	CO	01E	121
HREN TIMOTHY LOUIS	WI	53W	43
HRINKO WILLIAM JOHN	OH	05E	104
HRISOULIS ROBERT	MI	05W	58
HRUTKAY MICHAEL STEPHEN	PA	16W	45
HU PATRICK HOP SUNG	HI	15W	129
HUARD JAMES LINTON	MI	01W	56
HUART MARTIN REINHOLD JR	IL	04W	80
HUBARD THOMAS CARR JEFFER	MD	31E	58
HUBBARD ALFRED WILLIE	AL	21W	60
HUBBARD CHARLES AUSTIN	OK	21E	62
HUBBARD CORNELIUS FRANCIS	MA	20W	76
HUBBARD DAVID LEE JR	OK	01E	118
HUBBARD DENNIS LEROY	IN	19E	107
HUBBARD GEORGE ALLEN	OH	26W	14
HUBBARD GERALD MONROE	NM	13E	10
HUBBARD GLEN DAVID	MA	46E	35
HUBBARD GREGORY GEORGE	CA	28E	103
HUBBARD JAMES RAY	TN	15E	105
HUBBARD JOHN R	CT	17E	52
HUBBARD LAMAR	GA	44W	57
HUBBARD MARVIN PETER	LA	50W	1
HUBBARD MEREDITH GERALD	MI	09E	40
HUBBARD MERLE GRIFFIN	PA	14W	78
HUBBARD NATHANIEL	TX	08E	49
HUBBARD ROBERT STEPHEN PO	MO	57E	4
HUBBARD ROBERT WALKER	AL	37E	23
HUBBARD ROGER LEE	AR	28E	104
HUBBARD ROGER LEROY	MO	02E	111
HUBBARD SAMUEL BURNELL	VA	17E	36
HUBBARD THEODORE JR	OK	50E	29
HUBBARD THOMAS	NY	32E	17
HUBBARD THOMAS LEE	FL	62E	19
HUBBARD TONY GENE	FL	38W	35
HUBBARD W D	TX	04E	91
HUBBARD WAYNE GENE	IA	16W	49
HUBBARD WILLIAM HOBSON	NJ	06E	13
HUBBELL DAN ROBERT	CA	08W	9
HUBBELL THOMAS SIMCOCK	MI	32E	74
HUBBLE WILLIAM BAKER	KY	34E	37
HUBBS DANNY EUGENE	TN	28W	12
HUBBS DONALD RICHARD	NJ	45E	12
HUBER LEO JOHN III	LA	24W	43
HUBER LEON FAIRDEN	FL	36E	74
HUBER RANDY S	PA	64W	11
HUBER STEPHEN LEE	FL	41E	38
HUBER WILLIAM FREDRICK JR	TX	29E	101
HUBERT MICHAEL NEIL	KS	31W	36
HUBERT STEVEN JAMES	MN	27W	18
HUBERTH ERIC JAMES	CA	10W	33
HUBERTY DAVID JEROME	MN	11W	131
HUBERTY WILLIAM M	MN	11E	82
HUBICSAK FRANK CHARLES	MA	11E	3
HUBIS BRIAN ANDREW	MA	19W	126
HUBISZ JAMES FRANCIS	MA	05E	86
HUBLER EDWARD LINCOLN JR	PA	11W	14
HUBLER GEORGE LAWRENCE	UT	40E	75
HUBNER DAVID ERVIN	CA	10W	33
HUBRINS EDDIE BARRY	CA	02W	39
HUBSCHMITT ELBERT R JR	NY	08E	11
HUCKABA THOMAS JAMES	CA	27W	49
HUCKABEE JAMES EDWARD	TX	23E	100
HUCKABY DENNIS C	CA	19W	101
HUCKLEBERRY JAMES ROBERT	KY	19E	59
HUCKS LLOYD JUNIOR	SC	33W	86
HUCKS WALTER HERMAN	NY	41E	9
HUCZEK GERALD ALBERT	MI	38E	77
HUDAK ANDREW MICHAEL	OH	32E	57
HUDAK FRANK PAUL	OH	10E	40
HUDDLE CHARLES EDWIN JR	WV	01E	97
HUDDLESON RODNEY LEROY	OH	32E	23
HUDDLESTON LYNN RAGLE	TX	27E	16
HUDDLESTON ROBERT JOSEPH	TN	10W	25
HUDDLESTON THOMAS PATE	GA	30E	27
HUDDY DANNY JOE	OH	26E	25
HUDELSON JAMES E	OR	01W	60
HUDGENS EDWARD MONROE	OK	12W	30
HUDGENS JOHN WAYNE	AL	20E	29
HUDGINS CARL WILLIAM JR	MO	23W	110
HUDIS JAMES BRIAN	WI	11E	111
HUDNALL WILLIAM LEON	VA	09W	102
HUDSON BOBBY	MS	13E	30
HUDSON CALVIN CLIFFORD	GA	29E	73
HUDSON DALE FRANCIS	MO	03E	80
HUDSON DANNY CHARLES	NE	38W	18
HUDSON DENNIS NYE	CA	17W	110
HUDSON GARY DUANE	MO	06W	68
HUDSON GARY LEE	MO	56E	25
HUDSON GEORGE ALEX JR	NY	50E	29
HUDSON GEORGE HOWARD	OH	43E	22
HUDSON HENRY JR	CA	13W	58
HUDSON JAMES JR	NC	26W	25
HUDSON JAMES WILLIAM	MS	08W	59
HUDSON JERRY DOUGLAS	TX	23E	12
HUDSON JIMMY DALE	AL	12E	112
HUDSON JOE DAVID	GA	02W	131
HUDSON JOHN BARDEN	NY	51E	8
HUDSON JOHNNY	AL	06E	65
HUDSON JOSEPH JR	FL	40E	53
HUDSON JOSEPH ROBERT JR	PA	36W	51
HUDSON JOSEPH WILLIAM	MS	29W	61
HUDSON KENNETH WAYNE	TX	38E	1
HUDSON LEONARD PAUL	CA	01E	73
HUDSON LESSAINT PETER	NY	04E	97
HUDSON NATHANIEL	NC	27W	45
HUDSON PHILIP LONNIE	MO	24E	67
HUDSON RAYMOND HOYT	TX	08E	49
HUDSON RICHARD GREY	IL	42E	66
HUDSON ROBERT BENJAMIN	OK	41E	9
HUDSON ROBERT LARRY	CA	06W	77
HUDSON RONALD CHARLES	IN	18W	75
HUDSON ROY	GA	36E	16
HUDSON SAMUEL BERNARD	GA	43E	55
HUDSON THOMAS GORDON	MO	49W	14
HUDSON THOMAS HAROLD	MO	05W	19
HUDSON WILLIE JUNIOR	VA	30W	25
HUDSPETH JAMES L	OK	06E	51
HUEBNER BURREL DALE	IN	03E	49
HUEBNER HERMAN HENRY	CA	21W	65
HUEBNER TERENCE ARTHUR	OH	22W	112
HUEFFNER RICHARD ALAN	NY	40E	75
HUELSKAMP RONALD JAMES	AZ	42W	41
HUERD LAUREN DALE	MN	50E	5
HUERTA TOMMY	CA	20W	50
HUESTIS JOHN EDWARD	NY	24W	76
HUESTIS ROGER EDWARD	NY	31E	92
HUEY DONALD RAYMOND	NY	07W	53
HUEY GUY WINFRED	OH	13E	101
HUEY HERMAN LEROY	MI	05E	11
HUFF BRUCE NORMAN	IL	56E	9
HUFF CHARLES FRANK	IL	60W	2
HUFF FRANK C	OH	16E	45
HUFF JACKIE EUGENE	AZ	02E	112
HUFF JAMES A	AR	49W	10
HUFF JAMES EDMOND	AL	28E	82
HUFF JAMES HENRY	OH	27W	5
HUFF LOUIS HOWARD II	PA	44E	27
HUFF PAUL LLOYD	VA	48W	27
HUFF RAY GENE	OH	20W	50
HUFF RICHARD ELLIOT	CA	27W	56
HUFF ROBERT RANDEL	CA	63W	7
HUFF TERRY KENNETH	MO	51W	2
HUFF WILLIAM EDWARD	PA	41E	22
HUFFER ALBERT EUGENE	OH	11E	49
HUFFER KENNETH KIPLING	IN	04E	28
HUFFINE DENNIS WILLARD	AR	08W	17
HUFFINE MELVIN THOMAS	TN	10E	70
HUFFMAN DAVID JAY	CA	28W	47
HUFFMAN DAVID KEITH	IN	44W	24
HUFFMAN EDDIE GRAY	WV	36E	52
HUFFMAN GERALD	OH	26W	63
HUFFMAN GERALD DON	OR	20E	16
HUFFMAN GLEN MICHAEL	OH	45W	41
HUFFMAN ISAAC PAUL	WV	27E	90
HUFFMAN RICHARD ALLEN	PA	57E	24
HUFFMAN RONALD PETER	NY	17W	36
HUFFMAN SAMUEL LEWIS	OH	09E	74
HUFFMAN WALTER LEE	TN	10W	51
HUFFSTUTLER KEITH VINCENT	CO	29E	3
HUFFSTUTLER STEVEN RILEY	CA	24W	43
HUFSCHMID ROBERT GEORGE	NY	39W	8
HUFSTETLER JAMES THOMAS	GA	22E	88
HUGGANS KENNETH RICHARD	CA	57W	27
HUGGETT RICHARD THOMAS	VA	57W	10
HUGGINS BOBBY GENE	AL	09W	8
HUGGINS EUGENE	SC	09W	84
HUGGINS FRAZIER DANIEL	FL	23E	42
HUGGINS GORDON SAMUEL	SC	03E	13
HUGGINS JAMES FREDERICK	TX	05W	40
HUGGINS RICHARD VAN	NC	27E	73
HUGGS HAROLD SYLVESTER	NY	21W	23
HUGHART HAROLD GRANVILLE	FL	04E	110
HUGHART ROMEY EARL JR	WV	09E	127
HUGHENS FREDERICK EDWARD	LA	09W	95
HUGHES BEN ALLEN JR	TX	12W	6
HUGHES BILLY EUGENE II	TX	37W	6
HUGHES BRIAN GREGORY	CA	54E	25
HUGHES CARL LEROY JR	IN	15W	55
HUGHES CARL PATRICK	GA	18W	28
HUGHES CARL WAYNE	GA	29W	45
HUGHES CHARLES FREDRICK	WI	21W	60
HUGHES CHARLES GEORGE	PA	06W	51
HUGHES CHARLES WAYNE	NC	21W	118
HUGHES CHESTER STACY	TN	10E	119
HUGHES DAVID JAMES	MN	21E	1
HUGHES DENNIS FOX	IL	49E	11
HUGHES DUDLEY CARROLL JR	NC	32E	51
HUGHES EDWARD COWART III	CA	30E	97
HUGHES EDWARD JOHN JR	NY	57E	24
HUGHES ERNEST JOSEPH	MD	25W	72
HUGHES ERROL ARTHUR	AL	29W	99
HUGHES FERNANDO JAMES	MI	51E	46
HUGHES FRANCIS ALLEN	KY	23E	51
HUGHES FREDRICK JOSEPH	PA	06W	60
HUGHES FURMAN DAVID	IN	08W	125
HUGHES GORDON KAY	OH	41E	22
HUGHES GRAHAM	NY	24W	85
HUGHES GREGORY JOHN	MI	17W	9
HUGHES JAMES ALVIN	AR	13W	131
HUGHES JAMES EDWARD	VA	06E	3
HUGHES JAMES KENNETH	IL	06E	14
HUGHES JAMES OLIVER	TX	12E	63
HUGHES JEFFREY REX	FL	20E	60
HUGHES JERRY DANIEL	MO	27W	109
HUGHES JERRY LYNN	TX	23E	59
HUGHES JERRY NELSON	FL	04E	61
HUGHES JESSE HOWARD	GA	04E	73
HUGHES JESSE RAY JR	MO	02E	108
HUGHES JOHN CHARLES	CA	30E	73
HUGHES JOHN EDWARD D JR	PA	20W	97
HUGHES JOHN HOWARD	AZ	22W	1

NAME	STATE	PANEL NO.	LINE NO.
HUGHES JOHN JAMES	NY	38E	1
HUGHES JOHN RAYMOND III	TX	10W	85
HUGHES JOHN S JR	TX	09W	4
HUGHES JULIUS BRADLEY	PA	24E	28
HUGHES KENNETH RICHARD	OH	24E	100
HUGHES KENNETH ROCKWELL	MA	28W	70
HUGHES LEWIS EUGENE II	OH	09W	50
HUGHES MACKLIN OTIS	AL	51W	33
HUGHES MARION BENNETT JR	MD	37W	33
HUGHES MARVIN THOMAS	OH	13E	67
HUGHES MICHAEL DONALD	UT	21W	118
HUGHES MICHAEL NORMAN	TX	06W	83
HUGHES MITCHELL JR	KY	32E	74
HUGHES PAUL ARNOLD	CT	17W	105
HUGHES PAUL JOSEPH	MA	29E	10
HUGHES RICHARD RAMSEL	TX	18W	39
HUGHES ROBERT	NJ	20E	117
HUGHES ROBERT ALLEN	MI	15W	50
HUGHES ROBERT DOUGLAS	TX	46W	3
HUGHES ROBERT LAURENS	OH	39E	6
HUGHES ROBERT WAYNE	IL	56W	12
HUGHES SAM ZEB	FL	45E	34
HUGHES SAMUEL RUEBEN	CA	51E	21
HUGHES THOMAS EDWARD	MO	22W	60
HUGHES THOMAS GILBERT	CA	61W	2
HUGHES THOMAS STEVEN	OR	62E	6
HUGHES TONY HOWARD	NJ	06E	117
HUGHES WILLIAM BURDICK	KY	65E	9
HUGHES WILLIAM JOSEPH	OH	54E	9
HUGHEY CHESTER LYN	TN	15W	55
HUGHEY EDWARD WENDELL	AL	37E	8
HUGHEY LLOYD RAY	OH	25E	84
HUGHEY MICHAEL ALLEN	FL	13W	9
HUGHIE WARNER PRATER	GA	13W	118
HUGHLETT JOHN ALBERT	TN	03E	33
HUGO DONALD NEALE	IL	24E	28
HUGO FELICISIMO ARELIANO	HI	15E	96
HUICOCHEA-REYNA IGNACIO	CA	06E	11
HUIE LITCHFIELD PATTERSON	NC	15E	106
HUIE ROBERT ANDREW	AL	36E	17
HUIE ROBERT DOTSON JR	AR	26W	9
HUK PETER PAUL	IA	08W	38
HULBERT JEFFREY LEE	WA	19W	87
HULBERT JOHN ROY	WI	33E	86
HULINGS WALTER VINCENT	MD	16E	17
HULL ARNOLD MELVIN	NY	13E	53
HULL EDISON DENNIS	OH	17W	28
HULL GERALD EDWARD	OH	13W	14
HULL JAMES ALBERT JR	MO	24W	31
HULL JAMES LARRY	TX	05W	120
HULL RICKY LEE	OH	38E	52
HULLETT NATHAN EARL	AL	31W	5
HULLIHEN IRA HENRY	MD	33E	9
HULME JOHN WILLIAM	RI	21W	38
HULSE GARY WAYNE	CA	38W	27
HULSE GEORGE EDWARD III	NY	16E	40
HULSE RICHARD DAVID	AZ	12W	35
HULSE ROBERT MARK	CA	09E	68
HULSEY JAMES AUBREY	TX	12W	132
HULSEY LARRY BRYSON	GA	37E	58
HULSEY ROGER	GA	49W	41
HULSLANDER ROSS THOMAS	FL	43W	37
HULTQUIST EDWARD CHARLES	MI	20E	29
HULTQUIST LEONARD ASHBY	NE	05E	118
HULTS GARY DEAN	MO	10W	125
HULTS JEFFREY ANDREW	NC	39E	6
HULTS PHILLIP FRANK	CA	13W	32
HULWI WILLIAM GEORGE JR	MN	50E	15
HUMBERT JEAN PIERRE	WA	04W	118
HUMBLE CHARLES RAY	AR	23E	76
HUME CARL MICHAEL	CA	03E	87
HUME JOSEPH SYLVESTER JR	OH	26E	11
HUME KENNETH EDWARD	OH	01E	98
HUMES FRANK WILLIAM	NJ	21W	83
HUMES MAYNARD JEWEL	IL	12E	54
HUMM RONALD JOSEPH	PA	27E	29
HUMMEL HARRY LYNNE	OH	61W	3
HUMMEL JOHN FLOYD	TX	04W	28
HUMMINGBIRD FERRELL	CA	14E	27
HUMPHRES JIMMY DARREL	MS	03W	53
HUMPHREY CARL A	KY	15E	84
HUMPHREY CECIL HOWARD JR	IN	62W	11
HUMPHREY CHARLES EVERETT	TX	22E	104
HUMPHREY GALEN FRANCIS	MO	04E	129
HUMPHREY HARVEY EDWARD	VT	03W	56
HUMPHREY JAMES GILBERT	KS	39W	49
HUMPHREY JAROLD EDWARD	CA	33E	87
HUMPHREY JERRY DALE	MS	14E	48
HUMPHREY JOHN RICHARD	CA	12E	120
HUMPHREY JOHNNY WILLIAM	GA	41W	12
HUMPHREY KEVIN RICHARD	NJ	06W	40
HUMPHREY LAWRENCE JAMES	TN	19W	50
HUMPHREY RICHARD DAVID	MD	10W	33
HUMPHREY ROBERT LOY	TX	27W	109
HUMPHREY ROY DARRELL	VA	52E	19
HUMPHREY VICTOR JAMES	TX	56E	9
HUMPHREY WEDEN GARY	CA	36E	52
HUMPHREYS CHALMERS CLAUDE	MO	19W	54
HUMPHREYS GILMER EARL	MI	44W	48
HUMPHREYS LARRY DON	OK	58W	32
HUMPHRIES BENNIE FRANK	GA	49E	33
HUMPHRIES GARY DEAN	CA	34W	84
HUMPHRIES HAZEL H III	SC	24E	95
HUMPHRIES RONALD EDWARD	SC	10E	19
HUMPHRIES WAYNE WARREN	OK	03E	33
HUNDLEY JAMES FREEMAN	WV	19E	59
HUNDLEY MOSE CHILDS	IL	29W	100
HUNDLEY THEODORE LANGSTON	VA	12E	21
HUNDT ROGER LEE	NE	15W	22
HUNEYCUTT CHARLES J JR	NC	29E	67
HUNLEY JAMES WILLIAM	OH	24E	113
HUNNICUTT JASON DAVID	CA	23W	101
HUNSBARGER GERALD C III	CA	07E	133
HUNSICKER JAMES EDWARD	PA	01W	6
HUNSINGER CHARLES EDWARD	PA	22W	65
HUNSLEY DENNIS ROGER	MO	29W	45
HUNT ARTHUR WALTON III	FL	48E	53
HUNT BOB CLARENCE JR	AZ	04E	110
HUNT BOBBY EARNEST	TN	19E	5
HUNT BRUCE CHARLES	CA	06W	39
HUNT CALVIN GENE	CA	22W	89
HUNT DANIEL THOMAS	NY	15W	1
HUNT DAVID RAY	WV	25E	84
HUNT EUGENE	MS	18W	15
HUNT HOOD HAL	CA	43E	23
HUNT ISAAC E JR	TN	09E	98
HUNT JAMES ANTHONY	CA	42W	56
HUNT JAMES D	MT	41W	59
HUNT JAMES ROBERT	IN	08W	133
HUNT JOHN STUART	CA	07W	129
HUNT JOSEPH FRANCIS	PA	09E	80
HUNT JOSEPH THOMAS	MA	35E	47
HUNT LARRY FRANK	AL	33W	15
HUNT LEIGH WALLACE	AZ	17E	36
HUNT LEON ANDREW	KY	01W	43
HUNT MARSHALL WIMBERLY	FL	27E	53
HUNT MARTIN MOSHER	CA	24E	28
HUNT PHILIP MICHAEL	CA	30W	37
HUNT PHILIP WADE	MO	47W	28
HUNT RALPH EDWARD JR	OH	59W	23
HUNT RALPH WOMMACK	CA	08W	74
HUNT RICHARD	TX	47W	9
HUNT ROBERT EARL	TN	14W	112
HUNT ROBERT WILLIAM	WV	41E	67
HUNT RONALD ALAN	CO	19W	101
HUNT SAMUEL L	MS	28E	74
HUNT WILLIAM BALT	ID	12E	22
HUNT WILLIAM DICKSON	AL	18E	60
HUNT WILLIAM HOWARD	FL	31W	49
HUNT WILLIAM LARRIE	IN	03E	23
HUNT WILLIAM RAYMOND	CA	30E	97
HUNT WILLIAM SPRAGGINS	VA	44E	17
HUNTER ARLEN JOHN	SD	40W	44
HUNTER BARRY ALAN	MI	27E	81
HUNTER BILLY CHARLES	NC	38W	74
HUNTER BILLY RAY	MI	07W	31
HUNTER CHARLES LOUIS	MS	22W	78
HUNTER DAVID	IL	04E	91
HUNTER DELON	CA	43W	5
HUNTER DENNIS WAYNE	CA	11W	68
HUNTER DONALD EUGENE	PA	53E	34
HUNTER DONALD LEE	NJ	35E	47
HUNTER GERALD N	TX	34E	87
HUNTER HAROLD CLAYTON II	AR	02W	6
HUNTER HAROLD HENRY	MO	33W	2
HUNTER HENRY DAVID	NE	21W	83
HUNTER HERBERT PERRY	TX	23E	91
HUNTER JAMES D	TN	40W	54
HUNTER JAMES DOHERTY	VA	15E	70
HUNTER JOHN CLARK	OH	05W	124
HUNTER JOHN LOUIS	MO	06E	32
HUNTER JOHN ROBERT	AR	11W	74
HUNTER KENNETH RONALD	GA	29E	59
HUNTER LEROY	SC	11W	113
HUNTER LYNN ELMO	UT	15E	96
HUNTER MARVIN LYNN	NY	52W	44
HUNTER MELVIN TYRONE	MS	14E	67
HUNTER MICHAEL J	OK	16E	84
HUNTER MICHAEL RAY	MO	05W	111
HUNTER MICHAEL WOODROW	MI	14W	75
HUNTER MILTON CHARLES	AL	01W	86
HUNTER PAUL CARLING	PA	16E	101
HUNTER ROBERT GERALD	GA	07E	109
HUNTER RORY WILLIAM	CA	16W	95
HUNTER RUSSELL PALMER JR	CT	05E	22
HUNTER TROY HAZARD	CO	38E	1
HUNTER WASHINGTON	GA	38W	18
HUNTER WILLIAM KENNETH	VA	11W	16
HUNTER WILLIE HAYWARD	FL	42E	66
HUNTINGTON BRUCE	UT	26E	46
HUNTLEY EDWARD GLENN	IL	10W	41
HUNTLEY JOHN NORMAN	ME	17W	13
HUNTLEY MICHAEL ALAN	CA	24W	7
HUNTLEY THOMAS MATTHEW	CA	23E	110
HUNTOON RICHARD WARREN	MA	07E	53
HUNTZINGER GEORGE RAYMOND	PA	16W	2
HUOT RAYMOND CHARLES JR	MN	06W	44
HUPE RUSSELL EDWARD	CA	44E	37
HUPP JAMES EARL	PA	09W	130
HUPP RICHARD LEWIS JR	MO	20W	14
HURD CHARLES EVERETTE	WV	09E	103
HURD COLIN PLUMMER	ME	10W	6
HURD ERNEST LEON	FL	22E	54
HURD JAY ALLEN	NH	10E	60
HURD JERRY ALAN	AZ	39E	33
HURD JOHN LAWRENCE	OH	19W	94
HURD LAWRENCE ADAMS	AL	21E	106
HURD ROGER MICHAEL	MA	20E	75
HURD SAMUEL EUGENE	MI	01E	39
HURDLE PAUL EDWARD	DC	03E	80
HURIANEK JERRY ANTONE	ID	21W	23
HURKMANS WILHELM S JR	WI	51W	33
HURLBERT ROY DOUGLAS	CO	50E	15
HURLBUT THOMAS WILLARD	MI	21W	84
HURLEBAUS LESLIE VERNARD	OH	25E	102
HURLEY AILEY BERDEAN	IA	19E	82
HURLEY JAMES K	VA	01W	122
HURLEY JERRY LEE	OH	09W	39
HURLEY KEVIN MICHAEL	CO	35W	16
HURLEY NOEL	IL	40W	33
HURLEY TIMOTHY LAWRENCE	MO	30W	90
HURLEY WILLIAM PAUL JR	MA	47E	1
HURLIHE RICHARD RAYMOND	NY	32W	38
HURLOCK CURTIS WOODROW	FL	17E	57
HURLOCK PETER CLIFTON	FL	33W	79
HURNEY JOSEPH EMANUAL	SD	34W	7
HURRY SAMUEL GREEN	KY	36E	75
HURSE KENNETH CHARLES	OR	21E	94
HURST HOWARD EUGENE	CA	21E	122
HURST JAKE EDWARD	TX	36W	3
HURST JAMES RANDOLPH	FL	19W	55
HURST JOHN ALLEN	ID	14W	8
HURST JOHN CLARK	TX	52W	23
HURST QUENTIN FOXX	KS	42W	29
HURST ROBERT LEE	IL	03E	18
HURST RONALD CHARLES	MA	18E	18
HURST RONALD LYNN	NC	54E	40
HURST ROOSEVELT JR	AL	53W	20
HURST WILLIAM JOSEPH	AL	35E	72
HURSTON HORATIO WILLIAM	MI	19W	39
HURSTON HUGH LARRY	GA	20E	29
HURT DARRELL VON	IN	20W	7
HURT PAUL THOMAS III	MI	22W	78
HURT RONALD WAYNE	IN	12W	37
HURT VASSAR WILLIAM III	VA	11W	84
HURT WILLIAM C	NE	18E	29

NAME	STATE	PANEL NO.	LINE NO.
HURTA JOSEPH DANIEL	NM	17E	20
HURTADO ALBERT STEVEN	CA	10E	119
HURTADO JOHN BERNARD	CA	48E	28
HURTAULT CUTBURT	VI	22W	47
HUSCHER JOHN RANDOLPH	MI	40E	23
HUSK CLARENCE RAY	IN	19E	96
HUSKA MARTIN SAM	IL	11W	80
HUSKEY ESTEL	TN	07E	25
HUSKEY STEPHEN JOSEPH	MD	02W	57
HUSKON BENNY LEO	AZ	59W	23
HUSO WAYDE MURRAY	MN	19W	31
HUSS ROY ARTHUR	WI	37E	58
HUSSEY BILLY RAY	NC	12E	74
HUSSEY GEORGE ELLERY	MA	11W	95
HUSSEY SHERMAN JUNIOR	NC	53E	34
HUSSMANN KURT CHRISTOPHER	MD	38W	58
HUSTAD LARS PETER	MN	27W	18
HUSTEAD TERENCE MICHAEL	CA	44W	49
HUSTED GARY ARZA	MI	63W	7
HUSTER ROBERT RICHARD	NJ	17E	125
HUSTON CHARLES GREGORY	OH	46E	55
HUSTON DALE MARTIN	FL	46W	29
HUSTON HARRY D JR	OH	27E	6
HUSTON JOE STEPHEN	TX	29W	79
HUSTON TERRY FLOYD	ID	08E	17
HUTCHERSON GARY CAROL	SC	56W	4
HUTCHERSON JIMMIE CLAY	TN	07E	133
HUTCHERSON RONALD DAVID	TN	45W	52
HUTCHESON GEORGE DEWEY	FL	18W	20
HUTCHINGS ALVIN DALE	TN	09E	104
HUTCHINGS DAVID GEORGE	IN	08E	66
HUTCHINGS STEVEN WYLIE	TX	49W	19
HUTCHINS CHARLES E JR	OH	10E	47
HUTCHINS DALE EUGENE	NV	10W	97
HUTCHINS FRANK JOHN	NY	42E	33
HUTCHINS LUCIOUS	FL	43E	7
HUTCHINS MARION RAY	AR	17E	104
HUTCHINS TOLER LEE JR	AR	20E	75
HUTCHINSON ALLEN MELVIN	ME	14W	106
HUTCHINSON GEORGE ROBERT	NJ	42E	66
HUTCHINSON KENNETH P JR	WV	60W	18
HUTCHINSON PAUL LEE	PA	46E	7
HUTCHINSON RANDOLPH SCOTT	OH	13E	102
HUTCHINSON RICHARD JR	OH	16E	68
HUTCHINSON ROBERT S II	CA	39E	61
HUTCHINSON WALTER EUGENE	MI	18W	33
HUTCHINSON WAYNE ALLEN	FL	31E	47
HUTCHISON CHARLES RANDEL	AR	40W	37
HUTCHISON CHESTER K	FL	26E	60
HUTCHISON JOHN WILLIAM	SD	48W	56
HUTCHISON ROBERT LEE	WV	34E	20
HUTCHISON STANLEY ROBERT	IL	32E	45
HUTH PHILIP NICHOLAS II	TX	21W	108
HUTH RALPH CHARLES	IN	17E	92
HUTSON CARL RICKIE	AR	08E	104
HUTSON GEORGE GLENN	OH	05W	96
HUTSON MICHAEL GALE	CA	46W	50
HUTSON MICHAEL LOUIS	IL	01W	36
HUTSON RICKS ARBRA	AR	07W	131
HUTSON RONALD WAYNE	OK	15E	20
HUTTER ROBERT NELSON JR	MO	35E	73
HUTTIE FREDERICK E III	KS	08W	115
HUTTING ROY DONALD	FL	11E	15
HUTTO CURTIS WOODROW	GA	30E	27
HUTTON CHARLES PHILLIP	OK	07W	27
HUTTON EARL DEWITT	KS	12E	28
HUTTON JAMES EDWARD	IL	16E	60
HUTTON JOHN KENDRICK JR	VA	24E	100
HUTTON KENNETH KEITH	IA	41E	10
HUTTON WALTER WESLEY	NJ	07W	70
HUTTON WILLIAM JAMES	MO	29W	38
HUTTULA CARL RICHARD	WA	61E	12
HUTZELL JOHN FRANKLIN	MD	53E	15
HUWEL MICHAEL FRANCIS	OH	19E	31
HUWYLER JOSEF S	NY	02E	128
HUX THOMAS MICHAEL	MS	18W	59
HUXTABLE RONALD LESTER	MI	07W	70
HUYLER CECIL	FL	08E	75
HUYLER WILLIAM D JR	NJ	26E	72
HUZICKO CHARLES JAMES	OH	55W	35
HWANG GERALD RICHARD	CA	24W	7
HYATT GEORGE JACKSON	WA	27W	18
HYATT JACK EDWARD	NC	05W	19
HYATT JERALD MICHAEL	OH	20W	107
HYATT JOSEPH LAMAR	GA	29E	90
HYATT MICHAEL DALE	OK	30W	12
HYATT TRACY ROY	LA	09W	79
HYATT WAYNE REUBEN	AL	05W	116
HYDE DANNY EVERETT	UT	11E	94
HYDE JIMMY DON	OK	03E	127
HYDE LLOYD PATTERSON	GA	11E	111
HYDE MICHAEL LEWIS	CO	13E	22
HYDE ROBERT LEE	CO	10E	128
HYDE WAYNE	MO	08E	6
HYDEN DEE AARON	TX	15W	58
HYDER FLOYD ALLAN	MI	30E	56
HYETT KENNETH MONROE	MI	02E	106
HYLAND DENNIS MICHAEL	CO	49W	14
HYLAND JOHN PETER	CA	36E	52
HYLAND PAUL EDWARD	TX	45W	32
HYLEMAN MAUSBY EDWARD	NC	02E	101
HYLER NELSON MICHAEL	NY	09W	115
HYLMON JAMES EDWARD	TN	13W	97
HYMAN LINWOOD EARL	NJ	16W	127
HYMAN WALLACE	GA	09E	12
HYMAN WILLIAM ALTON	NY	21W	93
HYMERS CHARLES SUTHERLAND	PA	14E	117
HYMES JOHN LAMUEL	LA	10E	21
HYNDS WALLACE GOURLEY JR	SC	24E	68
HYNEK CARL FREDERICK III	PA	27E	54
HYNES ROBERT JOHN	NY	25W	39
HYSELL HOWARD ROBERT	SD	07E	13
HYSLOP LELAND WAYNE	OK	25E	1
HYSMITH HAROLD FRANKLIN	FL	17W	85
HYSON RAYMOND LEE	NY	23E	3
IANDOLI DONALD	NJ	30E	27
IANIERI RICHARD JOSEPH	PA	58W	10
IANNETTA LARRY ALBERT	OR	47E	1
IANNICELLI RICHARD LEE	CA	08E	80
IANNUZZI CHARLES EARNEST	NJ	02E	57
IASELLO DENNIS ANTHONY	NJ	23W	101
IBANEZ ALFONSO	TX	34E	49
IBANEZ ARISTOTOLES DEL R		40W	77
IBANEZ DI REYES	CA	21E	58
IBARRA MIKE GOMEZ	TX	29E	10
IBARRA RODRIGO FUENTES	TX	14W	114
IBROM ADRIAN JOSEPH	TX	13E	24
ICE WESLEY GENE	WV	24W	103
ICKE RALPH EDWARD II	CA	35W	35
IDE BEN HERVEY	CA	36W	45
IDE DONALD WILLIAM	DC	24W	103
IDING GREGORY THOMAS	OH	38E	52
IDLE THOMAS GEORGE	OH	54E	7
IDLETT JAMES	GA	25W	72
IDOM MAX RALPH	MS	29E	59
IGARTA BENITO JR	HI	06E	32
IGERT JOHN WILLIAM	MO	48W	33
IGGULDEN SCOTT WARREN	CA	16W	53
IGLESIAS JULIO A III	NY	25E	102
IGNACIO ROY	HI	03W	54
IGNASIAK DAVID JOSEPH	PA	12E	22
IGOE WILLIAM JOHN	PA	23E	52
IHNAT MICHAEL JOHN	NJ	02E	18
IHRIG GARRY LYNN	MO	30E	92
IJAMS DENNIS EARL	MO	51W	41
IKE THOMAS ROBERT	NJ	20E	104
ILAOA FALEAGAFULA	CA	01W	127
ILER KENNETH MARVIN	NE	63W	7
ILES BRUCE ADRION	CO	19E	125
ILGENFRITZ HERBERT E JR	FL	49W	30
ILLER RONALD	PA	26E	112
ILLI DANIEL JOHN	MI	12E	2
ILLINGWORTH JOHN JAMES	CT	13W	129
ILLMAN WILLIAM STEVE	CA	33E	19
ILSLEY ROBERT PATRICK	WA	28W	12
ILSTRUP JOHN ALVIN JR	MN	38E	52
IMAE HACHIRO	HI	08E	98
IMBACH JOHN III	CA	47W	19
IMBORNONE DARRELL DAVID	LA	17W	56
IMERESE JAMES DAVID	NY	22E	105
IMES HENRY EARL JR	NC	21W	65
IMLAH JACK SELWYN	OR	46W	60
IMLER HAROLD EUGENE JR	MD	03W	79
IMPELITHERE ALAN JOHN	NY	30E	70
IMPERIALE RONALD JOSEPH	MO	16E	92
IMPSON DOUGLAS GERALD	LA	44W	64
IMRIE JOHN CHARLES	WI	25E	12
INAY CHRISTOPHER HENRY	WA	41W	47
INBODEN JAMES RAY	IL	43E	7
INBODEN ROGER LEE	OH	59W	6
INBODEN STEVE LEE	IL	09W	105
INCASHOLA JEAN BAPTISTE	MT	12E	112
INCE JOHN DAVID	CO	22W	1
INCROCCI RICHARD LAFAYETT	CA	66W	8
INDRECC GREGORY THOMAS	MI	55E	18
INDYK FRANK ALAN	NH	31E	99
INFANZON-COLON RAMIRO	PR	36W	29
INFERRERA LOUIS JOSEPH	NJ	20E	61
ING HERBERT EDGAR III	NC	36W	69
INGALLS BENJAMIN HARRISON	IN	20E	8
INGALLS GEORGE ALAN	CA	18E	35
INGELS CHARLES WILLIAM	OH	28E	36
INGERSOLL DAVID PAUL	MA	21W	46
INGLE NATHAN LAMAR	TN	06W	17
INGLES DANNY LEE	OH	24E	107
INGLESTON STARET JOHN	NY	12W	57
INGLETT GERALD WAYNE	GA	21E	55
INGMAN BRUCE EDWIN	UT	21W	118
INGRAM ALLEN WADE	AZ	42W	5
INGRAM ARTIE	NY	63E	10
INGRAM CHARLIE BERNARD JR	AL	16E	17
INGRAM ELIJAH	FL	22W	90
INGRAM ISRAEL LONZO	OH	42E	66
INGRAM JERRY GRANT	FL	27E	20
INGRAM JIMMY ANDERSON	VA	22W	2
INGRAM JOHN LEE	OK	48E	41
INGRAM LAFE	WV	25W	6
INGRAM ROBERT HOWARD	CA	36W	57
INGRAM RONALD ERNEST	CA	53W	27
INGRAM WARREN G	MO	08W	28
INGRAM WILLIAM CARLYLE	WA	34W	59
INGRASSIA MICHAEL JOSEPH	IL	46W	50
INGRUM JOHN DANIEL	AR	12W	6
INGRUM JOSEPH HENRY	KS	59E	5
INGUILLO JOHN DEOGRACIAS	CA	23W	87
INIGUEZ DENNIS GLENN	CA	39W	27
INKEL GUY MARCEL	VT	19W	120
INLOW CHARLES EDWARD	MO	33W	41
INLOW RICKY GENE	OH	49E	2
INMAN HARRY CHARLES III	KY	07W	27
INMAN JAMES MACKENZIE	NC	33E	69
INMAN JAMES WESLEY	GA	56W	4
INMAN PHILLIP LEE	CA	44W	26
INMAN WILLIAM IVAN	OH	54E	25
INNES ROGER BURNS	IL	32E	74
INSALL BILLY GLEN	TX	50W	30
INSANA SALVATORE CARMELO	OH	51W	33
INSCORE ROGER VERNON	CA	20E	117
INSEL LAURENCE ALAN	CA	19E	6
INSLEE RAYMOND STEPHEN	NY	12W	57
INSPRUCKER GLENN EDWARD	CA	10E	106
INT-HOUT KURT	AK	02W	102
INTIHAR JOHN THOMAS	NY	52E	40
INTIHAR JOSEF PAUL	OH	46W	3
IOANNI LORENZO JOSEPH	NY	35E	47
IODICE TULLIO PATRICK JR	MD	11E	101
IOPA CHARLES MAHELONA	HI	02E	80
IORIO LEWIS PATRICK	NY	62E	19
IOZZIA SALVATORE	NY	23W	101
IRBY CHARLES WILLIAM	IL	34E	54
IRBY DONALD REECE	TX	43E	67
IRBY WILLIAM SAMUEL	NC	49W	30
IRELAN DANIEL ALBERT	OR	20W	87
IRELAN KENNETH RAY	MO	02E	84
IRELAND ELMER GLENN	ID	21W	42
IRELAND LEROY	GA	03E	80
IRELAND PHILLIP EARL	MD	20E	75
IRELAND ROBERT NEWELL	CA	11W	36
IRELAND RONALD WAYNE	IL	16W	84
IRIZARRY JOSE ANGEL	NY	23E	111
IRIZARRY-ACEVEDO DANIEL	PR	30W	77
IRIZARRY-HERNANDEZ ANGEL	PR	27E	101
IRIZARRY-PEREZ JAIME	PR	04E	67
IRONSIDE STEVEN PAUL	CA	52W	10
IRSCH WAYNE CHARLES	OK	34E	7
IRVIN OPHREY AUSTIN	OH	24W	104

NAME	STATE	PANEL NO.	LINE NO.
IRVIN PAUL EDWARD	FL	29W	24
IRVIN RICHARD LOWELL	OH	20W	97
IRVIN STEPHEN LEE	MO	26E	46
IRVIN THOMAS FRANKLIN	MS	05W	40
IRVING EARL ELESTER JR	IL	10E	86
IRVING JOHN WILLIAM JR	CA	01E	111
IRVING LEE	OH	26E	46
IRVING NATHANIEL	VA	33W	86
IRVING STANLEY NIXON	NY	21W	42
IRWIN RICHARD RAY JR	CA	27E	80
IRWIN ROBERT HARRY	NY	02W	107
IRWIN ROBERT JOSEPH	FL	58W	28
IRWIN THOMAS EDWARD	IL	25E	16
IRWIN VAN ALLEN	CA	50W	6
IRWIN WILLIAM EDWARD	OR	09E	127
ISAAC JAMES EDWARD JR	AL	25W	72
ISAAC ROCCO RENELL	PA	50W	14
ISAAC WILL JR	AL	10W	103
ISAACS DEAN ROBERT	MT	03W	61
ISAACS GARY NEAL	MI	33W	20
ISAACS JOHN PAUL	OH	06E	130
ISAACS MILO CLINTON	TX	06W	16
ISAACS ROYAL GEORGE JR	OK	01E	107
ISAACS SAMMY FLOYD	OK	04W	44
ISAACS WAYNE LEE	OH	27W	18
ISAACSON GARY ALLEN	WI	08E	75
ISAACSON GERALD EDWARD	MA	11E	61
ISAACSON MILFORD DON	IL	14W	62
ISABELLE LEMUEL	PA	31W	50
ISALES-BENITEZ JORGE LUIS	PR	08E	3
ISBELL DAVID GENE	TX	39E	34
ISBELL JAMES RUSSELL	MO	23E	12
ISBELL JIMMIE RAY	MS	04E	34
ISBELL MARSHALL HOWARD	GA	18E	69
ISBELL OTIS EDWARD	AR	61E	12
ISELY MICHAEL GENE	LA	12E	84
ISENHOUR RONALD WAITSEL	NC	06W	40
ISER KENNETH EUGENE	OH	53E	34
ISGRIG DENNIS EDWARD	MO	60E	24
ISHIHARA JAMES HIROSHI	HI	01E	19
ISHMAEL JOHNNIE LEROY	OK	14W	101
ISHMAN ALBERT JR	CA	59W	6
ISHMAN HUEY LEE	KS	16W	95
ISHMAN JOHN EDWARD	PA	40E	64
ISHMAN MICHAEL RAYMOND	PA	14E	15
ISLER CHARLES C JR	VA	54W	30
ISLER REID ALLEN	NM	62E	6
ISLEY CHARLES LESTER III	PA	12E	95
ISOM DAVID	KY	40E	75
ISOM DENNIS ROSS PAUL	PA	30W	25
ISOM THEODORE	TX	06W	73
ISON ARNOLD E	KY	05E	3
ISRAEL RALPH WALDO JR	CA	27W	94
ISSENMANN MICHAEL WILLIAM	CA	43W	16
ITALIANO HARRY RICHARD	MD	23W	53
ITRI DOUGLAS JOHN	MA	10W	6
ITUARTE ROBERTO	TX	04E	12
ITZOE ROBERT ANTHONY	MD	45E	12
IVAN ANDREW JR	NJ	02W	13
IVANOV WILBUR WILLIAM	VT	03E	41
IVENER TERRY LEE	IA	58W	26
IVERSON GERALD ALLEN	ND	29E	3
IVES DAVID ALLEN	CA	18E	75
IVES EDWIN ORRIN	PA	45E	12
IVES PHILLIP THOMAS	MO	21W	51
IVES RICHARD V	NJ	09E	113
IVES TIMOTHY JAMES	CO	18E	123
IVES WILLIAM ALLEN	IA	46E	7
IVEY DORRIS ALBERT	FL	04E	70
IVEY GLEN SIMMANG	NY	01W	14
IVEY HERMAN FRED	GA	06W	123
IVEY JOEL STEVENS JR	NC	02W	76
IVEY MARSHALL PERNELL	NC	15W	1
IVEY SAM	AK	02E	84
IVEY SHERMAN LEE	OH	10E	106
IVEY TOMMY HUBERT	FL	05W	57
IVORY KENNETH JOHN	PA	11E	82
IVORY MICHAEL THOMAS	TN	44W	26
IVY JESSE W JR	IL	15E	45
IVY LEONARD CLARENCE JR	IN	28W	60
IWASKO EDWARD BERNARD	IL	07W	122
IYNDELLIN EDWARD ALLEN	OR	08E	30
IYUA ARCHIE HUBERT JR	IL	29W	10
IZARD B C	TX	56W	34
IZARD PHILLIPS H JR	MS	49W	30
IZZARD SAMUEL JULIUS	DC	30W	77
JABLONSKI JOHN ANDREW	MA	49W	31
JABLONSKI MICHAEL JAMES	IL	21W	23
JABLONSKI ZYGMUNT PAUL JR	MA	40E	53
JABLONSKY EDMOND A JR	TX	54E	25
JACARUSO FRANK	NY	13W	118
JACK MICHAEL FRANCIS	MA	08E	119
JACK WILSON JR	LA	52W	44
JACKEMEYER ROBERT RAYMOND	MI	32E	51
JACKMAN ROGER DAHL	UT	08E	27
JACKOWIAK HENRY PATRICK	NY	27E	17
JACKOWSKI DENNIS EUGENE	NY	11W	7
JACKS GLENN GATES	MS	28E	40
JACKS MARK DOUGLAS	AR	49W	41
JACKSON ABRAHAM	NY	36E	17
JACKSON ABRAHAM	LA	59E	24
JACKSON ADAM	AL	09W	20
JACKSON ALEXANDER	DC	24E	109
JACKSON ALFRED	NY	50E	48
JACKSON ALLEN LEE	IN	25E	42
JACKSON ALLEN VERONE	GA	38W	36
JACKSON ALPHA RAY	TX	03E	81
JACKSON ALVIN EDWARD	PA	12E	88
JACKSON AMIL JR	TX	34W	76
JACKSON ANDREW	DC	43E	23
JACKSON ANGUS N	MD	14E	15
JACKSON ARELINN LEWIS	FL	34W	25
JACKSON ARNOLD BRYAN	TN	20W	50
JACKSON ARTHUR JAMES	CA	05E	86
JACKSON BARRY	CT	29W	69
JACKSON BEN JR	CA	08W	114
JACKSON BENJAMIN FRANKLIN	SC	13W	122
JACKSON BENNY CHARLES	NC	17W	97
JACKSON BILLY DALE	IL	43E	45
JACKSON BILLY LEE	AL	49E	2
JACKSON BOBBY GENE	MO	14E	22
JACKSON CALVIN OTIS	GA	38E	2
JACKSON CARL EDWIN	LA	02E	21
JACKSON CARROLL THOMAS	MD	01W	73
JACKSON CECIL JR	MO	07W	22
JACKSON CHARLES	LA	19E	59
JACKSON CHARLES ARTHUR	CT	35W	12
JACKSON CHARLES EDWARD	MS	63W	16
JACKSON CHARLES EDWARD	IN	18W	1
JACKSON CHARLES SID	TN	37E	8
JACKSON CHARLES WILLIAM	OH	10E	119
JACKSON CHESTER LEE	CA	18W	39
JACKSON CHRISTOPHER A	CA	19W	79
JACKSON CLARENCE	GA	29E	31
JACKSON CLARENCE JAMES	FL	49W	5
JACKSON CLINNIS HARRELL	NC	12E	37
JACKSON COLIN FRANK	CA	20E	29
JACKSON CRAWFORD JR	AL	48W	27
JACKSON CURTIS DARRELL	CA	22E	71
JACKSON DALE RAYMOND	MO	32W	6
JACKSON DALTON EARL	LA	11E	82
JACKSON DARRELL ASA	WA	11E	74
JACKSON DAVID ANDREW	CA	68E	3
JACKSON DAVID CHARLES M	IN	31W	68
JACKSON DAVID ERIC	IL	45E	12
JACKSON DAVID LEE JR	OH	04E	77
JACKSON DAVID LEON	TX	02W	53
JACKSON DAVID ROLLAND	AL	17W	7
JACKSON DAVID RUSSELL	OH	16W	44
JACKSON DEAN ALFRED	IA	03E	81
JACKSON DEARING MICHAEL	MO	15W	53
JACKSON DENNY MILBURN	CA	36E	17
JACKSON DONALD ALLEN	OH	12E	79
JACKSON DONALD EUGENE	VA	13E	23
JACKSON DONALD GENE	CA	51E	39
JACKSON DONNEY LYRCE	CA	33E	87
JACKSON DOUGLAS	MI	07E	19
JACKSON EDDIE LEE	FL	31E	99
JACKSON EDDIE LEE JR	NE	39W	17
JACKSON EDWARD HENRY JR	NY	15E	45
JACKSON EDWARD JR	NY	11E	82
JACKSON EDWARD JR	NC	11W	80
JACKSON EDWARD MERL	TX	45W	21
JACKSON FRED ORR JR	GA	18W	39
JACKSON FREDDIE	FL	01W	19
JACKSON FREDERICK G JR	NM	40W	20
JACKSON FREDERICK LEROY	DC	28E	9
JACKSON G B JR	CA	43W	16
JACKSON GARLAND DUANE	MI	59E	25
JACKSON GARY RAY	KS	18W	59
JACKSON GEORGE EMMETT	AL	33W	41
JACKSON GERALD ARTHUR	FL	14W	19
JACKSON GLEN ALAN III	IL	14W	86
JACKSON HARRY JOHN JR	NJ	16W	56
JACKSON HERMAN	FL	54E	26
JACKSON HOWARD WADE	WV	11E	15
JACKSON HUGH MAR	MO	24E	79
JACKSON JAMES ALBERT	CA	20E	75
JACKSON JAMES ARTHUR	CA	16W	57
JACKSON JAMES CHARLES	KY	03E	81
JACKSON JAMES CLEVELAND	SC	20W	58
JACKSON JAMES DONALD	TX	03W	74
JACKSON JAMES HERMAN	TX	68W	3
JACKSON JAMES TERRY	FL	02W	118
JACKSON JAMES WESLEY JR	GA	18W	121
JACKSON JEROME ELLIS	DC	04W	78
JACKSON JERRY LEE	OH	29E	15
JACKSON JOHN GLEN	PA	06E	65
JACKSON JOHN HERSTON	OH	37E	37
JACKSON JOHN RAYMOND	CO	24W	76
JACKSON JOHN RICHARD	KY	29W	10
JACKSON JOHN WENDELL	LA	19E	96
JACKSON JOHN WILLIAM	OH	15E	106
JACKSON JOHNNIE	NY	55W	13
JACKSON JOHNNIE BRUCE	TX	38E	30
JACKSON JOHNNY	NC	03W	72
JACKSON JOHNNY FRANKLIN	NC	46W	50
JACKSON JOSEPH EARL	NC	07W	53
JACKSON JOSEPH EUGENE	PA	04E	100
JACKSON JOSEPH LOUIS	NJ	43W	37
JACKSON KEITH MICHAEL	NJ	05W	72
JACKSON KENNETH EDWARD	WV	33W	64
JACKSON KENNETH MCKINLEY	MI	03E	119
JACKSON LAMOND JOSEPH	MO	09E	40
JACKSON LAMONT	NY	37W	81
JACKSON LARRY ALLEN	WV	39W	49
JACKSON LARRY ANTHONY	LA	29W	9
JACKSON LARRY RICHARD	KY	34E	8
JACKSON LAWRENCE	TX	54W	3
JACKSON LAWRENCE DAVID	OH	18W	75
JACKSON LAWRENCE EDWARD	WV	02E	75
JACKSON LAWRENCE HENRY	WV	20W	108
JACKSON LEHRON JR	PA	22E	25
JACKSON LEON JEROME	NY	03W	61
JACKSON LEONARD JR	IL	38E	30
JACKSON LEWIS JAMES	MO	08E	98
JACKSON LITTLE JAY	CA	43E	45
JACKSON LLOYD WILLIAM JR	CO	43W	37
JACKSON LLOYD WILNER	NV	11W	124
JACKSON MALAKIA JR	PA	07E	26
JACKSON MARK	FL	17W	128
JACKSON MAXIE JR	TX	26W	19
JACKSON MICHAEL CHARLES	CA	12W	13
JACKSON MICHAEL MEREDITH	SD	06E	44
JACKSON MICHELE LEE	KY	26W	92
JACKSON MURRAY JUNIOR	FL	26W	72
JACKSON NATHANIEL E L	SC	50E	15
JACKSON NATHANIEL HARVEY	CA	54E	9
JACKSON NATHANIEL JR	FL	18W	121
JACKSON NOBLE	NY	21E	5
JACKSON OTIS E	CA	12E	50
JACKSON PAUL EDWARD	CA	58E	9
JACKSON PAUL GRAY	NC	13E	84
JACKSON PAUL HOWARD JR	PA	29W	20
JACKSON PAUL NASH	NC	14W	62
JACKSON PAUL VERNON III	VA	01W	105
JACKSON RALFORD JOHN	AZ	24W	76
JACKSON RAY LEE	LA	46W	16
JACKSON RAYMOND COLUMBUS	NY	14E	35
JACKSON RICHARD ALBERT	MO	36E	17
JACKSON RICHARD BERNARD	PA	26E	11
JACKSON RICHARD CURTIS	FL	58E	22
JACKSON RICHARD THOMAS	WI	33E	58
JACKSON ROBERT ALAN	WA	39E	72
JACKSON ROBERT ANDREW	RI	34E	42
JACKSON ROBERT BUFORD	MS	10E	128

NAME	STATE	PANEL NO.	LINE NO.
JACKSON ROBERT ELEE	CA	39W	54
JACKSON ROBERT EUGENE	CO	42E	66
JACKSON ROBERT JR	MO	30W	55
JACKSON ROBERT LEONARD	NJ	46E	7
JACKSON RONALD	OH	04W	46
JACKSON ROY LEE	NC	35E	73
JACKSON SANFORD LEVON JR	NY	10E	9
JACKSON STANLEY ALLEN	NY	04W	2
JACKSON SYLVESTER JR	SC	05E	11
JACKSON TERRENCE TURNER	NY	06W	120
JACKSON TERRY KENT	GA	32W	27
JACKSON THOMAS CLAYTON	AL	12E	74
JACKSON THOMAS FRANCIS	MA	13E	53
JACKSON THOMAS PETER JR	NY	24W	67
JACKSON THOMAS WINFORD	AL	01W	48
JACKSON THORNTON ISHAM	FL	32E	74
JACKSON TOBY LEE	TX	21W	108
JACKSON TODD R	WI	35E	73
JACKSON TYRONE	IL	42W	29
JACKSON WALLACE MICHAEL	NC	25E	16
JACKSON WALTER PHILIP	IL	09E	123
JACKSON WILBUR DESMAR	IL	07E	65
JACKSON WILLIAM	NJ	29W	50
JACKSON WILLIAM BRAXTON	TX	23E	91
JACKSON WILLIAM EUGENE	MI	01E	42
JACKSON WILLIAMS OTIS	AL	17W	50
JACKSON WILLIE	GA	40E	64
JACKSON WILLIE	LA	46E	35
JACKSON WITHERS THEODORE	VA	16W	100
JACKYMACK RUDOLPH	MI	07E	26
JACO ARNOLD NOEL	KY	18W	47
JACOB PHILLIP	OH	24E	28
JACOB RANDALL GORDON	IL	25E	16
JACOB ROBERT MICHAEL	CT	48E	5
JACOBS AUBREY EUGENE JR	TN	41W	12
JACOBS BOBBY JOE	TX	07E	58
JACOBS CHRISTOPHER	NY	12W	113
JACOBS DANNIE DICK	TN	19E	82
JACOBS DAVID PAUL	MI	30W	45
JACOBS DEL RAY	NJ	19E	72
JACOBS DENNIS WAYNE	CA	41E	50
JACOBS DONALD WAYNE	PA	58W	26
JACOBS EDWARD DANIEL JR	NY	53W	43
JACOBS EDWARD JAMES JR	WA	25E	42
JACOBS ERNEST LINWOOD JR	SC	37E	23
JACOBS GARY ORLAND	FL	27W	81
JACOBS GEORGE EDGAR	TN	52E	30
JACOBS JAMES	NY	12W	61
JACOBS JEROME EDWARD	NJ	55E	18
JACOBS JOHN CHARLES	IN	08E	17
JACOBS JOHN EDWIN	NC	42W	57
JACOBS JOHN PAUL	MA	38E	2
JACOBS JOSEPH LEWIS	CA	15E	70
JACOBS PERRY OWEN	AL	41W	59
JACOBS PHILLIP HAROLD	UT	07W	96
JACOBS RALPH WAYNE	OH	24E	29
JACOBS RICHARD ALLEN	MI	25E	51
JACOBS RICHARD CHESTER	HI	13E	92
JACOBS RICKIE JEROME	OH	57W	18
JACOBS ROBERT MILTON	SD	58E	9
JACOBS THOMAS CARLYLE	IL	44W	49
JACOBS VERNON DUANE	WI	29W	61
JACOBS VINCENT LAWRENCE	NJ	35W	48
JACOBS WILLIAM JOHN	CA	41E	67
JACOBS WILLIE BREWSTER	GA	27W	88
JACOBSEN DONALD JAMES	MN	04E	110
JACOBSEN DONALD LEROY	IA	12E	37
JACOBSEN TIMOTHY JOHN	CA	01W	26
JACOBSEN WALLACE RAY	CA	04E	120
JACOBSGAARD DAVID KEITH	IL	31W	93
JACOBSON HARVEY GEORGE	WI	06W	129
JACOBSON JOHN W SR	MI	50W	35
JACOBSON JON CHRISTOPHER	NJ	07W	117
JACOBSON KENNETH JAMES	WA	30E	44
JACOBSON LARRY BRUCE	ND	07W	11
JACOBSON MARK NELS	WI	33W	2
JACOBSON SCOTT NELSON	IL	02W	112
JACOBSON WARNER CRAIG	CA	55W	18
JACOBUS WILLIAM THOMAS	NJ	33E	19
JACONETTI KENNETH RICHARD	NY	32E	17
JACQUES DONALD	NY	41E	22
JACQUES FELIX	CA	26W	25

NAME	STATE	PANEL NO.	LINE NO.
JACQUES JAMES JOSEPH	CO	01W	131
JACQUES JOSEPH ARTHUR	NM	06W	95
JACQUES KENNEDY	CA	24W	16
JACQUES ROBERT PAUL	MI	05W	81
JACQUEZ JOSEPH EDWARD	UT	25W	49
JAECK RICHARD ELMER	WI	01E	46
JAECKELS TOBY EDWARD	IL	18W	121
JAEGER JULIUS PATRICK	GA	12W	101
JAFFE BERNARD	TX	02E	83
JAGARD LARRY FRANK	CA	01W	59
JAGELER CHARLES DAVID	TX	17W	56
JAGER ROLAND VINCENT JR	CA	01E	74
JAGGERS THOMAS MURL	MS	19E	37
JAGIELO ALLEN DALE	CA	28E	25
JAHN DENNIS EARL	IL	04W	116
JAHNKE RONALD EDWARD	WI	04E	58
JAIME ANTONIO BARRERA	TX	41W	13
JAJTNER RAYMOND CHARLES	WI	07E	82
JAKEL CRAIG JAMES	NY	04W	3
JAKO JAMES LOUIS	MI	32E	74
JAKOBSEN PETER LAUST	CA	25W	23
JAKOVAC JOHN ANDREW	MI	21E	23
JALBERT DAVID MICHAEL	RI	37W	67
JALLOWAY STEPHEN FRANK	IL	13E	47
JAMACK CHARLES ANTHONY	MD	27E	24
JAMERSON KENNETH ROBERT	SD	17E	104
JAMERSON LARRY ALLEN	WA	50W	51
JAMERSON LARRY CARL	NC	51E	21
JAMES ARTHUR LEROY	IN	06E	65
JAMES BILLIE	NM	50E	3
JAMES BOBBY	GA	59E	24
JAMES BOBBY JOE	TX	08E	86
JAMES CHARLES ROBERT	CA	32W	59
JAMES CLAUDE RAY	CA	25E	51
JAMES CLAYTON WADE	VA	03W	29
JAMES CLIFFORD W	IL	18E	8
JAMES DAN NINKEY	GA	35W	4
JAMES DANIEL RAYMOND	NE	05E	80
JAMES DONALD JR	MI	19W	55
JAMES DUTLEY	NJ	18E	70
JAMES EDDIE LOUIS JR	SC	28E	82
JAMES EDWARD ARTHUR	RI	17W	124
JAMES EDWARD LUCAS II	KY	09W	47
JAMES ELVIN JR	NC	08W	116
JAMES EMMETT DWAINE	TX	17W	16
JAMES FRANKLIN THEODORE	MD	16W	22
JAMES GARY LYNN	TX	21E	13
JAMES GENERAL FIRD JR	VA	22E	105
JAMES GERALD	AL	63E	9
JAMES GERALD LYNN	MO	30W	58
JAMES HARRY LEE JR	VA	15E	9
JAMES HENRY	NJ	41W	40
JAMES JACK LLEWELLYN	IA	05E	51
JAMES JESSE JR	NJ	02E	16
JAMES JOE NEAL	CA	05E	65
JAMES JOHN HENRY JR	NY	17E	52
JAMES JOHN MATHAS	NC	06E	106
JAMES JOSEPH	NC	04E	91
JAMES KENNETH BRADLEY	FL	27W	10
JAMES KENNETH EARL	TX	18E	14
JAMES LEE ALLEN JR	NY	05E	12
JAMES LEE CHRISTOPHER JR	MO	19E	127
JAMES LEE ROY	KY	02E	76
JAMES MARC STEVEN	NY	27E	20
JAMES MARK EVERETT	GA	39E	48
JAMES MICHAEL RAY	MN	14W	26
JAMES MORRIS KEITH	WA	49E	35
JAMES PAUL JOSEPH	FL	13W	92
JAMES PERRY DEAN	MD	17E	36
JAMES RAY DON	TN	53E	15
JAMES RAYMON HORACE JR	AL	02W	65
JAMES RICHARD DALE	IN	37W	66
JAMES RICKY LYNN	OK	04W	19
JAMES ROBERT LEE	MO	07W	34
JAMES RODNEY ALVIN	NJ	09E	57
JAMES RONALD EUGENE	CA	37W	12
JAMES RUFUS LA DELL	TX	08E	11
JAMES SAMUEL ADAMS JR	NC	13E	10
JAMES SAMUEL JR	NY	13W	22
JAMES SAMUEL LARRY	TN	01W	117
JAMES SAMUEL REESE II	GA	49W	42
JAMES THELBERT ALLYSON	NY	35E	60

NAME	STATE	PANEL NO.	LINE NO.
JAMES THOMAS	NY	03E	81
JAMES WASHINGTON L	WV	46W	42
JAMES WILLIAM CALVIN	WV	16W	96
JAMES WILLIE JR	AL	03W	92
JAMES WILLIE LEE	IL	41E	39
JAMES WILLIE LEE	VA	40W	77
JAMESON DAVID ALLEN	KY	34E	87
JAMESON LARRY DUANE	IA	01E	30
JAMESON RODGER LEE	KS	19W	125
JAMIESON GARY LEE	NY	35W	34
JAMILSKI MARIAN	NY	39W	74
JAMISON DAVID	NV	14E	80
JAMISON ERNEST CECIL	PA	26W	40
JAMISON FRANK	PA	20E	117
JAMISON JAN DWAIN	AZ	45W	20
JAMISON ROCKWELL GRANT	CA	23E	60
JAMISON ROGER LEE	MI	25W	12
JAMISON TED RAY	OH	43W	38
JAMRO ROBERT JAMES	NY	22E	105
JAMROCK PHILIP ROBERT	IL	04W	49
JAMROCK STANLEY M	NY	39E	48
JAMROS RICHARD KENNETH	MN	06E	4
JAMROZY STANLEY MICHAEL	KY	20E	29
JANAK JOE JOHN	TX	59E	5
JANCA LOUIS EMIL	GA	07W	132
JANDERSHOVITZ PAUL WILLIA	PA	04E	38
JANEDA STEVEN MICHAEL	OH	10W	104
JANES NICKLOS BYRON	GA	29E	20
JANES WILLIAM CAREY	WA	32E	31
JANEWAY JERRY LEE	CA	55E	18
JANHUNEN DANIEL JOHN	MT	10E	61
JANIGIAN RICHARD ALLEN	OR	26E	103
JANISH DAVID WILLIAM	IA	13W	44
JANKA JAMES EDWARD	IL	30W	77
JANKA WILLIAM ROBERT	WI	16E	20
JANKE CHARLES JULIUS	WI	03E	44
JANKE KEITH BRIAN	WI	23W	9
JANKE THEODORE JR	KS	63E	11
JANKOWSKI LARRY FLOYD	IN	19E	60
JANKOWSKI RICHARD JOHN	NY	09E	19
JANKOWSKI WALTER JOSEPH	PA	12E	1
JANNETTA RODNEY ALAN	MN	21W	8
JANOSKA JOHN JAY JR	NY	14W	29
JANOUSEK RONALD JAMES	IL	20W	118
JANOWICZ JOSEPH ANTHONY	CA	49E	54
JANOWITZ ROBERT LAWRENCE	NJ	43W	28
JANOWSKY CARL EMIL JR	NY	21W	13
JANS ROBERT ALLEN	CA	41E	39
JANSEN ARTHUR RUSSELL	NY	35E	23
JANSEN JEROME EDDIE WALLY	CA	47W	9
JANSEN LARRY WAYNE	IL	44W	39
JANSEN MILES EDWARD	MN	24E	7
JANSENIUS RAYMOND LEE	FL	40W	58
JANSKI RICHARD JOSEPH	MN	32E	36
JANSONIUS FRED WALTER	ND	36E	74
JANSSEN ARNOLD	IL	36W	63
JANSSEN DOUGLAS DUANE	SD	34W	84
JANSSEN ROBERT DEAN	IL	60W	1
JANTO PAUL CHALMERS	OK	23W	45
JANTZ ROBERT WAYNE	KS	35W	20
JANTZEN LEONARD F	NY	17E	124
JAQUA MICHAEL DOUGLAS	OH	29E	3
JAQUINS CHARLES EGBERT	MA	02W	23
JAQUISH JAMES IVAN	MI	17W	7
JARA-VERANO ALBERTO I		13E	77
JARAMILLO JORGE M	CA	03E	127
JARANSON JAMES EDWARD	IL	23E	91
JARBOE LOWELL THOMAS	KY	11W	80
JARBOE WILLIAM LEE	IN	60W	2
JARDINE ROBERT AXEL JR	WI	12W	21
JARICK RUSSELL WILLIAM	CA	57E	24
JARMOLINSKI CHESTER JR	NJ	27W	94
JAROLIMEK JAMES MICHAEL	IL	05E	132
JARONIK ROBERT WALTER	IN	54W	17
JAROSCAK JOHN PAUL	IN	13W	81
JARRARD JERRY EDWIN	GA	44W	49
JARRAS STEPHEN THEODORE	MA	19E	128
JARRELL JOHN WAYNE	VA	11E	71
JARRELL JOSEPH DANIEL	MI	05E	34
JARRELL KENITH LEWIS	TX	19W	102
JARRELL RANDALL DAVID	TX	13E	27
JARRELL ROGER DALE	TN	06E	80

NAME	STATE	PANEL NO.	LINE NO.
JARRELL SIDNEY WADE	GA	10W	34
JARRELL WENDALL JOSEPH	MI	09W	124
JARRETT FREDERICK	HI	57E	4
JARRETT JAMES DALE	MI	11W	24
JARRETT LEMOYNDUE	IL	23E	111
JARRETT MICHAEL DONALD	OH	39W	74
JARRETT PHILLIP RONALD	NC	15E	33
JARRETT STEVEN ANDREW	VA	59E	5
JARVI RAYMOND LEE	MN	29E	59
JARVIS DANNY WAYNE	WA	26W	84
JARVIS DAVID LEONARD	NY	33E	19
JARVIS DEE RANDALL	UT	22E	105
JARVIS EDWARD CARL	MA	27E	95
JARVIS JEREMY MICHAEL	MI	23E	119
JARVIS LEE BRIAN	IL	26E	26
JARVIS PAUL ROGER	WA	33W	79
JARVIS RICHARD MARK	WA	48W	43
JARVIS ROGER ELLIS	IL	28E	13
JARVIS RONALD ALAN	KS	36W	51
JARVIS WILLIAM THOMAS	GA	37E	37
JARZENSKI JAMES HENRY	PA	03E	18
JASINSKI RONALD NORMAN	IL	05W	69
JASKIEWICZ DANIEL JOSEPH	MI	50E	15
JASMINE CHARLES	MO	31E	69
JASNOCHA ALFRED L JR	MA	60E	24
JASON BRUCE ELLSWORTH	MA	10E	91
JASPER DAVID CLAUD	IN	38W	11
JASSO JOHN	OH	07W	4
JASSO MARTIN	TX	39E	7
JASURA ROBERT WILLIAM	MI	39W	60
JATEFF WILLIAM ALBERT	OH	27E	65
JATICH GARY LEE	OH	43E	23
JAUER VICTOR CARL	PA	31W	37
JAUREGUI DAVID CRUZ	AZ	06W	87
JAVA DANIEL M	WI	13E	10
JAVINES JOSE JALOCON		01W	109
JAVORCHIK JOHN CHARLES	IL	21W	60
JAWOROWICZ LAWRENCE FRANK	MI	45W	41
JAY BRIAN EDWARD	GA	07W	22
JAY HARVEY LEON	FL	12W	43
JAY ROBERT VERN	CA	30W	48
JAYNES JAMES OAKLEY	TN	52E	6
JEALOUS-OF-HIM@ FRANK W	SD	22W	2
JEANTET FRANCIS LEON	CA	42E	33
JECMEN ANTON JAMES JR	IL	22W	120
JEDLICKA DONALD WILLIAM	IA	24E	29
JEDNAT ERIC JOHN	NY	53W	20
JEDNEAK DANIEL JOHN	MN	06W	51
JEDRZEJEWSKI HARRY FRANCI	PA	03E	81
JEFFERIS GARY DWIGHT	PA	10E	72
JEFFERS JOHN LARRY	SC	23E	119
JEFFERS ODES WINSTON	AR	01E	19
JEFFERSON BILLY RANDOLPH	VA	41W	24
JEFFERSON CARTER JR	LA	02W	70
JEFFERSON CLARENCE JR	LA	45E	34
JEFFERSON GARY DONALD	IN	12W	124
JEFFERSON HERMAN LOUIS JR	LA	03E	44
JEFFERSON JAMES MILTON	CA	19E	96
JEFFERSON JERRY WAYNE	KY	37W	12
JEFFERSON JIMMIE LEE	IL	50W	1
JEFFERSON LEROY	SC	32E	31
JEFFERSON LOUIS ALLN	VA	08E	36
JEFFERSON NELSON JR	GA	46W	4
JEFFERSON PERRY HENRY	CO	27W	5
JEFFERSON RANDOLPH THOMAS	PA	52W	44
JEFFERSON ROLAND IRA	MD	25E	38
JEFFORDS DERRELL BLACKBUR	AZ	04E	37
JEFFRIES CHARLES B JR	IL	06E	15
JEFFRIES GABRIEL AUGUS JR	VI	03W	8
JEFFRIES GERRIE GEORGE	MI	41E	10
JEFFRIES JAMES HERBERT	AR	29W	89
JEFFRIES MACK SIMPSON	MS	56E	25
JEFFS CLIVE GARTH	UT	04W	41
JELICH JOHN ANTHONY	WI	02W	126
JELINEK ALLEN LEO	OH	09E	40
JELKS CARLOS DENNIS	OH	05E	34
JEMISON JOHN L	PA	02E	57
JENCZYK FRANK PAUL JR	MA	58E	15
JENERSON RALPH MATTHEW	PA	12W	113
JENEWEIN MARK ARDELL	CA	13W	45
JENKINS ANDREW EARL	FL	27W	81
JENKINS ANTHONY LEROY	GA	18W	62
JENKINS BARNETTE GARTRELL	GA	05E	95
JENKINS BARRY DOUGLAS	NY	54W	37
JENKINS BERT McCREE	TX	26W	72
JENKINS CECIL RAYMOND	MD	19E	60
JENKINS CHARLES ARTHUR	VA	02E	17
JENKINS CHARLES OWEN JR	PA	02E	5
JENKINS CHARLES WAYNE	CA	29W	79
JENKINS CHARLIE EDWARD	LA	51W	26
JENKINS CLAUDE THOMAS	VA	27W	64
JENKINS CLAYTON DEAN	WI	23W	53
JENKINS CLIFFORD JR	NJ	58W	32
JENKINS DAN LAVERNE	NC	33W	17
JENKINS DENNIS ALAN	CA	03W	2
JENKINS DON	TX	07W	123
JENKINS DONALD RAY	OH	06W	118
JENKINS EARL DALE JR	IL	30E	3
JENKINS ERIC DORAN	CO	38W	75
JENKINS EUGENE RAY	OK	16W	34
JENKINS FRANK PAUL JR	AL	22E	25
JENKINS FRED CARLTON	FL	47E	40
JENKINS FRED HARVEY	SC	03E	82
JENKINS GERALD THOMAS	IN	03E	111
JENKINS GREGORY DALE	NC	19E	97
JENKINS ISADORE	NY	02W	86
JENKINS J CLIFFORD	KY	27W	10
JENKINS JAMES ALEX	NC	24W	60
JENKINS JAMES EARL	NC	29E	83
JENKINS JAMES LUCKY	FL	29E	28
JENKINS JERRY MALONE	VA	21E	112
JENKINS JERRY WAYNE	MS	39E	34
JENKINS JOHN ALLEN III	VA	42W	12
JENKINS JOYFUL J	AL	18W	47
JENKINS JULIUS EDGAR	PA	20E	84
JENKINS KENNETH BRUCE	SC	45W	53
JENKINS KENNETH CLIFFORD	OH	26W	20
JENKINS LANCE NORMAN	NJ	31E	48
JENKINS LARRY	FL	38W	49
JENKINS LARRY BARNEY	FL	49E	2
JENKINS LARRY RUFUS	MI	22W	2
JENKINS LEN MCKINLEY	TN	12E	50
JENKINS LEWIS FRANKLIN	VA	23E	52
JENKINS MICHAEL LEE	VA	31W	50
JENKINS MORRIS E	OH	03E	120
JENKINS PAUL LAVERNE	AR	09W	105
JENKINS PHILIP PAUL	MD	07E	38
JENKINS RANDALL LEE	OH	33W	41
JENKINS RAY G	UT	41E	67
JENKINS REGINALD ROCKEFEL	SC	63W	7
JENKINS ROBERT DONALD	TN	17E	20
JENKINS ROBERT DOUGLAS	MI	65W	10
JENKINS ROBERT EARL	KS	63E	11
JENKINS ROBERT HENRY JR	FL	30W	46
JENKINS ROBERT WILEY	GA	36E	17
JENKINS ROGER WARDELL	NC	07E	13
JENKINS ROLAND HAYES	TX	52W	35
JENKINS ROY LEE	NC	49W	36
JENKINS STEVEN LEE	CA	34W	8
JENKINS TERRY LEE	OH	23W	87
JENKINS VERNELL	TX	10E	128
JENKINS VINCENT EARL	VA	59E	24
JENKINS WAYNE DANIEL	NC	44W	38
JENKINS WILLIAM	SC	40E	23
JENKINS WILLIAM CLARENCE	AL	39E	34
JENKINS WILLIAM CLIFTON	VA	46E	7
JENKS GARY LEE	OH	08W	105
JENKS HARLEY JOHN	MI	53E	2
JENKS JAMES JOSEPH JR	MA	45W	14
JENKS JOSEPH WILLIAM	MI	16E	73
JENKS RICHARD DALE	CA	31E	89
JENKS ROBERT JAMES	MI	42E	33
JENNE ROBERT EARL	UT	57E	4
JENNER RICHARD LEE	MO	21E	122
JENNETT WILLIAM ROBERT	IN	52E	20
JENNETTE LEO MILLER	NC	47W	45
JENNIGES RONALD ARTHUR	MN	15W	122
JENNINGS BOBBY DALE	IL	28W	37
JENNINGS BOBBY JOHN	KY	15E	5
JENNINGS CHARLES WENDELL	NC	26W	63
JENNINGS DONALD MELVIN	MD	31W	8'
JENNINGS EARL WAYNE	OK	14E	112
JENNINGS ELTON LEE JR	GA	33W	2
JENNINGS GLENN ROBERT	MA	22W	98
JENNINGS JAMES DALE	MS	11W	113
JENNINGS JAMES JR	LA	17W	18
JENNINGS JAMES LEWIS	MD	57W	10
JENNINGS JASPER LEWIS	FL	19E	128
JENNINGS JIM FRANK	UT	22W	98
JENNINGS JOHN MICHAEL	NY	14W	40
JENNINGS LARRY JO	MO	51E	8
JENNINGS LAWRENCE MARTIN	NY	34E	77
JENNINGS MICHAEL	NJ	20W	44
JENNINGS ROBERT LEE	SC	23W	65
JENNINGS RUDOLPH	CA	55W	13
JENNINGS STEPHEN KENNETH	NM	20E	95
JENNINGS THOMAS ALVIN	IL	05E	118
JENNINGS THOMAS EDWARD	PA	43E	7
JENNINGS TIMOTHY PAUL	TX	26E	103
JENNINGS WILLIAM A III	TX	04E	15
JENNINGS WILLIAM CLARENCE	IL	03W	45
JENRY ROBERT EUGENE	MO	17W	70
JENS TERRY ROY JR	WA	49W	54
JENSEN ALAN THEODORE	WI	28E	26
JENSEN ARLIN ROGER	MN	03E	101
JENSEN BRUCE ALLAN	WY	25E	51
JENSEN DANA BRUCE	WA	27W	100
JENSEN DENNIS RAY	IA	16E	21
JENSEN DOUGLAS GARY	CA	34E	63
JENSEN FRANK ALFRED	AZ	32W	21
JENSEN GARY EDWARD	NJ	07W	4
JENSEN GEORGE WILLIAM	WA	07E	61
JENSEN HAROLD NORGAARD	IA	27W	74
JENSEN JAMES CHRISTIAN	UT	01W	21
JENSEN JAMES MAYNARD	CO	44E	59
JENSEN JAMES PAUL	UT	26W	9
JENSEN JOHN ACE	WA	25E	52
JENSEN JOHN JEFFREY	IL	27E	65
JENSEN KENNETH VERN	CA	27W	74
JENSEN LARRY SCOTT	WI	18E	29
JENSEN LLOYD BRUCE	ID	13E	38
JENSEN MICHAEL CHARLES	CA	06W	60
JENSEN NORMAN A	OR	32W	27
JENSEN PAUL ANDREW	NC	39E	57
JENSEN REED GEORGE	UT	01E	59
JENSEN RICHARD	WI	03E	111
JENSEN RICK V	NV	32W	7
JENSEN ROBERT ARTHUR	PA	38E	1
JENSEN ROGER DALE	MN	21W	28
JENSEN RONALD CHARLES	IL	33W	49
JENSEN RONALD JOHN	IL	39W	44
JENSEN TERANCE KAY	MN	02E	26
JENSEN WILLIAM NORMAN JR	OR	10W	81
JENSON MICHAEL GREGORY	MN	10W	6
JENT BILLY GENE	OK	33E	37
JEPSON ARTHUR C JR	IL	01E	118
JERDE GERALD DEAN	IL	25W	49
JERDET DENNIS CLARENCE	MN	41W	47
JEREMIA ALEKI	HI	40E	41
JEREMIAH RANDALL CRAIG	OR	63W	16
JEREMICZ GREGORY	PA	04E	24
JERGENSON RICKEY LAYNE	TX	10W	131
JERKINS WILLIAM EDGAR	FL	25E	102
JERMANY EMMETT JR	PA	20E	117
JERMANY RILEY	AR	09E	3
JERMYN BOBBY RAY	MS	20E	90
JERNBERG ROBERT STEVENS	CA	47E	12
JERNIGAN CHARLIE MIZZELLE	NY	51E	8
JERNIGAN MARK THOMAS	CA	09W	118
JERNIGAN RICHARD LEE	TX	44W	17
JERO DAVID WAYNE	CA	15W	64
JEROME PAUL ANDREW JR	RI	47W	28
JEROME STANLEY MILTON	MI	32W	56
JERRO WILLIAM GEORGE	NY	26E	79
JERSE WILLIAM EDWARD	CA	25W	72
JERSON JAMES RAY	LA	35W	9
JERSTAD LESLIE ARTHUR	TN	33W	49
JERVIS JOHN LEROY III	NJ	38E	30
JESKE JAMES ROBERT	WA	05W	103
JESKO STEPHEN EDWARD	TX	06W	3
JESSE CLIFFORD EARL	MI	11W	132
JESSE WILLIAM CLIFTON	OK	01W	11
JESSEE SAMUEL RICHARD	WV	17W	37
JESSEN ROBERT DUANE	NE	28E	60
JESSIE MARSHALL	NY	05E	86
JESSIMAN THAD BAZILY	CA	60E	23

NAME	STATE	PANEL NO.	LINE NO.
JESSMAN JAMES HENRY	NY	45W	6
JESTER RICHARD GARVER	VA	36W	22
JESTER THOMAS STORY	PA	43W	54
JESTER WAYNE CLIFFORD	DE	49E	11
JESZECK JOSEPH COBDEN	NY	11W	64
JETER BENTON ARTHUR	VA	46W	60
JETER CURTIS LEE	SC	13E	49
JETER DANNY WAYNE	CA	32E	57
JETERS DAROLD	IL	06W	131
JETT DANNY THOMAS	KY	02W	66
JETT JIMMIE JOE	CA	34E	63
JETT MICHAEL STEVEN	CA	10W	85
JETT RONALD GENE	MN	20W	25
JETT RUSSELL LANE	LA	24W	43
JETT WILLIAM HOWARD	CA	28E	43
JEWELL DAVID PRESTON	KY	31E	99
JEWELL EUGENE MILLARD	KS	02E	75
JEWELL JAMES CLARENCE JR	OH	63W	7
JEWELL PHILIP LAWRENCE	MN	16W	106
JEWELL RONALD DEE	IL	31W	68
JEWELL STEVEN THURLOW	IA	04E	97
JEWETT GUY LEONARD	FL	63E	11
JEWETT STEPHEN DYER	NH	04E	41
JEWITT BOB	CA	18E	109
JEZIORSKI DENNIS ALFRED	MI	32W	7
JILCOTT CHARLES B JR	IN	43E	55
JILEK LOUIS HENRY	OH	18E	5
JILES JAMES JR	MO	04W	123
JIM MARTIN JR	KS	05W	49
JIMENEZ ANASTACIO	NY	21W	89
JIMENEZ ANTONIO	TX	05E	119
JIMENEZ EDUARDO	KS	43E	55
JIMENEZ ISIDRO BRICENO	CA	56E	26
JIMENEZ JOSE FRANCISCO	AZ	18W	2
JIMENEZ JOSEPH ARTHUR	TX	19E	119
JIMENEZ JUAN MACIAS	TX	58E	22
JIMENEZ LUIS RAFAEL	PR	02E	35
JIMENEZ THOMAS ORTEGA JR	TX	50W	35
JIMENEZ-ACEVEDO WILLIAM	PR	02W	37
JIMENEZ-GONZALEZ ISABELO	PR	35W	16
JIMENEZ-LORENZO EDUARDO J	PR	17W	57
JIMENEZ-O'NEILL FRANCISCO	PR	16W	100
JIMENEZ-ROIG PAULINO FRANC	PR	02W	66
JINDRA ROBERT JAMES	OH	22E	14
JINDRICH STEVEN FREDERICK	CO	07W	85
JINES ROBERT ALLAN	MO	27W	50
JINKINS GEORGE W III	VA	18W	40
JINKS RAYMOND ARTHUR	GA	25W	102
JINKS WILLIAM DONALD	TX	20E	45
JIRSA PETER JOSEPH	NY	39W	20
JIVENS JERRY	GA	03E	58
JMAEFF GEORGE VICTOR		30W	4
JOANIS KENNETH JOSEPH	MO	24W	43
JOBE BOBBY W	TX	33E	87
JOBEY ANDREW JOHN		53E	2
JOBST KURT KARL JR	CT	46W	4
JODREY WILLIAM MICHAEL	MT	28W	61
JOE WILLIE LEE	SC	23W	88
JOECKEN RICHARD KENNETH	OH	18W	2
JOHANNES LYLE MAYNARD	ND	14W	79
JOHANNES URBAN HAROLD JR	IN	41W	47
JOHANNSEN GUSTAV ALFRED	NY	60W	1
JOHANSEN DONALD CHARLES	MA	01E	32
JOHANSEN JAMES ARTHUR	WA	34E	69
JOHANSEN RONALD	IL	18W	15
JOHANSON WAYNE	NY	28E	68
JOHN NOEL ALEXANDER	PR	26E	26
JOHN ROLAND RALPH	OH	15E	128
JOHN WILLIAM THOMAS	GA	06W	127
JOHNDRO RODNEY GEORGE	ME	08W	88
JOHNER KENNETH LEO	ND	17E	6
JOHNS CAREY LEE	AL	56W	23
JOHNS DONALD CECIL	FL	53W	36
JOHNS ERNEST LEE	FL	10W	34
JOHNS FRANK HOWARD	MD	46W	42
JOHNS JEFFREY JAY	MN	18W	81
JOHNS JOSEPH DARRYL	KY	12W	89
JOHNS LAMARR LEE	FL	28W	92
JOHNS MICHAEL WAYNE	AL	37E	59
JOHNS MICKY JAMES	NY	10E	124
JOHNS PAUL FREDERICK	IN	54W	11
JOHNS RONALD ELMER	FL	44E	59

NAME	STATE	PANEL NO.	LINE NO.
JOHNS VERNON ZIGMAN	MD	37E	5
JOHNSEN JOHNNIE WAYNE	CA	27W	95
JOHNSEN LARRY VERNON	WA	63E	11
JOHNSEN WILLIAM ARTHUR	NY	57W	10
JOHNSON AARON GILBERT	IL	43W	28
JOHNSON ADOCK VEISO	DC	14W	97
JOHNSON ADRIAN JOSEPH JR	TX	22W	40
JOHNSON ALAN HOWARD	NY	14W	107
JOHNSON ALAN PAUL	MA	13W	53
JOHNSON ALBERT JR	SC	24W	67
JOHNSON ALBERT LEE	NC	07W	11
JOHNSON ALEX LEE	TN	58W	19
JOHNSON ALEXANDER JR	AR	45W	42
JOHNSON ALFRED LEWIS	OH	05E	13
JOHNSON ALLEN ISAAC	MN	02E	29
JOHNSON ALLEN LOUIS	AL	01W	107
JOHNSON ALVIN SAMUEL	VA	33E	49
JOHNSON ANDREW	LA	22E	62
JOHNSON ANDY JR	KY	09E	114
JOHNSON ANTHONY	PA	29W	79
JOHNSON ANTHONY ERIC	CA	38W	75
JOHNSON ANTHONY KENT	NJ	23E	36
JOHNSON ANTHONY LEE	VA	32W	79
JOHNSON ARMSTEAD	AL	57E	4
JOHNSON ARNOLD EDWARD	IL	30E	3
JOHNSON ARTHUR ANTHONY	PA	15E	90
JOHNSON ARTHUR HARRY	NM	19W	94
JOHNSON ARTHUR LOUIS	VA	07E	40
JOHNSON ARTIE EUGENE	FL	13W	29
JOHNSON ASA THOMAS	PA	07W	1
JOHNSON AUGUST DAVID	TX	14E	112
JOHNSON BARTON WENDELL	MN	68W	3
JOHNSON BEN JR	IA	02E	108
JOHNSON BEN ODELL	TX	08W	127
JOHNSON BENJAMIN F III	TX	40E	23
JOHNSON BERNARD DEREK	NY	32E	57
JOHNSON BERNARD LEVERN II	VA	02W	109
JOHNSON BOBBY CAL	CA	21W	8
JOHNSON BOBBY GENE	LA	05E	42
JOHNSON BOBBY RAY	VA	26W	111
JOHNSON BRADLEY JAMES	WA	55W	14
JOHNSON BRUCE ERVIN	MN	27W	74
JOHNSON BRUCE GARDNER	MI	02E	5
JOHNSON BRUCE MARK	MN	08E	72
JOHNSON BRUCE MICHAEL	MI	36W	73
JOHNSON BUFORD GERALD	FL	51E	47
JOHNSON BYRON STEVEN	MA	34E	77
JOHNSON CAL DUAIN	TX	42E	34
JOHNSON CALVERT JAMES	VA	12E	42
JOHNSON CALVIN	VA	30W	102
JOHNSON CALVIN LEE	MT	14W	81
JOHNSON CALVIN RAY	LA	07W	54
JOHNSON CARL DAVID	IN	02W	105
JOHNSON CARL IRVING	MI	55W	19
JOHNSON CARL THOMAS	TX	21E	122
JOHNSON CARLTON JERRY	FL	30W	46
JOHNSON CARROLL MARSHALL	IL	27E	35
JOHNSON CHARLES	IL	05E	86
JOHNSON CHARLES A III	IA	06W	92
JOHNSON CHARLES AARON	CA	35W	27
JOHNSON CHARLES ALLEN	WI	26E	56
JOHNSON CHARLES BUFORD JR	GA	01E	23
JOHNSON CHARLES EDWARD	IL	21E	8
JOHNSON CHARLES EDWARD	NJ	22E	105
JOHNSON CHARLES EDWARD	LA	20W	57
JOHNSON CHARLES EDWARD	VA	11W	68
JOHNSON CHARLES EUGENE	OR	38E	30
JOHNSON CHARLES EUGENE	VA	53E	34
JOHNSON CHARLES EVERETT	IA	15W	36
JOHNSON CHARLES FRANKLIN	KS	19E	26
JOHNSON CHARLES FRENCH JR	SC	36E	18
JOHNSON CHARLES HOWARD	CA	22W	41
JOHNSON CHARLES JR	SC	06E	67
JOHNSON CHARLES LEO	WI	22E	54
JOHNSON CHARLES RAY	TX	26W	40
JOHNSON CHARLES TIMOTHY	MI	42E	67
JOHNSON CHARLES WALTER	MN	20W	34
JOHNSON CHARLES WILLIAM	NY	14E	16
JOHNSON CHARLES WILLIAM	PA	57E	24
JOHNSON CHRISTOPHER PAUL	MI	22E	88
JOHNSON CLARENCE EDWARD	MI	10E	124
JOHNSON CLAUDE L	TX	04E	9

NAME	STATE	PANEL NO.	LINE NO.
JOHNSON CLAYTON HENRY	LA	56W	23
JOHNSON CLAYTON WINSLOW	IL	20E	117
JOHNSON CLEVELAND OSBORNE	SC	14W	75
JOHNSON CLIFFORD ALVIN	PA	20E	30
JOHNSON CLIFFORD CURTIS	OK	04E	110
JOHNSON CLIFFORD THOMAS	GA	04E	110
JOHNSON CLIFFORD THOMAS	OR	05W	9
JOHNSON COLLIE JR	NY	04W	100
JOHNSON CURTIS	AL	48W	53
JOHNSON DALE ALONZO	TN	11E	119
JOHNSON DALE LLOYD	MI	23W	111
JOHNSON DALE WILLIAM	WY	38W	7
JOHNSON DALLAS LEMON	VA	48W	13
JOHNSON DANIEL COPE	CA	11W	85
JOHNSON DANIEL GENE	IL	60E	12
JOHNSON DANIEL JOSEPH	MA	33E	48
JOHNSON DANNIE LEWIS	MI	33E	3
JOHNSON DANNY WAYNE	IA	11W	31
JOHNSON DANNY WEST	NC	49W	17
JOHNSON DARRELL LEE	AZ	05E	119
JOHNSON DARYL LINN	OK	19E	26
JOHNSON DAVID ALLEN	OR	36W	77
JOHNSON DAVID ALLEN	IN	14W	85
JOHNSON DAVID ALVIN	AZ	39W	21
JOHNSON DAVID ARNOLD	NY	41W	13
JOHNSON DAVID ARTHUR	AZ	45E	2
JOHNSON DAVID CHARLES	CO	05W	79
JOHNSON DAVID CURTIS	VA	43W	38
JOHNSON DAVID E	MS	22E	42
JOHNSON DAVID EARL	AR	08W	38
JOHNSON DAVID FRANCIS	ND	10W	57
JOHNSON DAVID HAROLD	AR	23E	42
JOHNSON DAVID HENRY	IA	13W	15
JOHNSON DAVID JOSEPH	CA	20E	61
JOHNSON DAVID KEITH	MI	10W	104
JOHNSON DAVID LEE	GA	33E	69
JOHNSON DAVID LEE	KY	35W	43
JOHNSON DAVID RUDOLPH	MD	38E	2
JOHNSON DEAN HERBERT	VT	30W	77
JOHNSON DEAN RAYMOND	MN	26W	63
JOHNSON DENNING CICERO	NC	01W	121
JOHNSON DENNIS CHARLES	CA	21E	23
JOHNSON DENNIS GEORGE	OH	28W	71
JOHNSON DENNIS OGDEN	IA	39W	22
JOHNSON DENNIS VAN	OK	12W	69
JOHNSON DENNY LAYTON	LA	18W	24
JOHNSON DENNY LEE	TX	19E	60
JOHNSON DOHN WILLIAM	KY	39E	34
JOHNSON DONALD LEE	NJ	08E	3
JOHNSON DONALD PETER	WI	16E	73
JOHNSON DONALD RAY	TX	06E	89
JOHNSON DONALD RAY	TX	53E	16
JOHNSON DONALD VERN	TX	63E	11
JOHNSON DONEL RAY	NY	08E	37
JOHNSON DOUGLAS ANDREW	KY	09E	107
JOHNSON DOUGLAS RAY	CA	31E	88
JOHNSON DUANE AARON	TX	48W	6
JOHNSON DWIGHT DAWSON	PA	54E	35
JOHNSON EDWARD	TN	22W	22
JOHNSON EDWARD A JR	NY	04W	5
JOHNSON EDWARD BRUCE	NJ	14E	35
JOHNSON EDWARD DEWEY	MO	08W	51
JOHNSON EDWARD HARVEY	OR	01W	100
JOHNSON EDWARD LEE	MA	25E	52
JOHNSON EMMET LEE	MO	07E	85
JOHNSON EMORY FRANKLIN	GA	15E	84
JOHNSON ENOCH	MD	15E	66
JOHNSON ERIC BERNARD	IA	25W	102
JOHNSON ERIC WAYNE	FL	31E	48
JOHNSON EUGENE CHARLES	MN	45E	23
JOHNSON EUGENE MELVIN JR	MD	48E	42
JOHNSON EUGENE RICHARD	CT	02W	71
JOHNSON EVERETT EUGENE JR	OH	20E	45
JOHNSON EVERETT WILSON JR	TN	36E	18
JOHNSON EVERETTE R	WV	38E	2
JOHNSON FLOYD DEAN	NE	03E	49
JOHNSON FLOYD RAY	CA	13W	36
JOHNSON FOREST DENVER JR	GA	17W	71
JOHNSON FRANCIS DAVID LEO	MN	51W	41
JOHNSON FRANK EDWARD	MO	25W	73
JOHNSON FRANK JR	IL	37W	39
JOHNSON FRANKIE B JR	SC	51E	21

NAME	STATE	PANEL NO.	LINE NO.
JOHNSON FRANKIE RAY	WA	44E	47
JOHNSON FRANKLIN A	CA	29W	20
JOHNSON FRED ARTHUR	FL	14E	129
JOHNSON FRED LEROY	ND	14E	57
JOHNSON FREDDIE	LA	23E	3
JOHNSON FREDDIE LEE	AL	13E	18
JOHNSON FREDDIE LEE	GA	22E	71
JOHNSON FREDERICK P JR	KS	23W	21
JOHNSON FURMAN LEE	NC	33E	18
JOHNSON GARY ALAN	WI	26W	84
JOHNSON GARY DALE	KS	39E	61
JOHNSON GARY EUGENE	NC	31W	5
JOHNSON GARY L	TX	31W	93
JOHNSON GARY LEE	CA	05W	116
JOHNSON GARY LEE	NE	03W	81
JOHNSON GARY MORGAN	TX	33W	64
JOHNSON GARY RAY	OR	31E	92
JOHNSON GARY STEVEN	IL	51W	6
JOHNSON GEORGE	IA	46W	16
JOHNSON GEORGE	SC	09W	118
JOHNSON GEORGE ALBIAN JR	LA	14W	118
JOHNSON GEORGE DENNIS	FL	16E	92
JOHNSON GEORGE FRANKLIN	WV	36W	22
JOHNSON GEORGE HARRY	PA	21E	47
JOHNSON GEORGE MILTON	GA	41W	36
JOHNSON GEORGE RUSSELL	PA	07W	106
JOHNSON GEORGE STEPHEN	CA	50W	24
JOHNSON GERALD	CA	12E	74
JOHNSON GERALD	NY	04W	5
JOHNSON GERALD DEAN	MN	16W	43
JOHNSON GERALD JAMES	MN	33W	62
JOHNSON GERALD LEE	IN	55E	18
JOHNSON GERALD LEE	MI	55W	6
JOHNSON GERALD LYNN	CA	47E	22
JOHNSON GERALD V	PA	04E	57
JOHNSON GIDEON PICHA	HI	36E	18
JOHNSON GILTON WALTER	LA	34W	62
JOHNSON GORDON MICHAEL	FL	07W	55
JOHNSON GREGORY BERT	MO	16E	122
JOHNSON GREGORY RANDOLPH	CO	63W	18
JOHNSON GUFFEY SCOTT	VA	02W	57
JOHNSON GUS WINSLOW JR	OH	45W	53
JOHNSON GUY DAVID	WA	04E	30
JOHNSON GUY FREDERICK	NJ	28W	48
JOHNSON HAROLD BENJAMIN	CA	29W	89
JOHNSON HARRELL WAYNE	NC	62W	11
JOHNSON HARRY J	AL	22E	42
JOHNSON HARRY WILBUR	OH	66W	8
JOHNSON HARVEY DOUGLAS	AL	02W	60
JOHNSON HARVEY III	VA	12E	101
JOHNSON HAVART EARL	NJ	57W	1
JOHNSON HAYWOOD JR	NC	56E	9
JOHNSON HENRY	AR	27E	69
JOHNSON HENRY ALSTON	VA	21E	1
JOHNSON HENRY DAVID	WA	24W	85
JOHNSON HENRY L	IL	45E	2
JOHNSON HENRY LOUIS JR	NY	44W	38
JOHNSON HERBERT BURTON	NY	53W	20
JOHNSON HERBERT LAWRENCE	TX	09W	68
JOHNSON HERBERT NICHOLAS	NY	40W	54
JOHNSON HORACE JR	GA	48W	56
JOHNSON HOWARD LEON	TN	35E	11
JOHNSON HOWARD WARNER JR	NJ	25E	71
JOHNSON HOWARD WESTLEY JR	PA	01W	88
JOHNSON HUGH RICHARD JR	MA	38E	68
JOHNSON JACK	NY	04E	124
JOHNSON JACK DANIEL	NC	08E	98
JOHNSON JACK LEE	IN	24W	104
JOHNSON JACOB	SC	38W	2
JOHNSON JAMES ALBERT	IL	03W	110
JOHNSON JAMES ALLEN	NJ	21W	42
JOHNSON JAMES ALVIN	FL	40E	41
JOHNSON JAMES BRUCE SR	FL	24W	33
JOHNSON JAMES CARL	MS	27W	100
JOHNSON JAMES DEAN	IA	13W	78
JOHNSON JAMES DOYLE	TX	24W	110
JOHNSON JAMES EARL	OK	07E	38
JOHNSON JAMES EARL	OK	16W	43
JOHNSON JAMES EARL III	AL	05W	134
JOHNSON JAMES EDWARD	CA	66W	8
JOHNSON JAMES EDWARD JR	MA	26W	54
JOHNSON JAMES GORDON	IA	29W	79

NAME	STATE	PANEL NO.	LINE NO.
JOHNSON JAMES GRADY	TX	47E	51
JOHNSON JAMES HAROLD JR	DE	01E	29
JOHNSON JAMES J L	CA	16E	53
JOHNSON JAMES JR	OK	20E	76
JOHNSON JAMES JR	PA	37E	59
JOHNSON JAMES JR	MS	64E	14
JOHNSON JAMES JR	FL	06W	74
JOHNSON JAMES JUNA	NC	31W	94
JOHNSON JAMES KENNETH	MN	28W	26
JOHNSON JAMES LARRY	AL	19W	16
JOHNSON JAMES LOUIS	TX	21E	80
JOHNSON JAMES REED	IN	10E	24
JOHNSON JAMES ROBERT	VA	12E	79
JOHNSON JAMES WALTER JR	NC	22E	31
JOHNSON JAY DEAN	OR	25E	85
JOHNSON JEROME	AL	23E	86
JOHNSON JERRY	GA	30W	56
JOHNSON JERRY ALLEN	MN	02E	49
JOHNSON JERRY ALLEN	IL	03W	32
JOHNSON JERRY DEAN	OK	30E	63
JOHNSON JERRY HAMPTON	VA	57W	10
JOHNSON JERRY JACK	IL	08E	81
JOHNSON JERRY REED	AL	10W	118
JOHNSON JESSE	LA	29E	73
JOHNSON JESSE LEWIS	IL	21E	68
JOHNSON JESSIE LEE	VA	19E	39
JOHNSON JIMMIE LE ROY	KS	27E	59
JOHNSON JIMMIE LEE	IN	13W	71
JOHNSON JIMMY ALVIN	GA	11E	3
JOHNSON JIMMY DONALD	KY	26W	63
JOHNSON JIMMY EARL	AL	19E	108
JOHNSON JIMMY LEROY JR	NC	35E	40
JOHNSON JOE ALAN	TX	38W	75
JOHNSON JOE D JR	MI	13E	109
JOHNSON JOE EDWARD	AL	08E	124
JOHNSON JOE LOUIS	MS	32E	94
JOHNSON JOE THOMAS	PA	10E	132
JOHNSON JOHN ALVIN	VA	04E	124
JOHNSON JOHN ANDRES	IL	56E	8
JOHNSON JOHN ERNEST	NE	12E	5
JOHNSON JOHN FOSTER	MS	44E	8
JOHNSON JOHN HARRY	CA	23E	60
JOHNSON JOHN HENRY JR	MD	16E	11
JOHNSON JOHN KIRBY	OK	24E	68
JOHNSON JOHN MARTIN	OH	63W	8
JOHNSON JOHN PAUL	NE	07W	78
JOHNSON JOHN PETER	IL	33E	49
JOHNSON JOHN ROBERT	MA	12E	14
JOHNSON JOHN VICTOR JR	VA	51E	8
JOHNSON JOHN WAYNE	FL	45W	62
JOHNSON JOHNNY L	OH	40W	3
JOHNSON JOHNNY MALCOLM	WV	20E	74
JOHNSON JOHNNY VENT	TX	16W	109
JOHNSON JOSEPH JR	PA	36W	64
JOHNSON JOSEPH WALLACE	AL	04W	110
JOHNSON KEITH GEOFFREY	VA	39W	22
JOHNSON KENNETH	NY	17E	44
JOHNSON KENNETH	NY	38W	82
JOHNSON KENNETH CARL	IL	26E	46
JOHNSON KENNETH DUANE	KS	19W	102
JOHNSON KENNETH LEE	NE	52E	20
JOHNSON KENNETH MICHEAL	CA	21E	68
JOHNSON KENNETH PAUL	CA	34W	84
JOHNSON KENNETH RICHARD	MA	39E	62
JOHNSON KENNETH ROBERT	MA	31W	6
JOHNSON KIM WILLIAMS	CA	40E	77
JOHNSON LANE CARSTON	NE	39W	49
JOHNSON LARRY	FL	07W	55
JOHNSON LARRY ALLEN	IL	43W	47
JOHNSON LARRY DEAN	OH	43W	63
JOHNSON LARRY DEAN	NM	26W	46
JOHNSON LARRY DU WAYNE	UT	08W	42
JOHNSON LARRY HOWARD	IA	21W	70
JOHNSON LARRY LEE	CA	39W	68
JOHNSON LARRY PATRICK	KY	04W	24
JOHNSON LARRY RAY	CA	58E	21
JOHNSON LARRY RICHARD	OH	15W	56
JOHNSON LARRY TRAVIS	TX	54W	11
JOHNSON LARRY WAYNE	NY	44W	26
JOHNSON LAWRENCE	IL	42E	34
JOHNSON LAWRENCE EUGENE	MI	53W	21
JOHNSON LAWRENCE EVERETT	NY	05E	105

NAME	STATE	PANEL NO.	LINE NO.
JOHNSON LEDELL JR	AR	49W	9
JOHNSON LEE GRANT	OK	09E	89
JOHNSON LELAND CRAIG	WI	17W	62
JOHNSON LEMUEL	SC	42W	56
JOHNSON LEO FRED	FL	17W	67
JOHNSON LEONARD RICHARD	CA	25E	29
JOHNSON LEROY	NY	36E	52
JOHNSON LEROY	SC	53E	2
JOHNSON LESTER JR	NJ	33W	49
JOHNSON LESTER WESLEY JR	MT	38E	30
JOHNSON LILE LAMAR JR	AL	46W	60
JOHNSON LORENZO RAYNARD	VA	22W	120
JOHNSON LOUIS	MO	23W	21
JOHNSON LOWELL	KY	33E	38
JOHNSON LYLE ALBERT	MT	27E	54
JOHNSON MARION EDWARD	GA	12E	101
JOHNSON MARLIN JAMES	IL	11W	27
JOHNSON MARSHALL D	IL	63W	17
JOHNSON MARTIN RAYMOND	IL	35W	66
JOHNSON MARVIN RAY	NC	22E	120
JOHNSON MATTHEW JR	NY	29E	16
JOHNSON MAX ARDEN	RI	29W	89
JOHNSON MELVIN	GA	25W	29
JOHNSON MELVIN EDWARD	WA	27E	73
JOHNSON MICHAEL ARTHUR	IL	11W	113
JOHNSON MICHAEL ELLIOTT	HI	61E	12
JOHNSON MICHAEL JAMES	MI	56W	35
JOHNSON MICHAEL KIRK	IL	06W	64
JOHNSON MICHAEL LEE	OK	55E	18
JOHNSON MICHAEL NEAL	MD	16E	105
JOHNSON MILO PRESTON	GA	25E	78
JOHNSON MILTON	GA	23W	37
JOHNSON MILTON JAY	LA	52W	6
JOHNSON MYRON BLAINE	ND	04W	87
JOHNSON McARTHUR	NC	02E	29
JOHNSON McARTHUR	LA	12W	16
JOHNSON NAPOLEON	IL	03W	100
JOHNSON NATHAN JR	VA	28E	34
JOHNSON NATHANIEL LERVERN	SC	32W	54
JOHNSON NICHOLAS G SR	KY	08W	108
JOHNSON NORMAN WALLACE	PA	03E	128
JOHNSON NORRIS FELTON	FL	34E	21
JOHNSON OBBIE	AL	63W	8
JOHNSON OLIVER	IL	08E	37
JOHNSON OSCAR GIBSON JR	PA	28W	61
JOHNSON PAUL ALLEN	KY	08W	82
JOHNSON PAUL CONRAD	MN	53E	16
JOHNSON PAUL EDWARD	KY	29E	95
JOHNSON PAUL EDWARD	MI	21W	75
JOHNSON PAUL WILLIAM	OK	09E	57
JOHNSON PERRY DAVID	FL	33W	86
JOHNSON PETER WYETH	CT	39E	22
JOHNSON PHIL DAVID	KS	31W	47
JOHNSON PHILIP ALLEN	MI	32W	71
JOHNSON PHILIP HARRY	CA	14E	108
JOHNSON PHILLIP DALE	TX	26E	46
JOHNSON PRINCE ARTHUR JR	MS	35E	72
JOHNSON RALPH EDWARD	IN	30E	57
JOHNSON RALPH EDWARD	NJ	34W	76
JOHNSON RALPH EDWARD	AL	18W	11
JOHNSON RALPH HENRY	SC	43E	8
JOHNSON RALPH WILLIAM	MN	17W	112
JOHNSON RANDOLPH LEROY	WI	05W	124
JOHNSON RAY ELDRIEGE	CA	09E	105
JOHNSON RAY ELLSWORTH	OH	12E	101
JOHNSON RAYMOND EUGENE	FL	09E	40
JOHNSON RAYMOND JUNIOR	OH	48E	5
JOHNSON RAYMOND PAGE	LA	20W	118
JOHNSON RICHARD	NJ	42E	67
JOHNSON RICHARD ALLEN	MN	28E	68
JOHNSON RICHARD ARNO JR	CT	20W	123
JOHNSON RICHARD ARNOLD	MI	19E	52
JOHNSON RICHARD CHARLES	MA	11E	20
JOHNSON RICHARD HERMAN	NY	24E	29
JOHNSON RICHARD MICHAEL	MT	31W	68
JOHNSON RICHARD S JR	AL	17E	52
JOHNSON RICHARD SHERWIN	VA	01E	82
JOHNSON ROBERT ALAN	TX	19E	97
JOHNSON ROBERT ALLEN	CA	06E	100
JOHNSON ROBERT BRUCE	MI	06W	92
JOHNSON ROBERT CHARLES	IL	08E	67
JOHNSON ROBERT DENNISON	TX	25E	78

NAME	STATE	PANEL NO.	LINE NO.
JOHNSON ROBERT EDWARD	NY	15E	128
JOHNSON ROBERT EDWARD	IL	16E	69
JOHNSON ROBERT ERNEST	DE	23E	101
JOHNSON ROBERT FRED JR	KS	37E	9
JOHNSON ROBERT HENRY	TX	10W	25
JOHNSON ROBERT IRVIN	NJ	12E	5
JOHNSON ROBERT LAMAR	NC	14W	65
JOHNSON ROBERT LEE	MD	24E	61
JOHNSON ROBERT LEE	NY	34W	85
JOHNSON ROBERT LEE JR	OK	29E	60
JOHNSON ROBERT LEONARD JR	NY	51E	17
JOHNSON ROBERT MILTON	GA	09E	68
JOHNSON ROBERT THOMAS	AR	27W	6
JOHNSON ROBERT WAYNE	CO	05W	124
JOHNSON ROBERT WILLIAM JR	CA	53E	2
JOHNSON RODNEY DEAN	IL	15E	45
JOHNSON RODNEY W	MA	40E	76
JOHNSON ROG	AZ	05W	60
JOHNSON ROGER LEE JR	MO	42W	36
JOHNSON RONALD EUGENE	IA	23E	36
JOHNSON RONALD GENE	OH	38E	3
JOHNSON RONALD HAROLD	OR	18E	109
JOHNSON RONALD JAMES	WA	25E	7
JOHNSON RONALD JOE	CA	13E	53
JOHNSON RONALD JOHN	IA	38E	3
JOHNSON RONALD LEE	UT	18E	10
JOHNSON RONALD PETER	WI	03E	103
JOHNSON RONNIE LLOYD	OK	12W	124
JOHNSON RONNIE WAYNE	SD	24W	7
JOHNSON ROOSEVELT JR	DC	31W	50
JOHNSON ROSS ARNOLD JR	WI	35W	20
JOHNSON ROY ALBERT	SD	08W	8
JOHNSON ROY L	TX	46E	18
JOHNSON ROY MARVIN	WA	47W	9
JOHNSON RUSSELL CARL	MN	16E	17
JOHNSON RUSSELL LEE	GA	28W	92
JOHNSON SAMUEL ARLON	OH	23E	111
JOHNSON SAMUEL JR	VA	40W	37
JOHNSON SANFORD LEE	FL	08W	15
JOHNSON SANFORD STEVEN	AL	27E	40
JOHNSON STANLEY	OH	41E	22
JOHNSON STANLEY GARWOOD	CA	03E	121
JOHNSON STEPHEN AYER	CA	18W	89
JOHNSON STEPHEN DUANE	MN	23W	53
JOHNSON STERLING HENRY	DC	62E	6
JOHNSON STERLING PRICE	NV	43E	45
JOHNSON STEVE FREDDIE	HI	06W	120
JOHNSON STEVEN CHARLES	IA	07W	117
JOHNSON STEVEN EDWARD	OK	39W	70
JOHNSON STEVEN HOWARD	CA	30W	65
JOHNSON SYLVESTER	NJ	36W	57
JOHNSON TAYLOR DOUGLAS	TX	04E	103
JOHNSON TERRY ALAN	IN	39W	10
JOHNSON TERRY JAY	MN	42W	12
JOHNSON TERRY MELVIN	IL	35E	6
JOHNSON THEODORE	PA	26E	103
JOHNSON THEODORE FRED	MA	34E	69
JOHNSON THEODORE W	NY	30E	9
JOHNSON THOMAS ALAN	OH	19E	59
JOHNSON THOMAS ALAN	WV	39E	33
JOHNSON THOMAS ALLEN	AL	22E	31
JOHNSON THOMAS EUGENE	OH	42W	69
JOHNSON THOMAS EUGENE	IN	09W	2
JOHNSON THOMAS JOSEPH	VA	02E	67
JOHNSON THOMAS WAYNE	IN	10W	65
JOHNSON THOMAS WILLENE	OH	21W	60
JOHNSON TIMOTHY ALAN	CA	22E	14
JOHNSON TIMOTHY HOLTON	WI	03E	24
JOHNSON TOMMY	GA	31W	37
JOHNSON TURNER COLEMAN	OK	02W	115
JOHNSON VERNE DE WITT III	UT	28E	82
JOHNSON VERNE LYLE JR	IL	31E	88
JOHNSON VERNON JOE	OK	29E	73
JOHNSON VICTOR JR	LA	35E	60
JOHNSON VICTOR JR	MS	30W	65
JOHNSON W C	TX	30E	3
JOHNSON WALLACE B III	FL	46E	18
JOHNSON WALTER BILLY M	GA	27W	82
JOHNSON WALTER BOYCE	IA	04E	91
JOHNSON WARREN DEAN	MN	23E	116
JOHNSON WAYNE DAVID	MI	41W	5
JOHNSON WEBSTER BEREAL	NY	37W	33
JOHNSON WELLINGTON M	LA	22E	31
JOHNSON WILBERT HERSHELL	WV	03E	82
JOHNSON WILFRED C JR	WA	10E	70
JOHNSON WILLARD VERNON	NV	36E	75
JOHNSON WILLIAM	TX	05E	105
JOHNSON WILLIAM ALLEN	NC	11E	116
JOHNSON WILLIAM C JR	GA	27E	11
JOHNSON WILLIAM CHARLES	NC	21E	13
JOHNSON WILLIAM D JR	IN	53W	1
JOHNSON WILLIAM DARRELL	NC	34E	77
JOHNSON WILLIAM EDWARD	FL	11E	53
JOHNSON WILLIAM F	CA	13E	116
JOHNSON WILLIAM FRANK	MD	05W	40
JOHNSON WILLIAM HENRY	MI	06E	119
JOHNSON WILLIAM HORACE JR	AL	21E	94
JOHNSON WILLIAM JAMES	MO	02E	129
JOHNSON WILLIAM JOHN	CA	05W	99
JOHNSON WILLIAM LEROY	TN	02E	134
JOHNSON WILLIAM LOVETT	NY	29W	71
JOHNSON WILLIAM MELVIN	OR	17W	10
JOHNSON WILLIAM MICHAEL	MT	52W	23
JOHNSON WILLIAM NEWTON	MS	35E	47
JOHNSON WILLIAM THEODORE	FL	06E	71
JOHNSON WILLIAM THOMAS	NJ	05W	37
JOHNSON WILLIAM WAYNE	UT	54E	35
JOHNSON WILLIE	SC	13W	85
JOHNSON WILLIE C JR	GA	29E	58
JOHNSON WILLIE JR	MI	04W	83
JOHNSON WILLIS WAYNE	MA	15W	86
JOHNSON WYMAN TRUVOY	IL	11W	36
JOHNSON XAVIER	MO	20E	118
JOHNSON ZANE EVERETT	NM	28W	61
JOHNSON ZEBULON MURPHY JR	NY	05W	106
JOHNSTON BILLY NEAL JR	LA	08W	116
JOHNSTON BRUCE E III	MA	61W	3
JOHNSTON CHARLES KENNETH	TX	29E	25
JOHNSTON CHARLES W JR	IA	20E	17
JOHNSTON CLEMENT B JR	PA	07E	5
JOHNSTON DAVID ALLEN	OH	30W	25
JOHNSTON DAVID NEAL	OH	02W	111
JOHNSTON DAVID WILLIAM	AZ	07E	119
JOHNSTON DENNIS NEIL	OH	50E	19
JOHNSTON DONALD RAY	GA	29W	104
JOHNSTON DONALD REGINALD	VA	12E	21
JOHNSTON EDWARD CHARLES	OR	08W	108
JOHNSTON EVARISTO PACKECO	OH	38E	3
JOHNSTON GARY CLARENCE	TX	11W	14
JOHNSTON GARY FRANCIS	PA	43W	16
JOHNSTON GEORGE ELDON	MO	04E	37
JOHNSTON JACK CRAVEN JR	NC	20W	50
JOHNSTON JERRY BERNIS	CA	03E	128
JOHNSTON KENNETH DALE	CO	02E	67
JOHNSTON PAUL KINARD	LA	53W	36
JOHNSTON RANDY LEE	PA	27E	16
JOHNSTON RICHARD BRUCE	NH	22E	45
JOHNSTON RICHARD CRAIG	UT	27W	2
JOHNSTON RICHARD J	CA	22E	42
JOHNSTON RICHARD KEITH	TN	08W	118
JOHNSTON RICHARD WILLIAM	PA	50E	16
JOHNSTON ROBERT EARL JR	CA	36E	52
JOHNSTON ROBERT PATRICK	PA	54E	26
JOHNSTON RONALD LEE	PA	16E	69
JOHNSTON STEVEN BRYCE	OK	01W	108
JOHNSTON TERRY RANDALL	IL	22W	33
JOHNSTON THOMAS PATRICK	PA	05E	119
JOHNSTON TOMMY WAYNE	CA	58E	23
JOHNSTON WILLIAM E	CA	07W	121
JOHNSTONE JAMES M	SC	12E	86
JOHNSTONE KENT LEROY	WI	14E	117
JOINER WILLIAM FRANKLIN	GA	39E	7
JOJOLA HARRY DANIEL	CA	12W	103
JOLES RICHARD WADE	LA	49E	33
JOLIET DAVID LOUIS	PA	17W	83
JOLIVETTE MATHEW L	TX	21E	13
JOLLEY DAVID MARVIN JR	IN	07E	102
JOLLEY JOHN WILLIAM JR	PA	10E	129
JOLLY EUGENE	MO	09E	16
JOLLY ROBERT GERALD	NC	39W	27
JOLY MITCHELL LEWIS	MN	39W	37
JONES AARON BURR JR	NC	14E	22
JONES ABBOTT ROBERT	CA	13W	29
JONES ALAN PETER	TX	48E	53
JONES ALBERT JUNIOR	AL	21W	7
JONES ALDON CECIL	FL	48W	56
JONES ALLEN WINFRED	GA	04E	70
JONES ANTHONY BERNARD	FL	25W	6
JONES ARLAND JASPER	OK	21W	66
JONES ARTHUR ELLIOTT	OH	17E	62
JONES BENJAMIN ALLEN	WV	45E	57
JONES BENNIE FRANK	MA	05W	35
JONES BENNIE RAY	TN	62E	6
JONES BERNARD FRANCIS	WV	28E	15
JONES BILLY CHARLES	OK	14E	63
JONES BILLY JOE	KY	03W	45
JONES BOBBY EUGENE	NC	14W	81
JONES BOBBY JOE	GA	20W	102
JONES BOBBY MARVIN	GA	01W	93
JONES BOBBY RAY	NC	33E	87
JONES BOYD EUGENE	GA	32E	70
JONES BRENT R	ID	64E	15
JONES BRUCE DALE	AL	02W	114
JONES BRUCE EDWIN	MA	41E	22
JONES BRUCE R	OH	01E	4
JONES BYRON NORRIS	MI	49E	33
JONES CARL ALVIN	PA	35W	16
JONES CARROLL HENRY	VA	12E	101
JONES CECIL BEN JR	TN	33E	9
JONES CECIL LEE	OR	47E	32
JONES CHARLES A	SC	24E	91
JONES CHARLES ALEXANDER	CA	24W	75
JONES CHARLES CLIFTON	TX	19E	6
JONES CHARLES DONALD	IL	32W	60
JONES CHARLES JR	NY	58W	4
JONES CHARLES RAY	MS	24W	95
JONES CHARLES RICHARD	PA	15W	24
JONES CHARLES SPENCER	KY	32W	32
JONES CHARLES THOMAS	OH	03W	88
JONES CHARLES WAYNE	LA	43E	46
JONES CLARENCE	MS	63W	17
JONES CLARENCE EDWARD JR	IN	09E	131
JONES CLARENCE JR	IL	23W	27
JONES CLARENCE LLOYD	FL	01E	101
JONES CLEVELAND DAVID	GA	16E	45
JONES CLIFFORD ALAN	CA	19E	26
JONES CLIFFORD JR	NJ	35E	73
JONES CLIFFORD RAYMOND JR	MA	35W	5
JONES CLIFTON RANDAL	SC	35E	6
JONES CURRAN M	MO	26W	20
JONES CURTIS	GA	20W	44
JONES DANIEL CLEVELAND	GA	11E	25
JONES DANIEL JOHN JR	PA	21W	101
JONES DANNY LEE	MI	07E	48
JONES DANNY LEE	TN	14W	98
JONES DAVID ALLEN	KY	53E	35
JONES DAVID LAWRENCE	PA	10W	51
JONES DAVID LEE	IL	29E	50
JONES DAVID RUSSELL	CA	38E	53
JONES DAVID SAMUEL	ID	15W	125
JONES DAVID WILLIAMS	IA	15W	73
JONES DAVIES LEE	MS	26E	56
JONES DAVIS ALLEN	OH	29E	11
JONES DELMER R	WV	33E	65
JONES DENNIS KEITH	IL	59E	5
JONES DONALD ALBERT	NC	50W	14
JONES DONALD BYRON	CA	62E	19
JONES DONALD ERNEST	MD	43E	56
JONES DONALD EUGENE	IL	16E	112
JONES DOUGLAS LEE	TN	11E	68
JONES DOUGLAS ROBERT	WA	13W	97
JONES DOUGLAS WAYNE	MO	09E	114
JONES DOWARD LEROY JR	NC	46E	19
JONES DUBOIS ROBERT	MD	36E	18
JONES DWIGHT DALE	KY	15E	5
JONES DWIGHT HUBERT	FL	02W	29
JONES EARL TIMOTHY	CA	42E	6
JONES EDWARD CHARLES	IN	43W	47
JONES EDWIN	FL	16E	11
JONES ELIZABETH ANN	SC	05E	47
JONES EMANUEL JR	TN	22W	33
JONES ERVIN	FL	21W	70
JONES EVERETT SORRELL	MD	57E	23
JONES FRANK WARREN	DE	54W	24
JONES FREDDIE DAVID SR	KY	16E	126
JONES FREDDIE LEE	TX	59E	24

NAME	STATE	PANEL NO.	LINE NO.
JONES FREDERICK OLEN	FL	02W	34
JONES GARLAND	NJ	65W	10
JONES GARY ALLEN	TX	23W	88
JONES GARY BLAINE	IN	30E	101
JONES GARY C	GA	38E	53
JONES GARY CLAUD	OK	51W	19
JONES GARY HOWARD	OK	02E	123
JONES GARY LEE	IL	14E	117
JONES GARY WILLIAM	TX	08W	133
JONES GEORGE ALLEN JR	TX	14E	48
JONES GEORGE EDWARD JR	CT	14E	77
JONES GEORGE EDWARD JR	GA	38E	3
JONES GEORGE EMERSON	MS	23E	29
JONES GEORGE WALLACE	CA	13E	72
JONES GRANDVILLE R JR	VA	03E	128
JONES GRAYLAND	IN	16W	112
JONES GREGORY	PA	37E	59
JONES GREGORY THOMAS	OH	42W	69
JONES GRIFFITH ALFRED	CA	10W	25
JONES GUY THOMAS	IN	43E	56
JONES HALCOTT PRIDE JR	GA	33E	87
JONES HAROLD DANA	NY	01W	34
JONES HAROLD LEE	CO	34W	8
JONES HAROLD LESLIE	OK	25W	23
JONES HARRY	CO	22E	54
JONES HARVEY WAYNE	TX	05E	105
JONES HENRY JR	LA	42W	56
JONES HORACE	SC	35W	39
JONES HORATIO LEE	MI	32E	31
JONES HOWARD LAWRENCE	MD	03W	118
JONES HOWARD LEE	OK	12E	129
JONES HOWARD LEMUEL JR	ID	41E	10
JONES HOWARD WILLIAM	WV	22E	88
JONES HOWARD WILLIAM	OH	45W	26
JONES ISAAC	MA	08E	93
JONES ISAAC	MO	18E	94
JONES IVAN WAYNE	VA	34W	85
JONES JACK MARION	AL	47E	7
JONES JACK PAHL	IL	53W	21
JONES JACKIE DALLAS	IN	09E	17
JONES JAMES	MI	17W	121
JONES JAMES ANDREW	IL	26E	26
JONES JAMES BRUCE	NY	04E	93
JONES JAMES DALE	MI	06W	99
JONES JAMES E	GA	11E	42
JONES JAMES EDWARD	IN	37W	40
JONES JAMES GRADEY	AL	12E	63
JONES JAMES HARVEY	LA	14E	81
JONES JAMES HOWARD	MD	50W	43
JONES JAMES LESTER	CA	38W	18
JONES JAMES LYNN	FL	08W	2
JONES JAMES RANDALL	FL	41W	25
JONES JAMES RANDLE JR	WA	16W	118
JONES JAMES RAWLEY	NC	21E	122
JONES JAMES ROBERT	CA	28E	49
JONES JAMES WALTER	CA	45W	7
JONES JAMES WALTER	GA	21W	38
JONES JERALD LOUIS	SC	55W	28
JONES JEROME MICHAEL	DC	31W	81
JONES JERRELL RAY	AZ	17W	77
JONES JERRY	NY	42W	47
JONES JERRY DEAN	KY	33W	94
JONES JERRY DON	CA	29E	67
JONES JERRY ROBERT	OK	01E	115
JONES JIMMIE DOUGLAS	TX	40E	42
JONES JIMMIE JACK JR	PA	13W	92
JONES JIMMIE LEE	FL	21E	18
JONES JIMMIE LEE	AL	47E	12
JONES JIMMIE WAYNE	CA	28E	50
JONES JIMMY JAY	IL	63E	12
JONES JIMMY LEWIS	TN	19W	80
JONES JOE LOUIS	AL	40E	7
JONES JOHN FREDERICK	TN	27W	88
JONES JOHN HENRY	AL	11E	45
JONES JOHN HENRY JR	AL	35E	74
JONES JOHN HOWARD	OH	35W	27
JONES JOHN HUBERT	TN	25E	1
JONES JOHN IVORY JR	TN	09E	131
JONES JOHN LEE	KY	36E	75
JONES JOHN LEWIS	NJ	28E	45
JONES JOHN MONROE JR	NY	14W	75
JONES JOHN ORA JR	MO	11E	98

NAME	STATE	PANEL NO.	LINE NO.
JONES JOHN ROBERT	TX	03W	66
JONES JOHN WALLACE	CA	31E	48
JONES JOHNNY CARL	TX	16W	128
JONES JOHNNY CARROLL	TX	07W	84
JONES JOHNNY EUGENE	MO	03W	135
JONES JOHNNY MACK	AL	01W	6
JONES JON CARL	MI	44W	49
JONES JOSEPH BARRY	GA	37E	37
JONES JOSEPH JOHN	NC	53W	2
JONES JOSEPH MELVIN	GA	50E	16
JONES JOSEPH RICHARD	FL	53W	21
JONES JOSEPH WESTER III	TN	41W	30
JONES JOSHUA THOMAS	NC	12E	6
JONES JULIUS FRAZIER	FL	10E	95
JONES KENNETH HAROLD	OR	04W	28
JONES KENNETH LEE	UT	02W	19
JONES KENNETH LOREN	MO	35W	89
JONES KENNETH RAY	TX	50W	51
JONES KENNETH ROLAND	MD	11W	41
JONES LARRY	IN	66W	9
JONES LARRY ALLAN	CA	51E	47
JONES LARRY ALLEN	MI	45W	53
JONES LARRY HUGH	KY	37E	9
JONES LARRY NEAL	AL	11W	74
JONES LARRY PAUL	GA	25W	102
JONES LARRY WAYNE	IL	68W	4
JONES LARRY WILLIAM	NC	45E	45
JONES LAVOYN AUGUSTUS	VA	17W	62
JONES LAWRENCE EDWARD	CO	42E	52
JONES LEE FRANCIS	MI	60E	12
JONES LEMEN EARL	TX	15E	45
JONES LENNIS GODDARD JR	TN	16W	39
JONES LEONARD ALEXANDER	PA	03E	128
JONES LEROY ELTON	GA	04E	33
JONES LESTER	NY	09E	47
JONES LEWIS CARLTON JR	ME	33W	71
JONES LLOYD EDWARD	MD	27W	68
JONES LLOYD WESLEY	IA	27W	109
JONES LOREN CECIL	NC	29W	80
JONES LOUIS FARR	TX	31E	4
JONES LOUIS HENDERSON	AL	29W	100
JONES LOWEN LEON	IL	38E	3
JONES LOYD ELLIS	MN	44W	17
JONES LUTHER M	GA	22E	106
JONES LYNN	GA	02W	20
JONES MARCUS CLAUDE	FL	25E	57
JONES MARLIN MARK JR	OR	32W	55
JONES MARSHALL KEENE	KY	08W	125
JONES MARVIN CARL	NY	39W	17
JONES MARVIN HAROLD JR	MI	36E	18
JONES MARYUS NAPOLEON	VA	27W	64
JONES MELVIN LEWIS	LA	39E	34
JONES MERLE ELDON	KS	06E	53
JONES MICHAEL ALLEN	TN	27E	24
JONES MICHAEL BRUCE	AZ	59E	5
JONES MICHAEL CLAY	WA	23E	42
JONES MICHAEL EDWARD	MD	25E	39
JONES MICHAEL GILBERT	MO	09W	33
JONES MICHAEL LEON	PA	32E	75
JONES MICHAEL THOMAS	NM	14E	100
JONES MILFORD	FL	29E	90
JONES MILTON JOSEPH	IL	08W	3
JONES MITCHELL JR	GA	08W	47
JONES MONTE RICHARD	OH	22W	121
JONES MORRIS BLAINE	NC	33E	29
JONES MOSES EDWARD	MS	08W	118
JONES NEIL WADE	AL	02W	93
JONES NORMAN JR	OH	56W	23
JONES OMAR DAVID	IL	59E	6
JONES ORVILLE NELSON	NY	16E	79
JONES ORVIN CLARENCE JR	VA	01W	1
JONES OTIS CECIL JR	AR	14E	86
JONES OTIS ROBERT	KY	09W	96
JONES PAUL	FL	26W	107
JONES PAUL DAVIS	MI	22W	121
JONES PAUL ELDEN	VA	13W	1
JONES PERRY KINARD	PA	23E	38
JONES PHILIP ALFONSO	DC	06E	101
JONES PHILIP BOYD	IA	33W	7
JONES RALPH WAYNE	AL	04W	116
JONES RANDOLPH ROBERT	CA	34E	78
JONES RAY MORGAN KEITH	TN	29E	90

NAME	STATE	PANEL NO.	LINE NO.
JONES RAYMOND PARKER	VA	35W	39
JONES REESE ALVIN	PA	27E	90
JONES REGINALD WILLIAM	NC	22W	105
JONES REUBEN JR	LA	40E	7
JONES RICHARD ALFRED	MI	55W	29
JONES RICHARD JOSEPH JR	PA	64W	11
JONES RICHARD JUNIOR	VA	27E	103
JONES RICHARD LEE	KS	42W	29
JONES RICHARD STEPHEN	MI	28W	61
JONES RICHARD WARREN	OK	03W	90
JONES RICHARD WILLIAM	IL	28E	26
JONES ROBERT ARTHUR	OH	19W	87
JONES ROBERT EDWARD	MN	13E	33
JONES ROBERT EMMETT	CA	07E	53
JONES ROBERT ERNEST	MI	38W	68
JONES ROBERT EUGENE	IL	20W	97
JONES ROBERT HENRY OSBORN	VA	15E	106
JONES ROBERT LEE	GA	31W	6
JONES ROBERT LEE JR	OK	33E	58
JONES ROBERT LEWIS	MO	61W	14
JONES ROBERT LEWIS	NC	40W	25
JONES ROBERT MORRIS	IN	15E	74
JONES ROBERT NELSON	PA	57E	25
JONES ROBERT TAYLOR JR	IA	39W	67
JONES ROGER KENNETH	VA	61E	12
JONES ROGER LARRY	NY	16W	29
JONES ROMAN LEE	IN	02W	111
JONES RONALD	UT	54E	9
JONES RONALD	DC	28W	62
JONES RONALD RUSSELL	NY	23E	76
JONES RONALD TRENT	OH	08W	66
JONES RONALD WAYNE	VA	14W	27
JONES RONALD WEAVER	OH	06E	53
JONES RONNIE CLYDE	KY	08E	86
JONES RONNIE JOE	GA	54E	10
JONES RONNIE LEE	IL	08E	67
JONES RONNIE LEE	NY	60W	10
JONES ROOSEVELT	PA	34E	78
JONES ROY MITCHELL	AR	07E	113
JONES ROY MORGAN JR	NJ	18E	45
JONES RUDOLPH	VA	29W	53
JONES RUSSELL JR	GA	15W	9
JONES SAM	TX	58W	26
JONES SAM RAYMOND	TN	22E	55
JONES SAMMY JR	OK	12E	79
JONES SANDERFIERD ALLEN	TX	30W	46
JONES SCOTT WINFIELD	CA	04W	136
JONES SEABORN DAN	TX	35E	6
JONES SHERMAN LAWRENCE	FL	29E	31
JONES STEPHEN CRAWFORD	NJ	43E	56
JONES STEPHEN PERRY	IN	28E	83
JONES STERLING M JR	GA	31E	12
JONES STOKELY JAMES	NC	18W	102
JONES TERRY AGUSTA	MI	33E	3
JONES TERRY EDWARD	CA	27W	74
JONES THEODORE R JR	NE	03E	33
JONES THOMAS DEWITT	AL	19W	50
JONES THOMAS EDWARD JR	MD	29W	100
JONES THOMAS GEORGE	NY	20E	118
JONES THOMAS HOWARD	GA	15W	10
JONES THOMAS HUBERT	NJ	58W	26
JONES THOMAS JAKE	OR	23E	4
JONES THOMAS PAUL	NY	37E	59
JONES THOMAS STEVEN	GA	28E	60
JONES THOMAS WELDON	MD	25E	63
JONES TOMMY	CA	13E	5
JONES TOMMY ROY	NC	08E	109
JONES TRACY LEE	MI	15E	21
JONES VERNON DOUGLAS	KY	44W	49
JONES VICTOR LAWRENCE	NC	17W	67
JONES VICTOR WAYNE	TX	17W	47
JONES WALTER CHAPMAN III	NY	48E	5
JONES WALTER HOLT II	FL	13E	44
JONES WAYMON LOUIS JR	PA	29W	38
JONES WAYNE ELMER	AK	25E	7
JONES WAYNE IRA	MO	04E	69
JONES WILBERT EARL	NC	06W	5
JONES WILBERT EUGENE	NC	20W	77
JONES WILBERT JASPER JR	VA	08W	97
JONES WILLIAM	PA	04E	129
JONES WILLIAM ARCHIE JR	CO	14E	63
JONES WILLIAM ARTHUR	TX	44E	27

NAME	STATE	PANEL NO.	LINE NO.
JONES WILLIAM BARTON	NY	31W	50
JONES WILLIAM COY	NM	32E	31
JONES WILLIAM EDWARD	DE	08W	17
JONES WILLIAM EUGENE	TX	33E	49
JONES WILLIAM JR	IL	05E	97
JONES WILLIAM JR	GA	08E	61
JONES WILLIAM JUNIOR	SC	33W	2
JONES WILLIAM OLIVER	VA	25E	52
JONES WILLIAM STANLEY	FL	49W	5
JONES WILLIAM THOMAS	IL	64E	16
JONES WILLIE DONALD	FL	14E	6
JONES WILLIE GERALD	FL	37W	40
JONES WILLIE LEE JR	PA	26E	1
JONES WILLIE MORRIS	MS	17W	88
JONES WILLIS GEORGE	MI	59E	25
JONOZZO THOMAS CHARLES	OH	10E	113
JONSSON RONALD BRYNIEL	IL	42E	67
JOOSTEN CURTIS CHARLES	IA	17E	44
JOOSTEN ROBERT WALTER	WI	23E	80
JORDAN ALLAN H	NJ	10E	83
JORDAN ALLAN HAROLD	MA	48E	28
JORDAN ARTHUR	NJ	34E	21
JORDAN CHESTER GALE	TX	19E	27
JORDAN DANIEL WALTER	IN	23E	42
JORDAN DAVID MACKRAL	NC	21E	34
JORDAN DUDLEY NORMAN	MA	28E	40
JORDAN FRANCIS EUGENE	KS	60E	12
JORDAN GARY STEPHEN	KY	15E	84
JORDAN GRADY MERRIL	MI	32E	56
JORDAN HENRY CRAWLEY	NY	02E	57
JORDAN JACK JOSEPH JR	MS	42E	34
JORDAN JAMES ELDON JR	OH	53W	44
JORDAN JAMES SAMUEL	MO	25W	73
JORDAN JEFFREY ROBERT	WI	45E	34
JORDAN JERRY KENNETH	GA	24E	87
JORDAN JIMMY DALE	CA	07E	72
JORDAN JOE RITCHARD	OK	17E	6
JORDAN JOHN EDWARD	PA	13W	41
JORDAN JOSEPH LAMAR	GA	47E	51
JORDAN KENNETH BRADLEY	NH	17E	57
JORDAN KENT DOUGLAS	NJ	03E	15
JORDAN LARRY CHRISTOPHER	OH	03W	8
JORDAN LARRY LEON	SC	12W	39
JORDAN LARRY MICHAEL	CA	06E	106
JORDAN LAWRENCE WICKS	MO	01E	93
JORDAN LAWRENCE WILLIAM	AZ	02E	45
JORDAN LITAEL JR	CA	56W	23
JORDAN MACK ARTHUR	NC	13E	61
JORDAN PATRICK MICHAEL	NY	31E	92
JORDAN PAUL ROBERT	CA	34W	70
JORDAN RAYMOND ROBERT	TN	45E	63
JORDAN REGINALD ARCHIE	PA	26E	11
JORDAN RICHARD KENNETH	NC	02E	129
JORDAN ROBERT CLAYTON	TX	30W	37
JORDAN ROBERT LEROY JR	IL	45W	42
JORDAN ROBERT PATRICK	NY	03E	6
JORDAN ROGER FRANCIS	VT	64E	5
JORDAN ROY DOUGLAS	IN	05W	11
JORDAN STEPHEN ALAN	CA	46W	16
JORDAN STEVE EUGENE	CA	34W	76
JORDAN TEDDY ROOSEVELT	TX	11E	98
JORDAN TERENCE PATRICK	NY	33E	70
JORDAN THOMAS LEE	TX	40E	53
JORDAN WAYNE LAMONT	VA	16E	101
JORDAN WILLIAM ARLIN	AZ	42E	52
JORDAN WILLIAM E III	ME	04E	65
JORDAN-MOLERO ADRIEN MANU	PR	08E	104
JORDET RONALD GEORGE	MT	11E	22
JORDON ARTHUR L	SC	53E	2
JORDON ORVAL CLYDE III	IL	25W	73
JORENS EVERETT RALPH JR	MO	16W	80
JORGENSEN DAVID WAYNE	OH	56W	35
JORGENSEN EMORY LEE	UT	29E	31
JORGENSEN ROLF WALLACE	WA	09E	47
JORGENSEN SAMUEL JOSEPH	SD	13W	9
JORGENSON JEROME DVID	MN	24W	17
JORY EDWARD LEWIS JR	NM	25E	43
JOSE PAULL DAVID	MI	40W	77
JOSELANE HOWARD LEO	IL	38E	31
JOSEPH AUSTIN RAYMOND	NY	20E	64
JOSEPH JAMES	SC	33E	70
JOSEPH JEFFREY JOEL	CA	11W	24
JOSEPH MICHAEL ARNOLD	CA	63W	17
JOSEPH RONALD RAY	IN	20E	95
JOSEPH THOMAS EDWARD	IL	27E	39
JOSEPHS NOEL FITZROY	NY	23W	88
JOSEPHSON HARTLEY MICHAEL	CA	11E	57
JOSH WHYLEY E	WV	31E	11
JOSHUA JAMES EDWARD JR	AL	65E	11
JOSLEN PHILLIP DALE	MO	12E	1
JOSLIN TERRY LEROY	CA	15W	94
JOSLYN JAMES EUGENE	GA	11E	77
JOSSENDAL RICHARD L	IL	04E	39
JOUJON-ROCHE EDWARD	CA	03E	45
JOURDAN-FONT JORGE LUIS	PR	06W	86
JOURDANAIS THOMAS F JR	NY	35W	16
JOURDENAIS GEORGE HENRY	RI	17E	86
JOURNELL ROBERT MASON III	VA	08W	42
JOUVERT VICTOR MODESTO	NY	32W	79
JOWERS BEN JR	IL	37E	59
JOWERS RAY RAMSEY	TN	29W	69
JOY CHESTER JOSEPH	NY	20E	8
JOY DENNIS EARL	CA	13W	34
JOY EDGAR DALE	OH	60W	18
JOY RAYMOND STANLEY JR	TX	04E	18
JOY RICHARD DENNIS	NY	22W	98
JOY ROBERT HOLBROOK	WA	22W	112
JOY WILLIAM ARTHUR	NH	49W	48
JOY WILLIAM CHARLES	WV	18E	86
JOY WILLIAM CLYDE	NH	18W	103
JOYCE DANIEL THOMAS	NY	19E	119
JOYCE DERRELL WALTER	FL	40W	3
JOYCE GEORGE EDWARD	NH	03E	128
JOYCE JOHN GERARD	MA	31W	41
JOYCE JOHN H	MA	13E	68
JOYCE JOHN MORRIS	ND	27W	100
JOYCE JOHN MULLEN	MD	29E	50
JOYCE ROGER LEE	NC	22W	105
JOYCE THOMAS MICHAEL	IL	11E	112
JOYCE VAN JOHN	PA	04W	41
JOYCE WALTER ALOYSIUS	NY	32W	79
JOYCE WALTER EDWARD JR	MA	48E	28
JOYCE WILLIAM EDWARD JR	MA	12E	79
JOYCE WILLIAM FRANCIS	MA	06E	56
JOYNER CARL HENRY	FL	06E	44
JOYNER DONALD ARRINGTON	NC	01W	106
JOYNER KENNETH RUSSELL	MA	45E	57
JOYNER PAUL LOUIS	NC	56W	4
JOYNER STEPHEN DOUGLASS	CA	57W	27
JOYNES FRANK DENNIS JR	NJ	30W	56
JOYS JOHN WILLIAM	CA	10E	49
JOZEFOWSKI THOMAS JOSEPH	NY	01W	49
JOZWIAK ROGER EDWARD	MI	07E	86
JUAREZ GEORGE ALBERT	CA	45E	40
JUAREZ JESSE GOMEZ	CA	11W	114
JUAREZ JOE MANUEL	TX	37W	84
JUAREZ JOHN	CA	31E	35
JUAREZ MATEO	IL	06W	77
JUAREZ OSCAR REINA	TX	54W	9
JUCKETT ELMER L III	FL	13E	109
JUDD DAVID TERRENCE	MI	47W	37
JUDD DONALD R	NY	22E	42
JUDD GARY DEAN	NV	31W	1
JUDD MICHAEL BARRY	OH	22E	88
JUDGE CHARLES MARK JR	NJ	23E	60
JUDGE DARWIN LEE	IA	01W	124
JUDGE MARK WARREN	CA	26E	103
JUDGE WILLIAM CHARLES JR	NY	46E	47
JUDKINS LARRY DUANE	WI	15E	14
JUDKINS TERRY WILLIAM	OH	23E	19
JUDSON HAMPDEN CUTTS JR	MN	16E	21
JUDY DAVID LEROY	OR	14W	94
JUDY DAVID LYNN	IL	42W	49
JUDY HERMAN LEROY JR	VA	23W	15
JUEL DARRYL RICHARD	MT	22E	106
JUERGENS WILLIAM OWEN	IA	10E	76
JUERS ROY JAMES	NY	26E	60
JUETT WILLIAM LEE	KY	29E	50
JULES GEORGE HENRY	NY	25W	50
JULIA JON ALBERT	MD	40E	64
JULIAN JAMES JULIUS JR	MO	25W	102
JULIAN MICHAEL HENRY	OH	16E	123
JULIAN PERCY	OH	25E	89
JULIUS WILLIAM F III	PA	62E	7
JUMPER STEPHEN FRANKLIN	TX	29E	31
JUNE JEREMIAH	AL	24W	54
JUNE WILLIAM ALBERT	MO	22E	119
JUNEAU MICHAEL JOSEPH	LA	59E	25
JUNGA HAROLD JOSEPH	MI	16W	88
JUNGE JAMES CLARENCE	CA	08W	107
JUNGER WALTER JOSEPH JR	OK	27W	88
JUNK RICHARD HENRY	WI	64E	5
JUNKINS JOHNNY JUERGEN	GA	43E	56
JUNTILLA HARRY WILLIAM	MN	12E	1
JURADO AMBROSIOS SANTIAGO	PR	16E	45
JURADO ELIAS CASTRO JR	TX	49W	31
JURADO FRED V	TX	54W	30
JURADO RAMON	TX	40E	53
JURANIC FRANCIS JOSEPH JR	NJ	39W	54
JURCAK RICHARD ALAN	RI	16E	45
JURECKO DANIEL EDWARD	TX	57E	5
JUREK DALMER DOLAN	TX	05E	66
JUREK EDWARD JOSEPH II	CT	46E	19
JURGELLA JOSEPH PETER	WI	06W	22
JURGENS KENNETH WILLIAM	IA	16E	105
JURGENSEN DANIEL LEE	IA	16W	74
JURI ELGIN JOHN	CA	21W	33
JURICH WILLIAM AGNER	PA	09W	91
JURSZA WILLIAM JR	NJ	52E	30
JUST GERHARDT	ND	02E	67
JUSTICE DON McCLELLAND	KY	07W	44
JUSTICE DONALD LEE	OH	24W	77
JUSTICE EDWARD JAMES	OH	14W	13
JUSTICE EVERETT EUGENE JR	MD	38E	4
JUSTICE RALPH ROGER	IL	13E	119
JUSTICE RICHARD LEE	GA	50W	2
JUSTICE ROGER DALE	IN	39W	23
JUSTICE THOMAS LARRY	KY	20W	87
JUSTICE WALTER EUGENE SR	KS	26W	9
JUSTICE WILLIAM ALLEN	OH	09W	116
JUSTICE WILLIAM PAUL	NY	28W	71
JUSTIN WILLIAM BARRY	MA	24E	29
JUSTINIANO VICTOR A JR	NY	42E	52
JUSTIS RONALD HENRY	IN	07E	53
JUSTUS MICHAEL EUGENE	CA	12W	43
JUSTUS ROGER GALE	TX	31E	13
KAAIHUE KENNETH R	HI	08E	86
KAAKIMAKA ALGERNON P JR	HI	61W	1
KAASE FLOYD WAYNE	TX	21E	5
KAATZ BARNEY	MN	01E	8
KAAWA JOHN RICHARD	HI	33W	15
KABARA DENNIS FLOYD	IL	14W	23
KACHLINE JAMES LEE	PA	20E	96
KACHMAN EDWARD MICHAEL	PA	27W	38
KACSOCK WALTER JOSEPH JR	MA	08W	38
KADETZ GARY STEVEN	NY	07E	86
KADLEWICZ ZDZISLAW BRUNO	MA	21W	23
KADOUS DARYL LEE	IA	07E	9
KADOW PATRICK DENNIS	WA	09W	69
KAEBERLE DANA JAMES	KS	35W	55
KAELIN CHARLES WRAY	PA	14E	57
KAGEBEIN DALE LEONARD	IL	34W	50
KAHANA SAMUEL KAULUHAIMAI	HI	40W	77
KAHKONEN EDWIN MATTI JR	ME	28E	96
KAHLA VICTOR DAVISON JR	TX	29W	89
KAHLER CHARLES EDWARD	PA	29E	4
KAHLER HAROLD	NE	22W	47
KAHLER LE LUND MORRIS	SD	27W	39
KAHLSTORF KEITH ALAN	IA	24W	104
KAHRE DONALD LEE	IN	07W	65
KAIL ROBERT MORTON	IN	28E	50
KAIRAITIS FRANCIS	PA	38E	69
KAISER DENNIS DALE	PA	07E	42
KAISER FRANK MELVIN	MN	14W	108
KAISER HOWARD WALKER	NH	10E	91
KAISER LARRY KURT	TX	11W	74
KAISER RONALD HARRY	IA	09E	93
KAJIWARA JAMES TOSHI	CA	16E	60
KAKUK ALLEN JOHN	WI	09E	120
KALANI CHARLES MANUWAHL	HI	02W	94
KALB LOUIS WILSON	MD	39E	35
KALB MICHAEL DALE	CA	45E	2
KALE MICHAEL ROBERT	IL	56E	10
KALEIKINI THEODORE K JR	PA	34E	69
KALEN JOHN JOSEPH	MA	18W	95
KALER RICHARD DAVID	NY	09E	62

NAME	STATE	PANEL NO.	LINE NO.
KALETTA BARRY PAUL	OH	15W	78
KALFAS ALLAN GEORGE	CA	25E	85
KALHAGEN PHILIP ALFRED	WI	09W	69
KALIL JAMES NOBLE	IN	02E	58
KALILI MELVYN HAMANA	HI	12W	81
KALINA EDWARD CHARLES	AZ	18W	64
KALIS GERALD LEONARD	MN	09W	20
KALIVAS JOHN ANGELO	NJ	23W	101
KALKA CHARLES CLINTON	TX	54W	30
KALLAHER CHARLES THOMAS	TN	03W	20
KALSU JAMES ROBERT	OK	08W	38
KALTER JAMES MICHAEL	IL	30W	25
KALUA SOLOMON JR	HI	34E	88
KAMA FRED KAIMI NAAUAO	HI	26E	12
KAMALOLO JOEL KAHALEALOHA	HI	02W	1
KAMENICKY GEORGE WAYNE	TX	02W	31
KAMINSKI EDWARD J	NJ	42E	6
KAMINSKI JOSEPH M JR	DE	68E	3
KAMINSKI KENNETH	MI	46E	36
KAMINSKI RAYMOND DONALD	NE	05W	2
KAMINSKI RICHARD DENNIS	MI	17E	20
KAMINSKY JOHN PERRY	FL	10E	125
KAMP THOMAS KEITH	MA	16W	88
KAMPH MICHAEL CLYDE	OR	25E	52
KAMRATH JACK HARLAN	CA	59E	6
KANAAR LOUIS KENNETH	MI	04E	60
KANACZET JOHN FRANCIS JR	RI	37W	47
KANAMAN KENNETH HARVEY	WI	13W	78
KANDEL JAMES EDWARD	OH	50W	36
KANDLER TERRENCE ARTHUR	CA	57E	25
KANE BRUCE EDWARD	NY	20W	119
KANE CHARLES FRANKLIN JR	PA	02E	120
KANE CHARLES WILLIAM	MD	21E	58
KANE COLEMAN JOHN JR	NY	25E	35
KANE DENNIS JAMES	NY	32W	49
KANE FRANCIS XAVIER	PA	51E	22
KANE JOSEPH LEON	OH	06E	83
KANE LARRY WAYNE	OH	38E	4
KANE MICHAEL	CA	34E	70
KANE MOMI NUHI	HI	30E	16
KANE RICHARD RAYMOND	NJ	26E	61
KANE TERRANCE FREDERICK	MA	19W	2
KANE THOMAS JOSEPH	MA	10E	129
KANE THOMAS MICHAEL	IL	24E	29
KANE WILLIAM GERARD JR	NY	54W	24
KANEKO JULIO	CA	16E	101
KANESHIRO EDWARD NOBORU	HI	16E	28
KANESKI ROBERT ADAM	CA	45E	64
KANGAS ARTHUR NELSON	MI	11W	124
KANGAS CLIFFORD F D	UT	25E	30
KANGRO LAURI	NY	30W	37
KANNEL DONALD LEE	CA	18E	35
KANONCZYK RICHARD WALTER	PA	53E	35
KANOSH KENNARD KING	UT	07W	63
KANOSH WILBERT DWAYNE	UT	33W	20
KANSIK FREDERICK DANIEL	MI	34W	8
KANTER EDWARD LEE	OH	19W	2
KAOPUIKI ALEXANDER A JR	HI	20W	100
KAPALU GEORGE KUAMOO	HI	47W	19
KAPAS PETER JR	RI	04W	131
KAPELUCK JOHN MICHAEL	NJ	29E	51
KAPETANOPOULOS KOSMAS PET	MA	44E	37
KAPLAFKA MICHAEL JOHN	PA	57W	1
KAPLAN ALBERT	PA	40E	68
KAPLAN DANIEL JAMES	IA	38E	4
KAPLON PHILLIP FELIX JR	TX	39W	32
KAPOUN TIMOTHY JOHN	MN	40E	23
KAPP JOHN FRANCIS	PA	34W	8
KAPP PAUL LASLO	OH	53W	10
KAPP RICHARD WORRELL JR	SC	42E	18
KAPPMEYER PAUL JOSEPH	IN	10E	21
KAPPMEYER THEODORE C	CA	08W	92
KAPSHA RICHARD RUDOLPH	PA	02W	63
KAPUSTA EDWARD JOHN	PA	05W	42
KARAMAN FRED	NY	27W	100
KARAS PAUL RICHARD	VA	14E	112
KARAS WALTER	IL	20W	20
KARAS WILLIAM JAMES	IN	20W	80
KARASCH WOLFGANG WERNER	CA	10E	79
KARAU RONALD DEAN	MN	04W	61
KARDASH KENNETH MICHAEL	NY	46W	30
KARDELL DAVID ALLEN	CA	01E	112

NAME	STATE	PANEL NO.	LINE NO.
KARDOS JAMES MARION	VA	18W	33
KARDOS JOSEPH FRANCIS	PA	37E	9
KARES JOHN MICHAEL	IL	45E	40
KARGER BARRY EDWIN	CA	60E	13
KARGER GREGORY SCOTT	MN	05W	59
KARGER RICHARD TILDON	CA	09E	120
KARI JARMO ANTERO	MI	05E	20
KARICKHOFF WILLIS ARNOLD	WV	11E	122
KARINS JOSEPH JOHN JR	NY	16E	60
KARLIN DONALD DEAN	KS	04E	24
KARLSTROM SIGFRID R	WA	20E	118
KARN WAYNE DOUGLAS	NY	22E	25
KARNEHM STEVEN DALE	OH	02W	28
KARNES LESLIE LEROY	MO	05W	111
KAROPCZYC STEPHEN EDWARD	NY	16E	69
KARPENSKE DALE RODNEY	WI	43E	67
KARPIAK MICHAEL JR	PA	31E	65
KARPY JOSEPH RUBEN	PA	26W	112
KARR CHARLES LEE	MI	16W	29
KARR DAVID RAY	MO	45W	63
KARR GEORGE GEOFFREY	OR	13W	78
KARR JOHN PRESTON	LA	24W	104
KARR ROBERT EUGENE	IA	15E	91
KARRAS JAMES MICHAEL	PA	48W	57
KARST CARL FREDERICK	KS	39W	74
KARSZNIA LESZEK STANLEY	IL	08W	111
KASA KENNETH EUGENE	IN	18E	49
KASAI THOMAS TARO	NY	10E	21
KASCH FREDERICK MORRISON	CA	22E	106
KASER RANDALL FRANK	IN	19W	3
KASHIEMER CARL FREDERICK	MN	36W	51
KASIAH CLAUDE CHARLES	AR	22W	78
KASKE RICHARD ALAN	CT	32E	36
KASKI DONALD ALBERT	CA	36W	40
KASNOW EDWARD	MI	41E	23
KASPAUL ALFRED AUGUST	PA	11E	66
KASPER GREGORY JOSEPH	IL	27E	11
KASPER ROBERT EDWARD	CT	16E	35
KASPRZYK GERALD BENEDICT	TX	06E	130
KASSATKIN PAUL	NY	51E	47
KASTEN DANIEL MARK	WI	19E	52
KASTENDIECK WILLIAM PETER	NY	12W	69
KASTER JERRY LEE	IA	23E	19
KASTER LEONARD LEE	MA	01E	61
KASTER ROBERT LEE	MO	17E	10
KASTER STEPHEN JOSEPH	MN	06W	35
KASTLER CURTIS CHARLES	PA	02W	3
KASTNER RICHARD THOMAS	WY	16W	80
KASTRINOS JEROLD LLOYD	CO	31E	48
KASZUBOWSKI DANIEL F	IL	11W	22
KATAVOLOS ROBERT	NY	20E	76
KATONA JOHN JAMES JR	CT	21E	35
KATRENICS JAMES NOEL	IN	17E	124
KATTERHENRY LEROY W JR	OH	44E	60
KATTERHENRY TERRY FISHER	OH	04E	30
KATZ ALLAN HARVEY	CA	15E	96
KATZ ELKER GURTH	NY	15W	90
KATZ RONALD CHRISTOPHER	CO	29W	30
KATZENBERGER RAYMOND L	IN	18E	29
KAUFFER WILLIAM THOMAS	WV	17E	20
KAUFFMAN EARNEST LEE	MI	32W	65
KAUFFMAN KEITH WALTER	WA	06E	85
KAUFFMAN MICHAEL M II	IN	17E	116
KAUFFMAN RICHARD JOHN	PA	12W	113
KAUFMAN DAVID MITCHELL	LA	22W	53
KAUFMAN DONACIANO FRANCIS	NM	15E	109
KAUFMAN HAROLD JAMES	NY	30E	44
KAUFMAN JAY ALLEN	NY	23W	111
KAUFMAN THOMAS JAY	KY	11W	80
KAUFMAN WAYNE ELDON	IN	13W	10
KAUGARS JOHN	IL	10W	91
KAUHAIHAO JOHN KUULEI	HI	18W	40
KAUHANE ELIAS MAULILI	HI	10E	40
KAULBACK PETER JON	NY	62W	11
KAUPP CURTIS JAMES	SD	38W	27
KAUS HARRY LEONARD JR	NY	02E	58
KAUS WLADISLAW	NJ	12W	132
KAUSE WILLIAM RAYMOND	PA	43W	49
KAVICH ROBERT DALE	KY	06W	77
KAVULAK JOHN HENRY	NE	26E	103
KAWACHIKA ARTHUR KAORU	CA	04W	3
KAWAMURA GARY NOBORU	HI	19E	28

NAME	STATE	PANEL NO.	LINE NO.
KAWAMURA ROBERT KIYOSHI	CA	39E	49
KAWAMURA TERRY TERUO	HI	29W	90
KAY BRYAN THOMAS	MI	49W	24
KAY WALTER THOMAS JR	LA	28E	97
KAYE MARK SAMUEL	CA	38E	53
KAYGA WILLIAM DUANE	MI	19W	107
KAYS DAVID COLEMAN	IN	12W	117
KAYS JAMES G	GA	01W	127
KAYS JERRY ALLAN	KY	14W	19
KAYSER RUSSELL WILLIAM	SD	14W	5
KAZANOWSKI JOHN FRANCIS	MA	17W	47
KAZEKEVICIOUS JOSEPH HENR	NY	55E	17
KAZIKOWSKI JEFFREY G	CA	15E	45
KAZMIERCZAK ROBERT JOSEPH	NY	22W	47
KEA ANDREW MILLARD	OH	01E	119
KEA EDWARD KIKAU	HI	23E	43
KEAG ROBERT THOMAS	IL	37W	56
KEAHEY CARL JOHN III	OK	23W	111
KEAHI GENE LUTHER	HI	36E	53
KEAL CLEVELAND JR	TX	30E	27
KEAN BILLIE ORR	OH	45E	3
KEANE PATRICK BRENDAN	IL	15E	96
KEAO JOHN K III	CA	03E	24
KEARBY JEAN ARTHUR	MN	22W	121
KEARNEY CHARLES DARYL	CA	02E	32
KEARNEY DAVID GEORGE	PA	16E	61
KEARNEY DONALD BRIAN	NY	48E	5
KEARNEY ROBERT CURT	WA	33E	70
KEARNEY TIMOTHY WILLIAM	IL	19E	50
KEARNS BRENDAN JOHN	NJ	29E	67
KEARNS JAMES THOMAS	WI	02E	83
KEARNS JOSEPH THOMAS JR	NY	21E	47
KEARNS STEVEN JOHN	MA	03W	60
KEARSE JULIUS JOEY	NY	19E	60
KEARSLEY RONALD CHARLES	OH	51E	22
KEARSLEY TOMMY L	ID	11W	95
KEASLING ELMER LEO	TN	09W	34
KEATHLEY CHARLES BRIAN	FL	52W	28
KEATING ALLEN FRANCIS	MA	17W	91
KEATING DANIEL JAMES JR	NY	65E	12
KEATING RALPH AINSWORTH	MI	36E	75
KEATON DANNY GARTH	VA	09E	14
KEATON DAVID ROGER	WV	30E	3
KEATON EVERETT DENNIS	OH	14W	49
KEATON JOHN LAWRENCE	OH	27E	59
KEATS ROBERT GEORGE	IL	36E	76
KEAVENEY THOMAS ROBERT	NY	14E	49
KEBERLINE MICHAEL JOHN	VA	17W	22
KECK CARL RANDOLPH	TX	33W	41
KECK FRANK LESLIE	MI	28W	82
KECK GARTH WAYNE JR	OK	08E	3
KECK JAY LYNN	FL	17W	71
KECK RUSSELL FORREST	OK	20E	30
KECK WARREN EDWARD	KS	16E	53
KECKLER ROBERT L	CA	04E	9
KEDENBURG JOHN JAMES	NY	57W	17
KEDROSKI ALBERT ARTHUR JR	IL	26E	104
KEE DANIEL PETER III	PA	28E	76
KEE JULIAN STANLEY JR	FL	45W	14
KEE WILSON BEGAY	AZ	09W	60
KEEBLE EDWIN AUGUSTUS JR	NY	31W	94
KEEFE DENNIS MICHAEL	NC	38E	78
KEEFE DENNIS WRIGHT	WI	51W	11
KEEFE DOUGLAS O'NEIL	SC	20E	61
KEEFE FLOYD MILTON	AL	29W	80
KEEFE MARTIN RUSSELL	MA	31W	6
KEEFE PAUL PATRICK	MA	07W	93
KEEFE RICHARD CARLYSLE	TX	33E	70
KEEFER DAVID CHARLES	OH	49W	24
KEEFER KENNETH RAY	OH	21E	68
KEEGAN RICHARD MICHAEL	VA	37W	75
KEEHNER CARROL GENE	IA	32E	36
KEEL DAVID LATTIMORE	TX	03E	34
KEEL JOHN DAVID	NC	33W	2
KEELER BERT AUSTIN	IA	47E	12
KEELER DICKIE GAYLE	KY	32W	49
KEELER HARPER BROWN	TX	33W	20
KEELER JAMES EDMUND	IN	06E	23
KEELER LARRY DEAN	OK	15W	59
KEELER RALPH LEROY	CA	10E	68
KEELER WILLIAM CHARLES	NY	15W	13
KEELER WILLIAM GILBERT	NJ	37W	22

NAME	STATE	PANEL NO.	LINE NO.
KEELER WILLIAM HOWARD	NY	28W	27
KEELEY FREDDIE JOE	TN	28E	60
KEELING ARTHUR R	IL	31E	92
KEELING LARRY DEWAYNE	CA	22W	2
KEELS MARLOWE EUGENE	NY	40W	38
KEEN ALBERT MASON JR	VA	06E	44
KEEN ARTHUR	NJ	08E	101
KEEN DARYL LA VERNE	CA	02E	38
KEEN EDWIN THOMAS	CA	31W	6
KEEN JASPER LEE	TN	07E	86
KEENAN DENNIS JOSEPH	NY	21E	1
KEENAN DONALD WAYNE	PA	25E	78
KEENAN JOHN SCOTT	MA	11W	36
KEENAN LAWRENCE JOHN	IA	19E	15
KEENAN ROBERT JAMES	NJ	07E	1
KEENE DANIEL ARTHUR	OH	26W	64
KEENE GERALD BRICE	SC	24E	12
KEENE GLEN CAMERON JR	AL	21W	46
KEENE GRAT ALBERT	FL	47E	23
KEENE ROBERT MICHAEL	IL	46W	16
KEENE THOMAS WILLIAM	CA	02W	82
KEENE WALTER MARTIN	MI	34E	29
KEENER JAMES LEE	WV	25E	85
KEENER LARRY LEE	PA	05E	73
KEENER LAWTON ARVIL	NC	35W	77
KEENER ROBERT STEVEN	NC	14E	23
KEENER RONALD FLOYD	CA	15W	45
KEENEY GERALD ROBERT	MO	01E	78
KEENEY JOSEPH FRANK	MD	07W	68
KEEP DONALD WAYNE	IL	33E	85
KEEPNEWS JOHN ARTHUR	NY	59W	23
KEERAN WILLARD DAVID	OH	07E	107
KEESEE ARTHUR EARL	TX	39W	60
KEESEE JOSEPH TIMOTHY	VA	19E	128
KEESLER STEPHEN JOSEPH	PA	10W	25
KEESLING GERALD EDWARD	MO	16W	110
KEESLING JOHN ARTHUR	IN	25W	17
KEETER DONALD LARRY	NC	39W	60
KEETER MARVIN ROSS	AR	02W	82
KEETER MICHAEL YATES	NC	36E	53
KEETLE JEFFREY CHARLES	OH	04W	70
KEETON TOMMIE	TN	03E	66
KEEVEN LOUIS FERDINAND	MO	31E	35
KEFER CHARLES HENRY JR	IL	11W	80
KEFFALOS CHRIS ALBERT	NM	10W	76
KEGG DONNIE STANLEY	OH	53E	38
KEGLEWITSCH WILHELM LUDWI	IL	21E	106
KEGLEY JOE DAVID	MT	09E	80
KEGLOVITS EDWARD JOSEPH	PA	17E	72
KEGLOVITS RONALD EDWARD	PA	25E	47
KEHOE DOUGLAS BERNARD	NY	36W	11
KEHOE MICHAEL JOSEPH	NY	14E	23
KEHOE ROBERT ANTHONY	IL	48W	43
KEHRLI HERBERT ALBERT	FL	41E	67
KEIFER JOE HAROLD	AR	13E	114
KEIL DUANE RICHARD	MI	21W	52
KEIM JAMES ROBERT	AR	51W	31
KEIN ROBERT JOSEPH	NJ	20W	71
KEIPER GEORGE FREDERICK	CA	44W	65
KEIPER JOHN CHARLES	PA	12E	74
KEIRNS THOMAS LEE	MI	24E	30
KEISLING DERVIN JOHN	PA	54E	26
KEISTER DAVID EARL	OH	39E	49
KEISTER JOHN LOY	OH	08W	17
KEISTER LAWRENCE LEE	CA	34W	85
KEITH CLYDE LEE	MO	16E	31
KEITH DANIEL SCOTT	MI	27W	50
KEITH DANNY JOE	CA	21E	35
KEITH DENNIS MEVES	CA	33W	71
KEITH JAMES KELLY III	TN	16E	35
KEITH JIMMIE EUGENE	FL	20W	113
KEITH KENNETH ARCHIBALD	NY	11E	26
KEITH LEE ALBERT	TX	31W	2
KEITH MASON ALAN	WV	03W	93
KEITH MIGUEL	NE	11W	132
KEITH RICHARD HENRY	MO	10W	76
KEITH ROY BENJAMIN	IL	34E	29
KEITH WILLIE LEE	SC	17W	97
KEITHLINE RICHARD WARD	CT	31W	94
KEITT CHARLES JOSEPH	NY	16W	58
KEKAHUNA WILLIAM ANTONE	HI	56E	10
KEKEL JERRY EDWARD	OR	15W	4
KELBY WESLY ROBERT	WA	22E	78
KELEHER KEVIN REYNOLDS	AR	11W	74
KELL JAMES STEWART	CA	28E	36
KELL LYLE FRANCIS	IL	15W	19
KELLAM GEORGE LEE	VA	33W	65
KELLAMS GLENNIS RAY	IN	49E	43
KELLAR HARRY DAVID CHARLE		31W	51
KELLAS ROBERT LOUIS	VA	35E	55
KELLEMS RAYMOND EARL	IN	03E	129
KELLENBENZ BARRY CHARLES	WI	34W	38
KELLER BRUCE M	UT	05W	22
KELLER CHARLES HENRY II	MI	22W	121
KELLER CHARLES LEE	IL	17E	58
KELLER DAVID RICHARD	OH	60W	18
KELLER DODD CLIFTON	MN	04E	130
KELLER FRANCIS JOSEPH	NJ	10W	114
KELLER GARY DALE	WA	50W	39
KELLER GEORGE RICHARD	NM	10W	109
KELLER GREG	CA	08W	28
KELLER JACK ELMER	IL	06E	126
KELLER JAMES LOUIS	CA	50E	30
KELLER JAMES MASON	MA	11W	102
KELLER JOSEPH JOHN JR	NJ	27E	29
KELLER KENNETH LAVERN	NE	14W	126
KELLER KENNETH LEE	WI	10W	97
KELLER LAWRENCE OSWALD JR	IL	27W	88
KELLER LEONARD	NJ	13W	104
KELLER LEROY HENRY	NY	19E	97
KELLER NORMAN LAWRENCE	NY	60W	10
KELLER PETER JOSEPH JR	MI	14E	91
KELLER RAYMOND E JR	PA	49E	11
KELLER RICHARD ALDEN	PA	22W	66
KELLER RICHARD LEON	CA	26W	78
KELLER ROBERT CRITCHLEY	PA	11E	79
KELLER ROGER PRESBORN	NC	45E	56
KELLER RONALD DALE	IL	25W	35
KELLER RONALD NORMAN	NH	38E	53
KELLER TIMOTHY WAYNE	CT	57E	25
KELLER WAYNE ARNOLD	MD	50W	6
KELLER WENDELL RICHARD	ND	30W	5
KELLERMANN ALLAN HOWARD	IL	20E	118
KELLETT DANIEL MACARTHUR	MA	13E	22
KELLETT JOHN EDWARD	IL	56W	13
KELLEY BERNARD JAMES	NY	01E	122
KELLEY DANA RICHARD	CA	13E	130
KELLEY DANIEL MARTIN	MA	52E	6
KELLEY DANIEL THOMAS	TX	20E	1
KELLEY DAVID BRUCE	CA	51W	33
KELLEY DEWEY WILLIAM	SC	07E	105
KELLEY EDDIE RALPH	MI	29W	80
KELLEY FRED ALLAN	VA	23E	43
KELLEY FREDDIE RAY	TN	43W	6
KELLEY GEORGE ROBERT	OH	08W	43
KELLEY GLENN HOWELL	TN	01E	89
KELLEY HARVEY PAUL	NE	16W	100
KELLEY JAMES DANIEL	TN	43W	38
KELLEY JERRY CONRAD	CO	29E	83
KELLEY JOE C	OK	11E	33
KELLEY JOE FRANKLIN	CA	14E	92
KELLEY JOHN PATRICK	RI	52E	27
KELLEY JOHNNIE WOODROW	MI	25E	102
KELLEY JOSEPH HOWARD	MD	21W	42
KELLEY KARL ELTON JR	FL	40W	12
KELLEY KENDRICK KING III	FL	36E	76
KELLEY LARRY DEAN	AL	53E	35
KELLEY LARRY MILTON	AR	27W	33
KELLEY LOUIS JAMES	PA	22W	47
KELLEY MAHLON LEWIS	FL	09W	27
KELLEY MICHAEL JAMES	WI	46E	19
KELLEY MICHAEL PATRICK	IL	17E	52
KELLEY NATHANIEL	GA	41W	25
KELLEY OWEN C	MO	28E	36
KELLEY PATRICK GENE	OR	25E	103
KELLEY PAUL GLEN	TX	06W	81
KELLEY RICHARD JOSEPH	MA	40E	42
KELLEY RICHARD ROBERT	MA	25W	102
KELLEY ROGER VIRGIL	CA	27E	29
KELLEY RONALD JAMES	PA	38E	78
KELLEY THOMAS R	MI	25E	12
KELLEY VERNE CARL	NH	32W	21
KELLEY VICTOR BRUCE	AZ	01E	110
KELLEY VIRGIL KINNAIRD JR	KY	25E	103
KELLEY WILLIAM FRANCIS	FL	18W	11
KELLEY WILLIAM ROBERT	AL	10E	54
KELLISON DAVID GLENN	CA	26W	40
KELLOGG ALTON DELANEY	LA	36W	45
KELLOGG GREGORY JAMES	NY	45W	26
KELLOGG PETER PATRICK W	WA	10W	45
KELLUM NORMAN WADE	TX	31W	51
KELLUMS DENNIS ALLEN	IL	22W	2
KELLY BARNEY JOE	CT	16E	112
KELLY BENJAMIN EDWARD JR	SC	25E	69
KELLY BRIAN RICHARD	MA	23W	45
KELLY CARL EUGENE JR	TN	32W	55
KELLY CHARLES L	GA	01E	57
KELLY CHARLES PATRICK	CA	21E	122
KELLY CHARLES WESLEY	NJ	14E	44
KELLY CHRISTOPHER	LA	20W	92
KELLY DENNIS LEROY	CA	50W	51
KELLY DONALD GLENN	TX	24W	54
KELLY DONALD LYNN	AL	24W	55
KELLY DOUGLAS JOHN	MA	31E	35
KELLY DOUGLAS MILTON	ND	50W	24
KELLY EDDIE JR	TN	62E	7
KELLY EDMUND JOSEPH	NC	65E	12
KELLY ERIC MELVIN	CA	04W	117
KELLY ERIC STEVEN	WI	03W	129
KELLY ERNEST CALVIN	CO	04E	48
KELLY ERNEST JR	NC	13E	98
KELLY FATHIES JR	NY	32E	10
KELLY GEORGE THOMAS III	NC	11W	41
KELLY GERALD JOHN JR	PA	24W	7
KELLY GLENN ERROLL	NY	05W	27
KELLY GREGORY PAUL	CA	21E	83
KELLY GREGORY RICHARD	PA	48E	28
KELLY HARRY ALLEN	NC	23E	76
KELLY JAMES ANTHONY JR	PA	11E	112
KELLY JAMES EDWARD	VA	21W	52
KELLY JAMES KEVIN	NY	48W	57
KELLY JAMES MATHEW	AL	12E	43
KELLY JAMES MICHAEL	MD	35W	77
KELLY JAMES PATRICK	PA	02E	95
KELLY JAMES RAYMOND III	CA	17E	36
KELLY JEROME RICHARD	IN	39E	62
KELLY JOE DUSTIN	OR	06E	21
KELLY JOEL RAY	GA	25W	97
KELLY JOHN EDWARD JR	ND	20W	44
KELLY JOHN FRANKLIN	TX	45W	53
KELLY JOHN WILLIAM S G	MI	13W	15
KELLY LARRY LEE	CA	56E	10
KELLY LAWRENCE LEE	PA	03W	129
KELLY LEO JOHN III	PA	20E	45
KELLY MICHAEL DENNIS	MI	20W	102
KELLY MICHAEL EUGENE	IN	13W	71
KELLY MICHAEL JOHN	OH	39E	49
KELLY MICHAEL JOHN	MI	27W	25
KELLY MICHAEL JOSEPH JR	NY	26W	46
KELLY PATRICK JOSEPH JR	MA	05E	86
KELLY PAUL EDWARD JR	GA	21E	123
KELLY ROBERT FRANCIS	NY	48W	43
KELLY ROBERT MICHAEL	CA	12W	30
KELLY ROGER EDWARD	NY	36E	76
KELLY SEEBER J	FL	53E	16
KELLY STEPHEN ALLEN	GA	22E	43
KELLY STEPHEN GERE	IL	35W	83
KELLY STEPHEN JAMES	IL	19W	16
KELLY TERRY LEON	CA	03W	79
KELLY WILLARD DOUGLAS	NY	13W	1
KELLY WILLIAM MARTIN	NY	08E	76
KELLY WILLIAM PATRICK	MO	17E	105
KELLY WILLIE J	OH	16W	3
KELM LARRY ROBERT	MN	10E	40
KELMAN WAYNE H	MN	33E	38
KELNHOFER JOSEPH ALLEN	IL	35E	32
KELPINE RANDALL WAYNE	WI	66W	9
KELSALL BILLY ALLEN	GA	31E	75
KELSEY CLIFFORD EARL	MI	20E	91
KELSEY D J	OK	27W	6
KELSEY J C	MI	13E	6
KELSEY MILTON GEORGE	MN	29E	95
KELSEY RONALD KEITH	MI	06W	117
KELSEY STRAUGHAN D JR	FL	21E	47
KELSO JAMES MICHAEL	PA	07W	115
KELSO THOMAS JOSH JR	KY	10W	70

NAME	STATE	PANEL NO.	LINE NO.
KELSO TODD DUANE	MT	58W	20
KELTON RICHARD LANE	IL	06W	64
KEMBLE DONALD WILLIAM IV	MI	30E	101
KEMELMACHER ROBERT	NY	36E	19
KEMER ROBERT PATRICK	OH	43W	63
KEMERER THOMAS BLAIR	PA	09E	40
KEMMERER DONALD RICHARD	PA	24E	83
KEMMERLING JOE THOMAS	TN	47E	40
KEMP CHARLIE EDWARD	LA	47W	46
KEMP CLAYTON CHARLES JR	CO	14E	17
KEMP EDWARD	OH	02E	132
KEMP FREDDIE	NY	10E	16
KEMP FREDERICK DONALD	NY	57E	5
KEMP JERALD WAYNE	MI	30E	3
KEMP JIMMY	SC	21E	62
KEMP JOE MAC	NM	09E	69
KEMP JOHN ALDA	VA	09E	114
KEMP MARWICK LEROY	FL	32W	55
KEMP MITCHELL LYNN	KY	27E	73
KEMP ROBERT VICTOR	AR	24E	113
KEMP SAMUEL LEE	DC	10E	74
KEMP THOMAS WILLIAM	MI	63W	17
KEMPEL MICHAEL RICHARD	OH	07W	17
KEMPER JOHN RICHARD	OH	48E	6
KEMPF DENNIS JOSEPH	IN	16W	23
KEMPF DOUGLAS SCOTT	OH	18W	40
KEMPFF RONALD WARREN	LA	47W	10
KEMPKE SANTFORD BERNARD	OR	55E	19
KEMPKER PATRICK BENJAMIN	MO	21W	28
KEMPKES ROBERT LOUIS	NE	25E	103
KEMPLE GILBERT VERNON JR	OH	09E	1
KEMPNER MARION LEE	TX	12E	55
KEMSKI GARY DOUGLAS	CA	41W	48
KENAGA GARY LYLE	KS	22E	31
KENDALL ALBIN LEE	OK	02W	59
KENDALL COLEY LEE	KY	05W	116
KENDALL GEORGE PERCY JR	MT	37E	23
KENDALL JAMES D	CA	52E	7
KENDALL KENNETH BRUCE	IN	11W	125
KENDALL NEIL SCOTT	PA	04W	19
KENDLE RANDY TRUMAN	PA	25W	76
KENDRA GEORGE JOHN	PA	40W	58
KENDRICK HOMER PHILLIP	GA	25W	103
KENDRICK JAMES CALVIN	AL	13E	110
KENDRICK JAMES MICHAEL	NY	16E	61
KENDRICK RICHARD SMITH	VA	11W	125
KENDRICKS DOY RAY	TX	52W	10
KENEALLY CORNELIUS PAUL	NY	10E	94
KENEDY WILLIAM MICHAEL	MS	03W	46
KENEIPP WARREN OWINGS JR	IL	22E	106
KENERLY WARREN EUGENE	GA	36E	19
KENISON BENJAMIN ALBERT	NH	10E	101
KENNANN LARRY RUSSELL	CO	55W	7
KENNARD JAMES HORACE	NJ	12E	89
KENNEBREW JOHN C	MS	47W	28
KENNEDY ALLAN GORDON	CA	16W	30
KENNEDY ALTON RAY	VA	13E	53
KENNEDY ARLAN JOSEPH JR	PA	56W	35
KENNEDY BRUCE JAMES	MA	39W	67
KENNEDY BRUCE LEONARD	CA	11E	15
KENNEDY BRUCE THOMAS		46W	30
KENNEDY CHARLES F	AR	16E	35
KENNEDY CHARLES FLOYD	UT	28E	26
KENNEDY CURTIS LEE	NC	33E	38
KENNEDY DONALD LEE	MI	18W	103
KENNEDY EDWARD HENRY	CA	24W	85
KENNEDY GENE RANDOLF	MO	04W	59
KENNEDY GLENN ALEXANDER	MS	07E	34
KENNEDY JAMES	AL	37W	12
KENNEDY JAMES EDWARD	NJ	15W	81
KENNEDY JAMES JR	MD	07E	82
KENNEDY JOHN FRANKLIN	OH	56W	5
KENNEDY JOHN WILLIAM	VA	03W	132
KENNEDY JUDD WAYNE	TX	12E	6
KENNEDY LARRY SCOTT	WV	43E	23
KENNEDY LEE DONNIE	TX	15W	36
KENNEDY MARCUS TRUMAN	OK	27E	24
KENNEDY MATTHEW DEVANUGHA	SC	21E	94
KENNEDY MICHAEL JOSEPH	FL	56W	13
KENNEDY MILTON REGINALD	TN	07W	2
KENNEDY RAYMOND O	IN	41E	50
KENNEDY ROBERT JR	AL	17W	102
KENNEDY THOMAS JOSEPH JR	PA	08E	42
KENNEDY THOMAS MARTIN	TN	04W	59
KENNEDY TIMOTHY JOEL	WI	32E	63
KENNEDY WILLIAM D III	CA	06W	92
KENNEDY WILLIAM EDWARD	CA	12E	102
KENNEDY WILLIAM HENRY	TN	32E	36
KENNELL DANNY OWEN	MI	21E	94
KENNEY DAVID EDWARD	MA	22W	20
KENNEY EDWARD	NJ	01E	123
KENNEY ELMER FREDERICK	CA	23E	52
KENNEY HARRY JOHN	OH	39W	1
KENNEY JOHN JOSEPH	MA	31W	7
KENNEY JOSEPH HAYDEN	AL	21W	8
KENNEY OTIS	MO	34W	42
KENNEY TERRY JOE	IL	52E	20
KENNINGTON BILLY DON	NC	45E	34
KENNON DONALD NEAL	TX	32W	27
KENNY JOHN HENRY	NY	08E	86
KENNY ROBERT W		14E	74
KENNY RONALD MICHAEL	MD	05E	51
KENOFFEL STEPHEN MICHAEL	CA	12W	81
KENT DANIEL WILDER	MA	35E	23
KENT DOUGLAS BRIAN	CA	05W	27
KENT ERROL LYNN	MN	02W	59
KENT GREGORY PATRICK	MA	46E	55
KENT JESSE PHILLIP	MI	23W	15
KENT KENNETH ROSS	NY	30W	25
KENT LLOYD HENRY	MS	34E	37
KENT ROBERT DUANE	TX	36W	52
KENT RONALD LEROY	ND	14E	57
KENT WAYNE LEE	GA	06W	108
KENT WILLIAM WAYNE	TN	49W	54
KENTER MICHAEL WILLIAM	IL	28E	100
KENTON DONALD E	DE	43E	23
KENTON STANLEY CHARLES	CO	16W	23
KENYON DALE DEAN	SD	68E	4
KEO DANIEL WILLIAM	WA	52E	39
KEOGH MARTIN JEROME	NY	13W	74
KEOGH THOMAS PATRICK	PA	01W	53
KEOWN BLAIR LOGAN	UT	54W	12
KEPCZYK TADEUSZ MARIAN	FL	47W	50
KEPHART RUSSELL EDWARD	PA	37E	24
KEPPEN THOMAS ROGER	IN	53W	36
KEPPLER JOHN M	CA	26E	75
KEPSEL ELMER FRED	MI	15E	46
KERBL FRANK RONALD	NJ	27E	65
KERBY MARTIN JOHN	CA	20W	98
KERCHNER ROBERT BARD	PA	48E	28
KERCOUDE ANTHONY KONSTANT	MD	43W	55
KERCSMAR ROBERT CALVIN	PA	25W	50
KERI ROBERT CHARLES	NJ	14E	104
KERKHOFF RICHARD LEE	UT	22W	106
KERKSTRA HARRY WILLIAM	IL	25W	103
KERL MICHAEL JAMES	PA	05W	81
KERLEY ROYD STEVE JR	NC	18E	41
KERLIN WILLIS EUGENE JR	OH	02W	26
KERN BRUCE ALAN	FL	26E	65
KERN DANIEL OLMSTEAD	NY	11E	112
KERN DAVID JOSEPH	MN	06E	71
KERN DOUGLAS DUANE	MT	12E	79
KERN WILLIAM FRANCIS	IA	11E	61
KERNAHAN GREGORY P JR	NJ	43E	24
KERNAN MICHAEL ROBERT	NY	10W	97
KERNDL BRUCE EDGAR	NY	12E	22
KERNER RONALD BRIAN	OH	26E	47
KERNEY JOHN OSCAR	IN	26E	66
KERNS ARTHUR WILLIAM	TX	13E	74
KERNS DONALD RAY	MS	47W	46
KERNS FRED MICHAEL	WV	20W	71
KERNS GLENN DIRK	NC	29E	74
KERNS JOHN EDWARD	OH	05E	56
KERNS ROGER RAY	OH	37W	12
KEROHER GAYLAND EUGENE	MO	33W	79
KERR CHARLES DAVID	CT	32E	11
KERR CHARLES FRANKLIN	IL	41E	68
KERR EDWARD LEMOYNE	CO	12E	121
KERR ERNEST CLANEY JR	OH	46E	36
KERR EVERETT OSCAR	WV	08E	45
KERR GAYLORD GERALD	OH	23W	53
KERR J L JR	TX	18E	70
KERR JAMES CLAYTON	GA	37W	51
KERR JOHN CREIGHTON GILLE	FL	25E	30
KERR NORMAN THEODORE	MI	18E	23
KERR RICHARD ALLEN	PA	36E	19
KERR ROBERT GEORGE	WA	16E	53
KERR ROBERT WESLEY	IN	07W	106
KERR RONNIE ALBERT	CA	04W	123
KERR STANLEY JESSE	WA	27E	101
KERR WESLEY SHEPPARD	NY	29W	100
KERSEY ARDEN ELLSWORTH JR	TX	09W	51
KERSEY J D WILLIAM	AZ	25E	63
KERSEY MAX DUANE	AL	15W	129
KERSEY WILLIAM RUSSELL JR	FL	07W	31
KERSTEN LESTER JOSEPH	IL	03E	116
KERTIS HENRY LEE JR	AR	41W	13
KERVIN JOEL CHARLES	MN	19E	27
KERWIN REVELRY LAWRENCE	IL	23E	43
KESHNER KEO JOE	MO	23W	111
KESKI KEITH	MI	27W	101
KESLER LAWRENCE DAVID	GA	08E	93
KESLING RAYMON DALE	WV	15E	85
KESLING RONALD LEE	MD	32E	75
KESSEL MICHAEL HENRY	ND	10E	65
KESSEL ROBERT LESTER	PA	16E	123
KESSELHON JAMES EDWARD	WI	45E	48
KESSING THOMAS EDWARD JR	MD	07W	5
KESSINGER JOHN McFARLAND	WI	22E	106
KESSINGER KENNETH MARTIN	WA	17E	105
KESSLER JULIUS ALLEN III	NY	18E	123
KESSLER TIMOTHY ROBERT	IN	34E	54
KESTER FRED DUANE	OK	34W	42
KESTER JAMES JOSEPH	OH	19W	3
KESTER RICHARD LEE	NY	09W	5
KESTER THOMAS DUFAUX	MO	45W	33
KESTERSON CHARLES ROBERT	VA	07E	26
KESTERSON DAVID MICHAEL	OH	12W	82
KESTLER GARY LYLE	OR	64W	11
KESTLER JESSE LYNN	TX	06W	54
KETCH MICHAEL HAYWARD	OH	45E	41
KETCHIE SCOTT DOUGLAS	AL	02W	134
KETCHUM WILLIAM ARNOLD JR	CA	06W	93
KETELAAR ROBERT LEE	IL	19W	95
KETELS FLOYD DALE	CO	12W	73
KETHE HENRY JAMES	MO	10W	57
KETNER HAROLD K JR	VA	16E	46
KETT RANDOLPH CHARLES	FL	48W	44
KETTER TERRY LEE	CA	10W	12
KETTERER JAMES ALAN	WI	34E	88
KETTERING ROBERT PAUL	OH	12W	82
KETTMANN DANIEL RAY	IL	48E	29
KETTNER ALAN ARTHUR	MN	49E	43
KETZLER GILBERT JR	AK	17W	62
KEVER DWAYNE ELBERT	AR	48W	57
KEY ANDERSON HAROLD	SC	04E	70
KEY ANTHONY WAYNE	TX	19E	108
KEY HULUS EDGAR JR	GA	16W	19
KEY LESTER	FL	03E	114
KEY RICHARD JOHN	LA	21W	53
KEY ROGER EUGENE	AL	14W	52
KEYER DENNIS LEE	OH	07E	16
KEYES ARNELL	NY	05E	105
KEYES DANIEL DUANE	CA	60E	13
KEYES SCOTTY LEE	TX	25E	78
KEYES WILLIAM GEORGE	MI	51E	46
KEYS MICHAEL HENRY	WA	04W	3
KIAHA RODNEY SIU	HI	39W	27
KIATKIN NIKOLAI	NJ	45E	34
KIBBE GERRITH LOWELL	PA	22E	58
KIBBEY RICHARD ABBOTT	NY	14E	129
KIBEL CHARLEY CHESTER	CO	17E	99
KIBLER ALFRED JAMES	PA	11E	52
KICK DANIEL LEE	IL	40E	7
KICKLITER JAMES THOMAS	FL	47W	46
KIDD DENNIS CURTIS	NC	01E	60
KIDD DONALD EUGENE	KY	44E	47
KIDD DONNY RAMON	SD	42E	67
KIDD GEORGE R	FL	26W	47
KIDD JOHNNY LEE	OK	20W	7
KIDD KENNETH EDWARD	FL	60W	19
KIDD LEONARD WHITLEY	VA	08W	59
KIDD MELTON LAVONE	VA	58W	10
KIDD MICHAEL LOU	MD	54E	26
KIDD NORMAN RICHARD JR	CA	20E	118
KIDD PETER ALAN	NY	19W	95

NAME	STATE	PANEL NO.	LINE NO.
KIDD PHILLIP MERIDITH	NY	49E	3
KIDD RHEA MARSHALL	KY	10W	34
KIDD VICTOR ELDEN	PA	48E	42
KIDD WAYNE HUFFMAN	WV	01E	76
KIDWELL ROGER GENE	VA	14W	33
KIDWELL WAYNE MINOR	VA	43E	56
KIECKER PAUL FREDERICK	CO	21E	124
KIEFEL ERNST PHILIP JR	PA	05E	23
KIEFER STUART OTIS	TX	57W	19
KIEFFER WILLIAM LEWIS JR	MD	14W	126
KIEFHABER ANDREW JOHN	NY	31W	7
KIEHL MICHAEL RAYMOND	CA	07E	86
KIEHNE JAMES WESLEY	PA	02W	106
KIEL STEVEN TRACY	MI	34W	76
KIELLEY BYRON ALICK	WA	19E	108
KIELPIKOWSKI RONALD LEE	WI	31W	97
KIELY BILLY RAY	OK	57E	25
KIEME BRUCE DOUGLAS	FL	08W	49
KIENER KENNETH RICHARD	NY	15W	1
KIER CHARLES RICHARD	KS	04E	42
KIER LARRY GENE	NE	11W	112
KIERNAN JOSEPH M JR	NJ	21E	48
KIERZEK STANLEY P	MA	02E	41
KIERZNOWSKI TERRENCE E	IL	18W	77
KIES DAVID F	WI	14E	67
KIESELBURG GARY ROBERT	IL	11W	116
KIESER CHARLES DAVID	FL	24E	30
KIESLER RAYMOND JOSEPH	IL	17W	121
KIESLING GERALD DENNIS	IL	51W	34
KIESTLER JAMES LARRY	IL	23W	37
KIESWETTER GERARD MARTIN	CA	09E	75
KIEWLEN FRANK JOSEPH JR	CT	24W	77
KIEZKOWSKI EDWARD THOMAS	PA	23W	9
KIGAR LARRY EUGENE	MO	26W	99
KIGER DENNIS DELMAR	MN	11W	125
KIGER GEORGE ALAN	MO	23W	54
KIGER JAMES ANTHONY	AL	10E	107
KIGER JAMES ROBERT	IN	03W	23
KIGHT MICHAEL AARON	CT	20E	45
KIHL PATRICK JAMES	WI	05W	33
KIHNLEY GEORGE MATTHEW	KY	39E	73
KIJOWSKI ROBERT GEORGE	OH	26W	9
KIKER DOUGLAS HUGH	TX	38W	27
KIKKERT ROBERT MERRILL	IN	01W	78
KILBANE TERENCE JOSEPH	OH	23E	20
KILBANE TERRENCE PATRICK	OH	33W	72
KILBUCK GEORGE GREGORY	AK	02E	68
KILBURN WILLIAM HUNTER	SC	10W	125
KILBY RAYMOND MORGAN	VA	17W	23
KILCULLEN THOMAS MICHAEL	MD	25E	47
KILDARE WILLIAM JAMES	NE	26E	104
KILDERRY MICHAEL JOSEPH	PA	53W	27
KILDUFF MICHAEL JOHN	VA	02W	14
KILE JOHN TERRENCE	GA	06W	119
KILEY MICHAEL JAMES	CA	30E	44
KILGORE CHARLES HOWARD	TX	27E	39
KILGORE DANNY RAY	OR	50E	16
KILGORE GARY BREWSTER	TN	46W	4
KILGORE LARRY WYATT	MO	06W	12
KILKENNY FRANK JOSEPH	NY	21E	27
KILLABREW ROBERT LEROY	MO	04E	67
KILLEN JOHN DEWEY III	IA	22E	88
KILLENS RICHARD	OH	03E	129
KILLGORE GENE DOUGLAS	CA	38E	69
KILLIAN DAVID EDWARD	OH	06W	84
KILLIAN GARY MARTIN	MI	20E	61
KILLIAN MARVIN CLYDE	UT	09E	77
KILLIAN MELVIN JOSEPH	IA	02E	99
KILLILEA MARTIN FRANCIS	MA	07E	65
KILLING RONALD JAMES	MI	27W	65
KILLINGSWORTH SCOTT E	GA	09W	63
KILLION THOMAS JOSEPH JR	PA	38W	2
KILLMON FREDERICK RUSSELL	MD	07W	27
KILPATRICK DONALD ROBERT	PA	18W	24
KILPATRICK LARRY RONALD	GA	01W	45
KILROY MICHAEL WINSTON	NJ	07E	86
KILTON STANLEY ROY JR	NH	54W	12
KILUK EDWARD GEORGE JR	NH	08W	49
KILVER PHILLIP HENRY	IL	06W	21
KILWINE RICHARD JAMES	MT	19W	39
KIM EDWARD Y C	HI	04E	92
KIM HARRY	CA	49W	15

NAME	STATE	PANEL NO.	LINE NO.
KIMBALL PIERCE MALLORY	WA	41W	59
KIMBALL RICHARD NELSON JR	IL	30E	70
KIMBALL WILLIAM B JR	NJ	56E	10
KIMBALL WILLIAM ROBERT	TX	15W	42
KIMBER TERREL OLIN	UT	04W	92
KIMBLE CLEATUS PAUL	CA	16W	58
KIMBLE EDDIE CLAUDE	GA	39W	72
KIMBLE LESTER WILSON	IL	14W	103
KIMBLER LAWRENCE RUTHERFO	FL	24E	77
KIMBLEY ROBERT GLENN	MO	36W	85
KIMBRELL GORDON T JR	GA	09W	44
KIMBRELL LOUIS CLEVELAND	MO	54W	12
KIMBROUGH GOLSBY JR	PA	21W	70
KIMBROUGH HAROLD BRUCE	AR	07W	84
KIMES LOUIS D	WA	12E	89
KIMLING MILES WAYNE	TX	43E	8
KIMM CLARENCE ALFRED	NE	16E	73
KIMMEL EUGENE WILLIAM	SD	40W	20
KIMMEL GORDON LEE	PA	02W	8
KIMMEL LEWIS ALBERT JR	CA	05E	105
KIMMEL ROBERT CHARLES	NY	52E	7
KIMMEL ROBERT GENE	KS	29E	95
KIMMEL STANLEY REGAN	CA	10W	121
KIMMELL GEORGE SAMUEL	MD	21W	108
KIMPEL PHILIP JOHN	WI	16E	61
KIMSEY DONALD WAYNE	OH	18W	16
KIMSEY WILLIAM ARTHUR JR	TN	35E	7
KIMURA KAY KAZU	ID	13W	92
KIMZEY JOHN ALBERT	MI	12W	61
KINARD DIXON TALMADGE	HI	19W	113
KINARD LARRY VERGESS	PA	24E	30
KINARD LESTER STEPHEN	PA	35E	60
KINASZ MONTE CLIFFORD	GA	46E	19
KINCAID BARRY EDWARD	MD	55W	14
KINCAID PAUL EDDIE	WV	22E	71
KINCANNON RAYMOND OMER	CA	47E	33
KINCER ALFRED LEMUEL III	TX	04W	14
KINDEL JAMES CARL	NY	04E	16
KINDER BRADLEY ALLEN	CA	14W	115
KINDER LARRY WADE	FL	22W	121
KINDER WILLIAM ARTHUR	PA	04W	80
KINDLE WILLIAM DOYLE	MO	35W	5
KINDLE WILLIAM HENRY	MN	26W	64
KINDLEBERGER HAROLD PAUL	TX	07E	49
KINDRED LAWRENCE JOSEPH	MO	09E	123
KINDRED MICHAEL GEORGE	CA	38E	53
KINDRED RONNY KAY	OK	31E	93
KINDRICK BRYCE LEROY	CA	07W	99
KINDSVATTER WARREN EARL	OH	07W	113
KINDT THOMAS PATRICK	IN	10E	129
KINES EDWARD WRAY	GA	26E	47
KING ALEXANDER	GA	34W	42
KING ARGESTLAR JR	AL	47W	28
KING BILLY BROWN	KY	10E	133
KING BOBBY	TX	09E	12
KING BRADFORD STANLEY	AZ	29E	32
KING BRUCE THOMAS	TX	27W	45
KING CARSON MILO	TX	63E	12
KING CHARLES DOUGLAS	IA	36W	76
KING CHARLES LEE	NC	48E	6
KING CHARLES LEWIS	TX	23W	65
KING CHARLES MICHAEL JR	CA	16E	92
KING CHARLES RAY	GA	11W	55
KING DANNY EUGENE	TN	20E	30
KING DANNY RAYMOND	OH	03W	63
KING DAVID GLENN	CA	32W	66
KING DAVID MICHAEL	MO	12W	57
KING DE WAYNE	GA	49E	53
KING DENNIS DWAIN	WY	40E	42
KING DONALD GENE	CA	35W	17
KING DONALD LEWIS	MI	07E	59
KING DONNIE LUSTER	LA	21W	53
KING DOYLE GAYLON	AL	28E	2
KING EARL HUGO	FL	04W	111
KING EDWARD EARL	GA	23W	75
KING ELI J B	AR	22E	43
KING FELIX DELOACH JR	AL	03E	24
KING FLOYD D SR	WV	10E	68
KING FRANCIS J R	OK	28W	48
KING FREDRICK BEN	IN	38W	58
KING GARLAND BRYAN JR	AR	22W	90
KING GARRY EUGENE	MO	45E	32

NAME	STATE	PANEL NO.	LINE NO.
KING GEORGE LOUIS JR	OR	60W	19
KING GEORGE PAUL	IL	06E	42
KING GERALD EUGENE	TN	58E	10
KING GILBERT	CA	47W	29
KING GLEN EDWARDS	IL	02E	80
KING GUY RICHARD	MO	51W	11
KING HAROLD B	TN	18E	5
KING HAROLD JUNIOR JR	MD	13E	122
KING HAROLD WAYNE	VA	23E	52
KING HARRY CARLTON	KY	04W	55
KING IVAN CLAUS	MI	27E	38
KING JACK LLOYD	TX	04W	116
KING JAMES ALLEN	CA	59W	24
KING JAMES EDWARD	OH	22E	7
KING JAMES EDWARD	VA	38W	58
KING JAMES HENRY	FL	02E	110
KING JAMES ISRAEL	VA	30E	97
KING JAMES MICHEAL	IL	29W	101
KING JAMES ROGERS	MI	07W	31
KING JAMES ROY	MS	36W	52
KING JAY WILLIAM	WV	12W	69
KING JOHN CHESTER	CA	06W	35
KING JOHN EDWARD	IN	01E	76
KING JOHN TERRENCE	IL	17E	30
KING JOHNNY	GA	36W	11
KING JOHNNY LEE	NC	21W	108
KING JOHNNY RAY	AR	48E	53
KING JON MARC	NY	06W	93
KING JOSEPH CEPHUS JR	NY	61W	3
KING JOSEPH DEWARD	NC	20E	91
KING JOSEPH ROBERT JR	NC	30W	5
KING KENNETH WALTER	WY	60W	2
KING LARRY DOUGLAS	OK	37E	24
KING LARRY EUGENE	GA	42W	62
KING LAUNEY E	NC	40E	42
KING LAURENCE MICHAEL	FL	02E	97
KING LEE RAY	OH	37E	37
KING LEROY ALAN	OH	42W	30
KING LESLIE GENE	TX	02E	47
KING LESTER	NY	08W	77
KING LEWIS	FL	46W	4
KING LEWIS MILTON JR	WV	47W	19
KING LONNIE RALPH	TN	05E	93
KING LYELL FRANCIS	VA	05E	47
KING MICHAEL ELI	GA	04W	24
KING MICHAEL LEE	OH	07E	96
KING MONROE DEE	IL	11W	132
KING NORTON ZIGMUND	CA	36E	53
KING PATRICK WILLMER	CT	03E	129
KING PAUL CHESTER JR	MA	54E	41
KING RAYFORD HENRY	GA	04W	103
KING REGINALD DAVID	MO	32W	32
KING RICHARD LEE	OH	18E	60
KING ROBERT CARL	SC	27W	65
KING ROBERT D ORR	WA	34E	37
KING ROBERT DOUGLAS	IA	31E	36
KING ROBERT EARL	TN	21W	53
KING ROBERT EARL	SC	21W	89
KING ROBERT HENRY	AL	35E	33
KING ROBERT LARRY	OH	26W	47
KING ROBERT LEE	OH	21W	13
KING ROBERT LEE	MD	06W	105
KING ROBERT LEON	WV	15E	21
KING ROBERT LEWIS	VA	03W	105
KING ROBERT LOUIS	SC	09W	122
KING ROBERT SHELTON JR	MS	17W	57
KING ROBERT WAYNE	CA	09E	14
KING RONALD DEAN	WA	30E	28
KING RONALD REED	CA	26E	104
KING RONALD RICHARD	PA	23E	60
KING RONALD RUNYAN	CA	27E	44
KING STEVEN ROSS	MI	15E	28
KING THOMAS GEORGE	NY	22E	107
KING THOMAS KEITH	TX	06E	48
KING THOMAS PICKETT BYRD	SC	05W	83
KING THOMAS RAY	MD	32E	11
KING VERLON DONALD JR	OK	19W	120
KING WOODROW WILSON JR	MD	04E	92
KING WYLIE CLARENCE	SC	16W	128
KINGERY DONALD LEE	AR	15W	10
KINGERY PAUL JAY	OH	59E	25
KINGHAMMER STEVE WILLIAM	WA	14E	87

NAME	STATE	PANEL NO.	LINE NO.
KINGHORN STEPHEN JOHN	PA	22W	41
KINGMAN BARRY DEAN	CA	35W	5
KINGMAN DAN CHRISTIE JR	NE	01W	30
KINGREY EDWARD LEO	KY	21W	118
KINGSBURY DAVE ROYCE	OK	23E	52
KINGSLEY THOMAS EDWARD	OH	04W	61
KINGSTON GEORGE HENRY JR	NY	07W	132
KINGSTON THOMAS LLOYD	MN	35E	7
KINIRY ANDREW JOHN	PA	20W	65
KINIYALOCTS CHARLES M	OH	21W	33
KINK DAVID ROBERT	WI	20W	92
KINKADE WILLIAM LOUIS	OR	45W	20
KINKAID FRANK W JR	NE	17W	67
KINKEAD MAURICE HARRISON	MO	42W	18
KINKEADE RONALD JAY	MO	09E	48
KINKLE BOBBY GENE	OK	25E	103
KINMAN TERRY DEWAYNE	TX	06W	106
KINNAMON SAMMY EDWARD	KS	31W	68
KINNARD DANIEL LEE	OH	43E	67
KINNARD DENNIS RAY	OH	55W	21
KINNARD JAMES EDWARD	CA	30W	66
KINNARD WILLIAM LLOYD	CA	49E	23
KINNE ALLEN GENE	WA	11W	114
KINNEAR LAWRENCE FRANK	PA	11E	22
KINNETT GEORGE DELMER	IL	23W	102
KINNEY CHARLES WILLIAM	MI	54E	26
KINNEY DAVID WASHINGTON	WV	23W	28
KINNEY DELMER LANGLY	IL	20W	58
KINNEY DONALD MACK	KY	27W	31
KINNEY JOHN WADE	OK	40E	54
KINNEY LEE CHARLES	MN	38E	31
KINNEY MERLE ALLAN	IL	07E	16
KINNEY RANDLE	AL	12E	47
KINNEY RICHARD LEE	IL	18E	123
KINNY GERALD CARL	IA	36E	19
KINSER ARTHUR WILLIAM	IN	13W	10
KINSER JACOB LEE	CO	13W	97
KINSEY HARVEY JUNIOR	SC	23E	37
KINSEY JOE EDWARD	AZ	32E	96
KINSEY MICHAEL CHRISTOPHE	TX	40E	7
KINSKY RONALD CHARLES	PA	07E	128
KINSLER FREDERICK C JR	NJ	19W	103
KINSMAN ALLEN EUGENE	NE	04W	93
KINSMAN GERALD FRANCIS	MA	05W	45
KINSWORTHY LOYD EUGENE	CA	52E	31
KINTARO JOHN JULLIANO		02W	28
KINTON DONALD RAY	CO	46E	19
KINTON JOHN LEONARD	VA	13E	110
KINYON RODNEY EDWIN	OR	59W	24
KIPINA MARSHALL FREDERICK	MI	09E	20
KIPP DENNIS WALTER	CA	17W	97
KIPP DONALD LEE	CA	33W	86
KIPP RAYMOND SIDNEY	OK	12W	13
KIRACOFE BURLEY DARREL	MI	27W	19
KIRBY BOBBY ALEXANDER	GA	01W	100
KIRBY DONALD ROBERT III	CA	32E	75
KIRBY GEORGE H JR	KY	01E	110
KIRBY GERALD	TX	51W	34
KIRBY JAMES EUGENE	MI	32W	13
KIRBY LEWIS ROY	MI	12E	89
KIRBY MICHAEL CHARLES	FL	13E	34
KIRBY RANCE A	AL	17E	52
KIRBY STEVEN	PA	15E	84
KIRCHER ALFRED GEORGE	NY	20E	104
KIRCHGESLER DANIEL JAMES	SD	19W	87
KIRCHMAYER ANDREW GREGORY	WI	16W	93
KIRCHNER GARY ALLEN	MI	03W	26
KIRCHNER HENRY JOSEPH JR	KY	61E	11
KIRCHNER JOHN HENRY JR	PA	57E	30
KIRCHNER JOHN WARD	WI	23W	1
KIRCHOFF WILBUR GLEN	IA	05E	106
KIRIK MARTIN EUGENE	FL	19W	68
KIRK ARNOLD DAVID	MD	43E	46
KIRK DAVID GRANT	MD	63E	12
KIRK DAVID MICHAEL	CT	24W	17
KIRK HERBERT A	PA	44E	18
KIRK MELVIN LYNN	CA	50E	48
KIRK ROBERT LEE	NV	11W	114
KIRKBY JAMES KENT	NJ	14W	94
KIRKEBY DAVID LYNN	ND	58E	10
KIRKENDALL JOSEPH KEITH	IN	46W	42
KIRKENDOLL CLEE ANDREW	KS	45W	42
KIRKENDOLL JERRY WAYNE	KS	04W	50
KIRKES KENNETH LEE	TN	38E	54
KIRKHAM DONALD ALAN	WI	36E	53
KIRKLAND CHARLES S JR	MO	65E	12
KIRKLAND EUGENE H	NY	56E	10
KIRKLAND LARRY JAMES	TX	10W	76
KIRKLAND VIRGIL JR	TN	03E	45
KIRKLAND WILLIE LEE	FL	24W	44
KIRKPATRICK ELDON JOHN JR	OH	44E	18
KIRKPATRICK MICHAEL WARD	FL	20W	119
KIRKPATRICK RONALD IRVING	ME	20W	7
KIRKPATRICK RONALD RENE	FL	20W	108
KIRKPATRICK WILLIAM W	CA	04W	87
KIRKSEY JAMES WALTER	AZ	19W	61
KIRKSEY ROBERT LOUIS	AL	13E	110
KIRKSEY WILLIE JAMES	MO	29W	54
KIRKWOOD DERYL RAMON	LA	39E	7
KIRN JAMES EDWARD	KY	16E	92
KIRSCH WARREN MICHAEL	PA	56E	27
KIRSCHNER STEPHEN BENJAMI	NJ	33E	88
KIRSTEIN DANIEL LYNN	CA	19E	61
KISALA WALTER	IL	05E	29
KISCADEN MICHAEL EDWARD	PA	09W	108
KISCH ROBERT ANTHONY	NY	24E	30
KISELEWSKI VINCE ROBERT	IL	04W	80
KISER DAVID BUTLER	WV	08E	21
KISER JERRY ALLEN	OK	37W	17
KISER LEON EMMANUEL	GA	06W	31
KISER ROBERT JESSE	CT	04W	103
KISER ROBERT THOMAS	PA	04W	35
KISER WILLIAM BROOKS	AZ	27E	54
KISH CARY MICHAEL	MI	10E	47
KISH ERNEST	CA	18W	24
KISIELEWSKI JOHN WILLIAM	NJ	08W	94
KISNER THOMAS R	PA	32E	37
KISSAM EDWARD KNELL JR	NJ	01E	6
KISSELL BERNARD F JR	PA	40W	12
KISSINGER HAROLD JAMES	PA	43W	16
KISSINGER NORMAN CHARLES	WI	38E	50
KISSINGER RONALD CLAYTON	NY	14E	116
KISSLING BENJAMIN KAON	TX	49E	3
KISTLER BERNARD FRANCIS	PA	12E	43
KISTLER JAMES LEROY	IN	21E	95
KISTLER RUSSELL WILFORD	AL	04E	67
KISTNER GUY DALE	CA	32E	75
KISUCKY ANTHONY EDWARD	IL	31E	13
KITCHEN DAVID LEE	KS	26W	47
KITCHEN EDDIE JR	IL	43E	24
KITCHEN MICHAEL ROOSEVELT	IL	26W	107
KITCHEN ORVILLE EUGENE JR	OH	12W	82
KITCHEN RUSSELL HAROLD JR	MO	26W	14
KITCHENS FRANK M JR	AL	11W	17
KITCHENS HARRY MOSS	GA	09E	98
KITCHENS JOEL RHYNE	SC	21W	102
KITCHENS PERRY CASTELLION	GA	06W	37
KITE HARRY TURNER JR	PA	38W	49
KITNER RICHARD GRANVILLE	CA	09E	94
KITO DONALD HARRY	AK	23E	37
KITRILAKIS JOHN ANDREW	MI	12W	113
KITSON JOHN FRANCIS	NY	20W	36
KITTLE CECIL WILBERT JR	WV	03E	82
KITTLE FREDRICK MARTIN	PA	36E	19
KITTLE STEPHEN RANDALL	FL	09E	69
KITTLESON RANDY GENE	WA	10W	34
KITTLESON ROGER MICHAEL	MN	31W	51
KITTRELL LARRY DON	TX	42W	62
KITTS MARIO CLAYTON	IN	05E	119
KITZKE RONALD FREDERICK	WI	32E	76
KITZMILLER JOHN LESTER	CA	27E	11
KIVEL ELMER MARVIN	MI	39W	1
KIZER CARL SANFORD	PA	56W	35
KIZZIAH JERRY WAYNE	AL	34E	21
KIZZIE LEON EDWARD	VA	43W	17
KJELLERSON MYRON DALE	SD	22W	13
KJOS TERENCE MICHAEL	MN	08W	124
KLAAHSEN LAWRENCE JON	IA	42E	18
KLABUNDE ARTHUR JOHN JR	NE	35E	33
KLABUNDE JOHN PAUL	NE	26E	12
KLAGES ROBERT JOHN	MO	24E	61
KLAIBER FRANCIS EARL	PA	08W	15
KLANCKE CHARLES WILLIAM	MN	14W	19
KLANIECKI EDWARD MATTHEW	NJ	25W	30
KLANN MARTIN DOUGLAS	OH	34E	21
KLAPAK JOHN ROBERT JR	IN	26W	112
KLARIC TERRANCE EDWIN	PA	19E	90
KLARIK STEVE	IN	49E	16
KLASSEN FRANCIS JAMES	AR	02W	65
KLAUS ARTHUR LEE	KS	33W	86
KLAUS GEORGE PETER	IL	25E	1
KLAUSING RONALD LAVERN	CA	31E	99
KLAUSING THOMAS PATRICK	IL	52E	39
KLAVES JEFFREY JOHN	WI	11W	68
KLAWITTER WILLIAM RICHARD	OR	42E	18
KLCO JAMES EDWARD	MI	27W	6
KLEBER HARRY WILLIAM	FL	16E	29
KLECKLEY FREDDIE LEE	FL	09E	123
KLECZ STANLEY STEPHEN	NJ	20E	30
KLEFFMAN WILLIAM WALTER	IA	12W	103
KLEIBER GEORGE L JR	IN	18W	33
KLEIN DANIEL FRANCIS	MN	07W	39
KLEIN DENNIS W	NJ	43E	12
KLEIN DON ROBERT	MN	33W	8
KLEIN GARRY DEAN	ND	21E	1
KLEIN GEORGE PAUL	PA	51E	31
KLEIN GERALD DEAN	ND	54E	35
KLEIN GLEN CHARLES	OR	05W	25
KLEIN HENRY IRVING JR	NY	13E	5
KLEIN JACK WEBB SR	WV	01E	96
KLEIN JAMES MORTON	MO	12W	35
KLEIN JEROME DON	NM	04W	73
KLEIN JOSEPH	NJ	60W	19
KLEIN MICHAEL KENNETH	CA	40W	7
KLEIN RUSSELL LEO	IA	12W	93
KLEIN STEPHEN LOUIS	WA	09W	106
KLEIN SZOLTON SIGMOND	PA	23E	36
KLEINAU CARL EDWARD	IL	26W	85
KLEINBERG PETER SHELL	MA	33E	13
KLEINHANS LAWRENCE CHARLE	NY	41W	48
KLEINSMITH ROBERT LLOYD	OR	25W	73
KLEINT WILLIAM STANLEY	IN	44E	48
KLEIV MANFORD LLOYD	MT	01E	66
KLEMENCIC JOSEPH GORDON	MT	19E	72
KLEMM DONALD MARTIN	OH	21E	89
KLEMMER SYDNEY WILLIAM	MN	56E	6
KLEMP THOMAS JOHN	WI	12E	34
KLENDA DEAN ALBERT	KS	02E	85
KLENERT WILLIAM BLUE	NY	11E	99
KLENSKE HOWARD LEE	CA	50W	1
KLEPPIN KENNETH THOMAS	WI	14W	13
KLESTINEC ALBERT F JR	NY	09E	15
KLETINGER HANS	NY	33E	19
KLETT JOHN EARLE	MI	26E	104
KLEVENOWSKI ROBERT MICHAE	OH	13E	79
KLEVER MARK EDWARD	WI	09W	20
KLIGAR JOHN JOSEPH III	MI	07W	5
KLIMO JAMES ROBERT	MI	16W	30
KLIMPKE DENNIS LEE	WI	50E	5
KLINCK HARRISON HOYT	CA	30E	28
KLINDT DAN THOMAS	OR	32E	76
KLINE BRUCE EUGENE	FL	01W	30
KLINE DAVID BRUCE	ND	22E	107
KLINE DAVID SAMUEL	PA	16W	100
KLINE DENNIS	NJ	17E	6
KLINE GARY WAYNE	MI	21E	49
KLINE HAROLD FRANKLIN	MD	46W	4
KLINE HARVEY EDWARD II	CA	35E	33
KLINE JAMES JOSEPH	PA	60E	13
KLINE KENNETH GORDON	PA	16W	90
KLINE MARK LEE	MD	32W	28
KLINE ROBERT DANIEL	CA	32E	24
KLINE ROBERT EARL	PA	12E	10
KLINE ROBERT FRANCIS JR	CA	47E	13
KLINE ROBERT JAMES	MI	49E	12
KLINEFELTER GAYLORD NATHA	OR	05E	27
KLING LEROY JOHN OLIVER	LA	30E	9
KLINGAMAN BRUCE DAVID	NJ	13W	85
KLINGEN JOHN EDWARD	NY	18W	33
KLINGENSMITH CLYDEWALTER	PA	29E	20
KLINGENSMITH THEODORE R	PA	35W	27
KLINGER HENRY CHESTER	CA	15W	114
KLINGLER GARY LYNN	MI	45W	7
KLINGMAN RONALD ARTHUR	NY	17W	50
KLINGNER MICHAEL LEE	NE	12W	101
KLINK JAMES MARION	OH	12E	14

NAME	STATE	PANEL NO.	LINE NO.
KLINKE DONALD HERMAN	CA	01W	45
KLINKENBERG RICHARD CARL	MN	51E	22
KLINKER MARY THERESE	IN	01W	122
KLINSKI MICHAEL ROMAN	MI	52W	44
KLINZING THOMAS LEE	OH	36E	20
KLIPFEL JOE PAUL	MO	37W	48
KLIPPEL DAVID JOHN	MI	35E	16
KLIPPEN ARTHUR G	MD	10E	40
KLOC JOHN THOMAS	WI	19E	83
KLOEK LYLE ARCHIE	MN	08W	43
KLOESE WAYNE RICHARD	CA	25E	85
KLOOS RICHARD NICHOLAS	SD	44W	26
KLOOTWYK ROBERT IVAN	IA	24E	91
KLOPMEYER JAMES MARTIN	IL	32E	24
KLORAN THOMAS WALTER	PA	39E	73
KLOS DANIEL EDMUND JR	NY	29E	83
KLOS RONALD FRANK	MI	39E	35
KLOSE DOUGLAS CLEMENS	ND	40W	44
KLOSS THOMAS DONALD	CA	08W	12
KLOSSEK GERALD	NJ	30E	56
KLOSTER THOMAS HENRY	NY	39W	61
KLOTZ CRAIG GORDON	PA	17W	23
KLOTZ JOHN ROBERT	CA	42W	36
KLOTZ MICHAEL PETER	NY	21W	46
KLUEVER LARRY JOHN	DC	02W	7
KLUG HERBERT WHEELER	OH	13W	71
KLUG JOSEPH RONALD	WV	22E	25
KLUG PAUL FRANCIS	WV	13W	110
KLUG RICHARD DUANE	CA	29E	96
KLUGE JAMES DONALD	CA	24W	32
KLUGG JOSEPH RUSSELL	MI	06W	60
KLUKAS BRADLEY WILFRED	MN	21W	102
KLUMP JOHN THEODORE	OH	11E	5
KLUSENDORF HAROLD JOHN	MI	47W	46
KLUTE JERRY CRAIG	OH	22W	53
KLUTE KARL EDWIN	IN	06E	7
KLYNE JAMES ARNOLD	OH	21W	38
KMETYK JONATHAN PETER	NY	29E	96
KMETZ DAVID WILLIAM	WI	44E	18
KMIEC JOHN STANLEY	IL	34E	69
KMIT CHESTER JON	MA	33W	65
KNABB KENNETH KEITH JR	IL	40W	13
KNACK RICHARD CARL	VA	59W	24
KNADLE ROBERT EDWARD	MD	27E	81
KNADLER ROBERT STANLEY	TX	33W	94
KNAGGS JOHN CHRISTOPHER	MI	01E	70
KNAKE LLOYD E	MN	33E	71
KNAPIC BERNARD RICHARD	OH	17W	67
KNAPP DAVID BRUCE	NY	57E	5
KNAPP FREDRIC WOODROW	NY	29E	11
KNAPP HERMAN LUDWIG	NJ	18E	80
KNAPP KENTON DON	CA	14E	44
KNAPP MARTIN C	WV	03E	82
KNAPP RICHARD	TX	21E	71
KNAPP RICHARD CHARLES	OH	14W	79
KNAPP TOMMY DUANE	IA	48E	6
KNAPPER EDWARD WILLIAM	IA	44W	10
KNARIAN DANIEL	MI	07E	89
KNAUS JOHN RICHARD	NJ	11W	125
KNAUS RICHARD A	NY	13E	84
KNAUS WILLIAM CAMPBELL	OH	25W	74
KNEBEL DONALD JOSEPH	IN	05W	8
KNEBEL THOMAS EDWARD	AR	65E	12
KNECHT ADAM DYCKMAN	NY	56E	26
KNECHT PAUL HERBERT	IL	14W	126
KNECHTGES MICHAEL ALLEN	IL	18W	129
KNEECE CHARLES LEROY	OH	36W	30
KNEELAND PAUL JAMES	NY	18W	108
KNEPP GLENN DONALD JR	PA	18E	60
KNEPP JACK DALE	CA	15W	5
KNEPPER WARREN ORISON JR	AZ	08E	86
KNETSAR GEORGE ARTHUR	TX	06W	132
KNEVELBAARD ANDY	CA	59W	24
KNICKERBOCKER IRWIN LEE	NY	40W	20
KNICKERBOCKER RICHARD J	OH	05W	8
KNIEPER PHILIP GEORGE JR	LA	12W	25
KNIFFIN ARNOLD DEAN	OK	01E	53
KNIGHT ALBERT S III	NY	02E	16
KNIGHT ALVIN COY	KY	55E	19
KNIGHT BILLY	GA	40W	21
KNIGHT BILLY MELTON	AZ	03E	66
KNIGHT BRYAN THEOTIS	NY	10W	18

NAME	STATE	PANEL NO.	LINE NO.
KNIGHT CARLOS LARUE	FL	57W	1
KNIGHT CHESTER WILFORD	CA	11E	102
KNIGHT CLAUDE ARTHUR	PA	15W	122
KNIGHT DAVID MARSHALL	MO	06E	66
KNIGHT HENRY CLAY	CA	40W	7
KNIGHT HUBERT CHARLES	FL	61E	12
KNIGHT JAMES ROY	NY	37W	22
KNIGHT JAMES WILLIAM	TN	07W	55
KNIGHT JOHN WALLACE	ME	35E	7
KNIGHT JOHNNIE DAVID	KY	35W	13
KNIGHT KEVIN PETER	NY	05W	88
KNIGHT LARRY COLEMAN	OK	12W	114
KNIGHT LARRY DALE	OR	11E	57
KNIGHT LARRY WILLIAM	IL	21E	28
KNIGHT MACK ARTHUR	AL	10E	71
KNIGHT MARTIN ROY	MI	40E	23
KNIGHT MICHAEL KAY	VA	17W	48
KNIGHT MICHAEL PERRY	OK	17E	68
KNIGHT ORVILLE LEE	MD	27W	39
KNIGHT PETER STANLEY	FL	10E	40
KNIGHT RALPH MAX	AL	25E	69
KNIGHT RAYMOND HENRY	IA	17E	44
KNIGHT RICHARD	SC	15E	62
KNIGHT RICHARD VINCENT JR	FL	04W	87
KNIGHT RICK LEE	OH	08E	15
KNIGHT ROBERT LOUIS JR	NH	27W	56
KNIGHT RONALD EUGENE	PA	21W	53
KNIGHT RONALD HAROLD	TN	17W	50
KNIGHT ROY ABNER JR	TX	20E	45
KNIGHT TERRY VASCAL	TX	04W	106
KNIGHT THOMAS WILFORD	TX	10E	83
KNIGHT TROY LEE	GA	15E	46
KNIGHT WALTER GRANT	WV	13E	9
KNIGHTEN JACKEY VAN	AL	14W	72
KNIGHTON ELI WHITNEY JR	FL	20W	40
KNIGHTON HIRAM J JR	IL	09E	98
KNIGHTON PAUL GORDON	WA	23E	12
KNIPPEL LARRY DON	NE	13W	122
KNIPPELBERG IRVIN DALE	ND	07E	87
KNIPPERS WILLARD RUSSELL	AR	25E	78
KNISELY ROBERT LEE JR	WV	42W	56
KNISLEY RANDALL C	VA	06W	7
KNITTLE HAROLD JOSEPH	NV	61W	3
KNOBLES JAMES LEONARD	TX	07W	56
KNOBLOCH CRAIG GEOFFREY	MI	38E	78
KNOBLOCK GLEN LESTER	TX	11W	74
KNOBLOCK JOSEPH M JR	NY	44E	27
KNOCH DENNIS RICHARD	OH	27W	1
KNOCHEL CHARLES ALLEN	IN	10E	132
KNOEFERL KENNETH JOSEPH	IL	29W	69
KNOLL ANTHONY	MO	68W	4
KNOLL RAY EDWARD	MI	23W	38
KNOLL ROBERT EDWIN	MI	42W	30
KNOLLMEYER MARK ALAN	WA	43W	38
KNOPF JOHN FRANCIS	NY	12E	6
KNOPIK THOMAS ALLISON	MN	06W	68
KNOPPERT ANDRE LOUIS	UT	25W	23
KNORR JOHN ROY	WI	55E	19
KNOSKY RONALD WAYNE	NJ	19E	119
KNOTT DAVID LLOYD	CA	15W	94
KNOTT DENNIS LEE	CA	48E	42
KNOTT DOUGLAS HUGH	OH	09E	41
KNOTT JOHN CHARLES	MN	08W	34
KNOTT KEITH ROBERT	NY	07E	43
KNOUSE DAVID WALTER	WI	42E	54
KNOWLES CHARLES MILFORD	TX	11W	64
KNOWLES DAVID DU WAYNE	WA	27E	20
KNOWLES JAMES D	FL	21W	76
KNOWLES KENNETH JOSEPH	KS	64E	16
KNOWLES NATHANIEL	GA	25E	2
KNOWLES WILLIE JR	FL	32E	11
KNOWLTON BURNS WINSHIP JR	ME	11E	8
KNOWLTON DON GLENN	MN	02E	127
KNOWLTON GEORGE FRANK	RI	30E	28
KNOWLTON PAUL DARYLL	MA	41E	10
KNOWLTON WAYNE HOWARD	LA	34W	33
KNOX BRUCE NEAL	WI	37E	24
KNOX DAVID	IL	58W	4
KNOX DAVID ALLEN	NC	39W	50
KNOX EDDIE L	TN	06E	15
KNOX IRVILLE J	MI	32E	76
KNOX JAMES RICHARD	WI	34W	50

NAME	STATE	PANEL NO.	LINE NO.
KNOX LARRY WAYNE	MO	29W	90
KNOX LEONARD WAYNE	IL	07W	99
KNOX MICHAEL JOSEPH	IL	03W	103
KNOX WILLIAM EDWARD	OH	68E	4
KNUCKEY THOMAS WILLIAM	NJ	03W	56
KNUDSEN HAROLD EUGENE JR	CA	10E	95
KNUDSEN JOHN HENRY	IL	13E	28
KNUDSON KENNETH MAX	MT	06E	15
KNUDTSON ROGER DOUGLAS	ND	33W	58
KNUPP WAYNE WOOD	SC	54W	24
KNUTH LAWRENCE DOUGLAS	FL	07E	9
KNUTSEN DONALD PAUL	NY	04W	67
KNUTSON DENNIS CLARK	SD	09E	69
KNUTSON EARL WILLIAM JR	WI	13E	79
KNUTSON FELIX DELANO	IL	18W	33
KNUTSON JAMES KEITH	CA	48W	18
KNUTSON LARRY LEE	MN	16E	21
KNUTSON RICHARD ARTHUR	MN	01W	109
KNUTSON ROBERT BRUCE	VA	06E	54
KNUTSON VERNON G	MN	32W	44
KOBAYASHI ROY SHIGERU	HI	04E	84
KOBELIN JOHN WILLIAM II	WY	30W	56
KOBERLEIN CHARLES ERNEST	NY	07W	121
KOBOR FRANK LOUIS	IL	21W	53
KOCAK JOHN ANTHONY	OH	36W	45
KOCANDA JERRY JOSEPH III	NE	24W	67
KOCH DALE ROY	NE	22E	89
KOCH DARRYL JAY	WI	18E	30
KOCH DENNIS EARL	PA	33W	15
KOCH EDWARD STEPHEN	MD	17W	91
KOCH FRANKLIN LEROY	IL	23W	9
KOCH JAMES ANTHONY	MN	40E	64
KOCH KENNETH EDWIN	NY	14W	75
KOCH KENNETH JOHN	NJ	07W	109
KOCH LAWRENCE GEORGE	NY	38W	67
KOCH RONALD LEE	MI	37E	60
KOCH THOMAS MICHAEL	IN	07E	113
KOCHENDORFER MICHAEL J	MN	04E	111
KOCHENSPARGER JOHN EDWARD	OH	07E	102
KOCHER LAWRENCE HENRY	NJ	48E	6
KOCIPER ANTONINE GEORGE	CT	07E	20
KOCK EUGENE JOHN GEORGE	IA	28W	12
KOCKRITZ JEFFRY LETSON	FL	03E	2
KOEBERNICK ALLAN FRED	MN	43W	69
KOEBKE JOHN LEE	MI	50E	49
KOEFOD RODGER MAGNUS	ID	26W	64
KOEHLER DAVID JAMES	NY	23W	62
KOEHLER JAMES KEVIN	CA	21E	89
KOEHLER JOHN FRANCIS	IN	26W	32
KOEHLER NICKOLAS RAY	IA	01E	112
KOEHLER ROBERT THOMAS	PA	11W	59
KOEHLER RONALD LEE	MN	04E	3
KOEHLER WALTER ALLEN	IL	29W	11
KOEHLER WILLIAM EDWIN	VA	61E	13
KOEHLER WILSON COUCH	CA	14W	116
KOEHN ARLIN WAYNE	OK	30W	26
KOEHN BRIAN ROBERT	WI	05W	25
KOEHNE RODNEY HOWARD	MD	49E	43
KOELL DICKIE DEAN JR	CA	29W	54
KOELPER DONALD EDWARD	IL	01E	43
KOENIG DAREN LEE	MO	27W	25
KOENIG DAVID BRUCE	MI	19E	27
KOENIG EDWIN LEE	WA	13E	45
KOENIG JOHN MICHAEL	CA	14W	90
KOENIG ROY ROBERT	NY	41W	25
KOEPP DENNIS EDWARD	IA	41W	18
KOEPPE WALTER JR	CA	30E	85
KOEPPEN ERIC R	MN	52W	15
KOERNER FRANK MICHAEL	WV	33W	15
KOERNER RODNEY LEE	IA	09W	96
KOESTER JOEL REDERICK	AZ	34E	22
KOFLER SIEGFRIED	CA	23E	43
KOGER SIDNEY KEITH	MO	10W	51
KOHANKE LANCE JACK	TX	60E	13
KOHL DANIEL KAYE	CO	12W	63
KOHLAND RICHARD GLEN	NY	29E	67
KOHLBECK TERRENCE EUGENE	WI	56E	11
KOHLBECK VICTOR JOSEPH	WI	05E	55
KOHLER DELVIN LEE	CO	17W	28
KOHLER JOEL R	TX	24E	52
KOHLER LUDWIG PETER	CA	02E	43
KOHLER PAUL JEROME	MI	64W	11

NAME	STATE	PANEL NO.	LINE NO.
KOHLER TERRY	MI	01W	63
KOHLMEIR GEORGE JOHN III	NY	47E	38
KOHLMYER FRANK JOSEPH	NJ	05W	117
KOHLRUSCH WILLIAM FREDERI	NY	06E	71
KOHN ALAN SPENCE	SC	46E	36
KOHN ROBERT A	FL	01W	91
KOHN WAYNE EDWARD	WA	38W	3
KOHO WILLIAM HARMON	OR	16E	79
KOHR PAUL THEODORE	OH	19E	38
KOHR WILBUR LINWOOD	PA	13E	110
KOHUT ROGER SCOTT	MI	16E	80
KOITZSCH RONALD NORMAN	WA	57E	26
KOIVUPALO ROBERT W JR	MI	42E	67
KOJETIN ROGER JOHN	MT	02W	95
KOKALIS NICK	WI	28E	92
KOKESH ANDREW FRANK	MN	22W	106
KOKOSH GEORGE GERALD	MN	58E	23
KOLAKOWSKI HENRY JR	MI	57W	26
KOLAR JERRY JOSEPH JR	IL	14E	49
KOLAROV MICHAEL CAREY	OH	45W	53
KOLAS ROBERT ALLEN	CA	24E	114
KOLB CALVIN WILLIAM	OR	13W	126
KOLB LEROY JR	AR	06E	95
KOLB RONALD VICTOR	DC	12W	82
KOLBECK FRANZ JOSEPH	IL	05E	106
KOLEMAINEN MICHAEL WALTER	CA	12E	1
KOLENC WILLIAM JOSEPH	PA	30W	66
KOLENDA PAUL MICHAEL	MA	41W	37
KOLIBA HERBERT	TX	60E	24
KOLINSKI THOMAS GEORGE	MN	44E	48
KOLKA EDWARD LOUIS	MI	42E	34
KOLLENBERG CHARLES LOUIS	TX	06W	93
KOLLER HAROLD JUNIOR	PA	10E	62
KOLLER MICHAEL JOSEPH	MN	27E	29
KOLLMANN GLENN EDWARD	CA	44E	27
KOLLMANN RICHARD LEON	IL	15E	46
KOLLMEYER CARL	MN	55E	19
KOLMSTAD RONNIE GENE	MN	24W	96
KOLSTAD THOMAS CARL	MN	11E	98
KOLTER BRUCE	OH	22W	66
KOLVEK MARK ANDREW	IN	38E	31
KOLWYCK JOHN A	TN	19W	69
KOLY ROBERT JAMES	OH	06W	88
KOLZ JOHN JORDAN	MO	09E	114
KOMAN LAWRENCE RYLAND	PA	47E	13
KOMAROWSKI PETER MARK	NY	14W	108
KOMERS JOHN GEORGE	CA	68E	4
KOMMENDANT AADO	NJ	09E	114
KONECNY JAMES FRANK	MN	59W	24
KONEVAL ARTHUR PAUL	NY	28W	99
KONG BRIAN WALLACE	HI	05W	125
KONIGSFELD PHILIP LORNE	AZ	47E	51
KONING DOUGLAS LEE	MI	14W	94
KONOFF KENNETH GLEN	OH	18E	15
KONOPA CARL RAYMOND	AZ	19E	108
KONOW MICHAEL JACOB	IL	01W	35
KONWINSKI RONALD EUGENE	NE	37E	60
KONYU WILLIAM MICHAEL	NJ	27W	97
KOOB JOHN PETER	NJ	36W	35
KOOB THOMAS JOHN	MN	29W	30
KOOI JAMES WILLARD	MI	21E	90
KOOMAN GARY ROGER	NY	24E	95
KOON ALBERT LEWIS	OH	24W	17
KOON CHARLES MARION	OH	10W	26
KOON GEORGE KENNETH	MD	30E	4
KOONCE JEFFREY WAYNE	NJ	30E	28
KOONCE MICHAEL EARL	TN	18W	83
KOONCE ROBERT EDMUND	CA	07W	5
KOONCE TERRY TRELOAR	TX	32E	57
KOONE JACK RUSSELL	MI	07E	114
KOONS DALE FRANCIS	OH	02W	92
KOONS MICHAEL BOMBERGER	PA	25E	16
KOONTZ NOBE RAY JR	MA	48W	33
KOOS NORMAN LAVERN	MI	09E	69
KOOSER KENNETH BRIAN	PA	23E	29
KOPACSKA JOHN CARL	NY	19E	61
KOPCINSKI STANLEY JOHN	NJ	07E	59
KOPEC EDWARD	IL	02E	58
KOPETSKI MICHAEL BENJAMIN	FL	55W	7
KOPFER JOHN JEROME	CA	40E	54
KOPFLER JOSEPH STARNS III	LA	09E	69
KOPIK EDWARD STANLEY	NY	07E	130
KOPKA RICK EDWARD	IL	05E	83
KOPKE ROGER JOSEPH	WI	16W	5
KOPP BARRY LORENZ	MI	29W	80
KOPP PATRICK DANIEL	MN	53W	36
KOPPEL REDLICK SIMS	TN	44W	3
KOPRIVA JOHN GAYLORD	IA	22W	112
KOPRIVNIKAR JAMES JOSEPH	PA	31E	99
KOPSENG JAMES CLAIRE	ND	24W	7
KORANDO OLIVER KASPER	IL	58E	10
KORB DONALD DUANE	SD	55W	15
KORDASIEWICZ HARRY JAY	NY	48E	29
KORDOSKY THOMAS JAMES	MN	14W	65
KORECKI EUGENE M	OH	37E	9
KOREL EMERY LOUIS	VA	21W	28
KORINEK JOHN CHARLES	NE	40W	21
KORNICK FERDINAND J JR	PA	35E	23
KORNOVICH FRANK DENNIS	CA	07E	2
KOROLZYK RALPH STANLEY	TX	06E	95
KOROM ALLAN JAMES	ND	07E	102
KORONA ALBERT III	NJ	20E	30
KORPICS ANTHONY FRANCIS	PA	12E	98
KORPISZ ANTHONY JOSEPH JR	MD	17E	45
KORSMYER GARY ROBERT	OR	45W	33
KORSON GERALD EDWARD	MI	57W	19
KORTESMAKI PATRICK LEO	MN	48W	27
KOS JOHN JAMES	OH	14W	118
KOS JOHN JOSEPH	IL	14W	69
KOSAKOWSKI GERALD ANTHONY	MI	03E	82
KOSANKE PAUL JON	IA	11W	68
KOSAR RICHARD DENNIS	IL	58E	10
KOSCHAL GREGORY ANDREW	OH	22E	78
KOSCHKE MICHAEL EDWARD	TX	04W	61
KOSEBA DENNIS WILLIAM	MI	43W	69
KOSEL GENE MARLOW	MN	34E	88
KOSIK JOSEPH III	AZ	24E	30
KOSKI GENE RAYMOND	MI	19W	16
KOSKI LARRY CHARLES	MN	31W	69
KOSKI RICHARD ARNE	MN	43E	57
KOSKO WALTER	VA	02E	44
KOSKOVICH MICHAEL L	MN	40E	8
KOSKY RICHARD ALLEN	IL	13E	64
KOSKY WALTER HENRY JR	CA	15W	94
KOSLOSKY HOWARD MARK	AK	17W	30
KOSLOSKY WALTER NORMAN	PA	35W	43
KOSOVICH GEORGE C JR	CT	03E	13
KOSOWSKI KENNETH JOSEPH	IL	08W	127
KOSS FREDERICK M	OH	01W	53
KOSSOWSKI DAVID STANLEY	WI	50W	36
KOSTANSKI STEPHEN FRANCIS	MA	30W	56
KOSTER ANTHONY ALBERT	VA	33W	57
KOSTER JOHN KNOWLES	RI	37W	66
KOSTER KENNETH LEROY	GA	15E	46
KOSTICH ROBERT BOZO JR	CA	15W	1
KOSTICK PAUL FRANCIS	PA	19W	113
KOSTKA ROGER JOSEPH	WI	10W	131
KOSTROSKI MARVIN DAVID	WI	10E	47
KOT MYRON	NE	38E	5
KOTARSKI VINCENT R JR	CA	06W	12
KOTEWA FLOYD WILLIAM JR	MI	03W	131
KOTIK ROBERT JOHN	PA	18E	123
KOTKE LEO LEROY	MI	34W	38
KOTNIK WILLIAM MAX	WI	06W	5
KOTORA JOHN LEWIS	OH	11W	92
KOTRC JAMES CARL	NE	20W	71
KOTROUS EUDELL LEO	NE	11W	55
KOTT STEPHEN JAY	SC	28E	104
KOTTYAN GEORGE EDWARD	MI	39W	1
KOTULLA MICHAEL JERRARD	IL	18E	19
KOTYLUK KENNETH EUGENE	CA	51E	47
KOUHNS DENNIS BEN	IA	35E	74
KOUPE GREGORY LANCE	OK	31W	7
KOVAC DAVID ALLAN	WV	04E	42
KOVACEVICH THOMAS JAMES	MI	47E	23
KOVACH PETER FRANK	NJ	46W	5
KOVACS FRANCIS STEVEN	PA	26W	21
KOVACS ZOLTAN ALAJOS	CA	02E	6
KOVAL ROBERT GARY	WV	25W	50
KOVALCSIK RICHARD	MI	29E	93
KOVALOFF JOSEPH THOMAS	HI	53E	3
KOVANDA JOHN MARTIN	IL	31E	4
KOVAR JAMES RUSSELL	IL	07E	30
KOVARIK FRED GEORGE	IL	12W	52
KOWAL BOHDAN	NJ	17E	124
KOWALCZYK CZESLAW	NH	03E	129
KOWALESKI GREGORY STANLEY	NJ	64E	6
KOWALEWSKI ZYGMUNT	DC	36W	30
KOWALK CHARLES NORBERT	IL	03W	46
KOWALSKI LEONARD J JR	MI	07W	58
KOWALSKI ROBERT ALLEN	MI	04E	92
KOWALSKI ROBERT JOSEPH	PA	39W	70
KOWITZ DAVID RALPH	MI	04W	128
KOWSKI EDWARD JOHN JR	IL	37E	60
KOYL HARRY GLENN	MI	56E	26
KOZACH JOHN ALBERT	MA	43E	24
KOZAI KENNETH BRUCE K	NM	15W	5
KOZAK DAVID MICHAEL	NJ	10W	18
KOZDRON CHESTER JOSEPH	MI	31W	51
KOZEL PATRICK CHARLES	CA	13E	18
KOZIK RAYMOND JIM	TX	34W	42
KOZIOL JOHN THOMAS	MI	30E	10
KOZLOWSKI JAMES MICHAEL	MD	07W	5
KOZMA CARL NOEL	NY	32W	79
KRAABEL JOHN SPAULDING	WA	20W	15
KRAEMER FRED CHRIS	MN	07W	11
KRAEMER MAURICE PETER JR	MI	17W	62
KRAFT DONALD RAY	WA	25W	103
KRAFT JERRY BERNARD	MO	17E	58
KRAFT LARRY WILLIAM	OH	41E	23
KRAFT MICHAEL ALBERT	NY	13E	131
KRAFT MICHAEL EUGENE	IN	17E	124
KRAFT NOAH MORRIS	FL	06E	33
KRAFT ROBERT LEO	ND	20W	98
KRAGE BRUCE HERBERT	MN	26E	26
KRAGE LANNY RAY	SD	18E	61
KRAJESKI STEPHEN EDWARD	MA	09W	47
KRAJEWSKI DONALD JOSEPH	CT	31W	94
KRALICK KENNETH DONALD	MD	32E	11
KRALIK WILLIAM JOHN	CA	49E	44
KRALL ROBERT WILSON	PA	11E	83
KRALOWSKI JAMES EDWARD	MI	54E	36
KRAM HAROLD ANDREW JR	MO	37E	37
KRAMER ARTHUR THEODORE JR	KY	54E	36
KRAMER DENNIS DALE	CA	20E	31
KRAMER DOUGLAS LEE	WI	16E	29
KRAMER HOWARD MORRIS	MD	13E	105
KRAMER JAMES LEE	NV	15E	33
KRAMER JOHN DAVID	MD	07E	109
KRAMER JOSEPH P	RI	18E	10
KRAMER KEVIN CLINTON	KS	04W	35
KRAMER LEON JOSEPH	NJ	01E	17
KRAMER RAYMOND EUGENE	ND	36E	76
KRAMER ROBERT DEAN	OH	14W	36
KRAMER STEPHEN ARTHUR	VA	14W	71
KRANER DAVID STANLEY	CA	01W	37
KRANSHAN TIMOTHY MICHAEL	OH	15E	74
KRANSI RONALD T	MI	41E	61
KRANTZ FRANKLIN JOSHUA JR	MD	09W	51
KRANZ WILLIAM FRANCIS JR	NY	14E	81
KRASHES HAROLD DAVID	NY	02W	99
KRASNOFF ARNOLD ROSS	NY	12E	102
KRATZBERG JIMMIE LYNN	MO	48W	6
KRAUHS CURTIS JOHN	IL	42W	56
KRAUS JEAN MASON	MO	08W	86
KRAUS KENNETH C	MN	09E	15
KRAUS ROBERT LEE	PA	04E	46
KRAUS RONALD CALVIN	IN	02E	51
KRAUSE KENNETH J	WA	26E	5
KRAUSE MANFRED WALTER	CA	45E	57
KRAUSE RUSSELL EMIL	MN	08E	3
KRAUSMAN EDWARD L	CA	45E	3
KRAUSS RONALD IRWIN	NY	01E	122
KRAUSS WALTER JOSEPH JR	NY	22E	7
KRAUSSER ALBERT OTTO	MD	29W	101
KRAVCHAK MICHAEL STEVEN	NJ	41E	50
KRAVITZ JAMES STEPHEN	CA	39E	73
KRAWCZYK EDWARD CHESTER	RI	55E	20
KRAWCZYK JAN	MA	27E	6
KRAXNER FRANK IMRE	NY	08W	75
KRAYNAK JAMES CLYDE	PA	48W	44
KREBS FRANK J	MI	14E	45
KREBS JOHN THOMAS JR	WI	09W	28
KREBS KENNETH MARTIN	OR	42E	35
KREBS LARRY EDWARD	MN	14W	78
KREBS STANLEY GENE	MO	17W	62

NAME	STATE	PANEL NO.	LINE NO.
KREBSBACH RONALD ALPHONSE	MN	10W	114
KREC FRANK	NY	42E	35
KRECH MELVIN THOMAS	MN	06E	89
KRECH STEVEN DENNIS	CA	39W	41
KRECKEL JOHN WILLIAM	WI	08W	43
KREGELOH DONALD RICHARD	FL	18W	89
KREGER PAUL DENIS	WA	02W	108
KREH GARY HAROLD	MI	19E	61
KREHBIEL KENNETH DILLARD	KS	28E	40
KREIDLER JOHN ROBERT	PA	16E	61
KREIS SHERWOOD DAVID	IL	42W	40
KREISHER SIDNEY GEORGE	PA	17E	99
KREITZER DAVID A	NH	31E	24
KREK PHILIP JAMES JR	UT	46E	36
KREKELBERG RAYMOND JOSEPH	MN	34W	49
KRELL ROBERT GAIL	IL	25W	74
KRELL ROYAL TINDORF	MO	13E	14
KREMER DONALD PAUL	IA	37W	23
KRESESKIE FRANK THOMAS JR	MA	14E	41
KRESHO STACY	PA	15W	18
KRESIC JOSEPH JR	WI	37W	12
KRESSE WOLFGANG EDWARD	NY	20E	1
KRETSCHMANN WOLFRAM J	GA	31W	7
KRETSINGER DONALD MAURICE	IL	29E	51
KRETZCHMAR PETER	PA	33E	14
KREUSCHER DONALD EDWARD	NY	29E	101
KREUTZ KENNETH JOSEPH	MO	22W	3
KREUZIGER ROBERT ALAN	WI	06E	90
KRICK DONALD WILLIAM JR	OH	17E	73
KRIDER JACK GALE	IN	40E	76
KRIDLER BERNIE CHARLE III	MI	27E	74
KRIEG RONALD JAMES	OK	03W	105
KRIEGEL PAUL HENRY	OH	10W	34
KRIEGER ELDON EUGENE	OK	19E	83
KRIEGER FRANK ANTHONY	NY	29W	101
KRIG DAVID LEE	KS	20E	3
KRILL BRIAN STUART	PA	51W	26
KRILL RUSSELL WALTER	CA	38E	54
KRIMONT NICHOLAS	VA	18E	19
KRINKE STEPHEN MATHEWS	MN	46W	15
KRISAN DAVID ANTHONY	IL	26E	112
KRISCHE JOHN DANIEL	NY	28E	26
KRISELL JAMES LEE	AZ	63E	13
KRISKOVICH RAYMOND GEORGE	MT	49W	42
KRISPIN THOMAS ALBERT	MN	26E	52
KRISSMAN RUDY PAUL	CA	52W	10
KRIST MATTHEW JOHN	CO	10E	24
KRISTJANSON WILLIAM DAVIS	ND	13W	58
KRISTOF PETER FRANK	MA	20W	124
KRITZ EUGENE RICHARD	WI	18E	15
KROBETZKY RAYMOND GEORGE	NY	46W	17
KROBOTH STANLEY NEAL	GA	01W	104
KROEGER JOHN CURTIS	GA	14W	53
KROEHLER KENNETH RICHARD	AZ	14W	53
KROGER NEIL A	IL	03E	59
KROGH RICHARD OTIS	WA	46W	30
KROGMAN ALVA RAY	WY	14E	45
KROH CARL FRED	PA	19W	31
KROISENBACHER ADOLF J		30W	66
KROL JOHN LEWIS	NY	43W	38
KROLIKOWSKI JAMES JOSEPH	PA	20W	124
KROLIKOWSKI RICHARD	MI	29E	96
KROLL ERNEST NICK	OR	26E	79
KROM KENNETH LIONEL	MD	48W	44
KROM MICHAEL LEE	CA	21W	94
KROMMENHOEK JEFFREY MARTI	IA	28E	68
KROMREY DENNIS JOHN	WI	41E	39
KRONBERG CHARLES AUGUST	MI	36E	20
KRONTHALER PAUL JOHN	NY	25W	12
KROPIDLOWSKI GERALD	WI	29E	11
KROPP GORDON GENE	MI	24E	81
KROS ROGER ALLEN	IN	30E	28
KROSHUS LEONARD JOSEPH	WA	07E	128
KROSKE HAROLD WILLIAM JR	NJ	32W	13
KROSSEN RICHARD MARVIN	MN	26E	66
KROTZER DONALD MORGAN	CA	30E	85
KROTZER LYNN ROBBIN	OH	29W	101
KROUS KENNETH WAYNE	NE	14E	70
KROUSE JAMES CHARLES	CA	27E	44
KROUSLIS JOHN DAVID	NY	36W	35
KRUEGER CHARLES WILLIAM	WI	21E	23
KRUEGER DAVID RUSSEL	IL	12W	13
KRUEGER DEAN WILBUR	WI	04W	80
KRUEGER DUNCAN FREDERICK	WI	03E	83
KRUEGER GEORGE THOMAS	IL	10E	15
KRUEGER GREGORY KEITH	ND	08W	24
KRUEGER JOHN KENNETH	NJ	17W	73
KRUEGER LORNE COLEMAN	CA	45E	23
KRUEGER RANDALL LEE	OH	18W	110
KRUEGER WAYNE DALE	WI	46E	36
KRUG LINWOOD BROOKS	MD	08E	120
KRUG MICHAEL JOE	NM	27E	34
KRUG RAYMOND HENRY JR	WI	10W	41
KRUG STEPHEN PAUL	CA	05W	38
KRUGER FREDERICK LYLE	MI	45E	35
KRUGER ROBERT HENRY JR	NJ	19E	27
KRUKEMYER KENNETH WARREN	OH	24W	86
KRUKOW ARDEN LEE	IA	34W	59
KRUKOWSKI EDWARD EUGENE	NY	02E	6
KRUKOWSKI EDWARD STEPHEN	NY	01E	69
KRULL JAMES LEE	MN	08W	3
KRUMBINE LEO FREDERICK	WI	05E	60
KRUMM RICHARD HENRY	MN	20E	9
KRUMM ROBERT CHARLES	NY	40E	65
KRUMREI DONALD ALAN	OK	08W	22
KRUPA FREDERICK	PA	03W	14
KRUPA RICHARD DIDACUS	IL	18W	7
KRUPINSKI FREDERICK JOSEP	NJ	50W	24
KRUPINSKI RAYMOND JOHN	PA	26E	85
KRUPKIN STEVEN HAROLD	CA	07W	96
KRUPSKI WALTER BENJAMIN	FL	63E	12
KRUSE DALE LYNN	WA	53E	16
KRUSE JAMES ARTHUR	IA	22W	14
KRUSE KENDAL ROBERT	IA	47E	1
KRUSE PAUL HARLAN	MN	17W	29
KRUSI PETER HERMAN	UT	29E	16
KRUSSOW DONALD JOHN	TX	51W	34
KRYSKE LEO NEAL	IN	46W	17
KRYSTOSZEK GERALD MICHAEL	IL	18E	61
KRYSZAK THEODORE EUGENE	NY	08E	3
KRZMARCIK JOHN EDWARD	WI	23W	102
KRZYNOWEK PAUL S	MA	31E	48
KSIAZEK BENNIE	IN	42E	18
KUAHIWINUI MOSES IWANE JR	HI	19W	95
KUBE JOSEPH BERNARD	WI	47E	51
KUBELUS ANTHONY GEORGE JR	PA	08W	100
KUBIAK LEONARD	IL	23E	87
KUBICA THOMAS MICHAEL	PA	39W	33
KUBIK KENNETH ARTHUR	FL	17W	105
KUBINCIAK ROBERT JOSEPH	NY	23E	29
KUBISKY EDWARD	NJ	34E	88
KUBLER GARRY LEE	CA	27W	109
KUBLEY ROY ROBERT	WI	14E	100
KUCAS STEPHEN THOMAS	PA	42E	19
KUCERA RICHARD RALPH	MT	31E	59
KUCHCINSKI RALPH WARREN	CA	43W	6
KUCHEK RICHARD MICHAEL	MI	60E	13
KUCHTA JOHN VINCENT	PA	33W	72
KUCICH JOHN ANDREW	NY	32W	60
KUCWAY ROBERT JOHN	MI	59W	25
KUCZEWSKI WILLIAM ROBERT	WI	39W	71
KUCZYNSKI DAVID EDWARD	MI	17W	77
KUDLACEK EDWIN ALLEN	NE	02W	29
KUDRO TERRENCE JOSEPH	OH	25E	69
KUEBEL ANDREW MICHAEL	CA	27W	56
KUEBLER CLIFFORD A JR	MI	41W	62
KUEFNER JOHN ALAN	MN	19W	40
KUEHL PAUL DAVID	WI	46E	56
KUEHN DUANE JOSEPH	IA	44W	65
KUEHN LLOYD MARTIN	MN	16E	46
KUERSTEN JEFFERY DAVID	CA	06W	120
KUFFEL CONRAD JOSEPH	MN	35W	71
KUGELMANN ROBERT CHARLES	NJ	31E	84
KUGLER TERRY GUS	AL	02W	76
KUHLENHOELTER JIMMY	KY	17W	18
KUHLMAN MELVIN ERNEST	NE	23E	20
KUHLMAN ROBERT JOHN JR	IN	34W	25
KUHLMANN CHARLES FREDERIC	CT	43W	63
KUHN ANDREW ALAN	PA	22W	14
KUHN CHARLES EDWARD JR	OH	22W	122
KUHN CLIFFORD MARTIN	IN	38W	27
KUHN DAVID JAMES	ND	24W	86
KUHN ROBERT WILLIAM	IL	13W	45
KUHNE WILLIAM	NY	16E	80
KUHNKE WILLIAM ANDREW	IL	16W	124
KUHNLY GERALD LOREN	WI	04E	43
KUHNS DAVID ALLEN	MA	17W	34
KUHNS DAVID PAUL	PA	10E	88
KUHNS KURT LLOYD	FL	26E	35
KUHNS VICTOR EUGENE	PA	11E	36
KUHNS WILLIAM JOSEPH	MO	22W	92
KUHSE MICHAEL DARRELL	AL	62E	7
KUICK STANLEY J	MI	01W	54
KUILAN WENCESLEO	PR	04E	92
KUILAN-OLIVERAS RAMON	PR	03E	83
KUIPER JOHN FREDERICK	NY	36E	76
KUJAWA DONALD LEE	WA	32W	49
KUJAWA LARRY FRANK	LA	34E	29
KUKOWSKI THOMAS	NJ	03W	38
KUKTELIONIS JOHN LEON	PA	09E	5
KUKURUDA ANDREW JOSEPH	PA	29W	38
KULACZ DONALD EDWARD	MA	47E	33
KULACZKOWSKI LESZEK A	NJ	16W	111
KULAVIK RICHARD MARVIN	MN	32W	49
KULBATSKI FRANCIS KENNETH	NJ	32W	38
KULHANEK ARNOLD JOHN	TX	09W	2
KULICKE FREDERICK W III	PA	32W	80
KULIK CASIMIR	MI	15W	51
KULIKOWSKI EDWARD JOSEPH	PA	14W	121
KULL JOSEPH JOHN JR	PA	45W	54
KULLAND BYRON KENT	ND	02W	127
KULM GERALD ALBERT	WA	11W	102
KULPA RICHARD WALTER	NY	30W	14
KULTGEN ALAN JOSEPH	MT	11W	36
KULWICKI RICHARD STANLEY	PA	05W	83
KUMMELL ROBERT MICHAEL	OK	39W	33
KUMMINGS JAMES ALBERT	IN	23W	65
KUNER ROBERT MARTIN JR	PA	09W	56
KUNEY JERRY DEAN	OH	04W	41
KUNF JOHN THOMAS JR	PA	34W	38
KUNKEL ALFRED HENRY JR	CA	21W	23
KUNKEL JOHN ROBERT	CA	35W	27
KUNKEL ROBERT H	MN	03E	68
KUNKLER HARRY GROVER III	MI	22W	22
KUNNA FREDERICK CARMEN	MI	16E	123
KUNSHIER GARY LEE	MN	41W	5
KUNSMAN LEONARD PAUL JR	MD	06W	103
KUNST GENE ARTHUR	MI	55E	20
KUNTZ GENE RAY	CA	33E	50
KUNTZ RICHARD LORRAINE	PA	37E	38
KUNZ ANTHONY EDMOND	TX	19E	38
KUNZLER DARYL ROY	CA	01W	32
KUPCHINSKAS PAUL NORMAN	NY	25W	40
KUPFERER JACK JOSEPH	IN	34E	78
KUPIEC THOMAS MARK	MI	36W	36
KUPKA ANTHONY EDWARD	MA	27W	95
KUPKOWSKI JOHN WALTER	NY	04W	11
KUPPERSCHMIDT JEROME DEAN	IL	59W	25
KUPREVICH WILLIAM ALAN	PA	13E	64
KURDELSKI JAMES HOWARD	IN	06E	117
KURELLA MICHAEL J	IN	39E	35
KURI JACK	DC	18E	114
KURILICH ROBERT VASO	CA	59W	25
KURLIN WAYNE CARLTON	FL	55E	20
KUROPAS MICHAEL VINCENT	IL	11W	7
KURTH JAMES PETER	WI	12W	25
KURTIK RAYMOND PAUL	PA	21W	76
KURTOWICZ JAMES DAVID	NY	22W	14
KURTTI STEPHEN WILLIAM	OR	56W	13
KURTYKA GEORGE ALBERT	CT	34W	27
KURTZ ALVIN EDWARD	MN	13E	35
KURTZ CHARLES JOHN	NJ	31W	69
KURTZ CHRISTOPHER LANDIS	CA	65E	12
KURTZ LLOYD NELSON	DC	16E	92
KURTZ ROBERT WARNER	IN	22E	62
KURZ DENNIS LEE	NE	33W	16
KURZ JOHN PETER	MN	31E	4
KURZ SIDNEY ALLEN	WI	06W	7
KUSCH WILLIAM HOWARD	OK	08W	100
KUSHMAUL ROBERT EDWARD JR	MI	16W	84
KUSHNER DANIEL KENT	FL	02W	134
KUSICK JOSEPH GEORGE	PA	29E	51
KUSILEK LAWRENCE ROBERT	MN	15E	46
KUSPIEL KENNETH EDWARD	NJ	36E	53
KUSS FLORIAN HENRY	ND	33E	50
KUSTABORDER RONALD LEE	PA	41E	23

NAME	STATE	PANEL NO.	LINE NO.
KUSTABORDER THOMAS WILLIA	PA	32W	32
KUSTER STEVEN MARK	SD	14W	114
KUSTIGIAN MICHAEL JOHN	MA	56E	11
KUSY DAVID PAUL	MA	28E	46
KUTCHEY LAWRENCE DAVID	MI	38W	59
KUTKOWSKI GREGORY MITCHEL	NJ	06W	7
KUTSCHBACH STEPHEN RAY	OH	33W	32
KUTZER FREDERICK ROBERT	PA	28W	47
KUVIK GENE LAWRENCE	AZ	35E	61
KUYKENDALL HENRY JOSEPH	CA	41W	53
KUYKENDALL RICHARD WAYNE	VA	09W	49
KUYKENDALL WILLIE CLYDE	MS	03W	133
KUZAK TERRENCE MICHAEL	PA	15W	90
KUZER DENNIS	PA	24E	52
KUZILLA DONALD G	MI	10W	41
KUZMA MARC JOHN	MA	52E	20
KUZMANKO ROBERT J	PA	09E	100
KVERNES ROGER WENDELL	SD	15W	119
KWORTNIK JOHN CHARLES	PA	09E	94
KYAR LARRY CLARENCE	MN	46E	56
KYLE BARRY STUART	MA	32E	64
KYLE DONALD CHARLES	FL	53W	44
KYLE THOMAS ROBERT JR	NJ	10E	22
KYRICOS GEORGE ARTHUR	MA	47W	47
KYSER DOUGLAS MASON	NY	09E	47
KYSER JOHN THOMAS	IL	09E	33
KYZER RAYMOND BERT	NY	38W	36
L'HUILLIER JOSEPH ANDRE	NY	50W	7
LA BARBER JAMES J	CA	15E	70
LA BARBERA RICHARD F	NY	08E	87
LA BARR EDWARD LYNN	NY	24E	31
LA BELLE KERMIT HAROLD JR	AK	24E	12
LA BIANCA MICHAEL	NY	25W	30
LA BOHN GARY RUSSELL	MI	37W	13
LA BOUNTY GENE ALFRED	NY	64E	6
LA BRECQUE PAUL E JR	RI	05E	132
LA BRECQUE WILLIAM F JR	CT	09E	28
LA BUDA ROBERT ALAN	IN	38E	31
LA BUNDY JOHN ARTHUR	IL	56W	13
LA CAGNINA RALPH VINCENT	FL	08W	62
LA CHANCE ARTHUR ELVIN	PA	11W	92
LA CHANCE CLIFFORD DAMON	MA	09E	109
LA CHAPELLE GARY GEORGE	OH	41W	5
LA CHICA JOHN N	CA	23W	28
LA CLEAR JAMES PHILLIP	MI	07E	53
LA COMBE ROBERT LEE	TX	17W	88
LA COSSE JIMMY JOHN	MI	38W	81
LA COST REGNOLD JOSEPH	MI	09W	84
LA COSTE MICHAEL THOMAS	NY	40E	42
LA COSTE THOMAS EMILE	LA	12W	52
LA COURSE DAVID ANTHONY	VT	26W	107
LA DAGE DENNIS ALLEN	IA	09W	76
LA DUKE JOHN HENRY	NJ	18E	53
LA DUKE REX ALFRED	WI	21E	69
LA FASO JOSEPH STEPHEN	NJ	03E	83
LA FAVE RUSSELL THOMAS	NH	12W	70
LA FEVRE DARREL EUGENE	OK	40W	65
LA FIELD WILLIAM TRUMAN JR	TX	04W	41
LA FLAIR RICHARD LEON	NY	24E	31
LA FLAMME ROBERT JAMES	MA	05W	42
LA FLEMME DELBERT CHARLES	OR	01E	65
LA FLEUR GERALD JOHN	IL	52W	36
LA FLEUR GREGORY L	LA	17W	37
LA FLEUR JAMES GEORGE	NY	63W	17
LA FLEUR ROBERT WAYNE	LA	18W	47
LA FOUNTAIN ROBERT ALAN	NY	46E	56
LA FRANCE JON PATRICK	KS	35W	5
LA GRAND WILLIAM JOHN	OR	02E	75
LA GRANGE LANCE	NY	54W	37
LA GRAY ERNEST JAMES	NY	16W	74
LA GRONE WILLIAM NAPOLEON	MS	19W	50
LA GROU RAYMOND LOUIS JR	CA	47W	47
LA HAYE JAMES DAVID	WI	01E	112
LA JEUNESSE DAVID LYNDALL	UT	61W	9
LA LAND GEORGE EUGENE	NY	26E	104
LA LONDE HARRY FRANK JR	OH	18W	95
LA LONE JAMES CLIFTON	MI	16E	95
LA MARR PHILLIPS	CA	06E	110
LA MORTE ARTHUR WILLIAM	MD	38E	31
LA NORE DENNIS ARNOLD	MI	09E	58
LA PISH ROY ROBERT	PA	16E	17
LA PLANT KURT ELTON	KS	59W	6
LA PLANTE WILLIAM ROY III	MN	55W	10
LA POINT LARRY JOHN	LA	48W	44
LA POINTE JOSEPH GUY JR	OH	23W	45
LA POINTE LARRY W	CO	39E	7
LA POINTE RAYMOND ROLAND	MA	26E	47
LA POLLA JOHN ANTHONY	NY	27W	88
LA PORT LEONARD OSCAR	NY	18E	94
LA PORTE BRUCE STEPHEN	MI	15E	66
LA PORTE MICHAEL LOUIS	CA	26E	1
LA ROCCA VINCENT MICHAEL	MI	14W	126
LA ROCCO ANTHONY	NY	41E	39
LA ROCHE JOEL MITCHELL	CA	47W	47
LA ROCHELLE MARCEL ADELAR	CA	61W	4
LA ROCK REXFORD ADELBERT	NY	11E	8
LA ROSA MARION DOMINIC	CA	07W	34
LA ROSE JOSEPH RHUBEN	NY	19E	28
LA ROUCHE JAMES MICHAEL	MI	35E	74
LA SALLE LAWRENCE LEE	DE	16E	102
LA SCOLA VALENTINO J JR	RI	10W	83
LA TELLE RONALD LON	OH	12E	121
LA TORRE EDGARDO RAFAEL	OH	19W	80
LA VIGNE STEVEN BRUCE	MI	56W	23
LA VOO JOHN ALLEN	CO	43W	39
LAAN JACOB CLARK	WA	30W	26
LABAHN DARWIN LYN	SD	23W	54
LABANISH GEORGE MICHAEL	PA	19W	102
LABAY JOSEPH STANLEY	IL	22W	41
LABBE ROBERT BERG	OH	05E	106
LABER MERLIN JAMES	ND	24W	8
LABOMBARD CLIFFORD GEORGE	NY	27W	89
LABONTE DONALD ARTHUR	MA	41E	68
LABONTE GARY LEE	TX	52W	45
LABONTE ROGER EDWARD	ME	13E	22
LABONTE ROLAND CHARLES	NH	26W	9
LABOUNTY CHARLES RICHARD	TX	04W	136
LABOWSKI LEONARD WILLIAM	CA	28W	37
LABOY JAIME	NY	05W	34
LABOY NEFTALE JOHN	NY	56W	35
LABRECQUE ROBERT WILLIAM	FL	18W	110
LACAEYSE LARRY GENE	WI	30W	46
LACEY DAVID MICHAEL	OH	26W	47
LACEY EDWARD GENE	LA	21E	5
LACEY FRANK JAY	UT	46W	5
LACEY FRANKLIN D	KS	46E	56
LACEY PETER JOSEPH III	HI	16W	106
LACEY RICHARD JOSEPH	PA	36E	20
LACEY WILLIAM GIRARD	PA	16E	46
LACHER MARTIN JAMES	PA	06E	80
LACHNEY FLOYD CAMILLE	LA	34E	78
LACKAS MONTY GILBERT	NE	28W	27
LACKEY BILLY JAY	OH	61W	14
LACKEY JACK VERNON JR	KS	21W	94
LACKEY KEITH BERNELL	IL	14W	38
LACKEY PHILLIP LANS	IN	57E	26
LACKEY ROBERT EDGAR	CA	36W	3
LACKEY VERNON HARVIC	AZ	39E	46
LACKLAND LUTHER JAMES	MI	22W	66
LACKNER MICHAEL ALEXANDER	NY	21W	125
LACKS CORNELIUS CLAYTON	VA	28E	2
LACROIX PAUL DOUGLAS	VT	06W	129
LACUS GEORGE DONALD JR	MA	28E	75
LACY TIMOTHY HOWARD	IN	05W	14
LADD ALBERT ALLEN	MI	27W	101
LADD GARY MELVIN	OR	17E	21
LADD LARRY ROBERT	IL	09W	71
LADD LEAMON RAY	IL	13E	45
LADELL JOE EARL	TX	36W	11
LADENSACK ROBERT JOSEPH	AZ	02W	76
LADEROUTE MICHAEL JOHN	MA	41E	23
LADEWIG MELVIN EARL	CO	46W	5
LADNER JAY WESLY	FL	13W	93
LADOUCEUR LANNY GUY	NY	10W	65
LADSON LAFON WINSTON	FL	33E	50
LAFAYETTE JERRY OWEN	WA	02W	25
LAFAYETTE JOHN WAYNE	VT	06E	90
LAFFERTY DAVID NELSON	AL	32E	76
LAFFERTY JOHN ARTHUR	NY	55W	29
LAFFERTY THOMAS LEE	MI	06W	113
LAFLER JOHN JAMES	MI	07W	17
LAFON VAL LYNDON	UT	35W	73
LAFOND ROLAND ROBERT	CT	54E	10
LAFRAMBOISE PHILLIP DOUGL	CA	42E	7
LAFRENIERE PAUL JOSEPH JR	FL	18W	103
LAFROMBOISE MICHAEL S	WA	23W	88
LAGERWALL HARRY ROY	NY	01W	100
LAGODZINSKI ROGER THOMAS	NY	10W	65
LAGRAND ROBERT HENRY	AL	04E	111
LAGUER JOSE ENRIQUE	NY	05E	120
LAGUNA MARIO MONTES	CA	34W	85
LAHNA GARY WILLIAM	CA	18W	40
LAHNER THOMAS ALLAN	WI	01W	19
LAHR CLYDE DAVID	MI	23W	75
LAHTI JAMES WALTER	MI	45W	20
LAIDLAW WILLIAM CLIVE	MA	02E	58
LAIDLER ERNEST HAMMOND	MA	07W	93
LAIER STEPHEN EUGENE	IN	05E	38
LAIL VERNON EUGENE JR	NC	30W	26
LAINE WAYNE KEVIN	CA	39W	1
LAIPPLE JOHN ELDEN	WA	59E	6
LAIR ELLIS EDWARD	PA	44W	3
LAIRD DANIEL REX	WY	17E	62
LAIRD ERVIN LEONARD	OH	14E	104
LAIRD JAMES ALAN	NE	06W	32
LAIRD JAMES BYRON	IA	05E	87
LAIRD JAMES EUGENE	TX	45E	62
LAIRD JAMES FRANKLIN M	MI	31W	51
LAIRD JERRY PROCTOR	NJ	34W	59
LAIRD PATRICK STEVEN	CA	41W	48
LAIRD RICHARD FRANCIS	NY	29E	32
LAIRD ROBERT L	VA	02E	22
LAIRD ROBERT MURRAY	NY	02W	106
LAIS ROBERT WALLACE	AL	47W	10
LAJEUNESSE CLEMENT FOSTER	NY	25E	74
LAJKO ROBERT DENNIS	MI	13E	85
LAKASZUS HELMUT GUSTAV	SC	36E	20
LAKE JAMES LEE	IL	59E	6
LAKE JOHN ROACH JR	FL	17W	29
LAKE JOHN W	IN	02E	70
LAKE LARRY VERNON	CA	02E	110
LAKE LLOYD DEAN	KS	04E	74
LAKE RONALD FRANCIS	MA	17E	99
LAKE RONALD LEE	CA	23E	20
LAKE RONALD ROY	IA	46E	8
LAKER CARL JOHN	FL	09W	60
LAKEY DONALD KAY	IA	12E	6
LAKEY GEORGE LEO	MO	45E	48
LAKEY HOWARD WALLACE	OK	20W	66
LAKEY JAMES ERVIN	NC	19E	61
LAKEY LARRY LEE	NV	10E	133
LAKIN JOHN HAYES	FL	24W	96
LAKIN RICHARD DENMAN	OH	34E	8
LAKIN ROGER ALAN	KS	12W	43
LAKINS JAMES EARL	IN	14W	40
LAKWA EDWARD JOHN	IL	07W	87
LALAN LARRY RALPH	WI	39W	44
LALICH DAVID HUGH	CA	58W	27
LALLAVE ALFRED	NY	30W	46
LALLY MICHAEL JOHN	MN	11W	132
LAMA EDWARD BARTHOLOMEW	IL	28W	99
LAMA IVARS	SC	10E	87
LAMANNA JOHN MICHAEL	NJ	33W	32
LAMAR MELVIN STETTINIUS	MS	51W	11
LAMAR WILLIAM ERNEST	MI	03W	136
LAMAR WILLIE JAMES	OH	47W	47
LAMARR WALTER LOREN	WI	31W	52
LAMAS RAUL RUBEN	TX	38E	78
LAMB BILLY WAYNE	FL	13E	72
LAMB BRICEY ELROD	GA	26E	56
LAMB COLIN EDWARD	ID	53W	2
LAMB DONALD CAROL JR	GA	11W	37
LAMB EDWARD ALAN	MD	33W	26
LAMB ELWIN JAY	MI	22E	83
LAMB FLOYD WATSEL JR	TN	11W	96
LAMB GARY GRANT	OR	18W	125
LAMB HOWARD SIDNEY	AL	04W	12
LAMB LARRY NESBIT	GA	15W	129
LAMB MICHAEL HUGH	CO	18E	11
LAMB THEODORE	FL	01E	85
LAMB THOMAS ROBERT	CA	46W	50
LAMB WILLIAM HENRY	NC	23E	87
LAMB WILLIAM LLOYD	VA	60E	24
LAMBDIN DANIEL ALVEY	VA	09E	48
LAMBDIN MARVIN DOUGLAS	IN	09W	28
LAMBERSON CARL EDWARD JR	NJ	21W	47

NAME	STATE	PANEL NO.	LINE NO.
LAMBERT CECIL WAYNE	OH	19W	16
LAMBERT DALE LEE	WA	51E	47
LAMBERT DENNIS MICHAEL	NY	17W	29
LAMBERT DONALD RAY	IL	15W	98
LAMBERT DOUGLAS JOSEPH	CO	18W	54
LAMBERT ELDON EUGENE	NC	19E	119
LAMBERT FRED DONALD	NC	32E	37
LAMBERT GARY RAMOND	NY	04E	111
LAMBERT HENRY RAYMOND	RI	17W	112
LAMBERT JAMES CALEB JR	OH	11E	83
LAMBERT JEFFREY EARL	CA	50E	30
LAMBERT JERRY WILLIAM	TX	03W	32
LAMBERT LARRY RAYMOND	NC	10E	87
LAMBERT LEE MATHEWS	FL	46E	53
LAMBERT STEVE NATHANIEL	AZ	38E	4
LAMBERT TIMOTHY	CO	34E	8
LAMBERT WALTER DENNIS	TX	06W	102
LAMBERT WILLIAM DAVID	NC	13E	19
LAMBERT WILLIAM GLENN	FL	51E	8
LAMBERTON GEORGE MAGEE II	GA	43E	46
LAMBERTSON PAUL BRUCE	CA	10W	72
LAMBIE JOHN ALOYSIUS JR	MD	14E	74
LAMBOOY JOHN PATRICK	NE	18W	114
LAMBORN KENNETH HOWARD	CA	09W	34
LAMBTON BENNIE RICHARD	IN	08E	47
LAMBY CHARLES MICHAEL	NY	28W	92
LAMEIRAS RICHARD ARTHUR	MA	30W	90
LAMELZA MARIO	PA	24W	104
LAMERE ANTHONY JOHN	NE	03W	96
LAMEY LAVERN MICHAEL	MI	30W	47
LAMITIE TYRONE FRANCIS	NY	37E	38
LAMKIN FREDDIE LEE	SC	39W	54
LAMKIN LEWIS DEAN	VA	68W	4
LAMKIN STUART BASSETT	UT	13W	105
LAMM CECIL DWIGHT	NC	30E	92
LAMM JONATHAN LEE	MD	14W	127
LAMMERS DONALD GARY	IA	46W	5
LAMMERS WILLIAM JOSEPH	OH	03W	66
LAMMEY LLOYD GENE	TN	40E	8
LAMN JAMES FRANKLIN	FL	15E	119
LAMON FRANCIS WILLIAM JR	PA	50E	30
LAMON ROY ALLEN	KS	52E	20
LAMON WILLIAM CHARLES JR	NJ	16E	93
LAMONT PETER ALAN	MI	17E	93
LAMOREUX EDWARD DONALD	CT	28W	37
LAMOTHE GEORGE ANDREW	VT	24W	17
LAMOURT-TOSADO PEDRO LUIS	PR	08E	105
LAMP ARNOLD WILLIAM JR	OH	27W	65
LAMPERT ARLYN LORANZ	IA	15W	51
LAMPHIER LARRY GENE	IA	36W	22
LAMPLEY JAMES JR	PA	31E	69
LAMPLEY LEON PARNELL	OH	02E	104
LAMPMAN KENNETH WAYNE	NY	16E	21
LAMPRECHT MARK AUGUST	AZ	34E	43
LAMS ALLEN JAMES	MI	15W	99
LAMUSGA MICHAEL ALAN	MN	03W	64
LANCASTER DAVID CLYDE	WA	04W	63
LANCASTER EDDIE LYNN	TX	32E	28
LANCASTER HERMAN JR	VA	07W	90
LANCASTER JERRY DAVID	TN	28E	26
LANCASTER JOHN MANNING	KY	50W	25
LANCASTER KENNETH RAY	MD	33E	29
LANCASTER RICHARD P JR	NY	05E	56
LANCASTER ROBERT WEST	RI	08W	127
LANCE ALFRED FRANK	NJ	46E	20
LANCE JOHN HENRY	SC	28E	83
LANCE LARRY GAY	NC	26E	36
LANCE SAMUEL STEPHEN	GA	11W	81
LANCTOT RICHARD LOUIS	RI	31W	52
LAND CHARLES DWAYNE	CO	16E	46
LAND DAVID ALDEN	KS	34W	2
LAND DAVID ALFRED	FL	21E	69
LAND FRED EMERY	FL	48W	44
LAND LARRY ADRIAN	TN	16E	29
LAND LARRY PAUL	MO	04W	87
LAND RICHARD LEON	MO	20E	31
LAND SYLVESTER	NJ	16E	93
LANDER MARK ROBERT	MI	20E	62
LANDERS BILLIE DWAINE	WA	10E	107
LANDERS BLAINE WILSON	MO	22E	14
LANDERS CHARLES FRANCIS	IL	56W	5
LANDERS DONALD FRANCIS	NY	45E	64
LANDERS EDMOND JOHN	CA	60E	24
LANDERS JACKY EUGENE	CA	19W	45
LANDERS KEITH TERRELL	MA	31W	8
LANDERS KENNETH JEFFERSON	FL	28E	13
LANDERS RICHARD RAY	CA	54E	10
LANDERS RONNIE RAY	IL	19E	73
LANDERSHEIM LARRIE JOHN	FL	10W	86
LANDES DREK ALLEN	CO	44E	38
LANDES VICTOR REID	WY	33W	87
LANDI GEORGE FRANCIS	NY	23W	111
LANDIS BRUCE RANDOLPH JR	WA	06E	39
LANDIS CHARLES DAVID	KY	01W	1
LANDIS CLAUDE BRUCE II	PA	17W	121
LANDIS DUANE GERALD	IN	19W	125
LANDKAMER MICHAEL GEORGE	OK	38W	67
LANDMAN THOMAS PAUL	VA	23W	102
LANDON GARY JOSEPH	CA	36E	77
LANDON VINCENT P	MI	36E	83
LANDON WILLIAM GREGORY	IL	20E	121
LANDOR JOHN JOSEPH	NY	27E	40
LANDRINGHAM ROBERT GEORGE	NY	02E	23
LANDRUM JAMES ALFORD	OK	20W	71
LANDRUM THOMAS WILLIAM	OH	16W	65
LANDRY EDDIE LEE	LA	02E	58
LANDRY HOWARD DENNIS	LA	11W	17
LANDRY JOHN PATRICK	TN	28W	71
LANDRY JOSEPH RONALD	LA	04E	135
LANDRY PAUL JOSEPH	MA	18E	113
LANDRY PETER JOSEPH	MA	06W	40
LANDRY ROBERT ANTHONY	TX	57E	5
LANDWEHR DUANE HENRY JR	MI	23W	88
LANE ALAN	MI	19E	108
LANE ALBERT LEROY JR	MI	08W	22
LANE ALLEN GEORGE	PA	06E	47
LANE AUSTIN CLIFFORD	OR	30W	26
LANE BOBBY RAY	NC	56W	24
LANE CHARLES JR	SD	25E	33
LANE DAVID ALAN	ME	04E	98
LANE DENNIS EUGENE	CA	41E	23
LANE DENNIS WILLIAM	NY	64E	16
LANE ERNEST EDWARD JR	KY	07E	82
LANE FAMOUS LEE	MO	06E	124
LANE GERALD BRUCE	AL	30W	47
LANE GLEN OLIVER	TX	66E	10
LANE GLENN MCARTHUR	WV	02E	135
LANE JAMES EVERETT	TX	01E	11
LANE JAMES JOSEPH JR	IL	22W	78
LANE JAMES THOMAS	NY	27E	48
LANE JOHN TIMOTHY	WA	54E	36
LANE LEONARD FRANCIS	IN	10E	120
LANE LOUIS MICHAEL	NY	49E	3
LANE MICHAEL D	FL	01W	127
LANE MICHAEL S	SC	37E	38
LANE MITCHELL SIM	NM	35W	35
LANE NORMAN EDWARD JR	TN	47E	2
LANE RICHARD ARTHUR	CA	56W	5
LANE ROBERT CARL	PA	04E	54
LANE ROBERT HARRISON JR	TN	12W	70
LANE ROGER LEROY	NE	54W	31
LANE SHARON ANN	OH	23W	112
LANE SIDNEY DANIEL JR	MA	18E	115
LANE STEPHEN LESLIE	MA	13W	93
LANE THOMAS	GA	45W	43
LANE THOMAS ALLEN	MI	20E	119
LANE WARREN CLIFFORD	MI	44E	12
LANELLI JACK DANIEL	CA	02E	70
LANEY BILLY RAY	FL	21E	48
LANEY JERRY WAYNE	NC	34W	8
LANG ANDREW ALPHONSO	VI	55W	29
LANG BENJAMIN GAINES	NC	03W	16
LANG CHARLES VANDERBILT	NJ	07W	58
LANG DAVID ROBERT	IL	50W	7
LANG DEAN LAVERNE	WA	46W	5
LANG ERNEST ALPHONSO	FL	48E	18
LANG JAMES FRANKLIN	MO	52E	39
LANG JAMES L	NJ	38W	2
LANG MAINOR DAVID JR	GA	47W	19
LANG MICKEY DANIEL	AK	03W	41
LANG TIMOTHY MICHAEL	WA	01E	27
LANG WALTER ROBIN	IL	66W	9
LANG WILLIAM OTTO	WI	44W	4
LANGAN LARRY MILTON	NE	19E	61
LANGAUNET BRUCE MAGNUS	MT	20W	72
LANGE CONRAD THOMAS	IL	21E	79
LANGE DEAN RICHARD	NE	18W	28
LANGE HANS DIETRICK	IL	21E	74
LANGE KARL FERDINAND	WI	15W	42
LANGE RICHARD ROSS	MI	02W	69
LANGENFELD CHARLES THOMAS	SD	50E	30
LANGENFELD CHRISTIAN ALAN	WI	35E	47
LANGENHORST HERBERT CYRIL	IL	41W	74
LANGER ALAN KARL	MA	34W	85
LANGER FREDERICK PETER	PA	05E	12
LANGER MICHAEL WALTER	WI	43E	8
LANGERIO MICHAEL LUKE	PA	26E	12
LANGFORD ALVIN HUGH	NJ	48W	57
LANGFORD JAMES MINTER	TX	47E	52
LANGFORD LEWIS NELSON	VA	41E	24
LANGFORD RICHARD HENRY	AR	01E	107
LANGFORD ROBERT CANDLER	GA	35E	33
LANGFORD ROGER LEO	FL	34W	25
LANGH THOMAS EARL	CA	44W	17
LANGHAM HENRY JR	MS	24E	3
LANGHAM HOLLAND IRWIN	TX	54E	28
LANGHAM WILLIAM C	IL	30E	78
LANGHORN GARFIELD M	NY	34W	9
LANGHORNE LENNART G	CA	05W	75
LANGLER STEPHEN DOUGLAS	MI	36W	3
LANGLEY BILLY GUINN	GA	32W	14
LANGLEY DAVID FRANCIS	DC	53W	17
LANGLEY FRANCIS LEE	AL	14E	10
LANGLEY JERRY RAY	PA	26W	100
LANGLEY JODY MAC	TX	18E	11
LANGLEY WASHINGTON MORRIS	FL	17W	29
LANGLEY WESTON JOSEPH	ME	30E	45
LANGLINAIS JACK PETE	LA	29E	41
LANGLOIS JAMES THOMAS	OH	10E	9
LANGMAN WILLIAM JAMES	OR	07W	95
LANGNEHS MICHAEL WILLIAM	KY	04W	7
LANGROCK DENNIS RAY	CA	39E	23
LANGSJOEN RICHARD CLAYTON	WA	29E	25
LANGSLOW ROBERT MALCOLM	CA	34W	77
LANGSTON EVERETT EUGENE	AR	06E	101
LANGSTON JIMMY LEE	CT	15E	119
LANGSTON JOHN ALAN	OK	37W	33
LANGSTON MARK MITCHELL	OR	37E	38
LANGSTON MELVIN DOYLE	NE	59W	6
LANGSTON MICHAEL GARY	MO	19E	43
LANGSTON ROBERT EBERT	FL	23W	75
LANGWORTHY JAMES SCOTT	WA	53W	2
LANHAM DONALD GENE	WV	19W	69
LANIER CHARLIE LOUIS	MI	04W	50
LANIER DAYTON WAYNE	NC	57E	26
LANIER FRANKLIN MONROE	NC	29W	21
LANIER JAMES ARTHUR	GA	54E	27
LANIER JAMES PERRY	IN	36E	20
LANIER JAMMIE JAY	NC	06E	113
LANIER JERRY DON	AR	23E	60
LANIER LEE ROY	NC	42E	35
LANING JOHN EDWARD	MI	19E	62
LANINGER LEON LAVERNE	PA	22W	98
LANKASTER JOHN THOMAS JR	IN	11W	8
LANKFORD BILLY EUGENE	TN	32E	57
LANKFORD CHARLES BERNARD	IL	01E	33
LANKFORD EVELYN FRANKLIN	MS	05W	111
LANKFORD HENRY DEAN	SC	05E	120
LANKFORD JOHN WAYNE	IL	52E	39
LANKFORD ROBERT MITCHELL	TX	01W	61
LANKFORD WALTER MERL JR	TX	25E	57
LANMAN THOMAS DESMOND	CO	26E	84
LANNES SHERMAN DAVID JR	LA	12W	127
LANNING DAVID ALAN	IN	33W	32
LANNING HAROLD JAY	NJ	02E	122
LANNING RONALD BARRY	MN	40E	24
LANNOM GARY KENNETH	MS	41E	39
LANNOM RICHARD CLIVE	TN	42E	19
LANNOM WADE ANDREW JR	OK	24E	31
LANNON JOSEPH JR	PA	42W	57
LANNOYE NICHOLAS PIERRE	MN	17W	63
LANO LAWRENCE	ME	28E	97
LANSDEN THOMAS JACK	OK	57E	5
LANSKI JOSEPH WALTER	PA	03E	129
LANTEIGNE ARTHUR	MI	23E	4
LANTER KENNETH WAYNE	OH	05E	51

NAME	STATE	PANEL NO.	LINE NO.
LANTER RAYMOND EDWARD	OH	44W	50
LANTER RODGER PAUL	IL	26W	47
LANTOS LESLIE JOHN	WY	47E	52
LANTRY MERRILL LAGENE	MI	02E	73
LANTZ CHARLES WESLEY	WV	16E	102
LANTZ CHRISTOPHER JOSEPH	OH	05E	47
LANTZ GARY LEE	MN	61E	13
LANTZ PETER J	FL	30E	71
LANZARIN LEONARD ALLAN	CA	06W	39
LANZONE MARCHELLA RAYMOND	NJ	12E	121
LAPAN GEORGE FRANCIS	MA	34W	15
LAPARDO ANTHONY N	NY	32E	1
LAPE DAVID ALEN	AK	30E	97
LAPES DONALD ARTHUR	NY	20W	15
LAPHAM ROBERT GRANTHAN	MI	38E	32
LAPIERRE EDWARD ARTHUR	RI	21E	98
LAPLANTE NOEL CHARLES	OH	04W	106
LAPORTE DAHL J	NY	05E	106
LAPP HERBERT	ND	08E	125
LAPP MELVIN CHARLES	CA	28E	75
LAPPIN DENNY RAY	OH	19W	17
LARA APIMENIO	CA	63W	18
LARA ARTURO MENDOZA	CA	32E	88
LARA CHEVO GARCIA	CA	09E	123
LARA HUMBERTO	IL	31E	21
LARA LARRY CALUISTUS	CA	39W	76
LARA SABINO JR	CA	05W	128
LARABEE BENJAMIN CARLTON	MI	36W	40
LARACUENTE ERNESTO LUIS	NY	16W	30
LARAWAY WILLIAM DEAN	IN	18E	15
LARCHER ROGER WILLIAM	MN	33E	38
LARGE BRUCE EDWARD	MI	23E	119
LARGE GARY RAY	CO	13W	112
LARGE GEORGE WAYNE	PA	58W	27
LARGENT JOHN ALYN	MI	10W	12
LARGENT LOEL FLOYD	TX	27W	52
LARGENT WILLIAM ALAN	WV	05W	83
LARGO CALVIN DAVID	NM	43W	39
LARIMER KEITH WAYNE	CA	22W	90
LARIMORE JOHN RICHARD	PA	38W	50
LARISON ROBERT WILBUR	ID	29E	4
LARKIN JOHN PATRICK	NY	45E	24
LARKIN SAMUEL JAMES	WA	10E	41
LARKIN THOMAS JOHN II	OH	10W	41
LARKIN WILLIAM RONALD	NY	33W	49
LARKINS CHARLES KENNETH	IN	32W	14
LARKINS VIRGIL LEE	IN	25W	40
LARMAN CHARLES WILLARD	MD	20E	46
LARMON TIMOTHY ELTON	CA	17W	102
LAROCHE ERNEST ALBERT	NH	05E	81
LAROCQUE LESLIE HOWARD	VT	38W	75
LARRABEE FLOYD MICHAEL	KS	17E	53
LARRABEE STEVEN MICHAEL	CA	04W	73
LARRAGA ANGELO GENTRY	MA	08W	86
LARREMORE PAUL WILLIAM	TX	17W	35
LARRICK RICHARD ALLEN	MI	42W	18
LARRY JOHN DAVIS JR	AL	64E	6
LARSEN CHRIS JOHN III	WA	54E	10
LARSEN FREDRICK ELLIS	WA	43E	8
LARSEN GARY ALVIN	SD	42E	53
LARSEN JIMMY LEE	UT	29W	70
LARSEN JOE PAUL	WA	20E	31
LARSEN MICHAEL CONRAD	MI	51W	12
LARSEN STEPHEN EARL	NV	23W	102
LARSEN TERRY LEE	IL	25W	50
LARSEN THOMAS CHARLES	WI	07W	46
LARSON ANDREW MARTIN	TN	37E	60
LARSON BRUCE STANLEY	NY	43W	39
LARSON DALE K	ID	39W	54
LARSON DAVID ALLEN	ND	13W	63
LARSON DAVID NEIL	NE	01W	62
LARSON DAVID WAYNE	NE	07W	111
LARSON DUANE CLIFFORD	MN	14W	99
LARSON EDWARD DAVID	MN	11E	62
LARSON FRED DUANE	SD	11W	46
LARSON GARY WAYNE	VA	05W	99
LARSON GERALD LEE	ND	14E	124
LARSON JAMES EDWARD	WI	28E	27
LARSON JEFFRY ARTHUR	CO	33E	19
LARSON JOHN GILBERT	ID	13E	102
LARSON LARRY JOSEPH	CA	17E	55
LARSON LAWRENCE DONALD	OR	17W	81

NAME	STATE	PANEL NO.	LINE NO.
LARSON LOREN HENRY	KS	22W	98
LARSON MARK ALLAN	IA	06W	77
LARSON MARVIN DEAN	SD	17W	67
LARSON PAUL NOBLE	WA	50E	49
LARSON PETER SWINNERTON	CA	17E	6
LARSON RANDOLPH LOUIS	WI	19W	3
LARSON RICHARD ANDREW	SD	10W	81
LARSON RICHARD KEMP	CA	20W	50
LARSON ROBERT DARREL	MN	01E	5
LARSON ROBERT JOHN	MN	31E	75
LARSON ROBERT MERCHANT	MA	03W	108
LARSON ROGNER ANDRE	WA	13E	53
LARSON RONALD JOE	MN	03W	22
LARSON TERRANCE HENRY	WY	27E	74
LARSON THOMAS LLOYD	IL	18W	123
LARSON VERLE NORMAN	MN	20W	98
LARSON WILLIAM FRANCIS	OR	17W	113
LARUE DONALD EDWARD JR	NY	02W	17
LAS HERMES PHILIPPE LUC	MD	13W	10
LASATER LUTHER MCKIND III	TX	02W	106
LASCELLES DON HARRISON	IL	23W	89
LASCHE JAMES ALAN	IA	14E	130
LASER JAMES DALE	AZ	34W	25
LASHER ERNEST REGINALD JR	NY	11W	92
LASHER RICHARD ALLEN	TX	25E	19
LASHINSKY STEPHEN M JR	PA	55E	20
LASITER LAWRENCE RAY	OK	22E	14
LASKAY DONALD THOMAS	OH	22W	122
LASKEY JOHN BENNIE	OK	08E	18
LASKIN FRANK HOWARD	DC	14E	36
LASKOWSKI ANTHONY JAMES	KS	40W	38
LASKOWSKI JOHN JOSEPH	MA	24W	44
LASLIE JOSEPH TAYLOR JR	GA	68W	4
LASSEN DAVID HENRY	NY	12W	70
LASSETER KENNETH RAY	AL	14W	112
LASSITER DAVID STEVEN	GA	48W	33
LASSITER HERMAN EARL	VA	29W	101
LASSITER JOHN ALFRED	LA	41E	24
LASSITER KENNEY EARL	PA	19W	17
LASSITER RICHARD LEON	VA	25W	6
LASSITER WILLIAM O III	IL	10W	7
LASSITTER JOHN IRVING	AL	06W	106
LAST DONALD ROY	WI	23E	43
LASTER ALVIN MACK JR	CA	51W	6
LASURE DANNY LEWIS	OH	36E	21
LASZLO JOSEPH	AZ	47E	2
LATANOWICH THOMAS DANIEL	MA	55W	7
LATESSA ANDRE ROLAND	MA	25E	12
LATHAM DANNY RICHARD	TX	15W	36
LATHAM MICHAEL TERRY	IN	63W	8
LATHAM THOMAS EUGENE	TN	25W	74
LATHAN GEORGE	NY	53E	5
LATHON JAMES	AR	01W	27
LATHROPE ROBERT M		03E	108
LATIMER CLARENCE ALBERT	SC	28W	91
LATIMER RICHARD ELI JR	OK	37W	23
LATIMER ROBERT NATHANIEL	IL	23W	112
LATIMER WILBUR DALE	AR	05W	55
LATIMER WILLIAM ROYCE	IL	18E	86
LATINI GERALD LEOPOLD	GA	31E	5
LATORIA DAVID JOSEPH	IL	60E	25
LATOUR CARL JOSEPH	NY	08E	87
LATOURETTE PAUL E	NJ	28E	43
LATRAILLE DAVID JOHN	ND	43E	24
LATSCH DAVID RUDOLPH	PA	43W	55
LATSHAW HARRY KENNETH	PA	43E	25
LATTA CHARLES R	AL	24E	95
LATTIMORE CHARLES JR	VA	18E	15
LATTIN JOHN H JR	OH	32E	5
LATTMAN DONALD WAYNE	MN	42E	53
LAU CORNELIUS AFAI LAULII	CA	16E	123
LAU HOI TIN	CA	37E	10
LAU JOEL THOMAS	MN	16W	13
LAUBACHER ROBERT FRANCIS	OH	24W	8
LAUBER ROBERT DEAN	IL	28W	82
LAUCHMAN MICHAEL ALAN	PA	08W	59
LAUCK ELMER DALE	WY	44E	18
LAUCK HARRY ELMER	WV	08W	16
LAUDERDALE ARTHUR LEON	OK	33E	71
LAUDERDALE RONALD GENE	CA	16W	65
LAUDICINA JAMES RAY	MI	26E	39
LAUER CHARLES ARTHUR	OH	37W	51

NAME	STATE	PANEL NO.	LINE NO.
LAUER CHARLES RUSSELL	CA	22E	7
LAUER JOSEPH EDWARD	NJ	62W	12
LAUER MICHAEL DENNIS	PA	28E	97
LAUFFER BILLY LANE	AZ	10E	129
LAUGERMAN LLOYD CHARLES	PA	14E	16
LAUGHLIN THOMAS JOHN	PA	12W	132
LAUGHLIN THOMAS WILLIAM	PA	37E	38
LAUINGER JOSEPH MARK	OK	14W	14
LAUREANO-LOPEZ ISMAEL	NY	32W	72
LAUREL DESIDERIO C JR	TX	22E	34
LAURENCE JOE ROBERT	AZ	42W	57
LAURENCE WILLIAM H JR	TX	07W	12
LAURIE MICHAEL J	FL	17E	79
LAURITSEN DAVID WAYNE	WA	17E	124
LAUSCH DARRELL E	MI	12E	89
LAUSE DALE MICHAEL	MI	27E	34
LAUTERIO MANUEL ALONZO	CA	01W	110
LAUTNER FRANCIS ANTHONY	MI	62W	12
LAUTZENHEISER MICHAEL	IN	02W	51
LAUX MICHAEL DEANE	WI	06E	49
LAUZON LAWRENCE JOHN	WV	27W	101
LAUZON ROBERT WILLIAM	RI	41E	68
LAVALLEE KARL JOSEPH	CT	03W	46
LAVALLEE MICHAEL EUGENE	MN	28E	55
LAVALLEE ROBERT C JR	RI	30E	29
LAVELLE JOHN JOSEPH	NJ	08W	66
LAVELLE PATRICK JAMES	CA	36E	77
LAVELLE TERRENCE MICHAEL	OH	25E	43
LAVENDER RICHARD ALLEN	AR	21W	43
LAVENDER ROBERT EDWARD	AL	18W	117
LAVEROCK PAUL STUART	OH	26W	91
LAVERTY STEVE L J	MI	05W	17
LAVERY GREGG EUGENE	NY	45E	24
LAVERY OWEN THOMAS	CA	02E	127
LAVEZZOLI PAUL RICHARD	FL	16W	121
LAVIGNE GERARD ANDRE	CA	47E	33
LAVIGNE JOSEPH EVERETT	CT	24E	55
LAVIGNE STEWART JAMES	VT	19W	69
LAVIN THOMAS PATRICK	IL	03E	136
LAVINE KENNETH ANTHONY JR	CT	31W	69
LAVISH JOHN LARRY	IL	24E	61
LAVITE ANTHONY III	LA	27W	101
LAVOIE CLARENCE ROSAIRE	CT	10W	104
LAVOIE GERALD HENRY	RI	57W	28
LAVOY EUGENE LOUIS JR	ND	16E	11
LAW BRENT ROBIN	MI	08W	38
LAW EUGENE	NJ	34E	45
LAW JAMES DOUGLAS	IN	16E	102
LAW JAMES NEWTON	WV	19E	38
LAW JERALD LEE	CA	53W	36
LAW ROBERT DAVID	TX	32W	77
LAW WILLIAM LARRY	KY	55W	14
LAWENDOWSKI JOHN JACOB	NY	28E	75
LAWFIELD GLENN ROBERT	MI	42W	48
LAWHON CHARLES R	MO	07E	34
LAWHON MICHAEL HOWARD	IN	19W	3
LAWHORNE DONNIE JACKSON	VA	47W	10
LAWING JAMES MACK	NC	41W	6
LAWING PAUL HENDERSON JR	NC	01W	42
LAWLER DANIEL H	NC	20E	62
LAWLER JOHN E JR	IL	13E	34
LAWLER THOMAS FREDERICK	FL	17W	5
LAWLESS THOMAS ALOYSIUS	NJ	12E	14
LAWLESS WILLIAM RALPH JR	SC	13E	127
LAWLOR JAMES V	IL	18E	86
LAWLOR PATRICK EUGENE	NJ	10W	121
LAWLOR ROBERT JAMES	CO	10E	68
LAWRENCE BERT OTTO	TX	02W	81
LAWRENCE BILLY EVERETT	FL	10W	98
LAWRENCE BOBBY GENE	CA	25W	103
LAWRENCE BOBBY JOE	KY	32E	54
LAWRENCE BRUCE EDWARD	NJ	53W	21
LAWRENCE CLYDE WESLEY JR	OK	10W	52
LAWRENCE DELMAR LEON	MT	47E	33
LAWRENCE DENNIS ROLAND	GA	29W	64
LAWRENCE EARL DAWSON	TX	29E	51
LAWRENCE ERNEST FREDERICK	CA	39E	62
LAWRENCE FRANCIS M JR	FL	17E	93
LAWRENCE GARRY FRANK	AL	37E	24
LAWRENCE GORDON LEE	MD	35E	7
LAWRENCE GREGORY PAUL	AL	41W	13
LAWRENCE JAMES LARRY	MO	27E	66

NAME	STATE	PANEL NO.	LINE NO.
LAWRENCE JAMES LOYD JR	NC	57W	1
LAWRENCE JOHN FRANKLIN	VA	26W	85
LAWRENCE JOHN ROBERT	OK	40E	65
LAWRENCE JOHN WINSLOW JR	NH	02W	17
LAWRENCE JOHNNIE LEE	TX	11E	40
LAWRENCE JOHNNY HAROLD	IL	04W	106
LAWRENCE LARRY EUGENE	GA	21E	62
LAWRENCE MICHAEL D	UT	45E	64
LAWRENCE MICHAEL JAMES	NJ	19W	113
LAWRENCE RICHARD ALFRED	MI	15E	39
LAWRENCE SEWALL KENT	NY	06W	40
LAWRENCE TORY DRAKE	CA	07W	73
LAWRENCE WILLIAM AUBREY	WV	50E	32
LAWRENZ DAROL EDWARD	MN	45W	37
LAWS BILLY WAYNE	MO	11E	22
LAWS DELMER LEE	MO	09E	87
LAWS DWIGHT WILLIE	PA	11E	130
LAWS ISAIAH JR	MS	36E	54
LAWS JERRY DEE	UT	02W	134
LAWS LONNIE CHARLES	NC	45W	20
LAWS RICHARD LEE	CA	06E	80
LAWSON ALBERT C	NJ	26E	27
LAWSON AMOS DAVID	OH	56W	24
LAWSON BIRDEN JEROME	NJ	24W	44
LAWSON BOYCE EUGENE	VA	01E	16
LAWSON CHAMP JACKSON JR	VA	03E	18
LAWSON DALLAS	TN	01E	89
LAWSON DANIEL W	CA	30W	47
LAWSON DARRYL DEAN SMITH		26E	79
LAWSON DONALD VICTOR JR	CA	18E	19
LAWSON DONNY RAY	WA	24W	86
LAWSON FREDDIE DON	KY	24E	71
LAWSON GARY DON	CA	48W	27
LAWSON GERRY WAYNE	MO	15E	9
LAWSON JAMES GARFIELD	VA	26E	47
LAWSON JESSE HUGH	WA	02E	8
LAWSON JOHN DAVID	MA	07W	31
LAWSON JOHNNIE CARL JR	TX	27E	1
LAWSON KARL WADE	IN	49E	3
LAWSON LAMAR ALVIS	SC	34E	22
LAWSON LARRY EDWARD	SC	01W	117
LAWSON LEO CHARLES	CA	09E	75
LAWSON MICHAEL CARTER	IA	05W	93
LAWSON MICHAEL LESTER	OR	16E	124
LAWSON RAYMOND CHRISTOPHE	VA	38E	54
LAWSON RODNEY JOHN	WI	44E	28
LAWSON ROGER DALE	OH	20W	15
LAWSON ROGER W	IN	12E	102
LAWSON RONNIE	KY	21W	24
LAWSON STANLEY GARFIELD	KY	43W	53
LAWSON THOMAS ANDREW	TN	04E	111
LAWSON THOMAS JUNIOR	KY	50E	40
LAWSON TOMMY ROSS	OK	22W	3
LAWSON WARREN STEPHEN	FL	07W	93
LAWSON WILLIAM CHARLES	CA	46W	17
LAWSON WILLIAM E	CA	26E	39
LAWSON WILLIAM EDWARD JR	MI	18E	53
LAWSON WILLIAM ROY	AZ	31W	8
LAWTON BILLY JAMES	SC	19E	83
LAWTON EDWARD LESTER	WY	42W	30
LAWTON MICHAEL EUGENE	NY	37W	17
LAWVER DENNIS D	SD	53E	35
LAWYER ALFRED LEWIS	NY	25W	74
LAXSON RICHARD DOUGLAS	TX	19W	45
LAY GENE WENDELL	GA	27E	39
LAY JOHN EARL	TN	04E	111
LAY MELVIN W	MO	19W	113
LAY ROGER MINETT	OH	35E	33
LAY WILLIE RAY	AL	43W	64
LAYAOU ERNEST E JR	OH	12E	67
LAYE EDGAR CARTHA JR	IL	52E	7
LAYFIELD DONALD EDWARD	OH	09W	69
LAYMAN ROBERT EMMETT JR	CT	24W	77
LAYMON MICHAEL DIGNON	NY	25E	75
LAYNE BOB RAYMOND	UT	22E	79
LAYNE DAVID DANIEL	VA	30W	66
LAYNE DILLARD RAY	TN	53W	2
LAYNE HOWARD WILSON JR	MO	08W	17
LAYNE THOMAS ELSWORTH JR	TN	32E	52
LAYNE VICTOR LEE	TX	57E	6
LAYPORTE OSCAR ROBERT	OH	06W	29
LAYTON CALVIN JEROME	MS	12W	97
LAYTON DONALD DEAN	SD	08W	82
LAYTON JAMES RICHARD	AL	01W	58
LAYTON JON WALTER III	OR	54W	6
LAYTON PATRICK ARTHUR	MO	65W	10
LAYTON ROBERT ALLEN JR	NJ	21W	54
LAYTON RONALD DEAN	CO	27W	11
LAYTON RONALD DEAN	CA	23W	89
LAYTON STEVEN JAMES	WI	53E	36
LAYTON WEBB HERMAN JR	SC	15W	37
LAZAR DANIEL STEPHEN	MI	07W	123
LAZAR GEORGE FEODRO	CA	08E	45
LAZARO ROBERT JAMES	NJ	27E	82
LAZAROVICH JOHN F JR	MA	31E	36
LAZARUS ROBERT LANI	HI	17W	63
LAZARUS SIDNEY GILBERT JR	SC	19W	40
LAZEAR ROBERT LEROY	WV	18E	30
LAZICKI JOSEPH CHARLES	SC	13W	74
LAZICKI RONALD WAYNE	TX	42W	48
LAZZAROTTO ALBERT LOUIS	IL	44W	26
LE BARS STEVEN	CA	10W	45
LE BEAU ANDREW ERNEST JR	NV	38E	78
LE BEAU DAVID ALLEN	OH	26E	36
LE BLANC ALFRED LEROY	LA	50E	16
LE BLANC ELOY FELIPE ESTE	CA	36E	77
LE BLANC FRANCIS JOSEPH	CT	46W	30
LE BLANC FRED JOSEPH	NJ	14W	94
LE BLANC GERALD THOMAS	LA	62E	7
LE BLOND DONALD CHESTER	CT	31W	69
LE BOEUF MICHAEL JAMES	LA	06W	17
LE BOMBARB LONNIE GUY	KS	38E	54
LE BOSQUET CHARLES R	WI	19W	87
LE BOUEF ELTON JR	LA	19E	119
LE BOUEF WILTON PAUL	LA	10E	25
LE BRON LUIS ANGEL	NJ	14W	81
LE BRUN LAWRENCE P	PA	08E	87
LE CASTRE KENNETH JOHN	NY	19E	73
LE CATES ROBERT BURTON	AL	03W	46
LE CLAIR PRENTICE DALE	OK	24E	96
LE CLAIR TIMOTHY KIM	MO	24W	55
LE CLAIR WILLIAM GEORGE	MA	33W	27
LE CLERC PERRY ANDRE	OR	11W	92
LE COMPTE JOHN AULT	NM	54W	31
LE COMPTE RUSSELL MARTINEZ		16W	3
LE DESMA LOUR	CA	51E	39
LE DONNE LAWRENCE JOSEPH	NJ	45E	27
LE DUC THOMAS GLEN	MN	51W	6
LE FEBER WAYNE ROBERT	WI	49E	3
LE FEBURE RONALD DEAN	FL	06W	78
LE FEVER DAVID BRAUCH	PA	26E	12
LE FEVRE BRIAN FRANCIS	IL	51W	19
LE GRAND JOSEPH DALLAS JR	LA	20E	119
LE GRAND WILLIAM FRANCIS	OH	01E	110
LE GROW ARTHUR RUSSELL JR	MA	14E	28
LE HOULLIER PAUL RAYMOND	NH	27W	19
LE LEAUX MICHAEL JAMES	LA	09W	53
LE MASTER MICHAEL EUGENE	TX	26W	110
LE MAY PAUL LOUIS	IN	02E	126
LE MAY RICHARD DRIGGS JR	CT	44W	38
LE MOND DOUGLAS ALAN	IN	17W	78
LE NOUE BRUCE VERNON	MN	17E	73
LE PARD DONALD GEORGE	MI	28W	48
LE ROY HOWARD LLOYD JR	WA	17E	123
LE ROY JEROME EDWARD	IL	04W	67
LE TOURNEAU JACK DATE	CA	01E	6
LE VAN MELVIN VERNON	IL	03W	86
LE VASSEUR JEROME F JR	MN	32E	24
LE VESQUE LEO WILLIAM	MA	04E	15
LE VESQUE STEVEN DOUGLAS	VT	15W	28
LE VIER DAVID JAMES	OH	41W	66
LEA FRED STANLEY	TN	17E	26
LEA ROBERT EDWARD	OH	52E	21
LEACH ANTHONY MICHAEL	WA	24E	31
LEACH DEAN KENT	NE	01W	28
LEACH DICKIE LYNN	CA	49W	31
LEACH DOUGLAS HORACE	GA	03E	59
LEACH EARL GENE	WV	15W	95
LEACH GARY P	OH	20W	58
LEACH JAMES ANDREW	CA	26W	40
LEACH JAMES EDWARD	MI	20W	11
LEACH JAMES KENNETH	MD	56W	5
LEACH JAMES WILLIS	MS	12E	85
LEACH KENNETH RAYMOND	CA	16W	23
LEACH LARRY KEITH	WV	18E	102
LEACH RAY ALLEN	WV	24E	105
LEACH RICHARD STEPHEN	OH	16W	58
LEACH ROY HAMILTON	GA	25E	69
LEACH STEVEN LAWRENCE	OH	33W	32
LEACH TERRY VIRGIL	IN	25E	86
LEACH WALTER DARYLE	WA	13E	1
LEACH WILLIAM EDWARD	IL	10W	86
LEADBETTER ROGER GORDON	CA	38E	69
LEAF JACK B	CO	02E	121
LEAF JAMES WILLIAM	MD	31W	8
LEAGUE ROY BARRY	GA	54E	36
LEAHY DANIEL MICHAEL	NH	27W	109
LEAHY JAMES ALEXANDER	WI	49W	31
LEAHY RICHARD JAMES	NY	30W	56
LEAHY ROBERT MICHAEL	NY	59W	25
LEAK JERRY DAY	OH	41E	68
LEAKE JOHNNY H	NY	04E	50
LEAKE RONALD JAMES JR	CA	35W	48
LEAL ARMANDO GARZA JR	TX	25E	103
LEAL CHRISFINO DENNIS	CA	50E	17
LEAL FERNANDO	TX	14E	112
LEAL FRANK DANIEL	CA	23E	101
LEAL GUADALUPE MENDOZA	TX	50W	43
LEAL JOHN BORGES	CA	12E	80
LEAL SALVADOR JR	CA	08W	52
LEAMEN ROBERT EDWARD	OR	30W	57
LEAMON LARRY DEWAYNE	TN	04W	67
LEAMON WILLIAM EUGENE	IA	36E	54
LEANIO HILARIO B JR	HI	15E	58
LEAP THOMAS EDWARD JR	IN	27W	45
LEAPHART HAROLD PAUL	SC	10E	107
LEAR RICHARD DAVID	PA	17W	97
LEARY GARY HOYT	NC	49E	53
LEARY JOHN DENNIS	NJ	26W	64
LEARY PAUL EDWARD JR	TX	05W	49
LEARY SOLOMON	GA	50W	30
LEASE RICHARD FRANKLYN	OH	07E	103
LEASE WILLIAM FREDERICK	CA	16W	106
LEASER ROGER RAY	IN	14W	19
LEASURE DELBERT LOUIS	OH	40E	76
LEASURE JOHN EDWARD	OH	16W	75
LEATHERBURY DAVID WARREN	TX	34E	37
LEATHERBURY LOUIS ANTHONY	DE	17E	37
LEATHERS CLIFFORD W JR	OK	22E	32
LEATHERWOOD JAMES	AL	28E	83
LEATHERWOOD WILLIAM E JR	AL	05E	42
LEATUTUFU FAGALII LAITA	CA	39W	41
LEAVELL MELVIN RANDOLPH	GA	43E	68
LEAVELL RICHARD TYRONE	IN	27W	19
LEAVER JOHN MURRAY JR	MA	01W	14
LEAZER ABBIE EUGENE	NC	21W	54
LEAZER TERRY FRANKLIN	IA	20E	96
LEBEAU LOREN DALLAS	SD	05W	71
LEBITZ STEPHEN JR	NY	23E	111
LEBOFF JOHNNY HANS	GA	28E	92
LEBRON-DOMENECH OMAR	PR	32E	1
LEBRON-LOPEZ ISMAEL	PR	07E	82
LEBRON-MALDONADO ROGELIO	PR	40W	33
LEBRUN ROBERT NORMAND	RI	04W	68
LECHAK FREDERICK JAMES	OH	21E	101
LECHUGA MARTIN	TX	27W	57
LECRONE PAUL ALBERT	PA	12W	114
LEDBETTER DAVID WAYNE	AL	47W	19
LEDBETTER JAMES RILEY	MO	44E	28
LEDBETTER LARRY DOUGLAS	CA	18W	69
LEDBETTER ROGER DALE	IL	33E	70
LEDBETTER SANFORD JAMES	AR	19W	125
LEDBETTER THOMAS ISAAC	FL	01E	54
LEDDEN TERRANCE EDWARD	WI	18W	40
LEDE ROY LEO	CA	55E	20
LEDEBUR MICHAEL T	WI	09E	99
LEDEGAR RUSSELL OLE	WI	16E	93
LEDERER ANTHONY JOSEPH	PA	34E	22
LEDERHAUS DONALD HERMAN	WI	13E	85
LEDERLE MICHAEL ALAN	MO	34W	70
LEDERMAN MELVIN	NY	15W	5
LEDESMA ENCARNACION	TX	13W	100
LEDESMA JOSEPH JR	CA	20E	62
LEDFORD ALVIE JUNIOR JR	OK	27W	75
LEDFORD DANNY	NC	42E	19
LEDFORD DON KENNETH	SC	68W	4

NAME	STATE	PANEL NO.	LINE NO.
LEDFORD HENRY ALVERSON	VA	53W	22
LEDFORD JAMES HARVEY	TN	60E	25
LEDFORD JEFFERY LEE	MI	09E	94
LEDFORD RAY DOUGLAS	NC	04E	92
LEDFORD STEVE DENNIS	LA	48E	53
LEDFORD VIRGIL MADISON	MO	17E	7
LEDGER GILBERT	AL	03W	100
LEDGERWOOD DAVID GAIL	FL	53E	3
LEDIN DANIEL BING	MN	22W	66
LEDIN JAMES LARS	WI	09E	24
LEDLIE DONALD RALPH	IA	11W	75
LEE ADREN ANDREW	NC	19W	95
LEE ALAN JAMES	LA	21E	95
LEE ALBERT EUGENE	OH	02W	107
LEE ALFRED	VA	20E	76
LEE ANTHONY IRVIN	GA	52W	6
LEE BENJAMIN IV	TN	06E	18
LEE BILL GREGORY	AZ	29W	90
LEE BILLIE LEWIS	IN	36E	21
LEE BILLY	SC	11E	62
LEE BOBBY EUGENE	NJ	40E	8
LEE CALVIN RAY	TX	58E	10
LEE CHARLES EDWIN	TX	58W	29
LEE CHARLES RICHARD	CA	23E	39
LEE CHARLES THOMAS	MD	43E	25
LEE CHARLIE FRANK	AL	42E	35
LEE CHESTER LLOYD	AR	06E	72
LEE CLYDE MARVIN	MN	31E	36
LEE DANIEL L	VA	42W	66
LEE DAVID	PA	26W	25
LEE DENNIS VARIS	AZ	33W	8
LEE DOM E	IN	44E	48
LEE DONALD GERALD	CA	49E	12
LEE DONALD LAMAR	FL	13E	34
LEE DOUGLAS WAYNE	NC	17E	53
LEE EDGAR	FL	33W	79
LEE EDWARD GILBERT	MA	59E	25
LEE EWELL JR	KY	18E	70
LEE FRED VINCENT	VA	21E	28
LEE GARRETT FLORIS	IL	03E	83
LEE GARY ELTON	MI	51W	41
LEE GENE FRANCIS	OH	31E	88
LEE GEORGE BLUE	AL	22E	25
LEE GEORGE JR	FL	43W	17
LEE GLENN HUNG NIN	HI	10W	109
LEE GUY EUGENE	OH	40E	43
LEE HAROLD EUGENE	TN	14E	112
LEE HENRY C	TX	17E	7
LEE HOMER HARDY	TX	44E	8
LEE HOMER VIRGIL	GA	10W	125
LEE HOWARD W	TX	38E	32
LEE HUBERT LEON JR	AR	11E	103
LEE JACK CHARLES	IN	22W	22
LEE JAMES ALLEN	CA	24W	8
LEE JAMES ANDREW	AZ	11E	112
LEE JAMES FRANKLIN	AL	12W	89
LEE JAMES GEORGE	CA	03E	2
LEE JAMES HOWARD	NY	20W	1
LEE JAMES MARVIN	IA	29W	54
LEE JAMES RICHARD	KY	59E	2
LEE JERRY DWAIN	TX	06E	39
LEE JERRY TYRUS	NC	25W	95
LEE JOE LEWIS	FL	25E	39
LEE JOHN ALEX	MI	17W	74
LEE JOHN F	NH	09E	1
LEE JOHN PATRICK	CA	22E	15
LEE JOHN RAYMOND	OR	27E	96
LEE JOHN ROBERT	NC	10E	107
LEE JOHNNIE GENE	MS	01E	14
LEE JOHNNY ANDREW	TN	19E	83
LEE KENNETH MAC	NC	30W	78
LEE LARRY EUGENE	OH	14E	117
LEE LEONARD MURRAY	VA	32E	76
LEE LOREN VICTOR	CA	48W	33
LEE MARION LEONARD JR	TX	06E	39
LEE MARZEL RAY	NY	22W	122
LEE MELVIN	SC	27W	25
LEE MICHAEL DURYEA	CA	54E	10
LEE MILAN LAVOY	IN	07W	73
LEE MILTON ARTHUR	TX	52E	21
LEE MOSES CALVIN	GA	07E	5
LEE NATE FRANCIS	PA	62E	7
LEE NATHAN LARRY	NC	03W	33
LEE NATHANAEL	TX	02E	24
LEE NED	AZ	38E	29
LEE PAUL EDGAR	CA	05W	69
LEE PAUL RICHARD	MA	04E	112
LEE PHILLIP LEWIS	OH	03W	80
LEE RALPH NORRIS	CA	02W	39
LEE RICHARD NORMAN	CA	03W	88
LEE ROBERT	AZ	04W	96
LEE ROBERT CHARLES	LA	50W	25
LEE ROBERT EDWARD	AK	05E	42
LEE ROBERT LIST JR	FL	30E	71
LEE ROBERT MICHAEL	IL	31W	8
LEE ROGER GAIL	OK	39E	49
LEE RONALD PAUL	TX	49W	54
LEE RONALD WAYNE	NC	11E	53
LEE ROY RONALD	NC	30E	57
LEE STEPHEN MICHAEL	IL	19E	109
LEE STEVE DONALD	IL	48W	13
LEE TRAVIS BERTRAND JR	GA	27W	101
LEE VINCENT BURKE	MA	16W	112
LEE WALTER CLARENCE	MO	37W	56
LEE WILLIAM	IN	24E	31
LEE WILLIAM ALLEN	TX	39E	62
LEE WILLIAM ROBERT	VA	36E	21
LEE WILLIE B	NM	44E	28
LEECH ROBERT VOYD	MO	09E	87
LEED CARL ROBERT	PA	42E	6
LEEDS CLYDE A	NJ	10E	65
LEEK THOMAS JR	MO	11E	123
LEEMAN ROBERT ALLAN	CA	43E	25
LEEMHUIS DONALD J	OK	13E	54
LEEPER WALLACE WILSON	CO	31E	24
LEER JOHN EDWARD	FL	05E	4
LEES PAUL ERIC	OH	14W	104
LEESER LEONARD CHARLES	NY	14W	75
LEET DAVID LEVERETT	WI	02W	136
LEETUN DAREL DEAN	ND	10E	107
LEFEBVRE RUDOLPH H JR	MA	09E	33
LEFEVER DOUGLAS PAUL	OH	16W	34
LEFEVRE BERNARD LOUIS	CA	13W	58
LEFFLER RICHARD JOHN	FL	15W	5
LEFFLER RUSSELL ALAN	FL	18E	35
LEFLER BERT DOUGLAS	KY	34E	78
LEFLER CLIFFORD JOHN T	OH	23W	102
LEFLER DAVID ALLEN	IA	25W	74
LEFTWICH RAYMOND FRANCIS	KS	16E	46
LEFTWICH WILLIAM GROOM JR	TN	06W	68
LEGA JAMES GREGORY	CA	14W	23
LEGAT WILLIAM CHARLES	CA	16W	6
LEGATE RICHARD EDWARD	FL	17E	45
LEGAUX MERLIN PHILIP	LA	11E	49
LEGER GERALD ROGER	MA	46E	8
LEGER MALCOLM FRANCIS	LA	23W	112
LEGERE EMILE JOSEPH	MA	23E	55
LEGETTE O'NEAL	NJ	03E	130
LEGG JOHN DUANE	AL	19E	6
LEGG ROGER DALE	WV	13W	112
LEGGETT ALBERT GRAY	NC	25E	52
LEGGETT FRANKLIN ONEIL	NC	48E	6
LEGLER STEVEN EDWARD	CA	27E	45
LEGLEU SAMUEL	AZ	30E	98
LEGRAND MILTON HARRIS	NC	12E	96
LEHECKA JOHN ARTHUR	MS	14W	23
LEHEW DONALD LEE	NJ	10E	48
LEHMAN DAVID JOHAN III	TX	36W	22
LEHMAN DENNIS RAY	PA	12E	102
LEHMAN JIMMY FRANCIS	OH	42E	53
LEHMAN MILLARD WESLEY	AZ	09E	7
LEHMAN NELSON SAYLER JR	IL	16E	36
LEHMAN PETER ALLEN	NY	23W	89
LEHMANN DERLYN REYNOLD	MN	05E	12
LEHMANN PETER BODO	MI	21E	106
LEHNHOFF EDWARD WILLIA JR	KS	30E	16
LEHR DAVID RICHARD	CA	40E	76
LEHRKE STANLEY LAWRENCE	CA	01W	45
LEHUTA DONALD ALEXANDER	MT	21E	106
LEIBA LAWRENCE E	NY	31E	30
LEICHLEITER THOMAS ALLEN	NE	18W	122
LEICHLITER VYRL EUGENE JR	VA	09W	39
LEICHT ROMAN HENRY	WI	28W	82
LEIF MICHAEL WAYNE	IL	15W	37
LEIGH JOEL MILLER	NC	37W	75
LEIGH LAWRENCE GRAHAM JR	MA	41E	40
LEIGH NEWELL FERRELL JR	GA	47W	29
LEIGH THOMAS ANTHONY JR	NY	48W	45
LEIGHTON EARL LA ROY	NE	34W	26
LEIGHTON GARY WILLIARD	PA	23W	15
LEIGHTON GREGORY A	NH	10E	72
LEIGHTON RAYMOND ELTON	ME	06E	33
LEIGHTON THEODORE RICHARD	MI	14W	72
LEIJA LOUIE ZAPATA	TX	23W	16
LEIJA MARIANO JR	MI	19E	97
LEIKAM NORMAN ALEXIUS	KS	02E	132
LEIMBACH LARRY KENNETH	CA	07W	2
LEINDECKER LARRY JAMES	WI	53E	16
LEINEN GREGORY MICHAEL	CA	33W	94
LEINO GLENN KARL	MD	31W	81
LEINO VERNON LEROY	MN	20E	62
LEIS JOHN EUGENE	WI	03W	83
LEISING BRUCE CHARLES	WI	29E	32
LEISURE JACKIE GLEN	NM	59E	7
LEISY ROBERT RONALD	WA	15W	18
LEITCH LARRY DUANE	MI	13W	71
LEJEUNE HORACE JOSEPH JR	LA	45W	37
LEJEUNE THOMAS MILTON	PA	01W	37
LEKOVISH DONALD F	IL	13E	39
LELAND LEROY JR	AL	56W	24
LEMA ANTHONY LEROY	CA	35W	71
LEMAIRE DOUGLAS JAMES	MA	34E	22
LEMASTER LARRY D	NE	22W	53
LEMBKE MELVIN DENNIS	ND	36W	4
LEMCKE DAVID EARL	NY	64E	16
LEMIEUX WALTER JOHN	MA	30W	90
LEMING CHARLES R	IN	18W	47
LEMLEY BILLY JOE	KS	17W	121
LEMLEY JIMMY DAVIS	OK	45W	54
LEMMON RICHARD KEITH	OH	27W	65
LEMMOND WALTER VANN III	NC	18W	117
LEMMONS BRIT P	TX	26E	48
LEMMONS WILLIAM E	ID	22E	7
LEMOINE WILLIAM FRANCIS	LA	42W	16
LEMON JAMES RICHARD	CO	30E	85
LEMON JEFFREY CHARLES	IL	03W	12
LEMON JOE LEE	AR	13E	54
LEMONS BOBBY JOE	TN	10W	65
LEMONS ROBERT LEE	WV	10W	26
LEMUS CHARLES RUIZ JR	CA	40W	65
LENARTOWICZ CHARLES	PA	10E	92
LENCHNER DAVID ALLEN	VA	36W	26
LENDERMAN WAYNE MORRIS	IL	17W	71
LENGYEL DAVID GEORGE	OH	38W	36
LENHARD HOWARD THOMAS	NY	17W	41
LENIO DALE JAMES	OH	19W	125
LENLEY JESSE LEE	MO	07W	73
LENNARD BENJAMIN EDWIN JR	PA	49E	53
LENNER JACK RONALD	OH	19E	38
LENNON FREDERICK WILLIAM	IA	11E	83
LENNON JERRY	NY	54E	36
LENNON MARK STEVEN	IN	26W	55
LENOIR EUGENE	LA	16W	70
LENOVER WILLIAM JOSEPH	IL	17E	62
LENTO STANLEY JOHN	ME	20W	40
LENTZ DAVID BURNETT	OR	19W	45
LENTZ DOUGLAS ALAN	FL	42E	7
LENTZ EDWARD MARTIN	AZ	42E	68
LENTZ JERRY FRANCIS	NE	48E	42
LENZ GERALD FRANCIS	IN	34E	88
LENZ JAMES WARREN	WI	09W	84
LENZ LEE NEWLUN	WA	09W	111
LENZ THOMAS WAYNE	TX	26W	26
LENZSCH ROLF FRED	NJ	22E	79
LEO THEODORE THOMAS	NY	43E	46
LEON DE JESUS EFRAIN	PR	21E	75
LEON FELIX JR	PR	45E	12
LEON GUERRERO KINNY SAN N	CA	54W	17
LEON MARIO ROBERT	WI	28W	82
LEON PEDRO JR	MO	16E	19
LEON WILLIAM	NY	09E	18
LEONARD ARNOLD LEE JR	CA	56W	5
LEONARD BILLY	FL	13E	49
LEONARD CHARLES RAYMOND	KY	23E	107
LEONARD CHARLIE MURPHY	TN	46W	50
LEONARD EDWARD N	CA	04E	93

NAME	STATE	PANEL NO.	LINE NO.
LEONARD HENRY THOMAS	NC	12E	55
LEONARD JAMES MICHAEL	OK	23W	28
LEONARD JAMES STEVEN	CT	20E	32
LEONARD JERRY SMITH	NC	39W	1
LEONARD JOHN CHARLES	VA	27W	65
LEONARD KENNETH EDWARD	PA	18W	89
LEONARD KENT ALAN	NM	18E	80
LEONARD LEROY EDWARD	MD	17E	30
LEONARD LISTON RAPHEAL	VI	13W	45
LEONARD MARVIN MAURICE	MI	05W	107
LEONARD MATTHEW	AL	15E	119
LEONARD OLIN JENNES	NC	13W	118
LEONARD PAUL AUSTIN	MD	30E	101
LEONARD RICHARD JAMES	WI	08W	88
LEONARD ROBERT BRUCE	IA	17W	29
LEONARD RONALD FRED	NC	12W	26
LEONARD SIDNEY LAMAR	AL	38E	64
LEONARD WILLIAM	MA	14W	33
LEONARDI JERRY LEE	IA	09E	15
LEONARDIS STEPHEN WILLIAM	NJ	48W	27
LEONBERG ROBERT CHARLES	PA	24E	32
LEONE JOHN FRANK	NY	18E	109
LEONOR LEONARDO CAPISTRAN	NY	01W	81
LEOPARD JACK DAVID	OK	11W	102
LEOPOLD FREDERICK ERIC	PA	13W	45
LEOPOLD LESTER HAROLD	IL	18W	48
LEOPOLDINO LARRY GENE	HI	26W	48
LEOS LEONARDO	TX	20E	31
LEOS NARCISO JR	TX	35E	61
LEPAGE REYNALD GERARD	ME	20E	104
LEPAK DONALD CHESTER	WI	37W	13
LEPPKE LYLE GORDON	MN	20W	98
LEPTRONE FRANK	MI	33W	16
LERCH EARL ROGER	CA	60W	10
LERCH JOHN CHRISTIAN JR	NY	30E	85
LERMA GERONIMO	AZ	53W	28
LERMA GUADALUPE	TX	57W	28
LERMAN CONRAD	NM	58W	27
LERNER DAVID ATWOOD	VA	16W	100
LERNER IRWIN STUART	CT	01W	97
LERNER ROBERT HENRY	MD	10E	58
LESAGE ARMAND PAUL	VT	48E	42
LESAINE JIMMY WILSON	SC	34W	50
LESANDO NICHOLAS PETER JR	NY	42W	19
LESCARBEAU GEORGE GERALD	CT	39E	62
LESH TERRY LEE	PA	24W	17
LESHEN LEE MYRL		13W	1
LESKA ROBERT JOHN	CT	55E	21
LESKY CHRISTOPHER ALLAN	MI	25E	30
LESLIE PHILLIP WILLARD	NY	25E	59
LESLIE ROGER LAMAR	AL	09E	2
LESLIE WENDELL WAYNE	HI	26W	64
LESNIK WILLIAM ELGIE	PA	28E	61
LESS RANDALL PATRICK	MI	43W	64
LESS REUBEN ANTHONY	NY	10W	90
LESSEG JAMES ALFRED	OR	44E	9
LESSIG DANIEL KEPNER	PA	01E	29
LESTAGE WILLIAM FRED	VT	33W	50
LESTELLE JOHN ANDREW II	CA	29W	62
LESTER EARL ROY JR	OK	03W	75
LESTER EDWARD	WV	52W	6
LESTER GRADY RUDOLPH JR	VA	11W	86
LESTER JAMES LEROY JR	VA	19E	62
LESTER JAMES ROBERT	CA	22E	84
LESTER JAMES THOMAS	GA	08E	81
LESTER JIMMY DON	MO	27W	92
LESTER RODERICK BARNUM	WA	01W	68
LESTER THOMAS LYNN	IL	20E	62
LESTER WILLIAM WAYNE	WV	40W	21
LESTON THOMAS JEROME	IL	17E	117
LESURE ERNEST ESTELL	NY	49E	44
LESZCZYNSKI WITOLD JOHN	NY	30E	29
LETA DONALD	NJ	39E	22
LETBETTER BOBBY WELDON	TX	12E	102
LETCHWORTH EDWARD NORMAN	MT	15E	106
LETENDRE GERALD ARTHUR	MA	06E	51
LETENDRE RICHARD EDWARD	NH	41W	13
LETMATE GEORGE CAROLL	MD	54E	37
LETOURNEAU EDWARD R JR	MA	07E	14
LETSCH ROBERT DONALD JR	IA	52W	45
LETSON GARY WAYNE	CA	22W	79
LETTERMAN LAWRENCE ALLEN	WA	29E	90
LETTO ROGER WILLIAM	IL	44E	48
LEUNING VERNON LEE	WA	42E	68
LEUTENEGGER JOE CARL	IL	22E	107
LEUTHOLD DONALD FREDERICK	MO	08E	11
LEVAN ALVIN LEE	PA	11E	106
LEVANG CLEO LARRY	ND	13E	116
LEVATO FRANK	NY	21W	76
LEVENDIS WILLIAM MCNAMARA	VA	68W	5
LEVERING EDWIN HARRY	NJ	06E	101
LEVESQUE GEORGE ROBERT	MA	29W	30
LEVESQUE J B L	ME	28W	48
LEVESQUE ROLAND PHILLIP	CT	40E	65
LEVETT WILLIAM JAMES	CA	31W	37
LEVI LANE FATUTOA	47	11W	86
LEVICKIS EUGENE JAMES	IL	05W	59
LEVIN ROBERT PHILLIP	CA	31W	81
LEVINE ROBERT	NY	32E	1
LEVINGS JAMES M	ND	66E	10
LEVINGSTON JAMES ARTHUR	TX	07E	10
LEVINS FREDERICK RICHARD	FL	09W	57
LEVINSON JAY BARRY	NY	34W	71
LEVINTHOL JOHN JR	HI	47E	2
LEVIS CHARLES ALLEN	TX	02W	128
LEVIS DENNIS RICHARD	IA	08W	36
LEVULIS JOHN JOSEPH	NY	05W	128
LEVY BRUCE	NY	62E	19
LEVY GERALD	CT	04E	50
LEVY NORMAN STANLEY	NY	11E	112
LEVY WALTER NEVILLE	NY	02E	87
LEW SAI GIN	CA	06W	108
LEW VICTOR WALTER	CA	03W	99
LEW VINCENT GENE	CA	29W	11
LEWALLEN JACKIE LEE	KS	13W	45
LEWANDOWSKI LEONARD J JR	IL	11E	90
LEWANDOWSKY STANLEY ROBER	MI	43W	55
LEWELLEN WALTER EDWARD	IN	05W	117
LEWELLIN LAWRENCE FRANK	MN	18E	75
LEWER THOMAS CHARLES	MN	38E	32
LEWICKI STEVE WILLIAM	IN	39E	7
LEWIS ADRON LEE	CA	22W	122
LEWIS AL RICKEY	TN	68E	4
LEWIS ALFRED JOHN	MI	36E	2
LEWIS ALLEN LANUI	HI	22W	3
LEWIS ALLEN WAYNE	CA	56W	13
LEWIS ANDREW LEON	MD	08W	79
LEWIS ARTHUR	VA	18W	110
LEWIS ARTHUR EUGENE	OR	07E	72
LEWIS BARRY WAYNE	OH	57E	26
LEWIS BENJAMIN F JR	NJ	22W	33
LEWIS BENNY JOE	OK	62E	20
LEWIS BOBBY DWIGHT	TN	37W	33
LEWIS CALVIN	CA	35W	43
LEWIS CHARLES ALBERT JR	OH	03W	24
LEWIS CHARLES EDWARD	TX	27E	60
LEWIS CHARLES HUGH JR	MD	13E	34
LEWIS CHARLES RATES	KY	15E	48
LEWIS CHARLIE GRAY	NC	01E	121
LEWIS CLARENCE HENRY	LA	44E	63
LEWIS CLARENCE PAUL	KS	01W	28
LEWIS CONVERSE RISING III	TX	28E	75
LEWIS DANIEL	LA	20W	72
LEWIS DARREL GENE	TX	42E	68
LEWIS DAVID	OH	19W	62
LEWIS DAVID HARRY	OH	40E	24
LEWIS DAVID MARION	OR	28E	52
LEWIS DELBERT O	OH	32E	58
LEWIS DON ROBERT	FL	01E	87
LEWIS DONALD ALLEN	KS	10E	48
LEWIS DONALD GENE	NE	38W	58
LEWIS DONALD RANDELL	KY	31W	52
LEWIS DONNIE GORDON	OK	60E	14
LEWIS EARL LEROY	TX	32E	77
LEWIS EARL LLOYD	WA	29W	102
LEWIS ELTON WILLIAM	LA	07W	49
LEWIS ERIC OAKLEY	NY	14W	94
LEWIS FLETCHER LEON	VA	36E	4
LEWIS FRANK FREDERICK	MO	11W	115
LEWIS FRANKLIN CHARLES	NY	19E	53
LEWIS FREDDIE	LA	48W	6
LEWIS FREDERICK HARRY	TX	11E	87
LEWIS GARY	NY	05W	83
LEWIS GARY FRANKLIN	PA	04E	50
LEWIS GARY LEE	IA	44W	50
LEWIS GARY LYNN	CT	03W	95
LEWIS GRADY LEONARD	AL	16W	106
LEWIS HAROLD ST CLAIR	CA	31W	37
LEWIS HARRY JR	IL	05W	22
LEWIS HARVEY LEDREW	NC	10E	92
LEWIS JAMES C RALPH	CA	36W	16
LEWIS JAMES EARL	RI	26E	27
LEWIS JAMES FREDERICK	OH	60W	11
LEWIS JAMES HAROLD	VA	04E	9
LEWIS JAMES ROBBINS JR	FL	37W	57
LEWIS JAMES ROBERT	CA	23W	28
LEWIS JAMES WIMBERLEY	TX	01E	102
LEWIS JERRY D	OK	06E	15
LEWIS JESSIE ROY	KS	20W	7
LEWIS JIMMIE	SC	22E	107
LEWIS JOE	FL	23E	101
LEWIS JOHN EDWIN	CA	27W	95
LEWIS JOHN FREDERICK	IL	39E	73
LEWIS JOHN STEPHEN	CA	23W	103
LEWIS JOHN WESLEY JR	PA	04E	71
LEWIS JOHNNY ELMER	FL	17E	112
LEWIS JOSEPH ANTHONY	CA	29W	11
LEWIS KENNETH JERNIGAN	LA	32W	44
LEWIS LARRY GENE	NC	04W	8
LEWIS LAWRENCE EDWARD	KY	19E	97
LEWIS LEE	SC	15E	47
LEWIS LEONARD LEROY	MO	23W	38
LEWIS LESLIE A	TX	38W	43
LEWIS LESLIE ROSS	IL	41E	24
LEWIS MERRILL RAYMOND JR	IA	09E	48
LEWIS MICHAEL	IN	10E	26
LEWIS MICHAEL KEITH	IA	22W	41
LEWIS MICHAEL LEE	TX	19W	45
LEWIS MICHAEL LOUIS JR	NY	54W	17
LEWIS MOSES JOHN	NY	33E	9
LEWIS NATHANIEL	GA	06W	26
LEWIS OTIS	LA	15E	14
LEWIS PAUL	NY	68E	2
LEWIS RAYMOND ROY	WI	40E	8
LEWIS RICHARD EUGENE	CA	32E	77
LEWIS RICHARD GARY	NJ	55E	21
LEWIS RICHARD KENNETH	MI	20W	87
LEWIS ROBERT ALAN	GA	21W	54
LEWIS ROBERT DEAN	IN	25W	75
LEWIS ROBERT LEE	VA	03E	59
LEWIS ROBERT RAYMOND	VA	11W	50
LEWIS ROBERT RUSSELL	SD	34E	21
LEWIS RODGER DALE	CA	15E	96
LEWIS ROGER CHARLES	MN	25E	24
LEWIS ROGER DALE	OH	32W	35
LEWIS RONALD EUGENE	MO	01E	9
LEWIS RONALD EUGENE	IL	11E	45
LEWIS RONALD KEITH	CA	49W	5
LEWIS RONALD WILLIAM	DC	43W	47
LEWIS ROY ROBERT	AR	14W	27
LEWIS SINCLAIR BYRON JR	IL	25W	6
LEWIS STANLEY	PA	36E	22
LEWIS STEPHEN HERMAN	TX	53W	37
LEWIS STEPHEN MIX	CA	27W	57
LEWIS STEVEN	FL	55E	21
LEWIS TEDD MCCLUNE	TX	14W	19
LEWIS THOMAS	TN	03E	121
LEWIS THOMAS LAMAR	MA	36W	81
LEWIS THOMAS LEE	NC	01E	47
LEWIS WALTER WAYNE	SC	29E	32
LEWIS WAYNE EUGENE JR	PA	40E	8
LEWIS WILLIAM DAVID	MI	22E	108
LEWIS WILLIAM EWING	AR	08E	125
LEWIS WILLIAM RUSSELL JR	PA	02W	49
LEWIS WILLIE GEORGE JR	TX	17W	68
LEWTER DONALD EUGENE	CA	15W	129
LEWTER STANLEY REED	AL	42E	19
LEX MICHAEL EDWARD	WI	27W	95
LEYBA RAMON	NM	59W	25
LEYDE THEODORE EDWARD	MN	56E	11
LEYERLE BILLY BOB	WA	15W	59
LEYVA FRANK MONTANO	AZ	25E	53
LEYVA RICHARD	TX	20E	63
LEYVA-PARRA-FRIAS FELIX F F	CA	17E	125
LEZAMA JOSE JR	IN	28W	49
LHOTA ROBERT ALLAN	PA	43W	55

NAME	STATE	PANEL NO.	LINE NO.
LIA NICHOLAS ANTHONY	NY	36E	77
LIBBEE LARRY LEE	OH	12E	15
LIBBEY MALCOLM PIERCE	ME	27E	96
LIBBY JOHN H	ME	48E	43
LIBERATI PETER JOSEPH	IL	15E	62
LIBERSKY WILLIAM BERTRAM	WI	14W	27
LIBERTY RONALD EDWARD	IL	17E	73
LICATE DAVID LOUIS	OH	43W	64
LICEA FRANCISCO XAVIER	CA	48W	7
LICHOTA DENNIS	MI	03E	24
LICHTE JACK ROWLEY JR	MS	16E	124
LICIAGA-CONCEPCION LUIS A	PR	04E	43
LICKEY MICHAEL LEWIS	WA	25W	50
LICON FRANCISCO	TX	27W	82
LIDDELL BENJAMIN F III	MS	08E	72
LIDDELL ROBERT MORGAN	CO	12W	70
LIDDYCOAT WILLIAM ROWLAND	OR	35W	28
LIDER FRED RODRIGUEZ	CA	12E	67
LIEBERMAN JAY LESLIE	MN	53E	3
LIEBERMAN MAX	CA	13W	93
LIEBERNECHT VON MILES	CA	41W	40
LIEBESPECK JAMES WARREN	CA	64E	16
LIEBHABER KENNETH GEORGE	WI	32W	50
LIEBL DONALD ALVIN	MN	18W	89
LIEBNITZ JAMES TERRY	WI	31W	81
LIELMANIS ATIS KARLIS	PA	01E	34
LIEN JAMES LAWRENCE	SD	41E	51
LIESE TIMOTHY FRANCIS	MO	25E	63
LIESER ROBERT DARYL	FL	28W	49
LIEURANCE DAVEY ALAN	OH	18W	90
LIEWER RICHARD GEORGE	IA	52W	28
LIFRIERI PAUL J	NY	18E	23
LIGAMMARI NICHOLAS PAUL	NY	40E	43
LIGGETT DURAND GARFIELD	CA	19E	62
LIGGINS CLAYTON	LA	39E	50
LIGHT EVERETT EARL	VA	08E	7
LIGHT GLEE ROY	MT	56E	26
LIGHT JERRY CLIFTON	NJ	27E	90
LIGHT JOSEPH MARION	PA	10E	101
LIGHT WILLIAM MARVIN	MI	27W	19
LIGHTBOURNE RICHARD GREGO	NY	33E	88
LIGHTCAP JOSEPH MICHAEL	PA	38W	50
LIGHTFOOT BELVIN	TX	18E	103
LIGHTFOOT JAMES EDWARD	OH	26E	36
LIGHTFORD WILLIE JUNIOR	TN	25E	86
LIGHTMAN SAMUEL	PA	12E	10
LIGHTSEY DANNY LEE	GA	03W	114
LIGHTSEY JOHN HENRY	GA	08W	98
LIGONS DARYL LEE	CA	32E	64
LIGONS RAYMOND	MD	19W	46
LIKELY JAMES THOMAS	AL	27E	40
LIKELY RICHARD ALLEN	MA	03W	14
LIKENS ARTHUR EMMITT	TN	02W	112
LIKENS BOBBY DALE	WV	31E	13
LIKENS BOBBY JOE	IN	19W	69
LIKKEL DUANE ALLEN	WA	38W	67
LILE JOE CHARLES II	TX	05E	73
LILES EPHRIAM RUTLEDGE II	SC	21W	61
LILES LARRY JOE	NE	20E	104
LILES ROBERT LEONEL JR	LA	01W	101
LILIENTHAL MARK ALLEN	CT	11W	17
LILIENTHAL WILLIAM EDWARD	MN	44E	23
LILLA JOHN THOMAS	NY	24E	32
LILLEY DAVID WILLIAM	RI	05W	35
LILLEY FRANK JOHN	CT	16W	53
LILLEY JOSEPH EMMETT	AL	07E	59
LILLEY THOMAS EDWARD	NJ	40E	24
LILLIE JOE HENRY	FL	05W	38
LILLIE RICHARD ARTHUR	MT	05W	117
LILLIS RICHARD NED	MN	13E	98
LILLUND WILLIAM ALLAN	CA	27E	49
LILLY CARROLL BAXTER	WV	04W	114
LILLY DAVID ROSE	CA	44W	10
LILLY JOSEPH DARRELL	MN	42W	36
LILLY LAWRENCE EUGENE	CA	04W	55
LILLY ROBERT C	WV	05E	52
LILLY WILLIAM JOSEPH	CT	09E	24
LIMA KENNETH KAWIKA	HI	22E	43
LIMBACH HENRY LEE	NE	16W	85
LIMBACHER DURWARD ALLAN	IA	31E	49
LIMBERG DUANE EDWARD	IA	01E	35
LIMBRICK ALLEN ISSAC	TX	36W	64

NAME	STATE	PANEL NO.	LINE NO.
LIMERICK BOBBY FRANK	TX	02W	2
LIMINGA FREDERICK HUGO	MI	22E	43
LIMON ANDRES	TX	31E	81
LIMONES JESUS MARIO	TX	19E	62
LINAM MAXIE DEAN	OK	13W	29
LINCH LEE FRANCIS	PA	33W	34
LINCOLN GARY GENE	OH	28E	27
LIND FRED ANDREW	CT	09E	15
LIND JAMES JEROME	WI	33E	50
LIND MORTEN ARVID JR	CA	25W	75
LIND RALPH RICHARD JR	OH	06E	121
LIND THOMAS REINO	OH	46W	27
LINDABERRY JOHN LANCE	NJ	30E	4
LINDAHL JOHN CARL	KS	01W	109
LINDBERG BRIAN VICTOR	MN	48E	7
LINDBERG DALE RAYMOND	WA	28E	44
LINDBERG DAVID CARL	CA	20E	78
LINDBERG JOHN DAVID	OK	21W	71
LINDBERGH ROBERT RAYMOND	HI	33E	29
LINDBLOOM CHARLES DAVID	GA	47W	10
LINDE RICHARD VICTOR	OH	13E	68
LINDECAMP HOWARD S JR	PA	25E	69
LINDEL JOHN RICHARD	CA	65W	11
LINDELL LARRY ALBERT	NE	19E	50
LINDEMANN JAMES WILLIAM	MI	11W	8
LINDER GARRY HAROLD	CA	07E	49
LINDER GEORGE RICHARD	CA	20E	9
LINDER HERBERT III	IL	26E	48
LINDER JAMES JR	FL	19W	17
LINDERMAN MARK THOMAS	PA	23E	101
LINDERMAN MICHAEL EDWIN	WA	45E	57
LINDEWALD CHARLES W JR	IN	38E	5
LINDGREN ROBERT WILLIAM	MN	30E	57
LINDHOLM DAN VICTOR	KS	44W	4
LINDLAND DONALD FREDRICK	OR	01W	71
LINDLER JESSIE RAY	AR	05W	2
LINDLEY BOBBY PAT	TX	28W	49
LINDLEY MARVIN LEROY	UT	04E	124
LINDLEY RONNIE DEAN	TN	20W	87
LINDNER JOHN MICHAEL	IL	33E	50
LINDQUIST VIRGIL	IL	07E	20
LINDQUIST WILLIAM FRANCIS	KS	22W	122
LINDSAY BRUCE STUART	CA	54E	37
LINDSAY GARY WAYNE	ND	26E	27
LINDSAY GREGORY THAYER	FL	31W	8
LINDSAY JAMES RICKEY	AL	16W	75
LINDSAY MICHAEL CLAUDE	WA	36E	54
LINDSAY PHILIP TRIESTE	PA	49E	4
LINDSAY STEPHEN LEE	LA	05W	63
LINDSAY WASH JUNIOR	NC	23E	89
LINDSEY ARTHUR DALE	KY	30W	90
LINDSEY DANIEL HINSON	FL	31E	40
LINDSEY DENNIS PAUL	MI	16W	58
LINDSEY EDWARD BYRON	GA	54W	17
LINDSEY ELMER R JR	OH	48E	43
LINDSEY JACK WAYNE	TX	05E	106
LINDSEY JAMES KAHILILAUIN	HI	17E	99
LINDSEY JOHNNY WARNER	KY	34E	79
LINDSEY LARRY ALAN	OR	02E	77
LINDSEY MARVIN NELSON	LA	02E	24
LINDSEY REGINALD WALLACE	CA	15W	125
LINDSEY WILLIAM JEFFERSON	GA	03E	83
LINDSEY WILLIAM ROYAL	TX	68W	5
LINDSLEY DONALD PETER	NJ	18E	123
LINDSTROM PATRICK EUGENE	WA	40E	9
LINDSTROM RONNIE GEORGE	MN	15W	119
LINEBERGER HAROLD BENTON	TX	05W	67
LINEBERRY JERRY EUGENE	NC	13W	2
LINEBERRY RICHARD BRYAN	NC	01W	75
LINES RICHARD MICHAEL	LA	06E	134
LING WILLIAM CLIVE	OK	40E	65
LINGLE DALE DENNIS	IL	29W	102
LINGLE JOSEPH M JR	VA	18E	86
LINGLE ROBERT DEAN	MO	19W	95
LINGLEY NORMAN LEWIS	AK	12E	34
LININGER GARY LEE	PA	14E	39
LINK DAVID JOHN	MI	41E	40
LINK FREDERICK BEARD	NC	42E	19
LINK GARY WILLIAM	MI	57W	19
LINK GEORGE ARTHUR	PA	34E	89
LINK JOHN FRANCIS	IA	47E	13
LINK JOHN JOSEPH	NY	56W	36

NAME	STATE	PANEL NO.	LINE NO.
LINK RAYMOND PATRICK	PA	25E	58
LINK ROBERT CHARLES	DC	51E	22
LINK ROGER MARK	TX	46E	37
LINKS RICHARD FREDERICK	CT	47E	23
LINN DAVID WILLIAM	CA	19E	53
LINN JOHN HOLMES	MD	25W	51
LINN ROBERT LEWIS JR	MI	16E	112
LINNA STEVEN PAUL	MI	37E	24
LINNELL DENNIS RICHARD	WA	06W	52
LINNEN BENEDICT J III	OH	16W	82
LINSE KENNETH DAVID	GA	50W	36
LINSKI THEODORE PAUL	WI	24E	7
LINSON ROBERT WYLIE	TN	15E	31
LINT DARRELL CLIFFORD	MS	34E	59
LINT DONALD MICHAEL	IA	11W	37
LINTHICUM DON WILLIAM	FL	27E	60
LINTNER DARRYL CHARLES	MO	51E	15
LINTON LEE ROY EDWARD	WI	06W	93
LINVILLE DENNIS WAYNE	OH	50E	17
LINVILLE HAROLD LEE	NV	09W	84
LINVILLE MICHAEL THOMAS	MI	07W	78
LINVILLE ROBERT EDISON	OR	06W	32
LINVILLE SAMUEL SWANN	NC	57E	26
LIONETTA EDWARD ARTHUR	MA	44E	60
LIPAROTO LEONARD JOSEPH	MI	44W	38
LIPE JIMMY RUSSELL	NC	40W	44
LIPETZKY DANIEL JOHN	MN	22W	41
LIPINSKI VERNON RAYMOND	MD	32E	77
LIPPMAN GORDON JOSEPH	SD	04E	12
LIPSCOMB DAVID LEE	VA	45E	13
LIPSCOMB MELVIN	GA	16E	80
LIPSCOMB ROY LOLLIS	SC	26W	78
LIPSCOMB THOMAS DELANO	WV	24W	44
LIPSEY THOMAS WASHING III	MI	02W	104
LIPSIUS MICHAEL GLENN	CA	50E	49
LIPTAK CHARLES LEWIS	CA	27W	66
LIPTOCK MICHAEL	PA	02E	122
LIPTON JOSEPH PRICE	NY	19E	6
LIRA ALFRED GEORGE	TX	17E	105
LIRA ROBERT CHAGOYA	CA	27W	19
LIROT CHARLES PATRICK	IN	30E	92
LIS RICHARD JOHN	IL	31E	49
LISBOA RAFAEL	NY	27E	6
LISBON JOHNNY	SC	26W	92
LISCUM RONALD FRANCIS	NY	15W	104
LISENBY DONALD EUGENE	AL	47W	10
LISENBY JAMES ARNOLD	FL	48W	7
LISENBY MAX	OK	24W	111
LISERIO JOE FRANK	TX	06E	83
LISH GILBERT RAY	ID	36E	54
LISHCHYNSKY GEORGE	PA	09W	122
LISIEWSKI FREDRICK ALLEN	NY	21W	33
LISKOW LARRY LEE	MI	44W	27
LISLE JACK MCBRIDE	FL	01E	15
LISLE TERRILL MICHAEL	MN	27W	11
LISMENTS VILIS	IN	03E	108
LISOWSKI ANDREW ZBIGNIEW	IL	11W	103
LISS LARRY WILLIAM	CA	30W	66
LISTE DAVID ALLEN	LA	11E	113
LISTER JAMES JOHN	ID	29W	102
LISTORTI JOSEPH ANTHONY	PA	24E	104
LISZCZ ROBERT STANLEY	NY	16E	93
LITCHFIELD FRANK EDWARD	MA	20W	98
LITHERLAND THOMAS EDWARD	AZ	15E	5
LITKE JEROME WALTER	WI	08E	7
LITSEY MICHAEL LEWIS	KY	18W	41
LITTERIO ROBERT DALE	TX	45W	37
LITTLE CECIL EUGENE	OH	18E	53
LITTLE DANNY LEONARD	TX	11W	41
LITTLE DONNIE HUGH	GA	58W	10
LITTLE GARLAND PAUL	TX	25E	104
LITTLE GARY DEAN	KS	23E	37
LITTLE HENRY LEON	AL	21E	107
LITTLE JOHN EDGAR	AL	06E	90
LITTLE NORMAN EARL	TX	12W	49
LITTLE PAUL FREDERICK	NY	22W	90
LITTLE PETER	LA	12E	80
LITTLE PETER CLARK	OR	27W	96
LITTLE RANDELL BLAKE	MI	53W	2
LITTLE RODNEY DWIGHT	CA	19W	51
LITTLE SUN THOMAS LEE	OK	39E	63
LITTLE WALLACE SYLVESTER	AL	62E	20

NAME	STATE	PANEL NO.	LINE NO.
LITTLE WILLIAM F III	NJ	16W	58
LITTLE WILLIAM GREGORY	MT	14W	32
LITTLE WILLIAM HARRIS	MA	26E	74
LITTLE WILLIAM WALTER III	IL	29E	41
LITTLEFIELD ROBERT HENRY	AL	50E	17
LITTLEHALES ROY CHARLES	NJ	15E	47
LITTLEJOHN GREGORY LAWREN	PA	48E	43
LITTLEJOHN McGEARY	RI	03E	130
LITTLEJOHN TROY A	TN	36E	22
LITTLEPAGE THOMAS EARL	IN	14W	63
LITTLER JAMES L M III	HI	53W	3
LITTLETON DAVID ERNEST	KY	38E	55
LITTLETON JOHN WAYNE	AZ	03W	54
LITTLETON RICHARD WILLIAM	OH	08W	15
LITTON GARY WAYNE	KY	43E	8
LITTS JAMES GARRIS	PA	11E	45
LITWIN ROBERT RICHARD	MA	22E	43
LITZ TERRY RICHARD	PA	26E	24
LITZINGER DUANE EDWARD	MN	37E	60
LITZLER JAMES WILLIAM	AZ	57W	28
LIVELY BOBBY DEAN	NC	24E	87
LIVELY MARVIN EUGENE	TN	39W	38
LIVELY PAUL JOHNSON	KY	33E	88
LIVELY WARREN II	NJ	08W	9
LIVENGOOD STEVE ALLEN	FL	45W	54
LIVERMAN JOHN CLARENCE	MD	36W	4
LIVERMORE KEITH WARREN F	NY	25E	7
LIVERMORE ROSS WHITTIER	TN	35W	35
LIVESAY RALPH HOWARD	OH	06E	115
LIVINGSTON BILLY DALE	AR	41E	40
LIVINGSTON BRUCE BERNARD	OH	25E	86
LIVINGSTON ERSKIN DAN	SC	24E	109
LIVINGSTON JOHN DEWEY	NY	06W	4
LIVINGSTON JOHN JOSEPH	MO	12E	55
LIVINGSTON LARRY MONTEZ	KY	03W	92
LIVINGSTON LESLIE E III	MO	13W	37
LIVINGSTON NORMAN JAMES	MI	29E	68
LIVINGSTON PETER B	NY	38W	12
LIVINGSTON RICHARD ALLEN	WA	17W	30
LIVINGSTON WILLIAM MICHAE	OH	50W	7
LIVINGSTONE DAVID MICHAEL	MI	16W	19
LIZARRAGA MICHAEL WAYNE	CA	27W	50
LIZOTTE WARREN G H JR	IA	31W	69
LJUNG CARL LOUIS	NY	40E	11
LLAMAS JOSE	KS	19W	65
LLAMAZALES HUMBERTO	FL	20W	116
LLANES HAROLD LEROY	HI	52W	28
LLANTIN-ORTIZ JOSE MANUEL	PR	14W	83
LLEWELLYN JOHNNY WILLIAM	SC	09E	106
LLOYD ALLEN RICHARD	MN	05W	117
LLOYD DANIEL EDWARD	OR	50W	25
LLOYD DANIEL WILLIAM	MN	29W	29
LLOYD DONALD LEE	OK	39E	35
LLOYD DOUGLAS	NC	21E	5
LLOYD FREDDIE GEAN	MD	05E	40
LLOYD JAMES VERNON	AR	07W	116
LLOYD KENNETH EDWIN	OH	42E	35
LLOYD LOWELL RAY	IL	20E	119
LLOYD MARTIN ROGER	MO	03W	27
LLOYD ORLAND THOMAS	GA	12W	104
LLOYD RANDALL LYNN	OH	59E	7
LLOYD RODNEY DALE	AL	42E	20
LLOYD RONALD EDWARD	AL	33E	14
LO FORTI PAUL ROSARIO	CA	38W	44
LO GRASSO RALPH ANTHONY	NY	44E	9
LO MAURO ROBERT BRUCE	NY	15E	58
LOAN THOMAS LEE	OH	28W	27
LOANE ALLEN ROBERT	MA	27E	21
LOATMAN RODNEY ELLIS	NJ	35E	71
LOBACK THOMAS JOHN	NY	40E	24
LOBBEZOO DENNIS LEE	MI	59W	6
LOBKER DANN JOSEPH	MI	27W	11
LOBSINGER JOHN FORMAN	MN	35E	16
LOCATELLI VINCENT	CA	03E	84
LOCHER WALTER NORVEL	MT	22E	79
LOCHNER KEITH ALAN	IN	11W	37
LOCHNER VERNE ELDON	OR	27W	1
LOCHRIDGE ROBERT ERIC	WA	35E	74
LOCHTHOWE LEON LEROY	ND	27E	1
LOCK MOON WAI	WA	02E	22
LOCKARD ALAN CARROLL	MD	36W	16
LOCKARD DAVID LEE	KY	41W	59
LOCKARD LEONARD WAYNE	LA	01E	57
LOCKE GEORGE W JR	WV	27E	102
LOCKE JACK ELSWORTH	IN	04E	100
LOCKE JAMES LEE	OK	28W	49
LOCKE WILLIAM EDWARD	OR	03W	14
LOCKER JAMES DOUGLAS	OH	58W	10
LOCKET ROBERT JR	TX	12W	98
LOCKETT CLEO	AL	03E	34
LOCKETT EDWARD DEAN	CA	14W	121
LOCKETT JAMES EDWARD	WV	11W	28
LOCKETT LLOYD	LA	55E	23
LOCKETT WILLIAM NORRIS	MI	33E	3
LOCKHART CLARENCE	AL	13E	131
LOCKHART CURTIS	IL	02E	45
LOCKHART DOVER LEON	MI	25E	104
LOCKHART FLOYD BARNEY JR	TX	13W	122
LOCKHART FREDDIE LEWIS	WV	06W	83
LOCKHART GEORGE BARRY	TX	01W	101
LOCKHART HARLAN NATHANIEL	OH	12E	48
LOCKHART HARRY JAMES	TX	22E	108
LOCKHART JOHN THOMAS	NY	04W	38
LOCKHART KENNETH EUGENE	TN	24W	44
LOCKHART ROBERT LEE	WV	22W	23
LOCKHART RONALD JAY	KY	56W	14
LOCKHART ROY	CA	03E	59
LOCKHART WILLIAM LON	MO	25E	92
LOCKHORST JOHN ELDON JR	CA	13W	97
LOCKLAIR ALLISON WAYNE	SC	28W	61
LOCKLAR TED T	GA	12E	2
LOCKLEAR EDDIE LEE	NC	22W	112
LOCKLEAR FOSTER	NC	12W	21
LOCKLEAR GLEN	NC	27E	90
LOCKLEAR JIMMY	NC	45W	38
LOCKRIDGE JACK RAY	AL	36E	22
LOCKRIDGE JAMES T	TN	08E	42
LOCKWOOD DONALD PAUL	CO	03W	85
LOCKWOOD HAROLD SPENCER	MT	57W	19
LOCKWOOD JAMES ALTON	ID	10E	108
LOCKWOOD JOHN LARRY	IA	15E	6
LOCKWOOD KENNETH CHARLES	FL	42E	6
LOCKWOOD RICHARD JON	IA	04W	110
LODEN LARRY DAVID	TN	04W	25
LODGE ROBERT ALFRED	NY	01W	19
LODHOLM NORMAN ELLIOTT	WA	57W	8
LODISE JOSEPH FRANCIS JR	PA	53E	36
LODUHA GARY	WI	51E	40
LOECKER MARLOW MARTIN	NE	15E	47
LOEFFLER NORMAN F JR	OK	31E	13
LOEGERING DEAN CHARLES	MN	16E	112
LOEHLEIN ROBERT JOHN JR	MN	42W	12
LOERLEIN RONALD JOSEPH	PA	03E	114
LOESCHNER THEODORE R JR	NY	01E	108
LOEW DAVID WILLIAM	OR	22W	66
LOFARO MARCELLO JAMES	NY	35E	74
LOFFER TERRY ALLEN	IN	21W	14
LOFGREN JAMES ESKEL	NJ	03E	130
LOFMAN LANCE MICHAEL	FL	09W	98
LOFSTROM LELAND EDDY	ME	60E	25
LOFTHEIM DENNIS DEAN	FL	26E	39
LOFTIN TEDDY CARL	TX	27W	11
LOFTIS JOEL CONRAD	TX	23W	104
LOFTN JERRY WAYNE	MS	11W	3
LOFTON BOOKER T JR	TX	38W	75
LOFTON CHARLES EDWARD	DC	26E	102
LOFTON GLEN DORSE	TX	08E	37
LOFTON JOE EDDIE	MS	48W	57
LOFTON JOSEPH ALAN	OH	16W	65
LOFTON RAYFON	TN	10E	31
LOFTON RONALD HARRY	TX	24E	114
LOFTUS CRAIG JOHN	MN	35W	62
LOFTUS RAYMOND SHARP III	OH	53W	3
LOGAN BRADLEY JOHN	MI	16W	39
LOGAN CHARLIE LEE	IL	39W	50
LOGAN CHARLIE MATTHEW	VA	04W	68
LOGAN CLARENCE	NC	12W	70
LOGAN DONALD GORDON	MO	01E	26
LOGAN DOUGLAS ALFRED	MO	21E	123
LOGAN FRANCIS MARRION III	TX	16W	30
LOGAN GORDON WESLEY JR	WA	16W	65
LOGAN HALFORD	CA	02E	96
LOGAN JACK WILLIAM JR	OH	13E	28
LOGAN JACOB DRUMMOND	WA	03E	120
LOGAN JAMES DWIGHT	MI	31W	52
LOGAN JIMMY MORRIS	TN	43E	57
LOGAN JOHN TYLER	VA	11E	31
LOGAN JOSEPH LAWRENCE JR	MI	25W	75
LOGAN JOSEPH PATRICK JR	MA	63W	8
LOGAN RICHARD MATTHEW	OH	17W	122
LOGAN RONALD CHARLES	MO	06E	60
LOGAN RONNIE LEE	IN	25E	43
LOGAN WILLIAM LEON	IA	03W	128
LOGES JOHN EARL	FL	18W	48
LOGSDON CLIFFORD DOUGLAS	NY	44W	11
LOGSDON HERBERT JR	IN	21W	29
LOGUE JOHN EDWARD JR	PA	24W	67
LOGUE ROBERT DONALD	OH	03E	130
LOGWOOD CLARENCE	MO	15W	5
LOHEED HUBERT BRADFORD	MA	04E	130
LOHENRY ROBERT RAYMOND	IL	11W	125
LOHMAN HERMAN AUGUSTA JR	ID	48E	29
LOHMAN ROBERT THOMAS	CA	24E	91
LOHMEYER DOUGLAS EDWARD	CA	24W	33
LOHREY JAMES WILLIAM	IL	16E	125
LOHSE ARNOLD EDWIN HENRY	IA	24E	32
LOHSE RICHARD LEE	MN	59E	7
LOISEL JAMES LEE	MI	10W	42
LOISEL PATRICK MICHAEL	CA	20E	77
LOISELLE BRUCE WAYNE	FL	45E	3
LOISELLE RICHARD J	MI	19E	83
LOITZ MICHAEL NELSON	OH	38W	44
LOKENI FAGATOELE	SA	36W	81
LOKKEN GARY DAN	ND	49E	12
LOLLAR BYRON CLIFTON	MO	35E	40
LOLLAR THOMAS ARTHUR	MO	10W	104
LOLLIS CHARLES W	NJ	37E	61
LOMAS JOHNIE	MO	34W	50
LOMAX MALCOLM EUGENE	IN	38W	76
LOMAX RICHARD EUGENE	OH	46E	37
LOMBARD DURWOOD BERT	ME	44E	9
LOMBARDO RICHARD MYRON	OH	21E	35
LOMBAS DEXTER JOSEPH	LA	06W	64
LOMEN RALPH TERENCE	WA	23W	103
LONA GABRIEL	CA	29E	51
LONCON LARRY JOSEPH	LA	11W	59
LONDON DENNIS W	NV	01W	127
LONDON EARL	LA	34E	37
LONDON WILLIAM THOMAS	TN	11E	77
LONERGAN HAROLD SHERMAN	NY	31W	9
LONEY ASHTON NATHANIEL	NY	01W	131
LONG BILL BROOKS	TN	14W	79
LONG BILLIE MONROE	FL	40W	33
LONG BRIAN LEWIS	WV	16W	89
LONG CARL EDWIN	TX	15W	73
LONG CHARLES EDWARD	FL	24E	35
LONG CHARLES EDWARD	AL	29E	41
LONG CHARLES ELBERT	PA	18W	34
LONG CLYDE EDWARD JR	IL	22E	71
LONG DAN STEVEN	CA	27W	46
LONG DENNIS LANE	IL	03E	115
LONG DONALD EUGENE	MO	18E	11
LONG DONALD RUSSELL	OH	08E	112
LONG DOUGLAS EUGENE	MI	57W	28
LONG DOUGLAS LEONARD JR	GA	49E	44
LONG EARL WAYNE	PA	24E	114
LONG EDWARD EUGENE	OH	36E	54
LONG ELDON DALE	KS	05E	135
LONG FLOYD LESTER	CA	30E	16
LONG FREDDIE LERON	TN	15W	13
LONG GEORGE FRANCIS	NJ	63W	18
LONG GEORGE WENDELL	KS	59E	7
LONG HAL RANDOLPH	CA	38W	2
LONG HARRY LEROY	MO	22W	3
LONG HERLIHY TOWNSEND	GA	35E	48
LONG JAMES ALLEN	OH	35W	48
LONG JAMES ARTHUR	WA	05W	117
LONG JAMES DAVID	TN	02E	99
LONG JAMES MCKINLEY	MD	02E	108
LONG JAMES ROBERT	MI	50W	14
LONG JAMES ROBERT	PA	28W	62
LONG JAMES THOMAS	MA	41W	30
LONG JEROME ALBERT	KS	37W	40
LONG JERRY ROY	LA	17E	14
LONG JOE	MD	13W	63
LONG JOHN HENRY SOTHORON	PA	11E	88

NAME	STATE	PANEL NO.	LINE NO.
LONG JOHN WADE JR	CA	09W	39
LONG JOHNNY F	GA	09E	41
LONG JOSEPH LEROY	NY	34E	54
LONG LEONARD	CA	46E	37
LONG LEWIS BENTON	CA	04E	80
LONG LORIN ELWOOD	IN	47W	47
LONG MELVIN RAY	KS	44W	50
LONG MICHAEL DAVID	AL	38E	5
LONG NORMAN LACY JR	VA	36E	22
LONG PATRICK JEROME	NY	30E	4
LONG PAUL MICHAEL	PA	08E	115
LONG PERLEY MILFORD JR	VT	26E	72
LONG PHILLIP MICHAEL	VA	12W	118
LONG RAY FRANK	AL	15W	6
LONG RAY STEPHEN	MO	09E	88
LONG RAYMOND ERVIN	SC	28E	41
LONG RAYMOND LEON JR	AR	11W	115
LONG RICHARD LYTLE	NJ	33E	38
LONG RICHARD PAUL	OH	52W	15
LONG ROBERT DAVIS	OH	49W	15
LONG ROBERT LESTER	OH	03W	18
LONG ROBERT LYNNE	IN	32E	45
LONG ROBERT ORRIE	AZ	02E	59
LONG ROBERT WESLEY	OH	22W	3
LONG RONALD JAMES	WV	28W	104
LONG SAMMIE JAMES	IL	06W	93
LONG SHELBY MARCENE	OH	17W	105
LONG THOMAS ARNOLD	MO	08W	43
LONG THOMAS CALVIN JR	MD	24W	86
LONG THOMAS IRA	SC	54E	11
LONG THOMAS KENDRICK	IL	27W	96
LONG WAYNE THOMAS	TN	04E	42
LONG WILLIAM LOUIS	TX	22W	99
LONGABARDI MICHAEL JOSEPH	NY	38E	5
LONGANECKER RONALD LEE	OR	09E	7
LONGDAIL DENNIS LEE	AZ	11W	37
LONGFELLOW RONALD ANTHONY	PA	02W	99
LONGMIRE KENT WILLIAM	WI	11W	28
LONGO DENNIS MICHAEL	MO	56W	24
LONGORIA JOE GILBERT	TX	26W	10
LONGSTON HENRY RALPH	MO	29W	46
LONGTIN MARK WARREN	MN	43W	47
LONGTINE JERRY ALLEN	MN	68W	5
LONO LUTHER ALBERT	WA	17W	19
LONSDALE GEORGE EDWARD	CT	32E	77
LONSDALE JOHN DAVID	IA	11W	132
LONZO ANGELO ALBERT	CA	07E	87
LOO EDWARD LUKANA JR	HI	28W	104
LOOBEY MERLE E	WA	04W	33
LOOBY LAWRENCE CLARENCE	NE	32W	33
LOOMIS BILLIE CLIFFORD	CA	60W	2
LOOMIS RICKIE ALLAN	OR	21W	71
LOOMIS WILLIAM NICHOLAS	NH	26E	66
LOONEY DOUGLAS OSCAR	VA	30W	57
LOONEY EDWARD MICHAEL	NY	32E	1
LOONEY JAMES WESLEY	OH	20W	40
LOONEY JERRY WAYNE	CA	08E	37
LOONEY MILFORD JR	AL	29W	54
LOONEY PAUL THOMAS	MA	19E	84
LOONEY PHILLIP R	OH	05E	6
LOONEY ROBERT	TN	17W	68
LOOS THOMAS WALTER	MO	37E	25
LOPEMAN STEPHEN RAY	WA	25W	51
LOPER MILES HILTON JR	KY	03E	24
LOPES LAWRENCE RENALDO	RI	46E	47
LOPEZ ADRIAN SALOME	CA	40E	9
LOPEZ ALFREDO JR	TX	44W	17
LOPEZ ANTONIO JR	TX	68W	5
LOPEZ ARMANDO	CA	44W	27
LOPEZ ARTURO JR	TX	10W	114
LOPEZ AUGUSTINE JR	TX	12E	11
LOPEZ DONACIANO GUTIERREZ	OH	18E	115
LOPEZ EDDIE CESARIO	AZ	12E	115
LOPEZ EDWARD	CA	47W	48
LOPEZ EDWARD	MA	15W	59
LOPEZ EDWARD JOSEPH	CA	02W	76
LOPEZ FRANK JR	MI	05E	106
LOPEZ FREDERICK GEORGE	CA	39E	8
LOPEZ GEORGE LEONARD	CA	07W	53
LOPEZ HECTOR	NY	02E	110
LOPEZ HENRY ROBERT	IL	14E	123
LOPEZ JOHN	CA	31W	52

NAME	STATE	PANEL NO.	LINE NO.
LOPEZ JOHN EDWARD JR	CA	17W	57
LOPEZ JOSE	TX	28E	16
LOPEZ JOSE ANGEL JR	CA	50E	40
LOPEZ JOSE ANTONIO	CA	10E	74
LOPEZ JOSE DE JESUS	CA	34E	89
LOPEZ JOSE LIUS	NJ	35W	43
LOPEZ JOSEPH PAUL	CO	43W	39
LOPEZ LEOPOLDO AYALA	IL	10W	26
LOPEZ LUIS BELTRAN	SC	03E	130
LOPEZ LUPE PAUL	CA	32E	95
LOPEZ MANUEL	TX	10E	71
LOPEZ MANUEL TORRES	WI	54W	6
LOPEZ MAX ANDY	CA	16E	40
LOPEZ PAUL	CA	03W	100
LOPEZ PAULINO GUTIERREZ	TX	23E	106
LOPEZ PERFECTO NUNEZ	AZ	39E	22
LOPEZ PETE	TX	37W	75
LOPEZ PETER	PR	19W	99
LOPEZ PETER MITCHELL JR	CA	04W	6
LOPEZ RAMON	PR	44E	38
LOPEZ RAYMOND	CA	16E	61
LOPEZ RENE CERDA	KY	08E	42
LOPEZ RICARDO	NY	29W	102
LOPEZ RICHARD	TX	23E	116
LOPEZ RICHARD	TX	46E	47
LOPEZ RICHARD HENRY	CA	23E	29
LOPEZ ROBERT	IN	05E	94
LOPEZ ROBERT	WA	43E	25
LOPEZ ROBERT CHARLES	NM	58E	11
LOPEZ ROBERT DIAS	AZ	10W	131
LOPEZ ROBERT FRANCISCO	AZ	57W	29
LOPEZ RUDY	TX	58E	12
LOPEZ STEVE	CA	16E	124
LOPEZ VICTOR	CA	34W	26
LOPEZ-AGOSTO FELIX MANUEL	PR	14E	11
LOPEZ-COLON JUAN ANTONIO	PR	05E	42
LOPEZ-DEL TORO SAUL	PR	51E	39
LOPEZ-GARCIA GEOVEL	NY	39E	8
LOPEZ-MERCED RUBEN	PR	23W	38
LOPEZ-RAMOS LUIS ALFONSO	CA	60W	2
LOPEZ-VAZQUEZ LEONARDO	IL	56W	33
LOPINTO FRANK THOMAS	NJ	22E	108
LOPOCHONSKY JOHN HENRY JR	PA	03W	109
LOPP JAMES LEONARD	IL	38E	32
LOPRINO TERRY STEVEN	CA	14W	112
LORBER DONN MICHAEL	MD	12W	57
LORD ARTHUR JAMES	GA	50E	49
LORD BARRY DAVID	OH	49E	44
LORD ERIC ANTHONY	PA	18W	126
LORD NEAL ALEXANDER JR	CA	11W	126
LORD ROBERT RANDAL	MI	38E	4
LORD STEPHEN GEOFFREY	MI	05E	27
LORDEN DENNIS FRANKLIN	NH	21W	119
LORDI LOUIS ROBERT	PA	62E	8
LORDITCH PATRICK MICHAEL	MA	49W	20
LORENCE JOHN EDWARD	OH	23W	112
LORENZ TERRY WAYNE	WI	08E	52
LORENZINI DENNIS JOSEPH	PA	31W	9
LORENZO ROBERT J	CA	46E	8
LORIMER WILLIAM IV	MN	13W	105
LORTZ JOHN EDWARD III	CA	30W	102
LOSCHIAVO THOMAS LEE	KY	62W	12
LOSCUITO NED NATALE	NY	02E	64
LOSEL FRED GEORGE JR	CA	59E	7
LOSO JAMES MICHAEL	MI	21E	83
LOSOYA ERNEST FELIPE	CA	04E	28
LOSOYA RAUL	CA	02W	95
LOSPINUSO JAMES	MD	02W	96
LOSSING CLARENCE ERNEST	MN	23E	53
LOSTUTTER GEORGE FRANCIS	CA	20W	95
LOTHMAN JAMES EDWARD	OH	41W	6
LOTRIDGE GERALD STEPHEN	VA	20W	87
LOTT CHARLES ALLISON	NM	57E	27
LOTT DOUGLAS HUGH JR	GA	16W	6
LOTT HARVEY EUGENE	FL	32W	14
LOTT JAMES EDWARD		57E	6
LOTT JUNIOR EDWARD	AL	32E	24
LOTTA PHILLIP ANTHONY	CA	05E	77
LOTTES HERBERT JAMES	IN	21W	33
LOUALLEN JACK NEECE	SC	28W	92
LOUCKS HERBERT ALLEN	MI	26E	93
LOUDENBACK DOUGLAS FRANKL	KY	46E	57

NAME	STATE	PANEL NO.	LINE NO.
LOUDERMILK JAMES ELLIS	FL	32E	77
LOUDIN DALE RUSSELL	OH	29E	41
LOUGH ROBERT MELVIN JR	WV	31W	9
LOUGHLIN EDMUND MICHAEL	MA	10W	114
LOUGHRAN JOSEPH M JR	CT	54E	11
LOUGHRAN THOMAS WILLIAM	ME	34W	59
LOUGHREN MICHAEL EVAN	MI	45W	26
LOUIS ROBERT YOUGETE JR	TX	19E	28
LOUNDERMON RALPH E	VA	17W	37
LOUNSBURY WILLIAM DAVID	PA	20W	30
LOUT BILLY BURKE	LA	18E	36
LOUTHAN DAVID CARL	PA	12E	129
LOUVIERE MARVIN JOHN	LA	18W	34
LOUVRING CARL FREDRICK	OR	19E	109
LOUX JAMES ARTHUR	MI	04W	109
LOVAN PETER JOHN	NY	50W	51
LOVATO JOE JR	TX	28E	27
LOVATO LAURIANO LAWRENCE	CA	02E	114
LOVATO MICHAEL LEON	NM	38E	55
LOVATO RUDOLPH DANIEL	NM	12W	26
LOVE ANTHONY RAY	NC	56W	24
LOVE BURGESS ALLEN	PA	16E	29
LOVE CHARLES WILLIAM JR	FL	15W	99
LOVE CLARANCE LEE	TX	37W	23
LOVE CLYDE CURTIS	OR	01W	28
LOVE DANIEL HALEY	NY	19W	96
LOVE DARRELL STEVE	KS	39W	8
LOVE DON WAYNE	OK	08W	122
LOVE FREDERICK EUGENE	NJ	48E	29
LOVE GARY LEE	OH	25E	58
LOVE HARRY WILLIAM JR	NC	02E	25
LOVE HUGH ALLEN	TN	05E	42
LOVE J C	AL	11E	123
LOVE JAMES EDWARD	MD	03E	131
LOVE JAMES THOMAS	OH	53W	37
LOVE JOE L JR	TX	02W	70
LOVE JOHN ARTHUR	KS	25W	104
LOVE JOHN JR	CA	25W	75
LOVE JOHN WAYNE	OH	19E	109
LOVE KENNETH HARLEN	MD	06W	121
LOVE KERRY BRENT	WA	17W	109
LOVE LARRY DALE	TN	05W	45
LOVE RANDALL WAYNE	KY	11W	59
LOVE ROBERT	NC	35W	71
LOVE VERNON GLEN	OK	04W	62
LOVEDAHL CHARLES ROBERT	OH	45E	48
LOVEGREN DAVID EUGENE	OR	30W	5
LOVELACE CHARLES KENNEDY	NC	02E	16
LOVELACE KENNETH	OH	05W	60
LOVELACE ROBERT ALAN	TN	29E	20
LOVELACE ROBERT KENNETH	KY	05E	19
LOVELADY RONALD DAVID	AL	53E	36
LOVELAND RONALD RAY	CA	38E	5
LOVELL EDWARD API	OH	04E	43
LOVELL ERVIN	CA	19E	120
LOVELL JAMES RICHARD	AL	32W	7
LOVELL JERRY MICHAEL	TN	24W	45
LOVELL LEWIS RANDOLPH JR	VA	59W	7
LOVELL PATRICK DARREN	FL	09W	84
LOVELLETTE GARY VAUGHN	MN	15W	107
LOVELLETTE GEORGE RONALD	IL	30W	14
LOVENGUTH TERRANCE LEE	CA	01E	38
LOVETT BERNARD JAMES JR	MA	06W	4
LOVETT DONALD WALTER	OR	04E	2
LOVETT GLENN ALAN	OH	13W	93
LOVETT PETER LOUIS	NY	35E	23
LOVETT RONALD CRAIG	NC	08E	43
LOVETT RONNIE RAY	OR	06E	107
LOVETT TERRY WAYNE	AL	22W	33
LOVETTE SAMUEL D	NC	26W	85
LOVING MARTIN EDWIN	CO	03W	68
LOVINS ARNOLD	KY	03W	126
LOVITT DAVID GLEN	IA	30W	57
LOVLEY THOMAS GRANT	ME	13W	75
LOVSNES NEAL WALLACE JR	PA	27W	89
LOW GEORGE	NY	14E	63
LOW JAMES BERNARD	UT	04W	104
LOW KEVIN DOUGLAS		21W	29
LOWAS JOHN	PA	02E	102
LOWDEN THOMAS ALLEN	NJ	11E	22
LOWDER CLARENCE EDWARD	NC	18W	59
LOWDER JARVIS CRAWFORD	OH	09E	62

NAME	STATE	PANEL NO.	LINE NO.
LOWDER RICKY NORMAN	NC	13W	78
LOWDON GRAHAM NORRIS JR	DE	22E	79
LOWE AARON HARVEY	MO	25W	75
LOWE BARRY	MA	58W	10
LOWE CLAYTON BENTLEY JR	CA	21E	28
LOWE DONALD EVERETT	WA	55E	21
LOWE DONALD W	TX	02W	104
LOWE EARNEST LON	TN	41W	64
LOWE EDWARD LEONARD	CA	04E	39
LOWE FREDERICK MOLEE JR	NC	28E	46
LOWE JERE RONE	GA	17W	78
LOWE JOHN CHRISTOPHER	IA	21E	90
LOWE LOUIS CARDELL	AL	60E	14
LOWE ROBERT BREWSTER	FL	07E	10
LOWE ROBERT ERNEST	OH	10W	42
LOWE ROBERT KINLOCH	MI	05E	73
LOWE RONALD BRUCE	IL	53W	28
LOWE RONALD SIDNEY	VA	10W	7
LOWE ROY DALLAS JR	VA	48W	45
LOWE STEVEN RAY	IL	10W	125
LOWE THOMAS MICHAEL	NY	12W	118
LOWE WALTER BEDFORD JR	TX	18W	95
LOWE WILLIAM EARL	FL	24E	32
LOWE WILLIE LEE	KY	27W	20
LOWER LARRY LA MAR	MI	42W	19
LOWERANITIS JOHN LEON	PA	17E	73
LOWERY ALVIN LEROY	WA	29W	31
LOWERY CARL CECIL	KY	39E	73
LOWERY CHARLES WILLIAM	IL	16W	39
LOWERY CLEM SPENCER JR	VA	63W	16
LOWERY DALTON BUSTER	AL	13E	64
LOWERY DARYL LEE	IN	26W	10
LOWERY DONALD STEVEN	GA	15E	33
LOWERY FREDDIE LEON	OK	43W	29
LOWERY JAMES ALLEN	OR	37E	39
LOWERY LARRY DEAN	IL	26W	65
LOWERY MICHAEL AYR	CA	14E	123
LOWERY RICHARD HOMER	MD	13E	102
LOWERY ROGER DALE	CA	18W	83
LOWERY STEVE EDWIN	NC	30W	57
LOWERY WILLIAM LEE	VA	12W	98
LOWES RICHARD SMITH	FL	43E	9
LOWMAN JONATHAN FAYE	OH	20E	63
LOWMAN WILLIAM LOUIS	DE	14E	118
LOWNES CHARLES DAVID	PA	11W	81
LOWREY CHUBBY DEAN	MO	17W	126
LOWRY JAMES EARL	CA	15W	78
LOWRY JIMMY CLINT	FL	22E	44
LOWRY RONALD RAYMOND	PA	38W	67
LOWRY TYRRELL GORDON	OR	02E	12
LOWRY WILLIAM ALLISON	NC	37W	82
LOWTHER HAROLD WAYNE	LA	06E	85
LOWTHER LARRY JOSEPH	WV	09W	73
LOY JAMES RICHARD	WI	34E	30
LOY RANDELL HOOD	IN	45W	38
LOYA PAUL NELSON	NY	57W	11
LOYD HAROLD IVAN	MO	35E	23
LOYD LONNIE DOUGLAS JR	OK	32W	44
LOYD LONNY LEE	KS	38W	50
LOYD MELVIN	MO	20W	72
LOYD MICHAEL GLENN	TX	18W	54
LOZADA CARLOS JAMES	NY	30E	45
LOZADA-WICHY ANIBAL P	PR	07W	132
LOZANO CARLOS FELIPE MENDEZ	MI	32E	78
LOZANO DONALD JAMES	CA	40E	43
LOZANO EDWARD ROBERT	OH	22E	108
LOZANO FERNANDO LEONARD	CA	34W	77
LOZANO JOSE REYMUNDO	TX	15E	107
LOZANO JOSEPH ALFRED	IL	14W	5
LOZANO MATTHEW T JR	TX	23W	2
LOZANO PAUL RODRIGUEZ	TX	59E	24
LOZANO RICHARD BILL	TX	26E	1
LOZEAU NORMAN GERARD	NH	16E	47
LOZENSKI RICHARD ORDELL	CA	20E	46
LOZIER KENNETH WAYNE	IN	24E	33
LOZIER WILLIAM EARL	MI	36E	78
LUALLIN LEE ANDRES	CA	35E	16
LUBAS JAMES ALEX	IL	27E	2
LUBAVS KONSTANTINS ADOLFS	MI	05E	12
LUBBEHUSEN GERALD MARTIN	AZ	03W	53
LUBBERS THOMAS LAMBERT	MO	11W	64
LUBENO JEROME DEANE	WI	22W	47
LUBERDA ANDREW PATRICK	IL	28E	27
LUBESKY GEORGE A JR	CT	36E	55
LUBIN RICHARD MARC	CA	34W	86
LUBONSKI LAWRENCE FRANK	NJ	41E	51
LUC CHESTER ANTHONY	OH	02W	37
LUC FRANK LEO	CA	19E	90
LUCA PATRICK CHARLES	OH	41E	10
LUCAS ALAN FRANK	OH	11E	62
LUCAS ALLEN LEE	MD	39W	41
LUCAS ANDRE CAVARO	CA	08W	46
LUCAS BILLY RAY	KY	10W	66
LUCAS CLYDE AUSTIN	CA	28W	49
LUCAS DAVID GUY	WY	02E	14
LUCAS DONALD RAY	PA	35W	77
LUCAS GLENN ALLEN	NY	36E	55
LUCAS HERBERT GEORGE	CA	45W	27
LUCAS HOWARD LEWIS JR	IL	13W	63
LUCAS JAMES FRANCIS	NY	49W	31
LUCAS JOHN WILLIE	SC	30E	78
LUCAS JOSEPH JR	DC	33E	51
LUCAS KARL	CA	52E	7
LUCAS LARRY FRANCIS	WV	13E	64
LUCAS LARRY JACK	AR	26W	1
LUCAS MICHAEL ELSMERE	CA	17W	45
LUCAS MICHAEL RICHARD	AZ	52E	39
LUCAS MOSES B	PA	16W	49
LUCAS MYRON DONALD	CA	24E	8
LUCAS PATRICK DONOVAN	SC	23E	77
LUCAS PAUL DAVID	OK	18W	110
LUCAS PHILLIP WARREN	CA	41E	40
LUCAS ROBERT EUGENE	VA	46E	47
LUCAS STEVEN ERNEST	IN	07W	110
LUCAS WILBUR RAY	MO	07E	122
LUCAS WILLIAM HARVEY	MN	45W	38
LUCAS WILLIAM ROBERT	OH	30W	91
LUCCHESI GIANCARLO	NY	53E	17
LUCCHI AERIO JOSEPH JR	IL	04W	39
LUCCI CHRISTOPHER DUTCHER	FL	43W	29
LUCE PAUL FRANKLIN	CA	50W	51
LUCE RICHMOND ROSS	FL	21E	14
LUCERO ALBERTO A	CO	05E	107
LUCERO JAMES CLIFFORD	CA	22W	42
LUCERO PATRICK ARNOLD	CO	44E	48
LUCERO ROBERT FLORIENCIO	CO	38E	6
LUCIA STEPHEN WAYNE	CA	29W	38
LUCIANI LAWRENCE ANTHONY	WI	15W	108
LUCIDO JOSEPH BERT	CA	15E	85
LUCIER JOHN WILLIAM	MI	42W	70
LUCISANO ROCCO ROSARIO	NY	42W	57
LUCIW HENRY	NY	11E	119
LUCKENBACH RICHARD M JR	NY	25W	12
LUCKETT JAMES SAWYER II	OH	24W	86
LUCKETT LARRY JOE	CA	32W	14
LUCKEY JAMES ALFRED	FL	34W	77
LUCKI ALBIN EARL	UT	11W	41
LUCKSTEAD EDWIN JOSEF	IA	11E	8
LUCY ARCHIE THOMAS	AL	02W	77
LUDBAN GLEN CHARLES	IN	21W	39
LUDECKER ROBERT	NY	19E	62
LUDVIGSEN LEO JOHN JR	WI	11W	86
LUDWIG BYRON NELSON	OH	10E	9
LUDWIG CHARLES	NY	43E	9
LUDWIG FRANCIS JOSEPH	PA	23E	116
LUDWIG GALEN GEORGE	PA	12W	22
LUDWIG JAMES MICHAEL	MA	36W	30
LUDWIG LARRY GEORGE	NY	23E	12
LUDWIG LEONARD R	CA	24E	104
LUDWIG MICHAEL EUGENE	VA	65W	11
LUDWIG RAYMOND JAMES	DE	24E	8
LUEALLEN EDGAR BOWIE	AL	06E	117
LUEBBERS RALPH JOSEPH JR	MO	64W	11
LUEBKE JOHN CHARLES JR	IL	50W	2
LUEBKERT BERNARD MICHAEL	MO	20W	20
LUECK DOUGLAS ROY	MN	11E	36
LUECKE ROBERT WAYNE	OH	42E	36
LUECKING PAUL J	OH	02W	18
LUEDKE WILLIAM	NE	40W	49
LUERKENS MARVIN ALLEN	IA	05W	134
LUFF EDWARD RICHARD JR	PA	07E	10
LUGAR DENNIS WAYNE	MI	25E	79
LUGO ANTHONY SANTANA	CA	11W	22
LUGO-MOJICA HECTOR	PR	48W	45
LUHNOW GLENN EUGENE	CA	28E	2
LUIS GEORGE GREGORIO	HI	02E	130
LUJAN ENRIQUE	NM	14W	127
LUKAS JEROME KRISTIN	MI	25W	104
LUKASIEWSKI STEPHEN JAMES	CT	04E	24
LUKASIK BERNARD FRANCIS	PA	01E	44
LUKE ARNOLD WAYNE	CA	48W	1
LUKE JOHN ALBERT	WI	04W	28
LUKE RONALD HAROLD	FL	03E	19
LUKE STEVE RALPH	UT	37W	52
LUKENBACH MAX DUANE	AZ	04E	34
LUKENS DONALD GLEN	IL	10W	98
LUKER RICKIE	OR	61W	12
LUKER RUSSELL BURR	OH	04E	130
LUKERT EDWARD ROY	KS	21E	90
LUKES THOMAS BURTON	MI	52W	23
LUKEY GEOFFREY JOHN		17W	46
LUKINS PAUL ROGER	CA	25W	104
LUKITSCH FRANK JOSEPH JR	MO	05W	21
LUKOW MICHAEL EUGENE	CO	03W	106
LULL HOWARD BURDETTE JR	TX	02W	132
LULLA ROBERT ALLEN	OH	47E	33
LULOFS DENNIS JAY	MI	39E	74
LUM DAVID ANTHONY	HI	13E	63
LUMAN RONNIE DEAN	OK	62E	8
LUMLEY DONALD RICHARD	TN	05E	107
LUMM CHARLES LAVERN	NY	44W	50
LUMMUS FRANKLIN JACK	TX	13E	22
LUMPKIN GARY	NJ	13E	1
LUMPKIN HARRY JAMES	GA	07W	123
LUMPKINS LARRY RICHARD	AZ	16E	80
LUMSDEN WILLIAM WAYNE	MD	20E	77
LUNA ABEL	OK	40W	38
LUNA ADOLFO	MI	39E	63
LUNA ANGEL	TX	41W	41
LUNA ANGEL RAFAEL	NY	13E	54
LUNA ARMANDO CERVERA	TX	11W	96
LUNA CARTER PURVIS	MS	30W	102
LUNA DONALD ALFRED	TX	33W	33
LUNA FORTUNATO JR	TX	04E	112
LUNA FRANCISCO	TX	08E	79
LUNA HENRY THOMAS	CA	03E	84
LUNA JOE JR	CA	07W	18
LUNA JULIAN	TX	08W	3
LUNA ROBERT	CA	45E	58
LUNAPIENA NATHAN CHARLES	NJ	32W	80
LUND ARNOLD ATWOOD	AZ	12E	55
LUND HARRY D	WA	12E	28
LUND MICHAEL ORSON	CO	15W	129
LUND RALPH JAMES	NY	45W	59
LUND STEVEN DANNY	UT	18W	79
LUND TERRY BRUCE	WI	15W	113
LUND WILLARD SPENCER	NY	29W	70
LUND WILLIAM EDWARD	PA	17E	7
LUNDBERG PETER THOMAS	CA	18W	65
LUNDBERG WILLIAM RAYMOND	MI	18E	54
LUNDBY LORENCE MARION	IA	42E	72
LUNDE GREGORY HOWARD	ND	37E	61
LUNDELL JACKIE LINN	OH	12W	61
LUNDELL WAYNE THOMAS	MD	03E	84
LUNDEQUAM DONALD JAMES	MN	09W	14
LUNDGREN LAWRENCE EMIL	IN	13W	51
LUNDIN JOHN CHARLES	ND	11W	50
LUNDY ALBRO LYNN JR	CA	05W	5
LUNDY GERALD VERNON	MN	11W	126
LUNDY LONNIE EUGENE	AL	44W	27
LUNDY RANDY JOE	CO	19W	87
LUNDY RICHARD COLEN	VA	22E	15
LUNN EUGENE AUSTIN	MO	19W	70
LUNN TOMMIE RICHARD	WA	19E	28
LUNSFORD GLEN THOMAS	VA	37E	61
LUNSFORD HERBERT LAMAR	MS	23E	119
LUNSFORD JAMES ROBERT	TN	23E	4
LUNSFORD JAMES WILLIAM JR	OH	15W	6
LUNSFORD LEMMIE DEE	NC	39E	40
LUNSFORD PAUL R	OH	26W	45
LUNTSFORD JACK EDWARD	TN	21W	43
LUNZMANN LOWELL EUGENE	NV	43W	6
LUPAS GERALD ALLEN	OH	23E	93
LUPE EUGENE KENNETH	WI	62E	20
LUPIEN DAVID G	NY	41E	11
LUPO FRANCIS DAVID	LA	04W	28

NAME	STATE	PANEL NO.	LINE NO.
LUPO JOSEPH CHARLES	NY	25E	47
LUPOLI ALBERT FRANCIS JR	NY	54W	31
LUPU JOHN WILLIAM	NJ	17W	7
LURIE ROBERT MICHAEL	MS	51W	24
LURTH MELVILLE ALBERT JR	MN	23W	114
LUSCIER HOWARD HENRY	MA	44W	18
LUSCINSKI JAMES TIMOTHY	TN	17W	51
LUSCOMBE DOUGLAS EDWIN	CA	03W	85
LUSE KENNETH ALAN	IA	15W	6
LUSE MICHAEL JOHN	GA	04W	39
LUSHER THOMAS ROY	CO	03W	50
LUSK BERNARD MERLE	IN	25E	58
LUSK DONNIE RAY	CA	26E	79
LUSK SAMMY RAY	TX	53E	17
LUSSIER LARRY PAUL	CA	03E	2
LUSTER DALE ALAN	IL	42W	19
LUSTER LARRY	MI	21W	89
LUSTER MILTON BERNARD	SC	10E	92
LUSTER ROBERT LEE	OH	34W	65
LUTE HARRY GENE	TX	06E	92
LUTE JAMES ROBERT	OH	04E	57
LUTES MARK STANTON	FL	36W	77
LUTGE THOMAS ALBERT	CA	50W	10
LUTGEN CHESTER ARTHUR	IN	07E	131
LUTHER CLAYTON J	WI	09E	85
LUTHER NELSON CHARLES	PA	10W	7
LUTHER ROBERT BENJAMIN	NY	10W	13
LUTRICK DARRELL LEROY	AZ	42W	19
LUTTEL KENNETH BERNARD	IN	09W	2
LUTTGENS JAMES	NJ	08W	3
LUTTRELL BRUCE IRVING	ME	24W	60
LUTTRELL GARY ALLEN	IL	22E	44
LUTTRELL JAMES LEE	KY	55W	14
LUTTRELL JAMES MARTIN	NC	03W	29
LUTTRELL JOHN WALTER	IL	13W	112
LUTTRELL LLOYD IRVIN	KY	34W	73
LUTZ DONALD THOMAS	NC	57W	11
LUTZ GENE MILTON	OH	07E	90
LUTZ HANS PETER	NY	09E	15
LUTZ JOSEPH PATRICK	FL	09W	73
LUTZ LARRY EUGENE	OH	53E	17
LUTZ ROBERT EDWARD JR	OH	02W	105
LUTZ ROBERT STEVEN	WI	37E	61
LUTZ WERNER ERHARD	NJ	01E	130
LUTZ WILLIAM	PA	08E	76
LUTZ WILLIAM LEE	NC	25W	76
LUTZ WILMER THOMAS	MD	38W	12
LUTZE JOHN EDWIN	MI	39W	37
LUTZKE MICHAEL JON	WI	15E	97
LUX ANTHONY RAYMOND	IN	41W	74
LYBERGER ARDEN RUSSELL	VA	06W	114
LYBRAND CARL FREDERICK	PA	24W	96
LYDEN DENNIS M	MI	05E	120
LYDEN MICHAEL P	IL	24W	18
LYDIC DAVID ALLEN	PA	01W	20
LYDON RALPH JOSEPH JR	PA	59E	26
LYERLY RONALD WAYNE	NC	16E	29
LYKINS DANIEL CLYDE	OH	10E	41
LYLE ALAN DAVID	PA	57W	4
LYLE JOHN BRUCE	AL	22W	23
LYLE LARRY VANN	AL	29E	60
LYLE MICHAEL STEVEN	CO	20E	96
LYLE TERRANCE RICHARD	CA	12E	51
LYLES BELTON JR	SC	03E	2
LYLES CHARLIE JR	SC	12E	83
LYLES J L	IL	15E	48
LYLES MICHAEL ALLEN	IL	02E	53
LYLES OSCAR BURL JR	TN	15W	86
LYMAN ALAN RICHARD	TX	57W	12
LYMAN CHARLES LEE	NC	48W	7
LYMAN GERALD CLYDE	CA	04E	133
LYNAH TIMOTHY JOSEPH	MA	16E	22
LYNCH BERNARD	NY	08W	3
LYNCH BRUCE ANTHONY	OK	38W	59
LYNCH CARL DONALD	NY	23W	89
LYNCH CHARLES AARON	NY	22E	71
LYNCH DANIEL FRANCIS JR	MA	16W	66
LYNCH DANIEL MICHAEL	IL	18W	48
LYNCH FREDERICK GEORGE JR	PA	05E	119
LYNCH GERALD JAMES	PA	10W	14
LYNCH JAMES JOSEPH III	NY	27W	32
LYNCH JAMES MARTIN	PA	24E	33
LYNCH JAMES OLIVER	MI	27W	75
LYNCH JOHN CHARLES P	MI	11E	9
LYNCH JOHN EDWARD	PA	22W	54
LYNCH JOHN WILLIAM III	CA	05W	27
LYNCH JUSTIN MARSHALL	NC	03E	25
LYNCH KEVIN FRANCIS	MA	07W	49
LYNCH MICHAEL	NY	29W	46
LYNCH MICHAEL HENRY	KY	60E	14
LYNCH MICHAEL JOSEPH	NY	38E	55
LYNCH PETER	NY	22W	23
LYNCH PHILLIP EDMOND	IN	28W	37
LYNCH PINK MILTON JR	VA	11E	45
LYNCH REGINALD WAYNE	NC	14E	57
LYNCH RICHARD E	IN	02E	112
LYNCH RICHARD THOMAS	PA	01E	63
LYNCH ROBERT LAWRENCE	CA	16W	9
LYNCH SAMUEL ROY	TX	06W	130
LYNCH STEPHEN MICHAEL	WV	06W	130
LYNCH STEPHEN WILLIAM	AR	01W	39
LYNCH TIMOTHY JAMES	IN	03W	133
LYNCH WILLIAM AFFLEY JR	CA	12E	124
LYNE MICHAEL WILLIAM	NC	14W	8
LYNN ADRIAN LOUIS JR	TX	30E	71
LYNN DOYLE WILMER	PA	01E	125
LYNN HOMER MORGAN JR	IL	33W	65
LYNN JACK DALE	OH	03E	84
LYNN JAMES E	WI	32E	2
LYNN JOHN JOSEPH JR	IL	14E	1
LYNN JOHN THOMAS	WA	51W	27
LYNN JOHNNY RALPH	TN	30W	47
LYNN RICHARD ROBERT	PA	45E	24
LYNN ROBERT RAY	IL	01W	101
LYNN ROY EUGENE	OK	30W	31
LYNN STEPHEN DAVID	AL	15W	22
LYNN WELDON GEORGE	GA	32W	50
LYNN WILLIAM THOMAS	IN	23W	103
LYON CHRISTOPHER EDWIN	MI	37E	39
LYON DONAVAN LOREN	CA	45E	58
LYON FRANK ELLIOT	KY	26E	61
LYON JAMES MICHAEL	IN	14W	104
LYON JOHN PAUL	MA	26W	1
LYONS CARL	CA	45E	59
LYONS CHESTER GEORGE	CA	05W	125
LYONS FRANK ELLIS	NJ	08E	53
LYONS GARY DEAN	OH	22E	107
LYONS GEORGE MICHAEL	NJ	22W	112
LYONS JAMES ANDREW	MI	48W	7
LYONS JAMES E	PA	30E	16
LYONS JAMES JR	SC	08E	7
LYONS JOE L	TX	30E	29
LYONS JOHN JOSEPH	NY	12W	83
LYONS JOHN MICHAEL	PA	43W	6
LYONS JOSEPH WALTER	AZ	60W	19
LYONS LARRY JEROME	TN	48E	29
LYONS MALCOLM JOSEPH	LA	05W	53
LYONS MARION WAYNE	AR	31W	53
LYONS MONTAGUE	KY	31E	49
LYONS PATRICK NICHOLAS	WI	15E	119
LYONS QUILLARD FRANK	LA	49E	44
LYONS ROBERT PAUL	KS	27W	25
LYONS ROGER GENE	OH	38E	55
LYONS THOMAS JOSEPH	NY	21W	76
LYONS THOMAS KEVIN	PA	53E	36
LYONS WALTER JOHN	AR	21E	107
LYONS WILLIAM JOHN	CA	03E	19
LYONS WILLIAM MICHAEL III	NJ	18W	34
LYONS WILLIAM PERRY	IL	09W	118
LYSAGHT ROBERT JOHN	NY	09E	75
LYTAL JAMES FRANCIS	NJ	16E	53
LYTLE CLIFFORD JAMES	CA	29E	68
LYTLE MICHAEL LINN	IA	17W	122
LYTLE RICHARD WALTER	IN	16W	14
LYTTON BALFOUR OLIVER JR	MD	46E	20
LYVERE RONALD LEE	MI	18E	86
MAAG JOSEPH ANTHONY JR	IA	53E	3
MAAHS MILO GEORGE	MN	34W	51
MAAS CLARENCE F III	TX	40E	9
MAAS ROY FRANCIS	MN	26W	1
MABE CARL MARION	VA	47E	40
MABE ROGER DALE	VA	30E	45
MABE RONALD LEE	NC	63W	8
MABE TOMMY DARRELL	NC	45E	24
MABEE DOUGLAS CRAIGLOW	OH	12W	118
MABERRY CALVIN DWIGHT	TX	17E	21
MABERY DAVID MICHAEL	NC	37E	39
MABLE WASHINGTON CARVER	TX	31E	76
MABREY GARY MICHIEL	CA	49W	15
MABRY DONALD HENRY	TX	49W	24
MABRY RALPH EDGAR JR	OK	35E	75
MACAGBA EDILBERTO DULA	CA	44E	38
MACARELL MICHAEL JOSEPH	NJ	12E	66
MACCHIONI ALPHONSE JOSEPH	RI	63W	18
MACCIO DONALD J	NY	20W	57
MACE BRADLEY THOMAS	MN	13W	79
MACE DANA LEROY	ME	21W	76
MACE DAVID LESLIE	WA	42W	41
MACE JAMES DOYLE	UT	12W	114
MACEDONIO CARMINE ANGELO	NY	06W	113
MACEY EARL FRANCIS JR	NY	33E	9
MACHACEK WILLIAM ALLEN	IL	31E	76
MACHADO FRANCISCO JR	AZ	36E	78
MACHADO GARY ALLAEN	CA	09E	2
MACHADO ROBERTS	HI	12E	89
MACHALICA JOSEPH PAUL	IL	12E	6
MACHATA RUDOLPH GEORGE	CO	24W	87
MACHAU JOHNIE BOYD	OR	26E	48
MACHEN ARTHUR WEBSTER III	MD	06W	102
MACHEN BILLY WAYNE	TX	10E	19
MACHIE MICHAEL ALLEN	CT	62W	12
MACHOWSKI JOSEPH ANTHONY	CT	07E	108
MACHRISTIE ANDREW	PA	06W	107
MACHUL JOHN FRANCIS	MI	17W	10
MACHUT RICHARD RAY	IL	56W	14
MACIAS JOE	TX	35W	72
MACIAS ROBERTO JAVIER	TX	16W	30
MACIAS TRISTAL	TX	63W	9
MACIEL PETER JR	CO	14E	70
MACIMINIO ANTONIO PAUL	RI	07E	97
MACIUSZEK PAUL JOSEPH	CT	21E	35
MACK ALLEN GLENN	PA	48E	30
MACK ALVIN ANTHONY JR	OH	61E	13
MACK CALVIN DAVID	LA	05W	5
MACK DANIEL JAMES	SC	06E	85
MACK DANNY RAY	CA	29W	70
MACK DENNIS LEE	MI	68W	6
MACK DOUGLAS DULANE	TX	01E	104
MACK EARL	MD	39E	51
MACK FRANCIS WILLIAM	NJ	10E	16
MACK GARY LEIGH	WA	53E	4
MACK GEORGE JACOB	RI	07E	59
MACK HAROLD JR	SC	07E	97
MACK JAMES	LA	19W	102
MACK JOSEPH BINGHAM JR	GA	10E	108
MACK JOSEPH DEAN	MS	68E	5
MACK LARRY WESLEY	IL	51E	9
MACK ROBERT LEE	CA	06E	45
MACK ROBERT LEWIS	OH	05E	61
MACK WILLIAM JAMES	NY	14E	58
MACK WILLIE EDWARD	GA	09W	39
MACKAY NEILE COOPER	ID	14W	23
MACKAY PAUL ALFRED	NY	23E	87
MACKAY WILLIAM MICHAEL	NV	19W	70
MACKEDANZ LYLE EVERETT	MN	51E	22
MACKEN CHARLES DAVIS	GA	30W	78
MACKEY DAVID RANDELL	KY	18W	103
MACKEY DONALD ANDREW	NY	05W	93
MACKEY LARRY ALLEN	IL	07W	133
MACKEY ROBERT EUGENE	FL	45W	63
MACKEY TALTON LEE	OK	37W	75
MACKEY THOMAS EARL	CA	04W	123
MACKEY VERTIS L	GA	30E	78
MACKEY WILLIAM RUSSELL JR	MN	29W	1
MACKLIN RAYMOND LOUIS	MD	17E	45
MACKLIN RONALD WAYNE	CA	02E	127
MACKO CHARLES	NY	32W	80
MACOMB ORRIE E JR	NY	20E	32
MACOMBER CLIFFORD F JR	TX	10W	13
MACON JOSEPH	NC	44W	39
MACON SAMUEL CORNELIUS	FL	31W	53
MACY JAMES ROBERT	MD	35W	35
MACY JOSEPH DEAN	IN	27W	75
MACZULSKI WACLAW JOZEF	NJ	45E	51
MADDEN DAVID ALLEN	CA	22W	91
MADDEN DONALD EUGENE	TN	15E	97

NAME	STATE	PANEL NO.	LINE NO.
MADDEN ERNEST GARY	OH	19E	98
MADDEN FRANCIS BERNARD JR	NJ	22W	54
MADDEN JAMES FLOYD	AL	18E	5
MADDEN JOHN MARTIN JR	MA	26W	48
MADDEN JOHN PAUL	OH	20W	15
MADDEN LEON SHIRLEY	SC	21W	24
MADDEN PAUL BERNARD	NJ	10E	54
MADDEN RICHARD JR	OH	08E	4
MADDEN RORY ANTONIO	OK	27E	84
MADDEN THOMAS ANDREW II	IL	14W	69
MADDEN WILLIE ERSKINE	SC	30W	27
MADDOX HAROLD WAYNE	IL	15E	85
MADDOX JULIUS	MI	45E	58
MADDOX MARCUS WAYNE	TX	09W	58
MADDOX NOTLEY GWYNN	IL	20E	63
MADDOX PAUL RAY	OH	32E	52
MADDOX PHILIP NEIL	NE	07E	114
MADDOX RICHARD GREENE	CA	43W	69
MADDOX ROBERT BRUCE	MO	32W	13
MADDUX DAVID ALLEN	TX	45E	41
MADDUX DAVID THORNTON	WI	08W	98
MADDUX ROY RAYMOND JR	CA	41E	68
MADDY KENNETH LYNN	UT	11E	123
MADDY LARRY ROBERT	IL	33W	50
MADEL ROBERT THOMAS	NY	53E	36
MADER RICHARD MICHAEL	OH	14W	85
MADIGAN JOHN EDWARD JR	MA	27E	65
MADISON CYRIL HYMAN	TX	01W	27
MADISON FRANK ANTHONY	NY	18E	19
MADISON HENRY JR	NY	31W	82
MADISON JOHN B	IA	40E	24
MADISON RICHARD CARL	VA	55E	22
MADISON THOMAS VERNON	WI	09E	63
MADISON WILLIAM CURTIS	TN	18E	5
MADISON WILLIAM LOUIS	KY	07E	62
MADLAND ROBERT LOUIS	MN	25E	30
MADONNA DOMINICK JOSEPH	PA	19W	96
MADRID ADANO HERNENDEZ	CA	25W	76
MADRID ERNEST	AZ	36E	22
MADRID FRANK DODGE	NM	14W	76
MADRID FRANK JESSE LEE	NM	40E	65
MADRID GABRIEL HERNANDEZ	NM	26W	92
MADRID MICHAEL PHILLIP	CA	52W	45
MADRIGAL-CORDERO RAFAEL A JR	CA	45E	49
MADRUGA MANUEL DOMINIC	CA	36W	64
MADSEN MARK EUGENE	IL	36W	26
MADSEN MARLOW ERLING	MN	14E	49
MADSEN WILLIAM JOSEPH	IL	13E	59
MADSON ROBERT WARREN	IL	49E	17
MAES DANIEL JOHN	MI	05W	134
MAES PEDRO MIGUEL	CA	26W	111
MAESE JORGE V	TX	12W	6
MAESTAS GILBERT MERILL	CA	43W	29
MAGAHA DANNY ROY	SC	14W	101
MAGALLAN NOE	TX	11E	3
MAGBEE G W	SC	01E	24
MAGBY LLOYD BURNEY	NM	17E	86
MAGEE BOYD	LA	11W	50
MAGEE HERMAN PAUL	MS	51W	34
MAGEE JOHN EARL	CA	59E	8
MAGEE JOHN JOSEPH	MA	41E	24
MAGEE MITCHELL JR	IN	15W	94
MAGEE PATRICK JOSEPH	MT	05W	22
MAGEE RALPH WAYNE	LA	01E	2
MAGEL JAMES EDWARD	MO	01E	98
MAGER VINCENT LEO	WI	38W	76
MAGERR WILLIAM LEO III	PA	19W	70
MAGERS PAUL GERALD	NE	03W	61
MAGGARD DANNY JOE	ID	29W	70
MAGGARD LARRY DWIGHT	KY	60W	19
MAGGIO JOSEPH ANTHONY JR	IL	20E	104
MAGGIO RANDALL EUGENE	IL	02W	48
MAGGS ROBERT HOWARD	PA	02W	32
MAGISTRO ANTHONY PHILIP	NY	14E	45
MAGLIARO CHARLES LOUIS	NJ	25E	70
MAGNON MYRON WILLIAM	TX	38W	76
MAGNUSON DAVID JACK	IL	08W	36
MAGNUSON ERIC C JR	NJ	13E	102
MAGNUSSON FRED WAYNE	AL	34E	59
MAGNUSSON JAMES A JR	MA	01E	100
MAGRASS JOEL MICHAEL	MA	15W	130
MAGRI GIUSEPPE	NY	34W	15
MAGRIE DENNIS LOUIS	PA	35E	75
MAGRUDER DARRELL ZANE	PA	06E	123
MAGRUDER DAVID BYRON	KY	10W	52
MAGRUDER DOUGLAS GRAHAM	FL	30E	18
MAGSAMEN FREDERICK JOHN	MD	25W	32
MAGUIRE CALVIN GENE	PA	21W	109
MAGUIRE CHRISTOPHER J III	CA	22E	108
MAGUIRE DANIEL JOHN	NY	31E	81
MAGUIRE GERALD JOSEPH	PA	14E	98
MAGUIRE JACK IVAN	PA	25E	70
MAGUIRE KEVIN JAMES	NY	34E	59
MAGUIRE ROBERT STANLEY	CA	21E	123
MAGUIRE WILLIAM A JR	NJ	17W	17
MAGYAR BLAZE III	IL	33E	71
MAGYAROSI JOHN JOSEPH	UT	07E	72
MAHAN DARREL ULDRIC	TX	25E	17
MAHAN DAVID ALLAN	OH	44W	50
MAHAN DOUGLAS FRANK	MO	11W	28
MAHAN ROBERT CARY	KY	22W	99
MAHANA VANNY CHRIS	TX	15E	62
MAHARG EVERT RALPH	MI	18E	95
MAHER EDWARD MICHAEL JR	NJ	50W	52
MAHER HAROLD WILLIAM	PA	28W	62
MAHER LOUIS JOSEPH JR	IN	46E	8
MAHER MARTIN JOSEPH	OH	25W	7
MAHER PAUL IVAN	NY	05E	120
MAHL KENNETH ARTHUR	LA	21W	46
MAHLER JAMES WILLIAM	MA	02E	79
MAHNER LIN ALBERT	WI	24W	105
MAHON RICHARD MICHAEL	NY	15W	125
MAHONE HAYWOOD JR	VA	47W	48
MAHONE WILLIAM BENJAMIN	OH	25E	104
MAHONEY ALFRED RICHARD JR	CA	40W	65
MAHONEY ERNEST	OH	40E	25
MAHONEY HARRY CURTIS JR	DC	14E	64
MAHONEY JOHN MORRISON	WV	19W	17
MAHONEY MICHAEL THOMAS	PA	35E	61
MAHONEY RALPH GEORGE	OH	10E	92
MAHONEY RALPH MARTIN	CA	51E	23
MAHONEY RONALD J	WI	13E	23
MAHONEY THOMAS P III	CA	53W	27
MAHONEY TIMOTHY KEITH	TX	44W	65
MAHOWALD MICHAEL ALLEN	MN	22W	58
MAHURIN ELMER WAIN	MO	27E	90
MAHURTER LAWRENCE WILLIAM	NJ	26W	65
MAHY HAROLD EUGENE	SC	18E	23
MAIATO JAMES COSTA JR	MA	39W	55
MAIDENS MICHAEL ROBERT	MI	10W	109
MAIER DAVID ROY	CA	21W	112
MAIER GLENN ERVIN	ND	08W	10
MAILHES LAWRENCE SCOTT	AR	02E	50
MAILLOUX EARL ADELBERT	CA	35E	34
MAILLOUX JOHN JOSEPH	MA	38W	50
MAIN CHARLES REID	VA	32W	60
MAIN RICHARD HAROLD	NY	05E	1
MAIN ROBERT JAMES	MA	01E	22
MAIN WILLIAM GENE JR	OH	09E	83
MAIN WILLIAM TERRY	FL	06E	122
MAINARDY GEORGE WILLIAM	NY	02W	137
MAIORANA RONALD VINCENT	NY	30E	71
MAIR ALLAN LEON	UT	47E	23
MAISANO JOSEPH ANTHONY	MI	43W	69
MAISEY REGINALD VICTOR JR	CA	36E	23
MAIURO JOSEPH	NJ	25E	8
MAIZE WILSON JUNIOR	MO	10E	77
MAJER CHARLES ANTHONY	NY	49E	13
MAJESKI MICHAEL THOMAS	NJ	50W	19
MAJKOWSKI DONALD HENRY	IL	14W	58
MAJOR GERRY DEWAYNE	IA	44E	49
MAJOR KENNETH CARROLL JR	NY	36W	26
MAJOR LA MARRE ARTHUR	MI	16E	69
MAJOR ROBERT WARREN	CA	19W	40
MAJOR STEVEN ROBERT	IL	43W	56
MAJORS DANIEL WILLIAM	TN	18W	16
MAJORS JAMES RAY	TX	24E	68
MAJURE EUGENE JEHLEN	MS	10E	17
MAKAREWICZ DANIEL	MI	25E	13
MAKI FRANK RUDOLPH	MI	03W	86
MAKI GLEN ARVID	MI	26E	76
MAKI ROGER LEE	MN	05W	129
MAKIN ALLEN THEODORE II	AZ	16E	84
MAKIN JAMES BRIAN LAWRENC	SC	45E	3
MAKIN WOODROW JR	SC	64W	12
MAKINTAYA ALEJANDRO	TX	02W	14
MAKOWSKI WILLIAM JOHN	NY	02W	46
MAKSIN MIKE A	OH	33E	51
MAKSYMIW WALTER B	IL	38E	69
MAKUCK MICHAEL PATRICK	CA	52E	7
MAKUH FRANK JOSEPH	CA	59E	26
MALABE JULIO	NY	28W	84
MALABEY BENJAMIN KEALII	HI	05W	125
MALAPELLI JOHN WAYNE	KY	01E	87
MALARZ RENE LEE	WA	25E	39
MALASPINA RICHARD THOMAS	PA	11E	31
MALATESTA LARRY JOE	WA	08W	75
MALAVE-RIOS ABELARDO	NY	41E	51
MALBROUGH CHARLES RAY	LA	09E	35
MALCOLM JOHN DANIEL	CT	07W	5
MALCOLM WILLIAM EDWARD JR	OH	11W	103
MALCZYNSKI MATTHEW PAUL	IL	32E	64
MALDONADO ABRAEL	NY	32W	60
MALDONADO ANTHONY GILBERT	CA	36E	23
MALDONADO BALTAZAR A	TX	12E	121
MALDONADO CARLOS O	MI	30W	67
MALDONADO JORGE JOSEPH	NY	23E	53
MALDONADO JOSE	NY	02W	58
MALDONADO JUAN ARTURO	PR	34W	26
MALDONADO PATRICIO JR	TX	41E	69
MALDONADO-AGUILAR BENJAMIN	PR	33W	65
MALDONADO-LLUBERAS ALBERT	PR	13W	48
MALDONADO-TORRES LIONEL	PR	43W	17
MALEC DENNIS STANLEY	MI	51W	6
MALEC PAUL WILLIAM	AL	07E	59
MALECKE JAMES ALLEN	OH	17E	53
MALECKI ROBERT RICHARD	IL	25W	104
MALENFANT WILLIAM ARTHUR	NH	05W	46
MALESZEWSKI PAUL EDWARD	FL	39W	34
MALEWICZ EDWARD A JR	NY	02E	118
MALEWSKI DENIS W	OH	05E	133
MALEY CHARLES THOMAS	NY	14W	127
MALICEK DONALD JOSEPH	OH	24W	45
MALICHI BOBBY SPENCER	SC	36W	76
MALIN LOUIS NATHANIL	MO	27E	21
MALIN MICHAEL LEE	NY	28W	38
MALINOWSKI EDWARD	OH	09E	89
MALINS DAVID REAY	NM	27E	54
MALKUT STEFAN	MI	26W	20
MALL RONALD AVERY	NM	02W	136
MALLARD MORRIS A JR	GA	49W	24
MALLETT DOUGLAS MACKARTHE	MI	58W	5
MALLETTE AVON NORRIS	MS	06W	132
MALLINCKRODT ARTHUR T H JR	MO	25W	7
MALLOBOX JESSE ARMANDO	CA	25W	105
MALLON JAMES JOSEPH JR	IN	28E	61
MALLON RICHARD JOSEPH	OR	14W	76
MALLON THOMAS JOHN	NJ	16E	12
MALLON THOMAS WINSTON	CA	19E	15
MALLONEE KENNETH A	IA	11E	40
MALLORY CONNARD DARRELL	KY	37W	67
MALLORY DAVID ALLEN	AL	31W	53
MALLORY JERRY DOUGLAS	MI	37E	33
MALLORY WILLIAM EARL JR	IN	17E	7
MALLOY JAMES FRANCIS	MN	35W	44
MALLOY JOHN JOSEPH	MA	23E	20
MALLOY JOHN PERRY	GA	12W	30
MALLOY THOMAS VINCENT	NY	23E	37
MALLOY THOMAS WILLIAM	PA	32E	81
MALMANIS ULDIS JACK	NY	41W	36
MALMAY THOMAS SIMON	LA	07W	93
MALMQUIST PIERCE	PA	41W	30
MALNAR JOHN MARION	IL	54E	11
MALONE CHARLES KENNETH	PA	12E	103
MALONE CHARLES WALTER	KS	17W	42
MALONE CLIFTON	TN	47E	52
MALONE FELIX	CA	02W	23
MALONE HERBERT LEE	MS	26W	72
MALONE JAMES EDGAR	CA	37E	10
MALONE JIMMY MCDONALD	VA	07E	26
MALONE JOHN EDWARD	CA	50E	17
MALONE LAWRENCE MICHAEL	WA	33E	71
MALONE LEO FREDRICK	NY	48E	40
MALONE PHILIP NEWMAN	VA	30W	57
MALONE RICHARD CLAIR	IL	19E	53

NAME	STATE	PANEL NO.	LINE NO.
MALONE RICHARD LEE	NY	29W	90
MALONE ROBERT EARL	TX	50E	4
MALONE ROBERT GARY	KS	09E	83
MALONE SIDNEY JACK JR	CA	09E	70
MALONE WALLACE JAMES	NE	12E	106
MALONE WILLIAM FRANKLIN	TN	22W	106
MALONE WILLIAM WALTER	TX	05W	125
MALONE WILLIE EDWARD JR	TX	29W	54
MALONEY CHARLES DEO	PA	09W	60
MALONEY DANIEL JOSEPH	NY	09W	131
MALONEY JAMES PATRICK JR	NY	02W	64
MALONEY JEFFERY RAYMOND	CT	18E	95
MALONEY JOHN EDWARD JR	NY	36E	78
MALONEY JOHN FRANCIS JR	RI	09W	39
MALONEY MICHAEL KEVIN	IA	04W	4
MALONEY OSCAR	AZ	06W	35
MALONEY THOMAS ROBERT	NY	68W	5
MALOY GARY LEE	FL	48W	11
MALOY RICHARD FRANCIS	NY	06E	110
MALOY TERRY LEE	IN	28E	83
MALSEED FRANK JAMES JR	PA	46E	20
MALUEG MICHAEL PAUL	WI	30W	58
MAMBRETTI DANIEL IRVIN	OR	14W	82
MAMIE RICHARD NORMAN	OH	21W	9
MAMIYA JOHN MICHIO	HI	09E	88
MAMMOLITTI JOSEPH A	NY	10E	54
MAMON CESAR JABONILLO	CA	47W	1
MANAC DON	GA	08W	125
MANAREL CHARLES ROSS	CT	22W	23
MANCA RONALD JOHN	NY	02W	111
MANCHESTER GARY ORAL C	ME	15W	94
MANCHESTER JAY HARRISON	RI	29W	63
MANCHESTER JOHN SMYTHE	ME	52E	40
MANCILL DONALD BRYAN	PA	18W	48
MANCINI RICHARD MICHAEL	NY	34E	30
MANCINO SALVATORE JOHN	NY	50W	7
MANCUSO ANTHONY JOHN	NY	55W	36
MANCUSO JOSEPH ANTHONY	NY	20E	46
MANCUSO SALVATORE	NY	33W	66
MANDARINO JOSEPH	NY	38E	6
MANDERFELD KENNETH JAY	IL	25E	12
MANDERFELD THOMAS GEORGE	MN	27W	50
MANDEVILLE ROSS EDWARD	OK	19W	70
MANDLER JAMES THOMAS	OH	20E	1
MANDRACCHIA PAUL SCOTT	NY	11W	14
MANELA RANDALL PAUL	OR	06W	68
MANELLO FRANK RONALD	MD	40E	54
MANEMANN RICHARD RAYMOND	CA	16W	17
MANER HOWARD JOSEPH	MI	22W	79
MANESS ALAN CARSON	NC	18W	28
MANESS JAMES EMORY	AL	25E	86
MANESS MARTIN ROWLAND	OK	61W	4
MANESS STEVEN WAYNE	CA	04W	116
MANEY RALPH WARREN	MA	45E	58
MANFERDINI JOHN SEBASTIAN	MA	21W	54
MANGAN MICHAEL L	OH	22E	66
MANGAN MICHAEL ROBERT	CA	47W	20
MANGANELLO ANTHONY JR	NJ	46W	51
MANGAT FREDRICK CHARLES	OR	07E	72
MANGER JAMES ALLEN	IN	45W	7
MANGIN MARK DANIEL	ND	17W	23
MANGINO THOMAS ANGELO	OH	18E	61
MANGIOLARDO MICHAEL ANTHO	PA	36E	31
MANGOLD CARL JOSEPH	TX	02E	71
MANGOLD LEO JOSEPH	PA	30W	27
MANGRUM GEORGE THOMAS	AL	22E	84
MANGRUM RICHARD GALE	FL	33E	71
MANGUAL JOSE MANUEL	NY	14W	35
MANGUM ROBIN	SC	15W	32
MANGUM SAM HENRY	TX	16W	14
MANGUM THEODORE EDWARD JR	MD	20W	58
MANGUM WILLIAM THOMAS JR	MS	39E	74
MANGUS ARLIE ROBERT	PA	02W	61
MANHEIM VERNON ARTHUR JR	IL	10E	41
MANIAS ROBERT JAMES	NJ	03W	105
MANIERE MICHAEL JOHN	MI	10W	71
MANIGO EUGENE	FL	32E	37
MANINGER RAYMOND MARCINE	FL	08W	75
MANINO SALVATORE PATRICK	NY	25W	112
MANIS EDDIE	TN	19E	98
MANK ROYAL CHARLES	MI	57W	20
MANKA DOUGLAS THOMAS	MN	01W	91

NAME	STATE	PANEL NO.	LINE NO.
MANLEY RICHARD JOSEPH	MO	06E	101
MANLEY RONALD LEE	OH	16E	62
MANLY FREDERICK LEE	CO	33E	20
MANN CARL WILLIAM	AL	02E	92
MANN CHARLES CLIFTON JR	AR	39W	22
MANN DANIEL MCCARTHY	IL	17E	117
MANN DAVID LYLE	IA	23W	76
MANN DAVID ROY	IL	23W	10
MANN EDDIE MORRIS	GA	19E	73
MANN EDWARD HAROLD	MO	34W	43
MANN EDWARD LEONARD JR	ME	53E	14
MANN GARLAND RAY	AR	31E	49
MANN GLENN DILL	VA	03E	111
MANN HAROLD VAN JR	NC	14W	66
MANN JAMES EDWARD	CT	42W	70
MANN JOHN HAROLD	GA	31E	25
MANN NATHAN JAMES	MO	12W	71
MANN ROBERT BERNARD	NH	09E	17
MANN ROBERT JAMES	WI	13E	126
MANN ROBERT LEE	IN	02E	130
MANN RUSSELL CLAIR	NY	03W	98
MANN THOMAS CHARLES	PA	35W	72
MANNEROW PAUL DAVID	MI	25W	40
MANNERS DAVID PAUL	OK	07E	97
MANNERS RALPH WILLIAM	NY	46W	31
MANNERS VAN DYKE WILLIAM	NJ	15E	34
MANNERY RICHARD CHARLES	WA	50W	14
MANNIE ROGER MICHAEL	MN	03E	3
MANNINA MICHAEL CARMELO	NY	39W	44
MANNING BRUCE K	NY	21E	14
MANNING CHARLES EDWARD	TX	25W	76
MANNING DAVID KARL		35W	66
MANNING DAVID LAWRENCE	CO	09E	106
MANNING DENNIS CARROL	MI	04E	12
MANNING DENNIS DEWAIN	FL	50W	36
MANNING GLENN ROBERT	LA	15W	67
MANNING JAMES HOLDEN	CT	21W	84
MANNING JERRY	TX	21W	112
MANNING JERRY WAYNE	CA	17E	103
MANNING JOHN EDWARD	TX	35E	75
MANNING JOHN WARREN	CT	21W	77
MANNING PATRICK PEARSE	MO	02E	45
MANNING RALPH E	GA	08E	81
MANNING RALPH EDWARD	GA	24E	33
MANNING ROBERT THOMAS	NY	28W	27
MANNING RONALD	LA	09W	56
MANNING RONALD JAMES	OH	01W	131
MANNING THOMAS R	IN	15E	14
MANNING WILLIAM TERRY	AL	43E	57
MANNION AUGUST GORDIAN JR	MD	13E	65
MANNION DENNIS JOHN	MA	19E	43
MANNO MICHAEL RALPH	NY	43W	48
MANNS CHARLES EDWARD	VA	23E	20
MANNS EDWARD EMIL	NY	14E	108
MANNS ROGER D	IN	07E	49
MANNS ROY NANCE	TN	19E	27
MANOR JAMES	FL	02W	120
MANOS ARTHUR	FL	56E	27
MANOWSKI EDWARD	CA	37E	10
MANRING CURTIS JOHNSON	NC	07W	12
MANRIQUE RAMIRO JR	IL	09E	17
MANSELLE EUGENE L III	CT	56W	36
MANSERGH WILLIAM A JR	CA	26W	100
MANSFIELD BRUCE ELWIN	RI	08E	11
MANSFIELD CLAYTON JOHN JR	TX	02E	41
MANSFIELD DONALD LEWIS	ME	49E	45
MANSFIELD JOHN MICHAEL	CT	40W	45
MANSFIELD JOHN MONTAGUE	NY	16E	47
MANSFIELD PATRICK LEROY	AZ	59E	2
MANSFIELD WILLIAM GRANVIL	NY	11E	126
MANSIR PAUL WAYNE	TX	02E	81
MANSKE CHARLES JEROME	TX	24W	96
MANSKE DENNIS RUDOLPH	WI	21E	94
MANSKE PAUL EDWARD	WI	19E	109
MANSON DENNIS JAMES	ND	23W	89
MANSON JAMES EDWARD JR	PA	50W	8
MANSON JOHN EDWARD	IA	54E	27
MANSOR THOMAS NICKOLAS	PA	52W	39
MANSTIS ANTHONY WAYNE	IL	11W	31
MANTERNACH MARVIN GEORGE	IA	13E	75
MANTHEI JAMES WALTER	WI	04W	64
MANTHEY BARRY ARTHUR	NJ	48W	13

NAME	STATE	PANEL NO.	LINE NO.
MANTON BRUCE ARTHUR	OH	20E	63
MANTOOTH JIMMIE HUGH	TX	21E	83
MANTOOTH LEONARD HAYES JR	KY	02W	96
MANTOUVALES ANTHONY RALPH	MA	32E	25
MANUEL FRANCIS EVERETT	VA	57W	29
MANUEL JESSE STEPHEN JR	VA	23W	38
MANUEL LARRY GEORGE	IL	47E	13
MANUEL ROLAND WILL	NJ	30E	57
MANZ TERRY LEE	WI	14E	91
MANZANARES CHARLES EDWARD	CO	03E	131
MANZANARES JOSE ADORO	CO	34E	22
MANZANARES WILLIAM JR	TX	44W	51
MANZARO DANIEL VICTOR	MA	06E	72
MANZI JOHN PETER	NY	26E	27
MAPE JOHN CLEMENT	CA	06E	112
MAPES EDDIE D	ID	08W	12
MAPLE ARCHIE JAMES JR	MO	28E	9
MAPLE HOLLIS GARNELL	IN	18W	16
MAPLES FRANCIS LEROY	TX	29E	90
MAPLES PAUL EDWARD	TN	27W	26
MAQUILING LEONARD GIDEON	HI	02W	52
MARA JOSEPH P	IL	03E	103
MARABLE WALTER A JR	NY	28E	83
MARACZI ANTHONY	MO	22E	109
MARASCO JOSEPH ALLEN	NY	20W	34
MARASCO PHILIP	NY	50W	30
MARASCO WILLIAM FREDERICK	NY	37W	40
MARASON JOHN EDGAR	NJ	37W	23
MARATTA CRAIG	PA	07W	118
MARBUTT GARY THOMAS	GA	23E	80
MARCANO CARLOS ALBERTO	NY	50E	49
MARCANO WINSTON ELVETTE	NY	45W	27
MARCANO-DIAZ GAMALIEL	PR	12E	103
MARCANTEL ELBERT	LA	03W	84
MARCANTONI ROBERT JOHN	NJ	49E	9
MARCANTONIO JOSEPH FRANK	NY	08W	99
MARCAURELE LIONEL LUCIEN	CT	22W	79
MARCAVAGE ROBERT JOHN	PA	11E	77
MARCEAUX ERASTE JOHN	LA	50W	25
MARCELLO JOHN BERNARD	CA	68W	6
MARCH DONALD GEROLD	MI	08W	25
MARCH FRANK JR	FL	65E	13
MARCH FREDERICK LUTHER	MD	20E	63
MARCHAND THOMAS MICHAEL	PA	22W	34
MARCHAND WAYNE ELLSWORTH	NE	01E	8
MARCHANT PAUL LAFONTAINE	IL	17W	88
MARCHBANK LARRY OVERTON	VA	12W	6
MARCHBANKS R B JR	NM	07E	119
MARCHESE THOMAS VINCENT	NY	15W	51
MARCHESI JIMMY EUGENE	CO	06W	32
MARCHLEWICZ ARNOLD M	MI	40W	28
MARCHUT THOMAS ANDREW	NJ	37E	39
MARCIANO LOUIS VINCENT	NY	31W	9
MARCIN PAUL JOHN	MA	10W	58
MARCIN WILLIAM KEITH	NY	36E	55
MARCO JERRY ROY	MO	10W	7
MARCO ROBERT DONALD	WA	49E	13
MARCOMBE STEVE GARY	LA	21E	35
MARCONI FRANK JOSEPH	NY	34W	65
MARCOTTE ANDRE EDWARD	NH	22E	92
MARCOTTE DENNIS WILFRED	MI	27E	11
MARCOULIER LEO RENE	MA	23W	90
MARCRUM RONALD DEAN	CA	28E	10
MARCUM ERNEST DELBERT	WV	33E	9
MARCUM GILBERT GEORGE	MO	28E	61
MARCUM HAROLD LEE	OH	50W	44
MARCUM JERRY LEE	IN	43W	17
MARCUM JIMMY ALLEN	TN	05E	2
MARCUM KENNETH	IN	19W	2
MARCUM LEONARD GERALD	OR	24E	68
MARCUM WALTER	OH	11E	29
MARCUM WALTER VERNON	KY	06W	110
MARCUS MICHAEL BOOTH	CA	06W	130
MARCUSSEN GLENNON	AR	34E	8
MARCY WILLIAM LINCOLN	CT	24W	60
MARDIS JAMES ARNOLD JR	CA	23W	76
MAREADY TERRY KAY	OK	25W	52
MARECK RAYMOND DONALD	TX	11W	127
MAREK JOSEPH PENN	CA	29E	101
MAREK PAUL STEVEN	NY	45W	7
MARESH JAMES ANTHONY	TX	02W	9
MAREZ FREDERICK	NE	12W	83

NAME	STATE	PANEL NO.	LINE NO.
MARFURT RICHARD AGUST JR	NY	15W	87
MARGARITIS SOTORIOS MILTO	NH	24E	91
MARGLE THOMAS JOSEPH	PA	39E	50
MARGOLIS ROBERT LYNN	CA	19E	63
MARGRAVE DANIEL W II	MT	32W	80
MARGRO JAMES ANTHONY	NY	25W	105
MARHEFKA DUANE JOSEPH	OH	14W	66
MARIA CHARLES ANTHONY	MI	53W	3
MARIANI JOHN ROY	CA	10W	52
MARIANO JESUS ROSA	GM	02E	96
MARIER MAURICE JOHN		15E	48
MARIK CHARLES WELDON	MO	08E	93
MARIN FRANCISCO SANDOVAL	TX	22E	44
MARIN JULIAN	CA	18E	109
MARIN-RAMOS HECTOR RAMON	PR	49E	53
MARINE DAVID HARLON	TN	09W	8
MARINELLI ANTHONY JOHN	FL	21W	18
MARINELLI ELMO	CT	16E	69
MARINO ARIEL	NY	44W	51
MARINO CARL JOHN	CT	56E	27
MARINO NICHOLAS III	PA	44W	18
MARINSIC ALLEN HENRY	WA	30E	79
MARION CURTIS	GA	20W	72
MARION HARRY LEWIS	CA	14E	28
MARISKANISH CHARLES EDWAR	PA	57E	27
MARIZ ROBERT J	MN	35E	75
MARK RICHARD STRODE	PA	31W	9
MARK THOMAS RICHARD	PA	14E	118
MARKARIAN WILLIAM ARAM	CT	33E	72
MARKEL JAMES CALVIN JR	PA	50W	25
MARKEL RONALD JOE	MI	57E	27
MARKEN JOHN PAUL JR	CA	34E	79
MARKER MICHAEL WAYNE	TX	04W	21
MARKEVITCH ANTHONY G JR	WI	27W	96
MARKEY CHRISTOPHER HUGH	MI	14W	5
MARKEY JAMES PAUL JR	PA	05W	65
MARKHAM MARSHALL THOMAS	NC	17W	81
MARKHAM RAYMOND PAUL	IN	53E	37
MARKILLIE JOHN ROY	CA	08E	72
MARKLAND DONALD P III	FL	09W	40
MARKLAND GERALD DAVID	NM	36W	83
MARKLAND JAMES HARRY	TN	06W	103
MARKLE WILLIAM CARL JR	CO	33E	3
MARKOS GEORGE	TX	01E	85
MARKOSKI GERALD MICHAEL	PA	36E	37
MARKOVICH DOUGLAS JOSEPH	NJ	30W	9
MARKOWSKI HENRY JOSEPH JR	IN	17E	125
MARKS ANTONE PATRICK	MA	08E	11
MARKS DAVID ALAN	IN	35E	55
MARKS FRANK WILLIAM	IN	43E	58
MARKS GEORGE ALFRED JR	NY	39W	28
MARKS JOHN	CT	13W	15
MARKS MICHAEL DAVID	OH	33E	88
MARKS PHILLIP HADDON	CA	29W	55
MARKS RICHARD EDWARD	NY	05E	35
MARKS TOMMY LEE	GA	15W	99
MARKUM ROBERT BAILEY	NY	38W	3
MARKUNAS THOMAS WILLIAM	NY	25W	30
MARKUS JERRY	CT	35E	75
MARKUS LARRY FRANK	MN	20E	119
MARKUSEN TOBIAS EARL	CA	45W	7
MARKWELL EUGENE LYNN	CA	53W	11
MARKWITH GERALD WILLIAM	WA	42E	20
MARLAND INNES LEE	CA	38E	33
MARLAR DONNIE JOE	MS	39E	8
MARLAR OLIN DEWEY III	CA	04W	77
MARLATT ROY WAYNE	PA	08W	67
MARLEY KENNETH CHARLES	OH	19E	109
MARLIN EARL WILLIAM JR	IA	14W	5
MARLIN ELLIS SANFORD	MO	15W	110
MARLIN LEONARD THOMAS	TN	50W	44
MARLIN ROBERT DOUGLAS	TN	11E	77
MARLIN WILLIAM LUNN JR	TN	35E	24
MARLING BILLIE JAYE	NM	04W	64
MARLOW DONALD RAY	TN	11W	75
MARLOW JAMES EDWARD	NY	43W	17
MARLOW JOHN P	OK	24E	87
MARLOWE DANIEL PAUL	TX	11E	45
MARLOWE JACK WILLIAM	CA	50E	17
MARMIE ROBERT THEODORE	OH	20W	124
MAROON JAMES WILLMER	AR	16E	41
MAROSCHER ALBERT GEORGE	OH	50E	5

NAME	STATE	PANEL NO.	LINE NO.
MAROSITES BRUCE LOUIS	MI	05E	94
MARPLE REECE LESLIE	TN	58E	23
MARPLE TERRANCE DUANE	WV	08W	62
MARPO JOHN ERNEST	PA	31W	10
MARQUARDT MERLIN EUGENE	IN	02E	59
MARQUARDT WAYNE JOHN	NY	25E	86
MARQUEZ EDUARDO JR	TX	53E	17
MARQUEZ FLORENCIO Q	CA	17W	117
MARQUEZ GERALDO	AZ	31W	95
MARQUEZ JOHN	CA	10W	118
MARQUEZ JULIAN ERNEST	NM	05W	107
MARQUEZ MARTIN JR	CA	36E	23
MARQUEZ PAUL JOSEPH	CA	02E	79
MARQUEZ RONALD O	CO	33E	20
MARQUEZ VALENTINE	CO	03E	34
MARQUEZ-LOPEZ LUIS MANUEL	PR	31E	88
MARQUEZ-QUINONES RAIMUNDO	PR	29W	62
MARR GEORGE RICHARD JR	VA	05W	62
MARR JOHN AUSTIN	CA	10W	7
MARR NOEL DON	OK	07E	119
MARRERO-BAEZ FLOR	PR	17E	8
MARRERO-ESTRADA HERIBERTO	PR	24W	87
MARRERO-RIOS JOSE ANTONIO	PR	51E	18
MARRIETTA HAROLD JOSEPH	AZ	05E	12
MARRINGTON CRAIG THOMAS	WY	17W	97
MARRION JIMMIE CHARLES	MO	35E	61
MARRON BRUCE ALEN	MA	51W	19
MARRONE JOSEPH VIETO	NY	36E	24
MARROQUIN ELADIO R JR	PA	08E	22
MARROQUIN PEDRO JR	IL	16E	112
MARROQUIN TOMAS JR	TX	09E	127
MARRS CARL ROBERT	NE	09E	34
MARRS RONALD WAYNE	TX	25W	105
MARRUFO RODNEY ELMER JR	CA	66E	11
MARSCHALL ALAN FREDERIC	IL	29W	102
MARSDEN ROBERT PAUL	MA	05W	57
MARSDEN TYRONE CECIL	NY	30E	29
MARSH ALAN RICHARD	NE	21E	36
MARSH BOBBY JOE	AL	05E	127
MARSH CLARK LYNWOOD	AR	27E	25
MARSH DAVID JOSEPH	NY	56W	25
MARSH EDWARD K	PA	03E	131
MARSH FREDERICK CURTIS	NJ	11W	17
MARSH HAROLD CLIFTON	NC	06W	10
MARSH HERBERT LYNN	CA	13W	24
MARSH JOHN A	PA	26W	48
MARSH JOHN ROBERT	NY	41W	18
MARSH LARRY GLENN	OH	18W	83
MARSH LARRY LEE	MI	37W	66
MARSH LEE ERNEST JR	MD	09W	133
MARSH RICHARD ALBERT	OH	44E	9
MARSH RICHARD CHARLES	NY	13E	39
MARSH ROBERT ALLEN	NY	18W	20
MARSH RONALD ALTON	TX	04E	93
MARSH WILLIAM CLIFTON	TX	41E	24
MARSHALL BILLY RAY	LA	16W	101
MARSHALL BRIAN ALEXANDER	MI	44E	9
MARSHALL CHARLES RAY	CA	60E	25
MARSHALL CLIFFORD WAYNE	KY	05W	121
MARSHALL DANNY G	WV	01W	131
MARSHALL DENNIS CRAIG	OH	07W	60
MARSHALL DENNIS HARDIE	NH	26E	28
MARSHALL DOC HENRY	OH	37E	40
MARSHALL DONALD FISHER II	HI	40E	25
MARSHALL DONALD RICHARD	NJ	26E	36
MARSHALL EDDIE LESTER	NY	17E	105
MARSHALL FREDDIE JR	FL	16E	63
MARSHALL HAROLD B	PA	07E	14
MARSHALL JACKIE EVERETT	NY	59E	8
MARSHALL JAMES ALFRED	NY	02E	12
MARSHALL JAMES CONRAD	AL	36E	24
MARSHALL JAMES EDWARD	KY	49W	42
MARSHALL JAMES HENRY	AL	19W	17
MARSHALL JIMMIE RAY	KY	13W	33
MARSHALL JOHN GRADY	MO	47E	13
MARSHALL JOHN KEITH	WI	38W	2
MARSHALL JOSEPH HENRY III	MI	05W	118
MARSHALL JOSEPH LOUIS	RI	01W	38
MARSHALL LARRY HUNTER	MO	05W	77
MARSHALL LAWRENCE JAY	NH	01W	107
MARSHALL MARK DUANE	OH	28W	83
MARSHALL MICHAEL ALLAN	CA	30W	78

NAME	STATE	PANEL NO.	LINE NO.
MARSHALL RICHARD ALLAN	CA	05E	72
MARSHALL RICHARD CARLTON	IL	02E	76
MARSHALL RICHARD WILLIAM	PA	06W	12
MARSHALL ROBERT EDWARD	VA	38W	59
MARSHALL ROGER ROBERT	CA	30E	29
MARSHALL ROLAND TRENT	VA	62E	8
MARSHALL RONNIE SHINYA	OH	02W	11
MARSHALL SAMUEL THOMAS JR	KY	38E	6
MARSHALL THOMAS ROBERT	PA	15W	48
MARSHALL WILLARD DALE	CA	58W	27
MARSHALL WILLIE JUNIOR	NJ	35W	83
MARSHAND KENNETH LLOYD	OH	15W	56
MARSHMAN MICHAEL JON	MI	14E	58
MARSON RICKEY JOE	TX	48E	43
MARTEL NORMAND RICHARD	NH	19E	28
MARTELL GARY WILLIAM	OH	32E	78
MARTELL TERRY JACK	PA	03W	98
MARTENS STANLEY WAYNE	MO	21W	61
MARTER EZRA BUDD	NJ	12W	71
MARTHALER ROBERT FRANK	MN	10W	81
MARTHE RANDOLPH LEE	ND	04W	96
MARTICH THOMAS MARK	OH	36E	55
MARTIE ERNEST RAYMOND	OK	11E	15
MARTIN ALAN DAVID	OH	10W	58
MARTIN ALBERT	NY	40E	43
MARTIN ALPHONSO S	VA	36E	55
MARTIN ANTHONY TONY	LA	12E	109
MARTIN ARTHUR GLENN	IL	42W	62
MARTIN ARTHUR JUSTILIEN	LA	22W	23
MARTIN ASA JR	IL	33W	41
MARTIN AUBREY GRADY	TX	20W	20
MARTIN BENNIE LOUIS	GA	39E	36
MARTIN BILLY JOE RALPH	KY	23W	28
MARTIN BRUCE EDWARD	MA	13W	46
MARTIN BRUNO LEO	MI	08E	93
MARTIN BUDDY RAY	VA	23E	44
MARTIN CARL RAYMOND	MN	24W	68
MARTIN CHARLES EDWARD	AL	28W	83
MARTIN CHARLES FREDERICK	CO	25E	104
MARTIN CHARLES JEFFREY	IN	40E	25
MARTIN CHARLES LEROY	OR	03W	37
MARTIN CHARLES MICHAEL	NC	10E	93
MARTIN CHARLES ROBERT	NY	38E	55
MARTIN CHARLES THOMAS	GA	41E	25
MARTIN CLAYTON ARTHUR	ID	28E	16
MARTIN CLIFFORD B JR	AZ	63W	9
MARTIN CLYDE THOMAS	SC	25W	17
MARTIN DANNY GALE	TN	15W	13
MARTIN DARRELL G	WV	64E	17
MARTIN DAVID EARL	FL	17E	99
MARTIN DAVID LEE JR	CA	25E	33
MARTIN DAVID WAYNE	MS	13W	123
MARTIN DAVIE JOE	OH	15E	32
MARTIN DENNIS KEITH	IA	08W	8
MARTIN DENNIS PHILIP	NJ	13W	46
MARTIN DENNIS R	WI	05E	17
MARTIN DONAIL	MS	12E	127
MARTIN DONALD ARTHUR	OK	15W	52
MARTIN DONALD EDWARD	IN	36E	78
MARTIN DONALD LAWRENCE	LA	14W	43
MARTIN DONNIE JOE	IN	29W	46
MARTIN DONNIE RICHARD	TX	07W	129
MARTIN DOUGLAS KENT	TX	01W	117
MARTIN DUANE WHITNEY	CO	02E	91
MARTIN EDWARD DEAN	OH	26W	40
MARTIN EDWIN WOODS JR	AZ	22E	55
MARTIN ELMER	MI	53E	4
MARTIN EMERSON	NM	23W	16
MARTIN ERIE A JR	VA	02E	41
MARTIN ERNEST TYRONE	CA	34E	54
MARTIN EUGENE JOSEPH	PA	04E	14
MARTIN FLOYD NEWTON	VA	36W	52
MARTIN FREDDIE KAY	CA	47W	11
MARTIN FREDERICK L	NC	42E	7
MARTIN GARY ALAN	VA	42E	20
MARTIN GEORGE PAUL	CA	02W	77
MARTIN GEORGE ROLAND	PA	46E	8
MARTIN GEORGE WILLIS	TN	01E	66
MARTIN GERALD	CA	40W	49
MARTIN GREGORY LAWRENCE	CA	18E	49
MARTIN GUY WAYNE	NM	68W	6
MARTIN HAROLD DOUGLAS	MD	40W	25

NAME	STATE	PANEL NO.	LINE NO.
MARTIN HARRELD PIRTLE	KY	47W	48
MARTIN HARRY PEMBERTON	VA	58W	11
MARTIN HARRY WILLIAM	TX	18E	11
MARTIN HENRY CHARLEMONT	MI	12W	7
MARTIN HENRY OLIN III	GA	11E	31
MARTIN HENRY RONALD	GA	03W	28
MARTIN HOYLE	SC	43E	46
MARTIN HUBERT WILLIAM	AL	47W	20
MARTIN IRVIN EUGENE	TN	34W	71
MARTIN JAMES C JR	IL	21E	79
MARTIN JAMES EDWARD	UT	39E	74
MARTIN JAMES EMMETT	OR	39W	1
MARTIN JAMES HENRY	TN	51W	42
MARTIN JAMES LOUIS	MI	56W	6
MARTIN JAMES MICHAEL	NC	38W	19
MARTIN JEAN D	AR	29W	11
MARTIN JEFFREY LEA	CA	50W	30
MARTIN JERRY DEAN	IN	02W	61
MARTIN JERRY LEWIS	MI	09W	21
MARTIN JERRY WAYNE	UT	27W	20
MARTIN JIMMIE CARTER	CA	16E	30
MARTIN JOHN ANTHONY III	CA	25W	76
MARTIN JOHN BERNARD II	NJ	07W	115
MARTIN JOHN C	NJ	41E	11
MARTIN JOHN CHARLES	CA	49W	20
MARTIN JOHN D	TX	21W	113
MARTIN JOHN DAVID	TN	21W	84
MARTIN JOHN EUGENE	IL	15W	28
MARTIN JOHN FRANCIS	NY	36E	24
MARTIN JOHN JR	PA	33E	58
MARTIN JOHN MAJOR	CA	39E	23
MARTIN JOHN MURRAY	PA	30E	45
MARTIN JOHN SANFORD	FL	27E	74
MARTIN JOHN WARREN	GA	11E	41
MARTIN JOHNNY COCHRAN	AL	01W	24
MARTIN JOSEPH CRAIG	CA	35W	83
MARTIN JOSEPH THOMAS	CO	19E	91
MARTIN JOSEPH THOMAS	CA	22E	15
MARTIN JOSEPH VENSON	TN	05W	101
MARTIN KENNETH	MI	30W	47
MARTIN KENNETH LEROY	CA	44W	39
MARTIN KENNETH WAYNE	TN	09W	56
MARTIN KENNETH WILLIAM	CA	27E	16
MARTIN LARRY	IL	29E	74
MARTIN LARRY ALLEN	CA	34W	43
MARTIN LARRY CHARLES	OH	27W	75
MARTIN LARRY EUGENE	KS	52W	36
MARTIN LARRY EUGENE	FL	40W	28
MARTIN LARRY JOE	CA	31E	65
MARTIN LARRY RAYMOND	WV	22W	65
MARTIN LARRY WAYNE	TX	23W	103
MARTIN LAWRENCE	NY	16E	53
MARTIN LAWRENCE SAMUEL	PA	07W	41
MARTIN LEONARD JR	PA	18E	124
MARTIN LEONARD RAY	OH	37W	76
MARTIN LINWOOD DWIGHT	VA	45E	59
MARTIN LONNIE GENE	TX	37W	13
MARTIN MARVIN HENRY	NE	57E	27
MARTIN MERLE JAMES	WA	33W	8
MARTIN MICHAEL EMMETT	CA	42E	7
MARTIN MICHAEL JOSEPH	NY	01W	50
MARTIN MICHAEL PETER JR	PA	01E	37
MARTIN MICHAEL TERRY	NE	06W	78
MARTIN NAPOLEON	OH	44W	11
MARTIN PATRICK ROBERT	OH	15W	91
MARTIN PAUL RIVERS	VA	66E	11
MARTIN RALPH	TX	14W	104
MARTIN RAY THOMAS	NC	11W	37
MARTIN RAYMOND CHARLES	CA	06E	21
MARTIN RICHARD D	HI	53E	37
MARTIN RICHARD JODY	CA	43W	1
MARTIN RICHARD LE ROY	CO	41W	18
MARTIN RICHARD LEE	OH	05W	129
MARTIN RICHARD M	WY	54E	27
MARTIN ROBERT ALAN	IN	45E	25
MARTIN ROBERT DENNIS	IL	35W	49
MARTIN ROBERT ELMER	IL	16E	3
MARTIN ROBERT HARRISON JR	MD	23W	45
MARTIN ROBERT PHILLIPS JR	PA	04W	61
MARTIN ROBERT THOMAS JR	TN	22W	91
MARTIN ROBERT WILLIAM	RI	14E	104
MARTIN ROBERT WILLIE	NY	54E	11
MARTIN RONALD ANDREW	PA	27E	48
MARTIN RONALD LEE	IL	17W	74
MARTIN RONALD LYNN	TX	33E	14
MARTIN RONALD ROBERT	PA	03E	84
MARTIN RONALD STEVEN	MT	44W	39
MARTIN RUFUS MICHAEL	AL	53W	22
MARTIN RUSSELL DEAN	IA	08E	4
MARTIN SAMMY ARTHUR	TX	32E	78
MARTIN SAMUEL CALVIN	KY	62E	8
MARTIN STEPHAN JAMES	CA	06E	33
MARTIN STEVE LAIL	FL	10W	1
MARTIN STEVEN LARRY	CA	03W	32
MARTIN STEVEN LOUIS	KS	23W	29
MARTIN STEVEN WAYNE	VA	09E	78
MARTIN STEVEN WAYNE	NH	41W	48
MARTIN TERRY LEE	MN	27E	45
MARTIN TERRY LYNN	WI	34W	43
MARTIN THOMAS CHARLES	CA	42W	48
MARTIN TONY LEE	OH	22W	59
MARTIN VERNAL GLEN	WI	09E	115
MARTIN VINCENT PATRICK JR	AL	02W	68
MARTIN WALTER WESLEY	KS	34W	26
MARTIN WAYNE OSCAR	FL	28E	69
MARTIN WILEY LOUIS	OH	41W	54
MARTIN WILLIAM DAVIS	MS	19W	88
MARTIN WILLIAM DEAN	IL	25E	87
MARTIN WILLIAM EVERETT	AZ	21E	48
MARTIN WILLIAM GEORGE	FL	41W	60
MARTIN WILLIAM HAROLD	GA	06W	114
MARTIN WILLIAM PAUL	WI	17E	93
MARTIN WILLIAM REYNOLDS	VA	01E	72
MARTIN WILLIAM TORBERT	LA	21W	113
MARTINDALE PAUL VAUGHAN	AL	01W	9
MARTINE JAY BARKLOW JR	MI	23E	87
MARTINEAU MICHAEL WILLIAM	NJ	17E	100
MARTINEZ ADOLFO	PA	31W	82
MARTINEZ ADOLPH ALFRED	CO	54E	11
MARTINEZ ALEX EZEQUIEL	NM	20W	25
MARTINEZ ANGEL	TX	38E	6
MARTINEZ ANTHONY VINCENT	NY	08W	98
MARTINEZ ARMANDO DANIEL	TX	50W	39
MARTINEZ BILLY RICHARD	NM	13E	39
MARTINEZ BOBBY JOE	NM	58E	23
MARTINEZ CHRIS RONALD	CA	24W	111
MARTINEZ DANIEL TIOFILIO	NM	12E	7
MARTINEZ DONALD LYNWOOD	VA	18E	41
MARTINEZ EDDIE ANTHONY JR	NM	32W	7
MARTINEZ ENRIQUE	TX	24W	68
MARTINEZ ERNESTO	CA	44E	49
MARTINEZ ERNIE ROBLES	CA	21W	94
MARTINEZ ERNIE ROBLES	CA	02W	56
MARTINEZ EUGENE OSCAR	TX	17W	109
MARTINEZ EVARISTO III	TX	28E	81
MARTINEZ EZEKIAL	CA	12W	61
MARTINEZ FLORENTINO JR	TX	38W	59
MARTINEZ FRANK	NY	38W	7
MARTINEZ GEORGE FRANCIS	KS	23W	113
MARTINEZ GEORGE VINCENT	CA	44W	57
MARTINEZ GILIVALDO A JR	TX	03E	41
MARTINEZ GUADALUPE	TX	30E	10
MARTINEZ ISIDRO	TX	06E	85
MARTINEZ ISRAEL JR	NY	18W	11
MARTINEZ JAKE	TX	15W	24
MARTINEZ JESUS	TX	51E	9
MARTINEZ JIM DANIEL	NM	34E	23
MARTINEZ JOHN	TX	06W	130
MARTINEZ JOHN ANDREW	TX	56E	11
MARTINEZ JOHN ANTHONY	CA	09W	91
MARTINEZ JOHN JAMES	UT	30E	72
MARTINEZ JOHNNY SALAS	UT	37W	1
MARTINEZ JORGE	TX	50W	27
MARTINEZ JOSEPH RAYMOND	NY	14E	118
MARTINEZ JUAN HENRY	NM	33E	59
MARTINEZ JUAN JOSE	TX	41W	53
MARTINEZ JUAN PATRICIO	CO	55E	22
MARTINEZ LE ROY FELIX	CO	10W	98
MARTINEZ LOUIS ALVARADO	TX	40E	74
MARTINEZ MANUEL	NM	31W	82
MARTINEZ MANUEL FLOYD	CO	58W	11
MARTINEZ MANUEL GODINE	TX	17W	109
MARTINEZ MARGARITO	TX	43E	57
MARTINEZ MAURO	CO	50E	18
MARTINEZ PAUL DINNES JR	CA	25W	17
MARTINEZ PEDRO	TX	09E	53
MARTINEZ PETE MICHAEL	CO	09E	34
MARTINEZ PETER	KS	04E	82
MARTINEZ PETER JOHN JR	IL	11W	103
MARTINEZ PETER STEVEN	IL	25E	64
MARTINEZ RAFAEL	TX	47E	2
MARTINEZ REYNALDO	MI	21W	113
MARTINEZ RICARDO RAUL	NY	41W	74
MARTINEZ RICHARD EARL	WA	18W	2
MARTINEZ RICHARD PAUL	MO	63E	13
MARTINEZ ROBERT LEE	CO	11E	123
MARTINEZ ROBERT R	TX	13E	75
MARTINEZ RODNEY DEAN	CA	31E	25
MARTINEZ ROGELIO MANUEL	IL	33E	4
MARTINEZ SIXTO R JR	TX	30W	78
MARTINEZ STEVEN CATARINO	CA	47W	14
MARTINEZ SYLVESTER C	TX	03W	77
MARTINEZ THOMAS MICHAEL	FL	14E	108
MARTINEZ TOMAS VASQUEZ	MI	06E	45
MARTINEZ WILLIAM JOSEPH	WI	08W	32
MARTINEZ WILLIE DANIEN	NM	28W	62
MARTINEZ-FELICIANO JOSE L	PR	18E	110
MARTINEZ-MERCADO EDWIN J	NY	29E	74
MARTINEZ-QUILES JUAN A JR	PR	38W	44
MARTINEZ-SANTIAGO RAFAEL	PR	48E	18
MARTINEZ-SOTO JOSE	PR	10E	120
MARTINEZ-ZAYAS RUBEN	PR	07W	15
MARTINI GARY WAYNE	OR	18E	61
MARTINO STEPHEN LEE	OK	19W	70
MARTINO THOMAS JOSEPH	FL	20W	15
MARTINOVSKY MILOSLAV JOSE		35E	76
MARTINSEN LOREN DAUNE	CA	38W	76
MARTINSON DARRELL WAYNE	MN	07E	18
MARTINSON DELVIN CARL	MN	15W	2
MARTINSON LEROY CLAYTON	MN	37W	68
MARTIR-TORRES JULIO IGNAC	PR	11E	26
MARTORELLA GARY MARIO	NJ	62W	4
MARTURANO JOSEPH A JR	NY	43E	25
MARTZ DANIEL MORRIS JR	IN	05E	27
MARTZ MELVIN LEE	CA	35E	76
MARTZ MELVIN LOUIS	MI	20E	120
MARTZ WILLIAM HENRY JR	PA	27W	75
MARVIN GREGORY ALLEN	WA	30W	5
MARVIN JOSEPH	AL	23E	4
MARVIN ROBERT CLARENCE	MI	15E	28
MARVIN ROBERT GERALD	IN	66W	9
MARX ROBERT GARRY	CT	65W	11
MARXMILLER GARY EDWARD	TX	19W	32
MARYFIELD WILLIAM RICHARD	IL	44E	50
MARZENELL EDWARD JR	AL	55W	36
MASADAS BEN OBSENIARES	CA	48W	13
MASCARENAS ALCADIO NORBER	NM	08E	53
MASCARENAS JOE LEO	CO	39W	12
MASCARENAS ROBERT RAY	CO	36W	36
MASCARI PHILLIP LOUIS	NJ	26W	100
MASCHER BRENT THOMAS	UT	25W	105
MASCIALE VINCENT TOMMY	FL	19W	62
MASDEN STEPHEN KNIGHT	MO	03W	70
MASEDA GERALD LEE	FL	07W	107
MASEDA ROBERT	TX	08W	69
MASHBURN RAYMOND T	NC	28E	55
MASHBURN TSCHANN SCOTT	VA	11W	104
MASHLYKIN KENNETH HENRY	NY	42W	5
MASILLO JUAN	IL	40W	29
MASIN MERRILL HOWARD	NY	01W	64
MASINSKI JOHN GEORGE	NY	24W	18
MASK JOE JUNIOR	AR	54E	37
MASKE WILLIAM JAMES	NC	28W	71
MASLAK JOHN JOSEPH	KS	20W	108
MASLINSKI DWIGHT ANDREW	FL	12W	118
MASLYN EDWARD JAMES	FL	40W	45
MASNY BERNARD JOSEPH	IL	02E	104
MASON ALFRED LEE	VA	28E	84
MASON ALPHONZA	NJ	02W	77
MASON ALVIN PERNELL	DC	37E	61
MASON BENJAMIN H JR	NJ	25E	104
MASON BOBBY G	FL	02E	113
MASON CHARLES BUCKLEY	WA	62E	20
MASON CHARLES GILBERT	MD	15E	85
MASON CHARLES JOSEPH L	DC	42W	30
MASON DANIEL	AZ	51E	31

NAME	STATE	PANEL NO.	LINE NO.
MASON DAVID LEE	TX	16W	20
MASON DENNIS RAE	WI	64W	12
MASON DENNIS RAY	OK	53E	37
MASON EARNEST LEE JR	AL	53E	37
MASON GARY RICHARD	NC	18W	84
MASON GEORGE ARDEN	OK	11W	103
MASON HAROLD JR	NY	63W	9
MASON HARRY STANLEY JR	IL	06W	48
MASON JAMES PHILLIP	IL	41W	69
MASON JOHNNIE	NY	15E	63
MASON JOSEPH ANSON JR	IL	06E	45
MASON KENNETH ALLEN	SC	35W	39
MASON LARRY JOE SR	KY	38W	50
MASON LARRY MAURICE	VA	04W	64
MASON RAYMOND LEROY	MD	45E	49
MASON RICHARD FLOYD	NC	30E	72
MASON ROBERT	TN	26E	12
MASON ROBERT DAVID	MD	32E	37
MASON ROBERT ERNEST	FL	22E	26
MASON ROBERT SCOTT JR	NY	17W	57
MASON ROMAN GALE	MO	33W	3
MASON SVEN STERNING	CO	15W	64
MASON TERRY DEAN	WA	18W	41
MASON THEODORE RAYMOND	PA	05W	82
MASON WILLIAM HENDERSON	AR	65E	8
MASON WILLIAM PAUL	PA	42E	68
MASOTTI JAMES JOSEPH	NY	01E	125
MASSA DAVID LYNN	OH	53E	4
MASSA LUIS ALBERTO	NY	20W	114
MASSARI RICHARD D	NY	09W	48
MASSE RAYMOND GEORGE	MA	19W	46
MASSENGILL LARRY DALE	VA	43W	39
MASSETH ROBERT EUGENE	CA	11W	75
MASSEY HARRY	CT	23W	22
MASSEY JAMES	AR	02E	126
MASSEY JOHN WILLIAM JR	SC	30W	6
MASSEY MICHAEL JAY	GA	53E	37
MASSEY MICHAEL SEAN	CA	30W	74
MASSEY RALPH LAWRENCE	MI	10E	41
MASSEY SCOTTIE SHELVEN	NC	15W	115
MASSIE GEORGE EDGAR	MD	68E	5
MASSIE LARRY GLEN	OK	55W	7
MASSINE RICHARD PETER	ID	12E	96
MASSO-PEREZ JULIO	PR	18E	41
MASSONE MICHAEL STACY	CA	33W	50
MASSUCCI MARTIN JOHN	MI	02E	101
MAST RANDY LEE	IA	09W	15
MASTELLER ALLAN DEAN	CA	41E	74
MASTEN ARMAND DOMINIC	OH	26W	108
MASTEN JAMES ARTHUR	NJ	15E	79
MASTER WILLIAM STANLEY	PA	15E	6
MASTERS EDWARD ULYSES	FL	48E	30
MASTERS JAMES MADISON JR	FL	12W	7
MASTERS WILLIAM RICHARD	OH	11E	22
MASTERSON EDMUND MACEO	MI	04E	23
MASTERSON JOHN PATRICK	OH	68W	6
MASTERSON MICHAEL JOHN	WA	41W	61
MASTERSON ROBERT ALLEN	KY	10E	64
MASTRAMICO PHILIP	PA	21W	24
MASTROIANNI THOMAS FRANCIS	OH	16E	113
MASTROMATTEO FRANK JAMES	PA	48E	54
MASUDA ROBERT SUSUMU	CA	25W	106
MASUEN MICHAEL NICHOLAS	CA	19W	88
MATARAZZI JOHN JOSEPH JR	PA	49W	42
MATARAZZO EVERETT ROBERT	MI	22W	14
MATARAZZO PETER DAVID	NY	43W	40
MATARAZZO STEVEN	NY	32E	2
MATAYOSHI WALLACE KENJI	CA	04E	120
MATCHETT JAMES STEVEN	MI	35W	28
MATCHETT LESLIE DAVID	IN	34E	79
MATE DONALD RICHARD	IL	62E	20
MATEJA ALAN PAUL	KY	01W	1
MATEJECK WALTER LAWRENCE	FL	31E	36
MATEJOV JOSEPH ANDREW	NY	01W	115
MATEL RONALD JAMES	MN	22W	9
MATELSKI LEONARD JAMES	TX	02W	104
MATERN ROBERT SCHRACK	MA	21E	28
MATHEIS RICHARD ALAN	MN	10W	1
MATHENY BOBBY DANIEL	IL	38E	70
MATHENY LARRY DALE	IL	30W	91
MATHENY RUSSELL LEE	FL	51E	40
MATHER ALVIN EUGENE	KS	09W	8
MATHER HARRY MICHAEL	NM	51W	42
MATHERN EDWARD GERARD	CA	07W	36
MATHERS STEVEN ALLEN	IA	40W	38
MATHES EDWARD ARTHUR	OR	10W	109
MATHESON DOUGLAS ROY	MI	24W	82
MATHEW CECIL LEROY JR	OH	51W	12
MATTHEWS CHARLES DONALD	MI	07W	59
MATHEWS CHARLES L	IL	09W	22
MATHEWS CLAUDE WESLEY	NJ	04E	21
MATHEWS CLYDE JR	TX	17E	73
MATHEWS FRANK JAMES	OR	41E	40
MATHEWS GROVER C JR	OR	11E	23
MATHEWS HAROLD JOSEPH JR	NJ	44W	27
MATHEWS HENRY DON	AR	22W	91
MATHEWS JAMES LEONARD	IL	58E	11
MATHEWS JAMES MICHAEL	NJ	56W	25
MATHEWS PATRICK T	WA	01W	62
MATHEWS WILLIAM JEROME	IN	52W	20
MATHEWSON ROGER MICHAEL	OH	07E	49
MATHIAS JOSEPH VERNON	IL	18W	84
MATHIAS RANDY LEE	UT	56W	25
MATHIAS ROBERT	FL	34E	54
MATHIAS ROBERT P	CA	01W	127
MATHIAS STEVEN FRANKLIN	UT	22E	109
MATHIESEN ERHARDT WILLIAM	IL	30E	63
MATHIS ARNOLD	OH	23E	67
MATHIS BRENT EUGENE	CA	21E	123
MATHIS DAVID LINWOOD	AL	13W	113
MATHIS DONALD ROBERT	TN	03W	57
MATHIS FOY MANION	TX	04E	112
MATHIS HARRY JR	LA	15E	97
MATHIS JAMES RUFUS	NY	42E	36
MATHIS JIMMY CLIFTON	NM	30E	92
MATHIS ROGER EDWARD	GA	18E	46
MATHIS RONNIE THOMAS	GA	03E	85
MATHIS RUBIN II	GA	03W	88
MATHIS SAMUEL JUDSON	FL	20W	114
MATHIS WILLIAM LEE	NY	24E	61
MATHISON BRIAN JOHN	IL	47E	34
MATHISON MICHAEL ALFRED	MN	25W	73
MATHISON MICHAEL K	IL	03E	34
MATIAS WENCESLAO ROSAS JR	TX	36W	4
MATIAS-SANTANA FEDERICO	NY	37W	60
MATIER CURTIS OWENS	NC	20E	91
MATIS WALTER FRANCIS E JR	CT	50E	50
MATLOCK JOHN PHILLIP	KY	47E	23
MATLOCK McKENLEY ODIS	KY	47E	8
MATLOCK NELSON ALLEN	OK	16E	94
MATLOCK WILLIAM TRAVIS	TX	22W	34
MATOCHA DONALD JOHN	TX	48E	15
MATOS-CORREA JOSE ANTONIO	PR	48W	4
MATRANGA ROBERT	MA	23E	107
MATSON GARY LEE	CA	40W	58
MATSON HAROLD EUGENE	OR	10E	41
MATSON HOWARD V JR	WI	13E	11
MATSON ROBERT EDWIN	IL	14E	64
MATSON WILLMER ARDEN	NE	13W	131
MATSUURA ALAN YUKIO	HI	01E	48
MATT JOSEPH WALTER	VA	10E	80
MATTA BRUCE JOSEPH	MA	25W	106
MATTA MICHAEL ERNEST	CA	27W	57
MATTARO DONALD JAMES JR	MD	56E	26
MATTAROCCHIA JOHN F JR	MA	25W	17
MATTE ALAN LOUIS	MA	65W	11
MATTEI-SANTIAGO DANIEL	NY	40W	4
MATTER MARK ALLEN	WA	07W	103
MATTERA FRANK JOHN JOE	CA	29W	55
MATTERA GERALD	NY	59W	7
MATTERN CHARLES DUANE	OH	23E	120
MATTERN RICKY PALMER	WA	25E	93
MATTESON GLENN	TX	01E	2
MATTESON LYNN MICHAEL	CA	37W	76
MATTESON THOMAS WILLIAM	NY	48W	7
MATTHEI PETER KARL	MO	16W	101
MATTHEIS DENIS DUANE	IA	25E	48
MATTHEISEN JOHN CHARLES	MT	53E	18
MATTHES PETER RICHARD	OH	16W	118
MATTHEW HARRY ERIC	NY	39E	63
MATTHEWS AITKEN L JR	FL	05E	35
MATTHEWS ALAN LEE	CA	25E	87
MATTHEWS ALFRED RUSSELL	NY	06W	27
MATTHEWS BERNARD JULIAN	CA	20W	66
MATTHEWS CALVIN BERNARD	DC	15W	6
MATTHEWS CHARLES CROCKETT	NC	19W	32
MATTHEWS CHARLES TONEY	AL	05W	121
MATTHEWS DAVID BRUCE	IA	14E	16
MATTHEWS DAVID EARL	MS	18E	49
MATTHEWS EARL JR	SC	10E	81
MATTHEWS EARL MARTIN	MA	29W	103
MATTHEWS EDGAR DONALD	SD	09W	4
MATTHEWS FLOYD JOSEPH	CA	21W	61
MATTHEWS GENE FLETCHER	ME	20E	120
MATTHEWS GEORGE DENNIS	NC	59E	26
MATTHEWS GEORGE RUSSELL	NY	14W	122
MATTHEWS GILBERT LEWIS JR	SD	03W	87
MATTHEWS GORDON BRUCE	IA	37E	62
MATTHEWS HENRY ROBERT	NC	17E	8
MATTHEWS HOLLEY DEWITT	FL	34W	16
MATTHEWS JAMES ERICH	TX	23E	12
MATTHEWS JAMES NEWTON	CA	06E	66
MATTHEWS JAMES WASHINGTON	NC	08W	115
MATTHEWS JOSEPH	IL	20E	120
MATTHEWS KENT DOUGLAS	IL	14W	42
MATTHEWS KERMIT LESLIE	PA	06W	107
MATTHEWS MICHAEL FRANKLIN	CO	28E	37
MATTHEWS NATHANIAL CARL	PA	03W	128
MATTHEWS RICHARD LEE	ME	38W	26
MATTHEWS ROBERT JR	NC	29E	52
MATTHEWS ROBERT L	AL	17E	21
MATTHEWS ROBERT WILLIAM	PA	49W	15
MATTHEWS RONNIE EUGENE	FL	07E	19
MATTHEWS ROY GIBSON	SC	24W	68
MATTHEWS SETH HAYDEN III	FL	17W	110
MATTHEWS THOMAS W JR	TN	10W	35
MATTHEWS WILLIAM CLAY	KS	31W	70
MATTHEWS WILLIAM L JR	OH	50E	6
MATTHEWS WILLIS ALANZO	TN	17E	100
MATTIE ANDREW MARION	MI	31W	10
MATTINGLY GEORGE MICHAEL	MD	30E	45
MATTINGLY HARRY ALBERT JR	MD	34W	16
MATTINGLY JOHN EUGENE	OH	15W	6
MATTINGLY LARRY FRANKLIN	IN	11W	96
MATTINGLY OSBORNE JR	KY	09W	91
MATTINGLY TIMMY G	MO	13E	126
MATTIS WILLIAM CARROLL	CA	01E	95
MATTISON BENJAMIN FRANKLIN	SC	40E	9
MATTOCK JOHN LEE	TN	44E	28
MATTOCKS GEORGE ELI	MT	13W	46
MATTOX DENNIS MAYON	VA	19W	103
MATTOX DWAINE ELBYRNE	VA	08W	101
MATTOX JOHN RICHARD	GA	11W	51
MATTOX WILBUR FLORENCE	GA	52E	8
MATTRACION PHILIP REGINAL	NY	17E	106
MATTSON BERNARD CHARLES	IL	34E	38
MATTSON KENNETH EUGENE	CA	52W	7
MATTSON PAUL EDWARD	IL	51E	9
MATTSON ROBERT KENT	VA	26E	61
MATTSON TIMOTHY GEORGE	WA	49E	53
MATTY THOMAS RICHARD	PA	32E	37
MATULONIS JOHN	NY	32W	21
MATUSCSAK GEORGE EDWARD	NJ	09E	115
MATUSEK JOEL ALOIS	WI	30E	98
MATUSH THOMAS ERWIN	WI	14E	16
MATUSKA JOHN JAMES	OH	42W	42
MATYAS ANDREW	NJ	40E	10
MATYAS RICHARD EDWARD	WI	29W	1
MATYKIEWICZ DAVID BENJAMIN	PA	03W	46
MATYLEWICZ LEO JOHN	PA	46E	37
MAUGHAN GEORGE LEE SR	TX	53E	1
MAUL HENRY EUGENE	WY	36W	64
MAUL RICHARD ALLEN	IL	09E	28
MAULDEN LORENZO COLUMBUS	FL	09E	78
MAULDIN EDDIE LEE	CA	56W	25
MAULDIN MELVIN CALVIN JR	SC	41W	53
MAULDIN MICHAEL B	CA	07E	72
MAULDIN THOMAS JASPER	SC	10E	63
MAULTSBY THOMAS HENRY JR	NC	01E	57
MAUNAKEA RODNEY H	HI	25W	77
MAUNE FRANCIS EDWARD	MO	08W	39
MAUNEY GERALD CLINTON	MS	10W	49
MAUNEY RICKY DAVID	NC	27W	51
MAURER JAMES ROBERT	OH	60E	14
MAURER JEFFREY ALAN	IA	01W	39
MAURER JERRY EUGENE	TX	30E	17

NAME	STATE	PANEL NO.	LINE NO.
MAURER ROBERT FRANKLIN	WY	18W	7
MAURER WALTER LAWRENCE	CA	06W	33
MAURICE ROBERT CHARLES	TX	39E	23
MAURIN CHARLES DENNIS	UT	36W	73
MAURO VINCENT CARMEN JR	NJ	04W	61
MAURONE WILLIAM GREGORY	PA	02E	100
MAUSEN STEPHEN GREGORY	IN	21W	14
MAUTERER OSCAR	VA	05E	38
MAUTHE WILLIAM HAYES	PA	29W	90
MAVROUDIS ANTONIO MICHAEL	NY	28E	91
MAWDSLEY DANNY JOSEPH	MI	37W	33
MAXAM JAMES ALAN	MI	09E	88
MAXAM LARRY LEONARD	CA	36E	78
MAXEY EASON JASPER	NJ	39W	3
MAXHAM RALPH ARDEN JR	VT	05E	61
MAXIE CHARLES LEE	MN	10E	20
MAXIE NORMAN	GA	03W	111
MAXIM THIERRY TIMOTHY G	WA	07W	81
MAXSON CHARLES DANIEL	MI	31E	41
MAXSON JOHN ROBERT	IL	23W	76
MAXWELL CALVIN WALTER	NM	17W	63
MAXWELL CHARLES D	GA	14E	17
MAXWELL DENNIS RAY	MO	36W	45
MAXWELL ELBERT HENRY	NC	36E	56
MAXWELL EVERETT LEE	TX	30E	17
MAXWELL JAMES EDWARD	MS	02W	105
MAXWELL JAMES RICKEY	AR	01W	131
MAXWELL KEN SWAIN	UT	10W	121
MAXWELL ROBERT JAMES	CA	24E	96
MAXWELL SAMUEL CHAPMAN	NE	44W	38
MAXWELL WILLIAM EARL	OH	49E	34
MAXWELL WILLIAM ELBERT	AL	36W	81
MAY ALAN RICHARD	IL	20E	61
MAY ALFRED BYRON	TX	14E	95
MAY CHESTER HOWARD	TX	47W	48
MAY CLOVIS LEE	NM	24W	77
MAY CRAIG NOLAN	PA	33E	89
MAY DANIEL ARNOLD	IL	22W	67
MAY DAVID MURRAY	MD	05W	125
MAY DENNIS ARNOLD	IA	07E	10
MAY ERNEST	AR	32E	18
MAY FARRIS ELDON	AR	17W	51
MAY GARY WAYNE	MO	34W	86
MAY JAMES JR	CA	59W	7
MAY JOEL AUSBIN JR	TX	16W	75
MAY JOHN ALBERT	IL	29E	11
MAY LARRY ALLAN	TX	10W	86
MAY LEONARD DON	WY	06E	45
MAY MICHAEL FREDRICK	MI	30W	14
MAY RAYMOND ALLEN	MO	14W	20
MAY REED McKINLEY JR	PA	25E	64
MAY RICHARD EARL	MS	24W	32
MAY RICHARD GEORGE	FL	27W	32
MAY ROBERT WALTER	NY	39E	8
MAY ROY EDWARD	CA	38W	3
MAY THOMAS ANDREW	NY	15W	48
MAYBEE MICHAEL OWEN	MI	02W	77
MAYBERRY DONALD RICHARD	MO	30W	6
MAYBERRY GERALD WAYNE	KY	57E	6
MAYBERRY LARRY EUGENE	IL	39W	61
MAYBERRY MICHAEL JOSEPH	MO	11W	51
MAYBERRY RONALD JAMES	NV	29E	41
MAYBERRY SQUIRE N JR	OH	62W	13
MAYBURY THOMAS VINCENT	GA	39E	74
MAYE MICHAEL McKENZIE	LA	18W	48
MAYER ALEXANDER LEO	OK	17E	93
MAYER DWIGHT BENNIE	MN	16E	36
MAYER FRANCIS JOHN JR	NJ	36E	24
MAYER HOWARD HERCHER	NJ	37W	34
MAYER JUERGEN AUGUST	GA	10E	17
MAYER NORMAN ROBERT	NY	16E	62
MAYER OSCAR CLEMENT III	PA	23W	65
MAYER PAUL EVANS	AR	46E	57
MAYER ROBERT P	NY	18W	103
MAYER RODERICK LEWIS	ID	02E	125
MAYER THOMAS J	TX	12E	109
MAYER WALTER CHRISTIAN	TX	22E	44
MAYERCIK RONALD MICHAEL	NJ	30E	79
MAYERS RALPH EMERSON III	NY	30W	91
MAYES DAVE JR	LA	03E	48
MAYES HARRY LEROY	MO	42W	12
MAYES JAMES RUSSELL	DC	06W	27
MAYES JAMES WILLIAM	PA	03E	45
MAYES JOSEPH	SC	42E	20
MAYES RICHARD LE OTIS	MT	06E	57
MAYES ROBERT GRESHAM	VA	19E	63
MAYFIELD JIMMY GENE	TX	25E	93
MAYHAIR WILLIAM HERBERT	FL	08E	134
MAYHALL ALONZO EARL	NV	37E	62
MAYHEW ROBERT OLAN	WV	33W	87
MAYHUE DON N	AR	30E	101
MAYMI-MARTINEZ PEDRO ANTO	PR	52E	40
MAYMON DAVID MARK	IL	51W	34
MAYNARD BRUCE CALVIN	PA	23W	90
MAYNARD DARRELL WAYNE	KY	57W	20
MAYNARD GREGORY JOHN	OH	10W	98
MAYNARD GREGORY VALENTINE	NY	63E	13
MAYNARD JOHN	NY	14W	122
MAYNARD LESTER EUGENE	WV	39E	8
MAYNARD RALPH	WV	27W	89
MAYNARD RICHARD LEE JR	PA	06W	121
MAYNARD RICHARD RAY	SD	29W	87
MAYNARD ROBERT DEE	WA	02W	77
MAYNARD THOMAS HARRY	CA	03E	25
MAYNE STEPHEN WOODTHORPE	OR	34W	26
MAYO DUDLEY WAYNE	CA	01E	113
MAYO GEORGE OTHEL	WV	24W	77
MAYO GERALD FRANK	CA	27E	84
MAYO JAMES RUSSELL	VA	25E	105
MAYO JOHN	NC	12E	71
MAYO JOHNNIE MURRAY	NC	17E	8
MAYO MARVIN LACY	GA	46E	37
MAYO PIKE POWERS	TX	19E	47
MAYS AUBREY REID	VA	24W	87
MAYS CARL SHERRELL	MO	05E	13
MAYS E G JR	AR	32W	60
MAYS EMMITT JR	GA	06E	101
MAYS GEORGE M JR	CA	30W	6
MAYS JAMES EDWARD	OH	59E	26
MAYS JAMES JR	TN	19E	63
MAYS McELREE JR	AR	30E	63
MAYS PICARDO RAMONLZY	PA	07E	73
MAYS RAYMOND	TX	13W	24
MAYS RAYMOND RALIFORD	FL	03W	103
MAYS THOMAS CURTIS	MI	30E	87
MAYS THOMAS MONROE	UT	15W	79
MAYSEY LARRY WAYNE	NJ	29E	60
MAZAK STEFAN	DC	50E	40
MAZAL ROGER JAMES	NY	30W	67
MAZARIEGOS FRANCISCO ALBE	FL	22E	68
MAZE DAVID LEE	OH	10W	115
MAZITIS VICTOR ALLEN JR	OH	31E	65
MAZON THEODORE JR	CA	45E	25
MAZURSKY BERNARD RICHARD	WI	54E	37
MAZYCK RAYMOND JOHN JR	NY	43W	15
MAZZA ROBERT WILLIAM	MD	21E	83
MAZZA STEPHEN DARRELL	CA	38E	70
MAZZANTI JOSEPH EDMUND	LA	18W	110
MAZZILLO PETER JR	NJ	18E	124
MAZZONE JOSEPH MARK	NY	43W	64
MCATEE DON JAY	CA	26W	1
MEACHAM JACK BENNIE	AL	16E	113
MEACHAM RICHARD W JR	FL	10W	81
MEAD DALE WALTER	FL	05W	88
MEAD DENNIS MICHAEL	IN	43E	26
MEAD JEFFERY EVANS	WI	44E	29
MEAD LENUS EDWARD	MI	14W	8
MEAD NORMAN ARTHUR	NY	23E	92
MEAD PETER FRANCIS	NJ	07E	97
MEAD SAMMY LOUIS JR	MO	23W	54
MEAD THOMAS JOHN	IL	23W	54
MEADE DANIEL	NY	38E	33
MEADE DAVID ERNEST	OR	10W	46
MEADE JAMES ROBERT	KS	04W	101
MEADE JOHNSON ASHLEY	ME	04E	21
MEADE JOSEPH LYNN	TN	34W	77
MEADE THOMAS ALLERTON	NJ	37E	62
MEADOR BILLY JAY	MO	19E	110
MEADOR DANIEL R	VA	27E	45
MEADOR FRANCIS ELMORE	TX	01W	118
MEADOR KENNETH BRUCE	TX	15W	79
MEADOR LARRY JOE	CA	08W	79
MEADOR PHILLIP WAYNE	TX	12W	22
MEADOWS ARTIS WILBUR JR	GA	48E	44
MEADOWS CALVIN JR	PA	24W	45
MEADOWS CARROL FAYNE	SC	20W	21
MEADOWS CHAD DAVID	OH	55E	22
MEADOWS CHARLES THOMAS	OH	03W	36
MEADOWS DAVID LEWIS	IN	09W	128
MEADOWS EUGENE THOMAS	NC	11E	71
MEADOWS JERRY ROGER	KY	26W	100
MEADOWS JOHN WILLIAM	NM	16W	59
MEADOWS LEE DAVID	PA	07W	64
MEADOWS LESTER LEE JR	WV	27E	29
MEADOWS MERL RUSSELL	MI	68W	6
MEADOWS MILLARD FRANKLIN	MO	15E	9
MEADOWS ROY LESTER	GA	03W	53
MEADS HERBERT LYNN	AL	54E	12
MEADS KIM ELMER	IL	41E	25
MEAGHER CHRISTOPHER W	NY	32W	71
MEAGHER ROBERT JOHN	MI	67W	1
MEAKINS CHARLES HENRY	MN	07W	6
MEALER FERRELL EUGENE JR	VA	07W	59
MEALY DAVID HOWARD	PA	45E	13
MEANS DANA EDWRD	OH	19W	31
MEANS JOHN A	TX	12E	37
MEANS JOHNNY	FL	28E	75
MEANS MICHAEL EDWARD	SD	48W	18
MEANS RONALD LEE	CA	13W	24
MEANS RONALD LEROY	IA	37E	40
MEANS VERNON	GA	29E	91
MEARA WILLIAM DANIELS JR	NJ	39W	8
MEARES CECIL A	TX	27E	3
MEARNS ARTHUR STEWART	NY	12E	55
MEARNS GLENN RODNEY	CA	26W	102
MEARS CHARLES ROBERT	CA	21E	113
MEARS GUY LAMAR JR	GA	06W	5
MEARS JOSEPH HARRY	NY	30W	91
MEARS PETER JOSEPH JR	MA	47W	29
MEARS RALPH JUDSON JR	VA	23W	22
MEASELL KENNETH WILLIAM	MI	34W	25
MEASLEY HENRY HERBERT JR	IN	05E	27
MEAUX PAUL JAMES	LA	48W	32
MEBS FRANK MARTIN	PA	10W	110
MEBUST OWEN EDWARD	CA	36E	24
MECHEM JESSE	NM	39E	9
MECHLING DANIEL GARY	PA	04E	91
MECKEL JOHN BLOCKER	CA	05E	20
MECKLEY RONALD EUGENE	PA	23E	77
MEDARIS RICK EGGBURTUS	MI	16W	31
MEDEGUARI RENE	AZ	26W	101
MEDEIROS DENNIS JOSEPH	CA	43E	26
MEDEIROS MICHAEL JOHN	MA	32E	8
MEDEIROS WILLIAM CORREIA	MA	50E	18
MEDER PAUL OSWALD	NY	01W	101
MEDIATE ALAN WAYNE	CT	19W	8
MEDINA ALFREDO JR	TX	36E	56
MEDINA ARTHUR	TX	08W	133
MEDINA CARLOS	TX	15E	97
MEDINA CARLOS JUAN	NY	50E	31
MEDINA DANIEL MICHAEL	CA	34E	63
MEDINA DAVID PHILLIP	CA	03W	20
MEDINA ISRAEL	NY	03W	100
MEDINA JOHNNY	CO	36E	25
MEDINA ORLANDO	NY	36W	82
MEDINA RAYMOND	TX	14E	1
MEDINA-GONZALEZ RUPERTO	PR	55W	22
MEDINA-RIVERA ANGEL M	PR	26W	14
MEDINA-TORRES VINCENTE	PR	17E	112
MEDINE BERTRAND C JR	LA	08W	46
MEDJESKY VINCENT JOSEPH	IN	05W	135
MEDLEY CHARLES MICHAEL	KY	13W	37
MEDLEY CLARENCE	OH	05E	52
MEDLEY HOMER LANDUS	TN	61E	13
MEDLEY JOHN R	TX	44E	49
MEDLEY MICHAEL MILTON	MI	03E	34
MEDLEY TOMMY RAY	TX	38E	6
MEDLIN JACKIE MONROE	FL	38W	76
MEDLIN JOHN WILLIAM	TX	12E	38
MEDLIN PAUL CHARLES	CA	15W	56
MEDLIN RICKEY JOE	MI	16W	75
MEDRANO JOSE JR	TX	47E	2
MEDUNA DENNIS LEE	ND	03W	61
MEE MARION EUGENE	KY	06W	74
MEE RANDALL ALAN	WI	24W	56
MEECE MacHUGHLEN	KY	07E	30

NAME	STATE	PANEL NO.	LINE NO.
MEECHAN RICHARD JOSEPH	ID	01W	43
MEEHAN DALE PATRICK	CA	09W	91
MEEHAN DONALD LLOYD JR	IL	05W	84
MEEHAN JAMES MICHAEL	NY	06W	60
MEEHAN MICHAEL ALLEN	MI	13W	128
MEEHAN RAYMOND PATRICK	NY	02E	29
MEEHAN RICHARD WOODS	MD	09E	115
MEEHAN ROBERT EUGENE	PA	51E	40
MEEK CHARLES EDWARD	MI	12E	63
MEEK DONALD HOWARD	TN	02E	84
MEEK JAMES BRANNON	FL	30E	102
MEEK JOE LANELL	CA	02E	88
MEEK THOMAS OTIS	CA	39E	74
MEEK THOMAS WESLY	MI	17E	58
MEEK WILLIAM CHESTER	VA	07E	34
MEEKER EDWARD HOWARD JR	NJ	56W	25
MEEKER MARC JEFFERY	CT	04W	33
MEEKER RAMON ARTHUR	IL	38E	56
MEEKER ROBERT IRWIN	NY	32W	55
MEEKER TIMOTHY JAMES	OR	11E	127
MEEKINS RAYMOND C	VA	12W	63
MEEKS CHARLES HENRY JR	CA	27W	60
MEEKS DUSTAN WILLIAM	TX	28W	71
MEEKS JOHNNY LEE	NC	46W	51
MEEKS RICKY LEE	NC	18W	104
MEENAN THOMAS JAMES	WI	59W	7
MEERDINK GEORGE JR	TX	32W	81
MEERHOLZ CHARLES J JR	NY	51E	26
MEES WAYNE EDWARD	MN	16E	36
MEESTER EVERETT JACOB	NJ	40W	29
MEETZE DENNIS RAY	SC	23W	10
MEFFORD BOBBY RAY	KY	24E	83
MEFFORD HARRELL SAMUEL	KY	21W	34
MEGA JAMES FRANK	MN	55W	29
MEGAR HERBERT LEONARD JR	GA	21W	14
MEGEHEE JAMES WOOD	LA	18W	55
MEGGS MARION LEE	SC	30E	4
MEGINN MICHAEL MERIDITH	NV	37W	52
MEGIVERON EMIL GEORGE	MI	28E	27
MEGLIO ROBERT FRANK	NY	37E	62
MEGLIO WILLIAM MICHAEL JR	CT	03E	135
MEHAFFEY KEITH DALE	NC	17W	102
MEHEGAN RICHARD HAROLD	WA	29W	70
MEHL RICHARD EARL	OH	32E	25
MEHLHAFF RICHARD WAYNE	NM	10W	82
MEHLS LELAND McGEE	MT	07W	73
MEHNE RICHARD ALLEN	WI	29E	52
MEIDAM THOMAS LAWRENCE	WI	24E	78
MEIDINGER DARYL GENE	WA	26W	85
MEIER CARL FREDRIC	MO	09E	107
MEIER CARL LOUIS	TX	18W	59
MEIER CARROLL RODNEY	IA	64W	12
MEIER GARY MICHAEL	MN	55E	22
MEIER ROY ALAN	IA	42E	36
MEIER TERRANCE LEO	OR	24E	104
MEIEROTTO EDWARD RALPH	IL	29W	1
MEIGGS RICHARD RAY	VA	36W	70
MEIGHAN RICHARD JAMES	IA	45E	13
MEIN MICHAEL HOWARD	NY	37W	13
MEINECKE WILLIAM FREDERIC	WI	39W	34
MEINEN BERNARD PHILLIP JR	WI	32E	31
MEINERS PAUL ALBERT	UT	05E	96
MEIRNDORF BERNARD JAMES	MI	27E	82
MEIROSE DAVID ALLEN	NE	09W	15
MEIS DONALD DAVID	KS	61W	4
MEISBURGER JOSEPH STEVEN	PA	15E	10
MEISEL WILLIAM W JR	CT	41W	41
MEISHEID ALAN JAMES	FL	44W	18
MEISINGER JEROLD WERNER	NE	51W	6
MEISS ROBERT WARREN JR	PA	20E	64
MEISTER BERNARD EDWIN	TN	13W	10
MEISTER DAVID WILLIAM	PA	57E	6
MEISTER GEORGE FREDERICK	CA	26E	48
MEISTER WILLIAM ALFRED	NJ	11W	75
MEIXNER EDWIN GEORGE	OK	41E	69
MEJIA JESUS	TX	60E	14
MELADY RICHARD RAPHAEL	NJ	34W	27
MELAHN PETER T	NY	31E	81
MELCHOR JOHN GLENN	CA	07W	74
MELCZEK JOE ROGER	KY	50E	18
MELDAHL ALLEN ROBERT	MN	39W	71
MELDAHL CHARLES HOWARD	WA	40W	7

NAME	STATE	PANEL NO.	LINE NO.
MELECA FRANK	NY	27E	96
MELENDEZ CRISTOBAL	PR	11E	29
MELENDEZ HUMBERTO C E	TX	22W	24
MELENDEZ RAFAEL	NJ	33W	72
MELENDEZ RUDOLPH	CA	25E	19
MELENDEZ-GONZALEZ JOSE D	PR	42W	61
MELENDRES JOSEPH THOMAS	CA	16E	105
MELENDREZ ROBERT CHARLES	CA	29E	83
MELIM JON MICHAEL	CA	04W	119
MELISH ARNOLD EDWARD	NY	39E	9
MELIUS JOHN STERLING	AZ	10W	13
MELL FRANK RALPH JR	MI	45E	64
MELLAR FRANCIS JOHN JR	VA	27W	76
MELLINGER CARL B JR	PA	54W	37
MELLO ANTHONY JOSEPH	MD	55W	36
MELLO EDWARD THOMAS JR	MA	50E	50
MELLO ERHARD JAMES	PA	02W	102
MELLON MICHAEL OWEN	WI	46W	31
MELLOR FREDRIC MOORE	RI	02E	52
MELLOR MARK ELDREDGE	RI	63W	18
MELNICK JOEL	NY	07E	44
MELNICK PETE	PA	35E	76
MELNICK STEPHEN JOHN	CT	26E	85
MELNICK STEVEN BERNARD	MT	08W	119
MELNICK STEWART ARTHUR	NJ	45W	33
MELNYK JOSEPH JAMES JR	PA	43E	47
MELNYK MIKOLAW	NJ	27W	20
MELODY EDWARD BRUCE	AR	13W	49
MELONSON JOSEPH DUDLEY JR	TX	27W	76
MELOTT CHARLES EDWARD	OH	42E	36
MELOY JOHN PATRICK	IA	37W	82
MELOY LARRY JOHN	IL	24E	3
MELOY PAUL HOOVER	PA	49W	42
MELTON CHARLES EARL	MS	13W	15
MELTON CLIFFORD DEAN	GA	02E	42
MELTON DAVID LAWRENCE	DC	42E	36
MELTON DENNIS CAROL	GA	59W	7
MELTON EARL JR	MD	09E	99
MELTON EDGAR ROBERT	TX	01W	123
MELTON GEORGE CECIL	TX	24W	105
MELTON JACKIE LEE	FL	36E	56
MELTON JAMES ARTHUR JR	NC	36E	56
MELTON MICHAEL DENNIS	TX	24W	8
MELTON ROBERT FRANKLIN JR	NC	14E	36
MELTON ROBERT LEE JR	NC	49E	34
MELTON RODNEY WAYNE	PA	55E	22
MELTON RONALD DAVID	TN	34W	77
MELTON TODD MICHAEL	WI	01W	115
MELTON WESLEY EUGENE	NC	09W	65
MELTZER EDWARD ALAN	IL	28E	84
MELVILLE TIMOTHY JAMES	CA	44W	65
MELVIN BENJAMIN	NC	37W	34
MELVIN JAMES EDWIN JR	SC	15W	53
MELVIN JAMES LEONARD	MA	30E	92
MELVIN JOSEPH ERNEST	MI	25W	77
MELVIN MICHAEL WAYNE	CA	56E	12
MELVIN STANLEY TRACY	GA	21E	6
MEMORY AL DEWITT	FL	50W	52
MENA JOSEPH ANGEL	CA	59E	26
MENA SAMUEL	NJ	40W	4
MENANE JERRY BRUCE	CA	26E	61
MENARD DOUGLAS FRED	CO	30W	14
MENARD LOUIS UISVILLE JR	LA	49W	5
MENART JAMES JOSEPH	OH	20E	120
MENCHISE MICHAEL J JR	NY	23E	94
MENCONI WILLIAM LEE	RI	58E	23
MENDALL CARLTON JOSEPH	MA	05W	49
MENDELL ALLAN	CA	33E	72
MENDENHALL MICHAEL JOSEPH	OK	33E	73
MENDENHALL THOMAS DEAL	AZ	18E	46
MENDENHALL THOMAS JAMES	CA	19W	32
MENDENHALL WILLIAM G	CO	12E	7
MENDEZ ANGEL	NY	16E	94
MENDEZ DAVID	NY	12E	96
MENDEZ ERINEO MENDEZ	TX	13E	92
MENDEZ ISMAEL JR	NY	36W	85
MENDEZ JOHN WILLIAM	NJ	32W	27
MENDEZ JULIAN	TX	25E	58
MENDEZ MAURILIO	CA	09W	53
MENDEZ ROBERTO	TX	40W	45
MENDEZ SALVADOR JOE	AZ	47W	1
MENDEZ THEODORE SR	OH	21W	119

NAME	STATE	PANEL NO.	LINE NO.
MENDEZ WALTER XABIER	PR	05W	72
MENDEZ-MATOS JORGE LUIS	PR	25W	77
MENDEZ-ORTIZ FREDES VINDO	PR	24W	91
MENDEZ-QUINTANA EDWARD	NY	24W	88
MENDIAS MARIO JUAN	TX	30W	14
MENDIBLES RAYMOND G	CA	53E	38
MENDIOLA RICARDO	TX	14W	85
MENDIOLA ROBERT L G	GM	52E	38
MENDOZA ALBERT MANUEL	AZ	28W	11
MENDOZA ANTONIO	CA	18E	124
MENDOZA DAVID LOUIS	OH	03E	85
MENDOZA DAVID RAMIREZ	CA	04W	81
MENDOZA GILBERT	CA	50E	50
MENDOZA JOHN DEE	CA	39E	9
MENDOZA JOSE MEDEL	CA	32E	38
MENDOZA JOSEPH LOUIS	CA	15W	51
MENDOZA MARTIN ELBY	CA	38W	3
MENDOZA MILTON JOHN	LA	19W	79
MENDOZA PETER ACOSTA	CA	49E	34
MENDOZA RONNIE ALLEN	CA	01W	37
MENDY STAN		10W	26
MENEELY HERMAN RICHARD	IN	08E	37
MENEES RICHARD ALLEN	MS	17E	80
MENEFEE GENE ALLEN	AL	11E	69
MENENDEZ LEO JR	WV	32E	95
MENENDEZ-OCASIO ISMAEL	PR	41E	41
MENGEL KENNETH RAYMOND	WI	57W	2
MENGES GEORGE BRUCE	OH	13E	110
MENLEY EARNEST DALE	MO	26W	101
MENN ARTHUR JOHN	TX	06W	94
MENNINGER GEORGE EDWARD	TX	29W	103
MENNINGER ROBERT PATRICK	MO	30W	6
MENNONE MICHAEL GIOVANNI	CT	21W	24
MENO GEORGE SABLAN	WA	02W	85
MENO JESUS QUINENE	GM	37W	6
MENO ROY FLORES	HI	09E	56
MENOWSKY GLENN ALFRED	MA	17E	45
MENSCER WILLIAM DAVID	NC	10W	52
MENSCH CHARLES R	MO	36E	58
MENSEN ANTHONY JOSEPH	MN	02W	48
MENSHEK STEPHEN ALBERT	MN	22E	109
MENSING STANLEY ALFRED	IL	19W	18
MENTER JEROME	NJ	25W	77
MENTON ALBERT DAVID	TX	63W	13
MENTON CHARLES RUSSELL J	NC	61E	13
MENTZER GERALD LERVERNE	PA	09E	133
MENTZER ROBERT EDWIN JR	MD	47E	34
MENZ CLYDE RONALD	MN	37E	25
MENZIES ALEXANDER JOHN NE	NY	06E	75
MENZIES CLIFFORD LEROY JR	OR	20E	77
MEOLA ANTHONY PAUL	NY	14E	1
MERCADO DIEGO	NY	05E	107
MERCADO GEORGE	NY	13E	35
MERCADO-COLLADO LUIS ROLA	NY	53W	37
MERCADO-GUTIERREZ RUBEN D	PR	56W	36
MERCADO-SANTOS WILFREDO	NY	18E	16
MERCER CARL SINATRA	NC	13E	92
MERCER GARY LYNN	OK	09W	28
MERCER JACOB EDWARD	FL	01W	45
MERCER JIMMY HENRY	GA	08W	55
MERCER POLLARD HUGH JR	LA	34E	89
MERCER ROBERT JOHN	MA	45W	8
MERCER WILLIAM IVAN	CA	57W	29
MERCHANT CARL LEE	NY	45E	25
MERCHANT LONNIE VESTER	GA	18W	62
MERCIER JOHN CHARLES	WI	13E	23
MERCIER PATRICK TIMOTHY	MN	17E	80
MERCK ROGER EUGENE	SC	03E	86
MERCKE TERRANCE LEE	CA	37W	37
MERCURIO JOHN A	NY	30E	93
MEREDITH CLYDE PEYTON	TX	14W	30
MEREDITH HUBERT ARTHUR	TN	50W	44
MEREIDER ROBERT JOHN	DE	35E	55
MERENO MICHAEL	CA	14W	122
MERICANTANTE THOMAS LEE	CA	48W	28
MERIDITH GARY LEE	CA	33E	20
MERINGA GARY PAUL	MI	50E	18
MERINO LOUIS PHILLIP	NY	16E	54
MERKEL MICHAL ALVIN	IN	46E	9
MERKER RAND RUSSELL	IL	28W	50
MERKLE EDWARD DANIEL	NY	31W	10
MERKLE ELLIOTT LYNN	MO	04E	50

NAME	STATE	PANEL NO.	LINE NO.
MERLINO CARL STEVEN	NJ	02W	39
MERMEJO JOSEPH MICHAEL	UT	28W	83
MERONEY RAPHNELL J	TN	04E	112
MERONEY VIRGIL KERSH III	AR	30W	6
MERRELL DAVID RICHARD	IL	40W	33
MERRELL JAMES KEITH	IN	35W	49
MERRELL LOWELL HOWARD	TN	01E	107
MERRELL ROBERT DELL	TN	05E	73
MERRELL STEVEN DEE	ID	10W	46
MERRETT JAMES ALLEN	AZ	36W	12
MERRIAM DAVID HENRY	OH	38W	3
MERRICK JAMES LEE JR	IA	42W	70
MERRICK WALTER FORREST	ME	11E	113
MERRICKS ALVIN	FL	25W	30
MERRIHEW GLEN FREDERICK	FL	01E	7
MERRILL CHARLES LE ROY JR	PA	11W	8
MERRILL DAVID B	WI	14E	1
MERRILL DAVID LOUIS	IN	39W	29
MERRILL DENNIS LEE	CA	30E	102
MERRILL DOUGLAS CARROLL	MN	19W	62
MERRILL HUGH WALLACE	MI	05E	130
MERRILL JOSEPH ADELBERT	MA	37W	18
MERRILL LARRY ARTHUR	WA	25E	87
MERRILL ROBERT FRANKLIN	MA	12W	127
MERRILL WELDON BERNARD	NC	45E	3
MERRILL WILLIAM FRANKLIN	PA	16W	125
MERRIMAN CHARLES EDWARD	TN	23E	80
MERRIMAN JOHN DAVID	OK	25E	74
MERRIMAN JOHN SARGENT	PA	25W	24
MERRIMAN MICHAEL GENE	OH	07E	82
MERRIMAN REGINALD WALTER	TX	40W	50
MERRIMAN THOMAS BRUCE	OH	10W	13
MERRITT ALLEN TWIGGS IV	AL	36E	79
MERRITT CHARLES EVERETT	IA	15W	104
MERRITT EDWARD JEROME	PA	12E	22
MERRITT JOHN CLINTON	GA	04W	73
MERRITT TERRY LEE	LA	08W	46
MERRITT VERNON ALLEN	MI	05E	58
MERRIWEATHER GENE OPERIE	TN	30W	27
MERRIWEATHER NATHANIEL	WI	06E	85
MERRIWEATHER T Z	MS	17W	8
MERRY DONALD LEWIS	FL	55E	23
MERRYMAN DENNIS GARY	MI	30W	48
MERSCHEL LAWRENCE JAMES	PA	53E	35
MERSCHMAN JOHN WILLIAM	OH	10W	14
MERSCHROD LAWRENCE RICHAR	NJ	42W	30
MERSHON DANIEL LEE	CO	20W	95
MERSHON STEVEN VICTOR	IL	37W	34
MERTELL JAMES RICHARD JR	MO	26E	80
MERYS ROBERT KEITH	KS	37W	82
MERZ JAMES R JR	MI	09W	112
MESA JAMES GREGORY	CA	42W	48
MESA MANUEL E JR	FL	18E	101
MESA RICARDO	CA	03E	18
MESA TOMAS REYES	GM	40W	66
MESAROSH DONALD EARL	KY	20E	120
MESENBURG TERRANCE R	OH	23W	90
MESHIGAUD ANDREW HARRY	TX	02W	89
MESICH MICHAEL STEPHEN	WI	10W	76
MESOYEDZ HOWARD ANTHONY	WA	07E	134
MESQUITA FERNANDO OLIVAS	AZ	07E	43
MESSENGER JAMES EDWARD	WV	23E	77
MESSENGER KENNETH EDWARD	NY	55E	23
MESSER BOBBY GENE	OH	44W	57
MESSER DARRYL	AZ	02E	66
MESSER EARLEY JOSEPH	FL	15E	81
MESSER FERRELL EDWARD	OK	34W	33
MESSER JACK WILLIAM	SC	13W	119
MESSER JAMES ALLEN	MA	25E	30
MESSER JON LAIRD	CA	19E	15
MESSER SIGURD MARTIN	CA	23E	44
MESSER THOMAS HUBERT	VA	07W	19
MESSERLI STEVEN LOUIS	CA	45E	25
MESSERSMITH DEAN HAROLD	WA	28E	56
MESSICK JAMES AVERY	IL	13E	126
MESSING MITCHELL	CA	26W	48
MESSINO DAMIEN JOHN JAMES	PA	15W	99
MESTAS PETER VINCENT	CO	17W	92
MESZAR FRANK III	IN	30W	16
METCALF CARL JOSEPH JR	KY	36W	40
METCALF CHARLES EUGENE	AR	30E	79
METCALF CLAUDIE	MS	23W	76

NAME	STATE	PANEL NO.	LINE NO.
METCALF EDWARD WALTER	OR	03W	50
METCALF GERALD ERNEST	MA	07E	103
METCALF HAROLD	IN	44E	29
METCALF JERRY EUGENE	IL	21E	107
METCALF JIMMY ALLEN	TX	38E	33
METCALF LARRY DUANE	NY	31E	59
METCALF RICHARD LOUIS	CA	14W	53
METCALF TOM ANDREW	TN	15W	130
METOTT GERALD PATRICK	NY	03E	28
METOYER BRYFORD GLENN	LA	01E	42
METOYER JAMES EDWARD	LA	10E	58
METOYER MICHAEL ESPY	CA	26W	86
METROS CARL DEANE	IL	10E	77
METSKER THOMAS CURTIS	IN	03E	49
METTERT ROBERT ARNOLD	WA	19E	53
METTINGER ALBERT ELWOOD	NJ	07W	118
METTLING CRAIG STEVEN	MN	29W	31
METTY RAYMOND JAMES	NY	13E	79
METZ ALAN RUSSELL	NY	24E	33
METZ DANNY RAY	AR	18W	69
METZ GARY RAYMOND	MI	07W	28
METZ JAMES HARDIN	MO	50E	6
METZGER ANTHONY JOHN JR	PA	14W	95
METZGER GEORGE LEONARD	KS	18W	62
METZGER RUSSELL EDWARD	CA	08E	7
METZKER FRANKLIN H	MD	62E	8
METZLER CHARLES DAVID	CA	03W	85
METZLER JOHN EDWARD	PA	41W	53
METZLER PERRY	MI	05W	103
MEULEBROECK KENNETH JOHN	MN	20W	1
MEUSE JOHN RICHARD	MA	19E	29
MEUTE HOWARD MICHAEL	NM	28W	19
MEYER ARTHUR WILLIAM	AZ	47W	20
MEYER BURT JOSEPH JR	NY	31W	95
MEYER DAVID LEE	IA	05W	40
MEYER DAVID PAUL	IL	03W	25
MEYER EDWARD K	IL	20E	1
MEYER FRANKLIN DELANO	PA	09W	44
MEYER GARY ANTONE	CA	51W	35
MEYER GARY JON	IL	36W	38
MEYER GARY PAUL	CA	11E	23
MEYER GREGORY LEO	MO	20W	103
MEYER JAMES FREDRICK JR	WI	39E	75
MEYER JOHN FRANKLIN	MN	34W	86
MEYER JOHN JOSEPH	IN	30W	15
MEYER JOSEPH JOHN JR	PA	21W	61
MEYER KENNETH ALLEN	CA	05W	99
MEYER KENNETH ANTHONY	OH	18W	92
MEYER LEO ROLAND	WI	41W	14
MEYER LEWIS DONALD JR	MT	05W	88
MEYER LOWELL WAYNE	NY	24W	32
MEYER OTTO PAUL III	CA	19E	17
MEYER ROBERT JEROME	OH	14E	29
MEYER RONALD RAY	WA	28W	83
MEYER RONALD WILLIAM	IA	08E	53
MEYER TERRY LYNN	OH	34E	30
MEYER TERRY ROBERT	MI	48W	8
MEYER VAL GREGORY	IL	11W	31
MEYER VERLYN GWEN	SD	47W	29
MEYER WILLIAM MICHAEL	MI	18E	95
MEYERKORD HAROLD DALE	MO	01E	96
MEYERS CHARLES CARTER	PA	45W	15
MEYERS DAVID LEE	IN	24E	8
MEYERS GEORGE HENRY	IN	08W	122
MEYERS RAYMOND EILERT	HI	05E	87
MEYERS ROGER ALLEN	IL	33W	94
MEYERS VICTOR BERT	WI	49W	36
MEYHOFF MICHAEL FREDERICK	ND	33E	39
MEYSEMBOURG DANIEL LLOYD	WI	44E	18
MEZA JESUS JAMES	CA	13W	6
MEZERA TERRY FRANCIS	WI	05W	50
MEZZATESTA FREDERICK	NY	19W	55
MEZZLES TOMMY	TN	15E	116
MICAN ALLEN STANLEY	TX	17E	86
MICHAEL DAVID WILLIAM	IA	03E	111
MICHAEL DENNIS STEVEN	CA	40E	43
MICHAEL DON LESLIE	AL	17E	125
MICHAEL JAMES ALBERT	GA	05W	101
MICHAEL JAMES RICHARD	IL	20E	17
MICHAEL LEO GENE	MN	12E	103
MICHAEL LLOYD DONALD	CA	31E	65
MICHAEL THOMAS	NH	28W	72

NAME	STATE	PANEL NO.	LINE NO.
MICHAEL TIMOTHY SHAWN	NY	21W	61
MICHAEL VINFORD FRANKLYN	NY	05E	107
MICHAEL WILLIAM ARTHUR	MO	29E	32
MICHAELIS JOHN DAVID	OR	29E	4
MICHAELS JOHN JAY	PA	36W	52
MICHALAK WAYNE ALLEN	IN	37E	25
MICHALIK WILLY ROBERT	OK	49E	13
MICHALK ROBERT BRUCE	OH	05W	31
MICHALKE RUSSELL ARTHUR	MI	68E	5
MICHALOPOULOS RAYMOND WIL	RI	30E	57
MICHALOWICZ STANLEY JULUI	IL	49E	54
MICHALOWSKI RAYMOND JOHN	IL	36E	81
MICHALSKI JAMES	IN	23W	66
MICHALSKI JOHN MITCHELL	MI	58E	24
MICHALSKI JOHN STEVEN	NY	03E	9
MICHALSKI STEVEN	WI	27W	20
MICHAUD BENTON	ME	34E	23
MICHAUD LEO EDWARD	ME	34E	89
MICHAUD RONALD ALBERT	WI	22E	26
MICHEHL THOMAS CHARLES	CA	03W	61
MICHEL DANIEL VICTOR	NY	44E	29
MICHEL DAVID GEORGE	MN	22W	24
MICHEL JOHN S	MN	03E	59
MICHEL ROBERT ALFRED	NJ	41W	60
MICHEL WILLIAM FREDERICK	WA	09W	128
MICHEL WILLIAM LEIGH	TX	40W	42
MICHELLI ANGELO FRANCIS	PA	07E	20
MICHELS DONALD MATHEW JR	MI	33W	25
MICHELS JOHN JAY	PA	52W	15
MICHELS LESTER GEORGE	NJ	06E	33
MICHELS MICHAEL RONALD	SD	34W	86
MICHINOK FRANCIS MICHAEL	PA	24E	83
MICHLES EARL R	AR	57W	11
MICHULKA FRANK GEORGE	TX	32E	32
MICK FRED GEORGE	OH	01W	81
MICKA RUDOLF	NY	02W	108
MICKELSEN WILLIAM EMIL JR	MN	20W	124
MICKELSON DENNIS ERWIN	OR	36W	85
MICKENS CARL LAWRENCE	NJ	09W	119
MICKENS EDDIE JAMES	AL	17E	125
MICKLE JOHN RICHARD	OH	03W	70
MICKLE MOSES	SC	29E	4
MICKLES CHARLES EDWARD	VA	59W	8
MICKNA JOHN RONALD	NE	15E	80
MICKO MICHAEL ALBERT	NY	06W	27
MICLOSKEY KEN E	CT	34W	51
MICOLA DANA J	PA	06E	117
MICULS JANIS	MI	50E	50
MICUNEK MICHAEL MARK	MI	57E	27
MIDCALF THOMAS EDWARD	TN	20E	2
MIDCAP DAVID MICHAEL	CO	31E	49
MIDDLEBROOKS CARL MASON	MD	59W	23
MIDDLEBROOKS ROBERT NEAL	AL	04E	71
MIDDLEKAUFF DAVID	CA	32E	54
MIDDLETON CLAYTON	OH	16E	103
MIDDLETON DONALD ARTHUR	OH	25E	31
MIDDLETON HOMER RAY	TX	31E	5
MIDDLETON JAMES EDWARD	IN	28E	16
MIDDLETON KENNETH DALE	MI	05E	87
MIDDLETON RICHARD W	MO	30E	5
MIDDLETON RONALD	NY	55E	21
MIDDLETON STEVEN ALFRED	SC	44E	60
MIDDLETON TEDDY EUGENE	OH	20W	1
MIDDLETON WAYNE LEE	NY	18E	30
MIDGETT DEWEY ALLEN	VA	30E	86
MIDGETTE WILLIS LEANDREW	NC	35W	34
MIDGYETTE JOSEPH HARGROVE	NY	24E	55
MIDKIFF GARY BRUCE	OK	37E	25
MIDKIFF O L	KY	62W	13
MIDNIGHT FRANCIS BARNES	IN	25E	34
MIDTHUN ROGER WAYNE	MN	60E	25
MIDUSKI FRANCIS CHARLES	NJ	27E	54
MIECZKOWSKI JOSEPH	PA	18E	124
MIEDEMA MATTHEW GEORGE	MI	10E	42
MIEDZIELEC TIMOTHY R	MI	17W	68
MIELKE BRUCE EDWARD	IN	24E	62
MIETUS JOHN ANDREW	WI	20E	84
MIFFLIN JOHN RAY	IL	26W	33
MIGLIERINA ROBERT LEO	CT	41W	41
MIGLIORE LUCIEN JOSEPH	NY	08W	103
MIGNINI WILLIAM DOUGLAS	MD	25E	53
MIGUEL MICHAEL JOSEPH	CA	18E	16

NAME	STATE	PANEL NO.	LINE NO.
MIHALAKIS ELLAS LOUIS	IA	52W	7
MIHALEK ADELBERT F IV	FL	11E	130
MIHALOVICH JOHN MICHAEL	WI	46E	20
MIHORDIN DONALD STEPHEN	PA	38W	77
MIKA STEPHEN ADAM	OH	22E	44
MIKA VICTOR GEORGE	NJ	50E	31
MIKE STEVEN	NM	05W	29
MIKELS JAMES HERBERT JR	WV	41E	69
MIKESELL RONALD LEE	KY	16E	12
MIKITIS MICHEAL ALLEN	OH	35E	48
MIKOLAJCZYK DENNIS LEE	OH	07W	111
MIKOSZ WALTER JOSEPH JR	PA	35E	55
MIKRUT JOHN THOMAS	IL	18E	124
MIKULA CARL STEPHEN	PA	18W	24
MIKULA EMERY GEORGE	NJ	11E	71
MIKULECKY DONALD HENRY	OK	30E	93
MILADIN RAYMOND EDWARD	WI	29E	60
MILAM ARLIE BROOKS	WV	27W	102
MILAM CALVIN EDWARD	IL	05W	63
MILAM DALE E	WV	18E	6
MILAM LEWIS EDWARD	AL	17E	8
MILAM WILBUR LAWRENCE III	GA	32W	8
MILAN EDWARD WALTER	MA	42E	71
MILAN GEORGE LEONARD	NJ	25E	43
MILAN-ANAVITARTE LUIS ENR	NY	21E	69
MILANO JOSEPH JOHN	OH	19W	107
MILANOWSKI JOHN EDWARD	WI	40E	25
MILAR ALBERTO JR	HI	18W	55
MILBERGER RUSSELL DALE	OR	08W	4
MILBERRY RUSSELL E	MD	36E	25
MILBOURNE RALPH WILLIAM	VA	47W	5
MILBRADT DALE LA VERNE	KS	27W	57
MILBRANDT CHARLES J	SD	19E	110
MILBRATH ROBERT KEITH	MN	06W	40
MILBRODT GERALD LEE	MN	39E	63
MILBURN ALBERT	TX	10W	18
MILBURN MICHAEL DRENNEN	OH	37E	62
MILCO WILLIAM JOHN	IL	04W	88
MILDE DAVID W	MN	32E	38
MILDNER ROBERT MARC	CA	14W	38
MILEK MARTIN HEINRICH	PA	48E	30
MILENDER JOHN EMERSON	TN	04E	103
MILES BLAINE STANLEY JR	IL	42W	31
MILES BRUCE EDWARD	IL	13E	68
MILES DALE ARTHUR	CA	34E	55
MILES DAVID LEE	KY	14E	36
MILES ELIJAH JR	AL	36W	4
MILES GALEN SPINKS	SC	07W	49
MILES GLENN EDWARD	IN	40W	13
MILES HAROLD GENE	SC	19W	18
MILES JAMES EDWARD	VA	43E	27
MILES JOE JUNIOR	SC	32W	19
MILES JOHN CALVIN	NC	49W	48
MILES JOHN ELMER	FL	12E	28
MILES JOHN EMORY	IL	54W	38
MILES LARRY ALLEN	NY	28W	72
MILES LYNN LEROY	IA	14E	95
MILES MARK SCOTT	CA	13W	64
MILES MORRIS CALVIN JR	TX	14W	53
MILES PALMER BEACH	GA	03E	85
MILES PATRICK CHARLES	MI	47W	1
MILES PHILLIP ALBERT JR	PA	08W	12
MILES RAYMOND GENE	NY	14W	122
MILES RICHARD ROBERT	NY	10E	95
MILES ROBERT WAKE	NC	42W	70
MILES RONALD DAVID	CA	12E	122
MILES STEPHEN LEE	TN	15E	120
MILES THOMAS EDWARD	OH	06E	60
MILES WELDON JOHN	NJ	29E	74
MILEY BRUCE MICHAEL	NJ	40W	13
MILEY EUGENE	NJ	32E	25
MILEY FREDERICK JAMES JR	PA	27E	85
MILEY JOSEPH WAYNE	KY	05W	88
MILEY REUBEN JR	NY	42W	58
MILHORN LARRY DAYTON	TN	32W	1
MILICH JAMES HENRY	NY	38E	7
MILIKA GEORGE AUREL	PA	06W	23
MILIKIN RICHARD M III	FL	10E	23
MILIUS PAUL LLOYD	IA	41E	51
MILK ALLAN ARLYN	NY	12E	7
MILKS RICHARD ALLEN	MI	38W	44
MILLAN RICHARD	NJ	19W	32
MILLAN ROBERT DENNIS JR	MI	20E	119
MILLAR PETER EDMUND	NJ	20E	77
MILLARD CHARLES WORTH	NC	50E	50
MILLARD KENNETH ARTHUR	CA	22E	72
MILLARD LARRY DAVID	OH	35E	76
MILLARD LOREN RAY	WI	59W	8
MILLAY CHARLES FRANCI	KY	01E	104
MILLE WALTER	NY	15E	6
MILLEDGE FREDERICK RAYMON	ME	52W	7
MILLENDER ROBERT CLIFFORD	FL	13W	10
MILLER ALLEN PERDA	OK	13E	61
MILLER ALLEN ROBERT	NY	28W	26
MILLER ALVIN EDWARD	MS	35W	35
MILLER ANDREW J	WI	30E	79
MILLER ANTHONY	LA	45W	15
MILLER ARLEN JAY	PA	25W	106
MILLER ARNEZ FRANKLIN JR	AR	13E	127
MILLER ARTHUR JR	LA	33E	72
MILLER BENTON LEWIS	OH	06W	68
MILLER BERNHARDT WILLIAM	MT	29E	68
MILLER BERTMANN EARL	MO	29E	4
MILLER BILLY LEE	TN	17W	42
MILLER BURKE HOLBROOK	MO	08W	29
MILLER BURRNON ELIHUE	IN	26E	89
MILLER BURT EVERETT	OH	39W	17
MILLER CALVIN LEROY	CA	14E	81
MILLER CARL DEAN	MO	26E	2
MILLER CARL JEROME	AR	37W	67
MILLER CARL ROBERT	OK	50W	26
MILLER CARL SOCRATES JR	TN	04E	112
MILLER CARLETON PIERCE JR	MA	05W	29
MILLER CARY DUANE	IN	17W	46
MILLER CECIL VERNON	NY	21W	66
MILLER CHARLES	NY	06E	126
MILLER CHARLES	FL	18E	42
MILLER CHARLES CLAUDE	IA	48E	7
MILLER CHARLES DANIEL	OK	47E	24
MILLER CHARLES EDWARD	FL	26E	13
MILLER CHARLES EMIL	PA	17W	129
MILLER CHARLES EUGENE	OH	19E	6
MILLER CHARLES IRVIN	MI	59E	29
MILLER CHARLES RUSSELL	GA	66E	11
MILLER CHARLES WAYNE	MI	35E	24
MILLER CHARLES WILLARD JR	WV	33W	79
MILLER CHARLIE REUBEN JR	LA	40E	10
MILLER CHRISTOPHER A	WV	15W	82
MILLER CHRISTOPHER J J	MD	11E	92
MILLER CLARENCE ALVIE JR	IL	29E	33
MILLER CLARENCE DALE	MD	11E	113
MILLER CLARENCE STEPHEN	FL	31W	53
MILLER CLARK ALAN	MA	16E	94
MILLER CLAUDE PAUL	AL	23E	44
MILLER CLEVE DAVIS	CA	11W	14
MILLER CLINTON EUGENE	MO	18W	127
MILLER CURTIS DANIEL	TX	02W	122
MILLER CURTIS O'NEIL	VA	42W	62
MILLER DANA LEE	OH	25W	106
MILLER DANIEL AUGUST	PA	41W	19
MILLER DANIEL HAROLD	IL	24E	68
MILLER DARRELL EDWIN	OH	35W	72
MILLER DARYL L	IN	24E	83
MILLER DAVID BRUCE	MI	09W	112
MILLER DAVID EDWARD	IL	01E	49
MILLER DAVID HARVEY	CO	66W	9
MILLER DAVID MICHAEL	TX	19W	114
MILLER DAVID RAYMOND	MI	26E	2
MILLER DELANEY ERNEST JR	VA	08E	22
MILLER DENNIS CARL	IL	09W	51
MILLER DENNIS J	PA	36E	79
MILLER DONALD	NJ	64E	17
MILLER DONALD GENE	OR	17E	117
MILLER DONALD JOHN	NY	12E	129
MILLER DONALD ROBERT	KY	62W	13
MILLER DONALD WAYNE	KY	31E	36
MILLER DONALD WAYNE	VA	32W	71
MILLER DOUGLAS J	MI	13E	28
MILLER DOYCE GENE	TX	29W	11
MILLER EARL DAVID	IN	31E	20
MILLER EARNEST LEE	FL	56E	12
MILLER EDDIE LEE	TX	52E	21
MILLER EDWARD CHARLES	PA	54E	12
MILLER EDWARD CLINTON	IN	22E	109
MILLER EDWARD KENNETH	NJ	48W	34
MILLER EDWARD MARTIN	FL	10W	104
MILLER ERNEST LEE	MI	02E	88
MILLER EUGENE LEWIS	MO	19W	88
MILLER EUGENE STUART	MI	10W	86
MILLER EVERETT GENE	IN	04E	113
MILLER FOSTER BISHOP	OH	25E	105
MILLER FRANK HAROLD JR	OH	07W	74
MILLER FRANK LEONARD III	AL	02E	100
MILLER FRED ANTHONY	TX	52E	21
MILLER FREDERIC WILLIAM	WA	15E	10
MILLER FREDERICK C III	PA	29W	103
MILLER FREDRICK WAYNE	OH	06E	126
MILLER GARY AMES	CA	07E	131
MILLER GARY DEAN	CA	17E	75
MILLER GARY LEE	VA	32W	45
MILLER GARY LEONARD	PA	10E	120
MILLER GEORGE DANIEL	IN	22E	15
MILLER GEORGE DANIEL	MT	24E	33
MILLER GEORGE ERNEST	MI	16W	96
MILLER GEORGE LIVINGSTON	PA	15W	33
MILLER GEORGE WILLIAM	NJ	10E	120
MILLER GERALD CRAIG	IL	28E	46
MILLER GERALD LEON	IN	58W	11
MILLER GLENN EDWIN	CA	58E	11
MILLER GLENN RAY	IL	53W	22
MILLER GLENN STANFORD	TN	41W	67
MILLER GLENN WILLARD	DE	12W	104
MILLER GREEN EDWARD JR	AL	11W	104
MILLER GREGORY L	NY	13E	65
MILLER GURNEY LEN	NC	44W	11
MILLER HAROLD DWIGHT	OH	38W	36
MILLER HARRY J	PA	14E	64
MILLER HEBER JOSEPH	OH	29E	11
MILLER HERBERT	GA	03W	1
MILLER HERMAN A II	TX	49W	48
MILLER HERMAN EUGENE	NY	18E	23
MILLER HOLLIS GREGORY	FL	22W	79
MILLER HUBERT WAYNE	KY	41W	6
MILLER IRVIN GEORGE	MA	11E	83
MILLER IVAN DEAN JR	IN	31E	79
MILLER J C THEODORE	FL	15W	74
MILLER J D	GA	13W	19
MILLER JACK WAYNE	IN	33E	20
MILLER JAMES	SC	35E	22
MILLER JAMES BERNARD	FL	26E	13
MILLER JAMES CALVIN	WV	12W	71
MILLER JAMES EDWARD	MI	11E	16
MILLER JAMES EDWARD	PA	06W	24
MILLER JAMES GARRETT	OH	38E	56
MILLER JAMES GREGORY	OH	23W	66
MILLER JAMES HOWARD	OH	40E	10
MILLER JAMES IRVIN	OH	33E	89
MILLER JAMES LEE	DE	31E	93
MILLER JAMES LEROY	IA	34W	51
MILLER JAMES OLEN	CO	14E	130
MILLER JAMES RAY	WV	43W	7
MILLER JAMES RUSSELL	OH	31E	50
MILLER JAMES WALTER	MN	33E	20
MILLER JEFF	NC	14W	66
MILLER JEFFERY ALLEN	NY	08W	131
MILLER JEFFREY HAROLD	PA	09W	34
MILLER JERRY EUGENE	IN	41E	69
MILLER JERRY LAVON	OK	44W	11
MILLER JERRY LEE	SC	22E	109
MILLER JERRY LEE	UT	67W	1
MILLER JERRY RAY	WV	15E	59
MILLER JERRY ROBERT	CA	17E	117
MILLER JESSE J	PA	04E	78
MILLER JIMMIE	IL	19W	71
MILLER JIMMY ALLEN	CA	13E	116
MILLER JOEL LE ROY	IA	29W	39
MILLER JOHN EDWARD	IL	08E	38
MILLER JOHN EDWARD	VA	46W	6
MILLER JOHN JEROME JR	PA	02W	25
MILLER JOHN MICHAEL	IN	49E	23
MILLER JOHN ROBERT	MI	38W	28
MILLER JOHN RUSSELL	PA	05W	70
MILLER JOHN WILLIAM	KY	11E	62
MILLER JOHNNIE ROBERT	AL	18W	111
MILLER JOHNNY	NC	54E	12
MILLER JOSEPH ANTHONY JR	PA	39W	2

NAME	STATE	PANEL NO.	LINE NO.
MILLER JOSEPH JOHN JR	MD	50W	2
MILLER JOSEPH LLOYD	CO	10E	97
MILLER JOSEPH LORAN	KY	23E	61
MILLER KEITH ALLAN	CT	26E	28
MILLER KEITH NORMAN	WI	27W	39
MILLER KENNETH	MI	37W	57
MILLER KENNETH EDWARD	MI	30W	79
MILLER KENNETH WALTER	KS	42W	48
MILLER KENT FROEMMING	CA	55W	29
MILLER LARRY FLOYD	MO	02W	40
MILLER LARRY LEE	MO	03W	67
MILLER LARRY T	TX	58W	20
MILLER LAWRENCE SCOTT	MS	12W	17
MILLER LEO JUAN	IL	38W	36
MILLER LEON ABNER	KY	13W	37
MILLER LEON PETER	LA	31E	13
MILLER LEONARD CHARLES	LA	29W	1
MILLER LLOYD ASHTON	VA	19E	29
MILLER LOUIS CHARLES	CA	29E	33
MILLER MALCOLM THOMAS	FL	19E	84
MILLER MANFRED BERTOLD	CO	02E	126
MILLER MARK JEFFERY	CA	01W	112
MILLER MARLIN MCCLELLAND	PA	03W	84
MILLER MARSHALL	KY	05W	9
MILLER MARSHALL GREGORY	AZ	03W	86
MILLER MARVIN LEO	IN	40E	44
MILLER MARVIN RAY	CA	21W	24
MILLER MELVIN DALE	IA	08W	18
MILLER MERLIN EUGENE	IA	42W	42
MILLER MICHAEL ANDREW	AZ	28W	72
MILLER MICHAEL CLIFTON	CA	11E	104
MILLER MICHAEL J	IN	03E	85
MILLER MICHAEL JR	CA	36W	52
MILLER MICHAEL LEE	KY	27E	45
MILLER MICHAEL MERLIN	FL	28E	28
MILLER MICHAEL WESLEY	MO	49E	34
MILLER MILLS CRAFT	OH	16E	94
MILLER NORMAN ANTHONY	IL	37W	18
MILLER NORMAN NORWOOD	VA	06E	76
MILLER OREN KENNETH	CA	22E	62
MILLER ORMOND MITCHELL	AL	61E	14
MILLER PAUL	SC	08W	126
MILLER PAUL JAMES	MO	41E	51
MILLER PAUL LYNN	IL	53E	18
MILLER PAUL WAYNE	CA	23W	54
MILLER PETER RICHARD	CO	01W	9
MILLER PETER THOMAS	NY	42W	1
MILLER PHILIP CHANTRY JR	PA	31W	10
MILLER PHILIP DENNIS	CO	62E	11
MILLER PHILLIP	OK	11E	46
MILLER PHILLIP DANIEL	PA	64W	10
MILLER PIUS LEO	ND	04W	119
MILLER RALPH PETERSON III	MI	06W	10
MILLER RANDALL BRUCE	WV	15W	38
MILLER RAYMOND P II	MI	18W	122
MILLER RICHARD ARTHUR	NY	03E	108
MILLER RICHARD CHARLES	AL	18W	29
MILLER RICHARD DANCY	FL	04W	35
MILLER RICHARD DAVID	MI	26W	108
MILLER RICHARD DENNIS	TN	42E	20
MILLER RICHARD HERSHEL	CA	14W	95
MILLER RICHARD L	IN	34E	55
MILLER RICHARD LEE	SD	22W	24
MILLER RICHARD THOMAS	OR	25W	77
MILLER RICHARD W	FL	03E	121
MILLER ROBERT ARTHUR	NY	15E	97
MILLER ROBERT CHARLES	CA	46W	51
MILLER ROBERT EARL	FL	30E	30
MILLER ROBERT EDWIN III	IL	33W	27
MILLER ROBERT GAIL	CA	47W	48
MILLER ROBERT HENRY	IL	14W	40
MILLER ROBERT HERBERT	NY	18E	110
MILLER ROBERT J	MI	35E	24
MILLER ROBERT JACOB JR	OH	47W	49
MILLER ROBERT LEE	WA	52W	7
MILLER ROBERT LESTER	CA	16E	36
MILLER ROBERT MICHAEL	IL	21E	63
MILLER ROBERT RICHARD	LA	17W	57
MILLER ROBERT THEODORE	NJ	34W	38
MILLER ROBERT THOMAS	RI	32E	78
MILLER ROBERT WARREN JR	TX	29E	33
MILLER ROBIN BREWER	PA	30W	91
MILLER RONALD ALAN	TX	03E	85
MILLER RONALD DARRELL	OH	11E	66
MILLER RONALD JAY	MI	59E	8
MILLER RONALD JOHN	PA	17W	34
MILLER RONALD YATES	IL	38W	44
MILLER ROY WALDO JR	GA	39W	9
MILLER RUSSELL PERRY	IN	19E	84
MILLER STANLEY GENE	CO	15E	120
MILLER STANLEY JOSEPH JR	NJ	11W	59
MILLER STEPHEN PETER	PA	10E	113
MILLER STEVEN RICHARD	MN	22E	15
MILLER TED ROGER	PA	11W	69
MILLER TERRY BROWN	OH	26W	10
MILLER TERRY DEAN	IL	23W	90
MILLER TERRY LYNN	WV	44E	49
MILLER TERRY VERNON	IA	23W	16
MILLER THOMAS CRAIG	NJ	05W	72
MILLER THOMAS LEONARD	IL	56W	6
MILLER THOMAS PAUL	WA	02E	135
MILLER TIMMY LARRY	KS	38W	51
MILLER TOMMY NEAL	IL	31W	53
MILLER TOMMY ROGER	IN	05E	120
MILLER VERNELL HENRY JR	NC	65W	11
MILLER VERNON JOSEPH JR	MD	42E	7
MILLER VICTOR RAYMOND	OH	48E	30
MILLER WALTER CHARLES	IL	03E	105
MILLER WALTER PETER JR	NJ	16E	3
MILLER WALTER RAY JR	CA	22W	113
MILLER WAYNE TERRY	TN	16E	113
MILLER WILBUR JAMES JR	FL	30W	37
MILLER WILLIAM ANGUS	CO	12W	89
MILLER WILLIAM EDWARD	CT	28E	104
MILLER WILLIAM FRANKLIN	IL	26E	28
MILLER WILLIAM HARVEY	OH	33W	50
MILLER WILLIAM HOWARD	MO	22W	4
MILLER WILLIAM JR	NC	39W	44
MILLER WILLIAM JULIUS	MO	27E	102
MILLER WILLIAM LEE	UT	02E	133
MILLER WILLIAM LEE	OH	25E	24
MILLER WILLIAM LOUIS III	MI	01W	89
MILLER WILLIAM MICHAEL	NH	44W	65
MILLER WILLIAM N	VA	03E	45
MILLER WYATT JR	PA	07W	62
MILLETT LAURENCE ARTHUR	ME	18W	16
MILLETT STEVEN LAWRENCE	NY	21E	69
MILLETTE HARLENE EUGENE	SD	52W	36
MILLHOUSE KENNETH BRUCE	AK	36W	41
MILLIARD DENNIS EVANS	RI	16W	70
MILLICAN MALCOLM EDWARD	FL	03E	86
MILLIGAN GENE CHARLES	TX	05E	35
MILLIGAN JAMES ELDRIE	KY	24E	114
MILLIGAN JOHNSON MARCUS	AL	35E	34
MILLIGAN RANDALL GALE	CA	60E	27
MILLIKAN JOHN RUSSELL	PA	48W	48
MILLIMAN DAIN W	MI	12E	51
MILLINER ROBERT	NY	48W	28
MILLINER WILLIAM PATRICK	KY	04W	29
MILLING LARRY DEAN	WI	27W	26
MILLINGER GLEN ALLAN	OH	20W	92
MILLION RONALD LEE	KY	37W	52
MILLIRONS JAMES EUGENE	GA	21E	36
MILLISON DENNIS KEITH	PA	31W	66
MILLISON EDWARD JAMES III	PA	30W	98
MILLNER CARLTON BRANDARD	VA	14W	112
MILLNER CHARLES HEWETT	VA	50W	52
MILLNER MICHAEL	CA	31E	5
MILLS ANDREW LEE	AR	32W	66
MILLS ARTHUR LEE	SD	49E	34
MILLS AUDLEY DUANE	IN	02W	38
MILLS CARROLL RAY	CA	05W	81
MILLS CHARLES HOMER	ME	08E	112
MILLS DALE EDWARD	IN	31E	66
MILLS DAVID LEE	IL	23W	38
MILLS DAVID MICHAEL	NY	13E	47
MILLS DENZELL RAY	NY	28E	16
MILLS DONALD	NY	17E	45
MILLS FAIRLEY WAIN	WV	07E	26
MILLS GRAHAM LONNIE	VA	48E	44
MILLS GREG WENDELL	IL	28W	38
MILLS HANS LOTHAR	IL	24W	45
MILLS JAMES BURTON	CA	10E	130
MILLS JAMES DALE	TX	35E	61
MILLS JOHN PAUL	CA	41W	74
MILLS JOHNNY RAY	WV	35E	34
MILLS KARL WILLIAM	NJ	22W	27
MILLS KYNARD	DC	25E	87
MILLS LAWRENCE STEVEN	MO	27W	58
MILLS LEONARD MARK	TX	57W	2
MILLS LOUIS TRENT	NC	18W	29
MILLS PETER ROBERT	CA	19W	18
MILLS RICHARD THOMAS	IN	54E	37
MILLS RICKEY DUANE	CO	07W	49
MILLS ROBBIE RAY	AL	15E	34
MILLS ROBERT PERRY JR	TX	29E	12
MILLS ROBERT THOMAS	CA	01W	50
MILLS RODNEY KENNETH	MI	11W	104
MILLS ROGER BERTHA	MD	36E	25
MILLS ROGER DALE	IN	53E	18
MILLS RONNIE	KY	47E	34
MILLS STEVEN BERNARD	MI	08W	55
MILLS TED DOUGLAS	CA	29W	103
MILLS TERRY WAYNE	MO	01E	105
MILLS THOMAS WAYNE	OH	64W	14
MILLS VICTOR LANE	KY	26W	1
MILLS WARD WARREN JR	VA	08E	30
MILLSAP THOMAS III	NC	11W	38
MILLSPAUGH CECIL RAY	ID	46E	39
MILNE RONALD JAMES	MT	10W	26
MILNER MICHAEL WAYNE	IA	24W	8
MILOS JOSEPH LOUIS	NY	16E	22
MILOT LARRY JOSEPH	NH	47E	40
MILOVICH ROBIN PATRICK	CA	21E	90
MILSTEAD ANTONIO	TX	41W	6
MILTNOVICH EMIL MAX	WY	02W	25
MILTON CHARLES	MS	26E	93
MILTON CHARLES RUDOLPH JR	SC	20E	2
MILTON GARY ANDREW	TX	57W	11
MILTON RICHARD DWAYNE	SD	02W	132
MILUS EDWARD LEE	TX	45E	35
MIMBS BILLIE	GA	23E	82
MIMS FELTON LEE	TX	29W	21
MIMS GEORGE IVISON JR	SC	04E	30
MIMS KENNETH EDWARD	AL	04W	119
MINA JUAN VELASCO JR	WA	16E	106
MINAHAN DANIEL JOSEPH	MA	34W	60
MINARD EARL CHESTER	NY	44E	50
MINCE LYNN ELDON	CO	03E	49
MINCEY DORSEY III	GA	07W	6
MINCEY JAMES MARSHALL	SC	16W	106
MINCEY JOHN ELLIS	IL	52W	16
MINCEY JOHN H	FL	05E	20
MINCEY ROBERT EARLE	CA	10W	1
MINCH ROGER CARL	MI	43E	26
MINCKS JIMMIE LEE	IN	02E	118
MINDACH WILLIAM R	TX	09E	2
MINDOCK RICHARD WILLIAM	IL	08W	82
MINDYAS EDWARD ANDREW	PA	24E	34
MINEAR MARK WENDELL	FL	07W	22
MINEHAN MICHAEL PAUL	MA	61W	18
MINER GEORGE LOUIS	NY	19W	55
MINER JAMES ALLEN	KY	05W	135
MINER MICHAEL DAVID	PA	26E	67
MINER MICHAEL ROBERT	CA	25E	105
MINER STEVEN JAY	OR	59W	8
MINER WILLIAM DAVID	GA	04W	50
MINES JAMES JR	NJ	18E	125
MINETTO ROBERT NEIL	NV	57E	28
MINGLE ROBERT LOUIS	OH	22W	80
MINICK STEPHEN MICHAEL	PA	17E	55
MINIX CLYDE	IN	11E	11
MINK BOYD CARL	OH	51E	31
MINK DONALD KENNETH	IL	20W	21
MINKLER STEVEN JEFFERY	WA	03W	110
MINKO MICHAEL ANTHONY	CA	36W	64
MINKS RAYMOND CRANSTON	TX	34W	16
MINKUS DENNIS JAMES	PA	35W	83
MINNICH RICHARD WILLIS JR	PA	33E	39
MINNIEAR DWIGHT JED	CA	02W	99
MINNIEAR HAROLD NORMAN	OH	55W	8
MINNITEE JOHNSON JR	GA	32E	79
MINNIX LEROY FRANKLIN	OH	02E	120
MINNOCK JOSEPH PATRICK	NJ	03E	25
MINO ROBERT E	NY	41E	52
MINOGUE THOMAS FRANCIS	NY	17E	8

NAME	STATE	PANEL NO.	LINE NO.
MINOR ARMANDO ALVEREZ	TX	22W	48
MINOR CALVIN M	VA	22W	55
MINOR CARROL WILLIAM	SC	37W	76
MINOR DANIEL JAMES	WA	31W	82
MINOR JOHN MICHAEL	TX	02W	116
MINOR MATTHEW JR	AL	40W	7
MINOR MICHAEL JAMES	OH	32E	79
MINOR RANDY MICKEL	AL	21E	113
MINOR ROBERT PATRICK	PA	11E	9
MINOTTI ANTHONY JOHN	NY	24W	18
MINTER WILBUR LOVING JR	TX	44E	50
MINTON BOBBY	IN	21E	123
MINTON CHRISTOPHER ALAN H	CO	42W	5
MINTON DON WAYNE	TX	19E	39
MINTON PHILLIP EDWARD	TN	32W	55
MINUS RAYMOND BENJAMIN	MI	28E	28
MINUTOLI JOHN ROBERT	NY	17E	112
MIONE ANTHONY V	NJ	19W	96
MIOTKE STEVEN MICHAEL	WA	19W	55
MIRACLE DANIEL L	WV	13E	85
MIRACLE GARY RAYMOND	WI	31W	10
MIRACLE JAMES JR	KY	47E	52
MIRACLIA CHRISTOPHER G		07W	36
MIRAMONTES ARTHUR FRED	CA	28E	84
MIRAMONTEZ ENRIQUE	TX	22W	80
MIRAMONTEZ LEONARD	WA	23E	19
MIRANDA FILIBERTO GUILLER	TX	16E	71
MIRANDA JOE ALEMAN	CA	43E	26
MIRANDA MANUEL	CA	03W	76
MIRANDA MICHAEL	IL	26W	86
MIRANDA OSWALDO LUIS	NY	25E	105
MIRANDA PAUL ANDREW JR	IL	31E	50
MIRANDA PETER KALANI	NM	15W	33
MIRANDA ROBERT	MA	03W	121
MIRANDA WILLIAM	IN	19W	88
MIRANDA-CUEVAS LUIS ANTON	PR	02E	40
MIRANDA-ORTIZ JOSE LUIS	PR	31E	14
MIRANDA-PEREZ NOE	PR	04E	113
MIREMONT JAMES EDWARD	LA	10W	42
MIRICH JOHN	OH	34W	16
MIRICK STEVE JR	OH	31W	95
MIRRER ROBERT HENRY	NJ	05W	53
MIS RONALD HENRY	MI	11E	36
MISA TULELE	CA	23W	55
MISA VIANE SOFENI	CA	45E	25
MISCHEAUX RENE CLARENCE	CA	28W	38
MISCHLER HAROLD LOUIS	KS	01W	104
MISHEIKIS THEODORE N JR	IL	06E	52
MISHUK RICHARD EDWARD	MN	11E	90
MISIASZEK JOSEPH PETER	RI	62W	13
MISIUTA EDWARD MICHAEL	FL	42E	21
MISKIMMON JONATHAN JR	NY	33E	89
MISKOWSKI EDWARD A	MD	20W	58
MISNER KENNETH GENE	WA	27W	11
MISSAR JOSEPH CYRIL JR	MD	07E	35
MISTER DARNELL	IN	15W	18
MISTRETTA ERIC PAUL	LA	07W	19
MISZEWSKI DAVID MARTIN	MI	38W	37
MITCHAM CHARLES EMMETT	TX	12E	23
MITCHELL ALBERT COOK	NY	52E	8
MITCHELL ALBERT JEAN	IL	43E	27
MITCHELL ALEX LOUIS	TN	41W	12
MITCHELL ANDREW C III	AL	01E	20
MITCHELL ARTHUR G	OK	08E	105
MITCHELL BYRON JOSEPH	PA	46W	17
MITCHELL CARL BERG	KY	01E	40
MITCHELL CHARLES IRVIN	IL	16W	107
MITCHELL CHARLES LEROY JR	NY	03E	36
MITCHELL CHARLIE HOWARD	WV	18W	95
MITCHELL CHRIS ANTHONY JR	LA	11W	104
MITCHELL CHRISTOPHER	IL	33W	80
MITCHELL CLARENCE	TN	05E	81
MITCHELL CLARENCE E JR	OH	34E	89
MITCHELL CLYDE ULAND	NC	20E	32
MITCHELL CRAIG WESLEY	KS	58E	24
MITCHELL CURTIS	FL	25E	105
MITCHELL CYRIL JR	MA	44W	27
MITCHELL DANA WESSON	NY	18W	104
MITCHELL DANIEL LEE	MO	08W	75
MITCHELL DANNY JOE	WV	46W	17
MITCHELL DAVID ARTHUR	OH	29W	60
MITCHELL DAVID EUGENE	CA	09W	2
MITCHELL DAVID GEORGE	PA	51W	42
MITCHELL DAVID HENRY	NC	23E	53
MITCHELL DAVID LEE	SC	10W	95
MITCHELL DONALD THOMAS	SC	04E	93
MITCHELL DONALD WAYNE	KY	58E	11
MITCHELL ERNEST DARRELL	CA	09E	48
MITCHELL EUGENE EMMETT	AL	12E	103
MITCHELL FRED EVANS III	TN	53W	28
MITCHELL FRED W JR	GA	25E	13
MITCHELL GARY HENTON	GA	15W	39
MITCHELL GEORGE GROVER	TX	13W	24
MITCHELL GILBERT LOUIS	CA	43E	26
MITCHELL GLENN EDWARD	TN	15W	91
MITCHELL HARRY E	IN	56E	12
MITCHELL HENRY ALBERT	NY	52W	36
MITCHELL HOMER JR	AL	57E	28
MITCHELL HORACE GIBBS JR	IN	09E	5
MITCHELL ISAIAH JR	SC	63E	13
MITCHELL JAMES CARROLL JR	CA	14W	14
MITCHELL JAMES MCNALLY JR	CA	02E	70
MITCHELL JAMES RAY	NC	12W	49
MITCHELL JAMES STEPHEN	WI	51W	42
MITCHELL JAY ANDERSON	OK	19E	98
MITCHELL JOHN ALBERT	OH	06E	33
MITCHELL JOHN E S JR	ID	09W	112
MITCHELL JOHN EDWIN	TX	12E	51
MITCHELL JOHN LOUIS	OH	13W	24
MITCHELL JOSEPH ROBERT JR	AL	18E	125
MITCHELL JOSEPH WILLIAM	IL	19W	46
MITCHELL JULIUS AUGUSTA	FL	29W	1
MITCHELL KENNETH	DC	15E	129
MITCHELL LARRY GENE	CO	05W	130
MITCHELL LARRY LEON	GA	64E	6
MITCHELL LARRY LEVERN	AR	36E	79
MITCHELL LAWRENCE HOWARD	MA	21E	113
MITCHELL LEROY	GA	11W	22
MITCHELL LEROY GERALD	MI	17E	117
MITCHELL LONNIE RAY	ID	37W	52
MITCHELL LONNIE WAYNE	MD	02W	49
MITCHELL MACK LEE	SC	20W	21
MITCHELL MALCOLM EVERETT	TX	22W	48
MITCHELL MARK DAVID	CA	34W	27
MITCHELL MICHAEL DENNIS	TX	11E	58
MITCHELL MICHAEL JEFFREY	CA	46W	51
MITCHELL MICHAEL JOHN	NY	25W	78
MITCHELL MICHAEL LANG	TX	57E	28
MITCHELL MICHAEL LYNN	IN	33W	80
MITCHELL MICHAEL SIDNEY	CA	23E	44
MITCHELL MICHAEL THOMAS	CA	20W	21
MITCHELL PAUL HOLLAND JR	OH	11E	49
MITCHELL PAUL JOSEPH	PA	31W	11
MITCHELL PERRY ADKINS	AL	06W	60
MITCHELL PETER	NY	42E	53
MITCHELL PHILIP DANIEL	NY	34E	38
MITCHELL RALPH	NC	01E	68
MITCHELL RALPH BURTON	PA	08W	91
MITCHELL RICHARD A	NY	08E	38
MITCHELL ROBERT E JR	MI	20W	72
MITCHELL ROBERT LEE	IL	29W	71
MITCHELL ROBERT STEVENS	AR	19W	40
MITCHELL ROBERT WALTER	CT	17E	74
MITCHELL ROCHESTER	TN	07E	73
MITCHELL RODGER HYLER	VA	04W	124
MITCHELL ROGER C	CA	13E	117
MITCHELL RONALD EARL JR	TX	34W	39
MITCHELL STEPHEN PHILIP	IL	36E	57
MITCHELL STEVEN MICHAEL	IA	03W	47
MITCHELL THOMAS ALLAN	OH	43W	56
MITCHELL THOMAS BARRY	CO	65E	13
MITCHELL THOMAS C	WI	12E	74
MITCHELL THOMAS PETER	FL	17E	54
MITCHELL THOMAS VICTOR	PA	27W	32
MITCHELL THOMAS WILLIAM	NY	31E	25
MITCHELL TOMMIE LEE	OR	34W	65
MITCHELL TORRANCE JR	TX	23W	76
MITCHELL WILLIAM A II	PA	02E	82
MITCHELL WILLIAM BROOKS	PA	03E	59
MITCHELL WILLIAM BRUCE	CT	03E	15
MITCHELL WILLIE JAMES JR	SC	20E	46
MITCHELL WILLIE JR	DC	04E	31
MITCHELTREE ROBERT G JR	TX	14W	48
MITCHEM CHARLES CLIFFORD	VA	37E	63
MITTON WILLIAM JAMES	CA	11W	115
MITZEL LONNY LEROY	PA	14E	1
MIXSON JOSEPH GARY	TX	13E	28
MIXTER DAVID IVES	CT	05W	68
MIYAKE GARY NOBUO	HI	08E	115
MIYAZAKI RONALD KAZUO	HI	14E	101
MIZE CLIFFORD N	AR	22E	55
MIZE FREDDIE D	KY	12W	32
MIZE JAMES WESLEY JR	FL	05E	48
MIZE MELVIN LAMAR	FL	22W	80
MIZE WILLIAM DAVID	MI	28E	92
MIZELLE JOHN MARSHALL	TN	13E	123
MIZER LENTON EUGENE	KS	08W	20
MIZNER DARRELL CONDIE	OH	58W	11
MIZNER GARY LEE	IL	02W	34
MLODZINSKI BRUNO J JR	IL	22W	4
MLYNARSKI ROBERT LUCIAN	CT	30E	86
MOAK CLIFTON PEARCE	LA	66E	11
MOAKE CHARLES EDWARD JR	IL	16W	101
MOBILIA MICHAEL HOWARD	MA	22W	42
MOBLEY CLARENCE VERNON	NC	56W	26
MOBLEY DANIEL M	OH	13E	92
MOBLEY JENIES ISAAC	NC	50E	51
MOBLEY LAWRENCE	NC	54E	38
MOBLEY SUTTON JR	NC	54E	38
MOBLEY WARREN HERBERT	AL	06W	81
MOBLEY WILLIE ROY	GA	53W	22
MOBUS JOSEPH PATRICK	NJ	19W	71
MOCK DONALD RAY	OK	55E	23
MOCK JOEL WILLIAM	IN	17E	9
MOCK MAURICE KARL	WA	22E	110
MOCKER WILLIAM FRANCIS	NY	52W	9
MODDERMAN PHILIP JOHN	MI	24W	68
MODEN RICHARD SHELDON	NY	11W	103
MODESITT SAMUEL LEE	AR	21E	124
MODGLIN JOHN LARRY	IN	23E	88
MODISETTE THOMAS GLENN	TX	20E	77
MOE CHARLES MERLIN JR	MI	24W	32
MOE HAROLD JOHN	WI	27E	17
MOE LESTER JAMES	WA	04W	92
MOE RONALD JOHN	MT	38W	67
MOEGGENBORG LENARD F	MI	19W	107
MOEHRING DEAN WARD	IL	30W	27
MOELLER VINCENT GERALD ST	NY	08E	62
MOEN JOSEPH ALLEN	WA	11E	53
MOFFETT BILLY RAY	LA	07E	112
MOFFETT JAMES DELTON	OK	60W	11
MOFFETT JERRY LEE	VA	05W	43
MOFFETT MELVIN GLEN	CA	14E	124
MOFFITT THOMAS CARROLL D	MD	29W	31
MOGAN JOHN EDWARD	ME	32E	2
MOGCK DARYL MILTON	OR	19W	40
MOHAMED MACK PAUL	NY	26E	13
MOHAMMED NAZIR	NY	04W	41
MOHAREMOFF MICHAEL GEORGE	MI	40E	44
MOHL WOLFGANG TONY OTTO	HI	31E	37
MOHLER TIMOTHY ALLEN	KS	19W	71
MOHN LAURANCE RICHARD JR	TX	18W	16
MOHN RICHARD SAMUEL	PA	09E	28
MOHNIKE PHILLIP SHERMAN	CA	26W	65
MOHR RICHARD ALLEN	PA	12W	14
MOHR ROY JOHN	NE	64W	13
MOHR VICTOR ALLEN	NY	52E	8
MOHRHAUSER WILLIAM RICHAR	IA	34W	86
MOHRMANN DOUGLAS ROBERT	MA	44E	64
MOILANEN DALE BURTON	MI	02W	103
MOINESTER ROBERT WILLIAM	NY	36E	25
MOIREN RICHARD ALLEN	AL	11W	46
MOISE HERVE JEAN	CA	50E	18
MOKE RUSSELL EUGENE	IL	33W	80
MOKUAU KENNETH WILLIAM JR	NJ	34W	60
MOLAISON GORDON THOMAS	LA	63E	13
MOLANO CHARLES EDWARD	NY	27E	82
MOLDAVAN EDWARD A	GA	28E	84
MOLDENHAUER PETER JAMES	DC	17W	91
MOLDENHAUER RUSSELL	CA	31E	25
MOLE MALCOLM GEOFFREY	FL	35E	7
MOLES LEWIS DAYTON	WV	08W	94
MOLES THOMAS HARRY	VA	10W	82
MOLESE DENNIS PATRICK	NY	19E	121
MOLETTIERE BARRY ALAN	PA	13W	49
MOLETTIERE JOSEPH ANTHONY	PA	37E	40

NAME	STATE	PANEL NO.	LINE NO.
MOLINA AGAPITO JR	CA	09E	80
MOLINA GEORGE GERONIMO	CA	11E	26
MOLINA GILBERTO MENDEZ	TX	47W	49
MOLINA MICHAEL JOSEPH	CA	15E	120
MOLINA SIMON ROSALINO	AZ	29E	52
MOLINA-RODRIGUEZ EUGENIO	PR	15W	28
MOLINA-ROSARIO OCTAVIO	PR	59E	27
MOLINE KEVIN EUGENE	MI	40W	59
MOLINO EDDIE JR	NV	10W	14
MOLKENTINE RANDY WARREN	WI	30W	48
MOLL ROGER RALPH	MI	47W	49
MOLL STEVEN WILLIAM	IL	05W	59
MOLL WAYNE TYRONE	PA	27E	86
MOLLENHOUR ROBERT CARROL	OR	08W	88
MOLLER GLENN LOREN JR	MO	49E	35
MOLLETT CHESTER AUBREY	WV	13W	21
MOLLETTE JAMES RONNIE	KY	07E	10
MOLLEY CHESTER ANDREW	TN	26W	33
MOLLICA BENJAMIN GEORGE	NY	20E	121
MOLLICONE DONALD ALLAN	NY	01E	39
MOLLOHAN STEVEN P	WV	05E	7
MOLLOY JOSEPH JAMES	IL	34W	51
MOLNAR ALBERT RUSSELL	NJ	29E	18
MOLNAR FRANKIE ZOLY	NJ	20E	64
MOLNAR ISTVAN	KY	36E	51
MOLNAR NICHOLAS MICHAEL	MI	12W	60
MOLOSSI ROBERT JOHN	CA	34E	43
MOLPUS JAMES DAVIS	TX	54E	12
MOLTON KENNETH WAYNE	AL	37W	57
MOLTZAN WILLIAM JOHN	MN	58E	12
MOLYNEAUX JOHN LOUIS JR		45W	15
MOLZON ERNEST ALVIN	OH	63W	19
MOMCILOVICH MICHAEL JR	DE	55E	23
MONAGHAN JOHN JOSEPH JR	VA	67W	2
MONAGHAN JOSEPH THOMAS	PA	37W	82
MONAHAN DANIEL FRANCIS	PA	18E	26
MONAHAN EDWARD J JR	CT	03E	116
MONAHAN MICHAEL JAMES	MA	11E	113
MONAHAN MICHAEL JAMES	CA	16E	94
MONAHAN WILLIAM BRIAN	NY	23E	71
MONAHAN WILLIAM S III	NV	11W	21
MONAHON ROBERT EDWARD	NJ	21E	6
MONAT DONALD HENRY JR	OH	18E	87
MONCAVAGE DAVID JOHN	AZ	39E	36
MONCAYO JOSE ROBERTO	AZ	56W	26
MONCRIEF JAMES RAY	AL	48W	45
MONCRIEF WILLIAM GRADY	MN	53W	3
MONCUS BENNIE RAY	AL	42E	21
MONDAY ALVIN	LA	44W	13
MONDRAGON BENJAMIN ALLEN	CO	37E	25
MONDYKE CHARLES ANTHONY	MN	27E	25
MONEACHI DAVID KEITH	TX	18E	36
MONETTE NEAL E	VA	29W	12
MONETTE REGEN ALBERT		02W	113
MONEY WILLIAM WALLACE	NY	21E	23
MONEYSMITH HAROLD DEAN	IA	24E	8
MONFILS DENNIS EUGENE	CA	21E	48
MONFORE WILLIAM DAVID	IA	12E	15
MONFORT BENNIE FRANK	GA	56E	12
MONG WILBUR LEROY	NY	39W	55
MONGELLI ALEXANDER A	NY	24W	25
MONGER OTHA LEE	TN	25E	39
MONGILARDI PETER JR	NJ	02E	19
MONGILLO PAUL JOHN	NJ	32E	15
MONHOF AUGUST HAROLD	MI	31E	41
MONIA TERRY ROBERT	MO	29W	76
MONIN FRANCIS GEORGE	NY	23E	13
MONISH RONALD ANTHONY	NY	32W	38
MONISMITH WAYNE EUGENE	PA	43W	18
MONK SHERMAN DALTON	CA	18W	70
MONK THOMAS	NY	15E	86
MONKELBAAN TIMOTHY JAMES	NY	01W	31
MONKMAN DONALD EUGENE	IL	33E	72
MONKS JOHN	NY	04E	101
MONNETT LEONARD ALLEN	MD	05W	121
MONROE CARLTON LEE	VA	28W	50
MONROE CHARLES CALEB	AZ	21E	49
MONROE FRANCIS MARION	OH	16W	110
MONROE GREGORY JAMES	IL	05E	126
MONROE JAMES HOWARD	IL	15E	48
MONROE MARVIN EUGENE	IN	38E	56
MONROE ROCKNEY D	WA	18E	6
MONROE SAMMY FRANKLIN	NC	15E	107
MONROE VINCENT DUNCAN	NJ	62E	21
MONROE WILBER DEAN	AL	58W	26
MONROIG LUIS JOSE	PR	03W	112
MONSEBAIS LUPE	TX	49W	16
MONSEWICZ LLOYD JOEL	FL	03E	86
MONSKA BRUCE WILLIAM	MA	37E	40
MONSON JOSEPH	GA	12W	18
MONSON PHILLIP DEAN	WI	04W	50
MONTAG LEE EDWARD	OR	18W	41
MONTAGUE DENNIS EDWARD	NY	33E	39
MONTAGUE JESSE WILLARD JR	SC	02W	106
MONTAGUE STEPHEN GRIFFITH	CA	41W	64
MONTAGUE WILLIAM JOSEPH	NY	13W	2
MONTALVO MANUEL GUALVERTO	PA	21E	90
MONTALVO SIGIFREDO JR	TX	56E	27
MONTANA HAROLD LLOYD	FL	14E	32
MONTANA JIMMY CARLUS	CA	09W	54
MONTANA ROSENDO	TX	11W	8
MONTANEZ MIGUEL F	NM	38W	68
MONTANEZ PARIS WILLIAM	CA	33W	3
MONTANEZ PEDRO RODRIGUEZ	WY	30E	30
MONTANIO ANDREW	TX	20W	103
MONTANO ANTHONY	CA	39E	63
MONTANO FRANCISCO ANDREW	AZ	17E	121
MONTANO JOSE CLEMENTE	CO	09W	28
MONTANO WILLIAM ANDREW	NY	06W	71
MONTAPERT RONALD M	CA	27W	89
MONTE SALVADOR LOUIS JR	LA	31E	21
MONTEITH ROBERT F II	PA	10E	42
MONTELEONE ERNEST J JR	LA	02W	59
MONTELEONE GARY ROBERT	CA	01W	20
MONTELLANO MICHAEL A	CA	18W	70
MONTEMAYOR FRANK DE LEON	TX	19E	15
MONTEMAYOR JAMES MICHAEL	KS	34W	27
MONTEMAYOR JOSE SANCHEZ	TX	44E	29
MONTERO IGNACIO	NY	07W	100
MONTERROSO ALFONSO ALFRED	CA	26E	76
MONTERRUBIO ARMANDO	CA	10W	115
MONTES ANTHONY JOHN	PR	45W	54
MONTES JOSE L	PR	41W	25
MONTES LEONARD DANIEL	CA	03W	37
MONTES MIGUEL ALEJANDRO	IL	04W	133
MONTES RAUL	CA	17E	21
MONTEZ ANASTACIO	TX	24W	96
MONTEZ FRANK JAMES	CA	18W	117
MONTEZ JESSE BARRERA	TX	31W	13
MONTEZ JOE	TX	21E	34
MONTGOMERY CLARENCE WILLI	PA	17E	48
MONTGOMERY CLIFFORD	KY	15W	87
MONTGOMERY DONALD LEE	AL	42W	70
MONTGOMERY EDDIE JR	IL	24W	55
MONTGOMERY GEORGE WESLEY	NV	19E	120
MONTGOMERY GEORGE WESLEY	CA	50E	51
MONTGOMERY JACKIE GENE	MO	53E	38
MONTGOMERY JOHN THOMAS	OH	27W	5
MONTGOMERY LARRY	IN	50W	2
MONTGOMERY MICHAEL MALLOR	CA	55E	27
MONTGOMERY OWEN RAYMOND	KY	23E	59
MONTGOMERY ROBERT ALLEN	WA	17E	91
MONTGOMERY RONALD WAYNE	IN	17W	28
MONTGOMERY STANLEY DYKUS	IL	15W	82
MONTGOMERY STEVEN HUGH	CA	23W	104
MONTGOMERY WILLIAM EUGENE	CA	02E	49
MONTGOMERY WILLIAM JOHN	AZ	01E	51
MONTIJO MICHAEL	AZ	23W	45
MONTION ARTURO DANIEL	CA	48W	1
MONTONE KENNETH MICHAEL	NY	26E	105
MONTOYA ALEXANDER	CO	05E	13
MONTOYA ANTHONY JOHN JR	NY	42W	31
MONTOYA DAVID	TX	07W	17
MONTOYA EUSEBIO	NM	39W	55
MONTOYA GUADALUPE ESPARZA	IL	24W	63
MONTOYA JOE HERMAN	NM	07W	78
MONTOYA JOE NED	NM	24E	62
MONTOYA JOSE ALBINO	NM	21E	102
MONTOYA LOUIE GOOCH	CA	03W	72
MONTOYA LUIS ALBERTO	TX	22W	99
MONTOYA MANUEL TOMAS	AZ	13W	32
MONTOYA ROBERT EMILIO	CO	04E	17
MONTOYA ROBERT GONZALES	NM	27E	37
MONTOYA VICTOR H JR	NM	19E	98
MONTOYO-RODRIGUEZ NORBERT	PR	25W	18
MONTREY REAVIS A JR	MO	03E	66
MONTROSS BURTON CHARLES	MI	05E	66
MONTROSS CHARLES PAUL	PA	05W	96
MONTZ ROGER ELLIS	NY	63E	12
MOODY ADGER EUGENE	SC	29W	103
MOODY ALFRED JUDSONF	CT	16E	113
MOODY ANDREW LESLIE JR	WI	14E	40
MOODY ARTHUR R III	FL	03E	86
MOODY CHARLES WILBURN	IL	48E	30
MOODY FRANCIS	NY	03E	50
MOODY FRED ALLEN	NC	29W	21
MOODY HERBERT WAYNE	SC	67W	1
MOODY JERRY MARCUS	FL	16E	63
MOODY JIMMY DALE	MO	17E	37
MOODY JOHN ERNEST JR	NC	08W	15
MOODY LARRY GENE	AR	02E	32
MOODY PAUL JAMES	IL	46E	48
MOODY RICHARD FINISA	IL	04E	31
MOODY ROBERT WILCOX	IL	10E	102
MOODY STEPHEN TRUE	NY	21W	47
MOODY STEWART ROBBINS	CA	15W	122
MOODY THOMAS JOHN	ME	35E	9
MOOER GARY OWEN	MT	23E	111
MOOERS WILLIAM MATHIAS	CA	34W	60
MOOG PHILLIP JACOB	GA	09E	124
MOOMEY CHARLES RAY	IL	46E	38
MOON DEAN LEROY	ID	29W	81
MOON JERRY RUDOLPH	AL	26E	28
MOON LOWELL EDWIN	KY	09W	34
MOON MICHAEL JACK	IL	64W	13
MOON RAYMOND ROSS	UT	14W	127
MOON ROBERT WAYNE	TX	26W	33
MOON THEODORE EDWARD JR	NJ	28W	70
MOON THOMAS HENRY	OH	45W	27
MOON WALTER HUGH	AR	01E	4
MOON WILLIAM CHARLES	IL	53W	3
MOONEY CLARANCE ALLEN	OH	16E	95
MOONEY DWIGHT EDGAR	NC	49W	32
MOONEY FRED	OH	04W	10
MOONEY GENE ALLEN JR	FL	47W	1
MOONEY JAMES	AL	03E	26
MOONEY JOHN HOWARD JR	CA	13E	123
MOONEY MICHAEL JAMES	CA	20W	124
MOONEY PATRICK THOMAS	OH	08E	67
MOONEY ROBERT RAY	IL	25E	106
MOONEY TOMMIE LEE	MS	13E	34
MOONEY WALTER STEPHAN	MA	10E	71
MOONEYHAM BILLY FRANKLIN	TN	11E	62
MOORBERG MONTE LARUE	NE	13E	5
MOORE ABRAHAM LINCOLN	PA	17W	68
MOORE ALAN RANDAL	WV	14E	11
MOORE ALBERT JR	TX	24E	100
MOORE ALLAN JOHN	IN	10W	1
MOORE AMON FRANKLIN JR	TX	39E	72
MOORE ANTHONY LOUIS	LA	53E	4
MOORE BILLY DALE	TN	32W	22
MOORE BILLY EUGENE	CA	14W	53
MOORE BILLY RAY	KS	10E	72
MOORE CARLOS DAVID	KY	09E	81
MOORE CARTER LEE	NY	46E	48
MOORE CHARLES BERNARD	MI	15W	52
MOORE CHARLES EDWARD	KY	23W	55
MOORE CHARLES EDWARD JR	CA	53W	44
MOORE CHARLES EDWARD JR	NY	15W	115
MOORE CHARLES JAMES	MO	44W	58
MOORE CHARLES L	NY	08E	128
MOORE CHARLES LARRY	OR	23E	61
MOORE CHARLES RAY	AR	18W	49
MOORE CHARLES SARGENT	CA	18E	87
MOORE CHARLES THOMAS	MO	15W	130
MOORE CHARLES THOMAS JR	OH	03E	86
MOORE CLARENCE EARL	OK	02E	100
MOORE CLYDE VERNON	GA	27E	30
MOORE CURTIS WAYNE	MA	05W	46
MOORE DALE WILLIAM	IL	15E	63
MOORE DALLAS HENRY	AL	43E	27
MOORE DAN ROSS	ID	41W	69
MOORE DANIEL EUGENE JR	NE	15E	75
MOORE DAVID ALAN	IN	06W	4
MOORE DAVID ALLEN	MI	22E	79
MOORE DAVID CHARLES	MI	42E	37

NAME	STATE	PANEL NO.	LINE NO.
MOORE DAVID NED	VA	37W	67
MOORE DAVID T	FL	35W	72
MOORE DEAN	TX	30E	61
MOORE DENNIS EUGENE	CA	29E	42
MOORE DENNIS FRANCIS	NY	45E	26
MOORE DENNIS WESLEY	PA	14W	69
MOORE DENVER JR	IL	42W	71
MOORE DERRYL LEE	CA	48W	18
MOORE DONALD EUGENE	KS	38E	7
MOORE DONALD EUGENE	IL	18W	62
MOORE DONALD R JR	VA	17W	30
MOORE DOUGLAS EUGENE	NC	17E	46
MOORE DOUGLAS FILLEBROWN	MA	24W	78
MOORE EARL THOMAS JR	PA	31W	82
MOORE EDWARD LAMAR JR	GA	16E	81
MOORE EDWARD P	KY	08W	72
MOORE ELDON WAYNE	TX	12W	71
MOORE ELGAN LEROY	AZ	31E	38
MOORE ELLIOTT WAYNE	CA	33E	72
MOORE ERNEST LAWRENCE	MI	10W	14
MOORE FRANK HARRIS	PA	31E	66
MOORE FRANKLIN EDWARD	OK	46E	20
MOORE FRED JR	IN	03E	19
MOORE FULTON BEVERLY III	TN	30W	92
MOORE GALEN LEROY	CA	17E	21
MOORE GARY LEE	IA	26E	28
MOORE GARY LESLIE	KY	29W	21
MOORE GEORGE MONROE	IN	35E	19
MOORE GEORGE WASHINGTON	MS	49E	23
MOORE GILLIAM	NY	07E	90
MOORE GLENN DOUGLAS	CA	38E	33
MOORE HAROLD	MI	63E	14
MOORE HARRY TRUMAN	IL	62W	13
MOORE HERBERT HUBERT	NJ	06W	43
MOORE HERBERT LEE JR	TN	17W	113
MOORE HERBERT WILLIAM JR	PA	25E	93
MOORE HERCULES LEE	FL	66W	10
MOORE HERMAN A	FL	19E	44
MOORE HERMAN JR	MS	09W	79
MOORE HURIEL LEE	NC	53E	5
MOORE JACK DONALD JR	SC	04W	46
MOORE JAMES BUCKSON	PA	27E	85
MOORE JAMES CECIL	OH	41W	14
MOORE JAMES CHARLES JR	NY	26W	66
MOORE JAMES CURTIS	OK	15W	82
MOORE JAMES D	TX	26W	49
MOORE JAMES ELDON	NE	46E	21
MOORE JAMES EZRA	KS	43E	27
MOORE JAMES HARRISON	PA	29W	81
MOORE JAMES JR	MD	06E	75
MOORE JAMES LEE	CO	18W	41
MOORE JAMES LYNN	IN	49W	16
MOORE JAMES MICHAEL	NM	25E	74
MOORE JAMES MICHIAL	TN	16W	70
MOORE JAMES MINICK	NC	45W	20
MOORE JAMES ROBERT JR	GA	09W	51
MOORE JAMES RODNEY	NY	15E	120
MOORE JAMES RUSSELL	DC	34E	79
MOORE JAMES THOMAS	KY	21W	9
MOORE JAMES WILLIAM JR	KY	27W	82
MOORE JEROME	NJ	23E	71
MOORE JERRY LAWRENCE	NC	32W	45
MOORE JESSE LOUIS	MO	25E	53
MOORE JIMMY LEE	SC	66W	10
MOORE JIMMY RAY	CA	55E	24
MOORE JOHN BIGELOW	NY	36W	57
MOORE JOHN JOSEPH	NY	34E	90
MOORE JOHN MARSHALL JR	VA	22W	4
MOORE JOHN OTIS	DC	18W	122
MOORE JOHN TERRY JR	TX	58E	24
MOORE JOHNNY LEE	FL	09W	112
MOORE JOSEPH LEE	MO	34W	51
MOORE JOSEPH M	AL	13E	92
MOORE KENNETH CHARLES	LA	43E	58
MOORE KENNETH DEE	GA	45E	41
MOORE KEVIN WALKER	WI	47E	24
MOORE LARRY A	IA	31E	50
MOORE LARRY GENE	KY	50E	19
MOORE LARRY JAY	CA	44E	38
MOORE LARRY RICHARD	VA	40E	25
MOORE LAWRENCE HAMILTON	TX	32W	33
MOORE LAWRENCE MICHAEL	GA	09W	85
MOORE LEE ARTHUR JR	NC	06E	66
MOORE LEE ELMER JR	IL	35W	20
MOORE LEON DAVID	NJ	33W	3
MOORE LEONARD DAVID	AL	42E	37
MOORE LEONARD IRVIN	IN	17E	106
MOORE LEONARD LEE	SC	49W	32
MOORE LESTER LEWIS	CA	51E	31
MOORE LEWIS WAYNE	WV	44E	10
MOORE LLOYD WHITFIELD	NC	41E	25
MOORE LONNIE DEAN	OR	23W	55
MOORE LONZIA RAY	IN	25W	51
MOORE LOUIS CHARLES	MO	46W	61
MOORE LYLE THOMAS	UT	34W	1
MOORE MANUEL	NJ	53E	18
MOORE MAURICE	IL	46E	38
MOORE MAURICE HENRY	MD	59E	8
MOORE MICHAEL KEITH	PA	44E	38
MOORE NELSON ROGER	IL	07E	108
MOORE NORMAN JAMES	SC	15E	48
MOORE NORMAN LEE	WY	14E	23
MOORE PAUL MARTIN	OR	40W	34
MOORE PAUL VINCENT	MO	08W	91
MOORE PERCY	TN	26W	10
MOORE PETER CHARLES	PA	01E	49
MOORE PHILLIP ALEXANDER	OH	18E	70
MOORE RALPH EDWARD	IN	19E	29
MOORE RANDALL WHIT	PA	12E	43
MOORE RANDY COIS	IN	40E	77
MOORE RAYMOND GREGORY	OH	07W	123
MOORE RICHARD ALLEN	OH	33W	21
MOORE RICHARD LYNN	IL	20E	17
MOORE ROBERT CLAYTON	PA	09E	75
MOORE ROBERT DELL	CO	14E	28
MOORE ROBERT EVERETT	MA	29E	12
MOORE ROBERT GENE	IL	06W	99
MOORE ROBERT IRVIN	PA	34E	23
MOORE ROBERT JOSEPH	NJ	48E	7
MOORE ROBERT JR	NJ	16W	112
MOORE ROBERT LOUIS	AL	03E	60
MOORE ROBERT NED	CA	59W	8
MOORE ROBERT THOMAS	PA	01W	78
MOORE ROBERT VICTOR	NY	20W	16
MOORE ROBERT WAYNE	MO	14E	87
MOORE ROGER DEAN	IN	67W	1
MOORE ROLAND EDROY	MN	49E	4
MOORE RONALD ALLAN	CA	23E	92
MOORE RONALD JAMES	OH	20E	64
MOORE RONALD KELVIN	NY	39W	17
MOORE RONALD STANLEY	OR	45E	4
MOORE RONNIE GUNS	NE	51W	7
MOORE ROY LEE	AL	56W	6
MOORE SCOTT FERRIS JR	TX	13W	37
MOORE STANLEY LEROY	MI	08E	38
MOORE STEPHEN ALAN	WV	05W	72
MOORE STEPHEN DOUGLAS	CA	19W	96
MOORE TEDDY RAY	WV	25W	106
MOORE TERRY DWIGHT	IL	28W	50
MOORE TERRY ENGLEBERT	OK	53E	38
MOORE TERRY LEE	MO	56E	12
MOORE THOMAS	LA	03E	9
MOORE THOMAS ANTHONY	SC	15W	110
MOORE THOMAS DEWEY JR	TX	31E	14
MOORE THOMAS JON	NY	40E	26
MOORE THOMAS MICHAEL	WA	12E	7
MOORE THOMAS PHILIP	KY	33E	29
MOORE THOMAS RICHARD JR	MA	13W	46
MOORE THOMAS WAYNE JR	WV	16E	2
MOORE THOMAS WOODROW	MD	36E	25
MOORE WALTER LEE	TX	29W	12
MOORE WALTER LEE JR	TX	42W	42
MOORE WALTER ZAMPIER JR	CA	20E	85
MOORE WAVERY	OH	25W	78
MOORE WAYNE PAUL	MA	47E	14
MOORE WESLEY RICE JR	MD	36E	57
MOORE WILLIAM CHARLES JR	NC	32E	38
MOORE WILLIAM CLARENCE	VA	51W	27
MOORE WILLIAM HOWARD III	RI	35E	55
MOORE WILLIAM HYRAM	TN	31W	83
MOORE WILLIAM JAMES	WV	43W	7
MOORE WILLIAM JOHN	IL	07E	83
MOORE WILLIAM JUNE	PA	15E	75
MOORE WILLIAM JUNIOR JR	IN	67W	2
MOORE WILLIAM LEWIS	SC	42E	54
MOORE WILLIAM RAY	KS	17W	30
MOORE WILLIAM ROBERT	CA	04E	18
MOORE WILLIAM ROOSEVELT	NC	19E	29
MOORE WILLIAM VINCENT	MI	15W	14
MOORE WILLIE JAMES	FL	21E	72
MOOREHEAD JOE HOWARD	TN	11E	33
MOOREHEAD RICHARD L	MI	16W	35
MOOREHEAD RONALD JOHN	WV	07E	57
MOORER BOBBY	NJ	60E	26
MOORER CLARENCE LARRY	SC	01E	36
MOORES KENNETH FREDERICK	MA	41W	30
MOORHEAD MICHAEL EUGENE	OH	09W	54
MOORHOUSE WILLIAM CURTIS	NJ	13W	119
MOORMAN CECIL ROY	FL	26E	13
MOORMAN FRANK DAVID	NJ	34W	66
MOORMAN MICHAEL AUBREY	VA	24E	88
MOOTHART LARRY GRAYDON	CA	18W	96
MOPPERT EUGENE MEYERS	LA	41E	35
MORA ERNEST LOPEZ	CA	39W	51
MORA GREGORIO MANUEL	CA	22W	67
MORA JAMES J	CO	33E	73
MORA LUIS GUILLERMO		14E	108
MORA RAMIRO MICHAEL	CA	48W	28
MORA RAYMOND CASTILLO	KS	58W	28
MORA ROBERT CHARLES	TX	31W	11
MORACK GENE CHARLES	WI	59E	27
MORADO ANTONIO	TX	08E	81
MORADO DOMINGO FLORES	TX	25W	107
MORALES ALEXANDER M	CA	19W	103
MORALES ANGELO RAYMOND	CA	12W	46
MORALES ANTONIO JR	TX	28E	28
MORALES ANTONIO RUIZ	AZ	28W	50
MORALES BENITO	TX	26E	29
MORALES FELIPE	TX	06W	100
MORALES GILBERT	NM	52W	29
MORALES HAROLD WAYNE	FL	24E	8
MORALES JULIO VICTOR	PA	19E	110
MORALES RAMON J	IL	20E	121
MORALES SAMUEL	NM	51E	31
MORALES TOMMY	CA	10E	77
MORALES VICTOR	IN	09E	94
MORALES VICTOR DAVID	NY	25W	31
MORALES-GONZALEZ JULIO ER	PR	03E	80
MORALES-LUCAS LESLIE ISMA	PR	08E	120
MORALES-MERCADO JUAN BAUT	PR	36E	26
MORAN ALBERTO HECTOR	CA	26E	15
MORAN BERNARD JOSEPH JR	PA	02W	87
MORAN BRUCE JAMES	PA	33E	51
MORAN DANIEL HAGAN JR	IL	14E	36
MORAN DAVID ALFRED	NY	05W	99
MORAN EDGAR C II	PA	01W	128
MORAN JOE MICHAEL	TX	48E	7
MORAN JOHN FRANCIS	MA	57E	6
MORAN JOHN WILLIAM	PA	54E	38
MORAN LONZO JOSEPH JR	OK	44W	51
MORAN MICHAEL PETER	WI	04E	60
MORAN MICHAEL THOMAS	IL	34W	1
MORAN PAUL ROBERT	MA	13W	131
MORAN RAY EDWARD JR	CA	24E	96
MORAN RICHARD ALLAN	AR	09E	109
MORAN TERRENCE	NY	43W	40
MORAN VINCENT	NJ	28W	72
MORAN WALTER C B	MO	02W	100
MORAND BRAD WILLIAM	CA	09E	18
MORANO THOMAS LAWRENCE	NY	14W	116
MORAS ROBERT JOHN	MI	31E	37
MORASCINI JOHN V	CT	21W	119
MORBITZER CHRISTOPHER GEO	VA	03W	134
MORDEN BOBBY LEON	AR	08E	112
MORDEN ROBERT NELSON	NC	38E	33
MORE GARY KEITH	MI	07W	24
MOREAU EUGENE RAYMOND	MA	10E	50
MOREAU JOHN ALFRED	MA	14W	79
MOREAU THOMAS MICHAEL	AR	10W	46
MOREE BARRY RUSSELL	OH	45W	55
MOREHAM VINCENT PINAULA	GM	08W	70
MOREHOUSE DAVID LLOYD	SD	40E	46
MOREIDA MANUEL JESUS	TX	31E	26
MOREIRA RALPH ANGELO JR	PA	04W	25
MORELAND JAMES LESLIE	CA	38E	7
MORELAND JOHN LEE	OH	24E	90

NAME	STATE	PANEL NO.	LINE NO.
MORELAND LARRY WAYNE	LA	34W	39
MORELAND STEPHEN CRAIG	CA	59E	9
MORELAND TERRY LEE	OR	09W	48
MORELAND THOMAS LEE	WV	33W	8
MORELAND WILLIAM DAVID	CA	34E	59
MORELOCK REX DEWEY JR	OR	22W	51
MORELOCK WILLARD FRANKLIN	TN	42W	6
MORELOS CATARINO JR	CA	59W	8
MORENO ADOLFO VALENZUELA	CA	46W	43
MORENO ALFRED JR	AZ	28W	62
MORENO ANDRES JR	NM	07W	114
MORENO ANGEL JOSE	TX	06W	16
MORENO DAVID J	TX	51E	9
MORENO DENNIS RALPH	NE	06W	121
MORENO FRANCISCO HERNANDEZ	TX	10E	133
MORENO HILARIO	NM	38W	45
MORENO JESUS JR	TX	07W	41
MORENO JOE	TX	04E	9
MORENO JOHN BOBBY	CA	53W	37
MORENO JOHN HERBERT	MA	42E	21
MORENO JOSE LOUIS	TX	31E	5
MORENO JOSE LUIS	AZ	10E	54
MORENO MARTIN WALTER	CA	13E	117
MORENO MIGUEL ORTEGA	AZ	24W	45
MORENO RAMON	SC	26W	108
MORENO RICARDO LEON	CO	07E	119
MORENO RICHARD LAWRENCE	TX	30E	72
MORENO ROBERT	CA	03E	87
MORENO VICTOR AURELLIANO	IL	13W	11
MORETTI ANTONIO LOUIS	RI	10W	91
MOREU-LEON MARIO	PR	31E	50
MOREY ALDEN FRANK JR	IL	42E	21
MOREY DARRELL H	MI	30E	102
MOREY FRANK ERNEST JR	MA	31E	41
MORFORD LARRY HOWARD	CA	13W	2
MORFORD LOREN LEE	IN	26E	14
MORGAN ARTHUR EUGENE	VA	18W	41
MORGAN AUBRA ERLE JR	TX	34W	60
MORGAN BRUCE	NJ	03W	134
MORGAN BURKE HENDERSON	CO	25E	31
MORGAN CALVIN CARL	MI	15E	98
MORGAN CARL EUGENE	AL	20W	93
MORGAN CHARLES ELZY	CA	09E	2
MORGAN CHARLES LEWIS	SC	62W	14
MORGAN CHARLES RICHARD	LA	39E	22
MORGAN CHARLES VERNON	KY	01W	11
MORGAN CLYDE EDWARD	SC	43W	7
MORGAN DAVID ALLEN	OR	02E	93
MORGAN DAVID ELMER	NC	34W	43
MORGAN DAVID ROBERT	CA	30W	71
MORGAN DAVIS JUNIOR	MO	03W	67
MORGAN DENNIS EDWARD	NY	03W	18
MORGAN DENNIS EVERETT	IN	47W	49
MORGAN DENNIS LACO	FL	05E	7
MORGAN DONALD THOMAS	NJ	30E	30
MORGAN EDWIN EVERTON	NC	06E	4
MORGAN GARY WAYNE	WV	45W	8
MORGAN GEORGE	PA	16E	106
MORGAN GEORGE ALLEN	IL	05E	73
MORGAN GEORGE ROBERT	AL	04W	31
MORGAN GLENDELL	CA	19E	29
MORGAN GREGORY SCOTT	GA	04W	50
MORGAN HENRY LORANZE	NC	32E	95
MORGAN HUBERT HARROL JR	TN	24E	34
MORGAN JACKIE MARCELL	GA	39E	64
MORGAN JACKIE RAY	OK	30W	92
MORGAN JAMES EDWARD	AR	28E	44
MORGAN JAMES HENRY	DC	47E	36
MORGAN JAMES HENRY	TN	42W	13
MORGAN JAMES MARK	MI	34E	23
MORGAN JAMES PIERPONT	NC	06E	1
MORGAN JAMES RAYMOND	TN	17E	80
MORGAN JAMES SHEPPARD	AR	29E	68
MORGAN JERRY JR	NJ	26W	20
MORGAN JESSE FRANK	AL	04E	19
MORGAN JOHN D	NJ	08E	112
MORGAN JOHN HENRY	TN	07E	111
MORGAN JOHN LOUIS JR	CA	27W	51
MORGAN JOHN PATRICK JR	PA	07W	2
MORGAN JOSEPH JR	FL	32E	18
MORGAN JUNIOR RAY	IL	14E	28
MORGAN KENNETH DWIGHT	IL	07E	1
MORGAN LARRY GENE	OK	10W	1
MORGAN LARRY HAROLD	WI	59W	9
MORGAN LELAND RAY	KS	13E	9
MORGAN LEONARD	MD	10W	125
MORGAN LEONARD ANTHONY	MI	20E	85
MORGAN LOWELL EDWARD	TX	21E	49
MORGAN LUTHER JR	GA	24W	9
MORGAN LYNN MARTIN	AL	02W	18
MORGAN MAJOR BOONE JR	GA	19W	88
MORGAN MARK LAKE	CA	05E	87
MORGAN MELVIN DAVID JR	NY	35W	20
MORGAN MICHAEL LYNN	TN	07W	12
MORGAN MICHAEL ROY	NY	18E	125
MORGAN MILLER EDWARD	IL	16W	75
MORGAN OTIS CLEVELAND	NC	08W	63
MORGAN RAINER K	NJ	33E	89
MORGAN RICHARD	OH	04W	111
MORGAN ROBERT FRANCIS	IL	25E	106
MORGAN ROBERT LEROY JR	NV	26W	2
MORGAN ROBERT WEST	NJ	25E	70
MORGAN RODNEY EUGENE	WV	05W	27
MORGAN ROGER WAYNE	IL	53E	18
MORGAN RONALD CURTIS	OH	09W	51
MORGAN RONALD EDWARD	CA	23W	16
MORGAN SAMUEL FLOYD	IN	46W	46
MORGAN SHELTON	FL	20E	121
MORGAN STEPHEN EDWARD	CA	01E	80
MORGAN THEODORE JR	OH	31E	5
MORGAN THOMAS RAYMOND	OH	14E	81
MORGAN VAUGHAN SHAW	ME	25E	70
MORGAN WALTER WILLIAM	MA	27E	49
MORGAN WAYNE D	UT	15W	79
MORGAN WILLIAM DAVID	PA	31W	54
MORGAN WILLIAM JOOR	LA	02W	111
MORGAN WILLIAM LESLIE	CA	05W	63
MORGAN WILLIAM S II	NY	12E	35
MORGAN WILLIE LORENZO JR	AR	61W	15
MORGANFLASH ROBERT LEE	WY	03W	88
MORGENS CHRISTOPHER W	CA	06W	45
MORGERA DOMENICO JR	RI	39E	50
MORI BRUCE JUN	CA	37W	13
MORIARTY JAMES MICHAEL	WI	47W	29
MORIARTY PATRICK DALE	CA	43E	68
MORIARTY PATRICK O'NEAL	CT	18W	90
MORIARTY PETER GIBNEY	CT	04W	68
MORIARTY THOMAS WILLIAM	NY	10W	126
MORIN DONALD WILLIAM	VT	13W	20
MORIN JAMES THOMAS	PA	07W	107
MORIN RICHARD GIRARD	MA	36W	53
MORIN SILBANO	TX	10E	22
MORINA ANTHONY JOSEPH	NY	29W	46
MORISETTE CLEMENT JOSEPH	WA	11E	113
MORITZ MICHAEL PERRY	CA	02E	10
MORIWAKI KAZUTO	WA	39W	34
MORK THOMAS LEE	NY	42E	39
MORKA PETER JOSEPH	NY	20W	40
MORLEDGE WILLIAM RALPH	ID	43W	48
MORLEY CHARLES FRANK	MO	13W	29
MORLEY JAMES RICHARD	MI	10E	9
MORLEY JEFFREY PAUL	CA	37E	40
MORLEY JOHN JOSEPH JR	NJ	40W	29
MORMAN WILLIAM EUGENE JR	IN	39W	50
MORNEAU JEROME DALE	WI	22W	4
MORNINGSTAR DUANE LEE	MN	26E	29
MORNINGSTAR GEORGE AARON	FL	08E	28
MORNINGSTAR GEORGE LEE	NC	12W	7
MORNINGSTAR ROBERT LEE	PA	23E	13
MORONEY ROBERT JEROME	MI	04E	16
MORRELL DENNIS RICHARD	IN	16E	124
MORRELL WILLIAM ALEXANDER	CA	35W	84
MORRIGGI JOSEPH	NJ	21W	113
MORRILL BERNARD FRANCIS	ME	08W	101
MORRILL DAVID WHITTIER	CA	16E	106
MORRILL DENNIS LEROY	MA	12W	26
MORRILL EDWARD FRANCIS	MA	27W	6
MORRILL FRED WILLIAM	ME	60E	26
MORRILL MERWIN LAMPHREY	CA	25E	24
MORRIS ALVIN GARVIE	VA	11E	69
MORRIS ARCHIE W	WA	25E	25
MORRIS ARTHUR CYRUS JR	DE	06E	81
MORRIS BEDFORD MARK JR	NC	32W	28
MORRIS BILLY RAY	VA	40W	13
MORRIS BILLY VANCE	NC	02W	48
MORRIS CARL MICHAEL	PA	44E	39
MORRIS CHARLES H JR	WV	29E	84
MORRIS CHARLES RODNEY	WV	53W	28
MORRIS CLARENCE LUTHER	NC	20E	85
MORRIS CLENZELL	TX	37E	41
MORRIS DANIEL EUGENE	NJ	10E	22
MORRIS DAVID MICHAEL	MA	39W	67
MORRIS DONALD DURWOOD	TX	22E	16
MORRIS DONALD J	IL	10W	71
MORRIS DONALD WARREN	CA	53W	29
MORRIS DOYLE ANTHONY	MO	18W	7
MORRIS EDWARD	OK	21E	113
MORRIS ELROY	TX	31W	78
MORRIS EUGENE JR	LA	29E	42
MORRIS GARY KEVE	NY	64E	6
MORRIS GARY WILLIAM	OH	14W	34
MORRIS GEORGE WILLIAM JR	CA	01W	112
MORRIS HAROLD HERBERT	MA	14E	101
MORRIS HARRY LEO JR	CA	27W	32
MORRIS HERMAN RAY	CA	23W	113
MORRIS HOOVER	TX	03E	45
MORRIS JAMES ALBERT JR	MS	42W	31
MORRIS JAMES LOGAN	GA	10E	5
MORRIS JAMES ROBERT	NJ	36E	26
MORRIS JAMES THURMAN JR	DE	29E	16
MORRIS JEFFREY LYNN	PA	28E	46
MORRIS JESSE DON JR	TX	28W	104
MORRIS JIMMY TONY	GA	19W	120
MORRIS JOHN D	WI	32E	58
MORRIS JOHN FREDERICK	CA	29W	12
MORRIS JOHN HENRY JR	MO	03W	104
MORRIS JOHN LEE	TX	28W	19
MORRIS JOHN NATHAN	GA	09E	25
MORRIS JULIUS WILLIAM JR	TX	35E	34
MORRIS KELLY STUART	CA	20W	51
MORRIS KENNETH BRYAN	FL	18E	106
MORRIS LARRY LEE	IN	21E	69
MORRIS LEON LOPEZ	GA	20W	40
MORRIS LYLE WAYNE	CA	35E	41
MORRIS MARSHALL KENNETH	IA	19E	39
MORRIS MICHAEL EUGENE	OK	34E	79
MORRIS MICHAEL JOHN	NM	61E	14
MORRIS NEIL JAY	OH	41W	64
MORRIS PATRICK BENNETT	WA	03W	95
MORRIS RAYMOND LESTER	MI	23W	29
MORRIS RAYMOND MURPHY	GA	10W	9
MORRIS ROBERT DAVIS	GA	51W	12
MORRIS ROBERT DEAN	PA	12W	35
MORRIS ROBERT EDWARD JR	MA	06W	37
MORRIS ROBERT J	OR	46W	31
MORRIS ROBERT JOHN	NJ	35W	21
MORRIS ROBERT JOHN JR	MO	01W	105
MORRIS ROBERT JOSEPH	PA	08E	125
MORRIS ROBERT L	OH	31E	26
MORRIS ROBERT WESLEY	GA	46E	38
MORRIS RONALD EDWARDS	VA	37E	63
MORRIS RONALD LEWIS	VA	35W	49
MORRIS THOMAS HALL	GA	39E	64
MORRIS THOMAS RICHARD	MA	55W	36
MORRIS THOMAS W	CA	39W	61
MORRIS TOMMY GENE	MO	06W	119
MORRIS WALTER F	PA	18E	95
MORRIS WALTER JOSEPH	IN	26W	101
MORRIS WALTER KENNETH	KY	01E	33
MORRIS WAYMAN DEWEY	WV	62W	14
MORRIS WILLIAM	NY	08E	93
MORRIS WILLIAM HENRY JR	PA	17W	58
MORRIS WILLIAM T III	AL	59W	9
MORRIS WINSTON	IL	05E	66
MORRISON BILLY JOE	AL	31E	66
MORRISON BRUCE AUSTIN	VT	34E	43
MORRISON CARL PHILLIP	LA	26W	10
MORRISON CHARLES LLOYD	IL	37E	68
MORRISON CHRISTIAN HERMAN	PA	36E	28
MORRISON EDWARD ARNOLD	WI	36W	65
MORRISON EDWARD JR	IL	15W	91
MORRISON GENE FRANCIS	OH	60W	3
MORRISON GEORGE RAY	IL	02W	15
MORRISON GLEN MARK	CA	33E	89
MORRISON GLENN RAYMOND JR	IA	11E	114
MORRISON HOWARD GLENN	NV	11E	9

NAME	STATE	PANEL NO.	LINE NO.
MORRISON JACK ALLEN	MI	59E	9
MORRISON JACKIE LEE	OK	34W	78
MORRISON JAMES ALBERT	PA	34E	70
MORRISON JAMES ANTON	NE	26E	61
MORRISON JAMES JOHN	MI	33W	42
MORRISON JIMMY KEITH	NC	20E	121
MORRISON JOE HAROLD	CA	07W	118
MORRISON JOHN FRANKLIN JR	VA	33E	4
MORRISON JOSEPH CASTLEMAN	KY	38W	60
MORRISON JOSEPH WALTER	MO	16E	81
MORRISON PETER WHITCOMB	NH	21E	79
MORRISON RANDY STANTON	OK	09W	108
MORRISON RICHARD KEITH	MD	61E	14
MORRISON SAMMY RAY	NC	10W	91
MORRISON WENDELL ALBERT	MA	34W	16
MORRISON WILLIAM JOHN	MA	39W	2
MORRISSEY JAMES JOSEPH	PA	35W	5
MORRISSEY JOHN DENNIS	MD	21W	39
MORRISSEY RICHARD THOMAS	NY	19W	71
MORRISSEY ROBERT DAVID	NM	01W	90
MORRISSEY THOMAS J JR	NH	60W	20
MORROW BOYD ELLIS	PA	27E	102
MORROW BRIAN JOHN	WA	16W	10
MORROW DALE ARTHUR	CA	43W	10
MORROW EDWARD CY	PA	07W	34
MORROW HAROLD EUGENE	PA	23E	101
MORROW HERSHEL EUGENE	MS	45W	55
MORROW JAMES FRANCIS	MI	28E	10
MORROW JAMES RALPH	IN	18W	62
MORROW JOSEPH EDWARD JR	OR	26W	2
MORROW KENNETH PORTER	MI	55E	24
MORROW LARRY KANE	NC	01W	33
MORROW MERLE BRUCE	SC	30E	98
MORROW MICHAEL JOSEPH	NY	21E	124
MORROW RICHARD DAVID	CA	29E	12
MORROW SAMUEL THOMAS	NY	09E	63
MORROW TERRY PATRICK	OH	17E	9
MORROW WILLIAM DANNY	TN	65E	13
MORROW WILLIAM WALLACE	NY	09W	80
MORSE ANSEL WENDELL	NC	09W	28
MORSE CHARLES ALLEN	IA	17E	58
MORSE CHARLES FRANCIS JR	NJ	44E	50
MORSE DURWARD GLENNIE	VT	36W	16
MORSE EUGENE JOSEPH	PA	17W	63
MORSE HARRY MADISON	MD	04E	104
MORSE HOWARD EDWARD	MI	28E	69
MORSE JAMES EARL	NY	47E	14
MORSE LEONARD ALAN	IL	32W	1
MORSE REGINALD GEORGE	SC	16E	22
MORSE RICHARD DEAN	MO	25E	87
MORSE RICHARD LUCIAN	NY	24E	100
MORSE STEVEN PAUL	MO	30E	64
MORSE WILLIAM JOSEPH	NY	54E	12
MORT DANIEL LEON	MO	09E	30
MORTENSEN ALLAN DAVID	CA	29W	3
MORTENSEN GENE AL	UT	25E	106
MORTENSEN TERRENCE JOHN	IL	27W	85
MORTIBOY WILLIAM SHELTON	KS	17E	86
MORTICE THOMAS E III	IA	48W	2
MORTIMER EDWARD LEWIS JR	MD	03W	101
MORTON BILLY WAYNE	TX	06E	7
MORTON CHARLES TIENEREY	WA	06W	113
MORTON DAVID EUGENE	OH	50W	52
MORTON DOUGLAS GEORGE	AZ	48E	7
MORTON EDWARD EARL	CA	17E	62
MORTON GARY RAY	IN	20W	59
MORTON GEORGE WINSTON	KY	36W	36
MORTON JAMES EDWARD JR	TN	20W	92
MORTON JERREL CARL	FL	13E	14
MORTON JERRY WAYNE	TX	04E	51
MORTON MATTHEW EDWARD JR	AZ	30W	79
MORTON MITCHEL THOMAS	NC	29W	104
MORTON WILLIAM ACE BILLY	TX	09W	15
MORTON WILLIAM HOWARD	TX	63E	14
MORTUS PATRICK CLINTON	OH	34E	49
MORVAY JON RICHARD	NJ	28E	56
MOS RONALD BRUCE	CA	20E	64
MOSBACH MICHAEL P	NY	25E	34
MOSBURG HENRY LEE	OK	11E	20
MOSBY JERRY	NY	50E	31
MOSBY STATUE JR	CA	49W	36
MOSCHETTI BILL ARTHUR	CA	28W	19
MOSCRIP ARTHUR DAVID JR	PA	44W	51
MOSELEY DAVID WESLEY	WA	65E	13
MOSELEY HAROLD EUGENE	AR	44W	18
MOSELEY MURRAY SIMS	NC	07E	14
MOSELEY STEPHEN C	IL	31E	84
MOSELEY WILLIAM FRANCIS	NJ	31E	37
MOSER CECIL JOE	TX	51E	23
MOSER DAVID LLOYD GEORGE	PA	11E	53
MOSER GREGORY PHILLIP	WA	20E	46
MOSER HARRY JULIUS IV	PA	24E	110
MOSER JAMES MYRON	NE	46E	38
MOSER KEITH MILTON II	MI	21E	48
MOSER LEROY	SD	24E	34
MOSER MERRILL ANDREW	AL	57E	28
MOSER PAUL KIERSTEAD	CT	17W	30
MOSER SAMUEL RALPH	SC	09E	104
MOSER TERRY LEE	PA	13W	119
MOSES ABELL	LA	02E	108
MOSES CLIFTON	TN	48E	44
MOSES DONALD HARVEY	NJ	09E	12
MOSES DONALD SYLVESTER	MI	28E	69
MOSES JAMES JR	NY	13E	85
MOSES JAMES THOMAS	CA	18W	8
MOSES JESSE LEE	DE	08W	83
MOSES LESLIE DON	OK	12E	23
MOSES WALTER LEWIS JR	OH	29W	81
MOSES WILLIAM JOSHUA	NC	63W	9
MOSES WILLIE LEE	CA	19E	16
MOSGROVE JAMES MAURICE JR	MD	20E	47
MOSHER ALDEN GRAY JR	OH	32E	2
MOSHER ALEX ROY	MI	17W	51
MOSHER HARRY VAN ARNAM	NY	36E	57
MOSHER HARVEY MILFORD JR	TX	29E	21
MOSHER LARRY CLARENCE	WI	16W	66
MOSHER MAURICE WILLIAM	PA	01E	124
MOSHER ROBERT LLOYD	RI	20E	122
MOSHIER CHESTER JOHN JR	NY	50W	1
MOSHIER JIM EDWIN	CA	21E	91
MOSIER CLIVE VERE	MI	18E	80
MOSIER ROBERT KEAL	AL	01E	25
MOSIER ROBERT SHERMAN	KY	01E	90
MOSKOS PETER	MA	23E	29
MOSLEY A D	TX	06E	123
MOSLEY BERNIE JACK	AR	46E	48
MOSLEY EDWARD	AL	28E	10
MOSLEY GLEN HERBERT JR	MO	44E	37
MOSLEY IRVIN WILLIAM	TX	50W	9
MOSLEY JOHN CHARLES	MI	21W	46
MOSLEY RAYFORD JUNIOR	AL	11E	46
MOSLEY RICHARD JOHN	NY	14E	87
MOSLEY ROBERT LEE	GA	40E	10
MOSLEY WALLACE JEROME	MO	26W	78
MOSS CHARLES LEE JR	CA	21W	29
MOSS CHARLES LEWIS JR	NY	40W	29
MOSS CHARLES NATHAN	GA	28W	38
MOSS GARY REX	WV	28W	28
MOSS JACK JR	AL	07W	6
MOSS LARRY ALLEN	WA	13E	39
MOSS RICHARD LEE	FL	61E	14
MOSS ROBERT EUGENE	VA	42E	21
MOSS RONALD GENE	OK	31W	11
MOSS ROY THOMAS	NC	26W	11
MOSS THOMAS JOHN JR	OH	43E	27
MOSS WELDON DALE	WY	06E	76
MOSS WILEY BARRY	NC	28W	104
MOSS WILLIAM VANCE	NY	04E	33
MOSSEAU LLOYD FRANCIS	CA	54E	13
MOSSER CHARLES DENVER	WV	27W	1
MOSSFORD GREGORY FREDRICK	OH	45E	41
MOSSGROVE ROBERT BOYD	WV	13W	54
MOSSMAN HARRY SEEBER	NY	01W	68
MOSSMAN JOE RUSSELL	PA	02E	82
MOSSNER DAVID CAMPBELL	TX	10W	131
MOSSO ROBERT BRUCE	PA	46E	39
MOSTOWSKI THEODORE	PA	38W	37
MOTA PEDRO JUAN TOMAS	NY	45W	8
MOTE TERRY ALAN	MD	09W	109
MOTES CARL GILBERT	FL	22W	34
MOTES JAMES JACKSON	GA	20W	59
MOTLEY JOHN LARRY JR	AL	30W	79
MOTLEY LARRY KEITH	CA	21W	102
MOTLEY PAUL WILLIAM	TX	31W	11
MOTON EDDIE LEE JR	AL	22E	16
MOTSINGER JERRY WILLIAM	NC	58W	11
MOTT BARRY LEE	MN	09E	81
MOTT JAMES FRANKLIN	CT	18W	11
MOTT JOHN ARTHUR	KS	17E	22
MOTT JOHN JAMES	NY	01W	10
MOTT JOSEPH ANTHONY	NY	23W	104
MOTT TERRY WARD	NY	51E	10
MOTT WILLIAM LARRY	TN	33W	16
MOTTE GEORGE D	NC	25E	20
MOTTISHAW RONALD GRANT	ID	15E	48
MOTTO THOMAS NICHOLAS	NY	21W	54
MOTTOLA VINCENT ANTONIO	MA	40E	77
MOUDRY CHARLES RAY	TX	16E	41
MOUGIER JOHN EDGAR JR	LA	02E	16
MOULDEN JOHN	MD	37W	1
MOULDER LARRY THOMAS	MO	29W	100
MOULTINE CHARLES RAY	WA	29E	84
MOULTON LESTER NEAL	ID	10W	99
MOULTRIE CALVIN	FL	18W	70
MOULTRIE JOE DAVIS	SC	28E	32
MOULTRIE OXLEY CARRINGTON	MD	20E	122
MOUNCE BARRY MITCHELL	MI	13E	75
MOUNCE GEROLD LEE	NC	25E	31
MOUNT CHARLEY LE MEAR	OK	38W	60
MOUNT JOHN EDWARD	NJ	48E	44
MOUNTS BOBBIE JOE	OR	33E	51
MOUNTS JERRY DUANE	KS	39E	23
MOURGELAS DENNIS W	IL	59W	11
MOURITZEN DONALD ANDREW	NJ	21E	75
MOURTGIS ARTHUR C JR	NH	20E	2
MOUSEL WAYNE CHARLES	WI	09W	61
MOUTARDIER ODES HERMAN	FL	27E	82
MOUTON WILLIAM WAYNE	TX	50E	31
MOVCHAN DAVID EDWARD	IN	24W	46
MOWBRAY DOUGLAS RONALD	NY	10E	97
MOWER GARY RUEL	UT	10W	82
MOWER JOHN WAYNE	TX	17E	46
MOWERY CARL FRANCIS	OH	16E	22
MOWERY ROBERT ALLEN	PA	47E	41
MOWREY GLENN WILLIAM	OH	46E	39
MOWREY RICHARD LYNN	KS	13E	45
MOXLEY RICHARD STEPHEN	MA	46W	61
MOYA HERMANDO SANCHEZ	TX	07E	39
MOYA JOE	TX	21E	36
MOYA RAMON JR	TX	10W	27
MOYE FLOYD	NJ	13W	105
MOYE ROBERT DOUGLAS	NC	47W	30
MOYER BARRY LEE	PA	42E	37
MOYER CECIL GERALD JR	PA	06W	94
MOYER CHARLES ALBERT	NY	28E	92
MOYER DENNIS LEE	PA	29W	12
MOYER DOUGLAS ISAAC	PA	31E	81
MOYER LAWRENCE RICHARD	PA	25E	75
MOYER MERRHAGE MICHAEL	PA	14E	130
MOYER ROBERT W	OK	14E	118
MOYER WARREN JR	PA	53W	4
MOYERS MURL ALVIN	OK	12W	55
MOYERS RICHARD LEE	WV	39W	50
MOYERS RICHARD MICHAEL	MO	15E	6
MOYLAN DAVID JOHN	PA	09W	96
MOYLE WESLEY ALLEN	PA	32E	2
MOYNAHAN JOHN JAMES	CA	02W	116
MOZDZEN DALE MICHAEL	IL	04W	34
MRAVAK THOMAS A	NY	05W	75
MRAZIK JAMES PATRICK	MI	40W	29
MRDJENOVICH CHARLES	NC	51E	23
MROCZYNSKI RAYMOND CHARLE	NH	31W	75
MROSEWSKE ROY JAMES	MI	25W	40
MUCCI JOHN ROCCO	IL	06W	76
MUCHA HENRY JR	CA	23E	102
MUCHA HOWARD ALLEN	OH	21E	124
MUCHA LOUIS STEPHAN	IL	50E	31
MUCKLEROY JAMES RICHARD	FL	65E	14
MUDD LEROY BERNARD	PA	09W	102
MUEHE MARK RONALD	IL	15W	28
MUEHLBERG RONALD LEE	KS	48W	1
MUELLENBACH ROBERT JOSEPH	WI	08W	86
MUELLER CARL WILLIAM	KY	15E	25
MUELLER DAVID HAROLD	IA	11E	74
MUELLER JOSEPH BERNARD	WI	12W	31
MUELLER KURT JR	CO	52E	21

NAME	STATE	PANEL NO.	LINE NO.
MUELLER MARCO FRANCISCO	WI	60E	26
MUELLER MICHAEL DAVID	KY	58E	24
MUELLER RALPH THOMAS	MI	10W	71
MUELLER RANDY ROY	WI	30W	27
MUELLER ROBERT GILBERT	WI	06E	134
MUELLER ROBERT STEPHAN	MI	26E	105
MUELLER STEPHEN MICHAEL	OH	35E	48
MUELLER STEVEN AL	KS	14W	44
MUELLER STEVEN WAYNE	NE	32E	45
MUELLER TOM RICHARD	WI	33W	33
MUELLER WESLEY ERWIN	ND	20W	45
MUELLER WOODROW JOHN	MI	16E	49
MUENCH JOSEPH EARL	NY	17W	37
MUETING MICHAEL JOSEPH	TX	38E	79
MUGAVIN MARTIN M	OH	15E	80
MUHICH CRAIG STANLEY	MN	57W	20
MUHM ANTON LEONARD	SD	08E	21
MUHR WARREN FRANCIS	IL	15E	98
MUIR JAMES	AZ	63E	14
MUIR JOHN DAVID	FL	20W	83
MUIR JOSEPH EUGENE	WV	02E	81
MUIR THOMAS WAYNE	MD	14W	113
MUIR THOMAS WILSON	MD	06E	95
MUIR WILLIAM GUY	OR	29E	74
MUISENER JACK ELLSWORTH	CT	61W	15
MUKAI BRYAN THOMAS	WA	49E	13
MULARZ JOHN BRUCE	NY	48W	14
MULCAHY JOHN EDWIN CHARLE	MD	51E	48
MULCAHY JOHN MARTIN	FL	10W	131
MULCAHY MICHAEL LEE	WI	26E	66
MULDER RUSSELL WESLEY	WI	06W	19
MULDOVAN WILLIAM JEFFREY	NY	43E	47
MULDROW ROBERT LEE	OH	28E	100
MULFORD ALAN CRAIG	WA	05E	121
MULGREW KEVIN SPEAR	CA	49E	4
MULHAUSER HARVEY	VA	14E	101
MULHOLLAND ARNOLD LEE ROY	MI	38W	28
MULHOLLAND ROBERT ALTON	CA	28W	84
MULICK MICHAEL WILLIAM	CA	07E	114
MULKEY HERBERT EUGENE JR	MD	04W	17
MULKEY JEFF	KY	62W	14
MULKEY RALPH BUDDY JR	NC	38W	60
MULKEY TERRY LEE	GA	60W	20
MULL GERALD CRAWFORD	VA	49E	45
MULLAN CHARLES RICHARD JR	CA	22E	80
MULLAN JOHN TURNER	WA	25E	8
MULLEAVEY QUINTEN EMILE	NH	47E	52
MULLEN CLIFFORD TRUMAN	MO	35W	28
MULLEN DANIEL JERRY	FL	05W	77
MULLEN ELVIS EARL	TN	17W	42
MULLEN FRANK	LA	06E	7
MULLEN FREDERICK WILLIAM	PA	12E	28
MULLEN GILBERT GREGORY	PA	07E	73
MULLEN JOSEPH WILLIAM JR	CA	50E	32
MULLEN LARRY DONALD	CA	24W	111
MULLEN LEO ROBERT	RI	35W	52
MULLEN MICHAEL EUGENE	IA	13W	29
MULLEN WALTER STEPHEN	TX	01W	36
MULLEN WILLIAM FRANCIS	MA	07E	11
MULLENS ROBERT JOSEPH JR	NY	14W	58
MULLER ALLEN DONALD	CA	32W	15
MULLER DANIEL SCOTT	KS	23W	66
MULLER EDWARD JERRY	MO	17E	9
MULLER ERIC P	CT	26E	29
MULLER HAROLD BRADLEY	CA	44E	39
MULLER JAMES VAN NESS	NY	28E	104
MULLER STEPHEN PETER	IN	22E	110
MULLER WALTER JR	TX	09E	131
MULLERVY MICHAEL	NY	37E	63
MULLET STEVEN JAMES	IN	23E	102
MULLIN GERALD CARL	MI	39W	28
MULLIN RICHARD ROCCO	IL	26E	56
MULLIN WAYNE WILSON	MA	08W	126
MULLINAX HOMER LAMAR	TX	48W	32
MULLINAX JAMES CARLTON JR	SC	04W	51
MULLINAX RONALD ERNEST	NC	04E	33
MULLINEAUX BARRY THOMAS	PA	10W	27
MULLINEAUX STEVEN PAUL	IL	17W	17
MULLINS ARTHUR BRENT	AL	53W	29
MULLINS DANIEL LEE	VA	25E	75
MULLINS EARNEST RANDALL	KY	48W	8
MULLINS EDWARD PATRICK	PA	40W	45

NAME	STATE	PANEL NO.	LINE NO.
MULLINS HAROLD EUGENE	CO	08E	4
MULLINS JAMES EDWARD	FL	40E	26
MULLINS JAMES MICHAEL	TX	46E	21
MULLINS JAMES RAY	OH	63W	10
MULLINS JIMMY MERYL	OK	18E	61
MULLINS LARRY EUGENE	TN	12W	71
MULLINS RICHARD ALLEN	OH	51W	42
MULLINS STEPHEN RALPH	WV	35W	66
MULLINS WILLIAM DONALD	OK	13E	68
MULLINS WILLIAM F JR	NJ	28E	2
MULLIS CHARLES EDWARD	GA	28E	56
MULLIS JOHN BELK	NC	12W	114
MULLIS MARVIN BURNETT JR	GA	39W	9
MULROONEY GEORGE	NY	17W	38
MULTHAUPT JAMES WAYNE	CA	47E	3
MULVANEY JAMES RAYMOND JR	MN	34W	66
MULVANEY MICHAEL TERENCE		06E	72
MULVEY FRANCIS TRAINOR	WI	46W	18
MULVEY LAWRENCE PATRICK	NY	23W	77
MULWEE ISAIAH JR	CT	05E	66
MUMFORD JIMMY EARL	SC	14E	124
MUMMEL MICHAEL JERRY	NC	09E	41
MUMMERT ALLEN LAWRENCE	IL	38E	34
MUMMERT GEORGE LEONARD	PA	21W	84
MUMMERT ROBERT STERLING	CA	23E	13
MUNATONES JOSE JR	CA	60E	15
MUNCEY JAY ALLAN	NV	07W	19
MUNCH MICHAEL RAYMOND	IA	25W	107
MUNCY GILBERT HOWARD	CA	62E	21
MUNCY ROBERT WILLIAM	OK	34E	23
MUNDAY PHILLIP DEAN	KS	19E	16
MUNDELL GREGORY STAN	IN	43W	18
MUNDEN DONALD MARTIN	CA	22E	42
MUNDEN STEVEN DOUGLAS	MN	32E	95
MUNDHENKE DOUGLAS O	OR	16E	62
MUNDT HENRY GERALD II	TX	25W	24
MUNDY GEORGE LINWOOD JR	VA	60E	15
MUNDY HAROLD EUGENE	IN	19E	16
MUNDY REGINALD ALLAN	NC	25E	70
MUNDY ROBERT HAL	AL	56E	13
MUNGER JOHN ROBERT	SC	09W	40
MUNGER RONALD WILLIAM	KS	08W	127
MUNGIN LAWRENCE DAVID III	FL	13E	11
MUNIZ CARLOS NOBERTO	NY	14E	130
MUNIZ DANIEL HAROLD	NM	10W	58
MUNIZ-GARCIA LUIS ERNESTO	NY	06W	48
MUNN ALTON BERNARD	NC	08E	67
MUNN WILLIAM ARTHUR	MI	22E	45
MUNNS WALTER EARL	NC	17E	58
MUNOZ CARLOS GARCIA	CA	50W	31
MUNOZ DAVID	CA	10W	18
MUNOZ DAVID LOUIE	CA	25W	107
MUNOZ DOMINGO	TX	24E	13
MUNOZ ERNEST CEDILLO	TX	24W	110
MUNOZ GUILLERMO	TX	23E	71
MUNOZ JESUS ARTHUR	CA	06E	46
MUNOZ JOHNNY	TX	18W	2
MUNOZ JOSE	MI	13E	19
MUNOZ JOSE JR	CA	07W	98
MUNOZ JUAN	TX	09E	99
MUNOZ LARRY	CA	43E	28
MUNOZ LUIS R	NY	52E	40
MUNOZ PEDRO	TX	07E	54
MUNOZ ROJELIO OLIVAN II	AZ	48W	28
MUNOZ RUDOLPH PINA	OH	22W	80
MUNRO IVAN HALL	KY	22W	24
MUNSEY CARL L	WV	06E	66
MUNSEY RALPH CHARLES	MI	27W	96
MUNSON ALLEN ARTHUR	CO	10W	35
MUNSON ALVIN JAMES	NM	44E	39
MUNSON CHRIS DELANO	UT	42W	71
MUNSON EDWARD LOUIS	MI	54E	13
MUNSON RONALD LEE	IL	17W	31
MUNTZ GIRAUD DOMENICO	NY	14W	95
MURACA PATRICK JOHN	MA	31W	56
MURACO FRANCIS JOHN	MA	30E	72
MURCHISON JAMES EMANUEL	VA	45W	42
MURDEN STEPHEN BROOKS	WA	37E	10
MURDOCK CARL THOMAS	MI	60E	26
MURDOCK JOHN LEO	MA	22W	105
MURDOCK LARRY	TN	30W	38
MURDOCK MICHAEL GEORGE	WA	36E	57

NAME	STATE	PANEL NO.	LINE NO.
MURDOCK STANLEY	IL	36E	58
MUREN THOMAS RICHARD	CA	02W	129
MURFF WILLIAM EDWARD	AL	23E	103
MURNER PETER PATRICK JR	NJ	46W	31
MURPH SAMUEL ENNIS	LA	10E	132
MURPHEY DOUGLAS WAYNE	TN	20E	65
MURPHREE IRA JEROME	AL	31E	76
MURPHY ALFRED WALKER	TX	22E	63
MURPHY ARTHUR PATRICK JR	MA	51W	19
MURPHY B L JR	TN	32E	88
MURPHY BARRY DANIEL	FL	29W	69
MURPHY BILLY DAN	CA	29W	104
MURPHY BOBBY LOUIS	DC	22E	16
MURPHY CHARLES JOHN JR	MA	06E	113
MURPHY CORNELIUS F JR	NY	46W	23
MURPHY DANIEL JOSEPH	MN	45W	8
MURPHY DANIEL OWEN	NC	05W	118
MURPHY DAVID	GA	51E	40
MURPHY DAVID WAYNE	MA	40W	21
MURPHY DENNIS GERARD	NY	22W	79
MURPHY DENNIS JAMES	PA	18W	42
MURPHY DONALD JOSEPH	MI	09W	75
MURPHY DONALD LEROY	PA	52W	29
MURPHY EDWARD JOSEPH JR	MA	30E	6
MURPHY EDWARD THEODORE	NY	20E	85
MURPHY FRANK MONROE	TX	13E	19
MURPHY FREDERICK WILLIAM	MD	03W	97
MURPHY HERBERT BURGESS	WV	25W	41
MURPHY JAMES HOWARD	NY	13E	59
MURPHY JAMES JOHN	PA	29E	25
MURPHY JERRY RAY	CA	07E	27
MURPHY JESSE ALLEN	OK	47E	14
MURPHY JOHN FRANCIS	WA	20W	73
MURPHY JOHN JAMES	PA	13E	123
MURPHY JOHN LYLE	OH	37E	63
MURPHY JOHN PATRICK	NE	51W	35
MURPHY JOHN PAUL	PA	39W	45
MURPHY JOHN ROBERT	NY	38E	34
MURPHY JOHN WILLIAM	OR	06W	121
MURPHY JOHN WILLIAM III	MO	44E	10
MURPHY JON MICHAEL	MT	47E	3
MURPHY JOSEPH PATRICK	CA	17E	37
MURPHY JOSEPH THOMAS JR	NY	26W	112
MURPHY LARRON DAVID	GA	11W	41
MURPHY LLOYD ALBERT	CA	08W	89
MURPHY MICHAEL	MA	66W	10
MURPHY MICHAEL PATRICK	CA	10W	91
MURPHY MICHAEL THOMAS	FL	08E	30
MURPHY MICHAEL THOMAS	TX	36W	12
MURPHY PATRICK EDWARD	OR	25W	41
MURPHY PATRICK JAMES	NY	60E	26
MURPHY PATRICK MICHAEL	MI	38E	34
MURPHY PATRICK RONALD	LA	16E	81
MURPHY PATRICK WILLIAM	MI	39E	50
MURPHY PAUL WILLIAM JR	GA	18W	84
MURPHY RALPH OLIVER III	PA	10W	13
MURPHY RAY	IN	12W	14
MURPHY RICHARD BRIAN	MA	57W	29
MURPHY ROBERT D JR	TX	41E	45
MURPHY ROBERT DENNIS	NY	60E	15
MURPHY ROBERT DENNIS	NE	47W	49
MURPHY ROBERT EDWARD JR	OH	33E	14
MURPHY ROBERT EMMETT JR	CA	13E	68
MURPHY ROBERT L	NJ	20E	85
MURPHY RONALD JAMES	PA	49W	9
MURPHY ROY LYNWOOD	GA	01E	128
MURPHY STEVEN PATRICK	MT	47W	20
MURPHY TERENCE MEREDITH	NY	01E	103
MURPHY THOMAS JOSEPH	IA	17E	9
MURPHY THOMAS JOSEPH	WI	12W	72
MURPHY THOMAS RALPH	OH	12E	34
MURPHY TIMOTHY FRANCIS JR	MA	06W	32
MURPHY TIMOTHY JAMES	WI	41W	69
MURPHY TIMOTHY JOHN	NJ	22E	45
MURPHY TIMOTHY XAVIER	CA	17E	22
MURPHY VINCENT FRANCIS	MI	10E	114
MURPHY VINCENT PATRICK JR	CA	09W	15
MURPHY WALTER EDWARD JR	CA	31E	83
MURPHY WALTER MICHAEL	NY	36E	26
MURPHY WAYNE STEPHEN	OR	03W	89
MURPHY WILLIAM	PA	45E	26
MURPHY WILLIAM	NY	08W	91

NAME	STATE	PANEL NO.	LINE NO.
MURPHY WILLIAM CAMPBELL	MA	02E	109
MURPHY WILLIAM ELLIOTT	TX	03W	117
MURPHY WILLIAM HENRY III	WI	30E	25
MURPHY WILLIAM JOSEPH	MI	33W	21
MURPHY WILLIAM JOSEPH	DE	13W	20
MURPHY WILLIAM PATRICK	WA	47E	14
MURR CLYDE EDWARD	WA	06E	46
MURRAY ARTHUR JOSEPH JR	OH	24W	18
MURRAY BERNARD PHILLIP	MO	02E	94
MURRAY BRIAN THOMAS	OH	43E	9
MURRAY BRUCE ANDERSON	CA	53W	7
MURRAY CAESAR	SC	04W	59
MURRAY CARL EUGENE	KS	32E	30
MURRAY CECIL SCOTT	KY	52W	19
MURRAY CHARLES EDWARD	VA	16E	18
MURRAY DARNELL PATRICK	AL	49W	9
MURRAY DENNIS BRIAN	NY	22W	34
MURRAY DOUGLAS EARL	CA	12E	29
MURRAY GARY	TN	20E	96
MURRAY GEORGE THOMAS	WI	21E	124
MURRAY GORDON CHESTER	FL	30W	80
MURRAY HARRY WALTER	MD	13E	19
MURRAY JAMES EDWARD	OH	40E	44
MURRAY JAMES FRANCIS	MA	18E	95
MURRAY JOHN BUTLER	MA	53W	22
MURRAY JOSEPH VAUGHN	MO	05E	48
MURRAY LARRY	NC	20W	73
MURRAY LARRY DONNELL	GA	14W	54
MURRAY LESLIE EUGENE	WA	42E	22
MURRAY MARVIN WINSTON	NY	60W	3
MURRAY MERRITT LEWIS	NY	40W	56
MURRAY MICHAEL GARY	VA	06E	34
MURRAY MICHAEL VAN	GA	36E	26
MURRAY MICHIEL DAVID	MI	56W	6
MURRAY PATRICK PETER	MN	34E	80
MURRAY RICHARD LEMOYNE	IA	49E	14
MURRAY ROBERT CHARLES	NY	09W	24
MURRAY STEPHEN BRIAN	NJ	13W	79
MURRAY STEVEN	NY	57E	7
MURRAY STEVEN EDWARD	IN	24W	111
MURRAY THOMAS E	MO	03E	26
MURRAY THOMAS E	TX	26E	72
MURRAY THOMAS EDWARD	MA	04E	45
MURRAY THOMAS J	NY	45E	59
MURRAY VIRGIL ARTHUR	KS	06E	18
MURRAY WAYNE PAUL	NY	29E	91
MURRAY WILLIAM DONALD JR	MA	34W	87
MURRAY WILLIAM JOSEPH JR	PA	38W	7
MURRELL AARON CRUSOE	NC	03E	7
MURRELL ERVIN JEROME	AL	05W	2
MURRELL JIMMY ROGER	MI	03W	97
MURREY TRACY HENRY	MT	30E	46
MURRIETTA FRANK A	AZ	29E	96
MURRIN THOMAS JR	NY	66W	11
MURRY EUGENE	AL	19E	30
MURRY WILLIE JAMES	IL	26W	55
MURSCH JOHN WILLIAM	SC	09W	131
MURZIN WALTER ALECK	NH	11E	37
MUSA HENRY ALFRED JR	FL	02E	28
MUSCARA CARMEN	PA	18E	110
MUSCH DAVID IRA	IA	11E	31
MUSCO VINCENT JAMES	NY	19W	62
MUSCYNSKI FRANK	MI	07E	88
MUSE EDWARD GRADY	MS	36E	27
MUSE MARIO FOWLER JR	MD	62E	9
MUSE MICHAEL DENNIS	TX	19W	51
MUSER LOUIS CHARLES II	NJ	25E	64
MUSETTI JOSEPH TONY JR	ME	27E	25
MUSGROVE JOHN DAVID	OR	02E	106
MUSGUIRE GLEN ALAN	CA	12E	71
MUSICH JOHN PAUL	MI	06W	29
MUSICK FRANK FREDERICK	NY	37W	68
MUSICK MORRIS OLEN JR	CO	02E	64
MUSICK RAYMOND EARL JR	CA	47W	11
MUSICK THOMAS WAYNE	TX	48W	22
MUSIL CLINTON ALLEN SR	MN	03W	60
MUSKETT WAYNE	NM	19W	120
MUSS GLENN DAVID	KY	14E	6
MUSSELMAN DONALD L	CA	53E	5
MUSSELMAN HAROLD EARL	IN	30W	21
MUSSELMAN JAMES KEVIN	IN	08W	73
MUSSELMAN JOSEPH HENRY	NJ	19W	80

NAME	STATE	PANEL NO.	LINE NO.
MUSSELMAN ROBERT EUGENE	IN	28E	69
MUSSELMAN STEPHEN OWEN	TX	01W	72
MUSSENDEN GEORGE ADOLFO	NY	42E	8
MUSSER RICHARD LAVERNE	PA	30W	67
MUSSIN ROBERT JAMES	MI	11W	8
MUSSMAN DENNIS ERVIN	CO	40E	77
MUSTAIN JERRY WAYNE	MD	26E	76
MUSTIN LARRY STEVEN	NC	01W	20
MUSTO RICHARD FRANK	NY	11E	127
MUSZALSKI GREGORY ALLAN	IL	37E	42
MUSZYNSKI MICHAEL JOHN	NY	61W	4
MUTH JAMES RAY	OR	13W	94
MUTSCHLER JOHN LLOYD	MI	19W	71
MUTTER ALVIN GEORGE	PA	44W	58
MUTZ DENNIS HOWARD	MI	42E	69
MUVICH DENNIS ROBERT	IN	63E	14
MUZZEY CHARLES EDMOND	NH	34E	80
MYATT JOHN CARNUL	TX	01E	22
MYCKA TONEY FRANCIS JR	IA	22W	99
MYERS ALBERT C	OH	15E	86
MYERS BILLY EUGENE	IL	56E	27
MYERS CHARLES DEAN JR	CA	21E	107
MYERS CHARLES LEE	CA	15E	25
MYERS CHARLES LOUIS JR	IA	51W	27
MYERS CHESTER ARTHUR JR	WI	16E	54
MYERS DANIEL JOHN	NJ	14E	98
MYERS DANIEL LEROY	PA	12W	83
MYERS DAVID GEPHART	PA	21E	75
MYERS DAVID ROSS	PA	32E	38
MYERS DAVID WENDELL	IA	38W	19
MYERS DONALD WAYNE	TX	10W	110
MYERS EDWARD GEORGE	CA	07E	73
MYERS GARY FREDRICK	ND	59E	27
MYERS GENE ALLEN	KS	22W	5
MYERS GEORGE ARTHUR	MO	12E	117
MYERS GEORGE LAXLEY	NC	31E	84
MYERS GEORGE LEE	MD	47E	34
MYERS GEORGE LESTER JR	IL	54W	12
MYERS GEORGE NERVIN	PA	29W	81
MYERS GORDON E	MI	34W	78
MYERS GRAT G	WV	03E	12
MYERS HAROLD EDWIN	IL	04W	96
MYERS HOMER JULIUS	FL	20E	2
MYERS JAMES ALEXANDER JR	IN	39W	55
MYERS JAMES EDWARD	NJ	14E	83
MYERS JAMES HOWARD	OK	23W	77
MYERS JEFFERY PHILIP	MA	26E	29
MYERS JIMMY LEE	TX	31W	38
MYERS JOHN EARL	AR	14E	109
MYERS JOHN MAURICE	MI	04E	93
MYERS JOHN SAMUELS	VA	08W	8
MYERS LARRY DALE	MI	14E	13
MYERS LAWRENCE THOMAS	IL	41W	19
MYERS MICHAEL LEE	MI	15E	120
MYERS OLIVER WENDELL	MS	18E	16
MYERS PAUL DAVID	UT	07W	42
MYERS PAUL JUNIOR	OH	37E	41
MYERS PAUL RICHARD	OH	21E	98
MYERS PEARL WAYNE	IN	16E	93
MYERS R C	MS	25W	51
MYERS RICHARD VAUGHN	PA	29E	91
MYERS RICKY ALAN	CA	35E	62
MYERS ROBERT LESLIE	WA	63W	10
MYERS THOMAS WAYNE	NY	56E	28
MYERS THOMAS WAYNE	NJ	23W	2
MYERS TONY HOWARD	MO	06W	135
MYERS WALTER HARVEY JR	CT	12E	29
MYERS WAYNE CHESTER	NY	35E	49
MYERS WILLIAM HENRY	IN	19E	1
MYERS WILLIAM LATHEM JR	FL	15E	63
MYHR BARRY BERNDT	CO	12E	19
MYLANT STEVE VICTOR	OH	23E	44
MYLES ANTON CAESAR	IL	10W	115
MYLES JAMES WALTER	LA	03W	66
MYLES PHILLIP MURRY	LA	24E	9
MYLES ROBERT RAY	IN	09E	75
MYLLYMAKI CARL W III	RI	42W	63
MYNES THOMAS WILMER	VA	15W	111
MYRICK ALVA NORTEN II	CO	21E	113
MYRICK GEORGE FRANKLIN	CA	45E	13
MYRICK WILLIE J	OH	19E	7
MYSKYWEIZ RICHARD JOHN	NY	61E	14

NAME	STATE	PANEL NO.	LINE NO.
MacARTHUR DALE ALAN	WA	15W	39
MacBETH KENNETH NEIL	MI	08E	22
MacCALLUM STEPHEN MORLEY	WA	39W	61
MacCANN HENRY ELMER	MA	46E	57
MacDONALD ALLAN HERBERT	KS	08E	98
MacDONALD CHARLES JOSEPH	PA	18W	8
MacDONALD GEORGE DUNCAN	IL	01W	101
MacDONALD HAROLD LEE	MI	07W	64
MacDONALD JEROME JAMES	MA	33E	4
MacDONALD JOHN ALAN	OR	30E	64
MacDONALD LARRY EDWARD	MI	05E	88
MacDONALD LESTER EARL	ME	08E	22
MacDOUGAL JAMES HOWARD	CT	04W	124
MacFARLANE WILLIAM	NY	35W	84
MacFETTERS DUNCAN ALEXAN	LA	11E	37
MacGEARY FRED ERNEST	CA	28E	41
MacGLASHAN JOHN WILLIAM		24E	73
MacINTOSH DONALD GORDON	CA	35E	17
MacIVER NEIL KIRK	MD	01E	23
MacKAY CALVIN RONALD	MA	39E	9
MacKENNA JAMES JESSE	CO	07E	120
MacKILLOP NEIL HOWARD	ME	33W	33
MacLAUGHLIN DONALD C JR	MD	04E	51
MacLEAN JOHN DONALD KENNE	MA	37E	26
MacLEAN WESTON DAVID	NY	09E	56
MacLEOD PHILLIP LESLEY	CA	24W	33
MacLEOD ROBIN DOUGLAS	NY	22E	45
MacLEOD SIDNEY B JR	VA	57E	28
MacLURG DAVID WEBSTER	WA	07W	96
MacMANUS COLIN DAVID	NJ	15E	49
MacMANUS JAMES FRANCIS	CA	51E	10
MacMICHAEL CHARLES EDWAR	SC	10E	108
MacMILLAN GORDON ALAN	NY	22W	106
MacMILLAN THOMAS	MA	43E	28
MacNAMARA EDWIN JOSEPH	PA	08E	127
MacNAUGHT ROBERT WILLIAM	RI	08W	92
MacNEIL DOUGLAS GERALD	NY	12W	104
MacNEIL EDMUND LAMBER III	MA	03W	22
MacNUTT ROGER THOMAS	NC	12E	34
MacVEAN STEPHEN SHERWOOD	NJ	16W	2
MacVICKAR JAMES S JR	MD	24E	34
McADAMS EDGAR GREGORY	AL	29W	47
McADAMS GEROLD JEROME	NE	60W	3
McADAMS THOMAS ARTHUR	TX	31W	95
McADOO GLENN PAUL	CA	35W	28
McADOO MICHAEL DOUGLAS	MO	05W	9
McAFEE CARY FRANCIS	OH	44W	58
McAFEE CLYDE RICHARD	CA	39E	51
McAFEE DAVID ALFRED	MA	47W	30
McAFERTY ROBERT EUGENE	WA	28W	12
McALEER JAMES K III	PA	47W	30
McALISTER DONALD LYNN	CA	25E	106
McALISTER JAMES DAVID	NY	39E	68
McALISTER JOHN ULMER	NC	66E	11
McALLISTER ANGUS W JR	MS	31W	38
McALLISTER CAMERON TRENT	NE	18W	55
McALLISTER DONALD C JR	MD	48W	29
McALLISTER KENNETH RALPH	IL	44E	49
McALLISTER ROBERT ALLEN	IL	48W	46
McALLISTER ROGER J JR	NH	01E	112
McALLISTER WILLIAM DENNI	IN	30W	58
McALLISTER WILLIAM WALTE	CA	01E	106
McALUM ERNEST E	FL	08E	82
McANDREW JAMES DELMAS	NV	01E	16
McANDREW RICHARD T JR	MA	24E	88
McANDREW ROBERT CHARLES	CA	09W	44
McANDREWS JOHN JOSEPH	IN	24W	78
McANDREWS MICHAEL WILLIAM	FL	05W	2
McANINCH MICHAEL ALAN	TX	18W	2
McAPHEE SAMUEL LEE	AL	03W	118
McARDLE KEVIN JOSEPH	NY	48W	46
McARTHUR BRENT HAL	UT	16W	101
McARTHUR HENRY LEE	NC	24W	112
McARTHUR JAMES STEPHEN	CT	22E	64
McARTHUR JEROME DANNIE	MD	10E	120
McARTHUR JOHN DOUGLAS	MA	20W	77
McARTHUR MELVIN LLOYD	MI	49W	35
McARTHUR ROBERT LAMAR	TN	14W	85
McARTHUR STEVEN MICHAEL	ID	52E	40
McATEE WILLIAM JOSEPH	WY	37W	31
McATEER THOMAS JOSEPH	PA	12E	51
McAULEY GUY THOMAS	AL	14W	86

NAME	STATE	PANEL NO.	LINE NO.
McAULIFFE ALBERT JOSEPH	VI	13E	59
McAULIFFE EARLE EUGENE JR	ME	24E	34
McBEAIN DUANE MARVIN	IA	03W	96
McBEE CARL EDWARD	NC	01E	132
McBETH ROBERT STEVEN	IA	26E	14
McBETH RONALD GENE	TX	08E	94
McBRIDE ALBERT	NY	47W	50
McBRIDE ALBERT CAYRL	CO	18W	20
McBRIDE BEN K	OK	02E	134
McBRIDE CLAUDE WILLIAM	NJ	01E	27
McBRIDE DONALD WAYNE	MO	38W	19
McBRIDE EARL PAUL	PA	11E	98
McBRIDE EDWARD ERNEST	MS	38W	77
McBRIDE ELLIS A JR	FL	22E	55
McBRIDE FITZ-RANDOLPH BU	CA	18E	40
McBRIDE GRADY E III	AL	09W	15
McBRIDE HERMAN ALVIN	AL	31E	6
McBRIDE JAMES LARRY	OK	22E	110
McBRIDE KENNETH GERARD	NY	04E	101
McBRIDE MORRIS RALPH	MA	01E	45
McBRIDE PATRICK EUGENE	NJ	26E	48
McBRIDE THOMAS LEO	IN	60W	24
McBRIDE WILLIS LEONARD	VA	27E	82
McBROOM EDDIE ODONALD JR	TN	10E	42
McBROOM LOYD LINDAL	CA	17E	46
McBROOM WILLIAM STANLEY	NY	22E	45
McBROON JIMMY	UT	22E	110
McBURNETT LARRY TURNER	OK	28E	10
McBURROWS WENDELL	GA	39W	2
McBYNUM JIMMIE LLOYD	NC	02E	131
McCABE HUGH ROBERT	NY	23E	112
McCABE JAMES LOUIS JR	PA	14W	14
McCABE JOHN FRANCIS	NY	12E	109
McCABE LESTER	WY	17W	51
McCABE MARC WAYNE	CA	41E	70
McCABE MICHAEL RICHARD	NY	31W	12
McCABE PATRICK JOSEPH	ND	56E	13
McCABE ROBERT WARREN JR	OH	18W	3
McCADEN JAMES LEE	GA	26E	62
McCAFFERTY CORNELIUS A JR	OH	32W	50
McCAFFERTY MICHAEL LESTE	MA	42W	71
McCAFFREY CHARLES PATRIC	NY	38E	56
McCAFFREY GERALD WILLIAM	NY	41E	41
McCAFFREY JAMES J JR	PA	40W	46
McCAFFREY JAMES WILLIAM	NY	33E	21
McCAGG CARLTON F JR	NY	14W	39
McCAHAN MARLIN E	PA	01E	55
McCAHAN WALTER LEE	PA	44E	61
McCAIG ROBERT LEE	AL	07E	40
McCAIN JOHNNY WAYNE	TX	29E	68
McCAIN MARVIN RAYMOND JR	AL	55W	8
McCAIN MICHAEL CLINTON	AL	57E	29
McCALL ALLAN LEE	CA	41E	41
McCALL BILLIE RAY	FL	40E	66
McCALL CLAIBORNE PARKS	TN	08E	57
McCALL CLIFFORD	AL	10E	20
McCALL DIMITRIOUS CORTEZ	IL	42E	54
McCALL DOUGLAS HUDSON	CA	18E	70
McCALL GERALD ANTHONY	NJ	52W	29
McCALL PHILLIP GLEN	IL	19W	97
McCALL VICTOR GARNETT	NC	32W	83
McCALL WILLIAM ARTHUR JR	WA	26W	21
McCALLISTER ROBERT LYNN	MO	34E	30
McCALLUM PETER JOHN JR	NJ	28W	92
McCALVY JAMES A	WI	12E	96
McCAMBLE ROBERT LEE	AL	19E	8
McCAMMON DONALD WILLIS	PA	03E	131
McCAMMON GLENN EUGENE	OH	03E	87
McCAN CLAUDE JR	GA	51E	10
McCANDLESS MICHAEL DAVID	OH	21E	49
McCANDLIS OWEN TED	WA	14W	105
McCANN CECIL DARRELL	MI	16E	36
McCANN DONALD WAYNE	VA	12E	48
McCANN EDWARD DEAN	OH	10E	108
McCANN FRANCIS JOSEPH JR	PA	03W	13
McCANN JACK WILLIAM	PA	05W	11
McCANN JAMES KEVIN	IL	37E	10
McCANN MICHAEL ROSS	CA	20W	17
McCANN OWEN FRED	PA	05E	135
McCANN VINCENT OWEN JR	MA	15W	95
McCANN WILLIAM GEORGE	WI	11E	94
McCANTS ALFRED FRAZIER	CA	37W	6

NAME	STATE	PANEL NO.	LINE NO.
McCANTS JOSEPH JR	NJ	24W	32
McCANTS LELAND S III	VA	35W	9
McCAREY GUY HECTOR JR	FL	03E	116
McCARL ROBERT JAMES	IA	35E	24
McCARLEY CHARLES D JR	GA	13W	93
McCARN HAROLD DANIEL	NC	03E	87
McCARRELL JOHN EDWARD	TN	25W	52
McCARRICK WILLIAM W	PA	27E	45
McCARROLL IVY M JR	LA	20E	65
McCARROLL OREN B	OH	50E	47
McCARRON MICHAEL JOSEPH	VA	13W	100
McCARRON WILLIAM P JR	NY	15W	39
McCARTER JAMES W JR	LA	28E	3
McCARTER JERRY	TN	22W	54
McCARTER JIMMY CARL	TX	18E	30
McCARTER ROBERT LEONARD	TN	30E	56
McCARTER THOMAS LUTHER	TN	23E	21
McCARTHY BRIAN EDWARD	MI	10W	14
McCARTHY BRIAN FRANCIS	NY	29W	47
McCARTHY CARL RICHARD JR	NY	07W	78
McCARTHY DAVID PAUL	WV	30E	79
McCARTHY EDWARD CHARLES	MA	14E	109
McCARTHY EDWARD JOSEPH	IL	05E	88
McCARTHY EDWARD POLK III	MS	07W	100
McCARTHY HOWARD C JR	PA	09E	99
McCARTHY JAMES IRVIN JR	WA	15W	7
McCARTHY JAMES JOSEPH	NY	23E	112
McCARTHY JOHN EDWARD	MA	15E	66
McCARTHY JOHN HENRY	MA	46E	21
McCARTHY JOHN JOSEPH	NJ	11W	126
McCARTHY JOHN NEAL	NY	24W	97
McCARTHY JOSEPH F JR	CA	24W	105
McCARTHY LOYD VAN JR	TX	04W	52
McCARTHY PETER ROVERT	NY	17E	126
McCARTHY PHILIP JAMES	MD	03E	131
McCARTHY ROBERT ALAN	NY	31W	54
McCARTHY ROBERT JOHN	MA	39W	51
McCARTHY TERRY ALAN	CA	25W	52
McCARTHY THOMAS WELLER	MD	01E	45
McCARTHY TIMOTHY CLAY	MS	09W	89
McCARTHY TIMOTHY JOHN	NY	13E	65
McCARTHY WALTER R JR	NY	01E	10
McCARTHY WHILTON ANTHONY	NC	20E	14
McCARTHY WILLIAM FRANCIS	MA	32E	12
McCARTNEY ANDREW C	OH	10W	15
McCARTNEY DARRYL EUGENE	MO	30W	28
McCARTNEY HARRY C	WV	04E	100
McCARTNEY JOSEPH BYRON	TX	30W	28
McCARTNEY KEN ALLEN	TX	16W	33
McCARTNEY ROBERT ALLEN	WI	18E	30
McCARTY BILLY JOE	AL	65W	12
McCARTY DOUGLAS WAYNE	WV	49E	23
McCARTY EARL EDWARD	WY	04W	12
McCARTY EDWARD WESLEY	OH	16W	59
McCARTY FREDERICK DONALD	MS	46E	57
McCARTY GLENN MURRAY	NY	17E	63
McCARTY GLENN WELDON	TX	05W	126
McCARTY JAMES LON	TX	01W	49
McCARTY JOHN DAVIS	FL	14E	49
McCARTY JOHN LEIGH	CA	06E	57
McCARTY KENNETH LEON	CA	11W	1
McCARTY THOMAS HUBERT	MN	20W	36
McCARTY WILLIAM JOSEPH	NY	27E	96
McCARVEL STEPHEN LEWIS	MT	24W	98
McCARY CHARLES WAYMAN	AL	01E	19
McCASKEY ROBERT WALTER	NY	48E	44
McCASKILL FREDRIC CECIL	TX	56W	36
McCASKILL WILLIAM	GA	18E	96
McCASLIN GARY EUGENE	NC	10E	108
McCASLIN HAROLD JR	CO	01W	59
McCASLIN RAYMOND LOUIS	ID	15W	96
McCAULEY DALE MARTIN	OH	18E	26
McCAULEY DENNIS JAMES	NJ	24E	84
McCAULEY STEPHEN ARTHUR	CA	09W	14
McCAULEY WAYLAND F JR	VA	07W	59
McCHESNEY JOHN T III	AZ	35E	17
McCLAFFERTY JAMES EDWARD	MO	52W	29
McCLAFLIN ROBERT F	OR	19W	33
McCLAIN CECIL EVERETT	MS	12W	49
McCLAIN FRED JULOUS	FL	20W	51
McCLAIN GARY THOMAS	CA	13E	77
McCLAIN HARRY	DC	20E	105

NAME	STATE	PANEL NO.	LINE NO.
McCLAIN JAMES HARRY	MI	01E	59
McCLAIN JAMES LEWIS	VA	21E	95
McCLAIN KENNETH ALLEN	IA	50E	32
McCLAIN MICHAEL DEE	IL	42W	49
McCLAIN RICHARD AARON	IA	65E	14
McCLAIN RICHARD LARRY	NJ	42W	49
McCLAIN ROY HOWARD	NY	53W	4
McCLAIN WILLIAM DAVID	TX	61E	15
McCLAIN WILLIE JAMES JR	MI	64E	7
McCLAIN WILOFARD A II	TX	28W	74
McCLAMB HERMAN LEE	NC	36W	36
McCLANAHAN CLEATUS WAYNE	WV	49E	35
McCLANAHAN DONALD LEE	MD	46W	13
McCLANAHAN LARRY BYRON	WA	01E	90
McCLANAHAN TERRY LEE	WV	04W	29
McCLANE MICHAEL JAMES	IL	15W	43
McCLARY BENJAMIN FRANKLI	PA	34E	38
McCLARY GORDON STUART	VA	30E	80
McCLARY SAMUEL DONALD	SC	14E	118
McCLATCHEY JEWEL EDWARD	MO	33W	4
McCLATCHEY ROGER WAYNE	IA	36W	65
McCLATCHY JEFFERY JR	TX	42E	22
McCLATCHY PERCY W	TX	09E	133
McCLEAN JOHN HOWARD	NY	01E	26
McCLEARY GEORGE CARLTON	LA	03E	22
McCLEER TOMMY MIKE	IL	03W	120
McCLELLAN BRENT A	PA	05E	88
McCLELLAN BRUCE MAYO	OR	46W	31
McCLELLAN EDWARD EUGENE	MO	42E	8
McCLELLAN FRANK EDWARD	IN	09W	8
McCLELLAN M L	MS	05E	23
McCLELLAN MICHAEL JAMES	MN	16W	105
McCLELLAN PAUL TRUMAN JR	OR	03E	50
McCLELLAND AUBREY DAVID	TX	50E	19
McCLELLAND CHESTER RAY	IN	47W	46
McCLELLAND GEORGE	NJ	41E	25
McCLELLAND GEORGE DENNIS	OH	22W	123
McCLELLAND JAMES RICHARD	PA	49E	24
McCLELLAND MYRON	CA	05E	55
McCLELLAND RONALD EDWARD	PA	11E	123
McCLENDON JOHN NEWT JR	AL	09W	76
McCLENDON WILLIAM W JR	LA	35E	25
McCLENDON WILLIE JAMES	FL	36W	17
McCLENNAHAN CHARLES HENR	NY	13E	54
McCLENTON HENRY	FL	23W	55
McCLINTIC GEORGE PATRICK	PA	17W	78
McCLINTOCK GERALD	PA	57W	29
McCLINTOCK JAMES RICHARD	WA	36E	27
McCLINTOCK TED ERNEST	WA	34W	9
McCLOSKEY JOHN JAMES	MN	07E	45
McCLOSKEY ROBERT ALLEN	NJ	57W	30
McCLOSKEY SCOTT SIMONS	FL	19E	39
McCLOUD GARY LEE	CA	17W	74
McCLOUD LAWRENCE BEVERLY	MS	05E	83
McCLOUD STEVEN WILLIAM	IL	22W	5
McCLOUD WILLIE JR	MI	03W	124
McCLOYN JOSEPH	CA	41E	11
McCLUNG JIMMY HARRISON	VA	11W	9
McCLUNG JOHN AMBROSE	WV	48W	2
McCLUNG LARRY EARL	CO	31E	82
McCLUNG RONALD OLIN	WV	27E	5
McCLUNG WAYNE OLAND	OH	22W	54
McCLURE BILLIE JACK	NC	32W	66
McCLURE CHRISTABOL TOBY	NM	34W	17
McCLURE DWAYNE CHARLES	OR	49E	33
McCLURE JACK DALE	CA	04E	46
McCLURE JAMES M	OK	19E	16
McCLURE PATRICK RYAN	WI	25W	52
McCLURE THURLO MERIDA	GA	25E	2
McCLURG CHARLES D	MI	32E	58
McCLURG JAMES WALTER	NY	13W	97
McCLURG JOHN LLOYD	IA	08W	119
McCLUSKEY JOHN DAVID	MO	10W	8
McCLUSKEY KENNETH JAMES	PA	17W	11
McCLUSKEY PATRICK CHARLES	MN	07E	45
McCLUSKEY ROBERT WILLIAM	MA	33W	66
McCOIG DONALD B	CA	47E	3
McCOIN KENNETH DALE	MO	11E	103
McCOLLOUGH GARY	NC	24W	103
McCOLLUM DAVID VERNON	CA	46W	61
McCOLLUM JAMES PATRICK	NJ	66E	12
McCOLLUM ROBERT HENRY	GA	41E	49

NAME	STATE	PANEL NO.	LINE NO.
McCOLLUM RONALD LEE	KY	40E	10
McCOLLUM WAYNE ADELBERT	MN	12E	38
McCOMAS HOBART WILSON JR	OH	22E	16
McCOMB AUBURN DALE	FL	19E	120
McCOMB TERRY RUSSELL	MI	21E	59
McCOMBS DAVID LEROY	IA	17W	68
McCOMMONS MICHAEL RAY	CA	13E	36
McCONAHAY BRIAN DUAINE	IA	24E	35
McCONAHAY MICHAEL PAUL	CA	12E	111
McCONAHY THOMAS ARTHUR	PA	09E	25
McCONAUGHEAD HARVEY R JR	OH	15W	95
McCONKEY WAYNE ALLEN	IA	07W	66
McCONNAGHY WILLIAM P	CA	11W	47
McCONNAUGEHAY DAN DAILY	CA	05E	4
McCONNAUGHEY DAVID LYNN	OH	06E	67
McCONNEL GERALD WAYNE JR	WA	57E	7
McCONNELL DAVID WAYNE	CA	22W	80
McCONNELL GERARD ROBERT	NY	11E	124
McCONNELL JAMES PAUL	WI	36W	77
McCONNELL JAMES T III	NJ	52W	11
McCONNELL JERRY	NY	42W	6
McCONNELL JOHN STEVEN	OH	30E	4
McCONNELL ROBERT MUELLER	OH	34E	80
McCONNELL WILLIAM C IV	CO	13W	43
McCONNELL WILLIAM WALKER	CA	44E	50
McCONNICO DONALD	FL	07E	120
McCONNYHEAD JAMES JR	NY	22W	42
McCOOK GREGORY MADISON	GA	19E	73
McCORD BURTON KYLE	TX	06E	113
McCORD DAVID MICHAEL	CA	36W	70
McCORD DAVID PAUL	WV	46W	51
McCORD HAROLD RAYMOND JR	OH	10W	105
McCORD JOHN RICHARD	OH	15E	75
McCORD MICHAEL RAYE	IL	31E	88
McCORD ROGER CLAIR	IA	36W	41
McCORKEL JAMES EDWARD	AL	40W	21
McCORKLE BENNIE EUGENE	TN	39E	64
McCORKLE CHARLES THOMAS	MD	10E	56
McCORKLE CRAIG ERIC	NC	25E	88
McCORKLE DOUGLAS P JR	TX	11W	49
McCORKLE LESLIE LEROY	CA	24W	9
McCORKLE STEPHEN ALAN	OH	15E	59
McCORMACK HUGH JOHN	NY	15E	98
McCORMACK JAMES JOSEPH	NY	24E	114
McCORMACK WILLIAM EDWARD	MA	18W	25
McCORMICK BRUCE ALLEN	FL	15W	83
McCORMICK CARL OTTIS	IL	01W	81
McCORMICK CARL PHILIP	KY	29E	25
McCORMICK DENNIS LEE	WI	47W	2
McCORMICK DONNIE RAY	TN	38E	34
McCORMICK JAMES MILTON	IL	28E	50
McCORMICK JEROME LOMAC	NC	05E	56
McCORMICK JOHN VERN	MI	03E	119
McCORMICK JOHN W JR	PA	20E	31
McCORMICK LUTHER O'NEIL	NC	40W	49
McCORMICK MICHAEL P	OH	29W	91
McCORMICK MICHAEL TIMOTHY	HI	01W	110
McCORMICK PATRICK JOHN	NY	46W	18
McCORMICK RICHARD ALAN	DC	25E	24
McCORMICK RICHARD H JR	PA	25W	78
McCORMICK ROBERT PATRICK	PA	46W	43
McCORMICK RONALD LEE	WV	13W	62
McCORMICK RONNIE LEON	TN	14W	122
McCORMICK THOMAS A JR	MA	54E	38
McCORMICK WILLIAM C JR	PA	26W	49
McCORMICK WILLIAM L	NC	30W	67
McCORMICK WILLIAM T	WY	13W	119
McCORVEY EDWARD JR	FL	37E	11
McCORVEY GERALD	MI	25W	31
McCORVEY ROBERT KENNETH	OH	22E	8
McCOSAR WINFORD	CA	43E	28
McCOULLOUGH BEN JR	TN	43E	47
McCOWAN RALPH CHARLES	ND	47E	53
McCOWN ROBERT DEWAYNE	MO	12E	91
McCOY ALBERT JR	OH	03W	18
McCOY BOBBY LEE	OH	21W	47
McCOY BOOKER TEE JR	FL	09E	5
McCOY CARL THOMAS JR	TN	63W	10
McCOY DENNIS RAY	UT	54E	27
McCOY ELEC	SC	28E	69
McCOY EUGENE TAYLOR	IA	04E	124
McCOY GEORGE FRANKLIN	IN	05E	88

NAME	STATE	PANEL NO.	LINE NO.
McCOY HILDRA JR	NC	20E	78
McCOY JAMES GLENDALE	NY	22E	110
McCOY JAMES LARR	TN	38E	7
McCOY JAMES RAYMOND	SC	43W	29
McCOY JAMES WILLIAM	MO	12E	115
McCOY JOHN LOWERY	CA	01E	64
McCOY JOHN WILLIAM	OH	19E	54
McCOY LARRY	MS	03W	129
McCOY LARRY WILLIAM	FL	08W	128
McCOY MERIL OLEN JR	CA	06W	123
McCOY PETER JOSEPH	MO	10W	86
McCOY RALPH LINDSEY JR	AR	02W	24
McCOY RICKEY CLAUDE C	MI	33W	50
McCOY RONALD JAY	NC	40E	44
McCRACKEN JAMES MUIR	PA	02W	126
McCRACKEN RONALD	NY	10E	109
McCRAE JAMES HENRY	FL	29E	75
McCRANEY CLARENCE	IL	34W	39
McCRANIE DAVID CARROLL	GA	11W	126
McCRARY CLIFFORD PAUL	GA	19W	51
McCRARY DOUGLAS MacARTHUR	SC	15E	49
McCRARY JACK	TN	32E	95
McCRARY RONALD SMITH	MS	35W	28
McCRAW RONALD GENE	NM	44E	51
McCRAY EUGENE	FL	17E	112
McCRAY FRANK JR	FL	22E	46
McCRAY GARY DEAN	NC	24W	46
McCRAY GREGORY	IN	32E	25
McCRAY MELVIN	MS	08E	88
McCRAY PLEASANT JR	MO	08W	67
McCRAY THOMAS	NC	33E	39
McCREA LAWRENCE	MO	06E	86
McCREARY STANLEY EUGENE	MD	27W	32
McCREERY FLOYD SANFORD	MI	14W	54
McCREIGHT JOSEPH THOMAS	PA	13E	62
McCREIGHT TIMOTHY JOE	IL	15W	54
McCRIMMON ERNEST C JR	NC	61E	15
McCRIMMON HENRY THURMAN	NC	52E	8
McCROBIE GEORGE EDWARD	WV	15E	80
McCRONE JAMES ROLAND	TX	09W	58
McCRYSTAL JAMES LARRY	AR	09E	81
McCUAIG GLENN RICHARD	GA	24E	69
McCUBBIN GLENN DEWAYNE	KS	63E	14
McCUBBINS LARRY JAMES	KY	38E	34
McCUE GARY FRANCIS	MN	19E	63
McCUE JAMES EDWARD	MA	36E	27
McCUE WILLIAM JAMES	IL	25E	43
McCUEN WILLIAM DAVID JR	PA	05E	121
McCUISTON HARVEY RICHARD	NC	19W	72
McCULLOUGH ALBERT	CT	32W	81
McCULLOUGH ALFRED	PA	59W	9
McCULLOUGH BENJAMIN LEE	MI	23W	104
McCULLOUGH BILLY RAY	SC	10W	53
McCULLOUGH GARRY MICHAEL	TX	46W	18
McCULLOUGH JERRY WENDELL	TN	10E	99
McCULLOUGH JOHN EARNEST	SC	21E	114
McCULLOUGH JOHN JAMES	PA	09W	85
McCULLOUGH MARVIN L JR	MO	34W	1
McCULLOUGH MICHAEL EUGEN	CA	12E	38
McCULLOUGH PATRICK ELVIN	KS	33W	77
McCULLOUGH PREZEL	IL	03E	87
McCULLOUGH RONALD JAMES	AZ	14E	49
McCULLOUGH SYLVESTER	NY	40E	26
McCUMBER RAYMOND	TX	38W	77
McCUNE EDWARD JAMES	NY	22E	111
McCURDY JOHN A	NE	06E	115
McCURDY ROBERT LOWELL	WA	10W	105
McCURLEY TIMOTHY LEWIS	FL	14W	127
McCURRY ANDREAS	MI	23E	4
McCURTAIN CHARLES RAY JR	CA	39W	55
McCUTCHEN GEORGE	AL	03E	103
McCUTCHEN MARL W JR	NY	26E	27
McCUTCHEON ALLAN BRUCE	RI	16E	63
McCUTCHEON FRANK STAN III	IA	05W	74
McDAID JOHN MURL	MI	14W	47
McDANIEL ANDREW LEROY	TN	51E	40
McDANIEL ARCHIE HUGH JR	WA	20W	41
McDANIEL CARY ELZIEVAN	NC	05W	9
McDANIEL CHESTER	AR	43W	29
McDANIEL CRAIG ALLAN	CA	27E	30
McDANIEL EDGAR	PA	05W	91
McDANIEL FRANKIE B	MI	28W	50

NAME	STATE	PANEL NO.	LINE NO.
McDANIEL GEORGE WILLIAM	OH	18E	115
McDANIEL GILBERT ELLIS	OK	28W	12
McDANIEL JERRY JACKSON	GA	32E	88
McDANIEL JOHN LEWIS	NC	52E	22
McDANIEL JOHN THOMAS	MN	26E	49
McDANIEL JOHN THOMAS	IN	20W	59
McDANIEL JOHNNIE LEE	MO	19E	120
McDANIEL KENNETH REED	IN	19W	33
McDANIEL MICHAEL EUGENE	MO	17W	42
McDANIEL MORRIS L JR	GA	27E	49
McDANIEL MURAL	NY	39E	51
McDANIEL PATRICK ELSWOOD	PA	10W	122
McDANIEL RICHARD BYERS	CA	41E	25
McDANIEL ROBERT THOMAS	VA	23E	10
McDANIEL ROGER PAUL	WV	23E	21
McDANIEL ROY DEAN	MO	38E	35
McDANIEL SAMUEL WAYMON II	TX	03W	104
McDANIEL WAYNE IVAN	IN	25E	88
McDANIEL WILLIAM T	IL	26E	2
McDANIELS BILLY CLAYTON	SC	38W	12
McDANIELS CHARLES ALBERT	IN	16E	125
McDANIELS JOHNNY ANDERSO	MD	57W	30
McDANIELS WILLIAM LAWREN	IL	27E	30
McDAVID WILLIAM EARL	CA	49W	25
McDAVIS CALVIN LEE	TX	26E	59
McDAVITT GEORGE FRANCIS	NY	43W	7
McDERMOTT BERNARD A III	TN	18W	49
McDERMOTT JOHN FREDERICK	TX	03E	100
McDERMOTT JOHN PATRICK	KS	45W	63
McDERMOTT JOSEPH F III	MD	09W	131
McDERMOTT LEWIS E	MO	31E	50
McDERMOTT PATRICK THOMAS	NY	12E	48
McDERMOTT TERRENCE M	CT	20W	93
McDERMOTT THOMAS ANTHONY	NJ	31E	59
McDONALD ALBERT JR	OK	07W	56
McDONALD BILLY WALLACE	TX	22W	123
McDONALD CHARLIE RAY	TX	27W	14
McDONALD CLYDE D II	CA	06E	49
McDONALD D LANCE	CA	43W	8
McDONALD DANNY LEE	KS	11E	132
McDONALD DAVID HAROLD	FL	27W	12
McDONALD DAVID LETCHER	AL	55W	14
McDONALD DENNIS ELWOOD	WV	60E	15
McDONALD EMMETT RAYMOND	WA	07E	130
McDONALD GENIE LEE	IN	34E	8
McDONALD GEORGE COLUMBUS	CA	24E	32
McDONALD GEORGE E JR	MI	49E	4
McDONALD GERALD FRANCIS	MA	20E	122
McDONALD GERARD MORRIS	NY	41E	42
McDONALD HAROLD JOHN	NY	12W	82
McDONALD HAROLD WAYNE	NC	16W	101
McDONALD HENRY	NY	13E	35
McDONALD HENRY III	PA	41E	26
McDONALD JAMES	NJ	54E	13
McDONALD JAMES HOWARD	CA	12E	80
McDONALD JAMES MATTHEW	WV	12W	107
McDONALD JERRY CECIL	TX	30W	92
McDONALD JERRY DUANE	OR	30E	58
McDONALD JERRY SYLVESTER	SC	31W	95
McDONALD JERRY VERNON	AR	50E	51
McDONALD JOHN ETHRIDGE	GA	27W	90
McDONALD JOSEPH WAYNE	AL	14W	116
McDONALD JOSEPH WILLIAM	NY	01W	12
McDONALD KURT CASEY	WA	01E	80
McDONALD LARRY JAMES	MS	25E	44
McDONALD LEWIS LEVI	CA	30W	68
McDONALD LONZO O	TX	20W	114
McDONALD MARTIN TERRANCE	PA	04W	116
McDONALD MICHAEL JAY	KS	36W	57
McDONALD MICHAEL WILLIAM	NY	05E	61
McDONALD PHILL GENE	NC	59W	26
McDONALD ROBERT F II	VA	28W	35
McDONALD ROBERT WILFRED	IA	09W	58
McDONALD RONALD IRVIN	NY	11W	3
McDONALD ROY LAWRENCE	MD	25W	18
McDONALD SAMUEL LEE	PA	03E	60
McDONALD STEVEN JAMES	ID	02W	78
McDONALD THOMAS MICHAEL	OH	11W	104
McDONALD THOMAS R JR	GA	18W	67
McDONALD WALTER RAYMOND	CT	38E	56
McDONALD WILLIAM E	TN	30E	10
McDONALD WILLIAM EARL JR	PA	36W	85

NAME	STATE	PANEL NO.	LINE NO.
McDONALD WILLIAM FREDERI	WV	15E	59
McDONELL R D	TX	04W	77
McDONELL TERRY KEITH	OK	19W	46
McDONIAL WESLEY	IL	02E	127
McDONNELL JOEL WILLIAM	MN	13E	59
McDONNELL JOHN TERENCE	TX	30W	58
McDONNELL MARTIN GERARD	NY	32E	15
McDONNELL WILLIAM HERBER	PA	34W	71
McDONOUGH GEORGE WATSON	OK	27W	26
McDONOUGH JAMES M JR	ME	09E	99
McDONOUGH JAMES MICHAEL	NY	11W	38
McDONOUGH JAMES ROBERT	PA	56E	23
McDONOUGH JOHN RICHARD	NJ	08E	67
McDONOUGH ROBERT JAMES	MA	46W	61
McDORMAN DARL KENNETH	VA	60W	9
McDOUGAL BILLY DEAN	CA	45E	35
McDOUGALL HIMA DUNCAN JR	MT	07W	12
McDOWALL FRANCIS JR	GA	19W	18
McDOWELL CHARLES ELVIN	SC	38E	79
McDOWELL DONALD FRANCIS	NJ	32E	64
McDOWELL EARL WAYNE	OK	19W	41
McDOWELL GERALD LEE	GA	09W	99
McDOWELL HAROLD GUINN	SC	39E	64
McDOWELL JOHN CLARK	SD	34E	9
McDOWELL LARRY JAMES	IN	08W	59
McDOWELL LAURENCE THOMAS	PA	17W	19
McDOWELL MELVIN WARREN	CA	09E	81
McDOWELL ROBERT J JR	NY	24W	60
McDOWELL SAMUEL T JR	SC	38E	57
McDOWELL STEVEN DOUGLAS	IA	05W	91
McDOWELL WILLIAM CLAYTON	GA	04W	109
McDOWELL WILLIAM JOSEPH	CA	17E	74
McDUFFIE JAMES JR	NC	07W	104
McDUFFIE LARRY RAY	AL	28E	50
McDUFFIE RONALD LEE	IN	34E	56
McDUFFY ROBERT LOUIS	LA	52E	41
McDURMON CALVIN LAVON	GA	20W	41
McEACHERN LEO	NC	12W	125
McEACHERN RANCE ALDEN JR	ME	52W	29
McEACHIN JOHN JR	NY	22E	46
McEACHRON PAUL	MA	24E	115
McELENEY EDWARD RALPH JR	MA	01W	78
McELFRESH ALLEN KEITH	OH	05W	118
McELHANEY BOBBY GENE	AR	20E	32
McELHANEY LEE ROY	TN	42W	20
McELHANEY RODGER DENNIS	PA	20W	7
McELHANNON JAMES PHILLIP	OK	06E	90
McELHANNON KEVIN C JR	VA	07W	66
McELHANON MICHAEL OWEN	TX	48W	29
McELHANON WARREN SHELBY	TX	05E	133
McELRATH RALPH EDWARD	KY	03W	115
McELRATH WINSTON JR	GA	62W	14
McELREATH RANDALL LEE	OK	44E	26
McELROY DENNIS ARTHUR	CA	25W	78
McELROY GLENN DAVID	IL	16E	95
McELROY GRADY EDWARD	AR	12E	115
McELROY JOHN JAMES	PA	38E	70
McELROY JOHN LEE	NY	59E	9
McELROY RONALD LENEAR	TX	39E	75
McELROY THEODORE R JR	OH	13E	16
McELROY THOMAS LEE	TN	53W	23
McELVAIN JAMES RICHARD	CA	01W	94
McELWEE JACKIE RAY	IL	34E	43
McELYEA JAMES FRANK	CA	14E	124
McELYNN THOMAS JOSEPH	NY	31E	14
McENANY KEITH ALLEN	FL	28E	61
McENTEE NEIL CHARLES	CA	21E	114
McENTEE THOMAS	PA	06E	57
McEUEN RONALD CURTIS	CA	67W	2
McEWEN JAMES ARTHUR	PA	02E	131
McEWEN ROY CLIFFORD	ME	08E	63
McEWEN THOMAS C JR	TN	01E	93
McEWING HARRY	MA	09W	131
McFADDEN CARL JR	SC	46E	39
McFADDEN FLOYD	AR	43E	28
McFADDEN GREGORY WALTER	NJ	29E	42
McFADDEN HARRY BERNARD	SC	24E	81
McFADDEN PAUL RAY	NE	47E	3
McFADDIN LARRY RONALD	KY	68E	5
McFADYEN BRUCE SEARIGHT	NJ	34W	27
McFALL GARY RICHARD	CA	44W	51
McFALL KENNETH LEWIS	FL	22W	91
McFALL ROBERT DALE	MO	13W	105
McFALLS BILLY CESAR	AR	21E	14
McFALLS HARRY PRESTON	DE	34E	24
McFALLS JERRY ARNOLD	TN	34W	17
McFARLAND ARTHUR RAY	OK	24W	18
McFARLAND CHARLES HENRY	TX	23E	5
McFARLAND KENNETH EARL	CA	17E	112
McFARLAND LOUIE JUNNIE	IL	53W	44
McFARLAND LOUIS HENRY	CA	41E	52
McFARLAND RICHARD SCOTT	PA	16W	50
McFARLAND RICHARD WESLEY	OH	08W	101
McFARLAND RICK E	IN	04W	62
McFARLAND STEVEN LEE	CA	27W	51
McFARLAND SYLVESTER WARR	FL	39E	72
McFARLAND TERRENCE W	OH	34W	52
McFARLAND TOMMIE LOUIS	NY	06E	25
McFARLAND WILLIAM JOSEPH	VA	26W	65
McFARLAND WILLIAM LEROY	PA	29W	39
McFARLAND WILLIAM LLOYD	IL	43W	64
McFARLANE JOHN WILLIAM	UT	49E	24
McFARLANE RICHARD DEAN	NM	07W	79
McFARLIN CHARLES RICHARD	OH	04E	9
McFERON ERNEST	TX	01E	119
McFETRIDGE GARRY CLAYTON	IN	01E	14
McGAHA HAROLD F	SC	35E	8
McGAR BRIAN KENT	CA	21E	23
McGARRITY JAMES ERLEY JR	TN	18W	104
McGARRY JAMES BRIAN	MA	18W	104
McGARRY JEREMIAH D	MN	32E	32
McGARRY JOHN THOMAS	NY	22E	111
McGARRY THOMAS STEWART	TN	06W	13
McGARVEY CHARLES EDWARD	OH	09E	90
McGARVEY JAMES MAURICE	IN	18E	42
McGARVEY PATRICK GEORGE	WA	49E	35
McGARVEY RAYMOND LEE	PA	08E	125
McGARVEY WILLIAM BERNARD	PA	30E	17
McGAUGHEY PAUL JR	KY	13E	14
McGAUGHEY WILLIE LEE	AR	42E	37
McGEATH RICHARD ALLEN	IL	52W	30
McGEE BOLEN PONDEXDER	AR	52E	8
McGEE CARL BARRY	MI	04W	88
McGEE CHARLES ADAM	IL	05E	121
McGEE CHARLES EDWARD	MS	45E	47
McGEE CURTIS J	VA	05E	88
McGEE DANNY ALBERT	AL	36W	22
McGEE DANNY DEAN	GA	14E	70
McGEE DARRELL EUGENE	WI	21W	62
McGEE DARWIN DALE	OK	26W	41
McGEE FREDDY ALFORD	ME	34W	60
McGEE GEORGE FRANKLIN	NC	18W	70
McGEE GEORGE WILLIAM	OK	44W	28
McGEE HENRY HERBERT	NY	29E	42
McGEE HERMAN	IL	40E	66
McGEE JOSEPH O'NEIL	SC	07W	98
McGEE KENNETH WESLEY	MI	19E	84
McGEE PAT WELDON	TX	13E	14
McGEE RICHARD WAYNE	IN	08E	116
McGEE ROBERT JUNIOR	NC	42E	38
McGEE ROBERT LEE	MI	17E	74
McGEE ROBERT LEWIS JR	AL	55W	8
McGEE ROY DELL	MI	35E	60
McGEE SAMUEL RUSSELL III	GA	26E	14
McGEE STEPHEN DWAYNE	IN	57E	29
McGEE STEVEN WESLEY	NV	23E	21
McGEE THOMAS LEE	FL	16E	63
McGEE WILLIAM JAMES IV	NC	25E	88
McGEE WILLIAM ROYAL	MS	48E	45
McGEEVER THOMAS JOSEPH	AL	18E	103
McGEHEE JOHN ALBERT	CA	43W	56
McGEHEE NOBLE DOUGLAS	MS	04E	65
McGERTY MICHAEL JOHN	CA	07W	28
McGHEE BILLY WALKER	TN	37E	64
McGHEE DENNIS OLIVER	OH	17W	17
McGHEE GEORGE WILLIAM	TX	14E	58
McGHEE LARRY DALE	IL	20W	125
McGHEE RICHARD DALE	WV	30E	17
McGILL DAVID LOREN	FL	26W	11
McGILL JAMES BARRY	PA	20E	105
McGILL JOE LOUIS LOCKHAR	NC	57E	29
McGILL MICHAEL GREGORY	PA	19W	114
McGILL ROBERT ANDREW	GA	30W	38
McGILL ROBERT WARREN	OH	46W	6
McGILTON CALVIN EUGENE	CT	42W	71
McGILVARY DANIEL J JR	WI	15E	6
McGINLEY DONALD SMITH	ID	50W	31
McGINLEY GERALD GREYDON	CA	36W	86
McGINN EDWARD CHARLES	OR	23W	22
McGINN JOHN ARTHUR	MD	09W	100
McGINN WALTER WILLIAM	MA	44W	39
McGINNES CHARLES DENNIS	VA	04W	129
McGINNESS PAUL EDWARD	MA	40W	4
McGINNIS CHRISTOPHER MAR	AZ	23E	61
McGINNIS HARRY F JR	PA	17E	37
McGINNIS LEONARD DAVID	PA	64E	17
McGINNIS LESTER CLEO II	KS	41W	74
McGINNIS MICHAEL BRIAN	PA	18W	104
McGINNIS MICHAEL JOSEPH	NY	40E	45
McGINNIS ROBERT RAY	AR	21W	47
McGINNIS STEVEN LAVELLE	MS	21W	29
McGINNIS WILLIAM E II	MI	19E	38
McGINTY CALVIN A JR	AL	24E	62
McGINTY LAWRENCE MICHAEL	PA	56E	13
McGIVERN WILLIAM DAVID	CA	16W	81
McGLASSON JAMES CLARK	CA	19W	120
McGLEW JOHN JOSEPH	OH	50W	47
McGLOCHLIN DAVID EARL	CA	34E	24
McGLONE GERALD FIELD	IL	02W	35
McGLONE MICHAEL THOMAS	NH	18W	71
McGLOTHIN RAYMOND DENNIS	CA	33E	51
McGLOTHLEN JERRY WAYNE	WA	09W	34
McGLOTHLIN ALEXANDER J	CT	06E	110
McGLOTHLIN MICHAEL JOHN	IL	32W	15
McGOEY JAMES FRANCIS	NY	21E	36
McGOLDRICK MICHAEL JOSEP	NY	06E	118
McGONAGLE MICHAEL JOHN	ME	11E	81
McGONIGAL ALOYSIUS PAUL	DC	39E	75
McGONIGAL JOHN P JR	NY	59E	27
McGONIGLE CHARLES D	PA	03W	129
McGONIGLE WILLIAM DEE	KS	58E	11
McGOULDRICK FRANCIS J JR	CT	36W	17
McGOVERN CHARLES MANLEY	CA	33W	16
McGOVERN CHARLES VENTON	VA	06W	50
McGOVERN JAMES GERALD	MD	24E	35
McGOVERN JEROME GEORGE	KS	23E	61
McGOVERN KEVIN BERNARD	NY	52W	19
McGOVERN KEVIN MICHAEL	MA	31E	51
McGOVERN MICHAEL DONALD	NY	05W	96
McGOVERN MICHAEL JOHN JR	NY	18W	65
McGOVERN MICHAEL LEWIS	OH	15W	39
McGOVERN PATRICK EDWARD	MI	21W	66
McGOVERN RICHARD DALE	MN	59E	28
McGOVERN TERRANCE JAMES	IL	06W	46
McGOWAN FRANCIS RUSSELL	KY	23W	46
McGOWAN IRA EUGENE	AL	16W	50
McGOWAN PAUL JOSEPH	IL	16E	113
McGOWAN WILLIAM LEWIS	MD	24W	9
McGOWEN CHARLES FRANK	CO	56E	13
McGRADE GERARD	NY	23W	55
McGRANE DONALD PAUL	IA	23E	92
McGRATH CHARLES FRANCIS	PA	39E	50
McGRATH DANIEL EDWARD	OH	20W	25
McGRATH DANIEL WILLIAM	NY	20W	25
McGRATH EDWARD ALBERT	NY	48E	31
McGRATH EDWARD CHARLES	FL	27E	60
McGRATH JAMES PATRICK	NY	14E	104
McGRATH JAMES PATRICK	IL	24E	73
McGRATH JOHN AUGUST	MI	12E	63
McGRATH PAUL MARTIN	NY	59W	26
McGRATH THOMAS HOWARD	IL	31W	54
McGRATH WILLIAM DARRELL	CA	30E	10
McGRAW DONALD ORIN	OH	26W	31
McGRAW LARRY JOE	PA	16W	9
McGRAW THOMAS EDWARD	NY	04E	130
McGREGOR DONALD VERNON	UT	01E	26
McGREGOR RICHARD	NY	28E	5
McGREW LLOYD ARTHUR	WI	08W	25
McGREW WILLIAM WALLACE III	OH	30E	98
McGRIFF DANNY JAY	CA	05E	89
McGRUDER EDWARD	GA	23E	67
McGUCKIN JOSEPH	FL	07W	114
McGUIGON WILLIAM EDWARD	PA	54W	12
McGUIRE ANDY JR	IL	05E	89
McGUIRE DENNIS FRANCIS	PA	36W	53
McGUIRE FRANCIS MICHAEL	NJ	16E	125

NAME	STATE	PANEL NO.	LINE NO.
McGUIRE HARRY JOHN III	ME	20E	86
McGUIRE JAMES WILLIAM	CA	11W	69
McGUIRE JEFFREY DURON	KY	22E	58
McGUIRE JOHN EDDIE	MS	08W	115
McGUIRE JOHN WINCHESTER	NH	37E	11
McGUIRE MICHAEL JOSEPH	MO	12W	27
McGUIRE MITCHELL	OH	57E	29
McGUIRE MITCHELL LEE	NC	66W	10
McGUIRE PATRICK JOHN	NY	27E	11
McGUIRE RICHARD HAROLD	CA	20W	1
McGUIRE TIMOTHY PATRICK	IL	65W	12
McGUIRE TIMOTHY PAUL	CA	62W	14
McGUIRE WAYNE THOMAS	IA	42W	71
McGUIRE WILLIAM EDGAR	GA	36W	86
McGUIRK CHARLES ANTHONY	MO	09E	41
McGURTY TIMOTHY ARTHUR	WI	66E	12
McHALE JOHN BUNCE	NY	02E	136
McHAM RICHARD HUGH	CA	32E	38
McHANEY CARL JAMERSON	AL	29E	75
McHELLON GEORGE S	GA	03E	88
McHENRY EDWARD CURTIS	IL	36W	57
McHENRY JAMES CARTHELL	AR	35E	25
McHENRY PAUL VINCENT	PA	57W	30
McHUGH FRED C JR	MI	43E	28
McHUGH FREDERICK WILLIAM	ME	44W	4
McHUGH GARY ROBERT	IL	06W	27
McHUGH JOHN J	PA	36E	27
McHUGH TIMOTHY DAVID	PA	38E	7
McHUGO DONALD LYLE	WA	46E	21
McIE JOHNNY ELLIS	WV	21W	62
McILRAVY RONALD DEAN	SD	24E	35
McILROY DOUGLAS STEVEN	MI	34E	9
McILROY PATRICK C	MI	46E	21
McILVAIN EDWARD M III	PA	11E	88
McILVOY JAMES LEE	MI	33E	4
McILVOY JOSEPH RONALD	KY	22W	91
McILWEE JAMES R	VA	08E	68
McINERNEY PATRICK M	AK	29W	21
McINERNEY RICHARD NASH	NY	16E	63
McINERNY ROGER JAMES JR	MN	12W	72
McINNIS DALE RICHARD	SD	05E	13
McINNIS HENRY DAVID	MS	20E	78
McINNIS JOHN TERRY	NC	44W	58
McINNIS THEODORE VALENTI	CA	45E	59
McINTIRE DON RAY	OK	13W	20
McINTIRE HERMAN LEROY	IL	39W	22
McINTIRE SCOTT WINSTON	NM	02W	85
McINTIRE WALTER EDWIN JR	MI	04E	51
McINTOSH CHARLES GLENN	OH	09E	70
McINTOSH DONALD RAY	IN	13W	4
McINTOSH DONALD WILLIAM	KS	06W	46
McINTOSH ESTILL R	KY	10W	15
McINTOSH IAN		06W	79
McINTOSH JAMES CRABB	NY	13E	69
McINTOSH JOHN ARTHUR	MA	37E	41
McINTOSH JOHN RANDOLPH	WV	45W	15
McINTOSH RANDALL LEE	AZ	24E	100
McINTOSH RICHARD ROBERT	VA	19W	80
McINTOSH ROBERT A	FL	29W	71
McINTOSH ROBERT JAMES	IL	15W	18
McINTOSH RONALD	KY	31W	12
McINTOSH WALTER LESLI JR	IL	23E	120
McINTOSH WILLIE EDWARD	FL	16W	59
McINTURF SAMUEL DUANE	OH	41E	42
McINTYRE ARTHUR JAMES	MA	28W	28
McINTYRE DAVID ALLEN	OH	15W	54
McINTYRE DUNCAN B	CA	37W	23
McINTYRE GREGORY	NJ	40E	66
McINTYRE HOMER CLEO JR	DC	01E	60
McINTYRE JAMES ANTHONY	NY	05W	91
McINTYRE RAYMOND NEAL	OH	57W	23
McINTYRE ROBERT LEWIS	TX	23E	116
McIVER ALEXANDER	CA	01W	13
McJIMSEY WILLIAM ROBERT	CA	42E	22
McJUNKIN ROBERT TAYLOR	TN	52W	39
McJUNKIN RONALD LEE	OH	24E	35
McKAIN BOBBY LYN	KS	54E	27
McKAY DAVID GEORGE	CA	09W	8
McKAY EUGENE HENRY III	FL	05W	28
McKAY GERALD EUGENE	IL	11W	59
McKAY GERALD OTTO	KS	01E	132
McKAY GILMAN WILLIAM	NJ	12E	11
McKAY HOMER EUGENE	TX	37E	64
McKAY JOHN ROLAND JR	SC	15E	25
McKEAGUE GREGORY DEAN	MI	11E	41
McKEAN GUY EDWIN JR	NM	16W	102
McKEATHON DWIGHT PINZA	MI	20W	88
McKECHNIE DANIEL LEE	CA	38W	53
McKECHNIE JAMES ALLEN	ME	28W	13
McKEE CHARLIE MEARL	OH	26E	76
McKEE DAVID LEROY	IN	23W	113
McKEE DONALD WAYNE	IL	12W	39
McKEE JACK ROGER	CA	35E	76
McKEE JAMES EVERETT	TN	32W	15
McKEE JULIAN ALLAN	MO	16E	95
McKEE KENNETH DALE	MI	31E	14
McKEE LARRY WILLIAM	OH	04W	88
McKEE MILFORD GERALD	KY	23E	62
McKEE RICHARD CHARLES JR	WI	16E	22
McKEE ROBERT EARL	KY	18E	27
McKEE THOMAS EUGENE	CA	23E	21
McKEE WALTER ROY	FL	45W	15
McKEE WESLEY RAYMOND	OK	20E	67
McKEEL BILLY W	NC	14E	17
McKEEN GERALD CLAUDE	IA	11E	9
McKEEVER LEROY	MO	62E	21
McKEEVER MICHAEL EDWARD	MN	40E	75
McKELLAR DENNIS ALVIN	MI	11E	103
McKELLIP ROBERT JR	NY	57E	7
McKELLIPS RANDOLPH BURNS	FL	05W	132
McKELVEY JAMES DANIEL	AL	65W	12
McKELVEY WILLIAM R	PA	01W	128
McKENDRICK GARY RAYMOND	FL	50W	8
McKENNA JOHN MICHAEL	IL	17W	124
McKENNA KENNETH R JR	IL	09W	46
McKENNA NELSON WILLIAM	NY	31E	15
McKENNA ROBERT CHARLES	MI	16E	63
McKENNAN CLIFFORD ABDUL	NJ	06E	26
McKENNEY KENNETH DEWEY	MA	07E	62
McKENNEY NORMAN LAFOREST	ME	59W	9
McKENNEY PATRICK MICKAEL	MS	15E	121
McKENZIE DAVID DAYLE	MI	02E	35
McKENZIE DONALD FRANK	NC	37W	83
McKENZIE DOUGLAS N II	CA	43E	58
McKENZIE EDWARD AUSTIN	VT	47W	2
McKENZIE JACKIE RAY	GA	25W	12
McKENZIE JAMES ALLEN	CA	31E	59
McKENZIE JAMES CALVIN	CA	25E	106
McKENZIE JERALD THOMAS	TX	47W	50
McKENZIE JOHNNY RAY	GA	18W	96
McKENZIE LARRY DEAN	MN	23W	56
McKENZIE PAUL	NC	04W	126
McKENZIE RICHARD DOUGLAS	RI	22W	5
McKENZIE RICHARD WAYNE	CA	41E	26
McKENZIE WAYNE ROBERT	CT	20E	122
McKENZIE WENDELL HOWARD	OH	49W	40
McKENZIE WILLIE JAMES	GA	42W	58
McKEON JAMES PATRICK	NH	32W	28
McKEON JOSEPH THOMAS JR	IL	20E	32
McKERNS THOMAS PATRICK	PA	18W	3
McKIBBAN MICHAEL JAMES	OR	35W	17
McKIBBEN LARRY SIMS	TX	54E	13
McKIBBEN RAY	GA	37W	52
McKIBBEN WILLIAM RUSSELL	IA	11W	51
McKIBBIN HUGH R JR	VA	36E	79
McKIDDY GARY LEE	OH	11W	115
McKIE JACOB	SC	39W	9
McKIERNAN TIMOTHY JAMES	CA	35E	56
McKIETHAN DONALD FRANCIS	OH	03W	90
McKILLIP MERRIL ANDREW	HI	15E	15
McKILLOP LESLIE WAYNE	IN	25W	78
McKILLOP WILLIAM DION	OH	04E	25
McKIM EDWARD ALTON	TX	36E	27
McKIM WILLIAM RITCHIE	NJ	05E	35
McKINLEY ALLEN	IN	38E	35
McKINLEY GERALD WAYNE	CT	01E	99
McKINLEY JAMES MARION	FL	28W	83
McKINLEY LEVERNE WILLIAM	AR	02E	68
McKINLEY PATRICK JAMES	MI	35E	77
McKINLEY PAUL BLOUNT	TX	30E	64
McKINLEY STEPHEN WILLIAM	CA	34W	35
McKINLEY WAYNE HOUSTON	GA	64E	17
McKINNELL RICHARD LEE	KS	23E	5
McKINNEY ALBERT W JR	CA	36W	78
McKINNEY BERNARD B JR	WV	38E	35
McKINNEY CECIL CURTIS	TX	41W	14
McKINNEY CHARLES ANTHONY	LA	56W	37
McKINNEY CHARLES MICHAEL	TN	17E	126
McKINNEY CLEMIE	OH	02W	136
McKINNEY DALLAS ERVIN JR	NC	26W	26
McKINNEY DAVID LEE	VA	38E	35
McKINNEY DWIGHT A JR	MI	10W	90
McKINNEY EUGENE PHILLIP	MO	46E	9
McKINNEY FORREST ADRIAN	OH	29E	84
McKINNEY GERALD LEE	PA	30E	64
McKINNEY HOLLIS RAY JR	MS	25E	88
McKINNEY HUGH RUFUS	NY	32W	45
McKINNEY IVORY LEE	FL	11W	105
McKINNEY JAMES ODAS	LA	08E	53
McKINNEY JERRY LAYNE	NC	17E	126
McKINNEY JOSEPH STANLEY	WV	35E	17
McKINNEY LARRY ROBERT	IN	39E	76
McKINNEY MICHAEL GEORGE	LA	04W	33
McKINNEY NEIL BERNARD	IN	01E	28
McKINNEY RAYMOND BRUCE	KY	38W	60
McKINNEY RICHARD HENRY	NY	50W	36
McKINNEY ROBERT DALE	IN	03W	62
McKINNEY RONALD EUGENE	CA	18E	31
McKINNEY RONALD GENE	TX	04E	21
McKINNEY THOMAS ALAN	SC	11W	38
McKINNEY WESLEY JUNIOR	FL	33E	30
McKINNIE CHARLES W JR	FL	18E	103
McKINNIE HERMAN	GA	40E	26
McKINNIS CLARENCE EARL	MI	05E	133
McKINNON BOBBY RAY	MS	33E	73
McKINNON CLARENCE LEE	FL	33W	42
McKINNON JACK WILEY JR	CA	33E	30
McKINNON LARRY DEE	CA	22E	89
McKINNON TITUS JR	FL	12E	23
McKINSEY GERALD LEROY JR	CA	35E	8
McKINSON MICHAEL JAMES	IL	04E	48
McKINSTRY JAMES J JR	CA	52E	22
McKINZIE THOMAS LEON	OK	41W	70
McKITTRICK JAMES CLIFFORD	SC	22E	8
McKNIGHT GEORGE PARKER	LA	04E	13
McKNIGHT JAMES BRUCE	NV	33W	87
McKNIGHT JOSEPH PATRICK	MN	25W	79
McKNIGHT MATTHEW OWEN	FL	28E	37
McKNIGHT PAUL DAVID	PA	20W	80
McKNIGHT THOMAS EDWIN	NE	64E	7
McKNIGHT WILLIAM JR	NY	46W	52
McKOY LARRY D	NC	21W	109
McKOY WILLIAM OTHELLO	NC	29E	91
McLAIN JAY DARWIN	ID	21E	6
McLAIN JOHNIE WAYNE	NC	09E	100
McLAMB HARRY LAWRENCE	GA	09W	65
McLAREN ROBERT DALE	KS	01W	49
McLARNON THOMAS THEODORE	VA	01E	128
McLAUGHLIN ARTHUR VINCENT JR	MA	01W	96
McLAUGHLIN DANIEL P JR	MN	34E	84
McLAUGHLIN FRANCIS	VA	19W	62
McLAUGHLIN FREDERICK J	MA	32W	8
McLAUGHLIN JAMES BRUCE	ME	04W	129
McLAUGHLIN JAMES PAUL	CA	27E	10
McLAUGHLIN JOHN BERNARD	RI	01E	63
McLAUGHLIN JOHN ROBERT	PA	25W	51
McLAUGHLIN KIRK ALVIS	CA	11E	103
McLAUGHLIN LARRY HOLMES	NC	33E	37
McLAUGHLIN MARK MICHAEL	MA	15E	59
McLAUGHLIN MICHAEL PAUL	WA	48E	31
McLAUGHLIN OLEN BURKE	FL	23E	30
McLAUGHLIN PETER FRANCIS	PA	21W	94
McLAUGHLIN RUSSELL FRANK	WV	29E	97
McLAUGHLIN THOMAS MICHAE	NJ	23E	30
McLAUGHLIN WILLIAM F	MA	17W	38
McLAUGHLIN WILLIAM LAWRE	CA	13E	93
McLAUGHLIN WILLIAM LEE	PA	42W	68
McLAUREN CHARLES WILLIAM	LA	09W	85
McLAURIN CHARLES LONNELL	NC	51E	48
McLAURIN WILLIE JAMES	MS	07W	121
McLAWHORN CURTIS RAY	NC	23E	108
McLAY JOHN JACOB JR	PA	35W	11
McLEAN ALEX LEON	MD	17W	35
McLEAN DONALD KENT	MI	33W	80
McLEAN JAMES HENRY	CA	01E	87
McLEAN JAMES McMUARRY	MI	32E	39

NAME	STATE	PANEL NO.	LINE NO.
McLEAN RODNEY W	NY	28E	56
McLEAN RONALD WALSH	CA	23W	113
McLEAN TERRY R	MI	06E	76
McLEAN TIMOTHY L	OH	54W	3
McLEAN WILLIAM EDWARD	OH	05W	5
McLEARY ORVAL WADE	MO	56E	13
McLEESE KENNETH RICHARD	NE	19W	33
McLEISH CHARLES EDWARD	WI	08W	128
McLELLAN ARTHUR CHARLES	CT	47E	24
McLELLAN EMMETT DENEEN	IL	49W	25
McLELLAN JIMMY LEE	CA	24W	9
McLELLAN JOHN MALGER	FL	16W	70
McLELLAN STUART MURRAY	OH	47E	35
McLELLAND MARVIN EDWARD	CA	59W	10
McLEMORE DAVID EUGENE	TX	17E	9
McLEMORE JAMES ROBERT	TN	05E	89
McLEMORE JOHN WILSON JR	CA	04W	68
McLEMORE JOSEPH	OH	29E	39
McLEMORE TAYLOR HENRY	AL	21E	49
McLEMORE TILGHMAN RICHAR	FL	56E	14
McLENDON KENNETH HAYES	TX	15W	120
McLENDON MICHAEL RYAN	SC	10E	87
McLENDON RALPH WERNER	GA	50W	14
McLENNAN GARY ALFRED	MI	23E	102
McLENNAN ROY DEWAYNE	TX	19W	108
McLEOD ARTHUR EDWARD	NY	05W	100
McLEOD CHARLES WILLIAM	AL	18W	84
McLEOD DAVID VANCE JR	FL	01W	118
McLEOD LAMAR	AL	07W	134
McLEOD PATRICK ALAN	WA	14W	108
McLEOD ROBERT LEE	CA	30E	58
McLESTER SHERMAN DOUGLAS	AL	47W	50
McLHERN MICHAEL SHEA	IN	04W	97
McLIN LOUIS WILLIAM III	AL	13W	11
McLOUD DOUGLAS LYLE	NY	31E	51
McLOUGHLIN MILES JOSEPH	NY	17E	10
McLOUGHLIN ROBERT A JR	TN	56W	37
McMACKEN LESLIE T JR	CO	23W	29
McMACKINS REUBEN CARL JR	KY	49E	54
McMAHAN CHARLES DARNELL	LA	10W	27
McMAHAN CHARLES LARRY	SC	31W	12
McMAHAN DANIEL JACKSON	OH	09W	35
McMAHAN JOHN EDWARD	NC	07E	30
McMAHAN ROBERT CHARLES	IL	39E	36
McMAHAN THOMAS EDWARD JR	SC	02E	97
McMAHON CHARLES JR	MA	01W	124
McMAHON DOUGLAS DUANE	CA	48E	18
McMAHON FREDERICK ALFRED	MA	19E	39
McMAHON JAMES EDWARD	MD	22W	113
McMAHON JAMES HAROLD	MA	22W	5
McMAHON JOHN THOMAS	CA	21E	75
McMAHON LAWRENCE VINCENT	NY	10E	117
McMAHON RAYMOND PAUL	PA	09W	9
McMAHON THOMAS JOHN	MD	26E	49
McMAHON THOMAS JOSEPH	ME	29W	81
McMAHON THOMAS MARK JR	MI	15W	29
McMAHON THOMAS W JR	MO	22E	111
McMAHON TIMOTHY JAMES	WA	10E	114
McMAHON WILLIAM LAWRENCE	OH	40E	27
McMAINS DONALD HENRY JR	CA	20W	119
McMAKIN WALLACE THOMSON	SC	19W	19
McMANN ALVIN CHARLES JR	MI	17E	94
McMANUS CHARLES VERNE	AL	03E	60
McMANUS FRANK JOSEPH	NY	43W	18
McMANUS JERRY DOYNE	LA	52E	9
McMANUS JOHN	NY	29W	47
McMANUS MARK LAWRENCE	CA	20W	59
McMANUS MICHAEL GEORGE	MI	03E	117
McMANUS ROBERT FRANCIS	NJ	48W	1
McMANUS TRUMAN JOSEPH	CT	60W	20
McMASTER GLENN LEON	PA	32E	39
McMASTER JOHN WILLIAM	CA	27E	74
McMASTER MICHAEL LEE	ID	21W	26
McMASTER ROBERT PAUL	WI	07W	13
McMASTERS CHARLES ANTHON	CA	13E	35
McMASTERS JAMES THOMAS	IL	50E	6
McMATH DAVID LEE	IA	24E	104
McMEANS DENNIE	MI	23W	66
McMELLON ARTHUR NELLO	WV	03E	120
McMICAN M D	WA	01E	129
McMICKEN HARRY CARLYLE	WV	23E	112
McMILLAN BRUCE FRANCIS	CA	49E	24
McMILLAN DONALD FRANKLIN	KY	06E	76
McMILLAN EDDIE LEE JR	MS	47W	50
McMILLAN GERALD WAYNE	LA	28E	41
McMILLAN JAMES M JR	OK	12W	72
McMILLEN RONALD DEAN	IL	15W	64
McMILLIAN ROBERT DAVID	NC	43E	9
McMILLIAN SOLOMON LEON	AL	51W	27
McMILLIN DONNELL DEAN	AR	05E	109
McMILLIN GARY DON	MO	06W	43
McMILLIN ROBERT ALLEN	SC	16W	43
McMILLION CHARLES EUGENE	OH	23W	16
McMILLON JACKIE	WV	03E	46
McMINN DANNY LEE	CA	15E	34
McMINN RICHARD LEE	PA	11W	25
McMONEGAL JOHN JOSEPH JR	PA	25E	64
McMORRIS JIMMIE LUE	PA	29E	101
McMORROW JAMES JOSEPH	ME	16W	53
McMULLAN EDWARD MICHAEL	NY	20E	103
McMULLEN GENE SMEDLEY	PA	09E	29
McMULLEN GEORGE E III	GA	01W	128
McMULLEN LYMAN ALLISTER	OR	10E	17
McMULLIN CHARLES ERNEST	MO	62E	9
McMURDO JAMES ALFRED	CA	21E	63
McMURPHY JAY DARRELL	CA	45E	4
McMURRAY FRED HOWELL JR	SC	48E	45
McMURRAY JOHNNIE RAY	AL	27E	66
McMURRAY ODIE C	GA	25W	13
McMURRAY PETER HINCHMAN	MA	19W	125
McMURRY RODERICK DANE	WA	21E	29
McMURTREY WILLIAM NEWTON	AL	46W	6
McMURTRY RALPH DAVID	TN	27W	76
McNABB ALFRED LEE	IL	36E	80
McNABB DOUGLAS MEREDITH	MI	40E	77
McNABB JERRY WAYNE	AL	08E	100
McNABB JOHN JOSEPH	MA	31E	15
McNABB RICHARD DALE	FL	20W	30
McNAC DONALD CHARLES	FL	45E	13
McNAIR WILLIAM TERREL	TX	18W	105
McNAIR WILLIE CHARLES	MS	32E	25
McNALLY ARTHUR GERALD	NY	11E	84
McNALLY EDWARD	WY	36E	26
McNALLY EUGENE FLOYD	MT	10W	53
McNALLY HARRY MERLE	CA	28E	85
McNALLY JAMES WILLIAM	CA	01E	32
McNALLY PAUL FRANCIS	MA	02E	1
McNAMAR JIM CARL	ID	50E	32
McNAMARA DONALD WOODWARD	IA	23E	102
McNAMARA EDWARD MICHAEL	IL	63W	19
McNAMARA JOHN FRANCIS	NY	28E	41
McNAMARA WILLIAM JAMES	PA	65W	12
McNAMARA WILLIAM JAMES	MA	30W	68
McNARY FRANKLIN DELANO	ID	21E	98
McNAUGHTON MICHAEL DEAN	OH	42W	9
McNAY GUY ECKMAN JR	KY	20E	47
McNEAL MICHAEL E	WA	16E	106
McNEAL RICHARD	TN	26W	26
McNEAR TERRY LEE	WV	51W	20
McNEARNEY PATRICK VICTOR	CA	59E	28
McNEELY JAMES WILLIAM	CT	03E	116
McNEES DWIGHT ALLEN	MI	26W	55
McNEES GEORGE WILLIAM	KY	05E	66
McNEES RONALD HARVEY	CA	01E	131
McNEIL ALLEN W	UT	59E	11
McNEIL BRUCE ALAN	LA	06W	29
McNEIL DONALD K	WA	57E	29
McNEIL FREDDIE LEE	NC	56W	6
McNEIL HAROLD LOYD	TX	01E	61
McNEIL JOSEPH DANIEL	MA	62W	15
McNEIL SYLVESTER	IL	23E	21
McNEIL WILLIE DAVIS	MS	16W	89
McNEILL CLARENCE LEON	NC	33W	66
McNEILL DANIEL DIXON	NC	22W	59
McNEILL KENNETH REX	MI	23W	46
McNEILL LONNIE EARL	NC	37E	26
McNEILL MICHAEL SIDNEY	OK	01W	93
McNEILL RONALD PATRICK	ND	08W	83
McNEILL WILLIE B	NC	38E	70
McNEILLY JAMES H	NY	22W	113
McNEILLY RONALD WILLIAM	CA	14E	130
McNEISH RICHARD LEE	PA	28E	61
McNELIS FRANK CHARLES JR	TX	24E	36
McNELIS PATRICK ROBERT	PA	24W	25
McNELLIS ANTHONY FRANCIS	PA	51W	7
McNELLY WILLIAM ROBERT	CA	21W	62
McNETT JOE BILLY	IA	06W	54
McNEW BRIAN RICHARD	MI	24W	46
McNEW RALPH DENNIS	KY	15E	121
McNICHOLS RICHARD FRANCI	PA	09E	54
McNICOL GARY DOUGLAS	WV	13W	119
McNINCH PHILIP AARON	OR	17E	10
McNISH JAMES RONALD	TN	33W	66
McNULTY CHARLES RICHARD	VA	10W	53
McNULTY JOSEPH DENNIS	MA	10E	121
McNULTY MILTON KEITH	CA	02E	46
McNULTY WILLIAM FRANCIS	NY	08W	98
McNUTT CHARLES THOMAS	MA	50W	15
McNUTT FRANK ELLIOTT	FL	08W	23
McNUTT WINDOL WILSON	MO	03W	101
McPARLANE MICHAEL JOSEPH	NY	23W	56
McPETERS MICHAEL EDGAR	NC	04W	100
McPHAIL FRANKLIN LLOYD	CA	42W	49
McPHAIL MORRIS GENE	MI	32E	32
McPHAIL WILLIAM THOMAS	TN	65E	14
McPHEARSON JAMES CARL	CA	42E	5
McPHEE DONALD CAMERON	MI	02E	133
McPHEE DOUGLAS WAYNE	FL	22W	67
McPHEE RANDY NEAL	CA	18E	125
McPHERSON ALFRED	SC	10E	109
McPHERSON DAVID LEE	OH	38E	8
McPHERSON DAVID MICHAEL	NC	14E	28
McPHERSON DENNIS CRAIG	SD	29E	75
McPHERSON EVERETT ALVIN	VA	06E	21
McPHERSON FRED LAWER	CA	04E	104
McPHERSON JAMES EDWARD	NC	47E	15
McPHERSON LARRY RANDALL	CA	35W	29
McPHERSON MICHAEL LEE	MI	10W	2
McPHERSON ROBERT ALAN	PA	53E	19
McPHERSON STANLEY W	NM	26E	93
McPHERSON WILLIAM JOSEPH	FL	08W	71
McPHERSON WILLIAM RICHAR	WV	03E	122
McPHETERS CHET EUGENE	FL	44E	51
McPHILLIPS JAMES CRAIG	IL	17W	113
McPIKE JAMES EDWIN	OH	20W	22
McQUADE ARTHUR F JR	RI	53E	5
McQUADE JAMES RUSSELL	WA	01W	40
McQUADE WILLIAM VICTOR	MI	24E	36
McQUAY ROGER DILLON	NE	38E	8
McQUEEN CLAUDE EDWARD	DC	54E	14
McQUEEN FREDDIE	NY	42W	58
McQUEER MICHAEL PATRICK	MI	16W	59
McQUINN BYRON DEAN	IA	31W	38
McQUINN LEONARD LLOYD JR	IA	10E	71
McRAE ADELBERT EARL	NY	36W	58
McRAE CHARLES EDWARD	NC	08E	63
McRAE DAVID EDWARD	GA	13E	6
McRAE DAVID LE ROY	WA	45W	16
McRAE JIMMIE LEFON	SC	46E	57
McRAE LAWRENCE JOSEPH	PA	53E	19
McRAE WILLIAM JOSEPH	MA	24E	96
McRAY WAYNE DABNEY	VA	13W	11
McREE JOHN HENRY	TN	09E	83
McREYNOLDS GEORGE WAYNE	TN	35E	77
McRIGHT ROGER LYNN	IL	15W	29
McROBERTS CLIFFORD WAYNE	CA	05E	13
McROBIE NORMAN WAYNE	MD	12E	122
McSHAN DOYLE ALLEN	TX	13E	28
McSORLEY ROB GEORGE		12W	107
McSTOOTS THOMAS HOWARD	KY	22W	34
McSTRAVICK RICHARD P JR	OR	14E	104
McSWAIN BAYNES BALLEW JR	TX	41W	41
McSWAIN HARVEY JOSEPH	OH	24E	115
McSWEENY RICHARD JOSEPH	PA	09E	124
McSWINE JOHN HENRY	MO	26W	33
McSWINEY CHARLES A JR	FL	01W	87
McTAGGART WILLIAM JAMES	CA	09W	80
McTEER JEFFERY CLARK	KS	36E	28
McTIER KENNETH CHARLES	PA	14W	39
McVAY JOHN EARL	AL	20E	2
McVAY RICHARD WAYNE	PA	13E	24
McVAY THOMAS MARTIN	OK	49E	35
McVEA ROBERT MINOR	TX	43W	40
McVEA WILLIE DEE	TX	38W	12
McVEY JOHN WESLEY	OK	64W	13
McVEY LA VOY DON	CO	13W	75

NAME	STATE	PANEL NO.	LINE NO.
McVEY MICHAEL LEE	OH	07W	79
McWATERS DALTON HUBERT	FL	56E	28
McWETHY EDGAR LEE JR	CO	22E	32
McWHINNEY HARRY DEWITT JR	PA	02W	50
McWHIRTER JAMES GILBERT	IL	52W	30
McWHORTER JAMES DAVID	MS	20E	76
McWHORTER JAMES ELMER	OR	19W	97
McWHORTER JERRY MONROE	OK	06E	40
McWILLIAMS FREDDIE	LA	27E	30
McWILLIAMS GEORGE LINWOOD	NJ	08E	82
McWILLIAMS RICHARD EUGEN	OK	04E	17
McWILLIAMS ROBERT H JR	PA	32E	94
McWILLIAMS ROY M	GA	14E	58
McWILLIAMS WILLIAM G III	VA	11E	109
McWRIGHT DALE STEPHEN	TX	39E	76
McWRIGHT EDWARD ARTHUR	TX	12E	75
McZEAL MARTIN ALLEN	NY	22W	81
NAASZ EMIL JOHN	MT	07W	40
NAASZ LARRY DUANE	MT	12E	104
NABBEN ARTHUR S	MN	05W	58
NABORS J C	OK	14E	87
NABORS PAUL HOWARD	OK	50W	8
NABOURS JIMMIE FLOYD	NM	09W	106
NABOZNIAK MYRON RICHARD	MI	07W	87
NACCA CARL JR	CA	05W	126
NACHTIGALL DAVID JOSEPH	NE	13W	49
NACY JOHN O		35W	13
NADAL BALDOMERO ARTURO	CA	18E	31
NADANY FRANK JOSEPH JR	PA	03E	9
NADEAU ERIC DARYL	ND	24W	112
NADEAU HAROLD BRADLEY	NY	07E	73
NADEAU LARRY JOSEPH	ME	04E	48
NADEAU PAUL ERNEST	NH	10E	68
NADEAU ROBERT JOHN	ME	16W	121
NADEAU ROLAND HAROLD	ME	20W	88
NADEAU THOMAS DENNIS	NH	49W	48
NADOLSKI ROBERT	PA	13E	106
NAFE TIMOTHY MARK	PA	34E	80
NAFFZIGER MARSHALL EDWARD	IL	03W	124
NAGATO YOSHIIWA	CA	09E	42
NAGEL GORDON LAVERN	WI	17W	42
NAGELKIRK DENNIS DALE	MI	39E	9
NAGENGAST CARL DELANE	CA	20E	68
NAGY JOHN PAUL	IL	45E	49
NAGY ROBERT JOSEPH	OH	28E	28
NAGY STEVEN	IN	20W	59
NAHAN JOHN BENEDICT III	MI	24E	73
NAHER STEPHEN CHARLES	PA	07W	59
NAHODIL DONALD A JR	PA	42E	54
NAIL GARY DEAN	KS	06E	80
NAIL ROBERT MELVIN	FL	21E	76
NAILE THOMAS GLEN	MO	28E	93
NAILEN JAMES PATRICK	AL	16E	114
NAILLON DANNY L	ID	10E	88
NAILS EDDIE LEE JR	FL	10W	8
NAIMO JOSEPH PETER JR	FL	44W	58
NAJAR ADAM SERNA	CA	53E	20
NAJAR ALFRED SATURN JR	TX	41E	12
NAJAR MIGUEL FERNANDO	TX	11E	26
NAJARIAN MICHAEL ANTHONY	CA	08E	61
NAJERA MANUEL CHICK JR	CA	04W	127
NAJMOLA JOHN HENRY	OH	03W	47
NAKASHIMA MICHAEL SEIJI	HI	25W	52
NAKASHIMO MASASHI	CA	04W	9
NAKAYAMA JIMMY D	ID	03E	88
NAKI WILLIAM III	HI	05W	46
NAKKERUD ARNOLD OLAF	WA	24E	56
NALEY RICHARD HERBERT	FL	54E	14
NALL CARL DAVID	OH	28W	73
NALL JOHN TRUMAN	AL	20W	8
NALLEY CHARLES THOMAS	OH	38W	51
NALLS JOHN LAURENCE	DC	24W	46
NALLY ROBERT GERALD	WA	16E	102
NAMER MARTIN YALE	NY	17W	103
NANCE CHARLES THOMAS	IL	49W	19
NANCE DAVID EUGENE	CA	09E	17
NANCE ELMER MASON	VA	61E	15
NANCE KENNETH EDWIN	CA	01W	123
NANCE LEWIS	NC	46W	6
NANCE PAUL MARION JR	NC	53E	38
NANCE RICHARD ALAN	TX	11E	105
NANCE SHIRL BRAD	UT	35W	49

NAME	STATE	PANEL NO.	LINE NO.
NANEY REID MC DONALD	NC	31W	12
NANSEL JAMES DAVID	WA	53W	44
NAPIER DARREL GENE	OH	28W	39
NAPIER DAVID LAWRENCE	VA	16W	23
NAPIER LEE ALLAN	NE	24W	68
NAPIER ROBERT WAYNE	PA	07W	71
NAPIER ZACK WILLIAM	OH	59W	10
NAPIERATA NORMAN JOSEPH	MA	10E	133
NAPIERSKIE DANIEL	CA	18W	117
NAPOLI DANIEL LUKE	OH	34W	1
NAPPER CHARLES CRAWFORD	TN	16W	43
NAQUIN SIMIN ADOLPH	LA	26E	49
NARAMORE DAVID ZOHLEEH JR	AL	58W	20
NARANJO DAVID JESUS	CA	04W	31
NARANJO MIGUEL ERNEST JR	CO	05E	91
NARCISSE ALVIN RAY	CA	34W	73
NARCISSE PAUL	LA	41W	49
NARD JAMES PETER III	MS	10E	114
NARDELLI ROBERT JOSEPH	CA	38E	57
NARUM THOMAS LEROY	ND	14E	50
NARVAEZ PAUL REYES	TX	22W	81
NARVAEZ-MARRERO ANDRES LU	PR	51E	41
NARVARTE PETER E JR	TX	32E	45
NASCHEK MARVIN JOEL	NY	38W	28
NASH ANTHONY PRESTON	SC	35W	77
NASH CALVIN CURTIS	IN	02W	134
NASH DAVID EUGENE	CA	58W	12
NASH DAVID PAUL	KY	35W	6
NASH DAVID ROBERTSON	NJ	10W	35
NASH GEORGE ALFRED JR	IN	26E	14
NASH JAMES ROBERT	NJ	09E	71
NASH JAMES ROBERT	CA	49E	54
NASH JOHN MICHEL	IN	06E	11
NASH PETER GARY	MA	35E	35
NASH THOMAS STEVEN	GA	48E	45
NASHAWATY RICHARD JOHN	MA	25E	107
NASS WINFORD ALLEN	NY	31W	12
NASSER ROBERT BENJAMIN	CA	12E	23
NASTOR TONY VALDEZ	CA	60W	20
NASWORTHY MALVIN LOWE JR	GA	07E	65
NATALE NICHOLAS ANTHONY	NY	63W	10
NATALE PATRICK HENRY	NY	51E	10
NATALIE RONALD JOHN	MI	09W	128
NATARTE ROBERT ORTOGERO	HI	05E	38
NATHAN JOHN ARTHUR	CA	03E	35
NATHAN RALPH EUGENE	AL	31W	83
NATHE MICHAEL LEO	MT	46W	61
NATION JIMMY LEE	TX	50W	44
NATIONS JERRY LEE	LA	32E	26
NATIONS MICHAEL CLAY	GA	10E	109
NATIONS ROY LEE	LA	25W	79
NATOLI JOSEPH R	PA	24E	36
NATZKE NICHOLAS LEE	WI	27E	1
NAU JAMES CHRISTIAN	OH	46W	43
NAUGHTON JOHN R JR	IL	16W	122
NAUGHTON THOMAS DANIEL JR	MI	22W	81
NAUGLE RUSSELL WAYNE	PA	39E	51
NAUSS BRENT BRITTEN	MI	18W	25
NAVA FRANCIS XAVIER	NM	10E	77
NAVA SALVADOR MARTINEZ	CA	18E	11
NAVARRETE JOB JR	NC	03W	38
NAVARRO ARMANDO SANCHEZ	TX	46W	49
NAVARRO CARMELO	NY	38W	28
NAVARRO DANIEL LEON	TX	56E	28
NAVARRO FRANK GEA	CT	60E	27
NAVARRO JAMES LEE	GA	29E	52
NAVARRO NICHOLAS LEON	CO	14E	87
NAVE BILLY JOE	TN	08E	101
NAVONE VICTOR CHARLES JR	CA	32W	15
NAWROCKI ROBERT DENNIS	IL	35E	25
NAWROSKY MICHAEL ROBERT	NJ	53W	29
NAYAR WALTER HODGKINGSON	OK	04W	7
NAYLOR DENNIS EUGENE	CA	38W	61
NAYLOR EDWARD REYNOLDS JR	CO	30E	102
NAYLOR EUGENE	KY	28E	51
NAYLOR GEORGE EDWARD	TN	31E	21
NAYLOR LYNN PATTINSON	CA	32W	28
NAYLOR RAYMOND LUKE	KY	05E	52
NAZABAL ARTURO ALBERTO JR	CA	19W	51
NAZARIO JUAN JOSE	PR	45E	26
NEACE DENNIE	KY	21E	24
NEAD ELWOOD FRANKLIN JR	AZ	10E	66

NAME	STATE	PANEL NO.	LINE NO.
NEAL ARTHUR DARNELL	OK	09W	112
NEAL BARNEY KING JR	OK	07W	56
NEAL BURNETT JR	TX	18E	96
NEAL CARY	NY	13E	93
NEAL CHARLES MARION JR	OH	18E	87
NEAL CHARLES OTTIS	TN	27E	85
NEAL CHARLIE THOMAS	GA	25W	53
NEAL DENNIS PAUL	FL	20W	81
NEAL DENNIS WADE	WA	11W	9
NEAL EDWARD LEON	TN	15W	19
NEAL HARVEY RAY	VA	08W	60
NEAL JAMES RICHARD	NC	38E	35
NEAL JOHN HALL JR	NJ	35E	25
NEAL JOHNNY LEONARD	IL	11E	58
NEAL JONATHAN	IL	49E	14
NEAL JOSEPH E R	NY	50W	39
NEAL KENNETH LAWRENCE	CA	46E	9
NEAL NELSON DENFIELD	IL	26E	56
NEAL REUBEN JAMES	PA	20E	9
NEAL ROBERT EUGENE	OH	13W	19
NEAL ROBERT JUNIOR	IL	40E	66
NEAL RONALD FORREST	OR	34W	28
NEAL RONALD KEITH	WV	18E	62
NEAL RONALD WAYNE	IN	45W	33
NEAL ROY WILLIAM	TN	64W	13
NEAL STEPHEN BROWNING	CA	16E	102
NEAL THOMAS MARTIN	CT	32W	3
NEAL WILBERT HOYT JR	TN	48W	34
NEAL WILLIAM EDWARD	IN	04W	73
NEAL WILLIAM RICHARD	TX	47E	24
NEALE CHRISTOPHER JONATHA	CT	03W	22
NEALIS TOMMY R	KY	01W	128
NEALON JOHN MICHAEL	MA	32E	55
NEARY JOHN RUNYON II	TX	53E	39
NEAS STEPHEN EDWARD	WA	37W	68
NEASBITT LARRY DOUGLAS	TX	40E	45
NEASHAM ROBERT DEAN	OR	41W	60
NEAVES CLAYTON WILLARD	OH	09W	44
NEAVOR GARY ARNOLD	IA	24W	97
NEBEL THOMAS ALLEN	IA	23W	10
NEBLETT LYNELL	VA	27E	31
NECE HERBERT JAMES	OH	12E	130
NEDD HEYWARD WINDELL	SC	09E	5
NEDEDOG EMILIO NINAISEN	GM	04W	10
NEDERLK MICHAEL ALEXANDER	NY	31E	93
NEE PETER MARY	MA	28W	99
NEEDHAM RUSSELL DEAN	NE	20E	86
NEEF FREDERICK RICHARD	MD	06W	86
NEEL CHARLES HERBERT JR	CO	48E	18
NEEL FRANKLIN WYLIE	WV	15W	87
NEEL ROBERT RAY	TX	11W	86
NEELD BOBBY GENE	NM	35W	36
NEELEY DENNIS PAUL	IN	14E	16
NEELEY DONALD LEE	CO	17W	129
NEELEY EDDIE JOE	GA	36W	17
NEELEY LOWRENZO	GA	14W	58
NEELEY MARVIN EUGENE	IN	09W	24
NEELEY WILLIAM MERRITT	IL	51E	24
NEELY BILLY JOE	MS	15W	67
NEELY DAN LEE	AL	42E	22
NEELY DONALD LEE	OK	16E	124
NEELY JAMES ELGIN	TX	47W	51
NEELY PAUL JAMESON	DC	26W	66
NEER GERALD KING	KS	22W	67
NEESON BRUCE ROBERT	MI	09W	24
NEFF DAVID RUSSELL	OH	25W	79
NEFF LARRY LEE	PA	51E	10
NEFF PHILLIP ERNEST	PA	32E	60
NEGER ROGER LEE	CT	50E	30
NEGRANZA MARIANO R JR	CA	06E	91
NEGRINI WILLIAM LODI	CA	25W	13
NEGRO DANIEL LEE	MI	22E	46
NEGRON VICTOR MANUEL	NJ	26E	93
NEGRON-RODRIGUEZ JOSE	PR	04E	121
NEGRON-RODRIGUEZ MIGUEL A	PR	49W	10
NEGUS JACK THOMAS	MI	10W	65
NEHER ROBERT WILLIAM	OR	35E	62
NEHL JOSEPH ROBERT	MN	08W	60
NEHRING DENNIS DEAN	MN	37E	64
NEHRING LARRY JOSEPH	IA	14E	2
NEIBAUER ALEXANDER DUANE	MT	27W	82
NEIDLINGER JAMES JOSEPH	NY	45W	63

NAME	STATE	PANEL NO.	LINE NO.
NEIDRICK JACK LEE	PA	06E	17
NEIL SAMUEL THOMAS JR	MI	54E	38
NEILL JOE MELVIN	IL	40E	66
NEILL JOHN MAUTZ	OH	05W	65
NEILL LARRY WAYNE	TN	33W	42
NEILL TERRY JOSEPH PATRIC	PA	55W	22
NEIMAN GARY PRESTON	PA	26W	34
NEISESS JAMES A	WA	27E	40
NEISLAR DAVID PHILLIP	OK	32W	66
NEISS TERRY DUANE	MT	01W	20
NEISWENDER DANIEL LYNN	CA	38W	45
NEISZ CHARLES WARREN JR	VA	25E	17
NELLANS WILLIAM LEE	IN	26E	85
NELMS DANIEL EARNEST	TN	10W	82
NELMS PATRICK IRVIN	MO	39W	18
NELMS WILLIAM GARY JR	NC	18W	8
NELSEN DEAN RICHARD	OR	23E	120
NELSON ALBERT OSCAR JR	CA	24W	69
NELSON ALLAN JOSEPH JR	CA	13E	1
NELSON ARCHIE LEE JR	FL	48W	19
NELSON BENJAMIN ROY JR	CA	06W	99
NELSON BILLY DEAN	NE	09E	47
NELSON BOYD JEFFERY	CA	38E	8
NELSON BRADLEY ALBERT	OR	18E	80
NELSON BRUCE ANTHONY	MO	39E	51
NELSON BRUCE JEFFREY	MN	46W	19
NELSON CHARLES	AL	22W	5
NELSON CHARLES CARTER	MN	30E	30
NELSON CLIFFORD DALE	IA	23E	120
NELSON CLYDE KEITH	PA	01W	62
NELSON CURTIS LEE	NY	02W	5
NELSON DANA EDWARD	WV	28W	73
NELSON DANIEL ALAN	MI	40E	27
NELSON DANIEL CARTER	LA	26W	92
NELSON DANIEL EUGENE JR	CA	43W	56
NELSON DANIEL IVAN	MN	21E	18
NELSON DANIEL RAYMOND	RI	22W	123
NELSON DARROL OREN	AL	07E	126
NELSON DAVID BRUCE	MI	22E	120
NELSON DAVID CHARLES	NY	23W	22
NELSON DAVID ELLSWORTH	MI	19W	114
NELSON DAVID LINDFORD	WA	04W	25
NELSON DAVID REID	KS	53W	11
NELSON DAVID THOMAS	MN	27W	76
NELSON DENNIS LEROY	MN	07E	90
NELSON DENNIS ORVILLE	MN	16E	54
NELSON DENNIS WAYNE	NY	13W	2
NELSON DICKIE OWENS	SC	52E	41
NELSON DONALD CARL	WA	31E	93
NELSON DONALD ERWIN	MI	19W	121
NELSON DONALD EUGENE	CO	66E	12
NELSON DONALD LAWRENCE	CA	38E	8
NELSON DONALD LEE	MI	01E	52
NELSON DUANE MICHAEL	IA	02E	116
NELSON EARL	TN	05W	50
NELSON EARNEST GLYNN	MS	23E	13
NELSON EUGENE	SC	44E	51
NELSON FRANK WILLIAM JR	DE	31W	13
NELSON FRANKLIN KING	TX	08W	111
NELSON FRED ARTHUR	MI	16W	14
NELSON GARY NELS	CA	08E	7
NELSON GEORGE WASHINGTON	LA	31E	69
NELSON GRADY RAY	OR	38W	45
NELSON HARLAN CLAUDE	TX	16E	41
NELSON HAROLD BARNETT	MA	07E	134
NELSON HENRY J	CT	13E	54
NELSON HOMER DOUGLAS	WV	03E	3
NELSON HOWARD HAMILTON	MS	03W	82
NELSON HUGH REAVIS JR	NC	08E	12
NELSON JAMES LESLIE	MN	16W	45
NELSON JAMES RAYMOND	MI	21E	91
NELSON JAN HOUSTON	FL	12W	124
NELSON JOHN CHARLES	PA	25W	107
NELSON JOHN EDWARD	CA	49E	45
NELSON JOHN THOMAS	IL	28E	85
NELSON JULIUS DALE	VA	07W	44
NELSON LARRY	LA	04E	79
NELSON LARRY DOUGLAS	MI	48W	46
NELSON LARRY THOMAS	MO	09E	90
NELSON LAWSON DWIGHT	FL	28W	93
NELSON LEON GROVER	CA	22E	92
NELSON LEROY	AL	12W	114
NELSON LEROY A	IL	24E	9
NELSON LEWIS CHARLES	WA	52E	41
NELSON LOUIS HOWARD	MT	55E	24
NELSON MARSHALL DAYLE	TX	44E	10
NELSON MAX ALVIN	MN	41E	11
NELSON MELVIN DOUGLAS	MN	37W	83
NELSON MICHAEL ROY	CA	18E	6
NELSON MILES HENRY	GA	15E	17
NELSON NOEL STEVEN	MN	22E	89
NELSON ORLAN MARVIN	WI	31W	13
NELSON PAUL ALBERT	MN	20W	103
NELSON PAUL ARTHUR	MN	28W	73
NELSON PAUL VINCENT	NJ	23W	29
NELSON RAY LA GRANDE	MT	03E	101
NELSON RAYFORD	GA	48W	34
NELSON REX FRANKLIN JR	MI	25W	41
NELSON RICHARD ALLEN	MI	29E	97
NELSON RICHARD CRAWFORD	PA	43E	29
NELSON RICHARD DEAN	WA	10W	82
NELSON RICHARD WILLIAM	NY	19W	64
NELSON ROBERT ALLEN	IL	23E	112
NELSON ROBERT CHARLES	CT	23E	5
NELSON ROBERT DWAYNE	TN	27E	74
NELSON ROBERT JOSEPH	MA	39E	23
NELSON ROBERT MELVIN	FL	19W	72
NELSON ROBERT THOMAS	AL	03W	130
NELSON ROBERT WARREN	NE	24E	9
NELSON ROBERT WILLIAM	ID	07W	100
NELSON ROGER MILLER	SD	48E	45
NELSON ROGER THEODORE	MN	03E	88
NELSON ROGER TILTON	AL	44E	61
NELSON RONALD ELWOOD	MN	04E	57
NELSON ROY LANE	TX	03W	5
NELSON RUSSEL COURTNEY	MN	05W	31
NELSON SANFORD LEWIS	SC	13E	16
NELSON SCOTT THOMAS	CO	20W	103
NELSON STEPHAN JOSEPH	MN	26E	29
NELSON STEPHEN CARL	MT	18E	87
NELSON STEVEN HOWARD	MN	31E	76
NELSON SYLVESTER JR	TX	20W	105
NELSON TERRANCE WILLIAM	CA	20E	91
NELSON THEODORE RUSSELL	MN	20E	33
NELSON THOMAS LEON	MN	32E	52
NELSON TONEY JR	FL	26E	72
NELSON VERNON LEE	WI	34W	52
NELSON WAYNE HERMAN	NY	08E	72
NELSON WILLARD EDWARD	CA	35E	77
NELSON WILLIAM DE WITT	CA	39W	28
NELSON WILLIAM HUMPHREY	MI	09E	48
NELSON WILLIAM IRVIN II	FL	17E	37
NEMCHICK MICHAEL JOSEPH	PA	05E	61
NEMCHIK JOHN JOSEPH JR	NJ	20E	34
NEMETH ANTHONY JOHN	IL	56E	28
NEMETH JOSEPH JR	OH	35W	17
NEMETH JOSEPH STEVEN	IN	12W	118
NEMETH MICHAEL	NJ	38E	79
NERAD WALTER JOSEPH JR	OH	17E	74
NERECK LAWRENCE THOMAS	FL	16E	3
NERINI THOMAS HAROLD	IN	65W	12
NERIS-APONTE JOAQUIN	PR	63W	9
NERVEZA DELMORE BYRON	HI	03E	135
NERVIE KENNETH JOHN	OH	41W	10
NESBIT ROGER CHARLES	MI	32W	27
NESBITT CALVIN IAN	NY	52E	22
NESBITT HASKER LEE JR	NC	63E	15
NESBITT JOHNNY B	GA	46W	19
NESBITT JOSEPH	TN	27W	26
NESKE JOSEPH EDWIN	NY	30W	68
NESMITH LEROY	PA	16W	125
NESMITH NEWMAN RAY	GA	01E	37
NESOVANOVIC JOHN LAURENCE	WI	07W	107
NESS LESTER MILTON	PA	35E	48
NESS MICHAEL LESTER	OH	32W	8
NESS PATRICK LAWRENCE	MN	25E	34
NESSELROTTE JAMES MICHAEL	OH	22W	92
NESSET DAVID JON	ND	50E	51
NESTER ROGER	KY	52E	41
NESTERAK NORMAN LOUIS	PA	18W	29
NESTICH FRANK JOSEPH	OH	60W	3
NESTICO PHILIP FRANK	CT	61W	15
NESTLERODE GEORGE HERBERT	PA	42E	53
NESTOR FRANK RODNEY	NJ	19W	80
NETH DANNY A	WA	05E	121
NETH FRED ALBERT	KS	04E	75
NETHERLAND ROGER MORTON	PA	19E	84
NETHERLY ARTANZIE	CA	12W	108
NETO JOSE TORRES	NY	38W	61
NETTER DANNIEL JR	MS	27E	75
NETTESHEIM BRUCE PAUL	WI	52E	9
NETTLE WILLIAM LEROY	CA	09W	132
NETTLES VICTOR LEE JR	SC	05E	61
NETZOW EARL JEFFREY	WI	59E	28
NEU WILLIAM ALLEN	MO	07W	129
NEUBACHER BRANDT STEELE	CA	53W	29
NEUBAUER FRED ALLEN	NE	33W	66
NEUBAUER JAMES R	WI	05E	2
NEUBAUER JOHN FRANK	NY	05W	17
NEUBAUER RONALD GEORGE	FL	13W	11
NEUBIA WILLIAM JAMES	NY	36W	53
NEUBURGER DANIEL LEO	KS	48W	14
NEUDAHL MICHAEL LLOYD	MN	14W	101
NEUENSCHWANDER DAN LEE	ND	60E	27
NEUMAN RONALD M	PA	06E	49
NEUMANN MARK WILLARD	WI	25E	44
NEUMEIER TERRY JAMES	WI	02E	69
NEUMEYER JAMES EDWARD	IL	24E	36
NEUMYER OWEN FRANCIS	PA	13E	29
NEURA TED PETER JR	FL	01E	37
NEUSS WILLIAM HENRY	NY	27E	91
NEUTZLING WILLIAM P	OH	17E	126
NEVAREZ ALEXANDRO	CA	18E	125
NEVEL ROBERT JOSEPH	PA	26W	2
NEVELS JOHN ALTON	TX	40E	11
NEVES MANUEL CATANO	CA	31E	51
NEVIDOMSKY FRANK THEODORE	NY	65W	13
NEVILLE ANTHONY ANDREW	MD	21W	84
NEVILLE PATRICK MICHAEL	GA	12W	125
NEVILLE STEVEN WAYNE	WA	02W	26
NEVILLE WILLIAM EDWARD	CA	02E	12
NEVILLE WILLIAM ROY	IL	34W	87
NEVIN PATRICK CHRISTOPHER	IN	05E	67
NEVINS ELDON EUGENE	KS	43E	57
NEVINS FLOYD CHARLES	KS	24W	19
NEW CITY THEODORE C JR	TX	21E	50
NEW GEORGE JR	CA	24E	36
NEW MORRIS DWAINE	TX	20E	94
NEW ZACHARY PHILLIP	OH	49W	32
NEWBERG ROBERT MARION	CA	16W	102
NEWBERN MICHAEL R	WA	11E	99
NEWBERRY CLIFFORD LEE	KY	34W	78
NEWBERRY GRAYSON HENRY	GA	06W	94
NEWBERRY JASPER NEWTON JR	CA	20E	17
NEWBERRY LARRY GENE	IN	42W	49
NEWBERRY LEWIS JEWETT	MA	38E	8
NEWBERRY WAYNE ELLSWORTH	IL	42W	42
NEWBOLD BOYD KEITH	UT	20W	31
NEWBOULD WILLIAM GEORGE	IL	04W	55
NEWBRAND JERRY LESTER	UT	11E	16
NEWBROUGH GERALD RAYMOND	MN	31E	84
NEWBURN LARRY STEPHEN	IN	25E	64
NEWBY BOBBY GENE	KY	24W	46
NEWBY FREDERICK ALBERT JR	PA	24E	84
NEWBY GARY EUGENE	CA	24E	37
NEWBY KENNETH LEROY JR	WA	37W	76
NEWCOMB CLARENCE MATTHEWS	MD	02E	19
NEWCOMB CLIFTON CURTIS	TX	05W	79
NEWCOMB JAMES DWIGHT	AL	09E	30
NEWCOMB LARRY FRANKLIN	MS	36E	28
NEWCOMB WAYNE PAUL	MA	36E	80
NEWCOMBE ANDREW JACKSON	NC	05W	103
NEWCOMER JAMES HENRY	OH	02W	73
NEWELL CALVIN EUGENE	OH	18E	46
NEWELL CRAIG ALLEN	PA	22W	14
NEWELL EDWIN GRANT	OH	63E	19
NEWELL GREGG A	UT	15W	56
NEWELL MICHAEL THOMAS	NY	13E	45
NEWELL RONALD EUGENE	PA	21W	77
NEWELL TIM EDWIN	IA	07W	49
NEWENDORP JAMES VERNON	IA	02W	33
NEWFIELD JIMMY CHARLES	OK	57W	2
NEWHOUSE BERNARD JOSEPH	MI	51E	24
NEWHOUSE GARLAND ANDREW	WV	17E	10
NEWKIRK ARTHUR R	NC	24W	105
NEWKIRK JAMES EDWARD	FL	24E	37

NAME	STATE	PANEL NO.	LINE NO.
NEWKIRK MICHAEL A	NC	07E	5
NEWKIRK TERRY CURTIS	FL	15W	91
NEWKIRK THOMAS CLIFTON	NY	10E	83
NEWLAND LONNIE PITTS	FL	16W	14
NEWLAND MICHAEL DWAINE	OH	49E	4
NEWLIN MELVIN EARL	OH	23E	5
NEWMAN ALLEN TRUMAN	TX	21E	50
NEWMAN BOBBY JOE	IL	28W	28
NEWMAN CHARLES DAVID	PA	15W	70
NEWMAN CLIFFORD AUHUNA	HI	39W	51
NEWMAN CLYDE EDWARD	NV	19E	64
NEWMAN DANIEL JAMES JR	NY	17E	10
NEWMAN DENNIS EARL	CA	20W	1
NEWMAN ERMAN MILFORD JR	TX	09E	133
NEWMAN FRANK ALLEN	OH	01W	31
NEWMAN FRANK CHARLES	IL	13W	51
NEWMAN GARY KEN	TX	17E	46
NEWMAN GEORGE KENNARD	MD	05E	52
NEWMAN GREGORY EUGENE	WI	28W	20
NEWMAN JAMES CLIFFORD JR	TN	37E	64
NEWMAN JERRY LEE	KS	25E	59
NEWMAN JOSEPH ERNEST	MD	09E	42
NEWMAN LARRY EDWARD	TN	14W	98
NEWMAN LARRY JEROME	NE	01W	45
NEWMAN MAURICE GLENN JR	OH	40W	66
NEWMAN MICHAEL CARL	NE	14E	131
NEWMAN ROBERT NELSON	TX	25W	53
NEWMAN RONALD ELLIS	FL	11W	55
NEWMAN STANLEY HAROLD	FL	34W	87
NEWMAN STANLEY VICTOR	VA	08W	20
NEWMAN THOMAS MCKNETT	NJ	29W	104
NEWPORT GARY LEE	OR	08E	121
NEWPORT SCOTT HERBERT	OH	03W	42
NEWSOM BENJAMIN BYRD	VA	09E	63
NEWSOME DEAN OLIVER	IL	47W	2
NEWSOME JOHNNY	CA	17W	13
NEWSOME KENNETH RAY	KY	56E	14
NEWSOME ROY C	CT	24W	88
NEWSOME WILLIAM LESTER	NY	41E	26
NEWSON LEROY JR	CA	49W	37
NEWSTEAD THOMAS EUGENE	MI	40W	66
NEWTON BARRIE MYRON	NJ	25W	7
NEWTON CHARLES VERNON	TX	27W	102
NEWTON DONALD STEPHEN	CA	05E	81
NEWTON DONALD WILLIAM	MI	14E	37
NEWTON KENNETH PURCELL	NY	21E	70
NEWTON LEONARD LEE	CA	34E	80
NEWTON MELVIN DEW	AZ	47E	3
NEWTON RICHARD ERIC	OH	17E	113
NEWTON VERNON LEE	MI	36E	28
NEWTON WARREN EMERY	OR	34E	9
NEWTON WILLIAM J	CA	11E	101
NEWVILLE VAN HAROLD	AZ	27E	46
NEY DAVID C	PA	03E	56
NIBBELINK LEA EVERETT	CA	28W	84
NICASTRO CHARLES EDWARD	TN	07E	126
NICCOLI GREGORY JEROME	WA	33W	57
NICELY NELSON TALMADGE	VA	23E	112
NICEWANDER OSCAR FRANKLIN	OH	16E	125
NICHOLAS DAVID LAMPREY	PA	17W	87
NICHOLAS DAVID LYLE	WV	17W	69
NICHOLAS DEAN EDWARD	OH	52W	45
NICHOLAS DENIS	FL	14E	37
NICHOLAS JOHN ALVIE	TX	24W	31
NICHOLAS PAUL RUSSELL JR	TX	14E	29
NICHOLAS REGINALD	ME	02E	104
NICHOLAS ROBERT GEORGE	CA	22W	68
NICHOLAS TOMMY L	AL	05E	67
NICHOLES HAROLD JAMES	UT	65E	14
NICHOLL DALE ALLEN	MI	31W	13
NICHOLS BRUCE JOSEPH	PA	10W	77
NICHOLS CHARLES EDWARD	TN	02E	68
NICHOLS COLIN KEITH	PA	09E	49
NICHOLS DANIEL CLEMENT	NJ	25W	107
NICHOLS DARRELL EUGENE	WV	21W	55
NICHOLS DOUGLAS ELLSWORTH	CA	15E	107
NICHOLS ELI WAYNE	MI	05E	35
NICHOLS ERNEST JAMES JR	MI	33E	21
NICHOLS GARY BRUCE	MI	25W	18
NICHOLS HUBERT CAMPBEL JR	FL	10E	60
NICHOLS JAMES ARTHUR	CA	04W	121
NICHOLS JAMES WILLIAM JR	MN	41E	42

NAME	STATE	PANEL NO.	LINE NO.
NICHOLS JERRY ALLEN	WI	21W	19
NICHOLS JERRY RUSSELL	OH	49E	24
NICHOLS JOSEPH DAVID JR	IN	22E	80
NICHOLS LARRY DONALD	MD	38W	4
NICHOLS LARRY J	AL	06E	81
NICHOLS MAX E	NY	30E	11
NICHOLS McARTHUR	NC	10E	114
NICHOLS PHILIP GWYN	IL	25W	108
NICHOLS PHILIP LARRY	WV	39W	9
NICHOLS PHILLIP ARTHUR	MT	07W	133
NICHOLS RANDE LEE	CA	11W	31
NICHOLS RICHARD ALLEN	WA	22E	111
NICHOLS RICHARD ALLEN	NJ	38W	29
NICHOLS THOMAS EDWARD	TX	33W	33
NICHOLS WILLIAM WARD JR	NJ	02E	106
NICHOLSON DAVID DONELL	IL	33E	90
NICHOLSON DAVID LEONARD	CA	15W	10
NICHOLSON GEORGE JAMES	PA	46E	9
NICHOLSON GEORGE P	TN	35E	49
NICHOLSON GERALD W JR	FL	16W	14
NICHOLSON GERMAN LEE	MS	17E	10
NICHOLSON GLENN EDWARD	IL	55E	24
NICHOLSON JAMES ALEXANDER	CA	33W	3
NICHOLSON JAMES ARTHUR	CA	19E	121
NICHOLSON JAMES CLIFFORD	PA	35W	20
NICHOLSON JAMES PATON	ME	54E	14
NICHOLSON LARRY JAMES	WI	23W	90
NICK OTIS LEE	UT	42E	8
NICKEL WARREN F JR	CA	54E	28
NICKELS DARIS WAYNE	OH	32W	22
NICKELS LESLIE DAVID	IL	09E	115
NICKELSON MARTIN JOHN	MN	27W	90
NICKENS CECIL BERNARD	NJ	24E	96
NICKENS JAMES	SC	31W	38
NICKERSON BRADFORD SCOTT	ME	10E	60
NICKERSON CURTIS CARL	TX	06E	15
NICKERSON GENE BERTAN	MI	13W	59
NICKERSON GILBERT RONALD	WI	02E	62
NICKERSON LEWIS RAYMOND	PA	19E	40
NICKERSON MICHAEL KENT	IN	27W	80
NICKERSON PHILIP EUGENE	WA	22W	107
NICKERSON RONALD WILLIAM	NJ	04E	33
NICKERSON THOMAS CARROLL	MA	16E	85
NICKERSON WILLIAM BREWSTE	CT	06E	128
NICKERSON WILLIAM WALTER	FL	02E	59
NICKLAS GILBERT MICHAEL	NY	03E	50
NICKLEBERRY CLIFFORD	TX	13E	13
NICKLOW DANNY EUGENE	MD	16E	95
NICKLOW ROBERT JAMES	PA	23E	53
NICKLYN ROBERT JAMES	MI	03W	13
NICKOL ROBERT ALLEN	PA	02W	52
NICKS BENJAMIN ARNOLD III	KS	11W	42
NICODEMUS WILLIAM DEO	IN	05W	65
NICOL MICHAEL WILLIAM	MI	03W	93
NICOLA DENNIS GRANT	IL	13E	111
NICOLAI RUSSELL CHESTER	WI	21W	72
NICOLAISEN JAMES ELLSWORT	TX	50E	6
NICOLINI PETER JOSEPH	IL	20E	9
NICOLINI RICHARD DOMENIC	NY	47E	35
NIDDS DANIEL RUSSELL	NY	18E	62
NIDEVER DAVID FRANK	CA	04W	94
NIEBOER DOUGLAS ALAN	MI	07W	56
NIEBUR EDWARD LEROY	NE	41E	52
NIEDECKEN RAYMOND ALVIS	TX	32E	88
NIEDECKEN WILLIAM CLINTON	TX	32W	39
NIEDERHAUSE STEPHEN SCOTT	CA	31W	63
NIEDERMEIER ARTHUR ALAN	NJ	15E	99
NIEDERMEIER THOMAS DAVID	NY	21E	1
NIEDERMEYER JOHN GARY	FL	33E	90
NIEHAUS JAMES EDWARD	OH	54W	3
NIEKEN LARRY LEE	MN	09W	132
NIELSEN CHARLES JOSEPH	NY	49E	52
NIELSEN HAROLD RICHARD	CT	23E	103
NIELSEN MAGNUS CARL	FL	45W	16
NIELSEN MICHAEL CHARLES	WI	20W	51
NIELSEN ROBERT	NY	33E	73
NIELSEN ROLAND ALBERT	TX	27E	49
NIELSEN TERRY LEE	UT	05W	129
NIELSON JOHN LEIF	MD	36E	28
NIEMANN DAVID LEE	PA	20E	122
NIEMCZUK PETER RICHARD	IL	07E	97
NIEMEYER LOUIS ANDREW JR	MO	42W	6

NAME	STATE	PANEL NO.	LINE NO.
NIEMI JAMES ARNE	MN	14W	113
NIEMI MARTIN ROY	MI	60E	17
NIEMI ROGER LYLE	MI	15E	21
NIERER JOHN EDWARD	PA	14W	14
NIESPODZIANY CASIMIR	IL	14E	113
NIETO JESUS DIEZ JR	AZ	19W	108
NIEVES DAVID	NY	15W	28
NIEVES JORGE LUIS	OK	39W	75
NIEVES-COLON MARCELINO JR	PR	46W	52
NIEWAHNER RONALD LEO	KY	36W	13
NIEWENHOUS GERALD E JR	MD	15W	83
NIEZGODA MICHAEL ALLEN	MI	42W	6
NIGGLE HARRY TILLMAN	IN	33W	67
NIGH FREDRICK ELLIS	OH	43W	18
NIGHTENGALE TIMOTHY JAMES	NY	48E	31
NIGHTINGALE RANDALL JOHN	IL	45E	14
NIGRELLI THOMAS LYNWOOD	RI	21E	24
NIGRO ANTHONY JOSEPH	PA	11E	70
NIHILL RUSSELL EDWIN	RI	40W	13
NIHSEN DALLAS LEE	IA	02W	137
NILE MAURICE J	ME	25E	31
NILES JEFFERY CHARLES	WA	42W	26
NILES RONALD EDWARD	NC	19E	73
NILES RONALD ROBERT	WI	20W	81
NILSEN ERIC BJARNE	NY	46E	9
NIMAN ROBERT O'NEAL	OK	08W	131
NIMIROSKI JOSEPH ELWIN	MA	04E	25
NIMOX BENNY FRANK	MI	22E	111
NIMPHIE MAX EDWARD JR	MI	55E	25
NINO AMELIO	TX	60W	9
NINOW WILLIAM CHARLES	VA	30W	28
NIOUS ELVAIN ENNIS	CA	40E	67
NIPP STEVEN HAROLD	ID	33W	87
NIPPER DAVID	GA	01E	73
NIPPER DONALD EDWARD	TN	54E	39
NISEWONGER EDWARD EARL	AL	10W	46
NISHIYAMA MELVIN TETSUO	HI	08E	4
NISHIZAWA GLENN NOBUYKI	CA	62W	15
NISKANEN MARTIN KEITH	ME	02W	78
NISKI LEONARD EDWARD	NY	19E	85
NISSENBAUM MICHAEL DAVID	OH	31E	93
NITKA JOSEPH STANLEY	PA	48E	31
NITSCHE RICHARD EDMUND JR	MD	37W	40
NITZ ROBERT FRANKLIN	MI	29E	61
NITZSCHE LEONARD ARTHUR	IL	12W	108
NIX EDWARD LEWIS	AL	61E	15
NIX HENRY LEWIS	NY	39W	56
NIX JOHN DAVID	KY	03W	12
NIX ROBERT MICHAEL	TX	39E	10
NIX VERNON WALTER III	WY	53E	3
NIX WARREN PAUL	CA	25W	108
NIXON DONALD LEE	MO	28W	93
NIXON JEROME	MO	06E	42
NIXON JESSE ERNEST	FL	05W	53
NIXON JOHN ARLEIGH	VA	49E	24
NIXON LEN EVERETT	MI	12W	72
NIXON MASON JR	NC	67W	2
NIXON RAY	WA	15E	98
NIXON ROBERT JOHN	PA	38W	45
NIXON SAMUEL RAY	AR	45E	50
NIXON WILLIAM DALE	AR	57E	7
NOAH JOSH CAIN	OK	30E	46
NOAH MARVIN TIDWELL	OK	17E	38
NOBERT CRAIG ROLAND	CT	09E	49
NOBLE ALLEN EARL	AL	03W	109
NOBLE DANIEL JOSEPH	LA	40W	1
NOBLE DENNIS RAY	WA	08W	55
NOBLE GARY PAUL	WA	63E	15
NOBLE JAMES HERBERT	IN	17W	43
NOBLE JOHN RODNEY	CA	41W	41
NOBLE LEWIS RAULERSON	FL	39E	76
NOBLE MORRIS ALLAN	CA	21E	125
NOBLE RICHARD EDWIN	UT	57E	30
NOBLE RONALD GLEN	MI	46W	32
NOBLE THOMAS GREGORY	MN	05W	6
NOBLES AUBREY ELDON	TX	01W	83
NOBLES LAVELLE MILLARD	MS	02E	50
NOBLES NORMAN JAMES	PA	34W	52
NODDIN WILLIAM DAVID	IL	52E	9
NODEN TIMOTHY JOSEPH	PA	59E	28
NOE FLOYD RUSSELL	IN	23E	62
NOE FRANK RAY	AR	29E	6

NAME	STATE	PANEL NO.	LINE NO.
NOE GEORGE HOBERT	KY	24W	112
NOE JERRY LYNN	TN	22E	46
NOE MARVIN LEWIS	OK	25W	31
NOE TIM A	CA	08E	38
NOEL DONALD WILLIAM	WI	26W	55
NOEL DOUGLAS RAY	NC	24E	55
NOEL JOSEPH DONAT	RI	14E	29
NOEL JOSEPH PAUL	PA	60W	21
NOEL MAURICE THOMAS	NY	47E	4
NOEL MICHAEL DAVID	OH	07W	56
NOELDNER DANIEL MORRIS	SD	30W	55
NOELKE RICHARD ALLEN	CA	03E	26
NOELLSCH ROBERT DONALD	MO	42W	42
NOETZEL WILLIAM WESLEY	MD	11W	51
NOFFORD CLARENCE	NJ	30W	92
NOGGLE STEPHEN M	MN	21E	125
NOGIEWICH WILLIAM PETER	NY	33W	27
NOGUCHI ROCKNE MASAYOSHI	HI	19E	44
NOHE JOSEPH EDWARD JR	MD	30W	93
NOKES JOHN DARRELL	WA	16E	62
NOKES KENNETH CLIFFORD	CA	07W	96
NOLAN CHARLES ALBERT JR	PA	44W	52
NOLAN DAVID ALLEN	MN	24E	115
NOLAN JOSEPH PAUL JR	IL	01W	27
NOLAN MICHAEL FRANCIS JR	NY	34W	28
NOLAN PETER FRANCIS	MA	10W	2
NOLAN ROBERT FRANK	CT	56E	29
NOLAND JERRY LYNN	TX	07E	120
NOLAND KENNETH EUGENE	PA	55W	22
NOLDE WILLIAM BENEDICT	MI	01W	112
NOLDER CHARLES JAMES	PA	14W	44
NOLDIN RICHARD JOHN	NY	20W	114
NOLDNER RONALD LEE	SD	49W	32
NOLEN BOBBIE ELDON	AR	04E	94
NOLEN KENNETH JOE	KY	07W	46
NOLEN PAUL MICKLE	IN	04W	124
NOLES GARY EDWIN	FL	43W	41
NOLFF DANIEL BENSON	MI	11E	127
NOLL DAVID ROGER	MI	07W	31
NOLLEY LEE ROY	TX	27W	20
NOLT CALVIN EUGENE	PA	11W	81
NOLTE WILLIAM HARRY	NY	39W	75
NOMM TOIVO BERNHARD	MD	03W	87
NOON JACK ALDEN	MI	11W	81
NOONAN JOHN MICHAEL	MO	44E	39
NOONAN MICHAEL DENNIS	TX	21W	62
NOONAN THOMAS PATRICK JR	NY	33W	67
NOOTZ GAYLORD EUGENE	CA	23E	62
NOPP ROBERT GRAHAM	OR	09E	20
NORA RAYMOND VERNON	CA	62E	21
NORBERG WILLIAM GUNTHER	RI	08E	18
NORBUT GEORGE EDWARD	IL	25E	88
NORCIA JAMES JOSEPH	DC	14E	58
NORD DAVID LEE	IN	22W	123
NORDAHL LEE EDWARD	MT	04E	29
NORDELL JOHN EDWARD JR	CA	33W	67
NORDMAN ERIC REINHARD	NJ	09E	115
NORDQUIST GARY LEIGH	CA	35E	25
NORDQUIST JON HARRIS	MN	08W	75
NORDSTROM VICTOR CARL	CA	38E	9
NORE KENNETH HAROLD	MO	31E	6
NORFLEET BRIAN ROSS	MO	20E	97
NORFLEET HENRY JR	IL	42E	54
NORGAARD LARRY WAYNE	SD	37E	1
NORMAN ARTHUR EUGENE	TN	01E	82
NORMAN CALVIN JR	FL	30W	87
NORMAN CLAE TERRY	CA	08E	38
NORMAN GARY LESLIE	PA	32E	26
NORMAN GORDON JOSEPH	MA	15W	22
NORMAN JAMES MICHAEL	MN	30W	79
NORMAN JAY ROY	AR	25E	61
NORMAN LANNY JOSEPH	IN	39W	51
NORMAN MARION HENRY	TX	47E	15
NORMAN MICHAEL WARREN	FL	40E	27
NORMAN THOMAS WILEY JR	NC	18W	78
NORMAN TIMOTHY JOHN	WI	13W	33
NORMAN W H	FL	05E	67
NORMAN WILLIAM WILSON	NC	37E	64
NORMANDIN DUANE MICHAEL	MN	55E	25
NORRENBROCK WILLIAM A	KY	08W	29
NORRID HOLLIS RONNEY	GA	54W	31
NORRIS ALIN EMILE	NY	03W	20

NAME	STATE	PANEL NO.	LINE NO.
NORRIS BILLY RAYVON	FL	40E	27
NORRIS CALVIN ANDREW	TN	02W	61
NORRIS CHARLES BENJAMIN	SC	06E	127
NORRIS CHARLES RAYMOND	WV	47W	51
NORRIS CHARLES STEVEN	WA	15E	107
NORRIS DAVID LEE	NC	06W	118
NORRIS GEORGE CLYDE	IA	53E	19
NORRIS GRADY LEE	SC	08W	60
NORRIS JAMES ALAN	IA	19W	33
NORRIS JAMES RAPHAEL	KY	39W	12
NORRIS JERRY A	FL	19E	121
NORRIS JOHN ALEXANDER III	CA	27E	50
NORRIS JOSEPH ROBERT	FL	28E	93
NORRIS KENNETH EARL	VA	33W	27
NORRIS LINZA	MD	11E	131
NORRIS OTIS LESLIE JR	IL	40W	1
NORRIS ROBERT NORMAN	PA	15W	72
NORRIS RONNIE EUGENE	SC	13E	85
NORRIS THOMAS ANDREW	WV	39W	61
NORRIS TRUMAN DENNIS	VA	12W	14
NORRIS VAN ALLEN	AL	63W	10
NORRIS WIELAND CLYDE	CA	09W	5
NORRIS WILLIAM THEODORE	OH	16E	103
NORSWORTHY JIMMY LAYNE	AL	51W	27
NORTH BENNIE LEE	TX	03W	49
NORTH CLAUDE EUGENE	IN	38E	9
NORTH DALE EUGENE	MO	52W	7
NORTH DENNIS COLE	FL	32W	39
NORTH DONALD RICHARD JR	MI	61W	5
NORTH JOHN ALEX	WI	22W	11
NORTH MICHAEL WALTER	CA	20W	104
NORTHCUTT DANNY RAY	TX	36E	85
NORTHCUTT WILLIAM BUCKELE	TX	10E	31
NORTHERN FRANKIE		07W	47
NORTHERN JAMES ROBERT ALL	CA	12E	67
NORTHINGTON WILLIAM CLYDE	AL	30W	39
NORTHOUSE ROLLIE MELVIN	MI	53E	19
NORTHROP JAMES LEEROY	KS	08E	98
NORTHROP RONALD ROBERT	MO	04W	39
NORTHRUP MAURICE FREDRICK	MN	29E	52
NORTHUP DAVID WAYNE	CA	14E	105
NORTHUP EDWIN GILBERT	IA	01W	47
NORTON BENJAMIN PAUL	MI	10E	89
NORTON DAN BAKER	GA	42W	36
NORTON DEWIGHT EDWARDS	MI	05W	66
NORTON GEORGE HAROLD	NY	02E	52
NORTON GERALD OWEN	IA	01E	12
NORTON GERALD WAYNE	TX	33E	60
NORTON GREGORY BERNARD	MD	07E	87
NORTON JOHN EMORY	GA	05W	14
NORTON KENNETH BRADLEY	NC	57E	7
NORTON KENNETH DEAN	FL	17W	48
NORTON MICHAEL ROBERT	WV	16W	23
NORTON MITCHELL EARL	GA	21W	14
NORTON RICHARD L	MA	32E	3
NORTON ROBERT LYON	CT	37W	35
NORTON ROGER KAY	IL	23E	5
NORTON THOMAS	NY	38E	57
NORTON THOMAS FRANCIS	NY	51E	32
NORTON WARD III	PA	14W	47
NORVELL JEFFREY WOODROW	TN	45W	55
NORVELL RAYMOND FRANK	AZ	25W	81
NORVELLE CLYDE L JR	AZ	06E	67
NORWOOD HUGH	TX	24E	37
NORWOOD JOE WILLIAM	TX	19W	102
NORWOOD RICHARD DALE	CA	26E	96
NORWOOD THOMAS LEE JR	SC	14W	128
NORWOOD WILLIAM ARNOLD	SC	12W	7
NORZAGARAY SALVADOR LOPEZ	AZ	31W	70
NOSEFF RONNIE LEE	NM	11E	16
NOSEK WILLIAM ALLEN	IL	24E	78
NOSS JAMES THEODORE	WV	08E	128
NOSTADT FRANK JOHN JR	PA	03E	91
NOTEBOOM IVAN	SD	03E	104
NOTERMANN MICHAEL WILLIAM	MN	09W	69
NOTH WAYNE LOUIS	WI	22W	68
NOTHERN JAMES WILLIAM JR	AR	30E	46
NOTICH ANTHONY MICHAEL	PA	22W	59
NOTO ROBERT JOSEPH	MO	51E	11
NOTT BYRON LEE JR	CA	35W	13
NOTTAGE MICHAEL LEWIS	OH	13E	39
NOTTINGHAM RICHARD LANCE	CA	28W	73

NAME	STATE	PANEL NO.	LINE NO.
NOVAK BERNARD JOHN	MI	40E	67
NOVAK CLARENCE JOSEPH	NE	12W	98
NOVAK EDWARD JAMES	IL	08W	131
NOVAK GERALD FRANCIS	IL	16E	3
NOVAK LARRY DEAN	NE	68E	5
NOVAK MICHAEL JOSEPH	MI	40W	46
NOVAK RICHARD DANIEL	MN	48W	14
NOVAK THOMAS EUGENE	OH	36W	58
NOVAK WALTER MARK	PA	10W	35
NOVAKOVIC GEORGE D	WI	43E	9
NOVAKOVICH JERRY A	CA	38E	57
NOVEL CHARLES EDWARD	TN	38E	57
NOVELLO FRANCES F	MD	02E	74
NOVEMBER DWIGHT MYLES	NY	36E	58
NOVEMBRE CARMINE	NJ	52E	9
NOVISKI BERNIS J	TX	13E	75
NOVOBIELSKI DUANE ANDREW	WI	27E	50
NOVOSOD RAYMOND ORITIZ	MD	17W	81
NOVOTNY JAMES ROBERT	IL	16E	125
NOVOTNY JOHN RAYMOND	NY	29E	33
NOVOTNY RICHARD DENNIS	MI	15E	21
NOWACK THOMAS MICHAEL	MO	14E	131
NOWACZYNSKI NATALIE	MI	07W	84
NOWAK JOHN THOMAS	MI	12W	7
NOWAK LEONARD MICHAEL	WI	64W	13
NOWAK ROBERT VIRGIL	NE	40E	11
NOWAK RONALD MICHAEL	IL	32W	54
NOWAKOWSKI GLENN EDWARD	WI	01W	58
NOWAKOWSKI JOHN ALEXANDER	MI	30W	48
NOWAKOWSKI WALTER JOHN	IL	28E	70
NOWELL CHARLES KEITH JR	WV	31W	13
NOWICKI JOHN PAUL	VT	45W	21
NOWICKI ROBERT PHILIP	MA	06W	135
NOWLIN CHARLES DOUGLAS	TN	15E	63
NOWLIN FLETCHER JACOB JR	NY	23W	56
NOWRY RICHARD LOREN	MI	58W	12
NOYES RUSSELL WILLIS	MA	53E	19
NOYOLA RICHARD	CA	06E	102
NOZEWSKI ROBERT	MI	22W	107
NUBER RICHARD ANTHONY	MI	59E	9
NUCKLES C GREGORY	TX	29E	21
NUDENBERG DAVID ALAN	NJ	06W	55
NUEBEL WILLIAM GEORGE JR	NY	29E	101
NUEKU ROBERT LANI	HI	05E	121
NUESSE CHESTER KEITH	CA	16E	64
NUFER JAMES LEO	KS	44E	19
NUGENT HENRY FLOYD JR	NC	52W	1
NUGENT JAMES PATRICK	NJ	15W	59
NUGENT MICHAEL RAY	LA	05W	6
NUGENT RICHARD FRANCIS	NJ	05E	92
NUHFER WILLIAM DANIEL	PA	33W	3
NULL ARTHUR ELLIOTT JR	MO	59E	10
NULL HAROLD EDWARD	IL	17E	40
NULL RICKY LEE	PA	51E	11
NULL WILLIAM EUGENE	WV	31W	11
NULPH WILLIAM LEE JR	OH	29E	84
NULTON JAMES EDWARD II	NY	20W	22
NUNEZ DAVID GUERRERO JR	CA	57E	30
NUNEZ FRED CONTRERAS	CA	27E	46
NUNEZ GEORGE HENRY	NM	34E	81
NUNEZ JESSE MANUEL	TX	31W	14
NUNEZ JESUS CARLOS	CA	08W	12
NUNEZ RUDOLPH ALGAR	CA	08E	45
NUNEZ SANTOS SILVAS	TX	21W	55
NUNLEY JAMES E	IN	13E	86
NUNLEY WALTER WILLIAM JR	TN	14W	57
NUNN CHARLES ROBERT	KY	18E	76
NUNN JOSEPH LORAN	IN	11W	52
NUNN RODOLPH LEE JR	NC	59W	10
NUNN SAMUEL JOHN	NM	44W	19
NUNNALLY TIMOTHY CRAIG	CA	21W	47
NUNNERY CLARENCE E JR	SC	29W	2
NUNNERY TRAVIS EDWARD	TN	11E	33
NUNZIATO ANIELLO CARLO	NY	47E	1
NURISSO CHARLES WILLIAM	CA	07W	17
NURSE JOHN GORDON	IN	27W	51
NURZYNSKI JOSEPH ANTHONY	NY	25W	79
NUSCHKE EDGAR ERWIN	PA	14E	64
NUSSBAUMER JOHN JOSEPH	WA	11E	114
NUSSBAUMER STEVE OWEN	CA	46W	19
NUTE LEONARD KING	NH	20E	105
NUTE RONALD WADE	MA	02W	90

NAME	STATE	PANEL NO.	LINE NO.
NUTLY DANIEL THOMAS	NY	22E	16
NUTT RICHARD E	IL	05E	122
NUTT WALTER LEE III	IA	26W	72
NUTTER FREDERICK LEROY	OH	06W	8
NUTTER GREGORY LEROY	PA	40W	66
NUTWELL JOHN SYLVESTER	MD	07W	3
NUZIARD RICHARD LEE	IN	03E	35
NYBERG LEONARD ERIC	CA	12W	93
NYBLOM DUANE WILLARD	MN	24W	19
NYE AVERY MERRILL III	IN	12W	8
NYE DANIEL EUGENE	NY	02W	78
NYE HAROLD CURTIS	PA	22E	58
NYE JERRY WARREN	PA	10E	33
NYE WALLACE GREGORY	MN	21E	125
NYHOF RICHARD E	CA	01W	46
NYMAN LAWRENCE FREDERICK	WA	08E	87
NYMAN MICHAEL STUART	CT	30E	80
NYSTROM BRUCE AUGUST	OH	13E	6
NYSTROM THOMAS ALLEN	CA	53E	5
NYSTUL MICHAEL DEAN	MN	43W	56
NYSTUL WILLIAM CRAIG	CA	01W	124
O'BANION JAMES RUSS	KY	27W	39
O'BANNON ALBERT F JR	CA	57E	8
O'BANNON ROBERT III	CA	45E	26
O'BOYLE SHIRLEY WAYNE	WV	06E	49
O'BOYLE TERRENCE PATRICK	IN	06W	74
O'BRIEN ALAN JOSEPH	MA	10E	109
O'BRIEN ALDEN WALTON	KY	40W	14
O'BRIEN ARTHUR ALEN	AZ	14E	29
O'BRIEN CHESTER LAVERN JR	CA	05E	122
O'BRIEN CLYDE HAROLD	CT	14E	59
O'BRIEN DWIGHT PRESTON	WV	07W	13
O'BRIEN EDWARD STEPHEN	MA	31E	37
O'BRIEN EDWARD TE	IL	10W	105
O'BRIEN FRANK ANTHONY III	WV	46E	10
O'BRIEN GARY MALCOLM	FL	21E	50
O'BRIEN JOHN HENRY	OR	13E	111
O'BRIEN JOHN JOSEPH	WA	50E	6
O'BRIEN JOHN LAWRENCE	PA	12E	51
O'BRIEN JOHN MICHAEL	MO	19E	121
O'BRIEN KEVIN	NY	35W	61
O'BRIEN MARK JAMES	ID	36W	23
O'BRIEN MICHAEL MACKIE	TX	53E	43
O'BRIEN MICHAEL STEVEN	OR	25W	80
O'BRIEN PATRICK EDWARD	KS	15E	75
O'BRIEN PATRICK RORY	NY	08W	119
O'BRIEN PHILLIP ANTHONY	MA	19E	85
O'BRIEN RICHARD CONAWAY	CA	37E	65
O'BRIEN ROBERT EDWARD	RI	29W	104
O'BRIEN ROBERT PHILLIP	CA	10W	126
O'BRIEN STEPHEN	CA	09W	96
O'BRIEN T CHRISTOPHER FORD	MA	23E	39
O'BRIEN TERRENCE DALE	MS	12E	68
O'BRIEN TERRENCE PATRICK	MN	65E	14
O'BRIEN THEODORE	NY	34E	69
O'BRIEN WILLARD DONALD	AZ	10W	17
O'BRIEN WILLIAM JOSEPH	PA	17E	22
O'BRIEN WILLIAM JOSEPH	MA	17E	63
O'BYRN HERMAN JAMES	MI	17W	69
O'CALLAGHAN BRIAN JOSEPH	VA	14W	39
O'CALLAGHAN MAURICE JOSEP	NJ	18E	62
O'CONNELL DANIEL GERARD	NY	22W	92
O'CONNELL EUGENE GEORGE	NJ	67W	2
O'CONNELL KEVIN GERALD	NY	22E	84
O'CONNELL MICHAEL GRANT	IN	17W	124
O'CONNELL ROBERT GENE	MD	13W	17
O'CONNOR BRIAN RICHARD	MA	14E	1
O'CONNOR DANIEL JEROME	MN	52E	22
O'CONNOR DAVID CORNELIUS	IN	20W	88
O'CONNOR DAVID LEE	OH	10E	102
O'CONNOR DENIS	CA	27E	85
O'CONNOR DENNIS ALFRED	CA	22E	72
O'CONNOR DENNIS KENNETH	CA	39W	3
O'CONNOR EDMUND ANTHONY	NY	39E	11
O'CONNOR EDWIN THOMAS JR	VT	08E	57
O'CONNOR FREDERICK J JR	MA	41E	52
O'CONNOR GARRETT TIMOTHY	MI	57E	32
O'CONNOR GERARD FRANCIS	KS	11W	56
O'CONNOR JOHN FRANCIS	IL	10E	66
O'CONNOR JOHN THOMAS	IL	54W	18
O'CONNOR JOHN VINSON JR	CA	37W	76
O'CONNOR MICHAEL BARRY	FL	53E	39
O'CONNOR MICHAEL DONALD	IA	22E	46
O'CONNOR MICHAEL MAURICE	IA	23W	66
O'CONNOR MICHAEL PA	NY	30W	93
O'CONNOR MORTIMER LELANE	AZ	47E	35
O'CONNOR RICHARD EDWARD	NY	36E	29
O'CONNOR ROBERT ANTHONY	IL	19W	19
O'CONNOR ROBERT LEE	CA	10W	19
O'CONNOR THOMAS DUCKETT	SC	33E	30
O'CONNOR TIMOTHY JOHN	IN	06W	18
O'CONNOR WILLIAM EUGENE	SC	36W	58
O'CONNOR WILLIAM JAMES JR	IL	59E	10
O'DEA THOMAS FRANCIS JR	IL	36W	76
O'DEA THOMAS PATRICK	GA	24W	97
O'DELL TIMOTHY LEE	MS	52E	31
O'DONNELL BERNARD JACK	OH	12E	78
O'DONNELL DANIEL MARTIN	MI	21E	76
O'DONNELL DOUGLAS WILLIAM	DC	11E	95
O'DONNELL GEORGE MAURICE	TN	21E	114
O'DONNELL JOHN MIC	NY	24W	91
O'DONNELL JOHN PATRICK	OH	16E	4
O'DONNELL JOHN THOMAS	PA	57W	2
O'DONNELL ROBERT WAYNE	MI	44E	30
O'DONOVAN EDWARD T	IL	24W	106
O'FARRELL JOHN MICHAEL	PA	34W	2
O'FARRELL WILLIAM PATRICK	PA	50E	32
O'GRADY JOHN FRANCIS	NY	18E	12
O'GRADY MARTIN EDWARD	NY	33E	90
O'GUINN MICHAEL EUGENE	IL	08E	23
O'HALLORAN WILLIAM BRIAN	NY	66W	11
O'HAM ROCKY PEARSON	NC	10W	2
O'HARA JAMES LOYD	MO	21W	77
O'HARA JOHN PATRCK	TX	41W	11
O'HARA ROBERT CHARLES	IA	33W	72
O'HARE RICHARD JAMES	WI	43E	29
O'KANE JAMES B	MD	05E	8
O'KEEFE GARY MAURICE	OH	37W	47
O'KEEFE MICHAEL ANDREW JR	NY	15W	7
O'KEEFE MICHAEL JOSEPH	VA	18E	115
O'KEEFE PATRICK FRANCIS	NY	42E	69
O'KEEFE ROBERT WILLIAM	CA	22W	90
O'KEEFE RONALD THOMAS	MN	01E	70
O'KEEFE ROY TULANE	MD	37E	65
O'KEEFE TIMOTHY JOHN	GA	51E	11
O'KIEFF WILLIAM BRANDON	TN	06W	86
O'KUSKY HENRY JOSEPH JR	VA	54W	31
O'LAUGHLIN DANIEL THOMAS	MN	25E	34
O'LAUGHLIN JAMES FRANCIS	OH	42E	38
O'LEARY JAMES KEVIN	MA	09E	70
O'LEARY MICHAEL WILLIAM	IN	23W	103
O'LEARY PAUL FRANCIS	NY	47W	30
O'LEARY RICHARD LAUGHLIN	MA	27E	12
O'LEARY TIMOTHY MONROE	WA	13E	6
O'MALLEY FRED GILLESPIE	IL	21E	37
O'MEARA LAWRENCE W	IL	46E	58
O'NAIL ROBERT PAUL	OH	24E	3
O'NEAL DENNIS RAY	OH	14E	50
O'NEAL DOYD DEWAYNE	TX	01E	53
O'NEAL HAROLD JR	LA	44W	66
O'NEAL JAMES ELTON	TN	30E	80
O'NEAL JERRY LEE	MI	34W	90
O'NEAL LEROY	MO	24E	56
O'NEAL MARSHAL JUNIOR	MO	07E	96
O'NEAL MELVIN JR	NJ	19E	44
O'NEAL NELSON MONTAGUE	TN	33E	90
O'NEAL RICHARD MARK	MI	50W	15
O'NEAL ROY DAVID	OH	26E	30
O'NEAL TONY LEE	GA	17W	58
O'NEAL VICTOR HUBERT	AL	07E	74
O'NEIL RILEY CHARLES JR	KS	32E	3
O'NEIL ROBERT ANDREW	PA	17E	118
O'NEIL ROBERT WILLIAM	CA	34W	28
O'NEIL TERRENCE EDWARD	NY	66E	12
O'NEIL VAUGHN THOMAS	MI	30E	58
O'NEIL WALTER JAMES	MA	53W	11
O'NEIL WILLIAM WAYNE	NH	14W	54
O'NEILL ANTHONY JOSEPH	NY	24W	47
O'NEILL CARROLL PAUL	IA	32W	1
O'NEILL CHARLES LEO JR	MA	51W	12
O'NEILL DANIEL JOHN	MT	30W	93
O'NEILL DENNIS MICHAEL	MA	04E	133
O'NEILL GEORGE EDWARD	MA	11E	26
O'NEILL JAMES RAYMOND	NY	01E	18
O'NEILL JOHN JOSEPH JR	RI	09E	133
O'NEILL MICHAEL JAMES	MN	48W	46
O'NEILL THOMAS EDWARD JR	MA	05E	27
O'NEILL THOMAS PHILIP	NH	13W	128
O'NEILL TIMOTHY MICHAEL	MO	24W	106
O'REILLY ANTHONY PAUL	OH	60W	3
O'REILLY FRANCIS JOSEPH	MA	12W	119
O'REILLY JAMES C JR	MA	25E	107
O'REILLY TARRY THOMAS	ME	14W	123
O'REILLY TIMOTHY BOURKE	IL	25W	80
O'ROURKE RONALD PATRICK	FL	10E	42
O'SHAUGHNESSY JAMES JOHN	NJ	14W	104
O'SHAUGHNESSY JOHN FRANCI	NJ	05E	14
O'SHAUGHNESSY PATRICK J	WV	21W	34
O'SHEA JAMES CHARLES	IA	28W	99
O'SHEA STEPHEN JOHN	NY	20E	97
O'SHEA WILLIAM II	NJ	32W	61
O'SHELL DON MANUEL	TN	12W	46
O'SHELL DON THOMAS	MD	26E	30
O'STEEN CHARLES ROBERT	FL	33W	67
O'SULLIVAN CHRISTOPHER JO	NY	01E	128
O'TOOLE GEORGE PATRICK JR	MN	31E	85
O'TOOLE GERALD ARNOLD	TX	34E	90
O'TOOLE JAMES EDWARD JR	MA	51W	20
O'TOOLE LAWRENCE P II	NY	32W	81
O'TOOLE MICHAEL JOSEPH	MO	36W	54
O'TOOLE PETER JOSEPH	PA	43W	40
OAK GLEN EVERETT	MN	23E	88
OAKDEN TERRY LEE	NY	26E	96
OAKES ARNOLD GLEN	TN	34W	66
OAKES BRUCE DONALD	TX	34W	78
OAKES CHRISTOPHER COLUMBU	AL	10E	45
OAKES JACK WAYNE	PA	56W	12
OAKES PAUL LAVERNE JR	IA	56W	37
OAKEY JOHN RUSSELL	UT	08E	23
OAKLEY JAMES RONALD	NY	41E	4
OAKLEY LINUS LABIN	AR	02W	54
OAKLEY WILLIAM JOSEPH	CT	01E	126
OAKLEY WILLIAM LYNN	MD	05E	48
OAKS ROBERT LARRY	TX	16W	59
OAKS STEVEN BOYD	MO	29W	12
OAKS WILLIE JAMES	KY	02W	78
OATES EUGENE C III	TX	20W	95
OATES HENRY EATHEN	NC	27E	86
OATES ROBERT JAMES	OH	36E	80
OATES ROBERT WAYNE	CA	09E	124
OATES SAMUEL ARTHUR JR	PA	26E	14
OATMAN LEO CLARK	TX	03W	47
OATNEY ALLEN EUGENE	KS	09W	78
OBENLAND ROLAND ROBERT	MN	62E	21
OBENOUR RONALD MICHAEL	OH	43E	29
OBERDIER LYN DOUGLAS	OH	55E	25
OBERDING FRED JR	CA	01W	85
OBERG WILLIAM ARTHUR	OR	02E	27
OBERLE CHARLES G	PA	12E	75
OBERLE DAVID ALAN	CA	28E	39
OBERLE STEWART WILLIAM	NY	21W	39
OBERMEIER GEORGE RICHARD	NJ	18E	81
OBERSON FRANCIS SHERMAN	VA	30W	93
OBERT RICHARD ROBERT	CA	50W	19
OBEY DONALD ALTON	NY	44W	59
OBIE CLARENCE WILLIS III	VA	32E	46
OBMAN JOSEPH HOWARD	PA	15W	43
OBNEY RONNIE LEE	MI	57E	8
OBREGON RAUL ALBERT	CA	64W	14
OCAMPO ROBERT EGMEDIO	CA	17E	11
OCASIO FELIX	NY	54E	14
OCASIO VICTOR JR	IL	14W	94
OCHAB ROBERT	NY	14W	9
OCHOA ALFREDO JR	TX	22W	35
OCHOA JESUS	AZ	45W	55
OCHOA LOUIE	CA	28E	37
OCHOA LUPE P	TX	46W	6
OCHOA RALPH RICHARD	AZ	26W	20
OCHOA ROBERT	TX	30E	58
OCHS TIMOTHY CARL	NJ	35E	77
OCHS VALENTINE AMBROSE	PA	52E	41
OCKEY BRUCE GORDON	PA	22E	89
ODAFFER RICHARD DUANE	MN	40E	26
ODDO ANTHONY PHILIP	NY	14W	123
ODEGARD DELL COLEMAN	WA	35E	78
ODELL DENNIS LYNN	IA	29E	75

NAME	STATE	PANEL NO.	LINE NO.
ODELL JOHN MICHAEL	WA	53E	20
ODELL MICHAEL CHARLES	CO	22E	58
ODEN ROYAL PRESTON	WA	22W	81
ODENEAL JIMMY	IL	04W	42
ODENWELLER PETER EDWARD	MI	08E	111
ODIER STEVEN KENT	IN	14E	45
ODIERNO JOHN WILLIAM	NY	17E	11
ODIORNE GEORGE ALFRED	MA	13W	54
ODIOT EDGAR WILFREDO	NY	15E	34
ODLE JOHN CHARLES	IL	31W	38
ODOM HENRY DUANE	OK	05E	108
ODOM JOHN THOMAS	AL	15E	59
ODOM STEVEN CRAIG	GA	35E	78
ODOM VERN ERIC JR	IL	05W	6
ODOM WILLIAM CLINTON JR	AL	05W	118
ODONNELL MICHAEL DAVIS	IL	12W	40
ODONNELL SAMUEL JR	PA	01W	56
ODSTRCIL WILLIAM JOSEPH	TX	07W	100
ODUM JOSEPH BRITTON	GA	25E	20
ODUM MICHAEL RALPH R	FL	18W	71
OEHLER GEORGE HERMAN	IL	44E	19
OEN MICHAEL LYNN	OH	09W	35
OENS LA VERN OREN	CA	35W	40
OERTEL LARRY HUGH	WI	32E	58
OESTERREICH TILO RUDOLF	PA	48E	45
OESTREICHER PAUL ANTHONY	WI	27E	60
OESTRIECH JIM EDWARD	MN	17E	68
OFFERDAHL WILLIAM BRUCE	CA	35W	66
OFFIELD REX KAYE	MO	23E	45
OFFLEY JAMES CLIFTON	MA	20E	33
OFFUTT GARY PHELPS	MO	02E	101
OFSTEDAHL JERRY WAYNE	CA	19W	33
OGAMI TERRY Y	CA	40E	45
OGAS PHILLIP ARTHUR	CA	31E	14
OGATA TERRANCE AKI	HI	05W	133
OGBOURN GAYMAN CRANDALL	CO	18W	49
OGBURN FRANK JR	NJ	08E	121
OGBURN GLENN ROY	LA	23E	30
OGDEN DAVID ELLIS	CA	11W	115
OGDEN EDWARD PAUL	TX	34W	66
OGDEN HOWARD JR	NE	28E	37
OGDEN RUSSELL KEVIN	AZ	39W	56
OGDEN WILLIAM STEPHEN	PA	33W	72
OGEA WALLACE LEE	LA	30E	46
OGILVIE GORDON WILSON	AZ	42W	31
OGLE DAVID ROBERT	KS	42E	55
OGLE JOHNNY WAYNE	NC	08W	4
OGLE LEWIS MILTON	OK	29E	5
OGLES KENNETH WAYNE	GA	15E	49
OGLESBY CHARLES DOYLE	IN	06E	103
OGLESBY GERALD PHILLIP	MN	51W	12
OGLESBY JOHN R	CA	60E	27
OGLESBY LOOMIS III	NC	05E	97
OGLESBY RONALD	MD	51E	41
OGLESBY RONALD CHARLES	OK	44E	10
OGLETHORPE THOMAS JAY	CA	05E	74
OGLETREE YOUNG DAVID	AL	45E	2
OGREN JERRY LEWIS	CA	18W	96
OGRINC RONALD ROY	OH	24E	37
OGRIZEK JOHN ANTHONY	PA	07W	94
OHANESIAN VICTOR	NY	15E	129
OHARA STEVE MASAO	CA	45W	21
OHLER FREDERICK RICHARD	NY	49E	25
OHLER HERBERT	WV	03W	29
OHLINGER JAMES	NJ	12E	90
OHLSON GALEN ERICK	CA	40E	45
OHM DAVID JAMES	MN	51W	20
OHM ERIC GEORGE	NE	11W	32
OHMAN GARY ALAN	MN	19W	108
OHNESORGE THOMAS HERMAN	NE	22E	58
OJEDA JOE B	TX	15W	43
OJEDA NESTOR	NY	36E	29
OJILE MICHAEL RAYMOND	MO	21E	107
OKAMOTO DONALD RAY	CA	25E	68
OKAMOTO ROGER THOMAS	OR	06E	40
OKEEFE RICHARD WILLIAM	NY	05W	97
OKEMAH JOHN	OK	49E	41
OKER DAVID PAUL	MN	34W	44
OKERLUND THOMAS RICHARD	WA	05W	22
OKLAND VERNON LEO	IA	11W	105
OKUMURA EARL AKIO	HI	50W	42
OLAND DAVID MICHAEL	CA	08E	23
OLCOTT STEVEN JAMES	MN	05W	66
OLDFIELD CARL EVERETT	WI	17W	117
OLDFIELD JAMES STANLEY JR	TX	17E	75
OLDHAM JOHN SANDERS	NM	21E	91
OLDHAM KENNETH LINDLE	IN	42E	58
OLDHAM ROBERT LEE	TX	08W	6
OLDS ERNEST ARTHUR	MD	44E	19
OLDS JERRY DEAN	KY	08E	12
OLDS JOHN HENRY	PA	13E	25
OLEA FRANCISCO HERRERA	AZ	41W	36
OLEARNICK THOMAS	PA	30E	31
OLEKSA CHRISTOPHER JAMES	MI	19E	91
OLENICK JOHN DAVID	WV	24W	88
OLENZUK KENNETH FRANCIS	MI	32E	59
OLENZUK PAUL GREGORY	MI	49W	43
OLESEN RONALD ANDREW	SD	08W	43
OLESNANIK JOHN FRANCIS	PA	34E	30
OLESON JOSEPH JR	NJ	58W	12
OLETA JESUS C JR	CA	29W	82
OLGYAY ROY CHRISTOPHER	NY	07W	74
OLIN THOMAS M	MN	16E	85
OLINGER JAMES EDWARD JR	MI	09W	116
OLINSKY WALTER STANLEY JR	MA	18W	96
OLIPHANT JOSEPH B JR	NJ	31W	54
OLIVAR GILBERT	HI	01E	105
OLIVARES-MARTINEZ ARTURO	CA	52E	3
OLIVE DONALD LEWIS	MN	29W	82
OLIVE MILTON LEE III	IL	02E	131
OLIVER BERNARD GEORGE JR	NY	26W	21
OLIVER BOBBY GLENN	TN	22W	25
OLIVER CARL W	OH	28E	70
OLIVER CHARLES	MO	44E	10
OLIVER CHARLES EDWARD	OK	23E	113
OLIVER CHARLES OTIS	PA	27W	26
OLIVER CLIFTON	SC	61E	15
OLIVER DENNIS JERROD	GA	26W	34
OLIVER EDDIE VAN JR	OH	32W	66
OLIVER ERSKINE JAY	CA	23W	22
OLIVER FRANK GEORGE II	PA	01W	70
OLIVER FRED JR	IL	52E	31
OLIVER GARY LEE	TN	42E	22
OLIVER HENRY McCARTY	AL	44W	53
OLIVER KENNETH EARLSTON	NY	08W	105
OLIVER KENNETH ROY	OH	44W	4
OLIVER MICHAEL DEE	OR	54E	14
OLIVER MICHAEL PIERCE	TN	33E	90
OLIVER PAUL HAROLD	CA	34E	9
OLIVER RANDY DEWITT	SC	26W	92
OLIVER RICK ALTON	CA	32W	45
OLIVER ROBERT LYNN	TX	05W	23
OLIVER ROGER LEE	AL	24W	97
OLIVER ROMMIE	FL	54W	18
OLIVER THOMAS TUCKER	VA	38E	9
OLIVER TONY SYLVESTER	MD	42E	38
OLIVER TROY ROBERT JR	ID	63E	15
OLIVER WALTER B	OH	03E	19
OLIVERAS RUDY MICHAEL	CA	61W	5
OLIVO RAFAEL	NY	10W	99
OLIVO RAMIRO FROLIAN	TX	57E	25
OLLIKAINEN ROBERT JOHN	MI	17W	117
OLLILA DONALD WARREN	SD	09W	29
OLLIVIER JOSE ANTONIO	CA	31W	14
OLLOM ROBERT LEE	WA	51E	24
OLMEDA EDWIN JOSEPH	PA	18W	8
OLMOS ALFONSO	CA	20W	22
OLMOS LUIS	CA	13E	69
OLMSTEAD DALE FRANK	MN	17W	103
OLMSTEAD JOHN PAUL	IL	23E	77
OLMSTEAD ROBIN LEE	WA	24E	37
OLMSTEAD STANLEY EDWARD	OK	02E	125
OLMSTED GERALD RAY	WA	35W	66
OLMSTED JEROME EDWIN	WI	31E	15
OLNEY STEVEN IRA	MI	61W	15
OLOFSON PHILIP JOHN	MI	20E	33
OLSEN CECIL CHANCEY	IA	05W	34
OLSEN DONALD BRYAN	MI	39E	10
OLSEN DONALD WAYNE JR	IL	53W	5
OLSEN FLOYD WARREN	IL	51E	24
OLSEN GEORGE CHARLES	NY	53E	39
OLSEN GEORGE THOMAS	NY	13W	79
OLSEN GREGORY JON	WI	24W	106
OLSEN JAMES DANIEL	IL	06E	134
OLSEN JOHN ANDREW	NY	25W	31
OLSEN JOHN LOUIS	NY	22E	32
OLSEN KEITH	WA	22W	99
OLSEN OLAF THOMAS	IL	13W	113
OLSEN STEVEN WAYNE	CA	66E	12
OLSEN WILLIAM FRANK	ME	20W	8
OLSEN WILLIAM WHITBY	ID	24W	88
OLSON ALFRED RICHARD	MN	40E	45
OLSON ALLEN EDWIN	IL	32W	67
OLSON BARRY A	MN	42W	20
OLSON BENNETT WALFRED	ID	33E	91
OLSON BRUCE DENNIS	MN	04W	134
OLSON CARL ANDREW	GA	14W	95
OLSON CARL JOHN	IA	24E	38
OLSON CHARLES ANDREW	IL	38W	37
OLSON CHARLES EMMETTE	MN	40E	27
OLSON CHARLES ROBERT	WV	15W	123
OLSON CRAIG SEIMON	WI	35W	50
OLSON DELBERT AUSTIN	ND	34E	31
OLSON DENNIS GALE	IA	11E	127
OLSON DUANE ELMER	IA	22W	25
OLSON DUANE VIRGIL	WI	05E	15
OLSON ERICK OWEN	AZ	14W	108
OLSON GARY WAYNE	WI	16E	85
OLSON GENE JOHN	MN	15W	123
OLSON GERALD EVERETT	FL	06E	4
OLSON GROVER KONARD	OR	01E	41
OLSON HENRY LOUIS	MI	32E	15
OLSON JAMES ROBERT	FL	10W	19
OLSON JEROME ANDREW	MN	03W	47
OLSON KENNETH LEE	MN	59E	28
OLSON LARRY REX	ND	56W	37
OLSON MARK ALLEN	IL	07W	105
OLSON MEADDOW JOHN	IL	26W	26
OLSON RANDALL ALAN	IL	42W	20
OLSON RICHARD	MA	36W	41
OLSON RICHARD EMIL	MA	31W	14
OLSON RICHARD JAMES	ND	52E	22
OLSON RICHARD RALPH	MN	20W	114
OLSON ROBERT CHARLES JR	PA	32E	3
OLSON ROBERT EUGENE	MN	33W	67
OLSON ROBERT FRANKLIN	IA	20W	109
OLSON ROBERT GARY	CA	60E	27
OLSON RODNEY JAMES	WI	04E	125
OLSON ROGER LEWIS	IA	46E	38
OLSON RONALD LEON	NH	16W	118
OLSON STEVEN ALLAN	GA	08W	44
OLSON STEVEN RICKY	MO	51W	35
OLSON THOMAS PERCY	MN	04W	83
OLSON TIMOTHY ARTHUR	NY	15E	7
OLSON WILLIAM CRAIG	PA	34W	9
OLSON WILLIAM JAMES	IL	10W	35
OLSOWSKI GARY NEAL	TX	34W	28
OLSZEWSKI JOHN MICHAEL	PA	40E	46
OLSZEWSKI JOSEPH VERNE	CA	14W	72
OLT JOHN PAUL HARRIS	NY	09E	116
OLTMAN DEAN WILLIAM	IA	39W	23
OLVERA ADAN MONSIVAIS	TX	05E	62
OLZAK RAYMOND DENNIS	PA	13E	55
OLZER JAMES OSCAR JR	VA	13W	6
OMAN RICHARD ARLEN	TX	26W	66
OMELIA DENNIS WILLIAM	NC	05W	23
OMILIAN DENNIS ALLEN	MI	25E	107
OMMEN PETER RICHARD	SD	18E	126
OMSTEAD DAVID KING	CA	56W	7
ONAN JERRY LANG	KY	07E	27
ONANA RALPH WHEELER	CA	03E	13
ONCHI CURTIS	OR	28W	28
ONDERKO JOHN PATRICK	PA	37E	26
ONEAL STEVEN CLIFFORD	IN	03W	95
ONEILL DOUGLAS LEE	NJ	02W	129
ONEILL JAMES TIMOTHY	MD	01W	119
ONETO HARRY STEVEN JR	CA	44W	4
ONEY DANIEL LUTHER	OH	21W	25
ONISHEA JESSE JAMES	LA	12W	18
ONKALO PHILIP GORDON	MI	24E	81
ONLEY CLAUDE ALOYSIUS	DC	15E	17
ONOHAN LOUIS GEORGE	IN	01E	50
ONSLOW ROBERT CRANLEY	MN	58E	13
ONTIS BILLIE JOE	CO	38W	29
ONTIVEROS THOMAS J	CA	11E	27
OOCUMMA JOHN EDWARD	NC	15E	49

NAME	STATE	PANEL NO.	LINE NO.
OONK LESTER EUGENE	NE	08W	108
OOTHOUDT GARY ELDON	MN	08E	68
OPLINGER DAVID PAUL	PA	21E	114
OPPERMAN HUGH DANIEL	HI	05W	61
OPSAHL JAMES DEAN	SD	33W	58
OQUENDO FRUTO JAMES	NY	25W	13
OQUENDO JOHN ONOFRE JR	OH	10E	102
OQUENDO-GUTIERREZ RAMON	PR	58W	12
OQUINN ARVIN LEE	VA	26W	65
ORASH MICHAEL WILLIAM	MD	52E	31
ORBINO DENNIS MICHAEL	NY	28W	39
ORCUTT LARRY LEE	IN	32E	64
ORDNER JOHN ALBERT	MN	14W	24
ORDONEZ RAYMOND	IL	54W	18
ORDWAY WILLIAM DWIGHT	MA	34E	70
ORELL QUINLAN ROBERTS	OH	41W	60
OREM ALLEN WAYNE	TX	45W	43
ORENDORFF ERNEST E JR	PA	09E	104
ORETO JOSEPH ANTHONY	MD	27W	76
ORFIELD DAVID CHARLES	OR	13E	105
ORGERON PHILIP JOSEPH	LA	09W	124
ORISON LOUIS JAMES	PA	37E	65
ORLANDI JOSEPH ELISIO JR	NY	12W	8
ORLANDO ANTHONY MARIO	NY	16E	23
ORLANDO GASPER	NY	53E	39
ORLANDO RICHARD DUANE	OH	26W	66
ORLANDO SAMUEL GIZZI	MI	05E	108
ORLEMANN JOHN STEWART	MN	19W	72
ORLEY WALTER FRANK	PA	06E	90
ORLIKOWSKI DANIEL JOHN	WI	16E	37
ORLOWSKI CHARLES FRANCIS	WI	28W	1
ORLOWSKI HEDWIG DIANE	MI	31E	15
ORLOWSKI JOSEPH M	IL	27W	39
ORMOND DENNIS ALAN	IL	30W	94
ORN DEAN RUSSELL	IN	29W	13
ORNELAS BENJAMIN	TX	08E	116
ORNELAS CARL JOHN	KS	37E	41
ORNELAS JACK MICHAEL	NY	26W	49
ORNELAS-ARELLANO VICTOR M	CA	42W	72
ORNSBEY CHARLES RAY	MS	31W	14
OROPEZA MANUEL GARCIA	CA	54W	38
OROSCO LARRY J	CA	25E	13
OROSCO STEPHEN	NM	22W	81
OROSZ ANDREW JOHN	NY	30E	31
OROZCO ANTONIO	TX	44E	40
OROZCO REYNALDO NAVA	TX	49E	36
OROZCO TONY SALAZAR JR	AZ	49W	16
ORPHANOS THEOPHILOS	NY	03E	88
ORR BRIAN STANLEY	VT	10W	27
ORR BYRON DAVIS	UT	09E	94
ORR EMMETT SOMERS	KY	41W	42
ORR GEORGE JAMES	IL	04W	131
ORR JIMMIE RAY	TN	03E	3
ORR MERLIN GEORGE	NE	10W	2
ORR MICHAEL WALTER	MI	34E	44
ORR PATRICK OREILLY	KY	03W	18
ORR RAYMOND FRANKLIN JR	CA	39W	9
ORR RAYMOND SAMUEL	NC	14E	37
ORR ROBERT THOMAS	NY	29W	31
ORR THOMAS B JR	NC	35W	55
ORR THOMAS JOSEPH	CA	23W	10
ORR WARREN ROBERT JR	IL	59E	10
ORRICO JOHN THOMAS	CT	06W	35
ORRIS STEVE III	MI	03E	35
ORSINI JOHN JOSEPH JR	TX	05W	18
ORSINO JOHN GEORGE	PA	28E	76
ORSLAND GARY VARNER	CO	50W	32
ORSO PRINIS WILSON	LA	43W	48
ORSUA CHARLES DAVID	CA	20W	2
ORSUND RICHARD WAYNE	ND	46E	48
ORSZULAK KENNETH BENEDICT	IL	56E	29
ORT IVAN ALLEN JR	IN	33E	30
ORT STEVEN MICHAEL	OH	43W	30
ORTA RAUL	NJ	14E	105
ORTALS DAVID JOHN	PA	10W	83
ORTEGA ANIBAL JR	NY	61E	1
ORTEGA ERNEST	KS	13E	69
ORTEGA FRANK DENNIS	CA	41E	26
ORTEGA HILBERTO	TX	36E	80
ORTEGA JESUS F JR	NV	52W	30
ORTEGA JOE LUCIO JR	TX	05W	107
ORTEGA RAMON FELIX JR	NM	34W	79

NAME	STATE	PANEL NO.	LINE NO.
ORTEGA WILLIAM	NY	27W	102
ORTEGA WILLIAM JR	NY	17W	69
ORTEGO GERALD M	LA	38W	29
ORTEGON RICARDO JOSEPH	CA	30W	58
ORTIS JOSEPH RAYE	OR	14E	45
ORTIZ ALBERTO JR	TX	01W	3
ORTIZ ANTONIO OLIVAREZ	AZ	06W	132
ORTIZ ARTURO MARQUEZ	CA	38E	9
ORTIZ DOMINGO	NY	42E	55
ORTIZ ELIEZER	PA	60W	21
ORTIZ EUGENIO	NY	15W	130
ORTIZ JACOB	CO	29E	80
ORTIZ JOHN	IL	34E	63
ORTIZ JOHN MANUEL	IL	30E	46
ORTIZ JOSE ANGEL	TX	19W	108
ORTIZ JOSE ESPIRIDION	TX	17W	98
ORTIZ JOSE HECTOR	OH	22E	80
ORTIZ JOSE HECTOR	PR	11W	69
ORTIZ LAWRENCE JR	TX	36W	45
ORTIZ LOUIS THOMAS	PA	17W	20
ORTIZ MANUEL GALVAN	IL	44W	52
ORTIZ MARCELO JR	TX	50E	52
ORTIZ MELECIO	TX	19E	111
ORTIZ PEDRO	CA	19E	7
ORTIZ PEDRO MORENO	TX	56E	29
ORTIZ RANDALL ISAAC-JED	CO	19W	81
ORTIZ REINALDO SALVADOR	CA	20E	3
ORTIZ ROBERT WILSON	NJ	07W	34
ORTIZ ZENEIDO JR	OH	37W	41
ORTIZ-BURGOS JOSE ALBERTO	NJ	51W	44
ORTIZ-COLON ULISES	PR	11E	127
ORTIZ-CORREDOR LUIS	NJ	26E	105
ORTIZ-LEBRON ANDRES	PR	09W	21
ORTIZ-LOPEZ ALFONSO	PR	17E	113
ORTIZ-NEGRON JOSE JUAN	PR	38W	51
ORTIZ-ORTIZ CEFERINO ADRI	PR	14E	46
ORTIZ-PEREZ LUIS ANTONIO	PR	51E	48
ORTIZ-RAMIREZ JUAN	NY	25W	31
ORTIZ-RIVERA ANIBAL R	NY	52E	10
ORTIZ-RIVERA JUAN	PR	32E	88
ORTIZ-RODRIGUEZ ANGEL	PR	16E	47
ORTIZ-RODRIGUEZ JAIME	NY	48W	2
ORTMANN RALPH BERNARD	IL	21W	48
ORTON ELLIS JR	UT	12E	117
ORTON KENNETH WILLIAM JR	NY	18E	96
ORTON MATTHEW THEODORE	MO	15E	99
ORTWINE DENNIS ROYAL	MI	05E	122
ORVIS DOUGLAS GORDON	VT	50W	31
ORWIG DAVID THOMAS III	OH	46E	22
ORWIG MICHAEL JOHN	CA	11W	126
OSBON TOMMY EUGENE	TX	27E	21
OSBORN BARRY LEE	IN	21W	55
OSBORN CHARLES EDWARD	OK	45W	27
OSBORN DONALD KEITH	CO	04W	71
OSBORN EARL DOUGLAS	IA	41W	49
OSBORN GEOFFREY HOLMES	FL	02E	93
OSBORN JACK WILLIAM	TX	49E	25
OSBORN JERRY WAYNE	OH	01E	99
OSBORN LYNN ARTHUR	IN	12W	108
OSBORN RICHARD D	FL	31E	59
OSBORN ROBERT JAMES	OK	15W	87
OSBORN THOM THURSTON	MA	04E	104
OSBORN WILLIAM CHESTER	IN	01E	52
OSBORNE AMOS ROY	OR	26E	89
OSBORNE CHARLES EDWARD	KY	05E	14
OSBORNE DAVID FRANKLIN	MD	26W	101
OSBORNE DAVID WILLIAM	MD	08W	133
OSBORNE DONALD GWYN	MD	28E	76
OSBORNE DONALD RAY	OR	17W	74
OSBORNE EDWIN NELMS JR	FL	32E	96
OSBORNE ELVIS WELDON JR	TX	01W	39
OSBORNE GEORGE D	TN	41W	8
OSBORNE GEORGE JR	IN	30E	64
OSBORNE JAKE	KY	22W	35
OSBORNE JOHN WOODROW	NC	26W	86
OSBORNE JOSEPH JR	IL	38E	10
OSBORNE LAWRENCE ELSTON	NY	48E	8
OSBORNE RICHARD GENE	CA	22E	32
OSBORNE ROBERT ALLEN	KY	28W	22
OSBORNE RODNEY DEE	WA	04W	21
OSBORNE RONALD CHARLES	FL	13E	11
OSBORNE SAMUEL WILLIAM JR	SC	18E	103

NAME	STATE	PANEL NO.	LINE NO.
OSBORNE THOMAS YORK	NC	39E	36
OSBURN FRED HARRISON JR	CA	66E	1
OSCAR CECIL THOMAS	VA	59W	10
OSCELUS JOHN ALBERT	PA	49E	26
OSENBAUGH JAMES DALE	KS	33E	40
OSHEIM JON OWEN	IA	34W	17
OSHIRO WARREN SHIGEO	CA	03E	132
OSIER ROBERT DALE JR	MI	08W	55
OSINSKI RONALD ANTHONY	OH	36W	4
OSKILANEC WILLIAM JOSEPH	IL	43W	8
OSNESS VICTOR WILLIAM	UT	35W	17
OSSMEN JOHN DONALD	NJ	15E	71
OSTAPCHUK WALTER MICHAEL	OH	48E	19
OSTEEN MICHAEL STEVEN	FL	55E	25
OSTEEN RICHARD ARNOLD JR	FL	10E	56
OSTEEN THOMAS LELAND JR	VA	06W	71
OSTENFELD OTTO JOHN	NJ	14W	41
OSTENSON RONALD LE ROY	IL	33W	34
OSTER FRANK ALLEN	CA	42E	69
OSTERBERG BERNARD J JR	MI	65W	13
OSTERHOUDT CLIFFORD ROY	NY	04W	47
OSTERHOUS JOHN GARDNER	VA	29W	91
OSTERLOTH JAMES ALLAN	MT	46E	39
OSTERMEYER WILLIAM HENRY	FL	01W	25
OSTIFIN JOSEPH LYNN	PA	39E	10
OSTOLAZO-MALDONADO ALFREDO	PR	09E	116
OSTRAKOVIC GUSTAV	OH	44W	40
OSTRANDER MORRIS EDWARD	NE	54W	32
OSTROFF STEVEN LARRY	CA	28E	29
OSUNA ANTONIO RICHARD	CA	11E	4
OSUNA JOSE LUIS	CA	24W	19
OSUSKI ROBERT EUGENE	WI	41E	12
OSWALD DONALD ROY	PA	13E	75
OTAKE JOHN SADAO	HI	30W	68
OTIS SHERMAN ELDRIDGE	AL	03E	89
OTSEN DAVID BRYAN	CA	30E	65
OTT ALAN ROBERT	MI	60W	4
OTT DOUGLAS RALPH	MN	60W	21
OTT EDWARD LOUIS III	CT	25E	79
OTT JOSEPH STANLEY	NY	52W	30
OTT LARRY FREEMAN	OR	05W	107
OTT PATRICK LOUIS	CA	27E	41
OTT RAYMOND EARL	FL	12W	36
OTT RICHARD DEANE	MD	03E	89
OTT STEVEN ROBERT	WI	08W	116
OTT THOMAS DEVECMON II	MS	24E	38
OTT WAYNE HARRY	PA	24E	38
OTT WILLIAM AUGUST	CA	07W	119
OTTE KENNETH MICHAEL	NE	14E	40
OTTE RICHARD LEE	IL	13E	48
OTTE RICHARD LEE	MI	26E	30
OTTE THOMAS WILLIAM	WI	37E	11
OTTEY CARLTON MATTES	PA	25E	34
OTTMAN TODD WHITNEY	NY	07W	72
OTTMAR STANLEY JOHN	ND	27W	51
OTTMERS RAYMOND MAX JR	TX	25E	35
OTTO DALE LESTER	MN	19E	120
OTTO MICHAEL L	CO	21E	14
OTTO ROGER DEAN	WA	07W	47
OTTO WILLIAM FREDRICK	IL	07E	49
OUELLET DAVID GEORGE	MA	16E	30
OUELLETTE DANIEL P	ME	11W	17
OUELLETTE DAVID DENNIS	CT	28W	13
OUELLETTE DONALD ROLAND	CT	29E	33
OUELLETTE LEWIS CHARLES	NY	11W	1
OUILLETTE DONALD HENRY	RI	39W	2
OUILLETTE THOMAS ROBERT	MI	55E	25
OUTLAW CHARLES REUBEN JR	FL	30W	38
OUTMAN CHARLES EDGAR	MI	25W	24
OUTWATER ALBERT ALEYA JR	NJ	23E	102
OVAITT RICHARD ARTHUR	NJ	49W	33
OVALLE PORFIRIO M JR	TX	31W	58
OVERACKER EARL JOHN	SD	19W	46
OVERBAY CLARENCE M JR	VA	09W	91
OVERBECK PHILIP MOREY	WI	09W	40
OVERBEY MARION DEWAINE	MS	09W	61
OVERCASH WILLIAM TURNER	NC	36W	70
OVERKAMP NORBERT ALVIN JR	MO	25E	39
OVERLOCK JOHN FRANCIS	MA	48W	29
OVERMAN-RODRIGUEZ JOSE R	PR	31W	39
OVERMYER ROBERT JOE	IL	23E	6

NAME	STATE	PANEL NO.	LINE NO.
OVERPECK JAMES HARLEY	IN	21E	56
OVERRIGHT DANIEL LEE	IL	31W	83
OVERSHINE GEORGE EDWARD	TX	27E	30
OVERSTREET DAVID DEWAYNE	TX	28W	20
OVERSTREET ROGER WAYNE	GA	46E	48
OVERSTREET WILLIAM DANIEL	TX	29W	82
OVERSTREET WILLIAM LUTHER	KY	27W	46
OVERSTREET WILLIE JR	TX	58W	28
OVERTON DANNY JR	MI	50W	26
OVERTON DANNY WAYNE	FL	15W	125
OVERTON DOYLE WAYNE	IL	57W	21
OVERTON JEROME	NY	42W	20
OVERTON WILLIAM HILLIARD	AL	25W	1
OVERTON WINCE ISAAC JR	KY	45E	41
OVERTURF PHILIP GENE	IL	18E	54
OVERWEG GEORGE ALLEN	MI	03E	123
OVERWEG ROGER DALE	MI	07W	75
OVESON JAMES RAYMOND	UT	58E	12
OVIATT STEPHEN STANFORD	MT	15W	29
OVIEDO HIGINIO OVALLE	TX	17E	127
OVIEDO MICHAEL LESLIE	AZ	34W	66
OVIST DAVID EMANUEL	MI	28W	13
OVNAND CHESTER N	OK	01E	1
OVSAK GEORGE WILLIAM	NC	15E	75
OWCZARCZAK MELVIN JOSEPH	NY	45W	19
OWEN CHARLES THOMAS	TN	12E	90
OWEN CLYDE CHILTON	MO	06W	123
OWEN DAVID B	NJ	27E	50
OWEN DEAN GILMAN	MD	48E	31
OWEN JOHN WILSON	AZ	09W	116
OWEN LARRY JAMES	VA	37W	57
OWEN RAY WILLIAM	SC	59E	27
OWEN ROBERT DANEL JR	AR	08E	87
OWEN ROBERT DUVAL	VA	67E	1
OWEN ROBERT GARY	CA	41W	19
OWEN SAMUEL TAYLOR	TX	04W	42
OWEN STEPHEN BOYD	WA	56W	7
OWEN STEVEN CRAIG	CA	23W	29
OWEN THURMAN WAYNE	TX	06E	77
OWEN TIMOTHY SAMUEL	NY	54W	18
OWEN WILLIAM LEE JR	IL	27W	58
OWENBY CLYDE	GA	22E	47
OWENBY EUGENE OLIVER	GA	20E	47
OWENS ALBERT DANNY	CA	23W	113
OWENS BEN	IN	32E	79
OWENS BENNETT HOWELL JR	FL	06E	123
OWENS BILLY RAY	CA	10E	26
OWENS CARL EUGENE	NC	06W	29
OWENS CHARLES EDWARD	NC	43W	19
OWENS CLAUDE JAMES	LA	28W	51
OWENS DAVID LEE	MA	11E	50
OWENS DAVID RAY	AL	56E	29
OWENS DEWEY RAY	AL	45E	4
OWENS ELWOOD	NC	56W	26
OWENS FRED MONROE	OK	02E	3
OWENS GARY LEE	PA	37W	41
OWENS GEORGE ADAM	MD	47E	4
OWENS HAROLD EUGENE	FL	43W	48
OWENS HENRY LAWRENCE	SC	24W	9
OWENS HOWARD	TN	43W	57
OWENS JACK COLEMAN	CA	17E	63
OWENS JAMES DOUGLAS	SC	02W	126
OWENS JAMES EUGENE	SC	25E	107
OWENS JAMES HOWARD JR	IL	20W	96
OWENS JAMES JOSEPH	NY	18E	62
OWENS JERRY LYNN	AR	37W	68
OWENS JOHN WILLIAM	MI	05E	17
OWENS JOY LEONARD	WA	21E	70
OWENS KENNETH GRANT	FL	30E	65
OWENS LARRINGTON	VA	38E	10
OWENS LARRY RAY	WY	17W	51
OWENS LARRY THOMAS	TN	60W	6
OWENS MARTIN LEE	SC	67E	1
OWENS PERCIE EDWARD	NY	17E	11
OWENS RANDY LEE	CO	20W	81
OWENS REO	CA	09E	84
OWENS RICHARD LEE	CA	24E	38
OWENS ROBERT ERNEST	IL	16W	53
OWENS ROBERT FRANKLIN	IN	50E	19
OWENS ROBERT LEE	SC	58E	12
OWENS THOMAS BREVARD	MD	09W	132
OWENS THOMAS EARL	AL	22W	42
OWENS THOMAS RUDOLPH	GA	51W	43
OWENS TIMOTHY EUGENE	KS	50E	19
OWENS VERNELL	NY	56W	14
OWENS WALTER ALBERT	NY	31E	30
OWENS WILBERT	OH	35W	78
OWNBEY TIMOTHY ROBERT	OR	06W	21
OWNBY EDWARD ALLAN JOSEPH	CA	02E	2
OXENDINE CHARLES HEDRIC	NC	33W	81
OXENDINE HUGHIE	NC	32E	59
OXENDINE RODNEY GLENN	VA	19W	19
OXENDINE WILLIE F III	NC	63W	19
OXFORD HARRY EDWARD JR	NY	10E	5
OXLEY JAMES EDWARD	NC	12E	122
OXLEY JAMES EDWARD	AZ	18E	72
OXLEY JAMES KEITH	PA	31E	15
OXNER MARION LUTHER	SC	44W	40
OXX LAWRENCE MCFIE JR	NC	02W	101
OYOLA HECTOR DAVID	NY	08W	111
OYOLA-RABAGO ANIBAL	PR	32E	52
OZANNE JORDAN JAY	CA	57E	30
OZBUN JAMES D	CA	36W	73
OZGER ISLAM	NY	27W	16
OZIMEK RONALD ROBERT	NY	20W	125
OZUNA JUAN SANCHEZ	WA	32E	3
PAARZ GARY FREDRICK	NJ	18E	6
PABEY JOSE ANTHONY	IN	43W	48
PABST EUGENE MATTHEW	NY	11E	58
PACE DANNY WAYNE	AL	24E	38
PACE GARY LYNN	IN	28W	100
PACE GARY LYNN	SC	04W	95
PACE GEORGE ALEXANDER	MI	23E	6
PACE JAMES ALVIN	FL	47W	2
PACE JAMES RALPH	TN	06E	34
PACE JAMES TAYLOR	TX	13W	64
PACE RONALD EARL	CA	24W	33
PACE RONALD EUGENE	SC	09W	21
PACE RONALD GENE	TX	28W	93
PACETTA COSMO FRANCIS	NY	26E	2
PACHE HARLAN T	WI	34E	50
PACHECO ANDREW JOSE	NM	56W	27
PACHECO DONALD GONZALES	TX	50W	19
PACHECO EUGENE CARL	CO	25E	71
PACHECO FELIX	KS	10E	43
PACHECO FRANK MANUEL	RI	25E	75
PACHECO GEORGE ARTHUR	CO	04W	127
PACHECO JAIME	NM	01W	32
PACHECO JOSE ANTHONY	CA	06E	111
PACHECO MICHAEL JEROME	HI	18W	122
PACHECO ROBERT LEE	CA	37W	58
PACIO GEORGE HENRY	NY	06W	135
PACIOREK ROBERT EDWARD	OH	30E	47
PACK FRED WALTER	CA	16E	64
PACK JUNIOR B	TX	22E	84
PACK ROBERT VAN	OK	35W	50
PACK SANFORD GENE	MI	12W	43
PACK WILLARD ORVAL	TX	50W	31
PACKARD CARL EDWARD JR	CT	25W	80
PACKARD DAN BRUEN	FL	08E	31
PACKARD GEORGE RICHARD	IN	59W	10
PACKARD ROBERT FRANK	NY	12E	38
PACKARD RONALD LYLE	CO	24E	56
PACKER JOSEPH EVERETT JR	NJ	08E	53
PACO RICHARD MANUEL	CA	25W	53
PACOLBA ALFREDO	HI	18W	71
PADAYHAG AL SUMINGUIT		01E	7
PADBERG LARRY GENE	OK	25W	80
PADDLEFORD FRED HAROLD	FL	24W	47
PADDOCK DAVID ALLEN	NY	59W	26
PADDOCK GARY CLIFFTON	WA	15E	35
PADDOCK JOHN EVERETT	WA	10E	87
PADDOCK MICHAEL JAMES	CA	21W	29
PADDOCK MICHAEL L	CA	29W	47
PADGETT DALLAS LANDON	TX	35W	44
PADGETT DAVID EUGENE	IN	33W	73
PADGETT JON LESLIE	IN	11W	76
PADGETT ROBERT JERRY	GA	27E	66
PADGETT SAMUEL JOSEPH	OK	49E	14
PADIER WILTON JR	TX	16W	122
PADILLA ANTONIO DUARTE	CA	02E	65
PADILLA DAVID ESEQUIEL	TX	62E	22
PADILLA EDDIE JACK	CA	07W	44
PADILLA FIDEL	TX	25W	80
PADILLA GARY TEOFILIO	CA	04W	20
PADILLA GEORGE ISAAC	WA	14E	37
PADILLA GILBERTO	TX	11W	64
PADILLA JOSEPH ANTHONY	WY	62E	18
PADILLA MICHAEL DAVID	MT	51E	11
PADILLA MICHAEL RAYMOND	TX	16E	12
PADILLA PEDRO	NM	06E	57
PADILLA RALPH HENRY	CA	57W	2
PADILLA ROBERT LOUIS	CA	07E	74
PADILLA RONALD MATTHEW	HI	08E	48
PADILLA THOMAS	IL	12W	43
PADILLA-JORGE JAIME	PR	23W	39
PADRON IRENARDO FELIX	FL	25W	10
PADUA-LEDESMA AUGUSTO C	PR	11W	114
PADUCHOWSKI PAUL RICHARD	NY	37E	65
PAELE PETER JAMES	HI	28E	46
PAEPKE DUANE CARL JR	CA	30W	28
PAEZ JOSEPH FLAVIO	IL	27W	58
PAGADUAN GUILLERMO BAUTIS	PR	34E	90
PAGALING MICHAEL	CA	35W	21
PAGAN EDWIN PEREZ	IL	22W	107
PAGAN GARY DON	TX	38W	19
PAGAN MIGUEL	NY	61E	1
PAGAN-CARTAGENA JOSE RAMO	PR	04E	73
PAGAN-LOZADA WILFREDO	NY	15E	11
PAGAN-PAGAN AMALIO	PR	17E	59
PAGAN-RODRIGUEZ EVANGELIS	PR	12E	122
PAGCALIUAGAN CEIZHAR VALE	CA	42E	8
PAGE ADDISON WILLIAM JR	MA	02W	35
PAGE ALBERT LINWOOD JR	NH	24E	84
PAGE DAVID RONALD	IL	18E	96
PAGE EDGAR DE WITT	TX	52E	42
PAGE GEORGE MERRITT JR	CA	22W	35
PAGE GILBERT WAYNE	VA	24W	33
PAGE GORDON LEE	CA	05E	128
PAGE HENRY LINDSAY III	VA	55W	36
PAGE JAMES HENRY	WI	05E	122
PAGE JAMES ROBERT	IL	21E	85
PAGE JIM CAREY	OR	21W	85
PAGE JIMMY EDWARD	FL	19E	63
PAGE JOHN ARTHUR	CA	38E	58
PAGE JOHN GEORGE	NY	07W	59
PAGE JOHN MacARTHUR	IL	34W	44
PAGE JOHN WILLIE	TX	30E	11
PAGE LARRY LEE	MS	08E	76
PAGE LEWIS WAYNE	IL	48W	46
PAGE LUTHER JR	CA	39E	36
PAGE M C	TX	18W	96
PAGE MICHAEL RANSOM	CA	43W	57
PAGE PHILLIP ALLEN	SC	22W	59
PAGE RICHARD LEE	WA	03W	112
PAGE RONNIE	IL	18W	49
PAGE ROY DONALD	AL	42E	38
PAGE RUSSELL ELWARD	LA	22E	33
PAGE STEVE WILSON	CA	04E	94
PAGE THELBERT G	IL	30E	47
PAGE WILLIE LEE	NY	21E	63
PAGE WINGFIELD JR	DC	32W	81
PAGET MICHAEL GORDON	CA	01W	121
PAGLIARONI ALAN PAUL	NY	54E	28
PAGNANO ENRICO HENRY JR	MA	06E	21
PAHCHEKA ROBERT CARLOS	OK	40W	22
PAHISSA WILLIAM ANTHONY	AZ	08W	44
PAHL KENNETH ALLEN	MN	40W	22
PAHL RONALD G	IN	34E	81
PAHR WILLIAM JOHN JR	IL	36W	46
PAIALII PASIA	HI	02E	95
PAIER HELMUT WALTER	VA	17W	113
PAIGE DOUGLAS ALAN	NY	42W	20
PAIGE EZEKIEL	NC	47E	26
PAIGE ROBERT EDWARD	MO	16E	106
PAINE EDWARD ARTHUR	CA	20E	17
PAINE PAUL WARREN	MN	56E	29
PAINE VICTOR LLEWELLYN	CA	09E	5
PAINTER CURTIS WAYNE	SC	28E	85
PAINTER DAVID OLIVER	VA	44W	28
PAINTER DENNIS EARL	IL	50E	52
PAINTER GARY WILLIAM	GA	41E	70
PAINTER HOWARD LEROY	MI	38E	70
PAINTER JOHN RALPH JR	CA	21E	50
PAINTER JOHN ROBERT JR	MA	03W	81

NAME	STATE	PANEL NO.	LINE NO.
PAINTER MARVIN REED	OH	25W	13
PAINTER MICHAEL HARRIS	ID	20W	115
PAINTER ROBERT ALBERT JR	MD	07W	94
PAINTER ROBERT GLEN	PA	37E	11
PAINTER ROBERT LEE	CA	14E	29
PAINTER WAYNE ALLEN	OH	65W	13
PAIRAN WALTER ALLAN	OH	20E	47
PAIRIS ARNOLD	SC	50E	40
PAIZ JERRY	CA	31E	60
PAKELE FRED DALE	HI	05W	92
PAKULA THOMAS VINCENT	MI	15W	99
PALACIO GILBERT GONZALES	TX	25W	14
PALACIO JOE MAURICIO	CA	06W	102
PALACIO RAYMOND JESUS	CA	38E	58
PALACIOS CASIMIRO	CA	06E	81
PALACIOS LUIS FERNANDO	CA	59W	11
PALACIOS OSCAR H JR	TX	26E	36
PALACIOS TONY	CA	27W	40
PALANDRO RAYMOND JOSEPH	PA	20W	31
PALAZZOLA STEPHEN FRANK	NY	43E	29
PALCIC ERNEST PATRICK	NY	35E	26
PALCOWSKI RICHARD WAYNE	IL	07W	17
PALCZEWSKI EDMUND LAWRENC	CA	29E	16
PALEN CARL ANTHONY	IA	05W	23
PALENIK JAMES ANDRES JR	IL	49E	14
PALENSCAR ALEXANDER J III	NY	17E	59
PALENSCAR ROBERT JOSEPH	NY	63E	19
PALENSKE WILLIAM ALLEN	CA	12E	85
PALERMO GEORGE ROBERT	MA	23W	46
PALEY NORMAN FRED	OH	06W	82
PALISKIS EUGENE MICHAEL	OH	01E	72
PALK BOBBY LEE	TN	06W	130
PALL JOHN JOSEPH	NJ	47E	43
PALLADINO THOMAS ARTHUR	NY	13W	47
PALLAYE LOUIS DALE	OH	15W	25
PALM ALLEN NEIL	PA	37W	47
PALM DALE ARDEN	OH	44W	40
PALM DENNIS DU WAYNE	IL	25W	41
PALM JOSH JR	LA	11E	50
PALM TERRY ALAN	VA	08W	18
PALMA FRANCIS MICHAEL	PA	18E	126
PALMA GERARD VINCENT	NJ	26W	8
PALMA LUCO WILLIAM	MA	07W	72
PALMA RAYMOND BARELA	CA	32E	79
PALMENTA EDWARD VINCENT	CT	22W	25
PALMER ARNOLD RALPH	IA	23E	6
PALMER BRUCE CAMERON	MI	46W	43
PALMER CARL LEE	GA	03E	60
PALMER CLARENCE LEROY	MN	31E	16
PALMER DAVID LESLIE	CA	10W	30
PALMER DAVID SCOTT	MI	23E	14
PALMER DOUGLAS T	CT	10E	29
PALMER GARY JAMES	PA	41W	65
PALMER GILBERT SWAIN	AL	41E	53
PALMER HENRY LEE	KY	33W	87
PALMER HUBERT	FL	32W	39
PALMER JAMES	IL	32W	33
PALMER JAMES EDWARD	VA	02W	78
PALMER JAMES HESTER	MS	11W	60
PALMER JAMES KENNETH	TN	32E	89
PALMER JAMES LAMONT	PA	10E	93
PALMER JERRY ALLEN	AR	34W	67
PALMER JESSE JAMES	TX	44W	5
PALMER JOHNNY LEE	FL	30W	48
PALMER KENNETH OSCAR	RI	57W	12
PALMER LARRY DALE	PA	13W	37
PALMER LARRY RAY	IL	26E	49
PALMER LAYMON	AR	04W	88
PALMER LEON ALTON	GA	48W	35
PALMER LEROY JR	IL	67W	1
PALMER LYLE CLINT	UT	25W	79
PALMER MILLARD LAMAR	GA	52E	42
PALMER RONNY LEROY	CA	20E	33
PALMER SAMMY RAY	MS	36W	19
PALMER WALTER	NY	24W	34
PALMER WILLIAM HERSCHELL	AL	42W	13
PALMERI JAMES EDWARD	MA	31W	71
PALMGREN EDWIN DAVID	NC	51E	32
PALMIERI DAVID HAROLD	MA	22W	35
PALMIERI ERNEST	NY	13E	23
PALMIERI JOHN JOSEPH	CT	38E	58
PALMO JIMMIE CHARLES	TX	37E	65
PALMORE DONALD STEVEN	OH	63W	11
PALMORE ROBERT DUANE	TX	11W	76
PALMQUIST STEVEN LEONARD	CA	42W	63
PALOS ERASMO	TX	47E	25
PALOWSKI RICHARD EDWIN	CT	49W	6
PALUMBO ANTHONY PAUL	NY	59E	10
PALUMBO NICKOLAS R JR	OH	25E	65
PALUSCIO JOHN JOSEPH	PA	04E	121
PAMANET PAUL JOSEPH	WI	38W	29
PAMONICUTT MARTIN JAMES	WI	22W	123
PAMPEL LOREN LEE	IL	37E	66
PAMPLIN JOHN MAC	AR	61E	16
PANAK JOHN JR	PA	45W	16
PANAMAROFF WALTER JOHN	CA	44E	61
PANARESE ROLAND JOHN	NC	26W	11
PANEK ROBERT JOSEPH SR	IL	14W	76
PANELLA NICK JR	PA	22E	121
PANGAN ROGER ROGELIO	HI	20W	31
PANGANORAN ABRAHAM	HI	19E	99
PANGELINAN GREGORIO L	GM	30W	94
PANGELINAN PEDRO CABRERA	GM	05W	135
PANGLE WILLIAM MEDFORD	VA	51E	38
PANICCIA RONALD JAMES	NY	38W	37
PANKIEWICZ JAMES MICHAEL	IL	22W	100
PANKUCH BRUCE ALAN	OH	23W	104
PANNABECKER DAVID ERIC	PA	02W	120
PANNELL HARRY CLAYBURN	KY	38W	19
PANNELL JOSEPH	IL	30E	47
PANNELL PHILLIP RANDALL	TX	29W	39
PANNELL TYRONE SIDNEY	NY	03E	118
PANNELL WALTER THAXTON	GA	37E	66
PANNO DONALD DAVID	PA	37W	14
PANNO RONALD WILLIAM	MN	19W	56
PANQUERNE CHARLES PAUL	LA	03W	103
PANTALL JAMES ROBERT	PA	02W	61
PANTIER JAMES EDWARD	WY	51E	11
PANTOJA CIPRIANO J JR	TX	17E	118
PANULA REINO ARNE	IN	01E	79
PANZARELLA JAMES FRANCIS	RI	10E	125
PANZER RONALD LEE	MN	48W	2
PAOLANTONIO BENNIE JOE	PA	16E	123
PAOLETTI SAMUEL	DE	23E	83
PAONESSA MICHAEL DOMINIC	OH	40W	4
PAOPAO KEILA	CA	35E	56
PAPA FRANK J	NY	29E	16
PAPA WILLIAM JAMES	OH	55E	26
PAPALAS ANTHONY STEVEN	CA	23E	45
PAPALE ARTHUR LAWRENCE	MS	32W	45
PAPARELLO JOSEPH JOHN	CT	19W	81
PAPE FRANK ALBERT	IL	36E	58
PAPE JOHN CHARLES	NY	24W	49
PAPE JOHN DAVID	NJ	63W	19
PAPE ROBERT PAUL	PA	07W	34
PAPENFUS ALLEN DARYL	WI	16E	85
PAPESH DAVID C	MN	16E	11
PAPIN SAMUEL ALEXANDER JR	CA	19W	19
PAPKE THEODORE ARTHUR	NY	37E	42
PAPPAN BOBBY JACK	KS	45W	43
PAPPAS DON LEE	CA	13W	25
PAPPAS ELEFTHERIOS PANTEL	NY	12E	2
PAPPAS RALPH BYRON	CA	17E	75
PAPPENHEIM THOMAS HENRY	CO	08W	122
PAPPIN JOHN PATRICK	OK	13W	120
PAQUETTE BRUCE ARMAND	VT	27E	102
PAQUETTE RICHARD WALTER	IL	11W	96
PAQUIN HOWARD ROBERT	NY	26W	2
PAQUIN MICHAEL BRADLEY	CT	32E	3
PAQUIN PAUL EVERETTE JR	NJ	09W	99
PARADA EDWARD JOHN	PA	07W	18
PARADA-BARRERA ANTONIO	NY	07E	83
PARADIS RAYMOND LOUIS	NH	10W	8
PARADISE CHARLES ALONZO	TX	25E	107
PARAMATTO PAUL ANGELO	NY	64E	5
PARASILITI NICHOLAS	NY	44E	51
PARCEL JOHN WILLIAM	IN	51E	32
PARCELS REX LEWIS JR	CA	13W	100
PARCHER ROBERT HAROLD JR	KY	33W	88
PARDEE SCOTT KENTON	VA	12W	36
PARDO THOMAS ANTHONY	NY	08W	29
PAREDES ISMAEL JUSON	NJ	03E	89
PAREDEZ AUGUSTIN CHAVEZ	TX	03E	89
PARENT JEFFERY MARK	MA	25W	1
PARENT JOSEPH W	MO	06E	81
PARENT ROBERT WARREN	MA	51W	28
PARESA EDWARD KENNETH	HI	08E	101
PARHAM JAMES WAYNE	TX	34E	90
PARHAM JOHN HOLT III	GA	10W	115
PARHAM JOHN WILLIAM	TN	29W	71
PARHAM LOUIE SNYDER	TX	01E	96
PARHAM RICHARD LYNN	CA	14E	98
PARIS CRAWFORD BRIAN	CA	13E	12
PARISH CHARLES CARROLL	VA	50W	8
PARISH DAVID LEROY	IA	16E	83
PARISH EUGENE ALLEN	IN	28E	10
PARISH FRANK BRENNAN	CA	08E	61
PARISH MICHAEL LAWRENCE	CA	21E	29
PARISI GUILLERMO	CA	23W	56
PARK AUBREY G	TX	27E	37
PARK IRVING GEON	IN	13W	88
PARK JOSEPH CONARD JR	PA	46E	58
PARK MARVIN EDWARD	IA	25W	81
PARK RICHARD LEWIS	PA	04W	20
PARK ROBERT LEE	IN	26W	3
PARKEL GERALD PHILLIP	CA	27E	61
PARKER ALBERT EDEN	SC	16W	112
PARKER ALVIN G	TN	01E	86
PARKER ANDREW DAYTON JR	TN	02E	11
PARKER ARNOLD RAY	VA	41W	7
PARKER ARTHUR M III	SC	63W	11
PARKER BENNIE FRANK	CA	04E	120
PARKER BENNY BRUCE	AR	19W	63
PARKER BILLY RAY	KY	10W	66
PARKER CARL SYLVESTER	TX	08E	4
PARKER CARTER JR	AL	06W	19
PARKER CHARLES JOHN	MI	40W	25
PARKER CHARLES LESLIE JR	CA	01W	111
PARKER CHARLES THOMAS	NC	36E	81
PARKER DALE WARREN	FL	48E	32
PARKER DANNY LYNN	OK	23W	91
PARKER DAVID ALBERT	PA	31W	96
PARKER DAVID ALLEN	TX	48E	32
PARKER DAVID LLOYD	MN	36E	29
PARKER DAVID WAYNE	GA	33W	73
PARKER DONALD FREDRICK	GA	34E	91
PARKER DONALD LEE	OH	11W	86
PARKER EARL EPHRAIM	VA	41E	26
PARKER EDGAR EUGENE	SC	51W	43
PARKER ERIC	OH	50W	15
PARKER EUAN JOHN ERNEST	UT	24W	112
PARKER FRANK C III	PA	32E	96
PARKER FREDERICK G JR	MA	36W	73
PARKER GEORGE JOSEPH JR	NY	26W	15
PARKER HARVEY R	KS	13E	117
PARKER HERMAN JR	MO	45W	43
PARKER JAMES ALLEN	MD	13W	82
PARKER JAMES DALTON	OR	01E	34
PARKER JAMES EARL	NC	38E	36
PARKER JAMES EDWARD	NY	22W	100
PARKER JAMES LEONARD JR	NY	49E	45
PARKER JAMES LESTER	NC	17E	96
PARKER JAMES RONALD	NC	48W	19
PARKER JIMMIE EDWARD	CA	42E	55
PARKER JOHN BOYD	LA	22W	25
PARKER JOHN JACKSON	FL	13W	82
PARKER JOHNNY KENDRICK	AL	20W	26
PARKER JOHNNY RAY	OK	28W	28
PARKER JOSEPH E JR	MT	02E	26
PARKER KENNETH	CA	25W	14
PARKER KENNETH WAYNE	MO	02E	15
PARKER LARRY	NV	12W	31
PARKER LARRY THOMAS	CA	31E	16
PARKER LEON VICTOR	OH	21W	66
PARKER LESTER EUGENE	OH	09W	106
PARKER LEWIS JEFFERY	NC	34E	44
PARKER LONNIE EDWARD	AR	16E	73
PARKER LONNIE RONALD	AL	17W	8
PARKER LONNIE THOMAS	VA	40W	30
PARKER MARK EDWARD	NY	09E	116
PARKER MARVIN RUSSELL	MO	45W	8
PARKER MAXIM CHARLES	CA	16E	107
PARKER MICHAEL	NY	22E	72
PARKER MICHAEL LEE	AZ	32E	79
PARKER OTIS	FL	08W	30
PARKER PAUL ELMER	UT	47W	25

NAME	STATE	PANEL NO.	LINE NO.
PARKER PERLUM M JR	GA	20W	77
PARKER RALPH JOHN JR	CT	28E	104
PARKER RICHARD ANTHONY	GA	46W	7
PARKER RICHARD DENNIS	UT	04E	121
PARKER RICHARD EUGENE	NY	32W	67
PARKER RICHARD HOWARD	OK	30E	80
PARKER ROBERT	SC	44W	59
PARKER ROBERT KENNETH	MA	15W	10
PARKER ROGER LOUIS	OH	14E	53
PARKER RONALD WAYNE	WA	13E	119
PARKER RONNIE EARL	CA	24W	47
PARKER ROY EUGENE	CA	26W	72
PARKER RUDOLPH	LA	22W	42
PARKER SAMUEL LEE	OH	26E	30
PARKER STEPHEN VANCE	NY	25W	108
PARKER THOMAS AQUINAS	IN	17E	106
PARKER THOMAS EDWARD	CT	31W	55
PARKER UDON	AL	06E	4
PARKER VERNON HOWARD JR	PA	11E	16
PARKER VICTOR RALPH	CA	02E	119
PARKER WAYMON M	GA	25E	20
PARKER WESLEY	SC	23E	120
PARKER WILLIAM AVALON	AL	08W	55
PARKER WILLIAM E III	OH	35W	31
PARKER WILLIAM GENE	MI	49E	47
PARKER WILLIAM HILL	NY	59W	11
PARKER WILLIAM MONROE	CA	01W	123
PARKER WILLIAM THOMAS	CA	43W	19
PARKER WILLIAM THOMAS III	MD	21E	29
PARKER WINSTON GLEN	OH	57E	31
PARKER WOODROW WILSON II	FL	51E	48
PARKHILL FRANCIS EDWIN JR	PA	10W	99
PARKHURST GREIG ROBERT	WA	30E	98
PARKHURST VINCENT BERTRAM	IL	40E	46
PARKIN HAROLD LESLIE	MI	23W	77
PARKINSON GARY CONVERS	CA	42E	69
PARKS A L	OK	02E	85
PARKS ALAN HUGH	MI	10W	110
PARKS CALVIN ALAN	AZ	19E	64
PARKS CHARLES H JR	SC	19W	89
PARKS DAVID NORTON	CA	22E	59
PARKS DONALD JERALD	MD	41W	19
PARKS FLOYD JUNIOR	KY	24W	10
PARKS GLENN ALLEN	IL	09W	74
PARKS JAMES KERMIT	OH	37W	1
PARKS JERRY EMMET	MI	05E	122
PARKS JOE	TX	01E	78
PARKS JOSEPH L	MI	21E	91
PARKS RAYMOND FRANCIS	OH	01E	25
PARKS RAYMOND GEORGE	MI	18W	21
PARKS STEPHEN EARL	CA	28E	105
PARKS SYDNEY	OH	45E	26
PARKS WILLIE ALBERT	MI	21E	84
PARKULO DANNY RICHARD	WV	15E	121
PARLIAMENT KIM RANDLE	IN	50E	7
PARMELEE BRUCE CARLTON	MA	18E	62
PARMELEE JAMES EARL	MI	02E	37
PARMELEE JEFFREY MATHEW	NY	04W	77
PARMENTIER GERALD VICTOR	RI	20E	10
PARMENTIER ROGER DAVID	CO	08W	119
PARMERTER MICHAEL JAMES	NJ	22W	113
PARMETER GERALD THOMAS	CA	68E	6
PARMLEY DONALD WAYNE	MS	19W	114
PARNELL BILLY RAY	TX	04W	97
PARNELL KERMITT CHEVENE	NC	11E	119
PARNELL PETER PAUL JR	MO	15W	83
PARNELL RICHARD JAMES	NC	20W	31
PARNELL WILLIAM BRICE	NC	05E	62
PARNELLA JOHN	CA	06E	118
PARNELLE SAMUEL W III	NV	67W	3
PARO RANDY CHARLEY	HI	26W	93
PAROBEK SILAS WILLIAM	PA	26W	15
PAROLA JAY WAYNE	PA	40W	50
PAROPACIC JOHN PAUL	PA	18E	63
PAROUNAGIAN GEORGE JR	FL	41E	27
PARR KEITH MASON	IL	17W	122
PARR LARRY DOUGLAS	MI	26W	55
PARR MICHAEL GRAMBLING	TX	38W	77
PARR RONALD EUGENE	AL	53E	20
PARRA LIONEL JR	CA	52W	45
PARRA MANUEL FRANCISCO	CA	20W	115
PARRANTO LAWRENCE W JR	WA	26W	93

NAME	STATE	PANEL NO.	LINE NO.
PARRETT JAMES RAY	IN	03E	15
PARRILLA-CALDERON JAIME	PR	24E	78
PARRIS BOBBY JAMES	NC	06W	25
PARRIS DOUGLAS HAROLD	WA	06W	94
PARRIS JEROME JR	IL	62E	9
PARRISH BILLY JOE	WA	67E	1
PARRISH CONNIE WAYNE	AR	13W	16
PARRISH FRANK COLLINS	TX	34E	59
PARRISH IVORY PERRY	MI	16E	86
PARRISH LEONARD MONROE	NC	48W	14
PARRISH PHILIP OWEN	NC	21E	37
PARRISH ROGER ALAN	KS	22W	15
PARRISH RUDOLPH STEPHEN	NC	19W	89
PARRISH SAMUEL JOSEPH	VA	32W	8
PARROTT BRIAN GREGORY	WA	20W	66
PARROTT DEMPSEY WOODROW	NC	54E	39
PARROTT OSCAR ROBERT	TN	19E	40
PARSELLS JOHN WILLIAM	FL	07W	97
PARSLEY EDWARD MILTON	WV	04E	135
PARSLEY RONALD LEE	OH	14E	30
PARSON DOYLE HALL	NE	15W	109
PARSONS CHARLES EDWARD	MA	41E	70
PARSONS CHARLES WALTER	MD	08E	43
PARSONS CLIFFORD E JR	CT	08W	25
PARSONS DON BROWN JR	NY	10E	121
PARSONS DONALD EUGENE	IL	33W	73
PARSONS DOUGLAS BLANCHARD	CO	45E	27
PARSONS GARY LEE	NY	55E	26
PARSONS GARY REED	KS	11E	20
PARSONS GERALD LOYD	OK	53E	40
PARSONS GREGORY ALLEN	MN	13W	33
PARSONS HENRY BENNETT III	CA	15W	7
PARSONS JAMES LLOYD	MO	50E	52
PARSONS JOHN ROBERT	KY	41W	62
PARSONS LIONEL EUGENE	OK	16W	66
PARSONS MICHAEL DUANE	NV	05W	23
PARSONS PAUL GENE	OH	05E	108
PARSONS RONALD ALLEN	ME	32E	55
PARSONS RONALD NEAL	OH	12W	89
PARSONS ROY BROWN	OK	40E	46
PARSONS TERRY LEE	OH	55W	8
PARSONS WARREN CECIL JR	MO	51E	12
PARTEE JOHN LEROY	NC	28W	84
PARTEE WARDLOW WESLEY	MI	03E	46
PARTIDA ANDREW	MI	22W	15
PARTIDA CHARLIE LOPEZ	CA	43W	65
PARTIN DANIEL ROSS	FL	09W	5
PARTIN GEORGE EDWARD	DE	24E	110
PARTINGTON ROGER DALE	IL	16W	15
PARTINGTON WILLIAM JAY	NY	13W	75
PARTLOW KENNETH	NY	10E	50
PARTON CARL	NJ	19W	19
PARTON FLOYD EUGENE	NC	41W	30
PARTON JOHN EDWARD	AZ	01W	52
PARTRIDGE ALAN BRIAN	CA	14W	86
PARTRIDGE DOUGLAS ELWOOD	CA	19E	16
PARTRIDGE NORMAN WAYNE	KS	43W	8
PARTSAFAS TERRYL GLENN	OR	37W	7
PARZYNSKI HERBERT JOSEPH	IL	40W	56
PASCAL IVAN KIMOKEO	HI	67E	2
PASCALE GEORGE JOHN	CT	21W	119
PASCARELLA FRANK MARIO	IL	08W	62
PASCASCIO RODNEY GUSTAVUS	NY	36E	29
PASCH WILLIAM ERNEST	SD	58E	24
PASCHAL LESLIE CALVIN JR	MO	39W	68
PASCHALL LES HOWARD	IL	32E	39
PASCHALL RONALD PAGE	WA	02W	128
PASCO ALLEN	NY	53W	29
PASCOE ROBERT EDWARD	VA	23E	88
PASCUA DALMACIO P JR	HI	29W	22
PASCUAL FLORENDO B	HI	03E	15
PASEKOFF ROBERT EDWARD	PA	06E	4
PASHANO JACK POOLA	AZ	47W	2
PASHMAN STEPHEN MARK	CA	04E	94
PASILLAS HENRY	CA	51E	32
PASKINS WAYMAN E	NY	39E	37
PASKOWICZ DONALD	WI	23E	77
PASLEY HENRY	GA	04E	94
PASQUALUCCI EMIDIO	MD	22W	15
PASQUANTONIO JOHN EMIDIO	MA	53E	20
PASS JOHN III	PA	40E	28
PASSAFUME MICHAEL JAY	LA	38W	66

NAME	STATE	PANEL NO.	LINE NO.
PASSANANTE WILLIAM JAMES	PA	41W	67
PASSAVANTI JOSEPH J III	IL	68E	6
PASSERELLO ANTHONY JOSEPH	MA	25W	45
PASSIG DUANE RINEHARDT	IA	44E	51
PASTORE JAMES JOSEPH JR	CT	12W	115
PASTORE ROBERT JOSEPH	NY	39E	37
PASTORES GEVIN PESCOZO	CA	28W	46
PASTORINO MICHAEL ANTHONY	PA	16W	89
PASTRANA VICTOR RAPHAEL	NY	15E	86
PASTROVICH EUGENE ARTHUR	IL	18E	63
PASTULA STEPHEN JOSEPH	NC	31W	14
PASTVA MICHAEL JAMES	OH	31E	51
PATCH DONALD CHARLES	NM	02E	102
PATE GARY	GA	66E	3
PATE JOHN H JR	TN	55E	26
PATE MILTON DALE	TX	40W	66
PATE RICKY ALAN	IN	02W	38
PATE ROBERT LEE III	NC	17E	30
PATE RONALD DALE	SC	14W	104
PATE WILLIAM	FL	59E	10
PATE WILLIAM LAWRENCE	AL	61E	16
PATENAUDE HAROLD MICHAEL	NY	10E	84
PATENAUDE HENRY EDWARD	MA	17E	113
PATERSON ROSS JAMES	IL	05E	40
PATIENCE WILLIAM R JR	CT	01E	63
PATINO PABLO	WY	15E	60
PATINO ROBERTO LERMA	TX	06W	16
PATON RICHARD ALLEN	MI	32W	1
PATRICCA ANTHONY PASQUALE	PA	44W	52
PATRICK ALBERT EARL	FL	39E	37
PATRICK BILLY RAY	KY	07E	120
PATRICK BOBBY GENE	KY	29E	23
PATRICK CALVIN RAY	TX	24W	106
PATRICK DANIEL GARRY	WI	17E	106
PATRICK DANNY LEON	AL	27W	46
PATRICK DARYL WAYNE	KS	15W	59
PATRICK DEREK WILKERSON	TX	10W	42
PATRICK DONALD RAY	NC	03E	50
PATRICK DONNIE LEE	OH	61E	1
PATRICK DOUGLAS TYRONE	WY	09E	108
PATRICK J V	TX	04E	71
PATRICK JERRY	MO	33E	91
PATRICK JERRY KENT	CO	13E	29
PATRICK JERRY LEE	FL	47E	25
PATRICK JIMMIE LEE	GA	13E	25
PATRICK JIMMY RALPH	GA	15W	48
PATRICK MARINER	OH	03E	46
PATRICK MARION ELIJAH	GA	19E	17
PATRICK REESE MICHAEL	OR	24W	10
PATRICK RICHARD MICHAEL	CA	07E	74
PATRICK STANLEY KAY	NC	24E	39
PATRICK TEX DELANO	WV	22E	112
PATRILLO ALBERT JOHN	PA	20E	47
PATRIZI ANTHONY	IL	43E	29
PATRIZIO CHARLES JOSEPH	NY	40E	9
PATRONE JOHN THOMAS	NY	26W	49
PATTEN CARL EUGENE	TN	11W	69
PATTEN JEARL RAY	MO	48E	46
PATTEN JIMMIE	AZ	36E	29
PATTERSON BILLY J	TN	18E	50
PATTERSON BOOKER T JR	AL	27W	21
PATTERSON BRUCE DIXON	CA	14E	23
PATTERSON BRUCE MERLE	OR	24E	9
PATTERSON CHARLES EDWARD	MO	25E	13
PATTERSON CLEVELAND	IL	23E	54
PATTERSON DANIEL ARTHUR	CA	20E	99
PATTERSON DANIEL CHARLES	AZ	39W	3
PATTERSON DAVID Q	TX	32W	56
PATTERSON DONALD LEE	OR	21E	58
PATTERSON DWAYNE MAXIFIEL	CA	31E	30
PATTERSON EARL ALLEN	PA	01E	77
PATTERSON EDWARD LEON	CA	44E	52
PATTERSON FRED HENRY	VA	16E	114
PATTERSON GARY LEE	WA	68E	6
PATTERSON GEORGE FRANCIS	CA	12W	72
PATTERSON GEORGE WILLARD	MI	52W	19
PATTERSON GORDON LEE	TX	39W	75
PATTERSON JAMES BARNETT	MI	20E	97
PATTERSON JAMES GORDON	NJ	16E	96
PATTERSON JAMES KELLY	CA	20E	48
PATTERSON JAMES ROBERT	FL	30E	47
PATTERSON JAMES W JR	OH	27W	102

NAME	STATE	PANEL NO.	LINE NO.
PATTERSON JEFFERY SCOTT	NJ	60W	4
PATTERSON JEROME DEAN	KS	25E	59
PATTERSON JERRY LEROY	OK	50W	37
PATTERSON JOHNNIE	GA	04E	17
PATTERSON JOHNNIE HUGH	TN	24E	107
PATTERSON KEITH ALLEN	OH	17W	74
PATTERSON LARRY GENE	IN	58E	13
PATTERSON LARRY HART	CA	45W	16
PATTERSON MARK	TN	54W	3
PATTERSON MAXIE	GA	10E	43
PATTERSON MICHAEL RICHARD	MI	12W	69
PATTERSON OSCAR BERNARD	TX	09W	92
PATTERSON PATRICK CHASIE	SC	50E	7
PATTERSON RICHARD	NJ	17E	22
PATTERSON RICHARD ALAN	NY	10W	36
PATTERSON RICHARD LEE	TN	23W	17
PATTERSON RICHARD STUART	OH	03W	102
PATTERSON ROBERT DEWAYNE	PA	52E	10
PATTERSON ROBERT WAYNE	OK	29W	71
PATTERSON RONALD OREN	CA	08E	113
PATTERSON SAMUEL LEE	AL	25W	108
PATTERSON STANLEY	NY	33W	81
PATTERSON STANLEY F	IL	23E	30
PATTERSON STEVEN CRAIG	CA	17E	22
PATTERSON TERRY ALLEN	IL	16E	4
PATTERSON THOMAS	GA	17E	119
PATTERSON TIMOTHY COLEMAN	NC	18E	71
PATTERSON WALLIS GILBERT	IL	25W	16
PATTERSON WALTER MARCELLU	MI	40E	28
PATTERSON WAYNE O'NEAL	GA	05W	97
PATTERSON WILLIAM ANTHONY	WI	58W	16
PATTERSON WILLIAM WESLEY	AZ	17E	74
PATTILLO MINOR WESLEY	GA	28W	29
PATTILLO RALPH NATHAN	AL	05W	112
PATTISON JOHN JR	LA	16W	122
PATTISON RONALD ALAN	AR	26E	15
PATTON BARRY MICHAEL	WV	47E	41
PATTON CURTIS RAY	VA	37E	26
PATTON DAVID ALAN	PA	23W	105
PATTON DORRIS EDWARD	CA	09E	58
PATTON FRANCIS G	PA	25W	108
PATTON GEORGE	NY	22E	47
PATTON GUY WESLEY	KY	08W	119
PATTON JAMES ALAN	OH	45E	42
PATTON JERRY DON	TX	15W	37
PATTON JOHN HENRY	TN	33E	30
PATTON JOHN PERRY	CA	22E	47
PATTON KENNETH JAMES	PA	36E	81
PATTON ROGER WAYNE	MO	28W	63
PATTON RONALD WADE	OK	30E	72
PATTON THOMAS JAMES	OK	03W	29
PATTON WARD KARL	KS	50W	20
PATTY DUDLEY RANDOLPH	AL	17E	47
PATZWALL JAMES GEORGE	MD	05E	90
PAUL BRINSON IRA	TN	47W	11
PAUL CLYDE EVERTTE JR	KY	26E	85
PAUL CRAIG ALLAN	OH	01W	97
PAUL DANNY LEE	LA	21E	37
PAUL EDWARD JOSEPH	NJ	17E	113
PAUL ERNEST GEORGE	NH	07E	120
PAUL FRED JOHN	NJ	37W	35
PAUL GARY MICHAEL	MI	23W	17
PAUL HAMILTON JR	TX	07W	23
PAUL JAMES LEE	MI	05W	79
PAUL JAMES RICHARD	IN	14E	123
PAUL JAY	PA	13E	65
PAUL JOE CALVIN	OH	02E	63
PAULE PHILLIP ARTHUR	MO	08W	73
PAULETTE JOSEPH RONALD	MA	49E	5
PAULEY MARSHALL IRVIN	WV	06E	5
PAULEY WASHINGTON	SC	25W	81
PAULICH PATRICK JAMES	WI	06W	99
PAULIN JOHN THOMAS	KY	23W	105
PAULINO CARL ARTHUR	NY	56W	26
PAULK ELIAS JOHNSON	FL	43W	41
PAULK ROBERT MILTON	CA	68E	6
PAULL CHESTER DONALD	PA	22E	26
PAULLEY LARRY	NY	07E	74
PAULLEY OSCAR JR	KY	02W	79
PAULOS FRANK WOLGO	NY	01W	116
PAULSEN DAVID HENRY	IA	12E	63
PAULSEN GERARD FRANCIS	NY	31W	15
PAULSEN LAWRENCE EDWARD	MN	23W	77
PAULSEN MICHAEL	AZ	12W	104
PAULSEN NORMAN MACLEOD	NY	42W	13
PAULSEN WARREN	AK	21W	1
PAULSON JOHN PAUL JR	WI	31E	82
PAULSON MARVIN JR	WA	18E	126
PAULSON MERLYN LEROY	ND	02W	122
PAULUS ROBERT DUANE	IN	21W	34
PAVAN KENNETH ALAN	NY	24W	55
PAVAO RODNEY WAYNE	HI	34W	87
PAVEY CHESTER RAYMOND	IN	17E	47
PAVEY DALE RUSSELL	IL	22W	100
PAVLACKY LOUIS A JR	WI	13W	128
PAVLAKOVICH NICHOLAS ALLE	OH	20E	65
PAVLICEK JAMES EMIL JR	TX	29E	17
PAVLOCAK MICHAEL PETER JR	NJ	50E	7
PAWELKE RICHARD CHARLES	WI	02W	84
PAWLAK JAMES WILLIAM	MI	13E	93
PAWLAK RICHARD VICTOR	OH	13W	79
PAWLICK HENRY JOHN JR	NY	03E	29
PAWLISH GEORGE FRANCIS	CO	16E	41
PAWLOWICZ DENNIS WAYNE	MN	18E	63
PAWLOWSKI EDWARD WESLEY	NJ	28W	20
PAWLOWSKI THEODORE J JR	NY	31W	18
PAXSON STEVEN DUANE	KS	24W	78
PAXTON DONALD ELMER	IA	32W	82
PAYNE ANDREW JAMES JR	CA	50E	52
PAYNE DARNELL MILTON	VA	26W	34
PAYNE ELDON RAY	OK	13W	9
PAYNE ERNEST	LA	55E	26
PAYNE EUGENE JEROME III	MD	17E	63
PAYNE GARY LEE	GA	34W	61
PAYNE HERMAN GARFIELD	KY	47W	3
PAYNE HERMAN HOWARD	NC	18E	96
PAYNE HOWARD DAVID III	GA	03W	15
PAYNE HUBERT JACKSON	OH	30E	11
PAYNE JAMES CARL	AR	36E	81
PAYNE JAMES TERRY	NC	61E	16
PAYNE JEPPIE JOSEPH	TN	48W	29
PAYNE JOHN ALLEN	NY	16W	31
PAYNE JOHN FRANKLIN	IL	25W	42
PAYNE KENNETH RAY	KS	40W	59
PAYNE KYLIS THEROD	MD	01W	37
PAYNE LAWRENCE EDWARD	AL	13E	16
PAYNE LLOYD ADRIAN	GA	01E	38
PAYNE LOUIS SR	MD	05W	35
PAYNE MONTE LYNN	TN	17W	103
PAYNE NORMAN	OH	36W	46
PAYNE RICHARD JOSEPH	IA	32E	32
PAYNE RICHARD NORMAN	KS	09E	70
PAYNE ROBERT ELGIN	KS	20E	66
PAYNE ROBERT PAUL	IL	45E	24
PAYNE RONALD HARRY	GA	29E	43
PAYNE ROY CHARLES JR	MI	30E	47
PAYNE TERRY JOHN	WI	08W	85
PAYNE TROY DAVID JR	GA	18E	97
PAYNE WALTER FRANKLIN	MD	11E	50
PAYNE WENDLE L	MO	01W	123
PAYNE WILLARD FRANCIS	CA	03W	128
PAYNE WILLIE JAMES	SC	26E	55
PAYNTER ROBERT LEE	IL	05W	31
PAYNTER THOMAS BERNHARD	WA	24W	106
PAYSOUR DONALD BLAIR	NC	48E	8
PAYTON JAMES E	NC	13E	126
PAYTON VENUS DEWHIT JR	CA	41W	36
PAZDAN DENNIS SIGMUND	IL	21E	125
PEA EDWARD EARL	LA	44W	5
PEACE CHARLES LAMONT	PA	05W	84
PEACE JOHN DARLINGTON III	OH	33E	10
PEACH ROBERT ALAN	IL	08E	76
PEACOCK JACK ALLAN	FL	37E	11
PEACOCK JOHN ROBERT II	HI	01W	81
PEACOCK LEONARD EARL	GA	07E	121
PEACOCK NATHAN EDDLOW JR	FL	17E	127
PEACOCK THOMAS EDWARD F	OH	09W	5
PEAGLER LEROY W	PA	14E	88
PEAGLER WAYNE DONALD	SC	12W	8
PEAK DAVID FRANCIS	MN	35W	50
PEAK EARL ARCHER	MO	14W	39
PEAK LAWRENCE JOSEPH	KY	09E	108
PEAKE JOE LOUIS	NY	40E	52
PEALER ELIAS BENSON JR	CT	10W	2
PEARCE CHARLES HUBERT JR	AR	24W	69
PEARCE DALE ALLEN	OH	03W	39
PEARCE EDWIN JACK	PA	02W	122
PEARCE HENRY ELLWOOD II	NJ	34W	67
PEARCE JERRY DOYLE	TX	34W	9
PEARCE MARVIN ROBERT	CA	46W	19
PEARCE ROBIN ANDREW	CA	12W	8
PEARCE WAYNE WILLIAM	OH	46E	49
PEARCE WILLIAM CALVIN IV	MI	16E	81
PEARCY ROBERT LESLIE	CA	23W	67
PEARL RAYMOND JR	OK	11E	128
PEARL RICHARD MAX	OH	08W	39
PEARL RONALD LEE	OH	29W	47
PEARLSTEIN JERROLD S	CA	22W	92
PEARSALL HERBERT JR	NC	12E	104
PEARSALL RICHARD MARK	MI	29W	55
PEARSON ANTHONY JOSEPH	WA	40W	14
PEARSON ARNOLD C	CA	12E	96
PEARSON BRADLEY ALAN	WI	09E	49
PEARSON BRUCE FULLER	AZ	22W	6
PEARSON CARL OSCAR JR	AL	57E	3
PEARSON DAVID ALLEN	NY	51W	43
PEARSON DAVID L	IA	13E	117
PEARSON EARL THOMAS JR	IL	16W	54
PEARSON FRANCIS LAURY	MS	27W	7
PEARSON GEORGE B III	PA	10E	109
PEARSON GEORGE WILLIAM JR	CA	19W	72
PEARSON GREGORY JOHN	CA	21W	119
PEARSON JAMES CLIFFORD	NC	18E	50
PEARSON JAMES ROY	FL	12E	24
PEARSON JESSE JAMES	SC	29E	43
PEARSON JOHN HOWARD	CA	20W	60
PEARSON JOHN RUDOLPH	GA	10E	16
PEARSON KURT BYRON	NM	28E	3
PEARSON MICKEY DON	NE	11W	116
PEARSON NORMAN JAMES	MD	05W	92
PEARSON RICHARD ELLSWORTH	DC	18W	105
PEARSON ROBERT HARVEY	WA	21E	92
PEARSON ROBERT LEON	CA	13W	54
PEARSON ROBERT VERNER	IL	17E	118
PEARSON RODNEY SHAYNE	OR	39W	38
PEARSON RONALD RUSSELL	WA	28E	51
PEARSON RUDOLPH	MD	35W	84
PEARSON THOMAS RICKARD JR	CA	35E	17
PEARSON VAN HARVEY	CA	31W	71
PEARSON WAYNE EDWARD	IL	32W	82
PEARSON WILLIAM DELBERT	OR	50W	45
PEARSON WILLIAM ROY	NH	02W	132
PEASE HOMER LEFTERAGE	TN	12E	90
PEASE KENNETH WAYNE	KY	18W	97
PEASLEY GARY WAYNE	MI	13E	86
PEAT GARY LAVERNE	WI	09W	80
PEAVY THOMAS MICHAEL	CA	13W	85
PEAY DOUGLASS FRANKLIN	MD	23E	54
PEAY HARVEY A	KY	19W	20
PEAY JAMES EDMUND	TN	33E	73
PECHAITIS MATTHEW JOHN	OH	04E	62
PECK DARRELL VERNON	OR	23W	39
PECK JEFFREY LLOYD	NY	44E	19
PECK JOE RUSSELL	UT	45E	14
PECK ROBERT WILLIAM	MO	09E	16
PECK STEPHEN GRADY	CT	16E	30
PECK STEVEN RUSSELL	OK	04W	51
PECKHAM GEORGE ROBERT	MI	48E	8
PECORA JOSEPH ANTHONY JR	CT	07E	20
PECORARO FRANK ANTHONY	CA	14W	50
PEDA ROBERT CHARLES	NY	48E	46
PEDDICORD DONALD GLENN	IA	14E	71
PEDDLE MICHAEL RAY	NC	09W	122
PEDDY CHARLES LEE	CA	34W	88
PEDEN CLARK EDMUND	PA	42W	21
PEDERSEN CLARK RUSSELL	IL	13W	49
PEDERSEN DENNIS IRWIN	MN	61E	1
PEDERSEN FRED LEWIS	CA	14E	92
PEDERSEN KENNETH RALPH	CA	26W	34
PEDERSEN RUSSELL ALFORD	NY	44W	28
PEDERSEN WILLIAM A	CA	07W	66
PEDERSON ARTHUR CLIFFORD	MN	05E	90
PEDERSON JOE PALMER	CA	09W	85
PEDERSON KENNETH ALLEN	MN	30W	80
PEDERSON MARVIN CLIFFORD	WI	35W	44
PEDERSON ROGER ALLEN	WI	04W	92

NAME	STATE	PANEL NO.	LINE NO.
PEDICONE JEROME JOHN	IL	61E	16
PEDIGO CHARLES DANIEL	KY	09W	99
PEDINGS BILLY DEAN	FL	03W	77
PEDRICK CHARLES C II	CA	55W	30
PEDROSA CARLOS ALBERTO	NY	01W	84
PEDUE ROGER WILLIAM	IN	24W	26
PEEBLER CHRISTY ALBERT	CA	22W	43
PEEK DENNIS LEE	IL	14W	20
PEEK JOHN FOREMAN	MI	47E	29
PEEK JOHN THOMAS	NC	45W	21
PEEK RUSSELL JAMES	FL	08E	121
PEEKS LEE ROY ELDRED	FL	36E	30
PEEL JOHN CHARLES	MA	26E	85
PEEL LAWRENCE RAY	KS	03W	16
PEEL STEPHEN BLAKE	MO	20W	109
PEELE ELVERNON	NC	20W	51
PEELE LLOYD WILLIAM JR	VA	53E	6
PEELER GLOVER AUSTIN III	FL	15E	91
PEELER WILLIAM GERALD	IL	43W	65
PEEPLES BILLY HAMMOND	SC	06W	37
PEEPLES HARDY WINSTON	TX	14E	64
PEEPLES HARRY FRANK EDWAR	TN	39E	24
PEERY NORMAN DOUGLAS	CO	11W	18
PEETZKE RONALD EUGENE	NE	18W	55
PEFFER GREGORY LEE	IL	05W	61
PEGG DAVID BURTON	MD	11E	128
PEGGS ALBERT LEE	IL	37W	41
PEGRAM RICHARD EPPS JR	TN	47W	51
PEGROSS LEROY	TX	66W	11
PEGUERO RICHARD	CA	49E	46
PEHRSON DALE CHRISTOPHER	CA	31E	16
PEINA ERNEST DELBERT	NM	44W	52
PEIXOTO GILBERT COROA	MA	12W	58
PEKNY CHARLES DENNIS	IL	50W	9
PELAJIO ARTURO	TX	25W	20
PELCH MICHAEL J D	MI	44W	19
PELEIHOLANI HAYWARD K H	HI	19W	101
PELHAM EARL TIMOTHY JR	GA	55W	8
PELHAM LESTER LEON	CA	31E	70
PELIKAN ROGER	IL	02E	39
PELKEY RAYMOND NELSON	ME	14W	90
PELL RANDALL LEE	IN	12W	108
PELLEGRIN O'NEIL J JR	LA	14W	86
PELLEGRINO BERNARD MICHAEL	NY	54E	13
PELLEGRINO JOHN PETER	CT	41W	61
PELLEGRINO JOSEPH D	PA	07E	85
PELLEGRINO MICHAEL PHILIP	NY	40E	44
PELLETIER LAWRENCE JOSEPH	CT	17E	63
PELLETIER PAUL JOHN	MA	59W	11
PELLETIER RICHARD WILLIAM	NH	28W	30
PELLEW DAVID SEELEY	NY	29W	72
PELLICANO JEAN PIERRE V	CA	39W	23
PELLIZZARI LOUIS JOSEPH	NY	07E	11
PELLOSMA DAVID JOHN	MI	32W	82
PELLOT-RODRIGUEZ RAMON AL	PR	07E	4
PELTIER JAMES WARDEN	MI	17E	127
PELTON GLENN EUGENE	TX	20W	36
PELTON WILLIAM FRANK	WA	26E	49
PELULLO LEONARD SALVATORE	PA	15E	25
PELUSO PAUL RENATO JR	PA	14W	95
PELZER BENJAMIN F II	SC	21E	50
PELZMANN GERALD F	IL	37E	42
PEMBERTON ALVIN LEWIS	IL	08W	111
PEMBERTON GENE THOMAS	MO	09E	64
PEMBERTON JAMES ALEXANDER	WV	48E	19
PEMBERTON WILLIAM LARRY	TN	50W	32
PEMBLETON RONALD LEE	KY	38E	36
PENA DANIEL JR	TX	37E	16
PENA JESSE JOSEPH	IA	13W	3
PENA JOE JR	TX	32E	4
PENA JOE JR	TX	07W	79
PENA JOHN	NM	17E	38
PENA JOHN L	AZ	11W	47
PENA JOSE MANUEL	PR	46W	19
PENA MANUEL JUAN	TX	22W	6
PENA-CLASS RAUL	PR	44E	40
PENCE JAMES HOWARD	IA	15W	104
PENCE JAMES THOMAS	AL	32W	28
PENDARVIS ROBERT	SC	22E	84
PENDELL DAVID ALLEN	MI	15W	60
PENDELL JERALD WAYNE	IL	01E	12
PENDER DONALD L	WA	15E	99
PENDER JOHN FRANCIS	MD	27E	6
PENDER ORLAND JAMES JR	RI	01W	67
PENDERGAST ROBERT LEE	CT	11W	1
PENDERGIST RONALD LYNN	AR	14E	67
PENDERGRAFT RAY DANIEL	OH	22E	112
PENDERGRAFT RONNIE DEAN	CA	33E	91
PENDERGRASS JAMES WILLIAM	OK	32W	72
PENDERGRASS VERNON FRANKL	AL	42E	70
PENDERGRASS WILLIE CLEBER	AR	19E	99
PENDLETON GEORGE JR	FL	08E	8
PENDLEY ROBERT GLENN	FL	36W	5
PENDLEY WILLIAM GRANT	AL	53W	37
PENDOLA ANTHONY EUGENE	IL	03E	25
PENDYGRAFT GEORGE R	KY	08E	23
PENE RONALD EDWARD	CA	26E	97
PENFOLD PETER ALLAN	NY	28E	29
PENKE RICHARD ALLEN	MI	31W	15
PENLAND FRED DANIEL	OH	46W	20
PENLAND MARVIN KENNY	AL	07E	98
PENLAND RAY LEE JR	TX	66W	11
PENLEY CHARLES MARTIN JR	NC	25W	53
PENMAN JOHN RICHARD	GA	13W	98
PENMAN RONALD STIRLING	CA	27E	96
PENN CHARLES HUGHES	KY	06E	102
PENN CHARLES VARENCE	IL	15W	7
PENN EDWIN ALLAN	CO	45W	55
PENN FRANKLIN HAMILTON	SC	22E	112
PENN HERMAN	LA	06E	11
PENN RAYMOND BISHOP JR	PA	06W	102
PENN RONALD W	CA	21E	15
PENN ROOSEVELT FRANKLIN	AL	25W	18
PENNA JOHN ANTHONY	NY	21E	108
PENNAMON RICHARD STEVE	IL	50E	52
PENNEL LAWRENCE PAUL	MO	46E	40
PENNELL ARVIN DOUGLAS	TX	07E	109
PENNELL MICHAEL H	NC	12E	104
PENNELL WILBERT GENE	MI	15E	70
PENNETTI FRANCIS	PA	35E	26
PENNEY CHARLES OTIS	OH	39E	37
PENNEY DONALD THOMAS	NY	40W	50
PENNINGTON DALE ALLEN	IN	07W	32
PENNINGTON EDWARD LEE	TX	19W	41
PENNINGTON FRED MELVIN	AZ	12E	75
PENNINGTON JAMES E JR	IL	42W	7
PENNINGTON JOHN CHARLES	UT	58W	13
PENNINGTON KENNETH EDWARD	NC	17W	3
PENNINGTON PAUL PATRICK	MD	08E	15
PENNINGTON PHILIP EUGENE	VA	56E	14
PENNINGTON RICHARD W	IL	08W	56
PENNINGTON RONALD KEITH	WV	18E	104
PENNINGTON THOMAS JACK	MO	35E	49
PENNUCCI PETER JAMES	MA	10W	71
PENNY JAMES MELVEN	OH	02E	38
PENNY WILLIAM VICTOR	FL	27E	91
PENRY MARVIN EUGENE	IN	47E	4
PENSON DANIEL L	MD	42E	55
PENSON HAROLD EUGENE	IL	47E	4
PENSONEAU TERRY	IL	36W	29
PENSYL DONALD NEIL	NY	02W	6
PENTA STEPHEN JOSEPH	MA	19W	20
PENTLAND JAMES DOUGLAS	PA	40E	28
PEONIO STEPHEN JOSEPH	CO	23W	39
PEOPLES ALEXANDER A S	MS	33W	88
PEOPLES DAVID DOUGLAS JR	TX	04W	5
PEOPLES EDDIE DONALD	AL	12E	75
PEOPLES HOWARD GREGORY	AL	39W	41
PEOPLES JAMES DALE	PA	45W	27
PEOPLES JERRY WAYNE	LA	04W	51
PEOPLES PAUL JOSEPH	AL	29W	22
PEOPLES PERRY LEE	LA	18E	97
PEPE GEORGE WILLIAM	CT	18W	65
PEPIN JOHN FREDERICK	MI	03W	131
PEPPER ANTHONY JOHN	VA	48E	32
PEPPER JAMES THOMAS	MN	26E	13
PEPPER LARRY JAMES	OH	05W	70
PEPPER WILLIAM FRANKLIN	OH	45W	9
PEPPERS HAROLD DOUGLAS	IL	62E	22
PEPPERS WILLIE JEROME JR	NC	07E	46
PEPPIN DAVID DAWSON JR	VA	21W	94
PEPPLE CARL FRANKLIN JR	TX	19E	44
PEQUENO JUAN RODRIGUEZ	CA	32W	33
PERALEZ LOUIS FABIAN	NY	52W	1
PERALTA RAPHAEL ALEXANDER	LA	53E	40
PERCIVAL ALTON D	UT	33W	8
PERCY DONALD LEE	TX	07W	68
PERDOMO KRIS MITCHELL	CA	10W	8
PERDUE DON MELVIN	CA	20E	106
PERDUE DONALD M	KY	55E	26
PERDUE GEORGE EDWARD	TX	47W	51
PERDUE JOHN HARRY	WA	17E	127
PERDUE RICHARD W	OK	35E	78
PERDUE RICHARD WAYNE	VA	27W	21
PERDUE ROBERT DECKER	VA	05E	74
PERDUE WILLIAM CARMAN	IN	42W	43
PEREA EDWARD	NY	05E	133
PEREA ERNESTO SALVADOR	TX	46E	40
PEREA JUANITO	NM	41E	70
PEREA ROBERTO	TX	04W	121
PERECKO PAUL JOHN	PA	15E	15
PEREDA HENRY PANGELINAN	PR	06E	132
PEREIRA SOCORRO	PR	33E	59
PERETIATKO JERALD PAUL	OH	45W	43
PEREZ ADOLFO MORENO	TX	53E	8
PEREZ ALBERTO L	TX	63E	16
PEREZ ANTHONY	TX	28E	38
PEREZ ARTHUR CARLYLE	CA	19E	64
PEREZ ASCENSION ROSALES	TX	09W	52
PEREZ BENITO	TX	09E	100
PEREZ CARLOS AUGUSTO	PR	31E	22
PEREZ CELSO A	FL	21E	56
PEREZ DANIEL FLORES JR	TX	16E	96
PEREZ DANIEL TORRES	NY	18E	81
PEREZ DAVID	NY	22W	68
PEREZ ERNEST EUSTACE	CA	08E	113
PEREZ ERNESTO	IA	32E	4
PEREZ ESPIRIDION	TX	26W	86
PEREZ FREDERICO	TX	13E	113
PEREZ GUADALUPE	CA	26E	82
PEREZ HILARIO OCHOA	OH	10W	126
PEREZ HOMERO	TX	31E	22
PEREZ ISRAEL	TX	55E	24
PEREZ JAMES SANDERS	TX	25E	108
PEREZ JEFFREY	NY	34E	24
PEREZ JESUS ALBERT	CA	21W	9
PEREZ JESUS RAMON	TX	55W	30
PEREZ JOE FRANCISCO JR	CA	55W	37
PEREZ JOHN ANTHONY	GM	25W	109
PEREZ JOSE MANUEL	TX	08W	63
PEREZ JOSEPH ESPINO	CA	43E	68
PEREZ JUAN J	CA	33E	91
PEREZ LOUIS ANTONIO	NY	25W	19
PEREZ PETER	CA	58W	13
PEREZ RAUL BAUTISTA	TX	18E	71
PEREZ RAUL VICTOR	IL	29W	91
PEREZ RAYMOND	TX	30E	80
PEREZ RAYMOND LUNA	CA	47W	11
PEREZ RICARDO JAMES	LA	05E	62
PEREZ RICHARD	CA	38E	58
PEREZ RICHARD ELOY	WI	18W	49
PEREZ ROBERTO	TX	05E	21
PEREZ RODOLFO	TX	49W	16
PEREZ VICENTE DUENAS	GM	48W	8
PEREZ VICTOR JR	IL	42W	58
PEREZ WILFRED	NY	30W	59
PEREZ WILFRED M	NY	26E	86
PEREZ-CRUZ LUIS ANTONIO	PR	12E	24
PEREZ-PADIN JUAN RAMON	PR	19W	121
PEREZ-RIVERA MANUEL ANTON	PR	08E	73
PEREZ-RIVERA MILTON	NY	11W	87
PEREZ-VERDEJA RAFAEL	FL	02W	35
PEREZ-VERGARA ALBERTO	PR	06E	3
PERICH JOHN WHILDEN	CA	09E	58
PERILLO DONALD LEE	IL	48E	8
PERINOTTO ERNEST DAVID	PA	38W	4
PERISHO GORDON SAMUEL	IL	33E	10
PERITO JOSEPH	WV	07W	33
PERKETT DAVID LOUIS	MI	34E	60
PERKINS ALLEN DEAN	OR	16W	118
PERKINS BOBBY JAMES	NY	38W	68
PERKINS CALVIN MOORE	MD	42W	72
PERKINS CECIL CARRINGT JR	VA	02W	88
PERKINS CHARLES HAROLD	NY	62E	9
PERKINS CHARLIE JR	IL	47W	3
PERKINS CLYDE J	MS	12E	15

NAME	STATE	PANEL NO.	LINE NO.
PERKINS DALE ALLEN	OR	12E	15
PERKINS DANNY FRANKLIN	NC	28W	84
PERKINS DAVID DRAKE	AZ	11E	67
PERKINS DONALD DEAN JR	IL	36E	81
PERKINS DONALD ROBERT JR	OH	12W	119
PERKINS FREDERICK JOSEPH	MA	63W	11
PERKINS GARY ELDON	TN	07E	103
PERKINS GARY WILLIAM	OH	44E	30
PERKINS GEORGE PETER	MN	24W	19
PERKINS IRA HILTON JR	ME	08E	18
PERKINS JAMES BARNEY	AL	07W	47
PERKINS JOHNNIE KAY	KY	34E	38
PERKINS KEITH CHARLES	OR	24E	69
PERKINS LUTHER RIVES	LA	22W	6
PERKINS MICHAEL DAVID	OH	22E	59
PERKINS OFALEE	IN	26W	25
PERKINS RONALD JAMES	CA	30E	11
PERKINS STEPHEN JOHN	NV	10W	87
PERKINS WALLACE SAM	TX	07E	54
PERKINS WARDELL	AL	36W	30
PERKINS WILLIAM ARTHUR JR	MD	37W	18
PERKINS WILLIAM DEWITT JR	MS	10E	50
PERKINS WILLIAM THOMAS JR	CA	27E	97
PERKINS WILLIE JAMES	SC	27W	1
PERKO TERRY JOHN	OH	15E	71
PERLEWITZ BRIAN SCOTT	WI	45E	58
PERLEWITZ STEVEN OWEN	WI	15E	99
PERMALOFF CHARLES WASSEL	MI	36E	79
PERPETUA ROQUE JR	HI	13E	55
PERRAULT ALAN JAMES	MA	12E	29
PERREAULT DAVID B	NH	42W	72
PERREIRA ERROL WAYNE	HI	24W	78
PERRELLI KEITH FRANCIS	NJ	27E	12
PERRETTA JOHN ROCCO	NY	39E	52
PERRICHON DONALD HAROLD	NY	03E	104
PERRIGO STANLEY CHARLES	MI	02W	95
PERRIN RICHARD THOMAS	NE	08E	101
PERRINE ELTON LAWRENCE	NY	20E	86
PERRINS ROBERT RICHARD	PA	48E	8
PERRIS FELIZ	IL	02E	65
PERRODIN CURTIS JOSEPH	LA	07W	50
PERRON JOSEPH ADRIAN G	ME	10E	74
PERRON NORMAND PAUL	MD	32W	47
PERRONE JAMES PAUL JR	NJ	16E	71
PERRY ANDREW JR	IL	59W	9
PERRY ANTONE JR	CA	13E	74
PERRY BILLY EARL	TX	21W	77
PERRY CARROLL WAYNE	TX	14E	50
PERRY CASEY CLAYTON	CA	07W	129
PERRY CHARLES LEON	OH	54E	39
PERRY CLAUDE	KY	44W	59
PERRY CLYDE RANDOLPH JR	GA	24W	78
PERRY DANIEL	MA	52E	31
PERRY DENNIS MITCHELL	GA	22E	112
PERRY DONALD LEE	CA	40W	38
PERRY EARNEST	GA	61E	16
PERRY EDWARD LEE	OH	53E	20
PERRY ELMER JOSEPH JR	TX	53E	21
PERRY ELMER REID	AZ	13W	86
PERRY ERNEST MANUEL JR	RI	26W	41
PERRY FRANK MICHAEL JR	NY	10W	126
PERRY GEORGE EDWARD	AL	08E	48
PERRY GEORGE EVERETT III	VA	08E	59
PERRY GEORGE FRANCIS III	DE	20E	3
PERRY GERALD LESLIE	WV	10E	1
PERRY GORDON DEAN	WV	23W	23
PERRY GRAFTON LAWRENCE	NY	24W	98
PERRY HAL EDWARD	FL	13W	100
PERRY HARMON WAYNE	NC	42E	56
PERRY JACK ARMOND	MO	07W	121
PERRY JACKIE RAY	TX	31E	51
PERRY JAMES EARL	AL	16E	96
PERRY JOHN EVERETTE	OH	44W	40
PERRY KARL FREDERICK	NY	47E	41
PERRY KENNETH EDWARD	IL	15W	123
PERRY KENNETH LEE	OH	18W	114
PERRY KENNETH MERLE	IL	14W	105
PERRY KENNETH RICHARD	CA	02W	83
PERRY LARRY BRUCE	WV	16W	85
PERRY LOUIS EDWARD	NJ	17E	38
PERRY OTHA LEE	MI	02W	88
PERRY R C JR	TX	15E	26
PERRY R T	TN	41W	31
PERRY RANDALL EARL	TN	14W	63
PERRY RANDALL LAWRENCE	MI	17E	30
PERRY RANDOLPH ALLEN JR	MT	01W	97
PERRY RICHARD CLARK	NV	25E	75
PERRY RICHARD WILLIAM	AR	10E	121
PERRY ROBERT CONROY	MI	46W	57
PERRY ROBERT DALE	SC	06W	82
PERRY ROBERT KENT	WA	63W	11
PERRY ROBERT LEE	NC	10E	33
PERRY ROBERT LEE	IN	56E	15
PERRY ROBERT LEWIS	AL	10E	77
PERRY RODDIE LEE	TX	23W	56
PERRY RONALD DWIGHT	TN	01W	102
PERRY STEPHEN TUCKER	CT	24W	10
PERRY STEVE JOSEPH LEONE	CA	41W	29
PERRY STEVEN DALE	NC	41W	19
PERRY STEVEN J	UT	36W	86
PERRY THOMAS DAVID	IN	26W	27
PERRY THOMAS HEPBURN	CT	58E	13
PERRY TIMOTHY EUGENE	PA	15E	107
PERRY WILLARD ALTON JR	TX	53E	6
PERRY WILLIAM EDWARD	MI	19E	64
PERRYMAN DALLIS	OK	41E	70
PERRYMAN RONALD GLEN	KS	11E	105
PERRYMAN WILLIAM JOSEPH	MO	06W	71
PERSELY RICKY EDWARD	PA	10W	132
PERSHING RICHARD WARREN	NY	39E	76
PERSICKE ALLAN WAYNE	MI	18W	55
PERSINGER ROBERT MORRISON	WV	03W	2
PERSON DAVID EUGENE	TX	27E	1
PERSON JAMES ALFRED	MI	23W	114
PERSON ROBERT LEE	IN	18W	84
PERSONETTE MICHAEL DARWIN	MI	42W	1
PERSONS DANIEL BRUCE	MN	43W	47
PERSONS HENRY HARVEY	IN	36E	58
PERSYN RONALD FRANK	MI	08W	67
PERUSO LAWRENCE DAVID	PA	28W	74
PERYSIAN JOSEPH SALVATORE	IL	44E	52
PERZ TERRY LEE	WI	15W	65
PESCE PAUL JOHN	NY	01W	3
PESCHEL JAMES DOUGLAS	CO	31W	55
PESEK THOMAS JOHN	TX	26E	30
PESEWONIT RUSSELL EUGENE	OK	09E	59
PESIMER DANIEL	WV	47E	25
PESSIER STEVEN LEROY	SC	18W	34
PETAL JOHN DARRYL	OH	29W	91
PETANOVICH NICHOLAS C	CA	07W	50
PETCHNICK CHARLES RUSSELL	WA	18E	116
PETE FRANKLIN DANNY JR	AZ	65W	13
PETEET CHARLES LEONARD	TX	04E	125
PETELA THOMAS JOSEPH	MI	10W	42
PETER LE ROY ALVIN	IL	38E	36
PETERKIN THOMAS DOUGLAS	NY	17E	11
PETERLICH JOSEPH JAMES	WI	63E	16
PETERMAN THOMAS HOWARD	CA	41E	1
PETEROY BRUCE EDWARD	NY	25W	81
PETERS ALBERT JAMES	LA	46E	11
PETERS BERYL GENE	TX	14W	5
PETERS BILLY LEE	OH	17W	106
PETERS CARL HARMAN JR	OH	28W	20
PETERS CHARLES EDMUND	PA	12E	35
PETERS CHARLES HENRY	NE	08E	116
PETERS DANIEL ALLEN	OH	15W	29
PETERS DAVID ARTHUR	OK	48E	9
PETERS DAVID E	WI	09E	49
PETERS EDWARD KENT	IL	35E	53
PETERS EDWARD THEODORE JR	CA	27W	31
PETERS ELLIOTT LEE	WA	45E	27
PETERS EMMETT JACK	CO	19E	64
PETERS GEORGE CHARLES	IL	21W	1
PETERS GEORGE EDWARD JR	MT	53E	40
PETERS JOHN DENIS	CA	63W	11
PETERS JOHN THEODORE	NM	44W	59
PETERS JOSEPH CRAIG	FL	16W	102
PETERS JOSH	OK	20E	66
PETERS KENNETH WALTER	PA	34W	34
PETERS LARRY J	IL	25E	3
PETERS LAUVI PAUL PHILIP	CA	28W	13
PETERS LAWRENCE DAVID	NY	25E	108
PETERS LAWRENCE VINCENT	ME	06E	124
PETERS LEE RAYMOND	WI	08W	70
PETERS LYNN WAITMAN	WV	01E	124
PETERS MICHAEL	IL	28E	85
PETERS RALPH EDWARD	KY	39E	10
PETERS RICHARD EUGENE	IN	02E	132
PETERS ROBERT CHARLES	IL	35E	78
PETERS RODNEY WALTER	OR	39W	3
PETERS RONALD JAY	PA	04W	132
PETERS STEPHEN FREDERICK	AR	28E	76
PETERS STEVEN LLOYD	OR	13W	105
PETERS TOMMY RALPH	OH	25E	53
PETERS WALTER JOHN	CA	33E	40
PETERS WILBERT	AL	40E	54
PETERS WILLIAM LEE JR	IA	22W	107
PETERSDORF CHARLES H JR	CO	50W	9
PETERSEN CARL ROBERT	NY	35W	40
PETERSEN DANNY JOHN	KS	14W	20
PETERSEN DONALD ROGER JR	IL	26E	50
PETERSEN GALEN DEAN	CA	08E	101
PETERSEN GAYLORD DEAN	CA	26E	57
PETERSEN HARRY ALLEN	WA	41W	7
PETERSEN HARRY THOMAS	UT	06W	48
PETERSEN LAWRENCE LEE	CA	09W	96
PETERSEN MARK CARSON	IA	30E	31
PETERSEN PAUL JOSEPH	MI	21E	28
PETERSEN RAYMOND ALLAN	CA	24E	56
PETERSEN ROBERT BRUCE	WA	28E	38
PETERSEN ROGER ALLAN	SD	11E	74
PETERSEN WILLIAM DONN	ID	29E	102
PETERSEN WILLIAM ROBERT	CA	17E	80
PETERSON ALBERT ALLEN	PA	52E	23
PETERSON ALBERT EUGENE	NY	64E	17
PETERSON ALBERT EUGENE JR	GA	03W	111
PETERSON ANTHONY EARL	IA	21W	55
PETERSON BOBBY GENE	ID	24E	9
PETERSON BRADLEY EUGENE	MN	16E	64
PETERSON BURTON W JR	MA	48E	19
PETERSON CARL ALFRED	MA	20W	125
PETERSON CARL ELVING	WI	38E	71
PETERSON CARL JERROLD	NY	27W	1
PETERSON CHARLES C	WA	32E	46
PETERSON DARWIN STUART	WI	13W	123
PETERSON DAVID BRUCE	CA	28W	1
PETERSON DAVID MARTIN	MN	25W	32
PETERSON DELBERT RAY	MN	05E	133
PETERSON DENNIE DONALD	CA	26E	15
PETERSON DENNIS NEWELL	WI	02W	122
PETERSON DENNIS WILLIAM	CA	23E	92
PETERSON DILLARD ERIC	PA	51E	1
PETERSON DONALD CARL	IL	03E	89
PETERSON DONALD LEE	MN	53E	21
PETERSON DONALD MARTIN	CA	20E	3
PETERSON DUANE ARVID	MN	11W	105
PETERSON DUANE KENNETH	MT	16W	89
PETERSON EDGAR LEWIS JR	TX	02E	88
PETERSON FRANCOIS ACHILLE	VI	55W	15
PETERSON GARY WAYNE	MN	31E	70
PETERSON GERALD ROY	MA	39W	28
PETERSON HOWARD MATHIS	IL	24W	56
PETERSON JACK WALTER	MN	22E	55
PETERSON JAMES WILLIAM	FL	03W	50
PETERSON JEFFREY CHARLES	MN	19W	97
PETERSON JERRY LEE	IN	28W	21
PETERSON JESSE EARL	OH	05E	43
PETERSON JOE LEE	GA	17W	124
PETERSON JOHN ALFRED	WI	31W	15
PETERSON JOHN ARTHUR	SD	21E	6
PETERSON JOHN B JR	NJ	29W	2
PETERSON JOHN KENNETH	IL	22W	107
PETERSON JON DALE	ID	28W	104
PETERSON JULIUS LEE	AL	21W	48
PETERSON KENNETH AUBREY	TX	30E	48
PETERSON KERMIT C JR	IA	48W	14
PETERSON LEROY EMANUEL	MN	09E	42
PETERSON LOWELL TODD	WI	43E	49
PETERSON MARK ALLAN	OH	01W	113
PETERSON MARLIN TRENT	MN	14W	128
PETERSON MATTHEW	SC	19W	56
PETERSON MICHAEL EUGENE	CA	19E	121
PETERSON MICHAEL GERALD	MN	11E	114
PETERSON MICHAEL HARRELD	OH	06W	19
PETERSON MICHAEL VIRGIL	MN	35E	48
PETERSON RENOLD WILLIAM	MN	13E	72

NAME	STATE	PANEL NO.	LINE NO.
PETERSON RICHARD W	CA	04E	25
PETERSON ROBERT LEE	OR	40E	11
PETERSON ROBERT VERNON	MS	35E	77
PETERSON ROBERT WALKER	FL	21W	85
PETERSON ROY KEITH	NY	19W	97
PETERSON RUSSELL GEORGE	CO	51E	12
PETERSON STEPHEN EDWIN	MN	64W	14
PETERSON STEPHEN RUSSELL	CA	26W	34
PETERSON TED BARNETT	IL	17E	113
PETERSON TERRILL GENE	MN	08E	23
PETERSON THOMAS LAWRENCE	WA	38W	51
PETERSON THOMAS PAYNE	NY	36W	86
PETERSON THOMAS WAYNE	FL	66W	10
PETERSON TIMM CONRAD	WI	14E	6
PETERSON WALTER ARNOLD JR	MN	15W	54
PETERSON WARREN GARY	WA	05E	23
PETERSON WILLIAM J	WA	24W	47
PETETT LARRY WYNN	KS	41E	53
PETRACCO ROBERT	NJ	46W	20
PETRAGLIA ANGELO ANDREW	NY	36W	41
PETRAMALO THOMAS	NY	25E	25
PETRARCA JOSEPH A	PA	29W	63
PETRASHUNE MICHAEL JAMES	NY	06W	115
PETRAUSKAS KESTUTIS A	IL	44W	28
PETRE RONNIE JOSEPH	MI	18W	25
PETRECHKO EDMUND A JR	MO	13W	82
PETREY JAMES JIM	PA	36E	56
PETRIC JOHN ANTHONY	OH	30W	15
PETRICK FRANK EDWARD	NJ	25E	40
PETRICK RONALD PAUL	CA	02E	64
PETRIE JAMES ALLAN	CA	09W	97
PETRIE JOHN JAMES	MT	30W	94
PETRIE RICHARD JEFFREY	FL	42E	26
PETRILLA JOHN JOSEPH JR	PA	01W	11
PETRILLO JOHN JAMES	NY	37E	66
PETRIMOULX ROBERT GORDON	MI	13E	99
PETROLINE PAUL EDWARD	MI	22W	108
PETRONE LOUIS GENE JR	NJ	33E	74
PETROSSI WILLIAM JR	IL	32E	96
PETSCHKE ROBERT ELTON JR	MA	31W	83
PETSOS PHILLIP CHRIS	NY	21W	120
PETTAWAY LARRY CHARLES	OH	18E	63
PETTERSEN WAYNE ADOLPHUS	WA	21E	125
PETTERSON CHARLES STANLEY	IL	40W	49
PETTEYS CORNEL	NY	18W	21
PETTEYS JAMES BIRCH	PA	34W	9
PETTIE FLOYD WILLIAM III	CO	49E	38
PETTIEGREW JAMES PAUL	MS	02W	10
PETTIFORD JAMES LLOYD	PA	10E	130
PETTIGREW FRED LAFAY III	VA	32W	15
PETTIGREW KENNETH DALE	CA	24W	66
PETTIJOHN JAMES EARL	FL	17W	91
PETTIS BILLY WAYNE	AL	23W	30
PETTIS LORENZO RICHARD	FL	22W	35
PETTIS STEVEN GENE	VT	24W	10
PETTIS THOMAS EDWIN	AL	20E	91
PETTIT CRAIG STEVEN	CA	62W	15
PETTIT DENZIL DAL	CA	09E	100
PETTIT HUGH MICHAEL	MS	04W	117
PETTIT ROBERT HAROLD	NC	17E	106
PETTIT STANLEY RUSSELL	SC	44W	66
PETTITT DONALD ACE	CA	36W	18
PETTITT JAMES ALLEN	TN	49E	54
PETTITT JOHN THOMAS SR	IN	06W	43
PETTUS KENNETH	PA	17E	75
PETTWAY PATRICK HENRY II	TX	15E	21
PETTY ERNEST DE FOREST	MO	07W	50
PETTY ERNEST FLOYD	NE	23E	14
PETTY EUGENE	CA	26E	62
PETTY HOWARD PALMA	TN	44E	61
PETTY JERRY LEON	MO	62E	22
PETTY JOHN CABLE II	KS	10E	1
PETTY JOHN ROBERT JR	TN	02E	135
PETTY MICHAEL HARRIS	LA	05W	61
PETTY ROY ANDREW JR	OH	10W	58
PETTY ROY LYNN	TX	04W	6
PETTY WILLIAM CLARK	SC	22E	33
PETTY WILLIE JR	IL	33E	21
PEYTON WILLIAM ALLEN	IL	11W	127
PEZZULO JOHN FRANCIS	NY	17E	11
PFAFFMANN CHARLES BROOKS	CT	12W	115
PFEFER ARTHUR THOMAS	MN	20W	45

NAME	STATE	PANEL NO.	LINE NO.
PFEFFERLE WARREN W	NJ	05E	31
PFEIFER DENNIS WAYNE	CO	14W	118
PFEIFER RONALD EDWIN	NY	11E	53
PFEIFFER JOHN CLIFFORD	NY	20E	10
PFEISTER ROBERT	KY	34E	24
PFEUFER MICHAEL ANTHONY	NJ	16W	96
PFEUFFER MICHAEL LAWRENCE	TX	46E	22
PFEUFFER RONALD HOWARD	TX	24E	10
PFISTER DAN LEON	WI	56W	26
PFLASTER GARY LEWIS	CA	03W	73
PFLASTERER GEORGE ROBERT	GA	23E	14
PFORDT CHARLES C JR	PA	23W	17
PFOUTZ MYRON MCCLELLAND	PA	01E	126
PFROMMER STANLEY DENNIS	NJ	10E	72
PHAIR JAMES W	MI	08E	39
PHALP WILLIAM ANDERSON JR	KS	32W	8
PHARES KENNETH DUANE	OR	20E	34
PHARIS RONALD WASHINGTON	FL	46W	44
PHARRIS WILLIAM VALRIE	LA	09E	6
PHEARS RONALD GENE	TX	48E	9
PHEIFFER MICHAEL LAVERNE	IL	50E	33
PHELIX STEPHEN RAY	WV	04W	47
PHELPS DAVID CLAYTON	NY	26E	2
PHELPS DAVID HARLOW	NY	37W	58
PHELPS HERBERT LEE	GA	21W	85
PHELPS HERMAN ROY	TX	25E	108
PHELPS HUGER LEE	IN	32W	7
PHELPS JESSE DONALD	ID	04E	44
PHELPS LARRY DELTON	NM	61E	17
PHELPS LARRY LEE	MO	38E	58
PHELPS RANDALL CARL	WV	48E	54
PHELPS RAY WILLIARD JR	TN	41W	42
PHELPS RONALD JOSEPH	MI	29E	97
PHELPS RONNIE LOUIS	CA	19E	110
PHELPS WALTER WILLIAM	NY	07E	98
PHELPS WILLIAM	NY	02W	71
PHENEGAR WESLEY ROBERT JR	IL	24E	108
PHENNEY GEORGE S	MI	13E	107
PHIFER CLYDE EDWARD JR	WV	19W	81
PHIFER FREDDIE JOE	SC	31E	82
PHILBECK DONALD DEWAYNE	KY	40E	46
PHILBIN RICHARD GRIFFITH	CA	04E	133
PHILBRICK STEVEN JAY	NH	23W	91
PHILIBERT BRIAN HARDMAN	TX	51E	49
PHILIPS BURTON KEENEY JR	MO	16W	118
PHILIPSON JOSEPH BION JR	MA	41E	71
PHILLIPS ALTON RAY	KY	22W	55
PHILLIPS ANDREW MARK	PA	14W	34
PHILLIPS ANTHONY BRUCE	CA	10E	130
PHILLIPS AQUILLA ANTHONY	IL	38E	36
PHILLIPS BENJAMIN F JR	MD	27E	66
PHILLIPS BOYCE DEAN	IN	27W	21
PHILLIPS CARL WAYNE	IN	12E	90
PHILLIPS CHARLES EDWARD	MO	12E	91
PHILLIPS CHARLES EDWARD	NC	37E	66
PHILLIPS CHARLES W JR	SC	11W	116
PHILLIPS CLYDE RAYMOND	MS	33E	91
PHILLIPS DANIEL RAYMOND	PA	38E	10
PHILLIPS DAVID JEFFERY	NY	30W	80
PHILLIPS DAVID JOSEPH JR	FL	08E	126
PHILLIPS DEAN ANTHONY	OH	01W	20
PHILLIPS DENNIS L	OH	09E	6
PHILLIPS DENNIS MICHAEL	TX	23W	30
PHILLIPS DONNELL	TX	03E	60
PHILLIPS EARL GENE	WV	03E	26
PHILLIPS EDISON RICHARD	PA	24W	69
PHILLIPS ELBERT AUSTIN	AL	46W	52
PHILLIPS ERNEST	IL	24E	10
PHILLIPS GARY THOMAS	NC	15W	54
PHILLIPS GERALD ARTHUR	NC	56W	37
PHILLIPS GLENN ROSS JR	WA	10E	87
PHILLIPS GREGORY LEE	NM	39W	18
PHILLIPS HARRY V JR	MS	10E	1
PHILLIPS HENRY RICHARDSON	RI	43W	65
PHILLIPS HOWARD EDWARD	AL	04E	125
PHILLIPS JACK WARREN	KS	28E	3
PHILLIPS JAMES CLIFFORD	MI	19E	17
PHILLIPS JAMES EDWARD	VA	10E	9
PHILLIPS JAMES JR	MI	19E	17
PHILLIPS JAMES LESTER	AL	29W	72
PHILLIPS JAMES RILEY	MO	32W	9
PHILLIPS JERRY	TX	09E	128

NAME	STATE	PANEL NO.	LINE NO.
PHILLIPS JERRY ALFRED	SC	17E	29
PHILLIPS JERRY LEN	CO	39W	35
PHILLIPS JERRY NEWTON	FL	11W	87
PHILLIPS JOHN DAVID	CA	08W	133
PHILLIPS JOHN MICHAEL	CA	07E	20
PHILLIPS JOHN ROBERT	IL	32E	52
PHILLIPS JOHNNY WENDELL	TX	22W	108
PHILLIPS KERRY WAYNE	IN	06W	133
PHILLIPS LAWRENCE	SC	04W	81
PHILLIPS LEON MILTON	WI	43E	68
PHILLIPS LEONARD	AL	22E	56
PHILLIPS LEROY JACKSON	VA	26E	31
PHILLIPS LIONEL NESBIT JR	NC	39E	37
PHILLIPS LLOYD FREEMAN	IL	22E	121
PHILLIPS MARK JOHN	FL	19W	34
PHILLIPS MARLEN LE ROY	KS	45W	56
PHILLIPS MARSHALL W JR	OH	46W	62
PHILLIPS MARVIN FOSTER	TN	11E	20
PHILLIPS MICHAEL GENE	KS	28E	105
PHILLIPS MICHAEL LEON	DC	57W	12
PHILLIPS NATHANIEL JAMES	PA	08W	4
PHILLIPS NORRIS ARTHUR	TX	24W	19
PHILLIPS ORMAN DORR	AL	16E	23
PHILLIPS OSCAR C JR	OK	61W	5
PHILLIPS OTIS LAMONT	AR	37E	26
PHILLIPS PAT ELLIS	CA	19E	122
PHILLIPS PAUL HENRY	CT	08E	133
PHILLIPS RANDALL SCOTT	OK	11W	92
PHILLIPS RICHARD BRUCE	GA	28W	3
PHILLIPS RICHARD GREGORY	MO	20W	11
PHILLIPS ROBERT B	NC	17E	38
PHILLIPS ROBERT JAMES	OR	08E	28
PHILLIPS ROBERT LITTLETON	GA	11W	116
PHILLIPS ROBERT PAUL	OH	09W	85
PHILLIPS ROGER LEE	OH	29W	92
PHILLIPS ROGER LEE	TX	08W	4
PHILLIPS RONALD CHARLES	CA	24W	20
PHILLIPS ROY EDWIN	TX	50W	20
PHILLIPS ROY FRANKLIN	FL	34W	44
PHILLIPS ROY LEE	IL	36E	82
PHILLIPS SAMUEL C III	ID	27E	41
PHILLIPS SHEPHEN HIETT	MO	02E	39
PHILLIPS THEODORE BERT	CA	01E	68
PHILLIPS THOMAS FRANK	FL	15E	86
PHILLIPS THOMAS MILES	CA	44W	53
PHILLIPS TOMMIE	IL	31E	26
PHILLIPS WALTER MACK	OR	26E	15
PHILLIPS WARREN EVERETT	IA	04E	113
PHILLIPS WESLEY LEE	SC	05W	6
PHILLIPS WILEY LAVELL	MS	09E	100
PHILLIPS WILLIAM GRIGABY	OH	24E	74
PHILLIPS WILLIAM JOSEPH	CA	04E	94
PHILLIPS WILLIAM LEROY	GA	14W	50
PHILLIPS WILLIAM RONALD	NY	46E	1
PHILLIPS WILLIAM RUSSEL	AL	14E	113
PHILLIPS WYLIE ORIA	SC	33E	4
PHILLIS DONALD R JR	PA	52W	30
PHILPOTT HAROLD DEAN	TX	22E	121
PHILSON WILLARD ARLIN	NE	14E	105
PHILYAW LAWRENCE EDWARD	NC	47E	41
PHINN WILLIAM MARK	CA	29W	72
PHIPPS DONALD RAY	CA	27E	55
PHIPPS GENE RAY	NC	32E	89
PHIPPS HERBERT CHARLES	VA	10E	125
PHIPPS JAMES ALVIN	CA	58W	28
PHIPPS JAMES LARRY	IL	34E	9
PHIPPS JIMMY DOYLE	NC	11E	101
PHIPPS JIMMY WAYNE	CA	23W	2
PHIPPS LANNY WILLIAM	NJ	37W	58
PHIPPS LEONARD MORRIS	WA	40E	11
PHIPPS NORMAN IRA	VA	53E	21
PHIPPS ROBERT EARL	KY	09W	9
PHIPPS ROY LESTER	OH	11W	1
PHLEGER ROBERT CRAIN	OH	11W	127
PHOEBUS FREDERICK ALLEN	MD	08E	68
PHOENIX ALONZA WILLIE	SC	40W	7
PIACENTINO MICHAEL ALLEN	MD	17W	19
PIAMBINO JOSEPH ROBERT	NY	17E	23
PIANO RALPH ERNEST JR	NJ	17W	43
PIANTKOWSKI EDWARD JOSEPH	IL	12E	68
PIASCIK MICHAEL	NJ	09E	2
PIASECKI JOHN MICHAEL	IL	15W	7

NAME	STATE	PANEL NO.	LINE NO.
PIASKOWSKI WILLIAM FRANCI	AK	44E	52
PIATKOWSKI ROBERT J	PA	46E	29
PIATT CHARLES WILLIAM	OH	25E	108
PIATT RICHARD WEAVER	CA	18E	36
PIAZZA ROBERT GARY	NY	48E	33
PICANSO LEONARD JR	MA	19E	30
PICARAZZI JAMES VINCENT	NY	05W	100
PICARD MICHAEL W	MT	40E	47
PICARELLI JOSEPH HENRY	NJ	61E	1
PICCIANO TERRANCE ALAN	MI	59W	11
PICCOLELLA CHARLES VICTOR	NY	10E	30
PICELLE FRANK JOHN JR	OH	22W	55
PICHAUFFE CARL JOSEPH	LA	19W	41
PICHON HERMAN EDWARD	LA	04W	73
PICHON LOUIS ALPHONSE JR	LA	17E	39
PICK DONALD WILLIAM	WA	46W	44
PICKARD ALFRED	TX	15W	19
PICKARD DENNIS LEE	NY	35E	78
PICKARD HARRY DAVIS	NC	10W	122
PICKARD RICHARD JAMES	GA	25W	32
PICKART DWAYNE ROBERT	IA	25W	24
PICKART RONALD ERNEST	WI	14W	14
PICKEL GEORGE WILLIAM	NY	25W	109
PICKENS JOHNNIE JR	NY	10W	3
PICKERING DONALD WILLIAM	IA	57E	8
PICKERING RUSSELL THOMAS	IA	15W	19
PICKETT DARREL MONROE	AZ	07W	50
PICKETT HOMER LEE	OK	11E	46
PICKETT JOHN PRICE	WV	17W	75
PICKETT JOSEPH CHARLES JR	IL	54E	15
PICKETT KENNETH WALTER	KY	07E	74
PICKETT MALCOLM JEROME	IL	12W	44
PICKETT MORRIS CALVIN	GA	34E	10
PICKETT MORRISON LOUIS	OK	35E	79
PICKETT RICHARD DALE	MT	24W	79
PICKETT RODNEY DOUGLAS	VA	20E	97
PICKETT STEPHEN WILLIAM	NY	31E	94
PICKETT WILLIE CLARENCE	FL	03E	26
PICKETT WILTON RAY	CA	34E	10
PICKING FRANKLIN WILLIAM	IA	20W	36
PICKLE JIMMY DEE	MT	48E	9
PICKLES MICHAEL RICHARD	ME	11W	60
PICKWORTH JERRY LEE	OH	17E	23
PICONI PIETRO	PA	38W	68
PIERCE ALLEN LINN	OR	05E	74
PIERCE ANDREW STARRETT JR	WV	06W	44
PIERCE BERNARD LAWRENCE	CT	22W	92
PIERCE CALVIN BOB	IL	46W	20
PIERCE CLIFTON PALMER	WA	33E	40
PIERCE CLINTON DWIGHT	KS	16W	46
PIERCE DANNY RALPH	MO	41E	4
PIERCE DARREL GENE	MO	16W	46
PIERCE DAVID WAYNE	OH	36W	18
PIERCE DONALD JAMES JR	PA	12W	18
PIERCE DOUGLAS JACK	ND	02W	73
PIERCE EDWARD DAVIS	AL	06E	5
PIERCE EDWARD EARL	NC	17W	81
PIERCE GEORGE WASHINGTON	AL	20W	115
PIERCE HARRY W JR	DC	18W	42
PIERCE HERBERT LEE JR	OH	34W	67
PIERCE HOMER EARL JR	OH	34E	60
PIERCE IRVING CLARENCE JR	NJ	38E	79
PIERCE JAMES EVERETT	KY	33W	81
PIERCE JERRY DEAN	OK	41W	37
PIERCE JERRY LEE JR	WA	42W	72
PIERCE JIMMY RAY	AL	45E	14
PIERCE JOE JR	TX	50W	8
PIERCE JOHN ROBERT	IL	11E	64
PIERCE JOSEPH HOWARD JR	FL	32W	82
PIERCE JOSEPH ROBERT CLIN	IL	55E	27
PIERCE KENT DE WAYNE	IN	36W	82
PIERCE LARRY STANLEY	CA	02E	91
PIERCE LARRY WENDELL	PA	32E	55
PIERCE LEO	IL	22W	36
PIERCE LEON JOSEPH	CO	27W	96
PIERCE LOY WENDELL	CA	03W	127
PIERCE MERRICK ROBERT	OR	28E	85
PIERCE MICHAEL ABEL	TX	05W	20
PIERCE MORRIS WOODWARD JR	VA	04W	29
PIERCE OSCAR WAYNE	OK	16E	47
PIERCE PHILLIP MALCOLM JR	GA	09E	59
PIERCE RICHARD A	IN	13E	127

NAME	STATE	PANEL NO.	LINE NO.
PIERCE ROBERT DUANE	MI	02W	67
PIERCE ROBERT JAMES	GA	08W	103
PIERCE ROBERT LIVINGSTON	NM	11W	52
PIERCE ROGER LEE	IL	02W	100
PIERCE RONALD GERARD	RI	10E	73
PIERCE RONALD SHAFER	NY	25W	19
PIERCE SAMUEL HENRY JR	CA	19W	51
PIERCE TED	UT	17W	63
PIERCE TERRY PAUL	VA	12E	129
PIERCE WALTER MELVIN	PA	09W	40
PIERCE WILLIAM EARVIN	CA	05W	101
PIERCE WILLIAM WESLEY	TX	07E	60
PIERCY ROBERT CONOVER	MI	38E	10
PIERINI JOHN ROBERT	NV	48E	19
PIERPOINT DONALD EVERETT	WV	02W	30
PIERPONT WILLIAM MCGREGOR	MI	16W	66
PIERRE CARRIER	NY	03E	10
PIERRE NORMAN WALLACE	OH	34W	44
PIERSANTI ANTHONY J JR	NJ	06W	123
PIERSOL JOHN LAURENCE JR	PA	07W	13
PIERSON DENNIS LEROY	MN	02E	20
PIERSON GROVER CECIL JR	OH	04W	111
PIERSON LARRY JAMES	IN	66W	11
PIERSON LE ROY	OH	14E	23
PIERSON LYNN ALLEN	IN	51E	41
PIERSON ROBERT EMMETT	NJ	28W	1
PIERSON WILLIAM C III	WI	27W	77
PIERSON WILLIAM EDWIN	WI	32E	4
PIES JOHN DAVID FREDRICK	OH	14W	54
PIETRAS FRANK MARTIN	NY	23E	6
PIETRASZAK DAVID ALOYSIUS	OH	41W	53
PIETRZAK JOSEPH RAY	OH	05W	93
PIETRZYK MARK HAROLD	MI	39W	38
PIETSCH ROBERT EDWARD	OH	53E	21
PIFER ROGER LEE	PA	32W	67
PIGATT HARMON JULIOUS	SC	15E	22
PIGEON JOSEPH THOMAS JR	RI	47W	20
PIGFORD PHILLIP WAYNE	NC	43E	30
PIGG EDWARD WAYNE	IL	58E	27
PIGG THOMAS CHARLES	CA	23W	23
PIGNATARO JULIUS PHILIP	NY	28W	74
PIGNATO JOSEPH MICHAEL	MA	39W	29
PIGOTT CHARLES WILLIAM	RI	24W	48
PIGOTT JAMES HAROLD	OH	47W	31
PIKE DENNIS EUGENE	IL	11E	77
PIKE DENNIS STANLEY	AZ	02W	119
PIKE DONALD CLEAVER	KY	23E	22
PIKE EDWARD MORRIS	AL	36E	30
PIKE NIXON DEWAYNE	TX	13W	31
PIKE PETER XAVIER	NY	21W	109
PIKE RAYMOND HORACE JR	KS	36E	30
PILCHER WILLIAM GEORGE	MO	26E	105
PILK ROBERT HARRISON	FL	09W	70
PILKENTON CLARENCE WESLEY	TX	20E	66
PILKINGTON CARL EDWARD SR	IL	26W	49
PILKINGTON CHARLES H JR	TN	24W	10
PILKINGTON EDWARD PERCY	NC	04W	119
PILKINGTON THOMAS HOLT	IL	10E	121
PILLOW RONALD EDWARD	AR	52W	24
PILLSBURY JERRY DEAN	NH	11E	16
PILON ALAN EVERETT	CO	26E	62
PILOT STANLEY GEORGE JR	NC	01W	78
PILOTTE JOSEPH MARION	TX	13W	123
PILSNER JOHNNY MACK	TX	23W	30
PILSON THOMAS VICTOR	PA	31W	71
PILSON WALLACE EDWARD	WV	07E	121
PILTON GAVIN WILLIAM	RI	02W	114
PIMENTEL RONNIE CARDOZA	CA	45W	21
PIMENTEL TEOFILO CASTILLO	HI	05E	23
PINA FRANK DAVID	CA	42E	23
PINA GERALD MARTIN	FL	34E	31
PINA LOUIE PETE	NE	32E	26
PINA LUIZ JR	MA	13E	6
PINALES LAWRENCE	CA	53W	11
PINAMONTI ERNEST ANTHONY	CA	25W	81
PINATELLI THOMAS MICHAEL	CA	38E	71
PINCHOT CRAIG D	CA	27E	86
PINDER JOHN JOSEPH	NY	25E	71
PINE FREDERICK ANDREW	NJ	33E	21
PINEAU ROLAND ROBERT	MI	27E	75
PINEGAR WILLIAM DENNIS	NE	02E	111
PINER JOHN ROBERT	CA	13W	113

NAME	STATE	PANEL NO.	LINE NO.
PING ROY MARTIN	CA	22W	43
PINGEL WAYNE EDWARD	MI	41E	1
PINHEIRO JEFFREY ANTONE	MA	38E	79
PINION DOCK JEFFERSON	MS	12E	109
PINK JOSEPH PATRICK	CA	28E	56
PINKARD ROBERT LEE	TX	45W	33
PINKERTON BENJAMIN ROBERT	KY	03E	20
PINKERTON LLOYD D	IN	14E	6
PINKERTON MICHAEL DAVID	UT	22E	8
PINKNEY HARVEY TYRONE	MD	14W	31
PINKNEY ROBERTIS	MI	08W	116
PINKSTON ROBERT GENE	IL	44E	52
PINN ARNOLD	NY	30E	48
PINNEKER JERALD LEE	WI	06E	26
PINNELL ROBERT MERRITT JR	NJ	17E	12
PINNEY JOHN SCOTT	CA	32W	46
PINO ALFRED	NJ	16E	96
PINO ANTHONY CARLOS	NY	50W	26
PINOLE BABE	CA	37W	58
PINSON CLOYDE CYRIS JR	TX	19E	99
PINSON LARRY GUNNELL	GA	18W	114
PINSONAULT FRED JOHN	UT	34E	81
PINSONNAULT RICHARD NORMA	MA	53W	38
PINTA RICHARD THOMAS	NY	24E	39
PINTAR JAMES ALBERT	IN	33E	92
PINTER WILLIAM JAMES	VA	44W	40
PINTO CAESAR AUGUSTUS	MA	24E	97
PINTO JOSEPH JOHN	IL	19W	121
PINTO-PINTO SIGFREDO	PR	25E	20
PINTOLA JAMES MICHAEL	OH	29W	72
PIOTROWICZ DAVID	PA	36W	26
PIOTROWSKI DANIEL JOSEPH	MI	06E	77
PIPER CHARLES HERMAN JR	ND	01W	70
PIPER DONALD CHANDLER	VA	05E	74
PIPER EDWARD ROGER	AL	01E	127
PIPER JAMES DENNIS	CA	18E	16
PIPER ROBERT ANTHONY	GA	03W	119
PIPER SIDNEY JR	TX	10W	99
PIPER THOMAS LEIGH	MN	49W	25
PIPER WALTER JR	WA	05E	7
PIPES JAMES LEE JR	VA	43E	10
PIPHER CARL DALE	OH	33W	11
PIPKIN DENNIS NEWMAN	WA	12W	83
PIPKIN ERNEST GERALD	TN	11E	72
PIPKIN FRANK MEADOWS	CA	14E	119
PIPKIN THOMAS DEWEY JR	MO	27E	91
PIPPENBACH JOSEPH	NJ	11W	127
PIPPIN DAVID WAYNE	IL	39E	38
PIPPIN HENRY LEE	FL	20W	115
PIPPINS GUS	NY	07W	90
PIPPINS WILLIE SR	AR	05E	74
PIREZ-BERGES CARLOS	NY	11E	78
PIRKER VICTOR JOHN	MT	03E	108
PIRKLE WILLIAM ITHEL	FL	12W	36
PIRKOLA PAUL HENRY	MI	46W	20
PIRRMAN RAYMOND LEE	KY	21W	62
PIRRUCCELLO JOSEPH S JR	OH	37W	67
PISACRETA ROGER MELVIN		04W	35
PISCAR VINCENT JR	PA	51W	14
PISCIOTTA WAYNE CARLYLE	NJ	03W	104
PISCITELLO SALVATORE JOHN	MA	38W	79
PISENO RAYMOND RICHARD JR	MT	15W	49
PISHNER WILLIAM JR	CA	13W	106
PISKULA RICHARD	PA	20W	60
PITCHES JAMES SUTHERLAND	NY	18W	21
PITCHFORD L C	TN	04E	10
PITCOCK ELZIA RAY	MI	24E	62
PITMAN PETER POTTER	GA	19E	99
PITNER MONTE GALE	OR	35E	79
PITRE FLOYD LEON	LA	22W	25
PITRE JORY JOSEPH	LA	24W	48
PITRE KENNETH JOSEPH	LA	23W	105
PITSENBARGER DENNIS STOVE	VA	02E	24
PITSENBARGER WILLIAM HART	OH	06E	102
PITT ALBERT	NY	04E	85
PITT ROBERT LOUIS	CA	11E	105
PITT ROY SHARP	CA	08E	39
PITT WILLIAM LYNN	TN	46W	52
PITTARD DAVID HUNTER	NC	42W	32
PITTENGER DONALD ALAN	CA	19E	88
PITTIGREW JOHN FLOYD	WA	18W	90
PITTINGER CHARLES ROBERT	MD	16W	89

NAME	STATE	PANEL NO.	LINE NO.
PITTMAN CHARLES TERRELL	NC	05E	29
PITTMAN EDGAR STEVAN	GA	21W	1
PITTMAN JACK	OH	09E	76
PITTMAN JAMES SHERWIN	NY	11E	78
PITTMAN ROBERT EDWARD	FL	28E	38
PITTMAN ROBERT LOUIS	CA	35E	62
PITTMAN RONNIE RAY	KY	16E	48
PITTMAN WILLIAM T	GA	41E	27
PITTMANN ALAN DALE	IA	12E	80
PITTS BENJAMIN FREDERICK	IL	36E	30
PITTS BILLY JAY	KY	39W	12
PITTS CHARLES R	FL	30E	93
PITTS CLEVELAND	FL	15W	24
PITTS DANA ALLEN	MN	29E	12
PITTS DAVID ALLEN	MA	40E	28
PITTS DERWIN BROOKE	OK	19W	97
PITTS FRED EARL	OH	32W	9
PITTS FREDDIE RICHARD	FL	18E	126
PITTS JAMES ELSWORTH	FL	13E	16
PITTS JOSEPH WADE JR	PA	37W	41
PITTS RILEY LEROY	OK	28E	105
PITTS ROBERT ARDELL	TX	23W	2
PITTS ROBERT PATRICK	WA	19E	17
PITTS ROY EDWARD	CA	32W	50
PITTS TERRY DENNIS	CA	33E	21
PITTS WAYNE MONROE	FL	21E	70
PITZEN JOHN RUSSELL	IA	01W	67
PITZER RICHARD LYLE	WI	43E	30
PIVA JAMES EDWARD	ID	13W	64
PIXLEY RICHARD GORDON	NY	51W	20
PIZARRO VIC MANUEL	NY	43E	30
PIZARRO-COLON MARCOS	PR	08W	103
PIZER WESLEY IRWIN	CO	18E	71
PIZZANO JAMES ROBERT	MA	46W	53
PIZZI CHARLES DANIEL	NJ	02E	2
PIZZINO THOMAS CARMEN	OH	03E	90
PIZZUTI JOHN	MI	36W	5
PIZZUTO LOUIS EDWARD	NY	14E	20
PLACERES MOSES	CA	06W	30
PLACZEK PAUL GEORGE	IL	20W	125
PLAEP ALFRED EDGAR JR	OR	41E	1
PLAHN JACK CHARLES	NE	38E	59
PLAKE JAMES ROLAND	CA	28E	97
PLAMBECK PAUL WANDLING JR	TX	16W	70
PLANCHON RANDALL T II	CA	57W	30
PLANCK EVERETT ALLEN	KY	44W	53
PLANK JAMES DUANE	PA	14W	29
PLANTE GARY WILLIAM	MI	24W	26
PLANTE NORMAND AURELE	RI	18E	110
PLANTS OTIS EUGENE	AR	07W	38
PLANTS THOMAS LEE	OH	01E	130
PLASSMEYER BERNARD HERBER	MO	07W	57
PLASTER BILLY JOE JR	TX	05W	55
PLATA JOHNNY MORRIS	TX	28E	3
PLATA MARVIN JAMES	FL	36E	30
PLATE JAMES RICHARD	SD	16W	125
PLATERO RAYMOND	NM	14W	69
PLATH STEVEN DALE	MN	04W	88
PLATO JIMMIE LEON	NM	12E	75
PLATO ROBERT DEAN	OK	64E	7
PLATOSZ WALTER	CT	28E	29
PLATT BILLY WAYNE	TX	25E	31
PLATT DAVID BORNE	IN	23W	67
PLATT GARY W	CO	03E	15
PLATT JOHN HERBERT	IA	24W	97
PLATT LARRY DEAN	IN	21W	25
PLATT ROBERT LENWOOD JR	SC	21E	84
PLATT ROBERT LLOYD	PA	41E	71
PLATT WAYNE B	TX	41E	42
PLATTENBURGER SIDNEY E	NC	12W	73
PLATTER GEORGE RICHARD	MO	19W	20
PLATTNER ERNEST MELVIN	NY	39W	37
PLAVCAN KENNETH MICHAEL	OH	42W	59
PLAYFORD RONALD EDGAR	WA	28W	29
PLAZA BERNARD STANLEY	MA	12E	113
PLAZA JUAN JOSE	NY	06W	72
PLEASANT EDDIE LEE	MO	42E	56
PLEASANT MURPHY JR	WI	35W	21
PLEASANT STEPHEN DONALD	CA	17E	12
PLEASANT WILLIAM ANDREW	NJ	03E	90
PLECITY JAMES DONN	WI	31E	52
PLEDGER DONALD ALLEN	VA	36W	46
PLEIMAN JAMES EDWARD	OH	06E	7
PLEMMONS NORMAN LEE	NC	25W	1
PLEMMONS ROBERT COLQUITT	TX	44E	30
PLESAKOV LUCIANO PAUL	PA	19E	30
PLESH RAYMOND NICHOLAS	PA	24E	39
PLESS WILLIAM HUDSOL	TN	35W	36
PLETT LARRY JOE	AK	08W	36
PLIER EUGENE JOHN	WI	28E	29
PLILER LARRY DEAN	MO	62W	15
PLINER RICHARD DUANE	WI	09W	19
PLISKA MICHAEL DENNIS	PA	05E	90
PLOTE DALE EDWIN	IL	18E	6
PLOTKIN MARTIN LOUIS	NY	22E	1
PLOTKIN STEPHEN LEWIS	NY	26W	35
PLOTTS RICHARD	NJ	31E	60
PLOURDE CLAYTON	CT	02W	33
PLOURDE ROBERT JAMES	NH	64W	14
PLOURDE VICTOR M	ME	46W	53
PLOWMAN JAMES EDWIN	CA	17E	39
PLUCINSKI JACK ALBERT	IL	42W	21
PLUM BILLIE NEAL	MI	05E	82
PLUM CARROLL STEVEN	VA	07W	90
PLUMADORE KENNETH LEO	NY	26E	106
PLUMB CHARLES DONALD JR	MI	11W	127
PLUMB GARY ANTHONEY	CA	16E	64
PLUMB JACK CLARE	PA	45W	28
PLUMEY RAYMOND	NY	30E	58
PLUMLEE JAMES LEO JR	TX	21W	19
PLUMLEY JIMMIE LEE	GA	06E	124
PLUMM RICHARD DALE	MI	03W	50
PLUMMER CHARLES DEAN	WV	39W	68
PLUMMER HERBERT JR	TX	31E	94
PLUMMER JAMES ARMAND	IL	19E	45
PLUMMER JOHN DAVID	MO	19W	72
PLUMMER NEWTON RAY	IL	37W	18
PLUMMER RALPH WILLIAM III	OH	28E	97
PLUMMER REGGINALD WILLIAM	LA	15W	43
PLUMMER RICHARD EUGENE	FL	44W	59
PLUMMER SAMUEL RUDOLPH	GA	41W	60
PLUNKARD JOHN FRANCIS	MD	48E	54
PLUNKETT GERALD W	TN	44W	53
PLUNKETT RAYMOND LOUIS	DC	47E	15
PLUNKETT ROBERT STEPHEN	MA	35E	56
POBLOCK BERNARD FRANCIS	MI	32E	66
POCHEL GERALD DEVER	OR	45W	38
POCHER WILLIAM THORNTON	FL	20W	75
POCHRON RONALD EDWARD	WI	42W	59
POCKEY JAMES JODY	PA	02W	116
POCS LESLIE MARTIN	TX	18W	85
PODEBRADSKY ANTHONY JOHN	WI	39E	52
PODELL RICHARD W	IN	21E	80
PODGORNY DENNIS RICHARD	CA	29E	61
PODHAJSKY NORBERT ALBERT	IA	06W	94
PODLESNIK WAYNE A	PA	28E	7
PODMANICZKY CHRISTOPHER	MO	18E	65
PODNAR ROBERT JOHN	IA	09W	16
PODY JOHN CHRISTOPHER III	TN	24E	39
POE CHARLES ALTON	NV	20W	125
POE CLIFFORD EARL JR	TX	11W	116
POE JAMES WALKER	MI	23W	39
POE JERRY LYNN	GA	44W	66
POE JESSIE GERALD	IL	61W	15
POE JIMMIE CLYDE	SC	13E	35
POE JOHN RAYMOND	MD	08W	83
POE JOHN WAYNE	MI	32W	61
POE JOSEPH BYRON	AR	02W	22
POE ROBERT EDWIN	TN	42E	70
POE STEVEN MELVIN	IN	19W	81
POELING EUGENE FREDERICK	IL	20E	66
POELSTRA DENNIS PATRICK	CA	15W	56
POEPPING WILFRED NORBERT	MN	02W	68
POESCHL JOHN EDWIN	MO	03W	25
POESE NIGEL FREDERICK	NE	29W	92
POET LAWRENCE	MI	31W	15
POFF BILL DEAN	MO	60W	4
POFF DANIEL LOYD	WA	31W	16
POFF ELBERT DARRELL	WV	55E	27
POFF JERRY WAYNE	FL	21W	53
POFF JOHN ROBERT	WI	33W	51
POFFENBARGER WILLIAM OSCAR	CA	34E	35
POGGEMEYER JAMES ROBERT	NE	24E	56
POGGI MICHAEL LOUIS	NY	28W	73
POGRE BOB ELIA	CA	07E	11
POGREBA DEAN ANDREW	MT	02E	109
POGUE JOSEPH DONALD	CA	11W	42
POGUE MICHAEL ALAN	CA	36E	31
POHANCEK STEVE	IL	05W	6
POHJOLA JEFFREY WILLIS	MI	46W	20
POHL EHRHARD HANS KONRAD	TX	12W	34
POHL FLOYD WILLIAM	NY	04E	71
POHL RICHARD SHARON	OH	55W	30
POHL WILLIAM ANTHONY	CA	59E	29
POHLMAN CHARLES PAUL	IL	15E	15
POHLMAN JOHN HOWARD	CA	11W	9
POINDEXTER MOSES LEON	VA	20E	86
POINTER DARRYL WARREN ANT	IL	40E	47
POINTER RONALD JOSEPH	MA	43W	19
POINTER WALTER LEON	OK	07W	53
POIRIER PAUL EUGENE	MA	49E	46
POIRIER ROGER MILTON	CA	24E	69
POITRAS NORMAN GERALD JOS	ME	10E	27
POITROW EMERY NORMAN	ME	49E	5
POKE DONALD MAURICE	KS	03W	35
POKERJIM JOSEPH LOUIS	MT	27E	97
POKEY FRANK MICHEAL JR	WI	16E	96
POLAK PETER PAUL	WI	32W	72
POLANCO JOSE YBARRA JR	AZ	18W	90
POLAND HARRY TURNER	KY	13E	55
POLAND LEON LOVELL JR	ME	17E	54
POLAND RONALD LEE	OH	07W	40
POLASEK JOSEPH JAMES JR	MI	28W	93
POLASKI LEON CRAIG	WI	14W	79
POLCHOW WILLIAM ALFRED	NY	35E	18
POLDINO THOMAS	NY	29W	13
POLEFKA JOHN ARN	PA	18W	17
POLEGA GERRY ALBIN	MI	32W	29
POLENDO RAYNALDO	TX	28E	62
POLENSKI EDMOND CHESTER	MA	24W	48
POLESETSKY BRUCE	AZ	07W	111
POLETTI MICHAEL LEE	ID	44W	19
POLEY DAVID ALLAN	PA	30W	94
POLGLASE WILLIAM RAULISON	CT	35W	55
POLICASTRO MARK EDWARD	PA	41E	42
POLICH DAVID WILLIAM	IN	11E	17
POLING JACKIE RAY	OH	51W	35
POLING JOHN EARL	TX	41W	25
POLING KENNETH	OH	03E	105
POLING LARRY STERL	ND	17W	98
POLIQUIN MICHAEL EDWARD	ME	19W	73
POLISKY THOMAS RICHARD	MI	48W	8
POLITO GENE ALBERT	OH	33E	40
POLIZZI SALVATORE FRANK	NY	23E	62
POLK CHARLES QUINTEN	TX	15W	67
POLK GARY DON	AR	12W	49
POLK KENNETH ERBIE	AL	26W	73
POLK PRESTON WAYNE	MT	12E	97
POLK ROBERT LOUIS	TX	58W	13
POLKINGHORNE ROBERT ELISH	MI	11E	128
POLL MICHAEL JOHN	NC	16W	113
POLLACK JOHN JOSEPH	MI	14W	76
POLLARD GERALD RAY JR	MO	12W	73
POLLARD JAMES FREDERICK	WA	25E	108
POLLARD JAMES ROBERT JR	IL	29W	39
POLLARD RICHARD	LA	32W	82
POLLARD SIDNEY GERALD	FL	41W	70
POLLARD THOMAS LEROY	IA	47W	3
POLLARD WAYNE RICHARD	WA	27E	102
POLLARD WILLIAM ALFRED	DE	23E	103
POLLARD WILLIAM ISAAC	NJ	31E	38
POLLASTRO DOMINICK	NY	43W	19
POLLEY GARY PAT	OH	28E	41
POLLEY RICHARD ALAN	OH	60W	11
POLLEY ROGER DALE	OH	14E	11
POLLIN GEORGE JOHN	NJ	18E	116
POLLOCK DOUGLAS RAY	CO	30W	79
POLLOCK GARY JOE	UT	28W	74
POLLOCK LAWRENCE EDWARD	OH	17E	12
POLLOCK SEVENTY J	NJ	40E	28
POLNIAK ROBERT JOSEPH	NY	06W	95
POLONKO JOSEPH JOHN JR	NJ	07E	11
POLSON EDWARD LEE	KY	32E	42
POLSTER HARMON	OH	20W	2
POLSTON ERNEST ELIJAH	SC	24E	39
POLT ERWIN ANDREW	NE	46E	10

NAME	STATE	PANEL NO.	LINE NO.
POLUSNEY JAMES FRANCIS	PA	16W	90
POLZIN HENRY CLARENCE	MN	20W	81
POMERINKE RICHARD ALLEN	WA	08W	70
POMERLEAU JAMES GERARD	ME	18E	81
POMEROY ALEXANDER P	MT	20W	88
POMEROY CARLYLE B JR	CO	28E	98
POMEROY DAVID KEITH	MO	40E	12
POMEROY DEANE ALVA	TX	01E	53
POMEROY JACK WILLIAM	MI	16W	122
POMPELLA PATRICK OWEN	WA	13W	30
PONAK CORDELL JOSEPH	MI	16W	81
PONATH KURT FRANCIS	WI	44W	41
PONCE ANTONIO RAMON	MI	29E	85
PONCE BENITO ANDRADE	TX	13W	120
PONCE PAUL	CA	19W	47
PONCURAK RAYMOND JOSEPH	FL	10E	51
PONDER DERRELL LOIAL	FL	06W	27
PONDER JOHN DAVID	MO	61E	17
PONDER WILLIE LE EARL	DC	54E	28
PONDOFF JOHN CHRISTOPHER	IL	38E	36
PONGRATZ RONALD EUGENE	TX	26W	3
PONIKTERA STANLEY F JR	PA	64W	14
PONTIERE JOHN RANDALL	PA	23W	105
PONTING JOHN L	KS	30E	65
PONTIUS MARK DURWOOD	MI	10W	126
PONTO AUGUSTUS J III	NJ	21E	84
PONTUCK HOWARD SAMUEL	NY	43E	58
PONTY STEPHEN CHESTER JR	NJ	36W	86
POOCK MYRON JEROME	IA	51W	35
POOL CHARLES LEO	LA	40W	39
POOL CHARLES WINFRED JR	VA	26W	101
POOL GARY GLEN	UT	49W	48
POOL HAROLD LAVEROL	AL	18E	126
POOL JERRY LYNN	IL	12W	40
POOL LARRY GAY	AR	20W	34
POOL THOMAS JOHN	TX	22E	89
POOLAW PASCAL CLEATUS SR	OK	29E	43
POOLE CHARLES BURTON	KY	40E	12
POOLE CHARLIE SHERMAN	LA	01W	96
POOLE CONRAD EARL	AL	17E	114
POOLE EARL LEROY	GA	12W	52
POOLE FRANKLIN WILLIE	OK	39W	12
POOLE HARTWIG RALPH	OH	30E	17
POOLE JOHN EDWARD	AR	16W	81
POOLE MELVIN	GA	52W	31
POOLE ORIS LAMAR	GA	23E	45
POOLE OTHA LENSEY	TX	33W	68
POOLE PERRY LEE	AR	11E	80
POOLE RONALD DEAN	OH	57W	12
POOLE RONALD FELTON	TX	23E	78
POOLE THOMAS DEWITT	AL	39E	11
POOLE THOMAS LYNN	CA	09W	86
POOLE WILLIAM CLAUDE	TN	16E	30
POOLE WILLIAM DAVID JR	SC	25W	109
POOLE WILLIAM GUY III	TN	60W	18
POOLER JOHN SHELBY	IL	37W	7
POOR GEORGE ALBERT JR	NJ	22E	51
POOR RUSSELL ARDEN	IN	14E	119
POOR VICTOR LYNN	IN	31W	55
POORE LEONARD BURTON	TX	22E	47
POORE ROBERT EARL	MS	33W	9
POORE THOMAS WYATT	SC	20E	66
POPE CHARLES ALFRED JR	MO	06W	69
POPE CHARLES DEAN	AL	32E	80
POPE DEREK BOYD	CA	09E	116
POPE DONALD BURRIS	SC	15E	63
POPE EMMETT FELTON JR	GA	14E	53
POPE GEORGE RICHARD	NC	63E	16
POPE JAMES RUSSELL	MS	24E	10
POPE MORELL JOE	UT	26E	106
POPE ROBERT DALE	TX	46E	40
POPE SERVESTON DEVON	CA	49W	3
POPE THOMAS ROBERT	CA	44E	52
POPE WALTER GLENN	TN	53E	6
POPKIN STEVEN JAY	MA	41E	71
POPOWITZ GREGORY FRANCIS	PA	35E	26
POPP DAVID FRED	OR	29W	39
POPP DAVID JOSEPH	MN	44W	12
POPP JAMES ARTHUR	MI	17E	127
POPPA GERALD LELAND	CA	50W	45
POPPAW MICHAEL ROBERT	OH	07E	54
POPPEMA LEROY WARREN	IA	61E	17
POPPENGA PATRICK EDWARD	IL	23W	77
POPPLETON CHARLES ARTHUR	MO	02W	69
PORCARO SALVATORE VINCENT	MI	15E	61
PORCELLA STEPHEN RICHARD	MA	31E	16
PORCHIA BOBBY RAY	AR	55W	30
PORDEN LEE VICTOR JR	MI	37W	14
POREA ROBERT GEORGE	OH	27E	61
POROVICH STEVE	AZ	01W	5
PORRAS JUAN	KS	44W	19
PORRAZZO LOUIS EDWARD	MA	27E	21
PORT GARY CRAIG	CA	39E	24
PORT HYRUM BARRY	PA	04W	31
PORT WILLIAM DAVID	PA	34E	39
PORTA GERARD PAUL	MI	27W	40
PORTE ROBERT ANDREW	CA	27W	46
PORTELLO RODERICK CHARLES	CA	14E	74
PORTEOUS ROBERT RICHARD	IN	14E	124
PORTER ALLEN WAYNE	ND	18E	7
PORTER ARCHIE ANDREW	WV	28E	47
PORTER BOBBY L	OK	38E	10
PORTER CHARLES EDWARD	DE	06E	93
PORTER DAVID RANDLE	IN	23W	67
PORTER DELBERT RAY	IL	05W	46
PORTER DONALD JOHN	IL	23W	46
PORTER FRANK SOLIS	NM	45W	9
PORTER FRANKLIN DELANO	WV	01E	79
PORTER GARY THURSTON	MA	22E	26
PORTER JACK EUGENE	OH	57E	31
PORTER JAMES FRANK	PA	36E	31
PORTER JAMES HOLLAND	KS	34W	52
PORTER JOSEPH SAMUEL JR	VA	24E	88
PORTER KARL DENNIS	NH	02W	102
PORTER KEVIN ANTHONY	MA	30E	59
PORTER LARRY JAMES	SC	02W	46
PORTER LARRY MICHAEL	DC	22E	33
PORTER LAWRENCE EUGENE	OH	59W	12
PORTER LAWRENCE WILLIAM	OH	30W	7
PORTER LEO	LA	25E	14
PORTER MICHAEL GRANT	CA	27W	83
PORTER OSCAR KILPATRIC JR	GA	42W	21
PORTER RAYMOND JAMES	PA	19W	114
PORTER RICHARD CHARLES	NH	05W	64
PORTER RICHARD LEE	OH	27W	33
PORTER ROBERT LEE	GA	09W	74
PORTER ROBERT LEE	OK	07W	42
PORTER ROGER LEE	SD	09W	74
PORTER RONALD HARRY	MI	23W	105
PORTER RONALD WILLIAM	CA	04E	25
PORTER RONALD WILLIAM	NJ	17E	64
PORTER ROY LYNN	OH	18W	17
PORTER SANDY HILLY	FL	09W	124
PORTER STEVEN LINDSEY	ME	21W	90
PORTER THOMAS ALAN	IA	13W	38
PORTER THOMAS LAMAR	MS	08W	103
PORTER TIMOTHY MICHAEL	PA	40W	30
PORTER WILLIAM ROBERT JR	PA	35W	72
PORTER WILLIAM ROY	NY	09W	2
PORTERFIELD CHARLES WILBU	OR	46E	10
PORTERFIELD DALE KYETTE	CA	01W	12
PORTERFIELD DAVID EDWARD	NY	09E	34
PORTIS ANTHONY JEROME	MS	48W	19
PORTUGAL IGNACIO JR	CA	22E	17
PORTWOOD JAMES JR	KY	10W	43
POSCOVER GARY STUART	MO	36E	82
POSEY CHARLES ALBERT	KS	16W	35
POSEY DALE L	MO	62E	10
POSEY GEORGE RAY	IN	45W	42
POSEY RALPH EDWARD	CA	03W	51
POSEY ROBERT LEE JR	MD	14E	98
POSIUS ROBERT	MI	03E	90
POSO JOHN RICHARD	CA	38E	37
POSPISIL ALFRED FRANK	OK	03W	125
POSPISIL MARVIN LEROY	NE	31W	39
POSS GARY STEVEN	MO	17W	40
POSS TRAVIS O'NEAL	OH	03E	61
POST DANIEL GIBSON	PA	07E	98
POST DANIEL ZACHARY JR	TX	09E	92
POST DOUGLAS ARTHUR	PA	24E	40
POST JAMES HARVEY JR	CT	34E	64
POST KARL WALTER	OR	37E	66
POST THOMAS FRANK	NY	45W	34
POST VERNON JR	NJ	39E	24
POSTEN GERALD WAYNE	CA	23W	17
POSTIGLIONE JOSEPH JOHN	NY	13W	98
POSTON JAMES	SC	10E	81
POSTON RAYMOND ROGER	TX	05E	39
POSTON WILLIAM THOMAS	TX	30E	102
POSTORINO ERNEST	MD	46W	44
POTAS ALEXANDER FRANK	MI	12W	14
POTE FREDDIE CHARLES JR	IL	30W	82
POTEAT DENNIS MICHAEL	NC	47E	17
POTEET GLEN ERVIN	NC	21W	39
POTEET THOMAS JAMES	IL	17E	96
POTEMPA LOUIS WILLIAM	PA	12E	68
POTIER MILTON PHILLIP	LA	55E	27
POTTER ALBERT RAYMOND	NJ	08E	109
POTTER ALFRED N	RI	12W	119
POTTER DON	KY	29E	17
POTTER JAMES FRANK	NY	20W	88
POTTER JAMES RALPH	TN	18W	71
POTTER JERRY LEE	CO	03E	35
POTTER LARRY EMERSON	SC	09E	29
POTTER NEIL WARREN	MI	04E	14
POTTER PAUL D	NJ	47W	51
POTTER PAUL PRICE	MI	37W	3
POTTER RAYMOND GEORGE	OH	26E	50
POTTER RICHARD EDWARD	MA	20E	123
POTTER ROBERT ALLAN	WA	07E	75
POTTER ROBERT GLEN	LA	14W	31
POTTER WESLEY ROY	MI	34W	44
POTTER WILLIAM DON	IA	28W	63
POTTER WILLIAM JOSEPH JR	PA	32E	96
POTTER WILLIAM STEVEN	VA	31W	84
POTTER WILLIAM TOD	ND	37E	42
POTTER WILLIAM VERNON	CA	23E	88
POTTHOFF THOMAS ALBERT	MN	24W	69
POTTKOTTER JAMES VINCENT	OH	03E	13
POTTS BARTOW WESLEY JR	GA	05W	59
POTTS CLIFTON DENNIS	IL	27W	58
POTTS GEORGE HENRY	MI	03W	64
POTTS JERRY	PA	12E	122
POTTS JOHNNIE WYLIE	SC	40E	12
POTTS LARRY FLETCHER	DE	02W	132
POTTS LEONARD LEE	MO	18W	85
POTTS ROBERT JAMES	MD	05W	129
POTTS WILMER	CA	36E	82
POUGH EDDIE LEE	GA	03E	61
POULSON BRUCE WILLIAM	CA	48W	47
POUND THEUS JOSEPH	SC	33W	88
POUNDS ALVIN LEE	IL	50E	33
POUNDS RONNIE LOUIS	LA	42W	36
POUNDSTONE THOMAS RICHARD	IA	18W	94
POUSSON MICHAEL WAYNE	LA	43W	19
POVEY JOHN T	PA	03E	24
POWELL ABRAHAM	AL	04W	124
POWELL ALBERT CHARLES	AL	11W	47
POWELL ALFRED LEE	NY	49E	46
POWELL BOBBY WAYNE	KY	09W	58
POWELL BRYANT RUSSELL	NC	11E	67
POWELL CARROLL WAYNE	WA	11E	23
POWELL CHARLES THOMAS	GA	62W	15
POWELL DANIEL LEE	CA	66W	12
POWELL DAVID BRUCE JR	OK	06E	67
POWELL DAVID LEE	WV	55W	22
POWELL DAVID MICHAEL	MI	58E	13
POWELL DONALD KEITH	VA	47W	21
POWELL ELMER FRANKLIN	NJ	07E	35
POWELL ERWIN GILBERT JR	CA	45W	63
POWELL GARRY REGINALD	DC	39E	52
POWELL GEORGE EDWARD	TX	11W	32
POWELL GEORGE RALPH JR	WV	55W	15
POWELL GEORGE THOMAS	MD	18E	81
POWELL JAMES BENJAMIN JR	IN	06W	88
POWELL JAMES RICHARD	IN	09W	61
POWELL JAMES WILLIAM JR	DC	31E	85
POWELL JOHN DEE JR	TX	54W	24
POWELL JOHN PARKER	OH	08W	108
POWELL JOHNNIE EARL	FL	63W	19
POWELL JOSEPH LEWIS JR	VA	41W	58
POWELL LARRY DEAN	AZ	40E	67
POWELL LARRY GENE	GA	30E	66
POWELL LARRY KEITH	TX	38E	9
POWELL LESLIE ALLEN	CA	27W	102
POWELL LIONELL	LA	15E	49

NAME	STATE	PANEL NO.	LINE NO.
POWELL LYNN KESLER	UT	25E	25
POWELL MARION DAVID	KY	25W	82
POWELL MICHAEL ALLAN	MO	53W	12
POWELL MICHAEL ANTHONY	GA	24W	107
POWELL MORRIS	IL	53W	12
POWELL MORRIS JAMES	GA	05E	14
POWELL PETER EARL	OK	49E	25
POWELL RAYMOND ALAN	GA	43W	49
POWELL RAYMOND JR	MD	44W	12
POWELL RAYMOND LEE	MO	12E	64
POWELL REGINALD FOSTER	CA	56W	9
POWELL RICHARD EDWIN	PA	13E	62
POWELL RICHARD LEE	OH	46W	62
POWELL RICHARD WARREN JR	FL	52E	42
POWELL ROBERT	IL	55W	37
POWELL ROBERT ALLAN	ID	10E	122
POWELL ROBERT ALLEN	MO	08E	43
POWELL ROBERT CLYDE	TX	19E	30
POWELL RONALD L	MI	05E	60
POWELL RUSSELL J	CA	39W	29
POWELL SAMUEL HERBERT	OK	01W	41
POWELL STEPHEN ROLLEY	NC	60E	16
POWELL STEVEN REED	VA	30E	43
POWELL THOMAS STOKES	TX	01W	3
POWELL TONY GORDON	NY	43W	8
POWELL TROY EVERETT	KY	26W	102
POWELL WALTER MERRILL	MS	64W	12
POWELL WAVEL WAYNE	WV	26W	102
POWELL WAYLEN LEE	TX	23E	6
POWELL WILLIAM	GA	49E	14
POWELL WILLIAM	NY	52W	46
POWELL WILLIAM ELMO	TX	48W	35
POWER GEORGE PATRICK	NC	56W	7
POWER RICHARD DEAN	MN	09E	84
POWER RICHARD WILLIAM	MA	09E	117
POWERS BRADLEY LELAND	CA	15E	99
POWERS CHARLES RAY	MO	09E	117
POWERS DONALD HOWARD	TN	02W	90
POWERS EDWARD CLAUS	KY	26W	100
POWERS EDWARD DEAN	IL	32W	72
POWERS EDWARD DOYLE	TX	36W	26
POWERS FRANCIS EDWARD JR	MA	07W	129
POWERS HARRY LEE	MO	12E	104
POWERS JAMES CONRAD	IA	20E	123
POWERS JAMES WILLARD JR	PA	53E	6
POWERS JAMES WILLIAM	MI	05E	7
POWERS JOHN LYNN	ID	05W	107
POWERS JOHN ROGER	WA	11W	52
POWERS KENNETH	OH	05W	23
POWERS LOWELL STEPHEN	AZ	27W	2
POWERS MARK FREDERICK	FL	32W	34
POWERS MARTIN ROBERT	NY	31W	84
POWERS MONROE ALAN	VA	06W	57
POWERS RICHARD PAUL	WY	18W	42
POWERS ROBERT LAWRENCE	NY	41E	53
POWERS ROGER STEVEN	MS	16W	102
POWERS RONALD EUGENE	IL	41W	7
POWERS RONALD LEE	CA	46W	62
POWERS SPENCER BYRD JR	MS	38E	37
POWERS STEVEN CHARLES	CA	35E	79
POWERS STEVEN JAMES	MI	22E	112
POWERS TRENT RICHARD	MN	03E	10
POWERS VERNIE HOMER	MD	32E	55
POWERS WILLIAM JAMES	TX	35E	79
POWERS WILLIAM MAXWELL	PA	15E	76
POWLES DONALD EUGENE	IA	44W	52
POWLISTHA GERALD STEPHEN	IA	23W	78
POXON ROBERT LESLIE	MI	23W	46
POYNOR DANIEL ROBERTS	OK	02W	89
POZMANN ALEXANDER JR	OH	36W	5
PRADO GUADALUPE JR	TX	22W	6
PRAGMAN DONALD EUGENE	MO	48W	8
PRAIRIE LE ROY PAUL	IL	07E	134
PRANGE JOSEPH WILDER	CA	28E	4
PRANGE THOMAS CHARLES	MI	29W	22
PRANGER GLENN AIREN	IN	54W	38
PRASZYNSKI STEPHEN JAY	UT	16W	46
PRATER CALVIN RAY	CA	31W	55
PRATER DONALD HAROLD	CA	09W	122
PRATER HARVEY WILLIAM	KY	07E	35
PRATER LAWRENCE BUFORD	WV	28E	88
PRATER ROY DEWITT	OH	02W	131

NAME	STATE	PANEL NO.	LINE NO.
PRATHER CHRISTOPHER DAVID	MN	31W	16
PRATHER GARY W	MO	13E	99
PRATHER HENRY LEE III	LA	34E	24
PRATHER JAMES W	MD	28E	16
PRATHER LAVON NEIL	CA	21W	9
PRATHER MARTIN WILLIAM	KY	26E	3
PRATHER RONALD ROBERT JR	OR	38E	11
PRATHER WILLIAM HARLEY	OH	44W	41
PRATT CAREY JAY	IN	08W	13
PRATT DAVID ALVIN	FL	07W	45
PRATT DONALD WILLIAM	IL	52E	23
PRATT FRED OMAR	GA	46W	32
PRATT GUY LEON JR	OK	25W	32
PRATT JOHN LIONEL	MA	30W	29
PRATT JOHN MONROE	NC	25W	14
PRATT PHILIP AVERY	NH	23W	30
PRATT RICHARD CHESTER	CA	18E	87
PRATT RICHARD EMMETT	WA	31E	66
PRATT RODNEY TERRANCE	GA	36W	58
PRATT WALTER RAYMOND	MI	38E	37
PRATT WILLIAM TERRY	IL	43W	20
PRAY VERN LEE	OK	14E	3
PRAZINKO ROBERT JAMES	PA	14E	105
PRCHAL CHARLES ROBERT	NY	28W	85
PRCHLIK WILLIAM CHARLES	IN	08W	89
PREAUX THOMAS ALFRED	PA	18E	97
PRECOUR RICHARD FRANK	MI	59E	29
PREDDY ROBERT LEE	CA	22E	48
PREDIGER FRANZ GERHARD	CA	08E	113
PREDMORE DAVID MARTIN	TX	22E	92
PREDOVIC WILLIAM MARK	OH	07W	99
PREIRA DOMINIC J JR	CT	05E	48
PREIS MARK JOSEPH	MD	17W	102
PREISENDEFER HAROLD ALAN	PA	02E	129
PREISS ROBERT FRANCIS JR	NY	10W	28
PREJEAN KENNETH ANDREW	LA	26W	93
PREKKER GARY LEE	MN	17E	39
PREMENKO JOHN AL	CA	08W	112
PREMOCK DENNIS	NJ	56E	14
PRENDERGAST ARTHUR ONEILL	MD	46E	10
PRENGEL MICHAEL WAYNE	IL	15W	22
PRENTICE ALAN NEIL	MO	25W	82
PRENTICE DAVID GRAY	PA	09W	54
PRENTICE DAVID SHELTON	AK	24E	40
PRENTICE DENNIS ALBERT	CA	17E	23
PRENTICE EDWIN PAUL	NY	26E	3
PRENTICE GARY GALE	OR	04W	25
PRENTICE KENNETH MORTON	WA	17W	31
PRENTNER JERRY LEE	NC	11W	18
PRESBY THOMAS FRANK	CA	09E	71
PRESCOTT DENNIS LOUIS	CA	34E	10
PRESCOTT MILTON EMMETT JR	IL	18E	127
PRESCOTT STEVEN JAMES	NY	57E	8
PRESCOTT WILLARD SHERWIN	CA	21E	15
PRESIDENT ERNEST	FL	02E	116
PRESKENIS RICHARD JOSEPH	MA	06E	57
PRESLEY ANDREW LEE JR	AL	28W	21
PRESLEY AVEY	NJ	28W	39
PRESLEY DONNIE DWIGHT	MS	32E	39
PRESLEY JAMES HENRY	GA	61W	16
PRESLEY MELTON HOWARD	AL	43E	68
PRESLEY RONNIE CALVIN	TN	43E	30
PRESLIPSKI MICHAEL JR	PA	18W	17
PRESNALL CARL HAMBY	AL	22E	23
PRESS ROBERT M JR	IL	40W	67
PRESS VICTOR EUGENE	DE	17E	86
PRESSER PAUL MICHAEL	IL	43W	20
PRESSLER CHARLES EDWARD	OH	12W	8
PRESSLEY CORNELIUS	AL	40E	67
PRESSLEY JAMES EDWARD	GA	17E	87
PRESSON BILLIE TAYLOR	KY	26E	97
PRESSON JAMES DAVID	MO	13W	88
PRESSON WILLIAM PAUL JR	MO	11E	4
PRESTON ALVIN LEWIS	DC	57E	9
PRESTON JAMES ARTHUR	GA	07E	62
PRESTON JOHNNY CALVIN	GA	20E	97
PRESTON JOSEPH JR	SC	56W	7
PRESTON LEONARD LEE JR	KY	28W	1
PRESTON LUTHER ELMER	VA	29E	26
PRESTON MACK LEE JR	MO	23W	78
PRESTON ROBERT EDWARD	MA	39E	11
PRESTON ROSS MCCLLELAN	CA	55W	9

NAME	STATE	PANEL NO.	LINE NO.
PRESTON THOMAS RAY	OH	31W	16
PRESTWOOD BENNY RAY	NC	35W	61
PRETE ROBERT NICHOLAS	NY	27W	7
PRETNAR ALLEN JOHN	OH	49W	33
PRETTER THOMAS	NY	21E	76
PRETTY ROBERT ALTON	NC	31E	52
PREUSS CARL JOHN	MI	14W	67
PREVEDEL CHARLES FRANCIS	MO	27W	103
PREVOST ALBERT MICHAEL	CT	04E	130
PREVOST KENNETH WAYNE	CA	13W	123
PREWITT LARRY GENE	OK	17W	64
PREWITT WILLIAM EARL	KY	22W	68
PREWITT WILLIAM ROLAND	LA	24E	62
PREZIOSI JAMES LAWRENCE	NY	28E	98
PREZIOSI JOHN PATRICK	NJ	36E	31
PRICE ALTON DURHAM	NC	09E	100
PRICE ANTHONY ALOYSIUS	CT	03W	76
PRICE ARNOLD W	PA	40E	47
PRICE ARTHUR HOUSTON	AR	05W	10
PRICE BARRY CARLTON	PA	20E	65
PRICE BARRY FRANCIS	NY	17E	54
PRICE BILLY RAY JR	OH	05W	42
PRICE BOBBY WAYNE	KY	22E	17
PRICE BUNYAN DURANT JR	NC	11W	87
PRICE CHARLES ALLEN	TX	34W	39
PRICE CHARLES MITCHELL	NC	05W	31
PRICE DARREL L	UT	14E	6
PRICE DAVID EDGAR JR	VA	14E	125
PRICE DAVID J	OH	01W	60
PRICE DAVID MERRILL	WI	52W	36
PRICE DAVID S	WA	44E	19
PRICE DENNIS ALTON	OH	48W	2
PRICE DERRILL LE ROY JR	MO	24W	98
PRICE DWIGHT ANTHONY	CT	58W	28
PRICE ELBERT FORD JR	OH	29E	34
PRICE ELVIN	TX	09E	12
PRICE FRANK APPERSON III	NJ	28E	11
PRICE FREDERICK	PA	05E	135
PRICE GARRY OWEN	MO	21E	37
PRICE GARY DONALD	IL	18W	122
PRICE GARY WAYNE	IL	19E	51
PRICE GEORGE MICHAEL	NC	40W	54
PRICE HUBERT JR	OK	36E	82
PRICE HUMPHREY JAMES	MI	26E	15
PRICE JACK LEON	MI	20W	8
PRICE JACK RAY	NC	08E	39
PRICE JAMES ALLAN	WI	33E	22
PRICE JAMES ERWIN	KY	17E	75
PRICE JAMES HENRY	IL	23E	78
PRICE JAMES WHITEFORD JR	NC	21E	51
PRICE JAY ANTHONY	DC	50E	16
PRICE JHUE FRANK	TX	01E	113
PRICE JOHN CHAD	MO	39E	10
PRICE JOHN WILLIAM	NJ	29W	48
PRICE JOHNNY PAUL	VA	05E	21
PRICE JOSEPH MICHAEL	FL	24W	20
PRICE KENNETH RANDAL	OH	05W	101
PRICE LARRY JUNIOR	CO	05W	55
PRICE LARRY LEE	WA	21E	56
PRICE MARLIN LADON	AL	26E	62
PRICE MAXIE LANE	SC	35E	41
PRICE MICHAEL GLEN	LA	51E	32
PRICE MICHAEL KEATON	AL	17W	85
PRICE MILLARD ERNEST JR	MD	33E	92
PRICE PAUL LEE	KY	27E	3
PRICE RICHARD JOHN	MI	41W	61
PRICE ROBERT GLEN	TN	54E	39
PRICE RODNEY ALLEN	PA	33E	28
PRICE RONALD BRUCE	GA	16E	97
PRICE RUSSELL LEE	MD	08E	105
PRICE TERRY HUNTER	UT	04W	89
PRICE THOMAS GORDON	CA	31W	16
PRICE THOMAS J	MI	12W	128
PRICE THOMAS JOHN	MN	17W	19
PRICE WILLIAM DAVID	KY	45E	27
PRICE WILLIAM EDWARD	OH	44E	53
PRICE WILLIAM EUGENE	MD	31W	39
PRICE WILLIAM JOSEPH	KY	23E	22
PRICE WILLIAM MARSHALL	IL	01W	82
PRICE WILLIAM SIDWAY	DC	47E	5
PRICE WILLIE CAPAHAS	NY	41W	31
PRICHARD JOHN LEE	OK	35E	49

NAME	STATE	PANEL NO.	LINE NO.
PRIDDY RICHARD THOMAS	FL	10W	87
PRIDDY WILLIAM F	TN	13E	41
PRIDEAUX JAMES EARL	CO	37E	42
PRIDEMORE DALLAS REESE	OH	44W	1
PRIDEMORE JAMES LESLIE	IL	63W	12
PRIDGEN GARY MORGAN	AL	09W	99
PRIEBE JAMES EDWARD	OH	18E	127
PRIEN DON	CA	36E	23
PRIESER ROBERT SHERMAN	OH	44W	5
PRIEST DONALD JAMES	NY	09E	34
PRIEST DONALD WAYNE JR	OH	24W	11
PRIEST FRANKIE LEON	MO	12E	90
PRIEST JOHN HENRY JR	SC	22W	93
PRIEST MICHAEL LLOYD	ID	17E	128
PRIEST TERRENCE LEE	IN	25E	109
PRIESTHOFF JOHN HOWARD II	CA	43W	65
PRIESTHOFF THOMAS EUGENE	IN	32E	13
PRIETO ANTHONY RAYMOND	IN	59E	11
PRIETO RUBEN	KS	36W	58
PRIETO TRINIDAD GUTIERREZ	CA	13W	6
PRIMM SEVERO JAMES III	LA	01W	115
PRINCE DANNY DEAN	OH	09E	101
PRINCE DENNIS GLENN	MI	23W	47
PRINCE EUGENE JR	OK	06W	88
PRINCE GARRY GARNETT	AL	33E	40
PRINCE GARY DAVIS	NC	37W	7
PRINCE HARRY GORDON JR	AL	04W	47
PRINCE JOHN R	TN	14E	37
PRINCE JOSEPH DAVID JR	NC	20E	18
PRINCE JOSEPH STEPHEN	GA	10W	66
PRINCE RAYMOND LOUIS	DC	19E	85
PRINCE RONALD PERSHING	MO	29E	53
PRINCE STEPHEN ROBERT	WA	19W	4
PRINDLE ASHTON HAYWARD	CT	51E	41
PRINE ROBERT WAYNE	FL	39E	11
PRINGLE DONALD IRVEN	MI	15W	100
PRINGLE EMMETT TERENCE	CA	29W	72
PRINGLE JAMES EDWARD	NY	58W	13
PRINGLE JOE HAROLD	WV	36E	82
PRINZ RANDALL BOYD	MI	06E	102
PRIOR ANTHONY GEORGE	NY	65W	13
PRIP SOREN	IL	53E	21
PRISET JOHN FREDRICK	NJ	38W	20
PRITCHARD CLARENCE R JR	CA	06W	61
PRITCHARD DONALD RAY	OH	26E	50
PRITCHARD GALE STEWART	CO	18W	85
PRITCHARD ROBERT BRUCE	FL	10W	91
PRITCHARD VICTOR HEENAN	TX	28W	85
PRITCHARD WALTER LEO JR	RI	27W	66
PRITCHARD WILLIAM HENRY	IL	23E	37
PRITCHARD WILLIAM JOHN	CA	56E	15
PRITCHETT CARL WAYNE	GA	04W	89
PRITCHETT GREGORY GENE	CA	54E	28
PRITCHETT JULIUS DONALD	NC	64W	15
PRITT THOMAS EUGENE	MD	10W	115
PRIVIECH ROBERT MICHAEL	PA	24E	40
PRIVITAR RICHARD JOSEPH	NY	02W	45
PRIZGINTAS ANTANAS ARVIDA	NJ	35W	9
PROBART LEWIS DEVERN	ID	20W	11
PROBERTS WAYNE DOUGLAS	KS	03E	46
PROBST DELMAR WAYNE	PA	43E	58
PROCHASKA WILLARD FLOYD	VA	31W	16
PROCIDA RICHARD NICHOLAS	NY	43E	69
PROCINO NICHOLAS RALPH	KS	16W	46
PROCIV RICHARD MICHAEL	UT	11E	46
PROCK DANIEL LEE	CA	59W	12
PROCOPIO PETER LOUIS	NJ	13W	113
PROCTOR DANIEL VAUGHAN	OH	13W	64
PROCTOR ERVIN	TN	44W	53
PROCTOR FRANK MAURICE	MD	61W	5
PROCTOR GEORGE RICHARD	TX	61W	5
PROCTOR JAMES PATRICK	FL	24E	63
PROCTOR JOHNNY LEE	FL	59W	26
PROCTOR RICKEY ALLEN	CA	26W	56
PROCTOR SAMUEL JR	GA	20E	86
PROCTOR WAYNE SHELTON	SC	60W	12
PROCTOR WILLIAM AMBROSE	DC	18E	71
PROCTOR WILLIAM C JR	CA	20W	16
PROEHL PAUL ALLEN	MI	66E	1
PROFFER GEORGE FLOYD	MO	46E	10
PROFFIT JOHN BERNARD	NC	08W	80
PROFILET ROBERT C	IL	42W	63
PROFITT HARVEY JUNIOR	TN	08E	39
PROIETTI ANTHONY ALPHONSE	IL	27W	90
PROKOP FRANK JOSEPH	OH	26W	66
PROM WILLIAM RAYMOND	PA	32W	2
PROMBO JOHN ANTHONY	IL	33W	81
PROMMERSBERGER JAMES EDWI	OH	06E	118
PROPSON BERNARD AMBROSE	WI	18W	42
PROPSON MARVIN NORBERT	WI	39W	3
PROPST RICHARD HUGH	NC	12W	9
PROPST WILLIAM EARL	MD	49E	46
PROSCIA RICHARD MICHAEL	NY	32E	4
PROSE CHARLES WILLIAM JR	OH	18W	85
PROSE THOMAS DEAN	IL	02W	72
PROSE WILLIAM THOMAS	MO	30W	94
PROSKY LEVERET ROSCOE	CA	43W	57
PROSSER IRVIN WILLIS JR	NY	33W	28
PROSTELL RICHARD LOUIS	VA	52W	43
PROSZEK ANTON JR	MN	18E	104
PROTACK THOMAS JOHN	DE	14W	90
PROTAIN DAVID ALAN	OH	25W	42
PROTANO GUY JERRY JR	MA	33E	92
PROTHERO MICHAEL EUGENE	WI	55W	1
PROTHERO WILLIAM HENRY	NY	30E	93
PROTTO ROBERT B JR	CA	30W	95
PROTZ CLAUDE DOUGLAS	IL	57E	34
PROUDFOOT LEWIS H III	PA	26E	11
PROUDFOOT TIMOTHY COLE	CA	29W	31
PROUE JAMES THOMAS	MN	21W	43
PROVEAUX RICHARD BLAINE	WI	22W	36
PROVENCAL ROLAND ANDRE	MA	07E	121
PROVENCHER WAYNE THOMAS	NH	58E	12
PROVENZANO ROBERT LEE	IL	14E	50
PROVOST DAVID ARMAND	CT	60W	4
PRUDEN FREDERICK WILLIAM	FL	06W	35
PRUDEN RENE THOMAS	NY	51W	13
PRUDEN ROBERT JOSEPH	MN	16W	102
PRUDHOMME JOHN DOUGLAS	OH	04E	35
PRUETT DARREL EUGENE	IL	29E	54
PRUETT DONOVAN JESS	WA	06E	82
PRUETT JAMES RANDALL	MI	42W	21
PRUETT WILLIAM DAVID	VA	14W	76
PRUHS ROBERT L	VA	11E	74
PRUIETT THOMAS PIERRE JR	MI	47E	25
PRUITT CARL DUANE	NC	12E	24
PRUITT DAVID MONROE	SC	58W	29
PRUITT FRANCIS JOHN J	MD	13W	65
PRUITT GEORGE ALAN	MO	48E	54
PRUITT JAMES ELMER	KY	02E	96
PRUITT JAMES THOMAS	VA	07E	14
PRUITT OSIER LAWRENCE	SC	03W	48
PRUITT WILLIAM HENRY JR	OH	31E	52
PRUNER JOHN MARK	NY	24E	41
PRUNKA ALEXANDER E JR	NY	59E	29
PRUSH MONTY DOUGLAS	IN	55W	23
PRUSKO PAUL STANLEY	IL	04E	82
PRY JERRY EARL	IN	33E	92
PRYEAR JOHNNIE LEE	AL	04W	27
PRYOR DONALD RAY	TX	13E	59
PRYOR ERNEST PAUL	KY	11E	95
PRYOR JEROME	OH	54E	15
PRYOR LARRY ROY	MO	13W	3
PRYOR MELVIN SR	TX	52E	42
PRYOR ROBERT EDWIN	OR	02W	107
PRYOR THOMAS WILLIAM	MD	43E	10
PRYOR WILLIAM JACKIE	NJ	33W	68
PRYS ROBERT WILLIAM	CA	21E	15
PRZELOMSKI PAUL ANTHONY	MA	37E	12
PRZYBELSKI THOMAS F	WI	59E	29
PRZYBYLINSKI GERALD	MI	31W	56
PRZYBYLOWICZ WALTER JR	MI	22E	80
PTACEK TIMOTHY RICHARD	OH	24W	70
PTAK THOMAS JOHN	NJ	45E	59
PTASNICK WALTER JAMES	NY	18E	31
PUARIEA JAMES FREDERICK	MN	23W	91
PUCCI DANIEL LOUIS	OH	23W	47
PUCHALSKI WALTER MARTIN	OH	09W	109
PUCKETT DENNIS RAY	MO	17E	68
PUCKETT HARRY LEE	NM	41W	65
PUCKETT JEAN WAYNE	AL	36W	82
PUCKETT ROGER DALE	KY	36E	59
PUCKETT TROY MURL	SC	24E	74
PUDERBAUGH CHARLES KAY	NY	08W	105
PUDULS JURIS	OH	08E	88
PUENTES MANUEL RAMERIZ	TX	04W	78
PUENTES MIGUEL ANGEL	CA	33W	16
PUETZ MICHAEL DUANE	IL	14W	128
PUFF THOMAS JOE	CA	02W	68
PUFFENBARGER WILLIAM T	CA	43E	59
PUGGI JOSEPH DAVID	NJ	36E	83
PUGH DAVID JAMES	MA	29W	48
PUGH DENNIS GERARD	KS	12W	22
PUGH EVERETT CHARLES	DC	13W	72
PUGH GERALD RALPH	SC	21W	66
PUGH KENNETH LEE	CT	31E	82
PUGH KENNETH WARD	CA	06E	107
PUGH MICHAEL LAVERNE	TN	12E	7
PUGH MICHEL LEE	IN	19E	15
PUGH PERCY ISAIAH	LA	31W	84
PUGH RICHARD CARL	CA	36W	87
PUGH ROBERT EARL	FL	13E	48
PUGH ROBERT EARL	AR	28W	74
PUGH ROGER LESLIE	NY	17E	128
PUGH STEPHEN BRIAN	PA	42W	43
PUGLIESE FRANK	NY	37W	58
PUGMIRE MAX WELKER	ID	17W	113
PUHI DANIEL KIMOKEO	HI	31E	52
PUHI KEITH JON	HI	30W	59
PUISHIS DALE SCOTT	WA	35E	11
PULASKI PETER JR	NY	15W	126
PULASKI ROBERT ALLEN	MN	03W	122
PULLAM JAMES LEE	CA	11W	105
PULLARA ANGELO	FL	15E	50
PULLEN CLAUDE DOUGLAS	NC	24W	11
PULLEN MELVIN LEWIS	CA	09W	95
PULLEN ROBERT DALE	TX	33E	59
PULLEN THOMAS RICHARD	NY	50W	39
PULLEY JAMES EDWARD	OK	22W	48
PULLIAM CHARLES AUBREY	MD	01E	7
PULLIAM DALE ALLAN	KS	19E	123
PULLIAM EDGAR RUSSELL JR	OK	14W	27
PULLIAM ERIC VINCENT	MD	28W	75
PULLIAM ROBERT EDWARD JR	NC	09E	53
PULLIAM ROBERT LEE	VA	05W	68
PULLINS ROGERS JR	GA	27W	12
PULLUM HENRY JR	GA	30W	7
PULS ROBERT LAWRENCE	AZ	54W	32
PULSE DOYLE GEAN	OK	10W	46
PULSIFER NELSON F JR	CA	12E	71
PULTZ ROBERT LEWIS	OH	31E	52
PUMA WAYNE PAUL	NY	56E	30
PUMAREJO-COLON WILFREDO	PR	25E	33
PUMILLO MICHAEL	NY	38E	59
PUMPELLY WALTER LEE		07E	11
PUMPHREY CORNEALUS JR	CA	64E	7
PUMPHREY DONALD LEE	MO	48W	3
PUMPHREY EDWIN HOLLAND	MD	27W	52
PUMPHREY JAMES J L	TX	13W	72
PUNDSACK TERRY LYNN	WI	11E	17
PURCELL CHARLES KENT II	FL	19E	111
PURCELL DENNIS EDWARD	CA	52E	23
PURCELL GARY WILLIAM	CA	68E	6
PURCELL HOWARD PHILIP	PA	01E	28
PURCELL LARRY JOE	AL	48W	3
PURCELL MICHAEL JOSEPH	PA	47E	35
PURCELL RICHARD MICHAEL	MO	03W	100
PURDIE ROBERT DAVID	CA	47W	52
PURDIN PATRICK LAWRENCE	CA	16W	110
PURDON GERALD WAYNE	OH	12W	73
PURDUM RALPH SCOTT	MN	12W	9
PURDY LOUIS JAMES	CT	21E	109
PURDY RANDALL BREWARD	NY	32E	26
PURELIS JOSEPH KENNETH	NY	20E	98
PURGIEL ROBERT CHARLES	MI	27E	21
PURIFOY HUBERT J	AR	13E	127
PURIFOY RAY WARREN	TX	18W	42
PURKEY JAMES PAUL	MD	27E	103
PURNELL ADRIAN FLOYD	FL	12E	123
PURSEL THOMAS RONALD	WA	63E	16
PURSELL CHARLES ALAN	CA	12W	119
PURSER CHARLES EDWARD	AL	41E	2
PURSER DAVID ARTHUR	GA	45E	4
PURSER JAMES LEAVELL	CA	02E	14
PURTELL ROBERT BUCK	AR	47W	3
PURVIS ALFRED ALEXANDER	PA	32W	83

NAME	STATE	PANEL NO.	LINE NO.
PURVIS BERNARD GEORGE	NY	33W	4
PURVIS PHILIP ALAN	CO	12E	117
PURWIN ANTONI BOGUSLAW	MD	60E	1
PURYEAR JOSEPH A	NY	49E	15
PUSKARCIK RONALD JOSEPH	OH	51W	7
PUSSER THOMAS WILSON	SC	02E	131
PUTMAN THOMAS ANDREW	OH	16W	40
PUTNAM CHARLES LANCASTER	FL	16E	48
PUTNAM CHARLES RICHARD	GA	17E	80
PUTNAM RONALD VIRGIL	TN	12E	43
PUTNEY EDWARD ALLEN	MA	25W	42
PUTZ LAWRENCE JAMES JR	IN	38W	61
PUZYREWSKI LESLIE	IL	04E	10
PYE SAFFORD SMITH	PA	05E	25
PYLE CHARLES RICHARD	TX	45E	60
PYLE CHRIS MONROE	NM	23W	10
PYLE HOWARD MACDONALD JR	NY	19W	20
PYLE JERRY WILLIAM	IN	10W	19
PYLE JESSE ANDREW	OR	01E	86
PYLE JOHN WILLIAM	IL	39E	38
PYLE LARRY GENE	TX	27W	33
PYLE NICHOLAS IRVIN	OH	31W	17
PYLE TIMOTHY HOWARD	AL	26W	102
PYLE WILTON STROUD	CT	23W	17
PYLES HARLEY BOYD	OH	02E	125
PYNE ROGER DALE	MI	39E	65
PYNNONEN MICHAEL JONAS	MI	12W	58
PYPNIOWSKI LARRY	NJ	18W	97
PYRANT DONALD RAY	NC	46W	7
PYSHER GERALD JOHN	PA	20E	98
PYSZ ALEX DENNIS	PA	06W	25
QUAGLIERI PAUL VINCENZO	CA	29W	32
QUAITE DANNY JOE	MD	13W	75
QUALLS ARTHUR GERALD	TN	10W	72
QUALLS DAVID WAYNE	IL	23E	27
QUALLS TED WAYNE	TX	02E	70
QUAM JOHN ELLSWORTH	IA	15E	50
QUAMO GEORGE	NY	50E	1
QUAN KENNETH RAYMOND	MI	56E	15
QUANDT ROBERT FREDRICK	MI	02W	59
QUARLES FLOYD ELMER	NY	22E	48
QUARLES WAYNE ROBERT	NJ	27W	90
QUARTERMAN EARL QUINNON	IL	15E	12
QUAST WILLY VASCILLE	WI	13E	120
QUATRONE FERDINAND JOSEPH	NJ	29E	5
QUATTLEBAUM JOHN FRANKLIN	MI	48E	46
QUEALY MICHAEL JOSEPH	NY	12E	43
QUEBODEAUX WILLIAM C JR	LA	37E	12
QUEEN CARY PAUL	TX	25E	48
QUEEN CECIL WAYNE	TX	25W	82
QUEEN DONALD WAYNE	GA	47E	42
QUEEN WALTER LOUIS	NJ	20E	106
QUEENER ULYSSES GRANT JR	CA	34W	79
QUENGA JOHNNY CRUZ	GM	22E	63
QUERRY HOWARD EMERSON	IL	58E	13
QUERY ROBERT PETER	CA	16W	54
QUESADA JESUS	WI	33W	9
QUESENBERRY BOBBY RAY	MD	20W	109
QUESENBERRY JOHN QUINCY	MD	09E	12
QUESNEY JOSE MANUEL	AZ	43W	8
QUEVEDO ANGEL ALARID	NM	02W	58
QUEY DAVID MICHAEL	CT	14E	53
QUEZADA ARTHUR	CA	56W	27
QUICK ADRIAN ALLEN JR	NY	38E	11
QUICK GEORGE DEWEY JR	SC	14W	58
QUICK ISHAM IKE	NY	42W	32
QUICK JOHN JAMES	MI	42W	50
QUICK MICHAEL EDWARD	IL	07W	38
QUICK PAUL WAYNE III	DE	34E	31
QUICK RALPH RICHARD JR	MO	12W	49
QUICK ROBERT EUGENE	IN	55E	27
QUICK ROBERT GLYNN	MS	47E	42
QUICK ROBERT LEE	PA	38E	11
QUIDACHAY JESUS AQUININGO	GM	47E	26
QUIGLEY HENRY LEROY	FL	31W	71
QUIGLEY JAMES MICHAEL	CA	19E	74
QUIGLEY RONALD LEEROY	WA	31W	71
QUIGLEY TERRY LYNN	SC	22E	113
QUIGLEY TIMOTHY ERNEST	CA	13W	82
QUILALANG ANASTACIO DJ JR	CA	62W	16
QUILES-HERNANDEZ ANTONIO		04W	133
QUILICI PETER JR	NV	10E	31

NAME	STATE	PANEL NO.	LINE NO.
QUILL EDWARD BEEDING JR	CA	39E	52
QUILL PAUL FRANCIS	MA	34E	39
QUILLEN EARL THOMAS	TN	29W	62
QUILLEN JOHN EDWARD JR	NY	51E	12
QUILLEN LLOYD DANIEL	NY	27W	83
QUILLEN ROGER DELL	TN	35E	56
QUILLIN WILLIAM THOMAS	MN	16W	35
QUIMBY DANIEL LEE	OH	41W	26
QUIN CULLEN WOOD	IL	39E	65
QUINLAN DAVID PATRICK	WI	20W	73
QUINLAN FRANK JOSEPH JR	IA	09W	35
QUINN ANTHONY LOUIS	CA	33W	58
QUINN BOBBY JOE	TN	14E	2
QUINN DANIEL	NY	31E	30
QUINN DOUGLAS FRANK	CA	10E	102
QUINN GREGORY CORNELIUS	ME	30E	5
QUINN JAMES ANTHONY	PA	06W	28
QUINN JAMES JOSEPH III	WA	06W	5
QUINN JOHN ARNOLD	PA	17W	31
QUINN JOHN FRANCIS	TX	26W	56
QUINN JOHN MICHZEL	NY	04E	125
QUINN JOHN PHILIP JR	MA	02W	7
QUINN MELVIN DARYL	CA	12W	73
QUINN MICHAEL COURTNEY	TX	20E	98
QUINN MICHAEL EDWARD	MN	16W	110
QUINN MICHAEL PATRICK	MA	18W	8
QUINN PATRICK OWEN	CA	12E	117
QUINN PATRICK THOMAS	IL	09E	42
QUINN RAYMOND FRANCIS	PA	17E	87
QUINN RICHARD FLOYD	NY	08W	13
QUINN RICHARD JAMES	MA	35W	50
QUINN ROBERT	MI	50W	35
QUINN ROBERT FRANK	MS	19E	7
QUINN ROGER ALLAN	OH	47E	53
QUINN RONALD GENE	NY	19W	20
QUINN STEPHEN WAYNE	VA	62E	10
QUINN TERRY LEE	CA	06E	34
QUINN THOMAS WAYNE	MN	27W	12
QUINN WILLIAM DANIEL III	NY	25W	1
QUINONES DAVID	NY	37E	12
QUINONES EDWARD	NY	60W	5
QUINONES JOSE LUIS	NY	12W	74
QUINONES JUAN MANUEL	NY	46W	21
QUINONES JULIO JR	HI	20W	11
QUINONES-BORRAS NICHOLAS	PR	01W	37
QUINONES-RODRIGUEZ LUISAR	NY	04W	6
QUINT ANTHONY PETER	OH	02W	49
QUINTAL JOHN VINCENT	MA	55W	2
QUINTANA FRANKLIN HARRY A	CO	06E	119
QUINTANA JUAN CARLOS	CA	34W	40
QUINTANA SANTIAGO V E	NM	24W	89
QUINTANA-SOTO LUIS E	FL	19W	89
QUINTANILLA FRANCISCO JR	TX	04W	8
QUINTANILLA JEFFERY I	CA	04W	71
QUINTERO FERNANDO MENDOZA	AZ	41E	53
QUINTERO JOSE HERNANDEZ	CA	18E	42
QUIRION JOSEPH G L JR	ME	47E	53
QUIRK JEFFERY MICHAEL	WI	57E	9
QUIROGA ALEX LEON	CA	22E	113
QUIROS CARLOS MANUEL	CA	23E	14
QUIROZ ALEXANDER	TX	03W	29
QUIROZ ALFRED MAURO	CA	34W	43
QUIROZ JOSEPH ALBERT	IL	04E	113
QUITMEYER TONY JOHN	MN	34E	10
RAAB JAMES DONALD	NJ	57W	3
RAAUM JOHN VILNIS	ND	09E	13
RABACAL PATRICK WILLIAM	HI	02W	98
RABAIOTTI ANDREW CHARLES	MA	23E	31
RABB ROBERT IRA	GA	11W	105
RABEL LASZIO	MN	39W	62
RABEL VICTOR ART	MN	31W	17
RABER JOE EDWARD	MO	10W	53
RABER JOHN HAROLD	CT	08E	116
RABER PAUL J	WA	01W	128
RABER RALPH DONALD	WA	17W	35
RABEY KENNETH TILDEN	CA	45E	5
RABEY ROGER WILLIAM	TN	16E	54
RABIDEAU JOHN J	MA	18E	16
RABINOVITZ BARRY IVAN	PA	21W	30
RABINOVITZ JACK	MA	05E	67
RABON JOSEPH LEVERN	SC	12E	104
RABREN LARRY WAYNE	FL	11W	76

NAME	STATE	PANEL NO.	LINE NO.
RABURN WILLIAM FAY	IL	18W	3
RACCA WILLIAM	DC	27W	105
RACEY BRADFORD GREG	CO	12W	125
RACEY KENZEL MEREDITH	WV	29W	73
RACHAL CHARLES WILLIAM	LA	01E	119
RACHAL LIONEL THOMAS	IL	22W	6
RACHON CHARLES JOSEPH	NY	51E	33
RACINE FRANKLIN DOUGLAS	IL	02E	128
RACKHAUS JOHN PELL	IL	16W	85
RACKLEY INZAR WILLIAM JR	TX	11E	88
RACKOW ANDREW CHARLES	PA	49W	20
RADA TERRY GENE	SD	22W	7
RADABAUGH HAROLD W II	MI	22E	7
RADCLIFF DONALD GORDON	KY	02E	59
RADCLIFF ROBERT PAUL JR	OH	09W	113
RADECKI PHILIP HENRY	PA	56E	30
RADER ALAN REED	OH	15W	105
RADER CHARLES WAYNE	IL	05E	97
RADER FREDERICK M III	CT	06W	87
RADER GARY PHILIP	CA	11W	128
RADER JAMES DOIL	VA	31E	53
RADER REX EARL	OR	28W	105
RADES ROBERT RAYMOND	WI	39W	62
RADFORD GARY MONROE	TX	06E	93
RADGOWSKI CHESTER J JR	PA	58E	25
RADICS DONALD M	MI	36E	31
RADIL RONALD LUDWIG	NE	28E	4
RADLEY LELAND EUGENE	WI	46W	21
RADONSKI KENNETH WAYNE	WI	39E	76
RADTKE CARL LEONARD	CA	30W	15
RADTKE ERIC RUDOLPH	WI	26E	50
RADTKE LE ROY CARL JR	FL	23E	103
RADU STEVEN NICHOLAS	OH	32E	26
RADZELOVAGE JAMES MICHAEL	PA	09E	42
RADZIECKI MICHAEL ANTHONY	MI	34W	52
RAETZ ROBERT WILLIS	NY	18E	12
RAFFENSPERGER JAMES E JR	IA	29E	91
RAFFERTY BERNARD JOSEPH	PA	07W	102
RAFFERTY EDWARD JOHN	PA	27E	103
RAGANS HERBERT RANDOLPH	FL	18W	76
RAGER DANA LEE	WV	35W	50
RAGER WILLIAM EARL	KS	16E	54
RAGIN WILLIAM DAVID HOWSA	FL	01E	62
RAGLAND DAYTON WILLIAM	MO	07E	129
RAGLAND FRED MICHAEL	PA	20W	96
RAGLAND MASON ERWIN	LA	11W	52
RAGLAND ROBERT EUGENE	TX	10W	92
RAGLE JAMES WILLIAM	IN	25E	17
RAGLIN RONDA LEE	MI	09E	70
RAGO STEPHEN JOSEPH	MA	43E	69
RAGSDALE DONALD RAY O	OK	12W	74
RAGSDALE GARY WAYNE	CA	09W	54
RAGSDALE JOSEPH MICHAEL	AL	16W	93
RAGSDALE ROBERT LOUIS	TX	01E	55
RAGSDALE STEPHEN LEON	CA	15W	14
RAGUSA FRANK RICHARD	NY	21E	80
RAHILLY ANDREW STEPHEN	NY	23W	67
RAHM ARNOLD JOHN	LA	01W	3
RAHN DONALD KEITH	PA	63E	16
RAIFORD CHARLES LEROY JR	PA	13E	107
RAIFORD MARK PHILLIP	AL	09W	132
RAIH ROGER WILLIAM	WI	47E	35
RAILEY GEORGE EDMUND	SC	13W	88
RAILING CHARLES DAVID	PA	23E	62
RAILLA JEAN ANTHONY	CA	43E	30
RAIMEY CHRISTOPHER LA G	KS	05W	93
RAINAUD JEFFREY WILLIAM	MA	41W	49
RAINBOLT JAMES EDWARD	CA	51E	42
RAINE DAVID SHELTON	CA	22E	17
RAINER CURTIS HALL	TX	38W	68
RAINES CHARLES RANSOME	TN	15W	83
RAINES ROBERT STEPHEN	IN	15W	20
RAINES WARREN HENRY	NY	40W	67
RAINEY CHARLIE	FL	49E	5
RAINEY LARRY STEPHEN	IL	31W	84
RAINEY LLOYD STEVEN	AK	02W	87
RAINEY THOMAS BALLARD	FL	39W	50
RAINEY VERNON EDWARD	LA	05W	97
RAINEY WILLIAM GEORGE	GA	19E	50
RAINFORD EDWARD GEORGE	CA	54W	19
RAINS CHRISTOPHER LEE	OH	49W	43
RAINS CLYDE EDWARD	CA	30W	38

NAME	STATE	PANEL NO.	LINE NO.
RAINS FORREST DE VERE JR	SC	28E	98
RAINS MICHAEL EDWARD	IN	59W	27
RAINS VERNON BARTON	CA	32E	80
RAINVILLE RANDALL BRIAN	CA	18E	76
RAINWATER JAMES ALVIN JR	AL	23E	63
RAINWATER JAMES RONALD	TN	21W	48
RAINWATER JEWEL LEE	AR	47E	42
RAINWATER WILBUR DEAN	GA	10E	103
RAIOLO JAMES JOHN	MN	40W	4
RAISIS LEONIDAS	MA	04E	40
RAITT ALBERT HAROLD	NJ	02E	60
RAJALA STANLEY ROBERT	MI	20W	115
RAJCEVAC HANS ANTHONY	IL	08W	13
RAKENTINE KENNETH CARL	NY	26E	66
RAKER RONALD LEE	PA	32W	56
RAKUNAS RONALD EDWARD	IL	45E	50
RALEIGH LOUIS RAYMOND	MA	04E	39
RALICH RONALD	OH	07E	121
RALLS RAYMOND BERNARD	PA	66E	1
RALPH DAVID EDWARD	PA	26E	94
RALPH GARY RAY	CA	48W	29
RALPH JAMES TROY	IN	24W	70
RALPH THOMAS HENRY JR	TX	62E	10
RALSTON FRANK DELZELL III	CO	07E	60
RALSTON JAMES VINCENT	PA	14E	54
RALSTON THOMAS JOSEPH	OH	06E	91
RALSTON THOMAS MICHAEL	MA	19W	98
RALYA WARREN HENRY JR	FL	34E	91
RAM CORNELIUS HERBERT	NJ	05W	38
RAMAGE JAMES WAYNE	KY	21E	59
RAMAKER LAWRENCE FREDRICK	MN	04E	10
RAMBERG MICHAEL JOHN	FL	38E	71
RAMBERGER JERRY RAY	IN	04E	128
RAMBERT FRANKLIN	SC	44W	5
RAMBO ARTHUR JOHN	MT	16W	126
RAMBUR MICHAEL JAMES	CA	38W	52
RAMEY GLENN WILLIAM	NC	36E	83
RAMEY JOE DON	CA	10W	77
RAMEY JORDAN EUGENE	SC	33E	59
RAMEY ROY LINDSEY	WV	23W	91
RAMEY SONEY	OH	49W	25
RAMEY THOMAS RANDELL	KY	45E	27
RAMEY VERNON LEMAR	PA	11E	10
RAMIREZ ALBERTO ANTONIO	NY	03W	48
RAMIREZ ARMANDO	AZ	24W	89
RAMIREZ DAVID THOMAS	CA	15E	129
RAMIREZ DIEGO JR	TX	30E	93
RAMIREZ EDUARDO CRUZ	CA	06W	55
RAMIREZ FLORENCIO JR	TX	18W	97
RAMIREZ HILDEFONSO M	CA	33W	24
RAMIREZ HONORIO JR	MI	08E	82
RAMIREZ JESUS P	CA	38E	37
RAMIREZ JOHN ARTHUR	CA	29W	22
RAMIREZ JOSE HERIBERTO	TX	55W	32
RAMIREZ JOSEPH YBARRA JR	CA	33W	21
RAMIREZ JUAN	CA	26E	37
RAMIREZ JUAN JOSE	TX	19E	30
RAMIREZ LORENZO JR	CA	54W	13
RAMIREZ LOUIS JOSEPH	IL	41W	42
RAMIREZ LUIS ANTONIO	PR	13E	1
RAMIREZ MARIO	MI	14E	40
RAMIREZ NELSON	NY	32W	46
RAMIREZ NELSON R	NJ	55E	28
RAMIREZ RALPH ALBERT JR	CA	24W	20
RAMIREZ RAMIRO RIOS	TX	35E	26
RAMIREZ RICHARD JR	AZ	47W	3
RAMIREZ ROBERTO MANDOZA	AZ	24E	105
RAMIREZ SAMUEL MEDINA	NM	06E	50
RAMIREZ VINCENT ALBERT	CA	18E	24
RAMM FERENC JOHN	IL	06W	127
RAMON ANDRES LOPEZ	TX	05W	78
RAMON AURELIO R JR	TX	37E	67
RAMON DENNIS MICHAEL	OH	61W	16
RAMON EUGENE DOMINGUEZ	TX	24E	82
RAMOS ANGEL LUIS	NJ	41W	42
RAMOS ARMANDO	PR	11E	46
RAMOS BERNARDO KEALOHA	CA	04W	75
RAMOS BRINSLEY BERNARD	DC	02W	79
RAMOS EDWARD	TX	10E	110
RAMOS FELIX RICO JR	TX	10E	25
RAMOS FIDEL JR	TX	21E	37
RAMOS FORREST LEE	WA	22E	27
RAMOS FRANK JR	OH	38E	37
RAMOS GEORGE MICHAEL	CA	62W	16
RAMOS JOSE JR	TX	30E	99
RAMOS JOSE PABLO	TX	07W	66
RAMOS JUAN MANUEL	TX	21W	120
RAMOS LEONARDO JR	TX	67E	1
RAMOS LUIS	CA	07W	40
RAMOS PAUL LAJADA JR	NC	10W	36
RAMOS RAINER SYLVESTER	WA	34E	10
RAMOS RICHARD	CA	22W	113
RAMOS ROBERTO	NY	40W	55
RAMOS ROBERTO	CT	34W	10
RAMOS ROLAND ROLANDO	HI	20E	3
RAMOS SAMUEL	IL	24W	72
RAMOS STEPHEN KEALOHA	HI	09W	106
RAMOS-JIMENEZ RAUL	PR	57W	11
RAMOS-LOPEZ ROBERTO	PR	13W	82
RAMOS-RAMIREZ JOAQUIN	PR	21W	67
RAMP DAVID	MD	15W	91
RAMPLEY CHARLES HOWARD	GA	43E	47
RAMPULLA TERRY JAMES	PA	50E	20
RAMSAY CHARLES JAMES	NJ	35E	8
RAMSAY DAVID LEROY	MA	08W	120
RAMSBY JAMES EDWARD	MI	30W	61
RAMSDEN GERALD LEE	CA	35E	18
RAMSDEN RANDALL EDWARD	IL	15W	130
RAMSEY ALAN RYAN	IL	33W	36
RAMSEY ANTHONY LOUIS	LA	08W	102
RAMSEY BILL EDWARD JR	TX	40W	67
RAMSEY CALVIN WETZEL	VA	08W	94
RAMSEY CHARLES MARLIN	TX	23W	78
RAMSEY DON MICHAEL	TX	03W	62
RAMSEY ERNEST LEROY	IA	09W	45
RAMSEY HENRY CHARLES	TX	25W	7
RAMSEY JOHN LOUIS	MA	67W	3
RAMSEY MICHAEL WAYNE	CA	20E	87
RAMSEY MILTON HARDIN	KS	04W	14
RAMSEY RANDOLPH RAYMOND	OH	31W	56
RAMSEY RICHARD CHARLES	CA	40E	12
RAMSEY ROBERT LEE JR	AR	32W	16
RAMSEY ROCKE DARRELL	GA	25E	32
RAMSEY SAMUEL VIRGIL JR	OH	28W	85
RAMSEY STEVEN GEORGE	NJ	61W	6
RAMSEY THOMAS EARLE	NC	36W	27
RAMSEY VIRGUS FREDRICK JR	AR	16E	30
RAMSOWER IRVING BURNS II	TX	02W	124
RANALLO CHARLES EDWARD JR	PA	20E	34
RANC WILLIAM EDWARD	OH	37E	67
RANCE STEVEN PAUL	WI	42W	21
RAND DWIGHT FRANCIS	NJ	33E	41
RAND EARLIE	AL	19E	26
RAND MICHAEL	NY	11E	119
RAND RICHARD PAUL	MA	06E	72
RANDALL DELBERT BRYAN	TX	03W	127
RANDALL DONALD DAVID JR	MI	54E	15
RANDALL EDDIE SAM JR	IL	12W	1
RANDALL GARLAND JERONE	TX	28E	29
RANDALL JAMES ARTHUR	AL	18E	127
RANDALL JAMES GARY	GA	43E	48
RANDALL JAMES LAVERNE	NY	04W	36
RANDALL JOHN MICHAEL	AZ	24W	61
RANDALL LOUIS R	KY	11E	17
RANDALL LYNN MURRAY	CA	22W	48
RANDALL MICHAEL ALLEN SR	IN	40W	14
RANDALL MICHAEL EUGENE SR	IN	41W	42
RANDALL MICHAEL PAUL	CA	20E	34
RANDALL RICHARD DENNIS	MS	37W	35
RANDALL ROBERT BRUCE	MN	46W	62
RANDALL ROBERT JOHN JR	FL	24W	89
RANDALL RONALD MITCHELL	CT	65E	1
RANDALL SIMON	AL	51E	33
RANDALL TERRELL LYNN	IA	42E	70
RANDALL WAYNE MICHAEL	VT	27W	103
RANDAZZO EDWARD D	NY	24E	105
RANDAZZO JOSEPH ANTHONY	CA	04E	125
RANDLE GEORGE JR	MS	56E	31
RANDLES JOHN PETERS	WA	07E	75
RANDO JOSEPH PAUL	MA	19E	45
RANDOLPH CLIFFORD L	OH	23E	117
RANDOLPH CORTEZ ALLEN	MO	24W	98
RANDOLPH GEORGE	LA	22E	17
RANDOLPH HOWARD EDWARD	VA	43E	31
RANDOLPH JAMES TIMOTHY	NY	49W	43
RANDOLPH LIONEL	LA	06E	8
RANDOLPH MICHAEL JAMES	MD	12W	58
RANDOLPH RICHARD ALAN	CA	42E	9
RANDOLPH RICHARD DALE	MI	05W	73
RANDOLPH RICHARD MANFORD	IN	22W	26
RANDOLPH RICHARD WAYNE	KY	36W	31
RANDOLPH SETH EARL	TX	26W	56
RANDOLPH VAN LA SALLE JR	NY	37W	77
RANDOLPH VERNON CHESTER	IA	38E	11
RANDOLPH WILLIAM JR	TN	56E	30
RANDOLPH WILLIAM LEWIS	TN	14E	24
RANELLUCCI RAYMOND ANTHON	NY	06E	9
RANEY STEVEN LEON	IA	36E	83
RANGE THOMAS RONNIE JR	GA	43W	20
RANGEL FLORENTINO	OK	45W	1
RANGEL RICHARD	CA	05E	67
RANGES ROBERT HENRY JR	NJ	48E	10
RANK DENNIS ROBERT	WI	25W	53
RANKE ALLEN JAMES	OH	38W	5
RANKIN ANDREW BRYAN	MO	26W	79
RANKIN DAVID GEOFFREY	IN	29W	22
RANKIN DONALD IRVIN	KY	12E	115
RANKIN EDWARD GARRY	VA	10E	103
RANKIN EDWARD LEE	KY	25E	71
RANKIN JOHN ROBERT	NJ	16W	81
RANKIN KENNETH DEAN	OK	16W	85
RANKINS DONALD LEE	OK	57W	3
RANKINS JOSEPH McKINLEY	NC	35W	36
RANKINS SAMUAL KAYE	IL	07W	19
RANSBOTTOM FREDERICK JOEL	OK	59E	11
RANSBOTTOM MICHAEL LEE	WV	48E	46
RANSDELL CURTIS H	NM	09E	6
RANSHAW DOUGLAS LE ROY	MI	35W	67
RANSOM BRADLEY ROGERS	KY	17W	52
RANSOM ROBERT CRAWFORD JR	NY	58E	25
RANSOM RODNEY LEE	PA	45W	28
RANSOM ROY CARLAS	WV	11W	117
RANSON DAVID WILLIAM	IL	27W	33
RANSON JOHN NORMENT	VA	15W	83
RANSON MELVIN RENSELLAER	MD	43E	59
RANSON RODNEY KENT	WV	16W	103
RANSTEAD JAMES TERRY	OK	35E	11
RANTHUM DALE HAROLD	MN	36W	53
RAO GLENN BURLEIGH	LA	31W	72
RAPCZAK MARTIN JOSEPH	IL	67E	2
RAPER ALVIN LOUIS	AZ	39E	52
RAPEY JOHN WALTER	IL	16E	97
RAPP BILLY WAYNE	WV	28W	2
RAPP JOSEPH LOUIS	IL	07E	112
RAPP WILLIAM HENRY JR	OK	15W	111
RAPPAPORT HAROLD KENNETH	NY	14W	15
RAPPLEYEA TUNIS E JR	NY	30E	65
RAPPOLD ALBERT JOSEPH JR	OH	66W	12
RAPTIS ANGELO CESARE JR	NY	24E	110
RARIG ROBIN ARTHUR	CA	03E	112
RARRICK JOHN EDWARD	NY	12W	83
RASBERRY MIKE RAYMOND	AR	48E	9
RASCHEL THOMAS REGINALD	CA	22E	1
RASCHKE DEAN NELSON	CA	21E	114
RASCO KENNETH EDWARD	CA	35E	57
RASCOE WILLIE ROBERT JR	NC	12W	115
RASENYUCK JAN IVAN	MA	18W	3
RASEY LARRY WAYNE	CA	08W	56
RASH DONALD RAY	VA	47E	15
RASH HARRY DON	IL	14E	59
RASH LYNLEY LEE	WA	55E	28
RASH MELVIN DOUGLAS	VA	66E	1
RASH RONALD WAYNE	AR	09W	40
RASH WILLIAM GEORGE	MD	47W	21
RASMUSSEN DAVID NILSSON	UT	46W	7
RASMUSSEN JOHN WILLIAM	AZ	16W	43
RASMUSSEN JON SIDNEY	OR	33W	51
RASMUSSEN NEAL ARTHUR	CA	07E	35
RASMUSSEN PETER TERENCE	NJ	27W	91
RASMUSSEN ROBERT MICHAEL	IL	27W	40
RASMUSSON MICHAEL ALFRED	CA	09W	3
RASNIC OLEN WESLEY	VA	04E	80
RASNICK SIDNEY McARTHUR	MI	26E	67
RASORI CARL RAYMOND	CA	46E	11
RASPBERRY LAWRENCE	AL	21W	39
RASSANO WILLIAM	IL	42E	38

NAME	STATE	PANEL NO.	LINE NO.
RASSEL ROBERT HERMAN	MN	47E	42
RATAJCZAK ROBERT EDGAR	WI	04W	53
RATCLIFF JACKIE LEE	AL	27W	52
RATCLIFF LENOX LEE	OK	05W	89
RATCLIFF ROY	TX	13E	48
RATCLIFF TERRY WARD	CA	12W	74
RATCLIFFE CARL JR	MD	31E	60
RATH GARY KEITH	IA	25E	79
RATH ROBERT EMIL	TX	21W	19
RATHBUN CRAIG	MO	10W	72
RATHBUN GARY ALLEN	MN	20E	106
RATHBUN ROBERT FRANK	OH	13E	99
RATHBURN RICHARD ALLEN	LA	45E	5
RATHE PHILIP HENRY	IL	09E	43
RATHMANN EUGENE LE ROY	CA	35W	6
RATHMELL HENRY PORTER	PA	12W	128
RATLEDGE DANIEL P JR	CA	18W	85
RATLIFF BILLY HARRISON	KY	07W	87
RATLIFF BOBBIE JOE	WV	22E	17
RATLIFF CLARENCE CECIL	NC	54W	39
RATLIFF DALLAS	WV	26E	57
RATLIFF EVERETT DUEL	MD	09W	16
RATLIFF FRANKLIN DELANO	TN	53W	4
RATLIFF FRED ALEXANDER	CO	37W	59
RATLIFF FREDERICK R JR	OH	31W	56
RATLIFF JAMES LEE	LA	49W	20
RATLIFF JERRY SCOTT	TN	40W	46
RATLIFF JOHNNY	OH	06W	133
RATLIFF LARRY GENE	KY	37W	59
RATLIFF OSCAR E	FL	15E	29
RATLIFF PAUL WAYNE	CA	20E	48
RATLIFF TERRY DIXON	CA	42W	22
RATLIFF THOMAS HENRY	FL	04W	95
RATTA FELICE NICHOLS	MI	25W	82
RATTEE CARL ALLAN	MA	40E	29
RATTIN DENNIS MICHAEL	IL	17W	85
RATZEL WESLEY DALLAS	PA	01W	28
RAUB FRANKLIN HARRISON	MI	34E	25
RAUBACH WILLIAM PIERCE	NE	41E	71
RAUBER DALE EUGENE	WI	32W	72
RAUBER WILLIAM	PA	52E	10
RAUBOLT THOMAS EDWARD	MI	52E	23
RAUCH EDWARD HAROLD	CA	28E	30
RAUCH KIRK LESLIE	CA	08W	80
RAUEN JOHN VERNON	WA	05W	126
RAULERSON CLIFFORD H JR	GA	01E	119
RAULSTON CHARLES ALLEN	TN	12W	31
RAULSTON RILEY DAVID	MO	61E	2
RAUPACH KIM	OH	22W	49
RAUSCH JOHN ALEX	WI	42W	59
RAUSCH ROBERT ERNEST	NY	11W	14
RAUSCHENBERG DOUGLAS EDWA	OH	10E	66
RAUSCHER LARRY LEE	IN	29W	2
RAUSCHKOLB JAN	CO	24W	107
RAVA HENRY TONY	OR	13W	31
RAVELO-TORIBIO ELPIDIO J	FL	07W	114
RAVENCRAFT JAMES ALVIN	OH	56W	27
RAVENNA HARRY M III	TX	12E	72
RAVER CHARLES DAVID	NY	62E	10
RAWLIN ROY VERNON	CA	19W	4
RAWLING BRUCE H	WI	34W	67
RAWLINGS BENJAMIN JOSEPH	MD	30W	38
RAWLINGS JEROME	MO	53E	22
RAWLINS JAMES PATRICK	AL	43W	20
RAWLINSON TERRELL LEE	TX	07W	6
RAWLS CHARLES GLENN	SC	23W	106
RAWLS JERRY DOUGLAS	TN	16W	122
RAWLS ROBERT EDWARDS	MI	02E	88
RAWSON JAMES HILTON	MS	10W	28
RAWSON WILLIAM ALLEN	IL	21E	38
RAWSTHORNE EDGAR ARTHUR	CA	04E	45
RAY CARL BRUCE	NC	15W	21
RAY CHARLES	MI	18E	15
RAY DARRELL THOMAS	WA	05E	90
RAY DARWIN ESKER	CA	33E	31
RAY DAVID L	KY	43E	31
RAY DAVID ROBERT	TN	29W	82
RAY DENNIS MICHAEL	MS	26W	79
RAY DEWEY JUNIOR	MI	29W	63
RAY DEWEY VERN	MI	18W	87
RAY DURWARD FRANK	GA	02E	29
RAY EDWARD GEAN	MI	16E	23

NAME	STATE	PANEL NO.	LINE NO.
RAY FRANKLIN DANIEL	NC	41E	2
RAY FREDERICK FRANKLIN JR	PA	63W	12
RAY GUY EDWARD JR	VA	44E	36
RAY JACKIE	MI	01W	21
RAY JAMES FLOYD	GA	01E	81
RAY JAMES LEONARD	NC	20E	10
RAY JAMES MICHAEL	RI	45E	28
RAY JOHN EDWARD	MO	25W	109
RAY JOHN MACK	OK	31E	66
RAY KERMIT ANTHONY	VA	18E	97
RAY LANDON CLAIR	WV	15E	81
RAY MICHAEL GEORGE	WA	37W	77
RAY MICHAEL WAYNE	AR	10W	28
RAY NOLAN REED	DE	49E	36
RAY RANDY DAVID	KS	06W	108
RAY ROBERT BRECKENRIDGE	CA	52W	34
RAY ROLAND WOOLDRIEDGE	TX	15E	108
RAY RONALD EARL	TX	16W	71
RAY RONALD EDWIN	WA	35E	79
RAY RONALD JOHN	WI	19W	21
RAY RUFUS	TX	21E	80
RAY THOMAS FREDRICK JR	MI	40W	34
RAY THOMAS PAUL	CO	27E	86
RAY TIMOTHY	OH	07E	40
RAY WALTER DONALD	MA	30E	48
RAY WILLIAM CLAYTON	KY	09W	119
RAY WILLIAM COTTER	GA	16W	40
RAY WILLIAM DAVID	CA	38W	78
RAY WILLIAM LEE	TN	46E	22
RAY WILLIE JAMES	MS	07W	114
RAYBORN DANNY KEITH	IL	14W	2
RAYBURN EDWARD LEE	WA	04W	25
RAYBURN STEPHEN LOUIS	CA	01W	105
RAYCHEL JAMES DANIEL	IL	19W	121
RAYFIELD GREGORY RUSSELL	MO	52W	31
RAYMER CARROLL EDWARD JR	IN	08W	94
RAYMO WINSTON GLENWOOD	VI	19E	31
RAYMOND CARL ROGER	NY	07W	47
RAYMOND EDWARD ROBERT III	CA	23W	106
RAYMOND FRANK JR	MI	35E	49
RAYMOND FREDRICK CAROL JR	NC	08W	8
RAYMOND JOHN JAMES	MA	15E	35
RAYMOND LAWRENCE ROBERT	NH	46E	11
RAYMOND PAUL DARWIN	NY	26E	3
RAYMOND RICHARD PAUL	NH	19W	121
RAYMOND ROBERT KENNETH	OK	37E	67
RAYMOND THEODORE PAUL	CT	58W	29
RAYNO JOSEPH ANDREW	NH	13E	99
RAYNOR JAMES DANIEL	AL	45W	1
RAYSKI LARRY ALLAN HENRY	MO	03E	22
RAZ FRANK VINCENT	NY	30E	18
RAZO FRANK AMBROSE	AZ	07E	131
RAZZANO ROBERT THOMAS	NY	19W	89
REA BILLY McCALL	NM	44W	12
REA EMORY LEE	IN	15W	25
REA PHILLIP KENNETH	IL	03E	26
REACH WILLIAM THOMAS	GA	01E	81
READ ALAN THOMAS	IN	20E	48
READ CHARLES HAROLD W JR	FL	46W	7
READ ROBERT BERTON	CT	23W	11
READY JOHN III	SC	08W	18
READY ROBERT WILLIAM	CA	14W	69
REAGAN DICKIE WALTER	NC	11W	117
REAGAN JOHN WALTER	CA	09E	59
REAGAN NORMAN REX	TX	15E	29
REAGAN ROBERT WILLIAM	FL	02E	79
REAGLE JOHN LOUIS	PA	33W	9
REAID ROLLIE KEITH	AL	01W	102
REALE JOHN BATTISTE III	PA	46E	11
REALI GUIDO SILVESTRO JR	FL	38E	11
REAM ERIC ALLAN	PA	17W	11
REAM GARY LEE	PA	12E	15
REAM PAUL EUGENE	OH	17E	23
REAMER DONALD PAGE	NJ	47W	21
REAMER JAMES CHARLES	WI	03W	124
REAMS TERRY D	MI	08W	112
REAMS WILLIAM BLAIR JR	TN	39W	51
REARDON DENNIS JOSEPH	MA	15W	8
REARDON RICHARD JOHN	NY	26W	73
REASONER DAVID LEE	IN	26E	50
REASONER FRANK STANLEY	ID	02E	36
REASONS JAMES ALTON JR	TN	25W	30

NAME	STATE	PANEL NO.	LINE NO.
REASOR THOMAS W	IN	01W	61
REATHER WALLACE LEE JR	AR	35E	50
REATHERFORD LARRY REX	IL	20W	26
REAUME PAUL EDMUND	CA	16W	9
REAUME WADE RUSSELL	WA	46E	22
REAVES FRED JR	NC	40E	67
REAVES HOMER LEE	CA	14E	38
REAVES JAMES LOUIS	SC	31E	38
REAVES JOHN SHEPARD JR	SC	21W	85
REAVIS BRETT GRANT	IA	18W	43
REBELO JOAQUIM VAZ	NJ	19E	110
REBER KENNETH NEAL	OR	09W	129
REBER MICHAEL RICHARD	IL	04W	42
REBERG CHARLES WAYNE	WY	51E	24
REBITS JOHN RAYMOND	MI	33W	51
RECK DAVID LYNN	TX	15W	79
RECK JOHN	NJ	60E	1
RECTOR MICHAEL WILLIAM	IN	24W	11
RECTOR ROY JACK	TX	47W	21
RECTOR WILLIAM THOMAS JR	VA	30W	29
RECUPERO RICHARD ANTHONY	FL	06E	132
RED HAWK JESSE MILTON	SD	39W	45
REDD BOBBY EDWARD	KS	52W	25
REDD CHARLES EDWARD	WV	26W	67
REDDICK WILLIAM CARL	NJ	15W	115
REDDING CHARLES V III	MD	17W	111
REDDING WALTER LEE	FL	08W	103
REDDINGTON JAMES THOMAS	PA	17E	31
REDDIX MISTER JR	LA	33W	73
REDENIUS DAVID GARY	IL	50E	20
REDENIUS RONALD JAMES	MN	41W	15
REDFEARN DON ALLAN	IL	20E	18
REDFORD JAMES ROBERT	TX	48E	10
REDIC TERRY PETE	IN	08E	54
REDMAN SYLVESTER WILLIAM	WV	17W	52
REDMON LARRY RAY	KY	43E	61
REDMON STANLEY EUGENE	PA	05W	108
REDMOND CARTER	PA	07E	90
REDMOND DONALD MERLE	IL	49W	43
REDMOND JOSEPH VERN	IL	11W	128
REDMOND RALPH GEORGE	KS	01E	53
REDMOND WILLARD THOMAS	NY	51W	7
REDTKE DUANE FRANCIS	IL	56E	30
REECE HOWARD WAYNE	IA	15E	50
REECE PETER EDWARD	PA	27W	58
REECE RONNEY DEAN	GA	28E	30
REECE STACEY DANA	MO	41E	71
REECE WALTER JAMES	NC	63E	17
REECE WESTON HENRY	MT	14E	24
REED ALBERT MARSHALL	PA	07W	133
REED ANTHONY ERICH	NY	42E	70
REED BILLIE WAYNE	KY	23W	57
REED BRUCE EDWARD	NY	31W	96
REED CHARLES MICHAEL	NY	07W	53
REED CHARLES OSCAR	TN	20E	34
REED CHARLIE JR	MS	06E	86
REED CHRISTOPHER RAY	ID	22W	7
REED CLYDE JR	OH	18E	18
REED DAVID ALAN	MD	45W	44
REED DAVID NEAL	NY	15W	87
REED DELMA LEE	TX	22E	113
REED DENNIS DALE	CA	44E	20
REED DENNIS WAYNE	WI	49E	5
REED EARL DONALD	MO	65W	14
REED EDWARD ROGER	IL	23E	54
REED FLOYD LARDINO JR	AR	03E	61
REED GARY DEWAYNE	PA	45E	42
REED GARY ROBERT	VA	32W	16
REED GARY WALTON	CA	20W	11
REED GEORGE JOSEPH JR	PA	22W	59
REED GEORGE PARNELL	IL	15W	108
REED GREGG ERWIN	CA	11E	27
REED GUY RICHARD	AZ	07E	46
REED HAROLD B	DC	08E	128
REED ISREAL DALLAS	LA	38W	51
REED JACKIE KENNETH	TN	25E	109
REED JAMES CLAYTON	CA	29W	92
REED JAMES EDDIE	TN	36E	59
REED JAMES WILLIAM	OH	08W	49
REED JERRY DONNIE	GA	19W	34
REED JIMMIE LYNN	WA	23W	47
REED JOE ALLEN	TN	67W	3

NAME	STATE	PANEL NO.	LINE NO.
REED JOHN ARTHUR	OK	18W	114
REED JOHN BRUCE	PA	53W	12
REED JON EDWARD	WI	07W	42
REED KENNETH LEROY	IN	02E	9
REED LARRY	KY	13E	79
REED LARRY BRUCE	PA	59W	12
REED LEROY	LA	22E	1
REED LESLEY WAYNE	WV	30E	31
REED LOUIS JOSEPH	NY	11E	98
REED MARION EUGENE	FL	40W	25
REED MELVIN L JR	CA	35W	78
REED MICHAEL CHARLES	PA	10E	110
REED OTTIS	KY	22E	63
REED PAUL EDWARD	PA	06W	32
REED PAUL MARTIN	VA	10E	31
REED PHILIP PAUL	IL	58W	9
REED PHILLIP EUGENE	IN	28E	11
REED RALPH EUGENE	OH	11W	15
REED RICHARD LEON	IL	06W	113
REED ROBERT BRUCE	NJ	29E	34
REED ROBERT THOMAS	OH	12E	71
REED ROBERT WILLIAM	CA	17E	109
REED ROGER DALE	TN	06E	54
REED ROGER LEE	CA	42E	23
REED RONALD LEE	MI	06E	16
REED RONALD LEE	KY	39W	56
REED SAMUEL LEE	MN	09E	25
REED SCOTT DOUGLAS	PA	54E	29
REED SHELLIE JEAN	MS	32E	80
REED STANLEY MAJURE	NJ	31W	17
REED TED QUINTON JR	OR	30W	68
REED TERRY JOE	IA	05E	37
REED TERRY MICHAEL	TX	21W	1
REED WAYNE FRANCIS	IA	23E	81
REED WILBERT	TN	14W	80
REED WILLIAM CLEMON	OH	06W	55
REED WILLIAM ELBERT	OK	03W	81
REED WILLIAM VAL	TX	09W	29
REED WILLIE	AL	30E	18
REEDER BRENT ALEXANDER	NY	39W	71
REEDER DAVID LEE	CA	03E	101
REEDER EDWARD JAMES	PA	33E	74
REEDER JAMES EDWARD	OK	33W	21
REEDER MELVIN	SC	08E	28
REEDER PHILIP DALLAM	TX	42W	32
REEDER RONNIE ELLIS	TN	14E	96
REEDY GARY MARTIN	IN	46E	40
REEDY WILLIAM BOYD	VA	33W	73
REEDY WILLIAM HENRY JR	CA	34E	60
REEFER CHARLES LENARD	PA	20W	109
REEL J C	MI	28W	51
REEL WILLIAM EDWARD	IL	10E	78
REES DONALD BRUCE	PA	12W	31
REES JOSEPH MAURICE	OH	48E	46
REES RICHARD MORGAN	OH	01W	120
REES WILLIAM ALLEN	PA	55E	28
REES WILLIAM EDWARD	IA	27E	55
REESE ABRAHAM B	MI	15E	17
REESE CHESTER ROY JR	OK	07W	40
REESE DANIEL CORTEZ	VA	16E	48
REESE DANIEL JR	MS	33E	92
REESE DAVID PHILLIP	WA	07W	13
REESE DELBERT LEON	MO	36E	83
REESE DENNIS DEAN	NV	41W	1
REESE DENNIS EDWARD	NC	06W	24
REESE GOMER DAVID III	NY	11W	47
REESE JAMES HARRISON	DC	07E	90
REESE JAMES ROBERT	GA	37W	24
REESE JOHN WILLIAM JR	CA	07W	13
REESE PAUL HENRY	OH	17W	17
REESE RAYMOND RICHARD	PA	01W	64
REESE RUBEN DWIGHT	TX	15W	29
REESE WILLIAM PHILIP	NY	25E	8
REESE WILLIAM RICHARD JR	PA	08E	94
REESE WILLIAM ROBERT	TX	39E	38
REEVE DAVID LEO	UT	04E	113
REEVES ALVIS OREN	TX	13E	12
REEVES DENNIS LEE	TX	06E	113
REEVES DOYLE WELLS	FL	16E	64
REEVES GORDON MICHAEL	CA	25E	89
REEVES GREGORY KEITH	AR	53W	38
REEVES HAROLD RAY	TX	37E	27
REEVES HAROLD RAY	TX	36W	42
REEVES JOHN HOWARD		13E	76
REEVES LARRY RAY	TX	18E	50
REEVES LONNIE MICHAEL	MO	37W	1
REEVES LOREN STEVEN	IA	12E	56
REEVES M RAYMOND	PA	42E	56
REEVES MICHAEL DAVIS	NJ	64E	8
REEVES RAYMOND STANLEY JR	MN	38W	12
REEVES ROBERT LINTON	CO	41E	43
REEVES SAMUEL DAVID JR	TX	33W	15
REEVES WAYNE PAUL	NJ	45E	28
REEVES WILLIAM DOUGLAS JR	OH	29E	53
REEVS JOHN CURTIS	OK	18W	3
REFF CHARLES RICHARD	IN	48W	47
REGALADO RICARDO WAYNE	WA	16W	81
REGAN MARTIN JOSEPH	NY	28W	85
REGAN PHILIP THOMAS JR	MD	26W	67
REGAN RICHARD JAMES	CT	02E	50
REGAN THOMAS FRANCIS	VA	26E	89
REGAN WILLIAM KENNETH	MA	53W	38
REGENHARDT ROBERT JOHN JR	MI	29W	63
REGER WILLIAM LEWIS	WV	16W	46
REGGIO GERARD MICHAEL	NY	21W	56
REGIER RAYMOND DEAN	KS	14W	105
REGINALD ROBERT JAMEISON	NY	28E	93
REGISTER BILLY ELWOOD	FL	17E	23
REGISTER DORSIE EUGENE	MO	17E	128
REGISTER MAXIE DEAN	GA	19W	81
REGISTER ROY CARROLL	GA	46W	44
REGNOLDS JAMES RANDOLPH	CA	28W	2
REGO ARTHUR	NJ	04E	98
REGO JOHN H	HI	07E	35
REHBERG JAMES HERBERT	FL	26W	73
REHBERGER CHARLES GEORGE	MD	42E	37
REHDER ROBERT EDWARD	NY	40W	8
REHE RICHARD RAYMOND	CA	34E	11
REHLING GUNTHER H	CA	18W	50
REHM TERRY MICHAEL	PA	27E	75
REHN GARY LEE	MN	29E	62
REHWALD ROYSE WAYNE	IN	02W	16
REICH DONALD GEORGE	MI	13E	114
REICH MERRILL DALE JR	GA	65W	14
REICH THOMAS ALAN	PA	38W	4
REICH WILLIAM GOODRO	CA	38W	8
REICHARD GARRY LEE	MI	30E	18
REICHARDT STEVEN JOHN	MO	43W	20
REICHELT JAMES LOUIS	NY	32E	4
REICHERT JOSEPH R	NY	13E	113
REICHERT LAWRENCE JOHN	PA	18E	31
REICHERT ROBERT D	MI	46E	11
REICHERT STEVEN EDWARD	CO	39E	24
REICHERT WILLIAM FRANCIS	NY	05W	66
REICHLE DWIGHT GERALD	MI	53E	40
REICHLIN JOSEPH ALBERT JR	NY	58E	14
REID AUBREY ARCHIE JR	VA	26W	3
REID BENJAMIN HERSCHELL	GA	67E	2
REID CARL J	OK	41E	12
REID DANIEL FRANCIS	NV	48E	32
REID DANIEL GEORGE	MI	22W	26
REID DANNY ELIE	GA	27E	55
REID DARRELL LEE	OH	25E	21
REID DAVID DONALD	GA	38E	59
REID DAVID STIRLING	CA	13W	59
REID EDWARD ROWAN JR	CA	15E	129
REID GENE C	NC	41E	64
REID HAROLD ERICH	UT	26E	67
REID JAMES ALFRED	MD	59W	12
REID JAMES EDWARD	KS	10E	48
REID JAMES MURRY	PA	09E	25
REID JOHN LEE	IA	35E	37
REID JOHN MICHAEL	NJ	19E	85
REID JOHNNIE GENE	GA	53E	22
REID JON ERIC	AZ	05W	126
REID JOSEPH CLARK	LA	49E	46
REID JOSEPH H	NY	07E	36
REID KENNETH WAYNE	WA	47W	52
REID LEON	WA	37E	27
REID LEROY JR	FL	03W	132
REID PAUL FRANCIS	MA	29E	34
REID RALPH HENRY	VA	38E	80
REID ROBERT WOODSON	GA	08E	88
REID ROGER GLEN		04W	97
REID WILLIAM ALBERT	CA	01E	44
REID WINFIELD WALTER	LA	41E	72
REIDY MARTIN JOHN	IA	49E	15
REIFF MICHAEL DEAN	MO	38W	20
REIFSCHNEIDER ELMER J JR	MO	04E	114
REIGLE AARON HENRY	PA	39E	24
REIGSTAD DANNY RAY	MN	15E	99
REIKMANIS VIESTURS	NY	20W	104
REIL RONALD LE ROY	SD	43W	57
REILLY ALLAN VINCENT	CA	28E	30
REILLY DONALD JOSEPH	MO	04E	4
REILLY EDWARD DANIEL JR	PA	07E	2
REILLY EDWARD WILLIAM	PA	06E	103
REILLY JAMES JOSEPH JR	PA	02E	117
REILLY JAMES RICHMOND	NY	06E	19
REILLY JOHN CHARLES	RI	10W	81
REILLY JOHN FRANCIS	MN	13E	99
REILLY JOHN MICHEAL	IA	15W	115
REILLY JOHN NORMAN JR	NJ	38W	13
REILLY JOHN THOMAS	NY	40W	25
REILLY JOSEPH JOHN	NJ	05E	84
REILLY LAVERN GEORGE	MN	07E	62
REILLY MARTIN DANIEL	NY	07E	75
REILLY MICHAEL PATRICK	IL	15E	35
REILLY RAYMOND PATRICK	FL	45W	1
REILLY ROBERT JOHN JR	CA	04E	5
REILLY ROBERT JUDE	NY	01E	66
REILLY RONALD HENRY	WI	08W	23
REILLY WILLIAM F III	MD	52W	41
REILLY WILLIAM RAYMOND	NY	07E	111
REIMILLER THOMAS EVANS	PA	03W	121
REIN CHARLES FREDERICK	FL	38W	29
REINBOTT HAROLD W JR	MO	09E	81
REINECCIUS KARL LEWIS	AR	06W	24
REINECKE WAYNE CONRAD	OR	14E	17
REINEL RUSSELL EDWARD	GA	33W	68
REINER CHARLES EDWARD	NY	62E	10
REINHARDT ARTHUR WELKER	NY	25E	85
REINHARDT BARRY THOMAS	MN	55E	28
REINHARDT JAMES MICHAEL	PA	11W	1
REINHART PETER SIMMONS	PA	42E	39
REINHOLD MICHAEL J	AZ	40E	29
REINKE JACK RAYMOND	MN	49E	5
REINKE ROBERT HARVEY	WI	17E	12
REINKE RONALD RICHARD	WI	26E	16
REIPLINGER ROBERT LEE	IN	17W	106
REIS LUCIO JON	CA	05W	97
REIS TIAGO	MA	26E	106
REISER STEVE RONALD	NE	34W	10
REISING DALE	OH	10W	118
REISSIG LARRY LEROY	KS	19E	111
REISTROFFER DANIEL PHILLIP	IA	60E	1
REITER BRUCE MARTIN	NY	34W	28
REITER CLYDE ALVIN	MI	36W	87
REITER DEAN WESLEY	MO	11E	17
REITER GERALD ANDREW	PA	19E	99
REITER LESLEY STEVEN	NY	26W	67
REITER WILLIAM FRANCIS	OH	46W	32
REITHER PHILIP HENRY JR	MO	17W	20
REITHMANN TIMOTHY CHARLES	NY	37E	12
REITMANN THOMAS EDWARD	MN	03E	119
REITWIESNER JOHN CHARLES	CT	14W	54
REITZ KEITH HAROLD	MO	13W	101
REITZ MICHAEL ROBERT	NY	18W	34
REKAU HAROLD EDWARD	IL	42E	56
REKER ROBERT VINCENT	SD	22W	43
RELEFORD ISIEAH JR	GA	29W	32
RELF WILLIAM CHARLES	TX	17E	81
REMBERT HARVEY LEE	OK	32E	80
REMBERT LESLIE EUGENE	FL	12W	50
REMBOLDT RONALD PAUL	MO	02W	84
REMEDIES RICHARD JARRELL	LA	24E	63
REMEIKAS JOSEPH JOHN JR	VA	27W	77
REMELTS WILLIAM HENRY II	CA	06W	134
REMER CHARLES BRADLEY JR	CT	54E	15
REMER KEVIN RALPH	MN	48W	30
REMILLARD GARRY EDWARD	CA	38W	4
REMMEL HARMON L III	AR	38E	12
REMMERS KENNETH LEE	TX	02E	36
REMMLER MILTON WILLIAM JR	TX	25W	3
REMONDINI LEO ANGELO JR	MI	04E	53
REMPER GERALD NEAL	PA	54W	4

NAME	STATE	PANEL NO.	LINE NO.
REMULAR RUDOLPH	HI	14E	98
REMUTH LAWRENCE GUSTAVE	CT	15W	52
RENAUD ROBERT WILFRED	RI	33E	52
RENAULD RALPH VICTOR JR	MA	09E	25
RENCEVICZ CHESTER MICHAEL	NJ	50W	20
RENDER CECIL LAVON	IL	50E	40
RENDON GUADALUPE	AZ	21E	79
RENDON JOSEPH	CO	20W	81
RENDON RAPHAEL JOHNNY	IA	50W	26
RENDON THOMAS	TX	47E	5
RENELT WALTER A	SD	16W	103
RENFRO FRANKLIN JR	KY	49W	44
RENFRO JACK DENNIS	KS	12E	39
RENFRO NORMAN A	CA	16E	12
RENFRO RICHARD ALVIN	MO	49E	47
RENFROE MATHEREW DENNIS	MI	12E	44
RENFROW BILLY JOE	LA	17W	31
RENNE MYRON KEITH	MO	20W	37
RENNER JOHN MICHAEL	ND	20W	66
RENNER LYNN CARL	MI	04E	38
RENNER MATTHEW MARK	IN	04W	33
RENNER STEVEN RAY	IN	10W	28
RENNING RICHARD ANDREW	CA	35W	78
RENNOLET RICHARD FREDRICK	SD	50E	1
RENO DENNIS KEITH	IN	45W	44
RENO LAWRENCE GERALD	OH	69E	1
RENO RALPH JOSEPH	NC	08E	126
RENSHAW ANDERSON N III	TN	27W	71
RENSHAW FRANKLIN MASON	CT	11E	58
RENSHAW ROBERT FRANCIS	UT	28E	101
RENTAS JOSE CARMELO JR	NY	18W	126
RENTERIA LOUIS JESUS	CO	11E	124
RENTERIA RUDOLPH SOTELO	CA	46W	44
RENVILLE ARDEN KEITH	SD	51E	49
RENWICK HAROLD MCGILL JR	SC	41E	54
RENZ JAMES THOMAS	IL	13E	100
RENZ RAYMOND ALLAN	NJ	21E	38
REPACI DONALD SHELDON	CT	28W	29
REPETA HENRY JAMES	NY	01W	104
REPOLE RICHARD GLENN	CT	09W	132
RERA ROBERT	NY	44E	11
RESENDEZ AUGUSTINE	TX	18E	104
RESINGER DENNIS MICHAEL	PA	22W	109
RESKA CRAIG THOMAS	MI	06W	55
RESNICK ROBERT ALBERT	PA	53W	12
RESPASS HARMON THURSTON	NC	21E	115
RESPECKI DONALD GEORGE	MI	27W	66
RESPRESS THOMAS	OH	11E	128
RESTREPO JAIME	GA	06W	39
RETSCHULTE THOMAS HOWARD	KY	35E	8
RETSECK JOHN D JR	IN	14W	9
RETZLAFF ARTHUR CLIFTON	NJ	23E	45
RETZLOFF JAMES ROBERT JR	CA	47E	26
REUKAUF LEE EDWARD	KS	15E	121
REUTER NEIL GEORGE	WI	08E	133
REVAK ANTHONY NEAL	NY	47W	31
REVELL WILLIAM JAMES III	SC	22W	68
REVELLE GLENN	IL	26E	57
REVIER JOHN DAVID	CA	17W	103
REVIS CHARLES JAY	NC	29W	23
REVIS HUGH EDWARD	NC	20W	73
REVIS RONALD JAMES	CA	05W	63
REVLAND RICKEY DON	IA	19E	45
REVOIR RICHARD RUSSELL	MI	22W	26
REX ROBERT ALAN	UT	37W	68
REX ROBERT F	IA	30W	95
REXROAD LOEL FRANKLIN	WV	11W	18
REXROAD RONALD REUEL	IL	47E	58
REXROAT TERRY LYNN	IA	16W	126
REXRODE JACK LEE	WV	29W	83
REYES ALFREDO VICENTE	TX	22E	113
REYES ANGEL	PA	28W	13
REYES ANGEL LUIS JR	NY	45W	22
REYES ANTONIO	TX	34W	53
REYES DOUGLAS COOPER	TN	15E	55
REYES EDWARD THOMAS	CA	16W	47
REYES GILBERT	AZ	21E	15
REYES HAROLD	CO	27E	17
REYES HENRY R	CA	20W	2
REYES HUMBERTO	NY	54E	15
REYES JOSE ANGEL	TX	42E	39
REYES MOISES A JR	TX	35W	29

NAME	STATE	PANEL NO.	LINE NO.
REYES PETER C	TX	22E	121
REYES ROBERT ANTONIO	CA	36E	77
REYES RONALD	CA	47E	16
REYES RONALD DAVID	CA	23E	7
REYES RUBEN EVERARDO	CA	40W	14
REYES TOMAS GARCIA	GM	29E	61
REYES WILLIAM	MI	53W	23
REYMAN LAWRENCE FRANCIS	OK	28E	101
REYNA JOE JR	TX	08W	98
REYNA JUAN MANUEL	TX	08W	32
REYNA SAMUEL	TX	51E	13
REYNA THOMAS O	WA	54E	16
REYNER DAVID ELLIOT	TX	08E	94
REYNOLDS ARTHUR JR	PA	20E	18
REYNOLDS CARL MITCHELL	MI	09W	48
REYNOLDS DAVID MACK	OK	43E	59
REYNOLDS DAVID RICHARD	NY	30E	60
REYNOLDS DONALD J	FL	23E	38
REYNOLDS EARNEST LANE	OK	37W	69
REYNOLDS EDWARD LEE	MO	07W	72
REYNOLDS ELDON LEE	OK	21W	120
REYNOLDS FRANK EVERETT	IL	16E	18
REYNOLDS GARRY LEE	NC	08E	94
REYNOLDS GARY EDWARD	IL	32W	16
REYNOLDS GARY LEE	VA	04W	131
REYNOLDS GEORGE F JR	NY	28W	85
REYNOLDS GEORGE R JR	ME	10E	59
REYNOLDS GEORGE THOMAS	OH	06E	54
REYNOLDS HAROLD W	ME	14E	67
REYNOLDS HARVEY CLAUDE	KY	17W	106
REYNOLDS HARVEY MICHAEL	OH	04W	106
REYNOLDS JACK EDWARD	PA	54E	39
REYNOLDS JACKIE DEAN	IN	05E	108
REYNOLDS JAMES DEREK	IN	19E	111
REYNOLDS JAMES STEPHEN JR	AZ	31W	17
REYNOLDS JAY WILLARD	IN	08E	121
REYNOLDS JOHN DAVID	TN	26E	37
REYNOLDS JOHN EUGENE	PA	49W	25
REYNOLDS JOHN HENRY	AL	39E	65
REYNOLDS JOSEPH LEE	WA	31E	53
REYNOLDS JOSEPH RAY	CA	05E	108
REYNOLDS KENNETH ALDERSON	DC	05E	68
REYNOLDS LARRY ALLEN	TX	27W	21
REYNOLDS LARRY LEE	KY	11E	4
REYNOLDS LESLIE JR	OH	20W	12
REYNOLDS LEVI RAY	MD	53W	12
REYNOLDS LOUIS JAMES	WV	62W	1
REYNOLDS MARTIN DANIEL	CO	26W	35
REYNOLDS MICHAEL MONROE	CA	47E	16
REYNOLDS OLIVER EUGENE JR	TX	27W	52
REYNOLDS OSSIE	MI	32E	80
REYNOLDS RICHARD PETER JR	NY	34E	91
REYNOLDS ROBERT CLARENCE	OH	19E	50
REYNOLDS ROBERT GEORGE	NJ	21E	92
REYNOLDS ROBERT LEE JR	IN	08E	76
REYNOLDS ROBERT MICHEAL	PA	48W	30
REYNOLDS RONALD BURNS	TX	25W	21
REYNOLDS SHERWOOD	MD	41E	43
REYNOLDS THOMAS YORK	NY	46E	2
REYNOLDS WILLIAM	NC	29W	48
REYNOLDS WILLIAM DONALD	OK	01E	97
REYNOLDS WILLIAM LAWRENCE	KS	10W	116
REYNOSO RENE	CA	14E	17
REZA LEONARD	CA	03W	3
REZENDE DANIEL DIAS	CA	46W	21
REZENDES PAUL ALLEN	MA	22W	82
RHAMY RAYMOND DALE	OK	22E	63
RHASH BARRY ARTHUR	NC	04W	92
RHEA RANDOLPH VINCENT	CA	16W	66
RHEA SCOTTY HENRY	NC	11W	52
RHEAD JIM MARBLE	UT	07W	25
RHEAULT WILLIS CLIFFORD	MI	38E	59
RHEN DENNIS HENRY	PA	24W	34
RHINE RICHARD ALLEN	AZ	18E	46
RHINEHART CLYDE A	SC	38E	80
RHINEHART JOSEPH LEE	WV	21E	17
RHOADES CLINTON MORELL JR	MA	25E	79
RHOADES DAVID	OH	16E	97
RHOADES EUGENE BRUCE	OR	12E	81
RHOADES FRANCIS STEVEN	NJ	43W	41
RHOADES FREDERICK PAUL	AZ	42W	50
RHOADES LOUIS GEORGE	WI	59W	12

NAME	STATE	PANEL NO.	LINE NO.
RHOADS DANNY DAVID	CA	16E	70
RHOADS THOMAS VERNON	PA	34W	53
RHODE EDWARD ANTHONY	MO	50E	7
RHODEHAMEL JOHN RAY II	NV	17E	118
RHODEN TALMADGE	FL	19E	54
RHODES CLIFFORD G	FL	07E	75
RHODES CLIFFORD M JR	NY	19E	51
RHODES CURTIS ALLEN	MD	47E	36
RHODES DAVID FREDERICK	FL	37W	77
RHODES DONALD FRANK	NC	13E	123
RHODES DONALD RAY	IN	31W	84
RHODES FERRIS ANSEL JR	SC	05W	24
RHODES FRANK MOSS	WA	14E	88
RHODES GARY ARTHUR	OR	48E	19
RHODES GRANT A	OH	04E	53
RHODES HU BLAKEMORE	TN	69E	1
RHODES JAMES LAWRENCE	IL	17W	64
RHODES JAMES ROBERT	GA	14E	99
RHODES JIMMY LINWOOD	NC	12E	105
RHODES JOHN DAVID III	TN	23W	91
RHODES JOHN JOSEPH	NY	28E	51
RHODES JOHN OWEN	FL	17E	87
RHODES JOSEPH JOHN	OH	28E	57
RHODES JOSEPH LEE	MS	23W	11
RHODES KENNETH	SC	13E	40
RHODES LARRY WAYNE	KS	26W	73
RHODES RAY ANTHONY	AL	17E	12
RHODES RICHARD JAMES	IL	36E	32
RHODES ROBERT DAVID	MA	10W	110
RHODES RONALD JAMES	FL	42E	70
RHODES STANLEY RUFUS	MI	02W	16
RHODES THOMAS HENRY	VA	05E	28
RHODES TIMOTHY V	TX	25E	2
RHODES WAYNE A	OK	49E	47
RHODES WILLIAM BARTON	CA	05W	82
RHODES WILLIE JOE	NJ	22E	18
RHODES WILLIE MICHAEL	FL	24E	92
RHODUS RAY WESLEY	LA	17E	85
RHUDA ROBERT ARTHUR	CT	24E	40
RHUE CHARLES RUSSELL	FL	20E	48
RHUE MYRON EDWIN	NC	31W	17
RHYNES GLOUSTER	FL	69E	1
RIAL JAMES ALPHONSE	IA	01E	67
RIAL RICHARD FRED	NY	35E	80
RIALE RICHARD WILLIAM	NY	32W	22
RIBEIRO JOSEPH FRANCIS	NY	48W	30
RIBERA ANTONIO	NM	23E	88
RIBICH MICHAEL P		27W	101
RIBILLIA MARIANO JR	HI	34W	53
RIBITSCH ERIC	NY	08E	124
RIBUCAN VAN V	HI	39W	13
RICARD FRED LAYTON JR	PA	31W	54
RICARDO SALVADOR ORTENCIO	CA	32W	34
RICCI GERALD	MI	15E	22
RICCIARDO RONALD FRANCIS	NY	28W	75
RICCIONE STEVEN BLAINE	NY	27E	22
RICE ANDREW WILLIAM JR	AK	24W	89
RICE CALVIN CHARLES JR	PA	21W	14
RICE CAMERON A	CA	22E	18
RICE CLAUDE	GA	01E	30
RICE DENNIS KELLY	AZ	34E	44
RICE DONALD JEROME	GA	14W	60
RICE FINLEY AUSTIN	OH	05W	1
RICE FRANCIS DAVID	NY	11E	124
RICE FRANK LATIMER JR	NC	11W	87
RICE GEORGE WARREN	FL	04E	25
RICE GREGORY LLOYD	CA	34W	2
RICE HERBERT CHARLES	NY	17E	69
RICE HOWARD JACOB	NM	21E	76
RICE IRA ALBERT	MO	18E	72
RICE JACK WALTER	PA	39W	60
RICE JAMES BURNEL JR	MO	31W	15
RICE JAMES JOSEPH	MA	38E	12
RICE JAMES R	TX	10E	1
RICE JAMES ROY	WI	19W	21
RICE JEROME JAMES	IL	17W	69
RICE JERRY DAVID	MD	18W	111
RICE JESSE	IL	14E	40
RICE JOHN CLIMATH	WA	19E	31
RICE JOHN EDWARD	AR	50W	26
RICE JOHN MICHAEL	IN	14W	15
RICE JOHNIE EDWARD JR	KY	02E	30

NAME	STATE	PANEL NO.	LINE NO.
RICE LARRY ALLEN	MI	12E	24
RICE MAXIE ROSS	NV	36E	59
RICE MICHAEL PAUL	PA	01W	72
RICE MICHAEL PHILLIP	OH	33W	33
RICE MICHAEL RAY	FL	32E	65
RICE McKINLEY JR	FL	32W	9
RICE PATRICK L	TX	24W	48
RICE ROBERT	NY	50E	20
RICE ROBERT CHARLES	MI	28E	86
RICE ROBERT IVAN	AL	36E	84
RICE ROBERT THOMAS JR	OH	08W	94
RICE RONALD FRED	CA	07E	54
RICE THOMAS EVERETT	MN	05E	43
RICE THOMAS JR	SC	04E	44
RICE VIRGIL RAY	TX	34E	64
RICE WALTER GARLAND JR	OH	41W	26
RICETTI CHRISTOPHER JOHN	NY	21W	56
RICH CHARLES RAY	MO	24E	41
RICH CRAIG ARTHUR	IA	46W	32
RICH DANNY KAYE	CA	56E	14
RICH JOHN ALLAN	AZ	10E	43
RICH JON WILLIAM	MI	10W	77
RICH JOSEPH WALTER	SC	56W	14
RICH MICHAEL ROBERT	MI	39W	23
RICH PETER BERNARD	MA	44W	66
RICH RICHARD	CT	20E	43
RICH RONALD DUDLEY	AL	13E	93
RICH ROY WAYNE	TN	43W	41
RICHARD ANDREW GUS	IL	55W	1
RICHARD BYRON MATTHEW	LA	13W	106
RICHARD CURTIS	TX	06W	50
RICHARD DONALD WAYNE	TX	32E	59
RICHARD DUANE LAWRENCE	CA	14W	123
RICHARD JERRY GORDON	AL	45W	56
RICHARD JOHN WAYNE	OH	24W	70
RICHARD NORMAN LEO	FL	19W	103
RICHARD PHILIP EUGENE	OH	06W	84
RICHARD ROLAND ARMAND	CT	27W	40
RICHARD ROY JAMES	LA	07E	121
RICHARD WILLIAM W	MA	04E	33
RICHARDS CHARLES EDWARD	CT	37E	27
RICHARDS CHARLES H JR	PA	23E	81
RICHARDS DANIEL MARTIN	MI	01W	64
RICHARDS DANIEL PAUL	NY	12W	128
RICHARDS DENNIS R	OH	28W	39
RICHARDS DON JUNE	GA	07E	98
RICHARDS DONALD JUAN	NY	26E	106
RICHARDS DONALD LAWRENCE	MA	29E	102
RICHARDS DOUGLAS WAYNE	IL	27W	12
RICHARDS FRED EARL	MI	29W	23
RICHARDS GARY CHARLES	CT	15E	51
RICHARDS JAMES MICHAEL	NC	47W	31
RICHARDS JAMES PAUL	TN	13W	59
RICHARDS JOHNNY FRANKLIN	TX	45W	44
RICHARDS JOHNNY LEE	PA	36W	73
RICHARDS LEONARD JEFFREY	IL	30E	48
RICHARDS LON DAVIS	MO	47W	52
RICHARDS MICHAEL HUGH	ID	04W	51
RICHARDS MICHEAL EDWARD	AR	50W	38
RICHARDS PAUL ALLEN	TX	13W	106
RICHARDS RICKEY LEE	IN	47E	26
RICHARDS ROBERT	AL	56E	31
RICHARDS RONALD	GA	08E	39
RICHARDS STEPHEN RYAN	NC	50W	27
RICHARDS THOMAS JOSEPH JR	VA	58E	14
RICHARDS THOMAS STEPHEN	CT	29E	5
RICHARDS WAYNE	OK	60E	2
RICHARDSON ARLEN DEL	KS	13W	25
RICHARDSON ARPHALIA L JR	FL	32E	78
RICHARDSON ARTHUR GENE	IL	01E	30
RICHARDSON BENJAMIN	MI	20E	123
RICHARDSON BERNARD MCKINL	DC	46E	58
RICHARDSON BRUCE	NY	10W	127
RICHARDSON CHARLES A	CA	09W	16
RICHARDSON CHARLES HENRY	NJ	41W	31
RICHARDSON CHARLES WAYNE	IN	33W	28
RICHARDSON DALE WAYNE	WI	11W	87
RICHARDSON DANNY JOE	GA	47E	53
RICHARDSON DAREK NICHOLAU	TN	11W	28
RICHARDSON DAVID ALLEN	CA	18E	42
RICHARDSON DONALD HAROLD	CA	23W	57
RICHARDSON DONALD LOYE	TX	09E	128

NAME	STATE	PANEL NO.	LINE NO.
RICHARDSON DONALD WILLIAM	AL	35E	69
RICHARDSON EDMOND WILLIAM	WI	07W	62
RICHARDSON EUGENE	NY	01E	68
RICHARDSON EUGENE III	GA	55W	15
RICHARDSON EUGENE P JR	TN	13E	36
RICHARDSON FARRIS LEE	OH	45E	50
RICHARDSON FLOYD JR	MI	05W	74
RICHARDSON FLOYD WHITLEY	AK	16E	12
RICHARDSON FRED LEWIS	TN	07E	21
RICHARDSON GARY LYLE	CA	57W	12
RICHARDSON GARY WAYNE	KS	06W	30
RICHARDSON HAROLD OWEN	VA	12W	1
RICHARDSON HAROLD REED	NC	33W	58
RICHARDSON HARRY F JR	VA	36E	32
RICHARDSON HARRY TRACY JR	TX	08E	99
RICHARDSON HERMAN JR	PA	19W	122
RICHARDSON JAMES	PA	55W	23
RICHARDSON JAMES AUGUSTA	NC	09E	3
RICHARDSON JAMES DOUGLASS	LA	48E	47
RICHARDSON JAMES EVERT	MO	48E	33
RICHARDSON JEFFERY ALLEN	PA	24W	79
RICHARDSON JESSIE	LA	12E	81
RICHARDSON JIMMIE JENKINS	SC	46W	45
RICHARDSON JOHNNIE BRYANT	NY	61E	2
RICHARDSON LARRY EUGENE	TX	43W	21
RICHARDSON LEMOND	IL	29W	23
RICHARDSON LOUIS DOUGLAS	MS	03E	90
RICHARDSON MARVIN KEITH	MI	21W	102
RICHARDSON MARVIN NELSON	MO	43E	59
RICHARDSON MICHAEL WAYNE	LA	22W	82
RICHARDSON NELSON GRAFTON	ME	05W	78
RICHARDSON NORWOOD ROLAND	VA	14W	86
RICHARDSON OSSIE	IL	13W	89
RICHARDSON PHILIP OWEN	MN	19W	21
RICHARDSON RAYMOND LEE	MO	08E	121
RICHARDSON RAYMOND WILKIE	TN	15E	29
RICHARDSON RICHARD ELVIN	MO	11E	52
RICHARDSON RICKY WAYNE	HI	24E	40
RICHARDSON ROBERT	GA	21E	51
RICHARDSON ROBERT BROOKS	CA	40W	14
RICHARDSON ROBERT DANIEL	MO	08E	130
RICHARDSON ROBERT EARL	TX	12W	22
RICHARDSON ROBERT WAYNNE	TX	06W	133
RICHARDSON ROBIN WILLIAM	MO	29W	13
RICHARDSON ROGER PAUL	MT	16E	48
RICHARDSON RONALD DOUGLAS	MO	57E	9
RICHARDSON ROY LEE	UT	10W	9
RICHARDSON SCOTT DOUGLAS	FL	18E	127
RICHARDSON STEPHEN GOULD	WA	03E	118
RICHARDSON THEODORE	SC	02E	102
RICHARDSON WILLARD D JR	TN	19W	90
RICHARDSON WILLIAM F	TX	11W	32
RICHARDSON WILLIAM H JR	IN	29E	65
RICHARDSON WILLIAM L JR	FL	06E	77
RICHARDSON WILLIE LEE	GA	42E	23
RICHEE JAMES BURNUS	CA	46W	21
RICHEY KENNETH ALAN	IN	15W	37
RICHEY NEAL OLIN	MA	02E	128
RICHEY THOMAS EARL	GA	46W	21
RICHIE CHARLES HOWARD	KY	02W	68
RICHMOND JAMES ROSS	WV	57W	13
RICHMOND LAWRENCE DOUGLAS	WV	11W	18
RICHMOND ROBERT STANLEY	MI	12W	31
RICHMOND THOMAS GLEN	KY	10E	84
RICHMOND WILLIE BUREL	WV	46E	49
RICHTER DALE RAY	OR	46W	32
RICHTER DONALD JOSEPH	WI	28W	51
RICHTER JAY DEE	CA	51E	49
RICHTER KARL WENDELL	MI	24E	13
RICHTER MERVIN RALPH	IN	29W	83
RICHTMYRE CHARLES LAWRENC	IL	05E	30
RICHTSTEIG DAVID JOHN	UT	04E	2
RICK EUGENE MERLYN	MN	02E	117
RICK JOHN SCOTT	CA	12W	36
RICKARD RONALD LEE	OH	34E	81
RICKARD WALTER L	HI	01E	90
RICKARDS CLARENCE HOWARD	OH	15E	100
RICKARDS LINWOOD PRESTON	ME	52W	8
RICKEL DAVID J	FL	61E	18
RICKELS DAVID LEE	TX	37E	13
RICKELS FREDERICK DALE	FL	59E	11
RICKELS JAMES BURNELL	IA	44E	61

NAME	STATE	PANEL NO.	LINE NO.
RICKELS JOHN A	NM	35E	62
RICKER DARRELL BLANCHARD	CA	06W	79
RICKER WILLIAM ERNEST	OR	40W	50
RICKERSON ALBERT LEONARD	GA	45W	44
RICKERSON JAMES EDWARD	GA	21E	24
RICKERSON STEVEN ALLEN	PA	18W	91
RICKERT GLENN DALE	PA	10W	118
RICKERT ROGER ALLEN	WI	42W	32
RICKETTS JAMES E	VA	25W	25
RICKEY LAWRENCE DAVID	OH	27W	91
RICKLI RODNEY HOWARD	WI	15E	35
RICKMAN DWIGHT GRAY	MO	01W	105
RICKMAN WILLIAM JOEL	PA	17E	96
RICKMERS ROLF ERNST	NY	47W	52
RICKS JAMES LUTHER	NJ	04E	104
RICKS LARRY EUGENE	TX	37W	18
RICKS RONALD GLENN	TX	02W	31
RIDDICK DANIEL ALEXANDRIA	VA	38W	4
RIDDICK STERLING G W	NC	50E	41
RIDDLE BOBBY	AL	19W	63
RIDDLE CHARLES LLOYD	TX	14W	90
RIDDLE JOHN ROBERT	VA	07E	126
RIDDLE LARRY LYNN	MN	20W	74
RIDDLE LARRY RAY	GA	16E	37
RIDDLE MICHAEL DEAN	TN	03W	55
RIDDLE OLIVER JOHN	PA	13E	12
RIDDLE ROBERT THOMAS	TX	32E	81
RIDDLE WALTER RAY	OK	30E	31
RIDDLE WILLIAM MILLER	IL	35W	61
RIDEN FRANK LEE	MO	11W	15
RIDENHOUR DARWIN BRUCE	CA	47E	36
RIDENOUR EDWIN MICHAEL	AZ	43E	48
RIDENOUR WILLIAM ALBERT	OR	43W	21
RIDEOUT DAVID JAMES	CA	34W	17
RIDER ARNOLD TILMAN	GA	12W	90
RIDER EARL CONRAD JR	MI	29W	73
RIDER JAMES AUSTIN JR	WA	60E	1
RIDER SAMUEL DEWEY JR	WV	42E	56
RIDGE FELIX DENNIS	TX	37W	69
RIDGE JESSE LEE	OK	22W	7
RIDGE WILLIAM FRANCIS	NJ	19W	108
RIDGEWAY RICHARD	IL	01W	21
RIDGEWAY WILLIE JAMES	AL	12W	84
RIDGWAY CLYDE MOSES	CA	12E	76
RIDINGS LESTER LEON	MO	32E	27
RIDINGS LOUIS	CA	07E	105
RIDLEY GLENN THOMAS	TN	11W	25
RIDOUT CHARLES SAMUEL	DC	09E	49
RIEBLI JOSEPH ROBERT	WA	23E	31
RIECK JOHN JAMES JR	OH	22E	18
RIEDE RONALD EDGAR	MO	49E	25
RIEDEL ROBERT EUGENE	KS	02E	70
RIEDERER CARL JOSEPH	WI	31W	18
RIEDLBERGER GERALD FRANK	MN	33E	22
RIEGEL ARTHUR WILLIAM JR	NY	30E	94
RIEGEL JOHN FRANKLIN	PA	32E	27
RIEGEL TERRY LEE	IN	36E	32
RIEGER CHARLES A III	PA	28E	57
RIEGER RODNEY L	OK	15E	86
RIEHL HARLAN CYRUS	MN	06E	54
RIEK JEFFRY RANDAL	VA	13W	54
RIEKEN LARRY RIEK	NE	27W	22
RIELLY DAVID	OH	40W	26
RIEMER DAVID WALTER	OH	34W	79
RIEPE EVERETT DALE	IL	37W	51
RIES WILLIAM STUART	NY	05E	31
RIESBERG DANNY PAUL	MI	23E	14
RIETSCHY EDWARD CHARLES	MD	02W	135
RIFFE CHARLES DAVID	WV	08W	60
RIFFEY TRACY HARLEY	PA	27E	25
RIFFLE JOSEPH HENRY	MD	41W	65
RIFFLE STANLEY	OH	06E	34
RIGBY OLIS RAY	KS	30E	59
RIGDON RONALD MICHAEL	FL	05W	67
RIGDON WILLIAM FRANCIS	OH	21W	71
RIGG WILLIAM CECIL	CA	05E	48
RIGGINS BILLY G	NC	34E	25
RIGGINS EDDIE	OH	55W	23
RIGGINS GARY RONALD	CA	01E	66
RIGGINS JAMES PATRICK	TX	34W	79
RIGGINS ROBERT LUCIAN JR	TX	28W	2
RIGGINS ROBERT PAUL	IL	51E	33

NAME	STATE	PANEL NO.	LINE NO.
RIGGINS SIM HENRY JR	NJ	09E	43
RIGGLE JOSEPH DALE	PA	03E	132
RIGGLE MARK ANTHONY	IN	27E	67
RIGGLE ROBERT FRANKLIN	KY	45W	22
RIGGS DONALD STEPHEN	IN	31E	38
RIGGS DORSE	FL	06E	67
RIGGS JOSEPH BURNITT	MI	21W	1
RIGGS NIEL BURNS	UT	27E	31
RIGGS RICHARD VERNON	NC	60E	16
RIGGS ROBERT CHARLES	CT	34W	71
RIGGS STEVEN JAMES	NY	45W	34
RIGGS THOMAS FREDERICK	MI	21E	92
RIGGS WALTER RODERICK	CA	47E	26
RIGGS WILLARD WAYNE	CA	45W	9
RIGGS WILLIAM STEVEN	IN	32W	40
RIGHTER ROBERT LE ROY JR	OH	26E	37
RIGHTLER GORDON RAY	MI	16E	70
RIGHTMYER JACK LEE	PA	32W	46
RIGNEY LARRY JAMES	IN	10W	66
RIGSBY BARRY LANE	IN	39E	38
RIGSBY RANDY MARVIN	FL	04W	46
RIJOS TONY	NY	35E	80
RIKARD CHARLES DAVID	SC	16E	38
RIKER RICHARD JOHN	MI	32W	71
RILES DONALD EUGENE	MN	10W	53
RILES JAMES CALVIN	AR	35E	57
RILEY ALDEN LAVERNE	CA	12E	123
RILEY BOBBY LEE	FL	48W	15
RILEY CHARLES FRANKLIN	MO	29E	75
RILEY CHARLES JOHN	IL	11E	99
RILEY CURTIS RAY	OH	51E	1
RILEY DAVID CLARK	MI	11E	95
RILEY DENNIS HARLEN	IN	13W	86
RILEY DENNIS LEROY	PA	32W	46
RILEY DON ROBERT	FL	13W	107
RILEY EDDIE LEE	SC	44W	66
RILEY ERNST	KY	24E	63
RILEY EUGENE LEE	AR	53W	30
RILEY HARRY LEE JR	IL	61E	17
RILEY HOWARD GEORGE	PA	03E	90
RILEY JAMES CALVIN	CA	19E	86
RILEY JAMES FRANCIS	IA	06W	64
RILEY JAMES G	WI	31E	82
RILEY JAMES LEWIS	WV	03E	67
RILEY JAMES THOMAS	IL	40E	68
RILEY JOE ED JR	OK	58E	14
RILEY JOHN PATRICK	NY	49W	37
RILEY KIRK IRWIN	IL	03E	122
RILEY LARRY LLOYD	OK	69E	1
RILEY LESTER JR	MO	13W	106
RILEY MELVIN JOSEPH JR	MO	25E	79
RILEY NATHANIEL JULIUS JR	PA	16W	44
RILEY NEIL EDWARD	PA	10E	93
RILEY PAUL WILLIAM	NY	16E	13
RILEY RICHARD STEPHEN JR	NJ	40W	30
RILEY RICHARD WINFRED	VA	19W	126
RILEY RICKY VAUGHN	CA	54W	18
RILEY RONALD HOWARD	CA	26W	3
RILEY THOMAS EUGENE	MI	61W	16
RILEY THOMAS JAY	MN	30E	18
RILEY THOMAS JOHN	NY	22W	26
RILEY VERNON RAY	OH	11W	64
RILK HARLAN CARL	NJ	26E	80
RIMEL MELVIN LEWIS	PA	35E	9
RIMES TERRY MARTIN	GA	21E	51
RIMMER JAMES EDWARD	IL	11W	94
RIMMER JEARL EDWARD	TN	20E	33
RIMSON MARTIN LUTHER	MI	37E	43
RINARD KEVIN ALONZO	TX	03W	9
RINCK RICHARD JAMES	MI	17W	71
RINDONE MICHAEL GUSTAVE	IA	55W	9
RINDY GREGORY ARNOLD	MI	59E	11
RINEHART FRED GEROLD	CA	20W	104
RINEHART JAMES DALE	CA	43W	36
RINEHART JOSEPH LESTER	DC	37W	24
RINEHART RICHARD BENNETT	MA	05W	108
RINEHART TIMOTHY HOWARD	OH	32E	46
RINES EVERETT EDWARD	CT	12W	84
RING HAROLD KENNETH	KS	31W	18
RINGEL JAMES ROBERT	OH	60E	16
RINGENBERG JEROME JOSEPH	CO	14E	86
RINGENBERGER ROBERT E	IL	06W	25
RINGGOLD LAWRENCE L JR	MD	07E	76
RINGHOFER CURTIS EDWARD	MN	10W	36
RINGHOLM JOHN AZEL	NY	09W	89
RINGLE JAMES MYRON	WI	17E	81
RINGLER ROBERT LEWIS JR	PA	13E	55
RINGOEN MARVIN LEE	MN	13W	94
RINKER FRANCIS M	NY	18E	7
RION DONALD JOSEPH	IL	13E	29
RIORDAN GEORGE WILLIAM	NH	44E	53
RIORDAN JOHN MICHAEL	WA	12E	52
RIORDAN PATRICK CARLISLE	IL	63E	17
RIOS ARTURO RECIO	ID	51E	1
RIOS FIDENCIO GARZA JR	TX	09W	125
RIOS GERADO PEDRO	IL	19W	21
RIOS IGNACIO ELENO	TX	40W	8
RIOS JOSE TOMAS	NY	17W	106
RIOS NOEL LUIS	NJ	30W	69
RIOS PEDRO ANTONIO	PR	24W	70
RIOS ROBERTO PENA	TX	42E	71
RIOS SALVADOR DE LOS SANTOS	TX	32W	22
RIOS SEVERIANO	WI	12W	84
RIOS TEOFILO CARMONE	TX	12E	76
RIOS-MALDONADO FERNANDO	PR	11W	65
RIOS-ROSARIO TEODORITO	PR	46W	33
RIOS-VELAZQUEZ LEONARDO JR	PR	28W	14
RIPANTI JAMES LAWRENCE	DE	29W	40
RIPEL JOHN KENNETH	NY	39E	65
RIPKA HERBERT A	PA	21E	2
RIPLEY LARRY DEAN	OH	38E	12
RIPLEY WILLIAM L	PA	08W	109
RIPLIE GEORGE HENRY	OH	30W	15
RIPORTELLA FRANK J JR	VA	18E	97
RIPPE LARRY ALLAN	IN	10W	110
RIPPEE JON ALAN	MO	42W	22
RIPPEL EUGENE RAYMOND	GM	20W	31
RIPPETOE RAE KELLAND	TN	06W	61
RIPPY TERRY ALLEN	OR	06E	128
RISCH JAMES MICHAEL	WI	04W	81
RISCHE KARL BALTHASAR JR	WI	21E	51
RISH RICHARD LEE	IA	10W	106
RISHER CLARENCE IRWIN	WA	25W	82
RISHER CLARENCE T III	GA	36E	32
RISHER DAVID HORACE	DC	45W	51
RISING ALBERT CHARLES	NY	06E	58
RISINGER GERALD LEE	KY	09W	129
RISINGER JERRY LEROY	TX	11W	25
RISINGER PAUL WILLIAM	VA	29E	53
RISNER JOHN MILTON	NM	08E	99
RISNER WAYNE ERIC	PA	46E	41
RISOLDI VINCENT F	NJ	02E	22
RISSE WILLIAM JOHN	IL	12W	10
RISSI DONALD LOUIS	IL	01W	95
RIST GARY MICHAEL	CA	32E	33
RISTINE DOUGLAS CECIL	NE	47E	54
RISTINEN ARMAND ERVIN	IA	11W	53
RITCH ERNEST EUGENE	OH	34W	53
RITCH HAROLD JUNIOR	TX	02W	67
RITCH JOHN GWIN	AL	39W	45
RITCH MICHAEL EUGENE	NC	39W	13
RITCHEY CLAIR F JR	PA	66E	2
RITCHEY GARY WAYNE	OH	20E	67
RITCHEY LUTHER EDMOND JR	OH	01E	31
RITCHIE BERNARD FREDRICK	VT	26W	21
RITCHIE DAMON LIGOURI	NY	36E	32
RITCHIE DOUGLAS REID	CA	42E	39
RITCHIE EARNEST DEE	GA	23E	83
RITCHIE GLENN GARLAND JR	NC	07W	79
RITCHIE HERMAN HIRAM	OK	04E	71
RITER JAMES LEE	AZ	06W	134
RITSCHARD ROGER LEE	WI	06W	78
RITSEMA WARREN PETER	MI	04W	89
RITSICK EDWARD	PA	44E	20
RITTER ALLEN JEROME	MN	07E	103
RITTER DENNIS LEE	IA	09W	92
RITTER RICHARD FRANK	PA	16E	86
RITTICHIER JACK COLUMBUS	OH	58W	14
RITTLINGER DONALD ANDREW	NY	36W	65
RITZ DAVID GERALD	NY	16W	126
RITZ MARSHALL LEROY	PA	32E	18
RITZAU AUGUST KARL	OR	38W	78
RITZLER RICHARD PAUL	OH	31W	18
RITZSCHKE DAVID AARON	MN	23E	78
RIVARD RICHARD NORMAN	NH	50E	7
RIVAS ARTURO BROWN	TX	42W	22
RIVAS JOSE LUIS	TX	11W	9
RIVEIRA ROBERT CHARLES	HI	07W	86
RIVENBURGH RICHARD WILLIA	CA	01W	132
RIVERA ALFREDO	TX	31W	72
RIVERA ARNOLD JAVIER	TX	41E	27
RIVERA CARLOS JR	MA	06W	117
RIVERA CARLOS MANUEL	NY	49W	44
RIVERA DAVID	NY	18W	50
RIVERA EMILIO	NY	16W	6
RIVERA ERNEST ARBALLO JR	CA	14W	98
RIVERA EUCLIDES	NJ	33W	4
RIVERA FERNANDO A JR	NY	46W	33
RIVERA JAMES	NY	43E	69
RIVERA JESUS	NY	47W	21
RIVERA JOE LEWIS	TX	13W	54
RIVERA JOHN ASDRUBAL	NY	30W	69
RIVERA JOSE A	CA	09E	96
RIVERA JUAN	NY	33W	58
RIVERA JULIAN CABRAL	CA	33W	68
RIVERA MIGUEL ANGEL	NY	08E	18
RIVERA MIGUEL ANGEL	NY	28W	2
RIVERA RAUL	NY	08W	117
RIVERA RAYMOND NITO	AR	33W	42
RIVERA RUBEN	TX	19W	122
RIVERA SANTOS JR	NY	21W	90
RIVERA SILVESTRE MARTINEZ	CA	10W	43
RIVERA THOMAS ANTONIO	PR	21E	115
RIVERA THOMAS SALAS	GM	05E	14
RIVERA-AGOSTO EFRAIN	PR	01W	21
RIVERA-BALAGUER RAFAEL L	NY	21E	80
RIVERA-BARRETO JOSE FERMI	PR	07E	12
RIVERA-BERMUDEZ JOSE ANTO	CA	51W	13
RIVERA-COLON HECTOR	PR	65W	14
RIVERA-CRUZ CRISTOBAL	NY	09W	24
RIVERA-CRUZ MARCELINO	PR	19E	86
RIVERA-DELVALLE MANUEL A	NY	27W	67
RIVERA-FERNANDEZ SAMUEL	PR	33E	22
RIVERA-GALARZA BENIGNO	NY	40W	22
RIVERA-GARCIA WILLIAM	NY	32W	39
RIVERA-LOPEZ JAIME ALBERT		59E	9
RIVERA-MARTES CONFESOR	PR	17E	87
RIVERA-MELENDEZ JESUS D	PR	30E	59
RIVERA-MONTES EDICTOR	PR	07W	28
RIVERA-PAGAN EDUARDO	PR	16W	27
RIVERA-REYES JOSE ALBERTO	NY	04E	114
RIVERA-RUIZ ANDRES	CT	46W	22
RIVERA-TRINIDAD NESTOR JU	NY	26E	106
RIVERA-VELAZQUEZ ANGEL A	PR	40W	67
RIVERE ALVIN PIERIE	LA	28E	93
RIVERS CLARENCE	MI	27E	31
RIVERS HARRY EUGENE	PA	43W	9
RIVERS JETTIE JR	TN	23E	22
RIVERS JOHN WILSON	GA	23E	103
RIVERS MICHAEL ROSS	TX	42E	39
RIVERS NATHAN	SC	27E	55
RIVERS NELSON KEITH	VT	14E	82
RIVERS SANDY MITCHEL	PA	20E	98
RIVERS WILLIAM HOWARD	NC	19E	40
RIVES JOHN ARTHUR JR	IL	35W	55
RIVEST MARK HENRY	MA	09W	9
RIVET PAUL ROBERT	RI	03W	30
RIVIERE FRANK IRA	LA	23E	22
RIX DOUGLAS ALFRED	CA	15E	121
RIXMANN EDWARD HAROLD	WI	21E	29
RIZO ALBERT MARTINEZ	AZ	59E	12
RIZOR DAVID LEE	PA	02E	115
RIZZARDINI TIMOTHY JOSEPH	CA	62E	22
RIZZI RALPH JOSEPH	NY	22E	48
RIZZO JAMES PATRICK	OH	38E	38
RIZZO JOHN MICHAEL JR	NY	14W	34
RIZZO ROBERT CHARLES	CA	21W	48
ROACH CHARLES MICHAEL	IL	22E	1
ROACH FRED LEROY JR	NC	31W	18
ROACH JOHN HAROLD	OH	37W	2
ROACH JOHNNY FRANKLIN	TX	13W	86
ROACH MARION LEE	CA	16W	31
ROACH ORLANDO SILAS	SD	11E	120
ROACH RALPH EDWARD	IN	36W	5
ROACH RICHARD FRANKLIN	OH	08E	68
ROACH RONALD D	NH	39E	11

NAME	STATE	PANEL NO.	LINE NO.
ROACH SYLVESTER	NY	36W	78
ROACH TERENCE RAYMOND JR	MI	38E	38
ROACH THOMAS JOSEPH JR	MI	30W	80
ROADS DENNIS LEE	MS	27W	37
ROAR WILLIAM ARTHUR	AR	53E	7
ROARK ANUND C	CA	61E	18
ROARK EDWARD LEE	OH	07E	41
ROARK JAMES DAVID	VA	29E	85
ROARK ROY ROGERS	IN	12E	110
ROARK WILLIAM MARSHALL	NE	01E	102
ROAT RODNEY ALLEN	MI	41E	53
ROBALIN ALBERT SIMON JR	TX	02W	92
ROBAR STEPHEN FRANK	OH	34W	17
ROBB MARION C	UT	18W	71
ROBB RICHARD ALBERT	KY	14E	24
ROBBINS ARNOLD LEE	NY	10W	47
ROBBINS CHARLES LESTER	CA	15E	35
ROBBINS DENNIS TRUMAN	AR	46W	33
ROBBINS HENRY EARL	TX	14E	59
ROBBINS HUGH MILLER	IN	01E	129
ROBBINS JAMES WALTER	TX	20E	35
ROBBINS JAY LEE JR	CA	31W	19
ROBBINS JERRY CLAYTON	CA	30W	69
ROBBINS JOHN WILLIAM	CO	05E	56
ROBBINS JON PIUS	ND	31W	19
ROBBINS LARRY OLIVER	UT	27W	77
ROBBINS LAWRENCE STEPHEN	OK	07E	91
ROBBINS LEROY BRIAN	AR	43E	69
ROBBINS LESTER WAYNE	NC	15E	64
ROBBINS LONNIE JUNIOR	TN	26E	89
ROBBINS RICHARD JOSEPH	OH	06E	123
ROBBINS RONALD	NJ	19W	4
ROBBINS RUSSELL LINDSEY	TX	19E	18
ROBBINS WAYNE DUSTIN	CT	38E	12
ROBBINS WILLIAM D	GA	13E	12
ROBBINS WILLIAM JAY	MT	14E	131
ROBBLEY RICHARD PHILLIP	IL	03E	41
ROBENA CHARLES EDWARD	NY	41E	27
ROBERG JAMES AUSTIN	MN	22W	114
ROBERGE EDMUND EDWARD	NH	04W	53
ROBERSON ARTHUR PAUL	CA	03W	83
ROBERSON DONALD RADFORD	LA	14E	2
ROBERSON JIMMY DARRELL	MS	13W	128
ROBERSON JIMMY DON	TX	30E	32
ROBERSON JOHN TARRY	FL	40E	29
ROBERSON JOHN WILL	TX	22W	114
ROBERSON JOSEPH THOMAS	AL	11W	60
ROBERSON LARRY MICHAEL	NC	45E	60
ROBERSON LEONARD WADE	WA	24E	92
ROBERSON ROBERT SIDNEY JR	TX	45W	9
ROBERSON SAMUEL ALBERT	NC	28W	63
ROBERSON SAMUEL LOUIS	MO	12W	93
ROBERSON WILBURN	SC	11E	10
ROBERSON WILLIAM THOMAS	TX	33W	23
ROBERTS ALAN RICHARD	MI	45E	42
ROBERTS ALBERT C	OK	05E	90
ROBERTS ALBERT FRED	FL	02E	13
ROBERTS ALTON REESE	NC	04W	122
ROBERTS ARCHIE JAMES JR	CA	58E	25
ROBERTS ARTHUR JAMES JR	OH	36E	33
ROBERTS BEN	GA	19E	31
ROBERTS BILLY DALE	TX	32W	34
ROBERTS BILLY JACK	TX	13W	69
ROBERTS BOBBY LEE	TX	19W	109
ROBERTS CHARLES ALAN	TX	04E	40
ROBERTS CHARLES CAMILLE	TN	09E	8
ROBERTS CHARLES DWAINE	OK	19W	8
ROBERTS CHARLES G	PA	30E	66
ROBERTS CHARLES LEROY	OR	12E	47
ROBERTS CHARLES PRICE	CO	01W	64
ROBERTS CHARLES W JR	GA	03W	110
ROBERTS CHARLES WADDELL	LA	26E	107
ROBERTS CLAUDE	FL	49E	26
ROBERTS CLIFFORD ALTON	CA	02E	34
ROBERTS CLIFFORD JOSEPH	CA	39W	22
ROBERTS CYRUS S IV	NY	05E	127
ROBERTS DANNY RAY	TN	14W	102
ROBERTS DAVID JOHN	FL	55E	28
ROBERTS DAVID OWEN	IN	36E	33
ROBERTS DAVID WILLIAM	OR	16E	126
ROBERTS DENNIS RAY	IN	20W	93
ROBERTS EDDIE LEROY	AR	24E	41
ROBERTS ERVIN BRADLEY	OH	47W	22
ROBERTS FRANK JAMES	FL	39W	52
ROBERTS FREDDIE JOE	NM	45E	5
ROBERTS GARY KENNETH	SC	59W	13
ROBERTS GARY LEE	NJ	27E	7
ROBERTS GERALD JASON JR	CT	25E	76
ROBERTS GERALD RAY	TX	03E	120
ROBERTS HARLEY RICHARD	NY	53W	38
ROBERTS HAROLD JAMES JR	OR	02E	11
ROBERTS HERBERT JR	TN	32E	33
ROBERTS HERMAN DAVID	KY	52W	13
ROBERTS HOWARD TAYLOR	TX	62W	16
ROBERTS JAMES AARON F JR	AZ	07W	101
ROBERTS JAMES ALLEN	PA	17W	129
ROBERTS JAMES RICHARD	VA	35W	85
ROBERTS JERRY ARDELL	KY	08E	133
ROBERTS JERRY LEE	MI	02E	72
ROBERTS JERRY MARCO	NM	31E	83
ROBERTS JOE RAYMOND JR	MS	06W	2
ROBERTS JOHN ALLEN	TX	28E	86
ROBERTS JOHN CLYDE	TX	36W	23
ROBERTS JOHN EDWARD JR	WV	29W	48
ROBERTS JOHN HENRY	NY	05E	91
ROBERTS JOHN J	AZ	20E	35
ROBERTS JOHN LEONARD	TN	03W	121
ROBERTS JOHN LESLIE	IN	53W	30
ROBERTS JOHN WAYNE	ME	28E	4
ROBERTS JOHN WILSON III	MD	13W	47
ROBERTS JOSEPH RAY	IL	04E	77
ROBERTS JULIUS JR	NY	03E	132
ROBERTS KENNETH DAVID	WI	14E	125
ROBERTS KENNETH EUGENE	SC	33W	81
ROBERTS KENNETH RAY	CA	48E	20
ROBERTS KERMIT BRUCE	FL	24W	48
ROBERTS LESTER LEE	FL	08E	12
ROBERTS LLOYD VERNON	SC	20E	98
ROBERTS LONNIE BARRY	GA	11W	76
ROBERTS LOUIS WADE	CA	36W	78
ROBERTS MARVIN JAMES	LA	28W	75
ROBERTS MICHAEL ALLEN	CA	26E	107
ROBERTS MICHAEL EDWARD	OH	40W	15
ROBERTS MICHAEL LAND	MS	34E	31
ROBERTS MICHAEL STEPHEN	NC	22W	69
ROBERTS NOEL WAYNE	AR	26E	86
ROBERTS PAUL MICHAEL	IN	34E	91
ROBERTS PAUL MICHAEL	FL	19W	47
ROBERTS RICHARD DANIEL	PA	21W	9
ROBERTS RICHARD DEAN	MI	28W	40
ROBERTS RICHARD STEPHEN	KS	40E	29
ROBERTS RONALD EUGENE	IL	35W	6
ROBERTS RONNY DEAN	UT	30E	70
ROBERTS STEPHEN LORD	CA	23W	67
ROBERTS TERRY	IA	32E	33
ROBERTS THEODORE IRWIN	KY	11W	97
ROBERTS THOMAS JOHN	WI	08W	131
ROBERTS THOMAS WARREN	OH	44W	28
ROBERTS THURSTON CRAIG	TX	05W	18
ROBERTS VIRGIL JESSIE	NM	34W	61
ROBERTS WALLACE	OH	09W	97
ROBERTS WALTER EUGENE	TX	21W	90
ROBERTS WALTER JAMES	MI	06W	41
ROBERTS WAYNE LEROY	FL	45E	50
ROBERTS WILLIAM	NE	14E	128
ROBERTS WILLIAM CLAUDE	NC	45E	28
ROBERTS WILLIAM JACKSON	TN	35E	50
ROBERTS WILLIAM JOHN	OH	18W	97
ROBERTSON ALLEN HARVEY	TN	23W	57
ROBERTSON ALVIN WARNER	OH	36W	87
ROBERTSON ANDREW JAMES	IN	12E	11
ROBERTSON BENJAMIN F JR	AL	22E	1
ROBERTSON BOBBY LEE	SC	06W	108
ROBERTSON BRISTOL JR	MA	28E	98
ROBERTSON CHARLES EDWARD	WV	30E	32
ROBERTSON CHARLES WILLIAM	MA	14E	2
ROBERTSON CLIFTON BOYD JR	CA	25E	53
ROBERTSON DAVID WILLIAM	NJ	54W	6
ROBERTSON DON MARK	OK	26W	56
ROBERTSON DONALD REED	VA	28W	51
ROBERTSON ELLIS ANDRE		29W	83
ROBERTSON GEORGE LORD	MD	05W	65
ROBERTSON GERALD WILLIAM	AR	39E	38
ROBERTSON JAMES WAYNE	LA	16W	37
ROBERTSON JIMMY KARON	IL	37E	13
ROBERTSON JOE CARROL	CA	02E	13
ROBERTSON JOHN CHESTER	FL	06E	40
ROBERTSON JOHN CRAIG	NE	67E	1
ROBERTSON JOHN ERNEST	CA	05W	89
ROBERTSON JOHN HARTLEY	AL	64E	8
ROBERTSON JOHN LEIGHTON	WA	10E	103
ROBERTSON JOHNNY BILL JR	GA	23W	114
ROBERTSON KENNETH LEE	NM	06W	100
ROBERTSON LEONARD	NY	01W	54
ROBERTSON MARK JOHN	MI	05W	94
ROBERTSON MARSHALL EUGENE	VA	19W	122
ROBERTSON MARVIN KENT	MT	55W	37
ROBERTSON MERLE ELDON	CA	44W	18
ROBERTSON PAUL ALLEN	MS	03E	136
ROBERTSON PIERCE IRVING	CT	11E	64
ROBERTSON RAYMOND L JR	MT	10W	118
ROBERTSON ROBERT ALLAN	CA	01W	39
ROBERTSON ROBERT GLENN	PA	14E	88
ROBERTSON RONALD EDWARD	VA	21W	40
ROBERTSON RONNIE LEE	NC	19W	47
ROBERTSON ROY ALLEN JR	KY	19E	18
ROBERTSON THOMAS HARRY	IL	27W	66
ROBERTSON TOMMY WAYNE	TX	07W	84
ROBERTSON WILLIAM LEE	OH	09E	18
ROBERTSON WILLIAM S III	CA	17E	128
ROBESON EVART EUGENE	SD	30E	86
ROBEY RICHARD NEAL	OH	23E	7
ROBICHAUD ROGER EDWARD	NH	19W	122
ROBILLARD LARRY KENNETH	CA	18W	56
ROBILLARD WILFRED ROLAND	NH	02E	117
ROBILOTTO GEORGE FRANCIS	NY	42E	40
ROBIN DAVID ALAN	CA	22E	18
ROBINETTE CHARLES EDWARD	AZ	37W	77
ROBINETTE DANNY LEON	TX	09W	86
ROBINS JAMES MILTON	IA	49W	26
ROBINSON ALAN JOSEPH	MO	52W	31
ROBINSON ALFRED WILLIAM	VA	20E	35
ROBINSON BRUCE ALLEN	CA	39W	13
ROBINSON BRUCE ELTON	VA	32W	83
ROBINSON CALVIN	SC	35W	78
ROBINSON CHARLES DAVID	AZ	27W	103
ROBINSON CHARLES HARVEY	IN	30E	19
ROBINSON CHARLES HENRY	SC	21W	25
ROBINSON CHARLES JOHN	MA	35W	51
ROBINSON CHARLES WAYNE	MS	06W	57
ROBINSON CHARLIE JR	AL	22W	26
ROBINSON CLARENCE	AR	33E	31
ROBINSON CLARENCE JR	MD	32W	73
ROBINSON CLIFFORD LEROY	IL	08E	8
ROBINSON CLINTON CURTIS	MD	05W	35
ROBINSON DALLAS DEAN	TN	04W	89
ROBINSON DONALD FREDERICK	NY	20W	128
ROBINSON DONALD RAYFORD	VA	44W	6
ROBINSON DONALD RICHARD	TN	10E	67
ROBINSON EDWARD	MO	13W	101
ROBINSON EUGENE FRANCIS	MA	05E	134
ROBINSON EUGENE MAJOR		20W	76
ROBINSON FLOYD HENRY	KS	29W	23
ROBINSON FLOYD IRWIN	CA	28E	105
ROBINSON FRANCIS JOSEPH	LA	55E	29
ROBINSON FRANK EUGENE	TX	26E	37
ROBINSON FREDDIE LEE	SC	20E	10
ROBINSON GEORGE	MD	26W	50
ROBINSON GEORGE BERNARD	OK	11W	2
ROBINSON GEORGE RAY	NY	30W	29
ROBINSON GERALD ARDEN	WI	20E	10
ROBINSON GORDON LEE	TX	01E	73
ROBINSON GUS BLAKELY	CA	12W	128
ROBINSON HAROLD JACK JR	IL	37W	35
ROBINSON HENRY MILLARD JR	CT	31W	19
ROBINSON HERMAN DAVID	GA	46W	1
ROBINSON HERMAN RAY	AL	16E	86
ROBINSON HORACE VALLEY JR	AR	38W	21
ROBINSON HORRIS GENE	MS	41E	2
ROBINSON HOWARD CLINTON	CT	11E	120
ROBINSON JAMES DELANO	NC	37W	24
ROBINSON JAMES EDWARD	TN	38E	12
ROBINSON JAMES LLOYD	OH	27E	55
ROBINSON JAMES MARCUS	NC	33W	43
ROBINSON JAMES P	NJ	33E	60
ROBINSON JAMES WILLIAM JR	IL	06E	103

NAME	STATE	PANEL NO.	LINE NO.
ROBINSON JERRY ALVIN	NC	15E	50
ROBINSON JERRY LYNN	AZ	45W	28
ROBINSON JIMMIE LEE	SC	36W	76
ROBINSON JIMMIE LEE	AL	09W	117
ROBINSON JOEQUIN	MS	18W	43
ROBINSON JOHN	NY	09W	29
ROBINSON JOHN CALVIN II	GA	49W	44
ROBINSON JOHN JACKLON	DC	16W	82
ROBINSON JOHN LEO	AL	04E	58
ROBINSON JOHN WILLIAM JR	SC	41W	39
ROBINSON JOHNNY LEE	MS	32E	89
ROBINSON JOSEPH BRUCE	KY	38E	39
ROBINSON JOSEPH EARL	MI	45E	50
ROBINSON JOSEPH LUTHER	VA	05E	75
ROBINSON JOSEPH ROBERT	NH	17E	64
ROBINSON KENNETH DALE	IN	10E	57
ROBINSON KENNETH JAMES	CA	29W	13
ROBINSON LANCE ALLEN	WI	04W	71
ROBINSON LARRY LEE	MD	03W	39
ROBINSON LARRY MICHEAL	MI	19W	34
ROBINSON LARRY WARREN	NE	14W	1
ROBINSON LEONARD JR	TX	14E	106
ROBINSON LEROY	NY	07E	114
ROBINSON LEWIS MERRITT	MI	21E	56
ROBINSON LIONEL LARUE	DE	49E	15
ROBINSON LOYD EUGENE	WV	03W	72
ROBINSON LUCIEN	SC	40E	55
ROBINSON LUTHER	OH	21E	51
ROBINSON MARK EDWARD	CA	14E	82
ROBINSON MARSHALL LEE	NC	35E	50
ROBINSON MARTIN ROBERT	PA	07E	3
ROBINSON MARVIN RAY	TX	18W	72
ROBINSON MELVIN	SC	03W	55
ROBINSON MICHAEL BERNARD	KS	14W	9
ROBINSON MICHAEL JAMES	NJ	16W	72
ROBINSON MITCHELL	NJ	11W	117
ROBINSON NATHAN LYEN	KY	41E	31
ROBINSON O'DELL	MO	05E	76
ROBINSON PAUL WILLIAM	MS	34E	81
ROBINSON PHILIP OWEN	WY	06E	50
ROBINSON RALPH LEWIS	MD	01W	79
ROBINSON RANDALL CHARLES	OH	22W	27
ROBINSON RAYMOND CARL	MI	06E	66
ROBINSON RAYMOND DOUGLAS	WI	52W	24
ROBINSON REMBRANDT CECIL	PA	01W	15
ROBINSON ROBERT DOUGLAS	TX	46E	22
ROBINSON ROBERT EDWARD	IL	11E	23
ROBINSON ROBERT EUGENE	IL	19E	111
ROBINSON ROBERT JAMES	NJ	21W	2
ROBINSON RONALD EUGENE	NC	14W	91
ROBINSON ROY RAY	OH	40E	55
ROBINSON SAMUEL PERCELL	MD	43E	31
ROBINSON SHEPPARD JR	FL	05E	49
ROBINSON STANLEY A JR	NY	14E	96
ROBINSON TERRY ALAN	NY	50W	31
ROBINSON THOMAS DALE	OK	32E	46
ROBINSON THOMAS LEON	MI	29W	63
ROBINSON TIMOTHY CHARLES	MT	17W	106
ROBINSON TIMOTHY GEORGE	MN	51E	1
ROBINSON TOMMY LEE	FL	29W	13
ROBINSON VAL CLARK	UT	06W	125
ROBINSON WALTER	IL	40E	55
ROBINSON WALTER R JR	TX	18E	127
ROBINSON WARREN JAMES	MN	49E	47
ROBINSON WILLARD MICHAEL	PA	48E	47
ROBINSON WILLIAM D JR	MD	43W	30
ROBINSON WILLIE CLYDE JR	GA	25E	44
ROBINSON WILLIE JAMES	AL	04E	65
ROBINSON WINSTON TERRY	AR	26E	16
ROBIRDS PATRICK DALE	OK	21W	15
ROBISON DAVID LEE	WV	37W	47
ROBISON DONALD ROBERT	AK	44E	30
ROBISON EDWARD KEITH	AR	33E	31
ROBISON GARY HERBERT	MI	04W	36
ROBISON JIM BRUCE	CA	05E	14
ROBISON LARRY WAYNE	AL	16W	40
ROBISON WILLIAM RANDALL	PA	03W	107
ROBITAILLE PAUL EDWARD	MA	41E	2
ROBLE JOSEPH EDWARD	PA	43W	9
ROBLEDO EFRAIN JULIO	TX	26E	63
ROBLEDO JESUS JR	TX	47W	22
ROBLEDO RAUL	LA	44E	53
ROBLES CECILIO JR	NY	10W	87
ROBLES JOAQUIN	PR	44W	66
ROBLES-MIRANDA JOSE ANTON	NY	16E	126
ROBSON TIMOTHY FRANCIS	WI	24W	61
ROBSON WILLIAM REID		37E	67
ROBUSTELLINI DAVID W	CA	10E	61
ROBY CHARLES DONALD	TX	16E	13
ROCCO RICHARD MICHAEL	NY	29W	57
ROCCO WILLIAM FRANK	PA	26W	35
ROCHA DANIEL ALBERT	CO	48E	33
ROCHA FELICIANO	CA	20W	60
ROCHA GEORGE XAVIER	CA	32E	18
ROCHA JOSE MARIE	WI	05W	84
ROCHA RAYMOND GONZALEZ	TX	44E	20
ROCHA ROBERT SILAS	CA	06W	59
ROCHA ROBERTO JR	TX	08E	61
ROCHA RUBEN LOPEZ	TX	07E	3
ROCHA RUDOLFO LEONARD JR	TX	46E	12
ROCHACZ RICHARD JOHN	IL	32W	73
ROCHE JOHN	CA	15W	60
ROCHE JOHN DONALD	MI	32E	5
ROCHE JON PATRICK	NY	35W	54
ROCHE KENNETH WAYNE	IA	40E	64
ROCHE MATTHEW PETER JR	NY	15W	123
ROCHEZ ESTEBAN VALERIANO	NY	05W	11
ROCHKES FRANCIS ALBERT	IL	24E	97
ROCHOWICZ WAYNE CARL	PA	02W	12
ROCK ALLEN CLARENCE	VT	10E	22
ROCK DON LESLIE	WA	16W	96
ROCK GERALD FRANCIS	MI	38W	5
ROCKEFELLER RONALD EDWARD	NY	59W	27
ROCKENBAUGH WAYNE M	MD	22E	92
ROCKENSTYRE RICHARD	NY	25E	76
ROCKETT ALTON CRAIG JR	AL	21E	38
ROCKEY MICHAEL CRAIG	MI	09W	25
ROCKOWER HENRY NEIL	PA	12W	84
ROCKY ROBERT EDWARD	NJ	10E	110
ROCZEN ALEXANDER ANTHONY	NY	53W	13
ROD RONALD FRANCIS	LA	03E	123
RODARTE ALEXANDER D	CA	06E	23
RODDAM RODDNEY ALLEN	CA	63W	12
RODDICK WILLIAM HENRY	CA	21W	19
RODDY DONALD BARRETT	MI	03E	61
RODEN GEORGE COLUMBUS JR	KY	02E	113
RODEN JOHN JOSEPH WILLIAM	TX	17W	69
RODENBECK RODERICK JAMES	IL	15E	17
RODENBERG JOHN FREDERICK	MD	24E	101
RODERICK RONALD	MA	37E	27
RODERICK SCOTT JAMES	ME	14W	55
RODERIGUES PAUL IRVING	MA	24W	20
RODGERS BILLY GENE	OK	23E	104
RODGERS BOBBY RAY	AL	33E	52
RODGERS CARROLL L	LA	12E	127
RODGERS GARY GENE	CA	45W	9
RODGERS GREGORY WAYNE	PA	43W	65
RODGERS HAYWOOD	NC	03W	131
RODGERS JAMES HAMILTON	GA	27W	2
RODGERS JERRY PAUL	TX	24E	41
RODGERS JOHN ARLINGTON	CA	51E	12
RODGERS JOHN CARL	NC	19W	63
RODGERS JOHN JOSEPH	NJ	14E	38
RODGERS JOHN THOMAS	CA	14W	87
RODGERS JOHNNY MICHAEL	TX	08W	32
RODGERS LARRY JOE	TX	45E	14
RODGERS LARRY MORGAN	PA	30W	59
RODGERS LUIA	NM	42E	9
RODGERS MARTIN LEROY	TX	08W	56
RODGERS MOSES	NC	22W	27
RODGERS ROBERT LOUIS	MO	27W	97
RODGERS TILLMAN DAVID JR	SC	18W	68
RODKEY WILLIAM EUGENE	PA	25E	40
RODMAN DAVID B	PA	57E	9
RODNEY CARLISLE ANTHONY	NY	62W	16
RODOWICZ MICHAEL JOHN	DE	17W	118
RODREICK RONALD NELSON	CA	30E	32
RODRICK ROBERT LAWRENCE	MA	57W	20
RODRIGUES DANIEL EVERETTE	MA	33E	53
RODRIGUES EUGENIO	CA	23E	113
RODRIGUES GARY WAYNE	CA	19E	45
RODRIGUES JOE G JR	TX	30W	29
RODRIGUES JOHN NETO	CA	12E	116
RODRIGUES JOSEPH MICHAEL	CA	36E	84
RODRIGUES RICHARD	MA	10W	99
RODRIGUES RONALD	NV	16W	50
RODRIGUEZ ALBERT EDUARDO	NY	44E	20
RODRIGUEZ ARTURO	TX	15E	29
RODRIGUEZ ARTURO SERNA	HI	58W	4
RODRIGUEZ BENITO BOBO	CA	48E	32
RODRIGUEZ CALIXTRO S	TX	30W	59
RODRIGUEZ CARLOS MARIO	NY	13E	127
RODRIGUEZ CASIMIRO JR	TX	51E	1
RODRIGUEZ CESAR RODRIGO	IL	32W	9
RODRIGUEZ COLON RICARDO	NY	06E	59
RODRIGUEZ DAVID	NY	33W	28
RODRIGUEZ DENNIS JAMES	IL	17W	43
RODRIGUEZ DOMINGO JR	TX	43E	31
RODRIGUEZ EDWARD	NY	32E	48
RODRIGUEZ ELIAS RANGEL	TX	10E	125
RODRIGUEZ ENCARNASION	CA	18W	105
RODRIGUEZ FRANCISCO JR	TX	26W	79
RODRIGUEZ FRANK LOUIS	HI	47E	6
RODRIGUEZ GEORGE	WA	10W	87
RODRIGUEZ GUILLERMO	PR	06W	115
RODRIGUEZ ISRAEL	NY	22W	93
RODRIGUEZ JACK CHARLES	NY	05E	36
RODRIGUEZ JESSE EMITERIO	CA	33E	31
RODRIGUEZ JESSE NICKLUS	TX	03E	91
RODRIGUEZ JOE	TX	23W	18
RODRIGUEZ JOE	MI	17W	19
RODRIGUEZ JOE IGNACIO	CA	21W	120
RODRIGUEZ JOE STELO	AZ	42E	9
RODRIGUEZ JOEL	TX	05E	124
RODRIGUEZ JOSE ESTABAN	NY	30E	59
RODRIGUEZ JOSEPH	IL	50E	20
RODRIGUEZ JUAN ARMANDO	TX	26E	107
RODRIGUEZ JULIAN ROBLES	TX	14W	6
RODRIGUEZ LOUIS	PA	36W	54
RODRIGUEZ LOUIS	CA	23W	52
RODRIGUEZ LUCAS HERRERA	PR	41W	31
RODRIGUEZ MANUEL JOE	CA	28E	62
RODRIGUEZ MANUEL JR	TX	23W	47
RODRIGUEZ MARGARITO JR	TX	08W	86
RODRIGUEZ MATIAS T JR	TX	10E	122
RODRIGUEZ NICK NATHANIEL	NY	02W	48
RODRIGUEZ OSCAR FRANCISCO	CA	14W	47
RODRIGUEZ PAUL DAVID	CO	06E	86
RODRIGUEZ PAUL M JR	AZ	22E	72
RODRIGUEZ PEDRO ANGEL	IN	62W	2
RODRIGUEZ PEDRO JUAN	TX	47W	31
RODRIGUEZ RALPH O	NY	33E	93
RODRIGUEZ RAMON SAUL	NY	39E	53
RODRIGUEZ RAYMOND	NY	40E	29
RODRIGUEZ REGINALD JOSEPH	CA	32W	52
RODRIGUEZ REINALDO REIN	PR	05W	50
RODRIGUEZ REYNALDO SALAIS	TX	20W	51
RODRIGUEZ ROBERT	TX	12W	9
RODRIGUEZ ROGER ESPINOZA	CA	07E	122
RODRIGUEZ ROMAN DURAN	MI	13W	16
RODRIGUEZ ROMIRO C	CA	03E	119
RODRIGUEZ RUDOLPH	CA	03E	27
RODRIGUEZ SAMMY PINA	TX	08W	95
RODRIGUEZ VICENTE QUINTAN	TX	07E	54
RODRIGUEZ-ACEVEDO JOSE	PR	42E	32
RODRIGUEZ-COTTO ANGEL L	PR	20W	77
RODRIGUEZ-ESTREMERA ANGEL	PR	07E	104
RODRIGUEZ-GUZMAN ABELARDO	PR	20W	126
RODRIGUEZ-LEBRON SANTIAGO	PR	54E	40
RODRIGUEZ-RIVERA JAIME	PR	11W	60
RODRIGUEZ-RODRIGUEZ PEDRO	PR	20W	8
RODRIQUEZ ARTURO CANTU	CA	16W	90
RODRIQUEZ FELIX	TX	03E	101
RODRIQUEZ JOAQUIN	NY	38W	8
RODRIQUEZ LEONDIS ENRIQUE	TX	47W	52
RODRIQUEZ PEDRO S JR	TX	43W	40
RODRIQUEZ SAMUEL	PA	33W	17
RODRIQUEZ SAMUEL HENRI	ID	63E	17
RODRIQUEZ TOBY S JR	TX	26W	35
RODZEN BERNARD JAMES	OH	07E	21
ROE DONALD JAY	TX	55W	31
ROE JEFFREY TERRY	MI	10E	84
ROE JERRY LEE	TX	39E	12
ROE JOHN ELMER	TX	48W	30
ROE JOHN MARSHALL	WI	06W	64
ROE JOHN PHELEN	NY	20W	41

NAME	STATE	PANEL NO.	LINE NO.
ROE KENNETH ALLEN	MI	31E	7
ROE LINUS ROBERT	CA	32W	16
ROE PHILLIP WILLARD	CA	22E	113
ROE ROYCE EVERT	WI	31W	56
ROE TIMOTHY ROY	IN	13W	59
ROEBUCK ROBERT LENNON	TN	31W	72
ROECKL CHARLES	NY	29W	83
ROECKL JOHN DANIEL	MS	09E	102
ROEDER CHARLES THOMAS	PA	40W	55
ROEDERER JOHN STEPHEN	NY	22E	121
ROEDIGER CHRISS LESLIE	CA	17W	52
ROEGLIN WILLIAM JOHN	WI	16W	24
ROEHL ELWOOD JOHN	WI	18W	129
ROEHMER ROBERT PAUL	MD	27W	97
ROEHRICH RONALD L	AR	34E	70
ROELL MICHAEL CONRAD	NJ	20E	123
ROEMER DONALD PETER	NY	40E	30
ROENTSCH ROBERT QUENTIN	NH	05E	52
ROEPKE PHILLIP WRAY	MO	13E	128
ROERINK GARY DOYLE	MI	30E	73
ROESCH HEINZ KURT	NY	02W	16
ROESE ALAN JOHN	NY	22E	2
ROESLER ARTHUR CLEON	IL	28E	71
ROESLER JOHN ONDERDONK	CO	35E	26
ROESLER RICHARD ALFRED	WI	60W	12
ROESNER DANA HYLAND	OR	42E	40
ROEST DOUGLAS RAY	WI	13W	123
ROG EDWARD JOSEPH JR	IL	04W	104
ROGALLA GEORGE HENRY	MI	06W	36
ROGALSKE PAUL FRANK	WI	11W	81
ROGAN JAMES PAUL	UT	43E	60
ROGERS ALLEN TEBBS JR	TN	20E	67
ROGERS ARCHIE DEE	OH	35W	78
ROGERS BILLY LEE	IN	15W	14
ROGERS BOBBY DALE	MD	33W	29
ROGERS CHARLES DAVID	NC	29W	14
ROGERS CHARLES EDWARD	IN	19E	40
ROGERS CHARLES LEE	KY	14E	40
ROGERS CLARANCE W JR	GA	21E	115
ROGERS CLARK FRANKLIN	NC	09W	29
ROGERS CLAUDE BENTON	AR	15W	10
ROGERS CLAYTON GEORGE JR	AL	03E	91
ROGERS CORDELL BRUCE	IA	23W	1
ROGERS CRAIG RAY	IA	14W	9
ROGERS DANIEL GORDON	TX	05E	30
ROGERS DAVID ALAN	CT	13W	38
ROGERS DAVID CLYDE	MO	17E	13
ROGERS DAVID ROBERT	NV	53E	22
ROGERS DEAN FRANCIS	OR	08W	104
ROGERS DOUGLAS EUGENE	WY	30E	73
ROGERS DOUGLAS MANUEL	NJ	62W	11
ROGERS EDWARD FRANCIS	MA	44E	30
ROGERS EDWARD LEROY	GA	15W	88
ROGERS GARY HENDERSON	FL	08E	77
ROGERS GEORGE PATRICK	IA	19E	54
ROGERS GUINN JUNELL	AR	14E	71
ROGERS HARVEY DAVID JR	CA	11W	18
ROGERS HENRY LEWIS	KY	37W	9
ROGERS HERSHEL GALE	IL	02W	28
ROGERS HORACE POPE JR	NC	08E	88
ROGERS HOWARD LEONARD JR	VA	29E	53
ROGERS JACK	MT	31E	16
ROGERS JAMES STEVEN	CA	18W	91
ROGERS JERRY EUGENE	GA	22W	108
ROGERS JERRY LEE	OH	26E	63
ROGERS JIMMIE DALE	TX	29E	76
ROGERS JOHN AVERY	TN	34E	82
ROGERS JOHN DAVID	NM	20E	123
ROGERS KENNETH FAULKNER	OH	10W	28
ROGERS KENNETH LEE	PA	36E	59
ROGERS LARRY LEE	OH	03W	15
ROGERS LESTER A	MO	05E	91
ROGERS MICHAEL DEAN	NC	37W	19
ROGERS MICHAEL FREDRICK	CA	21W	102
ROGERS ORVILLE CURTIS JR	TX	06W	69
ROGERS PHILLIP	NY	55W	37
ROGERS RANDAL LEE	WA	32W	83
ROGERS RICHARD LEO	MA	36W	23
ROGERS ROBERT CHARLES	IL	29W	82
ROGERS ROBERT DAVID	MI	32W	46
ROGERS ROBERT GENE	CA	14W	66
ROGERS ROBERT JAMES	IL	05W	82
ROGERS ROBERT LEE	TN	34E	44
ROGERS ROBERT LEE	LA	11W	56
ROGERS ROBERT RICHARD	WY	26E	31
ROGERS ROBERT RUSSELL	GA	21E	52
ROGERS RODNEY ROBERT	IL	14W	20
ROGERS RONALD DEAN	IL	18W	17
ROGERS RONALD EDWIN	IN	09W	5
ROGERS RONALD LEE	CA	56E	15
ROGERS RONNIE VAGO	AL	05W	28
ROGERS ROY JAMES	FL	13W	55
ROGERS ROY RUMSEY	MI	08E	116
ROGERS SCOTT CAMERON	OR	44E	11
ROGERS THOMAS FRANKLIN JR	TN	16W	90
ROGERS THOMAS SAMUEL	NJ	08W	18
ROGERS WAYNE JOHNATHEN	CA	38W	78
ROGERS WILLIAM FRANCIS	NC	59E	12
ROGERS WILLIAM HENRY	MI	43E	31
ROGERS WILLIAM JAMES IV	NY	28W	52
ROGERS WILLIAM LOUIS	TX	41W	7
ROGERS WILLIAM PAUL JR	WV	19E	98
ROGERS WILLIAM T IV	AL	43E	32
ROGERS WILLIE JR	TN	18W	91
ROGERS WILLIS JR	IL	21W	56
ROGERSON CHARLES ROLAND	FL	21E	24
ROGERSON GARRY EARL	UT	40E	47
ROGGOW NORMAN LEE	IA	27E	75
ROGIERS CHARLES JOSEPH	IL	27E	46
ROGNE WILLIAM ROBERT	NV	13W	98
ROGOFF JAMES BILL	CA	04E	121
ROGONE JOHN PIO	CA	54W	19
ROGOWSKI RONALD CHESTER	IL	27E	12
ROGUS ANDREW JOSEPH JR	IL	09W	106
ROHAN FREDERICK LEO	IL	61E	17
ROHAN WILLIAM JAMES	WI	10E	103
ROHDE LLOYD HANS	OR	12E	131
ROHLEDER DONALD WILLIAM	MD	11E	69
ROHLER SIDNEY EARL	OH	12W	52
ROHLFSEN LYLE ERVIN	IA	21E	115
ROHLINGER JOSEPH EARL	VA	06W	33
ROHN HERSHEL HILLARY JR	FL	24E	84
ROHR JOHN WILLARD	MA	12W	98
ROHRING KEVIN MICHAEL	NY	17E	59
ROHRKASTE RONALD EDWARD	IL	38E	59
ROHTVALI ARVI	NY	55W	37
ROHWELLER ROBERT TIM	FL	26W	21
ROKASKI MARK CHARLES	PA	63W	12
ROKER JONATHAN CECIL	FL	08E	45
ROLAND CHARLES EDWARD	FL	24E	41
ROLAND GEORGE RAY	CA	26E	3
ROLAND HULAN DUANE	MS	26E	51
ROLAND JAMES CURTISS	GA	13W	124
ROLAND JOHN P	TX	03E	124
ROLAND LARUS WAYNE	OR	29E	97
ROLAND THOMAS MILTON	UT	50W	20
ROLDAN WILLIAM JUNIOR	PA	18E	128
ROLEN SAMUEL FLOYD	OK	61E	18
ROLES JOHN WAYNE	CA	15W	8
ROLEY HERBERT WALLACE	CA	52W	1
ROLF GERALD R	OH	08E	105
ROLF TOMMIE ALLEN	TX	64E	8
ROLFE DARYL EDSON	MI	21E	95
ROLFE GARY FAY	KS	30W	45
ROLFE MICHAEL DUANE	MD	43E	60
ROLFS GERHARD M	CT	18W	76
ROLLASON WILLIAM DAVID	CA	08W	29
ROLLE JOHN BERKLEY	FL	35W	79
ROLLE MELVIN	FL	09E	124
ROLLEN CLARENCE EDWARD	LA	16E	82
ROLLER BENJAMIN C JR	PA	10E	43
ROLLER CHARLES BENNETT JR	TX	16W	40
ROLLER WILLIAM EUGENE	FL	07W	45
ROLLINGS JIMMY	FL	06E	95
ROLLINS ARBAL JR	IL	10E	54
ROLLINS BOBBY JOHN	OK	30W	95
ROLLINS DALE FRANKLIN	MT	39W	62
ROLLINS EDWIN CHARLES	TN	08E	68
ROLLINS GLENN HASKELL	TN	34W	72
ROLLINS HOBERT TRUMAN	TN	39E	25
ROLLINS LEWIS CHARLES	WV	07E	129
ROLLINS WADE HAMPTON	MD	05W	121
ROLLINS WILLIAM BLAINE JR	WV	34W	34
ROLLINS WILLIAM PAUL	TX	42W	43
ROLSTAD THEODORE S	WA	26W	11
ROMACK WILLIAM ROBERT	CO	07E	43
ROMAGOSA LAYNE JOSEPH	LA	07W	82
ROMAINE THOMAS GILBERT	NJ	27W	77
ROMAN EULALIO ARTURO	NJ	45E	28
ROMAN JEREMIAS	NY	42E	71
ROMAN MARK JOSEPH	NY	54E	16
ROMAN VICTOR MUNOZ	NM	21W	28
ROMAN-AGUILAR CARMELO	NJ	11E	5
ROMAN-RODRIGUEZ EDWIN	PR	24W	112
ROMANCHUK MICHAEL GEORGE	PA	13E	81
ROMANELLI LOUIS VINCENT	PA	29W	55
ROMANIELLO ANTHONY JOSEPH	CT	16E	97
ROMANKO DANIEL ROBERT	PA	02E	96
ROMANKO MICHAEL JAMES	MN	42W	1
ROMANO AUGUST	NY	58W	14
ROMANO GERALD MICHAEL	NY	01E	130
ROMANO MICHAEL JR	NJ	29E	17
ROMANO MICHAEL STEPHEN	NY	35E	34
ROMANO NICHOLAS ANTHONY	VA	54W	29
ROMANO WILLIAM ROSS	IL	02E	119
ROMANSHEK JOHN CHARLES	WI	31E	53
ROMANSKI JAMES HENRY	OR	52W	24
ROME ROOSEVELT SNOW	IL	04E	101
ROMEO DUANE CLARK	NY	31W	19
ROMERO ARTHUR WILFRED	CO	51E	42
ROMERO BENNIE	CO	04E	28
ROMERO CHARLES ANTHONY	NM	18W	43
ROMERO GLENN WAYNE	LA	35W	51
ROMERO HECTOR MANUEL	TX	28E	93
ROMERO JOSEPH	CO	33W	43
ROMERO JOSEPH MICHAEL	CA	46E	1
ROMERO MANUEL VILLAREAL	TX	48E	33
ROMERO MICHAEL ANDREW	AZ	12W	1
ROMERO PEDRO JR	CA	58E	14
ROMERO RICARDO IBRAHIN	NJ	27W	73
ROMERO RICHARD	CO	42E	40
ROMERO ROBERT ANTHONY	AZ	50W	20
ROMERO ROBERT EUGENE	WY	15W	23
ROMERO ROBERT LUIS	AZ	23W	78
ROMERO ROBERT WILLIAM	CA	52E	42
ROMERO ROBERTO ANDRESS	CA	33W	17
ROMERO RONALD JAMES	LA	45E	51
ROMERO RONALD M	TX	36W	5
ROMERO SAMMY CHACON	NM	38W	45
ROMERO TIMOTEO FRED	NM	10W	116
ROMERO TRINE JR	NM	22E	48
ROMERO VICTOR	CA	45E	35
ROMERO WALTER DAVID	OK	16W	82
ROMERO-DE-JESUS BENJAMIN	NY	25E	25
ROMERO-OYOLA HERIBERTO	PR	15E	91
ROMERO-PEREZ PORFIRIO	PR	08W	80
ROMESSER RICHARD JAMES	NY	15W	95
ROMIG EDWARD LEON	PA	08E	57
ROMIG LEROY HENRY	PA	36W	6
ROMINE ALBERT W	KS	61E	18
ROMINE ROGER DALE	WV	28E	51
ROMMEL MICHAEL RAY	IN	31W	85
ROMO FRANK GONZALES	CA	22E	2
ROMO JOHN ROGER	AZ	19W	104
ROMO ROBERT ALLEN	CA	54E	16
RON GRIJALBA HUMBERTO	NY	02E	113
RONALD THOMAS ALAN	OH	20E	49
RONAN PATRICK JOSEPH	PA	32W	56
RONCA ROBERT FRANCIS	PA	01E	93
RONDO RONALD LEE	MI	43W	21
RONE JAMES ROBERT	AR	42W	59
RONGA ROBERT FRANK JR	MA	07W	97
RONIGER JUNIOR FLOYD	IL	32W	67
RONJE JOE LUIS	TX	11E	72
RONNEBERG HUGH JULIUS	MD	12W	18
RONZANI CHARLES KENNETH	IL	52W	24
ROOD CRAIG ALLEN	MN	55E	29
ROONEY TERRENCE MANN	CO	12E	56
ROOP FRANK	FL	04E	116
ROOSSIEN ROBERT ALLEN	MI	25W	83
ROOT CLARENCE ROBERT	PA	54W	20
ROOT CLYDE DEAN	OH	13W	38
ROOT EDWARD CHARLES	KS	52E	10
ROOT JAMES MICHAEL	MI	31W	57
ROOT ROGER DALE	MI	25E	25
ROOT RUSSELL LEE	MI	16E	114

NAME	STATE	PANEL NO.	LINE NO.
ROOT THOMAS RICHARD	HI	20W	60
ROOT VERN ERNEST	MI	29W	40
ROOTH CHARLES WILLIAM	NE	08E	31
ROPCHOCK THEODORE MATTATW	PA	13W	94
ROPER CLAUDE TILLMAN	GA	41W	1
ROPER JOEL CLYDE	GA	27E	83
ROPER JOHN MORTON	WA	12E	130
ROPER ROBERT CLARANCE	TX	26E	107
ROPETER LESTER EARL	NY	43W	42
ROQUE FLORENTINO R	FL	11E	37
RORABACK KENNETH M	NY	01E	34
RORICK KENNETH ROY	CA	18E	72
ROSA JOHN MICHAEL	NY	16W	80
ROSA JUAN ANTONIO	NY	35E	27
ROSA-SEIN ROSARIO	PR	10E	1
ROSA-URBINA VICENTE	PR	25W	14
ROSADO ERNEST SR	NY	55E	29
ROSADO-BORGES JOSE F	PR	19W	109
ROSADO-RODRIGUEZ EUGENIO	PR	09E	39
ROSALES BERNIE JR	MI	44W	19
ROSALES MARTIN ANGEL	KS	26E	51
ROSANOVA DANIEL FRANK	IL	26W	35
ROSAR ROBERT JOHN	CA	62E	11
ROSARIO AGUSTIN	NY	36W	6
ROSARIO-CRUZ MIGUEL JR	PR	43W	49
ROSARIO-SALABERRIOS ELMO	PR	10E	112
ROSARIO-SOTO ERNESTO JR	PR	23W	92
ROSAS JOSE ANTONIO	TX	19E	65
ROSAS-SANZ SAMUEL	PR	43W	66
ROSATO JOSEPH FRANK	OH	07E	134
ROSBECK RICHARD A	MA	11E	41
ROSE ALBERT EUGENE	MI	43W	21
ROSE ALBERT JAMES	MA	18E	111
ROSE ANDREW CLAYTON	NY	23W	57
ROSE BARNES WARLAND JR	CA	29E	21
ROSE CARLOS JAMES	MA	25W	83
ROSE CHARLES WILLIAM	MD	02E	137
ROSE DANA GALE	CA	13E	105
ROSE DANIEL PATRICK	CA	33W	9
ROSE DANNY LEE	UT	40W	1
ROSE DAVID EARL	MI	07W	14
ROSE DAVID JON	CA	11E	10
ROSE DAVID LEE	CA	02E	39
ROSE DONALD RAY	TX	15W	60
ROSE FRANK JAMES JR	CA	23E	63
ROSE GARY LEE	IN	08W	67
ROSE GERALD BRUCE	WV	01E	94
ROSE HARRY QUINCY	VA	32W	73
ROSE JAMES ELDON	OK	43E	32
ROSE JERRY GENE	OH	21W	113
ROSE JESSE BEA	AR	17E	13
ROSE JOHN CHARLES	NJ	12W	121
ROSE JOHNNY JR	KY	41E	12
ROSE JOSEPH SHEPHERD JR	OH	26E	72
ROSE LARRY EMMETT	IL	06E	77
ROSE LAWRENCE CARROLL	IL	45W	28
ROSE LAWRENCE OLIVER	NY	58W	20
ROSE LEO JAMES	CA	05W	40
ROSE LEONARD DALE	CA	34W	67
ROSE LUTHER LEE	TX	08E	2
ROSE MARK RICHARD	WA	16W	67
ROSE MELVILLE BRICE III	NC	33W	34
ROSE MICHAEL ALLEN	CA	47E	5
ROSE NATHANIEL ROBERT	CA	33E	41
ROSE NORMAN EARL III	NC	38E	13
ROSE ONSBY RAY	VA	07E	83
ROSE PAUL WARREN	CA	13W	124
ROSE RAYMOND ALFRED	OH	03W	122
ROSE ROBERT FRANCIS	OR	23W	30
ROSE ROBERT JAMES	IN	19E	31
ROSE ROBERT LEE	KY	15W	111
ROSE ROGER CLARKE	CA	26E	37
ROSE THOMAS ELDEN	OH	20W	22
ROSE WESLEY HAROLD	IN	01W	79
ROSEBERRY MICHELE McCORD	OH	34E	91
ROSEBERRY ROGER DUANE	IN	17E	13
ROSEBRUGH FRANCIS PAUL	NY	11E	101
ROSEDIETCHER HOWARD	NY	21W	15
ROSEKRANS LESLIE DONALD	MI	37W	35
ROSEMAN MICHAEL DENNIS	IN	10E	125
ROSEMOND JOHN L	TX	24W	98
ROSEN DANIEL ELMER	IL	24W	3
ROSEN MAX EMMANUEL	PA	17W	52
ROSEN PATRICK DEAN	TX	06W	41
ROSENBACH ROBERT PAGE	MO	13W	86
ROSENBAUM GERALD GEORGE	IA	42E	23
ROSENBERG KENNETH	NY	01W	19
ROSENBERGER DAVID ARTHUR	CA	48E	10
ROSENBERGER ROGER DALE	MI	22W	69
ROSENBERRY FRED BRYAN	PA	04W	104
ROSENBUSCH CHARLES RICHARD	MA	57E	31
ROSENLUND NELS VERN II	CA	18W	121
ROSENOW ROBERT JAMES	WI	23W	18
ROSENOW THOMAS ARTHUR	WI	20W	126
ROSENSTOCK MARK LAMONT	AZ	07E	50
ROSENSTREICH AARON LIEB	CT	25W	54
ROSENTHAL MICHAEL D JR	LA	16W	10
ROSENWALD ROBERT JOHN	PA	40E	55
ROSENWASSER LEE EDWARD	FL	04E	67
ROSETO JOHN	NY	10E	103
ROSHON ROBERT BROWN	OH	10W	116
ROSOLIE WALTER WILLIAM	NY	47E	24
ROSS ALAN	MO	10W	92
ROSS ARTHUR JAMES JR	NJ	39W	18
ROSS CARLTON	TN	42W	22
ROSS CHARLES BRENT	IN	18W	72
ROSS CHARLES GREGORY	IL	42E	57
ROSS CONRAD E	IN	37E	67
ROSS DALE RAY	MO	24E	42
ROSS DAVID LYLE	OR	46E	58
ROSS DAVID SETH	NY	24W	89
ROSS DENNIS WAYNE	KS	16W	67
ROSS DON LEWIS	WV	25W	2
ROSS DONALD EDWARD	WV	26W	36
ROSS DOUGLAS ALAN	CA	34W	61
ROSS ELMER TIM	WV	04W	122
ROSS ERNEST EDWARD	NC	12E	83
ROSS FRANK MILAN JR	TN	45E	28
ROSS GENE AUTRY	LA	35E	80
ROSS GENE K	CA	48E	9
ROSS GEORGE BACON JR	NY	16E	126
ROSS GERALD RAYDINE	IN	15W	40
ROSS GREGORY MARK	OH	55W	9
ROSS HARVEY TURNER JR	MS	09W	45
ROSS JAMES ARTHUR	OH	16W	15
ROSS JAMES LEE	NC	15E	122
ROSS JERRY WAYNE	AR	11E	21
ROSS JIMMIE CALVIN	MS	15E	129
ROSS JLYNN JR	MI	45E	14
ROSS JOSEPH SHAW	KY	50W	45
ROSS KENNETH	NY	14W	123
ROSS KENNETH EDWARD	CA	26W	93
ROSS KEVIN HENRY	NY	60E	2
ROSS LARRY DAVID	MI	15E	60
ROSS LARRY EDWARD	CA	15E	122
ROSS LARRY THOMAS	CA	32W	68
ROSS LEWIS DEWAYNE	FL	18W	63
ROSS LUTHER JULIAN JR	AL	51W	36
ROSS MICHAEL ROBERT	TX	25W	109
ROSS MILTON ALAN	NE	32W	2
ROSS MORRIS JEROME	WA	41W	36
ROSS MYRON RUDOLPH II	NJ	41W	1
ROSS PAUL R	CA	22W	36
ROSS PHILLIP K	NC	42E	69
ROSS RAYMOND JEFFERSON JR	CA	11E	84
ROSS REID REX JR	PA	37W	41
ROSS ROBERT GARRY	CA	19E	86
ROSS ROBERT JAMES	NC	54W	32
ROSS ROBERT LEE	LA	29E	92
ROSS ROBERT LEE	CO	45W	22
ROSS ROBERT LESLIE	MA	47W	31
ROSS ROBERT W	CA	01W	129
ROSS ROGER ALAN	NJ	36W	74
ROSS ROGER DALE	CA	25W	110
ROSS RONALD ALAN	WI	16W	9
ROSS RONALD CARL	OH	51W	7
ROSS RONNIE ALLEN	LA	04W	112
ROSS SAMUEL	WV	04E	114
ROSS SANDY LEE	GA	14E	11
ROSS STANLEY DENNIS	IA	17W	98
ROSS THOMAS ARTHUR	OH	27W	7
ROSS THOMAS EDWARD	TX	04W	14
ROSS THOMAS MICHAEL	OH	36E	84
ROSS WALTER JR	VA	08W	4
ROSS WILLIAM ALLEN	GA	30E	32
ROSS WILLIAM GRAY	TN	57W	31
ROSS WILLIAM KEITH	OH	63E	17
ROSS WILLIAM ROBERT JR	WV	35E	80
ROSS WILLIAM SIDNEY JR	TN	23E	113
ROSS WILLIE JAMES	MD	62W	1
ROSSANO RICHARD JOSEPH	NY	04W	78
ROSSELL FRANCIS L JR	NJ	40W	50
ROSSER EDWARD JOHN	MA	25E	2
ROSSER ERNIE WAYNE	KY	13E	36
ROSSER GARY EDWARD	OH	10E	126
ROSSI ALDO JR	IL	04E	98
ROSSI RUDOLPH	NY	24W	49
ROSSI THOMAS LOUIS	CA	32W	34
ROSSI VINCENT LOUIS SR	NY	06W	62
ROSSIGNOL RICHARD W	ME	28W	86
ROSSINI RONALD STEPHEN	NY	27W	50
ROSSON PHILLIP ENOS	AR	31W	96
ROSSOTTO VINCENT JOSEPH	NY	54W	5
ROSSOW GERALD JOHN	WI	19W	115
ROST JAMES FRANCIS JR	NY	16W	90
ROST LEROY ALPHUS	IL	29E	92
ROSTAMO THOMAS DAVID	MN	42E	24
ROTGER GUSTAVO JR	NY	41E	28
ROTH BILLIE LEROY	IL	02E	21
ROTH BRUCE JONATHAN	IL	32E	97
ROTH FRANK THEODORE	PA	18E	128
ROTH FRED STEWART	WA	20E	97
ROTH IVAN DAVID	IL	30E	19
ROTH JOHN HOWARD	MI	16E	48
ROTH LA ROY FREDERICH	IA	14W	9
ROTH RONALD ARTHUR BERT	MI	06E	103
ROTHAR PHILLIP EDWARD JR	FL	26W	73
ROTHEL LARRY WAYNE	TX	03W	26
ROTHENBUHLER LYNN HARLEY	IN	01E	39
ROTHER ROBERT DAWSON JR	MO	08W	134
ROTHERY RICHARD ALAN	IL	41E	11
ROTHHAAR BRUCE LEE	PA	19E	112
ROTHRING HOWARD EARL JR	IN	06E	113
ROTKO RUSSELL JOSEPH JR	CT	40W	59
ROTONNELLI JOHN	NY	61E	18
ROTTER RALPH LEE	ID	33E	22
ROTTON JOHNNY STEVE	GA	27E	12
ROUBA EDWARD S	PA	21E	24
ROUCHON ALAN MICHAEL	KS	22W	93
ROUGHGARDEN RICHARD J	NJ	18W	86
ROULETT JAMES HOUSTON	TN	54W	7
ROULIER RUSSELL RENE	MA	22E	33
ROUM STEVEN JEROME	WI	33W	4
ROUNDTREE RICHARD RALPH	WA	07E	119
ROUNDTREE WILLIE JUNIUS	NC	11E	58
ROUNSEVILLE JOSEPH WILFRE	RI	38E	60
ROUNTREE GLEN EVERETT	KY	35W	84
ROUNTREE HARVEY F JR	NY	20W	2
ROUNTREE RONALD CORBIN	CA	38E	38
ROUSCHER JOHN MARTIN	PA	35W	73
ROUSE CLARENCE LEON	OK	29W	14
ROUSE FREDERICK EUGENE	OK	42W	37
ROUSE GORDON ARTHUR JR	NY	18E	71
ROUSE GREGORY MICHAEL	CO	50W	9
ROUSE JEROME MICHAEL	WI	06W	36
ROUSE JOHN WILLIAM	PA	62W	1
ROUSE PHILLIP LEONARD	VA	19E	45
ROUSE WILLIAM CLARENCE	OH	25E	93
ROUSH ROBERT ROGERS	IL	21E	102
ROUSH RONNIE RAY	PA	36E	33
ROUSH SAMUEL EMMERSON	AZ	56E	31
ROUSH WILLIAM WAKEFIELD	TX	41E	54
ROUSKA DENNIS LEON	WA	06W	113
ROUSSEAU DUANE MICHAEL	TN	20W	66
ROUSSEAU RICHARD LEE	FL	51W	43
ROUSSELL CLARENCE A JR	NY	43E	32
ROUSSELL RALPH S JR	LA	09W	16
ROUSSOS WILLIAM ROBERT	MI	11E	84
ROVINSKY RICHARD MICHAEL	PA	12W	50
ROVITO GILBERT ALLAN	PA	01W	119
ROWDEN JAMES HERBERT	OR	05E	123
ROWDEN JOHN WAYNE	OR	38E	71
ROWE ARTHUR MORTIMER	NJ	61W	6
ROWE BRUCE PHILLIP	CA	02W	108
ROWE CHESTER EARL JR	PA	17E	107
ROWE DOUGLAS NOEL	ID	30W	95

NAME	STATE	PANEL NO.	LINE NO.
ROWE ERNEST LEROY	PA	42W	10
ROWE JAMES GRAY JR	CA	54W	19
ROWE MICHAEL THOMAS	GA	32W	63
ROWE OLIVER GILMAN JR	NC	15E	17
ROWE RUSSELL ALLEN	MD	08W	33
ROWE SALVATORE ALFRED	NJ	36W	18
ROWE SHARBER MAYFIELD	NM	53W	38
ROWE WILLIAM EDWIN	CA	28W	2
ROWELL DAVID LOU	TX	19E	65
ROWELL FRANKLIN DELANO	SC	19W	73
ROWELL KEITH WILLIAM	TX	46W	22
ROWELL LEE MILTON	MN	41E	2
ROWELL RICHARD A	IL	16E	65
ROWELL ROGER JAMES	GA	13W	72
ROWEN GERALD LOYD II	CA	32E	65
ROWLAND GEORGE CLAYTON JR	KY	38W	5
ROWLAND GEORGE JR	KY	15E	108
ROWLAND HARVEY LYN	MI	10E	69
ROWLAND JOHN WILLIAM JR	FL	04E	83
ROWLAND RICHARD LEE JR	AZ	47W	53
ROWLAND ROGER LEE	MN	56E	15
ROWLAND THOMAS PATRICK	WA	03E	3
ROWLAND THOMAS W	GA	37W	24
ROWLAND WAYNE HULEN	OH	06E	120
ROWLAND WILLIAM MICHAEL	CA	57W	3
ROWLAND ZACK OSCAR	MT	37E	13
ROWLES ALLEN DUANE	PA	54E	16
ROWLES STEVEN ROBERT	CA	34W	18
ROWLETT GARY PAUL	PA	52W	46
ROWLETT GARY STEVEN	TN	16E	97
ROWLETT HAL JONES	OK	13E	119
ROWLETT JAMES WESLEY	TX	11E	23
ROWLETT JIMMIE HENRY	KY	10E	115
ROWLEY CHARLES STODDARD	CT	11W	38
ROWLEY DONALD ALBERT	MI	09W	86
ROWLEY HARRY EMILUS	LA	01E	90
ROWLEY JOSEPH PATRICK	MD	27E	78
ROWLEY THEODORE TEXAS	OH	07W	130
ROWSEY RONALD DUANE	WV	05W	56
ROWSON GEOFFREY THOMAS	CT	55W	1
ROY ALLEN JAYSON	CT	28E	38
ROY BILLY DUANE	OK	48W	47
ROY CHARLES SULLIVAN	WY	51W	44
ROY CLIFTON DOUGLAS	MD	36E	33
ROY DANIEL THOMAS	OH	19W	41
ROY DAVID PAUL	MA	26W	86
ROY DAVID PAUL	TX	12W	93
ROY GERALD RAYMOND	NY	45W	1
ROY HENRY JOHN JR	TX	20W	49
ROY JAMES DEAN	IL	57E	9
ROY JAMES WILLIE III	CA	33E	41
ROY LEONARD ALLAN	IN	67W	3
ROY PATRICK ROBERT	PA	32E	12
ROY PETER WILLIAM	MA	31E	41
ROY RICHARD W	CT	09E	117
ROY ROBERT RICHARD	ME	05E	2
ROYAL COUNCIL LEE	VA	40W	15
ROYAL FRANCIS PATRICK	MO	11E	37
ROYAL JAMES NORMAN	FL	15W	11
ROYAL JERRY CHARLES	OK	26E	16
ROYAL WILLIAM EARL	GA	04W	62
ROYALL LESLIE WILLIAM III	CA	53W	39
ROYALTY AMEL DOUGLAS	IL	52E	43
ROYBAL ANTHONY WILFRED	CO	20E	78
ROYBAL THOMAS MICHAEL JR	AZ	51W	8
ROYDES KRAG BARRY	OH	29E	43
ROYE GEORGE EDWARD	VA	06W	50
ROYER RICHARD HOWARD	PA	07E	109
ROYER ROBERT HENRY	PA	03W	23
ROYSTER DOUGLAS	PA	08E	99
ROYSTER HUBERT JR	NC	33E	74
ROYSTER JOSEPH EDWARD	TN	18E	88
ROYSTON ALAN MICHAEL	WI	31W	39
ROYSTON LOUIS DON JR	KS	02E	72
ROYSTON ROY LEE	TX	15W	65
ROZANSKI EDWARD CHARLES	IL	25E	109
ROZELL EDWARD ARNOLD	NY	14W	87
ROZELLE DAVID THOMAS	PA	35E	9
ROZO JAMES MILAN	NY	09W	86
ROZOW JOHN	IN	25W	83
ROZZI WILLIAM ALLEN	CT	40E	55
RUANE MICHAEL PATRICK	NY	32E	19

NAME	STATE	PANEL NO.	LINE NO.
RUBADO CHARLES FRANCIS	NY	51W	13
RUBBO KENNETH WILLIAM	PA	37W	59
RUBERG CHRISTOPHER EUGENE	CA	05E	58
RUBIN HERMAN FRANCIS	MN	36W	6
RUBIN ROY GARLAND	NY	28W	75
RUBINS JOHN CHARLES	NY	29E	97
RUBIO EURIPIDES JR	PR	12E	44
RUBIO JUAN AMADOR	TX	13W	49
RUBIO PETER PAUL	CA	22W	55
RUBIO RUBEN	NM	03W	102
RUBY BLANE MARKWOOD	MD	60W	21
RUBY STEPHEN CHARLES	NJ	02W	81
RUCH FRANCIS WILLIAM II	NY	07E	4
RUCH ROBERT STEPHEN	PA	03E	7
RUCHTI HEINZ	CA	44W	29
RUCKER CARLOS WILSON	NV	28W	52
RUCKER EMMETT JR	TX	69E	1
RUCKER JOHN MARSHALL	GA	25W	54
RUCKER JOHN ONEAL	TX	01W	113
RUCKER JOHN WILLIAM	VA	06W	121
RUCKER KENNETH RAY	TX	65W	14
RUCKER MACEY LEE	TN	15W	72
RUCKER RICHARD LEE	OH	62W	1
RUCKER RICKY LEE	MD	01W	79
RUCKLE CLINTON GEAN	KS	14W	6
RUCKS OTIS JAMES	AR	21W	19
RUCKTAESCHEL GARY ARDEN	MN	28E	86
RUD KENNETH HANS	WA	14E	131
RUDD CHARLES NIVEN	MD	06E	50
RUDD DONALD LEE	MI	30W	29
RUDD JAMES EARL	PA	49W	20
RUDD JAMES WALLACE	VA	51E	25
RUDD RICHARD JOHN JR	IA	51E	25
RUDD ROBERT CHARLES	TX	28E	4
RUDDAN WILLIAM ANDREW	CA	17W	88
RUDEEN PAUL E JR	NC	05E	127
RUDDELL ALAN JAMES	MO	20E	124
RUDEN MATTHEW ALBERT	IA	39W	13
RUDERSON ANDERSON LINWOOD	NY	34E	44
RUDINEC JOHN JOSEPH	PA	15E	71
RUDISILL DAYTON LUTHER	KS	05E	36
RUDITYS EDWARD MICHAEL	MI	31W	35
RUDLONG THELMER ARTHUR	MN	31E	41
RUDOLF MARK PHILLIP	WI	14W	31
RUDOLPH RICHARD JOSEPH	GA	59W	13
RUDOLPH ROBERT DAVID	CA	02E	78
RUDOLPH ROBERT GEORGE	GA	12E	91
RUDOLPH RONALD CLEMENCE	VA	17W	75
RUDOLPH WALTER WILLIAM	NY	30W	30
RUDON JOSE ANTONIO	NY	37W	83
RUDY PAUL CHARLES	NY	33W	43
RUDZIAK ERIK NILES	PA	34W	19
RUEBEL JOSEPH PETER	CA	20W	74
RUEHLE DOUGLAS DUANE	MI	23W	58
RUEHLE MEDARD A J	OH	18E	17
RUELAS MATEO	TX	10W	54
RUENGER CARL DENNIS	WI	11W	60
RUEPPEL RONALD BENTON	ID	02W	28
RUETH JOHN LEONARD	WI	29W	62
RUFF GARY LYNN	MI	07W	36
RUFF GILBERT OLIVER JR	MO	04W	1
RUFF RONALD CALVIN	AL	05W	103
RUFF THOMAS VALENTINE JR	MD	19E	65
RUFF WILLIAM HERMAN	WA	15W	96
RUFF WILLIE JEROME	SC	41E	28
RUFFIN CHARLES NATHANIEL	DC	12W	128
RUFFIN JAMES JUNIUS	NC	16E	114
RUFFIN JAMES THOMAS	AL	05E	49
RUFFNER RUSSELL MILES JR	CA	19W	73
RUFTY JOE HEARNE	NC	14W	80
RUGAR STEVEN DALE	MI	61E	3
RUGENSTEIN GREGORY P	MI	16W	44
RUGGE LLOYD TAYLOR	CA	14E	82
RUGGERI ANTONINO	CA	32W	20
RUGGERO VICTOR JOSEPH JR	NY	16E	70
RUGGIERO ROBERT JOHN	NY	09E	6
RUGGLES JOHN RICHARD III	TN	41E	72
RUGGLES LARRY DEAN	OH	27W	2
RUGGLES ROBERT HOYT	VA	14W	55
RUGGS RANDALL	FL	26W	41
RUGH FRED PLYMOUTH	OH	45W	44
RUHL ROBERT JACK JR	MO	39E	12

NAME	STATE	PANEL NO.	LINE NO.
RUHL ROBERT WAYNE	MD	09E	39
RUHLAND KLAUS DIETER R	OK	40W	15
RUHLMANN HEINRICH	MO	25W	48
RUHLOFF GARY CARL	IL	13E	114
RUHTER MICHAEL ALLEN	NE	20W	37
RUIS DEWEY DOLEN JR	FL	33W	68
RUIS FRANKLIN DWIGHT	GA	16E	114
RUITER JERRY LEE	MI	12E	65
RUIZ ANDREW ANDY	CA	38W	37
RUIZ ANGEL O	NY	35E	18
RUIZ ANTONIO ELIZONDO	TX	29W	40
RUIZ CARLOS HERIBERTO	NY	03E	132
RUIZ FELIX ALVARDO	TX	36E	84
RUIZ GILBERT	CA	28W	3
RUIZ HECTOR LOPEZ	WA	30E	81
RUIZ JOHN FRANCO	MI	35E	63
RUIZ JOSE	NY	50E	20
RUIZ JOSE JR	NY	47E	16
RUIZ JOSE MANUEL	PR	43W	9
RUIZ MANUEL	CA	47E	5
RUIZ MARTIN JR	TX	13E	29
RUIZ PASTOR FRANCISCO	FL	13W	21
RUIZ PETER GEORGE	AZ	54W	19
RUIZ RAMON RODRIGUEZ	CA	57E	31
RUIZ RAYMOND	CA	23E	78
RUIZ RICHARD PETER	TX	27E	41
RUIZ SALVADORE INIGUEZ	CA	23W	31
RUIZ THOMAS	NY	54W	32
RUIZ WILLIAM JR	CA	05W	56
RUIZ-BERNARD GUILLERMO A	PR	49E	25
RUIZ-DEL PILAR RAFAEL ANG	PR	36E	33
RUIZ-PEREZ ROBERTO	PR	34W	68
RULE TED JAMES	IA	37W	7
RULISON DANIEL GRANT	MI	17W	82
RUMBAUGH ELWOOD EUGENE	PA	01W	132
RUMBLE GEROULD MCLEAN III	NC	16W	35
RUMBLE JON MAC GILLIVRAY	VA	36W	77
RUMINSKI PHILIP EDWARD JR	NY	33E	74
RUMINSKI ROBERT PAUL	WI	17E	88
RUMLEY RICHARD ALLEN	CA	33E	93
RUMMAGE JAMES FELIX	NC	36W	59
RUMMEL DONALD EUGENE	NY	47W	12
RUMMEL FRANCIS CLAIR	PA	08E	24
RUMMEL JAMES DOUGLAS	MT	09W	50
RUMMERFIELD JAMES C JR	CA	16W	76
RUMRILL PAUL WILLIAM	MA	34E	25
RUMSEY JAY DEE	NY	34W	79
RUMSEY MELVIN DARRYL	GA	38W	20
RUMSON SAMUEL JAMES JR	MA	43E	60
RUNDLE CARY FRANK	PA	39W	4
RUNDLE DANNY RAY	CA	10E	115
RUNDLE JAMES JR	NY	23W	106
RUNEY LAWRENCE F	PA	08E	105
RUNGE FRANKLIN JAMES	WI	29W	23
RUNGE ROBERT CARL	CA	06W	79
RUNION MARION GILMER	VA	14E	109
RUNK GARY WESLEY	PA	33E	52
RUNKEL RONALD L	IN	05E	82
RUNKLE DANIEL C	IN	46E	23
RUNKLE ROBERT LESLIE	KS	48E	10
RUNNELLS EVERETT PORTER	NH	10E	51
RUNNELLS GLYN LINAL JR	AL	22E	90
RUNNELS JAMES MIKEL	FL	24E	42
RUNNELS LLOYD CHISOLM JR	CA	30E	73
RUNSER ROBERT JOSEPH	IL	20W	52
RUNYON BARRY LEE	NJ	32E	15
RUNYON STEVEN THOMAS	IN	32E	12
RUNZO RICHARD FRANCIS	OH	21W	95
RUOFF ROGER DALE	OH	12E	81
RUOHO JOHN RONALD	WI	31E	30
RUONAVAARA ROBERT EDWIN	CA	17E	69
RUPCIC RAYMOND ELLSWORTH	OH	01E	101
RUPE DONALD LEE	IA	30W	81
RUPERT JOHN MICHAEL	NY	39E	12
RUPERT LEO FRANKLIN	MO	57E	32
RUPINSKI BERNARD FRANCIS	PA	56W	8
RUPKE DARYL JAMES	CO	16W	85
RUPLE HOMER ALFRED JR	MI	36E	84
RUPP JEFFREY DAVID	OH	34W	29
RUPPERT FRANCIS GROVER	MD	22W	108
RUSCH STEPHEN ARTHUR	NJ	02W	113
RUSCITO JOHN ANDREW	NY	42W	22

NAME	STATE	PANEL NO.	LINE NO.
RUSEK RONALD LEE	OH	50W	27
RUSH CHARLES GLYNN JR	TN	26W	22
RUSH CLAUDE BENJAMIN JR	TX	13E	100
RUSH CLIFFORD JAMES	MO	17W	114
RUSH DAVID CLYDE	CA	34W	88
RUSH ERVIN LEE	CA	47E	54
RUSH GEORGE HENRY JR	MI	25E	54
RUSH JACK RAYMOND	WI	22E	114
RUSH JAMES EDWARD JR	MS	47W	22
RUSH JAMES LEROY	OH	15E	36
RUSH JAMES THEODORE	OH	35W	79
RUSH JOSEPH BRADLEY	VA	33W	29
RUSH KENNETH	KY	05E	15
RUSH LARRY ALLEN	IN	22W	58
RUSH MARVIN GENE	TN	50E	21
RUSH ROLAND EDWARD	GA	20E	67
RUSH THEODORE MARSHALL	AL	33W	43
RUSH THOMAS CLYDE JR	VA	18W	50
RUSH WILLIAM ARDIE	CA	19E	112
RUSHA GARY EDWARD	MI	50E	42
RUSHER ROBERT CHARLES	CA	33E	74
RUSHIN LESTER	GA	01W	60
RUSHING EDWARD FRANKLIN	MS	15E	27
RUSHING GARY GRANT	NC	11E	120
RUSHING GEORGE WILLIAM	TX	40E	47
RUSHING JAMES MONROE	FL	36W	31
RUSHING KENNETH ROGER	GA	05W	32
RUSHING MICHAEL GEAN	AL	21E	15
RUSHING STEPHEN ABRAM	IA	08W	70
RUSHING WILLIAM LENDELL	TX	56E	16
RUSHLOW RICHARD LEONARD	MI	05W	41
RUSHTON BRIAN WAYNE	TN	23E	63
RUSHTON WAYNE STERLING	OH	05W	18
RUSNAK GEORGE BERNARD	PA	17E	24
RUSNAK ROBERT JOSEPH	PA	44W	12
RUSNELL DANIEL JOSEPH	MI	11E	10
RUSS ALFRED BAYARD	NH	34E	45
RUSS BILLIE GROVER	NC	39W	45
RUSS JAMES ALVIN	FL	11W	61
RUSS JAMES ERWIN	MI	10W	87
RUSS JAMES LEE JR	OH	32E	65
RUSS JOSEPH BLAIS	PA	07E	36
RUSS LEE HENDERSON	CA	19E	32
RUSS PAUL EDWARD	NY	13W	129
RUSS RICHARD ARNOLD	NC	31E	38
RUSS RICHARD JR	FL	02W	8
RUSS THOMAS EDISON	NC	26E	3
RUSS WILLIAM R	NC	29E	43
RUSSAW PRESTON IVORY	TX	38E	13
RUSSEK JOHN JOSEPH	MN	36W	18
RUSSELL ALLEN BARTLEY	CA	20E	67
RUSSELL ARTHUR JAMES	AR	08E	12
RUSSELL BERNARD	MD	14W	91
RUSSELL BOBBY	OH	02E	6
RUSSELL BRIAN PATRICK	NY	05W	46
RUSSELL CARL ERIC	IL	14E	106
RUSSELL CECIL LEE	IL	38E	13
RUSSELL CHARLES E III	NC	36W	6
RUSSELL CHARLES GLENN	KY	45W	64
RUSSELL CHARLES M III	GA	16W	119
RUSSELL CHARLES PIERCE	KY	02W	83
RUSSELL CHARLES TERRY	AL	14W	55
RUSSELL CLARENCE DEAN	MO	31W	19
RUSSELL DAVID ADAMS	DC	43E	69
RUSSELL DAVID ALLEN	MD	29W	64
RUSSELL DAVID GORDON	OR	06E	77
RUSSELL DAVID PAUL	MI	20W	26
RUSSELL DONALD MYRICK	ME	31E	42
RUSSELL DONNIE HOWARD	CA	09W	116
RUSSELL EDWARD T	ME	07E	14
RUSSELL FLOYD H JR	AL	21E	108
RUSSELL FRED CALVIN	TN	15E	15
RUSSELL GARY LEE	NY	60W	5
RUSSELL GORDON WARREN	MA	14E	106
RUSSELL GREGORY ALLEN	CA	58E	25
RUSSELL HENRY EUGENE	VA	25W	17
RUSSELL HOLLIE BOYD	IN	12E	123
RUSSELL JAMES A III	TN	63W	12
RUSSELL JAMES LEROY	TX	18E	76
RUSSELL JAMES LOWELL	OH	44E	20
RUSSELL JAMES ROBERT	CA	33W	21
RUSSELL JERRY WILLIAM	MN	13W	89
RUSSELL JOE TRAVIS	FL	41W	37
RUSSELL JOHN ERNEST	TX	47W	22
RUSSELL JOHN JOSEPH	OH	08W	77
RUSSELL JOHN MALCOLM JR	VT	43E	32
RUSSELL KENNETH MUREL	AR	34W	18
RUSSELL KENNETH TRUMAN	OK	15E	51
RUSSELL LARRY GENE	IL	50E	33
RUSSELL LYNN JORDAN	ME	12E	27
RUSSELL PATRICK ANTHONY	GA	21W	56
RUSSELL PETER FRANSSON	NJ	24W	90
RUSSELL PETER JOHN	NY	50W	45
RUSSELL PETER LOWELL	TX	47W	33
RUSSELL RANDALL KERWIN	MO	23E	22
RUSSELL RICHARD DUANE	IL	12E	91
RUSSELL RICHARD LEE	CA	55W	22
RUSSELL RICHARD LEE	TX	01W	7
RUSSELL RICHARD SHANNON	CA	35E	63
RUSSELL ROBERT THOMAS II	TX	15W	57
RUSSELL RONALD JAMES	WA	09E	95
RUSSELL RONALD PATRICK	CA	30W	39
RUSSELL RONNIE LEN	IL	40W	48
RUSSELL ROY DEAN	SD	03W	107
RUSSELL SAMUEL	TN	54W	33
RUSSELL WAYNE	CA	21W	2
RUSSELL WAYNE HOWARD	NJ	28W	98
RUSSELL WILLIAM JOHN JR	OH	38W	30
RUSSIN DONALD JOHN JR	OH	37E	68
RUSSO AUGUSTINE DANIEL	PA	11E	47
RUSSO DENNIS JOSEPH	NY	37W	36
RUSSO JOSEPH CHARLES	NY	30W	69
RUSSO MICHAEL CANDIDO	NY	46E	49
RUSSO MICHAEL L III	NY	41W	67
RUSSO MICHAEL PHILLIP	NY	03E	36
RUSSO RONALD SALVATORE	NY	35E	52
RUSSO THOMAS PETER	PA	42E	57
RUSSO WILLIAM	NJ	64W	15
RUST GARY ALFRED	MA	39W	52
RUST HENRY WILSON JR	AR	12E	125
RUST JAMES HENRY	NY	26E	16
RUSTINE DOUGLAS C	NE	47E	42
RUSZKIEWICZ PAUL FRANK	MI	18E	82
RUTBERG FRANKLIN STEVEN	PA	19E	74
RUTGERS DAVID LYNN	IA	31W	57
RUTH ALFRED DARNELL	LA	19W	122
RUTH DENNIS	NJ	22E	2
RUTH TERRY AUSTIN	IN	44W	6
RUTHERFORD DANNY LEWIS	KY	09E	50
RUTHERFORD ERNEST WAYNE	KY	52W	16
RUTHERFORD LARRY SCOTT	KY	14W	70
RUTHERFORD LEROY	VT	18W	30
RUTHERFORD MELVIN NEAL	KY	09W	74
RUTHERFORD MICHAEL TOXEY	AL	16W	36
RUTHERFORD RICHARD EUGENE	MO	09W	9
RUTIGLIANO ANTHONY	NY	24E	4
RUTLAND WARREN LESTER	SC	41W	8
RUTLEDGE GEORGE EDWARD	IN	06E	120
RUTLEDGE JAMES BENSON	OH	34E	55
RUTLEDGE JAMES ROBERT	OK	05E	56
RUTLEDGE JAMES ROBERT JR	TN	14W	15
RUTOWSKI DENNIS DAVID	WI	03E	36
RUTTAN JAMES EARL	NY	19W	82
RUTTER JOSEPH DELMAR JR	OH	67E	2
RUTTER LYNNE HARLAN	NJ	06W	41
RUTTER THOMAS CLAYTON	NJ	36W	6
RUTTIMANN ALLAN	CA	13W	124
RUTTLE ROBERT PRESTON JR	PA	23W	70
RUVALCABA-LOPEZ MIGUEL AN	TX	55E	29
RUVOLIS EDWARD JOSEPH	NJ	59E	12
RUYBAL DANNY GILBERT	CO	12W	125
RUYFF RONALD PAUL	CA	27E	76
RUZICKA JOSEP L JR	SC	01W	61
RUZILA PETER JR	NJ	03E	13
RYALS JIMMIE DALE	MI	08W	105
RYAN BERNARD STEVEN	CA	36E	85
RYAN DANIEL JOSEPH	CA	28E	51
RYAN DELBERT LEROY	KS	07E	132
RYAN DONALD JAMES	NY	27E	86
RYAN EDWARD KENNETH	WI	44W	54
RYAN FRANK D JR	CA	12W	120
RYAN FREDERICK LEE	OH	08E	72
RYAN GERALD SCOTT	UT	28E	44
RYAN JERRY VAN	CA	18W	72
RYAN JOHN ALOYSIUS JR	NY	28E	44
RYAN JOHN ROGER JR	IL	38W	78
RYAN JOHN THOMAS	NY	21W	20
RYAN JOSEPH ROBERT JR	OH	04W	90
RYAN LAWRENCE BRENDAN	NY	54W	25
RYAN LIONEL ALVAREZ	TX	45W	45
RYAN MICHAEL JOHN	CT	34E	55
RYAN ROBERT ANTHONY	PA	19W	115
RYAN ROBERT DALE	TX	51W	20
RYAN ROBERT EDWARD	MA	02W	56
RYAN RONALD ROYCE	CA	43E	32
RYAN SAMUEL FRANKLIN	OH	26W	102
RYAN TERRENCE PATRICK	NJ	14W	27
RYAN THOMAS KEVIN	NY	20W	89
RYAN THOMAS LAWRENCE	MN	12W	14
RYAN WILLARD R	MA	07E	106
RYAN WILLIAM CORNELIUS JR	NJ	25W	54
RYAN WILLIAM DEAN	IL	30W	7
RYBAK FRANCIS PAUL	NY	33E	52
RYBERG CHARLES EDWARD	MN	26E	31
RYBICKI FRANK ANTHONY JR	PA	19E	74
RYBOLT DONALD RAY	IN	21E	6
RYCKAERT ANTHONY LEE	MI	02W	15
RYCKO RAYMOND ADAM	IL	17E	31
RYCROFT LARRY WAYNE	OK	38W	46
RYDEN GARY ARDEAN	MI	47E	54
RYDER ALDO EUGENE	CT	60W	12
RYDER CARL EDWARD	PA	23E	104
RYDER EDWIN BYRON	ME	18W	17
RYDER JOHN LESLIE	MN	09W	35
RYDLEWICZ JOHN MICHAEL	WI	03W	130
RYE BRYAN A	CT	01W	121
RYE DILLARD GALE	CA	38E	71
RYGG CHARLES ALLEN	CA	56W	8
RYKACZEWSKI STANLEY K	PA	34W	29
RYKOSKEY EDWARD JAY	PA	10E	17
RYLAND WILLIAM PATRICK	TN	46W	8
RYLANDER ROBERT J	TX	46E	41
RYLEE JAMES SIDNEY	PA	58E	26
RYMOND NICHOLAS JAMES	CA	18W	12
RYNEARSON KARL FRANCIS	PA	29E	5
RYNKIEWICZ RICHARD ROBERT	PA	04E	72
RYNNING KENNETH DEAN	CO	60E	16
RYON JOHN W	CT	01W	92
RYSE ROY LOUIS JR	CA	03E	88
RYTTER PAUL E	CA	02E	88
RYZA WAYNE DAVID	TX	32E	1
SAARELA WILLIAM GEORGE	MN	01W	64
SAATHOFF RAYMOND JOSEPH	MN	04W	53
SAAVEDRA LUIS FORERO	NY	41W	54
SAAVEDRA ROBERT	AZ	52E	43
SABA LESTER PAUL	MN	13W	114
SABATINELLI VINCENT F	MA	20W	45
SABATINI ROBERT JOSEPH	AR	03W	96
SABEC DAVID LOUIS	OH	05E	123
SABEL JOEL MICHAEL	CA	23E	45
SABENS JERRY DEAN	IN	12E	105
SABIN RONALD	IN	33W	43
SABINE JOHN SHAW IV	WA	06E	68
SABLAN ANTONIO QUICHOCHO	GM	06E	47
SABLAN FRANK AGUAN	AL	04W	15
SABLAN IGNACIO ESPINOSA	GM	24E	75
SABLAN JOHN TENERIO	GM	01W	21
SABLAN THOMAS QUICHOCHO	GM	14E	88
SABLE BROOKS EDWARD	WV	23W	58
SABLOTNY RICHARD ALAN	OH	40W	46
SABO ANDREW ROBERT	IL	25W	83
SABO LARRY MICHAEL	CA	42W	64
SABO LESLIE HALASZ JR	PA	10W	15
SACCO EDWARD STEVEN	IL	23E	78
SACCO JAMES DOMINICK	NY	34E	43
SACCOMEN EDMOND RAY	OH	18W	91
SACHARANSKI FRANK ERIC	NJ	12W	44
SACHASCHIK JAMES HARRY	IL	13W	52
SACHEN WILLIAM GEORGE JR	MI	63E	17
SACK GERALD DUANE	MN	50W	37
SACKETT DAVID LEE	WV	17W	114
SACKETT ERIC	TX	04E	95
SACKS JAY CHARLES	IL	19W	41
SADBERRY BENJAMIN	GA	39W	52
SADBERRY SEYMOUR PATRICK	MA	03E	6
SADICK RICHARD JOHN	OH	34W	72

NAME	STATE	PANEL NO.	LINE NO.
SADLER CARL J	TN	03E	3
SADLER HOWARD JR	TX	37E	13
SADLER JOHN WELDON	WI	26W	50
SADLER MITCHELL OLEN JR	CA	09W	107
SADLER ROBERT LEE	NC	26E	17
SADLER RONALD FRANCIS	NY	46E	12
SADLER THOMAS WAYNE	CA	25W	110
SADOWSKY LLOYD J	PA	12E	64
SAEGAERT DONALD RUSSELL	CT	02E	6
SAENZ ALFREDO JOSE	TX	13E	101
SAENZ EDWARD LLOYD	KS	42W	63
SAENZ FRANCISCO XAVIER	CA	02E	10
SAENZ HECTOR MARIO	NM	22E	48
SAENZ RICHARD	NM	41W	20
SAENZ RODOLFO ANDRES	TX	20E	78
SAEZ-RAMIREZ ANGEL PERFIR	PR	16E	13
SAFFELL RONALD CORY	TX	36W	31
SAFFLE EDGAR JOE JR	CA	14E	46
SAFRIT WILLIAM JULIUS	IN	55E	29
SAGAN SYLVESTER STANLEY	MI	29E	85
SAGE LELAND CHARLES COOKE	IL	21W	2
SAGE REX RUSSELL	GA	44W	6
SAGE ROBERT DAVID	NY	13E	29
SAGE TERENCE FAIRCHILD	KS	36E	34
SAGEN THOMAS A	WI	03E	19
SAGERIAN BRUCE ELLIOTT	MA	27E	2
SAGERS RONALD RAY	IA	10W	83
SAGON RUDY MANTIAD	HI	04E	10
SAGON STANLEY INCILLO	HI	07E	91
SAHLBERG GREGORY IRVING	MN	03W	109
SAIDE DAVID ALLIE	MI	06W	65
SAILOR EDDIE	MO	15W	108
SAIN DON RUE	CA	09E	88
SAIN JEROME ROBERT	PA	14W	55
SAIN LARRY DEAN	NC	45E	29
SAINT CLAIR ELISHA R	VA	06W	79
SAITO SAMUEL RYOICHI	CA	06W	82
SAIZ FRED ROMAN	NM	09E	101
SAIZ RONALD JAMES	CO	22E	18
SAKAI ERNEST SEICHI	HI	55W	1
SAKELLARIS MICHAEL GEORGE	MD	61W	6
SALA JAMES DONALD	IL	03E	136
SALAMONE JAMES ALBERT	WI	28W	100
SALANITRO GARY CHARLES	NY	22W	83
SALAS DANIEL STEPHEN	CO	02W	46
SALAS FELIX JUAN	TX	26W	93
SALAS ORLANDO ALBERTO	NY	36W	18
SALAZAR ALFREDO	TX	05W	18
SALAZAR ARTURO	TX	22W	43
SALAZAR CRES PADILLA	NM	53W	30
SALAZAR ELIAS JR	TX	47W	22
SALAZAR ERNESTO VICTOR	NY	07W	54
SALAZAR FIDEL GARCIA		17W	31
SALAZAR GILBERT SOLANO	CA	25E	109
SALAZAR JOHN	HI	60W	5
SALAZAR JOSE	MI	27E	95
SALAZAR JOSE LUIS	TX	22W	100
SALAZAR MEL ERNEST JR	NM	14W	47
SALAZAR PATRICK	NM	37W	24
SALAZAR RENE JAVIER	TX	36W	46
SALAZAR RICHARD FRANK	WA	28W	14
SALAZAR ROBERTO	TX	17W	1
SALAZAR ROY	IL	11E	37
SALAZAR RUDY JESSIE	TX	48E	33
SALCIDO GEORGE ARTHUR	AZ	52W	46
SALDANA FERMIN JR	TX	07E	106
SALDANA FERNANDO SAENZ	CA	26W	87
SALDANA RICHARD DAVID	CA	04W	17
SALDANA RICHARD E	PA	43E	33
SALDANO VINCENT	CA	17W	107
SALDIVAR JOSE ANGEL	TX	41E	3
SALE HAROLD REEVES JR	SC	21E	70
SALEAUMUA UINIFARETI	HI	15E	50
SALEH CHRISTOPHER RUBEN	CO	27E	61
SALEMA GEORGE STANLEY	HI	28E	17
SALEMI VINCENT RALPH	NJ	36W	7
SALERNO ANTHONY JOHN	NJ	20E	124
SALERNO PAUL LOUIS	WV	08W	25
SALERNO RALPH DENNIS	PA	20E	11
SALES CHARLES CARROLL	KY	55W	38
SALES HARLIS CALVIN	OK	22W	109
SALES NATHAN RAY	MI	43W	66
SALIMAN NORMAN SHELDON	CO	29W	20
SALINAS ANTONIO MONTANO	AZ	23E	115
SALINAS DAVID GREGORY	MI	51E	2
SALINAS JAIME ARTURO	TX	20W	37
SALINAS JOE MANUEL	CA	02E	41
SALINAS JOSE CONTRERAS	TX	17W	64
SALINAS MERCEDES PEREZ	TX	04E	13
SALINAS PHILLIP LOUIE	KS	37E	68
SALINAS RAMIRO LOPEZ	TX	49W	9
SALINAS ROBERT LONGORIA	TX	20E	1
SALINAS ROY RODRIGUEZ	TX	05W	50
SALISBERRY LARRY GORDON	PA	24E	69
SALISBURY GARY EUGENE	MI	38E	60
SALISBURY JAMES RUSSELL	OR	56W	27
SALISBURY ROBERT JAMES	WV	16W	54
SALLEE DOYLE EUGENE	IN	39W	56
SALLEE RICHARD JR	KY	03W	98
SALLER DONALD VINCENT	TN	32W	83
SALLEY JAMES JR	SC	04W	97
SALLEY WALTER JUNIOR	PA	07E	122
SALLY HANK	KY	23W	79
SALMELA ROBERT EARL	FL	60E	2
SALMIERI JOHN DOMINICK	NY	22E	114
SALMINEN PAUL JOHN	MI	20W	41
SALMON LARRY ANTHONY	CA	09W	9
SALMOND RICHARD WILLIAM	MI	06W	62
SALONIES EDWARD JR	IL	36W	59
SALONISH EDWARD GEORGE	PA	11E	84
SALTER CHARLES LOWELL	AL	17E	107
SALTER DWAYNE LAMONT	AL	47W	32
SALTER FRANK DEMON	AL	10W	66
SALTER JAMES WILLIAM	NY	14W	25
SALTER ROBERT WAYNE	AL	47W	54
SALTER SCOTT BRUCE	UT	65W	14
SALTERS LEE EARNEST	MS	07W	14
SALTMARSH JAMES JOHN	NY	23E	113
SALTMARSH THOMAS JOHN	NH	44E	53
SALTZ ERIC DONN	NY	19W	98
SALTZ MARION NELSON	IN	45E	42
SALUGA STEPHEN JOHN III	NJ	40W	5
SALVANIA RONALD LANDON	NY	42E	40
SALVATORE THOMAS ANTHONY	HI	18W	50
SALVESON SELMER ERNEST	MN	36E	85
SALVO JOSEPH MICHAEL	NY	25E	93
SALYARDS PATRICK JOHN	NE	13E	25
SALYER BILLY RAY	IN	26E	67
SALYER FRED LAMARR	KY	37E	63
SALYER STANLEY WILLIAM	MT	07E	106
SALZARULO RAYMOND PAUL JR	WV	10E	69
SALZER GENE LEO	MN	31W	20
SALZMAN LAVERN LEO	CA	28E	70
SAM WILFRED GERALD	NV	27W	33
SAMANIEGO JOE HENRY	TX	19E	46
SAMANIEGO ROBERTO	TX	02E	15
SAMANS WALTER A JR	VA	23E	46
SAMARAS PETER NICHOLAS	MA	16E	115
SAMARIPA JESSE	TX	12E	11
SAMFORD JESSE LEROY	TX	52E	10
SAMOLEJ GERALD	MI	41W	32
SAMORAY RICHARD MARTIN	NY	48W	15
SAMPERS JAMES WILLIAM	IA	18W	56
SAMPLE MICHAEL RAY	MO	17W	98
SAMPLE RONALD NEIL	IL	33W	20
SAMPLE STEPHEN GEORGE	IN	14W	31
SAMPLER LEWIS EUGENE	FL	28W	40
SAMPLES HERBERT CLEVELAND	WV	24E	92
SAMPLES LARRY JUNIOR	AL	66E	2
SAMPLES STEPHEN HENRY	NY	40W	39
SAMPSELL JOEL WARREN	CA	13W	21
SAMPSON GERALD HILBERT	PA	18W	4
SAMPSON JOSEPH C JR	OH	09E	82
SAMPSON LESLIE VERNE	MT	01E	2
SAMPSON MICHAEL JOHN	MN	07W	110
SAMPSON RANDOLPH	FL	45W	56
SAMPT JOHN FRANCIS	CT	05E	43
SAMS JOHN WILBUR JR	IA	12W	34
SAMS MICHAEL DOUGLAS	FL	30W	30
SAMS RICHARD BARRY	KY	16E	65
SAMSON FRANCISCO LEO JR	CA	21E	108
SAMSON JERRY ERNEST	MI	29W	73
SAMSON MICHAEL ROMAN	CA	09E	84
SAMUELS DONALD RAY	VA	13W	72
SAMUELS ELZIE EUGENE	FL	27E	41
SAMUELS GEORGE LEROY	KS	06E	94
SAMUELS ISAIAH	SC	17E	31
SAMUELS JAMES	NY	30E	99
SAMUELSON ROBERT L	NY	48E	43
SAMUELSON RONALD EARL	NE	08W	89
SAMZ FRANCIS MARK	WI	27W	41
SAN MARCOS EDMOND	CA	13E	62
SAN NICOLAS RUFO SANTOS	GM	07W	35
SAN NICOLAS VICTOR P	GM	14W	67
SANABIA OSCAR ENRIQUE	NY	36W	24
SANAZARO ERNEST JR	MO	55W	23
SANBORN JACK RICHARD	MI	50W	9
SANBOWER RONALD LEE	MD	04W	124
SANCEVERINO GARY ANTHONY	NY	11W	61
SANCHEZ ALBERTO VASQUEZ	TX	55W	38
SANCHEZ ANGEL LUIS	OH	66E	2
SANCHEZ ANGEL MANUEL	NY	16E	80
SANCHEZ BENNY KUMIYAMA	CA	44E	17
SANCHEZ CAMILO JAMES	NM	42E	71
SANCHEZ CARLOS J		06E	86
SANCHEZ CESAR ERNESTO	NY	15E	100
SANCHEZ CHARLES ANTHONY	NM	03W	74
SANCHEZ CRESENCIO PAUL	NM	05E	109
SANCHEZ DAVID	NY	24E	69
SANCHEZ EDWARD CHARLES	TX	31W	96
SANCHEZ EDWARD JR	CA	34E	45
SANCHEZ ERNESTO JR	TX	21E	108
SANCHEZ FRANKIE	KS	05E	68
SANCHEZ GEORGE SANTIAGO	GM	33W	34
SANCHEZ HECTOR LOUIS	OH	30E	99
SANCHEZ HERMAN PAUL	LA	14W	1
SANCHEZ IGNACIO	MA	38W	9
SANCHEZ JAVIER ARTURO E	TX	19E	32
SANCHEZ JESSE	CA	30E	49
SANCHEZ JIMMY PINEDA	CA	05E	123
SANCHEZ JOSE ANGEL	CA	03W	65
SANCHEZ JOSE GUADALUPE JR	TX	39W	23
SANCHEZ JOSE L	NM	23W	39
SANCHEZ JOSE RAMON	NY	59W	13
SANCHEZ JOSEPH SEBASTIAN	TX	09W	21
SANCHEZ JUAN DIEGO	NM	09E	59
SANCHEZ JUAN OSCAR	TX	43W	21
SANCHEZ MACARIO JR	TX	06W	87
SANCHEZ MICHAEL	TX	07W	74
SANCHEZ NICK ENRIQUE	CO	07W	19
SANCHEZ PABLO DEMEO	TX	47E	43
SANCHEZ PAUL FRANK	AZ	62W	17
SANCHEZ PEDRO JR	TX	37W	83
SANCHEZ RALPH JR	CA	57E	32
SANCHEZ REYNALDO AYALA	TX	51E	30
SANCHEZ ROBERT HUERTA	TX	41W	54
SANCHEZ ROBERT PAUL JR	CA	03W	64
SANCHEZ ROBERTO	WI	54E	16
SANCHEZ RUDOLPHO	AZ	45E	51
SANCHEZ SANTOS	CA	08E	94
SANCHEZ THOMAS JOSEPH	CA	16E	31
SANCHEZ UVALDO	NM	18E	64
SANCHEZ VIDAL JR	NJ	19E	112
SANCHEZ WILBERTO CABRERA	TX	09E	53
SANCHEZ-BERRIOS CARMELO	PR	06E	11
SANCHEZ-ORTIZ DIONISIO	PR	36W	65
SANCHEZ-ROHENA HECTOR M	PR	29W	83
SANCHEZ-SALIVA RAFAEL	PR	62E	9
SAND JAMES EDWARD	NY	52E	43
SAND RALPH THOMAS	CA	27W	13
SANDBERG CHARLES H	PA	60E	2
SANDBERG JOEL ALEXIS	CT	15W	74
SANDEFUR BILLIE E	OR	30E	99
SANDEFUR TOMMY GERALD	OK	36E	59
SANDEL RONALD S	WI	27E	83
SANDER JAMES KIETH	CA	38W	38
SANDER MICHAEL DENNIS	CA	32E	5
SANDER THOMAS WOODROW	OH	32W	51
SANDERLIN WILLIAM DALE	TX	15W	18
SANDERS ALAN EARL	TX	21W	10
SANDERS ARTHUR EDWIN	MO	05E	18
SANDERS ARTHUR JACKSON	KY	30E	33
SANDERS CHARLES	IN	43E	10
SANDERS CHARLES WILLIAM	IL	16E	107
SANDERS CLYDE DOUGLAS	TX	09W	41
SANDERS DARRELL W	WV	03E	91

NAME	STATE	PANEL NO.	LINE NO.
SANDERS DAUNT BRUNELL	WA	20W	60
SANDERS DONALD RAY	AK	17E	47
SANDERS DONALD ROBERT JR	OH	25W	43
SANDERS EDWARD LEON	AR	45W	1
SANDERS ELZIE JR	KY	29E	85
SANDERS FRANCIS EUGENE	MI	32E	59
SANDERS FRANK BART	CA	07W	82
SANDERS FREDERICK WRIGHT	OK	31E	53
SANDERS GEORGE AUSTIN	OH	13E	30
SANDERS GERARD JUDE	PA	53W	23
SANDERS GLENN EDWARD	AL	22E	85
SANDERS HARVEY RICHARD	CA	19E	101
SANDERS HENRY CLYDE	IL	29W	24
SANDERS JACK ALAN JR	FL	49E	26
SANDERS JACKIE LYNN	IN	22E	73
SANDERS JAMES ALBERT	AR	25W	32
SANDERS JAMES EDGAR JR	LA	46W	8
SANDERS JAMES GARLAND	NM	40W	34
SANDERS JERRY J	MO	03E	79
SANDERS JESSIE FRANKLIN	AL	10W	47
SANDERS JIMMY DOYLE	OK	15W	123
SANDERS JOHNNY CRAWFORD	MS	01E	39
SANDERS JON HUBBARD	FL	02W	137
SANDERS JULIUS MITCHELL	NM	10E	43
SANDERS KENNETH EUGENE	OK	12E	12
SANDERS LARRY TRUMAN	TX	18W	56
SANDERS LEO MELVIN	DC	08W	5
SANDERS LOYD HOWARD	NC	08W	40
SANDERS MACK ROYAL	NE	07E	55
SANDERS MARVIN HOWARD	MO	15W	20
SANDERS MELVIN HILTON	CT	39E	53
SANDERS PHILLIP DUANE	OK	24W	20
SANDERS RICHARD LEE	CA	30E	81
SANDERS RICHARD WAYNE	OH	42W	59
SANDERS ROBERT BRUCE	NV	47W	32
SANDERS ROBERT EARL	NC	57W	3
SANDERS ROBERT HERNDON	LA	62W	2
SANDERS ROBERT JAMES	PA	30E	33
SANDERS ROBERT NEIL	NE	36W	31
SANDERS RODNEY RAYFORD	AL	10W	127
SANDERS RONALD LLOYD	OK	31W	20
SANDERS RONALD WALTER	MI	19E	65
SANDERS STANLEY	MD	22E	114
SANDERS STEVEN ROY	MT	19W	115
SANDERS TERRY LEE	MI	09W	116
SANDERS THOMAS	NY	19E	86
SANDERS THOMAS ANDREW	NY	02E	30
SANDERS WAYNE JACKSON	AR	18W	50
SANDERS WILLIAM JACOB	OH	25E	54
SANDERS WILLIAM LEROY	CO	19E	100
SANDERS WILLIAM RAYMOND	IL	15E	80
SANDERS WILLIAM STEPHEN	ME	09W	107
SANDERSEN WILLIAM LEONARD	CO	47W	4
SANDERSON BOBBY	SC	31W	20
SANDERSON GAIL GENE	IA	23W	3
SANDERSON JACK JOHNSTONE	NY	38W	52
SANDERSON JOHN DANIEL	MS	10E	32
SANDERSON JOHNNIE D	WI	27E	22
SANDERSON SANDER CHRIS	CA	14E	18
SANDFER WILLIE J JR	NM	28W	29
SANDFORD BRADLEY ELLIOTT	NH	05W	12
SANDIDGE THEODORE WILLIAM	IL	47E	58
SANDIFER RICHARD WELLS	MI	29E	17
SANDLIN RONALD LEE	MS	34E	92
SANDLIN STEVEN RAY	CA	11W	62
SANDMAN MITCHELL HARVEY	NY	23W	58
SANDMANN RONALD LEE	MN	31E	77
SANDNER ROBERT LOUIS	FL	08E	18
SANDNES LARRY GORDON	PA	37W	69
SANDOVAL ALAN PAUL	CA	20W	45
SANDOVAL DANIEL FLORE	CA	50E	10
SANDOVAL EVARISTO	TX	26E	63
SANDOVAL GEORGE	CA	43W	22
SANDOVAL HECTOR MONTALVO	IL	07W	14
SANDOVAL JOSE RAMON	CO	05W	41
SANDOVAL LOUIE JOE	CA	61E	19
SANDOVAL PHILLIP JAMES	NM	05W	92
SANDOVAL RANDALL JACK	AZ	30W	69
SANDOVAL THOMAS FREDRICK	CA	31E	1
SANDOVAL VICENTE DIAZ	ID	17E	128
SANDOVALL ANTONIO RAMOS	TX	01W	129
SANDS EDDIE BERNARD	NC	56E	30

NAME	STATE	PANEL NO.	LINE NO.
SANDS JOSEPH GREGORY	MD	19W	22
SANDS KENNETH EARL	PA	47E	16
SANDS OKEY LEE	WV	06E	118
SANDS RICHARD EUGENE	IL	59E	12
SANDS THOMAS MICHAEL	CA	16E	31
SANDS WILLIAM D III	GA	17E	24
SANDSTEDT DANIEL JOSEPH	NE	22E	19
SANDSTROM HUGH THOMAS	NY	16E	86
SANDSTROM ROBERT RICHARD	CA	27E	56
SANDVE DONALD RAYMOND	SD	04E	60
SANDVIG DAVID JAMES	WA	29W	92
SANDVIG LAMOINE LOWELL	CO	23E	90
SANDVIG VERNON DALE	CA	46E	58
SANEDA JOHN	OH	48W	47
SANFILIPPO FRANK	NY	38W	46
SANFORD ALBERT RUSSELL	KY	47E	16
SANFORD ARNOLD	SC	26W	36
SANFORD DAVID AMON	MI	38E	13
SANFORD GARY BERNERD	MI	51W	8
SANFORD HENRY CHARLES JR	OH	57W	3
SANFORD HOLLIS COLEMAN JR	MS	08W	83
SANFORD JACKIE WILLARD	WV	02E	11
SANFORD JAMES IRA	GA	24W	71
SANFORD JAMES RUSSELL JR	OH	48E	34
SANFORD JAMES WALTER	SC	22E	49
SANFORD JOHN FRANCIS	PA	05E	15
SANFORD ROBERT RAY	WA	20W	26
SANGER STEPHEN CARROLL	NY	14E	113
SANGILLO WAYNE	ME	38W	8
SANGSTER GARY LAVERN	MN	08E	69
SANGSTER ROBERT LEONARD	GA	38W	46
SANKS JERRY WILLIE RAY	FL	07E	6
SANSBURY RICHARD H	MD	05W	34
SANSEVERINO ANTHONY	NY	18E	116
SANSING JERRY RUSSELL	FL	47W	12
SANSONE DOMINICK	NY	01E	76
SANSONE DONALD FRANK	IL	29E	34
SANSONE JAMES JOSEPH	MA	01W	62
SANTA CRUZ JOSE ANGEL	AZ	14W	91
SANTA-CRUZ DAVID FRANK	CA	10W	122
SANTANA ANTHONY JOHN	NY	47W	53
SANTANA FLORENTINO JOHN	IL	10E	115
SANTANA JOSE JR	NY	33E	10
SANTANA JOSE MANUEL	NY	29E	34
SANTANGELO SAMUEL JOHN	NY	39E	77
SANTANIELLO VINCENT BENOR	NY	46E	59
SANTEE HENRY EDWARD	MS	05W	7
SANTELLAN TEODORO	MI	42W	1
SANTELLANO LUIS ADRIAN	IL	11W	75
SANTIAGO ALAN ANGEL	NY	25E	59
SANTIAGO ALEXANDER P JR	NY	23W	79
SANTIAGO ANGELO CARMELO	PA	59W	13
SANTIAGO FELIPE OBED	NY	21W	56
SANTIAGO GERMAN ANTONIO	PR	69E	2
SANTIAGO HUMBERTO RUIZ JR	NY	21W	25
SANTIAGO JOSE JUAN	NY	39E	39
SANTIAGO LUIS SANTIAGO	NJ	08E	88
SANTIAGO ROBINSON	NY	31W	57
SANTIAGO TIMOTEO MUNOZ JR	TX	39W	24
SANTIAGO-APONTE NELSON	PR	60E	2
SANTIAGO-ARROYO ANSELMO	PR	20W	32
SANTIAGO-CASTILLO REINALDO JR	PR	14W	33
SANTIAGO-COLON HECTOR	NY	54W	13
SANTIAGO-CRUZ RAFAEL	NJ	03E	46
SANTIAGO-LUGO JOSE C JR	NY	27E	76
SANTIAGO-MALDONADO JUAN A	PR	11E	95
SANTIAGO-MARTINEZ ANDRES	PR	12W	32
SANTIAGO-VAZQUEZ BERNARDINO	NY	15E	22
SANTILLI RAYMO	PA	03E	47
SANTINAC LAWRENCE HAROLD	LA	13W	107
SANTINELLO RALPH MICHAEL	NY	25W	110
SANTISTEVAN BENNY M JR	CO	47E	43
SANTO PATRICK ANGELO	MI	18W	4
SANTONE JOSEPH ANTHONY	PA	16E	115
SANTOR ROBERT PAUL	AZ	11E	10
SANTORA RAYMOND PAUL	OH	38W	38
SANTORELLA ROBERT H	CO	06E	115
SANTORI JOSEPH	NJ	51E	42
SANTORO ROBERT JOHN		48W	15
SANTORO RONALD PETER	NJ	49W	6
SANTOROSKI MICHAEL PAUL	NY	27E	16
SANTOS ALBERT WILLARD	MA	25E	109

NAME	STATE	PANEL NO.	LINE NO.
SANTOS ENRIQUE ROSARIO	GM	04W	54
SANTOS ERNEST PABLO	GM	22E	33
SANTOS JAMES EDWARD ANDER	GM	16E	98
SANTOS JOHN F JR	CA	01E	50
SANTOS JOSE CARLOS	TX	39W	62
SANTOS JOSEPH	CA	37E	13
SANTOS LAYNE MICHAEL	CA	30W	30
SANTOS MICHAEL EUGENE	CA	53E	22
SANTOS RAFAEL SALAS	GM	12W	129
SANTOS RENE ANTHONY	TX	28W	1
SANTOS-IZAGAS DIOSDADO	PR	33W	4
SANTOS-LOPEZ JOSE LUIS	PR	13W	114
SANTOS-PINEDO PEDRO	PR	05E	57
SANTOS-TRUJILLO DANIEL	PR	03E	27
SANTOS-VEGA MARCELINO	PR	08E	58
SANTUCCI VINICIO FREDEK	IL	44W	29
SANTY STEVEN CRAIG	NH	52W	31
SANUT ALFREDO	HI	07W	107
SANVILLE ERNEST EUGENE	NH	45W	16
SANZONE ROBERT BENJAMIN	NY	20E	35
SANZOVERINO WILLIAM EUGEN	NY	56E	31
SAPINOSA ALFRED ROBERT	CA	45E	29
SAPORITO MICHAEL CHARLES	NY	41W	15
SAPORITO RONALD	NY	55E	30
SAPP ALFRED GEORGE SR	MD	18W	98
SAPP BENNY JAMES	OH	38W	20
SAPP CLARK EDWARD	CA	21E	19
SAPP FREDDY LEE	TX	08E	79
SAPP ISAAC	CT	23W	3
SAPP JEFFERY TRUETT	TX	27W	59
SAPP JON CHARLES	IL	11W	25
SAPP RONALD ALLEN	FL	06E	42
SAPP STANLEY L	TX	03E	124
SAPP WAYNE LEROY	CA	36E	80
SAPP WILLIAM DANIEL	AL	05W	108
SAPP WILLIAM EDWARD	GA	59W	27
SAPPINGFIELD FRANKLIN A	IN	45E	42
SARACINO FRANK DE PAUL JR	CO	29W	92
SARAH HUGH HENRY	MI	17W	1
SARAKAS RICHARD THOMAS	MO	19E	112
SARAKOV HARRY DANIEL	CA	24W	21
SARDINA FRANK	NY	41E	72
SARGENT BILLY RAY	KY	09W	75
SARGENT EDWARD RAY	NC	18W	25
SARGENT GARY LEE	OH	10E	2
SARGENT GEORGE THOMAS JR	AL	28W	3
SARGENT GORDON LEROY JR	NJ	30W	16
SARGENT JAMES RAY	WV	58E	14
SARGENT KENNETH EUGENE	WA	03E	104
SARGENT KENNETH PAGE	FL	15E	130
SARGENT ROLLIN CHESLEY JR	VT	01E	67
SARGENT RUPPERT LEON	VA	16E	86
SARGENT STANTON GERALD	MS	03W	1
SARGENT STEVAN ROY	WA	39E	53
SARJEANT DWIGHT CUTLER	OH	38W	78
SARMENTO HENRY MICHAEL	CT	20E	49
SARNA ARNOLD PAUL	MI	44E	40
SAROCAM JOSEPH	HI	43W	30
SAROSSY STEVE SANDOR	OH	34E	92
SARSFIELD HARRY CARL	CA	28E	30
SARTOR JOHN VICTOR	WI	50W	2
SARTOR LEONDA	SC	39W	75
SARVELA MERREL GERALD	MN	43W	66
SARVIS RICHARD LEE	NC	05W	131
SAS LOUIS	PA	16E	115
SAS ROBERT LOUIS	OH	30E	81
SAS THEODORE FRANCIS	MA	13W	16
SASAKI ALLYSON YUKIO	HI	30E	66
SASEK RICHARD JOHN	KS	23E	23
SASSE PATRICK T	SD	31E	53
SASSER GEORGE FREDERICK	TN	01W	104
SATCHELL RONALD EDWARD	PA	38E	80
SATCHER CHARLES SHERLEE	CA	05E	123
SATER REGINALD MARK	FL	20W	126
SATHER RICHARD CHRISTIAN	CA	01E	60
SATHOFF DALE ERVIN	MO	08W	71
SATO TAKESHI	CA	21W	57
SATTER DONALD STEPHEN	MN	59W	13
SATTERFIELD HARRY TRUMAN	NC	15E	122
SATTERFIELD HOWARD EUGENE	TX	07W	23
SATTERFIELD JOHN STEPHEN	AR	01W	108
SATTERFIELD ROBERT W	PA	27W	97

NAME	STATE	PANEL NO.	LINE NO.
SATTERFIELD WILLIAM HURLE	NJ	31W	20
SATTERTHWAITE RICHARD D	MT	29W	84
SATTERWHITE DWIGHT KING	TX	11E	11
SATTERWHITE RUFFIN J JR	PA	41E	54
SATTLER WILLIAM JOHN III	CA	11W	69
SAUBLE MARTIN G JR	PA	35W	13
SAUBLE THOMAS EUGENE	PA	16E	73
SAUCEDA JOE A	TX	17E	31
SAUCEDO ROGELIO	TX	17E	129
SAUCIER ROBERT ARTHUR	AR	22E	92
SAUER CHARLES EDWARD	CT	23E	31
SAUER PHILIP HOWARD	CA	18E	81
SAUER WALTER JR	OH	26E	107
SAUERS GERALD	PA	16W	47
SAUKAITIS JOSEPH STEPHEN	PA	12W	9
SAULER CHARLIE F		27E	50
SAULNIER JEREMIAH JOHN	RI	52W	37
SAULS ELBERT JAMES	AR	29W	40
SAULS GEORGE HAROLD JR	FL	43E	60
SAULS OLLIE LESLIE JR	MI	64W	1
SAULS ROBERT NED	GA	29W	14
SAULSBERRY CLARENCE L JR	IL	01W	22
SAUNDERS BASIL LEE	OK	28E	62
SAUNDERS BRUCE	NY	24W	21
SAUNDERS BRUCE ALLAN	VA	31W	57
SAUNDERS CLYDE WILLIAM	OH	18W	115
SAUNDERS DARRYL ELDRIDGE	IL	23E	23
SAUNDERS DONALD BARON	NJ	42E	71
SAUNDERS EARNEST ROLLIN	CT	61W	7
SAUNDERS EMANUEL LAWRENCE	DC	23W	47
SAUNDERS FREDERIC C JR	FL	02W	7
SAUNDERS GEOFFREY D R	FL	52E	23
SAUNDERS GEORGE THOMAS JR	WV	03E	10
SAUNDERS JOHN LLOYD	PA	41E	3
SAUNDERS JOHN WILBUR JR	CO	17W	5
SAUNDERS KEITH FRANK	NV	16W	20
SAUNDERS LOWELL RAY	WV	02W	72
SAUNDERS MICHAEL JORN	NH	31E	77
SAUNDERS MICHAEL JOSEPH	FL	52E	43
SAUNDERS NICHOLAS GABRIEL	CA	10W	62
SAUNDERS RALF IRVIN	IN	29E	35
SAUNDERS RANDALL LEROY	UT	39E	65
SAUNDERS RONALD	MD	55W	19
SAUNDERS TIMOTHY JUDD	WY	23E	15
SAUNDERS WILLIAM MICHAEL	OK	46E	1
SAUNDERS WILLIAM O JR	CA	34E	45
SAURINI JAMES PAUL	TX	30E	66
SAUSE BERNARD JACOB JR	MD	15E	108
SAUVE DANIEL LOUIS PAUL		06E	127
SAUX ROGER DOUGLAS	WA	50E	41
SAVACOOL PAUL ROSS JR	GA	49W	33
SAVAGE DANIEL	PA	14W	105
SAVAGE DOUGLAS PAUL	CA	21W	2
SAVAGE JAMES TERRY	GA	17W	78
SAVAGE JAMES WADDELL	VA	26E	97
SAVAGE MORGAN ELBERT	MD	14E	59
SAVAGE VARIS JR	TN	03E	27
SAVAGE WILLIAM ROSS	OK	08E	89
SAVAGEAU JOHN HENRY	MA	06E	26
SAVANUCK PAUL DAVID	MD	26W	2
SAVARE HOWARD LEROY	WA	46E	23
SAVAS SAM MICHAEL JR	FL	02E	120
SAVELL FLOYD GWEN	ID	15E	30
SAVELL MYLES CLAYTON	MS	10E	76
SAVICK JOSEPH JAMES JR	OH	02W	79
SAVIEO RICHARD HUGH	OH	07W	6
SAVILLE JOHN DERWOOD JR	MD	27E	76
SAVINO LAWRENCE NEIL	MA	24W	107
SAVOREN WILLIAM MARTIN	MN	03E	114
SAVOTH TERRY LEE	NJ	37W	25
SAVOY CLAYTON EDWARD	ME	10W	116
SAVOY M J	MO	08E	58
SAWAYA ROBERT MITCHELL	UT	32E	5
SAWICKI ANTHONY PETER	PA	26E	51
SAWICKI RICHARD P	NE	03E	91
SAWNEY JACKIE LEE	OK	05W	38
SAWRAN RICHARD ARTHUR	NJ	18W	76
SAWTELLE PAUL COBURN	NY	04W	129
SAWYER BRADFORD PRESTON	CT	33W	88
SAWYER DONALD SHERWOOD	NC	27W	61
SAWYER FRANK W JR	KY	22E	114
SAWYER JAMES EVERETT JR	NH	22W	49
SAWYER JAMES HOWARD	WV	02E	60
SAWYER JOHNNIE PAUL	SC	08E	31
SAWYER JONATHAN ANSEL	ME	22E	114
SAWYER KENNETH ROBERT	VA	32W	24
SAWYER MICHAEL KENNETH	VA	17W	85
SAWYER PAUL LEWIS JR	AL	48E	53
SAWYER ROBERT WILLIAM	NH	47W	53
SAWYER WILLIAM A	MI	37E	68
SAWYER WILLIAM LELON JR	FL	08W	50
SAWYERS CHARLES DOUGLAS	WV	29E	76
SAWYERS ROGER THURSTON	NM	27E	41
SAXBY JAMES FRANCIS	NY	06W	92
SAXON CLYDE EDWARD	GA	29W	73
SAXON FRANK ROBERT	MD	02E	83
SAXON JAMES RUSSELL	MD	03W	62
SAXON JOHNNY	NC	04W	133
SAXTON GARY LEE	CA	35E	11
SAXTON JAMES HERSHEL JR	FL	06W	48
SAYER ALBERT FRANCIS JR	KY	26E	38
SAYER JOHN STEPHEN	NY	13E	30
SAYER TERRY LYNN	NE	30W	60
SAYERS LARRY VENCIL	KY	21E	52
SAYERS PAUL FREDERICK	VA	11W	3
SAYERS THOMAS RALPH	OH	19W	98
SAYLOR CHARLES DUANE	IN	16E	67
SAYLOR SCOTT EDWARD	PA	24W	113
SAYLOR WAYMOND ANDREW	WV	40W	46
SAYLOR WILLIAM JR	SC	03W	48
SAYRE LESLIE BERKLEY	OH	45E	43
SCADUTO RICHARD LEE	PA	25E	65
SCAHILL EDWARD JOHN	MA	12E	105
SCAIFE KENNETH DOYLE	PA	01W	108
SCALA RICHARD MICHAEL	NY	41E	28
SCALES ASTOR JR	CA	55W	15
SCALES DOUGLAS	GA	52W	11
SCALF DARYL GENE	IL	33W	69
SCALF JAMES RAY	OK	18E	50
SCALISE EDWARD JOSEPH	CA	36W	59
SCALISE THOMAS RANDAL	PA	45W	2
SCALLIONS CARL WAYNE	TN	20E	87
SCAMARONI LUIS GUILLERMO	NY	48E	34
SCANLAN GEORGE JOSEPH	MI	13E	111
SCANLAN LAWRENCE WALKER	KS	44E	3
SCANLAN WARREN LEE JR	VA	10W	77
SCANLON MICHAEL JOHN	CT	14E	50
SCANLON WILLIAM MANUEL	CA	08W	95
SCARANO CHARLES PATRICK		47E	54
SCARBERRY DONALD YOUNG	MI	23W	4
SCARBERRY LARRY DALE	WV	04E	5
SCARBORO THOMAS ALLEN	NC	12W	108
SCARBOROUGH EDMUND BAGWEL	VA	58E	15
SCARBOROUGH ELMER WAYNE	MI	08E	130
SCARBOROUGH GEORGE THOMAS	GA	13W	107
SCARBOROUGH GRIFFIN ELI	NC	59E	15
SCARBOROUGH JACK WADE JR	WV	51W	43
SCARBOROUGH JAMES ARTHUR	AZ	35W	21
SCARBOROUGH RUSSELL WILLI	FL	48E	34
SCARBROUGH ARTHUR BENJAMI	AL	10E	48
SCARBROUGH DAVID CLIFTON	OH	41E	28
SCARBROUGH ENNIS RALPH	AL	07E	55
SCARBROUGH ROGER ALLEN	IL	07W	28
SCARMEAS JAMES SAM JR	MI	24W	71
SCARPINATO JOHN ANDREW	CA	59W	27
SCARPULLA FRANK MARK JR	MD	21E	16
SCATES CHARLES EDWARD JR	KS	63E	1
SCATES CHARLIE KENNETH	WV	05E	57
SCATUORCHIO DOMINIC N JR	NJ	13W	106
SCAVELLA ALLAN NAPOLEON	NY	34W	18
SCAVELLA JESSE ELLISON JR	NY	44E	11
SCAVUZZO PETER GARY	NJ	05E	107
SCHAAF JOHN RAYMOND	MN	50E	21
SCHAAF RICHARD ALLAN	MD	09E	117
SCHAAF RONALD JOSEPH	OH	08W	56
SCHAAF WILLIAM JOHN	MD	30W	30
SCHACHNER DAVID BRENNAN	NC	24W	11
SCHACHTNER JAMES ALOYSIUS	WI	09W	102
SCHADDELEE WILLIAM D	IL	14E	106
SCHAEFER ALAN FRANCIS	NY	13E	124
SCHAEFER CHARLES HAROLD	IL	19W	109
SCHAEFER DAVID ROY	WI	26W	94
SCHAEFER JOHN STEVE	TX	12W	10
SCHAEFER KENNETH LEE	WI	08E	127
SCHAEFER ROGER BERNARD	MN	16W	123
SCHAEFER ROY ANTHONY JR	WI	16E	23
SCHAEFER SYLVESTER ANTONY	MN	08E	77
SCHAEFER THOMAS KOENIG	MN	30W	30
SCHAEFER WILLIAM ERIC	IL	25W	83
SCHAEFER WILLIAM HAYS	KY	39W	56
SCHAEFFER ARLON GLENN	CO	42W	7
SCHAEFFER FREDERICK WILLI	CA	22E	13
SCHAEFFER GEROLD	WI	08E	30
SCHAEFFER GUY LAWRENCE	NJ	03E	92
SCHAEFFER PAUL HENRY	PA	22W	93
SCHAFER CHARLES EDWARD	CO	09E	8
SCHAFER DONALD FRED	MI	20E	49
SCHAFER DONALD RAYMOND	OR	53E	40
SCHAFER GARY RAY	MD	26E	108
SCHAFER JOSEPH RICHARD	WV	03W	25
SCHAFER MARVIN ALBERT	KY	18E	128
SCHAFERNOCKER MICHAEL E	TX	26W	74
SCHAFFER BILLY JOE	SC	12W	74
SCHAFFER BLAINE CLARENCE	PA	49W	16
SCHAFFER DAVID THOMAS	AZ	18W	4
SCHAFFER JOHN FERDINAND	AR	39W	34
SCHAFFNER JACK DOHN	KY	37W	69
SCHAFFNER MARSHALL GUST	ID	45E	29
SCHAICH DONALD BRUCE	OH	36E	34
SCHALIPP MURVIN JR	KS	03E	92
SCHALK THOMAS MICHAEL SR	OH	09W	80
SCHALL CHARLES NELSON JR	PA	41W	8
SCHALTENBRAND WAYNE KEITH	FL	24W	12
SCHAMPIER ROBERT BRUCE	NY	43E	33
SCHANCK HENRY EDWARD	MN	33E	32
SCHANCK WILLIAM G JR	RI	22W	109
SCHANEBERG LEROY CLYDE	IL	09W	107
SCHAP FRANK JOSEPH	MD	39E	39
SCHAPANICK CHESTER	NY	07E	98
SCHARES ROBERT JOHN	IA	16W	93
SCHARF CHARLES JOSEPH	CA	02E	101
SCHARF RONALD JAMES	OH	20W	61
SCHARFF LENNIE HAROLD	CA	40E	56
SCHARIBONE DAVID JOHN	NJ	19E	112
SCHARLACH STEVEN EDWARD	NY	21E	52
SCHARNBERG RONALD OLIVER	AR	04W	56
SCHARON ROBERT E III	MD	29E	61
SCHAROSCH PATRICK FRANCIS	CA	50E	8
SCHASRE DAVID M	CA	40E	12
SCHATZLEY MICHAEL DONN	IL	06E	46
SCHATZMAN ROBERT JAMES	PA	62W	19
SCHAUB TERRY LEE	OH	40E	33
SCHAUBLE KENNETH WILLIAM	NJ	59W	14
SCHAUERMANN ARTHUR GARRY	OR	53E	22
SCHAUTTEET LOUIS L JR	TX	33E	93
SCHAVELIN HUGH ERNEST	NJ	50E	21
SCHECK CLIFFORD HENRY	IN	52W	20
SCHECKLER PAUL	PA	53W	4
SCHEELER VICTOR RAY	OH	30W	39
SCHEELY ROBERT JAMES	OH	16W	37
SCHEETZ JOHN ELLWOOD	PA	20E	18
SCHEIB LAWRENCE ELWOOD JR	PA	07W	23
SCHEIB RALPH EUGENE	NY	18E	64
SCHEIBER RICHARD ALAN	IN	29E	92
SCHEIBER WILLIAM HENRY JR	KY	35E	50
SCHEIDEL ROBERT L JR	CT	27W	59
SCHEIDT WILLIAM H	CA	08E	106
SCHELL DUANE CHARLES	WA	02E	89
SCHELL EDWARD EARL	MI	15E	1
SCHELL RANDY STEPHEN	PA	56W	27
SCHELL RICHARD JOHN	MN	25E	40
SCHELL ROBERT CHARLES JR	NY	19W	109
SCHELL TERRY LEE	IL	12W	74
SCHELL WILLIAM LEROY	PA	04W	71
SCHELLER JEFFREY LYNN	NJ	01W	79
SCHELLIN JAMES WILLARD F	SC	06W	63
SCHELLING CHARLES HOWARD	CA	02W	116
SCHELVAN DAVID ERIC	WA	18E	98
SCHEMEL GARY LEROY	MO	02E	95
SCHEMEL JERRY L	MI	09E	82
SCHENA ROBERT PETER	MA	14E	12
SCHENE TERRANCE RICHARD	MO	03W	42
SCHEPP DALE ALLEN	WI	15W	43
SCHERDIN ROBERT FRANCIS	NJ	35W	6
SCHERER CHRISTOPHER J	NY	63E	2
SCHERER JAMES LEE	TX	33E	32

NAME	STATE	PANEL NO.	LINE NO.
SCHERER JAMES MICHAEL	PA	05W	53
SCHERF MICHAEL GREGORY	CO	23W	58
SCHERLAG ROBERT	NY	18E	27
SCHERLE WILLIAM JOSEPH JR	KY	20E	99
SCHERMANN HERMAN WILLIAM	PA	49W	17
SCHERRER LAWRENCE FRANCIS	MO	20E	49
SCHERTZ JOHN EDWARD	IL	58E	26
SCHETTIG ROBERT SCOTT	NY	03W	99
SCHETTL DAVID LEROY	WI	62E	11
SCHETTLER HARRY ROBERT	MD	07W	68
SCHEU GUNTER WILFRIED	PA	03W	116
SCHEUBLE MELVIN JOHN	MN	53W	5
SCHEUER BOBBY DALE	OH	17W	5
SCHEULEN GARY JEROME J	MO	24W	49
SCHEURICH THOMAS EDWIN	NE	42E	24
SCHIAVONE RALPH	NY	41W	1
SCHIBI JAMES LEE	AZ	46W	33
SCHICKEL MICHAEL JOSEPH	FL	34W	88
SCHIELE CRAIG BRIAN	OH	06W	19
SCHIELE JAMES FRANCIS	UT	23E	65
SCHIERMEYER WILLIAM D JR	CA	14W	113
SCHIESL GERALD RAYMOND	WI	28W	30
SCHIESS THOMAS CHARLES	NJ	07W	123
SCHIEVE PAUL EVERETT	MI	62W	1
SCHIFFHAUER JOHN CHARLES	PA	30W	7
SCHIFRIN RAYMOND RICHARD	NY	22W	27
SCHILLER JOSEPH FREDERICK	NY	56W	8
SCHILLER MARTIN SULLY JR	TN	14W	34
SCHILLING GEORGE DON	TX	55W	23
SCHIMANSKI KENNETH ALFRED	WA	17W	17
SCHIMBERG JAMES PHILIP	IA	04E	60
SCHIMMEL STEVEN GEORGE	IN	23W	58
SCHIMMELS EDDIE RAY	CA	32W	56
SCHIMPF JOSEPH FRANCIS	PA	28W	30
SCHINDLER EUGENE DONALD	MN	51W	36
SCHINDLER THOMAS JAMES	MD	02E	109
SCHIRO GERALD ANTHONY	IL	47E	17
SCHLAMP GARY OLIN	CA	55E	30
SCHLECHT JOHN III	NY	03E	92
SCHLEE HARRY LEE	PA	28E	86
SCHLEY ROBERT JAMES	WI	18E	128
SCHLICHT JEROME JOSEPH	MN	33W	22
SCHLICHTING VICTOR STEVEN	MI	32W	73
SCHLICK JOSEPH FRANCIS	IL	46E	59
SCHLIE KENNETH MARTIN	VA	06W	13
SCHLIEBEN KLAUS DIETER	VA	12W	75
SCHLIESMAN JERROLD JOSEPH	WI	03E	92
SCHLIEWE FLOYD ABNER	WI	06W	13
SCHLINGER JAMES IRWIN	NJ	39W	8
SCHLOEMER CARL WAYNE	MO	09E	26
SCHLOSSER STEVEN MICHAEL	IL	49W	44
SCHLOTE LOUIS CHRIS	CA	50E	21
SCHLOTT DENNIS GUY	MD	13E	100
SCHLOTTMAN ALVERN WARREN	MO	11E	59
SCHLOTTMAN JAMES EDWARD	CA	25E	32
SCHLUEB STEVEN MICHAEL	OH	47W	32
SCHLUTERMAN DAVID FRANK	AR	22W	43
SCHLUTTER WILLIAM DAVID	WI	04W	56
SCHMALE WILLIAM OTTO	AL	47W	53
SCHMALTZ DOUGLAS RALPH	OH	05W	84
SCHMALZ CARL FREDRICK JR	NJ	63E	1
SCHMAUTZ FRANCIS PHILLIP	MA	28E	87
SCHMECKER JOHN LEONARD	CT	13E	73
SCHMEES WILLIAM F JR	OH	29E	21
SCHMELING ERWIN ROSS	MN	12W	15
SCHMELTZ JERRY E	IL	13E	86
SCHMELZLE JOHN JOSEPH	KS	27W	78
SCHMICH JOSEPH JR	MO	30W	31
SCHMID JAY JULIUS	NJ	37W	59
SCHMID JOHN STEPHEN	WI	04E	44
SCHMID ROBERT ANTHONY	NY	10E	13
SCHMID RONALD KENNETH	WI	13E	93
SCHMIDT ALLAN LEE	IA	39W	29
SCHMIDT DALE HOWARD	IA	37E	14
SCHMIDT DALE W JR	TX	09E	78
SCHMIDT DANIEL THOMAS	MI	21E	29
SCHMIDT DANNY RAY	IN	09W	48
SCHMIDT DARYL JAY	NY	22W	82
SCHMIDT DAVID JEROME	WI	12W	75
SCHMIDT DENIS GORDON	MI	24W	26
SCHMIDT DENNIS RICHARD	NJ	09E	117
SCHMIDT DENNIS ROBERT	WI	31E	1
SCHMIDT DONALD FRANK	MI	08E	69
SCHMIDT DONALD HAROLD	MN	46E	23
SCHMIDT EDMUND JOSEPH	MT	35W	17
SCHMIDT FREDERICK CHARLES	MO	18E	76
SCHMIDT GARY RUSSELL	NE	27E	12
SCHMIDT GERALD BERNARD	IL	06E	26
SCHMIDT HERBERT ELLIS	MO	69E	2
SCHMIDT JAMES DREW	WA	08W	25
SCHMIDT JOHN GEORGE	MO	34E	64
SCHMIDT JOHN JOSEPH	AR	19W	115
SCHMIDT JOSEPH	OH	45W	61
SCHMIDT JOSEPH VINCENT	MO	24W	26
SCHMIDT KARL ALBERT JR	FL	11E	17
SCHMIDT KENNETH WAYNE	NE	03E	16
SCHMIDT LARRY ROMAN	WI	19W	22
SCHMIDT LAWRENCE EDWARD	WI	16W	31
SCHMIDT MARK VEDDER	NY	32E	81
SCHMIDT MICHAEL	NY	02W	95
SCHMIDT NORMAN	CA	10E	60
SCHMIDT PAUL EDWARD	CO	36W	3
SCHMIDT PETER ALDEN	WI	08W	115
SCHMIDT RICHARD CARL	NY	14W	1
SCHMIDT RICHARD HERMAN	PA	07E	76
SCHMIDT RICHARD LEROY	NE	46E	49
SCHMIDT RICHARD MARTIN	NY	29W	14
SCHMIDT RICKFORD RAY	CA	14E	3
SCHMIDT ROBERT GUSTAVE	NY	23W	11
SCHMIDT RONALD EUGENE	IL	10W	43
SCHMIDT SCOTT LAWRENCE	CA	06W	105
SCHMIDT STEVEN WARREN	CA	34E	25
SCHMIDT WALTER JAMES	NJ	12E	44
SCHMIDT WALTER ROY JR	NY	58W	14
SCHMIDT WILFRED F JR	IL	27W	78
SCHMIDT WILLIAM JAMES	CA	19W	22
SCHMITT FRANCIS BARON	FL	62E	11
SCHMITT FREDERICK	WI	33W	34
SCHMITT GARY WALTER	CO	29E	54
SCHMITT JOHN KENNETH JR	IA	49W	49
SCHMITT RICHIE HUMES	FL	04E	5
SCHMITTOU EUREKA LAVERN	TX	20E	92
SCHMITZ CRAIG ALAN	MO	07W	28
SCHMITZ LOREN MICHAEL	MN	19E	100
SCHMITZ PHILLIP NICHOLAS	MN	10W	15
SCHMITZ RICHARD ALBERT	CA	07E	57
SCHMITZ RICHARD TRAVIS	OH	18E	128
SCHMITZ ROBERT EUGENE	ND	18W	98
SCHMITZ WILLIAM DAVID	MN	32E	81
SCHMOLKE JOSEPH MICHAEL	LA	34W	80
SCHMOLL JAMES KENNETH	WI	05W	126
SCHMUDE JOHN ROBERT	MI	49W	10
SCHMUTZ ANTHONY MICHAEL	NJ	23E	7
SCHNABLY DONALD FRANCIS	WV	15W	14
SCHNABOLK HOWARD JON	NJ	24E	74
SCHNACK STEVEN SPENCER	CA	33E	60
SCHNAIDT RONALD RUSSELL	SD	17E	107
SCHNAKE RICHARD MARTIN	MI	24W	99
SCHNEBEL ROBERT FRED	OH	36W	54
SCHNEE DONALD LAWRENCE	OH	15E	51
SCHNEEMAN CLIFFORD W JR	OH	29E	26
SCHNEGG CHARLES GLENN	OH	31E	37
SCHNEIDER DAVID ALAN	OH	32W	61
SCHNEIDER DAVID FRANCIS	OH	39E	39
SCHNEIDER DENNIS PATRICK	OR	13W	50
SCHNEIDER GARY GENE	OH	13E	105
SCHNEIDER GARY LEE	KY	08W	18
SCHNEIDER GERARD JOSEPH	NY	19E	65
SCHNEIDER HARRY WARREN	WI	39E	66
SCHNEIDER JACK ARTHUR	IL	08E	8
SCHNEIDER JOHN MILLARD	FL	57E	32
SCHNEIDER KENNETH EUGENE	NY	38E	80
SCHNEIDER ROBERT DEAN	CO	06W	95
SCHNEIDER ROGER LLOYD	NE	36E	85
SCHNEIDER SCOTT EDWARD	WA	08W	120
SCHNEIDER TERRANCE H	MI	27E	50
SCHNEIDER THOMAS HERSCHAL	IN	38W	52
SCHNEIDER THOMAS JAMES	OH	21W	48
SCHNEIDER WILLIAM JOSEPH	WI	13E	2
SCHNELL JOSEPH RICHARD	VA	31W	57
SCHNELLER ANTHONY JOHN JR	IL	37E	45
SCHNELLER STEVEN OWEN	CA	41W	26
SCHNITGER GERARD GEORGE	LA	04E	17
SCHNOBRICH ANTON JOHN	MT	02W	48
SCHNURRER REINHARD J JR	MN	39W	4
SCHOBER JACK ERVIN	OH	18W	9
SCHOBORG GARY ALLEN	KY	11W	32
SCHOCK HAROLD HENRY	NY	03E	7
SCHODERER ERIC JOHN	NJ	12E	52
SCHOEBEN SCOTT DOUGLAS	MN	27W	67
SCHOEL RENNY DEAN	CA	32E	65
SCHOELIER TJEERD	NJ	27E	61
SCHOENBAUM CRAIG RAY	CA	21E	81
SCHOENBERG RICHARD C	NJ	06W	76
SCHOENER ROGER HARRY	NY	43W	49
SCHOENEWALD DAVID CHARLES	AZ	15W	24
SCHOENHOFF ROBERT JOHN	OH	04W	34
SCHOENIG EDMOND DAVID	PA	12E	56
SCHOEPFLIN CHARLES DUAINE	GA	64W	1
SCHOEPKE ANTON JOHN	CA	08W	76
SCHOEPPNER LEONARD JOHN	OH	13W	101
SCHOETTNER GEORGE CRAIG	NJ	20W	93
SCHOFER KARL ANDREW	NY	22W	7
SCHOFF LEO RICHARD	PA	29E	6
SCHOFIELD ALFRED VINCENT	MA	43W	9
SCHOFIELD CECIL CLAYTON	AL	10W	88
SCHOFIELD ROBERT LOUIS	FL	08W	117
SCHOFIELD THOMAS HARVEY	UT	54E	17
SCHOLD RAY ARTHUR	WI	25E	94
SCHOLES WILLIAM HADLEY	MA	06E	127
SCHOLL CLIFFORD LEO	KY	44W	41
SCHOLL CLIFFORD PAUL JR	PA	08W	26
SCHOLLARD JOHN ANDREW	FL	14E	3
SCHOLZ KLAUS DIETER	TX	37W	14
SCHON JOHN EDWARD	OR	20E	124
SCHONBERG DENNIS WAYNE	TX	33W	44
SCHONFIELD JEFFREY ALAN	MI	20W	122
SCHOOK GEORGE WASHINGTON	WA	24E	86
SCHOOLCRAFT CHARLES EARL	OH	32W	51
SCHOOLER STEVEN THOMAS	WA	16W	71
SCHOOLEY JAMES DANIEL	AL	04W	62
SCHOOLMEESTERS JOSEPH A	MN	04W	119
SCHOONMAKER LARRY	MI	07W	32
SCHOONOVER CHARLES DAVID	IN	04E	75
SCHOONVELD RICHARD JAY	IL	21W	120
SCHOPER GREGORY CARLYLLE	SC	13W	12
SCHOPMANN RAYMOND FRANK	NJ	46E	41
SCHOPPAUL ROBERT EARNEST	TX	16E	65
SCHOPPE FRANKLIN DALE	TX	17W	21
SCHOPPE SHERWIN CRESCENT	TX	07E	65
SCHORNDORF KENNETH FRANCI	NJ	47E	43
SCHOSSOW DENNIS ROBERT	ND	05W	61
SCHOTH WILLIAM WESLEY II	KS	28W	52
SCHOTT RICHARD SIMPSON	VI	02W	132
SCHOUVILLER THOMAS JOHN	MN	10E	97
SCHOUWBURG GERRIT JOHN	MI	22E	59
SCHOUWEILER DAVID LEE	OK	26E	94
SCHRADER FRANKLIN DANIEL	IA	14W	47
SCHRADER PETER ANTHONY	MO	29E	62
SCHRADER RONALD BRUCE	AZ	17E	100
SCHRADER RUDOLF AUGUST	FL	35E	18
SCHRAM FREDERICK LLOYD	CO	33E	93
SCHRAMEL KENNETH MICHAEL	MN	23E	71
SCHRAMM BROCK ROWLAND	CA	52E	11
SCHRAMM CHRISTOPHER JOSEP	PA	60E	1
SCHRAMM PETER FRYE	MA	07E	131
SCHRAMM WILLIAM GEORGE	NY	33E	75
SCHRAND ROBERT LEE	MO	13W	42
SCHRANK KARL F	MI	07E	16
SCHRECKENGOST FRED THOMAS	OH	01E	54
SCHRECKENGOST HAROLD LEE	PA	34E	45
SCHRECONGOST FREDERIC LEE	MI	26W	56
SCHREFFLER CLEON LARRY	PA	19E	32
SCHRENK DONALD GEORGE	CO	27E	51
SCHRINER JUNIOR LEE	OH	32E	27
SCHRIVER STEPHEN PAUL	ME	06W	16
SCHRIVER THOMAS CLYDE	OR	58E	6
SCHROBILGEN WARREN H JR	CA	22E	49
SCHROCK PHILIP JOHN	MI	15W	33
SCHROCK VERNON EARL	OR	10W	105
SCHRODER JACK WAYNE	NE	28E	30
SCHROEDER ALFRED M JR	IL	43W	30
SCHROEDER DONALD BENJAMIN	WY	32W	29
SCHROEDER DONALD LEE	IL	16E	115
SCHROEDER DONALD RAY	IN	48E	47
SCHROEDER GARY LEE	WI	06W	13

NAME	STATE	PANEL NO.	LINE NO.
SCHROEDER GEORGE H JR	MD	61E	19
SCHROEDER GLENN MICHAEL	OH	17W	103
SCHROEDER JERRY DEAN	CA	33E	32
SCHROEDER JOE LAWRENCE	TX	16E	98
SCHROEDER LYLE WILLIAM	MN	34W	88
SCHROEDER MICHAEL ALLEN	IA	25W	54
SCHROEDER NICHOLAS LEE	CA	49W	26
SCHROEDER RICHARD GLEN	IL	09E	20
SCHROEDER ROBERT EMIL JR	WI	16W	20
SCHROEDER STANLEY A	CA	63E	18
SCHROEDER TIMOTHY RICHARD	PA	42E	72
SCHROEDER WILLIAM RAY	IL	08W	71
SCHROEFFEL THOMAS ANTHONY	PA	05E	49
SCHROLLER LEO JOE JR	TX	27W	27
SCHROM JOHN FRANCIS	MN	39W	13
SCHROM KENNETH R	MN	13E	128
SCHROYER LAWSON J III	MD	39W	28
SCHRYVER PETER EDWARD	FL	41W	49
SCHUBERT GARY EDWARD	WV	31E	94
SCHUBERT JOEL LUTHER	CA	28E	62
SCHUBERT WILLIS JUNIOR	PA	28E	94
SCHUCK DONALD PHILIP	IN	64W	15
SCHUELLER JAMES PATRICK	WI	22E	2
SCHUEREN DANIEL RICHARD	IL	41E	28
SCHUETT JEROME ALAN	WI	39E	25
SCHUETTE DAVID FRANCIS	WI	14W	123
SCHUH ARNOLD RAYMOND	WI	17W	98
SCHUH DAVID MICHAEL	WI	43E	33
SCHUKAR GENE LEROY	CO	34W	40
SCHUKAR RONALD KEITH	IL	02E	117
SCHULER GARY FREDERICK	NY	17E	81
SCHULER HAROLD RICHARD	PA	13W	3
SCHULER ROBERT HARRY JR	NY	02E	124
SCHULMAN SHELDON BORIS	IL	22E	19
SCHULTE ALVIN CLAYTON	KY	28W	75
SCHULTE HENRY GERARD	NY	33W	35
SCHULTE NORMAN DOUGLAS	TX	19W	34
SCHULTZ ALAN ROBERT	PA	24E	101
SCHULTZ CHARLES JOSEPH	NJ	21E	52
SCHULTZ CHESTER JOSEPH	MI	41W	26
SCHULTZ DANNY CARL	MT	05E	25
SCHULTZ DAVID ALAN	CA	26E	4
SCHULTZ DAVID CHARLES	MI	54E	40
SCHULTZ DAVID CHARLES	WI	40W	51
SCHULTZ DAVID JOEL	WA	48E	10
SCHULTZ DAVID PAUL	TX	08W	9
SCHULTZ DENNIS MELVIN	IL	12W	53
SCHULTZ EDWARD AUGUST	CA	42E	72
SCHULTZ ERNEST M III	FL	01E	90
SCHULTZ GARY A	CA	04W	81
SCHULTZ GEORGE CLIFTON JR	MA	10W	58
SCHULTZ GEORGE JOSEPH	PA	40E	68
SCHULTZ GERALD WAYNE	WI	30W	31
SCHULTZ JACK ELSWORTH	OR	33W	88
SCHULTZ JAMES CHESTER	IL	43W	42
SCHULTZ JAMES RONALD	NE	43W	49
SCHULTZ JOHN JOSEPH JR	MI	07E	55
SCHULTZ JOHN LA VERN	MI	24W	21
SCHULTZ JOHN ROBERT	CT	12E	68
SCHULTZ KENNETH EUGENE	IL	13E	55
SCHULTZ LOWELL EUGENE	WA	12E	52
SCHULTZ MICHAEL DOUGLAS	IA	17E	32
SCHULTZ ROBERT CHARLES	NY	39E	12
SCHULTZ ROBERT WILLIAM	IA	36E	34
SCHULTZ RONALD JAMES	KS	08W	39
SCHULTZ RONNIE DEAN	CO	42E	9
SCHULTZ SHELDON D	PA	33E	53
SCHULTZ STEVEN OWEN	MN	09E	63
SCHULTZ THOMAS RUSSELL	PA	08W	44
SCHULTZ WILLIAM JOHN	IL	10E	23
SCHULTZ WILLIAM LEE	KS	11E	63
SCHULZ ALLAN HENRY	OH	13E	106
SCHULZ JAMES WILLIAM	NY	52W	31
SCHULZ RONALD DOUGLAS	KS	11W	4
SCHULZ RONALD KENNETH	WA	02W	39
SCHULZ WILLIAM ARTHUR	NJ	28E	11
SCHULZE DAVID EDWARD	IL	30W	7
SCHULZE ROBERT EUGENE	CA	03W	116
SCHUMACHER DONALD EUGENE	IA	09E	76
SCHUMACHER JEFFREY DAVID	NY	03W	75
SCHUMACHER LARRY DEAN	TX	01W	96
SCHUMACHER MICHAEL WAYNE	WI	32W	16
SCHUMACHER ROBERT JAMES	OR	04W	90
SCHUMACHER RONALD KENNETH	IL	23E	95
SCHUMACHER STEPHEN LAWREN	MN	32W	34
SCHUMACHER WAYNE THOMAS	MN	22E	19
SCHUMANN JOHN ROBERT	MN	02E	11
SCHUMMER DALE CLARENCE	MN	14E	46
SCHUNEMANN JAMES EDWARD	NH	12W	26
SCHURCH RONALD LEE	IL	22E	66
SCHURRER JON RODNEY	WI	56W	28
SCHUSSLER WILLIAM JAMES	PA	17W	114
SCHUSTER DANIEL CARL	WI	53W	5
SCHUSTER FRANK	NJ	46E	49
SCHUSTER JOSEPH JOHN	NY	03E	4
SCHUSTER JOSEPH WILLIAM	PA	07E	131
SCHUTT RANDALL KARL	IA	36E	34
SCHUTZ PETER JOHN	MI	16E	13
SCHUTZ RICHARD JAMES	IL	23E	104
SCHUYLER RONALD LEE	CA	40W	67
SCHWAB RICHARD MICHAEL	OR	07W	42
SCHWAB THOMAS PAUL	OH	38W	21
SCHWAGEL KENNETH FRANCIS	MN	48W	47
SCHWALBACH GEORGE AUSTIN	IL	39W	75
SCHWAN DANIEL GEORGE	OH	47W	54
SCHWANGER FREDERICK JAY	PA	02E	20
SCHWARTZ ALLAN EDWARD	NE	40W	34
SCHWARTZ CALVIN ELLIOT	NY	17E	24
SCHWARTZ CHARLES GLENNON	MO	15W	33
SCHWARTZ DANNY GILBERT	CO	35W	68
SCHWARTZ DAVID EARL	CA	37W	53
SCHWARTZ GARY STEVEN	CA	02W	133
SCHWARTZ JOHN GUSTAVE	PA	03W	3
SCHWARTZ KENNETH DALE	CA	50E	8
SCHWARTZ MARTIN PETER	IL	32E	47
SCHWARTZ RANDALL FRANK	IL	31W	21
SCHWARTZ RUSSELL ALBERT	WI	21W	85
SCHWARTZ SAMUEL BRUCE	PA	25W	55
SCHWARTZ TERRY E	MI	03W	3
SCHWARTZ WAYNE GILMORE	PA	01E	115
SCHWARZ DONALD EDWIN	AZ	32W	30
SCHWARZ FRANCIS ANTHONY	IL	48W	15
SCHWARZ LARRY EDWARD	MT	40W	60
SCHWARZ ROGER LEE	IA	47W	4
SCHWARZKOPF ALLAN ALBERT	MN	12E	24
SCHWEBEL MICHAEL PHILIP	IL	03E	132
SCHWEBKE LARRY CHARLES	IA	54E	17
SCHWEFEL DALE WAYNE	WI	33W	44
SCHWEIG VICTOR JOHN	IL	62E	11
SCHWEIGHOFER REED JAY	PA	43E	10
SCHWEIKL JEFFREY ALLAN	WA	17E	129
SCHWELLENBACH GARY RALPH	CA	32E	81
SCHWENDLER RICHARD WILLIA	WI	03E	67
SCHWENDY RANDALL JAMES	NY	37E	68
SCHWERDTFEGER JOSEPH ALLE	IA	07E	22
SCHWESINGER RAYMOND PAUL	PA	07E	36
SCHWEYHER JOHN WILLIAM JR	NJ	22E	27
SCHWICHOW RICHARD JOSEPH	IL	28W	80
SCHWICK MARTIN FRANK JR	IL	02E	91
SCHWIDERSKI RICHARD DEAN	IL	21W	114
SCHWINTZ BOBBITT	WA	13W	3
SCHWORER RONALD PAUL	NV	49E	15
SCHWUCHOW GERALD LEE	IN	14W	35
SCHYSKA LEROY FLOYD	IL	31E	54
SCIARRETTI VINTURE	PA	12W	75
SCIBELLI THOMAS ANTHONY	NY	15W	100
SCIBILIA ROBERT PETER	NH	24W	90
SCICUTELLA JOSEPH	NY	12E	105
SCISLO ROBERT TED	OH	12W	50
SCISNEY MICHAEL LYNN	IN	18E	24
SCIVOLINO ANTHONY CHRISTO	NJ	13E	40
SCOBEL UWE-THORSTEN	MD	01E	47
SCOBY RICHARD WILLIAM	WA	05W	3
SCOFIELD HARVEY DREW	FL	24E	42
SCOFIELD JOHN CHARLES	CA	51W	8
SCOFIELD ROBERT LEE	IN	02E	60
SCOGGIN ALLEN DEAN	CO	03W	35
SCOGGINS FRANKLIN GRAHAM	NC	09W	122
SCOGGINS JOHN PAUL	CA	15E	108
SCOGGINS ROYCE GLENN	TX	05E	124
SCOGGINS TONY EUGENE	NC	18W	86
SCOGNAMILIO PATRICK JOHN	NY	53W	31
SCOLLEY BENJAMIN ELMER	IN	07E	55
SCOLNICK DAVID	NY	26W	57
SCORSONE DONALD FLOYD	NC	24W	56
SCORSONE GEORGE ANTHONY	AZ	54W	25
SCOTELLARO MICHAEL BERTRA	NY	22E	2
SCOTT ALVIN JOSEPH	LA	06W	57
SCOTT ARTHUR EDWARD	GA	25W	84
SCOTT BARRY FRANK	MI	16W	126
SCOTT BILLY EDWARD	PA	40W	34
SCOTT BILLY JOE	OH	44W	29
SCOTT BRUCE RICHARD	WI	23E	54
SCOTT BUSTER LEROY	CA	09W	6
SCOTT CHARLES F	PA	01W	120
SCOTT CHARLES LOUIS JR	MD	04E	59
SCOTT CLARENCE WALTER	GA	29E	35
SCOTT DAIN VANDERLIN	PA	25E	24
SCOTT DANIEL R	MO	40E	13
SCOTT DANNY RAY	TX	35W	51
SCOTT DARRYL KENNETH	CA	06W	10
SCOTT DAVE RUSSELL	KS	35E	27
SCOTT DAVID AMOS	IN	07E	36
SCOTT DAVID LEE	MI	24E	88
SCOTT DAVID LEE	IL	52E	11
SCOTT DAVID LEE	MO	01W	79
SCOTT DAYNE YORK	CA	41W	70
SCOTT DENNIS LEE	NY	32E	82
SCOTT DON RUSSELL	FL	11W	38
SCOTT DONALD BLUE	NJ	49W	1
SCOTT DONALD EUGENE	IA	17W	5
SCOTT DONALD EUGENE	OK	03W	117
SCOTT DORTY HINCHMAN JR	IL	36E	60
SCOTT DUANE CARL	NY	17W	14
SCOTT EDDIE JAMES	GA	15E	22
SCOTT EDWARD DRAKE	PA	57W	4
SCOTT EDWARD EARL JR	OH	05W	131
SCOTT EUGENE C	MO	03E	92
SCOTT GARY ARNOLD	NY	47E	5
SCOTT GARY JAMES	NY	64W	1
SCOTT GAYLAND OMER	IL	40W	15
SCOTT GRADY	DC	40E	30
SCOTT GREG BRADFORD	AZ	17W	58
SCOTT GREGORY EDWARD	WA	18W	63
SCOTT GREGORY JOHN	PA	25E	110
SCOTT HAROLD	NY	03E	93
SCOTT HERBERT WILLIAM III	FL	57W	4
SCOTT HUGH DON	MI	30E	19
SCOTT IRA EDWARD	NE	21E	81
SCOTT JAMES BERNARD	PA	43W	66
SCOTT JAMES ELLISON	TN	31W	55
SCOTT JAMES ELVIN	FL	18W	86
SCOTT JAMES FRANK	AL	38E	38
SCOTT JAMES GEORGE	CA	22E	66
SCOTT JAMES GUINAN	NY	40W	55
SCOTT JAMES HOWARD	CO	14E	125
SCOTT JAMES LEE	OH	27E	17
SCOTT JAMES RAYMOND	FL	05E	109
SCOTT JEREMIAH	FL	36E	60
SCOTT JIMMIE L	AL	07E	132
SCOTT JOHN MELVILLE JR	MI	10E	82
SCOTT JOHN WALTER	IL	09E	21
SCOTT JOHNNY FRED	GA	08W	39
SCOTT JOHNNY MAJOR JR	AL	60W	23
SCOTT JOSEPH ROBERT	FL	23W	48
SCOTT KENNETH DAVID	NC	40E	68
SCOTT KENNETH LEROY	IN	10E	81
SCOTT KENNETT KEITH	IA	11E	91
SCOTT LARRY	GA	28W	3
SCOTT LARRY EUGENE	KS	22W	7
SCOTT LARRY ROBERT	IA	15E	87
SCOTT LAWRENCE EDWARD	SC	06W	83
SCOTT LEONARD STANLEY JR	GA	24E	105
SCOTT LEROY HARRY	PA	22W	60
SCOTT LLOYD M JR	MO	22W	8
SCOTT MARTIN RONALD	OK	06E	12
SCOTT MARTIN T II	MI	30W	49
SCOTT MARVIN	MI	55W	2
SCOTT MICHAEL	OH	20W	22
SCOTT MICHAEL FREDRICK	TX	15E	11
SCOTT MICHAEL JON	IL	44E	40
SCOTT MICHAEL MONROE	NE	04W	109
SCOTT MIKE JOHN	NJ	25W	110
SCOTT NATHANIEL	VA	15W	2
SCOTT O D	CA	30E	5
SCOTT PATRICK RAY	TX	21W	71

NAME	STATE	PANEL NO.	LINE NO.
SCOTT PATTERSON JR	AL	14E	51
SCOTT PAUL	TX	43E	10
SCOTT PERRY JAY	OK	26W	3
SCOTT PETER W	NJ	32E	59
SCOTT PRESTON ROOSEVELT	FL	55W	31
SCOTT RANDOLPH	SC	13W	114
SCOTT RANDOLPH CLINTON	SC	07E	83
SCOTT RICHARD ALLEN	MA	48W	3
SCOTT RICHARD LEE	MI	14W	30
SCOTT RICKEY LEROY	IN	09W	133
SCOTT ROBERT EUGENE	DC	10W	106
SCOTT ROBERT JAMES		24E	92
SCOTT ROBERT L	PA	25E	44
SCOTT ROBERT LEE	LA	35E	41
SCOTT ROBERT LEE	MS	44W	29
SCOTT ROBERT MILLER	IL	55W	38
SCOTT ROGER LEE	WY	14W	50
SCOTT RONALD	VA	21W	10
SCOTT ROOSEVELT	FL	16E	70
SCOTT SAMMY LEE	KY	66E	2
SCOTT STEVEN CLAYTON	IA	08W	109
SCOTT STEVEN JOSEPH	MI	52W	32
SCOTT TERRENCE DUANE	OH	06E	132
SCOTT THOMAS LASANDA	NY	16E	37
SCOTT THOMAS LEE	CA	29E	54
SCOTT THOMAS WILLIAM	IL	45E	5
SCOTT TRAVIS HENRY JR	AL	11W	9
SCOTT VERNON ELBERT	SC	30W	31
SCOTT VINCENT CALVIN JR	VA	26W	27
SCOTT WALTER MICHAEL	IN	38E	80
SCOTT WARREN TAYLOR	OH	26E	97
SCOTT WILLIAM	NY	22E	93
SCOTT WILLIAM	PA	16W	67
SCOTT WILLIAM ALEXANDER	NJ	23E	46
SCOTT WILLIAM BENFORD	NC	19W	22
SCOTT WILLIAM BLAKE	WA	32W	73
SCOTT WILLIAM GRAVELLE JR	NY	32W	23
SCOTT WILLIAM HENRY	TN	13W	79
SCOTT WILLIAM HENRY M	MI	22W	69
SCOTT WILLIAM NORMAN	FL	22E	19
SCOTT WILLIE CHARLES	GA	39E	12
SCOVILL GARY ALAN	MI	18E	64
SCOVILLE HOWARD JAMES	FL	06W	107
SCOVILLE WILLIAM WARD	MI	27E	46
SCOWDEN CURTIS DEAN	MO	37E	69
SCOWDEN DUANE NEVADA	MI	20W	116
SCRAGG BRUCE HASSELL	WV	18E	129
SCRANTON ALLEN FRANK JR	WA	08E	12
SCREEN MARVIN EDMUND	FL	18W	29
SCRIBER LEON R	CO	07E	87
SCRIBNER GARY DAVID	MI	35E	27
SCRIMSHAW WAYNE GREGORY	FL	22W	44
SCRITCHFIELD DAVID ALLEN	NY	26E	57
SCRIVEN SAMUEL T	FL	19E	7
SCRIVENER STEPHEN RUSSELL	FL	04W	55
SCRIVER JAMES MICHAEL	WI	07W	50
SCRIVNER BROOKS MICHAEL	AR	36W	33
SCROGGIN MICHAEL THOMAS	IL	15E	30
SCROGGINS CARREY EUGENE	TX	41W	26
SCROGGINS DOUGLAS SIDNEY	AL	48W	45
SCROGGINS JAMES LELAND	IL	01W	116
SCROGGS JERRELL DAVID	TX	08W	21
SCROGUM JIMMIE CHARLES	OK	21W	90
SCRUGGS ALBERT JOSEPH	FL	17W	1
SCRUGGS DAVID L	MO	24E	57
SCRUGGS JAMES ARTHUR	TX	09W	65
SCRUGGS JOSEPH ALLEN	KY	17E	107
SCRUGGS STUART JACKSON JR	GA	12W	9
SCRUTON KENNETH CHARLES	NY	33E	53
SCUCCHI JOHN GLENN	AR	39W	24
SCUDIERO PATRICK FRANK	IL	13E	7
SCUITIER JAMES	NJ	41E	72
SCULL GARY BERNARD	IA	13W	120
SCULL JOHN FELLOWS JR	IL	06E	34
SCULLEN THOMAS JAMES	OH	42E	41
SCULLY EDWARD ANTHONY	NY	29E	92
SCULLY JOHN MICHAEL	OH	34E	46
SCULLY KENNETH WILLIAM	MA	10W	105
SCULLY PATRICK R JR	IL	52W	47
SCULLY RUSSELL CRAIG	IA	07W	32
SCUNGIO VINCENT ANTHONY	PA	12E	25
SCURFIELD DANNY VINSON	RI	41W	63
SCURLOCK LEE D JR	OH	32E	39
SCURR KENNETH WESLEY	CA	23W	31
SEABLOM EARL FRANCIS	MI	51W	8
SEABORN WILLIAM HERMAN JR	AL	05W	61
SEABORNE FREDERICK VERNON	MA	47W	4
SEABOURNE BENNY ELLIS	MO	22E	122
SEABRIDGE RICHARD ROY	MI	17W	1
SEABROOK ROY MICHAEL	NY	03W	59
SEABROOKS ARTHUR	MI	48W	48
SEADORE LARRY LEWIS	NE	08W	26
SEADORF MICHAEL J	MI	28E	105
SEAGRAVES MELVIN DOUGLAS	TX	01W	10
SEAGROVES MICHAEL ANTHONY	IL	22W	114
SEALL GEORGE MELVIN	OH	18E	121
SEALS CLIFFORD	OK	19W	56
SEALS WALTER	MS	48W	35
SEAMAN DONALD JOSEPH	PA	01E	119
SEAMAN HAROLD LA VERN	MO	30W	60
SEAMAN JOHN CHARLES JR	CA	45E	29
SEAMAN JOSEPH ANDREW	MA	08W	32
SEAMANS OTTO ANDREAE JR	VA	20E	35
SEAMSTER WILLIE PURFOY	LA	57W	31
SEARBY BARRY MARTIN	CA	12W	10
SEARCY ELTON LLOYD	FL	26W	50
SEARFUS WILLIAM HENRY	CA	30E	86
SEARGENT ROBERT LEE	IL	09W	58
SEARIGHT JAMES ARNOLD	NY	16E	74
SEARING JACK EDWARD	IL	02W	40
SEARLE JOSEPH KENT	UT	42W	7
SEARLES CHARLES PETER	CA	53W	13
SEARLES JEFFREY PAUL	IA	11W	25
SEARS EARNEST G	KY	03E	47
SEARS GORDON BERT	CA	06W	41
SEARS LEON	CT	28W	21
SEARS MICHAEL	WI	43E	33
SEARS STEVEN DWIGHT	IA	29E	6
SEASE WILLIAM DANIEL	SC	26E	38
SEASHOLTZ RONALD J	PA	06E	103
SEASTROM WILLIAM LEONAR	CA	13E	56
SEATON CHARLES EVERETT	MO	37W	25
SEATON DAVID THOMAS	KY	42W	13
SEATON ROBERT WAYNE	KY	40E	30
SEAVERS STANLEY JOSEPH	AR	24E	63
SEAVEY DOUGLAS REX	CA	38W	39
SEAWEL WARREN PAUL	MO	04W	71
SEAWRIGHT WALTER LEE	PA	59W	14
SEAWRIGHT WILLIAM J JR	AL	12E	76
SEAY BOBBY DAREL	IL	06W	95
SEAY TONY ELWOOD	VA	17W	82
SEAY WILLIAM WAYNE	FL	46W	22
SEBAST WILLIAM MICHAEL	NY	36E	33
SEBASTIAN ALTON BROWNING	CT	37E	43
SEBASTIAN BILLY JOE	KY	11W	53
SEBASTIAN JOSEPH WILLIAM	OH	42W	14
SEBASTIAN LOUIS JOSEPH	NY	29E	21
SEBENS GAYLORD JAMES	CA	36E	85
SEBERS FREDERICK THEODORE	WA	29E	44
SEBRING RONALD WAYNE	TX	54W	38
SEBURG DONALD PAUL JR	MI	23W	23
SECANTI RICHARD MICHAEL	CA	25E	17
SECHREST JAMES RONALD	IN	10E	10
SECOR GILBERT ARTHUR	NJ	47W	54
SECOR WILLIAM DALE	WA	09W	113
SECRESS HARLAN	KY	35W	13
SECREST EDWARD WILLIAM	PA	45W	56
SECREST JACK MCCOMBS JR	TX	15E	10
SECRIST FRED JASON	OR	34E	11
SEDA FERNANDO JR	NY	04E	38
SEDA PABLO ISREAL	NY	07W	66
SEDDIG WALTER S	NY	23W	59
SEDGWICK RICHARD BRUCE	PA	18E	111
SEDGWICK ROBERT CHARLES	CT	29E	61
SEDIES RICHARD SAMUEL	WA	17E	24
SEDILLO JUAN NATIVIDAD	AZ	48E	54
SEE EDWARD EUGENE	PA	16W	10
SEE MICHAEL DUANE	TX	41W	2
SEE OTTO WILLIAM	WV	48E	47
SEE RICHARD CHARLES	CA	35W	61
SEE WARD EUGENE	IN	42W	58
SEEBER FLETCHER JR	TN	22E	34
SEEBODE JOHN CONRAD	LA	67W	3
SEEDES HARRY BATON III	PA	30W	26
SEEFELDT CHARLES L JR	NY	19E	54
SEEKAMP ROBERT LEE ROY	WI	20W	23
SEEKFORD DANIEL LEONARD	MD	16W	60
SEEKFORD JOSEPH LEVI	VA	32E	47
SEEL JOHN CHARLES	NY	11W	70
SEEL WALTER PHILLIP JR	PA	31W	58
SEELEY DOUGLAS MILTON	OH	04W	56
SEELEY JOHN STUART	CA	08E	101
SEELEY WILLIAM ARTHUR	NY	07W	32
SEELIG GERD FRANZ	OR	15E	100
SEELY RICHARD CLAIR	PA	35W	22
SEEMAN JERI CALVIN	CA	31E	60
SEEMAN STEVEN CARL	MN	10W	29
SEERY JONN JOSEPH	OH	32W	61
SEFRHANS JAMES	IL	37E	69
SEGAL JEFFREY BERNARD	NY	65E	1
SEGAR CALVIN RUSSELL	AZ	07W	85
SEGAR CHARLES JR	SC	55W	9
SEGARRA LUIS ERNESTO JR	NY	20E	68
SEGARS TOMMY QUINN JR	GA	26W	22
SEGER VERNON JOSEPH	OH	17W	114
SEGERS ROGER DALE	FL	23E	71
SEGICH MICHAEL PAUL	PA	10W	29
SEGINE RONALD EUGENE	TN	63W	13
SEGLEM RICHARD NOYCE	KS	07W	88
SEGOVIA RAUL LERMA	TX	33W	22
SEGUNDO PETE SPRULE	CA	18W	43
SEGURA MANUEL TIODORO	NM	37E	14
SEGURA STEVEN REY	CA	30W	8
SEHESTED RONALD ALLEN	OK	27W	34
SEHI GEORGE STEPHEN	CA	34E	5
SEIBER DAVID ANDREW	TN	30W	31
SEIBERLING KARLHEINZ S	PA	05W	102
SEIBERT JOSEPH DEAN	WI	43E	33
SEIBERT MICHAEL ROBERT	IL	20W	119
SEIBERT RICHARD J	NJ	34E	15
SEIBERT WILLIAM ROBERT	PA	40E	30
SEIDEL CRAIG LEE	IN	57W	13
SEIDEL DONALD WILLIAM	MT	51W	44
SEIDEL KENNETH WAYNE	IL	54W	13
SEIDEL WALTER JAMES	CA	39W	4
SEIDENSTICKER JAMES	NY	36E	35
SEIFERT THOMAS LEONARD	OH	61E	2
SEIFERTH STEPHEN ERIC	OH	50E	21
SEIGLE WILLIAM ARTHUR	OK	23W	3
SEIGLER STEVEN LEE	TX	05W	102
SEILER CLYDE	CO	28W	64
SEILER WILLIAM JOSEPH	NY	21W	26
SEILHEIMER HOWARD ALLEN	TX	04E	114
SEISSER KENNETH ANTHONY	IL	02E	35
SEITZ CHRISTOPHER RICHARD	FL	02W	106
SEK MITCHELL FRANCIS	IL	41E	54
SEKLECKI THOMAS MARTIN	MA	17E	13
SEKNE SYLVESTER VICTOR	OH	27W	67
SEKVA ROBERT GLENN	CA	22W	24
SELAK JOHN RAYMOND	MD	05W	129
SELANIKIO LEONARD	NY	45W	57
SELBY DE WAYNE MICHAEL	ND	66W	12
SELBY ROBERT B	MD	40E	68
SELDEN FRANK WILLIAM	WA	09E	104
SELDERS EUGENE	LA	09W	10
SELDERS WILLIAM DEAN	WY	37E	43
SELDON DAVID SCOTT	MD	18W	65
SELDON JAMES LENVER	MS	18W	98
SELENKA RUDOLPH CARL JR	MN	08E	77
SELF EUGENE LAWRENCE	NJ	11E	88
SELF IRVING ALBERT	CA	01E	52
SELF JAMES EDWARD	TN	47W	32
SELGRADE STEPHEN FRANK	PA	38W	52
SELIG RONALD JOHN	NJ	36E	86
SELIX JAMES MICHAEL	CO	02W	56
SELKEY DONALD ANTHONY JR	MI	15W	84
SELKREGG EDWARD M III	PA	27E	85
SELL CLIFFORD LLOYD	PA	51E	2
SELL JOSEPH WAYNE JR	WV	22W	100
SELLER JOSEPH JOHN	MN	21E	38
SELLERS CHARLES RAYFORD	AL	06W	65
SELLERS FLOYD EUGENE	FL	50W	37
SELLERS JERRY ALAN	FL	32E	60
SELLERS LLOYD ANDREW III	OH	22E	20
SELLERS MELVIN LOUIS	AL	31W	85
SELLERS PHILIP DOYLE	AL	01W	60

NAME	STATE	PANEL NO.	LINE NO.
SELLERS RICHARD TAYLOR JR	CA	21W	30
SELLERS ROBERT	SC	32W	81
SELLERS WILLIAM CLESSON	NJ	01E	109
SELLETT STEPHEN CHARLES	IL	06W	102
SELLITTO MICHAEL JOSEPH	NJ	28W	52
SELLNER CHARLES EDWARD	MN	35W	22
SELLS JIMMY DWAYNE	NC	24W	49
SELLS ROBERT DEE JR	IA	19E	66
SELLS TERRY STEPHEN	TX	08W	77
SELMAN CHARLES GEORGE	MI	12W	115
SELTZER JACKIE RALPH	PA	59E	13
SEMANS THOMAS EDWARD	CA	18W	4
SEMENIUK LARRY STEPHEN		34E	64
SEMENTELLI DOMINIC M JR	PA	28W	40
SEMERARO DAVID ALEXANDER	OH	20W	26
SEMIDEY HECTOR LUIS	NY	40E	69
SEMINARA CHARLES BENJAMIN	NY	20W	127
SEMLER STANLEY KENTON	CA	04E	115
SEMMER PETER ANTHONY	CA	01E	92
SEMMLER DAVID ALBERT	NY	05W	79
SEMON KENNETH RONALD	LA	67W	4
SEMORE BOBBY ALLEN	CA	19E	74
SEMPLE WILLIAM EUGENE	OH	14W	60
SEMPSROTT BRUCE GORDON	IN	06W	129
SENA BENNY	NM	09E	76
SENA FRED JR	CO	52E	11
SENECHEK JOHN	NH	02W	18
SENESE CHRISTOPHER LEIGH	NY	27W	78
SENG RICHARD MICHAEL	PA	57E	10
SENGER MICHAEL MELVIN	CA	32E	47
SENGSTOCK GARY DAVID	WI	08W	95
SENN THOMAS LARRY	AL	40E	13
SENNE THOMAS ALFRED	ND	40W	39
SENNETT ROBERT RUSSELL	CA	04E	83
SENOR JOHN JOSEPH	NY	33W	44
SENS PHILIP MARION	OH	03E	7
SENSAT MORRIS JOSEPH	LA	28E	4
SENSING JOHN LESLIE	TN	11W	76
SENTERS BOBBY	KY	08E	69
SENTERS CHARLES DONALD	KY	04E	101
SENTI DONALD LEE	CO	05W	62
SENTMAN DONALD WARREN	PA	36W	70
SENZ DENNIS LEON	WI	32E	19
SEPULVEDA JESUS GARCIA	TX	01W	42
SEPULVEDA LAWRENCE KENNET	GA	33E	75
SEPUT FREDERICK WILLIAM	IL	17E	13
SERAIN CALVIN ERNESTO	HI	13W	48
SERATTE JOHN STEVEN	CA	20W	127
SERAVALLI JOHN ANTHONY	NY	15E	122
SERCOVICH JOSEPH GEORGE	LA	04E	77
SERENA JAMES DAVID	OH	37E	27
SERENIL RICARDO	TX	14W	20
SEREX HENRY MUIR	LA	02W	128
SERIO ROBERT FRANK	NY	50E	33
SERNA ERNEST	CO	16W	60
SERNA HERMAN	AZ	10W	43
SERNA LEOPOLDO PEREA	CA	19E	20
SERNA PHILIP JOSEPH	TX	07E	91
SERNA RAYMOND	NM	18W	76
SERRANO FILEMON	NM	29W	93
SERRANO GILBERT	CA	46E	23
SERRANO JOHN REYITO	NY	50W	27
SERRANO MARCO ANTONIO JR	NY	16E	74
SERRANO RENE	NY	47W	4
SERRANO RODOLFO CARRILLO	CA	47E	34
SERRANO THOMAS ROBERT	MN	12E	91
SERRANO-ECHEVARRIA RAUL	NY	58E	9
SERRANO-GIRAL CANDIDO	PR	21E	3
SERRANO-RIVERA JULIO	PR	58W	19
SERREM MARK MACDONALD	CA	36E	35
SERSHON LAURENCE G	AZ	23E	63
SERVANTEZ JOSEPH ANTHONY	MI	18W	101
SERVEN PAUL ELLIOTT	NJ	04W	83
SERVENT HENRY JOSEPH JR	MA	45E	5
SERVERA BAEZ RAMON AURELIO	CT	05W	21
SERVICE JOHN ANDREW	NJ	02W	12
SERWINOWSKI RICHARD EARL	NY	26E	17
SESLER JOHN JOSEPH	TN	21W	67
SESSA MICHAEL JR	NY	20E	36
SESSIONS WILLIAM ROBERT	PA	24W	34
SESSOMS HOWARD ARNOLD	NC	22E	34
SESSUMS KENNETH BRUCE	MD	15W	40
SESTER EUGENE	KY	21E	115
SESTITO ANTHONY JOHN	MA	23W	79
SETH CHARLES WILLIAM	PA	44W	60
SETKA STANTON JAMES	IA	25E	65
SETTER JAMES ADRIAN	MI	17E	54
SETTER RICHARD ALLEN	NY	39W	18
SETTERQUIST FRANCIS LESLI	MN	47W	54
SETTIMI RONALD MARK	NY	25W	84
SETTLE FRANK LEROY	FL	01W	46
SETTLE WILLIAM FOY	CA	08W	23
SETTLEMIRE WILLIAM DAVID	IL	05E	21
SETTLEMYRE JEFFERY COLIN	MI	60E	12
SETZENFAND CHARLES FREDER	PA	05E	123
SETZER JERRY PHILIP	MD	15E	22
SETZER PAUL RAY	CA	05E	2
SEU MILTON J S	CA	08E	8
SEUELL JOHN WAYNE	MO	01W	38
SEUFERT ROBERT JOHANN	NY	06W	110
SEVELL ROBERT LEE	NJ	41E	72
SEVENBERGEN JERRY L	CA	06E	16
SEVENEY WILLIAM FRANCIS	MA	24E	42
SEVENSKI ALFRED	NJ	12E	29
SEVERINO WAYNE THOMAS	MA	39E	66
SEVERLOH PAUL BRUCE	CA	14E	92
SEVERSON DONALD JON	WI	08W	44
SEVERSON JOHN EDGAR	MN	43E	60
SEVERSON PAUL ROY	IL	46W	22
SEVERSON ROBERT DARYL	NY	03W	123
SEVERSON THOMAS EUGENE	WI	13W	107
SEVICK JOHN FRANCIS	KS	36E	60
SEVIER DAVID HOWARD	IN	45E	15
SEVIGNY GEORGE WOLFGANG	VA	02W	115
SEWARD KENNITH MARION	CO	23W	3
SEWARD WILLIAM HENRY	GA	43E	34
SEWELL DONALD MELVIN	CA	29E	62
SEWELL JOHN FRANCIS JR	MD	10E	130
SEWELL JOHNNIE BRUCE	AL	50W	10
SEWELL LORENZO	AL	48W	48
SEWELL MONTY RAE	MO	23E	7
SEWELL RAYFORD NEAL	TX	30E	94
SEWELL WILLIAM JERRY	MD	23W	31
SEXTON ANDREW BOWMAN	MI	16W	47
SEXTON CARL HOWARD JR	VA	64W	1
SEXTON CLARENCE LEE	NC	09E	90
SEXTON DAVID MASON	OH	04W	51
SEXTON EDWARD CICERO	MI	07E	122
SEXTON HUGH AMES JR	NC	03W	71
SEXTON JEFFREY ROSS	AZ	22E	49
SEXTON JIMMY CLYDE	FL	05E	68
SEXTON JOHN DAVID	TN	26W	94
SEXTON JOHN JUNIOR	OH	16W	119
SEXTON LARRY LEE	TN	25E	58
SEXTON LEONARD EARL	NJ	47W	4
SEXTON LUTHER MANLEY JR	FL	50W	32
SEXTON PHILLIP EDWARD	FL	43E	61
SEXTON RICHARD JARRETT II	PA	13W	16
SEXTON TROY LAVERNE	WA	23E	64
SEXTON WAYNE EDWARD	NC	52E	32
SEXTON WESLEY ROBERT	GA	23E	39
SEYBOLD GERALD CALVIN	NH	03W	16
SEYKORA WILLIAM JOSEPH	MN	52E	32
SEYMOE JOSEPH PHILLIP	TX	35E	8
SEYMORE PAUL JESSIE	VA	25W	33
SEYMORE RICHARD MORRIS	KY	08W	91
SEYMOUR GARY CARL	MI	57W	31
SEYMOUR JAMES THOMAS	NY	15E	71
SEYMOUR LEO EARL	PA	22E	123
SFERRAZZA ANGELO JOSEPH	CT	09E	17
SFERRUZZI WILLIAM LEE	IN	39W	10
SGAMBATI PAUL ANTHONY	OH	04W	20
SHACKELFORD DON R	IN	05E	21
SHACKELFORD IVAN J JR	OK	18E	64
SHACKELFORD RANDALL LEE	IA	29W	32
SHACKELFORD RICKY LEE	OK	58W	14
SHADBURNE BROOKE MCKAY	OR	17E	108
SHADDON ROY GENE	AR	03W	51
SHADE GEORGE EVERETT	PA	27E	103
SHADE WILLIAM STEVE	CO	17W	75
SHADWICK ALVIN LEE	TX	33W	89
SHAEFFER CHRISTOPHER L	OH	08W	21
SHAFER DONALD MAILY II	OH	05E	49
SHAFER FRANCIS LOE JR	OK	47E	15
SHAFER GARY CHRISTOPHER	FL	64W	1
SHAFER GLENN WESLEY	AL	17E	64
SHAFER JAMES DUDLEY	OH	29E	26
SHAFER LESLIE HOMER	OH	32W	84
SHAFER PHILIP RAYMOND	CO	51E	2
SHAFER ROBERT LAURENCE	IL	14E	119
SHAFER ROGER DALE	MI	51W	36
SHAFER ROYAL ROY	IN	16W	36
SHAFER THOMAS JAMES	OH	35W	62
SHAFF MAURICE ALBERT JR	IL	22E	3
SHAFF RONALD DEAN	ID	32W	62
SHAFFER BRUCE WILLIAM	IN	28W	76
SHAFFER CHARLES	PA	15E	60
SHAFFER EARL THOMAS SR	GA	37W	77
SHAFFER EDDIE LOU	WV	38W	46
SHAFFER JACK LEON	IL	13E	100
SHAFFER JOHN ANDREW	NY	14W	77
SHAFFER JONATHAN PETER	CA	32E	97
SHAFFER LAWRENCE ALLEN	IL	55W	9
SHAFFER RANDALL DALE	WV	29E	98
SHAFFER ROBERT EUGENE	IN	29W	24
SHAFFER ROBERT LEE	TN	36E	86
SHAFFER VICTOR THOMAS	OH	22W	93
SHAFFER WALLACE CLAIR JR	PA	33E	94
SHAFFER WILLIAM EMERSON	OH	55E	30
SHAFFER WILLIAM PAUL	NY	22E	20
SHAFFNER DAVID WAYNE	NC	21W	77
SHAGOVAC PETER WILLIAM JR	OH	47E	36
SHAIN ELWIN ROX	IA	50W	27
SHAIN JERRY WAYNE	KY	48E	11
SHAINA CONRAD WILLIAM	CA	09E	3
SHAKLEY GERALD WAYNE	PA	22W	15
SHALHOOB TERRY WAYNE	CA	13E	76
SHALLAH JOHN HERBERT	MA	16E	37
SHALLER RONALD WILLIAM	MA	52W	16
SHALLER WILLIAM HOWARD	MD	11W	106
SHAMBAUGH DALE K	KS	02E	60
SHAMBAUGH GREGORY RANDALL	MI	43E	34
SHAMBLIN KENNETH WAYNE	WV	03W	1
SHAMBLIN THEODORE	WV	03E	41
SHAMEL JOHN CLARENCE	CA	21E	109
SHAMP PAUL DAVID JR	FL	37E	69
SHANDS MICHAEL ANTHONY	WA	05E	109
SHANE WALLACE WILLIAM	PA	55E	30
SHANER MICHAEL IRA	IL	04E	131
SHANER STEPHEN PAUL	OH	20W	109
SHANG DONALD J	NC	36W	87
SHANK EDWIN GERALD JR	IN	01E	47
SHANK GARY LESLIE	KS	01W	59
SHANK JOHN B	IA	43E	34
SHANK RALPH	OH	04E	10
SHANK RODNEY GEORGE	ME	33W	82
SHANKS DONALD WILFRED	CA	11E	114
SHANKS JAMES EVERETT	IL	03W	20
SHANKS JAMES LEE	NY	69E	2
SHANKS THOMAS FRANK	PA	26E	63
SHANLEY MICHAEL HENRY JR	CA	15W	20
SHANNON BILLY EUGENE	MO	01E	120
SHANNON EARL EDWIN	GA	06W	119
SHANNON GARRY MONZEL	WV	09W	107
SHANNON GEORGE DAVID	MO	43W	22
SHANNON GUY GENE JR	CA	04W	97
SHANNON JAMES HERVEY JR	MS	12E	35
SHANNON JESSIE EDWIN	GA	08E	40
SHANNON JOHN PATRICK JR	CA	18W	86
SHANNON KENNETH ARTHUR	VA	01E	47
SHANNON KENNETH MICHAEL	CA	40E	13
SHANNON LEROY JR	GA	65E	2
SHANNON PATRICK L	OK	44E	21
SHANNON RANDELL FRANK	CA	11E	27
SHANNON RICHARD DEAN JR	KS	25W	84
SHANNON ROBERT CONRAD	UT	51W	21
SHANNON ROBERT JOSEPH	IA	11W	77
SHANNON STEPHEN CRAIG	CA	45E	60
SHANNON THOMAS ERIC	MN	17E	24
SHANOR GERALD DELMAR	MN	13W	120
SHANOWER TIMOTHY EDWARD	OH	45W	34
SHAPARD MICHAEL ROBERT	CO	31E	78
SHAPIRO MILTON	CA	31W	85
SHAPLAND KENNETH WAYNE	MI	40E	13
SHAPLEY ELDON LYLE	CO	02W	37
SHAPPEE JAMES MONFRE	FL	15E	60

NAME	STATE	PANEL NO.	LINE NO.
SHARAR RONALD LEE	FL	20E	68
SHARBER JOHN JR	MS	22E	49
SHAREK FRANK JOSEPH JR	NH	51W	44
SHARK EARL ERIC	CA	44W	41
SHARLOW GUST J	MN	14E	18
SHARMAN CHARLES W III	GA	18W	56
SHARP ALLEN MORRIS	KY	31W	58
SHARP BRUCE DAVID	NJ	36E	35
SHARP BURTON IRVING	MI	20E	49
SHARP CURTIS HENRY JR	OH	37W	78
SHARP DANIEL FRANKLIN	MO	06E	8
SHARP DAVID JACKSON	CA	53W	39
SHARP DERRELL KEITH	MS	10E	10
SHARP JOHN DAVID	MD	23W	92
SHARP KEITH FRANCIS	IL	25E	101
SHARP LARRY DOUGLAS	CA	29E	62
SHARP LUFKIN SCOTT	GA	55W	2
SHARP MICHAEL ANTHONY	TX	08E	24
SHARP PHILIP DEAN	CA	03W	52
SHARP PRESTON DOUGLAS	TX	12W	22
SHARP RAY LAVERN	MI	34W	53
SHARP RICHARD DENNIS	OH	03E	8
SHARP SAMUEL ARTHUR JR	CA	19E	86
SHARP STEPHEN ALLEN	KY	08W	117
SHARP STEPHEN CARL	TX	12E	130
SHARP STEPHEN LAMONT	OH	17W	89
SHARP TED LEROY	OR	38W	13
SHARP THOMAS BOYD	TX	18E	88
SHARP VALDEZ	TX	30E	65
SHARPE CHARLES DENNIS	MI	10W	100
SHARPE DENNIS CLAUDE	TN	19W	115
SHARPE EDWARD GERALD		18E	88
SHARPE JAYE ARTHUR	AR	63E	18
SHARPE MACK DONALD	GA	28W	86
SHARPE RICHARD ALLAN	MN	40E	31
SHARPE ROBERT ERNEST	OR	05W	47
SHARPE RONNIE	AL	02W	71
SHARPE THOMAS EDWARD	MI	63E	1
SHARPE WILLIAM A JR	AZ	12W	109
SHARPLESS JOHN PAUL	GA	09W	100
SHARPLESS ROBERT LEON	CA	38E	60
SHARPLEY LEONARD COSBY	LA	53W	39
SHARPNACK MATTHEW F	PA	30E	81
SHARROCK EDWARD ALVA	OH	46E	1
SHARTZ FRANK JR	OH	30W	39
SHARTZER JOSEPH CLARENCE	VA	24E	42
SHASTEEN KENNETH PARKER	TN	55E	30
SHATTUCK BERNARD MERLE	NY	29E	35
SHATTUCK HAROLD LEON JR	MA	22W	54
SHATTUCK RONALD LAWRENCE	NY	35W	10
SHATTUCK RONNY DEAN	WA	13W	120
SHAUGER HARRISON BENJAMIN	NJ	42W	50
SHAUGHNESSY EDWARD JEROME	CA	22W	27
SHAUGHNESSY JAMES J JR	CA	45W	22
SHAUGHNESSY JOHN F JR	TX	01E	18
SHAUM RAY THOMAS JR	OH	30W	33
SHAUVER TERRY DEAN	MI	17E	54
SHAVEL FREDRICK STANLEY	NY	27W	97
SHAVER CLINTON WILLIAM JR	AZ	26W	79
SHAVER RONALD LEE	OH	55W	20
SHAVIES GEORGE ARTHUR	CT	38W	69
SHAW CHARLES E	VA	47E	17
SHAW CLAIBORNE LAVELLE	LA	10E	110
SHAW CLARENCE LEE	OK	29E	44
SHAW EDWARD BRENDAN	RI	02E	76
SHAW GARY FRANCIS	OH	29E	76
SHAW GORDON ALLEN	IN	10W	38
SHAW JAMES DOUGLAS	AL	39E	25
SHAW JAMES ROBERT	CA	05W	34
SHAW JEFFREY MICHAEL	OH	06W	20
SHAW JOE CARL	NM	19W	90
SHAW JOHN ANDY	GA	03E	93
SHAW JOHN DILLINGER	MS	02E	30
SHAW JOHN JAMES	NJ	14E	94
SHAW KRIS EDWARD	IL	20W	74
SHAW LARRY LEE	OH	19W	4
SHAW LEE ROY	IL	19W	22
SHAW RICHARD EARL	NY	33E	53
SHAW ROBERT ERNEST	NH	28W	100
SHAW ROBERT FLOYD	FL	28E	57
SHAW ROLAND JUNIOR	OK	16E	65
SHAW RONNIE DEAN	OK	23W	92
SHAW ROY EDWARD JR	FL	06W	110
SHAW STANLEY SERGEANT	OH	01E	43
SHAW STEPHEN WILLIAM	IN	56W	15
SHAW THOMAS	WI	12E	76
SHAW THOMAS FRANCIS	WI	01W	8
SHAW THOMAS WILLIAM	CA	05W	2
SHAW WADE THOMAS	TN	36W	46
SHAW WILLIAM FREDERICK JR	SC	08W	89
SHAW WILLIAM MARSHALL JR	AL	19E	66
SHAWN RAYMOND BEN	TX	53W	13
SHAWNEE CLARK VERNON	OK	04W	90
SHAY DONALD EMERSON JR	MD	07W	120
SHAY LAWRENCE WILLIAM JR	ME	08E	49
SHAY THOMAS WILLIAM	CT	08E	49
SHEA DANIEL JOHN	CT	24W	12
SHEA GARY JOHN	NY	61E	2
SHEA HAROLD JOSEPH	MA	10W	127
SHEA JAMES PATRICK	CA	01E	106
SHEA JOHN FRANCIS	CT	01E	45
SHEA LARRY	KY	19W	109
SHEA MICHAEL FRANCIS	NV	25E	110
SHEA MICHAEL JOHN	TX	01W	124
SHEA THOMAS COLLINS	ME	14E	18
SHEA THOMAS WELCH	MO	08W	92
SHEAFFER DAVID LAWRENCE	MI	02W	24
SHEAHAN MICHAEL DAVID	CA	41E	29
SHEARER DON TYRONE	OK	53W	13
SHEARES JOHNNIE N JR	NY	36E	87
SHEARIN DAN ROGERS	NC	04E	126
SHEARIN JOSEPH EARL	NC	08E	48
SHEARIN WILLIAM CLIFTON	NC	50E	41
SHEDD ALTON	AL	20E	50
SHEEHAN ALLEN PAUL	NY	45E	9
SHEEHAN CHARLES J III	MA	37E	43
SHEEHAN DANIEL MORELAND	CO	20W	12
SHEEHAN PAUL HENRY	MA	21W	78
SHEEHY DAVID LAWRENCE	CT	13E	128
SHEEHY DONALD JAMES	NY	19E	46
SHEEHY RONALD J	CT	13E	86
SHEELER GREGORY WILLIAM	MI	10W	116
SHEELY ROBERT PAUL	IN	17W	110
SHEEN WILLIAM EDWARD	OH	20W	61
SHEER PAUL ARTHUR	OR	04W	89
SHEETS ORVILLE ALLAN	MO	39E	39
SHEETS WINFRIED ALBERT	WA	34E	64
SHEFF JAMES LEWIS	NC	03W	33
SHEFFEY RONALD DAVID	PA	29E	6
SHEFFIELD ANTHONY D	AL	04E	5
SHEFFIELD EARNEST EARL	FL	36W	27
SHEFFIELD FREDRICK WAYNE	FL	10W	36
SHEFFIELD JAMES TIMOTHY	FL	37W	36
SHEFFIELD JOHN NOBLE	TN	16E	115
SHEFFIELD LARRY GENE	NC	11E	11
SHEFFIELD ROY HENRY	FL	36W	42
SHEGOG WILLIE LEE	MO	31E	6
SHEGOGUE ROBERT STEPHEN	MD	20W	16
SHEHL MICHAEL JOHN	OH	23E	68
SHEHORN TOMMY LOREN	IL	55E	31
SHEIBLEY CLARENCE DAVID	PA	26E	108
SHEKELL STEVEN EDWARD	IN	32E	82
SHELBY JAMES BENJAMIN	IL	24W	61
SHELBY JAY CLAYTON	IL	15E	130
SHELDON CHARLES MILLS	VA	06E	94
SHELDON EDWARD CLARENCE	VT	46E	23
SHELDON KIMBALL HAYES	FL	12W	63
SHELDON LEROY ELLSWORTH	NE	31W	40
SHELDON WILLIAM CHARLES	IL	55E	31
SHELINE ALLEN CURTIS	OH	51W	8
SHELL JOHN ROBERT		36E	50
SHELL MARVIN	TN	12W	46
SHELLEM ROBERT PATRICK	NJ	52E	43
SHELLEMAN KENNETH HYDE	WV	33W	44
SHELLEY DELMAR	IL	39W	68
SHELLEY GREGORY ALLEN	NJ	59W	27
SHELLEY MICHAEL OWEN	CA	21E	16
SHELLEY STEPHEN ANDREW	FL	41E	29
SHELLIE DARREL ANDRE	MI	36E	60
SHELLITO WALTER CHARLES	OH	41E	73
SHELLMAN VERNON LINDLY	KY	04E	52
SHELLUM JOHN CHARLES	WI	26W	4
SHELTON ARTHUR ALEXANDER	CA	01E	75
SHELTON ARTHUR DAVID	WV	43E	34
SHELTON BOBBY JAMES	TN	27E	31
SHELTON CHARLES ERVIN	KY	01E	111
SHELTON CHARLES H	MI	08E	40
SHELTON CHARLES HOWARD	AL	26W	103
SHELTON CHARLES MURRY	GA	14E	119
SHELTON CHARLES THOMAS	CA	13E	119
SHELTON CLYDE DOUGLAS JR	VA	21E	57
SHELTON CRAIG STEPHEN	NE	14E	77
SHELTON DALLAS C JR	NC	22W	101
SHELTON DARWIN HUGH	TX	42W	7
SHELTON DAVID PRESTON	KY	02W	123
SHELTON EARL S	IL	07E	37
SHELTON EDWARD ARNOLD	OH	10E	69
SHELTON EDWARD LEE	DC	21W	121
SHELTON EDWARD MINOT JR	CA	53E	23
SHELTON FRANK TIMOTHY	TN	07E	84
SHELTON HAROLD DAVID	MD	20E	50
SHELTON HENRY EARL	CA	66W	12
SHELTON JAMES DALLAS	TX	37E	44
SHELTON JAMES EDWARD	MO	20W	82
SHELTON JAMES HARVEY	OK	18E	64
SHELTON JEROLD JEROME	CT	33W	10
SHELTON JOSEPH HENRY III	AL	08W	122
SHELTON LARRY DEAN	OR	07W	126
SHELTON LESLIE LEWIS	VA	15W	105
SHELTON MATTHEWS	OH	03E	93
SHELTON RICHARD POWELL	CA	19W	116
SHELTON ROBERT SCOTT	CA	46E	59
SHELTON ROBERT WAYNE	IN	14W	63
SHELTON RONALD THOMAS	IL	06E	96
SHELTON SHERRELL VANCE	TX	39W	14
SHELTON TIMOTHY JOHN	NY	21W	15
SHELTON WESLEY STEWART	IL	02W	43
SHELTON WILLIAM ARTHUR	TN	02W	45
SHELTON WILLIE	TN	47E	55
SHEMORY KENNETH CHARLES	PA	66E	2
SHENEP KARL EDMOND	TN	18E	36
SHENK LESLIE FRED	PA	16W	54
SHEPARD HARRY CLIFTON JR	ME	17W	64
SHEPARD JAMES MERRILL JR	WI	22E	73
SHEPARD LAWRENCE ROBERT	CA	25W	84
SHEPARD MORRIS RAYMONE JR	FL	48E	11
SHEPARD RAYMOND ANDREW	IL	09E	104
SHEPARD RONALD WAYNE	TX	57E	32
SHEPERSKY VINCENT LLOYD	MN	19W	45
SHEPHERD BLAINE JOSEPH	UT	42W	43
SHEPHERD CLIFFORD	OH	21E	52
SHEPHERD EDWARD	NC	07E	99
SHEPHERD FRANKLIN STEVE	NC	23E	46
SHEPHERD GORDON	OH	06E	19
SHEPHERD HARRY JOSEPH JR	FL	12E	97
SHEPHERD LARRY EUGENE	OH	31E	6
SHEPHERD MICHAEL ALLEN	KY	32W	23
SHEPHERD PETER MERRILL	OR	59W	14
SHEPHERD RICHARD DEWITT B	NY	15E	1
SHEPHERD ROGER EUGENE	OH	39W	4
SHEPHERD RONALD DEAN	WI	23E	15
SHEPHERD RONALD STEVE	IN	02W	5
SHEPHERD THOMAS CHRIST SR	NY	04W	74
SHEPHERD THOMAS GLENN	SC	15E	76
SHEPLER ANTHONY GEORGE JR	IL	05E	39
SHEPPARD BEN OGILVIE JR	AR	01W	65
SHEPPARD GARRY DAYMON	NC	40E	13
SHEPPARD GLENN ANDRE	NY	16E	28
SHEPPARD JOHNNIE ARNOLD	OH	62W	17
SHEPPARD LONNIE JR	NJ	59W	14
SHEPPARD ROBERT LEE JR	NJ	17W	48
SHEPPARD ROBERT PORTER	NJ	11W	128
SHEPPARD RONALD EUGENE	MO	43W	50
SHEPPARD THOMAS EDWARD	FL	38W	38
SHEPPERDSON GARY ROBERT	MI	42W	50
SHERADIN ROBERT DONALD	NY	15W	100
SHERBURN HUGH LESLIE	WA	33W	69
SHERECK JAMES JOHN	MN	04W	22
SHEREDOS ROLAND MIKE	NY	52W	1
SHERELS CURLEY JR	IN	02E	60
SHERFIELD BRUCE JR	GA	67W	4
SHERIDAN EUGENE RAYMOND	NY	28W	93
SHERIDAN MICHAEL FRANKLIN	PA	20W	127
SHERIDAN PHILIP FRANCIS	NY	50E	1
SHERIDAN ROBERT EDWARD	CA	28W	52
SHERIDAN ROBERT ROY	NY	23W	114

NAME	STATE	PANEL NO.	LINE NO.
SHERIFF JAMES CHARLES JR	GA	02E	27
SHERIN JOHN C III		42W	64
SHERLIN FREDDIE MICHAEL	TN	20W	116
SHERLOCK DAVID HENRY	IA	20W	92
SHERLOCK JOSEPH V III	CA	30E	66
SHERLOCK ROBERT EUGENE	PA	33W	51
SHERLOCK STEPHEN ANDREW	NY	27W	2
SHERMAN ANDREW MARCO	OH	09E	116
SHERMAN DANIEL L	KS	04E	60
SHERMAN HARLEY EDWARD	IN	13E	81
SHERMAN JOHN BROOKS	CT	06E	50
SHERMAN JOHN CALVIN	CA	11W	88
SHERMAN JOHN HAROLD	WA	18E	50
SHERMAN KENNETH LARMAR	FL	35W	29
SHERMAN LARRY DEE	IN	44E	41
SHERMAN PETER WOODBURY	OH	21E	84
SHERMAN REX MARCEL	WV	16W	96
SHERMAN ROBERT CARL	IL	22E	59
SHERMAN RONALD EARL	MA	06E	68
SHERMAN ROOSEVELT JR	CA	51W	21
SHERMAN STEVEN ROSS	MD	09E	78
SHERMAN THOMAS ALAN	MI	35W	36
SHERMAN VICTOR P JR	NY	38E	72
SHERMAN WILLIAM WARREN	MO	28W	3
SHERMOS JOHN DANIEL	MI	39W	52
SHEROKE JOHN RICHARD JR	PA	49W	26
SHERRELL DAVID FRANK	CA	21E	63
SHERRELL MELVIN LEON	VA	13E	41
SHERRILL AMOS CHESTER II	KS	51W	13
SHERRILL HERBERT	NY	22E	85
SHERRILL JAMES J	TN	36E	35
SHERRILL JIMMY L	KY	45E	29
SHERRILL JOHN OTIS	OK	46E	24
SHERRILL RICHARD WAYNE	AR	18W	80
SHERRILL VANN DWAIN	NC	02E	133
SHERROD DONALD ANCKER	TN	09E	118
SHERROD EDWARD HERBERT	OK	18W	1
SHERROD LOUIS	DC	03E	27
SHERROD WALTER JR	MI	41W	15
SHERRY THOMAS	OR	10W	29
SHERWOOD JAMES ROBERT	MI	41W	27
SHERWOOD RICHARD GUY	MI	31E	60
SHERWOOD ROBERT JAMES JR	PA	17E	96
SHETRON WILLIAM MACKS	MI	11E	4
SHETTERS JOHN HENRY	TN	09E	118
SHEVLIN HUGH JOHN	AZ	06W	46
SHEW DENNIS WAYNE	WI	18W	72
SHEWMAKE JOHN DANIEL SR	AR	02W	62
SHEWMAN RONALD JAMES	CA	69E	2
SHIANNA LOUIE JOHN	IL	26W	4
SHIBATA GLENN TEUGIO	HI	28W	86
SHIEFER JOHN FREDERICK	ID	07W	23
SHIELDS ALAN HARRY	CA	12E	64
SHIELDS DAVID	NJ	05E	124
SHIELDS DAVID THOMAS	CA	54W	20
SHIELDS ELMER MATTHEW	IL	16W	32
SHIELDS GARY DON	IL	14E	12
SHIELDS JAMES CURTIS	OK	17W	58
SHIELDS JIMMY LEE	CA	38W	21
SHIELDS MARTIN DEAN	VA	38W	5
SHIELDS MARVIN GLEN	WA	02E	7
SHIELDS MELVIN LEROY	MI	20E	36
SHIELDS RICHARD DALE	CA	30W	95
SHIELDS ROBERT EARL	PA	26E	17
SHIELDS ROBERT HAZEN II	MD	19W	47
SHIELDS RONALD WAYNE	OK	39E	21
SHIELDS RUSSELL ALLEN	CO	14W	108
SHIELDS STEPHEN EDWARD	MD	01W	47
SHIELDS WILLIAM JOHN	PA	24E	43
SHIER RONALD JAMES	MI	30W	32
SHIFFLETT ALVIN MARION JR	KY	11E	115
SHIFLETT DAVID HENRY	WV	25W	55
SHIKO RAYMOND JOSEPH	PA	01W	22
SHILLER ALBERT	PA	47E	43
SHILLING DEAN RICHARD	OH	15W	11
SHILT RICHARD EUGENE	IL	25E	8
SHIMABUKURO KENYU	HI	47W	33
SHIMEK ALBERT LAWRENCE	TX	01E	48
SHIMEK SAMUEL DALE	PA	37W	78
SHIMODA WESLEY	CO	12E	77
SHIMP ANDREW HARRY	IL	21E	81
SHINAULT JOHN MICHAEL	TN	25W	19

NAME	STATE	PANEL NO.	LINE NO.
SHINE ANTHONY CAMERON	NY	01W	93
SHINE DENNIS FRANCIS	MA	19W	73
SHINE JONATHAN CAMERON	NY	06W	2
SHINELDECKER RAYMOND MACK	MI	24W	61
SHINER JOHN ROBERT	IL	40W	26
SHINGLEDECKER ARMON D	OH	07E	129
SHINGLER ROY DELL	MS	05W	108
SHINGLETON THEODORE JR	WV	38E	13
SHINKAWA ROY YASUSHI	HI	04W	1
SHINN GARY JAMES	MI	03W	60
SHINN WILLIAM CHARLES	CA	14W	77
SHIPE THOMAS ALLEBACH	PA	07W	75
SHIPLEY DREW DOUGLAS	OK	31E	77
SHIPLEY ROGER WILLIAM	OR	59W	14
SHIPLEY RONALD EUGENE	IL	19W	52
SHIPLEY THOMAS FREDERICK	TN	16W	47
SHIPLEY WALTER W JR	PA	10E	44
SHIPMAN JAMES ROBERT	NY	19W	123
SHIPMAN MARVIN LEROY	IL	04E	31
SHIPMAN ROBERT DUANE	IL	13W	89
SHIPMAN WILLIE FRAZER	NC	41E	3
SHIPP KEITH LEROY	OR	06E	78
SHIRAKA JOHN EDWARD	MA	29W	14
SHIREMAN PAUL JR	AR	50W	32
SHIRK STEVEN GLEN	IN	43W	66
SHIRLEY CARL DOUGLAS	NC	20W	34
SHIRLEY CARL EUGENE	KY	63E	1
SHIRLEY DALE EDWARD	OK	44E	21
SHIRLEY DONALD LEE	TN	30W	96
SHIRLEY HAROLD GENE	FL	37E	69
SHIRMANG RICHARD	IL	16W	44
SHIRODA ROBERT LOUIS JR	MI	31W	40
SHIVELY DENNIS CARL	OR	46E	12
SHIVER CHARLES JR	TX	18E	129
SHIVER HENRY ARNOLD	FL	06E	103
SHIVER RICHARD WAYNE	FL	34E	26
SHOAPS KENNETH DUANE	MI	24W	90
SHOBER TIMOTHY ALLEN	PA	22W	101
SHOCK JACK DEAN	NV	34W	2
SHOCKLEY BOBBY JOE	MO	10E	2
SHOCKLEY DON LEE	MD	17E	64
SHOCKLEY RONALD DAVID	CA	46W	8
SHOCKLEY THURMAN B JR	TN	04E	101
SHOEMAKER DAVID HOWARD	CA	29E	12
SHOEMAKER DONALD ELTON	NY	14E	68
SHOEMAKER JOHN STOUDT	PA	31W	20
SHOEMAKER KENNETH R JR	KY	31E	17
SHOEMAKER RAYMOND A II	OH	16W	41
SHOEMAKER ROBERT DALE	TN	32W	23
SHOEMAKER ROBERT LEE	PA	01E	131
SHOGAN PAUL FRANCIS	PA	08E	31
SHOLAR EDWIN FRANKLIN	KY	23W	68
SHOLL ROBERT LEE	PA	15E	77
SHOMAKER JEROME CHARLES	CA	30E	50
SHOMPANY ERNEST VON	VT	55W	24
SHONECK JOHN REGINALD	CT	11E	88
SHONKA DARYL DAVID	IA	08W	87
SHOOK BOYD LEROY	NJ	08W	63
SHOOK GEORGE LEONARD JR	CA	02E	93
SHOOK ROBERT LYNN	GA	20W	89
SHOOP JACK HENRY JR	PA	30E	33
SHOOPMAN KENNETH DOYLE	OK	36W	78
SHOOPMAN PHILLIP RAY	KY	15E	87
SHOOT TERRY WILLIAM	IL	51E	48
SHORACK THEODORE JAMES JR	OR	08E	28
SHORES DANNY JEAN	OK	07W	116
SHORES MALTON GENE	AR	23E	46
SHORT ANDREW JONAH III	MS	20E	18
SHORT BARRY JAN	WI	18E	129
SHORT BILLY DALE	MO	17W	43
SHORT CHARLES DUDLEY	CA	26W	4
SHORT J C LESLIE	MI	06E	104
SHORT JAMES EVERRTTE	KY	21W	20
SHORT JOSEPH WILLIAM	TN	49E	47
SHORT LARRY RAY	OK	31W	21
SHORT LEWIS LEROY	CA	20W	110
SHORT MITCHELL CONRAD	CA	02E	61
SHORT PAUL THEODORE JR	PA	14E	113
SHORT RANDALL CHARLES	OH	03W	52
SHORT RONALD LEE	CA	19W	23
SHORT WILLIAM MICHAEL	OH	21W	72
SHORTALL STEPHEN ADAMS	CT	32W	23

NAME	STATE	PANEL NO.	LINE NO.
SHORTEN TIMOTHY JOHN	NY	47E	27
SHORTER JOHN JOSEPH	MD	55W	24
SHORTER ROBERT LEE	FL	41E	73
SHORTLEY DOUGLAS LYLE	MN	12W	18
SHORTS WILLIAM VINCENT	NY	13E	12
SHORTSLEEVES WILLIAM JOSE	MA	46E	18
SHORTT WALTER RUBEN	MO	06E	35
SHORTT WILLIAM	NJ	16E	4
SHOTWELL JAMES HUNTER	MA	67W	4
SHOUFF JOHNNY EDWARD	DC	19W	126
SHOULDERS DONALD RAY	IN	22W	8
SHOUP ROY NEAL	OH	16E	98
SHOUP WILLIAM K	NY	06E	34
SHOVER BRUCE CHARLES	OH	05W	50
SHOVER WILLIAM	OH	14E	51
SHOVLIN FRANK JOSEPH	PA	21E	70
SHOWALTER JAMES EDWARD	PA	10E	10
SHOWALTER WALDEMAR D	CO	08E	109
SHOWERS DENNIS KARL	CA	46E	24
SHOWERS JOHN ELLSWORTH JR	PA	27E	76
SHOWMAKER RONALD EUGENE	IL	26E	76
SHOWS JAMES JERRY	MS	41W	49
SHRACK ROBERT VENARD JR	OH	28W	53
SHRADER HAROLD WILLIAM	NE	02E	49
SHRADER JAMES GAYLORD	PA	10W	29
SHRAMKO MICHAEL ANGELO	NY	43E	61
SHREVE JOSEPH LYNWOOD JR	CA	53E	41
SHREWSBERRY ROGER LYNN	WA	45W	22
SHREWSBURY PAUL WAYNE	VA	29W	15
SHRINER ROBERT LEE	CA	06W	74
SHRINER THOMAS JOHN	WA	12W	63
SHRIVER JERRY MICHAEL	CA	26W	41
SHRIVER ROBERT S JR	OR	03E	93
SHROBA THOMAS MICHAEL	IL	17W	38
SHROPSHIRE GLEN EMERY	ID	24E	57
SHROPSHIRE RONALD LEE	NY	25W	55
SHROUT SANFORD JR	CA	25E	89
SHROYER ALAN CRAIG	IN	16E	18
SHROYER PERRY VERNANDO	OH	41E	73
SHRUM KENNETH EDWARD	TN	11E	78
SHRUM LEON JERRY	KY	36E	35
SHRUM WILLIAM LAWRENCE	AZ	51W	37
SHUBBUCK ROLLAND BERNARD	NY	04E	75
SHUBERT DARNAY	PA	32E	82
SHUBERT EDWIN LENARD JR	FL	22E	80
SHUBERT JACKIE ECHOLS	FL	28E	31
SHUBIAK JOSEPH EDWARD	PA	25E	8
SHUCK RICHARD LEE	MD	31W	40
SHUCK ROBERT LE ROY	WY	12E	8
SHUE DONALD MONROE	NC	16W	24
SHUE RUSSELL DALE	KS	09W	10
SHUEMAKER MICHAEL THOMAS	PA	21W	63
SHUEY GLENN COLIN	NE	15W	74
SHUFELT GEORGE JERRY	MA	05E	15
SHUFFITT KENNETH LEN	KY	14E	18
SHUGART LYNN DOYLE	CA	24W	71
SHUH FREDERICK JOHN	MO	17E	39
SHUKAS JAMES CHRIS	IL	12W	129
SHULER HAROLD WILLIAM	GA	14W	125
SHULER ROGER DALE	NC	35W	85
SHULL SANDY LEE	TN	39E	66
SHULTS ROY EARL JR	WA	18E	24
SHULTS WALTER GLENN	CA	06E	35
SHULTZ CHARLES EDGAR	CA	17W	118
SHULTZ DALE EDWARD	PA	05W	3
SHULTZ JERRY LEE	OH	51W	36
SHULTZ WILLIAM HARRY	PA	24W	21
SHUMAN ERNEST MAXWELL JR	GA	09E	95
SHUMAN MICHAEL BERNARD	MA	46W	36
SHUMAN WILLIAM CONRAD	ME	41W	27
SHUMATE BERLIN ROBERT	CA	56E	31
SHUMATE NILE DEAN	WV	61W	6
SHUMATE WILLIAM CLAYTON	GA	40E	31
SHUMBARGER DALE EARL	IL	29E	35
SHUMBRIS EUGENE PAUL	NY	15W	44
SHUMINSKI STANLEY JOHN	OH	19W	4
SHUMPERT CHARLES McCLAME	MS	14W	128
SHUMPERT JOE THOMAS	SC	32E	60
SHUMWAY GEOFFREY RAYMOND	NY	01W	49
SHUPE HERBERT CARSON	WV	12E	92
SHUPTRINE ROBERT M	LA	06W	22
SHURR ROBERT JAMES	MN	11W	2

NAME	STATE	PANEL NO.	LINE NO.
SHURTLEFF BRUCE WARREN	WA	09W	119
SHUSTER DARRYL WAYNE	CA	31W	21
SHUTT CARL ALVIN JR	NY	46E	50
SHUTTERS PATRICK ALAN	IN	44E	62
SHUYLER JAMES EARNEST	OK	08E	29
SHY GARY NOLAN	OH	43E	59
SIAMBONES GUS	IN	19W	73
SIBAYAN FRANKLIN DANIEL	HI	20W	67
SIBERT DARRELL WAYNE	OH	38E	60
SIBILLY JOHN RICHARD	NY	26E	31
SIBLEY RALPH	IL	46E	41
SIBSON SCOTT MEYER	PA	31W	21
SICILIA BRIGGS KINNEY	CA	35W	18
SICILIANO JOSEPH A JR	OH	20E	106
SICKEL JOHN AULDE III	MA	16E	38
SICKELS ROBERT T	KY	17E	100
SICKLER CHARLES STEVEN	NJ	34E	46
SICKLER HARRY JOSEPH	NY	01E	70
SICKLES JAMES ARTHUR	PA	18W	91
SICKLES JOHN ANDREW	MI	21E	116
SICKLES RICHARD LEE	NC	25W	84
SICKLES ROBERT PAUL	NY	57E	30
SIDDALL JIMMIE	VA	20E	106
SIDDONS JAMES GARLAND	IL	05W	100
SIDELKO GEORGE	NY	26W	87
SIDENER WESLEY MELVIN	KS	16W	110
SIDERS MARVIN ISAAC	IN	39W	29
SIDES CHARLES KENNETH	OK	01E	98
SIDES HAROLD ERWIN	TX	07W	79
SIDOR MICHAEL EDWARD	MI	31W	21
SIEBE GERALD WILLIAM	IL	11E	115
SIEBEN EDWARD MICHAEL	IL	09E	101
SIEBEN THOMAS RICHARD	OR	14E	7
SIEBENALLER ROBERT CHARLE	OH	40W	47
SIEBERT FREDERICK W JR	LA	15W	14
SIEDENTOPF MARK	CA	33W	74
SIEGEL DAVID DOUGLAS	IA	45W	46
SIEGEL DENNIS LEE	WI	41E	3
SIEGEL THEODORE FRANK	KY	27W	83
SIEGER RAYMOND MARTIN	IL	20E	107
SIEGERT WILLIAM FRY	TX	10E	110
SIEGLER BOBBY TRUMAN	MO	12W	23
SIEGLER WILLIE JAMES	OH	28W	94
SIEGRIST WILBUR JERRY	PA	35W	62
SIEGRIST WILLIAM LEROY	VA	01E	80
SIEGWALT MARLIN LYNN	NY	40W	60
SIEGWARTH DONALD EDWIN	NJ	08E	58
SIEKIERKA DONALD BERNARD	IL	38E	72
SIEMANOWSKI DAVID ALBERT	WI	06E	52
SIEMON DAVID ALAN	PA	17E	76
SIENGO RONALD JAMES	PA	32E	60
SIERCHIO ALFONSO DONATO	NJ	18E	51
SIETING STANLEY LAWTON	MI	45W	17
SIETSEMA DENNIS RAYMOND	IL	50E	8
SIETZ RICHARD MARTIN	PA	24E	43
SIEVERS DALE GLENN JR	CA	26E	90
SIEVERS FRANCIS EUGENE JR	PA	29W	56
SIEVERS JOHN ROBERT	CO	09W	125
SIGAFOOS WALTER HARRI III	PA	03W	12
SIGALAS GEORGE CURTIS	MS	32E	47
SIGEL LEWIS WILLIAM	PA	32E	48
SIGG JOHN CHARLES	PA	01E	127
SIGHOLTZ ROBERT H JR	VA	24W	113
SIGLER ADRIAN EDWARD	MD	40E	31
SIGMAN CHRISTOPHER SCOTT	NY	15E	1
SIGMON HAROLD WAYNE	OH	33E	94
SIGMON WILLIAM SPENCER JR	NC	11W	82
SIGNA ANTHONY ROBERT	NY	43W	9
SIGNETT JAMES GUERDON	VA	48E	11
SIGSBEE MICHAEL JAMES	IN	28E	38
SIGURDSON JOHNNY ALLEN	WA	29E	102
SIGWORTH RICHARD JACOB	OH	23W	40
SIJAN LANCE PETER	WI	29E	62
SIKES BOBBIE EARL	LA	40E	31
SIKES CHARLES MICHAEL	FL	20W	67
SIKES THOMAS GARY	FL	36W	53
SIKICH MICHAEL MATTHEW	MN	05W	3
SIKKINK ROY DEAN	OK	20W	23
SIKON ROBERT ARCHIBALD	PA	32E	66
SIKORSKI DANIEL	WI	28E	31
SIKORSKI ELMER GERALD	OH	36W	59
SIKORSKI LARRY JOSEPH	ND	31W	58
SIKORSKI LEO PETER	MI	18W	105
SIKORSKI SIGMOND MICHAEL	NY	29W	24
SILAS THEODORE BUCHANAN	CA	04E	72
SILBA ANTHONY	RI	06E	58
SILBAS ROSENDO FLORES	CA	12W	125
SILBERBERGER PAUL JOHN	TN	42W	7
SILBERSACK RONALD VINCENT	KY	06E	124
SILBERT LEO VINCENT	NY	14E	51
SILER GARY HUBERT	AR	18E	17
SILER JIMMY LOUIS	NC	39E	53
SILER MANLEY EUGENE JR	TX	17W	64
SILFEE JAMES EVERETT	PA	48E	34
SILLAWAY CHARLES EUGENE	OK	28E	31
SILLER PETER LENHART	CA	35E	41
SILLIMAN JACK LLOYD	NM	23W	59
SILLS DAREL LEE	OR	11E	72
SILLS FRANK RICHARD	OH	15E	81
SILLS KENNETH HOWARD	WA	41W	27
SILLS TOMMIE LEE	GA	06E	82
SILMAN GARY WILLIS	LA	23W	68
SILON JOSEPH ARTHUR JR	NY	04W	22
SILOS FRANKLIN ROSADO	NY	02W	37
SILVA ANTONIO	CA	09W	10
SILVA CLAUDE ARNOLD	CO	14E	96
SILVA FEDERICO	CA	04E	26
SILVA GEORGE LEE	CA	31W	22
SILVA JOE REYES	TX	04W	120
SILVA JOSEPH ANTHONY	VT	07W	94
SILVA MANUEL	TX	29E	98
SILVA RITO	TX	56W	30
SILVA ROBERT JOHN	MA	16W	127
SILVA THOMAS JOSEPH	CA	12W	90
SILVA WILLIAM GREGORY	RI	21E	16
SILVAS JORGE ALVARADO	AZ	45W	10
SILVEE HERMAN WILLIAM	TX	02E	47
SILVEIRA JOSE A C	CA	33E	22
SILVEIRA LEONEL MENDONCA	NY	18W	123
SILVER EDWARD DEAN	OR	53W	23
SILVER GARETH MacKENZIE	CA	08W	40
SILVER JOHN CLYDE	MN	20E	11
SILVER LAWRENCE JAY	CT	21E	99
SILVER LEE VERN	NC	32W	51
SILVER LONNIE LEE	GA	30E	94
SILVER WILLIAM F JR	VA	25W	110
SILVER WILLIAM ROBERT	FL	12E	97
SILVERBERG ARVID OSCAR JR	MA	34W	68
SILVERI DENNIS MICHAEL	HI	28W	29
SILVERII LOUIS ZANE	CA	31E	31
SILVERMAN SHELDON	CT	07W	2
SILVERNAIL DOUGLAS HAROLD	NY	07W	118
SILVERS MITCHELL FRANK	CA	35E	35
SILVERSTEIN GERALD LEON	NY	19W	74
SILVESAN DENNIS RAY	WA	10W	92
SILVEY HAROLD RAY	MO	53W	5
SILVIA CLIFFORD WILLIAM	RI	23E	83
SIMANCAS LUIS JOSE	NY	22W	95
SIMBOLA JOSE SCOTTY	NM	08E	58
SIMCHOCK THOMAS PETER	NJ	04E	45
SIME ROBERT JOY	ND	28E	57
SIMEONE CRAIG MICHAEL	MA	23W	23
SIMEONOFF FREDERICK M	AK	11W	19
SIMES ROBERT GARLAND JR	WA	08W	134
SIMETH THOMAS JAMES SR	CA	17W	1
SIMIELE DONATO JOSEPH	NY	58W	14
SIMISON TERRY CLEO	MI	34W	29
SIMKAITIS ERICH	FL	02E	80
SIMKO ANDREW MICHAEL	OH	12W	98
SIMMERMON ROBERT JOHN	IL	07E	55
SIMMERS GAROLD RAY	SC	31W	40
SIMMERS GEORGE WILLIAM JR	VA	18W	118
SIMMETH MAXIMILIAN HEINRI	MD	36E	36
SIMMONDS JERRY LEE	CA	46W	22
SIMMONS ARTHUR D	TX	12W	10
SIMMONS BENNIE LEE	MS	05E	75
SIMMONS BILLY JOE	AZ	33W	17
SIMMONS BRADLEY JOSEPH	NY	19W	23
SIMMONS BURNELL	GA	28E	11
SIMMONS CHARLIE JR	GA	18W	5
SIMMONS CHESTER JOHN	LA	09E	59
SIMMONS CLARENCE JIMMIE	PA	19E	18
SIMMONS DAVID LEROY	MI	45E	6
SIMMONS DONALD LEE	MO	06E	112
SIMMONS EDDIE LEE	SC	42W	60
SIMMONS EDGAR LEE	AR	47E	55
SIMMONS EDWARD LAMAR	GA	03E	93
SIMMONS ELLIOTT JR	NY	09E	109
SIMMONS ELROY	IL	08W	33
SIMMONS FAY CLYDE III	SC	53W	5
SIMMONS FRANK RUDOLPH	GA	51E	49
SIMMONS GLENN HAROLD	OR	32E	40
SIMMONS HAROLD JOSEPH	MO	46E	41
SIMMONS HARRY JENNINGS JR	PA	17E	129
SIMMONS HEROLIN THADUS	NC	09E	26
SIMMONS ISIAH	SC	46W	8
SIMMONS JAKE A	TX	11E	105
SIMMONS JAMES BENJAMIN	NY	14E	59
SIMMONS JAMES CHARLES DAN	AZ	43W	42
SIMMONS JAMES ROBERT	WV	28E	5
SIMMONS JOHN STEPHEN	KS	42E	24
SIMMONS JOHN WAYNE	CO	03W	30
SIMMONS KENNETH JEROME	MI	08W	30
SIMMONS MACK DANIEL III	NC	20E	87
SIMMONS MICHAEL LEE	OH	38W	61
SIMMONS NATHAN BEDFORD	GA	25W	85
SIMMONS NATHANIEL	LA	04E	104
SIMMONS NOLAN LESTER	TX	37E	69
SIMMONS NORBERT GENE	IA	08E	50
SIMMONS OBIE CLYDE	AL	07E	91
SIMMONS RANDALL ROBERT	IL	11W	11
SIMMONS RICHARD	SC	55W	38
SIMMONS RICHARD CHARLES	TX	28W	105
SIMMONS RICHARD STANLEY	PA	50W	10
SIMMONS ROBERT EUGENE	NY	02W	123
SIMMONS ROBERT LEE	WV	03W	71
SIMMONS ROBERT LOUIS	SC	41E	29
SIMMONS RONALD WAYNE	OK	25E	89
SIMMONS ROSEVELT JR	FL	11E	63
SIMMONS ROY LEE	MI	06W	131
SIMMONS SERGE BENSON	UT	16W	24
SIMMONS TOM WILLIS JR	TX	35E	12
SIMMONS TRAVIS A JR	TX	16E	98
SIMMONS WAYNE CARL	MA	01E	99
SIMMONS WILLIAM	NJ	59W	15
SIMMONS WILLIAM PRESTWOOD	MS	10E	67
SIMMONS WILLIAM S JR	NC	24E	63
SIMMONS WILLIE JAMES	MI	29E	92
SIMMS JAMES WILLIAM	MO	31W	72
SIMMS LEON	MI	25E	110
SIMOES ANTHONY	MA	47E	36
SIMON CURLEY JOHN	LA	23E	39
SIMON DAVID LOWELL	MA	33E	41
SIMON DONALD ROBERT	VA	08W	52
SIMON JAMES MARTIN	KY	05W	112
SIMON JOSEPH LOUIS JOHN	NJ	30E	81
SIMON MICHAEL WAYNE	KY	60W	22
SIMON PAUL JOSEPH	CA	04E	15
SIMON PAUL JOSEPH	LA	23E	31
SIMON PAUL RICHARD	NY	27E	61
SIMON RALPH	MD	08E	40
SIMON RICHARD CHARLES	WI	39W	15
SIMON ROBERT LEE JR	VA	01E	91
SIMON TERENCE EDWARD	MI	20E	19
SIMON THOMAS JAMES	TX	19W	23
SIMON VICTOR	NY	63W	13
SIMONDS HAROLD RILEY	NY	25W	55
SIMONE DENIS LAVERN	NJ	40W	26
SIMONE JOSEPH RALPH	NY	11E	93
SIMONS AINSLEY CUDIE	DC	36W	23
SIMONS DAVID RICHARD	PA	33E	41
SIMONS EDWARD JUNIOR	WV	28E	5
SIMONS ERNEST EUGENE	CA	06E	118
SIMONS GARVIS KEITH	TX	33W	10
SIMONS GERALD SHIELDS	NM	09E	118
SIMONS LEROY EUGENE	OH	06E	58
SIMONS RAY OTIS JR	PA	35E	42
SIMONS ROBERT VINCENT	MI	48W	19
SIMONSEN RICHARD HAROLD	OR	26W	22
SIMONSON DONALD WAYNE	SD	45W	2
SIMONSON LARRY ARNOLD	WA	04W	78
SIMPKIN WALLACE FREDERICK	NM	36W	37
SIMPKINS ROBERT LEE JR	PA	13E	117
SIMPKINS TIMOTHY HAYES	NY	21W	4
SIMPKINS WILMER FRANKLIN	AL	53W	39
SIMPSON ADAM ERNEST JR	TX	02E	104

NAME	STATE	PANEL NO.	LINE NO.
SIMPSON ALFRED FRANKLIN	CA	24E	97
SIMPSON BLAIR H	UT	08W	105
SIMPSON BOBBY GENE	MO	36W	7
SIMPSON BRUCE LAMAR	FL	11E	89
SIMPSON CHESTER PAUL	KY	15E	3
SIMPSON DANNY ROY	KY	09E	6
SIMPSON DOUGLAS EDWARD	OH	10W	127
SIMPSON EDWARD MONROE	IL	58E	26
SIMPSON ELMORE ROBERT	TX	46E	59
SIMPSON GERRY GLEN	WV	30E	73
SIMPSON JAMES R	NC	21E	30
SIMPSON JOHN HARRISON	TN	19E	113
SIMPSON JOHN WILLIAM JR	GA	52W	39
SIMPSON JOHNNY CLEVELAND	GA	43W	42
SIMPSON JOSEPH LOUIS	CO	59E	13
SIMPSON LARRY DOUGLAS	CA	27W	41
SIMPSON LOYDE HAROLD	TX	41W	15
SIMPSON MAX COLEMAN	NM	14E	74
SIMPSON MELVIN RICHARD	TX	64W	2
SIMPSON MICHAEL	OH	07E	27
SIMPSON MICHAEL PAUL	IL	43W	50
SIMPSON MORRIS ALFRED	TX	04W	12
SIMPSON OTIS RAYMOND	GA	39W	18
SIMPSON ROBERT LEWIS		01E	10
SIMPSON ROGER LEE	WV	21W	20
SIMPSON RONALD EARL	KY	22W	94
SIMPSON WALTER STEPHEN	NJ	66E	3
SIMPSON WILLIAM JAMES	IL	38W	77
SIMRAU ROGER ALLEN	MI	03E	94
SIMS CHARLES WAYNE	GA	05E	91
SIMS CLIFFORD CHESTER	FL	40E	56
SIMS CLINT JOSEPH	AL	11W	70
SIMS EDWARD CLEO	GA	65E	1
SIMS ERWIN BRUCE	OH	42E	41
SIMS FREDERICK AUGUSTAS	TN	14E	77
SIMS HARRY	NY	35W	56
SIMS HENRY JAMES	FL	05W	18
SIMS JAMES LARRY	GA	13E	94
SIMS JAMES WALTER	IN	10E	81
SIMS JEROME	FL	23E	88
SIMS JERRY G	CA	37E	70
SIMS JOHN CHARLES JR	TX	19W	5
SIMS KIRK WAYNE	TX	07W	42
SIMS LARRY ROY	IL	44W	41
SIMS MICHAEL EUGENE	AL	15E	108
SIMS PONDER RAY	AR	23E	104
SIMS THOMAS JAMES	AL	25W	25
SIMS WILLIAM A	TX	39E	14
SIMS WILLIAM JESS	AR	20W	8
SINCAVAGE MICHAEL JOSEPH	IL	33W	71
SINCAVAGE RICHARD	NJ	36W	23
SINCERE JAMES WALTER	CT	38W	38
SINCHAK ANDREW RICHARD JR	OH	36W	12
SINCHAK WILLIAM ANDREW	PA	21E	38
SINCLAIR GARY PHILIP	NY	15W	79
SINCLAIR JOHN JAMES	NY	19W	23
SINCLAIR LEE ELDEN	HI	23W	18
SINCLAIR PATRICK EUGENE	LA	45W	57
SINCLAIR ROBERT HENRY JR	NY	35W	14
SINE HARRY RICHARD JR	WV	15W	92
SINEGAL HUBERT JR	LA	35W	40
SINEGAL LARRY JAMES	TX	66W	12
SINER WALLACE KINGSLEY	TX	04E	55
SINES TIMOTHY DAVID	OH	42W	50
SINGER ALAN EDWARD	WI	25W	2
SINGER DONALD MAURICE	PA	10E	15
SINGER KENNETH EDWIN	TX	19W	104
SINGER MICHAEL ERNEST	OH	53W	39
SINGER MORTON HAROLD	NY	36W	37
SINGER NORMAN PAUL	OK	24W	47
SINGER SAMUEL ARNOLD	PA	53E	23
SINGERHOUSE ROBERT ALLEN	KS	03E	122
SINGLER DELBERT LEO JR	PA	30W	32
SINGLETARY ALTON LAMER	FL	65E	1
SINGLETARY HILBERT M JR	SC	12E	81
SINGLETARY JAMES SAMUEL	FL	57E	10
SINGLETARY NEELY JAMES	PA	19E	91
SINGLETARY ROY LEE	GA	21W	86
SINGLETON ARTHUR DWIGHT	KY	34E	65
SINGLETON CHARLIE JR	LA	08W	5
SINGLETON CLIFFORD RICHARD	NY	13E	27
SINGLETON DANIEL EVERETT	OH	34W	88
SINGLETON EDWARD JR	MD	41E	29
SINGLETON ELWIN EARL	TX	20W	9
SINGLETON GEORGE JAMES	LA	54E	29
SINGLETON GERALD BLAINE	CA	08W	44
SINGLETON J D	OK	26E	17
SINGLETON JAMES ARNOLD	AR	39W	10
SINGLETON JAMES PERRY	VA	43E	61
SINGLETON JESSE W JR	GA	22W	8
SINGLETON RAYMOND	SC	37W	47
SINGLETON THOMAS ARNOLD	TX	57E	33
SINGLETON WALTER KEITH	TN	17E	39
SINIBALDI MICHAEL WILLIAM	NJ	48W	15
SININGER TEDDY RAY	OH	36W	27
SINK CHARLES ROBERT	IL	26W	57
SINK MELVIN FRANCIS	IN	27E	101
SINK OTIS BEVERLEY	VA	15E	109
SINKEWICZ JOSEPH MICHAEL	PA	41E	43
SINKLER MARVIN JOHN	MI	20E	4
SINKS LARRY EUGENE	IL	41E	54
SINKSEN ARTHUR DALE	IL	61W	16
SINN BRADLEY LOUIS	AZ	19W	5
SINNETT ALBERT MERREL	WV	07E	17
SINNOCK JOHN ROBERT	OH	62W	2
SINNOTT DANIEL BERNARD	IN	21W	49
SINTIC GREGORY JOHN	IL	35E	57
SINTONI JOSEPH EUGENE	MA	46E	50
SIOW GALE ROBERT	CA	34E	31
SIP RAYMOND LEE	SD	35W	40
SIPE ROBERT ERNEST	NJ	27E	3
SIPE ROBERT VINCENT	NY	27E	37
SIPES RICHARD EARL	CA	13E	100
SIPKA RONALD WAYNE	IL	09W	41
SIPOS WILLIAM GEORGE	NY	17E	111
SIPP PETER ELMER	CT	25W	42
SIPP RODGER WILLIAM	IL	39E	25
SIPPEL WILLIAM JAMES	NY	22E	20
SIPPERLEY LORNE JAY	MI	26W	67
SIPPEY WAYNE KEITH	PA	15E	100
SIPPLE CONRAD ALAN	IN	05E	124
SIQUEIROS MANUEL MENDOZA	AZ	50W	15
SIRATT JACOB F III	CA	51W	14
SIRBAUGH THOMAS EDWARD	MD	40W	68
SIRCHER PAUL CHARLES	IL	26E	90
SIRES ROBERT JOHN	MN	21W	109
SIRIANNI DANIEL EDWARD	NY	38E	39
SIRIANNI PAUL JR	IL	06W	33
SIRMANS ALBERT WILSON JR	GA	43W	22
SIRMANS RUFUS	GA	26W	74
SIROCCO WILLIAM DAVID JR	VA	16W	15
SIROIS LAWRENCE EVERETT	MA	38W	52
SIROIS MAURICE LEO	FL	42E	9
SIRON JAMES LLOYD	MO	35E	9
SIROUSA MICHAEL ANGELO	IL	13W	3
SISARIO FELIX ANTHONY	NY	33E	14
SISCO ARTHUR CLARENCE JR	NJ	15E	109
SISCO BILLY JOE	AR	52W	16
SISCO JERRY DONALD JR	CA	40E	31
SISK HARRY DUNCAN	AL	59E	13
SISK ROBERT ALAN	NM	05W	70
SISK ROBERT DONALD	FL	11E	92
SISLER GEORGE KENTON	MO	15E	7
SISLER WILLIAM DOUGLAS	WV	55W	2
SISLEY RUSSELL JAY	IA	08E	54
SISLEY WILLIAM EDWARD	NY	21W	86
SISNEROS ARTURO SYLVESTER	NM	25W	43
SISNEROS ROMAN	NM	25E	65
SISSEL CHARLES EDWARD	IA	04E	46
SISSON BENNIE JOE	TX	45E	60
SISSON DONALD HENRY	RI	31W	22
SISSON RONALD PAUL	NY	04E	19
SISSON WINFIELD WADE	CA	02E	125
SISTRUNK CANOY LEWIS	MS	21W	103
SISTRUNK CREIGHTON WAYNE	MS	09W	29
SISTRUNK DONALD WAYNE	LA	12W	120
SITEK THOMAS WALTER	NY	25E	35
SITLER BARRY JAMES	CA	04E	11
SITO RICHARD ANTHONY SR	NY	39W	76
SITTEN JOHNNY WAYNE	GA	63E	2
SITTNER RONALD NICHOLIS	OH	25E	35
SITTON DAVID THOMAS	CO	22W	49
SITTON TROY NELSON	OK	33W	74
SITZ EDWARD R	TN	01W	117
SIVATTA MARC ANTHONY	NY	08E	69
SIVERLY DAVID LEE	IA	12E	127
SIVITS CHARLES E	PA	13E	25
SIVO ANTHONY JOHN	RI	50W	3
SIX CHRISTOPHER JAMES ROY	CA	04W	10
SIZELOVE EDWARD LEROY	IN	61W	16
SIZEMORE CLARENCE	KY	24W	71
SIZEMORE DONALD EUGENE	FL	29W	32
SIZEMORE DONALD RAY	SC	47W	12
SIZEMORE DONNIE RAY	CA	09W	52
SIZEMORE JACK SR	NC	42W	1
SIZEMORE JAMES ELMO	CA	21W	86
SIZEMORE JAMES WILLIAM	MS	03E	20
SIZEMORE ROBERT RALPH JR	FL	07W	48
SIZEMORE THOMAS JEFFERSON	OH	21W	78
SIZEMORE WILLIAM D	GA	22E	81
SKAAR WILBUR ARNOLD	WI	62E	12
SKAGGS FLOYD PETER	OH	33E	23
SKAGGS FREDERICK BRIAN	KY	10E	44
SKAGGS HAROLD ALONZO	AZ	23W	68
SKAGGS LONNIE G	IN	18E	104
SKAGGS RAYMOND GENE	OH	39W	30
SKAGGS RICHARD ALLAN	CA	56W	28
SKAGGS WILLARD JR	IN	42E	41
SKAGGS WILLIAM FRANK	MN	24W	107
SKAKEL GEORGE WALTER	CA	43E	34
SKALA DAVID FRANCIS	OH	13W	30
SKALBA JOHN JOSEPH	MI	04E	54
SKALLY THOMAS MICHAEL	MO	32W	57
SKANSON LOUIS JAMES	MN	53W	14
SKAPINSKY GEORGE JOSEPH	MA	06E	125
SKARMAN ORVAL HARRY	MN	34E	56
SKARPHOL ROBERT WAYNE	CA	16E	41
SKAVARIL THOMAS JOSEPH	NE	33E	53
SKEBECK EDWARD JOHN JR	NY	18E	111
SKEEN RICHARD ROBERT	CA	10W	54
SKEEN STEVEN JAMES	CO	21W	3
SKEET PATRICK	NM	41E	29
SKEINS RODRICK ALLAN	CA	09W	65
SKELLY STEVEN G	CA	16W	71
SKELTON PAUL DARRELL II	TX	20E	124
SKELTON RONALD ALBERT	MA	51W	37
SKEWES ROBERT JOSEPH	UT	04W	95
SKIBBE DAVID WILLIAM	IL	13W	75
SKIDGEL DONALD SIDNEY	ME	18W	86
SKIDMORE VERLE JENNINGS	ID	58E	15
SKILES JAMES ARTHUR	NJ	16E	13
SKILES THEODORE VAN	TX	18W	106
SKILES THOMAS WILLIAM	WY	02W	89
SKINNER BRIAN KAY	CO	01E	75
SKINNER CLAIBORNE JOHN	LA	45W	2
SKINNER COURTNEY A	MO	26W	74
SKINNER DAVID LEE	IN	11E	84
SKINNER DONALD ALVAH	NJ	20E	92
SKINNER ERNEST MACK	MI	18E	54
SKINNER GORDON A II	MA	48W	30
SKINNER HERBERT KIRK	CA	37W	59
SKINNER JAMES ALLEN	AL	10E	10
SKINNER JAMES CRAWFORD	ME	02W	52
SKINNER KENNETH W III	OK	56W	8
SKINNER LARRY RICKFORD	MO	18W	123
SKINNER OWEN GEORGE	OH	06W	117
SKINNER PHILLIP CRAIG	IL	19E	32
SKINNER RICHARD AARON	MD	09E	125
SKINNER ROBERT CLARENCE	MI	16W	86
SKINNER WALTER FRANCIS	CA	41E	30
SKIPPER HUGH G	CA	13E	86
SKIPPER JAMES EARL	GA	33W	51
SKIPPER MICHAEL RAY	SC	26W	27
SKIRVIN JOHN DARREL	IA	09W	133
SKIRVIN ORVAL L	CA	28E	12
SKIVINGTON WILLIAM E JR	NV	59E	13
SKLODOSKI LAWRENCE	IN	46E	34
SKOCH EUGENE RICHARD	NY	46W	23
SKOCICH FRANK ALBERT	PA	43W	23
SKODMIN ANTHONY	NJ	04E	81
SKOGERBOE DENNIS MICHAEL	IA	19W	110
SKOLITS WAYNE E	NY	38W	30
SKOMSKI JAMES MARK	NY	33W	89
SKONIECKI LEONARD F JR	PA	43W	57
SKORO JOHN PETER JR	IN	10E	93
SKOUBY RICHARD LOWELL	MN	33W	89

NAME	STATE	PANEL NO.	LINE NO.
SKOVIAK RONALD FRANK	MI	01E	31
SKOVRAN WILLIAM MICHAEL	OH	27E	31
SKRINE WILLIE B JR	GA	20E	124
SKUMURSKI DAVID LEONARD	NY	47E	56
SKUNDA EDMUND	PA	35E	27
SKUTT DENNIS DWAYNE	MI	23E	54
SKUZA ARVID BURDEEN	MN	38E	39
SKYLES GORDON RAY	TN	08E	89
SKYLES NYLES BERNARD	OH	56W	15
SLABINGER PETER WALTER	IL	48W	3
SLACK CHARLES LEROY JR	PA	15E	36
SLACK DENTON RAY	KY	22E	115
SLACK DONALD FRANCIS JR	IN	48W	48
SLACK LLOYD	MI	31E	94
SLACK RICHARD DON JR	MA	01E	73
SLACK STEVEN GEORGE	CT	39E	39
SLADE BILLY RAY	NC	06E	8
SLADE JAMES L JR	TX	06E	86
SLADE WILLIAM	NC	44W	29
SLAGEL JAMES ALLAN	IL	17E	108
SLAGER CHARLES ALBERT	IL	11E	89
SLAGLE DAVID RODDY	MO	01W	12
SLAGLE LARRY RAY	PA	11W	10
SLAGOWSKI BENJAMIN EUGENE	WY	04W	42
SLANAKER ROBERT JAY	MI	20W	12
SLANDER RICKEY ALLAN	MN	04W	1
SLANE LYLE EDWARD	IL	54W	33
SLANE RONALD ALLEN	OR	42E	41
SLANE WILLIAM LLEWELLYN	IL	26E	38
SLANKARD WAYNE ALBERT	MO	49E	15
SLATE DONALD ANTHONY	WV	06W	95
SLATER DONALD EUGENE	MI	54E	40
SLATER FREDDIE LEON	MD	01W	13
SLATER JAMES ALLEN	NE	21W	10
SLATER JERALD ALBERT	NJ	27E	25
SLATER JOHN EDWARD	IA	36W	27
SLATER KENNETH EUGENE	IN	29E	6
SLATON ALVIN MAYNARD	GA	30W	49
SLATTERY JAMES DENNIS	NY	18W	111
SLATTERY ROBERT JOHN	NJ	23E	23
SLAUGHTER FREDDIE L JR	MS	01W	61
SLAUGHTER HARVEY NEWTON	VA	22W	49
SLAUGHTER KENNETH WESLEY	NC	08W	45
SLAUGHTER PHILLIP EDWARD	MO	44W	30
SLAUGHTER WILLIAM A JR	MD	03E	1
SLAUGHTER WILLIAM SHELLEY	VA	25W	56
SLAVEN RICHARD E	NY	28W	86
SLAVENS WENDELL LEE	IN	20E	19
SLAVENSKY JOSEPH JR	WV	17W	52
SLAVIN RICHARD NEAL	NY	15E	23
SLAWEK JOSEPH DENNIS JR	IL	27W	13
SLAY RONNIE GLYNN	TX	52E	44
SLAYMAKER LARRY STEPHEN	TX	16W	6
SLAYTON CHARLES DEWANN	NY	10W	9
SLAYTON RONALD DENNIS	MO	34W	10
SLEDGE DOUGLAS ROY	TX	30W	39
SLEEPER DAVID FREDERICK	MA	46W	34
SLEIGH DUNCAN BALFOUR	MA	39W	30
SLEMP FREDERICK ALBERT	VA	05E	75
SLEMSEK FRED ALBERT	CA	19W	82
SLESH JOHN DANIEL JR	PA	19E	66
SLICHTER DONALD JAMES	PA	51W	21
SLIFKA JOHN JOSEPH	IL	61E	2
SLIFKA JOSEPH JOHN JR	MT	02W	99
SLIGH ALVIN C	NC	03E	27
SLIM JIMMIE FARRELL	AZ	09W	119
SLINGERLAND GERALD HOWARD	NY	28E	74
SLINGERLAND HAROLD J JR	NY	35W	71
SLOAN ARTHUR JR	FL	31E	1
SLOAN BOBBY LOUIS	PA	19E	66
SLOAN DOUGLAS DEAN	CA	50W	3
SLOAN GEORGE MICHAEL	IN	16E	4
SLOAN HAROLD MARTIN	TN	21W	121
SLOAN JOHNNIE LEE	OK	02E	97
SLOAN LARRY EUGENE	TX	50E	8
SLOAN LESLIE RAY	CA	31E	70
SLOAN LEWIS LEONARD	GA	30E	5
SLOAN MAX EUGENE	GA	13E	73
SLOAN MICHAEL LEE	OK	47E	6
SLOAN MONTE THOMAS	MN	13E	30
SLOAN ROBERT LELAND	CA	30W	40
SLOAN TERRY PATRICK	IA	12E	48
SLOAN THOMAS NEWTON	MN	04E	20
SLOAN VERNAR	SC	50W	13
SLOAT BENNY DAVID	MI	12W	23
SLOAT DONALD PAUL	OK	14W	41
SLOAT GREGORY ALEC	ME	05W	118
SLOCUM QUENTON EDWARD JR	PA	62E	12
SLOCUM STEPHEN ELLIS	WY	03W	113
SLOCUM WILLIAM SCOTT	AZ	30E	99
SLOMIANY KAZIMIERZ HENRYK	NJ	22E	20
SLOPPYE ROBERT ROYCE	CA	34W	68
SLOUGH RUSSELL EUGENE	TX	09W	89
SLUDER DONALD TED	TN	28E	37
SLUSHER STEVEN	MT	35W	56
SLUSSEAR ALEXANDER MARTIN	PA	48W	24
SLUSSER CHARLES RODNEY	WA	42W	23
SLUSSER HARLAN RAY	TX	21E	102
SLY JOHNNIE RAE	MO	03W	9
SLY RICHARD STEPHEN	IL	26W	94
SLYE GEORGE DALE	WA	11W	88
SMALL ALFRED JOHN	MA	38W	53
SMALL BURT CHAUNCY JR	GA	16E	31
SMALL BURTON EUGENE	IA	17W	78
SMALL CLAUDIUS AUGUSTUS	PR	04W	64
SMALL DONALD BRUCE	NY	36E	86
SMALL EUGENE	FL	45E	43
SMALL KENNETH LLOYD	ID	23W	106
SMALL NORMAN EUGENE	KS	48E	20
SMALL ROBERT RAYMOND	IN	54E	40
SMALL SAM JARRELL JR	OH	19W	5
SMALL SAMUEL OLIVER	KY	02W	6
SMALL TERRY SIDNEY	PA	18W	35
SMALL VERNARD JAY	IA	02E	46
SMALL WILLIAM DALE	TN	20W	2
SMALLIDGE JEFFREY RONALD	NY	10E	98
SMALLING CHARLES LEE	TN	11W	77
SMALLS BENJAMIN ALONZA	SC	29W	48
SMALLS BERNARD AUGUSTUS	FL	67W	4
SMALLS JOSEPH	SC	33E	52
SMALLWOOD ERRAL DALE	GA	27E	7
SMALLWOOD EUGENE FENTON	DC	18W	59
SMALLWOOD JAMES FRANCIS	MD	07E	60
SMALLWOOD JIMMY ANDREW	MD	42W	63
SMALLWOOD JOHN JACKIE	GA	01W	119
SMALLWOOD THOMAS J JR	FL	16W	10
SMARR ALBERT WARD JR	SC	02W	111
SMARR KENNETH WAYNE	GA	15W	45
SMARSH JOSEPH II	MI	62W	17
SMART ARVEL RAY	OK	20W	116
SMART CEDRICK LOUVANE	MA	36W	31
SMART FRED STEVEN	ID	09W	70
SMART LESTER EDWARD JR	CA	39E	26
SMART ROBERT HALL	TX	27W	59
SMARTT MICHAEL CHRISTOPHE	CA	01W	108
SMASO JACK	NY	20E	125
SMAY ATLAS JASPER MORENE	MD	10E	111
SMEAD CARL ROY	CA	06E	46
SMEAL ROBERT	NY	44E	62
SMEDLEY LARRY EUGENE	FL	32E	40
SMEESTER DANIEL RAYMOND	WI	22E	93
SMELSER ROGER MYERS	TN	01W	51
SMELSER ROGER WAYNE	TX	30W	81
SMELTZER CHARLES E III	PA	13W	6
SMENYAK MARK ANDREW	IN	35W	10
SMERIGLIO ALBERT PETER	CT	40W	68
SMEVOLD EMIL HAROLD	CA	45W	38
SMIDDY KYLE	OH	22E	67
SMIDSTRA CHARLES RICHARD	IA	42W	64
SMIGLIANI DOMENIC	MA	03W	116
SMILES WALTER LEROY	IL	17W	6
SMILEY EDWARD ROWE JR	WA	15W	25
SMILEY FRANCIS EDWARD	PA	25E	54
SMILEY FRANKIE LEE	FL	46W	23
SMILEY GEORGE ROBERT	AL	64W	2
SMILEY JIMMIE TAVY	GA	06E	21
SMILEY RONALD OWEN	ME	10W	15
SMILEY STANLEY KUTZ	NE	20W	27
SMILEY WILLIAM THOMAS	CA	55E	31
SMILIE BLAINE PATRICK	CO	11W	61
SMITH AARON BRUCE	KS	19W	23
SMITH AARON CHARLES	LA	30W	96
SMITH AARON LEE	TX	29W	2
SMITH ADRIAN JAMES	FL	31W	22
SMITH ALAN IVAN	CT	11E	99
SMITH ALAN JOHN	MA	25E	71
SMITH ALAN RAY	OH	37E	44
SMITH ALBERT CHARLES	TX	11W	97
SMITH ALBERT DOUGLAS	KY	47W	12
SMITH ALBERT EDWARD JR	IL	28W	4
SMITH ALBERT EDWIN	PA	57E	33
SMITH ALBERT HEUGH	WA	14E	39
SMITH ALBERT JOSEPH	OK	22W	60
SMITH ALBERT MERRIMAN	DC	05E	49
SMITH ALBERT PRESLEY	DC	50W	28
SMITH ALFRED DOUGLAS JR	MD	48E	34
SMITH ALFRED JAMES	NJ	25E	72
SMITH ALFRED JOHN	TX	05E	109
SMITH ALLAN EUGENE	LA	11E	85
SMITH ALLAN LESLIE	OK	10W	16
SMITH ALLEN DEWAYNE	OH	27E	13
SMITH ALLEN JAY	OK	06W	2
SMITH ALLEN LLOYD	NY	51W	21
SMITH ALLEN THOMAS	MD	39E	35
SMITH ALTON	VA	16E	104
SMITH ALTON	MI	17E	88
SMITH AMMONS EWING JR	CA	26W	94
SMITH ANDREW DAVID III	RI	10W	119
SMITH ANDREW RICHARD JR	OH	45E	49
SMITH ANDREW WILLIAM	AZ	13W	94
SMITH ANTHONY	TN	34E	50
SMITH ANTHONY ROOSEVELT	NY	51E	13
SMITH ARCHIE D	CA	43E	11
SMITH ARIEL JAMES	ID	16W	48
SMITH ARTHUR ALBERT	CT	05W	67
SMITH ARTHUR BURMAN	VA	47E	27
SMITH ARTHUR WAYNE	OH	56E	32
SMITH ARTHUR WHORLOW	FL	26W	27
SMITH AUDRON L	MS	61W	17
SMITH AUTHOR C	AL	47E	17
SMITH AVERY GENE	KY	08E	20
SMITH BARNEY McCOY	FL	15W	120
SMITH BARRY JAMES	NY	16W	103
SMITH BARRY LEE	PA	02W	100
SMITH BARRY WAYNE	MD	32W	62
SMITH BENNIE ALLEN	NC	31E	1
SMITH BENNY JAMES	CA	36E	36
SMITH BENNY LEON	MS	09E	84
SMITH BERNARD EDWARD	IL	40E	32
SMITH BILLIE HAYWOOD	GA	09E	95
SMITH BILLY	KY	46W	8
SMITH BILLY EUGENE	GA	35W	56
SMITH BILLY GENE	ID	29E	85
SMITH BILLY JAKE	WV	13W	4
SMITH BOBBY DALE	IN	24E	57
SMITH BOBBY LEE	FL	27E	7
SMITH BOOKER JR	PA	11E	29
SMITH BOYD WAYNE	TN	11W	106
SMITH BRIAN FREDERICK	FL	13E	65
SMITH BRUCE MARTIN	NY	10E	56
SMITH CAREY WAYNE	GA	31W	58
SMITH CARL ARTHUR	NY	19E	7
SMITH CARL GENE	IL	15E	26
SMITH CARY CARSON	MO	40E	69
SMITH CARY JOSEPH	SC	51E	2
SMITH CECIL RAY JR	DC	12W	94
SMITH CHARLES ALLAN	KY	41E	73
SMITH CHARLES CLARENCE JR	CA	26W	4
SMITH CHARLES DANIEL	MD	45E	30
SMITH CHARLES DANIEL	GA	57W	31
SMITH CHARLES EARL	NC	21W	78
SMITH CHARLES EDWARD	PA	14E	38
SMITH CHARLES EDWARD JR	TN	18W	12
SMITH CHARLES ERNEST	OR	33W	10
SMITH CHARLES EUGENE	GA	41W	65
SMITH CHARLES EVERETT	NC	09E	30
SMITH CHARLES FRANK	PA	46W	34
SMITH CHARLES FRANKLIN	MO	06W	24
SMITH CHARLES HERBERT	GA	33E	94
SMITH CHARLES LEE	GA	38W	30
SMITH CHARLES LENET	CA	37W	69
SMITH CHARLES LESLIE	OK	30W	40
SMITH CHARLES MARCELLEUS	FL	18E	65
SMITH CHARLES PORTER JR	VA	25W	43
SMITH CHARLES ROBERT	OH	01E	123
SMITH CHARLES WALLACE	TN	59W	15

NAME	STATE	PANEL NO.	LINE NO.
SMITH CHARLES WARREN	AL	11E	131
SMITH CHARLES WENDLE	IA	09E	50
SMITH CHRISTOPHER SCOTT	CA	33W	85
SMITH CLARENCE ELVIN	TN	29W	93
SMITH CLAUDE ALLEN	PA	27E	4
SMITH CLEO	MS	03E	112
SMITH CLIFFORD	IN	13E	2
SMITH CLIFTON BRADLEY	AL	31E	17
SMITH CLIFTON THOMAS	TX	13W	2
SMITH CLINTON ARNOLD	CT	16E	87
SMITH CLINTON DANIEL	AL	27W	13
SMITH CRAIG LEWIS	IA	53W	4
SMITH CURTIS	IL	10W	100
SMITH CURTIS DWAINE	NC	20W	67
SMITH CURTIS ORAN JR	TX	44W	30
SMITH DALE GENE	IL	24W	61
SMITH DANIEL J	NY	36E	36
SMITH DANIEL JEFFREY	CA	16W	54
SMITH DANNY LE MOYNE	NM	08E	113
SMITH DARRELL	KY	12W	53
SMITH DARRELL JACK	KY	14W	109
SMITH DAVID ARLIE	OH	23E	83
SMITH DAVID FRANCIS	PA	20W	104
SMITH DAVID GERALD	SC	28W	40
SMITH DAVID HUGH	CA	04W	39
SMITH DAVID II	NC	55W	24
SMITH DAVID LEE	OR	15W	74
SMITH DAVID LELAND	PA	08W	122
SMITH DAVID LEON	MI	05E	29
SMITH DAVID LEON	LA	41E	43
SMITH DAVID RONALD	OH	33E	23
SMITH DAVID ROSCOE	OH	29W	56
SMITH DAVID WALTER	WA	10W	57
SMITH DAVID WAYNE	VA	24E	43
SMITH DAVID WAYNE	SC	32W	23
SMITH DAVID WESLEY	SC	38W	79
SMITH DAVID WILLARD	AL	18W	123
SMITH DAVID WILLIAM	MO	65W	1
SMITH DAVID WILLIAM	IN	11W	88
SMITH DEAN JR	GA	16E	87
SMITH DEANE FRANKLYN JR	TX	23W	114
SMITH DELBERT RAY	MI	18W	43
SMITH DENNIS	OH	03E	8
SMITH DENNIS	NJ	48E	11
SMITH DENNIS ALLEN	CA	29W	93
SMITH DENNIS ARTHUR	OH	04W	3
SMITH DENNIS CAROL	MN	32E	97
SMITH DENNIS GERALD	MS	13W	107
SMITH DENNIS JR	FL	15W	11
SMITH DENNIS MICHAEL	CO	06W	100
SMITH DENNIS WAYNE	WY	16E	23
SMITH DENNIS WAYNE	TN	14W	66
SMITH DON	TN	29W	64
SMITH DONALD ALLEN JR	MI	11E	47
SMITH DONALD BOYD	OK	10E	55
SMITH DONALD BRUCE	CA	12W	109
SMITH DONALD C	MO	50E	22
SMITH DONALD CLAYTON	TX	04E	31
SMITH DONALD EMMETT	KY	02W	13
SMITH DONALD EUGENE	CA	01E	71
SMITH DONALD EUGENE	GA	30E	32
SMITH DONALD GRAY	NC	57W	4
SMITH DONALD JAMES	CA	52W	47
SMITH DONALD JOSEPH	IN	34W	40
SMITH DONALD LAMAR	GA	36E	36
SMITH DONALD LAVERN	WI	32E	40
SMITH DONALD LEE	VA	59W	15
SMITH DONALD P	FL	12E	85
SMITH DONALD RAY	CA	08E	69
SMITH DONALD RAY	CA	22W	8
SMITH DONALD RICHARD	TX	07W	20
SMITH DONALD WAYNE	TX	05E	84
SMITH DONALD WAYNE	AL	05W	44
SMITH DONALD WOODROW	IL	10W	16
SMITH DONNIE PAUL	TX	08W	131
SMITH DOUGLAS BANE	NC	54E	35
SMITH DOUGLAS MARK	NY	44W	30
SMITH DOUGLAS WAYNE	TX	41E	30
SMITH DUANE CHARLES	CO	02E	123
SMITH EARL	MI	08E	114
SMITH EARL FREDERICK	OR	14E	82
SMITH EDDIE LEE	GA	22W	8
SMITH EDDIE LOUIS	MO	01E	64
SMITH EDGAR ARMSTRONG	NY	43W	42
SMITH EDGAR LARUE	GA	41W	17
SMITH EDMOND EUGENE III	NY	14W	96
SMITH EDWARD ARTHUR	KY	22E	4
SMITH EDWARD BRUCE	NY	04E	95
SMITH EDWARD DEWILTON JR	NY	02W	123
SMITH EDWARD FRANCIS	MA	14E	119
SMITH EDWARD JR	MO	34W	68
SMITH EDWARD SPENCER	DC	54E	17
SMITH ELDON WAYNE	ME	41W	20
SMITH ELIJAH HENRY	OH	17E	32
SMITH ELLIOTT ROBERT	MI	45E	30
SMITH ELMELINDO RODRIGUES	HI	15E	51
SMITH EMORY MOREL	GA	57W	13
SMITH ERNEST WILLIAM	NJ	50E	22
SMITH ERVIN DALE	OK	37W	78
SMITH EUGENE	TX	43W	30
SMITH EUGENE IVAN	KY	05W	20
SMITH EUGENE WILLARD	MD	22W	16
SMITH EVERETT HAROLD JR	OR	42W	14
SMITH FERROL SHANE	OR	28W	63
SMITH FORREST LLOYD	GA	23W	11
SMITH FORTUNE	NJ	10E	44
SMITH FRANK	NC	08W	23
SMITH FRANK GEORGE	IA	20W	77
SMITH FRANK JOHN	CA	42W	64
SMITH FRANK LEE	WA	14E	41
SMITH FRANK NORMAN	OH	36W	37
SMITH FRANKLIN WAYNE	OH	08E	13
SMITH FRED D	WI	28W	94
SMITH FRED DOUGLAS JR	DC	10E	10
SMITH FRED WINSTON	GA	18W	21
SMITH FREDERICK E	DE	05E	81
SMITH FREDERICK JOSEPH	PA	07W	85
SMITH FREDERICK PHILLIP	OK	05W	102
SMITH FREDRICK JOE	IN	53W	30
SMITH GALEN MINOR	GA	17W	109
SMITH GARRY GREGORY	MI	19W	24
SMITH GARY	AL	13W	12
SMITH GARY CLARENCE	ID	41W	43
SMITH GARY D	TN	03E	94
SMITH GARY EDWARD	MO	19E	122
SMITH GARY HOLDEN	KY	41W	37
SMITH GARY KENNETH	CA	15E	109
SMITH GARY KENT	MI	24W	116
SMITH GARY LEE	OH	44W	54
SMITH GARY MARTIN	MI	20E	125
SMITH GARY MICHAEL	MT	15W	80
SMITH GARY RAY	TN	39E	78
SMITH GARY ROY	NH	26W	67
SMITH GARY WAYNE	OR	05W	3
SMITH GARY WENDELL	WI	31W	40
SMITH GARY WILLIAM	MS	13E	22
SMITH GENE ALBERT	UT	08E	102
SMITH GENE DARRELL	VA	18E	129
SMITH GENERAL DEWAYNE	TX	03W	1
SMITH GEOFFREY STEPHEN	NJ	20W	27
SMITH GEORGE ARTHUR	OH	54E	17
SMITH GEORGE CRAIG	MO	01E	100
SMITH GEORGE EUGENE	NY	23E	53
SMITH GEORGE FREETH	AR	18E	111
SMITH GEORGE HENRY	FL	26W	12
SMITH GEORGE JOHN JR	DC	42W	23
SMITH GEORGE JULIUS JR	NY	29W	16
SMITH GEORGE W III	PA	13E	41
SMITH GEORGE W JR	MS	46W	9
SMITH GERALD ALLEN	UT	18W	9
SMITH GERRAL AUBREY	TN	27W	41
SMITH GILBERT JR	FL	02E	66
SMITH GILBERT NOLAN	CA	16E	116
SMITH GREGG ALLISON	NY	08W	73
SMITH GREGORY ALLAN	IA	03W	43
SMITH GUS JR	WA	11W	53
SMITH HALLIE WILLIAM	OR	33E	94
SMITH HARDING EUGENE SR	CA	08E	5
SMITH HARLEY ALBERT JR	PA	26W	27
SMITH HAROLD	PA	33E	59
SMITH HAROLD JOHN	MN	30W	16
SMITH HAROLD LEE	IA	38E	60
SMITH HAROLD MCRAE	SC	03E	36
SMITH HAROLD ROGER	VT	47E	55
SMITH HAROLD VICTOR	IL	05E	128
SMITH HARRY CHARLES	PA	04E	2
SMITH HARRY ERNEST	WA	48E	55
SMITH HARRY WINFIELD	LA	16W	67
SMITH HARVIE G	IL	25E	72
SMITH HENRY BEALL JR	AL	45W	17
SMITH HENRY EDWARD	PA	19E	74
SMITH HENRY FLOYD	GA	47W	54
SMITH HENRY FONZO	NC	03E	94
SMITH HERBERT EUGENE	FL	09E	89
SMITH HERBERT JR	GA	02E	32
SMITH HERSHEL CLIFFORD	OH	16W	15
SMITH HOMER LEROY	WV	20E	68
SMITH HOWARD BRUCE	CT	45E	6
SMITH HOWARD HORTON	OK	42W	51
SMITH HUBERT RAY	NC	06E	26
SMITH HUGH EDWIN	MS	25E	3
SMITH HURLEY ALVIN	AL	36E	86
SMITH IVAN RAY	IN	01E	114
SMITH J T	MI	13E	25
SMITH JACK A	AL	06E	91
SMITH JACK HOWARD	MD	16E	71
SMITH JACK MILTON	OK	29E	86
SMITH JACK RAE	IA	12W	63
SMITH JACK RUSSELL	WI	10W	43
SMITH JACK STEPHEN	FL	50W	16
SMITH JACKIE GLENN	TN	38E	14
SMITH JACKIE LEE	CA	20W	3
SMITH JAMES ALBERT	KY	02E	61
SMITH JAMES ALFRED	IL	63W	13
SMITH JAMES ALLEN	ME	67E	2
SMITH JAMES ALVIN	OH	23E	46
SMITH JAMES ANDERSEN	ID	44W	43
SMITH JAMES ANDREW	MO	11E	115
SMITH JAMES BRYAN	KY	24W	12
SMITH JAMES BUFORD	AL	22E	20
SMITH JAMES CHRISTOPHER	AR	52E	24
SMITH JAMES DAVID	AL	03E	61
SMITH JAMES DAVID	OH	10E	133
SMITH JAMES DELVIN	OH	11W	106
SMITH JAMES DOUGLAS	CA	51W	44
SMITH JAMES EDWARD	RI	21E	2
SMITH JAMES EDWARD	MS	31W	59
SMITH JAMES EDWARD	MS	28W	4
SMITH JAMES GORDON	CT	61W	17
SMITH JAMES HENRY	FL	13E	36
SMITH JAMES HERBERT JR	NV	43E	35
SMITH JAMES HOWARD	KY	21W	117
SMITH JAMES HOWELL	OK	23W	59
SMITH JAMES LEE	NY	34W	40
SMITH JAMES LEE	IL	29W	32
SMITH JAMES LEONARD	WI	05W	13
SMITH JAMES LEROY	WV	05W	108
SMITH JAMES PRATT	FL	48E	48
SMITH JAMES RICHARD	CO	26E	80
SMITH JAMES ROBERT	OK	26E	51
SMITH JAMES ROBERT	NY	33W	82
SMITH JAMES RONALD	OK	15W	8
SMITH JAMES WALTER	PA	19E	46
SMITH JAMES WARREN	TX	47W	53
SMITH JAMES WESLEY	MO	18W	65
SMITH JAMES WILLIAM JR	NY	32W	9
SMITH JEFFERY NOLAN	NM	15W	44
SMITH JEFFERY W	AL	10E	13
SMITH JEFFREY EARL	IL	43E	48
SMITH JEROME JOSEPH	IA	11E	41
SMITH JERROLD PATRICK	MN	42E	10
SMITH JERRY DEAN	UT	16W	86
SMITH JERRY LYNN	GA	33E	32
SMITH JERRY LYNN	TN	10W	100
SMITH JERRY WALTON	TX	40E	69
SMITH JERRY WAYNE	TX	54E	17
SMITH JESSE E	GA	30E	59
SMITH JESSE LEE	CA	39E	26
SMITH JIM L	AL	09E	8
SMITH JIMMY DON	AR	08W	56
SMITH JIMMY HERMAN	FL	58W	20
SMITH JIMMY JOE	AR	17E	100
SMITH JIMMY V	NC	31W	22
SMITH JOE CLARENCE	GA	35E	51
SMITH JOE WILKINS	AL	46E	42
SMITH JOHN ALEXANDER	MN	14W	81

NAME	STATE	PANEL NO.	LINE NO.
SMITH JOHN ARCHER	FL	38E	39
SMITH JOHN BYRON	IN	45W	2
SMITH JOHN CALVIN	CA	10E	2
SMITH JOHN CALVIN	CA	21W	3
SMITH JOHN CHARLES	IL	62E	12
SMITH JOHN CLIFFORD III	SC	42W	23
SMITH JOHN CURTIS JR	IL	64W	15
SMITH JOHN DARRELL	WV	08E	8
SMITH JOHN DAVID	NJ	09E	128
SMITH JOHN GERDES	WV	19W	47
SMITH JOHN JR	LA	14W	15
SMITH JOHN LEE	AL	12W	75
SMITH JOHN LEWIS	OH	27W	91
SMITH JOHN LEWIS	SC	01W	72
SMITH JOHN MARSHALL	IL	14W	102
SMITH JOHN MICHAEL	WA	16W	128
SMITH JOHN RAYMOND	GA	11W	77
SMITH JOHN ROBERT JR	DC	41E	73
SMITH JOHN RUSSELL	IL	11E	50
SMITH JOHN THOMAS	NY	36E	36
SMITH JOHN WILLIAM	OH	30E	49
SMITH JOHNNIE CECIL JR	OH	56E	16
SMITH JOHNNIE EARL	MS	09E	60
SMITH JOHNNIE JR	MI	07E	4
SMITH JOHNNY JEROME	VA	10W	72
SMITH JOHNNY LEE	TX	28W	21
SMITH JOHNNY WILLIAM	WV	18E	36
SMITH JOL NEBANE	NM	08W	95
SMITH JOSEPH BERNARD JR	NY	43E	11
SMITH JOSEPH EARNEST	NY	47W	12
SMITH JOSEPH EWING	TX	45W	45
SMITH JOSEPH FRANK	NY	06E	104
SMITH JOSEPH FREDERICK JR	FL	22W	82
SMITH JOSEPH JOHN	NJ	33W	59
SMITH JOSEPH JOHN	NY	10W	132
SMITH JOSEPH PRESTON	VA	20E	125
SMITH JOSEPH RAYMOND	MD	18E	43
SMITH JOSEPH STANLEY	IL	04W	106
SMITH JOSIAH JR	NC	43E	11
SMITH KENNETH DOUGLAS	GA	57W	21
SMITH KENNETH EUGENE	WI	10W	47
SMITH KENNETH LAVELLE	MS	24W	79
SMITH KENNETH RAYMOND	MO	12W	40
SMITH KENNETH SHELDON JR	OH	33E	75
SMITH KENNETH WAYNE	KS	35E	57
SMITH KENNETH WILLIAM	MI	23W	4
SMITH KENT ANDREW	UT	09E	50
SMITH L C JR	TX	33W	22
SMITH LARRY ALAN	WI	27W	95
SMITH LARRY CURTIS	MI	38E	14
SMITH LARRY DEAN	MO	43W	22
SMITH LARRY DEAN	GA	29W	93
SMITH LARRY EARL	NY	14E	109
SMITH LARRY ELDON	FL	14E	109
SMITH LARRY ELLSWORTH	MI	04W	11
SMITH LARRY EUGENE	NE	58W	15
SMITH LARRY EUGENE	IA	26W	57
SMITH LARRY F	LA	11E	105
SMITH LARRY HAYS	MS	54W	20
SMITH LARRY JAMES	MI	42W	32
SMITH LARRY MAX	MT	30W	96
SMITH LARRY MICHAEL	IN	19E	1
SMITH LARRY MICHAEL	CA	47W	55
SMITH LARRY WAYNE	CA	24W	21
SMITH LAWRENCE CLAUDE	CA	02W	73
SMITH LAWRENCE LEON	WV	28W	14
SMITH LEO BRIAN	PA	28W	21
SMITH LEON BOYD II	FL	04E	66
SMITH LEONARD DALE JR	MS	33W	44
SMITH LEONARD HOWARD	GA	18E	88
SMITH LESLIE R	IN	08E	109
SMITH LEWIS BENJAMIN	NY	30E	33
SMITH LEWIS PHILIP II	PA	62W	2
SMITH LLEWELLYN ANTONIO	VI	10E	98
SMITH LLOYD EDGAR	NM	22E	49
SMITH LLOYD HENRY	FL	43W	23
SMITH LLOYD STEVEN	WI	12E	50
SMITH LONNIE LEO	TX	20E	68
SMITH LOUGHTON	AL	23E	95
SMITH LOWELL VETTER	NC	41E	12
SMITH LUKE ANDREW JR	IL	65W	1
SMITH LUTHER AUGUSTUS	FL	28E	31
SMITH LYLE ELTON	IN	05W	121
SMITH LYNN HUDSON	WI	36E	61
SMITH LYNN LEROY	IN	06E	120
SMITH MALCOLM CARLIS	AL	14E	82
SMITH MARCUS	LA	06W	1
SMITH MARK EDWARD	CA	42E	41
SMITH MARK JR	PA	20E	36
SMITH MARLIN	CA	37W	42
SMITH MARSHALL R	CA	05E	68
SMITH MARSHALL ROY	OH	38W	69
SMITH MARVIN	VA	32E	15
SMITH MARVIN BONNEY JR	VA	04E	65
SMITH MARVIN GENE	IL	18E	12
SMITH MARVIN R	OR	30E	33
SMITH MATTHEW EDWARD	CA	27W	59
SMITH MAYNARD LEE	KS	38E	14
SMITH MELTON EDWARD	NC	28W	94
SMITH MELVIN	LA	31E	77
SMITH MICHAEL	NY	07W	126
SMITH MICHAEL ANTHONY	GA	56E	32
SMITH MICHAEL BRUCE	CA	23E	31
SMITH MICHAEL DAVID	CT	22E	115
SMITH MICHAEL EDWARD	OH	13E	77
SMITH MICHAEL EUGENE	IN	49W	37
SMITH MICHAEL FRANCIS	NY	16E	107
SMITH MICHAEL FRANCIS	NE	52E	44
SMITH MICHAEL FRANK	CA	20E	36
SMITH MICHAEL JOSEPH	KS	18E	20
SMITH MICHAEL LA VERN	MI	27W	66
SMITH MICHAEL RAY	NC	19E	113
SMITH MICHAEL REX	CA	09E	34
SMITH MICHAEL STEPHEN	IN	64W	15
SMITH MICHAEL THOMAS	NY	03E	94
SMITH MICKEL MELVIN	TX	29E	76
SMITH MILTON FRANCIS	FL	12E	56
SMITH MILTON WARREN	MT	32E	97
SMITH MITCHELL BRUCE	WA	05W	130
SMITH MOSE JR	AL	08E	109
SMITH MURRAY LAWRENCE	NH	32E	40
SMITH MYRON FRANCIS	OK	32E	16
SMITH NEAL ARTHUR	FL	18W	51
SMITH NELSON LEE	OH	30W	70
SMITH NOAH LELAND	NC	38W	46
SMITH NORRIS RAY	AL	26E	17
SMITH OLEN WAINWRIGHT	PA	25W	85
SMITH OTIS THOMAS	FL	29E	102
SMITH PATRICK EDWARD JR	OH	38W	69
SMITH PATRICK JACKSON	UT	32E	5
SMITH PATRICK LEROY	KY	13W	52
SMITH PAUL ALLEN	IN	27W	22
SMITH PAUL LESLIE	CA	41W	16
SMITH PAUL RICHARD	NE	01E	24
SMITH PAUL RICHARD JR	PA	16E	31
SMITH PAUL WESLEY	CA	55E	31
SMITH PEDRO ANDRE	MI	15E	36
SMITH PERRY MONROE	NC	05W	54
SMITH PHILIP CORY	IL	06E	60
SMITH PHILIP EDWIN JR	OR	14W	41
SMITH PHILIP JEREMIAH	CA	14E	113
SMITH PHILIP JR	CA	66E	3
SMITH PHILIP THOMAS	TX	19W	34
SMITH PHILLIP CHARLES	CA	20W	93
SMITH PHILLIP JOE	OH	10W	3
SMITH PHILLIP ROBERT	WA	08E	24
SMITH PRESTON LEE	MI	07W	40
SMITH R J	SC	24W	12
SMITH RALPH EDWARD	PA	21E	39
SMITH RALPH JAMES	MD	17E	55
SMITH RALPH MACK	TX	17W	125
SMITH RALPH NATHANIEL	NC	03E	28
SMITH RALPH R	NC	08E	46
SMITH RALPH WENTZ	PA	21E	39
SMITH RAYBURN LESTER III	TX	07W	75
SMITH RAYMOND JULIUS	PA	52E	24
SMITH REGINALD EDWARD	NY	26E	108
SMITH RICHARD	PA	04E	132
SMITH RICHARD ALAN SR	FL	17W	58
SMITH RICHARD ALBERT	NY	11E	31
SMITH RICHARD CLIFTON	MD	06E	91
SMITH RICHARD DEAN	KS	01E	95
SMITH RICHARD DEANE	WA	10W	100
SMITH RICHARD EDWARD	MI	29E	13
SMITH RICHARD EUGENE	OH	47W	23
SMITH RICHARD FLOYD	NY	06E	16
SMITH RICHARD JOHN	CA	48E	55
SMITH RICHARD JR	FL	24E	10
SMITH RICHARD LEE	SC	09W	123
SMITH RICHARD ROBERT	NY	25E	2
SMITH RICHARD TERRY	MS	24E	43
SMITH RICHARD VROMAN	NY	27E	97
SMITH RICHARD WILLIAM	MN	29W	40
SMITH RICKEY DOVIE	OK	53E	41
SMITH RICKY EDWARD	TN	49W	2
SMITH RICKY GENE	AL	19E	1
SMITH ROBERT	LA	47E	55
SMITH ROBERT BARRY	NJ	16E	14
SMITH ROBERT CARL	IA	14W	113
SMITH ROBERT CARROLL	CA	50W	32
SMITH ROBERT CHARLES	NY	25E	48
SMITH ROBERT CHARLES	NY	36E	37
SMITH ROBERT EARL JR	MD	07E	62
SMITH ROBERT EUGENE	MS	37E	44
SMITH ROBERT EUGENE JR	CA	36W	54
SMITH ROBERT GEORGE	OH	04E	52
SMITH ROBERT HAROLD	PA	14E	73
SMITH ROBERT JAMES	NY	50E	41
SMITH ROBERT JEREMIAH	NY	27E	32
SMITH ROBERT JOE	FL	17E	14
SMITH ROBERT JOHN	ME	02E	19
SMITH ROBERT JOSEPH	GA	46W	34
SMITH ROBERT JR	PA	07E	111
SMITH ROBERT L	TN	10E	44
SMITH ROBERT LEE	WV	04E	115
SMITH ROBERT LEE	OH	67W	6
SMITH ROBERT LEE	MI	62W	17
SMITH ROBERT LEE	OH	45W	28
SMITH ROBERT LEE	IL	15W	111
SMITH ROBERT LEE JR	VA	05E	110
SMITH ROBERT LEWIS	KY	59W	15
SMITH ROBERT LINDO	NC	05E	43
SMITH ROBERT LOUIS	NC	16E	42
SMITH ROBERT MICHAEL	IL	13W	108
SMITH ROBERT NORMAN	PA	19W	74
SMITH ROBERT SR	LA	11E	96
SMITH ROBERT T	IN	27W	67
SMITH ROBERT WALTER	MS	34W	45
SMITH ROBERT WILBUR	DC	11W	19
SMITH ROBERT WILLIAM	MO	12E	64
SMITH RODNEY HOWE	VA	21E	53
SMITH ROGER LEE	OH	41W	2
SMITH RONALD C	MI	16E	14
SMITH RONALD CARLTON	PA	50E	1
SMITH RONALD EUGENE	IN	06W	89
SMITH RONALD GORDON	TN	30E	60
SMITH RONALD LARRY	GA	31W	24
SMITH RONALD LEE	IN	65W	1
SMITH RONNIE WAYNE	AL	64W	16
SMITH RONNY	MS	25W	43
SMITH ROY	AL	20E	65
SMITH ROY MILTON	TX	05W	122
SMITH RUSSELL FRANCIS	MD	17W	107
SMITH RUSSELL LAMAR	GA	37W	2
SMITH SAMMY RAY	OK	50E	22
SMITH SAMUEL DAVID	AL	58E	26
SMITH SAMUEL JEROME	IL	31E	78
SMITH SAMUEL THOMAS JR	AL	52W	32
SMITH SAMUEL WALLACE	MD	12E	105
SMITH SCOTT GARY	MO	50W	45
SMITH SCOTT PHILIP	MI	18W	106
SMITH SIDNEY COURTNEY MIC	NY	03E	94
SMITH SPENCER	MS	13W	16
SMITH STANLEY BRUCE	IL	44E	11
SMITH STANLEY RICHARD	PA	09E	30
SMITH STANLEY RICHARD	IA	58E	26
SMITH STEPHEN JAY	IL	27E	83
SMITH STEPHEN JAY W	OH	09W	76
SMITH STEPHEN LEE	KS	04W	15
SMITH STEPHEN SCOTT	NY	30E	67
SMITH STEPHEN THOMAS	IN	07W	82
SMITH STEVEN ADRIAN	OR	28E	76
SMITH STEVEN DEAN	OH	50E	9
SMITH STEVEN EUGENE	OH	38E	14
SMITH STEVEN JAMES	WI	27W	23
SMITH STEVEN LEE	IN	36E	87

NAME	STATE	PANEL NO.	LINE NO.
SMITH STEVEN MARTY	WA	06E	83
SMITH STEVEN ROBERT	MI	35E	81
SMITH TERRANCE EDWARD	NJ	46E	12
SMITH TERRENCE GLEN	AZ	35E	9
SMITH TERRY CLEVELAND	NC	47E	6
SMITH TERRY HUGH	WA	57W	4
SMITH TERRY LEE	SC	11E	124
SMITH TERRY LEE	TN	40E	48
SMITH THEODORE	MO	39W	38
SMITH THOMAS ALEXANDER	MD	18E	7
SMITH THOMAS CLINTON JR	GA	12W	109
SMITH THOMAS DAVID	OH	44W	30
SMITH THOMAS EMINGS	MI	02W	108
SMITH THOMAS EUGENE	OH	15E	100
SMITH THOMAS F JR	NJ	42E	57
SMITH THOMAS FRANKLIN	NM	36W	17
SMITH THOMAS HERBERT	WI	39W	4
SMITH THOMAS JOEL	RI	55W	38
SMITH THOMAS KING	TX	47W	33
SMITH THOMAS LEROY	NE	18W	73
SMITH THOMAS LLOYD	CA	45E	30
SMITH THOMAS MONTGOMERY	MO	27W	83
SMITH THOMAS PAUL	MI	07W	43
SMITH THOMAS TIMOTHY	AL	11W	93
SMITH THURMAN HORACE	VA	43W	67
SMITH TIMOTHY JOHN	WI	44W	12
SMITH TIMOTHY N JR	CA	26E	51
SMITH TOMMY DAVE	OK	03W	9
SMITH TOMMY LEE	GA	21E	99
SMITH TULLIE ROSCOE JR	CA	37W	19
SMITH VARDE WESTON III	TX	25E	110
SMITH VENNIE LEE	CA	14E	3
SMITH VERNON PARR	CA	37E	44
SMITH VICTOR ARLON	MD	34W	29
SMITH WALKER JR	MO	31E	77
SMITH WALTER DANIEL	TN	28W	94
SMITH WALTER LEE	VA	10E	56
SMITH WALTER LEWIS	TN	02E	63
SMITH WALTER THOMAS	PA	13W	69
SMITH WARDELL	IN	53W	14
SMITH WARREN ALLEN	MI	43W	23
SMITH WARREN PARKER JR	TX	08E	77
SMITH WAYNE KEITH	CA	10W	3
SMITH WAYNE MICHAEL	NY	55W	39
SMITH WILBUR ALLEN	WV	23W	48
SMITH WILBUR EUGENE JR	SC	56E	17
SMITH WILLIAM	FL	14W	104
SMITH WILLIAM ARTHUR JR	MI	42W	33
SMITH WILLIAM CARY	AL	30E	82
SMITH WILLIAM DAVID	LA	04W	74
SMITH WILLIAM DOUGLAS	MO	16W	32
SMITH WILLIAM EDWARD	TX	63W	13
SMITH WILLIAM EUGENE	WV	36E	37
SMITH WILLIAM EUGENE	MS	10W	106
SMITH WILLIAM FRANKLIN JR	PA	27E	42
SMITH WILLIAM GARY	IN	40E	56
SMITH WILLIAM GENE	OK	40W	39
SMITH WILLIAM HARRY	SC	12W	115
SMITH WILLIAM HENRY JR	NY	38E	14
SMITH WILLIAM HENRY JR	NC	14W	87
SMITH WILLIAM HOYT	AL	27W	103
SMITH WILLIAM MARK	MA	30W	32
SMITH WILLIAM MARTIN JR	TN	10E	44
SMITH WILLIAM PAUL	NY	34E	32
SMITH WILLIAM PROSPER JR	VA	38W	20
SMITH WILLIAM ROBERT	PA	60E	17
SMITH WILLIAM TAFT	AR	03W	48
SMITH WILLIAM THOMAS	SC	19W	24
SMITH WILLIAM THOMAS	WI	12W	84
SMITH WILLIAM THOMAS	WA	12W	90
SMITH WILLIAM WALTER	MO	24W	71
SMITH WILLIAM WARD	AR	09E	64
SMITH WILLIE FRANKLIN	TX	31W	59
SMITH WILLIE JAMES	MS	47E	56
SMITH WILLIE JAMES	MS	17W	8
SMITH WILLIE JAMES JR	MI	03E	4
SMITH WILLIS WILSON JR	MS	51E	3
SMITH WINFRED LEE	VA	09W	30
SMITH WINSTON JOHN	LA	13W	17
SMITH WINSTON OSBORNE	TN	24W	12
SMITH WISELEE	CA	27E	18
SMITH YANCEY JR	TN	54W	13
SMITHEE RONALD GAIL	TX	25W	85
SMITHERMAN FRANK DONALD	MI	34W	80
SMITHSON CRAIG DENNIS	MN	15W	74
SMITHSON PAUL WINTHROP	MD	38W	21
SMITHWICK DAVID GEORGE	WI	02W	57
SMITS HERMAN JR	IA	53W	23
SMOAK JAMES THURSTON JR	SC	16W	107
SMOCK DARYL EUGENE	NE	12E	97
SMOCK TERRY DANE	IN	45W	4
SMOCK WILLIAM HASKELL	AR	45W	10
SMOCZYNSKI THOMAS JOSEPH	IL	42W	3
SMOGER MICHAEL ARTHUR	MN	69E	2
SMOKE BRUCE ALLEN	OH	11W	10
SMOLAREK EDWIN JOSEPH JR	NY	19W	63
SMOLAREK KENNETH JAMES	MI	16W	128
SMOLIK VERNON KENNETH JR	AZ	09W	129
SMOOT CURTIS RICHARD	LA	04W	36
SMOOT MONT STEVE	NC	01W	34
SMOOT RAYMOND EUGENE	OK	12E	85
SMOOT ROBERT GENE	CA	33E	54
SMOOTS NORMAN CARTER	TX	28W	40
SMOTHERS DANNY LEE	NV	43E	61
SMOYER JOSEPH RONALD	PA	11W	47
SMOYER WILLIAM STANLEY	NJ	50W	28
SMRTNIK DONALD EUGENE	IL	50E	42
SMYK FRANK BARTH	MI	33E	54
SMYLY DUNCAN PADGETT	SC	30E	34
SMYRYCHYNSKI GEORGE MICHA	NJ	11E	72
SMYTHE JAMES EDWARD	MO	12E	106
SNAITH THOMAS RANKIN	NJ	14E	83
SNAKOVSKY LOUIS ALLAN JR	OH	60W	12
SNAVELY ROBERT AMMON	PA	25E	14
SNEAD BERNARD JAMES JR	MD	58W	29
SNEAD DOUGLAS LEE	VA	15W	105
SNEAD LEONARD HARRISON JR	VA	34E	32
SNEAD WALTER MURRELL	IN	17E	108
SNEE FRANCIS JOSEPH JR	CA	15W	126
SNEED CARL MICHAEL	OK	22W	36
SNEED SAMMIE RAY JR	SC	44E	53
SNEED WARD GRAY	TN	21W	72
SNELL ESMOND EMERSON JR	CA	50E	22
SNELL HERBERT DONALD	PA	62W	2
SNELL MARC EDWARD	PA	45W	34
SNELL RALEIGH JOHN JR	NY	15W	65
SNELL ROBERT MICHAEL	TX	22W	49
SNELSON JOHN WILLIAM	OH	11W	42
SNELSON TERRIL WAYDE	CA	15W	40
SNETHEN ROBERT CARL	IA	21W	15
SNIDER CHARLES CALVIN JR	MT	02W	13
SNIDER HUGHIE FRANKLIN	WV	11W	65
SNIDER MARVIN DALE	OH	09W	92
SNIDER RONNIE M	IN	24E	101
SNIDOW STEPHEN ALLEN	AR	19W	24
SNIPES BILLY EUGENE	KY	07E	75
SNIPES BILLY LEE	NC	27E	37
SNIPES EDDIE WENDELL	DC	24W	22
SNIPES JERRY ARTHUR	NC	49E	48
SNITCH JOHN HERBERT	OH	16E	87
SNITCHLER HOWARD WILLIAM	FL	52E	44
SNITKER CURTIS DEAN	IA	36E	61
SNITKO JOE ANTHONY	TX	57W	13
SNODGRASS DALLAS RAY	IL	15W	120
SNODGRASS GEORGE EDWARD	NJ	06E	12
SNODGRASS JACK LEE	OK	54E	18
SNODGRASS NORMAN EDWARD	MO	02E	53
SNODGRASS WILLIAM LEONARD	MD	53W	13
SNOOK JAMES ARTHUR	OK	31E	7
SNOVER DAVID DARRELL	CO	09W	48
SNOW CHARLES HARRY	OR	22E	50
SNOW CRAWFORD	UT	19E	122
SNOW EARL PATRICK	WA	26W	109
SNOW JOHN FRANCIS	NY	24E	43
SNOW KELLYNN VAL	UT	39E	26
SNOW LONNIE DALE	KS	02E	46
SNOW MILTON JR	NY	27E	91
SNOW RONALD M	NY	05E	15
SNOWDEN BEN DAVID	TX	21E	108
SNOWDEN THOMAS EDWARD	HI	03W	36
SNOWDON RICHARD ATWOOD	SC	18W	106
SNYDER BOBBY CLYDE	CA	37W	83
SNYDER CHARLES DAVID	MI	30W	81
SNYDER CHARLES JOHN	NY	46W	45
SNYDER CHARLES OWEN	PA	28W	76
SNYDER DALE MARVIN	NY	04W	20
SNYDER DUANE HAROLD	OH	41E	55
SNYDER EARL SPENCER	MI	29W	24
SNYDER FREDERICK DON	UT	10W	59
SNYDER GARY FOSTER	OH	11W	117
SNYDER GEORGE EUGENE	MI	19W	24
SNYDER GERALD ALLISON	PA	01E	120
SNYDER GUY FORD	MA	05E	10
SNYDER HAROLD JR	NY	24E	64
SNYDER JAMES DALE	OH	32W	51
SNYDER JAMES RALPH	PA	22E	73
SNYDER JERRY WAYNE	MT	40W	8
SNYDER JOHN HERBERT	CA	28E	12
SNYDER JOHN MARSHALL JR	MO	48E	48
SNYDER LAWRENCE DAVID	OH	31E	17
SNYDER LAWRENCE JAMES	PA	51E	3
SNYDER LORA WILLIAM	IL	11W	70
SNYDER MICHAEL ALLAN	ID	48E	35
SNYDER MICHAEL BRYANT	MO	49W	44
SNYDER PRESTON JOHN	CA	07E	84
SNYDER RICHARD ANDREWS	MI	19E	66
SNYDER ROBERT DUANE	OH	22E	81
SNYDER ROBERT LEE	IL	19E	87
SNYDER ROBERT WILLIAM	UT	27W	34
SNYDER ROCKY RAND	MI	17E	76
SNYDER RODGER CLAYBORN	MD	15E	7
SNYDER ROY HARRISON	NY	11W	70
SNYDER ROY JASPER	WY	10W	100
SNYDER STEPHEN FRANCIS	PA	10E	34
SNYDER TERRANCE LEE	MD	31W	72
SNYDER TERRY LEE	IL	11E	32
SNYDER THOMAS DEAN	TN	20W	127
SNYDER THOMAS LYNN	OH	18W	87
SNYDER THOMAS WAYNE	NJ	27W	98
SNYDER WOODROW WILSON JR	LA	15W	75
SOARES MANUEL AGUIAR	MA	41W	32
SOBACKI PETE WILLIAM	IL	44W	20
SOBCZAK JOSEPH S II	OH	40E	22
SOBEL IRWIN ROSS	NY	46E	50
SOBOLIK KARL DAVID	NE	12E	123
SOBOTA DANIEL JAMES	IL	03E	35
SOBY DONALD JEAN	ND	23E	32
SOCHACKI NICHOLES	NY	05E	77
SOCHUREK FERDINAND J III	MD	13W	12
SOCKEY RONALD	OK	46E	24
SODAITIS GEORGE FRANK	NY	24E	97
SODEN ROBERT HARRY	IN	38E	15
SODERSTROM MICHAEL DENNIS	HI	60W	12
SODERSTROM WILLIAM E	OR	07E	37
SODOWSKY MELVIN DEWAYNE	OK	31E	78
SOGNIER JOHN WOODWARD JR	GA	31E	54
SOKAL IRWIN NORMAN	NY	37W	36
SOKALSKY STEPHEN W JR	PA	21E	59
SOKOLOF HARVEY GERALD	CA	05W	21
SOKOLOWSKI FRANK MICHAEL	MA	11E	59
SOLA-MALDONADO YLDEFONSO	PR	49E	16
SOLANO MIKE ANTHONY	AZ	38W	8
SOLANO PORFIRIO SAM	CO	57W	13
SOLANO RICHARD JOHN	CA	09W	86
SOLARI STEVEN	NJ	34E	70
SOLBERG KALE ARLAN	MN	04E	131
SOLCZYK RICHARD JOHN	IL	32E	82
SOLDATO SHANE NUNZIO	NC	10W	88
SOLER RAFAEL	NY	39W	30
SOLES DONALD RAYMOND	FL	06W	43
SOLIS ANTONIO ABEL	PA	13E	36
SOLIS DAVID TOBIAS	AZ	12W	47
SOLIS EUSEBIO	CA	53E	41
SOLIS EXTRUMBERTO	TX	46E	50
SOLIS FELIX	NY	14W	15
SOLIS ISMAEL	FL	25W	33
SOLIS OSCAR ABREGO	TX	10W	9
SOLIVAN LOUIS	GA	25W	8
SOLIZ ENRIQUE LORENZO	CA	40E	32
SOLIZ GEORGE	TX	51W	14
SOLIZ JULIAN	TX	54E	29
SOLIZ ROLANDO LUIS	TX	10E	89
SOLIZ THOMAS	CA	26E	18
SOLLARS FRANKLIN ELLWOOD	OH	34E	82
SOLLENBERGER DENNIS MILTO	PA	65W	1
SOLLERS FRANCIS CRAIG	OR	36W	70

NAME	STATE	PANEL NO.	LINE NO.
SOLLEY JOHN JOSEPH	CA	05E	18
SOLOMON DOUGLAS EDWARD	AR	29E	53
SOLOMON ECKWOOD HAROLD JR	FL	09E	82
SOLOMON FLOYD DEAN	TX	06W	131
SOLOMON JAMES VERDELL	IL	50E	41
SOLOMON LEAVY CARLTON	GA	35W	73
SOLOMON MICHAEL VERNON	TX	06W	15
SOLOMON MILTON	PA	03E	133
SOLOMON ROBERT GEORGE	NJ	19W	74
SOLOMON SAMUEL K JR	HI	12E	16
SOLOMON SIDNEY MORTON	NY	10W	54
SOLOMON WILFRED L SR	NE	38E	38
SOLORZANO ROBERT ANGELO	LA	03E	16
SOLTAN LAWRENCE WILLIAM	NY	34W	89
SOLTOW NORMAN WILLIAM	IL	03E	95
SOLTYS MICHAEL THADDEUS	MD	15W	67
SOMA THOMAS EDWARD	MN	15W	112
SOMBATI ROBERT STEPHEN	OH	14W	1
SOMBELON ALBERT EDWARD	TX	07E	63
SOMERO KENNETH EDWIN	MI	08E	43
SOMERS FRANK J		14E	77
SOMERS GENE WILLIAM JR	WV	29W	84
SOMERS GREGORY S	VA	05W	77
SOMERS RICHARD KEITH	MI	04W	6
SOMERVILLE WILLIAM HAROLD	IN	19W	48
SOMES RONALD REE	MI	26W	108
SOMMA RYUZO	NY	30W	40
SOMMER DOUGLAS JOHN	UT	24W	90
SOMMERER ROBERT JOHN	NY	16E	49
SOMMERHAUSER JOSEPH ALLYN	MN	65E	1
SOMMERHOF EARL THOMAS	NC	17W	23
SOMMERS LARRY EUGENE	CA	39W	57
SOMMERS STEVEN ALLEN	CA	57E	33
SONAGGERA FREDDIE LEON	OK	50E	33
SONDERMAN THOMAS LEE	KS	04W	112
SONES JOHN LESTER	CA	03W	90
SONGLE CLAYTON ANDREW	MN	30W	49
SONGNE DARNELL JOSEPH	LA	43W	23
SONNEBERGER RICHARD G	OH	21W	57
SONNENBERG ARDEN GENE	WI	46W	18
SONNER EUGENE VINCENT	NY	38E	68
SONNER KALEY ALFRED	WA	39E	13
SONNICHSEN EDWIN CHARLES	OH	47W	23
SONNIER ALBERT WILBER	TX	03E	62
SONNIER FOSTER LEE	LA	25W	14
SONNKALB CHARLES DAVID JR	OH	48W	31
SONSTEIN PAUL PHILLIP	CA	40E	56
SONSTENG DENNIS WAYNE	MT	36E	37
SONY THOMAS ANTHONY	TX	05W	86
SOOTER GARY ERCIL	MO	05E	124
SOPER JOHN CAMDEN	NY	24E	84
SOPER RICHARD ORRIN	MI	47W	55
SOPKO ROBERT MICHAEL	PA	64W	16
SORANNO VINCENT MICHAEL	NY	40E	15
SORCHINI ANDRES	CA	39E	77
SORCI MARK TIMOTHY	NY	07W	112
SORENSEN DALE EDWARD	OR	03W	5
SORENSEN DONALD ROBERT	CA	19E	51
SORENSEN KENNETH JAY	UT	08W	101
SORENSEN KENNETH LEE	KS	03E	124
SORENSEN ODIN EDGAR	CA	04E	2
SORENSEN RICHARD LEE	UT	38E	81
SORENSEN ROBERT WILLIAM	MN	33E	42
SORENSON EUGENE A	CA	39E	66
SORIANO JAMES GABRIEL	HI	40W	35
SORICK STEVEN PAUL	CA	40W	15
SORIM ROLLEEN C	IL	27E	103
SORNSON EDWIN HAROLD	DE	08E	70
SOROKA DOUGLAS MARTIN	NJ	35E	57
SOROVETZ MICHAEL	MI	21E	7
SORRELL SHERMAN AMOS	NY	32E	6
SORRELLS BOBBY HORACE	GA	23E	95
SORRENTI JOHN ANTHONY	MA	30W	40
SORRENTINO GERALD DAVID	NY	59W	18
SORROW CHARLES FINNEY JR	CA	32E	40
SORTER MICHAEL VINCENT	LA	55W	1
SOSA ARISTIDES	NY	42E	43
SOSA GEORGE RAMIRO	TX	64W	3
SOSA JORGE	TX	21E	53
SOSA MARCOS JR	NY	32E	12
SOSA SECUNDINO GARCIA JR	TX	29E	44
SOSA VICTORIANO PEREZ JR	TX	22E	3
SOSA-CAMEJO FELIX	FL	39E	26
SOSA-HIRALDO CARMELO	PR	46W	9
SOSINSKI JOSEPH	NY	28E	57
SOSNIAK TADEUSZ		45W	10
SOSNOSKI RONALD FRANCIS	MI	51W	14
SOSNOWSKI JAMES FRANCIS	NJ	39E	66
SOSSAMON EDWARD DE CAMP	SC	11W	15
SOTAK TIBOR	PA	26W	14
SOTELO LUIS ALONZO	CA	20W	29
SOTH MICHAEL JOSEPH	CA	08E	73
SOTO ARTHUR OLOGUE	CA	46W	45
SOTO BRAVIE	AZ	26E	4
SOTO CHARLES	NY	46W	53
SOTO EFRAIN SR	NY	42W	33
SOTO FELIX F	NY	18E	116
SOTO ISMAEL	NY	12W	100
SOTO JOHNNY	NY	03W	84
SOTO JOSEPH MARTINEZ	IL	06W	39
SOTO MARTIN JESUS	CA	43E	48
SOTO RICARDO HINOJOSA	CA	06E	72
SOTO THOMAS GABRIEL	NE	24W	49
SOTO-CONCEPCION JOSE	NY	25W	15
SOTO-FIGUEROA JOSE ANTONIO	PR	03W	9
SOTO-GARCIA GILBERTO	PR	08E	125
SOTO-RODRIGUEZ ANGEL MIGU	PR	19E	100
SOTZEN HAROLD JAMES	MI	28E	62
SOUCY RONALD PHILIP	IN	20E	92
SOUHRADA TERRENCE LEE	IL	05E	68
SOULE CHARLES HOWARD	ME	05W	89
SOULE JOSEPH PAUL	OH	12W	53
SOULE RONALD GLEN	CA	06E	111
SOULE WILLIAM D	ME	25E	26
SOULE WILLIAM FRED	WA	48W	19
SOULIER DUWAYNE	WI	19E	8
SOURS BRUCE MICHAEL	CA	27W	60
SOUSA LAURENCE NELSON	MA	04E	74
SOUSA ROBERT PATRICK	CA	09E	16
SOUTAR WALTER JACK	CA	35E	81
SOUTH JOHN HERSHEL	TN	51E	49
SOUTH OSWALD CLAYTON JR	IN	16E	126
SOUTHALL JOHN GEORGE	KS	56W	8
SOUTHARD CHARLES A III	AZ	05E	62
SOUTHARD HAROLD ELLSWORTH	ME	22E	59
SOUTHARD JERRY LEE	OH	21W	13
SOUTHER DOUGLAS S JR	NH	27W	34
SOUTHER JAMES ALLEN	VA	03W	77
SOUTHER JOHN MARTIN	CA	04W	7
SOUTHER WALTER ALVIN III	LA	55W	31
SOUTHERLAND CECIL WAYNE	KY	05W	54
SOUTHERLAND ROY EDWARD	TN	32E	6
SOUTHERLAND VERNON DAVEY	GA	19W	56
SOUTHERN EDWARD CHARLES	KS	31W	73
SOUTHERN RICKEY DALE	IN	18E	98
SOUTHEY JAMES RUSSELL	IL	54E	29
SOUTHWICK HAROLD KENNETH	MO	16E	4
SOUTHWICK JOHN PAUL	WA	17W	91
SOUTHWORTH RONALD HUBERT	NY	17E	81
SOUZA CHRIS ANTHONY	CA	28W	4
SOUZA FRANCIS LOUIS	CA	25W	111
SOUZA RAYMOND JOSEPH	CA	10W	37
SOUZON JEAN PIERRE	PA	12W	10
SOVA CONRAD ANDREW	MI	23W	3
SOVEY ELWOOD CHARLES JR	MI	19E	40
SOVIZAL ROBERT JAMES	PA	47E	56
SOWA JAMES ANDREW	MI	41W	54
SOWARD DOUGLAS	CA	52W	1
SOWARD LOUIS RAY	KY	15E	36
SOWARDS DAVID MICHAEL	KY	44W	42
SOWDER BERNARD ALLEN	TX	15W	126
SOWDERS BARRY GENE	IN	31W	73
SOWELL COTIES R	TX	30E	19
SOWELL DONALD BRITTON	GA	06W	8
SOWELL HARRY LEE JR	SC	51E	42
SOWELL RONALD	PA	17W	114
SOWER DONALD MICHAEL	UT	24E	70
SOWERS CHARLES HENRY II	AZ	44E	54
SOWERS JAMES RODNEY	ME	25W	85
SOWERS RANDAL GENE	OH	09W	131
SOWERS ROBERT LEE	IN	01W	8
SOWINSKI ROBERT JOSEPH	MA	49E	16
SOWLE NED ALEXANDER	NY	13E	128
SOYLAND DAVID PECOR	SD	03W	39
SOZA REYNALDO	TX	33W	17
SPACH JIMMY RUSSELL	NC	48E	35
SPADARO THOMAS	NY	42E	24
SPADARO VICTOR ANTHONY	PA	24E	52
SPAFFORD GALON GENE	CA	38W	39
SPAFFORD JOHN WAYNE	WA	33W	69
SPAHN DENNIS M	PA	13E	94
SPAIN ERVIN	IL	30E	49
SPAIN HUGH FRED	TN	04E	62
SPAINHOUR WALTER J JR	NC	10E	98
SPAINHOWER CLAYTON MARQUI	FL	31E	54
SPAK GEORGE STEPHEN JR	OH	26E	18
SPAKES ESTEL DENNY	TN	44E	31
SPALDING AARON BERNARD	KY	22E	67
SPANGLER CARL C	TN	07E	104
SPANGLER GEORGE OWEN	TX	63E	18
SPANGLER JOHN FLANAGAN	OH	09W	133
SPANGLER LARRY KIETH	OH	39E	13
SPANGLER MAX RAY	TX	34E	39
SPANGLER MICHAEL ROBERT	OH	35W	84
SPANGLER RICHARD ALLEN	TX	12E	30
SPANGLER STANLEY E JR	PA	57W	1
SPANN JAMES HALL	CA	02W	74
SPANN LYNN	MS	09E	26
SPARE WAYNE JOHN	MD	39E	26
SPARENBERG BENARD JOHN	MD	05E	5
SPARK MICHAEL MELVIN	NY	34W	10
SPARKMAN ISAAC	SC	51W	21
SPARKMAN LEONARD PETER	WA	19W	24
SPARKS CHARLES PIERCE	TX	01E	69
SPARKS CLIFFORD EDWARD	FL	16E	24
SPARKS DAVID LEO	CO	40W	30
SPARKS DONALD LEE	IA	22W	69
SPARKS GLENN LOUIS	CA	29W	84
SPARKS HENRY EUGENE	CA	21W	95
SPARKS JAMES EDWARD	CA	36W	42
SPARKS JAMES HENRY	TX	22E	90
SPARKS JOHN W	WA	14W	21
SPARKS JON MICHAEL	ID	04W	58
SPARKS PAUL ALLAN	TX	19W	74
SPARKS PETER ALLAN	MN	27E	51
SPARKS RICHARD L	OH	43W	43
SPARKS RICKIE D	MI	30E	19
SPARKS ROGER HOWARD	WA	54E	29
SPARKS RONALD DAVID	VA	48E	35
SPARKS STEPHEN DUANE SR	OK	44W	30
SPARKS STEVEN LEE	OH	48E	35
SPARKS THOMAS JAMES	TX	38E	61
SPARKS WILLIAM DOUGLAS	OH	22W	9
SPARRE LYN DWIGHT	MI	41W	32
SPARROW CARL WILLIAM	OH	57E	10
SPATAFORE DONALD JAMES	MI	29W	33
SPATES WILLIAM RICHARD JR	MD	02E	134
SPAULDING DEAN FRANCIS JR	MI	36W	28
SPAULDING JACK DOUGLAS	NY	11E	75
SPAULDING LARRY EUGENE	OH	25W	85
SPAULDING RICHARD LEE	CO	26E	52
SPAW JAMES ODIS	CA	48W	48
SPEAK ERIC B	CA	15E	36
SPEAKMAN RICHARD PAUL JR	OH	21W	20
SPEAKS MAC WAYNE	AL	46E	50
SPEAKS PAUL EDWARD	OH	24W	79
SPEAR EDWARD BRUCE	PA	41W	16
SPEAR FRED HAROLD	MI	35E	42
SPEAR HOWARD JOSEPH	OH	55E	31
SPEAR JOHN RANDALL	CA	26W	36
SPEAR MICHAEL JOHN	IL	33W	89
SPEAR MICHAEL SHELDON	NY	09W	61
SPEARE WALTER RICHARD III	OR	12E	54
SPEARMAN DAVID GLENN	VA	22E	115
SPEARMAN GORDON KEITH JR	OR	04W	36
SPEARMAN WILLIAM T III	IL	30W	96
SPEARMON J B	TX	43W	31
SPEARS BENJAMIN GEORGE	GA	05E	129
SPEARS DAVID PAUL	TN	09E	71
SPEARS JERRY WAYNE	TN	21W	71
SPEARS JOHNNY CLARENCE	TX	05W	70
SPEARS MILTON EARL	WA	56E	16
SPEARS RONDALL PRESTON	OH	17W	82
SPEATH DAVID PAUL	CT	51E	42
SPECK DENNIS JEROME	MI	51W	45
SPECK GEORGE EDGAR	OH	41E	55

NAME	STATE	PANEL NO.	LINE NO.
SPEER BYRON MORROW	CA	21E	99
SPEER JAMES WALTER	IA	24W	90
SPEER LOUIS LEON	IN	55E	32
SPEER RICHARD MICHAEL	FL	11W	39
SPEER ROBERT FRITZ	TX	03W	9
SPEIDEL LOUIS JOHN	OH	03W	89
SPEIGHT FRANKLIN ELLIOTT	NC	45E	43
SPEIGHT JOHNNIE MOSES JR	NC	18W	76
SPEIGHT WILLIAM ROBERT	GA	19W	98
SPEIGHT WILLIAM RUFUS	NC	10W	67
SPEIGHTS ROOSEVELT	SC	40W	30
SPEIR DALE LLOYD	OH	21E	63
SPELLER JAMES RONALD	NC	30E	34
SPELLMAN JOSEPH VICTOR	CO	39E	67
SPELLMAN WAYNE JUDE	LA	06E	107
SPENARD NORMAN JOSEPH GEO	CT	03E	133
SPENCE ALEX C JR	NY	09W	75
SPENCE DONALD EDWIN	MN	16W	94
SPENCE EDGAR CLAY	LA	42E	10
SPENCE GEORGE ANTHONY	NY	04W	22
SPENCE JAMES MAYNARD	GA	05E	84
SPENCE JOHN ANDREW III	PA	07W	130
SPENCE JOSEPH C JR	VA	05W	7
SPENCE RICHARD BRUCE	PA	14W	28
SPENCE ROGER JAMES	NJ	30W	70
SPENCE RONALD LEE	OH	15W	2
SPENCER ARLIE JR	MI	10W	47
SPENCER BOBBY LEE	NC	42W	2
SPENCER BUFORD RONALD	VA	09W	77
SPENCER CORDELL	AL	03E	36
SPENCER DANIEL EUGENE JR	OR	39W	57
SPENCER DANNY RAY	MO	17W	59
SPENCER DEAN CALVIN III	WV	59W	28
SPENCER EDWARD ODELL	VA	34E	82
SPENCER EUGENE	KY	40W	68
SPENCER FLOYD BROWN JR	TX	36E	23
SPENCER FLOYD TYRONE	NC	44E	21
SPENCER FRANK III	NE	14W	61
SPENCER GENE B	WI	08E	82
SPENCER GLENN EUGENE	PA	51W	45
SPENCER HARRY HERBERT	OH	30E	49
SPENCER HAYWARD CARL	ME	16E	65
SPENCER HERBERT CHARLES	IL	29W	84
SPENCER JAMES ALBERT JR	SC	26W	22
SPENCER JAMES FREDERICK	MI	16W	20
SPENCER JAMES HERBERT	OH	23E	72
SPENCER JAMES PRICE	KY	14E	75
SPENCER JERRY LEE	IN	24E	85
SPENCER JOHNNIE JR	IL	15E	71
SPENCER KENNETH CLINTON	WV	42W	2
SPENCER KENNETH DARRELL	VA	24W	72
SPENCER KENNETH GLENN	NC	52E	11
SPENCER KENNETH JAMES	MI	01W	87
SPENCER LEANDREW JR	CA	04E	79
SPENCER LEROY JR	FL	38W	13
SPENCER NORMAN	KY	08E	54
SPENCER PAUL MATTHEW	NC	50E	42
SPENCER PHILIP GLENN	MI	52W	11
SPENCER RICHARD CHARLES	WA	42E	57
SPENCER ROBERT DALE	TX	08W	80
SPENCER STEPHEN ALAN	IL	03W	10
SPENCER WARREN RICHARD	CA	01W	97
SPENCER WENDELL	IL	14E	114
SPENCER WILLIAM EDWARD	ME	15W	108
SPENELLI DENNIS ARTHUR	MI	18W	51
SPENGLER HENRY MERSHO III	VA	02W	129
SPENS WILLIAM EDWARD III	MI	47W	33
SPENSKO LOUIS PAUL	UT	60E	3
SPERB WILLIAM LYLE	OR	27W	83
SPERL DONALD WALTER	AK	57E	11
SPERLING WESLEY WILLIAM	NE	48E	20
SPERRY WILLIAM FORSYTH	GA	12E	68
SPEYER ALFRED WILLIAM	MA	42E	57
SPICER DONALD FAYE	NY	22E	81
SPICER EUGENE DOUGLAS	MN	19E	32
SPICER JERRY EUGENE	IL	65E	2
SPICER JERRY LOUIS	IN	14E	114
SPICER JONATHAN NATHANIEL	FL	44E	54
SPICER MICHAEL BRUCE	OH	42E	24
SPICZKA ALOYSIUS F JR	MN	57W	34
SPIDER ALVIN RICHARD	SD	20E	36
SPIEGEL ROBERT EUGENE	IL	29W	49
SPIEKER GARY LYNN	TX	10W	119
SPIELMAN JOHN MARK	PA	41E	43
SPIER HARRY DIWAIN	TX	23E	47
SPIEROWSKI RUSSELL DEAN	MN	52W	25
SPIERS FRANK	MS	28W	14
SPIERS RANDOLPH	MO	09W	120
SPIERS STEPHEN ARTHUR	MA	13W	109
SPIESS JOHN CHARLES	KS	24E	44
SPIKER PATRICK JR	WA	02E	38
SPIKES A V	MS	07E	99
SPIKES STANLEY	NJ	49E	48
SPILKER JAMES DENNIS	OH	19W	82
SPILKER KENNETH ALFRED	IL	35E	81
SPILLANE PAUL DONALD	MA	50W	16
SPILLER CLIFTON	OH	42W	37
SPILLER LEROY III	TX	25E	66
SPILLERS GEORGE THOMAS	GA	14W	67
SPILLERS WILLIAM ROBERT	PA	15W	68
SPILLMAN CHARLES OTTO	MN	41E	74
SPILLMAN HAROLD RAY	KY	07W	62
SPILLNER ROBERT K	HI	19W	63
SPILMAN DYKE AUGUSTUS	NJ	11E	24
SPINA ELMER FRANK	PA	13E	111
SPINA FRED CONCETTO	NJ	44W	31
SPINALI DAVID JOHN	CA	28E	12
SPINDLER JOHN GATES	MO	51E	25
SPINELLI DOMENICK ANTHONY	OH	42W	51
SPINK WARREN LEE	WA	34W	45
SPINKS ALLEN ROBERT	TX	04E	53
SPINLER DARRELL JOHN	MN	22E	32
SPINLER RAYMOND PAUL	MN	46W	9
SPINNER ALFRED WILLIAM	VA	26W	68
SPINNICCHIA JOSEPH FRANK	MO	27W	52
SPINO ANTHONY LAWRANCE	IL	40W	68
SPINUZZI JAMES CARL	CO	04E	85
SPIRES JOHN ALBERT	NY	01W	58
SPIRES JOHN MILTON	VA	26E	18
SPIRES ROBERT EVERETT	MA	29W	25
SPIRES ROBERT LEE	GA	16E	24
SPIRITO ANTHONY JOSEPH JR	CT	37E	44
SPISTO JUSTIN RICHARD	NY	13W	83
SPITLER FORREST F S	VA	41E	30
SPITLER JERRY ROBERT	OH	23E	64
SPITLER NELSON EVERETT	OH	24E	44
SPITTLER IRA JAMES III	CA	14E	125
SPITZ GEORGE ROSS	HI	01W	114
SPITZER HOWARD RAY	MI	63E	1
SPITZER KENNETH LYLE	CA	24E	82
SPITZER THOMAS EDMUND	ND	11E	115
SPITZFADEN ALFRED LOUIS	NY	04E	34
SPIVEY EDDIE LEE	GA	15W	120
SPIVEY ELMER LYNN	TX	26W	78
SPIVEY HARLEY EDWIN	AL	20E	79
SPIVEY JAMES WILLIAM	FL	34W	54
SPIVEY JOHNNY WAYNE	GA	24E	44
SPIVEY WILLARD EARL	KY	15W	68
SPIVEY WILLIE DALPHUS	SC	39W	24
SPOEHR WINFIELD AUGUST JR	WI	32E	27
SPOHN JOHN SCOTT	IL	12W	64
SPOHN KENNETH RAYMOND	OR	25E	3
SPONG ERNEST ALLAN	MN	33W	52
SPOONER EUGENE EDWARD	MI	13W	124
SPOTANSKI SERGE WALTER	GA	37W	53
SPOTSWOOD MICHAEL CARR	IA	35W	6
SPOTWOOD FRANK JR	CA	56W	9
SPRADLIN EDDIE EUGENE	MI	39W	5
SPRADLIN GERALD DOUGLAS	AL	01W	33
SPRADLIN JERRY DEAN	OH	31W	23
SPRADLIN ROGER WAYNE	FL	03E	133
SPRAGG HAROLD DEAN	IL	34E	71
SPRAGINS CARROLL WAYNE	KS	13W	108
SPRAGUE STANLEY GEORGE	SD	10E	89
SPRATLEY GLENN EUGENE	TX	08E	131
SPRATLIN MICHAEL STEPHEN	AR	20W	120
SPRAY VICTOR GENE	FL	15E	1
SPRENKLE DENNIS ALLEN	PA	11W	106
SPREWELL JOHN SPURGEON	GA	10W	67
SPRICK DOYLE ROBERT	NE	04E	85
SPRIGGS OTHA THOMAS JR	MD	24W	50
SPRING BRUCE WAYNE	OH	06W	108
SPRING HOMER DOYLE	TX	34E	71
SPRING TIMOTHY LANZER	OH	40W	8
SPRINGER CHARLES A	TN	29E	86
SPRINGER GERALD WAYNE	KS	45W	3
SPRINGER JAMES ROBERT	WI	39W	34
SPRINGER LOUIS DANIEL	TX	23E	64
SPRINGER ROBERT L	TX	55E	32
SPRINGER TIMOTHY MICHAEL	IL	08W	71
SPRINGFIELD ALFRED C JR	PA	29E	54
SPRINGFIELD CHARLES DEAN	TN	37W	79
SPRINGFIELD THOMAS EARL	FL	27E	62
SPRINGFIELD WILLIAM VAL	OH	25W	111
SPRINGS ANDREW	SC	45E	30
SPRINGS RALPH RONALD JR	TN	16E	47
SPRINGSTEADAH DONALD K	NJ	44E	21
SPRINGSTEEN DENNIS EUGENE	WA	11E	69
SPRINGSTON THEODORE JR	CA	21E	53
SPRINKLE JAMES LARRY	NC	19W	48
SPRINKLE MICHAEL DUANE	FL	21W	90
SPRINKLE ROGER DALE	NC	35W	10
SPRINKLE STEVEN KENNETH	NC	23W	31
SPRINKLE THOMAS THOMA	PA	53W	40
SPRINKLE VERNON PATRICK	OR	29E	93
SPRINKLES WILFORD LESLIE	TN	10E	25
SPROTT ARTHUR ROY JR	FL	35W	67
SPROUL RAYMOND RONALD	ME	41E	3
SPROUL ROBERT LEE	OR	57W	14
SPROULE WILLIAM C JR	PA	58E	15
SPROUSE JERRY WAYNE	IL	14E	38
SPROUSE LEE ROY DAVID	WV	55W	39
SPROUSE LONNIE DAVID	GA	11E	27
SPROUSE RONALD EDWARD	SC	51E	33
SPROUT RICHARD MICHAEL	PA	46W	34
SPROWL JAMES EDWARD	OH	45E	30
SPRUILL JAMES POLK	NC	01E	49
SPRUILL OVELL	NJ	08W	83
SPUDIS RONALD ANTHONY	MD	02W	86
SPURGEON ROY STEPHEN	NM	41E	44
SPURLEY JAMES VIRGIL JR	WI	25W	86
SPURLIN DANIEL RAYMOND	GA	43W	43
SPURLOCK JOHN	IL	41E	4
SPURLOCK LON ARNOLD II	WV	28W	76
SQUAIRE JAMES EDWARD	FL	18W	12
SQUARE GREGORY	DC	13W	69
SQUARRELL SAMUEL LUVENE	MD	38E	15
SQUIER WILLIAM RUSSELL JR	KS	18W	80
SQUIERS GARY LADD	IA	33W	10
SQUIRE BOYD EDWIN	CA	23E	64
SQUIRES DAVID RAY	KY	60W	5
SQUIRES ROY BENJAMIN	WV	45W	57
SQUIRES SIDNEY CHESTER	NY	55W	10
SRADER CHARLES WESLEY JR	MO	52W	40
SRAL LEONARD WALTER	PA	03E	62
SRB ERVIN RYNOLT JR	MT	20W	67
SROKA JOHN MICHAEL JR	NY	20W	32
SROKA RICHARD MARION	NY	01E	58
SROKA STEPHEN EUGENE	MD	20W	94
SRSEN STEVE ALBERT	CA	14E	89
ST PIERRE DEAN PAUL	IL	66E	3
STAAB KURT CLARENCE	CA	19E	67
STAAB RICHARD EUGENE	CO	24W	34
STAATS GERALD MARTIN	OH	13W	59
STABLER JOHN LESLIE	AL	47W	55
STACEY GARY ROSS	MO	12W	27
STACEY JAMES SHELTON	MI	20W	89
STACEY RALPH MCGUIN JR	CA	23E	95
STACHOWSKI ARTHUR THOMAS	NY	25E	9
STACK JOSEPH VINCENT	CA	38W	61
STACKHOUSE HUBERT	NC	28E	12
STACKHOUSE JOHN E	MO	10E	93
STACKS RAYMOND CLARK	TN	37W	14
STACY MICHAEL LEIGH	IL	29W	49
STACY WALTER ROBERT	NY	24W	22
STACY WILLIAM ARTHUR JR	MD	06E	35
STADDON PETER BRUCE	AZ	06W	28
STADEL CHUCK MICHAEL	IL	27W	22
STADING GARY ALAN	CA	52E	11
STAEHLI BRUCE WAYNE	IN	53E	23
STAFF JOHN STANLEY	PA	23W	106
STAFFORD FORREST MONTGOME	NC	19E	122
STAFFORD FRED PATRICK	TX	54E	30
STAFFORD FREDERICK	PA	09E	118
STAFFORD HAROLD RICHARD	MD	36E	37
STAFFORD HENRY LEE	DC	21W	43

NAME	STATE	PANEL NO.	LINE NO.
STAFFORD JAMES HUBERT	CA	05W	112
STAFFORD LEE ROY	MO	44E	1
STAFFORD PHILIP CLARK	CA	28W	105
STAFFORD ROBERT BERYL	TN	36E	38
STAFFORD RONALD DEAN	NE	01W	92
STAFFORD RONALD WADE	FL	13W	65
STAFFORD THOMAS STEPHEN	MI	15W	80
STAGER KENNETH L	NM	21E	19
STAGGS LARRY DEAN	AR	31W	23
STAGGS ROBERT DALE	IL	20W	32
STAHL ALVIN THORNTON	KY	29W	41
STAHL DONALD EUGENE	PA	08E	102
STAHL EDWARD ARNOLD	KS	20E	107
STAHL GEORGE HENRY JR	PA	07E	91
STAHL JOHN JOSEPH	NY	31W	23
STAHL JOHN WELFRED	OH	42W	23
STAHL PHILLIP THOMAS	FL	05E	134
STAHL ROBERT HENRY	MN	44W	67
STAHL ROGER WILLIAM	PA	04W	68
STAHLECKER GARY ROBERT	NY	22W	28
STAHLSTROM ALLAN EMILE	TX	25W	43
STAINBACK MACK DONALD JR	VA	05E	125
STAINER WILLIAM EDWARD	OH	33E	23
STAINES ERNEST MICHAEL	GA	21W	34
STAIR GLENN ROBERT	OH	30W	81
STAIR WILBUR THOMAS	PA	14E	77
STAKE KENDALL ALBERT	NM	48E	20
STALEVICZ GREGORY HENRY	NJ	61W	7
STALEY FREDDY KEITH	MI	17W	23
STALEY JOHN ARTHUR	TX	03W	30
STALEY ROBERT E	AZ	57E	33
STALEY ROBERT LEE JR	IN	35E	81
STALEY RONALD ALEX	GA	09W	17
STALEY THOMAS W JR	GA	01W	69
STALINSKI STEFAN ZBIGNIEW		02E	32
STALL WILLIAM ROBB	TX	34E	71
STALLARD DON GENE	VA	03E	133
STALLARD GILES WARREN	VA	41W	20
STALLCUP ALVIN WAYNE	CA	18W	5
STALLINGS FRANKLIN DELANO	DC	19E	41
STALLINGS JAMES D	TN	11E	18
STALLINGS JOHN LARRY	AL	06W	103
STALLINGS ROBERT ELVIS	WA	09E	60
STALLINGS RONALD CLARK	KY	31E	78
STALLS ELTON STANTON	NC	54W	5
STALNAKER LAWRENCE ARNOLD	GA	28E	106
STALNAKER LEONARD ALLEN	IN	38E	39
STALNECKER WILLIAM JOHN	PA	05E	7
STALTER JOHN RAYMOND	CA	16E	14
STAMAN TERRY LA VERN	OR	28W	14
STAMATO VINCENT JAMES JR	PA	62E	12
STAMEY JIMMY EDWARD	AL	12E	106
STAMM ERNEST ALBERT	OR	38W	62
STAMM MONTE LEWIS	KY	15W	60
STAMP GEORGE RILEY	MO	19E	41
STAMPER DAVID HIRAM	WV	02W	137
STAMPER FRANK RAYMOND	IN	05E	2
STAMPER RICHARD G JR	OH	31E	6
STAMPFLI THEODORE ARTHUR	CA	41E	55
STAMPS GEORGE HARRELL	MI	37W	25
STAMPS JOHNNY GREEN	AL	29W	34
STAMPS OLIVER CLIFTON	MD	14W	10
STANBERRY JERRY WAYNE	OK	31W	23
STANCELL JAMES JR	PA	36E	38
STANCHEK EDWARD MILTON	PA	06E	87
STANCIL GREGORY HALE	VA	35W	40
STANCIL KENNETH LEON	TN	04E	44
STANCIL REGINALD ALFONSO	PA	35E	42
STANCIU KENNETH ALLAN	PA	43E	35
STANCROFF DENNIS CHARLES	MI	04E	38
STANDEFER JAMES GLENN	TX	40E	14
STANDEFORD JAMES MICHAEL	KS	37W	19
STANDERWICK ROBERT L SR	KS	05W	76
STANDIFER ANTHONY	MI	18W	111
STANDLEY THOMAS GARY	TN	10W	3
STANDRIDGE HARLEY ROY	OK	32E	13
STANDRIDGE JERRY WAYNE	CA	30E	74
STANDRIDGE PAUL RICHARD	AL	57E	33
STANDRING LAUREN WALTER	CA	08W	45
STANDS DANIEL GILBERT JR	AZ	06E	22
STANEART RONALD KEITH	OH	11E	47
STANEK ROBERT LEE	TN	37E	28
STANFIELD GARY KELVIN	KS	18W	87
STANFORD BOBBY GAYLE	LA	19E	101
STANFORD EARL MICHAEL	IL	16W	123
STANFORD ERNEST LEE	GA	20W	78
STANGEL LAWRENCE NORBART	WI	36E	41
STANICH NADE MICHAEL	MI	09W	120
STANISZEWSKI WLADYSLAW	MA	23E	32
STANKEVICH EDWARD JOHN	PA	36W	82
STANKIEWICZ KENNETH DAVID	NY	02E	61
STANKO ROBERT GEORGE	OH	40W	68
STANKO WALTER LEE	MI	07W	47
STANLEY BOBBY DWAYNE	TX	55W	2
STANLEY BUDDY ALFONZA	IN	12E	77
STANLEY CHARLES GERALD	NJ	38W	63
STANLEY CHARLES HUBERT	IN	41E	50
STANLEY CHARLES IRVIN	OH	33W	74
STANLEY DAVID CARL	PA	26E	73
STANLEY DENNIS JOHN	CA	35W	29
STANLEY DENNIS RALPH	VA	35E	58
STANLEY DON SCOTT	NM	54W	33
STANLEY EARL	DC	06E	134
STANLEY EURAL JR	CA	39E	53
STANLEY FRANKIE	IL	19W	123
STANLEY JACKIE G	OH	22E	81
STANLEY JAMES MITCHELL	AL	13W	81
STANLEY JAMES STEVEN	AL	12W	11
STANLEY JOE HARRY	AL	38W	30
STANLEY MARION HENRY	FL	02W	8
STANLEY MICHAEL JOHN	PA	45W	29
STANLEY RAYMOND ERNEST	NH	53E	23
STANLEY RICHARD ALLEN	AZ	18W	35
STANLEY ROBERT WILLIAM	OR	17E	88
STANLEY THEODUS MORRIS	OH	19W	25
STANLEY THOMAS LEE	VA	38W	31
STANLEY VICKEY EARL	NC	11E	24
STANLEY VIRGIL JR	GA	15E	109
STANLEY WILLIAM CHARLES	RI	20E	79
STANNARD DARYL KENNETH	NY	07E	60
STANSBARGER RICHARD LAURE	IA	04W	93
STANSBURY DAVID JOE	IN	38W	69
STANSBURY RAYMOND L II	GA	08W	120
STANSBURY THOMAS RODGERS	TX	02W	32
STANSELL GERRALD AUNDRE	NC	05E	18
STANSELL RICHARD NORRIS	CA	14E	83
STANTON EDGAR DOUGLAS JR	OH	43W	10
STANTON EDWARD RYLAND II	MI	12E	39
STANTON EMMETT CHARLES	AR	41E	74
STANTON HAROLD E	IL	34E	60
STANTON JAMES	PA	19W	25
STANTON RICHARD EUGENE	MO	37E	14
STANTON RONALD	OH	40W	8
STANTON SCOTT NEAL	CA	18W	60
STANUSH THOMAS JOSEPH	TX	02W	37
STAPELMAN RONALD LEE	ID	21E	84
STAPLES ALTON LEON III	OH	59W	28
STAPLES GREGORY JOE	OR	54E	18
STAPLES JAMES ARTHUR	MI	27W	34
STAPLES LOUIS FRANKLIN	VA	37E	45
STAPLES THOMAS HAROLD	MI	36E	38
STAPLES THOMAS TRAMMEL II	GA	33W	45
STAPLETON CLIFFORD	OH	60W	5
STAPLETON LAWRENCE GEORGE	OH	24E	78
STAPLETON OLLIE RAY	CA	41W	65
STARBUCK ROBERT FRENCH	NY	14E	121
STARCHER DAVID WAYNE	FL	03W	30
STARCHER EDDIE DEAN	WV	12E	77
STARCKS JEROME STEVEN	IL	53W	31
STARK ALFRED	TX	26W	22
STARK COY FOSTER	CA	57W	5
STARK GERRY LYLE	WA	24E	44
STARK GORDON WILLIAM	IL	15E	2
STARK HERBERT D	MN	01W	63
STARK JAMES ALEXANDER	MA	35E	27
STARK LARRY ALLEN	NE	29W	49
STARK LAWRENCE J	OH	28E	50
STARK STEPHEN WILLIAM	WY	36E	38
STARK WILLIE ERNEST	NE	13E	7
STARKEL MAX PAUL	WA	17E	32
STARKES JOHN MILTON JR	NY	02E	120
STARKES ROBERT B JR	VA	25W	56
STARKEY BLAIR WILLIAM	OH	25E	59
STARKEY DANIEL LEE	OH	16W	10
STARKEY HENRY MORGAN	CA	05E	36
STARKEY JAMES WAYNE	CA	65E	2
STARKEY KURT L	WA	32W	40
STARKEY LLOYD MARTAIN	VA	61W	17
STARKEY RICHARD WILLIAM	NY	18W	106
STARKS GEORGE LARRY	OH	45E	31
STARKS JAMES EDWARD	SC	22E	3
STARKS WARNER	MO	12W	58
STARKWEATHER JEROME FRANK	CO	21E	81
STARLEY JAMES ARTHUR	GA	01E	94
STARLING WALTER LEO	FL	36W	12
STARNES CULLEN GEORGE JR	GA	27E	32
STARNES JAMES CECIL	NC	06W	96
STARNES KEITH NEWTON JR	NC	24W	70
STARNES MILBURN HINES	TX	12E	16
STARNS DAN CLIFTON JR	TX	23E	89
STARR ALLEN EUGENE	TX	20W	35
STARR BENNY ARNOLD	WA	13E	37
STARR EDWARD IRWIN	NY	13E	103
STARR KIERAN JOHN	CA	22E	63
STARR RONALD DEAN	OH	20E	69
STARRETT JOHN DELBERT	OK	07W	112
STARRY DOUGLAS C	MI	27E	13
STASHONSKY JOHN RAY	TN	20W	78
STASIO RICHARD PETER	NY	55W	31
STASKO PAUL JR	PA	40E	56
STASKO THOMAS WILLIAM	CO	05E	50
STASSI JAMES STEPHEN	IL	22E	74
STATECZNY HARRY JOHN JR	IL	08E	127
STATELMAN EDWARD CHARLES	NY	26E	90
STATEN ROBERT JOSEPH	CA	38E	15
STATEN TYRONE JOSEPH	IN	26W	15
STATES DAVID PERSHING	PA	11E	85
STATES JOHN WAYNE	MD	42W	23
STATES WILLIAM CODAR	WV	26W	15
STATH ALLEN WAYNE	IN	20E	127
STATON DAVID WALDEN	SC	11W	77
STATON FRANK LYNN	IA	13W	65
STATON PAUL RAY	IL	27E	13
STATON ROBERT GARY	KY	20E	107
STATON ROBERT MILTON JR	NC	29E	76
STATON RODNEY DALE	WV	13E	87
STAUD ROBERT NICOLAS	CA	16E	32
STAUDOHAR TERRENCE EDWARD	IL	37E	70
STAUDT RUSSELL MARVIN	FL	19W	35
STAUFF ERIC LOUIS WILLIAM	MI	61E	19
STAUFFER GORDON CHARLES	MI	12W	11
STAUFFER HERBERT HOLLINGE	PA	32W	68
STAUFFER ROBERT EARL	PA	22E	27
STAUNTON JOEL PAUL	WA	23E	113
STAVINOHA ROBERT JAMES	TX	51E	25
STAVLAS PANORMITIS	FL	02W	101
STAYER HARRY SHERMAN	PA	47E	37
STAYROOK DONALD GLENN	PA	28E	65
STAYTON COY G	OK	33E	34
STEAD VERNON ROBERT	MI	44E	41
STEADMAN JAMES EUGENE	CO	02W	73
STEADMAN STERLING DWIGHT	WA	23E	114
STEAGALL EDSEL WAYNE	TN	25W	86
STEARNS ALLAN JULIUS	PA	23E	95
STEARNS FRANK EDWIN	IL	09W	120
STEARNS HARREL EARL	TX	22W	60
STEARNS JERRY SHELDON	OR	04W	127
STEARNS LLOYD PALMER	WA	17E	129
STEARNS MICHAEL FORRESTER	CA	16E	49
STEARNS ROGER HORACE	CO	18W	73
STEBBINS HARDY WESLEY JR	IN	12E	48
STEBNER ROBERT LYLE JR	OH	25E	89
STEC FRANK LOUIS	IL	38E	81
STEC ROBERT MICHAEL	NY	35W	30
STECKBAUER CURTIS JOHN	WI	01E	24
STECKER DENNIS EUGENE	WI	06W	66
STECKER JOHN CHARLES	WI	20E	50
STECKER RICHARD E	OH	35E	12
STEDL WILLIAM JOHN	WI	29W	3
STEDMAN LEE ALLEN	OK	11W	26
STEDMAN PAUL FRANCIS	FL	41E	44
STEED GERALD	NY	08E	9
STEED JERRY LYNE	TX	22E	60
STEED WILLIAM OWEN	TN	27W	41
STEEL JOHN ALLEN	MA	12W	47
STEEL KENNETH LEE	NE	15E	122

NAME	STATE	PANEL NO.	LINE NO.
STEEL RICHARD EDWARD	TX	03E	19
STEEL ROBERT JAMES		11E	47
STEELE DANIEL SCOTT	OR	31E	7
STEELE DAVID MARK	OK	22W	69
STEELE EDWARD BERNARD	WY	31W	23
STEELE GARY LYN	ID	01E	105
STEELE PATRICK MATTHEW	MI	64W	2
STEELE RAYMOND THOMAS	NY	60W	13
STEELE ROBERT CHARLES	OR	54W	4
STEELE ROBERT FRANKLIN	IA	09W	70
STEELE ROBERT HUGH	FL	25E	60
STEELE ROGER ALLEN	NV	16W	60
STEELE STEVEN PATRICK	CA	11W	28
STEELE THOMAS DONALD	PA	06E	104
STEELE THOMAS WILLIAM	CO	44W	31
STEELE TOWNSER JR	AL	27W	41
STEELE WALTER CHARLES	CA	47W	23
STEELE WALTER EDWIN	OK	24E	44
STEELE WILLIAM DAVIS	NC	20W	23
STEELE WILLIE LEE	MS	09W	30
STEELEY MARK M	MN	26W	50
STEELMAN TEDDY WAYNE	IL	15E	106
STEEN ANTHONY MICHAEL	NY	18W	80
STEEN JAMES NELSON	IN	19W	105
STEEN MARTIN WILLIAM	ND	07E	129
STEER JOHN CLIFTON	NH	28E	106
STEFANIAK STEPHEN ROBERT	NJ	53W	14
STEFANIC RUDOLPH MICHAEL	OH	22W	60
STEFANICH NICHOLAS C	MN	07W	26
STEFANIK EDWARD PETER	MA	12E	33
STEFANSKI STEVEN RUSSELL	CA	09W	17
STEFFANS MARSHALL GEORGE	NY	22E	115
STEFFE MICHAEL WILLIAM	MD	16W	24
STEFFEK EDWARD STEPHEN	NY	04E	48
STEFFEN ALAN RALPH	OH	12E	123
STEFFEN CARL ROBERT	NJ	04E	39
STEFFEN FREDERICK GEORGE	MI	69E	3
STEFFENS WALTER FREDERICK	MI	26E	67
STEFFES WILLIAM JOSEPH	MN	36E	39
STEFFLER CHARLES ERVIN	MI	11W	10
STEFFUS GARY PAUL	IN	21E	25
STEFKO WILLIAM CHARLES	NJ	14W	17
STEGALL ALLAN JR	GA	06E	12
STEGALL ALTON LESKER	GA	08W	57
STEGALL DOUGLAS WAYNE	TX	16E	70
STEGALL LINDELL RAY	SC	17E	97
STEGALL LORENZO	IN	53E	7
STEGELAND JOHN JOSEPH III	NY	01W	4
STEGER DAVID NAYLOR	MD	05W	1
STEGER JAMES ALVIN	WI	31E	17
STEGMAN THOMAS	MD	41E	74
STEHLE HERBERT NEIL	MI	58W	27
STEIBEL FRANK DALE	IL	16W	50
STEIDLER JOHNSON AUGUSTUS	NJ	22E	50
STEIER WILLIAM EDWARD	NY	08E	89
STEIGER WILLIAM FREDRICK	NY	13E	9
STEIGHNER JAMES THOMAS	PA	20E	79
STEIGLEMAN DERWOOD D JR	PA	08E	33
STEIMBACH JOSEPH JOHN	FL	49E	36
STEIMEL GREGG FRANCIS	KS	08W	73
STEIMER ROBERT FENTON	CA	21E	102
STEIMER THOMAS JACK	CA	19E	67
STEIN ALAN ALBERT	OH	22E	34
STEIN ANDREW PAUL JR	NY	23E	15
STEIN ARMOND JOSEPH JR	LA	60E	3
STEIN CLAUDE JOSEPH	LA	31E	67
STEIN DONALD VEARL	OH	10E	48
STEIN LEON CHARLES	PA	02E	33
STEIN PAUL ANDREW	IL	38W	38
STEIN PAUL HENRY JR	IL	48E	20
STEIN PHILIP CLARENCE	WI	27W	13
STEIN RICHARD WILLIAM	WI	28E	77
STEIN RONALD MARVIN	IA	19E	75
STEINBACH THOMAS RAYMOND	TX	37W	4
STEINBACHER STEVEN MICHAE	IN	33W	10
STEINBERG GEORGE CHARLES	WI	06E	104
STEINBRUNNER DONALD THOMA	WA	23E	96
STEINDAM RUSSELL ALBERT	TX	14W	88
STEINEKE JAMES LEE	SD	14E	92
STEINER CHARLES THOMAS	MD	03E	95
STEINER JOSEPH R III	NY	48W	35
STEINER LARRY ALLEN	MD	37W	25

NAME	STATE	PANEL NO.	LINE NO.
STEINER LAWRENCE TERRELL	TX	09E	125
STEINER MARK STEPHEN	UT	38W	53
STEINER TERRY MICHAEL	WI	13W	114
STEINFELD HOWARD MARSHALL	TX	02W	65
STEINHEBEL KENNETH ERWIN	IL	31W	24
STEINKIRCHNER JAMES LEWIS	NY	04W	9
STEINKIRCHNER KENNETH M	MD	05W	109
STEINSIECK ROBERT T JR	MA	31E	31
STEIRO ROBERT EDWARD	MN	14E	99
STELL JAMES ARTHUR	PA	51W	22
STELLE GERALD CAIN	CA	21E	99
STELLMACH STANLEY R JR	PA	50E	1
STELPFLUG MERLIN CLARENCE	WI	26E	102
STELTER NYMAN WILLIAM JR	TX	30W	81
STELZER CURTIS EDWIN	CA	09W	102
STEMAC STEPHEN JOSEPH	CA	10E	51
STEMBRIDGE WAYLAND DAN	MT	20W	23
STEMEN FREDERICK MILTON	OH	38E	61
STEMMONS BIRCH UDELL	MO	09W	41
STEMPER PHILIP JON	NY	12W	75
STENBERG JERRY OSCAR	OR	35E	10
STENBERG JOHN MARVIN	MN	24W	113
STENDER PAUL ALAN	IL	36E	87
STENGEM PETER MICHAEL	MT	26W	75
STENHOUSE J LYNN JR	SC	18W	115
STEPAN JACOB FRANCIS	MT	16E	55
STEPANOV ROBERT DUANE	OH	02E	28
STEPHAN LARRY ROY	CA	19E	8
STEPHANAC MARK JOHN	NJ	18W	87
STEPHEN PHILIPPE BRUCE	PA	16E	24
STEPHEN VIRGIL LYNN	TX	02E	40
STEPHENS ALLEY OAKLEY	IL	28W	22
STEPHENS ANDREW LEWIS	TX	12E	106
STEPHENS ARTHUR ALLYN	MO	38E	15
STEPHENS ARTHUR CHARLE JR	WI	03W	38
STEPHENS BEN WESLEY	TX	49W	26
STEPHENS BENNIE VORICE JR	TX	16W	32
STEPHENS BING FOREST	MO	22E	85
STEPHENS BOYD ADAM JR	CA	09W	117
STEPHENS CLYDE J	KY	23E	96
STEPHENS CLYDE WAYNE	TX	22E	21
STEPHENS CURTIS ADRON	OK	21W	78
STEPHENS DANNY LYNN	LA	47E	27
STEPHENS DAVID ALLEN	FL	22E	50
STEPHENS DENNIS ARTHUR	MI	09W	45
STEPHENS DONALD HENRY	NC	56W	9
STEPHENS GARY BENNETT	PA	24E	108
STEPHENS GEORGE JOSEPH	NJ	03E	95
STEPHENS GERALD WAYNE	AL	26W	23
STEPHENS HARRY EDWARD	VA	30E	34
STEPHENS HAYS CHARLES	CA	27W	13
STEPHENS JAMES	OH	32W	17
STEPHENS JAMES CALVIN	PA	18E	111
STEPHENS JAMES ROWE	AL	07E	76
STEPHENS JAMES WILLIAMS	MT	02E	82
STEPHENS JASPER JR	MI	07E	12
STEPHENS JOHNNIE PERRY JR	FL	26W	28
STEPHENS LARRY ALAN	MO	18W	21
STEPHENS LARRY ALLAN	CA	33W	18
STEPHENS LARRY EUGENE	AL	35W	56
STEPHENS LESTER AL	KS	35W	79
STEPHENS LLOYD ISAAC	DC	16E	5
STEPHENS MARVIN GENE	KY	17W	2
STEPHENS MICHAEL EUGENE	WV	35E	28
STEPHENS MICHAEL JEFF	NY	18E	98
STEPHENS NATHANIEL H JR	CO	18E	98
STEPHENS ROGER DEAN	CA	60E	15
STEPHENS SONNIE	NC	43E	62
STEPHENS THOMAS ALLEN	TN	10W	29
STEPHENS TOMMY LEE	WA	45E	15
STEPHENS WILLIAM F JR	TX	12W	76
STEPHENS WILLIE DOUGLAS	FL	13W	89
STEPHENSEN MARK LANE	UT	18E	116
STEPHENSON BRUCE DONALD	CA	03W	10
STEPHENSON DAVID RICHARD	OK	22E	50
STEPHENSON DONALD RAY	TN	55E	32
STEPHENSON FREDERICK DALE	IL	51W	37
STEPHENSON GARY LUCKY	RI	19W	25
STEPHENSON HOWARD DAVID	MA	02W	123
STEPHENSON KEITH POWELL	TN	17E	14
STEPHENSON KENNETH RAY	MO	42E	10
STEPHENSON KURT PATRICK	IA	49W	45

NAME	STATE	PANEL NO.	LINE NO.
STEPHENSON LYNN LADELLE	PA	25W	25
STEPHENSON RICHARD C	OH	14W	105
STEPHENSON ROBERT CLAYTON	WV	18E	76
STEPHENSON RONALD DEE	PA	05W	58
STEPHENSON WAYMOND NELSON	AL	05E	39
STEPHENSON WILLIAM JAMES	NJ	05E	69
STEPHENSON WILLIAM WILLAR	OR	31E	31
STEPP CHARLES HAROLD	MO	01W	70
STEPP DONALD EUGENE	OH	18W	66
STEPP DOW E	IL	26E	58
STEPP EUGENE HENRY	OH	45W	45
STEPP JOEL RICHARD	TN	14W	124
STEPP JOHN PAUL	WV	41W	7
STEPP PAUL ROBERT JR	NC	12W	58
STEPP WILLIAM D	MS	26W	50
STEPP WILLIAM HOWARD	KY	10W	122
STEPPEE LARRY ELMER	TN	04W	107
STEPSIE RONALD STEVENS	PA	36W	12
STEPTOE RAYMOND	TX	10E	11
STERITI STEPHEN JOSEPH	MA	07E	41
STERLING CHARLES WESLEY	NJ	04W	98
STERLING DAVID WALTER	MI	34W	89
STERLING JOHN CHARLES	CA	18W	44
STERLING RICHARD JOE	AR	15E	101
STERLING ROBERT ALLEN	IA	01W	1
STERLING ROBERT JAMES	RI	18E	88
STERN GARY WAYNE	PA	23E	104
STERN LARRY	NY	67W	5
STERN LONNIE LEE	SD	05W	24
STERN ROBERT ALAN	NY	02W	132
STERNIN EDWARD MARVIN	NJ	44E	3
STERNS RANDOLPH JOEL	AL	57E	34
STERRY RAYMOND EDWARD	ME	22E	116
STERUD MARTIN FREDERICK	CA	29E	36
STETSON KENNETH EARL	CO	39E	77
STETTEN G LYLE	MI	14E	12
STETTER RONALD THOMAS	NY	52E	12
STEUER FRED MARTIN	IN	01E	5
STEVENS ALLYN TROY	IL	22W	108
STEVENS CHARLES WAYNE	FL	02E	105
STEVENS DAVID JR	PA	07E	12
STEVENS DENNIS LEE	CA	16W	76
STEVENS DENNIS MICHAEL	MI	31E	83
STEVENS DONNY RAY	LA	02E	122
STEVENS EDRICK KENNETH	CA	29E	36
STEVENS EDWARD HOWARD	MO	22E	21
STEVENS FORESTAL ALONZO	OH	46W	23
STEVENS FRANCIS GEORGE	ME	08E	110
STEVENS GARY LYNN	IN	19E	113
STEVENS GERALD	VA	14E	24
STEVENS HAROLD KENNETH JR	NH	02E	2
STEVENS HOWARD STANLEY	MD	17E	64
STEVENS JOHN BRADFORD	CA	41W	32
STEVENS JOHN WARNER JR	AZ	42E	72
STEVENS JOSEPH NELSON	MD	11E	75
STEVENS LARRY JAMES	CA	32W	33
STEVENS MARVIN OWENS	IL	23E	15
STEVENS MICHAEL DAVID	OR	26W	108
STEVENS PHILIP HUGH	HI	01W	65
STEVENS PHILIP PAUL	MI	34E	32
STEVENS RAYMOND JOHN	MN	41W	37
STEVENS RICHARD CRAIG	IN	38W	47
STEVENS RICHARD DURAND	NY	41W	20
STEVENS ROBERT FRANCIS	CT	21E	85
STEVENS ROBERT LOUIS JR	MI	22E	50
STEVENS RODNEY FRANKLIN	OH	20W	96
STEVENS RUDOLPH	LA	03W	110
STEVENS TAMADGE CECIL JR	CA	18E	59
STEVENS THOMAS ARTHUR JR	IN	64W	16
STEVENS WALTER BRUCE	CA	07E	122
STEVENS WAYNE ALAN	MD	26W	94
STEVENS WESLEY WARREN	MN	25W	111
STEVENSON BILLY EDWARD	TN	08E	77
STEVENSON BOBBY DALE	MI	27E	76
STEVENSON BOBBY GENE	SC	35W	22
STEVENSON CHARLES ROBERT	TX	37E	45
STEVENSON CHARLES ROYCE	KY	10W	101
STEVENSON CLEMENT OLIN JR	NJ	08E	58
STEVENSON DON EDDIE	LA	15W	25
STEVENSON GARY GEORGE	CA	58W	15
STEVENSON GEORGE MARK	AR	17E	65
STEVENSON GREG DOUGLAS	TX	08W	50

NAME	STATE	PANEL NO.	LINE NO.
STEVENSON JAMES DERRILL	IL	17W	118
STEVENSON JAMES RALPH	MS	25W	86
STEVENSON JESSE BRENT	UT	30W	96
STEVENSON JOHN RAYMOND	CA	41E	30
STEVENSON LARRY	OH	33W	82
STEVENSON LAWRENCE EDWARD	MD	47W	32
STEVENSON MELVIN L	IL	01W	73
STEVENSON RICHARD CHARLES	DE	31W	22
STEVENSON RUFUS NEWTON JR	MI	24W	13
STEVENSON THOMAS G JR	FL	31W	24
STEVENSON WILLIAM LUTHER	KY	22E	115
STEVENSON WILLIAM MAYO	WV	15W	75
STEVER JAMES MITCHELL	CA	01W	87
STEVERSON SIM SMEDDLEY	MS	31E	89
STEWARD ANDREW RICHARD JR	OH	04W	93
STEWARD FLOYD LESTER	WV	22W	101
STEWARD JERRY WAINE	VA	07W	104
STEWARD STEVE LEE	OK	12W	101
STEWART ARNOLD LEE	WV	55E	32
STEWART BILLY GRAY	NC	57E	31
STEWART BYRON DUNCAN	WV	21W	103
STEWART CHARLES LEROY JR	MI	01W	87
STEWART CHARLIE ACES JR	AL	37E	16
STEWART DAN ROGERS	SC	10W	9
STEWART DAVID GLENN	TN	34E	46
STEWART DAVID SHERMAN	IL	26E	4
STEWART DAVID WAYNE	KY	08E	40
STEWART DENNIS RAY	CA	02W	84
STEWART DONALD DAVID	NC	04E	11
STEWART DONNY RAY	FL	43W	59
STEWART EDWARD	LA	49W	45
STEWART EDWARD LARRY	WV	02E	121
STEWART EDWARD SAMUEL	FL	47W	55
STEWART FRANCIS ERNEST	NE	26W	83
STEWART GARY LEE	OH	09W	22
STEWART GEORGE CURTIS	IL	14E	110
STEWART GEORGE EDWARD	MO	11E	89
STEWART GERALD HILAND	CT	13E	17
STEWART GREGORY WILLIAM	AZ	41W	38
STEWART HARRY RAY	TN	16E	55
STEWART HENRY MATT JR	OH	18W	123
STEWART HOWARD WARREN	GA	56W	15
STEWART JACK THOMAS	DC	17E	40
STEWART JAMES BARTIE	WA	14E	110
STEWART JAMES HERBERT JR	OH	07E	123
STEWART JAMES JOSEPH	MA	39E	54
STEWART JAMES JR	GA	09E	92
STEWART JAMES LLOYD	KY	28W	53
STEWART JAMES WESLEY	PA	14W	96
STEWART JERRY DEAN	MO	05E	53
STEWART JIMMY GOETHEL	OH	07E	84
STEWART JOHN EMANUEL	LA	05W	34
STEWART JOHN FRANCIS	VA	26W	103
STEWART JOHN JOSEPH	PA	12E	126
STEWART JOHN LEONARD	WA	41E	44
STEWART JOHN WALLACE	MI	25W	8
STEWART LAWRENCE	NY	32E	6
STEWART LELAND	CA	33E	60
STEWART LEONARD KEITH	KS	51W	29
STEWART LESLIE JAMES	PA	26W	95
STEWART LONNY LAWRENCE	CA	56E	16
STEWART MANFORD DALVIS	KY	25E	111
STEWART MICHAEL EDWARD	VA	19E	113
STEWART MICHAEL HENRY	KS	57E	10
STEWART MORGAN EUGENE	TX	33E	32
STEWART PAUL CLARK	CA	05W	89
STEWART PAUL JOHN	MA	44W	20
STEWART PAUL LEO	MA	15E	76
STEWART PETER JOSEPH	FL	06E	12
STEWART RALPH CARSON	FL	54E	18
STEWART RICHARD	IN	03W	19
STEWART RICHARD CORTLANDT	NJ	04E	135
STEWART RICHARD JAMES	CA	17E	88
STEWART RICHARD JOHN	ME	44E	31
STEWART RICK JAMES	MI	22E	73
STEWART ROBERT ALLAN	DC	19E	101
STEWART ROBERT COLE	NC	15E	37
STEWART ROBERT HENRY	SC	11E	128
STEWART ROBERT LEE	CA	61E	19
STEWART RONALD RICHARD	WY	09W	70
STEWART RONALD WAYNE	IL	04W	47
STEWART ROY KENNETH	NY	02W	79

NAME	STATE	PANEL NO.	LINE NO.
STEWART SAM WILLIAM	AL	40E	48
STEWART SAMUEL KAY	CA	42E	10
STEWART SAMUEL R III	FL	38E	81
STEWART STEPHEN JAMES	MO	33E	94
STEWART TOMMY LANE	DC	38E	40
STEWART ULYSSES	LA	39E	13
STEWART VIRGIL GRANT	LA	24W	34
STEWART WAYNE YEARWOOD	GA	27W	34
STEWART WENDELL WARREN	SD	24E	74
STEWART WILBERT JR	MD	12E	106
STEWART WILLIAM JAMES	MD	03E	133
STEWART WILLIAM LOUIS JR	VA	27E	77
STEWART WILLIAM STEVEN	KS	06W	123
STEWART WILLIAM WESLEY	CA	18E	82
STIBBINS MILO BENETT	PA	02E	8
STICE LARRY DOUGLAS	CO	05E	57
STICH VERNON GENE	WI	24E	89
STICHER JOHN THOMAS	VA	03E	136
STICKEL BRUCE JACOB	WA	07W	107
STICKEL GARY STEPHEN	OH	32E	48
STICKELS MARK GALEN	IA	48E	11
STICKLAND BILLIE GRANVIL	FL	43W	23
STICKLE TIMOTHY DAVID	OH	36W	7
STICKLER CLARK D	CA	60W	4
STICKLER ROBERT ALLEN	IN	24E	45
STICKNEY PHILLIP JOSEPH	NH	07E	129
STICKS STEVEN MICHAEL	WI	21W	63
STIDHAM ERNEST JAMES	CA	36W	66
STIEFERMAN CURTIS EDWARD	TX	29E	22
STIEHLER GEORGE DENNIS	IL	35E	81
STIERWALT LADDIE C	NV	20E	125
STIEVE WILLIAM JOHN	NY	11W	70
STIGALL ARTHUR DONALD	LA	29E	44
STIGALL CHARLES BENNETT	TN	30E	94
STIGEN WAYNE DOUGLAS	IL	25W	91
STIGER GREG PATTERSON	NY	39W	63
STIGER HAROLD EUGENE	OH	15E	7
STIGGINS DOUGLAS LEE	KS	20W	41
STIGLICH MICHAEL LEON	VA	17W	53
STIGLITZ DENNIS LAWRENCE	MI	67W	5
STILES CHARLES WALTER	CA	02E	23
STILES DONALD LAVEREN	PA	47E	41
STILES JAMES LEO	OH	55W	10
STILES MICHAEL PAUL	KY	52E	24
STILES THOMAS NELSON	TX	32E	82
STILES VERRELL DANIEL	NC	17E	65
STILL FLOYD LAVERNE	SC	45W	57
STILL FRED HAROLD	SC	09E	101
STILL JERRY MELTON	SC	07W	7
STILL JIMMIE DALE	IA	15W	115
STILL RICHARD LOUIS	OH	13W	101
STILLEY JOHN WAYNE	TX	33E	5
STILLEY RONALD JOSEPH	PA	42E	42
STILLIONS RONALD BRUCE	IN	11W	32
STILLS HAROLD CLIFFORD	TN	37W	53
STILLWAGONER RALPH LLOYD	WV	16E	38
STILWELL ROY MILES	MO	16W	113
STIMPSON PAUL LEWIS	ME	18E	72
STIMSON JOHN THOMPSON JR	NY	40W	69
STINDL RICHARD WILLIAM	WI	24W	22
STINE JOSEPH MILLARD	PA	11E	24
STINGLEY JAMES	MS	19W	116
STINN JOHN RICHARD	IA	10W	47
STINNETT JIMMY CLIFORD	VA	01E	122
STINNETT RICHARD DOIL	OR	23E	114
STINSON FLOYD ALBERT	KY	39W	38
STINSON GEORGE WILLIAM JR	OK	13E	56
STINSON RODNEY LEROY	VA	25E	35
STINSON WILLIAM CLYDE JR	GA	30W	32
STINSON WILLIAM SHERRIL	AL	01W	110
STIRLING ELGIN LEROY	CA	02E	36
STIRLING JOHN F	CA	16E	42
STIRNKORB CYRIL EDWARD	OH	24E	106
STIRPE JOHN	NY	42W	60
STIRRUP WILLIAM DAVID	NY	61E	3
STITELY CARL MICHAEL	PA	45E	51
STITES JAMES JOHN	IL	43W	43
STITH DARYL LA DON	CA	64E	8
STITH PETER LEWIS	WA	27W	60
STITT GREGORY CARLYLE	UT	08W	109
STITT RICHARD WESLEY	CA	29W	73
STIVERS GEORGE EDWARD	OK	29E	77

NAME	STATE	PANEL NO.	LINE NO.
STIYER DAVID ALAN	MN	24W	13
STIZZA JOHN BONAT	OK	14W	55
STOAKLEY GORDON ALAN	MI	05W	112
STOCHAJ PAUL JOHN	MA	05E	69
STOCK DALE LOUIS	OH	28W	4
STOCKARD ROBERT FERRELL	NC	36W	37
STOCKBAUER CHARLES THOMAS	MO	21W	95
STOCKBURGER ARTHUR LEE	MT	46W	45
STOCKDALE JAMES BYRON	MI	18W	80
STOCKDALE JOHN ROBERT	OK	52W	11
STOCKDALE MELVIN JAMES	MN	04E	115
STOCKER DANIEL LEO	TX	58W	5
STOCKETT RICHARD LEE	AZ	04W	17
STOCKFEDER MARTIN	NY	01E	58
STOCKHOLM DWIGHT ROSS	MI	20E	11
STOCKLIN CURTIS ROBERT	OH	35W	67
STOCKLIN GARY DENNIS	MO	22W	16
STOCKMAN DAVID LYNN	MD	55W	10
STOCKMAN GENE WALLACE	PA	02W	54
STOCKMAN JOHN FRANK	PA	06W	69
STOCKS WILLIAM REED	MD	32W	29
STOCKSTILL WALLACE A JR	LA	14W	98
STOCKTON CLIFFORD GEOFFRE	PA	42E	42
STOCKTON DON EUGENE JR	OR	15W	60
STOCKWELL BRYAN B	IL	10E	126
STOCKWELL DENNIS BERNARD	SD	17E	14
STOCKWELL EDWARD E JR	LA	34W	18
STOCKWELL PAUL MARION	MO	46W	53
STODARD WILLIAM TERRY	MS	05W	24
STODDARD CLARENCE W JR	TX	10E	95
STODDARD JAN MARTINE	FL	37E	70
STODDARD KEITH ARTHUR	MI	05W	73
STODDARD MARCUS WILLIAM	NY	26W	57
STODDARD NORMAN R JR	CT	06W	65
STODDARD RUSSELL MERRILL	MO	13W	50
STODDART GREGORY WILLIAM	WI	12W	102
STOEBERL JAMES ARNOLD	WI	27E	67
STOEHR DAVID LOREN	NE	58W	15
STOELT HAROLD EDWIN	MI	06E	2
STOEN MARCUS SHERWIN	MN	04W	47
STOFFER BENJAMIN F II	OH	31W	73
STOFFREGEN ROY DIXON	AL	32W	62
STOFKO STEVEN MICHAEL	IN	24E	64
STOFLET GORDON WAYNE	WI	22E	85
STOFLET MICHAEL HOWARD	WI	12E	8
STOGSDILL DELBERT RAY	MI	47W	23
STOGSDILL JACKIE DEAN	CA	03W	53
STOHLMEYER CHARLES JOSEPH	WA	33W	22
STOJINSKI JOSEPH JOHN JR	PA	06W	13
STOKEN CHARLES ALBERT	MI	18E	7
STOKER HUELYN BERNARD	TX	27E	22
STOKER KENNETH GRANT	CA	23E	92
STOKER RONALD EDWARD	MD	34W	45
STOKES BARTLEY THOMAS III	FL	26E	18
STOKES CHARLES EUGENE	CA	10E	111
STOKES COLBEN BENJAMIN JR	MS	35E	82
STOKES DAVID ALAN	IA	60W	22
STOKES DONNIE MONROE	FL	37W	36
STOKES FRANK EDWARD	NY	30E	50
STOKES GUY LYNN JR	GA	10W	54
STOKES HAROLD DEAN	IN	38E	61
STOKES JAMES DOUGLAS	TN	07E	21
STOKES JAMES DOYLE	MO	31E	17
STOKES JAMES MICHAEL	FL	09W	3
STOKES JEFFREY RANDALL	CA	02W	34
STOKES KENNETH LARRY	AL	14W	44
STOKES ODELL JR	NC	33E	23
STOKES PAUL AMOS	AR	02W	42
STOKES ROBERT LEE	UT	03E	62
STOKES RONALD T	NY	32E	12
STOKES ROY E	MI	01E	131
STOKES WAYNE JOSEPH	GA	31E	26
STOKKERMAN JON WILLIAM	MI	16W	20
STOLARUN RICHARD RAYMOND	CT	17W	71
STOLINSKI JAMES FRANCIS	NE	46E	42
STOLL DAVID LOUIS	NM	28E	87
STOLL GEORGE GERALD	OH	12E	30
STOLL GEORGE LUDWIG	TX	07E	31
STOLL WILLIAM KEEN JR	KY	08E	61
STOLLAR LARRY DAVID	OH	26W	103
STOLLEY WILLIAM R JR	MI	29W	41
STOLPA RAYMOND VINCENT	CO	45W	45

NAME	STATE	PANEL NO.	LINE NO.
STOLTENBERG REID WILLIAM	IA	17E	38
STOLTENBURG MARK ERNEST	IA	09E	54
STOLTENOW RONALD GILBERT	ND	29E	45
STOLTZ DONALD ROBERT	WI	37W	42
STOLTZ STEVEN RAY	IA	09W	66
STOLTZMAN GEORGE LEO	MN	03E	118
STOLZ JAMES EDWARD JR	NY	06W	69
STOLZ LAWRENCE GENE	IN	02W	92
STOLZ ROBERT LARRY	OH	34E	71
STOMMES KENNETH CLARENCE	MN	28E	87
STONE BEN WADE	TN	19W	25
STONE BYRON CLARK	TX	01E	62
STONE CHARLES H	MO	02W	103
STONE DANIEL MELVIN	NY	39E	67
STONE DAVID	GA	28W	53
STONE DAVID RONALD	SC	08E	127
STONE DEE WAYNE JR	NY	12E	57
STONE EDWARD THOMAS JR	MA	47E	27
STONE EDWARD WILSON	IL	11W	93
STONE FOREST MICHAEL	IN	09W	123
STONE GEORGE DAVIDSON	KS	50E	2
STONE GORDON ELLIOTT	VA	01W	29
STONE GREGORY MARTIN	CA	04W	74
STONE HARMON S JR	IL	30E	20
STONE HAROLD ALVIN	IL	60E	3
STONE HARRY JAMES	CA	10W	62
STONE JAMES EDWARD	SC	38W	21
STONE JAMES EMMETT	OH	30E	5
STONE JAMES LAWRENCE	AR	10E	27
STONE JAMES MARVIN	FL	33E	75
STONE JERRY MICHAEL	FL	62W	3
STONE JOSEPH CHARLES	PA	24W	62
STONE JOSEPH LAMAR	CA	05W	76
STONE LARRY EVANS	NC	10W	67
STONE LARRY GEORGE	NV	20E	87
STONE LESTER RAY JR	NY	30W	33
STONE LEWIS LYNN	VA	01E	17
STONE MELVIN LOUIS JR	OH	11E	51
STONE ORMAN	KY	34W	34
STONE OTTO JR	IA	07W	25
STONE PAUL AARON	OH	34W	2
STONE RAYMOND EDWARD JR	NV	31E	94
STONE RICHARD ARLAN	CA	29E	36
STONE ROBERT DOUGLAS	VT	51W	28
STONE RODNEY HAROLD	VA	11W	88
STONE ROGER ALLEN	AL	03E	95
STONE THOMAS DAVID	OH	18W	9
STONE WILLIAM EARL	CA	40W	55
STONE WILLIAM J B	CO	11E	78
STONE WILLIAM MARVIN JR	MD	22W	70
STONEBRAKER KENNETH ARNOLD	IN	40W	51
STONEBURNER JOHN FREDRICK	OH	01E	75
STONEHOUSE ALFRED LEE	NY	10E	84
STONEKING DANNY MIRE	MD	42E	42
STONEKING HERBERT RALPH	MO	02W	89
STONEMAN DONALD LOUIS	VA	36W	37
STONEMETZ GERALD DUANE	PA	35W	57
STONER CLARENCE MOODY JR	TX	22W	44
STONER JAMES CONLEY	GA	19W	5
STONER LARRY LEE	NE	29W	15
STONER WILLIAM DENNIS	MO	03W	15
STONESIFER DONALD LEE	CA	49W	49
STONESIFER HARRY NELSON	MD	26W	87
STONGE THOMAS GORDON	MI	26W	51
STOOPS JONATHAN LYNN	IN	59W	16
STOPHER GALE JR	IN	12W	120
STOPPELWERTH DAVID HENRY	OH	14W	44
STOPPLEWORTH DENNIS M	WI	09W	75
STOPYRA THOMAS JOHN	MA	46W	23
STORBO RONALD LAWRENCE	CA	23W	92
STORCH WILLIAM FRANK JR	HI	17E	65
STORELLI JOHN	NY	14E	120
STOREY CHARLES WILLIAM	AL	03E	95
STOREY ROBERT LEE	ND	38W	31
STORIE WILLARD GENE	MO	06W	82
STORK ROBERT JOHN JR	CA	27W	3
STORM EDWARD REYNOLD	OR	15W	105
STORM RALPH DORMAN	CA	20W	61
STORY CHESLEY ALEXANDER	NC	45E	51
STORY EDDIE B		17W	120
STORY FRED DELL	MI	08W	80
STORY J C	AL	33E	93

NAME	STATE	PANEL NO.	LINE NO.
STORY JAMES CLELLON	IL	22W	44
STORZ GEORGE WILLIAM	CA	43E	62
STORZ RONALD EDWARD	NY	01E	110
STOTLER LARRY PAUL	IN	28E	17
STOTLER MICHAEL DEAN	CO	36E	87
STOTLER RAY W	WV	24E	70
STOTSBERY RICHARD PAUL	OH	15W	112
STOTTS DONALD MAURICE	MI	04W	90
STOTTS JAMES MARTIN	CA	23W	40
STOUDT GORDON EDWARD	PA	19E	1
STOUDT JOSEPH GEORGE	PA	05E	125
STOUT CLIFFORD RUSSELL	NJ	12E	103
STOUT EUGENE EDWARD	WV	13E	94
STOUT JAMES ROBERT	KY	03W	22
STOUT JERRY LEE	MI	13W	53
STOUT JOHN HENRY	AR	22E	3
STOUT KEVIN ARLEY	TX	12W	120
STOUT MITCHELL WILLIAM	NC	13W	121
STOUT SAM EUGENE	TN	08W	134
STOUT TERRY LEE	CA	44W	20
STOUT WILLIAM HENRY III	MI	26W	74
STOVALL ALVIN RAMSEY JR	TN	17W	92
STOVALL CARL ROGERS	FL	20E	92
STOVALL CHARLES ALLEN	AL	39E	40
STOVALL GUS JR	MA	16E	49
STOVALL JAMES TUCKER	TX	39W	35
STOVALL WILBERT	PA	44E	1
STOVALL WILLIAM DALE	FL	40W	69
STOVER DAVID DONALD	NY	01W	2
STOVER DOUGLAS EARL	NH	28W	53
STOVER JAMES EDWARD	MI	37E	43
STOVER SHELBY DEAN	WV	17W	2
STOVER TOMMY GENE	CA	33E	24
STOVES MERRITT III	AL	14E	7
STOW JOHN LEWIS	NY	39E	19
STOW LILBURN RAY	OK	52E	24
STOWE JEFFREY CHARLES	AZ	25W	111
STOWE LUTHER TONY	CA	23E	55
STOWE ROY	NC	36W	19
STOWERS AUBREY EUGENE JR	OK	45E	52
STOWERS JOE D	WV	17E	81
STOZEK GERALD STANLEY	WI	42W	37
STRACHOTA JOHN GREGORY	WI	06W	57
STRACK LAWRENCE	NY	16E	14
STRACNER WILLIAM ELLIS	AL	05W	41
STRADER CHARLES EDWARD	KY	05E	3
STRADTMAN THOMAS LEE	MN	19W	64
STRAFACE JEFFREY DENNIS	WV	34E	46
STRAFELLO CHARLES FRANKLIN	MA	40W	5
STRAHAN LARRY	MI	29W	15
STRAHAN WALTER SPERRING	FL	27W	53
STRAHIN ARTHUR RONALD	WV	26W	80
STRAHL RICHARD WILLIAM	AZ	16E	5
STRAHM PAUL DOUGLAS	OH	34E	50
STRAHM ROBERT EUGENE	OH	12E	83
STRAIN EDWARD W	IA	12W	120
STRAIN JAMES PAUL	TX	38E	61
STRAIN KENNETH DALE	CA	24E	45
STRAIT BENNIE HOWARD	OH	17E	88
STRAIT DAVID LEON	TX	26E	68
STRAIT DOUGLAS FRANK	WA	06W	8
STRAIT LAFFEY FRANKLIN	MO	31E	18
STRAKER GARY ENNIS	MO	43W	31
STRALEY JOHN LEROY	PA	01E	42
STRAND PHILIP STANLEY JR	CA	34E	1
STRANDBERG ERVIND CARL	MN	13E	113
STRANDE THOMAS ALVIN	IL	53W	6
STRANGE FLOYD WAYNE	CA	31E	25
STRANGE PAUL ROBERT MACK	IN	26E	68
STRANGE RICHARD LEE	VA	08E	95
STRANGE ROBERT ALLEN	MI	23E	64
STRANGE ROBERT GREER	CA	14E	38
STRANGEWAY JAMES J JR	NJ	52W	8
STRANO JAMES CLINTON	CT	35E	18
STRASSHOFER STEVE OTTO	OH	21W	26
STRASSNER CORNELIUS WILLI	NY	41E	55
STRASZEWSKI GEORGE STEPHEN	IN	37W	14
STRATE BRUCE EDGAR	IN	38E	16
STRATE JOHN DELBERT	NY	48W	31
STRATEGOS PETER STEPHEN	IL	37W	70
STRATHMANN THOMAS WILLIAM	PA	23W	112
STRATTON CHARLES WAYNE	TX	05W	24

NAME	STATE	PANEL NO.	LINE NO.
STRATTON EVERETT JR	KY	24E	76
STRATTON MILO HERSEY	OR	57W	14
STRATTON SIDNEY TAYLOR	TX	41E	30
STRATTON THOMAS ALLAN	PA	25W	86
STRAUB CONRAD FRANCIS	KS	15E	110
STRAUB JOHN EDWIN	PA	06W	26
STRAUB MARK ALAN	TN	13W	4
STRAUB TERRY GORDON	PA	20E	87
STRAUDOVSKIS JOHN	IA	19E	101
STRAUGHN WILLIAM HERSCHEL	KY	14E	101
STRAUS ALLEN ARTHUR	NE	56E	16
STRAUSBAUGH HOWARD ALBERT	OH	44E	1
STRAUSER JOHN CHARLES	OR	05W	74
STRAUSS HOWARD DAVID	PA	11E	115
STRAUSS KLAUS JOSEF	TX	38E	40
STRAUSS ROBERT STEPHAN	VA	47W	13
STRAUSSER DARRY RICHARD	MN	34E	39
STRAUSSER PAUL JOSEPH	TN	09E	71
STRAW BARRY MERCER	CA	04W	26
STRAWBRIDGE JOSEPH EDWARD	OH	35W	3
STRAWN JOHN THOMAS	OR	04W	22
STRAYER LAWRENCE EDWARD	OH	25W	33
STRAYER PATRICK JOSEPH	OH	36E	39
STRAZZANTI ALAN PETER	OH	19W	116
STREAMER FRANK MARION	CO	20W	120
STRECHA JAMES JR	MI	47E	44
STRECKERT RONALD JOHN	WI	32E	89
STREEKS FRANK MORRIS JR	MD	27E	2
STREET BRENT ANTHONY	CA	12W	76
STREET DOUGLAS GERALD	MT	15E	123
STREET LENARD JR	OK	47E	56
STREET MICHAEL RAY	NC	03W	68
STREET ROBERT ANDREW	MO	06E	5
STREET TOBY WINDFIELD	CA	34W	34
STREHLE ERNEST WILLIAM	IL	08E	95
STREMLER DAVID ALLEN	MI	53E	41
STRENGTH NORMAN HOWARD	WA	12W	47
STRIBBLING GWYMAN	AL	20W	120
STRIBLING JESSE B	AR	09E	29
STRIBLING VICTOR BERNARD	CA	14W	56
STRIBLING VICTOR MICHAEL	MS	39E	13
STRICKLAND BILLY LEWIS	NC	35E	28
STRICKLAND CHARLIE R JR	NC	43E	35
STRICKLAND DOUGLAS LEE	CA	22W	28
STRICKLAND GAIL LYNN	TX	03W	130
STRICKLAND HIRAM DILLARD	NC	04E	131
STRICKLAND JAMES S JR	FL	41E	1
STRICKLAND JOHN LEE	WV	14E	12
STRICKLAND JOSEPH ODELL	SC	33W	90
STRICKLAND LESSIE KEITH	NC	02E	61
STRICKLAND RANDY ALBERT	GA	24W	79
STRICKLAND ROBERT CECIL	LA	47E	38
STRICKLAND THOMAS NEIL	MI	26W	103
STRICKLAND WAYNE THAD	GA	11E	11
STRICKLER DAVID FRANCIS	VA	53E	7
STRICKLER JOHN CLINE JR	DC	04E	81
STRICKLIN ROBERT GUY	CA	23W	115
STRICKLIN THOMAS GRADY	MN	52E	44
STRIDE JAMES DANIEL JR	TX	41W	16
STRIDIRON GEORGE THOMAS	NY	07E	15
STRIEPE PAUL RAYMOND	IA	33E	33
STRINGER ANTHONY ODELL	GA	42E	25
STRINGER ISAAC JR	FL	31W	73
STRINGER JOHN CURTIS II	KY	06W	99
STRINGER OTTIS EDWARD	TX	21W	109
STRINGER ROY LEE	KY	14W	80
STRINGER WILLIAM FRANKLIN	MS	21W	16
STRINGFELLOW JOHN D JR	TN	47W	33
STRINGHAM WILLIAM STERLIN	CA	01W	114
STRIPLING JOHN DAVID III	OH	18E	89
STRIPPOLI JOSEPH PAT JR	NY	45E	15
STRITTMATER KENNETH LEROY	WI	30W	16
STRIZZI PHILLIP ARTHUR	OH	19E	1
STRNAD FRANK JAY	IL	55W	19
STROBBE DANIEL EDWIN	CA	56E	32
STROBEL WILLIAM ERIC	NY	23E	39
STROBLE COY EDWARD	AR	57W	14
STROBLE JAMES JOHN	CA	16W	51
STROBO HENRY RONALD	GA	31W	24
STROBRIDGE RODNEY LYNN	CA	01W	24
STROCK CHARLES FREDERICK	CA	41E	4
STROHL BILLIE RICHARD	IL	06W	109

NAME	STATE	PANEL NO.	LINE NO.
STROHLEIN MADISON ALEXAND	PA	03W	86
STROHM TIMOTHY LAWRENCE	OR	61W	17
STROHMAIER JOHN RICHARD	OH	44E	31
STROISCH LOYD EDWARD	OH	49E	36
STROM LARRY A	IL	13E	81
STROMBACK GLENN CHARLES	IL	46W	24
STROMBECK EDWARD EARL	HI	22E	4
STROME JOHN CLARENCE	OK	46W	24
STRONG ANDREW CARNEGI III	NY	03W	62
STRONG CALVIN MORRIS	VA	30E	74
STRONG DANIEL LEROY	CA	11E	116
STRONG DAVID ALLEN	TX	20W	37
STRONG GRIDLEY BARSTOW	CA	51E	25
STRONG HAROLD E JR	OH	01E	83
STRONG HENRY HOOKER JR	PA	01W	33
STRONG JACK MERRIEL	NY	50W	33
STRONG JAMES LARRY	TN	07W	70
STRONG RICHARD WILLIAM JR	WA	40W	16
STRONG STANLEY GRANT	CA	43E	35
STROOMER RONALD LEE	WA	34E	62
STROSCHEIN RONALD ROBERT	IA	43W	58
STROSHANE MICHAEL ALLEN	MN	33E	1
STROTHER CHATWIN ARNOLD	IL	10W	119
STROTHER CLAUD PAUL	TX	01W	8
STROTHERS THOMAS F JR	PA	53E	41
STROUB STEVEN JOHN	MN	37E	45
STROUD ABLE CROOM III	NC	33E	24
STROUD ALLEN RALPH	MD	09W	133
STROUD ALLEN SHEFFIELD	NC	56W	15
STROUD DENNIS CARROLL	SC	17E	76
STROUD EDWARD EUGENE	AR	60E	4
STROUD ROGER LEE	TX	53W	40
STROUD SANDERS KEY II	TX	29E	22
STROUD STEVEN ARNOLD	TX	40W	39
STROUD WILLIAM HAROLD	WI	06W	1
STROUSE GARY LEE	NY	52W	12
STROUSE HOWARD DALE	WI	11E	54
STROUSE LARRY DALE	CA	18W	111
STROUSE PAUL EDWIN	FL	30W	60
STROUT PHILIP WILLIAM	ME	24W	91
STROUT ROGER HENRY	MA	36W	38
STROVEN WILLIAM HARRY	MI	40W	51
STROYE FERDINAND	TN	37W	2
STROYMAN ARTHUR	MA	19W	82
STRUBE JAMES CLARENCE	KS	22W	28
STRUBE STEVEN DREW	NE	13W	51
STRUBLE STANLEY DEAN	IA	06W	72
STRUCEL JOSEPH JOHN	MI	30W	49
STRUCHEN THOMAS MICHAEL	OH	28W	22
STRUEBING DEWEY IRVIN	NE	32W	2
STRUNK WILLIAM LOCKE	CO	15E	87
STRUPP DAVID ALAN	NJ	49E	37
STRUSS LARRY ANTHONY	MN	13W	108
STRYCHARZ STEPHEN S JR	CT	09E	26
STRYKER ROBERT FRANCIS	NY	29E	45
STUART EDWARD HAROLD	OR	38E	72
STUART JAMES HENRY	OR	26E	31
STUART JOE BEN JR	CO	31W	96
STUART JOHN DESMOND JR	MN	36W	32
STUART JOHN FRANKLIN	IN	01W	97
STUART LEE DAVIS JR	MS	05W	51
STUART MARVIN BLAIR JR	WV	03W	113
STUART MILES BOYD	NY	41E	44
STUBBE WILLIAM LEROY	NE	11E	34
STUBBERFIELD ROBERT AUSTI	NC	01E	111
STUBBLEFIELD JAMES EDWARD	MI	06W	96
STUBBLEFIELD KENNETH R	IA	31E	89
STUBBS BILLY RAY	AZ	25W	2
STUBBS WILLIAM W W	WA	17W	99
STUBE RICHARD HURRELL	MT	07W	80
STUBSTAD GERALD EDWARD	IL	09E	26
STUCK LAWRENCE MILTON	GA	24W	72
STUCK RANSOM LEE	IN	41E	44
STUCKEY BENNY DAVIS	TX	21W	34
STUCKEY HENRY JAMES	NY	14E	7
STUCKEY JOHN STEINER JR	IN	29E	77
STUCKEY WALTER	CA	37W	2
STUCKY RONALD	MI	42W	51
STUDARDS ROBERT LARRY	MI	09E	71
STUDDARD DANNY GERALD	NV	03W	78
STUDDARD FINIS RONEY	AL	03E	96
STUDER FLOYD	PA	01E	4
STUDER LOREN FRANCIS	IA	62W	18
STUDIER RICHARD ERWIN	NY	05W	113
STUDWAY DEWITT JR	MS	35W	85
STUESSEL JAMES DAVID	CA	34W	61
STUEWE CHRISTOPHER S	UT	17W	87
STUHL ALOYSIUS JOHN	PA	12E	110
STUIFBERGEN GENE PAUL	MI	38W	79
STUKES ISAIAH TRUMAN	SC	25W	87
STULL JAY WEBSTER	CT	41E	69
STULL LARRY WARREN	OH	37E	70
STULLER JOHN CHARLES	VA	59E	13
STULTS EVEANS JERRY	IN	10E	62
STULTZ CHARLES GILBERT	KS	25W	87
STUMP EDWARD EARL	MO	16W	76
STUMP HAROLD OLIVER	SC	20W	78
STUMPP ALMA JACK	WY	02E	137
STUPAR MITCHELL NICK	MI	21E	64
STURDEVANT WILLIAM DEAN	SD	39W	10
STURDIVANT JASPER DEAN	CA	08E	127
STURDY ALAN MacDONALD	CA	22E	116
STURGAL THOMAS JOHN	WI	45E	60
STURGEON DONALD FREDERIC	CT	40W	51
STURGEON IRA JACKIE	KY	25W	111
STURGEON WALTER	AR	31W	24
STURGILL HAROLD J JR	VA	27E	13
STURGILL MICHAEL JAMES	MI	25W	87
STURM HERMAN VICTOR JR	NC	08W	99
STURMA CHARLES FRANK	AL	30W	97
STURTEVANT THEODORE JAMES	IL	38E	72
STURTZ DARWIN CLIFFORD	MN	62W	18
STUTES JAMES RONALD	LA	09W	22
STUTES KENNETH JOHN	LA	23E	15
STUTES WILLIAM BYRON	CA	26E	52
STUTLER DANIEL WAYNE	WV	08E	131
STUTTS THOMAS RICHARD	MS	37W	19
STYBEL CONRAD ANTHONY	NJ	26E	86
STYER FREDERIC CLARENCE	WI	21E	7
STYERS REID TYRONE	WV	65W	1
STYLES DAVID IRA	OR	28W	81
STYMUS GARY LEE	NY	20E	108
STYS STANLEY ALBERT	PA	43E	35
SUAPAIA DAVID KEALOHA	HI	19E	87
SUAREZ ENCARNACION ALEGRE	CA	34W	41
SUAREZ EUGENE RAVN	MI	42W	60
SUAREZ JOSE WILFREDO	CA	03E	104
SUAREZ RAYMOND JR	CT	31W	25
SUAREZ VALENTINE BERRONES	TX	17W	89
SUBER RANDOLPH BOTHWELL	MO	16W	71
SUBERT GEORGE THOMAS	IL	17E	108
SUBLER GERALD FRANCIS	OH	42W	51
SUBLETT JOHN KENNETH JR	TX	30W	49
SUBLETT MICHEL KENT	AR	42W	14
SUBLETTE GARY LYNN	CO	12E	8
SUCCI MICHAEL LAWRENCE	NH	44E	54
SUCHKA BRADLEY EUGENE	IN	34W	89
SUCHOMEL FREDERICK V	WI	27W	91
SUCHON CLARENCE MYRON	WI	04W	69
SUDBOROUGH MICHAEL G	OR	17E	7
SUDBRINK DONALD ALBERT	WI	15W	116
SUDDUTH ROBERT THOMAS	AZ	13W	33
SUDLER DERRICK	MD	11W	106
SUDLER EDMUND LAWRENCE	DE	06E	43
SUDLESKY THOMAS FRANCIS	PA	43W	51
SUDSBURY PAUL EARL	ME	09E	125
SUEDMEYER MERILL LAWRENCE	IL	22E	21
SUEDMYER LARRY DEAN III	CA	04W	107
SUETOS GILBERT BRIAN	HI	06E	115
SUGDEN WILLIAM JAMES	PA	36W	7
SUGGS JAMES DAVID	AL	30E	20
SUGGS JOHN FENTON JR	MO	39W	24
SUGHRUE PATRICK J	PA	28E	52
SUGIMOTO LEONARD JAMES	CA	15W	65
SUGIURA TOM DENNIS	CA	45W	29
SUHAR WALTER	OH	12E	124
SUHR ALFRED HENRY	MO	28W	54
SUIAUNOA TUIOALELE T	CA	35E	83
SUIT GROVER LYNN	GA	44W	7
SUKARA MICHAEL THEODORE	OH	08E	40
SUKOWATEY STANLEY JOSEPH	WI	60E	3
SULANDER DANIEL ARTHUR	MN	13E	7
SULATYCKI HENRYK TADUESZ		48W	16
SULLENS GEORGE BUSTER JR	OK	29E	5
SULLINGER JAMES EDWARD	OH	57W	32
SULLINGER WILTON JAMES JR	TX	40E	32
SULLIVAN ALLAN FRANCIS	NH	41E	4
SULLIVAN ARNOLD HOSEA	AL	34E	2
SULLIVAN BENJAMIN JOSEPH	IL	20W	9
SULLIVAN CHARLES A JR	MI	18E	20
SULLIVAN CHARLES E JR	ME	22E	85
SULLIVAN DANIEL	MS	21W	87
SULLIVAN DANIEL JOHN	NY	23E	23
SULLIVAN DAVID OWEN	MA	32W	35
SULLIVAN DAVID PATRICK	MT	45W	39
SULLIVAN DONALD SHERRIL	NC	14E	96
SULLIVAN DOUGLAS J	MN	13E	128
SULLIVAN EDDIE LEE	GA	15E	2
SULLIVAN EDWARD MICHAEL	MA	58W	15
SULLIVAN EMERY CAPERS III	NC	26E	58
SULLIVAN FARRELL JUNIOR	TX	01W	50
SULLIVAN FRANCIS C JR	MA	35W	14
SULLIVAN FRANCIS JORDAN	CT	07W	94
SULLIVAN GERALD DEWAYNE	SC	36E	39
SULLIVAN GLENN	FL	43E	36
SULLIVAN HAROLD	KY	32W	68
SULLIVAN HUGH JOHN JR	PA	01E	131
SULLIVAN JAMES EDWARD	MA	01W	85
SULLIVAN JAMES MICHAEL	NY	28W	76
SULLIVAN JEREMIAH JOSEPH	PA	28E	55
SULLIVAN JOHN ANTHONY	WA	38E	81
SULLIVAN JOHN BERNARD III	PA	08E	73
SULLIVAN JOHN FRANCIS	WI	48W	49
SULLIVAN JOHN JOSEPH	MA	43E	62
SULLIVAN JOHN MICHAEL	CA	31W	59
SULLIVAN JOHN MILLER	MA	14E	30
SULLIVAN JOSEPH HARRY	SC	10E	98
SULLIVAN LAWRENCE MICHAEL	TN	07W	133
SULLIVAN LEO JOSEPH JR	MA	19E	67
SULLIVAN MARTIN JOSEPH	MA	15E	23
SULLIVAN MELVIN	MO	15W	80
SULLIVAN MICHAEL JAMES	KS	30E	60
SULLIVAN MICHAEL NELSON	VA	13W	114
SULLIVAN MICHAEL XAVIER	MA	38E	40
SULLIVAN MIKAL JAMES	WI	59W	16
SULLIVAN NEIL BRIAN	AR	63E	2
SULLIVAN PAUL JOSEPH	MA	49W	37
SULLIVAN PETER MICHAEL	MA	15E	10
SULLIVAN PIERRE LEROY	PA	54E	18
SULLIVAN R D	TN	47W	23
SULLIVAN RAYMOND WALTER	CA	34W	72
SULLIVAN RICHARD ARTHUR	CA	04E	85
SULLIVAN RICHARD D JR	CA	50W	40
SULLIVAN ROBERT JOSEPH	NH	23E	63
SULLIVAN ROBERT JOSEPH	OH	26E	63
SULLIVAN ROBERT MICHAEL	MI	35W	14
SULLIVAN STANLEY HOUSTON	TN	23E	7
SULLIVAN STEPHEN THOMAS	MA	64W	16
SULLIVAN TERRENCE COLIN	NH	20E	69
SULLIVAN THOMAS EMERSON	IL	08E	78
SULLIVAN THOMAS HOWARD	CA	16W	76
SULLIVAN THOMAS MICHAEL	ME	17E	82
SULLIVAN TIMOTHY EMMETT	MN	11W	20
SULLIVAN WILLIAM ANDERSON	NC	03E	25
SULLIVAN WILLIAM LEE	CO	09W	120
SULLIVAN WILLIS M JR	PA	21E	116
SULSER DAVID WESLEY	OH	01W	22
SUMERLIN TERRY LEE	OR	26E	32
SUMICH FRANKLIN JOHN	OR	21E	92
SUMIDA JERALD KATSUJI	HI	23E	79
SUMLIN THOMAS EARL	MS	15W	44
SUMMERFIELD SAMUEL REED	WV	43W	10
SUMMERLIN J C	AL	03W	48
SUMMERLIN JOHN WRIGHT	VA	28W	76
SUMMERLIN STEVE MONROE	NC	28E	77
SUMMERS CHARLES G H	NY	17E	82
SUMMERS DONALD L	NM	10E	11
SUMMERS EUGENE C	WV	04E	95
SUMMERS FRANKLIN DALLAS	TX	12W	129
SUMMERS HARRY LEE	VA	01E	91
SUMMERS JOHN THOMAS III	MD	46E	60
SUMMERS JON RAY	MT	24W	62
SUMMERS PHILLIP PAUL	MO	31E	22
SUMMERS ROBERT RANDOLPH	MO	19E	113
SUMMERS RONALD LEE	TX	41W	32
SUMMERS WILLIAM ELVIN	TX	02W	66

NAME	STATE	PANEL NO.	LINE NO.
SUMMERSILL EARL PHILLIP	FL	52E	24
SUMMERVILLE FREDERICK BRU	MI	03W	102
SUMMERVILLE WILLIE JR	MS	33W	69
SUMNER BUFORD ELLIS	VA	12W	32
SUMNER JAMES HOWELL	IN	26W	103
SUMPTER BOBBY RECE	KY	44W	6
SUMPTER EDDY GALE	AR	38W	30
SUMPTER JOSEPH BOYD	KY	26E	40
SUMRALL ROGER DALE	MS	09W	113
SUMTER FORREST DARRYL	OK	12W	11
SUND TERRENCE LEE	WI	31E	54
SUNDAY JAMES MICHAEL	OH	27E	32
SUNDEEN TERRY ALLAN	OR	24W	107
SUNDELL LARS PEDER	CA	48E	12
SUNDET GARY LEE	SD	09E	19
SUNDQUIST DAVID HARRY	MN	31W	25
SUNDQUIST JACK DONALD	UT	46E	51
SUNDQUIST JOHN OLAF	MN	11E	96
SUNIGA JOHN ANTHONY JR	CO	08W	50
SUNIGA MICHAEL EDWARD	CA	32E	48
SUNIGA RUBEN BOSQUEZ	TX	07W	116
SUPERCZYNSKI JOHN PAUL JR	IL	47W	55
SUPINGER CLAUDE CARROLL	VA	12E	30
SUPINO LOUIS VINCENT	NY	37E	70
SUPNET EMILIO CABRERA JR	CA	10W	54
SUPNET RICHARD ARELLANO	CA	02W	24
SUPPLE JOHN PHILIP	NY	48E	21
SUPRENANT CHARLES E JR	FL	12W	85
SURBER HERBERT DONALD	FL	13E	79
SURBER MARK WAYNE	MI	18W	126
SURBER SAMMUEL EDGAR	NC	14W	36
SURETTE PAUL JOSEPH	MA	08E	110
SURETTE WILLIAM WARREN JR	NY	14W	50
SURGALSKI JOHN ANTHONY	PA	38E	15
SURLES LOREN CLEVELAND	NY	20E	126
SURMA STEVEN JOHN	SD	18E	31
SURPRENANT NORMAN ROGER	CT	31W	60
SURWALD MICHAEL EDWARD	IL	10E	111
SUSI ANDREW PAUL	NY	10W	111
SUSI RAYMOND PETER	NY	11W	65
SUSMARSKI KENNETH JOHN	PA	22W	109
SUSSMEIER JAMES JOSEPH	NY	23E	38
SUSTERSIC LOUIS ROBERT	OH	16W	24
SUTER JERRY TIMOTHY	AZ	10E	98
SUTERA LOUIS JR	GA	33E	5
SUTHARD CHARLES LEE JR	VA	33W	74
SUTHERLAND BOBBY COLLINS	GA	39E	13
SUTHERLAND CHARLES EDWARD	MO	45E	31
SUTHERLAND HERBERT LEE	CA	07E	37
SUTHERLAND JAMES EDWARD	CA	04W	101
SUTHERLAND JOHN ALVIN	FL	20E	107
SUTHERLAND REGINALD J	NY	15W	46
SUTHERLAND RICHARD EUGENE	IA	26E	108
SUTHERLAND SCOTT EUGENE	WA	10W	19
SUTHERLIN WILLIAM REGINAL	MO	07E	88
SUTHONS MELVIN HAROLD		02E	13
SUTPHEN JACK B	UT	35E	35
SUTT GEORGE STEVEN	IN	21E	19
SUTTER FREDERICK JOHN	KS	02W	93
SUTTER RICHARD FURLONG	GA	23E	105
SUTTLE FREDERICK N JR	VA	01W	34
SUTTLE WILLIAM EARL	AL	20W	3
SUTTLEHAN LAURENCE CHRIST	NY	29E	54
SUTTON ARTHUR LAVERN	OK	06W	44
SUTTON BEN FREDERICK	FL	18W	30
SUTTON BRYAN JAMES	CA	04W	56
SUTTON DENNIS LEE	CA	60W	22
SUTTON DOUGLAS ROLLAND	NC	65W	2
SUTTON EDMOND CEASAR	MD	22E	51
SUTTON EUGENE MORGAN JR	NC	63E	18
SUTTON FRANK	AZ	33E	75
SUTTON GARRETT GARLAND JR	MS	11E	24
SUTTON GEORGE STANLEY	VA	38E	73
SUTTON HUBERT DANIEL	MA	17W	40
SUTTON JACK LENN	TN	18E	82
SUTTON JACK RICHARD	IL	14E	30
SUTTON JAMES KENNETH	AL	31W	59
SUTTON JAMES THOMAS	MI	50E	34
SUTTON LAREST CLENNON	NC	16W	111
SUTTON LARRY IVAN	WI	23E	114
SUTTON LAWRENCE EDWIN	OR	12W	76
SUTTON LOWHMAN SOLON	OK	50W	37
SUTTON MATTHEW EARL JR	PA	54E	18
SUTTON RONALD MARTIN	NC	06E	22
SUTTON TERRY JAMES	NE	40E	14
SUTTON TERRY WAYNE	NC	41E	13
SUTTON TRAVIS ROBERT	AL	32E	55
SUTTON VICTOR BLAKE	NC	23W	92
SUTTON WILLIAM CARL	NC	14W	77
SUTTON WILLIAM JOSEPH	VA	22E	116
SUVARA FRANK CARL JR	PA	14E	30
SUYDAM JAMES LAWRENCE	NJ	07W	124
SUYDAM JOHN HOWARD III	CA	39E	14
SUZUKI KENNY RYOSUKE	CA	13E	45
SVANOE KENNARD ERROL	OH	23W	48
SVEEN BRENT WILLIAM	ND	07W	45
SVIR ROGER LEE	ND	02W	26
SVOBODNY LAWRENCE MARVIN	MN	26E	68
SWAB RICHARD EUGENE	MD	54W	20
SWABBY BRENT LESLIE	CA	69E	3
SWAFFORD KENNETH WAYNE	OH	24E	108
SWAFFORD ROBERT WAYNE	MO	26E	18
SWAGER GENE STANLEY	WI	11W	10
SWAGLER CRAIG EVERETT	NY	31W	85
SWAIM ALLAN GREGORY	CA	50W	46
SWAIM BRUCE ALAN	IN	40E	69
SWAIM CHARLES MICHAEL	MO	15E	15
SWAIM JAMES LEE	NE	15W	84
SWAIM RONALD GAIL	IA	64E	8
SWAIN CRAIG FRANCIS	MA	49W	1
SWAIN LEE WESLEY JR	AL	48W	49
SWAIN MILTON TRUMAN	MS	12W	76
SWAIN ROBERT HATCHER	MD	24E	45
SWAIN ROBERT RAY	IN	15W	105
SWAIN TOMMY HERMAN	GA	12W	36
SWAIN WALTER LEE	FL	18E	94
SWALLEY ROBERT EUGENE	WA	34E	92
SWAN DAVID MARTIN	CT	20W	99
SWAN JERALD DAVID	WA	51E	13
SWAN LEO EDWARD JR	MA	51E	13
SWAN ROBERT RONALD	IL	25E	80
SWAN WAYNE ROBERT	NY	28W	87
SWANCEY RANDALL FILLMORE	GA	51W	14
SWANCY JAMES ANDREW	TX	27E	4
SWANE BRIAN EDWARD	NY	25W	15
SWANEY LARRY DEAN	OH	58W	21
SWANEY RICKEY EUGENE	IA	19W	42
SWANGIN MICHAEL DEWITT	NJ	12E	92
SWANGO JAMES RAY	IN	09W	61
SWANGUARIM LAWRENCE ALFRE	MO	48E	36
SWANHART RUSSELL JAMES	PA	26E	64
SWANKER NELSON CHRISTAN	NY	57E	34
SWANN ELLSWORTH	KY	31E	96
SWANN HOWARD ERNEST	MO	21E	81
SWANN JAMES CECIL	VA	42E	68
SWANN JOHNNY DELBERT	GA	18W	44
SWANN THOMAS FREDRICK JR	NC	58E	16
SWANSON BOBBY GENE JR	TX	12W	53
SWANSON DARREL THOMAS	MN	33W	82
SWANSON DONALD LLOYD	CA	14W	87
SWANSON JAMES CLIFFORD SR	OH	27W	104
SWANSON JOHN EARNEST JR	IA	54E	32
SWANSON JOHN WILLARD JR	IL	21E	109
SWANSON JON EDWARD	CO	04W	7
SWANSON KEITH LYLE	CA	40W	40
SWANSON LAWRENCE HARRY	MN	38E	16
SWANSON LYNN CURTIS	MN	25W	112
SWANSON NELS WILLIAM	IL	04E	29
SWANSON RAYMOND WILLIAM	NY	22W	16
SWANSON ROBERT EDWIN	ND	02E	136
SWANSON ROGER WESLEY	MN	40W	69
SWANSON TODD EARLE	CA	44E	41
SWANSON WILLIAM EDWARD	MN	01E	103
SWANSON WILLIAM HENRY	TN	25W	56
SWANSTROM DOUGLAS GAYLORD	NY	24W	72
SWANTAK DENNIS RAY	WA	67W	5
SWARBRICK LAWRENCE GORDON	CA	08W	109
SWART WALDON JEROME	MN	35W	30
SWARTZ CHARLES DELANO	OH	04E	62
SWARTZ GARY LEE	PA	13W	65
SWARTZ JAMES ALBERT JR	PA	12W	85
SWARTZ WILLIAM JOSEPH	NY	12W	19
SWARTZLANDER ELIE EDWARD	AR	38W	9
SWATEK STEVEN PAUL	WI	42E	25
SWATSELL DONNIE JAY	TN	14W	96
SWATSLEY MICKEY LYNN	IL	44W	6
SWAYKOS WILLIAM ERNEST	NJ	01E	83
SWAYZE GERALD CLIFFORD	SD	15W	112
SWAYZE JOSEPH J	NJ	07E	27
SWAYZE RICHARD DAVID	CA	06E	35
SWAZICK DANNY GEORGE	KS	42E	42
SWEAT DONALD JEANE	TX	54E	41
SWEAT HERBERT HOOVER JR	FL	32W	74
SWEAT LORAN EDGAR JR	VA	11W	42
SWEAT NORMAN ROGER	GA	17W	46
SWEATT CLYDE STANLEY	SC	28W	15
SWEATT GEORGE EDWARD	KY	43E	48
SWEATT THEODORE ALFRED	IN	38W	79
SWED ROY FRANCIS	NY	39E	54
SWEDA JOSEPH R	NY	02E	134
SWEDEEN RICHARD ALLEN	MN	36E	87
SWEDENBURG ROBERT JOHN	MN	15W	44
SWEENEY BRUCE ROBERT J N	NY	38W	39
SWEENEY CLARENCE JOSEPH	WA	15E	7
SWEENEY JOHN EDWARD	VT	51W	9
SWEENEY JOSEPH EDWARD	PA	03W	58
SWEENEY MICHAEL BERNARD	NH	32E	56
SWEENEY MICHAEL MURPHY	SC	38E	81
SWEENEY PATRICK JOHN	IL	23E	89
SWEENEY RICHARD JOHN	WY	31W	25
SWEENEY ROBERT MICHAEL	IL	04E	47
SWEENEY THOMAS JAMES	PA	41E	45
SWEENEY THOMAS PAUL	MA	47E	27
SWEENEY TIMOTHY JAMES	IL	01W	74
SWEESY JOHN EARL	OH	19E	33
SWEET DAVID ARTHUR	OH	14W	40
SWEET DONN LAFAYETTE	VA	50W	10
SWEET EUGENE FREDERICK JR	NH	33E	42
SWEET JAMES NEWTON	NY	41W	70
SWEET JERRY ALAN	NY	50E	24
SWEET JOHN HARLAN	FL	20W	99
SWEET LARRY EUGENE	TX	18W	87
SWEET RICHARD DONALD	MN	25W	2
SWEET ROGER WILLIAM	FL	06W	122
SWEET RONALD STEVEN	IA	26E	68
SWEETEN R C EARL	OK	16W	67
SWEETLAND RONALD KENNETH	MI	02W	79
SWEGER RICHARD HAUSE	PA	35W	22
SWEINSBERGER THOMAS EDWAR	OH	02W	11
SWENCK ROBERT BENNETT	KY	02W	72
SWENDER JACK SHIVELY	KS	04E	26
SWENSGARD WILLIAM ELLING	MT	26E	109
SWENSON PEDRO ARNADO	PA	14E	92
SWENSON SWANTE AUGUST	NJ	34E	32
SWIDONOVICH NICHOLAS JOHN	NY	34W	10
SWIECZKOWSKI MICHAEL JOHN	NY	64E	9
SWIFT DERALD DEAN	OR	13E	19
SWIFT EUGENE EDWARD	MD	44E	2
SWIFT JAMES THEALBEART JR	PA	11W	61
SWIFT RICHARD C	IA	38W	39
SWIGART PAUL EUGENE JR	CA	33W	69
SWIGART ROBERT WILLIAMS	PA	23E	8
SWIGER BERNARD LEROY	OH	06W	115
SWIGER HARRY RAY	WV	01E	122
SWIGER RICHARD JACKSON	WV	18W	56
SWIGGUM LARRY WILLIAM	WI	49W	26
SWIHART DAVID EUGENE	OH	62W	3
SWIM PAUL EUGENE	GA	07E	41
SWINDELL BOBBY DALE	TX	07E	76
SWINDELL WILBUR EUGENE	PA	10E	96
SWINDLE ROBERT EAL	FL	19W	35
SWINFORD FRANK LEVI III	TX	26E	19
SWINFORD RONALD DEAN	OH	07W	38
SWINFORD SYLVESTER JR	MS	07E	123
SWINK JACKIE LEE	KS	17W	79
SWINNEA THOMAS HENRY	TX	35E	82
SWINNEY GEORGE EDWARD	AR	11E	80
SWINSON LONNIE MELROE	WA	07W	57
SWINT CHARLES JUNIOR	TN	33W	75
SWISHER CLIFFORD LEE	CA	28W	15
SWISHER LARRY RAYMOND	NY	29W	56
SWISHER WILLIAM HENRY	IN	35W	67
SWITZER JERROLD ALLEN	IL	45E	31
SWOFFORD DANNY RAY	SC	63E	8
SWONER ERNEST WILLIAM	TN	31W	25
SWONKE EDWARD ANTONE JR	TX	45E	15

NAME	STATE	PANEL NO.	LINE NO.
SWOOPE RUDOLPH	IL	31W	86
SWOPE CHARLES FREDERICK	KY	12E	49
SWORDS JOHN ARTHUR	GA	29W	84
SWORDS SMITH III	CA	33E	5
SWOVELAND WILLIAM ALAN	MI	46W	24
SWYMER GEORGE T	GA	42E	58
SYBERT ROSCOE	VA	11W	107
SYDOR DENNIS WILLIAM	NJ	21W	63
SYGNATUR JOSEPH JOHN	NY	18E	51
SYINTSAKOS PETER CHARLES	RI	23E	72
SYKES DANA MICHAEL	NC	24W	50
SYKES DERRI	IL	34E	11
SYKES DON CARLOS	GA	47E	55
SYKES DON RICHARD	NC	19W	25
SYKES HAMP JUROME JR	IL	06E	82
SYKES JONATHAN EDWARD	NJ	37E	71
SYKES KENNETH BERNARD	PA	07E	132
SYLVESTRE ARMAND ALVIN	CA	52W	37
SYLVIA JERRY	NJ	18W	51
SYLVIA MICHAEL ALAN	RI	22W	36
SYLVIA WAYNE JOHN	MA	23E	105
SYLWANOWICZ CASIMIR SYLWA	MI	15E	23
SYMANK TOMMIE LEE	TX	44E	54
SYNKOWSKI VALENTINE JOHN	PA	61E	3
SYNOD MICHAEL JOHN	MI	39W	5
SYROVATKA ARNOLD DEAN	SD	28E	12
SYSAK CRAIG ALAN	CA	05W	36
SZABO ISTVAN	MD	11E	24
SZAHLENDER JULIUS NICHOLA	OH	41E	13
SZAWALUK NICKOLAS	NJ	60W	6
SZCZEPANCZYK GEORGE V	NJ	45W	29
SZCZUPAJ JAMES WALTER	IL	41W	43
SZEKELY AKOS DEZSO	MD	44W	31
SZEKELY JOSEPH CHARLES	MS	02W	135
SZEYLLER EDWARD PHILIP	PA	17E	101
SZIDOR JOSEPH DANIEL	FL	38W	47
SZIJJARTO STEPHEN JOSEPH	KS	13E	56
SZLAPA JOHN FRANK III	MI	06W	124
SZOR HENRY	NY	37W	36
SZOSZOREK GERALD JAMES	PA	36W	38
SZPONDER ROBERT ALLAN	FL	08W	67
SZUTZ BRAD JOHN	CA	35E	82
SZYDLO THOMAS JOSEPH	RI	24E	1
SZYMANSKI FRANK ADAM IV	OH	41E	31
SZYMANSKI JOHN STEPHEN	NJ	17E	32
SZYMANSKI ROBERT THOMAS	WI	30E	50
SZYSZPUTOWSKI GERALD ADAM	PA	56W	7
StAMAND RICHARD CARL	MA	41W	61
StCLAIR BRADLEY ANDREW	IN	45W	57
StCLAIR CHARLES DAVID	KY	05W	51
StCLAIR CLARENCE H JR	FL	18W	5
StCLAIR LEONARD RAY	TX	15E	101
StCYR JAMES AUGUSTINE	MA	06E	52
StGEORGE FRED DAVID	VT	26E	52
StGERMAINE RONALD HUBERT	GA	20W	99
StJEAN BERNARD EDWARD	MA	13E	69
StJOHN DAVID MICHAEL	MA	48W	49
StJOHN RONALD GEORGE	ME	10E	104
StJOHN WILLIAM LUKE	CT	34W	61
StLAURENT LANCE WILFRED	WA	21W	63
StLAWRENCE ALBERT ALFRED	MA	09W	27
StLOUIS BRUCE WAYNE	CA	32E	27
StONGE MICHAEL JOSEPH	DC	31W	25
StPETER ROBERT EUGENE	IL	04E	115
StPETERS JOHN DONALD	IL	22E	21
StPIERRE MICHAEL LEONARD	MA	20W	45
TABABOO DANIEL JOHN JR	OR	59E	14
TABB PHIL	GA	06E	6
TABER JERRY DEAN	OK	12E	30
TABER MARTIN LESTER	FL	19W	82
TABET HENRY MARSIAL	CA	39E	54
TABLER ROY TOM	AR	01W	106
TABOADA ADOLFO ANTONIO JR	CA	02E	133
TABOADA FRANK OLIVARES	TX	33E	42
TABOR BRUCE WAYNE	CO	55E	32
TABOR CLAUDE EDWARD	IL	20W	61
TABOR CLIFFORD JR	GA	25W	2
TABOR DENNIS RICHARD	MN	08E	41
TABOR EVERETT LEROY	IL	13E	114
TABOR MOSES CLARK	TN	03E	108
TABOR RICHARD EUGENE	WY	05W	32
TABRON BOBBY RAY	NC	24E	45

NAME	STATE	PANEL NO.	LINE NO.
TACKETT CLARENCE E	KY	24E	92
TACKETT GARY DOUGLAS	OH	12E	25
TACKETT GEORGE EDWARD	KY	24W	50
TACKETT RUBEN NOAH	KY	44E	41
TACTAY EUGENE RICARDO JR	CA	11E	131
TADENA ESTEBAN WALLACE	HI	29E	45
TADEVIC RALPH DULANE	IL	17W	129
TADEVICH EMIL JEROME	MA	04E	47
TADIOS LEONARD MASAYON	HI	01E	76
TAFAO FA'ASAVILIGA V	CA	22E	51
TAFF GEORGE THOMAS JR	TX	05W	127
TAFFE THOMAS LEO	MI	46E	51
TAFOLLA NABOR RICHARD	IA	37E	71
TAFOYA FLORENTINO JR	NM	29E	22
TAFOYA FRANK	NM	20E	4
TAFOYA FRANK LEROY	UT	30E	67
TAFOYA GEORGE ELOY	NM	38E	82
TAFOYA JOHN OLIVIO	NM	34W	72
TAFOYA JOSEPH ERNEST	CA	46W	53
TAFOYA MARK ALVAN	NM	07W	108
TAFOYA VICTOR ARNALDO	UT	09W	25
TAFT PHILIP JEFFREY	VA	41W	38
TAFT ROBERT EDMUND	IL	03E	62
TAFT THOMAS HAROLD	IN	03W	10
TAGATA LAAVALE FUATAU	CA	03E	122
TAGGART ISAAC	IL	43W	31
TAGGART LARRY JOEL	CO	44E	62
TAGGART WINSTON ADAMS	NH	32E	28
TAGLIEBER LEONARD JOSEPH	PA	23E	16
TAGLIONE ROBERT	MI	02E	61
TAGMAN JOHNNY RAY	OK	09E	16
TAGUE JOHN ROBERT	ND	56W	9
TAGUE NICHOLAS ALLEN	CA	19E	87
TAILLON JOHN PHILLIPS	MA	16E	14
TAIRA CLIFFORD KAZUMI	HI	25W	56
TAISLER JOSEPH ANDREW	NY	21W	103
TAITAGUE JOHNNY SALAS	GM	51E	34
TAJCHMAN ADOLPH WILLIAM	TX	38W	39
TAKACS THEODORE NELSON JR	OH	27E	62
TAKEHARA YOSHIO	HI	05W	109
TAKEMOTO KENNETH JAMES	HI	33E	42
TAKETA KEN HARRIS	CA	03W	116
TALAN ARISTON R JR	HI	19E	46
TALBERT CLAUDE JR	TN	02E	113
TALBOT THOMAS PAUL	UT	10W	67
TALBOTT JAMES FRANKLIN	IN	20W	104
TALBURT RAYMOND THURL	KS	23W	107
TALIAFERRO GLEN JOHNSON	KS	03W	122
TALIAFERRO NAPOLEON ENOCH	PA	57W	32
TALIANA JOHN BARRY	PA	11E	129
TALKEN GEORGE FRANCIS	CA	20W	89
TALKINGTON DENNIS LEE	TX	05E	97
TALL WARREN LEE	MS	42E	43
TALLENT GARRY GLENN	NC	25E	21
TALLENT HERSHALL	SC	58E	16
TALLENTIRE GARY LEE	OH	37E	71
TALLEY BILLY J	AR	03E	67
TALLEY FLOYD G	KY	15W	40
TALLEY GARY LEE	CA	43E	11
TALLEY HAROLD LEE	CA	17E	108
TALLEY JAMES LANE	GA	02E	15
TALLEY JERRY WAYNE	MS	34W	80
TALLEY LARRY JAMES	VA	20W	127
TALLEY TEDDY GENE	AR	20E	126
TALLION JOHN MICHAEL	OH	17E	59
TALLMAN DANIEL FERREL	WV	03E	112
TALLMAN DONALD CHARLES	OH	02W	57
TALLMAN GEORGE	CA	18E	7
TALLMAN RICHARD JOSEPH	PA	01W	55
TALLMAN ROGER LEE	MI	16W	60
TALLON DOUGLAS WAYNE	MT	19E	18
TALMADGE THOMAS ROBERT	NJ	17E	14
TALMON PETER GEORGE III	CA	22E	116
TALTON BOBBY RAY	LA	40E	48
TALTY PATRICK ANTHONY	CO	02W	133
TAMAGNINI JOSEPH EDWARD	NJ	57W	32
TAMAYO FRANCISCO MARIO JR	CA	13E	17
TAMAYO JOEL	TX	07E	99
TAMBURRI JOHN RICHARD JR	NY	07W	70
TAMER RICHARD EDWARD	OH	24W	72
TAMEYOZA NOE	TX	39W	10
TAMEZ NOE	TX	22W	70

NAME	STATE	PANEL NO.	LINE NO.
TAMILIO THOMAS	NY	15E	37
TAMM RICHARD DAVID	MI	37W	42
TAMMEN WILLIAM DWIGHT	IL	08E	126
TAMS ROBERT NIELSEN	DE	07E	46
TANAKA MINORU	HI	31E	1
TANASSO AMBROSE P JR	MA	36W	74
TANDY MICHAEL GORDON	CA	10E	78
TANGARIE JOSEPH THOMAS	NJ	46E	24
TANGEMAN JAMES LEROY	MI	50W	33
TANGEN TERENCE RONALD	MI	08E	32
TANGUAY ALAN MICHAEL	WA	05E	135
TANIMOTO MILES T	HI	09E	76
TANK CHARLES LOUIS	MI	26W	12
TANK PHILIP LEONARD	MI	44W	42
TANKERSLEY JAMES ESTILL	MI	25W	42
TANKSLEY CLIFTON	TN	31E	61
TANKSLEY ROBERT WILLIE	GA	35E	42
TANNEHILL CHARLES DEVEAUX	MS	26W	36
TANNEHILL RAY EDWIN	MO	01W	65
TANNENBAUM DONALD CHARLES	NC	12W	116
TANNER CHARLES ELBERT	NC	02E	133
TANNER DAVID ARLINGTON	ID	31E	67
TANNER DONALD JAY	TX	03E	124
TANNER DOUGLAS HOWARD	MI	14W	124
TANNER KENNETH PAUL	FL	08W	47
TANNER RAY EUGENE	OH	06W	74
TANNER RAYMOND	TN	06W	37
TANNER RAYMOND MARSHALL	TX	40W	47
TANNER ROGER LEE	OH	15E	2
TANNER RONALD RUSSELL	MT	10W	127
TANNER STEVEN DALE	KY	32W	62
TANNER WILLIAM LA MARR	GA	29W	49
TANNEY JOHN MICHAEL	NY	42W	2
TANTON CHARLIE THOMAS	AL	03W	91
TANZOLA CARL JOSEPH JR	NY	33W	70
TAPIA MOISES	CA	28W	15
TAPIO HEINZ ARNOLD	CA	23E	108
TAPP JOHN BETHEL	KY	06E	43
TAPP MARION NEAL	MD	52W	20
TAPP MARSHALL LANDIS	CA	07E	63
TAPP NEWTON LEE	IL	12W	64
TAPPAN FREDERICK HOWARD	CA	47W	13
TAPPE KENNETH WILLIAM JR	NY	28E	106
TAPPER FREDDIE LESLIE	IN	07W	101
TAPSCOTT KENNITH WALKER	SC	08W	89
TARANGO ERNESTO	CA	32E	89
TARANGO MAGDALENO	NM	16E	24
TARANTO DAVID WILLIAM	NY	41W	54
TARANTO ROBERT JOSEPH	NY	37W	8
TARANTOWICZ JOHN EDWARD	PA	17E	129
TARASUK VICTOR	WV	13E	73
TARASZKIEWICZ JOSEPH G	MI	31W	26
TARBELL CLIFFORD LAWRENCE	NY	12W	126
TARBELL WILLIAM M	NY	05E	82
TARBERT CHARLES STANLEY	IL	15W	44
TARDIO RONALD ENRIQUE		11E	116
TARIN EDWARD JAMES	TX	41E	45
TARIN ELISEO ESPINOZA	TX	20E	69
TARJANY RANDOLPH MICHAEL	IL	50W	3
TARKENTON JAMES C III	TX	16E	116
TARKINGTON CURTIS RAY	AZ	02E	110
TARKINGTON RICHARD JR	OK	15E	51
TARPLEY NORMAN WESLEY	OH	50E	23
TARPLEY WILLIAM JUNIOR	VA	61E	19
TARRANCE JAMES CURTIS	FL	37W	42
TARRANCE WILLIAM BLAIR	CA	32W	86
TARSI WILLIAM JAMES	CT	10E	34
TART CLIFTON LEE	NY	05E	91
TARTE JAMES LAFON	TN	46W	9
TARTER BOBBY LEE	KY	19W	110
TARTT CARLOS LEROY	MS	29W	15
TARVER EDWARD	LA	08W	106
TARVER LLOYD ROBERT	OK	06E	69
TASCH JON	CA	19W	26
TASCHEK KARL JOSEPH JR	WI	29W	93
TASHNER WALTER A	OR	29E	102
TASKER DAVID LEROY	CA	30E	94
TASKER JAMES BRUCE	OH	55W	33
TASKER KENNETH EARL	MD	09E	125
TASSEY MALCOLM FAIRCHILD	NJ	22E	116
TASTE WADE	NC	07E	99
TATARSKI LESLIE MILES	NY	09W	49

NAME	STATE	PANEL NO.	LINE NO.
TATARYN GEORGE LUBOMYR	IL	36W	74
TATE ALENN MERRITT	VA	04E	98
TATE ALEXANDER JR	NY	53E	7
TATE ANTHONY GARY	TX	02E	24
TATE BERNIE LEE	MI	23E	65
TATE BRADLEY HAYNES	VA	09E	118
TATE CHARLES EDWARD	TN	53E	23
TATE CHARLES THOMAS JR	NY	35E	82
TATE DANIEL HARRISON	TX	05W	97
TATE FENNELL	CA	13E	129
TATE FRED EUGENE	CA	19E	87
TATE GARY DENTON	IL	20W	42
TATE JACKIE LEE	MO	27W	42
TATE JAMES E	TN	04E	75
TATE JOHN CULLEN	WA	19E	87
TATE KENNETH WAYNE	IL	26E	40
TATE LEE BERNARD	MO	06E	61
TATE LYLE SCOTT	OR	19E	75
TATE RICHARD LEE	NC	06W	18
TATE ROBERT ARNOLD JR	WV	29W	94
TATE ROBERT GERALD	MI	43W	43
TATE ROBERT LEE	NC	48E	48
TATE SCIP	NJ	03E	37
TATE TODD III	IL	31E	39
TATE TONY LARUE	LA	44E	22
TATE WALTER REAVES JR	SC	09E	50
TATE WILLIE JAMES	SC	36W	66
TATEM HAROLD PAUL	VA	26W	87
TATNALL CLYDE BENJAMIN	GA	13W	38
TATNEY ERNEST JR	LA	25E	80
TATSUNO ALBERT HIROSHI	HI	04E	115
TATUM DORSEY L	GA	06E	12
TATUM HAROLD DEAN	GA	26E	109
TATUM HERBERT ARTHUR	IL	29W	74
TATUM IVRA ALLEN	AR	23E	32
TATUM JOSEPH STEPHEN	OH	11W	82
TATUM LAWRENCE BYRON	TN	10E	85
TATUM RICHARD LEE	MO	49W	21
TAUAESE VALENTINO	CA	21E	109
TAUALA TAGIPO VAOGA	WA	05W	109
TAUANUU PELESASA SOLOMONA	HI	64W	16
TAUBERMAN CHARLES G SR	IL	04W	12
TAUFI AOULIULITAU FAITUPE	CA	19W	90
TAULBEE DANNY JOE	KY	10W	20
TAURISANO JAMES VINCENT	MA	04E	81
TAUSCHEK LEONARD JOHN	WI	26E	32
TAVARES BELMIRO JR	MA	11E	38
TAVARES CHARLES ALBERT	MA	31W	86
TAVARES MANUEL ANTONIO D	MA	14W	21
TAVAREZ JOSE RAFAEL	NY	41E	56
TAWIL AARON	NY	38W	5
TAWNEY GARY WAYNE	WV	02W	96
TAYLOR ALBERT RUSSELL II	CA	56W	28
TAYLOR ALONZO HUGHES	CA	09W	45
TAYLOR ANDREW JAMES	WI	11W	88
TAYLOR ANTHONY	NJ	53E	42
TAYLOR BERNELL	MS	64W	17
TAYLOR BILLY JOE	MI	49W	1
TAYLOR BOBBY ALLEN	NM	37E	14
TAYLOR CALVIN LEROY	GA	20E	37
TAYLOR CECIL FRANKLIN	SC	24W	99
TAYLOR CHARLES FRANKLIN	MI	18W	44
TAYLOR CHARLES MINOR III	AR	30E	60
TAYLOR CHARLES STOCKTON	AL	21W	3
TAYLOR CHARLIE WILLIAM	NJ	08W	120
TAYLOR CLARENCE	AL	23W	11
TAYLOR CLIFFORD McARTHUR	TN	28W	4
TAYLOR CLIFTON THOMAS	AL	67E	3
TAYLOR CLYDE DAVID	OK	04E	55
TAYLOR DANIEL MORRIS	IL	17E	25
TAYLOR DANNY GENE	MO	11E	27
TAYLOR DARRELL DUANE	MI	19W	98
TAYLOR DARRYL WADE	DC	03W	92
TAYLOR DAVID ADOLPHUS	GA	16E	24
TAYLOR DAVID BERNARD	MI	55W	16
TAYLOR DAVID EARL	TX	34W	45
TAYLOR DAVID F III	AR	17E	89
TAYLOR DAVID STUART JR	FL	40W	52
TAYLOR DAVID THORNTON	CA	05W	127
TAYLOR DE WAYNE	AL	31W	26
TAYLOR DEANE ARTHUR JR	GA	34W	11
TAYLOR DENNIS GILBERT	CT	09E	120
TAYLOR DENNIS LEE	CA	23W	79
TAYLOR DENNIS WAYNE	TN	56W	9
TAYLOR DONALD CLAUDE	IL	13W	86
TAYLOR DONALD RICHARD	PA	01E	43
TAYLOR DONALD THOMAS	MI	25W	8
TAYLOR DONNIE CARL	MI	04W	110
TAYLOR DUNCAN JR	LA	61E	3
TAYLOR DWIGHT JOSEPH	NY	38W	9
TAYLOR EARL EUGENE	OH	30W	82
TAYLOR EDD DAVID	AR	02E	68
TAYLOR EDMUND BATTELLE JR	OH	01W	15
TAYLOR EDWARD EUGENE	OH	02W	101
TAYLOR ELMER JACK	AL	06E	68
TAYLOR EMORY LE ROY	WV	18E	43
TAYLOR ERIC WYCKOFF	NY	13W	30
TAYLOR ERNEST EDWARD	WY	03E	96
TAYLOR ERNEST RAY	OK	61W	7
TAYLOR ERNEST RAY JR	OH	30E	49
TAYLOR ERNEST VERNON	TX	37E	45
TAYLOR FRED	VA	02E	37
TAYLOR FREDERICK WAYNE	OH	61E	3
TAYLOR GARY DEAN	CA	17W	38
TAYLOR GARY LEE	OH	21E	96
TAYLOR GARY LYNN	IL	22W	44
TAYLOR GARY LYNN	OH	10W	93
TAYLOR GEOFFREY RAYMOND	CA	54E	20
TAYLOR GEORGE DAVID	TN	24E	110
TAYLOR GEORGE DENNIS	TN	45W	64
TAYLOR GEORGE MICHAEL	WA	20E	69
TAYLOR GEORGE THOMAS JR	SC	03W	49
TAYLOR GERALD K	FL	29E	77
TAYLOR GLENN DEAN	WA	36E	61
TAYLOR GORDON LEE	WV	02E	98
TAYLOR GRANT CARL	OH	21E	59
TAYLOR GROVER R	WV	06E	125
TAYLOR HAROLD	OH	23E	32
TAYLOR HARRY EDWARD	NY	16E	32
TAYLOR HARRY EUGENE	KY	07W	101
TAYLOR HENRY LUSCIOUS	OH	14W	34
TAYLOR HERBERT GORDAN	NC	42W	33
TAYLOR HERMAN L	CA	58E	16
TAYLOR HOMER JR	TN	40E	14
TAYLOR HOWARD FRANKLIN	VA	19W	99
TAYLOR JACK CLINTON	OR	36E	86
TAYLOR JACK EDWIN	NY	08W	52
TAYLOR JAMES	FL	53W	25
TAYLOR JAMES ALTON	GA	46W	34
TAYLOR JAMES EDWARD	IN	06E	58
TAYLOR JAMES EDWARD	FL	33W	35
TAYLOR JAMES ERWIN	NC	08W	57
TAYLOR JAMES GLENN	TN	02W	118
TAYLOR JAMES HARRY	CA	05W	109
TAYLOR JAMES LAWRENCE	WV	05E	135
TAYLOR JAMES OTIS	MO	43E	36
TAYLOR JAMES R	NJ	06E	111
TAYLOR JAMES RANDEL	MD	30W	16
TAYLOR JAMES ROBERT	FL	04E	105
TAYLOR JAMES TIMOTHY	OH	32E	13
TAYLOR JAMES WADE	NC	27W	91
TAYLOR JEROME MILTON	MI	17W	53
TAYLOR JERRY LEE	GA	01E	44
TAYLOR JERRY LEWIS	CA	31W	26
TAYLOR JESSE ALLEN	TX	25E	66
TAYLOR JESSE JUNIOR	CA	03E	96
TAYLOR JIMMIE ELLIS	GA	11E	106
TAYLOR JIMMY B	AL	06E	78
TAYLOR JOE KENNETH	TN	05E	62
TAYLOR JOHN FRANCIS	NC	28W	105
TAYLOR JOHN HENRY	TN	17W	89
TAYLOR JOHN LEWIS	LA	14W	113
TAYLOR JOHN RAYMOND	CA	23W	59
TAYLOR JOHN STEWART	CT	24W	62
TAYLOR JOHN VERNON JR	MO	29E	22
TAYLOR JOSEPH GORDON	VA	36W	87
TAYLOR KARL GORMAN	PA	37W	70
TAYLOR KEITH DEGERO	NV	56W	28
TAYLOR KENNA CLYDE	OH	07W	82
TAYLOR KENT CHILDS	UT	10W	44
TAYLOR KERRY LAMONT	MN	14W	56
TAYLOR LANDUS S JR	GA	23W	31
TAYLOR LARRY	OK	50W	21
TAYLOR LARRY DEAN	IL	10E	58
TAYLOR LARRY GENE	CA	07W	29
TAYLOR LARRY ROBERT	CO	02E	80
TAYLOR LEE CURTIS	MS	07W	104
TAYLOR LEE ROY	NC	23E	32
TAYLOR LEE ROY	KY	24E	45
TAYLOR LESTER KEITH JR	NE	12W	15
TAYLOR LOUIS ANTHONY	NJ	38W	40
TAYLOR LOUIS GAINES	NY	43E	36
TAYLOR LOUIS ROBERT	TN	01W	94
TAYLOR MARK ALLAN	MI	34W	62
TAYLOR MARK RANDALL	IN	03W	62
TAYLOR MARVIN JUSTIN	CA	18W	60
TAYLOR MICHAEL GEORGE	TX	28W	105
TAYLOR MICHAEL PATRICK	MD	32W	17
TAYLOR NEIL BROOKS	ME	02E	83
TAYLOR NORMAN ALFRED	GA	13W	17
TAYLOR ORIS CAMILLUS	PA	45E	43
TAYLOR PAUL CLIVE O	CA	04E	42
TAYLOR PHILIP CHARLES	NY	03W	56
TAYLOR PHILIP JOSEPH	MA	30W	33
TAYLOR PHILLIP EARL	NC	10E	115
TAYLOR PHILLIP EDWARD	MN	30W	50
TAYLOR PRESTON JR	SC	23W	48
TAYLOR RALPH LEE	MD	15W	30
TAYLOR RANDY LEE	DC	25E	9
TAYLOR RAY	TN	32E	24
TAYLOR RAYMOND NOVELL	MD	11W	89
TAYLOR RAYMOND RALPH JR	NY	13W	42
TAYLOR RICHARD ALLEN	MI	07W	94
TAYLOR RICHARD BERRY	NC	52W	32
TAYLOR RICHARD HENRY	PA	24E	46
TAYLOR RICHARD KENNETH	CA	61W	7
TAYLOR RICHARD LEE	OH	18E	43
TAYLOR ROBERT	NY	27E	22
TAYLOR ROBERT ALLEN	GA	18E	24
TAYLOR ROBERT DWIGHT	CA	30E	95
TAYLOR ROBERT ELWOOD	WV	05W	73
TAYLOR ROBERT EMERSON	MD	06E	8
TAYLOR ROBERT EUGENE	IN	12E	30
TAYLOR ROBERT HILDRETH	AL	37E	71
TAYLOR ROBERT L	GA	48E	13
TAYLOR ROBERT LEE JR	MO	43E	62
TAYLOR ROBERT LYMAN	FL	01E	42
TAYLOR ROBERT THOMAS	WV	25W	87
TAYLOR ROBERT THOMAS	RI	13W	65
TAYLOR ROBERT WAYNE	OR	08W	63
TAYLOR RODNEY ALAN	TX	11W	97
TAYLOR RODNEY EUGENE	NC	07W	38
TAYLOR RONALD BURTON	IL	49W	10
TAYLOR RONALD JAMES	SD	15W	46
TAYLOR RONALD LEE	OH	10E	122
TAYLOR ROYNALD EDWARD	GA	02E	89
TAYLOR RUDY RONNIE	CA	35W	67
TAYLOR RUSSELL ALLEN	WV	19W	123
TAYLOR SELVWYN RISHER	TX	29W	56
TAYLOR SHERMAN RAY	CA	04W	8
TAYLOR STANLEY EDWARD	VA	15W	80
TAYLOR STANLEY WADE	LA	02W	52
TAYLOR STEVEN EARL	OR	50E	2
TAYLOR STEVEN LESTER	IN	01W	89
TAYLOR STEVIE	AL	17W	59
TAYLOR TED JAMES	SC	03W	108
TAYLOR TERRY DEAN	IN	31W	41
TAYLOR TERRY LEE	PA	29W	56
TAYLOR THEODORE F JR	MD	05E	26
TAYLOR THEODORE JR	OH	33E	43
TAYLOR THOMAS EUGENE	WA	09W	45
TAYLOR THOMAS MARCELLUS	SC	16W	119
TAYLOR TOMMY LEE	SC	51E	3
TAYLOR TOMMY LEE	TN	55E	33
TAYLOR TYRONE	TN	31E	54
TAYLOR VINCENT ANDREW	NY	27W	42
TAYLOR WALTER JOSEPH JR	MS	06W	111
TAYLOR WALTER LEE JR	KS	11W	4
TAYLOR WALTER MINOR	TN	27W	104
TAYLOR WAYNE OLIVER	CA	26W	95
TAYLOR WENDELL	NC	06W	36
TAYLOR WENDELL GENE	TN	45E	16
TAYLOR WILLIAM A	WA	22E	86
TAYLOR WILLIAM DOUGLAS	CA	45W	23
TAYLOR WILLIAM EDWARD	FL	10E	11
TAYLOR WILLIAM EUGENE	MT	12W	37

NAME	STATE	PANEL NO.	LINE NO.
TAYLOR WILLIAM HENRY	NC	67E	3
TAYLOR WILLIAM JOHN III	MI	03E	104
TAYLOR WILLIAM KERRY	OH	03W	67
TAYLOR WILLIAM ROBERT	HI	49W	1
TAYLOR WILLIAM RUSSELL	KY	10E	52
TAZELAAR JAMES ALLEN	MI	08E	106
TCHAKIRIDES IRVING BURR	CT	49W	17
TEAGUE ALONZO ALLEN	KY	11E	99
TEAGUE BRUCE EDWARD	CA	61E	20
TEAGUE CHARLES E	TX	49W	49
TEAGUE JAMES ERLAN	AR	30E	34
TEAGUE JOHN WALTER	SC	07E	76
TEAGUE MICHAEL AUTREY	TX	54E	19
TEAGUE THOMAS NICKELL	WA	60E	4
TEAL FRED THOMAS	CA	23W	93
TEAL RAYMOND WILSON	FL	13W	121
TEAR GEORGE BERNARD	MI	21W	103
TEARL MARK FRANCIS	MD	16W	91
TEAS CLARENCE A	AR	06E	119
TEASLEY HENRY EZRA	PA	14E	25
TEASLEY ROBERT	NY	36W	8
TEATSWORTH GARREL LEE	IA	18E	55
TEBAULT BENJAMIN LEE	OR	01W	35
TEBBE RONALD JOE	IL	52W	17
TEBBETTS TERRY LEE	CA	52E	25
TEBOW WILLIAM JENNINGS	GA	02E	136
TECCO MICHAEL JAMES	OH	05W	7
TECHMEIR LARRY LESTER	WI	21W	121
TEDDS MERVYN DONALD	CA	25E	111
TEDESCO JAMES JOSEPH	IA	47E	37
TEDESCO LEONARD VITO	OH	22E	21
TEDFORD ROBERT CHARLES	MA	28W	15
TEDRICK WARREN GAMBIEL JR	AZ	43E	49
TEDROW DANIEL CLINE	ID	38W	79
TEEPLE WAYNE WINSTON	MI	30W	33
TEER WILLIAM EDWARD	SC	10E	94
TEETER GARY ALAN	MI	34E	1
TEETER HILBERT WALTER	IN	03W	10
TEETER KENNETH WARREN	NM	14E	39
TEETER NORMAN WADE	AR	22W	4
TEETER ROGER LYNN	NC	05W	13
TEETH AUSTIN	MT	26W	75
TEETOR JOHN HAROLD	OR	53E	42
TEEVENS RICHARD PAUL	MI	30E	11
TEFFS JAMES RICHARD	OK	07W	85
TEFFT GEORGE EDWARD	OK	07W	14
TEFTELLER GORDON RAY	AR	15E	110
TEGELMAN DALE FRANCIS	WI	23E	83
TEGLAS GEZA	DC	03E	1
TEGTMEIER LA VERN WILLIAM	NE	16W	41
TEGTMEIER LESLIE JON	IL	49W	33
TEICH DAVID LEE	MN	16W	76
TEJADA HENRY LEROY	NM	40W	5
TEJANO RICARDO ROBERT	WA	60W	22
TELA MOLIMAU ASOMALIU	CA	06E	111
TELFER ROBERT RAY	NY	09E	27
TELFORD JOHN WILLIAM	UT	25E	9
TELL BRITT JR	AR	07E	31
TELLEFSEN TIMOTHY MARTIN	MI	34W	11
TELLES PAUL GEORGE	CA	33W	29
TELLEZ DANIEL	TX	36W	8
TELLING JACK EDWIN	MI	25E	111
TELLIS ANDREW JESENEK	IL	33E	76
TELLIS WILLIAM JAMES	MI	50W	16
TELLO JOAQUIN RODRIGUEZ	TX	23W	26
TEMPLE KIRK IRWIN	OR	14W	109
TEMPLE LAMAR HAYES	TX	25E	3
TEMPLE MALONE BENNETT	NY	33W	52
TEMPLE THOMAS RICHARD	PA	11E	91
TEMPLES KENNETH RAY	FL	08E	63
TEMPLETON BILLY	GA	29E	63
TEMPLETON CLARENCE WAYNE	MO	11W	11
TEMPLETON DAVID LEE	WV	05W	12
TEMPLETON DONALD LEE	TN	43W	58
TEMPLETON GARY DALE	MI	53W	24
TEMPLETON JOHN ASHLEY	IL	51W	9
TEMPLETON RAYMOND WOODROW	CA	58W	29
TEMPLIN ERWIN BENARD JR	TX	04E	83
TEN HUSKIE YAZZIE B	AZ	37E	23
TENCZA ANTHONY JOHN	NJ	01E	11
TENHOFF TRACY STEPHEN	MN	12E	69

NAME	STATE	PANEL NO.	LINE NO.
TENNANT BYRON LEE	VA	31W	97
TENNANT JOHN RANDY	WV	31W	71
TENNANT WILLIAM ALLAN	MI	33W	59
TENNILL LARRY EARL	MO	04E	62
TENNIS THOMAS ROY	IL	14W	70
TENNISON ALVIN GENE	MN	14E	114
TENON JOHNNIE MERRITT	GA	06E	19
TENORIO JIMMY JOE	CA	19W	104
TENORIO RAFAEL GABRIEL	NM	21W	20
TENORIO SAM	NM	31E	2
TENSLEY CLYDE LEWIS	NC	08W	70
TEO FIATELE TAULAGO	67	03W	83
TERAN REFUGIO THOMAS	MI	11W	117
TEREJKO BENJAMIN JOHN JR	NY	38E	61
TERESINSKI JOSEPH ALVIN	WI	05W	82
TERHORST BERNARD REINHOLD	MN	26W	12
TERHUNE CHARLES PATRICK	IN	16E	82
TERHUNE DARYL BERT JR	LA	43E	36
TERLA LOTHAR GUSTAV T	PA	13W	101
TERLECKI WALTER ALEXANDER	CT	05E	50
TERMINI JAMES MICHAEL	MA	05E	77
TERRAZAS JUAN LUIS	CA	21W	91
TERRAZAS NICHOLAS E	TX	14E	102
TERRELL ALVA RAY	AZ	34W	54
TERRELL CALVIN LEE	KY	56W	29
TERRELL DAVID WILLIS	LA	08E	131
TERRELL EDDIE GEAN	IL	11W	97
TERRELL GORDON LEE	OR	55E	34
TERRELL JOHN WESLY	OH	30E	12
TERRELL KEAVIN LEE	LA	17W	32
TERRELL LEMUEL EBB	MS	26W	109
TERRELL LOUIS WAYNE	TX	16E	66
TERRELL ROBERT EARL	FL	52E	25
TERRELL WILLIAM LEE	GA	43E	36
TERRILL PHILIP BRADFORD	NY	04W	98
TERRONEZ DOMINGO MENDOZA	TX	44W	13
TERRY ALLEN LEE	TX	53E	24
TERRY ANCEL JAMES	KY	11W	71
TERRY ARIE	AL	53E	24
TERRY ARLIE	OH	43E	37
TERRY BILL HENRY JR	AL	21W	57
TERRY CHESTER H JR	MS	28W	94
TERRY CONDON HUNTER	TX	01E	24
TERRY CORNELIUS	MS	13W	66
TERRY DANIEL LEE	IN	21W	35
TERRY DELTON EUGENE	OK	24E	46
TERRY EDDIE THOMAS	GA	59W	28
TERRY FREDERICK G JR	NJ	53W	14
TERRY HOYLE JR	TN	46E	42
TERRY JAMES WILLIE	NJ	52E	25
TERRY JOHN FRANCIS JR	IL	28E	52
TERRY MARVIN HALL	CA	40E	14
TERRY MICHAEL DEAN	IN	17W	72
TERRY ORAL RAY	IL	54E	30
TERRY PATRICK WAYNE	GA	03W	5
TERRY PHILIP ALLEN	KY	37W	70
TERRY RALPH PAUL	KY	35W	62
TERRY ROBERT ISAAC III	TX	31E	42
TERRY ROBERT LOUIS	FL	05E	82
TERRY RONALD TERRANCE	NY	04E	116
TERRY RONNIE LEE	TX	38E	16
TERRY THOMAS L	WV	23E	8
TERRY TOMMY J	MI	15E	52
TERRY WILLIAM JAMES	AL	01W	80
TERSTEEGE PAUL FRANCIS	AZ	34W	72
TERWILLIGER DAVID WILLIAM	MI	06E	131
TERWILLIGER RODGER EDSON	CO	11E	78
TERWILLIGER VIRGIL BYRON	OH	16E	74
TESAURO JOHN APOLLO	MD	49W	50
TESCHENDORF RONNIE CARL	MN	06W	96
TESH DAVID MILTON	NC	08W	33
TESILLO ARMANDO	CA	04E	126
TESKE BERNARD ALBERT III	MN	07E	50
TESORO RICHARD RAMIREZ	HI	44E	62
TESSADRI JIMMY JOE	CO	46E	25
TESSARO MICHAEL JOHN	IL	35W	61
TESSIER LUCIEN CHARLES	NH	40E	32
TESSMAN CLARENCE CLEMENT	CA	01E	26
TESSMAN RICHARD CARL	CT	01W	80
TESSMER DAVID LEE	WI	23W	4
TESTA DONALD ANTHONY	NY	56E	32
TESTA RICHARD	NY	03E	62

NAME	STATE	PANEL NO.	LINE NO.
TESTORFF THOMAS EDWARD	MO	04W	57
TETER RANDALL KEITH	NM	15W	106
TETKOSKI LEON ANTHONY	NJ	11W	77
TETREAULT ROBERT NAZAIRE	MA	09E	13
TETTE JOHN BERNARD	NY	02E	62
TETTLETON DAVID DEWAYNE	AR	14W	30
TEUTSCH DAVID CHARLES	OH	29W	16
TEW JERRY EUGENE	IA	02W	55
TEWKSBURY JAMES LEE	MI	06E	73
TEWKSBURY ROBERT W	ME	31E	61
TEWS ERNEST WILLIAM	WI	26W	88
TEWS HENRY JAMES WILLIAM	ID	35W	7
TH-UOT HUBERT OWEN	MI	15E	123
THACKER FREDRICK ANTHONY	AR	02W	20
THACKER GRADY	GA	49E	49
THACKER JAMES	NY	20W	84
THACKERSON McCLURE	NC	18E	1
THACKERSON WALTER A JR	AL	07E	99
THACKREY WADE E JR	TX	39E	54
THADEN GARY DENNIS	CO	09W	120
THAIN HARRY LINDSAY	FL	01W	31
THALIN NEAL ROBERT	MA	21E	39
THAMES JAMES FRANKLIN	FL	05W	57
THANE ROBERT LEE	MI	17W	92
THARALDSON JEFFRY RAY	CA	48E	48
THARP ALEXANDER	NV	10E	51
THARP CLAUDE WILLIAM	KY	04E	79
THARP EARL WATSON JR	MO	09W	97
THARP GERALD LEROY	IL	29W	25
THARP HAROLD ALLEN JR	NM	49E	37
THARP JERRY DONALD	TX	02E	62
THARP PAUL ARNOLD	IN	09W	109
THARP TERRY EDWARD	MS	29W	49
THARPE SAMUEL CHARLES	VA	25W	112
THARRINGTON ROOSEVELT JR	NC	47E	56
THATCHER GARY DAVID	MT	14W	109
THATCHER THOMAS MILTON	MI	27E	7
THAXTON DAVID EDWARD	IL	31W	26
THAXTON JOHNNY R JR	GA	51W	45
THAYER JOHN MERL	OH	06W	6
THAYER THOMAS EDWARD JR	KY	03E	37
THEDFORD LUTHER JAMES	OH	47W	56
THEIS FREDDIE EDWARD	OH	20E	108
THEIS LAWRENCE WILLIAM	OH	10W	83
THEISEN GEORGE DANIEL	FL	13E	42
THEISEN JAMES ELMER	MN	21E	39
THEISEN WILLIAM ANTHONY	WI	15W	92
THELEN LE ROY EDMUND	WI	08W	5
THELEN ROBERT JOSEPH	MI	05W	130
THEMMEN MICHAEL JAMES	NV	21W	26
THEOBALD DAVID EDWARD	OH	30W	82
THEODORE J ATHAN	WA	44E	41
THERIAULT HARRY EVERETT	ME	25W	87
THERIAULT PAUL RAYMOND	MA	69E	3
THERIAULT SAMUEL SILVER	NH	30E	100
THERIOT PHILLIP FINNAN	LA	23W	93
THEURKAUF HARRY LEE	CA	60W	23
THEYERL CLAYTON JOSEPH	WI	41E	31
THIBAULT JAMES WILLIAM	MI	21W	110
THIBAULT JEFFERY ALLEN	NJ	57W	32
THIBAULT KENNETH M	MA	17E	94
THIBAULT RICHARD GARY	WA	25E	21
THIBEAULT FRANCIS JOHN	RI	28E	63
THIBEAULT GILBERT	CT	42E	10
THIBEAULT JOHN LORNIE	MA	03E	134
THIBODEAU DAVID PAUL	ME	51W	13
THIBODEAU WALLATE FRED	NY	20W	23
THIBODEAUX EDWARD JOSEPH	LA	40W	6
THIBODEAUX MICHAEL L	LA	08W	32
THIBOU ALLAN COURTNEY	NY	21W	103
THICK HOMER DANIEL	MI	21W	3
THIEL JOHN EDWARD	OH	31E	67
THIELE JOHN ARTHUR JR	FL	67W	5
THIELEN JOHN ROGER	CA	29W	74
THIELEN MICHAEL JOSEPH	FL	53W	24
THIELGES CHARLES THEODORE	NY	18W	35
THIEM WILLIAM RAYMOND	NE	38W	80
THIERY JOHN	CA	27W	67
THIESFELDT-COLLAZO WILLIAM J	PR	49W	27
THIEX RONALD CHARLES	WI	30W	33
THIGPEN WILLIAM HASSELL	NC	05W	51
THIGPEN WILLIE JUNIOR	FL	07W	48

NAME	STATE	PANEL NO.	LINE NO.
THIGPEN WILLIE LEE	MS	22E	3
THIMM JOSEPH MICHAEL	MI	04E	26
THIRKETTLE MICHAEL JOHN	CA	30E	95
THIROWAY PATRICK JAMES JR	PA	63E	15
THIRY SCOTT LOUIS	WI	28E	106
THODE LAWRENCE GREGORY	WA	12W	109
THOELE NICHOLAS EUGENE	IL	10W	92
THOENNES MICHAEL WALTER	KS	21E	19
THOMA CHARLES JOHN	WI	14E	18
THOMAN FLOYD NICKOLAS	MO	46E	25
THOMAN THEODORE VAIL	CA	27W	7
THOMAN TYRONE GARY	PA	29W	25
THOMAS AARON LEON	PA	12E	18
THOMAS ALGERNON PAUL	OH	17E	15
THOMAS ALLEN	OH	32W	84
THOMAS ALLEN WALKER	TX	39W	39
THOMAS ALLISON LEWIS JR	GA	26E	19
THOMAS ALTON JR	NJ	44E	2
THOMAS ANDREW JACKSON	CA	60W	6
THOMAS ANTHONY	MS	15E	12
THOMAS ARTHUR ISIAH	VA	29E	7
THOMAS ARTHUR WAYNE	FL	55W	31
THOMAS BARRY DON	CO	19E	54
THOMAS BENJAMIN ANDREW	MD	26E	4
THOMAS BERNARD MONROE	MN	17E	119
THOMAS BILLY DEAN	WV	30W	70
THOMAS BILLY LEE	OK	24W	108
THOMAS BRUCE EDWARD	KY	07W	90
THOMAS BRUCE MAYNARD	CT	34E	7
THOMAS CHARLES BLAKE	CA	56W	29
THOMAS CHARLES EDWARD	KY	06W	6
THOMAS CHARLES EDWARD JR	OH	13W	12
THOMAS CHARLES ELBERT	OK	20E	107
THOMAS CHARLES ELLIS	FL	26W	12
THOMAS CHARLES F IV	FL	04W	113
THOMAS CHARLES FRANKLIN	GA	35W	44
THOMAS CHARLES JR	LA	25W	88
THOMAS CHARLES WAYNE	IN	30W	50
THOMAS CHARLIE BERNARD	LA	48E	12
THOMAS CLYDE	TX	04W	52
THOMAS CLYDE EUGENE	OH	15W	8
THOMAS DALE DANIEL	OH	01E	60
THOMAS DANIEL	NY	45E	52
THOMAS DANIEL PATRICK JR	NY	23W	32
THOMAS DANIEL WAYNE	IA	03W	102
THOMAS DARWIN JOEL	CA	11E	75
THOMAS DAVID CARL	IN	47E	57
THOMAS DAVID EUGENE	MO	29E	17
THOMAS DAVID EUGENE	GA	31W	60
THOMAS DAVID GEORGE	MI	58E	16
THOMAS DAVID JOHN	TX	02E	62
THOMAS DAVID ROY	OH	49W	45
THOMAS DONALD LEROY	PA	24E	85
THOMAS DOUGLAS MCARTHUR	TX	14E	39
THOMAS EARL	OH	56W	29
THOMAS EARL WILLIAM JR	TX	36W	59
THOMAS EDGAR DURPHY	VA	03W	64
THOMAS ELMER WAYNE	TX	67W	5
THOMAS FRANK HERBERT JR	FL	17E	76
THOMAS FRED L	GA	10E	11
THOMAS FRED LOUIS JR	IN	31W	26
THOMAS FREDDIE LEE	OH	38E	40
THOMAS FREDDIE LEE JR	FL	29E	63
THOMAS GARY JOSEPH	MI	63E	3
THOMAS GEORGE DOLBRYN	VA	24W	26
THOMAS GEORGE JR	OH	62E	12
THOMAS GERALD LYNN	TX	33W	59
THOMAS GLENN WILLIAM	OH	27W	27
THOMAS GREEN	OH	10W	117
THOMAS GREGORY JOSEPH	PA	14W	37
THOMAS GREGORY WAYNE	NC	65E	2
THOMAS HARRY EUGENE	CA	02E	52
THOMAS HARRY JR	NY	59W	16
THOMAS HENRY BENNY	PA	07W	29
THOMAS HENRY EARL	MS	44E	2
THOMAS HOUSTON FRANKLIN	AR	33W	59
THOMAS HOWARD RAY JR	AL	29W	16
THOMAS ISAAC JR	FL	23W	107
THOMAS ISIAH	LA	46W	54
THOMAS JACK JR	SC	04E	126
THOMAS JACKSON	TN	14E	114
THOMAS JAMES CALVEN	AZ	47E	57

NAME	STATE	PANEL NO.	LINE NO.
THOMAS JAMES CARL	WV	13E	66
THOMAS JAMES EDWARD	TX	02E	105
THOMAS JAMES EDWARD JR	CA	14E	92
THOMAS JAMES ERNEST	NC	41E	74
THOMAS JAMES LAWRENCE	IL	62W	3
THOMAS JAMES LEON JR	IN	41W	55
THOMAS JAMES MYER	SC	32E	13
THOMAS JAMES OLIVER	IL	29E	45
THOMAS JAMES RICHARD	GA	25W	44
THOMAS JAMES RICHARD	FL	02W	72
THOMAS JAMES RONALD	LA	04W	131
THOMAS JAMES WELDON	NY	33W	18
THOMAS JERRY DENVER	IN	24W	22
THOMAS JERRY GALE	OH	02W	60
THOMAS JERRY LEE	TX	26E	20
THOMAS JERRY LYNN	OH	03W	69
THOMAS JERRY T	CA	22E	64
THOMAS JESS	FL	38E	62
THOMAS JIMMIE LEE	FL	20E	37
THOMAS JIMMY RAY	AL	62W	18
THOMAS JOE MINOR	OK	27E	7
THOMAS JOHN CHARLES	WA	09E	35
THOMAS JOHN CHARLES	MD	48W	35
THOMAS JOHN DAVID	FL	11W	15
THOMAS JOHN DERRAL	WV	40W	16
THOMAS JOHN HENRY JR	PA	06W	1
THOMAS JOHN JOSEPH	PA	19E	46
THOMAS JOHN RAYMOND	CA	37W	42
THOMAS JOHN WILLIAM	PA	04E	62
THOMAS JOHN WILLIE	NC	32W	84
THOMAS JOHNIE B	MI	36E	39
THOMAS JONATHON E JR	TX	14E	69
THOMAS JOSEPH EUGENE	MA	53W	40
THOMAS JOSEPH HAROLD	NY	42W	8
THOMAS JOSEPH MICHAEL	MI	09E	78
THOMAS JULIUS	TX	34E	39
THOMAS KENNETH BEN	CA	11W	93
THOMAS KENNETH DEANE JR	IL	07E	31
THOMAS KENNETH LEE	LA	45W	29
THOMAS KENNETH LEON	OR	48W	49
THOMAS L V JR	TX	06E	68
THOMAS LARRY BENJAMIN	AL	34W	11
THOMAS LARRY EDWARD	WI	24W	13
THOMAS LEE DANIEL	PA	30W	70
THOMAS LEO TARLTON JR	KY	02W	90
THOMAS LEONARD ALAN	NY	29E	86
THOMAS LEWIS MCCOY	TX	06E	114
THOMAS MARSHALL FLOYD	IL	17W	65
THOMAS MATTHEW ALONZO JR	TX	16W	94
THOMAS MELVIN RAY	MI	10W	48
THOMAS MICHAEL CLAIR	PA	11E	85
THOMAS MICHAEL DALE	WV	35W	73
THOMAS MICHAEL EDWARD	CA	52W	8
THOMAS MICHAEL FRANCIS	KY	12W	85
THOMAS MICHAEL HERMAN	AR	18W	88
THOMAS MICHAEL HOWARD	OK	34E	92
THOMAS MICHAEL JONES	NC	19W	35
THOMAS MICHAEL OLIVER	VA	20W	52
THOMAS MILTON HUMPHERY JR	PA	21E	85
THOMAS MONTE VERNON	CA	17E	15
THOMAS MORRIS E	NV	65W	2
THOMAS MURREL D	KY	01E	123
THOMAS NATHAN	GA	57W	32
THOMAS NATHANIEL	NY	14W	63
THOMAS NORMAN ARNOLD	NY	24E	46
THOMAS NORMAN EUGENE	IL	41E	13
THOMAS NORMAN EUGENE	OH	16W	91
THOMAS OSCAR LEE	FL	30E	95
THOMAS OSCAR LOW JR	FL	28E	58
THOMAS OTHEL	GA	18E	43
THOMAS PAUL EDWARD	KS	12W	99
THOMAS PEARLY JUNIOR	NC	39E	67
THOMAS RAYMOND BRUCE	PA	18W	44
THOMAS REGINALD MICHAEL	IL	13E	57
THOMAS RICHARD ALAN	CA	14W	21
THOMAS RICHARD GEORGE	OH	05E	28
THOMAS RICHARD LYNN	CA	07W	62
THOMAS ROBERT ERVIN JR	IL	02W	33
THOMAS ROBERT JAMES	FL	01W	95
THOMAS ROBERT JOHN	MD	20E	37
THOMAS ROBERT JOSEPH	MT	12W	15
THOMAS ROBERT LEE	TN	25W	1

NAME	STATE	PANEL NO.	LINE NO.
THOMAS ROBERT VIRGIL	OH	14E	89
THOMAS ROBERT WAYNE	OH	51W	28
THOMAS RONALD GENE	CO	21W	121
THOMAS RONALD MEDFORD II	ME	18E	5
THOMAS ROY EDWARD	AL	05E	8
THOMAS ROY STEPHEN	MT	25W	44
THOMAS RUDOLPH CALVIN	SC	05W	44
THOMAS RUFUS ALFONZO JR	CA	26E	94
THOMAS STEPHEN EVANS	KY	07E	37
THOMAS STEPHEN NEIL	NC	30E	67
THOMAS TENNYSON AARON	AL	37E	71
THOMAS TERENCE PIERCE	ID	44E	22
THOMAS THEODORE DAVE JR	TX	28E	31
THOMAS TIM	CA	39E	27
THOMAS TIMOTHY ARMA	CA	01W	88
THOMAS TOBY ARTHUR	MO	09W	87
THOMAS TOM MICHAEL	OH	46W	54
THOMAS TOMMY ROY	CA	17W	13
THOMAS WALTER REED	IL	15E	110
THOMAS WAYNE EARL	FL	47W	34
THOMAS WAYNE LEWIS	TX	31W	41
THOMAS WAYNE ROY	WI	22W	70
THOMAS WILLIAM ARCHABLE	WV	15E	52
THOMAS WILLIAM ARTHUR JR	PA	53E	42
THOMAS WILLIAM DEWAYNE	CA	39E	40
THOMAS WILLIAM HENRY JR	GA	12W	44
THOMAS WILLIAM MICHAEL	NM	33W	11
THOMAS WILLIAM PHILIP	WI	26W	104
THOMAS WILSON DECOSTA	VA	22W	55
THOMAS WILTON HERMAN	AL	39E	77
THOMAS WYATT STEPHEN	NY	39W	57
THOMASON JAMES CALVIN	TN	41E	1
THOMASON KENNETH ARTHUR	IA	04W	103
THOMPKINS MICHAEL LAROY	MO	04W	98
THOMPKINS RONALD WINSTON	MO	28W	54
THOMPSON ALBERT C	SC	25W	112
THOMPSON ALFRED L	NC	06E	68
THOMPSON BARRY ALLAN	MI	32E	33
THOMPSON BARRY NEAL	KY	21W	16
THOMPSON BENJAMIN A JR	AL	40W	35
THOMPSON BERNARD DAVID JR	CA	36E	39
THOMPSON BILLY ALBERT	PA	06E	133
THOMPSON BRUCE WAYNE	CA	30W	32
THOMPSON CALVIN EUGENE JR	NJ	15W	23
THOMPSON CARL	SC	25W	88
THOMPSON CARL ALLEN	MI	16W	77
THOMPSON CARL WAYNE	VA	02W	35
THOMPSON CARROLL U	SC	12E	57
THOMPSON CECIL TRUMAN	KS	14E	2
THOMPSON CHARLES CLAIR	CA	49E	26
THOMPSON CHARLES LEE	SC	04W	121
THOMPSON CHARLES MICHAEL	PA	43W	5
THOMPSON CHARLIE EARL	TX	16E	107
THOMPSON CHARLIE VANCE	NC	56W	29
THOMPSON DALE EARL	NV	23W	107
THOMPSON DALE EUGENE	IN	17W	104
THOMPSON DALLAS EUGENE	OH	25E	60
THOMPSON DANIEL FRANCIS	NJ	67E	3
THOMPSON DANNY STEWART	SC	46E	12
THOMPSON DAVID	NC	01E	42
THOMPSON DAVID BENTON	VA	15W	61
THOMPSON DAVID MATHEW	PA	01W	66
THOMPSON DENNIS EUGENE	CA	55W	39
THOMPSON DENNIS HUGH	MO	42E	58
THOMPSON DENNIS MICHAEL	WA	15E	70
THOMPSON DENNIS WAYNE	NJ	63E	2
THOMPSON DON CARTHAL JR	TX	28E	17
THOMPSON DONALD ARTHUR	IA	39W	68
THOMPSON DONALD BRUCE	TX	08W	1
THOMPSON DONALD EARL	NY	14E	120
THOMPSON DONALD R	CO	38E	16
THOMPSON DONALD WAYNE	IA	31E	26
THOMPSON DOUGLAS	OH	08W	112
THOMPSON DOUGLAS GERALD	NC	49E	6
THOMPSON EDGAR WAYNE	CA	26E	47
THOMPSON EVERETT BARL	WA	03E	101
THOMPSON EVERETTE ARTHUR	MI	09E	125
THOMPSON FARLEY DEE	AL	13E	76
THOMPSON FRANCIS JAMES	NY	14E	75
THOMPSON FRANCIS LLOYD	VT	23W	93
THOMPSON FRANK ALBERT	OK	18E	32
THOMPSON FREDDIE JR	LA	11W	26

NAME	STATE	PANEL NO.	LINE NO.
THOMPSON FREDERICK C JR	FL	24W	57
THOMPSON GEORGE JR	KY	04W	79
THOMPSON GEORGE RAY	OK	04E	14
THOMPSON GEORGE WINTON	WV	07E	63
THOMPSON GERALD RICHARD	OH	28W	5
THOMPSON GERALD RONALD	NJ	16E	25
THOMPSON GREGORY CARL	WA	08W	57
THOMPSON GREGORY MALCOLM	NV	20E	19
THOMPSON GROVER WILLIS	VA	35W	80
THOMPSON HARRY NATHANIEL	NY	23W	59
THOMPSON HARRY STEWART	IN	03E	134
THOMPSON HERBERT LEON	FL	28E	42
THOMPSON HOWARD MICHAEL	OH	54E	19
THOMPSON JAMES	WV	25E	94
THOMPSON JAMES EDWARD	NJ	05E	30
THOMPSON JAMES EDWARD	MO	33E	10
THOMPSON JAMES ESCOL	OH	04E	26
THOMPSON JAMES MICHAEL	MO	25W	112
THOMPSON JAMES PATRICK	WA	05W	109
THOMPSON JENNINGS MILROY	OH	19E	123
THOMPSON JEROME	DC	29E	77
THOMPSON JERRALD RICH	OH	08E	54
THOMPSON JERRY ELMER	NM	26W	80
THOMPSON JERRY LENWOOD	MA	10W	128
THOMPSON JIM ALLEN	OH	25W	33
THOMPSON JIMMIE MALCOLM	OR	37W	70
THOMPSON JIMMY LEE	MA	11W	107
THOMPSON JOHN BRYAN	NY	51E	13
THOMPSON JOHN CLYDE JR	NE	03W	130
THOMPSON JOHN FRANKLIN	WA	25W	88
THOMPSON JOHN H	LA	05E	3
THOMPSON JOHN KIRKLAND	VA	12E	113
THOMPSON JOHN L JR	NY	10W	119
THOMPSON JOHN LEE	FL	11W	4
THOMPSON JOHN MICHAEL	TX	42E	43
THOMPSON JOHN PATRICK	MD	59W	16
THOMPSON JOHN ROY	LA	08E	41
THOMPSON JOHN WALTER	MD	33E	33
THOMPSON JOHNNY WAYNE	IN	42W	24
THOMPSON JOSEPH DAVID	TX	19W	83
THOMPSON JOSEPH WAYNE	VA	25E	90
THOMPSON KARL LUDWIG	CO	04E	78
THOMPSON KENDALL WILLIAM	CA	60W	6
THOMPSON KENNETH DAVID	OH	49E	26
THOMPSON LAWRENCE CURTIS	NY	21E	85
THOMPSON LELAND HERBERT	OR	20E	37
THOMPSON LEONARD DEAN	WI	18E	89
THOMPSON LEONARD LUKE	MI	39W	71
THOMPSON LESLIE DALE	FL	30W	50
THOMPSON LOUIS KENNETH	CA	53W	24
THOMPSON LYLE JOHN	MN	30W	60
THOMPSON MELVIN CARL	GA	37E	72
THOMPSON MELVIN EUGENE	IA	38W	31
THOMPSON MICHAEL GUY	MI	55W	30
THOMPSON MICHAEL KELLY	MI	28W	5
THOMPSON MORGAN	FL	29W	50
THOMPSON MYRON	KY	49W	33
THOMPSON NATHANIEL	MO	30E	50
THOMPSON NATHANIEL ANTHON	OK	29E	77
THOMPSON NEIL STEWART	MI	42E	42
THOMPSON ODIS	MO	10E	27
THOMPSON OLIVER NATHAN	TN	16W	77
THOMPSON ONNIE JR	GA	38E	40
THOMPSON OTHAT	TX	04E	42
THOMPSON OTIS FRANKLIN	NJ	31E	31
THOMPSON PERRY EDDISON	LA	50W	3
THOMPSON PETER GARLAND	TX	40W	5
THOMPSON PHILIP BRUCE	KY	28W	5
THOMPSON RALPH LAYTON JR	DE	36E	61
THOMPSON RANDALL ALAN	OH	43W	7
THOMPSON RANDALL ALAN	IN	04W	78
THOMPSON RAYMOND MASSIE	VA	10E	45
THOMPSON RICHARD LEE	WA	12E	82
THOMPSON RICHARD LEWIS JR	AZ	29W	25
THOMPSON RICHARD MARTIN	CA	15W	34
THOMPSON RICHARD VICKERS	CA	14E	89
THOMPSON RICHARD W	KS	30E	34
THOMPSON ROBERT ACQUINN	GA	24E	97
THOMPSON ROBERT ALAN	CA	24W	56
THOMPSON ROBERT BRUCE	OR	51E	12
THOMPSON ROBERT CHARLES	NE	10W	30
THOMPSON ROBERT DEWEY	WV	20E	92
THOMPSON ROBERT EUGENE	KS	07E	27
THOMPSON ROBERT EUGENE	LA	21E	102
THOMPSON ROBERT EUGENE	CA	29W	94
THOMPSON ROBERT JAMES	CT	12W	109
THOMPSON ROBERT JR	CA	18E	1
THOMPSON ROBERT MICHAEL	WA	32E	83
THOMPSON ROBERT NOEL	OR	12W	27
THOMPSON ROBERT R	CA	48E	21
THOMPSON ROBERT RAYMOND	OH	50W	3
THOMPSON ROBERT VINCENT	NY	11W	97
THOMPSON ROGER ALLEN	TX	42E	25
THOMPSON ROGER DARRIEL	GA	20E	19
THOMPSON RONALD EUGENE	OK	35E	83
THOMPSON ROY EUGENE	TX	02W	137
THOMPSON RUDY MICHEL	OK	50E	34
THOMPSON RUSSELL LEE	TN	51E	3
THOMPSON SAMMY LEE	MO	03E	112
THOMPSON SAMUEL DWIGHT	MI	15E	2
THOMPSON SOLOMON EUGENE	AR	22W	83
THOMPSON STANLEY JAMES	MI	05E	1
THOMPSON STANLEY WENDELL	MN	28E	44
THOMPSON STEPHEN MICHAEL	MD	25W	105
THOMPSON TERRY LEE	OR	35W	44
THOMPSON TERRY NEIL	MS	26W	80
THOMPSON THELBERT K JR	IL	06E	123
THOMPSON THEODORE A JR	MA	44W	7
THOMPSON THERMALL	SC	43W	58
THOMPSON THOMAS DONALD JR	CA	30W	15
THOMPSON THOMAS MICHAEL	VA	22E	117
THOMPSON TIMOTHY JOSEPH	OH	06W	119
THOMPSON TOMMY RAY	OH	31E	27
THOMPSON TROY MILLER JR	NC	02E	95
THOMPSON TURNER L JR	OK	09E	43
THOMPSON VENEY EWELL	OK	13W	121
THOMPSON VICTOR HUGO III	TX	16E	87
THOMPSON WALTER LEE	CA	42E	25
THOMPSON WAYLAND KENT	TX	28E	17
THOMPSON WESLEY ROBERT	MN	15W	57
THOMPSON WILLIAM ARTHUR	AK	52W	20
THOMPSON WILLIAM BERNARD	NY	63E	19
THOMPSON WILLIAM DARRELL	FL	02W	80
THOMPSON WILLIAM DEWEY JR	CA	32E	6
THOMPSON WILLIAM F JR	MA	04W	74
THOMPSON WILLIAM FRANK	SC	24E	47
THOMPSON WILLIAM HOWARD	IL	15E	123
THOMPSON WILLIAM JAMES	TX	50W	46
THOMPSON WILLIAM JOSEPH	KS	34E	60
THOMPSON WILLIAM JOSEPH	FL	34W	54
THOMPSON WILLIAM MATT	NY	48E	36
THOMPSON WILLIAM NATHANIE	NC	06E	16
THOMPSON WILLIAM P JR	KY	28W	63
THOMPSON WILLIE RAY	TX	54W	4
THOMSEN GAIL WARD	WA	29E	45
THOMSON ROBERT BRIAN	CO	39E	67
THOMSON STUART HAROLD	WI	35E	63
THOMURE LARRY LEE	MO	25W	88
THONEN JAMES LEO	WV	14W	41
THONUES GUENTER ROBERT	CA	37W	48
THORESEN DONALD NELLIS	MI	34E	28
THORIK PAUL JR	CT	53E	24
THORMODSGARD ARVID PALMER	SD	04W	22
THORN CLIFTON CARDELL	TX	35W	1
THORN JOSEPH MEREL	NJ	62W	18
THORNBURG SCOTT WILLIAM	TN	23W	32
THORNBURG VINCENT ROBERT	CA	14W	99
THORNE CHARLES GORDON	NC	13W	6
THORNE JOSEF LLOYD	SD	01E	105
THORNE JOSEPH CLAYTON JR	MD	29W	64
THORNE KEVIN GARNER	OH	04W	10
THORNE LARRY ALAN	CT	02E	126
THORNE ROBERT WALTER	CO	04W	42
THORNE-THOMSEN CARL SPAUL	IL	28E	70
THORNELL EDMUND FRANCIS	CA	10E	85
THORNELL LESTER JEFFERSON	MS	06E	78
THORNELL RICHARD LLOYD	MI	16E	82
THORNHILL JOHN R III	VA	56E	32
THORNHILL WILLIAM JOHN	MD	23W	12
THORNHILL WILLIAM JOSEPH	NY	40E	15
THORNLEY REX EDWIN	CA	09W	46
THORNLOW GARY WILLIAM	NY	26W	16
THORNTON ALAN WAYNE	CA	29W	41
THORNTON CARL LEE	GA	02W	80
THORNTON CHARLES EDWARD	TX	09W	70
THORNTON CURTIS FRANCIS	NY	34W	29
THORNTON DAVID LESLIE	CA	39W	35
THORNTON DWIGHT JACKSON	GA	17W	118
THORNTON EVANS JEROME	LA	22W	70
THORNTON FRANK JR	GA	01E	52
THORNTON JAMES HOLMES	VA	03E	16
THORNTON JAMES VINCENT	PA	41E	31
THORNTON JOHN BRUCE	UT	39W	14
THORNTON JOHN THOMAS	MS	09W	30
THORNTON JOSEPH RAY	MS	37W	48
THORNTON KENNETH CHARLES	OH	06W	17
THORNTON KENNETH EUGENE	OH	12E	77
THORNTON LARRY C	ID	04E	38
THORNTON LARRY LEE	UT	54W	20
THORNTON LEO KEITH	NM	10E	51
THORNTON LEON	NC	20E	37
THORNTON LYNWOOD KEETON	GA	14W	41
THORNTON MATTHEW WINSTON	VA	35W	73
THORNTON ROBERT EDWARD	FL	25E	66
THORNTON RODNEY GARDNER	UT	11E	50
THORNTON STEPHEN H	NM	29E	98
THORNTON TERRY ALLEN	OK	15W	106
THORNTON TERRY LEE	IL	22W	28
THORNTON WILLIAM A JR	CA	36E	46
THORNTON WILLIAM D JR	NY	14E	93
THORP JOHN WILLIAM	NY	44W	7
THORPE DAVID ALBERT	NY	11E	41
THORPE DAVID LOUIS	CA	09E	119
THORPE DENNIS RAY	CA	50E	9
THORPE FRANCIS JOSEPH	MA	05W	41
THORPE FRANKLIN ROOSEVELT	NC	21E	109
THORPE FRED ROBERT	CA	17W	59
THORPE GARY WILFORD	UT	41E	5
THORPE WILLIAM DAVID	IA	07W	14
THORSON ERNEST LEROY	MN	11W	54
THORSON WALLACE R JR	MI	63E	19
THORSTEINSON VERNON JOSEP	NY	24E	104
THOTLAND JOHN ALFRED	MN	42E	1
THOUVENELL ARMAND RENE	CO	21E	16
THRASHER JOHN DOUGLAS	AZ	16W	32
THRASHER LARRY GLEN	TX	10E	96
THREADGILL DAVID ELLIS	TX	12E	39
THREATS GEORGE EDWARD	PA	09E	80
THREET HOWARD ANDREW	MO	56E	17
THREET PIERRE ANATOLE	NY	26E	94
THREET TROY TONY	OH	38E	73
THRESHER KENNETH EUGENE	WI	32E	53
THRIFT FRED LEWIS	AL	64W	17
THROCKMORTON GARY GRAY	NC	38W	62
THROWER FREDRICK LAMAR	AR	25E	111
THRUSH OLIN RICHARD	NY	11E	5
THRUSTON ROBERT READE III	VA	01E	77
THUET STEPHEN PAUL	MN	40E	48
THULIN DONALD FREDRICK	WA	17E	101
THUM RICHARD COBB	OH	38W	62
THUNMAN RICHARD GWINN	IL	35W	45
THURMAN CURTIS FRANK	MO	39E	78
THURMAN LARRY PRESTON	TX	30E	12
THURMAN RAYMOND DALE	OK	35W	23
THURMOND EDWARD SCOTT	GA	37E	72
THURMOND JAMES	OH	67W	6
THURNHAM JOHN BRENT	MI	22W	70
THURSBY RICHARD ALLEN	AZ	28W	106
THURSTON CLAIR HALL JR	ME	03E	37
THURSTON DANIEL TUCKER	PA	22W	9
THURSTON WESLEY GEORGE	NY	37E	46
TIBBETT CALVIN B	MO	01W	92
TIBBETTS BRUCE HAROLD	ME	22W	28
TIBBETTS CLINTON E	ME	20W	61
TIBBETTS DAVID RAMSEY	CA	19W	64
TIBBETTS GORDON EDMUND	ME	04W	81
TIBBS EUGENE COSTELLA	MD	44W	31
TICE EDWARD JOSEPH III	PA	18E	65
TICE FRED ROST	PA	02E	89
TICE GARY DALE	CA	52W	47
TICE JIMMIE RAY	TX	31W	74
TICE PAUL DOUGLAS	NY	11E	18
TICE WAYNE ARTAMUS	NM	38W	13
TICHENOR QUINN WILLIAM	KY	29E	63
TICHNELL KENNETH EUGENE	WV	39E	14
TIDERENCEL JOHN WERNER	CA	26W	36

NAME	STATE	PANEL NO.	LINE NO.
TIDERMAN JOHN MARK	KS	06E	35
TIDWELL DONNY GAY	TX	49E	37
TIDWELL EARL CARL E JR	TX	13W	12
TIDWELL ERICH LINWOOD	CA	18W	106
TIDWELL JOSEPH STANLEY	DE	05W	54
TIDWELL ROBERT PAUL	GA	26W	80
TIDWELL VOYD EUGENE	MI	42E	72
TIEFENTHALER JOSEPH THOMA	NJ	19E	114
TIEMAN EDWARD LEWIS	IL	20E	108
TIEMAN WILLIAM EDWARD	NJ	34E	1
TIENDA DANIEL	TX	06E	36
TIERNEY BRIAN EDWARD	CT	65E	2
TIERNEY KENNETH PETER	MI	10E	32
TIERNO JAMES	NY	32E	6
TIFFANY CLARENCE JAMES	PA	31E	7
TIFFANY DAVID L	CA	23W	12
TIFFANY JOHN MICHAEL	OK	55E	33
TIFFANY RAYMOND ELLIS	FL	34W	18
TIFFIN RAINFORD	CA	09E	54
TIFFT DANNY WILLIAM	OK	36W	42
TIGHE CHARLES JOSEPH	CA	18E	77
TIGHE JAMES EDWARD	MA	03W	47
TIGHE JOHN ROY	CA	20E	19
TIGHE RAYMOND HOWARD	CA	20E	50
TIGHE THOMAS DANIEL	CT	14W	24
TIGLAS THOMAS LEE	MI	13E	76
TIGNER JEFFREY SANDERS	CT	45W	3
TIGNER JOHN HENRY	GA	35E	83
TIGNER LEE MORROW	DC	01W	68
TIGUE PAUL EDWARD JR	PA	24E	98
TIJERINA ALBERT JR	TX	04W	15
TIJERINA ARTHUR CASTILLO	TX	58E	16
TIJERINA HOMERO ELIUD	TX	08E	131
TIJERINA JOSE BENIGNO	TX	17E	25
TILGHMAN BENJAMIN	MD	51W	45
TILGHMAN JIMMIE MACK	TX	27W	3
TILL JOHN JEREMIAH	WA	50W	28
TILL RALPH GARY	TX	11E	28
TILL WILLARD HAROLD JR	NC	26W	37
TILLEMAN PAUL ROBERT	MO	23W	79
TILLER ROBERT	AL	04E	95
TILLER WALTER LEON	FL	31E	31
TILLERY JERRY THOMAS	PA	37E	72
TILLERY RONALD DEAN	MO	19W	56
TILLEY HUBERT SAMUEL JR	NC	25W	55
TILLEY JAMES A	MI	34E	71
TILLINGHAST BRADLEY OLEN	CA	23E	65
TILLITSON STANLEY SCOTT	CA	02W	135
TILLMAN CECIL WAYNE	TN	29W	3
TILLMAN JOHN III	NC	42E	25
TILLMON WILLIE SANDFORD	GA	45E	43
TILLOTSON ROBERT VIRTUS	MT	52W	12
TILLOU JOHN FREDERICK JR	AZ	09W	10
TILLQUIST ROBERT ARNOLD	CT	03E	20
TILLSON GARDNER JR	MA	19E	75
TILSON LANE ABERHAM	NC	32E	41
TIMBERLAKE DWIGHT ELMER	MI	20E	79
TIMBOE ARTHUR RICHARD	CA	36E	62
TIMIAN FRANK EDWARD	NY	27W	68
TIMM DAVID WILLIAM	WI	48E	21
TIMMER AKKE JANS JR	IA	20W	105
TIMMERMAN ALLAN DAVID	IL	14E	13
TIMMERMAN PETER STEVEN	OR	32W	74
TIMMONS BOBBY DANIEL	SC	32W	84
TIMMONS BRUCE ALLAN	FL	12E	77
TIMMONS DENNIS EDWARD	CA	16W	68
TIMMONS EDWARD HUGH	CA	06E	94
TIMMONS JAMES MICHAEL	OH	39W	30
TIMMONS MICHAEL VINCENT	OH	04E	58
TIMMONS RICHARD RUSSELL	WI	08W	23
TIMMS ALFRED	NY	29E	69
TIMMS TERRY LYNN	OH	41W	63
TIMOTHY WAYNE ELLIOTT	CA	51W	45
TIMPA JOSEPH JR	NY	06E	111
TIMS ANDRE BARRY	NY	04W	64
TIMS FREDERICK HOWARD	MO	25E	26
TIMSON DAVID OLIVER	IL	37W	25
TINAJERO JOSE ANTONIO	TX	32E	36
TINDALL BRUCE GARLAND	AL	07W	3
TINDALL CORBIN CLARK	IA	27W	64
TINDELL JAMES FRANKLIN	FL	18E	27
TINDLE DANIEL WAYNE	MO	29W	16
TINE JOHN RICHARD	MD	26W	95
TINES FRANZ	NY	44W	33
TINGLE KENNETH WAYNE	CA	29E	55
TINGLE TOM KERMIT	MS	06E	96
TINGLEY JOHN CHARLES	ND	34E	26
TINGLEY PHILIP ALLISON JR	NY	33E	15
TINGLEY THOMAS JAMES	CT	33E	5
TINKER GARY LYNN	MI	20W	52
TINKER JOHN GREGG	IL	28E	94
TINKER NORMAN LEE	PA	35E	35
TINKO GEORGE DONALD	PA	32W	74
TINKUM ETHER ARNOLD	KS	44W	67
TINNEY DONALD WARREN JR	NY	11W	4
TINNEY JOHNNY MACK	TX	05W	89
TINNIN EUGENE SANFORD	TX	47W	13
TINO JOHN FRANCIS JR	CT	19E	1
TINSEY DAVID FREDERICK	MI	07W	108
TINSLEY FRANK DANIEL	NC	06W	82
TINSLEY FRANKLIN DENIS	NY	41W	21
TINSLEY JAMES E	MO	38E	82
TINSLEY RONALD ETHRIDGE	TX	09E	72
TINSON PAUL DRAKE	MD	37E	72
TIPPERY TERRY LEE	NE	35W	85
TIPPETS LENNY MAURICE	UT	11W	128
TIPPETT ALBERT ALLEN	NC	39E	40
TIPPING HENRY ALBERT	PA	54W	39
TIPSY HAYWOOD WADE JR	TN	26E	73
TIPTON CHARLES ROY	LA	16W	15
TIPTON FREDDIE LEON	TX	31W	27
TIPTON JAY C	KY	12E	110
TIPTON JOHN EDWARD	NJ	30W	8
TIPTON LYNWOOD AUSTIN	FL	16E	32
TIPTON MARTINIS GENE	OK	61W	6
TIPTON TIMOTHY TAYLOR	CA	26W	4
TIRADO DANIEL	NY	25W	19
TIRICO RICHARD LOUIS	NY	55W	16
TISCHLER HOMER ERICK	TX	09E	13
TISCHLER THOMAS JOSEPH	OH	26W	28
TISCORNIA JOHN JOSEPH	CA	29E	78
TISDALE DONALD WAYNE	VA	43E	49
TISDALE HENRY CARLOS	AL	06E	127
TISDALE LEON	NC	30W	82
TISDALL GARY DEAN	CA	53W	6
TISSIER RICHARD HENRY	NY	16E	5
TITCOMB ROBERT PAUL	NH	18W	63
TITMAS JAMES III	CA	24W	113
TITSWORTH CARREL JEAN	MO	42E	43
TITSWORTH KENNETH CARL	CA	15E	52
TITTLE WILLIAM EDWARD	FL	18W	29
TITUS CHARLES M	FL	14E	93
TITUS DONALD ROBERT	MD	43E	62
TITUS FIRMAN ANDREW	OH	29W	64
TITUS JAMES ELROY	OH	31W	59
TITUS KARL WILLIAM	NY	07W	108
TITUS TERRENCE RICHARD	OH	02E	8
TITUS TOUSSAINT LEO	TX	69E	3
TIVIS JOHNNY EARL	CA	05W	70
TIZZIO PASQUALE JOSEPH	NY	28E	32
TJERNBERG ROGER BLAKE	WA	14E	114
TOADVINE DENNIS ARRON	IL	44E	22
TOAL ALONZO R	PA	33E	60
TOBER PAUL HENRY	WI	31W	27
TOBEY MICHAEL JAMES	MA	42W	24
TOBIAS BILLY LEE	TX	21E	64
TOBIAS JOHN CHILICOTT	IN	09W	54
TOBIE DAVID CARL	MI	21W	122
TODARELLO FRANCIS VINCENT	NY	59W	16
TODD CARL EDWARD	SC	28W	41
TODD CARLOS FRANKLIN	AL	08W	9
TODD CHARLES MICHAEL	OH	12E	41
TODD FRANKLIN GODFEY	NY	05E	5
TODD FREDRICK WELTON	TX	31E	61
TODD GEORGE ALBERT	AZ	51W	22
TODD JEROME DEAN	KS	02W	25
TODD JIMMIE LESTER	KS	42E	1
TODD JOHN ANDREW	GA	01W	54
TODD JOHN CALVIN	IN	21W	86
TODD KENNETH WAYNE	KY	15W	116
TODD LARRY RICHARD	GA	52E	25
TODD ROBERT JACY	MA	19E	75
TODD ROBERT JAMES	CA	39W	5
TODD VERNON BERNARD	MO	12E	57
TODD WILLIAM ANTHONY	NY	02W	124
TODI JOHN ANTHONY	NY	17E	82
TODTENBIER JAMES LOUIS	KY	23W	93
TOENNIES NORMAN GEORGE	IL	13E	69
TOENYAN FRANCIS HENRY	MN	22E	86
TOEPRITZ RICHARD	IL	17E	109
TOFFERI CHARLES EHNSTROM	MA	11E	92
TOGNAZZINI MILFORD MARVIN	CA	20W	111
TOGNERI DANIEL ERNEST	NY	20E	11
TOIA MATAU JR	CA	60W	13
TOINS FRED	MI	02E	121
TOKARSKI STANLEY RICHARD	NY	17W	110
TOLBERT CLARENCE ORFIELD	OK	01W	89
TOLBERT DALE WILLIAM	OR	20E	50
TOLBERT DELANCY DU BARRY	NJ	19E	85
TOLBERT PAUL EDWARD	IN	03E	97
TOLBERT REGINALD GAY	AL	47W	34
TOLBERT RODERICK KENNETH	AL	09W	6
TOLEDO THOMAS AMBROSE	NM	04W	29
TOLENTINO CLARENCE	CA	56W	15
TOLER DAVID BRUCE	KY	07W	67
TOLER EDMOND RAY	NC	48W	9
TOLER JOSEPH BERNARD	DC	27W	7
TOLER RICHARD GEORGE	MI	04W	132
TOLER ROBERT WILBER JR	GA	06W	109
TOLER STANLEY GRAY	NC	10E	62
TOLESON THOMAS NORMAN	CA	17E	25
TOLETTE RICHARD ROSS	CA	50W	7
TOLIVER WILLIAM LEE	TX	21W	95
TOLLEFSON DWIGHT DUANE	MN	05E	110
TOLLESON LYNDOL EARL	TX	26E	32
TOLLETT ELIJAH GOAR JR	TN	04E	68
TOLLEY CALVIN COOLIDGE JR	VA	04E	116
TOLLEY EDWARD ROBERT	OH	25W	88
TOLLEY LEE G	VA	40E	69
TOLLEY MICHAEL	TN	43E	1
TOLLIVER JIMMY ELLISON	KY	39E	67
TOLLIVER LARRY LEE	MD	57E	34
TOLLIVER SAMUEL STANLEY	VA	03E	37
TOLLIVER THOMAS JAMES	MO	02E	89
TOLPA ROBERT RICHARD	MA	46W	9
TOLPAROFF ALEX ROBERT	CA	39E	27
TOLSMA RAYMOND EARL	AL	30W	17
TOLZMANN TED NORMAN	MA	12E	39
TOM GEORGE WILLIAM	TX	11W	61
TOMA RICHARD HISAO	HI	16E	25
TOMAKOSKI JAMES ROMAN	MI	06E	107
TOMALKA VINCENT MILO	OH	16E	87
TOMAS DAVID RAY	TX	08W	86
TOMASCHEK ARTHUR	PA	02W	7
TOMASEK MICHAEL JOSEPH	NY	26E	19
TOMASINI RICHARD E JR	CA	15E	101
TOMASKO DAMIAN THOMAS	PA	35W	41
TOMASOVIC STANLEY ROBERT	NY	11E	124
TOMASZEWSKI PHILIP PAUL	IN	17W	21
TOMASZEWSKI STANLEY JR	NY	23E	87
TOMASZEWSKI THOMAS DAVID	NY	17W	115
TOMASZEWSKI ZBIGNIEW JOHN	IL	65E	3
TOMBLIN TROY FRANKLIN	WV	15E	72
TOMCHESSON TEDDY JAMES	TX	55E	33
TOMCZAK THOMAS JAMES	WI	51W	46
TOMCZYK VICTOR DAVID	WI	33E	24
TOMEK GLEN DALE	MO	26W	5
TOMENY JOHN HAROLD	NJ	66E	1
TOMIKEL DAVID HAROLD	MD	34W	34
TOMKINS JOHN MICHAEL	CA	43E	64
TOMKO JOSEPH ANDREW	PA	21E	30
TOMLIN BARRY COLEY	AL	01W	23
TOMLIN CARL DELBERT JR	MI	02W	58
TOMLINSON CLEMMIE JAMES	GA	14E	54
TOMLINSON DAVID CULLEN	CA	52W	20
TOMLINSON DAVID MARLOW	CA	49E	27
TOMLINSON EDGAR LEE	KY	44W	42
TOMLINSON GARY PRESTON	AL	03W	99
TOMLINSON GERALD DOUGLAS	MI	14W	102
TOMLINSON JAMES HOWARD SR	FL	28E	101
TOMLINSON JAMES RICHARD	OK	43E	1
TOMLINSON JONES EUGENE	HI	49E	37
TOMLINSON MICHAEL JAMES	CA	26E	58
TOMLINSON ROBERT DALE	CA	41W	1
TOMON F RONALD	PA	59W	17
TOMPKINS ERNEST GALE	OH	05E	36

NAME	STATE	PANEL NO.	LINE NO.
TOMPKINS GLENN ALAN	IL	30W	34
TOMPKINS HAROLD	GA	49E	16
TOMPKINS HARVEY JOSEPH	IL	46E	42
TOMPKINS JAMES ERVIN	DC	17W	8
TOMPKINS PHILLIP WARREN	AZ	44W	60
TOMS DENNIS LEROY	MN	03E	106
TOMSIC MICHAEL PATRICK	CO	09W	35
TOMSIC THOMAS T	OH	15W	68
TONER LOUIS JOSEPH	PA	43E	37
TONEY WILLIE LEE	TX	45W	58
TONGEN GEORGE ELWOOD	ND	65E	3
TONGRET THOMAS EDWARD	OH	52E	12
TONI EUGENE J		07W	121
TONON JAMES ANTHONY	OH	17W	13
TONTI MARK EDWARD	OH	14W	44
TOOGOOD MANSFIELD M JR	DC	14E	81
TOOKE JOHN KARL	NJ	29E	36
TOOLE TERRY EDWARD	NY	23W	115
TOOLEY JAMES EDWARD	ID	13E	62
TOOLOOSE DALE LEROY	MO	02E	73
TOOMBS ALVIN CARNALL JR	VA	30W	8
TOOMBS WILLIAM HAYWARD	GA	22E	117
TOOMES WILLIS ALBERT	KS	43W	58
TOOMEY JOSEPH PATRICK	PA	49W	34
TOOMEY SAMUEL KAMU III	MO	37W	15
TOON JERRY WAYNE	KY	02E	52
TOONKEL BENJAMIN RICHARD	NY	45W	58
TOOPS FRANCIS IVAN	OH	02E	113
TOOTHAKER JAMES ALLAN	CO	10E	59
TOPHAM ROBERT WILLIAM JR	MA	32W	85
TOPOLINSKI DENNIS MICHAEL	MI	14W	45
TOPORCER ANDREW JAMES JR	NY	37W	2
TOPPI CHRISTOPHER JOHN	ME	35E	51
TOPPS RONNIE NEAL	IL	01W	90
TORBETT STEPHEN JUSTENE	TN	19W	42
TORCIVIA ANTHONY RICHARD	PA	39W	5
TORELLO CARL HARVEY	NY	04E	40
TORESON ROBERT WAYNE	CA	27W	104
TORGERSON BARRENT OTTO	WI	17W	129
TORI THOMAS JOSEPH	NY	28E	17
TORLIATT CHARLES PETER JR	CA	38E	62
TORO JOSE MIGUEL	NY	22W	109
TORPIE WILLIAM JAMES	NY	28W	41
TORRANCE FREDDY LEE	NY	09E	3
TORRE FRANCIS SAN NICOLAS	GM	40E	33
TORRE PASQUALE	NY	24W	62
TORRENCE JAMES EDWARD	PA	03W	40
TORRENCE WILLIE CHARLES	AR	38E	73
TORREROS JOSE	TX	29W	74
TORRES ANGELO	IL	17E	89
TORRES ANTHONY WILFRED	NJ	54E	41
TORRES ARCADIO	PR	09W	10
TORRES ARCADIO JR	CA	47W	34
TORRES DAVID	OR	20W	90
TORRES DAVID	CA	16W	91
TORRES ESTEVAN	KY	45E	61
TORRES EZEQUIEL JR	TX	16W	1
TORRES FERNANDO LUIS JR	NY	12E	31
TORRES FRANK CHICO JR	CA	19E	47
TORRES GILBERT GARCIA	TX	34W	1
TORRES HIGINIO RODRIGUEZ	CA	02W	9
TORRES IGNACIO JR	TX	30E	20
TORRES JESUS M	NY	23E	47
TORRES JOE D	TX	06W	107
TORRES JOSE	TX	05E	89
TORRES JOSE ENRIQUE	NY	43E	1
TORRES JUAN	TX	12E	69
TORRES LOUIS FERNDEZ	TX	16E	38
TORRES MANUEL PRIETO	CA	38E	42
TORRES MANUEL ROMERO	AZ	11W	56
TORRES MANUEL VEGA	WA	21E	99
TORRES MICHAEL ANGEL	CA	28W	30
TORRES PRISHARDO J T	GM	08E	78
TORRES RAMON HERNANDEZ	TX	30E	82
TORRES RAYMOND	CA	21W	95
TORRES REYNALDO LERMA JR	TX	59W	28
TORRES REYNALDO SANDOVAL	TX	23E	81
TORRES ROBERT	PA	37E	46
TORRES ROBERTO	NY	45W	29
TORRES SANTIAGO JR	NY	44E	2
TORRES SANTIAGO JR	NY	51W	15
TORRES VICTOR LUIS	NY	14E	46
TORRES VINCENT	NY	13E	115
TORRES-ACEVEDO JUVENCIO	PR	04E	52
TORRES-LOPEZ RIGOBERTO	PR	56W	10
TORRES-OYOLA ORLANDO	PR	08W	113
TORRES-RIVERA RAFAEL	PR	01E	102
TORRES-RODRIGUEZ JOSE R	PR	26W	95
TORRES-RODRIGUEZ JULIO A	PR	19E	33
TORRES-SERRANO LUIS	PR	20W	3
TORRESRAMOS REY FRANCISCO	PR	03W	66
TORREY RAYMOND D	NY	13E	56
TORREY STEVEN MICHAEL	IA	12W	99
TORREZ LAWRENCE DANIEL	WY	25E	111
TORREZ MANUEL ANTONIO	NM	15E	101
TORRINGTON THOMAS JACOB	MD	36E	40
TORSIELLO WAYNE LOUIS	NJ	11W	98
TORTORICI BRUCE	CA	48E	21
TORTORICI FRANK	NY	23W	80
TORZOK JOSEPH	PA	08E	24
TOSA ANTONIO TONY	NM	03W	133
TOSADO-HERNANDEZ VICTOR M	PR	10E	55
TOSCHI RICHARD WILLIAM	WA	24E	52
TOSCHIK MARK JOSEPH	AZ	08W	104
TOSH BRENT JOHN	FL	39E	54
TOSH JAMES C III	AL	19W	89
TOSH MICHAEL CLAY	IN	28E	63
TOSTENSON MICHAEL LEE	MN	37E	28
TOTCOFF DENNIS STEVEN	IL	54E	19
TOTH ANDREW JOSEPH JR	OH	04W	18
TOTH BERTALAN JAMES	CA	25W	89
TOTH DAVID McBRIDE	OH	28E	71
TOTH DONALD BONNEY	PA	01E	17
TOTH JOHN PAUL	OH	42E	2
TOTH ROBERT GENE	IN	50E	34
TOTH RONALD C	CO	26E	32
TOTH WILLIAM CHARLES	AZ	01E	69
TOTORA CHRIS ANTHONY	IL	28E	70
TOTTEN KENNETH ROMAINE JR	NY	47E	17
TOTTEN RANDY GENE	MI	07E	77
TOTTY DELBERT CHAN	CA	17E	82
TOUART FOSTER JEWELL G JR	VA	26E	19
TOUART JOHN ELLIOTT	AL	07W	74
TOUCHBERRY MILES D JR	SC	27W	68
TOUSEY GEARWIN PHILLIP	WI	41E	27
TOUSLEY GEORGE HENRY III	MO	02W	105
TOVAR ATILANO URIEGAS	CA	12W	23
TOVEY DONALD LEE	OR	21W	49
TOWARD RONALD JOSEPH	VA	27W	53
TOWATER JERALD RILEY	KY	06E	61
TOWE EDWARD SCOTT	NY	18E	99
TOWER KENNETH KEITH JR	IL	45W	3
TOWERY HERMAN	NC	01E	67
TOWLE GARY CHESTER	NH	24W	99
TOWLE JOHN CLINE	IL	11W	39
TOWNE PETER CLARK	CT	02E	62
TOWNE TERRY ALLEN	MI	41W	8
TOWNER ALLEN RAY	MI	14W	61
TOWNER JOHN GARTH	PA	04E	40
TOWNES LEROY	NY	50E	23
TOWNES MORTON ELMER JR	AL	14E	115
TOWNES ROBERT FRANCIS JR	MA	01W	54
TOWNLEY CYRIL HARRIS	NY	16W	72
TOWNLEY JAMES EDWARD SR	MI	15W	112
TOWNSEND BRUCE	FL	21E	110
TOWNSEND BURDETTE D JR	NY	01W	46
TOWNSEND CHARLES DWYNE	TX	32E	90
TOWNSEND CHARLES ROLAND	FL	12W	129
TOWNSEND CHESTER DAVIS	SC	01E	35
TOWNSEND DELMAS SHERWOOD	WV	08E	89
TOWNSEND FRANCIS WAYNE	TX	01W	66
TOWNSEND FRANKLIN ARTHUR	MI	57E	34
TOWNSEND GARY RAY	NY	42W	51
TOWNSEND GEORGE HARRY	PA	28E	32
TOWNSEND JAMES LEE	IN	24E	46
TOWNSEND JOHN A JR	NH	37W	43
TOWNSEND JONATHAN	MS	15W	20
TOWNSEND ROBERT FRANKLIN	MI	03E	20
TOWNSEND ROOSEVELT	AL	56W	16
TOWNSEND STEPHEN LANCE	CA	42W	24
TOWNSEND WILLIAM PAUL JR	CA	53E	42
TOWNSLEY STEVEN DOUGLAS	OH	61W	7
TOWNSLEY THOMAS EDWARD	NY	13E	118
TOWNSON ARTHUR CLARENCE	PA	58W	15
TOWSLEE EDWARD LAWRENCE	OH	48E	12
TOY GERALD OSCAR	CA	12E	128
TOYER LEE ARTHUR	AL	28E	47
TOYIAS CHARLES LESLIE	CA	41W	8
TOZER ELDON WILLIAM	MA	16W	103
TOZOUR MARVIN GEORGE	NJ	60E	4
TRAASETH LARRY DUANE	WI	32E	19
TRACY DOUGLAS LEE	MD	14E	83
TRACY GARY DALE	ME	02E	1
TRACY GERALD FRANCIS	MN	41E	31
TRACY JOHN LEO	IA	45W	10
TRACY JOHN WAYNE	OK	18W	112
TRACY JOHN WILLIAM	MN	42E	11
TRACY PATRICK	MI	13W	98
TRACY ROBERT LOUIS	DE	34E	72
TRAIL RANDELL GENE	KY	02E	136
TRAIL ROBERT HILL III	MD	31W	60
TRAIN STEVE WARREN	KS	12W	85
TRAIN WILLIAM FREW III	GA	01E	10
TRAINER DORRIS WAYNE	KY	12W	19
TRAINHAM JOHNNY WILLIAM	AL	16W	107
TRAINHAM THOMAS NEIL	LA	42W	8
TRAINOR PAUL WILLIAM	MA	49W	2
TRAINOR TERRY LEO	NM	44E	42
TRAMEL WALTER OTHO	MN	02E	89
TRAMELL DANIEL	CA	23E	114
TRAMMELL HARRY MICHAEL	OH	24W	80
TRAMMELL RODGER LEON	MO	07E	64
TRAMPSKI DONALD JOSEPH	IN	18W	98
TRANI FREDERICK EUGENE JR	NY	42W	24
TRANT STEVEN ALLEN	SD	01W	57
TRANTHAM DONALD RAY	CA	62W	18
TRANTHAM RAYMOND FARLEY	NC	63E	15
TRANTHAM VAN VERNON III	MS	24E	89
TRAPANI ANDREW	MI	16E	66
TRAPP BOBBY RAY	SC	56W	29
TRASK LEWIS ARTHUR	NV	27E	62
TRASTER RICHARD EUGENE	OR	45W	6
TRAUGHBER STEPHEN LEE	IN	26E	52
TRAVER CRAWFORD HENRY	MI	04W	93
TRAVER JOHN GROVE III	FL	04W	69
TRAVERS LOUIS WESLEY	FL	05W	58
TRAVERS WALLACE OLDHAM JR	MO	48W	49
TRAVIESO JOSE ANTONIO	NY	37E	72
TRAVIS DALLAS RAY	IN	52W	47
TRAVIS EDMUND BURKE	IN	22E	73
TRAVIS JAMES DAVID JR	TN	26E	58
TRAVIS JAMES LEONARD JR	KY	30E	67
TRAVIS JON PAUL	NY	04E	98
TRAVIS LYNN MICHAEL	AR	37E	73
TRAVIS MICHAEL RICHARD	KS	42E	43
TRAVIS MICHAEL WARREN	IN	59W	28
TRAVIS WILLIAM HARRY	MI	19E	101
TRAVNICEK EDWIN RAY	TX	08E	62
TRAW JIM SILAS	WA	58E	1
TRAXLER TOMMY JR	MS	10E	73
TRAYLOR FRED EDWARD	AL	22W	71
TRAYLOR JAMES DOUGLAS	NC	17W	104
TRAYLOR MARTHELL JR	MD	43W	10
TRAYLOR WAYNE MCKENNELY	AL	07E	50
TRAYNOR STEPHEN MICHAEL	MI	05W	78
TRBOVICH DAVID JOHN	PA	17W	82
TREADWAY KENNETH EARL	MI	28E	47
TREADWAY THOMAS CHARLES	TN	48W	3
TREADWAY WILLIAM MICHAEL	MI	19W	26
TREADWELL EUGENE DURWOOD	VT	37E	15
TREADWELL MILLARD LEON JR	GA	21E	53
TREAS RICHARD LEE	KS	47W	34
TREASURE ROBERT JOSEPH	CA	41W	67
TREAT FLOYD GENE	OK	24E	52
TRECINSKI LEON	IL	17W	59
TREDINNICK CHARLES NICHOL	PA	35E	63
TREECE JAMES ALLEN	TN	11E	59
TREEN HARLIN PERRY	OK	48W	4
TREESH JAMES M	IN	11W	93
TREEST NORMAN EUGENE	IL	23E	16
TREGRE LARRY PETER	LA	27W	89
TREIBLE THOMAS CHARLES	WI	24W	55
TREIBLEY KENNETH EUGENE	PA	26E	73
TREJO JOHN MICHAEL	CA	34W	11
TREJO JOSE MANUEL	TX	32W	2
TREJO JOSEPH JR	CA	23W	107

NAME	STATE	PANEL NO.	LINE NO.
TREJO MIGUEL	TX	02E	131
TREMAINE CURTIS LLEWELLYN	WI	21E	53
TREMAYNE JAMES RONALD	IL	18E	43
TREMBLAY ALAIN JOSEPH	NY	53W	40
TREMBLAY JAMES ALLAN	MD	50E	9
TREMBLAY PATRICK JOSEPH	NY	45E	16
TREMBLAY RICHARD	NJ	16E	42
TREMBLEY J FORREST GEORGE	WA	25E	26
TRENT ALAN ROBERT	OH	10W	37
TRENT JIMMIE EDWARD	OK	34W	30
TRENT LESLIE ROLAND	IL	15W	23
TRENT WILLIAM DERRILL	IL	57E	11
TRESCOTT CHARLES ROBERT	MI	07E	21
TRESSLER DANIEL ARK JR	DE	33W	45
TRESTER DAVID ALEXANDER	CA	05W	24
TREVARTON LARRY GEORGE	CO	52W	12
TREVATHAN ROBERT LEWIS	TN	50E	9
TREVINO CARLOS V	TX	44E	31
TREVINO ESTEBAN ANGEL JR	TX	25W	89
TREVINO FAUSTINO	TX	48E	12
TREVINO GREGORIO JR	TX	36W	8
TREVINO JUAN RAMON	CA	06E	61
TREVINO MANUEL VAILLIDO	TX	14E	65
TREVINO RODOLFO	TX	32E	7
TREVINO RUDOLPH ROBERT	IL	23W	34
TREVINO SAVAS ESCAMILLA	TX	23W	48
TREVISANO ANTHONY	MO	09E	30
TREWEEK CHARLES JOHN	WI	64W	2
TREZEK JERRY ALLEN	IL	44W	13
TRIANA SALVADOR PUGA	TX	23W	32
TRIBBETT LLOYD EUGENE	IN	57E	11
TRIBBLE PRESTON JR	GA	25W	89
TRICKER CHARLES RUPERT	CA	04W	11
TRICKEY JOE H JR	TX	12E	124
TRIDLE LEON PAUL	CA	07W	25
TRIER KENNETH ROBERT	NY	35E	35
TRIER ROBERT DOUGLAS	TN	04E	32
TRIEST LEON BUTLER	FL	11E	103
TRIEVEL CLYDE EDWARD JR	PA	05E	125
TRIGALET ROBERT ERNEST	OK	26W	104
TRIGG ROBERT CARL	KY	11W	26
TRIGGS FOSTER F	TX	01E	127
TRIGGS WAYMON LEON	TX	41W	43
TRIM JACK RILEY	MS	15E	101
TRIMBLE DENNIS ARTHUR	WA	19E	102
TRIMBLE JAMES MITCHELL	CA	48E	35
TRIMBLE LARRY ALLEN	WA	01W	1
TRIMBLE TOMMY LEE	TX	29W	25
TRIMM ARCHIE EDWARD	NY	09W	17
TRIMNAL GREGORY NEESE	NC	18W	12
TRINCHITELLA FRANCIS A	NY	15W	80
TRINKALA DAVID ALLEN	PA	25W	56
TRINKLER DICKIE DAVIS	MO	07E	43
TRIPLETT GORDON MARSHAL	WA	21E	7
TRIPLETT GRADY THOMAS	CA	01W	67
TRIPLETT JAMES MICHAEL	FL	27W	104
TRIPLETT JOHNNY RAY	SC	02E	41
TRIPLETT MARK LEON	IL	43W	43
TRIPLETT RALPH MORGAN	OH	09W	66
TRIPODO BENEDICT JOHN	NY	34W	68
TRIPP ALFRED LEONARD	RI	50W	10
TRIPP DENNIS ROBERT	CO	40W	35
TRIPP DONALD DELMORE	MA	19W	83
TRIPP PETER LEADBETTER	CT	30W	80
TRIPPLETT A W	IL	12E	92
TRISDALE ROBERT LEE	TN	26W	57
TRISKE RICHARD FRANK	ND	61W	17
TRISKO WALTER HENRY	NM	01W	92
TRISLER RICHARD LEE	CA	53W	31
TRISSELL WOODROW N JR	IN	21W	10
TRISTAN ALBERT FLORES	TX	09W	125
TRITICO MICHAEL JOSEPH	TX	07E	12
TRITSCH PHILIP ALON	CA	33W	11
TRITT JAMES FRANCIS	PA	23E	33
TRITTSCHUH GERALD F	OH	09E	101
TRIVELPIECE STEVE MAURICE	CA	48E	12
TRIVETTE JOHN THOMAS	NC	20E	93
TRIVISONNO ROBERT	NJ	39W	71
TRIZZA SAM RICHARD JR	OK	21E	39
TROCK THEODORE ALLEN	IL	18W	115
TRODDEN PATRICK JOHN	IL	17E	119
TROELSTRUP THOMAS LEE	CA	13E	111

NAME	STATE	PANEL NO.	LINE NO.
TROGDON RONALD GALE	NC	22E	22
TROGLEN JACKIE WAYNE	TN	24W	99
TROIANELLO CLEMENT JOSEPH	IL	08W	57
TROJAHN DARRELL CARL	NY	38E	16
TROLIA MICHAEL PATRICK	IL	46W	35
TROLLINGER JIMMY MICHAEL	TX	41E	56
TROMBETTA TONY	CA	54W	33
TROMBLEY MICHAEL LAWRENCE	MI	24E	70
TROMP WILLIAM LESLIE	MI	06E	120
TRONERUD STEPHEN LYLE	MN	35W	51
TRONNES ALVIN PHILLIP	MN	28E	94
TROSPER JACKIE EDWARD	KY	27E	34
TROTT DONALD HERMON	ME	17W	79
TROTTA FRANCIS JEFFREY	OH	07W	67
TROTTER DOUGLAS EARL	WA	02W	94
TROTTER PATRICK JOSEPH	IA	05W	78
TROTTER RICHARD BARRY	NY	42W	25
TROTTER SHELBY MILES	MO	21W	78
TROTTER THOMAS MICHAEL	IL	23W	40
TROUGHTON PHILLIP NIEL	MI	09E	84
TROUP RODRICK	GA	03W	124
TROUPE HERMAN LEE	AL	10E	18
TROUT BRADFORD LEE	IN	37E	73
TROUT MICHAEL RICHARD	OR	42W	8
TROUTT LOUIE JAY JR	MI	31W	86
TROVATO ROSS ANGELO	NY	03W	91
TROWBRIDGE DUSTIN COWLES	IL	15W	96
TROWER GARY RAY	KS	24W	50
TROXEL CHARLES LEONARD	KS	19W	52
TROXEL EDWIN NEWTON	OR	03W	122
TROXEL MARLON WADE	MN	29W	57
TROXELL DONALD RICHARD	OH	20E	126
TROXELL ROGER LEE	OH	35W	36
TROY PETER JOHN	MN	18W	57
TROYAN MICHAEL JOSEPH JR	MI	21W	122
TROYANO ROLAND DEAN	CA	05W	85
TROYE DANIEL ROBERT	IL	12W	53
TROYER JOHN MICHAEL	OH	13E	17
TROYER RODNEY PHILLIP	OK	38E	41
TRUANCE FRANCIS PATTON	PA	37W	26
TRUBE DELBERT LEROY JR	KS	05E	110
TRUCANO ALAN DALE	IL	49W	34
TRUDEAU ALBERT RAYMOND	WI	02W	52
TRUDEAU RAYMOND L	NH	09E	72
TRUE MALCOLM ROSCOE JR	FL	36W	66
TRUELOVE JAMES MELVIN	AL	27W	42
TRUELOVE JERRY ALLEN	AR	39W	63
TRUELOVE THOMAS WILLIAM	TN	02W	23
TRUELUCK GEORGE GUTHRIE	MI	09E	102
TRUESDALE CHARLES KENNETH	SC	13W	124
TRUESDALE LARRY LEE	OH	02E	90
TRUESDALE STANLEY E	CA	01E	21
TRUESDELL JOHN LEROY	OK	04W	62
TRUETT QUINCY HIGHTOWER	FL	34W	46
TRUETT WILLIAM RANDAL	OH	37E	1
TRUEX GLENN ELLSWORTH	NJ	19W	123
TRUGLIO ROBERT	NY	07W	120
TRUHLER BRUCE LEE	MN	52W	25
TRUITT JERRY BOB	MO	52E	1
TRUJILLO FELIX MARCIAL	CA	04W	104
TRUJILLO FRANCISCO M	CA	15W	19
TRUJILLO GABRIEL	NM	05W	110
TRUJILLO GARY LEON	CO	31E	7
TRUJILLO GREGORIO JR	NM	13E	13
TRUJILLO JACOB ROMO	AZ	49W	17
TRUJILLO JOSEPH FELIX	NM	10E	67
TRUJILLO PAUL	NM	02W	62
TRUJILLO RAYMOND ANTHONY	CA	02W	80
TRUJILLO RICHARD TOBY	UT	08E	19
TRUJILLO ROBERT STEVEN	NM	33E	76
TRUJILLO VICTOR DAVID	CO	47W	5
TRUJILLO WILLIAM OWEN	IN	52W	12
TRUJILLO-TRUJILLO ABRAHAM	PR	36W	24
TRUMBLAY LEONARD JAMES	IL	04W	110
TRUMBLE DARRELL LYNN	TX	48W	9
TRUNKHAHN PEKKA	WI	07E	66
TRUSHAW JAMES EDWARD	FL	26E	109
TRUSLEY JASPER H JR	WA	22W	9
TRUSSELL LARRY HUGH	OR	14W	91
TRUSSELL ROYCE WILLIAM JR	CA	15W	40
TRUSTY MICHAEL JEFFERSON	SC	18W	51
TRUSTY WILLIAM ROBERT JR	IL	41E	13

NAME	STATE	PANEL NO.	LINE NO.
TRYGG STANLEY HERBERT JR	IL	06W	61
TRYON FRED ALBERT JR	CA	04E	26
TRYON GARY PAUL	NY	35W	85
TRYON LEE JR	CA	20W	27
TRYPUS FRANK DONALD	PA	03E	102
TSCHAMBERS JOSEPH L	MO	02E	73
TSCHERTER VERNON S	MN	39E	40
TSCHUMI WILLIAM JOHN	CA	30E	82
TSCHUMPER ROBERT G	MN	28E	58
TSIROS ALEXANDER	OH	53E	24
TSIROVASILES PETER	MA	08E	1
TSOSIE ALBERT	AZ	08W	9
TSOSIE LEE DINO	AZ	50W	11
TUAZON SIMEON ANDRADE JR		28E	63
TUBB JAMES CALVIN JR	OR	04W	26
TUBBS EDWIN FRANKLIN	PA	35W	79
TUBBS GLENN ERNEST	TX	14W	31
TUBBY ROBERT WILLIAM	NY	24E	82
TUBRE STEPHEN RENIER	CA	45W	17
TUCCI ROBERT LEON	MI	16W	68
TUCH JIMMIE	TX	12E	71
TUCK HUBERT JR	TN	11E	89
TUCK JAMES WILLIAM JR	NC	33W	59
TUCKER ALVIN BERNARD	NC	12E	107
TUCKER ARTHUR L	IL	46E	60
TUCKER BARRY GLENN	OH	09W	66
TUCKER BOBBY DAN	TX	44E	42
TUCKER BYRON CLAIR	WI	48W	20
TUCKER CARL WESLEY	FL	10E	23
TUCKER CHARLES GILBERT	TN	01E	102
TUCKER DANNY EUGENE	WV	46E	1
TUCKER DARRELL LEE	WA	21W	72
TUCKER DAVID	SC	29E	7
TUCKER DAVID BRUCE	NY	27E	38
TUCKER DONNY LYNN	NC	07W	124
TUCKER EARNEST ALFRED JR	GA	07E	28
TUCKER EDWIN BYRON	MA	18E	82
TUCKER EUGENE	MS	19W	52
TUCKER GEORGE LESLIE JR	WV	09W	30
TUCKER GERALD ALEXANDER	MI	39E	14
TUCKER GREGORY CHARLES	CA	34W	73
TUCKER JAMES EDWARD JR	TX	05W	122
TUCKER JAMES ERIC	FL	31W	60
TUCKER JAMES HALE	OK	07E	2
TUCKER JAMES TAYLOR	MS	18W	126
TUCKER JEROME ERNIE	OH	21W	40
TUCKER JERRY JAMES	FL	25E	17
TUCKER JOE NATHAN	SC	13W	83
TUCKER KENNETH WAYNE	IA	05W	110
TUCKER MELVIN EUGENE	IL	07W	126
TUCKER MICHAEL RAYMOND	MI	25W	89
TUCKER OLLIE	GA	15E	12
TUCKER OTTO DALE	TX	16E	103
TUCKER RICHARD EUGENE	GA	04E	61
TUCKER ROBERT EUGENE	KS	06W	69
TUCKER THOMAS CECIL	TN	16E	32
TUCKER THOMAS EDWIN	MS	03E	63
TUCKER TIMOTHY MICHAEL	CO	02W	91
TUCKER TOMAS C	TN	16W	48
TUCKER VALENTINE	IL	51W	36
TUCKER WESLEY GRIFFIN	TX	33E	10
TUCKER WILLIAM EUGENE JR	MD	07E	21
TUCKER WILLIE JAMES	OH	10E	22
TUCKER WILLIE JR	NC	62W	17
TUCKER WILLIE ROBERT	KY	40W	27
TUELL DANIEL PAUL	ME	13E	15
TUELL ROBERT LEE III	OK	18W	115
TUELLER JAMES ALBERT	UT	36W	71
TUFF MICHAEL STEPHEN	CA	10W	3
TUFTS ROBERT BRUCE	NJ	22W	50
TUGGLE JACK DE WAYNE JR	FL	11W	19
TUGGLE LORENZO	GA	21W	67
TUHOLSKI GREGORY ALLEN	IN	31E	39
TUINSTRA DENNIS	WI	23W	49
TULL MARTIN NELSON	OK	20E	51
TULLER DENNIS J	CA	05E	28
TULLER ERIC LAWRENCE	MA	11W	43
TULLIER LONNIE JOSEPH	LA	48W	4
TULLIS JAMES CLEVELAND	MO	54W	38
TULLY ROBERT EDWARD	VA	56W	10
TULLY STEPHEN MEREDITH	KY	48W	36
TULLY WALTER BUSILL JR	NJ	30W	17

NAME	STATE	PANEL NO.	LINE NO.
TULLY WILLIAM BOYD	KY	01E	14
TULP GUYLER NEIL	NJ	26W	88
TUMINO JOHN JOSEPH	NY	07E	41
TUMMINIA GIOVANNINO	MS	06E	69
TUNALL STANLEY WILLIAM	CA	28E	77
TUNGATE DAVID JESSEE	IN	03E	134
TUNGATE NORMAN LEE	MI	25W	57
TUNICK FRANKLIN MICHAEL	NJ	11E	116
TUNISON GEORGE ROBERT	IL	40W	52
TUNNELL JOHN WALLACE	CA	08E	70
TUNNEY MICHAEL JOSEPH	LA	01E	13
TUNNY NICHOLAS RANDLE	IN	06W	41
TUNSTILL FRANK JR	CA	16E	116
TUOHY JACKIE ALLEN	AZ	26E	90
TURBERT FRANCIS XAVIER	MA	44E	11
TURBERVILLE CHARLES WAYNE	AL	02W	27
TURBITT RICHARD JOHN JR	IL	51E	14
TURCHI LOUIS	PA	11E	75
TURCOTTE DANIEL JOSEPH	MI	08W	45
TURCOTTE PETER RUDOLPH	MA	55E	33
TURCOTTE RALPH JEAN	CA	19E	75
TURIANO BENJAMIN ROBERT	NY	28W	30
TURK CHRISTOPHER HAROLD	OH	02W	107
TURK EDWIN FRANCIS JR	IL	22W	82
TURK JOHN GEOFFREY	CA	33E	43
TURK JON PETER	IL	28E	87
TURK JOSEPH MICHAEL	TX	45W	46
TURKSTRA ARTHUR JOHN	IL	42E	11
TURLEY CHARLES VAN	VA	08E	29
TURLEY MORVAN DARRELL	MO	14E	25
TURLEY RICHARD LYNN	IL	26W	58
TURN HENRY LON	TX	19E	41
TURNAGE EARNEST LEE	FL	22E	117
TURNAGE THOMAS ALFRED	AR	03E	37
TURNBOUGH CHARLES DANNIE	WA	25E	72
TURNBULL GARY ALLEN	CA	10W	16
TURNBULL JOSEPH PARKHILL	FL	40E	15
TURNBULL JUSTIN GLASTON	NY	45E	52
TURNBULL ROBERT CHESTER	NJ	38E	17
TURNER ALAN BRADFORD	CA	16W	93
TURNER ALFRED LEE	WA	16W	113
TURNER ANDERSON	AL	29E	78
TURNER ARTHUR JOSEPH	MN	15E	110
TURNER ARTHUR JR	SC	30E	50
TURNER ARTHUR TRAVIS	AR	58W	5
TURNER BERNARD EMERSON	LA	02E	26
TURNER BRENDAN XAVIER	NY	23W	80
TURNER CHARLES	TN	01W	4
TURNER CHARLES HERBERT JR	MD	54E	19
TURNER CHARLES WONDREWS	NY	11E	21
TURNER CLARENCE S III	TX	14W	35
TURNER CLAUDE TYLER	AL	04E	116
TURNER DANIEL ROBERT	MA	19W	57
TURNER DAVID LEE	AL	36E	40
TURNER DAVID ROBERT	CA	37W	70
TURNER DON ELDRIDGE	MA	37W	60
TURNER DONALD EUGENE	WA	43W	31
TURNER DONALD JOHN	MA	34W	54
TURNER EARL RALPH JR	FL	24W	35
TURNER EDDIE D	CA	28E	58
TURNER EDWARD PHILLIP JR	PA	42W	43
TURNER EUGENE	OK	03E	47
TURNER EUGENE	CA	46W	24
TURNER FREDDIE	LA	03W	97
TURNER FREDRICK RAY	OH	39W	30
TURNER GEORGE ALLEN	AL	12E	107
TURNER GILBERT CRAIG JR	ME	18W	51
TURNER HAYZELL CALVIN	MS	17E	15
TURNER JAMES EARL	KS	49W	27
TURNER JAMES EDDY	VA	23E	8
TURNER JAMES HENRY	OH	07W	124
TURNER JAMES LOUIS	CO	52E	25
TURNER JAMES MACK	GA	01W	107
TURNER JAMES PAUL	MI	33E	61
TURNER JEFFREY ARTHUR	CA	44E	22
TURNER JOHN HAROLD	KS	64E	9
TURNER JOHN MICHAEL	AZ	28W	54
TURNER JOHN RICHARD	NY	06E	27
TURNER JOHNNY CHARLES	TX	37W	78
TURNER JON ARNOLD	MN	16W	103
TURNER KELTON RENA	CA	01W	130
TURNER KENNETH EUGENE	ID	06E	133
TURNER KENNETH LEON	IL	27E	8
TURNER LARRY BURNS	NC	22E	51
TURNER LARRY EUGENE	OH	29E	44
TURNER LARRY THOMAS	AR	27W	60
TURNER LAWRENCE FRANK	FL	59E	14
TURNER LINDSAY CLINTON	SC	20W	128
TURNER LLOYD KENNETH	VA	38W	6
TURNER LOUIS G	AL	07E	66
TURNER MARCUS SHARPE JR	SC	15E	27
TURNER MERLE DEANE	MO	25E	112
TURNER MICHAEL BARRY	GA	40E	14
TURNER MICHAEL BRUCE	WI	58E	27
TURNER MICHAEL DENNIS	OH	37W	3
TURNER MICHAEL DENTIS	MO	23W	68
TURNER MICHAEL GLENN	OR	51E	26
TURNER MILAN ELLIOT	GA	49W	6
TURNER OTIS	TX	61W	8
TURNER PHILIP GERALD	GA	69E	3
TURNER PRESTON HARRY JR	NJ	21E	54
TURNER RANDY VAN	WA	17W	8
TURNER RAYMOND RIVERS	FL	18E	72
TURNER RICHARD	DC	62E	13
TURNER RICHARD EUGENE	OH	40W	60
TURNER RICHARD MATHIAS	OH	18W	107
TURNER ROBERT ALLAN	ME	20E	38
TURNER ROBERT ELDON	KS	25W	25
TURNER ROBERT JOSEPH	NC	32W	29
TURNER ROBERT LAWRENCE	SC	38E	82
TURNER RODNEY CARL	ID	16W	48
TURNER STANLEY	GA	24W	99
TURNER STEPHEN FREDRICK	FL	56W	30
TURNER THOMAS GAINES	MD	30W	97
TURNER THOMAS GEORGE	IL	53W	24
TURNER TONY RAY	TX	15W	33
TURNER VAN SYLVESTER JR	MS	14W	48
TURNER WILLIAM BRENT	OH	12W	105
TURNER WILLIAM COY	KY	20E	20
TURNER WILLIAM IRVIN JR	NC	52W	2
TURNER WILLIAM OLIVER	AL	42E	1
TURNER WILLIAM RICHARD JR	NY	43W	44
TURNER WILLIE GEORGE	NY	16W	71
TURNEY JAMES FRED	NC	60E	17
TURNHAM CLAY SAMUEL	MO	22E	93
TURONE NORMAN MICHAEL	IL	60W	23
TUROSE MICHAEL STEPHEN	OH	01W	74
TUROWSKI JOSEPH MARION JR	MD	09W	81
TURPIN GORDON JAMES JR	TN	19W	83
TURPIN RICHARD FLOYD III	MI	56E	17
TURRI CHARLES JOSEPH	OH	29W	26
TURSKEY HAROLD SEAN	IL	24E	89
TURSO DONALD ARTHUR	NY	24W	56
TURZILLI STEPHEN EDWARD	NY	23W	33
TUSKEY ROBERT WILLIAM SR	MN	41W	43
TUTEN MICHAEL HAMILTON	SC	46W	54
TUTEN RICHARD BAILEY	GA	27W	84
TUTHILL CARROLL LAVERNE	OH	08E	89
TUTHILL CHARLES PRESTON	NY	01E	31
TUTOR REX FRANKLIN	OH	39E	55
TUTTLE ALFRED JOSEPH	VT	02W	14
TUTTLE ARLEN CLIFTON	KY	03E	22
TUTTLE CLETUS DALE	IL	55W	24
TUTTLE ERVIN LEE	TX	13W	76
TUTTLE HERBERT LEROY JR	NY	58E	2
TUTTLE JAMES WALTER	TN	26W	80
TUTTLE KENNETH ALLEN	OH	35W	14
TUTTLE LAWRENCE KAY	IN	38E	41
TUTTLE McCREA BENEDICT	OH	44E	2
TUTTLE NELSON PAYNE	TX	08W	21
TUTTLE ROBERT ERVIN	TN	57E	11
TUYES DONALD GLENN	LA	38E	17
TWEED JAMES LEE	OH	26E	40
TWEEDLE KEVIN EDWARD	TX	32W	85
TWEEDY STUART KING	PA	04E	27
TWEEDY VERNON RUBEN	LA	43E	11
TWEHOUS GENE LEANDER	NE	26E	86
TWIGG JOSEPH RICHARD JR	MD	35W	1
TWIGG MICHAEL WILLIAM	PA	17E	47
TWING ROBERT ANTHONY	IL	13E	30
TWINN LOUIS BELL SR	TX	04E	47
TWIST ROBERT JAMES	MD	46W	35
TWITTY DANIEL RAY	CA	48E	36
TWO CROW@ BLAIR WILLIAM	SD	37W	43
TWOEAGLE GABRIEL LAWRENCE	SD	04W	133
TWOMEY RAYMOND LEE	FL	18E	82
TWOREK GERALD JOHN	NY	05W	90
TWOREK JOHN RENFIELD	OR	44E	1
TWYFORD THOMAS LIONEL	CA	53E	7
TYCZ JAMES NEIL	WI	19E	88
TYE MICHAEL JAMES	MO	17W	32
TYES ROBERT LEE	CA	54W	19
TYLER ADOLPHUS NORWOOD	MD	19W	90
TYLER ALLAN ROBERT	IL	39W	19
TYLER ALLEN	VA	25W	26
TYLER EARTHELL	SC	03E	96
TYLER EDWARD	OK	58E	1
TYLER ERNEST KENNETH	TX	03W	78
TYLER GEORGE EDWARD	MI	40W	31
TYLER JESSIE JAMES	SC	20W	116
TYLER JOHN DEVON	VA	09E	53
TYLER LARRY JEROME	TX	49W	34
TYLER LARRY JOSH	CA	41E	32
TYLER LESTER	NY	30E	51
TYLER MARK DENNIS	MI	57W	33
TYLER MITCHEL RAY	TX	38W	48
TYLER SYLVESTER GEORGE	DC	62E	13
TYLER WILLIE	MS	15E	130
TYMESON RAYMOND W JR	NY	37W	22
TYNDALL JOHN HARVEY JR	NC	18E	20
TYNE JEFFREY GORDON	MA	07E	123
TYNER JAMES ANTHONY	OK	11W	10
TYNER JAMES DANIEL	MS	12E	69
TYNER JAMES PHILEMON	SC	04E	59
TYNER ROBERT EMMETT	FL	40E	33
TYNER ROGER MARTIN	NC	31W	27
TYNES EARL KENNETH	FL	07E	123
TYNES GREGORY ALLAN	FL	04W	127
TYNES REGINALD BERNARD	VA	57W	33
TYNES WILBERT A JR	VA	26E	94
TYPE WALTER JOHN JR	FL	07E	4
TYRCZ WALTER FREDRICK JR	NY	44E	54
TYREE EARL EDWARD	MA	32E	47
TYREE WILLIAM EVERETT	VA	21E	82
TYRELL THOMAS JUDD	CT	28W	95
TYRKA PETER STEVEN	IL	44W	20
TYRON WILLIAM DAVID	MO	27W	14
TYRONE WILLIE DONALD	TX	01E	128
TYRRELL JOHN FRANKLIN	OH	39E	41
TYRRELL WALTER RIPLEY	NY	33W	82
TYSON CHARLES FLOYD III	FL	22W	110
TYSON CLIFFORD EARL	WA	53E	8
TYSON DENNIS LEE	IN	44W	13
TYSON HAROLD RAY	GA	32W	40
TYSON LARRY PRESTON	TX	42E	11
TYSON STUART HANCKEL	VA	23W	107
TYSZKA EDWARD MICHAEL	CT	35W	74
TYSZKIEWICZ ARTHUR KASIMI	TX	14E	30
TYUS JAMES DREWERY JR	GA	31W	27
U REN FRED THOMPSON	MI	61E	20
UBERMAN RODNEY RAY	TX	12W	15
UCKER DAVID JOHN	CA	27E	92
UDELL EDGAR JOHN	OR	32E	60
UDELL MARK FOSTER	TN	07E	87
UDING STANLEY ROY	CA	27E	56
UEBLER ROY NICHOLAS JR	MI	51W	46
UECKER DAVID ARNOLD	MN	36W	82
UELI PENI	CA	04E	75
UFFORD ROBERT LYNN	UT	14W	102
UGARTE CARLOS	NY	15E	2
UGELSTAD BRUCE ALLEN	MN	16W	1
UGINO JOHN JOSEPH	NY	34E	1
UGLAND DAVID LEONARD	MN	03E	38
UHL RAYMOND RIEDE	CO	09W	44
UHL ROBERT DALE	CA	04W	15
UHL THOMAS FRANCIS	NY	28E	87
UHLER GORDON ROBERT	OH	01W	50
UHLIG MICHAEL STEVEN	CA	15E	52
UHLMANSIEK RALPH EDWARD	OH	21E	92
UHLS WILLIS GRANT	SD	05W	98
UHREN BERNARD JEFFERY	MT	42W	60
ULBRICH JOHN HAROLD	MI	58W	4
ULFERS JOHN BURDETTE	IA	38W	80
ULI SASA	HI	22W	61
ULIBARRI EDWARD ANTHONY	CA	17W	24
ULICNI JOHN	MI	08W	30

NAME	STATE	PANEL NO.	LINE NO.
ULLBERG VICTOR VANCE	OR	15E	87
ULLMER WILLIAM ARTHUR JR	CA	19E	123
ULLOA HUGO HECTOR	TX	23W	80
ULLOA MANUEL GURROLA	CA	33W	90
ULM DOUGLAS RAYMOND	OR	09W	3
ULMAN EDWARD DELBERT	MI	51E	14
ULMER DAVID JOSEPH	MS	39W	24
ULMER HOWARD D JR	GA	11E	42
ULMER JAN ALAN	VT	50E	42
ULREY KESTER	VA	37E	28
ULRICH GEORGE HENRY	NY	27E	32
ULRICH JAMES CRAIG	OH	15E	26
ULRICH JAYSON FRED	WI	19W	57
ULRICH RAY LEONARD	PA	23W	49
ULRICKSON PETER EDWARD	MI	21W	91
ULSTAD DENNIS ELMER	MT	34W	89
UMBENHAUER DALE E	PA	07E	77
UMDENSTOCK MICHAEL LANE	OK	49W	6
UMEL MICHAEL PETER	ME	49E	16
UMHOLTZ DARRELL RAYMOND	VA	42E	11
UMSTOT CLARENCE EDWARD	MD	11W	26
UMSTOT SAMUEL GILMORE JR	WV	44W	42
UNCAPHER VALENTINE DANIEL	IN	24E	115
UNCKRICH WILLIAM F	OH	17W	65
UNDERDOWN GEORGE MICHAEL	NY	12W	76
UNDERHILL BENJAMIN S	TN	39E	55
UNDERHILL DAVID J	VT	06E	122
UNDERWOOD ANDREW FILLEBRO	TX	01W	38
UNDERWOOD BILLY LOUIS	NC	31W	27
UNDERWOOD DANIEL LEDARE	AL	61E	20
UNDERWOOD EUGENE	IL	10E	126
UNDERWOOD FRANKLIN W JR	MD	21W	3
UNDERWOOD GEORGE WARREN	MA	01E	59
UNDERWOOD HARRY EDWARD	VA	16W	42
UNDERWOOD HARRY WILLIAM	MO	44W	60
UNDERWOOD JACKIE SHIRL	TN	39W	69
UNDERWOOD JAMES EDWARD	MT	01E	120
UNDERWOOD JERRY DWAYNE	KY	02E	90
UNDERWOOD KENNETH FRANK	NC	15E	92
UNDERWOOD PAUL GERARD	NY	06E	16
UNDERWOOD PERRY LUKE	WA	21W	4
UNDERWOOD ROBERT STEPHEN	MO	47W	56
UNDERWOOD RONALD EUGENE	FL	09W	74
UNDERWOOD THOMAS WAYNE	OH	12W	30
UNDERWOOD WATSON JR	WV	47E	44
UNDERWOOD WILLIAM HENRY J	CA	38E	62
UNFRIED BARRY LON	CA	23W	49
UNGARO DOMINIC JR	FL	55W	39
UNGER DON LEE	FL	01W	13
UNGER LESTER EUGENE JR	OH	12E	107
UNGERECHT RICHARD ALFRED	MN	07E	88
UNRUE ROBERT DANIEL	VA	10W	62
UNRUH JAMES HOWARD	PA	10W	128
UNSINN MICHAEL JOSEPH	WI	35W	30
UNZICKER GREGORY DEAN	MO	08W	24
UPCHURCH JAMES GLENN	OK	28W	41
UPCHURCH RODNEY CLEVELAND	CA	09E	89
UPCHURCH WILLIAM HARDY JR	NC	26E	98
UPLINGER BARTON JOHN	CA	40E	33
UPLINGER GARRY LYNN	OH	24W	50
UPNER EDWARD CHARLES	AL	03E	134
UPP JEFF HAROLD	IN	22W	51
UPRIGHT BRIAN DALE	PA	07W	112
UPRIGHT EDWIN FRANCIS	NY	24E	75
UPRIGHT RUSSELL EDWARD	CA	16W	77
UPSHAW OLEN LEE	AR	07W	110
UPTAIN DAVIS	AL	03E	38
UPTIGROVE JESSE	LA	21W	86
UPTON CARLETON WEBSTER	MA	01E	46
UPTON DANIEL CARL	IA	08W	112
UPTON STEPHEN LOUIS	RI	23W	12
UR STANLEY EUGENE	GA	31W	97
URBAN ALEXANDER JOHN JR	MI	21W	96
URBAN DAVID LEE	OH	37W	34
URBAN JOHN ROBERT	MT	01E	87
URBAN PAUL RICHARD JR	WV	40E	48
URBAN RICHARD EDWARD	CT	50W	28
URBAN ROBERT LEE	KS	41W	33
URBANCZYK JOSEPH MICHAEL	NY	29W	33
URBANI ROGER STANLEY	VA	06W	66
URBANIAK EDWARD	IL	29E	78
URBANOVSKY ROBERT EUGENE	TX	06E	46

NAME	STATE	PANEL NO.	LINE NO.
URBANSKI RONALD MICHAEL	PA	40E	49
URBAS STANLEY FRANK	WI	34W	89
URBASSIK ROBERT JOHN	OH	10W	67
URBELIS JOHN EDWARD	IN	40W	69
URDIALES ALFRED JR	IL	38E	17
URDIALES CHARLES A JR	IL	60E	4
URDIALEZ RUBEN	TX	22W	50
URIAS DAVID SOQUI	AZ	51E	26
URIBE EDWARD ANTHONY	CA	11E	34
URICK JOHN WILLIAM	VA	19E	34
URMANN JOSEPH HERMAN	PA	21E	101
URNES JAMES LEE	CA	25W	3
URQUHART GLENN ROSS JR	MI	33W	70
URQUHART PAUL DEAN	PA	03W	57
URQUHART THOMAS	NY	13W	125
URRABAZO HOMER	CA	15E	76
URRUTIA ANTHONY JOHN	NY	28W	64
URSERY MICHAEL TERRY	TX	21E	116
URSIN WILLIAM NORMAND	CT	48W	20
USHER FREDDIE	GA	31W	74
USHER TERRY MAXWELL	WA	04W	1
USILTON JOHN CLANNAHAN	PA	21W	110
USSERY CARL RICHARD	MO	42W	37
USSERY MICHAEL MONROE	OH	10W	8
USZAKOW JEAN	NC	11E	9
UTECHT ROBERT STEPHEN	IL	09W	117
UTEGAARD THOMAS HAROLD	WI	22W	44
UTHEMANN ROBERT ERICK	WI	09W	11
UTLEY DAVID WAYNE	MO	05E	63
UTLEY MICHAEL LEWIS	MO	15E	77
UTLEY RUSSEL KEITH	CA	34W	90
UTRIAINEN GARY ALBERT	MI	09W	46
UTTER JAMES ROBERT	IN	18E	32
UTTER KEITH EDWARD	MT	08W	19
UTTER MICHAEL JOSEPH	IA	30E	60
UTTER THOMAS DUANE	IL	17E	32
UTTERMARK JAMES FREDERIC	MN	31W	28
UTTS WILLIAM WARNER	NE	29W	85
UTZ GARY DOUGLAS	OH	45E	31
UUTELA DERRIS LEE	MN	60W	23
UYESAKA ROBERT JOSEPH	CA	47W	56
UZZELL FRANK NELSON	TN	35E	51
VACENOVSKY DENNIS EDWARD	FL	07W	114
VACHON WILBUR JOSEPH III	ME	20W	12
VACZI ALEX E	MI	05E	8
VAD HENRY JOSEPH	NY	16W	41
VADAKIN DONALD KEITH	OH	36W	8
VADBUNKER JAMES PATRICK	IL	16E	88
VADEN ROBERT LEE	CO	06E	114
VADEN ROBERT WILLIAM	MD	33E	76
VADEN WILLIAM KENNETH JR	TX	06W	46
VADEN WOODROW WILSON	TN	01E	76
VADIRODRIGUEZ ALBERTO	PR	02W	116
VAGNONE MICHAEL JOHN	CT	11W	23
VAGNONE RICHARD BERNARD	CA	19E	41
VAICKUS ANTHONY JOSEPH JR	IL	28E	32
VAIL THOMAS EARL	WI	08W	33
VAIL WALTER WILBER	NC	42E	1
VAILLANCOURT EDWARD JOHN	RI	13W	69
VALADEZ RICHARD PAUL	CA	23W	93
VALADEZ TIMMY	CA	17W	18
VALANDINGHAM EVERETT JOSE	TX	43E	1
VALASQUEZ PETE ANTHONY	CO	04E	16
VALDEZ ALFRED	CA	40E	33
VALDEZ DANIEL VIRAMONTES	CA	22E	47
VALDEZ DAVID MEDINA	CA	20W	103
VALDEZ FERNANDO MARCELO	HI	50W	16
VALDEZ FRANCIS PEDRO	WI	09W	25
VALDEZ FRANCISCO NEVARES	IN	05W	122
VALDEZ FRANK	NM	16E	116
VALDEZ GREGORIO JR	TX	04E	121
VALDEZ ISMAEL JOSE JR	CA	54E	20
VALDEZ JOHN BEN	CO	19W	35
VALDEZ JUAN PEDRO	CO	49E	48
VALDEZ LEROY EDWARD	FL	37E	1
VALDEZ LEROY FRANK	NM	58E	25
VALDEZ MODESTO	AZ	43W	67
VALDEZ PHIL ISADORE	NM	14E	97
VALDEZ RODOLFO	TX	02W	3
VALE CHARLES	FL	23W	60
VALE TONY	TX	03E	116
VALENCIA AMADO ACOSTA	TX	24W	22

NAME	STATE	PANEL NO.	LINE NO.
VALENCIA CLEMENT JR	CA	23W	60
VALENCIA FRANCISCO MACEDO	CA	18E	32
VALENCIA RALPH MARIO	CA	31E	78
VALENCIA ROSALIO	AZ	65W	2
VALENCICH PETER LYLE	MI	20E	88
VALENTA RUDOLPH GLENN	WI	02W	36
VALENTE ANTHONY NICHOLAS	NY	41E	56
VALENTE GLENN CURTIS	PA	05W	28
VALENTIN MARTINIANO JR	NY	48W	50
VALENTIN MIGUEL ANGEL JR	NY	01E	13
VALENTIN RAFAEL	NY	19E	122
VALENTIN-PEREZ HECTOR M	PR	22W	9
VALENTINE DONALD LYNN	IN	06W	58
VALENTINE FRANK MICHAEL	OH	11W	78
VALENTINE JAMES RUSSELL	PA	19E	67
VALENTINE JERON FRANKLIN	VA	56E	33
VALENTINE JOHN WESLEY	WV	41W	55
VALENTINE JOSEPH RONALD	LA	60W	6
VALENTINE LEWIS RUSSELL	PA	32W	40
VALENTINE LLOYD EARL	MO	45W	45
VALENTINE PERVIS B JR	MA	51E	3
VALENTINE WILLIAM MARTIN	VA	42W	37
VALENTINO ANTHONY ROBERT	NY	05E	39
VALENZUELA CARLOS	CA	14W	103
VALENZUELA HENRY JR	CA	33E	24
VALENZUELA JUAN	TX	25E	26
VALENZUELA OSCAR JR	CA	57W	33
VALENZUELA PEDRO	AZ	49E	6
VALENZUELA RODOLFO	AZ	42E	26
VALERIO DAVID N	PA	40E	49
VALERIO THOMAS	NY	04W	32
VALERIUS MILLARD RUSSELL	MI	01E	127
VALERO JOHN JUAN	CA	28W	5
VALESKO JOSEPH JR	NY	23W	80
VALINT JULIUS JOSEPH JR	PA	06E	36
VALKER GEORGE ERNEST III	ND	49W	45
VALKOS FRANCIS J	PA	01E	91
VALLANCE DAVID CLARK	MT	28W	15
VALLE ELOY RUBEN	TX	08W	36
VALLE FRANCISCO LOUIS	GA	44E	31
VALLE GUILLERMO	NY	07W	43
VALLE HECTOR	NY	20W	16
VALLE MANUEL BURROLA	AZ	17E	89
VALLECILLO EDGAR HENRY	NJ	21E	64
VALLEE JOSEPH LEO	MA	09E	79
VALLELONGA LARRY COSIMO	MI	21W	40
VALLEN DONALD WILLIAM JR	NY	24W	13
VALLERAND LARKIN OSCAR	CA	08E	90
VALLIERE STEPHEN CHARLES	NY	07E	6
VALLONE FRANK	NY	44W	32
VALLONE RICHARD JOSEPH	NJ	24E	47
VALO HENRY LOUIS JR	AZ	13W	52
VALOV JAMES DAMION	CA	26W	59
VALPAIS-MORALES RAFAEL A	PR	32E	33
VALRIE DWIGHT THEODORE	FL	63E	19
VALSTAD CLYDE JULIUS	CA	54E	19
VALT RALPH WESLEY	NJ	13E	73
VALTIERRA JUAN BORJA	CA	04E	55
VALTR JAMES ROBERT	TX	03W	78
VALUNAS MICHAEL	PA	28W	31
VALUSEK DENNIS WAYNE	TX	09W	31
VAN AKIN CRAIG ALDEN	OH	12W	110
VAN ALLEN CHARLES CLIFFOR	WA	61E	20
VAN ALST HARRY L JR	NY	44W	32
VAN ALSTINE MERLE O	IN	01E	91
VAN ANDEL CLAUDE RICHARD	NE	23W	4
VAN ANTWERP WILLIAM M JR	NY	26E	80
VAN ARTSDALEN CLIFFORD DA	PA	58E	1
VAN AVERY RONALD FRANCIS	OR	51E	26
VAN BALLEGOOYEN ROBERT A	IA	28E	3
VAN BARRIGER RONALD ERNES	NJ	37W	26
VAN BEBER ELDON CHRIST	CO	08E	13
VAN BEUKERING MARK ALAN	MI	17W	59
VAN BEUKERING RONALD DALE	MI	11W	118
VAN BLARCOM RICHARD WILLI	PA	59E	14
VAN BUREN GERALD GORDON	OH	32E	97
VAN BUSKIRK HAROLD DENNIS	MO	18E	8
VAN CAMPEN THOMAS CHARLES	CA	02E	17
VAN CEDARFIELD JAMES RAY	CT	13E	40
VAN CLAKE JOHN WILLIAM	OH	14E	71
VAN CLEAVE WALTER SHELBY	TX	26W	28
VAN CLEAVE WILLIAM F	MI	16W	126

NAME	STATE	PANEL NO.	LINE NO.
VAN CLIEF LARRY	NY	09E	54
VAN COOK DONALD F JR	NY	23W	68
VAN DALSEM MARC GREGORY	IA	51W	37
VAN DAM BRUCE ALLAN	MI	05W	85
VAN DANIKER JOSEPH MICHAE	MD	31W	28
VAN DE HEI JOSEPH ROBERT	WI	29W	85
VAN DE VENTER BLYTHE NOE	ND	12W	77
VAN DE WARKER RICHARD L	MI	11W	107
VAN DEN HEUVEL DAVID F	WI	30W	17
VAN DER SCHANS DONALD ED	NY	47E	37
VAN DEUSEN FREDERICK FREN	VA	53W	1
VAN DEUSEN PHILLIP ANDREN	NY	21E	68
VAN DONKELAAR GERALD WAYN	MI	45W	11
VAN DRIESSCHE JOHN	IN	07E	39
VAN DUSEN JOHN PHILLIP	NY	43W	50
VAN DUSEN ROBERT EDWARD	MI	28W	106
VAN DUYN JON FRANCIS	IL	48E	55
VAN DUYNE ROBERT SCHUYLER	CA	07E	50
VAN DUYNHOVEN PATRICK FRA	NY	49E	27
VAN DUZER RONALD LEE	OH	21W	2
VAN DYKE DEANE S JR	PA	07E	6
VAN DYKE RICHARD HAVEN	UT	44W	32
VAN DYKE STEPHEN DENNIS	MI	22W	94
VAN EVERY EDWARD JR	IA	10W	132
VAN FLEET DONALD WILLIAM	CA	43E	63
VAN FREDENBERG ALLEN JOHN	AZ	18W	30
VAN GELDER WILLIAM H JR	NY	08W	116
VAN GESSEL LARRY EUGENE	MI	48W	16
VAN GIESON ROBERT LESTER	CA	16E	71
VAN GILDER ROBERT RANDALL	MI	37E	15
VAN GORDER WILLIAM JOSEPH	IL	55W	16
VAN GUNDY NELSON EARL	IL	02E	3
VAN HAITSMA RANDALL CRAIG	MI	10W	71
VAN HATTEM JAMES ROBERT	MI	16W	77
VAN HOOK JAMES DOUGLAS	CA	37E	1
VAN HOOK RANDOLPH MARTIN	OH	09W	36
VAN HOOSE PAUL EDWIN	KY	15E	87
VAN HOOSIER JAMES D	IL	31E	42
VAN HORN ALBERT JAMES	MI	25W	33
VAN HORN BARRY WILLIAM	CA	53E	42
VAN HORN CHARLES ALBERT	CA	13W	94
VAN HORN DONALD THOMAS	MO	15E	110
VAN HORN EDWARD LINDLEY	WA	43E	12
VAN HORN JOHN RICHMOND	IL	61W	18
VAN HOUTEN NELSON OMAR	NJ	27W	78
VAN HOUTEN THOMAS EDWARD	NJ	14E	75
VAN HOY KENNETH EDWARD	NC	24W	35
VAN KEUREN ALLEN L	WI	31E	95
VAN KEUREN DEPUY RAYMOND	PA	02E	65
VAN LANT WAYNE G	CA	24E	57
VAN LEEUWEN ROBERT JAMES	MI	19E	51
VAN LEW KENNETH LESLIE	PA	09E	13
VAN LONE MURRAY WAYNE SR	WI	34E	92
VAN LOON FRANK C JR	AZ	41W	44
VAN MATER WILLIAM WAYNE	WI	43W	67
VAN METER JAKE HAROLD JR	WV	27E	67
VAN METER LARRY EUGENE	OH	41W	27
VAN NORMAN JOHN R III	FL	21E	103
VAN OCHTEN TERRY JOSEPH	MI	08W	26
VAN ORDEN EDWIN WARD JR	TX	30E	35
VAN PATTEN ROBERT ANDREW	CA	30E	87
VAN POLL HUBERT CLARENCE	OR	21E	110
VAN RAEMDONCK RONALD FRAN	MI	10E	130
VAN REGENMORTER RONALD RA	SD	14E	19
VAN RENSELAAR LARRY JACK	NV	42W	52
VAN REYPEN ROBERT JULIUS	NY	06E	54
VAN RIESEN ALVIN CHRIS	IA	65W	2
VAN SANT JOHN WILLARD	TX	42E	58
VAN SESSEN RONALD A	IN	12E	2
VAN STAVEREN THEODORE D	UT	49E	12
VAN TASSEL WILLIAM D JR	NY	41W	27
VAN TASSELL JAMES WARREN	NY	53W	24
VAN TOL GARY LEON	CA	57W	14
VAN TONGEREN TIMOTHY RAY	MI	26W	23
VAN VACTOR VICTOR HAROLD	KY	17E	53
VAN VALKENBURG CLYDE W JR	CA	17W	82
VAN VLECK JOHN JOSEPH	FL	23E	23
VAN VLEET JEFFERY HAROLD	MN	46E	13
VAN VLEET ROBERT CLAY	UT	24W	114
VAN VLIET HOWARD ELMER	NJ	40W	16
VAN WAMBEKE RONALD ARTHUR	IL	33W	23
VAN WIEREN JACK ALAN	MI	13W	69
VAN WINKLE CURTIS GLENN	KY	03W	106
VAN WINKLE GERALD VINCENT	OH	02W	19
VAN WINKLE HAROLD J JR	NJ	32W	47
VAN WINKLE JESS H JR	KS	18W	57
VAN WYK JOHN H	IO	03E	40
VAN ZANDT RAY LOUIS	TX	21E	40
VAN ZANDT THOMAS MILTON	TX	32E	66
VANASSE PHILIP RICHARD	MA	19E	67
VANATTA RANDALL ALLEN	IA	13E	46
VANBENDEGOM JAMES LEE	WI	23E	65
VANCE DANNY RAY	OH	33E	76
VANCE DARRELL VERNON	IN	59E	14
VANCE DE WITT STANLEY	MI	15W	68
VANCE DENNIS LEE	KY	15W	20
VANCE JAMES SIDNEY	TX	15W	126
VANCE JERRY DUANE	IN	01W	65
VANCE KERRY LAVERNE	AZ	11W	33
VANCE REGGIE LEE	OH	40E	70
VANCE SHERMAN DALE	IL	53W	6
VANCE THEODORE ROOSEVELT	OR	19E	102
VANCE WILLIAM CHARLES	MI	48E	13
VANCE WILLIAM JR	KY	47E	28
VANCELLETTE DAVID MICHAEL	MA	03E	98
VANCIL MICHAEL	MI	08E	59
VANCOSKY MICHAEL ANTHONY	PA	11W	98
VANDE GEER RICHARD	OH	01W	132
VANDE VEGTE DOUGLAS LEE	CA	27W	22
VANDEN BERG JOHN EDWARD	MI	16W	16
VANDEN BOSCH DWAINE WILM	MI	44E	8
VANDEN EYKEL MARTIN D II	IL	15W	21
VANDENACRE HOWARD DANIEL	MT	18E	27
VANDENBERG RONALD JAY	MI	30W	34
VANDER DUSSEN GEORGE	CA	52W	9
VANDER HAAG ALBERT JACOB	MI	06W	135
VANDER HEYDEN CHARLES G	WI	47W	24
VANDER STERREN CORNELIS	WI	44W	54
VANDER WEG PETER MICHAEL	WI	08W	52
VANDER WEG PHILLIP JOHN	MI	03E	115
VANDERBOOM PAUL WARD JR	WI	19W	64
VANDERBROOK GARY LAURENCE	NY	31W	86
VANDERCOOK DAVID FRANKLIN	MI	15E	92
VANDERFORD GERHARD W C	MS	35W	30
VANDERGRIFF ROBERT EUGENE	OH	15W	11
VANDERGRIFF RODGER ALAN	TN	25W	89
VANDERHEID MARK EDWARD	NY	54W	8
VANDERHOFF GEORGE A JR	NJ	41W	68
VANDERHOOF ALLEN WALTER	NJ	65E	3
VANDERKLOOT HARRY CORNELI	IL	31E	18
VANDERMUELEN ROBERT LYNN	OH	49E	6
VANDERPOOL EDWARD LEE	KY	36W	74
VANDERPOOL JOE WAYNE	AK	42E	26
VANDERSKI NORMAN JAMES	NJ	30E	86
VANDERVORT EDWARD PAUL	CA	33W	60
VANDERVORT WILLIAM F JR	PA	52E	26
VANDERZICHT JOHN ROBERT	FL	26E	40
VANDEVENDER JERRY WAYNE	TX	64W	3
VANDEVENDER JOSEPH TOMMY	RI	61W	18
VANDEVENTER JAMES CHARLES	CA	26W	95
VANDEVENTER JOHN WILTON	VT	18E	77
VANDEWALLE GREGORY JEROME	TX	19E	123
VANDIVER FRED GERALD	CA	08W	21
VANDIVER HARRY MELBORN JR	MO	02W	81
VANDIVIER JOHN DANIEL	IN	11W	65
VANEREM DAN ALLEN	WI	35W	41
VANGELISTI MICHAEL J	IL	11W	66
VANGUNDY GEORGE JEFFERSON	IL	04W	135
VANHULLE ANTHONY F II	WA	36E	40
VANLANDINGHAM RONALD LEE	TX	01W	88
VANN CARL REGINALD	VA	27W	42
VANN GARY STEVEN	NM	24W	51
VANN RONALD BRYSON	TX	26W	51
VANNATTA JON DAVID	IN	02E	59
VANNATTER LLOYD ALLEN	VA	04E	11
VANNOY DAN PAGE	PA	60E	3
VANOVER EDWARD CHARLES	PA	52W	13
VANOVER PAUL PHILLIP	CA	09E	76
VANSKIKE MONTE EUGENE	MO	41E	45
VANWEY WILLIAM EARL	CO	36W	19
VAQUERA ALBERT ALVARADO	TX	20W	90
VARA PAUL MARTINEZ	TX	44W	13
VARANSKY JAMES NELSON	OH	11W	39
VARDNER JOHN JOSEPH	RI	09W	41
VARDY ALEX VICTOR	OH	13W	108
VARELA DANIEL	CT	30E	35
VARGAS FRANKIE LEYBA	CO	04E	74
VARGAS JORGE	TX	22W	110
VARGAS JULIO CESAR	NY	11E	51
VARGAS LAWRENCE JAMES	CO	49E	48
VARGAS MARCELINO JR	IL	13W	109
VARGAS RAUL JOHN	CA	16W	55
VARGAS-VARGAS ISRAEL	PR	04E	78
VARGO ROBERT	OH	22E	117
VARICK ROBERT KITTRIDGE	IL	50E	42
VARNADO CLARENCE	AR	15E	111
VARNADO MICHAEL BANARD	LA	11W	89
VARNER CHARLES ALFRED	NJ	13W	125
VARNER DOUGLAS ALLEN	CA	04W	120
VARNER HARRY KAY	AZ	12E	97
VARNER JERRY DANIEL	CA	27E	92
VARNER RAYMOND ROBERT JR	IL	57W	5
VARNER THOMAS ALLISON JR	TN	32E	83
VARNEY KENNETH ARTHUR	NY	19E	8
VARNEY ROBIN LEE	WA	27E	23
VARNEY RONALD T	KY	31W	41
VARNEY WILLIE ROSS	MD	61E	4
VARNI HOWARD STEVEN	CA	47W	56
VARS JONATHAN R	NJ	20W	12
VARVELL DAVID LEE	MO	03E	102
VASCONCELLOS RICHARD JOHN	MA	10E	11
VASEY WILLIAM CHARLES	PA	05W	32
VASIL THOMAS JOSEPH	OH	27W	35
VASILOPULOS JOHN WILLIAM	IL	32E	13
VASKO RICHARD MARTIN	OH	38E	17
VASPORY WILLIAM LOUIS	OH	12W	85
VASQUES SELVESTER JOE	CA	16E	15
VASQUEZ ALBERTO RIOS JR	TX	25W	90
VASQUEZ ANGEL RUDY	NY	43E	1
VASQUEZ CARMELO	NY	46W	24
VASQUEZ CHARLES V JR	CA	56W	10
VASQUEZ DAVID	CA	17E	25
VASQUEZ DEAN	MN	54E	20
VASQUEZ EDDIE	NY	08E	70
VASQUEZ ENRIQUE	TX	37E	46
VASQUEZ EPHRAIM	TX	08E	13
VASQUEZ JESUS ROBERTO	TX	35E	83
VASQUEZ JIMMY	CA	13E	56
VASQUEZ JOSE MARIA	AZ	20E	79
VASQUEZ MARK ANTHONY	CA	16E	116
VASQUEZ MARTIN MENDOZA	AZ	02W	62
VASQUEZ MAX V III	CA	08E	32
VASQUEZ MICHAEL	UT	13E	94
VASQUEZ PATRICK JOHN	CA	23E	105
VASQUEZ RODOLFO ARTURO	TX	41E	5
VASQUEZ TONY MARIA	UT	17W	60
VASSAUR FRANKIE CARL	TX	10W	4
VASSEY GEORGE CREIGHTON	VA	49W	10
VASTINE LARRY CHARLES	OH	17W	11
VATER DIETER RUDOLF	CA	39W	5
VATISTAS DENNIS NICK	NH	05W	1
VAUGHAN CARVER JOE	TX	05W	12
VAUGHAN COUNCIL DELANO	VA	06W	63
VAUGHAN DANIEL JOSEPH	CA	10W	20
VAUGHAN DONALD CHARLES	CA	12E	69
VAUGHAN DONALD FRANKLIN	NY	02W	53
VAUGHAN DONALD SYLVESTER	PA	15E	123
VAUGHAN DOUGLAS DEAN	IL	24W	62
VAUGHAN EGBERT R	GA	54E	41
VAUGHAN HARRY KENNETH	GA	43E	49
VAUGHAN HOWARD JAMES	OH	36W	54
VAUGHAN JAMES ODELL	MD	03E	97
VAUGHAN JOHN DAVID	OH	40E	70
VAUGHAN JOHN W	OH	22E	4
VAUGHAN MICHAEL PATRICK	MA	55W	32
VAUGHAN MILTON LEE	VA	10E	52
VAUGHAN RAYMOND WALTER JR	CT	18W	25
VAUGHAN ROBERT LESTER	WA	32E	83
VAUGHAN ROBERT REDDINGTON	CA	28E	5
VAUGHAN RONNIE GORDON	MA	05W	60
VAUGHAN THOMAS CECIL	OK	40E	33
VAUGHN CLAUDE FRANKLIN	GA	46W	25
VAUGHN CLIFTON FLOYD	MS	10E	47
VAUGHN DELBERT LEE JR	TX	01E	65
VAUGHN DENNIS WAYNE	TN	42W	33
VAUGHN DONALD WILBANKS	CA	39E	55

NAME	STATE	PANEL NO.	LINE NO.
VAUGHN GENE	TX	19E	19
VAUGHN HERBERT LEE	OR	67W	6
VAUGHN HOWARD GREGORY	IL	37E	15
VAUGHN JEFFREY PAUL	OH	11E	18
VAUGHN JOHN CARL	FL	09W	36
VAUGHN JOHN MYRON	PA	51E	23
VAUGHN JOHN PATRICK	CA	05E	16
VAUGHN JOSEPH DOUGLAS	GA	08W	21
VAUGHN KELLY PATRICK	TN	28W	5
VAUGHN RICHARD WILLIAM	CA	31E	55
VAUGHN ROBERT LEE JR	PA	24W	73
VAUGHN WENDELL GLEN	MI	26E	20
VAUGHN WILLIAM OREL	TN	15W	112
VAUGHT CRAIG STEPHEN	CA	15E	77
VAUGHT HAROLD TIMOTHY	MD	15E	123
VAUGHT JOHNNIE L JR	TN	42W	44
VAUGHT MICHAEL EUGENE	TX	34E	2
VAUGHT WILLIAM H III	IN	10W	88
VAULTZ JIMMY LEE	IL	16W	60
VAUSE JAMES EDWARD	NJ	08E	122
VAUTOUR DAVID	CT	25E	3
VAVRIN FRANK NEAL	GA	07W	48
VAVROSKY PAUL PETER	IL	30W	60
VAZQUEZ FELIX JR	NY	51E	26
VAZQUEZ JOSE ANGEL	NY	12E	8
VAZQUEZ JOSE GILBERTO	PR	11W	56
VAZQUEZ JUAN FRANCISCO	PR	37E	28
VAZQUEZ WILLIAM	CA	44E	3
VAZQUEZ-BERRIOS RUBEN ANT	PR	15E	30
VAZQUEZ-GONZALEZ PEDRO	PR	06E	13
VAZQUEZ-NIEVES RAMON LUIS	PR	23W	12
VAZQUEZ-SANTIAGO EFRAIN	PR	19W	126
VEACH JAROLD A	OH	08E	122
VEACH RICHARD ELZIE	CA	21E	7
VEACH ROBERT EUGENE	IN	55W	3
VEALE RALPH DEAN	MO	30W	82
VEARA JOHN VINCENT	TX	47W	5
VEDDER RICHARD JEROME	MN	16E	103
VEDRO EDMUND RONALD	MI	15E	55
VEDROS RANDOLPH PAUL	CA	06E	110
VEGA ANGEL	TX	32E	48
VEGA ANTONIO	IN	16E	74
VEGA FRANCISCO	NY	06W	104
VEGA-DIAZ HECTOR MANUEL	NY	30W	83
VEGA-LOPEZ CARLOS	PR	38W	80
VEGA-MAYSONET RAFAEL	PR	12E	44
VEHLING ROBERT WAYNE	IN	02W	96
VEIHL JOHN	MI	64E	1
VELA VITALIO JR	TX	39E	41
VELARDO ANTHONY GUY	MA	06E	55
VELASCO MIKE RALPH	CA	34E	65
VELASQUEZ ANTONIO	CA	17E	40
VELASQUEZ CHARLES	CA	19W	35
VELASQUEZ DAVID ROBERT	KS	05E	8
VELASQUEZ JOHN ROBERT	CO	56E	17
VELASQUEZ JOSE HILARIO	CO	21E	93
VELASQUEZ JULIAN VICTOR	NM	27W	3
VELASQUEZ ROBERT	CA	08W	87
VELASQUEZ ROBERT JEROME	FL	24E	47
VELAZQUEZ FRANK	MO	33E	15
VELAZQUEZ-FELICIANO RODRIGO JR	PR	42E	55
VELAZQUEZ-LOPEZ VICTOR R	PR	29E	69
VELAZQUEZ-ORTIZ CARLOS A	PR	37W	53
VELEZ BERT	NY	31E	55
VELEZ JUAN ANTONIO	CT	24E	47
VELEZ LUIS FELIPE	NY	38E	73
VELEZ PAUL	NY	48W	50
VELEZ VICTORIANO	NY	18E	20
VELEZ-HERNANDEZ JOSE A	PR	15W	25
VELEZ-RIVERA LUIS ALFONSO	PR	41W	9
VELEZ-RODRIGUEZ ELLIOTT	PR	34W	54
VELEZ-VILLAMIL JUAN MANUE	PR	32W	74
VELILLA WILLIAM	NY	30E	5
VELLANCE RICHARD PAUL	MI	39E	55
VELOZ EDUARDO	CA	49W	17
VELTMAN TIMOTHY ANDREW	FL	09E	106
VELVET WALTER C JR	VA	42E	44
VENABLE BILLY RAY	MO	46W	35
VENABLE ELTON RAY	OK	32W	62
VENABLE JOSEPH ALVIN	LA	44W	54
VENABLE WESTOVEL	NJ	04E	95

NAME	STATE	PANEL NO.	LINE NO.
VENCEL ALBERT ALLEN	OH	04W	82
VENCILL EDDIE WAYNE	VA	04W	44
VENDELIN THOMAS LESLIE	CA	29W	33
VENDITTI NICHOLAS LOUIS	PA	20W	3
VENEGAS VERNON BERNABE	IL	34E	2
VENEKAMP PHILLIP ROBERT	IN	22E	8
VENENGA DARRELL DEAN	SD	30E	12
VENET GLEN ORVILLE	WI	31W	97
VENNARD JOHN JOSEPH	NY	50E	34
VENNIK ROBERT NICHOLAS	NJ	02W	3
VENTERS ROGER LEE	CA	15W	30
VENTLINE LUKAS JOHN	MI	40E	15
VENUTI VINCENT JR	CA	35W	68
VER HELST JAMES LAYMAN	IL	17E	55
VER LIHAY FRANK T JR	PA	10W	88
VER LINDEN CRAIG ALDEN	CA	27E	51
VER PAULT KEVIN EDWARD	NY	40E	35
VERA ABELARDO	TX	45E	44
VERA PEDRO ANGEL	NY	47W	13
VERA VENANCIO	IN	20W	90
VERA-DURAN MIGUEL DE JESUS	PR	03E	97
VERASTIQUE JOHNNY RALPH	TX	35W	46
VERBILLA DAVID	PA	19E	33
VERCOUTEREN EDWARD ARNOLD	NY	21E	71
VERCRUYSSE GREGORY PAUL	WA	21E	71
VERDINEK GEORGE THOMAS	PA	02E	48
VERDUGO ADALBERTO R E	CA	31W	37
VERDUGO DANIEL ALEXANDER	CA	32E	41
VERGALLITO JOHN ANTHONY	NY	06E	27
VERGAMINI DOUGLAS SILVIO	IA	09W	97
VERGANO ROBERT THOMAS	CA	08E	102
VERGARA ELISEO	TX	18W	98
VERGARA-ARBIL AUGUSTINE	NY	43E	12
VERHAEGHE MICHAEL J	WI	27W	46
VERMEESCH WESLEY WILLIAM	ID	16W	6
VERNER SCOTT MITCHELL	PA	18W	12
VERNES ROBERT FRANK	CA	15E	52
VERNO JOHN ARTHUR	AZ	10W	20
VERNON BROADUS WAYNE	NC	37W	43
VERNON DONALD GENE	FL	12E	107
VERNON PAUL LAWRENCE	PA	15E	88
VERNOR JAMES EDWIN	WA	49W	27
VERON MURRAY LEE	IN	36E	40
VERRETT DURWOOD WAYNE	LA	58E	1
VERRETT KENNETH EMERY	MI	28W	100
VERRY FREDERICK ALFRED	NY	23W	69
VERSACE HUMBERT ROQUE	VA	01E	33
VERSCHEURE JOHNNY DELBERT	IL	06W	117
VERSTRAETE MICHAEL JAMES	MO	03W	64
VERWERS ROGER LEE	MN	18E	73
VESCELIUS MILTON JAMES JR	MI	26E	109
VESELY JOSEPH STANLEY JR	OH	08E	63
VESER EDWARD	WI	11W	118
VESEY CHARLES HANSEN	CA	26W	13
VESEY JERROLD LOUIS	CA	07W	7
VESS LESTER STANLEY	NC	06W	30
VESSELL WAYNE JACKSON	GA	52W	32
VESSELS CHARLES ROBERT	NC	11E	86
VEST DAVID WAYNE	KY	30E	68
VEST ROBERT LEE	OR	12E	31
VESTAL STEVE ALAN	CO	09W	125
VESTER FREDRICK HAZER	ME	08E	73
VETRANO GERALD MICHAEL	NY	08W	64
VETTER ERNEST JR	OK	50E	43
VEVERA PHILIP JOHN	IL	19W	104
VEZEAU THOMAS JOSEPH	NH	13W	55
VIADO REYNALDO ROCILLO		17W	32
VIALPANDO JOHN A	CO	37W	60
VIBBERT CARLOS DYRAL	KY	45W	64
VICALVI TIMOTHY LAWRENCE	MA	28E	39
VICE FARRELL JAMES	LA	24W	100
VICHOSKY WALTER JOSEPH JR	NJ	03W	125
VICICH ALBERT LEE	IL	11E	51
VICICH CHARLES EDWARD	NY	21E	116
VICK ALBERT JR	NC	20W	46
VICK RICHARD DEWEY	MN	40E	50
VICK ROSCOE L	NC	05E	110
VICK WILLIAM LEON	KY	45W	5
VICKERS BILLY JOE	WV	48E	55
VICKERS CHARLES GRIFFIN	PA	21W	4
VICKERS DAVID ERWIN	FL	02W	97
VICKERS ROBERT LEE	GA	43E	37

NAME	STATE	PANEL NO.	LINE NO.
VICKERS ROGER LEE	OH	34W	80
VICKERY FREDERICK M III	FL	48W	50
VICKERY GARRY FRANCIS	NY	38E	82
VICKERY MICHAEL CLARENCE	TN	14W	16
VICKREY CHARLES CRAIG	FL	28W	54
VICKREY CLARKE KEMBLE	TX	17W	125
VICKS EDWARD JAMES JR	NY	50E	34
VICTOR GEORGE M	HI	56E	33
VICTORIA FREDERICK PEARCE	NY	12E	85
VICTORY JOHN JOSEPH	IL	07E	6
VICTORY WILLIAM THOMAS	VA	03E	63
VIDALES ALEXANDER	VA	15E	76
VIDLER MURRAY DEAN	ND	32E	28
VIDRINE TERREL JAMES	LA	38W	47
VIEGRA LUZ	KS	03E	124
VIEHMANN GEORGE JOHN JR	NJ	20W	3
VIEHWEG MICHAEL	IL	29E	7
VIEIRA JOSEPH	MA	35E	17
VIEL ALFRED	NH	36W	66
VIELBAUM JAMES MICHAEL	WI	36E	40
VIERAS JOSE LOUIS	CA	58E	17
VIEREGGE WALTER III	TX	27E	35
VIERHELLER HAROLD J JR	OH	53E	24
VIERRA JOSEPH	CA	16E	5
VIESTENZ KREG ARTHUR	OR	43W	31
VIGGIANO ROBERT EDWARD	NJ	25E	18
VIGH ALEXANDER JOSEPH	MI	13E	62
VIGIL ALEXANDER	CA	17W	99
VIGIL ANTHONY	WA	30E	35
VIGIL ARTHUR VERNON	CA	21E	2
VIGIL DAVID LORENZO	CO	10W	72
VIGIL FREDERICK ANTHONY	CO	05W	62
VIGIL HENRY ORLANDO	UT	24E	115
VIGIL LAURENCIO	NM	19W	5
VIGIL LOUIS DAVID	CO	19E	53
VIGO-NEGRIN LUIS	PR	15E	53
VIKTORYN JOHN WILLIAM JR	OH	57E	11
VILANO EVARISTO	TX	18E	1
VILARDO RONALD ALLAN	CA	27E	69
VILAS GERALD FRANK	MI	02W	20
VILKAS ALLEN RUDOLPH	IL	24E	89
VILLA ARMANDO	CA	23E	79
VILLA FELIBERTO	TX	06E	78
VILLA RAUL	TX	19E	76
VILLAFRANCO RODOLFO	TX	43E	63
VILLALOBOS ARTHUR GARCIA	CA	24W	23
VILLALOBOS ELISEO MORALES	TX	26W	16
VILLALOBOS HENRY ESTRELLA	AZ	20W	74
VILLALOBOS IGNACIO L	CA	23W	115
VILLALOBOS JAIME	MI	67W	4
VILLALOBOS JUAN JESUS	CA	28E	88
VILLALOBOS PAUL RUBIO	CA	05W	10
VILLALPANDO RAYMOND JR	CA	61W	14
VILLAMOR ROMAN ROZEL JR	MI	17E	78
VILLANUEVA ALFREDO JULIAN	TX	32W	68
VILLANUEVA FELIPE	OR	09E	19
VILLANUEVA FLORENCIO G	HI	34E	1
VILLANUEVA FRANCISCO JR	CA	25W	3
VILLANUEVA HILARIO PIZARR	NY	23E	33
VILLANUEVA JOSE EDWARDO	CA	13W	17
VILLANUEVA LARRY	SC	14W	1
VILLAROSA PAUL HERMAN	CA	33E	43
VILLARREAL ERNESTO	MI	30E	51
VILLARREAL JOHNNY	TX	31E	76
VILLARREAL MICHAEL	IA	39W	76
VILLARREAL RICARDO	CA	51E	14
VILLARREAL ROLANDO G	TX	29W	55
VILLASANA FERNANDO	TX	06W	70
VILLASENOR GONZALO H	TX	27W	57
VILLEGAS DANIEL JOHN	CA	38E	82
VILLEGAS RALPH PAUL	CA	26E	20
VILLEGAS-VILA HECTOR	PR	16W	123
VILLEPONTEAUX JAMES H JR	SC	07E	47
VILLIARD JOSEPH GEORGE	NH	06E	45
VILLON CASIMIRO	HI	34E	72
VILONE PHILIP JR	WV	08E	54
VINAL RICHARD ALDEN	CA	18E	32
VINAS GARY LIONEL	PA	10E	2
VINASSA MICHAEL	CA	07E	104
VINCENT DONALD W	MI	04E	5
VINCENT GEORGE	CA	03E	38
VINCENT HALTON RAMSEY	LA	02W	32

NAME	STATE	PANEL NO.	LINE NO.
VINCENT IVAN L JR	MI	46W	10
VINCENT JOHN LEROY	MO	51E	43
VINCENT KEITH DAN	OK	58E	27
VINCENT MARK DEE	UT	14W	21
VINCENT NORMAN WAYNE	MN	13E	112
VINCENT RICHARD ELSWORTH	WV	44E	3
VINCIGUERRA JAMES VINCENT	OH	14W	67
VINES CLEVELAND	VA	07E	100
VINES RICHARD LARRY	CA	60W	22
VINEYARD GEORGE MICKEL	TX	28E	58
VINGE RICHARD LONNIE	WA	60W	23
VINGE TERRY LEE	CA	41E	45
VINLUAN DOMINGO BALANSAY		03E	14
VINNEDGE JOHN ROBERT	MI	17W	44
VINSCOTSKI ROBERT VALENTI	NY	33E	43
VINSON AARON	AR	07W	64
VINSON ALBERT GAMALIEL	OH	36W	74
VINSON BOBBY C	TN	03E	97
VINSON BOBBY GENE	TX	52E	1
VINSON DONALD RAY	IN	02E	37
VINSON HENRY MITCHELL	AL	06E	78
VINSON WALTER WAYNE	AL	22E	90
VINTER STEVEN CHARLES	CA	47W	56
VINTON ROBERT ALFRED JR	OH	53E	25
VIOLA CARL DANIEL	LA	07E	125
VIOLETT JAMES EDWARD	GM	37E	73
VIRBICKAS ANTHONY A	NJ	16W	107
VIRGILIO LAWRENCE JOSEPH	NJ	23E	117
VIRGONA JOHN ANGELO	NY	44E	55
VIRUET JOSE GALENO	NY	36E	41
VIS JOHN PAUL	WI	26E	90
VISCONTI FRANCIS EDWARD	NY	03E	109
VISCONTI LAWRENCE GUY	CT	19E	19
VISE GEORGE FRANCIS	WA	49E	37
VISINTIN KENNETH HENRY	WA	28W	87
VISKER THOMAS PETER	WA	47E	57
VISSER JOHN JOSEPH	MI	43W	34
VITACCO MICHAEL	NY	14E	71
VITALE MICHAEL NICHOLAS	PA	27W	84
VITALE WILLIAM MILLER	IL	37W	8
VITANZA CHARLES JOSEPH	PA	15E	12
VITCH RALPH ALLAN	FL	24W	108
VITELLO JOHN MATHEW JR	OH	36W	27
VITRO VITO	NY	31W	94
VIVETTE LEON LOUIS	WA	23E	24
VIVIAN JOHN HALL	TX	47E	6
VIVILACQUA THEODORE R	CA	25W	113
VIX STEPHEN AUGUST JR	AL	26W	104
VIZER GERALD ARLENE	WI	21E	19
VLAHAKOS PETER GEORGE	ME	04E	131
VLASAK WILLIAM JAMES JR	IL	19E	19
VLIEK RONALD CRAIG	MI	18W	44
VLISIDES GEORGE FREDERICK	MI	01E	84
VOEGTLI JOHN SARGEANT	CT	05E	23
VOELKER MARVIN ALDRID JR	KY	16W	123
VOGEL DONALD FRANCIS	IL	61E	4
VOGEL DUANE ARLEN	WI	13E	76
VOGEL EDWARD BARRY	NJ	38W	80
VOGEL GARRITY	MN	43E	37
VOGEL HAROLD RAYMOND	PA	57W	21
VOGEL LAWRENCE SMITH	MI	14E	89
VOGEL TIMOTHY PETERSON	PA	25E	54
VOGELI RALPH LEE	WI	35W	45
VOGELPOHL REX ALAN	IN	05W	41
VOGELSANG JOHN KIM	MN	23W	94
VOGET DONALD GUSTAV	CA	05W	102
VOGLER GALE KURK	IL	16E	66
VOGLER GREGORY RAYMOND	MO	23W	60
VOGRINEC JOSEPH GARY	UT	35E	63
VOGT LEONARD FREDERICK JR	OH	02E	90
VOHRINGER WILLIAM THOMAS	NJ	12W	2
VOHS WILLIAM FRANCIS	NY	09E	64
VOIGT ARNO JOSEPH	TX	09W	11
VOIGT THEODORE HAROLD	SD	26E	41
VOIGTS RICHARD SCOTT	IL	01W	31
VOILES GASPER ALLEN	TN	25E	44
VOJIR JAMES PAUL	NY	39E	14
VOKES RICHARD HENRY	CA	08W	52
VOKISH JERALD ANTHONY	PA	21E	25
VOLENTINE PHILIP ALVIN	LA	31E	32
VOLHEIM MICHAEL CORY	CA	23W	18
VOLK BARCLAY LEONARD	MT	11W	19
VOLK DENNIS RICHARD	SD	60W	20
VOLK GEORGE FRANCIS	ID	18E	65
VOLK RICHARD ANTHONY	ND	29W	85
VOLKE CLIFFORD JAMES II	CA	35E	19
VOLLHARDT PHILIPP R	CT	05W	74
VOLLMAR CHRISTOPHER LEE	MI	03W	10
VOLLMAR GEORGE THOMAS	NY	15E	102
VOLLMAR SAMMIE J	TX	21E	30
VOLLMER DAVID STEPHEN	NY	38W	6
VOLLMER DONALD GENE	ND	16W	18
VOLLMER VALENTINE BERNARD	WI	39E	68
VOLLMERHAUSEN JOHN M JR	FL	24W	51
VOLLRATH JOHNNY DEWEY	GA	16W	16
VOLNER JOHN DELANE	TN	15E	55
VOLPONE DANTE	NJ	23E	114
VOLTNER DONALD CHARLES	WI	31W	97
VOLTZ ROBERT CARL	PA	16E	66
VOLZ ROGER WAYNE	UT	64W	17
VOLZ STEPHEN THOMAS	CA	39W	39
VON AHRENS NORMAN LEE	OH	35W	68
VON BISCHOFFSHAUSEN ROBERT A	NJ	49W	34
VON DER HOFF RALPH HENRY	MI	07W	20
VON KLEIST AUSTIN RICHARD	MD	32E	14
VONASEK RICHARD JAMES	MN	40E	15
VONDERCHEK WALTER EARL	NY	40E	49
VONTOR THOMAS JOSEPH	PA	09E	13
VOORHEES DONALD LEE	NC	11W	89
VOORHEES RICHARD ALLEN	MI	37E	73
VOORHEIS HAROLD ROBERT	NY	47W	57
VOORHIES EMORY DAVID	OH	58W	16
VORE KENNETH STEPHEN	OH	10W	73
VORE RODNEY ALLEN	MI	28W	64
VORENKAMP DAVID R	MI	21W	49
VORIES JOHN LLOYD	AR	55E	34
VORIS RUSSEL EARL	MO	09W	89
VOS KENNETH RICHARD	MI	02W	123
VOSS CURTIS MALROY	SD	14E	8
VOSS MICHAEL ALAN	CO	32W	85
VOSS RALPH	TX	52E	1
VOSS RAYMOND ALLAN	WA	22W	94
VOSS ROBERT J	IA	02E	32
VOSS WILLIAM ARTHUR	MO	42W	44
VOSSEN STANLEY JOSEPH	CA	56E	17
VOSYLIUS VINCENT	IL	26W	58
VOTAVA JAMES J JR	IL	02E	66
VOTAW MARVIN LYNN	TX	50E	2
VOUGHT WARREN DEMAREST JR	CT	17E	47
VOWLES JOHN WESLEY	IL	34W	55
VOYLES FLOYD	AL	39E	1
VOYLES JOHN WALTER	IL	19W	74
VOYT EDWARD	OH	22W	56
VOYTKO DAVID LEE	OH	54W	21
VRABEL JOHN ROBIN	VA	19E	123
VRABLICK MICHAEL STEPHEN	CA	07W	104
VRANKOVICH NICHOLAS SAMUE	PA	70E	1
VRBA JAMES MATHEW JR	TX	36E	41
VRBA RAYMOND JOE JR	TX	01E	124
VROMAN MERLIN HOWARD	PA	23E	105
VROOM JAMES LEE	IN	31W	98
VROOMAN NICHOLAS WHITTIER	CA	10W	93
VRUGGINK JOEL	MI	39W	31
VUGA STEPHEN MICHAEL	PA	32E	65
VULLO MICHAEL PHILLIP	CA	08W	10
VULTAGGIO ANTHONY	NY	21W	87
VURLUMIS CHRIS C	CA	08E	25
WAALEN JOHN HOWARD	WA	10W	73
WABLE SAMUEL LEE	OK	25W	90
WABSCHALL ARCHIE CARL III	OR	13W	60
WACKER JOSEPH HENRY	TX	35W	80
WACKERFUSS RICHARD WILLIAM	MN	55E	33
WADDELL BOBBY LEE	MI	13E	66
WADDELL JAMES DARRELL	TX	04W	125
WADDELL LARRY JONATHAN	OH	16E	49
WADDELL ROBERT DOUGLAS	OH	30E	74
WADDELL WILLIAM THOMAS	NC	11W	128
WADDLE SAMMIE WAYNE	AL	24W	13
WADDLE WILLIAM SAMUEL	PA	15W	126
WADE ARCHIE NORMAN	WA	13W	4
WADE BARTON SCOTT	IN	01W	102
WADE BICKETT ORLANDO JR	NC	20E	11
WADE BOYD LEE	OK	14W	18
WADE CHARLES FREDERICK	OH	34W	11
WADE DONALD JAMES	CA	13W	55
WADE DOUGLAS BUREM	TN	38E	62
WADE DOUGLAS JOHN	ID	05E	53
WADE FRANKIE DON	NC	17E	46
WADE GERALD ROBERT	OR	15W	88
WADE JAMES LEE JR	GA	31E	55
WADE KENNETH EARL	NC	31W	28
WADE LARRY	PA	29E	78
WADE LINDBERG	NC	24W	23
WADE MELVIN ALEXANDER	NY	19E	68
WADE MICHAEL ALLEN	IL	04W	95
WADE NATHANIEL	GA	56W	28
WADE RICHARD ALLEN	IA	25W	44
WADE RICHARD EDWARD	TN	29E	22
WADE ROBERT JOHN	NJ	15E	92
WADE ROBERT LE ROY	IN	12W	126
WADE ROBERT MILTON	VA	27E	97
WADE STEVEN MICHAEL	AL	08W	92
WADE THOMAS JOE	OK	30E	51
WADE THOMAS LEE	VA	58E	27
WADE WILLIAM GLENN	OH	06E	36
WADEN JOHN F	MA	12E	107
WADKINS WOOTS EARL	OH	31W	28
WADLEY JACK DALE	TX	32W	17
WADLEY JOE ALTON	GA	22W	101
WADLINGTON LOUIS WAYNE	KY	31E	95
WADSWORTH CHARLES DAVID	WV	05E	110
WADSWORTH DEAN AMICK	TX	01E	32
WADSWORTH HARRY MARSHALL	AL	20E	12
WADSWORTH JOHN LANIER	CA	08W	1
WAFER DAVID EARL	CA	54W	21
WAFFORD RONALD L	CA	06E	56
WAFORD HUBERT EARL	KY	49E	36
WAGENAAR DANIEL LEONARD	WA	21W	110
WAGENER DAVID RAYMOND	MI	11E	92
WAGER RICHARD JAMES	MI	25E	60
WAGES JAMES LEWIS	OK	36E	38
WAGES JERRY LEON	GA	17W	115
WAGES JESSE FLOYD	IN	07E	77
WAGIE DENNIS RICHARD	WI	26W	104
WAGMAN JEFFREY BURTON	IL	10E	6
WAGMAN NICHOLAS OWEN	KY	25E	90
WAGNER BRUCE ALLEN	MI	29E	78
WAGNER BRUCE DAVID	PA	08W	113
WAGNER CECIL BOYD JR	OH	42W	44
WAGNER CLIFTON FRED	OR	30W	83
WAGNER DAN JR	KY	32E	7
WAGNER DAVID FREDERICK	CA	49E	6
WAGNER DAVID LEE	GA	01W	27
WAGNER EDWARD JOHN JR	WA	20E	51
WAGNER FARL DUANE	OK	35W	7
WAGNER GREY H	IA	34E	26
WAGNER HARRY EDWARD	NJ	17E	109
WAGNER JAMES EDWARD	MN	35E	58
WAGNER JAMES JOSEPH	MD	26W	41
WAGNER JERRY LOUIS	NC	18E	112
WAGNER JOHN LAWRENCE	CA	07W	108
WAGNER KENNETH JAMES	MN	04W	23
WAGNER LEE CELIN JR	OH	01E	120
WAGNER MARVIN LEROY	CA	08W	40
WAGNER MICHAEL JAMES	WI	13W	47
WAGNER PHILIP ROBERT	WI	02W	30
WAGNER RANDALL WILLIAM	WI	38W	80
WAGNER RAYMOND ANTHONY	IN	02W	120
WAGNER RICHARD ALLEN	CA	05E	125
WAGNER RICHARD EDWARD	OH	39E	15
WAGNER ROBERT ALFRED	NE	61E	21
WAGNER ROBERT JAMES	IL	19W	75
WAGNER ROBERT KAY	CA	48W	20
WAGNER ROY CARL	ND	27E	42
WAGNER RUSSELL MARK	CA	14E	93
WAGNER WALTER ADOLPH	CA	21E	76
WAGNER WAYNE DOUGLAS	CA	16E	32
WAGNER WILLIAM JOHN JR	PA	28E	94
WAGNER WILLIAM OSCAR	MN	48E	55
WAGNER WILLIAM PETER III	WA	22E	34
WAGNER WILLIAM WALTER	NY	37W	54
WAGSTAFF JAMES DONALD	NY	46W	45
WAGSTAFF STEVEN RAY	IL	22E	117
WAGUESPACK GARY LOUIS	LA	23E	65
WAHL DENNIS JAMES	OH	23E	105

NAME	STATE	PANEL NO.	LINE NO.
WAHL JAN BERNARD	OH	40E	70
WAHL JOHNNIE MITCHELL	AZ	16W	129
WAHL PHILIP RAYMOND	PA	29E	63
WAHLEN GERALD JOHN	PA	17E	65
WAHLER PAUL WINTON JR	WI	30E	20
WAID BILLY GENE	TX	25W	44
WAID DALE ARDEN	OH	11E	38
WAIDE DONALD GILES	NM	56E	33
WAIDMAN WILLIAM HERMAN JR	MD	18W	107
WAINIO ALEXANDER GEORGE	NH	20E	126
WAINSCOTT DAVID HENRY	OH	29E	63
WAINWRIGHT DAVID BARD	IL	27E	51
WAINWRIGHT MICHAEL ALBERT	IL	10W	59
WAINWRIGHT MICHAEL JAMES	WA	12W	59
WAINZ ROBERT MICHAEL	NY	18E	83
WAIT BERNARD JOSEPH	NY	04E	114
WAITE CAROLD REX	MO	16E	33
WAITE DONALD STEVEN	NE	38E	62
WAITERS LAWRENCE	SC	46W	54
WAITES SHERMAN RAY	TX	22E	118
WAJDA PHILIP JOHN	IL	43W	44
WAKE RUSSELL DEAN	MO	53W	40
WAKEFIELD CARL DANIEL	MA	49W	2
WAKEFIELD JOSEPH JR	OH	12W	44
WAKLEE DUANE A	NY	07E	104
WAKULICH GREGORY PAUL	NY	14W	116
WALANGITANG BENJAMIN T	OH	19W	99
WALBER RONALD JAMES	CA	52E	12
WALBRIDGE GEORGE WILCOX	AL	38E	73
WALBRIDGE WILLIAM ROBERT	VT	11W	23
WALD GUNTHER HERBERT	NJ	16W	25
WALDEN DANIEL EDGAR	TN	06E	104
WALDEN DARRELL EDWARD	IL	27W	35
WALDEN DAVID	GA	12W	11
WALDEN JAMES LARRY	FL	14W	109
WALDEN JAMES ROBERT	FL	37E	73
WALDEN LARRY HUSTON	MS	42E	44
WALDEN MARION FRANK JR	FL	36W	19
WALDEN ROBERT DAVID	SC	12W	1
WALDEN TRAVIS GARY	MO	15E	111
WALDERA DAVID ARLEN	ND	27W	3
WALDING JARED BRUCE	GA	13W	80
WALDON TOMMY ANDREW	IN	45E	44
WALDORF ARTHUR LOUIS	OR	66E	3
WALDORF GARY ALAN	WI	44W	32
WALDOWSKI JAMES RICHARD	WA	19W	83
WALDREP JIMMY RAY	AL	10E	122
WALDRON DUANE EVERETT	CA	08W	112
WALDRON GEORGE ALLEN	CA	11E	40
WALDRON HOWARD BERT	ID	43E	37
WALDRON JAMES TAYLOR	MN	07W	62
WALDRON JERRY MONROE	FL	64E	1
WALDRON KARL MERRITT JR	MN	39E	55
WALDRON STEVEN	CA	15E	13
WALDROP KYLE	KY	29W	26
WALDROP RAYMOND CLARENCE	AL	40W	5
WALDROP RONALD TERRY	CA	20E	51
WALDVOGEL ROBERT E	MN	03E	96
WALENSKY GORDON DAVID	MN	49E	12
WALERZAK WILLIAM THOMAS	MI	04W	1
WALINSKI BERNARD GORDON	MD	08E	126
WALJESKI CHARLES	IL	26E	53
WALKER AARON	IL	15W	65
WALKER ARTIE DELL	MI	12E	31
WALKER BARRY RONALD	IL	08E	59
WALKER BRADLEY A	AZ	19E	8
WALKER BRUCE CHARLES	CO	02W	133
WALKER BURTON KIMBALL	NM	14W	118
WALKER CARL LYNN	PA	21W	79
WALKER CECIL	KY	12E	65
WALKER CHARLES	MO	28W	77
WALKER CHARLES BUTNER JR	KS	18W	30
WALKER CHARLES CLARENCE	AL	28W	87
WALKER CHARLES EDWARD	AR	07E	123
WALKER CHARLIE C	GA	06E	17
WALKER CHARLIE LEWIS	AL	22E	51
WALKER CLARENCE	AR	53W	6
WALKER CLARK L	MI	14E	75
WALKER CLIFFORD C	AL	47W	13
WALKER CLIFFORD WAYNE	CA	40E	16
WALKER CLIFTON	GA	48E	36
WALKER CLOVIS BERNARD	VA	21W	40
WALKER DALE ALLEN	MI	04W	8
WALKER DOUGLAS ALEXANDER	MA	63E	3
WALKER EDDIE LEE	IL	17W	92
WALKER EDWARD	SC	58E	27
WALKER ELBERT BERTON	NE	47E	57
WALKER EVANS S	SC	28E	18
WALKER FRANK MARK	MI	14W	6
WALKER GARY LAYNE	CA	62E	13
WALKER GARY WAYNE	NC	08W	123
WALKER GEORGE EDWARD JR	VT	10W	106
WALKER GEORGE NELSON	KY	64W	17
WALKER GEORGE THOMAS LLOY	CA	56E	33
WALKER GERARD JOSEPH	NJ	15W	96
WALKER HARDEN BERT	GA	07E	28
WALKER HAROLD EVERETT JR	ME	43E	63
WALKER HENSON FRANK	UT	22W	45
WALKER HOLLIS ALLEN	TX	08E	90
WALKER HOWARD LESLIE	NC	12E	25
WALKER IRVIN	NJ	36W	78
WALKER ISUM MERRILL	FL	18E	12
WALKER J C JR	TX	10E	42
WALKER JACKIE CARROLL	TN	16W	104
WALKER JACKIE DALE	OK	51E	43
WALKER JAMES ALFRED JR	FL	28W	6
WALKER JAMES DANIEL	CA	23W	80
WALKER JAMES EDWARD	MS	07E	77
WALKER JAMES EDWARD	LA	43W	50
WALKER JAMES EDWARD JR	CA	53E	8
WALKER JAMES LLOYD	ID	11E	131
WALKER JAMES RICHARD	PA	15E	72
WALKER JERRY DOYLE	MS	06W	105
WALKER JERRY LEE	CA	02W	61
WALKER JOE FRANKLIN	VA	14E	120
WALKER JOHN DAVID	WA	16W	77
WALKER JOHN FREDERICK	NY	31W	28
WALKER JOHN HENRY	SC	10E	74
WALKER JOHN HENRY JR	TN	26E	32
WALKER JOHN JOSEPH	NY	18W	90
WALKER JOHN RAYMOND	NH	02W	117
WALKER JOHN WESLEY	CA	18W	107
WALKER JOHNNIE	DC	28E	88
WALKER JOSEPH BENSON	WY	22W	37
WALKER JULIUS LEMUEL JR	IL	54E	20
WALKER KENNETH EARL	MI	01E	64
WALKER KURTESS HOWARD	UT	10W	128
WALKER LA VERNE	CO	18E	37
WALKER LARRY ALLEN	CA	07W	133
WALKER LARRY WAYNE	NC	48W	50
WALKER LAVALLE	MO	33W	11
WALKER LAWRENCE PERCELL	NJ	14W	129
WALKER LESLIE ELROY	UT	20W	67
WALKER LESTER TIMOTHY	IA	52E	1
WALKER LINWOOD ALFERONIA	MD	11W	71
WALKER LLOYD FRANCIS	OR	14E	102
WALKER LUTHER JR	SC	20W	128
WALKER M B JR	IL	41E	13
WALKER MANLEY GLEN	TN	45W	30
WALKER MARTIN JR	OH	13W	55
WALKER MICHAEL ALLEN	NE	08W	29
WALKER MICHAEL CLYDE	CO	37W	71
WALKER MICHAEL DWAYNE	FL	19E	88
WALKER MICHAEL EARL	OH	54W	7
WALKER MICHAEL FREDERICK	CA	33E	61
WALKER MICHAEL STEPHEN	LA	20W	4
WALKER NEELY CLARENCE	GA	14W	56
WALKER ORIEN JUDSON JR	MA	01E	124
WALKER RALPH BAMFORD II	TX	21E	16
WALKER RANDALL EDWARD	MO	15E	81
WALKER RICHARD DUANE	NY	22W	50
WALKER RICHARD HAROLD	WA	34E	56
WALKER RICHARD HOWARD	NV	26W	58
WALKER RICHARD JR	IL	30E	35
WALKER RICHARD LEE	MD	22E	74
WALKER ROBERT DONALD	TX	01E	105
WALKER ROBERT HARVEY	TX	43E	2
WALKER ROBERT LAMONT JR	PA	05W	34
WALKER ROBERT LEE	FL	23E	117
WALKER ROBERT LEE	MI	41E	45
WALKER ROBERT LEE JR	AL	13W	4
WALKER ROSS JEROME	MO	16E	50
WALKER ROY	TX	12W	121
WALKER ROY LEACY	WV	23W	115
WALKER RUSSELL BERNDT	WA	10E	71
WALKER SAMUEL FRANKLIN JR	PA	36W	19
WALKER STEPHEN ARCHIE	NC	55W	17
WALKER STEPHEN CHRISTIAN	FL	33W	60
WALKER THOMAS	FL	09E	79
WALKER THOMAS DAVID	WI	36W	79
WALKER THOMAS EDWARD	SC	60W	24
WALKER THOMAS JAMES	CA	31E	27
WALKER THOMAS JAMES	NC	46W	25
WALKER THOMAS MICHAEL	CA	54E	20
WALKER THOMAS RAY	CA	18E	24
WALKER THOMAS TAYLOR	OR	06E	93
WALKER TOMMY DALE	TX	49E	17
WALKER TROY LEE	MS	18W	30
WALKER VERNON LEWIS	TN	41E	56
WALKER WALTER LEWIS	GA	08W	1
WALKER WAYNE HOWARD	PA	15W	92
WALKER WILLIAM GREGORY II	OH	07W	35
WALKER WILLIAM JOHN	CA	51E	14
WALKER WILLIAM WAYMAN	FL	08W	95
WALKER WILLIE	LA	13E	103
WALKER WILLIE B JR	GA	15W	120
WALKER WILLIE C	NC	36W	13
WALKER WILLIE TERRY JR	AL	12W	26
WALKER WINSTON CHARLES	MS	12W	99
WALKINSHAW GEORGE MYRON	CA	21E	5
WALKLEY ROBERT MARK	MI	28W	31
WALKO DANIEL STEVEN	PA	08W	96
WALKOWSKI PAUL DOUGLAS	NY	07E	100
WALL ALBERT CHARLES JR	PA	22W	94
WALL ARLON DANIEL JR	TX	26E	41
WALL CARL HORACE JR	NC	27E	62
WALL DONALD LEE	NC	48E	36
WALL GEORGE ELTON	TX	24E	47
WALL GEORGE MICHAEL	MS	11W	39
WALL GEORGE ROBERT	GA	09W	87
WALL JAMES ALLEN	SC	33E	61
WALL JAMES ARTHUR	TX	04W	135
WALL JAMES HOWELL	NC	30W	97
WALL JAMES NEIL	FL	20W	4
WALL JERRY LEE	NC	26W	28
WALL JERRY MACK	TX	07E	84
WALL JIMMIE PAUL	AR	35E	82
WALL JOHN WALTER	IA	18E	65
WALL PAUL EVERETT	CA	17W	83
WALL ROBERT ALBERT	PA	11W	23
WALL SAMUEL RAY	OH	31W	61
WALL STERLING AIDEN	MA	25E	40
WALL THOMAS JR	DC	08W	13
WALL WILLIAM PENN III	WA	12W	77
WALLACE ARNOLD BRIAN	CA	14E	78
WALLACE BARTLEY ALLEN	OK	01W	34
WALLACE BRIAN FRANCIS	NY	24E	116
WALLACE CHARLES FRANKLIN	MS	25E	60
WALLACE CHARLES JAMES	NV	41W	2
WALLACE CHARLES JR	FL	34E	82
WALLACE DANIEL LEON	FL	13W	76
WALLACE DIXIE DE	AZ	60E	4
WALLACE DONALD DEAN	KS	09E	95
WALLACE DOUGLAS DELANO	VA	18E	117
WALLACE EDDIE	MI	35W	86
WALLACE EPHRON JR	LA	02E	109
WALLACE EUGENE KENNETH	NC	22W	83
WALLACE FRANKIE LEE	AL	05E	1
WALLACE GARY ANTHONY	KY	24W	100
WALLACE GARY FRANK	AL	23E	96
WALLACE GEORGE DAVID	VA	21E	54
WALLACE GEORGE F JR	MS	39W	25
WALLACE GILBERT EARL	IN	16W	16
WALLACE HARRY WILLIAM	MA	26E	64
WALLACE HOBART MCKINLEY JR	WV	34E	82
WALLACE JACKIE ELMORE	FL	57W	33
WALLACE JAMES CLARENCE	MI	08E	50
WALLACE JAMES EARL	TX	10E	78
WALLACE JAMES LEROY	IL	51E	43
WALLACE JAMES RALPH	IN	19W	75
WALLACE JERALD D	TX	13E	87
WALLACE JIMMIE CARL	MS	29E	69
WALLACE JIMMIE LEWIS JR	MO	06E	23
WALLACE JOHN CLAYTON	MO	42W	25
WALLACE JOHN EDWARD	OR	27W	42
WALLACE JOHN THOMAS	MI	04W	136

NAME	STATE	PANEL NO.	LINE NO.
WALLACE KEM L	TX	20W	13
WALLACE LANNY JOHN	KS	08W	40
WALLACE LEMON JR	FL	52W	13
WALLACE LEROY	FL	10W	44
WALLACE MERVIN EDEN		50W	11
WALLACE MICHAEL D	CA	10E	2
WALLACE MICHAEL JOHN	MI	51E	2
WALLACE MICHAEL WALTER	UT	46E	60
WALLACE RICHARD COURTNEY	VA	39W	39
WALLACE RICHARD DEAN	MI	37W	19
WALLACE RICHARD F	IL	06E	7
WALLACE ROBERT CHARLES	NY	26E	20
WALLACE ROBERT MICHAEL	OH	24E	57
WALLACE RONALD RAY	MN	64W	3
WALLACE ROOSEVELT	GA	17W	48
WALLACE RUSSELL LEWIS	CO	43E	63
WALLACE ULYSSES	TN	16W	129
WALLACE VERNON MARTIN	LA	46W	35
WALLACE WENDELL LEVERN	WV	05W	19
WALLACE WILLARD BOSTON	OH	30E	74
WALLACE WILLIAM ROBERT	IN	05E	37
WALLACE WILLIAM THOMAS JR	GA	09W	11
WALLACE WILLIE LEWIS	AL	31W	85
WALLEN ERNIE LEE	IN	18W	13
WALLEN GARY LEE	IL	23W	33
WALLEN JOSEPH ROBERT	MA	14E	83
WALLENBECK FRANK C	NY	20W	36
WALLER CASEY OWEN	VA	12W	77
WALLER CHARLES ROBERT	OH	19E	76
WALLER HAROLD DEAN	MO	03W	41
WALLER JAMES	PA	46W	10
WALLER JAMES HARRELL	FL	19E	114
WALLER JAMES LEONARD	CO	38E	17
WALLER JERRY GORDON	GA	20E	126
WALLER JOHN BUSSEY	CA	28W	64
WALLER ROBERT WILLIE	FL	22E	74
WALLER THERMAN MORRIS	AR	04E	135
WALLEY TERRY CLINTON	TX	33E	61
WALLICK RICHARD ALLEN	PA	31W	74
WALLIN DENNIS RAY	GA	37E	74
WALLIN DOUGLAS DEWEY	MN	25E	48
WALLING CHARLES MILTON	AZ	09E	119
WALLING HARRY ALLEN	WA	01E	54
WALLING LEWIS METCALFE JR	RI	01E	7
WALLING ROGER PAUL	MO	16W	47
WALLING WILLIAM	IL	11E	116
WALLINGTON GEORGE HEYWARD	SC	61E	21
WALLNER FRANZ XAVIER	NY	08E	41
WALLS ALBERT CALVIN JR	NY	24W	108
WALLS CARL WILLIAM	PA	24W	23
WALLS JERRY FRANKLIN	MO	27E	77
WALLS JOHN THOMAS	GA	33W	52
WALLS KENNETH MARION JR	IL	10W	44
WALLS ROBERT LEE	LA	32E	41
WALLS RONALD RAY	PA	42W	24
WALLS TERRY LEE	OH	12E	31
WALLS THURMAN TRACY	WV	51E	34
WALLS WALTER LEE	KY	49W	27
WALLS WILLIAM HENRY	PA	04E	85
WALMSLEY WILLIAM MORRIS	WA	12W	94
WALROD RICHARD ARTHUR	CA	03E	50
WALSH ALLAN RAY	MI	42W	64
WALSH BLAINE HENRY	WI	16W	129
WALSH CASPAR MARVIN III	IL	12E	45
WALSH CHARLES SUMNER	PA	44E	62
WALSH DAVID WILLIAM	DC	22W	16
WALSH DONALD KEVIN	CT	31W	60
WALSH FRANCIS ANTHONY JR	CT	01W	102
WALSH GORDON O'DELL	TN	18E	37
WALSH JAMES EDWARD	OH	36E	41
WALSH JAMES MICHAEL	MA	49W	34
WALSH JEFFREY MICHAEL	PA	38E	41
WALSH JEROME WILLIAM	NY	29E	79
WALSH JOHN MICHAEL	NY	26W	28
WALSH MICHAEL PATRICK	NY	36W	47
WALSH RICHARD AMBROSE III	MN	32W	39
WALSH RICHARD DAVID	MA	15W	106
WALSH ROBERT DALE	MD	11W	62
WALSH ROBERT PAUL	MI	44W	60
WALSH ROBERT STEPHEN	MA	29E	46
WALSH ROBERT THOMAS	WI	09E	126
WALSH THOMAS CHARLES	OR	10E	85
WALSH THOMAS ROY	NY	23E	33
WALSH TRUMAN J	MT	31W	61
WALSH WAYNE EMERICK JR	PA	08W	96
WALSH WILLIAM THOMAS JR	IL	03W	76
WALSTER THOMAS GAVIN	UT	06E	94
WALSTON RUBY KENNETH	NC	45W	58
WALTER ALBERT MARION	NM	47W	57
WALTER CLIFTON MARTIN	PA	10E	32
WALTER CLYDE ELMER JR	PA	07W	127
WALTER HERBERT	LA	17W	21
WALTER WARD GUNARD	ND	31E	8
WALTERMAN LARRY JOHN	WA	42E	11
WALTERS BOBBY JOE	IN	28W	64
WALTERS BRUCE ELLIOT	NY	16W	68
WALTERS CHARLES ALLEN	MS	12W	15
WALTERS CRAIG COLLINS	AZ	55E	34
WALTERS DAVID MORGAN	KY	09W	92
WALTERS DONALD EDWARD JR	IL	20E	88
WALTERS DONALD WESLEY	CA	16E	117
WALTERS DONOVAN KEITH	NE	01W	102
WALTERS EUGENE	SC	36W	8
WALTERS FREDERICK F	FL	60E	5
WALTERS FREDRICK STEPHEN	GA	24W	80
WALTERS GERALD LEROY	NE	54W	25
WALTERS J D	OH	41W	50
WALTERS JACK JR	NC	20E	51
WALTERS JAMES REESE	NY	25W	113
WALTERS JIM JAMES	IA	24W	108
WALTERS JOHN BRADY	CA	24E	93
WALTERS JOHN EDMOND	KS	30W	17
WALTERS JOHN EDWARD	IN	50E	9
WALTERS KENNETH LEE	IN	19E	19
WALTERS MICHAEL	IN	20W	68
WALTERS MICHAEL ARTHUR	NJ	25W	57
WALTERS RICHARD EDWIN	SC	16W	97
WALTERS RICHARD FLOYD	SC	11E	35
WALTERS ROBERT DANIEL	MO	04W	75
WALTERS ROBERT JAMES	TX	09W	99
WALTERS ROBERT LOUIS	AR	26W	104
WALTERS RONALD C	NJ	06W	125
WALTERS SHERMAN LEE	PA	48W	50
WALTERS THOMAS JERRY	MS	64W	2
WALTERS TIM LEROY	IN	30W	97
WALTERS WILLIAM	CA	07E	77
WALTERS WILLIAM	PA	25W	44
WALTERS WILLIAM FRANCIS	AK	09W	49
WALTERS WILLIAM HAROLD	MO	27E	35
WALTERS WILLIAM OWEN	KY	30W	34
WALTERS WILLIAM PORTER	WV	03W	93
WALTHALL CHARLES EDWARD	GA	65E	3
WALTHERS FRANK DANIEL	IL	20W	84
WALTHOUR SAMUEL W JR	IA	20W	78
WALTMAN JESSE LYLE	CA	12E	121
WALTMAN RICHARD A	MS	10E	12
WALTON CRAIG LESLIE	CA	39W	35
WALTON EUGENE	TN	50E	2
WALTON GEORGE SAMUEL	NC	15E	102
WALTON HAROLD LEE	GA	53W	41
WALTON HARRY THOMAS JR	KY	03W	93
WALTON JIMMY RONALD	LA	08W	123
WALTON JOSEPH	MS	35W	45
WALTON JOSEPH HERBERT	IL	10E	23
WALTON LAWRENCE RICHARD	OH	33E	76
WALTON LEWIS ALAN	IN	02W	85
WALTON LEWIS CLARK	RI	03W	30
WALTON LOUIS EUGENE	MI	08E	102
WALTON RICHARD FREEMAN	NY	14W	109
WALTON ROGER EDWIN	NY	27E	98
WALTON WILLIAM HENRY JR	VA	03W	23
WALTON WILLIAM LEROY	NM	06E	135
WALTRICH ROBERT JOHN	IL	17E	76
WALTZ JAMES ROBERT	PA	60E	5
WALTZ LARRY THOMAS	PA	39W	6
WALZ GARY THOMAS	WI	25W	90
WALZ NICHOLAS GEORGE	WI	32E	53
WANAMAKER DANNY WAYNE	CA	09E	79
WANAMAKER JOHNNY WAYNE	TN	46E	43
WANBAUGH RONALD NELSON	CA	52E	12
WANDLER LOUIS JOHN	MT	14E	65
WANDRO JAMES MATTHEW	CA	22W	29
WANER LOUIS BERNARD II	LA	28W	20
WANG ANDREW JACOB	RI	61W	18
WANGERIN LEON ARTHUR	WI	20E	69
WANGESHIK MELVIN UDELSON	MI	40E	34
WANGLER LOSSY RAY	CA	06E	27
WANKA CARL JEFFREY	MN	06W	1
WANN DONALD LYNN	OK	03W	63
WANNER CARL JOSEPH	PA	24W	51
WANTO JOHN PAUL	PA	12W	32
WANZEL CHARLES JOSEPH III	NY	02W	124
WAPINSKI DANIEL KEITH	VA	21W	35
WARBINGTON HOWARD OTTO	MS	04W	104
WARBIS LARRY LYLE	ND	41W	21
WARBRITTON JERRY LEE	IN	34W	35
WARCZAK DAVID JAMES	VA	30W	40
WARD ALAN CURTIS	OH	25W	113
WARD ALBERT	MO	41E	32
WARD ALEXANDER KEARNEY	MD	39E	68
WARD ALLAN CURT	WI	53E	25
WARD ALLEN LEA	ME	48W	9
WARD BEN CALHOUN	SC	17W	83
WARD BRENT F	UT	56E	18
WARD CARL GENE	AL	64W	3
WARD CARL RAY	NE	57W	33
WARD CARL RAY JR	OK	20W	90
WARD CHARLES DWIGHT	TX	23E	79
WARD CHARLES EDWARD	KY	64W	17
WARD CLYDE ANDERSON	TN	20E	80
WARD CRAIG NELSON	OH	06W	89
WARD DANNY EDWARD	CA	61W	8
WARD DANNY RUSSELL	KY	03E	38
WARD DAVID EUGENE	MO	28E	47
WARD DAVID JAMES	NV	53W	14
WARD DENNIS CHARLES	CA	14W	61
WARD DONALD ROLAND	MD	26E	19
WARD DONNIE LEE	NC	15E	26
WARD EARNEST SHELBY	MS	42E	58
WARD EUGENE AMBROSE	IA	20E	70
WARD FORREST EDWARD	NY	57W	14
WARD GARRY WALLACE	AR	12W	126
WARD GARY EDWIN	GA	14E	97
WARD GEORGE HOWARD	MS	06E	105
WARD GEORGE ROBERT JR	TN	29W	41
WARD GEORGE WARREN	CA	12W	23
WARD HERSCHEL RUDOLPH	SC	08E	9
WARD IVORY JR	MO	03E	63
WARD JAMES CALVIN	WI	02E	119
WARD JAMES CLINTON	VA	25W	34
WARD JAMES CRAIG	CA	04W	44
WARD JAMES HOWARD	IL	33W	35
WARD JAMES LARRY	FL	33W	83
WARD JAMES PATRICK	MD	21W	104
WARD JIMMY LEE	ID	31E	18
WARD JOHN DOUGLAS JR	TN	36E	41
WARD JOHN FRANCIS	NY	17W	46
WARD JOHN LAWRENCE	NY	11W	62
WARD JOHNNY LEE	ID	18W	73
WARD JOHNNY NEWTON JR	FL	05W	51
WARD KURT EUGEN	OH	51W	9
WARD LEONARD DANIEL	OK	21W	72
WARD LEROY	MO	21W	73
WARD LUTHER BURNETT JR	NY	02W	57
WARD MARK HEYWOOD	MD	19W	75
WARD NEAL CLINTON	TX	22W	39
WARD PATRICK EDWARD	PA	47W	34
WARD PATRICK MICHAEL	CA	18W	73
WARD PAUL	OH	08W	132
WARD RALPH LELAND	OH	04W	26
WARD RANDOLPH BUCK	UT	16E	82
WARD RANDY NEAL	TN	35E	51
WARD RICHARD HENRY	NY	11W	29
WARD ROBERT DAVID	CA	04E	61
WARD ROBERT WILLIAM	CA	08W	53
WARD ROGER ELGIN	MI	48E	21
WARD ROGER LEE	IN	26W	74
WARD RONALD JACK	OK	01W	95
WARD RONALD RAY	KS	24W	88
WARD RONALD WAYNE	VA	20E	88
WARD RUDOLPH NATHINAL	VA	30E	35
WARD TERRY J	UT	36W	66
WARD TERRY MICHAEL	IN	61E	21
WARD THEODORE DAVISON	OH	25W	26
WARD THOMAS LESLIE	MS	33E	77
WARD TIMMIE JOE	IA	01W	65

NAME	STATE	PANEL NO.	LINE NO.
WARD TOM	OH	01E	62
WARD TONY ROBERT	GA	10W	73
WARD WALTER LEONARD	IL	21E	71
WARD WAYNE LEVOYER	AL	42E	12
WARD WILLIAM	IL	24W	80
WARD WILLIAM JAMES JR	NC	04W	127
WARD WILLIAM LEE	OK	13E	2
WARDELL HORACE LEE	PA	08W	126
WARDEN RICHARD JOHN	WI	09W	121
WARDLOW JAMES DILLON	TX	44W	54
WARDROBE RICHARD ALFRED	FL	26E	53
WARDROP THOMAS III	IN	05E	111
WARDS DAN THOMAS	KS	33E	66
WARDWELL ERIC MICHAEL	ME	25E	112
WARE BEVERLY COSTNER	NC	26W	58
WARE CECIL Y	WV	05E	75
WARE CLIFFORD OTIS	WA	34E	50
WARE DON HAMUEL	AL	02W	109
WARE FRANCIS LOUIS III	OH	13W	89
WARE GENE LAMAR	GA	24W	87
WARE JOE L	IL	59E	14
WARE JOHN ALAN	OR	16W	32
WARE KEITH LINCOLN	CA	44W	55
WARE MACK ARTHUR	AL	03E	98
WARE MATTHEW	AL	12E	83
WARE OLIVER ARGYLE	WV	20E	38
WARE ORTEN LEE	OK	51E	14
WARE RICHARD ALEXANDRA	MS	46W	10
WARE ROBERT DENNIS	VA	14E	115
WARF LAWRENCE ROBERT	CA	15W	124
WARFIELD DENNIS GORDON	MI	26W	88
WARFIELD PHILLIP RAY	TN	11W	118
WARGO DAVID ROY	MI	11E	4
WARGO DENNIS MICHAEL	PA	19E	76
WARGO VINCENT JOSEPH JR	PA	44W	67
WARING GEORGE BADEN	MD	01W	69
WARK CARLISLE OGDEN JR	MD	25W	57
WARK DANIEL EDWARD	HI	47W	24
WARK WILLIAM EDWARD III	PA	44W	32
WARLICK SAM DIXON	NC	31E	18
WARMBRODT JON FREDERICK	CA	34W	80
WARMSLEY HAROLD JAMES	TX	23W	4
WARNE DENNIS EUGENE	OH	29E	93
WARNER ARTHUR LEE	SC	37W	37
WARNER BRUCE BYERLY	CT	06E	2
WARNER CHARLES WILLIAM F	CA	24E	1
WARNER CHARLES WILLIAM JR	FL	03W	12
WARNER DAN EDISON	CO	27E	77
WARNER DAVID HOWARD	WA	39E	78
WARNER DOUGLAS LEROY	FL	37W	8
WARNER GARY ALLEN	OH	36W	24
WARNER HENRY LUKE III	DC	46W	46
WARNER HERBERT ALVIN JR	CA	21E	103
WARNER JAMES LEO	RI	43W	59
WARNER LEWIS WILLIAM JR	KY	32W	40
WARNER MICHAEL LEE	OH	34W	62
WARNER MICHAEL PATRICK	PA	22W	110
WARNER RICHARD THOMAS	VA	27W	27
WARNER ROBERT ALLEN	MI	35E	83
WARNER STEPHEN HENRY	NJ	05W	104
WARNER THOMAS CRAIG	PA	31W	61
WARNER WILFRED WESLEY JR	IN	08W	47
WARNETT RONALD LEONARD	NJ	30W	50
WARNICK JERONE JAMES	MD	27W	92
WARNICK LEONARD CHARLES	NE	09W	25
WARNICK MICHAEL GENE	OK	07W	108
WARNOCK LARRY LYMAN	WY	17E	15
WARNOCK ROBERT MERRILL	CA	14W	99
WARR JAMES MILTON	TX	44E	22
WARRELMANN KLAUS	CA	12E	8
WARREN ARTHUR LEONARD	OH	13E	15
WARREN BAXTER		12W	50
WARREN BENJAMIN IRVIN	LA	11E	42
WARREN COLEMAN LITCHFIELD	MI	11E	104
WARREN DAVID BRANIARD	PA	05E	111
WARREN DONALD ALBERT	CA	47E	18
WARREN ERVIN	PA	08E	5
WARREN GALEN EUGENE	WA	20E	70
WARREN GRAY DAWSON	IA	17W	122
WARREN JAMES ROBERT JR	IN	28E	88
WARREN JEIDER JACKSON	LA	41E	56
WARREN JIMMIE SHERRILL	MI	31W	29
WARREN JOHN ALBERT	OH	16W	7
WARREN JOHN EARL JR	NY	34W	3
WARREN JOHN OWEN	GA	06W	125
WARREN LARRY	PA	24W	23
WARREN LARRY DEAN	KS	50E	23
WARREN MANASSEH BROCK	DC	04W	72
WARREN MICHAEL JAY	IL	52E	12
WARREN MICHAEL WALTER	CO	40E	34
WARREN RICHARD JOHN	NY	29E	86
WARREN RICHARD MICHAEL	NV	04W	120
WARREN ROBERT GLENN	GA	15W	116
WARREN ROBERT MARION	PA	26E	33
WARREN RODIS JOHN	LA	18E	54
WARREN RONALD JOHN	MO	01E	127
WARREN SAMMIE LEE	AR	25W	26
WARREN STEPHEN EDWARD	NY	05W	72
WARREN THOMAS ALLEN	PA	49W	11
WARREN THOMAS WAYNE	VA	38W	47
WARREN TOMMY RAY	TX	14W	37
WARREN WILLIAM THOMAS JR	KY	02W	83
WARREN WILLIE CRAIG	TX	22E	52
WARRICK CLARENCE RAY	TN	64E	3
WARRINGTON CHARLES W JR	CA	29W	57
WARSHAWSKY JOEL BARRY	NY	27E	1
WARSING CHARLES GRAFFIOUS	PA	64W	3
WARTCHOW DENNIS RUSSELL	WY	18W	45
WARTH WOODROE WARREN	IA	57E	10
WARTHAN ALBERT WILLIAM	IN	48E	56
WARTMAN CHESTER JAMES	KY	25W	57
WARWICK DUNCAN ALBERT	LA	20W	32
WARZECHA GERALD WALTER	IL	08E	57
WASCHICK WALTER RAYMOND	WI	38E	63
WASH NATHAN JR	TX	50E	23
WASHAM DENNY LEE	TN	37W	71
WASHBURN DAVID ANDREW	PA	61W	18
WASHBURN FRED ZIMRI	MA	42W	65
WASHBURN JOHNNY LEE	CA	16E	117
WASHBURN LARRY EUGENE	TX	08E	59
WASHBURN ROBERT GLEN	CA	46W	46
WASHBURN WAYNE ARTHUR	IL	37E	29
WASHENIK GARY LEE	FL	08W	117
WASHINGTON ALBERT ALLEYNE	NY	25E	9
WASHINGTON ALBERT B JR	NJ	23W	40
WASHINGTON ANTHONY FELIX	IL	38W	31
WASHINGTON ARTHUR DOUGLAS	DC	14E	39
WASHINGTON BOOKER THOMAS	FL	13E	87
WASHINGTON CARL	MI	35W	45
WASHINGTON CHARLES L	DC	15W	66
WASHINGTON CLARENCE EDWAR	MS	19E	88
WASHINGTON CLARENCE H JR	IN	58E	2
WASHINGTON COLEY LOUIS JR	NY	06E	108
WASHINGTON DAN THOMAS	LA	14E	115
WASHINGTON DONALD LEROY	OK	55W	32
WASHINGTON DONALD RAY	TX	17W	79
WASHINGTON DOUGLAS MAC	LA	59W	17
WASHINGTON EDWARD W JR	MS	52W	3
WASHINGTON ERICK LEE	NY	28E	86
WASHINGTON GEORGE RAYMOND	SC	35E	36
WASHINGTON GLENN	NY	17W	79
WASHINGTON JAMES B	TX	55W	24
WASHINGTON JAMES BELL	TX	03E	47
WASHINGTON JAMES C JR	GA	06W	72
WASHINGTON JAMES ERVIN	IL	19E	102
WASHINGTON JAMES LEROY SR	LA	25W	8
WASHINGTON JOHN	AR	35E	1
WASHINGTON JOHN WILLIE	GA	31W	29
WASHINGTON KING DAVID	LA	37W	15
WASHINGTON LARRY EDWARD	TN	10E	115
WASHINGTON LAWRENCE O	KY	14W	80
WASHINGTON LEONARD B JR	IL	30E	20
WASHINGTON LOUIS WELDON	VT	40W	40
WASHINGTON MAURICE JOEL	IL	28W	54
WASHINGTON NATHANIEL	PA	04E	15
WASHINGTON RALPH LEVON	VA	44E	32
WASHINGTON ROBERT	NY	10W	106
WASHINGTON ROBERT ALLAN	VA	19W	36
WASHINGTON ROBERT JAMES	IN	46W	55
WASHINGTON SHERMAN THOMAS	PA	47E	28
WASHINGTON SYLVESTER	MS	60E	5
WASHINGTON THOMAS MELVIN	VA	54W	33
WASHINGTON WILLIAM F JR	AL	61W	8
WASHINGTON WILLIE J JR	PA	38W	8
WASHINGTON WILLIE JAMES	NY	18W	52
WASHKUHN JAMES WILLIAMS	WI	12E	45
WASHUT WALTER JUNIOR	WY	20E	70
WASILOW JOHN STEPHEN	SC	38W	53
WASSENICH STEPHEN GEORGE	OH	22E	74
WASSERMAN MICHAEL LEON	ID	41W	55
WASSON STEVEN EDWARD	WI	11W	107
WASZKIEWICZ DENNIS LAVERN	MI	04W	79
WATANABE JAMES RYOICHIRO	CA	27E	17
WATERBURY RICHARD MEAD	FL	17E	89
WATERFIELD RICHARD F	MO	15W	30
WATERLOO MICHAEL JEFFERY	IL	21W	10
WATERMAN CRAIG HOUSTON	MA	24E	53
WATERMAN CRAIG THOMAS	IA	07W	37
WATERMAN DENNIS WALTER	IA	11E	73
WATERMAN MICHAEL J	MA	22E	52
WATERMAN THOMAS L	VA	12W	121
WATERS CLARENCE EDGAR	LA	26E	64
WATERS ELIJAH	NC	31E	95
WATERS GLENDON LEE	TX	23E	33
WATERS LEON ELDRED JR	NY	41E	14
WATERS MELVIN LESTER	IL	01E	91
WATERS MICHAEL	IL	08E	55
WATERS MICHAEL ROY	GA	09W	108
WATERS ROBERT MITCHELL	MD	11E	18
WATERS SAMUEL EDWIN JR	NC	13E	42
WATERS TROY LEE	AR	01E	123
WATERS WILLIAM WALTER JR	VA	46W	54
WATHEN FREDERICK ALLEN	OH	09E	20
WATINGTON RALPH H JR	NY	19E	68
WATKINS ALTON LAMOTTE JR	MD	33E	23
WATKINS ANTHONY RONALD	OK	34E	2
WATKINS BILLY JOE	KY	22E	35
WATKINS BRUCE LAMAR	GA	06E	36
WATKINS CHARLES EMANUEL	TN	13E	46
WATKINS CHARLES HENRY JR	VA	34W	87
WATKINS DAVID EUGENE	CA	67W	6
WATKINS EARL WELDON JR	GA	37E	74
WATKINS FRANKLIN ROOSEVEL	VA	15E	80
WATKINS GARY WINSTON	TX	42E	44
WATKINS GERALD EDWARD	DC	22E	35
WATKINS GLENN ALLEN	MO	21E	77
WATKINS GREGORY H	NY	49E	1
WATKINS HAROLD DAVID	OH	24E	46
WATKINS HAROLD EUGENE	AL	03E	47
WATKINS HARRY LEE JR	MD	34E	7
WATKINS JAMES LEE	TX	14E	93
WATKINS JERYL LINN	OH	54E	21
WATKINS JOEL KEITH	AL	31W	74
WATKINS JOHN WILLIAM	TN	06E	105
WATKINS KENNETH MAURICE	DC	44E	32
WATKINS LARRY LANCE	IL	11W	98
WATKINS LARRY WAYNE	NC	25W	34
WATKINS LAWRENCE D JR	VA	10E	20
WATKINS MAHLON HUGH	PA	25W	26
WATKINS MARION	KY	12E	92
WATKINS MARTIN LEE	CA	08E	9
WATKINS MICHAEL	NY	03W	107
WATKINS REGINALD ALVIN	NC	03E	63
WATKINS ROBERT JAMES JR	MD	17W	53
WATKINS SAMUEL EUGENE	UT	55E	34
WATKINS SHERDIN JAY	CA	05E	43
WATKINS TOBY JACK	CO	44W	33
WATROUS ROBERT ROLAND	OR	25E	4
WATSON ALBERT CLAY JR	WI	28E	106
WATSON ALFONZA	CA	19E	9
WATSON AMOS CARLTON	NC	01E	114
WATSON ARTHUR	NC	47W	5
WATSON ARTHUR	NY	34W	46
WATSON ARTHUR JR	CA	10E	111
WATSON BILLY FRANK	TX	25E	26
WATSON BILLY JOE	OK	03W	84
WATSON CARNELL EARL	TX	20E	51
WATSON CHARLES BRYANT JR	SC	20E	52
WATSON CLARENCE EDWARD	TN	51W	15
WATSON COLUMBUS JR	FL	02W	117
WATSON CURTIS LEE JR	MO	07E	60
WATSON DAVID JAMES	WI	02W	64
WATSON DAVID WARREN	TX	26W	51
WATSON DELMIS CLAYTON	VA	18W	26
WATSON DENNIS ALLEN	PA	15W	15
WATSON DONALD DAVID	WI	02E	46

NAME	STATE	PANEL NO.	LINE NO.
WATSON DONNIE EDWARD	FL	42W	2
WATSON ERNEST	MI	05E	40
WATSON FRANK PETER	OK	02E	14
WATSON GARY EUGENE	TX	47E	57
WATSON GEORGE WILLIAM	OR	01E	38
WATSON GREGORY ALTON	NJ	29E	18
WATSON HARRY ALLEN	IN	06W	96
WATSON HARVEY RAYMOND	MD	20W	52
WATSON J V	CA	08W	53
WATSON JAMES ANTHONY	MD	03E	125
WATSON JAMES ARTHUR	PA	30E	61
WATSON JAMES CHARLES	TN	02W	91
WATSON JAMES EDWARD	CA	15E	92
WATSON JAMES FRANKLIN	TN	46W	25
WATSON JAMES HAROLD	TN	28W	53
WATSON JAMES OSMOND	CA	15W	116
WATSON JAMES THOMAS	NY	12W	54
WATSON JIMMY LEE	NC	44E	42
WATSON JOE NATHAN	AR	17W	99
WATSON JOE NATHAN	TN	13W	13
WATSON JOHN ELMO	NY	10E	52
WATSON JOHNNY MACK	AL	09W	71
WATSON JOSEPH MICHAEL	GA	34E	2
WATSON KENNETH GARY	CO	53W	41
WATSON KENNETH LAWRENCE	MO	29W	33
WATSON KENNETH MICHAEL	OH	49E	49
WATSON LARRY ELLIOTT	SC	15W	8
WATSON LARRY WILLIAM	MN	41W	33
WATSON LEE ARTHUR	NC	48E	37
WATSON LESLIE JAMES	CA	11W	2
WATSON LESTER ARTHUR	SD	51W	22
WATSON LORING WILLIAM	ME	29W	85
WATSON MARVIN LEROI	NJ	22W	71
WATSON PAUL EDWARD	MD	61E	20
WATSON PERCY EARL	NC	19E	89
WATSON RICHARD COLON	NC	20W	89
WATSON RICHARD DALE	WA	18E	37
WATSON RICHARD WAYNE	NC	23W	60
WATSON RONALD LEE	OK	10E	45
WATSON RONALD LEONARD	TX	05W	119
WATSON RONALD R	CA	33E	43
WATSON RUSSEL LEE	ID	15E	3
WATSON SAMMIE LEE JR	MO	37W	3
WATSON STANLEY EUGENE	CA	39E	1
WATSON SULLIVAN WALL	IL	26W	16
WATSON THOMAS ARTHUR	GA	23W	33
WATSON THOMAS EDWARD	CA	09W	89
WATSON TOMMIE	GA	19W	6
WATSON TYRONE CALVIN	PA	07W	63
WATSON ULMER JOE	GA	04W	129
WATSON WILLIAM B	TN	26W	5
WATSON WILLIAM B JR	NC	05E	69
WATSON WILLIAM L	KY	41E	14
WATSON WILMER	CA	31E	18
WATT ROBERT LEE	TX	23W	23
WATT SAMMIE LEE	MS	17E	89
WATT WILLIAM ROY	TX	42E	12
WATTERS CHARLES JOSEPH	NJ	30E	36
WATTERS PHILLIP DONALD	MN	35W	30
WATTERSON DENNIS RAY	CA	05W	35
WATTS AFTON M	TX	55E	34
WATTS ASTER	KY	07E	84
WATTS BRADLEY KEITH	TN	44W	67
WATTS FLOYD	KY	21W	63
WATTS FRANK TAYLOR	FL	46E	60
WATTS HENRY LINCOLN SR	GA	03W	31
WATTS JOHN RAYMOND	AL	19W	75
WATTS LARRY DEAN	KS	16E	37
WATTS RALPH O	MA	12E	69
WATTS RICHARD ALLEN	NY	15W	30
WATTS RICHARD JOE	FL	07W	115
WATTS ROBERT LEE	IL	41E	46
WATTS ROBERT WESLEY	KY	30E	67
WATTS ROY DELANO	AL	06E	125
WATTS RUSSELL DAVID	IL	10W	92
WATTS SCHYLER	KY	02W	83
WATTS THEARTIS JR	PA	48W	36
WATTS THOMAS JAMES	CA	26W	37
WATTS THOMAS ROGER	CA	34E	55
WATTS WAYNE ALAN	ME	26E	53
WATTS WILLIAM E	TX	52W	19
WATTS WILLIAM SCOTT	TX	38W	31

NAME	STATE	PANEL NO.	LINE NO.
WAUCHOPE DOUGLAS	NY	02E	25
WAUGH GRANT REED	WA	08W	102
WAUGH JOHN LOUIS	NY	37W	60
WAUGH MARION EDWARD	TX	55E	35
WAUGH RANDALL MICHAEL	CA	53W	25
WAUGH RONNEL LOUIE	TN	31W	61
WAULK JAMES HAROLD JR	OH	13W	38
WAWERSIK KENNETH WILLIAM	MI	13E	46
WAX DAVID J	MA	04E	32
WAXMAN SAUL	NY	11E	29
WAXMAN TEDDY	MD	31E	19
WAXTON WILBERT EUGENE	AL	07E	12
WAY CLARENCE L	SC	18E	73
WAY THOMAS URBAN	NY	27E	79
WAYCASTER RICHARD LEE	NC	32W	61
WAYMAN ALBERT ORLANDO JR	WY	17W	115
WAYMAN BOBBY RAY	IN	05E	37
WAYMAN DONALD MICHAEL	CT	22W	37
WAYMIRE BILLY JOE	AR	12E	86
WAYMIRE JACKIE L	WV	14E	3
WAYMIRE MICHAEL KARL	IN	09W	123
WAYNE JAMES CLARK	IN	02W	53
WAYRYNEN DALE EUGENE	MN	20E	52
WAYSACK WILLIAM JOHN	CA	58E	2
WAYT CHARLES M	OH	15E	37
WAYT SCOTT WILLIAM	OR	03W	63
WEAKS MELVIN LEE	NC	03W	134
WEAKS TIMOTHY HOWARD	OH	39W	19
WEAMER ALLEN RAY	WA	57W	15
WEANT TERRANCE LEE	OH	30W	70
WEAR DENNIS WILLIAM	MT	44W	20
WEARING MARION BERNARD	NY	32E	16
WEARMOUTH RONALD VERNON	IA	57W	21
WEARS JAMES CRAIG	WV	23E	47
WEATHERBY JACK WILTON	TX	02E	45
WEATHERBY JOHN GEOFFREY	PA	29E	7
WEATHERFORD JERRY GLENN	TX	27W	68
WEATHERFORD JOHN MICHAEL	TX	52E	1
WEATHERFORD ROY JULIAN JR	SC	36W	9
WEATHERHEAD GARY ROBERT	MI	35W	86
WEATHERLY JACKIE DON	CA	22E	22
WEATHERS BOBBY LYNN	TX	45E	16
WEATHERS NATHANIEL	OH	35E	12
WEATHERS WILLIAM B III	OH	52W	47
WEATHERSBEE ERNEST MURRAL	CA	39E	41
WEATHERSBY JAMES EARL	MS	05W	66
WEAVER ALLEN PRICE	TX	47W	35
WEAVER BARRY KENT	OH	09W	69
WEAVER CHARLES EDWARD	TX	29E	64
WEAVER CLINTON JAMES	GA	19W	26
WEAVER DALE LARRY	PA	51W	1
WEAVER DOYLE WAYNE	CA	10W	44
WEAVER FRANKLIN FLOYD	PA	06E	87
WEAVER GARRY LYNN	TN	07W	130
WEAVER GARY LEE	MI	32E	49
WEAVER GEORGE ANTHONY	MI	36W	38
WEAVER GEORGE ROBERT JR	PA	12E	9
WEAVER GREG	TX	07E	112
WEAVER HAYDEN EDWARD	WI	01E	120
WEAVER HENRY LUE	PA	18E	73
WEAVER JACK	GA	13E	8
WEAVER JAMES ONLEY	NC	36W	9
WEAVER JERALD BRUCE	NY	24E	116
WEAVER JERRY LEE	TN	52W	25
WEAVER JERRY MICHAEL	MI	08W	24
WEAVER JOHN FORREST	MO	34W	62
WEAVER JOHN HERBERT	GA	34W	30
WEAVER JOHN SIMMONS	IL	05W	51
WEAVER JOSEPH ROBERT JR	GA	39E	41
WEAVER PHILIP WARREN	GA	46W	35
WEAVER RICHARD ALLAN	CA	37W	8
WEAVER RICHARD MICHAEL	OH	64E	9
WEAVER ROBERT DUANE	MN	11E	104
WEAVER RONALD LEE	PA	41E	5
WEAVER SAMMY LANE	LA	02W	117
WEAVER TERRY LEE	IN	42E	44
WEAVER TIMOTHY PATRICK	CA	41W	44
WEAVER WILLIAM CARRELL	TX	18W	18
WEBB ALFONSO AUGUSTUS	TN	26W	59
WEBB ALFRED JR	MN	27W	60
WEBB BILL ALAN	OK	47W	11
WEBB BRUCE DOUGLAS	IL	02E	63

NAME	STATE	PANEL NO.	LINE NO.
WEBB DANIEL DAVID	FL	43E	47
WEBB DONALD	WV	04E	76
WEBB DONALD FRANKLIN	OH	33E	33
WEBB DONALD RAY	CA	41W	55
WEBB DONALD RAY	IA	13W	102
WEBB EARL KENNON	LA	30E	51
WEBB EARL RAY JR	DE	09W	6
WEBB FRANK WRIGHT	VA	55E	35
WEBB FREDERIC PEERS	OR	32E	41
WEBB GARY ALAN	KS	15E	102
WEBB GARY JOSEPH	MA	22W	114
WEBB GEORGE GRANT KING JR	HI	05E	22
WEBB GREGORY LYNN	MI	24E	48
WEBB HOWARD LEE	DE	21E	77
WEBB JACKIE JOE	TN	29W	85
WEBB JAMES ARTHUR	NJ	16E	5
WEBB JAMES EDWARD	TX	12E	120
WEBB JAMES WILLIAM JR	MO	42W	25
WEBB JOHN FRIEL	NC	02W	9
WEBB JOHNNY LEE	WI	09W	46
WEBB JOHNNY ROBERT	KS	50E	43
WEBB LARRY DALE	TN	46E	51
WEBB LEONARD JR	MO	36W	60
WEBB LEROY BOYD	GA	18E	12
WEBB MARK JAMES	IN	08W	36
WEBB MICHAEL DEAN	NC	21W	73
WEBB MICHAEL RAY	OR	04E	57
WEBB MICHAEL WILLIAM	OR	61E	4
WEBB NORVELL JOHNATHAN	IL	52W	21
WEBB OLIVER KENNETH	GA	30W	34
WEBB PAUL HENLEY	KY	33E	77
WEBB ROBERT JAMES	WA	38E	18
WEBB ROBERT MITCHELL JR	GA	02W	42
WEBB STEVEN CHARLES	IL	21W	114
WEBB TERRY EMERSON	OH	44E	42
WEBB THEODORE WOOD	VA	18W	99
WEBB VIRGIL JUNIOR	OH	42W	33
WEBB WALLIS WAYNE	MO	05W	76
WEBB WILLIAM MATTHEW	TX	37W	26
WEBB WILLIAM WINTON	VA	08E	13
WEBB WILSON LEWIS JR	NC	11W	71
WEBBER BRIAN LEE	NM	37W	71
WEBBER FLOYD DEAN	TX	12W	1
WEBBER FREDERICK CARL	NY	41E	32
WEBBER JAMES THOMAS	WI	09W	101
WEBBER SCOTT STILLMAN	CA	13E	60
WEBER CRAIG HOWARD	OH	17W	104
WEBER DANNY A	IN	35E	64
WEBER DAVID ALLAN	MN	28W	41
WEBER DAVID FRANK	MN	04E	74
WEBER DAVID GERALD	CA	09W	36
WEBER DELBERT ELLIS	FL	21W	11
WEBER DENNIS LEE	IA	04E	6
WEBER GREGORY JOHN	TN	41W	28
WEBER JEROME PAUL	PA	30E	61
WEBER JOHN KNUTE	MN	37E	15
WEBER JOSEPH ALAN	PA	31W	41
WEBER KARL EDWIN	WI	39W	69
WEBER LESTER WILLIAM	IL	31W	29
WEBER PATRICK	CA	03W	51
WEBER PAUL FREDERICK	CA	23W	49
WEBER RAYMOND N	CA	34E	56
WEBER ROGER DALE	OH	59W	17
WEBER TERRY LEE	IN	12E	70
WEBER WILLIAM EUGENE	IA	47W	35
WEBER WILLIAM JAMES	MN	39E	15
WEBER WILLIAM PAUL	NJ	53W	41
WEBER WILLIS WILLIAM	ND	03E	40
WEBER WILTSE LEE	WA	08W	50
WEBORG JOHN CHARLES	CA	14E	72
WEBSTER CHRISTOPHER C	MT	19W	26
WEBSTER DAVID	VA	01E	19
WEBSTER DAVID O'NEIL	AZ	11E	47
WEBSTER DENNIS WADE	RI	05W	19
WEBSTER FRANCIS MARION	UT	61E	4
WEBSTER FRANK ANTHONY	CA	09W	113
WEBSTER FRANKLIN	MD	32E	83
WEBSTER HENRY WAYNE	OK	14E	25
WEBSTER HOWARD GREGORY	CA	29W	16
WEBSTER JAMES ROBERT JR	TX	40E	34
WEBSTER JAY DENNIS JR	PA	19W	57
WEBSTER JOHN THOMAS	NC	34E	26

NAME	STATE	PANEL NO.	LINE NO.
WEBSTER MICHAEL WARREN	TX	37E	75
WEBSTER REGERNAILD	TN	15W	100
WEBSTER RHENA CHARLES	CA	32W	85
WEBSTER RICHARD	OH	04E	116
WEBSTER ROBERT LEWIS	IL	13W	90
WEBSTER THOMAS MONTROSE	OH	32E	28
WEBSTER WILBERT MICHAEL	CA	30W	8
WECKER HARRY HERR	PA	18W	22
WEDDENDORF ROBERT GEORGE	CA	55E	35
WEDDINGTON PHILLIP MURRY	KY	54W	1
WEDGEWORTH WILLIAM THOMAS	OH	56W	16
WEDHORN DAVID EARL	MI	38E	18
WEDLAKE BRIAN FRANCIS	NJ	54E	21
WEDLOW KENNETH EDWIN	CA	13W	108
WEDMAN KENNETH ALBERT	CA	44W	43
WEDRICK LONNIE MARK	WA	60W	13
WEED DONALD EDMOND	CA	35E	51
WEED JAMES ALLAN	WA	21E	54
WEED MORGAN WILLIAM	AL	10W	20
WEED RODNEY RICHARD	WA	16E	117
WEEDEN LARRY LEE	IN	25W	57
WEEDEN ROBERT LEE	WI	54E	21
WEEDER RICHARD D	CA	28E	28
WEEDO VINCENT JAMES JR	NJ	14E	93
WEEKFALL EDDIE LEE	IL	31E	39
WEEKLEY CLIFFORD WAYNE	CA	21W	114
WEEKLEY GARY LEE	OH	28W	31
WEEKLEY GARY WAYNE	WV	12W	94
WEEKLEY RUSSELL JOSEPH	LA	58W	30
WEEKS CURTIS MILLER JR	AZ	16W	36
WEEKS DAVID L	NY	01W	120
WEEKS GEORGE DALE	TX	08E	1
WEEKS HOWARD DANIEL	FL	46E	60
WEEKS MICHAEL DALE	UT	18W	107
WEEKS MICHAEL DOUGLAS	OR	34W	62
WEEKS WALKER NORWOOD	MO	10E	27
WEEKS WALTER DARRYL	MI	56W	10
WEEMS RICHARD QUENTIN	NY	29E	36
WEEMS RONALD CLIFTON	MS	32W	85
WEESE RALPH JUNIOR	OH	43E	38
WEESE RONNIE GENE	MO	25W	58
WEEST JAMES JOSEPH	PA	24E	93
WEGER JOHN JR	CA	02E	132
WEGNER DENNIS RAY	WA	37W	82
WEHDE GERALD ALBERT	MO	24E	48
WEHNER BRIAN CHARLES	MD	15E	111
WEHR DONALD GENE	OH	16W	16
WEHR JAMES LE ROY	CA	17E	90
WEHR JOHN LESLIE	OH	32W	2
WEHR MARVIN FRANCIS	IA	34W	12
WEHRHEIM CHARLES GEORGE	IL	07W	15
WEHRHEIM LOUIS JOSEPH	FL	27W	79
WEHRHEIN RICHARD JOSEPH	IA	24E	10
WEHRS DAVID WILBERT	MN	14E	115
WEHRS DENNIS DUANE	WI	67W	6
WEHUNT BILLY DEAN	GA	09W	41
WEHUNT ROBERT LEONARD	NC	15W	88
WEIAND RAYMOND D	PA	05E	57
WEICHE LAWRENCE MICHAEL	MO	33W	29
WEID RICHARD GEORGE JR	MI	10W	122
WEIDEMIER PETER JOSEPH	CA	60W	7
WEIDENBACH EDWARD JOSEPH	ID	19E	44
WEIDERMAN CLAUDE FREDRICK	WA	09E	119
WEIDINGER WILLIAM JOSEPH	OH	45E	44
WEIDLE ROBERT JAMES	PA	07W	35
WEIDNER DAVID EDWARD	MO	25W	90
WEIDNER FREDERICK WILLIAM	IA	64E	9
WEIDNER RICHARD DALE	OH	17E	65
WEIDNER RICHARD JOHN	NY	67W	7
WEIGAND PAUL GARY	MT	10E	85
WEIGHTMAN GREG EUGENE	WA	10W	27
WEIGHTMAN KENNETH G JR	VT	08E	32
WEIGLE THOMAS HERMAN	NY	27W	12
WEIGNER DAVID RALPH	PA	08W	60
WEIGT STEPHEN LENN	CA	28W	6
WEIHER DOUGLAS RICHARD	WI	49E	38
WEIHER ROBERT LESTER	MI	28W	77
WEIK MICHAEL JOSEPH	TX	11W	19
WEIKAL WILLIAM BYRON JR	CA	22E	4
WEIL LARRY STEVEN	MI	24W	14
WEIL RICHARD ANTHONY JR	CA	22W	110
WEILL JOHN BRUCE	KY	46E	13
WEIMAN EDWARD OTTO	FL	41W	16
WEIMER JERRY ALAN	CO	47W	57
WEIMER WILLIAM PATRICK	IL	32W	1
WEIMORTS ROBERT FRANKLIN	AL	06E	129
WEINBERG DENNIS EDWARD	WI	12E	116
WEINMAN DONALD FREDERICK	FL	04E	72
WEINPER ARTHUR J	NY	48E	56
WEINTRAUB NEIL WILLIAM	PA	55W	19
WEIR DAVID ANTHONY	RI	15W	46
WEIR GARY WAYNE	IA	40W	47
WEIR JOHN RANDOLPH	CA	29W	15
WEIR PHILIP GRANT	PA	23W	33
WEIS KENNETH D	KS	26E	68
WEISBROD JOHN	OH	25W	113
WEISE RICHARD RAYMOND	MN	31E	42
WEISHEIT LONNIE HAROLD	IN	09W	77
WEISMAN ALAN N	NY	12E	92
WEISMAN DONALD EUGENE	MD	03W	17
WEISMAN KURT FREDERICK	IN	01W	8
WEISNER FRANKLIN LEE	GA	17W	61
WEISNER GREGORY CHARLES	IN	38E	41
WEISS DAVID EARL	IL	22W	61
WEISS DOUGLAS JOHN	FL	07E	36
WEISS FRANK ENZER	PA	45E	31
WEISS HOWARD DENNIS	OH	07E	28
WEISS RAYMOND DOUGLAS	CA	36W	24
WEISS RICHARD EARL	VA	21W	4
WEISS ROBERT RALPH	OH	44W	43
WEISS RODERICK LEE	KY	23E	117
WEISS STEPHEN LEE	IN	09E	128
WEISS THOMAS JOSEPH	PA	63E	3
WEISS THOMAS RAY	WI	06W	14
WEISS WALTER	NJ	15E	72
WEISS WILLIAM CONRAD JR	PA	11W	118
WEISSER ROBERT LEE	WA	02W	6
WEISSERT MICHAEL FRANCIS	IN	27E	91
WEISSMAN VICTOR BARRY	WV	37W	26
WEISSMUELLER COURTNEY EDW	FL	15E	23
WEISTER RONALD KEITH	OH	53W	7
WEITKAMP EDGAR WILKEN JR	PA	01E	2
WEITZ DONALD EDWARD	IL	44E	55
WEITZ HENRY KENNARD	WA	12W	102
WEITZ MONEK	MA	24W	108
WEITZEL BILLY DEAN	MN	18W	35
WEITZEL GEORGE MARTIN	AZ	48E	48
WEITZEL KELLY WAYNE	CA	31W	29
WEIXEL DANIEL JOSEPH	PA	63W	13
WELBORN JOE THOMAS	TX	03E	20
WELBORN MELVIN O'NEAL	AL	29E	46
WELBORNE SCOTT TERRY	NC	06E	87
WELCH ARTHUR NORMAN	LA	16W	78
WELCH BLAINE ALFRED	UT	47W	35
WELCH CLYDE RAY	TX	11E	111
WELCH DAVID	FL	12W	77
WELCH DAVID ELMER	MD	16E	82
WELCH DAVID RUSSELL	CO	13W	121
WELCH DONALD WALTER	PA	47W	57
WELCH E J JR	MS	15W	95
WELCH GARY MAX	OK	18E	77
WELCH GREGORY JOHN	UT	23W	108
WELCH HAROLD HUGH	NC	35E	64
WELCH JACK ALLEN	IL	09E	119
WELCH JODIE VARNER JR	KS	17E	40
WELCH JOHN HAROLD	MO	29E	7
WELCH JOHN HENRY III	CT	14E	106
WELCH JOSHUA JR	FL	13E	37
WELCH LARRY EUGENE	IL	44E	55
WELCH LELAND DOUGLAS	MN	59W	29
WELCH MICHAEL ALLEN	CA	18E	1
WELCH MICHAEL JOHN	IL	02W	100
WELCH NORMAN GENE	TX	23W	81
WELCH RANDALL EDWARD	KY	40W	1
WELCH RICHARD DENNIS	NY	41E	57
WELCH RICHARD ERNEST	CA	12E	124
WELCH RICHARD M	IA	42W	65
WELCH RICHARD WILLIAM	MA	44W	55
WELCH ROBERT EDWARD	MT	60E	5
WELCH ROBERT JOHN	MI	14E	41
WELCH ROBERT LEROY	MI	09W	117
WELCH STEPHEN MARTIN	NY	17W	101
WELCH TERRY	FL	18E	20
WELCH THOMAS EDWARD	LA	39W	14
WELD JULIO CESAR	LA	29W	17
WELDIN JACOB ROBINSON	DE	59W	17
WELDING CLIFFORD KAY	NE	38W	32
WELDON LIBERT JAMES JR	SC	31E	19
WELDON ROBERT P	KS	01W	129
WELDON TERRENCE WAYNE	OH	05W	76
WELDY GEORGE W JR	TX	31W	61
WELENOFSKY ERICK RUDOLPH	NY	02W	112
WELESKI MARTIN W III	PA	34E	12
WELGE BRUCE RICHARD	IL	34W	90
WELIN DANIEL KENNETH	MN	12W	94
WELK LAWRENCE NORMAN	MN	20E	93
WELKER ABRAM JOSEPH	PA	27E	92
WELKER THOMAS A	ND	24E	11
WELKER THOMAS EDWARD	NY	44W	33
WELLER DAVID HOWARD	NH	21E	40
WELLER ROBERT ALLEN II	CA	29E	103
WELLER TERRY LEE	PA	04E	126
WELLINGHOFF RALPH ALVIN	IL	21W	122
WELLINGS EDWARD ALFRED	PA	10E	129
WELLMAN CECIL ALBERT	OK	06W	1
WELLMAN KENYON GARY	TX	32E	49
WELLMAN RICHARD DOUGLAS	NC	19W	36
WELLMAN WILLIAM MARTIN JR	OH	23W	69
WELLMANN DENNIS WELDON	MN	10E	32
WELLONS HUGH WILLIAM	SC	11E	73
WELLONS PHILLIP ROGERSON	NC	08W	120
WELLS ALLEN GLAINE	OR	10E	16
WELLS BARRY SCOTT	IL	45W	39
WELLS BENJAMIN GARETH	AL	20E	108
WELLS BILLY	AL	41W	2
WELLS BOBBY GENE	GA	23E	115
WELLS BRIAN LEE	KS	32W	41
WELLS CONNIE VERGEL	GA	47E	6
WELLS DAVID CLAUD	TX	58E	28
WELLS EDWARD WILLIAM	WA	18E	77
WELLS ELROY FREDERICK	OK	05W	10
WELLS EVERETT EARL JR	FL	08W	134
WELLS FRANK JR	CA	42W	60
WELLS GENE GORDON	KY	14W	10
WELLS HARRY LEON	TN	40W	52
WELLS JAMES ALLEN	MI	02W	18
WELLS JAMES EDWARD	IN	45W	3
WELLS JAMES EDWARD	CA	31W	62
WELLS JAMES RANDALL	GA	48E	49
WELLS JERRY DAN	OR	35E	12
WELLS JOHN CHARLES	MO	39W	31
WELLS JOHN CURTIS	MI	45E	61
WELLS JOHN ELMORE	MS	09W	11
WELLS JUDSON ARTHUR JR	TX	24E	48
WELLS KENNETH RAY	VA	45E	6
WELLS KENNETH WAYNE	IL	16E	25
WELLS LARRY DEAN	CO	34E	46
WELLS LUCION PERRY	OH	36E	42
WELLS MICHAEL ALONZO	WV	21W	26
WELLS ORVILLE D	HI	09E	64
WELLS RALPH NORWOOD	NC	48E	49
WELLS RICHARD ARTHUR	KY	10W	10
WELLS RICHARD FOY	AR	55E	35
WELLS RICHARD KENNETH	CA	22E	27
WELLS ROBERT JAMES	PA	09E	60
WELLS ROBERT JAMES JR	NY	50E	23
WELLS ROBERT OLIVER	TX	28W	55
WELLS ROGER ORRIE	PA	07W	71
WELLS ROY VON	AR	14E	68
WELLS RUSSELL LEE JR	TX	36W	77
WELLS THOMAS RALPH	VA	47W	35
WELLS TINSLEY JACK JR	KY	12W	27
WELLS WALTER LOUIS	LA	11E	1
WELLS WILLIAM	NY	20E	38
WELSCH CLARENCE LEON JR	KS	35W	1
WELSCH GERALD	NY	04W	43
WELSFORD JOHN AUGUST JR	WA	21W	67
WELSH DANIEL	IL	26W	75
WELSH EARL RAYMOND JR	PA	51W	15
WELSH ELBERT ARTHUR	OH	02W	18
WELSH FREDERICK	OH	20W	110
WELSH JAMES RAYMOND	PA	11E	117
WELSH JOHN O'NEIL JR	PA	14E	12
WELSH LARRY DON	KS	35W	52
WELSH LARRY MICHAEL	WI	52W	37
WELSH LEWIS NEAL	PA	07E	78

NAME	STATE	PANEL NO.	LINE NO.
WELSH RUTHERFORD J		09E	82
WELSH STEPHEN JACKSON	SC	45E	52
WELSH THOMAS H	NJ	07E	66
WELSHAN JOHN THOMAS	TN	42E	59
WELTY CARROLL LEON	MO	05E	57
WELTY TERRY CHIP	OH	45W	46
WELTZ HERBERT F JR	PA	46E	25
WEMETTE SCOTT FRANCIS	NY	08W	40
WEMHOFF MICHAEL LYNN	NE	04W	129
WEMPLE EARL SCOTT	NJ	26W	23
WENAAS GORDON JAMES	ND	33E	1
WENBAN BRUCE R	CA	51W	46
WENCKER CLIFFORD L	FL	25E	76
WENCL DAVID ALLAN	MN	39W	14
WENDEL RICHARD LOUIS	MI	37E	1
WENDER TERRY ARTHUR	MI	25W	113
WENDEROTH GERALD F P	FL	26E	41
WENDLER RUSSELL WILLIAM	MA	32W	51
WENDOLOWSKI JAMES FRANCIS	IL	13E	70
WENDT CHARLES DONALD	ND	60W	24
WENDT ROBERT WAYNE	TX	02W	30
WENGER DAVID ALLEN	PA	58W	12
WENGER JEFF LYNN	MO	15W	30
WENGER ROBERT LEE	MI	09E	63
WENNES ROBERT ALLEN	MN	31E	27
WENRICK CLYDE ALLEN	MI	17W	32
WENRICK PHILIP BRUCE	GA	47E	7
WENSEL MILFORD HOMER	PA	23W	81
WENSEL NORMAN BYRON	CA	13E	115
WENSINGER RALPH ROBERT	CA	40W	16
WENTE DANIEL LEWIS	IL	17E	94
WENTWORTH JOHN VESTER	CA	04W	121
WENTZ DONALD RAY	PA	38W	32
WENTZ FREDERICK ANTHONY	OH	06E	87
WENTZ MITCHELL ALLEN	CA	59W	29
WENTZEL MERLYN LEE	CO	08W	121
WENTZEL RALPH MICHAEL	PA	17E	25
WENTZEL WILLIAM CHARLES	MI	26E	110
WENTZELL JEFFREY RAYMOND	CA	39E	41
WENZEL CARL RICHARD	NY	01E	109
WENZEL JAMES EDWARD	IN	01E	27
WENZEL MARK ANDREW	MN	56W	30
WENZEL ROBERT LEE	PA	50W	11
WENZL RONALD ALBERT	CA	01W	47
WENZLER JOSEPH R	PA	44E	42
WERBISKI PHILIP MICHAEL	IL	19W	75
WERDEHOFF MICHAEL RAY	OH	51E	4
WERDERMAN JAMES EDWARD	IL	22E	9
WERLE HAROLD FRANCIS	IL	21E	40
WERLEY ROBERT WAYNE	MO	57W	15
WERMAN EDWARD ALEC	ND	03W	63
WERNER ANTHONY ROBERT	OH	25W	26
WERNER GREGORY EDMUND	NY	33E	11
WERNER JOHN FREDRICK	IA	08W	134
WERNER NORBERT OTTO	CA	40W	69
WERNER ODELL JACK	CA	16E	127
WERNER STUART ARTHUR	CA	52E	2
WERNER THOMAS MARTIN	OH	55W	7
WERNER WALLACE BRUCE	CA	53W	41
WERNET DAVID PAUL	FL	25E	14
WERNIG RANDY RICHARD	NY	51W	46
WERNSDORFER GERALD FRANCI	MD	44E	23
WERSCHING ADAM EDWARD	IL	16E	6
WERTMAN JOHN THOMAS	MD	27E	56
WERTMAN MICHAEL LEE	PA	27W	22
WERTS GREGORY IRA	PA	22W	37
WERTZ STEVE EDWARD	OH	37W	43
WESCOTT FREDERICK DEVILLA	PA	50E	43
WESCOTT RICHARD LEE	PA	24E	48
WESCOTT ROBERT HYATT JR	PA	26W	81
WESIGHAN LESTER ARTHUR	NY	05E	111
WESKAMP ROBERT LARRY	CO	18E	84
WESKE RICHARD ALWIN	CA	65E	3
WESLEY ERNEST LAMAR	GA	59W	29
WESLEY MARVIN JR	AL	41W	50
WESLEY ROBERT EARL	TX	42E	1
WESOLICK HAROLD JAMES JR	TX	34E	12
WESOLOWSKI ALVIN JOHN JR	CA	35E	84
WESOLOWSKI JEFFREY SCOTT	CA	03W	83
WESSEL MICHAEL DANIEL	NV	24E	11
WESSEL RICHARD	IN	16E	33
WESSEL STEVEN ARTHUR	OH	35W	37

NAME	STATE	PANEL NO.	LINE NO.
WESSELLS WILLIAM DAVID	VA	15E	53
WESSELMAN GARY LEROY	CA	18E	51
WESSELS EDWARD JOHN	MI	24E	48
WESSINGER LARRY ALLEN	TX	31W	62
WESSLER DANIEL GUY	WA	29W	86
WESSON LANNY LAMAR	GA	36W	47
WEST ALDERMAN CARROWAY JR	NC	49W	27
WEST BENNIE LEE	NM	25E	76
WEST BOBBY	CA	35E	10
WEST CARL LYNN	TN	37E	3
WEST CHARLES EDWARD	WA	22E	4
WEST CHARLES ROBERT	MI	10W	10
WEST DALLAS ARNOLD	MD	57W	5
WEST DANIEL FLOYD	NV	38W	53
WEST DANNY GENE	OK	40W	52
WEST DANNY RAY	AR	53E	39
WEST DARRELL CHARLES	OH	25W	90
WEST DAVID EUGENE	IL	06W	10
WEST DAVID RICHARD	TX	12E	93
WEST DONALD FREDERICK	NJ	03W	17
WEST EDGAR LEO JR	FL	05W	44
WEST EDWARD TYRONE	NJ	47W	24
WEST EUGENE EDWARD	GA	18E	73
WEST FREDERICK THOMAS	OH	18E	66
WEST GARFIELD JR	OR	25E	18
WEST GEORGE A	TX	02E	85
WEST GRAYSON JERALD	IA	04E	19
WEST HOMER	KY	33W	23
WEST HOWARD CECIL	NC	13E	37
WEST JAMES CLIFFORD JR	CA	28W	77
WEST JAMES DENNIS	OH	20E	4
WEST JAMES EDWARD	PA	10E	85
WEST JAMES EDWARD JR	VA	62W	19
WEST JAMES LARRY	GA	40E	49
WEST JAMES OSCAR	CA	47E	28
WEST JAMES RUSSELL	ME	35E	28
WEST JAMES WILLIAM	IA	32E	14
WEST JERALD DALE	MI	14W	87
WEST JESSE LEONARD	NC	12W	23
WEST JIMMY DON	OK	21W	64
WEST JOHN EDWARD JR	TN	32W	30
WEST JOHN HAYDEN	NJ	30W	67
WEST JOHN MICHAEL	KS	17E	83
WEST JOHN THOMAS	MD	15W	117
WEST KENNETH PETER	MT	22W	114
WEST KENNETH WADE	FL	11E	48
WEST LARRY CHANDLER	IL	14E	25
WEST LARRY JOE	AZ	62E	4
WEST MELFORD WAYNE	MS	33E	33
WEST MOUNCE EDWARD	AR	30W	8
WEST NOEL THOMAS	WA	22E	22
WEST PAUL BRADLEY	LA	28W	95
WEST PAUL EDWARD	KS	42E	44
WEST PAUL ROBERT	ME	12E	125
WEST RAYMOND JOHN	MA	36W	20
WEST RICHARD ANDRESEN	OH	27E	77
WEST ROBERT LEWIS	TX	61W	19
WEST ROBERT WILKS	CA	61E	4
WEST ROY ROGERS	NC	45W	3
WEST RUSSELL UDELL	CA	67E	3
WEST SETH LEE JR	NC	50E	24
WEST STANLEY EUGENE	WA	42W	8
WEST STEPHEN ALAN	OH	43E	38
WEST WILLIAM EDWARD	CT	37E	46
WEST WILLIAM RICHARD	WA	06E	58
WESTBAY GAYLORD LEE	CA	26E	38
WESTBERG RICHARD CHARLES	IA	44E	12
WESTBERRY VINCENT DOUGLAS	CA	44E	12
WESTBROOK DENNIS FRANKLIN	AL	50E	35
WESTBROOK DONALD ELLIOT	TX	44E	43
WESTBROOK JAMES BARRINGTO	TN	46W	25
WESTBROOK JIMMY WAYNE	CO	07W	109
WESTBROOK ROY THOMAS	AL	47W	1
WESTBROOK THEODORE ELBA	MI	23E	84
WESTBROOKS ALLISON A JR	MO	35E	1
WESTCOTT GARY PATRICK	CA	02W	125
WESTCOTT RODNEY WAYNE	LA	09E	60
WESTER ALBERT DWAYNE	TX	41W	16
WESTER DONALD LEE	KY	42W	65
WESTER WILBURN EDWARD	GA	39E	78
WESTERBERG KENNETH GLEN	MN	03W	49
WESTERFIELD FRANK BROWN	TX	23E	16

NAME	STATE	PANEL NO.	LINE NO.
WESTERGARD TERRY MICHAEL	IA	39W	57
WESTERN AARON HAROLD	CA	02E	11
WESTERN RICHARD ALAN	NY	64E	10
WESTERVELT JOHNNIE BOWEN	MT	24W	73
WESTFALL BRONSON LEE	VA	28E	88
WESTFALL RICHARD EARL	MT	15W	68
WESTFALL ROBERT LEE	PA	01E	7
WESTFALL ROBERT LOUIS JR	MO	16E	108
WESTFALL RUBIN WILBERT JR	MO	08W	106
WESTLAKE CLAIR LLOYD JR	MO	35W	18
WESTLAKE WILLIAM ARNOLD	IN	42W	25
WESTLIE DANIEL LEE	WI	35W	64
WESTLY CYRIL JEFFREY	IA	17E	55
WESTMAN MYLES DALEN	MN	25W	114
WESTMORELAND BRUCE WAYNE	NC	34W	71
WESTMORELAND JIMMY ROGER	NC	27W	43
WESTON JAMES EDWARD	TX	03W	15
WESTON OSCAR BRANCH JR	VA	01E	3
WESTON ROBERT HUGH	CA	08W	109
WESTON THOMAS JR	GA	18E	44
WESTON WENDELL ALLEN	VT	25W	91
WESTOVER DAVID EDWIN	KS	20W	68
WESTPHAL GARY LEE	WI	03W	74
WESTPHAL GLENN A	IN	48E	49
WESTPHAL JAMES FRANCIS	NY	14W	6
WESTPHAL JERELD EUGENE	KS	21E	54
WESTPHAL RONALD DALE	IL	17W	122
WESTPHAL SCOTT BRIAN	WI	02W	109
WESTPHAL STEPHEN JOHN	WI	49E	49
WESTPHALL VICTOR D III	NM	66E	4
WESTPOINT THOMAS LEE	SC	11E	29
WESTRA DIRK JON	MN	53W	15
WESTRA LEROY JAMES	PA	03W	55
WESTRATE ROBERT JAY	MI	59W	29
WESTWOOD NORMAN PHILIP JR	CT	10W	59
WETHINGTON DAVID L JR	OH	42E	45
WETJEN GORDON JOHN	IA	38E	18
WETMORE DOUGLAS MCARTHUR	KY	04E	131
WETTERGREN STEVEN EDWARD	MN	27W	68
WETZEL CHARLES ROBERT	NJ	05E	111
WETZEL JOHN THOMAS	MI	15E	124
WETZEL WALTER JOSEPH	NY	07E	124
WETZLER ROBIN KIRMEYER	UT	21W	96
WEYANDT IRVIN GRANT	PA	23E	96
WEYKER DONALD DENNIS	IA	37W	48
WEYMOUTH THEODORE GAY	CA	64E	1
WHALEN CHARLES ARTHUR	KY	46W	36
WHALEN EDWARD EUGENE	PA	51E	34
WHALEN GARLAND GUY	CO	33W	29
WHALEN MICHAEL CORNELIUS	MA	31W	98
WHALEN MICHAEL JAMES	CO	04W	130
WHALEN RICHARD D	NY	28E	5
WHALEN ROBERT JAMES	FL	27W	104
WHALEN RODRICK PIUS	CO	11E	34
WHALER ARCHIE LEON	AR	12W	40
WHALEY CARSON LEO JR	NC	25E	45
WHALEY HENRY LEE	CT	06E	69
WHALEY JAMES GOODWIN	CA	31E	89
WHALEY LOY NEAL	CA	59W	29
WHALEY WILLIAM ELDRED III	KY	24W	57
WHAN VORIN EDWIN JR	AL	38E	18
WHARTON HENRY MARVIN JR	MD	26E	53
WHARTON THOMAS MICHAEL	PA	09W	66
WHARTON WAYNE ALLEN	WV	32W	68
WHATLEY CHARLES	OH	13W	90
WHEAT GENE JOSEPH	LA	40E	70
WHEAT PRYOR L	AR	26E	20
WHEAT ROY MITCHELL	MS	24E	101
WHEAT WENDELL RAY	TX	05E	18
WHEATLEY JOHN ALBION	VI	10W	107
WHEATLEY WILLIAM GEORGE	CA	02E	122
WHEATON ALLEN THOMAS	VA	07E	56
WHEATON JAMES	NY	02E	98
WHEELER BOBBY LEE	WV	63W	1
WHEELER CARL EUGENE	OK	15W	57
WHEELER CHARLES EDWARD	MO	29W	86
WHEELER CLINTON LEE	OK	30W	61
WHEELER CONRAD JACK	TX	16W	5
WHEELER DARRELL EUGENE	CA	42E	45
WHEELER EUGENE LACY	OH	11W	33
WHEELER FREDERICK GEORGE	NJ	17E	26
WHEELER JAMES	IL	15E	130

NAME	STATE	PANEL NO.	LINE NO.
WHEELER JAMES ATLEE	AZ	01E	103
WHEELER JAMES CHRISTOPHER	NY	10W	73
WHEELER JAMES KENNETH	MA	59W	17
WHEELER JOHN CLARK	OR	57W	5
WHEELER JOHN MELVIN	GA	17W	75
WHEELER JOHNNY CECIL	GA	25E	36
WHEELER JOSEPH KEITH	NY	47E	28
WHEELER KENNITH WAYNE	TX	25W	45
WHEELER LARRY JAY	OR	19W	26
WHEELER LARRY KENNETH	GA	32W	17
WHEELER LOUIS GERARD	PA	29W	57
WHEELER MELVIN CARTER JR	IL	04W	107
WHEELER MICHEL T	ID	45E	6
WHEELER MILLARD PRESTON	OH	19W	27
WHEELER MORRIS CRAIG	KS	14E	7
WHEELER MORRIS EUGENE	PA	03E	28
WHEELER NICOLAS	CA	07W	63
WHEELER OSCAR LEE	TX	25W	34
WHEELER RALPH D III	PA	35E	52
WHEELER RAYMOND LEE	MO	11E	42
WHEELER WILLIAM EUGENE	MI	08W	22
WHEELER WILLIAM TIMOTHY	WV	29W	26
WHEELHOUSE CLIFTON P JR	VA	12W	77
WHELAN JOSEPH VINCENT	NJ	17W	115
WHELAN MICHAEL PATRICK	CA	44W	7
WHELCHEL RUSSELL DESMOND	KS	26E	33
WHELESS DOUGLASS TERRELL	LA	06W	78
WHELESS JIMMY RAY	TX	58E	1
WHELIHAN THOMAS MEAKIN	NC	43W	1
WHELPLEY RAYMOND LAWRENCE	MI	45W	58
WHETHAM VERNON E	MT	31E	19
WHETSEL JACK ALLEN JR	TX	53E	25
WHETZEL HARRY THOMAS	OH	11E	59
WHICKER DENNIS RAY	MO	33W	52
WHIDDON TOMMY LEON	FL	11W	118
WHIKEHART MARK ANDREW	VA	12W	16
WHILES FRED LAMAR JR	OK	58E	2
WHINERY ROGER LEE	KS	21E	30
WHINNERY DAVID VERNON	MI	53E	8
WHIPKEY RICHARD ALLEN	CA	51W	15
WHIPPLE CLIFFORD LEROY	CA	04E	27
WHIPPLE GARY EUGENE	PA	18E	1
WHIPPLE GARY NORMAN	NH	37W	43
WHIPPLE STEPHEN JOHN	ME	32E	7
WHIPS FLETCHER DANNY	CO	21E	71
WHIRLOW ROGER DALE	TX	04W	90
WHISENANT JOHN WILLIAM	CA	20W	74
WHISENANT PERRY SHELTON	FL	44W	11
WHISENANT STEPHEN LEE	NC	05W	92
WHISENHUNT JAMES HENRY	CA	19E	1
WHISMAN ERMIL LEE	KY	34W	12
WHISNAN JAMES CARL	OR	44E	55
WHITAKER DONALD EUGENE	MO	41E	32
WHITAKER FRED DARREL	IN	32W	41
WHITAKER FREDDIE	NJ	51E	4
WHITAKER G W	CA	09E	7
WHITAKER JERE LEE	CA	53W	30
WHITAKER JERRY	SC	58E	17
WHITAKER JOSEPH LEON JR	OR	25E	66
WHITAKER KELLY EUGENE	TN	03E	38
WHITAKER MICHAEL JOSEPH	CA	03W	89
WHITAKER RUDOLPH	NC	08E	83
WHITAKER STEVE RANDAL	KY	28W	55
WHITAKER THOMAS EARL	NY	40E	70
WHITBECK ROBERT EARL	VA	35E	84
WHITBY JOE ALAN	WA	16E	25
WHITBY THOMAS ALVIN	MI	25W	91
WHITCHER CLAYTON DONALD	OH	12W	105
WHITCOME LARRY WILLIAM	MI	11E	18
WHITE ALBERT DEWELL	GA	38E	18
WHITE ALBERT RONALD	MA	05E	76
WHITE ALGER LAWRENCE JR	MI	38E	19
WHITE ALLEN EUGENE	TN	37W	15
WHITE ALLEN JOSEPH	IA	24E	49
WHITE ALLEN THOMAS	OK	11W	43
WHITE ARNOLD SYLVANUS	PA	50E	10
WHITE AULDON KEITH	LA	10W	132
WHITE BARNEY JOE	TX	39W	19
WHITE BEDFORD FREDERICK	MI	18W	75
WHITE BEN	SC	23E	47
WHITE BOBBY BLAKE	FL	02W	54
WHITE CALVIN PERRY	FL	16E	55

NAME	STATE	PANEL NO.	LINE NO.
WHITE CARROLL EUGENE	VA	41W	44
WHITE CARROLL WAYNE	TN	42W	44
WHITE CHARLES	AR	10E	12
WHITE CHARLES BOYD	MI	07E	15
WHITE CHARLES CLINTON	MN	58W	30
WHITE CHARLES EDWARD	AL	35E	64
WHITE CHARLES FRANKLIN	WV	28W	6
WHITE CHARLES HENRY	MN	17E	53
WHITE CHARLES MOTT SR	CA	35E	28
WHITE CHARLES THERON	TX	34E	56
WHITE COLEY PHILLIP	WV	12E	93
WHITE CORDIS RAY	MO	18W	112
WHITE CRAIG PRESTON	PA	34E	3
WHITE DANFORTH ELLITHORPE	PA	28W	101
WHITE DANIEL WESLEY	VA	21E	54
WHITE DANNY CARL	WV	11E	79
WHITE DAVID LEE	VA	43W	59
WHITE DONALD EUGENE	MO	16E	25
WHITE DONALD HERBERT	CA	19W	27
WHITE DONALD LEE	CO	21E	2
WHITE DONALD MERLE JR	AZ	26E	53
WHITE DONALD NISLER	AR	07W	127
WHITE DONALD RICHARD	AL	10W	37
WHITE DONNIE RAYMOND	TN	45W	58
WHITE DOUGLAS EDWARD	CT	06W	63
WHITE EDDIE JOE	OH	53E	25
WHITE EDDY EUGENE	VA	09W	107
WHITE ERNEST BERTIE	NC	17W	75
WHITE EUGENE	PA	14E	31
WHITE FRANKLIN RALPH	CA	01E	29
WHITE FRED DONALD	AZ	24E	49
WHITE GARSON FRANKLIN	MS	32W	30
WHITE GARY RICHARD	WV	10W	55
WHITE GARY SIDNEY	OK	04W	69
WHITE GENE ARCARO	OH	23E	106
WHITE GENE LEWIS	IL	27W	8
WHITE GENERAL	PA	06E	43
WHITE GEORGE PRESTON	FL	30W	34
WHITE GLENN EARL	KS	29E	37
WHITE GORDON GLENN		29W	26
WHITE GREGORY LEE	NY	06W	52
WHITE HAROLD LEE	GA	48W	11
WHITE HARRY RAY JR	FL	31E	79
WHITE HERBERT FRANKLIN	NJ	46E	43
WHITE HERMAN JR	OH	20W	68
WHITE ISAIAH	SC	35E	52
WHITE JACK LEE	WA	62E	13
WHITE JAMES BLAIR	FL	16W	119
WHITE JAMES BROADUS	PA	33W	45
WHITE JAMES DARRELL JR	IL	04E	117
WHITE JAMES DAVID	MN	20W	94
WHITE JAMES DAVIS	AL	46E	51
WHITE JAMES E	FL	53E	25
WHITE JAMES HARDY	LA	44W	43
WHITE JAMES LEE	NY	31W	29
WHITE JAMES LEO	IL	02E	64
WHITE JEFFREY MERLE	CA	07W	97
WHITE JERRY DEAN	AR	18W	66
WHITE JERRY MORGAN	TX	36W	20
WHITE JOHN ARTHUR	FL	11W	107
WHITE JOHN CLYDE III	OH	39W	6
WHITE JOHN CULLIN	MA	34E	61
WHITE JOHN EDWARD	MA	45E	44
WHITE JOHN HERBERT JR	CA	42E	26
WHITE JOHN MICHAEL	MO	42W	2
WHITE JOHN OLIVER	AL	35E	12
WHITE JOHN WILLIE	PA	02E	3
WHITE JOHNNY BRYAN	CA	11W	15
WHITE JOSEPH	NY	24E	4
WHITE JOSEPH RUMMEL JR	NY	50W	33
WHITE KENNETH LEROY	IL	26W	96
WHITE KURNEY JOSEPH JR	LA	20E	108
WHITE LARIS JR	FL	03E	21
WHITE LARRY FREDERICK	IL	35E	10
WHITE LARRY JOE	TX	21W	41
WHITE LAWRENCE LEALAND	OH	22W	16
WHITE LEAMUEL ARTIS	AL	43E	38
WHITE LEE OWENS JR	IL	12E	108
WHITE LENWOOD JR	TX	27W	3
WHITE LEON	SC	23W	108
WHITE LEONARD RAY	CA	57W	15
WHITE LEROY JR	GA	02W	62

NAME	STATE	PANEL NO.	LINE NO.
WHITE LOREN DOUGLAS	OR	61W	8
WHITE LOWELL FRANKLIN	NJ	04E	57
WHITE LUCKY GAYLEN	IL	53E	8
WHITE MARCUS DELMAR	KY	15E	18
WHITE MARVIN CHARLES	CA	22W	61
WHITE MARVIN RAY	IN	18E	117
WHITE MELVIN ELIJAH	SC	23W	94
WHITE MELVIN RICHARD	WA	54W	7
WHITE MICHAEL ALAN	KS	22W	10
WHITE MICHAEL DALE	OH	45W	46
WHITE MICHAEL EUGENE	AL	07W	7
WHITE MICHAEL JAMES	MN	34W	55
WHITE MICHAEL LA VERN	KS	17W	2
WHITE MICHAEL LAWRENCE	WI	44E	43
WHITE MICHAEL MATTHEW	PA	57W	5
WHITE MILES EUGENE	WA	23E	24
WHITE MONETTE VON	CA	05W	94
WHITE MOUSE JOSEPH LEWIS	SD	04W	113
WHITE NATHAN JR	SC	63E	3
WHITE NATHAN MONROE	GA	31E	55
WHITE OSCAR LEE	CO	21W	96
WHITE OWEN JR	IL	44W	33
WHITE RALPH ERIC	CA	35E	84
WHITE RANDALL RAY	GA	23W	60
WHITE RAYMOND	AL	34E	3
WHITE RAYMOND AUSTIN III	TX	14W	10
WHITE RICHARD ALLEN	CA	28W	87
WHITE RICHARD EDWARD	WA	55W	3
WHITE RICHARD JOSEPH	MN	19W	110
WHITE RICHARD NEAL	MN	24W	109
WHITE ROBERT ALEXANDER	VA	05E	16
WHITE ROBERT FREDERICK	NH	25E	9
WHITE ROBERT HENRY	HI	03E	123
WHITE ROBERT JAMES	CT	20E	109
WHITE ROBERT LEE	MO	01E	84
WHITE ROBERT LEE	IL	27E	104
WHITE ROBERT RANDOLPH JR	GA	51E	34
WHITE ROBERT RICHARD	PA	57W	20
WHITE ROBERT WAYNE	AL	14E	8
WHITE ROBERT WESLEY	VA	21W	104
WHITE ROGER DUWAINE	MI	13E	87
WHITE RONALD GENE SR	MO	54W	39
WHITE RONALD LEE	NJ	12W	40
WHITE RONNIE RUDOLPH	NC	28W	6
WHITE ROOSEVELT	MS	57E	12
WHITE SAMUEL MARLAR JR	AZ	22W	71
WHITE STANLEY DEAN	IA	35W	29
WHITE STEPHEN MARK	IN	01W	51
WHITE STEPHEN O'MEARA	IL	35W	10
WHITE STEPHEN ROBERT	NY	53E	6
WHITE STEVEN RUDOLPH	IN	04W	45
WHITE SYLVAIN LARRY	KY	64W	4
WHITE TED ARNOLD	AL	35W	31
WHITE TERRY ROGER	WV	46E	13
WHITE THEODORE G JR	MD	09E	128
WHITE THOMAS MITCHELL	GA	53E	43
WHITE TIMOTHY ALLEN	MI	08W	64
WHITE TIMOTHY CHAMPREAUX	LA	15W	88
WHITE TIMOTHY LEE	IL	37E	2
WHITE TOMMIE VAUGHN	TX	22E	118
WHITE TOMMY LEE	MI	06E	87
WHITE TOMMY RYAN	MO	07E	56
WHITE TONY LEE VAN	NC	26E	33
WHITE ULYSSES	FL	13E	77
WHITE WESLEY WILLIAM	NJ	47E	44
WHITE WHITNEY LEE	NY	56W	10
WHITE WILLIAM EDMOND III	FL	35E	64
WHITE WILLIAM ERNEST JR	DC	19E	47
WHITE WILLIAM GEORGE	NJ	22W	61
WHITE WILLIAM HENRY	IL	51W	46
WHITE WILLIAM HENRY	CA	43W	11
WHITE WILLIAM IVAN	PA	28E	6
WHITE WILLIAM JOSEPH JR	CA	10W	111
WHITE WILLIAM SAMPSON	NY	23E	108
WHITE WILLIE	SC	27E	18
WHITEAKER JOHNNY LAVERNE	TN	47W	24
WHITED JAMES LAFAYETTE	OK	12E	93
WHITEFIELD CHARLES ELMER	MD	12E	57
WHITEHEAD ALFRED EVARTS	KY	56W	11
WHITEHEAD CHARLES F JR	CA	01E	31
WHITEHEAD CLARENCE ALBERT	GA	06E	51
WHITEHEAD ESAU JR	NY	43E	49

NAME	STATE	PANEL NO.	LINE NO.
WHITEHEAD JEFF	GA	29W	57
WHITEHEAD LARRY GENE	TN	32W	29
WHITEHEAD MORRIS ALFRED	VA	41E	14
WHITEHEAD RICKEY JACKSON	WI	31W	74
WHITEHEAD THOMAS LEROY	KS	34E	72
WHITEHEAD WILLIAM C JR	PA	54W	22
WHITEHEAD WILLIAM J	AZ	48E	49
WHITEHILL DAVID HUGH	NY	70E	1
WHITEHOUSE GREGORY KENT	TX	43E	38
WHITEHOUSE RICHARD JAMES	PA	21W	57
WHITELAW GEORGE DAVID	MI	41E	32
WHITELEY WAYNE ANTHONY	NY	33E	61
WHITEMAN RICHARD LEE	CA	12W	119
WHITEMAN WAYNE FRANK	IA	28E	52
WHITEMAN WILLIAM EARL II	PA	02W	42
WHITERS DONALD EMERY	KS	56W	30
WHITES ROBERT JOSEPH	SD	20W	42
WHITESELL DENHAM A JR	VA	37W	27
WHITESIDE JOHN CURTIS	AL	19W	36
WHITESIDE ROY RUDOLPH	KY	17W	70
WHITESIDES RICHARD LEBROU	CA	01E	48
WHITFIELD CHARLES CURTIS	NC	05E	75
WHITFIELD CHARLES F JR	NY	10E	49
WHITFIELD CICERO JR	NC	25E	32
WHITFIELD JAMES LEMAR	GA	23E	106
WHITFIELD LAWRENCE ALLEN	GA	23E	47
WHITFIELD RICHARD K	OK	19E	41
WHITFIELD THOMAS MICHAEL	IL	38W	62
WHITFIELD WILLIE JR	MS	48W	4
WHITFORD LAWRENCE W JR	IA	16W	21
WHITFORD LYNN CECIL	NY	28W	16
WHITING J C JR	TN	47W	14
WHITING JUSTIN RICE IV	NJ	02E	66
WHITING MALCOLM D III	CA	21W	96
WHITING RICHARD EDWARD	CA	08E	70
WHITINGTON LARRY E	IL	10E	23
WHITIS LARRY MICHAEL	IN	29W	94
WHITLATCH GAIL LEE	IL	20W	35
WHITLATCH WILLIAM CARL JR	WV	15W	51
WHITLEY ARSELL	MD	22E	93
WHITLEY EMMANUEL DAVID	CA	06E	116
WHITLEY FREDDIE LEE	MO	47W	57
WHITLEY ROBERT LEE	NY	36E	42
WHITLOCK ALAN D	TX	14E	8
WHITLOCK DONALD BENED III	PR	03W	123
WHITLOCK HALLEY DON	TX	11E	63
WHITLOCK HARRY OWENS JR	VA	28E	59
WHITLOCK IVAN PRESTON	LA	01E	8
WHITLOCK JIMMIE DALE	OK	41E	14
WHITLOCK PATRICK A	WA	37E	29
WHITLOCK THEODORE JAY	NV	50W	46
WHITLOCK THOMAS DANIEL	MI	01E	71
WHITLOW LEROY ALLEN	VA	48W	20
WHITLOW RONALD DAVID	NM	49W	21
WHITLOW THOMAS JAMES JR	CA	13W	95
WHITMAN DAVID STEWART	TN	31W	86
WHITMAN JERRY RONALD	FL	56E	18
WHITMAN RAYMOND LEE	MN	19W	96
WHITMAN THOMAS MICHAEL	NY	16E	108
WHITMER ALFRED VAN	AZ	49E	48
WHITMER KENNETH EUGENE	OH	12W	41
WHITMIRE WARREN TAYLOR JR	VA	53E	43
WHITMORE GARLAND D II	VA	26E	4
WHITMORE GREGORY BRIAN	PA	49W	11
WHITMORE JAMES CALVIN	OH	29E	64
WHITMORE JAMES ROBERT	FL	15W	127
WHITMORE RICHARD ALLEN	CA	13W	34
WHITMORE WILLIAM LEE	OR	08W	102
WHITNEY ARTHUR JOSEPH JR	AK	19E	47
WHITNEY BLAKE DOMINIC	IL	05W	92
WHITNEY DICK EDWARD	OR	23W	12
WHITNEY HARLEY DAIRREL	IL	13W	76
WHITNEY PHILIP LEONARD	CO	53W	7
WHITNEY ROBERT ARNOLD	WA	67W	7
WHITNEY ROBERT WALTER	IL	32W	47
WHITNEY WILLIAM ARTHUR	UT	29E	55
WHITSON JIMMY ALAN	CA	15W	127
WHITT BROADUS ALFRED	SC	46E	25
WHITT JAMES EDWARD	IL	02W	119
WHITT MARK ALAN	CA	22E	118
WHITTAKER HAROLD CHARLES	MA	42E	12
WHITTAKER TERRY JAMES	NH	18E	8
WHITTED BOYD LEE	NC	19W	48
WHITTED CURTIS	VA	10W	107
WHITTED JOE RAY	MO	61E	5
WHITTED ROBERT ALBIN	CA	14W	112
WHITTEKER RICHARD LEE	PA	46E	51
WHITTEMORE FREDERICK H	NV	49E	20
WHITTEN DAVID ELGA	CA	05E	44
WHITTEN MILAN ELMER	ME	11E	129
WHITTEN PATRICK ANTHONY	CA	18W	73
WHITTEN ROBERT EUGENE	FL	57E	12
WHITTEN ROBERT FRANKLIN	IN	28W	22
WHITTEN THOMAS WILLIAM	VA	28W	6
WHITTEN TOMMIE JOE	TX	19E	76
WHITTHORNE PAUL LUCIUS JR	TN	49E	49
WHITTICOM JONATHAN CHARLE	NH	22E	74
WHITTIER JAMES BENJAMIN	NY	54W	7
WHITTIER MARK CROSBY	CA	43E	38
WHITTINGTON JOHN HEZEKIAH	MD	16W	119
WHITTINGTON MERREL P	WA	30E	51
WHITTINGTON PAUL TIMOTHY	TN	07E	15
WHITTINGTON PERRY LEE	DC	58E	28
WHITTINGTON RUSSEL JOSEPH	IL	36W	42
WHITTLE ALBERT ALLAN	PA	25W	34
WHITTLE JUNIOR LEE	IN	11E	11
WHITTLESEY ROY LEE	TX	54W	34
WHITTON EDWARD JAMES	OR	08W	71
WHITTON TEDDY GENE	AR	31E	55
WHITWORTH SAMMY HOWARD	GA	22W	61
WHOOLERY TRACY LEE	MD	29E	13
WHORFF JOHN DENNIS	CT	25E	66
WHORTON DWAYNE JEFFERSON	CA	37W	3
WHYNAUGHT JEFFREY LYLE	CA	29W	46
WHYTE CHARLES JAMES	WA	63W	1
WHYTE RICHARD ALAN	SD	25W	86
WIAR JOSEPH CLERMAN JR	MI	33E	77
WIBBENS JOHN EDWARD	OR	19W	52
WICHMAN ROGER EDWARD	OH	39W	41
WICK GERALD PAUL	NY	05W	110
WICK MICHAEL RAYMOND	NY	22W	10
WICK RICHARD GALE	OH	03E	109
WICKAM JERRY WAYNE	IL	33E	62
WICKEL KENNETH WILLIAM	PA	07E	124
WICKENBERG ERIK BERNARD	MN	23E	24
WICKER EUGENE WESLEY	NC	45W	46
WICKER HENRY RAY	KY	19E	68
WICKER WALTER GUY JR	NC	17W	76
WICKERSHAM HARRY W JR	TX	39W	45
WICKHAM DAVID WALLACE II	WV	04E	21
WICKHAM JOHN EUGENE	OH	46W	36
WICKHAM RALPH ARTHUR	NY	18E	27
WICKLACE RANDALL JAMES	MN	34W	19
WICKLIFFE JOHN NORMAN	AR	24E	74
WICKLIFFE ROBERT LOGAN	MS	35E	13
WICKLINE DONALD LEE JR	NJ	22W	56
WICKS WILLIAM ARTHUR	NY	08W	13
WICKWARD WILLIAM J	NJ	19W	126
WIDDER DAVID JOHN WICK	WI	01E	97
WIDDIS JAMES WESLEY JR	NJ	28W	22
WIDDISON IMLAY SCOTT	UT	59E	15
WIDDOWS JOHN WILLIAM	IL	07W	15
WIDEMAN ELVIN JOSEPH	MO	12E	93
WIDEN JOHN GEORGE	MN	11W	119
WIDENER JAMES EDWARD	NY	21E	93
WIDENER JOHN EDWARD	CA	13E	37
WIDENER LARRY ALLEN	OH	42E	45
WIDENER MICHAEL EDWARD	PA	02E	18
WIDERQUIST THOMAS CARL	IL	01W	12
WIDGER GEORGE JAMES	NY	15E	16
WIDICK MAURICE GENE	NE	26E	77
WIDMANN RAYMOND	NY	08E	131
WIDMER KIM WILLIAM	WA	06W	21
WIDMER RICHARD JAMES	MI	12W	27
WIDNER DANNY LEE	TX	59E	12
WIDOMSKI DANIEL ALBIN	NY	31W	75
WIDON KENNETH HARRY	MI	34E	33
WIDTFELDT PAUL FRANK JR	IA	11E	63
WIEBEN OTTO TOM	FL	04W	82
WIEBURG WILLIAM WARREN	TX	44E	12
WIECHERT ROBERT CHARLES	UT	39W	76
WIECKOWICZ ANTHONY JOSEPH	WI	34W	69
WIEDEMAN ROBERT ARTHUR	NY	41E	33
WIEDEMANN ROBERT JOSEPH	IN	46E	25
WIEGAND DEAN MICHAEL JR	PA	08W	128
WIEGAND ROY VICTOR	IL	33E	62
WIEGEL LLOYD GEORGE	WI	07E	88
WIEGERT LARRY ROBERT	OK	25E	27
WIEHR RICHARD DANIEL	MN	01W	111
WIELAND DAVID ERIC	FL	27E	78
WIELER JAMES LAWRENCE	PA	04W	32
WIELINSKI DONALD JAMES	MN	39E	64
WIELKOPOLAN DONALD DAVID	MI	34E	72
WIENCKOSKI DAVID RAYMOND	NJ	43E	39
WIENEKE CARL JOSHUA	IL	37E	74
WIER MICHAEL BRODERICK	NY	27W	69
WIERZBA EDWIN RUDOLPH	IL	37E	46
WIESE ROBERT JAMES	MO	13W	21
WIESE THOMAS ARTHUR	NE	28W	88
WIESENDANGER LAWRENCE LOU	LA	03W	23
WIESER LYNN JAY	NE	25W	114
WIESKUS WILLIAM CLEMENS	IN	49W	35
WIESNEIFSKI PETER ROBERT	NY	13W	60
WIESNETH ROBERT PAUL	NE	18W	74
WIEST DONALD R	IL	02E	92
WIEST JOHN ROBIN	MT	41W	55
WIGFALL HERBERT JR	SC	21E	110
WIGFALL NEOPOLIS	MD	03E	98
WIGFIELD RONALD LEE	OH	61E	5
WIGGIN ROBERT JAMES	ME	39E	27
WIGGINS ALFRED FRANCIS JR	NJ	09W	17
WIGGINS AUBREY ALAN	FL	14W	46
WIGGINS DAVID ROGER	AL	27W	27
WIGGINS HIRAM ELI MARVIN	VA	14E	60
WIGGINS JERRY LEE	MO	29E	23
WIGGINS JOSEPH	FL	15E	53
WIGGINS OVID KEITH	VA	02E	52
WIGGINS RONALD HOWARD	FL	01W	2
WIGGINS STEPHAN MAX	FL	47E	18
WIGGINS THOMAS WAYNE	LA	05W	110
WIGGINS TOMMY AUSTIN	IL	37E	74
WIGGINS VERNON MIKELL	FL	14W	67
WIGGINS WALLACE LUTTRELL	CA	37E	15
WIGHT ALONZO WILLIAM	ME	32W	86
WIGHT CHARLES EDWIN	WA	53W	31
WIGHT RALPH CHESTER JR	MA	48E	37
WIGHTMAN DAVID LLOYD III	CA	24E	75
WIGINTON GARY RAY	AL	46E	26
WIGINTON LARRY MICHAEL	MI	08E	32
WIGLESWORTH ERNEST W JR	NC	44E	49
WIGTON PHILIP GREGORY	NE	58E	2
WIKANDER DAVID JOSEPH	OH	09W	92
WIKE JOHN MICHAEL	IL	13W	60
WIKLE RICKY LYNN	CA	34W	59
WILBANKS DONALD MELVEN	OK	45W	59
WILBANKS HILLIARD ALMOND	GA	15E	88
WILBANKS JAMES HARDY	TX	13W	13
WILBANKS LESLIE JOE	AZ	10W	16
WILBANKS TIMOTHY MARCIA	TX	49W	11
WILBER WILLIAM FREDRICK	MN	07E	66
WILBERTON HAROLD JR	IL	35W	23
WILBORN CHARLEY ANDREW	VA	07W	115
WILBRECHT KURT MICHAEL	MN	09W	25
WILBUR DENNIS	VT	14E	120
WILBUR JACK LEROY	OH	13E	57
WILBUR WILLIAM JR	PA	62W	3
WILBURN JOHN EDWARD	OK	51E	4
WILBURN WILLIAM LEVY JR	TN	34W	12
WILBURN WOODROW HOOVER	TX	14E	121
WILCOX ARMOUR DAVID III	OH	37W	71
WILCOX CHARLES CHESTER	NY	31E	61
WILCOX CHARLES EARL JR	LA	49E	17
WILCOX CHARLES KIRBY	MO	34E	12
WILCOX CHARLES THOMAS	OH	03W	27
WILCOX DAVID JOHN	WI	38W	40
WILCOX GARY LEE	NY	17E	56
WILCOX JOHN ARTHUR JR	GA	38E	41
WILCOX RAYMOND LEE	MI	19W	83
WILCOX RICK ALAN	OH	11W	11
WILCOX RUSSELL LEE	OH	34E	72
WILCOX THOMAS DEWEY	IA	60W	13
WILCOX WAYNE ALAN	IN	32W	41
WILCOX WILLIAM EIDMAN JR	NY	58E	17
WILCOXSON ROBERT FRANKLIN	OK	01W	32
WILDAUER PAUL ARTHUR	CA	01E	44
WILDE ERSKINE BUFORD	VA	09E	83

NAME	STATE	PANEL NO.	LINE NO.
WILDE RAYMOND CHARLES	MN	01E	17
WILDER ARLOS CLAYTON	CA	07E	78
WILDER AVERY	NY	61W	19
WILDER BENNETT G	NC	27E	32
WILDER BRUCE JEFFREY	MI	59E	15
WILDER CHARLIE LARRY	GA	31W	30
WILDER FRANK	MS	30W	5
WILDER LUTHER TOMMY	NC	48E	13
WILDER RONALD FREDERICK	TX	20W	33
WILDER STEVE CLIFTON	AL	54E	21
WILDERS WILLIAM JAMES	NY	12E	81
WILDERSPIN DEAN ALLYN	MI	14W	7
WILDERSPIN VERNON CHARLES	MI	36E	42
WILDES MICHAEL LAYTEN	FL	02E	10
WILDMAN MELVIN ALVIN	AR	61E	5
WILDMAN MILES GREGORY	PA	40W	40
WILDMAN RICHARD LYNN	OH	07E	92
WILDMAN STEVEN EARL	IA	49W	35
WILDY SHIRLEY JR	FL	63W	1
WILENSKI STANLEY JR	NY	11W	26
WILES ALVIN EUGENE	TN	60E	5
WILES JOHNNY	AR	22W	50
WILES MARVIN BENJAMIN CHR	CA	01W	14
WILES TERRY LEE	IN	08E	32
WILEY FRANK DAVID	TX	16E	18
WILEY GILBERT	NY	48E	49
WILEY JAMES JOSEPH	GA	34W	55
WILEY JOHN DUDLEY	NC	24E	75
WILEY MICHAEL RAY	MD	51W	22
WILEY PHILLIP TONY	CO	13E	31
WILEY RICHARD DENNIS	IL	01W	41
WILEY THOMAS J	LA	01W	25
WILFONG GIL STEVENS	IL	19W	42
WILFONG ROBERT WESLEY	IN	24E	49
WILFONG ROGER DALE	MD	28E	89
WILFORD PERCY LEE	WA	17E	66
WILHELM DAVID KENNETH	WA	40W	40
WILHELM FREDERICK	OH	18W	74
WILHELM JOHN LESTER	PA	14E	65
WILHELM LAWRENCE M JR	LA	28W	55
WILHELM MACK HOUSTON	TX	32W	63
WILHELM RICHARD THOMAS	NY	18W	13
WILHELM WILLIAM LESTER	OH	07W	43
WILHELMI HENRY JOSEPH JR	PA	21E	85
WILHITE TROY DEAN	CO	17W	46
WILHOIT HOWARD RAY JR	KY	38W	47
WILHOIT ROBERT STEVE	FL	49W	2
WILHOITE HENRY O'NEIL	KY	20W	16
WILK CHARLES LEE	MS	30E	82
WILK JOSEPH ANTHONY JR	VA	34W	63
WILK THOMAS JOHN	MA	22W	45
WILK WILLIAM ANTHONY	MD	24E	49
WILKE ROBERT FREDERICK	WI	34E	65
WILKEN BRYAN LEE	NE	03W	105
WILKENING ARNOLD G III	WA	20E	127
WILKENS JOHN HERMAN	NY	63W	1
WILKERSON CHARLES ROBERT	IN	25E	72
WILKERSON DAVID HUNTER	IA	24W	63
WILKERSON DAVID LEE	FL	46E	13
WILKERSON GEORGE OLIVER	IL	09W	36
WILKERSON JUNIOR	CT	17E	26
WILKERSON LARRY WAYNE	TX	18E	54
WILKERSON LAWRENCE	TX	03W	101
WILKERSON RICHARD LEE	IL	12W	90
WILKERSON STEVEN DOUGLAS	NE	36W	81
WILKERSON WILLIAM MHOON	MI	44W	21
WILKERSON WILLIE WOODSON	NC	09E	64
WILKES EULIS NEIL JR	AZ	35E	1
WILKES JOHN GRADY	TN	13W	42
WILKES ROBERT LEE	CA	45W	17
WILKEY BLAIR CECIL	UT	23W	40
WILKEY EMMITT JAMES JR	TX	10E	78
WILKIE ARTHUR WAYNE	NC	14E	41
WILKIE CHARLES DAVID	NY	31E	67
WILKIE DOUGLAS WILMER	MI	19W	57
WILKIE ROBERT GEORGE	MI	13E	70
WILKINS ALLAN FRANCIS	VT	04W	113
WILKINS ALTON III	VA	10E	59
WILKINS BEN HENRY JR	KY	30W	9
WILKINS BOBBY RAY	NJ	21W	35
WILKINS CALVIN WAYNE	TX	33W	90
WILKINS GARY LEE	WA	64E	2

NAME	STATE	PANEL NO.	LINE NO.
WILKINS GEORGE HENRY	NC	09E	18
WILKINS HAROLD EUGENE	NC	03E	48
WILKINS JAMES MARVIN	MI	50W	40
WILKINS MICHAEL LEE	OR	28W	88
WILKINS RANDOLPH RECARDO	NJ	58E	17
WILKINS RICHARD EDWARD	WA	20E	125
WILKINS ROBERT JOHN	MO	04E	27
WILKINS TERRY KENNETH	NV	08E	126
WILKINS WILLIAM GEORGE	PA	47E	44
WILKINSON BILLIE WELDON	TX	39W	19
WILKINSON CLYDE DAVID	TX	05W	100
WILKINSON DALE SLOAN	FL	20W	128
WILKINSON DENNIS EDWARD	FL	01W	22
WILKINSON DONALD ALFRED	MA	27E	75
WILKINSON GARY	KY	55W	25
WILKINSON HARLAND LYLE	NE	17W	11
WILKINSON JACK WILLIAM	NY	25E	72
WILKINSON JAMES JOSEPH JR	NY	10W	63
WILKINSON JOHN TERRELL	TN	47E	58
WILKINSON JOSEPH E III	AL	14E	4
WILKINSON RICHARD THOMAS	MI	17W	86
WILKINSON RONALD JAMES	RI	31W	30
WILKINSON STEPHEN DAVID	CT	27W	43
WILKINSON WILLIAM GILBERT	MS	32E	14
WILKOWSKY WILLIAM JR	NH	07E	15
WILKS GREGARY ALAN	UT	06W	20
WILKS JAMES ALAN	TN	17W	125
WILKS JAMES LEE	SC	24W	80
WILKS JOHNNY LEE	MS	44W	55
WILKS WALTER ALBERT	IL	20E	52
WILL FREDERICK REED	CA	52W	8
WILL GORDON WALDEMAR	WI	28E	42
WILL WILLIAM ANTHONY	PA	08E	134
WILLARD ALAN WAYNE	MA	40E	16
WILLARD CHARLES R JR	NC	14W	10
WILLARD FREDERICK R JR	CA	18E	66
WILLARD HUGH GREY	SC	32E	50
WILLARD JAMES MONROE	NM	18W	99
WILLARD KENNETH EUGENE JR	IN	45E	32
WILLARD LEON DAVID	VA	48W	9
WILLARD LLOYD LOREN	MN	67W	7
WILLARD RALPH JOHN	MA	51W	28
WILLARD ROBERT LEROY	MD	03W	117
WILLARD THOMAS ALAN	NH	22W	83
WILLBANKS CHARLES EDWARDS	GA	30E	68
WILLEFORD FRANKLIN PATRIC	OK	36W	21
WILLEFORD JAMES ROBERT	IL	12E	128
WILLEFORD JIMMY WAYNE	TX	16W	51
WILLEKE GARY ROBERT	OH	51W	37
WILLEMS JOHN GUSTAVE	WI	18W	28
WILLERT DIETER ERIC	IL	22W	83
WILLETT FRANKLIN DAVID	AZ	26E	77
WILLETT LOUIS EDWARD	NY	15E	37
WILLETT RICHARD JAMES	CA	09E	107
WILLETT ROBERT LEE	IL	14W	45
WILLETT ROBERT VINCENT JR	MT	27W	103
WILLEY ALDEN BERTRAM	NH	06E	55
WILLEY BURR MCBRIDE	VA	01W	46
WILLEY DONALD MORRIS	CT	37E	29
WILLEY JOHN JAMES	CA	11W	119
WILLEY PETER RAY	MN	34E	57
WILLEY ROBERT LEON	ID	25W	45
WILLHITE HOWARD K JR	NC	05W	113
WILLIAM RONALD WAYNE	KS	12W	32
WILLIAMS ALAN EDWIN		27E	42
WILLIAMS ALEXANDER	FL	03E	63
WILLIAMS ALFONZIA	FL	41E	5
WILLIAMS ALFRED LACY	MA	15W	88
WILLIAMS ALLAN JAMES	FL	04E	117
WILLIAMS ALLEN	NJ	60W	7
WILLIAMS AMOS LEVERN	NY	21W	57
WILLIAMS ARTHUR C JR	AR	49E	27
WILLIAMS ARTHUR JR	GA	37W	27
WILLIAMS ARTHUR PAUL	MA	10E	49
WILLIAMS AUBREY	IL	10W	55
WILLIAMS AUGUSTUS LOUIS	TX	48W	20
WILLIAMS BARRY HENNETT	CA	26E	95
WILLIAMS BEN	SC	10W	128
WILLIAMS BEN HAROLD	FL	43E	64
WILLIAMS BILL FRED JR	NC	35W	57
WILLIAMS BILL GENE	ID	09W	6
WILLIAMS BILLIE JOE	KS	01W	94

NAME	STATE	PANEL NO.	LINE NO.
WILLIAMS BILLIE JOE	MO	01W	94
WILLIAMS BILLY	SC	08E	43
WILLIAMS BILLY JOE	KY	11W	119
WILLIAMS BOBBIE LEE	AL	05W	25
WILLIAMS BOBBY LEE	TX	12E	125
WILLIAMS BOBBY RAY	MS	13E	101
WILLIAMS BOBBY RAY	TX	55E	35
WILLIAMS BOBBY RAY	OK	07W	101
WILLIAMS BRIAN JOHN	CA	12W	105
WILLIAMS BRUCE REGINALD	MI	18E	99
WILLIAMS BURNELL JR	AR	51E	15
WILLIAMS C W RICHARD	NJ	45E	61
WILLIAMS CAL WILLIS	GA	61W	8
WILLIAMS CALVIN	SC	10W	128
WILLIAMS CAROL EDWARD	SC	45W	59
WILLIAMS CARTER LEE JR	MS	05E	92
WILLIAMS CHARLES	MD	13E	101
WILLIAMS CHARLES CLINTON	GA	08E	83
WILLIAMS CHARLES EDWARD	NC	41E	57
WILLIAMS CHARLES JAMES	CA	29E	79
WILLIAMS CHARLES RAY	LA	05E	18
WILLIAMS CHARLES ROBERT	CA	56E	18
WILLIAMS CHARLES ROSS	GA	09E	18
WILLIAMS CHRISTIAN LARS	CA	27E	42
WILLIAMS CHRISTOPHER	VA	23W	18
WILLIAMS CLARENCE	OH	05E	63
WILLIAMS CLARK LEE VERN	SC	22W	29
WILLIAMS CLAUDE ARTHUR	TN	03W	1
WILLIAMS CLAUDE NATHANIEL	OK	12E	118
WILLIAMS CLIFFORD DAN	MI	53E	43
WILLIAMS CLIFFORD LEROY	OH	46E	52
WILLIAMS COLERIDGE JR	DC	20E	99
WILLIAMS CRAIG EMERY	CA	30W	61
WILLIAMS CURTIS F JR	FL	28E	107
WILLIAMS CURTIS JOHN	KY	13E	13
WILLIAMS CURTIS LEE	MO	43E	2
WILLIAMS CURTIS LELAND	SD	05W	82
WILLIAMS DALE EDWARD	OH	09W	55
WILLIAMS DANIEL EUGENE	ID	27W	61
WILLIAMS DANIEL III	SC	40E	16
WILLIAMS DANNY	OK	41W	9
WILLIAMS DAVID	TX	05E	19
WILLIAMS DAVID BERYL	LA	01W	13
WILLIAMS DAVID CHARLES	CA	39E	15
WILLIAMS DAVID CLARK	TN	60W	7
WILLIAMS DAVID EDWARD	MA	18E	37
WILLIAMS DAVID EDWARD	TX	26W	29
WILLIAMS DAVID GEORGE	CA	26E	110
WILLIAMS DAVID III	CA	16W	111
WILLIAMS DAVID JR	GA	34W	35
WILLIAMS DAVID LEIGH	MN	48E	13
WILLIAMS DAVID MICHAEL	VA	35W	74
WILLIAMS DAVID RICHARD	TN	17E	90
WILLIAMS DEMPSEY H III	NC	01E	95
WILLIAMS DENNIS ALAN	NM	28W	31
WILLIAMS DENNIS CRAIG	CA	16E	81
WILLIAMS DENNIS LEE	CA	11E	42
WILLIAMS DENNIS MICHAEL	OH	21W	4
WILLIAMS DENNIS NEIL	IA	12E	110
WILLIAMS DEREX JR	FL	25E	36
WILLIAMS DEWAYNE THOMAS	MI	43W	25
WILLIAMS DONALD	GA	19E	68
WILLIAMS DONALD D JR	VA	55W	10
WILLIAMS DONALD LEE	AL	37E	75
WILLIAMS DONALD WINSLOW	AL	56E	33
WILLIAMS DORSEY BURWIN	TN	19E	2
WILLIAMS DOUGLAS CANDIT	UT	40E	34
WILLIAMS DOYLE	SC	47E	44
WILLIAMS DUANE GREGORY	PA	15W	116
WILLIAMS EARNEST	IL	06W	89
WILLIAMS EDDIE	NC	45W	23
WILLIAMS EDDIE EARL	TX	23E	66
WILLIAMS EDDIE JONES JR	TN	26W	105
WILLIAMS EDDIE KENNETH	SC	08E	114
WILLIAMS EDDIE LEE	FL	11E	40
WILLIAMS EDGAR W JR	NC	35W	31
WILLIAMS EDWARD J	VA	04E	65
WILLIAMS EDWARD WAYNE	FL	02W	129
WILLIAMS EDWIN JEROME	MI	22E	52
WILLIAMS ELBERT THOMAS	NC	23E	72
WILLIAMS ERIC	LA	06E	105
WILLIAMS ERNEST C JR	LA	67W	7

NAME	STATE	PANEL NO.	LINE NO.
WILLIAMS EUGENE MELVIN	OH	34E	33
WILLIAMS EUGENE VERNON	IL	36E	62
WILLIAMS FLOYD CHARLES	LA	23E	66
WILLIAMS FLOYD LEE JR	CO	70E	1
WILLIAMS FRANK A	MI	29E	103
WILLIAMS FRANK CURTIS	FL	26W	5
WILLIAMS FRANK DUVALL	CA	01E	77
WILLIAMS FRANK EDWARD	MI	61W	9
WILLIAMS FRANK EMANUEL	FL	02W	102
WILLIAMS FRANK NORMAN	SC	17W	76
WILLIAMS FRANK WAYNE JR	FL	04E	96
WILLIAMS FRANKIE ROSS	CT	33W	60
WILLIAMS FRANKLIN BRUCE	PA	14E	120
WILLIAMS FRANKLIN DEAN	IN	19W	6
WILLIAMS FRED ALBERT	NC	06W	126
WILLIAMS FRED JOSEPH JR	OR	12E	45
WILLIAMS FRED THOMAS	NJ	26W	88
WILLIAMS FREDDY ROOSEVELT	GA	48W	51
WILLIAMS FREDDY THOMAS	TX	35W	31
WILLIAMS FREDERICK JOSEPH	CA	21E	110
WILLIAMS FREDERICK THOMAS	NY	41E	33
WILLIAMS FREDRICK H JR	CA	65W	2
WILLIAMS GARY LYNN	IA	09E	110
WILLIAMS GARY ROBERT	IL	06W	14
WILLIAMS GAYLE EDWARD	TX	16W	25
WILLIAMS GENE WILLIAM	AL	02E	121
WILLIAMS GENRETT	FL	04E	126
WILLIAMS GEORGE ANTHONY	MO	08E	70
WILLIAMS GEORGE DAVIS JR	IN	24W	23
WILLIAMS GEORGE HARDY JR	VA	03W	5
WILLIAMS GEORGE HARVEY	DE	20E	12
WILLIAMS GEORGE JOSEPH	NY	33E	6
WILLIAMS GERALD DAN	TX	38W	22
WILLIAMS GERALD MARK	GA	06W	26
WILLIAMS GERALD PATRICK	CA	38E	63
WILLIAMS GERALD STUART	MI	53E	26
WILLIAMS GLEN RAYMOND	NJ	29E	23
WILLIAMS GOLER JUNIOR	NC	29E	86
WILLIAMS GREGORY J	UT	49E	7
WILLIAMS HAROLD ALLEN	VA	58W	16
WILLIAMS HAROLD DAVID	NC	32E	60
WILLIAMS HAROLD DAVID	CA	20W	84
WILLIAMS HARRIS LEE	SC	04W	98
WILLIAMS HARVEY LEE	AR	18W	107
WILLIAMS HENRY BRAXTON JR	MS	44E	23
WILLIAMS HERBERT	TX	39W	19
WILLIAMS HIAWATHA HENRY	OH	03W	70
WILLIAMS HILLARD EVANS	TX	31E	2
WILLIAMS HOLLIS JR	OH	43E	39
WILLIAMS HOWARD	GA	40E	50
WILLIAMS HOWARD	NY	03W	35
WILLIAMS HOWARD C JR	TX	50E	35
WILLIAMS HOWARD CLAYTON	LA	52W	2
WILLIAMS HOWARD EUGENE JR	GA	15W	37
WILLIAMS HOWARD KEITH	OH	45E	32
WILLIAMS HUEY	LA	30W	97
WILLIAMS IRA WINARD	GA	22E	75
WILLIAMS J C	OH	08E	41
WILLIAMS J C JR	IN	44W	43
WILLIAMS JACK ELWIN	CA	30W	83
WILLIAMS JAMES	VA	07E	37
WILLIAMS JAMES	OK	24E	79
WILLIAMS JAMES A	KY	48W	9
WILLIAMS JAMES ALEC	CA	54W	34
WILLIAMS JAMES BERNARD JR	GA	23W	19
WILLIAMS JAMES EARL	MS	42E	59
WILLIAMS JAMES EDGAR	SC	40W	9
WILLIAMS JAMES EDWARD JR	OK	32E	83
WILLIAMS JAMES ELLIS	MS	07E	63
WILLIAMS JAMES GORDON	FL	19E	33
WILLIAMS JAMES JOSEPH	CT	54W	39
WILLIAMS JAMES PRITCHARD	TN	06E	23
WILLIAMS JAMES RANDALL	NC	33E	1
WILLIAMS JAMES RAYMOND	MI	51W	1
WILLIAMS JAMES S	KY	06E	22
WILLIAMS JAMES THOMAS	GA	19E	124
WILLIAMS JAMES THOMAS JR	NY	04W	15
WILLIAMS JAMES U III	SC	36W	71
WILLIAMS JAMES WESLEY	TX	44E	12
WILLIAMS JERRY HIOTT	SC	08E	90
WILLIAMS JERRY LEONARD	OK	65W	3
WILLIAMS JIMMIE	GA	11E	106
WILLIAMS JIMMIE KEITH	IN	37W	71
WILLIAMS JIMMY	LA	45W	11
WILLIAMS JIMMY DARRELL	NC	26E	54
WILLIAMS JIMMY LAVERNE	AL	07E	78
WILLIAMS JOE BUCK	TX	51W	1
WILLIAMS JOE JR	GA	18E	99
WILLIAMS JOEL JR	AR	23E	33
WILLIAMS JOHN CHARLES	KS	19W	6
WILLIAMS JOHN DAVID	CA	11E	1
WILLIAMS JOHN DEWEY	IL	28E	6
WILLIAMS JOHN DILLARD	MO	42W	57
WILLIAMS JOHN GRADY JR	NC	01E	86
WILLIAMS JOHN KIRBY	PA	24E	98
WILLIAMS JOHN RAY	WV	37W	9
WILLIAMS JOHN VINSON JR	CA	07W	116
WILLIAMS JOHN WILLIAM	LA	05E	94
WILLIAMS JOHNNIE LEE JR	FL	18W	126
WILLIAMS JOHNNY	CA	15E	26
WILLIAMS JOHNNY	NC	34E	12
WILLIAMS JOHNNY	IN	16W	21
WILLIAMS JOHNNY BEE	TX	43W	11
WILLIAMS JOHNNY EDWARD	SC	10E	122
WILLIAMS JOHNNY GLEN	IL	31W	62
WILLIAMS JOHNNY JR	AL	26E	69
WILLIAMS JOSEPH JEREMIAH	NY	24W	51
WILLIAMS JOSEPH JEROME	MO	42E	45
WILLIAMS JOSEPH MICHAEL	IL	64E	10
WILLIAMS JOSEPH PIERCE	FL	17E	107
WILLIAMS JOSEPH THOMAS	PA	11E	5
WILLIAMS KENNETH CORNEY	OH	02W	97
WILLIAMS KENNETH JERRY	GA	37E	2
WILLIAMS KENNETH R JR	WA	44E	1
WILLIAMS KERMIT LOUIS	NC	43W	32
WILLIAMS KERRY LEE	PA	05E	125
WILLIAMS LABON RAPHAEL	TN	16W	21
WILLIAMS LAMAR LONGO	FL	04W	122
WILLIAMS LARRY DALE	MN	55E	36
WILLIAMS LARRY DOUGLAS	AL	08E	83
WILLIAMS LARRY ELLIS	CA	36E	62
WILLIAMS LARRY GLEN	OK	31E	27
WILLIAMS LARRY JOE	MO	17E	40
WILLIAMS LARRY KEITH	CA	29E	93
WILLIAMS LARRY LEE	KY	20E	70
WILLIAMS LARRY LEE	TX	30E	75
WILLIAMS LAURENCE E	FL	37W	1
WILLIAMS LAVESTER LEE	OK	01E	20
WILLIAMS LAWRENCE	DC	52E	32
WILLIAMS LAWRENCE C JR	TX	07W	72
WILLIAMS LAWRENCE DEAN	CO	35E	36
WILLIAMS LAWRENCE H JR	DC	14W	110
WILLIAMS LAWRENCE JR	LA	11E	19
WILLIAMS LEE ARTHUR	AR	22W	17
WILLIAMS LEMUEL TAYLOR	MO	30E	52
WILLIAMS LEONARD	SC	04E	96
WILLIAMS LEONARD TAYLOR	VA	24E	1
WILLIAMS LEROY	OH	10E	81
WILLIAMS LEROY	MS	27E	13
WILLIAMS LEROY C	FL	24W	109
WILLIAMS LEROY JR	NJ	02E	105
WILLIAMS LEROY WALTER	IN	07E	46
WILLIAMS LESLIE WAYNE	CO	17W	6
WILLIAMS LESTER JR	NJ	39W	6
WILLIAMS LESTER LEE	MO	32E	53
WILLIAMS LONNIE	IL	38W	81
WILLIAMS LONNIE CLIFFORD	PA	07E	100
WILLIAMS LOUIS	IL	50E	8
WILLIAMS MACK WILBERT	OK	54W	1
WILLIAMS MALCOLM GEORGE	CT	13W	47
WILLIAMS MARK EVERETT	OK	13W	70
WILLIAMS MARSHALL WAYNE	TX	02W	44
WILLIAMS MAURICE THERON	FL	39E	78
WILLIAMS MAXIE R JR	TN	49E	17
WILLIAMS MELVIN JAMES	AL	03W	6
WILLIAMS MELVIN JOE	AL	36E	42
WILLIAMS MICHAEL EARL	IL	05W	67
WILLIAMS MICHAEL WALTER	CA	66E	4
WILLIAMS MILLIGAN RUDOLPH	GA	19E	124
WILLIAMS MORRIS EDWARD	ID	14W	110
WILLIAMS MOSES	GA	23E	66
WILLIAMS NATHAN C	NY	13E	129
WILLIAMS NATHANIEL JR	IL	43E	50
WILLIAMS NATHANIEL MEARLO	AR	50E	22
WILLIAMS NEIL STEPHEN	NY	15E	111
WILLIAMS NOAH	OH	30E	21
WILLIAMS NOEL DEAN	OK	40E	16
WILLIAMS NORMAN COLUMBUS	TX	02E	8
WILLIAMS NORMAN PAUL	ND	31E	56
WILLIAMS OSCAR BURDETT	NC	02W	5
WILLIAMS OTTAWAY LARSON	IL	15W	52
WILLIAMS PAUL EDWARD	IL	24E	58
WILLIAMS PAUL EDWARD	AL	47E	7
WILLIAMS PHILLIP W	FL	26W	75
WILLIAMS PLUMMER	AR	13E	81
WILLIAMS PONDEXTUER E	FL	08W	96
WILLIAMS RALPH GENE	OR	08E	29
WILLIAMS RALPH LEROY	MT	39E	56
WILLIAMS RALPH MAURICE	IL	06E	79
WILLIAMS RANDALL LEE	SD	61W	19
WILLIAMS RAY	GA	66E	4
WILLIAMS RAY FRANCIS	FL	13E	88
WILLIAMS RAY LEE	TX	16E	75
WILLIAMS RAY MILTON	LA	33W	45
WILLIAMS RAYFIELD	TX	37E	75
WILLIAMS RAYMOND CHARLES	IL	44W	7
WILLIAMS RAYMOND LEON	DC	08W	78
WILLIAMS RAYMOND LEROY	VA	25W	114
WILLIAMS RAYMOND LEWIS	IL	12W	116
WILLIAMS RAYNER EDWARD	MD	45W	54
WILLIAMS REGINALD JR	NY	50E	43
WILLIAMS REMER GARTH	NC	30E	36
WILLIAMS REUBEN CHARLES	TN	25E	73
WILLIAMS RICHARD ALLEN	IL	18E	13
WILLIAMS RICHARD C	PA	15W	127
WILLIAMS RICHARD D	CA	41E	46
WILLIAMS RICHARD EARL	MN	48E	22
WILLIAMS RICHARD FRANK	CA	43W	32
WILLIAMS RICHARD HARRY	PA	21W	96
WILLIAMS RICHARD JR	TX	14W	70
WILLIAMS RICHARD OLIVER	MS	33E	54
WILLIAMS RICHARD WARREN	MI	14W	92
WILLIAMS ROBERT	OH	02W	88
WILLIAMS ROBERT A JR	OR	06W	107
WILLIAMS ROBERT ALTON	NJ	28E	89
WILLIAMS ROBERT ALWYN	CA	22W	94
WILLIAMS ROBERT CLEVEN	AL	21W	5
WILLIAMS ROBERT CURTIS	FL	06E	13
WILLIAMS ROBERT CYRIL	IL	08E	117
WILLIAMS ROBERT D JR	TN	05E	81
WILLIAMS ROBERT EARL	IL	19E	76
WILLIAMS ROBERT EARL	FL	39E	27
WILLIAMS ROBERT EARL	FL	11W	62
WILLIAMS ROBERT ENOCH	OH	42W	3
WILLIAMS ROBERT EUGENE	TN	53W	25
WILLIAMS ROBERT FLOYD	NE	50E	2
WILLIAMS ROBERT JOHN	NY	05W	76
WILLIAMS ROBERT JOHN	AL	01W	24
WILLIAMS ROBERT JR	AZ	49W	49
WILLIAMS ROBERT L	FL	33E	24
WILLIAMS ROBERT LEE	DC	53E	26
WILLIAMS ROBERT LEE	MS	51W	15
WILLIAMS ROGER DALE	VA	70E	1
WILLIAMS ROGER RALPH	KS	16E	15
WILLIAMS RONAL LOYD	WV	13W	30
WILLIAMS RONALD	MA	31E	39
WILLIAMS RONALD AARON	PA	16E	26
WILLIAMS RONALD ANTHONY	SC	21E	72
WILLIAMS ROOSEVELT	GA	41W	18
WILLIAMS ROY CHARLES	TX	59E	15
WILLIAMS ROY COLON JR	NC	18W	22
WILLIAMS ROY KENNETH JR	MI	21W	16
WILLIAMS RUFUS TIMOTHY	TX	22E	64
WILLIAMS RUSSELL LOWELL	IL	09W	81
WILLIAMS SAMMY	OH	13E	112
WILLIAMS SAMUEL	FL	62W	19
WILLIAMS SAMUEL HARRY	TX	15W	69
WILLIAMS SAMUEL LOUIS JR	MD	21W	67
WILLIAMS SAMUEL WILLIE	NY	08W	57
WILLIAMS SHERMAN ELLIOT	AL	02E	34
WILLIAMS STEPHEN	PA	32E	84
WILLIAMS STEVEN GARY	IL	03W	99
WILLIAMS STEVEN JAMES	OR	12W	78
WILLIAMS TED	MI	16E	98
WILLIAMS TERRY ALLEN	OR	43E	64
WILLIAMS TERRY CHARLES	NC	26E	5

NAME	STATE	PANEL NO.	LINE NO.
WILLIAMS TERRY DOUGLAS	GA	29E	37
WILLIAMS TERRY EUGENE	TN	08W	5
WILLIAMS TERRY JOE	WI	36E	42
WILLIAMS TERRY LUTHER	AR	40W	55
WILLIAMS TERRY WAYNE	TN	39E	28
WILLIAMS THADDEUS E JR	AL	14E	7
WILLIAMS THEODORE ALFORD	IL	13W	25
WILLIAMS THEODORE JR	IL	08E	132
WILLIAMS THOMAS ALBERT	PA	13W	30
WILLIAMS THOMAS EARL JR	FL	26W	105
WILLIAMS THOMAS HANSFORD	CO	43E	39
WILLIAMS THOMAS HENRY	OR	46W	10
WILLIAMS THOMAS HOWARD	CA	54W	34
WILLIAMS THOMAS JOHN	CA	12W	54
WILLIAMS THOMAS JOSEPH	MS	23W	81
WILLIAMS THOMAS MURRAY		09E	35
WILLIAMS THOMAS RALPH	NM	22W	101
WILLIAMS THOMAS VERNON JR	KS	46W	55
WILLIAMS TIMOTHY LEROY	DC	34W	3
WILLIAMS TIMOTHY RONALD	OH	51E	27
WILLIAMS TIMOTHY TAYLOR	OH	21W	97
WILLIAMS TOMMIE DORSEY	OH	50E	35
WILLIAMS TOMMIE LEE	AL	05E	76
WILLIAMS TROY BYRON	WV	03E	39
WILLIAMS VAN	NY	02E	117
WILLIAMS VANCE GEORGE	TX	17E	94
WILLIAMS VERE LOYD JR	CO	42E	23
WILLIAMS VICTOR DEMOTT	IL	02W	55
WILLIAMS VINCENT RICHARD	CA	17E	15
WILLIAMS VIRGIL LAWRENCE	CO	42E	46
WILLIAMS WALDO ALVA	IA	15W	127
WILLIAMS WALLACE	NY	17E	77
WILLIAMS WALTER	LA	22W	110
WILLIAMS WALTER ALEXANDER	NC	45E	23
WILLIAMS WALTER DOUGLAS	MD	23E	48
WILLIAMS WALTER JOSEPH JR	VA	58E	3
WILLIAMS WALTER JR	OH	08E	29
WILLIAMS WALTER JR	VA	11E	19
WILLIAMS WARREN	FL	26W	29
WILLIAMS WAYNE CHARLES	TN	54W	4
WILLIAMS WAYNE RICHARDSON	VA	03W	38
WILLIAMS WILBERT JR	NY	12E	128
WILLIAMS WILBUR LEO JR	MA	47E	18
WILLIAMS WILLARD LOYD	MO	66E	4
WILLIAMS WILLEY EDGAR JR	NY	35W	22
WILLIAMS WILLIAM CHARLES	MS	37W	44
WILLIAMS WILLIAM JACK	TN	22E	75
WILLIAMS WILLIAM LYNN	NJ	05W	98
WILLIAMS WILLIAM SMYLY JR	NC	44E	63
WILLIAMS WILLIE AMOS	SC	44E	23
WILLIAMS WILLIE LEE	MS	31W	30
WILLIAMS WILLIE ROGERS	NY	03W	126
WILLIAMS WILLIS WHITE	GA	18E	17
WILLIAMS WOODROW	PA	19E	45
WILLIAMSON ALBERTIS	NC	38E	74
WILLIAMSON BENJAMIN JEFFE	SC	60W	13
WILLIAMSON BENTON CLAUDE	TX	06W	6
WILLIAMSON CHARLES ALTON	WV	02E	19
WILLIAMSON CHARLIE C JR	TN	25W	15
WILLIAMSON DAVID THOMAS	VA	06W	17
WILLIAMSON DON CLAUDE	UT	67W	7
WILLIAMSON DON IRA	KY	02E	30
WILLIAMSON DONALD LEE	WA	16W	82
WILLIAMSON DONALD RAY	CA	52W	33
WILLIAMSON EDWARD LARUE	MS	21W	49
WILLIAMSON EDWARD LOUIS	SC	31E	19
WILLIAMSON ERVIN HOWARD	PA	25W	45
WILLIAMSON HOWARD LANIER	AL	09W	6
WILLIAMSON JAMES CALVIN	AL	02W	117
WILLIAMSON JAMES D	WA	33E	54
WILLIAMSON JOEL STEPHEN	NY	30E	36
WILLIAMSON JOHN CLARENCE	CA	24W	51
WILLIAMSON JOHNNY GORDON	TX	03W	11
WILLIAMSON LARRY ALLEN	WI	20E	80
WILLIAMSON LARRY GAIL	OH	13W	114
WILLIAMSON MILLARD LEROY	GA	08E	71
WILLIAMSON PAUL DOUGLAS	NC	21E	25
WILLIAMSON PETE ELLIS	KY	05W	16
WILLIAMSON RICHARD WESLEY	VA	09E	126
WILLIAMSON ROBERT GREGORY	ME	12E	52
WILLIAMSON ROBERT JOE	IN	36E	43
WILLIAMSON THOMAS DARRELL	TX	04E	117

NAME	STATE	PANEL NO.	LINE NO.
WILLIAMSON WILLIAM CURTIS	NY	28W	95
WILLIAMSON WILLIAM N	NC	14W	56
WILLIBER GERALD PAUL	LA	64E	1
WILLIFORD ELSWORTH	NC	44E	43
WILLING EDWARD ARLE	DE	51W	29
WILLINGHAM CHARLES WATSON	MS	41W	17
WILLINGHAM ELDON WAYNE	CA	25E	45
WILLINGHAM JOHN DAVIS	MD	37E	29
WILLINGHAM NATHANIEL	PA	47E	1
WILLINGHAM PRESTON T JR	IL	08W	5
WILLINGHAM WILLIAM EARL	WV	27E	35
WILLINGHAM WILMER JAY	LA	11E	131
WILLIS ARCHIE VAUGHN	MI	40E	34
WILLIS BENJAMIN GALU	06	47W	35
WILLIS DONALD CLYDE	CA	31E	95
WILLIS DONNIS GLEN	IL	28W	55
WILLIS GLENN LEE	GA	10W	132
WILLIS HAROLD EUGENE	CA	04E	96
WILLIS HINEY	TX	42W	14
WILLIS HOWARD DANIEL	MS	43E	50
WILLIS JAMES RONALD	NV	50W	43
WILLIS JOEL THOMAS	CA	21E	93
WILLIS JOHN HENRY	PA	16E	105
WILLIS JOSEPH F	MI	28W	55
WILLIS KENNETH MAX	VA	20W	6
WILLIS LARRY JOE	IL	13E	88
WILLIS LARRY WAYNE	AL	21W	21
WILLIS LEDELL	LA	08E	99
WILLIS M L	TX	10E	89
WILLIS PAUL MITCHELL	MO	54E	21
WILLIS RAYMOND CONLUIS	AL	25W	3
WILLIS RICHARD A	OH	03E	62
WILLIS STEVEN CRAIG	IN	06W	109
WILLIS THOMAS MURTEN	ID	21E	59
WILLIS WATSON	OH	05E	37
WILLIS WILLIAM SHERRILL	NC	01W	122
WILLIS WILLIE CLIFTON	MO	18E	37
WILLISON FRANKLIN JOE	AR	10W	107
WILLMAN GARY LYNN	TX	44E	56
WILLOUGHBY EARL CHARLES	PA	02E	77
WILLOUGHBY JESSE LAVERN	IL	49E	17
WILLOUGHBY JIMMY STEWART	OR	63W	14
WILLOUGHBY JULIAN B	MI	07E	13
WILLOW ROBERT GLENN	PA	26E	21
WILLS DAVID COLLIER JR	GA	07E	46
WILLS FRANCIS DESALES	MD	05E	82
WILLS ROBERT EMERY	ME	12W	64
WILLS ROBERT JOHN	PA	57W	31
WILLS ROBSON WARD	TX	18W	99
WILLS ROY SHANNON	TN	21W	122
WILLSON LOYD MEREDITH	TX	40E	71
WILMOTH LEWIS DIXON	WV	24E	1
WILSFORD MICHAEL STEPHEN	IN	26E	69
WILSHER EVERETT NELSON	FL	32W	74
WILSHER JOSEPH MICHAEL	TX	04W	3
WILSON ADAM	CA	16W	82
WILSON ALBERT RICHARD	WA	07E	83
WILSON ALFRED MAC	TX	30W	35
WILSON ARTHUR JR	WV	04W	75
WILSON BILLIE JOE	KS	14W	118
WILSON BILLIE JOE	MS	04W	112
WILSON BILLY JOE	MS	03E	105
WILSON BILLY LEO	OK	48W	36
WILSON BILLY WAYNE	TX	37E	2
WILSON BOBBY	IN	41E	33
WILSON BOBBY JOE	IN	14E	19
WILSON BRIAN LYLE	OR	13W	83
WILSON BRYAN LEE	IA	39W	14
WILSON CALVIN RAY	MA	14E	51
WILSON CARL RICHARD JR	DC	28W	7
WILSON CHARLES E JR	MS	25W	91
WILSON CHARLES EDWIN	TX	31W	30
WILSON CHARLES JACKSON	MO	26W	23
WILSON CHESTER WAYNE	TN	38E	74
WILSON CLARENCE CORNELIUS	OH	05E	134
WILSON CLAUDE DAVID JR	CA	13E	46
WILSON DALE KEITH	AL	43E	63
WILSON DANIEL KEITH	MN	09W	81
WILSON DANIEL L	CA	09E	14
WILSON DARRELL WAYNE	WA	13E	57
WILSON DAVID	AR	57W	6
WILSON DAVID ALLEN	CA	34W	3

NAME	STATE	PANEL NO.	LINE NO.
WILSON DAVID HENRY II	CA	20W	99
WILSON DAVID LEWIS	CA	45W	11
WILSON DAVID OLSEN	MO	28W	65
WILSON DAVID RALPH	PA	36E	43
WILSON DAVID REYNOLDS	MI	47E	18
WILSON DAVID WALTER	NY	41W	17
WILSON DAVID WAYNE	VA	24W	35
WILSON DEAN CHARLES	CA	21W	11
WILSON DELVIN KEITH	MI	26W	51
WILSON DONALD CHARLES	IN	53W	41
WILSON DONALD MAURICE	IN	24E	79
WILSON DONALD WAYNE	IA	12W	11
WILSON EARL CLIFFORD	IN	47W	58
WILSON EARL LEE	MI	29W	58
WILSON EARNEST	OH	44E	63
WILSON EDMOND Q JR	KY	33W	37
WILSON EDWIN EUGENE	UT	15E	13
WILSON ELROY	NJ	27W	69
WILSON ERNEST HOWARD	KY	14E	13
WILSON EUGENE	MS	59W	18
WILSON FRANK LEONARD	CA	07W	124
WILSON FRANK WILLARD	OH	02E	1
WILSON FRED	AL	55W	3
WILSON GAIL FRANCIS	TX	25E	94
WILSON GALEN LLOYD	NE	15E	27
WILSON GAROLD THOMAS	OH	28E	63
WILSON GARY DUANE	CA	02W	80
WILSON GARY ROBERT	IL	26E	73
WILSON GEORGE A	GA	03E	97
WILSON GEORGE L	VA	48E	37
WILSON GERALD ANTHONY	NY	48W	4
WILSON GERALD LEE	GA	24W	73
WILSON GERALD W	AL	17E	118
WILSON GORDON SCOTT	IN	12E	110
WILSON HAROLD STANLEY	FL	15E	64
WILSON HAROLD THOMAS	NC	13E	112
WILSON HAROLD WENDELL	TN	06E	36
WILSON HARRY CONARD II	PA	30E	21
WILSON HARRY TRUMAN	TX	09W	11
WILSON HERBERT JR	NY	16E	15
WILSON IRVING MCKINLEY JR	MD	06E	105
WILSON ISAIAH HERMAN	OK	09E	27
WILSON JACK PYEATT JR	CA	37E	2
WILSON JAMES CLAIBORNE	MO	25W	58
WILSON JAMES CLAIR	OK	26E	54
WILSON JAMES DAVID	CA	38E	74
WILSON JAMES EDWARD	MD	08E	122
WILSON JAMES HAROLD	IL	28W	101
WILSON JAMES HENRY JR	NC	28E	101
WILSON JAMES MILTON	NC	13E	11
WILSON JAMES MURL	KY	26E	33
WILSON JAMES ROBERT	NC	12E	39
WILSON JAMES WILLIAM	LA	39E	42
WILSON JAMES WILLIE	CA	27W	84
WILSON JAN FRANKLIN	MD	43E	50
WILSON JEFFREY LYNN	IA	13W	90
WILSON JEROME I	FL	51E	4
WILSON JERRY BARBER	ID	13E	46
WILSON JERRY LEE	MO	48W	31
WILSON JOHN CHARLES	OK	11E	80
WILSON JOHN HENRY	PA	16W	25
WILSON JOHN JOSEPH	IA	06W	126
WILSON JOHN LANNING JR	OR	04W	128
WILSON JOHN LEE	KS	11W	129
WILSON JOHN RAY	OH	50W	4
WILSON JOHN ROBERT	FL	40W	31
WILSON JOHN STANTON	NM	31W	30
WILSON JOHN STEPHENSON	OH	09W	49
WILSON JOHN THOMAS	AZ	20E	38
WILSON JOHN WALTER JR	MN	04E	11
WILSON JOHN WESLEY	TN	03W	6
WILSON JOHN WILLIAM	AZ	19W	84
WILSON JOHN WILLIAM	TN	12W	90
WILSON JOHN WILLIAM JR	PA	29E	55
WILSON JONATHAN TRAXLER	VA	05W	25
WILSON JOSEPH	MD	07E	104
WILSON JOSEPH G III	VA	34W	3
WILSON JUAN JAY	NM	32W	35
WILSON KEITH LESLIE	IA	45W	17
WILSON KENNETH PETE	NC	28E	32
WILSON KENNETH RICHARD	CA	64E	2
WILSON KERRY FRANK	TX	33W	90

NAME	STATE	PANEL NO.	LINE NO.
WILSON LARRY EUGENE	MN	22E	5
WILSON LAVON STEPHEN	NM	01E	92
WILSON LAWRENCE HUMES JR	OR	09E	44
WILSON LAWRENCE W	SC	23E	34
WILSON LEON	GA	27W	43
WILSON LEVI JAMES	AL	04W	113
WILSON LEWIS BRACY	TN	43E	50
WILSON LLOYD CALVERIA	PA	05E	126
WILSON LORNE JOHN	MD	28W	77
WILSON LOUIS HENRY	MS	11W	11
WILSON MARION EARL	OH	37E	16
WILSON MARVIN JAMES	MN	05E	69
WILSON MICHAEL	IL	04E	134
WILSON MICHAEL	OH	32W	67
WILSON MICHAEL DONVIAN	OH	45W	35
WILSON MICHAEL JACK	WV	32W	3
WILSON MICHAEL JAY	WI	41W	63
WILSON MICHAEL JOSEPH	NE	19E	102
WILSON MICHAEL LANCE	OR	33E	77
WILSON MICHAEL LUND	KS	60W	7
WILSON MICHAEL RICHARD	MO	49W	49
WILSON MICHAEL ROY	MO	03W	89
WILSON MICKEY ALLEN	CA	01W	110
WILSON MICKEY LOUIS	TX	03W	31
WILSON MONTY NORRIS	MD	24E	64
WILSON NATHANIEL	NY	08E	78
WILSON NELSON EDDIE	OH	02E	72
WILSON NORMAN RAYMOND	WA	08E	50
WILSON PAUL	CA	29W	86
WILSON PAUL JOSIAH	IA	34W	30
WILSON PETER JOE	NY	06W	10
WILSON PHILLIP ALLEN	MI	06W	126
WILSON PHILLIP MARK	TX	11E	93
WILSON RAY GENE	OK	31W	31
WILSON RAYMOND WESLEY	FL	06E	40
WILSON REGINALD EUGENE	NY	23E	106
WILSON REXFORD EARLE	VA	09W	113
WILSON RICHARD EDWIN	MI	04E	42
WILSON RICHARD HERBERT	NC	12W	16
WILSON RICHARD JR	AR	03W	77
WILSON RICHARD LEE	OK	20W	110
WILSON RICHARD LEWIS	MS	02W	97
WILSON ROBERT ALLAN	MI	01W	46
WILSON ROBERT ALLYN	PA	56E	18
WILSON ROBERT BRUCE IV	NC	30E	36
WILSON ROBERT CHARLES	NY	34E	3
WILSON ROBERT EUGENE	TX	47E	18
WILSON ROBERT GRANT	NY	12E	35
WILSON ROBERT HENERSON JR	MO	06W	70
WILSON ROBERT LAURENCE	AZ	24E	64
WILSON ROBERT LEE	IL	13W	40
WILSON ROBERT LEE JR	VA	37E	75
WILSON ROBERT THOMAS	AL	06W	4
WILSON RODNEY DAVID	KS	21W	58
WILSON RODNEY JOSEPH	TX	10E	67
WILSON RODNEY WAYNE	DE	10W	101
WILSON ROGER EUGENE	VA	01W	41
WILSON ROGER GLENN	OK	39E	56
WILSON ROGER LEE	IL	35E	1
WILSON RONALD ALTON	CA	57W	15
WILSON RONALD EUGENE	OH	47E	37
WILSON RONALD KELLEY	CA	26W	75
WILSON RONALD LEE	IL	26E	73
WILSON ROY HASKEL	TN	40W	22
WILSON ROY LEE	OH	10W	20
WILSON ROYCE HAROLD JR	CA	36E	62
WILSON RUDOLPH	GA	30W	92
WILSON STEVEN WAYNE	VA	18W	52
WILSON SYLVESTER	NC	29W	41
WILSON SYLVESTER WILLIAM	NJ	30E	75
WILSON THOMAS EDWARD	MI	12W	78
WILSON THOMAS LESLIE	OH	52W	2
WILSON TOMMY ROBERT	TN	03E	120
WILSON VIRGIL HENRY JR	MD	41W	50
WILSON VOMER OVID JR	LA	19E	68
WILSON WALTER GENE	WA	46E	60
WILSON WALTER LEE JR	NC	13W	52
WILSON WAYNE MICHAEL	OK	23W	24
WILSON WAYNE VASTER	NC	22E	118
WILSON WENDELL LEWIS	KY	11E	125
WILSON WILLARD EUGENE	MI	18W	99
WILSON WILLIAM BERNARD	NY	31W	75
WILSON WILLIAM BRUCE	CO	10E	75
WILSON WILLIAM D	MO	31E	19
WILSON WILLIAM DEAN	OK	67W	8
WILSON WILLIAM EARL	OH	27E	33
WILSON WILLIAM EARL	SC	58W	21
WILSON WILLIAM HENRY JR	MI	58W	16
WILSON WILLIAM JEFFREY	CA	08E	5
WILSON WILLIAM LARRY	OR	64E	2
WILSON WILLIAM MICHEAL	WY	21W	25
WILSON WILLIAM NEIL	AZ	02E	63
WILSON WILLIAM RALPH	MO	23W	115
WILSON WILLIAM REED JR	MS	20W	82
WILSON WILLIAM ROBERT	AR	28W	41
WILSON WILLIAM WAYNE	WV	49E	49
WILSON WILLIE GENE	AL	49E	7
WILSON WILMER DWAYNE	TX	50E	24
WILSON WOODROW	NC	45E	35
WILT JOHN WILLIAM JR	TX	06E	52
WILT RICHARD JAMES	OH	41E	46
WILTON STANLEY FRANK	CA	39W	76
WILTSE JAMES B JR	CA	24E	93
WILTSE RONALD ELLIS	CA	60E	6
WILTSIE JOSEPH CARL	NY	23W	33
WIMBERLY ARNOLD BRUCE	MI	43W	11
WIMBERLY BENNY EARL	TX	11E	28
WIMBROW NUTTER JEROME III	MD	01W	105
WIMER FLOYD DANIEL	CA	14W	73
WIMER ROBERT ARNOLD	CA	23W	116
WIMMER JAMES ALLEN	WA	09W	100
WIMMER ROY DEAN	VA	30W	83
WIMMER SCOTT THOMAS	WI	41W	63
WIMMER WILLARD ALVON	MD	30W	35
WIMMERGREN EDMOND DALE	MN	20W	110
WIMP ROBERT G	CO	32W	63
WINBORNE JOHN HUTCHINGS	NC	07W	109
WINCH GERALD JAMES	OH	44E	63
WINCHELL CHESTER A JR	WV	29E	79
WINCHELL DOUGLAS JAMES JR	NE	32W	86
WINCHESTER JIMMY DALE	KY	40E	35
WINCHESTER LARRY ALDEN	AL	52E	26
WINCKLER DONALD LEWIS	MI	19E	42
WINDBIGLER RICHARD EDWARD	IN	43E	2
WINDELER CHARLES CARL JR	GA	02W	130
WINDER DAVID FRANCIS	OH	10W	37
WINDER WALTER RIDGEWAY JR	DC	51E	34
WINDFELDER JOHN EDWARD	PA	02W	80
WINDHAM JAMES EUGENE JR	NY	11E	54
WINDHAM MELVIN GEORGE	TX	58E	3
WINDLE PAUL RALPH	KS	02E	26
WINDSHEIMER RICHARD LEE	PA	20W	79
WINDSOR DAVID WARREN JR	GA	03W	16
WINE HARRISON JR	SC	29W	17
WINER ROY LEE	OK	37E	29
WINES THOMAS LOWELL	WV	55W	25
WINFIELD GEORGE EDWARD	TX	49E	50
WINFIELD LUCIUS	MS	26E	54
WINFREY AUTHRAN WAYNE	OR	24W	24
WINFREY DOUGLAS NELSON	GA	11W	98
WINFREY JAMES ARTHUR	MO	20W	111
WINFREY JOHNNIE PAUL	TX	02E	90
WINFREY RAYMOND MICHAEL	CA	27W	47
WING ROBERT CHARLES	OH	27E	104
WINGATE RICHARD EDWARD	NC	02E	92
WINGENBACH GLENN S JR	OH	30W	61
WINGENFELD ROBERT JOHN	NY	09W	121
WINGER JON RICHARD	IA	55W	3
WINGERT DOUGLAS GENE	WA	27E	104
WINGERT JAMES ALBERT	PA	19W	100
WINGET HAROLD WILLIAM	OK	15E	27
WINGET KENNETH WAYNE	CO	42E	46
WINGFIELD ALBERT GREEN JR	MD	36W	66
WININGHAM JERRY LYNN	TX	41E	33
WINK MELVIN RALPH	PA	10W	133
WINKEL WILLIAM DANIEL	MO	33W	30
WINKELVOSS THOMAS JOHN	PA	07E	111
WINKEMPLECK GEORGE HAROLD	CA	27E	87
WINKLE DAVID RYAN	UT	03W	37
WINKLER BOBBY JOE	MO	33E	25
WINKLER DAVID DE SALES	MD	17W	123
WINKLER GARY JOHN	NY	22W	10
WINKLER JOHN ANTHONY	VA	03E	109
WINKLES GEORGE WILLIAM JR	WA	03W	32
WINKLES HARVIE PERRY III	NM	37W	72
WINKLES JAMES WILLIAM	GA	54W	21
WINLAND PRESTON PAUL JR	IN	08W	30
WINN DONALD DEAN	KS	05W	20
WINNER BRIAN CARL	MI	58W	1
WINNINGHAM CLIFTON	KS	05E	126
WINNINGHAM JOHN QUITMAN	CA	01W	101
WINNINGHAM RICHARD DANIEL	MI	35W	49
WINOWITCH THEODORE ALAN	PA	01E	79
WINSLOW JERRY G	CO	06E	17
WINSLOW JOHN KEMPE	NY	20W	79
WINSLOW LARRY A	MI	31E	61
WINSLOW WILLIAM DAVID	FL	50E	27
WINSON JAMES JOSEPH	IL	03W	135
WINSTON ALVESTER LEE	MD	31E	39
WINSTON CHARLES C III	NY	24E	64
WINSTON ERNEST GREGORY	FL	59W	15
WINSTON JAMES CLENNON	AL	14E	121
WINSTON THURMAN WILLIAM	MD	50W	11
WINSTON WILLIAM CURTIS	AL	39W	52
WINSTON WILLIAM OVERTON	GA	24E	65
WINTER CARL J	MI	38W	48
WINTER EDWIN THOMAS	PA	09W	42
WINTER GARY GLEN	OH	08W	87
WINTER GARY JAMES	OR	08W	102
WINTER JOHN WESLEY	AL	36E	62
WINTER PETER LOUIS	TX	04W	100
WINTER ROY ALAN	MO	58W	30
WINTERHALTER HUGH FRANCIS	NY	13E	101
WINTERMOYER TERRY	MD	03E	109
WINTERS ALLEN LANE	MI	36E	43
WINTERS CHRISTOPHER MICHA	NJ	03W	36
WINTERS DANIEL EARL	TX	41W	33
WINTERS DARRYL GORDON	CA	09E	44
WINTERS DAVID MARSHALL	CA	18E	66
WINTERS GENE TALBERT	IN	12E	31
WINTERS JEROME CORDELL	FL	09E	77
WINTERS JOHN	NJ	24W	109
WINTERS JOHN EDWARD	KS	06W	30
WINTERS JOHN LANE	TX	22E	22
WINTERS MICHAEL JOHN	NY	26W	29
WINTERS ROBERT J	NY	29E	64
WINTERS RONALD PAUL	MO	25E	4
WINTERS STEVEN ANDREW	OK	45W	64
WINTERS TERRY LEROY	OH	24E	53
WINTERS TINEY W	TX	41E	5
WINTERS WALTER RAY	FL	07W	110
WINTERS WILLIAM FREDRICK	PA	07E	92
WINTERS WILLIAM JOHN	NY	24W	14
WINTERTON LARRY DEAN	SD	51W	1
WIRE EUGENE CHARLES	HI	41E	6
WIRICK WILLIAM CHARLES	OH	37W	72
WIRKS ROBERT BLANE	OH	07W	90
WIRT DENNIS ARTHUR	MI	41W	2
WIRT DENNIS HAROLD	MI	51W	22
WIRT LARRY FRANCIS	VA	06E	130
WIRTH GORDON LEE JR	OR	05W	36
WIRTH JOSEPH WILLIAM	MA	13W	76
WISCH ROBERT JAMES	WI	27E	87
WISCHEMANN DAVID EDWARDS	HI	01W	88
WISDOM JESSE ALLAN	TX	14W	110
WISDOM KERRY DEAN	KY	24E	49
WISDOM SELWIN DEROY	OR	04E	78
WISE DONALD A	WA	13E	17
WISE EDWARD JOSEPH	MD	24E	11
WISE ELWIN CLAUDE	WA	06E	53
WISE GORDON SCOTT	MN	08W	110
WISE JAMES CARL JR	GA	04E	35
WISE JAMES DAVID	PA	26E	80
WISE JAMES EDWARD	TN	31W	62
WISE JAMES JOSEPH	MI	23W	34
WISE JAMES LEROY JR	PA	37E	74
WISE JOSEPH ROBERT	AZ	36E	43
WISE RICHARD MARVIN	AL	19W	42
WISE ROBERT EVANS	WA	16E	26
WISE RODNEY DALE	OH	33W	75
WISE SCOTT EDWARD	IL	19W	57
WISE WILBUR MEARL	OH	04E	102
WISELY DANIEL LEE	IA	33E	62
WISEMAN BAIN WENDELL JR	NM	05W	4
WISEMAN JOHN SAMUEL	MO	51E	43
WISEMAN LANE WAYNE	OR	13W	129

NAME	STATE	PANEL NO.	LINE NO.
WISEMAN MALCOLM RICHARD	TN	26E	97
WISEMAN RICHARD LEE	IN	12W	19
WISHAM CHARLES RICHARD	NC	20E	109
WISHAM GEORGE MERRITT JR	CA	33E	44
WISHER HERBERT JAMES	NY	41W	56
WISHON DONALD RAY	MI	13W	95
WISKOW INGO JULIUS ROBERT	OH	47E	45
WISKUR JAMES CLYDE	IL	07E	13
WISNIER GARY	NY	53E	9
WISNIEWSKI CHARLES J JR	CT	08E	13
WISNIEWSKI DAVID	MD	12E	126
WISNIEWSKI DENNIS EUGENE	IL	30W	9
WISNIOWICZ THOMAS LEO	IL	20W	17
WISSELL LAWRENCE JAMES	IL	36W	60
WISSIG EDWARD SIMON	NY	05W	100
WISSINK STEVEN LEE	IA	32W	30
WISSLER RICHARD LAVERN JR	PA	17W	32
WISSMAN RONALD EDWARD	MA	20E	80
WISTRAND ROBERT CARL	NY	01E	112
WISWELL SAMMY RAY	KS	12E	93
WITANEK CHESTER LAWREN JR	MA	50W	11
WITCHER ALBERT	VA	03E	64
WITCHER LEONARD III	IL	10E	99
WITCHER SAMUEL EARNEST	VA	23E	8
WITCHET FRED DOUGLAS	TX	03E	98
WITEK EDWARD JOSEPH	IL	14W	45
WITEK WILLIAM FRANK	IL	36E	63
WITHAM JAMES GEORGE	VT	24W	27
WITHAM KENNETH LEROY	FL	28W	65
WITHEE CLYDE WILLIAM	ME	05E	77
WITHEE EDWARD WILLIAM	ME	07W	116
WITHEE JAMES MONTGOMERY	IN	21W	64
WITHERELL GARY LEE	CA	64E	2
WITHERS GARY WAYNE	IL	18W	9
WITHERS STEVEN RICHARD	MO	16E	83
WITHERSPOON CHARLES E	MD	05W	85
WITHERSPOON JAMES MARTIN	IL	50W	33
WITHERSPOON JOE	IN	15W	31
WITHERSPOON JOHNELL	FL	06W	38
WITHERSPOON LEON DUGAN	VA	08W	37
WITHERSPOON MARION	SC	34W	12
WITHERSPOON THOMAS JR	NY	27E	78
WITHEY HOWARD HUGH	AR	21E	64
WITHROW MICHAEL DENNIS	TX	21E	8
WITHROW PAUL RICHARD	WV	03W	103
WITKO DANIEL ANDREW	PA	56W	30
WITKOP MICHAEL ERWIN	NY	40W	35
WITKOWSKI DENNIS EDWARD	PA	43W	32
WITMER KENNETH EUGENE	PA	25W	114
WITMER NOEL BRUCE	CA	03W	31
WITMER OMAR DAVID JR	PA	26E	86
WITT CHARLES DON	TX	20E	99
WITT DANNY KEITH	MS	13W	47
WITT EARNEST LYNN	TN	63W	1
WITT JAMES	NJ	45E	16
WITT JAMES PATRICK	OH	32W	35
WITT JERRY PAUL	IL	12E	9
WITT KENNETH LEE	MN	30E	6
WITT MARK STEVEN	NE	18W	18
WITT MICHAEL ROBERT	OH	48W	51
WITT MORRIS BOWDOIN	TX	18E	25
WITTBRACHT MARK CHARLES	MI	06W	114
WITTE ROGER EARL	IL	03W	81
WITTEVRONGEL MICHAEL CAMI	IL	60E	6
WITTKOP JOE ALLEN	MN	48E	22
WITTLER LARRY ELDON	CA	36E	63
WITTMAN GORDON RICHARD	NY	04E	59
WITTMAN NARVIN OTTO JR	CA	24E	89
WITTMAN ROBERT KEITH	FL	21W	21
WITTMAN WILLIAM	NY	44W	42
WITTS JOHN JOSEPH JR	PA	26W	37
WITTY ROBERT WILLIAM	OH	22W	71
WITYCYAK GLEN ROBERT	PA	11W	93
WITZEL ROBERT CHARLES	NY	51W	47
WITZIG RAYMOND GEORGE	IL	56E	18
WITZKOSKI BILLY JOE	TX	17E	26
WIXSON RALPH MICHAEL	WI	20E	12
WOBBE DENNIS MICHAEL	IL	52W	24
WOBLE JOHN B	CT	17E	90
WODARCZYK MATT JOHN	PA	04W	113
WOEHLCKE BERNARD RICHARD	PA	37W	57
WOEHNKER HARRISON E JR	MN	51W	9
WOEHRL MICHAEL JOHN	IL	25W	11
WOFFORD WILLIAM PHILLIP	MI	26W	37
WOGAN WILLIAM MICHAEL	NY	32W	47
WOHLFORD LLOYD CYRUS JR	IA	22E	5
WOHLGAMUTH BILLY ROBERT	OH	28E	77
WOHLMAN STANLEY ROCKY	NY	49W	45
WOHLRAB BRUCE	NJ	04W	34
WOHRER JAMES FIELDING	IL	20W	53
WOJAHN ARTHUR EDWARD	WI	18W	45
WOJCICKY JOHN LEO	MD	60E	6
WOJCIK LAWRENCE ADAM	IL	28E	6
WOJTKIEWICZ JEREMY ROBERT	WI	34W	30
WOJTKIEWICZ RONALD JOSEPH	NE	49E	18
WOJTYNA ROBERT ANTHONY	PA	27W	28
WOLCHESKI RICHARD JOHN	CT	05E	89
WOLD BRUCE LLOYD	ND	11W	33
WOLF DEWITT JOSEPH	GA	34E	40
WOLF DURWYN LEE	IL	10W	129
WOLF JACK MORSE	NE	46E	59
WOLF JOHN ROBY	WA	30E	52
WOLF KENT CARTER	IA	08W	81
WOLF MICHAEL FERDINAND	ND	26E	54
WOLF PAUL DEIHL	PA	58E	3
WOLF ROBERT CLARENCE	WI	33E	78
WOLF ROY EDWIN	OH	34E	50
WOLF WILLIAM BISHOP	OH	02E	124
WOLFE ABRA JOSEPH JR	LA	47E	19
WOLFE ALFRED MELVIN	WV	53E	26
WOLFE BRIAN EDWARD	CA	20W	126
WOLFE DANIEL EDWARD	OH	51E	35
WOLFE DAVID NORMAN	WV	14E	72
WOLFE DONALD FINDLING	MT	27E	78
WOLFE FRANK JESSE	PA	41E	9
WOLFE HIRAM MICHAEL IV	VA	15W	26
WOLFE HULSA D	OK	19E	114
WOLFE JACK LEE	FL	09W	100
WOLFE JIMMY RAY	TN	06E	112
WOLFE JOEL DAVID	IL	38W	81
WOLFE JOHN THOMAS	NJ	61W	4
WOLFE JOSEPH GEORGE	OR	55E	36
WOLFE JOSEPH KENT	CA	43W	50
WOLFE KENNETH WAYNE	CA	07E	2
WOLFE MATHEW	NE	36E	63
WOLFE MELVIN EDWARD	OH	01W	84
WOLFE PATRICK ROBERT JR	MI	34E	83
WOLFE PAUL EDWARD	NM	06W	103
WOLFE RICHARD EDWARD	IN	33E	62
WOLFE RICHARD LAWRENCE	MI	19E	9
WOLFE RICHARD OGDEN	KS	15W	11
WOLFE RONALD GALE	WA	11E	93
WOLFE THOMAS HUBERT	MO	08E	106
WOLFE THURMAN WILLIAM	LA	11W	11
WOLFE WILLIAM EDWARD	CA	03W	49
WOLFE WILLIAM EDWARD JR	AR	45W	11
WOLFENDALE EDWARD JAMES	MA	31W	42
WOLFENDEN HARRY	NY	05W	85
WOLFF RICHARD GLEN	NJ	42W	9
WOLFF WARREN KENNETH	IA	02W	69
WOLFINGTON RICHARD JR	IN	16E	103
WOLFKEIL WAYNE BENJAMIN	PA	49W	37
WOLFORD BILLARA	OH	55E	36
WOLFORD CRAIG BENTON	IA	01E	19
WOLFORD MARSHALL DAVID	OH	49W	28
WOLFRIES LOWELL ASTLEY	NY	14E	41
WOLFRUM LARRY VIRGIL	OH	24W	14
WOLK BARRY LEE	MA	37E	14
WOLOS PAUL HARVEY	ND	18E	112
WOLOSONOWICH LARRY JAMES	MI	39W	42
WOLOSZYK DONALD JOSEPH	MI	05E	94
WOLPE JACK	NY	24E	75
WOLPERT LARRY MICHAEL	MI	48E	37
WOLTER ARTHUR GEORGE WILL	LA	36E	63
WOLTER JAMES LESTER	MN	35W	52
WOLTER RONALD ALAN	OK	40W	70
WOLTER STEVEN ROSS	HI	47E	28
WOLTERMAN GERARD THEODORE	UT	58W	30
WOLTERS EUGENE EBEN	ID	07W	25
WOLTERS THEODORE ANTHONY	IL	07W	20
WOMACK ROBERT LEE	LA	02E	119
WOMACK ROY ARNOLD	AR	28W	95
WOMBLE DAVID LEE	NC	09W	26
WOMBLE WILLIAM THOMAS JR	VA	19E	34
WONDERLICH MICHAEL KAYE	IL	43W	44
WONER JOHN PERRY	IL	13W	102
WONG EDWARD PUCK KOW JR	CA	02W	120
WONN JAMES CHARLES	PA	39E	77
WONNACOTT WALTER L	CA	13E	94
WOOD AARON LEE	WI	62E	14
WOOD ALVY EUGENE	MT	59E	15
WOOD ARTHUR MURRY	TN	08E	102
WOOD ARTHUR WINDELL	MO	37W	72
WOOD BARRY RUSSELL	VT	12E	11
WOOD BERTRAM JR	MD	07W	88
WOOD BOBBY CLYDE	LA	60E	6
WOOD CALVIN KNIGHT JR	TX	66E	4
WOOD CARL MITCHELL	CO	05W	80
WOOD CHARLES	GA	38E	74
WOOD DANIEL LEWIS	VA	14W	35
WOOD DARRELL GEORGE JR	OR	13W	34
WOOD DAVID BEAVERS	GA	03W	14
WOOD DAVID MITCHELL	AL	22E	22
WOOD DELBERT ROY	AZ	01W	89
WOOD DENNIS MELVIN	WI	36W	9
WOOD DENNIS PAUL	OH	32E	49
WOOD DON CHARLES	UT	04E	76
WOOD DONALD	OH	03W	78
WOOD DONALD CHARLES	PA	64E	10
WOOD DONALD FRANK	MI	47E	38
WOOD DONALD FRED	IA	19W	76
WOOD DONALD ROY	GA	27E	24
WOOD EDWARD CHARLES	NY	07E	63
WOOD FREDERICK DERL	MO	24E	85
WOOD HAROLD SHELBY JR	KY	45E	36
WOOD JAMES ALBERT	MS	06E	49
WOOD JAMES ANTHONY	MI	41E	33
WOOD JAMES C	VA	49E	27
WOOD JAMES EDWIN	SC	21E	40
WOOD JAMES LEONARD	IL	09W	55
WOOD JAMES LEWIS	MO	39E	56
WOOD JAMES SCHENLER	MO	59W	18
WOOD JAMES WATSON	IL	08W	121
WOOD JAMES WILBURN	TX	44E	13
WOOD JOE IRVIN	OR	38W	81
WOOD JOHN ALLEN	MI	42W	34
WOOD JOHN CLIFFORD	CO	21W	64
WOOD JOHNNY MACK	TX	17E	94
WOOD LARRY DAVID	AL	13W	39
WOOD LARRY LESTER	GA	15W	75
WOOD LARRY T	TN	13E	82
WOOD LAWRENCE JEFFREY	MI	26E	81
WOOD LEROY	TX	52W	25
WOOD LESTER LEE	TX	44W	44
WOOD LEWIS EDWARD	AL	18W	66
WOOD LLOYD JOSEPH SR	KS	26W	88
WOOD LOREN EDWIN JR	MO	27W	69
WOOD MELVIN	NY	64E	10
WOOD PATRICK HARDY	MO	15E	1
WOOD PATRICK LEE	CA	14E	11
WOOD PETER LORENZ	CA	35E	1
WOOD RAYMOND CHARLES	NY	24W	35
WOOD REX STEWART	IA	21E	40
WOOD RICHARD ALAN	NJ	14E	121
WOOD RICHARD DALE	IN	60E	7
WOOD RICHARD STEVEN	UT	16E	66
WOOD ROBERT ABBOTT	GA	12W	2
WOOD ROBERT DELUN	IL	57W	21
WOOD ROBERT HAROLD	MN	20W	4
WOOD ROBERT HELM	GA	49E	7
WOOD ROBERT TINSLEY	TX	10W	37
WOOD ROBERT VICTOR	NY	14E	25
WOOD ROBERT WAYNE	GA	23E	106
WOOD RODNEY GLEN	MI	09W	62
WOOD RONALD WILLIAM	TX	37E	30
WOOD ROSS W JR	OK	25E	73
WOOD STEPHEN DUANE	MO	41W	28
WOOD STRATHER FRANKLIN	OR	05W	119
WOOD STUART JOHN	WA	51W	23
WOOD THOMAS DANIEL JR	GA	01W	29
WOOD THOMAS EUGENE	WA	01W	22
WOOD TODD LOUIS	CA	35W	62
WOOD WALTER SUTTON	NC	07E	19
WOOD WILLIAM COMMODORE JR	TN	01W	70
WOOD WILLIAM ESLEY JR	SC	03W	2
WOOD WILLIAM LEE	OH	14W	70

NAME	STATE	PANEL NO.	LINE NO.
WOOD WILLIAM MILTON JR	CA	05E	36
WOOD WILLIAM WAYNE	OH	13W	39
WOOD WILLIS LEROY	GA	26E	69
WOODALL CHARLES MINOR JR	AL	34W	81
WOODALL GEORGE WALLY	CA	05E	78
WOODALL JERRY	OH	13E	124
WOODALL JERRY RUSS	FL	36E	43
WOODALL JOHN BRAXTON	IL	19E	2
WOODALL RALPH TRAYLOR JR	GA	16E	108
WOODARD HARRY DONALD	AL	06E	95
WOODARD JACKIE LAVANDA	TN	21W	97
WOODARD JOHN DOUGLAS	NC	48E	13
WOODARD JOHNIE KENNETH	TN	03W	12
WOODARD JON ROBERT	IL	53W	25
WOODARD JOSEPH	FL	25W	15
WOODARD JOSEPH WILBERT JR	TN	25W	91
WOODARD MICHAEL DAVID	TN	04W	63
WOODARD PAUL LEROY	NJ	44E	63
WOODARD ROBERT BRAXTON	NC	27W	84
WOODARD STEPHEN LEE	IA	61E	21
WOODARD WAYNE HOWARD	PA	19E	2
WOODBURN LARRY ALBERT	MD	05W	80
WOODCOCK MICHAEL KEITH	TX	06W	118
WOODCOCK STEVEN JON	CA	21W	35
WOODEN CHARLIE K	GA	49E	28
WOODEN DAVID WAYNE	MO	30E	100
WOODEN JOE PETE JR	OH	20E	52
WOODEN VICTOR ROBERT	OR	28E	99
WOODFIN DONALD PIERCE	VA	12W	102
WOODFORD WESLEY LEE	OH	40E	71
WOODHOUSE ROBERT F JR	NY	09W	129
WOODLAND DOUGLAS MEAD	AZ	07W	95
WOODLAND THOMAS S JR	MD	47E	45
WOODLAND WAYNE KARL	PA	14W	116
WOODMAN STUART ALAN	ME	10W	129
WOODMANSEE RONNY LOUIS	TX	01E	37
WOODROFFE TERRY SCOTT	OR	09W	22
WOODROW ROBERT A	NJ	23E	8
WOODRUFF ALTON DARNELL	GA	26W	58
WOODRUFF DAVID GLENN	KY	26E	1
WOODRUFF DONALD COLES	FL	09E	50
WOODRUFF EDWARD WARREN	CA	12E	94
WOODRUFF JAMES AMMONS	MS	23W	41
WOODRUFF WAYNE THOMAS	OH	15E	72
WOODRUM JOHN JAMES	TX	03W	28
WOODS ABRAHAM	AL	27E	8
WOODS ADVERT JR	SC	19W	27
WOODS ALBERT CLARENCE JR	MT	40E	49
WOODS ALONZO DALE	CA	19E	19
WOODS ALVIN RICHARD JR	IN	04E	47
WOODS ARTHUR LEE	CA	25W	3
WOODS CARL JULIUS	ND	02E	97
WOODS CHARLES GORDON	CA	08E	50
WOODS CHARLES M	OH	06E	69
WOODS CLAYTON LEON	IA	05W	122
WOODS CORDELL EMANUEL	IL	39E	68
WOODS CURTIS STEVEN	WI	27W	69
WOODS DAVID ALEXANDER	MO	29E	8
WOODS DAVID EDWARD	NC	45W	39
WOODS DAVID WALTER	OH	02W	62
WOODS DUREL STEVENS	LA	20W	24
WOODS EARL	IL	58E	28
WOODS EDWARD JOHN	NY	46W	25
WOODS FLOYD WILLIAM	OK	03W	85
WOODS GARY DORVIN	IL	55W	3
WOODS GERALD	PA	36W	83
WOODS GERALD ERNEST	OR	05W	119
WOODS GREGORY	MO	47W	58
WOODS GREGORY WAYNE	PA	19E	47
WOODS JAMES ARLIE	AL	53W	25
WOODS JAMES BAKER III	NC	05E	8
WOODS JAMES BERNARD JR	NJ	17W	6
WOODS JAMES CLARK	CA	17W	92
WOODS JAMES ROBERT	OR	19W	6
WOODS JAMES THOMAS	NC	22W	95
WOODS JERRY OTIS	AL	44E	3
WOODS JOHN KEVIN	IL	39E	1
WOODS JOHN WILLIE JR	TN	11E	130
WOODS LARRY JAMES	CA	02W	120
WOODS LAWRENCE	TN	01E	68
WOODS LAWRENCE DANE	CT	08E	90
WOODS MATTHEW	IN	50W	46
WOODS PATRICK LEONARD	OR	36W	75
WOODS RANDLE TOM	TN	03E	28
WOODS RAY HOUSTON	GA	42E	59
WOODS ROBERT EARL	MI	02W	10
WOODS ROBERT EDWIN	FL	32E	66
WOODS ROBERT FRANCIS	UT	54W	4
WOODS ROBERT M	PA	56W	31
WOODS ROBERT WALTER	NJ	48W	10
WOODS RONALD LEE	KY	10E	3
WOODS SAMUEL LEE	MS	04E	29
WOODS STEPHEN FORREST	IL	43E	39
WOODS STERLING SADLER	VA	19E	89
WOODS THEODORE R JR	WI	17E	16
WOODS WILLARD PAUL	GA	26E	110
WOODS WILLIAM STEPHEN	SC	04W	5
WOODSIDE MICHAEL LEE	CA	30W	59
WOODSMALL MAX MARVIN	IN	12E	108
WOODSON ARNOLD	NJ	06E	88
WOODSON BILLY BARNELL	TN	13E	7
WOODSON EUGENE MERRILL	TN	49W	32
WOODSON GEORGE WILSON JR	PA	06E	130
WOODSON JAMES LIONEL JR	MO	26E	95
WOODSON JOHNNY	CA	08E	117
WOODSON LAURENCE OLIVER	MA	44W	21
WOODSON RAYMOND DALE	OH	07W	86
WOODSON RICHARD EUGENE	IL	24E	65
WOODWARD DOUGLAS MORRIS	VA	13W	67
WOODWARD JAMES	OH	36W	9
WOODWARD RICHARD HENRY	TX	45E	52
WOODWARD RICHARD RANDOLPH	VA	05E	19
WOODWARD STANLEY KAMAKI	HI	37E	47
WOODWORTH CLARK NEWELL JR	MI	05E	92
WOODWORTH JAMES LEROY	IN	33W	35
WOODWORTH MARC ALAN	NY	32W	35
WOODWORTH SAMUEL ALEXANDE	OK	01E	103
WOODY JOHN HENRY	GA	03E	98
WOODY THURMAN JR	VA	02W	117
WOODY VERNON WAYNE	TX	14W	82
WOODY WILLARD EVERETT	KS	05W	36
WOOLARD JAMES HARRY	OH	16W	25
WOOLBRIGHT DONALD EUGENE	MS	09E	21
WOOLBRIGHT JOHN WAYNE	IL	45W	59
WOOLCOTT RANDALL ALAN	WI	39E	15
WOOLDRIDGE LAWRENCE O	VA	20W	105
WOOLDRIDGE PAUL M JR	IL	20E	127
WOOLEY DONALD	AL	34E	3
WOOLEY HENRY EUGENE	AR	57W	15
WOOLF ALTON KENNETH JR	TX	51W	28
WOOLF DWIGHT D	MO	24E	77
WOOLFOLK JIMMY LEE	TX	32E	28
WOOLFORD PAUL BURNELL	IL	16W	55
WOOLHEATER JOHN STEVEN	PA	14E	89
WOOLIVER CHARLES WILLIAM	TN	07E	24
WOOLLARD RUSSELL DAN	TX	32W	17
WOOLLEY JAMES NED	TX	16W	7
WOOLLEY KIRK ALLEN	KY	32W	18
WOOLLEY MACK LEE JR	CA	27E	23
WOOLRIDGE LARRY ROGER	WI	39W	72
WOOLRIDGE THOMAS ALPHONSE	AZ	51W	1
WOOLRIDGE THORNTON LEWIS	WV	04W	59
WOOLSEY HILTON EDWARD	AL	40W	47
WOOLSEY JACK LEE	OK	58W	16
WOOLSEY WILLIAM JAY	CA	27W	35
WOOLUM LARRY LEE	OH	31W	62
WOOLUMS EVERETT EARL JR	OH	16W	120
WOOSLEY PERRY LEE	KY	11W	12
WOOSTER ROGER EDSON	MI	25W	92
WOOTEN BOBBIE GENE	MO	22W	50
WOOTEN DAVID DARYL	FL	07W	91
WOOTEN JOHN WESLEY	WV	30E	52
WOOTEN PHILIP MILTON	TX	59E	16
WOOTON GARY LEE	WV	15E	66
WOOTTEN CARL DEE	CA	11W	82
WOPINSKI BARRY MILTON	IL	41E	34
WORCESTER JOHN BOWERS	MI	02E	126
WORD WILLIAM KENEITH	CA	23W	13
WORDEN ROBERT LEE	PA	24W	24
WORK GEORGE ALLEN	IL	21W	114
WORKMAN DAVID FRANK	PA	40W	60
WORKMAN DONALD RENAY	MO	08W	39
WORKMAN GLENN ROGER	WV	21W	58
WORKMAN JAMES ARNOLD	IN	20E	38
WORKMAN JAMES EDWARD	WV	24W	91
WORKMAN JAMES HERBERT	PA	21W	40
WORKMAN JOSEPH MYRON	IL	03E	99
WORKMAN LANCE DAVIS	TN	03W	106
WORKMAN LARRY E	IN	46E	26
WORKMAN LIONEL	KY	20W	110
WORKMAN TIMOTHY E	WA	14E	51
WORKS JONATHAN P	CT	04E	105
WORL LESLIE WAYNE	CA	28W	65
WORLDS JAMES ALLEN	FL	40W	40
WORLEY DON F	AR	44E	23
WORLEY GARRY LEE	TN	11W	43
WORLEY JAMES RONALD	TN	53E	26
WORLEY KENNETH LEE	CA	48W	1
WORLEY MICHAEL GREGG	NC	22W	29
WORLEY ROBERT FRANKLIN	CA	51W	47
WORLEY ROBERT KEITH	VA	05E	30
WORLEY ROBERT LEE	NV	56E	19
WORLEY ROM	NC	18E	104
WORLEY STEPHEN MICHAEL	WV	44E	13
WORLEY STEPHEN RAY	LA	28E	6
WORLEY THOMAS JAMES JR	MI	51E	27
WORLEY WILLIAM PAUL	PA	44E	43
WORMAN CHESTER EUGENE JR	PA	04E	29
WORMAN KENNETH GLEN	PA	20E	88
WORMDAHL RICHARD GENE	IL	13E	70
WORREL THOMAS DUANE	IN	11W	42
WORRELL DAVID ALLEN	MO	22W	48
WORRELL GARY PAUL	CA	14E	60
WORRELL HURSTON EDWARD	AL	37W	7
WORRELL JAMES R	FL	30E	75
WORRELL MILTON JERRY	GA	34W	19
WORRELL PAUL LAURANCE	PA	13E	7
WORRELL ROBERT EARL	VA	21W	114
WORRELL ROBERT LEE	CO	52E	26
WORSHINSKI ROBERT MATTHEW	NJ	47W	36
WORST KARL EDWARD	AR	05E	96
WORTH JAMES FREDERICK	MD	02W	127
WORTH RICHARD A	TX	25E	112
WORTH ROBERT EARL	TX	06W	133
WORTH ROY EDWARD	IN	38E	19
WORTH TIMOTHY LANE	TN	36E	44
WORTHAM MURRAY LAMAR	TX	33E	6
WORTHEN LARRY EUGENE	GA	21E	72
WORTHEN ROBERT KENT	UT	16W	108
WORTHEY DAVID ALLEN	IL	60E	7
WORTHEY DONNIE LEON	IL	36W	47
WORTHEY ED	OH	38E	63
WORTHEY OWEN WAYNE	MS	07E	38
WORTHINGTON EDWARD LLEWEL	TX	40E	71
WORTHINGTON JAMES AUTHOR	DC	26W	37
WORTHINGTON LAURENCE D	CA	35W	74
WORTHINGTON RICHARD C JR	WA	09W	125
WORTHINGTON ROBERT LEE	PA	36W	60
WORTHINGTON ROBERT LEROY	CA	27W	69
WORTHINGTON ROBERT WARD	NJ	11W	108
WORTHLEY KENNETH WAYNE	MN	19W	123
WORTHY JERRY DEAN	SC	14E	105
WORTMAN DOUGLAS FREDERICK	MI	11W	33
WORTMANN FREDERICK EDWARD	TX	11W	71
WOSICK DENNIS STANLEY	ND	22W	10
WOYNARSKI RICHARD MICHAEL	NY	28E	39
WOZENCRAFT WARREN LYNN	MS	10W	73
WOZNIAK FREDERICK JOSEPH	MI	14E	46
WOZNIAK JAMES KENNETH	WI	18W	22
WOZNIAK RICHARD LOUIS	IN	64E	1
WOZNIAK ROBERT ANDREW	NY	34E	47
WOZNICKI DAVID JAMES	WI	31E	62
WRANOSKY ROBERT WAYNE	TX	04E	1
WRATTEN GARY PATTERSON	NY	12E	25
WRAY JIM ALLEN	KY	21W	49
WRAY STEVEN CHARLES	MO	04W	100
WRAY VAN THOMAS	NC	10W	36
WRAY WILLIAM CLAYTON	NY	42W	3
WRAZEN GERALD	NY	32W	84
WRENN FRED MELVIN	NC	33E	54
WRENN LARRY CURTIS	NC	17W	11
WRIGHT ALBERT FLOYD JR	MD	24E	70
WRIGHT ALBERT N JR	TN	17W	93
WRIGHT ANDREW SAMUEL	DC	20E	109
WRIGHT ARKIE JUNIOR	OH	40E	35
WRIGHT ARTHUR	MI	15E	72

NAME	STATE	PANEL NO.	LINE NO.
WRIGHT ARTHUR EMERSON III	MA	12E	118
WRIGHT ARTHUR P	TX	07E	78
WRIGHT BILLY LEE	TN	36E	63
WRIGHT BOOKER T	MS	44W	55
WRIGHT BRADFORD DWAIN	MN	42W	34
WRIGHT BRUCE WILLIAM	IA	07W	32
WRIGHT CHARLES FRED	CA	47W	58
WRIGHT CHARLES HENRY	MS	14W	99
WRIGHT CHARLES HERMAN	WV	18W	115
WRIGHT CHARLES KEITH	OH	08E	73
WRIGHT CHESTER ANTON	OH	49W	1
WRIGHT CLAYTON DAVIS	VA	52W	32
WRIGHT CLIFFORD DEVON	FL	21W	27
WRIGHT CLIFFORD IVAN	IL	07W	130
WRIGHT CLIFTON	SC	13W	109
WRIGHT CURTIS RONALD	SC	52E	2
WRIGHT DARREL ZANE	WA	37E	75
WRIGHT DARRYL WHITNEY	WA	43E	39
WRIGHT DAVID DANIEL	CA	21W	79
WRIGHT DAVID IRVIN	MD	06W	58
WRIGHT DAVID LEO	MD	47W	36
WRIGHT DELBERT PAT	NE	25W	41
WRIGHT DENNIS HAROLD	CA	25W	92
WRIGHT DENNIS PAUL	CA	12E	125
WRIGHT DONALD LEE	MD	16W	120
WRIGHT DONALD WOODSON	NC	18W	22
WRIGHT EDWARD TAYLOR	CA	58W	30
WRIGHT FRANK JR	LA	18W	57
WRIGHT FRANKLIN EARL	NC	16W	55
WRIGHT FRED YOUEL JR	IN	06E	40
WRIGHT FREDERICK W III	NJ	01W	90
WRIGHT GARLAND FLENDOLPH	VA	09E	60
WRIGHT GARRY	MI	08E	9
WRIGHT GARY GENE	CA	14E	47
WRIGHT GARY WAYNE	VA	26W	109
WRIGHT GEORGE NATHAN	OR	20E	80
WRIGHT GROVER C JR	VA	50E	43
WRIGHT HARVEY WAYNE	NC	04W	30
WRIGHT HENRY ARTHUR	CA	37E	76
WRIGHT HENRY BERTRAM	FL	14W	96
WRIGHT HERBERT COLEMAN JR	NC	22E	118
WRIGHT HERMAN W O JR	CT	38W	9
WRIGHT HOWARD EUGENE	MD	32W	63
WRIGHT HOWARD OLIVER JR	MD	06E	69
WRIGHT JACK LEE	TX	12W	116
WRIGHT JAMES	GA	09E	129
WRIGHT JAMES	SC	03W	130
WRIGHT JAMES ALFRED	OR	23W	34
WRIGHT JAMES AMBLER	VA	40W	35
WRIGHT JAMES DAVID JR	FL	28W	16
WRIGHT JAMES EARL	AL	31E	79
WRIGHT JAMES FRANK	TN	35E	2
WRIGHT JAMES GREER SR	DC	35W	1
WRIGHT JAMES JOSEPH	CA	29E	13
WRIGHT JAMES L	CA	12E	32
WRIGHT JAMES PAIGE	SD	01E	55
WRIGHT JAMES WALTER	FL	31W	98
WRIGHT JAMES WILLIAM II	CA	55E	36
WRIGHT JAY L	CA	31E	95
WRIGHT JEFFERY LYNN	AZ	02W	32
WRIGHT JERDY ALBERT JR	TX	05E	129
WRIGHT JERRY DEAN	CA	66E	5
WRIGHT JERRY GORDON	FL	24E	50
WRIGHT JOE DAVID	SC	15W	61
WRIGHT JOHN EDWARD	OH	17W	2
WRIGHT JOHN PAUL	CO	16W	1
WRIGHT JOHN WESLEY	MO	57W	22
WRIGHT JOHN WILLIAM	MO	25E	90
WRIGHT JOHNIE J JR	TN	15E	64
WRIGHT JOHNNY WAYNE	VA	11E	104
WRIGHT KAY WILLIAM	NC	23E	9
WRIGHT KENNETH HAROLD	TX	19E	20
WRIGHT KENNETH MICHAEL	IL	22E	81
WRIGHT KENNETH RAY	KY	22E	75
WRIGHT LANNY GAYLE	MO	16E	38
WRIGHT LARRY	FL	35E	50
WRIGHT LEE ROY	CO	56E	19
WRIGHT LEROY NORRIS	NJ	54E	22
WRIGHT LESLIE EDWARD	MI	12E	45
WRIGHT LESTER ALLEN	PA	09E	92
WRIGHT LINCOLN ROY	TX	01W	14
WRIGHT MARTIN WILLARD	NY	08W	53
WRIGHT MELVIN ROY	TN	22E	93
WRIGHT MICHAEL DALE	PA	04W	75
WRIGHT MICHAEL LEE	WA	09W	55
WRIGHT MICHAEL VINCEN	TX	41E	46
WRIGHT O'NEAL	NY	36E	44
WRIGHT PAUL THOMAS	PA	47E	53
WRIGHT PHILLIP GERALD	KY	08W	41
WRIGHT RANDY BLAKE	KY	12E	9
WRIGHT RAYMOND EARL	TN	52W	40
WRIGHT RICHARD HUGH	KS	06E	79
WRIGHT RICHARD JOHN	TX	15E	10
WRIGHT ROBERT	NY	50E	24
WRIGHT ROBERT CARROL	OK	15W	121
WRIGHT ROBERT EDWARD	CA	38E	63
WRIGHT ROBERT FRANK	WA	22E	23
WRIGHT ROBERT G	OH	03E	99
WRIGHT ROBERT JOSEPH	TX	45W	47
WRIGHT ROBERT LEE	TN	12E	26
WRIGHT ROBERT LEROY	IL	34E	3
WRIGHT ROBERT NORMAN	WA	49E	18
WRIGHT ROBERT RICHARD JR	PA	40W	16
WRIGHT RODERICK MICHAEL	MI	37E	76
WRIGHT ROGER DALE	MS	19W	84
WRIGHT RONALD LEE	TN	44E	60
WRIGHT ROSCOE JR	OK	13E	87
WRIGHT RUSSELL L III	VA	45W	34
WRIGHT SCOTT ALAN	IL	51E	15
WRIGHT SILAS CLIFFTON	CA	20W	46
WRIGHT STEPHEN LOUIS	IN	52W	5
WRIGHT STEVEN JAMES	CA	25E	112
WRIGHT SYLVESTER JR	LA	46E	43
WRIGHT TERRY TIM	IN	02E	118
WRIGHT THOMAS CLAY	CA	41E	57
WRIGHT THOMAS THAWSON	IN	41E	57
WRIGHT TOMMY DEE	MO	24W	60
WRIGHT TYRONE	CA	29E	64
WRIGHT TYRONE MELVIN	PA	34W	63
WRIGHT VERNON ARTHUR	IA	07W	41
WRIGHT VINCENT	WI	03W	80
WRIGHT WALTER CLARENCE	NV	27E	46
WRIGHT WILLARD GERALD	NC	39E	15
WRIGHT WILLIAM ANDREW	KY	26E	98
WRIGHT WILLIAM CLAY JR	NY	07E	106
WRIGHT WILLIE ALFRED	IL	29E	37
WRIGHT WILLIE JOSEPH	MA	03E	134
WRIGHT WYLEY JR	FL	01E	46
WRISBERG JOHN HOLGER III	IA	34E	61
WROBEL ROBERT JOSEPH	NY	12W	86
WROBLESKI WALTER FRANCIS	NJ	20E	80
WRONSKI JOHN C	MN	06E	82
WRYE BLAIR CHARLTON	MA	09E	131
WUCINSKI RICHARD THOMAS	WI	14E	72
WUERTENBERGER CHARLES EDG	NY	34E	65
WUERTZ ROBERT DAMIAN	OH	08E	95
WUEST LOUIS ARTHUR JR	NY	36W	75
WUESTENBERG LEWIS CURTIS	SC	36W	67
WULFF ROBERT WAYNE	WA	16E	108
WULFFERT JOHN LAWRENCE	NY	32E	53
WUNDER ROBERT LEE	MI	04W	78
WUNDERLICH HENRY	NY	52E	44
WUNSCH MICHAEL CHARLES	PA	20W	68
WURTENBERG JOHN RICHARD	NY	09W	42
WURTZ EMIL JOHN	IL	40E	71
WUSTERBARTH CLINTON CARL	WI	45E	32
WUTZKE WAYNE GARY	IA	10W	59
WYANT ALFRED LEROY	PA	49W	2
WYANT WILLIAM DOUGLAS	IL	38E	63
WYATT ALVIE CLINTON	CA	14E	13
WYATT BILLY HERDON	CA	03W	67
WYATT BILLY JOE	MO	58W	31
WYATT CHARLES REMBERT	GA	46W	10
WYATT EDWARD W	TX	20W	62
WYATT EVERETT ALBERT JR	TX	38E	19
WYATT JAMES EDWARD	MO	44E	4
WYATT JOHN WESLEY JR	CA	37E	30
WYATT MARVIN LEON	VA	56W	16
WYATT PHILLIP EDGAR	FL	63W	2
WYATT RICHARD COLEMAN	VA	55E	36
WYATT ROBERT PAUL	FL	23E	48
WYATT RONALD	NJ	11E	125
WYATT TOMMY LLOYD	LA	32W	86
WYCINSKY GEORGE JR	PA	11E	1
WYDRA MILAN CHAUNCEY	MI	33E	33
WYKOFF THEODORE LEONARD	CA	18W	92
WYLES DONALD CLAIR	PA	08E	33
WYLEY NATHANIEL	MS	12E	45
WYLIE GLENN ROBERT	PA	30E	6
WYLIE JOSEPH DUNN II	IL	18E	66
WYMAN JERRY ALAN	MI	55E	37
WYMAN MICHAEL JAMES	IL	32W	41
WYMAN MURRAY JOHN	CA	16W	11
WYMER JAMES NELSON	OH	13E	48
WYMER WILLIAM CLIFFORD JR	OH	38W	1
WYMER WILLIAM WAYNE	OH	50E	24
WYNDER CLEVELAND GYE	VA	10W	44
WYNDER EDWARD ORLANDO	NJ	47E	37
WYNN FLOYD	KY	01E	92
WYNN GERARD MICHAEL	NJ	29E	98
WYNN HARVEY EUGENE	GA	24E	98
WYNN JOSEPH RAY JR	GA	01E	114
WYNN LEONARD ANDREA	FL	21E	17
WYNN ROBERT LEE	IL	02W	81
WYNNE JERRY PETER	OH	25E	54
WYNNE JOHN ROBERT	NY	12W	47
WYNNE LARRY B	IL	15E	64
WYNNE PATRICK EDWARD	FL	09E	119
WYNNE THOMAS EDWARD	NY	13W	39
WYRICK DAVID HUGH	OH	45E	32
WYRICK DAVID KEITH	FL	50E	35
WYRICK MICHAEL ALLEN	KS	28E	47
WYROSDIC WILLIAM EVERETT	AL	41W	33
WYSEL MITCHELL BLAINE	CA	22W	56
WYSOCKI WOJCIECH	NY	33E	78
WYSONG JOSEPH WALTER	IN	30W	98
WYSZOMIRSKI JOHN DONALD	NY	09E	132
XAVIER AUGUSTO MARIA	CA	06E	1
YABES MAXIMO	OR	15E	102
YABIKU TAKESHI	CA	35W	80
YACKS RONALD G	MI	26E	87
YADOCK DANIEL JOSEPH	PA	10W	21
YAGER JOHN CORWIN	CA	28E	98
YAGHOOBIAN CHARLES JR	RI	28E	6
YAGLE THOMAS NEIL	MI	06E	119
YAGUES ROBERT GENE	ID	19E	34
YALE RONALD FREDERICK	OH	04W	74
YAMANAKA ROGER KIMO	CA	43E	2
YAMANE BENJI	CA	45E	6
YAMASHIRO EDWARD SATORU	HI	21E	72
YAMASHIRO NAOTO	HI	25E	36
YAMASHITA AKIRA	CA	09E	89
YAMASHITA KENJI JERRY	CA	58E	28
YAMASHITA MELVIN MASAICHI	HI	17W	115
YAMASHITA RICK	MI	29W	34
YAMASHITA SHOJIRO	CA	09W	42
YANCEY CRAIG MARTIN	OK	10W	68
YANCHAR RONALD ALBERT	OH	39W	77
YANCHUK RICHARD PHILIP JR	CA	34W	3
YANCY JOSEPH STANLEY	NY	24E	101
YANEZ JESUS JR	TX	24E	105
YANEZ VICTOR MANUEL	CA	25W	58
YANKOSKI ROBERT ALLEN	MN	01W	83
YANO RODNEY JAMES TAKASHI	HI	35W	18
YANTIS KENNETH RICHARD	PA	47E	29
YAPSUGA EDWARD F JR	PA	13W	109
YARBER DAVID WAYNE	IL	54W	21
YARBER MICHAEL JEROME	IL	24E	116
YARBER VERNON LEE	FL	46W	33
YARBINITZ BERNARD FRANCIS	PA	67W	8
YARBORO DONALD RAY	NC	14W	63
YARBROUGH BILLY EDWARD	TX	47W	36
YARBROUGH DAN BURGESS	UT	21W	104
YARBROUGH GEORGE ALLEN	TN	43W	22
YARBROUGH JAMES LAMAR	GA	29W	2
YARBROUGH LESTER GARNELL	GA	36E	44
YARBROUGH LEVERETT E	GA	07W	104
YARBROUGH WILLIAM P JR	TX	14E	54
YARD BENJAMIN EDWIN JR	PA	02W	98
YARDLEY RODNEY BIRDELL	UT	38W	81
YARGER JEFFREY J	OH	45E	36
YARGER JOHN ROBERT	MT	28W	23
YARNELL DANIEL DAVID	CA	12E	64
YARRINGTON DONALD P JR	UT	28E	45
YARTYMYK MICHAEL HARRY	PA	29E	79
YASENOSKY ANDREW RICHARD	PA	13E	9